The Complete Works *of*

William Shakespeare

The Alexander Text
introduced by Peter Ackroyd

Collins

HarperCollins Publishers
1 London Bridge Street, London SE1 9GF

www.collins.co.uk

Collins is a registered trademark of HarperCollins Publishers Ltd.

The Alexander Text of the Complete Works of William Shakespeare was first published in 1951.
Reset edition published 1994
This edition published 2006
Reprinted 2007, 2008, 2010

Hardback Edition: ISBN 978-0-00-720830-2

Paperback Edition: ISBN 978-0-00-720831-9

Leather Edition: ISBN 978-0-00-721490-7

A catalogue record for this book is available from the British Library.

Printed and bound in China

The Complete Works *of*

William Shakespeare

Contents

Sonnets and Poems

The Contributors

Peter Ackroyd was born in London in 1949 and is a highly regarded novelist, biographer and poet. He is the author of *London: The Biography* (2000) and *Albion: The Origins of the English Imagination* (2002); acclaimed biographies of T. S. Eliot, Dickens, Blake, and Thomas More; and several successful novels. His most recent book has been *Shakespeare: The Biography* (2005). He is a Fellow of the Royal Society of Literature, and has won a number of distinguished literary awards.

Germaine Greer was born in Australia in 1939, and became one of the most influential writers of modern times following the publication in 1970 of her analysis of sexual stereotyping, *The Female Eunuch*. Other works include *The Obstacle Race* (1979), *Sex and Destiny: the Politics of Human Fertility* (1984), *Shakespeare* (1986), *The Change* (1991), *The Whole Woman* (1999) and *The Beautiful Boy* (2003). In 2005 she retired as Professor of English and Comparative Studies at the University of Warwick.

Anthony Burgess was born in Manchester in 1917 and died in 1993, shortly after completing the introduction to Shakespeare's theatre for this edition of the Alexander text. One of the most highly regarded novelists and critics of the 20th century, his many works include the novels *A Clockwork Orange* (1962), *Inside Mr Enderby* (1963), *The Malayan Trilogy* (1964) and *Nothing Like the Sun* (1964), the latter work being a fictionalised biography of Shakespeare. Other works include the autobiography *Little Wilson and Big God* (1987) and the biography *Shakespeare* (1970).

The introductions to the plays, poems and sonnets were written by a team from Glasgow University's Department of English Literature, in which department Peter Alexander was Professor Emeritus of English Language and Literature. The contributors are Susan Anthony, Robert Cummings, Catherine E. Durie, Stuart Gillespie, Robert Grant, Philip Hobsbaum, Ralph Jessop, Donald Mackenzie, Dorothy McMillan, Robert Maslen, David Newell, Patrick Reilly and Alec Yearling.

The introduction to the Alexander text was written by Alec Yearling, and the introductions by the Glasgow University team were organised by David Newell.

Reading Shakespeare Today

by Peter Ackroyd

In recent years it has become all the more necessary to read William Shakespeare. We live in a visual, rather than an oral, culture. Shakespeare's first audiences were used to the long sermon, as well as to the 'mighty line' of the newly popular playwrights. The audiences of the twenty-first century are ill-equipped to listen to Shakespeare's plays, even in the most benign circumstances. They cannot follow the dialogue, even if they can more or less comprehend the plot. Half the significance is lost to them. That is why contemporary directors feel it necessary to provide their own interest, and laughter, with various theatrical devices that have nothing to do with Shakespeare himself.

It all becomes much clearer when you read him. We may for once leave behind the argument that there is no pristine text for any of the plays. The dramas themselves were no doubt endlessly changed and shortened at rehearsals; at a later date contemporary allusions and lines for specific actors were removed. There is no 'clean copy' of any of the plays, which were probably played differently every time they were performed. What we have instead is an approximate transcript, a rough guide to Shakespeare's language and intentions. In that sense it is probably the best possible introduction to Shakespeare's imagination, which seems always to have been in a fluid and provisional shape.

He wrote quickly but never carelessly. As his contemporary, Ben Jonson, observed he had a free wit and a copious imagination; according to Jonson, 'hee never blotted out line'. Words, and combinations of words, came easily to him. The effect is like that of a comet, burning all the brighter as it passes through the cosmos. He gathers strength as he writes, forming characters in the act of creation and fashioning meaning from the chance association of words and cadences. Shakespeare did not know where the words came from; he only knew that they came. It is as if we are gazing upon the spectacle of language in the act of expressing itself.

Much of his own writing is borrowed or stolen from other books. That much is certain. But this is not a question of plagiarism or pastiche. He did not steal words; he rescued them from inferiors. In his act of remembering and restoration, all of the resources of his imagination clustered around the words and images so that they were immeasurably strengthened and deepened. They became 'Shakespearian' with that unique and irreplaceable presence which is so hard to characterise or to define.

His speed is one of the characteristics that seems little short of astonishing. One gets the impression of restless and rapid creation. He hardly ever punctuated as he wrote, leaving that task to later. He misplaces or leaves out stage directions. They could wait to rehearsals. He confuses the speakers. He did not mark act or scene divisions. Yet there are times when he hesitated, pen over paper, ready to strike out a word or improve it with a better one. There are times when he will lose his way with a piece of prose or verse, and so then he returns to the beginning and starts all over again. We know that because there are passages where both first and second thoughts have been included by the printer. There are moments, in the white heat of creation, when he did not know or care whether he was writing prose or verse. And there are times when he runs verse lines together in order to save space. He was in every sense a professional writer. Indeed he can even be considered to be the first professional writer in England – a writer, that is, who was tied to a specific market for whom he had to produce a series of works in order to earn his living. He had no patron, in the conventional sense, except the many-headed multitude who filled the Globe and the Theatre and the Curtain.

His writing comes from sources that were too deep, and obscure, for him to understand. That is why his own character seems to lead ineluctably to the characters he created. There will be some relation between the two, however universal and multifarious his range of characters might be. There is something of Shakespeare within them. Otherwise he would not have been able to give them life. All of them have an exultant and self-sufficient energy that lifts them above the realm of nature. That is why the greatest tragic characters are close to comedy. Their expansiveness and self-assertion provoke delight.

That is also why Shakespeare betrays no real interest in motive. His characters are fully alive as soon as they walk upon the stage, and no excuse or reason for their conduct is ever necessary. As far as the great tragic heroes are concerned, too, there is a corresponding belief in the ruling power of the self. Their destiny does not dwell in the stars, and least of all in any concept of divine providence. Their capacity for life is astonishing. They have a mental, as well as a physical energy. Even Macbeth retains a mysterious optimism. They are at one with the forces of the universe.

Shakespeare's true villains are pessimists, denying human energy and the capacity for human greatness. They are self-absorbed and melancholy, the enemies of movement and vitality. And here, if anywhere, the true sympathies of Shakespeare's own nature are to be found. They are not governed by rational choices; their logic is always the logic of intuition or dream. Their dilemma often concerns the role they must play in the world, the part they must assume, His characters are witty, and cryptic, and whimsical. They are sometimes inscrutable and more than a little fantastical. Can we not see the face of Shakespeare somewhere behind them?

Yet this biographical speculation is probably out of place in any introduction to these extraordinary and memorable dramas that will live as long as the English language itself. They are in fact embedded deep within the fabric of that language itself, so that in studying these plays you will encounter the whole array and panoply of the English imagination. Read him.

William Shakespeare

A biography by Germaine Greer

There can be no doubt that there once lived a man called William Shakespeare and that he wrote a number of extraordinary plays. We know from the hysterical attack on him in Greene's *Groatsworth of Wit* that by 1592 he was already known to his fellow writers, at least one of whom bitterly resented his success. How long he had been practising successfully as a playwright is not so clear. No play of his was published before 1594, when *Titus Andronicus* appeared in quarto but in 1593 *Venus and Adonis*, a highly finished narrative poem, was published in a good edition with Shakespeare's name appearing in full as the signatory of the dedicatory epistle addressed to the young Earl of Southampton. Though scholars are embarrassed by this opulent poem, which is amongst the least studied of Shakespeare's works, the more literate of his contemporaries greatly admired it. The first printing sold out, to be followed by another in the same year, another in each of the next three years, and two in 1599. At least sixteen editions appeared over the next fifty years, making *Venus and Adonis* a publishing success unsurpassed by any of Shakespeare's rivals.

Venus and Adonis demonstrates that Shakespeare knew his Ovid intimately, both in spirit and to the letter, that he was a master of versification and could handle an intricate stanza form with mercurial changes of tone, mood and pace at least as well as more pretentious poets, and that he was a self-conscious artist who, when he was responsible for his own text, produced clear, clean copy. *Venus and Adonis* bears no resemblance at all to native woodnotes wild; almost every topos in the poem can be traced to a literary precedent. A year later *The Rape of Lucrece*, even less popular with scholars, consolidated Shakespeare's claim to literary reputation.

In 1593 the 'man Shakespeare', as Countess Russell is supposed to have called him, thus consciously or unconsciously distinguishing him from a gentleman, was a nobody. The baptismal entry in the register of Holy Trinity Church, Stratford-upon-Avon, for April 26, 1564, 'Guglielmus filius Johannes Shakespeare', adds to the mystery of his rise to literary eminence rather than dispelling it. John Shakespeare is almost certainly the same man who was fined for allowing muck to accumulate outside his house in Henley Street ('the Birthplace') in 1552, and who was described as a glover in a lawsuit of 1556. As a glover he must have prospered for he was able to buy two properties in that year and to enlarge his house, possibly in preparation for his marriage to Mary Arden, who inherited a farm from her father in 1557 and was probably married to John in the same year. If these are the poet's parents, it is the more surprising that they both appear to have been illiterate. The Shakespeare-Arden family have left the usual paper trail of entries in parish registers, and records of fines, lawsuits and wills, providing a pattern of rich and poor relations, and rises and falls in prosperity, but none of it explains the Shakespeare phenomenon.

The Shakespeares christened two children before William, and six children after him, of whom only Joan, Gilbert, Richard and Edmund survived to adulthood. None was married but Joan, to a hatter who could not provide for his numerous offspring.

John Shakespeare prospered, adding trading in wool to his activities as a glover, buying and renting out houses. He was appointed an ale-taster, a constable, an assessor of fines and a burgess; in 1568 he became an alderman, but by 1576 he was beginning to default in his public duties and in his financial dealings. The severe recession of the 1590s brought worse problems and Shakespeare had much ado to remain solvent but when he died in 1601, the big house in Henley Street was still in his possession, to be left to his poet son.

Of the years that intervened between Shakespeare's christening and his appearance on the London stage nothing is known. He must have gone at least to dame school and, as one would expect of the son of a Stratford alderman, from the age of six or seven to the King's New Grammar School. Though the masters, being university men, are themselves documented, not one makes reference to anyone called Shakespeare, while the poet's references to school and schoolboys give no very attractive picture of either. In the lower school, rote learning of Latin, supported by Lily's grammar, first from the *Sententiae Pueriles*, and then from Plautus and Terence, was the staple. In the upper school he would have studied rhetoric and logic, Cicero, Quintilian, Ovid, Virgil and Horace and have begun the study of Greek. These studies were all the literary training that any Elizabethan poet received; universities trained men up for the church, for the law-courts and in medicine, such as it was.

In the 1590s there was no profession of letters. Poetry was practised as an accomplished pastime by gentlemen and scholars. In the years before copyright, the only way that the author of a text could make money from its publication was by selling the text outright (for relatively little) and offering a dedication to a rich patron, who would graciously confer a couple of guineas on the author. All the income from book sales went to the printers and booksellers, who enjoyed much narrower profit margins in the centuries before cheap paper became a possibility. After leaving school, a clever student could look for employment as a secretary in a great house, making fair copies of the scribbled letters of a nobleman or functionary, or as a tutor, while he published his own poetic effusions on the side. If Shakespeare had done this, his entire career would have been documented. We have literally no idea how the child baptised in 1564 developed into the author of *Venus and Adonis* in 1593.

The only documented event in the years between is the rather unconventional marriage of William Shakespeare aged eighteen with Anne Hathaway, an heiress, six or seven years older and pregnant. Because it was November and the penitential season of Advent when marriages could not be solemnised was at hand, application had to be made to the consistory court of the see of Worcester for a special licence. The entry for the licence itself mistakes Anne's surname, a circumstance that has stimulated the fantasy of some male commentators who have imagined a 'budding virgin pure and fresh and sweet' whom Shakespeare was being forced to give up because he had been seduced by an aged, wanton, cunning shrew. The son of an ex-alderman too embarrassed by debt to show up at church was actually lucky to find a well-to-do bride; the fact of her pregnancy would have removed any objection that her family might have felt and provided Shakespeare with a helpmeet he could not have secured any other way. Speculation about the Shakespeares' relationship is merely that and, as such, reveals more about the speculator than about Shakespeare. Suffice it to point out that the marriage lasted and that Shakespeare invested all the considerable earnings from his theatre enterprises in maintaining and enlarging a large establishment at Stratford which, because he was so often in London, must have been managed for him by Anne Shakespeare. There may be more than coincidence in the fact that his one authentic monument, the First Folio, was published just after Anne died in 1623. The creator of Shakespeare's vocal, loyal and courageous female characters probably knew at least one such woman; the one he knew best was Anne Shakespeare. The only other documentation we have before 1592 relates to the children Anne bore William, Susanna in May, 1583 and the twins, Hamnet and Judith in 1585.

Tosspot, deerstealer, papist, schoolmaster, soldier, lawyer, tutor, travelling player, Shakespeare has been described as all of them, and may have been none of them, during the lost years. We find no trace of him until late 1592 when Robert Greene reviles him in his *Groatsworth of Wit* as the 'upstart crow', the 'Shakes-scene' who 'with his tiger heart wrapped in a player's hide supposes he is as well able to bombast out a blank verse as the best'. Greene libels Shakespeare in the most flattering way with a distorted quotation from *Henry VI Part Three.* Henry Chettle, the editor of Greene's *Groatsworth,* attempted to make amends by an apology in *Kind Heart's Dream* by testifying to 'his demeanour no less civil than he excellent in the quality he professes: besides divers of worship have reported, his uprightness of dealing, which argues his honesty, and his facetious grace in writing, that approves his art.' Chettle's wording is more mysterious than informative, but it provides further evidence that Shakespeare was already conspicuously active in the theatre as a writer and possibly also as an entrepreneur.

The title page of *Titus Andronicus* does not name the author, saying simply that it had been played by 'the Earl of Derby, Earl of Pembroke and Earl of Sussex their servants'. Likewise, the quarto of *Henry VI Part Two,* published in 1594 as *The First Part of the Contention betwixt the two famous Houses of York and Lancaster* is anonymous, as is the quarto of the third part, called *The true Tragedie of Richard Duke of York* published the following year. An admiring comment in Nashe's *Pierce Penilesse* (1592) tells us that at least part of the trilogy had been played with great success, almost certainly by the Admiral's Men at the Rose in the spring and summer of 1592.

The publication of two non-dramatic poems by Shakespeare in 1593 and 1594 is usually taken to be an indirect consequence of the closing of the playhouses in the summer of 1592 on account of an outbreak of plague in London. That Shakespeare dedicated both to the young Earl of Southampton is taken to be evidence of an actual association between them, especially in view of the closing lines of the dedicatory epistle to *Lucrece*: 'What I have done is yours, what I have to do is yours, being part in all I have, devoted, yours.' To compare this with the usual language of dedications from marked social inferiors, as for example, Emilia Lanier, dedicating her collection called *Salve Rex Judaeorum* to assorted noblewomen in 1601, is to realise that it need not signify even the slightest degree of intimacy.

Internal evidence has been taken to indicate that most of Shakespeare's Sonnets date from the same period as the narrative poems; proponents of the theory of an attachment, Platonic or otherwise, between the nobleman and the player are more likely to find evidence of such dating than are others. The sonnets were never intended as versified biography, which is an entirely anachronistic idea. As printed by Thomas Thorpe in 1609, *Shakespeares Sonnets* appears to represent a collection of incomplete sequences. If the dedication 'To the only begetter of these ensuing sonnets Mr. W. H.' could have been taken by contemporaries to refer to 'Lord H. W.' i.e. Henry Wriothesley, third Earl of Southampton, the printer must have been a jackass and totally unafraid of a whipping. Though floods of ink have been devoted to unravelling the Sonnets they remain as ravelled, and as compelling therefore, as ever. No earl, however pretty, ever had such *billets doux*. More puzzling is the fact that Shakespeare neither assisted with the publication of the Sonnets (judging from the messiness of the texts) nor deplored it. He seems to have ignored the publication, which had none of the success of his narrative poems.

In March, 1595 Shakespeare was named in the Declared Accounts of the Royal Chamber as one of three leaders of the Lord Chamberlain's Men receiving payment for a Christmas entertainment at Greenwich. The Lord Chamberlain's Men, then newly reorganised and housed at Burbage's Theatre in Shoreditch, were rivalled in prestige only by the Admiral's Men, whose chief playwright, Christopher Marlowe, had been killed the year before. As this eminence represents the top of a player's profession, it is reasonable to assume that in 1595 Shakespeare was no beginner in the theatrical profession. In 1596, he made application, probably on behalf of his father, for a coat of arms; before it was confirmed in October 1596, Shakespeare's son Hamnet died. The next year he bought New Place, one of the finest houses in Stratford; he was to acquire another cottage and garden, altogether 107 acres of arable land, farmed by tenants, and make a considerable investment in tithes. As a consequence of these and other dealings his name figures regularly in the Stratford records, where he is never identified as poet, performer, producer or playwright.

In 1596 Shakespeare was also recorded as a resident of the Bishopsgate ward, close to the Theatre. In 1598 his name appeared at the head of the cast for a performance of Ben Jonson's *Every man in his Humour* playing at the Curtain because, after protracted negotiations, the Theatre had lost its lease and was to be taken down. The timbers were ferried over the river to the Bankside to build a new theatre to be called The Globe, the first playhouse to be part-owned by the players. On 21 February, 1599, the lease shows Shakespeare as holding a tenth share, and the Burbage brothers half; later that share was increased to a seventh until the post-mortem accounts of the landlord show Shakespeare as principal tenant. At the same time he moved his lodgings; the tax records show him living nearby in the Liberty of the Clink.

In 1598 Francis Meres named Shakespeare as the leading playwright in a 'Comparative Discourse of our Modern Poets' appended to his *Palladis Tamia.*

> The sweet witty soul of Ovid lives in mellifluous and honey-tongued Shakespeare, witness his *Venus and Adonis,* his *Lucrece,* his sugared sonnets among his private friends, &c. As Plautus and Seneca are accounted the best for comedy and tragedy among the Latins, so Shakespeare among the English is the most excellent in both kinds for the stage; for comedy witness his *Gentlemen of Verona,* his *Errors,* his *Love Labour's Lost,* his *Love Labour Won,* his *Midsummer's Night Dream,* and his *Merchant of Venice;* for tragedy, his *Richard the Second, Richard the Third, Henry the Fourth, King John, Titus Andronicus,* and his *Romeo and Juliet.*

As Shakespeare's name was now a selling point, it began to appear on the published versions of his work and sometimes of the work of others. In 1599, William Jaggard published a compilation of twenty poems called *The Passionate Pilgrim by W. Shakespeare* Only five of the poems were Shakespeare's; two are versions of his sonnets, and the other three of the young lords' poems in *Love's Labour's Lost.* The second printings of *Richard III* and *Love's Labour's Lost* carried his name; *Henry VI Part One* had to wait until the third printing in 1599. Four plays, *Henry IV Part Two, The Merchant of Venice, Midsummer Night's Dream* and *Much Ado* all carried Shakespeare's name when they were published in 1600; *Henry V* did not. The general rule was that play texts were the stock-in-trade of the companies rather than the authors, whose identities were not the point. That Shakespeare's work was often unattributed is less surprising than that his authorship was so often acknowledged.

The flurry of Shakespeare publishing in the late 1590s almost certainly represents a gathering up of work produced over the formative years of Shakespeare's professional career. By 1600, first publication might be assumed to have more or less caught up with composition, but the dating of the composition of all of Shakespeare's plays remains a matter for speculation. To complicate matters further, only two of the thirteen plays Shakespeare wrote after Queen Elizabeth's death were published in his lifetime, probably because the company under his direction took steps to protect its property from exploitation by its rivals. They would have been better able to accomplish this because in 1603 King James had granted the company a formal Patent under the Great Seal. The Lord Chamberlain's Men were now the King's Men and were issued with red cloth to be made up into the livery of Grooms of the Chamber.

The King's Men were required regularly to perform at court, in very different circumstances from those that prevailed at the Globe; between November 1, 1604, and 12 February, 1605, for example, they performed eleven times, presenting ten plays, seven of them by Shakespeare. This was the year of *Othello,* to be followed by *King Lear* and *Macbeth*. In 1608 the company took over the Blackfriars theatre, so that they could play during the winter on a stage lit by candlelight. For a time daylight virtually disappeared from Shakespeare's plays, to return in the late plays as sunlight remembered, in the bitter-sweet mode of pastoral.

Running two theatres and producing court performances was rewarding, in a pecuniary sense at least, but strenuous. We do not know when Shakespeare retired to Stratford; as he is mentioned frequently in the records in both London and Stratford, it is no easy matter to decide when he ceased making visits to London. (The Stratford Shakespeare and the London Shakespeare have never been positively identified as the same person.)

In the winter of 1615–16 Shakespeare turned his mind to making his will which was completed and signed by him on March 25. The will has been the cause of some dismay, both because it makes no mention of books or papers, and because of the famous afterthought by which Anne Hathaway was left his second-best bed, which was probably the bed they had always slept in, the best being kept for visitors of rank. On April 23, 1616, aged 52 years to the day, Shakespeare died and was buried in Holy Trinity Church Stratford.

His monument in the church has been altered so many times that it cannot be said to be a likeness of anyone. The engraving by Martin Droeshout for the title page of the First Folio is more authentic but so inept that it too has little value as a likeness. Nowadays the Chandos portrait in the National Portrait Gallery is thought to have the best claim though it represents neither the figure on the monument nor the sitter for Martin Droeshout. We are left with no option but to follow Ben Jonson's advice:

Reader, Looke
Not on his Picture, but his Booke.

Shakespeare's Theatre

Introduction by Anthony Burgess

Once again we are invited to read the Complete Works of William Shakespeare. That is a term which, as the poet knew well, his contemporaries would hardly have tolerated. Ben Jonson dared to publish his plays as his Works and was derided for his presumption. *Venus and Adonis* and *The Rape of Lucrece* were intended as Shakespeare's contribution to literature. *Hamlet* and *King Lear* were merely plays. It was a bold venture on the part of Heminges and Condell to produce the first Folio of the complete plays in 1623, seven years after the death of the author, their friend and fellow-actor. Shakespeare himself, preoccupied with the concerns of a small country magnate, would not have thought of it. If, during his lifetime, his plays appeared in quarto form, singletons in *editions de poche,* this had nothing to do with their eternisation as literature. The plays belonged not to himself but to the theatrical company of which he was a member (the Lord Chamberlain's Men, elevated in 1603 to the King's Men). They had to be published as a mode of protection. There were pirates in those days, printers who paid shorthand-writers to transcribe plays as they were performed and then published them, however garbled. The public could be expected to prefer the genuine to the spurious, hence the rushing out of the poet's own text. One has only to compare the so-called bad quarto of *Hamlet* with the good quarto put out by the Lord Chamberlain's Men to be made aware of the need of publication as a kind of sanitation.

Some work has been done on that bad quarto of *Hamlet,* and it seems likely that the transcription was the work of a co-opted player who took the role of Reynaldo. He produces acceptable paraphrases of Shakespeare's lines when himself speaking them, or when physically close enough to the action to have a clear notion of the lines, but he fails wretchedly with the soliloquy beginning, in his version, 'To live or to die, aye, there's a point'. Clearly, the shorthand used was not, like Gregg or Pitman, phonetic; it was roughly ideo-grammatic, like Chinese, and hence a ready killer of the well-made phrase. The Lord Chamberlain's Men saw their plays as literary artefacts of a sort, not to be deformed by meddlers, but there were good historical reasons why they were not to be evaluated in terms proper to Plautus or Seneca. Strictly, there was in England no tradition of dramatic literature: Shakespeare was nearly in at the beginning of the founding of one.

Literature may be defined as the exploitation of language to an aesthetic end. Traditionally – that is, in ancient Greece and Rome – such exploitation had been confined to verse; prose was considered a pedestrian medium suitable for law and letters, physics and metaphysics. Aeschylus, Euripides and Sophocles were great poets as well as great dramatists – great distillers of universal truth in memorable lines springing out of the theatrical particularity of a chosen myth. Seneca in Rome took those same myths and developed a poetic style destined to be influential in the Elizabethan drama, but only, as it were, cosmetically. The creation of a native theatre entailed wrestling with the native language and drawing on the native stock of history and myth.

The drama is peculiar in that it can function without those elements we term literary. It is possible to write a play without any display of literary talent, and indeed the tradition which developed in the nineteenth century eschewed the poetic and abhorred verse, though verse is highly practical for the line-learning actor. The plays of Ibsen – other than his poetic dramas *Peer Gynt* and *Brand* – are in pedestrian prose that matches the pedestrian lives drably delineated on the stage. This is what is mostly expected in the drama of the day. The poetic drama, revived by T. S. Eliot, W. H. Auden and others, was an embarrassment. So, to some audiences, is Shakespeare. Plain speech is wanted, as in Harold Pinter. Pinter is good to hear but excruciating to read.

A drama that was pedestrian enough, though it used verse, had existed in England from about 1311 till the coming of the Reformation. Pope Urban IV instituted the feast of Corpus Christi and decreed that it be observed with all due ceremony. In England this came to mean the performance of religious plays by the trade guilds. These are often termed mystery plays, *mystery* signifying not an inexplicable religious truth but the arcana of a trade. The term survives in the French *métier* and the Italian *mestiere*.

The guilds would choose episodes from the Bible for dramatisation, and the choice would usually be appropriate to the trade practised. Thus the Chester guilds had the Last Supper acted by the Bakers, the Passion and Crucifixion of Christ by the Fletchers (or Arrowmakers), Coopers and Ironmongers, and the Descent into Hell by the Cooks. Each guild had its decorated cart, called a *pageant*, a sort of portable stage to be dragged through the town, set up at different spots, and, at the end of the long day's acting, dragged back to its shed for another year. The plays were presented in strict chronological sequence, starting with the Fall of Lucifer or the Creation of the World and ending with the Day of Judgment. The total number of plays performed in Chester on Corpus Christi was about twenty-four, but Wakefield could have thirty-three, Coventry forty-two, and York fifty-four. The actors and audience needed the long summer daylight to get through so formidable a schedule.

These were amateur productions, and the texts themselves, though sometimes brutally realistic and rarely devoid of low humour, have none of the qualities that might please the cultivated. Yet the guild dramas had nearly three centuries of life before Henry VIII's Reformation rang down the curtain on them for good. They could give little to the development of a later, secular, drama – save perhaps the memory of characters like Pontius Pilate and Herod, whose tearing of a passion to tatters, to very rags, is condemned by Hamlet. Nevertheless, there is a Pilatic or Herodian quality in Marlowe's Tamburlaine and Barabas, larger-than-life figures whose villainy, and language to match it, touches the apocalyptic. The secular dramas that followed the guild plays – moralities and interludes – could teach very little to the Elizabethan age. They were amateurish works, though performed by professionals – a professional being defined as someone who will willingly perform, however badly, for money, however little.

The morality play did not take its subject from the Bible: it was a dramatised sermon more than a good plain narrative. Moral abstractions were personified. Wisdom, Mischief, Pleasure, Folly, Backbiting, Indignation, Sturdiness, Malice, Revenge, Discord and a general abstraction named the Vice stalked the stage in a presentation usually dull, didactic, ill-made, lacking in genuine conflict and human interest. The titles are off-putting enough – *Mind, Will and Understanding*; *Mankind*; *The Castle of Perseverance.* Only the very moving *Everyman* succeeds in touching the heart of drama: we recognise ourselves in the eponymous hero; the abstract virtues and vices take on a kind of human substance. In other plays, vice itself, or the Vice, assumes the form of a low comedian, armed with slapstick and deplorable japes. Feste in *Twelfth Night* remembers him, as does Prince Hal in *Henry IV*. As a personification of insouciant immorality he is the raw lump that may some day be moulded into Falstaff.

It is not easy to distinguish between the morality and the interlude. The chief difference lies not in theme or treatment but in place and occasion of performance. An interlude, as the name indicates, was a kind of incidental entertainment, a short play presented as an adjunct to a feast or other ceremonial occasion, with an educated audience of some sophistication. A demotic and an aristocratic development of the same dramatic form subsist, it seems, side by side. The players in a great house may well be indentured servants wearing their master's livery. The masterless wanderers who take round the hat on the village green or in the innyard would gladly have such a gesture of permanence and protection. The two kinds of players need to merge.

The aristocratic morality play, calling itself an interlude, can often be assigned to a named author, and men like Rastell, Medwall and Bale, who continue to be unknown in the great world, have attained at least the small immortality that scholarly histories grant. Bale, in his *Interlude of God's Promises,* points to the future with a formal act division, and his dull didactic disquisition on free will and divine grace has, at least, a prosodic rigour and a certain linguistic elegance. Medwall wrote *Fulgens and Lucrece,* whose title already suggests an Elizabethan historical drama, though his aim in choosing a Roman story is all too didactic a lengthy illustration of the nature of true nobility. Surprisingly, we find the play almost readable. We are never likely to know if it is also actable. The same may be said of the trifles of John Heywood, whose bubbly *Play of the Weather* and *The Four P's* (mere gossip between a palmer, a pardoner, a 'pothecary and a pedlar) totally lack a moral content. Sheer diversion, unfastened to any didactic purpose, is appearing not on the village green but in the manor house.

The acting troupes that sought their audiences in London needed something other than an open space on which to unload their property carts. They found that innyards were highly suitable from many aspects. With increasing floods of visitors from the provinces and, indeed, from Europe, London's inns were beginning to fill. Here were readymade audiences. The square yard was enclosed by an upper gallery, on to which the bedchambers opened. The visitors could bring out their chairs. In the yard itself was standing room only. The stage could be an improvised platform at one end of the innyard, and the fixed gallery above could also be used as an acting area. Foreseeing large profits in plays, some entrepreneurs – of the James Burbage and Philip Henslowe type – might be encouraged to build playhouses modelled on innyards, retaining only one amenity of the inn itself – a licence to sell intoxicants. Everyone remembers how, when the Globe theatre burnt down in 1613, a groundling whose breeches caught fire had the flame doused with pottle-ale.

The stage now became a fixed structure, covered with a canopy known as the heavens and jutting into the auditorium. The apron stage, as it is called, has been revived in our own age, but plays are mostly written for a stage thrust back from the audience, enclosed, like a picture, by a proscenium arch. The Elizabethan acting troupes, performing in daylight, saw their audiences all too clearly, could not pretend they were not there, and hence, on that jutting apron, drew them into the action. There were even stools on the stage for the accommodation of the better sort of spectator. There were a couple of doors, left and right, for exits and entrances, a trap-door, and a curtained recess for intimate scenes known as the study. The upper gallery, very much an acting area, was called the tarrass, and above this was a musicians' gallery which could also be employed in the action. The opening scene of *The Tempest* could easily imitate a ship at sea, with ship's boy at the summit and fearful passengers going below. The view of dramatic action was then vertical. We have not reverted from the horizontal since the Gallicised drama of the Restoration.

The dramatic company with which Shakespeare is mainly associated had established its personnel by the year 1600, the year of *Hamlet*. We know the names of the actors, though we do not know well which played what kind of part. The head of the troupe was Richard Burbage, evidently a very great actor to whom all the major parts were entrusted. Then there were Jack Heminges, Gus Philips, Tom Pope, George Bryan, Harry Condell, Will Sly, Dick Cowly, Jack Lowin, Sam Cross, Alex Cook, Sam Gilburne, Robin Armin, Will Ostler, Nat Field, Jack Underwood, Nick Tooley, Will Ecclestone, Joseph Taylor, Robin Benfield and Robin Gough, Dicky Robinson (Ben Jonson's favourite actor), Jack Shank and Jack Rice. One name is missing from the list which certainly would have been there if Shakespeare's notion of comedy had not undergone a seismic revision. Will Kemp was a famous clown in his day, but he would not learn lines and he leered and capered and tripped. He was replaced by Robin Armin, the Feste of *Twelfth Night*, the Fool of *King Lear*, a subtle comedian with a sweet voice. This company, on court occasions, wore the livery first of the Lord Chamberlain, who was the nominal master; later, as the King's Men, they rather more than nominally served King James VI and I and officially performed as Grooms of the Bedchamber.

Shakespeare, then, as resident playwright of his company and as a major shareholder, knew, with whatever play it was deemed fitting for him to write, exactly which actors he was writing for. As for the craft of dramaturgy, this, as I have indicated, could learn nothing from miracle, morality or interlude. The rather crude rhymed structures which had served the old texts would not do. A dramatic prosody was needed which, by sheer chance, had been made available seven years before Shakespeare's birth, when Henry Earl of Surrey published his *Certain Bokes of Virgiles Aeneis*, a fairly close translation of part of the *Aeneid* in a new and experimental metric:

> They whisted all, with fixed face attent
> When Prince Aeneas from the royal seat
> Thus gan to speak, O Queene, it is thy will,
> I should renew a woe can not be told:
> How that the Grekes did spoile and overthrow
> The Phrygian wealth, and wailful realm of Troy,
> Those ruthful things that I myself beheld.

This, of course, is blank verse. With it Surrey sought an English equivalent for Virgil's hexameters, which did not rhyme. The new dramatists could see its virtues – its closeness to speech, for one thing – and found it especially appropriate when, as they had to, they leaned heavily on the Roman Seneca for plot, mood and, above all, violence. Without the example of Seneca, whom Shakespeare undoubtedly read and perhaps acted while at school, there would have been no Elizabethan tragedy. 1561, three years before Shakespeare's birth, may be taken as a key-year in our dramatic history, for it saw the production of *Gorboduc*, in Surreyesque blank verse, at the Inner Temple of the Inns of Court. The authors were Thomas Norton and Thomas Sackville, and they took their story from the *History of the Britons* by Geoffrey of Monmouth, the medieval chronicler. It tells of the quarrel between Ferrex and Porrex, sons of King Gorboduc and Queen Videna, over the division of the kingdom of Britain. Porrex kills Ferrex, and Queen Videna kills Porrex. The Duke of Albany tries to assume control of the country, and civil war breaks out. There are what are known as Senecan properties, such as ghosts and reported horrors. Seneca honoured the Athenian tradition whereby rape, mutilation and murder could be recounted but not shown. Norton and Sackville made sufficient use of messengers coming on to announce ever new horrors, but this kind of restraint was not to be typical of the popular tragedy of blood which regaled the groundlings, as well as the better sort, at the Theatre or the Curtain, playhouses where Shakespeare did his first work.

There were, in fact, three distinct ways of drawing on the great example of Seneca. One was to go straight to his Latin texts and attempt to transmit his spirit through English. This was the way of the young learned amateurs who wrote for the Inns of Court. The way of the intellectuals who clustered about the Earl of Pembroke, or his formidable mother, was that of the French dramatist Garnier: here was refined dilution of the true fierce Senecan rhetoric: it was not likely to appeal in the popular theatre. Samuel Daniel anticipated Shakespeare by writing a tragedy called *Cleopatra* for the delectation of the Pembroke crowd, but it lacks rhetorical savour and does not compensate for this with violence of action. The Elizabethans of the playhouses preferred to follow the Italian Senecan tradition, in which the stage was littered with corpses, preferably tongueless, headless, or limbless. The most popular play of the day was Thomas Kyd's *The Spanish Tragedy*, in which Hieronimo bites out his tongue, ghosts shriek, and terrible revenges are taken. Neither Marlowe nor Shakespeare learned all that much from Seneca. Marlowe derived his stage violence from the fancied destructive doctrines of Machiavelli and, for *Tamburlaine*, from history itself. Shakespeare, in *Titus Andronicus*, went too far, blatantly emptying on to the stage a cornucopia of mutilation, rape, burial alive, cannibalism and mass murder. From then on, his Senecanism was more restrained, limited to rhetorical tropes and, according to T. S. Eliot, an infusion of Senecan stoicism. Seneca, once tutor to Nero, finally ordered to slit his veins in his bath, was not primarily a dramatist. He followed the stoical philosophy of the Greeks, in which the pursuit of virtue transcended worship of the gods and patience rather than violence confronted the tyranny of such as his own imperial master. In the plays, a character believes that his survival is ensured, while the very heavens fall, by the mere fact of his virtue. The gods can be vicious. Medea cries '*Medea superest!*' – Medea lives on. In *Hamlet*, the prince, who has created a measure of chaos in Denmark, demands as he dies that his just cause be reported aright to the unsatisfied. This, according to Eliot, is pure Senecan stoicism.

The other mask of drama, the comic one, owed something to the Romans Plautus and Terence. Again, Shakespeare drained the possibilities of an alien form in *The Comedy of Errors*, modelled on Plautus's *Menechmi* but much more complicated. It might be considered enough to have the confusion of identical twin brothers without adding a pair of servants in the same situation. It must seem to any reader that, in the early phase of his career, Shakespeare was indulging in a kind of mockery of the classic Roman dramaturges. With a tragedy like *Romeo and Juliet* or a comedy like *The Merchant of Venice*, in both of which the comic-tragic division is not clearly drawn, an original talent is at work, Shakespeare is launched.

We must assume that Shakespeare was satisfied with his trade. He made money from it and retired to Stratford as owner of its finest house and of many productive acres. Yet a tradition grew up in the nineteenth century, and perhaps especially among the romantic artists of the Continent, to the effect that Shakespeare was too good for his trade, that he transcended the crude Elizabethan playhouse, and that he ought to be remade after another pattern. Thus, Hector Berlioz found it necessary to exalt this idol into pure music, even spiritualising Romeo and Juliet into wordless melody. Shakespeare's dramatic goal, so it is implied by Goethe, should have been *Faust* Parts I and II. Even in England, where it was accepted that Shakespeare was a professional playwright, the heavy realism of theatrical productions contradicted everything the Globe had stood for. The speed of the cinema has better shown the Shakespearean essence, though at the expense of much of the language. The language, of course, is of paramount importance, and yet a good deal of it has to be cut in both film and stage production. This tends to confirm readers of Shakespeare in the belief that he wrote a text not primarily to be acted, and that its being butchered for performance would not have pleased him. The truth was probably that too much was better than too little and that Shakespeare preferred Burbage's knife or red pencil to petulant demands for more lines.

I think that these Complete Works ought to be read in the context of the circumstances of their first production. These women are really boys; that sequence of lines is to cover a descent from the tarrass to the main stage; 'Hercules and his globe too' is a direct reference to what all the audience can see – the flying flag of the playhouse, Hercules bearing the earth upon it, the motto '*Totus mundus agit histrionem*' (All the world acts a play, is a stage), the name of the theatre itself. And yet no playwright has been less resistant to the forced migration of his dramas to other times and places: modern-dress Shakespeare very nearly always works, abetted by the playwright's own indifference to historical validity (striking clocks and hats in ancient Rome; Ulysses quoting Aristotle). But there is an undoubted danger in the assumption that actors in non-Elizabethan dress are speaking a language that rides above the time of its origin.

For Shakespeare's English, though classified as Early Modern, is not quite ours. We need a glossary to hold us from thinking that a politician was a member of parliament and not a plotting Jesuit, that 'naughty' is rather an inept word to describe a wicked man, that the suburbs are clean, moneyed, and leafy and not the wretched brothel district of the city. The connotations of words whose primary meaning we do not mistake are tied to Shakespeare's own age: the 'hangman's hands' of Macbeth are clotted with entrails as well as blood. It is, one supposes, remarkable that so much of the language hits home as it does. One wonders whether the sound of Shakespeare in his own day, reproduced in ours, would militate against serious acceptance. It is useless reading Chaucer with twentieth-century phonemes – translation is a different matter – and, in an age which has decided on authenticity of musical performance even in Brahms and Dvorak, there are grounds for resuscitating the plays of Shakespeare as the sonic experience that audience knew in the Globe.

We know the phonemic inventory of Elizabethan English, though this is not the place for a detailed catalogue. Word-play in Shakespeare often depends on pronunciations now only found in regional dialects. That reasons should be as plentiful as blackberries depends on 'reasons' being a homophone of 'raisins'. The pun on 'Mousetrap' and 'tropically' in *Hamlet* should remind us that, as in modern American English, a rounded 'o' at the bottom of the mouth was not acceptable in Standard Elizabethan. Generations nourished on the Higher Thespian of Lord Olivier and Sir John Gielgud would find Authentic Shakespeare altogether provincial, even bumpkinishly rural. Much depends on how far we can accept the reality of the situation. A daily exercise in acceptance would be the repetition of Shakespeare's name with its Tudor vowels, which also happen to be the 'grave e' and 'acute e' of modern French.

Of the universality of Shèkespére, of his poetic brilliance, his complexity, even his quite frequent unintelligibility, we have never been in doubt, but it is as well to relate his greatness to the standards of his own time. Ben Jonson, contributing a panegyric to the First Folio, saw that he was greater than Lyly, Kyd and Marlowe, and was even prepared to ask Seneca to make room for him. That he was, in fact, greater than Marlowe may be argued: Marlowe did things Shakespeare never dared to attempt. Other university men, such as Robert Greene, knew that learning could not compete with unschooled genius but were unwilling to admit it. In the Jacobean period, with the appearance of playwrights like Middleton, Tourneur, Webster and possibly Marston, we see skill approximating to that of the Stratford man approaching retirement, though we may consider what they have all learnt from Shakespeare. It was, and one yawns reiterating it, a great age for drama, and we need more than these Complete Works in assessing one particular playwright's genius: we need to dig, even though shallowly, into Peele and Dekker and Beaumont and Fletcher. Shakespeare was a remarkable phenomenon but no miracle. In our own day, of course, he would be.

The Alexander Text

Introduction by Alec Yearling

When it was first published in 1951 Peter Alexander's was the first independently edited single-volume Shakespeare to have appeared in Britain for some fifty years. It continues to provide a reliable and straightforward text for the reader.

Reader should be stressed, for a reader's requirements are different from those of the men who first handled Shakespeare's freshly written pages. They were the actors, members of Shakespeare's company, receiving the raw material for performance. Though none of Shakespeare's major theatrical manuscripts has survived,[1] contemporary evidence indicates that what playwrights wrote at that time were players' scripts: assigned speeches and dialogue, with little in the way of punctuation or stage directions. Movements, points of emphasis, pauses, what props or furniture were involved, were practical matters for the staging process rather than for being inscribed in the text. Even the 'book' – essentially a prompt-copy – prepared by a scribe for use in the playhouse, would lack many of the features required by a reader, especially one separated by some four hundred years from the conventions of Shakespeare's theatre.

Editing Shakespeare, therefore, resembles performing him in being a necessary act of interpretation. The page-*vs*-stage opposition falters when we consider that 'Shakespeare's plays' are and always were words requiring mediation. Historically, that mediation has been imperfect in its details, and sometimes in larger matters. Printers in Shakespeare's day habitually altered spelling and inserted punctuation. Mistakes were made through carelessness or the difficulty of reading manuscript copy. For half of Shakespeare's canon, we have only one printed text – that of the 1623 First Folio – to refer to. This was printed after Shakespeare's death; and there is no sign that the author took any part in proof-reading those plays, or the sonnets, printed in his lifetime. Since the eighteenth century, editors have emended the readings of those early editions in an effort to restore what they think Shakespeare must have meant. Some of their alterations have been inspired, and many highhanded or prejudiced or myopic. A modem editor, with a general idea of the likely characteristics of a Shakespearean or scribal manuscript, and aware of what could happen in the printing-house, has to establish what we may call 'a reading version of the plays containing the words Shakespeare is thought to have written, with the addition of sufficient aids, in layout and stage directions, to allow readers to recreate in their minds something like the dramatic process apparently envisioned by the playwright' – a good deal of which must needs be educated guesswork, since in places Shakespeare's precise words are lost to us.

Consider three examples of lost words. An error arose in the printing of the account of Falstaff's death in *Henry V* [1.3.16], where the Folio (the sole substantially reliable text) has: 'his Nose was as sharpe as a Pen, and a Table of greene fields.' To make sense of that *Table*, Lewis Theobald suggested in 1726 that the passage should read 'a [=he] babbled of green fields', a convincing emendation followed by subsequent editors, since handwritten *babld* could be misread as *table* (though *talkd* is another, plainer, possibility). Elsewhere plausible solutions have been less forthcoming. In *Coriolanus* [2.3.112] the hero disparages his gown of humility as 'this wolvish toge' (Alexander; the Folio has 'this Wooluish tongue', the printer at sea over both adjective and noun). But there seems nothing wolfish about a gown of humility, and one may find *woolish*, *foolish*, and *womanish* among editors' replacement readings. Again, in *Measure for Measure* [3.1.95, 98] the Folio twice uses the word *prenzie* to describe Angelo and his qualities; apparently meaningless, it was replaced in the Second Folio by *Princely*, and in Alexander's and most modern editions by *precise*, a term used earlier of Angelo, and a plausible reading. But whether it is right, and how the repeated mistake arose, we do not know.

Faced with these and plentiful other cruxes, some editors in previous centuries were carried away in their earnest efforts to correct what were seen as errors in texts debauched by players' additions and contaminated wholesale by printers' botching. Modern editors tend to tread more warily in seeking to provide an intelligible text which diverges relatively little from the original. The reasons for this caution are complex: scientific procedures in bibliography and textual criticism, together with a post-Romantic deference to the author, and a twentieth-century awareness of literature's capacity for difficulty, all foster editorial conservatism.

The texts, though, continue to present their range of imperfections. *The Taming of the Shrew* is incomplete, lacking the close of its framing action. *Timon of Athens* is more patchily unfinished. An editor can do no more than make maimed texts presentable, as too with *Pericles*, which has its peculiar problems. Omitted for reasons unknown from the First Folio, it appeared in the Third Folio of 1664, reprinted from the latest in a series of Quarto reprints of which the earliest is dated 1609. That text, for at least the first third of its length, is faulty. In the sixth line of its first scene a stage direction (*Music*) has become incorporated into the dialogue ('Musicke bring in our daughter ...'), and matters go on from there. It is still a point of debate whether these early scenes are by another's hand, or represent a garbled Shakespearean original. And if garbled, how, and to what extent? An editor's mediation here assumes major proportions. Other plays exist in more than one version. The 1604 Quarto and the Folio texts of *Hamlet* each contain passages not in the other; an earlier, unreliable Quarto contains in distorted form yet other material. The play, it seems, had been differently cut on different occasions. But were the cuts theatrical exigencies, or the dramatist's later shapings of a long and complex play? And which version superseded which? Alexander's is like most modern editions in opting for safety, including everything by conflating the two authoritative versions: lacking Shakespearean guidance, this is the path of humility. One might, however, conceive of this as a well-intentioned misrepresentation if it incorporated material intended for deletion. The same problem arises with *King Lear*, where the differences between Quarto and Folio go far beyond printers' errors and divergent transcriptions of a single original text: indeed, it would seem that the play was at some point rewritten. Scenes are trimmed, sentences dropped, phrases altered. Thus in the Folio, Lear addresses Cordelia as 'our last and least' daughter, and in the Quarto says that she is 'Although the last, not least in our deere loue': there is a clear difference of emphasis and yet another editorial choice to be made. (Alexander, 1.1.82, follows the Folio reading.) But again, which version represents Shakespeare's later thoughts? And can one speak of a 'final version' when dealing with scripts for performances and revivals under changeable circumstances?

A reader may ask how far all this makes any real difference. Often the difference is, in the larger context, marginal. Whether Angelo is prenzie or princely or precise, the dialogue hereabouts is essentially unaffected, with the heroine and her brother still expressing shock at the contrast between Angelo's public and private faces. Sometimes, though, the blurred spot is closer to the play's central concerns. In *Hamlet* [1.4.36–38] the prince reflects on how a natural fault may unbalance a man's reputation: 'the dram of eale/Doth all the noble substance of a doubt/To his own scandle.' So reads the Quarto – the passage is absent from the Folio – and while it makes sense of a sort, it is not good sense. The play shows the prince himself as mixed in his qualities, and tender of his good name; the passage matters, and despite teasing by some of its editors, it will not come clear.

Assessment of a play's shape may also be affected by textual anomalies. Hamlet more than once berates himself for delaying his revenge, though mostly this takes place in the first half of the play when he is also seeking proof of his uncle's guilt. One soliloquy in this vein, however, comes later, [4.4] ('How all occasions do inform against me ...'), prompted by the sight of Fortinbras going to war. This passage has been thought odd at this point in the action, since Hamlet is effectively powerless, under guard and being sent to England. How significant is it then that one text, the Folio, omits it? The difference is between a Hamlet whose mind adapts to changing circumstances, and one stuck in a fixed mode of self-condemnation. Was the Folio cut to prevent just such fixity?

Throughout, Alexander includes dubious or debated material when it forms part of the traditionally received canon. While *Macbeth* is, compared to the other tragedies, notably short, with our (Folio) text possibly an abbreviated one, it is also thought that the Hecate scenes [3.5; 4.1] were added by Middleton for a later revival. But we lack certitude, and informed readers can make up their own minds from a conservative text. When faced with a manifest error, but with nothing authoritative to put in its place, Alexander simply registers it, as with the bracketed phrase in the second line of Sonnet 146, where an error of repetition in the 1609 printing leaves no clue to the proper reading.

Dealing, then, with such originals, this edition follows a middle course between straight reproduction of the texts, and the interventionist editorial practice once common. Spelling is modernised, a wise procedure despite attendant problems.[2]

Punctuation, shaping the syntax, is unfussy but necessarily heavier than that of the printing house. Context dictates the amount of stage-direction: where the dialogue points strongly, Alexander supplies reinforcement (the action and sound sequence in *The Winter's Tale* [3.3.46–69] where the baby is abandoned while a hunt impinges nearby); where it is content to hint (Malvolio fingering his chain of office in *Twelfth Night* 2.5.57), he lets the hint speak for itself. Act and scene divisions are based on those of the Folio and of earlier editors. Location directions orientate without being over-elaborate. In *The Merchant of Venice* we find '*Venice. A Street*' and '*Belmont. Portia's house*', where the first printings allow settings to be inferred from the characters present or from what they say ('This is the pent-house ...'. 2.6.1). These formal demarcations, though not authorial, facilitate the location of particular passages. A necessary price is paid in that they occasionally obscure the fluidity of the originals' scenic conception, as when in *Romeo and Juliet* Act 1 Scenes 4, 5 the Folio's smooth transition as the young men gatecrash the Capulets' party ('They march about the Stage, and Seruing men come forth with their napkins') becomes a complete change of scene, though with the 'march' retained since the dialogue suggests just such a mock-serious procession. When in this connection an intractable episode arises, Alexander's response, though open to question, indicates his care for the reader. In *Antony and Cleopatra* [5.2] Cleopatra is captured by the Roman soldiers. She is in her 'monument', in Act 4 Scene 14 explicitly presented as an upper acting area[3]. Alexander assumes consistency, and follows earlier editors in inserting an elaborate stage direction involving a ladder as the queen is 'surpris'd.' The Folio, probably through a mishap, lacks any direction. If the monument-location has shifted to the lower stage, the soldiers need only enter at the back; but Alexander, considering the readers' likely envisioning of the scene, provides a version which is both a possible staging in Jacobean terms, and a re-creation for imaginations attuned to the conventions of novel and film, where things and places have a solidity and continuity, unlike the word- and action-orientated Renaissance stage. It is this kind of tactful aid, reinforced by sound scholarship, which makes the Alexander Shakespeare continuingly useful.

Notes

[1] See Appendix on the passage from the composite play *Sir Thomas More.*

[2] For a judicious defence of modern-spelling editions, see Stanley Wells, *Re-Editing Shakespeare for the Modern Reader*, Ch. 1, 'Old and Modern Spelling.' (Oxford, 1984)

[3] The staging of the monument receives detailed consideration in Appendix IV of M. R. Ridley's Arden edition of the play. (Methuen, 1954)

Introduction to the 1951 Edition*

by Peter Alexander

It is still true in the study of Shakespeare that 'the dispersion of error is the first step in the discovery of truth'. The scholarly criticism of his plays, which found but casual expression in his lifetime and took systematic shape only in the eighteenth century when men of letters and scholars found the editing of his works a source of profit or reputation, began by remarking that he ignored the Rules. These rules or laws of the drama were generalizations from the practice of the Greek dramatists; and Renaissance critics and their eighteenth century disciples regarded plays that failed to conform to these Laws as deficient in Art. Shakespeare ignored the Rules so constantly that his critics, however much they admired his natural powers, could not accept him as a great Artist. This opinion is still maintained to-day by men of distinction in letters; but it is an opinion born of a fashion in European thought that has passed away, and it survives only as a prejudice that will no longer bear critical examination.

It is now realised that this demand for the scholarly imitation of the external or accidental features of classical masterpieces is an appeal to the letter not to the spirit of Art. No one to-day will argue that Westminster Abbey is inferior as a work of art to St. Paul's because the Gothic builders were not so familiar as Wren with 'the four regular orders of Greece'. Indeed, the complete revolution wrought by the progress of European criticism is best seen in the attitude of the French, who were the most jealous guardians of what they considered 'classical' form. The French were in this phase of their culture as severe in their denunciations of their own early architecture as they were of the lawless Shakespeare. Now France is proud to reckon the buildings they once despised as Gothic as their greatest and most original contribution to the art of the

*To spare the reader a succession of footnotes, I mention here some of the studies I should otherwise have to refer him to in passing. J. S. Smart's *Shakespeare: Truth and Tradition*, 'a new landmark in Shakespeare scholarship' is the best introduction to a study of *A Life of Shakespeare* by J. Quincy Adams; the student will then be in a position to profit by *Shakespeare: A Study of Facts and Problems* by Sir Edmund Chambers. The best idea of the structure of Shakespeare's theatre is given by *The Globe Playhouse* by John C. Adams, of Shakespeare's Audience by Alfred Harbage's *Shakespeare's Audience*. On dramatic questions Granville-Barker's *Prefaces* are most helpful. Bradley's *Shakespearean Tragedy* is still an important guide in interpretation, and those who fancy that recent 'historical or objective' criticism has outmoded his method should read Alfred Harbage's *As They Liked It*. Dr. Tillyard's *Shakespeare's History Plays* is a valuable study of Shakespeare's attitude to his material and of the implications it suggests; and in Dr. Ivor Brown's *Shakespeare* can be seen the reactions to academic opinion of one familiar with the modern theatre. All Dr. Hotson's works have added valuable touches to the social background of Shakespeare's life and his *Shakespeare's Sonnets Dated* makes further apology for the dates here suggested for Shakespeare's 'First Period' unnecessary. Pollard's *Shakespeare's Fight with the Pirates* is the ideal preparation for Sir Walter Greg's *The Editorial Problem in Shakespeare*, an authoritative review that will enable the reader to study with advantage Professor Dover Wilson's *Introductions* to the Cambridge 'New Shakespeare'. The views summarized in the introduction now before the reader will be found argued in some detail in the writer's *Shakespeare's Life and Art*.

world. And for the very same reasons the English may now claim that Shakespeare is the greatest artist to whom their race has so far given birth – a dramatist unsurpassed, as all acknowledge, in the gifts that nature alone can bestow, but as unsurpassed for the judgment that gives to work almost as various as nature itself the unity and commanding power found only in the world's supreme masterpieces.

When Rowe in 1709 and Pope in 1725 ventured on the systematic criticism of Shakespeare, so important did the Rules seem to them and their contemporaries that they deduced from Shakespeare's practice three important conclusions that were long accepted as almost self-evident. First: Shakespeare could not have received any instruction worthy of the name of education, and consequently Stratford where he was born and brought up must have been peopled merely by ignorant and unbookish rustics. Second: the form in which Shakespeare cast his dramas, not being prescribed by the Rules of Art, was dictated by the dramatist's desire to gratify, in his pursuit of gain, an ignorant and untaught audience. Third: so little interest, except financial, did Shakespeare and his even more ignorant fellow-actors take in his works that his plays were transmitted to posterity in so sadly mangled a condition, so full of interpolations from hands other than his own, that it was hardly possible to judge in many instances which were and which were not his writings, or to believe that we had them in a form even approximating to that in which he left them.

On the first and third of these issues modern criticism has shown that in general the truth is the very opposite to what was once so confidently maintained; on the second the wiser judgments of the great critics of the past are being gradually confirmed and developed.

STRATFORD

In Elizabethan England every self-respecting community made careful provision for the education of its children. Measured by this standard the inhabitants of Stratford could claim an honourable place amongst their countrymen. Education had in its beginnings in England been the business of the Church, but, like many other functions of the Church, education had in the course of the Middle Ages been transferred to lay administration; and the school at Stratford had passed from the Church into the keeping of the Guild of the Holy Cross, the organisation in which the social instincts of the locality, according to the fashion of the time, found expression. There has been a long-standing belief that the schools of England were largely the creation of the Reformation, but this serious historical error was exposed by A. F. Leach; and in his *Social History of England* Sir George Trevelyan has summarised the true course of events when he says that it was not the Reformation that made the Schools of England but the schools that made the Reformation. In 1553 the school at Stratford was renamed The King's New School of Stratford-upon-Avon; but the school owed nothing to Edward VI or his Council, and was not new by some centuries.

This renaming of the school merely marks the change from the old Guild system to a more modern form of administration in which Stratford became by Royal Charter a corporate borough under a Bailiff, Alderman, and Burgesses. The new Common Council, whose original members had all served on the Guild, now paid the Vicar and the School-master and administered the property and revenues of the Guild. It was during this period of transition that the poet's father, John Shakespeare, came to Stratford.

John Shakespeare must have left his father's home in Snitterfield, some four miles to the north of Stratford – where his father Richard Shakespeare worked as a yeoman farmer – at least seven years before 1552. In that year is found the first mention of him in Stratford records, and he is already in business as a glover in Henley Street; and to become a member of the Craft of Glovers, Whitetawers and Collarmakers, he must have served a seven year apprenticeship. By 1557 John Shakespeare had so prospered in business that he was able to return to the district of his birth to marry the youngest daughter of Robert Arden, the gentleman from whom his father, Richard Shakespeare, rented his land.

Further than Richard Shakespeare no one has yet traced with any certainty the poet's paternal connections. But on his mother's side he was related to one of the great families of the West Country, for Robert Arden came of a younger branch of the Ardens of Park Hall, a family settled in the Arden district of Warwickshire, from which they took their name, from before the Norman Conquest.

Of the marriage of John Shakespeare and Mary Arden there were eight children – four sons and four daughters. William, the third child and first son, was christened on 26th April 1564. The only member of this group to survive the poet was his younger sister Joan, who is mentioned in his will. The other three girls died in infancy, and though his brothers reached manhood they too predeceased him.

In the year of his marriage John Shakespeare was elected to the Common Council and soon took a leading part in its affairs. He acted as Chamberlain for four years – a term of office without precedent in Stratford – presumably because he was specially qualified for keeping the borough accounts. In 1568 he became Bailiff, and by virtue of his office a gentleman entitled to his coat of arms. In 1577, however, after twenty years of continuous service, he suddenly ceased to attend the Council meetings.

It has been conjectured that in his zeal for public affairs he had neglected his own business; and he certainly, at this time, was or wished to be taken for a poor man, mortgaging as he did a valuable property inherited by his wife. The authorities however took a different view of his circumstances: in 1580 he was summoned before the Queen's Bench in Westminster and fined £20 for failing to provide security that he would keep the Queen's peace; and on the same day he was fined another £20, as he had stood surety for another man in the same position as himself. That this was the outcome of the measures of John Whitgift, the new Bishop of Worcester, who had come to Worcester as he was later to go to Canterbury to restore church discipline, there can be little doubt. John Shakespeare's troubles therefore were probably political not financial, and that he was a 'recusant' there is no doubt, though the grounds of his discontent are unknown.

In 1582 his son William married Ann Hathaway, the daughter of an old family friend. The licence was issued in November 1582; the first child of the marriage, Susanna, was born in May 1583. All attempts to show from an examination of the Bishop's *Register* and the circumstances of the marriage that it reflects discredit on either party rest on the unhistorical conjecture that the church ceremony was then, as it would be now, the marriage ceremony. The church ceremony, for which the licence was obtained, was in respectable Elizabethan society frequently no more than an after-ceremony to the marriage proper; the licence is in no respect out of the ordinary. Ann Hathaway may have been eight years older than her husband, but this is not absolutely certain, and even if it were this would be no proof of irregularity. Those who still insist that there was some impropriety in the matter may be asked to produce their evidence. In February 1585, the twins, Hamnet and Judith, were christened at Stratford.

How Shakespeare intended to support a wife and family is a natural question, and fortunately the only tradition about Shakespeare's youth that has any trustworthy pedigree behind it supplies the answer. The group of traditions that gathers round Rowe's account of Shakespeare's deer-stealing and of his prosecution by Sir Thomas Lucy has not only no pedigree but is contradicted by the fact that there was no deer-park at Charlecote at that time, the Lucy family establishing one there only in the next generation. The passage from the first scene of *The Merry Wives of Windsor* that is regularly cited as Shakespeare's reminiscence of this adventure is more probably the origin of the story itself; and, as Professor Hotson has shown, any personal reference in the lines may be directed towards a man very different in character from Sir Thomas Lucy. This and the other popular stories about Shakespeare's youth are the kind of conjecture commonly drawn in to fill the vacuum that biographers naturally abhor. The story however that the youthful Shakespeare was a country schoolmaster rests on a quite different foundation. The antiquary John Aubrey, who made a valuable series of notes on the men of Shakespeare's generation, was advised to visit William Beeston, then an old man, but well informed about the history of the stage, for he, like his father, Christopher Beeston, had been an actor and actor-manager. His father, Christopher, had actually been in the same company as Shakespeare for a number of years. That Aubrey discussed with Beeston the observation by Jonson on Shakespeare's 'small Latin and less Greek' is revealed in Aubrey's note: 'Though as Ben Jonson says of him that he had but little Latin and less Greek, he understood Latin pretty well, for he had been in his younger years a schoolmaster in the country'. In the margin Aubrey recorded that his authority was Mr. Beeston.

Shakespeare's next step – his departure to London – is a venture that needs no fanciful embroidery to make it intelligible. Conscious, like a later country school-master, of the genius within him, he naturally sought the field where alone his talents could find their full employment.

LONDON

Those who think of Shakespeare as an ignorant youth driven by a wrathful landlord from his careless rustic existence have now to explain how he started on his new and very different career in London. It is not surprising that some look elsewhere, to Bacon or to Lord Oxford, for the author of *Hamlet* or the *Sonnets*; for the explanation usually offered is as improbable as the transformation it attempts to account for. Shakespeare began, we are told, by rewriting the plays of others, among them those of Robert Greene. Why the works of a writer who boasted of a degree from both Universities should have been turned over to an illiterate new-comer is hardly to be understood; and the evidence that was for long advanced by scholars in support of this story is now seen to indicate a different and more natural course of events.

Those, however, who accept Beeston's statement that Shakespeare had been a schoolmaster find no difficulty in understanding his beginnings and progress as a dramatist. No miracle except that of genius, no hidden hand, whether that of Bacon or Lord Oxford, need be invoked. Shakespeare began as any educated young man might have begun by adapting for his purposes the models prescribed by the fashion of his time, the Latin authors familiar to him from his schooling.

Before grouping his plays in the approximate order of their composition one important observation that emerges from such a chronological arrangement as almost self-evident must be considered. Viewed as a whole and as the successive episodes in the life of one creative mind his plays reveal in their creator powers of development and self-criticism found, whether the medium be music, or painting, or literature, only in the greatest masters – those who gave to their art the devotion of a life-time. To suppose that this development could come by chance or from the mere desire to gain the applause or money of the ignorant is to deny the evidence of experience. Shakespeare had of course to make the major contribution to the fortunes of a large and important Company of actors, and at times this part of his task affected his work, but such plays as *Hamlet* and *Othello* are clearly the creations of a man who had thought long and deeply about his art. A later and in its own opinion better instructed generation did not hesitate to deny to Shakespeare even the rudiments of stage craft. The more carefully, however, this side of Shakespeare's work is examined the more clearly it is seen to be skilfully contrived for his own stage; and, what is more important, the more clearly it is seen that his craft is not an end in itself but the technical mastery inseparable from any powerful manifestation of art.

Beginning then with plays fashioned on the models then approved – plays so little like his masterpieces that they are frequently attributed to other hands – Shakespeare soon developed an original style of his own that commanded the applause of a wide public. In spite, however, of his popularity and success he was not content to repeat himself but from about his thirty-fifth year started on the series of tragic masterpieces, matched, if at all, only by the drama of ancient Athens. Nor do the works of his later years echo in feebler tones these triumphs but bring with their colouring and glow the splendid evening to the noon-day intensity of his genius – a conclusion visionary and apocalyptic.

First Period

From Shakespeare's arrival in London (1584) to his joining the Lord Chamberlain's men (1594)

No definite date can be given for Shakespeare's arrival in London; but by 1594 he had a body of work to his credit that must have occupied a considerable number of years. Naturally no details survive of his London connections when he was still unknown to the world, but what evidence there is indicates that he was for a time at least a member of Lord Pembroke's Company, and that for them he wrote some of his early plays.

Before the end of this period Shakespeare had established himself as a popular dramatist and as a poet of whom much was expected. The first reference to him in print, from the pen of the poet and dramatist Robert Greene, provides, indirectly, evidence of his success. Greene had failed to find in London the reward he expected for his work, and his irregular life was closing in misery and want. He felt with much bitterness that a writer received but a small return for his plays compared with the drawings taken by the performers; and on his death-bed he wrote for publication a letter to some playwrights with whom he claimed acquaintance, warning them by his own fate against depending on such ungrateful employers as the actors. 'Base minded men all three of you, if by my misery you be not warn'd; for unto none of you (like me) sought those burrs to cleave – those Puppets (I mean) that spake from our mouths, those Anticks garnisht in our colours.'

Greene then, as the allusions indicate, goes on to attack Shakespeare not merely as an actor but also as an actor-dramatist whose success, though undeserved, was making it more difficult for Greene and his friends to gain a living. 'Yes trust them not; for there is an upstart Crow, beautified with our feathers, that with his *Tiger's heart wrapt in a Player's hide* supposes he is as well able to bombast out a blank verse as the best of you; and being an absolute *Johannes fac totum* is in his own conceit the only Shake-scene in a country.'

Soon after Greene's death his friend Chettle printed this letter in a pamphlet entitled *Greene's Groatsworth of Wit bought with a Million of Repentance.*

Marlowe, with whom Greene claimed acquaintance, was naturally displeased with the letter, for Greene like many self-confessed sinners found satisfaction in proclaiming the faults of his friends. Shakespeare also was annoyed. Chettle, three months later, in a preface to his own *Kind-Heart's Dream* refused to admit he had wronged Marlowe but made full apology for what he confessed was an unwarranted attack on Shakespeare. 'I am as sorry as if the original fault had been my fault, because myself have seen his demeanour no less civil than he excellent in the quality he professes. Besides, divers of worship have reported his uprightness of dealing, which argues his honesty, and his facetious grace in writing, that approves his Art.'

Approximate order of composition of Shakespeare's Works

Period	Comedies	Histories	Tragedies
1584	Comedy of Errors	1, 2, 3 Henry VI	Titus Andronicus
	Taming of the Shrew	Richard III	
	Two Gentlemen of Verona	King John	
I	1592		
		poems	
		Venus and Adonis	
	Love's Labour's Lost	Rape of Lucrece	
1594			
	Midsummer-Night's Dream	Richard II	Romeo and Juliet
	Merchant of Venice	1 Henry IV	
II	Merry Wives of Windsor	2 Henry IV	
	Much Ado About Nothing		
	As You Like It	Henry V	
1599			
	Twelfth Night		Julius Cæsar
	Troilus and Cressida		Hamlet
	Measure for Measure		Othello
	All's Well		Timon of Athens
III			Lear
			Macbeth
			Antony and Cleopatra
			Coriolanus
1608			
	Pericles		
IV	Cymbeline		
	Winter's Tale		
1613	Tempest	Henry VIII	

As Chettle's words indicate, Shakespeare was already highly thought of in courtly circles; and this is confirmed by the publication of his *Venus and Adonis* in 1593 and the *Rape of Lucrece* in 1594, with dedications to Lord Southampton, whose gracious entertainment of the poet is publicly and warmly acknowledged in the dedicatory epistle to *Lucrece*. Further evidence of Shakespeare's familiarity with courtly and learned circles is found in his *Love's Labour's Lost* with its copious allusion to personalities, events, and fashions, then current topics in such society. Shakespeare's poems were no doubt written during the years 1591-93 when the plague and other troubles had closed the London theatres and the Companies had to tour the provinces for a living. Shakespeare can hardly have been on tour during this period of composition, and it was not till the return to London of the leading companies, and after the extensive regrouping that it made necessary, that he joined the Lord Chamberlain's men.

Venus and Adonis, although Shakespeare's first published work, was that of a writer of recognised reputation. His success had been made on the stage; but actors were very unwilling to publish their pieces, partly owing to lack of copyright protection, partly owing to their belief that publication would lessen their takings at the theatre. In this policy Shakespeare acquiesced throughout his life-time, never hastening into print with new pieces. The straitened circumstances of the actors however during their enforced absence from London gave the publishers a chance to pick up some of these much desired productions, and versions, good and bad, of certain of Shakespeare's plays now appeared in print.

From this and related evidence one can with some confidence assign to the period before the poems: his first tragedy, *Titus Andronicus*; his comedies, *The Comedy of Errors, The Taming of the Shrew, The Two Gentlemen of Verona*; his history plays, *Henry VI* (in three parts), and possibly *Richard III*. The assumption that Shakespeare did not begin his work as a dramatist till 1591 rests on the misinterpretation by Malone of Greene's attack on Shakespeare. Malone interpreted it as a charge of plagiarism. Now that this interpretation is rejected the conclusions drawn from it are unsupported, and indeed contradicted not only by the evidence of Greene and Chettle but by the circumstances in which his Poems and early plays were printed. Shakespeare must have been working as a dramatist for some years before 1590. This period of successful work explains how by 1594 he could take a leading place in the first company of the age.

Second Period

From Shakespeare's joining the Lord Chamberlain's men in 1594 to the opening of the Globe Theatre in 1599

The Company which Shakespeare now joined included Richard Burbage, who was to prove himself in the roles Shakespeare provided for him the greatest tragic actor of his age, Will Kemp the popular comedian, and John Heminge and Henry Condell, who became the Company's managers and later Shakespeare's first editors. Their headquarters were at The Theatre, the first play-house to be built in England for theatrical performances.

During this period Shakespeare was living, as the subsidy rolls indicate, in easy circumstances in London; and there still survives a letter to him from a friend of his father, Richard Quiney, who was twice Bailiff of Stratford, that confirms the evidence of the subsidies. In 1596 John Shakespeare obtained from the College of Heralds a grant of arms. He was entitled to this as a former Bailiff of Stratford, but although nearly thirty years before the actual grant he had taken the preliminary steps towards this dignity, he had allowed the matter to lapse. It was no doubt considered proper in view of the poet's position in London to complete the necessary formalities, and the family shield now showed 'in a field of gold upon a bend sable, a spear of the first, the point upward, headed argent', and above as crest 'a falcon, with his wings displayed, standing on a wreath of his colours, supporting a spear, armed, headed, and steeled silver'. The motto was 'NON SANS DROICT'. In 1597 Shakespeare bought New Place at Stratford.

Whatever his interests at this time in his personal and private affairs, Shakespeare's mind must have been unsparingly given to his work in the theatre. In 1598 Francis Meres in his *Palladis Tamia* describes him as 'the most excellent in both kinds (comedy and tragedy) for the stage', and adds 'for comedy, witnes his *Gentlemen of Verona*, his *Errors*, his *Love labours lost*, his *Love labours wonne*, his *Midsummer night's dreame*, and his *Merchant of Venice*: for tragedy his *Richard II, Richard III, Henry IV, King John, Titus Andronicus*, and his *Romeo and Juliet*.' He also mentions his poems and 'his sugred Sonnets among his private friends'.

The period opens with a group of 'poetical plays', *Midsummer-Night's Dream, Richard II*, and *Romeo and Juliet*. The comedy is perfect in its kind and unsurpassed for the marvellous harmony it establishes among so many apparently discordant elements. The tragedy is another of the early masterpieces and anticipates in its spacious design and intensity of handling the works of Shakespeare's full maturity. But for some years to come comedy and prose were the main interest, and this, in the figure of Falstaff, overwhelms even the historical interest in the two parts of *Henry IV*. With Falstaff gone, there is little left for *Henry V* but pageantry; yet this opportunity for costume effects and patriotic verse may have been not unwelcome to Shakespeare as a suitable opening for the new Globe Theatre in 1599.

Third Period

From the opening of the Globe (1599) to the taking over of the Blackfriars Theatre (1608)

The Globe Theatre was opened about May 1599. With the lease of the ground on which the Theatre stood nearing an end, the Burbages bought the old dining-hall of the Blackfriars and furnished it as a theatre, but an influential circle who lived in the vicinity had this project defeated. The Burbages then acquired ground just over London Bridge on the Bankside. To this side, south of the river, they transferred some of the main timbers from the Theatre; force was necessary for the landlord hoped to retain their building for his own profit. To meet this additional expense they took into partnership as 'householders' five of the leading 'sharers' of the company, of whom Shakespeare was one. The Blackfriars they leased to the Children of the Queen's Revels. The actors were choir boys and their theatre was described as 'private' to distinguish it from ordinary theatres where the charges were not beyond the vulgar purse.

Near the beginning of this period Shakespeare's father died, in 1601; at the end, his mother, in 1608. His daughter Susanna married the well-known physician John Hall in 1607. The great public event of the time was the death of Queen Elizabeth and the arrival of James in London in May 1603. The King at once took over the Lord

Chamberlain's Company and they were now known as the King's Men. The senior members became Grooms of the Royal Chamber and in that capacity formed part of the entourage of the Spanish Ambassador who came in August 1604, to negotiate a peace between England and Spain.

During part of this period, as Professor Wallace has shown, Shakespeare lodged with a Huguenot family in Silver Street. He was now in a position to make considerable purchases of land at Stratford and investments in the tithes of the parish. As before, however, Shakespeare must have given unremitting attention to his art, for he was now from his thirty-fifth year to engage in the most sustained and intense effort of his career. The plays that were to make the name of the Globe for ever famous were very different from *Henry V*. During the next ten years Shakespeare produced there his seven great tragedies: *Julius Cæsar, Hamlet, Othello, Lear, Macbeth, Antony and Cleopatra*, and *Coriolanus*.

Many explanations have been offered for this apparently sudden shift in Shakespeare's interest. Some have blamed the dark lady of the Sonnets and the conduct of the friend for inducing a mood of gloom and misanthropy; others have dwelt on Shakespeare's connections with Essex and Southampton, and the former's death on the block, as the cause of his disillusionment and pessimism; others again see in this tragic mood Shakespeare's infection with the spirit of a new age. The accidents of life undoubtedly provide the material on which the imagination operates; but the relationship between this accidental and the universal element in art is not so simple as cause and effect. The process of transformation is even more complicated and vital than that of digestion. But it is unnecessary to attempt an analysis of this psychological problem here, for the tragedies rightly interpreted do not reveal a spirit of gloom and disillusionment.

Many critics have dwelt on the bitterness and disgust in the works of this period. And it is true that nowhere can one find a fiercer invective and more withering scorn than that poured by these plays on the baser side of our nature. The picture of man dressed in a little brief authority playing his fantastic tricks before high heaven with an effrontery that makes the angels weep has never been drawn with more penetrating irony. And as a background we have the cowardly or malignant complacency in our natures that tolerates such shameless wickedness. Passage after passage emphasizes the degradation to which men can sink. It is summed up in one terrible line from *King Lear*: 'A dog's obey'd in office.'

King Lear has been described as a tragedy of ingratitude – an ingratitude that divides parent from child and splits the very core of human existence. And the elements seem to take part in the confusion as the old and cast-off father rages on the heath with a fury that out-tongues the elements. But those who find in this fury the climax of the drama have missed half the vision and the half that is greater than the whole. The design on which the drama is constructed is one familiar to great spirits in all ages, and is perhaps exhibited in its simplest elements in the old story of Elijah fleeing from Jezebel's vengeance and how as he stood at the mouth of a cave 'a great and strong wind rent the mountains and brake in pieces the rocks before the Lord; but the Lord was not in the wind; and after the wind an earthquake, but the Lord was not in the earthquake; and after the earthquake a fire, but the Lord was not in the fire; and after the fire a still small voice'.

The heart of Shakespeare's drama is not reached till the storm and tempest are over and we come on the stillness of Lear's reconciliation with Cordelia. Here at last he recognises goodness for what it is in its own right. And the play's real theme is the gratitude of the converted heart at such a revelation. To see the virtues struggling in a world where their very virtue is the cause of their undoing is to be aware of tragedy; but – and this is the touch of nature that makes the reader kin with the poet – this makes us love the virtues not less but more. Had Shakespeare not seen so clearly the hollowness of the world he could not have created with such passionate brooding those spirits whom his art has made the dwellers for all time in the imaginations of men. He is not confounded by his terrible visions, for he sees in the midst of them what walks unscathed; and we read his plays because, however unconsciously, we share in that triumph, and have at least a sense, however our intelligence or conduct may later deny it, of what the soul hungers to attain to.

This revelation which is the consummation of his art did not come to Shakespeare suddenly or because a woman was false or a friend disloyal. It is born of the modest and ceaseless years of thought and labour which are not without their intimations of the final triumph of this period. Viewed in retrospect the humour and comedy, which his earlier critics found more natural to his genius, are only another aspect, a partial realisation, of his tragic vision. Philosophers have indeed maintained that tragedy and comedy have another and finer connection than that of contrast; but, though there have been great tragic artists and great comic artists before and since Shakespeare's time, nowhere are they found united as in his work, and in such a manner that each but adds a new force to its apparent opposite.

Viewed after the event, the tragic period is seen as the natural development of the previous periods and to be explained only in so far as we can explain to ourselves the growth and nature of Shakespeare's art.

Fourth Period

From the taking over of the Blackfriars (1608) to the burning of the Globe Theatre (1613)

The manager of the Children at the Blackfriars theatre was foolish enough to allow indiscreet stage allusions to royalty that led to the suppression of his company. The Burbages and a group of actors as 'householders' that included Shakespeare took over from him his lease, and the King's men now acted at the Blackfriars during the winter months instead of in the open Globe Theatre, to the very substantial increase in their takings. The King's men were now too well established in official favour for the old objections to their presence there to be raised again.

The plays of this period have happy endings; but to distinguish their peculiar colouring from that of his earlier comedies they have been called Romances. Once again critics have dwelt on the contrasts between this and the previous period and denied any spiritual continuity between them, or have paradoxically asserted that the Romances are the flight into a world of make-believe that alone could save the poet from the madness in which his tragic thoughts would inevitably have engulfed him. Or again the fashion of the time is thought by some to have directed Shakespeare's interest to this type of play.

But the tragedies are the foundation on which the Romances rest. If Shakespeare had found the heart of man wanting in the fiery trial of the tragedies, what would be the hopes and aspirations in which human nature reclothes itself with every new generation as regularly as the flowers return with the spring – what would these hopes and aspirations be but will-o'-the-wisps to lure mankind to its destruction, or to leave it, should it survive, bogged in disillusion and a dreary materialism?

If fashion had anything to do with Shakespeare's return to comedy, it was because it gave him an opportunity for the expression of something he had now very much at heart, something that came naturally after the struggle of the tragedies, as naturally as Prospero's sympathies with Miranda's hopes and fears.

There can be little doubt that the *Tempest*, considered in conjunction with what we know of Shakespeare's arrangements at this date for taking over his house in Stratford from his cousin Thomas Greene, the town-clerk, indicates that he intended it to be his farewell to the stage. Persuaded no doubt by the importunity of his old colleagues he returned to take a final bow in *Henry VIII*. During the first performance of the piece, on 29th June 1613, the Globe was burnt to the ground; and this accident, for lack of more precise knowledge, may be taken as marking the conclusion of Shakespeare's work as an actor and dramatist.

STRATFORD

Shakespeare seems to have passed his last days quietly at Stratford, though there is a record of at least one visit to London. He made his will in January 1615 or 1616, and revised it on 25th March 1616, after the marriage of his second daughter Judith to Thomas Quiney in February 1616. He remembers amongst other friends his old colleagues, Burbage, Heminge and Condell, the last survivors of the group with which he had acted for some twenty years. He makes provision for Judith and for his sister Joan Hart, but the bulk of his estate is settled on his daughter Susanna and her heirs. His wife was obviously going to live with her daughter, who was, if what she put on her mother's grave gives any echo of truth, devoted to her.

Shakespeare died on St. George's day, 23rd April 1616, and was buried, having this right as a tithe-holder, in the Chancel of the Church at Stratford. The monument on the north wall was erected sometime before 1623. In 1623 his wife was buried beside him, and his daughter Susanna not far away in 1649. She left a daughter Elizabeth Hall who had married Thomas Nash and, on his death, Sir John Bernard, but was to die without issue. Judith Shakespeare had three sons who all died childless before her. From his sister only, and that through her second son Thomas, can those living today who are related to Shakespeare claim their descent.

THE FIRST FOLIO

In 1623, seven years after Shakespeare's death, his old friends and fellow-actors, John Heminge and Henry Condell, gave the world the first collected edition of Shakespeare's plays. This is now known as the First Folio, because of its format and to distinguish it from the Second, Third, and Fourth Folios, issued in 1632, 1663, and 1685 respectively. Each of these later Folios is in turn based on its predecessor. Heminge and Condell attributed thirty-six plays to Shakespeare, all that are included in the present volume except *Pericles*, for *Pericles*, although its omission by Shakespeare's colleagues is good evidence that it is not wholly his, undoubtedly contains scenes from his pen.

Their long friendship with Shakespeare, their admiration for his genius, their position of authority in the company, for they had acted as its managers for many years, made Heminge and Condell in some respects well qualified for their task. They, if anyone did, must have known what was by Shakespeare and what was not; their office in the company had made them familiar with his manuscripts. Yet their edition has presented students with problems for which reasonable solutions have been found only in recent years; problems that may be summarized here in the questions: Why did Shakespeare himself not supervise the printing of his plays; and why, since Heminge and Condell claimed to be Shakespeare's literary executors and to have used his papers, is the First Folio not accepted as the last and final authority for the text of all the plays? Why have there been so many subsequent editors, a line that begins with Rowe in 1709, and includes Pope (1725), Theobald (1733), Johnson (1765), Capell (1768) and Malone (1790), and threatens, like the phantom procession that appalled Macbeth, to stretch out to the crack of doom.

Shakespeare did not print his plays when he produced them because the actors did not favour such a procedure. They feared that publication might affect adversely their takings at the theatre, and the financial return from such publications, at least to the author or actors, was insufficient to overcome this fear. It was not because there was no reading public; publishers were only too ready to print his plays; but there was nothing in the nature of modern copyright to protect the author's interest; and to dispose for a pittance of plays that were drawing good houses did not seem sound policy. Yet in spite of these considerations nineteen of Shakespeare's plays were printed in some form or other during his lifetime, and a twentieth just before 1623.

THE QUARTOS

THE Quartos, so called from their format, contained single plays and sold at sixpence apiece, compared with the pound charged for the First Folio. For their printing the initiative lay with the publishers rather than with the actors. Enterprising if unscrupulous printers were ready to issue even imperfect versions of the plays, whether put together by needy actors who had had parts in them, or vamped up by someone who had carried away from performances the drift of the plot. Seven plays were published in this manner: *The Contention, The True Tragedy* (these were pirated versions of 2 and 3 *Henry VI*), *A Shrew, Romeo and Juliet, Merry Wives of Windsor, Henry V*, and *Hamlet* – and *The Troublesome Reign of King John* may be an eighth. These are now known as the Bad Quartos.

This attack on their property inevitably provoked a reaction in Shakespeare and his company. They published in reply the genuine text of *Romeo and Juliet* and *Hamlet*, and they were not unwilling to print plays that had become well known through frequent performance. In contrast, then, to the seven or eight mutilated or distorted versions stand fourteen authorised or authoritative texts: *Titus Andronicus, Love's Labour's Lost, Romeo and Juliet, Richard II, Richard III*, 1 and 2 *Henry IV, Merchant of Venice, Midsummer-Night's Dream, Much Ado, Hamlet, Troilus and Cressida, King Lear, Othello.* These are the Good Quartos. Even they, however, were treated as in some measure provisional publications. Shakespeare never revised the proofs for any of them, and the printer, although he was in quite a number working from a manuscript in Shakespeare's own hand, found difficulties (*see* p. 1402) he failed to master. The Good Quartos are therefore in places faulty or corrupt, and Shakespeare died before he cared to mend matters.

The actors, when at last they came to their task, had to provide the publisher with copy that extends in print to nearly 900 pages in double column. Their knowledge that many of the Good Quartos were set up from the author's manuscript or an authorised transcript prompted their use of some printed versions as copy for their own text; they took the precaution, however, of having the printed versions compared with manuscripts in their possession, but too casually to exclude all error. The manuscript copy they had to provide for the other plays was also defective for much the same reasons that the Quarto prints were not faultless: the scribe prepared his draft from material not originally designed for the printer's use, and only careful supervision could have prevented his not infrequent stumblings.

To the printed record of this large body of theatrical copy, often entangled as it were in Quarto and Folio, a modern editor has to address himself in an attempt to remove its corruptions. Heminge and Condell discharged their task honestly and with all the skill that could be expected of them; posterity can never be too grateful for their care and pains; but only those who read their Shakespeare regularly in the early versions can know how much the general reader owes to the subsequent editorial labours of those whom Johnson defined as harmless drudges.

Acknowledgements

'All trustworthy restoration of corrupted texts is founded on a study of their history.' This principle, long established in the recension of classical and biblical texts, is implicit in the work of Shakespeare's earlier editors, but its full implications were first made completely explicit in the criticism of A. W. Pollard, R. B. McKerrow and Sir Walter Greg. Their study of Elizabethan books and theatrical documents in the light of collateral evidence hitherto neglected or misinterpreted enabled them to redraw on more probable and intelligible lines the history of the versions in which Shakespeare's work has been transmitted to us. The gap the earlier editors left between Shakespeare and his text, they closed: minutiae – such as the original punctuation – once considered negligible, they have made relevant for the interpretation of the text.

This development in critical method has prompted the present revision of the text of Shakespeare that Messrs. Collins first published nearly ninety years ago. That edition was based on the work of the earlier editors, and their contribution to the elucidation of the text is naturally still invaluable. The lines are now numbered as in the great Cambridge edition of Clark and Wright. They were the first editors to provide so simple but necessary a means of reference; and by this and their authoritative survey of all previous editions, digested in a compendious textual apparatus, they greatly facilitated subsequent work on the text. It is unfortunate that the standard concordance follows the line-numbering of their Globe edition, for there the references no longer always correspond with that of the apparatus, so indispensable to all students of the text, of their major edition.

The range of detail that now confronts a general editor is so extensive that he is necessarily indebted not merely to previous editors but more and more to scholars who have made an intensive study of some aspect or portion of the text. Of the many special contributions that I have found most helpful I must name Dr. Greg's *The Variants in the First Quarto of 'King Lear'*, and its sequel, Professor G. I. Duthie's 'old-spelling' edition of the play; Professor David Patrick's *The Textual History of 'Richard III'*, a study of a text that shares a peculiar history with *Lear*; Professor J. Dover Wilson's *The Manuscript of 'Hamlet'*, and its sequel, the critical study of the play by Professor Thomas Parrott and Professor Hardin Craig, an edition admirably adapted *editorum in usum*. In the interpretation of the punctuation of the early texts – for to reproduce this punctuation would merely confuse and mislead the general reader – I am indebted to Dr. Percy Simpson's *Shakespearian Punctuation* and to the studies of the late Alfred Thiselton. To the glossaries of Dr. C. J. Onions and R. J. Cunliffe I am conscious of owing much; and I have found helpful matter in the work of Professor M. A. Shaaber and Dr. Richard Flatter.

The complete editions I have consulted with advantage include those by Mr. M. R. Ridley and G. L. Kittredge and that by W. A. Neilson and Professor C. J. Hill. Lastly I must mention the edition still in progress edited by Professor J. Dover Wilson, although my debt to him is not the least I have to acknowledge; for whenever I have ventured to disagree with him on general principles or their particular application,

I have not spared myself the expense of second thoughts.

My personal thanks are due to Mr. George F. Maine, 'the onlie begetter' of this revision, for his constant encouragement and assistance; to Mr. James C. Harrison and the caseroom staff for their courtesy and patience in spite of my many requests; to Mrs. Hilda Bone for all her care and pains in the task; and to Sir Walter Greg and the Syndics of the Cambridge University Press for their generous permission to reproduce the special transcript of Shakespeare's contribution to *Sir Thomas More*.

The Preliminary Matter to the First Folio (1623)

Introduction

Heminge and Condell, who edited the first collected edition of Shakespeare's plays, arranged their contents in three sections: Comedies, Histories, and Tragedies. That arrangement as well as the order in which they placed the pieces in each section is preserved in this edition.

To their text the editors prefixed the preliminary matter here reproduced. Opposite the engraved portrait of Shakespeare which stood as frontispiece – now known as the Droeshout engraving after the name of the engraver – they placed Ben Jonson's lines *To the Reader*. Then follow their dedicatory epistle and the address to 'the great variety of readers'. They also included Ben Jonson's famous lines to Shakespeare's memory and short tributes from Leonard Digges and John Mabbe, both of Oxford University, and verses from the sister University of Cambridge by Hugh Holland.

Their 'Catalogue' does not mention *Troilus and Cressida*, for they were able to include this play, in a kind of no man's land, between the Histories and the Tragedies, only at the last moment and after the settlement of a dispute with the publishers who had issued the Quarto version in 1609. Heminge and Condell originally intended to place *Troilus and Cressida* among the Tragedies immediately after *Romeo and Juliet*.

TO THE READER

This Figure, that thou here seest put,
It was for gentle Shakespeare cut;
Wherein the Grauer had a strife
with Nature, to out-doo the life:
O, could he but haue drawne his wit
As well in brasse, as he hath hit
His face; the Print would then surpasse
All, that vvas euer vvrit in brasse.
But, since he cannot, Reader, looke
Not on his Picture, but his Booke.
B.I.

TO THE MOST NOBLE AND INCOMPARABLE PAIRE OF BRETHREN, WILLIAM, EARLE OF PEMBROKE, &c., LORD CHAMBERLAINE TO THE KINGS MOST EXCELLENT MAIESTY, AND PHILIP, EARLE OF MONTGOMERY, &c., GENTLEMAN OF HIS MAIESTIES BEDCHAMBER; BOTH KNIGHTS OF THE MOST NOBLE ORDER OF THE GARTER, AND OUR SINGULAR GOOD LORDS.

Right Honourable,

Whilst we studie to be thankful in our particular, for the many fauors we haue received from your L.L. we are falne vpon the ill fortune, to mingle two the most diuerse things that can bee, feare, and rashnesse; rashnesse in the enterprize, and feare of the successe. For, when we valew the places your H.H. sustaine, we cannot but know their dignity greater, then to descend to the reading of these trifles: and, while we name them trifles, we haue depriu'd our selues of the defence of our Dedication. But since your L.L. haue beene pleas'd to thinke these trifles some-hing, heeretofore; and haue prosequuted both them, and their Author liuing, with so much fauour: we hope, that (they out-liuing him, and he not hauing the fate, common with some, to be exequutor to his owne writings) you will vse the like indulgence toward them, you haue done vnto their parent. There is a great difference, whether any Booke choose his Patrones, or finde them: This hath done both. For, so much were your L.L. likings of the seuerall parts, when they were acted, as before they were published, the Volume ask'd to be yours. We haue but collected them, and done an office to the dead, to procure his Orphanes, Guardians; without ambition either of selfe-profit, or fame: onely to keepe the memory of so worthy a Friend, & Fellow aliue, as was our *Shakespeare*, by humble offer of his playes, to your most noble patronage. Wherein, as we haue iustly obserued, no man to come neere your L.L. but with a kind of religious addresse; it hath bin the height of our care, who are the Presenters, to make the present worthy of your H.H. by the perfection. But, there we must also craue our abilities to be considerd, my Lords. We cannot go beyond our owne powers. Country hands reach foorth milke, creame, fruites, or what they haue: and many Nations (we haue heard) that had not gummes & incense, obtained their requests with a leauened Cake. It was no fault to approach their Gods, by what meanes they could: And the most, though meanest, of things are made more precious, when they are dedicated to Temples. In that name therefore, we most humbly consecrate to your H.H. these remaines of your seruant *Shakespeare;* that what delight is in them, may be euer your L.L. the reputation his, & the faults ours, if any be committed, by a payre so carefull to shew their gratitude both to the liuing, and the dead, as is

Your Lordshippes most bounden,

IOHN HEMINGE.
HENRY CONDELL.

TO THE GREAT VARIETY OF READERS

From the most able, to him that can but spell: There you are number'd. We had rather you were weighd. Especially, when the fate of all Bookes depends vpon your capacities: and not of your heads alone, but of your purses. Well! it is now publique, & you wil stand for your priuiledges wee know: to read, and censure. Do so, but buy it first. That doth best commend a Booke, the Stationer saies. Then, how odde soeuer your braines be, or your wisedomes, make your licence the same, and spare not. Iudge your sixe-pen'orth, your shillings worth, your fiue shillings worth at a time, or higher, so you rise to the iust rates, and welcome. But, what euer you do, Buy. Censure will not driue a Trade, or make the Iacke go. And though you be a Magistrate of wit, and sit on the Stage at *Black-Friers*, or the *Cock-pit*, to arraigne Playes dailie, know, these Playes haue had their triall alreadie, and stood out all Appeales; and do now come forth quitted rather by a Decree of Court, then any purchas'd Letters of commendation.

It had bene a thing, we confesse, worthie to haue bene wished, that the Author himselfe had liu'd to haue set forth, and ouerseen his owne writings; But since it hath bin ordain'd otherwise, and he by death departed from that right, we pray you do not envie his Friends, the office of their care, and paine, to haue collected & publish'd them; and so to haue publish'd them, as where (before) you were abus'd with diuerse stolne, and surreptitious copies, maimed, and deformed by the frauds and stealthes of iniurious imposters, that expos'd them: euen those, are now offer'd to your view cur'd, and perfect of their limbes; and all the rest, absolute in their numbers, as he conceiued them. Who, as he was a happie imitator of Nature, was a most gentle expresser of it. His mind and hand went together: And what he thought, he vttered with that easiness, that wee haue scarse receiued from him a blot in his papers. But it is not our prouince, who onely gather his works, and giue them you, to praise him. It is yours that reade him. And there we hope, to your diuers capacities, you will finde enough, both to draw, and hold you: for his wit can no more lie hid, then it could be lost. Reade him, therefore; and againe, and againe: And if then you doe not like him, surely you are in some manifest danger, not to vnderstand him. And so we leaue you to other of his Friends, whom if you need, can bee your guides: if you neede them not, you can leade your selues, and others. And such Readers we wish him.

IOHN HEMINGE.
HENRIE CONDELL.

TO THE MEMORY OF MY BELOUED, THE AVTHOR MR. WILLIAM SHAKESPEARE: AND WHAT HE HATH LEFT VS.

To draw no enuy (*Shakespeare*) on thy name,
  Am I thus ample to thy Booke, and Fame:
While I confesse thy writings to be such,
  As neither *Man*, nor *Muse*, can praise too much.
'Tis true, and all mens suffrage. But these wayes
  Were not the paths I meant vnto thy praise:
For seeliest Ignorance on these may light,
  Which, when it sounds at best, but eccho's right;
Or blinde Affection, which doth ne're aduance
  The truth, but gropes, and vrgeth all by chance;
Or crafty Malice, might pretend this praise,
  And thinke to ruine, where it seem'd to raise.
These are, as some infamous Baud, or Whore,
  Should praise a Matron. What could hurt her more?
But thou art proofe against them, and indeed
  Aboue th' ill fortune of them, or the need.
I, therefore will begin. Soule of the Age!
  The applause! delight! the wonder of our Stage!
My *Shakespeare*, rise; I will not lodge thee by
  Chaucer, or *Spenser*, or bid *Beaumont* lye
A little further, to make thee a roome:
  Thou art a Moniment, without a tombe,
And art aliue still, while thy Booke doth liue,
  And we haue wits to read, and praise to giue.
That I not mixe thee so, my braine excuses;
  I meane with great, but disproportion'd *Muses:*
For, if I thought my judgement were of yeeres,
  I should commit thee surely with thy peeres,
And tell, how farre thou didst our *Lily* out-shine,
  Or sporting *Kid*, or *Marlowes* mighty line.
And though thou hadst small *Latine*, and lesse *Greeke*,
  From thence to honour thee, I would not seeke
For names; but call forth thund'ring *Æschilus*,
  Euripides, and *Sophocles* to vs,
Paccuuius, Accius, him of *Cordoua* dead,
  To life againe, to heare thy Buskin tread,
And shake a Stage: Or, when thy Sockes were on,
  Leaue thee alone, for the comparison
Of all, that insolent *Greece*, or haughtie *Rome*

sent forth, or since did from their ashes come.
Triumph, my *Britaine*, thou hast one to showe,
To whom all Scenes of *Europe* homage owe.
He was not of an age, but for all time!
And all the *Muses* still were in their prime,
When like *Apollo* he came forth to warme
Our eares, or like a *Mercury* to charme!
Nature her selfe was proud of his designes,
And ioy'd to weare the dressing of his lines!
Which were so richly spun, and wouen so fit,
As, since, she will vouchsafe no other Wit.
The merry *Greeke*, tart *Aristophanes*,
Neat *Terence*, witty *Plautus*, now not please;
But antiquated, and deserted lye
As they were not of Natures family.
Yet must I not giue Nature all: Thy Art,
My gentle *Shakespeare*, must enioy a part.
For though the *Poets* matter, Nature be,
His Art doth giue the fashion. And, that he,
Who casts to write a liuing line, must sweat,
(such as thine are) and strike the second heat
Vpon the *Muses* anuile: turne the same,
(And himself with it) that he thinkes to frame;
Or for the lawrell, he may gaine a scorne,
For a good *Poet's* made, as well as borne.
And such wert thou. Looke how the fathers face
Liues in his issue, euen so, the race
Of *Shakespeares* minde, and manners brightly shines
In his well torned, and true-filed lines:
In each of which, he seemes to shake a Lance,
As brandish't at the eyes of Ignorance.
Sweet Swan of *Auon!* what a sight it were
To see thee in our waters yet appeare,
And make those flights vpon the bankes of *Thames*,
That so did take *Eliza*, and our *Iames!*
But stay, I see thee in the *Hemisphere*
Aduanc'd, and made a Constellation there!
Shine forth, thou Starre of *Poets*, and with rage,
Or influence, chide, or cheere the drooping Stage;
Which, since thy flight from hence, hath mourn'd like night,
And despaires day, but for thy Volumes light.

BEN: IONSON.

VPON THE LINES AND LIFE OF THE FAMOUS SCENICKE POET,
MASTER WILLIAM SHAKESPEARE

Those hands, which you so clapt, go now, and wring
You *Britaines* braue; for done are *Shakespeares* dayes:
His dayes are done, that made the dainty Playes,
Which made the Globe of heau'n and earth to ring.
Dry'de is that veine, dry'd is the *Thespian* Spring,
Turn'd all to teares, and *Phœbus* clouds his rayes:
That corp's, that coffin now besticke those bayes,
Which crown'd him *Poet* first, then *Poets* King.
If *Tragedies* might any *Prologue* haue,
All those he made, would scarse make one to this:
Where *Fame*, now that he gone is to the graue
(Deaths publique tyring-house) the *Nuncius* is.
For though his line of life went soone about,
The life yet of his lines shall neuer out.

HVGH HOLLAND.

TO THE MEMORIE OF THE DECEASED AUTHOR
MAISTER W. SHAKESPEARE.

SHAKE-SPEARE, at length thy pious fellowes giue
The world thy Workes: thy Workes, by which, out-liue
Thy Tombe, thy name must: when that stone is rent,
And Time dissolues thy *Stratford* Moniment,
Here we aliue shall view thee still. This Booke,
When Brasse and Marble fade, shall make thee looke
Fresh to all Ages: when Posteritie
Shall loath what's new, thinke all is prodegie
That is not *Shake-speares;* eu'ry Line, each Verse
Here shall reuiue, redeeme thee from they Herse.
Nor Fire, nor cankring Age, as *Naso* said,
Of his, thy wit-fraught Booke shall once inuade.
Nor shall I e're beleeue, or thinke thee dead
(Though mist) vntill our bankrout Stage be sped
(Impossible) with some new straine t' out-do
Passions of *Juliet,* and her *Romeo;*
Or till I heare a Scene more nobly take,
Then when thy half-Sword parlying *Romans* spake.

Till these, till any of they Volumes rest
Shall with more fire, more feeling be exprest,
Be sure, our *Shake-speare*, thou canst neuer dye,
But crown'd with Lawrell, liue eternally.

L. DIGGES.

TO THE MEMORIE OF
M. W. *SHAKE-SPEARE*

WEE wondred (*Shake-speare*) that thou went'st so soone
From the Worlds-Stage, to the Graues-Tyring-roome.
Wee thought thee dead, but this thy printed worth,
Tels thy Spectators, that thou went'st but forth
To enter with applause. An Actors Art,
Can dye, and liue, to acte a second part.
That's but an *Exit* of Mortalitie;
This, a Re-entrance to a Plaudite.

I. M.

THE WORKES OF WILLIAM SHAKESPEARE,
CONTAINING ALL HIS COMEDIES, HISTORIES, AND TRAGEDIES:
TRUELY SET FORTH, ACCORDING TO THEIR FIRST ORIGINALL.

THE NAMES OF THE PRINCIPALL ACTORS IN ALL THESE PLAYES.

William Shakespeare.
Richard Burbadge.
John Hemmings.
Augustine Phillips.
William Kempt.
Thomas Poope.
George Bryan.
Henry Condell.
William Slye.
Richard Cowly.
John Lowine.
Samuell Crosse.
Alexander Cooke.
Samuel Gilburne.
Robert Armin.
William Ostler.
Nathan Field.
John Underwood.
Nicholas Tooley.
William Ecclestone.
Joseph Taylor.
Robert Benfield.
Robert Goughe.
Richard Robinson.
Iohn Shancke.
Iohn Rice.

A CATALOGVE OF THE SEUERALL COMEDIES, HISTORIES, AND TRAGEDIES CONTAINED IN THIS VOLUME.

The Tempest

Introduction by ROBERT GRANT

The Tempest is generally thought to be Shakespeare's last single-handed play, and the only one apart from *Love's Labour's Lost* to boast an original plot. It dates from between September 1610, when some of its source material (the so-called Bermuda pamphlets) first reached England, and Hallowmas (1st November) 1611, when it received, at Court, its first recorded performance. Some scholars have supposed that the masque of Ceres in Act 4 was added for the second recorded performance, again at Court, in the winter of 1612–13, as part of the festivities preceding the Princess Elizabeth's wedding in February.

Be that as it may, *The Tempest*'s prevailing idealism is certainly appropriate to the celebration of an aristocratic marriage (one such being anticipated on stage). Unclouded by the brooding, nihilistic equivocation of much Jacobean drama (including some by Shakespeare), the play movingly articulates what Lionel Trilling, in a different Shakespearean context, called a lucid moral lyricism, something inherited from the courtly Renaissance humanists and subsequently passed on to Cavalier poets such as Lovelace.

The Tempest is a digest, in mythic or fairy-tale mode, of its author's profoundest reflections on the nature and ends of life. A work of masterly invention, faultless economy, and the most exquisite artifice, it contains scenes of surpassing dramatic poignancy and verse which, consistently gripping in its taut suggestiveness and athletic celerity, rises in the great set-piece speeches to an earth-shaking rhetorical and imaginative power.

Like the Duke in *Measure for Measure*, Prospero is the play's prime mover and controlling, quasi-dramaturgical presence. He is also its moral centre, and the more interesting for being no saint. His goodness, nobility, wisdom and magnanimity are not God-given. They testify, rather, to the godlike rationality and self-command of one who is both naturally impatient and accustomed to expect obedience. Prospero's virtue nevertheless seems entirely unforced. It resembles, indeed, that of his friend and saviour, the gentle, grandfatherly Gonzalo, in stemming from a spirit of reverence and gratitude wholly free from intimations of servility. Both Prospero and Gonzalo detect something hidden from the witty but wicked and trivial-minded cynics Antonio and Sebastian, namely, a providential pattern in events, in the light of which even one's own misfortunes form part of an ultimately benign cosmic order.

Prospero's expulsion from Milan (so he tells his daughter Miranda) was the tragic consequence of his negligence, which enabled his brother Antonio to usurp the dukedom. But Providence turns tragedy to comedy, as it does misfortune to deliverance, and evil to good (though a realistic note is struck in Antonio's final impotent but impenitent silence). For Prospero's negligence was the result, in turn, of his absorption in magic, a study without whose continued pursuit (Gonzalo having provided him with his books) Prospero could not subsequently have survived on the island, still less bring his enemy Alonso to a reconciliation and marry Miranda to

Alonso's son Ferdinand. In contriving the latter event, moreover, Prospero makes his heirs the future rulers of Naples, the very kingdom to which, in exchange for Alonso's help in deposing him, Antonio has subjected Milan.

In keeping with this labyrinthine logic, the play is a Chinese puzzle of interlocking hierarchies, correspondences and contrasts. Antonio's conspiracy against Alonso recapitulates the original one against Prospero; that of the drunkard Stephano burlesques both. Ariel, being discarnate, is literally a free spirit. Consequently, though he loves Prospero in his own teasing, featherweight fashion, he can only guess at the deeper emotional ties by which embodied rational beings, men and women, willingly bind themselves to duty and their kind. His diametric opposite is the earthy, carnal and savage Caliban, who, lacking self-restraint, is fit only (as in Aristotle) for slavery, be it under Prospero or (by his own choice) Stephano. Yet Caliban shows real aesthetic sensitivity and, like Gonzalo, a child-like capacity for wonder, seeming eventually, if only through his native intelligence and shame-filled disillusionment with Stephano, to be redeemed.

In one sense, *The Tempest* is a meditation upon authority. At sea even the royal party are subject, for good practical reasons, to the boatswain's orders. Stephano's grotesque, caricaturally populist authority derives from his hidden butt of sack. Prospero's authority is variously derived, and is perhaps symbolised in, as it is certainly exercised through, his magical powers. Their chief purpose and justification (Ariel's and Caliban's subordination apart) are moral and educational. The young lovers' ordeal, like Prospero's solemn adjurations to sexual restraint, is necessary in order to test and strengthen their love. That of the royal party is designed to bring the wicked to repentance (it is wholly successful only with Alonso), thence to forgiveness, and overall to self-knowledge and a new life.

This 'proper self', to which Ariel, Prospero and Gonzalo all allude, involves our realisation not only of what we have been, but also of what it is still our natural destiny, obligation and fulfilment to be, willing agents for good in the great universal drama, of which this beautiful and profoundly moving play is a kind of microcosm. Once we have been brought to it, as to adulthood, further compulsion is superfluous, and Prospero (or whatever his real-life equivalent may be) can safely break his staff, drown his book, and set us all free, himself included.

The Tempest

DRAMATIS PERSONAE

ALONSO
King of Naples
SEBASTIAN
his brother
PROSPERO
the right Duke of Milan
ANTONIO
his brother, the usurping Duke of Milan
FERDINAND
son to the King of Naples
GONZALO
an honest old counsellor
ADRIAN, FRANCISCO
lords
CALIBAN
a savage and deformed slave
TRINCULO
a jester
STEPHANO
a drunken butler
Master of a Ship
Boatswain
Mariners
MIRANDA
daughter to Prospero
ARIEL
an airy spirit
IRIS, CERES, JUNO, *Nymphs, Reapers*
spirits
Other Spirits attending on Prospero

THE SCENE: A SHIP AT SEA; AFTERWARDS AN UNINHABITED ISLAND

ACT ONE

SCENE I. *On a ship at sea; a tempestuous noise of thunder and lightning heard.*

Enter a Shipmaster and a Boatswain.

MASTER Boatswain!

BOATSWAIN Here, master; what cheer?

MASTER Good! Speak to th' mariners; fall to 't yarely, or we run ourselves aground; bestir, bestir. [*Exit.*

Enter Mariners.

BOATSWAIN Heigh, my hearts! cheerly, cheerly, my hearts! yare, yare! Take in the topsail. Tend to th' master's whistle. Blow till thou burst thy wind, if room enough.

Enter ALONSO, SEBASTIAN, ANTONIO, FERDINAND, GONZALO, and Others.

ALONSO Good boatswain, have care.
Where's the master? Play the men.

BOATSWAIN I pray now, keep below.

ANTONIO Where is the master, boson?

BOATSWAIN Do you not hear him? You mar our labour; keep your cabins; you do assist the storm.

GONZALO Nay, good, be patient.

BOATSWAIN When the sea is. Hence! What cares these roarers for the name of king? To cabin! silence! Trouble us not.

GONZALO Good, yet remember whom thou hast aboard.

BOATSWAIN None that I more love than myself. You are a counsellor; if you can command these elements to silence, and work the peace of the present, we will not hand a rope more. Use your authority; if you cannot, give thanks you have liv'd so long, and make yourself ready in your cabin for the mischance of the hour, if it so hap. – Cheerly, good hearts! – Out of our way, I say. [*Exit.*

GONZALO I have great comfort from this fellow. Methinks he hath no drowning mark upon him; his complexion is perfect gallows. Stand fast, good Fate, to his hanging; make the rope of his destiny our cable, for our own doth little advantage. If he be not born to be hang'd, our case is miserable. [*Exeunt.*

Re-enter Boatswain.

BOATSWAIN Down with the topmast. Yare, lower, lower! Bring her to try wi'th' main-course. [*A cry within*] A plague upon this howling! They are louder than the weather or our office.

Re-enter SEBASTIAN, ANTONIO, and GONZALO.

Yet again! What do you here? Shall we give o'er, and drown? Have you a mind to sink?

SEBASTIAN A pox o' your throat, you bawling, blasphemous, incharitable dog!

BOATSWAIN Work you, then.

ANTONIO Hang, cur; hang, you whoreson, insolent noise-maker; we are less afraid to be drown'd than thou art.

GONZALO I'll warrant him for drowning, though

the ship were no stronger than a nutshell, and as leaky as an unstanched wench.

BOATSWAIN Lay her a-hold, a-hold; set her two courses; off to sea again; lay her off.

Enter Mariners, wet.

MARINERS All lost! to prayers, to prayers! all lost!
[*Exeunt.*

BOATSWAIN What, must our mouths be cold?
GONZALO The King and Prince at prayers!
Let's assist them,
For our case is as theirs.
SEBASTIAN I am out of patience.
ANTONIO We are merely cheated of our lives by drunkards.
This wide-chopp'd rascal – would thou mightest lie drowning
The washing of ten tides!
GONZALO He'll be hang'd, yet,
Though every drop of water swear against it,
And gape at wid'st to glut him.
[*A confused noise within*: Mercy on us!
We split, we split! Farewell, my wife and children!
Farewell, brother! We split, we split, we split!
ANTONIO Let's all sink wi' th' King.
SEBASTIAN Let's take leave of him.
[*Exeunt Antonio and Sebastian.*

GONZALO Now would I give a thousand furlongs of sea for an acre of barren ground – long heath, brown furze, any thing. The wills above be done, but I would fain die a dry death. [*Exeunt.*

SCENE II. *The island. Before Prospero's cell.*

Enter PROSPERO and MIRANDA.

MIRANDA If by your art, my dearest father, you have
Put the wild waters in this roar, allay them.
The sky, it seems, would pour down stinking pitch,
But that the sea, mounting to th' welkin's cheek,
Dashes the fire out. O, I have suffered
With those that I saw suffer! A brave vessel,
Who had no doubt some noble creature in her,
Dash'd all to pieces! O, the cry did knock
Against my very heart! Poor souls, they perish'd.
Had I been any god of power, I would
Have sunk the sea within the earth or ere
It should the good ship so have swallow'd and
The fraughting souls within her.
PROSPERO Be collected;
No more amazement; tell your piteous heart
There's no harm done.
MIRANDA O, woe the day!
PROSPERO No harm.
I have done nothing but in care of thee,
Of thee, my dear one, thee, my daughter, who
Art ignorant of what thou art, nought knowing
Of whence I am, nor that I am more better
Than Prospero, master of a full poor cell,
And thy no greater father.
MIRANDA More to know
Did never meddle with my thoughts.
PROSPERO 'Tis time
I should inform thee farther. Lend thy hand,
And pluck my magic garment from me. So,
[*Lays down his mantle.*

Lie there my art. Wipe thou thine eyes; have comfort.
The direful spectacle of the wreck, which touch'd
The very virtue of compassion in thee,
I have with such provision in mine art
So safely ordered that there is no soul –
No, not so much perdition as an hair
Betid to any creature in the vessel
Which thou heard'st cry, which thou saw'st sink. Sit down,
For thou must now know farther.
MIRANDA You have often
Begun to tell me what I am; but stopp'd,
And left me to a bootless inquisition,
Concluding 'Stay; not yet'.
PROSPERO The hour's now come;
The very minute bids thee ope thine ear.
Obey, and be attentive. Canst thou remember
A time before we came unto this cell?
I do not think thou canst; for then thou wast not
Out three years old.
MIRANDA Certainly, sir, I can.
PROSPERO By what? By any other house, or person?
Of any thing the image, tell me, that
Hath kept with thy remembrance?
MIRANDA 'Tis far off,
And rather like a dream than an assurance
That my remembrance warrants. Had I not
Four, or five, women once, that tended me?
PROSPERO Thou hadst, and more, Miranda. But how is it
That this lives in thy mind? What seest thou else
In the dark backward and abysm of time?
If thou remem'brest aught, ere thou cam'st here,
How thou cam'st here thou mayst.
MIRANDA But that I do not.
PROSPERO Twelve year since, Miranda, twelve year since,
Thy father was the Duke of Milan, and
A prince of power.

MIRANDA Sir, are not you my father?
PROSPERO Thy mother was a piece of virtue, and
She said thou wast my daughter; and thy father
Was Duke of Milan, and his only heir
And princess no worse issued.
MIRANDA O, the heavens!
What foul play had we that we came from
thence?
Or blessed was't we did?
PROSPERO Both, both, my girl.
By foul play, as thou say'st, were we heav'd
thence;
But blessedly holp hither.
MIRANDA O, my heart bleeds
To think o' th' teen that I have turn'd you to,
Which is from my remembrance. Please you,
farther.
PROSPERO My brother and thy uncle, call'd
Antonio –
I pray thee, mark me that a brother should
Be so perfidious. He, whom next thyself
Of all the world I lov'd, and to him put
The manage of my state; as at that time
Through all the signories it was the first,
And Prospero the prime duke, being so reputed
In dignity, and for the liberal arts
Without a parallel, those being all my study –
The government I cast upon my brother
And to my state grew stranger, being
transported
And rapt in secret studies. Thy false uncle –
Dost thou attend me?
MIRANDA Sir, most heedfully.
PROSPERO Being once perfected how to grant
suits,
How to deny them, who t' advance, and who
To trash for over-topping, new created
The creatures that were mine, I say, or chang'd
'em,
Or else new form'd 'em; having both the key
Of officer and office, set all hearts i' th' state
To what tune pleas'd his ear; that now he was
The ivy which had hid my princely trunk
And suck'd my verdure out on't. Thou attend'st
not.
MIRANDA O, good sir, I do!
PROSPERO I pray thee, mark me.
I thus neglecting worldly ends, all dedicated
To closeness and the bettering of my mind
With that which, but by being so retir'd,
O'er-priz'd all popular rate, in my false brother
Awak'd an evil nature; and my trust,
Like a good parent, did beget of him
A falsehood, in its contrary as great
As my trust was; which had indeed no limit,
A confidence sans bound. He being thus lorded,
Not only with what my revenue yielded,
But what my power might else exact, like one
Who having into truth, by telling of it,
Made such a sinner of his memory,
To credit his own lie – he did believe
He was indeed the Duke; out o' th' substitution,
And executing th' outward face of royalty
With all prerogative. Hence his ambition
growing –
Dost thou hear?
MIRANDA Your tale, sir, would cure deafness.
PROSPERO To have no screen between this part
he play'd
And him he play'd it for, he needs will be
Absolute Milan. Me, poor man – my library
Was dukedom large enough – of temporal
royalties
He thinks me now incapable; confederates,
So dry he was for sway, wi' th' King of Naples,
To give him annual tribute, do him homage,
Subject his coronet to his crown, and bend
The dukedom, yet unbow'd – alas, poor
Milan! –
To most ignoble stooping.
MIRANDA O the heavens!
PROSPERO Mark his condition, and th' event,
then tell me
If this might be a brother.
MIRANDA I should sin
To think but nobly of my grandmother:
Good wombs have borne bad sons.
PROSPERO Now the condition:
This King of Naples, being an enemy
To me inveterate, hearkens my brother's suit;
Which was, that he, in lieu o' th' premises,
Of homage, and I know not how much tribute,
Should presently extirpate me and mine
Out of the dukedom, and confer fair Milan
With all the honours on my brother. Whereon,
A treacherous army levied, one midnight
Fated to th' purpose, did Antonio open
The gates of Milan; and, i' th' dead of darkness,
The ministers for th' purpose hurried thence
Me and thy crying self.
MIRANDA Alack, for pity!
I, not rememb'ring how I cried out then,
Will cry it o'er again; it is a hint
That wrings mine eyes to't.
PROSPERO Hear a little further,
And then I'll bring thee to the present business
Which now's upon 's; without the which this
story
Were most impertinent.
MIRANDA Wherefore did they not
That hour destroy us?
PROSPERO Well demanded, wench!
My tale provokes that question. Dear, they durst
not,

So dear the love my people bore me; nor set
A mark so bloody on the business; but
With colours fairer painted their foul ends.
In few, they hurried us aboard a bark;
Bore us some leagues to sea, where they prepared
A rotten carcass of a butt, not rigg'd,
Nor tackle, sail, nor mast; the very rats
Instinctively have quit it. There they hoist us,
To cry to th' sea, that roar'd to us; to sigh
To th' winds, whose pity, sighing back again,
Did us but loving wrong.

MIRANDA Alack, what trouble
Was I then to you!

PROSPERO O, a cherubin
Thou wast that did preserve me! Thou didst smile,
Infused with a fortitude from heaven,
When I have deck'd the sea with drops full salt,
Under my burden groan'd; which rais'd in me
An undergoing stomach, to bear up
Against what should ensue.

MIRANDA How came we ashore?

PROSPERO By Providence divine.
Some food we had and some fresh water that
A noble Neapolitan, Gonzalo,
Out of his charity, who being then appointed
Master of this design, did give us, with
Rich garments, linens, stuffs, and necessaries,
Which since have steaded much; so, of his gentleness,
Knowing I lov'd my books, he furnish'd me
From mine own library with volumes that
I prize above my dukedom.

MIRANDA Would I might
But ever see that man!

PROSPERO Now I arise.

[*Puts on his mantle.*

Sit still, and hear the last of our sea-sorrow.
Here in this island we arriv'd; and here
Have I, thy schoolmaster, made thee more profit
Than other princess' can, that have more time
For vainer hours, and tutors not so careful.

MIRANDA Heavens thank you for't! And now, I pray you, sir,
For still 'tis beating in my mind, your reason
For raising this sea-storm?

PROSPERO Know thus far forth:
By accident most strange, bountiful Fortune,
Now my dear lady, hath mine enemies
Brought to this shore; and by my prescience
I find my zenith doth depend upon
A most auspicious star, whose influence
If now I court not, but omit, my fortunes
Will ever after droop. Here cease more questions;
Thou art inclin'd to sleep; 'tis a good dullness,
And give it way. I know thou canst not choose.

[*Miranda sleeps.*

Come away, servant; come; I am ready now.
Approach, my Ariel. Come.

Enter ARIEL.

ARIEL All hail, great master! grave sir, hail! I come
To answer thy best pleasure; be't to fly,
To swim, to dive into the fire, to ride
On the curl'd clouds. To thy strong bidding task
Ariel and all his quality.

PROSPERO Hast thou, spirit,
Perform'd to point the tempest that I bade thee?

ARIEL To every article.
I boarded the King's ship; now on the beak,
Now in the waist, the deck, in every cabin,
I flam'd amazement. Sometime I'd divide,
And burn in many places; on the topmast,
The yards, and bowsprit, would flame distinctly,
Then meet and join. Jove's lightning, the precursors
O' th' dreadful thunder-claps, more momentary
And sight-outrunning were not; the fire and cracks
Of sulphurous roaring the most mighty Neptune
Seem to besiege, and make his bold waves tremble,
Yea, his dread trident shake.

PROSPERO My brave spirit!
Who was so firm, so constant, that this coil
Would not infect his reason?

ARIEL Not a soul
But felt a fever of the mad, and play'd
Some tricks of desperation. All but mariners
Plung'd in the foaming brine, and quit the vessel,
Then all afire with me; the King's son, Ferdinand,
With hair up-staring – then like reeds, not hair –
Was the first man that leapt; cried 'Hell is empty,
And all the devils are here'.

PROSPERO Why, that's my spirit!
But was not this nigh shore?

ARIEL Close by, my master.

PROSPERO But are they, Ariel, safe?

ARIEL Not a hair perish'd;
On their sustaining garments not a blemish,
But fresher than before; and, as thou bad'st me,
In troops I have dispers'd them 'bout the isle.
The King's son have I landed by himself,
Whom I left cooling of the air with sighs
In an odd angle of the isle, and sitting,
His arms in this sad knot.

PROSPERO Of the King's ship,
The mariners, say how thou hast dispos'd,
And all the rest o' th' fleet?
ARIEL Safely in harbour
Is the King's ship; in the deep nook, where once
Thou call'dst me up at midnight to fetch dew
From the still-vex'd Bermoothes, there she's hid;
The mariners all under hatches stowed,
Who, with a charm join'd to their suffred labour,
I have left asleep; and for the rest o' th' fleet,
Which I dispers'd, they all have met again,
And are upon the Mediterranean flote
Bound sadly home for Naples,
Supposing that they saw the King's ship wreck'd,
And his great person perish.
PROSPERO Ariel, thy charge
Exactly is perform'd; but there's more work.
What is the time o' th' day?
ARIEL Past the mid season.
PROSPERO At least two glasses. The time 'twixt six and now
Must by us both be spent most preciously.
ARIEL Is there more toil? Since thou dost give me pains,
Let me remember thee what thou hast promis'd,
Which is not yet perform'd me.
PROSPERO How now, moody?
What is 't thou canst demand?
ARIEL My liberty.
PROSPERO Before the time be out? No more!
ARIEL I prithee,
Remember I have done thee worthy service,
Told thee no lies, made thee no mistakings, serv'd
Without or grudge or grumblings. Thou didst promise
To bate me a full year.
PROSPERO Dost thou forget
From what a torment I did free thee?
ARIEL No.
PROSPERO Thou dost; and think'st it much to tread the ooze
Of the salt deep,
To run upon the sharp wind of the north,
To do me business in the veins o' th' earth
When it is bak'd with frost.
ARIEL I do not, sir.
PROSPERO Thou liest, malignant thing. Hast thou forgot
The foul witch Sycorax, who with age and envy
Was grown into a hoop? Hast thou forgot her?
ARIEL No, sir.
PROSPERO Thou hast. Where was she born?
Speak; tell me.
ARIEL Sir, in Argier.
PROSPERO O, was she so? I must
Once in a month recount what thou hast been,
Which thou forget'st. This damn'd witch Sycorax,
For mischiefs manifold, and sorceries terrible
To enter human hearing, from Argier
Thou know'st was banish'd; for one thing she did
They would not take her life. Is not this true?
ARIEL Ay, sir.
PROSPERO This blue-ey'd hag was hither brought with child,
And here was left by th' sailors. Thou, my slave,
As thou report'st thyself, wast then her servant;
And, for thou wast a spirit too delicate
To act her earthy and abhorr'd commands,
Refusing her grand hests, she did confine thee,
By help of her more potent ministers,
And in her most unmitigable rage,
Into a cloven pine; within which rift
Imprison'd thou didst painfully remain
A dozen years; within which space she died,
And left thee there, where thou didst vent thy groans
As fast as mill-wheels strike. Then was this island –
Save for the son that she did litter here,
A freckl'd whelp, hag-born – not honour'd with
A human shape.
ARIEL Yes, Caliban her son.
PROSPERO Dull thing, I say so; he, that Caliban
Whom now I keep in service. Thou best know'st
What torment I did find thee in; thy groans
Did make wolves howl, and penetrate the breasts
Of ever-angry bears; it was a torment
To lay upon the damn'd, which Sycorax
Could not again undo. It was mine art,
When I arriv'd and heard thee, that made gape
The pine, and let thee out.
ARIEL I thank thee, master.
PROSPERO If thou more murmur'st, I will rend an oak
And peg thee in his knotty entrails, till
Thou hast howl'd away twelve winters.
ARIEL Pardon, master;
I will be correspondent to command,
And do my spriting gently.
PROSPERO Do so; and after two days
I will discharge thee.
ARIEL That's my noble master!
What shall I do? Say what. What shall I do?
PROSPERO Go make thyself like a nymph o' th' sea; be subject
To no sight but thine and mine, invisible
To every eyeball else. Go take this shape,

And hither come in 't. Go, hence with diligence!
[Exit Ariel.
Awake, dear heart, awake; thou hast slept well;
Awake.

MIRANDA The strangeness of your story put
Heaviness in me.

PROSPERO Shake it off. Come on,
We'll visit Caliban, my slave, who never
Yields us kind answer.

MIRANDA 'Tis a villain, sir,
I do not love to look on.

PROSPERO But as 'tis,
We cannot miss him: he does make our fire,
Fetch in our wood, and serves in offices
That profit us. What ho! slave! Caliban!
Thou earth, thou! Speak.

CALIBAN *[Within]* There's wood enough within.

PROSPERO Come forth, I say; there's other business for thee.
Come, thou tortoise! when?

Re-enter ARIEL like a water-nymph.

Fine apparition! My quaint Ariel,
Hark in thine ear.

ARIEL My lord, it shall be done. *[Exit.*

PROSPERO Thou poisonous slave, got by the devil himself
Upon thy wicked dam, come forth!

Enter CALIBAN.

CALIBAN As wicked dew as e'er my mother brush'd
With raven's feather from unwholesome fen
Drop on you both! A south-west blow on ye
And blister you all o'er!

PROSPERO For this, be sure, to-night thou shalt have cramps,
Side-stitches that shall pen thy breath up; urchins
Shall, for that vast of night that they may work,
All exercise on thee; thou shalt be pinch'd
As thick as honeycomb, each pinch more stinging
Than bees that made 'em.

CALIBAN I must eat my dinner.
This island's mine, by Sycorax my mother,
Which thou tak'st from me. When thou cam'st first,
Thou strok'st me and made much of me, wouldst give me
Water with berries in't, and teach me how
To name the bigger light, and how the less,
That burn by day and night; and then I lov'd thee,
And show'd thee all the qualities o' th' isle,
The fresh springs, brine-pits, barren place and fertile.
Curs'd be I that did so! All the charms
Of Sycorax, toads, beetles, bats, light on you!
For I am all the subjects that you have,
Which first was mine own king; and here you sty me
In this hard rock, whiles you do keep from me
The rest o' th' island.

PROSPERO Thou most lying slave,
Whom stripes may move, not kindness! I have us'd thee,
Filth as thou art, with human care, and lodg'd thee
In mine own cell, till thou didst seek to violate
The honour of my child.

CALIBAN O ho, O ho! Would't had been done.
Thou didst prevent me; I had peopl'd else
This isle with Calibans.

MIRANDA Abhorred slave,
Which any print of goodness wilt not take,
Being capable of all ill! I pitied thee,
Took pains to make thee speak, taught thee each hour
One thing or other. When thou didst not, savage,
Know thine own meaning, but wouldst gabble like
A thing most brutish, I endow'd thy purposes
With words that made them known. But thy vile race,
Though thou didst learn, had that in't which good natures
Could not abide to be with; therefore wast thou
Deservedly confin'd into this rock, who hadst
Deserv'd more than a prison.

CALIBAN You taught me language, and my profit on't
Is, I know how to curse. The red plague rid you
For learning me your language!

PROSPERO Hag-seed, hence!
Fetch us in fuel. And be quick, thou 'rt best,
To answer other business. Shrug'st thou, malice?
If thou neglect'st, or dost unwillingly
What I command, I'll rack thee with old cramps,
Fill all thy bones with aches, make thee roar,
That beasts shall tremble at thy din.

CALIBAN No, pray thee.
[Aside] I must obey. His art is of such pow'r,
It would control my dam's god, Setebos,
And make a vassal of him.

PROSPERO So, slave; hence!
[Exit Caliban.

Re-enter ARIEL invisible, playing and singing; FERDINAND following.

Ariel's Song.

Come unto these yellow sands,
And then take hands;
Curtsied when you have and kiss'd,
The wild waves whist,
Foot it featly here and there,
And, sweet sprites, the burden bear.
Hark, hark!
Burden dispersedly. Bow-wow.
The watch dogs bark.
Burden dispersedly. Bow-wow.
Hark, hark! I hear
The strain of strutting chanticleer
Cry, Cock-a-diddle-dow.

FERDINAND Where should this music be? I' th' air or th' earth?
It sounds no more; and sure it waits upon
Some god o' th' island. Sitting on a bank,
Weeping again the King my father's wreck,
This music crept by me upon the waters,
Allaying both their fury and my passion
With its sweet air; thence I have follow'd it,
Or it hath drawn me rather. But 'tis gone.
No, it begins again.

Ariel's Song.

Full fathom five thy father lies;
Of his bones are coral made;
Those are pearls that were his eyes;
Nothing of him that doth fade
But doth suffer a sea-change
Into something rich and strange.
Sea-nymphs hourly ring his knell:
Burden. Ding-dong.
Hark! now I hear them – Ding-dong bell.

FERDINAND The ditty does remember my drown'd father.
This is no mortal business, nor no sound
That the earth owes. I hear it now above me.

PROSPERO The fringed curtains of thine eye advance,
And say what thou seest yond.

MIRANDA What is't? a spirit?
Lord, how it looks about! Believe me, sir,
It carries a brave form. But 'tis a spirit.

PROSPERO No, wench; it eats and sleeps and hath such senses
As we have, such. This gallant which thou seest
Was in the wreck; and but he's something stain'd
With grief, that's beauty's canker, thou mightst call him
A goodly person. He hath lost his fellows,
And strays about to find 'em.

MIRANDA I might call him
A thing divine; for nothing natural
I ever saw so noble.

PROSPERO [*Aside*] It goes on, I see,
As my soul prompts it. Spirit, fine spirit! I'll free thee
Within two days for this.

FERDINAND Most sure, the goddess
On whom these airs attend! Vouchsafe my pray'r
May know if you remain upon this island,
And that you will some good instruction give
How I may bear me here. My prime request,
Which I do last pronounce, is, O you wonder!
If you be maid or no?

MIRANDA No wonder, sir;
But certainly a maid.

FERDINAND My language? Heavens!
I am the best of them that speak this speech,
Were I but where 'tis spoken.

PROSPERO How? the best?
What wert thou, if the King of Naples heard thee?

FERDINAND A single thing, as I am now, that wonders
To hear thee speak of Naples. He does hear me;
And that he does I weep. Myself am Naples,
Who with mine eyes, never since at ebb, beheld
The King my father wreck'd.

MIRANDA Alack, for mercy!

FERDINAND Yes, faith, and all his lords, the Duke of Milan
And his brave son being twain.

PROSPERO [*Aside*] The Duke of Milan
And his more braver daughter could control thee,
If now 'twere fit to do't. At the first sight
They have chang'd eyes. Delicate Ariel,
I'll set thee free for this. [*To Ferdinand*] A word, good sir;
I fear you have done yourself some wrong; a word.

MIRANDA Why speaks my father so ungently? This
Is the third man that e'er I saw; the first
That e'er I sigh'd for. Pity move my father
To be inclin'd my way!

FERDINAND O, if a virgin,
And your affection not gone forth, I'll make you
The Queen of Naples.

PROSPERO Soft, sir! one word more.
[*Aside*] They are both in either's pow'rs; but this swift business
I must uneasy make, lest too light winning
Make the prize light. [*To Ferdinand*] One word more; I charge thee
That thou attend me; thou dost here usurp
The name thou ow'st not; and hast put thyself
Upon this island as a spy, to win it
From me, the lord on't.

FERDINAND No, as I am a man.
MIRANDA There's nothing ill can dwell in such a temple.
If the ill spirit have so fair a house,
Good things will strive to dwell with't.
PROSPERO Follow me.
Speak not you for him; he's a traitor. Come;
I'll manacle thy neck and feet together.
Sea-water shalt thou drink; thy food shall be
The fresh-brook mussels, wither'd roots, and husks
Wherein the acorn cradled. Follow.
FERDINAND No;
I will resist such entertainment till
Mine enemy has more power.
[*He draws, and is charmed from moving.*
MIRANDA O dear father,
Make not too rash a trial of him, for
He's gentle, and not fearful.
PROSPERO What, I say,
My foot my tutor? Put thy sword up, traitor;
Who mak'st a show but dar'st not strike, thy conscience
Is so possess'd with guilt. Come from thy ward;
For I can here disarm thee with this stick
And make thy weapon drop.
MIRANDA Beseech you, father!
PROSPERO Hence! Hang not on my garments.
MIRANDA Sir, have pity;
I'll be his surety.
PROSPERO Silence! One word more
Shall make me chide thee, if not hate thee. What!
An advocate for an impostor! hush!
Thou think'st there is no more such shapes as he,
Having seen but him and Caliban. Foolish wench!
To th' most of men this is a Caliban,
And they to him are angels.
MIRANDA My affections
Are then most humble; I have no ambition
To see a goodlier man.
PROSPERO Come on; obey.
Thy nerves are in their infancy again,
And have no vigour in them.
FERDINAND So they are;
My spirits, as in a dream, are all bound up.
My father's loss, the weakness which I feel,
The wreck of all my friends, nor this man's threats
To whom I am subdu'd, are but light to me,
Might I but through my prison once a day
Behold this maid. All corners else o' th' earth
Let liberty make use of; space enough
Have I in such a prison.
PROSPERO [*Aside*] It works. [*To Ferdinand*] Come on. –
Thou hast done well, fine Ariel! [*To Ferdinand*] Follow me.
[*To Ariel*] Hark what thou else shalt do me.
MIRANDA Be of comfort;
My father's of a better nature, sir,
Than he appears by speech; this is unwonted
Which now came from him.
PROSPERO [*To Ariel*] Thou shalt be as free
As mountain winds; but then exactly do
All points of my command.
ARIEL To th' syllable.
PROSPERO [*To Ferdinand*] Come, follow.
[*To Miranda*] Speak not for him. [*Exeunt.*

ACT TWO

SCENE 1. *Another part of the island.*

Enter ALONSO, SEBASTIAN, ANTONIO, GONZALO, ADRIAN, FRANCISCO, and Others.

GONZALO Beseech you, sir, be merry; you have cause,
So have we all, of joy; for our escape
Is much beyond our loss. Our hint of woe
Is common; every day, some sailor's wife,
The masters of some merchant, and the merchant,
Have just our theme of woe; but for the miracle,
I mean our preservation, few in millions
Can speak like us. Then wisely, good sir, weigh
Our sorrow with our comfort.
ALONSO Prithee, peace.

SEBASTIAN He receives comfort like cold porridge.

ANTONIO The visitor will not give him o'er so.

SEBASTIAN Look, he's winding up the watch of his wit; by and by it will strike.

GONZALO Sir –

SEBASTIAN One – Tell.

GONZALO When every grief is entertain'd that's offer'd,
Comes to th' entertainer –

SEBASTIAN A dollar.

GONZALO Dolour comes to him, indeed; you have spoken truer than you purpos'd.

SEBASTIAN You have taken it wiselier than I meant you should.

GONZALO Therefore, my lord –

ANTONIO Fie, what a spendthrift is he of his tongue!

ALONSO I prithee, spare.

GONZALO Well, I have done; but yet –

SEBASTIAN He will be talking.

ANTONIO Which, of he or Adrian, for a good wager, first begins to crow?

SEBASTIAN The old cock.

ANTONIO The cock'rel.

SEBASTIAN Done. The wager?

ANTONIO A laughter.

SEBASTIAN A match!

ADRIAN Though this island seem to be desert –

ANTONIO Ha, ha, ha!

SEBASTIAN So, you're paid.

ADRIAN Uninhabitable, and almost inaccessible –

SEBASTIAN Yet –

ADRIAN Yet –

ANTONIO He could not miss't.

ADRIAN It must needs be of subtle, tender, and delicate temperance.

ANTONIO Temperance was a delicate wench.

SEBASTIAN Ay, and a subtle; as he most learnedly deliver'd.

ADRIAN The air breathes upon us here most sweetly.

SEBASTIAN As if it had lungs, and rotten ones.

ANTONIO Or, as 'twere perfum'd by a fen.

GONZALO Here is everything advantageous to life.

ANTONIO True; save means to live.

SEBASTIAN Of that there's none, or little.

GONZALO How lush and lusty the grass looks! how green!

ANTONIO The ground indeed is tawny.

SEBASTIAN With an eye of green in't.

ANTONIO He misses not much.

SEBASTIAN No; he doth but mistake the truth totally.

GONZALO But the rarity of it is, which is indeed almost beyond credit –

SEBASTIAN As many vouch'd rarities are.

GONZALO That our garments, being, as they were, drench'd in the sea, hold, notwithstanding, their freshness and glosses, being rather newdy'd, than stain'd with salt water.

ANTONIO If but one of his pockets could speak, would it not say he lies?

SEBASTIAN Ay, or very falsely pocket up his report.

GONZALO Methinks our garments are now as fresh as when we put them on first in Afric, at the marriage of the King's fair daughter Claribel to the King of Tunis.

SEBASTIAN 'Twas a sweet marriage, and we prosper well in our return.

ADRIAN Tunis was never grac'd before with such a paragon to their queen.

GONZALO Not since widow Dido's time.

ANTONIO Widow! a pox o' that! How came that 'widow' in? Widow Dido!

SEBASTIAN What if he had said 'widower Aeneas' too? Good Lord, how you take it!

ADRIAN 'Widow Dido' said you? You make me study of that. She was of Carthage, not of Tunis.

GONZALO This Tunis, sir, was Carthage.

ADRIAN Carthage?

GONZALO I assure you, Carthage.

ANTONIO His word is more than the miraculous harp.

SEBASTIAN He hath rais'd the wall, and houses too.

ANTONIO What impossible matter will he make easy next?

SEBASTIAN I think he will carry this island home in his pocket, and give it his son for an apple.

ANTONIO And, sowing the kernels of it in the sea, bring forth more islands.

GONZALO Ay.

ANTONIO Why, in good time.

GONZALO Sir, we were talking that our garments seem now as fresh as when we were at Tunis at the marriage of your daughter, who is now Queen.

ANTONIO And the rarest that e'er came there.

SEBASTIAN Bate, I beseech you, widow Dido.

ANTONIO O, widow Dido! Ay, widow Dido.

GONZALO Is not, sir, my doublet as fresh as the first day I wore it? I mean, in a sort.

ANTONIO That 'sort' was well fish'd for.

GONZALO When I wore it at your daughter's marriage?

ALONSO You cram these words into mine ears against
The stomach of my sense. Would I had never
Married my daughter there; for, coming thence,
My son is lost; and, in my rate, she too,
Who is so far from Italy removed
I ne'er again shall see her. O thou mine heir
Of Naples and of Milan, what strange fish
Hath made his meal on thee?

FRANCISCO Sir, he may live;
I saw him beat the surges under him,
And ride upon their backs; he trod the water,
Whose enmity he flung aside, and breasted
The surge most swoln that met him; his bold head
'Bove the contentious waves he kept, and oared
Himself with his good arms in lusty stroke
To th' shore, that o'er his wave-worn basis bowed,
As stooping to relieve him. I not doubt
He came alive to land.

ALONSO No, no, he's gone.
SEBASTIAN Sir, you may thank yourself for this great loss,
That would not bless our Europe with your daughter,
But rather lose her to an African;
Where she, at least, is banish'd from your eye,
Who hath cause to wet the grief on't.
ALONSO Prithee, peace.
SEBASTIAN You were kneel'd to, and importun'd otherwise
By all of us; and the fair soul herself
Weigh'd between loathness and obedience at
Which end o' th' beam should bow. We have lost your son,
I fear, for ever. Milan and Naples have
Moe widows in them of this business' making,
Than we bring men to comfort them;
The fault's your own.
ALONSO So is the dear'st o' th' loss.
GONZALO My lord Sebastian,
The truth you speak doth lack some gentleness,
And time to speak it in; you rub the sore,
When you should bring the plaster.
SEBASTIAN Very well.
ANTONIO And most chirurgeonly.
GONZALO It is foul weather in us all, good sir,
When you are cloudy.
SEBASTIAN Fowl weather?
ANTONIO Very foul.
GONZALO Had I plantation of this isle, my lord –
ANTONIO He'd sow 't with nettle-seed.
SEBASTIAN Or docks, or mallows.
GONZALO And were the king on't, what would I do?
SEBASTIAN Scape being drunk for want of wine.
GONZALO I' th' commonwealth I would by contraries
Execute all things; for no kind of traffic
Would I admit; no name of magistrate;
Letters should not be known; riches, poverty,
And use of service, none; contract, succession,
Bourn, bound of land, tilth, vineyard, none;
No use of metal, corn, or wine, or oil;
No occupation; all men idle, all;
And women too, but innocent and pure;
No sovereignty –
SEBASTIAN Yet he would be king on't.
ANTONIO The latter end of his commonwealth forgets the beginning.
GONZALO All things in common nature should produce
Without sweat or endeavour. Treason, felony,
Sword, pike, knife, gun, or need of any engine,
Would I not have; but nature should bring forth,
Of it own kind, all foison, all abundance,
To feed my innocent people.
SEBASTIAN No marrying 'mong his subjects?
ANTONIO None, man; all idle; whores and knaves.
GONZALO I would with such perfection govern, sir,
T' excel the golden age.
SEBASTIAN Save his Majesty!
ANTONIO Long live Gonzalo!
GONZALO And – do you mark me, sir?
ALONSO Prithee, no more; thou dost talk nothing to me.
GONZALO I do well believe your Highness; and did it to minister occasion to these gentlemen, who are of such sensible and nimble lungs that they always use to laugh at nothing.
ANTONIO 'Twas you we laugh'd at.
GONZALO Who in this kind of merry fooling am nothing to you; so you may continue, and laugh at nothing still.
ANTONIO What a blow was there given!
SEBASTIAN An it had not fall'n flat-long.
GONZALO You are gentlemen of brave mettle; you would lift the moon out of her sphere, if she would continue in it five weeks without changing.

Enter ARIEL, invisible, playing solemn music.

SEBASTIAN We would so, and then go a-bat-fowling.
ANTONIO Nay, good my lord, be not angry.
GONZALO No, I warrant you; I will not adventure my discretion so weakly. Will you laugh me asleep, for I am very heavy?
ANTONIO Go sleep, and hear us.

[*All sleep but Alonso, Sebastian and Antonio*

ALONSO What, all so soon asleep! I wish mine eyes
Would, with themselves, shut up my thoughts; I find
They are inclin'd to do so.
SEBASTIAN Please you, sir,
Do not omit the heavy offer of it:
It seldom visits sorrow; when it doth,
It is a comforter
ANTONIO We two, my lord,
Will guard your person while you take your rest,
And watch your safety.
ALONSO Thank you – wondrous heavy!

[*Alonso sleeps. Exit Ariel.*

SEBASTIAN What a strange drowsiness possesses them!
ANTONIO It is the quality o' th' climate.
SEBASTIAN Why
Doth it not then our eyelids sink? I find not

Myself dispos'd to sleep.
ANTONIO Nor I; my spirits are nimble.
They fell together all, as by consent;
They dropp'd, as by a thunder-stroke. What might,
Worthy Sebastian? O, what might! No more!
And yet methinks I see it in thy face,
What thou shouldst be; th' occasion speaks thee; and
My strong imagination sees a crown
Dropping upon thy head.
SEBASTIAN What, art thou waking?
ANTONIO Do you not hear me speak?
SEBASTIAN I do; and surely
It is a sleepy language, and thou speak'st
Out of thy sleep. What is it thou didst say?
This is a strange repose, to be asleep
With eyes wide open; standing, speaking, moving,
And yet so fast asleep.
ANTONIO Noble Sebastian,
Thou let'st thy fortune sleep – die rather; wink'st
Whiles thou art waking.
SEBASTIAN Thou dost snore distinctly;
There's meaning in thy snores.
ANTONIO I am more serious than my custom; you
Must be so too, if heed me; which to do
Trebles thee o'er.
SEBASTIAN Well, I am standing water.
ANTONIO I'll teach you how to flow.
SEBASTIAN Do so: to ebb,
Hereditary sloth instructs me.
ANTONIO O,
If you but knew how you the purpose cherish,
Whiles thus you mock it! how, in stripping it,
You more invest it! Ebbing men indeed,
Most often, do so near the bottom run
By their own fear or sloth.
SEBASTIAN Prithee say on.
The setting of thine eye and cheek proclaim
A matter from thee; and a birth, indeed,
Which throes thee much to yield.
ANTONIO Thus, sir:
Although this lord of weak remembrance, this
Who shall be of as little memory
When he is earth'd, hath here almost persuaded –
For he's a spirit of persuasion, only
Professes to persuade – the King his son's alive,
'Tis as impossible that he's undrown'd
As he that sleeps here swims.
SEBASTIAN I have no hope
That he's undrown'd.
ANTONIO O, out of that 'no hope'
What great hope have you! No hope that way is
Another way so high a hope, that even
Ambition cannot pierce a wink beyond,
But doubt discovery there. Will you grant with me
That Ferdinand is drown'd?
SEBASTIAN He's gone.
ANTONIO Then tell me,
Who's the next heir of Naples?
SEBASTIAN Claribel.
ANTONIO She that is Queen of Tunis; she that dwells
Ten leagues beyond man's life; she that from Naples
Can have no note, unless the sun were post,
The Man i' th' Moon's too slow, till newborn chins
Be rough and razorable; she that from whom
We all were sea-swallow'd, though some cast again,
And by that destiny, to perform an act
Whereof what's past is prologue, what to come
In yours and my discharge.
SEBASTIAN What stuff is this! How say you?
'Tis true, my brother's daughter's Queen of Tunis;
So is she heir of Naples; 'twixt which regions
There is some space.
ANTONIO A space whose ev'ry cubit
Seems to cry out 'How shall that Claribel
Measure us back to Naples? Keep in Tunis,
And let Sebastian wake'. Say this were death
That now hath seiz'd them; why, they were no worse
Than now they are. There be that can rule Naples
As well as he that sleeps; lords that can prate
As amply and unnecessarily
As this Gonzalo; I myself could make
A chough of as deep chat. O, that you bore
The mind that I do! What a sleep were this
For your advancement! Do you understand me?
SEBASTIAN Methinks I do.
ANTONIO And how does your content
Tender your own good fortune?
SEBASTIAN I remember
You did supplant your brother Prospero.
ANTONIO True.
And look how well my garments sit upon me,
Much feater than before. My brother's servants
Were then my fellows; now they are my men.
SEBASTIAN But, for your conscience –
ANTONIO Ay, sir; where lies that? If 'twere a kibe,
'Twould put me to my slipper; but I feel not
This deity in my bosom; twenty consciences
That stand 'twixt me and Milan, candied be they
And melt, ere they molest! Here lies your brother,

No better than the earth he lies upon,
If he were that which now he's like – that's dead;
Whom I with this obedient steel, three inches of it,
Can lay to bed for ever; whiles you, doing thus,
To the perpetual wink for aye might put
This ancient morsel, this Sir Prudence, who
Should not upbraid our course. For all the rest,
They'll take suggestion as a cat laps milk;
They'll tell the clock to any business that
We say befits the hour.

SEBASTIAN Thy case, dear friend,
Shall be my precedent; as thou got'st Milan,
I'll come by Naples. Draw thy sword. One stroke
Shall free thee from the tribute which thou payest;
And I the King shall love thee.

ANTONIO Draw together;
And when I rear my hand, do you the like,
To fall it on Gonzalo.

SEBASTIAN O, but one word.
[*They talk apart.*

Re-enter ARIEL, invisible, with music and song.

ARIEL My master through his art foresees the danger
That you, his friend, are in; and sends me forth –
For else his project dies – to keep them living.
[*Sings in Gonzalo's ear.*

While you here do snoring lie,
Open-ey'd conspiracy
His time doth take.
If of life you keep a care,
Shake off slumber, and beware.
Awake, awake!

ANTONIO Then let us both be sudden.

GONZALO Now, good angels
Preserve the King! [*They wake.*

ALONSO Why, how now? – Ho, awake! –
Why are you drawn?
Wherefore this ghastly looking?

GONZALO What's the matter?

SEBASTIAN Whiles we stood here securing your repose,
Even now, we heard a hollow burst of bellowing
Like bulls, or rather lions; did't not wake you?
It struck mine ear most terribly.

ALONSO I heard nothing.

ANTONIO O, 'twas a din to fright a monster's ear,
To make an earthquake! Sure it was the roar
Of a whole herd of lions.

ALONSO Heard you this, Gonzalo?

GONZALO Upon mine honour, sir, I heard a humming,
And that a strange one too, which did awake me;
I shak'd you, sir, and cried; as mine eyes open'd,
I saw their weapons drawn – there was a noise,
That's verily. 'Tis best we stand upon our guard,
Or that we quit this place. Let's draw our weapons.

ALONSO Lead off this ground; and let's make further search
For my poor son.

GONZALO Heavens keep him from these beasts!
For he is, sure, i' th' island.

ALONSO Lead away.

ARIEL Prospero my lord shall know what I have done;
So, King, go safely on to seek thy son. [*Exeunt.*

SCENE II. *Another part of the island.*

Enter CALIBAN, with a burden of wood.

A noise of thunder heard.

CALIBAN All the infections that the sun sucks up
From bogs, fens, flats, on Prosper fall, and make him
By inch-meal a disease! His spirits hear me,
And yet I needs must curse. But they'll nor pinch,
Fright me with urchin-shows, pitch me i' th' mire,
Nor lead me, like a firebrand, in the dark
Out of my way, unless he bid 'em; but
For every trifle are they set upon me;
Sometime like apes that mow and chatter at me,
And after bite me; then like hedgehogs which
Lie tumbling in my barefoot way, and mount
Their pricks at my footfall; sometime am I
All wound with adders, who with cloven tongues
Do hiss me into madness.

Enter TRINCULO.

Lo, now, lo!
Here comes a spirit of his, and to torment me
For bringing wood in slowly. I'll fall flat;
Perchance he will not mind me.

TRINCULO Here's neither bush nor shrub to bear off any weather at all, and another storm brewing; I hear it sing i' th' wind. Yond same black cloud, yond huge one, looks like a foul bombard that would shed his liquor. If it should thunder as it did before, I know not where to hide my head. Yond same cloud cannot choose but fall by pailfuls. What have we here? a man or a fish? dead or alive? A fish: he smells like a fish; a very ancient and fish-like smell; a kind of not-of-the-newest Poor-John. A strange fish! Were I in England now, as once I was, and had but this fish painted, not a holiday

fool there but would give a piece of silver. There would this monster make a man; any strange beast there makes a man; when they will not give a doit to relieve a lame beggar, they will lay out ten to see a dead Indian. Legg'd like a man, and his fins like arms! Warm, o' my troth! I do now let loose my opinion; hold it no longer: this is no fish, but an islander, that hath lately suffered by a thunderbolt.
[*Thunder*] Alas, the storm is come again! My best way is to creep under his gaberdine; there is no other shelter hereabout. Misery acquaints a man with strange bedfellows. I will here shroud till the dregs of the storm be past.

Enter STEPHANO singing; a bottle in his hand.

STEPHANO I shall no more to sea, to sea,
Here shall I die ashore –
This is a very scurvy tune to sing at a man's funeral; well, here's my comfort. [*Drinks.*

The master, the swabber, the boatswain, and I,
The gunner, and his mate,
Lov'd Mall, Meg, and Marian, and Margery,
But none of us car'd for Kate;
For she had a tongue with a tang,
Would cry to a sailor 'Go hang!'
She lov'd not the savour of tar nor of pitch,
Yet a tailor might scratch her where'er she did itch.
Then to sea, boys, and let her go hang!

This is a scurvy tune too; but here's my comfort. [*Drinks.*

CALIBAN Do not torment me. O!

STEPHANO What's the matter? Have we devils here? Do you put tricks upon 's with savages and men of Ind? Ha! I have not scap'd drowning to be afeard now of your four legs; for it hath been said: As proper a man as ever went on four legs cannot make him give ground; and it shall be said so again, while Stephano breathes at nostrils.

CALIBAN The spirit torments me. O!

STEPHANO This is some monster of the isle with four legs, who hath got, as I take it, an ague. Where the devil should he learn our language? I will give him some relief, if it be but for that. If I can recover him, and keep him tame, and get to Naples with him, he's a present for any emperor that ever trod on neat's leather.

CALIBAN Do not torment me, prithee; I'll bring my wood home faster.

STEPHANO He's in his fit now, and does not talk after the wisest. He shall taste of my bottle; if he have never drunk wine afore, it will go near to remove his fit. If I can recover him, and keep him tame, I will not take too much for him; he shall pay for him that hath him, and that soundly.

CALIBAN Thou dost me yet but little hurt; thou wilt anon, I know it by thy trembling; now Prosper works upon thee.

STEPHANO Come on your ways; open your mouth; here is that which will give language to you, cat. Open your mouth; this will shake your shaking, I can tell you, and that soundly; you cannot tell who's your friend. Open your chaps again.

TRINCULO I should know that voice; it should be – but he is drown'd; and these are devils. O, defend me!

STEPHANO Four legs and two voices; a most delicate monster! His forward voice, now, is to speak well of his friend; his backward voice is to utter foul speeches and to detract. If all the wine in my bottle will recover him, I will help his ague. Come – Amen! I will pour some in thy other mouth.

TRINCULO Stephano!

STEPHANO Doth thy other mouth call me? Mercy, mercy! This is a devil, and no monster; I will leave him; I have no long spoon.

TRINCULO Stephano! If thou beest Stephano, touch me, and speak to me; for I am Trinculo – be not afeard – thy good friend Trinculo.

STEPHANO If thou beest Trinculo, come forth; I'll pull thee by the lesser legs; if any be Trinculo's legs, these are they. Thou art very Trinculo indeed! How cam'st thou to be the siege of this moon-calf? Can he vent Trinculos?

TRINCULO I took him to be kill'd with a thunderstroke. But art thou not drown'd, Stephano? I hope now thou are not drown'd. Is the storm overblown? I hid me under the dead moon-calf's gaberdine for fear of the storm. And art thou living, Stephano? O Stephano, two Neapolitans scap'd!

STEPHANO Prithee, do not turn me about; my stomach is not constant.

CALIBAN [*Aside*] These be fine things, an if they be not sprites.
That's a brave god, and bears celestial liquor.
I will kneel to him.

STEPHANO How didst thou scape? How cam'st thou hither? Swear by this bottle how thou cam'st hither – I escap'd upon a butt of sack, which the sailors heaved o'erboard – by this bottle, which I made of the bark of a tree, with mine own hands, since I was cast ashore.

CALIBAN I'll swear upon that bottle to be thy true subject, for the liquor is not earthly.

STEPHANO Here; swear then how thou escap'dst.

TRINCULO Swum ashore, man, like a duck; I can swim like a duck, I'll be sworn.

STEPHANO [*Passing the bottle*] Here, kiss the book. Though thou canst swim like a duck, thou art made like a goose.

TRINCULO O Stephano, hast any more of this?

STEPHANO The whole butt, man; my cellar is in a rock by th' seaside, where my wine is hid. How now, moon-calf! How does thine ague?

CALIBAN Hast thou not dropp'd from heaven?

STEPHANO Out o' th' moon, I do assure thee; I was the Man i' th' Moon, when time was.

CALIBAN I have seen thee in her, and I do adore thee. My mistress show'd me thee, and thy dog and thy bush.

STEPHANO Come, swear to that; kiss the book. I will furnish it anon with new contents. Swear.

[*Caliban drinks.*

TRINCULO By this good light, this is a very shallow monster! I afeard of him! A very weak monster! The Man i' th' Moon! A most poor credulous monster! Well drawn, monster, in good sooth!

CALIBAN I'll show thee every fertile inch o' th' island; and I will kiss thy foot. I prithee be my god.

TRINCULO By this light, a most perfidious and drunken monster! When 's god's asleep he'll rob his bottle.

CALIBAN I'll kiss thy foot; I'll swear myself thy subject.

STEPHANO Come on, then; down, and swear.

TRINCULO I shall laugh myself to death at this puppy-headed monster. A most scurvy monster! I could find in my heart to beat him –

STEPHANO Come, kiss.

TRINCULO But that the poor monster's in drink. An abominable monster!

CALIBAN I'll show thee the best springs; I'll pluck thee berries;
I'll fish for thee, and get thee wood enough.
A plague upon the tyrant that I serve!
I'll bear him no more sticks, but follow thee,
Thou wondrous man.

TRINCULO A most ridiculous monster, to make a wonder of a poor drunkard!

CALIBAN I prithee let me bring thee where crabs grow;
And I with my long nails will dig thee pignuts;
Show thee a jay's nest, and instruct thee how
To snare the nimble marmoset; I'll bring thee
To clust'ring filberts, and sometimes I'll get thee
Young scamels from the rock. Wilt thou go with me?

STEPHANO I prithee now, lead the way without any more talking. Trinculo, the King and all our company else being drown'd, we will inherit here. Here, bear my bottle. Fellow Trinculo, we'll fill him by and by again.

CALIBAN [*Sings drunkenly*] Farewell, master; farewell, farewell!

TRINCULO A howling monster; a drunken monster!

CALIBAN No more dams I'll make for fish;
Nor fetch in firing
At requiring,
Nor scrape trenchering, nor wash dish.
'Ban 'Ban, Ca – Caliban,
Has a new master – Get a new man.

Freedom, high-day! high-day, freedom! freedom, high-day, freedom!

STEPHANO O brave monster! Lead the way.

[*Exeunt.*

ACT THREE

SCENE I. *Before Prospero's cell.*

Enter FERDINAND, bearing a log.

FERDINAND There be some sports are painful, and their labour
Delight in them sets off; some kinds of baseness
Are nobly undergone, and most poor matters
Point to rich ends. This my mean task
Would be as heavy to me as odious, but
The mistress which I serve quickens what's dead,
And makes my labours pleasures. O, she is
Ten times more gentle than her father's crabbed;
And he's compos'd of harshness. I must remove
Some thousands of these logs, and pile them up,
Upon a sore injunction; my sweet mistress
Weeps when she sees me work, and says such baseness
Had never like executor. I forget;
But these sweet thoughts do even refresh my labours,
Most busy, least when I do it.

Enter MIRANDA; and PROSPERO at a distance, unseen.

MIRANDA Alas, now; pray you,
Work not so hard; I would the lightning had
Burnt up those logs that you are enjoin'd to pile.
Pray, set it down and rest you; when this burns,
'Twill weep for having wearied you. My father

Is hard at study; pray, now, rest yourself;
He's safe for these three hours.
FERDINAND O most dear mistress,
The sun will set before I shall discharge
What I must strive to do.
MIRANDA If you'll sit down,
I'll bear your logs the while; pray give me that;
I'll carry it to the pile.
FERDINAND No, precious creature;
I had rather crack my sinews, break my back,
Than you should such dishonour undergo,
While I sit lazy by.
MIRANDA It would become me
As well as it does you; and I should do it
With much more ease; for my good will is to it,
And yours it is against.
PROSPERO [*Aside*] Poor worm, thou art infected!
This visitation shows it.
MIRANDA You look wearily.
FERDINAND No, noble mistress; 'tis fresh morning with me
When you are by at night. I do beseech you,
Chiefly that I might set it in my prayers,
What is your name?
MIRANDA Miranda – O my father,
I have broke your hest to say so!
FERDINAND Admir'd Miranda!
Indeed the top of admiration; worth
What's dearest to the world! Full many a lady
I have ey'd with best regard; and many a time
Th' harmony of their tongues hath into bondage
Brought my too diligent ear; for several virtues
Have I lik'd several women, never any
With so full soul, but some defect in her
Did quarrel with the noblest grace she ow'd,
And put it to the foil; but you, O you,
So perfect and so peerless, are created
Of every creature's best!
MIRANDA I do not know
One of my sex; no woman's face remember,
Save, from my glass, mine own; nor have I seen
More that I may call men than you, good friend,
And my dear father. How features are abroad,
I am skilless of; but, by my modesty,
The jewel in my dower, I would not wish
Any companion in the world but you;
Nor can imagination form a shape,
Besides yourself, to like of. But I prattle
Something too wildly, and my father's precepts
I therein do forget.
FERDINAND I am, in my condition,
A prince, Miranda; I do think, a king –
I would not so! – and would no more endure
This wooden slavery than to suffer
The flesh-fly blow my mouth. Hear my soul speak:
The very instant that I saw you, did
My heart fly to your service; there resides
To make me slave to it; and for your sake
Am I this patient log-man.
MIRANDA Do you love me?
FERDINAND O heaven, O earth, bear witness to this sound,
And crown what I profess with kind event,
If I speak true! If hollowly, invert
What best is boded me to mischief! I,
Beyond all limit of what else i' th' world,
Do love, prize, honour you.
MIRANDA I am a fool
To weep at what I am glad of.
PROSPERO [*Aside*] Fair encounter
Of two most rare affections! Heavens rain grace
On that which breeds between 'em!
FERDINAND Wherefore weep you?
MIRANDA At mine unworthiness, that dare not offer
What I desire to give, and much less take
What I shall die to want. But this is trifling;
And all the more it seeks to hide itself,
The bigger bulk it shows. Hence, bashful cunning!
And prompt me plain and holy innocence!
I am your wife, if you will marry me;
If not, I'll die your maid. To be your fellow
You may deny me; but I'll be your servant,
Whether you will or no.
FERDINAND My mistress, dearest;
And I thus humble ever.
MIRANDA My husband, then?
FERDINAND Ay, with a heart as willing
As bondage e'er of freedom. Here's my hand.
MIRANDA And mine, with my heart in't. And now farewell
Till half an hour hence.
FERDINAND A thousand thousand!
[*Exeunt Ferdinand and Miranda severally.*
PROSPERO So glad of this as they I cannot be,
Who are surpris'd withal; but my rejoicing
At nothing can be more. I'll to my book;
For yet ere supper time must I perform
Much business appertaining. [*Exit.*

SCENE II. *Another part of the island.*

Enter CALIBAN, STEPHANO and TRINCULO.

STEPHANO Tell not me – when the butt is out we will drink water, not a drop before; therefore bear up, and board 'em. Servant-monster, drink to me.

TRINCULO Servant-monster! The folly of this island! They say there's but five upon this isle: we are three of them; if th' other two be brain'd like us, the state totters.

STEPHANO Drink, servant-monster, when I bid

thee; thy eyes are almost set in thy head.

TRINCULO Where should they be set else? He were a brave monster indeed, if they were set in his tail.

STEPHANO My man-monster hath drown'd his tongue in sack. For my part, the sea cannot drown me; I swam, ere I could recover the shore, five and thirty leagues, off and on. By this light, thou shalt be my lieutenant, monster, or my standard.

TRINCULO Your lieutenant, if you list; he's no standard.

STEPHANO We'll not run, Monsieur Monster.

TRINCULO Nor go neither; but you'll lie like dogs, and yet say nothing neither.

STEPHANO Moon-calf, speak once in thy life, if thou beest a good moon-calf.

CALIBAN How does thy honour? Let me lick thy shoe.
I'll not serve him; he is not valiant.

TRINCULO Thou liest, most ignorant monster: I am in case to justle a constable. Why, thou debosh'd fish, thou, was there ever man a coward that hath drunk so much sack as I to-day? Wilt thou tell a monstrous lie, being but half a fish and half a monster?

CALIBAN Lo, how he mocks me! Wilt thou let him, my lord?

TRINCULO 'Lord' quoth he! That a monster should be such a natural!

CALIBAN Lo, lo again! Bite him to death, I prithee.

STEPHANO Trinculo, keep a good tongue in your head; if you prove a mutineer – the next tree! The poor monster's my subject, and he shall not suffer indignity.

CALIBAN I thank my noble lord. Wilt thou be pleas'd to hearken once again to the suit I made to thee?

STEPHANO Marry will I; kneel and repeat it; I will stand, and so shall Trinculo.

Enter ARIEL, invisible.

CALIBAN As I told thee before, I am subject to a tyrant, a sorcerer, that by his cunning hath cheated me of the island.

ARIEL Thou liest.

CALIBAN Thou liest, thou jesting monkey, thou;
I would my valiant master would destroy thee.
I do not lie.

STEPHANO Trinculo, if you trouble him any more in's tale, by this hand, I will supplant some of your teeth.

TRINCULO Why, I said nothing.

STEPHANO Mum, then, and no more. Proceed.

CALIBAN I say, by sorcery he got this isle;
From me he got it. If thy greatness will
Revenge it on him – for I know thou dar'st,
But this thing dare not –

STEPHANO That's most certain.

CALIBAN Thou shalt be lord of it, and I'll serve thee.

STEPHANO How now shall this be compass'd?
Canst thou bring me to the party?

CALIBAN Yea, yea my lord; I'll yield him thee asleep,
Where thou mayst knock a nail into his head.

ARIEL Thou liest; thou canst not.

CALIBAN What a pied ninny's this! Thou scurvy patch!
I do beseech thy greatness, give him blows,
And take his bottle from him. When that's gone
He shall drink nought but brine; for I'll not show him
Where the quick freshes are.

STEPHANO Trinculo, run into no further danger; interrupt the monster one word further and, by this hand, I'll turn my mercy out o' doors, and make a stock-fish of thee.

TRINCULO Why, what did I? I did nothing. I'll go farther off.

STEPHANO Didst thou not say he lied?

ARIEL Thou liest.

STEPHANO Do I so? Take thou that. [*Beats him*]
As you like this, give me the lie another time.

TRINCULO I did not give the lie. Out o' your wits and hearing too? A pox o' your bottle! This can sack and drinking do. A murrain on your monster, and the devil take your fingers!

CALIBAN Ha, ha, ha!

STEPHANO Now, forward with your tale. –
Prithee stand further off.

CALIBAN Beat him enough; after a little time, I'll beat him too.

STEPHANO Stand farther. Come, proceed.

CALIBAN Why, as I told thee, 'tis a custom with him
I' th' afternoon to sleep; there thou mayst brain him,
Having first seiz'd his books; or with a log
Batter his skull, or paunch him with a stake,
Or cut his wezand with thy knife. Remember
First to possess his books; for without them
He's but a sot, as I am, nor hath not
One spirit to command; they all do hate him
As rootedly as I. Burn but his books.
He has brave utensils – for so he calls them –
Which, when he has a house, he'll deck withal.
And that most deeply to consider is
The beauty of his daughter; he himself
Calls her a nonpareil. I never saw a woman
But only Sycorax my dam and she;
But she as far surpasseth Sycorax
As great'st does least.

STEPHANO Is it so brave a lass?
CALIBAN Ay, lord; she will become thy bed, I warrant,
And bring thee forth brave brood.

STEPHANO Monster, I will kill this man; his daughter and I will be King and Queen – save our Graces! – and Trinculo and thyself shall be viceroys. Dost thou like the plot, Trinculo?

TRINCULO Excellent.

STEPHANO Give me thy hand; I am sorry I beat thee; but while thou liv'st, keep a good tongue in thy head.

CALIBAN Within this half hour will he be asleep.
Wilt thou destroy him then?
STEPHANO Ay, on mine honour.
ARIEL This will I tell my master.
CALIBAN Thou mak'st me merry; I am full of pleasure.
Let us be jocund; will you troll the catch
You taught me but while-ere?

STEPHANO At thy request, monster, I will do reason, any reason. Come on, Trinculo, let us sing. *[Sings.*

Flout 'em and scout 'em,
And scout 'em and flout 'em;
Thought is free.

CALIBAN That's not the tune.

[Ariel plays the tune on a tabor and pipe.

STEPHANO What is this same?

TRINCULO This is the tune of our catch, play'd by the picture of Nobody.

STEPHANO If thou beest a man, show thyself in thy likeness; if thou beest a devil, take't as thou list.

TRINCULO O, forgive me my sins!

STEPHANO He that dies pays all debts. I defy thee. Mercy upon us!

CALIBAN Art thou afeard?

STEPHANO No, monster, not I.

CALIBAN Be not afeard. The isle is full of noises,
Sounds, and sweet airs, that give delight, and hurt not.
Sometimes a thousand twangling instruments
Will hum about mine ears; and sometime voices,
That, if I then had wak'd after long sleep,
Will make me sleep again; and then, in dreaming,
The clouds methought would open and show riches
Ready to drop upon me, that, when I wak'd
I cried to dream again.

STEPHANO This will prove a brave kingdom to me, where I shall have my music for nothing.

CALIBAN When Prospero is destroy'd.

STEPHANO That shall be by and by, I remember the story.

TRINCULO The sound is going away; let's follow it, and after do our work.

STEPHANO Lead, monster; we'll follow. I would I could see this taborer; he lays it on.

TRINCULO Wilt come? I'll follow, Stephano

[Exeunt.

SCENE III. *Another part of the island.*

Enter ALONSO, SEBASTIAN, ANTONIO, GONZALO, ADRIAN, FRANCISCO, and Others.

GONZALO By'r lakin, I can go no further, sir;
My old bones ache. Here's a maze trod, indeed,
Through forth-rights and meanders! By your patience,
I needs must rest me.
ALONSO Old lord, I cannot blame thee,
Who am myself attach'd with weariness
To th' dulling of my spirits; sit down and rest.
Even here I will put off my hope, and keep it
No longer for my flatterer; he is drown'd
Whom thus we stray to find, and the sea mocks
Our frustrate search on land. Well, let him go.
ANTONIO *[Aside to Sebastian]* I am right glad that he's so out of hope.
Do not, for one repulse, forgo the purpose
That you resolv'd t' effect.
SEBASTIAN *[Aside to Antonio]* The next advantage
Will we take throughly.
ANTONIO *[Aside to Sebastian]* Let it be to-night;
For, now they are oppress'd with travel, they
Will not, nor cannot, use such vigilance
As when they are fresh.
SEBASTIAN *[Aside to Antonio]* I say, to-night; no more.

Solemn and strange music; and PROSPERO on the top, invisible. Enter several strange Shapes, bringing in a banquet; and dance about it with gentle actions of salutations; and inviting the King, etc., to eat, they depart.

ALONSO What harmony is this? My good friends, hark!
GONZALO Marvellous sweet music!
ALONSO Give us kind keepers, heavens! What were these?
SEBASTIAN A living drollery. Now I will believe
That there are unicorns; that in Arabia
There is one tree, the phoenix' throne, one phoenix
At this hour reigning there.
ANTONIO I'll believe both;
And what does else want credit, come to me,
And I'll be sworn 'tis true; travellers ne'er did lie,
Though fools at home condemn 'em.
GONZALO If in Naples

I should report this now, would they believe me?
If I should say, I saw such islanders,
For certes these are people of the island,
Who though they are of monstrous shape yet, note,
Their manners are more gentle-kind than of
Our human generation you shall find
Many, nay, almost any.

PROSPERO [*Aside*] Honest lord,
Thou hast said well; for some of you there present
Are worse than devils.

ALONSO I cannot too much muse
Such shapes, such gesture, and such sound, expressing,
Although they want the use of tongue, a kind
Of excellent dumb discourse.

PROSPERO [*Aside*] Praise in departing.

FRANCISCO They vanish'd strangely.

SEBASTIAN No matter, since
They have left their viands behind; for we have stomachs.
Will't please you taste of what is here?

ALONSO Not I.

GONZALO Faith, sir, you need not fear. When we were boys,
Who would believe that there were mountaineers,
Dewlapp'd like bulls, whose throats had hanging at 'em
Wallets of flesh? or that there were such men
Whose heads stood in their breasts? which now we find
Each putter-out of five for one will bring us
Good warrant of.

ALONSO I will stand to, and feed,
Although my last; no matter, since I feel
The best is past. Brother, my lord the Duke,
Stand to, and do as we.

Thunder and lightning. Enter ARIEL, like a harpy; claps his wings upon the table; and, with a quaint device, the banquet vanishes.

ARIEL You are three men of sin, whom Destiny,
That hath to instrument this lower world
And what is in't, the never-surfeited sea
Hath caus'd to belch up you; and on this island
Where man doth not inhabit – you 'mongst men
Being most unfit to live. I have made you mad;
And even with such-like valour men hang and drown
Their proper selves.

[*Alonso, Sebastian etc., draw their swords.*

You fools! I and my fellows
Are ministers of Fate; the elements
Of whom your swords are temper'd may as well
Wound the loud winds, or with bemock'd-at stabs
Kill the still-closing waters, as diminish
One dowle that's in my plume; my fellow-ministers
Are like invulnerable. If you could hurt,
Your swords are now too massy for your strengths
And will not be uplifted. But remember –
For that's my business to you – that you three
From Milan did supplant good Prospero;
Expos'd unto the sea, which hath requit it,
Him, and his innocent child; for which foul deed
The pow'rs, delaying, not forgetting, have
Incens'd the seas and shores, yea, all the creatures,
Against your peace. Thee of thy son, Alonso,
They have bereft; and do pronounce by me
Ling'ring perdition, worse than any death
Can be at once, shall step by step attend
You and your ways; whose wraths to guard you from –
Which here, in this most desolate isle, else falls
Upon your heads – is nothing but heart's sorrow,
And a clear life ensuing,

He vanishes in thunder; then, to soft music, enter the Shapes again, and dance, with mocks and mows, and carrying out the table.

PROSPERO Bravely the figure of this harpy hast thou
Perform'd, my Ariel; a grace it had, devouring.
Of my instruction hast thou nothing bated
In what thou hadst to say; so, with good life
And observation strange, my meaner ministers
Their several kinds have done. My high charms work,
And these mine enemies are all knit up
In their distractions. They now are in my pow'r;
And in these fits I leave them, while I visit
Young Ferdinand, whom they suppose is drown'd,
And his and mine lov'd darling.

[*Exit above.*

GONZALO I' th' name of something holy, sir, why stand you
In this strange stare?

ALONSO O, it is monstrous, monstrous!
Methought the billows spoke, and told me of it;
The winds did sing it to me; and the thunder,
That deep and dreadful organ-pipe, pronounc'd
The name of Prosper; it did bass my trespass.
Therefore my son i' th' ooze is bedded; and
I'll seek him deeper than e'er plummet sounded,
And with him there lie mudded. [*Exit.*

SEBASTIAN But one fiend at a time,
I'll fight their legions o'er.
ANTONIO I'll be thy second.
[Exeunt Sebastian and Antonio.

GONZALO All three of them are desperate; their great guilt,
Like poison given to work a great time after,
Now gins to bite the spirits. I do beseech you,
That are of suppler joints, follow them swiftly,
And hinder them from what this ecstasy
May now provoke them to.
ADRIAN Follow, I pray you. *[Exeunt.*

ACT FOUR

SCENE I. *Before Prospero's cell.*

Enter PROSPERO, FERDINAND, and MIRANDA.

PROSPERO If I have too austerely punish'd you,
Your compensation makes amends; for I
Have given you here a third of mine own life,
Or that for which I live; who once again
I tender to thy hand. All thy vexations
Were but my trials of thy love, and thou
Hast strangely stood the test; here, afore heaven,
I ratify this my rich gift. O Ferdinand!
Do not smile at me that I boast her off,
For thou shalt find she will outstrip all praise,
And make it halt behind her.
FERDINAND I do believe it
Against an oracle.
PROSPERO Then, as my gift, and thine own acquisition
Worthily purchas'd, take my daughter. But
If thou dost break her virgin-knot before
All sanctimonious ceremonies may
With full and holy rite be minist'red,
No sweet aspersion shall the heavens let fall
To make this contract grow; but barren hate,
Sour-ey'd disdain, and discord, shall bestrew
The union of your bed with weeds so loathly
That you shall hate it both. Therefore take heed,
As Hymen's lamps shall light you.
FERDINAND As I hope
For quiet days, fair issue, and long life,
With such love as 'tis now, the murkiest den,
The most opportune place, the strong'st suggestion
Our worser genius can, shall never melt
Mine honour into lust, to take away
The edge of that day's celebration,
When I shall think or Phoebus' steeds are founder'd
Or Night kept chain'd below.
PROSPERO Fairly spoke.
Sit, then, and talk with her; she is thine own.
What, Ariel! my industrious servant, Ariel!

Enter ARIEL.

ARIEL What would my potent master? Here I am
PROSPERO Thou and thy meaner fellows your last service
Did worthily perform; and I must use you
In such another trick. Go bring the rabble,
O'er whom I give thee pow'r, here to this place.
Incite them to quick motion; for I must
Bestow upon the eyes of this young couple
Some vanity of mine art; it is my promise,
And they expect it from me.
ARIEL Presently?
PROSPERO Ay, with a twink.
ARIEL Before you can say 'come' and 'go',
And breathe twice, and cry 'so, so',
Each one, tripping on his toe,
Will be here with mop and mow.
Do you love me, master? No?
PROSPERO Dearly, my delicate Ariel. Do not approach
Till thou dost hear me call.
ARIEL Well! I conceive. *[Exit.*

PROSPERO Look thou be true; do not give dalliance
Too much the rein; the strongest oaths are straw
To th' fire i' th' blood. Be more abstemious,
Or else good night your vow!
FERDINAND I warrant you, sir,
The white cold virgin snow upon my heart
Abates the ardour of my liver.
PROSPERO Well!
Now come, my Ariel, bring a corollary,
Rather than want a spirit; appear, and pertly.
No tongue! All eyes! Be silent. *[Soft music.*

Enter IRIS

IRIS Ceres, most bounteous lady, thy rich leas
Of wheat, rye, barley, vetches, oats, and pease;
Thy turfy mountains, where live nibbling sheep,
And flat meads thatch'd with stover, them to keep;
Thy banks with pioned and twilled brims,
Which spongy April at thy hest betrims,
To make cold nymphs chaste crowns; and thy broom groves,
Whose shadow the dismissed bachelor loves,
Being lass-lorn; thy pole-clipt vineyard;
And thy sea-marge, sterile and rocky-hard,
Where thou thyself dost air – the Queen o' th' sky,

Whose wat'ry arch and messenger am I,
Bids thee leave these; and with her sovereign grace,
Here on this grass-plot, in this very place,
To come and sport. Her peacocks fly amain.

Juno descends in her car.

Approach, rich Ceres, her to entertain.

Enter CERES.

CERES Hail, many-coloured messenger, that ne'er
Dost disobey the wife of Jupiter;
Who, with thy saffron wings, upon my flow'rs
Diffusest honey drops, refreshing show'rs;
And with each end of thy blue bow dost crown
My bosky acres and my unshrubb'd down,
Rich scarf to my proud earth – why hath thy Queen
Summon'd me hither to this short-grass'd green?

IRIS A contract of true love to celebrate,
And some donation freely to estate
On the blest lovers.

CERES Tell me, heavenly bow,
If Venus or her son, as thou dost know,
Do now attend the Queen? Since they did plot
The means that dusky Dis my daughter got,
Her and her blind boy's scandal'd company
I have forsworn.

IRIS Of her society
Be not afraid. I met her Deity
Cutting the clouds towards Paphos, and her son
Dove-drawn with her. Here thought they to have done
Some wanton charm upon this man and maid,
Whose vows are that no bed-rite shall be paid
Till Hymen's torch be lighted; but in vain.
Mars's hot minion is return'd again;
Her waspish-headed son has broke his arrows,
Swears he will shoot no more, but play with sparrows,
And be a boy right out. [*Juno alights.*

CERES Highest Queen of state,
Great Juno, comes; I know her by her gait.

JUNO How does my bounteous sister? Go with me
To bless this twain, that they may prosperous be,
And honour'd in their issue.

They sing.

JUNO Honour, riches, marriage-blessing,
Long continuance, and increasing,
Hourly joys be still upon you!
Juno sings her blessings on you.

CERES Earth's increase, foison plenty,
Barns and garners never empty;
Vines with clust'ring bunches growing,
Plants with goodly burden bowing;
Spring come to you at the farthest,
In the very end of harvest!
Scarcity and want shall shun you,
Ceres' blessing so is on you.

FERDINAND This is a most majestic vision, and
Harmonious charmingly. May I be bold
To think these spirits?

PROSPERO Spirits, which by mine art
I have from their confines call'd to enact
My present fancies.

FERDINAND Let me live here ever;
So rare a wond'red father and a wise
Makes this place Paradise.

[*Juno and Ceres whisper, and send Iris on employment.*

PROSPERO Sweet now, silence;
Juno and Ceres whisper seriously.
There's something else to do; hush, and be mute,
Or else our spell is marr'd.

IRIS You nymphs, call'd Naiads, of the wind'ring brooks,
With your sedg'd crowns and ever harmless looks,
Leave your crisp channels, and on this green land
Answer your summons; Juno does command.
Come, temperate nymphs, and help to celebrate
A contract of true love; be not too late.

Enter certain Nymphs.

You sun-burnt sicklemen, of August weary,
Come hither from the furrow, and be merry;
Make holiday; your rye-straw hats put on,
And these fresh nymphs encounter every one
In country footing.

Enter certain Reapers, properly habited; they join with the Nymphs in a graceful dance; towards the end whereof Prospero starts suddenly, and speaks; after which, to a strange, hollow, and confused noise, they heavily vanish.

PROSPERO [*Aside*] I had forgot that foul conspiracy
Of the beast Caliban and his confederates
Against my life; the minute of their plot
Is almost come. [*To the Spirits*] Well done; avoid; no more!

FERDINAND This is strange; your father's in some passion
That works him strongly.

MIRANDA Never till this day
Saw I him touch'd with anger so distemper'd.

PROSPERO You do look, my son, in a mov'd sort,
As if you were dismay'd; be cheerful, sir.
Our revels now are ended. These our actors,
As I foretold you, were all spirits, and

Are melted into air, into thin air;
And, like the baseless fabric of this vision,
The cloud-capp'd towers, the gorgeous palaces,
The solemn temples, the great globe itself,
Yea, all which it inherit, shall dissolve,
And, like this insubstantial pageant faded,
Leave not a rack behind. We are such stuff
As dreams are made on; and our little life
Is rounded with a sleep. Sir, I am vex'd;
Bear with my weakness; my old brain is troubled;
Be not disturb'd with my infirmity.
If you be pleas'd, retire into my cell
And there repose; a turn or two I'll walk
To still my beating mind.

FERDINAND, MIRANDA We wish your peace. *[Exeunt.*

PROSPERO Come, with a thought. I thank thee, Ariel; come.

Enter ARIEL.

ARIEL Thy thoughts I cleave to. What's thy pleasure?

PROSPERO Spirit,
We must prepare to meet with Caliban.

ARIEL Ay, my commander. When I presented 'Ceres',
I thought to have told thee of it; but I fear'd
Lest I might anger thee.

PROSPERO Say again, where didst thou leave these varlets?

ARIEL I told you, sir they were red-hot with drinking;
So full of valour that they smote the air
For breathing in their faces; beat the ground
For kissing of their feet; yet always bending
Towards their project. Then I beat my tabor,
At which like unback'd colts they prick'd their ears,
Advanc'd their eyelids, lifted up their noses
As they smelt music; so I charm'd their ears,
That calf-like they my lowing follow'd through
Tooth'd briers, sharp furzes, pricking goss, and thorns,
Which ent'red their frail shins. At last I left them
I' th' filthy mantled pool beyond your cell,
There dancing up to th' chins, that the foul lake
O'erstunk their feet.

PROSPERO This was well done, my bird.
Thy shape invisible retain thou still.
The trumpery in my house, go bring it hither
For stale to catch these thieves.

ARIEL I go, I go. *[Exit.*

PROSPERO A devil, a born devil, on whose nature
Nurture can never stick; on whom my pains,
Humanely taken, all, all lost, quite lost;
And as with age his body uglier grows,
So his mind cankers. I will plague them all,
Even to roaring.

Re-enter ARIEL, loaden, with glistering apparel, etc.

Come, hang them on this line.

Prospero and Ariel remain, invisible. Enter CALIBAN, STEPHANO, and TRINCULO, all wet.

CALIBAN Pray you, tread softly, that the blind mole may not
Hear a foot fall; we now are near his cell.

STEPHANO Monster, your fairy, which you say is a harmless fairy, has done little better than play'd the Jack with us.

TRINCULO Monster, I do smell all horse-piss at which my nose is in great indignation.

STEPHANO So is mine. Do you hear, monster? If I should take a displeasure against you, look you –

TRINCULO Thou wert but a lost monster.

CALIBAN Good my lord, give me thy favour still.
Be patient, for the prize I'll bring thee to
Shall hoodwink this mischance; therefore speak softly.
All's hush'd as midnight yet.

TRINCULO Ay, but to lose our bottles in the pool!

STEPHANO There is not only disgrace and dishonour in that, monster, but an infinite loss.

TRINCULO That's more to me than my wetting; yet this is your harmless fairy, monster.

STEPHANO I will fetch off my bottle, though I be o'er ears for my labour.

CALIBAN Prithee, my king, be quiet. Seest thou here,
This is the mouth o' th' cell; no noise, and enter.
Do that good mischief which may make this island
Thine own for ever, and I, thy Caliban,
For aye thy foot-licker.

STEPHANO Give me thy hand. I do begin to have bloody thoughts.

TRINCULO O King Stephano! O peer! O worthy Stephano! Look what a wardrobe here is for thee!

CALIBAN Let it alone, thou fool; it is but trash.

TRINCULO O, ho, monster; we know what belongs to a frippery. O King Stephano!

STEPHANO Put off that gown, Trinculo; by this hand, I'll have that gown.

TRINCULO Thy Grace shall have it.

CALIBAN The dropsy drown this fool! What do you mean
To dote thus on such luggage? Let't alone,
And do the murder first. If he awake,
From toe to crown he'll fill our skins with pinches;
Make us strange stuff.

STEPHANO Be you quiet, monster. Mistress line,

is not this my jerkin? Now is the jerkin under the line; now, jerkin, you are like to lose your hair, and prove a bald jerkin.

TRINCULO Do, do. We steal by line and level, an't like your Grace.

STEPHANO I thank thee for that jest; here's a garment for't. Wit shall not go unrewarded while I am King of this country. 'Steal by line and level' is an excellent pass of pate; there's another garment for't.

TRINCULO Monster, come, put some lime upon your fingers, and away with the rest.

CALIBAN I will have none on't. We shall lose our time,
And all be turn'd to barnacles, or to apes
With foreheads villainous low.

STEPHANO Monster, lay-to your fingers; help to bear this away where my hogshead of wine is, or I'll turn you out of my kingdom. Go to, carry this.

TRINCULO And this.

STEPHANO Ay, and this.

A noise of hunters heard. Enter divers Spirits, in shape of dogs and hounds, hunting them about; Prospero and Ariel setting them on.

PROSPERO Hey, Mountain, hey!
ARIEL Silver! there it goes, Silver!
PROSPERO Fury, Fury! There, Tyrant, there!
Hark, hark!

[*Caliban, Stephano, and Trinculo are driven out.*

Go charge my goblins that they grind their joints
With dry convulsions, shorten up their sinews
With aged cramps, and more pinch-spotted make them
Than pard or cat o' mountain.
ARIEL Hark, they roar.
PROSPERO Let them be hunted soundly. At this hour
Lies at my mercy all mine enemies.
Shortly shall all my labours end, and thou
Shalt have the air at freedom; for a little
Follow, and do me service. [*Exeunt.*

ACT FIVE

SCENE I. *Before Prospero's cell.*

Enter PROSPERO in his magic robes, and ARIEL.

PROSPERO Now does my project gather to a head;
My charms crack not, my spirits obey; and time
Goes upright with his carriage. How's the day?
ARIEL On the sixth hour; at which time, my lord,
You said our work should cease.
PROSPERO I did say so,
When first I rais'd the tempest. Say, my spirit,
How fares the King and 's followers?
ARIEL Confin'd together
In the same fashion as you gave in charge;
Just as you left them; all prisoners, sir,
In the line-grove which weather-fends your cell;
They cannot budge till your release. The King,
His brother, and yours, abide all three distracted,
And the remainder mourning over them,
Brim full of sorrow and dismay; but chiefly
Him you term'd, sir, 'the good old lord, Gonzalo';
His tears run down his beard, like winter's drops
From eaves of reeds. Your charm so strongly works 'em
That if you now beheld them your affections
Would become tender.
PROSPERO Dost thou think so, spirit?
ARIEL Mine would, sir, were I human.
PROSPERO And mine shall.
Hast thou, which art but air, a touch, a feeling
Of their afflictions, and shall not myself,
One of their kind, that relish all as sharply,
Passion as they, be kindlier mov'd than thou art?
Though with their high wrongs I am struck to th' quick,
Yet with my nobler reason 'gainst my fury
Do I take part; the rarer action is
In virtue than in vengeance; they being penitent,
The sole drift of my purpose doth extend
Not a frown further. Go release them, Ariel;
My charms I'll break, their senses I'll restore,
And they shall be themselves.
ARIEL I'll fetch them, sir. [*Exit.*
PROSPERO Ye elves of hills, brooks, standing lakes, and groves;
And ye that on the sands with printless foot
Do chase the ebbing Neptune, and do fly him
When he comes back; you demi-puppets that
By moonshine do the green sour ringlets make,
Whereof the ewe not bites; and you whose pastime
Is to make midnight mushrooms, that rejoice
To hear the solemn curfew; by whose aid –
Weak masters though ye be – I have be-dimm'd
The noontide sun, call'd forth the mutinous winds,

And 'twixt the green sea and the azur'd vault
Set roaring war. To the dread rattling thunder
Have I given fire, and rifted Jove's stout oak
With his own bolt; the strong-bas'd promontory
Have I made shake, and by the spurs pluck'd up
The pine and cedar. Graves at my command
Have wak'd their sleepers, op'd, and let 'em forth,
By my so potent art. But this rough magic
I here abjure; and, when I have requir'd
Some heavenly music – which even now I do –
To work mine end upon their senses that
This airy charm is for, I'll break my staff,
Bury it certain fathoms in the earth,
And deeper than did ever plummet sound
I'll drown my book. [*Solemn music.*

Here enters ARIEL before; then ALONSO, with a frantic gesture, attended by GONZALO; SEBASTIAN and ANTONIO in like manner, attended by ADRIAN and FRANCISO. They all enter the circle which Prospero had made, and there stand charm'd; which Prospero observing, speaks.

A solemn air, and the best comforter
To an unsettled fancy, cure thy brains,
Now useless, boil'd within thy skull! There stand,
For you are spell-stopp'd.
Holy Gonzalo, honourable man,
Mine eyes, ev'n sociable to the show of thine,
Fall fellowly drops. The charm dissolves apace,
And as the morning steals upon the night,
Melting the darkness, so their rising senses
Begin to chase the ignorant fumes that mantle
Their clearer reason. O good Gonzalo,
My true preserver, and a loyal sir
To him thou follow'st! I will pay thy graces
Home both in word and deed. Most cruelly
Didst thou, Alonso, use me and my daughter;
Thy brother was a furtherer in the act.
Thou art pinch'd for 't now, Sebastian. Flesh and blood,
You, brother mine, that entertain'd ambition,
Expell'd remorse and nature, who, with Sebastian –
Whose inward pinches therefore are most strong –
Would here have kill'd your king, I do forgive thee,
Unnatural though thou art. Their understanding
Begins to swell, and the approaching tide
Will shortly fill the reasonable shore
That now lies foul and muddy. Not one of them
That yet looks on me, or would know me. Ariel,
Fetch me the hat and rapier in my cell;
I will discase me, and myself present
As I was sometime Milan. Quickly, spirit;
Thou shalt ere long be free.

ARIEL, on returning, sings and helps to attire him.

Where the bee sucks, there suck I;
In a cowslip's bell I lie;
There I couch when owls do cry.
On the bat's back I do fly
After summer merrily.
Merrily, merrily shall I live now
Under the blossom that hangs on the bough.

PROSPERO Why, that's my dainty Ariel! I shall miss thee;
But yet thou shalt have freedom. So, so, so.
To the King's ship, invisible as thou art;
There shalt thou find the mariners asleep
Under the hatches; the master and the boatswain
Being awake, enforce them to this place;
And presently, I prithee.

ARIEL I drink the air before me, and return
Or ere your pulse twice beat. [*Exit.*

GONZALO All torment, trouble, wonder and amazement,
Inhabits here. Some heavenly power guide us
Out of this fearful country!

PROSPERO Behold, Sir King,
The wronged Duke of Milan, Prospero.
For more assurance that a living prince
Does now speak to thee, I embrace thy body;
And to thee and thy company I bid
A hearty welcome.

ALONSO Whe'er thou be'st he or no,
Or some enchanted trifle to abuse me,
As late I have been, I not know. Thy pulse
Beats, as of flesh and blood; and, since I saw thee,
Th' affliction of my mind amends, with which,
I fear, a madness held me. This must crave –
An if this be at all – a most strange story.
Thy dukedom I resign, and do entreat
Thou pardon me my wrongs. But how should Prospero
Be living and be here?

PROSPERO First, noble friend,
Let me embrace thine age, whose honour cannot
Be measur'd or confin'd.

GONZALO Whether this be
Or be not, I'll not swear.

PROSPERO You do yet taste
Some subtleties o' th' isle, that will not let you
Believe things certain. Welcome, my friends all!
[*Aside to Sebastian and Antonio*] But you, my brace of lords, were I so minded,

I here could pluck his Highness' frown upon you,
And justify you traitors; at this time
I will tell no tales.
SEBASTIAN [*Aside*] The devil speaks in him.
PROSPERO No.
For you, most wicked sir, whom to call brother
Would even infect my mouth, I do forgive
Thy rankest fault – all of them; and require
My dukedom of thee, which perforce I know
Thou must restore.
ALONSO If thou beest Prospero,
Give us particulars of thy preservation;
How thou hast met us here, whom three hours since
Were wreck'd upon this shore; where I have lost –
How sharp the point of this remembrance is! –
My dear son Ferdinand.
PROSPERO I am woe for't, sir.
ALONSO Irreparable is the loss; and patience
Says it is past her cure.
PROSPERO I rather think
You have not sought her help, of whose soft grace
For the like loss I have her sovereign aid,
And rest myself content.
ALONSO You the like loss!
PROSPERO As great to me as late; and, supportable
To make the dear loss, have I means much weaker
Than you may call to comfort you, for I
Have lost my daughter.
ALONSO A daughter!
O heavens, that they were living both in Naples,
The King and Queen there! That they were, I wish
Myself were mudded in that oozy bed
Where my son lies. When did you lose your daughter?
PROSPERO In this last tempest. I perceive these lords
At this encounter do so much admire
That they devour their reason, and scarce think
Their eyes do offices of truth, their words
Are natural breath; but, howsoe'er you have
Been justled from your senses, know for certain
That I am Prospero, and that very duke
Which was thrust forth of Milan; who most strangely
Upon this shore, where you were wreck'd, was landed
To be the lord on't. No more yet of this;
For 'tis a chronicle of day by day,
Not a relation for a breakfast, nor
Befitting this first meeting. Welcome, sir;
This cell's my court; here have I few attendants,
And subjects none abroad; pray you, look in.
My dukedom since you have given me again,
I will requite you with as good a thing;
At least bring forth a wonder, to content ye
As much as me my dukedom.

Here Prospero discovers FERDINAND and MIRANDA playing at chess.

MIRANDA Sweet lord, you play me false.
FERDINAND No, my dearest love,
I would not for the world.
MIRANDA Yes, for a score of kingdoms you should wrangle,
And I would call it fair play.
ALONSO If this prove
A vision of the island, one dear son
Shall I twice lose.
SEBASTIAN A most high miracle!
FERDINAND Though the seas threaten, they are merciful;
I have curs'd them without cause. [*Kneels.*
ALONSO Now all the blessings
Of a glad father compass thee about!
Arise, and say how thou cam'st here.
MIRANDA O, wonder!
How many goodly creatures are there here!
How beauteous mankind is! O brave new world
That has such people in't!
PROSPERO 'Tis new to thee.
ALONSO What is this maid with whom thou wast at play?
Your eld'st acquaintance cannot be three hours;
Is she the goddess that hath sever'd us,
And brought us thus together?
FERDINAND Sir, she is mortal;
But by immortal Providence she's mine.
I chose her when I could not ask my father
For his advice, nor thought I had one. She
Is daughter to this famous Duke of Milan,
Of whom so often I have heard renown
But never saw before; of whom I have
Receiv'd a second life; and second father
This lady makes him to me.
ALONSO I am hers.
But, O, how oddly will it sound that I
Must ask my child forgiveness!
PROSPERO There, sir, stop;
Let us not burden our remembrances with
A heaviness that's gone.
GONZALO I have inly wept,
Or should have spoke ere this. Look down, you gods,
And on this couple drop a blessed crown;
For it is you that have chalk'd forth the way
Which brought us hither.
ALONSO I say, Amen, Gonzalo!

GONZALO Was Milan thrust from Milan, that his issue
Should become Kings of Naples? O, rejoice
Beyond a common joy, and set it down
With gold on lasting pillars: in one voyage
Did Claribel her husband find at Tunis;
And Ferdinand, her brother, found a wife
Where he himself was lost; Prospero his dukedom
In a poor isle; and all of us ourselves
When no man was his own.

ALONSO *[To Ferdinand and Miranda]* Give me your hands.
Let grief and sorrow still embrace his heart
That doth not wish you joy.

GONZALO Be it so. Amen!

Re-enter ARIEL, with the Master and Boat-swain amazedly following.

O look, sir; look, sir! Here is more of us!
I prophesied, if a gallows were on land,
This fellow could not drown. Now, blasphemy,
That swear'st grace o'erboard, not an oath on shore?
Hast thou no mouth by land? What is the news?

BOATSWAIN The best news is that we have safely found
Our King and company; the next, our ship –
Which but three glasses since we gave out split –
Is tight and yare, and bravely rigg'd, as when
We first put out to sea.

ARIEL *[Aside to Prospero]* Sir, all this service
Have I done since I went.

PROSPERO *[Aside to Ariel]* My tricksy spirit!

ALONSO These are not natural events; they strengthen
From strange to stranger. Say, how came you hither?

BOATSWAIN If I did think, sir, I were well awake,
I'd strive to tell you. We were dead of sleep,
And – how, we know not – all clapp'd under hatches;
Where, but even now, with strange and several noises
Of roaring, shrieking, howling, jingling chains,
And moe diversity of sounds, all horrible,
We were awak'd; straightway at liberty;
Where we, in all her trim, freshly beheld
Our royal, good, and gallant ship; our master
Cap'ring to eye her. On a trice, so please you,
Even in a dream, were we divided from them,
And were brought moping hither.

ARIEL *[Aside to Prospero]* Was't well done?

PROSPERO *[Aside to Ariel]* Bravely, my diligence. Thou shalt be free.

ALONSO This is as strange a maze as e'er men trod;
And there is in this business more than nature
Was ever conduct of. Some oracle
Must rectify our knowledge.

PROSPERO Sir, my liege,
Do not infest your mind with beating on
The strangeness of this business; at pick'd leisure,
Which shall be shortly, single I'll resolve you,
Which to you shall seem probable, of every
These happen'd accidents; till when, be cheerful
And think of each thing well. *[Aside to Ariel]* Come hither, spirit;
Set Caliban and his companions free;
Untie the spell. *[Exit Ariel]* How fares my gracious sir?
There are yet missing of your company
Some few odd lads that you remember not.

Re-enter ARIEL, driving in CALIBAN, STEPHANO, and TRINCULO, in their stolen apparel.

STEPHANO Every man shift for all the rest, and let no man take care for himself; for all is but fortune. Coragio, bully-monster, coragio!

TRINCULO If these be true spies which I wear in my head, here's a goodly sight.

CALIBAN O Setebos, these be brave spirits indeed!
How fine my master is! I am afraid
He will chastise me.

SEBASTIAN Ha, ha!
What things are these, my lord Antonio?
Will money buy 'em?

ANTONIO Very like; one of them
Is a plain fish, and no doubt marketable.

PROSPERO Mark but the badges of these men, my lords,
Then say if they be true. This mis-shapen knave –
His mother was a witch, and one so strong
That could control the moon, make flows and ebbs,
And deal in her command without her power.
These three have robb'd me; and this demi-devil –
For he's a bastard one – had plotted with them
To take my life. Two of these fellows you
Must know and own; this thing of darkness I
Acknowledge mine.

CALIBAN I shall be pinch'd to death.

ALONSO Is not this Stephano, my drunken butler?

SEBASTIAN He is drunk now; where had he wine?

ALONSO And Trinculo is reeling ripe; where should they
Find this grand liquor that hath gilded 'em?

How cam'st thou in this pickle?
TRINCULO I have been in such a pickle since I saw you last that, I fear me, will never out of my bones. I shall not fear flyblowing.
SEBASTIAN Why, how now, Stephano!
STEPHANO O, touch me not; I am not Stephano, but a cramp.
PROSPERO You'd be king 'o the isle, sirrah?
STEPHANO I should have been a sore one, then.
ALONSO [*Pointing to Caliban*] This is as strange a thing as e'er I look'd on.
PROSPERO He is as disproportion'd in his manners
As in his shape. Go, sirrah, to my cell;
Take with you your companions; as you look
To have my pardon, trim it handsomely.
CALIBAN Ay, that I will; and I'll be wise hereafter,
And seek for grace. What a thrice-double ass
Was I to take this drunkard for a god,
And worship this dull fool!
PROSPERO Go to; away!
ALONSO Hence, and bestow your luggage where you found it.
SEBASTIAN Or stole it, rather.
[*Exeunt Caliban, Stephano, and Trinculo.*
PROSPERO Sir, I invite your Highness and your train
To my poor cell, where you shall take your rest
For this one night; which, part of it, I'll waste
With such discourse as, I not doubt, shall make it
Go quick away – the story of my life,
And the particular accidents gone by
Since I came to this isle. And in the morn
I'll bring you to your ship, and so to Naples,
Where I have hope to see the nuptial
Of these our dear-belov'd solemnized,
And thence retire me to my Milan, where
Every third thought shall be my grave.
ALONSO I long
To hear the story of your life, which must
Take the ear strangely.
PROSPERO I'll deliver all;
And promise you calm seas, auspicious gales,
And sail so expeditious that shall catch
Your royal fleet far off. [*Aside to Ariel*] My Ariel, chick,
That is thy charge. Then to the elements
Be free, and fare thou well! – Please you, draw near. [*Exeunt.*

EPILOGUE

SPOKEN BY PROSPERO

Now my charms are all o'erthrown,
And what strength I have's mine own,
Which is most faint. Now 'tis true,
I must be here confin'd by you,
Or sent to Naples. Let me not,
Since I have my dukedom got,
And pardon'd the deceiver, dwell
In this bare island by your spell;
But release me from my bands
With the help of your good hands.
Gentle breath of yours my sails
Must fill, or else my project fails,
Which was to please. Now I want
Spirits to enforce, art to enchant;
And my ending is despair
Unless I be reliev'd by prayer,
Which pierces so that it assaults
Mercy itself, and frees all faults.
As you from crimes would pardon'd be,
Let your indulgence set me free.

The Two Gentlemen of Verona

Introduction by ALEC YEARLING

Two gentlemen, their two ladies, their two servants; and of these pairings and doublings Shakespeare makes patterns of parallel and contrast. One gentleman is a lover; the other travels and becomes a lover too; the first follows him, abandoning his own beloved to steal his friend's mistress. There are separations: the ladies follow their gentlemen, one in male disguise, the other not. When everyone is together in the last scene a flicker of sexual danger is subsumed in a sudden glow of generous male friendship before everyone pairs off as they had been paired early in Act 2. The figure has been danced through, despite some false steps, moving towards a harmony more mechanical than truly dynamic.

Patterns are present everywhere in this romantic comedy. The characters, well-born lovers or coarse clowns, weave words together with intense relish. Phrases, lines and sentences pair off in counterchange. Lists rise to climaxes. Puns yank the dialogue sideways along fault-lines of linguistic logic. Everything is grist to the mill: no matter whether a personage is in love, or betrayed, or despairing, a rhetorical occasion is made of it. Shakespeare varies his wares: if your taste does not run to lovers' verse-alternations in the most orthodox ornate late-Elizabethan manner, you may be better pleased by the more impolite but equally schematic ruminations of the servant-clown Launce.

This may be the earliest of Shakespeare's comedies, combining frank delight in linguistic excess with a startling dramatic crudity. Motivation and action are basic. Characters baldly announce what has happened, how they feel, and what they will do about it: Proteus at the opening of 4.2 is a good example. Basic also is such theatrical expertise as is on view. If nothing much is left to the imagination, neither is a situation left hanging for long in the air. No sooner has Proteus said that he intends to forget Julia, than we see Julia preparing to follow him. The moment Proteus has betrayed Valentine's intended elopement to the girl's father, Valentine enters to be exposed with his letter and ladder. Construction is episodic. From time to time Launce strolls in, assisted by his dog, to deliver an amiable comic monologue. He and Speed, the other servant, go in for extended duels of low-grade wit. Most untidy of all, a wholly new element is introduced in Act 4, in the form of a band of outlaws who adopt Valentine as their leader (since he looks personable, and can cope with foreign languages) and proceed to take prisoner everyone else who matters before their mass rehabilitation at Valentine's behest. The outlaws' quaint and clumsy treatment may indicate parodic intentions on Shakespeare's part: certainly the lovers' final showdown concerns us little when surrounded by these desperadoes who contrive to be dashing and pious at the same time.

Crude stuff, one may be tempted to call it; and often it is. It formed a kind of seedbed for Shakespeare's later romantic comedies: the crisscrossing sets of lovers of *A Midsummer Night's Dream* and *Love's Labour's Lost*; the confession of love by a fictitious proxy in *Twelfth Night*; the adoption of cross-dressing for a hazardous journey in *As You*

Like It; the juxtaposition of the more-or-less cynical clown's sentiments with the elevated feelings of lovers and gentlefolk. If Launce was conceived as integral to the play from the first – and some critics have questioned this – it was also the occasion of Shakespeare's discovering the dramatic potential of letting nothing much happen while a well-defined character with a thoroughly imagined linguistic register is thrust forward at the audience. Bottom is here provided with a parent; also Falstaff.

The notorious moment in the final scene when Valentine magnanimously hands Sylvia over to the liar, betrayer and would-be rapist Proteus has been seen as indicating a debate-theme about the claims of male friendship being valued above those of love. This was a Renaissance commonplace, and might fit with the chauvinistic notions routinely on view, as when Valentine in Act 3 Scene 1 is sure that girls mean yes when they say no, but there is little elsewhere in the play to substantiate such an overall reading. The gentlemen end as friends but more emphatically as successful lovers. The theme is best regarded as one element in a pot-pourri of some energy and much stock material.

The Two Gentlemen of Verona

DRAMATIS PERSONAE

DUKE OF MILAN
father to Silvia
VALENTINE, PROTEUS
the two gentlemen
ANTONIO
father to Proteus
THURIO
a foolish rival to Valentine
EGLAMOUR
agent for Silvia in her escape
SPEED
a clownish servant to Valentine
LAUNCE
the like to Proteus
PANTHINO
servant to Antonio
Host where Julia lodges in Milan
Outlaws with Valentine
JULIA
a lady of Verona, beloved of Proteus
SILVIA
the Duke's daughter, beloved of Valentine
LUCETTA
waiting-woman to Julia
Servants
Musicians

THE SCENE: VERONA; MILAN; THE FRONTIERS OF MANTUA

ACT ONE

SCENE I. *Verona. An open place.*

Enter VALENTINE and PROTEUS.

VALENTINE Cease to persuade, my loving Proteus:
Home-keeping youth have ever homely wits.
Were't not affection chains thy tender days
To the sweet glances of thy honour'd love,
I rather would entreat thy company
To see the wonders of the world abroad,
Than, living dully sluggardiz'd at home,
Wear out thy youth with shapeless idleness.
But since thou lov'st, love still, and thrive therein,
Even as I would, when I to love begin.

PROTEUS Wilt thou be gone? Sweet Valentine, adieu!
Think on thy Proteus, when thou haply seest
Some rare noteworthy object in thy travel.
Wish me partaker in thy happiness
When thou dost meet good hap; and in thy danger,
If ever danger do environ thee,
Commend thy grievance to my holy prayers,
For I will be thy beadsman, Valentine.

VALENTINE And on a love-book pray for my success?

PROTEUS Upon some book I love I'll pray for thee.

VALENTINE That's on some shallow story of deep love:
How young Leander cross'd the Hellespont.

PROTEUS That's a deep story of a deeper love;
For he was more than over shoes in love.

VALENTINE 'Tis true; for you are over boots in love,
And yet you never swum the Hellespont.

PROTEUS Over the boots! Nay, give me not the boots.

VALENTINE No, I will not, for it boots thee not.

PROTEUS What?

VALENTINE To be in love – where scorn is bought with groans,
Coy looks with heart-sore sighs, one fading moment's mirth
With twenty watchful, weary, tedious nights;
If haply won, perhaps a hapless gain;
If lost, why then a grievous labour won;
However, but a folly bought with wit,
Or else a wit by folly vanquished.

PROTEUS So, by your circumstance, you call me fool.

VALENTINE So, by your circumstance, I fear you'll prove.

PROTEUS 'Tis love you cavil at; I am not Love.

VALENTINE Love is your master, for he masters you;
And he that is so yoked by a fool,
Methinks, should not be chronicled for wise.

PROTEUS Yet writers say, as in the sweetest bud
The eating canker dwells, so eating love

Inhabits in the finest wits of all.

VALENTINE And writers say, as the most forward bud
Is eaten by the canker ere it blow,
Even so by love the young and tender wit
Is turn'd to folly, blasting in the bud,
Losing his verdure even in the prime,
And all the fair effects of future hopes.
But wherefore waste I time to counsel thee
That art a votary to fond desire?
Once more adieu. My father at the road
Expects my coming, there to see me shipp'd.

PROTEUS And thither will I bring thee, Valentine.

VALENTINE Sweet Proteus, no; now let us take our leave.
To Milan let me hear from thee by letters
Of thy success in love, and what news else
Betideth here in absence of thy friend;
And I likewise will visit thee with mine.

PROTEUS All happiness bechance to thee in Milan!

VALENTINE As much to you at home; and so farewell! [*Exit Valentine.*

PROTEUS He after honour hunts, I after love;
He leaves his friends to dignify them more:
I leave myself, my friends, and all for love.
Thou, Julia, thou hast metamorphis'd me,
Made me neglect my studies, lose my time,
War with good counsel, set the world at nought;
Made wit with musing weak, heart sick with thought.

Enter SPEED.

SPEED Sir Proteus, save you! Saw you my master?

PROTEUS But now he parted hence to embark for Milan.

SPEED Twenty to one then he is shipp'd already,
And I have play'd the sheep in losing him.

PROTEUS Indeed a sheep doth very often stray,
An if the shepherd be awhile away.

SPEED You conclude that my master is a shepherd then, and I a sheep?

PROTEUS I do.

SPEED Why then, my horns are his horns, whether I wake or sleep.

PROTEUS A silly answer, and fitting well a sheep.

SPEED This proves me still a sheep.

PROTEUS True; and thy master a shepherd.

SPEED Nay, that I can deny by a circumstance.

PROTEUS It shall go hard but I'll prove it by another.

SPEED The shepherd seeks the sheep, and not the sheep the shepherd; but I seek my master, and my master seeks not me; therefore, I am no sheep.

PROTEUS The sheep for fodder follow the shepherd; the shepherd for food follows not the sheep: thou for wages followest thy master; thy master for wages follows not thee. Therefore, thou art a sheep.

SPEED Such another proof will make me cry 'baa'.

PROTEUS But dost thou hear? Gav'st thou my letter to Julia?

SPEED Ay, sir; I, a lost mutton, gave your letter to her, a lac'd mutton; and she, a lac'd mutton, gave me, a lost mutton, nothing for my labour.

PROTEUS Here's too small a pasture for such store of muttons.

SPEED If the ground be overcharg'd, you were best stick her.

PROTEUS Nay, in that you are astray: 'twere best pound you.

SPEED Nay, sir, less than a pound shall serve me for carrying your letter.

PROTEUS You mistake; I mean the pound – a pinfold.

SPEED From a pound to a pin? Fold it over and over,
'Tis threefold too little for carrying a letter to your lover.

PROTEUS But what said she?

SPEED [*Nodding*] Ay.

PROTEUS Nod-ay. Why, that's 'noddy'.

SPEED You mistook, sir; I say she did nod; and you ask me if she did nod; and I say 'Ay'.

PROTEUS And that set together is 'noddy'.

SPEED Now you have taken the pains to set it together, take it for your pains.

PROTEUS No, no; you shall have it for bearing the letter.

SPEED Well, I perceive I must be fain to bear with you.

PROTEUS Why, sir, how do you bear with me?

SPEED Marry, sir, the letter, very orderly; having nothing but the word 'noddy' for my pains.

PROTEUS Beshrew me, but you have a quick wit.

SPEED And yet it cannot overtake your slow purse.

PROTEUS Come, come, open the matter; in brief, what said she?

SPEED Open your purse, that the money and the matter may be both at once delivered.

PROTEUS Well, sir, here is for your pains. What said she?

SPEED Truly, sir, I think you'll hardly win her.

PROTEUS Why, couldst thou perceive so much from her?

SPEED Sir, I could perceive nothing at all from her; no, not so much as a ducat for delivering your letter; and being so hard to me that brought your mind, I fear she'll prove as hard to you in telling your mind. Give her no token but stones, for she's as hard as steel.

PROTEUS What said she? Nothing?

SPEED No, not so much as 'Take this for thy pains'. To testify your bounty, I thank you, you have testern'd me; in requital whereof, henceforth carry your letters yourself; and so, sir, I'll commend you to my master.

PROTEUS Go, go, be gone, to save your ship from wreck,
Which cannot perish, having thee aboard,
Being destin'd to a drier death on shore.

[*Exit Speed.*

I must go send some better messenger.
I fear my Julia would not deign my lines,
Receiving them from such a worthless post.

[*Exit.*

SCENE II. *Verona. The garden of Julia's house.*

Enter JULIA and LUCETTA.

JULIA But say, Lucetta, now we are alone,
Wouldst thou then counsel me to fall in love?

LUCETTA Ay, madam; so you stumble not unheedfully.

JULIA Of all the fair resort of gentlemen
That every day with parle encounter me,
In thy opinion which is worthiest love?

LUCETTA Please you, repeat their names; I'll show my mind
According to my shallow simple skill.

JULIA What think'st thou of the fair Sir Eglamour?

LUCETTA As of a knight well-spoken, neat, and fine;
But, were I you, he never should be mine.

JULIA What think'st thou of the rich Mercatio?

LUCETTA Well of his wealth; but of himself, so so.

JULIA What think'st thou of the gentle Proteus?

LUCETTA Lord, Lord! to see what folly reigns in us!

JULIA How now! what means this passion at his name?

LUCETTA Pardon, dear madam; 'tis a passing shame
That I, unworthy body as I am,
Should censure thus on lovely gentlemen.

JULIA Why not on Proteus, as of all the rest?

LUCETTA Then thus: of many good I think him best.

JULIA Your reason?

LUCETTA I have no other but a woman's reason:
I think him so, because I think him so.

JULIA And wouldst thou have me cast my love on him?

LUCETTA Ay, if you thought your love not cast away.

JULIA Why, he, of all the rest, hath never mov'd me.

LUCETTA Yet he, of all the rest, I think, best loves ye.

JULIA His little speaking shows his love but small.

LUCETTA Fire that's closest kept burns most of all.

JULIA They do not love that do not show their love.

LUCETTA O, they love least that let men know their love.

JULIA I would I knew his mind.

LUCETTA Peruse this paper, madam.

JULIA 'To Julia' – Say, from whom?

LUCETTA That the contents will show.

JULIA Say, say, who gave it thee?

LUCETTA Sir Valentine's page; and sent, I think, from Proteus.
He would have given it you; but I, being in the way,
Did in your name receive it; pardon the fault, I pray.

JULIA Now, by my modesty, a goodly broker!
Dare you presume to harbour wanton lines?
To whisper and conspire against my youth?
Now, trust me, 'tis an office of great worth,
And you an officer fit for the place.
There, take the paper; see it be return'd;
Or else return no more into my sight.

LUCETTA To plead for love deserves more fee than hate.

JULIA Will ye be gone?

LUCETTA That you may ruminate.

[*Exit.*

JULIA And yet, I would I had o'erlook'd the letter.
It were a shame to call her back again,
And pray her to a fault for which I chid her.
What fool is she, that knows I am a maid
And would not force the letter to my view!
Since maids, in modesty, say 'No' to that
Which they would have the profferer construe 'Ay'.
Fie, fie, how wayward is this foolish love,
That like a testy babe will scratch the nurse,
And presently, all humbled, kiss the rod!
How churlishly I chid Lucetta hence,
When willingly I would have had her here!
How angerly I taught my brow to frown,
When inward joy enforc'd my heart to smile!
My penance is to call Lucetta back
And ask remission for my folly past.
What ho! Lucetta!

Re-enter LUCETTA.

LUCETTA What would your ladyship?

JULIA Is 't near dinner time?

LUCETTA I would it were,
That you might kill your stomach on your meat
And not upon your maid.
JULIA What is't that you took up so gingerly?
LUCETTA Nothing.
JULIA Why didst thou stoop then?
LUCETTA To take a paper up that I let fall.
JULIA And is that paper nothing?
LUCETTA Nothing concerning me.
JULIA Then let it lie for those that it concerns.
LUCETTA Madam, it will not lie where it concerns,
Unless it have a false interpreter.
JULIA Some love of yours hath writ to you in rhyme.
LUCETTA That I might sing it, madam, to a tune.
Give me a note; your ladyship can set.
JULIA As little by such toys as may be possible.
Best sing it to the tune of 'Light o' Love'.
LUCETTA It is too heavy for so light a tune.
JULIA Heavy! belike it hath some burden then.
LUCETTA Ay; and melodious were it, would you sing it.
JULIA And why not you?
LUCETTA I cannot reach so high.
JULIA Let's see your song. [*Lucetta withholds the letter*] How now, minion!
LUCETTA Keep tune there still, so you will sing it out.
And yet methinks I do not like this tune.
JULIA You do not!
LUCETTA No, madam; 'tis too sharp.
JULIA You, minion, are too saucy.
LUCETTA Nay, now you are too flat
And mar the concord with too harsh a descant;
There wanteth but a mean to fill your song.
JULIA The mean is drown'd with your unruly bass.
LUCETTA Indeed, I bid the base for Proteus.
JULIA This babble shall not henceforth trouble me.
Here is a coil with protestation!
[*Tears the letter.*]
Go, get you gone; and let the papers lie.
You would be fing'ring them, to anger me.
LUCETTA She makes it strange; but she would be best pleas'd
To be so ang'red with another letter. [*Exit.*
JULIA Nay, would I were so ang'red with the same!
O hateful hands, to tear such loving words!
Injurious wasps, to feed on such sweet honey
And kill the bees that yield it with your stings!
I'll kiss each several paper for amends.
Look, here is writ 'kind Julia'. Unkind Julia,
As in revenge of thy ingratitude,
I throw thy name against the bruising stones,
Trampling contemptuously on thy disdain.
And here is writ 'love-wounded Proteus'.
Poor wounded name! my bosom, as a bed,
Shall lodge thee till thy wound be throughly heal'd;
And thus I search it with a sovereign kiss.
But twice or thrice was 'Proteus' written down.
Be calm, good wind, blow not a word away
Till I have found each letter in the letter –
Except mine own name; that some whirlwind bear
Unto a ragged, fearful, hanging rock,
And throw it thence into the raging sea.
Lo, here in one line is his name twice writ:
'Poor forlorn Proteus, passionate Proteus,
To the sweet Julia'. That I'll tear away;
And yet I will not, sith so prettily
He couples it to his complaining names.
Thus will I fold them one upon another;
Now kiss, embrace, contend, do what you will.

Re-enter LUCETTA.

LUCETTA Madam,
Dinner is ready, and your father stays.
JULIA Well, let us go.
LUCETTA What, shall these papers lie like tell-tales here?
JULIA If you respect them, best to take them up.
LUCETTA Nay, I was taken up for laying them down;
Yet here they shall not lie for catching cold.
JULIA I see you have a month's mind to them.
LUCETTA Ay, madam, you may say what sights you see;
I see things too, although you judge I wink.
JULIA Come, come; will't please you go? [*Exeunt.*

SCENE III. *Verona. Antonio's house.*

Enter ANTONIO and PANTHINO.

ANTONIO Tell me, Panthino, what sad talk was that
Wherewith my brother held you in the cloister?
PANTHINO 'Twas of his nephew Proteus, your son.
ANTONIO Why, what of him?
PANTHINO He wond'red that your lordship
Would suffer him to spend his youth at home.
While other men, of slender reputation,
Put forth their sons to seek preferment out:
Some to the wars, to try their fortune there;
Some to discover islands far away;
Some to the studious universities.
For any, or for all these exercises,
He said that Proteus, your son, was meet;
And did request me to importune you
To let him spend his time no more at home,

Which would be great impeachment to his age,
In having known no travel in his youth.

ANTONIO Nor need'st thou much importune me to that
Whereon this month I have been hammering.
I have consider'd well his loss of time,
And how he cannot be a perfect man,
Not being tried and tutor'd in the world:
Experience is by industry achiev'd,
And perfected by the swift course of time.
Then tell me whither were I best to send him.

PANTHINO I think your lordship is not ignorant
How his companion, youthful Valentine,
Attends the Emperor in his royal court.

ANTONIO I know it well.

PANTHINO 'Twere good, I think, your lordship sent him thither:
There shall he practise tilts and tournaments,
Hear sweet discourse, converse with noblemen,
And be in eye of every exercise
Worthy his youth and nobleness of birth.

ANTONIO I like thy counsel; well hast thou advis'd;
And that thou mayst perceive how well I like it,
The execution of it shall make known:
Even with the speediest expedition
I will dispatch him to the Emperor's court.

PANTHINO To-morrow, may it please you, Don Alphonso
With other gentlemen of good esteem
Are journeying to salute the Emperor,
And to commend their service to his will.

ANTONIO Good company; with them shall Proteus go.

Enter PROTEUS.

And – in good time! – now will we break with him.

PROTEUS Sweet love. sweet lines! sweet life!
Here is her hand, the agent of her heart;
Here is her oath for love, her honour's pawn.
O that our fathers would applaud our loves,
To seal our happiness with their consents!
O heavenly Julia!

ANTONIO How now! What letter are you reading there?

PROTEUS May't please your lordship, 'tis a word or two
Of commendations sent from Valentine,
Deliver'd by a friend that came from him.

ANTONIO Lend me the letter; let me see what news.

PROTEUS There is no news, my lord; but that he writes
How happily he lives, how well-belov'd
And daily graced by the Emperor;
Wishing me with him, partner of his fortune.

ANTONIO And how stand you affected to his wish?

PROTEUS As one relying on your lordship's will,
And not depending on his friendly wish.

ANTONIO My will is something sorted with his wish.
Muse not that I thus suddenly proceed;
For what I will, I will, and there an end.
I am resolv'd that thou shalt spend some time
With Valentinus in the Emperor's court;
What maintenance he from his friends receives,
Like exhibition thou shalt have from me.
To-morrow be in readiness to go –
Excuse it not, for I am peremptory.

PROTEUS My lord, I cannot be so soon provided;
Please you, deliberate a day or two.

ANTONIO Look, what thou want'st shall be sent after thee.
No more of stay; to-morrow thou must go.
Come on, Panthino; you shall be employ'd
To hasten on his expedition.

[Exeunt Antonio and Panthino.

PROTEUS Thus have I shunn'd the fire for fear of burning,
And drench'd me in the sea, where I am drown'd.
I fear'd to show my father Julia's letter,
Lest he should take exceptions to my love;
And with the vantage of mine own excuse
Hath he excepted most against my love.
O, how this spring of love resembleth
The uncertain glory of an April day,
Which now shows all the beauty of the sun,
And by and by a cloud takes all away!

Re-enter PANTHINO.

PANTHINO Sir Proteus, your father calls for you;
He is in haste; therefore, I pray you, go.

PROTEUS Why, this it is: my heart accords thereto;
And yet a thousand times it answers 'No'.

[Exeunt.

ACT TWO

SCENE I. *Milan. The Duke's palace.*

Enter VALENTINE and SPEED.

SPEED Sir, your glove.

VALENTINE Not mine: my gloves are on.

SPEED Why, then, this may be yours; for this is but one.

VALENTINE Ha! let me see; ay, give it me, it's mine;
Sweet ornament that decks a thing divine!
Ah, Silvia! Silvia!

SPEED [*Calling*] Madam Silvia! Madam Silvia!

VALENTINE How now, sirrah?

SPEED She is not within hearing, sir.

VALENTINE Why sir, who bade you call her?

SPEED Your worship, sir; or else I mistook.

VALENTINE Well, you'll still be too forward.

SPEED And yet I was last chidden for being too slow.

VALENTINE Go to, sir; tell me, do you know Madam Silvia?

SPEED She that your worship loves?

VALENTINE Why, how know you that I am in love?

SPEED Marry, by these special marks: first, you have learn'd, like Sir Proteus, to wreath your arms like a malcontent; to relish a love-song, like a robin redbreast; to walk alone, like one that had the pestilence; to sigh, like a school-boy that had lost his A B C; to weep, like a young wench that had buried her grandam; to fast, like one that takes diet; to watch, like one that fears robbing; to speak puling, like a beggar at Hallowmas. You were wont, when you laughed, to crow like a cock; when you walk'd, to walk like one of the lions; when you fasted, it was presently after dinner; when you look'd sadly, it was for want of money. And now you are metamorphis'd with a mistress, that, when I look on you, I can hardly think you my master.

VALENTINE Are all these things perceiv'd in me?

SPEED They are all perceiv'd without ye.

VALENTINE Without me? They cannot.

SPEED Without you! Nay, that's certain; for, without you were so simple, none else would; but you are so without these follies that these follies are within you, and shine through you like the water in an urinal, that not an eye that sees you but is a physician to comment on your malady.

VALENTINE But tell me, dost thou know my lady Silvia?

SPEED She that you gaze on so, as she sits at supper?

VALENTINE Hast thou observ'd that? Even she, I mean.

SPEED Why, sir, I know her not.

VALENTINE Dost thou know her by my gazing on her, and yet know'st her not?

SPEED Is she not hard-favour'd, sir?

VALENTINE Not so fair, boy, as well-favour'd.

SPEED Sir, I know that well enough.

VALENTINE What dost thou know?

SPEED That she is not so fair as, of you, well favour'd.

VALENTINE I mean that her beauty is exquisite, but her favour infinite.

SPEED That's because the one is painted, and the other out of all count.

VALENTINE How painted? and how out of count?

SPEED Marry, sir, so painted, to make her fair, that no man counts of her beauty.

VALENTINE How esteem'st thou me? I account of her beauty.

SPEED You never saw her since she was deform'd.

VALENTINE How long hath she been deform'd?

SPEED Ever since you lov'd her.

VALENTINE I have lov'd her ever since I saw her, and still I see her beautiful.

SPEED If you love her, you cannot see her.

VALENTINE Why?

SPEED Because Love is blind. O that you had mine eyes; or your own eyes had the lights they were wont to have when you chid at Sir Proteus for going ungarter'd!

VALENTINE What should I see then?

SPEED Your own present folly and her passing deformity; for he, being in love, could not see to garter his hose; and you, being in love, cannot see to put on your hose.

VALENTINE Belike, boy, then you are in love; for last morning you could not see to wipe my shoes.

SPEED True, sir; I was in love with my bed. I thank you, you swing'd me for my love, which makes me the bolder to chide you for yours.

VALENTINE In conclusion, I stand affected to her.

SPEED I would you were set, so your affection would cease.

VALENTINE Last night she enjoin'd me to write some lines to one she loves.

SPEED And have you?

VALENTINE I have.

SPEED Are they not lamely writ?

VALENTINE No, boy, but as well as I can do them.

Enter SILVIA.

Peace! here she comes.

SPEED [*Aside*] O excellent motion! O exceeding puppet! Now will he interpret to her.
VALENTINE Madam and mistress, a thousand good morrows.
SPEED [*Aside*] O, give ye good ev'n!
Here's a million of manners.
SILVIA Sir Valentine and servant, to you two thousand.
SPEED [*Aside*] He should give her interest, and she gives it him.
VALENTINE As you enjoin'd me, I have writ your letter
Unto the secret nameless friend of yours;
Which I was much unwilling to proceed in,
But for my duty to your ladyship.
SILVIA I thank you, gentle servant. 'Tis very clerkly done.
VALENTINE Now trust me, madam, it came hardly off;
For, being ignorant to whom it goes,
I writ at random, very doubtfully.
SILVIA Perchance you think too much of so much pains?
VALENTINE No, madam; so it stead you, I will write,
Please you command, a thousand times as much;
And yet –
SILVIA A pretty period! Well, I guess the sequel;
And yet I will not name it – and yet I care not.
And yet take this again – and yet I thank you –
Meaning henceforth to trouble you no more.
SPEED [*Aside*] And yet you will; and yet another 'yet'.
VALENTINE What means your ladyship? Do you not like it?
SILVIA Yes, yes; the lines are very quaintly writ;
But, since unwillingly, take them again.
Nay, take them. [*Gives back the letter.*
VALENTINE Madam, they are for you.
SILVIA Ay, ay, you writ them, sir, at my request;
But I will none of them; they are for you:
I would have had them writ more movingly.
VALENTINE Please you, I'll write your ladyship another.
SILVIA And when it's writ, for my sake read it over;
And if it please you, so; if not, why, so.
VALENTINE If it please me, madam, what then?
SILVIA Why, if it please you, take it for your labour.
And so good morrow, servant. [*Exit Silvia.*
SPEED O jest unseen, inscrutable, invisible,
As a nose on a man's face, or a weather-cock on a steeple!
My master sues to her; and she hath taught her suitor,
He being her pupil, to become her tutor.
O excellent device! Was there ever heard a better,
That my master, being scribe, to himself should write the letter?
VALENTINE How now, sir! What are you reasoning with yourself?
SPEED Nay, I was rhyming: 'tis you that have the reason.
VALENTINE To do what?
SPEED To be a spokesman from Madam Silvia?
VALENTINE To whom?
SPEED To yourself; why, she woos you by a figure.
VALENTINE What figure?
SPEED By a letter, I should say.
VALENTINE Why, she hath not writ to me.
SPEED What need she, when she hath made you write to yourself? Why, do you not perceive the jest?
VALENTINE No, believe me.
SPEED No believing you indeed, sir. But did you perceive her earnest?
VALENTINE She gave me none except an angry word.
SPEED Why, she hath given you a letter.
VALENTINE That's the letter I writ to her friend.
SPEED And that letter hath she deliver'd, and there an end.
VALENTINE I would it were no worse.
SPEED I'll warrant you 'tis as well.
'For often have you writ to her; and she, in modesty,
Or else for want of idle time, could not again reply;
Or fearing else some messenger that might her mind discover,
Herself hath taught her love himself to write unto her lover.'
All this I speak in print, for in print I found it.
Why muse you, sir? 'Tis dinner time.
VALENTINE I have din'd.
SPEED Ay, but hearken, sir; though the chameleon Love can feed on the air, I am one that am nourish'd by my victuals, and would fain have meat. O, be not like your mistress! Be moved, be moved. [*Exeunt.*

SCENE II. *Verona. Julia's house.*

Enter PROTEUS and JULIA.

PROTEUS Have patience, gentle Julia.
JULIA I must, where is no remedy.
PROTEUS When possibly I can, I will return.
JULIA If you turn not, you will return the sooner.
Keep this remembrance for thy Julia's sake. [*Giving a ring.*

PROTEUS Why, then, we'll make exchange. Here, take you this.
JULIA And seal the bargain with a holy kiss.
PROTEUS Here is my hand for my true constancy;
And when that hour o'erslips me in the day
Wherein I sigh not, Julia, for thy sake,
The next ensuing hour some foul mischance
Torment me for my love's forgetfulness!
My father stays my coming; answer not;
The tide is now – nay, not thy tide of tears:
That tide will stay me longer than I should.
Julia, farewell! [*Exit Julia.*
What, gone without a word?
Ay, so true love should do: it cannot speak;
For truth hath better deeds than words to grace it.

Enter PANTHINO.

PANTHINO Sir Proteus, you are stay'd for.
PROTEUS Go; I come, I come.
Alas! this parting strikes poor lovers dumb.
[*Exeunt.*

SCENE III. *Verona. A street.*

Enter LAUNCE, leading a dog.

LAUNCE Nay, 'twill be this hour ere I have done weeping; all the kind of the Launces have this very fault. I have receiv'd my proportion, like the Prodigious Son, and am going with Sir Proteus to the Imperial's court. I think Crab my dog be the sourest-natured dog that lives: my mother weeping, my father wailing, my sister crying, our maid howling, our cat wringing her hands, and all our house in a great perplexity; yet did not this cruel-hearted cur shed one tear. He is a stone, a very pebble stone, and has no more pity in him than a dog. A Jew would have wept to have seen our parting; why, my grandam having no eyes, look you, wept herself blind at my parting. Nay, I'll show you the manner of it. This shoe is my father; no, this left shoe is my father; no, no, this left shoe is my mother, nay, that cannot be so neither; yes, it is so, it is so, it hath the worser sole. This shoe with the hole in it is my mother, and this my father. A vengeance on 't! There 'tis. Now, sir, this staff is my sister, for, look you, she is as white as a lily and as small as a wand; this hat is Nan our maid; I am the dog; no, the dog is himself, and I am the dog – O, the dog is me, and I am myself; ay, so, so. Now come I to my father: 'Father, your blessing'. Now should not the shoe speak a word for weeping; now should I kiss my father; well, he weeps on. Now come I to my mother. O that she could speak now like a wood woman! Well, I kiss her – why there 'tis; here's my mother's breath up and down. Now come I to my sister; mark the moan she makes. Now the dog all this while sheds not a tear, nor speaks a word; but see how I lay the dust with my tears.

Enter PANTHINO.

PANTHINO Launce, away, away aboard! Thy master is shipp'd, and thou art to post after with oars. What's the matter? Why weep'st thou, man? Away, ass! You'll lose the tide if you tarry any longer.
LAUNCE It is no matter if the tied were lost; for it is the unkindest tied that ever any man tied.
PANTHINO What's the unkindest tide?
LAUNCE Why, he that's tied here, Crab, my dog.
PANTHINO Tut, man, I mean thou'lt lose the flood, and, in losing the flood, lose thy voyage, and, in losing thy voyage, lose thy master, and, in losing thy master, lose thy service, and, in losing thy service – Why dost thou stop my mouth?
LAUNCE For fear thou shouldst lose thy tongue.
PANTHINO Where should I lose my tongue?
LAUNCE In thy tale.
PANTHINO In thy tail!
LAUNCE Lose the tide, and the voyage, and the master, and the service, and the tied! Why, man, if the river were dry, I am able to fill it with my tears; if the wind were down, I could drive the boat with my sighs.
PANTHINO Come, come away, man; I was sent to call thee.
LAUNCE Sir, call me what thou dar'st.
PANTHINO Wilt thou go?
LAUNCE Well I will go. [*Exeunt.*

SCENE IV. *Milan. The Duke's Palace.*

Enter SILVIA, VALENTINE, THURIO, and SPEED.

SILVIA Servant!
VALENTINE Mistress?
SPEED Master, Sir Thurio frowns on you.
VALENTINE Ay, boy, it's for love.
SPEED Not of you.
VALENTINE Of my mistress, then.
SPEED 'Twere good you knock'd him. [*Exit.*
SILVIA Servant, you are sad.
VALENTINE Indeed, madam, I seem so.
THURIO Seem you that you are not?
VALENTINE Haply I do.
THURIO So do counterfeits.
VALENTINE So do you.
THURIO What seem I that I am not?
VALENTINE Wise.
THURIO What instance of the contrary?

VALENTINE Your folly.

THURIO And how quote you my folly?

VALENTINE I quote it in your jerkin.

THURIO My jerkin is a doublet.

VALENTINE Well, then, I'll double your folly.

THURIO How?

SILVIA What, angry, Sir Thurio! Do you change colour?

VALENTINE Give him leave, madam; he is a kind of chameleon.

THURIO That hath more mind to feed on your blood than live in your air.

VALENTINE You have said, sir.

THURIO Ay, sir, and done too, for this time.

VALENTINE I know it well, sir; you always end ere you begin.

SILVIA A fine volley of words, gentlemen, and quickly shot off.

VALENTINE 'Tis indeed, madam; we thank the giver.

SILVIA Who is that, servant?

VALENTINE Yourself, sweet lady; for you gave the fire. Sir Thurio borrows his wit from your ladyship's looks, and spends what he borrows kindly in your company.

THURIO Sir, if you spend word for word with me, I shall make your wit bankrupt.

VALENTINE I know it well, sir; you have an exchequer of words, and, I think, no other treasure to give your followers; for it appears by their bare liveries that they live by your bare words.

Enter DUKE.

SILVIA No more, gentlemen, no more. Here comes my father.

DUKE Now, daughter Silvia, you are hard beset.
Sir Valentine, your father is in good health.
What say you to a letter from your friends
Of much good news?

VALENTINE My lord, I will be thankful
To any happy messenger from thence.

DUKE Know ye Don Antonio, your countryman?

VALENTINE Ay, my good lord, I know the gentleman
To be of worth and worthy estimation,
And not without desert so well reputed.

DUKE Hath he not a son?

VALENTINE Ay, my good lord; a son that well deserves
The honour and regard of such a father.

DUKE You know him well?

VALENTINE I knew him as myself; for from our infancy
We have convers'd and spent our hours together;
And though myself have been an idle truant,
Omitting the sweet benefit of time
To clothe mine age with angel-like perfection,
Yet hath Sir Proteus, for that's his name,
Made use and fair advantage of his days:
His years but young, but his experience old;
His head unmellowed, but his judgment ripe;
And, in a word, for far behind his worth
Comes all the praises that I now bestow,
He is complete in feature and in mind,
With all good grace to grace a gentleman.

DUKE Beshrew me, sir, but if he make this good,
He is as worthy for an empress' love
As meet to be an emperor's counsellor.
Well, sir, this gentleman is come to me
With commendation from great potentates,
And here he means to spend his time awhile.
I think 'tis no unwelcome news to you.

VALENTINE Should I have wish'd a thing, it had been he.

DUKE Welcome him, then, according to his worth –
Silvia, I speak to you, and you, Sir Thurio;
For Valentine, I need not cite him to it.
I will send him hither to you presently.

[*Exit Duke.*

VALENTINE This is the gentleman I told your ladyship
Had come along with me but that his mistress
Did hold his eyes lock'd in her crystal looks.

SILVIA Belike that now she hath enfranchis'd them
Upon some other pawn for fealty.

VALENTINE Nay, sure, I think she holds them prisoners still.

SILVIA Nay, then, he should be blind; and, being blind,
How could he see his way to seek out you?

VALENTINE Why, lady, Love hath twenty pair of eyes.

THURIO They say that Love hath not an eye at all.

VALENTINE To see such lovers, Thurio, as yourself;
Upon a homely object Love can wink.

[*Exit Thurio.*

Enter PROTEUS.

SILVIA Have done, have done; here comes the gentleman.

VALENTINE Welcome, dear Proteus! Mistress, I beseech you
Confirm his welcome with some special favour.

SILVIA His worth is warrant for his welcome hither,
If this be he you oft have wish'd to hear from.

VALENTINE Mistress, it is; sweet lady, entertain him

To be my fellow-servant to your ladyship.
SILVIA Too low a mistress for so high a servant.
PROTEUS Not so, sweet lady; but too mean a servant
To have a look of such a worthy mistress.
VALENTINE Leave off discourse of disability;
Sweet lady, entertain him for your servant.
PROTEUS My duty will I boast of, nothing else.
SILVIA And duty never yet did want his meed.
Servant, you are welcome to a worthless mistress.
PROTEUS I'll die on him that says so but yourself.
SILVIA That you are welcome?
PROTEUS That you are worthless.

Re-enter THURIO.

THURIO Madam, my lord your father would speak with you.
SILVIA I wait upon his pleasure. Come, Sir Thurio,
Go with me. Once more, new servant, welcome.
I'll leave you to confer of home affairs;
When you have done we look to hear from you.
PROTEUS We'll both attend upon your ladyship.

[*Exeunt Silvia and Thurio.*

VALENTINE Now, tell me, how do all from whence you came?
PROTEUS Your friends are well, and have them much commended.
VALENTINE And how do yours?
PROTEUS I left them all in health.
VALENTINE How does your lady, and how thrives your love?
PROTEUS My tales of love were wont to weary you;
I know you joy not in a love-discourse.
VALENTINE Ay, Proteus, but that life is alter'd now;
I have done penance for contemning Love,
Whose high imperious thoughts have punish'd me
With bitter fasts, with penitential groans,
With nightly tears, and daily heart-sore sighs;
For, in revenge of my contempt of love,
Love hath chas'd sleep from my enthralled eyes
And made them watchers of mine own heart's sorrow.
O gentle Proteus, Love's a mighty lord,
And hath so humbled me as I confess
There is no woe to his correction,
Nor to his service no such joy on earth.
Now no discourse, except it be of love;
Now can I break my fast, dine, sup, and sleep,
Upon the very naked name of love.
PROTEUS Enough; I read your fortune in your eye.
Was this the idol that you worship so?
VALENTINE Even she; and is she not a heavenly saint?
PROTEUS No; but she is an earthly paragon.
VALENTINE Call her divine.
PROTEUS I will not flatter her.
VALENTINE O, flatter me; for love delights in praises!
PROTEUS When I was sick you gave me bitter pills,
And I must minister the like to you.
VALENTINE Then speak the truth by her; if not divine,
Yet let her be a principality,
Sovereign to all the creatures on the earth.
PROTEUS Except my mistress.
VALENTINE Sweet, except not any;
Except thou wilt except against my love.
PROTEUS Have I not reason to prefer mine own?
VALENTINE And I will help thee to prefer her too:
She shall be dignified with this high honour –
To bear my lady's train, lest the base earth
Should from her vesture chance to steal a kiss
And, of so great a favour growing proud,
Disdain to root the summer-swelling flow'r
And make rough winter everlastingly.
PROTEUS Why, Valentine, what braggardism is this?
VALENTINE Pardon me, Proteus; all I can is nothing
To her, whose worth makes other worthies nothing;
She is alone.
PROTEUS Then let her alone.
VALENTINE Not for the world! Why, man, she is mine own;
And I as rich in having such a jewel
As twenty seas, if all their sand were pearl,
The water nectar, and the rocks pure gold.
Forgive me that I do not dream on thee,
Because thou seest me dote upon my love.
My foolish rival, that her father likes
Only for his possessions are so huge,
Is gone with her along; and I must after,
For love, thou know'st, is full of jealousy.
PROTEUS But she loves you?
VALENTINE Ay, and we are betroth'd; nay more, our marriage-hour,
With all the cunning manner of our flight,
Determin'd of – how I must climb her window,
The ladder made of cords, and all the means
Plotted and 'greed on for my happiness.
Good Proteus, go with me to my chamber,
In these affairs to aid me with thy counsel.
PROTEUS Go on before; I shall enquire you forth;
I must unto the road to disembark
Some necessaries that I needs must use;
And then I'll presently attend you.

VALENTINE Will you make haste?
PROTEUS I will. [*Exit Valentine.*
Even as one heat another heat expels
Or as one nail by strength drives out another,
So the remembrance of my former love
Is by a newer object quite forgotten.
Is it my mind, or Valentinus' praise,
Her true perfection, or my false transgression,
That makes me reasonless to reason thus?
She is fair; and so is Julia that I love –
That I did love, for now my love is thaw'd;
Which like a waxen image 'gainst a fire
Bears no impression of the thing it was.
Methinks my zeal to Valentine is cold,
And that I love him not as I was wont.
O! but I love his lady too too much,
And that's the reason I love him so little.
How shall I dote on her with more advice
That thus without advice begin to love her!
'Tis but her picture I have yet beheld,
And that hath dazzled my reason's light;
But when I look on her perfections,
There is no reason but I shall be blind.
If I can check my erring love, I will;
If not, to compass her I'll use my skill. [*Exit.*

SCENE V. *Milan. A street.*

Enter SPEED and LAUNCE severally.

SPEED Launce! by mine honesty, welcome to Padua.

LAUNCE Forswear not thyself, sweet youth, for I am not welcome. I reckon this always, that a man is never undone till he be hang'd nor never welcome to a place till some certain shot be paid, and the hostess say 'Welcome!'

SPEED Come on, you madcap; I'll to the alehouse with you presently; where, for one shot of five pence, thou shalt have five thousand welcomes. But, sirrah, how did thy master part with Madam Julia?

LAUNCE Marry after they clos'd in earnest, they parted very fairly in jest.

SPEED But shall she marry him?

LAUNCE No.

SPEED How then? Shall he marry her?

LAUNCE No, neither.

SPEED What, are they broken?

LAUNCE No, they are both as whole as a fish.

SPEED Why then, how stands the matter with them?

LAUNCE Marry, thus: when it stands well with him, it stands well with her.

SPEED What an ass art thou! I understand thee not.

LAUNCE What a block art thou that thou canst not! My staff understands me.

SPEED What thou say'st?

LAUNCE Ay, and what I do too; look thee, I'll but lean, and my staff understands me.

SPEED It stands under thee, indeed.

LAUNCE Why, stand-under and understand is all one.

SPEED But tell me true, will't be a match?

LAUNCE Ask my dog. If he say ay, it will; if he say no, it will; if he shake his tail and say nothing, it will.

SPEED The conclusion is, then, that it will.

LAUNCE Thou shalt never get such a secret from me but by a parable.

SPEED 'Tis well that I get it so. But, Launce, how say'st thou that my master is become a notable lover?

LAUNCE I never knew him otherwise.

SPEED Than how?

LAUNCE A notable lubber, as thou reportest him to be.

SPEED Why, thou whoreson ass, thou mistak'st me.

LAUNCE Why, fool, I meant not thee, I meant thy master.

SPEED I tell thee my master is become a hot lover.

LAUNCE Why, I tell thee I care not though he burn himself in love. If thou wilt, go with me to the alehouse; if not, thou art an Hebrew, a Jew, and not worth the name of a Christian.

SPEED Why?

LAUNCE Because thou hast not so much charity in thee as to go to the ale with a Christian. Wilt thou go?

SPEED At thy service. [*Exeunt.*

SCENE VI. *Milan. The Duke's palace.*

Enter PROTEUS.

PROTEUS To leave my Julia, shall I be forsworn;
To love fair Silvia, shall I be forsworn;
To wrong my friend, I shall be much forsworn;
And ev'n that pow'r which gave me first my oath
Provokes me to this threefold perjury:
Love bade me swear, and Love bids me forswear.
O sweet-suggesting Love, if thou hast sinn'd,
Teach me, thy tempted subject, to excuse it!
At first I did adore a twinkling star,
But now I worship a celestial sun.
Unheedful vows may heedfully be broken;
And he wants wit that wants resolved will
To learn his wit t' exchange the bad for better.
Fie, fie, unreverend tongue, to call her bad
Whose sovereignty so oft thou hast preferr'd
With twenty thousand soul-confirming oaths!
I cannot leave to love, and yet I do;
But there I leave to love where I should love

Julia I lose, and Valentine I lose;
If I keep them, I needs must lose myself;
If I lose them, thus find I by their loss:
For Valentine, myself; for Julia, Silvia.
I to myself am dearer than a friend;
For love is still most precious in itself;
And Silvia – witness heaven, that made her fair! –
Shows Julia but a swarthy Ethiope.
I will forget that Julia is alive,
Rememb'ring that my love to her is dead;
And Valentine I'll hold an enemy,
Aiming at Silvia as a sweeter friend.
I cannot now prove constant to myself
Without some treachery us'd to Valentine.
This night he meaneth with a corded ladder
To climb celestial Silvia's chamber window,
Myself in counsel, his competitor.
Now presently I'll give her father notice
Of their disguising and pretended flight,
Who, all enrag'd, will banish Valentine,
For Thurio, he intends, shall wed his daughter;
But, Valentine being gone, I'll quickly cross
By some sly trick blunt Thurio's dull proceeding.
Love, lend me wings to make my purpose swift,
As thou hast lent me wit to plot this drift.

[*Exit.*

SCENE VII. *Verona. Julia's house.*

Enter JULIA and LUCETTA.

JULIA Counsel, Lucetta; gentle girl, assist me;
And, ev'n in kind love, I do conjure thee,
Who art the table wherein all my thoughts
Are visibly character'd and engrav'd,
To lesson me and tell me some good mean
How, with my honour, I may undertake
A journey to my loving Proteus.

LUCETTA Alas, the way is wearisome and long!

JULIA A true-devoted pilgrim is not weary
To measure kingdoms with his feeble steps;
Much less shall she that hath Love's wings to fly,
And when the flight is made to one so dear,
Of such divine perfection, as Sir Proteus.

LUCETTA Better forbear till Proteus make return.

JULIA O, know'st thou not his looks are my soul's food?
Pity the dearth that I have pined in
By longing for that food so long a time.
Didst thou but know the inly touch of love,
Thou wouldst as soon go kindle fire with snow
As seek to quench the fire of love with words.

LUCETTA I do not seek to quench your love's hot fire,
But qualify the fire's extreme rage,
Lest it should burn above the bounds of reason.

JULIA The more thou dam'st it up, the more it burns.
The current that with gentle murmur glides,
Thou know'st, being stopp'd, impatiently doth rage;
But when his fair course is not hindered,
He makes sweet music with th' enamell'd stones,
Giving a gentle kiss to every sedge
He overtaketh in his pilgrimage;
And so by many winding nooks he strays,
With willing sport, to the wild ocean.
Then let me go, and hinder not my course.
I'll be as patient as a gentle stream,
And make a pastime of each weary step,
Till the last step have brought me to my love;
And there I'll rest as, after much turmoil,
A blessed soul doth in Elysium.

LUCETTA But in what habit will you go along?

JULIA Not like a woman, for I would prevent
The loose encounters of lascivious men;
Gentle Lucetta, fit me with such weeds
As may beseem some well-reputed page.

LUCETTA Why then, your ladyship must cut your hair.

JULIA No, girl; I'll knit it up in silken strings
With twenty odd-conceited true-love knots –
To be fantastic may become a youth
Of greater time than I shall show to be.

LUCETTA What fashion, madam, shall I make your breeches?

JULIA That fits as well as 'Tell me, good my lord,
What compass will you wear your farthingale'.
Why ev'n what fashion thou best likes, Lucetta.

LUCETTA You must needs have them with a codpiece, madam.

JULIA Out, out, Lucetta, that will be ill-favour'd.

LUCETTA A round hose, madam, now's not worth a pin,
Unless you have a codpiece to stick pins on.

JULIA Lucetta, as thou lov'st me, let me have
What thou think'st meet, and is most mannerly.
But tell me, wench, how will the world repute me
For undertaking so unstaid a journey?
I fear me it will make me scandaliz'd.

LUCETTA If you think so, then stay at home and go not.

JULIA Nay, that I will not.

LUCETTA Then never dream on infamy, but go.
If Proteus like your journey when you come,
No matter who's displeas'd when you are gone.
I fear me he will scarce be pleas'd withal.

JULIA That is the least, Lucetta, of my fear:
A thousand oaths, an ocean of his tears,
And instances of infinite of love,
Warrant me welcome to my Proteus.

LUCETTA All these are servants to deceitful men.
JULIA Base men that use them to so base effect!
But truer stars did govern Proteus' birth;
His words are bonds, his oaths are oracles,
His love sincere, his thoughts immaculate,
His tears pure messengers sent from his heart,
His heart as far from fraud as heaven from earth.
LUCETTA Pray heav'n he prove so when you come to him.
JULIA Now, as thou lov'st me, do him not that wrong
To bear a hard opinion of his truth;
Only deserve my love by loving him.
And presently go with me to my chamber,
To take a note of what I stand in need of
To furnish me upon my longing journey.
All that is mine I leave at thy dispose,
My goods, my lands, my reputation;
Only, in lieu thereof, dispatch me hence.
Come, answer not, but to it presently;
I am impatient of my tarriance. [*Exeunt.*

ACT THREE

SCENE I. *Milan. The Duke's palace.*

Enter DUKE, THURIO, and PROTEUS.

DUKE Sir Thurio, give us leave, I pray, awhile;
We have some secrets to confer about.
[*Exit Thurio.*
Now tell me, Proteus, what's your will with me?
PROTEUS My gracious lord, that which I would discover
The law of friendship bids me to conceal;
But, when I call to mind your gracious favours
Done to me, undeserving as I am,
My duty pricks me on to utter that
Which else no worldly good should draw from me.
Know, worthy prince, Sir Valentine, my friend,
This night intends to steal away your daughter;
Myself am one made privy to the plot.
I know you have determin'd to bestow her
On Thurio, whom your gentle daughter hates;
And should she thus be stol'n away from you,
It would be much vexation to your age.
Thus, for my duty's sake, I rather chose
To cross my friend in his intended drift
Than, by concealing it, heap on your head
A pack of sorrows which would press you down,
Being unprevented, to your timeless grave.
DUKE Proteus, I thank thee for thine honest care,
Which to requite, command me while I live.
This love of theirs myself have often seen,
Haply when they have judg'd me fast asleep,
And oftentimes have purpos'd to forbid
Sir Valentine her company and my court;
But fearing lest my jealous aim might err
And so, unworthily, disgrace the man,
A rashness that I ever yet have shunn'd,
I gave him gentle looks, thereby to find
That which thyself hast now disclos'd to me.
And, that thou mayst perceive my fear of this,
Knowing that tender youth is soon suggested,
I nightly lodge her in an upper tow'r,
The key whereof myself have ever kept;
And thence she cannot be convey'd away.
PROTEUS Know, noble lord, they have devis'd a mean
How he her chamber window will ascend
And with a corded ladder fetch her down;
For which the youthful lover now is gone,
And this way comes he with it presently;
Where, if it please you, you may intercept him.
But, good my lord, do it so cunningly
That my discovery be not aimed at;
For love of you, not hate unto my friend,
Hath made me publisher of this pretence.
DUKE Upon mine honour, he shall never know
That I had any light from thee of this.
PROTEUS Adieu, my lord; Sir Valentine is coming. [*Exit.*

Enter VALENTINE.

DUKE Sir Valentine, whither away so fast?
VALENTINE Please it your Grace, there is a messenger
That stays to bear my letters to my friends,
And I am going to deliver them.
DUKE Be they of much import?
VALENTINE The tenour of them doth but signify
My health and happy being at your court.
DUKE Nay, then, no matter; stay with me awhile;
I am to break with thee of some affairs
That touch me near, wherein thou must be secret.
'Tis not unknown to thee that I have sought
To match my friend Sir Thurio to my daughter.
VALENTINE I know it well, my lord; and, sure, the match
Were rich and honourable; besides, the gentleman
Is full of virtue, bounty, worth, and qualities
Beseeming such a wife as your fair daughter.

Cannot your Grace win her to fancy him?
DUKE No, trust me; she is peevish, sullen, forward,
Proud, disobedient, stubborn, lacking duty;
Neither regarding that she is my child
Nor fearing me as if I were her father;
And, may I say to thee, this pride of hers,
Upon advice, hath drawn my love from her;
And, where I thought the remnant of mine age
Should have been cherish'd by her childlike duty,
I now am full resolv'd to take a wife
And turn her out to who will take her in.
Then let her beauty be her wedding-dow'r;
For me and my possessions she esteems not.
VALENTINE What would your Grace have me to do in this?
DUKE There is a lady, in Verona here,
Whom I affect; but she is nice, and coy,
And nought esteems my aged eloquence.
Now, therefore, would I have thee to my tutor –
For long agone I have forgot to court;
Besides, the fashion of the time is chang'd –
How and which way I may bestow myself
To be regarded in her sun-bright eye.
VALENTINE Win her with gifts, if she respect not words:
Dumb jewels often in their silent kind
More than quick words do move a woman's mind.
DUKE But she did scorn a present that I sent her.
VALENTINE A woman sometimes scorns what best contents her.
Send her another; never give her o'er,
For scorn at first makes after-love the more.
If she do frown, 'tis not in hate of you,
But rather to beget more love in you;
If she do chide, 'tis not to have you gone,
For why the fools are mad if left alone.
Take no repulse, whatever she doth say;
For 'Get you gone' she doth not mean 'Away!'
Flatter and praise, commend, extol their graces;
Though ne'er so black, say they have angels' faces.
That man that hath a tongue, I say, is no man,
If with his tongue he cannot win a woman.
DUKE But she I mean is promis'd by her friends
Unto a youthful gentleman of worth;
And kept severely from resort of men,
That no man hath access by day to her.
VALENTINE Why then I would resort to her by night.
DUKE Ay, but the doors be lock'd and keys kept safe,
That no man hath recourse to her by night.
VALENTINE What lets but one may enter at her window?
DUKE Her chamber is aloft, far from the ground,
And built so shelving that one cannot climb it
Without apparent hazard of his life.
VALENTINE Why then a ladder, quaintly made of cords,
To cast up with a pair of anchoring hooks,
Would serve to scale another Hero's tow'r,
So bold Leander would adventure it.
DUKE Now, as thou art a gentleman of blood,
Advise me where I may have such a ladder.
VALENTINE When would you use it? Pray, sir, tell me that.
DUKE This very night; for Love is like a child,
That longs for everything that he can come by.
VALENTINE By seven o'clock I'll get you such a ladder.
DUKE But, hark thee; I will go to her alone;
How shall I best convey the ladder thither?
VALENTINE It will be light, my lord, that you may bear it
Under a cloak that is of any length.
DUKE A cloak as long as thine will serve the turn?
VALENTINE Ay, my good lord.
DUKE Then let me see thy cloak.
I'll get me one of such another length.
VALENTINE Why, any cloak will serve the turn, my lord.
DUKE How shall I fashion me to wear a cloak?
I pray thee, let me feel thy cloak upon me.
What letter is this same? What's here? 'To Silvia'!
And here an engine fit for my proceeding!
I'll be so bold to break the seal for once.
[*Reads.*

'My thoughts do harbour with my Silvia nightly,
And slaves they are to me, that send them flying.
O, could their master come and go as lightly,
Himself would lodge where senseless, they are lying!
My herald thoughts in thy pure bosom rest them,
While I, their king, that thither them importune,
Do curse the grace that with such grace hath blest them,
Because myself do want my servants' fortune.
I curse myself, for they are sent by me,
That they should harbour where their lord should be.'
What's here?
'Silvia, this night I will enfranchise thee.'
'Tis so; and here's the ladder for the purpose.

Why, Phaethon – for thou art Merops' son –
Wilt thou aspire to guide the heavenly car,
And with thy daring folly burn the world?
Wilt thou reach stars because they shine on thee?
Go, base intruder, over-weening slave,
Bestow thy fawning smiles on equal mates;
And think my patience, more than thy desert,
Is privilege for thy departure hence.
Thank me for this more than for all the favours
Which, all too much, I have bestow'd on thee.
But if thou linger in my territories
Longer than swiftest expedition
Will give thee time to leave our royal court,
By heaven! my wrath shall far exceed the love
I ever bore my daughter or thyself.
Be gone; I will not hear thy vain excuse,
But, as thou lov'st thy life, make speed from hence. [*Exit Duke.*

VALENTINE And why not death rather than living torment?
To die is to be banish'd from myself,
And Silvia is myself; banish'd from her
Is self from self, a deadly banishment.
What light is light, if Silvia be not seen?
What joy is joy, if Silvia be not by?
Unless it be to think that she is by,
And feed upon the shadow of perfection.
Except I be by Silvia in the night,
There is no music in the nightingale;
Unless I look on Silvia in the day,
There is no day for me to look upon.
She is my essence, and I leave to be
If I be not by her fair influence
Foster'd, illumin'd, cherish'd, kept alive.
I fly not death, to fly his deadly doom:
Tarry I here, I but attend on death;
But fly I hence, I fly away from life.

Enter PROTEUS and LAUNCE.

PROTEUS Run, boy, run, run, and seek him out.

LAUNCE So-ho, so-ho!

PROTEUS What seest thou?

LAUNCE Him we go to find: there's not a hair on 's head but 'tis a Valentine.

PROTEUS Valentine?

VALENTINE No.

PROTEUS Who then? his spirit?

VALENTINE Neither.

PROTEUS What then?

VALENTINE Nothing.

LAUNCE Can nothing speak? Master, shall I strike?

PROTEUS Who wouldst thou strike?

LAUNCE Nothing.

PROTEUS Villain, forbear.

LAUNCE Why, sir, I'll strike nothing. I pray you –

PROTEUS Sirrah, I say, forbear. Friend Valentine, a word.

VALENTINE My ears are stopp'd and cannot hear good news,
So much of bad already hath possess'd them.

PROTEUS Then in dumb silence will I bury mine,
For they are harsh, untuneable, and bad.

VALENTINE Is Silvia dead?

PROTEUS No, Valentine.

VALENTINE No Valentine, indeed, for sacred Silvia.
Hath she forsworn me?

PROTEUS No, Valentine.

VALENTINE No Valentine, if Silvia have forsworn me.
What is your news?

LAUNCE Sir, there is a proclamation that you are vanished.

PROTEUS That thou art banished – O, that's the news! –
From hence, from Silvia, and from me thy friend.

VALENTINE O, I have fed upon this woe already,
And now excess of it will make me surfeit.
Doth Silvia know that I am banished?

PROTEUS Ay, ay; and she hath offered to the doom –
Which, unrevers'd, stands in effectual force –
A sea of melting pearl, which some call tears;
Those at her father's churlish feet she tender'd;
With them, upon her knees, her humble self,
Wringing her hands, whose whiteness so became them
As if but now they waxed pale for woe.
But neither bended knees, pure hands held up,
Sad sighs, deep groans, nor silver-shedding tears,
Could penetrate her uncompassionate sire –
But Valentine, if he be ta'en, must die.
Besides, her intercession chaf'd him so,
When she for thy repeal was suppliant,
That to close prison he commanded her,
With many bitter threats of biding there.

VALENTINE No more; unless the next word that thou speak'st
Have some malignant power upon my life;
If so, I pray thee breathe it in mine ear,
As ending anthem of my endless dolour.

PROTEUS Cease to lament for that thou canst not help,
And study help for that which thou lament'st.
Time is the nurse and breeder of all good.
Here if thou stay thou canst not see thy love;
Besides, thy staying will abridge thy life.
Hope is a lover's staff; walk hence with that,
And manage it against despairing thoughts.

Thy letters may be here, though thou art hence,
Which, being writ to me, shall be deliver'd
Even in the milk-white bosom of thy love.
The time now serves not to expostulate.
Come, I'll convey thee though the city gate;
And, ere I part with thee, confer at large
Of all that may concern thy love affairs.
As thou lov'st Silvia, though not for thyself,
Regard thy danger, and along with me.

VALENTINE I pray thee, Launce, an if thou seest my boy,
Bid him make haste and meet me at the Northgate.

PROTEUS Go, sirrah, find him out. Come, Valentine.

VALENTINE O my dear Silvia! Hapless Valentine!

[*Exeunt Valentine and Proteus.*

LAUNCE I am but a fool, look you, and yet I have the wit to think my master is a kind of a knave; but that's all one if he be but one knave. He lives not now that knows me to be in love; yet I am in love; but a team of horse shall not pluck that from me; nor who 'tis I love; and yet 'tis a woman; but what woman I will not tell myself; and yet 'tis a milkmaid; yet 'tis not a maid, for she hath had gossips; yet 'tis a maid, for she is her master's maid and serves for wages. She hath more qualities than a water-spaniel – which is much in a bare Christian. Here is the cate-log [*Pulling out a paper*] of her condition. 'Inprimis: she can fetch and carry.' Why, a horse can do no more; nay, a horse cannot fetch, but only carry; therefore is she better than a jade. 'Item: She can milk.' Look you, a sweet virtue in a maid with clean hands.

Enter SPEED.

SPEED How now, Signior Launce! What news with your mastership?

LAUNCE With my master's ship? Why, it is at sea.

SPEED Well, your old vice still: mistake the word. What news, then, in your paper?

LAUNCE The black'st news that ever thou heard'st.

SPEED Why, man? how black?

LAUNCE Why, as black as ink.

SPEED Let me read them.

LAUNCE Fie on thee, jolt-head; thou canst not read.

SPEED Thou liest; I can.

LAUNCE I will try thee. Tell me this: Who begot thee?

SPEED Marry, the son of my grandfather.

LAUNCE O illiterate loiterer. It was the son of thy grandmother. This proves that thou canst not read.

SPEED Come, fool, come; try me in thy paper.

LAUNCE [*Handing over the paper*] There; and Saint Nicholas be thy speed.

SPEED [*Reads*] 'Inprimis: She can milk.'

LAUNCE Ay, that she can.

SPEED 'Item: She brews good ale.'

LAUNCE And thereof comes the proverb: Blessing of your heart, you brew good ale.

SPEED 'Item: She can sew.'

LAUNCE That's as much as to say 'Can she so?'

SPEED 'Item: She can knit.'

LAUNCE What need a man care for a stock with a wench, when she can knit him a stock.

SPEED 'Item: She can wash and scour.'

LAUNCE A special virtue; for then she need not be wash'd and scour'd.

SPEED 'Item: She can spin.'

LAUNCE Then may I set the world on wheels, when she can spin for her living.

SPEED 'Item: She hath many nameless virtues.'

LAUNCE That's as much as to say 'bastard virtues'; that indeed know not their fathers, and therefore have no names.

SPEED 'Here follow her vices.'

LAUNCE Close at the heels of her virtues.

SPEED 'Item: She is not to be kiss'd fasting, in respect of her breath.'

LAUNCE Well, that fault may be mended with a breakfast. Read on.

SPEED 'Item: She hath a sweet mouth.'

LAUNCE That makes amends for her sour breath.

SPEED 'Item: She doth talk in her sleep.'

LAUNCE It's no matter for that, so she sleep not in her talk.

SPEED 'Item: She is slow in words.'

LAUNCE O villain, that set this down among her vices! To be slow in words is a woman's only virtue. I pray thee, out with't; and place it for her chief virtue.

SPEED 'Item: she is proud.'

LAUNCE Out with that too; it was Eve's legacy, and cannot be ta'en from her.

SPEED 'Item: She hath no teeth.'

LAUNCE I care not for that neither, because I love crusts.

SPEED 'Item: She is curst.'

LAUNCE Well, the best is, she hath no teeth to bite.

SPEED 'Item: She will often praise her liquor.'

LAUNCE If her liquor be good, she shall; if she will not, I will; for good things should be praised.

SPEED 'Item: She is too liberal.'

LAUNCE Of her tongue she cannot, for that's writ down she is slow of; of her purse she shall not, for that I'll keep shut. Now of another thing she may, and that cannot I help. Well, proceed.

SPEED 'Item: She hath more hair than wit, and

more faults than hairs, and more wealth than faults.'

LAUNCE Stop there; I'll have her; she was mine, and not mine, twice or thrice in that last article. Rehearse that once more.

SPEED 'Item: She hath more hair than wit' –

LAUNCE More hair than wit. It may be; I'll prove it: the cover of the salt hides the salt, and therefore it is more than the salt; the hair that covers the wit is more than the wit, for the greater hides the less. What's next?

SPEED 'And more faults than hairs' –

LAUNCE That's monstrous. O that that were out!

SPEED 'And more wealth than faults.'

LAUNCE Why, that word makes the faults gracious. Well, I'll have her; an if it be a match, as nothing is impossible –

SPEED What then?

LAUNCE Why, then will I tell thee – that thy master stays for thee at the Northgate.

SPEED For me?

LAUNCE For thee! ay, who art thou? He hath stay'd for a better man than thee.

SPEED And must I go to him?

LAUNCE Thou must run to him, for thou hast stay'd so long that going will scarce serve the turn.

SPEED Why didst not tell me sooner? Pox of your love letters! [*Exit.*

LAUNCE Now will he be swing'd for reading my letter. An unmannerly slave that will thrust himself into secrets! I'll after, to rejoice in the boy's correction. [*Exit.*

SCENE II. *Milan. The Duke's palace.*

Enter DUKE and THURIO.

DUKE Sir Thurio, fear not but that she will love you
Now Valentine is banish'd from her sight.

THURIO Since his exile she hath despis'd me most,
Forsworn my company and rail'd at me,
That I am desperate of obtaining her.

DUKE This weak impress of love is as a figure
Trenched in ice, which with an hour's heat
Dissolves to water and doth lose his form.
A little time will melt her frozen thoughts,
And worthless Valentine shall be forgot.

Enter PROTEUS.

How now, Sir Proteus! Is your countryman,
According to our proclamation, gone?

PROTEUS Gone, my good lord.

DUKE My daughter takes his going grievously.

PROTEUS A little time, my lord, will kill that grief.

DUKE So I believe; but Thurio thinks not so.
Proteus, the good conceit I hold of thee –
For thou hast shown some sign of good desert –
Makes me the better to confer with thee.

PROTEUS Longer than I prove loyal to your Grace
Let me not live to look upon your Grace.

DUKE Thou know'st how willingly I would effect
The match between Sir Thurio and my daughter.

PROTEUS I do, my lord.

DUKE And also, I think, thou art not ignorant
How she opposes her against my will.

PROTEUS She did, my lord, when Valentine was here.

DUKE Ay, and perversely she persevers so.
What might we do to make the girl forget
The love of Valentine, and love Sir Thurio?

PROTEUS The best way is to slander Valentine
With falsehood, cowardice, and poor descent –
Three things that women highly hold in hate.

DUKE Ay, but she'll think that it is spoke in hate.

PROTEUS Ay, if his enemy deliver it;
Therefore it must with circumstance be spoken
By one whom she esteemeth as his friend.

DUKE Then you must undertake to slander him.

PROTEUS And that, my lord, I shall be loath to do:
'Tis an ill office for a gentleman,
Especially against his very friend.

DUKE Where your good word cannot advantage him,
Your slander never can endamage him;
Therefore the office is indifferent,
Being entreated to it by your friend.

PROTEUS You have prevail'd, my lord; if I can do it
By aught that I can speak in his dispraise,
She shall not long continue love to him.
But say this weed her love from Valentine,
It follows not that she will love Sir Thurio.

THURIO Therefore, as you unwind her love from him,
Lest it should ravel and be good to none,
You must provide to bottom it on me;
Which must be done by praising me as much
As you in worth dispraise Sir Valentine.

DUKE And, Proteus, we dare trust you in this kind,
Because we know, on Valentine's report,
You are already Love's firm votary
And cannot soon revolt and change your mind.
Upon this warrant shall you have access
Where you with Silvia may confer at large –
For she is lumpish, heavy, melancholy,
And, for your friend's sake, will be glad of you –
Where you may temper her by your persuasion
To hate young Valentine and love my friend.

PROTEUS As much as I can do I will effect.
But you, Sir Thurio, are not sharp enough;
You must lay lime to tangle her desires
By wailful sonnets, whose composed rhymes
Should be full-fraught with serviceable vows.
DUKE Ay,
Much is the force of heaven-bred poesy.
PROTEUS Say that upon the altar of her beauty
You sacrifice your tears, your sighs, your heart;
Write till your ink be dry, and with your tears
Moist it again, and frame some feeling line
That may discover such integrity;
For Orpheus' lute was strung with poets' sinews,
Whose golden touch could soften steel and stones,
Make tigers tame, and huge leviathans
Forsake unsounded deeps to dance on sands.
After your dire-lamenting elegies,
Visit by night your lady's chamber window
With some sweet consort; to their instruments
Tune a deploring dump – the night's dead silence
Will well become such sweet-complaining grievance.
This, or else nothing, will inherit her.
DUKE This discipline shows thou hast been in love.
THURIO And thy advice this night I'll put in practice;
Therefore, sweet Proteus, my direction-giver,
Let us into the city presently
To sort some gentlemen well skill'd in music.
I have a sonnet that will serve the turn
To give the onset to thy good advice.
DUKE About it, gentlemen!
PROTEUS We'll wait upon your Grace till after supper,
And afterward determine our proceedings.
DUKE Even now about it! I will pardon you.
[*Exeunt.*

ACT FOUR

SCENE I. *The frontiers of Mantua. A forest.*

Enter certain Outlaws.

1 OUTLAW Fellows, stand fast; I see a passenger.
2 OUTLAW If there be ten, shrink not, but down with 'em.

Enter VALENTINE and SPEED.

3 OUTLAW Stand, sir, and throw us that you have about ye;
If not, we'll make you sit, and rifle you.
SPEED Sir, we are undone; these are the villains
That all the travellers do fear so much.
VALENTINE My friends –
1 OUTLAW That's not so, sir; we are your enemies.
2 OUTLAW Peace! we'll hear him.
3 OUTLAW Ay, by my beard, will we; for he is a proper man.
VALENTINE Then know that I have little wealth to lose;
A man I am cross'd with adversity;
My riches are these poor habiliments,
Of which if you should here disfurnish me,
You take the sum and substance that I have.
2 OUTLAW Whither travel you?
VALENTINE To Verona.
1 OUTLAW Whence came you?
VALENTINE From Milan.
3 OUTLAW Have you long sojourn'd there?
VALENTINE Some sixteen months, and longer might have stay'd,
If crooked fortune had not thwarted me.
1 OUTLAW What, were you banish'd thence?
VALENTINE I was.
2 OUTLAW For what offence?
VALENTINE For that which now torments me to rehearse:
I kill'd a man, whose death I much repent;
But yet I slew him manfully in fight,
Without false vantage or base treachery.
1 OUTLAW Why, ne'er repent it, if it were done so.
But were you banish'd for so small a fault?
VALENTINE I was, and held me glad of such a doom.
2 OUTLAW Have you the tongues?
VALENTINE My youthful travel therein made me happy,
Or else I often had been miserable.
3 OUTLAW By the bare scalp of Robin Hood's fat friar,
This fellow were a king for our wild faction!
1 OUTLAW We'll have him. Sirs, a word.
SPEED Master, be one of them; it's an honourable kind of thievery.
VALENTINE Peace, villain!
2 OUTLAW Tell us this: have you anything to take to?
VALENTINE Nothing but my fortune.
3 OUTLAW Know, then, that some of us are gentlemen,
Such as the fury of ungovern'd youth

Thrust from the company of awful men;
Myself was from Verona banished
For practising to steal away a lady,
An heir, and near allied unto the Duke.

2 OUTLAW And I from Mantua, for a gentleman
Who, in my mood, I stabb'd unto the heart.

1 OUTLAW And I for such-like petty crimes as these.
But to the purpose – for we cite our faults
That they may hold excus'd our lawless lives;
And, partly, seeing you are beautified
With goodly shape, and by your own report
A linguist, and a man of such perfection
As we do in our quality much want –

2 OUTLAW Indeed, because you are a banish'd man,
Therefore, above the rest, we parley to you.
Are you content to be our general –
To make a virtue of necessity,
And live as we do in this wilderness?

3 OUTLAW What say'st thou? Wilt thou be of our consort?
Say 'ay' and be the captain of us all.
We'll do thee homage, and be rul'd by thee,
Love thee as our commander and our king.

1 OUTLAW But if thou scorn our courtesy thou diest.

2 OUTLAW Thou shalt not live to brag what we have offer'd.

VALENTINE I take your offer, and will live with you,
Provided that you do no outrages
On silly women or poor passengers.

3 OUTLAW No, we detest such vile base practices.
Come, go with us; we'll bring thee to our crews,
And show thee all the treasure we have got;
Which, with ourselves, all rest at thy dispose.
[*Exeunt.*

SCENE II. *Milan. Outside the Duke's palace, under Silvia's window.*

Enter PROTEUS.

PROTEUS Already have I been false to Valentine,
And now I must be as unjust to Thurio.
Under the colour of commending him
I have access my own love to prefer;
But Silvia is too fair, too true, too holy,
To be corrupted with my worthless gifts.
When I protest true loyalty to her,
She twits me with my falsehood to my friend;
When to her beauty I commend my vows,
She bids me think how I have been forsworn
In breaking faith with Julia whom I lov'd;
And notwithstanding all her sudden quips,
The least whereof would quell a lover's hope,
Yet, spaniel-like, the more she spurns my love
The more it grows and fawneth on her still.

Enter THURIO and Musicians.

But here comes Thurio. Now must we to her window,
And give some evening music to her ear.

THURIO How now, Sir Proteus, are you crept before us?

PROTEUS Ay, gentle Thurio; for you know that love
Will creep in service where it cannot go.

THURIO Ay, but I hope, sir, that you love not here.

PROTEUS Sir, but I do; or else I would be hence.

THURIO Who? Silvia?

PROTEUS Ay, Silvia – for your sake.

THURIO I thank you for your own. Now, gentlemen,
Let's tune, and to it lustily awhile.

Enter at a distance, Host, and JULIA *in boy's clothes.*

HOST Now, my young guest, methinks you're allycholly; I pray you, why is it?

JULIA Marry, mine host, because I cannot be merry.

HOST Come, we'll have you merry; I'll bring you where you shall hear music, and see the gentleman that you ask'd for.

JULIA But shall I hear him speak?

HOST Ay, that you shall. [*Music plays.*

JULIA That will be music.

HOST Hark, hark!

JULIA Is he among these?

HOST Ay; but peace! let's hear 'em.

Song.

Who is Silvia? What is she,
That all our swains commend her?
Holy, fair, and wise is she;
The heaven such grace did lend her,
That she might admired be.

Is she kind as she is fair?
For beauty lives with kindness.
Love doth to her eyes repair,
To help him of his blindness;
And, being help'd, inhabits there.

Then to Silvia let us sing
That Silvia is excelling;
She excels each mortal thing
Upon the dull earth dwelling.
To her let us garlands bring.

HOST How now, are you sadder than you were before? How do you, man? The music likes you not.

JULIA You mistake; the musician likes me not.

HOST Why, my pretty youth?

JULIA He plays false, father.

HOST How, out of tune on the strings?
JULIA Not so; but yet so false that he grieves my very heart-strings.
HOST You have a quick ear.
JULIA Ay, I would I were deaf; it makes me have a slow heart.
HOST I perceive you delight not in music.
JULIA Not a whit, when it jars so.
HOST Hark, what fine change is in the music!
JULIA Ay, that change is the spite.
HOST You would have them always play but one thing?
JULIA I would always have one play but one thing.
But, Host, doth this Sir Proteus, that we talk on,
Often resort unto this gentlewoman?
HOST I tell you what Launce, his man, told me: he lov'd her out of all nick.
JULIA Where is Launce?
HOST Gone to seek his dog, which tomorrow, by his master's command, he must carry for a present to his lady.
JULIA Peace, stand aside; the company parts.
PROTEUS Sir Thurio, fear not you; I will so plead
That you shall say my cunning drift excels.
THURIO Where meet we?
PROTEUS At Saint Gregory's well.
THURIO Farewell.

[Exeunt Thurio and Musicians.

Enter SILVIA above, at her window.

PROTEUS Madam, good ev'n to your ladyship.
SILVIA I thank you for your music, gentlemen.
Who is that that spake?
PROTEUS One, lady, if you knew his pure heart's truth,
You would quickly learn to know him by his voice.
SILVIA Sir Proteus, as I take it.
PROTEUS Sir Proteus, gentle lady, and your servant.
SILVIA What's your will?
PROTEUS That I may compass yours.
SILVIA You have your wish; my will is even this,
That presently you hie you home to bed.
Thou subtle, perjur'd, false, disloyal man,
Think'st thou I am so shallow, so conceitless,
To be seduced by thy flattery
That hast deceiv'd so many with thy vows?
Return, return, and make thy love amends.
For me, by this pale queen of night I swear,
I am so far from granting thy request
That I despise thee for thy wrongful suit,
And by and by intend to chide myself
Even for this time I spend in talking to thee.
PROTEUS I grant, sweet love, that I did love a lady;
But she is dead.
JULIA *[Aside]* 'Twere false, if I should speak it;
For I am sure she is not buried.
SILVIA Say that she be; yet Valentine, thy friend,
Survives, to whom, thyself art witness,
I am betroth'd; and art thou not asham'd
To wrong him with thy importunacy?
PROTEUS I likewise hear that Valentine is dead.
SILVIA And so suppose am I; for in his grave
Assure thyself my love is buried.
PROTEUS Sweet lady, let me rake it from the earth.
SILVIA Go to thy lady's grave, and call hers thence;
Or, at the least, in hers sepulchre thine.
JULIA *[Aside]* He heard not that.
PROTEUS Madam, if your heart be so obdurate,
Vouchsafe me yet your picture for my love,
The picture that is hanging in your chamber;
To that I'll speak, to that I'll sigh and weep;
For, since the substance of your perfect self
Is else devoted, I am but a shadow;
And to your shadow will I make true love.
JULIA *[Aside]* If 'twere a substance, you would, sure, deceive it
And make it but a shadow, as I am.
SILVIA I am very loath to be your idol, sir;
But since your falsehood shall become you well
To worship shadows and adore false shapes,
Send to me in the morning, and I'll send it;
And so, good rest.
PROTEUS As wretches have o'ernight
That wait for execution in the morn.

[Exeunt Proteus and Silvia.

JULIA Host, will you go?
HOST By my halidom, I was fast asleep.
JULIA Pray you, where lies Sir Proteus?
HOST Marry, at my house. Trust me, I think 'tis almost day.
JULIA Not so; but it hath been the longest night
That e'er I watch'd, and the most heaviest.

[Exeunt.

SCENE III. *Under Silvia's window.*

Enter EGLAMOUR.

EGLAMOUR This is the hour that Madam Silvia
Entreated me to call and know her mind;
There's some great matter she'd employ me in.
Madam, madam!

Enter SILVIA above, at her window.

SILVIA Who calls?
EGLAMOUR Your servant and your friend;
One that attends your ladyship's command.
SILVIA Sir Eglamour, a thousand times good morrow!

EGLAMOUR As many, worthy lady, to yourself!
According to your ladyship's impose,
I am thus early come to know what service
It is your pleasure to command me in.

SILVIA O Eglamour, thou art a gentleman –
Think not I flatter, for I swear I do not –
Valiant, wise, remorseful, well accomplish'd.
Thou art not ignorant what dear good will
I bear unto the banish'd Valentine;
Nor how my father would enforce me marry
Vain Thurio, whom my very soul abhors.
Thyself hast lov'd; and I have heard thee say
No grief did ever come so near thy heart
As when thy lady and thy true love died,
Upon whose grave thou vow'dst pure chastity.
Sir Eglamour, I would to Valentine,
To Mantua, where I hear he makes abode;
And, for the ways are dangerous to pass,
I do desire thy worthy company,
Upon whose faith and honour I repose.
Urge not my father's anger, Eglamour,
But think upon my grief, a lady's grief,
And on the justice of my flying hence
To keep me from a most unholy match,
Which heaven and fortune still rewards with plagues.
I do desire thee, even from a heart
As full of sorrows as the sea of sands,
To bear me company and go with me;
If not, to hide what I have said to thee,
That I may venture to depart alone.

EGLAMOUR Madam, I pity much your grievances;
Which since I know they virtuously are plac'd,
I give consent to go along with you,
Recking as little what betideth me
As much I wish all good befortune you.
When will you go?

SILVIA This evening coming.

EGLAMOUR Where shall I meet you?

SILVIA At Friar Patrick's cell,
Where I intend holy confession.

EGLAMOUR I will not fail your ladyship. Good
morrow, gentle lady.

SILVIA Good morrow, kind Sir Eglamour.

[*Exeunt.*

SCENE IV. *Under Silvia's window.*

Enter LAUNCE, with his dog.

LAUNCE When a man's servant shall play the cur with him, look you, it goes hard – one that I brought up of a puppy; one that I sav'd from drowning, when three or four of his blind brothers and sisters went to it. I have taught him, even as one would say precisely 'Thus I would teach a dog'. I was sent to deliver him as a present to Mistress Silvia from my master; and I came no sooner into the dining-chamber, but he steps me to her trencher and steals her capon's leg. O, 'tis a foul thing when a cur cannot keep himself in all companies! I would have, as one should say, one that takes upon him to be a dog indeed, to be, as it were, a dog at all things. If I had not had more wit than he, to take a fault upon me that he did, I think verily he had been hang'd for't; sure as I live, he had suffer'd for't. You shall judge. He thrusts me himself into the company of three or four gentleman-like dogs under the Duke's table; he had not been there, bless the mark, a pissing while but all the chamber smelt him. 'Out with the dog' says one; 'What cur is that?' says another; 'Whip him out' says the third; 'Hang him up' says the Duke. I, having been acquainted with the smell before, knew it was Crab, and goes me to the fellow that whips the dogs. 'Friend,' quoth I 'you mean to whip the dog.' 'Ay, marry do I' quoth he. 'You do him the more wrong;' quoth I ''twas I did the thing you wot of.' He makes me no more ado, but whips me out of the chamber. How many masters would do this for his servant? Nay, I'll be sworn, I have sat in the stocks for puddings he hath stol'n, otherwise he had been executed; I have stood on the pillory for geese he hath kill'd, otherwise he had suffer'd for't. Thou think'st not of this now. Nay, I remember the trick you serv'd me when I took my leave of Madam Silvia. Did not I bid thee still mark me and do as I do? When didst thou see me heave up my leg and make water against a gentlewoman's farthingale? Didst thou ever see me do such a trick?

Enter PROTEUS and JULIA in boy's clothes.

PROTEUS Sebastian is thy name? I like thee well,
And will employ thee in some service presently.

JULIA In what you please; I'll do what I can.

PROTEUS I hope thou wilt. [*To Launce*] How now,
you whoreson peasant!
Where have you been these two days loitering?

LAUNCE Marry, sir, I carried Mistress Silvia the dog you bade me.

PROTEUS And what says she to my little jewel?

LAUNCE Marry, she says your dog was a cur, and tells you currish thanks is good enough for such a present.

PROTEUS But she receiv'd my dog?

LAUNCE No, indeed, did she not; here have I brought him back again.

PROTEUS What, didst thou offer her this from me?

LAUNCE Ay, sir; the other squirrel was stol'n from me by the hangman's boys in the market-place; and then I offer'd her mine own, who is a dog as big as ten of yours, and therefore the gift the greater.

PROTEUS Go, get thee hence and find my dog again,
Or ne'er return again into my sight.
Away, I say. Stayest thou to vex me here?
[Exit Launce.
A slave that still an end turns me to shame!
Sebastian, I have entertained thee,
Partly that I have need of such a youth
That can with some discretion do my business,
For 'tis no trusting to yond foolish lout,
But chiefly for thy face and thy behaviour,
Which, if my augury deceive me not,
Witness good bringing up, fortune, and truth;
Therefore, know thou, for this I entertain thee.
Go presently, and take this ring with thee,
Deliver it to Madam Silvia –
She lov'd me well deliver'd it to me.

JULIA It seems you lov'd not her, to leave her token.
She is dead, belike?

PROTEUS Not so; I think she lives.

JULIA Alas!

PROTEUS Why dost thou cry 'Alas'?

JULIA I cannot choose
But pity her.

PROTEUS Wherefore shouldst thou pity her?

JULIA Because methinks that she lov'd you as well
As you do love your lady Silvia.
She dreams on him that has forgot her love:
You dote on her that cares nor for your love.
'Tis pity love should be so contrary;
And thinking on it makes me cry 'Alas!'

PROTEUS Well, give her that ring, and therewithal
This letter. That's her chamber. Tell my lady
I claim the promise for her heavenly picture.
Your message done, hie home unto my chamber,
Where thou shalt find me sad and solitary.
[Exit Proteus.

JULIA How many women would do such a message?
Alas, poor Proteus, thou hast entertain'd
A fox to be the shepherd of thy lambs.
Alas, poor fool, why do I pity him
That with his very heart despiseth me?
Because he loves her, he despiseth me;
Because I love him, I must pity him.
This ring I gave him, when he parted from me,
To bind him to remember my good will;
And now am I, unhappy messenger,
To plead for that which I would not obtain,
To carry that which I would have refus'd,
To praise his faith, which I would have disprais'd.
I am my master's true confirmed love,
But cannot be true servant to my master
Unless I prove false traitor to myself.
Yet will I woo for him, but yet so coldly
As, heaven it knows, I would not have him speed.

Enter SILVIA, attended.

Gentlewoman, good day! I pray you be my mean
To bring me where to speak with Madam Silvia.

SILVIA What would you with her, if that I be she?

JULIA If you be she, I do entreat your patience
To hear me speak the message I am sent on.

SILVIA From whom?

JULIA From my master, Sir Proteus, madam.

SILVIA O, he sends you for a picture?

JULIA Ay, madam.

SILVIA Ursula, bring my picture there.
Go, give your master this. Tell him from me,
One Julia, that his changing thoughts forget,
Would better fit his chamber than this shadow.

JULIA Madam, please you peruse this letter.
Pardon me, madam; I have unadvis'd
Deliver'd you a paper that I should not.
This is the letter to your ladyship.

SILVIA I pray thee let me look on that again.

JULIA It may not be; good madam, pardon me.

SILVIA There, hold!
I will not look upon your master's lines.
I know they are stuff'd with protestations,
And full of new-found oaths, which he will break
As easily as I do tear his paper.

JULIA Madam, he sends your ladyship this ring.

SILVIA The more shame for him that he sends it me;
For I have heard him say a thousand times
His Julia gave it him at his departure.
Though his false finger have profan'd the ring,
Mine shall not do his Julia so much wrong.

JULIA She thanks you.

SILVIA What say'st thou?

JULIA I thank you, madam, that you tender her.
Poor gentlewoman, my master wrongs her much.

SILVIA Dost thou know her?

JULIA Almost as well as I do know myself.
To think upon her woes, I do protest
That I have wept a hundred several times.

SILVIA Belike she thinks that Proteus hath forsook her.

JULIA I think she doth, and that's her cause of sorrow.

SILVIA Is she not passing fair?
JULIA She hath been fairer, madam, than she is.
When she did think my master lov'd her well,
She, in my judgment, was as fair as you;
But since she did neglect her looking-glass
And threw her sun-expelling mask away,
The air hath starv'd the roses in her cheeks
And pinch'd the lily-tincture of her face,
That now she is become as black as I.
SILVIA How tall was she?
JULIA About my stature; for at Pentecost,
When all our pageants of delight were play'd,
Our youth got me to play the woman's part,
And I was trimm'd in Madam Julia's gown;
Which served me as fit, by all men's judgments,
As if the garment had been made for me;
Therefore I know she is about my height.
And at that time I made her weep agood,
For I did play a lamentable part.
Madam, 'twas Ariadne passioning
For Theseus' perjury and unjust flight;
Which I so lively acted with my tears
That my poor mistress, moved therewithal,
Wept bitterly; and would I might be dead
If I in thought felt not her very sorrow.
SILVIA She is beholding to thee, gentle youth.
Alas, poor lady, desolate and left!
I weep myself, to think upon thy words.
Here, youth, there is my purse; I give thee this
For thy sweet mistress' sake, because thou lov'st her.
Farewell. [*Exit Silvia with attendants.*
JULIA And she shall thank you for't, if e'er you know her.
A virtuous gentlewoman, mild and beautiful!
I hope my master's suit will be but cold,
Since she respects my mistress' love so much.
Alas, how love can trifle with itself!
Here is her picture; let me see. I think,
If I had such a tire, this face of mine
Were full as lovely as is this of hers;
And yet the painter flatter'd her a little,
Unless I flatter with myself too much.
Her hair is auburn, mine is perfect yellow;
If that be all the difference in his love,
I'll get me such a colour'd periwig.
Her eyes are grey as glass, and so are mine;
Ay, but her forehead's low, and mine's as high.
What should it be that he respects in her
But I can make respective in myself,
If this fond Love were not a blinded god?
Come, shadow, come, and take this shadow up,
For 'tis thy rival. O thou senseless form,
Thou shalt be worshipp'd, kiss'd, lov'd, and ador'd!
And were there sense in his idolatry
My substance should be statue in thy stead.
I'll use thee kindly for thy mistress' sake,
That us'd me so; or else, by Jove I vow,
I should have scratch'd out your unseeing eyes,
To make my master out of love with thee.
[*Exit.*

ACT FIVE

SCENE I. *Milan. An abbey.*

Enter EGLAMOUR.

EGLAMOUR The sun begins to gild the western sky,
And now it is about the very hour
That Silvia at Friar Patrick's cell should meet me.
She will not fail, for lovers break not hours
Unless it be to come before their time,
So much they spur their expedition.

Enter SILVIA.

See where she comes. Lady, a happy evening!
SILVIA Amen, amen! Go on, good Eglamour,
Out at the postern by the abbey wall;
I fear I am attended by some spies.
EGLAMOUR Fear not. The forest is not three leagues off;
If we recover that, we are sure enough.
[*Exeunt.*

SCENE II. *Milan. The Duke's palace.*

Enter THURIO, PROTEUS, and JULIA as Sebastian.

THURIO Sir Proteus, what says Silvia to my suit?
PROTEUS O, sir, I find her milder than she was;
And yet she takes exceptions at your person.
THURIO What, that my leg is too long?
PROTEUS No; that it is too little.
THURIO I'll wear a boot to make it somewhat rounder.
JULIA [*Aside*] But love will not be spurr'd to what it loathes.
THURIO What says she to my face?
PROTEUS She says it is a fair one.
THURIO Nay, then, the wanton lies; my face is black.
PROTEUS But pearls are fair; and the old saying is:
Black men are pearls in beauteous ladies' eyes.
JULIA [*Aside*] 'Tis true, such pearls as put out ladies' eyes;
For I had rather wink than look on them.

THURIO How likes she my discourse?
PROTEUS Ill, when you talk of war.
THURIO But well when I discourse of love and peace?
JULIA [*Aside*] But better, indeed, when you hold your peace.
THURIO What says she to my valour?
PROTEUS O, sir, she makes no doubt of that.
JULIA [*Aside*] She needs not, when she knows it cowardice.
THURIO What says she to my birth?
PROTEUS That you are well deriv'd.
JULIA [*Aside*] True; from a gentleman to a fool.
THURIO Considers she my possessions?
PROTEUS O, ay; and pities them.
THURIO Wherefore?
JULIA [*Aside*] That such an ass should owe them.
PROTEUS That they are out by lease.
JULIA Here comes the Duke.

Enter DUKE.

DUKE How now, Sir Proteus! how now, Thurio!
Which of you saw Sir Eglamour of late?
THURIO Not I.
PROTEUS Nor I.
DUKE Saw you my daughter?
PROTEUS Neither.
DUKE Why then,
She's fled unto that peasant Valentine;
And Eglamour is in her company.
'Tis true; for Friar Lawrence met them both
As he in penance wander'd through the forest;
Him he knew well, and guess'd that it was she,
But, being mask'd, he was not sure of it;
Besides, she did intend confession
At Patrick's cell this even; and there she was not.
These likelihoods confirm her flight from hence;
Therefore, I pray you, stand not to discourse,
But mount you presently, and meet with me
Upon the rising of the mountain foot
That leads toward Mantua, whither they are fled.
Dispatch, sweet gentlemen, and follow me. [*Exit*

THURIO Why, this it is to be a peevish girl
That flies her fortune when it follows her.
I'll after, more to be reveng'd on Eglamour
Than for the love of reckless Silvia. [*Exit.*
PROTEUS And I will follow, more for Silvia's love
Than hate of Eglamour, that goes with her. [*Exit.*
JULIA And I will follow, more to cross that love
Than hate for Silvia, that is gone for love. [*Exit.*

SCENE III. *The frontiers of Mantua. The forest.*

Enter Outlaws with SILVIA.

1 OUTLAW Come, come,
Be patient; we must bring you to our captain.
SILVIA A thousand more mischances than this one
Have learn'd me how to brook this patiently.
2 OUTLAW Come, bring her away.
1 OUTLAW Where is the gentleman that was with her?
2 OUTLAW Being nimble-footed, he hath outrun us,
But Moyses and Valerius follow him.
Go thou with her to the west end of the wood;
There is our captain; we'll follow him that's fled.
The thicket is beset; he cannot 'scape.
1 OUTLAW Come, I must bring you to our captain's cave;
Fear not; he bears an honourable mind,
And will not use a woman lawlessly.
SILVIA O Valentine, this I endure for thee! [*Exeunt.*

SCENE IV. *Another part of the forest.*

Enter VALENTINE.

VALENTINE How use doth breed a habit in a man!
This shadowy desert, unfrequented woods,
I better brook than flourishing peopled towns.
Here can I sit alone, unseen of any,
And to the nightingale's complaining notes
Tune my distresses and record my woes.
O thou that dost inhabit in my breast,
Leave not the mansion so long tenantless,
Lest, growing ruinous, the building fall
And leave no memory of what it was!
Repair me with thy presence, Silvia;
Thou gentle nymph, cherish thy forlorn swain.
What halloing and what stir is this to-day?
These are my mates, that make their wills their law,
Have some unhappy passenger in chase.
They love me well; yet I have much to do
To keep them from uncivil outrages.
Withdraw thee, Valentine. Who's this comes here? [*Steps aside.*

Enter PROTEUS, SILVIA, and JULIA as Sebastian.

PROTEUS Madam, this service I have done for you,
Though you respect not aught your servant doth,
To hazard life, and rescue you from him
That would have forc'd your honour and your

love.
Vouchsafe me, for my meed, but one fair look;
A smaller boon than this I cannot beg,
And less than this, I am sure, you cannot give.

VALENTINE [*Aside*] How like a dream is this I see and hear!
Love, lend me patience to forbear awhile.

SILVIA O miserable, unhappy that I am!

PROTEUS Unhappy were you, madam, ere I came;
But by my coming I have made you happy.

SILVIA By thy approach thou mak'st me most unhappy.

JULIA [*Aside*] And me, when he approacheth to your presence.

SILVIA Had I been seized by a hungry lion,
I would have been a breakfast to the beast
Rather than have false Proteus rescue me.
O, heaven be judge how I love Valentine,
Whose life's as tender to me as my soul!
And full as much, for more there cannot be,
I do detest false, perjur'd Proteus.
Therefore be gone; solicit me no more.

PROTEUS What dangerous action, stood it next to death,
Would I not undergo for one calm look?
O, 'tis the curse in love, and still approv'd,
When women cannot love where they're belov'd!

SILVIA When Proteus cannot love where he's belov'd!
Read over Julia's heart, thy first best love,
For whose dear sake thou didst then rend thy faith
Into a thousand oaths; and all those oaths
Descended into perjury, to love me.
Thou hast no faith left now, unless thou'dst two,
And that's far worse than none; better have none
Than plural faith, which is too much by one.
Thou counterfeit to thy true friend!

PROTEUS In love,
Who respects friend?

SILVIA All men but Proteus.

PROTEUS Nay, if the gentle spirit of moving words
Can no way change you to a milder form,
I'll woo you like a soldier, at arms' end,
And love you 'gainst the nature of love – force ye.

SILVIA O heaven!

PROTEUS I'll force thee yield to my desire.

VALENTINE Ruffian! let go that rude uncivil touch;
Thou friend of an ill fashion!

PROTEUS Valentine!

VALENTINE Thou common friend, that's without faith or love –
For such is a friend now; treacherous man,
Thou hast beguil'd my hopes; nought but mine eye
Could have persuaded me. Now I dare not say
I have one friend alive: thou wouldst disprove me.
Who should be trusted, when one's own right hand
Is perjured to the bosom? Proteus,
I am sorry I must never trust thee more,
But count the world a stranger for thy sake.
The private wound is deepest. O time most accurst!
'Mongst all foes that a friend should be the worst!

PROTEUS My shame and guilt confounds me.
Forgive me, Valentine; if hearty sorrow
Be a sufficient ransom for offence,
I tender 't here; I do as truly suffer
As e'er I did commit.

VALENTINE Then I am paid;
And once again I do receive thee honest.
Who by repentance is not satisfied
Is nor of heaven nor of earth, for these are pleas'd;
By penitence th' Eternal's wrath's appeas'd.
And, that my love may appear plain and free,
All that was mine in Silvia I give thee.

JULIA O me unhappy! [*Swoons.*

PROTEUS Look to the boy.

VALENTINE Why, boy! why, wag! how now!
What's the matter? Look up; speak.

JULIA O good sir, my master charg'd me to deliver a ring to Madam Silvia, which, out of my neglect, was never done.

PROTEUS Where is that ring, boy?

JULIA Here 'tis; this is it.

PROTEUS How! let me see. Why, this is the ring I gave to Julia.

JULIA O, cry you mercy, sir, I have mistook;
This is the ring you sent to Silvia. 94

PROTEUS But how cam'st thou by this ring?
At my depart I gave this unto Julia.

JULIA And Julia herself did give it me;
And Julia herself have brought it hither.

PROTEUS How! Julia!

JULIA Behold her that gave aim to all thy oaths,
And entertain'd 'em deeply in her heart.
How oft hast thou with perjury cleft the root!
O Proteus, let this habit make thee blush!
Be thou asham'd that I have took upon me
Such an immodest raiment – if shame live
In a disguise of love.
It is the lesser blot, modesty finds,
Women to change their shapes than men their minds.

PROTEUS Than men their minds! 'tis true. O heaven, were man
But constant, he were perfect! That one error
Fills him with faults; makes him run through all th' sins:
Inconstancy falls off ere it begins.
What is in Silvia's face but I may spy
More fresh in Julia's with a constant eye?
VALENTINE Come, come, a hand from either.
Let me be blest to make this happy close;
'Twere pity two such friends should be long foes.
PROTEUS Bear witness, heaven, I have my wish for ever.
JULIA And I mine.

Enter Outlaws, with DUKE and THURIO.

OUTLAWS A prize, a prize, a prize!
VALENTINE Forbear, forbear, I say; it is my lord the Duke.
Your Grace is welcome to a man disgrac'd,
Banished Valentine.
DUKE Sir Valentine!
THURIO Yonder is Silvia; and Silvia's mine.
VALENTINE Thurio, give back, or else embrace thy death;
Come not within the measure of my wrath;
Do not name Silvia thine; if once again,
Verona shall not hold thee. Here she stands
Take but possession of her with a touch –
I dare thee but to breathe upon my love.
THURIO Sir Valentine, I care not for her, I;
I hold him but a fool that will endanger
His body for a girl that loves him not.
I claim her not, and therefore she is thine.
DUKE The more degenerate and base art thou
To make such means for her as thou hast done
And leave her on such slight conditions.
Now, by the honour of my ancestry,
I do applaud thy spirit, Valentine,
And think thee worthy of an empress' love.
Know then, I here forget all former griefs,
Cancel all grudge, repeal thee home again,
Plead a new state in thy unrivall'd merit,
To which I thus subscribe: Sir Valentine,
Thou art a gentleman, and well deriv'd;
Take thou thy Silvia, for thou hast deserv'd her
VALENTINE I thank your Grace; the gift hath made me happy.
I now beseech you, for your daughter's sake,
To grant one boon that I shall ask of you.
DUKE I grant it for thine own, whate'er it be.
VALENTINE These banish'd men, that I have kept withal,
Are men endu'd with worthy qualities;
Forgive them what they have committed here,
And let them be recall'd from their exile:
They are reformed, civil, full of good,
And fit for great employment, worthy lord.
DUKE Thou hast prevail'd; I pardon them and thee;
Dispose of them as thou know'st their deserts.
Come, let us go; we will include all jars
With triumphs, mirth, and rare solemnity.
VALENTINE And, as we walk along, I dare be bold
With our discourse to make your Grace to smile.
What think you of this page, my lord?
DUKE I think the boy hath grace in him; he blushes.
VALENTINE I warrant you, my lord – more grace than boy.
DUKE What mean you by that saying?
VALENTINE Please you, I'll tell you as we pass along,
That you will wonder what hath fortuned.
Come, Proteus, 'tis your penance but to hear,
The story of your loves discovered.
That done, our day of marriage shall be yours;
One feast, one house, one mutual happiness!
[*Exeunt.*

The Merry Wives of Windsor

Introduction by RALPH JESSOP

Two Windsor wives make merry with the obese Sir John Falstaff's feeble initiative to seduce them. Defying the contraries of a testing jealous suspicion and an unbridled freedom, Mrs Ford and Mrs Page will prove that comic wives can have their way in merry-making deceits and still be true to their husbands. Mr Page trusts his wife absolutely. Dreading the cuckold's horns, Mr Ford becomes ridiculously entrapped by the collision of his plot to verify Mrs Ford's guilt with Falstaff's own scheme to substantiate it. Both husbands deploy deceit. Obsessed with testing his wife's faithfulness, Ford re-names himself Brook, disguises himself as his wife's would-be seducer, and patronises Falstaff to debauch her. Page, against the wishes of his wife, attempts to marry off his daughter Anne to the unsuitable Abraham Slender. Mrs Page will also deceive her husband both in her scheme for marrying Anne to that other mismatched suitor, Dr Caius, and in colluding with Mrs Ford's deceptions. Party to deception, conflicting interests, and the course of true love, Dr Caius' servant, Mrs Quickly, crucially acts as go-between. She assists in tricking Falstaff and does what only she can for each of Anne's suitors, Slender, Caius, and Fenton. The Pages' mutual deceptions miscarry. Anne Page elopes with Fenton and is married to him by the Welsh parson Sir Hugh Evans. After the climax of his public humiliation, the arrow of the uniting forces of the married couples momentarily glances off Falstaff and gives way to the possibility of his inclusion in the Windsor community.

Revenge, money, jealousy, cuckoldry, mirth, comic incongruities, are the play's driving energies. Justice Shallow begins *The Merry Wives* with a demand for redressing wrongs done to him by Falstaff. Pinched for cash, Falstaff puns on his gross waist and initiates measures for thrift – the projected seductions of Mrs Page and Mrs Ford are means to his financial ends. Money-motives are also connected with all of Anne's suitors – even her true love, Fenton, claims to have replaced an initial interest in her father's wealth for the riches of herself. Cast off by Falstaff, Nym and Pistol aim at revenge through incensing jealousies. Providing ample mirth, Mrs Page and Mrs Ford exact revenge on Falstaff, forcing him to escape Ford in a buck-basket full of the foulest laundry. Dressed as the old woman of Brainford he escapes a second interrupted liaison while Ford, mistaking him for a witch, thrashes him. Falstaff is finally tricked into disguising himself as Herne the Hunter with antlers on his head in a scene that echoes Bottom's transformation in *A Midsummer Night's Dream*. Doubling mockery at this public ridicule of Falstaff, Caius and Slender are each cheated of their planned elopements with Anne when they discover that costumes, supposedly signifying her hidden identity, conceal boys. Caius storms off stage with a threat that hints at being revenged on the whole pack of them. The financially motivated love-suits all fail as the play expunges the sexually weak or suspect, the orally suave yet impotent Falstaff, the threat of cuckoldry, and the rule of divided parenthood – individualism in the course of true love appears to triumph with a communal blessing.

In *The Merry Wives* words are mismatched with meanings, tragedy consorts with comedy. Falstaff's oily physical grossness and decadence draws him near to a pitiful, unaccommodated state as he plots seduction and is seduced into follies of unwarranted sexual confidence. As disguises manifest and hide identities, Mrs Quickly hints of truths and her own plots within a language of malapropisms and unknowing knowingness. Her final role as Fairy Queen hints at witchcraft, an occult presence steering sexual fates. This witchcraft emasculates men yet fosters marriage. It makes imposters and would-be cuckolders cuckold through licensed deceits that secure the marriages of Fenton, Ford and Page – Falstaff and not Ford is finally made to wear the cuckold's horns. Other hints are given a more public currency as the pass-words of subterfuge that suggest political satire and result in the disclosure of gender. 'Mum' and 'budget' are uttered and lead to the silencing of financial interests in the disclosure of male identities within female garments. The example of Christopher Sly in *The Taming of the Shrew* suggests that a dazed and simple-minded audience, unaware of the Elizabethan play's use of boy actors for female parts, mistakes male actors for women. But if all the women on Shakespeare's stage are page-boys, all the wives of Windsor are deceptive. This provides a rich joke which runs through the whole play into the very last line.

The Merry Wives of Windsor

DRAMATIS PERSONAE

SIR JOHN FALSTAFF
FENTON
a young gentleman
SHALLOW
a country justice
SLENDER
cousin to Shallow
FORD, PAGE
gentlemen to Windsor
WILLIAM PAGE
a boy, son to Page
SIR HUGH EVANS
a Welsh parson
DOCTOR CAIUS
a French physician
Host of the Garter Inn
BARDOLPH, PISTOL, NYM
followers of Falstaff
ROBIN
page to Falstaff
SIMPLE
servant to Slender
RUGBY
servant to Doctor Caius
MISTRESS FORD
MISTRESS PAGE
MISTRESS ANNE PAGE
her daughter
MISTRESS QUICKLY
servant to Doctor Caius
Servants to Page, Ford, etc.

THE SCENE: WINDSOR, AND THE NEIGHBOURHOOD

ACT ONE

SCENE I. *Windsor. Before Page's house.*

Enter JUSTICE SHALLOW, SLENDER and SIR HUGH EVANS.

SHALLOW Sir Hugh, persuade me not; I will make a Star Chamber matter of it; if he were twenty Sir John Falstaffs, he shall not abuse Robert Shallow, esquire.

SLENDER In the county of Gloucester, Justice of Peace, and Coram.

SHALLOW Ay, cousin Slender, and Custalorum.

SLENDER Ay, and Ratolorum too; and a gentleman born, Master Parson, who writes himself 'Armigero' in any bill, warrant, quittance, or obligation – 'Armigero'.

SHALLOW Ay, that I do; and have done any time these three hundred years.

SLENDER All his successors, gone before him, hath done't; and all his ancestors, that come after him, may: they may give the dozen white luces in their coat.

SHALLOW It is an old coat.

EVANS The dozen white louses do become an old coat well; it agrees well, passant; it is a familiar beast to man, and signifies love.

SHALLOW The luce is the fresh fish; the salt fish is an old coat.

SLENDER I may quarter, coz.

SHALLOW You may, by marrying.

EVANS It is marring indeed, if he quarter it.

SHALLOW Not a whit.

EVANS Yes, py'r lady! If he has a quarter of your coat, there is but three skirts for yourself, in my simple conjectures; but that is all one. If Sir John Falstaff have committed disparagements unto you, I am of the church, and will be glad to do my benevolence, to make atonements and compremises between you.

SHALLOW The Council shall hear it; it is a riot.

EVANS It is not meet the Council hear a riot; there is no fear of Got in a riot; the Council, look you, shall desire to hear the fear of Got, and not to hear a riot; take your vizaments in that.

SHALLOW Ha! o' my life, if I were young again, the sword should end it.

EVANS It is petter that friends is the sword and end it; and there is also another device in my prain, which peradventure prings goot discretions with it. There is Anne Page, which is daughter to Master George Page, which is pretty virginity.

SLENDER Mistress Anne Page? She has brown hair, and speaks small like a woman.

EVANS It is that fery person for all the orld, as just as you will desire; and seven hundred pounds of moneys, and gold, and silver, is her grandsire upon his death's-bed – Got deliver to a joyful resurrections ! – give, when she is able to overtake seventeen years old. It were a goot motion if we leave our pribbles and prabbles, and desire a marriage between Master Abraham and Mistress Anne Page.

SHALLOW Did her grandsire leave her seven hundred pound?

EVANS Ay, and her father is make her a petter penny.

SHALLOW I know the young gentlewoman; she has good gifts.

EVANS Seven hundred pounds, and possibilities, is goot gifts.

SHALLOW Well, let us see honest Master Page. Is Falstaff there?

EVANS Shall I tell you a lie? I do despise a liar as I do despise one that is false; or as I despise one that is not true. The knight Sir John is there; and, I beseech you, be ruled by your well-willers. I will peat the door for Master Page. [*Knocks*] What, hoa! Got pless your house here!

PAGE [*Within*] Who's there?

Enter PAGE.

EVANS Here is Got's plessing, and your friend, and Justice Shallow; and here young Master Slender, that peradventures shall tell you another tale, if matters grow to your likings.

PAGE I am glad to see your worships well. I thank you for my venison, Master Shallow.

SHALLOW Master Page, I am glad to see you; much good do it your good heart! I wish'd your venison better; it was ill kill'd. How doth good Mistress Page? – and I thank you always with my heart, la! with my heart.

PAGE Sir, I thank you.

SHALLOW Sir, I thank you; by yea and no, I do.

PAGE I am glad to see you, good Master Slender.

SLENDER How does your fallow greyhound, sir? I heard say he was outrun on Cotsall.

PAGE It could not be judg'd, sir.

SLENDER You'll not confess, you'll not confess.

SHALLOW That he will not. 'Tis your fault; 'tis your fault; 'tis a good dog.

PAGE A cur, sir.

SHALLOW Sir, he's a good dog, and a fair dog. Can there be more said? He is good, and fair. Is Sir John Falstaff here?

PAGE Sir, he is within; and I would I could do a good office between you.

EVANS It is spoke as a Christians ought to speak.

SHALLOW He hath wrong'd me, Master Page.

PAGE Sir, he doth in some sort confess it.

SHALLOW If it be confessed, it is not redressed; is not that so, Master Page? He hath wrong'd me; indeed he hath; at a word, he hath, believe me; Robert Shallow, esquire, saith he is wronged.

PAGE Here comes Sir John.

Enter SIR JOHN FALSTAFF, BARDOLPH, NYM and PISTOL.

FALSTAFF Now, Master Shallow, you'll complain of me to the King?

SHALLOW Knight, you have beaten my men, kill'd my deer, and broke open my lodge.

FALSTAFF But not kiss'd your keeper's daughter.

SHALLOW Tut, a pin! this shall be answer'd.

FALSTAFF I will answer it straight: I have done all this. That is now answer'd.

SHALLOW The Council shall know this.

FALSTAFF 'Twere better for you if it were known in counsel: you'll be laugh'd at.

EVANS Pauca verba, Sir John; goot worts.

FALSTAFF Good worts! good cabbage! Slender, I broke your head; what matter have you against me?

SLENDER Marry, sir, I have matter in my head against you; and against your cony-catching rascals, Bardolph, Nym, and Pistol. They carried me to the tavern, and made me drunk, and afterward pick'd my pocket.

BARDOLPH You Banbury cheese!

SLENDER Ay, it is no matter.

PISTOL How now, Mephostophilus!

SLENDER Ay, it is no matter.

NYM Slice, I say! pauca, pauca; slice! That's my humour.

SLENDER Where's Simple, my man? Can you tell, cousin?

EVANS Peace, I pray you. Now let us understand. There is three umpires in this matter, as I understand: that is, Master Page, fidelicet Master Page; and there is myself, fidelicet myself; and the three party is, lastly and finally, mine host of the Garter.

PAGE We three to hear it and end it between them.

EVANS Fery goot. I will make a prief of it in my note-book; and we will afterwards ork upon the cause with as great discreetly as we can.

FALSTAFF Pistol!

PISTOL He hears with ears.

EVANS The tevil and his tam! What phrase is this, 'He hears with ear'? Why, it is affectations.

FALSTAFF Pistol, did you pick Master Slender's purse?

SLENDER Ay, by these gloves, did he – or I would I might never come in mine own great chamber again else! – of seven groats in mill-sixpences, and two Edward shovelboards that cost me two shilling and two pence apiece of Yead Miller, by these gloves.

FALSTAFF Is this true, Pistol?

EVANS No, it is false, if it is a pick-purse.

PISTOL Ha, thou mountain-foreigner! Sir John,
and master mine,
I combat challenge of this latten bilbo.
Word of denial in thy labras here!
Word of denial! Froth and scum, thou liest.

SLENDER By these gloves, then, 'twas he.

NYM Be avis'd, sir, and pass good humours; I will say 'marry trap' with you, if you run the nuthook's humour on me; that is the very note of it.

SLENDER By this hat, then, he in the red face had it; for though I cannot remember what I did when you made me drunk, yet I am not altogether an ass.

FALSTAFF What say you, Scarlet and John?

BARDOLPH Why, sir, for my part, I say the gentleman had drunk himself out of his five sentences.

EVANS It is his five senses; fie, what the ignorance is!

BARDOLPH And being fap, sir, was, as they say, cashier'd; and so conclusions pass'd the careers.

SLENDER Ay, you spake in Latin then too; but 'tis no matter; I'll ne'er be drunk whilst I live again, but in honest, civil, godly company, for this trick. If I be drunk, I'll be drunk with those that have the fear of God, and not with drunken knaves.

EVANS So Got udge me, that is a virtuous mind.

FALSTAFF You hear all these matters deni'd, gentlemen; you hear it.

Enter MISTRESS ANNE PAGE with wine; MISTRESS FORD and MISTRESS PAGE, following.

PAGE Nay, daughter, carry the wine in; we'll drink within. *[Exit Anne Page.*

SLENDER O heaven! this is Mistress Anne Page.

PAGE How now, Mistress Ford!

FALSTAFF Mistress Ford, by my troth, you are very well met; by your leave, good mistress. *[Kisses her.*

PAGE Wife, bid these gentlemen welcome. Come, we have a hot venison pasty to dinner; come, gentlemen, I hope we shall drink down all unkindness.

[Exeunt all but Shallow, Slender, and Evans.

SLENDER I had rather than forty shillings I had my Book of Songs and Sonnets here.

Enter SIMPLE.

How now, Simple! Where have you been? I must wait on myself, must I? You have not the Book of Riddles about you, have you?

SIMPLE Book of Riddles! Why, did you not lend it to Alice Shortcake upon All-hallowmas last, a fortnight afore Michaelmas?

SHALLOW Come, coz; come, coz; we stay for you. A word with you, coz; marry, this, coz: there is, as 'twere, a tender, a kind of tender, made afar off by Sir Hugh here. Do you understand me?

SLENDER Ay, sir, you shall find me reasonable; if it be so, I shall do that that is reason.

SHALLOW Nay, but understand me.

SLENDER So I do, sir.

EVANS Give ear to his motions: Master Slender, I will description the matter to you, if you be capacity of it.

SLENDER Nay, I will do as my cousin Shallow says; I pray you pardon me; he's a justice of peace in his country, simple though I stand here.

EVANS But that is not the question. The question is concerning your marriage.

SHALLOW Ay, there's the point, sir.

EVANS Marry is it; the very point of it; to Mistress Anne Page.

SLENDER Why, if it be so, I will marry her upon any reasonable demands.

EVANS But can you affection the oman? Let us command to know that of your mouth or of your lips; for divers philosophers hold that the lips is parcel of the mouth. Therefore, precisely, can you carry your good will to the maid?

SHALLOW Cousin Abraham Slender, can you love her?

SLENDER I hope, sir, I will do as it shall become one that would do reason.

EVANS Nay, Got's lords and his ladies! you must speak possitable, if you can carry her your desires towards her.

SHALLOW That you must. Will you, upon good dowry, marry her?

SLENDER I will do a greater thing than that upon your request, cousin, in any reason.

SHALLOW Nay, conceive me, conceive me, sweet coz; what I do is to pleasure you, coz. Can you love the maid?

SLENDER I will marry her, sir, at your request; but if there be no great love in the beginning, yet heaven may decrease it upon better acquaintance, when we are married and have more occasion to know one another. I hope upon familiarity will grow more contempt. But if you say 'marry her', I will marry her; that I am freely dissolved, and dissolutely.

EVANS It is a fery discretion answer, save the fall is in the ord 'dissolutely': the ort is, according to our meaning, 'resolutely'; his meaning is good.

SHALLOW Ay, I think my cousin meant well.

SLENDER Ay, or else I would I might be hang'd, la!

Re-enter ANNE PAGE.

SHALLOW Here comes fair Mistress Anne. Would I were young for your sake, Mistress Anne!

ANNE The dinner is on the table; my father desires your worships' company.

SHALLOW I will wait on him, fair Mistress Anne!

EVANS Od's plessed will! I will not be absence at the grace. [*Exeunt Shallow and Evans.*

ANNE Will't please your worship to come in, sir?

SLENDER No, I thank you, forsooth, heartily; I am very well.

ANNE The dinner attends you, sir.

SLENDER I am not a-hungry, I thank you, forsooth. Go, sirrah, for all you are my man, go wait upon my cousin Shallow. [*Exit Simple*] A justice of peace sometime may be beholding to his friend for a man. I keep but three men and a boy yet, till my mother be dead. But what though? Yet I live like a poor gentleman born.

ANNE I may not go in without your worship; they will not sit till you come.

SLENDER I' faith, I'll eat nothing; I thank you as much as though I did.

ANNE I pray you, sir, walk in.

SLENDER I had rather walk here, I thank you. I bruis'd my shin th' other day with playing at sword and dagger with a master of fence – three veneys for a dish of stew'd prunes – and, I with my ward defending my head, he hot my shin, and, by my troth, I cannot abide the smell of hot meat since. Why do your dogs bark so? Be there bears i' th' town?

ANNE I think there are, sir; I heard them talk'd of.

SLENDER I love the sport well; but I shall as soon quarrel at it as any man in England. You are afraid, if you see the bear loose, are you not?

ANNE Ay, indeed, sir.

SLENDER That's meat and drink to me now. I have seen Sackerson loose twenty times, and have taken him by the chain; but, I warrant you, the women have so cried and shriek'd at it that it pass'd; but women, indeed, cannot abide 'em; they are very ill-favour'd rough things.

Re-enter PAGE.

PAGE Come, gentle Master Slender, come; we stay for you.

SLENDER I'll eat nothing, I thank you, sir.

PAGE By cock and pie, you shall not choose, sir! Come, come.

SLENDER Nay, pray you lead the way.

PAGE Come on, sir.

SLENDER Mistress Anne, yourself shall go first.

ANNE Not I, sir; pray you keep on.

SLENDER Truly, I will not go first; truly, la! I will not do you that wrong.

ANNE I pray you, sir.

SLENDER I'll rather be unmannerly than troublesome. You do yourself wrong indeed, la! [*Exeunt.*

SCENE II. *Before Page's house.*

Enter SIR HUGH EVANS and SIMPLE.

EVANS Go your ways, and ask of Doctor Caius' house which is the way; and there dwells one Mistress Quickly, which is in the manner of his nurse, or his dry nurse, or his cook, or his laundry, his washer, and his wringer.

SIMPLE Well, sir.

EVANS Nay, it is petter yet. Give her this letter; for it is a oman that altogether's acquaintance with Mistress Anne Page; and the letter is to desire and require her to solicit your master's desires to Mistress Anne Page. I pray you be gone. I will make an end of my dinner; there's pippins and cheese to come. [*Exeunt.*

SCENE III. *The Garter Inn.*

Enter FALSTAFF, HOST, BARDOLPH, NYM, PISTOL and ROBIN.

FALSTAFF Mine host of the Garter!

HOST What says my bully rook? Speak scholarly and wisely.

FALSTAFF Truly, mine host, I must turn away some of my followers.

HOST Discard, bully Hercules; cashier; let them wag; trot, trot.

FALSTAFF I sit at ten pounds a week.

HOST Thou'rt an emperor – Caesar, Keiser, and Pheazar. I will entertain Bardolph; he shall draw, he shall tap; said I well, bully Hector?

FALSTAFF Do so, good mine host.

HOST I have spoke; let him follow. [*To Bardolph*] Let me see thee froth and lime. I am at a word; follow. [*Exit Host.*

FALSTAFF Bardolph, follow him. A tapster is a good trade; an old cloak makes a new jerkin; a wither'd serving-man a fresh tapster. Go; adieu.

BARDOLPH It is a life that I have desir'd; I will thrive.

PISTOL O base Hungarian wight! Wilt thou the spigot wield? [*Exit Bardolph.*

NYM He was gotten in drink. Is not the humour conceited?

FALSTAFF I am glad I am so acquit of this tinder-box: his thefts were too open; his filching was like an unskilful singer – he kept not time.

NYM The good humour is to steal at a minute's rest.

PISTOL 'Convey' the wise it call. 'Steal' foh! A fico for the phrase!

FALSTAFF Well, sirs, I am almost out at heels.

PISTOL Why, then, let kibes ensue.

FALSTAFF There is no remedy; I must cony-catch; I must shift.

PISTOL Young ravens must have food.

FALSTAFF Which of you know Ford of this town?

PISTOL I ken the wight; he is of substance good.

FALSTAFF My honest lads, I will tell you what I am about.

PISTOL Two yards, and more.

FALSTAFF No quips now, Pistol. Indeed, I am in the waist two yards about; but I am now about no waste; I am about thrift. Briefly, I do mean to make love to Ford's wife; I spy entertainment in her; she discourses, she carves, she gives the leer of invitation; I can construe the action of her familiar style; and the hardest voice of her behaviour, to be English'd rightly, is 'I am Sir John Falstaff's'.

PISTOL He hath studied her well, and translated her will out of honesty into English.

NYM The anchor is deep; will that humour pass?

FALSTAFF Now, the report goes she has all the rule of her husband's purse; he hath a legion of angels.

PISTOL As many devils entertain; and 'To her, boy' say I.

NYM The humour rises; it is good; humour me the angels.

FALSTAFF I have writ me here a letter to her; and here another to Page's wife, who even now gave me good eyes too, examin'd my parts with most judicious oeillades; sometimes the beam of her view gilded my foot, sometimes my portly belly.

PISTOL Then did the sun on dunghill shine.

NYM I thank thee for that humour.

FALSTAFF O, she did so course o'er my exteriors with such a greedy intention that the appetite of her eye did seem to scorch me up like a burning-glass! Here's another letter to her. She bears the purse too; she is a region in Guiana, all gold and bounty. I will be cheaters to them both, and they shall be exchequers to me; they shall be my East and West Indies, and I will trade to them both. Go, bear thou this letter to Mistress Page; and thou this to Mistress Ford. We will thrive, lads, we will thrive.

PISTOL Shall I Sir Pandarus of Troy become,
And by my side wear steel? Then Lucifer take all!

NYM I will run no base humour. Here, take the humour-letter; I will keep the haviour of reputation.

FALSTAFF [*To Robin*] Hold, sirrah; bear you these letters tightly;
Sail like my pinnace to these golden shores.
Rogues, hence, avaunt! vanish like hailstones, go;
Trudge, plod away i' th' hoof; seek shelter, pack!
Falstaff will learn the humour of the age;
French thrift, you rogues; myself, and skirted page. [*Exeunt Falstaff and Robin.*

PISTOL Let vultures gripe thy guts! for gourd and fullam holds,
And high and low beguiles the rich and poor;
Tester I'll have in pouch when thou shalt lack,
Base Phrygian Turk!

NYM I have operations in my head which be humours of revenge.

PISTOL Wilt thou revenge?

NYM By welkin and her star!

PISTOL With wit or steel?

NYM With both the humours, I.
I will discuss the humour of this love to Page.

PISTOL And I to Ford shall eke unfold
How Falstaff, varlet vile,
His dove will prove, his gold will hold,
And his soft couch defile.

NYM My humour shall not cool; I will incense Page to deal with poison; I will possess him with yellowness; for the revolt of mine is dangerous. That is my true humour.

PISTOL Thou art the Mars of malcontents;
I second thee; troop on. [*Exeunt.*

SCENE IV. *Doctor Caius's house.*

Enter MISTRESS QUICKLY, SIMPLE and RUGBY.

QUICKLY What, John Rugby! I pray thee go to the casement and see if you can see my master, Master Doctor Caius, coming. If he do, i' faith, and find anybody in the house, here will be an old abusing of God's patience and the King's English.

RUGBY I'll go watch.

QUICKLY Go; and we'll have a posset for't soon at night, in faith, at the latter end of a sea-coal fire. [*Exit Rugby*] An honest, willing, kind fellow, as ever servant shall come in house withal; and, I warrant you, no tell-tale nor no breed-bate; his worst fault is that he is given to prayer; he is something peevish that way; but nobody but has his fault; but let that pass. Peter Simple you say your name is?

SIMPLE Ay, for fault of a better.

QUICKLY And Master Slender's your master?

SIMPLE Ay, forsooth.

QUICKLY Does he not wear a great round beard,

like a glover's paring-knife?

SIMPLE No, forsooth; he hath but a little whey face, with a little yellow beard, a Cain-colour'd beard.

QUICKLY A softly-sprighted man, is he not?

SIMPLE Ay, forsooth; but he is as tall a man of his hands as any is between this and his head; he hath fought with a warrener.

QUICKLY How say you? O, I should remember him. Does he not hold up his head, as it were, and strut in his gait?

SIMPLE Yes, indeed, does he.

QUICKLY Well, heaven send Anne Page no worse fortune! Tell Master Parson Evans I will do what I can for your master. Anne is a good girl, and I wish –

Re-enter RUGBY.

RUGBY Out, alas! here comes my master.

QUICKLY We shall all be shent. Run in here, good young man; go into this closet. [*Shuts Simple in the closet*] He will not stay long. What, John Rugby! John! what John, I say! Go, John, go inquire for my master; I doubt he be not well that he comes not home. [*Singing.*

And down, down, adown-a, etc.

Enter DOCTOR CAIUS.

CAIUS Vat is you sing? I do not like des toys. Pray you, go and vetch me in my closet un boitier vert – a box, a green-a box. Do intend vat I speak? A green-a box.

QUICKLY Ay, forsooth, I'll fetch it you. [*Aside*] I am glad he went not in himself; if he had found the young man, he would have been horn-mad.

CAIUS Fe, fe, fe, fe! ma foi, il fait fort chaud. Je m'en vais à la cour – la grande affaire.

QUICKLY Is it this, sir?

CAIUS Oui; mette le au mon pocket: dépêche, quickly. Vere is dat knave, Rugby?

QUICKLY What, John Rugby! John!

RUGBY Here, sir.

CAIUS You are John Rugby, and you are Jack Rugby. Come, take-a your rapier, and come after my heel to the court.

RUGBY 'Tis ready, sir, here in the porch.

CAIUS By my trot, I tarry too long. Od's me! Qu'ai j' oublié? Dere is some simples in my closet dat I vill not for the varld I shall leave behind.

QUICKLY Ay me, he'll find the young man there, and be mad!

CAIUS O diable, diable! vat is in my closet? Villainy! larron! [*Pulling Simple out*] Rugby, my rapier!

QUICKLY Good master, be content.

CAIUS Wherefore shall I be content-a?

QUICKLY The young man is an honest man.

CAIUS What shall de honest man do in my closet? Dere is no honest man dat shall come in my closet.

QUICKLY I beseech you, be not so phlegmatic; hear the truth of it. He came of an errand to me from Parson Hugh.

CAIUS Vell?

SIMPLE Ay, forsooth, to desire her to –

QUICKLY Peace, I pray you.

CAIUS Peace-a your tongue. Speak-a your tale.

SIMPLE To desire this honest gentlewoman, your maid, to speak a good word to Mistress Anne Page for my master, in the way of marriage.

QUICKLY This is all, indeed, la! but I'll ne'er put my finger in the fire, and need not.

CAIUS Sir Hugh send-a you? Rugby, baillez me some paper. Tarry you a little-a-while. [*Writes.*

QUICKLY [*Aside to Simple*] I am glad he is so quiet; if he had been throughly moved, you should have heard him so loud and so melancholy. But notwithstanding, man, I'll do you your master what good I can; and the very yea and the no is, the French doctor, my master – I may call him my master, look you, for I keep his house; and I wash, wring, brew, bake, scour, dress meat and drink, make the beds, and do all myself –

SIMPLE [*Aside to Quickly*] 'Tis a great charge to come under one body's hand.

QUICKLY [*Aside to Simple*] Are you avis'd o' that? You shall find it a great charge; and to be up early and down late; but notwithstanding – to tell you in your ear, I would have no words of it – my master himself is in love with Mistress Anne Page; but notwithstanding that, I know Anne's mind – that's neither here nor there.

CAIUS You jack'nape; give-a this letter to Sir Hugh; by gar, it is a shallenge; I will cut his troat in de park; and I will teach a scurvy jack-a-nape priest to meddle or make. You may be gone; it is not good you tarry here. By gar, I will cut all his two stones; by gar, he shall not have a stone to throw at his dog. [*Exit Simple.*

QUICKLY Alas, he speaks but for his friend.

CAIUS It is no matter-a ver dat. Do not you tell-a me dat I shall have Anne Page for myself? By gar, I vill kill de Jack priest; and I have appointed mine host of de Jarteer to measure our weapon. By gar, I will myself have Anne Page.

QUICKLY Sir, the maid loves you, and all shall be well. We must give folks leave to prate. What the good-year!

CAIUS Rugby, come to the court with me. By gar, if I have not Anne Page, I shall turn your head out of my door. Follow my heels, Rugby.

[Exeunt Caius and Rugby.

QUICKLY You shall have – An fool's-head of your own. No, I know Anne's mind for that; never a woman in Windsor knows more of Anne's mind than I do; nor can do more than I do with her, I thank heaven.

FENTON *[Within]* Who's within there? ho!

QUICKLY Who's there, I trow? Come near the house, I pray you.

Enter FENTON.

FENTON How now, good woman, how dost thou?

QUICKLY The better that it pleases your good worship to ask.

FENTON What news? How does pretty Mistress Anne?

QUICKLY In truth, sir, and she is pretty, and honest, and gentle; and one that is your friend, I can tell you that by the way; I praise heaven for it.

FENTON Shall I do any good, think'st thou? Shall I not lose my suit?

QUICKLY Troth, sir, all is in His hands above; but notwithstanding, Master Fenton, I'll be sworn on a book she loves you. Have not your worship a wart above your eye?

FENTON Yes, marry, have I; what of that?

QUICKLY Well, thereby hangs a tale; good faith, it is such another Nan; but, I detest, an honest maid as ever broke bread. We had an hour's talk of that wart; I shall never laugh but in that maid's company! But, indeed, she is given too much to allicholy and musing; but for you – well, go to.

FENTON Well, I shall see her to-day. Hold, there's money for thee; let me have thy voice in my behalf. If thou seest her before me, commend me.

QUICKLY Will I? I'faith, that we will; and I will tell your worship more of the wart the next time we have confidence; and of other wooers.

FENTON Well, farewell; I am in great haste now.

QUICKLY Farewell to your worship. *[Exit Fenton]* Truly, an honest gentleman; but Anne loves him not; for I know Anne's mind as well as another does. Out upon 't, what have I forgot?

[Exit.

ACT TWO

SCENE I. *Before Page's house.*

Enter MISTRESS PAGE, with a letter.

MRS. PAGE What! have I scap'd love-letters in the holiday-time of my beauty, and am I now a subject for them? Let me see. *[Reads.*

'Ask me no reason why I love you; for though Love use Reason for his precisian, he admits him not ior his counsellor. You are not young, no more am I; go to, then, there's sympathy. You are merry, so am I; ha! ha! then there's more sympathy. You love sack, and so do I; would you desire better sympathy? Let it suffice thee, Mistress Page – at the least, if the love of soldier can suffice – that I love thee. I will not say, Pity me: 'tis not a soldier-like phrase; but I say, Love me. By me,

Thine own true knight,
By day or night,
Or any kind of light,
With all his might,
For thee to fight,
JOHN FALSTAFF.'

What a Herod of Jewry is this! O wicked, wicked world! One that is well-nigh worn to pieces with age to show himself a young gallant! What an unweighed behaviour hath this Flemish drunkard pick'd – with the devil's name! – out of my conversation, that he dares in this manner assay me? Why, he hath not been thrice in my company! What should I say to him? I was then frugal of my mirth. Heaven forgive me! Why, I'll exhibit a bill in the parliament for the putting down of men. How shall I be reveng'd on him? for reveng'd I will be, as sure as his guts are made of puddings.

Enter MISTRESS FORD.

MRS. FORD Mistress Page! trust me, I was going to your house.

MRS. PAGE And, trust me, I was coming to you. You look very ill.

MRS. FORD Nay, I'll ne'er believe that; I have to show to the contrary.

MRS. PAGE Faith, but you do, in my mind.

MRS. FORD Well, I do, then; yet, I say, I could show you to the contrary. O Mistress Page, give me some counsel.

MRS. PAGE What's the matter, woman?

MRS. FORD O woman, if it were not for one trifling respect, I could come to such honour!

MRS. PAGE Hang the trifle, woman; take the honour. What is it? Dispense with trifles; what is it?

MRS. FORD If I would but go to hell for an eternal moment or so, I could be knighted.

MRS. PAGE What? Thou liest. Sir Alice Ford!

These knights will hack; and so thou shouldst not alter the article of thy gentry.

MRS. FORD We burn daylight. Here, read, read; perceive how I might be knighted. I shall think the worse of fat men as long as I have an eye to make difference of men's liking. And yet he would not swear; prais'd women's modesty, and gave such orderly and well-behaved reproof to all uncomeliness that I would have sworn his disposition would have gone to the truth of his words; but they do no more adhere and keep place together than the Hundredth Psalm to the tune of 'Greensleeves'. What tempest, I trow, threw this whale, with so many tuns of oil in his belly, ashore at Windsor? How shall I be revenged on him? I think the best way were to entertain him with hope, till the wicked fire of lust have melted him in his own grease. Did you ever hear the like?

MRS. PAGE Letter for letter, but that the name of Page and Ford differs. To thy great comfort in this mystery of ill opinions, here's the twin-brother of thy letter; but let thine inherit first, for, I protest, mine never shall. I warrant he hath a thousand of these letters, writ with blank space for different names – sure, more! – and these are of the second edition. He will print them, out of doubt; for he cares not what he puts into the press when he would put us two. I had rather be a giantess and lie under Mount Pelion. Well, I will find you twenty lascivious turtles ere one chaste man.

MRS. FORD Why, this is the very same; the very hand, the very words. What doth he think of us?

MRS. PAGE Nay, I know not; it makes me almost ready to wrangle with mine own honesty. I'll entertain myself like one that I am not acquainted withal; for, sure, unless he know some strain in me that I know not myself, he would never have boarded me in this fury.

MRS. FORD 'Boarding' call you it? I'll be sure to keep him above deck.

MRS. PAGE So will I; if he come under my hatches, I'll never to sea again. Let's be reveng'd on him; let's appoint him a meeting, give him a show of comfort in his suit, and lead him on with a fine-baited delay, till he hath pawn'd his horses to mine host of the Garter.

MRS. FORD Nay, I will consent to act any villainy against him that may not sully the chariness of our honesty. O that my husband saw this letter! It would give eternal food to his jealousy.

MRS. PAGE Why, look where he comes; and my good man too; he's as far from jealousy as I am from giving him cause; and that, I hope, is an unmeasurable distance.

MRS. FORD You are the happier woman.

MRS. PAGE Let's consult together against this greasy knight. Come hither. [*They retire.*

Enter FORD with PISTOL, and PAGE with NYM.

FORD Well, I hope it be not so.

PISTOL Hope is a curtal dog in some affairs.
Sir John affects thy wife.

FORD Why, sir, my wife is not young.

PISTOL He woos both high and low, both rich and poor,
Both young and old, one with another, Ford;
He loves the gallimaufry. Ford, perpend.

FORD Love my wife!

PISTOL With liver burning hot. Prevent, or go thou,
Like Sir Actaeon he, with Ringwood at thy heels.
O, odious is the name!

FORD What name, sir?

PISTOL The horn, I say. Farewell.
Take heed, have open eye, for thieves do foot by night;
Take heed, ere summer comes, or cuckoo birds do sing.
Away, Sir Corporal Nym.
Believe it, Page; he speaks sense. [*Exit Pistol.*

FORD [*Aside*] I will be patient; I will find out this.

NYM [*To Page*] And this is true; I like not the humour of lying. He hath wronged me in some humours; I should have borne the humour'd letter to her; but I have a sword, and it shall bite upon my necessity. He loves your wife; there's the short and the long.
My name is Corporal Nym; I speak, and I avouch;
'Tis true. My name is Nym, and Falstaff loves your wife.
Adieu! I love not the humour of bread and cheese; and there's the humour of it. Adieu. [*Exit Nym.*

PAGE 'The humour of it' quoth 'a! Here's a fellow frights English out of his wits.

FORD I will seek out Falstaff.

PAGE I never heard such a drawling, affecting rogue.

FORD If I do find it – well.

PAGE I will not believe such a Cataian though the priest o' th' town commended him for a true man.

FORD 'Twas a good sensible fellow. Well.

[*Mrs. Page and Mrs. Ford come forward.*

PAGE How now, Meg!

MRS. PAGE Whither go you, George? Hark you.

MRS. FORD How now, sweet Frank, why art thou melancholy?

FORD I melancholy! I am not melancholy. Get you home; go.

MRS. FORD Faith, thou hast some crotchets in thy head now. Will you go, Mistress Page?

Enter MISTRESS QUICKLY.

MRS. PAGE Have with you. You'll come to dinner, George? [*Aside to Mrs. Ford*] Look who comes yonder; she shall be our messenger to this paltry knight.

MRS. FORD [*Aside to Mrs. Page*] Trust me, I thought on her; she'll fit it.

MRS. PAGE You are come to see my daughter Anne?

QUICKLY Ay, forsooth; and, I pray, how does good Mistress Anne?

MRS. PAGE Go in with us and see; we have an hour's talk with you.

[*Exeunt Mrs. Page, Mrs. Ford, and Mrs. Quickly.*

PAGE How now, Master Ford!

FORD You heard what this knave told me, did you not?

PAGE Yes; and you heard what the other told me?

FORD Do you think there is truth in them?

PAGE Hang 'em, slaves! I do not think the knight would offer it; but these that accuse him in his intent towards our wives are a yoke of his discarded men; very rogues, now they be out of service.

FORD Were they his men?

PAGE Marry, were they.

FORD I like it never the better for that. Does he lie at the Garter?

PAGE Ay, marry, does he. If he should intend this voyage toward my wife, I would turn her loose to him; and what he gets more of her than sharp words, let it lie on my head.

FORD I do not misdoubt my wife; but I would be loath to turn them together. A man may be too confident. I would have nothing lie on my head. I cannot be thus satisfied.

Enter HOST.

PAGE Look where my ranting host of the Garter comes. There is either liquor in his pate or money in his purse when he looks so merrily. How now, mine host!

HOST How now, bully rook! Thou'rt a gentleman. [*To Shallow following*] Cavaleiro Justice, I say.

Enter SHALLOW.

SHALLOW I follow, mine host, I follow. Good even and twenty, good Master Page! Master Page, will you go with us? We have sport in hand.

HOST Tell him, Cavaleiro Justice; tell him, bully rook.

SHALLOW Sir, there is a fray to be fought between Sir Hugh the Welsh priest and Caius the French doctor.

FORD Good mine host o' th' Garter, a word with you.

HOST What say'st thou, my bully rook?

[*They go aside.*

SHALLOW [*To Page*] Will you go with us to behold it? My merry host hath had the measuring of their weapons; and, I think, hath appointed them contrary places; for, believe me, I hear the parson is no jester. Hark, I will tell you what our sport shall be.

[*They converse apart.*

HOST Hast thou no suit against my knight, my guest-cavaleiro.

FORD None, I protest; but I'll give you a pottle of burnt sack to give me recourse to him, and tell him my name is Brook – only for a jest.

HOST My hand, bully; thou shalt have egress and regress – said I well? – and thy name shall be Brook. It is a merry knight. Will you go, Mynheers?

SHALLOW Have with you, mine host.

PAGE I have heard the Frenchman hath good skill in his rapier.

SHALLOW Tut, sir, I could have told you more. In these times you stand on distance, your passes, stoccadoes, and I know not what. 'Tis the heart, Master Page; 'tis here, 'tis here. I have seen the time with my long sword I would have made you four tall fellows skip like rats.

HOST Here, boys, here, here! Shall we wag?

PAGE Have with you. I had rather hear them scold than fight. [*Exeunt all but Ford.*

FORD Though Page be a secure fool, and stands so firmly on his wife's frailty, yet I cannot put off my opinion so easily. She was in his company at Page's house, and what they made there I know not. Well, I will look further into 't, and I have a disguise to sound Falstaff. If I find her honest, I lose not my labour; if she be otherwise, 'tis labour well bestowed. [*Exit.*

SCENE II. *A room in the Garter Inn.*

Enter FALSTAFF and PISTOL.

FALSTAFF I will not lend thee a penny.

PISTOL I will retort the sum in equipage.

FALSTAFF Not a penny.

PISTOL Why, then the world's mine oyster,
Which I with sword will open.

FALSTAFF Not a penny. I have been content, sir, you should lay my countenance to pawn. I have grated upon my good friends for three reprieves for you and your coach-fellow, Nym; or else you had look'd through the grate, like a geminy of baboons. I am damn'd in hell for swearing to gentlemen my friends you were good soldiers and tall fellows; and when Mistress Bridget lost the handle of her fan, I took 't upon mine honour thou hadst it not.

PISTOL Didst not thou share? Hadst thou not fifteen pence?

FALSTAFF Reason, you rogue, reason. Think'st thou I'll endanger my soul gratis? At a word, hang no more about me, I am no gibbet for you. Go – a short knife and a throng! – to your manor of Pickt-hatch; go. You'll not bear a letter for me, you rogue! You stand upon your honour! Why, thou unconfinable baseness, it is as much as I can do to keep the terms of my honour precise. I, I, I myself sometimes, leaving the fear of God on the left hand, and hiding mine honour in my necessity, am fain to shuffle, to hedge, and to lurch; and yet you, rogue, will ensconce your rags, your cat-a-mountain looks, your red-lattice phrases, and your bold-beating oaths, under the shelter of your honour! You will not do it, you!

PISTOL I do relent; what would thou more of man?

Enter ROBIN.

ROBIN Sir, here's a woman would speak with you.

FALSTAFF Let her approach.

Enter MISTRESS QUICKLY.

QUICKLY Give your worship good morrow.

FALSTAFF Good morrow, good wife.

QUICKLY Not so, an't please your worship.

FALSTAFF Good maid, then.

QUICKLY I'll be sworn;
As my mother was, the first hour I was born.

FALSTAFF I do believe the swearer. What with me?

QUICKLY Shall I vouchsafe your worship a word or two?

FALSTAFF Two thousand, fair woman; and I'll vouchsafe thee the hearing.

QUICKLY There is one Mistress Ford, sir – I pray, come a little nearer this ways. I myself dwell with Master Doctor Caius.

FALSTAFF Well, on: Mistress Ford, you say –

QUICKLY Your worship says very true. I pray your worship come a little nearer this ways.

FALSTAFF I warrant thee nobody hears – mine own people, mine own people.

QUICKLY Are they so? God bless them, and make them his servants!

FALSTAFF Well; Mistress Ford, what of her?

QUICKLY Why, sir, she's a good creature. Lord, Lord, your worship's a wanton! Well, heaven forgive you, and all of us, I pray.

FALSTAFF Mistress Ford; come, Mistress Ford –

QUICKLY Marry, this is the short and the long of it: you have brought her into such a canaries as 'tis wonderful. The best courtier of them all, when the court lay at Windsor, could never have brought her to such a canary. Yet there has been knights, and lords, and gentlemen, with their coaches; I warrant you, coach after coach, letter after letter, gift after gift; smelling so sweetly, all musk, and so rushling, I warrant you, in silk and gold; and in such alligant terms; and in such wine and sugar of the best and the fairest, that would have won any woman's heart; and, I warrant you, they could never get an eye-wink of her. I had myself twenty angels given me this morning; but I defy all angels, in any such sort, as they say, but in the way of honesty; and, I warrant you, they could never get her so much as sip on a cup with the proudest of them all; and yet there has been earls, nay, which is more, pensioners; but, I warrant you, all is one with her.

FALSTAFF But what says she to me? Be brief, my good she-Mercury.

QUICKLY Marry, she hath receiv'd your letter; for the which she thanks you a thousand times; and she gives you to notify that her husband will be absence from his house between ten and eleven.

FALSTAFF Ten and eleven?

QUICKLY Ay, forsooth; and then you may come and see the picture, she says, that you wot of. Master Ford, her husband, will be from home. Alas, the sweet woman leads an ill life with him! He's a very jealousy man; she leads a very frampold life with him, good heart.

FALSTAFF Ten and eleven. Woman, commend me to her; I will not fail her.

QUICKLY Why, you say well. But I have another messenger to your worship. Mistress Page hath her hearty commendations to you too; and let me tell you in your ear, she's as fartuous a civil modest wife, and one, I tell you, that will not miss you morning nor evening prayer, as any is in Windsor, whoe'er be the other; and she bade me tell your worship that her husband is seldom from home, but she hopes there will come a time. I never knew a woman so dote upon a man; surely I think you have charms, la! Yes, in truth.

FALSTAFF Not I, I assure thee; setting the attraction of my good parts aside, I have no other charms.

QUICKLY Blessing on your heart for 't!

FALSTAFF But, I pray thee, tell me this: has Ford's wife and Page's wife acquainted each other how they love me?

QUICKLY That were a jest indeed! They have not so little grace, I hope – that were a trick indeed!

But Mistress Page would desire you to send her your little page of all loves. Her husband has a marvellous infection to the little page; and truly Master Page is an honest man. Never a wife in Windsor leads a better life than she does; do what she will, say what she will, take all, pay all, go to bed when she list, rise when she list, all is as she will; and truly she deserves it; for if there be a kind woman in Windsor, she is one. You must send her your page; no remedy.

FALSTAFF Why, I will.

QUICKLY Nay, but do so then; and, look you, he may come and go between you both; and in any case have a nay-word, that you may know one another's mind, and the boy never need to understand any thing; for 'tis not good that children should know any wickedness. Old folks, you know, have discretion, as they say, and know the world.

FALSTAFF Fare thee well; commend me to them both. There's my purse; I am yet thy debtor. Boy, go along with this woman. [*Exeunt Quickly and Robin*] This news distracts me.

PISTOL [*Aside*] This punk is one of Cupid's
carriers;
Clap on more sails; pursue; up with your fights;
Give fire; she is my prize, or ocean whelm them
all! [*Exit Pistol.*

FALSTAFF Say'st thou so, old Jack; go thy ways; I'll make more of thy old body than I have done. Will they yet look after thee? Wilt thou, after the expense of so much money, be now a gainer? Good body, I thank thee. Let them say 'tis grossly done; so it be fairly done, no matter.

Enter BARDOLPH.

BARDOLPH Sir John, there's one Master Brook below would fain speak with you, and be acquainted with you; and hath sent your worship a morning's draught of sack.

FALSTAFF Brook is his name?

BARDOLPH Ay, sir.

FALSTAFF Call him in. [*Exit Bardolph*] Such Brooks are welcome to me, that o'erflows such liquor. Ah, ha! Mistress Ford and Mistress Page, have I encompass'd you? Go to; via!

Re-enter BARDOLPH, with FORD disguised.

FORD Bless you, sir!

FALSTAFF And you, sir! Would you speak with me?

FORD I make bold to press with so little preparation upon you.

FALSTAFF You're welcome. What's your will? Give us leave, drawer. [*Exit Bardolph.*

FORD Sir, I am a gentleman that have spent much; my name is Brook.

FALSTAFF Good Master Brook, I desire more acquaintance of you.

FORD Good Sir John, I sue for yours – not to charge you; for I must let you understand I think myself in better plight for a lender than you are; the which hath something embold'ned me to this unseason'd intrusion; for they say, if money go before, all ways do lie open.

FALSTAFF Money is a good soldier, sir, and will on.

FORD Troth, and I have a bag of money here troubles me; if you will help to bear it, Sir John, take all, or half, for easing me of the carriage.

FALSTAFF Sir, I know not how I may deserve to be your porter.

FORD I will tell you, sir, if you will give me the hearing.

FALSTAFF Speak, good Master Brook; I shall be glad to be your servant.

FORD Sir, I hear you are a scholar – I will be brief with you – and you have been a man long known to me, though I had never so good means as desire to make myself acquainted with you. I shall discover a thing to you, wherein I must very much lay open mine own imperfection; but, good Sir John, as you have one eye upon my follies, as you hear them unfolded, turn another into the register of your own, that I may pass with a reproof the easier, sith you yourself know how easy is it to be such an offender.

FALSTAFF Very well, sir; proceed.

FORD There is a gentlewoman in this town, her husband's name is Ford.

FALSTAFF Well, sir.

FORD I have long lov'd her, and, I protest to you, bestowed much on her; followed her with a doting observance; engross'd opportunities to meet her; fee'd every slight occasion that could but niggardly give me sight of her; not only bought many presents to give her, but have given largely to many to know what she would have given; briefly, I have pursu'd her as love hath pursued me; which hath been on the wing of all occasions. But whatsoever I have merited, either in my mind or in my means, meed, I am sure, I have received none, unless experience be a jewel; that I have purchased at an infinite rate, and that hath taught me to say this:
'Love like a shadow flies when substance love
pursues;
Pursuing that that flies, and flying what
pursues'.

FALSTAFF Have you receiv'd no promise of satisfaction at her hands?

FORD Never.

FALSTAFF Have you importun'd her to such a purpose?

FORD Never.

FALSTAFF Of what quality was your love, then?

FORD Like a fair house built on another man's ground; so that I have lost my edifice by mistaking the place where I erected it.

FALSTAFF To what purpose have you unfolded this to me?

FORD When I have told you that, I have told you all. Some say that though she appear honest to me, yet in other places she enlargeth her mirth so far that there is shrewd construction made of her. Now, Sir John, here is the heart of my purpose: you are a gentleman of excellent breeding, admirable discourse, of great admittance, authentic in your place and person, generally allow'd for your many war-like, court-like, and learned preparations.

FALSTAFF O, sir!

FORD Believe it, for you know it. There is money; spend it, spend it; spend more; spend all I have; only give me so much of your time in exchange of it as to lay an amiable siege to the honesty of this Ford's wife; use your art of wooing, win her to consent to you; if any man may, you may as soon as any.

FALSTAFF Would it apply well to the vehemency of your affection, that I should win what you would enjoy? Methinks you prescribe to yourself very preposterously.

FORD O, understand my drift. She dwells so securely on the excellency of her honour that the folly of my soul dares not present itself; she is too bright to be look'd against. Now, could I come to her with any detection in my hand, my desires had instance and argument to commend themselves; I could drive her then from the ward of her purity, her reputation, her marriage vow, and a thousand other her defences, which now are too too strongly embattl'd against me. What say you to 't, Sir John?

FALSTAFF Master Brook, I will first make bold with your money; next, give me your hand; and last, as I am a gentleman, you shall, if you will, enjoy Ford's wife.

FORD O good sir!

FALSTAFF I say you shall.

FORD Want no money, Sir John; you shall want none.

FALSTAFF Want no Mistress Ford, Master Brook; you shall want none. I shall be with her, I may tell you, by her own appointment; even as you came in to me her assistant, or go-between, parted from me; I say I shall be with her between ten and eleven; for at that time the jealous rascally knave, her husband, will be forth. Come you to me at night; you shall know how I speed.

FORD I am blest in your acquaintance. Do you know Ford, sir?

FALSTAFF Hang him, poor cuckoldly knave! I know him not; yet I wrong him to call him poor; they say the jealous wittolly knave hath masses of money; for the which his wife seems to me well-favour'd. I will use her as the key of the cuckoldly rogue's coffer; and there's my harvest-home.

FORD I would you knew Ford, sir, that you might avoid him if you saw him.

FALSTAFF Hang him, mechanical salt-butter rogue! I will stare him out of his wits; I will awe him with my cudgel; it shall hang like a meteor o'er the cuckold's horns. Master Brook, thou shalt know I will predominate over the peasant, and thou shalt lie with his wife. Come to me soon at night. Ford's a knave, and I will aggravate his style; thou, Master Brook, shalt know him for knave and cuckold. Come to me soon at night. [*Exit.*

FORD What a damn'd Epicurean rascal is this! My heart is ready to crack with impatience. Who says this is improvident jealousy? My wife hath sent to him; the hour is fix'd; the match is made. Would any man have thought this? See the hell of having a false woman! My bed shall be abus'd, my coffers ransack'd, my reputation gnawn at; and I shall not only receive this villainous wrong, but stand under the adoption of abominable terms, and by him that does me this wrong. Terms! names! Amaimon sounds well; Lucifer, well; Barbason, well; yet they are devils' additions, the names of fiends. But cuckold! Wittol! Cuckold! the devil himself hath not such a name. Page is an ass, a secure ass; he will trust his wife; he will not be jealous; I will rather trust a Fleming with my butter, Parson Hugh the Welshman with my cheese, an Irishman with my aqua-vitae bottle, or a thief to walk my ambling gelding, than my wife with herself. Then she plots, then she ruminates, then she devises; and what they think in their hearts they may effect, they will break their hearts but they will effect. God be prais'd for my jealousy! Eleven o'clock the hour. I will prevent this, detect my wife, be reveng'd on Falstaff, and laugh at Page. I will about it; better three hours too soon than a minute too late. Fie, fie, fie! cuckold! cuckold! cuckold! [*Exit.*

SCENE III. *A field near Windsor.*

Enter CAIUS and RUGBY.

CAIUS Jack Rugby!

RUGBY Sir?

CAIUS Vat is de clock, Jack?

RUGBY 'Tis past the hour, sir, that Sir Hugh promis'd to meet.

CAIUS By gar, he has save his soul dat he is no come; he has pray his Pible well dat he is no come; by gar, Jack Rugby, he is dead already, if he be come.

RUGBY He is wise, sir; he knew your worship would kill him if he came.

CAIUS By gar, de herring is no dead so as I vill kill him. Take your rapier, Jack; I vill tell you how I vill kill him.

RUGBY Alas, sir, I cannot fence!

CAIUS Villainy, take your rapier.

RUGBY Forbear; here's company.

Enter HOST, SHALLOW, SLENDER and PAGE.

HOST Bless thee, bully doctor!

SHALLOW Save you, Master Doctor Caius!

PAGE Now, good Master Doctor!

SLENDER Give you good morrow, sir.

CAIUS Vat be all you, one, two, tree, four, come for?

HOST To see thee fight, to see thee foin, to see thee traverse; to see thee here, to see thee there; to see thee pass thy punto, thy stock, thy reverse, thy distance, thy montant. Is he dead, my Ethiopian? Is he dead, my Francisco? Ha, bully! What says my Aesculapius? my Galen? my heart of elder? Ha! is he dead, bully stale? Is he dead?

CAIUS By gar, he is de coward Jack priest of de vorld; he is not show his face.

HOST Thou art a Castalion-King-Urinal. Hector of Greece, my boy!

CAIUS I pray you, bear witness that me have stay six or seven, two tree hours for him, and he is no come.

SHALLOW He is the wiser man, Master Doctor: he is a curer of souls, and you a curer of bodies; if you should fight, you go against the hair of your professions. Is it not true, Master Page?

PAGE Master Shallow, you have yourself been a great fighter, though now a man of peace.

SHALLOW Bodykins, Master Page, though I now be old, and of the peace, if I see a sword out, my finger itches to make one. Though we are justices, and doctors, and churchmen, Master Page, we have some salt of our youth in us; we are the sons of women, Master Page.

PAGE 'Tis true, Master Shallow.

SHALLOW It will be found so, Master Page. Master Doctor Caius, I am come to fetch you home. I am sworn of the peace; you have show'd yourself a wise physician, and Sir Hugh hath shown himself a wise and patient churchman. You must go with me, Master Doctor.

HOST Pardon, Guest Justice. A word, Mounseur Mockwater.

CAIUS Mock-vater! Vat is dat?

HOST Mockwater, in our English tongue, is valour, bully.

CAIUS By gar, then I have as much mockvater as de Englishman. Scurvy jack-dog priest! By gar, me vill cut his ears.

HOST He will clapper-claw thee tightly, bully.

CAIUS Clapper-de-claw! Vat is dat?

HOST That is, he will make thee amends.

CAIUS By gar, me do look he shall clapper-de-claw me; for, by gar, me vill have it.

HOST And I will provoke him to 't, or let him wag.

CAIUS Me tank you for dat.

HOST And, moreover, bully – but first: [*Aside to the others*] Master Guest, and Master Page, and eke Cavaleiro Slender, go you through the town to Frogmore.

PAGE [*Aside*] Sir Hugh is there, is he?

HOST [*Aside*] He is there. See what humour he is in; and I will bring the doctor about by the fields. Will it do well?

SHALLOW [*Aside*] We will do it.

PAGE, SHALLOW, AND SLENDER Adieu, good Master Doctor.

[*Exeunt Page, Shallow, and Slender.*

CAIUS By gar, me vill kill de priest; for he speak for a jack-an-ape to Anne Page.

HOST Let him die. Sheathe thy impatience; throw cold water on thy choler; go about the fields with me through Frogmore; I will bring thee where Mistress Anne Page is, at a farm-house, a-feasting; and thou shalt woo her. Cried game! Said I well?

CAIUS By gar, me dank you vor dat; by gar, I love you; and I shall procure-a you de good guest, de earl, de knight, de lords, de gentlemen, my patients.

HOST For the which I will be thy adversary toward Anne Page. Said I well?

CAIUS By gar, 'tis good; vell said.

HOST Let us wag, then.

CAIUS Come at my heels, Jack Rugby.

[*Exeunt.*

ACT THREE

SCENE I. *A field near Frogmore.*

Enter SIR HUGH EVANS and SIMPLE.

EVANS I pray you now, good Master Slender's serving-man, and friend Simple by your name, which way have you look'd for Master Caius, that calls himself Doctor of Physic?

SIMPLE Marry, sir, the pittie-ward, the park-ward; every way; old Windsor way, and every way but the town way.

EVANS I most fehemently desire you you will also look that way.

SIMPLE I will, sir. [*Exit.*

EVANS Pless my soul, how full of chollors I am, and trempling of mind! I shall be glad if he have deceived me. How melancholies I am! I will knog his urinals about his knave's costard when I have goot opportunities for the ork. Pless my soul! [*Sings.*

To shallow rivers, to whose falls
Melodious birds sings madrigals;
There will we make our peds of roses,
And a thousand fragrant posies.
To shallow –

Mercy on me! I have a great dispositions to cry. [*Sings.*

Melodious birds sing madrigals –
Whenas I sat in Pabylon –
And a thousand vagram posies.
To shallow, etc.

Re-enter SIMPLE.

SIMPLE Yonder he is, coming this way, Sir Hugh.

EVANS He's welcome. [*Sings.*

To shallow rivers, to whose falls –

Heaven prosper the right! What weapons is he?

SIMPLE No weapons, sir. There comes my master, Master Shallow, and another gentleman, from Frogmore, over the stile, this way.

EVANS Pray you give me my gown; or else keep it in your arms. [*Takes out a book.*

Enter PAGE, SHALLOW, and SLENDER.

SHALLOW How now, Master Parson! Good morrow, good Sir Hugh. Keep a gamester from the dice, and a good student from his book, and it is wonderful.

SLENDER [*Aside*] Ah, sweet Anne Page!

PAGE Save you, good Sir Hugh!

EVANS Pless you from his mercy sake, all of you!

SHALLOW What, the sword and the word! Do you study them both, Master Parson?

PAGE And youthful still, in your doublet and hose, this raw rheumatic day!

EVANS There is reasons and causes for it.

PAGE We are come to you to do a good office, Master Parson.

EVANS Fery well; what is it?

PAGE Yonder is a most reverend gentleman, who, belike having received wrong by some person, is at most odds with his own gravity and patience that ever you saw.

SHALLOW I have lived fourscore years and upward; I never heard a man of his place, gravity, and learning, so wide of his own respect.

EVANS What is he?

PAGE I think you know him: Master Doctor Caius, the renowned French physician.

EVANS Got's will and his passion of my heart! I had as lief you would tell me of a mess of porridge.

PAGE Why?

EVANS He has no more knowledge in Hibocrates and Galen, and he is a knave besides – a cowardly knave as you would desires to be acquainted withal.

PAGE I warrant you, he's the man should fight with him.

SLENDER [*Aside*] O sweet Anne Page!

SHALLOW It appears so, by his weapons. Keep them asunder; here comes Doctor Caius.

Enter HOST, CAIUS, and RUGBY.

PAGE Nay, good Master Parson, keep in your weapon.

SHALLOW So do you, good Master Doctor.

HOST Disarm them, and let them question; let them keep their limbs whole and hack our English.

CAIUS I pray you, let-a me speak a word with your ear. Verefore vill you not meet-a me?

EVANS [*Aside to Caius*] Pray you use your patience; in good time.

CAIUS By gar, you are de coward, de Jack dog, John ape.

EVANS [*Aside to Caius*] Pray you, let us not be laughing-stocks to other men's humours; I desire you in friendship, and I will one way or other make you amends. [*Aloud*] I will knog your urinals about your knave's cogscomb for missing your meetings and appointments.

CAIUS Diable! Jack Rugby – mine Host de Jarteer – have I not stay for him to kill him? Have I not, at de place I did appoint?

EVANS As I am a Christians soul, now, look you, this is the place appointed. I'll be judgment by mine host of the Garter.

HOST Peace, I say, Gallia and Gaul, French and Welsh, soul-curer and body-curer.

CAIUS Ay, dat is very good! excellent!

HOST Peace, I say. Hear mine host of the Garter. Am I politic? am I subtle? am I a Machiavel? Shall I lose my doctor? No; he gives me the potions and the motions. Shall I lose my parson, my priest, my Sir Hugh? No; he gives me the proverbs and the noverbs. Give me thy hand, terrestrial; so. Give me thy hand, celestial; so. Boys of art, I have deceiv'd you both; I have directed you to wrong places; your hearts are mighty, your skins are whole, and let burnt sack be the issue. Come, lay their swords to pawn. Follow me, lads of peace; follow, follow, follow.

SHALLOW Trust me, a mad host. Follow, gentlemen, follow.

SLENDER [*Aside*] O sweet Anne Page!

[*Exeunt all but Caius and Evans.*

CAIUS Ha, do I perceive dat? Have you make-a de sot of us, ha, ha?

EVANS This is well; he has made us his vlouting-stog. I desire you that we may be friends; and let us knog our prains together to be revenge on this same scall, scurvy, cogging companion, the host of the Garter.

CAIUS By gar, with all my heart. He promise to bring me where is Anne Page; by gar, he deceive me too.

EVANS Well, I will smite his noddles. Pray you follow. [*Exeunt.*

SCENE II. *The street in Windsor.*

Enter MISTRESS PAGE and ROBIN.

MRS. PAGE Nay, keep your way, little gallant; you were wont to be a follower, but now you are a leader. Whether had you rather lead mine eyes, or eye your master's heels?

ROBIN I had rather, forsooth, go before you like a man than follow him like a dwarf.

MRS. PAGE O, you are a flattering boy; now I see you'll be a courtier.

Enter FORD.

FORD Well met, Mistress Page. Whither go you?

MRS. PAGE Truly, sir, to see your wife. Is she at home?

FORD Ay; and as idle as she may hang together, for want of company. I think, if your husbands were dead, you two would marry.

MRS. PAGE Be sure of that – two other husbands.

FORD Where had you this pretty weather-cock?

MRS. PAGE I cannot tell what the dickens his name is my husband had him of. What do you call your knight's name, sirrah?

ROBIN Sir John Falstaff.

FORD Sir John Falstaff!

MRS. PAGE He, he; I can never hit on 's name. There is such a league between my good man and he! Is your wife at home indeed?

FORD Indeed she is.

MRS. PAGE By your leave, sir. I am sick till I see her. [*Exeunt Mrs. Page and Robin.*

FORD Has Page any brains? Hath he any eyes? Hath he any thinking? Sure, they sleep; he hath no use of them. Why, this boy will carry a letter twenty mile as easy as a cannon will shoot pointblank twelve score. He pieces out his wife's inclination; he gives her folly motion and advantage; and now she's going to my wife, and Falstaff's boy with her. A man may hear this show'r sing in the wind. And Falstaff's boy with her! Good plots! They are laid; and our revolted wives share damnation together. Well; I will take him, then torture my wife, pluck the borrowed veil of modesty from the so seeming Mistress Page, divulge Page himself for a secure and wilful Actaeon; and to these violent proceedings all my neighbours shall cry aim. [*Clock strikes*] The clock gives me my cue, and my assurance bids me search; there I shall find Falstaff. I shall be rather prais'd for this than mock'd; for it is as positive as the earth is firm that Falstaff is there. I will go.

Enter PAGE, SHALLOW, SLENDER, HOST, SIR HUGH EVANS, CAIUS, and RUGBY.

SHALLOW, PAGE, ETC. Well met, Master Ford.

FORD Trust me, a good knot; I have good cheer at home, and I pray you all go with me.

SHALLOW I must excuse myself, Master Ford.

SLENDER And so must I, sir; we have appointed to dine with Mistress Anne, and I would not break with her for more money than I'll speak of.

SHALLOW We have linger'd about a match between Anne Page and my cousin Slender, and this day we shall have our answer.

SLENDER I hope I have your good will, father Page.

PAGE You have, Master Slender; I stand wholly for you. But my wife, Master Doctor, is for you altogether.

CAIUS Ay, be-gar; and de maid is love-a me; my nursh-a Quickly tell me so mush.

HOST What say you to young Master Fenton? He capers, he dances, he has eyes of youth, he writes verses, he speaks holiday, he smells April and May; he will carry 't, he will carry't; 'tis in his buttons; he will carry 't.

PAGE Not by my consent, I promise you. The
gentleman is of no having: he kept company
with the wild Prince and Poins; he is of too high
a region, he knows too much. No, he shall not
knit a knot in his fortunes with the finger of my
substance; if he take her, let him take her
simply; the wealth I have waits on my consent,
67 and my consent goes not that way.

FORD I beseech you, heartily, some of you go
home with me to dinner: besides your cheer,
you shall have sport; I will show you a monster.
Master Doctor, you shall go; so shall you,
71 Master Page; and you, Sir Hugh.

SHALLOW Well, fare you well; we shall have the
freer wooing at Master Page's.
[Exeunt Shallow and Slender.

CAIUS Go home, John Rugby; I come anon.
[Exit Rugby.

HOST Farewell, my hearts; I will to my honest
knight Falstaff, and drink canary with him.
[Exit Host.

FORD *[Aside]* I think I shall drink in pipe-wine
first with him; I'll make him dance. Will you go,
78 gentles?

ALL Have with you to see this monster. *[Exeunt.*

SCENE III. *Ford's house.*

Enter MISTRESS FORD and MISTRESS PAGE.

MRS. FORD What, John! what, Robert!

MRS. PAGE Quickly, quickly! Is the buck-basket –

MRS. FORD I warrant. What, Robin, I say!

Enter Servants with a basket.

MRS. PAGE Come, come, come.

MRS. FORD Here, set it down.

MRS. PAGE Give your men the charge; we must be
brief.

MRS. FORD Marry, as I told you before, John and
Robert, be ready here hard by in the brew-
house; and when I suddenly call you, come
forth, and, without any pause or staggering, take
this basket on your shoulders. That done,
trudge with it in all haste, and carry it among
the whitsters in Datchet Mead, and there empty
13 it in the muddy ditch close by the Thames side.

MRS. PAGE You will do it?

MRS. FORD I ha' told them over and over; they
lack no direction. Be gone, and come when you
16 are call'd. *[Exeunt Servants.*

MRS. PAGE Here comes little Robin.

Enter ROBIN.

MRS. FORD How now, my eyas-musket, what
19 news with you?

ROBIN My master Sir John is come in at your
back-door, Mistress Ford, and requests your
company.

MRS. PAGE You little Jack-a-Lent, have you been
true to us? 23

ROBIN Ay, I'll be sworn. My master knows not of
your being here, and hath threat'ned to put me
into everlasting liberty, if I tell you of it; for he
swears he'll turn me away.

MRS. PAGE Thou 'rt a good boy; this secrecy of
thine shall be a tailor to thee, and shall make
thee a new doublet and hose. I'll go hide me. 29

MRS. FORD Do so. Go tell thy master I am alone.
[Exit Robin] Mistress Page, remember you your
cue. 31

MRS. PAGE I warrant thee; if I do not act it, hiss
me. *[Exit Mrs. Page.*

MRS. FORD Go to, then; we'll use this
unwholesome humidity, this gross wat'ry
pumpion; we'll teach him to know turtles from
jays. 35

Enter FALSTAFF.

FALSTAFF Have I caught thee, my heavenly
jewel?
Why, now let me die, for I have liv'd long
enough; this is the period of my ambition.
O this blessed hour!

MRS. FORD O sweet Sir John! 39

FALSTAFF Mistress Ford, I cannot cog, I cannot
prate, Mistress Ford. Now shall I sin in my wish;
I would thy husband were dead; I'll speak
it before the best lord, I would make thee my
lady.

MRS. FORD I your lady, Sir John? Alas, I should
be a pitiful lady. 45

FALSTAFF Let the court of France show me such
another. I see how thine eye would emulate the
diamond; thou hast the right arched beauty of
the brow that becomes the ship-tire, the tire-
valiant, or any tire of Venetian admittance. 49

MRS. FORD A plain kerchief, Sir John; my brows
become nothing else, nor that well neither. 51

FALSTAFF By the Lord, thou art a tyrant to say so;
thou wouldst make an absolute courtier, and
the firm fixture of thy foot would give an
excellent motion to thy gait in a semi-circled
farthingale. I see what thou wert, if Fortune thy
foe were, not Nature, thy friend. Come, thou
canst not hide it. 56

MRS. FORD Believe me, there's no such thing in
me.

FALSTAFF What made me love thee? Let that
persuade thee there's something extraordinary
in thee. Come, I cannot cog, and say thou art
this and that, like a many of these lisping
hawthorn-buds that come like women in men's
apparel, and smell like Bucklersbury in simple

time; I cannot; but I love thee, none but thee; and thou deserv'st it.

MRS. FORD Do not betray me, sir; I fear you love Mistress Page.

FALSTAFF Thou mightst as well say I love to walk by the Counter-gate, which is as hateful to me as the reek of a lime-kiln.

MRS. FORD Well, heaven knows how I love you; and you shall one day find it.

FALSTAFF Keep in that mind; I'll deserve it.

MRS. FORD Nay, I must tell you, so you do; or else I could not be in that mind.

ROBIN [*Within*] Mistress Ford, Mistress Ford! here's Mistress Page at the door, sweating and blowing and looking wildly, and would needs speak with you presently.

FALSTAFF She shall not see me; I will ensconce me behind the arras.

MRS. FORD Pray you, do so; she's a very tattling woman. [*Falstaff hides himself.*

Re-enter MISTRESS PAGE and ROBIN.

What's the matter? How now!

MRS. PAGE O Mistress Ford, what have you done? You're sham'd, y'are over-thrown, y'are undone for ever.

MRS. FORD What's the matter, good Mistress Page?

MRS. PAGE O well-a-day, Mistress Ford, having an honest man to your husband, to give him such cause of suspicion!

MRS. FORD What cause of suspicion?

MRS. PAGE What cause of suspicion? Out upon you, how am I mistook in you!

MRS. FORD Why, alas, what's the matter?

MRS. PAGE Your husband's coming hither, woman, with all the officers in Windsor, to search for a gentleman that he says is here now in the house, by your consent, to take an ill advantage of his absence. You are undone.

MRS. FORD 'Tis not so, I hope.

MRS. PAGE Pray heaven it be not so that you have such a man here; but 'tis most certain your husband 's coming, with half Windsor at his heels, to search for such a one. I come before to tell you. If you know yourself clear, why, I am glad of it; but if you have a friend here, convey, convey him out. Be not amaz'd; call all your senses to you; defend your reputation, or bid farewell to your good life for ever.

MRS. FORD What shall I do? There is a gentleman, my dear friend; and I fear not mine own shame so much as his peril. I had rather than a thousand pounds he were out of the house.

MRS. PAGE For shame, never stand 'you had rather' and 'you had rather'! Your husband's here at hand; bethink you of some conveyance; in the house you cannot hide him. O, how have you deceiv'd me! Look, here is a basket; if he be of any reasonable stature, he may creep in here; and throw foul linen upon him, as if it were going to bucking, or – it is whiting-time – send him by your two men to Datchet Mead.

MRS. FORD He's too big to go in there. What shall I do?

FALSTAFF [*Coming forward*] let me see 't, let me see 't. O, let me see 't! I'll in, I'll in; follow your friend's counsel; I'll in.

MRS. PAGE What, Sir John Falstaff! [*Aside to Falstaff*] Are these your letters, knight?

FALSTAFF [*Aside to Mrs. Page*] I love thee and none but thee; help me away. – Let me creep in here; I'll never –

[*Gets into the basket; they cover him with foul linen.*]

MRS. PAGE Help to cover your master, boy. Call your men, Mistress Ford. You dissembling knight!

MRS. FORD What, John! Robert! John! [*Exit Robin.*

Re-enter Servants.

Go, take up these clothes here, quickly; where's the cowl-staff? Look how you drumble. Carry them to the laundress in Datchet Mead; quickly, come.

Enter FORD, PAGE, CAIUS, and SIR HUGH EVANS.

FORD Pray you come near. If I suspect without cause, why then make sport at me, then let me be your jest; I deserve it. How now, whither bear you this?

SERV To the laundress, forsooth.

MRS. FORD Why, what have you to do whither they bear it? You were best meddle with buck-washing.

FORD Buck? I would I could wash myself of the buck! Buck, buck, buck! ay, buck! I warrant you, buck; and of the season too, it shall appear. [*Exeunt Servants with the basket*] Gentlemen, I have dream'd to-night; I'll tell you my dream. Here, here, here be my keys; ascend my chambers, search, seek, find out. I'll warrant we'll unkennel the fox. Let me stop this way first. [*Locking the door*] So, now uncape.

PAGE Good Master Ford, be contented; you wrong yourself too much.

FORD True, Master Page. Up, gentlemen, you shall see sport anon; follow me, gentlemen. [*Exit.*

EVANS This is fery fantastical humours and jealousies.

CAIUS By gar, 'tis no the fashion of France; it is not jealous in France.

PAGE Nay, follow him, gentlemen; see the issue of his search.

[*Exeunt Evans, Page, and Caius.*

MRS. PAGE Is there not a double excellency in this?

MRS. FORD I know not which pleases me better, that my husband is deceived, or Sir John.

MRS. PAGE What a taking was he in when your husband ask'd who was in the basket!

MRS. FORD I am half afraid he will have need of washing; so throwing him into the water will do him a benefit.

MRS. PAGE Hang him, dishonest rascal! I would all of the same strain were in the same distress.

MRS. FORD I think my husband hath some special suspicion of Falstaff's being here, for I never saw him so gross in his jealousy till now.

MRS. PAGE I will lay a plot to try that, and we will yet have more tricks with Falstaff. His dissolute disease will scarce obey this medicine.

MRS. FORD Shall we send that foolish carrion, Mistress Quickly, to him, and excuse his throwing into the water, and give him another hope, to betray him to another punishment?

MRS. PAGE We will do it; let him be sent for to-morrow eight o'clock, to have amends.

Re-enter FORD, PAGE, CAIUS, and SIR HUGH EVANS.

FORD I cannot find him; may be the knave bragg'd of that he could not compass.

MRS. PAGE [*Aside to Mrs. Ford*] Heard you that?

MRS. FORD You use me well, Master Ford, do you?

FORD Ay, I do so.

MRS. FORD Heaven make you better than your thoughts!

FORD Amen.

MRS. PAGE You do yourself mighty wrong, Master Ford.

FORD Ay, ay; I must bear it.

EVANS If there be any pody in the house, and in the chambers, and in the coffers, and in the presses, heaven forgive my sins at the day of judgment!

CAIUS Be gar, nor I too; there is no bodies.

PAGE Fie, fie, Master Ford, are you not asham'd? What spirit, what devil suggests this imagination? I would not ha' your distemper in this kind for the wealth of Windsor Castle.

FORD 'Tis my fault, Master Page; I suffer for it.

EVANS You suffer for a pad conscience. Your wife is as honest a omans as I will desires among five thousand, and five hundred too.

CAIUS By gar, I see 'tis an honest woman.

FORD Well, I promis'd you a dinner. Come, come, walk in the Park. I pray you pardon me; I will hereafter make known to you why I have done this. Come, wife, come, Mistress Page; I pray you pardon me; pray heartly, pardon me.

PAGE Let's go in, gentlemen; but, trust me, we'll mock him. I do invite you tomorrow morning to my house to breakfast; after, we'll a-birding together; I have a fine hawk for the bush. Shall it be so?

FORD Any thing.

EVANS If there is one, I shall make two in the company.

CAIUS If there be one or two, I shall make-a the turd.

FORD Pray you go, Master Page.

EVANS I pray you now, remembrance to-morrow on the lousy knave, mine host.

CAIUS Dat is good; by gar, with all my heart.

EVANS A lousy knave, to have his gibes and his mockeries!

[*Exeunt.*

SCENE IV. *Before Page's house.*

Enter FENTON and ANNE PAGE.

FENTON I see I cannot get thy father's love;
Therefore no more turn me to him, sweet Nan.

ANNE Alas, how then?

FENTON Why, thou must be thyself.
He doth object I am too great of birth;
And that, my state being gall'd with my expense,
I seek to heal it only by his wealth.
Besides these, other bars he lays before me,
My riots past, my wild societies;
And tells me 'tis a thing impossible
I should love thee but as a property.

ANNE May be he tells you true.

FENTON No, heaven so speed me in my time to come!
Albeit I will confess thy father's wealth
Was the first motive that I woo'd thee, Anne;
Yet, wooing thee, I found thee of more value
Than stamps in gold, or sums in sealed bags;
And 'tis the very riches of thyself
That now I aim at.

ANNE Gentle Master Fenton,
Yet seek my father's love; still seek it, sir.
If opportunity and humblest suit
Cannot attain it, why then – hark you hither.

[*They converse apart.*

Enter SHALLOW, SLENDER, and MISTRESS QUICKLY.

SHALLOW Break their talk, Mistress Quickly; my kinsman shall speak for himself.

SLENDER I'll make a shaft or a bolt on 't; 'slid, 'tis but venturing.

SHALLOW Be not dismay'd.

SLENDER No, she shall not dismay me. I care not for that, but that I am afeard.

QUICKLY Hark ye, Master Slender would speak a word with you.

ANNE I come to him. [*Aside*] This is my father's choice.
O, what a world of vile ill-favour'd faults
Looks handsome in three hundred pounds a year!

QUICKLY And how does good Master Fenton? Pray you, a word with you.

SHALLOW She's coming; to her, coz. O boy, thou hadst a father!

SLENDER I had a father, Mistress Anne; my uncle can tell you good jests of him. Pray you, uncle, tell Mistress Anne the jest how my father stole two geese out of a pen, good uncle.

SHALLOW Mistress Anne, my cousin loves you.

SLENDER Ay, that I do; as well as I love any woman in Gloucestershire.

SHALLOW He will maintain you like a gentlewoman.

SLENDER Ay, that I will come cut and long-tail, under the degree of a squire.

SHALLOW He will make you a hundred and fifty pounds jointure.

ANNE Good Master Shallow, let him woo for himself.

SHALLOW Marry, I thank you for it; I thank you for that good comfort. She calls you, coz; I'll leave you.

ANNE Now, Master Slender –

SLENDER Now, good Mistress Anne –

ANNE What is your will?

SLENDER My will! 'Od's heartlings, that's a pretty jest indeed! I ne'er made my will yet, I thank heaven; I am not such a sickly creature, I give heaven praise.

ANNE I mean, Master Slender, what would you with me?

SLENDER Truly, for mine own part I would little or nothing with you. Your father and my uncle hath made motions; if it be my luck, so; if not, happy man be his dole! They can tell you how things go better than I can. You may ask your father; here he comes.

Enter PAGE and MISTRESS PAGE.

PAGE Now, Master Slender! Love him, daughter Anne –
Why, how now, what does Master Fenton here?
You wrong me, sir, thus still to haunt my house.
I told you, sir, my daughter is dispos'd of.

FENTON Nay, Master Page, be not impatient.

MRS. PAGE Good Master Fenton, come not to my child.

PAGE She is no match for you.

FENTON Sir, will you hear me?

PAGE No, good Master Fenton.
Come, Master Shallow; come, son Slender; in.
Knowing my mind, you wrong me, Master Fenton. [*Exeunt Page, Shallow, and Slender.*

QUICKLY Speak to Mistress Page.

FENTON Good Mistress Page, for that I love your daughter
In such a righteous fashion as I do,
Perforce, against all checks, rebukes, and manners,
I must advance the colours of my love,
And not retire. Let me have your good will.

ANNE Good mother, do not marry me to yond fool.

MRS. PAGE I mean it not; I seek you a better husband.

QUICKLY That's my master, Master Doctor.

ANNE Alas, I had rather be set quick i' th' earth,
And bowl'd to death with turnips.

MRS. PAGE Come, trouble not yourself. Good Master Fenton,
I will not be your friend, nor enemy;
My daughter will I question how she loves you,
And as I find her, so am I affected;
Till then, farewell, sir; she must needs go in;
Her father will be angry.

FENTON Farewell, gentle mistress; farewell, Nan.

[*Exeunt Mrs. Page and Anne.*

QUICKLY This is my doing now: 'Nay,' said I 'will you cast away your child on a fool, and a physician? Look on Master Fenton'. This is my doing.

FENTON I thank thee; and I pray thee, once to-night
Give my sweet Nan this ring. There's for thy pains.

QUICKLY Now Heaven send thee good fortune! [*Exit Fenton*] A kind heart he hath; a woman would run through fire and water for such a kind heart. But yet I would my master had Mistress Anne; or I would Master Slender had her; or, in sooth, I would Master Fenton had her; I will do what I can for them all three, for so I have promis'd, and I'll be as good as my word; but speciously for Master Fenton. Well, I must of another errand to Sir John Falstaff from my two mistresses. What a beast am I to slack it! [*Exit.*

SCENE V. *The Garter Inn.*

Enter FALSTAFF and BARDOLPH.

FALSTAFF Bardolph, I say!

BARDOLPH Here, sir.

FALSTAFF Go fetch me a quart of sack; put a toast

in 't. [*Exit Bardolph*] Have I liv'd to be carried in a basket, like a barrow of butcher's offal, and to be thrown in the Thames? Well, if I be serv'd such another trick, I'll have my brains ta'en out and butter'd, and give them to a dog for a new-year's gift. The rogues slighted me into the river with as little remorse as they would have drown'd a blind bitch's puppies, fifteen i' th' litter; and you may know by my size that I have a kind of alacrity in sinking; if the bottom were as deep as hell I should down. I had been drown'd but that the shore was shelvy and shallow – a death that I abhor; for the water swells a man; and what a thing should I have been when I had been swell'd! I should have been a mountain of mummy.

Re-enter BARDOLPH, with sack.

BARDOLPH Here's Mistress Quickly, sir, to speak with you.

FALSTAFF Come, let me pour in some sack to the Thames water; for my belly's as cold as if I had swallow'd snow-balls for pills to cool the reins. Call her in.

BARDOLPH Come in, woman.

Enter MISTRESS QUICKLY.

QUICKLY By your leave; I cry you mercy. Give your worship good morrow.

FALSTAFF Take away these chalices. Go, brew me a pottle of sack finely.

BARDOLPH With eggs, sir?

FALSTAFF Simple of itself; I'll no pullet-sperm in my brewage. [*Exit Bardolph*] How now!

QUICKLY Marry, sir, I come to your worship from Mistress Ford.

FALSTAFF Mistress Ford! I have had ford enough; I was thrown into the ford; I have my belly full of ford.

QUICKLY Alas the day, good heart, that was not her fault! She does so take on with her men; they mistook their erection.

FALSTAFF So did I mine, to build upon a foolish woman's promise.

QUICKLY Well, she laments, sir, for it, that it would yearn your heart to see it. Her husband goes this morning a-birding; she desires you once more to come to her between eight and nine; I must carry her word quickly. She'll make you amends, I warrant you.

FALSTAFF Well, I will visit her. Tell her so; and bid her think what a man is. Let her consider his frailty, and then judge of my merit.

QUICKLY I will tell her.

FALSTAFF Do so. Between nine and ten, say'st thou?

QUICKLY Eight and nine, sir.

FALSTAFF Well, be gone; I will not miss her.

QUICKLY Peace be with you, sir. [*Exit.*

FALSTAFF I marvel I hear not of Master Brook; he sent me word to stay within. I like his money well. O, here he comes.

Enter FORD disguised.

FORD Bless you, sir!

FALSTAFF Now, Master Brook, you come to know what hath pass'd between me and Ford's wife?

FORD That, indeed, Sir John, is my business.

FALSTAFF Master Brook, I will not lie to you: I was at her house the hour she appointed me.

FORD And sped you, sir?

FALSTAFF Very ill-favouredly, Master Brook.

FORD How so, sir; did she change her determination?

FALSTAFF No, Master Brook; but the peaking cornuto her husband, Master Brook, dwelling in a continual 'larum of jealousy, comes me in the instant of our encounter, after we had embrac'd, kiss'd, protested, and, as it were, spoke the prologue of our comedy; and at his heels a rabble of his companions, thither provoked and instigated by his distemper, and, forsooth, to search his house for his wife's love.

FORD What, while you were there?

FALSTAFF While I was there.

FORD And did he search for you, and could not find you?

FALSTAFF You shall hear. As good luck would have it, comes in one Mistress Page, gives intelligence of Ford's approach; and, in her invention and Ford's wife's distraction, they convey'd me into a buck-basket.

FORD A buck-basket!

FALSTAFF By the Lord, a buck-basket! Ramm'd me in with foul shirts and smocks, socks, foul stockings, greasy napkins, that, Master Brook, there was the rankest compound of villainous smell that ever offended nostril.

FORD And how long lay you there?

FALSTAFF Nay, you shall hear, Master Brook, what I have suffer'd to bring this woman to evil for your good. Being thus cramm'd in the basket, a couple of Ford's knaves, his hinds, were call'd forth by their mistress to carry me in the name of foul clothes to Datchet Lane; they took me on their shoulders; met the jealous knave their master in the door; who ask'd them once or twice what they had in their basket. I quak'd for fear lest the lunatic knave would have search'd it; but Fate, ordaining he should be a cuckold, held his hand. Well, on went he for a search, and away went I for foul clothes. But mark the sequel, Master Brook – I suffered the pangs of three several deaths: first, an

intolerable fright to be detected with a jealous rotten bell-wether; next, to be compass'd like a good bilbo in the circumference of a peck, hilt to point, heel to head; and then, to be stopp'd in, like a strong distillation, with stinking clothes that fretted in their own grease. Think of that – a man of my kidney. Think of that – that am as subject to heat as butter; a man of continual dissolution and thaw. It was a miracle to scape suffocation. And in the height of this bath, when I was more than half-stew'd in grease, like a Dutch dish, to be thrown into the Thames, and cool'd, glowing hot, in that surge, like a horse-shoe; think of that – hissing hot. Think of that,
108 Master Brook.

FORD In good sadness, sir, I am sorry that for my sake you have suffer'd all this. My suit, then, is
111 desperate; you'll undertake her no more.

FALSTAFF Master Brook, I will be thrown into Etna, as I have been into Thames, ere I will leave her thus. Her husband is this morning gone a-birding; I have received from her another embassy of meeting; 'twixt eight and nine is the hour, Master Brook.

FORD 'Tis past eight already, sir. 117

FALSTAFF Is it? I will then address me to my appointment. Come to me at your convenient leisure, and you shall know how I speed; and the conclusion shall be crowned with your enjoying her. Adieu. You shall have her, Master Brook; Master Brook, you shall cuckold Ford.

[*Exit.* 122

FORD Hum! ha! Is this a vision? Is this a dream? Do I sleep? Master Ford, awake; awake, Master Ford. There's a hole made in your best coat, Master Ford. This 'tis to be married; this 'tis to have linen and buck-baskets! Well, I will proclaim myself what I am; I will now take the lecher; he is at my house. He cannot scape me; 'tis impossible he should; he cannot creep into a halfpenny purse nor into a pepper box. But, lest the devil that guides him should aid him, I will search impossible places. Though what I am I cannot avoid, yet to be what I would not shall not make me tame. If I have horns to make one mad, let the proverb go with me – I'll be horn mad. [*Exit.* 134

ACT FOUR

SCENE I. *Windsor. A street.*

Enter MISTRESS PAGE, MISTRESS QUICKLY, and WILLIAM

MRS. PAGE Is he at Master Ford's already, think'st thou?

QUICKLY Sure he is by this; or will be presently; but truly he is very courageous mad about his throwing into the water. Mistress Ford desires you to come suddenly.

MRS. PAGE I'll be with her by and by; I'll but bring my young man here to school. Look where his
8 master comes; 'tis a playing day, I see.

Enter SIR HUGH EVANS.

How now, Sir Hugh, no school to-day?

EVANS No; Master Slender is let the boys leave to play.

12 **QUICKLY** Blessing of his heart!

MRS. PAGE Sir Hugh, my husband says my son profits nothing in the world at his book; I pray
15 you ask him some questions in his accidence.

EVANS Come hither, William; hold up your head; come.

MRS. PAGE Come on, sirrah; hold up your head; answer your master; be not afraid.

EVANS William, how many numbers is in nouns?

20 **WILLIAM** Two.

QUICKLY Truly, I thought there had been one number more, because they say 'Od's nouns'.

EVANS Peace your tattlings. What is 'fair', William?

WILLIAM Pulcher.

QUICKLY Polecats! There are fairer things than polecats, sure. 26

EVANS You are a very simplicity oman; I pray you, peace. What is 'lapis', William?

WILLIAM A stone.

EVANS And what is 'a stone', William?

WILLIAM A pebble. 31

EVANS No, it is 'lapis'; I pray you remember in your prain.

WILLIAM Lapis.

EVANS That is a good William. What is he, William, that does lend articles? 36

WILLIAM Articles are borrowed of the pronoun, and be thus declined: Singulariter, nominativo; hic, haec, hoc.

EVANS Nominativo, hig, hag, hog; pray you, mark: genitivo, hujus. Well, what is your accusative case? 40

WILLIAM Accusativo, hinc.

EVANS I pray you, have your remembrance, child. Accusativo, hung, hang, hog.

QUICKLY 'Hang-hog' is Latin for bacon, I warrant you.

EVANS Leave your prabbles, oman.

What is the focative case, William?

WILLIAM O – vocativo, O.

EVANS Remember, William: focative is caret.

QUICKLY And that's a good root.

EVANS Oman, forbear.

MRS. PAGE Peace.

EVANS What is your genitive case plural, William?

WILLIAM Genitive case?

EVANS Ay.

WILLIAM Genitive: horum, harum, horum.

QUICKLY Vengeance of Jenny's case; fie on her! Never name her, child, if she be a whore.

EVANS For shame, oman.

QUICKLY You do ill to teach the child such words. He teaches him to hick and to hack, which they'll do fast enough of themselves; and to call 'horum'; fie upon you!

EVANS Oman, art thou lunatics? Hast thou no understandings for thy cases, and the numbers of the genders? Thou art as foolish Christian creatures as I would desires.

MRS. PAGE Prithee hold thy peace.

EVANS Show me now, William, some declensions of your pronouns.

WILLIAM Forsooth, I have forgot.

EVANS It is qui, quae, quod; if you forget your qui's, your quae's, and your quod's, you must be preeches. Go your ways and play; go.

MRS. PAGE He is a better scholar than I thought he was.

EVANS He is a good sprag memory. Farewell, Mistress Page.

MRS. PAGE Adieu, good Sir Hugh. [*Exit Evans*] Get you home, boy. Come, we stay too long.

[*Exeunt.*

SCENE II. *Ford's house.*

Enter FALSTAFF and MISTRESS FORD.

FALSTAFF Mistress Ford, your sorrow hath eaten up my sufferance. I see you are obsequious in your love, and I profess requital to a hair's breadth; not only, Mistress Ford, in the simple office of love, but in all the accoutrement, complement, and ceremony of it. But are you sure of your husband now?

MRS. FORD He's a-birding, sweet Sir John.

MRS. PAGE [*Within*] What hoa, gossip Ford, what hoa!

MRS. FORD Step into th' chamber, Sir John.

[*Exit Falstaff.*

Enter MISTRESS PAGE.

MRS. PAGE How now, sweetheart, who's at home besides yourself?

MRS. FORD Why, none but mine own people.

MRS. PAGE Indeed?

MRS. FORD No, certainly. [*Aside to her*] Speak louder.

MRS. PAGE Truly, I am so glad you have nobody here.

MRS. FORD Why?

MRS. PAGE Why, woman, your husband is in his old lunes again. He so takes on yonder with my husband; so rails against all married mankind; so curses all Eve's daughters, of what complexion soever; and so buffets himself on the forehead, crying 'Peer-out, peer-out!' that any madness I ever yet beheld seem'd but tameness, civility, and patience, to this his distemper he is in now. I am glad the fat knight is not here.

MRS. FORD Why, does he talk of him?

MRS. PAGE Of none but him; and swears he was carried out, the last time he search'd for him, in a basket; protests to my husband he is now here; and hath drawn him and the rest of their company from their sport, to make another experiment of his suspicion. But I am glad the knight is not here; now he shall see his own foolery.

MRS. FORD How near is he, Mistress Page?

MRS. PAGE Hard by, at street end; he will be here anon.

MRS. FORD I am undone: the knight is here.

MRS. PAGE Why, then, you are utterly sham'd, and he's but a dead man. What a woman are you! Away with him, away with him; better shame than murder.

MRS. FORD Which way should he go? How should I bestow him? Shall I put him into the basket again?

Re-enter FALSTAFF.

FALSTAFF No, I'll come no more i' th' basket. May I not go out ere he come?

MRS. PAGE Alas, three of Master Ford's brothers watch the door with pistols, that none shall issue out; otherwise you might slip away ere he came. But what make you here?

FALSTAFF What shall I do? I'll creep up into the chimney.

MRS. FORD There they always use to discharge their birding-pieces.

MRS. PAGE Creep into the kiln-hole.

FALSTAFF Where is it?

MRS. FORD He will seek there, on my word. Neither press, coffer, chest, trunk, well, vault, but he hath an abstract for the remembrance of such places, and goes to them by his note. There is no hiding you in the house.

FALSTAFF I'll go out then.

MRS. PAGE If you go out in your own semblance,

you die, Sir John. Unless you go out disguis'd.

MRS. FORD How might we disguise him?

MRS. PAGE Alas the day, I know not! There is no woman's gown big enough for him; otherwise he might put on a hat, a muffler, and a kerchief, and so escape.

FALSTAFF Good hearts, devise something; any extremity rather than a mischief.

MRS. FORD My maid's aunt, the fat woman of Brainford, has a gown above.

MRS. PAGE On my word, it will serve him; she's as big as he is; and there's her thrumm'd hat, and her muffler too. Run up, Sir John.

MRS. FORD Go, go, sweet Sir John. Mistress Page and I will look some linen for your head.

MRS. PAGE Quick, quick; we'll come dress you straight. Put on the gown the while.

[Exit Falstaff.

MRS. FORD I would my husband would meet him in this shape; he cannot abide the old woman of Brainford; he swears she's a witch, forbade her my house, and hath threat'ned to beat her.

MRS. PAGE Heaven guide him to thy husband's cudgel; and the devil guide his cudgel afterwards!

MRS. FORD But is my husband coming?

MRS. PAGE Ay, in good sadness is he; and talks of the basket too, howsoever he hath had intelligence.

MRS. FORD We'll try that; for I'll appoint my men to carry the basket again, to meet him at the door with it as they did last time.

MRS. PAGE Nay, but he'll be here presently; let's go dress him like the witch of Brainford.

MRS. FORD I'll first direct my men what they shall do with the basket. Go up; I'll bring linen for him straight.

[Exit.

MRS. PAGE Hang him, dishonest varlet! we cannot misuse him enough.
We'll leave a proof, by that which we will do,
Wives may be merry and yet honest too.
We do not act that often jest and laugh;
'Tis old but true: Still swine eats all the draff.

[Exit.

Re-enter MISTRESS FORD, with two Servants.

MRS. FORD Go, sirs, take the basket again on your shoulders; your master is hard at door; if he bid you set it down, obey him; quickly, dispatch.

[Exit.

1 SERVANT Come, come, take it up.

2 SERVANT Pray heaven it be not full of knight again.

1 SERVANT I hope not; I had lief as bear so much lead.

Enter FORD, PAGE, SHALLOW, CAIUS, and SIR HUGH EVANS.

FORD Ay, but if it prove true, Master Page, have you any way then to unfool me again? Set down the basket, villain! Somebody call my wife. Youth in a basket! O you panderly rascals, there's a knot, a ging, a pack, a conspiracy against me. Now shall the devil be sham'd. What, wife, I say! Come, come forth; behold what honest clothes you send forth to bleaching.

PAGE Why, this passes, Master Ford; you are not to go loose any longer; you must be pinion'd.

EVANS Why, this is lunatics. This is mad as a mad dog.

SHALLOW Indeed, Master Ford, this is not well, indeed.

FORD So say I too, sir.

Re-enter MISTRESS FORD.

Come hither, Mistress Ford; Mistress Ford, the honest woman, the modest wife, the virtuous creature, that hath the jealous fool to her husband! I suspect without cause, mistress, do I?

MRS. FORD Heaven be my witness, you do, if you suspect me in any dishonesty.

FORD Well said, brazen-face; hold it out. Come forth, sirrah. *[Pulling clothes out of the basket.*

PAGE This passes!

MRS. FORD Are you not asham'd? Let the clothes alone.

FORD I shall find you anon.

EVANS 'Tis unreasonable. Will you take up your wife's clothes? Come away.

FORD Empty the basket, I say.

MRS. FORD Why, man, why?

FORD Master Page, as I am a man, there was one convey'd out of my house yesterday in this basket. Why may not he be there again? In my house I am sure he is; my intelligence is true; my jealousy is reasonable. Pluck me out all the linen.

MRS. FORD If you find a man there, he shall die a flea's death.

PAGE Here's no man.

SHALLOW By my fidelity, this is not well, Master Ford; this wrongs you.

EVANS Master Ford, you must pray, and not follow the imaginations of your own heart; this is jealousies.

FORD Well, he's not here I seek for.

PAGE No, nor nowhere else but in your brain.

FORD Help to search my house this one time. If I find not what I seek, show no colour for my extremity; let me for ever be your table sport; let them say of me 'As jealous as Ford, that search'd a hollow walnut for his wife's leman'. Satisfy me once more; once more search with me.

MRS. FORD What, hoa, Mistress Page! Come you and the old woman down; my husband will come into the chamber.

FORD Old woman? What old woman's that?

MRS. FORD Why, it is my maid's aunt of Brainford.

FORD A witch, a quean, an old cozening quean! Have I not forbid her my house? She comes of errands, does she? We are simple men; we do not know what's brought to pass under the profession of fortune-telling. She works by charms, by spells, by th' figure, and such daub'ry as this is, beyond our element. We know nothing. Come down, you witch, you hag you; come down, I say.

MRS. FORD Nay, good sweet husband! Good gentlemen, let him not strike the old woman.

Re-enter FALSTAFF in woman's clothes, and MISTRESS PAGE.

MRS. PAGE Come, Mother Prat; come, give me your hand.

FORD I'll prat her. [*Beating him*] Out of my door, you witch, you hag, you baggage, you polecat, you ronyon! Out, out! I'll conjure you, I'll fortune-tell you. [*Exit Falstaff.*

MRS. PAGE Are you not asham'd? I think you have kill'd the poor woman.

MRS. FORD Nay, he will do it. 'Tis a goodly credit for you.

FORD Hang her, witch!

EVANS By yea and no, I think the oman is a witch indeed; I like not when a oman has a great peard; I spy a great peard under his muffler.

FORD Will you follow, gentlemen? I beseech you follow; see but the issue of my jealousy; if I cry out thus upon no trail, never trust me when I open again.

PAGE Let's obey his humour a little further. Come, gentlemen.

[*Exeunt all but Mrs. Ford and Mrs. Page.*

MRS. PAGE Trust me, he beat him most pitifully.

MRS. FORD Nay, by th' mass, that he did not; he beat him most unpitifully me-thought.

MRS. PAGE I'll have the cudgel hallow'd and hung o'er the altar; it hath done meritorious service.

MRS. FORD What think you? May we, with the warrant of womanhood and the witness of a good conscience, pursue him with any further revenge?

MRS. PAGE The spirit of wantonness is sure scar'd out of him; if the devil have him not in fee-simple, with fine and recovery, he will never, I think, in the way of waste, attempt us again.

MRS. FORD Shall we tell our husbands how we have serv'd him?

MRS. PAGE Yes, by all means; if it be but to scrape the figures out of your husband's brains. If they can find in their hearts the poor unvirtuous fat knight shall be any further afflicted, we two will still be the ministers.

MRS. FORD I'll warrant they'll have him publicly sham'd; and methinks there would be no period to the jest, should he not be publicly sham'd.

MRS. PAGE Come, to the forge with it then; shape it. I would not have things cool.

[*Exeunt.*

SCENE III. *The Garter Inn.*

Enter HOST and BARDOLPH.

BARDOLPH Sir, the Germans desire to have three of your horses; the Duke himself will be tomorrow at court, and they are going to meet him.

HOST What duke should that be comes so secretly? I hear not of him in the court. Let me speak with the gentlemen; they speak English?

BARDOLPH Ay, sir; I'll call them to you.

HOST They shall have my horses, but I'll make them pay; I'll sauce them; they have had my house a week at command; I have turn'd away my other guests. They must come off; I'll sauce them. Come. [*Exeunt.*

SCENE IV. *Ford's house.*

Enter PAGE, FORD, MISTRESS PAGE, MISTRESS FORD, and SIR HUGH EVANS.

EVANS 'Tis one of the best discretions of a oman as ever I did look upon.

PAGE And did he send you both these letters at an instant?

MRS. PAGE Within a quarter of an hour.

FORD Pardon me, wife. Henceforth, do what thou wilt;
I rather will suspect the sun with cold
Than thee with wantonness. Now doth thy honour stand,
In him that was of late an heretic,
As firm as faith.

PAGE 'Tis well, 'tis well; no more.
Be not as extreme in submission as in offence;
But let our plot go forward. Let our wives
Yet once again, to make us public sport,
Appoint a meeting with this old fat fellow,
Where we may take him and disgrace him for it.

FORD There is no better way than that they spoke of.

PAGE How? To send him word they'll meet him in the Park at midnight? Fie, fie! he'll never come!

EVANS You say he has been thrown in the rivers; and has been grievously peaten as an old oman; methinks there should be terrors in him, that he should not come; methinks his flesh is punish'd; he shall have no desires.

PAGE So think I too.

MRS. FORD Devise but how you'll use him when he comes,
And let us two devise to bring him thither.

MRS. PAGE There is an old tale goes that Herne the Hunter,
Sometime a keeper here in Windsor Forest,
Doth all the winter-time, at still midnight,
Walk round about an oak, with great ragg'd horns;
And there he blasts the tree, and takes the cattle,
And makes milch-kine yield blood, and shakes a chain
In a most hideous and dreadful manner.
You have heard of such a spirit, and well you know
The superstitious idle-headed eld
Receiv'd, and did deliver to our age,
This tale of Herne the Hunter for a truth.

PAGE Why yet there want not many that do fear
In deep of night to walk by this Herne's oak.
But what of this?

MRS. FORD Marry, this is our device –
That Falstaff at that oak shall meet with us,
Disguis'd, like Herne, with huge horns on his head.

PAGE Well, let it not be doubted but he'll come,
And in this shape. When you have brought him thither,
What shall be done with him? What is your plot?

MRS. PAGE That likewise have we thought upon, and thus:
Nan Page my daughter, and my little son,
And three or four more of their growth, we'll dress
Like urchins, ouphes, and fairies, green and white,
With rounds of waxen tapers on their heads,
And rattles in their hands; upon a sudden,
As Falstaff, she, and I, are newly met,
Let them from forth a sawpit rush at once
With some diffused song; upon their sight
We two in great amazedness will fly.
Then let them all encircle him about,
And fairy-like, to pinch the unclean knight;
And ask him why, that hour of fairy revel,
In their so sacred paths he dares to tread
In shape profane.

MRS. FORD And till he tell the truth,
Let the supposed fairies pinch him sound,
And burn him with their tapers.

MRS. PAGE The truth being known,
We'll all present ourselves; dis-horn the spirit,
And mock him home to Windsor.

FORD The children must
Be practis'd well to this or they'll nev'r do 't.

EVANS I will teach the children their behaviours; and I will be like a jack-an-apes also, to burn the knight with my taber.

FORD That will be excellent. I'll go buy them vizards.

MRS. PAGE My Nan shall be the Queen of all the Fairies,
Finely attired in a robe of white.

PAGE That silk will I go buy. [*Aside*] And in that time
Shall Master Slender steal my Nan away,
And marry her at Eton. – Go, send to Falstaff straight.

FORD Nay, I'll to him again, in name of Brook;
He'll tell me all his purpose. Sure, he'll come.

MRS. PAGE Fear not you that. Go get us properties
And tricking for our fairies.

EVANS Let us about it. It is admirable pleasures, and fery honest knaveries.

[*Exeunt Page, Ford, and Evans.*

MRS. PAGE Go, Mistress Ford,
Send Quickly to Sir John to know his mind.

[*Exit Mrs. Ford.*

I'll to the Doctor; he hath my good will,
And none but he, to marry with Nan Page.
That Slender, though well landed, is an idiot;
And he my husband best of all affects.
The Doctor is well money'd, and his friends
Potent at court; he, none but he, shall have her,
Though twenty thousand worthier come to crave her.

[*Exit.*

SCENE V. *The Garter Inn.*

Enter HOST and SIMPLE.

HOST What wouldst thou have, boor? What, thick-skin? Speak, breathe, discuss; brief, short, quick, snap.

SIMPLE Marry, sir, I come to speak with Sir John Falstaff from Master Slender.

HOST There's his chamber, his house, his castle, his standing-bed and truckle-bed; 'tis painted about with the story of the Prodigal, fresh and new. Go, knock and call; he'll speak like an Anthropophaginian unto thee. Knock, I say.

SIMPLE There's an old woman, a fat woman, gone up into his chamber; I'll be so bold as stay, sir, till she come down; I come to speak with her, indeed.

HOST Ha! a fat woman? The knight may be robb'd. I'll call. Bully knight! Bully Sir John! Speak from thy lungs military. Art thou there? It is thine host, thine Ephesian, calls.

FALSTAFF [*Above*] How now, mine host?

HOST Here's a Bohemian-Tartar tarries the coming down of thy fat woman. Let her descend, bully, let her descend; my chambers are honourable. Fie, privacy, fie!

Enter FALSTAFF.

FALSTAFF There was, mine host, an old fat woman even now with me; but she's gone.

SIMPLE Pray you, sir, was't not the wise woman of Brainford?

FALSTAFF Ay, marry was it, mussel-shell. What would you with her?

SIMPLE My master, sir, my Master Slender, sent to her, seeing her go thorough the streets, to know, sir, whether one Nym, sir, that beguil'd him of a chain, had the chain or no.

FALSTAFF I spake with the old woman about it.

SIMPLE And what says she, I pray, sir?

FALSTAFF Marry, she says that the very same man that beguil'd Master Slender of his chain cozen'd him of it.

SIMPLE I would I could have spoken with the woman herself; I had other things to have spoken with her too, from him.

FALSTAFF What are they? Let us know.

HOST Ay, come; quick.

SIMPLE I may not conceal them, sir.

FALSTAFF Conceal them, or thou diest.

SIMPLE Why, sir, they were nothing but about Mistress Anne Page: to know if it were my master's fortune to have her or no.

FALSTAFF 'Tis, 'tis his fortune.

SIMPLE What, sir?

FALSTAFF To have her, or no. Go; say the woman told me so.

SIMPLE May I be bold to say so, sir?

FALSTAFF Ay, sir; like who more bold?

SIMPLE I thank your worship; I shall make my master glad with these tidings. [*Exit Simple.*

HOST Thou art clerkly, thou art clerkly, Sir John. Was there a wise woman with thee?

FALSTAFF Ay, that there was, mine host; one that hath taught me more wit than ever I learn'd before in my life; and I paid nothing for it neither, but was paid for my learning.

Enter BARDOLPH.

BARDOLPH Out, alas, sir, cozenage, mere cozenage!

HOST Where be my horses? Speak well of them, varletto.

BARDOLPH Run away with the cozeners; for so soon as I came beyond Eton, they threw me off from behind one of them, in a slough of mire; and set spurs and away, like three German devils, three Doctor Faustuses.

HOST They are gone but to meet the Duke, villain; do not say they be fled. Germans are honest men.

Enter SIR HUGH EVANS.

EVANS Where is mine host?

HOST What is the matter, sir?

EVANS Have a care of your entertainments. There is a friend of mine come to town tells me there is three cozen-germans that has cozen'd all the hosts of Readins, of Maidenhead, of Colebrook, of horses and money. I tell you for good will, look you; you are wise, and full of gibes and vlouting-stogs, and 'tis not convenient you should be cozened. Fare you well. [*Exit.*

Enter DOCTOR CAIUS.

CAIUS Vere is mine host de Jarteer?

HOST Here, Master Doctor, in perplexity and doubtful dilemma.

CAIUS I cannot tell vat is dat; but it is tell-a me dat you make grand preparation for a Duke de Jamany. By my trot, dere is no duke that the court is know to come; I tell you for good will. Adieu. [*Exit.*

HOST Hue and cry, villain, go! Assist me, knight; I am undone. Fly, run, hue and cry, villain; I am undone. [*Exeunt Host and Bardolph.*

FALSTAFF I would all the world might be cozen'd, for I have been cozen'd and beaten too. If it should come to the ear of the court how I have been transformed, and how my transformation hath been wash'd and cudgell'd, they would melt me out of my fat, drop by drop, and liquor fishermen's boots with me; I warrant they would whip me with their fine wits till I were as crest-fall'n as a dried pear. I never prosper'd since I forswore myself at primero. Well, if my wind were but long enough to say my prayers, I would repent.

Enter MISTRESS QUICKLY.

Now! whence come you?

QUICKLY From the two parties, forsooth.

FALSTAFF The devil take one party and his dam the other! And so they shall be both bestowed. I have suffer'd more for their sakes, more than the villainous inconstancy of man's disposition is able to bear.

QUICKLY And have not they suffer'd? Yes, I warrant; speciously one of them; Mistress Ford, good heart, is beaten black and blue, that you cannot see a white spot about her.

FALSTAFF What tell'st thou me of black and blue? I was beaten myself into all the colours of the rainbow; and I was like to be apprehended for the witch of Brainford. But that my admirable dexterity of wit, my counterfeiting the action of an old woman, deliver'd me, the knave constable had set me i' th' stocks, i' th' common stocks, for a witch.

QUICKLY Sir, let me speak with you in your chamber; you shall hear how things go, and, I warrant, to your content. Here is a letter will say somewhat. Good hearts, what ado here is to bring you together! Sure, one of you does not serve heaven well, that you are so cross'd.

FALSTAFF Come up into my chamber.

[*Exeunt.*

SCENE VI. *The Garter Inn.*

Enter FENTON and HOST.

HOST Master Fenton, talk not to me; my mind is heavy; I will give over all.

FENTON Yet hear me speak. Assist me in my purpose,
And, as I am a gentleman, I'll give thee
A hundred pound in gold more than your loss.

HOST I will hear you, Master Fenton; and I will, at the least, keep your counsel.

FENTON From time to time I have acquainted you
With the dear love I bear to fair Anne Page;
Who, mutually, hath answer'd my affection,
So far forth as herself might be her chooser,
Even to my wish. I have a letter from her
Of such contents as you will wonder at;
The mirth whereof so larded with my matter
That neither, singly, can be manifested
Without the show of both. Fat Falstaff
Hath a great scene. The image of the jest
I'll show you here at large. Hark, good mine host:
To-night at Herne's oak, just 'twixt twelve and one,
Must my sweet Nan present the Fairy Queen –
The purpose why is here – in which disguise,
While other jests are something rank on foot,
Her father hath commanded her to slip
Away with Slender, and with him at Eton
Immediately to marry; she hath consented.
Now, sir,
Her mother, even strong against that match
And firm for Doctor Caius, hath appointed
That he shall likewise shuffle her away
While other sports are tasking of their minds,
And at the dean'ry, where a priest attends,
Straight marry her. To this her mother's plot
She seemingly obedient likewise hath
Made promise to the doctor. Now thus it rests:
Her father means she shall be all in white;
And in that habit, when Slender sees his time
To take her by the hand and bid her go,
She shall go with him; her mother hath intended,
The better to denote her to the doctor –
For they must all be mask'd and vizarded –
That quaint in green she shall be loose enrob'd,
With ribands pendent, flaring 'bout her head;
And when the doctor spies his vantage ripe,
To pinch her by the hand, and, on that token,
The maid hath given consent to go with him.

HOST Which means she to deceive, father or mother?

FENTON Both, my good host, to go along with me.
And here it rests – that you'll procure the vicar
To stay for me at church, 'twixt twelve and one,
And in the lawful name of marrying,
To give our hearts united ceremony.

HOST Well, husband your device; I'll to the vicar.
Bring you the maid, you shall not lack a priest.

FENTON So shall I evermore be bound to thee;
Besides, I'll make a present recompense.

[*Exeunt.*

ACT FIVE

SCENE I. *The Garter Inn.*

Enter FALSTAFF and MISTRESS QUICKLY.

FALSTAFF Prithee, no more prattling; go. I'll hold. This is the third time; I hope good luck lies in odd numbers. Away, go; they say there is divinity in odd numbers, either in nativity, chance, or death. Away.

QUICKLY I'll provide you a chain, and I'll do what I can to get you a pair of horns.

FALSTAFF Away, I say; time wears; hold up your head, and mince. [*Exit Mrs. Quickly.*

Enter FORD, disguised.

How now, Master Brook! Master Brook, the matter will be known to-night or never. Be you in the Park about midnight, at Herne's oak, and you shall see wonders.

FORD Went you not to her yesterday, sir, as you told me you had appointed?

FALSTAFF I went to her, Master Brook, as you

see, like a poor old man; but I came from her, Master Brook, like a poor old woman. That same knave Ford, her husband, hath the finest mad devil of jealousy in him, Master Brook, that ever govern'd frenzy. I will tell you – he beat me grievously in the shape of a woman; for in the shape of man, Master Brook, I fear not Goliath with a weaver's beam; because I know also life is a shuttle. I am in haste; go along with me; I'll tell you all, Master Brook. Since I pluck'd geese, play'd truant, and whipp'd top, I knew not what 'twas to be beaten till lately. Follow me. I'll tell you strange things of this knave Ford, on whom tonight I will be revenged, and I will deliver his wife into your hand. Follow. Strange things in hand, Master Brook! Follow. [*Exeunt.*

SCENE II. *Windsor Park.*

Enter PAGE, SHALLOW, and SLENDER.

PAGE Come, come; we'll couch i' th' Castle ditch till we see the light of our fairies. Remember, son Slender, my daughter.

SLENDER Ay, forsooth; I have spoke with her, and we have a nay-word how to know one another. I come to her in white and cry 'mum'; she cries 'budget'; and by that we know one another.

SHALLOW That's good too; but what needs either your mum or her budget? The white will decipher her well enough. It hath struck ten o'clock.

PAGE The night is dark; light and spirits will become it well. Heaven prosper our sport! No man means evil but the devil, and we shall know him by his horns. Let's away; follow me. [*Exeunt.*

SCENE III. *A street leading to the Park.*

Enter MISTRESS PAGE, MISTRESS FORD, and DOCTOR CAIUS.

MRS. PAGE Master Doctor, my daughter is in green; when you see your time, take her by the hand, away with her to the deanery, and dispatch it quickly. Go before into the Park; we two must go together.

CAIUS I know vat I have to do; adieu.

MRS. PAGE Fare you well, sir. [*Exit Caius*] My husband will not rejoice so much at the abuse of Falstaff as he will chafe at the doctor's marrying my daughter; but 'tis no matter; better a little chiding than a great deal of heart-break.

MRS. FORD Where is Nan now, and her troop of fairies, and the Welsh devil, Hugh?

MRS. PAGE They are all couch'd in a pit hard by Herne's oak, with obscur'd lights; which, at the very instant of Falstaff's and our meeting, they will at once display to the night.

MRS. FORD That cannot choose but amaze him.

MRS. PAGE If he be not amaz'd, he will be mock'd; if he be amaz'd, he will every way be mock'd.

MRS. FORD We'll betray him finely.

MRS. PAGE Against such lewdsters and their lechery,
Those that betray them do no treachery.

MRS. FORD The hour draws on. To the oak, to the oak! [*Exeunt.*

SCENE IV. *Windsor Park.*

Enter SIR HUGH EVANS like a satyr, with Others as fairies.

EVANS Trib, trib, fairies; come; and remember your parts. Be pold, I pray you; follow me into the pit; and when I give the watch-ords, do as I pid you. Come, come; trib, trib. [*Exeunt.*

SCENE V. *Another part of the Park.*

Enter FALSTAFF disguised as Herne.

FALSTAFF The Windsor bell hath struck twelve; the minute draws on. Now the hot-blooded gods assist me! Remember, Jove, thou wast a bull for thy Europa; love set on thy horns. O powerful love! that in some respects makes a beast a man; in some other a man a beast. You were also, Jupiter, a swan, for the love of Leda. O omnipotent love! how near the god drew to the complexion of a goose! A fault done first in the form of a beast – O Jove, a beastly fault! – and then another fault in the semblance of a fowl – think on't, Jove, a foul fault! When gods have hot backs what shall poor men do? For me, I am here a Windsor stag; and the fattest, I think, i' th' forest. Send me a cool rut-time, Jove, or who can blame me to piss my tallow? Who comes here? my doe?

Enter MISTRESS FORD and MISTRESS PAGE.

MRS. FORD Sir John! Art thou there, my deer, my male deer.

FALSTAFF My doe with the black scut! Let the sky rain potatoes; let it thunder to the tune of Greensleeves, hail kissing-comfits, and snow eringoes; let there come a tempest of provocation, I will shelter me here. [*Embracing her.*

MRS. FORD Mistress Page is come with me, sweetheart.

FALSTAFF Divide me like a brib'd buck, each a haunch; I will keep my sides to myself, my shoulders for the fellow of this walk, and my horns I bequeath your husbands. Am I a woodman, ha? Speak I like Herne the Hunter? Why, now is Cupid a child of conscience; he makes restitution. As I am a true spirit, welcome! [*A noise of horns.*

MRS. PAGE Alas! what noise?

MRS. FORD Heaven forgive our sins!

FALSTAFF What should this be?

MRS. FORD, MRS. PAGE Away, away.

[*They run off.*

FALSTAFF I think the devil will not have me damn'd, lest the oil that's in me should set hell on fire; he would never else cross me thus.

Enter SIR HUGH EVANS like a satyr, ANNE PAGE as a fairy, and Others as the Fairy Queen, fairies, and Hobgoblin; all with tapers.

FAIRY QUEEN Fairies, black, grey, green, and white,
You moonshine revellers, and shades of night,
You orphan heirs of fixed destiny,
Attend your office and your quality.
Crier Hobgoblin, make the fairy oyes.

PUCK Elves, list your names; silence, you airy toys.
Cricket, to Windsor chimneys shalt thou leap;
Where fires thou find'st unrak'd, and hearths unswept,
There pinch the maids as blue as bilberry;
Our radiant Queen hates sluts and sluttery.

FALSTAFF They are fairies; he that speaks to them shall die.
I'll wink and couch; no man their works must eye. [*Lies down upon his face.*

EVANS Where's Pede? Go you, and where you find a maid
That, ere she sleep, has thrice her prayers said,
Raise up the organs of her fantasy,
Sleep she as sound as careless infancy;
But those as sleep and think not on their sins,
Pinch them, arms, legs, backs, shoulders, sides, and shins.

FAIRY QUEEN About, about;
Search Windsor castle, elves, within and out;
Strew good luck, ouphes, on every sacred room,
That it may stand till the perpetual doom
In state as wholesome as in state 'tis fit,
Worthy the owner and the owner it.
The several chairs of order look you scour
With juice of balm and every precious flower;
Each fair instalment, coat, and sev'ral crest,
With loyal blazon, evermore be blest!
And nightly, meadow-fairies, look you sing,
Like to the Garter's compass, in a ring;
Th' expressure that it bears, green let it be,
More fertile-fresh than all the field to see;
And 'Honi soit qui mal y pense' write
In em'rald tufts, flow'rs purple, blue and white;
Like sapphire, pearl, and rich embroidery,
Buckled below fair knighthood's bending knee.
Fairies use flow'rs for their charactery.
Away, disperse; but till 'tis one o'clock,
Our dance of custom round about the oak
Of Herne the Hunter let us not forget.

EVANS Pray you, lock hand in hand; yourselves in order set;
And twenty glow-worms shall our lanterns be,
To guide our measure round about the tree.
But, stay. I smell a man of middle earth.

FALSTAFF Heavens defend me from that Welsh fairy, lest he transform me to a piece of cheese!

PUCK Vile worm, thou wast o'erlook'd even in thy birth.

FAIRY QUEEN With trial-fire touch me his finger-end;
If he be chaste, the flame will back descend,
And turn him to no pain; but if he start,
It is the flesh of a corrupted heart.

PUCK A trial, come.

EVANS Come, will this wood take fire?

[*They put the tapers to his fingers, and he starts.*

FALSTAFF Oh, oh, oh!

FAIRY QUEEN Corrupt, corrupt, and tainted in desire!
About him, fairies; sing a scornful rhyme;
And, as you trip, still pinch him to your time.

The Song.

Fie on sinful fantasy!
Fie on lust and luxury!
Lust is but a bloody fire,
Kindled with unchaste desire,
Fed in heart, whose flames aspire,
As thoughts do blow them, higher and higher.
Pinch him, fairies, mutually;
Pinch him for his villainy;
Pinch him and burn him and turn him about,
Till candles and star-light and moonshine be out.

During this song they pinch Falstaff. DOCTOR CAIUS comes one way, and steals away a fairy in green; SLENDER another way, and takes off a fairy in white; and FENTON steals away Anne Page. A noise of hunting is heard within. All the fairies run away. Falstaff pulls off his buck's head, and rises.

Enter PAGE, FORD, MISTRESS PAGE, MISTRESS FORD, and SIR HUGH EVANS.

PAGE Nay, do not fly; I think we have watch'd you now.
Will none but Herne the Hunter serve your turn?

MRS. PAGE I pray you, come, hold up the jest no higher.
Now, good Sir John, how like you Windsor wives?
See you these, husband? Do not these fair yokes
Become the forest better than the town?

FORD Now, sir, who's a cuckold now? Master Brook, Falstaff's a knave, a cuckoldly knave; here are his horns, Master Brook; and, Master Brook, he hath enjoyed nothing of Ford's but his buck-basket, his cudgel, and twenty pounds of money, which must be paid to Master Brook; his horses are arrested for it, Master Brook.

MRS. FORD Sir John, we have had ill luck; we could never meet. I will never take you for my love again; but I will always count you my deer.

FALSTAFF I do begin to perceive that I am made an ass.

FORD Ay, and an ox too; both the proofs are extant.

FALSTAFF And these are not fairies? I was three or four times in the thought they were not fairies; and yet the guiltiness of my mind, the sudden surprise of my powers, drove the grossness of the foppery into a receiv'd belief, in despite of the teeth of all rhyme and reason, that they were fairies. See now how wit may be made a Jack-a-Lent when 'tis upon ill employment.

EVANS Sir John Falstaff, serve Got, and leave your desires, and fairies will not pinse you.

FORD Well said, fairy Hugh.

EVANS And leave you your jealousies too, I pray you.

FORD I will never mistrust my wife again, till thou art able to woo her in good English.

FALSTAFF Have I laid my brain in the sun, and dried it, that it wants matter to prevent so gross o'er-reaching as this? Am I ridden with a Welsh goat too? Shall I have a cox-comb of frieze? 'Tis time I were chok'd with a piece of toasted cheese.

EVANS Seese is not good to give putter; your belly is all putter.

FALSTAFF 'Seese' and 'putter'! Have I liv'd to stand at the taunt of one that makes fritters of English? This is enough to be the decay of lust and late-walking through the realm.

MRS. PAGE Why, Sir John, do you think, though we would have thrust virtue out of our hearts by the head and shoulders, and have given ourselves without scruple to hell, that ever the devil could have made you our delight?

FORD What, a hodge-pudding? a bag of flax?

MRS. PAGE A puff'd man?

PAGE Old, cold, wither'd, and of intolerable entrails?

FORD And one that is as slanderous as Satan?

PAGE And as poor as Job?

FORD And as wicked as his wife?

EVANS And given to fornications, and to taverns, and sack, and wine, and metheglins, and to drinkings, and swearings, and starings, pribbles and prabbles?

FALSTAFF Well, I am your theme; you have the start of me; I am dejected; I am not able to answer the Welsh flannel; ignorance itself is a plummet o'er me; use me as you will.

FORD Marry, sir, we'll bring you to Windsor, to one Master Brook, that you have cozen'd of money, to whom you should have been a pander. Over and above that you have suffer'd, I think to repay that money will be a biting affliction.

PAGE Yet be cheerful, knight; thou shalt eat a posset to-night at my house, where I will desire thee to laugh at my wife, that now laughs at thee. Tell her Master Slender hath married her daughter.

MRS. PAGE [*Aside*] Doctors doubt that; if Anne Page be my daughter, she is, by this, Doctor Caius' wife.

Enter SLENDER.

SLENDER Whoa, ho, ho, father Page!

PAGE Son, how now! how now, son! Have you dispatch'd?

SLENDER Dispatch'd! I'll make the best in Gloucestershire know on't; would I were hang'd, la, else!

PAGE Of what, son?

SLENDER I came yonder at Eton to marry Mistress Anne Page, and she's a great lubberly boy. If it had not been i' th' church, I would have swing'd him, or he should have swing'd me. If I did not think it had been Anne Page, would I might never stir! – and 'tis a postmaster's boy.

PAGE Upon my life, then, you took the wrong.

SLENDER What need you tell me that? I think so, when I took a boy for a girl. If I had been married to him, for all he was in woman's apparel, I would not have had him.

PAGE Why, this is your own folly. Did not I tell you how you should know my daughter by her garments?

SLENDER I went to her in white and cried 'mum' and she cried 'budget' as Anne and I had appointed; and yet it was not Anne, but a postmaster's boy.

MRS. PAGE Good George, be not angry. I know of your purpose; turn'd my daughter into green; and, indeed, she is now with the Doctor at the dean'ry, and there married.

Enter CAIUS.

CAIUS Vere is Mistress Page? By gar, I am cozened; I ha' married un garcon, a boy; un paysan, by gar, a boy; it is not Anne Page; by gar, I am cozened.

MRS. PAGE Why, did you take her in green?

CAIUS Ay, be gar, and 'tis a boy; be gar, I'll raise all Windsor. [*Exit Caius.*

FORD This is strange. Who hath got the right Anne?

PAGE My heart misgives me; here comes Master Fenton.

Enter FENTON and ANNE PAGE.

How now, Master Fenton!

ANNE Pardon, good father. Good my mother, pardon.

PAGE Now, Mistress, how chance you went not with Master Slender?

MRS. PAGE Why went you not with Master Doctor, maid?

FENTON You do amaze her. Hear the truth of it.
You would have married her most shamefully,
Where there was no proportion held in love.
The truth is, she and I, long since contracted,
Are now so sure that nothing can dissolve us.
Th' offence is holy that she hath committed;
And this deceit loses the name of craft,
Of disobedience, or unduteous title,
Since therein she doth evitate and shun
A thousand irreligious cursed hours,
Which forced marriage would have brought upon her.

FORD Stand not amaz'd; here is no remedy.
In love, the heavens themselves do guide the state;
Money buys lands, and wives are sold by fate.

FALSTAFF I am glad, though you have ta'en a special stand to strike at me, that your arrow hath glanc'd.

PAGE Well, what remedy? Fenton, heaven give thee joy!
What cannot be eschew'd must be embrac'd.

FALSTAFF When night-dogs run, all sorts of deer are chas'd.

MRS. PAGE Well, I will muse no further. Master Fentcn,
Heaven give you many, many merry days!
Good husband, let us every one go home,
And laugh this sport o'er by a country fire;
Sir John and all.

FORD Let it be so. Sir John,
To Master Brook you yet shall hold your word;
For he, to-night, shall lie with Mistress Ford.

[*Exeunt.*

Measure for Measure

Introduction by DOROTHY McMILLAN

The action of *Measure for Measure* is on the face of it motivated by Duke Vincentio's desire to clean up Vienna without having to get his own hands dirty; the duke's additional motive, declared only to Friar Thomas, is to find out what people, Angelo in particular, are really like beneath their public facades. He has some success in the latter project, albeit that it might be objected that he already had reason to be suspicious of Angelo, but since it is scarcely achieved by an institutionalisable method, it does not look like being much help in the future. Nor does the duke appear to have managed the cleansing of the city nor clarified the means by which this might occur. The place and function of judgment in a commonwealth seems as hazy at the end as at the beginning; the play dissolves in a series of refusals and pious hopes for the future that display the duke almost in the character of the vacillating parent who says he really means it this time and ends up buying some sweets to keep the immediate peace. Can it be wisdom to hope that Barnardine will 'provide/For better times to come', that marrying his whore will smarten Lucio up or that Angelo will be redeemed by the love of a good woman? 'Judge not, that ye be not judged', the Bible tells us; but we must judge – the audience of *Measure for Measure* is apparently being asked to take pleasure from the contemplation of the conjunction of necessity and impossibility.

It is, of course, precisely this conjunction that is forced upon Isabella who is given a choice which is defined by not being one. A modern generation, schooled in the belief that charity is more important than chastity has sometimes felt that Isabella's attachment to her chastity (she does not say 'virginity') is evidence of reprehensible frigidity which seeks unnaturally to protect itself in a convent. It is not clear exactly how Shakespeare's audience would have responded to a nun on the stage but some of them would surely have had aunts who had been nuns and would perhaps not have found them unnatural. In any case she is being asked to make a filthy bargain with unjust authority and Angelo's subsequent determination to execute Claudio any way shows clearly what happens when such bargains are struck. Even the disproportionate vehemence of her condemnation of Claudio's perfectly understandable youthful desire for life at any price need not result in disapproval of Isabella. She, like Claudio himself, is young and isolated, has no one to appeal to for support other than the very brother that she must damage. And if she acquiesces too readily in the dubious morality of the bed trick, let s/he who has never wished for a fairy-tale solution to a moral dilemma cast the first stone.

But even if one may somewhat defuse the sexual issue as far as Isabella's choice is concerned, it will not do to try to displace sex as a major concern of the play; and not very wholesome sex at that. Claudio and Juliet can scarcely be presented as romantic lovers; Juliet's pregnancy is given in a less warm light than that of Helen in *All's Well That Ends Well*, and the nuptials have been delayed after all to secure a dowry – that is unromantically cautious. The presentation of Angelo's sexuality goes some way to supporting the contention of twentieth-century feminists that rape is about degradation and domination rather than pleasure. And there is little in the way of qualification of Lucio's view of prostitutes as punks. Perhaps sexuality is yet another of these necessary impossibilities that seem to characterise this play.

To counteract this apparent miasma of negativity and disgust I want to return to that notion of the love of a good woman which I seemed initially to mock. When the duke tests Mariana's love for Angelo by offering her the means to 'buy a better husband', she replies, 'O my dear lord,/I crave no other, nor no better man'. Can there be any more moving or more energetic acceptance of things as they are, any more convincing forgiveness of a man for being merely what he is? Since I do not want to explain the play away in a welter of sentimental approval of mercy, I want to stress the energy of Mariana's appeal, the absoluteness of her commitment which makes her ask for Isabella's supporting voice even before the duke suggests it might be a powerful one. And it is in energy that I find the positives of this play. Claudio's plea for life may not be theologically admirable but the future of his child depends on the vehemence of such desire; Angelo's sentiments are never lukewarm and may now find a proper channel. If Isabella lends the duke her energy as she may give him her hand, then at least forgiveness within the commonwealth will proceed from capability not from exhaustion.

Measure for Measure

DRAMATIS PERSONAE

VINCENTIO
the Duke
ANGELO
the Deputy
ESCALUS
an ancient Lord
CLAUDIO
a young gentleman
LUCIO
a fantastic
Two other like gentlemen
VARRIUS
a gentleman, servant to the Duke
PROVOST
THOMAS, PETER
two friars
PETER
A JUSTICE
ELBOW
a simple constable
FROTH
a foolish gentleman
POMPEY
a clown and servant to Mistress Overdone
ABHORSON
an executioner
BARNARDINE
a dissolute prisoner
ISABELLA
sister to Claudio
MARIANA
betrothed to Angelo
JULIET
beloved of Claudio
FRANCISCA
a nun
MISTRESS OVERDONE
a bawd
Lords, Officers, Citizens, a Boy, and Attendants

THE SCENE: VIENNA

ACT ONE

SCENE I. *The Duke's palace.*

Enter DUKE, ESCALUS, Lords, and Attendants.

DUKE Escalus!
ESCALUS My lord.
DUKE Of government the properties to unfold
Would seem in me t' affect speech and discourse,
Since I am put to know that your own science
Exceeds, in that, the lists of all advice
My strength can give you; then no more remains
But that to your sufficiency – as your worth is able –
And let them work. The nature of our people,
Our city's institutions, and the terms
For common justice, y'are as pregnant in
As art and practice hath enriched any
That we remember. There is our commission,
From which we would not have you warp.
Call hither,
I say, bid come before us Angelo.
[*Exit an Attendant.*
What figure of us think you he will bear?
For you must know we have with special soul
Elected him our absence to supply;
Lent him our terror, dress'd him with our love,
And given his deputation all the organs
Of our own power. What think you of it?
ESCALUS If any in Vienna be of worth
To undergo such ample grace and honour,
It is Lord Angelo.

Enter ANGELO.

DUKE Look where he comes.
ANGELO Always obedient to your Grace's will,
I come to know your pleasure.
DUKE Angelo,
There is a kind of character in thy life
That to th' observer doth thy history
Fully unfold. Thyself and thy belongings
Are not thine own so proper as to waste
Thyself upon thy virtues, they on thee.
Heaven doth with us as we with torches do,
Not light them for themselves; for if our virtues
Did not go forth of us, 'twere all alike
As if we had them not. Spirits are not finely touch'd
But to fine issues; nor Nature never lends
The smallest scruple of her excellence
But, like a thrifty goddess, she determines
Herself the glory of a creditor,
Both thanks and use. But I do bend my speech
To one that can my part in him advertise.
Hold, therefore, Angelo –
In our remove be thou at full ourself;
Mortality and mercy in Vienna
Live in thy tongue and heart. Old Escalus,

Though first in question, is thy secondary.
Take thy commission.

ANGELO Now, good my lord,
Let there be some more test made of my metal,
Before so noble and so great a figure
Be stamp'd upon it.

DUKE No more evasion!
We have with a leaven'd and prepared choice
Proceeded to you; therefore take your honours.
Our haste from hence is of so quick condition
That it prefers itself, and leaves unquestion'd
Matters of needful value. We shall write to you,
As time and our concernings shall importune,
How it goes with us, and do look to know
What doth befall you here. So, fare you well.
To th' hopeful execution do I leave you
Of your commissions.

ANGELO Yet give leave, my lord,
That we may bring you something on the way.

DUKE My haste may not admit it;
Nor need you, on mine honour, have to do
With any scruple: your scope is as mine own,
So to enforce or qualify the laws
As to your soul seems good. Give me your hand;
I'll privily away I love the people,
But do not like to stage me to their eyes;
Though it do well, I do not relish well
Their loud applause and Aves vehement;
Nor do I think he man of safe discretion
That does affect it. Once more, fare you well.

ANGELO The heavens give safety to your purposes!

ESCALUS Lead forth and bring you back in happiness!

DUKE I thank you. Fare you well. *[Exit.*

ESCALUS I shall desire you, sir, to give me leave
To have free speech with you; and it concerns me
To look into the bottom of my place:
A pow'r I have, but of what strength and nature
I am not yet instructed.

ANGELO 'Tis so with me. Let us withdraw together
And we may soon our satisfaction have
Touching that point.

ESCALUS I'll wait upon your honour.
[Exeunt.

SCENE II. *A street.*

Enter LUCIO and two other Gentlemen.

LUCIO If the Duke, with the other dukes, come not to composition with the King of Hungary, why then all the dukes fall upon the King.

1 GENTLEMAN Heaven grant us its peace, but not the King of Hungary's!

2 GENTLEMAN Amen.

LUCIO Thou conclud'st like the sanctimonious pirate that went to sea with the Ten Commandments, but scrap'd one out of the table.

2 GENTLEMAN 'Thou shalt not steal'?

LUCIO Ay, that he raz'd.

1 GENTLEMAN Why, 'twas a commandment to command the captain and all the rest from their functions: they put forth to steal. There's not a soldier of us all that, in the thanksgiving before meat, do relish the petition well that prays for peace.

2 GENTLEMAN I never heard any soldier dislike it.

LUCIO I believe thee; for I think thou never wast where grace was said.

2 GENTLEMAN No? A dozen times at least.

1 GENTLEMAN What, in metre?

LUCIO In any proportion or in any language.

1 GENTLEMAN I think, or in any religion.

LUCIO Ay, why not? Grace is grace, despite of all controversy; as, for example, thou thyself art a wicked villain, despite of all grace.

1 GENTLEMAN Well, there went but a pair of shears between us.

LUCIO I grant; as there may between the lists and the velvet. Thou art the list.

1 GENTLEMAN And thou the velvet; thou art good velvet; thou 'rt a three-pil'd piece, I warrant thee. I had as lief be a list of an English kersey as be pil'd, as thou art pil'd, for a French velvet. Do I speak feelingly now?

LUCIO I think thou dost; and, indeed, with most painful feeling of thy speech. I will, out of thine own confession, learn to begin thy health; but, whilst I live, forget to drink after thee.

1 GENTLEMAN I think I have done myself wrong, have I not?

2 GENTLEMAN Yes, that thou hast, whether thou art tainted or free.

Enter MISTRESS OVERDONE.

LUCIO Behold, behold, where Madam Mitigation comes! I have purchas'd as many diseases under her roof as come to –

2 GENTLEMAN To what, I pray?

1 GENTLEMAN Judge.

2 GENTLEMAN To three thousand dolours a year.

1 GENTLEMAN Ay, and more.

LUCIO A French crown more.

1 GENTLEMAN Thou art always figuring diseases in me, but thou art full of error; I am sound.

LUCIO Nay, not, as one would say, healthy; but so sound as things that are hollow: thy bones are hollow; impiety has made a feast of thee.

1 GENTLEMAN How now! Which of your hips has the most profound sciatica?

MRS. OVERDONE Well, well! there's one yonder arrested, and carried to prison was worth five thousand of you all.

1 GENTLEMAN Who's that, I pray thee?

MRS. OVERDONE Marry, sir, that's Claudio, Signior Claudio.

1 GENTLEMAN Claudio to prison? 'Tis not so.

MRS. OVERDONE Nay, but I know 'tis so: I saw him arrested saw him carried away; and, which is more, within these three days his head to be chopp'd off.

LUCIO But, after all this fooling, I would not have it so. Art thou sure of this?

MRS. OVERDONE I am too sure of it; and it is for getting Madam Julietta with child.

LUCIO Believe me, this may be; he promis'd to meet me two hours since, and he was ever precise in promise-keeping.

2 GENTLEMAN Besides, you know, it draws something near to the speech we had to such a purpose.

1 GENTLEMAN But most of all agreeing with the proclamation.

LUCIO Away; let's go learn the truth of it.

[Exeunt Lucio and Gentlemen.

MRS. OVERDONE Thus, what with the war, what with the sweat, what with the gallows, and what with poverty, I am custom-shrunk.

Enter POMPEY.

How now! what's the news with you?

POMPEY Yonder man is carried to prison.

MRS. OVERDONE Well, what has he done?

POMPEY A woman.

MRS. OVERDONE But what's his offence?

POMPEY Groping for trouts in a peculiar river.

MRS. OVERDONE What! is there a maid with child by him?

POMPEY No; but there's a woman with maid by him. You have not heard of the proclamation, have you?

MRS. OVERDONE What proclamation, man?

POMPEY All houses in the suburbs of Vienna must be pluck'd down.

MRS. OVERDONE And what shall become of those in the city?

POMPEY They shall stand for seed; they had gone down too, but that a wise burgher put in for them.

MRS. OVERDONE But shall all our houses of resort in the suburbs be pull'd down?

POMPEY To the ground, mistress.

MRS. OVERDONE Why, here's a change indeed in the commonwealth! What shall become of me?

POMPEY Come, fear not you: good counsellors lack no clients. Though you change your place you need not change your trade; I'll be your tapster still. Courage, there will be pity taken on you; you that have worn your eyes almost out in the service, you will be considered.

MRS. OVERDONE What's to do here, Thomas Tapster? Let's withdraw.

POMPEY Here comes Signior Claudio, led by the provost to prison; and there's Madam Juliet.

[Exeunt.

Enter PROVOST, CLAUDIO, JULIET, and Officers; LUCIO following.

CLAUDIO Fellow, why dost thou show me thus to th' world?
Bear me to prison, where I am committed.

PROVOST I do it not in evil disposition,
But from Lord Angelo by special charge.

CLAUDIO Thus can the demigod Authority
Make us pay down for our offence by weight
The words of heaven: on whom it will, it will;
On whom it will not, so; yet still 'tis just.

LUCIO Why, how now, Claudio, whence comes this restraint?

CLAUDIO From too much liberty, my Lucio, liberty;
As surfeit is the father of much fast,
So every scope by the immoderate use
Turns to restraint. Our natures do pursue,
Like rats that ravin down their proper bane,
A thirsty evil; and when we drink we die.

LUCIO If I could speak so wisely under an arrest, I would send for certain of my creditors; and yet, to say the truth, I had as lief have the foppery of freedom as the morality of imprisonment. What's thy offence, Claudio?

CLAUDIO What but to speak of would offend again.

LUCIO What, is't murder?

CLAUDIO No.

LUCIO Lechery?

CLAUDIO Call it so.

PROVOST Away, sir; you must go.

CLAUDIO One word, good friend. Lucio, a word with you.

LUCIO A hundred, if they'll do you any good. Is lechery so look'd after?

CLAUDIO Thus stands it with me: upon a true contract
I got possession of Julietta's bed.
You know the lady; she is fast my wife,
Save that we do the denunciation lack
Of outward order; this we came not to,
Only for propagation of a dow'r
Remaining in the coffer of her friends.
From whom we thought it meet to hide our love
Till time had made them for us. But it chances
The stealth of our most mutual entertainment,

With character too gross, is writ on Juliet.
LUCIO With child, perhaps?
CLAUDIO Unhappily, even so.
And the new deputy now for the Duke –
Whether it be the fault and glimpse of newness,
Or whether that the body public be
A horse whereon the governor doth ride,
Who, newly in the seat, that it may know
He can command, lets it straight feel the spur;
Whether the tyranny be in his place,
Or in his eminence that fills it up,
I stagger in. But this new governor
Awakes me all the enrolled penalties
Which have, like unscour'd armour, hung by th' wall
So long that nineteen zodiacs have gone round
And none of them been worn; and, for a name,
Now puts the drowsy and neglected act
Freshly on me. 'Tis surely for a name.

LUCIO I warrant it is; and thy head stands so tickle on thy shoulders that a milkmaid, if she be in love, may sigh it off.
Send after the Duke, and appeal to him.

CLAUDIO I have done so, but he's not to be found.
I prithee, Lucio, do me this kind service:
This day my sister should the cloister enter,
And there receive her approbation;
Acquaint her with the danger of my state;
Implore her, in my voice, that she make friends
To the strict deputy; bid herself assay him.
I have great hope in that; for in her youth
There is a prone and speechless dialect
Such as move men; beside, she hath prosperous art
When she will play with reason and discourse,
And well she can persuade.

LUCIO I pray she may; as well for the encouragement of the like, which else would stand under grievous imposition, as for the enjoying of thy life, who I would be sorry should be thus foolishly lost at a game of tick-tack. I'll to her.

CLAUDIO I thank you, good friend Lucio.
LUCIO Within two hours.
CLAUDIO Come, officer, away.
[*Exeunt*

SCENE III. *A monastery.*

Enter DUKE and FRIAR THOMAS.

DUKE No, holy father; throw away that thought;
Believe not that the dribbling dart of love
Can pierce a complete bosom. Why I desire thee
To give me secret harbour hath a purpose
More grave and wrinkled than the aims and ends
Of burning youth.
FRIAR THOMAS May your Grace speak of it?
DUKE My holy sir, none better knows than you
How I have ever lov'd the life removed,
And held in idle price to haunt assemblies
Where youth, and cost, a witless bravery keeps.
I have deliver'd to Lord Angelo,
A man of stricture and firm abstinence,
My absolute power and place here in Vienna,
And he supposes me travell'd to Poland;
For so I have strew'd it in the common ear,
And so it is receiv'd. Now, pious sir,
You will demand of me why I do this.
FRIAR THOMAS Gladly, my lord.
DUKE We have strict statutes and most biting laws,
The needful bits and curbs to headstrong steeds,
Which for this fourteen years we have let slip;
Even like an o'ergrown lion in a cave,
That goes not out to prey. Now, as fond fathers,
Having bound up the threat'ning twigs of birch,
Only to stick it in their children's sight
For terror, not to use, in time the rod
Becomes more mock'd than fear'd; so our decrees,
Dead to infliction, to themselves are dead;
And liberty plucks justice by the nose;
The baby beats the nurse, and quite athwart
Goes all decorum.
FRIAR THOMAS It rested in your Grace
To unloose this tied-up justice when you pleas'd;
And it in you more dreadful would have seem'd
Than in Lord Angelo.
DUKE I do fear, too dreadful.
Sith 'twas my fault to give the people scope,
'Twould be my tyranny to strike and gall them
For what I bid them do; for we bid this be done,
When evil deeds have their permissive pass
And not the punishment. Therefore, indeed, my father,
I have on Angelo impos'd the office;
Who may, in th' ambush of my name, strike home,
And yet my nature never in the fight
To do in slander. And to behold his sway,
I will, as 'twere a brother of your order,
Visit both prince and people. Therefore, I prithee,
Supply me with the habit, and instruct me
How I may formally in person bear me
Like a true friar. Moe reasons for this action
At our more leisure shall I render you.
Only, this one: Lord Angelo is precise;
Stands at a guard with envy; scarce confesses
That his blood flows, or that his appetite
Is more to bread than stone. Hence shall we see,

If power change purpose, what our seemers be.
[*Exeunt.*

SCENE IV. *A nunnery.*

Enter ISABELLA and FRANCISCA.

ISABELLA And have you nuns no farther privileges?
FRANCISCA Are not these large enough?
ISABELLA Yes, truly I speak not as desiring more,
But rather wishing a more strict restraint
Upon the sisterhood, the votarists of Saint Clare.
LUCIO [*Within*] Ho! Peace be in this place!
ISABELLA Who's that which calls?
FRANCISCA It is a man's voice. Gentle Isabella,
Turn you the key, and know his business of him;
You may, I may not; you are yet unsworn;
When you have vow'd, you must not speak with men
But in the presence of the prioress;
Then, if you speak, you must not show your face,
Or, if you show your face, you must not speak.
He calls again; I pray you answer him.
[*Exit Francisca.*
ISABELLA Peace and prosperity! Who is't that calls?

Enter LUCIO.

LUCIO Hail, virgin, if you be, as those cheek-roses
Proclaim you are no less. Can you so stead me
As bring me to the sight of Isabella,
A novice of this place, and the fair sister
To her unhappy brother Claudio?
ISABELLA Why her 'unhappy brother'? Let me ask
The rather, for I now must make you know
I am that Isabella, and his sister.
LUCIO Gentle and fair, your brother kindly greets you.
Not to be weary with you, he's in prison.
ISABELLA Woe me! For what?
LUCIO For that which, if myself might be his judge,
He should receive his punishment in thanks:
He hath got his friend with child.
ISABELLA Sir, make me not your story.
LUCIO It is true.
I would not – though 'tis my familiar sin
With maids to seem the lapwing, and to jest,
Tongue far from heart – play with all virgins so:
I hold you as a thing enskied and sainted,
By your renouncement an immortal spirit,
And to be talk'd with in sincerity,
As with a saint.
ISABELLA You do blaspheme the good in mocking me.
LUCIO Do not believe it. Fewness and truth, 'tis thus:
Your brother and his lover have embrac'd.
As those that feed grow full, as blossoming time
That from the seedness the bare fallow brings
To teeming foison, even so her plenteous womb
Expresseth his full tilth and husbandry.
ISABELLA Some one with child by him? My cousin Juliet?
LUCIO Is she your cousin?
ISABELLA Adoptedly, as school-maids change their names
By vain though apt affection.
LUCIO She it is.
ISABELLA O, let him marry her!
LUCIO This is the point.
The Duke is very strangely gone from hence;
Bore many gentlemen, myself being one,
In hand, and hope of action; but we do learn,
By those that know the very nerves of state,
His givings-out were of an infinite distance
From his true-meant design. Upon his place,
And with full line of his authority,
Governs Lord Angelo, a man whose blood
Is very snow-broth, one who never feels
The wanton stings and motions of the sense,
But doth rebate and blunt his natural edge
With profits of the mind, study and fast.
He – to give fear to use and liberty,
Which have for long run by the hideous law,
As mice by lions – hath pick'd out an act
Under whose heavy sense your brother's life
Falls into forfeit; he arrests him on it,
And follows close the rigour of the statute
To make him an example. All hope is gone,
Unless you have the grace by your fair prayer
To soften Angelo. And that's my pith of business
'Twixt you and your poor brother.
ISABELLA Doth he so seek his life?
LUCIO Has censur'd him
Already, and, as I hear, the Provost hath
A warrant for his execution.
ISABELLA Alas! what poor ability's in me
To do him good?
LUCIO Assay the pow'r you have.
ISABELLA My power, alas, I doubt!
LUCIO Our doubts are traitors,
And make us lose the good we oft might win
By fearing to attempt. Go to Lord Angelo,
And let him learn to know, when maidens sue,
Men give like gods; but when they weep and kneel,
All their petitions are as freely theirs
As they themselves would owe them.
ISABELLA I'll see what I can do.

LUCIO But speedily.

ISABELLA I will about it straight;
No longer staying but to give the Mother
Notice of my affair. I humbly thank you.
Commend me to my brother; soon at night
I'll send him certain word of my success.

LUCIO I take my leave of you.

ISABELLA Good sir, adieu.

[*Exeunt.*

ACT TWO

SCENE I. *A hall in Angelo's house*

Enter ANGELO, ESCALUS, a JUSTICE, PROVOST, Officers, and other Attendants.

ANGELO We must not make a scarecrow of the law,
Setting it up to fear the birds of prey,
And let it keep one shape till custom make it
Their perch, and not their terror.

ESCALUS Ay, but yet
Let us be keen, and rather cut a little
Than fall and bruise to death. Alas! this gentleman,
Whom I would save, had a most noble father.
Let but your honour know,
Whom I believe to be most strait in virtue,
That, in the working of your own affections,
Had time coher'd with place, or place with wishing,
Or that the resolute acting of our blood
Could have attain'd th' effect of your own purpose,
Whether you had not sometime in your life
Err'd in this point which now you censure him,
And pull'd the law upon you.

ANGELO 'Tis one thing to be tempted, Escalus,
Another thing to fall. I not deny
The jury, passing on the prisoner's life,
May in the sworn twelve have a thief or two
Guiltier than him they try. What's open made to justice,
That justice seizes. What knows the laws
That thieves do pass on thieves? 'Tis very pregnant,
The jewel that we find, we stoop and take 't,
Because we see it; but what we do not see
We tread upon, and never think of it.
You may not so extenuate his offence
For I have had such faults; but rather tell me,
When I, that censure him, do so offend,
Let mine own judgment pattern out my death,
And nothing come in partial. Sir, he must die.

ESCALUS Be it as your wisdom will.

ANGELO Where is the Provost?

PROVOST Here, if it like your honour.

ANGELO See that Claudio
Be executed by nine to-morrow morning;
Bring him his confessor; let him be prepar'd;
For that's the utmost of his pilgrimage.

[*Exit Provost.*

ESCALUS [*Aside*] Well, heaven forgive him! and forgive us all!
Some rise by sin, and some by virtue fall;
Some run from breaks of ice, and answer none,
And some condemned for a fault alone.

Enter ELBOW and Officers with FROTH and POMPEY.

ELBOW Come, bring them away; if these be good people in a commonweal that do nothing but use their abuses in common houses, I know no law; bring them away.

ANGELO How now, sir! What's your name, and what's the matter?

ELBOW If it please your honour, I am the poor Duke's constable, and my name is Elbow; I do lean upon justice, sir, and do bring in here before your good honour two notorious benefactors.

ANGELO Benefactors! Well – what benefactors are they? Are they not malefactors?

ELBOW If it please your honour, I know not well what they are; but precise villains they are, that I am sure of, and void of all profanation in the world that good Christians ought to have.

ESCALUS This comes off well; here's a wise officer.

ANGELO Go to; what quality are they of? Elbow is your name? Why dost thou not speak, Elbow?

POMPEY He cannot, sir; he's out at elbow.

ANGELO What are you, sir?

ELBOW He, sir? A tapster, sir; parcel-bawd; one that serves a bad woman; whose house, sir, was, as they say, pluck'd down in the suburbs; and now she professes a hot-house, which, I think, is a very ill house too.

ESCALUS How know you that?

ELBOW My wife, sir, whom I detest before heaven and your honour –

ESCALUS How! thy wife!

ELBOW Ay, sir; whom, I thank heaven, is an honest woman –

ESCALUS Dost thou detest her therefore?

ELBOW I say, sir, I will detest myself also, as well as she, that this house, if it be not a bawd's house, it is pity of her life, for it is a naughty house.

ESCALUS How dost thou know that, constable?

ELBOW Marry, sir, by my wife; who, if she had been a woman cardinally given, might have been accus'd in fornication, adultery, and all uncleanliness there.

ESCALUS By the woman's means?

ELBOW Ay, sir, by Mistress Overdone's means; but as she spit in his face, so she defied him.

POMPEY Sir, if it please your honour, this is not so.

ELBOW Prove it before these varlets here, thou honourable man, prove it.

ESCALUS Do you hear how he misplaces?

POMPEY Sir, she came in great with child; and longing, saving your honour's reverence, for stew'd prunes. Sir, we had but two in the house, which at that very distant time stood, as it were, in a fruit dish, a dish of some three pence; your honours have seen such dishes; they are not China dishes, but very good dishes.

ESCALUS Go to, go to; no matter for the dish, sir.

POMPEY No, indeed, sir, not of a pin; you are therein in the right; but to the point. As I say, this Mistress Elbow, being, as I say, with child, and being great-bellied, and longing, as I said, for prunes; and having but two in the dish, as I said, Master Froth here, this very man, having eaten the rest, as I said, and, as I say, paying for them very honestly; for, as you know, Master Froth, I could not give you three pence again –

FROTH No, indeed.

POMPEY Very well; you being then, if you be rememb'red, cracking the stones of the foresaid prunes –

FROTH Ay, so I did indeed.

POMPEY Why, very well; I telling you then, if you be rememb'red, that such a one and such a one were past cure of the thing you wot of, unless they kept very good diet, as I told you –

FROTH All this is true.

POMPEY Why, very well then –

ESCALUS Come, you are a tedious fool. To the purpose: what was done to Elbow's wife that he hath cause to complain of? Come me to what was done to her.

POMPEY Sir, your honour cannot come to that yet.

ESCALUS No, sir, nor I mean it not.

POMPEY Sir, but you shall come to it, by your honour's leave. And, I beseech you, look into Master Froth here, sir, a man of fourscore pound a year; whose father died at Hallowmas – was't not at Hallowmas, Master Froth?

FROTH All-hallond eve.

POMPEY Why, very well; I hope here be truths. He, sir, sitting, as I say, in a lower chair, sir; 'twas in the Bunch of Grapes, where, indeed, you have a delight to sit, have you not?

FROTH I have so; because it is an open room, and good for winter.

POMPEY Why, very well then; I hope here be truths.

ANGELO This will last out a night in Russia,
When nights are longest there; I'll take my leave,
And leave you to the hearing of the cause,
Hoping you'll find good cause to whip them all.

ESCALUS I think no less. Good morrow to your lordship.

[*Exit Angelo.*

Now, sir, come on; what was done to Elbow's wife, once more?

POMPEY Once? – sir. There was nothing done to her once.

ELBOW I beseech you, sir, ask him what this man did to my wife.

POMPEY I beseech your honour, ask me.

ESCALUS Well, sir, what did this gentleman to her?

POMPEY I beseech you, sir, look in this gentleman's face. Good Master Froth, look upon his honour; 'tis for a good purpose. Doth your honour mark his face?

ESCALUS Ay, sir, very well.

POMPEY Nay, I beseech you, mark it well.

ESCALUS Well, I do so.

POMPEY Doth your honour see any harm in his face?

ESCALUS Why, no.

POMPEY I'll be suppos'd upon a book his face is the worst thing about him. Good then; if his face be the worst thing about him, how could Master Froth do the constable's wife any harm? I would know that of your honour.

ESCALUS He's in the right, constable; what say you to it?

ELBOW First, an it like you, the house is a respected house; next, this is a respected fellow; and his mistress is a respected woman.

POMPEY By this hand, sir, his wife is a more respected person than any of us all.

ELBOW Varlet, thou liest; thou liest, wicked varlet; the time is yet to come that she was ever respected with man, woman, or child.

POMPEY Sir, she was respected with him before he married with her.

ESCALUS Which is the wiser here, Justice or Iniquity? Is this true?

ELBOW O thou caitiff! O thou varlet! O thou wicked Hannibal! I respected with her before I was married to her! If ever I was respected with her, or she with me, let not your worship think me the poor Duke's officer. Prove this, thou wicked Hannibal, or I'll have mine action of batt'ry on thee.

ESCALUS If he took you a box o' th' ear, you might have your action of slander too.

ELBOW Marry, I thank your good worship for it. What is't your worship's pleasure I shall do with this wicked caitiff?

ESCALUS Truly, officer, because he hath some offences in him that thou wouldst discover if thou couldst, let him continue in his courses till thou know'st what they are.

ELBOW Marry, I thank your worship for it. Thou seest, thou wicked varlet, now, what's come upon thee: thou art to continue now, thou varlet; thou art to continue.

ESCALUS Where were you born, friend?

FROTH Here in Vienna, sir.

ESCALUS Are you of fourscore pounds a year?

FROTH Yes, an't please you, sir.

ESCALUS So. What trade are you of, sir?

POMPEY A tapster, a poor widow's tapster.

ESCALUS Your mistress' name?

POMPEY Mistress Overdone.

ESCALUS Hath she had any more than one husband?

POMPEY Nine, sir; Overdone by the last.

ESCALUS Nine! Come hither to me, Master Froth. Master Froth, I would not have you acquainted with tapsters: they will draw you, Master Froth, and you will hang them. Get you gone, and let me hear no more of you.

FROTH I thank your worship. For mine own part, I never come into any room in a taphouse but I am drawn in.

ESCALUS Well, no more of it, Master Froth; farewell. [*Exit Froth*] Come you hither to me, Master Tapster; what's your name, Master Tapster?

POMPEY Pompey.

ESCALUS What else?

POMPEY Bum, sir.

ESCALUS Troth, and your bum is the greatest thing about you; so that, in the beastliest sense, you are Pompey the Great. Pompey, you are partly a bawd, Pompey, howsoever you colour it in being a tapster. Are you not? Come, tell me true; it shall be the better for you.

POMPEY Truly, sir, I am a poor fellow that would live.

ESCALUS How would you live, Pompey – by being a bawd? What do you think of the trade, Pompey? Is it a lawful trade?

POMPEY If the law would allow it, sir.

ESCALUS But the law will not allow it, Pompey; nor it shall not be allowed in Vienna.

POMPEY Does your worship mean to geld and splay all the youth of the city?

ESCALUS No, Pompey.

POMPEY Truly, sir, in my poor opinion, they will to't then. If your worship will take order for the drabs and the knaves, you need not to fear the bawds.

ESCALUS There is pretty orders beginning, I can tell you: it is but heading and hanging.

POMPEY If you head and hang all that offend that way but for ten year together, you'll be glad to give out a commission for more heads; if this law hold in Vienna ten year, I'll rent the fairest house in it, after threepence a bay. If you live to see this come to pass, say Pompey told you so.

ESCALUS Thank you, good Pompey; and, in requital of your prophecy, hark you: I advise you, let me not find you before me again upon any complaint whatsoever – no, not for dwelling where you do; if I do, Pompey, I shall beat you to your tent, and prove a shrewd Caesar to you; in plain dealing, Pompey, I shall have you whipt. So for this time, Pompey, fare you well.

POMPEY I thank your worship for your good counsel; [*Aside*] but I shall follow it as the flesh and fortune shall better determine.
Whip me? No, no; let carman whip his jade;
The valiant heart's not whipt out of his trade.
[*Exit.*

ESCALUS Come hither to me, Master Elbow; come hither, Master Constable. How long have you been in this place of constable?

ELBOW Seven year and a half, sir.

ESCALUS I thought, by the readiness in the office, you had continued in it some time. You say seven years together?

ELBOW And a half, sir.

ESCALUS Alas, it hath been great pains to you! They do you wrong to put you so oft upon't. Are there not men in your ward sufficient to serve it?

ELBOW Faith, sir, few of any wit in such matters; as they are chosen, they are glad to choose me for them; I do it for some piece of money, and go through with all.

ESCALUS Look you, bring me in the names of some six or seven, the most sufficient of your parish.

ELBOW To your worship's house, sir?

ESCALUS To my house. Fare you well. [*Exit Elbow*] What's o'clock, think you?

JUSTICE Eleven sir.

ESCALUS I pray you home to dinner with me.

JUSTICE I humbly thank you.

ESCALUS It grieves me for the death of Claudio;
But there's no remedy.

JUSTICE Lord Angelo is severe.
ESCALUS It is but needful:
Mercy is not itself that oft looks so;
Pardon is still the nurse of second woe.
But yet, poor Claudio! There is no remedy.
Come, sir. *[Exeunt.*

SCENE II. *Another room in Angelo's house.*

Enter PROVOST and a Servant.

SERVANT He's hearing of a cause; he will come straight.
I'll tell him of you.
PROVOST Pray you do. *[Exit Servant*
I'll know
His pleasure; may be he will relent. Alas,
He hath but as offended in a dream!
All sects, all ages, smack of this vice; and he
To die for 't!

Enter ANGELO.

ANGELO Now, what's the matter, Provost?
PROVOST Is it your will Claudio shall die to-morrow?
ANGELO Did not I tell thee yea? Hadst thou not order?
Why dost thou ask again?
PROVOST Lest I might be too rash;
Under your good correction, I have seen
When, after execution, judgment hath
Repented o'er his doom.
ANGELO Go to; let that be mine.
Do you your office, or give up your place,
And you shall well be spar'd.
PROVOST I crave your honour's pardon.
What shall be done, sir, with the groaning Juliet?
She's very near her hour.
ANGELO Dispose of her
To some more fitter place, and that with speed.

Re-enter Servant.

SERVANT Here is the sister of the man condemn'd
Desires access to you.
ANGELO Hath he a sister?
PROVOST Ay, my good lord; a very virtuous maid,
And to be shortly of a sisterhood,
If not already.
ANGELO Well, let her be admitted.
[Exit Servant.
See you the fornicatress be remov'd;
Let her have needful but not lavish means;
There shall be order for't.

Enter LUCIO and ISABELLA.

PROVOST *[Going]* Save your honour!
ANGELO Stay a little while. *[To Isabella]*
Y'are welcome; what's your will?
ISABELLA I am a woeful suitor to your honour,
Please but your honour hear me.
ANGELO Well; what's your suit?
ISABELLA There is a vice that most I do abhor,
And most desire should meet the blow of justice;
For which I would not plead, but that I must;
For which I must not plead, but that I am
At war 'twixt will and will not.
ANGELO Well; the matter?
ISABELLA I have a brother is condemn'd to die;
I do beseech you, let it be his fault,
And not my brother.
PROVOST *[Aside]* Heaven give thee moving graces!
ANGELO Condemn the fault and not the actor of it!
Why, every fault 's condemn'd ere it be done;
Mine were the very cipher of a function,
To fine the faults whose fine stands in record,
And let go by the actor.
ISABELLA O just but severe law!
I had a brother, then. Heaven keep your honour!
LUCIO *[To Isabella]* Give't not o'er so; to him again, entreat him,
Kneel down before him, hang upon his gown;
You are too cold: if you should need a pin,
You could not with more tame a tongue desire it.
To him, I say.
ISABELLA Must he needs die?
ANGELO Maiden, no remedy.
ISABELLA Yes; I do think that you might pardon him,
And neither heaven nor man grieve at the mercy.
ANGELO I will not do't.
ISABELLA But can you, if you would?
ANGELO Look, what I will not, that I cannot do.
ISABELLA But might you do't, and do the world no wrong,
If so your heart were touch'd with that remorse
As mine is to him?
ANGELO He's sentenc'd; 'tis too late.
LUCIO *[To Isabella]* You are too cold.
ISABELLA Too late? Why, no; I, that do speak a word,
May call it back again. Well, believe this:
No ceremony that to great ones longs,
Not the king's crown nor the deputed sword,
The marshal's truncheon nor the judge's robe,
Become them with one half so good a grace
As mercy does.

If he had been as you, and you as he,
You would have slipp'd like him; but he, like you,
Would not have been so stern.

ANGELO Pray you be gone.

ISABELLA I would to heaven I had your potency,
And you were Isabel! Should it then be thus?
No; I would tell what 'twere to be a judge
And what a prisoner.

LUCIO [*To Isabella*] Ay, touch him; there's the vein.

ANGELO Your brother is a forfeit of the law,
And you but waste your words.

ISABELLA Alas! alas!
Why, all the souls that were were forfeit once;
And He that might the vantage best have took
Found out the remedy. How would you be
If He, which is the top of judgement, should
But judge you as you are? O, think on that;
And mercy then will breathe within your lips,
Like man new made.

ANGELO Be you content, fair maid.
It is the law, not I condemn your brother.
Were he my kinsman, brother, or my son,
It should be thus with him. He must die to-morrow.

ISABELLA To-morrow! O, that's sudden! Spare him, spare him.
He's not prepar'd for death. Even for our kitchens
We kill the fowl of season; shall we serve heaven
With less respect than we do minister
To our gross selves? Good, good my lord, bethink you.
Who is it that hath died for this offence?
There's many have committed it.

LUCIO [*Aside*] Ay, well said.

ANGELO The law hath not been dead, though it hath slept.
Those many had not dar'd to do that evil
If the first that did th' edict infringe
Had answer'd for his deed. Now 'tis awake,
Takes note of what is done, and, like a prophet,
Looks in a glass that shows what future evils –
Either now or by remissness new conceiv'd,
And so in progress to be hatch'd and born –
Are now to have no successive degrees,
But here they live to end.

ISABELLA Yet show some pity.

ANGELO I show it most of all when I show justice;
For then I pity those I do not know,
Which a dismiss'd offence would after gall,
And do him right that, answering one foul wrong,
Lives not to act another. Be satisfied;
Your brother dies to-morrow; be content.

ISABELLA So you must be the first that gives this sentence,
And he that suffers. O, it is excellent
To have a giant's strength! But it is tyrannous
To use it like a giant.

LUCIO [*To Isabella*] That's well said.

ISABELLA Could great men thunder
As Jove himself does, Jove would never be quiet,
For every pelting petty officer
Would use his heaven for thunder,
Nothing but thunder. Merciful Heaven,
Thou rather, with thy sharp and sulphurous bolt,
Splits the unwedgeable and gnarled oak
Than the soft myrtle. But man, proud man,
Dress'd in a little brief authority,
Most ignorant of what he's most assur'd,
His glassy essence, like an angry ape,
Plays such fantastic tricks before high heaven
As makes the angels weep; who, with our spleens,
Would all themselves laugh mortal.

LUCIO [*To Isabella*] O, to him, to him, wench! He will relent;
He's coming; I perceive 't.

PROVOST [*Aside*] Pray heaven she win him.

ISABELLA We cannot weigh our brother with ourself.
Great men may jest with saints: 'tis wit in them;
But in the less foul profanation.

LUCIO [*To Isabella*] Thou'rt i' th' right, girl; more o' that.

ISABELLA That in the captain's but a choleric word
Which in the soldier is flat blasphemy.

LUCIO [*To Isabella*] Art avis'd o' that? More on't.

ANGELO Why do you put these sayings upon me?

ISABELLA Because authority, though it err like others,
Hath yet a kind of medicine in itself
That skins the vice o' th' top. Go to your bosom,
Knock there, and ask your heart what it doth know
That's like my brother's fault. If it confess
A natural guiltiness such as is his,
Let it not sound a thought upon your tongue
Against my brother's life.

ANGELO [*Aside*] She speaks, and 'tis
Such sense that my sense breeds with it. –
Fare you well.

ISABELLA Gentle my lord, turn back.

ANGELO I will bethink me. Come again tomorrow.

ISABELLA Hark how I'll bribe you; good, my lord, turn back.
ANGELO How, bribe me?
ISABELLA Ay, with such gifts that heaven shall share with you.
LUCIO [*To Isabella*] You had marr'd all else.
ISABELLA Not with fond sicles of the tested gold,
Or stones, whose rate are either rich or poor
As fancy values them; but with true prayers
That shall be up at heaven and enter there
Ere sun-rise, prayers from preserved souls,
From fasting maids, whose minds are dedicate
To nothing temporal.
ANGELO Well; come to me to-morrow.
LUCIO [*To Isabella*] Go to; 'tis well; away.
ISABELLA Heaven keep your honour safe!
ANGELO [*Aside*] Amen; for I
Am that way going to temptation
Where prayers cross.
ISABELLA At what hour to-morrow
Shall I attend your lordship?
ANGELO At any time 'fore noon.
ISABELLA Save your honour!

[*Exeunt all but Angelo.*

ANGELO From thee; even from thy virtue!
What's this, what's this? Is this her fault or mine?
The tempter or the tempted, who sins most?
Ha!
Not she; nor doth she tempt; but it is I
That, lying by the violet in the sun,
Do as the carrion does, not as the flow'r,
Corrupt with virtuous season. Can it be
That modesty may more betray our sense
Than woman's lightness? Having waste ground enough,
Shall we desire to raze the sanctuary,
And pitch our evils there? O, fie, fie, fie!
What dost thou, or what art thou, Angelo?
Dost thou desire her foully for those things
That make her good? O, let her brother live!
Thieves for their robbery have authority
When judges steal themselves. What, do I love her,
That I desire to hear her speak again,
And feast upon her eyes? What is't I dream on?
O cunning enemy, that, to catch a saint,
With saints dost bait thy hook! Most dangerous
Is that temptation that doth goad us on
To sin in loving virtue. Never could the strumpet,
With all her double vigour, art and nature,
Once stir my temper; but this virtuous maid
Subdues me quite. Ever till now,
When men were fond, I smil'd and wond'red how.

[*Exit.*

SCENE III. *A prison.*

Enter, severally, DUKE, disguised as a Friar, and PROVOST.

DUKE Hail to you, Provost! so I think you are.
PROVOST I am the Provost. What's your will, good friar?
DUKE Bound by my charity and my blest order,
I come to visit the afflicted spirits
Here in the prison. Do me the common right
To let me see them, and to make me know
The nature of their crimes, that I may minister
To them accordingly.
PROVOST I would do more than that, if more were needful.

Enter JULIET.

Look, here comes one; a gentlewoman of mine,
Who, falling in the flaws of her own youth,
Hath blister'd her report. She is with child;
And he that got it, sentenc'd – a young man
More fit to do another such offence
Than die for this.
DUKE When must he die?
PROVOST As I do think, to-morrow.
[*To Juliet*] I have provided for you; stay awhile
And you shall be conducted.
DUKE Repent you, fair one, of the sin you carry?
JULIET I do; and bear the shame most patiently.
DUKE I'll teach you how you shall arraign your conscience,
And try your penitence, if it be sound
Or hollowly put on.
JULIET I'll gladly learn.
DUKE Love you the man that wrong'd you?
JULIET Yes, as I love the woman that wrong'd him.
DUKE So then, it seems, your most offenceful act
Was mutually committed.
JULIET Mutually.
DUKE Then was your sin of heavier kind than his.
JULIET I do confess it, and repent it, father.
DUKE 'Tis meet so, daughter; but lest you do repent
As that the sin hath brought you to this shame,
Which sorrow is always toward ourselves, not heaven,
Showing we would not spare heaven as we love it,
But as we stand in fear –
JULIET I do repent me as it is an evil,
And take the shame with joy.
DUKE There rest.
Your partner, as I hear, must die to-morrow,
And I am going with instruction to him.
Grace go with you! Benedicite! [*Exit.*
JULIET Must die to-morrow! O, injurious law,

That respites me a life whose very comfort
Is still a dying horror!

PROVOST 'Tis pity of him. [*Exeunt.*

SCENE IV. *Angelo's house.*

Enter ANGELO.

ANGELO When I would pray and think, I think and pray
To several subjects. Heaven hath my empty words,
Whilst my invention, hearing not my tongue,
Anchors on Isabel. Heaven in my mouth,
As if I did but only chew his name,
And in my heart the strong and swelling evil
Of my conception. The state whereon I studied
Is, like a good thing being often read,
Grown sere and tedious; yea, my gravity,
Wherein – let no man hear me – I take pride,
Could I with boot change for an idle plume
Which the air beats for vain. O place, O form,
How often dost thou with thy case, thy habit,
Wrench awe from fools, and tie the wiser souls
To thy false seeming! Blood, thou art blood.
Let's write 'good angel' on the devil's horn;
'Tis not the devil's crest.

Enter Servant.

How now, who's there?

SERVANT One Isabel, a sister, desires access to you.

ANGELO Teach her the way. [*Exit Servant*] O heavens!
Why does my blood thus muster to my heart,
Making both it unable for itself
And dispossessing all my other parts
Of necessary fitness?
So play the foolish throngs with one that swoons;
Come all to help him, and so stop the air
By which he should revive; and even so
The general subject to a well-wish'd king
Quit their own part, and in obsequious fondness
Crowd to his presence, where their untaught love
Must needs appear offence.

Enter ISABELLA.

How now, fair maid?

ISABELLA I am come to know your pleasure.

ANGELO That you might know it would much better please me
Than to demand what 'tis. Your brother cannot live.

ISABELLA Even so! Heaven keep your honour!

ANGELO Yet may he live awhile, and, it may be,
As long as you or I; yet he must die.

ISABELLA Under your sentence?

ANGELO Yea.

ISABELLA When? I beseech you; that in his reprieve,
Longer or shorter, he may be so fitted
That his soul sicken not.

ANGELO Ha! Fie, these filthy vices! It were as good
To pardon him that hath from nature stol'n
A man already made, as to remit
Their saucy sweetness that do coin heaven's image
In stamps that are forbid; 'tis all as easy
Falsely to take away a life true made
As to put metal in restrained means
To make a false one.

ISABELLA 'Tis set down so in heaven, but not in earth.

ANGELO Say you so? Then I shall pose you quickly.
Which had you rather – that the most just law
Now took your brother's life; or, to redeem him,
Give up your body to such sweet uncleanness
As she that he hath stain'd?

ISABELLA Sir, believe this:
I had rather give my body than my soul.

ANGELO I talk not of your soul; our compell'd sins
Stand more for number than for accompt.

ISABELLA How say you?

ANGELO Nay, I'll not warrant that; for I can speak
Against the thing I say. Answer to this:
I, now the voice of the recorded law,
Pronounce a sentence on your brother's life;
Might there not be a charity in sin
To save this brother's life?

ISABELLA Please you to do't,
I'll take it as a peril to my soul
It is no sin at all, but charity.

ANGELO Pleas'd you to do't at peril of your soul,
Were equal poise of sin and charity.

ISABELLA That I do beg his life, if it be sin,
Heaven let me bear it! You granting of my suit,
If that be sin, I'll make it my morn prayer
To have it added to the faults of mine,
And nothing of your answer.

ANGELO Nay, but hear me;
Your sense pursues not mine; either you are ignorant
Or seem so, craftily; and that's not good.

ISABELLA Let me be ignorant, and in nothing good
But graciously to know I am no better.

ANGELO Thus wisdom wishes to appear most bright

When it doth tax itself; as these black masks
Proclaim an enshielded beauty ten times louder
Than beauty could, display'd. But mark me:
To be received plain, I'll speak more gross –
Your brother is to die.

ISABELLA So.

ANGELO And his offence is so, as it appears,
Accountant to the law upon that pain.

ISABELLA True.

ANGELO Admit no other way to save his life,
As I subscribe not that, nor any other,
But, in the loss of question, that you, his sister,
Finding yourself desir'd of such a person
Whose credit with the judge, or own great place,
Could fetch your brother from the manacles
Of the all-binding law; and that there were
No earthly mean to save him but that either
You must lay down the treasures of your body
To this supposed, or else to let him suffer –
What would you do?

ISABELLA As much for my poor brother as myself;
That is, were I under the terms of death,
Th' impression of keen whips I'd wear as rubies,
And strip myself to death as to a bed
That longing have been sick for, ere I'd yield
My body up to shame.

ANGELO Then must your brother die.

ISABELLA And 'twere the cheaper way:
Better it were a brother died at once
Than that a sister, by redeeming him,
Should die for ever.

ANGELO Were not you, then, as cruel as the sentence
That you have slander'd so?

ISABELLA Ignominy in ransom and free pardon
Are of two houses: lawful mercy
Is nothing kin to foul redemption.

ANGELO You seem'd of late to make the law a tyrant;
And rather prov'd the sliding of your brother
A merriment than a vice.

ISABELLA O, pardon me, my lord! It oft falls out,
To have what we would have, we speak not what we mean:
I something do excuse the thing I hate
For his advantage that I dearly love.

ANGELO We are all frail.

ISABELLA Else let my brother die,
If not a fedary but only he
Owe and succeed thy weakness.

ANGELO Nay, women are frail too.

ISABELLA Ay, as the glasses where they view themselves,
Which are as easy broke as they make forms.
Women, help heaven! Men their creation mar
In profiting by them. Nay, call us ten times frail;
For we are soft as our complexions are,
And credulous to false prints.

ANGELO I think it well;
And from this testimony of your own sex,
Since I suppose we are made to be no stronger
Than faults may shake our frames, let me be bold.
I do arrest your words. Be that you are,
That is, a woman; if you be more, you're none;
If you be one, as you are well express'd
By all external warrants, show it now
By putting on the destin'd livery.

ISABELLA I have no tongue but one; gentle, my lord,
Let me intreat you speak the former language.

ANGELO Plainly conceive, I love you.

ISABELLA My brother did love Juliet,
And you tell me that he shall die for't.

ANGELO He shall not, Isabel, if you give me love.

ISABELLA I know your virtue hath a license in't,
Which seems a little fouler than it is,
To pluck on others.

ANGELO Believe me, on mine honour,
My words express my purpose.

ISABELLA Ha! little honour to be much believ'd,
And most pernicious purpose! Seeming, seeming!
I will proclaim thee, Angelo, look for't.
Sign me a present pardon for my brother
Or, with an outstretch'd throat, I'll tell the world aloud
What man thou art.

ANGELO Who will believe thee, Isabel?
My unsoil'd name, th' austereness of my life,
My vouch against you, and my place i' th' state,
Will so your accusation overweigh
That you shall stifle in your own report,
And smell of calumny. I have begun,
And now I give my sensual race the rein:
Fit thy consent to my sharp appetite;
Lay by all nicety and prolixious blushes
That banish what they sue for; redeem thy brother
By yielding up thy body to my will;
Or else he must not only die the death,
But thy unkindness shall his death draw out
To ling'ring sufferance. Answer me to-morrow,
Or, by the affection that now guides me most,
I'll prove a tyrant to him. As for you,
Say what you can: my false o'erweighs your true.

[*Exit.*

ISABELLA To whom should I complain? Did I tell this,
Who would believe me? O perilous mouths
That bear in them one and the self-same tongue

Either of condemnation or approof,
Bidding the law make curtsy to their will;
Hooking both right and wrong to th' appetite,
To follow as it draws! I'll to my brother.
Though he hath fall'n by prompture of the blood,
Yet hath he in him such a mind of honour
That, had he twenty heads to tender down
On twenty bloody blocks, he'd yield them up
Before his sister should her body stoop
To such abhorr'd pollution.
Then, Isabel, live chaste, and, brother, die:
More than our brother is our chastity.
I'll tell him yet of Angelo's request,
And fit his mind to death, for his soul's rest.
[Exit.

ACT THREE

SCENE I. *The prison.*

Enter DUKE, disguised as before, CLAUDIO, and PROVOST.

DUKE So, then you hope of pardon from Lord Angelo?

CLAUDIO The miserable have no other medicine
But only hope:
I have hope to live, and am prepar'd to die.

DUKE Be absolute for death; either death or life
Shall thereby be the sweeter. Reason thus with life.
If I do lose thee, I do lose a thing
That none but fools would keep. A breath thou art,
Servile to all the skyey influences,
That dost this habitation where thou keep'st
Hourly afflict. Merely, thou art Death's fool;
For him thou labour'st by thy flight to shun
And yet run'st toward him still. Thou art not noble;
For all th' accommodations that thou bear'st
Are nurs'd by baseness. Thou 'rt by no means valiant;
For thou dost fear the soft and tender fork
Of a poor worm. Thy best of rest is sleep,
And that thou oft provok'st; yet grossly fear'st
Thy death, which is no more. Thou art not thyself;
For thou exists on many a thousand grains
That issue out of dust. Happy thou art not;
For what thou hast not, still thou striv'st to get,
And what thou hast, forget'st. Thou art not certain;
For thy complexion shifts to strange effects,
After the moon. If thou art rich, thou'rt poor;
For, like an ass whose back with ingots bows,
Thou bear'st thy heavy riches but a journey,
And Death unloads thee. Friend hast thou none;
For thine own bowels which do call thee sire,
The mere effusion of thy proper loins,
Do curse the gout, serpigo, and the rheum,
For ending thee no sooner. Thou hast nor youth nor age,
But, as it were, an after-dinner's sleep,
Dreaming on both; for all thy blessed youth
Becomes as aged, and doth beg the alms
Of palsied eld; and when thou art old and rich,
Thou hast neither heat, affection, limb, nor beauty,
To make thy riches pleasant. What's yet in this
That bears the name of life? Yet in this life
Lie hid moe thousand deaths; yet death we fear,
That makes these odds all even.

CLAUDIO I humbly thank you.
To sue to live, I find I seek to die;
And, seeking death, find life. Let it come on.

ISABELLA *[Within]* What, ho! Peace here; grace and good company!

PROVOST Who's there? Come in; the wish deserves a welcome.

DUKE Dear sir, ere long I'll visit you again.

CLAUDIO Most holy sir, I thank you.

Enter ISABELLA.

ISABELLA My business is a word or two with Claudio.

PROVOST And very welcome. Look, signior, here's your sister.

DUKE Provost, a word with you.

PROVOST As many as you please.

DUKE Bring me to hear them speak, where I may be conceal'd. *[Exeunt Duke and Provost.*

CLAUDIO Now, sister, what's the comfort?

ISABELLA Why,
As all comforts are; most good, most good, indeed.
Lord Angelo, having affairs to heaven,
Intends you for his swift ambassador,
Where you shall be an everlasting leiger.
Therefore, your best appointment make with speed;
To-morrow you set on.

CLAUDIO Is there no remedy?

ISABELLA None, but such remedy as, to save a head,
To cleave a heart in twain.

CLAUDIO But is there any?

ISABELLA Yes, brother, you may live:
There is a devilish mercy in the judge,
If you'll implore it, that will free your life,
But fetter you till death.
CLAUDIO Perpetual durance?
ISABELLA Ay, just; perpetual durance, a restraint,
Though all the world's vastidity you had,
To a determin'd scope.
CLAUDIO But in what nature?
ISABELLA In such a one as, you consenting to't,
Would bark your honour from that trunk you bear,
And leave you naked.
CLAUDIO Let me know the point.
ISABELLA O, I do fear thee, Claudio; and I quake,
Lest thou a feverous life shouldst entertain,
And six or seven winters more respect
Than a perpetual honour. Dar'st thou die?
The sense of death is most in apprehension;
And the poor beetle that we tread upon
In corporal sufferance finds a pang as great
As when a giant dies.
CLAUDIO Why give you me this shame?
Think you I can a resolution fetch
From flow'ry tenderness? If I must die,
I will encounter darkness as a bride
And hug it in mine arms.
ISABELLA There spake my brother; there my father's grave
Did utter forth a voice. Yes, thou must die:
Thou art too noble to conserve a life
In base appliances. This outward-sainted deputy,
Whose settled visage and deliberate word
Nips youth i' th' head, and follies doth enew
As falcon doth the fowl, is yet a devil;
His filth within being cast, he would appear
A pond as deep as hell.
CLAUDIO The precise Angelo!
ISABELLA O, 'tis the cunning livery of hell
The damned'st body to invest and cover
In precise guards! Dost thou think, Claudio,
If I would yield him my virginity
Thou mightst be freed?
CLAUDIO O heavens ! it cannot be.
ISABELLA Yes, he would give't thee, from this rank offence,
So to offend him still. This night's the time
That I should do what I abhor to name,
Or else thou diest to-morrow.
CLAUDIO Thou shalt not do't.
ISABELLA O, were it but my life!
I'd throw it down for your deliverance
As frankly as a pin.
CLAUDIO Thanks, dear Isabel.
ISABELLA Be ready, Claudio, for your death to-morrow.
CLAUDIO Yes. Has he affections in him
That thus can make him bite the law by th' nose
When he would force it? Sure it is no sin;
Or of the deadly seven it is the least.
ISABELLA Which is the least?
CLAUDIO If it were damnable, he being so wise,
Why would he for the momentary trick
Be perdurably fin'd? – O Isabel!
ISABELLA What says my brother?
CLAUDIO Death is a fearful thing.
ISABELLA And shamed life a hateful.
CLAUDIO Ay, but to die, and go we know not where;
To lie in cold obstruction, and to rot;
This sensible warm motion to become
A kneaded clod; and the delighted spirit
To bathe in fiery floods or to reside
In thrilling region of thick-ribbed ice;
To be imprison'd in the viewless winds,
And blown with restless violence round about
The pendent world; or to be worse than worst
Of those that lawless and incertain thought
Imagine howling – 'tis too horrible.
The weariest and most loathed worldly life
That age, ache, penury, and imprisonment,
Can lay on nature is a paradise
To what we fear of death.
ISADELLA Alas, alas!
CLAUDIO Sweet sister, let me live.
What sin you do to save a brother's life,
Nature dispenses with the deed so far
That it becomes a virtue.
ISABELLA O you beast!
O faithless coward! O dishonest wretch!
Wilt thou be made a man out of my vice?
Is't not a kind of incest to take life
From thine own sister's shame? What should I think?
Heaven shield my mother play'd my father fair!
For such a warped slip of wilderness
Ne'er issu'd from his blood. Take my defiance;
Die; perish. Might but my bending down
Reprieve thee from thy fate, it should proceed.
I'll pray a thousand prayers for thy death,
No word to save thee.
CLAUDIO Nay, hear me, Isabel.
ISABELLA O fie, fie, fie!
Thy sin's not accidental, but a trade.
Mercy to thee would prove itself a bawd;
'Tis best that thou diest quickly.
CLAUDIO O hear me, Isabella.

Re-enter DUKE.

DUKE Vouchsafe a word, young sister, but one word.
ISABELLA What is your will?
DUKE Might you dispense with your leisure, I

would by and by have some speech with you; the satisfaction I would require is likewise your own benefit.

ISABELLA I have no superfluous leisure; my stay must be stolen out of other affairs; but I will attend you awhile. [*Walks apart.*

DUKE Son, I have overheard what hath pass'd between you and your sister. Angelo had never the purpose to corrupt her; only he hath made an assay of her virtue to practise his judgment with the disposition of natures. She, having the truth of honour in her, hath made him that gracious denial which he is most glad to receive. I am confessor to Angelo, and I know this to be true; therefore prepare yourself to death. Do not satisfy your resolution with hopes that are fallible; to-morrow you must die; go to your knees and made ready.

CLAUDIO Let me ask my sister pardon. I am so out of love with life that I will sue to be rid of it.

DUKE Hold you there. Farewell. [*Exit Claudio*] Provost, a word with you.

Re-enter PROVOST.

PROVOST What's your will, father?

DUKE That, now you are come, you will be gone. Leave me a while with the maid; my mind promises with my habit no loss shall touch her by my company.

PROVOST In good time. [*Exit Provost.*

DUKE The hand that hath made you fair hath made you good; the goodness that is cheap in beauty makes beauty brief in goodness; but grace, being the soul of your complexion, shall keep the body of it ever fair. The assault that Angelo hath made to you, fortune hath convey'd to my understanding; and, but that frailty hath examples for his falling, I should wonder at Angelo. How will you do to content this substitute, and to save your brother?

ISABELLA I am now going to resolve him; I had rather my brother die by the law than my son should be unlawfully born. But, O, how much is the good Duke deceiv'd in Angelo! If ever he return, and I can speak to him, I will open my lips in vain, or discover his government.

DUKE That shall not be much amiss; yet, as the matter now stands, he will avoid your accusation: he made trial of you only. Therefore fasten your ear on my advisings; to the love I have in doing good a remedy presents itself. I do make myself believe that you may most uprighteously do a poor wronged lady a merited benefit; redeem your brother from the angry law; do no stain to your own gracious person; and much please the absent Duke, if peradventure he shall ever return to have hearing of this business.

ISABELLA Let me hear you speak farther; I have spirit to do anything that appears not foul in the truth of my spirit.

DUKE Virtue is bold, and goodness never fearful. Have you not heard speak of Mariana, the sister of Frederick, the great soldier who miscarried at sea?

ISABELLA I have heard of the lady, and good words went with her name.

DUKE She should this Angelo have married; was affianced to her by oath, and the nuptial appointed; between which time of the contract and limit of the solemnity her brother Frederick was wreck'd at sea, having in that perished vessel the dowry of his sister. But mark how heavily this befell to the poor gentlewoman: there she lost a noble and renowned brother, in his love toward her ever most kind and natural; with him the portion and sinew of her fortune, her marriage-dowry; with both, her combinate husband, this well-seeming Angelo.

ISABELLA Can this be so? Did Angelo so leave her?

DUKE Left her in her tears, and dried not one of them with his comfort; swallowed his vows whole, pretending in her discoveries of dishonour; in few, bestow'd her on her own lamentation, which she yet wears for his sake; and he, a marble to her tears, is washed with them, but relents not.

ISABELLA What a merit were it in death to take this poor maid from the world! What corruption in this life that it will let this man live! But how out of this can she avail?

DUKE It is a rupture that you may easily heal; and the cure of it not only saves your brother, but keeps you from dishonour in doing it.

ISABELLA Show me how, good father.

DUKE This forenamed maid hath yet in her the continuance of her first affection; his unjust unkindness, that in all reason should have quenched her love, hath, like an impediment in the current, made it more violent and unruly. Go you to Angelo; answer his requiring with a plausible obedience; agree with his demands to the point; only refer yourself to this advantage: first, that your stay with him may not be long; that the time may have all shadow and silence in it; and the place answer to convenience. This being granted in course – and now follows all: we shall advise this wronged maid to stead up your appointment, go in your place. If the encounter acknowledge itself hereafter, it may compel him to her recompense; and here, by this, is your brother saved, your honour untainted, the poor Mariana advantaged, and the corrupt deputy scaled. The maid will I frame and make fit for his attempt. If you think well to carry this as you may, the doubleness of the benefit defends the deceit from reproof. What think you of it?

ISABELLA The image of it gives me content already; and I trust it will grow to a most prosperous perfection.

DUKE It lies much in your holding up. Haste you speedily to Angelo; if for this night he entreat you to his bed, give him promise of satisfaction. I will presently to Saint Luke's; there, at the moated grange, resides this dejected Mariana. At that place call upon me; and dispatch with Angelo, that it may be quickly.

ISABELLA I thank you for this comfort. Fare you well, good father. [*Exeunt severally.*

SCENE II. *The street before the prison.*

Enter, on one side, DUKE disguised as before; on the other, ELBOW, and Officers with POMPEY.

ELBOW Nay, if there be no remedy for it, but that you will needs buy and sell men and women like beasts, we shall have all the world drink brown and white bastard.

DUKE O heavens! what stuff is here?

POMPEY 'Twas never merry world since, of two usuries, the merriest was put down, and the worser allow'd by order of law a furr'd gown to keep him warm; and furr'd with fox on lamb-skins too, to signify that craft, being richer than innocency, stands for the facing.

ELBOW Come your way, sir. Bless you, good father friar.

DUKE And you, good brother father.
What offence hath this man made you, sir?

ELBOW Marry, sir, he hath offended the law; and, sir, we take him to be a thief too, sir, for we have found upon him, sir, a strange picklock, which we have sent to the deputy.

DUKE Fie, sirrah, a bawd, a wicked bawd!
The evil that thou causest to be done,
That is thy means to live. Do thou but think
What 'tis to cram a maw or clothe a back
From such a filthy vice; say to thyself
'From their abominable and beastly touches I
drink, I eat, array myself, and live'.
Canst thou believe thy living is a life,
So stinkingly depending? Go mend, go mend.

POMPEY Indeed, it does stink in some sort, sir; but yet, sir, I would prove –

DUKE Nay, if the devil have given thee proofs for sin,
Thou wilt prove his. Take him to prison, officer;
Correction and instruction must both work
Ere this rude beast will profit.

ELBOW He must before the deputy, sir; he has given him warning. The deputy cannot abide a whoremaster; if he be a whoremonger, and comes before him, he were as good go a mile on his errand.

DUKE That we were all, as some would seem to be,
From our faults, as his faults from seeming, free.

ELBOW His neck will come to your waist – a cord, sir.

Enter LUCIO.

POMPEY I spy comfort; I cry bail. Here's a gentleman, and a friend of mine.

LUCIO How now, noble Pompey! What, at the wheels of Caesar? Art thou led in triumph? What, is there none of Pygmalion's images, newly made woman, to be had now for putting the hand in the pocket and extracting it clutch'd? What reply, ha? What say'st thou to this tune, matter, and method? Is't not drown'd i' th' last rain, ha? What say'st thou, trot? Is the world as it was, man? Which is the way? Is it sad, and few words? or how? The trick of it?

DUKE Still thus, and thus; still worse!

LUCIO How doth my dear morsel, thy mistress? Procures she still, ha?

POMPEY Troth, sir, she hath eaten up all her beef, and she is herself in the tub.

LUCIO Why, 'tis good; it is the right of it; it must be so; ever your fresh whore and your powerder'd bawd – an unshunn'd consequence; it must be so. Art going to prison, Pompey?

POMPEY Yes, faith, sir.

LUCIO Why, 'tis not amiss, Pompey. Farewell; go, say I sent thee thither. For debt, Pompey – or how?

ELBOW For being a bawd, for being a bawd.

LUCIO Well, then, imprison him. If imprisonment be the due of a bawd, why, 'tis his right. Bawd is he doubtless, and of antiquity, too; bawd-born. Farewell, good Pompey. Commend me to the prison, Pompey. You will turn good husband now, Pompey; you will keep the house.

POMPEY I hope, sir, your good worship will be my bail.

LUCIO No, indeed, will I not, Pompey; it is not the wear. I will pray, Pompey, to increase your bondage. If you take it not patiently, why, your mettle is the more. Adieu, trusty Pompey. Bless you, friar.

DUKE And you.

LUCIO Does Bridget paint still, Pompey, ha?

ELBOW Come your ways, sir; come.

POMPEY You will not bail me then, sir?

LUCIO Then, Pompey, nor now. What news abroad, friar? what news?

ELBOW Come your ways, sir; come.

LUCIO Go to kennel, Pompey, go.

[*Exeunt Elbow, Pompey and Officers.*

What news, friar, of the Duke?

DUKE I know none. Can you tell me of any?

LUCIO Some say he is with the Emperor of Russia; other some, he is in Rome; but where is he, think you?

DUKE I know not where; but wheresoever, I wish him well.

LUCIO It was a mad fantastical trick of him to steal from the state and usurp the beggary he was never born to. Lord Angelo dukes it well in his absence; he puts transgression to't.

DUKE He does well in't.

LUCIO A little more lenity to lechery would do no harm in him. Something too crabbed that way, friar.

DUKE It is too general a vice, and severity must cure it.

LUCIO Yes, in good sooth, the vice is of a great kindred; it is well allied; but it is impossible to extirp it quite, friar, till eating and drinking be put down. They say this Angelo was not made by man and woman after this downright way of creation. Is it true, think you?

DUKE How should he be made, then?

LUCIO Some report a sea-maid spawn'd him; some, that he was begot between two stock-fishes. But it is certain that when he makes water his urine is congeal'd ice; that I know to be true. And he is a motion generative; that's infallible.

DUKE You are pleasant, sir, and speak apace.

LUCIO Why, what a ruthless thing is this in him, for the rebellion of a codpiece to take away the life of a man! Would the Duke that is absent have done this? Ere he would have hang'd a man for the getting a hundred bastards, he would have paid for the nursing a thousand. He had some feeling of the sport; he knew the service, and that instructed him to mercy.

DUKE I never heard the absent Duke much detected for women; he was not inclin'd that way.

LUCIO O, sir, you are deceiv'd.

DUKE 'Tis not possible.

LUCIO Who – not the Duke? Yes, your beggar of fifty; and his use was to put a ducat in her clack-dish. The Duke had crotchets in him. He would be drunk too; that let me inform you.

DUKE You do him wrong, surely.

LUCIO Sir, I was an inward of his. A shy fellow was the Duke; and I believe I know the cause of his withdrawing.

DUKE What, I prithee, might be the cause?

LUCIO No, pardon; 'tis a secret must be lock'd within the teeth and the lips; but this I can let you understand: the greater file of the subject held the Duke to be wise.

DUKE Wise? Why, no question but he was.

LUCIO A very superficial, ignorant, unweighing fellow.

DUKE Either this is envy in you, folly, or mistaking; the very stream of his life, and the business he hath helmed, must, upon a warranted need, give him a better proclamation. Let him be but testimonied in his own bringings-forth, and he shall appear to the envious a scholar, a statesman, and a soldier. Therefore you speak unskilfully; or, if your knowledge be more, it is much dark'ned in your malice.

LUCIO Sir, I know him, and I love him.

DUKE Love talks with better knowledge, and knowledge with dearer love.

LUCIO Come, sir, I know what I know.

DUKE I can hardly believe that, since you know not what you speak. But, if ever the Duke return, as our prayers are he may, let me desire you to make your answer before him. If it be honest you have spoke, you have courage to maintain it; I am bound to call upon you; and I pray you your name?

LUCIO Sir, my name is Lucio, well known to the Duke.

DUKE He shall know you better, sir, if I may live to report you.

LUCIO I fear you not.

DUKE O, you hope the Duke will return no more; or you imagine me too unhurtful an opposite. But, indeed, I can do you little harm: you'll forswear this again.

LUCIO I'll be hang'd first. Thou art deceiv'd in me, friar. But no more of this.
Canst thou tell if Claudio die to-morrow or no?

DUKE Why should he die, sir?

LUCIO Why? For filling a bottle with a tun-dish. I would the Duke we talk of were return'd again. This ungenitur'd agent will unpeople the province with continency; sparrows must not build in his house-eaves because they are lecherous. The Duke yet would have dark deeds darkly answered; he would never bring them to light. Would he were return'd! Marry, this Claudio is condemned for untrussing. Farewell, good friar; I prithee pray for me. The Duke, I say to thee again, would eat mutton on Fridays. He's not past it yet; and, I say to thee, he would mouth with a beggar though she smelt brown bread and garlic. Say that I said so. Farewell.

[*Exit.*

DUKE No might nor greatness in mortality

Can censure scape; back-wounding calumny
The whitest virtue strikes. What king so strong
Can tie the gall up in the slanderous tongue?
But who comes here?

Enter ESCALUS, PROVOST, and OFFICERS with MISTRESS OVERDONE.

ESCALUS Go, away with her to prison.

MRS. OVERDONE Good my lord, be good to me; your honour is accounted a merciful man; good my lord.

ESCALUS Double and treble admonition, and still forfeit in the same kind! This would make mercy swear and play the tyrant.

PROVOST A bawd of eleven years' continuance, may it please your honour.

MRS. OVERDONE My lord, this is one Lucio's information against me. Mistress Kate Keepdown was with child by him in the Duke's time; he promis'd her marriage. His child is a year and a quarter old come Philip and Jacob; I have kept it myself; and see how he goes about to abuse me.

ESCALUS That fellow is a fellow of much license. Let him be call'd before us. Away with her to prison. Go to; no more words. [*Exeunt Officers with Mrs. Overdone*.] Provost, my brother Angelo will not be alter'd: Claudio must die to-morrow. Let him be furnish'd with divines, and have all charitable preparation. If my brother wrought by my pity, it should not be so with him.

PROVOST So please you, this friar hath been with him, and advis'd him for th' entertainment of death.

ESCALUS Good even, good father.

DUKE Bliss and goodness on you!

ESCALUS Of whence are you?

DUKE Not of this country, though my chance is now
To use it for my time. I am a brother
Of gracious order, late come from the See
In special business from his Holiness.

ESCALUS What news abroad i' th' world?

DUKE None, but that there is so great a fever on goodness that the dissolution of it must cure it. Novelty is only in request; and, as it is, as dangerous to be aged in any kind of course as it is virtuous to be constant in any undertaking. There is scarce truth enough alive to make societies secure; but security enough to make fellowships accurst. Much upon this riddle runs the wisdom of the world. This news is old enough, yet it is every day's news. I pray you, sir, of what disposition was the Duke?

ESCALUS One that, above all other strifes, contended especially to know himself.

DUKE What pleasure was he given to?

ESCALUS Rather rejoicing to see another merry than merry at anything which profess'd to make him rejoice; a gentleman of all temperance. But leave we him to his events, with a prayer they may prove prosperous; and let me desire to know how you find Claudio prepar'd. I am made to understand that you have lent him visitation.

DUKE He professes to have received no sinister measure from his judge, but most willingly humbles himself to the determination of justice. Yet had he framed to himself, by the instruction of his frailty, many deceiving promises of life; which I, by my good leisure, have discredited to him, and now is he resolv'd to die.

ESCALUS You have paid the heavens your function, and the prisoner the very debt of your calling. I have labour'd for the poor gentleman to the extremest shore of my modesty; but my brother justice have I found so severe that he hath forc'd me to tell him he is indeed Justice.

DUKE If his own life answer the straitness of his proceeding, it shall become him well; wherein if he chance to fail, he hath sentenc'd himself.

ESCALUS I am going to visit the prisoner. Fare you well.

DUKE Peace be with you!

[*Exeunt Escalus and Provost.*

He who the sword of heaven will bear
Should be as holy as severe;
Pattern in himself to know,
Grace to stand, and virtue go;
More nor less to others paying
Than by self-offences weighing.
Shame to him whose cruel striking
Kills for faults of his own liking!
Twice treble shame on Angelo,
To weed my vice and let his grow!
O, what may man within him hide,
Though angel on the outward side!
How may likeness, made in crimes,
Make a practice on the times,
To draw with idle spiders' strings
Most ponderous and substantial things!
Craft against vice I must apply.
With Angelo to-night shall lie
His old betrothed but despised;
So disguise shall, by th' disguised,
Pay with falsehood false exacting,
And perform an old contracting. [*Exit.*

ACT FOUR

SCENE I. *The moated grange at Saint Luke's.*

Enter MARIANA; and Boy singing.

Song

Take, O, take those lips away,
That so sweetly were forsworn;
And those eyes, the break of day,
Lights that do mislead the morn;
But my kisses bring again, bring again;
Seals of love, but seal'd in vain, seal'd in vain.

Enter DUKE, disguised as before.

MARIANA Break off thy song, and haste thee quick away;
Here comes a man of comfort, whose advice
Hath often still'd my brawling discontent.
[*Exit Boy.*
I cry you mercy, sir, and well could wish
You had not found me here so musical.
Let me excuse me, and believe me so,
My mirth it much displeas'd, but pleas'd my woe.

DUKE 'Tis good; though music oft hath such a charm
To make bad good and good provoke to harm.
I pray you tell me hath anybody inquir'd for me here to-day. Much upon this time have I promis'd here to meet.

MARIANA You have not been inquir'd after;
I have sat here all day.

Enter ISABELLA.

DUKE I do constantly believe you. The time is come even now. I shall crave your forbearance a little. May be I will call upon you anon, for some advantage to yourself.

MARIANA I am always bound to you. [*Exit.*

DUKE Very well met, and well come.
What is the news from this good deputy?

ISABELLA He hath a garden circummur'd with brick,
Whose western side is with a vineyard back'd;
And to that vineyard is a planched gate
That makes his opening with this bigger key;
This other doth command a little door
Which from the vineyard to the garden leads.
There have I made my promise.
Upon the heavy middle of the night
To call upon him.

DUKE But shall you on your knowledge find this way?

ISABELLA I have ta'en a due and wary note upon't;
With whispering and most guilty diligence,
In action all of precept, he did show me
The way twice o'er.

DUKE Are there no other tokens
Between you 'greed concerning her observance?

ISABELLA No, none, but only a repair i' th' dark;
And that I have possess'd him my most stay
Can be but brief; for I have made him know
I have a servant comes with me along,
That stays upon me; whose persuasion is
I come about my brother.

DUKE 'Tis well borne up.
I have not yet made known to Mariana
A word of this. What ho, within! come forth.

Re-enter MARIANA.

I pray you be acquainted with this maid;
She comes to do you good.

ISABELLA I do desire the like.

DUKE Do you persuade yourself that I respect you?

MARIANA Good friar, I know you do, and have found it.

DUKE Take, then, this your companion by the hand,
Who hath a story ready for your ear.
I shall attend your leisure; but make haste;
The vaporous night approaches.

MARIANA Will't please you walk aside?
[*Exeunt Mariana and Isabella.*

DUKE O place and greatness! Millions of false eyes
Are stuck upon thee. Volumes of report
Run with these false, and most contrarious quest
Upon thy doings. Thousand escapes of wit
Make thee the father of their idle dream,
And rack thee in their fancies.

Re-enter MARIANA and ISABELLA.

Welcome, how agreed?

ISABELLA She'll take the enterprise upon her, father,
If you advise it.

DUKE It is not my consent,
But my entreaty too.

ISABELLA Little have you to say,
When you depart from him, but, soft and low,
'Remember now my brother'.

MARIANA Fear me not.

DUKE Nor, gentle daughter, fear you not at all.
He is your husband on a pre-contract.
To bring you thus together 'tis no sin,
Sith that the justice of your title to him

Doth flourish the deceit. Come, let us go;
Our corn's to reap, for yet our tithe's to sow.
[*Exeunt.*

SCENE II. *The prison.*

Enter PROVOST and POMPEY.

PROVOST Come hither, sirrah. Can you cut off a man's head?

POMPEY If the man be a bachelor, sir, I can; but if he be a married man, he's his wife's head, and I can never cut off a woman's head.

PROVOST Come, sir, leave me your snatches and yield me a direct answer. To-morrow morning are to die Claudio and Barnardine. Here is in our prison a common executioner, who in his office lacks a helper; if you will take it on you to assist him, it shall redeem you from your gyves; if not, you shall have your full time of imprisonment, and your deliverance with an unpitied whipping, for you have been a notorious bawd.

POMPEY Sir, I have been an unlawful bawd time out of mind; but yet I will be content to be a lawful hangman. I would be glad to receive some instruction from my fellow partner.

PROVOST What ho, Abhorson! Where's Abhorson there?

Enter ABHORSON.

ABHORSON Do you call, sir?

PROVOST Sirrah, here's a fellow will help you to-morrow in your execution. If you think it meet, compound with him by the year, and let him abide here with you; if not, use him for the present, and dismiss him. He cannot plead his estimation with you; he hath been a bawd.

ABHORSON A bawd, sir? Fie upon him! He will discredit our mystery.

PROVOST Go to, sir; you weigh equally; a feather will turn the scale. [*Exit.*

POMPEY Pray, sir, by your good favour – for surely, sir, a good favour you have but that you have a hanging look – do you call, sir, your occupation a mystery?

ABHORSON Ay, sir; a mystery.

POMPEY Painting, sir, I have heard say, is a mystery; and your whores, sir, being members of my occupation, using painting, do prove my occupation a mystery; but what mystery there should be in hanging, if I should be hang'd, I cannot imagine.

ABHORSON Sir, it is a mystery.

POMPEY Proof?

ABHORSON Every true man's apparel fits your thief: if it be too little for your thief, your true man thinks it big enough; if it be too big for your thief, your thief thinks it little enough; so every true man's apparel fits your thief.

Re-enter PROVOST.

PROVOST Are you agreed?

POMPEY Sir, I will serve him; for I do find your hangman is a more penitent trade than your bawd; he doth oftener ask forgiveness.

PROVOST You, sirrah, provide your block and your axe to-morrow four o'clock.

ABHORSON Come on, bawd; I will instruct thee in my trade; follow.

POMPEY I do desire to learn, sir; and I hope, if you have occasion to use me for your own turn, you shall find me yare; for truly, sir, for your kindness I owe you a good turn.

PROVOST Call hither Barnardine and Claudio.
[*Exeunt Abhorson and Pompey.*

Th' one has my pity; not a jot the other,
Being a murderer, though he were my brother.

Enter CLAUDIO.

Look, here's the warrant, Claudio, for thy death;
'Tis now dead midnight, and by eight to-morrow
Thou must be made immortal. Where's Barnardine?

CLAUDIO As fast lock'd up in sleep as guiltless labour
When it lies starkly in the traveller's bones.
He will not wake.

PROVOST Who can do good on him?
Well, go, prepare yourself. [*Knocking within*]
But hark, what noise?
Heaven give your spirits comfort!
[*Exit Claudio.*
[*Knocking continues*] By and by.
I hope it is some pardon or reprieve
For the most gentle Claudio.

Enter DUKE, disguised as before.

Welcome, father.

DUKE The best and wholesom'st spirits of the night
Envelop you, good Provost! Who call'd here of late?

PROVOST None, since the curfew rung.

DUKE Not Isabel?

PROVOST No.

DUKE They will then, ere't be long.

PROVOST What comfort is for Claudio?

DUKE There's some in hope.

PROVOST It is a bitter deputy.

DUKE Not so, not so; his life is parallel'd
Even with the stroke and line of his great justice;

He doth with holy abstinence subdue
That in himself which he spurs on his pow'r
To qualify in others. Were he meal'd with that
Which he corrects, then were he tyrannous;
But this being so, he's just. [*Knocking within*]
Now are they come. [*Exit Provost*.
This is a gentle provost; seldom when
The steeled gaoler is the friend of men.
[*Knocking within*.
How now, what noise! That spirit's possess'd with haste
That wounds th' unsisting postern with these strokes.

Re-enter PROVOST.

PROVOST There he must stay until the officer
Arise to let him in; he is call'd up.
DUKE Have you no countermand for Claudio yet
But he must die to-morrow?
PROVOST None, sir, none.
DUKE As near the dawning, Provost, as it is,
You shall hear more ere morning.
PROVOST Happily
You something know; yet I believe there comes
No countermand; no such example have we.
Besides, upon the very siege of justice,
Lord Angelo hath to the public ear
Profess'd the contrary.

Enter a Messenger.

This is his lordship's man.
DUKE And here comes Claudio's pardon.

MESSENGER My lord hath sent you this note; and by me this further charge, that you swerve not from the smallest article of it, neither in time, matter, or other circumstance. Good morrow; for as I take it, it is almost day.

PROVOST I shall obey him. [*Exit Messenger*.
DUKE [*Aside*] This is his pardon, purchas'd by such sin
For which the pardoner himself is in;
Hence hath offence his quick celerity,
When it is borne in high authority.
When vice makes mercy, mercy's so extended.
That for the fault's love is th' offender friended.
Now, sir, what news?

PROVOST I told you: Lord Angelo, belike thinking me remiss in mine office, awakens me with this unwonted putting-on; methinks strangely, for he hath not us'd it before.

DUKE Pray you, let's hear.

PROVOST [*Reads*]'Whatsoever you may hear to the contrary, let Claudio be executed by four of the clock, and, in the afternoon, Barnardine. For my better satisfaction, let me have Claudio's head sent me by five. Let this be duly performed, with a thought that more depends on it than we must yet deliver. Thus fail not to do your office, as you will answer it at your peril.'

What say you to this, sir?

DUKE What is that Barnardine who is to be executed in th' afternoon?

PROVOST A Bohemian born; but here nurs'd up and bred. One that is a prisoner nine years old.

DUKE How came it that the absent Duke had not either deliver'd him to his liberty or executed him? I have heard it was ever his manner to do so.

PROVOST His friends still wrought reprieves for him; and, indeed, his fact, till now in the government of Lord Angelo, came not to an undoubtful proof.

DUKE It is now apparent?

PROVOST Most manifest, and not denied by himself.

DUKE Hath he borne himself penitently in prison? How seems he to be touch'd?

PROVOST A man that apprehends death no more dreadfully but as a drunken sleep; careless, reckless, and fearless, of what's past, present, or to come; insensible of mortality and desperately mortal.

DUKE He wants advice.

PROVOST He will hear none. He hath evermore had the liberty of the prison; give him leave to escape hence, he would not; drunk many times a day, if not many days entirely drunk. We have very oft awak'd him, as if to carry him to execution, and show'd him a seeming warrant for it; it hath not moved him at all.

DUKE More of him anon. There is written in your brow, Provost, honesty and constancy. If I read it not truly, my ancient skill beguiles me; but in the boldness of my cunning I will lay myself in hazard. Claudio, whom here you have warrant to execute, is no greater forfeit to the law than Angelo who hath sentenc'd him. To make you understand this in a manifested effect, I crave but four days' respite; for the which you are to do me both a present and a dangerous courtesy.

PROVOST Pray, sir, in what?

DUKE In the delaying death.

PROVOST Alack! How may I do it, having the hour limited, and an express command, under penalty, to deliver his head in the view of Angelo? I may make my case as Claudio's, to cross this in the smallest.

DUKE By the vow of mine order, I warrant you, if my instructions may be your guide. Let this Barnardine be this morning executed, and his head borne to Angelo.

PROVOST Angelo hath seen them both, and will

165 discover the favour.

DUKE O, death's a great disguiser; and you may add to it. Shave the head and tie the beard; and say it was the desire of the penitent to be so bar'd before his death. You know the course is common. If anything fall to you upon this more than thanks and good fortune, by the saint whom I profess, I will plead against it with my life.

PROVOST Pardon me, good father; it is against
172 my oath.

DUKE Were you sworn to the Duke, or to the deputy?

PROVOST To him and to his substitutes.

DUKE You will think you have made no offence if
176 the Duke avouch the justice of your dealing?

PROVOST But what likelihood is in that?

DUKE Not a resemblance, but a certainty. Yet since I see you fearful, that neither my coat, integrity, nor persuasion, can with ease attempt you, I will go further than I meant, to pluck all fears out of you. Look you, sir, here is the hand and seal of the Duke. You know the character, I doubt not; and the signet is not strange to you.

184 PROVOST I know them both.

DUKE The contents of this is the return of the Duke; you shall anon over-read it at your pleasure, where you shall find within these two days he will be here. This is a thing that Angelo knows not; for he this very day receives letters of strange tenour, perchance of the Duke's death, perchance entering into some monastery; but, by chance, nothing of what is writ. Look, th' unfolding star calls up the shepherd. Put not yourself into amazement how these things should be: all difficulties are but easy when they are known. Call your executioner, and off with Barnardine's head. I will give him a present shrift, and advise him for a better place. Yet you are amaz'd, but this shall absolutely resolve you. Come away; it is almost clear dawn. [*Exeunt.*

SCENE III. *The prison.*

Enter POMPEY.

POMPEY I am as well acquainted here as I was in our house of profession; one would think it were Mistress Overdone's own house, for here be many of her old customers. First, here's young Master Rash; he's in for a commodity of brown paper and old ginger, nine score and seventeen pounds, of which he made five marks ready money. Marry, then ginger was not much in request, for the old women were all dead. Then is there here one Master Caper, at the suit of Master Threepile the mercer, for some four suits of peach-colour'd satin, which now peaches him a beggar. Then have we here young Dizy, and young Master Deepvow, and Master Copperspur, and Master Starvelackey, the rapier and dagger man, and young Dropheir that kill'd lusty Pudding, and Master Forthlight the tilter, and brave Master Shootie the great traveller, and wild Halfcan that stabb'd Pots, and, I think, forty more – all great doers in our trade, and are
now 'for the Lord's sake'. 18

Enter ABHORSON.

ABHORSON Sirrah, bring Barnardine hither.

POMPEY Master Barnardine! You must rise and be
hang'd, Master Barnardine! 21

ABHORSON What ho, Barnardine!

BARNARDINE [*Within*] A pox o'your throats! Who makes that noise there? What are you?

POMPEY Your friends, sir; the hangman. You must be so good, sir, to rise and be put to
death. 26

BARNARDINE [*Within*] Away, you rogue, away; I am sleepy.

ABHORSON Tell him he must awake, and that quickly too.

POMPEY Pray, Master Barnardine, awake till you
are executed, and sleep afterwards. 30

ABHORSON Go in to him, and fetch him out.

POMPEY He is coming, sir, he is coming; I hear his straw rustle.

Enter BARNARDINE.

ABHORSON Is the axe upon the block, sirrah?

POMPEY Very ready, sir. 35

BARNARDINE How now, Abhorson, what's the news with you?

ABHORSON Truly, sir, I would desire you to clap into your prayers; for look you, the warrant's come.

BARNARDINE You rogue, I have been drinking all
night; I am not fitted for't. 40

POMPEY O, the better, sir! For he that drinks all night and is hanged betimes in the morning may
sleep the sounder all the next day. 43

Enter DUKE, disguised as before.

ABHORSON Look you, sir, here comes your ghostly father. Do we jest now, think you?

DUKE Sir, induced by my charity, and hearing how hastily you are to depart, I am come to
advise you, comfort you, and pray with you. 48

BARNARDINE Friar, not I; I have been drinking hard all night, and I will have more time to prepare me, or they shall beat out my brains with billets. I will not consent to die this day,
that's certain. 52

DUKE O, sir, you must; and therefore I beseech you
Look forward on the journey you shall go.

BARNARDINE I swear I will not die to-day for any man's persuasion.
DUKE But hear you –
BARNARDINE Not a word; if you have anything to say to me, come to my ward; for thence will not I to-day. *[Exit.*
DUKE Unfit to live or die. O gravel heart!
After him, fellows; bring him to the block.
[Exeunt Abhorson and Pompey.

Enter PROVOST.

PROVOST Now, sir, how do you find the prisoner?
DUKE A creature unprepar'd, unmeet for death;
And to transport him in the mind he is
Were damnable.
PROVOST Here in the prison, father,
There died this morning of a cruel fever
One Ragozine, a most notorious pirate,
A man of Claudio's years; his beard and head
Just of his colour. What if we do omit
This reprobate till he were well inclin'd,
And satisfy the deputy with the visage
Of Ragozine, more like to Claudio?
DUKE O, 'tis an accident that heaven provides!
Dispatch it presently; the hour draws on
Prefix'd by Angelo. See this be done,
And sent according to command; whiles I
Persuade this rude wretch willingly to die.
PROVOST This shall be done, good father, presently.
But Barnardine must die this afternoon;
And how shall we continue Claudio,
To save me from the danger that might come
If he were known alive?
DUKE Let this be done:
Put them in secret holds, both Barnardine and Claudio.
Ere twice the sun hath made his journal greeting
To the under generation, you shall find
Your safety manifested.
PROVOST I am your free dependant.
DUKE Quick, dispatch, and send the head to Angelo. *[Exit Provost.*
Now will I write letters to Angelo –
The Provost, he shall bear them – whose contents
Shall witness to him I am near at home,
And that, by great injunctions, I am bound
To enter publicly. Him I'll desire
To meet me at the consecrated fount,
A league below the city; and from thence,
By cold gradation and well-balanc'd form,
We shall proceed with Angelo.

Re-enter PROVOST.

PROVOST Here is the head; I'll carry it myself.
DUKE Convenient it is. Make a swift return;
For I would commune with you of such things
That want no ear but yours.
PROVOST I'll make all speed. *[Exit.*
ISABELLA *[Within]* Peace, ho, be here!
DUKE The tongue of Isabel. She's come to know
If yet her brother's pardon be come hither;
But I will keep her ignorant of her good,
To make her heavenly comforts of despair
When it is least expected.

Enter ISABELLA.

ISABELLA Ho, by your leave!
DUKE Good morning to you, fair and gracious daughter.
ISABELLA The better, given me by so holy a man.
Hath yet the deputy sent my brother's pardon?
DUKE He hath releas'd him, Isabel, from the world.
His head is off and sent to Angelo.
ISABELLA Nay, but it is not so.
DUKE It is no other.
Show your wisdom, daughter, in your close patience.
ISABELLA O, I will to him and pluck out his eyes!
DUKE You shall not be admitted to his sight.
ISABELLA Unhappy Claudio! Wretched Isabel!
Injurious world! Most damned Angelo!
DUKE This nor hurts him nor profits you a jot;
Forbear it, therefore; give your cause to heaven.
Mark what I say, which you shall find
By every syllable a faithful verity.
The Duke comes home to-morrow. Nay, dry your eyes.
One of our covent, and his confessor,
Gives me this instance. Already he hath carried
Notice to Escalus and Angelo,
Who do prepare to meet him at the gates,
There to give up their pow'r. If you can, pace your wisdom
In that good path that I would wish it go,
And you shall have your bosom on this wretch,
Grace of the Duke, revenges to your heart,
And general honour.
ISABELLA I am directed by you.
DUKE This letter, then, to Friar Peter give;
'Tis that he sent me of the Duke's return.
Say, by this token, I desire his company
At Mariana's house to-night. Her cause and yours
I'll perfect him withal; and he shall bring you
Before the Duke; and to the head of Angelo
Accuse him home and home. For my poor self,
I am combined by a sacred vow,
And shall be absent. Wend you with this letter.
Command these fretting waters from your eyes
With a light heart; trust not my holy order,

If I pervert your course. Who's here?

Enter LUCIO.

LUCIO Good even. Friar, where's the Provost?

DUKE Not within, sir.

LUCIO O pretty Isabella, I am pale at mine heart to see thine eyes so red. Thou must be patient. I am fain to dine and sup with water and bran; I dare not for my head fill my belly; one fruitful meal would set me to't. But they say the Duke will be here to-morrow. By my troth, Isabel, I lov'd thy brother. If the old fantastical Duke of dark corners had been at home, he had lived.

[Exit Isabella.

DUKE Sir, the Duke is marvellous little beholding to your reports; but the best is, he lives not in them.

LUCIO Friar, thou knowest not the Duke so well as I do; he's a better woodman than thou tak'st him for.

DUKE Well, you'll answer this one day. Fare ye well.

LUCIO Nay, tarry; I'll go along with thee; I can tell thee pretty tales of the Duke.

DUKE You have told me too many of him already, sir, if they be true; if not true, none were enough.

LUCIO I was once before him for getting a wench with child.

DUKE Did you such a thing?

LUCIO Yes, marry, did I; but I was fain to forswear it: they would else have married me to the rotten medlar.

DUKE Sir, your company is fairer than honest.
Rest you well.

LUCIO By my troth, I'll go with thee to the lane's end. If bawdy talk offend you, we'll have very little of it. Nay, friar, I am a kind of burr; I shall stick.

[Exeunt.

SCENE IV. *Angelo's house.*

Enter ANGELO and ESCALUS.

ESCALUS Every letter he hath writ hath disvouch'd other.

ANGELO In most uneven and distracted manner. His actions show much like to madness; pray heaven his wisdom be not tainted! And why meet him at the gates, and redeliver our authorities there?

ESCALUS I guess not.

ANGELO And why should we proclaim it in an hour before his ent'ring that, if any crave redress of injustice, they should exhibit their petitions in the street?

ESCALUS He shows his reason for that: to have a dispatch of complaints; and to deliver us from devices hereafter, which shall then have no power to stand against us.

ANGELO Well, I beseech you, let it be proclaim'd;
Betimes i' th' morn I'll call you at your house;
Give notice to such men of sort and suit
As are to meet him.

ESCALUS I shall, sir; fare you well.

ANGELO Good night. *[Exit Escalus.*

This deed unshapes me quite, makes me unpregnant
And dull to all proceedings. A deflow'red maid!
And by an eminent body that enforc'd
The law against it! But that her tender shame
Will not proclaim against her maiden loss,
How might she tongue me! Yet reason dares her no;
For my authority bears a so credent bulk
That no particular scandal once can touch
But it confounds the breather. He should have liv'd,
Save that his riotous youth, with dangerous sense,
Might in the times to come have ta'en revenge,
By so receiving a dishonour'd life
With ransom of such shame. Would yet he had liv'd!
Alack, when once our grace we have forgot,
Nothing goes right; we would, and we would not. *[Exit.*

SCENE V. *Fields without the town.*

Enter DUKE in his own habit, and FRIAR PETER.

DUKE These letters at fit time deliver me.

[Giving letters.

The Provost knows our purpose and our plot.
The matter being afoot, keep your instruction
And hold you ever to our special drift;
Though sometimes you do blench from this to that
As cause doth minister. Go, call at Flavius' house,
And tell him where I stay; give the like notice
To Valentinus, Rowland, and to Crassus,
And bid them bring the trumpets to the gate;
But send me Flavius first.

FRIAR PETER It shall be speeded well.

[Exit Friar.

Enter VARRIUS.

DUKE I thank thee, Varrius; thou hast made good haste.
Come, we will walk. There's other of our friends
Will greet us here anon. My gentle Varrius!

[Exeunt.

SCENE VI. *A street near the city gate.*

Enter ISABELLA and MARIANA.

ISABELLA To speak so indirectly I am loath;
I would say the truth; but to accuse him so,
That is your part. Yet I am advis'd to do it;
He says, to veil full purpose.
MARIANA Be rul'd by him.
ISABELLA Besides, he tells me that, if peradventure
He speak against me on the adverse side,
I should not think it strange; for 'tis a physic
That's bitter to sweet end.
MARIANA I would friar Peter –

Enter FRIAR PETER.

ISABELLA O, peace! the friar is come.
FRIAR PETER Come, I have found you out a stand most fit,
Where you may have such vantage on the Duke
He shall not pass you. Twice have the trumpets sounded;
The generous and gravest citizens
Have hent the gates, and very near upon
The Duke is ent'ring; therefore, hence, away.

[Exeunt.

ACT FIVE

SCENE I. *The city gate.*

Enter at several doors DUKE, VARRIUS, Lords; ANGELO, ESCALUS, LUCIO, PROVOST, Officers, and Citizens.

DUKE My very worthy cousin, fairly met!
Our old and faithful friend, we are glad to see you.
ANGELO, ESCALUS Happy return to be your royal Grace!
DUKE Many and hearty thankings to you both.
We have made inquiry of you, and we hear
Such goodness of your justice that our soul
Cannot but yield you forth to public thanks,
Forerunning more requital.
ANGELO You make my bonds still greater.
DUKE O, your desert speaks loud; and I should wrong it
To lock it in the wards of covert bosom,
When it deserves, with characters of brass,
A forted residence 'gainst the tooth of time
And razure of oblivion. Give me your hand,
And let the subject see, to make them know
That outward courtesies would fain proclaim
Favours that keep within. Come, Escalus,
You must walk by us on our other hand;
And good supporters are you.

Enter FRIAR PETER and ISABELLA.

FRIAR PETER Now is your time; speak loud, and kneel before him.
ISABELLA Justice, O royal Duke! Vail your regard
Upon a wrong'd – I would fain have said a maid!
O worthy Prince, dishonour not your eye
By throwing it on any other object
Till you have heard me in my true complaint,
And given me justice, justice, justice, justice.
DUKE Relate your wrongs. In what? By whom? Be brief.
Here is Lord Angelo shall give you justice;
Reveal yourself to him.
ISABELLA O worthy Duke,
You bid me seek redemption of the devil!
Hear me yourself; for that which I must speak
Must either punish me, not being believ'd,
Or wring redress from you. Hear me, O, hear me, here!
ANGELO My lord, her wits, I fear me, are not firm;
She hath been a suitor to me for her brother,
Cut off by course of justice –
ISABELLA By course of justice!
ANGELO And she will speak most bitterly and strange.
ISABELLA Most strange, but yet most truly, will I speak.
That Angelo's forsworn, is it not strange?
That Angelo's a murderer, is't not strange?
That Angelo is an adulterous thief,
An hypocrite, a virgin-violator,
Is it not strange and strange?
DUKE Nay, it is ten times strange.
ISABELLA It is not truer he is Angelo
Than this is all as true as it is strange;
Nay, it is ten times true; for truth is truth
To th' end of reck'ning.
DUKE Away with her. Poor soul,
She speaks this in th' infirmity of sense.
ISABELLA O Prince! I conjure thee, as thou believ'st
There is another comfort than this world,
That thou neglect me not with that opinion
That I am touch'd with madness. Make not impossible
That which but seems unlike: 'tis not impossible
But one, the wicked'st caitiff on the ground,
May seem as shy, as grave, as just, as absolute,
As Angelo; even so may Angelo,
In all his dressings, characts, titles, forms,
Be an arch-villain. Believe it, royal Prince,

If he be less, he's nothing; but he's more,
Had I more name for badness.

DUKE By mine honesty,
If she be mad, as I believe no other,
Her madness hath the oddest frame of sense,
Such a dependency of thing on thing,
As e'er I heard in madness.

ISABELLA O gracious Duke,
Harp not on that; nor do not banish reason
For inequality; but let your reason serve
To make the truth appear where it seems hid,
And hide the false seems true.

DUKE Many that are not mad
Have, sure, more lack of reason. What would you say?

ISABELLA I am the sister of one Claudio,
Condemn'd upon the act of fornication
To lose his head; condemn'd by Angelo.
I, in probation of a sisterhood,
Was sent to by my brother; one Lucio
As then the messenger –

LUCIO That's I, an't like your Grace.
I came to her from Claudio, and desir'd her
To try her gracious fortune with Lord Angelo
For her poor brother's pardon.

ISABELLA That's he, indeed.

DUKE You were not bid to speak.

LUCIO No, my good lord;
Nor wish'd to hold my peace.

DUKE I wish you now, then;
Pray you take note of it; and when you have
A business for yourself, pray heaven you then
Be perfect.

LUCIO I warrant your honour.

DUKE The warrant's for yourself; take heed to't.

ISABELLA This gentleman told somewhat of my tale.

LUCIO Right.

DUKE It may be right: but you are i' the wrong
To speak before your time. Proceed.

ISABELLA I went
To this pernicious caitiff deputy.

DUKE That's somewhat madly spoken.

ISABELLA Pardon it;
The phrase is to the matter.

DUKE Mended again. The matter – proceed.

ISABELLA In brief – to set the needless process by,
How I persuaded, how I pray'd, and kneel'd,
How he refell'd me, and how I replied,
For this was of much length – the vile conclusion
I now begin with grief and shame to utter:
He would not, but by gift of my chaste body
To his concupiscible intemperate lust,
Release my brother; and, after much debatement,
My sisterly remorse confutes mine honour,
And I did yield to him. But the next morn betimes,
His purpose surfeiting, he sends a warrant
For my poor brother's head.

DUKE This is most likely!

ISABELLA O that it were as like as it is true!

DUKE By heaven, fond wretch, thou know'st not what thou speak'st,
Or else thou art suborn'd against his honour
In hateful practice. First, his integrity
Stands without blemish; next, it imports no reason
That with such vehemency he should pursue
Faults proper to himself. If he had so offended,
He would have weigh'd thy brother by himself,
And not have cut him off. Some one hath set you on;
Confess the truth, and say by whose advice
Thou cam'st here to complain.

ISABELLA And is this all?
Then, O you blessed ministers above,
Keep me in patience; and, with ripened time,
Unfold the evil which is here wrapt up
In countenance! Heaven shield your Grace from woe,
As I, thus wrong'd, hence unbelieved go!

DUKE I know you'd fain be gone. An officer!
To prison with her! Shall we thus permit
A blasting and a scandalous breath to fall
On him so near us? This needs must be a practice.
Who knew of your intent and coming hither?

ISABELLA One that I would were here, friar Lodowick.

DUKE A ghostly father, belike. Who knows that Lodowick?

LUCIO My lord, I know him; 'tis a meddling friar.
I do not like the man; had he been lay, my lord,
For certain words he spake against your Grace
In your retirement, I had swing'd him soundly.

DUKE Words against me? This's a good friar, belike!
And to set on this wretched woman here
Against our substitute! Let this friar be found.

LUCIO But yesternight, my lord, she and that friar,
I saw them at the prison; a saucy friar,
A very scurvy fellow.

FRIAR PETER Blessed be your royal Grace!
I have stood by, my lord, and I have heard
Your royal ear abus'd. First, hath this woman
Most wrongfully accus'd your substitute;
Who is as free from touch or soil with her
As she from one ungot.

DUKE We did believe no less.
Know you that friar Lodowick that she speaks of?

FRIAR PETER I know him for a man divine and holy;
Not scurvy, nor a temporary meddler,
As he's reported by this gentleman;
And, on my trust, a man that never yet
Did, as he vouches, misreport your Grace.

LUCIO My lord, most villainously; believe it.

FRIAR PETER Well, he in time may come to clear himself;
But at this instant he is sick, my lord,
Of a strange fever. Upon his mere request –
Being come to knowledge that there was complaint
Intended 'gainst Lord Angelo – came I hither
To speak, as from his mouth, what he doth know
Is true and false; and what he, with his oath
And all probation, will make up full clear,
Whensoever he's convented. First, for this woman –
To justify this worthy nobleman,
So vulgarly and personally accus'd –
Her shall you hear disproved to her eyes,
Till she herself confess it.

DUKE Good friar, let's hear it.

[Exit Isabella guarded.

Do you not smile at this, Lord Angelo?
O heaven, the vanity of wretched fools!
Give us some seats. Come, cousin Angelo;
In this I'll be impartial; be you judge
Of your own cause.

Enter MARIANA veiled.

Is this the witness friar?
First let her show her face, and after speak.

MARIANA Pardon, my lord; I will not show my face
Until my husband bid me.

DUKE What, are you married?

MARIANA No, my lord.

DUKE Are you a maid?

MARIANA No, my lord.

DUKE A widow, then?

MARIANA Neither, my lord.

DUKE Why, you are nothing then; neither maid, widow, nor wife.

LUCIO My lord, she may be a punk; for many of them are neither maid, widow, nor wife.

DUKE Silence that fellow. I would he had some cause
To prattle for himself.

LUCIO Well, my lord.

MARIANA My lord, I do confess I ne'er was married,
And I confess, besides, I am no maid.
I have known my husband; yet my husband
Knows not that ever he knew me.

LUCIO He was drunk, then, my lord; it can be no better.

DUKE For the benefit of silence, would thou wert so too!

LUCIO Well, my lord.

DUKE This is no witness for Lord Angelo.

MARIANA Now I come to't, my lord:
She that accuses him of fornication,
In self-same manner doth accuse my husband;
And charges him, my lord, with such a time
When I'll depose I had him in mine arms,
With all th' effect of love.

ANGELO Charges she moe than me?

MARIANA Not that I know.

DUKE No? You say your husband.

MARIANA Why, just, my lord, and that is Angelo,
Who thinks he knows that he ne'er knew my body,
But knows he thinks that he knows Isabel's.

ANGELO This is a strange abuse. Let's see thy face.

MARIANA My husband bids me; now I will unmask.

[Unveiling.

This is that face, thou cruel Angelo,
Which once thou swor'st was worth the looking on;
This is the hand which, with a vow'd contract,
Was fast belock'd in thine; this is the body
That took away the match from Isabel,
And did supply thee at thy garden-house
In her imagin'd person.

DUKE Know you this woman?

LUCIO Carnally, she says.

DUKE Sirrah, no more.

LUCIO Enough, my lord.

ANGELO My lord, I must confess I know this woman;
And five years since there was some speech of marriage
Betwixt myself and her; which was broke off,
Partly for that her promised proportions
Came short of composition; but in chief
For that her reputation was disvalued
In levity. Since which time of five years
I never spake with her, saw her, nor heard from her,
Upon my faith and honour.

MARIANA Noble Prince,
As there comes light from heaven and words from breath,
As there is sense in truth and truth in virtue,
I am affianc'd this man's wife as strongly
As words could make up vows. And, my good lord,
But Tuesday night last gone, in's garden-house,

He knew me as a wife. As this is true,
Let me in safety raise me from my knees,
Or else for ever be confixed here,
A marble monument!

ANGELO I did but smile till now.
Now, good my lord, give me the scope of justice;
My patience here is touch'd. I do perceive
These poor informal women are no more
But instruments of some more mightier member
That sets them on. Let me have way, my lord,
To find this practice out.

DUKE Ay, with my heart;
And punish them to your height of pleasure.
Thou foolish friar, and thou pernicious woman,
Compact with her that's gone, think'st thou thy oaths,
Though they would swear down each particular saint,
Were testimonies against his worth and credit,
That's seal'd in approbation? You, Lord Escalus,
Sit with my cousin; lend him your kind pains
To find out this abuse, whence 'tis deriv'd.
There is another friar that set them on;
Let him be sent for.

FRIAR PETER Would he were here, my lord! For he indeed
Hath set the women on to this complaint.
Your provost knows the place where he abides,
And he may fetch him.

DUKE Go, do it instantly.
[Exit Provost.
And you, my noble and well-warranted cousin,
Whom it concerns to hear this matter forth,
Do with your injuries as seems you best
In any chastisement. I for a while will leave you;
But stir not you till you have well determin'd
Upon these slanderers.

ESCALUS My lord, we'll do it throughly.
[Exit Duke.
Signior Lucio, did not you say you knew that friar Lodowick to be a dishonest person?

LUCIO 'Cucullus non facit monachum': honest in nothing but in his clothes; and one that hath spoke most villainous speeches of the Duke.

ESCALUS We shall entreat you to abide here till he come, and enforce them against him. We shall find this friar a notable fellow.

LUCIO As any in Vienna, on my word.

ESCALUS Call that same Isabel here once again; I would speak with her. *[Exit an Attendant]* Pray you, my lord, give me leave to question; you shall see how I'll handle her.

LUCIO Not better than he, by her own report.

ESCALUS Say you?

LUCIO Marry, sir, I think, if you handled her privately, she would sooner confess; perchance, publicly, she'll be asham'd.

Re-enter Officers with ISABELLA; and PROVOST with the DUKE in his friar's habit.

ESCALUS I will go darkly to work with her.

LUCIO That's the way; for women are light at midnight.

ESCALUS Come on, mistress; here's a gentlewoman denies all that you have said.

LUCIO My lord, here comes the rascal I spoke of, here with the Provost.

ESCALUS In very good time. Speak not you to him till we call upon you.

LUCIO Mum.

ESCALUS Come, sir; did you set these women on to slander Lord Angelo? They have confess'd you did.

DUKE 'Tis false.

ESCALUS How! Know you where you are?

DUKE Respect to your great place! and let the devil
Be sometime honour'd for his burning throne!
Where is the Duke? 'Tis he should hear me speak.

ESCALUS The Duke's in us; and we will hear you speak;
Look you speak justly.

DUKE Boldly, at least. But, O, poor souls,
Come you to seek the lamb here of the fox,
Good night to your redress! Is the Duke gone?
Then is your cause gone too. The Duke's unjust
Thus to retort your manifest appeal,
And put your trial in the villain's mouth
Which here you come to accuse.

LUCIO This is the rascal; this is he I spoke of.

ESCALUS Why, thou unreverend and unhallowed friar,
Is't not enough thou hast suborn'd these women
To accuse this worthy man, but, in foul mouth,
And in the witness of his proper ear,
To call him villain; and then to glance from him
To th' Duke himself, to tax him with injustice?
Take him hence; to th' rack with him! We'll touze you
Joint by joint, but we will know his purpose.
What, 'unjust'!

DUKE Be not so hot; the Duke
Dare no more stretch this finger of mine than he
Dare rack his own; his subject am I not,
Nor here provincial. My business in this state
Made me a looker-on here in Vienna,
Where I have seen corruption boil and bubble
Till it o'errun the stew: laws for all faults,

But faults so countenanc'd that the strong statutes
Stand like the forfeits in a barber's shop,
As much in mock as mark.

ESCALUS Slander to th' state! Away with him to prison!

ANGELO What can you vouch against him, Signior Lucio?
Is this the man that you did tell us of?

LUCIO 'Tis he, my lord. Come hither, good-man bald-pate. Do you know me?

DUKE I remember you, sir, by the sound of your voice. I met you at the prison, in the absence of the Duke.

LUCIO O did you so? And do you remember what you said of the Duke?

DUKE Most notedly, sir.

LUCIO Do you so, sir? And was the Duke a fleshmonger, a fool, and a coward, as you then reported him to be?

DUKE You must, sir, change persons with me ere you make that my report; you, indeed, spoke so of him; and much more, much worse.

LUCIO O thou damnable fellow! Did not I pluck thee by the nose for thy speeches?

DUKE I protest I love the Duke as I love myself.

ANGELO Hark how the villain would close now, after his treasonable abuses!

ESCALUS Such a fellow is not to be talk'd withal. Away with him to prison! Where is the Provost? Away with him to prison! Lay bolts enough upon him; let him speak no more. Away with those giglets too, and with the other confederate companion!

[The Provost lays hands on the Duke.

DUKE Stay, sir; stay awhile.

ANGELO What, resists he? Help him, Lucio.

LUCIO Come, sir; come, sir; come, sir; foh, sir! Why, you bald-pated lying rascal, you must be hooded, must you? Show your knave's visage, with a pox to you! show your sheep-biting face, and be hang'd an hour! Will't not off?

[Pulls off the friar's hood, and discovers the Duke.

DUKE Thou art the first knave that e'er mad'st a duke.
First, Provost, let me bail these gentle three.
[*To Lucio*] Sneak not away, sir, for the friar and you
Must have a word anon. Lay hold on him.

LUCIO This may prove worse than hanging.

DUKE [*To Escalus*] What you have spoke I pardon; sit you down.
We'll borrow place of him. [*To Angelo*] Sir, by your leave.
Hast thou or word, or wit, or impudence,
That yet can do thee office? If thou hast,
Rely upon it till my tale be heard,
And hold no longer out.

ANGELO O my dread lord,
I should be guiltier than my guiltiness,
To think I can be undiscernible,
When I perceive your Grace, like pow'r divine,
Hath look'd upon my passes. Then, good Prince,
No longer session hold upon my shame,
But let my trial be mine own confession;
Immediate sentence then, and sequent death,
Is all the grace I beg.

DUKE Come hither, Mariana.
Say, wast thou e'er contracted to this woman?

ANGELO I was, my lord.

DUKE Go, take her hence and marry her instantly.
Do you the office, friar; which consummate,
Return him here again. Go with him, Provost.

[Exeunt Angelo, Mariana, Friar Peter, and Provost.

ESCALUS My lord, I am more amaz'd at his dishonour
Than at the strangeness of it.

DUKE Come hither, Isabel.
Your friar is now your prince. As I was then
Advertising and holy to your business,
Not changing heart with habit,I am still
Attorney'd at your service.

ISABELLA O, give me pardon,
That I, your vassal, have employ'd and pain'd
Your unknown sovereignty.

DUKE You are pardon'd Isabel.
And now, dear maid, be you as free to us.
Your brother's death, I know, sits at your heart;
And you may marvel why I obscur'd myself,
Labouring to save his life, and would not rather
Make rash remonstrance of my hidden pow'r
Than let him so be lost. O most kind maid,
It was the swift celerity of his death,
Which I did think with slower foot came on,
That brain'd my purpose. But peace be with him!
That life is better life, past fearing death,
Than that which lives to fear. Make it your comfort,
So happy is your brother.

ISABELLA I do, my lord.

Re-enter ANGELO, MARIANA, FRIAR

PETER, and PROVOST.

DUKE For this new-married man approaching here,
Whose salt imagination yet hath wrong'd
Your well-defended honour, you must pardon
For Mariana's sake; but as he adjudg'd your brother –

Being criminal in double violation
Of sacred chastity and of promise-breach,
Thereon dependent, for your brother's life –
The very mercy of the law cries out
Most audible, even from his proper tongue,
'An Angelo for Claudio, death for death!'
Haste still pays haste, and leisure answers leisure;
Like doth quit like, and Measure still for Measure.
Then, Angelo, thy fault's thus manifested,
Which, though thou wouldst deny, denies thee vantage.
We do condemn thee to the very block
Where Claudio stoop'd to death, and with like haste.
Away with him!

MARIANA O my most gracious lord,
I hope you will not mock me with a husband.

DUKE It is your husband mock'd you with a husband.
Consenting to the safeguard of your honour,
I thought your marriage fit; else imputation,
For that he knew you, might reproach your life,
And choke your good to come. For his possessions,
Although by confiscation they are ours,
We do instate and widow you withal,
To buy you a better husband.

MARIANA O my dear lord,
I crave no other, nor no better man.

DUKE Never crave him; we are definitive.

MARIANA Gentle, my liege – *[Kneeling.*

DUKE You do but lose your labour.
Away with him to death! *[To Lucio]* Now, sir, to you.

MARIANA O my good lord! Sweet Isabel, take my part;
Lend me your knees, and all my life to come
I'll lend you all my life to do you service.

DUKE Against all sense you do importune her.
Should she kneel down in mercy of this fact,
Her brother's ghost his paved bed would break,
And take her hence in horror.

MARIANA Isabel,
Sweet Isabel, do yet but kneel by me;
Hold up your hands, say nothing; I'll speak all.
They say best men are moulded out of faults;
And, for the most, become much more the better
For being a little bad; so may my husband.
O Isabel, will you not lend a knee?

DUKE He dies for Claudio's death.

ISABELLA *[Kneeling]* Most bounteous sir,
Look, if it please you, on this man condemn'd,
As if my brother liv'd. I partly think
A due sincerity govern'd his deeds
Till he did look on me; since it is so,
Let him not to die. My brother had but justice,
In that he did the thing for which he died;
For Angelo,
His act did not o'ertake his bad intent,
And must be buried but as an intent
That perish'd by the way. Thoughts are no subjects;
Intents but merely thoughts.

MARIANA Merely, my lord.

DUKE Your suit's unprofitable; stand up, I say.
I have bethought me of another fault.
Provost, how came it Claudio was beheaded
At an unusual hour?

PROVOST It was commanded so.

DUKE Had you a special warrant for the deed?

PROVOST No, my good lord; it was by private message.

DUKE For which I do discharge you of your office;
Give up your keys.

PROVOST Pardon me, noble lord;
I thought it was a fault, but knew it not;
Yet did repent me, after more advice;
For testimony whereof, one in the prison,
That should by private order else have died,
I have reserv'd alive.

DUKE What's he?

PROVOST His name is Barnardine.

DUKE I would thou hadst done so by Claudio.
Go fetch him hither; let me look upon him.
[Exit Provost.

ESCALUS I am sorry one so learned and so wise
As you, Lord Angelo, have still appear'd,
Should slip so grossly, both in the heat of blood
And lack of temper'd judgment afterward.

ANGELO I am sorry that such sorrow I procure;
And so deep sticks it in my penitent heart
That I crave death more willingly than mercy;
'Tis my deserving, and I do entreat it.

Re-enter PROVOST, with BARNARDINE, CLAUDIO [muffled], and JULIET.

DUKE Which is that Barnardine?

PROVOST This, my lord.

DUKE There was a friar told me of this man.
Sirrah, thou art said to have a stubborn soul,
That apprehends no further than this world,
And squar'st thy life according. Thou'rt condemn'd;
But, for those earthly faults, I quit them all,
And pray thee take this mercy to provide
For better times to come. Friar, advise him;
I leave him to your hand. What muffl'd fellow's that?

PROVOST This is another prisoner that I sav'd,

Who should have died when Claudio lost his head;
As like almost to Claudio as himself.
[*Unmuffles Claudio.*

DUKE [*To Isabella*] If he be like your brother, for his sake
Is he pardon'd; and for your lovely sake,
Give me your hand and say you will be mine,
He is my brother too. But fitter time for that.
By this Lord Angelo perceives he's safe;
Methinks I see a quick'ning in his eye.
Well, Angelo, your evil quits you well.
Look that you love your wife; her worth worth yours.
I find an apt remission in myself;
And yet here's one in place I cannot pardon.
[*To Lucio*] You, sirrah, that knew me for a fool, a coward,
One all of luxury, an ass, a madman!
Wherein have I so deserv'd of you
That you extol me thus?

LUCIO Faith, my lord, I spoke it but according to the trick. If you will hang me for it, you may; but I had rather it would please you I might be whipt.

DUKE Whipt first, sir, and hang'd after.
Proclaim it, Provost, round about the city,
If any woman wrong'd by this lewd fellow –
As I have heard him swear himself there's one
Whom he begot with child, let her appear,
And he shall marry her. The nuptial finish'd,
Let him be whipt and hang'd.

LUCIO I beseech your Highness, do not marry me to a whore. Your Highness said even now I made you a duke; good my lord, do not recompense me in making me a cuckold.

DUKE Upon mine honour, thou shalt marry her.
Thy slanders I forgive; and therewithal
Remit thy other forfeits. Take him to prison;
And see our pleasure herein executed.

LUCIO Marrying a punk, my lord, is pressing to death, whipping, and hanging.

DUKE Slandering a prince deserves it.
[*Exeunt Officers with Lucio.*

She, Claudio, that you wrong'd, look you restore.
Joy to you, Mariana! Love her, Angelo;
I have confess'd her, and I know her virtue.
Thanks, good friend Escalus, for thy much goodness;
There's more behind that is more gratulate.
Thanks, Provost, for thy care and secrecy;
We shall employ thee in a worthier place.
Forgive him, Angelo, that brought you home
The head of Ragozine for Claudio's:
Th' offence pardons itself. Dear Isabel,
I have a motion much imports your good;
Whereto if you'll a willing ear incline,
What's mine is yours, and what is yours is mine.
So, bring us to our palace, where we'll show
What's yet behind that's meet you all should know.
[*Exeunt.*

The Comedy of Errors

Introduction by DAVID NEWELL

The Comedy of Errors is the first of Shakespeare's 'family reunion' comedies. The temporal fragility and underlying resilience of the family is a pervasive theme in the Shakespearean comic world, climaxing in the exquisite magic of *The Winter's Tale*. The consequences of Egeon's search for his lost sons, slaves and wife are condensed into the dramatic tightness of one day, beginning with exposition (the frozen quality of the opening scene highlights the subsequent explosion into the very physical, kinetic world of farce) and ending appropriately with a cluster of joyful last-minute revelations, one of which – the identity of the abbess – is a surprise even to the audience.

The errors of the play's title are a complex series of mistaken identities created by the presence in one town, but unbeknown to each other, of two sets of identical (and identically named) twins. This unlikely expansion of a classical formula is fun for the audience but a nightmare for its victims. The bewildering experiences of the visiting Antipholus convince him that Ephesus is a hot-bed of sorcery and deception. While he speculates on the nature of illusion ('Am I in earth, in heaven, or in hell?') his servant Dromio, obsessed with the fairy-tale terrors of 'goblins, owls, and sprites', is more concerned about being pinched 'black and blue', a plausible threat in a society where, for slaves at least, the most effective method of communication is apparently by hand.

The irony of the play is that all these errors are innocent. There is no magic, no madness, and no real malice in Ephesus. On the contrary, this commercial centre is populated by the dullest pillars of Elizabethan respectability: merchants, goldsmiths, officers, schoolmasters, servants, and housewives. Nature alone has conspired to ridicule human complacency, for out of the sea, that Shakespearean symbol of the mysterious and uncontrollable, come two doppelgängers. There is nothing like the natural mimicry of twins to pull the plug on solemnity and dignity. As a consequence every sphere of life – domestic, social, commercial and legal – is plunged into anarchy. Even at the very end, when all is known, the possibility of confusion lingers. Both the duke ('Stay, stand apart; I know not which is which') and the Syracusan Dromio still have difficulty distinguishing Egeon's sons. The mayhem of the plot originates ultimately in the joyful, natural magic of childbirth.

The play's brevity (a mere 1800 lines) brings its own problems, for it inhibits development. Characters and episodes struggle within their limitations. While the plot calls for Adriana to be the typical nagging wife ('My wife is shrewish' is her husband's first comment on her) she is constantly slipping the leash to manifest touches of real feeling. Hearing that her supposed husband has been making advances, albeit delicate ones, towards her own sister, she erupts:

> He is deformed, crooked, old, and sere,
> Ill-fac'd, worse bodied, shapeless everywhere. [4.2.19–20]

Yet this comic if mechanical thesaurus of insults is undermined by her confession, 'I think him better than I say ... My heart prays for him, though my tongue do curse'. And her later genuine distress at his apparent lunacy is touching indeed.

Luciana, representing the traditional values of womanly obedience, transcends that role in the tactful distinction she maintains between private criticism of and public loyalty to her sister. If Adriana is no shrew then she is no prig. Indeed, the entire cast is treated sympathetically, with the exception of Dr Pinch, who is subjected to the verbal and physical abuse which Shakespeare seems to reserve specially for the teaching profession.

As with character so with situation. The embryonic courtship between Antipholus of Syracuse and Luciana, simultaneously absurd and moving, is left unexplored. Even the final revelations receive short shrift, for farce allows little breathing space. The long-lost Antipholus brothers are silent, husband and wife exchange formalities, and only the Dromios seem fascinated by their mirror-images. There is none of the breath-taking wonder which accompanies the reunion of the *Twelfth Night* twins, or the religious ceremonial of Hermione's simulated resurrection in *The Winter's Tale*.

But despite this *The Comedy of Errors* has much to offer. A perfectly paced farce, it alternates swiftly between pathos and comedy, between the seen and the reported. Hard on the heels of Antipholus's burgeoning romance with Luciana comes the distraught Dromio, whose off-stage encounter with a kitchen wench parodies his master's formal Petrarchan wooing. The greasy, globular and geographically extensive Dowsabel ('she is spherical ... I could find out countries in her') is the more gloriously grotesque for being invisible. One only regrets Shakespeare's failure to dramatise Ephesian Antipholus's escape from the awful Dr Pinch, a feat worthy of Sexton Blake at his best:

> And in a dark and dankish vault at home
> There left me and my man, both bound together;
> Till, gnawing with my teeth my bonds in sunder,
> I gain'd my freedom. [5.1.247–50]

Now that *would* have been worth seeing on stage!

The Comedy of Errors

DRAMATIS PERSONAE

SOLINUS
Duke of Ephesus
AEGEON
a merchant of Syracuse
ANTIPHOLUS of Syracuse, ANTIPHOLUS of Ephesus
twin brothers, and sons to Aegeon and Aemilia
DROMIO of Ephesus, DROMIO of Syracuse
twin brothers, and attendants on the two Antipholuses
BALTHAZAR
a merchant
ANGELO
a goldsmith
First Merchant friend to Antipholus of Syracuse
Second Merchant to whom Angelo is a debtor

PINCH
a schoolmaster
AEMILIA
wife to Aegeon; an abbess at Ephesus
ADRIANA
wife to Antipholus of Ephesus
LUCIANA
her sister
LUCE
servant to Adriana
A Courtezan
A Gaoler, Officers, and Attendants

THE SCENE: EPHESUS

ACT ONE

SCENE I. *A hall in the duke's palace.*

Enter the DUKE OF EPHESUS, AEGEON, The Merchant of Syracusa, Gaoler, Officers, and other Attendants.

AEGEON Proceed, Solinus, to procure me fall,
And by the doom of death end woes and all.
DUKE Merchant of Syracusa, plead no more;
I am not partial to infringe our laws.
The enmity and discord which of late
Sprung from the rancorous outrage of your duke
To merchants, our well-dealing countrymen,
Who, wanting guilders to redeem their lives,
Have seal'd his rigorous statutes with their bloods,
Excludes all pity from our threat'ning looks.
For, since the mortal and intestine jars
'Twixt thy seditious countrymen and us,
It hath in solemn synods been decreed,
Both by the Syracusians and ourselves,
To admit no traffic to our adverse towns;
Nay, more: if any born at Ephesus
Be seen at any Syracusian marts and fairs;
Again, if any Syracusian born
Come to the bay of Ephesus – he dies,
His goods confiscate to the Duke's dispose,
Unless a thousand marks be levied,
To quit the penalty and to ransom him.
Thy substance, valued at the highest rate,
Cannot amount unto a hundred marks;
Therefore by law thou art condemn'd to die.
AEGEON Yet this my comfort: when your words are done,
My woes end likewise with the evening sun.
DUKE Well, Syracusian, say in brief the cause
Why thou departed'st from thy native home,
And for what cause thou cam'st to Ephesus.
AEGEON A heavier task could not have been impos'd
Than I to speak my griefs unspeakable;
Yet, that the world may witness that my end
Was wrought by nature, not by vile offence,
I'll utter what my sorrow gives me leave.
In Syracusa was I born, and wed
Unto a woman, happy but for me,
And by me, had not our hap been bad.
With her I liv'd in joy; our wealth increas'd
By prosperous voyages I often made
To Epidamnum; till my factor's death,
And the great care of goods at random left,
Drew me from kind embracements of my spouse;
From whom my absence was not six months old,
Before herself, almost at fainting under
The pleasing punishment that women bear,
Had made provision for her following me,
And soon and safe arrived where I was.
There had she not been long but she became
A joyful mother of two goodly sons;
And, which was strange, the one so like the other
As could not be distinguish'd but by names.

That very hour, and in the self-same inn,
A mean woman was delivered
Of such a burden, male twins, both alike.
Those, for their parents were exceeding poor,
I bought, and brought up to attend my sons.
My wife, not meanly proud of two such boys,
Made daily motions for our home return;
Unwilling I agreed. Alas! too soon
We came aboard.
A league from Epidamnum had we sail'd
Before the always-wind-obeying deep
Gave any tragic instance of our harm;
But longer did we not retain much hope,
For what obscured light the heavens did grant
Did but convey unto our fearful minds
A doubtful warrant of immediate death;
Which though myself would gladly have embrac'd,
Yet the incessant weepings of my wife,
Weeping before for what she saw must come,
And piteous plainings of the pretty babes,
That mourn'd for fashion, ignorant what to fear,
Forc'd me to seek delays for them and me.
And this it was, for other means was none:
The sailors sought for safety by our boat,
And left the ship, then sinking-ripe, to us;
My wife, more careful for the latter-born,
Had fast'ned him unto a small spare mast,
Such as sea-faring men provide for storms;
To him one of the other twins was bound,
Whilst I had been like heedful of the other.
The children thus dispos'd, my wife and I,
Fixing our eyes on whom our care was fix'd,
Fast'ned ourselves at either end the mast,
And, floating straight, obedient to the stream,
Was carried towards Corinth, as we thought.
At length the sun, gazing upon the earth,
Dispers'd those vapours that offended us;
And, by the benefit of his wished light,
The seas wax'd calm, and we discovered
Two ships from far making amain to us –
Of Corinth that, of Epidaurus this.
But ere they came – O, let me say no more!
Gather the sequel by that went before.

DUKE Nay, forward, old man, do not break off so;
For we may pity, though not pardon thee.

AEGEON O, had the gods done so, I had not now
Worthily term'd them merciless to us!
For, ere the ships could meet by twice five leagues,
We were encount'red by a mighty rock,
Which being violently borne upon,
Our helpful ship was splitted in the midst;
So that, in this unjust divorce of us,
Fortune had left to both of us alike
What to delight in, what to sorrow for.
Her part, poor soul, seeming as burdened
With lesser weight, but not with lesser woe,
Was carried with more speed before the wind;
And in our sight they three were taken up
By fishermen of Corinth, as we thought.
At length another ship had seiz'd on us;
And, knowing whom it was their hap to save,
Gave healthful welcome to their shipwreck'd guests,
And would have reft the fishers of their prey,
Had not their bark been very slow of sail;
And therefore homeward did they bend their course.
Thus have you heard me sever'd from my bliss,
That by misfortunes was my life prolong'd,
To tell sad stories of my own mishaps.

DUKE And, for the sake of them thou sorrowest for,
Do me the favour to dilate at full
What have befall'n of them and thee till now.

AEGEON My youngest boy, and yet my eldest care,
At eighteen years became inquisitive
After his brother, and importun'd me
That his attendant – so his case was like,
Reft of his brother, but retain'd his name –
Might bear him company in the quest of him;
Whom whilst I laboured of a love to see,
I hazarded the loss of whom I lov'd.
Five summers have I spent in farthest Greece,
Roaming clean through the bounds of Asia,
And, coasting homeward, came to Ephesus;
Hopeless to find, yet loath to leave unsought
Or that or any place that harbours men.
But here must end the story of my life;
And happy were I in my timely death,
Could all my travels warrant me they live.

DUKE Hapless Aegeon, whom the fates have mark'd
To bear the extremity of dire mishap!
Now, trust me, were it not against our laws,
Against my crown, my oath, my dignity,
Which princes, would they, may not disannul,
My soul should sue as advocate for thee.
But though thou art adjudged to the death,
And passed sentence may not be recall'd
But to our honour's great disparagement,
Yet will I favour thee in what I can.
Therefore, merchant, I'll limit thee this day
To seek thy help by beneficial hap.
Try all the friends thou hast in Ephesus;
Beg thou, or borrow, to make up the sum,
And live; if no, then thou art doom'd to die.
Gaoler, take him to thy custody.

GAOLER I will, my lord.

AEGEON Hopeless and helpless doth Aegeon wend,
But to procrastinate his lifeless end. [*Exeunt.*

SCENE II. *The mart.*

Enter ANTIPHOLUS of Syracuse, DROMIO of Syracuse, and First Merchant.

FIRST MERCHANT Therefore, give out you are of Epidamnum,
Lest that your goods too soon be confiscate.
This very day a Syracusian merchant
Is apprehended for arrival here;
And, not being able to buy out his life,
According to the statute of the town,
Dies ere the weary sun set in the west.
There is your money that I had to keep.

S. ANTIPHOLUS Go bear it to the Centaur, where we host,
And stay there, Dromio, till I come to thee.
Within this hour it will be dinner-time;
Till that, I'll view the manners of the town,
Peruse the traders, gaze upon the buildings,
And then return and sleep within mine inn;
For with long travel I am stiff and weary.
Get thee away.

S. DROMIO Many a man would take you at your word,
And go indeed, having so good a mean.
[*Exit S. Dromio.*

S. ANTIPHOLUS A trusty villain, sir, that very oft,
When I am dull with care and melancholy,
Lightens my humour with his merry jests.
What, will you walk with me about the town,
And then go to my inn and dine with me?

FIRST MERCHANT I am invited, sir, to certain merchants,
Of whom I hope to make much benefit;
I crave your pardon. Soon at five o'clock,
Please you, I'll meet with you upon the mart,
And afterward consort you till bed time.
My present business calls me from you now.

S. ANTIPHOLUS Farewell till then. I will go lose myself,
And wander up and down to view the city.

FIRST MERCHANT Sir, I commend you to your own content. [*Exit First Merchant.*

S. ANTIPHOLUS He that commends me to mine own content
Commends me to the thing I cannot get.
I to the world am like a drop of water
That in the ocean seeks another drop,
Who, falling there to find his fellow forth,
Unseen, inquisitive, confounds himself.
So I, to find a mother and a brother,
In quest of them, unhappy, lose myself.

Enter DROMIO of Ephesus.

Here comes the almanac of my true date.
What now? How chance thou art return'd so soon?

E. DROMIO Return'd so soon! rather approach'd too late.
The capon burns, the pig falls from the spit;
The clock hath strucken twelve upon the bell –
My mistress made it one upon my cheek;
She is so hot because the meat is cold,
The meat is cold because you come not home,
You come not home because you have no stomach,
You have no stomach, having broke your fast;
But we, that know what 'tis to fast and pray,
Are penitent for your default to-day.

S. ANTIPHOLUS Stop in your wind, sir; tell me this, I pray:
Where have you left the money that I gave you?

E. DROMIO O – sixpence that I had a Wednesday last
To pay the saddler for my mistress' crupper?
The saddler had it, sir; I kept it not.

S. ANTIPHOLUS I am not in a sportive humour now;
Tell me, and dally not, where is the money?
We being strangers here, how dar'st thou trust
So great a charge from thine own custody?

E. DROMIO I pray you jest, sir, as you sit at dinner.
I from my mistress come to you in post;
If I return, I shall be post indeed,
For she will score your fault upon my pate.
Methinks your maw, like mine, should be your clock,
And strike you home without a messenger.

S. ANTIPHOLUS Come, Dromio, come, these jests are out of season;
Reserve them till a merrier hour than this.
Where is the gold I gave in charge to thee?

E. DROMIO To me, sir? Why, you gave no gold to me.

S. ANTIPHOLUS Come on, sir knave, have done your foolishness,
And tell me how thou hast dispos'd thy charge.

E. DROMIO My charge was but to fetch you from the mart
Home to your house, the Phoenix, sir, to dinner.
My mistress and her sister stays for you.

S. ANTIPHOLUS Now, as I am a Christian, answer me
In what safe place you have bestow'd my money,
Or I shall break that merry sconce of yours,
That stands on tricks when I am undispos'd.
Where is the thousand marks thou hadst of me?

E. DROMIO I have some marks of yours upon my pate,
Some of my mistress' marks upon my shoulders,
But not a thousand marks between you both.

If I should pay your worship those again,
Perchance you will not bear them patiently.

S. ANTIPHOLUS Thy mistress' marks! What mistress, slave, hast thou?

E. DROMIO Your worship's wife, my mistress at the Phoenix;
She that doth fast till you come home to dinner,
And prays that you will hie you home to dinner.

S. ANTIPHOLUS What, wilt thou flout me thus unto my face,
Being forbid? There, take you that, sir knave.
[Beats him.

E. DROMIO What mean you, sir? For God's sake hold your hands!
Nay, an you will not, sir, I'll take my heels.
[Exit E. Dromio.

S. ANTIPHOLUS Upon my life, by some device or other
The villain is o'erraught of all my money.
They say this town is full of cozenage;
As, nimble jugglers that deceive the eye,
Dark-working sorcerers that change the mind,
Soul-killing witches that deform the body,
Disguised cheaters, prating mountebanks,
And many such-like liberties of sin;
If it prove so, I will be gone the sooner.
I'll to the Centaur to go seek this slave.
I greatly fear my money is not safe. *[Exit.*

ACT TWO

SCENE I. *The house of Antipholus of Ephesus.*

Enter ADRIANA, wife to Antipholus of Ephesus, with LUCIANA, her sister.

ADRIANA Neither my husband nor the slave return'd
That in such haste I sent to seek his master!
Sure, Luciana, it is two o'clock.

LUCIANA Perhaps some merchant hath invited him,
And from the mart he's somewhere gone to dinner;
Good sister, let us dine, and never fret.
A man is master of his liberty;
Time is their master, and when they see time,
They'll go or come. If so, be patient, sister.

ADRIANA Why should their liberty than ours be more?

LUCIANA Because their business still lies out o' door.

ADRIANA Look, when I serve him so, he takes it ill.

LUCIANA O, know he is the bridle of your will.

ADRIANA There's none but asses will be bridled so.

LUCIANA Why, headstrong liberty is lash'd with woe.
There's nothing situate under heaven's eye
But hath his bound, in earth, in sea, in sky.
The beasts, the fishes, and the winged fowls,
Are their males' subjects, and at their controls.
Man, more divine, the master of all these,
Lord of the wide world and wild wat'ry seas,
Indu'd with intellectual sense and souls,
Of more pre-eminence than fish and fowls,
Are masters to their females, and their lords;
Then let your will attend on their accords.

ADRIANA This servitude makes you to keep unwed.

LUCIANA Not this, but troubles of the marriage-bed.

ADRIANA But, were you wedded, you would bear some sway.

LUCIANA Ere I learn love, I'll practise to obey.

ADRIANA How if your husband start some other where?

LUCIANA Till he come home again, I would forbear.

ADRIANA Patience unmov'd! no marvel though she pause:
They can be meek that have no other cause.
A wretched soul, bruis'd with adversity,
We bid be quiet when we hear it cry;
But were we burd'ned with like weight of pain,
As much, or more, we should ourselves complain.
So thou, that hast no unkind mate to grieve thee,
With urging helpless patience would relieve me;
But if thou live to see like right bereft,
This fool-begg'd patience in thee will be left.

LUCIANA Well, I will marry one day, but to try.
Here comes your man, now is your husband nigh.

Enter DROMIO of Ephesus.

ADRIANA Say, is your tardy master now at hand?

E. DROMIO Nay, he's at two hands with me, and that my two ears can witness.

ADRIANA Say, didst thou speak with him? Know'st thou his mind?

E. DROMIO Ay, ay, he told his mind upon mine ear.
Beshrew his hand, I scarce could understand it.

LUCIANA Spake he so doubtfully thou couldst not feel his meaning?
E. DROMIO Nay, he struck so plainly I could too well feel his blows; and withal so doubtfully that I could scare understand them.
ADRIANA But say, I prithee, is he coming home?
It seems he hath great care to please his wife.
E. DROMIO Why, mistress, sure my master is horn-mad.
ADRIANA Horn-mad, thou villain!
E. DROMIO I mean not cuckold-mad;
But, sure, he is stark mad.
When I desir'd him to come home to dinner,
He ask'd me for a thousand marks in gold.
''Tis dinner time' quoth I; 'My gold!' quoth he.
'Your meat doth burn' quoth I; 'My gold!' quoth he.
'Will you come home?' quoth I; 'My gold!' quoth he
'Where is the thousand marks I gave thee, villain?'
'The pig' quoth I 'is burn'd'; 'My gold!' quoth he.
'My mistress, sir' quoth I; 'Hang up thy mistress;
I know not thy mistress; out on thy mistress.'
LUCIANA Quoth who?
E. DROMIO Quoth my master.
'I know' quoth he 'no house, no wife, no mistress.'
So that my errand, due unto my tongue,
I thank him, I bare home upon my shoulders;
For, in conclusion, he did beat me there.
ADRIANA Go back again, thou slave, and fetch him home.
E. DROMIO Go back again, and be new beaten home?
For God's sake, send some other messenger.
ADRIANA Back, slave, or I will break thy pate across.
E. DROMIO And he will bless that cross with other beating;
Between you I shall have a holy head.
ADRIANA Hence, prating peasant! Fetch thy master home.
E. DROMIO Am I so round with you, as you with me,
That like a football you do spurn me thus?
You spurn me hence, and he will spurn me hither;
If I last in this service, you must case me in leather. [*Exit.*

LUCIANA Fie, how impatience loureth in your face!
ADRIANA His company must do his minions grace,
Whilst I at home starve for a merry look.
Hath homely age th' alluring beauty took
From my poor cheek? Then he hath wasted it.
Are my discourses dull? Barren my wit?
If voluble and sharp discourse be marr'd,
Unkindness blunts it more than marble hard.
Do their gay vestments his affections bait?
That's not my fault; he's master of my state.
What ruins are in me that can be found
By him not ruin'd? Then is he the ground
Of my defeatures. My decayed fair
A sunny look of his would soon repair.
But, too unruly deer, he breaks the pale,
And feeds from home; poor I am but his stale.
LUCIANA Self-harming jealousy! fie, beat it hence.
ADRIANA Unfeeling fools can with such wrongs dispense.
I know his eye doth homage otherwhere;
Or else what lets it but he would be here?
Sister, you know he promis'd me a chain;
Would that alone a love he would detain,
So he would keep fair quarter with his bed!
I see the jewel best enamelled
Will lose his beauty; yet the gold bides still
That others touch and, often touching, will
Where gold; and no man that hath a name
By falsehood and corruption doth it shame.
Since that my beauty cannot please his eye,
I'll weep what's left away, and weeping die.
LUCIANA How many fond fools serve mad jealousy! [*Exeunt.*

SCENE II. *The mart.*

Enter ANTIPHOLUS of Syracuse.

S. ANTIPHOLUS The gold I gave to Dromio is laid up
Safe at the Centaur, and the heedful slave
Is wand'red forth in care to seek me out.
By computation and mine host's report
I could not speak with Dromio since at first
I sent him from the mart. See, here he comes.

Enter DROMIO of Syracuse.

How now, sir, is your merry humour alter'd?
As you love strokes, so jest with me again.
You know no Centaur! You receiv'd no gold!
Your mistress sent to have me home to dinner!
My house was at the Phoenix! Wast thou mad,
That thus so madly thou didst answer me?
S. DROMIO What answer, sir? When spake I such a word?
S. ANTIPHOLUS Even now, even here, not half an hour since.
S. DROMIO I did not see you since you sent me hence,

Home to the Centaur, with the gold you gave me.
S. ANTIPHOLUS Villain, thou didst deny the gold's receipt,
And told'st me of a mistress and a dinner;
For which, I hope, thou felt'st I was displeas'd.
S. DROMIO I am glad to see you in this merry vein.
What means this jest? I pray you, master, tell me.
S. ANTIPHOLUS Yea, dost thou jeer and flout me in the teeth?
Think'st thou I jest? Hold, take thou that, and that. [*Beating him.*
S. DROMIO Hold, sir, for God's sake! Now your jest is earnest.
Upon what bargain do you give it me?
S. ANTIPHOLUS Because that I familiarly sometimes
Do use you for my fool and chat with you,
Your sauciness will jest upon my love,
And make a common of my serious hours.
When the sun shines let foolish gnats make sport,
But creep in crannies when he hides his beams.
If you will jest with me, know my aspect,
And fashion your demeanour to my looks,
Or I will beat this method in your sconce.
S. DROMIO Sconce, call you it? So you would leave battering, I had rather have it a head. An you use these blows long, I must get a sconce for my head, and insconce it too; or else I shall seek my wit in my shoulders. But I pray, sir, why am I beaten?
S. ANTIPHOLUS Dost thou not know?
S. DROMIO Nothing, sir, but that I am beaten.
S. ANTIPHOLUS Shall I tell you why?
S. DROMIO Ay, sir, and wherefore; for they say every why hath a wherefore.
S. ANTIPHOLUS Why, first for flouting me; and then wherefore,
For urging it the second time to me.
S. DROMIO Was there ever any man thus beaten out of season,
When in the why and the wherefore is neither rhyme nor reason?
Well, sir, I thank you.
S. ANTIPHOLUS Thank me, sir! for what?
S. DROMIO Marry, sir, for this something that you gave me for nothing.
S. ANTIPHOLUS I'll make you amends next, to give you nothing for something. But say, sir, is it dinner-time?
S. DROMIO No, sir; I think the meat wants that I have.
S. ANTIPHOLUS In good time, sir, what's that?
S. DROMIO Basting.
S. ANTIPHOLUS Well, sir, then 'twill be dry.
S. DROMIO If it be, sir, I pray you eat none of it.
S. ANTIPHOLUS Your reason?
S. DROMIO Lest it make you choleric, and purchase me another dry basting.
S. ANTIPHOLUS Well, sir, learn to jest in good time; there's a time for all things.
S. DROMIO I durst have denied that, before you were so choleric.
S. ANTIPHOLUS By what rule, sir?
S. DROMIO Marry, sir, by a rule as plain as the plain bald pate of Father Time himself.
S. ANTIPHOLUS Let's hear it.
S. DROMIO There's no time for a man to recover his hair that grows bald by nature.
S. ANTIPHOLUS May he not do it by fine and recovery?
S. DROMIO Yes, to pay a fine for a periwig, and recover the lost hair of another man.
S. ANTIPHOLUS Why is Time such a niggard of hair, being, as it is, so plentiful an excrement?
S. DROMIO Because it is a blessing that he bestows on beasts, and what he hath scanted men in hair he hath given them in wit.
S. ANTIPHOLUS Why, but there's many a man hath more hair than wit.
S. DROMIO Not a man of those but he hath the wit to lose his hair.
S. ANTIPHOLUS Why, thou didst conclude hairy men plain dealers without wit.
S. DROMIO The plainer dealer, the sooner lost; yet he loseth it in a kind of jollity.
S. ANTIPHOLUS For what reason?
S. DROMIO For two; and sound ones too.
S. ANTIPHOLUS Nay, not sound I pray you.
S. DROMIO Sure ones, then.
S. ANTIPHOLUS Nay, not sure, in a thing falsing.
S. DROMIO Certain ones, then.
S. ANTIPHOLUS Name them.
S. DROMIO The one, to save the money that he spends in tiring; the other, that at dinner they should not drop in his porridge.
S. ANTIPHOLUS You would all this time have prov'd there is no time for all things.
S. DROMIO Marry, and did, sir; namely, no time to recover hair lost by nature.
S. ANTIPHOLUS But your reason was not substantial, why there is no time to recover.
S. DROMIO Thus I mend it: Time himself is bald, and therefore to the world's end will have bald followers.
S. ANTIPHOLUS I knew 'twould be a bald conclusion. But, soft, who wafts us yonder?

Enter ADRIANA and LUCIANA.

ADRIANA Ay, ay, Antipholus, look strange and frown.

Some other mistress hath thy sweet aspects;
I am not Adriana, nor thy wife.
The time was once when thou unurg'd wouldst vow
That never words were music to thine ear,
That never object pleasing in thine eye,
That never touch well welcome to thy hand,
That never meat sweet-savour'd in thy taste,
Unless I spake, or look'd, or touch'd, or carv'd to thee.
How comes it now, my husband, O, how comes it,
That thou art then estranged from thyself?
Thyself I call it, being strange to me,
That, undividable, incorporate,
Am better than thy dear self's better part.
Ah, do not tear away thyself from me;
For know, my love, as easy mayst thou fall
A drop of water in the breaking gulf,
And take unmingled thence that drop again
Without addition or diminishing,
As take from me thyself, and not me too.
How dearly would it touch thee to the quick,
Shouldst thou but hear I were licentious,
And that this body, consecrate to thee,
By ruffian lust should be contaminate!
Wouldst thou not spit at me and spurn at me,
And hurl the name of husband in my face,
And tear the stain'd skin off my harlot-brow,
And from my false hand cut the wedding-ring.
And break it with a deep-divorcing vow?
I know thou canst, and therefore see thou do it.
I am possess'd with an adulterate blot;
My blood is mingled with the crime of lust;
For if we two be one, and thou play false,
I do digest the poison of thy flesh,
Being strumpeted by thy contagion.
Keep then fair league and truce with thy true bed;
I live dis-stain'd, thou undishonoured.

S. ANTIPHOLUS Plead you to me, fair dame? I know you not:
In Ephesus I am but two hours old,
As strange unto your town as to your talk,
Who, every word by all my wit being scann'd,
Wants wit in all one word to understand.

LUCIANA Fie, brother, how the world is chang'd with you!
When were you wont to use my sister thus?
She sent for you by Dromio home to dinner.

S. ANTIPHOLUS By Dromio?

S. DROMIO By me?

ADRIANA By thee; and this thou didst return from him –
That he did buffet thee, and in his blows
Denied my house for his, me for his wife.

S. ANTIPHOLUS Did you converse, sir, with this gentlewoman?
What is the course and drift of your compact?

S. DROMIO I, sir? I never saw her till this time.

S. ANTIPHOLUS Villain, thou liest; for even her very words
Didst thou deliver to me on the mart.

S. DROMIO I never spake with her in all my life.

S. ANTIPHOLUS How can she thus, then, call us by our names,
Unless it be by inspiration?

ADRIANA How ill agrees it with your gravity
To counterfeit thus grossly with your slave,
Abetting him to thwart me in my mood!
Be it my wrong you are from me exempt,
But wrong not that wrong with a more contempt.
Come, I will fasten on this sleeve of thine;
Thou art an elm, my husband, I a vine,
Whose weakness, married to thy stronger state,
Makes me with thy strength to communicate.
If aught possess thee from me, it is dross,
Usurping ivy, brier, or idle moss;
Who all, for want of pruning, with intrusion
Infect thy sap, and live on thy confusion.

S. ANTIPHOLUS To me she speaks; she moves me for her theme.
What, was I married to her in my dream?
Or sleep I now, and think I hear all this?
What error drives our eyes and ears amiss?
Until I know this sure uncertainty,
I'll entertain the offer'd fallacy.

LUCIANA Dromio, go bid the servants spread for dinner.

S. DROMIO O, for my beads! I cross me for a sinner.
This is the fairy land. O spite of spites!
We talk with goblins, owls, and sprites.
If we obey them not, this will ensue:
They'll suck our breath, or pinch us black and blue.

LUCIANA Why prat'st thou to thyself, and answer'st not?
Dromio, thou drone, thou snail, thou slug, thou sot!

S. DROMIO I am transformed, master, am not I?

S. ANTIPHOLUS I think thou art in mind, and so am I.

S. DROMIO Nay, master, both in mind and in my shape.

S. ANTIPHOLUS Thou hast thine own form.

S. DROMIO No, I am an ape.

LUCIANA If thou art chang'd to aught, 'tis to an ass.

S. DROMIO 'Tis true; she rides me, and I long for grass.
'Tis so, I am an ass; else it could never be

But I should know her as well as she knows me.
ADRIANA Come, come, no longer will I be a fool,
To put the finger in the eye and weep,
Whilst man and master laughs my woes to scorn.
Come, sir, to dinner. Dromio, keep the gate.
Husband, I'll dine above with you to-day,
And shrive you of a thousand idle pranks.
Sirrah, if any ask you for your master,
Say he dines forth, and let no creature enter.
Come, sister. Dromio, play the porter well.
S. ANTIPHOLUS Am I in earth, in heaven, or in hell?
Sleeping or waking, mad or well-advis'd?
Known unto these, and to myself diguis'd!
I'll say as they say, and persever so,
And in this mist at all adventures go.
S. DROMIO Master, shall I be porter at the gate?
ADRIANA Ay; and let none enter, lest I break your pate.
LUCIANA Come, come, Antipholus, we dine too late. [*Exeunt.*

ACT THREE

SCENE I. *Before the house of Antipholus of Ephesus.*

Enter ANTIPHOLUS of Ephesus, DROMIO of Ephesus, ANGELO, and BALTHAZAR.

E. ANTIPHOLUS Good Signior Angelo, you must excuse us all;
My wife is shrewish when I keep not hours.
Say that I linger'd with you at your shop
To see the making of her carcanet,
And that to-morrow you will bring it home.
But here's a villain that would face me down
He met me on the mart, and that I beat him,
And charg'd him with a thousand marks in gold,
And that I did deny my wife and house.
Thou drunkard, thou, what didst thou mean by this?
E. DROMIO Say what you will, sir, but I know what I know.
That you beat me at the mart I have your hand to show;
If the skin were parchment, and the blows you gave were ink,
Your own handwriting would tell you what I think.
E. ANTIPHOLUS I think thou art an ass.
E. DROMIO Marry, so it doth appear
By the wrongs I suffer and the blows I bear.
I should kick, being kick'd; and being at that pass,
You would keep from my heels, and beware of an ass.
E. ANTIPHOLUS Y'are sad, Signior Balthazar; pray God our cheer
May answer my good will and your good welcome here.
BALTHAZAR I hold your dainties cheap, sir, and your welcome dear.
E. ANTIPHOLUS O, Signior Balthazar, either at flesh or fish,
A table full of welcome makes scarce one dainty dish.
BALTHAZAR Good meat, sir, is common; that every churl affords.
E. ANTIPHOLUS And welcome more common; for that's nothing but words.
BALTHAZAR Small cheer and great welcome makes a merry feast.
E. ANTIPHOLUS Ay, to a niggardly host and more sparing guest.
But though my cates be mean, take them in good part;
Better cheer may you have, but not with better heart.
But, soft, my door is lock'd; go bid them let us in.
E. DROMIO Maud, Bridget, Marian, Cicely, Gillian, Ginn!
S. DROMIO [*Within*] Mome, malt-horse, capon, coxcomb, idiot, patch!
Either get thee from the door, or sit down at the hatch.
Dost thou conjure for wenches, that thou call'st for such store,
When one is one too many? Go get thee from the door.
E. DROMIO What patch is made our porter? My master stays in the street.
S. DROMIO [*Within*] Let him walk from whence he came, lest he catch cold on's feet.
E. ANTIPHOLUS Who talks within there? Ho, open the door!
S. DROMIO [*Within*] Right, sir; I'll tell you when, an you'll tell me wherefore.
E. ANTIPHOLUS Wherefore? For my dinner; I have not din'd to-day.
S. DROMIO [*Within*] Nor to-day here you must not; come again when you may.
E. ANTIPHOLUS What art thou that keep'st me out from the house I owe?
S. DROMIO [*Within*] The porter for this time, sir, and my name is Dromio.

E. DROMIO O villain, thou hast stol'n both mine office and my name!
The one ne'er got me credit, the other mickle blame.
If thou hadst been Dromio to-day in my place,
Thou wouldst have chang'd thy face for a name, or thy name for an ass.

Enter LUCE, within.

LUCE [*Within*] What a coil is there, Dromio? Who are those at the gate?

E. DROMIO Let my master in, Luce.

LUCE [*Within*] Faith, no, he comes too late;
And so tell your master.

E. DROMIO O Lord, I must laugh!
Have at you with a proverb: Shall I set in my staff?

LUCE [*Within*] Have at you with another: that's – when? can you tell?

S. DROMIO [*Within*] If thy name be called Luce – Luce, thou hast answer'd him well.

E. ANTIPHOLUS Do you hear, you minion? You'll let us in, I hope?

LUCE [*Within*] I thought to have ask'd you.

S. DROMIO [*Within*] And you said no.

E. DROMIO So, come, help; well struck! there was blow for blow.

E. ANTIPHOLUS Thou baggage, let me in.

LUCE [*Within*] Can you tell for whose sake?

E. DROMIO Master, knock the door hard.

LUCE [*Within*] Let him knock till it ache.

E. ANTIPHOLUS You'll cry for this, minion, if I beat the door down.

LUCE [*Within*] What needs all that, and a pair of stocks in the town?

Enter ADRIANA, within.

ADRIANA [*Within*] Who is that at the door, that keeps all this noise?

S. DROMIO [*Within*] By my troth, your town is troubled with unruly boys.

E. ANTIPHOLUS Are you there, wife? You might have come before.

ADRIANA [*Within*] Your wife, sir knave! Go get you from the door.

E. DROMIO If you went in pain, master, this 'knave' would go sore.

ANGELO Here is neither cheer, sir, nor welcome; we would fain have either.

BALTHAZAR In debating which was best, we shall part with neither.

E. DROMIO They stand at the door, master; bid them welcome hither.

E. ANTIPHOLUS There is something in the wind, that we cannot get in.

E. DROMIO You would say so, master, if your garments were thin.
Your cake here is warm within; you stand here in the cold;
It would make a man mad as a buck to be so bought and sold.

E. ANTIPHOLUS Go fetch me something; I'll break ope the gate.

S. DROMIO [*Within*] Break any breaking here, and I'll break your knave's pate.

E. DROMIO A man may break a word with you, sir; and words are but wind;
Ay, and break it in your face, so he break it not behind.

S. DROMIO [*Within*] It seems thou want'st breaking; out upon thee, hind!

E. DROMIO Here's too much 'out upon thee!' I pray thee let me in.

S. DROMIO [*Within*] Ay, when fowls have no feathers and fish have no fin.

E. ANTIPHOLUS Well, I'll break in; go borrow me a crow.

E. DROMIO A crow without feather? Master, mean you so?
For a fish without a fin, there's a fowl without a feather;
If a crow help us in, sirrah, we'll pluck a crow together.

E. ANTIPHOLUS Go get thee gone; fetch me an iron crow.

BALTHAZAR Have patience, sir; O, let it not be so!
Herein you war against your reputation,
And draw within the compass of suspect
Th' unviolated honour of your wife.
Once this – your long experience of her wisdom,
Her sober virtue, years, and modesty,
Plead on her part some cause to you unknown;
And doubt not, sir, but she will well excuse
Why at this time the doors are made against you.
Be rul'd by me: depart in patience,
And let us to the Tiger all to dinner;
And, about evening, come yourself alone
To know the reason of this strange restraint.
If by strong hand you offer to break in
Now in the stirring passage of the day,
A vulgar comment will be made of it,
And that supposed by the common rout
Against your yet ungalled estimation
That may with foul intrusion enter in
And dwell upon your grave when you are dead;
For slander lives upon succession,
For ever hous'd where it gets possession.

E. ANTIPHOLUS You have prevail'd. I will depart in quiet,
And in despite of mirth mean to be merry.
I know a wench of excellent discourse,
Pretty and witty; wild, and yet, too, gentle;

There will we dine. This woman that I mean,
My wife – but, I protest, without desert –
Hath oftentimes upbraided me withal;
To her will we to dinner. [*To Angelo*] Get you home
And fetch the chain; by this I know 'tis made.
Bring it, I pray you, to the Porpentine;
For there's the house. That chain will I bestow –
Be it for nothing but to spite my wife –
Upon mine hostess there; good sir, make haste.
Since mine own doors refuse to entertain me,
I'll knock elsewhere, to see if they'll disdain me.

ANGELO I'll meet you at that place some hour hence.

E. ANTIPHOLUS Do so; this jest shall cost me some expense. [*Exeunt.*

SCENE II. *Before the house of Antipholus of Ephesus.*

Enter LUCIANA with ANTIPHOLUS of Syracuse.

LUCIANA And may it be that you have quite forgot
A husband's office? Shall, Antipholus,
Even in the spring of love, thy love-springs rot?
Shall love, in building, grow so ruinous?
If you did wed my sister for her wealth,
Then for her wealth's sake use her with more kindness;
Or, if you like elsewhere, do it by stealth;
Muffle your false love with some show of blindness;
Let not my sister read it in your eye;
Be not thy tongue thy own shame's orator;
Look sweet, speak fair, become disloyalty;
Apparel vice like virtue's harbinger;
Bear a fair presence, though your heart be tainted;
Teach sin the carriage of a holy saint;
Be secret-false. What need she be acquainted?
What simple thief brags of his own attaint?
'Tis double wrong to truant with your bed
And let her read it in thy looks at board;
Shame hath a bastard fame, well managed;
Ill deeds is doubled with an evil word.
Alas, poor women! make us but believe,
Being compact of credit, that you love us;
Though others have the arm, show us the sleeve;
We in your motion turn, and you may move us.
Then, gentle brother, get you in again;
Comfort my sister, cheer her, call her wife.
'Tis holy sport to be a little vain
When the sweet breath of flattery conquers strife.

S. ANTIPHOLUS Sweet mistress – what your name is else, I know not,
Nor by what wonder you do hit of mine –
Less in your knowledge and your grace you show not
Than our earth's wonder – more than earth, divine.
Teach me, dear creature, how to think and speak;
Lay open to my earthy-gross conceit,
Smoth'red in errors, feeble, shallow, weak,
The folded meaning of your words' deceit.
Against my soul's pure truth why labour you
To make it wander in an unknown field?
Are you a god? Would you create me new?
Transform me, then, and to your pow'r I'll yield.
But if that I am I, then well I know
Your weeping sister is no wife of mine,
Nor to her bed no homage do I owe;
Far more, far more, to you do I decline.
O, train me not, sweet mermaid, with thy note,
To drown me in thy sister's flood of tears.
Sing, siren, for thyself, and I will dote;
Spread o'er the silver waves thy golden hairs,
And as a bed I'll take them, and there lie;
And in that glorious supposition think
He gains by death that hath such means to die.
Let Love, being light, be drowned if she sink.

LUCIANA What, are you mad, that you do reason so?

S. ANTIPHOLUS Not mad, but mated; how, I do not know.

LUCIANA It is a fault that springeth from your eye.

S. ANTIPHOLUS For gazing on your beams, fair sun, being by.

LUCIANA Gaze where you should, and that will clear your sight.

S. ANTIPHOLUS As good to wink, sweet love, as look on night.

LUCIANA Why call you me love? Call my sister so.

S. ANTIPHOLUS Thy sister's sister.

LUCIANA That's my sister.

S. ANTIPHOLUS No;
It is thyself, mine own self's better part;
Mine eye's clear eye, my dear heart's dearer heart,
My food, my fortune, and my sweet hope's aim,
My sole earth's heaven, and my heaven's claim.

LUCIANA All this my sister is, or else should be.

S. ANTIPHOLUS Call thyself sister, sweet, for I am thee;
Thee will I love, and with thee lead my life;
Thou hast no husband yet, nor I no wife.
Give me thy hand.

LUCIANA O, soft, sir, hold you still;

I'll fetch my sister to get her good will. *[Exit Luciana.*

Enter DROMIO of Syracuse.

S. ANTIPHOLUS Why, how now, Dromio! Where run'st thou so fast?

S. DROMIO Do you know me, sir? Am I Dromio? Am I your man? Am I myself?

S. ANTIPHOLUS Thou art Dromio, thou art my man, thou art thyself.

S. DROMIO I am an ass, I am a woman's man, and besides myself.

S. ANTIPHOLUS What woman's man, and how besides thyself?

S. DROMIO Marry, sir, besides myself, I am due to a woman – one that claims me, one that haunts me, one that will have me.

S. ANTIPHOLUS What claim lays she to thee?

S. DROMIO Marry, sir, such claim as you would lay to your horse; and she would have me as a beast: not that, I being a beast, she would have me; but that she, being a very beastly creature, lays claim to me.

S. ANTIPHOLUS What is she?

S. DROMIO A very reverent body; ay, such a one as a man may not speak of without he say 'Sir-reverence'. I have but lean luck in the match, and yet is she a wondrous fat marriage.

S. ANTIPHOLUS How dost thou mean a fat marriage?

S. DROMIO Marry, sir, she's the kitchen-wench, and all grease; and I know not what use to put her to but to make a lamp of her and run from her by her own light. I warrant, her rags and the tallow in them will burn a Poland winter. If she lives till doomsday, she'll burn a week longer than the whole world.

S. ANTIPHOLUS What complexion is she of?

S. DROMIO Swart, like my shoe; but her face nothing like so clean kept; for why she sweats, a man may go over shoes in the grime of it.

S. ANTIPHOLUS That's a fault that water will mend.

S. DROMIO No, sir, 'tis in grain; Noah's flood could not do it.

S. ANTIPHOLUS What's her name?

S. DROMIO Nell, sir; but her name and three quarters, that's an ell and three quarters, will not measure her from hip to hip.

S. ANTIPHOLUS Then she bears some breadth?

S. DROMIO No longer from head to foot than from hip to hip: she is spherical, like a globe; I could find out countries in her.

S. ANTIPHOLUS In what part of her body stands Ireland?

S. DROMIO Marry, sir, in her buttocks; I found it out by the bogs.

S. ANTIPHOLUS Where Scotland?

S. DROMIO I found it by the barrenness, hard in the palm of the hand.

S. ANTIPHOLUS Where France?

S. DROMIO In her forehead, arm'd and reverted, making war against her heir.

S. ANTIPHOLUS Where England?

S. DROMIO I look'd for the chalky cliffs, but I could find no whiteness in them; but I guess it stood in her chin, by the salt rheum that ran between France and it.

S. ANTIPHOLUS Where Spain?

S. DROMIO Faith, I saw it not, but I felt it hot in her breath.

S. ANTIPHOLUS Where America, the Indies?

S. DROMIO O, sir, upon her nose, all o'er embellished with rubies, carbuncles, sapphires, declining their rich aspect to the hot breath of Spain; who sent whole armadoes of caracks to be ballast at her nose.

S. ANTIPHOLUS Where stood Belgia, the Netherlands?

S. DROMIO O, sir, I did not look so low. To conclude: this drudge or diviner laid claim to me; call'd me Dromio; swore I was assur'd to her; told me what privy marks I had about me, as, the mark of my shoulder, the mole in my neck, the great wart on my left arm, that I, amaz'd, ran from her as a witch.
And, I think, if my breast had not been made of faith, and my heart of steel,
She had transform'd me to a curtal dog, and made me turn i' th' wheel.

S. ANTIPHOLUS Go hie thee presently post to the road;
An if the wind blow any way from shore,
I will not harbour in this town to-night.
If any bark put forth, come to the mart,
Where I will walk till thou return to me.
If every one knows us, and we know none,
'Tis time, I think, to trudge, pack, and be gone.

S. DROMIO As from a bear a man would run for life,
So fly I from her that would be my wife. *[Exit.*

S. ANTIPHOLUS There's none but witches do inhabit here,
And therefore 'tis high time that I were hence.
She that doth call me husband, even my soul
Doth for a wife abhor. But her fair sister,
Possess'd with such a gentle sovereign grace,
Of such enchanting presence and discourse,
Hath almost made me traitor to myself;
But, lest myself be guilty to self-wrong,
I'll stop mine ears against the mermaid's song.

Enter ANGELO with the chain.

ANGELO Master Antipholus!

S. ANTIPHOLUS Ay, that's my name.
ANGELO I know it well, sir. Lo, here is the chain.
I thought to have ta'en you at the Porpentine;
The chain unfinish'd made me stay thus long.
S. ANTIPHOLUS What is your will that I shall do with this?
ANGELO What please yourself, sir; I have made it for you.
S. ANTIPHOLUS Made it for me, sir! I bespoke it not.
ANGELO Not once nor twice, but twenty times you have.
Go home with it, and please your wife withal;
And soon at supper-time I'll visit you,
And then receive my money for the chain.
S. ANTIPHOLUS I pray you, sir, receive the money now,
For fear you ne'er see chain nor money more.
ANGELO You are a merry man, sir; fare you well. [*Exit.*
S. ANTIPHOLUS What I should think of this I cannot tell;
But this I think, there's no man is so vain
That would refuse so fair an offer'd chain.
I see a man here needs not live by shifts,
When in the streets he meets such golden gifts.
I'll to the mart, and there for Dromio stay;
If any ship put out, then straight away. [*Exit.*

ACT FOUR

SCENE I. *A public place.*

Enter Second Merchant, ANGELO, and an Officer.

SECOND MERCHANT You know since Pentecost the sum is due,
And since I have not much importun'd you;
Nor now I had not, but that I am bound
To Persia, and want guilders for my voyage;
Therefore make present satisfaction,
Or I'll attach you by this officer.
ANGELO Even just the sum that I do owe to you
Is growing to me by Antipholus;
And in the instant that I met with you
He had of me a chain; at five o'clock
I shall receive the money for the same.
Pleaseth you walk with me down to his house,
I will discharge my bond, and thank you too.

Enter ANTIPHOLUS of Ephesus, and DROMIO of Ephesus, from the courtezan's.

OFFICER That labour may you save; see where he comes.
E. ANTIPHOLUS While I go to the goldsmith's house, go thou
And buy a rope's end; that will I bestow
Among my wife and her confederates,
For locking me out of my doors by day.
But, soft, I see the goldsmith. Get thee gone;
Buy thou a rope, and bring it home to me.
E. DROMIO I buy a thousand pound a year; I buy a rope. [*Exit Dromio.*
E. ANTIPHOLUS A man is well holp up that trusts to you!
I promised your presence and the chain;
But neither chain nor goldsmith came to me.
Belike you thought our love would last too long,
If it were chain'd together, and therefore came not.
ANGELO Saving your merry humour, here's the note
How much your chain weighs to the utmost carat,
The fineness of the gold, and chargeful fashion,
Which doth amount to three odd ducats more
Than I stand debted to this gentleman.
I pray you see him presently discharg'd,
For he is bound to sea, and stays but for it.
E. ANTIPHOLUS I am not furnish'd with the present money;
Besides, I have some business in the town.
Good signior, take the stranger to my house,
And with you take the chain, and bid my wife
Disburse the sum on the receipt thereof.
Perchance I will be there as soon as you.
ANGELO Then you will bring the chain to her yourself?
E. ANTIPHOLUS No; bear it with you, lest I come not time enough.
ANGELO Well, sir, I will. Have you the chain about you?
E. ANTIPHOLUS An if I have not, sir, I hope you have;
Or else you may return without your money.
ANGELO Nay, come, I pray you, sir, give me the chain;
Both wind and tide stays for this gentleman,
And I, to blame, have held him here too long.
E. ANTIPHOLUS Good Lord! you use this dalliance to excuse
Your breach of promise to the Porpentine;
I should have chid you for not bringing it,
But, like a shrew, you first begin to brawl.
SECOND MERCHANT The hour steals on; I pray you, sir, dispatch.
ANGELO You hear how he importunes me – the chain!

E. ANTIPHOLUS Why, give it to my wife, and fetch your money.

ANGELO Come, come, you know I gave it you even now.
Either send the chain or send by me some token.

E. ANTIPHOLUS Fie, now you run this humour out of breath!
Come, where's the chain? I pray you let me see it.

SECOND MERCHANT My business cannot brook this dalliance.
Good sir, say whe'r you'll answer me or no;
If not, I'll leave him to the officer.

E. ANTIPHOLUS I answer you! What should I answer you?

ANGELO The money that you owe me for the chain.

E. ANTIPHOLUS I owe you none till I receive the chain.

ANGELO You know I gave it you half an hour since.

E. ANTIPHOLUS You gave me none; you wrong me much to say so.

ANGELO You wrong me more, sir, in denying it.
Consider how it stands upon my credit.

SECOND MERCHANT Well, officer, arrest him at my suit.

OFFICER I do; and charge you in the Duke's name to obey me.

ANGELO This touches me in reputation.
Either consent to pay this sum for me,
Or I attach you by this officer.

E. ANTIPHOLUS Consent to pay thee that I never had!
Arrest me, foolish fellow, if thou dar'st.

ANGELO Here is thy fee; arrest him, officer.
I would not spare my brother in this case,
If he should scorn me so apparently.

OFFICER I do arrest you, sir; you hear the suit.

E. ANTIPHOLUS I do obey thee till I give thee bail.
But, sirrah, you shall buy this sport as dear
As all the metal in your shop will answer.

ANGELO Sir, sir, I shall have law in Ephesus,
To your notorious shame, I doubt it not.

Enter DROMIO of Syracuse, from the bay.

S. DROMIO Master, there's a bark of Epidamnum
That stays but till her owner comes aboard,
And then, sir, she bears away. Our fraughtage, sir,
I have convey'd aboard; and I have bought
The oil, the balsamum, and aqua-vitae.
The ship is in her trim; the merry wind
Blows fair from land; they stay for nought at all
But for their owner, master, and yourself.

E. ANTIPHOLUS How now! a madman? Why, thou peevish sheep,
What ship of Epidamnum stays for me?

S. DROMIO A ship you sent me to, to hire waftage.

E. ANTIPHOLUS Thou drunken slave, I sent thee for a rope;
And told thee to what purpose and what end.

S. DROMIO You sent me for a rope's end as soon –
You sent me to the bay, sir, for a bark.

E. ANTIPHOLUS I will debate this matter at more leisure,
And teach your ears to list me with more heed.
To Adriana, villain, hie thee straight;
Give her this key, and tell her in the desk
That's cover'd o'er with Turkish tapestry
There is a purse of ducats; let her send it.
Tell her I am arrested in the street,
And that shall bail me; hie thee, slave, be gone.
On, officer, to prison till it come.

[Exeunt all but Dromio.

S. DROMIO To Adriana! that is where we din'd,
Where Dowsabel did claim me for her husband.
She is too big, I hope, for me to compass.
Thither I must, although against my will,
For servants must their masters' minds fulfil.

[Exit.

SCENE II. *The house of Antipholus of Ephesus.*

Enter ADRIANA and LUCIANA.

ADRIANA Ah, Luciana, did he tempt thee so?
Mightst thou perceive austerely in his eye
That he did plead in earnest? Yea or no?
Look'd he or red or pale, or sad or merrily?
What observation mad'st thou in this case
Of his heart's meteors titling in his face?

LUCIANA First he denied you had in him no right.

ADRIANA He meant he did me none – the more my spite.

LUCIANA Then swore he that he was a stranger here.

ADRIANA And true he swore, though yet forsworn he were.

LUCIANA Then pleaded I for you.

ADRIANA And what said he?

LUCIANA That love I begg'd for you he begg'd of me.

ADRIANA With what persuasion did he tempt thy love?

LUCIANA With words that in an honest suit might move.
First he did praise my beauty, then my speech.

ADRIANA Didst speak him fair?

LUCIANA Have patience, I beseech.

ADRIANA I cannot, nor I will not hold me still;

My tongue, though not my heart, shall have his will.
He is deformed, crooked, old, and sere,
Ill-fac'd, worse bodied, shapeless everywhere;
Vicious, ungentle, foolish, blunt, unkind;
Stigmatical in making, worse in mind.

LUCIANA Who would be jealous then of such a one?
No evil lost is wail'd when it is gone.

ADRIANA Ah, but I think him better than I say,
And yet would herein others' eyes were worse.
Far from her nest the lapwing cries away;
My heart prays for him, though my tongue do curse.

Enter DROMIO of Syracuse.

S. DROMIO Here go – the desk, the purse. Sweet now, make haste.

LUCIANA How hast thou lost thy breath?

S. DROMIO By running fast.

ADRIANA Where is thy master, Dromio? Is he well?

S. DROMIO No, he's in Tartar limbo, worse than hell.
A devil in an everlasting garment hath him;
One whose hard heart is button'd up with steel;
A fiend, a fairy, pitiless and rough;
A wolf, nay worse, a fellow all in buff;
A back-friend, a shoulder-clapper, one that countermands
The passages of alleys, creeks, and narrow lands;
A hound that runs counter, and yet draws dry-foot well;
One that, before the Judgment, carries poor souls to hell.

ADRIANA Why, man, what is the matter?

S. DROMIO I do not know the matter; he is 'rested on the case.

ADRIANA What, is he arrested? Tell me, at whose suit?

S. DROMIO I know not at whose suit he is arrested well;
But he's in a suit of buff which 'rested him, that can I tell.
Will you send him, mistress, redemption, the money in his desk?

ADRIANA Go fetch it, sister. [*Exit Luciana*] This I wonder at:
Thus he unknown to me should be in debt.
Tell me, was he arrested on a band?

S. DROMIO Not on a band, but on a stronger thing,
A chain, a chain. Do you not hear it ring?

ADRIANA What, the chain?

S. DROMIO No, no, the bell; 'tis time that I were gone.
It was two ere I left him, and now the clock strikes one.

ADRIANA The hours come back! That did I never hear.

S. DROMIO O yes. If any hour meet a sergeant, 'a turns back for very fear.

ADRIANA As if Time were in debt! How fondly dost thou reason!

S. DROMIO Time is a very bankrupt, and owes more than he's worth to season.
Nay, he's a thief too: have you not heard men say
That Time comes stealing on by night and day?
If 'a be in debt and theft, and a sergeant in the way,
Hath he not reason to turn back an hour in a day?

Re-enter LUCIANA with a purse.

ADRIANA Go, Dromio, there's the money; bear it straight,
And bring thy master home immediately.
Come, sister; I am press'd down with conceit –
Conceit, my comfort and my injury. [*Exeunt.*

SCENE III. *The mart.*

Enter ANTIPHOLUS of Syracuse.

S. ANTIPHOLUS There's not a man I meet but doth salute me
As if I were their well-acquainted friend;
And every one doth call me by my name.
Some tender money to me, some invite me,
Some other give me thanks for kindnesses,
Some offer me commodities to buy;
Even now a tailor call'd me in his shop,
And show'd me silks that he had bought for me,
And therewithal took measure of my body.
Sure, these are but imaginary wiles,
And Lapland sorcerers inhabit here.

Enter DROMIO of Syracuse.

S. DROMIO Master, here's the gold you sent me for. What, have you got the picture of old Adam new-apparell'd?

S. ANTIPHOLUS What gold is this? What Adam dost thou mean?

S. DROMIO Not that Adam that kept the Paradise, but that Adam that keeps the prison; he that goes in the calf's skin that was kill'd for the Prodigal; he that came behind you, sir, like an evil angel, and bid you forsake your liberty.

S. ANTIPHOLUS I understand thee not.

S. DROMIO No? Why, 'tis a plain case: he that went, like a bass-viol, in a case of leather; the man, sir, that, when gentlemen are tired, gives them a sob, and rests them; he, sir, that takes pity on decayed men, and gives them suits of durance; he that sets up his rest to do more exploits with his mace than a morris-pike.

S. ANTIPHOLUS What, thou mean'st an officer?

S. DROMIO Ay, sir, the sergeant of the band; he that brings any man to answer it that breaks his band; one that thinks a man always going to bed, and says 'God give you good rest!'

S. ANTIPHOLUS Well, sir, there rest in your foolery. Is there any ship puts forth tonight? May we be gone?

S. DROMIO Why, sir, I brought you word an hour since that the bark Expedition put forth to-night; and then were you hind'red by the sergeant, to tarry for the hoy Delay. Here are the angels that you sent for to deliver you.

S. ANTIPHOLUS The fellow is distract, and so am I;
And here we wander in illusions.
Some blessed power deliver us from hence!

Enter a Courtezan.

COURTEZAN Well met, well met, Master Antipholus.
I see, sir, you have found the goldsmith now.
Is that the chain you promis'd me to-day?

S. ANTIPHOLUS Satan, avoid! I charge thee, tempt me not.

S. DROMIO Master, is this Mistress Satan?

S. ANTIPHOLUS It is the devil.

S. DROMIO Nay, she is worse, she is the devil's dam, and here she comes in the habit of a light wench; and thereof comes that the wenches say 'God damn me!' That's as much to say 'God make me a light wench!' It is written they appear to men like angels of light; light is an effect of fire, and fire will burn; ergo, light wenches will burn. Come not near her.

COURTEZAN Your man and you are marvellous merry, sir.
Will you go with me? We'll mend our dinner here.

S. DROMIO Master, if you do, expect spoon-meat, or bespeak a long spoon.

S. ANTIPHOLUS Why, Dromio?

S. DROMIO Marry, he must have a long spoon that must eat with the devil.

S. ANTIPHOLUS Avoid then, fiend! What tell'st thou me of supping?
Thou art, as you are all, a sorceress;
I conjure thee to leave me and be gone.

COURTEZAN Give me the ring of mine you had at dinner,
Or, for my diamond, the chain you promis'd,
And I'll be gone, sir, and not trouble you.

S. DROMIO Some devils ask but the parings of one's nail,
A rush, a hair, a drop of blood, a pin,
A nut, a cherry-stone;
But she, more covetous, would have a chain.
Master, be wise; an if you give it her,
The devil will shake her chain, and fright us with it.

COURTEZAN I pray you, sir, my ring, or else the chain;
I hope you do not mean to cheat me so.

S. ANTIPHOLUS Avaunt, thou witch! Come, Dromio, let us go.

S. DROMIO 'Fly pride' says the peacock.
Mistress, that you know.

[*Exeunt S. Antipholus and S. Dromio.*

COURTEZAN Now, out of doubt, Antipholus is mad,
Else would he never so demean himself.
A ring he hath of mine worth forty ducats,
And for the same he promis'd me a chain;
Both one and other he denies me now.
The reason that I gather he is mad,
Besides this present instance of his rage,
Is a mad tale he told to-day at dinner
Of his own doors being shut against his entrance.
Belike his wife, acquainted with his fits,
On purpose shut the doors against his way.
My way is now to hie home to his house,
And tell his wife that, being lunatic,
He rush'd into my house and took perforce
My ring away. This course I fittest choose,
For forty ducats is too much to lose. [*Exit.*

SCENE IV. *A street.*

Enter ANTIPHOLUS of Ephesus with the Officer.

E. ANTIPHOLUS Fear me not, man; I will not break away.
I'll give thee, ere I leave thee, so much money,
To warrant thee, as I am 'rested for.
My wife is in a wayward mood to-day,
And will not lightly trust the messenger.
That I should be attach'd in Ephesus,
I tell you 'twill sound harshly in her ears.

Enter DROMIO of Ephesus, with a rope's-end.

Here comes my man; I think he brings the money.
How now, sir! Have you that I sent you for?

E. DROMIO Here's that, I warrant you, will pay them all.

E. ANTIPHOLUS But where's the money?

E. DROMIO Why, sir, I gave the money for the rope.

E. ANTIPHOLUS Five hundred ducats, villain, for a rope?

E. DROMIO I'll serve you, sir, five hundred at the rate.

E. ANTIPHOLUS To what end did I bid thee hie thee home?

E. DROMIO To a rope's-end, sir; and to that end am I return'd.

E. ANTIPHOLUS And to that end, sir, I will welcome you.

[*Beating him.*

OFFICER Good sir, be patient.

E. DROMIO Nay, 'tis for me to be patient; I am in adversity.

OFFICER Good now, hold thy tongue.

E. DROMIO Nay, rather persuade him to hold his hands.

E. ANTIPHOLUS Thou whoreson, senseless villain!

E. DROMIO I would I were senseless, sir, that I might not feel your blows.

E. ANTIPHOLUS Thou art sensible in nothing but blows, and so is an ass.

E. DROMIO I am an ass indeed; you may prove it by my long 'ears. I have served him from the hour of my nativity to this instant, and have nothing at his hands for my service but blows. When I am cold he heats me with beating; when I am warm he cools me with beating. I am wak'd with it when I sleep; rais'd with it when I sit; driven out of doors with it when I go from home; welcom'd home with it when I return; nay, I bear it on my shoulders as a beggar wont her brat; and I think, when he hath lam'd me, I shall beg with it from door to door.

Enter ADRIANA, LUCIANA, the Courtezan, and a Schoolmaster call'd PINCH.

E. ANTIPHOLUS Come, go along; my wife is coming yonder.

E. DROMIO Mistress, 'respice finem', respect your end; or rather, to prophesy like the parrot, 'Beware the rope's-end'.

E. ANTIPHOLUS Wilt thou still talk?

[*Beating him.*

COURTEZAN How say you now? Is not your husband mad?

ADRIANA His incivility confirms no less.
Good Doctor Pinch, you are a conjurer:
Establish him in his true sense again,
And I will please you what you will demand.

LUCIANA Alas, how fiery and how sharp he looks!

COURTEZAN Mark how he trembles in his ecstasy.

PINCH Give me your hand, and let me feel your pulse.

E. ANTIPHOLUS There is my hand, and let it feel your ear.

[*Striking him.*

PINCH I charge thee, Satan, hous'd within this man,
To yield possession to my holy prayers,
And to thy state of darkness hie thee straight.
I conjure thee by all the saints in heaven.

E. ANTIPHOLUS Peace, doting wizard, peace! I am not mad.

ADRIANA O, that thou wert not, poor distressed soul!

E. ANTIPHOLUS You minion, you, are these your customers?
Did this companion with the saffron face
Revel and feast it at my house to-day,
Whilst upon me the guilty doors were shut,
And I denied to enter in my house?

ADRIANA O husband, God doth know you din'd at home,
Where would you had remain'd until this time,
Free from these slanders and this open shame!

E. ANTIPHOLUS Din'd at home! Thou villain, what sayest thou?

E. DROMIO Sir, sooth to say, you did not dine at home.

E. ANTIPHOLUS Were not my doors lock'd up and I shut out?

E. DROMIO Perdie, your doors were lock'd and you shut out.

E. ANTIPHOLUS And did not she herself revile me there?

E. DROMIO Sans fable, she herself revil'd you there.

E. ANTIPHOLUS Did not her kitchen-maid rail, taunt, and scorn me?

E. DROMIO Certes, she did; the kitchen-vestal scorn'd you.

E. ANTIPHOLUS And did not I in rage depart from thence?

E. DROMIO In verity, you did. My bones bear witness,
That since have felt the vigour of his rage.

ADRIANA Is't good to soothe him in these contraries?

PINCH It is no shame; the fellow finds his vein,
And, yielding to him, humours well his frenzy.

E. ANTIPHOLUS Thou hast suborn'd the goldsmith to arrest me.

ADRIANA Alas, I sent you money to redeem you,
By Dromio here, who came in haste for it.

E. DROMIO Money by me! Heart and good-will you might,
But surely, master, not a rag of money.

E. ANTIPHOLUS Went'st not thou to her for a purse of ducats?

ADRIANA He came to me, and I deliver'd it.

LUCIANA And I am witness with her that she did.

E. DROMIO God and the rope-maker bear me witness

That I was sent for nothing but a rope!
PINCH Mistress, both man and master is possess'd;
I know it by their pale and deadly looks.
They must be bound, and laid in some dark room.
E. ANTIPHOLUS Say, wherefore didst thou lock me forth to-day?
And why dost thou deny the bag of gold?
ADRIANA I did not, gentle husband, lock thee forth.
E. DROMIO And, gentle master, I receiv'd no gold;
But I confess, sir, that we were lock'd out.
ADRIANA Dissembling villain, thou speak'st false in both.
E. ANTIPHOLUS Dissembling harlot, thou art false in all,
And art confederate with a damned pack
To make a loathsome abject scorn of me;
But with these nails I'll pluck out these false eyes
That would behold in me this shameful sport.
ADRIANA O, bind him, bind him; let him not come near me.
PINCH More company! The fiend is strong within him.

Enter three or four, and offer to bind him. He strives.

LUCIANA Ay me, poor man, how pale and wan he looks!
E. ANTIPHOLUS What, will you murder me? Thou gaoler, thou,
I am thy prisoner. Wilt thou suffer them
To make a rescue?
OFFICER Masters, let him go;
He is my prisoner, and you shall not have him.
PINCH Go bind this man, for he is frantic too.

[*They bind Dromio.*

ADRIANA What wilt thou do, thou peevish officer?
Hast thou delight to see a wretched man
Do outrage and displeasure to himself?
OFFICER He is my prisoner; if I let him go,
The debt he owes will be requir'd of me.
ADRIANA I will discharge thee ere I go from thee;
Bear me forthwith unto his creditor,
And, knowing how the debt grows, I will pay it.
Good Master Doctor, see him safe convey'd
Home to my house. O most unhappy day!
E. ANTIPHOLUS O most unhappy strumpet!
E. DROMIO Master, I am here ent'red in bond for you.
E. ANTIPHOLUS Out on thee, villain! Wherefore dost thou mad me?
E. DROMIO Will you be bound for nothing?
Be mad, good master; cry 'The devil!'
LUCIANA God help, poor souls, how idly do they talk!
ADRIANA Go bear him hence. Sister, go you with me.

[*Exeunt all but Adriana, Luciana, Officer, and Courtezan.*

Say now, whose suit is he arrested at?
OFFICER One Angelo, a goldsmith; do you know him?
ADRIANA I know the man. What is the sum he owes?
OFFICER Two hundred ducats.
ADRIANA Say, how grows it due?
OFFICER Due for a chain your husband had of him.
ADRIANA He did bespeak a chain for me, but had it not.
COURTEZAN When as your husband, all in rage, to-day
Came to my house, and took away my ring –
The ring I saw upon his finger now –
Straight after did I meet him with a chain.
ADRIANA It may be so, but I did never see it.
Come, gaoler, bring me where the goldsmith is;
I long to know the truth hereof at large.

Enter ANTIPHOLUS of Syracuse, with his rapier drawn, and DROMIO of Syracuse.

LUCIANA God, for they mercy! they are loose again.
ADRIANA And come with naked swords.
Let's call more help to have them bound again.
OFFICER Away, they'll kill us!

[*Exeunt all but S. Antipholus and S. Dromio as fast as may be, frighted.*

S. ANTIPHOLUS I see these witches are afraid of swords.
S. DROMIO She that would be your wife now ran from you.
S. ANTIPHOLUS Come to the Centaur; fetch our stuff from thence.
I long that we were safe and sound aboard.
S. DROMIO Faith, stay here this night; they will surely do us no harm; you saw they speak us fair, give us gold; methinks they are such a gentle nation that, but for the mountain of mad flesh that claims marriage of me, I could find in my heart to stay here still and turn witch.
S. ANTIPHOLUS I will not stay to-night for all the town;
Therefore away, to get our stuff aboard.

[*Exeunt.*

ACT FIVE

SCENE I. *A street before a priory.*

Enter Second Merchant and ANGELO.

ANGELO I am sorry, sir, that I have hind'red you;
But I protest he had the chain of me,
Though most dishonestly he doth deny it.

SECOND MERCHANT How is the man esteem'd here in the city?

ANGELO Of very reverent reputation, sir,
Of credit infinite, highly belov'd,
Second to none that lives here in the city;
His word might bear my wealth at any time.

SECOND MERCHANT Speak softly; yonder, as I think, he walks.

Enter ANTIPHOLUS of Syracuse and DROMIO of Syracuse.

ANGELO 'Tis so; and that self chain about his neck
Which he forswore most monstrously to have.
Good sir, draw near to me, I'll speak to him.
Signior Antipholus, I wonder much
That you would put me to this shame and trouble;
And, not without some scandal to yourself,
With circumstance and oaths so to deny
This chain, which now you wear so openly.
Beside the charge, the shame, imprisonment,
You have done wrong to this my honest friend;
Who, but for staying on our controversy,
Had hoisted sail and put to sea to-day.
This chain you had of me; can you deny it?

S. ANTIPHOLUS I think I had; I never did deny it.

SECOND MERCHANT Yes, that you did, sir, and forswore it too.

S. ANTIPHOLUS Who heard me to deny it or forswear it?

SECOND MERCHANT These ears of mine, thou know'st, did hear thee.
Fie on thee, wretch! 'tis pity that thou liv'st
To walk where any honest men resort.

S. ANTIPHOLUS Thou art a villain to impeach me thus;
I'll prove mine honour and mine honesty
Against thee presently, if thou dar'st stand.

SECOND MERCHANT I dare, and do defy thee for a villain. [*They draw.*

Enter ADRIANA, LUCIANA, the Courtezan, and Others.

ADRIANA Hold, hurt him not, for God's sake! He is mad.
Some get within him, take his sword away;
Bind Dromio too, and bear them to my house.

S. DROMIO Run, master, run; for God's sake take a house.
This is some priory. In, or we are spoil'd.

[*Exeunt S. Antipholus and S. Dromio to the priory.*

Enter the Lady Abbess.

ABBESS Be quiet, people. Wherefore throng you hither?

ADRIANA To fetch my poor distracted husband hence.
Let us come in, that we may bind him fast,
And bear him home for his recovery.

ANGELO I knew he was not in his perfect wits.

SECOND MERCHANT I am sorry now that I did draw on him.

ABBESS How long hath this possession held the man?

ADRIANA This week he hath been heavy, sour, sad,
And much different from the man he was;
But till this afternoon his passion
Ne'er brake into extremity of rage.

ABBESS Hath he not lost much wealth by wreck of sea?
Buried some dear friend? Hath not else his eye
Stray'd his affection in unlawful love?
A sin prevailing much in youthful men
Who give their eyes the liberty of gazing.
Which of these sorrows is he subject to?

ADRIANA To none of these, except it be the last;
Namely, some love that drew him oft from home.

ABBESS You should for that have reprehended him.

ADRIANA Why, so I did.

ABBESS Ay, but not rough enough.

ADRIANA As roughly as my modesty would let me.

ABBESS Haply in private.

ADRIANA And in assemblies too.

ABBESS Ay, but not enough.

ADRIANA It was the copy of our conference.
In bed, he slept not for my urging it;
At board, he fed not for my urging it;
Alone, it was the subject of my theme;
In company, I often glanced it;
Still did I tell him it was vile and bad.

ABBESS And thereof came it that the man was mad.
The venom clamours of a jealous woman
Poisons more deadly than a mad dog's tooth.
It seems his sleeps were hind'red by thy railing,
And thereof comes it that his head is light.
Thou say'st his meat was sauc'd with thy unbraidings:

Unquiet meals make ill digestions;
Thereof the raging fire of fever bred;
And what's a fever but a fit of madness?
Thou say'st his sports were hind'red by thy brawls.
Sweet recreation barr'd, what doth ensure
But moody and dull melancholy,
Kinsman to grim and comfortless despair,
And at her heels a huge infectious troop
Of pale distemperatures and foes to life?
In food, in sport, and life-preserving rest,
To be disturb'd would mad or man or beast.
The consequence is, then, thy jealous fits
Hath scar'd thy husband from the use of wits.

LUCIANA She never reprehended him but mildly,
When he demean'd himself rough, rude, and wildly.
Why bear you these rebukes, and answer not?

ADRIANA She did betray me to my own reproof.
Good people, enter, and lay hold on him.

ABBESS No, not a creature enters in my house.

ADRIANA Then let your servants bring my husband forth.

ABBESS Neither; he took this place for sanctuary,
And it shall privilege him from your hands
Till I have brought him to his wits again,
Or lose my labour in assaying it.

ADRIANA I will attend my husband, be his nurse,
Diet his sickness, for it is my office,
And will have no attorney but myself;
And therefore let me have him home with me.

ABBESS Be patient; for I will not let him stir
Till I have us'd the approved means I have,
With wholesome syrups, drugs, and holy prayers,
To make of him a formal man again.
It is a branch and parcel of mine oath,
A charitable duty of my order;
Therefore depart, and leave him here with me.

ADRIANA I will not hence and leave my husband here;
And ill it doth beseem your holiness
To separate the husband and the wife.

ABBESS Be quiet, and depart; thou shalt not have him. [*Exit Abbess.*

LUCIANA Complain unto the Duke of this indignity.

ADRIANA Come, go; I will fall prostrate at his feet,
And never rise until my tears and prayers
Have won his Grace to come in person hither
And take perforce my husband from the Abbess.

SECOND MERCHANT By this, I think, the dial points at five;
Anon, I'm sure, the Duke himself in person
Comes this way to the melancholy vale,
The place of death and sorry execution,
Behind the ditches of the abbey here.

ANGELO Upon what cause?

SECOND MERCHANT To see a reverend Syracusian merchant,
Who put unluckily into this bay
Against the laws and statutes of this town,
Beheaded publicly for his offence.

ANGELO See where they come; we will behold his death.

LUCIANA Kneel to the Duke before he pass the abbey.

Enter the DUKE, attended; AEGEON, bareheaded; with the Headsman and other Officers.

DUKE Yet once again proclaim it publicly,
If any friend will pay the sum for him,
He shall not die; so much we tender him.

ADRIANA Justice, most sacred Duke, against the Abbess!

DUKE She is a virtuous and a reverend lady;
It cannot be that she hath done thee wrong.

ADRIANA May it please your Grace, Antipholus, my husband,
Who I made lord of me and all I had
At your important letters – this ill day
A most outrageous fit of madness took him,
That desp'rately he hurried through the street,
With him his bondman all as mad as he,
Doing displeasure to the citizens
By rushing in their houses, bearing thence
Rings, jewels, anything his rage did like.
Once did I get him bound and sent him home,
Whilst to take order for the wrongs I went,
That here and there his fury had committed.
Anon, I wot not by what strong escape,
He broke from those that had the guard of him,
And with his mad attendant and himself,
Each one with ireful passion, with drawn swords,
Met us again and, madly bent on us,
Chas'd us away; till, raising of more aid,
We came again to bind them. Then they fled
Into this abbey, whither we pursu'd them;
And here the Abbess shuts the gates on us,
And will not suffer us to fetch him out,
Nor send him forth that we may bear him hence.
Therefore, most gracious Duke, with thy command
Let him be brought forth and borne hence for help.

DUKE Long since thy husband serv'd me in my wars,
And I to thee engag'd a prince's word,
When thou didst make him master of thy bed,
To do him all the grace and good I could.

Go, some of you, knock at the abbey gate,
And bid the Lady Abbess come to me.
I will determine this before I stir.

Enter a Messenger.

MESSENGER O mistress, mistress, shift and save yourself!
My master and his man are both broke loose,
Beaten the maids a-row and bound the doctor,
Whose beard they have sing'd off with brands of fire;
And ever, as it blaz'd, they threw on him
Great pails of puddled mire to quench the hair.
My master preaches patience to him, and the while
His man with scissors nicks him like a fool;
And sure, unless you send some present help,
Between them they will kill the conjurer.

ADRIANA Peace, fool! thy master and his man are here,
And that is false thou dost report to us.

MESSENGER Mistress, upon my life, I tell you true;
I have not breath'd almost since I did see it.
He cries for you, and vows, if he can take you,
To scorch your face, and to disfigure you.

[Cry within

Hark, hark, I hear him, mistress; fly, be gone!

DUKE Come, stand by me; fear nothing. Guard with halberds.

ADRIANA Ay me, it is my husband! Witness you
That he is borne about invisible.
Even now we hous'd him in the abbey here,
And now he's there, past thought of human reason.

Enter ANTIPHOLUS of Ephesus and DROMIO of Ephesus.

E. ANTIPHOLUS Justice, most gracious Duke; O, grant me justice!
Even for the service that long since I did thee,
When I bestrid thee in the wars, and took
Deep scars to save thy life; even for the blood
That then I lost for thee, now grant me justice.

AEGEON Unless the fear of death doth make me dote,
I see my son Antipholus, and Dromio.

E. ANTIPHOLUS Justice, sweet Prince, against that woman there!
She whom thou gav'st to me to be my wife,
That hath abused and dishonoured me
Even in the strength and height of injury.
Beyond imagination is the wrong
That she this day hath shameless thrown on me.

DUKE Discover how, and thou shalt find me just.

E. ANTIPHOLUS This day, great Duke, she shut the doors upon me,
While she with harlots feasted in my house.

DUKE A grievous fault. Say, woman, didst thou so?

ADRIANA No, my good lord. Myself, he, and my sister,
To-day did dine together. So befall my soul
As this is false he burdens me withal!

LUCIANA Ne'er may I look on day nor sleep on night
But she tells to your Highness simple truth!

ANGELO O perjur'd woman! They are both forsworn.
In this the madman justly chargeth them.

E. ANTIPHOLUS My liege, I am advised what I say;
Neither disturbed with the effect of wine,
Nor heady-rash, provok'd with raging ire,
Albeit my wrongs might make one wiser mad.
This woman lock'd me out this day from dinner;
That goldsmith there, were he not pack'd with her,
Could witness it, for he was with me then;
Who parted with me to go fetch a chain,
Promising to bring it to the Porpentine,
Where Balthazar and I did dine together.
Our dinner done, and he not coming thither,
I went to seek him. In the street I met him,
And in his company that gentleman.
There did this perjur'd goldsmith swear me down
That I this day of him receiv'd the chain,
Which, God he knows, I saw not; for the which
He did arrest me with an officer.
I did obey, and sent my peasant home
For certain ducats; he with none return'd.
Then fairly I bespoke the officer
To go in person with me to my house.
By th' way we met my wife, her sister, and a rabble more
Of vile confederates. Along with them
They brought one Pinch, a hungry lean-fac'd villain,
A mere anatomy, a mountebank,
A threadbare juggler, and a fortune-teller,
A needy, hollow-ey'd, sharp-looking wretch,
A living dead man. This pernicious slave,
Forsooth, took on him as a conjurer,
And gazing in mine eyes, feeling my pulse,
And with no face, as 'twere, outfacing me,
Cries out I was possess'd. Then all together
They fell upon me, bound me, bore me thence,
And in a dark and dankish vault at home
There left me and my man, both bound together;
Till, gnawing with my teeth my bonds in sunder,
I gain'd my freedom, and immediately

Ran hither to your Grace; whom I beseech
To give me ample satisfaction
For these deep shames and great indignities.

ANGELO My lord, in truth, thus far I witness with him,
That he din'd not at home, but was lock'd out.

DUKE But had he such a chain of thee, or no?

ANGELO He had, my lord, and when he ran in here,
These people saw the chain about his neck.

SECOND MERCHANT Besides, I will be sworn these ears of mine
Heard you confess you had the chain of him,
After you first forswore it on the mart;
And thereupon I drew my sword on you,
And then you fled into this abbey here,
From whence, I think, you are come by miracle.

E. ANTIPHOLUS I never came within these abbey walls,
Nor ever didst thou draw thy sword on me;
I never saw the chain, so help me Heaven!
And this is false you burden me withal.

DUKE Why, what an intricate impeach is this!
I think you all have drunk of Circe's cup.
If here you hous'd him, here he would have been;
If he were mad, he would not plead so coldly.
You say he din'd at home: the goldsmith here
Denies that saying. Sirrah, what say you?

E. DROMIO Sir, he din'd with her there, at the Porpentine.

COURTEZAN He did; and from my finger snatch'd that ring.

E. ANTIPHOLUS 'Tis true, my liege; this ring I had of her.

DUKE Saw'st thou him enter at the abbey here?

COURTEZAN As sure, my liege, as I do see your Grace.

DUKE Why, this is strange. Go call the Abbess hither.
I think you are all mated or stark mad.

[Exit one to the Abbess.

AEGEON Most mighty Duke, vouchsafe me speak a word:
Haply I see a friend will save my life
And pay the sum that may deliver me.

DUKE Speak freely, Syracusian, what thou wilt.

AEGEON Is not your name, sir, call'd Antipholus?
And is not that your bondman Dromio?

E. DROMIO Within this hour I was his bondman, sir,
But he, I thank him, gnaw'd in two my cords;
Now am I Dromio and his man unbound.

AEGEON I am sure you both of you remember me.

E. DROMIO Ourselves we do remember, sir, by you;
For lately we were bound as you are now.
You are not Pinch's patient, are you, sir?

AEGEON Why look you strange on me? You know me well.

E. ANTIPHOLUS I never saw you in my life till now.

AEGEON O! grief hath chang'd me since you saw me last;
And careful hours with time's deformed hand
Have written strange defeatures in my face.
But tell me yet, dost thou not know my voice?

E. ANTIPHOLUS Neither.

AEGEON Dromio, nor thou?

E. DROMIO No, trust me, sir, nor I.

AEGEON I am sure thou dost.

E. DROMIO Ay, sir, but I am sure I do not; and whatsoever a man denies, you are now bound to believe him.

AEGEON Not know my voice! O time's extremity,
Hast thou so crack'd and splitted my poor tongue
In seven short years that here my only son
Knows not my feeble key of untun'd cares?
Though now this grained face of mine be hid
In sap-consuming winter's drizzled snow,
And all the conduits of my blood froze up,
Yet hath my night of life some memory,
My wasting lamps some fading glimmer left,
My dull deaf ears a little use to hear;
All these old witnesses – I cannot err –
Tell me thou art my son Antipholus.

E. ANTIPHOLUS I never saw my father in my life.

AEGEON But seven years since, in Syracusa, boy,
Thou know'st we parted; but perhaps, my son,
Thou sham'st to acknowledge me in misery.

E. ANTIPHOLUS The Duke and all that know me in the city
Can witness with me that it is not so:
I ne'er saw Syracusa in my life.

DUKE I tell thee, Syracusian, twenty years
Have I been patron to Antipholus,
During which time he ne'er saw Syracusa.
I see thy age and dangers make thee dote.

Re-enter the Abbess, with ANTIPHOLUS of Syracuse and DROMIO of Syracuse.

ABBESS Most mighty Duke, behold a man much wrong'd.

[All gather to see them.

ADRIANA I see two husbands, or mine eyes deceive me.

DUKE One of these men is genius to the other;
And so of these. Which is the natural man,
And which the spirit? Who deciphers them?

S. DROMIO I, sir, am Dromio; command him away.
E. DROMIO I, sir, am Dromio; pray let me stay.
S. ANTIPHOLUS Aegeon, art thou not? or else his ghost?
S. DROMIO O, my old master! who hath bound him here?
ABBESS Whoever bound him, I will loose his bonds,
And gain a husband by his liberty.
Speak, old Aegeon, if thou be'st the man
That hadst a wife once call'd Aemilia,
That bore thee at a burden two fair sons.
O, if thou be'st the same Aegeon, speak,
And speak unto the same Aemilia!
AEGEON If I dream not, thou art Aemilia.
If thou art she, tell me where is that son
That floated with thee on the fatal raft?
ABBESS By men of Epidamnum he and I
And the twin Dromio, all were taken up;
But by and by rude fishermen of Corinth
By force took Dromio and my son from them,
And me they left with those of Epidamnum.
What then became of them I cannot tell;
I to this fortune that you see me in.
DUKE Why, here begins his morning story right.
These two Antipholus', these two so like,
And these two Dromios, one in semblance –
Besides her urging of her wreck at sea –
These are the parents to these children,
Which accidentally are met together.
Antipholus, thou cam'st from Corinth first?
S. ANTIPHOLUS No, sir, not I; I came from Syracuse.
DUKE Stay, stand apart; I know not which is which.
E. ANTIPHOLUS I came from Corinth, my most gracious lord.
E. DROMIO And I with him.
E. ANTIPHOLUS Brought to this town by that most famous warrior,
Duke Menaphon, your most renowned uncle.
ADRIANA Which of you two did dine with me to-day?
S. ANTIPHOLUS I, gentle mistress.
ADRIANA And are not you my husband?
E. ANTIPHOLUS No; I say nay to that.
S. ANTIPHOLUS And so do I, yet did she call me so;
And this fair gentlewoman, her sister here,
Did call me brother. [*To Luciana*] What I told you then,
I hope I shall have leisure to make good;
If this be not a dream I see and hear.
ANGELO That is the chain, sir, which you had of me.
S. ANTIPHOLUS I think it be, sir; I deny it not.
E. ANTIPHOLUS And you, sir, for this chain arrested me.
ANGELO I think I did, sir; I deny it not.
ADRIANA I sent you money, sir, to be your bail,
By Dromio; but I think he brought it not.
E. DROMIO No, none by me.
S. ANTIPHOLUS This purse of ducats I receiv'd from you,
And Dromio my man did bring them me.
I see we still did meet each other's man,
And I was ta'en for him, and he for me,
And thereupon these ERRORS are arose.
E. ANTIPHOLUS These ducats pawn I for my father here.
DUKE It shall not need; thy father hath his life.
COURTEZAN Sir, I must have that diamond from you.
E. ANTIPHOLUS There, take it; and much thanks for my good cheer.
ABBESS Renowned Duke, vouchsafe to take the pains
To go with us into the abbey here,
And hear at large discoursed all our fortunes;
And all that are assembled in this place
That by this sympathized one day's error
Have suffer'd wrong, go keep us company,
And we shall make full satisfaction.
Thirty-three years have I but gone in travail
Of you, my sons; and till this present hour
My heavy burden ne'er delivered.
The Duke, my husband, and my children both,
And you the calendars of their nativity,
Go to a gossips' feast, and go with me;
After so long grief, such nativity!
DUKE With all my heart, I'll gossip at this feast.
[*Exeunt all but S. Antipholus, E. Antipholus, S. Dromio, and E. Dromio.*
S. DROMIO Master, shall I fetch your stuff from shipboard?
E. ANTIPHOLUS Dromio, what stuff of mine hast thou embark'd?
S. DROMIO Your goods that lay at host, sir, in the Centaur.
S. ANTIPHOLUS He speaks to me. I am your master, Dromio.
Come, go with us; we'll look to that anon.
Embrace thy brother there; rejoice with him.
[*Exeunt S. Antipholus and E. Antipholus.*
S. DROMIO There is a fat friend at your master's house,
That kitchen'd me for you to-day at dinner;
She now shall be my sister, not my wife.
E. DROMIO Methinks you are my glass, and not my brother;
I see by you I am a sweet-fac'd youth.

Will you walk in to see their gossiping?

S. DROMIO Not I, sir; you are my elder.

E. DROMIO That's a question; how shall we try it?

S. DROMIO We'll draw cuts for the senior; till then, lead thou first.

E. DROMIO Nay, then, thus:
We came into the world like brother and brother,
And now let's go hand in hand, not one before another.
[*Exeunt.*

Much Ado About Nothing

Introduction by SUSAN ANTHONY

Superficially, *Much Ado About Nothing* is the lightest and most sparkling of comedies. But if something so important to individual happiness as lifelong sexual pairing is 'nothing', then the play figures an alarming conformity to oppressive institutions vested in elderly male authority, property rights – and proprietorial rights in women: 'Well, niece, I trust you will be ruled by your father'.

Pronounced 'noting', the title suggests watching (the city watch provides the comic chorus); prying; checking-up – on financial prospects, and on that ultimately uncheckable 'thing', female chastity. Leonato seizes on the fact that his daughter, unusually, lay alone, without an alibi, on the night before her wedding, as proof that she is unchaste: 'Confirm'd, confirm'd!'.

Much Ado is confined within the everyday: to family life in a small town in Italy. In an urban play without escapes, society supervises love, which takes curious guises thus restrained. Though the audience delights in the love-play (masking as antipathy) between Beatrice and Benedick, they offend each other. And the jealous insecurity Claudio's decorously delegated courtship hides breeds alarming hatred, unbalancing the comedy.

The masked dance [2.1.], which licenses covert communication between the sexes, is ambiguous. Claudio dare not claim his Hero, who accepts him not of her own choice, but in docile obedience to authority. Their only communication is a silent kiss, which she would as placidly bestow on any man her father directed. Hero's modest pliancy – she is a girl wholly constructed by family and society, without one spark of individual will – perversely supports Don John's base insinuation: 'every man's Hero'.

Messina, without wives or mothers, is a town full of nervous men. Claudio romanticises his own sexuality, and deprecates Hero's. Don John's malice activates these buried fears. Her own father's agonised but acquiescent reaction to Claudio's accusation against his only daughter defines the prejudices of his world. To defend her never occurs to him: he joins with her accusers. He wishes he had no daughter: he wishes her dead.

But it is all much ado about *nothing*. In the magic world of comedy, which the play after all inhabits, a benign friar, and most inactive watch can avert disaster. When, chastened, Claudio accepts a masked and unknown bride on trust, he finds old love miraculously restored. 'The former Hero, Hero that is dead'. And Hero for the first time finds her tongue, which Beatrice and Benedick never lost (he calls her 'my Lady Tongue'). Benedick is the jester for his male friends' hidden fears. Beatrice defies subjection.

> Would it not grieve a woman to be overmastered with a piece of valiant dust? . . .
> No, uncle, I'll none: Adam's sons are my brethren, and truly I hold it a sin to
> match in my kindred. [2.1.50–52]

But her disarming playfulness is strategic, allowable 'women's language': like Benedick, she is actually lonely. Both are more anxious than they seem. They change as soon as they find new selves in the mirror of love their friends contrive. That their conversions are genuine, their penitent frankness assures us.

> . . . Benedick, love on, I will requite thee,
> Taming my wild heart to thy loving hand. [3.1.111–112]

Having dared to voice their feelings, they dare risk plain language.

> Beatrice: 'Kill Claudio!'
> Benedick: 'Ha, not for the wide world.' [4.1.287–288]

A new and unbridgable gap seems opened between them by contradictory loyalties. But because this is no conventional romance test, but a necessary challenge, Benedick undertakes (and the comedy averts) it. Sexual vitality and honesty, human decency and good faith (Benedick's instinct is to trust, he waits to hear what Beatrice can say for Hero instead of clanning with the other men), redress the overpowering masculine repressiveness of Messina – though Dogberry remains a man with 'everything handsome' about him.

Doubts linger. Comic machinery cannot effectively dispel Claudio's convincing nastiness. But the play ends cheerfully in a noisy, plain, resounding dance: and that is the lasting impression remaining on our minds.

Much Ado About Nothing

DRAMATIS PERSONAE

DON PEDRO
Prince of Arragon
DON JOHN
his bastard brother
CLAUDIO
a young lord of Florence
BENEDICK
a young lord of Padua
LEONATO
Governor of Messina
ANTONIO
his brother
BALTHASAR
attendant on Don Pedro
BORACHIO, CONRADE
followers of Don John
FRIAR FRANCIS
DOGBERRY
a constable
VERGES
a headborough
A Sexton
A Boy
HERO
daughter to Leonato
BEATRICE
niece to Leonato
MARGARET, URSULA
gentlewomen attending on Hero
Messengers, a Watch, and Attendants

THE SCENE: MESSINA

ACT ONE

SCENE I. *Before Leonato's house.*

Enter LEONATO, HERO, and BEATRICE, with a Messenger.

LEONATO I learn in this letter that Don Pedro of Arragon comes this night to Messina.

MESSENGER He is very near by this; he was not three leagues off when I left him.

LEONATO How many gentlemen have you lost in this action?

MESSENGER But few of any sort, and none of name.

LEONATO A victory is twice itself when the achiever brings home full numbers. I find here that Don Pedro hath bestowed much honour on a young Florentine called Claudio.

MESSENGER Much deserv'd on his part, and equally rememb'red by Don Pedro. He hath borne himself beyond the promise of his age, doing, in the figure of a lamb, the feats of a lion; he hath, indeed, better bett'red expectation than you must expect of me to tell you how.

LEONATO He hath an uncle here in Messina will be very much glad of it.

MESSENGER I have already delivered him letters, and there appears much joy in him; even so much that joy could not show itself modest enough without a badge of bitterness.

LEONATO Did he break out into tears?

MESSENGER In great measure.

LEONATO A kind overflow of kindness. There are no faces truer than those that are so wash'd. How much better is it to weep at joy than to joy at weeping!

BEATRICE I pray you, is Signior Mountanto return'd from the wars or no?

MESSENGER I know none of that name, lady; there was none such in the army of any sort.

LEONATO What is he that you ask for, niece?

HERO My cousin means Signior Benedick of Padua.

MESSENGER O, he's return'd, and as pleasant as ever he was.

BEATRICE He set up his bills here in Messina, and challeng'd Cupid at the flight; and my uncle's fool, reading the challenge, subscrib'd for Cupid, and challeng'd him at the bird-bolt. I pray you, how many hath he kill'd and eaten in these wars? But how many hath he kill'd? For, indeed, I promised to eat all of his killing.

LEONATO Faith, niece, you tax Signior Benedick too much; but he'll be meet with you, I doubt it not.

MESSENGER He hath done good service, lady, in these wars.

BEATRICE You had musty victual, and he hath holp to eat it; he is a very valiant trencherman; he hath an excellent stomach.

MESSENGER And a good soldier too, lady.

BEATRICE And a good soldier to a lady; but what is he to a lord?

MESSENGER A lord to a lord, a man to a man; stuff'd with all honourable virtues.

BEATRICE It is so, indeed; he is no less than a

stuff'd man; but for the stuffing – well, we are all mortal.

LEONATO You must not, sir, mistake my niece: there is a kind of merry war betwixt Signior Benedick and her; they never meet but there's a skirmish of wit between them.

BEATRICE Alas, he gets nothing by that. In our last conflict four of his five wits went halting off, and now is the whole man govern'd with one; so that if he have wit enough to keep himself warm, let him bear it for a difference between himself and his horse; for it is all the wealth that he hath left, to be known a reasonable creature. Who is his companion now? He hath every month a new sworn brother.

MESSENGER Is't possible?

BEATRICE Very easily possible: he wears his faith but as the fashion of his hat; it ever changes with the next block.

MESSENGER I see, lady, the gentleman is not in your books.

BEATRICE No; an he were, I would burn my study. But, I pray you, who is his companion? Is there no young squarer now that will make a voyage with him to the devil?

MESSENGER He is most in the company of the right noble Claudio.

BEATRICE O Lord! He will hang upon him like a disease; he is sooner caught than the pestilence, and the taker runs presently mad. God help the noble Claudio! If he have caught the Benedick, it will cost him a thousand pound ere 'a be cured.

MESSENGER I will hold friends with you, lady.

BEATRICE Do, good friend.

LEONATO You will never run mad, niece.

BEATRICE No, not till a hot January.

MESSENGER Don Pedro is approach'd.

Enter DON PEDRO, CLAUDIO, BENEDICK, BALTHASAR, and JOHN the Bastard.

DON PEDRO Good Signior Leonato, are you come to meet your trouble? The fashion of the world is to avoid cost, and you encounter it.

LEONATO Never came trouble to my house in the likeness of your Grace; for trouble being gone comfort should remain; but when you depart from me sorrow abides, and happiness takes his leave.

DON PEDRO You embrace your charge too willingly. I think this is your daughter.

LEONATO Her mother hath many times told me so.

BENEDICK Were you in doubt, sir, that you ask'd her?

LEONATO Signior Benedick, no; for then were you a child.

DON PEDRO You have it full, Benedick; we may guess by this what you are, being a man. Truly, the lady fathers herself. Be happy, lady, for you are like an honourable father.

BENEDICK If Signior Leonato be her father, she would not have his head on her shoulders for all Messina, as like him as she is.

BEATRICE I wonder that you will still be talking, Signior Benedick; nobody marks you.

BENEDICK What, my dear Lady Disdain! Are you yet living?

BEATRICE Is it possible disdain should die while she hath such meet food to feed it as Signior Benedick? Courtesy itself must convert to disdain if you come in her presence.

BENEDICK Then is courtesy a turncoat. But it is certain I am loved of all ladies, only you excepted; and I would I could find in my heart that I had not a hard heart, for, truly, I love none.

BEATRICE A dear happiness to women! They would else have been troubled with a pernicious suitor. I thank God, and my cold blood, I am of your humour for that: I had rather hear my dog bark at a crow than a man swear he loves me.

BENEDICK God keep your ladyship still in that mind! So some gentleman or other shall scape a predestinate scratch'd face.

BEATRICE Scratching could not make it worse, an 'twere such a face as yours were.

BENEDICK Well, you are a a rare parrot-teacher.

BEATRICE A bird of my tongue is better than a beast of yours.

BENEDICK I would my horse had the speed of your tongue, and so good a continuer. But keep your way a God's name, I have done.

BEATRICE You always end with a jade's trick; I know you of old.

DON PEDRO That is the sum of all, Leonato. Signior Claudio and Signior Benedick, my dear friend Leonato hath invited you all. I tell him we shall stay here at the least a month; and he heartily prays some occasion may detain us longer. I dare swear he is no hypocrite, but prays from his heart.

LEONATO If you swear, my lord, you shall not be forsworn. [*To Don John*] Let me bid you welcome, my lord – being reconciled to the Prince your brother, I owe you all duty.

DON JOHN I thank you; I am not of many words, but I thank you.

LEONATO Please it your Grace lead on?

DON PEDRO Your hand, Leonato; we will go together.

[*Exeunt all but Benedick and Claudio.*

CLAUDIO Benedick, didst thou note the daughter of Signior Leonato?

BENEDICK I noted her not, but I look'd on her.

CLAUDIO Is she not a modest young lady?

BENEDICK Do you question me, as an honest man should do, for my simple true judgment; or would you have me speak after my custom, as being a professed tyrant to their sex?

CLAUDIO No, I pray thee speak in sober judgment.

BENEDICK Why, i' faith, methinks she's too low for a high praise, too brown for a fair praise, and too little for a great praise; only this commendation I can afford her, that were she other than she is, she were unhandsome, and being no other but as she is, I do not like her.

CLAUDIO Thou thinkest I am in sport; I pray thee tell me truly how thou lik'st her.

BENEDICK Would you buy her, that you inquire after her?

CLAUDIO Can the world buy such a jewel?

BENEDICK Yea, and a case to put it into. But speak you this with a sad brow, or do you play the flouting Jack, to tell us Cupid is a good hare-finder, and Vulcan a rare carpenter? Come, in what key shall a man take you to go in the song?

CLAUDIO In mine eye she is the sweetest lady that ever I look'd on.

BENEDICK I can see yet without spectacles, and I see no such matter; there's her cousin, an she were not possess'd with a fury, exceeds her as much in beauty as the first of May doth the last of December. But I hope you have no intent to turn husband, have you?

CLAUDIO I would scarce trust myself, though I had sworn the contrary, if Hero would be my wife.

BENEDICK Is't come to this? In faith, hath not the world one man but he will wear his cap with suspicion? Shall I never see a bachelor of threescore again? Go to, i' faith; an thou wilt needs thrust thy neck into a yoke, wear the print of it, and sigh away Sundays. Look, Don Pedro is returned to seek you.

Re-enter DON PEDRO

DON PEDRO What secret hath held you here, that you followed not to Leonato's?

BENEDICK I would your Grace would constrain me to tell.

DON PEDRO I charge thee on thy allegiance.

BENEDICK You hear, Count Claudio; I can be secret as a dumb man, I would have you think so; but on my allegiance, mark you this, on my allegiance – he is in love. With who? now that is your Grace's part. Mark how short his answer is: with Hero, Leonato's short daughter.

CLAUDIO If this were so, so were it utt'red.

BENEDICK Like the old tale, my lord: 'It is not so, nor 'twas not so; but, indeed, God forbid it should be so!'

CLAUDIO If my passion change not shortly, God forbid it should be otherwise!

DON PEDRO Amen, if you love her; for the lady is very well worthy.

CLAUDIO You speak this to fetch me in, my lord?

DON PEDRO By my troth, I speak my thought.

CLAUDIO And, in faith, my lord, I spoke mine.

BENEDICK And, by my two faiths and troths, my lord I spoke mine.

CLAUDIO That I love her, I feel.

DON PEDRO That she is worthy, I know.

BENEDICK That I neither feel how she should be loved, nor know how she should be worthy, is the opinion that fire cannot melt out of me; I will die in it at the stake.

DON PEDRO Thou wast ever an obstinate heretic in the despite of beauty.

CLAUDIO And never could maintain his part but in the force of his will.

BENEDICK That a woman conceived me, I thank her; that she brought me up, I likewise give her most humble thanks; but that I will have a recheat winded in my forehead, or hang my bugle in an invisible baldrick, all women shall pardon me. Because I will not do them the wrong to mistrust any, I will do myself the right to trust none; and the fine is, for the which I may go the finer, I will live a bachelor.

DON PEDRO I shall see thee, ere I die, look pale with love.

BENEDICK With anger, with sickness, or with hunger, my lord; not with love. Prove that ever I lose more blood with love than I will get again with drinking, pick out mine eyes with a ballad-maker's pen, and hang me up at the door of a brothel-house for the sign of blind Cupid.

DON PEDRO Well, if ever thou dost fall from this faith, thou wilt prove a notable argument.

BENEDICK If I do, hang me in a bottle like a cat, and shoot at me; and he that hits me, let him be clapp'd on the shoulder and call'd Adam.

DON PEDRO Well, as time shall try.
'In time the savage bull doth bear the yoke.'

BENEDICK The savage bull may; but if ever the sensible Benedick bear it, pluck off the bull's horns and set them in my forehead, and let me be vilely painted; and in such great letters as they write 'Here is good horse to hire' let them signify under my sign 'Here you may see Benedick the married man'.

CLAUDIO If this should ever happen, thou wouldst be horn-mad.

DON PEDRO Nay, if Cupid have not spent all his

quiver in Venice, thou wilt quake for this shortly.

BENEDICK I look for an earthquake too, then.

DON PEDRO Well, you will temporize with the hours. In the meantime, good Signior Benedick, repair to Leonato's; commend me to him, and tell him I will not fail him at supper; for, indeed, he hath made great preparation.

BENEDICK I have almost matter enough in me for such an embassage; and so I commit you –

CLAUDIO To the tuition of God. From my house – if I had it –

DON PEDRO The sixth of July. Your loving friend, Benedick.

BENEDICK Nay, mock not, mock not. The body of your discourse is sometime guarded with fragments, and the guards are but slightly basted on neither; ere you flout old ends any further, examine your conscience; and so I leave you.

[*Exit Benedick.*

CLAUDIO My liege, your Highness now may do me good.

DON PEDRO My love is thine to teach; teach it but how,
And thou shalt see how apt it is to learn
Any hard lesson that may do thee good.

CLAUDIO Hath Leonato any son, my lord?

DON PEDRO No child but Hero; she's his only heir.
Dost thou affect her, Claudio?

CLAUDIO O, my lord,
When you went onward on this ended action,
I look'd upon her with a soldier's eye,
That lik'd, but had a rougher task in hand
Than to drive liking to the name of love;
But now I am return'd, and that war-thoughts
Have left their places vacant, in their rooms
Come thronging soft and delicate desires,
All prompting me how fair young Hero is,
Saying I lik'd her ere I went to wars.

DON PEDRO Thou wilt be like a lover presently,
And tire the hearer with a book of words.
If thou dost love fair Hero, cherish it;
And I will break with her, and with her father,
And thou shalt have her. Was't not to this end
That thou began'st to twist so fine a story?

CLAUDIO How sweetly you do minister to love,
That know love's grief by his complexion!
But lest my liking might too sudden seem,
I would have salv'd it with a longer treatise.

DON PEDRO What need the bridge much broader than the flood?
The fairest grant is the necessity.
Look what will serve is fit. 'Tis once, thou lovest;
And I will fit thee with the remedy.
I know we shall have revelling to-night;
I will assume thy part in some disguise,
And tell fair Hero I am Claudio;
And in her bosom I'll unclasp my heart,
And take her hearing prisoner with the force
And strong encounter of my amorous tale.
Then, after, to her father will I break;
And the conclusion is she shall be thine.
In practice let us put it presently. [*Exeunt.*

SCENE II. *Leonato's house.*

Enter, severally, LEONATO and ANTONIO.

LEONATO How now, brother! Where is my cousin, your son? Hath he provided this music?

ANTONIO He is very busy about it. But, brother, I can tell you strange news that you yet dreamt not of.

LEONATO Are they good?

ANTONIO As the event stamps them; but they have a good cover; they show well outward. The Prince and Count Claudio, walking in a thick-pleached alley in mine orchard, were thus much overheard by a man of mine: the Prince discovered to Claudio that he loved my niece your daughter, and meant to acknowledge it this night in a dance; and, if he found her accordant, he meant to take the present time by the top, and instantly break with you of it.

LEONATO Hath the fellow any wit that told you this?

ANTONIO A good sharp fellow; I will send for him, and question him yourself.

LEONATO No, no; we will hold it as a dream, till it appear itself; but I will acquaint my daughter withal, that she may be the better prepared for an answer, if peradventure this be true. Go you and tell her of it. [*Several persons cross the stage*] Cousins, you know what you have to do. O, I cry you mercy, friend; go with me, and I will use your skill. Good cousin, have a care this busy time. [*Exeunt.*

SCENE III. *Leonato's house.*

Enter DON JOHN and CONRADE.

CONRADE What the good-year, my lord! Why are you thus out of measure sad?

DON JOHN There is no measure in the occasion that breeds; therefore the sadness is without limit.

CONRADE You should hear reason.

DON JOHN And when I have heard it, what blessing brings it?

CONRADE If not a present remedy, at least a patient sufferance.

DON JOHN I wonder that thou, being, as thou say'st thou art, born under Saturn, goest about to apply a moral medicine to a mortifying mischief. I cannot hide what I am; I must be sad when I have cause, and smile at no man's jests; eat when I have stomach, and wait for no man's leisure; sleep when I am drowsy, and tend on no man's business; laugh when I am merry, and claw no man in his humour.

CONRADE Yea, but you must not make the full show of this till you may do it without controlment. You have of late stood out against your brother, and he hath ta'en you newly into his grace; where it is impossible you should take true root but by the fair weather that you make yourself; it is needful that you frame the season for your own harvest.

DON JOHN I had rather be a canker in a hedge than a rose in his grace; and it better fits my blood to be disdain'd of all than to fashion a carriage to rob love from any. In this, though I cannot be said to be a flattering honest man, it must not be denied but I am a plain-dealing villain. I am trusted with a muzzle and enfranchis'd with a clog; therefore I have decreed not to sing in my cage. If I had my mouth, I would bite; if I had my liberty, I would do my liking; in the meantime let me be that I am, and seek not to alter me.

CONRADE Can you make no use of your discontent?

DON JOHN I make all use of it, for I use it only. Who comes here?

Enter BORACHIO.

What news, Borachio?

BORACHIO I came yonder from a great supper. The Prince, your brother, is royally entertain'd by Leonato; and I can give you intelligence of an intended marriage.

DON JOHN Will it serve for any model to build mischief on? What is he for a fool that betroths himself to unquietness?

BORACHIO Marry, it is your brother's right hand.

DON JOHN Who? The most exquisite Claudio?

BORACHIO Even he.

DON JOHN A proper squire! And who, and who? Which way looks he?

BORACHIO Marry, on Hero, the daughter and heir of Leonato.

DON JOHN A very forward March-chick! How came you to this?

BORACHIO Being entertain'd for a perfumer, as I was smoking a musty room, comes me the Prince and Claudio hand in hand, in sad conference. I whipt me behind the arras, and there heard it agreed upon that the Prince should woo Hero for himself, and, having obtain'd her, give her to Count Claudio.

DON JOHN Come, come, let us thither; this may prove food to my displeasure; that young start-up hath all the glory of my overthrow. If I can cross him any way, I bless myself every way. You are both sure, and will assist me?

CONRADE To the death, my lord.

DON JOHN Let us to the great supper; their cheer is the greater that I am subdued. Would the cook were o' my mind! Shall we go prove what's to be done?

BORACHIO We'll wait upon your lordship.

[*Exeunt.*

ACT TWO

SCENE I. *A hall in Leonato's house.*

Enter LEONATO, ANTONIO, HERO, BEATRICE, MARGARET, URSULA, and Others.

LEONATO Was not Count John here at supper?

ANTONIO I saw him not.

BEATRICE How tartly that gentleman looks! I never can see him but I am heart-burn'd an hour after.

HERO He is of a very melancholy disposition.

BEATRICE He were an excellent man that were made just in the mid-way between him and Benedick: the one is too like an image and says nothing, and the other too like my lady's eldest son, evermore tattling.

LEONATO Then half Signior Benedick's tongue in Count John's mouth, and half Count John's melancholy in Signior Benedick's face –

BEATRICE With a good leg and a good foot, uncle, and money enough in his purse, such a man would win any woman in the world, if 'a could get her good-will.

LEONATO By my troth, niece, thou wilt never get thee a husband if thou be so shrewd of thy tongue.

ANTONIO In faith, she's too curst.

BEATRICE Too curst is more than curst. I shall lessen God's sending that way; for it is said 'God sends a curst cow short horns'; but to a cow too curst he sends none.

LEONATO So, by being too curst, God will send you no horns.

BEATRICE Just, if he send me no husband; for the which blessing I am at him upon my knees every morning and evening. Lord! I could not endure a husband with a beard on his face; I had rather lie in the woollen.

LEONATO You may light on a husband that hath no beard.

BEATRICE What should I do with him? Dress him in my apparel, and make him my waiting gentlewoman? He that hath a beard is more than a youth, and he that hath no beard is less than a man; and he that is more than a youth is not for me, and he that is less than a man I am not for him; therefore I will even take sixpence in earnest of the berrord, and lead his apes into hell.

LEONATO Well then, go you into hell?

BEATRICE No; but to the gate, and there will the devil meet me, like an old cuckold, with horns on his head, and say 'Get you to heaven, Beatrice, get you to heaven; here's no place for you maids'. So deliver I up my apes and away to Saint Peter for the heavens; he shows me where the bachelors sit, and there live we as merry as the day is long.

ANTONIO [*To Hero*] Well, niece, I trust you will be rul'd by your father.

BEATRICE Yes, faith; it is my cousin's duty to make curtsy, and say 'Father, as it please you'. But yet for all that, cousin, let him be a handsome fellow, or else make another curtsy and say 'Father, as it please me.'

LEONATO Well, niece, I hope to see you one day fitted with a husband.

BEATRICE Not till God make men of some other metal than earth. Would it not grieve a woman to be over-master'd with a piece of valiant dust, to make an account of her life to a clod of wayward marl? No, uncle, I'll none: Adam's sons are my brethren; and, truly, I hold it a sin to match in my kindred.

LEONATO Daughter, remember what I told you: if the Prince do solicit you in that kind, you know your answer.

BEATRICE The fault will be in the music, cousin, if you be not wooed in good time. If the Prince be too important, tell him there is measure in every thing, and so dance out the answer. For, hear me, Hero: wooing, wedding, and repenting, is as a Scotch jig, a measure, and a cinquepace; the first suit is hot and hasty, like a Scotch jig, and full as fantastical; the wedding, mannerly modest, as a measure, full of state and ancientry; and then comes repentance, and, with his bad legs, falls into the cinquepace faster and faster, till he sink into his grave.

LEONATO Cousin, you apprehend passing shrewdly.

BEATRICE I have a good eye, uncle; I can see a church by daylight.

LEONATO The revellers are ent'ring, brother; make good room. [*Antonio masks.*

Enter DON PEDRO, CLAUDIO, BENEDICK, BALTHASAR, DON JOHN, and BORACHIO, as maskers, with a drum.

DON PEDRO Lady, will you walk about with your friend?

HERO So you walk softly, and look sweetly, and say nothing, I am yours for the walk; and, especially, when I walk away.

DON PEDRO With me in your company?

HERO I may say so, when I please.

DON PEDRO And when please you to say so?

HERO When I like your favour; for God defend the lute should be like the case!

DON PEDRO My visor is Philemon's roof; within the house is Jove.

HERO Why, then, your visor should be thatch'd.

DON PEDRO Speak low, if you speak love. [*Takes her aside.*

BALTHASAR Well, I would you did like me.

MARGARET So would not I, for your own sake; for I have many ill qualities.

BALTHASAR Which is one?

MARGARET I say my prayers aloud.

BALTHASAR I love you the better; the hearers may cry Amen.

MARGARET God match me with a good dancer!

BALTHASAR Amen.

MARGARET And God keep him out of my sight when the dance is done! Answer, clerk.

BALTHASAR No more words; the clerk is answered.

URSULA I know you well enough; you are Signior Antonio.

ANTONIO At a word, I am not.

URSULA I know you by the waggling of your head.

ANTONIO To tell you true, I counterfeit him.

URSULA You could never do him so ill-well unless you were the very man. Here's his dry hand up and down; you are he, you are he.

ANTONIO At a word, I am not.

URSULA Come, come; do you think I do not know you by your excellent wit? Can virtue hide itself? Go to; mum; you are he; graces will appear, and there's an end.

BEATRICE Will you not tell me who told you so?

BENEDICK No, you shall pardon me.

BEATRICE Nor will you not tell me who you are?

BENEDICK Not now.

BEATRICE That I was disdainful, and that I had

my good wit out of the 'Hundred Merry Tales' – well, this was Signior Benedick that said so.

BENEDICK What's he?

BEATRICE I am sure you know him well enough.

BENEDICK Not I, believe me.

BEATRICE Did he never make you laugh?

BENEDICK I pray you, what is he?

BEATRICE Why, he is the Prince's jester, a very dull fool; only his gift is in devising impossible slanders; none but libertines delight in him, and the commendation is not in his wit but in his villainy; for he both pleases men and angers them, and then they laugh at him and beat him. I am sure he is in the fleet; I would he had boarded me.

BENEDICK When I know the gentleman, I'll tell him what you say.

BEATRICE Do, do; he'll but break a comparison or two on me; which, peradventure, not mark'd, or not laugh'd at, strikes him into melancholy; and then there's a partridge wing saved, for the fool will eat no supper that night. [*Music*] We must follow the leaders.

BENEDICK In every good thing.

BEATRICE Nay, if they lead to any ill, I will leave them at the next turning.

[*Dance. Then exeunt all but Don John, Borachio, and Claudio.*

DON JOHN Sure, my brother is amorous on Hero, and hath withdrawn her father to break with him about it. The ladies follow her, and but one visor remains.

BORACHIO And that is Claudio; I know him by his bearing.

DON JOHN Are not you Signior Benedick?

CLAUDIO You know me well; I am he.

DON JOHN Signior, you are very near my brother in his love; he is enamour'd on Hero; I pray you dissuade him from her; she is no equal for his birth. You may do the part of an honest man in it.

CLAUDIO How know you he loves her?

DON JOHN I heard him swear his affection.

BORACHIO So did I too; and he swore he would marry her to-night.

DON JOHN Come, let us to the banquet.

[*Exeunt Don John and Borachio.*

CLAUDIO Thus answer I in name of Benedick,
But hear these ill news with the ears of Claudio.
'Tis certain so: the Prince woos for himself.
Friendship is constant in all other things
Save in the office and affairs of love;
Therefore all hearts in love use their own tongues.
Let every eye negotiate for itself.
And trust no agent; for beauty is a witch
Against whose charms faith melteth into blood.
This is an accident of hourly proof,
Which I mistrusted not. Farewell, therefore, Hero.

Re-enter BENEDICK.

BENEDICK Count Claudio?

CLAUDIO Yea, the same.

BENEDICK Come, will you go with me?

CLAUDIO Whither?

BENEDICK Even to the next willow, about your own business, County. What fashion will you wear the garland of? About your neck, like an usurer's chain, or under your arm, like a lieutenant's scarf? You must wear it one way, for the Prince hath got your Hero.

CLAUDIO I wish him joy of her.

BENEDICK Why, that's spoken like an honest drovier; so they sell bullocks. But did you think the Prince would have served you thus?

CLAUDIO I pray you leave me.

BENEDICK Ho! now you strike like the blind man; 'twas the boy that stole your meat, and you'll beat the post.

CLAUDIO If it will not be, I'll leave you. [*Exit.*

BENEDICK Alas, poor hurt fowl! Now will he creep into sedges. But that my Lady Beatrice should know me, and not know me! The Prince's fool! Ha! It may be I go under that title because I am merry. Yea, but so I am apt to do myself wrong; I am not so reputed; it is the base, though bitter, disposition of Beatrice that puts the world into her person, and so gives me out. Well, I'll be revenged as I may.

Re-enter DON PEDRO.

DON PEDRO Now, signior, where's the Count? Did you see him?

BENEDICK Troth, my lord, I have played the part of Lady Fame. I found him here as melancholy as a lodge in a warren; I told him, and I think I told him true, that your Grace had got the good will of this young lady; and I off'red him my company to a willow tree, either to make him a garland, as being forsaken, or to bind him up a rod, as being worthy to be whipt.

DON PEDRO To be whipt! What's his fault?

BENEDICK The flat transgression of a schoolboy, who, being overjoyed with finding a bird's nest, shows it his companion, and he steals it.

DON PEDRO Wilt thou make a trust a transgression? The transgression is in the stealer.

BENEDICK Yet it had not been amiss the rod had been made, and the garland too; for the garland he might have worn himself, and the rod he might have bestowed on you, who, as I take it, have stol'n his bird's nest.

DON PEDRO I will but teach them to sing, and restore them to the owner.

BENEDICK If their singing answer your saying, by my faith, you say honestly.

DON PEDRO The Lady Beatrice hath a quarrel to you; the gentleman that danc'd with her told her she is much wrong'd by you.

BENEDICK O, she misus'd me past the endurance of a block; an oak but with one green leaf on it would have answered her; my very visor began to assume life and scold with her. She told me, not thinking I had been myself, that I was the Prince's jester, that I was duller than a great thaw; huddling jest upon jest with such impossible conveyance upon me that I stood like a man at a mark, with a whole army shooting at me. She speaks poniards, and every word stabs; if her breath were as terrible as her terminations, there were no living near her; she would infect to the north star. I would not marry her though she were endowed with all that Adam had left him before he transgress'd; she would have made Hercules have turn'd spit, yea, and have cleft his club to make the fire too. Come, talk not of her; you shall find her the infernal Ate in good apparel. I would to God some scholar would conjure her; for certainly, while she is here, a man may live as quiet in hell as in a sanctuary; and people sin upon purpose, because they would go thither; so, indeed, all disquiet, horror, and perturbation, follows her.

Re-enter CLAUDIO and BEATRICE, LEONATO and HERO.

DON PEDRO Look, here she comes.

BENEDICK Will your Grace command me any service to the world's end? I will go on the slightest errand now to the Antipodes that you can devise to send me on; I will fetch you a toothpicker now from the furthest inch of Asia; bring you the length of Prester John's foot; fetch you a hair off the great Cham's beard; do you any embassage to the Pigmies – rather than hold three words' conference with this harpy. You have no employment for me?

DON PEDRO None, but to desire your good company.

BENEDICK O God, sir, here's a dish I love not; I cannot endure my Lady Tongue. *[Exit.*

DON PEDRO Come, lady, come; you have lost the heart of Signior Benedick.

BEATRICE Indeed, my lord, he lent it me awhile; and I gave him use for it, a double heart for his single one; marry, once before he won it of me with false dice, therefore your Grace may well say I have lost it.

DON PEDRO You have put him down, lady, you have put him down.

BEATRICE So I would not he should do me, my lord, lest I should prove the mother of fools. I have brought Count Claudio, whom you sent me to seek.

DON PEDRO Why, how now, Count! Wherefore are you sad?

CLAUDIO Not sad, my lord.

DON PEDRO How then, sick?

CLAUDIO Neither, my lord.

BEATRICE The Count is neither sad, nor sick, nor merry, nor well; but civil count – civil as an orange, and something of that jealous complexion.

DON PEDRO I' faith, lady, I think your blazon to be true, though I'll be sworn, if he be so, his conceit is false. Here, Claudio, I have wooed in thy name, and fair Hero is won. I have broke with her father, and his good will obtained. Name the day of marriage, and God give thee joy!

LEONATO Count, take of me my daughter, and with her my fortunes; his Grace hath made the match, and all grace say Amen to it!

BEATRICE Speak, Count, 'tis your cue.

CLAUDIO Silence is the perfectest herald of joy: I were but little happy if I could say how much. Lady, as you are mine, I am yours; I give away myself for you, and dote upon the exchange.

BEATRICE Speak, cousin; or, if you cannot, stop his mouth with a kiss, and let not him speak neither.

DON PEDRO In faith, lady, you have a merry heart.

BEATRICE Yea, my lord; I thank it, poor fool, it keeps on the windy side of care. My cousin tells him in his ear that he is in her heart.

CLAUDIO And so she doth, cousin.

BEATRICE Good Lord, for alliance! Thus goes every one to the world but I, and I am sunburnt; I may sit in a corner and cry 'Heigh-ho for a husband!'

DON PEDRO Lady Beatrice, I will get you one.

BEATRICE I would rather have one of your father's getting. Hath your Grace ne'er a brother like you? Your father got excellent husbands, if a maid could come by them.

DON PEDRO Will you have me, lady?

BEATRICE No, my lord, unless I might have another for working-days; your Grace is too costly to wear every day. But, I beseech your Grace, pardon me; I was born to speak all mirth and no matter.

DON PEDRO Your silence most offends me, and to

be merry best becomes you; for, out o' question, you were born in a merry hour.

BEATRICE No, sure, my lord, my mother cried; but then there was a star danc'd, and under that was I born. Cousins, God give you joy!

LEONATO Niece, you will look to those things I told you of?

BEATRICE I cry your mercy, uncle. By your Grace's pardon. *[Exit Beatrice.*

DON PEDRO By my troth, a pleasant-spirited lady.

LEONATO There's little of the melancholy element in her, my lord; she is never sad but when she sleeps, and not ever sad then; for I have heard my daughter say she hath often dreamt of unhappiness, and wak'd herself with laughing.

DON PEDRO She cannot endure to hear tell of a husband.

LEONATO O, by no means; she mocks all her wooers out of suit.

DON PEDRO She were an excellent wife for Benedick.

LEONATO O Lord, my lord, if they were but a week married, they would talk themselves mad.

DON PEDRO County Claudio, when mean you to go to church?

CLAUDIO To-morrow, my lord. Time goes on crutches till love have all his rites.

LEONATO Not till Monday, my dear son, which is hence a just seven-night; and a time too brief, too, to have all things answer my mind.

DON PEDRO Come, you shake the head at so long a breathing; but I warrant thee, Claudio, the time shall not go dully by us. I will in the interim undertake one of Hercules' labours; which is, to bring Signior Benedick and the Lady Beatrice into a mountain of affection th' one with th' other. I would fain have it a match; and I doubt not but to fashion it if you three will but minister such assistance as I shall give you direction.

LEONATO My lord, I am for you, though it cost me ten nights' watchings.

CLAUDIO And I, my lord.

DON PEDRO And you too, gentle Hero?

HERO I will do any modest office, my lord, to help my cousin to a good husband.

DON PEDRO And Benedick is not the unhopefullest husband that I know. Thus far can I praise him: he is of a noble strain, of approved valour, and confirm'd honesty. I will teach you how to humour your cousin that she shall fall in love with Benedick; and I, with your two helps, will so practise on Benedick that, in despite of his quick wit and his queasy stomach, he shall fall in love with Beatrice. If we can do this, Cupid is no longer an archer; his glory shall be ours, for we are the only love-gods. Go in with me, and I will tell you my drift. *[Exeunt.*

SCENE II. *Leonato's house.*

Enter DON JOHN and BORACHIO.

DON JOHN It is so: the Count Claudio shall marry the daughter of Leonato.

BORACHIO Yea, my lord, but I can cross it.

DON JOHN Any bar, any cross, any impediment, will be med'cinable to me. I am sick in displeasure to him; and whatsoever comes athwart his affection ranges evenly with mine. How canst thou cross this marriage?

BORACHIO Not honestly, my lord; but so covertly that no dishonesty shall appear in me.

DON JOHN Show me briefly how.

BORACHIO I think I told your lordship a year since how much I am in the favour of Margaret, the waiting gentlewoman to Hero.

DON JOHN I remember.

BORACHIO I can at any unseasonable instant of the night appoint her to look out at her lady's chamber window.

DON JOHN What life is in that, to be the death of this marriage?

BORACHIO The poison of that lies in you to temper. Go you to the Prince your brother; spare not to tell him that he hath wronged his honour in marrying the renowned Claudio – whose estimation do you mightily hold up – to a contaminated stale, such a one as Hero.

DON JOHN What proof shall I make of that?

BORACHIO Proof enough to misuse the Prince, to vex Claudio, to undo Hero, and kill Leonato. Look you for any other issue?

DON JOHN Only to despite them I will endeavour anything.

BORACHIO Go, then; find me a meet hour to draw Don Pedro and the Count Claudio alone; tell them that you know that Hero loves me; intend a kind of zeal both to the Prince and Claudio – as in love of your brother's honour, who hath made this match, and his friend's reputation, who is thus like to be cozen'd with the semblance of a maid – that you have discover'd thus. They will scarcely believe this without trial; offer them instances; which shall bear no less likelihood than to see me at her chamber window; hear me call Margaret Hero; hear Margaret term me Borachio; and bring them to see this the very night before the intended wedding – for in the meantime I will so fashion the matter that Hero shall be absent – and there shall appear such seeming truth of Hero's disloyalty that jealousy shall be call'd assurance, and all the preparation overthrown.

DON JOHN Grow this to what adverse issue it can, I will put it in practice. Be cunning in the working this, and thy fee is a thousand ducats.

BORACHIO Be you constant in the accusation, and my cunning shall not shame me.

DON JOHN I will presently go learn their day of marriage. [*Exeunt.*

SCENE III. *Leonato's orchard.*

Enter BENEDICK, alone.

BENEDICK Boy!

BOY [*Within*] Signior?

BENEDICK In my chamber-window lies a book; bring it hither to me in the orchard.

BOY [*Above, at chamber window*] I am here already, sir.

BENEDICK I know that; but I would have thee hence and here again. [*Boy brings book; Exit*] I do much wonder that one man, seeing how much another man is a fool when he dedicates his behaviours to love, will, after he hath laugh'd at such shallow follies in others, become the argument of his own scorn by falling in love; and such a man is Claudio. I have known when there was no music with him but the drum and the fife, and now had he rather hear the tabor and the pipe; I have known when he would have walk'd ten mile afoot to see a good armour, and now will he lie ten nights awake carving the fashion of a new doublet. He was wont to speak plain and to the purpose, like an honest man and a soldier, and now is he turn'd orthography; his words are a very fantastical banquet, just so many strange dishes. May I be so converted, and see with these eyes? I cannot tell; I think not. I will not be sworn but love may transform me to an oyster; but I'll take my oath on it, till he have made an oyster of me he shall never make me such a fool. One woman is fair, yet I am well; another is wise, yet I am well; another virtuous, yet I am well; but till all graces be in one woman, one woman shall not come in my grace. Rich she shall be, that's certain; wise, or I'll none; virtuous, or I'll never cheapen her; fair, or I'll never look on her; mild, or come not near me; noble, or not I for an angel; of good discourse, an excellent musician, and her hair shall be of what colour it please God. Ha! the Prince and Monsieur Love! I will hide me in the arbour. [*Withdraws.*

Enter DON PEDRO, LEONATO, and CLAUDIO.

DON PEDRO Come, shall we hear this music?

CLAUDIO Yea, my good lord. How still the evening is,
As hush'd on purpose to grace harmony!

DON PEDRO See you where Benedick hath hid himself?

CLAUDIO O, very well, my lord; the music ended,
We'll fit the kid-fox with a pennyworth.

Enter BALTHASAR, with music.

DON PEDRO Come, Balthasar, we'll hear that song again.

BALTHASAR O, good my lord, tax not so bad a voice
To slander music any more than once.

DON PEDRO It is the witness still of excellency
To put a strange face on his own perfection.
I pray thee sing, and let me woo no more.

BALTHASAR Because you talk of wooing, I will sing,
Since many a wooer doth commence his suit
To her he thinks not worthy; yet he woos,
Yet will he swear he loves.

DON PEDRO Nay, pray thee, come;
Or if thou wilt hold longer argument,
Do it in notes.

BALTHASAR Note this before my notes:
There's not a note of mine that's worth the noting.

DON PEDRO Why, these are very crotchets that he speaks;
Note notes, forsooth, and nothing! [*Music.*

BENEDICK Now, divine air! now is his soul ravish'd. Is it not strange that sheeps' guts should hale souls out of men's bodies? Well, a horn for my money, when all's done.

Balthasar sings.

Sigh no more, ladies, sigh no more,
Men were deceivers ever,
One foot in sea and one on shore,
To one thing constant never.
Then sigh not so, but let them go,
And be you blithe and bonny;
Converting all your sounds of woe
Into Hey nonny nonny.
Sing no more ditties, sing no moe
Of dumps so dull and heavy;
The fraud of men was ever so,
Since summer first was leavy.
Then sigh not so, etc.

DON PEDRO By my troth, a good song.

BALTHASAR And an ill singer, my lord.

CLAUDIO Ha, no; no, faith; thou sing'st well enough for a shift.

BENEDICK An he had been a dog that should have howl'd thus, they would have hang'd him; and I pray God his bad voice bode no mischief. I had as lief have heard the night-raven, come what plague could have come after it.

DON PEDRO Yea, marry; dost thou hear,

Balthasar? I pray thee get us some excellent music; for to-morrow night we would have it at the Lady Hero's chamber window.

BALTHASAR The best I can, my lord.

DON PEDRO Do so; farewell. [*Exit Balthasar*] Come hither, Leonato. What was it you told me of to-day – that your niece Beatrice was in love with Signior Benedick?

CLAUDIO O ay; stalk on, stalk on; the fowl sits. I did never think that lady would have loved any man.

LEONATO No, nor I neither; but most wonderful that she should so dote on Signior Benedick, whom she hath in all outward behaviours seem'd ever to abhor.

BENEDICK Is't possible? Sits the wind in that corner?

LEONATO By my troth, my lord, I cannot tell what to think of it; but that she loves him with an enraged affection – it is past the infinite of thought.

DON PEDRO May be she doth but counterfeit.

CLAUDIO Faith, like enough.

LEONATO O God, counterfeit! There was never counterfeit of passion came so near the life of passion as she discovers it.

DON PEDRO Why, what effects of passion shows she?

CLAUDIO Bait the hook well; this fish will bite.

LEONATO What effects, my lord? She will sit you – you heard my daughter tell you how.

CLAUDIO She did, indeed.

DON PEDRO How, how, I pray you? You amaze me; I would have thought her spirit had been invincible against all assaults of affection.

LEONATO I would have sworn it had, my lord; especially against Benedick.

BENEDICK I should think this a gull, but that the white-bearded fellow speaks it; knavery cannot, sure, hide himself in such reverence.

CLAUDIO He hath ta'en th' infection; hold it up.

DON PEDRO Hath she made her affection known to Benedick?

LEONATO No; and swears she never will; that's her torment.

CLAUDIO 'Tis true, indeed; so your daughter says. 'Shall I,' says she 'that have so oft encount'red him with scorn, write to him that I love him?'

LEONATO This says she now, when she is beginning to write to him; for she'll be up twenty times a night; and there will she sit in her smock till she have writ a sheet of paper. My daughter tells us all.

CLAUDIO Now you talk of a sheet of paper, I remember a pretty jest your daughter told us of.

LEONATO O, when she had writ it, and was reading it over, she found 'Benedick' and 'Beatrice' between the sheet!

CLAUDIO That.

LEONATO O, she tore the letter into a thousand halfpence; rail'd at herself that she should be so immodest to write to one that she knew would flout her. 'I measure him' says she 'by my own spirit; for I should flout him if he writ to me; yea, though I love him, I should.'

CLAUDIO Then down upon her knees she falls, weeps, sobs, beats her heart, tears her hair, prays, curses – 'O sweet Benedick! God give me patience!'

LEONATO She doth indeed; my daughter says so; and the ecstasy hath so much overborne her that my daughter is sometime afeard she will do a desperate outrage to herself. It is very true.

DON PEDRO It were good that Benedick knew of it by some other, if she will not discover it.

CLAUDIO To what end? He would make but a sport of it, and torment the poor lady worse.

DON PEDRO An he should, it were an alms to hang him. She's an excellent sweet lady, and, out of all suspicion, she is virtuous.

CLAUDIO And she is exceeding wise.

DON PEDRO In everything but in loving Benedick.

LEONATO O my lord, wisdom and blood combating in so tender a body, we have ten proofs to one that blood hath the victory. I am sorry for her, as I have just cause, being her uncle and her guardian.

DON PEDRO I would she had bestowed this dotage on me; I would have daff'd all other respects and made her half myself. I pray you, tell Benedick of it, and hear what 'a will say.

LEONATO Were it good, think you?

CLAUDIO Hero thinks surely she will die; for she says she will die if he love her not; and she will die ere she make her love known; and she will die if he woo her, rather than she will bate one breath of her accustomed crossness.

DON PEDRO She doth well; if she should make tender of her love, 'tis very possible he'll scorn it; for the man, as you know all, hath a contemptible spirit.

CLAUDIO He is a very proper man.

DON PEDRO He hath, indeed, a good outward happiness.

CLAUDIO Before God, and in my mind, very wise!

DON PEDRO He doth, indeed, show some sparks that are like wit.

LEONATO And I take him to be valiant.

DON PEDRO As Hector, I assure you; and in the managing of quarrels you may say he is wise, for either he avoids them with great discretion, or undertakes them with a most Christian-like fear.

LEONATO If he do fear God, 'a must necessarily keep peace; if he break the peace, he ought to enter into a quarrel with fear and trembling.

DON PEDRO And so will he do; for the man doth fear God, howsoever it seems not in him by some large jests he will make. Well, I am sorry for your niece. Shall we go seek Benedick, and tell him of her love?

CLAUDIO Never tell him, my lord; let her wear it out with good counsel.

LEONATO Nay, that's impossible; she may wear her heart out first.

DON PEDRO Well, we will hear further of it by your daughter; let it cool the while. I love Benedick well; and I could wish he would modestly examine himself, to see how much he is unworthy so good a lady.

LEONATO My lord, will you walk? Dinner is ready.

CLAUDIO If he do not dote on her upon this, I will never trust my expectation.

DON PEDRO Let there be the same net spread for her; and that must your daughter and her gentlewomen carry. The sport will be when they hold one an opinion of another's dotage, and no such matter; that's the scene that I would see, which will be merely a dumb show. Let us send her to call him in to dinner.

[*Exeunt Don Pedro, Claudio, and Leonato.*

BENEDICK [*Coming forward*] This can be no trick: the conference was sadly borne; they have the truth of this from Hero; they seem to pity the lady; it seems her affections have their full bent. Love me! Why, it must be requited. I hear how I am censur'd: they say I will bear myself proudly if I perceive the love come from her; they say, too, that she will rather die than give any sign of affection. I did never think to marry. I must not seem proud; happy are they that hear their detractions and can put them to mending. They say the lady is fair; 'tis a truth, I can bear them witness; and virtuous; 'tis so, I cannot reprove it; and wise, but for loving me. By my troth, it is no addition to her wit; nor no great argument of her folly, for I will be horribly in love with her. I may chance have some odd quirks and remnants of wit broken on me because I have railed so long against marriage; but doth not the appetite alter? A man loves the meat in his youth that he cannot endure in his age. Shall quips, and sentences, and these paper bullets of the brain, awe a man from the career of his humour? No; the world must be peopled. When I said I would die a bachelor, I did not think I should live till I were married. Here comes Beatrice. By this day, she's a fair lady; I do spy some marks of love in her.

Enter BEATRICE.

BEATRICE Against my will I am sent to bid you come in to dinner.

BENEDICK Fair Beatrice, I thank you for your pains.

BEATRICE I took no more pains for those thanks than you take pains to thank me; if it had been painful, I would not have come.

BENEDICK You take pleasure, then, in the message?

BEATRICE Yea, just so much as you may take upon a knife's point, and choke a daw withal. You have no stomach, signior; fare you well.

[*Exit.*

BENEDICK Ha! 'Against my will I am sent to bid you come in to dinner' – there's a double meaning in that. 'I took no more pains for those thanks than you took pains to thank me' – that's as much as to say 'Any pains that I take for you is as easy as thanks'. If I do not take pity of her, I am a villain; if I do not love her, I am a Jew. I will go get her picture.

[*Exit.*

ACT THREE

SCENE I. *Leonato's orchard.*

Enter HERO, MARGARET, and URSULA.

HERO Good Margaret, run thee to the parlour;
There shalt thou find my cousin Beatrice
Proposing with the Prince and Claudio.
Whisper her ear, and tell her I and Ursula
Walk in the orchard, and our whole discourse
Is all of her; say that thou overheard'st us;
And bid her steal into the pleached bower,
Where honeysuckles, ripened by the sun,
Forbid the sun to enter – like favourites,
Made proud by princes, that advance their pride
Against that power that bred it. There will she hide her
To listen our propose. This is thy office;
Bear thee well in it, and leave us alone.

MARGARET I'll make her come, I warrant you, presently.

[*Exit.*

HERO Now, Ursula, when Beatrice doth come,
As we do trace this alley up and down,

Our talk must only be of Benedick.
When I do name him, let it be thy part
To praise him more than ever man did merit;
My talk to thee must be how Benedick
Is sick in love with Beatrice. Of this matter
Is little Cupid's crafty arrow made,
That only wounds by hearsay. Now begin;

Enter BEATRICE, behind.

For look where Beatrice, like a lapwing, runs
Close by the ground, to hear our conference.

URSULA The pleasant'st angling is to see the fish
Cut with her golden oars the silver stream,
And greedily devour the treacherous bait.
So angle we for Beatrice; who even now
Is couched in the woodbine coverture.
Fear you not my part of the dialogue.

HERO Then go we near her, that her ear lose nothing
Of the false sweet bait that we lay for it.

[*They advance to the bower.*

No, truly, Ursula, she is too disdainful;
I know her spirits are as coy and wild
As haggards of the rock.

URSULA But are you sure
That Benedick loves Beatrice so entirely?

HERO So says the Prince and my new-trothed lord.

URSULA And did they bid you tell her of it, madam?

HERO They did entreat me to acquaint her of it;
But I persuaded them, if they lov'd Benedick,
To wish him wrestle with affection,
And never to let Beatrice know of it.

URSULA Why did you so? Doth not the gentleman
Deserve as full as fortunate a bed
As ever Beatrice shall couch upon?

HERO O god of love! I know he doth deserve
As much as may be yielded to a man;
But nature never fram'd a woman's heart
Of prouder stuff than that of Beatrice.
Disdain and scorn ride sparkling in her eyes,
Misprising what they look on; and her wit
Values itself so highly that to her
All matter else seems weak. She cannot love,
Nor take no shape nor project of affection,
She is so self-endeared.

URSULA Sure, I think so;
And therefore, certainly, it were not good
She knew his love, lest she'll make sport at it.

HERO Why, you speak truth. I never yet saw man,
How wise, how noble, young, how rarely featur'd,
But she would spell him backward. If fair-fac'd,
She would swear the gentleman should be her sister;
If black, why, Nature, drawing of an antic,
Made a foul blot; if tall, a lance ill-headed;
If low, an agate very vilely cut;
If speaking, why, a vane blown with all winds;
If silent, why, a block moved with none.
So turns she every man the wrong side out,
And never gives to truth and virtue that
Which simpleness and merit purchaseth.

URSULA Sure, sure, such carping is not commendable.

HERO No; not to be so odd and from all fashions,
As Beatrice is, cannot be commendable;
But who dare tell her so? If I should speak,
She would mock me into air; O, she would laugh me
Out of myself, press me to death with wit!
Therefore let Benedick, like cover'd fire,
Consume away in sighs, waste inwardly.
It were a better death than die with mocks,
Which is as bad as die with tickling.

URSULA Yet tell her of it; hear what she will say.

HERO No; rather I will go to Benedick
And counsel him to fight against his passion;
And, truly, I'll devise some honest slanders
To stain my cousin with. One doth not know
How much an ill word may empoison liking.

URSULA O, do not do your cousin such a wrong!
She cannot be so much without true judgment –
Having so swift and excellent a wit
As she is priz'd to have – as to refuse
So rare a gentleman as Signior Benedick.

HERO He is the only man of Italy,
Always excepted my dear Claudio.

URSULA I pray you be not angry with me, madam,
Speaking my fancy: Signior Benedick,
For shape, for bearing, argument, and valour,
Goes foremost in report through Italy.

HERO Indeed, he hath an excellent good name.

URSULA His excellence did earn it ere he had it.
When are you married, madam?

HERO Why, every day – to-morrow. Come, go in;
I'll show thee some attires, and have thy counsel
Which is the best to furnish me to-morrow.

URSULA She's lim'd, I warrant you; we have caught her, madam.

HERO If it prove so, then loving goes by haps:
Some Cupid kills with arrows, some with traps.

[*Exeunt Hero and Ursula.*

BEATRICE [*Coming forward*] What fire is in mine ears? Can this be true?
Stand I condemn'd for pride and scorn so much?
Contempt, farewell! and maiden pride, adieu!

No glory lives behind the back of such.
And, Benedick, love on; I will requite thee,
Taming my wild heart to thy loving hand;
If thou dost love, my kindness shall incite thee
To bind our loves up in a holy band;
For others say thou dost deserve, and I
Believe it better than reportingly. *[Exit.*

SCENE II. *Leonato's house.*

Enter DON PEDRO, CLAUDIO, BENEDICK, and LEONATO.

DON PEDRO I do but stay till your marriage be consummate, and then go I toward Arragon.

CLAUDIO I'll bring you thither, my lord, if you'll vouchsafe me.

DON PEDRO Nay, that would be as great a soil in the new gloss of your marriage as to show a child his new coat, and forbid him to wear it. I will only be bold with Benedick for his company; for, from the crown of his head to the sole of his foot, he is all mirth; he hath twice or thrice cut Cupid's bow-string, and the little hangman dare not shoot at him; he hath a heart as sound as a bell, and his tongue is the clapper; for what his heart thinks, his tongue speaks.

BENEDICK Gallants, I am not as I have been.

LEONATO So say I; methinks you are sadder.

CLAUDIO I hope he be in love.

DON PEDRO Hang him, truant! There's no true drop of blood in him to be truly touch'd with love; if he be sad, he wants money.

BENEDICK I have the toothache.

DON PEDRO Draw it.

BENEDICK Hang it!

CLAUDIO You must hang it first and draw it afterwards.

DON PEDRO What! sigh for the toothache?

LEONATO Where is but a humour or a worm.

BENEDICK Well, every one can master a grief but he that has it.

CLAUDIO Yet, say I, he is in love.

DON PEDRO There is no appearance of fancy in him, unless it be a fancy that he hath to strange disguises; as to be a Dutchman today, a Frenchman to-morrow; or in the shape of two countries at once, as a German from the waist downward, all slops, and a Spaniard from the hip upward, no doublet. Unless he have a fancy to this foolery, as it appears he hath, he is no fool for fancy, as you would have it appear he is.

CLAUDIO If he be not in love with some woman, there is no believing old signs: 'a brushes his hat o' mornings; what should that bode?

DON PEDRO Hath any man seen him at the barber's?

CLAUDIO No, but the barber's man hath been seen with him; and the old ornament of his cheek hath already stuff'd tennis-balls.

LEONATO Indeed, he looks younger than he did, by the loss of a beard.

DON PEDRO Nay, 'a rubs himself with civet. Can you smell him out by that?

CLAUDIO That's as much as to say the sweet youth's in love.

DON PEDRO The greatest note of it is his melancholy.

CLAUDIO And when was he wont to wash his face?

DON PEDRO Yea, or to paint himself? For the which I hear what they say of him.

CLAUDIO Nay, but his jesting spirit, which is now crept into a lute-string, and now govern'd by stops.

DON PEDRO Indeed, that tells a heavy tale for him; conclude, conclude, he is in love.

CLAUDIO Nay, but I know who loves him.

DON PEDRO That would I know too; I warrant, one that knows him not.

CLAUDIO Yes, and his ill conditions; and, in despite of all, dies for him.

DON PEDRO She shall be buried with her face upwards.

BENEDICK Yet is this no charm for the toothache. Old signior, walk aside with me; I have studied eight or nine wise words to speak to you, which these hobby-horses must not hear.

[Exeunt Benedick and Leonato.

DON PEDRO For my life, to break with him about Beatrice.

CLAUDIO 'Tis even so. Hero and Margaret have by this played their parts with Beatrice; and then the two bears will not bite one another when they meet.

Enter DON JOHN

DON JOHN My lord and brother, God save you!

DON PEDRO Good den, brother.

DON JOHN If your leisure serv'd, I would speak with you.

DON PEDRO In private?

DON JOHN If it please you; yet Count Claudio may hear, for what I would speak of concerns him.

DON PEDRO What's the matter?

DON JOHN *[To Claudio]* Means your lordship to be married to-morrow?

DON PEDRO You know he does.

DON JOHN I know not that, when he knows what I know.

CLAUDIO If there be any impediment, I pray you discover it.

DON JOHN You may think I love you not; let that appear hereafter, and aim better at me by that I now will manifest. For my brother, I think he holds you well, and in dearness of heart hath holp to effect your ensuing marriage – surely suit ill spent, and labour ill bestowed.

DON PEDRO Why, what's the matter?

DON JOHN I came hither to tell you; and, circumstances short'ned, for she has been too long a talking of, the lady is disloyal.

CLAUDIO Who? Hero?

DON JOHN Even she – Leonato's Hero, your Hero, every man's Hero.

CLAUDIO Disloyal?

DON JOHN The word is too good to paint out her wickedness; I could say she were worse; think you of a worse title, and I will fit her to it. Wonder not till further warrant; go but with me to-night, you shall see her chamber window ent'red, even the night before her wedding-day. If you love her then, to-morrow wed her; but it would better fit your honour to change your mind.

CLAUDIO May this be so?

DON PEDRO I will not think it.

DON JOHN If you dare not trust that you see, confess not that you know. If you will follow me, I will show you enough; and when you have seen more, and heard more, proceed accordingly.

CLAUDIO If I see anything to-night why I should not marry her, to-morrow in the congregation where I should wed, there will I shame her.

DON PEDRO And, as I wooed for thee to obtain her, I will join with thee to disgrace her.

DON JOHN I will disparage her no farther till you are my witnesses; bear it coldly but till midnight, and let the issue show itself.

DON PEDRO O day untowardly turned!

CLAUDIO O mischief strangely thwarting!

DON JOHN O plague right well prevented! So will you say when you have seen the sequel. [*Exeunt.*

SCENE III. *A street.*

Enter DOGBERRY and his compartner VERGES, with the Watch.

DOGBERRY Are you good men and true?

VERGES Yea, or else it were pity but they should suffer salvation, body and soul.

DOGBERRY Nay, that were a punishment too good for them, if they should have any allegiance in them, being chosen for the Prince's watch.

VERGES Well, give them their charge, neighbour Dogberry.

DOGBERRY First, who think you the most desartless man to be constable?

1 WATCH Hugh Oatcake, sir, or George Seacoal; for they can write and read.

DOGBERRY Come hither, neighbour Seacoal. God hath bless'd you with a good name. To be a well-favoured man is the gift of fortune; but to write and read comes by nature.

2 WATCH Both which, Master Constable –

DOGBERRY You have; I knew it would be your answer. Well, for your favour, sir, why, give God thanks, and make no boast of it; and for your writing and reading, let that appear when there is no need of such vanity. You are thought here to be the most senseless and fit man for the constable of the watch; therefore bear you the lantern. This is your charge: you shall comprehend all vagrom men; you are to bid any man stand, in the Prince's name.

2 WATCH How if 'a will not stand?

DOGBERRY Why, then, take no note of him, but let him go; and presently call the rest of the watch together, and thank God you are rid of a knave.

VERGES If he will not stand when he is bidden, he is none of the Prince's subjects.

DOGBERRY True, and they are to meddle with none but the Prince's subjects. You shall also make no noise in the streets; for for the watch to babble and to talk is most tolerable and not to be endured.

2 WATCH We will rather sleep than talk; we know what belongs to a watch.

DOGBERRY Why, you speak like an ancient and most quiet watchman, for I cannot see how sleeping should offend; only, have a care that your bills be not stol'n. Well, you are to call at all the ale-houses, and bid those that are drunk get them to bed.

2 WATCH How if they will not?

DOGBERRY Why, then, let them alone till they are sober; if they make you not then the better answer, you may say they are not the men you took them for.

2 WATCH Well, sir.

DOGBERRY If you meet a thief, you may suspect him, by virtue of your office, to be no true man; and, for such kind of men, the less you meddle or make with them, why, the more is for your honesty.

2 WATCH If we know him to be a thief, shall we not lay hands on him?

DOGBERRY Truly, by your office you may, but I think they that touch pitch will be defil'd; the most peaceable way for you, if you do take a thief, is to let him show himself what he is, and steal out of your company.

VERGES You have been always called a merciful man, partner.

DOGBERRY Truly, I would not hang a dog by my

will, much more a man who hath any honesty in him.

VERGES If you hear a child cry in the night, you must call to the nurse and bid her still it.

2 WATCH How if the nurse be asleep and will not hear us?

DOGBERRY Why, then, depart in peace, and let the child wake her with crying; for the ewe that will not hear her lamb when it baes will never answer a calf when he bleats.

VERGES 'Tis very true.

DOGBERRY This is the end of the charge: you, constable, are to present the Prince's own person; if you meet the Prince in the night, you may stay him.

VERGES Nay, by'r lady, that I think 'a cannot.

DOGBERRY Five shillings to one on't, with any man that knows the statues, he may stay him; marry, not without the Prince be willing; for, indeed, the watch ought to offend no man, and it is an offence to stay a man against his will.

VERGES By'r lady, I think it be so.

DOGBERRY Ha, ah, ha! Well, masters, good night; an there be any matter of weight chances, call up me; keep your fellows' counsels and your own, and good night. Come, neighbour.

2 WATCH Well, masters, we hear our charge; let us go sit here upon the church bench till two, and then all to bed.

DOGBERRY One word more, honest neighbours: I pray you watch about Signior Leonato's door; for the wedding being there to-morrow, there is a great coil to-night. Adieu; be vigitant, I beseech you. [*Exeunt Dogberry and Verges.*

Enter BORACHIO and CONRADE.

BORACHIO What, Conrade!

2 WATCH [*Aside*] Peace, stir not.

BORACHIO Conrade, I say!

CONRADE Here, man, I am at thy elbow.

BORACHIO Mass, and my elbow itch'd; I thought there would a scab follow.

CONRADE I will owe thee an answer for that; and now forward with thy tale.

BORACHIO Stand thee close then under this penthouse, for it drizzles rain; and I will, like a true drunkard, utter all to thee.

2 WATCH [*Aside*] Some treason, masters; yet stand close.

BORACHIO Therefore know I have earned of Don John a thousand ducats.

CONRADE Is it possible that any villainy should be so dear?

BORACHIO Thou shouldst rather ask if it were possible any villainy should be so rich; for when rich villains have need of poor ones, poor ones may make what price they will.

CONRADE I wonder at it.

BORACHIO That shows thou art unconfirm'd. Thou knowest that the fashion of a doublet, or a hat, or a cloak, is nothing to a man.

CONRADE Yes, it is apparel.

BORACHIO I mean the fashion.

CONRADE Yes, the fashion is the fashion.

BORACHIO Tush! I may as well say the fool's the fool. But seest thou not what a deformed thief this fashion is?

2 WATCH [*Aside*] I know that Deformed; 'a has been a vile thief this seven year; 'a goes up and down like a gentleman; I remember his name.

BORACHIO Didst thou not hear somebody?

CONRADE No; 'twas the vane on the house.

BORACHIO Seest thou not, I say, what a deformed thief this fashion is, how giddily 'a turns about all the hot bloods between fourteen and five and thirty, sometimes fashioning them like Pharaoh's soldiers in the reechy painting, sometime like god Bel's priests in the old church-window, sometime like the shaven Hercules in the smirch'd worm-eaten tapestry, where his codpiece seems as massy as his club?

CONRADE All this I see; and I see that the fashion wears out more apparel than the man. But art not thou thyself giddy with the fashion too, that thou hast shifted out of thy tale into telling me of the fashion?

BORACHIO Not so neither; but know that I have to-night wooed Margaret, the Lady Hero's gentlewoman, by the name of Hero; she leans me out at her mistress' chamber-window, bids me a thousand times good night – I tell this tale vilely. I should first tell thee how the Prince, Claudio, and my master, planted and placed and possessed by my master Don John, saw afar off in the orchard this amiable encounter.

CONRADE And thought they Margaret was Hero?

BORACHIO Two of them did, the Prince and Claudio; but the devil my master knew she was Margaret; and partly by his oaths, which first possess'd them, partly by the dark night, which did deceive them, but chiefly by my villainy, which did confirm any slander that Don John had made, away went Claudio enrag'd; swore he would meet her, as he was appointed, next morning at the temple, and there, before the whole congregation, shame her with what he saw o'er night, and send her home again without a husband.

2 WATCH We charge you in the Prince's name, stand.

1 WATCH Call up the right Master Constable; we have here recover'd the most dangerous piece of lechery that ever was known in the commonwealth.

2 WATCH And one Deformed is one of them; I know him, 'a wears a lock.

CONRADE Masters, masters!

2 WATCH You'll be made bring Deformed forth, I warrant you.

CONRADE Masters –

1 WATCH Never speak, we charge you; let us obey you to go with us.

BORACHIO We are like to prove a goodly commodity, being taken up of these men's bills.

CONRADE A commodity in question, I warrant you. Come, we'll obey you. *[Exeunt.*

SCENE IV. *Hero's apartment.*

Enter HERO, MARGARET, and URSULA.

HERO Good Ursula, wake my cousin Beatrice, and desire her to rise.

URSULA I will, lady.

HERO And bid her come hither.

URSULA Well. *[Exit Ursula.*

MARGARET Troth, I think your other rabato were better.

HERO No, pray thee, good Meg, I'll wear this.

MARGARET By my troth's not so good; and I warrant your cousin will say so.

HERO My cousin's a fool, and thou art another; I'll wear none but this.

MARGARET I like the new tire within excellently, if the hair were a thought browner; and your gown's a most rare fashion, i' faith. I saw the Duchess of Milan's gown that they praise so.

HERO O, that exceeds, they say.

MARGARET By my troth's but a night-gown in respect of yours – cloth o' gold, and cuts, and lac'd with silver, set with pearls, down sleeves, side sleeves, and skirts, round underborne with a bluish tinsel; but for a fine, quaint, graceful, and excellent fashion, yours is worth ten on't.

HERO God give me joy to wear it, for my heart is exceeding heavy.

MARGARET 'Twill be heavier soon, by the weight of a man.

HERO Fie upon thee! art not ashamed?

MARGARET Of what, lady, of speaking honourably? Is not marriage honourable in a beggar? Is not your lord honourable without marriage? I think you would have me say 'saving your reverence, a husband'; an bad thinking do not wrest true speaking I'll offend nobody. Is there any harm in 'the heavier for a husband'? None, I think, an it be the right husband and the right wife; otherwise 'tis light, and not heavy. Ask my Lady Beatrice else; here she comes.

Enter BEATRICE.

HERO Good morrow, coz.

BEATRICE Good morrow, sweet Hero.

HERO Why, how now! do you speak in the sick tune?

BEATRICE I am out of all other tune, methinks.

MARGARET Clap's into 'Light o' love'; that goes without a burden. Do you sing it, and I'll dance it.

BEATRICE Ye light o' love with your heels! Then if your husband have stables enough, you'll see he shall lack no barnes.

MARGARET O illegitimate construction! I scorn that with my heels.

BEATRICE 'Tis almost five o'clock, cousin; 'tis time you were ready. By my troth, I am exceeding ill. Heigh-ho!

MARGARET For a hawk, a horse, or a husband?

BEATRICE For the letter that begins them all – H.

MARGARET Well, an you be not turn'd Turk, there's no more sailing by the star.

BEATRICE What means the fool, trow?

MARGARET Nothing I; but God send every one their heart's desire!

HERO These gloves the Count sent me; they are an excellent perfume.

BEATRICE I am stuff'd, cousin, I cannot smell.

MARGARET A maid and stuff'd! There's goodly catching of cold.

BEATRICE O, God help me! God help me! How long have you profess'd apprehension?

MARGARET Ever since you left it. Doth not my wit become me rarely?

BEATRICE It is not seen enough; you should wear it in your cap. By my troth, I am sick.

MARGARET Get you some of this distill'd Carduus Benedictus, and lay it to your heart; it is the only thing for a qualm.

HERO There thou prick'st her with a thistle.

BEATRICE Benedictus! why Benedictus? You have some moral in this 'Benedictus'.

MARGARET Moral? No, by my troth, I have no moral meaning; I meant plain holy-thistle. You may think, perchance, that I think you are in love. Nay, by'r lady, I am not such a fool to think what I list; nor I list not to think what I can; nor, indeed, I cannot think, if I would think my heart out of thinking, that you are in love, or that you will be in love, or that you can be in love. Yet Benedick was such another, and now is he become a man; he swore he would never marry, and yet now, in despite of his heart, he eats his meat without grudging. And how you may be converted I know not; but methinks you look with your eyes as other women do.

BEATRICE What pace is this that thy tongue keeps?

MARGARET Not a false gallop.

Re-enter URSULA.

URSULA Madam, withdraw; the Prince, the Count, Signior Benedick, Don John, and all the gallants of the town, are come to fetch you to church.

HERO Help to dress me, good coz, good Meg, good Ursula. *[Exeunt.*

SCENE V. *Leonato's house.*

Enter LEONATO, with DOGBERRY and VERGES.

LEONATO What would you with me, honest neighbour?

DOGBERRY Marry, sir, I would have some confidence with you that decerns you nearly.

LEONATO Brief, I pray you; for you see it is a busy time with me.

DOGBERRY Marry, this it is, sir

VERGES Yes, in truth it is, sir.

LEONATO What is it, my good friends?

DOGBERRY Goodman Verges, sir, speaks a little off the matter – an old man, sir, and his wits are not so blunt as, God help, I would desire they were; but, in faith, honest as the skin between his brows.

VERGES Yes, I thank God I am as honest as any man living that is an old man and no honester than I.

DOGBERRY Comparisons are odorous; palabras, neighbour Verges.

LEONATO Neighbours, you are tedious.

DOGBERRY It pleases your worship to say so, but we are the poor Duke's officers; but, truly, for mine own part, if I were as tedious as a king, I could find in my heart to bestow it all of your worship.

LEONATO All thy tediousness on me, ah?

DOGBERRY Yea, an 'twere a thousand pound more than 'tis; for I hear as good exclamation on your worship as of any man in the city; and though I be but a poor man, I am glad to hear it.

VERGES And so am I.

LEONATO I would fain know what you have to say.

VERGES Marry, sir, our watch to-night, excepting your worship's presence, ha' ta'en a couple of as arrant knaves as any in Messina.

DOGBERRY A good old man, sir, he will be talking; as they say 'When the age is in the wit is out'. God help us, it is a world to see! Well said, i' faith, neighbour Verges; well, God's a good man; an two men ride of a horse, one must ride behind. An honest soul, i' faith, sir, by my troth he is, as ever broke bread; but God is to be worshipp'd; all men are not alike; alas, good neighbour!

LEONATO Indeed, neighbour, he comes too short of you.

DOGBERRY Gifts that God gives.

LEONATO I must leave you.

DOGBERRY One word, sir: our watch, sir, have indeed comprehended two aspicious persons, and we would have them this morning examined before your worship.

LEONATO Take their examination yourself, and bring it me; I am now in great haste, as it may appear unto you.

DOGBERRY It shall be suffigance.

LEONATO Drink some wine ere you go; fare you well.

Enter a Messenger.

MESSENGER My lord, they stay for you to give your daughter to her husband.

LEONATO I'll wait upon them; I am ready. *[Exeunt Leonato and Messenger.*

DOGBERRY Go, good partner, go, get you to Francis Seacoal; bid him bring his pen and inkhorn to the gaol; we are now to examination these men

VERGES And we must do it wisely.

DOGBERRY We will spare for no wit, I warrant you; here's that shall drive some of them to a non-come; only get the learned writer to set down our excommunication, and meet me at the gaol. *[Exeunt.*

ACT FOUR

SCENE I. *A church.*

Enter DON PEDRO, DON JOHN, LEONATO, FRIAR FRANCIS, CLAUDIO, BENEDICK, HERO, BEATRICE, and Attendants.

LEONATO Come, Friar Francis, be brief; only to the plain form of marriage, and you shall recount their particular duties afterwards.

FRIAR You come hither, my lord, to marry this lady?

CLAUDIO No.

LEONATO To be married to her, friar! You come to marry her.

FRIAR Lady, you come hither to be married to this count?

HERO I do.

FRIAR If either of you know any inward impediment why you should not be conjoined, I charge you, on your souls, to utter it.

CLAUDIO Know you any, Hero?

HERO None, my lord.

FRIAR Know you any, Count?

LEONATO I dare make his answer, None.

CLAUDIO O, what men dare do! What men may do! What men daily do, not knowing what they do!

BENEDICK How now! Interjections? Why, then, some be of laughing, as, ah, ha, he!

CLAUDIO Stand thee by, friar. Father, by your leave:
Will you with free and unconstrained soul
Give me this maid, your daughter?

LEONATO As freely, son, as God did give her me.

CLAUDIO And what have I to give you back whose worth
May counterpoise this rich and precious gift?

DON PEDRO Nothing, unless you render her again.

CLAUDIO Sweet Prince, you learn me noble thankfulness.
There, Leonato, take her back again;
Give not this rotten orange to your friend;
She's but the sign and semblance of her honour.
Behold how like a maid she blushes here.
O, what authority and show of truth
Can cunning sin cover itself withal!
Comes not that blood as modest evidence
To witness simple virtue? Would you not swear,
All you that see her, that she were a maid
By these exterior shows? But she is none:
She knows the heat of a luxurious bed;
Her blush is guiltiness, not modesty.

LEONATO What do you mean, my lord?

CLAUDIO Not to be married,
Not to knit my soul to an approved wanton.

LEONATO Dear, my lord, if you, in your own proof,
Have vanquish'd the resistance of her youth,
And made defeat of her virginity –

CLAUDIO I know what you would say. If I have known her,
You will say she did embrace me as a husband,
And so extenuate the 'forehand sin.
No, Leonato,
I never tempted her with word too large
But, as a brother to his sister, show'd
Bashful sincerity and comely love.

HERO And seem'd I ever otherwise to you?

CLAUDIO Out on thee! Seeming! I will write against it.
You seem to me as Dian in her orb,
As chaste as is the bud ere it be blown;
But you are more intemperate in your blood
Than Venus, or those pamp'red animals
That rage in savage sensuality.

HERO Is my lord well, that he doth speak so wide?

LEONATO Sweet Prince, why speak not you?

DON PEDRO What should I speak?
I stand dishonour'd that have gone about
To link my dear friend to a common stale.

LEONATO Are these things spoken, or do I but dream?

DON JOHN Sir, they are spoken, and these things are true.

BENEDICK This looks not like a nuptial.

HERO True! O God!

CLAUDIO Leonato, stand I here?
Is this the Prince? Is this the Prince's brother?
Is this face Hero's? Are our eyes our own?

LEONATO All this is so; but what of this, my lord?

CLAUDIO Let me but move one question to your daughter;
And, by that fatherly and kindly power
That you have in her, bid her answer truly.

LEONATO I charge thee do so, as thou art my child.

HERO O, God defend me! how am I beset!
What kind of catechising call you this?

CLAUDIO To make you answer truly to your name.

HERO Is it not Hero? Who can blot that name
With any just reproach?

CLAUDIO Marry, that can Hero;
Hero itself can blot out Hero's virtue.
What man was he talk'd with you yester-night
Out at your window, betwixt twelve and one?
Now, if you are a maid, answer to this.

HERO I talk'd with no man at that hour, my lord.

DON PEDRO Why, then are you no maiden. Leonato,
I am sorry you must hear: upon mine honour,
Myself, my brother, and this grieved Count,
Did see her, hear her, at that hour last night,
Talk with a ruffian at her chamber window;
Who hath, indeed, most like a liberal villain,
Confess'd the vile encounters they have had
A thousand times in secret.

DON JOHN Fie, fie! they are not to be nam'd, my lord,
Not to be spoke of;
There is not chastity enough in language
Without offence to utter them. Thus, pretty lady,
I am sorry for thy much misgovernment.

CLAUDIO O Hero, what a Hero hadst thou been,
If half thy outward graces had been placed
About thy thoughts and counsels of thy heart!

But fare thee well, most foul, most fair! Farewell,
Thou pure impiety and impious purity!
For thee I'll lock up all the gates of love,
And on my eyelids shall conjecture hang,
To turn all beauty into thoughts of harm,
And never shall it more be gracious.

LEONATO Hath no man's dagger here a point for me? [*Hero swoons.*

BEATRICE Why, how now, cousin! Wherefore sink you down?

DON JOHN Come, let us go. These things, come thus to light,
Smother her spirits up.
[*Exeunt Don Pedro, Don John, and Claudio.*

BENEDICK How doth the lady?

BEATRICE Dead, I think. Help, uncle!
Hero! why, Hero! Uncle! Signior Benedick! Friar!

LEONATO O Fate, take not away thy heavy hand!
Death is the fairest cover for her shame
That may be wish'd for.

BEATRICE How now, cousin Hero!

FRIAR Have comfort, lady.

LEONATO Dost thou look up?

FRIAR Yea; wherefore should she not?

LEONATO Wherefore! Why, doth not every earthly thing
Cry shame upon her? Could she here deny
The story that is printed in her blood?
Do not live, Hero; do not ope thine eyes;
For, did I think thou wouldst not quickly die,
Thought I thy spirits were stronger than thy shames,
Myself would, on the rearward of reproaches,
Strike at thy life. Griev'd I I had but one?
Chid I for that at frugal nature's frame?
O, one too much by thee! Why had I one?
Why ever wast thou lovely in my eyes?
Why had I not, with charitable hand,
Took up a beggar's issue at my gates,
Who smirched thus and mir'd with infamy,
I might have said 'No part of it is mine;
This shame derives itself from unknown loins'?
But mine, and mine I lov'd, and mine I prais'd,
And mine that I was proud on; mine so much
That I myself was to myself not mine,
Valuing of her – why, she, O, she is fall'n
Into a pit of ink, that the wide sea
Hath drops too few to wash her clean again,
And salt too little which may season give
To her foul tainted flesh!

BENEDICK Sir, sir, be patient.
For my part, I am so attir'd in wonder,
I know not what to say.

BEATRICE O, on my soul, my cousin is belied!

BENEDICK Lady, were you her bedfellow last night?

BEATRICE No, truly not; although, until last night,
I have this twelvemonth been her bedfellow.

LEONATO Confirm'd, confirm'd! O, that is stronger made
Which was before barr'd up with ribs of iron!
Would the two princes lie; and Claudio lie,
Who lov'd her so, that, speaking of her foulness,
Wash'd it with tears? Hence from her! let her die.

FRIAR Hear me a little;
For I have only been silent so long,
And given way unto this course of fortune,
By noting of the lady: I have mark'd
A thousand blushing apparitions
To start into her face, a thousand innocent shames
In angel whiteness beat away those blushes;
And in her eye there hath appear'd a fire
To burn the errors that these princes hold
Against her maiden truth. Call me a fool;
Trust not my reading nor my observations,
Which with experimental seal doth warrant
The tenour of my book; trust not my age,
My reverence, calling, nor divinity,
If this sweet lady lie not guiltless here
Under some biting error.

LEONATO Friar, it cannot be.
Thou seest that all the grace that she hath left
Is that she will not add to her damnation
A sin of perjury; she not denies it.
Why seek'st thou then to cover with excuse
That which appears in proper nakedness?

FRIAR Lady, what man is he you are accus'd of?

HERO They know that do accuse me; I know none.
If I know more of any man alive
Than that which maiden modesty doth warrant,
Let all my sins lack mercy! O my father,
Prove you that any man with me convers'd
At hours unmeet, or that I yesternight
Maintain'd the change of words with any creature,
Refuse me, hate me, torture me to death.

FRIAR There is some strange misprision in the princes.

BENEDICK Two of them have the very bent of honour;
And if their wisdoms be misled in this,
The practice of it lives in John the bastard,
Whose spirits toil in frame of villainies.

LEONATO I know not. If they speak but truth of her,

These hands shall tear her; if they wrong her honour,
The proudest of them shall well hear of it.
Time hath not yet so dried this blood of mine,
Nor age so eat up my invention,
Nor fortune made such havoc of my means,
Nor my bad life reft me so much of friends,
But they shall find awak'd in such a kind
Both strength of limb and policy of mind,
Ability in means and choice of friends,
To quit me of them throughly.

FRIAR Pause awhile,
And let my counsel sway you in this case.
Your daughter here the princes left for dead;
Let her awhile be secretly kept in,
And publish it that she is dead indeed;
Maintain a mourning ostentation,
And on your family's old monument
Hang mournful epitaphs, and do all rites
That appertain unto a burial.

LEONATO What shall become of this? What will this do?

FRIAR Marry, this, well carried, shall on her behalf
Change slander to remorse; that is some good.
But not for that dream I on this strange course,
But on this travail look for greater birth.
She dying, as it must be so maintain'd,
Upon the instant that she was accus'd,
Shall be lamented, pitied, and excus'd,
Of every hearer; for it so falls out
That what we have we prize not to the worth
Whiles we enjoy it, but being lack'd and lost,
Why, then we rack the value, then we find
The virtue that possession would not show us
Whiles it was ours. So will it fare with Claudio.
When he shall hear she died upon his words,
Th' idea of her life shall sweetly creep
Into his study of imagination,
And every lovely organ of her life
Shall come apparell'd in more precious habit,
More moving, delicate, and full of life,
Into the eye and prospect of his soul,
Than when she liv'd indeed. Then shall he mourn,
If ever love had interest in his liver,
And wish he had not so accused her –
No, though he thought his accusation true.
Let this be so, and doubt not but success
Will fashion the event in better shape
Than I can lay it down in likelihood.
But if all aim but this be levell'd false,
The supposition of the lady's death
Will quench the wonder of her infamy.
And if it sort not well, you may conceal her,
As best befits her wounded reputation,
In some reclusive and religious life,
Out of all eyes, tongues, minds, and injuries.

BENEDICK Signior Leonato, let the friar advise you;
And though you know my inwardness and love
Is very much unto the Prince and Claudio,
Yet, by mine honour, I will deal in this
As secretly and justly as your soul
Should with your body.

LEONATO Being that I flow in grief
The smallest twine may lead me.

FRIAR 'Tis well consented. Presently away;
For to strange sores strangely they strain the cure.
Come, lady, die to live; this wedding day
Perhaps is but prolong'd; have patience and endure.

[Exeunt all but Benedick and Beatrice.

BENEDICK Lady Beatrice, have you wept all this while?

BEATRICE Yea, and I will weep a while longer.

BENEDICK I will not desire that.

BEATRICE You have no reason; I do it freely.

BENEDICK Surely I do believe your fair cousin is wronged.

BEATRICE Ah, how much might the man deserve of me that would right her!

BENEDICK Is there any way to show such friendship?

BEATRICE A very even way, but no such friend.

BENEDICK May a man do it?

BEATRICE It is a man's office, but not yours.

BENEDICK I do love nothing in the world so well as you. Is not that strange?

BEATRICE As strange as the thing I know not. It were as possible for me to say I lov'd nothing so well as you; but believe me not, and yet I lie not; I confess nothing, nor I deny nothing. I am sorry for my cousin.

BENEDICK By my sword, Beatrice, thou lovest me.

BEATRICE Do not swear, and eat it.

BENEDICK I will swear by it that you love me; and I will make him eat it that says I love not you.

BEATRICE Will you not eat your word?

BENEDICK With no sauce that can be devised to it; I protest I love thee.

BEATRICE Why, then, God forgive me!

BENEDICK What offence, sweet Beatrice?

BEATRICE You have stayed me in a happy hour; I was about to protest I loved you.

BENEDICK And do it with all thy heart?

BEATRICE I love you with so much of my heart that none is left to protest.

BENEDICK Come, bid me do anything for thee.

BEATRICE Kill Claudio.

BENEDICK Ha! not for the wide world.

BEATRICE You kill me to deny it. Farewell.

BENEDICK Tarry, sweet Beatrice.

BEATRICE I am gone though I am here; there is no love in you; nay, I pray you, let me go.

BENEDICK Beatrice –

BEATRICE In faith, I will go.

BENEDICK We'll be friends first.

BEATRICE You dare easier be friends with me than fight with mine enemy.

BENEDICK Is Claudio thine enemy?

BEATRICE Is 'a not approved in the height a villain that hath slandered, scorned, dishonoured, my kinswoman? O that I were a man! What! bear her in hand until they come to take hands, and then with public accusation, uncover'd slander, unmitigated rancour – O God, that I were a man! I would eat his heart in the market-place.

BENEDICK Hear me, Beatrice.

BEATRICE Talk with a man out at a window! A proper saying!

BENEDICK Nay, but, Beatrice –

BEATRICE Sweet Hero! She is wrong'd, she is sland'red, she is undone.

BENEDICK Beat –

BEATRICE Princes and Counties! Surely, a princely testimony, a goodly count, Count Comfect; a sweet gallant, surely! O that I were a man for his sake! or that I had any friend would be a man for my sake! But manhood is melted into curtsies, valour into compliment, and men are only turn'd into tongue, and trim ones too. He is now as valiant as Hercules that only tells a lie and swears it. I cannot be a man with wishing, therefore I will die a woman with grieving.

BENEDICK Tarry, good Beatrice. By this hand, I love thee.

BEATRICE Use it for my love some other way than swearing by it.

BENEDICK Think you in your soul the Count Claudio hath wrong'd Hero?

BEATRICE Yea, as sure as I have a thought or a soul.

BENEDICK Enough, I am engag'd; I will challenge him; I will kiss your hand, and so I leave you. By this hand, Claudio shall render me a dear account. As you hear of me, so think of me. Go comfort your cousin; I must say she is dead; and so, farewell. *[Exeunt.*

SCENE II. *A prison.*

Enter DOGBERRY, VERGES, and SEXTON, in gowns; and the Watch, with CONRADE and BORACHIO.

DOGBERRY Is our whole dissembly appear'd?

VERGES O, a stool and a cushion for the sexton!

SEXTON Which be the malefactors?

DOGBERRY Marry, that am I and my partner.

VERGES Nay, that's certain; we have the exhibition to examine.

SEXTON But which are the offenders that are to be examin'd? Let them come before Master Constable.

DOGBERRY Yea, marry, let them come before me. What is your name, friend?

BORACHIO Borachio.

DOGBERRY Pray write down Borachio. Yours, sirrah?

CONRADE I am a gentleman, sir, and my name is Conrade.

DOGBERRY Write down Master Gentleman Conrade. Masters, do you serve God?

CONRADE, BORACHIO Yea, sir, we hope.

DOGBERRY Write down that they hope they serve God; and write God first; for God defend but God should go before such villains! Masters, it is proved already that you are little better than false knaves, and it will go near to be thought so shortly. How answer you for yourselves?

CONRADE Marry, sir, we say we are none.

DOGBERRY A marvellous witty fellow, I assure you; but I will go about with him. Come you hither, sirrah; a word in your ear: sir, I say to you it is thought you are false knaves.

BORACHIO Sir, I say to you we are none.

DOGBERRY Well, stand aside. Fore God, they are both in a tale. Have you writ down that they are none?

SEXTON Master Constable, you go not the way to examine; you must call forth the watch that are their accusers.

DOGBERRY Yea, marry, that's the eftest way. Let the watch come forth. Masters, I charge you in the Prince's name, accuse these men.

1 WATCH This man said, sir, that Don John, the Prince's brother, was a villain.

DOGBERRY Write down Prince John a villain. Why, this is flat perjury, to call a prince's brother villain.

BORACHIO Master Constable –

DOGBERRY Pray thee, fellow, peace; I do not like thy look, I promise thee.

SEXTON What heard you him say else?

2 WATCH Marry, that he had received a thousand ducats of Don John for accusing the Lady Hero wrongfully.

DOGBERRY Flat burglary as ever was committed.

VERGES Yea, by mass, that it is.

SEXTON What else, fellow?

1 WATCH And that Count Claudio did mean, upon his words, to disgrace Hero before the whole assembly, and not marry her.

DOGBERRY O villain! thou wilt be condemn'd

into everlasting redemption for this.

SEXTON What else?

2 WATCH This is all.

SEXTON And this is more, masters, than you can deny. Prince John is this morning secretly stol'n away; Hero was in this manner accus'd, in this very manner refus'd and upon the grief of this suddenly died. Master Constable, let these men be bound and brought to Leonato's; I will go before and show him their examination.

[Exit.

DOGBERRY Come, let them be opinion'd.

VERGES Let them be in the hands.

CONRADE Off, coxcomb.

DOGBERRY God's my life, where's the sexton? Let him write down the Prince's officer coxcomb. Come, bind them. Thou naughty varlet!

CONRADE Away! you are an ass, you are an ass.

DOGBERRY Dost thou not suspect my place? Dost thou not suspect my years? O that he were here to write me down an ass! But, masters, remember that I am an ass; though it be not written down, yet forget not that I am an ass. No, thou villain, thou art full of piety, as shall be prov'd upon thee by good witness. I am a wise fellow; and, which is more, an officer; and, which is more, a householder; and, which is more, as pretty a piece of flesh as any is in Messina; and one that knows the law, go to; and a rich fellow enough, go to; and a fellow that hath had losses; and one that hath two gowns, and everything handsome about him. Bring him away. O that I had been writ down an ass!

[Exeunt.

ACT FIVE

SCENE I. *Before Leonato's house.*

Enter LEONATO and ANTONIO.

ANTONIO If you go on thus, you will kill yourself,
And 'tis not wisdom thus to second grief
Against yourself.

LEONATO I pray thee cease thy counsel,
Which falls into mine ears as profitless
As water in a sieve. Give not me counsel;
Nor let no comforter delight mine ear
But such a one whose wrongs do suit with mine.
Bring me a father that so lov'd his child,
Whose joy of her is overwhelm'd like mine,
And bid him speak of patience;
Measure his woe the length and breadth of mine,
And let it answer every strain for strain;
As thus for thus, and such a grief for such,
In every lineament, branch, shape, and form.
If such a one will smile and stroke his beard,
And sorrow wag, cry 'hem!' when he should groan,
Patch grief with proverbs, make misfortune drunk
With candle-wasters – bring him yet to me,
And I of him will gather patience.
But there is no such man; for, brother, men
Can counsel and speak comfort to that grief
Which they themselves not feel; but, tasting it,
Their counsel turns to passion, which before
Would give preceptial medicine to rage,
Fetter strong madness in a silken thread,
Charm ache with air and agony with words.
No, no; 'tis all men's office to speak patience
To those that wring under the load of sorrow,
But no man's virtue nor sufficiency
To be so moral when he shall endure
The like himself. Therefore, give me no counsel;
My griefs cry louder than advertisement.

ANTONIO Therein do men from children nothing differ.

LEONATO I pray thee peace; I will be flesh and blood;
For there was never yet philosopher
That could endure the toothache patiently,
However they have writ the style of gods,
And made a push at chance and sufferance.

ANTONIO Yet bend not all the harm upon yourself;
Make those that do offend you suffer too.

LEONATO There thou speak'st reason; nay, I will do so.
My soul doth tell me Hero is belied;
And that shall Claudio know; so shall the Prince,
And all of them that thus dishonour her.

ANTONIO Here comes the Prince and Claudio hastily.

Enter DON PEDRO and CLAUDIO.

DON PEDRO Good den, good den.

CLAUDIO Good day to both of you.

LEONATO Hear you, my lords!

DON PEDRO We have some haste, Leonato.

LEONATO Some haste, my lord! Well, fare you well, my lord.
Are you so hasty now? Well, all is one.

DON PEDRO Nay, do not quarrel with us, good old man.

ANTONIO If he could right himself with quarrelling,
Some of us would lie low.
CLAUDIO Who wrongs him?
LEONATO Marry, thou dost wrong me; thou dissembler, thou!
Nay, never lay thy hand upon thy sword;
I fear thee not.
CLAUDIO Marry, beshrew my hand
If it should give your age such cause of fear!
In faith, my hand meant nothing to my sword.
LEONATO Tush, tush, man; never fleer and jest at me;
I speak not like a dotard nor a fool,
As under privilege of age to brag
What I have done being young, or what would do
Were I not old. Know, Claudio, to thy head,
Thou hast so wrong'd mine innocent child and me
That I am forc'd to lay my reverence by,
And with grey hairs and bruise of many days
Do challenge thee to trial of a man.
I say thou hast belied mine innocent child;
Thy slander hath gone through and through her heart,
And she lies buried with her ancestors –
O! in a tomb where never scandal slept,
Save this of hers, fram'd by thy villainy.
CLAUDIO My villainy!
LEONATO Thine, Claudio; thine, I say.
DON PEDRO You say not right, old man.
LEONATO My lord, my lord,
I'll prove it on his body if he dare,
Despite his nice fence and his active practice,
His May of youth and bloom of lustihood.
CLAUDIO Away! I will not have to do with you.
LEONATO Canst thou so daff me? Thou hast kill'd my child;
If thou kill'st me, boy, thou shalt kill a man.
ANTONIO He shall kill two of us, and men indeed;
But that's no matter; let him kill one first.
Win me and wear me; let him answer me.
Come, follow me, boy; come, sir boy, come follow me;
Sir boy, I'll whip you from your foining fence;
Nay, as I am a gentleman, I will.
LEONATO Brother –
ANTONIO Content yourself. God knows I lov'd my niece;
And she is dead, slander'd to death by villains,
That dare as well answer a man indeed
As I dare take a serpent by the tongue.
Boys, apes, braggarts, Jacks, milksops!
LEONATO Brother Antony –
ANTONIO Hold you content. What, man! I know them, yea,
And what they weigh, even to the utmost scruple –
Scambling, out-facing, fashion-monging boys,
That lie and cog and flout, deprave and slander,
Go anticly, and show outward hideousness,
And speak off half a dozen dang'rous words,
How they might hurt their enemies, if they durst;
And this is all.
LEONATO But, brother Antony –
ANTONIO Come, 'tis no matter;
Do not you meddle; let me deal in this.
DON PEDRO Gentlemen both, we will not wake your patience.
My heart is sorry for your daughter's death;
But, on my honour, she was charg'd with nothing
But what was true, and very full of proof.
LEONATO My lord, my lord –
DON PEDRO I will not hear you.
LEONATO No?
Come, brother, away. I will be heard.
ANTONIO And shall, or some of us will smart for it. [*Exeunt Leonato and Antonio.*
DON PEDRO See, see; here comes the man we went to seek.

Enter BENEDICK.

CLAUDIO Now, signior, what news?
BENEDICK Good day, my lord.
DON PEDRO Welcome, signior; you are almost come to part almost a fray.
CLAUDIO We had lik'd to have had our two noses snapp'd off with two old men without teeth.
DON PEDRO Leonato and his brother. What think'st thou? Had we fought, I doubt we should have been too young for them.
BENEDICK In a false quarrel there is no true valour. I came to seek you both.
CLAUDIO We have been up and down to seek thee; for we are high-proof melancholy, and would fain have it beaten away. Wilt thou use thy wit?
BENEDICK It is in my scabbard; shall I draw it?
DON PEDRO Dost thou wear thy wit by thy side?
CLAUDIO Never any did so, though very many have been beside their wit. I will bid thee draw, as we do the minstrels – draw to pleasure us.
DON PEDRO As I am an honest man, he looks pale. Art thou sick or angry?
CLAUDIO What, courage, man! What though care kill'd a cat, thou hast mettle enough in thee to kill care.
BENEDICK Sir, I shall meet your wit in the career, an you charge it against me. I pray you choose another subject.

CLAUDIO Nay, then, give him another staff; this last was broke cross.

DON PEDRO By this light, he changes more and more; I think he be angry indeed.

CLAUDIO If he be, he knows how to turn his girdle.

BENEDICK Shall I speak a word in your ear?

CLAUDIO God bless me from a challenge!

BENEDICK *[Aside to Claudio]* You are a villain; I jest not; I will make it good how you dare, with what you dare, and when you dare. Do me right, or I will protest your cowardice. You have kill'd a sweet lady, and her death shall fall heavy on you. Let me hear from you.

CLAUDIO Well, I will meet you, so I may have good cheer.

DON PEDRO What, a feast? a feast?

CLAUDIO I' faith, I thank him; he hath bid me to a calf's head and a capon, the which if I do not carve most curiously, say my knife's naught. Shall I not find a woodcock too?

BENEDICK Sir, your wit ambles well; it goes easily.

DON PEDRO I'll tell thee how Beatrice prais'd thy wit the other day. I said thou hadst a fine wit. 'True,' said she 'a fine little one.' 'No,' said I 'a great wit.' 'Right,' says she 'a great gross one.' 'Nay,' said I 'a good wit.' 'Just,' said she 'it hurts nobody.' 'Nay,' said I 'the gentleman is wise.' 'Certain,' said she 'a wise gentleman.' 'Nay,' said I 'he hath the tongues.' 'That I believe,' said she 'for he swore a thing to me on Monday night, which he forswore on Tuesday morning. There's a double tongue; there's two tongues.' Thus did she, an hour together, trans-shape thy particular virtues; yet, at last, she concluded, with a sigh, thou wast the proper'st man in Italy.

CLAUDIO For the which she wept heartily, and said she cared not.

DON PEDRO Yea, that she did; but yet, for all that, an if she did not hate him deadly, she would love him dearly. The old man's daughter told us all.

CLAUDIO All, all; and, moreover, 'God saw him when he was hid in the garden'.

DON PEDRO But when shall we set the savage bull's horns on the sensible Benedick's head?

CLAUDIO Yea, and text underneath, 'Here dwells Benedick the married man'?

BENEDICK Fare you well, boy; you know my mind. I will leave you now to your gossip-like humour; you break jests as braggarts do their blades, which, God be thanked, hurt not. My lord, for your many courtesies I thank you. I must discontinue your company. Your brother the bastard is fled from Messina. You have among you kill'd a sweet and innocent lady. For my Lord Lackbeard there, he and I shall meet; and till then, peace be with him.

[Exit Benedick.

DON PEDRO He is in earnest.

CLAUDIO In most profound earnest; and I'll warrant you for the love of Beatrice.

DON PEDRO And hath challeng'd thee?

CLAUDIO Most sincerely.

DON PEDRO What a pretty thing man is when he goes in his doublet and hose and leaves off his wit!

CLAUDIO He is then a giant to an ape; but then is an ape a doctor to such a man.

DON PEDRO But, soft you, let me be; pluck up, my heart, and be sad. Did he not say my brother was fled?

Enter DOGBERRY, VERGES, and the Watch, with CONRADE and BORACHIO.

DOGBERRY Come, you, sir; if justice cannot tame you, she shall ne'er weigh more reasons in her balance; nay, an you be a cursing hypocrite once, you must be look'd to.

DON PEDRO How now! two of my brother's men bound – Borachio one.

CLAUDIO Hearken after their offence, my lord.

DON PEDRO Officers, what offence have these men done?

DOGBERRY Marry, sir, they have committed false report; moreover, they have spoken untruths; secondarily, they are slanders; sixth and lastly, they have belied a lady; thirdly, they have verified unjust things; and to conclude, they are lying knaves.

DON PEDRO First, I ask thee what they have done; thirdly, I ask thee what's their offence; sixth and lastly, why they are committed; and to conclude, what you lay to their charge.

CLAUDIO Rightly reasoned, and in his own division; and, by my troth, there's one meaning well suited.

DON PEDRO Who have you offended, masters, that you are thus bound to your answer? This learned constable is too cunning to be understood. What's your offence?

BORACHIO Sweet Prince, let me go no farther to mine answer; do you hear me, and let this Count kill me. I have deceived even your very eyes. What your wisdoms could not discover, these shallow fools have brought to light; who, in the night, overheard me confessing to this man how Don John your brother incensed me to slander the Lady Hero; how you were brought into the orchard, and saw me court Margaret in Hero's garments; how you disgrac'd her, when you should marry her. My villainy they have upon record; which I had rather seal with my death than repeat over to my shame. The lady is dead upon mine and my master's false accusation; and, briefly, I desire nothing but the reward of a villain.

DON PEDRO Runs not this speech like iron through your blood?

CLAUDIO I have drunk poison whiles he utter'd it.

DON PEDRO But did my brother set thee on to this?

BORACHIO Yea, and paid me richly for the practice of it.

DON PEDRO He is compos'd and fram'd of treachery,
And fled he is upon this villainy.

CLAUDIO Sweet Hero, now thy image doth appear
In the rare semblance that I lov'd it first.

DOGBERRY Come, bring away the plaintiffs; by this time our sexton hath reformed Signior Leonato of the matter. And, masters, do not forget to specify, when time and place shall serve, that I am an ass.

VERGES Here, here comes Master Signior Leonato and the sexton too.

Re-enter LEONATO and ANTONIO, with the Sexton.

LEONATO Which is the villain? Let me see his eyes,
That when I note another man like him
I may avoid him. Which of these is he?

BORACHIO If you would know your wronger, look on me.

LEONATO Art thou the slave that with thy breath hast kill'd
Mine innocent child?

BORACHIO Yea, even I alone.

LEONATO No, not so, villain; thou beliest thyself;
Here stand a pair of honourable men,
A third is fled, that had a hand in it.
I thank you, princes, for my daughter's death;
Record it with your high and worthy deeds;
'Twas bravely done, if you bethink you of it.

CLAUDIO I know not how to pray your patience,
Yet I must speak. Choose your revenge yourself;
Impose me to what penance your invention
Can lay upon my sin; yet sinn'd I not
But in mistaking.

DON PEDRO By my soul, nor I;
And yet, to satisfy this good old man,
I would bend under any heavy weight
That he'll enjoin me to.

LEONATO I cannot bid you bid my daughter live –
That were impossible; but, I pray you both,
Possess the people in Messina here
How innocent she died; and, if your love
Can labour aught in sad invention,
Hang her an epitaph upon her tomb,
And sing it to her bones; sing it to-night.
To-morrow morning come you to my house;
And since you could not be my son-in-law,
Be yet my nephew. My brother hath a daughter,
Almost the copy of my child that's dead;
And she alone is heir to both of us.
Give her the right you should have giv'n her cousin,
And so dies my revenge.

CLAUDIO O noble sir!
Your over-kindness doth wring tears from me.
I do embrace your offer; and dispose
For henceforth of poor Claudio.

LEONATO To-morrow, then, I will expect your coming;
To-night I take my leave. This naughty man
Shall face to face be brought to Margaret,
Who, I believe, was pack'd in all this wrong,
Hir'd to it by your brother.

BORACHIO No, by my soul, she was not;
Nor knew not what she did when she spoke to me;
But always hath been just and virtuous
In anything that I do know by her.

DOGBERRY Moreover, sir, which indeed is not under white and black, this plaintiff here, the offender, did call me ass; I beseech you, let it be rememb'red in his punishment. And also, the watch heard them talk of one Deformed; they say he wears a key in his ear and a lock hanging by it, and borrows money in God's name; the which he hath us'd so long, and never paid, that now men grow hard-hearted, and will lend nothing for God's sake. Pray you examine him upon that point.

LEONATO I thank thee for thy care and honest pains.

DOGBERRY Your worship speaks like a most thankful and reverend youth, and I praise God for you.

LEONATO There's for thy pains.

DOGBERRY God save the foundation!

LEONATO Go; I discharge thee of thy prisoner, and I thank thee.

DOGBERRY I leave an arrant knave with your worship; which I beseech your worship to correct yourself, for the example of others. God keep your worship! I wish your worship well; God restore you to health! I humbly give you leave to depart; and if a merry meeting may be wish'd, God prohibit it! Come, neighbour.

[*Exeunt Dogberry and Verges.*

LEONATO Until to-morrow morning, lords, farewell.

ANTONIO Farewell, my lords; we look for you to-morrow.

DON PEDRO We will not fail.

CLAUDIO To-night I'll mourn with Hero.

[*Exeunt Don Pedro and Claudio.*

LEONATO [To the Watch] Bring you these
315 fellows on. We'll talk with Margaret
How her acquaintance grew with this lewd fellow. [*Exeunt severally.*

SCENE II. *Leonato's orchard.*

Enter BENEDICK and MARGARET, meeting.

BENEDICK Pray thee, sweet Mistress Margaret, deserve well at my hands by helping me to the speech of Beatrice.

MARGARET Will you then write me a sonnet in
4 praise of my beauty?

BENEDICK In so high a style, Margaret, that no man living shall come over it; for, in most
7 comely truth, thou deservest it.

MARGARET To have no man come over me! Why, shall I always keep below stairs?

BENEDICK Thy wit is as quick as the grey-
11 hound's mouth; it catches.

MARGARET And yours as blunt as the fencer's foils, which hit, but hurt not.

BENEDICK A most manly wit, Margaret; it will not hurt a woman; and so, I pray thee, call
16 Beatrice. I give thee the bucklers.

MARGARET Give us the swords; we have bucklers of our own.

BENEDICK If you use them, Margaret, you must put in the pikes with a vice; and they are
19 dangerous weapons for maids.

MARGARET Well, I will call Beatrice to you, who, I think, hath legs. [*Exit Margaret.*

BENEDICK And therefore will come.

[*Sings*]
The god of love,
That sits above,
25 And knows me, and knows me,
How pitiful I deserve –

I mean in singing; but in loving – Leander the good swimmer, Troilus the first employer of panders, and a whole bookful of these quondam carpet-mongers, whose names yet run smoothly in the even road of a blank verse, why, they were never so truly turn'd over and over as my poor self in love. Marry, I cannot show it in rhyme; I have tried; I can find out no rhyme to 'lady' but 'baby' – an innocent rhyme; for 'scorn', 'horn' – a hard rhyme; for 'school', 'fool' – a babbling rhyme; very ominous endings. No, I was not born
under a rhyming planet, nor I cannot woo in 37
festival terms.

Enter BEATRICE.

Sweet Beatrice, wouldst thou come when I call'd thee?

BEATRICE Yea, signior, and depart when you bid me.

BENEDICK O, stay but till then! 40

BEATRICE 'Then' is spoken; fare you well now. And yet, ere I go, let me go with that I came, which is, with knowing what hath pass'd between you and Claudio.

BENEDICK Only foul words; and thereupon I will
kiss thee. 44

BEATRICE Foul words is but foul wind, and foul wind is but foul breath, and foul breath is
noisome; therefore I will depart unkiss'd. 47

BENEDICK Thou hast frighted the word out of his right sense, so forcible is thy wit. But, I must tell thee plainly, Claudio undergoes my challenge; and either I must shortly hear from him, or I will subscribe him a coward. And, I pray thee now, tell me for which of my bad parts didst
thou first fall in love with me? 53

BEATRICE For them all together; which maintain'd so politic a state of evil that they will not admit any good part to intermingle with them. But for which of my good parts did you
first suffer love for me? 57

BENEDICK Suffer love – a good epithet! I do suffer love indeed, for I love thee against my will.

BEATRICE In spite of your heart, I think; alas, poor heart! If you spite it for my sake, I will spite it for yours; for I will never love that which
my friend hates. 62

BENEDICK Thou and I are too wise to woo peaceably.

BEATRICE It appears not in this confession: there's not one wise man among twenty that will
praise himself. 65

BENEDICK An old, an old instance, Beatrice, that liv'd in the time of good neighbours; if a man do not erect in this age his own tomb ere he dies, he shall live no longer in monument than the bell rings and the widow weeps.

BEATRICE And how long is that, think you? 69

BENEDICK Question: why, an hour in clamour, and a quarter in rheum. Therefore is it most expedient for the wise, if Don Worm, his conscience, find no impediment to the contrary, to be the trumpet of his own virtues, as I am to myself. So much for praising myself, who, I myself will bear witness, is praiseworthy. And now tell me, how doth your cousin?

BEATRICE Very ill.

BENEDICK And how do you?

BEATRICE Very ill too.

BENEDICK Serve God, love me, and mend; there will I leave you too, for here comes one in haste.

Enter URSULA.

URSULA Madam, you must come to your uncle. Yonder's old coil at home. It is proved my Lady Hero hath been falsely accus'd, the Prince and Claudio mightily abus'd; and Don John is the author of all, who is fled and gone. Will you come presently?

BEATRICE Will you go hear this news, signior?

BENEDICK I will live in thy heart, die in thy lap, and be buried in thy eyes; and, more over, I will go with thee to thy uncle's. *[Exeunt.*

SCENE III. *A churchyard.*

Enter DON PEDRO, CLAUDIO, and three or four with tapers.

CLAUDIO Is this the monument of Leonato?

A LORD It is, my lord.

CLAUDIO *[Reads from a scroll]*

Epitaph.

'Done to death by slanderous tongues
Was the Hero that here lies;
Death, in guerdon of her wrongs,
Gives her fame which never dies.
So the life that died with shame
Lives in death with glorious fame.'
Hang thou there upon the tomb,
Praising her when I am dumb.
Now, music, sound, and sing your solemn hymn.

Song.

Pardon, goddess of the night,
Those that slew thy virgin knight;
For the which, with songs of woe,
Round about her tomb they go.
Midnight, assist our moan;
Help us to sigh and groan,
Heavily, heavily.
Graves, yawn, and yield your dead,
Till death be uttered,
Heavily, heavily.

CLAUDIO Now, unto thy bones good night.
Yearly will I do this rite.

DON PEDRO Good morrow, masters; put your torches out;
The wolves have prey'd; and look, the gentle day,
Before the wheels of Phoebus, round about
Dapples the drowsy east with spots of grey.
Thanks to you all, and leave us. Fare you well.

CLAUDIO Good morrow, masters; each his several way.

DON PEDRO Come, let us hence, and put on other weeds;
And then to Leonato's we will go.

CLAUDIO And Hymen now with luckier issue speed's
Than this for whom we rend'red up this woe.

[Exeunt.

SCENE IV. *Leonato's house.*

Enter LEONATO, ANTONIO, BENEDICK, BEATRICE, MARGARET, URSULA, FRIAR FRANCIS, and HERO.

FRIAR Did I not tell you she was innocent?

LEONATO So are the Prince and Claudio, who accus'd her
Upon the error that you heard debated.
But Margaret was in some fault for this,
Although against her will, as it appears
In the true course of all the question.

ANTONIO Well, I am glad that all things sorts so well.

BENEDICK And so am I, being else by faith enforc'd
To call young Claudio to a reckoning for it.

LEONATO Well, daughter, and you gentlewomen all,
Withdraw into a chamber by yourselves;
And when I send for you, come hither mask'd.
The Prince and Claudio promis'd by this hour
To visit me. You know your office, brother:
You must be father to your brother's daughter,
And give her to young Claudio.

[Exeunt Ladies.

ANTONIO Which I will do with confirm'd countenance.

BENEDICK Friar, I must entreat your pains, I think.

FRIAR To do what, signior?

BENEDICK To bind me, or undo me – one of them.
Signior Leonato, truth it is, good signior,
Your niece regards me with an eye of favour.

LEONATO That eye my daughter lent her. 'Tis most true.

BENEDICK And I do with an eye of love requite her.

LEONATO The sight whereof, I think, you had from me,
From Claudio, and the Prince. But what's your will?

BENEDICK Your answer, sir, is enigmatical.

But, for my will, my will is your good will
May stand with ours, this day to be conjoin'd
In the state of honourable marriage;
In which, good friar, I shall desire your help.

LEONATO My heart is with your liking.

FRIAR And my help.
Here comes the Prince and Claudio.

Enter DON PEDRO and CLAUDIO, with Attendants.

DON PEDRO Good morrow to this fair assembly.

LEONATO Good morrow, Prince; good morrow, Claudio;
We here attend you. Are you yet determin'd
To-day to marry with my brother's daughter?

CLAUDIO I'll hold my mind were she an Ethiope.

LEONATO Call her forth, brother; here's the friar ready. [*Exit Antonio.*

DON PEDRO Good morrow, Benedick. Why, what's the matter
That you have such a February face,
So full of frost, of storm, and cloudiness?

CLAUDIO I think he thinks upon the savage bull.
Tush, fear not, man; we'll tip thy horns with gold,
And all Europa shall rejoice at thee,
As once Europa did at lusty Jove,
When he would play the noble beast in love.

BENEDICK Bull Jove, sir, had an amiable low;
And some such strange bull leap'd your father's cow,
And got a calf in that same noble feat
Much like to you, for you have just his bleat.

Re-enter ANTONIO, with the Ladies masked.

CLAUDIO For this I owe you. Here comes other reck'nings.
Which is the lady I must seize upon?

ANTONIO This same is she, and I do give you her.

CLAUDIO Why, then she's mine. Sweet, let me see your face.

LEONATO No, that you shall not, till you take her hand
Before this friar, and swear to marry her.

CLAUDIO Give me your hand; before this holy friar
I am your husband, if you like of me.

HERO And when I liv'd I was your other wife; [*Unmasking.*
And when you lov'd you were my other husband.

CLAUDIO Another Hero!

HERO Nothing certainer.
One Hero died defil'd; but I do live,
And, surely as I live, I am a maid.

DON PEDRO The former Hero! Hero that is dead!

LEONATO She died, my lord, but whiles her slander liv'd.

FRIAR All this amazement can I qualify,
When, after that the holy rites are ended,
I'll tell you largely of fair Hero's death.
Meantime let wonder seem familiar,
And to the chapel let us presently.

BENEDICK Soft and fair, friar. Which is Beatrice?

BEATRICE I answer to that name. [*Unmasking*]
What is your will?

BENEDICK Do not you love me?

BEATRICE Why no, no more than reason.

BENEDICK Why, then your uncle, and the Prince, and Claudio,
Have been deceived: they swore you did.

BEATRICE Do not you love me?

BENEDICK Troth no, no more than reason.

BEATRICE Why, then my cousin, Margaret, and Ursula,
Are much deceiv'd; for they did swear you did.

BENEDICK They swore that you were almost sick for me.

BEATRICE They swore that you were well-nigh dead for me.

BENEDICK 'Tis no such matter. Then you do not love me?

BEATRICE No, truly, but in friendly recompense.

LEONATO Come, cousin, I am sure you love the gentleman.

CLAUDIO And I'll be sworn upon't that he loves her;
For here's a paper written in his hand,
A halting sonnet of his own pure brain,
Fashion'd to Beatrice.

HERO And here's another,
Writ in my cousin's hand, stol'n from her pocket,
Containing her affection unto Benedick.

BENEDICK A miracle! here's our own hands against our hearts. Come, I will have thee; but, by this light, I take thee for pity.

BEATRICE I would not deny you; but, by this good day, I yield upon great persuasion; and partly to save your life, for I was told you were in a consumption.

BENEDICK Peace; I will stop your mouth. [*Kissing her.*

DON PEDRO How dost thou, Benedick the married man?

BENEDICK I'll tell thee what, Prince: a college of wit-crackers cannot flout me out of my humour. Dost thou think I care for a satire or an epigram? No. If a man will be beaten with brains, 'a shall wear nothing handsome about him. In brief, since I do purpose to marry, I will think nothing to any purpose that the world can say against it; and therefore never flout at me for what I have said against it; for man is a giddy thing, and this is my conclusion. For thy part, Claudio, I did think to have beaten thee; but in that thou art like to be my kinsman, live unbruis'd, and love my cousin.

CLAUDIO I had well hop'd thou wouldst have denied Beatrice, that I might have cudgell'd thee out of thy single life, to make thee a double dealer; which out of question thou wilt be, if my cousin do not look exceeding narrowly to thee.

BENEDICK Come, come, we are friends. Let's have a dance ere we are married, that we may lighten our own hearts and our wives' heels.

LEONATO We'll have dancing afterward.

BENEDICK First, of my word; therefore play, music. Prince, thou art sad; get thee a wife, get thee a wife. There is no staff more reverend than one tipp'd with horn.

Enter a Messenger.

MESSENGER My lord, your brother John is ta'en in flight,
And brought with armed men back to Messina.

BENEDICK Think not on him till to-morrow.
I'll devise thee brave punishments for him.
Strike up, pipers.

[*Dance. Exeunt.*

Love's Labour's Lost

Introduction by DONALD MACKENZIE

This is a play of extremes. Love is preposterous and a tyranny [3.1.170f]: love educates and inspires [4.3.286f]. The leering pedant Holofernes we enjoy (if at all) as simply a buffoon: yet, relentlessly baited in the final scene by his social superiors, he exits with a single unanswerable line of wounded rebuke: 'This is not generous, not gentle, not humble.' The plot is minimal; the setting static, sometimes emblematic: the curious-knotted garden, the Princess taking her place for the deer hunt. Plot and setting together create an enclosed space for word-play which is pursued more strenuously than in any other Shakespearean comedy – but pursued into a renouncing of all verbal richness and an abrupt breaking of the comic frame in the final scene.

One key to this locking of extremes can be found in the closing lines of Berowne, the most alert of the play's verbal jugglers: 'our wooing doth not end like an old play:/Jack hath not Jill. These ladies' courtesy/Might well have made our sport a comedy.' 'Sport' here is the playing of verbal and courtship games. Like all play (cf. Huizinga, 1949) it moves in an artificial space marked off from ordinary experience. It blends the improvised or spontaneous with the rigorously stylised. And, like much play, it can sheath aggression . As the comedy advances – or, rather, continues to fence within its enclosed play-space – the strained or the frustrated turns recurrently unpleasant. The wit-combats can dance themselves down into the squalid [4.1.101f] or take on an edge of the savage as in the ragging of the Worthies by the humiliated wooers. Marriage would release all the blocked energies of the play in the conventional climax of a Shakespearean comedy whose generic conventions, with the expectations they raise and satisfy, rest on the wider conventions of human bonding, commitment and promise ('the world-without-end bargain' of the Princess's ponderable phrase). And such a release is what the wooers and we are refused. The most ostentatiously verbal and artificial of Shakespearean comedies finally turns on its own artifice.

This ending is unique in the comedies. But it only drives to an extreme one key pattern in Shakespeare's work of the 1590s where an elegantly self-enclosed style (of language and life) is challenged, broken open by the destructive energies of experience: sexual passion, violence, the power of time (Goldman, 1972). These in turn are met by what seeks to transcend them: the immortalising promised by art, the absolute commitment of love. This is the pattern of *Venus and Adonis* or *Romeo and Juliet*. The Sonnets explore it more searchingly; it is given a steely refashioning at the end of the decade in the relationship of Falstaff and Hal. *Love's Labour's Lost* examines it through the indulgence and critique of word-play. It is at once entranced by, and deeply suspicious of, language, its mutliplicity, its innate capacity for excess, its quicksilver instability (cf Steiner, 1992: cc 2–3).

The capacity for excess can lead to the laboured (Armado, Holofernes) or the irresponsible and self-indulgent (Berowne). Instability can lead to a tiresome quibbling, if not deception and betrayal. Against it is set the self-binding of promise ('We arrest your word' says the Princess to the King in their first encounter); against the indulgence of verbal excess the discipline Rosaline imposes on Berowne.

This ambivalence towards language *Love's Labour's Lost* refuses finally to resolve. Like *Two Gentlemen of Verona* and *The Comedy of Errors* it clashes styles and elaborates stylistic set-pieces but does so with an extremism that no reading of it as parody or critique can save from being, at times, pedantic or strained. This calls out a renunciation, a verbal puritanism not less extreme and perhaps dissatisfying. (Does it smack of self-flagellation? Do the women have the moral authority to demand it?) With his usual creative thrift Shakespeare recycled and transformed key elements of this jagged climax in the harmonious and ironical last scene of *A Midsummer Night's Dream* as he recycled and extended the group of young men broken in upon by love in *Romeo and Juliet* or *Much Ado*. Yet the final scene of *Love's Labour's Lost* is in its own right as masterfully orchestrated as anything in early Shakespeare. And as for word-play and its excesses: Armado can spin, on occasion, a silkily beautiful verbal cocoon; Berowne's quibbling can surge into his marshalled celebration of love; and this static, fantastical, parodic comedy finally debouches into the lyrics of spring and winter which are at once enchanting and completely mundane.

Love's Labour's Lost

DRAMATIS PERSONAE

FERDINAND
King of Navarre
BEROWNE, LONGAVILLE, DUMAIN
lords attending on the King
BOYET, MARCADE
lords attending on the Princess of France
DON ADRIANO DE ARMADO
a fantastical Spaniard
SIR NATHANIEL
a curate
HOLOFERNES
a schoolmaster
DULL
a constable
COSTARD
a clown
MOTH
page to Armado
A Forester
THE PRINCESS OF FRANCE
ROSALINE, MARIA, KATHARINE
ladies attending on the Princess
JAQUENETTA
a country wench
Lords, Attendants, etc.

THE SCENE: NAVARRE

ACT ONE

SCENE I. *Navarre. The King's park.*

Enter the KING, BEROWNE, LONGAVILLE, and DUMAIN.

KING Let fame, that all hunt after in their lives,
Live regist'red upon our brazen tombs,
And then grace us in the disgrace of death;
When, spite of cormorant devouring Time,
Th' endeavour of this present breath may buy
That honour which shall bate his scythe's keen edge,
And make us heirs of all eternity.
Therefore, brave conquerors – for so you are
That war against your own affections
And the huge army of the world's desires –
Our late edict shall strongly stand in force:
Navarre shall be the wonder of the world;
Our court shall be a little Academe,
Still and contemplative in living art.
You three, Berowne, Dumain, and Longaville,
Have sworn for three years' term to live with me
My fellow-scholars, and to keep those statutes
That are recorded in this schedule here.
Your oaths are pass'd; and now subscribe your names,
That his own hand may strike his honour down
That violates the smallest branch herein.
If you are arm'd to do as sworn to do,
Subscribe to your deep oaths, and keep it too.
LONGAVILLE I am resolv'd; 'tis but a three years' fast.
The mind shall banquet, though the body pine.
Fat paunches have lean pates; and dainty bits
Make rich the ribs, but bankrupt quite the wits.
DUMAIN My loving lord, Dumain is mortified.
The grosser manner of these world's delights
He throws upon the gross world's baser slaves;
To love, to wealth, to pomp, I pine and die,
With all these living in philosophy.
BEROWNE I can but say their protestation over;
So much, dear liege, I have already sworn,
That is, to live and study here three years.
But there are other strict observances,
As: not to see a woman in that term,
Which I hope well is not enrolled there;
And one day in a week to touch no food,
And but one meal on every day beside,
The which I hope is not enrolled there;
And then to sleep but three hours in the night
And not be seen to wink of all the day –
When I was wont to think no harm all night,
And make a dark night too of half the day –
Which I hope well is not enrolled there.
O, these are barren tasks, too hard to keep,
Not to see ladies, study, fast, not sleep!
KING Your oath is pass'd to pass away from these.
BEROWNE Let me say no, my liege, an if you please:
I only swore to study with your Grace,
And stay here in your court for three years' space.
LONGAVILLE You swore to that, Berowne, and to the rest.
BEROWNE By yea and nay, sir, then I swore in jest.
What is the end of study, let me know.
KING Why, that to know which else we should not know.

BEROWNE Things hid and barr'd, you mean, from common sense?
KING Ay, that is study's god-like recompense.
BEROWNE Come on, then; I will swear to study so,
To know the thing I am forbid to know,
As thus: to study where I well may dine,
When I to feast expressly am forbid;
Or study where to meet some mistress fine,
When mistresses from common sense are hid;
Or, having sworn too hard-a-keeping oath,
Study to break it, and not break my troth.
If study's gain be thus, and this be so,
Study knows that which yet it doth not know.
Swear me to this, and I will ne'er say no.
KING These be the stops that hinder study quite,
And train our intellects to vain delight.
BEROWNE Why, all delights are vain; but that most vain
Which, with pain purchas'd, doth inherit pain,
As painfully to pore upon a book
To seek the light of truth; while truth the while
Doth falsely blind the eyesight of his look.
Light, seeking light, doth light of light beguile;
So, ere you find where light in darkness lies,
Your light grows dark by losing of your eyes.
Study me how to please the eye indeed,
By fixing it upon a fairer eye;
Who dazzling so, that eye shall be his heed,
And give him light that it was blinded by.
Study is like the heaven's glorious sun,
That will not be deep-search'd with saucy looks;
Small have continual plodders ever won,
Save base authority from others' books.
These earthly godfathers of heaven's lights
That give a name to every fixed star
Have no more profit of their shining nights
Than those that walk and wot not what they are.
Too much to know is to know nought but fame;
And every godfather can give a name.
KING How well he's read, to reason against reading!
DUMAIN Proceeded well, to stop all good proceeding!
LONGAVILLE He weeds the corn, and still lets grow the weeding.
BEROWNE The spring is near, when green geese are a-breeding.
DUMAIN How follows that?
BEROWNE Fit in his place and time.
DUMAIN In reason nothing.
BEROWNE Something then in rhyme.
LONGAVILLE Berowne is like an envious sneaping frost
That bites the first-born infants of the spring.
BEROWNE Well, say I am; why should proud summer boast
Before the birds have any cause to sing?
Why should I joy in any abortive birth?
At Christmas I no more desire a rose
Than wish a snow in May's new-fangled shows;
But like of each thing that in season grows;
So you, to study now it is too late,
Climb o'er the house to unlock the little gate.
KING Well, sit you out; go home, Berowne; adieu.
BEROWNE No, my good lord; I have sworn to stay with you;
And though I have for barbarism spoke more
Than for that angel knowledge you can say,
Yet confident I'll keep what I have swore,
And bide the penance of each three years' day.
Give me the paper; let me read the same;
And to the strictest decrees I'll write my name.
KING How well this yielding rescues thee from shame!
BEROWNE [*Reads*] 'Item. That no woman shall come within a mile of my court' –
Hath this been proclaimed?
LONGAVILLE Four days ago.
BEROWNE Let's see the penalty. [*Reads*] '– on pain of losing her tongue.' Who devis'd this penalty?
LONGAVILLE Marry, that did I.
BEROWNE Sweet lord, and why?
LONGAVILLE To fright them hence with that dread penalty.
BEROWNE A dangerous law against gentility.
[*Reads*] 'Item. If any man be seen to talk with a woman within the term of three years, he shall endure such public shame as the rest of the court can possibly devise.'
This article, my liege, yourself must break;
For well you know here comes in embassy
The French king's daughter, with yourself to speak –
A maid of grace and complete majesty –
About surrender up of Aquitaine
To her decrepit, sick, and bedrid father;
Therefore this article is made in vain,
Or vainly comes th' admired princess hither.
KING What say you, lords? Why, this was quite forgot.
BEROWNE So study evermore is over-shot.
While it doth study to have what it would,
It doth forget to do the thing it should;
And when it hath the thing it hunteth most,
'Tis won as towns with fire – so won, so lost.
KING We must of force dispense with this decree;
She must lie here on mere necessity.
BEROWNE Necessity will make us all forsworn
Three thousand times within this three years' space;

For every man with his affects is born,
Not by might mast'red, but by special grace.
If I break faith, this word shall speak for me:
I am forsworn on mere necessity.
So to the laws at large I write my name;
[*Subscribes.*
And he that breaks them in the least degree
Stands in attainder of eternal shame.
Suggestions are to other as to me;
But I believe, although I seem so loath,
I am the last that will last keep his oath.
But is there no quick recreation granted?

KING Ay, that there is. Our court, you know, is haunted
With a refined traveller of Spain,
A man in all the world's new fashion planted,
That hath a mint of phrases in his brain;
One who the music of his own vain tongue
Doth ravish like enchanting harmony;
A man of complements, whom right and wrong
Have chose as umpire of their mutiny.
This child of fancy, that Armado hight,
For interim to our studies shall relate,
In high-born words, the worth of many a knight
From tawny Spain lost in the world's debate.
How you delight, my lords, I know not, I;
But I protest I love to hear him lie,
And I will use him for my minstrelsy.

BEROWNE Armado is a most illustrious wight,
A man of fire-new words, fashion's own knight.

LONGAVILLE Costard the swain and he shall be our sport;
And so to study three years is but short.

Enter DULL, a constable, with a letter, and COSTARD.

DULL Which is the Duke's own person?

BEROWNE This, fellow. What wouldst?

DULL I myself reprehend his own person, for I am his Grace's farborough; but I would see his own person in flesh and blood.

BEROWNE This is he.

DULL Signior Arme – Arme – commends you. There's villainy abroad; this letter will tell you more.

COSTARD Sir, the contempts thereof are as touching me.

KING A letter from the magnificent Armado.

BEROWNE How low soever the matter, I hope in God for high words.

LONGAVILLE A high hope for a low heaven. God grant us patience!

BEROWNE To hear, or forbear hearing?

LONGAVILLE To hear meekly, sir, and to laugh moderately; or, to forbear both.

BEROWNE Well, sir, be it as the style shall give us cause to climb in the merriness.

COSTARD The matter is to me, sir, as concerning Jaquenetta. The manner of it is, I was taken with the manner.

BEROWNE In what manner?

COSTARD In manner and form following, sir; all those three: I was seen with her in the manor-house, sitting with her upon the form, and taken following her into the park; which, put together, is in manner and form following. Now, sir, for the manner – it is the manner of a man to speak to a woman. For the form – in some form.

BEROWNE For the following, sir?

COSTARD As it shall follow in my correction; and God defend the right!

KING Will you hear this letter with attention?

BEROWNE As we would hear an oracle.

COSTARD Such is the simplicity of man to hearken after the flesh.

KING [*Reads*] 'Great deputy, the welkin's vicegerent and sole dominator of Navarre, my soul's earth's god and body's fost'ring patron' –

COSTARD Not a word of Costard yet.

KING [*Reads*] 'So it is' –

COSTARD It may be so; but if he say it is so, he is, in telling true, but so.

KING Peace!

COSTARD Be to me, and every man that dares not fight!

KING No words!

COSTARD Of other men's secrets, I beseech you.

KING [*Reads*] 'So it is, besieged with sable-coloured melancholy, I did commend the black oppressing humour to the most wholesome physic of thy health-giving air; and, as I am a gentleman, betook myself to walk. The time When? About the sixth hour; when beasts most graze, birds best peck, and men sit down to that nourishment which is called supper. So much for the time When. Now for the ground Which? which, I mean, I walk'd upon; it is ycleped thy park. Then for the place Where? where, I mean, I did encounter that obscene and most prepost'rous event that draweth from my snow-white pen the ebon-coloured ink which here thou viewest, beholdest, surveyest, or seest. But to the place Where? It standeth north-north-east and by east from the west corner of thy curious-knotted garden. There did I see that low-spirited swain, that base minnow of thy mirth,'

COSTARD Me?

KING 'that unlettered small-knowing soul,'

COSTARD Me?

KING 'that shallow vassal,'

COSTARD Still me?

KING 'which, as I remember, hight Costard,'

COSTARD O, me!

KING 'sorted and consorted, contrary to thy established proclaimed edict and continent canon; which, with, O, with – but with this I passion to say wherewith –'

COSTARD With a wench.

KING 'with a child of our grandmother Eve, a female; or, for thy more sweet understanding, a woman. Him I, as my ever-esteemed duty pricks me on, have sent to thee, to receive the meed of punishment, by thy sweet Grace's officer, Antony Dull, a man of good repute, carriage, bearing, and estimation.'

DULL Me, an't shall please you; I am Antony Dull.

KING 'For Jaquenetta – so is the weaker vessel called, which I apprehended with the aforesaid swain – I keep her as a vessel of thy law's fury; and shall, at the least of thy sweet notice, bring her to trial. Thine, in all compliments of devoted and heart-burning heat of duty,

DON ADRIANO DE ARMADO.'

BEROWNE This is not so well as I look'd for, but the best that ever I heard.

KING Ay, the best for the worst. But, sirrah, what say you to this?

COSTARD Sir, I confess the wench.

KING Did you hear the proclamation?

COSTARD I do confess much of the hearing it, but little of the marking of it.

KING It was proclaimed a year's imprisonment to be taken with a wench.

COSTARD I was taken with none, sir; I was taken with a damsel.

KING Well, it was proclaimed damsel.

COSTARD This was no damsel neither, sir; she was a virgin.

KING It is so varied too, for it was proclaimed virgin.

COSTARD If it were, I deny her virginity; I was taken with a maid.

KING This 'maid' will not serve your turn, sir.

COSTARD This maid will serve my turn, sir.

KING Sir, I will pronounce your sentence: you shall fast a week with bran and water.

COSTARD I had rather pray a month with mutton and porridge.

KING And Don Armado shall be your keeper.
My Lord Berowne, see him delivered o'er;
And go we, lords, to put in practice that
Which each to other hath so strongly sworn.

[*Exeunt King, Longaville, and Dumain.*

BEROWNE I'll lay my head to any good man's hat
These oaths and laws will prove an idle scorn.
Sirrah, come on.

COSTARD I suffer for the truth, sir; for true it is I was taken with Jaquenetta, and Jaquenetta is a true girl; and therefore welcome the sour cup of prosperity! Affliction may one day smile again; and till then, sit thee down, sorrow. [*Exeunt.*

SCENE II. *The park.*

Enter ARMADO and MOTH, his page.

ARMADO Boy, what sign is it when a man of great spirit grows melancholy?

MOTH A great sign, sir, that he will look sad.

ARMADO Why, sadness is one and the self-same thing, dear imp.

MOTH No, no; O Lord, sir, no!

ARMADO How canst thou part sadness and melancholy, my tender juvenal?

MOTH By a familiar demonstration of the working, my tough signior.

ARMADO Why tough signior? Why tough signior?

MOTH Why tender juvenal? Why tender juvenal?

ARMADO I spoke it, tender juvenal, as a congruent epitheton appertaining to thy young days, which we may nominate tender.

MOTH And I, tough signior, as an appertinent title to your old time, which we may name tough.

ARMADO Pretty and apt.

MOTH How mean you, sir? I pretty, and my saying apt? or I apt, and my saying pretty?

ARMADO Thou pretty, because little.

MOTH Little pretty, because little. Wherefore apt?

ARMADO And therefore apt, because quick.

MOTH Speak you this in my praise, master?

ARMADO In thy condign praise.

MOTH I will praise an eel with the same praise.

ARMADO What, that an eel is ingenious?

MOTH That an eel is quick.

ARMADO I do say thou art quick in answers; thou heat'st my blood.

MOTH I am answer'd, sir.

ARMADO I love not to be cross'd.

MOTH [*Aside*] He speaks the mere contrary: crosses love not him.

ARMADO I have promised to study three years with the Duke.

MOTH You may do it in an hour, sir.

ARMADO Impossible.

MOTH How many is one thrice told?

ARMADO I am ill at reck'ning; it fitteth the spirit of a tapster.

MOTH You are a gentleman and a gamester, sir.

ARMADO I confess both; they are both the varnish of a complete man.

MOTH Then I am sure you know how much the gross sum of deuce-ace amounts to.

ARMADO It doth amount to one more than two.

MOTH Which the base vulgar do call three.

ARMADO True.

MOTH Why, sir, is this such a piece of study? Now here is three studied ere ye'll thrice wink; and how easy it is to put 'years' to the word 'three', and study three years in two words, the dancing horse will tell you.

ARMADO A most fine figure!

MOTH [*Aside*] To prove you a cipher.

ARMADO I will hereupon confess I am in love. And as it is base for a soldier to love, so am I in love with a base wench. If drawing my sword against the humour of affection would deliver me from the reprobate thought of it, I would take Desire prisoner, and ransom him to any French courtier for a new-devis'd curtsy. I think scorn to sigh; methinks I should out-swear Cupid. Comfort me, boy; what great men have been in love?

MOTH Hercules, master.

ARMADO Most sweet Hercules! More authority, dear boy, name more; and, sweet my child, let them be men of good repute and carriage.

MOTH Samson, master; he was a man of good carriage, great carriage, for he carried the town gates on his back like a porter; and he was in love.

ARMADO O well-knit Samson! strong-jointed Samson! I do excel thee in my rapier as much as thou didst me in carrying gates. I am in love too. Who was Samson's love, my dear Moth?

MOTH A woman, master.

ARMADO Of what complexion?

MOTH Of all the four, or the three, or the two, or one of the four.

ARMADO Tell me precisely of what complexion.

MOTH Of the sea-water green, sir.

ARMADO Is that one of the four complexions?

MOTH As I have read, sir; and the best of them too.

ARMADO Green, indeed, is the colour of lovers; but to have a love of that colour, methinks Samson had small reason for it. He surely affected her for her wit.

MOTH It was so, sir; for she had a green wit.

ARMADO My love is most immaculate white and red.

MOTH Most maculate thoughts, master, are mask'd under such colours.

ARMADO Define, define, well-educated infant.

MOTH My father's wit and my mother's tongue assist me!

ARMADO Sweet invocation of a child; most pretty, and pathetical!

MOTH If she be made of white and red,
Her faults will ne'er be known;
For blushing cheeks by faults are bred,
And fears by pale white shown.
Then if she fear, or be to blame,
By this you shall not know;
For still her cheeks possess the same
Which native she doth owe.

A dangerous rhyme, master, against the reason of white and red.

ARMADO Is there not a ballad, boy, of the King and the Beggar?

MOTH The world was very guilty of such a ballad some three ages since; but I think now 'tis not to be found; or if it were, it would neither serve for the writing nor the tune.

ARMADO I will have that subject newly writ o'er, that I may example my digression by some mighty precedent. Boy, I do love that country girl that I took in the park with the rational hind Costard; she deserves well.

MOTH [*Aside*] To be whipt; and yet a better love than my master.

ARMADO Sing, boy; my spirit grows heavy in love.

MOTH And that's great marvel, loving a light wench.

ARMADO I say, sing.

MOTH Forbear till this company be past.

Enter DULL, COSTARD, and JAQUENETTA.

DULL Sir, the Duke's pleasure is that you keep Costard safe; and you must suffer him to take no delight nor no penance; but 'a must fast three days a week. For this damsel, I must keep her at the park; she is allow'd for the day-woman. Fare you well.

ARMADO I do betray myself with blushing. Maid!

JAQUENETTA Man!

ARMADO I will visit thee at the lodge.

JAQUENETTA That's hereby.

ARMADO I know where it is situate.

JAQUENETTA Lord, how wise you are!

ARMADO I will tell thee wonders.

JAQUENETTA With that face?

ARMADO I love thee.

JAQUENETTA So I heard you say.

ARMADO And so, farewell.

JAQUENETTA Fair weather after you!

DULL Come, Jaquenetta, away.

[*Exeunt Dull and Jaquenetta.*

ARMADO Villain, thou shalt fast for thy offences ere thou be pardoned.

COSTARD Well, sir, I hope when I do it I shall do it on a full stomach.

ARMADO Thou shalt be heavily punished.

COSTARD I am more bound to you than your fellows, for they are but lightly rewarded.

ARMADO Take away this villain; shut him up.

MOTH Come, you transgressing slave, away.

COSTARD Let me not be pent up, sir; I will fast, being loose.

MOTH No, sir; that were fast and loose. Thou shalt to prison.

COSTARD Well, if ever I do see the merry days of desolation that I have seen, some shall see.

MOTH What shall some see?

COSTARD Nay, nothing, Master Moth, but what they look upon. It is not for prisoners to be too silent in their words, and therefore I will say nothing. I thank God I have as little patience as another man, and therefore I can be quiet.

[Exeunt Moth and Costard.

ARMADO I do affect the very ground, which is base, where her shoe, which is baser, guided by her foot, which is basest, doth tread. I shall be forsworn – which is a great argument of falsehood – if I love. And how can that be true love which is falsely attempted? Love is a familiar; Love is a devil. There is no evil angel but Love. Yet was Samson so tempted, and he had an excellent strength; yet was Solomon so seduced, and he had a very good wit. Cupid's butt-shaft is too hard for Hercules' club, and therefore too much odds for a Spaniard's rapier. The first and second cause will not serve my turn; the passado he respects not, the duello he regards not; his disgrace is to be called boy, but his glory is to subdue men. Adieu, valour; rust, rapier; be still, drum; for your manager is in love; yea, he loveth. Assist me, some extemporal god of rhyme, for I am sure I shall turn sonnet. Devise, wit; write, pen; for I am for whole volumes in folio.

[Exit.

ACT TWO

SCENE I. *The park.*

Enter the PRINCESS OF FRANCE, with three attending ladies, ROSALINE, MARIA, KATHARINE, BOYET, and two other Lords.

BOYET Now, madam, summon up your dearest spirits.
Consider who the King your father sends,
To whom he sends, and what's his embassy:
Yourself, held precious in the world's esteem,
To parley with the sole inheritor
Of all perfections that a man may owe,
Matchless Navarre; the plea of no less weight
Than Aquitaine, a dowry for a queen.
Be now as prodigal of all dear grace
As Nature was in making graces dear,
When she did starve the general world beside
And prodigally gave them all to you.

PRINCESS Good Lord Boyet, my beauty, though but mean,
Needs not the painted flourish of your praise.
Beauty is bought by judgment of the eye,
Not utt'red by base sale of chapmen's tongues;
I am less proud to hear you tell my worth
Than you much willing to be counted wise
In spending your wit in the praise of mine.
But now to task the tasker: good Boyet,
You are not ignorant all-telling fame
Doth noise abroad Navarre hath made a vow,
Till painful study shall outwear three years,
No woman may approach his silent court.
Therefore to's seemeth it a needful course,
Before we enter his forbidden gates,
To know his pleasure; and in that behalf,
Bold of your worthiness, we single you
As our best-moving fair solicitor.
Tell him the daughter of the King of France,
On serious business, craving quick dispatch,
Importunes personal conference with his Grace.
Haste, signify so much; while we attend,
Like humble-visag'd suitors, his high will.

BOYET Proud of employment, willingly I go.

PRINCESS All pride is willing pride, and yours is so. *[Exit Boyet.*
Who are the votaries, my loving lords,
That are vow-fellows with this virtuous duke?

1 LORD Lord Longaville is one.

PRINCESS Know you the man?

MARIA I know him, madam; at a marriage feast,
Between Lord Perigort and the beauteous heir
Of Jaques Falconbridge, solemnized
In Normandy, saw I this Longaville.
A man of sovereign parts, peerless esteem'd,
Well fitted in arts, glorious in arms;
Nothing becomes him ill that he would well.
The only soil of his fair virtue's gloss,
If virtue's gloss will stain with any soil,
Is a sharp wit match'd with too blunt a will,
Whose edge hath power to cut, whose will still wills
It should none spare that come within his power.

PRINCESS Some merry mocking lord, belike; is't so?

MARIA They say so most that most his humours know.

PRINCESS Such short-liv'd wits do wither as they grow.
Who are the rest?
KATHARINE The young Dumain, a well-accomplish'd youth,
Of all that virtue love for virtue loved;
Most power to do most harm, least knowing ill;
For he hath wit to make an ill shape good,
And shape to win grace though he had no wit.
I saw him at the Duke Alençon's once;
And much too little of that good I saw
Is my report to his great worthiness.
ROSALINE Another of these students at that time
Was there with him, if I have heard a truth.
Berowne they call him; but a merrier man,
Within the limit of becoming mirth,
I never spent an hour's talk withal.
His eye begets occasion for his wit,
For every object that the one doth catch
The other turns to a mirth-moving jest,
Which his fair tongue, conceit's expositor,
Delivers in such apt and gracious words
That aged ears play truant at his tales,
And younger hearings are quite ravished;
So sweet and voluble is his discourse.
PRINCESS God bless my ladies! Are they all in love,
That every one her own hath garnished
With such bedecking ornaments of praise?
1 LORD Here comes Boyet.

Re-enter BOYET.

PRINCESS Now, what admittance, lord?
BOYET Navarre had notice of your fair approach,
And he and his competitors in oath
Were all address'd to meet you, gentle lady,
Before I came. Marry, thus much I have learnt:
He rather means to lodge you in the field,
Like one that comes here to besiege his court,
Than seek a dispensation for his oath,
To let you enter his unpeopled house.
[The ladies-in-waiting mask.

Enter KING, LONGAVILLE, DUMAIN, BEROWNE, and Attendants.

Here comes Navarre.
KING Fair Princess, welcome to the court of Navarre.
PRINCESS 'Fair' I give you back again; and 'welcome' I have not yet. The roof of this court is too high to be yours, and welcome to the wide fields too base to be mine.
KING You shall be welcome, madam, to my court.
PRINCESS I will be welcome then; conduct me thither.
KING Hear me, dear lady: I have sworn an oath –
PRINCESS Our Lady help my lord! He'll be forsworn.
KING Not for the world, fair madam, by my will.
PRINCESS Why, will shall break it; will, and nothing else.
KING Your ladyship is ignorant what it is.
PRINCESS Were my lord so, his ignorance were wise,
Where now his knowledge must prove ignorance.
I hear your Grace hath sworn out house-keeping.
'Tis deadly sin to keep that oath, my lord,
And sin to break it.
But pardon me, I am too sudden bold;
To teach a teacher ill beseemeth me.
Vouchsafe to read the purpose of my coming,
And suddenly resolve me in my suit.
[Giving a paper.
KING Madam, I will, if suddenly I may.
PRINCESS You will the sooner that I were away,
For you'll prove perjur'd if you make me stay.
BEROWNE Did not I dance with you in Brabant once?
KATHARINE Did not I dance with you in Brabant once?
BEROWNE I know you did.
KATHARINE How needless was it then to ask the question!
BEROWNE You must not be so quick.
KATHARINE 'Tis long of you, that spur me with such questions.
BEROWNE Your wit 's too hot, it speeds too fast, 'twill tire.
KATHARINE Not till it leave the rider in the mire.
BEROWNE What time o' day?
KATHARINE The hour that fools should ask.
BEROWNE Now fair befall your mask!
KATHARINE Fair fall the face it covers!
BEROWNE And send you many lovers!
KATHARINE Amen, so you be none.
BEROWNE Nay, then will I be gone.
KING Madam, your father here doth intimate
The payment of a hundred thousand crowns;
Being but the one half of an entire sum
Disbursed by my father in his wars.
But say that he or we, as neither have,
Receiv'd that sum, yet there remains unpaid
A hundred thousand more, in surety of the which,
One part of Aquitaine is bound to us,
Although not valued to the money's worth.
If then the King your father will restore
But that one half which is unsatisfied,
We will give up our right in Aquitaine,
And hold fair friendship with his Majesty.
But that, it seems, he little purposeth,
For here he doth demand to have repaid

A hundred thousand crowns; and not demands,
On payment of a hundred thousand crowns,
To have his title live in Aquitaine;
Which we much rather had depart withal,
And have the money by our father lent,
Than Aquitaine so gelded as it is.
Dear Princess, were not his requests so far
From reason's yielding, your fair self should make
A yielding 'gainst some reason in my breast,
And go well satisfied to France again.

PRINCESS You do the King my father too much wrong,
And wrong the reputation of your name,
In so unseeming to confess receipt
Of that which hath so faithfully been paid.

KING I do protest I never heard of it;
And, if you prove it, I'll repay it back
Or yield up Aquitaine.

PRINCESS We arrest your word.
Boyet, you can produce acquittances
For such a sum from special officers
Of Charles his father.

KING Satisfy me so.

BOYET So please your Grace, the packet is not come,
Where that and other specialties are bound;
To-morrow you shall have a sight of them.

KING It shall suffice me; at which interview
All liberal reason I will yield unto.
Meantime receive such welcome at my hand
As honour, without breach of honour, may
Make tender of to thy true worthiness.
You may not come, fair Princess, within my gates;
But here without you shall be so receiv'd
As you shall deem yourself lodg'd in my heart,
Though so denied fair harbour in my house.
Your own good thoughts excuse me, and farewell.
To-morrow shall we visit you again.

PRINCESS Sweet health and fair desires consort your Grace!

KING Thy own wish wish I thee in every place.
[*Exit with attendants.*

BEROWNE Lady, I will commend you to mine own heart.

ROSALINE Pray you, do my commendations; I
would be glad to see it.

BEROWNE I would you heard it groan.

ROSALINE Is the fool sick?

BEROWNE Sick at the heart.

ROSALINE Alack, let it blood.

BEROWNE Would that do it good?

ROSALINE My physic says 'ay'.

BEROWNE Will you prick't with your eye?

ROSALINE No point, with my knife.

BEROWNE Now, God save thy life!

ROSALINE And yours from long living!

BEROWNE I cannot stay thanksgiving.
[*Retiring.*

DUMAIN Sir, I pray you, a word: what lady is that same?

BOYET The heir of Alencon, Katharine her name.

DUMAIN A gallant lady! Monsieur, fare you well.
[*Exit.*

LONGAVILLE I beseech you a word: what is she in the white?

BOYET A woman sometimes, an you saw her in the light.

LONGAVILLE Perchance light in the light. I desire her name.

BOYET She hath but one for herself; to desire that were a shame.

LONGAVILLE Pray you, sir, whose daughter?

BOYET Her mother's, I have heard.

LONGAVILLE God's blessing on your beard!

BOYET Good sir, be not offended;
She is an heir of Falconbridge.

LONGAVILLE Nay, my choler is ended.
She is a most sweet lady.

BOYET Not unlike, sir; that may be.
[*Exit Longaville.*

BEROWNE What's her name in the cap?

BOYET Rosaline, by good hap.

BEROWNE Is she wedded or no?

BOYET To her will, sir, or so.

BEROWNE You are welcome, sir; adieu!

BOYET Farewell to me, sir, and welcome to you.
[*Exit Berowne. Ladies unmask.*

MARIA That last is Berowne, the merry mad-cap lord;
Not a word with him but a jest.

BOYET And every jest but a word.

PRINCESS It was well done of you to take him at his word.

BOYET I was as willing to grapple as he was to board.

KATHARINE Two hot sheeps, marry!

BOYET And wherefore not ships?
No sheep, sweet lamb, unless we feed on your lips.

KATHARINE You sheep and I pasture – shall that finish the jest?

BOYET So you grant pasture for me.
[*Offering to kiss her.*

KATHARINE Not so, gentle beast;
My lips are no common, though several they be.

BOYET Belonging to whom?

KATHARINE To my fortunes and me.
PRINCESS Good wits will be jangling; but, gentles, agree;
This civil war of wits were much better used
On Navarre and his book-men, for here 'tis abused.
BOYET If my observation, which very seldom lies,
By the heart's still rhetoric disclosed with eyes,
Deceive me not now, Navarre is infected.
PRINCESS With what?
BOYET With that which we lovers entitle 'affected'.
PRINCESS Your reason?
BOYET Why, all his behaviours did make their retire
To the court of his eye, peeping thorough desire.
His heart, like an agate, with your print impressed,
Proud with his form, in his eye pride expressed;
His tongue, all impatient to speak and not see,
Did stumble with haste in his eyesight to be;
All senses to that sense did make their repair,
To feel only looking on fairest of fair.
Methought all his senses were lock'd in his eye,
As jewels in crystal for some prince to buy;
Who, tend'ring their own worth from where they were glass'd,
Did point you to buy them, along as you pass'd.
His face's own margent did quote such amazes
That all eyes saw his eyes enchanted with gazes.
I'll give you Aquitaine and all that is his,
An you give him for my sake but one loving kiss.
PRINCESS Come, to our pavilion. Boyet is dispos'd.
BOYET But to speak that in words which his eye hath disclos'd;
I only have made a mouth of his eye,
By adding a tongue which I know will not lie.
MARIA Thou art an old love-monger, and speakest skilfully.
KATHARINE He is Cupid's grandfather, and learns news of him.
ROSALINE Then was Venus like her mother; for her father is but grim.
BOYET Do you hear, my mad wenches?
MARIA No.
BOYET What, then; do you see?
MARIA Ay, our way to be gone.
BOYET You are too hard for me.

[*Exeunt.*

ACT THREE

SCENE I. *The park.*

Enter ARMADO and MOTH

ARMADO Warble, child; make passionate my sense of hearing.

[*Moth sings* Concolinel.

ARMADO Sweet air! Go, tenderness of years, take this key, give enlargement to the swain, bring him festinately hither; I must employ him in a letter to my love.

MOTH Master, will you win your love with a French brawl?

ARMADO How meanest thou? Brawling in French?

MOTH No, my complete master; but to jig off a tune at the tongue's end, canary to it with your feet, humour it with turning up your eyelids, sigh a note and sing a note, sometime through the throat, as if you swallowed love with singing love, sometime through the nose, as if you snuff'd up love by smelling love, with your hat penthouse-like o'er the shop of your eyes, with your arms cross'd on your thin-belly doublet, like a rabbit on a spit, or your hands in your pocket, like a man after the old painting; and keep not too long in one tune, but a snip and away. These are complements, these are humours; these betray nice wenches, that would be betrayed without these; and make them men of note – do you note me? – that most are affected to these.

ARMADO How hast thou purchased this experience?

MOTH By my penny of observation.

ARMADO But O – but O –

MOTH The hobby-horse is forgot.

ARMADO Call'st thou my love 'hobby-horse'?

MOTH No, master; the hobby-horse is but a colt, and your love perhaps a hackney. But have you forgot your love?

ARMADO Almost I had.

MOTH Negligent student! learn her by heart.

ARMADO By heart and in heart, boy.

MOTH And out of heart, master; all those three I will prove.

ARMADO What wilt thou prove?

MOTH A man, if I live; and this, by, in, and without, upon the instant. By heart you love her, because your heart cannot come by her; in heart you love her, because your heart is in love with her; and out of heart you love her, being out of heart that you cannot enjoy her.

ARMADO I am all these three.

MOTH And three times as much more, and yet nothing at all.

ARMADO Fetch hither the swain; he must carry me a letter.

MOTH A message well sympathiz'd – a horse to be ambassador for an ass.

ARMADO Ha, ha, what sayest thou?

MOTH Marry, sir, you must send the ass upon the horse, for he is very slow-gaited. But I go.

ARMADO The way is but short; away.

MOTH As swift as lead, sir.

ARMADO The meaning, pretty ingenious? Is not lead a metal heavy, dull, and slow?

MOTH Minime, honest master; or rather, master, no.

ARMADO I say lead is slow.

MOTH You are too swift, sir, to say so:
Is that lead slow which is fir'd from a gun?

ARMADO Sweet smoke of rhetoric!
He reputes me a cannon; and the bullet, that's he;
I shoot thee at the swain.

MOTH Thump, then, and I flee.

[*Exit.*

ARMADO A most acute juvenal; volable and free of grace!
By thy favour, sweet welkin, I must sigh in thy face;
Most rude melancholy, valour gives thee place.
My herald is return'd.

Re-enter MOTH with COSTARD.

MOTH A wonder, master! here's a costard broken in a shin.

ARMADO Some enigma, some riddle; come, thy l'envoy; begin.

COSTARD No egma, no riddle, no l'envoy; no salve in the mail, sir. O, sir, plantain, a plain plantain; no l'envoy, no l'envoy; no salve, sir, but a plantain!

ARMADO By virtue thou enforcest laughter; thy silly thought, my spleen; the heaving of my lungs provokes me to ridiculous smiling. O, pardon me, my stars! Doth the inconsiderate take salve for l'envoy, and the word 'l'envoy' for a salve?

MOTH Do the wise think them other? Is not l'envoy a salve?

ARMADO No, page; it is an epilogue or discourse to make plain
Some obscure precedence that hath tofore been sain.
I will example it:
The fox, the ape, and the humble-bee,
Were still at odds, being but three.
There's the moral. Now the l'envoy.

MOTH I will add the l'envoy. Say the moral again.

ARMADO The fox, the ape, and the humble-bee,
Were still at odds, being but three.

MOTH Until the goose came out of door,
And stay'd the odds by adding four.
Now will I begin your moral, and do you follow with my l'envoy.
The fox, the ape, and the humble-bee,
Were still at odds, being but three.

ARMADO Until the goose came out of door,
Staying the odds by adding four.

MOTH A good l'envoy, ending in the goose; would you desire more?

COSTARD The boy hath sold him a bargain, a goose, that's flat.
Sir, your pennyworth is good, an your goose be fat.
To sell a bargain well is as cunning as fast and loose;
Let me see: a fat l'envoy; ay, that's a fat goose.

ARMADO Come hither, come hither. How did this argument begin?

MOTH By saying that a costard was broken in a shin.
Then call'd you for the l'envoy.

COSTARD True, and I for a plantain. Thus came your argument in;
Then the boy's fat l'envoy, the goose that you bought;
And he ended the market.

ARMADO But tell me: how was there a costard broken in a shin?

MOTH I will tell you sensibly.

COSTARD Thou hast no feeling of it, Moth; I will speak that l'envoy.
I, Costard, running out, that was safely within,
Fell over the threshold and broke my shin.

ARMADO We will talk no more of this matter.

COSTARD Till there be more matter in the shin.

ARMADO Sirrah Costard, I will enfranchise thee.

COSTARD O, marry me to one Frances! I smell some l'envoy, some goose, in this.

ARMADO By my sweet soul, I mean setting thee at liberty, enfreedoming thy person; thou wert immured, restrained, captivated, bound.

COSTARD True, true; and now you will be my purgation, and let me loose.

ARMADO I give thee thy liberty, set thee from durance; and, in lieu thereof, impose on thee nothing but this: bear this significant [*giving a letter*] to the country maid Jaquenetta; there is remuneration, for the best ward of mine honour is rewarding my dependents. Moth, follow.

[*Exit.*

MOTH Like the sequel, I. Signior Costard, adieu.
COSTARD My sweet ounce of man's flesh, my incony Jew!

[Exit Moth.

Now will I look to his remuneration. Remuneration! O, that's the Latin word for three farthings. Three farthings – remuneration. 'What's the price of this inkle?' – 'One penny.' – 'No, I'll give you a remuneration.' Why, it carries it. Remuneration! Why, it is a fairer name than French crown. I will never buy and sell out of this word.

Enter BEROWNE.

BEROWNE My good knave Costard, exceedingly well met!
COSTARD Pray you, sir, how much carnation ribbon may a man buy for a remuneration?
BEROWNE What is a remuneration?
COSTARD Marry, sir, halfpenny farthing.
BEROWNE Why, then, three-farthing worth of silk.
COSTARD I thank your worship. God be wi' you!
BEROWNE Stay, slave; I must employ thee.
As thou wilt win my favour, good my knave,
Do one thing for me that I shall entreat.
COSTARD When would you have it done, sir?
BEROWNE This afternoon.
COSTARD Well, I will do it, sir; fare you well.
BEROWNE Thou knowest not what it is.
COSTARD I shall know, sir, when I have done it.
BEROWNE Why, villain, thou must know first.
COSTARD I will come to your worship to-morrow morning.
BEROWNE It must be done this afternoon.
Hark, slave, it is but this:
The Princess comes to hunt here in the park,
And in her train there is a gentle lady;
When tongues speak sweetly, then they name her name,
And Rosaline they call her. Ask for her,
And to her white hand see thou do commend
This seal'd-up counsel. There's thy guerdon; go.

[Giving him a shilling.

COSTARD Gardon, O sweet gardon! better than remuneration; a 'leven-pence farthing better; most sweet Gardon! I will do it, sir, in print. Gardon – remuneration! *[Exit.*

BEROWNE And I, forsooth, in love; I, that have been love's whip;
A very beadle to a humorous sigh;
A critic, nay, a night-watch constable;
A domineering pedant o'er the boy,
Than whom no mortal so magnificent!
This wimpled, whining, purblind, wayward boy,
This senior-junior, giant-dwarf, Dan Cupid;
Regent of love-rhymes, lord of folded arms,
Th' anointed sovereign of sighs and groans,
Liege of all loiterers and malcontents,
Dread prince of plackets, king of codpieces,
Sole imperator, and great general
Of trotting paritors. O my little heart!
And I to be a corporal of his field,
And wear his colours like a tumbler's hoop!
What! I love, I sue, I seek a wife –
A woman, that is like a German clock,
Still a-repairing, ever out of frame,
And never going aright, being a watch,
But being watch'd that it may still go right!
Nay, to be perjur'd, which is worst of all;
And, among three, to love the worst of all,
A whitely wanton with a velvet brow,
With two pitch balls stuck in her face for eyes;
Ay, and, by heaven, one that will do the deed,
Though Argus were her eunuch and her guard.
And I to sigh for her! to watch for her!
To pray for her! Go to; it is a plague
That Cupid will impose for my neglect
Of his almighty dreadful little might.
Well, I will love, write, sigh, pray, sue, and groan:
Some men must love my lady, and some Joan.

[Exit.

ACT FOUR

SCENE I. *The park.*

Enter the PRINCESS, ROSALINE, MARIA, KATHARINE, BOYET, Lords, Attendants, and a Forester.

PRINCESS Was that the King that spurr'd his horse so hard
Against the steep-up rising of the hill?
BOYET I know not; but I think it was not he.
PRINCESS Whoe'er 'a was, 'a show'd a mounting mind.
Well, lords, to-day we shall have our dispatch;
On Saturday we will return to France.
Then, forester, my friend, where is the bush
That we must stand and play the murderer in?
FORESTER Hereby, upon the edge of yonder coppice;
A stand where you may make the fairest shoot.
PRINCESS I thank my beauty I am fair that shoot,

And thereupon thou speak'st the fairest shoot.
FORESTER Pardon me, madam, for I meant not so.
PRINCESS What, what? First praise me, and again say no?
O short-liv'd pride! Not fair? Alack for woe!
FORESTER Yes, madam, fair.
PRINCESS Nay, never paint me now;
Where fair is not, praise cannot mend the brow.
Here, good my glass, take this for telling true: [*Giving him money.*
Fair payment for foul words is more than due.
FORESTER Nothing but fair is that which you inherit.
PRINCESS See, see, my beauty will be sav'd by merit.
O heresy in fair, fit for these days!
A giving hand, though foul, shall have fair praise.
But come, the bow. Now mercy goes to kill,
And shooting well is then accounted ill;
Thus will I save my credit in the shoot:
Not wounding, pity would not let me do't;
If wounding, then it was to show my skill,
That more for praise than purpose meant to kill.
And, out of question, so it is sometimes:
Glory grows guilty of detested crimes,
When, for fame's sake, for praise, an outward part,
We bend to that the working of the heart;
As I for praise alone now seek to spill
The poor deer's blood that my heart means no ill.
BOYET Do not curst wives hold that self-sovereignty
Only for praise sake, when they strive to be
Lords o'er their lords?
PRINCESS Only for praise; and praise we may afford
To any lady that subdues a lord.

Enter COSTARD.

BOYET Here comes a member of the commonwealth.
COSTARD God dig-you-den all! Pray you, which is the head lady?
PRINCESS Thou shalt know her, fellow, by the rest that have no heads.
COSTARD Which is the greatest lady, the highest?
PRINCESS The thickest and the tallest.
COSTARD The thickest and the tallest! It is so; truth is truth.
An your waist, mistress, were as slender as my wit,
One o' these maids' girdles for your waist should be fit.
Are not you the chief woman? You are the thickest here.
PRINCESS What's your will, sir? What's your will?
COSTARD I have a letter from Monsieur Berowne to one Lady Rosaline.
PRINCESS O, thy letter, thy letter! He's a good friend of mine.
Stand aside, good bearer. Boyet, you can carve.
Break up this capon.
BOYET I am bound to serve.
This letter is mistook; it importeth none here.
It is writ to Jaquenetta.
PRINCESS We will read it, I swear.
Break the neck of the wax, and every one give ear.
BOYET [*Reads*] 'By heaven, that thou art fair is most infallible; true that thou art beauteous; truth itself that thou art lovely. More fairer than fair, beautiful than beauteous, truer than truth itself, have commiseration on thy heroical vassal. The magnanimous and most illustrate king Cophetua set eye upon the pernicious and indubitate beggar Zenelophon; and he it was that might rightly say, 'Veni, vidi, vici'; which to annothanize in the vulgar, – O base and obscure vulgar! – videlicet, He came, saw, and overcame. He came, one; saw, two; overcame, three. Who came? – the king. Why did he come? – to see. Why did he see? – to overcome. To whom came he? – to the beggar. What saw he? – the beggar. Who overcame he? – the beggar. The conclusion is victory; on whose side? – the king's. The captive is enrich'd; on whose side? – the beggar's. The catastrophe is a nuptial; on whose side? – the king's. No, on both in one, or one in both. I am the king, for so stands the comparison; thou the beggar, for so witnesseth thy lowliness. Shall I command thy love? I may. Shall I enforce thy love? I could. Shall I entreat thy love? I will. What shalt thou exchange for rags? – robes, for titles? – titles, for thyself? – me. Thus expecting thy reply, I profane my lips on thy foot, my eyes on thy picture, and my heart on thy every part.
Thine in the dearest design of industry,
DON ADRIANO DE ARMADO.'

'Thus dost thou hear the Nemean lion roar
'Gainst thee, thou lamb, that standest as his prey;
Submissive fall his princely feet before,
And he from forage will incline to play.
But if thou strive, poor soul, what art thou then?
Food for his rage, repasture for his den.'
PRINCESS What plume of feathers is he that indited this letter?

What vane? What weathercock? Did you ever hear better?

BOYET I am much deceived but I remember the style.

PRINCESS Else your memory is bad, going o'er it erewhile.

BOYET This Armado is a Spaniard, that keeps here in court;
A phantasime, a Monarcho, and one that makes sport
To the Prince and his book-mates.

PRINCESS Thou fellow, a word.
Who gave thee this letter?

COSTARD I told you: my lord.

PRINCESS To whom shouldst thou give it?

COSTARD From my lord to my lady.

PRINCESS From which lord to which lady?

COSTARD From my Lord Berowne, a good master of mine,
To a lady of France that he call'd Rosaline.

PRINCESS Thou hast mistaken his letter. Come lords, away.
[*To Rosaline*] Here, sweet, put up this; 'twill be thine another day.

[*Exeunt Princess and Train.*

BOYET Who is the shooter? Who is the shooter?

ROSALINE Shall I teach you to know?

BOYET Ay, my continent of beauty.

ROSALINE Why, she that bears the bow.
Finely put off!

BOYET My lady goes to kill horns; but, if thou marry,
Hang me by the neck, if horns that year miscarry.
Finely put on!

ROSALINE Well then, I am the shooter.

BOYET And who is your deer?

ROSALINE If we choose by the horns, yourself come not near.
Finely put on indeed!

MARIA You still wrangle with her, Boyet, and she strikes at the brow.

BOYET But she herself is hit lower. Have I hit her now?

ROSALINE Shall I come upon thee with an old saying, that was a man when King Pepin of France was a little boy, as touching the hit it?

BOYET So I may answer thee with one as old, that was a woman when Queen Guinever of Britain was a little wench, as touching the hit it.

ROSALINE [*Singing*]
Thou canst not hit it, hit it, hit it,
Thou canst not hit it, my good man.

BOYET An I cannot, cannot, cannot,
An I cannot, another can.

[*Exeunt Rosaline and Katharine*

COSTARD By my troth, most pleasant! How both did fit it!

MARIA A mark marvellous well shot; for they both did hit it.

BOYET A mark! O, mark but that mark! A mark, says my lady!
Let the mark have a prick in't, to mete at, if it may be.

MARIA Wide o' the bow-hand! I' faith, your hand is out.

COSTARD Indeed, 'a must shoot nearer, or he'll ne'er hit the clout.

BOYET An if my hand be out, then belike your hand is in.

COSTARD Then will she get the upshoot by cleaving the pin.

MARIA Come, come, you talk greasily; your lips grow foul.

COSTARD She's too hard for you at pricks, sir; challenge her to bowl.

BOYET I fear too much rubbing; good-night, my good owl.

[*Exeunt Boyet and Maria.*

COSTARD By my soul, a swain, a most simple clown!
Lord, Lord! how the ladies and I have put him down!
O' my troth, most sweet jests, most incony vulgar wit!
When it comes so smoothly off, so obscenely, as it were, so fit.
Armado a th' t'one side – O, a most dainty man!
To see him walk before a lady and to bear her fan!
To see him kiss his hand, and how most sweetly 'a will swear!
And his page a t' other side, that handful of wit!
Ah, heavens, it is a most pathetical nit!
Sola, sola!

[*Exit Costard.*

SCENE II. *The park.*

From the shooting within, enter HOLOFERNES, SIR NATHANIEL, and DULL.

NATHANIEL Very reverent sport, truly; and done in the testimony of a good conscience.

HOLOFERNES The deer was, as you know, sanguis, in blood; ripe as the pomewater, who now hangeth like a jewel in the ear of caelo, the sky, the welkin, the heaven; and anon falleth like a crab on the face of terra, the soil, the land, the earth.

NATHANIEL Truly, Master Holofernes, the epithets are sweetly varied, like a scholar at the least; but, sir, I assure ye it was a buck of the first head.

HOLOFERNES Sir Nathaniel, haud credo.

DULL 'Twas not a haud credo; 'twas a pricket.

HOLOFERNES Most barbarous intimation! yet a kind of insinuation, as it were, in via, in way, of explication; facere, as it were, replication, or rather, ostentare, to show, as it were, his inclination, after his undressed, unpolished, uneducated, unpruned, untrained, or rather unlettered, or ratherest unconfirmed fashion, to insert again my haud credo for a deer.

DULL I said the deer was not a haud credo; 'twas a pricket.

HOLOFERNES Twice-sod simplicity, bis coctus!
O thou monster Ignorance, how deformed dost
thou look!

NATHANIEL Sir, he hath never fed of the dainties
that are bred in a book;
He hath not eat paper, as it were; he hath not drunk ink; his intellect is not replenished; he is only an animal, only sensible in the duller parts;
And such barren plants are set before us that we
thankful should be –
Which we of taste and feeling are – for those
parts that do fructify in us more than he.
For as it would ill become me to be vain,
indiscreet, or a fool,
So, were there a patch set on learning, to see
him in a school.
But, omne bene, say I, being of an old father's
mind:
Many can brook the weather that love not the
wind.

DULL You two are book-men: can you tell me by
your wit
What was a month old at Cain's birth that's not
five weeks old as yet?

HOLOFERNES Dictynna, goodman Dull;
Dictynna, goodman Dull.

DULL What is Dictynna?

NATHANIEL A title to Phoebe, to Luna, to the
moon.

HOLOFERNES The moon was a month old when
Adam was no more,
And raught not to five weeks when he came to
five-score.
Th' allusion holds in the exchange.

DULL 'Tis true, indeed; the collusion holds in the exchange.

HOLOFERNES God comfort thy capacity! I say th' allusion holds in the exchange.

DULL And I say the polusion holds in the exchange; for the moon is never but a month old; and I say, beside, that 'twas a pricket that the Princess kill'd.

HOLOFERNES Sir Nathaniel, will you hear an extemporal epitaph on the death of the deer? And, to humour the ignorant, call the deer the Princess kill'd a pricket.

NATHANIEL Perge, good Master Holofernes, perge, so it shall please you to abrogate scurrility.

HOLOFERNES I will something affect the letter, for it argues facility.

The preyful Princess pierc'd and prick'd a pretty
pleasing pricket.
Some say a sore; but not a sore
till now made sore with shooting.
The dogs did yell; put el to sore,
then sorel jumps from thicket –
Or pricket sore, or else sorel;
the people fall a-hooting.
If sore be sore, then L to sore
makes fifty sores o' sorel.
Of one sore I an hundred make
by adding but one more L.

NATHANIEL A rare talent!

DULL [*Aside*] If a talent be a claw, look how he claws him with a talent.

HOLOFERNES This is a gift that I have, simple, simple; a foolish extravagant spirit, full of forms, figures, shapes, objects, ideas, apprehensions, motions, revolutions. These are begot in the ventricle of memory, nourish'd in the womb of pia mater, and delivered upon the mellowing of occasion. But the gift is good in those in whom it is acute, and I am thankful for it.

NATHANIEL Sir, I praise the Lord for you, and so may my parishioners; for their sons are well tutor'd by you, and their daughters profit very greatly under you. You are a good member of the commonwealth.

HOLOFERNES Mehercle, if their sons be ingenious, they shall want no instruction; if their daughters be capable, I will put it to them; but, vir sapit qui pauca loquitur. A soul feminine saluteth us.

Enter JAQUENETTA and COSTARD.

JAQUENETTA God give you good morrow, Master Person.

HOLOFERNES Master Person, quasi pers-one.
And if one should be pierc'd, which is the one?

COSTARD Marry, Master Schoolmaster, he that is likest to a hogshead.

HOLOFERNES Piercing a hogshead! A good lustre of conceit in a turf of earth; fire enough for a flint, pearl enough for a swine; 'tis pretty; it is well.

JAQUENETTA Good Master Parson, be so good as read me this letter; it was given me by Costard, and sent me from Don Armado. I beseech you read it.

HOLOFERNES Fauste, precor gelida quando pecus omne sub umbra
Ruminat –
and so forth. Ah, good old Mantuan! I may speak of thee as the traveller doth of Venice:
Venetia, Venetia,
Chi non ti vede, non ti pretia.
Old Mantuan, old Mantuan! Who understandeth thee not, loves thee not –
Ut, re, sol, la, mi, fa.
Under pardon, sir, what are the contents? or rather as Horace says in his – What, my soul, verses?

NATHANIEL Ay, sir, and very learned.

HOLOFERNES Let me hear a staff, a stanze, a verse; Lege, domine.

NATHANIEL [*Reads*] 'If love make me forsworn, how shall I swear to love?
Ah, never faith could hold, if not to beauty vowed!
Though to myself forsworn, to thee I'll faithful prove;
Those thoughts to me were oaks, to thee like osiers bowed.
Study his bias leaves, and makes his book thine eyes,
Where all those pleasures live that art would comprehend.
If knowledge be the mark, to know thee shall suffice;
Well learned is that tongue that well can thee commend;
All ignorant that soul that sees thee without wonder;
Which is to me some praise that I thy parts admire.
Thy eye Jove's lightning bears, thy voice his dreadful thunder,
Which, not to anger bent, is music and sweet fire.
Celestial as thou art, O, pardon love this wrong,
That singes heaven's praise with such an earthly tongue.'

HOLOFERNES You find not the apostrophas, and so miss the accent: let me supervise the canzonet. Here are only numbers ratified; but, for the elegancy, facility, and golden cadence of poesy, caret. Ovidius Naso was the man. And why, indeed, 'Naso' but for smelling out the odoriferous flowers of fancy, the jerks of invention? Imitari is nothing: so doth the hound his master, the ape his keeper, the tired horse his rider. But damosella virgin, was this directed to you?

JAQUENETTA Ay, sir, from one Monsieur Berowne, one of the strange queen's lords.

HOLOFERNES I will overglance the superscript: 'To the snow-white hand of the most beauteous Lady Rosaline'. I will look again on the intellect of the letter, for the nomination of the party writing to the person written unto: 'Your Ladyship's in all desired employment, Berowne'. Sir Nathaniel, this Berowne is one of the votaries with the king; and here he hath framed a letter to a sequent of the stranger queen's which accidentally, or by the way of progression, hath miscarried. Trip and go, my sweet; deliver this paper into the royal hand of the King; it may concern much. Stay not thy compliment; I forgive thy duty. Adieu.

JAQUENETTA Good Costard, go with me. Sir, God save your life!

COSTARD Have with thee, my girl.

[*Exeunt Costard and Jaquenetta.*

NATHANIEL Sir, you have done this in the fear of God, very religiously; and, as a certain father saith–

HOLOFERNES Sir, tell not me of the father; I do fear colourable colours. But to return to the verses: did they please you, Sir Nathaniel?

NATHANIEL Marvellous well for the pen.

HOLOFERNES I do dine to-day at the father's of a certain pupil of mine; where, if, before repast, it shall please you to gratify the table with a grace, I will, on my privilege I have with the parents of the foresaid child or pupil, undertake your ben venuto; where I will prove those verses to be very unlearned, neither savouring of poetry, wit, nor invention. I beseech your society.

NATHANIEL And thank you too; for society, saith the text, is the happiness of life.

HOLOFERNES And certes, the text most infallibly concludes it. [*To Dull*] Sir, I do invite you too; you shall not say me nay: pauca verba. Away; the gentles are at their game, and we will to our recreation. [*Exeunt.*

SCENE III. *The park.*

Enter BEROWNE, with a paper in his hand, alone.

BEROWNE The King he is hunting the deer: I am coursing myself. They have pitch'd a toil: I am toiling in a pitch – pitch that defiles. Defile! a foul word. Well, 'set thee down, sorrow!' for so they say the fool said, and so say I, and I am the fool. Well proved, wit. By the Lord, this love is as mad as Ajax: it kills sheep; it kills me – I a sheep. Well proved again o' my side. I will not love; if I do, hang me. I' faith, I will not. O, but her eye! By this light, but for her eye, I would not love her – yes for her two eyes. Well, I do nothing in the world but lie, and lie in my throat. By heaven, I do love; and it hath taught me to rhyme, and to be melancholy; and here is part of my rhyme, and here my melancholy. Well, she hath one o' my sonnets already; the clown bore it, the fool sent it, and the lady hath it: sweet clown, sweeter fool, sweetest lady! By the world, I would not care a pin if the other three were in. Here comes one with a paper; God give him grace to groan!

[*Climbs into a tree.*

Enter the KING, with a paper.

KING Ay me!

BEROWNE Shot, by heaven! Proceed, sweet Cupid; thou hast thump'd him with thy bird-bolt under the left pap. In faith, secrets!

KING [*Reads*]
'So sweet a kiss the golden sun gives not
To those fresh morning drops upon the rose,
As thy eye-beams, when their fresh rays have smote
The night of dew that on my cheeks down flows;
Nor shines the silver moon one half so bright
Through the transparent bosom of the deep,
As doth thy face through tears of mine give light.
Thou shin'st in every tear that I do weep;
No drop but as a coach doth carry thee;
So ridest thou triumphing in my woe.
Do but behold the tears that swell in me,
And they thy glory through my grief will show.
But do not love thyself; then thou wilt keep
My tears for glasses, and still make me weep.
O queen of queens! how far dost thou excel
No thought can think nor tongue of mortal tell.'
How shall she know my griefs? I'll drop the paper –
Sweet leaves, shade folly. Who is he comes here? [*Steps aside.*

Enter LONGAVILLE, with a paper.

What, Longaville, and reading! Listen, ear.

BEROWNE Now, in thy likeness, one more fool appear!

LONGAVILLE Ay me, I am forsworn!

BEROWNE Why, he comes in like a perjure, wearing papers.

KING In love, I hope; sweet fellowship in shame!

BEROWNE One drunkard loves another of the name.

LONGAVILLE Am I the first that have been perjur'd so?

BEROWNE I could put thee in comfort: not by two that I know;
Thou makest the triumviry, the corner-cap of society,
The shape of Love's Tyburn that hangs up simplicity.

LONGAVILLE I fear these stubborn lines lack power to move.
O sweet Maria, empress of my love!
These numbers will I tear, and write in prose.

BEROWNE O, rhymes are guards on wanton Cupid's hose:
Disfigure not his slop.

LONGAVILLE This same shall go.

[*He reads the sonnet.*

'Did not the heavenly rhetoric of thine eye,
'Gainst whom the world cannot hold argument,
Persuade my heart to this false perjury?
Vows for thee broke deserve not punishment.
A woman I forswore; but I will prove,
Thou being a goddess, I forswore not thee:
My vow was earthly, thou a heavenly love;
Thy grace being gain'd cures all disgrace in me.
Vows are but breath, and breath a vapour is;
Then thou, fair sun, which on my earth dost shine,
Exhal'st this vapour-vow; in thee it is.
If broken, then it is no fault of mine;
If by me broke, what fool is not so wise
To lose an oath to win a paradise?'

BEROWNE This is the liver-vein, which makes flesh a deity,
A green goose a goddess – pure, pure idolatry.
God amend us, God amend! We are much out o' th' way.

Enter DUMAIN, with a paper.

LONGAVILLE By whom shall I send this? – Company! Stay. [*Steps aside.*

BEROWNE 'All hid, all hid' – an old infant play.
Like a demigod here sit I in the sky,
And wretched fools' secrets heedfully o'er-eye.
More sacks to the mill! O heavens, I have my wish!
Dumain transformed! Four woodcocks in a dish!

DUMAIN O most divine Kate!

BEROWNE O most profane coxcomb!

DUMAIN By heaven, the wonder in a mortal eye!

BEROWNE By earth, she is not, corporal; there you lie.

DUMAIN Her amber hairs for foul hath amber quoted.

BEROWNE An amber-colour'd raven was well noted.

DUMAIN As upright as the cedar.

BEROWNE Stoop, I say;
Her shoulder is with child.

DUMAIN As fair as day.

BEROWNE Ay, as some days; but then no sun must shine.

DUMAIN O that I had my wish!
LONGAVILLE And I had mine!
KING And I mine too, good Lord!
BEROWNE Amen, so I had mine! Is not that a good word?
DUMAIN I would forget her; but a fever she
Reigns in my blood, and will remember'd be.
BEROWNE A fever in your blood? Why, then incision
Would let her out in saucers. Sweet misprision!
DUMAIN Once more I'll read the ode that I have writ.
BEROWNE Once more I'll mark how love can vary wit.
DUMAIN [*Reads*]
'On a day – alack the day! –
Love, whose month is ever May,
Spied a blossom passing fair
Playing in the wanton air.
Through the velvet leaves the wind,
All unseen, can passage find;
That the lover, sick to death,
Wish'd himself the heaven's breath.
"Air," quoth he "thy cheeks may blow;
Air, would I might triumph so!
But, alack, my hand is sworn
Ne'er to pluck thee from thy thorn;
Vow, alack, for youth unmeet,
Youth so apt to pluck a sweet.
Do not call it sin in me
That I am forsworn for thee;
Thou for whom Jove would swear
Juno but an Ethiope were;
And deny himself for Jove,
Turning mortal for thy love."
This will I send; and something else more plain
That shall express my true love's fasting pain.
O, would the King, Berowne and Longaville,
Were lovers too! Ill, to example ill,
Would from my forehead wipe a perjur'd note;
For none offend where all alike do dote.
LONGAVILLE [*Advancing*] Dumain, thy love is far from charity,
That in love's grief desir'st society;
You may look pale, but I should blush, I know,
To be o'er heard and taken napping so.
KING [*Advancing*] Come, sir, you blush; as his, your case is such.
You chide at him, offending twice as much:
You do not love Maria! Longaville
Did never sonnet for her sake compile;
Nor never lay his wreathed arms athwart
His loving bosom, to keep down his heart.
I have been closely shrouded in this bush,
And mark'd you both, and for you both did blush.
I heard your guilty rhymes, observ'd your fashion,
Saw sighs reek from you, noted well your passion.
'Ay me!' says one. 'O Jove!' the other cries.
One, her hairs were gold; crystal the other's eyes.
[*To Longaville.*] You would for paradise break faith and troth;
[*To Dumain.*] And Jove for your love would infringe an oath.
What will Berowne say when that he shall hear
Faith infringed which such zeal did swear?
How will he scorn, how will he spend his wit!
How will he triumph, leap, and laugh at it!
For all the wealth that ever I did see,
I would not have him know so much by me.
BEROWNE [*Descending*] Now step I forth to whip hypocrisy.
Ah, good my liege, I pray thee pardon me.
Good heart, what grace hast thou thus to reprove
These worms for loving, that art most in love?
Your eyes do make no coaches; in your tears
There is no certain princess that appears;
You'll not be perjur'd; 'tis a hateful thing;
Tush, none but minstrels like of sonneting.
But are you not ashamed? Nay, are you not,
All three of you, to be thus much o'ershot?
You found his mote; the King your mote did see;
But I a beam do find in each of three.
O, what a scene of fool'ry have I seen,
Of sighs, of groans, of sorrow, and of teen!
O me, with what strict patience have I sat,
To see a king transformed to a gnat!
To see great Hercules whipping a gig,
And profound Solomon to tune a jig,
And Nestor play at push-pin with the boys,
And critic Timon laugh at idle toys!
Where lies thy grief, O, tell me, good Dumain?
And, gentle Longaville, where lies thy pain?
And where my liege's? All about the breast.
A caudle, ho!
KING Too bitter is thy jest.
Are we betrayed thus to thy over-view?
BEROWNE Not you by me, but I betrayed to you.
I that am honest, I that hold it sin
To break the vow I am engaged in;
I am betrayed by keeping company
With men like you, men of inconstancy.
When shall you see me write a thing in rhyme?
Or groan for Joan? or spend a minute's time
In pruning me? When shall you hear that I
Will praise a hand, a foot, a face, an eye,
A gait, a state, a brow, a breast, a waist,
A leg, a limb –
KING Soft! whither away so fast?

A true man or a thief that gallops so?
BEROWNE I post from love; good lover, let me go.

Enter JAQUENETTA and COSTARD.

JAQUENETTA God bless the King!
KING What present hast thou there?
COSTARD Some certain treason.
KING What makes treason here?
COSTARD Nay, it makes nothing, sir.
KING If it mar nothing neither,
The treason and you go in peace away together.
JAQUENETTA I beseech your Grace, let this letter be read;
Our person misdoubts it; 'twas treason he said.
KING Berowne, read it over.
[Berowne reads the letter.
Where hadst thou it?
JAQUENETTA Of Costard.
KING Where hadst thou it?
COSTARD Of Dun Adramadio, Dun Adramadio.
[Berowne tears the letter.
KING How now! What is in you? Why dost thou tear it?
BEROWNE A toy, my liege, a toy! Your Grace needs not fear it.
LONGAVILLE It did move him to passion, and therefore let's hear it.
DUMAIN It is Berowne's writing, and here is his name.
[Gathering up the pieces.
BEROWNE [*To Costard*] Ah, you whoreson loggerhead, you were born to do me shame.
Guilty, my lord, guilty! I confess, I confess.
KING What?
BEROWNE That you three fools lack'd me fool to make up the mess;
He, he, and you – and you, my liege! – and I
Are pick-purses in love, and we deserve to die.
O, dismiss this audience, and I shall tell you more.
DUMAIN Now the number is even.
BEROWNE True, true, we are four.
Will these turtles be gone?
KING Hence, sirs away.
COSTARD Walk aside the true folk, and let the traitors stay. [*Exeunt Costard and Jaquenetta.*
BEROWNE Sweet lords, sweet lovers, O, let us embrace!
As true we are as flesh and blood can be.
The sea will ebb and flow, heaven show his face;
Young blood doth not obey an old decree.
We cannot cross the cause why we were born,
Therefore of all hands must we be forsworn.
KING What, did these rent lines show some love of thine?
BEROWNE 'Did they?' quoth you. Who sees the heavenly Rosaline
That, like a rude and savage man of Inde
At the first op'ning of the gorgeous east,
Bows not his vassal head and, strucken blind,
Kisses the base ground with obedient breast?
What peremptory eagle-sighted eye
Dares look upon the heaven of her brow
That is not blinded by her majesty?
KING What zeal, what fury hath inspir'd thee now?
My love, her mistress, is a gracious moon;
She, an attending star, scarce seen a light.
BEROWNE My eyes are then no eyes, nor I Berowne.
O, but for my love, day would turn to night!
Of all complexions the cull'd sovereignty
Do meet, as at a fair, in her fair cheek,
Where several worthies make one dignity,
Where nothing wants that want itself doth seek.
Lend me the flourish of all gentle tongues –
Fie, painted rhetoric! O, she needs it not!
To things of sale a seller's praise belongs:
She passes praise; then praise too short doth blot.
A wither'd hermit, five-score winters worn,
Might shake off fifty, looking in her eye.
Beauty doth varnish age, as if new-born,
And gives the crutch the cradle's infancy.
O, 'tis the sun that maketh all things shine!
KING By heaven, thy love is black as ebony.
BEROWNE Is ebony like her? O wood divine!
A wife of such wood were felicity.
O, who can give an oath? Where is a book?
That I may swear beauty doth beauty lack,
If that she learn not of her eye to look.
No face is fair that is not full so black.
KING O paradox! Black is the badge of hell,
The hue of dungeons, and the school of night;
And beauty's crest becomes the heavens well.
BEROWNE Devils soonest tempt, resembling spirits of light.
O, if in black my lady's brows be deckt,
It mourns that painting and usurping hair
Should ravish doters with a false aspect;
And therefore is she born to make black fair.
Her favour turns the fashion of the days;
For native blood is counted painting now;
And therefore red that would avoid dispraise
Paints itself black, to imitate her brow.
DUMAIN To look like her are chimney-sweepers black.
LONGAVILLE And since her time are colliers counted bright.
KING And Ethiopes of their sweet complexion crack.

DUMAIN Dark needs no candles now, for dark is light.
BEROWNE Your mistresses dare never come in rain
For fear their colours should be wash'd away.
KING 'Twere good yours did; for, sir, to tell you plain,
I'll find a fairer face not wash'd to-day.
BEROWNE I'll prove her fair, or talk till doomsday here.
KING No devil will fright thee then so much as she.
DUMAIN I never knew man hold vile stuff so dear.
LONGAVILLE Look, here's thy love: my foot and her face see.

[*Showing his shoe.*

BEROWNE O, if the streets were paved with thine eyes,
Her feet were much too dainty for such tread!
DUMAIN O vile! Then, as she goes, what upward lies
The street should see as she walk'd overhead.
KING But what of this? Are we not all in love?
BEROWNE Nothing so sure; and thereby all forsworn.
KING Then leave this chat; and, good Berowne, now prove
Our loving lawful, and our faith not torn.
DUMAIN Ay, marry, there; some flattery for this evil.
LONGAVILLE O, some authority how to proceed;
Some tricks, some quillets, how to cheat the devil!
DUMAIN Some salve for perjury.
BEROWNE 'Tis more than need.
Have at you, then, affection's men-at-arms.
Consider what you first did swear unto:
To fast, to study, and to see no woman –
Flat treason 'gainst the kingly state of youth.
Say, can you fast? Your stomachs are too young,
And abstinence engenders maladies.
And where that you have vow'd to study, lords,
In that each of you have forsworn his book,
Can you still dream, and pore, and thereon look?
For when would you, my lord, or you, or you,
Have found the ground of study's excellence
Without the beauty of a woman's face?
From women's eyes this doctrine I derive:
They are the ground, the books, the academes,
From whence doth spring the true Promethean fire.
Why, universal plodding poisons up
The nimble spirits in the arteries,
As motion and long-during action tires
The sinewy vigour of the traveller.
Now, for not looking on a woman's face,
You have in that forsworn the use of eyes,
And study too, the causer of your vow;
For where is any author in the world
Teaches such beauty as a woman's eye?
Learning is but an adjunct to ourself,
And where we are our learning likewise is;
Then when ourselves we see in ladies' eyes,
With ourselves,
Do we not likewise see our learning there?
O, we have made a vow to study, lords,
And in that vow we have forsworn our books.
For when would you, my liege, or you, or you,
In leaden contemplation have found out
Such fiery numbers as the prompting eyes
Of beauty's tutors have enrich'd you with?
Other slow arts entirely keep the brain;
And therefore, finding barren practisers,
Scarce show a harvest of their heavy toil;
But love, first learned in a lady's eyes,
Lives not alone immured in the brain,
But with the motion of all elements
Courses as swift as thought in every power,
And gives to every power a double power,
Above their functions and their offices.
It adds a precious seeing to the eye:
A lover's eyes will gaze an eagle blind.
A lover's ear will hear the lowest sound,
When the suspicious head of theft is stopp'd.
Love's feeling is more soft and sensible
Than are the tender horns of cockled snails;
Love's tongue proves dainty Bacchus gross in taste.
For valour, is not Love a Hercules,
Still climbing trees in the Hesperides?
Subtle as Sphinx; as sweet and musical
As bright Apollo's lute, strung with his hair.
And when Love speaks, the voice of all the gods
Make heaven drowsy with the harmony.
Never durst poet touch a pen to write
Until his ink were temp'red with Love's sighs;
O, then his lines would ravish savage ears,
And plant in tyrants mild humility.
From women's eyes this doctrine I derive.
They sparkle still the right Promethean fire;
They are the books, the arts, the academes,
That show, contain, and nourish, all the world,
Else none at all in aught proves excellent.
Then fools you were these women to forswear;
Or, keeping what is sworn, you will prove fools.
For wisdom's sake, a word that all men love;
Or for Love's sake, a word that loves all men;
Or for men's sake, the authors of these women;
Or women's sake, by whom we men are men –
Let us once lose our oaths to find ourselves,
Or else we lose ourselves to keep our oaths.

It is religion to be thus forsworn;
For charity itself fulfils the law,
And who can sever love from charity?

KING Saint Cupid, then! and, soldiers, to the field!

BEROWNE Advance your standards, and upon them, lords;
Pell-mell, down with them! But be first advis'd,
In conflict, that you get the sun of them.

LONGAVILLE Now to plain-dealing; lay these glozes by.
Shall we resolve to woo these girls of France?

KING And win them too; therefore let us devise
Some entertainment for them in their tents.

BEROWNE First, from the park let us conduct them thither;
Then homeward every man attach the hand
Of his fair mistress. In the afternoon
We will with some strange pastime solace them,
Such as the shortness of the time can shape;
For revels, dances, masks, and merry hours,
Forerun fair Love, strewing her way with flowers.

KING Away, away! No time shall be omitted
That will betime, and may by us be fitted.

BEROWNE Allons! allons! Sow'd cockle reap'd no corn,
And justice always whirls in equal measure.
Light wenches may prove plagues to men forsworn;
If so, our copper buys no better treasure.

[Exeunt.

ACT FIVE

SCENE I. *The park.*

Enter HOLOFERNES, SIR NATHANIEL, and DULL.

HOLOFERNES Satis quod sufficit.

NATHANIEL I praise God for you, sir. Your reasons at dinner have been sharp and sententious; pleasant without scurrility, witty without affection, audacious without impudency, learned without opinion, and strange without heresy. I did converse this quondam day with a companion of the King's, who is intituled, nominated, or called, Don Adriano de Armado.

HOLOFERNES Novi hominem tanquam te. His humour is lofty, his discourse peremptory, his tongue filed, his eye ambitious, his gait majestical, and his general behaviour vain, ridiculous, and thrasonical. He is too picked, too spruce, too affected, too odd, as it were, too peregrinate, as I may call it.

NATHANIEL A most singular and choice epithet.

[Draws out his table-book.

HOLOFERNES He draweth out the thread of his verbosity finer than the staple of his argument. I abhor such fanatical phantasimes, such insociable and point-devise companions; such rackers of orthography, as to speak 'dout' fine, when he should say 'doubt'; 'det' when he should pronounce 'debt' – d, e, b, t, not d, e, t. He clepeth a calf 'cauf', half 'hauf'; neighbour vocatur 'nebour'; 'neigh' abbreviated 'ne'. This is abhominable – which he would call 'abbominable'. It insinuateth me of insanie: ne intelligis, domine? to make frantic, lunatic.

NATHANIEL Laus Deo, bone intelligo.

HOLOFERNES 'Bone'? – 'bone' for 'bene'.
Priscian a little scratch'd; 'twill serve.

Enter ARMADO, MOTH, and COSTARD.

NATHANIEL Videsne quis venit?

HOLOFERNES Video, et gaudeo.

ARMADO *[To Moth]* Chirrah!

HOLOFERNES Quare 'chirrah', not 'sirrah'?

ARMADO Men of peace, well encount'red.

HOLOFERNES Most military sir, salutation.

MOTH *[Aside to Costard]* They have been at a great feast of languages and stol'n the scraps.

COSTARD O, they have liv'd long on the alms-basket of words. I marvel thy master hath not eaten thee for a word, for thou are not so long by the head as honorificabilitudinitatibus; thou art easier swallowed than a flap-dragon.

MOTH Peace! the peal begins.

ARMADO *[To Holofernes]* Monsieur, are you not lett'red?

MOTH Yes, yes; he teaches boys the hornbook. What is a, b, spelt backward with the horn on his head?

HOLOFERNES Ba, pueritia, with a horn added.

MOTH Ba, most silly sheep with a horn.
You hear his learning.

HOLOFERNES Quis, quis, thou consonant?

MOTH The third of the five vowels, if You repeat them; or the fifth, if I.

HOLOFERNES I will repeat them: a, e, I –

MOTH The sheep; the other two concludes it: o, U.

ARMADO Now, by the salt wave of the Mediterraneum, a sweet touch, a quick venue of wit – snip, snap, quick and home. It rejoiceth my intellect. True wit!

MOTH Offer'd by a child to an old man; which is wit-old.

HOLOFERNES What is the figure? What is the figure?

MOTH Horns.

HOLOFERNES Thou disputes like an infant; go whip thy gig.

MOTH Lend me your horn to make one, and I will whip about your infamy *circum circa* – a gig of a cuckold's horn.

COSTARD An I had but one penny in the world, thou shouldst have it to buy gingerbread. Hold, there is the very remuneration I had of thy master, thou halfpenny purse of wit, thou pigeon-egg of discretion. O, an the heavens were so pleased that thou wert but my bastard, what a joyful father wouldest thou make me! Go to; thou hast it *ad dunghill*, at the fingers' ends, as they say.

HOLOFERNES O, I smell false Latin; 'dunghill' for *unguem*.

ARMADO Arts-man, preambulate; we will be singuled from the barbarous. Do you not educate youth at the charge-house on the top of the mountain?

HOLOFERNES Or *mons*, the hill.

ARMADO At your sweet pleasure, for the mountain.

HOLOFERNES I do, sans question.

ARMADO Sir, it is the King's most sweet pleasure and affection to congratulate the Princess at her pavilion, in the posteriors of this day; which the rude multitude call the afternoon.

HOLOFERNES The posterior of the day, most generous sir, is liable, congruent, and measurable, for the afternoon. The word is well cull'd, chose, sweet, and apt, I do assure you, sir, I do assure.

ARMADO Sir, the King is a noble gentleman, and my familiar, I do assure ye, very good friend. For what is inward between us, let it pass. I do beseech thee, remember thy courtesy. I beseech thee, apparel thy head. And among other importunate and most serious designs, and of great import indeed, too – but let that pass; for I must tell thee it will please his grace, by the world, sometime to lean upon my poor shoulder, and with his royal finger thus dally with my excrement, with my mustachio; but, sweet heart, let that pass. By the world, I recount no fable: some certain special honours it pleaseth his greatness to impart to Armado, a soldier, a man of travel, that hath seen the world; but let that pass. The very all of all is – but, sweet heart, I do implore secrecy – that the King would have me present the Princess, sweet chuck, with some delightful ostentation, or show, or pageant, or antic, or firework. Now, understanding that the curate and your sweet self are good at such eruptions and sudden breaking-out of mirth, as it were, I have acquainted you withal, to the end to crave your assistance.

HOLOFERNES Sir, you shall present before her the Nine Worthies. Sir Nathaniel, as concerning some entertainment of time, some show in the posterior of this day, to be rend'red by our assistance, the King's command, and this most gallant, illustrate, and learned gentleman, before the Princess – I say none so fit as to present the Nine Worthies.

NATHANIEL Where will you find men worthy enought to present them?

HOLOFERNES Joshua, yourself; myself, Alexander; this gallant gentleman, Judas Maccabaeus; this swain, because of his great limb or joint, shall pass Pompey the Great; the page, Hercules.

ARMADO Pardon, sir; error: he is not quantity enough for that Worthy's thumb; he is not so big as the end of his club.

HOLOFERNES Shall I have audience? He shall present Hercules in minority: his enter and exit shall be strangling a snake; and I will have an apology for that purpose.

MOTH An excellent device! So, if any of the audience hiss, you may cry 'Well done, Hercules; now thou crushest the snake!' That is the way to make an offence gracious, though few have the grace to do it.

ARMADO For the rest of the Worthies?

HOLOFERNES I will play three myself.

MOTH Thrice-worthy gentleman!

ARMADO Shall I tell you a thing?

HOLOFERNES We attend.

ARMADO We will have, if this fadge not, an antic. I beseech you, follow.

HOLOFERNES Via, goodman Dull! Thou hast spoken no word all this while.

DULL Nor understood none neither, sir.

HOLOFERNES Allons! we will employ thee.

DULL I'll make one in a dance, or so; or I will play
On the tabor to the Worthies, and let them dance the hay.

HOLOFERNES Most dull, honest Dull! To our sport, away. [*Exeunt.*

SCENE II. *The park.*

Enter the PRINCESS, MARIA, KATHARINE, and ROSALINE.

PRINCESS Sweet hearts, we shall be rich ere we depart,
If fairings come thus plentifully in.

A lady wall'd about with diamonds!
Look you what I have from the loving King.
ROSALINE Madam, came nothing else along with that?
PRINCESS Nothing but this! Yes, as much love in rhyme
As would be cramm'd up in a sheet of paper
Writ o' both sides the leaf, margent and all,
That he was fain to seal on Cupid's name.
ROSALINE That was the way to make his godhead wax;
For he hath been five thousand year a boy.
KATHARINE Ay, and a shrewd unhappy gallows too.
ROSALINE You'll ne'er be friends with him: 'a kill'd your sister.
KATHARINE He made her melancholy, sad, and heavy;
And so she died. Had she been light, like you,
Of such a merry, nimble, stirring spirit,
She might 'a been a grandam ere she died.
And so may you; for a light heart lives long.
ROSALINE What's your dark meaning, mouse, of this light word?
KATHARINE A light condition in a beauty dark.
ROSALINE We need more light to find your meaning out.
KATHARINE You'll mar the light by taking it in snuff;
Therefore I'll darkly end the argument.
ROSALINE Look what you do, you do it still i' th' dark.
KATHARINE So do not you; for you are a light wench.
ROSALINE Indeed, I weigh not you; and therefore light.
KATHARINE You weigh me not? O, that's you care not for me.
ROSALINE Great reason; for 'past cure is still past care'.
PRINCESS Well bandied both; a set of wit well play'd.
But, Rosaline, you have a favour too?
Who sent it? and what is it?
ROSALINE I would you knew.
An if my face were but as fair as yours,
My favour were as great: be witness this.
Nay, I have verses too, I thank Berowne;
The numbers true, and, were the numb'ring too,
I were the fairest goddess on the ground.
I am compar'd to twenty thousand fairs.
O, he hath drawn my picture in his letter!
PRINCESS Anything like?
ROSALINE Much in the letters; nothing in the praise.
PRINCESS Beauteous as ink – a good conclusion.
KATHARINE Fair as a text B in a copy-book.
ROSALINE Ware pencils, ho! Let me not die your debtor,
My red dominical, my golden letter:
O that your face were not so full of O's!
KATHARINE A pox of that jest! and I beshrew all shrows!
PRINCESS But, Katharine, what was sent to you from fair Dumain?
KATHARINE Madam, this glove.
PRINCESS Did he not send you twain?
KATHARINE Yes, madam; and, moreover,
Some thousand verses of a faithful lover;
A huge translation of hypocrisy,
Vilely compil'd profound simplicity.
MARIA This, and these pearl, to me sent Longaville;
The letter is too long by half a mile.
PRINCESS I think no less. Dost thou not wish in heart
The chain were longer and the letter short?
MARIA Ay, or I would these hands might never part.
PRINCESS We are wise girls to mock our lovers so.
ROSALINE They are worse fools to purchase mocking so.
That same Berowne I'll torture ere I go.
O that I knew he were but in by th' week!
How I would make him fawn, and beg, and seek,
And wait the season, and observe the times,
And spend his prodigal wits in bootless rhymes,
And shape his service wholly to my hests,
And make him proud to make me proud that jests!
So pertaunt-like would I o'ersway his state
That he should be my fool, and I his fate.
PRINCESS None are so surely caught, when they are catch'd,
As wit turn'd fool; folly, in wisdom hatch'd,
Hath wisdom's warrant and the help of school,
And wit's own grace to grace a learned fool.
ROSALINE The blood of youth burns not with such excess
As gravity's revolt to wantonness.
MARIA Folly in fools bears not so strong a note
As fool'ry in the wise when wit doth dote,
Since all the power thereof it doth apply
To prove, by wit, worth in simplicity.

Enter BOYET.

PRINCESS Here comes Boyet, and mirth is in his face.
BOYET O, I am stabb'd with laughter! Where's her Grace?
PRINCESS Thy news, Boyet?
BOYET Prepare, madam, prepare!

Arm, wenches, arm! Encounters mounted are
Against your peace. Love doth approach disguis'd,
Armed in arguments; you'll be surpris'd.
Muster your wits; stand in your own defence;
Or hide your heads like cowards, and fly hence.

PRINCESS Saint Dennis to Saint Cupid! What are they
That charge their breath against us? Say, scout, say.

BOYET Under the cool shade of a sycamore
I thought to close mine eyes some half an hour;
When, lo! to interrupt my purpos'd rest,
Toward that shade I might behold addrest
The King and his companions; warily
I stole into a neighbour thicket by,
And overheard what you shall overhear –
That, by and by, disguis'd they will be here.
Their herald is a pretty knavish page,
That well by heart hath conn'd his embassage.
Action and accent did they teach him there:
'Thus must thou speak' and 'thus thy body bear',
And ever and anon they made a doubt
Presence majestical would put him out;
'For' quoth the King 'an angel shalt thou see;
Yet fear not thou, but speak audaciously'.
The boy replied 'An angel is not evil;
I should have fear'd her had she been a devil'.
With that all laugh'd, and clapp'd him on the shoulder,
Making the bold wag by their praises bolder.
One rubb'd his elbow, thus, and fleer'd, and swore
A better speech was never spoke before.
Another with his finger and his thumb
Cried 'Via! we will do't, come what will come'.
The third he caper'd, and cried 'All goes well'.
The fourth turn'd on the toe, and down he fell.
With that they all did tumble on the ground,
With such a zealous laughter, so profound,
That in this spleen ridiculous appears,
To check their folly, passion's solemn tears.

PRINCESS But what, but what, come they to visit us?

BOYET They do, they do; and are apparell'd thus,
Like Muscovites or Russians, as I guess.
Their purpose is to parley, court, and dance;
And every one his love-feat will advance
Unto his several mistress; which they'll know
By favours several which they did bestow.

PRINCESS And will they so? The gallants shall be task'd,
For, ladies, we will every one be mask'd;
And not a man of them shall have the grace,
Despite of suit, to see a lady's face.
Hold, Rosaline, this favour thou shalt wear,
And then the King will court thee for his dear;
Hold, take thou this, my sweet, and give me thine,
So shall Berowne take me for Rosaline.
And change you favours too; so shall your loves
Woo contrary, deceiv'd by these removes.

ROSALINE Come on, then, wear the favours most in sight.

KATHARINE But, in this changing, what is your intent?

PRINCESS The effect of my intent is to cross theirs.
They do it but in mocking merriment,
And mock for mock is only my intent.
Their several counsels they unbosom shall
To loves mistook, and so be mock'd withal
Upon the next occasion that we meet
With visages display'd to talk and greet.

ROSALINE But shall we dance, if they desire us to't?

PRINCESS No, to the death, we will not move a foot,
Nor to their penn'd speech render we no grace;
But while 'tis spoke each turn away her face.

BOYET Why, that contempt will kill the speaker's heart,
And quite divorce his memory from his part.

PRINCESS Therefore I do it; and I make no doubt
The rest will ne'er come in, if he be out.
There's no such sport as sport by sport o'erthrown,
To make theirs ours, and ours none but our own;
So shall we stay, mocking intended game,
And they well mock'd depart away with shame.
[*Trumpet sounds within.*

BOYET The trumpet sounds; be mask'd; the maskers come. [*The Ladies mask.*

Enter Blackamoors with music, MOTH as Prologue, the KING and his Lords as maskers, in the guise of Russians.

MOTH *All hail, the richest beauties on the earth!*

BOYET Beauties no richer than rich taffeta.

MOTH *A holy parcel of the fairest dames*
[*The Ladies turn their backs to him.*
That ever turn'd their – backs – to mortal views!

BEROWNE *Their eyes*, villain, *their eyes.*

MOTH *That ever turn'd their eyes to mortal views!*
Out –

BOYET True; *out* indeed.

MOTH *Out of your favours, heavenly spirits, vouchsafe*
Not to behold –

BEROWNE *Once to behold*, rogue.

MOTH *Once to behold with your sun-beamed eyes – with your sun-beamed eyes –*

BOYET They will not answer to that epithet;
You were best call it 'daughter-beamed eyes'.

MOTH They do not mark me, and that brings me out.

BEROWNE Is this your perfectness? Be gone, you rogue. [*Exit Moth.*

ROSALINE What would these strangers? Know their minds, Boyet.
If they do speak our language, 'tis our will
That some plain man recount their purposes.
Know what they would.

BOYET What would you with the Princess?

BEROWNE Nothing but peace and gentle visitation.

ROSALINE What would they, say they?

BOYET Nothing but peace and gentle visitation.

ROSALINE Why, that they have; and bid them so be gone.

BOYET She says you have it, and you may be gone.

KING Say to her we have measur'd many miles
To tread a measure with her on this grass.

BOYET They say that they have measur'd many a mile
To tread a measure with you on this grass.

ROSALINE It is not so. Ask them how many inches
Is in one mile? If they have measured many,
The measure, then, of one is eas'ly told.

BOYET If to come hither you have measur'd miles,
And many miles, the Princess bids you tell
How many inches doth fill up one mile.

BEROWNE Tell her we measure them by weary steps.

BOYET She hears herself.

ROSALINE How many weary steps
Of many weary miles you have o'ergone
Are numb'red in the travel of one mile?

BEROWNE We number nothing that we spend for you;
Our duty is so rich, so infinite,
That we may do it still without accompt.
Vouchsafe to show the sunshine of your face,
That we, like savages, may worship it.

ROSALINE My face is but a moon, and clouded too.

KING Blessed are clouds, to do as such clouds do.
Vouchsafe, bright moon, and these thy stars, to shine,
Those clouds removed, upon our watery eyne.

ROSALINE O vain petitioner! beg a greater matter;
Thou now requests but moonshine in the water.

KING Then in our measure do but vouchsafe one change.
Thou bid'st me beg; this begging is not strange.

ROSALINE Play, music, then. Nay, you must do it soon.
Not yet? No dance! Thus change I like the moon.

KING Will you not dance? How come you thus estranged?

ROSALINE You took the moon at full; but now she's changed.

KING Yet still she is the Moon, and I the Man.
The music plays; vouchsafe some motion to it.

ROSALINE Our ears vouchsafe it.

KING But your legs should do it.

ROSALINE Since you are strangers, and come here by chance,
We'll not be nice; take hands. We will not dance.

KING Why take we hands then?

ROSALINE Only to part friends.
Curtsy, sweet hearts; and so the measure ends.

KING More measure of this measure; be not nice.

ROSALINE We can afford no more at such a price.

KING Price you yourselves. What buys your company?

ROSALINE Your absence only.

KING That can never be.

ROSALINE Then cannot we be bought; and so adieu –
Twice to your visor and half once to you.

KING If you deny to dance, let's hold more chat.

ROSALINE In private then.

KING I am best pleas'd with that.
[*They converse apart.*

BEROWNE White-handed mistress, one sweet word with thee.

PRINCESS Honey, and milk, and sugar; there is three.

BEROWNE Nay, then, two treys, an if you grow so nice,
Metheglin, wort, and malmsey; well run, dice!
There's half a dozen sweets.

PRINCESS Seventh sweet, adieu!
Since you can cog, I'll play no more with you.

BEROWNE One word in secret.

PRINCESS Let it not be sweet.

BEROWNE Thou grievest my gall.

PRINCESS Gall! bitter.

BEROWNE Therefore meet.
[*They converse apart.*

DUMAIN Will you vouchsafe with me to change a word?

MARIA Name it.

DUMAIN Fair lady –

MARIA Say you so? Fair lord –
Take that for your fair lady.

DUMAIN Please it you,
As much in private, and I'll bid adieu.
[They converse apart.

KATHARINE What, was your vizard made without a tongue?

LONGAVILLE I know the reason, lady, why you ask.

KATHARINE O for your reason! Quickly, sir; I long.

LONGAVILLE You have a double tongue within your mask,
And would afford my speechless vizard half.

KATHARINE 'Veal' quoth the Dutchman. Is not 'veal' a calf?

LONGAVILLE A calf, fair lady!

KATHARINE No, a fair lord calf.

LONGAVILLE Let's part the word.

KATHARINE No, I'll not be your half.
Take all and wean it; it may prove an ox.

LONGAVILLE Look how you butt yourself in these sharp mocks!
Will you give horns, chaste lady? Do not so.

KATHARINE Then die a calf, before your horns do grow.

LONGAVILLE One word in private with you ere I die.

KATHARINE Bleat softly, then; the butcher hears you cry. *[They converse apart.*

BOYET The tongues of mocking wenches are as keen
As is the razor's edge invisible,
Cutting a smaller hair than may be seen,
Above the sense of sense; so sensible
Seemeth their conference; their conceits have wings,
Fleeter than arrows, bullets, wind, thought, swifter things.

ROSALINE Not one word more, my maids; break off, break off.

BEROWNE By heaven, all dry-beaten with pure scoff!

KING Farewell, mad wenches; you have simple wits. *[Exeunt King, Lords, and Blackamoors.*

PRINCESS Twenty adieus, my frozen Muscovits.
Are these the breed of wits so wondered at?

BOYET Tapers they are, with your sweet breaths puff'd out.

ROSALINE Well-liking wits they have; gross, gross; fat, fat.

PRINCESS O poverty in wit, kingly-poor flout!
Will they not, think you, hang themselves to-night?
Or ever but in vizards show their faces?
This pert Berowne was out of count'nance quite.

ROSALINE They were all in lamentable cases!
The King was weeping-ripe for a good word.

PRINCESS Berowne did swear himself out of all suit.

MARIA Dumain was at my service, and his sword.
'No point' quoth I; my servant straight was mute.

KATHARINE Lord Longaville said I came o'er his heart;
And trow you what he call'd me?

PRINCESS Qualm, perhaps.

KATHARINE Yes, in good faith.

PRINCESS Go, sickness as thou art!

ROSALINE Well, better wits have worn plain statute-caps.
But will you hear? The King is my love sworn.

PRINCESS And quick Berowne hath plighted faith to me.

KATHARINE And Longaville was for my service born.

MARIA Dumain is mine, as sure as bark on tree.

BOYET Madam, and pretty mistresses, give ear:
Immediately they will again be here
In their own shapes; for it can never be
They will digest this harsh indignity.

PRINCESS Will they return?

BOYET They will, they will, God knows,
And leap for joy, though they are lame with blows:
Therefore, change favours; and, when they repair,
Blow like sweet roses in this summer air.

PRINCESS How blow? how blow? Speak to be understood.

BOYET Fair ladies mask'd are roses in their bud:
Dismask'd, their damask sweet commixture shown,
Are angels vailing clouds, or roses blown.

PRINCESS Avaunt, perplexity! What shall we do
If they return in their own shapes to woo?

ROSALINE Good madam, if by me you'll be advis'd,
Let's mock them still, as well known as disguis'd.
Let us complain to them what fools were here,
Disguis'd like Muscovites, in shapeless gear;
And wonder what they were, and to what end
Their shallow shows and prologue vilely penn'd,
And their rough carriage so ridiculous,
Should be presented at our tent to us.

BOYET Ladies, withdraw; the gallants are at hand.

PRINCESS Whip to our tents, as roes run o'er land.

[Exeunt Princess, Rosaline, Katharine, and Maria.

Re-enter the KING, BEROWNE, LONGAVILLE, and DUMAIN, in their proper habits.

KING Fair sir, God save you! Where's the Princess?

BOYET Gone to her tent. Please it your Majesty
Command me any service to her thither?
KING That she vouchsafe me audience for one word.
BOYET I will; and so will she, I know, my lord.
[*Exit.*
BEROWNE This fellow pecks up wit as pigeons pease,
And utters it again when God doth please.
He is wit's pedlar, and retails his wares
At wakes, and wassails, meetings, markets, fairs;
And we that sell by gross, the Lord doth know,
Have not the grace to grace it with such show.
This gallant pins the wenches on his sleeve;
Had he been Adam, he had tempted Eve.
'A can carve too, and lisp; why this is he
That kiss'd his hand away in courtesy;
This is the ape of form, Monsieur the Nice,
That, when he plays at tables, chides the dice
In honourable terms; nay, he can sing
A mean most meanly; and in ushering,
Mend him who can. The ladies call him sweet;
The stairs, as he treads on them, kiss his feet.
This is the flow'r that smiles on every one,
To show his teeth as white as whales-bone;
And consciences that will not die in debt
Pay him the due of 'honey-tongued Boyet'.
KING A blister on his sweet tongue, with my heart,
That put Armado's page out of his part!

Re-enter the PRINCESS, ushered by BOYET; ROSALINE, MARIA, and KATHARINE.

BEROWNE See where it comes! Behaviour, what wert thou
Till this man show'd thee? And what art thou now?
KING All hail, sweet madam, and fair time of day!
PRINCESS 'Fair' in 'all hail' is foul, as I conceive.
KING Construe my speeches better, if you may.
PRINCESS Then wish me better; I will give you leave.
KING We came to visit you, and purpose now
To lead you to our court; vouchsafe it then.
PRINCESS This field shall hold me, and so hold your vow:
Nor God, nor I, delights in perjur'd men.
KING Rebuke me not for that which you provoke.
The virtue of your eye must break my oath.
PRINCESS You nickname virtue: vice you should have spoke;
For virtue's office never breaks men's troth.
Now by my maiden honour, yet as pure
As the unsullied lily, I protest,
A world of torments though I should endure,
I would not yield to be your house's guest;
So much I hate a breaking cause to be
Of heavenly oaths, vowed with integrity.
KING O, you have liv'd in desolation here,
Unseen, unvisited, much to our shame.
PRINCESS Not so, my lord; it is not so, I swear;
We have had pastimes here, and pleasant game;
A mess of Russians left us but of late.
KING How, madam! Russians!
PRINCESS Ay, in truth, my lord;
Trim gallants, full of courtship and of state.
ROSALINE Madam, speak true. It is not so, my lord.
My lady, to the manner of the days,
In courtesy gives undeserving praise.
We four indeed confronted were with four
In Russian habit; here they stayed an hour
And talk'd apace; and in that hour, my lord,
They did not bless us with one happy word.
I dare not call them fools; but this I think,
When they are thirsty, fools would fain have drink.
BEROWNE This jest is dry to me. Fair gentle sweet,
Your wit makes wise things foolish; when we greet,
With eyes best seeing, heaven's fiery eye,
By light we lose light; your capacity
Is of that nature that to your huge store
Wise things seem foolish and rich things but poor.
ROSALINE This proves you wise and rich, for in my eye –
BEROWNE I am a fool, and full of poverty.
ROSALINE But that you take what doth to you belong,
It were a fault to snatch words from my tongue.
BEROWNE O, I am yours, and all that I possess.
ROSALINE All the fool mine?
BEROWNE I cannot give you less.
ROSALINE Which of the vizards was it that you wore?
BEROWNE Where? when? what vizard? Why demand you this?
ROSALINE There, then, that vizard; that superfluous case
That hid the worse and show'd the better face.
KING We were descried; they'll mock us now downright.
DUMAIN Let us confess, and turn it to a jest.
PRINCESS Amaz'd, my lord? Why looks your Highness sad?
ROSALINE Help, hold his brows! he'll swoon! Why look you pale?
Sea-sick, I think, coming from Muscovy.
BEROWNE Thus pour the stars down plagues for perjury.
Can any face of brass hold longer out?

Here stand I, lady – dart thy skill at me,
Bruise me with scorn, confound me with a flout,
Thrust thy sharp wit quite through my ignorance,
Cut me to pieces with thy keen conceit;
And I will wish thee never more to dance,
Nor never more in Russian habit wait.
O, never will I trust to speeches penn'd,
Nor to the motion of a school-boy's tongue,
Nor never come in vizard to my friend,
Nor woo in rhyme, like a blind harper's song.
Taffeta phrases, silken terms precise,
Three-pil'd hyperboles, spruce affectation,
Figures pedantical – these summer-flies
Have blown me full of maggot ostentation.
I do forswear them; and I here protest,
By this white glove – how white the hand, God knows! –
Henceforth my wooing mind shall be express'd
In russet yeas, and honest kersey noes.
And, to begin, wench – so God help me, law! –
My love to thee is sound, sans crack or flaw.

ROSALINE Sans 'sans', I pray you.

BEROWNE Yet I have a trick
Of the old rage; bear with me, I am sick;
I'll leave it by degrees. Soft, let us see –
Write 'Lord have mercy on us' on those three;
They are infected; in their hearts it lies;
They have the plague, and caught it of your eyes.
These lords are visited; you are not free,
For the Lord's tokens on you do I see.

PRINCESS No, they are free that gave these tokens to us.

BEROWNE Our states are forfeit; seek not to undo us.

ROSALINE It is not so; for how can this be true,
That you stand forfeit, being those that sue?

BEROWNE Peace; for I will not have to do with you.

ROSALINE Nor shall not, if I do as I intend.

BEROWNE Speak for yourselves; my wit is at an end.

KING Teach us, sweet madam, for our rude transgression
Some fair excuse.

PRINCESS The fairest is confession.
Were not you here but even now, disguis'd?

KING Madam, I was.

PRINCESS And were you well advis'd

KING Madam, I was.

PRINCESS When you then were here,
What did you whisper in your lady's ear?

KING That more than all the world I did respect her.

PRINCESS When she shall challenge this, you will reject her.

KING Upon mine honour, no.

PRINCESS Peace, peace, forbear;
Your oath once broke, you force not to forswear.

KING Despise me when I break this oath of mine.

PRINCESS I will; and therefore keep it. Rosaline,
What did the Russian whisper in your ear?

ROSALINE Madam, he swore that he did hold me dear
As precious eyesight, and did value me
Above this world; adding thereto, moreover,
That he would wed me, or else die my lover.

PRINCESS God give thee joy of him! The noble lord
Most honourably doth uphold his word.

KING What mean you, madam? By my life, my troth,
I never swore this lady such an oath.

ROSALINE By heaven, you did; and, to confirm it plain,
You gave me this; but take it, sir, again.

KING My faith and this the Princess I did give;
I knew her by this jewel on her sleeve.

PRINCESS Pardon me, sir, this jewel did she wear;
And Lord Berowne, I thank him, is my dear.
What, will you have me, or your pearl again?

BEROWNE Neither of either; I remit both twain.
I see the trick on't: here was a consent,
Knowing aforehand of our merriment,
To dash it like a Christmas comedy.
Some carry-tale, some please-man, some slight zany,
Some mumble-news, some trencher-knight, some Dick,
That smiles his cheek in years and knows the trick
To make my lady laugh when she's dispos'd,
Told our intents before; which once disclos'd,
The ladies did change favours; and then we,
Following the signs, woo'd but the sign of she.
Now, to our perjury to add more terror,
We are again forsworn in will and error.
Much upon this it is; [*To Boyet*] and might not you
Forestall our sport, to make us thus untrue?
Do not you know my lady's foot by th' squier,
And laugh upon the apple of her eye?
And stand between her back, sir, and the fire,
Holding a trencher, jesting merrily?
You put our page out. Go, you are allow'd;
Die when you will, a smock shall be your shroud.
You leer upon me, do you? There's an eye
Wounds like a leaden sword.

BOYET Full merrily
Hath this brave manage, this career, been run.

BEROWNE Lo, he is tilting straight! Peace; I have done.

Enter COSTARD.

Welcome, pure wit! Thou part'st a fair fray.

COSTARD O Lord, sir, they would know
Whether the three Worthies shall come in or no?

BEROWNE What, are there but three?

COSTARD No, sir; but it is vara fine,
For every one pursents three.

BEROWNE And three times thrice is nine.

COSTARD Not so, sir; under correction, sir, I hope it is not so.
You cannot beg us, sir, I can assure you, sir; we know what we know;
I hope, sir, three times thrice, sir –

BEROWNE Is not nine.

COSTARD Under correction, sir, we know whereuntil it doth amount.

BEROWNE By Jove, I always took three threes for nine.

COSTARD O Lord, sir, it were pity you should get your living by reck'ning, sir.

BEROWNE How much is it?

COSTARD O Lord, sir, the parties themselves, the actors, sir, will show whereuntil it doth amount. For mine own part, I am, as they say, but to parfect one man in one poor man, Pompion the Great, sir.

BEROWNE Art thou one of the Worthies?

COSTARD It pleased them to think me worthy of Pompey the Great; for mine own part, I know not the degree of the Worthy; but I am to stand for him.

BEROWNE Go, bid them prepare.

COSTARD We will turn it finely off, sir; we will take some care. [*Exit Costard.*

KING Berowne, they will shame us; let them not approach.

BEROWNE We are shame-proof, my lord, and 'tis some policy
To have one show worse than the King's and his company.

KING I say they shall not come.

PRINCESS Nay, my good lord, let me o'errule you now.
That sport best pleases that doth least know how;
Where zeal strives to content, and the contents
Dies in the zeal of that which it presents.
Their form confounded makes most form in mirth,
When great things labouring perish in their birth.

BEROWNE A right description of our sport, my lord.

Enter ARMADO.

ARMADO Anointed, I implore so much expense of thy royal sweet breath as will utter a brace of words.

[*Converses apart with the King, and delivers a paper.*

PRINCESS Doth this man serve God?

BEROWNE Why ask you?

PRINCESS 'A speaks not like a man of God his making.

ARMADO That is all one, my fair, sweet, honey monarch; for, I protest, the school-master is exceeding fantastical; too too vain, too too vain; but we will put it, as they say, to fortuna de la guerra. I wish you the peace of mind, most royal couplement! [*Exit Armado.*

KING Here is like to be a good presence of Worthies. He presents Hector of Troy; the swain, Pompey the Great; the parish curate, Alexander; Armado's page, Hercules; the pedant, Judas Maccabaeus.
And if these four Worthies in their first show thrive,
These four will change habits and present the other five.

BEROWNE There is five in the first show.

KING You are deceived, 'tis not so.

BEROWNE The pedant, the braggart, the hedge-priest, the fool, and the boy;
Abate throw at novum, and the whole world again
Cannot pick out five such, take each one in his vein.

KING The ship is under sail, and here she comes amain.

Enter COSTARD, *armed for Pompey.*

COSTARD *I Pompey am* –

BEROWNE You lie, you are not he.

COSTARD *I Pompey am* –

BOYET With libbard's head on knee.

BEROWNE Well said, old mocker; I must needs be friends with thee.

COSTARD *I Pompey am, Pompey surnam'd the Big* –

DUMAIN The *Great.*

COSTARD It is *Great*, sir.
Pompey surnam'd the Great,
That oft in field, with targe and shield, did make my foe to sweat;
And travelling along this coast, I here am come by chance,
And lay my arms before the legs of this sweet lass of France.
If your ladyship would say 'Thanks, Pompey', I had done.

PRINCESS Great thanks, great Pompey.

COSTARD 'Tis not so much worth; but I hope I was perfect. I made a little fault in Great.

BEROWNE My hat to a halfpenny, Pompey proves the best Worthy.

Enter SIR NATHANIEL, for Alexander.

NATHANIEL *When in the world I liv'd, I was the world's commander;*
By east, west, north, and south, I spread my conquering might.
My scutcheon plain declares that I am Alisander –

BOYET Your nose says, no, you are not; for it stands too right.

BEROWNE Your nose smells 'no' in this, most tender-smelling knight.

PRINCESS The conqueror is dismay'd. Proceed, good Alexander.

NATHANIEL *When in the world I liv'd, I was the world's commander –*

BOYET Most true, 'tis right, you were so, Alisander.

BEROWNE Pompey the Great!

COSTARD Your servant, and Costard.

BEROWNE Take away the conqueror, take away Alisander.

COSTARD [*To Sir Nathaniel*] O, sir, you have overthrown Alisander the conqueror! You will be scrap'd out of the painted cloth for this. Your lion, that holds his poleaxe sitting on a close-stool, will be given to Ajax. He will be the ninth Worthy. A conqueror and afeard to speak! Run away for shame, Alisander. [*Sir Nathaniel retires*] There, an't shall please you, a foolish mild man; an honest man, look you, and soon dash'd. He is a marvellous good neighbour, faith, and a very good bowler; but for Alisander – alas! you see how 'tis – a little o'erparted. But there are Worthies a-coming will speak their mind in some other sort.

PRINCESS Stand aside, good Pompey.

Enter HOLOFERNES, for Judas; and MOTH, for Hercules.

HOLOFERNES *Great Hercules is presented by this imp,*
Whose club kill'd Cerberus, that three-headed canus;
And when he was a babe, a child, a shrimp,
Thus did he strangle serpents in his manus..
Quoniam he seemeth in minority,
Ergo I come with this apology.

Keep some state in thy exit, and vanish. [*Moth retires.*

Judas I am –

DUMAIN A Judas!

HOLOFERNES Not Iscariot, sir.
Judas I am, ycliped Maccabaeus.

DUMAIN Judas Maccabaeus clipt is plain Judas.

BEROWNE A kissing traitor. How art thou prov'd Judas?

HOLOFERNES *Judas I am –*

DUMAIN The more shame for you, Judas!

HOLOFERNES What mean you, sir?

BOYET To make Judas hang himself.

HOLOFERNES Begin, sir; you are my elder.

BEROWNE Well followed: Judas was hanged on an elder.

HOLOFERNES I will not be put out of countenance.

BEROWNE Because thou hast no face.

HOLOFERNES What is this?

BOYET A cittern-head.

DUMAIN The head of a bodkin.

BEROWNE A death's face in a ring.

LONGAVILLE The face of an old Roman coin, scarce seen.

BOYET The pommel of Caesar's falchion.

DUMAIN The carv'd-bone face on a flask.

BEROWNE Saint George's half-cheek in a brooch.

DUMAIN Ay, and in a brooch of lead.

BEROWNE Ay, and worn in the cap of a tooth-drawer. And now, forward; for we have put thee in countenance.

HOLOFERNES You have put me out of countenance

BEROWNE False: we have given thee faces.

HOLOFERNES But you have outfac'd them all.

BEROWNE An thou wert a lion we would do so.

BOYET Therefore, as he is an ass, let him go.
And so adieu, sweet Jude! Nay, why dost thou stay?

DUMAIN For the latter end of his name.

BEROWNE For the ass to the Jude; give it him – Jud-as, away.

HOLOFERNES This is not generous, not gentle, not humble.

BOYET A light for Monsieur Judas! It grows dark, he may stumble. [*Holofernes retires.*

PRINCESS Alas, poor Maccabaeus, how hath he been baited!

Enter ARMADO, for Hector.

BEROWNE Hide thy head, Achilles; here comes Hector in arms.

DUMAIN Though my mocks come home by me, I will now be merry.

KING Hector was but a Troyan in respect of this.

BOYET But is this Hector?

DUMAIN I think Hector was not so clean-timber'd.

LONGAVILLE His leg is too big for Hector's.

DUMAIN More calf, certain.
BOYET No; he is best indued in the small.
BEROWNE This cannot be Hector.
DUMAIN He's a god or a painter, for he makes faces.
ARMADO *The armipotent Mars, of lances the almighty,*
Gave Hector a gift –
DUMAIN A gilt nutmeg.
BEROWNE A lemon.
LONGAVILLE Stuck with cloves.
DUMAIN No, cloven.
ARMADO Peace!
The armipotent Mars, of lances the almighty,
Gave Hector a gift, the heir of Ilion;
A man so breathed that certain he would fight ye,
From morn till night out of his pavilion.
I am that flower –
DUMAIN That mint.
LONGAVILLE That columbine.
ARMADO Sweet Lord Longaville, rein thy tongue.
LONGAVILLE I must rather give it the rein, for it runs against Hector.
DUMAIN Ay, and Hector's a greyhound.
ARMADO The sweet war-man is dead and rotten; sweet chucks, beat not the bones of the buried; when he breathed, he was a man. But I will forward with my device. [*To the Princess*] Sweet royalty, bestow on me the sense of hearing.

[*Berowne steps forth, and speaks to Costard.*

PRINCESS Speak, brave Hector; we are much delighted.
ARMADO I do adore thy sweet Grace's slipper.
BOYET [*Aside to Dumain*] Loves her by the foot.
DUMAIN [*Aside to Boyet*] He may not by the yard.
ARMADO *This Hector far surmounted Hannibal –*
COSTARD The party is gone, fellow Hector, she is gone; she is two months on her way.
ARMADO What meanest thou?
COSTARD Faith, unless you play the honest Troyan, the poor wench is cast away. She's quick; the child brags in her belly already; 'tis yours.
ARMADO Dost thou infamonize me among potentates? Thou shalt die.
COSTARD Then shall Hector be whipt for Jaquenetta that is quick by him, and hang'd for Pompey that is dead by him.
DUMAIN Most rare Pompey!
BOYET Renowned Pompey!
BEROWNE Greater than Great! Great, great, great Pompey! Pompey the Huge!
DUMAIN Hector trembles.
BEROWNE Pompey is moved. More Ates, more Ates! Stir them on! stir them on!
DUMAIN Hector will challenge him.
BEROWNE Ay, if 'a have no more man's blood in his belly than will sup a flea.
ARMADO By the North Pole, I do challenge thee.
COSTARD I will not fight with a pole, like a Northren man; I'll slash; I'll do it by the sword. I bepray you, let me borrow my arms again.
DUMAIN Room for the incensed Worthies!
COSTARD I'll do it in my shirt.
DUMAIN Most resolute Pompey!
MOTH Master, let me take you a button-hole lower. Do you not see Pompey is uncasing for the combat? What mean you? You will lose your reputation.
ARMADO Gentlemen and soldiers, pardon me; I will not combat in my shirt.
DUMAIN You may not deny it: Pompey hath made the challenge.
ARMADO Sweet bloods, I both may and will.
BEROWNE What reason have you for 't?
ARMADO The naked truth of it is: I have no shirt; I go woolward for penance.
BOYET True, and it was enjoined him in Rome for want of linen; since when, I'll be sworn, he wore none but a dish-clout of Jaquenetta's, and that 'a wears next his heart for a favour.

Enter as messenger, MONSIEUR MARCADE.

MARIA God save you, madam!
PRINCESS Welcome, Marcade;
But that thou interruptest our merriment.
MARIA I am sorry, madam; for the news I bring
Is heavy in my tongue. The King your father –
PRINCESS Dead, for my life!
MARIA Even so; my tale is told.
BEROWNE Worthies, away; the scene begins to cloud.
ARMADO For mine own part, I breathe free breath. I have seen the day of wrong through the little hole of discretion, and I will right myself like a soldier. [*Exeunt Worthies.*

KING How fares your Majesty?
PRINCESS Boyet, prepare; I will away to-night.
KING Madam, not so; I do beseech you stay.
PRINCESS Prepare, I say. I thank you, gracious lords,
For all your fair endeavours, and entreat,
Out of a new-sad soul, that you vouchsafe
In your rich wisdom to excuse or hide
The liberal opposition of our spirits,
If over-boldly we have borne ourselves
In the converse of breath – your gentleness
Was guilty of it. Farewell, worthy lord.
A heavy heart bears not a nimble tongue.
Excuse me so, coming too short of thanks
For my great suit so easily obtain'd.

KING The extreme parts of time extremely forms
All causes to the purpose of his speed;
And often at his very loose decides
That which long process could not arbitrate.
And though the mourning brow of progeny
Forbid the smiling courtesy of love
The holy suit which fain it would convince,
Yet, since love's argument was first on foot,
Let not the cloud of sorrow justle it
From what it purpos'd; since to wail friends lost
Is not by much so wholesome-profitable
As to rejoice at friends but newly found.
PRINCESS I understand you not; my griefs are double.
BEROWNE Honest plain words best pierce the ear of grief;
And by these badges understand the King.
For your fair sakes have we neglected time,
Play'd foul play with our oaths; your beauty, ladies,
Hath much deformed us, fashioning our humours
Even to the opposed end of our intents;
And what in us hath seem'd ridiculous,
As love is full of unbefitting strains,
All wanton as a child, skipping and vain;
Form'd by the eye and therefore, like the eye,
Full of strange shapes, of habits, and of forms,
Varying in subjects as the eye doth roll
To every varied object in his glance;
Which parti-coated presence of loose love
Put on by us, if in your heavenly eyes
Have misbecom'd our oaths and gravities,
Those heavenly eyes that look into these faults
Suggested us to make. Therefore, ladies,
Our love being yours, the error that love makes
Is likewise yours. We to ourselves prove false,
By being once false for ever to be true
To those that make us both – fair ladies, you;
And even that falsehood, in itself a sin,
Thus purifies itself and turns to grace.
PRINCESS We have receiv'd your letters, full of love;
Your favours, the ambassadors of love;
And, in our maiden council, rated them
At courtship, pleasant jest, and courtesy,
As bombast and as lining to the time;
But more devout than this in our respects
Have we not been; and therefore met your loves
In their own fashion, like a merriment.
DUMAIN Our letters, madam, show'd much more than jest.
LONGAVILLE So did our looks.
ROSALINE We did not quote them so.
KING Now, at the latest minute of the hour,
Grant us your loves.
PRINCESS A time, methinks, too short
To make a world-without-end bargain in.
No, no, my lord, your Grace is perjur'd much,
Full of dear guiltiness; and therefore this,
If for my love, as there is no such cause,
You will do aught – this shall you do for me:
Your oath I will not trust; but go with speed
To some forlorn and naked hermitage,
Remote from all the pleasures of the world;
There stay until the twelve celestial signs
Have brought about the annual reckoning.
If this austere insociable life
Change not your offer made in heat of blood,
If frosts and fasts, hard lodging and thin weeds,
Nip not the gaudy blossoms of your love,
But that it bear this trial, and last love,
Then, at the expiration of the year,
Come, challenge me, challenge me by these deserts;
And, by this virgin palm now kissing thine,
I will be thine; and, till that instant, shut
My woeful self up in a mournful house,
Raining the tears of lamentation
For the remembrance of my father's death.
If this thou do deny, let our hands part,
Neither intitled in the other's heart.
KING If this, or more than this, I would deny,
To flatter up these powers of mine with rest,
The sudden hand of death close up mine eye!
Hence hermit then, my heart is in thy breast.
BEROWNE *And what to me, my love? and what to me?*
ROSALINE *You must be purged too, your sins are rack'd;*
You are attaint with faults and perjury;
Therefore, if you my favour mean to get,
A twelvemonth shall you spend, and never rest,
But seek the weary beds of people sick.
DUMAIN But what to me, my love? but what to me?
A wife?
KATHARINE A beard, fair health, and honesty;
With threefold love I wish you all these three.
DUMAIN O, shall I say I thank you, gentle wife?
KATHARINE Not so, my lord; a twelvemonth and a day
I'll mark no words that smooth-fac'd wooers say.
Come when the King doth to my lady come;
Then, if I have much love, I'll give you some.
DUMAIN I'll serve thee true and faithfully till then.
KATHARINE Yet swear not, lest ye be forsworn again.
LONGAVILLE What says Maria?
MARIA At the twelvemonth's end
I'll change my black gown for a faithful friend.

LONGAVILLE I'll stay with patience; but the time is long.
MARIA The liker you; few taller are so young.
BEROWNE Studies my lady? Mistress, look on me;
Behold the window of my heart, mine eye,
What humble suit attends thy answer there.
Impose some service on me for thy love.
ROSALINE Oft have I heard of you, my Lord Berowne,
Before I saw you; and the world's large tongue
Proclaims you for a man replete with mocks,
Full of comparisons and wounding flouts,
Which you on all estates will execute
That lie within the mercy of your wit.
To weed this wormwood from your fruitful brain,
And therewithal to win me, if you please,
Without the which I am not to be won,
You shall this twelvemonth term from day to day
Visit the speechless sick, and still converse
With groaning wretches; and your task shall be,
With all the fierce endeavour of your wit,
To enforce the pained impotent to smile.
BEROWNE To move wild laughter in the throat of death?
It cannot be; it is impossible;
Mirth cannot move a soul in agony.
ROSALINE Why, that's the way to choke a gibing spirit,
Whose influence is begot of that loose grace
Which shallow laughing hearers give to fools.
A jest's prosperity lies in the ear
Of him that hears it, never in the tongue
Of him that makes it; then, if sickly ears,
Deaf'd with the clamours of their own dear groans,
Will hear your idle scorns, continue then,
And I will have you and that fault withal.
But if they will not, throw away that spirit,
And I shall find you empty of that fault,
Right joyful of your reformation.
BEROWNE A twelvemonth? Well, befall what will befall,
I'll jest a twelvemonth in an hospital.
PRINCESS *[To the King]* Ay, sweet my lord, and so I take my leave.
KING No, madam; we will bring you on your way.
BEROWNE Our wooing doth not end like an old play:
Jack hath not Jill. These ladies' courtesy
Might well have made our sport a comedy.
KING Come, sir, it wants a twelvemonth an' a day,
And then 'twill end.
BEROWNE That's too long for a play.

Re-enter ARMADO.

ARMADO Sweet Majesty, vouchsafe me –
PRINCESS Was not that Hector?
DUMAIN The worthy knight of Troy.
ARMADO I will kiss thy royal finger, and take leave. I am a votary: I have vow'd to Jaquenetta to hold the plough for her sweet love three year. But, most esteemed greatness, will you hear the dialogue that the two learned men have compiled in praise of the Owl and the Cuckoo? It should have followed in the end of our show.
KING Call them forth quickly; we will do so.
ARMADO Holla! approach.

Enter All.

This side is Hiems, Winter; this Ver, the Spring – the one maintained by the Owl, th' other by the Cuckoo. Ver, begin.

Spring.

When daisies pied and violets blue
And lady-smocks all silver-white
And cuckoo-buds of yellow hue
Do paint the meadows with delight,
The cuckoo then on every tree
Mocks married men, for thus sings he:
'Cuckoo;
Cuckoo, cuckoo' – O word of fear,
Unpleasing to a married ear!

When shepherds pipe on oaten straws,
And merry larks are ploughmen's clocks;
When turtles tread, and rooks and daws,
And maidens bleach their summer smocks;
The cuckoo then on every tree
Mocks married men, for thus sings he:
'Cuckoo;
Cuckoo, cuckoo' – O word of fear,
Unpleasing to a married ear!

Winter.

When icicles hang by the wall,
And Dick the shepherd blows his nail,
And Tom bears logs into the hall,
And milk comes frozen home in pail,
When blood is nipp'd, and ways be foul,
Then nightly sings the staring owl:
'Tu-who;
Tu-whit, Tu-who' – A merry note,
While greasy Joan doth keel the pot.

When all aloud the wind doth blow,
And coughing drowns the parson's saw,
And birds sit brooding in the snow,
And Marian's nose looks red and raw,

When roasted crabs hiss in the bowl,
Then nightly sings the staring owl:
'Tu-who;
Tu-whit, To-who' – A merry note,
While greasy Joan doth keel the pot.

ARMADO The words of Mercury are harsh after the songs of Apollo. You that way: we this way.

[*Exeunt.*

A Midsummer Night's Dream

Introduction by ALEC YEARLING

Of the handful of plays where the material seems to have been essentially of Shakespeare's own invention, *A Midsummer Night's Dream* is by some way the most sturdily put together. Within a framing situation of the impending nuptials of Theseus and Hippolita, three actions are juxtaposed, alternating and inter-connecting – the story of the four lovers being the most elaborate in terms of plot, and that of the rehearsing Mechanicals the most rudimentary. Into both of these the wilfulness of the fairy world intrudes: temporarily in the transformation of Bottom, permanently in the continuing enchantment of Demetrius which allows the lovers' initial ragged ensemble to emerge as symmetrical pairing. The various actions echo each other without falling into too schematic a pattern of parallel or contrast. Theseus and Hippolita have come through antagonism to mutual love; Oberon bests Titania by humiliating her until she seeks his love and protection; the mortal lovers endure the hazards common to their kind – parental opposition, passion unrequited, infidelity, betrayal – until they and their situation are satisfactorily adjusted; and the Mechanicals play out a miniature *Romeo and Juliet* which would be tragedy were it not inadvertently presented as farce.

It would, in fact, be easy to summarise many incidents so as to make the play seem darker and more threatening than it proves: Titania degraded by an amorous involvement with a bestial clown; Hermia threatened with death or the nunnery; old friendships ripped up in sexual rivalry; sado-masochistic tendencies in the world's rulers. As it is, 'merriments' is what Theseus commands on first entrance, and on the way towards the final fairy-benediction our overriding response is laughter. Everything provokes it: our Puck-like superiority to characters' conditioned responses, our recognition of actuality in the acrimonious verbal exchanges, above all our (almost) invariable pleasure taken in the performance of what is one of Shakespeare's most bounteous gifts to the acting profession.

What binds it all together is an imaginative wholeness wherein the early Shakespeare's free lyrical flow is directed towards a unified vision which proves to be both ironic and celebratory. Night, dreams, and the moon are invoked at the outset, and come increasingly to be linked with the idea of irrational sight, sight which is at odds both with what the object is, and is known to be. Shakespeare teases out this theme until it embraces the audience as well as every element of the play. 'I would my father look'd but with my eyes' says Hermia [1.1.56], and it is of course upon the eyes that the juice of the purple flower is squeezed. All see what they are inclined to see; the inclination is sometimes involuntary, sometimes willed, sometimes coerced. Oberon's and Puck's enchantment stands for the delusive powers of darkness and dreaming, or for lunacy, or for the vagaries of the heart. Lysander and Demetrius are agreed in the first scene to be much of a muchness; Hermia and Helena have names that denote the potential interchangeability which will become actual in the chaotic middle of the play, with at any point one beloved and one not. The mysteries of inclination are not to be solved by objective scrutiny. And meanwhile what the spectators are encouraged to see is not by any means what they scrutinize: while the text repeatedly evokes a miniaturised fairy world which is delicate and tenebrous and sometimes invisible, what is seen are full-sized human beings – even boys being not especially miniature. Moreover, what the original audiences presumably saw was daylit and without benefit of scenery. Suspension of disbelief, like inclination, is a potent thing. The Mechanicals' efforts are subject to the same enhancement. Hippolita's initial resistance to their play is rebuked by her husband:

> – This is the silliest stuff that ever I heard.
> – The best in this kind are but shadows; and the worst are no worse,
> if imagination amend them.
> – It must be your imagination then, and not theirs. [5.1.209–12]

By line 282 her imagination, and with it her feelings, have been engaged:

> – Beshrew my heart, but I pity the man.

We may remember that at the start of this act Theseus likened poetic creation to the delusions of lovers and madmen: something the play at once illustrates and demonstrates. It is a more insidious, even subliminal, version of what *Henry V*'s Chorus exhorts us: 'Piece out our imperfections with your thoughts'; – not that there are many imperfections in what has proved to be the most enduringly popular, and genuinely comic, of Shakespeare's earlier comedies.

A Midsummer Night's Dream

DRAMATIS PERSONAE

THESEUS
Duke of Athens
EGEUS
father to Hermia
LYSANDER, DEMETRIUS
in love with Hermia
PHILOSTRATE
Master of the Revels to Theseus
QUINCE
a carpenter
SNUG
a joiner
BOTTOM
a weaver
FLUTE
a bellows-mender
SNOUT
a tinker
STARVELING
a tailor
HIPPOLYTA
Queen of the Amazons, betrothed to Theseus
HERMIA
daughter to Egeus, in love with Lysander
HELENA
in love with Demetrius
OBERON
King of the Fairies
TITANIA
Queen of the Fairies
PUCK or ROBIN GOODFELLOW
PEASEBLOSSOM, COBWEB, MOTH, MUSTARDSEED
fairies
PROLOGUE *presented by* QUINCE
PYRAMUS *presented by* BOTTOM
THISBY *presented by* FLUTE
WALL *presented by* SNOUT
MOONSHINE *presented by* STARVELING
LION *presented by* SNUG
Other Fairies attending their King and Queen.
Attendants on Theseus and Hippolyta.

THE SCENE: ATHENS AND A WOOD NEAR IT.

ACT ONE

SCENE I. *Athens. The palace of Theseus.*

Enter THESEUS, HIPPOLYTA, PHILOSTRATE, and Attendants.

THESEUS Now, fair Hippolyta, our nuptial hour
Draws on apace; four happy days bring in
Another moon; but, O, methinks, how slow
This old moon wanes! She lingers my desires,
Like to a step-dame or a dowager,
Long withering out a young man's revenue.
HIPPOLYTA Four days will quickly steep themselves in night;
Four nights will quickly dream away the time;
And then the moon, like to a silver bow
New-bent in heaven, shall behold the night
Of our solemnities.
THESEUS Go, Philostrate,
Stir up the Athenian youth to merriments;
Awake the pert and nimble spirit of mirth;
Turn melancholy forth to funerals;
The pale companion is not for our pomp.
[*Exit Philostrate.*
Hippolyta, I woo'd thee with my sword,
And won thy love doing thee injuries;
But I will wed thee in another key,
With pomp, with triumph, and with revelling.

Enter EGEUS, and his daughter HERMIA, LYSANDER, and DEMETRIUS.

EGEUS Happy be Theseus, our renowned Duke!
THESEUS Thanks, good Egeus; what's the news with thee?
EGEUS Full of vexation come I, with complaint
Against my child, my daughter Hermia.
Stand forth, Demetrius. My noble lord,
This man hath my consent to marry her.
Stand forth, Lysander. And, my gracious Duke,
This man hath bewitch'd the bosom of my child.
Thou, thou, Lysander, thou hast given her rhymes,
And interchang'd love-tokens with my child;
Thou hast by moonlight at her window sung,
With feigning voice, verses of feigning love,
And stol'n the impression of her fantasy

With bracelets of thy hair, rings, gawds, conceits,
Knacks, trifles, nosegays, sweetmeats – messengers
Of strong prevailment in unhardened youth;
With cunning hast thou filch'd my daughter's heart;
Turn'd her obedience, which is due to me,
To stubborn harshness. And, my gracious Duke,
Be it so she will not here before your Grace
Consent to marry with Demetrius,
I beg the ancient privilege of Athens:
As she is mine I may dispose of her;
Which shall be either to this gentleman
Or to her death, according to our law
Immediately provided in that case.

THESEUS What say you, Hermia? Be advis'd, fair maid.
To you your father should be as a god;
One that compos'd your beauties; yea, and one
To whom you are but as a form in wax,
By him imprinted, and within his power
To leave the figure, or disfigure it.
Demetrius is a worthy gentleman.

HERMIA So is Lysander.

THESEUS In himself he is;
But, in this kind, wanting your father's voice,
The other must be held the worthier.

HERMIA I would my father look'd but with my eyes.

THESEUS Rather your eyes must with his judgment look.

HERMIA I do entreat your Grace to pardon me.
I know not by what power I am made bold,
Nor how it may concern my modesty
In such a presence here to plead my thoughts;
But I beseech your Grace that I may know
The worst that may befall me in this case,
If I refuse to wed Demetrius.

THESEUS Either to die the death, or to abjure
For ever the society of men.
Therefore, fair Hermia, question your desires,
Know of your youth, examine well your blood,
Whether, if you yield not to your father's choice,
You can endure the livery of a nun,
For aye to be in shady cloister mew'd,
To live a barren sister all your life,
Chanting faint hymns to the cold fruitless moon.
Thrice-blessed they that master so their blood
To undergo such maiden pilgrimage;
But earthlier happy is the rose distill'd
Than that which withering on the virgin thorn
Grows, lives, and dies, in single blessedness.

HERMIA So will I grow, so live, so die, my lord,
Ere I will yield my virgin patent up
Unto his lordship, whose unwished yoke
My soul consents not to give sovereignty.

THESEUS Take time to pause; and by the next new moon –
The sealing-day betwixt my love and me
For everlasting bond of fellowship –
Upon that day either prepare to die
For disobedience to your father's will,
Or else to wed Demetrius, as he would,
Or on Diana's altar to protest
For aye austerity and single life.

DEMETRIUS Relent, sweet Hermia; and, Lysander, yield
Thy crazed title to my certain right.

LYSANDER You have her father's love, Demetrius;
Let me have Hermia's; do you marry him.

EGEUS Scornful Lysander, true, he hath my love;
And what is mine my love shall render him;
And she is mine; and all my right of her
I do estate unto Demetrius.

LYSANDER I am, my lord, as well deriv'd as he,
As well possess'd; my love is more than his;
My fortunes every way as fairly rank'd,
If not with vantage, as Demetrius';
And, which is more than all these boasts can be,
I am belov'd of beauteous Hermia.
Why should not I then prosecute my right?
Demetrius, I'll avouch it to his head,
Made love to Nedar's daughter, Helena,
And won her soul; and she, sweet lady, dotes,
Devoutly dotes, dotes in idolatry,
Upon this spotted and inconstant man.

THESEUS I must confess that I have heard so much,
And with Demetrius thought to have spoke thereof;
But, being over-full of self-affairs,
My mind did lose it. But, Demetrius, come;
And come, Egeus; you shall go with me;
I have some private schooling for you both.
For you, fair Hermia, look you arm yourself
To fit your fancies to your father's will,
Or else the law of Athens yields you up –
Which by no means we may extenuate –
To death, or to a vow of single life.
Come, my Hippolyta; what cheer, my love?
Demetrius, and Egeus, go along;
I must employ you in some business
Against our nuptial, and confer with you
Of something nearly that concerns yourselves.

EGEUS With duty and desire we follow you.

[*Exeunt all but Lysander and Hermia.*

LYSANDER How now, my love! Why is your cheek so pale?
How chance the roses there do fade so fast?

HERMIA Belike for want of rain, which I could well
Beteem them from the tempest of my eyes.
LYSANDER Ay me! for aught that I could ever read,
Could ever hear by tale or history,
The course of true love never did run smooth;
But either it was different in blood –
HERMIA O cross! too high to be enthrall'd to low.
LYSANDER Or else misgraffed in respect of years –
HERMIA O spite! too old to be engag'd to young.
LYSANDER Or else it stood upon the choice of friends –
HERMIA O hell! to choose love by another's eyes.
LYSANDER Or, if there were a sympathy in choice,
War, death, or sickness, did lay siege to it,
Making it momentary as a sound,
Swift as a shadow, short as any dream,
Brief as the lightning in the collied night
That, in a spleen, unfolds both heaven and earth,
And ere a man hath power to say 'Behold!'
The jaws of darkness do devour it up;
So quick bright things come to confusion.
HERMIA If then true lovers have been ever cross'd,
It stands as an edict in destiny.
Then let us teach our trial patience,
Because it is a customary cross,
As due to love as thoughts and dreams and sighs,
Wishes and tears, poor Fancy's followers.
LYSANDER A good persuasion; therefore, hear me, Hermia:
I have a widow aunt, a dowager
Of great revenue, and she hath no child –
From Athens is her house remote seven leagues –
And she respects me as her only son.
There, gentle Hermia, may I marry thee;
And to that place the sharp Athenian law
Cannot pursue us. If thou lovest me then,
Steal forth thy father's house to-morrow night;
And in the wood, a league without the town,
Where I did meet thee once with Helena
To do observance to a morn of May,
There will I stay for thee.
HERMIA My good Lysander!
I swear to thee by Cupid's strongest bow,
By his best arrow, with the golden head,
By the simplicity of Venus' doves,
By that which knitteth souls and prospers loves,
And by that fire which burn'd the Carthage Queen,
When the false Troyan under sail was seen,
By all the vows that ever men have broke,
In number more than ever women spoke,
In that same place thou hast appointed me,
To-morrow truly will I meet with thee.
LYSANDER Keep promise, love. Look, here comes Helena.

Enter HELENA.

HERMIA God speed fair Helena! Whither away?
HELENA Call you me fair? That fair again unsay.
Demetrius loves your fair. O happy fair!
Your eyes are lode-stars and your tongue's sweet air
More tuneable than lark to shepherd's ear,
When wheat is green, when hawthorn buds appear.
Sickness is catching; O, were favour so,
Yours would I catch, fair Hermia, ere I go!
My ear should catch your voice, my eye your eye,
My tongue should catch your tongue's sweet melody.
Were the world mine, Demetrius being bated,
The rest I'd give to be to you translated.
O, teach me how you look, and with what art
You sway the motion of Demetrius' heart!
HERMIA I frown upon him, yet he loves me still.
HELENA O that your frowns would teach my smiles such skill!
HERMIA I give him curses, yet he gives me love.
HELENA O that my prayers could such affection move!
HERMIA The more I hate, the more he follows me.
HELENA The more I love, the more he hateth me.
HERMIA His folly, Helena, is no fault of mine.
HELENA None, but your beauty; would that fault were mine!
HERMIA Take comfort: he no more shall see my face;
Lysander and myself will fly this place.
Before the time I did Lysander see,
Seem'd Athens as a paradise to me.
O, then, what graces in my love do dwell,
That he hath turn'd a heaven unto a hell!
LYSANDER Helen, to you our minds we will unfold:
To-morrow night, when Phoebe doth behold
Her silver visage in the wat'ry glass,
Decking with liquid pearl the bladed grass,
A time that lovers' flights doth still conceal,
Through Athens' gates have we devis'd to steal.
HERMIA And in the wood where often you and I
Upon faint primrose beds were wont to lie,
Emptying our bosoms of their counsel sweet,
There my Lysander and myself shall meet;
And thence from Athens turn away our eyes,

To seek new friends and stranger companies.
Farewell, sweet playfellow; pray thou for us,
And good luck grant thee thy Demetrius!
Keep word, Lysander; we must starve our sight
From lovers' food till morrow deep midnight.

LYSANDER I will, my Hermia.

[Exit Hermia.

Helena adieu;
As you on him, Demetrius dote on you!

[Exit Lysander.

HELENA How happy some o'er other some can be!
Through Athens I am thought as fair as she.
But what of that? Demetrius thinks not so;
He will not know what all but he do know.
And as he errs, doting on Hermia's eyes,
So I, admiring of his qualities.
Things base and vile, holding no quantity,
Love can transpose to form and dignity.
Love looks not with the eyes, but with the mind;
And therefore is wing'd Cupid painted blind.
Nor hath Love's mind of any judgment taste;
Wings and no eyes figure unheedy haste;
And therefore is Love said to be a child,
Because in choice he is so oft beguil'd.
As waggish boys in game themselves forswear,
So the boy Love is perjur'd everywhere;
For ere Demetrius look'd on Hermia's eyne,
He hail'd down oaths that he was only mine;
And when this hail some heat from Hermia felt,
So he dissolv'd, and show'rs of oaths did melt.
I will go tell him of fair Hermia's flight;
Then to the wood will he to-morrow night
Pursue her; and for this intelligence
If I have thanks, it is a dear expense.
But herein mean I to enrich my pain,
To have his sight thither and back again.

[Exit.

SCENE II. *Athens. Quince's house.*

Enter QUINCE, SNUG, BOTTOM, FLUTE, SNOUT and STARVELING.

QUINCE Is all our company here?

BOTTOM You were best to call them generally, man by man, according to the scrip.

QUINCE Here is the scroll of every man's name which is thought fit, through all Athens, to play in our interlude before the Duke and the Duchess on his wedding-day at night.

BOTTOM First, good Peter Quince, say what the play treats on; then read the names of the actors; and so grow to a point.

QUINCE Marry, our play is 'The most Lamentable Comedy and most Cruel Death of Pyramus and Thisby'.

BOTTOM A very good piece of work, I assure you, and a merry. Now, good Peter Quince, call forth your actors by the scroll. Masters, spread yourselves.

QUINCE Answer, as I call you. Nick Bottom, the weaver.

BOTTOM Ready. Name what part I am for, and proceed.

QUINCE You, Nick Bottom, are set down for Pyramus.

BOTTOM What is Pyramus? A lover, or a tyrant?

QUINCE A lover, that kills himself most gallant for love.

BOTTOM That will ask some tears in the true performing of it. If I do it, let the audience look to their eyes; I will move storms; I will condole in some measure. To the rest – yet my chief humour is for a tyrant. I could play Ercles rarely, or a part to tear a cat in, to make all split.

'The raging rocks
And shivering shocks
Shall break the locks
Of prison gates;
And Phibbus' car
Shall shine from far,
And make and mar
The foolish Fates.'

This was lofty. Now name the rest of the players. This is Ercles' vein, a tyrant's vein: a lover is more condoling.

QUINCE Francis Flute, the bellows-mender.

FLUTE Here, Peter Quince.

QUINCE Flute, you must take Thisby on you.

FLUTE What is Thisby? A wand'ring knight?

QUINCE It is the lady that Pyramus must love.

FLUTE Nay, faith, let not me play a woman; I have a beard coming.

QUINCE That's all one; you shall play it in a mask, and you may speak as small as you will.

BOTTOM An I may hide my face, let me play Thisby too. I'll speak in a monstrous little voice: 'Thisne, Thisne!' [*Then speaking small*] 'Ah Pyramus, my lover dear! Thy Thisby dear, and lady dear!'

QUINCE No, no, you must play Pyramus; and, Flute, you Thisby.

BOTTOM Well; proceed.

QUINCE Robin Starveling, the tailor.

STAR Here, Peter Quince.

QUINCE Robin Starveling, you must play Thisby's mother. Tom Snout, the tinker.

SNOUT Here, Peter Quince.

QUINCE You, Pyramus' father; myself, Thisby's father; Snug, the joiner, you, the lion's part. And, I hope, here is a play fitted.

SNUG Have you the lion's part written? Pray you, if it be, give it me, for I am slow of study.

QUINCE You may do it extempore, for it is nothing but roaring.

BOTTOM Let me play the lion too. I will roar that I will do any man's heart good to hear me; I will roar that I will make the Duke say 'Let him roar again, let him roar again'.

QUINCE An you should do it too terribly, you would fright the Duchess and the ladies, that they would shriek; and that were enough to hang us all.

ALL That would hang us, every mother's son.

BOTTOM I grant you, friends, if you should fright the ladies out of their wits, they would have no more discretion but to hang us; but I will aggravate my voice so, that I will roar you as gently as any sucking dove; I will roar you an 'twere any nightingale.

QUINCE You can play no part but Pyramus; for Pyramus is a sweet-fac'd man; a proper man, as one shall see in a summer's day; a most lovely gentleman-like man; therefore you must needs play Pyramus.

BOTTOM Well, I will undertake it. What beard were I best to play it in?

QUINCE Why, what you will.

BOTTOM I will discharge it in either your straw-colour beard, your orange-tawny beard, your purple-in-grain beard, or your French-crown-colour beard, your perfect yellow.

QUINCE Some of your French crowns have no hair at all, and then you will play bare-fac'd. But, masters, here are your parts; and I am to entreat you, request you, and desire you, to con them by to-morrow night; and meet me in the palace wood, a mile without the town, by moonlight; there will we rehearse; for if we meet in the city, we shall be dogg'd with company, and our devices known. In the meantime I will draw a bill of properties, such as our play wants. I pray you, fail me not.

BOTTOM We will meet; and there we may rehearse most obscenely and courageously. Take pains; be perfect; adieu.

QUINCE At the Duke's oak we meet.

BOTTOM Enough; hold, or cut bow-strings.

[*Exeunt.*

ACT TWO

SCENE I. *A wood near Athens.*

Enter a Fairy at one door, and PUCK at another.

PUCK How now, spirit! whither wander you?

FAIRIES Over hill, over dale,
Thorough bush, thorough brier,
Over park, over pale,
Thorough flood, thorough fire,
I do wander every where,
Swifter than the moon's sphere;
And I serve the Fairy Queen,
To dew her orbs upon the green.
The cowslips tall her pensioners be;
In their gold coats spots you see;
Those be rubies, fairy favours,
In those freckles live their savours.
I must go seek some dewdrops here,
And hang a pearl in every cowslip's ear.
Farewell, thou lob of spirits; I'll be gone.
Our Queen and all her elves come here anon.

PUCK The King doth keep his revels here to-night;
Take heed the Queen come not within his sight;
For Oberon is passing fell and wrath,
Because that she as her attendant hath
A lovely boy, stolen from an Indian king.
She never had so sweet a changeling;
And jealous Oberon would have the child
Knight of his train, to trace the forests wild;
But she perforce withholds the loved boy,
Crowns him with flowers, and makes him all her joy.
And now they never meet in grove or green,
By fountain clear, or spangled starlight sheen,
But they do square, that all their elves for fear
Creep into acorn cups and hide them there.

FAIRIES Either I mistake your shape and making quite,
Or else you are that shrewd and knavish sprite
Call'd Robin Goodfellow. Are not you he
That frights the maidens of the villagery,
Skim milk, and sometimes labour in the quern,
And bootless make the breathless housewife churn,
And sometime make the drink to bear no barm,
Mislead night-wanderers, laughing at their harm?
Those that Hobgoblin call you, and sweet Puck,
You do their work, and they shall have good luck.
Are not you he?

PUCK Thou speakest aright:
I am that merry wanderer of the night.
I jest to Oberon, and make him smile
When I a fat and bean-fed horse beguile,
Neighing in likeness of a filly foal;
And sometime lurk I in a gossip's bowl
In very likeness of a roasted crab,
And, when she drinks, against her lips I bob,

And on her withered dewlap pour the ale.
The wisest aunt, telling the saddest tale,
Sometime for three-foot stool mistaketh me;
Then slip I from her bum, down topples she,
And 'tailor' cries, and falls into a cough;
And then the whole quire hold their hips and laugh,
And waxen in their mirth, and neeze, and swear
A merrier hour was never wasted there.
But room, fairy, here comes Oberon.

FAIRIES And here my mistress. Would that he were gone!

Enter OBERON at one door, with his Train, and TITANIA, at another, with hers.

OBERON Ill met by moonlight, proud Titania.

TITANIA What, jealous Oberon! Fairies, skip hence;
I have forsworn his bed and company.

OBERON Tarry, rash wanton; am not I thy lord?

TITANIA Then I must be thy lady; but I know
When thou hast stolen away from fairy land,
And in the shape of Corin sat all day,
Playing on pipes of corn, and versing love
To amorous Phillida. Why art thou here,
Come from the farthest steep of India,
But that, forsooth, the bouncing Amazon,
Your buskin'd mistress and your warrior love,
To Theseus must be wedded, and you come
To give their bed joy and prosperity?

OBERON How canst thou thus, for shame, Titania,
Glance at my credit with Hippolyta,
Knowing I know thy love to Theseus?
Didst not thou lead him through the glimmering night
From Perigouna, whom he ravished?
And make him with fair AEgles break his faith,
With Ariadne and Antiopa?

TITANIA These are the forgeries of jealousy;
And never, since the middle summer's spring,
Met we on hill, in dale, forest, or mead,
By paved fountain, or by rushy brook,
Or in the beached margent of the sea,
To dance our ringlets to the whistling wind,
But with thy brawls thou hast disturb'd our sport.
Therefore the winds, piping to us in vain,
As in revenge, have suck'd up from the sea
Contagious fogs; which, falling in the land,
Hath every pelting river made so proud
That they have overborne their continents.
The ox hath therefore stretch'd his yoke in vain,
The ploughman lost his sweat, and the green corn
Hath rotted ere his youth attain'd a beard;
The fold stands empty in the drowned field,
And crows are fatted with the murrion flock;
The nine men's morris is fill'd up with mud,
And the quaint mazes in the wanton green,
For lack of tread, are undistinguishable.
The human mortals want their winter here;
No night is now with hymn or carol blest;
Therefore the moon, the governess of floods,
Pale in her anger, washes all the air,
That rheumatic diseases do abound.
And thorough this distemperature we see
The seasons alter: hoary-headed frosts
Fall in the fresh lap of the crimson rose;
And on old Hiems' thin and icy crown
An odorous chaplet of sweet summer buds
Is, as in mockery, set. The spring, the summer,
The childing autumn, angry winter, change
Their wonted liveries; and the mazed world,
By their increase, now knows not which is which.
And this same progeny of evils comes
From our debate, from our dissension;
We are their parents and original.

OBERON Do you amend it, then; it lies in you.
Why should Titania cross her Oberon?
I do but beg a little changeling boy
To be my henchman.

TITANIA Set your heart at rest;
The fairy land buys not the child of me.
His mother was a vot'ress of my order;
And, in the spiced Indian air, by night,
Full often hath she gossip'd by my side;
And sat with me on Neptune's yellow sands,
Marking th' embarked traders on the flood;
When we have laugh'd to see the sails conceive,
And grow big-bellied with the wanton wind;
Which she, with pretty and with swimming gait
Following – her womb then rich with my young squire –
Would imitate, and sail upon the land,
To fetch me trifles, and return again,As from a voyage, rich with merchandise.
But she, being mortal, of that boy did die;
And for her sake do I rear up her boy;
And for her sake I will not part with him.

OBERON How long within this wood intend you stay?

TITANIA Perchance till after Theseus' wedding-day.
If you will patiently dance in our round,
And see our moonlight revels, go with us;
If not, shun me, and I will spare your haunts.

OBERON Give me that boy and I will go with thee.

TITANIA Not for thy fairy kingdom. Fairies, away.
We shall chide downright if I longer stay.

[*Exit Titania with her Train.*

OBERON Well, go thy way; thou shalt not from this grove
Till I torment thee for this injury.
My gentle Puck, come hither. Thou remembr'rest
Since once I sat upon a promontory,
And heard a mermaid on a dolphin's back
Uttering such dulcet and harmonious breath
That the rude sea grew civil at her song,
And certain stars shot madly from their spheres
To hear the sea-maid's music.

PUCK I remember.

OBERON That very time I saw, but thou couldst not,
Flying between the cold moon and the earth
Cupid, all arm'd; a certain aim he took
At a fair vestal, throned by the west,
And loos'd his love-shaft smartly from his bow,
As it should pierce a hundred thousand hearts;
But I might see young Cupid's fiery shaft
Quench'd in the chaste beams of the wat'ry moon;
And the imperial vot'ress passed on,
In maiden meditation, fancy-free.
Yet mark'd I where the bolt of Cupid fell.
It fell upon a little western flower,
Before milk-white, now purple with love's wound,
And maidens call it Love-in-idleness.
Fetch me that flow'r, the herb I showed thee once.
The juice of it on sleeping eyelids laid
Will make or man or woman madly dote
Upon the next live creature that it sees.
Fetch me this herb, and be thou here again
Ere the leviathan can swim a league.

PUCK I'll put a girdle round about the earth
In forty minutes. *[Exit Puck.*

OBERON Having once this juice,
I'll watch Titania when she is asleep,
And drop the liquor of it in her eyes;
The next thing then she waking looks upon,
Be it on lion, bear, or wolf, or bull,
On meddling monkey, or on busy ape,
She shall pursue it with the soul of love.
And ere I take this charm from off her sight,
As I can take it with another herb,
I'll make her render up her page to me.
But who comes here? I am invisible;
And I will overhear their conference.

Enter DEMETRIUS, HELENA following him.

DEMETRIUS I love thee not, therefore pursue me not.
Where is Lysander and fair Hermia?
The one I'll slay, the other slayeth me.
Thou told'st me they were stol'n unto this wood,
And here am I, and wood within this wood,
Because I cannot meet my Hermia.
Hence, get thee gone, and follow me no more.

HELENA You draw me, you hard-hearted adamant;
But yet you draw not iron, for my heart
Is true as steel. Leave you your power to draw.
And I shall have no power to follow you.

DEMETRIUS Do I entice you? Do I speak you fair?
Or, rather, do I not in plainest truth
Tell you I do not nor I cannot love you?

HELENA And even for that do I love you the more.
I am your spaniel; and, Demetrius,
The more you beat me, I will fawn on you.
Use me but as your spaniel, spurn me, strike me,
Neglect me, lose me; only give me leave,
Unworthy as I am, to follow you.
What worser place can I beg in your love,
And yet a place of high respect with me,
Than to be used as you use your dog?

DEMETRIUS Tempt not too much the hatred of my spirit;
For I am sick when I do look on thee.

HELENA And I am sick when I look not on you.

DEMETRIUS You do impeach your modesty too much
To leave the city and commit yourself
Into the hands of one that loves you not;
To trust the opportunity of night,
And the ill counsel of a desert place,
With the rich worth of your virginity.

HELENA Your virtue is my privilege for that:
It is not night when I do see your face,
Therefore I think I am not in the night;
Nor doth this wood lack worlds of company,
For you, in my respect, are all the world.
Then how can it be said I am alone
When all the world is here to look on me?

DEMETRIUS I'll run from thee and hide me in the brakes,
And leave thee to the mercy of wild beasts.

HELENA The wildest hath not such a heart as you.
Run when you will; the story shall be chang'd:
Apollo flies, and Daphne holds the chase;
The dove pursues the griffin; the mild hind
Makes speed to catch the tiger – bootless speed,
When cowardice pursues and valour flies.

DEMETRIUS I will not stay thy questions; let me go;
Or, if thou follow me, do not believe
But I shall do thee mischief in the wood.

HELENA Ay, in the temple, in the town, the field,
You do me mischief. Fie, Demetrius!
Your wrongs do set a scandal on my sex.
We cannot fight for love as men may do;
We should be woo'd, and were not made to woo. *[Exit Demetrius.*

I'll follow thee, and make a heaven of hell,
To die upon the hand I love so well.
[Exit Helena.

OBERON Fare thee well, nymph; ere he do leave this grove,
Thou shalt fly him, and he shall seek thy love.
Re-enter PUCK.
Hast thou the flower there? Welcome, wanderer.

PUCK Ay, there it is.

OBERON I pray thee give it me.
I know a bank where the wild thyme blows,
Where oxlips and the nodding violet grows,
Quite over-canopied with luscious wood-bine,
With sweet musk-roses, and with eglantine;
There sleeps Titania sometime of the night,
Lull'd in these flowers with dances and delight;
And there the snake throws her enamell'd skin,
Weed wide enough to wrap a fairy in;
And with the juice of this I'll streak her eyes,
And make her full of hateful fantasies.
Take thou some of it, and seek through this grove:
A sweet Athenian lady is in love
With a disdainful youth; anoint his eyes;
But do it when the next thing he espies
May be the lady. Thou shalt know the man
By the Athenian garments he hath on.
Effect it with some care, that he may prove
More fond on her than she upon her love.
And look thou meet me ere the first cock crow.

PUCK Fear not, my lord; your servant shall do so.
[Exeunt.

SCENE II. *Another part of the wood.*

Enter TITANIA, with her Train.

TITANIA Come now, a roundel and a fairy song;
Then, for the third part of a minute, hence:
Some to kill cankers in the musk-rose buds;
Some war with rere-mice for their leathern wings,
To make my small elves coats; and some keep back
The clamorous owl that nightly hoots and wonders
At our quaint spirits. Sing me now asleep;
Then to your offices, and let me rest.

The Fairies sing.

1 FAIRY You spotted snakes with double tongue,
Thorny hedgehogs, be not seen;
Newts and blind-worms, do no wrong,
Come not near our fairy Queen.

CHORUS Philomel with melody
Sing in our sweet lullaby.
Lulla, lulla, lullaby; lulla, lulla, lullaby.
Never harm
Nor spell nor charm
Come our lovely lady nigh.
So good night, with lullaby.

2 FAIRY Weaving spiders, come not here;
Hence, you long-legg'd spinners, hence.
Beetles black, approach not near;
Worm nor snail do no offence.

CHORUS Philomel with melody, etc.
[Titania sleeps.

1 FAIRY Hence away; now all is well.
One aloof stand sentinel.
[Exeunt Fairies.

Enter OBERON and squeezes the flower on Titania's eyelids.

OBERON What thou seest when thou dost wake,
Do it for thy true-love take;
Love and languish for his sake.
Be it ounce, or cat, or bear,
Pard, or boar with bristled hair,
In thy eye that shall appear
When thou wak'st, it is thy dear.
Wake when some vile thing is near. *[Exit.*

Enter LYSANDER and HERMIA.

LYSANDER Fair love, you faint with wand'ring in the wood;
And, to speak troth, I have forgot our way;
We'll rest us, Hermia, if you think it good,
And tarry for the comfort of the day.

HERMIA Be it so, Lysander: find you out a bed,
For I upon this bank will rest my head.

LYSANDER One turf shall serve as pillow for us both;
One heart, one bed, two bosoms, and one troth.

HERMIA Nay, good Lysander; for my sake, my dear,
Lie further off yet; do not lie so near.

LYSANDER O, take the sense, sweet, of my innocence!
Love takes the meaning in love's conference.
I mean that my heart unto yours is knit,
So that but one heart we can make of it;
Two bosoms interchained with an oath,
So then two bosoms and a single troth.
Then by your side no bed-room me deny,
For lying so, Hermia, I do not lie.

HERMIA Lysander riddles very prettily.
Now much beshrew my manners and my pride,
If Hermia meant to say Lysander lied!
But, gentle friend, for love and courtesy
Lie further off, in human modesty;
Such separation as may well be said

Becomes a virtuous bachelor and a maid,
So far be distant; and good night, sweet friend.
Thy love ne'er alter till thy sweet life end!

LYSANDER Amen, amen, to that fair prayer say I;
And then end life when I end loyalty!
Here is my bed; sleep give thee all his rest!

HERMIA With half that wish the wisher's eyes be press'd! [*They sleep.*

Enter PUCK.

PUCK Through the forest have I gone,
But Athenian found I none
On whose eyes I might approve
This flower's force in stirring love.
Night and silence – Who is here?
Weeds of Athens he doth wear:
This is he, my master said,
Despised the Athenian maid:
And here the maiden, sleeping sound,
On the dank and dirty ground.
Pretty soul! she durst not lie
Near this lack-love, this kill-courtesy.
Churl, upon thy eyes I throw
All the power this charm doth owe:
When thou wak'st let love forbid
Sleep his seat on thy eyelid.
So awake when I am gone:
For I must now to Oberon. [*Exit.*

Enter DEMETRIUS and HELENA, running.

HELENA Stay, though thou kill me, sweet Demetrius.

DEMETRIUS I charge thee, hence, and do not haunt me thus.

HELENA O, wilt thou darkling leave me? Do not so.

DEMETRIUS Stay on thy peril; I alone will go. [*Exit Demetrius.*

HELENA O, I am out of breath in this fond chase!
The more my prayer, the lesser is my grace.
Happy is Hermia, wheresoe'er she lies,
For she hath blessed and attractive eyes.
How came her eyes so bright? Not with salt tears;
If so, my eyes are oft'ner wash'd than hers.
No, no, I am as ugly as a bear,
For beasts that meet me run away for fear;
Therefore no marvel though Demetrius
Do, as a monster, fly my presence thus.
What wicked and dissembling glass of mine
Made me compare with Hermia's sphery eyne?
But who is here? Lysander! on the ground!
Dead, or asleep? I see no blood, no wound.
Lysander, if you live, good sir, awake.

LYSANDER [*Waking*] And run through fire I will for thy sweet sake.
Transparent Helena! Nature shows art,
That through thy bosom makes me see thy heart.
Where is Demetrius? O, how fit a word
Is that vile name to perish on my sword!

HELENA Do not say so, Lysander; say not so.
What though he love your Hermia? Lord, what though?
Yet Hermia still loves you; then be content.

LYSANDER Content with Hermia! No; I do repent
The tedious minutes I with her have spent.
Not Hermia but Helena I love:
Who will not change a raven for a dove?
The will of man is by his reason sway'd,
And reason says you are the worthier maid.
Things growing are not ripe until their season;
So I, being young, till now ripe not to reason;
And touching now the point of human skill,
Reason becomes the marshal to my will,
And leads me to your eyes, where I o'erlook
Love's stories, written in Love's richest book.

HELENA Wherefore was I to this keen mockery born?
When at your hands did I deserve this scorn?
Is't not enough, is't not enough, young man,
That I did never, no, nor never can,
Deserve a sweet look from Demetrius' eye,
But you must flout my insufficiency?
Good troth, you do me wrong, good sooth, you do,
In such disdainful manner me to woo.
But fare you well; perforce I must confess
I thought you lord of more true gentleness.
O, that a lady of one man refus'd
Should of another therefore be abus'd! [*Exit.*

LYSANDER She sees not Hermia. Hermia, sleep thou there;
And never mayst thou come Lysander near!
For, as a surfeit of the sweetest things
The deepest loathing to the stomach brings,
Or as the heresies that men do leave
Are hated most of those they did deceive,
So thou, my surfeit and my heresy,
Of all be hated, but the most of me!
And, all my powers, address your love and might
To honour Helen, and to be her knight! [*Exit.*

HERMIA [*Starting*] Help me, Lysander, help me; do thy best
To pluck this crawling serpent from my breast.
Ay me, for pity! What a dream was here!
Lysander, look how I do quake with fear.
Methought a serpent eat my heart away,
And you sat smiling at his cruel prey.
Lysander! What, remov'd? Lysander! lord!

What, out of hearing gone? No sound, no word?
Alack, where are you? Speak, an if you hear;
Speak, of all loves! I swoon almost with fear.
No? Then I well perceive you are not nigh.
Either death or you I'll find immediately.

[*Exit.*

ACT THREE

SCENE I. *The wood. Titania lying asleep.*

Enter QUINCE, SNUG, BOTTOM, FLUTE, SNOUT, and STARVELING.

BOTTOM Are we all met?

QUINCE Pat, pat; and here's a marvellous convenient place for our rehearsal. This green plot shall be our stage, this hawthorn brake our tiring-house; and we will do it in action, as we will do it before the Duke.

BOTTOM Peter Quince!

QUINCE What sayest thou, bully Bottom?

BOTTOM There are things in this comedy of Pyramus and Thisby that will never please. First, Pyramus must draw a sword to kill himself; which the ladies cannot abide. How answer you that?

SNOUT By'r lakin, a parlous fear.

STAR I believe we must leave the killing out, when all is done.

BOTTOM Not a whit; I have a device to make all well. Write me a prologue; and let the prologue seem to say we will do no harm with our swords, and that Pyramus is not kill'd indeed; and for the more better assurance, tell them that I Pyramus am not Pyramus but Bottom the weaver. This will put them out of fear.

QUINCE Well, we will have such a prologue; and it shall be written in eight and six.

BOTTOM No, make it two more; let it be written in eight and eight.

SNOUT Will not the ladies be afeard of the lion?

STAR I fear it, I promise you.

BOTTOM Masters, you ought to consider with yourself to bring in – God shield us! – a lion among ladies is a most dreadful thing; for there is not a more fearful wild-fowl than your lion living; and we ought to look to't.

SNOUT Therefore another prologue must tell he is not a lion.

BOTTOM Nay, you must name his name, and half his face must be seen through the lion's neck; and he himself must speak through, saying thus, or to the same defect: 'Ladies,' or 'Fair ladies, I would wish you' or 'I would request you' or 'I would entreat you not to fear, not to tremble. My life for yours! If you think I come hither as a lion, it were pity of my life. No, I am no such thing; I am a man as other men are'. And there, indeed, let him name his name, and tell them plainly he is Snug the joiner.

QUINCE Well, it shall be so. But there is two hard things – that is, to bring the moonlight into a chamber; for, you know, Pyramus and Thisby meet by moonlight.

SNOUT Doth the moon shine that night we play our play?

BOTTOM A calendar, a calendar! Look in the almanack; find out moonshine, find out moonshine.

QUINCE Yes, it doth shine that night.

BOTTOM Why, then may you leave a casement of the great chamber window, where we play, open; and the moon may shine in at the casement.

QUINCE Ay; or else one must come in with a bush of thorns and a lantern, and say he comes to disfigure or to present the person of Moonshine. Then there is another thing: we must have a wall in the great chamber; for Pyramus and Thisby, says the story, did talk through the chink of a wall.

SNOUT You can never bring in a wall. What say you, Bottom?

BOTTOM Some man or other must present Wall; and let him have some plaster, or some loam, or some rough-cast about him, to signify wall; and let him hold his fingers thus, and through that cranny shall Pyramus and Thisby whisper.

QUINCE If that may be, then all is well. Come, sit down, every mother's son, and rehearse your parts. Pyramus, you begin; when you have spoken your speech, enter into that brake; and so every one according to his cue.

Enter PUCK behind.

PUCK What hempen homespuns have we swagg'ring here,
So near the cradle of the Fairy Queen?
What, a play toward! I'll be an auditor;
An actor too perhaps, if I see cause.

QUINCE Speak, Pyramus. Thisby, stand forth.

BOTTOM *Thisby, the flowers of odious savours sweet* –

QUINCE 'Odious' – odorous!

BOTTOM – – *odours savours sweet;*
So hath thy breath, my dearest Thisby dear.
But hark, a voice! Stay thou but here awhile,
And by and by I will to thee appear. [*Exit.*

PUCK A stranger Pyramus than e'er played here! [*Exit.*

FLUTE Must I speak now?

QUINCE Ay, marry, must you; for you must understand he goes but to see a noise that he heard, and is to come again.

FLUTE *Most radiant Pyramus, most lily-white of hue,*
Of colour like the red rose on triumphant brier,
Most brisky juvenal, and eke most lovely Jew,
As true as truest horse, that yet would never tire,
I'll meet thee, Pyramus, at Ninny's tomb.

QUINCE 'Ninus' tomb', man! Why, you must not speak that yet; that you answer to Pyramus. You speak all your part at once, cues and all. Pyramus enter: your cue is past; it is 'never tire'.

FLUTE O – *As true as truest horse, that yet would never tire.*

Re-enter PUCK, and BOTTOM with an ass's head.

BOTTOM *If I were fair, Thisby, I were only thine.*

QUINCE O monstrous! O strange! We are haunted. Pray master! fly, masters! Help! [*Exeunt all but Bottom and Puck.*

PUCK I'll follow you; I'll lead you about a round,
Through bog, through bush, through brake, through brier;
Sometime a horse I'll be, sometime a hound,
A hog, a headless bear, sometime a fire;
And neigh, and bark, and grunt, and roar, and burn,
Like horse, hound, hog, bear, fire, at every turn. [*Exit.*

BOTTOM Why do they run away? This is a knavery of them to make me afeard.

Re-enter SNOUT.

SNOUT O Bottom, thou art chang'd! What do I see on thee?

BOTTOM What do you see? You see an ass-head of your own, do you? [*Exit Snout.*

Re-enter QUINCE.

QUINCE Bless thee, Bottom, bless thee! Thou art translated. [*Exit.*

BOTTOM I see their knavery: this is to make an ass of me; to fright me, if they could. But I will not stir from this place, do what they can; I will walk up and down here, and I will sing, that they shall hear I am not afraid. [*Sings.*

The ousel cock, so black of hue,
With orange-tawny bill,
The throstle with his note so true,
The wren with little quill.

TITANIA What angel wakes me from my flow'ry bed?

BOTTOM [*Sings*]
The finch, the sparrow, and the lark,
The plain-song cuckoo grey,
Whose note full many a man doth mark,
And dares not answer nay –

for, indeed, who would set his wit to so foolish a bird? Who would give a bird the lie, though he cry 'cuckoo' never so?

TITANIA I pray thee, gentle mortal, sing again.
Mine ear is much enamoured of thy note;
So is mine eye enthralled to thy shape;
And thy fair virtue's force perforce doth move me,
On the first view, to say, to swear, I love thee.

BOTTOM Methinks, mistress, you should have little reason for that. And yet, to say the truth, reason and love keep little company together now-a-days. The more the pity that some honest neighbours will not make them friends. Nay, I can gleek upon occasion.

TITANIA Thou art as wise as thou art beautiful.

BOTTOM Not so, neither; but if I had wit enough to get out of this wood, I have enough to serve mine own turn.

TITANIA Out of this wood do not desire to go;
Thou shalt remain here whether thou wilt or no.
I am a spirit of no common rate;
The summer still doth tend upon my state;
And I do love thee; therefore, go with me.
I'll give thee fairies to attend on thee;
And they shall fetch thee jewels from the deep,
And sing, while thou on pressed flowers dost sleep;
And I will purge thy mortal grossness so
That thou shalt like an airy spirit go.
Peaseblossom! Cobweb! Moth! and Mustardseed!

Enter PEASEBLOSSOM, COBWEB, MOTH, and MUSTARDSEED.

PEASEBLOSSOM Ready.

COBWEB And I.

MOTH And I.

MUSTARDSEED And I.

ALL Where shall we go?

TITANIA Be kind and courteous to this gentleman;
Hop in his walks and gambol in his eyes;
Feed him with apricocks and dewberries,
With purple grapes, green figs, and mulberries;
The honey bags steal from the humble-bees,
And for night-tapers crop their waxen thighs,
And light them at the fiery glow-worm's eyes,
To have my love to bed and to arise;

And pluck the wings from painted butterflies,
To fan the moonbeams from his sleeping eyes.
Nod to him, elves, and do him courtesies.

PEASEBLOSSOM Hail, mortal!

COBWEB Hail!

MOTH Hail!

MUSTARDSEED Hail!

BOTTOM I cry your worships mercy, heartily; I beseech your worship's name.

COBWEB Cobweb.

BOTTOM I shall desire you of more acquaintance, good Master Cobweb. If I cut my finger, I shall make bold with you. Your name, honest gentleman?

PEASEBLOSSOM Peaseblossom.

BOTTOM I pray you, commend me to Mistress Squash, your mother, and to Master Peascod, your father. Good Master Peaseblossom I shall desire you of more acquaintance too. Your name, I beseech you, sir?

MUSTARDSEED Mustardseed.

BOTTOM Good Master Mustardseed, I know your patience well. That same cowardly giant-like ox-beef hath devour'd many a gentleman of your house. I promise you your kindred hath made my eyes water ere now. I desire you of more acquaintance, good Master Mustardseed.

TITANIA Come, wait upon him; lead him to my bower.
The moon, methinks, looks with a wat'ry eye;
And when she weeps, weeps every little flower,
Lamenting some enforced chastity.
Tie up my love's tongue, bring him silently.

[Exeunt.

SCENE II. *Another part of the wood.*

Enter OBERON.

OBERON I wonder if Titania be awak'd;
Then, what it was that next came in her eye,
Which she must dote on in extremity.

Enter PUCK.

Here comes my messenger. How now, mad spirit!
What night-rule now about this haunted grove?

PUCK My mistress with a monster is in love.
Near to her close and consecrated bower,
While she was in her dull and sleeping hour,
A crew of patches, rude mechanicals,
That work for bread upon Athenian stalls,
Were met together to rehearse a play
Intended for great Theseus' nuptial day.
The shallowest thickskin of that barren sort,
Who Pyramus presented, in their sport
Forsook his scene and ent'red in a brake;
When I did him at this advantage take,
An ass's nole I fixed on his head.
Anon his Thisby must be answered,
And forth my mimic comes. When they him spy,
As wild geese that the creeping fowler eye,
Or russet-pated choughs, many in sort,
Rising and cawing at the gun's report,
Sever themselves and madly sweep the sky,
So at his sight away his fellows fly;
And at our stamp here, o'er and o'er one falls;
He murder cries, and help from Athens calls.
Their sense thus weak, lost with their fears thus strong,
Made senseless things begin to do them wrong,
For briers and thorns at their apparel snatch;
Some sleeves, some hats, from yielders all things catch.
I led them on in this distracted fear,
And left sweet Pyramus translated there;
When in that moment, so it came to pass,
Titania wak'd, and straightway lov'd an ass.

OBERON This falls out better than I could devise.
But hast thou yet latch'd the Athenian's eyes
With the love-juice, as I did bid thee do?

PUCK I took him sleeping – that is finish'd too –
And the Athenian woman by his side;
That, when he wak'd, of force she must be ey'd.

Enter DEMETRIUS and HERMIA.

OBERON Stand close; this is the same Athenian.

PUCK This is the woman, but not this the man.

DEMETRIUS O, why rebuke you him that loves you so?
Lay breath so bitter on your bitter foe.

HERMIA Now I but chide, but I should use thee worse,
For thou, I fear, hast given me cause to curse.
If thou hast slain Lysander in his sleep,
Being o'er shoes in blood, plunge in the deep,
And kill me too.
The sun was not so true unto the day
As he to me. Would he have stolen away
From sleeping Hermia? I'll believe as soon
This whole earth may be bor'd, and that the moon
May through the centre creep and so displease
Her brother's noontide with th' Antipodes.
It cannot be but thou hast murd'red him;
So should a murderer look – so dead, so grim.

DEMETRIUS So should the murdered look; and so should I,
Pierc'd through the heart with your stern cruelty;
Yet you, the murderer, look as bright, as clear,
As yonder Venus in her glimmering sphere.

HERMIA What's this to my Lysander? Where is he?

Ah, good Demetrius, wilt thou give him me?

DEMETRIUS I had rather give his carcass to my hounds.

HERMIA Out, dog! out, cur! Thou driv'st me past the bounds
Of maiden's patience. Hast thou slain him, then?
Henceforth be never numb'red among men!
O, once tell true; tell true, even for my sake!
Durst thou have look'd upon him being awake,
And hast thou kill'd him sleeping? O brave touch!
Could not a worm, an adder, do so much?
An adder did it; for with doubler tongue
Than thine, thou serpent, never adder stung.

DEMETRIUS You spend your passion on a mispris'd mood:
I am not guilty of Lysander's blood;
Nor is he dead, for aught that I can tell.

HERMIA I pray thee, tell me then that he is well.

DEMETRIUS And if I could, what should I get therefore?

HERMIA A privilege never to see me more.
And from thy hated presence part I so;
See me no more whether he be dead or no. [*Exit.*

DEMETRIUS There is no following her in this fierce vein;
Here, therefore, for a while I will remain.
So sorrow's heaviness doth heavier grow
For debt that bankrupt sleep doth sorrow owe;
Which now in some slight measure it will pay,
If for his tender here I make some stay. [*Lies down.*

OBERON What hast thou done? Thou hast mistaken quite,
And laid the love-juice on some true-love's sight.
Of thy misprision must perforce ensue
Some true love turn'd, and not a false turn'd true.

PUCK Then fate o'er-rules, that, one man holding troth,
A million fail, confounding oath on oath.

OBERON About the wood go swifter than the wind,
And Helena of Athens look thou find;
All fancy-sick she is and pale of cheer,
With sighs of love that costs the fresh blood dear.
By some illusion see thou bring her here;
I'll charm his eyes against she do appear.

PUCK I go, I go; look how I go,
Swifter than arrow from the Tartar's bow. [*Exit.*

OBERON Flower of this purple dye,
Hit with Cupid's archery,
Sink in apple of his eye.
When his love he doth espy,
Let her shine as gloriously
As the Venus of the sky.
When thou wak'st, if she be by,
Beg of her for remedy.

Re-enter PUCK.

PUCK Captain of our fairy band,
Helena is here at hand,
And the youth mistook by me
Pleading for a lover's fee;
Shall we their fond pageant see?
Lord, what fools these mortals be!

OBERON Stand aside. The noise they make
Will cause Demetrius to awake.

PUCK Then will two at once woo one.
That must needs be sport alone;
And those things do best please me
That befall prepost'rously.

Enter LYSANDER and HELENA.

LYSANDER Why should you think that I should woo in scorn?
Scorn and derision never come in tears.
Look when I vow, I weep; and vows so born,
In their nativity all truth appears.
How can these things in me seem scorn to you,
Bearing the badge of faith, to prove them true?

HELENA You do advance your cunning more and more.
When truth kills truth, O devilish-holy fray!
These vows are Hermia's. Will you give her o'er?
Weigh oath with oath, and you will nothing weigh:
Your vows to her and me, put in two scales,
Will even weigh; and both as light as tales.

LYSANDER I had no judgment when to her I swore.

HELENA Nor none, in my mind, now you give her o'er.

LYSANDER Demetrius loves her, and he loves not you.

DEMETRIUS [*Awaking*] O Helen, goddess, nymph, perfect, divine!
To what, my love, shall I compare thine eyne?
Crystal is muddy. O, how ripe in show
Thy lips, those kissing cherries, tempting grow!
That pure congealed white, high Taurus' snow,
Fann'd with the eastern wind, turns to a crow
When thou hold'st up thy hand. O, let me kiss
This princess of pure white, this seal of bliss!

HELENA O spite! O hell! I see you all are bent
To set against me for your merriment.
If you were civil and knew courtesy,
You would not do me thus much injury.

Can you not hate me, as I know you do,
But you must join in souls to mock me too?
If you were men, as men you are in show,
You would not use a gentle lady so:
To vow, and swear, and superpraise my parts,
When I am sure you hate me with your hearts.
You both are rivals, and love Hermia;
And now both rivals, to mock Helena.
A trim exploit, a manly enterprise,
To conjure tears up in a poor maid's eyes
With your derision! None of noble sort
Would so offend a virgin, and extort
A poor soul's patience, all to make you sport.

LYSANDER You are unkind, Demetrius; be not so;
For you love Hermia. This you know I know;
And here, with all good will, with all my heart,
In Hermia's love I yield you up my part;
And yours of Helena to me bequeath,
Whom I do love and will do till my death.

HELENA Never did mockers waste more idle breath.

DEMETRIUS Lysander, keep thy Hermia; I will none.
If e'er I lov'd her, all that love is gone.
My heart to her but as guest-wise sojourn'd,
And now to Helen is it home return'd,
There to remain.

LYSANDER Helen, it is not so.

DEMETRIUS Disparage not the faith thou dost not know,
Lest, to thy peril, thou aby it dear.
Look where thy love comes; yonder is thy dear.

Enter HERMIA.

HERMIA Dark night, that from the eye his function takes,
The ear more quick of apprehension makes;
Wherein it doth impair the seeing sense,
It pays the hearing double recompense.
Thou art not by mine eye, Lysander, found;
Mine ear, I thank it, brought me to thy sound.
But why unkindly didst thou leave me so?

LYSANDER Why should he stay whom love doth press to go?

HERMIA What love could press Lysander from my side?

LYSANDER Lysander's love, that would not let him bide –
Fair Helena, who more engilds the night
Than all yon fiery oes and eyes of light.
Why seek'st thou me? Could not this make thee know
The hate I bare thee made me leave thee so?

HERMIA You speak not as you think; it cannot be.

HELENA Lo, she is one of this confederacy!
Now I perceive they have conjoin'd all three
To fashion this false sport in spite of me.
Injurious Hermia! most ungrateful maid!
Have you conspir'd, have you with these contriv'd,
To bait me with this foul derision?
Is all the counsel that we two have shar'd,
The sisters' vows, the hours that we have spent,
When we have chid the hasty-footed time
For parting us – O, is all forgot?
All school-days' friendship, childhood innocence?
We, Hermia, like two artificial gods,
Have with our needles created both one flower,
Both on one sampler, sitting on one cushion,
Both warbling of one song, both in one key;
As if our hands, our sides, voices, and minds,
Had been incorporate. So we grew together,
Like to a double cherry, seeming parted,
But yet an union in partition,
Two lovely berries moulded on one stem;
So, with two seeming bodies, but one heart;
Two of the first, like coats in heraldry,
Due but to one, and crowned with one crest.
And will you rent our ancient love asunder,
To join with men in scorning your poor friend?
It is not friendly, 'tis not maidenly;
Our sex, as well as I, may chide you for it,
Though I alone do feel the injury.

HERMIA I am amazed at your passionate words;
I scorn you not; it seems that you scorn me.

HELENA Have you not set Lysander, as in scorn,
To follow me and praise my eyes and face?
And made your other love, Demetrius,
Who even but now did spurn me with his foot,
To call me goddess, nymph, divine, and rare,
Precious, celestial? Wherefore speaks he this
To her he hates? And wherefore doth Lysander
Deny your love, so rich within his soul,
And tender me, forsooth, affection,
But by your setting on, by your consent?
What though I be not so in grace as you,
So hung upon with love, so fortunate,
But miserable most, to love unlov'd?
This you should pity rather than despise.

HERMIA I understand not what you mean by this.

HELENA Ay, do – persever, counterfeit sad looks,
Make mouths upon me when I turn my back,
Wink each at other; hold the sweet jest up;
This sport, well carried, shall be chronicled.
If you have any pity, grace, or manners,
You would not make me such an argument.
But fare ye well; 'tis partly my own fault,
Which death, or absence, soon shall remedy.

LYSANDER Stay, gentle Helena; hear my excuse;
My love, my life, my soul, fair Helena!

HELENA O excellent!

HERMIA Sweet, do not scorn her so.

DEMETRIUS If she cannot entreat, I can compel.

LYSANDER Thou canst compel no more than she entreat;
Thy threats have no more strength than her weak prayers.
Helen, I love thee, by my life I do;
I swear by that which I will lose for thee
To prove him false that says I love thee not.
DEMETRIUS I say I love thee more than he can do.
LYSANDER If thou say so, withdraw, and prove it too.
DEMETRIUS Quick, come.
HERMIA Lysander, whereto tends all this?
LYSANDER Away, you Ethiope!
DEMETRIUS No, no, he will
Seem to break loose – take on as you would follow,
But yet come not. You are a tame man; go!
LYSANDER Hang off, thou cat, thou burr; vile thing, let loose,
Or I will shake thee from me like a serpent.
HERMIA Why are you grown so rude? What change is this,
Sweet love?
LYSANDER Thy love! Out, tawny Tartar, out!
Out, loathed med'cine! O hated potion, hence!
HERMIA Do you not jest?
HELENA Yes, sooth; and so do you.
LYSANDER Demetrius, I will keep my word with thee.
DEMETRIUS I would I had your bond; for I perceive
A weak bond holds you; I'll not trust your word.
LYSANDER What, should I hurt her, strike her, kill her dead?
Although I hate her, I'll not harm her so.
HERMIA What! Can you do me greater harm than hate?
Hate me! wherefore? O me! what news, my love?
Am not I Hermia? Are not you Lysander?
I am as fair now as I was erewhile.
Since night you lov'd me; yet since night you left me.
Why then, you left me – O, the gods forbid! –
In earnest, shall I say?
LYSANDER Ay, by my life!
And never did desire to see thee more.
Therefore be out of hope, of question, of doubt;
Be certain, nothing truer; 'tis no jest
That I do hate thee and love Helena.
HERMIA O me! you juggler! you cankerblossom!
You thief of love! What! Have you come by night,
And stol'n my love's heart from him?
HELENA Fine, i' faith!
Have you no modesty, no maiden shame,
No touch of bashfulness? What! Will you tear
Impatient answers from my gentle tongue?
Fie, fie! you counterfeit, you puppet you!
HERMIA 'Puppet!' why so? Ay, that way goes the game.
Now I perceive that she hath made compare
Between our statures; she hath urg'd her height;
And with her personage, her tall personage,
Her height, forsooth, she hath prevail'd with him.
And are you grown so high in his esteem
Because I am so dwarfish and so low?
How low am I, thou painted maypole? Speak.
How low am I? I am not yet so low
But that my nails can reach unto thine eyes.
HELENA I pray you, though you mock me, gentlemen,
Let her not hurt me. I was never curst;
I have no gift at all in shrewishness;
I am a right maid for my cowardice;
Let her not strike me. You perhaps may think,
Because she is something lower than myself,
That I can match her.
HERMIA 'Lower' hark, again.
HELENA Good Hermia, do not be so bitter with me.
I evermore did love you, Hermia,
Did ever keep your counsels, never wrong'd you;
Save that, in love unto Demetrius,
I told him of your stealth unto this wood.
He followed you; for love I followed him;
But he hath chid me hence, and threat'ned me
To strike me, spurn me, nay, to kill me too;
And now, so you will let me quiet go,
To Athens will I bear my folly back,
And follow you no further. Let me go.
You see how simple and how fond I am.
HERMIA Why, get you gone! Who is't that hinders you?
HELENA A foolish heart that I leave here behind.
HERMIA What! with Lysander?
HELENA With Demetrius.
LYSANDER Be not afraid; she shall not harm thee, Helena.
DEMETRIUS No, sir, she shall not, though you take her part.
HELENA O, when she is angry, she is keen and shrewd;
She was a vixen when she went to school;
And, though she be but little, she is fierce.
HERMIA 'Little' again! Nothing but 'low' and 'little'!
Why will you suffer her to flout me thus?
Let me come to her.
LYSANDER Get you gone, you dwarf;
You minimus, of hind'ring knot-grass made;
You bead, you acorn.

DEMETRIUS You are too officious
In her behalf that scorns your services.
Let her alone; speak not of Helena;
Take not her part; for if thou dost intend
Never so little show of love to her,
Thou shalt aby it.

LYSANDER Now she holds me not.
Now follow, if thou dar'st, to try whose right,
Of thine or mine, is most in Helena.

DEMETRIUS Follow! Nay, I'll go with thee, cheek by jowl.

[Exeunt Lysander and Demetrius.

HERMIA You, mistress, all this coil is long of you.
Nay, go not back.

HELENA I will not trust you, I;
Nor longer stay in your curst company.
Your hands than mine are quicker for a fray;
My legs are longer though, to run away.
[*Exit*.

HERMIA I am amaz'd, and know not what to say.

[Exit.

OBERON This is thy negligence. Still thou mistak'st,
Or else committ'st thy knaveries wilfully.

PUCK Believe me, king of shadows, I mistook.
Did not you tell me I should know the man
By the Athenian garments he had on?
And so far blameless proves my enterprise
That I have 'nointed an Athenian's eyes;
And so far am I glad it so did sort,
As this their jangling I esteem a sport.

OBERON Thou seest these lovers seek a place to fight.
Hie therefore, Robin, overcast the night;
The starry welkin cover thou anon
With drooping fog as black as Acheron,
And lead these testy rivals so astray
As one come not within another's way.
Like to Lysander sometime frame thy tongue,
Then stir Demetrius up with bitter wrong;
And sometime rail thou like Demetrius;
And from each other look thou lead them thus,
Till o'er their brows death-counterfeiting sleep
With leaden legs and batty wings doth creep.
Then crush this herb into Lysander's eye;
Whose liquor hath this virtuous property,
To take from hence all error with his might
And make his eyeballs roll with wonted sight.
When they next wake, all this derision
Shall seem a dream and fruitless vision;
And back to Athens shall the lovers wend
With league whose date till death shall never end.
Whiles I in this affair do thee employ,
I'll to my queen, and beg her Indian boy;
And then I will her charmed eye release
From monster's view, and all things shall be peace.

PUCK My fairy lord, this must be done with haste,
For night's swift dragons cut the clouds full fast;
And yonder shines Aurora's harbinger,
At whose approach ghosts, wand'ring here and there,
Troop home to churchyards. Damned spirits all,
That in cross-ways and floods have burial,
Already to their wormy beds are gone,
For fear lest day should look their shames upon;
They wilfully themselves exil'd from light,
And must for aye consort with black-brow'd night.

OBERON But we are spirits of another sort:
I with the Morning's love have oft made sport;
And, like a forester, the groves may tread
Even till the eastern gate, all fiery red,
Opening on Neptune with fair blessed beams,
Turns into yellow gold his salt green streams.
But, notwithstanding, haste, make no delay;
We may effect this business yet ere day.

[Exit Oberon.

PUCK Up and down, up and down,
I will lead them up and down.
I am fear'd in field and town.
Goblin, lead them up and down.

Here comes one.

Enter LYSANDER.

LYSANDER Where art thou, proud Demetrius? Speak thou now.

PUCK Here, villain, drawn and ready. Where art thou?

LYSANDER I will be with thee straight.

PUCK Follow me, then,
To plainer ground.

[Exit Lysander as following the voice.

Enter DEMETRIUS.

DEMETRIUS Lysander, speak again.
Thou runaway, thou coward, art thou fled?
Speak! In some bush? Where dost thou hide thy head?

PUCK Thou coward, art thou bragging to the stars,
Telling the bushes that thou look'st for wars,
And wilt not come? Come, recreant, come, thou child;
I'll whip thee with a rod. He is defil'd
That draws a sword on thee.

DEMETRIUS Yea, art thou there?

PUCK Follow my voice; we'll try no manhood here.

[Exeunt.

Re-enter LYSANDER.

LYSANDER He goes before me, and still dares me on;
When I come where he calls, then he is gone.
The villain is much lighter heel'd than I.
I followed fast, but faster he did fly,
That fallen am I in dark uneven way,
And here will rest me. [*Lies down*] Come, thou gentle day.
For if but once thou show me thy grey light,
I'll find Demetrius, and revenge this spite.
[*Sleeps.*

Re-enter PUCK and DEMETRIUS.

PUCK Ho, ho, ho! Coward, why com'st thou not?
DEMETRIUS Abide me, if thou dar'st; for well I wot
Thou run'st before me, shifting every place,
And dar'st not stand, nor look me in the face.
Where art thou now?
PUCK Come hither; I am here.
DEMETRIUS Nay, then, thou mock'st me. Thou shalt buy this dear,
If ever I thy face by daylight see;
Now, go thy way. Faintness constraineth me
To measure out my length on this cold bed.
By day's approach look to be visited.
[*Lies down and sleeps.*

Enter HELENA.

HELENA O weary night, O long and tedious night,
Abate thy hours! Shine comforts from the east,
That I may back to Athens by daylight,
From these that my poor company detest.
And sleep, that sometimes shuts up sorrow's eye,
Steal me awhile from mine own company.
[*Sleeps.*
PUCK Yet but three? Come one more;
Two of both kinds makes up four.
Here she comes, curst and sad.
Cupid is a knavish lad,
Thus to make poor females mad.

Enter HERMIA.

HERMIA Never so weary, never so in woe,
Bedabbled with the dew, and torn with briers,
I can no further crawl, no further go;
My legs can keep no pace with my desires.
Here will I rest me till the break of day.
Heavens shield Lysander, if they mean a fray!
[*Lies down and sleeps.*
PUCK On the ground
Sleep sound;
I'll apply
To your eye,
Gentle lover, remedy.
[*Squeezing the juice on Lysander's eyes.*
When thou wak'st,
Thou tak'st
True delight
In the sight
Of thy former lady's eye;
And the country proverb known,
That every man should take his own,
In your waking shall be shown.
Jack shall have Jill;
Nought shall go ill;
The man shall have this mare again, and all shall be well.
[*Exit.*

ACT FOUR

SCENE I. *The wood. Lysander, Demetrius, Helena, and Hermia, lying asleep.*

Enter TITANIA and BOTTOM; PEASEBLOSSOM, COBWEB, MOTH, MUSTARDSEED and other Fairies attending; OBERON behind, unseen.

TITANIA Come, sit thee down upon this flow'ry bed,
While I thy amiable cheeks do coy,
And stick musk-roses in thy sleek smooth head,
And kiss thy fair large ears, my gentle joy.
BOTTOM Where's Peaseblossom?
PEASEBLOSSOM Ready.
BOTTOM Scratch my head, Peaseblossom. Where's Mounsieur Cobweb?
COBWEB Ready.
BOTTOM Mounsieur Cobweb; good mounsieur, get you your weapons in your hand and kill me a red-hipp'd humble-bee on the top of a thistle; and, good mounsieur, bring me the honey-bag. Do not fret yourself too much in the action, mounsieur; and, good mounsieur, have a care the honey-bag break not; I would be loath to have you overflowen with a honey-bag, signior. Where's Mounsieur Mustardseed?
MUSTARDSEED Ready.
BOTTOM Give me your neaf, Mounsieur Mustardseed. Pray you, leave your curtsy, good mounsieur.
MUSTARDSEED What's your will?
BOTTOM Nothing, good mounsieur, but to help Cavalery Cobweb to scratch. I must to the barber's, mounsieur; for methinks I am marvellous hairy about the face; and I am such a

tender ass, if my hair do but tickle me I must scratch.

TITANIA What, wilt thou hear some music, my sweet love?

BOTTOM I have a reasonable good ear in music. Let's have the tongs and the bones.

TITANIA Or say, sweet love, what thou desirest to eat.

BOTTOM Truly, a peck of provender; I could munch your good dry oats. Methinks I have a great desire to a bottle of hay. Good hay, sweet hay, hath no fellow.

TITANIA I have a venturous fairy that shall seek
The squirrel's hoard, and fetch thee new nuts.

BOTTOM I had rather have a handful or two of dried peas. But, I pray you, let none of your people stir me; I have an exposition of sleep come upon me.

TITANIA Sleep thou, and I will wind thee in my arms.
Fairies, be gone, and be all ways away.

[*Exeunt Fairies.*

So doth the woodbine the sweet honeysuckle
Gently entwist; the female ivy so
Enrings the barky fingers of the elm.
O, how I love thee! how I dote on thee!

[*They sleep.*

Enter PUCK.

OBERON [*Advancing*] Welcome, good Robin.
Seest thou this sweet sight?
Her dotage now I do begin to pity;
For, meeting her of late behind the wood,
Seeking sweet favours for this hateful fool,
I did upbraid her and fall out with her.
For she his hairy temples then had rounded
With coronet of fresh and fragrant flowers;
And that same dew which sometime on the buds
Was wont to swell like round and orient pearls
Stood now within the pretty flowerets' eyes,
Like tears that did their own disgrace bewail.
When I had at my pleasure taunted her,
And she in mild terms begg'd my patience,
I then did ask of her changeling child;
Which straight she gave me, and her fairy sent
To bear him to my bower in fairy land.
And now I have the boy, I will undo
This hateful imperfection of her eyes.
And, gentle Puck, take this transformed scalp
From off the head of this Athenian swain,
That he awaking when the other do
May all to Athens back again repair,
And think no more of this night's accidents
But as the fierce vexation of a dream.
But first I will release the Fairy Queen.

[*Touching her eyes.*

Be as thou wast wont to be;
See as thou was wont to see.
Dian's bud o'er Cupid's flower
Hath such force and blessed power.
Now, my Titania; wake you, my sweet queen.

TITANIA My Oberon! What visions have I seen!
Methought I was enamour'd of an ass.

OBERON There lies your love.

TITANIA How came these things to pass?
O, how mine eyes do loathe his visage now!

OBERON Silence awhile. Robin, take off this head.
Titania, music call; and strike more dead
Than common sleep of all these five the sense.

TITANIA Music, ho, music, such as charmeth sleep!

PUCK Now when thou wak'st with thine own fool's eyes peep.

OBERON Sound, music. Come, my Queen, take hands with me, [*Music.*
And rock the ground whereon these sleepers be.
Now thou and I are new in amity,
And will to-morrow midnight solemnly
Dance in Duke Theseus' house triumphantly,
And bless it to all fair prosperity.
There shall the pairs of faithful lovers be
Wedded, with Theseus, all in jollity.

PUCK Fairy King, attend and mark;
I do hear the morning lark.

OBERON Then, my Queen, in silence sad,
Trip we after night's shade.
We the globe can compass soon,
Swifter than the wand'ring moon.

TITANIA Come, my lord; and in our flight,
Tell me how it came this night
That I sleeping here was found
With these mortals on the ground.

[*Exeunt.*

To the winding of horns, enter THESEUS, HIPPOLYTA, EGEUS, and Train.

THESEUS Go, one of you, find out the forester;
For now our observation is perform'd,
And since we have the vaward of the day,
My love shall hear the music of my hounds.
Uncouple in the western valley; let them go.
Dispatch, I say, and find the forester.

[*Exit an attendant.*

We will, fair Queen, up to the mountain's top,
And mark the musical confusion
Of hounds and echo in conjunction.

HIPPOLYTA I was with Hercules and Cadmus once
When in a wood of Crete they bay'd the bear
With hounds of Sparta; never did I hear

Such gallant chiding, for, besides the groves,
The skies, the fountains, every region near,
Seem'd all one mutual cry. I never heard
So musical a discord, such sweet thunder.

THESEUS My hounds are bred out of the Spartan kind,
So flew'd, so sanded; and their heads are hung
With ears that sweep away the morning dew;
Crook-knee'd and dew-lapp'd like Thessalian bulls;
Slow in pursuit, but match'd in mouth like bells,
Each under each. A cry more tuneable
Was never holla'd to, nor cheer'd with horn,
In Crete, in Sparta, nor in Thessaly.
Judge when you hear. But, soft, what nymphs are these?

EGEUS My lord, this is my daughter here asleep.
And this Lysander, this Demetrius is,
This Helena, old Nedar's Helena.
I wonder of their being here together.

THESEUS No doubt they rose up early to observe
The rite of May; and, hearing our intent,
Came here in grace of our solemnity.
But speak, Egeus; is not this the day
That Hermia should give answer of her choice?

EGEUS It is, my lord.

THESEUS Go, bid the huntsmen wake them with their horns.

[Horns and shout within. The sleepers awake and kneel to Theseus.

Good-morrow, friends. Saint Valentine is past;
Begin these wood-birds but to couple now?

LYSANDER Pardon, my lord.

THESEUS I pray you all, stand up.
I know you two are rival enemies;
How comes this gentle concord in the world
That hatred is so far from jealousy
To sleep by hate, and fear no enmity?

LYSANDER My lord, I shall reply amazedly,
Half sleep, half waking; but as yet, I swear,
I cannot truly say how I came here,
But, as I think – for truly would I speak,
And now I do bethink me, so it is –
I came with Hermia hither. Our intent
Was to be gone from Athens, where we might,
Without the peril of the Athenian law –

EGEUS Enough, enough, my Lord; you have enough;
I beg the law, the law upon his head.
They would have stol'n away, they would, Demetrius,
Thereby to have defeated you and me:
You of your wife, and me of my consent,
Of my consent that she should be your wife.

DEMETRIUS My lord, fair Helen told me of their stealth,
Of this their purpose hither to this wood;
And I in fury hither followed them,
Fair Helena in fancy following me.
But, my good lord, I wot not by what power –
But by some power it is – my love to Hermia,
Melted as the snow, seems to me now
As the remembrance of an idle gaud
Which in my childhood I did dote upon;
And all the faith, the virtue of my heart,
The object and the pleasure of mine eye,
Is only Helena. To her, my lord,
Was I betroth'd ere I saw Hermia.
But, like a sickness, did I loathe this food;
But, as in health, come to my natural taste,
Now I do wish it, love it, long for it,
And will for evermore be true to it.

THESEUS Fair lovers, you are fortunately met;
Of this discourse we more will hear anon.
Egeus, I will overbear your will;
For in the temple, by and by, with us
These couples shall eternally be knit.
And, for the morning now is something worn,
Our purpos'd hunting shall be set aside.
Away with us to Athens, three and three;
We'll hold a feast in great solemnity.
Come, Hippolyta.

[Exeunt Theseus, Hippolyta, Egeus and Train.

DEMETRIUS These things seem small and undistinguishable,
Like far-off mountains turned into clouds.

HERMIA Methinks I see these things with parted eye,
When every thing seems double.

HELENA So methinks;
And I have found Demetrius like a jewel,
Mine own, and not mine own.

DEMETRIUS Are you sure
That we are awake? It seems to me
That yet we sleep, we dream. Do not you think
The Duke was here, and bid us follow him?

HERMIA Yea, and my father.

HELENA And Hippolyta.

LYSANDER And he did bid us follow to the temple.

DEMETRIUS Why, then, we are awake; let's follow him;
And by the way let us recount our dreams.

[Exeunt.

BOTTOM *[Awaking]* When my cue comes, call me, and I will answer. My next is 'Most fair Pyramus'. Heigh-ho! Peter Quince! Flute, the bellows-mender! Snout, the tinker! Starveling! God's my life, stol'n hence, and left me asleep! I have had a most rare vision. I have had a dream, past the wit of man to say what dream it was.

Man is but an ass if he go about to expound this dream. Methought I was – there is no man can tell what. Methought I was, and methought I had, but man is but a patch'd fool, if he will offer to say what methought I had. The eye of man hath not heard, the ear of man hath not seen, man's hand is not able to taste, his tongue to conceive, nor his heart to report, what my dream was. I will get Peter Quince to write a ballad of this dream. It shall be call'd 'Bottom's Dream', because it hath no bottom; and I will sing it in the latter end of a play, before the Duke. Peradventure, to make it the more gracious, I shall sing it at her death.

[*Exit.*

SCENE II. *Athens. Quince's house.*

Enter QUINCE, FLUTE, SNOUT, and STARVELING.

QUINCE Have you sent to Bottom's house? Is he come home yet?

STAR He cannot be heard of. Out of doubt he is transported.

FLUTE If he come not, then the play is marr'd; it goes not forward, doth it?

QUINCE It is not possible. You have not a man in all Athens able to discharge Pyramus but he.

FLUTE No; he hath simply the best wit of any handicraft man in Athens.

QUINCE Yea, and the best person too; and he is a very paramour for a sweet voice.

FLUTE You must say 'paragon'. A paramour is – God bless us! – a thing of naught.

Enter SNUG.

SNUG Masters, the Duke is coming from the temple; and there is two or three lords and ladies more married. If our sport had gone forward, we had all been made men.

FLUTE O sweet bully Bottom! Thus hath he lost sixpence a day during his life; he could not have scaped sixpence a day. An the Duke had not given him sixpence a day for playing Pyramus, I'll be hanged. He would have deserved it: sixpence a day in Pyramus, or nothing.

Enter BOTTOM.

BOTTOM Where are these lads? Where are these hearts?

QUINCE Bottom! O most courageous day! O most happy hour!

BOTTOM Masters, I am to discourse wonders; but ask me not what; for if I tell you, I am not true Athenian. I will tell you everything, right as it fell out.

QUINCE Let us hear, sweet Bottom.

BOTTOM Not a word of me. All that I will tell you is, that the Duke hath dined. Get your apparel together; good strings to your beards, new ribbons to your pumps; meet presently at the palace; every man look o'er his part; for the short and the long is, our play is preferr'd. In any case, let Thisby have clean linen; and let not him that plays the lion pare his nails, for they shall hang out for the lion's claws. And, most dear actors, eat no onions nor garlic, for we are to utter sweet breath; and I do not doubt but to hear them say it is a sweet comedy. No more words. Away, go, away!

[*Exeunt.*

ACT FIVE

SCENE I. *Athens. The palace of Theseus.*

Enter THESEUS, HIPPOLYTA, PHILOSTRATE, Lords and Attendants.

HIPPOLYTA 'Tis strange, my Theseus, that these lovers speak of.
THESEUS More strange than true. I never may believe
These antique fables, nor these fairy toys.
Lovers and madmen have such seething brains,
Such shaping fantasies, that apprehend
More than cool reason ever comprehends.
The lunatic, the lover, and the poet,
Are of imagination all compact.
One sees more devils than vast hell can hold;
That is the madman. The lover, all as frantic,
Sees Helen's beauty in a brow of Egypt.
The poet's eye, in a fine frenzy rolling,
Doth glance from heaven to earth, from earth to heaven;
And as imagination bodies forth
The forms of things unknown, the poet's pen
Turns them to shapes, and gives to airy nothing
A local habitation and a name.
Such tricks hath strong imagination
That, if it would but apprehend some joy,
It comprehends some bringer of that joy,
Or in the night, imagining some fear,
How easy is a bush suppos'd a bear?
HIPPOLYTA But all the story of the night told over,
And all their minds transfigur'd so together,
More witnesseth than fancy's images,
And grows to something of great constancy,
But howsoever strange and admirable.

Enter LYSANDER, DEMETRIUS, HERMIA, and HELENA.

THESEUS Here come the lovers, full of joy and mirth.
Joy, gentle friends, joy and fresh days of love
Accompany your hearts!
LYSANDER More than to us
Wait in your royal walks, your board, your bed!
THESEUS Come now; what masques, what dances shall we have,
To wear away this long age of three hours
Between our after-supper and bed-time?
Where is our usual manager of mirth?
What revels are in hand? Is there no play
To ease the anguish of a torturing hour?
Call Philostrate.
PHILOSTRATE Here mighty Theseus.
THESEUS Say, what abridgment have you for this evening?
What masque? what music? How shall we beguile
The lazy time, if not with some delight?
PHILOSTRATE There is a brief how many sports are ripe;
Make choice of which your Highness will see first. *[Giving a paper.*
THESEUS 'The battle with the Centaurs, to be sung
By an Athenian eunuch to the harp.'
We'll none of that: that have I told my love,
In glory of my kinsman Hercules.
'The riot of the tipsy Bacchanals,
Tearing the Thracian singer in their rage.'
That is an old device, and it was play'd
When I from Thebes came last a conqueror.
'The thrice three Muses mourning for the death
Of Learning, late deceas'd in beggary.'
That is some satire, keen and critical,
Not sorting with a nuptial ceremony.
'A tedious brief scene of young Pyramus
And his love Thisby; very tragical mirth.'
Merry and tragical! tedious and brief!
That is hot ice and wondrous strange snow.
How shall we find the concord of this discord?
PHILOSTRATE A play there is, my lord, some ten words long,
Which is as brief as I have known a play;
But by ten words, my lord, it is too long,
Which makes it tedious; for in all the play
There is not one word apt, one player fitted.
And tragical, my noble lord, it is;
For Pyramus therein doth kill himself.
Which when I saw rehears'd, I must confess,
Made mine eyes water; but more merry tears
The passion of loud laughter never shed.
THESEUS What are they that do play it?
PHILOSTRATE Hard-handed men that work in Athens here,
Which never labour'd in their minds till now;
And now have toil'd their unbreathed memories
With this same play against your nuptial.
THESEUS And we will hear it.
PHILOSTRATE No, my noble lord,
It is not for you. I have heard it over,
And it is nothing, nothing in the world;
Unless you can find sport in their intents,
Extremely stretch'd and conn'd with cruel pain,
To do you service.
THESEUS I will hear that play;
For never anything can be amiss
When simpleness and duty tender it.
Go, bring them in; and take your places, ladies.
[Exit Philostrate.

HIPPOLYTA I love not to see wretchedness o'er-charged,
And duty in his service perishing.
THESEUS Why, gentle sweet, you shall see no such thing.
HIPPOLYTA He says they can do nothing in this kind.
THESEUS The kinder we, to give them thanks for nothing.
Our sport shall be to take what they mistake;
And what poor duty cannot do, noble respect
Takes it in might, not merit.
Where I have come, great clerks have purposed
To greet me with premeditated welcomes;
Where I have seen them shiver and look pale,
Make periods in the midst of sentences,
Throttle their practis'd accent in their fears,
And, in conclusion, dumbly have broke off,
Not paying me a welcome. Trust me, sweet,
Out of this silence yet I pick'd a welcome;
And in the modesty of fearful duty
I read as much as from the rattling tongue
Of saucy and audacious eloquence.
Love, therefore, and tongue-tied simplicity
In least speak most to my capacity.

Re-enter PHILOSTRATE.

PHILOSTRATE So please your Grace, the Prologue is address'd.
THESEUS Let him approach. *[Flourish of trumpets.*

Enter QUINCE as the PROLOGUE.

PROLOGUE *If we offend, it is with our good will.*
That you should think, we come not to offend,
But with good will. To show our simple skill,
That is the true beginning of our end.
Consider then, we come but in despite.
We do not come, as minding to content you,
Our true intent is. All for your delight

We are not here. That you should here repent you,
The actors are at hand; and, by their show,
You shall know all, that you are like to know,

THESEUS This fellow doth not stand upon points.

LYSANDER He hath rid his prologue like a rough colt; he knows not the stop. A good moral my lord: it is not enough to speak, but to speak true.

HIPPOLYTA Indeed he hath play'd on this prologue like a child on a recorder – a sound, but not in government.

THESEUS His speech was like a tangled chain; nothing impaired, but all disordered. Who is next?

Enter, with a Trumpet before them, as in dumb show, PYRAMUS and THISBY, WALL, MOONSHINE, and LION.

PROLOGUE *Gentles, perchance you wonder at this show;*
But wonder on, till truth make all things plain.
This man is Pyramus, if you would know;
This beauteous lady Thisby is certain.
This man, with lime and rough-cast, doth present
Wall, that vile Wall which did these lovers sunder;
And through Wall's chink, poor souls, they are content
To whisper. At the which let no man wonder.
This man, with lanthorn, dog, and bush of thorn,
Presenteth Moonshine; for, if you will know,
By moonshine did these lovers think no scorn
To meet at Ninus' tomb, there, there to woo.
This grisly beast, which Lion hight by name,
The trusty Thisby, coming first by night,
Did scare away, or rather did affright;
And as she fled, her mantle she did fall;
Which Lion vile with bloody mouth did stain.
Anon comes Pyramus, sweet youth and tall,
And finds his trusty Thisby's mantle slain;
Whereat with blade, with bloody blameful blade,
He bravely broach'd his boiling bloody breast;
And Thisby, tarrying in mulberry shade,
His dagger drew, and died. For all the rest,
Let Lion, Moonshine, Wall, and lovers twain,
At large discourse while here they do remain.

[*Exeunt Prologue, Pyramus, Thisby, Lion, and Moonshine.*

THESEUS I wonder if the lion be to speak.

DEMETRIUS No wonder, my lord: one lion may, when many asses do.

WALL *In this same interlude it doth befall*
That I, one Snout by name, present a wall;
And such a wall as I would have you think
That had in it a crannied hole or chink,
Through which the lovers, Pyramus and Thisby,
Did whisper often very secretly.
This loam, this rough-cast, and this stone, doth show
That I am that same wall; the truth is so;
And this the cranny is, right and sinister,
Through which the fearful lovers are to whisper.

THESEUS Would you desire lime and hair to speak better?

DEMETRIUS It is the wittiest partition that ever I heard discourse, my lord.

Enter PYRAMUS.

THESEUS Pyramus draws near the wall; silence.

PYRAMUS *O grim-look'd night! O night with hue so black!*
O night, which ever art when day is not!
O night, O night, alack, alack, alack,
I fear my Thisby's promise is forgot!
And thou, O wall, O sweet, O lovely wall,
That stand'st between her father's ground and mine;
Thou wall, O wall, O sweet and lovely wall,
Show me thy chink, to blink through with mine eyne. [*Wall holds up his fingers.*
Thanks, courteous wall. Jove shield thee well for this!
But what see I? No Thisby do I see.
O wicked wall, through whom I see no bliss;
Curs'd be thy stones for thus deceiving me!

THESEUS The wall, methinks, being sensible, should curse again.

PYRAMUS No, in truth, sir, he should not. Deceiving me is Thisby's cue. She is to enter now, and I am to spy her through the wall. You shall see it will fall pat as I told you; yonder she comes.

Enter THISBY.

THISBY *O wall, full often hast thou heard my moans,*
For parting my fair Pyramus and me!
My cherry lips have often kiss'd thy stones,
Thy stones with lime and hair knit up in thee.

PYRAMUS *I see a voice; now will I to the chink,*
To spy an I can hear my Thisby's face.
Thisby!

THISBY *My love! thou art my love, I think.*

PYRAMUS *Think what thou wilt, I am thy lover's grace;*
And like Limander am I trusty still.

THISBY *And I like Helen, till the Fates me kill.*

PYRAMUS *Not Shafalus to Procrus was so true.*

THISBY *As Shafalus to Procrus, I to you.*

PYRAMUS *O, kiss me through the hole of this vile wall.*

THISBY *I kiss the wall's hole, not your lips at all.*

PYRAMUS *Wilt thou at Ninny's tomb meet me straightway?*

THISBY *Tide life, tide death, I come without delay.*

[*Exeunt Pyramus and Thisby.*

WALL *Thus have I, Wall, my part discharged so;*
And, being done, thus Wall away doth go.

[*Exit Wall.*

THESEUS Now is the moon used between the two neighbours.

DEMETRIUS No remedy, my lord, when walls are so wilful to hear without warning.

HIPPOLYTA This is the silliest stuff that ever I heard.

THESEUS The best in this kind are but shadows; and the worst are no worse, if imagination amend them.

HIPPOLYTA It must be your imagination then, and not theirs.

THESEUS If we imagine no worse of them than they of themselves, they may pass for excellent men. Here come two noble beasts in, a man and a lion.

Enter LION and MOONSHINE.

LION *You, ladies, you, whose gentle hearts do fear*
The smallest monstrous mouse that creeps on floor,
May now, perchance, both quake and tremble here,
When lion rough in wildest rage doth roar.
Then know that I as Snug the joiner am
A lion fell, nor else no lion's dam;
For, if I should as lion come in strife
Into this place, 'twere pity on my life.

THESEUS A very gentle beast, and of a good conscience.

DEMETRIUS The very best at a beast, my lord, that e'er I saw.

LYSANDER This lion is a very fox for his valour.

THESEUS True; and a goose for his discretion.

DEMETRIUS Not so, my lord; for his valour cannot carry his discretion, and the fox carries the goose.

THESEUS His discretion, I am sure, cannot carry his valour; for the goose carries not the fox. It is well. Leave it to his discretion, and let us listen to the Moon.

MOONSHINE *This lanthorn doth the horned moon present –*

DEMETRIUS He should have worn the horns on his head.

THESEUS He is no crescent, and his horns are invisible within the circumference.

MOONSHINE *This lanthorn doth the horned moon present;*
Myself the Man i' th' Moon do seem to be.

THESEUS This is the greatest error of all the rest; the man should be put into the lantern. How is it else the man i' th' moon?

DEMETRIUS He dares not come there for the candle; for, you see, it is already in snuff.

HIPPOLYTA I am aweary of this moon. Would he would change!

THESEUS It appears, by his small light of discretion, that he is in the wane; but yet, in courtesy, in all reason, we must stay the time.

LYSANDER Proceed, Moon.

MOONSHINE All that I have to say is to tell you that the lanthorn is the moon; I, the Man i' th' Moon; this thorn-bush, my thorn-bush; and this dog, my dog.

DEMETRIUS Why, all these should be in the lantern; for all these are in the moon. But silence; here comes Thisby.

Re-enter THISBY.

THISBY *This is old Ninny's tomb. Where is my love?*

LION [*Roaring*] O – [*Thisby runs off.*

DEMETRIUS Well roar'd, Lion.

THESEUS Well run, Thisby.

HIPPOLYTA Well shone, Moon. Truly, the moon shines with a good grace.

[*The Lion tears Thisby's mantle, and exit.*

THESEUS Well mous'd, Lion.

Re-enter PYRAMUS.

DEMETRIUS And then came Pyramus.

LYSANDER And so the lion vanish'd.

PYRAMUS *Sweet Moon, I thank thee for thy sunny beams;*
I thank thee, Moon, for shining now so bright;
For, by thy gracious, golden, glittering gleams,
I trust to take of truest Thisby sight.
But stay, O spite!
But mark, poor knight,
What dreadful dole is here!
Eyes, do you see?
How can it be?
O dainty duck! O dear!
Thy mantle good,
What! stain'd with blood?
Approach, ye Furies fell.
O Fates! come, come;
Cut thread and thrum;
Quail, crush, conclude, and quell.

THESEUS This passion, and the death of a dear friend, would go near to make a man look sad.

HIPPOLYTA Beshrew my heart, but I pity the man.

PYRAMUS *O wherefore, Nature, didst thou lions frame?*
Since lion vile hath here deflower'd my dear;
Which is – no, no – which was the fairest dame

That liv'd, that lov'd, that lik'd, that look'd with cheer.
Come, tears, confound;
Out, sword, and wound
The pap of Pyramus;
Ay, that left pap,
Where heart doth hop.
[*Stabs himself.*
Thus die I, thus, thus, thus.
Now am I dead,
Now am I fled;
My soul is in the sky.
Tongue, lose thy light;
Moon, take thy flight.
[*Exit Moonshine.*
Now die, die, die, die, die. [*Dies.*

DEMETRIUS No die, but an ace, for him; for he is but one.

LYSANDER Less than an ace, man; for he is dead; he is nothing.

THESEUS With the help of a surgeon he might yet recover and yet prove an ass.

HIPPOLYTA How chance Moonshine is gone before Thisby comes back and finds her lover?

Re-enter THISBY.

THESEUS She will find him by starlight. Here she comes; and her passion ends the play.

HIPPOLYTA Methinks she should not use a long one for such a Pyramus; I hope she will be brief.

DEMETRIUS A mote will turn the balance, which Pyramus, which Thisby, is the better – he for a man, God warrant us: she for a woman, God bless us!

LYSANDER She hath spied him already with those sweet eyes.

DEMETRIUS And thus she moans, videlicet: –

THISBY *Asleep, my love?*
What, dead, my dove?
O Pyramus, arise,
Speak, speak. Quite dumb?
Dead, dead? A tomb
Must cover thy sweet eyes.
These lily lips,
This cherry nose,
These yellow cowslip cheeks,
Are gone, are gone;
Lovers, make moan;
His eyes were green as leeks.
O Sisters Three,
Come, come to me,
With hands as pale as milk;
Lay them in gore,
Since you have shore
With shears his thread of silk.
Tongue, not a word.
Come, trusty sword;
Come, blade, my breast imbrue.
[*Stabs herself.*
And farewell, friends;
Thus Thisby ends;
Adieu, adieu, adieu.
[*Dies.*

THESEUS Moonshine and Lion are left to bury the dead.

DEMETRIUS Ay, and Wall too.

BOTTOM [*Starting up*] No, I assure you; the wall is down that parted their fathers. Will it please you to see the Epilogue, or to hear a Bergomask dance between two of our company?

THESEUS No epilogue, I pray you; for your play needs no excuse. Never excuse; for when the players are all dead there need none to be blamed. Marry, if he that writ it had played Pyramus, and hang'd himself in Thisby's garter, it would have been a fine tragedy. And so it is, truly; and very notably discharg'd. But come, your Bergomask; let your epilogue alone.
[*A dance.*
The iron tongue of midnight hath told twelve.
Lovers, to bed; 'tis almost fairy time.
I fear we shall out-sleep the coming morn,
As much as we this night have overwatch'd.
This palpable-gross play hath well beguil'd
The heavy gait of night. Sweet friends, to bed.
A fortnight hold we this solemnity,
In nightly revels and new jollity.
[*Exeunt.*

Enter PUCK with a broom.

PUCK Now the hungry lion roars,
And the wolf behowls the moon;
Whilst the heavy ploughman snores,
All with weary task fordone.
Now the wasted brands do glow,
Whilst the screech-owl, screeching loud,
Puts the wretch that lies in woe
In remembrance of a shroud.
Now it is the time of night
That the graves, all gaping wide,
Every one lets forth his sprite,
In the church-way paths to glide.
And we fairies, that do run
By the triple Hecate's team
From the presence of the sun,
Following darkness like a dream,

Now are frolic. Not a mouse
Shall disturb this hallowed house.
I am sent with broom before,
To sweep the dust behind the door.

Enter OBERON and TITANIA, with all their Train.

OBERON Through the house give glimmering light,
By the dead and drowsy fire;
Every elf and fairy sprite
Hop as light as bird from brier;
And this ditty, after me,
Sing and dance it trippingly.

TITANIA First, rehearse your song by rote,
To each word a warbling note;
Hand in hand, with fairy grace,
Will we sing, and bless this place.

leading, the Fairies sing and dance.

OBERON Now, until the break of day,
Through this house each fairy stray.
To the best bride-bed will we,
Which by us shall blessed be;
And the issue there create
Ever shall be fortunate.
So shall all the couples three
Ever true in loving be;
And the blots of Nature's hand
Shall not in their issue stand;
Never mole, hare-lip, nor scar,
Nor mark prodigious, such as are
Despised in nativity,
Shall upon their children be.
With this field-dew consecrate,
Every fairy take his gait,
And each several chamber bless,
Through this palace, with sweet peace;
And the owner of it blest
Ever shall in safety rest.
Trip away; make no stay;
Meet me all by break of day

[Exeunt all but Puck.

PUCK If we shadows have offended,
Think but this, and all is mended,
That you have but slumb'red here
While these visions did appear
And this weak and idle theme,
No more yielding but a dream,
Gentles, do not reprehend.
If you pardon, we will mend.
And, as I am an honest Puck,
If we have unearned luck
Now to scape the serpent's tongue,
We will make amends ere long;
Else the Puck a liar call.
So, good night unto you all.
Give me your hands, if we be friends,
And Robin shall restore amends. *[Exit.*

The Merchant of Venice

Introduction by DAVID NEWELL

In March 1814, Jane Austen took her niece to see Edmund Kean perform in *The Merchant of Venice*, 'a good play for Fanny – she cannot be much affected, I think'. Perhaps she considered comedy less likely than tragedy to arouse strong passions. Times have changed. There can be no question now as to this play's ability to kindle late-twentieth-century emotions. One recent essay brands it 'profoundly and crudely anti-Semitic' (Cohen, 1988).

Opposing views of *The Merchant of Venice* take their cue from the play's rival centres of control, for it is a drama with two directors, each pulling strongly for different generic destinations. Shylock will have a tragic melodrama, with himself as knife-whetting villain and Antonio as victim. The latter indeed seems not unattracted to a role which allows him a momentary centrality denied him in the rest of the play. Portia, on the other hand, manoeuvres the plot and its characters inexorably towards a comic resolution.

On the structural level *The Merchant of Venice* unquestionably *is* a comedy. It contains all the standard elements: lyrical courtship, fairy-tale plot, obstructions to overcome, and a happy ending in the escapist world of Belmont. But as it proceeds, the play invites us to reassess our opinions, to revalue the very conventions on which it builds. Romance is both glamorous and superficial. We are assailed by the discrepancy between what is reported (Shylock ludicrously confusing daughter and ducats) and what is seen (Shylock grieving over memories of a ring), between expectation and disappointment (a masque is arranged only to be abandoned at the last moment). Nor can we overlook the niggling co-existence of the attractive and the repellent: Bassanio is lover *and* thoughtless spendthrift, Antonio respected merchant *and* anti-Semite, Portia intelligent heroine *and* calculating deceiver. But Shylock himself is the play's sternest challenge to comic optimism.

The growing tension between light comedy and something darker is reflected in the contest between speech styles which comes to a head in the trial scene (4.1). The language of up-market Venice and Belmont draws on the earlier comedies and the Sonnets: a rhetoric of romance, chiselled metaphor and self-conscious wit. Against this Shylock articulates a slow, gritty language of almost scientific precision, fiscal prudence, and grave austerity. The Duke's conciliatory words aim to steer him from vengeance to mercy by means of the rhetoric of public approbation and veiled threat: the world, he insists, looks for 'remorse', 'human gentleness and love', 'an eye of pity', 'tender courtesy', and 'a gentle answer'. Othello, another outsider in Renaissance Italy, has deliberately cultivated the Venetian graces: Shylock, just as resolutely, has not. His 'answer' (a word he reiterates like a remorselessly prodding finger) would wither any olive branch. A wilfully ugly diction, barren of metaphor, displays his contempt for Venetian elegance: 'rat', 'gaping pig', 'cat', 'bagpipe', 'urine' – these are *his* verbal counters. And Antonio putrifies before our very eyes into 'a weight of carrion flesh'. While the young lovers in the play happily discover both romance *and* riches, Shylock proves unexpectedly indifferent to financial gain. All he has is 'a lodged hate and a certain loathing' – inexplicable and therefore beyond the reach of rational, economic or emotional appeal. His proud Jewish separatism divorces him not only from Venetian vocabulary but ultimately from common humanity.

Such malevolence should settle our loyalties. Yet it is not as simple as that. Shylock's exclusion from the glittering society of the play brings him strangely closer to the audience. Comedy conventionally distances so as to highlight large-scale patterns and social groupings. But Shylock, alienated by voice and profession, race and religion, stands nearer to a century equally uncertain about the values of Renaissance civilisation. And the play's refusal to become *his* tragedy isolates him further: not a tragic Jew, but one despoiled, cheated, deprived of dramatic weight, robbed finally of any function in a play which proceeds calmly without him. If Antonio is not to be the lamb for the slaughter, then Shylock must be the scapegoat. There is always a cost: even comedy must expel its dissidents.

Thus the final Act retreats doggedly into a beautiful but brittle fantasy world where lovers unite, fathers relent, games conclude, and ships come home. The play which began with 'a lady richly left' ends aptly with the news of a deed of gift 'from the rich Jew'. The symmetry is ironic. Reduced by the triumphant Portia into an off-stage benefactor Shylock becomes part of the mechanism of the comic world. But that world will never be quite the same again. Unlike Fanny, we cannot but be much affected.

The Merchant of Venice

DRAMATIS PERSONAE

THE DUKE OF VENICE
THE PRINCE OF MOROCCO, THE PRINCE OF ARRAGON
suitors to Portia
ANTONIO
a merchant of Venice
BASSANIO
his friend, suitor to Portia
SOLANIO, SALERIO, GRATIANO
friends to Antonio and Bassanio
LORENZO
in love with Jessica
SHYLOCK
a rich Jew
TUBAL
a Jew, his friend
LAUNCELOT GOBBO
a clown, servant to Shylock
OLD GOBBO
father to Launcelot
LEONARDO
servant to Bassanio
BALTHASAR, STEPHANO
servants to Portia
STEPHANO
PORTIA
a rich heiress
NERISSA
her waiting-maid
JESSICA
daughter to Shylock
Magnificoes of Venice, Officers of the Court of Justice, a Gaoler, Servants, and other Attendants.

THE SCENE: VENICE, AND PORTIA'S HOUSE AT BELMONT.

ACT ONE

SCENE I. *Venice. A street.*

Enter ANTONIO, SALERIO, and SOLANIO.

ANTONIO In sooth, I know not why I am so sad.
It wearies me; you say it wearies you;
But how I caught it, found it, or came by it,
What stuff 'tis made of, whereof it is born,
I am to learn;
And such a want-wit sadness makes of me
That I have much ado to know myself.

SALERIO Your mind is tossing on the ocean;
There where your argosies, with portly sail –
Like signiors and rich burghers on the flood,
Or as it were the pageants of the sea –
Do overpeer the petty traffickers,
That curtsy to them, do them reverence,
As they fly by them with their woven wings.

SOLANIO Believe me, sir, had I such venture forth,
The better part of my affections would
Be with my hopes abroad. I should be still
Plucking the grass to know where sits the wind,
Peering in maps for ports, and piers, and roads;
And every object that might make me fear
Misfortune to my ventures, out of doubt,
Would make me sad.

SALERIO My wind, cooling my broth,
Would blow me to an ague when I thought
What harm a wind too great might do at sea.
I should not see the sandy hour-glass run
But I should think of shallows and of flats,
And see my wealthy Andrew dock'd in sand,
Vailing her high top lower than her ribs
To kiss her burial. Should I go to church
And see the holy edifice of stone,
And not bethink me straight of dangerous rocks,
Which, touching but my gentle vessel's side,
Would scatter all her spices on the stream,
Enrobe the roaring waters with my silks,
And, in a word, but even now worth this,
And now worth nothing? Shall I have the thought
To think on this, and shall I lack the thought
That such a thing bechanc'd would make me sad?
But tell not me; I know Antonio
Is sad to think upon his merchandise.

ANTONIO Believe me, no; I thank my fortune for it,
My ventures are not in one bottom trusted,
Nor to one place; nor is my whole estate
Upon the fortune of this present year;
Therefore my merchandise makes me not sad.

SOLANIO Why then you are in love.

ANTONIO Fie, fie!

SOLANIO Not in love neither? Then let us say you are sad
Because you are not merry; and 'twere as easy
For you to laugh and leap and say you are merry,

Because you are not sad. Now, by two-headed Janus,
Nature hath fram'd strange fellows in her time:
Some that will evermore peep through their eyes,
And laugh like parrots at a bag-piper;
And other of such vinegar aspect
That they'll not show their teeth in way of smile
Though Nestor swear the jest be laughable.

Enter BASSANIO, LORENZO, and GRATIANO.

Here comes Bassanio, your most noble kinsman,
Gratiano and Lorenzo. Fare ye well;
We leave you now with better company.

SALERIO I would have stay'd till I had made you merry,
If worthier friends had not prevented me.

ANTONIO Your worth is very dear in my regard.
I take it your own business calls on you,
And you embrace th' occasion to depart.

SALERIO Good morrow, my good lords.

BASSANIO Good signiors both, when shall we laugh? Say when.
You grow exceeding strange; must it be so?

SALERIO We'll make our leisures to attend on yours.

[Exeunt Salerio and Solanio.

LORENZO My Lord Bassanio, since you have found Antonio,
We two will leave you; but at dinner-time,
I pray you, have in mind where we must meet.

BASSANIO I will not fail you.

GRATIANO You look not well, Signior Antonio;
You have too much respect upon the world;
They lose it that do buy it with much care.
Believe me, you are marvellously chang'd.

ANTONIO I hold the world but as the world, Gratiano –
A stage, where every man must play a part,
And mine a sad one.

GRATIANO Let me play the fool.
With mirth and laughter let old wrinkles come;
And let my liver rather heat with wine
Than my heart cool with mortifying groans.
Why should a man whose blood is warm within
Sit like his grandsire cut in alabaster,
Sleep when he wakes, and creep into the jaundice,
By being peevish? I tell thee what, Antonio –
I love thee, and 'tis my love that speaks –
There are a sort of men whose visages
Do cream and mantle like a standing pond,
And do a wilful stillness entertain,
With purpose to be dress'd in an opinion
Of wisdom, gravity, profound conceit;
As who should say 'I am Sir Oracle,
And when I ope my lips let no dog bark'.
O my Antonio, I do know of these
That therefore only are reputed wise
For saying nothing; when, I am very sure,
If they should speak, would almost damn those ears
Which, hearing them, would call their brothers fools.
I'll tell thee more of this another time.
But fish not with this melancholy bait
For this fool gudgeon, this opinion.
Come, good Lorenzo. Fare ye well awhile;
I'll end my exhortation after dinner.

LORENZO Well, we will leave you then till dinner-time.
I must be one of these same dumb wise men,
For Gratiano never lets me speak.

GRATIANO Well, keep me company but two years moe,
Thou shalt not know the sound of thine own tongue.

ANTONIO Fare you well; I'll grow a talker for this gear.

GRATIANO Thanks, i' faith, for silence is only commendable
In a neat's tongue dried, and a maid not vendible.

[Exeunt Gratiano and Lorenzo.

ANTONIO Is that anything now?

BASSANIO Gratiano speaks an infinite deal of nothing, more than any man in all Venice. His reasons are as two grains of wheat hid in two bushels of chaff: you shall seek all day ere you find them, and when you have them they are not worth the search.

ANTONIO Well; tell me now what lady is the same
To whom you swore a secret pilgrimage,
That you to-day promis'd to tell me of?

BASSANIO 'Tis not unknown to you, Antonio,
How much I have disabled mine estate
By something showing a more swelling port
Than my faint means would grant continuance;
Nor do I now make moan to be abridg'd
From such a noble rate; but my chief care
Is to come fairly off from the great debts
Wherein my time, something too prodigal,
Hath left me gag'd. To you, Antonio,
I owe the most, in money and in love;
And from your love I have a warranty
To unburden all my plots and purposes
How to get clear of all the debts I owe.

ANTONIO I pray you, good Bassanio, let me know it;

And if it stand, as you yourself still do,
Within the eye of honour, be assur'd
My purse, my person, my extremest means,
Lie all unlock'd to your occasions.

BASSANIO In my school-days, when I had lost one shaft,
I shot his fellow of the self-same flight
The self-same way, with more advised watch,
To find the other forth; and by adventuring both
I oft found both. I urge this childhood proof,
Because what follows is pure innocence.
I owe you much; and, like a wilful youth,
That which I owe is lost; but if you please
To shoot another arrow that self way
Which you did shoot the first, I do not doubt,
As I will watch the aim, or to find both,
Or bring your latter hazard back again
And thankfully rest debtor for the first.

ANTONIO You know me well, and herein spend but time
To wind about my love with circumstance;
And out of doubt you do me now more wrong
In making question of my uttermost
Than if you had made waste of all I have.
Then do but say to me what I should do
That in your knowledge may by me be done,
And I am prest unto it; therefore, speak.

BASSANIO In Belmont is a lady richly left,
And she is fair and, fairer than that word,
Of wondrous virtues. Sometimes from her eyes
I did receive fair speechless messages.
Her name is Portia – nothing undervalu'd
To Cato's daughter, Brutus' Portia.
Nor is the wide world ignorant of her worth;
For the four winds blow in from every coast
Renowned suitors, and her sunny locks
Hang on her temples like a golden fleece,
Which makes her seat of Belmont Colchos' strond,
And many Jasons come in quest of her.
O my Antonio, had I but the means
To hold a rival place with one of them,
I have a mind presages me such thrift
That I should questionless be fortunate.

ANTONIO Thou know'st that all my fortunes are at sea;
Neither have I money nor commodity
To raise a present sum; therefore go forth,
Try what my credit can in Venice do;
That shall be rack'd, even to the uttermost,
To furnish thee to Belmont to fair Portia.
Go presently inquire, and so will I,
Where money is; and I no question make
To have it of my trust or for my sake. [*Exeunt.*

SCENE II. *Belmont. Portia's house.*

Enter PORTIA with her waiting-woman, NERISSA.

PORTIA By my troth, Nerissa, my little body is aweary of this great world.

NERISSA You would be, sweet madam, if your miseries were in the same abundance as your good fortunes are; and yet, for aught I see, they are as sick that surfeit with too much as they that starve with nothing. It is no mean happiness, therefore, to be seated in the mean: superfluity comes sooner by white hairs, but competency lives longer.

PORTIA Good sentences, and well pronounc'd.

NERISSA They would be better, if well followed.

PORTIA If to do were as easy as to know what were good to do, chapels had been churches, and poor men's cottages princes' palaces. It is a good divine that follows his own instructions; I can easier teach twenty what were good to be done than to be one of the twenty to follow mine own teaching. The brain may devise laws for the blood, but a hot temper leaps o'er a cold decree; such a hare is madness the youth, to skip o'er the meshes of good counsel the cripple. But this reasoning is not in the fashion to choose me a husband. O me, the word 'choose'! I may neither choose who I would nor refuse who I dislike; so is the will of a living daughter curb'd by the will of a dead father. Is it not hard, Nerissa, that I cannot choose one, nor refuse none?

NERISSA Your father was ever virtuous, and holy men at their death have good inspirations; therefore the lott'ry that he hath devised in these three chests, of gold, silver, and lead – whereof who chooses his meaning chooses you – will no doubt never be chosen by any rightly but one who you shall rightly love. But what warmth is there in your affection towards any of these princely suitors that are already come?

PORTIA I pray thee over-name them; and as thou namest them, I will describe them; and according to my description, level at my affection.

NERISSA First, there is the Neapolitan prince.

PORTIA Ay, that's a colt indeed, for he doth nothing but talk of his horse; and he makes it a great appropriation to his own good parts that he can shoe him himself; I am much afear'd my lady his mother play'd false with a smith.

NERISSA Then is there the County Palatine.

PORTIA He doth nothing but frown, as who should say 'An you will not have me, choose'. He hears merry tales and smiles not. I fear he will prove the weeping philosopher when he grows old, being so full of unmannerly sadness in his youth. I had rather be married to a death's-head with a bone in his mouth than to either of these. God defend me from these two!

NERISSA How say you by the French lord, Monsieur Le Bon?

PORTIA God made him, and therefore let him pass for a man. In truth, I know it is a sin to be a mocker, but he – why, he hath a horse better than the Neapolitan's, a better bad habit of frowning than the Count Palatine; he is every man in no man. If a throstle sing he falls straight a-cap'ring; he will fence with his own shadow; if I should marry him, I should marry twenty husbands. If he would despise me, I would forgive him; for if he love me to madness, I shall never requite him.

NERISSA What say you then to Falconbridge, the young baron of England?

PORTIA You know I say nothing to him, for he understands not me, nor I him: he hath neither Latin, French, nor Italian, and you will come into the court and swear that I have a poor pennyworth in the English. He is a proper man's picture; but, alas, who can converse with a dumb-show? How oddly he is suited! I think he bought his doublet in Italy, his round hose in France, his bonnet in Germany, and his behaviour everywhere.

NERISSA What think you of the Scottish lord, his neighbour?

PORTIA That he hath a neighbourly charity in him, for he borrowed a box of the ear of the Englishman, and swore he would pay him again when he was able; I think the Frenchman became his surety, and seal'd under for another.

NERISSA How like you the young German, the Duke of Saxony's nephew?

PORTIA Very vilely in the morning when he is sober; and most vilely in the afternoon when he is drunk. When he is best, he is a little worse than a man, and when he is worst, he is little better than a beast. An the worst fall that ever fell, I hope I shall make shift to go without him.

NERISSA If he should offer to choose, and choose the right casket, you should refuse to perform your father's will, if you should refuse to accept him.

PORTIA Therefore, for fear of the worst, I pray thee set a deep glass of Rhenish wine on the contrary casket; for if the devil be within and that temptation without, I know he will choose it. I will do anything, Nerissa, ere I will be married to a sponge.

NERISSA You need not fear, lady, the having any of these lords; they have acquainted me with their determinations, which is indeed to return to their home, and to trouble you with no more suit, unless you may be won by some other sort than your father's imposition, depending on the caskets.

PORTIA If I live to be as old as Sibylla, I will die as chaste as Diana, unless I be obtained by the manner of my father's will. I am glad this parcel of wooers are so reasonable; for there is not one among them but I dote on his very absence, and I pray God grant them a fair departure.

NERISSA Do you not remember, lady, in your father's time, a Venetian, a scholar and a soldier, that came hither in company of the Marquis of Montferrat?

PORTIA Yes, yes, it was Bassanio; as I think, so was he call'd.

NERISSA True, madam; he, of all the men that ever my foolish eyes look'd upon, was the best deserving a fair lady.

PORTIA I remember him well, and I remember him worthy of thy praise.

Enter a Servant.

How now! what news?

SERVANT The four strangers seek for you, madam, to take their leave; and there is a forerunner come from a fifth, the Prince of Morocco, who brings word the Prince his master will be here to-night.

PORTIA If I could bid the fifth welcome with so good heart as I can bid the other four farewell, I should be glad of his approach; if he have the condition of a saint and the complexion of a devil, I had rather he should shrive me than wive me.
Come, Nerissa. Sirrah, go before.
Whiles we shut the gate upon one wooer,
another knocks at the door. *[Exeunt.*

SCENE III. *Venice. A public place.*

Enter BASSANIO with SHYLOCK the Jew.

SHYLOCK Three thousand ducats – well.

BASSANIO Ay, sir, for three months.

SHYLOCK For three months – well.

BASSANIO For the which, as I told you, Antonio shall be bound.

SHYLOCK Antonio shall become bound – well.

BASSANIO May you stead me? Will you pleasure me? Shall I know your answer?

SHYLOCK Three thousand ducats for three months, and Antonio bound.

BASSANIO Your answer to that.

SHYLOCK Antonio is a good man.

BASSANIO Have you heard any imputation to the contrary?

SHYLOCK Ho, no, no, no, no; my meaning in saying he is a good man is to have you understand me that he is sufficient; yet his means are in supposition: he hath an argosy bound to Tripolis, another to the Indies; I understand, moreover, upon the Rialto, he hath a third at Mexico, a fourth for England – and other ventures he hath, squand'red abroad. But ships are but boards, sailors but men; there be land-rats and water-rats, water-thieves and land-thieves – I mean pirates; and then there is the peril of waters, winds, and rocks. The man is, notwithstanding, sufficient. Three thousand ducats – I think I may take his bond.

BASSANIO Be assur'd you may.

SHYLOCK I will be assur'd I may; and, that I may be assured, I will bethink me. May I speak with Antonio?

BASSANIO If it please you to dine with us.

SHYLOCK Yes, to smell pork, to eat of the habitation which your prophet, the Nazarite, conjured the devil into! I will buy with you, sell with you, talk with you, walk with you, and so following; but I will not eat with you, drink with you, nor pray with you. What news on the Rialto? Who is he comes here?

Enter ANTONIO.

BASSANIO This is Signior Antonio.

SHYLOCK [*Aside*] How like a fawning publican he looks!
I hate him for he is a Christian;
But more for that in low simplicity
He lends out money gratis, and brings down
The rate of usance here with us in Venice.
If I can catch him once upon the hip,
I will feed fat the ancient grudge I bear him.
He hates our sacred nation; and he rails,
Even there where merchants most do congregate,
On me, my bargains, and my well-won thrift,
Which he calls interest. Cursed be my tribe
If I forgive him!

BASSANIO Shylock, do you hear?

SHYLOCK I am debating of my present store,
And, by the near guess of my memory,
I cannot instantly raise up the gross
Of full three thousand ducats. What of that?
Tubal, a wealthy Hebrew of my tribe,
Will furnish me. But soft! how many months
Do you desire? [*To Antonio*] Rest you fair, good signior;
Your worship was the last man in our mouths.

ANTONIO Shylock, albeit I neither lend nor borrow
By taking nor by giving of excess,
Yet, to supply the ripe wants of my friend,
I'll break a custom. [*To Bassanio*] Is he yet possess'd
How much ye would?

SHYLOCK Ay, ay, three thousand ducats.

ANTONIO And for three months.

SHYLOCK I had forgot – three months; you told me so.
Well then, your bond; and, let me see – but hear you,
Methoughts you said you neither lend nor borrow
Upon advantage.

ANTONIO I do never use it.

SHYLOCK When Jacob graz'd his uncle Laban's sheep –
This Jacob from our holy Abram was,
As his wise mother wrought in his behalf,
The third possessor; ay, he was the third –

ANTONIO And what of him? Did he take interest?

SHYLOCK No, not take interest; not, as you would say,
Directly int'rest; mark what Jacob did:
When Laban and himself were compromis'd
That all the eanlings which were streak'd and pied
Should fall as Jacob's hire, the ewes, being rank,
In end of autumn turned to the rams;
And when the work of generation was
Between these woolly breeders in the act,
The skilful shepherd pill'd me certain wands,
And, in the doing of the deed of kind,
He stuck them up before the fulsome ewes,
Who, then conceiving, did in eaning time
Fall parti-colour'd lambs, and those were Jacob's.
This was a way to thrive, and he was blest;
And thrift is blessing, if men steal it not.

ANTONIO This was a venture, sir, that Jacob serv'd for;
A thing not in his power to bring to pass,
But sway'd and fashion'd by the hand of heaven.
Was this inserted to make interest good?
Or is your gold and silver ewes and rams?

SHYLOCK I cannot tell; I make it breed as fast.
But note me, signior.

ANTONIO [*Aside*] Mark you this, Bassanio,
The devil can cite Scripture for his purpose.
An evil soul producing holy witness
Is like a villain with a smiling cheek,
A goodly apple rotten at the heart.
O, what a goodly outside falsehood hath!

SHYLOCK Three thousand ducats – 'tis a good round sum.
Three months from twelve; then let me see, the rate –

ANTONIO Well, Shylock, shall we be beholding to you?

SHYLOCK Signior Antonio, many a time and oft

In the Rialto you have rated me
About my moneys and my usances;
Still have I borne it with a patient shrug,
For suff'rance is the badge of all our tribe;
You call me misbeliever, cut-throat dog,
And spit upon my Jewish gaberdine,
And all for use of that which is mine own.
Well then, it now appears you need my help;
Go to, then; you come to me, and you say
'Shylock, we would have moneys'. You say so –
You that did void your rheum upon my beard
And foot me as you spurn a stranger cur
Over your threshold; moneys is your suit.
What should I say to you? Should I not say
'Hath a dog money? Is it possible
A cur can lend three thousand ducats?' Or
Shall I bend low and, in a bondman's key,
With bated breath and whisp'ring humbleness,
Say this:
'Fair sir, you spit on me on Wednesday last,
You spurn'd me such a day; another time
You call'd me dog; and for these courtesies
I'll lend you thus much moneys'?

ANTONIO I am as like to call thee so again,
To spit on thee again, to spurn thee too.
If thou wilt lend this money, lend it not
As to thy friends – for when did friendship take
A breed for barren metal of his friend? –
But lend it rather to thine enemy,
Who if he break thou mayst with better face
Exact the penalty.

SHYLOCK Why, look you, how you storm!
I would be friends with you, and have your love,
Forget the shames that you have stain'd me with,
Supply your present wants, and take no doit
Of usance for my moneys, and you'll not hear me.
This is kind I offer.

BASSANIO This were kindness.

SHYLOCK This kindness will I show.
Go with me to a notary, seal me there
Your single bond, and, in a merry sport,
If you repay me not on such a day,
In such a place, such sum or sums as are
Express'd in the condition, let the forfeit
Be nominated for an equal pound
Of your fair flesh, to be cut off and taken
In what part of your body pleaseth me.

ANTONIO Content, in faith; I'll seal to such a bond,
And say there is much kindness in the Jew.

BASSANIO You shall not seal to such a bond for me;
I'll rather dwell in my necessity.

ANTONIO Why, fear not, man; I will not forfeit it;
Within these two months – that's a month before
This bond expires – I do expect return
Of thrice three times the value of this bond.

SHYLOCK O father Abram, what these Christians are,
Whose own hard dealings teaches them suspect
The thoughts of others! Pray you, tell me this:
If he should break his day, what should I gain
By the exaction of the forfeiture?
A pound of man's flesh taken from a man
Is not so estimable, profitable neither,
As flesh of muttons, beefs, or goats. I say,
To buy his favour, I extend this friendship;
If he will take it, so; if not, adieu;
And, for my love, I pray you wrong me not.

ANTONIO Yes, Shylock, I will seal unto this bond.

SHYLOCK Then meet me forthwith at the notary's;
Give him direction for this merry bond,
And I will go and purse the ducats straight,
See to my house, left in the fearful guard
Of an unthrifty knave, and presently I'll be with you.

ANTONIO Hie thee, gentle Jew.

[*Exit Shylock*.

The Hebrew will turn Christian: he grows kind.

BASSANIO I like not fair terms and a villain's mind.

ANTONIO Come on; in this there can be no dismay;
My ships come home a month before the day.

[*Exeunt*.

ACT TWO

SCENE I. *Belmont. Portia's house.*

Flourish of cornets. Enter the PRINCE OF MOROCCO, a tawny Moor all in white, and three or four Followers accordingly, with PORTIA, NERISSA, and Train.

MOROCCO Mislike me not for my complexion,
The shadowed livery of the burnish'd sun,
To whom I am a neighbour, and near bred.
Bring me the fairest creature northward born,
Where Phoebus' fire scarce thaws the icicles,
And let us make incision for your love
To prove whose blood is reddest, his or mine.
I tell thee, lady, this aspect of mine
Hath fear'd the valiant; by my love, I swear
The best-regarded virgins of our clime
Have lov'd it too. I would not change this hue,
Except to steal your thoughts, my gentle queen.

PORTIA In terms of choice I am not solely led
By nice direction of a maiden's eyes;
Besides, the lott'ry of my destiny
Bars me the right of voluntary choosing.
But, if my father had not scanted me,
And hedg'd me by his wit to yield myself
His wife who wins me by that means I told you,
Yourself, renowned Prince, then stood as fair
As any comer I have look'd on yet
For my affection.

MOROCCO Even for that I thank you.
Therefore, I pray you, lead me to the caskets
To try my fortune. By this scimitar,
That slew the Sophy and a Persian prince,
That won three fields of Sultan Solyman,
I would o'erstare the sternest eyes that look,
Outbrave the heart most daring on the earth,
Pluck the young sucking cubs from the she-bear,
Yea, mock the lion when 'a roars for prey,
To win thee, lady. But, alas the while!
If Hercules and Lichas play at dice
Which is the better man, the greater throw
May turn by fortune from the weaker hand.
So is Alcides beaten by his page;
And so may I, blind Fortune leading me,
Miss that which one unworthier may attain,
And die with grieving.

PORTIA You must take your chance,
And either not attempt to choose at all,
Or swear before you choose, if you choose wrong,
Never to speak to lady afterward
In way of marriage; therefore be advis'd.

MOROCCO Nor will not; come, bring me unto my chance.

PORTIA First, forward to the temple. After dinner
Your hazard shall be made.

MOROCCO Good fortune then,
To make me blest or cursed'st among men!

[*Cornets, and exeunt.*

SCENE II. *Venice. A street.*

Enter LAUNCELOT GOBBO.

LAUNCELOT Certainly my conscience will serve me to run from this Jew my master. The fiend is at mine elbow and tempts me, saying to me 'Gobbo, Launcelot Gobbo, good Launcelot' or 'good Gobbo' or 'good Launcelot Gobbo, use your legs, take the start, run away'. My conscience says 'No; take heed, honest Launcelot, take heed, honest Gobbo' or, as aforesaid, 'honest Launcelot Gobbo, do not run; scorn running with thy heels'. Well, the most courageous fiend bids me pack. 'Via!' says the fiend; 'away!' says the fiend. 'For the heavens, rouse up a brave mind' says the fiend 'and run.' Well, my conscience, hanging about the neck of my heart, says very wisely to me 'My honest friend Launcelot, being an honest man's son' or rather 'an honest woman's son'; for indeed my father did something smack, something grow to, he had a kind of taste – well, my conscience says 'Launcelot, budge not'. 'Budge' says the fiend. 'Budge not' says my conscience. 'Conscience,' say I 'you counsel well.' 'Fiend,' say I 'you counsel well.' To be rul'd by my conscience, I should stay with the Jew my master, who – God bless the mark! – is a kind of devil; and, to run away from the Jew, I should be ruled by the fiend, who – saving your reverence! – is the devil himself. Certainly the Jew is the very devil incarnation; and, in my conscience, my conscience is but a kind of hard conscience to offer to counsel me to stay with the Jew. The fiend gives the more friendly counsel. I will run, fiend; my heels are at your commandment; I will run.

Enter OLD GOBBO, with a basket.

OLD GOBBO Master young man, you, I pray you, which is the way to master Jew's?

LAUNCELOT [*Aside*] O heavens! This is my true-begotten father, who, being more than sand-blind, high-gravel blind, knows me not. I will try confusions with him.

OLD GOBBO Master young gentleman, I pray you, which is the way to master Jew's?

LAUNCELOT Turn up on your right hand at the next turning, but, at the next turning of all, on your left; marry, at the very next turning, turn of no hand, but turn down indirectly to the Jew's house.

OLD GOBBO Be God's sonties, 'twill be a hard way to hit! Can you tell me whether one Launcelot, that dwells with him, dwell with him or no?

LAUNCELOT Talk you of young Master Launcelot? [*Aside*] Mark me now; now will I raise the waters. – Talk you of young Master Launcelot?

OLD GOBBO No master, sir, but a poor man's son; his father, though I say't, is an honest exceeding poor man, and, God be thanked, well to live.

LAUNCELOT Well, let his father be what 'a will, we talk of young Master Launcelot.

OLD GOBBO Your worship's friend, and Launcelot, sir.

LAUNCELOT But I pray you, ergo, old man, ergo, I beseech you, talk you of young Master Launcelot?

OLD GOBBO Of Launcelot, an't please your mastership.

LAUNCELOT Ergo, Master Launcelot. Talk not of Master Launcelot, father; for the young gentleman, according to Fates and Destinies and such odd sayings, the Sisters Three and such branches of learning, is indeed deceased; or, as you would say in plain terms, gone to heaven.

OLD GOBBO Marry, God forbid! The boy was the very staff of my age, my very prop.

LAUNCELOT Do I look like a cudgel or a hovelpost, a staff or a prop? Do you know me, father?

OLD GOBBO Alack the day, I know you not, young gentleman; but I pray you tell me, is my boy – God rest his soul! – alive or dead?

LAUNCELOT Do you not know me, father?

OLD GOBBO Alack, sir, I am sand-blind; I know you not.

LAUNCELOT Nay, indeed, if you had your eyes, you might fail of the knowing me: it is a wise father that knows his own child. Well, old man, I will tell you news of your son. Give me your blessing; truth will come to light; murder cannot be hid long; a man's son may, but in the end truth will out.

OLD GOBBO Pray you, sir, stand up; I am sure you are not Launcelot my boy.

LAUNCELOT Pray you, let's have no more fooling about it, but give me your blessing; I am Launcelot, your boy that was, your son that is, your child that shall be.

OLD GOBBO I cannot think you are my son.

LAUNCELOT I know not what I shall think of that; but I am Launcelot, the Jew's man, and I am sure Margery your wife is my mother.

OLD GOBBO Her name is Margery, indeed. I'll be sworn, if thou be Launcelot, thou art mine own flesh and blood. Lord worshipp'd might he be, what a beard hast thou got! Thou hast got more hair on thy chin than Dobbin my fill-horse has on his tail.

LAUNCELOT It should seem, then, that Dobbin's tail grows backward; I am sure he had more hair of his tail than I have of my face when I last saw him.

OLD GOBBO Lord, how art thou chang'd! How dost thou and thy master agree? I have brought him a present. How 'gree you now?

LAUNCELOT Well, well; but, for mine own part, as I have set up my rest to run away, so I will not rest till I have run some ground. My master's a very Jew. Give him a present! Give him a halter. I am famish'd in his service; you may tell every finger I have with my ribs. Father, I am glad you are come; give me your present to one Master Bassanio, who indeed gives rare new liveries; if I serve not him, I will run as far as God has any ground. O rare fortune! Here comes the man. To him, father, for I am a Jew, if I serve the Jew any longer.

Enter BASSANIO, with LEONARDO, with a Follower or two.

BASSANIO You may do so; but let it be so hasted that supper be ready at the farthest by five of the clock. See these letters delivered, put the liveries to making, and desire Gratiano to come anon to my lodging. [*Exit a servant.*

LAUNCELOT To him, father.

OLD GOBBO God bless your worship!

BASSANIO Gramercy; wouldst thou aught with me?

OLD GOBBO Here's my son, sir, a poor boy –

LAUNCELOT Not a poor boy, sir, but the rich Jew's man, that would, sir, as my father shall specify –

OLD GOBBO He hath a great infection, sir, as one would say, to serve –

LAUNCELOT Indeed, the short and the long is, I serve the Jew, and have a desire, as my father shall specify –

OLD GOBBO His master and he, saving your worship's reverence, are scarce cater-cousins –

LAUNCELOT To be brief, the very truth is that the Jew, having done me wrong, doth cause me, as my father, being I hope an old man, shall frutify unto you –

OLD GOBBO I have here a dish of doves that I would bestow upon your worship; and my suit is –

LAUNCELOT In very brief, the suit is impertinent to myself, as your worship shall know by this honest old man; and, though I say it, though old man, yet poor man, my father.

BASSANIO One speak for both. What would you?
LAUNCELOT Serve you, sir.
OLD GOBBO That is the very defect of the matter, sir.
BASSANIO I know thee well; thou hast obtain'd thy suit.
Shylock thy master spoke with me this day,
And hath preferr'd thee, if it be preferment
To leave a rich Jew's service to become
The follower of so poor a gentleman.

LAUNCELOT The old proverb is very well parted between my master Shylock and you, sir: you have the grace of God, sir, and he hath enough.

BASSANIO Thou speak'st it well. Go, father, with thy son.
Take leave of thy old master, and inquire
My lodging out. [*To a servant*] Give him a livery
More guarded than his fellows'; see it done.

LAUNCELOT Father, in. I cannot get a service, no! I have ne'er a tongue in my head! [*Looking on his palm*] Well; if any man in Italy have a fairer table which doth offer to swear upon a book – I shall have good fortune. Go to, here's a simple line of life; here's a small trifle of wives; alas, fifteen wives is nothing; a'leven widows and nine maids is a simple coming-in for one man. And then to scape drowning thrice, and to be in peril of my life with the edge of a feather-bed – here are simple scapes. Well, if Fortune be a woman, she's a good wench for this gear. Father, come; I'll take my leave of the Jew in the twinkling. [*Exeunt Launcelot and Old Gobbo.*

BASSANIO I pray thee, good Leonardo, think on this.
These things being bought and orderly bestowed,
Return in haste, for I do feast to-night
My best esteem'd acquaintance; hie thee, go.
LEONARDO My best endeavours shall be done herein.

Enter GRATIANO.

GRATIANO Where's your master?
LEONARDO Yonder, sir, he walks. [*Exit.*
GRATIANO Signior Bassanio!
BASSANIO Gratiano!
GRATIANO I have suit to you.
BASSANIO You have obtain'd it.
GRATIANO You must not deny me: I must go with you to Belmont.
BASSANIO Why, then you must. But hear thee, Gratiano:
Thou art too wild, too rude, and bold of voice –
Parts that become thee happily enough,
And in such eyes as ours appear not faults;
But where thou art not known, why there they show
Something too liberal. Pray thee, take pain
To allay with some cold drops of modesty
Thy skipping spirit; lest through thy wild behaviour
I be misconst'red in the place I go to
And lose my hopes.
GRATIANO Signior Bassanio, hear me:
If I do not put on a sober habit,
Talk with respect, and swear but now and then,
Wear prayer-books in my pocket, look demurely,
Nay more, while grace is saying hood mine eyes
Thus with my hat, and sigh, and say amen,
Use all the observance of civility
Like one well studied in a sad ostent
To please his grandam, never trust me more.
BASSANIO Well, we shall see your bearing.
GRATIANO Nay, but I bar to-night; you shall not gauge me
By what we do to-night.
BASSANIO No, that were pity;
I would entreat you rather to put on
Your boldest suit of mirth, for we have friends
That purpose merriment. But fare you well;
I have some business.
GRATIANO And I must to Lorenzo and the rest;
But we will visit you at supper-time. [*Exeunt.*

SCENE III. *Venice. Shylock's house.*

Enter JESSICA and LAUNCELOT.

JESSICA I am sorry thou wilt leave my father so.
Our house is hell; and thou, a merry devil,
Didst rob it of some taste of tediousness.
But fare thee well; there is a ducat for thee;
And, Launcelot, soon at supper shalt thou see
Lorenzo, who is thy new master's guest.
Give him this letter; do it secretly.
And so farewell. I would not have my father
See me in talk with thee.

LAUNCELOT Adieu! tears exhibit my tongue. Most beautiful pagan, most sweet Jew! If a Christian do not play the knave and get thee, I am much deceived. But, adieu! these foolish drops do something drown my manly spirit; adieu!

JESSICA Farewell, good Launcelot. [*Exit.*
Alack, what heinous sin is it in me
To be asham'd to be my father's child!
But though I am a daughter to his blood,
I am not to his manners. O Lorenzo,
If thou keep promise, I shall end this strife,
Become a Christian and thy loving wife. [*Exit.*

SCENE IV. *Venice. A street.*

Enter GRATIANO, LORENZO, SALERIO, and SOLANIO.

LORENZO Nay, we will slink away in suppertime,
Disguise us at my lodging, and return
All in an hour.
GRATIANO We have not made good preparation.
SALERIO We have not spoke us yet of torch-bearers.
SOLANIO 'Tis vile, unless it may be quaintly ordered;
And better in my mind not undertook.
LORENZO 'Tis now but four o'clock; we have two hours
To furnish us.

Enter LAUNCELOT, with a letter.

Friend Launcelot, what's the news?

LAUNCELOT An it shall please you to break up this, it shall seem to signify.

LORENZO I know the hand; in faith, 'tis a fair hand,
And whiter than the paper it writ on
Is the fair hand that writ.
GRATIANO Love-news, in faith!
LAUNCELOT By your leave, sir.
LORENZO Whither goest thou?

LAUNCELOT Marry, sir, to bid my old master, the Jew, to sup to-night with my new master, the Christian.

LORENZO Hold, here, take this. Tell gentle Jessica
I will not fail her; speak it privately.
Go, gentlemen, [*Exit Launcelot.*
Will you prepare you for this masque to-night?
I am provided of a torch-bearer.
SALERIO Ay, marry, I'll be gone about it straight.
SOLANIO And so will I.
LORENZO Meet me and Gratiano
At Gratiano's lodging some hour hence.
SALERIO 'Tis good we do so.
[*Exeunt Salerio and Solanio.*

GRATIANO Was not that letter from fair Jessica?
LORENZO I must needs tell thee all. She hath directed
How I shall take her from her father's house;
What gold and jewels she is furnish'd with;
What page's suit she hath in readiness.
If e'er the Jew her father come to heaven,
It will be for his gentle daughter's sake;
And never dare misfortune cross her foot,
Unless she do it under this excuse,
That she is issue to a faithless Jew.
Come, go with me, peruse this as thou goest;
Fair Jessica shall be my torch-bearer. [*Exeunt.*

SCENE V. *Venice. Before Shylock's house.*

Enter SHYLOCK and LAUNCELOT.

SHYLOCK Well, thou shalt see; thy eyes shall be thy judge,
The difference of old Shylock and Bassanio. –
What, Jessica! – Thou shalt not gormandize
As thou hast done with me – What, Jessica! –
And sleep and snore, and rend apparel out –
Why, Jessica, I say!
LAUNCELOT Why, Jessica!
SHYLOCK Who bids thee call? I do not bid thee call.

LAUNCELOT Your worship was wont to tell me I could do nothing without bidding.

Enter JESSICA.

JESSICA Call you? What is your will?
SHYLOCK I am bid forth to supper, Jessica;
There are my keys. But wherefore should I go?
I am not bid for love; they flatter me;
But yet I'll go in hate, to feed upon
The prodigal Christian. Jessica, my girl,
Look to my house. I am right loath to go;
There is some ill a-brewing towards my rest,
For I did dream of money-bags to-night.

LAUNCELOT I beseech you, sir, go; my young master doth expect your reproach.

SHYLOCK So do I his.

LAUNCELOT And they have conspired together; I will not say you shall see a masque, but if you do, then it was not for nothing that my nose fell a-bleeding on Black Monday last at six o'clock i' th' morning, falling out that year on Ash Wednesday was four year, in th' afternoon.

SHYLOCK What, are there masques? Hear you me, Jessica:
Lock up my doors, and when you hear the drum,
And the vile squealing of the wry-neck'd fife,
Clamber not you up to the casements then,
Nor thrust your head into the public street
To gaze on Christian fools with varnish'd faces;
But stop my house's ears – I mean my casements;
Let not the sound of shallow fopp'ry enter
My sober house. By Jacob's staff, I swear
I have no mind of feasting forth to-night;
But I will go. Go you before me, sirrah;
Say I will come.

LAUNCELOT I will go before, sir. Mistress, look out at window for all this.

There will come a Christian by
Will be worth a Jewess' eye. [*Exit.*

SHYLOCK What says that fool of Hagar's offspring, ha?
JESSICA His words were 'Farewell, mistress';

nothing else.
SHYLOCK The patch is kind enough, but a huge feeder,
Snail-slow in profit, and he sleeps by day
More than the wild-cat; drones hive not with me,
Therefore I part with him; and part with him
To one that I would have him help to waste
His borrowed purse. Well, Jessica, go in;
Perhaps I will return immediately.
Do as I bid you, shut doors after you.
Fast bind, fast find –
A proverb never stale in thrifty mind. [*Exit.*
JESSICA Farewell; and if my fortune be not crost,
I have a father, you a daughter, lost. [*Exit.*

SCENE VI. *Venice. Before Shylock's house.*

Enter the maskers, GRATIANO and SALERIO.

GRATIANO This is the pent-house under which Lorenzo
Desired us to make stand.
SALERIO His hour is almost past.
GRATIANO And it is marvel he out-dwells his hour,
For lovers ever run before the clock.
SALERIO O, ten times faster Venus' pigeons fly
To seal love's bonds new made than they are wont
To keep obliged faith unforfeited!
GRATIANO That ever holds: who riseth from a feast
With that keen appetite that he sits down?
Where is the horse that doth untread again
His tedious measures with the unbated fire
That he did pace them first? All things that are
Are with more spirit chased than enjoy'd.
How like a younker or a prodigal
The scarfed bark puts from her native bay,
Hugg'd and embraced by the strumpet wind;
How like the prodigal doth she return,
With over-weather'd ribs and ragged sails,
Lean, rent, and beggar'd by the strumpet wind!

Enter LORENZO.

SALERIO Here comes Lorenzo; more of this hereafter.
LORENZO Sweet friends, your patience for my long abode!
Not I, but my affairs, have made you wait.
When you shall please to play the thieves for wives,
I'll watch as long for you then. Approach;
Here dwells my father Jew. Ho! who's within?

Enter JESSICA, above, in boy's clothes.

JESSICA Who are you? Tell me, for more certainty,
Albeit I'll swear that I do know your tongue.
LORENZO Lorenzo, and thy love.
JESSICA Lorenzo, certain; and my love indeed;
For who love I so much? And now who knows
But you, Lorenzo, whether I am yours?
LORENZO Heaven and thy thoughts are witness that thou art.
JESSICA Here, catch this casket; it is worth the pains.
I am glad 'tis night, you do not look on me,
For I am much asham'd of my exchange;
But love is blind, and lovers cannot see
The pretty follies that themselves commit,
For, if they could, Cupid himself would blush
To see me thus transformed to a boy.
LORENZO Descend, for you must be my torch-bearer.
JESSICA What! must I hold a candle to my shames?
They in themselves, good sooth, are too too light.
Why, 'tis an office of discovery, love,
And I should be obscur'd.
LORENZO So are you, sweet,
Even in the lovely garnish of a boy.
But come at once,
For the close night doth play the runaway,
And we are stay'd for at Bassanio's feast.
JESSICA I will make fast the doors, and gild myself
With some moe ducats, and be with you straight. [*Exit above.*
GRATIANO Now, by my hood, a gentle, and no Jew.
LORENZO Beshrew me, but I love her heartily,
For she is wise, if I can judge of her,
And fair she is, if that mine eyes be true,
And true she is, as she hath prov'd herself;
And therefore, like herself, wise, fair, and true,
Shall she be placed in my constant soul.

Enter JESSICA, below.

What, art thou come? On, gentlemen, away;
Our masquing mates by this time for us stay.
[*Exit with Jessica and Salerio.*

Enter ANTONIO.

ANTONIO Who's there?
GRATIANO Signior Antonio?
ANTONIO Fie, fie, Gratiano, where are all the rest?
'Tis nine o'clock; our friends all stay for you;
No masque to-night; the wind is come about;
Bassanio presently will go abroad;
I have sent twenty out to seek for you.

GRATIANO I am glad on't; I desire no more delight
Than to be under sail and gone to-night. [*Exeunt.*

SCENE VII. *Belmont. Portia's house.*

Flourish of Cornets. Enter PORTIA, with the PRINCE OF MOROCCO, and their Trains.

PORTIA Go draw aside the curtains and discover
The several caskets to this noble Prince.
Now make your choice.
MOROCCO The first, of gold, who this inscription bears:
'Who chooseth me shall gain what many men desire'.
The second, silver, which this promise carries:
'Who chooseth me shall get as much as he deserves'.
This third, dull lead, with warning all as blunt:
'Who chooseth me must give and hazard all he hath'.
How shall I know if I do choose the right?
PORTIA The one of them contains my picture, Prince;
If you choose that, then I am yours withal.
MOROCCO Some god direct my judgment! Let me see;
I will survey th' inscriptions back again.
What says this leaden casket?
'Who chooseth me must give and hazard all he hath.'
Must give – for what? For lead? Hazard for lead!
This casket threatens; men that hazard all
Do it in hope of fair advantages.
A golden mind stoops not to shows of dross;
I'll then nor give nor hazard aught for lead.
What says the silver with her virgin hue?
'Who chooseth me shall get as much as he deserves.'
As much as he deserves! Pause there, Morocco,
And weigh thy value with an even hand.
If thou beest rated by thy estimation,
Thou dost deserve enough, and yet enough
May not extend so far as to the lady;
And yet to be afeard of my deserving
Were but a weak disabling of myself.
As much as I deserve? Why, that's the lady!
I do in birth deserve her, and in fortunes,
In graces, and in qualities of breeding;
But more than these, in love I do deserve.
What if I stray'd no farther, but chose here?
Let's see once more this saying grav'd in gold:
'Who chooseth me shall gain what many men desire'.
Why, that's the lady! All the world desires her;
From the four corners of the earth they come
To kiss this shrine, this mortal-breathing saint.
The Hyrcanian deserts and the vasty wilds
Of wide Arabia are as throughfares now
For princes to come view fair Portia.
The watery kingdom, whose ambitious head
Spits in the face of heaven, is no bar
To stop the foreign spirits, but they come
As o'er a brook to see fair Portia.
One of these three contains her heavenly picture.
Is't like that lead contains her? 'Twere damnation
To think so base a thought; it were too gross
To rib her cerecloth in the obscure grave.
Or shall I think in silver she's immur'd,
Being ten times undervalued to tried gold?
O sinful thought! Never so rich a gem
Was set in worse than gold. They have in England
A coin that bears the figure of an angel
Stamp'd in gold; but that's insculp'd upon.
But here an angel in a golden bed
Lies all within. Deliver me the key;
Here do I choose, and thrive I as I may!
PORTIA There, take it, Prince, and if my form lie there,
Then I am yours.
[*He opens the golden casket.*
MOROCCO O hell! what have we here?
A carrion Death, within whose empty eye
There is a written scroll! I'll read the writing.
'All that glisters is not gold,
Often have you heard that told;
Many a man his life hath sold
But my outside to behold.
Gilded tombs do worms infold.
Had you been as wise as bold,
Young in limbs, in judgment old,
Your answer had not been inscroll'd.
Fare you well, your suit is cold.'
Cold indeed, and labour lost,
Then farewell, heat, and welcome, frost.
Portia, adieu! I have too griev'd a heart
To take a tedious leave; thus losers part.
[*Exit with his train. Flourish of cornets.*
Portia. A gentle riddance. Draw the curtains, go.
Let all of his complexion choose me so.
[*Exeunt.*

SCENE VIII. *Venice. A street.*

Enter SALERIO and SOLANIO.

SALERIO Why, man, I saw Bassanio under sail;
With him is Gratiano gone along;
And in their ship I am sure Lorenzo is not.
SOLANIO The villain Jew with outcries rais'd the Duke,

Who went with him to search Bassanio's ship.

SALERIO He came too late, the ship was under sail;
But there the Duke was given to understand
That in a gondola were seen together
Lorenzo and his amorous Jessica;
Besides, Antonio certified the Duke
They were not with Bassanio in his ship.

SOLANIO I never heard a passion so confus'd,
So strange, outrageous, and so variable,
As the dog Jew did utter in the streets.
'My daughter! O my ducats! O my daughter!
Fled with a Christian! O my Christian ducats!
Justice! the law! My ducats and my daughter!
A sealed bag, two sealed bags of ducats,
Of double ducats, stol'n from me by my daughter!
And jewels – two stones, two rich and precious stones,
Stol'n by my daughter! Justice! Find the girl;
She hath the stones upon her and the ducats.'

SALERIO Why all the boys in Venice follow him,
Crying, his stones, his daughter, and his ducats.

SOLANIO Let good Antonio look he keep his day,
Or he shall pay for this.

SALERIO Marry, well rememb'red;
I reason'd with a Frenchman yesterday,
Who told me, in the narrow seas that part
The French and English, there miscarried
A vessel of our country richly fraught.
I thought upon Antonio when he told me,
And wish'd in silence that it were not his.

SOLANIO You were best to tell Antonio what you hear;
Yet do not suddenly, for it may grieve him.

SALERIO A kinder gentleman treads not the earth.
I saw Bassanio and Antonio part.
Bassanio told him he would make some speed
Of his return. He answered 'Do not so;
Slubber not business for my sake, Bassanio,
But stay the very riping of the time;
And for the Jew's bond which he hath of me,
Let it not enter in your mind of love;
Be merry, and employ your chiefest thoughts
To courtship, and such fair ostents of love
As shall conveniently become you there'.
And even there, his eye being big with tears,
Turning his face, he put his hand behind him,
And with affection wondrous sensible
He wrung Bassanio's hand; and so they parted.

SOLANIO I think he only loves the world for him.
I pray thee, let us go and find him out,
And quicken his embraced heaviness
With some delight or other.

SALERIO Do we so.

[Exeunt.

SCENE IX. *Belmont. Portia's house.*

Enter NERISSA, and a Servitor.

NERISSA Quick, quick, I pray thee, draw the curtain straight;
The Prince of Arragon hath ta'en his oath,
And comes to his election presently.

Flourish of Cornets. Enter the PRINCE OF ARRAGON, PORTA, and their Trains.

PORTIA Behold, there stand the caskets, noble Prince.
If you choose that wherein I am contain'd,
Straight shall our nuptial rites be solemniz'd;
But if you fail, without more speech, my lord,
you must be gone from hence immediately.

ARRAGON I am enjoin'd by oath to observe three things:
First, never to unfold to any one
Which casket 'twas I chose; next, if I fail
Of the right casket, never in my life
To woo a maid in way of marriage;
Lastly,
If I do fail in fortune of my choice,
Immediately to leave you and be gone.

PORTIA To these injunctions every one doth swear
That comes to hazard for my worthless self.

ARRAGON And so have I address'd me. Fortune now
To my heart's hope! Gold, silver, and base lead.
'Who chooseth me must give and hazard all he hath.'
You shall look fairer ere I give or hazard.
What says the golden chest? Ha! let me see:
'Who chooseth me shall gain what many men desire'.
What many men desire – that 'many' may be meant
By the fool multitude, that choose by show,
Not learning more than the fond eye doth teach;
Which pries not to th' interior, but, like the martlet,
Builds in the weather on the outward wall,
Even in the force and road of casualty.
I will not choose what many men desire,
Because I will not jump with common spirits
And rank me with the barbarous multitudes.
Why, then to thee, thou silver treasure-house!
Tell me once more what title thou dost bear.
'Who chooseth me shall get as much as he deserves.'
And well said too; for who shall go about
To cozen fortune, and be honourable
Without the stamp of merit? Let none presume
To wear an undeserved dignity.

O that estates, degrees, and offices,
Were not deriv'd corruptly, and that clear honour
Were purchas'd by the merit of the wearer!
How many then should cover that stand bare!
How many be commanded that command!
How much low peasantry would then be gleaned
From the true seed of honour! and how much honour
Pick'd from the chaff and ruin of the times,
To be new varnish'd! Well, but to my choice.
'Who chooseth me shall get as much as he deserves.'
I will assume desert. Give me a key for this,
And instantly unlock my fortunes here.

[He opens the silver casket.

PORTIA *[Aside]* Too long a pause for that which you find there.

ARRAGON What's here? The portrait of a blinking idiot
Presenting me a schedule! I will read it.
How much unlike art thou to Portia!
How much unlike my hopes and my deservings!
'Who chooseth me shall have as much as he deserves.'
Did I deserve no more than a fool's head?
Is that my prize? Are my deserts no better?

PORTIA To offend and judge are distinct offices
And of opposed natures.

ARRAGON What is here? *[Reads.*

'The fire seven times tried this;
Seven times tried that judgment is
That did never choose amiss.
Some there be that shadows kiss,
Such have but a shadow's bliss.
There be fools alive iwis
Silver'd o'er, and so was this.
Take what wife you will to bed,
I will ever be your head.
So be gone; you are sped.'
Still more fool I shall appear
By the time I linger here.
With one fool's head I came to woo,
But I go away with two.
Sweet, adieu! I'll keep my oath,
Patiently to bear my wroth.

[Exit with his Train.

PORTIA Thus hath the candle sing'd the moth.
O, these deliberate fools! When they do choose,
They have the wisdom by their wit to lose.

NERISSA The ancient saying is no heresy:
Hanging and wiving goes by destiny.

PORTIA Come, draw the curtain, Nerissa.

Enter a Servant.

SERVANT Where is my lady?

PORTIA Here; what would my lord?

SERVANT Madam, there is alighted at your gate
A young Venetian, one that comes before
To signify th' approaching of his lord,
From whom he bringeth sensible regreets;
To wit, besides commends and courteous breath,
Gifts of rich value. Yet I have not seen
So likely an ambassador of love.
A day in April never came so sweet
To show how costly summer was at hand
As this fore-spurrer comes before his lord.

PORTIA No more, I pray thee; I am half afeard
Thou wilt say anon he is some kin to thee,
Thou spend'st such high-day wit in praising him.
Come, come, Nerissa, for I long to see
Quick Cupid's post that comes so mannerly.

NERISSA Bassanio, Lord Love, if thy will it be!

[Exeunt.

ACT THREE

SCENE I. *Venice. A street.*

Enter SOLANIO and SALERIO.

SOLANIO Now, what news on the Rialto?

SALERIO Why, yet it lives there uncheck'd that Antonio hath a ship of rich lading wreck'd on the narrow seas; the Goodwins I think they call the place, a very dangerous flat and fatal, where the carcases of many a tall ship lie buried, as they say, if my gossip Report be an honest woman of her word.

SOLANIO I would she were as lying a gossip in that as ever knapp'd ginger or made her neighbours believe she wept for the death of a third husband. But it is true, without any slips of prolixity or crossing the plain highway of talk, that the good Antonio, the honest Antonio — O that I had a title good enough to keep his name company! —

SALERIO Come, the full stop.

SOLANIO Ha! What sayest thou? Why, the end is, he hath lost a ship.

SALERIO I would it might prove the end of his losses.

SOLANIO Let me say amen betimes, lest the devil cross my prayer, for here he comes in the likeness of a Jew.

Enter SHYLOCK.

How now, Shylock? What news among the merchants?

SHYLOCK You knew, none so well, none so well as you, of my daughter's flight.

SALERIO That's certain; I, for my part, knew the tailor that made the wings she flew withal.

SOLANIO And Shylock, for his own part, knew the bird was fledge; and then it is the complexion of them all to leave the dam.

SHYLOCK She is damn'd for it.

SALERIO That's certain, if the devil may be her judge.

SHYLOCK My own flesh and blood to rebel!

SOLANIO Out upon it, old carrion! Rebels it at these years?

SHYLOCK I say my daughter is my flesh and my blood.

SALERIO There is more difference between thy flesh and hers than between jet and ivory; more between your bloods than there is between red wine and Rhenish. But tell us, do you hear whether Antonio have had any loss at sea or no?

SHYLOCK There I have another bad match: a bankrupt, a prodigal, who dare scarce show his head on the Rialto; a beggar, that was us'd to come so smug upon the mart. Let him look to his bond. He was wont to call me usurer; let him look to his bond. He was wont to lend money for a Christian courtesy; let him look to his bond.

SALERIO Why, I am sure, if he forfeit, thou wilt not take his flesh. What's that good for?

SHYLOCK To bait fish withal. If it will feed nothing else, it will feed my revenge. He hath disgrac'd me and hind'red me half a million; laugh'd at my losses, mock'd at my gains, scorned my nation, thwarted my bargains, cooled my friends, heated mine enemies. And what's his reason? I am a Jew. Hath not a Jew eyes? Hath not a Jew hands, organs, dimensions, senses, affections, passions, fed with the same food, hurt with the same weapons, subject to the same diseases, healed by the same means, warmed and cooled by the same winter and summer, as a Christian is? If you prick us, do we not bleed? If you tickle us, do we not laugh? If you poison us, do we not die? And if you wrong us, shall we not revenge? If we are like you in the rest, we will resemble you in that. If a Jew wrong a Christian, what is his humility? Revenge. If a Christian wrong a Jew, what should his sufferance be by Christian example? Why, revenge. The villainy you teach me I will execute; and it shall go hard but I will better the instruction.

Enter a Man from Antonio.

MAN Gentlemen, my master Antonio is at his house, and desires to speak with you both.

SALERIO We have been up and down to seek him.

Enter TUBAL.

SOLANIO Here comes another of the tribe; a third cannot be match'd, unless the devil himself turn Jew.

[Exeunt Solanio, Salerio, and Man.

SHYLOCK How now, Tubal, what news from Genoa? Hast thou found my daughter?

TUBAL I often came where I did hear of her, but cannot find her.

SHYLOCK Why there, there, there, there! A diamond gone, cost me two thousand ducats in Frankfort! The curse never fell upon our nation till now; I never felt it till now. Two thousand ducats in that, and other precious, precious jewels. I would my daughter were dead at my foot, and the jewels in her ear; would she were hears'd at my foot, and the ducats in her coffin! No news of them? Why, so – and I know not what's spent in the search. Why, thou – loss upon loss! The thief gone with so much, and so much to find the thief; and no satisfaction, no revenge; nor no ill luck stirring but what lights o' my shoulders; no sighs but o' my breathing; no tears but o' my shedding!

TUBAL Yes, other men have ill luck too: Antonio, as I heard in Genoa –

SHYLOCK What, what, what? Ill luck, ill luck?

TUBAL Hath an argosy cast away coming from Tripolis.

SHYLOCK I thank God, I thank God. Is it true, is it true?

TUBAL I spoke with some of the sailors that escaped the wreck.

SHYLOCK I thank thee, good Tubal. Good news, good news – ha, ha! – head in Genoa.

TUBAL Your daughter spent in Genoa, as I heard, one night, fourscore ducats.

SHYLOCK Thou stick'st a dagger in me – I shall never see my gold again. Fourscore ducats at a sitting! Fourscore ducats!

TUBAL There came divers of Antonio's creditors in my company to Venice that swear he cannot choose but break.

SHYLOCK I am very glad of it; I'll plague him, I'll torture him; I am glad of it.

TUBAL One of them showed me a ring that he had of your daughter for a monkey.

SHYLOCK Out upon her! Thou torturest me, Tubal. It was my turquoise; I had it of Leah when I was a bachelor; I would not have given it

for a wilderness of monkeys.
TUBAL But Antonio is certainly undone.
SHYLOCK Nay, that's true; that's very true. Go, Tubal, fee me an officer; bespeak him a fortnight before. I will have the heart of him, if he forfeit; for, were he out of Venice, I can make what merchandise I will. Go, Tubal, and meet me at our synagogue; go, good Tubal; at our synagogue, Tubal. *[Exeunt.*

SCENE II. *Belmont. Portia's house.*

Enter BASSANIO, PORTIA, GRATIANO, NERISSA,, and all their Trains.

PORTIA I pray you tarry; pause a day or two
Before you hazard; for, in choosing wrong,
I lose your company; therefore forbear a awhile.
There's something tells me – but it is not love –
I would not lose you; and you know yourself
Hate counsels not in such a quality.
But lest you should not understand me well –
And yet a maiden hath no tongue but thought –
I would detain you here some month or two
Before you venture for me. I could teach you
How to choose right, but then I am forsworn;
So will I never be; so may you miss me;
But if you do, you'll make me wish a sin,
That I had been forsworn. Beshrew your eyes!
They have o'erlook'd me and divided me;
One half of me is yours, the other half yours –
Mine own, I would say; but if mine, then yours,
And so all yours. O! these naughty times
Puts bars between the owners and their rights;
And so, though yours, not yours. Prove it so,
Let fortune go to hell for it, not I.
I speak too long, but 'tis to peize the time,
To eke it, and to draw it out in length,
To stay you from election.
BASSANIO Let me choose;
For as I am, I live upon the rack.
PORTIA Upon the rack, Bassanio? Then confess
What treason there is mingled with your love.
BASSANIO None but that ugly treason of mistrust,
Which makes me fear th' enjoying of my love;
There may as well be amity and life
'Tween snow and fire as treason and my love.
PORTIA Ay, but I fear you speak upon the rack,
Where men enforced do speak anything.
BASSANIO Promise me life, and I'll confess the truth.
PORTIA Well then, confess and live.
BASSANIO 'Confess' and 'love'
Had been the very sum of my confession.
O happy torment, when my torturer
Doth teach me answers for deliverance!
But let me to my fortune and the caskets.
PORTIA Away, then; I am lock'd in one of them.
If you do love me, you will find me out.
Nerissa and the rest, stand all aloof;
Let music sound while he doth make his choice;
Then, if he lose, he makes a swan-like end,
Fading in music. That the comparison
May stand more proper, my eye shall be the stream
And wat'ry death-bed for him. He may win;
And what is music then? Then music is
Even as the flourish when true subjects bow
To a new-crowned monarch; such it is
As are those dulcet sounds in break of day
That creep into the dreaming bridegroom's ear
And summon him to marriage. Now he goes,
With no less presence, but with much more love,
Than young Alcides when he did redeem
The virgin tribute paid by howling Troy
To the sea-monster. I stand for sacrifice;
The rest aloof are the Dardanian wives,
With bleared visages come forth to view
The issue of th' exploit. Go, Hercules!
Live thou, I live. With much much more dismay
I view the fight than thou that mak'st the fray.

A Song, the whilst Bassanio comments on the caskets to himself.

Tell me where is fancy bred,
Or in the heart or in the head,
How begot, how nourished?
Reply, reply.
It is engend'red in the eyes,
With gazing fed; and fancy dies
In the cradle where it lies.
Let us all ring fancy's knell:
I'll begin it – Ding, dong, bell.

ALL Ding, dong, bell.
BASSANIO So may the outward shows be least themselves;
The world is still deceiv'd with ornament.
In law, what plea so tainted and corrupt
But, being season'd with a gracious voice,
Obscures the show of evil? In religion,
What damned error but some sober brow
Will bless it, and approve it with a text,
Hiding the grossness with fair ornament?
There is no vice so simple but assumes
Some mark of virtue on his outward parts.
How many cowards, whose hearts are all as false
As stairs of sand, wear yet upon their chins
The beards of Hercules and frowning Mars;
Who, inward search'd, have livers white as milk!
And these assume but valour's excrement
To render them redoubted. Look on beauty
And you shall see 'tis purchas'd by the weight,
Which therein works a miracle in nature,

Making them lightest that wear most of it;
So are those crisped snaky golden locks
Which makes such wanton gambols with the wind
Upon supposed fairness often known
To be the dowry of a second head –
The skull that bred them in the sepulchre.
Thus ornament is but the guiled shore
To a most dangerous sea; the beauteous scarf
Veiling an Indian beauty; in a word,
The seeming truth which cunning times put on
To entrap the wisest. Therefore, thou gaudy gold,
Hard food for Midas, I will none of thee;
Nor none of thee, thou pale and common drudge
'Tween man and man; but thou, thou meagre lead,
Which rather threaten'st than dost promise aught,
Thy plainness moves me more than eloquence,
And here choose I. Joy be the consequence!

PORTIA *[Aside]* How all the other passions fleet to air,
As doubtful thoughts, and rash-embrac'd despair,
And shudd'ring fear, and green-ey'd jealousy!
O love, be moderate, allay thy ecstasy,
In measure rain thy joy, scant this excess!
I feel too much thy blessing. Make it less,
For fear I surfeit.

BASSANIO *[Opening the leaden casket]* What find I here?
Fair Portia's counterfeit! What demi-god
Hath come so near creation? Move these eyes?
Or whether riding on the balls of mine
Seem they in motion? Here are sever'd lips,
Parted with sugar breath; so sweet a bar
Should sunder such sweet friends. Here in her hairs
The painter plays the spider, and hath woven
A golden mesh t' entrap the hearts of men
Faster than gnats in cobwebs. But her eyes –
How could he see to do them? Having made one,
Methinks it should have power to steal both his,
And leave itself unfurnish'd. Yet look how far
The substance of my praise doth wrong this shadow
In underprizing it, so far this shadow
Doth limp behind the substance. Here's the scroll,
The continent and summary of my fortune.

'You that choose not by the view,
Chance as fair and choose as true!
Since this fortune falls to you,
Be content and seek no new.
If you be well pleas'd with this,
And hold your fortune for your bliss,
Turn you where your lady is
And claim her with a loving kiss.'

A gentle scroll. Fair lady, by your leave;
I come by note, to give and to receive.
Like one of two contending in a prize,
That thinks he hath done well in people's eyes,
Hearing applause and universal shout,
Giddy in spirit, still gazing in a doubt
Whether those peals of praise be his or no;
So, thrice-fair, lady, stand I even so,
As doubtful whether what I see be true,
Until confirm'd, sign'd, ratified by you.

PORTIA You see me, Lord Bassanio, where I stand,
Such as I am. Though for myself alone
I would not be ambitious in my wish
To wish myself much better, yet for you
I would be trebled twenty times myself,
A thousand times more fair, ten thousand times more rich,
That only to stand high in your account
I might in virtues, beauties, livings, friends,
Exceed account. But the full sum of me
Is sum of something which, to term in gross,
Is an unlesson'd girl, unschool'd, unpractis'd;
Happy in this, she is not yet so old
But she may learn; happier than this,
She is not bred so dull but she can learn;
Happiest of all is that her gentle spirit
Commits itself to yours to be directed,
As from her lord, her governor, her king.
Myself and what is mine to you and yours
Is now converted. But now I was the lord
Of this fair mansion, master of my servants,
Queen o'er myself; and even now, but now,
This house, these servants, and this same myself,
Are yours – my lord's. I give them with this ring,
Which when you part from, lose, or give away,
Let it presage the ruin of your love,
And be my vantage to exclaim on you.

BASSANIO Madam, you have bereft me of all words;
Only my blood speaks to you in my veins;
And there is such confusion in my powers
As, after some oration fairly spoke
By a beloved prince, there doth appear
Among the buzzing pleased multitude,
Where every something, being blent together,
Turns to a wild of nothing, save of joy
Express'd and not express'd. But when this ring
Parts from this finger, then parts life from hence;

O, then be bold to say Bassanio's dead!
NERISSA My lord and lady, it is now our time
That haye stood by and seen our wishes prosper
To cry 'Good joy'. Good joy, my lord and lady!
GRATIANO My Lord Bassanio, and my gentle
lady,
I wish you all the joy that you can wish,
For I am sure you can wish none from me;
And, when your honours mean to solemnize
The bargain of your faith, I do beseech you
Even at that time I may be married too.
BASSANIO With all my heart, so thou canst get a
wife.
GRATIANO I thank your lordship you have got
me one.
My eyes, my lord, can look as swift as yours:
You saw the mistress, I beheld the maid;
You lov'd, I lov'd; for intermission
No more pertains to me, my lord, than you.
Your fortune stood upon the caskets there,
And so did mine too, as the matter falls;
For wooing here until I sweat again,
And swearing till my very roof was dry
With oaths of love, at last – if promise last –
I got a promise of this fair one here
To have her love, provided that your fortune
Achiev'd her mistress.
PORTIA Is this true, Nerissa?
NERISSA Madam, it is, so you stand pleas'd
withal.
BASSANIO And do you, Gratiano, mean good
faith?
GRATIANO Yes, faith, my lord.
BASSANIO Our feast shall be much honoured in
your marriage.
GRATIANO We'll play with them: the first boy for
a thousand ducats.
NERISSA What, and stake down?
GRATIANO No; we shall ne'er win at that sport,
and stake down –
But who comes here? Lorenzo and his infidel?
What, and my old Venetian friend, Salerio!

Enter LORENZO, JESSICA, and SALERIO, a messenger from Venice.

BASSANIO Lorenzo and Salerio, welcome hither,
If that the youth of my new int'rest here
Have power to bid you welcome. By your
leave,
I bid my very friends and countrymen,
Sweet Portia, welcome.
PORTIA So do I, my lord;
They are entirely welcome.
LORENZO I thank your honour. For my part, my
lord,
My purpose was not to have seen you here;
But meeting with Salerio by the way,
He did entreat me, past all saying nay,
To come with him along.
SALERIO I did, my lord,
And I have reason for it. Signior Antonio
Commends him to you.
[Gives Bassanio a letter.
BASSANIO Ere I ope his letter,
I pray you tell me how my good friend doth.
SALERIO Not sick, my lord, unless it be in mind;
Nor well, unless in mind; his letter there
Will show you his estate.
[Bassanio opens the letter.
GRATIANO Nerissa, cheer yond stranger; bid her
welcome.
Your hand, Salerio. What's the news from
Venice?
How doth that royal merchant, good Antonio?
I know he will be glad of our success:
We are the Jasons, we have won the fleece.
SALERIO I would you had won the fleece that he
hath lost.
PORTIA There are some shrewd contents in yond
same paper
That steals the colour from Bassanio's cheek:
Some dear friend dead, else nothing in the
world
Could turn so much the constitution
Of any constant man. What, worse and worse!
With leave, Bassanio: I am half yourself,
And I must freely have the half of anything
That this same paper brings you.
BASSANIO O sweet Portia,
Here are a few of the unpleasant'st words
That ever blotted paper! Gentle lady,
When I did first impart my love to you,
I freely told you all the wealth I had
Ran in my veins – I was a gentleman;
And then I told you true. And yet, dear lady,
Rating myself at nothing, you shall see
How much I was a braggart. When I told you
My state was nothing, I should then have told
you
That I was worse than nothing; for indeed
I have engag'd myself to a dear friend,
Engag'd my friend to his mere enemy,
To feed my means. Here is a letter, lady,
The paper as the body of my friend,
And every word in it a gaping wound
Issuing life-blood. But it is true, Salerio?
Hath all his ventures fail'd? What, not one hit?
From Tripolis, from Mexico, and England,
From Lisbon, Barbary, and India,
And not one vessel scape the dreadful touch
Of merchant-marring rocks?
SALERIO Not, one, my lord.

Besides, it should appear that, if he had
The present money to discharge the Jew,
He would not take it. Never did I know
A creature that did bear the shape of man
So keen and greedy to confound a man.
He plies the Duke at morning and at night,
And doth impeach the freedom of the state,
If they deny him justice. Twenty merchants,
The Duke himself, and the magnificoes
Of greatest port, have all persuaded with him;
But none can drive him from the envious plea
Of forfeiture, of justice, and his bond.

JESSICA When I was with him, I have heard him swear
To Tubal and to Chus, his countrymen,
That he would rather have Antonio's flesh
Than twenty times the value of the sum
That he did owe him; and I know, my lord,
If law, authority, and power, deny not,
It will go hard with poor Antonio.

PORTIA Is it your dear friend that is thus in trouble?

BASSANIO The dearest friend to me, the kindest man,
The best condition'd and unwearied spirit
In doing courtesies; and one in whom
The ancient Roman honour more appears
Than any that draws breath in Italy.

PORTIA What sum owes he the Jew?

BASSANIO For me, three thousand ducats.

PORTIA What! no more?
Pay him six thousand, and deface the bond;
Double six thousand, and then treble that,
Before a friend of this description
Shall lose a hair through Bassanio's fault.
First go with me to church and call me wife,
And then away to Venice to your friend;
For never shall you lie by Portia's side
With an unquiet soul. You shall have gold
To pay the petty debt twenty times over.
When it is paid, bring your true friend along.
My maid Nerissa and myself meantime
Will live as maids and widows. Come, away;
For you shall hence upon your wedding-day.
Bid your friends welcome, show a merry cheer;
Since you are dear bought, I will love you dear.
But let me hear the letter of your friend.

BASSANIO [*Reads*] 'Sweet Bassanio, my ships have all miscarried, my creditors grow cruel, my estate is very low, my bond to the Jew is forfeit; and since, in paying it, it is impossible I should live, all debts are clear'd between you and I, if I might but see you at my death. Notwithstanding, use your pleasure; if your love do not persuade you to come, let not my letter.'

PORTIA O love, dispatch all business and be gone!

BASSANIO Since I have your good leave to go away,
I will make haste; but, till I come again,
No bed shall e'er be guilty of my stay,
Nor rest be interposer 'twixt us twain.

[*Exeunt.*

SCENE III. *Venice. A street.*

Enter SHYLOCK, SOLANIO, ANTONIO, and Gaoler.

SHYLOCK Gaoler, look to him. Tell not me of mercy
This is the fool that lent out money gratis.
Gaoler, look to him.

ANTONIO Hear me yet, good Shylock.

SHYLOCK I'll have my bond; speak not against my bond.
I have sworn an oath that I will have my bond.
Thou call'dst me dog before thou hadst a cause,
But, since I am a dog, beware my fangs;
The Duke shall grant me justice. I do wonder,
Thou naughty gaoler, that thou art so fond
To come abroad with him at his request.

ANTONIO I pray thee hear me speak.

SHYLOCK I'll have my bond. I will not hear thee speak;
I'll have my bond; and therefore speak no more.
I'll not be made a soft and dull-ey'd fool,
To shake the head, relent, and sigh, and yield,
To Christian intercessors. Follow not;
I'll have no speaking; I will have my bond.

[*Exit.*

SOLANIO It is the most impenetrable cur
That ever kept with men.

ANTONIO Let him alone;
I'll follow him no more with bootless prayers.
He seeks my life; his reason well I know:
I oft deliver'd from his forfeitures
Many that have at times made moan to me;
Therefore he hates me.

SOLANIO I am sure the Duke
Will never grant this forfeiture to hold.

ANTONIO The Duke cannot deny the course of law;
For the commodity that strangers have
With us in Venice, if it be denied,
Will much impeach the justice of the state,
Since that the trade and profit of the city
Consisteth of all nations. Therefore, go;
These griefs and losses have so bated me
That I shall hardly spare a pound of flesh
To-morrow to my bloody creditor.
Well, gaoler, on; pray God Bassanio come
To see me pay his debt, and then I care not.

[*Exeunt.*

SCENE IV. *Belmont. Portia's house.*

Enter PORTIA, NERISSA, LORENZO, JESSICA, and BALTHASAR.

LORENZO Madam, although I speak it in your presence,
You have a noble and a true conceit
Of godlike amity, which appears most strongly
In bearing thus the absence of your lord.
But if you knew to whom you show this honour,
How true a gentleman you send relief,
How dear a lover of my lord your husband,
I know you would be prouder of the work
Than customary bounty can enforce you.

PORTIA I never did repent for doing good,
Nor shall not now; for in companions
That do converse and waste the time together,
Whose souls do bear an equal yoke of love,
There must be needs a like proportion
Of lineaments, of manners, and of spirit,
Which makes me think that this Antonio,
Being the bosom lover of my lord,
Must needs be like my lord. If it be so,
How little is the cost I have bestowed
In purchasing the semblance of my soul
From out the state of hellish cruelty!
This comes too near the praising of myself;
Therefore, no more of it; hear other things.
Lorenzo, I commit into your hands
The husbandry and manage of my house
Until my lord's return; for mine own part,
I have toward heaven breath'd a secret vow
To live in prayer and contemplation,
Only attended by Nerissa here,
Until her husband and my lord's return.
There is a monastery two miles off,
And there we will abide. I do desire you
Not to deny this imposition,
The which my love and some necessity
Now lays upon you.

LORENZO Madam, with all my heart
I shall obey you in all fair commands.

PORTIA My people do already know my mind,
And will acknowledge you and Jessica
In place of Lord Bassanio and myself.
So fare you well till we shall meet again.

LORENZO Fair thoughts and happy hours attend on you!

JESSICA I wish your ladyship all heart's content.

PORTIA I thank you for your wish, and am well pleas'd
To wish it back on you. Fare you well, Jessica.
[Exeunt Jessica and Lorenzo.
Now, Balthasar,
As I have ever found thee honest-true,
So let me find thee still. Take this same letter,
And use thou all th' endeavour of a man
In speed to Padua; see thou render this
Into my cousin's hands, Doctor Bellario;
And look what notes and garments he doth give thee,
Bring them, I pray thee, with imagin'd speed
Unto the traject, to the common ferry
Which trades to Venice. Waste no time in words,
But get thee gone; I shall be there before thee.

BALTHASAR Madam, I go with all convenient speed. *[Exit.*

PORTIA Come on, Nerissa, I have work in hand
That you yet know not of; we'll see our husbands
Before they think of us.

NERISSA Shall they see us?

PORTIA They shall, Nerissa; but in such a habit
That they shall think we are accomplished
With that we lack. I'll hold thee any wager,
When we are both accoutred like young men,
I'll prove the prettier fellow of the two,
And wear my dagger with the braver grace,
And speak between the change of man and boy
With a reed voice; and turn two mincing steps
Into a manly stride; and speak of frays
Like a fine bragging youth; and tell quaint lies,
How honourable ladies sought my love,
Which I denying, they fell sick and died –
I could not do withal. Then I'll repent,
And wish, for all that, that I had not kill'd them.
And twenty of these puny lies I'll tell,
That men shall swear I have discontinued school
Above a twelvemonth. I have within my mind
A thousand raw tricks of these bragging Jacks,
Which I will practise.

NERISSA Why, shall we turn to men?

PORTIA Fie, what a question's that,
If thou wert near a lewd interpreter!
But come, I'll tell thee all my whole device
When I am in my coach, which stays for us
At the park gate; and therefore haste away,
For we must measure twenty miles to-day.
[Exeunt.

SCENE V. *Belmont. The garden.*

Enter LAUNCELOT and JESSICA.

LAUNCELOT Yes, truly; for, look you, the sins of the father are to be laid upon the children; therefore, I promise you, I fear you. I was always plain with you, and so now I speak my agitation of the matter; therefore be o' good cheer, for truly I think you are damn'd. There is but one hope in it that can do you any good, and that is but a kind of bastard hope neither.

JESSICA And what hope is that, I pray thee?

LAUNCELOT Marry, you may partly hope that your father got you not – that you are not the Jew's daughter.

JESSICA That were a kind of bastard hope indeed; so the sins of my mother should be visited upon me.

LAUNCELOT Truly then I fear you are damn'd both by father and mother; thus when I shun Scylla, your father, I fall into Charybdis, your mother; well, you are gone both ways.

JESSICA I shall be sav'd by my husband; he hath made me a Christian.

LAUNCELOT Truly, the more to blame he; we were Christians enow before, e'en as many as could well live one by another. This making of Christians will raise the price of hogs; if we grow all to be pork-eaters, we shall not shortly have a rasher on the coals for money.

Enter LORENZO.

JESSICA I'll tell my husband, Launcelot, what you say; here he comes.

LORENZO I shall grow jealous of you shortly, Launcelot, if you thus get my wife into corners.

JESSICA Nay, you need nor fear us, Lorenzo; Launcelot and I are out; he tells me flatly there's no mercy for me in heaven, because I am a Jew's daughter; and he says you are no good member of the commonwealth, for in converting Jews to Christians you raise the price of pork.

LORENZO I shall answer that better to the commonwealth than you can the getting up of the negro's belly; the Moor is with child by you, Launcelot.

LAUNCELOT It is much that the Moor should be more than reason; but if she be less than an honest woman, she is indeed more than I took her for.

LORENZO How every fool can play upon the word! I think the best grace of wit will shortly turn into silence, and discourse grow commendable in none only but parrots. Go in, sirrah; bid them prepare for dinner.

LAUNCELOT That is done, sir; they have all stomachs.

LORENZO Goodly Lord, what a wit-snapper are you! Then bid them prepare dinner.

LAUNCELOT That is done too, sir, only 'cover' is the word.

LORENZO Will you cover, then, sir?

LAUNCELOT Not so, sir, neither; I know my duty.

LORENZO Yet more quarrelling with occasion! Wilt thou show the whole wealth of thy wit in an instant? I pray thee understand a plain man in his plain meaning: go to thy fellows, bid them cover the table, serve in the meat, and we will come in to dinner.

LAUNCELOT For the table, sir, it shall be serv'd in; for the meat, sir, it shall be cover'd; for your coming in to dinner, sir, why, let it be as humours and conceits shall govern. [*Exit.*

LORENZO O dear discretion, how his words are suited!
The fool hath planted in his memory
An army of good words; and I do know
A many fools that stand in better place,
Garnish'd like him, that for a tricksy word
Defy the matter. How cheer'st thou, Jessica?
And now, good sweet, say thy opinion,
How dost thou like the Lord Bassanio's wife?

JESSICA Past all expressing. It is very meet
The Lord Bassanio live an upright life,
For, having such a blessing in his lady,
He finds the joys of heaven here on earth;
And if on earth he do not merit it,
In reason he should never come to heaven.
Why, if two gods should play some heavenly match,
And on the wager lay two earthly women,
And Portia one, there must be something else
Pawn'd with the other; for the poor rude world
Hath not her fellow.

LORENZO Even such a husband
Hast thou of me as she is for a wife.

JESSICA Nay, but ask my opinion too of that.

LORENZO I will anon; first let us go to dinner.

JESSICA Nay, let me praise you while I have a stomach.

LORENZO No, pray thee, let it serve for table-talk;
Then howsome'er thou speak'st, 'mong other things
I shall digest it.

JESSICA Well, I'll set you forth.

[*Exeunt.*

ACT FOUR

SCENE I. *Venice. The court of justice.*

Enter the DUKE, *the Magnificoes,* ANTONIO, BASSANIO, GRATIANO, SALERIO, *and Others.*

DUKE What, is Antonio here?

ANTONIO Ready, so please your Grace.

DUKE I am sorry for thee; thou art come to answer
A stony adversary, an inhuman wretch,
Uncapable of pity, void and empty

From any dram of mercy.
ANTONIO I have heard
Your Grace hath ta'en great pains to qualify
His rigorous course; but since he stands obdurate,
And that no lawful means can carry me
Out of his envy's reach, I do oppose
My patience to his fury, and am arm'd
To suffer with a quietness of spirit
The very tyranny and rage of his.
DUKE Go one, and call the Jew into the court.
SALERIO He is ready at the door; he comes, my lord.

Enter SHYLOCK.

DUKE Make room, and let him stand before our face.
Shylock, the world thinks, and I think so too,
That thou but leadest this fashion of thy malice
To the last hour of act; and then, 'tis thought,
Thou'lt show thy mercy and remorse, more strange
Than is thy strange apparent cruelty;
And where thou now exacts the penalty,
Which is a pound of this poor merchant's flesh,
Thou wilt not only loose the forfeiture,
But, touch'd with human gentleness and love,
Forgive a moiety of the principal,
Glancing an eye of pity on his losses,
That have of late so huddled on his back –
Enow to press a royal merchant down,
And pluck commiseration of his state
From brassy bosoms and rough hearts of flint,
From stubborn Turks and Tartars, never train'd
To offices of tender courtesy.
We all expect a gentle answer, Jew.
SHYLOCK I have possess'd your Grace of what I purpose,
And by our holy Sabbath have I sworn
To have the due and forfeit of my bond.
If you deny it, let the danger light
Upon your charter and your city's freedom.
You'll ask me why I rather choose to have
A weight of carrion flesh than to receive
Three thousand ducats. I'll not answer that,
But say it is my humour – is it answer'd?
What if my house be troubled with a rat,
And I be pleas'd to give ten thousand ducats
To have it ban'd? What, are you answer'd yet?
Some men there are love not a gaping pig;
Some that are mad if they behold a cat;
And others, when the bagpipe sings i' th' nose,
Cannot contain their urine; for affection,
Mistress of passion, sways it to the mood
Of what it likes or loathes. Now, for your answer:
As there is no firm reason to be rend'red
Why he cannot abide a gaping pig;
Why he, a harmless necessary cat;
Why he, a woollen bagpipe, but of force
Must yield to such inevitable shame
As to offend, himself being offended;
So can I give no reason, nor I will not,
More than a lodg'd hate and a certain loathing
I bear Antonio, that I follow thus
A losing suit against him. Are you answered?
BASSANIO This is no answer, thou unfeeling man,
To excuse the current of thy cruelty.
SHYLOCK I am not bound to please thee with my answers.
BASSANIO Do all men kill the things they do not love?
SHYLOCK Hates any man the thing he would not kill?
BASSANIO Every offence is not a hate at first.
SHYLOCK What, wouldst thou have a serpent sting thee twice?
ANTONIO I pray you, think you question with the Jew.
You may as well go stand upon the beach
And bid the main flood bate his usual height;
You may as well use question with the wolf,
Why he hath made the ewe bleat for the lamb;
You may as well forbid the mountain pines
To wag their high tops and to make no noise
When they are fretten with the gusts of heaven;
You may as well do any thing most hard
As seek to soften that – than which what's harder? –
His Jewish heart. Therefore, I do beseech you,
Make no moe offers, use no farther means,
But with all brief and plain conveniency
Let me have judgment, and the Jew his will.
BASSANIO For thy three thousand ducats here is six.
SHYLOCK If every ducat in six thousand ducats
Were in six parts, and every part a ducat,
I would not draw them; I would have my bond.
DUKE How shalt thou hope for mercy, rend'ring none?
SHYLOCK What judgment shall I dread, doing no wrong?
You have among you many a purchas'd slave,
Which, like your asses and your dogs and mules,
You use in abject and in slavish parts,
Because you bought them; shall I say to you
'Let them be free, marry them to your heirs –
Why sweat they under burdens? – let their beds
Be made as soft as yours, and let their palates
Be season'd with such viands'? You will answer
'The slaves are ours'. So do I answer you:
The pound of flesh which I demand of him

Is dearly bought, 'tis mine, and I will have it.
If you deny me, fie upon your law!
There is no force in the decrees of Venice.
I stand for judgment; answer; shall I have it?

DUKE Upon my power I may dismiss this court,
Unless Bellario, a learned doctor,
Whom I have sent for to determine this,
Come here to-day.

SALERIO My lord, here stays without
A messenger with letters from the doctor,
New come from Padua.

DUKE Bring us the letters; call the messenger.

BASSANIO Good cheer, Antonio! What, man, courage yet!
The Jew shall have my flesh, blood, bones, and all,
Ere thou shalt lose for me one drop of blood.

ANTONIO I am a tainted wether of the flock,
Meetest for death; the weakest kind of fruit
Drops earliest to the ground, and so let me.
You cannot better be employ'd, Bassanio,
Than to live still, and write mine epitaph.

Enter NERISSA, dressed like a lawyer's clerk.

DUKE Came you from Padua, from Bellario?

NERISSA From both, my lord. Bellario greets your Grace. [*Presents a letter.*

BASSANIO Why dost thou whet thy knife so earnestly?

SHYLOCK To cut the forfeiture from that bankrupt there.

GRATIANO Not on thy sole, but on thy soul, harsh Jew,
Thou mak'st thy knife keen; but no metal can,
No, not the hangman's axe, bear half the keenness
Of thy sharp envy. Can no prayers pierce thee?

SHYLOCK No, none that thou hast wit enough to make.

GRATIANO O, be thou damn'd, inexecrable dog!
And for thy life let justice be accus'd.
Thou almost mak'st me waver in my faith,
To hold opinion with Pythagoras
That souls of animals infuse themselves
Into the trunks of men. Thy currish spirit
Govern'd a wolf who, hang'd for human slaughter,
Even from the gallows did his fell soul fleet,
And, whilst thou layest in thy unhallowed dam,
Infus'd itself in thee; for thy desires
Are wolfish, bloody, starv'd, and ravenous.

SHYLOCK Till thou canst rail the seal from off my bond,
Thou but offend'st thy lungs to speak so loud;
Repair thy wit, good youth, or it will fall
To cureless ruin. I stand here for law.

DUKE This letter from Bellario doth commend
A young and learned doctor to our court.
Where is he?

NERISSA He attendeth here hard by
To know your answer, whether you'll admit him.

DUKE With all my heart. Some three or four of you
Go give him courteous conduct to this place.
Meantime, the court shall hear Bellario's letter.

CLERK [*Reads*] 'Your Grace shall understand that at the receipt of your letter I am very sick; but in the instant that your messenger came, in loving visitation was with me a young doctor of Rome – his name is Balthazar. I acquainted him with the cause in controversy between the Jew and Antonio the merchant; we turn'd o'er many books together; he is furnished with my opinion which, bettered with his own learning – the greatness whereof I cannot enough commend – comes with him at my importunity to fill up your Grace's request in my stead. I beseech you let his lack of years be no impediment to let him lack a reverend estimation, for I never knew so young a body with so old a head. I leave him to your gracious acceptance, whose trial shall better publish his commendation.'

Enter PORTIA for BALTHASAR, dressed like a Doctor of Laws.

DUKE You hear the learn'd Bellario, what he writes;
And here, I take it, is the doctor come.
Give me your hand; come you from old Bellario?

PORTIA I did, my lord.

DUKE You are welcome; take your place.
Are you acquainted with the difference
That holds this present question in the court?

PORTIA I am informed throughly of the cause.
Which is the merchant here, and which the Jew?

DUKE Antonio and old Shylock, both stand forth.

PORTIA Is your name Shylock?

SHYLOCK Shylock is my name.

PORTIA Of a strange nature is the suit you follow;
Yet in such rule that the Venetian law
Cannot impugn you as you do proceed.
You stand within his danger, do you not?

ANTONIO Ay, so he says.

PORTIA Do you confess the bond?

ANTONIO I do.

PORTIA Then must the Jew be merciful.

SHYLOCK On what compulsion must I? Tell me that.

PORTIA The quality of mercy is not strain'd;
It droppeth as the gentle rain from heaven

Upon the place beneath. It is twice blest:
It blesseth him that gives and him that takes.
'Tis mightiest in the mightiest; it becomes
The throned monarch better than his crown;
His sceptre shows the force of temporal power,
The attribute to awe and majesty,
Wherein doth sit the dread and fear of kings;
But mercy is above this sceptred sway,
It is enthroned in the hearts of kings,
It is an attribute to God himself;
And earthly power doth then show likest God's
When mercy seasons justice. Therefore, Jew,
Though justice be thy plea, consider this –
That in the course of justice none of us
Should see salvation; we do pray for mercy,
And that same prayer doth teach us all to render
The deeds of mercy. I have spoke thus much
To mitigate the justice of thy plea,
Which if thou follow, this strict court of Venice
Must needs give sentence 'gainst the merchant there.

SHYLOCK My deeds upon my head! I crave the law,
The penalty and forfeit of my bond.

PORTIA Is he not able to discharge the money?

BASSANIO Yes; here I tender it for him in the court;
Yea, twice the sum; if that will not suffice,
I will be bound to pay it ten times o'er
On forfeit of my hands, my head, my heart;
If this will not suffice, it must appear
That malice bears down truth. And, I beseech you,
Wrest once the law to your authority;
To do a great right do a little wrong,
And curb this cruel devil of his will.

PORTIA It must not be; there is no power in Venice
Can alter a decree established;
'Twill be recorded for a precedent,
And many an error, by the same example,
Will rush into the state; it cannot be.

SHYLOCK A Daniel come to judgment! Yea, a Daniel!
O wise young judge, how I do honour thee!

PORTIA I pray you, let me look upon the bond.

SHYLOCK Here 'tis, most reverend Doctor; here it is.

PORTIA Shylock, there's thrice thy money off'red thee.

SHYLOCK An oath, an oath! I have an oath in heaven.
Shall I lay perjury upon my soul?
No, not for Venice.

PORTIA Why, this bond is forfeit;
And lawfully by this the Jew may claim
A pound of flesh, to be by him cut off
Nearest the merchant's heart. Be merciful.
Take thrice thy money; bid me tear the bond.

SHYLOCK When it is paid according to the tenour.
It doth appear you are a worthy judge;
You know the law; your exposition
Hath been most sound; I charge you by the law,
Whereof you are a well-deserving pillar,
Proceed to judgment. By my soul I swear
There is no power in the tongue of man
To alter me. I stay here on my bond.

ANTONIO Most heartily I do beseech the court
To give the judgment.

PORTIA Why then, thus it is:
You must prepare your bosom for his knife.

SHYLOCK O noble judge! O excellent young man!

PORTIA For the intent and purpose of the law
Hath full relation to the penalty,
Which here appeareth due upon the bond.

SHYLOCK 'Tis very true. O wise and upright judge,
How much more elder art thou than thy looks!

PORTIA Therefore, lay bare your bosom.

SHYLOCK Ay, his breast –
So says the bond; doth it not, noble judge?
'Nearest his heart', those are the very words.

PORTIA It is so. Are there balance here to weigh
The flesh?

SHYLOCK I have them ready.

PORTIA Have by some surgeon, Shylock, on your charge,
To stop his wounds, lest he do bleed to death.

SHYLOCK Is it so nominated in the bond?

PORTIA It is not so express'd, but what of that?
'Twere good you do so much for charity.

SHYLOCK I cannot find it; 'tis not in the bond.

PORTIA You, merchant, have you anything to say?

ANTONIO But little: I am arm'd and well prepar'd.
Give me your hand Bassanio; fare you well.
Grieve not that I am fall'n to this for you,
For herein Fortune shows herself more kind
Than is her custom. It is still her use
To let the wretched man outlive his wealth,
To view with hollow eye and wrinkled brow
An age of poverty; from which ling'ring penance
Of such misery doth she cut me off.
Commend me to your honourable wife;
Tell her the process of Antonio's end;
Say how I lov'd you; speak me fair in death;
And, when the tale is told, bid her be judge
Whether Bassanio had not once a love.
Repent but you that you shall lose your friend,
And he repents not that he pays your debt;
For if the Jew do cut but deep enough,

I'll pay it instantly with all my heart.
BASSANIO Antonio, I am married to a wife
Which is as dear to me as life itself;
But life itself, my wife, and all the world,
Are not with me esteem'd above thy life;
I would lose all, ay, sacrifice them all
Here to this devil, to deliver you.
PORTIA Your wife would give you little thanks for that,
If she were by to hear you make the offer.
GRATIANO I have a wife who I protest I love;
I would she were in heaven, so she could
Entreat some power to change this currish Jew.
NERISSA 'Tis well you offer it behind her back;
The wish would make else an unquiet house.
SHYLOCK [*Aside*] These be the Christian husbands! I have a daughter –
Would any of the stock of Barrabas
Had been her husband, rather than a Christian! –
We trifle time; I pray thee pursue sentence.
PORTIA A pound of that same merchant's flesh is thine.
The court awards it and the law doth give it.
SHYLOCK Most rightful judge!
PORTIA And you must cut this flesh from off his breast.
The law allows it and the court awards it.
SHYLOCK Most learned judge! A sentence! Come, prepare.
PORTIA Tarry a little; there is something else.
This bond doth give thee here no jot of blood:
The words expressly are 'a pound of flesh'.
Take then thy bond, take thou thy pound of flesh;
But, in the cutting it, if thou dost shed
One drop of Christian blood, thy lands and goods
Are, by the laws of Venice, confiscate
Unto the state of Venice.
GRATIANO O upright judge! Mark, Jew. O learned judge!
SHYLOCK Is that the law?
PORTIA Thyself shalt see the act;
For, as thou urgest justice, be assur'd
Thou shalt have justice, more than thou desir'st.
GRATIANO O learned judge! Mark, Jew. A learned judge!
SHYLOCK I take this offer then: pay the bond thrice,
And let the Christian go.
BASSANIO Here is the money.
PORTIA Soft!
The Jew shall have all justice. Soft! No haste.
He shall have nothing but the penalty.
GRATIANO O Jew! an upright judge, a learned judge!
PORTIA Therefore, prepare thee to cut off the flesh.
Shed thou no blood, nor cut thou less nor more
But just a pound of flesh; if thou tak'st more
Or less than a just pound – be it but so much
As makes it light or heavy in the substance,
Or the divison of the twentieth part
Of one poor scruple; nay, if the scale do turn
But in the estimation of a hair –
Thou diest, and all thy goods are confiscate.
GRATIANO A second Daniel, a Daniel, Jew!
Now, infidel, I have you on the hip.
PORTIA Why doth the Jew pause? Take thy forfeiture.
SHYLOCK Give me my principal, and let me go.
BASSANIO I have it ready for thee; here it is.
PORTIA He hath refus'd it in the open court;
He shall have merely justice, and his bond.
GRATIANO A Daniel still say I, a second Daniel!
I thank thee, Jew, for teaching me that word.
SHYLOCK Shall I not have barely my principal?
PORTIA Thou shalt have nothing but the forfeiture
To be so taken at thy peril, Jew.
SHYLOCK Why, then the devil give him good of it!
I'll stay no longer question.
PORTIA Tarry, Jew.
The law hath yet another hold on you.
It is enacted in the laws of Venice,
If it be prov'd against an alien
That by direct or indirect attempts
He seek the life of any citizen,
The party 'gainst the which he doth contrive
Shall seize one half his goods; the other half
Comes to the privy coffer of the state;
And the offender's life lies in the mercy
Of the Duke only, 'gainst all other voice.
In which predicament, I say, thou stand'st;
For it appears by manifest proceeding
That indirectly, and directly too,
Thou hast contrived against the very life
Of the defendant; and thou hast incurr'd
The danger formerly by me rehears'd.
Down, therefore, and beg mercy of the Duke.
GRATIANO Beg that thou mayst have leave to hang thyself;
And yet, thy wealth being forfeit to the state,
Thou hast not left the value of a cord;
Therefore thou must be hang'd at the state's charge.
DUKE That thou shalt see the difference of our spirit,
I pardon thee thy life before thou ask it.
For half thy wealth, it is Antonio's;
The other half comes to the general state,
Which humbleness may drive unto a fine.

PORTIA Ay, for the state; not for Antonio.
SHYLOCK Nay, take my life and all, pardon not that.
You take my house when you do take the prop
That doth sustain my house; you take my life
When you do take the means whereby I live.
PORTIA What mercy can you render him, Antonio?
GRATIANO A halter gratis; nothing else, for God's sake!
ANTONIO So please my lord the Duke and all the court
To quit the fine for one half of his goods;
I am content, so he will let me have
The other half in use, to render it
Upon his death unto the gentleman
That lately stole his daughter –
Two things provided more: that, for this favour,
He presently become a Christian;
The other, that he do record a gift,
Here in the court, of all he dies possess'd
Unto his son Lorenzo and his daughter.
DUKE He shall do this, or else I do recant
The pardon that I late pronounced here.
PORTIA Art thou contented, Jew? What dost thou say?
SHYLOCK I am content.
PORTIA Clerk, draw a deed of gift.
SHYLOCK I pray you, give me leave to go from hence;
I am not well; send the deed after me
And I will sign it.
DUKE Get thee gone, but do it.
GRATIANO In christ'ning shalt thou have two god-fathers;
Had I been judge, thou shouldst have had ten more,
To bring thee to the gallows, not to the font.

[Exit Shylock.

DUKE Sir, I entreat you home with me to dinner.
PORTIA I humbly do desire your Grace of pardon;
I must away this night toward Padua,
And it is meet I presently set forth.
DUKE I am sorry that your leisure serves you not.
Antonio, gratify this gentleman,
For in my mind you are much bound to him.

[Exeunt Duke, Magnificoes, and Train.

BASSANIO Most worthy gentleman, I and my friend
Have by your wisdom been this day acquitted
Of grievous penalties; in lieu whereof
Three thousand ducats, due unto the Jew,
We freely cope your courteous pains withal.
ANTONIO And stand indebted, over and above,
In love and service to you evermore.
PORTIA He is well paid that is well satisfied,
And I, delivering you, am satisfied,
And therein do account myself well paid.
My mind was never yet more mercenary.
I pray you, know me when we meet again;
I wish you well, and so I take my leave.
BASSANIO Dear sir, of force I must attempt you further;
Take some remembrance of us, as a tribute,
Not as fee. Grant me two things, I pray you,
Not to deny me, and to pardon me.
PORTIA You press me far, and therefore I will yield.
[*To Antonio*] Give me your gloves, I'll wear them for your sake.
[*To Bassanio*] And, for your love, I'll take this ring from you.
Do not draw back your hand: I'll take no more,
And you in love shall not deny me this.
BASSANIO This ring, good sir – alas, it is a trifle;
I will not shame myself to give you this.
PORTIA I will have nothing else but only this;
And now, methinks, I have a mind to it.
BASSANIO There's more depends on this than on the value.
The dearest ring in Venice will I give you,
And find it out by proclamation;
Only for this, I pray you, pardon me.
PORTIA I see, sir, you are liberal in offers;
You taught me first to beg, and now, methinks,
You teach me how a beggar should be answer'd.
BASSANIO Good sir, this ring was given me by my wife;
And, when she put it on, she made me vow
That I should neither sell, nor give, nor lose it.
PORTIA That 'scuse serves many men to save their gifts.
An if your wife be not a mad woman,
And know how well I have deserv'd this ring,
She would not hold out enemy for ever
For giving it to me. Well, peace be with you!

[Exeunt Portia and Nerissa.

ANTONIO My Lord Bassanio, let him have the ring.
Let his deservings, and my love withal,
Be valued 'gainst your wife's commandment.
BASSANIO Go, Gratiano, run and overtake him;
Give him the ring, and bring him, if thou canst,
Unto Antonio's house. Away, make haste.

[Exit Gratiano.

Come, you and I will thither presently;
And in the morning early will we both
Fly toward Belmont. Come, Antonio. *[Exeunt.*

SCENE II. *Venice. A street.*

Enter PORTIA and NERISSA.

PORTIA Inquire the Jew's house out, give him this deed,
And let him sign it; we'll away to-night,
And be a day before our husbands home.
This deed will be well welcome to Lorenzo.

Enter GRATIANO.

GRATIANO Fair sir, you are well o'erta'en.
My Lord Bassanio, upon more advice,
Hath sent you here this ring, and doth entreat
Your company at dinner.

PORTIA That cannot be.
His ring I do accept most thankfully,
And so, I pray you, tell him. Furthermore,
I pray you show my youth old Shylock's house.

GRATIANO That will I do.

NERISSA Sir, I would speak with you.
[*Aside to Portia*] I'll see if I can get my husband's ring,
Which I did make him swear to keep for ever.

PORTIA [*To Nerissa*] Thou mayst, I warrant.
We shall have old swearing
That they did give the rings away to men;
But we'll outface them, and outswear them too.
[*Aloud*] Away, make haste, thou know'st where I will tarry.

NERISSA Come, good sir, will you show me to this house? [*Exeunt.*

ACT FIVE

SCENE I. *Belmont. The garden before Portia's house.*

Enter LORENZO and JESSICA.

LORENZO The moon shines bright. In such a night as this,
When the sweet wind did gently kiss the trees,
And they did make no noise – in such a night,
Troilus methinks mounted the Troyan walls,
And sigh'd his soul toward the Grecian tents,
Where Cressid lay that night.

JESSICA In such a night
Did Thisby fearfully o'ertrip the dew,
And saw the lion's shadow ere himself,
And ran dismayed away.

LORENZO In such a night
Stood Dido with a willow in her hand
Upon the wild sea-banks, and waft her love
To come again to Carthage.

JESSICA In such a night
Medea gathered the enchanted herbs
That did renew old Aeson.

LORENZO In such a night
Did Jessica steal from the wealthy Jew,
And with an unthrift love did run from Venice
As far as Belmont.

JESSICA In such a night
Did young Lorenzo swear he lov'd her well,
Stealing her soul with many vows of faith,
And ne'er a true one.

LORENZO In such a night
Did pretty Jessica, like a little shrew,
Slander her love, and he forgave it her.

JESSICA I would out-night you, did no body come;
But, hark, I hear the footing of a man.

Enter STEPHANO.

LORENZO Who comes so fast in silence of the night?

STEPHANO A friend.

LORENZO A friend! What friend? Your name, I pray you, friend?

STEPHANO Stephano is my name, and I bring word
My mistress will before the break of day
Be here at Belmont; she doth stray about
By holy crosses, where she kneels and prays
For happy wedlock hours.

LORENZO Who comes with her?

STEPHANO None but a holy hermit and her maid.
I pray you, is my master yet return'd?

LORENZO He is not, nor we have not heard from him.
But go we in, I pray thee, Jessica,
And ceremoniously let us prepare
Some welcome for the mistress of the house.

Enter LAUNCELOT.

LAUNCELOT Sola, sola! wo ha, ho! sola, sola!

LORENZO Who calls?

LAUNCELOT Sola! Did you see Master Lorenzo?
Master Lorenzo! Sola, sola!

LORENZO Leave holloaing, man. Here!

LAUNCELOT Sola! Where, where?

LORENZO Here!

LAUNCELOT Tell him there's a post come from my master with his horn full of good news; my master will be here ere morning. [*Exit.*

LORENZO Sweet soul, let's in, and there expect their coming.
And yet no matter – why should we go in?
My friend Stephano, signify, I pray you,
Within the house, your mistress is at hand;

And bring your music forth into the air.
[*Exit Stephano.*
How sweet the moonlight sleeps upon this bank!
Here will we sit and let the sounds of music
Creep in our ears; soft stillness and the night
Become the touches of sweet harmony.
Sit, Jessica. Look how the floor of heaven
Is thick inlaid with patines of bright gold;
There's not the smallest orb which thou behold'st
But in his motion like an angel sings,
Still quiring to the young-ey'd cherubins;
Such harmony is in immortal souls,
But whilst this muddy vesture of decay
Doth grossly close it in, we cannot hear it.

Enter Musicians.

Come, ho, and wake Diana with a hymn;
With sweetest touches pierce your mistress' ear,
And draw her home with music. [*Music.*

JESSICA I am never merry when I hear sweet music.
LORENZO The reason is your spirits are attentive;
For do but note a wild and wanton herd,
Or race of youthful and unhandled colts,
Fetching mad bounds, bellowing and neighing loud,
Which is the hot condition of their blood –
If they but hear perchance a trumpet sound,
Or any air of music touch their ears,
You shall perceive them make a mutual stand,
Their savage eyes turn'd to a modest gaze
By the sweet power of music. Therefore the poet
Did feign that Orpheus drew trees, stones, and floods;
Since nought so stockish, hard, and full of rage,
But music for the time doth change his nature.
The man that hath no music in himself,
Nor is not mov'd with concord of sweet sounds,
Is fit for treasons, stratagems, and spoils;
The motions of his spirit are dull as night,
And his affections dark as Erebus.
Let no such man be trusted. Mark the music.

Enter PORTIA and NERISSA.

PORTIA That light we see is burning in my hall.
How far that little candle throws his beams!
So shines a good deed in a naughty world.
NERISSA When the moon shone, we did not see the candle.
PORTIA So doth the greater glory dim the less:
A substitute shines brightly as a king
Until a king be by, and then his state
Empties itself, as doth an inland brook
Into the main of waters. Music! hark!
NERISSA It is your music, madam, of the house.
PORTIA Nothing is good, I see, without respect;
Methinks it sounds much sweeter than by day.
NERISSA Silence bestows that virtue on it, madam.
PORTIA The crow doth sing as sweetly as the lark
When neither is attended; and I think
The nightingale, if she should sing by day,
When every goose is cackling, would be thought
No better a musician than the wren.
How many things by season season'd are
To their right praise and true perfection!
Peace, ho! The moon sleeps with Endymion,
And would not be awak'd. [*Music ceases.*

LORENZO That is the voice,
Or I am much deceiv'd, of Portia.
PORTIA He knows me as the blind man knows the cuckoo,
By the bad voice.
LORENZO Dear lady, welcome home.
PORTIA We have been praying for our husbands' welfare,
Which speed, we hope, the better for our words.
Are they return'd?
LORENZO Madam, they are not yet;
But there is come a messenger before,
To signify their coming.
PORTIA Go in, Nerissa;
Give order to my servants that they take
No note at all of our being absent hence;
Nor you, Lorenzo; Jessica, nor you.
[*A tucket sounds.*

LORENZO Your husband is at hand; I hear his trumpet.
We are no tell-tales, madam, fear you not.
PORTIA This night methinks is but the daylight sick;
It looks a little paler; 'tis a day
Such as the day is when the sun is hid.

Enter BASSANIO, ANTONIO, GRATIANO, and their Followers.

BASSANIO We should hold day with the Antipodes,
If you would walk in absence of the sun.
PORTIA Let me give light, but let me not be light,
For a light wife doth make a heavy husband,
And never be Bassanio so for me;
But God sort all! You are welcome home, my lord.
BASSANIO I thank you, madam; give welcome to my friend.
This is the man, this is Antonio,
To whom I am so infinitely bound.
PORTIA You should in all sense be much bound to him.

For, as I hear, he was much bound for you.
ANTONIO No more than I am well acquitted of.
PORTIA Sir, you are very welcome to our house.
It must appear in other ways than words,
Therefore I scant this breathing courtesy.
GRATIANO [*To Nerissa*] By yonder moon I swear you do me wrong;
In faith, I gave it to the judge's clerk.
Would he were gelt that had it, for my part,
Since you do take it, love, so much at heart.
PORTIA A quarrel, ho, already! What's the matter?
GRATIANO About a hoop of gold, a paltry ring
That she did give me, whose posy was
For all the world like cutler's poetry
Upon a knife, 'Love me, and leave me not'.
NERISSA What talk you of the posy or the value?
You swore to me, when I did give it you,
That you would wear it till your hour of death,
And that it should lie with you in your grave;
Though not for me, yet for your vehement oaths,
You should have been respective and have kept it.
Gave it a judge's clerk! No, God's my judge,
The clerk will ne'er wear hair on's face that had it.
GRATIANO He will, an if he live to be a man.
NERISSA Ay, if a woman live to be a man.
GRATIANO Now by this hand I gave it to a youth,
A kind of boy, a little scrubbed boy
No higher than thyself, the judge's clerk;
A prating boy that begg'd it as a fee;
I could not for my heart deny it him.
PORTIA You were to blame, I must be plain with you,
To part so slightly with your wife's first gift,
A thing stuck on with oaths upon your finger
And so riveted with faith unto your flesh.
I gave my love a ring, and made him swear
Never to part with it, and here he stands;
I dare be sworn for him he would not leave it
Nor pluck it from his finger for the wealth
That the world masters. Now, in faith, Gratiano,
You give your wife too unkind a cause of grief;
An 'twere to me, I should be mad at it.
BASSANIO [*Aside*] Why, I were best to cut my left hand off,
And swear I lost the ring defending it.
GRATIANO My Lord Bassanio gave his ring away
Unto the judge that begg'd it, and indeed
Deserv'd it too; and then the boy, his clerk,
That took some pains in writing, he begg'd mine;
And neither man nor master would take aught
But the two rings.
PORTIA What ring gave you, my lord?
Not that, I hope, which you receiv'd of me.
BASSANIO If I could add a lie unto a fault,
I would deny it; but you see my finger
Hath not the ring upon it; it is gone.
PORTIA Even so void is your false heart of truth;
By heaven, I will ne'er come in your bed
Until I see the ring.
NERISSA Nor I in yours
Till I again see mine.
BASSANIO Sweet Portia,
If you did know to whom I gave the ring,
If you did know for whom I gave the ring,
And would conceive for what I gave the ring,
And how unwillingly I left the ring,
When nought would be accepted but the ring,
You would abate the strength of your displeasure.
PORTIA If you had known the virtue of the ring,
Or half her worthiness that gave the ring,
Or your own honour to contain the ring,
You would not then have parted with the ring.
What man is there so much unreasonable,
If you had pleas'd to have defended it
With any terms of zeal, wanted the modesty
To urge the thing held as a ceremony?
Nerissa teaches me what to believe:
I'll die for't but some woman had the ring.
BASSANIO No, by my honour, madam, by my soul,
No woman had it, but a civil doctor,
Which did refuse three thousand ducats of me,
And begg'd the ring; the which I did deny him,
And suffer'd him to go displeas'd away –
Even he that had held up the very life
Of my dear friend. What should I say, sweet lady?
I was enforc'd to send it after him;
I was beset with shame and courtesy;
My honour would not let ingratitude
So much besmear it. Pardon me, good lady;
For by these blessed candles of the night,
Had you been there, I think you would have begg'd
The ring of me to give the worthy doctor.
PORTIA Let not that doctor e'er come near my house;
Since he hath got the jewel that I loved,
And that which you did swear to keep for me,
I will become as liberal as you;
I'll not deny him anything I have,
No, not my body, nor my husband's bed.
Know him I shall, I am well sure of it.
Lie not a night from home; watch me like Argus;
If you do not, if I be left alone,
Now, by mine honour which is yet mine own,
I'll have that doctor for mine bedfellow.

NERISSA And I his clerk; therefore be well advis'd
How you do leave me to mine own protection.
GRATIANO Well, do you so, let not me take him then;
For, if I do, I'll mar the young clerk's pen.
ANTONIO I am th' unhappy subject of these quarrels.
PORTIA Sir, grieve not you; you are welcome notwithstanding.
BASSANIO Portia, forgive me this enforced wrong;
And in the hearing of these many friends
I swear to thee, even by thine own fair eyes,
Wherein I see myself ——
PORTIA Mark you but that!
In both my eyes he doubly sees himself,
In each eye one; swear by your double self,
And there's an oath of credit.
BASSANIO Nay, but hear me.
Pardon this fault, and by my soul I swear
I never more will break an oath with thee.
ANTONIO I once did lend my body for his wealth,
Which, but for him that had your husband's ring,
Had quite miscarried; I dare be bound again,
My soul upon the forfeit, that your lord
Will never more break faith advisedly.
PORTIA Then you shall be his surety. Give him this,
And bid him keep it better than the other.
ANTONIO Here, Lord Bassanio, swear to keep this ring.
BASSANIO By heaven, it is the same I gave the doctor!
PORTIA I had it of him. Pardon me, Bassanio,
For, by this ring, the doctor lay with me.
NERISSA And pardon me, my gentle Gratiano,
For that same scrubbed boy, the doctor's clerk,
In lieu of this, last night did lie with me.
GRATIANO Why, this is like the mending of highways
In summer, where the ways are fair enough.
What, are we cuckolds ere we have deserv'd it?
PORTIA Speak not so grossly. You are all amaz'd.
Here is a letter; read it at your leisure;
It comes from Padua, from Bellario;
There you shall find that Portia was the doctor,
Nerissa there her clerk. Lorenzo here
Shall witness I set forth as soon as you,
And even but now return'd; I have not yet
Enter'd my house. Antonio, you are welcome;
And I have better news in store for you
Than you expect. Unseal this letter soon;
There you shall find three of your argosies
Are richly come to harbour suddenly.
You shall not know by what strange accident
I chanced on this letter.
ANTONIO I am dumb.
BASSANIO Were you the doctor, and I knew you not?
GRATIANO Were you the clerk that is to make me cuckold?
NERISSA Ay, but the clerk that never means to do it,
Unless he live until he be a man.
BASSANIO Sweet Doctor, you shall be my bedfellow;
When I am absent, then lie with my wife.
ANTONIO Sweet lady, you have given me life and living;
For here I read for certain that my ships
Are safely come to road.
PORTIA How now, Lorenzo!
My clerk hath some good comforts too for you.
NERISSA Ay, and I'll give them him without a fee.
There do I give to you and Jessica,
From the rich Jew, a special deed of gift,
After his death, of all he dies possess'd of.
LORENZO Fair ladies, you drop manna in the way
Of starved people.
PORTIA It is almost morning,
And yet I am sure you are not satisfied
Of these events at full. Let us go in,
And charge us there upon inter'gatories,
And we will answer all things faithfully.
GRATIANO Let it be so. The first inter'gatory
That my Nerissa shall be sworn on is,
Whether till the next night she had rather stay,
Or go to bed now, being two hours to day.
But were the day come, I should wish it dark,
Till I were couching with the doctor's clerk.
Well, while I live, I'll fear no other thing
So sore as keeping safe Nerissa's ring. [*Exeunt*.

As You Like It

Introduction by PHILIP HOBSBAUM

As You Like It is a pastoral, in which no naturalistic business of life distracts the attention of the audience from the emotions deployed among the various characters. The central character is Rosalind, daughter of a Duke exiled to the Forest of Arden, in turn herself expelled from her father's former dominion. She is accompanied by her cousin, Celia, and by a singularly loutish clown.

Rosalind has disguised herself as a boy. In this guise, she good-humouredly interrogates various characters, finding out who they are and exposing their various absurdities. There is, for example, a shepherdess who scorns her faithful lover. She is shrewdly told by Rosalind, 'Down on your knees,/And thank heaven, fasting, for a good man's love'. Another character thus catechised is Jaques, a worldly-wise cynic, whose satire is reductive and therefore no match for Rosalind's wholesome comedy. Jaques declares 'Why, 'tis good to be sad and say nothing' to be met with Rosalind's retort, 'Why then, 'tis good to be a post'.

But the crucial dialogues are those with Orlando, a young man from a surbordinate fiefdom, expelled, like the Duke, by a wicked brother. In her disguise as a boy, Rosalind enters into a mock-courtship, as it must necessarily be. But mock or not, this is a way of testing Orlando out, finding out who he really is. Rosalind, in her 'holiday humour', demands 'What would you say to me now, an I were your very very Rosalind?' to which he replies, in his romantic innocence, 'I would kiss before I spoke'. This romantic attitude is instantly debunked, in a decidedly pithy prose: 'Nay, you were better speak first; and when you were gravelled for lack of matter, you might take occasion to kiss. Very good orators, when they are out, they will spit; and for lovers lacking – God warn us! – matter, the cleanliest shift is to kiss'. That is not romantic, not redolent of Arden, but very much down to earth and of this world. Rosalind is not against love, but she is definitely against nonsense; as, indeed, is the play itself.

It is an interesting irony that Shakespeare uses the form of the pastoral to put forward a highly unpastoral set of attitudes. The medium is mostly prose, though prose of a racy and cheerful kind, as instanced in Rosalind's various rejoinders. The point can best be made if we contrast the language of *As You Like It* with that of *Rosalynde* by Thomas Lodge, from which it was adapted: ''Tis good, forester, to love, but not to overlove, lest in loving her that likes not thee, thou fold thyself in an endless labyrinth'.

Rosalynde is just a tale for the tale's own sake. *As You Like It*, on the other hand, has a definite pattern, though the text as we have it seems not quite finished, so there are some loose ends and internal contradictions. In the main, however, the worthwhile characters are chivvied from sensibility into sense, while the less worthwhile characters fall victim to various tricks. For example, the egregious Jaques seeks out a guru, who will no doubt addle his brains still further, and the loutish clown, Touchstone, marries one of the very 'country copulatives' whom he has, up till now, scorned.

The whole ends with an epilogue, spoken by Rosalind in her woman's dress once more: 'I charge you, O women, for the love you bear to men, to like as much of this play as please you'. This goes along with the title, *As You Like It*. The argument may seem circular, but the import is clear: test out fancy by acquaintance, and ignore the dictates of fashion. The Forest of Arden is a good place for self-discovery, but, once the 'self' is discovered, the characters troop back to town.

As You Like It

DRAMATIS PERSONAE

DUKE
living in exile
FREDERICK
his brother, and usurper of his dominions
AMIENS, JAQUES
lords attending on the banished Duke
LE BEAU
a courtier attending upon Frederick
CHARLES
wrestler to Frederick
OLIVER, JAQUES, ORLANDO
sons of Sir Rowland de Boys
ADAM, DENNIS
servants to Oliver
TOUCHSTONE
the court jester
SIR OLIVER MARTEXT
a vicar
CORIN, SILVIUS
shepherds
WILLIAM
a country fellow, in love with Audrey
A person representing HYMEN
ROSALIND
daughter to the banished Duke
CELIA
daughter to Frederick
PHEBE
a shepherdess
AUDREY
a country wench
Lords, Pages, Foresters, and Attendants

THE SCENE: OLIVER'S HOUSE; FREDERICK'S COURT; AND THE FOREST OF ARDEN.

ACT ONE

SCENE I. *Orchard of Oliver's house.*

Enter ORLANDO and ADAM.

ORLANDO As I remember, Adam, it was upon this fashion bequeathed me by will but poor a thousand crowns, and, as thou say'st, charged my brother, on his blessing, to breed me well; and there begins my sadness. My brother Jaques he keeps at school, and report speaks goldenly of his profit. For my part, he keeps me rustically at home, or, to speak more properly, stays me here at home unkept; for call you that keeping for a gentleman of my birth that differs not from the stalling of an ox? His horses are bred better; for, besides that they are fair with their feeding, they are taught their manage, and to that end riders dearly hir'd; but I, his brother, gain nothing under him but growth; for the which his animals on his dunghills are as much bound to him as I. Besides this nothing that he so plentifully gives me, the something that nature gave me his countenance seems to take from me. He lets me feed with his hinds, bars me the place of a brother, and as much as in him lies, mines my gentility with my education. This is it, Adam, that grieves me; and the spirit of my father, which I think is within me, begins to mutiny against this servitude. I will no longer endure it, though yet I know no wise remedy how to avoid it.

Enter OLIVER.

ADAM Yonder comes my master, your brother.

ORLANDO Go apart, Adam, and thou shalt hear how he will shake me up. [*Adam retires.*

OLIVER Now, sir! what make you here?

ORLANDO Nothing; I am not taught to make any thing.

OLIVER What mar you then, sir?

ORLANDO Marry, sir, I am helping you to mar that which God made, a poor unworthy brother of yours, with idleness.

OLIVER Marry, sir, be better employed, and be nought awhile.

ORLANDO Shall I keep your hogs, and eat husks with them? What prodigal portion have I spent that I should come to such penury?

OLIVER Know you where you are, sir?

ORLANDO O, sir, very well; here in your orchard.

OLIVER Know you before whom, sir?

ORLANDO Ay, better than him I am before knows me. I know you are my eldest brother; and, in the gentle condition of blood, you should so know me. The courtesy of nations allows you my better in that you are the first-born; but the same tradition takes not away my blood, were there twenty brothers betwixt us. I have as much of my father in me as you, albeit I confess your coming before me is nearer to his reverence.

OLIVER What, boy! [*Strikes him.*

ORLANDO Come, come, elder brother, you are too young in this.

OLIVER Wilt thou lay hands on me, villain?

ORLANDO I am no villain; I am the youngest son of Sir Rowland de Boys. He was my father; and he is thrice a villain that says such a father begot villains. Wert thou not my brother, I would not take this hand from thy throat till this other had pull'd out thy tongue for saying so. Thou has rail'd on thyself.

ADAM [*Coming forward*] Sweet masters, be patient; for your father's remembrance, be at accord.

OLIVER Let me go, I say.

ORLANDO I will not, till I please; you shall hear me. My father charg'd you in his will to give me good education: you have train'd me like a peasant, obscuring and hiding from me all gentleman-like qualities. The spirit of my father grows strong in me, and I will no longer endure it; therefore allow me such exercises as may become a gentleman, or give me the poor allottery my father left me by testament; with that I will go buy my fortunes.

OLIVER And what wilt thou do? Beg, when that is spent? Well, sir, get you in. I will not long be troubled with you; you shall have some part of your will. I pray you leave me.

ORLANDO I will no further offend you than becomes me for my good.

OLIVER Get you with him, you old dog.

ADAM Is 'old dog' my reward? Most true, I have lost my teeth in your service. God be with my old master! He would not have spoke such a word. [*Exeunt Orlando and Adam.*

OLIVER Is it even so? Begin you to grow upon me? I will physic your rankness, and yet give no thousand crowns neither. Holla, Dennis!

Enter DENNIS.

DENNIS Calls your worship?

OLIVER Was not Charles, the Duke's wrestler, here to speak with me?

DENNIS So please you, he is here at the door and importunes access to you.

OLIVER Call him in. [*Exit Dennis*] 'Twill be a good way; and to-morrow the wrestling is.

Enter CHARLES.

CHARLES Good morrow to your worship.

OLIVER Good Monsieur Charles! What's the new news at the new court?

CHARLES There's no news at the court, sir, but the old news; that is, the old Duke is banished by his younger brother the new Duke; and three or four loving lords have put themselves into voluntary exile with him, whose lands and revenues enrich the new Duke; therefore he gives them good leave to wander.

OLIVER Can you tell if Rosalind, the Duke's daughter, be banished with her father?

CHARLES O, no; for the Duke's daughter, her cousin, so loves her, being ever from their cradles bred together, that she would have followed her exile, or have died to stay behind her. She is at the court, and no less beloved of her uncle than his own daughter; and never two ladies loved as they do.

OLIVER Where will the old Duke live?

CHARLES They say he is already in the Forest of Arden, and a many merry men with him; and there they live like the old Robin Hood of England. They say many young gentlemen flock to him every day, and fleet the time carelessly, as they did in the golden world.

OLIVER What, you wrestle to-morrow before the new Duke?

CHARLES Marry, do I, sir; and I came to acquaint you with a matter. I am given, sir, secretly to understand that your younger brother, Orlando, hath a disposition to come in disguis'd against me to try a fall. To-morrow, sir, I wrestle for my credit; and he that escapes me without some broken limb shall acquit him well. Your brother is but young and tender; and, for your love, I would be loath to foil him, as I must, for my own honour, if he come in; therefore, out of my love to you, I came hither to acquaint you withal, that either you might stay him from his intendment, or brook such disgrace well as he shall run into, in that it is a thing of his own search and altogether against my will.

OLIVER Charles, I thank thee for thy love to me, which thou shalt find I will most kindly requite. I had myself notice of my brother's purpose herein, and have by underhand means laboured to dissuade him from it; but he is resolute. I'll tell thee, Charles, it is the stubbornest young fellow of France; full of ambition, an envious emulator of every man's good parts, a secret and villainous contriver against me his natural brother. Therefore use thy discretion: I had as lief thou didst break his neck as his finger. And thou wert best look to't; for if thou dost him any slight disgrace, or if he do not mightily grace himself on thee, he will practise against thee by poison, entrap thee by some treacherous device, and never leave thee till he hath ta'en thy life by some indirect means or other; for, I assure thee, and almost with tears I speak it, there is not one so young and so villainous this day living. I speak but brotherly of him; but should I anatomize him to thee as he is, I must blush and weep, and thou must look pale and wonder.

CHARLES I am heartily glad I came hither to you.

If he come to-morrow I'll give him his payment. If ever he go alone again, I'll never wrestle for prize more. And so, God keep your worship! [*Exit.*

OLIVER Farewell, good Charles. Now will I stir this gamester. I hope I shall see an end of him; for my soul, yet I know not why, hates nothing more than he. Yet he's gentle; never school'd and yet learned; full of noble device; of all sorts enchantingly beloved; and, indeed, so much in the heart of the world, and especially of my own people, who best know him, that I am altogether misprised. But it shall not be so long; this wrestler shall clear all. Nothing remains but that I kindle the boy thither, which now I'll go about. [*Exit.*

SCENE II. *A lawn before the Duke's palace.*

Enter ROSALIND and CELIA.

CELIA I pray thee, Rosalind, sweet my coz, be merry.

ROSALIND Dear Celia, I show more mirth than I am mistress of; and would you yet I were merrier? Unless you could teach me to forget a banished father, you must not learn me how to remember any extraordinary pleasure.

CELIA Herein I see thou lov'st me not with the full weight that I love thee. If my uncle, thy banished father, had banished thy uncle, the Duke my father, so thou hadst been still with me, I could have taught my love to take thy father for mine; so wouldst thou, if the truth of thy love to me were so righteously temper'd as mine is to thee.

ROSALIND Well, I will forget the condition of my estate, to rejoice in yours.

CELIA You know my father hath no child but I, nor none is like to have; and, truly, when he dies thou shalt be his heir; for what he hath taken away from thy father perforce, I will render thee again in affection. By mine honour, I will; and when I break that oath, let me turn monster; therefore, my sweet Rose, my dear Rose, be merry.

ROSALIND From henceforth I will, coz, and devise sports. Let me see; what think you of falling in love?

CELIA Marry, I prithee, do, to make sport withal; but love no man in good earnest, nor no further in sport neither than with safety of a pure blush thou mayst in honour come off again.

ROSALIND What shall be our sport, then?

CELIA Let us sit and mock the good housewife Fortune from her wheel, that her gifts may henceforth be bestowed equally.

ROSALIND I would we' could do so; for her benefits are mightily misplaced; and the bountiful blind woman doth most mistake in her gifts to women.

CELIA 'Tis true; for those that she makes fair she scarce makes honest; and those that she makes honest she makes very ill-favouredly.

ROSALIND Nay; now thou goest from Fortune's office to Nature's: Fortune reigns in gifts of the world, not in the lineaments of Nature.

Enter TOUCHSTONE.

CELIA No; when Nature hath made a fair creature, may she not by Fortune fall into the fire? Though Nature hath given us wit to flout at Fortune, hath not Fortune sent in this fool to cut off the argument?

ROSALIND Indeed, there is Fortune too hard for Nature, when Fortune makes Nature's natural the cutter-off of Nature's wit.

CELIA Peradventure this is not Fortune's work neither, but Nature's, who perceiveth our natural wits too dull to reason of such goddesses, and hath sent this natural for our whetstone; for always the dullness of the fool is the whetstone of the wits. How now, wit! Whither wander you?

TOUCHSTONE Mistress, you must come away to your father.

CELIA Were you made the messenger?

TOUCHSTONE No, by mine honour; but I was bid to come for you.

ROSALIND Where learned you that oath, fool?

TOUCHSTONE Of a certain knight that swore by his honour they were good pancakes, and swore by his honour the mustard was naught. Now I'll stand to it, the pancakes were naught and the mustard was good, and yet was not the knight forsworn.

CELIA How prove you that, in the great heap of your knowledge?

ROSALIND Ay, marry, now unmuzzle your wisdom.

TOUCHSTONE Stand you both forth now: stroke your chins, and swear by your beards that I am a knave.

CELIA By our beards, if we had them, thou art.

TOUCHSTONE By my knavery, if I had it, then I were. But if you swear by that that is not, you are not forsworn; no more was this knight, swearing by his honour, for he never had any; or if he had, he had sworn it away before ever he saw those pancakes or that mustard.

CELIA Prithee, who is't that thou mean'st?

TOUCHSTONE One that old Frederick, your father, loves.

CELIA My father's love is enough to honour him. Enough, speak no more of him; you'll be whipt for taxation one of these days.

TOUCHSTONE The more pity that fools may not speak wisely what wise men do foolishly.

CELIA By my troth, thou sayest true; for since the little wit that fools have was silenced, the little foolery that wise men have makes a great show. Here comes Monsieur Le Beau.

Enter LE BEAU.

ROSALIND With his mouth full of news.

CELIA Which he will put on us as pigeons feed their young.

ROSALIND Then shall we be news-cramm'd.

CELIA All the better; we shall be the more marketable. Bon jour, Monsieur Le Beau. What's the news?

LE BEAU Fair Princess, you have lost much good sport.

CELIA Sport! of what colour?

LE BEAU What colour, madam? How shall I answer you?

ROSALIND As wit and fortune will.

TOUCHSTONE Or as the Destinies decrees.

CELIA Well said; that was laid on with a trowel.

TOUCHSTONE Nay, if I keep not my rank –

ROSALIND Thou losest thy old smell.

LE BEAU You amaze me, ladies. I would have told you of good wrestling, which you have lost the sight of.

ROSALIND Yet tell us the manner of the wrestling.

LE BEAU I will tell you the beginning, and, if it please your ladyships, you may see the end; for the best is yet to do; and here, where you are, they are coming to perform it.

CELIA Well, the beginning that is dead and buried.

LE BEAU There comes an old man and his three sons –

CELIA I could match this beginning with an old tale.

LE BEAU Three proper young men, of excellent growth and presence.

ROSALIND With bills on their necks: 'Be it known unto all men by these presents' –

LE BEAU The eldest of the three wrestled with Charles, the Duke's wrestler; which Charles in a moment threw him, and broke three of his ribs, that there is little hope of life in him. So he serv'd the second, and so the third. Yonder they lie; the poor old man, their father, making such pitiful dole over them that all the beholders take his part with weeping.

ROSALIND Alas!

TOUCHSTONE But what is the sport, monsieur, that the ladies have lost?

LE BEAU Why, this that I speak of.

TOUCHSTONE Thus men may grow wiser every day. It is the first time that ever I heard breaking of ribs was sport for ladies.

CELIA Or I, I promise thee.

ROSALIND But is there any else longs to see this broken music in his sides? Is there yet another dotes upon rib-breaking? Shall we see this wrestling, cousin?

LE BEAU You must, if you stay here; for here is the place appointed for the wrestling, and they are ready to perform it.

CELIA Yonder, sure, they are coming. Let us now stay and see it.

Flourish. Enter DUKE FREDERICK, Lords, ORLANDO, CHARLES, and Attendants.

DUKE FREDERICK Come on; since the youth will not be entreated, his own peril on his forwardness.

ROSALIND Is yonder the man?

LE BEAU Even he, madam.

CELIA Alas, he is too young; yet he looks successfully.

DUKE FREDERICK How now, daughter and cousin! Are you crept hither to see the wrestling?

ROSALIND Ay, my liege; so please you give us leave.

DUKE FREDERICK You will take little delight in it, I can tell you, there is such odds in the man. In pity of the challenger's youth I would fain dissuade him, but he will not be entreated. Speak to him, ladies; see if you can move him.

CELIA Call him hither, good Monsieur Le Beau.

DUKE FREDERICK Do so; I'll not be by.

[*Duke Frederick goes apart.*

LE BEAU Monsieur the Challenger, the Princess calls for you.

ORLANDO I attend them with all respect and duty.

ROSALIND Young man, have you challeng'd Charles the wrestler?

ORLANDO No, fair Princess; he is the general challenger. I come but in, as others do, to try, with him the strength of my youth.

CELIA Young gentleman, your spirits are too bold for your years. You have seen cruel proof of this man's strength; if you saw yourself with your eyes, or knew yourself with your judgment, the fear of your adventure would counsel you to a more equal enterprise. We pray you, for your own sake, to embrace your own safety and give over this attempt.

ROSALIND Do, young sir; your reputation shall not therefore be misprised: we will make it our suit to the Duke that the wrestling might not go forward.

ORLANDO I beseech you, punish me not with your hard thoughts, wherein I confess me much guilty to deny so fair and excellent ladies any thing. But let your fair eyes and gentle wishes go with me to my trial; wherein if I be foil'd, there is but one sham'd that was never gracious; if kill'd, but one dead that is willing to be so. I shall do my friends no wrong, for I have none to lament me; the world no injury, for in it I have nothing; only in the world I fill up a place, which may be better supplied when I have made it empty.

ROSALIND The little strength that I have, I would it were with you.

CELIA And mine to eke out hers.

ROSALIND Fare you well. Pray heaven I be deceiv'd in you!

CELIA Your heart's desires be with you!

CHARLES Come, where is this young gallant that is so desirous to lie with his mother earth?

ORLANDO Ready, sir; but his will hath in it a more modest working.

DUKE FREDERICK You shall try but one fall.

CHARLES No, I warrant your Grace, you shall not entreat him to a second, that have so mightily persuaded him from a first.

ORLANDO You mean to mock me after; you should not have mock'd me before; but come your ways.

ROSALIND Now, Hercules be thy speed, young man!

CELIA I would I were invisible, to catch the strong fellow by the leg. *[They wrestle.*

ROSALIND O excellent young man!

CELIA If I had a thunderbolt in mine eye, I can tell who should down.

[Charles is thrown. Shout.

DUKE FREDERICK No more, no more.

ORLANDO Yes, I beseech your Grace; I am not yet well breath d.

DUKE FREDERICK How dost thou, Charles?

LE BEAU He cannot speak, my lord.

DUKE FREDERICK Bear him away. What is thy name, young man?

ORLANDO Orlando, my liege; the youngest son of Sir Rowland de Boys.

DUKE FREDERICK I would thou hadst been son to some man else.
The world esteem'd thy father honourable,
But I did find him still mine enemy.
Thou shouldst have better pleas'd me with this deed,
Hadst thou descended from another house.
But fare thee well; thou art a gallant youth;
I would thou hadst told me of another father.

[Exeunt Duke, Train, and Le Beau.

CELIA Were I my father, coz, would I do this?

ORLANDO I am more proud to be Sir Rowland's son,
His youngest son – and would not change that calling
To be adopted heir to Frederick.

ROSALIND My father lov'd Sir Rowland as his soul,
And all the world was of my father's mind;
Had I before known this young man his son,
I should have given him tears unto entreaties
Ere he should thus have ventur'd.

CELIA Gentle cousin,
Let us go thank him, and encourage him;
My father's rough and envious disposition
Sticks me at heart. Sir, you have well deserv'd;
If you do keep your promises in love
But justly as you have exceeded all promise,
Your mistress shall be happy.

ROSALIND Gentleman,

[Giving him a chain from her neck.

Wear this for me; one out of suits with fortune,
That could give more, but that her hand lacks means.
Shall we go, coz?

CELIA Ay. Fare you well, fair gentleman.

ORLANDO Can I not say 'I thank you'? My better parts
Are all thrown down; and that which here stands up
Is but a quintain, a mere lifeless block.

ROSALIND He calls us back. My pride fell with my fortunes;
I'll ask him what he would. Did you call, sir?
Sir, you have wrestled well, and overthrown
More than your enemies.

CELIA Will you go, coz?

ROSALIND Have with you. Fare you well.

[Exeunt Rosalind and Celia.

ORLANDO What passion hangs these weights upon my tongue?
I cannot speak to her, yet she urg'd conference.
O poor Orlando, thou art overthrown!
Or Charles or something weaker masters thee.

Re-enter LE BEAU.

LE BEAU Good sir, I do in friendship counsel you
To leave this place. Albeit you have deserv'd
High commendation, true applause, and love,
Yet such is now the Duke's condition
That he misconstrues all that you have done.
The Duke is humorous; what he is, indeed,
More suits you to conceive than I to speak of.

ORLANDO I thank you, sir; and pray you tell me this:

Which of the two was daughter of the Duke
That here was at the wrestling?

LE BEAU Neither his daughter, if we judge by manners;
But yet, indeed, the smaller is his daughter;
The other is daughter to the banish'd Duke,
And here detain'd by her usurping uncle,
To keep his daughter company; whose loves
Are dearer than the natural bond of sisters.
But I can tell you that of late this Duke
Hath ta'en displeasure 'gainst his gentle niece,
Grounded upon no other argument
But that the people praise her for her virtues
And pity her for her good father's sake;
And, on my life, his malice 'gainst the lady
Will suddenly break forth. Sir, fare you well.
Hereafter, in a better world than this,
I shall desire more love and knowledge of you.

ORLANDO I rest much bounden to you; fare you well. [*Exit Le Beau.*
Thus must I from the smoke into the smother;
From tyrant Duke unto a tyrant brother.
But heavenly Rosalind! [*Exit.*

SCENE III. *The Duke's palace.*

Enter CELIA and ROSALIND.

CELIA Why, cousin! why, Rosalind! Cupid have mercy! Not a word?

ROSALIND Not one to throw at a dog.

CELIA No, thy words are too precious to be cast away upon curs; throw some of them at me; come, lame me with reasons.

ROSALIND Then there were two cousins laid up, when the one should be lam'd with reasons and the other mad without any.

CELIA But is all this for your father?

ROSALIND No, some of it is for my child's father. O, how full of briers is this working-day world!

CELIA They are but burs, cousin, thrown upon thee in holiday foolery; if we walk not in the trodden paths, our very petticoats will catch them.

ROSALIND I could shake them off my coat: these burs are in my heart.

CELIA Hem them away

ROSALIND I would try, if I could cry 'hem' and have him.

CELIA Come, come, wrestle with thy affections.

ROSALIND O, they take the part of a better wrestler than myself.

CELIA O, a good wish upon you! You will try in time, in despite of a fall. But, turning these jests out of service, let us talk in good earnest. Is it possible, on such a sudden, you should fall into so strong a liking with old Sir Rowland's youngest son?

ROSALIND The Duke my father lov'd his father dearly.

CELIA Doth it therefore ensue that you should love his son dearly? By this kind of chase I should hate him, for my father hated his father dearly; yet I hate not Orlando.

ROSALIND No, faith, hate him not, for my sake.

CELIA Why should I not? Doth he not deserve well?

Enter DUKE FREDERICK, with Lords.

ROSALIND Let me love him for that; and do you love him because I do. Look, here comes the Duke.

CELIA With his eyes full of anger.

DUKE FREDERICK Mistress, dispatch you with your safest haste,
And get you from our court.

ROSALIND Me, uncle?

DUKE FREDERICK You, cousin.
Within these ten days if that thou beest found
So near our public court as twenty miles,
Thou diest for it.

ROSALIND I do beseech your Grace,
Let me the knowledge of my fault bear with me.
If with myself I hold intelligence,
Or have acquaintance with mine own desires;
If that I do not dream, or be not frantic –
As I do trust I am not – then, dear uncle,
Never so much as in a thought unborn
Did I offend your Highness.

DUKE FREDERICK Thus do all traitors;
If their purgation did consist in words,
They are as innocent as grace itself.
Let it suffice thee that I trust thee not.

ROSALIND Yet your mistrust cannot make me a traitor.
Tell me whereon the likelihood depends.

DUKE FREDERICK Thou art thy father's daughter; there's enough.

ROSALIND So was I when your Highness took his dukedom;
So was I when your Highness banish'd him.
Treason is not inherited, my lord;
Or, if we did derive it from our friends,
What's that to me? My father was no traitor.
Then, good my liege, mistake me not so much
To think my poverty is treacherous.

CELIA Dear sovereign, hear me speak.

DUKE FREDERICK Ay, Celia; we stay'd her for your sake,
Else had she with her father rang'd along.

CELIA I did not then entreat to have her stay;
It was your pleasure, and your own remorse;
I was too young that time to value her,
But now I know her. If she be a traitor,
Why so am I: we still have slept together,

Rose at an instant, learn'd, play'd, eat together;
And wheresoe'er we went, like Juno's swans,
Still we went coupled and inseparable.

DUKE FREDERICK She is too subtle for thee; and her smoothness,
Her very silence and her patience,
Speak to the people, and they pity her.
Thou art a fool. She robs thee of thy name;
And thou wilt show more bright and seem more virtuous
When she is gone. Then open not thy lips.
Firm and irrevocable is my doom
Which I have pass'd upon her; she is banish'd.

CELIA Pronounce that sentence, then, on me, my liege;
I cannot live out of her company.

DUKE FREDERICK You are a fool. You, niece, provide yourself.
If you outstay the time, upon mine honour,
And in the greatness of my word, you die.
[*Exeunt Duke and Lords.*

CELIA O my poor Rosalind! Whither wilt thou go?
Wilt thou change fathers? I will give thee mine.
I charge thee be not thou more griev'd than I am.

ROSALIND I have more cause.

CELIA Thou hast not, cousin.
Prithee be cheerful. Know'st thou not the Duke
Hath banish'd me, his daughter?

ROSALIND That he hath not.

CELIA No, hath not? Rosalind lacks, then, the love
Which teacheth thee that thou and I am one.
Shall we be sund'red? Shall we part, sweet girl?
No; let my father seek another heir.
Therefore devise with me how we may fly,
Whither to go, and what to bear with us;
And do not seek to take your charge upon you,
To bear your griefs yourself, and leave me out;
For, by this heaven, now at our sorrows pale,
Say what thou canst, I'll go along with thee.

ROSALIND Why, whither shall we go?

CELIA To seek my uncle in the Forest of Arden.

ROSALIND Alas, what danger will it be to us,
Maids as we are, to travel forth so far!
Beauty provoketh thieves sooner than gold.

CELIA I'll put myself in poor and mean attire,
And with a kind of umber smirch my face;
The like do you; so shall we pass along,
And never stir assailants.

ROSALIND Were it not better,
Because that I am more than common tall,
That I did suit me all points like a man?
A gallant curtle-axe upon my thigh,
A boar spear in my hand; and – in my heart
Lie there what hidden woman's fear there will –
We'll have a swashing and a martial outside,
As many other mannish cowards have
That do outface it with their semblances.

CELIA What shall I call thee when thou art a man?

ROSALIND I'll have no worse a name than Jove's own page,
And therefore look you call me Ganymede.
But what will you be call'd?

CELIA Something that hath a reference to my state:
No longer Celia, but Aliena.

ROSALIND But, cousin, what if we assay'd to steal
The clownish fool out of your father's court?
Would he not be a comfort to our travel?

CELIA He'll go along o'er the wide world with me;
Leave me alone to woo him. Let's away,
And get our jewels and our wealth together;
Devise the fittest time and safest way
To hide us from pursuit that will be made
After my flight. Now go we in content
To liberty, and not to banishment. [*Exeunt.*

ACT TWO

SCENE I. *The Forest of Arden.*

Enter DUKE SENIOR, AMIENS, and two or three LORDS, like foresters.

DUKE SENIOR Now, my co-mates and brothers in exile,
Hath not old custom made this life more sweet
Than that of painted pomp? Are not these woods
More free from peril than the envious court?
Here feel we not the penalty of Adam,
The seasons' difference; as the icy fang
And churlish chiding of the winter's wind,
Which when it bites and blows upon my body,
Even till I shrink with cold, I smile and say
'This is no flattery; these are counsellors
That feelingly persuade me what I am'.
Sweet are the uses of adversity;
Which, like the toad, ugly and venomous,
Wears yet a precious jewel in his head;
And this our life, exempt from public haunt,
Finds tongues in trees, books in the running brooks,
Sermons in stones, and good in everything.
I would not change it.

AMIENS Happy is your Grace,
That can translate the stubbornness of fortune
Into so quiet and so sweet a style.
DUKE SENIOR Come, shall we go and kill us venison?
And yet it irks me the poor dappled fools,
Being native burghers of this desert city,
Should, in their own confines, with forked heads
Have their round haunches gor'd.
1 LORD Indeed, my lord,
The melancholy Jaques grieves at that;
And, in that kind, swears you do more usurp
Than doth your brother that hath banish'd you.
To-day my Lord of Amiens and myself
Did steal behind him as he lay along
Under an oak whose antique root peeps out
Upon the brook that brawls along this wood!
To the which place a poor sequest'red stag,
That from the hunter's aim had ta'en a hurt,
Did come to languish; and, indeed, my lord,
The wretched animal heav'd forth such groans
That their discharge did stretch his leathern coat
Almost to bursting; and the big round tears
Cours'd one another down his innocent nose
In piteous chase; and thus the hairy fool,
Much marked of the melancholy Jaques,
Stood on th' extremest verge of the swift brook,
Augmenting it with tears.
DUKE SENIOR But what said Jaques?
Did he not moralize this spectacle?
1 LORD O, yes, into a thousand similes.
First, for his weeping into the needless stream:
'Poor deer,' quoth he 'thou mak'st a testament
As worldlings do, giving thy sum of more
To that which had too much'. Then, being there alone,
Left and abandoned of his velvet friends:
''Tis right;' quoth he 'thus misery doth part
The flux of company'. Anon, a careless herd,
Full of the pasture, jumps along by him
And never stays to greet him. 'Ay,' quoth Jaques
'Sweep on, you fat and greasy citizens;
'Tis just the fashion. Wherefore do you look
Upon that poor and broken bankrupt there?'
Thus most invectively he pierceth through
The body of the country, city, court,
Yea, and of this our life; swearing that we
Are mere usurpers, tyrants, and what's worse,
To fright the animals, and to kill them up
In their assign'd and native dwelling-place.
DUKE SENIOR And did you leave him in this contemplation?
2 LORD We did, my lord, weeping and commenting
Upon the sobbing deer.
DUKE SENIOR Show me the place;
I love to cope him in these sullen fits,
For then he's full of matter.
1 LORD I'll bring you to him straight. [*Exeunt.*

SCENE II. *The Duke's palace.*

Enter DUKE FREDERICK, with Lords.

DUKE FREDERICK Can it be possible that no man saw them?
It cannot be; some villains of my court
Are of consent and sufferance in this.
1 LORD I cannot hear of any that did see her.
The ladies, her attendants of her chamber,
Saw her abed, and in the morning early
They found the bed untreasur'd of their mistress.
2 LORD My lord, the roynish clown, at whom so oft
Your Grace was wont to laugh, is also missing.
Hisperia, the Princess' gentlewoman,
Confesses that she secretly o'erheard
Your daughter and her cousin much commend
The parts and graces of the wrestler
That did but lately foil the sinewy Charles;
And she believes, wherever they are gone,
That youth is surely in their company.
DUKE FREDERICK Send to his brother; fetch that gallant hither.
If he be absent, bring his brother to me;
I'll make him find him. Do this suddenly;
And let not search and inquisition quail
To bring again these foolish runaways. [*Exeunt.*

SCENE III. *Before Oliver's house.*

Enter ORLANDO and ADAM, meeting.

ORLANDO Who's there?
ADAM What, my young master? O my gentle master!
O my sweet master! O you memory
Of old Sir Rowland! Why, what make you here?
Why are you virtuous? Why do people love you?
And wherefore are you gentle, strong, and valiant?
Why would you be so fond to overcome
The bonny prizer of the humorous Duke?
Your praise is come too swiftly home before you.
Know you not, master, to some kind of men
Their graces serve them but as enemies?
No more do yours. Your virtues, gentle master,
Are sanctified and holy traitors to you.
O, what a world is this, when what is comely

Envenoms him that bears it!

ORLANDO Why, what's the matter?

ADAM O unhappy youth!
Come not within these doors; within this roof
The enemy of all your graces lives.
Your brother – no, no brother; yet the son –
Yet not the son; I will not call him son
Of him I was about to call his father –
Hath heard your praises; and this night he means
To burn the lodging where you use to lie,
And you within it. If he fail of that,
He will have other means to cut you off;
I overheard him and his practices.
This is no place; this house is but a butchery;
Abhor it, fear it, do not enter it.

ORLANDO Why, whither, Adam, wouldst thou have me go?

ADAM No matter whither, so you come not here.

ORLANDO What, wouldst thou have me go and beg my food,
Or with a base and boist'rous sword enforce
A thievish living on the common road?
This I must do, or know not what to do;
Yet this I will not do, do how I can.
I rather will subject me to the malice
Of a diverted blood and bloody brother.

ADAM But do not so. I have five hundred crowns,
The thrifty hire I sav'd under your father,
Which I did store to be my foster-nurse,
When service should in my old limbs lie lame,
And unregarded age in corners thrown.
Take that, and He that doth the ravens feed,
Yea, providently caters for the sparrow,
Be comfort to my age! Here is the gold;
All this I give you. Let me be your servant;
Though I look old, yet I am strong and lusty;
For in my youth I never did apply
Hot and rebellious liquors in my blood,
Nor did not with unbashful forehead woo
The means of weakness and debility;
Therefore my age is as a lusty winter,
Frosty, but kindly. Let me go with you;
I'll do the service of a younger man
In all your business and necessities.

ORLANDO O good old man, how well in thee appears
The constant service of the antique world,
When service sweat for duty, not for meed!
Thou art not for the fashion of these times,
Where none will sweat but for promotion,
And having that do choke their service up
Even with the having; it is not so with thee.
But, poor old man, thou prun'st a rotten tree
That cannot so much as a blossom yield
In lieu of all thy pains and husbandry.
But come thy ways, we'll go along together,
And ere we have thy youthful wages spent
We'll light upon some settled low content.

ADAM Master, go on; and I will follow thee
To the last gasp, with truth and loyalty.
From seventeen years till now almost four-score
Here lived I, but now live here no more.
At seventeen years many their fortunes seek,
But at fourscore it is too late a week;
Yet fortune cannot recompense me better
Than to die well and not my master's debtor.

[Exeunt.

SCENE IV. *The Forest of Arden.*

Enter ROSALIND for GANYMEDE, CELIA for ALIENA, and Clown alias TOUCHSTONE.

ROSALIND O Jupiter, how weary are my spirits!

TOUCHSTONE I care not for my spirits, if my legs were not weary.

ROSALIND I could find in my heart to disgrace my man's apparel, and to cry like a woman; but I must comfort the weaker vessel, as doublet and hose ought to show itself courageous to petticoat; therefore, courage, good Aliena.

CELIA I pray you bear with me; I cannot go no further.

TOUCHSTONE For my part, I had rather bear with you than bear you; yet I should bear no cross if I did bear you; for I think you have no money in your purse.

ROSALIND Well, this is the Forest of Arden.

TOUCHSTONE Ay, now am I in Arden; the more fool I; when I was at home I was in a better place; but travellers must be content.

Enter CORIN and SILVIUS.

ROSALIND Ay, be so, good Touchstone. Look you, who comes here, a young man and an old in solemn talk.

CORIN That is the way to make her scorn you still.

SILVIUS O Corin, that thou knew'st how I do love her!

CORIN I partly guess; for I have lov'd ere now.

SILVIUS No, Corin, being old, thou canst not guess,
Though in thy youth thou wast as true a lover
As ever sigh'd upon a midnight pillow.
But if thy love were ever like to mine,
As sure I think did never man love so,
How many actions most ridiculous
Hast thou been drawn to by thy fantasy?

CORIN Into a thousand that I have forgotten.

SILVIUS O, thou didst then never love so heartily!
If thou remember'st not the slightest folly
That ever love did make thee run into,
Thou hast not lov'd;

Or if thou hast not sat as I do now,
Wearing thy hearer in thy mistress' praise,
Thou hast not lov'd;
Or if thou hast not broke from company
Abruptly, as my passion now makes me,
Thou hast not lov'd.
O Phebe, Phebe, Phebe! *[Exit Silvius.*

ROSALIND Alas, poor shepherd! searching of thy wound,
I have by hard adventure found mine own.

TOUCHSTONE And I mine. I remember, when I was in love, I broke my sword upon a stone, and bid him take that for coming a-night to Jane Smile; and I remember the kissing of her batler, and the cow's dugs that her pretty chopt hands had milk'd; and I remember the wooing of a peascod instead of her; from whom I took two cods, and, giving her them again, said with weeping tears 'Wear these for my sake'. We that are true lovers run into strange capers; but as all is mortal in nature, so is all nature in love mortal in folly.

ROSALIND Thou speak'st wiser than thou art ware of.

TOUCHSTONE Nay, I shall ne'er be ware of mine own wit till I break my shins against it.

ROSALIND Jove, Jove! this shepherd's passion
Is much upon my fashion.

TOUCHSTONE And mine; but it grows something stale with me.

CELIA I pray you, one of you question yond man
If he for gold will give us any food;
I faint almost to death.

TOUCHSTONE Holla, you clown!

ROSALIND Peace, fool; he's not thy kinsman.

CORIN Who calls?

TOUCHSTONE Your betters, sir.

CORIN Else are they very wretched.

ROSALIND Peace, I say. Good even to you, friend.

CORIN And to you, gentle sir, and to you all.

ROSALIND I prithee, shepherd, if that love or gold
Can in this desert place buy entertainment,
Bring us where we may rest ourselves and feed.
Here's a young maid with travel much oppress'd,
And faints for succour.

CORIN Fair sir, I pity her,
And wish, for her sake more than for mine own,
My fortunes were more able to relieve her;
But I am shepherd to another man,
And do not shear the fleeces that I graze.
My master is of churlish disposition,
And little recks to find the way to heaven
By doing deeds of hospitality.
Besides, his cote, his flocks, and bounds of feed,
Are now on sale; and at our sheepcote now,
By reason of his absence, there is nothing
That you will feed on; but what is, come see,
And in my voice most welcome shall you be.

ROSALIND What is he that shall buy his flock and pasture?

CORIN That young swain that you saw here but erewhile,
That little cares for buying any thing.

ROSALIND I pray thee, if it stand with honesty,
Buy thou the cottage, pasture, and the flock,
And thou shalt have to pay for it of us.

CELIA And we will mend thy wages. I like this place,
And willingly could waste my time in it.

CORIN Assuredly the thing is to be sold.
Go with me; if you like upon report
The soil, the profit, and this kind of life,
I will your very faithful feeder be,
And buy it with your gold right suddenly.
[Exeunt

SCENE V. *Another part of the Forest.*

Enter AMIENS, JAQUES, and Others.

Song.

AMIENS Under the greenwood tree
Who loves to lie with me,
And turn his merry note
Unto the sweet bird's throat,
Come hither, come hither, come hither.
Here shall he see
No enemy
But winter and rough weather.

JAQUES More, more, I prithee, more.

AMIENS It will make you melancholy, Monsieur Jaques.

JAQUES I thank it. More, I prithee, more. I can suck melancholy out of a song, as a weasel sucks eggs. More, I prithee, more.

AMIENS My voice is ragged; I know I cannot please you.

JAQUES I do not desire you to please me; I do desire you to sing. Come, more; another stanzo. Call you 'em stanzos?

AMIENS What you will, Monsieur Jaques.

JAQUES Nay, I care not for their names; they owe me nothing. Will you sing?

AMIENS More at your request than to please myself.

JAQUES Well then, if ever I thank any man, I'll thank you; but that they call compliment is like th' encounter of two dog-apes; and when a man thanks me heartily, methinks I have given him a penny, and he renders me the beggarly thanks. Come, sing; and you that will not, hold your tongues.

AMIENS Well, I'll end the song. Sirs, cover the while; the Duke will drink under this tree. He hath been all this day to look you.

JAQUES And I have been all this day to avoid him. He is too disputable for my company. I think of as many matters as he; but I give heaven thanks, and make no boast of them. Come, warble, come.

Song.

All together here.

Who doth ambition shun,
And loves to live i' th' sun,
Seeking the food he eats,
And pleas'd with what he gets,
Come hither, come hither, come hither.
Here shall he see
No enemy
But winter and rough weather.

JAQUES I'll give you a verse to this note that I made yesterday in despite of my invention.

AMIENS And I'll sing it.

JAQUES Thus it goes:

If it do come to pass
That any man turn ass,
Leaving his wealth and ease
A stubborn will to please,
Ducdame, ducdame, ducdame;
Here shall he see
Gross fools as he,
An if he will come to me.

AMIENS What's that 'ducdame'?

JAQUES 'Tis a Greek invocation, to call fools into a circle. I'll go sleep, if I can; if I cannot, I'll rail against all the first-born of Egypt.

AMIENS And I'll go seek the Duke; his banquet is prepar'd. [*Exeunt severally.*

SCENE VI. *The forest.*

Enter ORLANDO and ADAM.

ADAM Dear master, I can go no further. O, I die for food! Here lie I down, and measure out my grave. Farewell, kind master.

ORLANDO Why, how now, Adam! No greater heart in thee? Live a little; comfort a little; cheer thyself a little. If this uncouth forest yield anything savage, I will either be food for it or bring it for food to thee. Thy conceit is nearer death than thy powers. For my sake be comfortable; hold death awhile at the arm's end. I will here be with thee presently; and if I bring thee not something to eat, I will give thee leave to die; but if thou diest before I come, thou art a mocker of my labour. Well said! thou look'st cheerly; and I'll be with thee quickly. Yet thou liest in the bleak air. Come, I will bear thee to some shelter; and thou shalt not die for lack of a dinner, if there live any thing in this desert. Cheerly, good Adam! [*Exeunt.*

SCENE VII. *The forest.*

A table set out. Enter DUKE SENIOR, AMIENS, and Lords, like outlaws.

DUKE SENIOR I think he be transform'd into a beast;
For I can nowhere find him like a man.

1 LORD My lord, he is but even now gone hence;
Here was he merry, hearing of a song.

DUKE SENIOR If he, compact of jars, grow musical,
We shall have shortly discord in the spheres.
Go seek him; tell him I would speak with him.

Enter JAQUES.

1 LORD He saves my labour by his own approach.

DUKE SENIOR Why, how now, monsieur! what a life is this,
That your poor friends must woo your company?
What, you look merrily!

JAQUES A fool, a fool! I met a fool i' th' forest,
A motley fool. A miserable world!
As I do live by food, I met a fool,
Who laid him down and bask'd him in the sun,
And rail'd on Lady Fortune in good terms,
In good set terms – and yet a motley fool.
'Good morrow, fool' quoth I; 'No, sir,' quoth he
'Call me not fool till heaven hath sent me fortune.'
And then he drew a dial from his poke,
And, looking on it with lack-lustre eye,
Says very wisely 'It is ten o'clock;
Thus we may see' quoth he 'how the world wags;
'Tis but an hour ago since it was nine;
And after one hour more 'twill be eleven;
And so, from hour to hour, we ripe and ripe,
And then, from hour to hour, we rot and rot;
And thereby hangs a tale'. When I did hear
The motley fool thus moral on the time,
My lungs began to crow like chanticleer
That fools should be so deep contemplative;
And I did laugh sans intermission
An hour by his dial. O noble fool!
A worthy fool! Motley's the only wear.

DUKE SENIOR What fool is this?

JAQUES O worthy fool! One that hath been a courtier,
And says, if ladies be but young and fair,
They have the gift to know it; and in his brain,
Which is as dry as the remainder biscuit

After a voyage, he hath strange places cramm'd
With observation, the which he vents
In mangled forms. O that I were a fool!
I am ambitious for a motley coat.

DUKE SENIOR Thou shalt have one.

JAQUES It is my only suit,
Provided that you weed your better judgments
Of all opinion that grows rank in them
That I am wise. I must have liberty
Withal, as large a charter as the wind,
To blow on whom I please, for so fools have;
And they that are most galled with my folly,
They most must laugh. And why, sir, must they so?
The why is plain as way to parish church:
He that a fool doth very wisely hit
Doth very foolishly, although he smart,
Not to seem senseless of the bob; if not,
The wise man's folly is anatomiz'd
Even by the squand'ring glances of the fool.
Invest me in my motley; give me leave
To speak my mind, and I will through and through
Cleanse the foul body of th' infected world,
If they will patiently receive my medicine.

DUKE SENIOR Fie on thee! I can tell what thou wouldst do.

JAQUES What, for a counter, would I do but good?

DUKE SENIOR Most mischievous foul sin, in chiding sin;
For thou thyself hast been a libertine,
As sensual as the brutish sting itself;
And all th' embossed sores and headed evils
That thou with licence of free foot hast caught
Wouldst thou disgorge into the general world.

JAQUES Why, who cries out on pride
That can therein tax any private party?
Doth it not flow as hugely as the sea,
Till that the wearer's very means do ebb?
What woman in the city do I name
When that I say the city-woman bears
The cost of princes on unworthy shoulders?
Who can come in and say that I mean her,
When such a one as she such is her neighbour?
Or what is he of basest function
That says his bravery is not on my cost,
Thinking that I mean him, but therein suits
His folly to the mettle of my speech?
There then! how then? what then? Let me see wherein
My tongue hath wrong'd him: if it do him right,
Then he hath wrong'd himself; if he be free,
Why then my taxing like a wild-goose flies,
Unclaim'd of any man. But who comes here?

Enter ORLANDO, with his sword drawn.

ORLANDO Forbear, and eat no more.

JAQUES Why, I have eat none yet.

ORLANDO Nor shalt not, till necessity be serv'd.

JAQUES Of what kind should this cock come of?

DUKE SENIOR Art thou thus bolden'd, man, by thy distress?
Or else a rude despiser of good manners,
That in civility thou seem'st so empty?

ORLANDO You touch'd my vein at first: the thorny point
Of bare distress hath ta'en from me the show
Of smooth civility; yet am I inland bred,
And know some nurture. But forbear, I say;
He dies that touches any of this fruit
Till I and my affairs are answered.

JAQUES An you will not be answer'd with reason, I must die.

DUKE SENIOR What would you have? Your gentleness shall force
More than your force move us to gentleness.

ORLANDO I almost die for food, and let me have it.

DUKE SENIOR Sit down and feed, and welcome to our table.

ORLANDO Speak you so gently? Pardon me, I pray you;
I thought that all things had been savage here,
And therefore put I on the countenance
Of stern commandment. But whate'er you are
That in this desert inaccessible,
Under the shade of melancholy boughs,
Lose and neglect the creeping hours of time;
If ever you have look'd on better days,
If ever been where bells have knoll'd to church,
If ever sat at any good man's feast,
If ever from your eyelids wip'd a tear,
And know what 'tis to pity and be pitied,
Let gentleness my strong enforcement be;
In the which hope I blush, and hide my sword.

DUKE SENIOR True is it that we have seen better days,
And have with holy bell been knoll'd to church,
And sat at good men's feasts, and wip'd our eyes
Of drops that sacred pity hath engend'red;
And therefore sit you down in gentleness,
And take upon command what help we have
That to your wanting may be minist'red.

ORLANDO Then but forbear your food a little while,
Whiles, like a doe, I go to find my fawn,
And give it food. There is an old poor man
Who after me hath many a weary step
Limp'd in pure love; till he be first suffic'd,
Oppress'd with two weak evils, age and hunger,
I will not touch a bit.

DUKE SENIOR Go find him out.
And we will nothing waste till you return.

ORLANDO I thank ye; and be blest for your good comfort! [*Exit.*

DUKE SENIOR Thou seest we are not all alone unhappy:
This wide and universal theatre
Presents more woeful pageants than the scene
Wherein we play in.

JAQUES All the world's a stage,
And all the men and women merely players;
They have their exits and their entrances;
And one man in his time plays many parts,
His acts being seven ages. At first the infant,
Mewling and puking in the nurse's arms;
Then the whining school-boy, with his satchel
And shining morning face, creeping like snail
Unwillingly to school. And then the lover,
Sighing like furnace, with a woeful ballad
Made to his mistress' eyebrow. Then a soldier,
Full of strange oaths, and bearded like the pard,
Jealous in honour, sudden and quick in quarrel,
Seeking the bubble reputation
Even in the cannon's mouth. And then the justice,
In fair round belly with good capon lin'd,
With eyes severe and beard of formal cut,
Full of wise saws and modern instances;
And so he plays his part. The sixth age shifts
Into the lean and slipper'd pantaloon,
With spectacles on nose and pouch on side,
His youthful hose, well sav'd, a world too wide
For his shrunk shank; and his big manly voice,
Turning again toward childish treble, pipes
And whistles in his sound. Last scene of all,
That ends this strange eventful history,
Is second childishness and mere oblivion;
Sans teeth, sans eyes, sans taste, sans every thing.

Re-enter ORLANDO with ADAM.

DUKE SENIOR Welcome. Set down your venerable burden.
And let him feed.

ORLANDO I thank you most for him.

ADAM So had you need;
I scarce can speak to thank you for myself.

DUKE SENIOR Welcome; fall to. I will not trouble you
As yet to question you about your fortunes.
Give us some music; and, good cousin, sing.

Song.

Blow, blow, thou winter wind,
Thou art not so unkind
As man's ingratitude;
Thy tooth is not so keen,
Because thou are not seen,
Although thy breath be rude.
Heigh-ho! sing heigh-ho! unto the green holly!
Most friendship is feigning, most loving mere folly.
Then, heigh-ho, the holly!
This life is most jolly.
Freeze, freeze, thou bitter sky,
That dost not bite so nigh
As benefits forgot;
Though thou the waters warp,
Thy sting is not so sharp
As friend rememb'red not.
Heigh-ho! sing, etc.

DUKE SENIOR If that you were the good Sir Rowland's son,
As you have whisper'd faithfully you were,
And as mine eye doth his effigies witness
Most truly limn'd and living in your face,
Be truly welcome hither. I am the Duke
That lov'd your father. The residue of your fortune,
Go to my cave and tell me. Good old man,
Thou art right welcome as they master is.
Support him by the arm. Give me your hand,
And let me all your fortunes understand. [*Exeunt.*

ACT THREE

SCENE I. *The palace.*

Enter DUKE FREDERICK, OLIVER, and Lords.

DUKE FREDERICK Not see him since! Sir, sir, that cannot be.
But were I not the better part made mercy,
I should not seek an absent argument
Of my revenge, thou present. But look to it:
Find out thy brother wheresoe'er he is;
Seek him with candle; bring him dead or living
Within this twelvemonth, or turn thou no more
To seek a living in our territory.
Thy lands and all things that thou dost call thine
Worth seizure do we seize into our hands,
Till thou canst quit thee by thy brother's mouth
Of what we think against thee.

OLIVER O that your Highness knew my heart in this!
I never lov'd my brother in my life.

DUKE FREDERICK More villain thou. Well, push him out of doors;

And let my officers of such a nature
Make an extent upon his house and lands.
Do this expediently, and turn him going.
[*Exeunt.*

SCENE II. *The forest.*

Enter ORLANDO, with a paper.

ORLANDO Hang there, my verse, in witness of my love;
And thou, thrice-crowned Queen of Night, survey
With thy chaste eye, from thy pale sphere above,
Thy huntress' name that my full life doth sway.
O Rosalind! these trees shall be my books,
And in their barks my thoughts I'll character,
That every eye which in this forest looks
Shall see thy virtue witness'd every where.
Run, run, Orlando; carve on every tree,
The fair, the chaste, and unexpressive she.
[*Exit.*

Enter CORIN and TOUCHSTONE.

CORIN And how like you this shepherd's life, Master Touchstone?

TOUCHSTONE Truly, shepherd, in respect of itself; it is a good life; but in respect that it is a shepherd's life, it is nought. In respect that it is solitary, I like it very well; but in respect that it is private, it is a very vile life. Now in respect it is in the fields, it pleaseth me well; but in respect it is not in the court, it is tedious. As it is a spare life, look you, it fits my humour well; but as there is no more plenty in it, it goes much against my stomach. Hast any philosophy in thee, shepherd?

CORIN No more but that I know the more one sickens the worse at ease he is; and that he that wants money, means, and content, is without three good friends; that the property of rain is to wet, and fire to burn; that good pasture makes fat sheep; and that a great cause of the night is lack of the sun; that he that hath learned no wit by nature nor art may complain of good breeding, or comes of a very dull kindred.

TOUCHSTONE Such a one is a natural philosopher. Wast ever in court, shepherd?

CORIN No, truly.

TOUCHSTONE Then thou art damn'd.

CORIN Nay, I hope.

TOUCHSTONE Truly, thou art damn'd, like an ill-roasted egg, all on one side.

CORIN For not being at court? Your reason.

TOUCHSTONE Why, if thou never wast at court thou never saw'st good manners; if thou never saw'st good manners, then thy manners must be wicked; and wickedness is sin, and sin is damnation. Thou art in a parlous state, shepherd.

CORIN Not a whit, Touchstone. Those that are good manners at the court are as ridiculous in the country as the behaviour of the country is most mockable at the court. You told me you salute not at the court, but you kiss your hands; that courtesy would be uncleanly if courtiers were shepherds.

TOUCHSTONE Instance, briefly; come, instance.

CORIN Why, we are still handling our ewes; and their fells, you know, are greasy.

TOUCHSTONE Why, do not your courtier's hands sweat? And is not the grease of a mutton as wholesome as the sweat of a man? Shallow, shallow. A better instance, I say; come.

CORIN Besides, our hands are hard.

TOUCHSTONE Your lips will feel them the sooner. Shallow again. A more sounder instance; come.

CORIN And they are often tarr'd over with the surgery of our sheep; and would you have us kiss tar? The courtier's hands are perfum'd with civet.

TOUCHSTONE Most shallow man! thou worm's meat in respect of a good piece of flesh indeed! Learn of the wise, and perpend: civet is of a baser birth than tar – the very uncleanly flux of a cat. Mend the instance, shepherd.

CORIN You have too courtly a wit for me; I'll rest.

TOUCHSTONE Wilt thou rest damn'd? God help thee, shallow man! God make incision in thee! thou art raw.

CORIN Sir, I am a true labourer: I earn that I eat, get that I wear; owe no man hate, envy no man's happiness; glad of other men's good, content with my harm; and the greatest of my pride is to see my ewes graze and my lambs suck.

TOUCHSTONE That is another simple sin in you: to bring the ewes and the rams together, and to offer to get your living by the copulation of cattle; to be bawd to a bell-wether, and to betray a she-lamb of a twelvemonth to a crooked-pated, old, cuckoldly ram, out of all reasonable match. If thou beest not damn'd for this, the devil himself will have no shepherds; I cannot see else how thou shouldst scape.

CORIN Here comes young Master Ganymede, my new mistress's brother.

Enter ROSALIND, reading a paper.

ROSALIND 'From the east to western Inde,
No jewel is like Rosalinde.
Her worth, being mounted on the wind,

Through all the world bears
Rosalinde.
All the pictures fairest lin'd
Are but black to Rosalinde.
Let no face be kept in mind
But the fair of Rosalinde.'

TOUCHSTONE I'll rhyme you so eight years together, dinners, and suppers, and sleeping hours, excepted. It is the right butter-women's rank to market.

ROSALIND Out, fool!

TOUCHSTONE For a taste:
If a hart do lack a hind,
Let him seek out Rosalinde.
If the cat will after kind,
So be sure will Rosalinde.
Winter garments must be lin'd,
So must slender Rosalinde.
They that reap must sheaf and
bind,
Then to cart with Rosalinde.
Sweetest nut hath sourest rind,
Such a nut is Rosalinde.
He that sweetest rose will find
Must find love's prick and
Rosalinde.
This is the very false gallop of verses; why do you infect yourself with them?

ROSALIND Peace, you dull fool! I found them on a tree.

TOUCHSTONE Truly, the tree yields bad fruit.

ROSALIND I'll graff it with you, and then I shall graff it with a medlar. Then it will be the earliest fruit i' th' country; or you'll be rotten ere you be half ripe, and that's the right virtue of the medlar.

TOUCHSTONE You have said; but whether wisely or no, let the forest judge.

Enter CELIA, with a writing.

ROSALIND Peace!
Here comes my sister, reading; stand aside.

CELIA 'Why should this a desert be?
For it is unpeopled? No;
Tongues I'll hang on every tree
That shall civil sayings show.
Some, how brief the life of man
Runs his erring pilgrimage,
That the stretching of a span
Buckles in his sum of age;
Some, of violated vows
'Twixt the souls of friend and friend;
But upon the fairest boughs,
Or at every sentence end,
Will I Rosalinda write,
Teaching all that read to know
The quintessence of every sprite
Heaven would in little show.
Therefore heaven Nature charg'd
That one body should be fill'd
With all graces wide-enlarg'd.
Nature presently distill'd
Helen's cheek, but not her heart,
Cleopatra's majesty,
Atalanta's better part,
Sad Lucretia's modesty.
Thus Rosalinde of many parts
By heavenly synod was devis'd,
Of many faces, eyes, and hearts,
To have the touches dearest priz'd.
Heaven would that she these gifts should
have,
And I to live and die her slave.'

ROSALIND O most gentle pulpiter! What tedious homily of love have you wearied your parishioners withal, and never cried 'Have patience, good people'.

CELIA How now! Back, friends; shepherd, go off a little; go with him, sirrah.

TOUCHSTONE Come, shepherd, let us make an honourable retreat; though not with bag and baggage, yet with scrip and scrippage.

[*Exeunt Corin and Touchstone.*

CELIA Didst thou hear these verses?

ROSALIND O, yes, I heard them all, and more too; for some of them had in them more feet than the verses would bear.

CELIA That's no matter; the feet might bear the verses.

ROSALIND Ay, but the feet were lame, and could not bear themselves without the verse, and therefore stood lamely in the verse.

CELIA But didst thou hear without wondering how thy name should be hang'd and carved upon these trees?

ROSALIND I was seven of the nine days out of the wonder before you came; for look here what I found on a palm-tree. I was never so berhym'd since Pythagoras' time that I was an Irish rat, which I can hardly remember.

CELIA Trow you who hath done this?

ROSALIND Is it a man?

CELIA And a chain, that you once wore, about his neck. Change you colour?

ROSALIND I prithee, who?

CELIA O Lord, Lord! it is a hard matter for friends to meet; but mountains may be remov'd with earthquakes, and so encounter.

ROSALIND Nay, but who is it?

CELIA Is it possible?

ROSALIND Nay, I prithee now, with most petitionary vehemence, tell me who it is.

CELIA O wonderful, wonderful, and most

wonderful wonderful, and yet again wonderful,
and after that, out of all whooping!
ROSALIND Good my complexion! dost thou
think, though I am caparison'd like a man, I
have a doublet and hose in my disposition? One
inch of delay more is a South Sea of discovery. I
prithee tell me who is it quickly, and speak
apace. I would thou couldst stammer, that thou
mightst pour this conceal'd man out of thy
mouth, as wine comes out of a narrow-mouth'd
bottle – either too much at once or none at all. I
prithee take the cork out of thy mouth that I
189 may drink thy tidings.
CELIA So you may put a man in your belly.
ROSALIND Is he of God's making? What manner
of man? Is his head worth a hat or his chin
worth a beard?
193 **CELIA** Nay, he hath but a little beard.
ROSALIND Why, God will send more if the man
will be thankful. Let me stay the growth of his
beard, if thou delay me not the knowledge of his
196 chin.
CELIA It is young Orlando, that tripp'd up the
wrestler's heels and your heart both in an
instant.
ROSALIND Nay, but the devil take mocking!
200 Speak sad brow and true maid.
CELIA I' faith, coz, 'tis he.
ROSALIND Orlando?
203 **CELIA** Orlando.
ROSALIND Alas the day! what shall I do with my
doublet and hose? What did he when thou
saw'st him? What said he? How look'd he?
Wherein went he? What makes he here? Did he
ask for me? Where remains he? How parted he
with thee? And when shalt thou see him again?
209 Answer me in one word.
CELIA You must borrow me Gargantua's mouth
first; 'tis a word too great for any mouth of this
age's size. To say ay and no to these particulars
213 is more than to answer in a catechism.
ROSALIND But doth he know that I am in this
forest, and in man's apparel? Looks he
216 as freshly as he did the day he wrestled?
CELIA It is as easy to count atomies as to resolve
the propositions of a lover; but take a taste of
my finding him, and relish it with good
observance. I found him under a tree, like a
220 dropp'd acorn.
ROSALIND It may well be call'd Jove's tree, when
it drops forth such fruit.
CELIA Give me audience, good madam.
ROSALIND Proceed.
CELIA There lay he, stretch'd along like a
226 wounded knight.
ROSALIND Though it be pity to see such a sight, it
well becomes the ground.
CELIA Cry 'Holla' to thy tongue, I prithee; it
curvets unseasonably. He was furnish'd like a
hunter. 230
ROSALIND O, ominous! he comes to kill my
heart.
CELIA I would sing my song without a burden;
thou bring'st me out of tune.
ROSALIND Do you not know I am a woman?
When I think, I must speak. Sweet, say on.
CELIA You bring me out. Soft! comes he not
here? 236

Enter ORLANDO and JAQUES.

ROSALIND 'Tis he; slink by, and note him.
JAQUES I thank you for your company; but, good
faith, I had as lief have been myself alone.
ORLANDO And so had I; but yet, for fashion sake,
I thank you too for your society. 241
JAQUES God buy you; let's meet as little as we
can.
ORLANDO I do desire we may be better strangers.
JAQUES I pray you mar no more trees with
writing love songs in their barks. 245
ORLANDO I pray you mar no moe of my verses
with reading them ill-favouredly.
JAQUES Rosalind is your love's name?
ORLANDO Yes, just.
JAQUES I do not like her name. 250
ORLANDO There was no thought of pleasing you
when she was christen'd.
JAQUES What stature is she of?
ORLANDO Just as high as my heart. 254
JAQUES You are full of pretty answers. Have you
not been acquainted with goldsmiths' wives,
and conn'd them out of rings? 257
ORLANDO Not so; but I answer you right painted
cloth, from whence you have studied your
questions. 259
JAQUES You have a nimble wit; I think 'twas
made of Atalanta's heels. Will you sit down with
me? and we two will rail against our mistress
the world, and all our misery. 262
ORLANDO I will chide no breather in the world
but myself, against whom I know most faults.
JAQUES The worst fault you have is to be in love. 265
ORLANDO 'Tis a fault I will not change for your
best virtue. I am weary of you.
JAQUES By my troth, I was seeking for a fool
when I found you.
ORLANDO He is drown'd in the brook; look but
in, and you shall see him. 271
JAQUES There I shall see mine own figure.
ORLANDO Which I take to be either a fool or a
cipher.
JAQUES I'll tarry no longer with you; farewell,
good Signior Love. 275
ORLANDO I am glad of your departure; adieu,

good Monsieur Melancholy. *[Exit Jaques.*

ROSALIND *[Aside to Celia]* I will speak to him like a saucy lackey, and under that habit play the knave with him. – Do you hear, forester?

ORLANDO Very well; what would you?

ROSALIND I pray you, what is't o'clock?

ORLANDO You should ask me what time o' day; there's no clock in the forest.

ROSALIND Then there is no true lover in the forest, else sighing every minute and groaning every hour would detect the lazy foot of Time as well as a clock.

ORLANDO And why not the swift foot of Time? Had not that been as proper?

ROSALIND By no means, sir. Time travels in divers paces with divers persons. I'll tell you who Time ambles withal, who Time trots withal, who Time gallops withal, and who he stands still withal.

ORLANDO I prithee, who doth he trot withal?

ROSALIND Marry, he trots hard with a young maid between the contract of her marriage and the day it is solemniz'd; if the interim be but a se'nnight, Time's pace is so hard that it seems the length of seven year.

ORLANDO Who ambles Time withal?

ROSALIND With a priest that lacks Latin and a rich man that hath not the gout; for the one sleeps easily because he cannot study, and the other lives merrily because he feels no pain; the one lacking the burden of lean and wasteful learning, the other knowing no burden of heavy tedious penury. These Time ambles withal.

ORLANDO ho doth he gallop withal?

ROSALIND With a thief to the gallows; for though he go as softly as foot can fall, he thinks himself too soon there.

ORLANDO Who stays it still withal?

ROSALIND With lawyers in the vacation; for they sleep between term and term, and then they perceive not how Time moves.

ORLANDO Where dwell you, pretty youth?

ROSALIND With this shepherdess, my sister; here in the skirts of the forest, like fringe upon a petticoat.

ORLANDO Are you native of this place?

ROSALIND As the coney that you see dwell where she is kindled.

ORLANDO Your accent is something finer than you could purchase in so removed a dwelling.

ROSALIND I have been told so of many; but indeed an old religious uncle of mine taught me to speak, who was in his youth an inland man; one that knew courtship too well, for there he fell in love. I have heard him read many lectures against it; and I thank God I am not a woman, to be touch'd with so many giddy offences as he hath generally tax'd their whole sex withal.

ORLANDO Can you remember any of the principal evils that he laid to the charge of women?

ROSALIND There were none principal; they were all like one another as halfpence are; every one fault seeming monstrous till his fellow-fault came to match it.

ORLANDO I prithee recount some of them.

ROSALIND No; I will not cast away my physic but on those that are sick. There is a man haunts the forest that abuses our young plants with carving 'Rosalind' on their barks; hangs odes upon hawthorns and elegies on brambles; all, forsooth, deifying the name of Rosalind. If I could meet that fancy-monger, I would give him some good counsel, for he seems to have the quotidian of love upon him.

ORLANDO I am he that is so love-shak'd; I pray you tell me your remedy.

ROSALIND There is none of my uncle's marks upon you; he taught me how to know a man in love; in which cage of rushes I am sure you are not prisoner.

ORLANDO What were his marks?

ROSALIND A lean cheek, which you have not; a blue eye and sunken, which you have not; an unquestionable spirit, which you have not; a beard neglected, which you have not; but I pardon you for that, for simply your having in beard is a younger brother's revenue. Then your hose should be ungarter'd, your bonnet unbanded, your sleeve unbutton'd, your shoe untied, and every thing about you demonstrating a careless desolation. But you are no such man; you are rather point-device in your accoutrements, as loving yourself than seeming the lover of any other.

ORLANDO Fair youth, I would I could make thee believe I love.

ROSALIND Me believe it! You may as soon make her that you love believe it; which, I warrant, she is apter to do than to confess she does. That is one of the points in the which women still give the lie to their consciences. But, in good sooth, are you he that hangs the verses on the trees wherein Rosalind is so admired?

ORLANDO I swear to thee, youth, by the white hand of Rosalind, I am that he, that unfortunate he.

ROSALIND But are you so much in love as your rhymes speak?

ORLANDO Neither rhyme nor reason can express how much.

ROSALIND Love is merely a madness; and, I tell you, deserves as well a dark house and a whip as madmen do; and the reason why they are not so punish'd and cured is that the lunacy is so ordinary that the whippers are in love too. Yet I profess curing it by counsel.

ORLANDO Did you ever cure any so?

ROSALIND Yes, one; and in this manner. He was to imagine me his love, his mistress; and I set him every day to woo me; at which time would I, being but a moonish youth, grieve, be effeminate, changeable, longing and liking, proud, fantastical, apish, shallow, inconstant, full of tears, full of smiles; for every passion something and for no passion truly anything, as boys and women are for the most part cattle of this colour; would now like him, now loathe him; then entertain him, then forswear him; now weep for him, then spit at him; that I drave my suitor from his mad humour of love to a living humour of madness; which was, to forswear the full stream of the world and to live in a nook merely monastic. And thus I cur'd him; and this way will I take upon me to wash your liver as clean as a sound sheep's heart, that there shall not be one spot of love in 't.

ORLANDO I would not be cured, youth.

ROSALIND I would cure you, if you would but call me Rosalind, and come every day to my cote and woo me.

ORLANDO Now, by the faith of my love, I will. Tell me where it is.

ROSALIND Go with me to it, and I'll show it you; and, by the way, you shall tell me where in the forest you live. Will you go?

ORLANDO With all my heart, good youth.

ROSALIND Nay, you must call me Rosalind. Come, sister, will you go? [*Exeunt.*

SCENE III. *The forest.*

Enter TOUCHSTONE and AUDREY; JAQUES behind.

TOUCHSTONE Come apace, good Audrey; I will fetch up your goats, Audrey. And how, Audrey, am I the man yet? Doth my simple feature content you?

AUDREY Your features! Lord warrant us! What features?

TOUCHSTONE I am here with thee and thy goats, as the most capricious poet, honest Ovid, was among the Goths.

JAQUES [*Aside*] O knowledge ill-inhabited, worse than Jove in a thatch'd house!

TOUCHSTONE When a man's verses cannot be understood, nor a man's good wit seconded with the forward child understanding, it strikes a man more dead than a great reckoning in a little room. Truly, I would the gods had made thee poetical.

AUDREY I do not know what 'poetical' is. Is it honest in deed and word? Is it a true thing?

TOUCHSTONE No, truly; for the truest poetry is the most feigning, and lovers are given to poetry; and what they swear in poetry may be said as lovers they do feign.

AUDREY Do you wish, then, that the gods had made me poetical?

TOUCHSTONE I do, truly, for thou swear'st to me thou art honest; now, if thou wert a poet, I might have some hope thou didst feign.

AUDREY Would you not have me honest?

TOUCHSTONE No, truly, unless thou wert hard-favour'd; for honesty coupled to beauty is to have honey a sauce to sugar.

JAQUES [*Aside*] A material fool!

AUDREY Well, I am not fair; and therefore I pray the gods make me honest.

TOUCHSTONE Truly, and to cast away honesty upon a foul slut were to put good meat into an unclean dish.

AUDREY I am not a slut, though I thank the gods I am foul.

TOUCHSTONE Well, praised be the gods for thy foulness; sluttishness may come hereafter. But be it as it may be, I will marry thee; and to that end I have been with Sir Oliver Martext, the vicar of the next village, who hath promis'd to meet me in this place of the forest, and to couple us.

JAQUES [*Aside*] I would fain see this meeting.

AUDREY Well, the gods give us joy!

TOUCHSTONE Amen. A man may, if he were of a fearful heart, stagger in this attempt; for here we have no temple but the wood, no assembly but horn-beasts. But what though? Courage! As horns are odious, they are necessary. It is said: 'Many a man knows no end of his goods'. Right! Many a man has good horns and knows no end of them. Well, that is the dowry of his wife; 'tis none of his own getting. Horns? Even so. Poor men alone? No, no; the noblest deer hath them as huge as the rascal. Is the single man therefore blessed? No; as a wall'd town is more worthier than a village, so is the forehead of a married man more honourable than the bare brow of a bachelor; and by how much defence is better than no skill, by so much is a horn more precious than to want. Here comes Sir Oliver.

Enter SIR OLIVER MARTEXT.

Sir Oliver Martext, you are well met. Will you dispatch us here under this tree, or shall we go with you to your chapel?

SIR OLIVER Is there none here to give the woman?

TOUCHSTONE I will not take her on gift of any man.

SIR OLIVER Truly, she must be given, or the marriage is not lawful.

JAQUES [*Discovering himself*] Proceed, proceed; I'll give her.

TOUCHSTONE Good even, good Master What-ye-call't; how do you, sir? You are very well met. Goddild you for your last company. I am very glad to see you. Even a toy in hand here, sir. Nay; pray be cover'd.

JAQUES Will you be married, motley?

TOUCHSTONE As the ox hath his bow, sir, the horse his curb, and the falcon her bells, so man hath his desires; and as pigeons bill, so wedlock would be nibbling.

JAQUES And will you, being a man of your breeding, be married under a bush, like a beggar? Get you to church and have a good priest that can tell you what marriage is; this fellow will but join you together as they join wainscot; then one of you will prove a shrunk panel, and like green timber warp, warp.

TOUCHSTONE [*Aside*] I am not in the mind but I were better to be married of him than of another; for he is not like to marry me well; and not being well married, it will be a good excuse for me hereafter to leave my wife.

JAQUES Go thou with me, and let me counsel thee.

TOUCHSTONE Come, sweet Audrey;
We must be married or we must live in bawdry.
Farewell, good Master Oliver. Not –
O sweet Oliver,
O brave Oliver,
Leave me not behind thee.
But –
Wind away,
Begone, I say,
I will not to wedding with thee.

[*Exeunt Jaques, Touchstone, and Audrey.*

SIR OLIVER 'Tis no matter; ne'er a fantastical knave of them all shall flout me out of my calling. [*Exit.*

SCENE IV. *The forest.*

Enter ROSALIND and CELIA.

ROSALIND Never talk to me; I will weep.

CELIA Do, I prithee; but yet have the grace to consider that tears do not become a man.

ROSALIND But have I not cause to weep?

CELIA As good cause as one would desire; therefore weep.

ROSALIND His very hair is of the dissembling colour.

CELIA Something browner than Judas's. Marry, his kisses are Judas's own children.

ROSALIND I'faith, his hair is of a good colour.

CELIA An excellent colour: your chestnut was ever the only colour.

ROSALIND And his kissing is as full of sanctity as the touch of holy bread.

CELIA He hath bought a pair of cast lips of Diana. A nun of winter's sisterhood kisses not more religiously; the very ice of chastity is in them.

ROSALIND But why did he swear he would come this morning, and comes not?

CELIA Nay, certainly, there is no truth in him.

ROSALIND Do you think so?

CELIA Yes; I think he is not a pick-purse nor a horse-stealer; but for his verity in love, I do think him as concave as a covered goblet or a worm-eaten nut.

ROSALIND Not true in love?

CELIA Yes, when is he in; but I think he is not in.

ROSALIND You have heard him swear downright he was.

CELIA 'Was' is not 'is'; besides, the oath of a lover is no stronger than the word of a tapster; they are both the confirmer of false reckonings. He attends here in the forest on the Duke, your father.

ROSALIND I met the Duke yesterday, and had much question with him. He asked me of what parentage I was; I told him, of as good as he; so he laugh'd and let me go. But what talk we of fathers when there is such a man as Orlando?

CELIA O, that's a brave man! He writes brave verses, speaks brave words, swears brave oaths, and breaks them bravely, quite traverse, athwart the heart of his lover; as a puny tilter, that spurs his horse but on one side, breaks his staff like a noble goose. But all's brave that youth mounts and folly guides. Who comes here?

Enter CORIN.

CORIN Mistress and master, you have oft enquired
After the shepherd that complain'd of love,
Who you saw sitting by me on the turf,
Praising the proud disdainful shepherdess
That was his mistress.

CELIA Well, and what of him?

CORIN If you will see a pageant truly play'd
Between the pale complexion of true love
And the red glow of scorn and proud disdain,
Go hence a little, and I shall conduct you,
If you will mark it.

ROSALIND O, come, let us remove!
The sight of lovers feedeth those in love.

Bring us to this sight, and you shall say
I'll prove a busy actor in their play. [*Exeunt.*

SCENE V. *Another part of the forest.*

Enter SILVIUS and PHEBE.

SILVIUS Sweet Phebe, do not scorn me; do not, Phebe.
Say that you love me not; but say not so
In bitterness. The common executioner,
Whose heart th' accustom'd sight of death makes hard,
Falls not the axe upon the humbled neck
But first begs pardon. Will you sterner be
Than he that dies and lives by bloody drops?

Enter ROSALIND, CELIA, and CORIN, at a distance.

PHEBE I would not be thy executioner;
I fly thee, for I would not injure thee.
Thou tell'st me there is murder in mine eye.
'Tis pretty, sure, and very probable,
That eyes, that are the frail'st and softest things,
Who shut their coward gates on atomies,
Should be call'd tyrants, butchers, murderers!
Now I do frown on thee with all my heart;
And if mine eyes can wound, now let them kill thee.
Now counterfeit to swoon; why, now fall down;
Or, if thou canst not, O, for shame, for shame,
Lie not, to say mine eyes are murderers.
Now show the wound mine eye hath made in thee.
Scratch thee but with a pin, and there remains
Some scar of it; lean upon a rush,
The cicatrice and capable impressure
Thy palm some moment keeps; but now mine eyes,
Which I have darted at thee, hurt thee not;
Nor, I am sure, there is not force in eyes
That can do hurt.

SILVIUS O dear Phebe,
If ever – as that ever may be near –
You meet in some fresh cheek the power of fancy,
Then shall you know the wounds invisible
That love's keen arrows make.

PHEBE But till that time
Come not thou near me; and when that time comes,
Afflict me with thy mocks, pity me not;
As till that time I shall not pity thee.

ROSALIND [*Advancing*] And why, I pray you?
Who might be your mother,
That you insult, exult, and all at once,
Over the wretched? What though you have no beauty –
As, by my faith, I see no more in you
Than without candle may go dark to bed –
Must you be therefore proud and pitiless?
Why, what means this? Why do you look on me?
I see no more in you than in the ordinary
Of nature's sale-work. 'Od's my little life,
I think she means to tangle my eyes too!
No, faith, proud mistress, hope not after it;
'Tis not your inky brows, your black silk hair,
Your bugle eyeballs, nor your cheek of cream,
That can entame my spirits to your worship.
You foolish shepherd, wherefore do you follow her,
Like foggy south, puffing with wind and rain?
You are a thousand times a properer man
Than she a woman. 'Tis such fools as you
That makes the world full of ill-favour'd children.
'Tis not her glass, but you, that flatters her;
And out of you she sees herself more proper
Than any of her lineaments can show her.
But, mistress, know yourself. Down on your knees,
And thank heaven, fasting, for a good man's love;
For I must tell you friendly in your ear:
Sell when you can; you are not for all markets.
Cry the man mercy, love him, take his offer;
Foul is most foul, being foul to be a scoffer.
So take her to thee, shepherd. Fare you well.

PHEBE Sweet youth, I pray you chide a year together;
I had rather hear you chide than this man woo.

ROSALIND He's fall'n in love with your foulness, and she'll fall in love with my anger. If it be so, as fast as she answers thee with frowning looks, I'll sauce her with bitter words. Why look you so upon me?

PHEBE For no ill will I bear you.

ROSALIND I pray you do not fall in love with me,
For I am falser than vows made in wine;
Besides, I like you not. If you will know my house,
'Tis at the tuft of olives here hard by.
Will you go, sister? Shepherd, ply her hard.
Come, sister. Shepherdess, look on him better,
And be not proud; though all the world could see,
None could be so abus'd in sight as he.
Come, to our flock.

[*Exeunt Rosalind, Celia, and Corin.*

PHEBE Dead shepherd, now I find thy saw of might:
'Who ever lov'd that lov'd not at first sight?'

SILVIUS Sweet Phebe.

PHEBE Ha! What say'st thou, Silvius?

SILVIUS Sweet Phebe, pity me.

PHEBE Why, I am sorry for thee, gentle Silvius.
SILVIUS Wherever sorrow is, relief would be.
If you do sorrow at my grief in love,
By giving love, your sorrow and my grief
Were both extermin'd.
PHEBE Thou hast my love; is not that neighbourly?
SILVIUS I would have you.
PHEBE Why, that were covetousness.
Silvius, the time was that I hated thee;
And yet it is not that I bear thee love;
But since that thou canst talk of love so well,
Thy company, which erst was irksome to me,
I will endure; and I'll employ thee too.
But do not look for further recompense
Than thine own gladness that thou art employ'd
SILVIUS So holy and so perfect is my love,
And I in such a poverty of grace,
That I shall think it a most plenteous crop
To glean the broken ears after the man
That the main harvest reaps; loose now and then
A scatt'red smile, and that I'll live upon.
PHEBE Know'st thou the youth that spoke to me erewhile?
SILVIUS Not very well; but I have met him oft;
And he hath bought the cottage and the bounds
That the old carlot once was master of.
PHEBE Think not I love him, though I ask for him;
'Tis but a peevish boy; yet he talks well.
But what care I for words? Yet words do well
When he that speaks them pleases those that hear.
It is a pretty youth – not very pretty;
But, sure, he's proud; and yet his pride becomes him.
He'll make a proper man. The best thing in him
Is his complexion; and faster than his tongue
Did make offence, his eye did heal it up.
He is not very tall; yet for his years he's tall;
His leg is but so-so; and yet 'tis well.
There was a pretty redness in his lip,
A little riper and more lusty red
Than that mix'd in his cheek; 'twas just the difference
Betwixt the constant red and mingled damask.
There be some women, Silvius, had they mark'd him
In parcels as I did, would have gone near
To fall in love with him; but, for my part,
I love him not, nor hate him not; and yet
I have more cause to hate him than to love him;
For what had he to do to chide at me?
He said mine eyes were black, and my hair black,
And, now I am remembr'red, scorn'd at me.
I marvel why I answer'd not again;
But that's all one: omittance is no quittance.
I'll write to him a very taunting letter,
And thou shalt bear it; wilt thou, Silvius?
SILVIUS Phebe, with all my heart.
PHEBE I'll write it straight;
The matter's in my head and in my heart;
I will be bitter with him and passing short.
Go with me, Silvius.

[*Exeunt*.

ACT FOUR

SCENE I. *The forest.*

Enter ROSALIND, CELIA, and JAQUES.

JAQUES I prithee, pretty youth, let me be better acquainted with thee.

ROSALIND They say you are a melancholy fellow.

JAQUES I am so; I do love it better than laughing.

ROSALIND Those that are in extremity of either are abominable fellows, and betray themselves to every modern censure worse than drunkards.

JAQUES Why, 'tis good to be sad and say nothing.

ROSALIND Why then, 'tis good to be a post.

JAQUES I have neither the scholar's melancholy, which is emulation; nor the musician's, which is fantastical; nor the courtier's, which is proud; nor the soldier's, which is ambitious; nor the lawyer's, which is politic; nor the lady's, which is nice; nor the lover's, which is all these; but it is a melancholy of mine own, compounded of many simples, extracted from many objects, and, indeed, the sundry contemplation of my travels; in which my often rumination wraps me in a most humorous sadness.

ROSALIND A traveller! By my faith, you have great reason to be sad. I fear you have sold your own lands to see other men's; then to have seen much and to have nothing is to have rich eyes and poor hands.

JAQUES Yes, I have gain'd my experience.

Enter ORLANDO.

ROSALIND And your experience makes you sad. I had rather have a fool to make me merry than experience to make me sad – and to travel for it too.

ORLANDO Good day, and happiness, dear Rosalind!

JAQUES Nay, then, God buy you, an you talk in

blank verse.

ROSALIND Farewell, Monsieur Traveller; look you lisp and wear strange suits, disable all the benefits of your own country, be out of love with your nativity, and almost chide God for making you that countenance you are; or I will scarce think you have swam in a gondola. [*Exit Jaques*] Why, how now, Orlando! where have you been all this while? You a lover! An you serve me such another trick, never come in my sight more.

ORLANDO My fair Rosalind, I come within an hour of my promise.

ROSALIND Break an hour's promise in love! He that will divide a minute into a thousand parts, and break but a part of the thousand part of a minute in the affairs of love, it may be said of him that Cupid hath clapp'd him o' th' shoulder, but I'll warrant him heart-whole.

ORLANDO Pardon me, dear Rosalind.

ROSALIND Nay, an you be so tardy, come no more in my sight. I had as lief be woo'd of a snail.

ORLANDO Of a snail!

ROSALIND Ay, of a snail; for though he comes slowly, he carries his house on his head – a better jointure, I think, than you make a woman; besides, he brings his destiny with him.

ORLANDO What's that?

ROSALIND Why, horns; which such as you are fain to be beholding to your wives for; but he comes armed in his fortune, and prevents the slander of his wife.

ORLANDO Virtue is no horn-maker; and my Rosalind is virtuous.

ROSALIND And I am your Rosalind.

CELIA It pleases him to call you so; but he hath a Rosalind of a better leer than you.

ROSALIND Come, woo me, woo me; for now I am in a holiday humour, and like enough to consent. What would you say to me now, an I were your very very Rosalind?

ORLANDO I would kiss before I spoke.

ROSALIND Nay, you were better speak first; and when you were gravell'd for lack of matter, you might take occasion to kiss. Very good orators, when they are out, they will spit; and for lovers lacking – God warn us! – matter, the cleanliest shift is to kiss.

ORLANDO How if the kiss be denied?

ROSALIND Then she puts you to entreaty, and there begins new matter.

ORLANDO Who could be out, being before his beloved mistress?

ROSALIND Marry, that should you, if I were your mistress; or I should think my honesty ranker than my wit.

ORLANDO What, of my suit?

ROSALIND Not out of your apparel, and yet out of your suit. Am not I your Rosalind?

ORLANDO I take some joy to say you are, because I would be talking of her.

ROSALIND Well, in her person, I say I will not have you.

ORLANDO Then, in mine own person, I die.

ROSALIND No, faith, die by attorney. The poor world is almost six thousand years old, and in all this time there was not any man died in his own person, videlicet, in a love-cause. Troilus had his brains dash'd out with a Grecian club; yet he did what he could to die before, and he is one of the patterns of love. Leander, he would have liv'd many a fair year, though Hero had turn'd nun, if it had not been for a hot midsummer-night; for, good youth, he went but forth to wash him in the Hellespont, and, being taken with the cramp, was drown'd; and the foolish chroniclers of that age found it was – Hero of Sestos. But these are all lies: men have died from time to time, and worms have eaten them, but not for love.

ORLANDO I would not have my right Rosalind of this mind; for, I protest, her frown might kill me.

ROSALIND By this hand, it will not kill a fly. But come, now I will be your Rosalind in a more coming-on disposition; and ask me what you will, I will grant it.

ORLANDO Then love me, Rosalind.

ROSALIND Yes, faith, will I, Fridays and Saturdays, and all.

ORLANDO And wilt thou have me?

ROSALIND Ay, and twenty such.

ORLANDO What sayest thou?

ROSALIND Are you not good?

ORLANDO I hope so.

ROSALIND Why then, can one desire too much of a good thing? Come, sister, you shall be the priest, and marry us. Give me your hand, Orlando. What do you say, sister?

ORLANDO Pray thee, marry us.

CELIA I cannot say the words.

ROSALIND You must begin 'Will you, Orlando' –

CELIA Go to. Will you, Orlando, have to wife this Rosalind?

ORLANDO I will.

ROSALIND Ay, but when?

ORLANDO Why, now; as fast as she can marry us.

ROSALIND Then you must say 'I take thee, Rosalind, for wife'.

ORLANDO I take thee, Rosalind, for wife.

ROSALIND I might ask you for your commission; but – I do take thee, Orlando, for my husband. There's a girl goes before the priest; and, certainly, a woman's thought runs before her actions.

ORLANDO So do all thoughts; they are wing'd

ROSALIND Now tell me how long you would have her, after you have possess'd her.

ORLANDO For ever and a day.

ROSALIND Say 'a day' without the 'ever'. No, no, Orlando; men are April when they woo, December when they wed: maids are May when they are maids, but the sky changes when they are wives. I will be more jealous of thee than a Barbary cock-pigeon over his hen, more clamorous than a parrot against rain, more new-fangled than an ape, more giddy in my desires than a monkey. I will weep for nothing, like Diana in the fountain, and I will do that when you are dispos'd to be merry; I will laugh like a hyen, and that when thou art inclin'd to sleep.

ORLANDO But will my Rosalind do so?

ROSALIND By my life, she will do as I do.

ORLANDO O, but she is wise.

ROSALIND Or else she could not have the wit to do this. The wiser, the waywarder. Make the doors upon a woman's wit, and it will out at the casement; shut that, and 'twill out at the key-hole; stop that, 'twill fly with the smoke out at the chimney.

ORLANDO A man that had a wife with such a wit, he might say 'Wit, whither wilt?'

ROSALIND Nay, you might keep that check for it, till you met your wife's wit going to your neighbour's bed.

ORLANDO And what wit could wit have to excuse that?

ROSALIND Marry, to say she came to seek you there. You shall never take her without her answer, unless you take her without her tongue. O, that woman that cannot make her fault her husband's occasion, let her never nurse her child herself, for she will breed it like a fool!

ORLANDO For these two hours, Rosalind, I will leave thee.

ROSALIND Alas, dear love, I cannot lack thee two hours!

ORLANDO I must attend the Duke at dinner; by two o'clock I will be with thee again.

ROSALIND Ay, go your ways, go your ways. I knew what you would prove; my friends told me as much, and I thought no less. That flattering tongue of yours won me. 'Tis but one cast away, and so, come death! Two o'clock is your hour?

ORLANDO Ay, sweet Rosalind.

ROSALIND By my troth, and in good earnest, and so God mend me, and by all pretty oaths that are not dangerous, if you break one jot of your promise, or come one minute behind your hour, I will think you the most pathetical break-promise, and the most hollow lover, and the most unworthy of her you call Rosalind, that may be chosen out of the gross band of the unfaithful. Therefore beware my censure, and keep your promise.

ORLANDO With no less religion than if thou wert indeed my Rosalind; so, adieu.

ROSALIND Well, Time is the old justice that examines all such offenders, and let Time try. Adieu. *[Exit Orlando.*

CELIA You have simply misus'd our sex in your love-prate. We must have your doublet and hose pluck'd over your head, and show the world what the bird hath done to her own nest.

ROSALIND O coz, coz, coz, my pretty little coz, that thou didst know how many fathom deep I am in love! But it cannot be sounded; my affection hath an unknown bottom, like the Bay of Portugal.

CELIA Or rather, bottomless; that as fast as you pour affection in, it runs out.

ROSALIND No; that same wicked bastard of Venus, that was begot of thought, conceiv'd of spleen, and born of madness; that blind rascally boy, that abuses every one's eyes because his own are out – let him be judge how deep I am in love. I'll tell thee, Aliena, I cannot be out of the sight of Orlando. I'll go find a shadow, and sigh till he come.

CELIA And I'll sleep. *[Exeunt.*

SCENE II. *The forest.*

Enter JAQUES and Lords, in the habit of foresters.

JAQUES Which is he that killed the deer?

LORD Sir, it was I.

JAQUES Let's present him to the Duke, like a Roman conqueror; and it would do well to set the deer's horns upon his head for a branch of victory. Have you no song, forester, for this purpose?

LORD Yes, sir.

JAQUES Sing it; 'tis no matter how it be in tune, so it make noise enough.

Song.

What shall he have that kill'd the deer?
His leather skin and horns to wear.

[The rest shall bear this burden:

Then sing him home.
Take thou no scorn to wear the horn;
It was a crest ere thou wast born.
Thy father's father wore it;
And thy father bore it.
The horn, the horn, the lusty horn,

Is not a thing to laugh to scorn.
[*Exeunt*.

SCENE III. *The forest.*

Enter ROSALIND and CELIA.

ROSALIND How say you now? Is it not past two o'clock? And here much Orlando!

CELIA I warrant you, with pure love and troubled brain, he hath ta'en his bow and arrows, and is gone forth – to sleep. Look, who comes here.

Enter SILVIUS

SILVIUS My errand is to you, fair youth;
My gentle Phebe did bid me give you this.
I know not the contents; but, as I guess
By the stern brow and waspish action
Which she did use as she was writing of it,
It bears an angry tenour. Pardon me,
I am but as a guiltless messenger.

ROSALIND Patience herself would startle at this letter,
And play the swaggerer. Bear this, bear all.
She says I am not fair, that I lack manners;
She calls me proud, and that she could not love me,
Were man as rare as Phoenix. 'Od's my will!
Her love is not the hare that I do hunt;
Why writes she so to me? Well, shepherd, well,
This is a letter of your own device.

SILVIUS No, I protest, I know not the contents;
Phebe did write it.

ROSALIND Come, come, you are a fool,
And turn'd into the extremity of love.
I saw her hand; she has a leathern hand,
A freestone-colour'd hand; I verily did think
That her old gloves were on, but 'twas her hands;
She has a huswife's hand – but that's no matter.
I say she never did invent this letter:
This is a man's invention, and his hand.

SILVIUS Sure, it is hers.

ROSALIND Why, 'tis a boisterous and a cruel style;
A style for challengers. Why, she defies me,
Like Turk to Christian. Women's gentle brain
Could not drop forth such giant-rude invention,
Such Ethiope words, blacker in their effect
Than in their countenance. Will you hear the letter?

SILVIUS So please you, for I never heard it yet;
Yet heard too much of Phebe's cruelty.

ROSALIND She Phebes me: mark how the tyrant writes.
[*Reads*.

'Art thou god to shepherd turn'd
That a maiden's heart hath burn'd?'

Can a woman rail thus?

SILVIUS Call you this railing?

ROSALIND 'Why, thy godhead laid apart,
War'st thou with a woman's heart?'

Did you ever hear such railing?

'Whiles the eye of man did woo me,
That could do no vengeance to me.'

Meaning me a beast.

'If the scorn of your bright eyne
Have power to raise such love in mine,
Alack, in me what strange effect
Would they work in mild aspect!
Whiles you chid me, I did love;
How then might your prayers move!
He that brings this love to thee
Little knows this love in me;
And by him seal up thy mind,
Whether that thy youth and kind
Will the faithful offer take
Of me and all that I can make;
Or else by him my love deny,
And then I'll study how to die.'

SILVIUS Call you this chiding?

CELIA Alas, poor shepherd!

ROSALIND Do you pity him? No, he deserves no pity. Wilt thou love such a woman? What, to make thee an instrument, and play false strains upon thee! Not to be endur'd! Well, go your way to her, for I see love hath made thee a tame snake, and say this to her – that if she love me, I charge her to love thee; if she will not, I will never have her unless thou entreat for her. If you be a true lover, hence, and not a word; for here comes more company. [*Exit Silvius*.

Enter OLIVER.

OLIVER Good morrow, fair ones; pray you, if you know,
Where in the purlieus of this forest stands
A sheep-cote fenc'd about with olive trees?

CELIA West of this place, down in the neighbour bottom.
The rank of osiers by the murmuring stream
Left on your right hand brings you to the place.
But at this hour the house doth keep itself;
There's none within.

OLIVER If that an eye may profit by a tongue,
Then should I know you by description –
Such garments, and such years: 'The boy is fair,
Of female favour, and bestows himself
Like a ripe sister; the woman low,
And browner than her brother'. Are not you
The owner of the house I did inquire for?

CELIA It is no boast, being ask'd, to say we are.

OLIVER Orlando doth commend him to you both;
And to that youth he calls his Rosalind
He sends this bloody napkin. Are you he?

ROSALIND I am. What must we understand by this?

OLIVER Some of my shame; if you will know of me
What man I am, and how, and why, and where,
This handkercher was stain'd.

CELIA I pray you, tell it.

OLIVER When last the young Orlando parted from you,
He left a promise to return again
Within an hour; and, pacing through the forest,
Chewing the food of sweet and bitter fancy,
Lo, what befell! He threw his eye aside,
And mark what object did present itself.
Under an oak, whose boughs were moss'd with age,
And high top bald with dry antiquity,
A wretched ragged man, o'ergrown with hair,
Lay sleeping on his back. About his neck
A green and gilded snake had wreath'd itself,
Who with her head nimble in threats approach'd
The opening of his mouth; but suddenly,
Seeing Orlando, it unlink'd itself,
And with indented glides did slip away
Into a bush; under which bush's shade
A lioness, with udders all drawn dry,
Lay couching, head on ground, with catlike watch,
When that the sleeping man should stir; for 'tis
The royal disposition of that beast
To prey on nothing that doth seem as dead.
This seen, Orlando did approach the man,
And found it was his brother, his elder brother.

CELIA O, I have heard him speak of that same brother;
And he did render him the most unnatural
That liv'd amongst men.

OLIVER And well he might so do,
For well I know he was unnatural.

ROSALIND But, to Orlando: did he leave him there,
Food to the suck'd and hungry lioness?

OLIVER Twice did he turn his back, and purpos'd so;
But kindness, nobler ever than revenge,
And nature, stronger than his just occasion
Made him give battle to the lioness,
Who quickly fell before him; in which hurtling
From miserable slumber I awak'd.

CELIA Are you his brother?

ROSALIND Was't you he rescu'd?

CELIA Was't you that did so oft contrive to kill him?

OLIVER 'Twas I; but 'tis not I. I do not shame
To tell you what I was, since my conversion
So sweetly tastes, being the thing I am.

ROSALIND But for the bloody napkin?

OLIVER By and by.
When from the first to last, betwixt us two,
Tears our recountments had most kindly bath'd,
As how I came into that desert place –
In brief, he led me to the gentle Duke,
Who gave me fresh array and entertainment,
Committing me unto my brother's love;
Who led me instantly unto his cave,
There stripp'd himself, and here upon his arm
The lioness had torn some flesh away,
Which all this while had bled; and now he fainted,
And cried, in fainting, upon Rosalind.
Brief, I recover'd him, bound up his wound,
And, after some small space, being strong at heart,
He sent me hither, stranger as I am,
To tell this story, that you might excuse
His broken promise, and to give this napkin,
Dy'd in his blood, unto the shepherd youth
That he in sport doth call his Rosalind.

[Rosalind swoons.

CELIA Why, how now, Ganymede! sweet Ganymede!

OLIVER Many will swoon when they do look on blood.

CELIA There is more in it. Cousin Ganymede!

OLIVER Look, he recovers.

ROSALIND I would I were at home.

CELIA We'll lead you thither.
I pray you, will you take him by the arm?

OLIVER Be of good cheer, youth. You a man!
You lack a man's heart.

ROSALIND I do so, I confess it. Ah, sirrah, a body would think this was well counterfeited. I pray you tell your brother how well I counterfeited. Heigh-ho!

OLIVER This was not counterfeit; there is too great testimony in your complexion that it was a passion of earnest.

ROSALIND Counterfeit, I assure you.

OLIVER Well then, take a good heart and counterfeit to be a man.

ROSALIND So I do; but, i' faith, I should have been a woman by right.

CELIA Come, you look paler and paler; pray you draw homewards. Good sir, go with us.

OLIVER That will I, for I must bear answer back
How you excuse my brother, Rosalind.

ROSALIND I shall devise something; but, I pray you, commend my counterfeiting to him. Will you go? *[Exeunt.*

ACT FIVE

SCENE I. *The forest.*

Enter TOUCHSTONE and AUDREY.

TOUCHSTONE We shall find a time, Audrey; patience, gentle Audrey.

AUDREY Faith, the priest was good enough, for all the old gentleman's saying.

TOUCHSTONE A most wicked Sir Oliver, Audrey, a most vile Martext. But, Audrey, there is a youth here in the forest lays claim to you.

AUDREY Ay, I know who 'tis; he hath no interest in me in the world; here comes the man you mean.

Enter WILLIAM.

TOUCHSTONE It is meat and drink to me to see a clown. By my troth, we that have good wits have much to answer for: we shall be flouting; we cannot hold.

WILLIAM Good ev'n, Audrey.

AUDREY God ye good ev'n, William.

WILLIAM And good ev'n to you, sir.

TOUCHSTONE Good ev'n, gentle friend. Cover thy head, cover thy head; nay, prithee be cover'd. How old are you, friend?

WILLIAM Five and twenty, sir.

TOUCHSTONE A ripe age. Is thy name William?

WILLIAM William, sir.

TOUCHSTONE A fair name. Wast born i' th' forest here?

WILLIAM Ay, sir, I thank God.

TOUCHSTONE 'Thank God.' A good answer. Art rich?

WILLIAM Faith, sir, so so.

TOUCHSTONE 'So so' is good, very good, very excellent good; and yet it is not; it is but so so. Art thou wise?

WILLIAM Ay, sir, I have a pretty wit.

TOUCHSTONE Why, thou say'st well. I do now remember a saying: 'The fool doth think he is wise, but the wise man knows himself to be a fool'. The heathen philosopher, when he had a desire to eat a grape, would open his lips when he put it into his mouth; meaning thereby that grapes were made to eat and lips to open. You do love this maid?

WILLIAM I do, sir.

TOUCHSTONE Give me your hand. Art thou learned?

WILLIAM No, sir.

TOUCHSTONE Then learn this of me: to have is to have; for it is a figure in rhetoric that drink, being pour'd out of a cup into a glass, by filling the one doth empty the other; for all your writers do consent that ipse is he; now, you are not ipse, for I am he.

WILLIAM Which he, sir?

TOUCHSTONE He, sir, that must marry this woman. Therefore, you clown, abandon – which is in the vulgar leave – the society – which in the boorish is company – of this female – which in the common is woman – which together is: abandon the society of this female; or, clown, thou perishest; or, to thy better understanding, diest; or, to wit, I kill thee, make thee away, translate thy life into death, thy liberty into bondage. I will deal in poison with thee, or in bastinado, or in steel; I will bandy with thee in faction; I will o'er-run thee with policy; I will kill thee a hundred and fifty ways; therefore tremble, and depart.

AUDREY Do, good William.

WILLIAM God rest you merry, sir. [*Exit.*

Enter CORIN.

CORIN Our master and mistress seeks you; come away, away.

TOUCHSTONE Trip, Audrey, trip, Audrey. I attend, I attend. [*Exeunt.*

SCENE II. *The forest.*

Enter ORLANDO and OLIVER.

ORLANDO Is't possible that on so little acquaintance you should like her? that but seeing you should love her? and loving woo? and, wooing, she should grant? and will you persever to enjoy her?

OLIVER Neither call the giddiness of it in question, the poverty of her, the small acquaintance, my sudden wooing, nor her sudden consenting; but say with me, I love Aliena; say with her that she loves me; consent with both that we may enjoy each other. It shall be to your good; for my father's house and all the revenue that was old Sir Rowland's will I estate upon you, and here live and die a shepherd.

ORLANDO You have my consent. Let your wedding be to-morrow. Thither will I invite the Duke and all's contented followers. Go you and prepare Aliena; for, look you, here comes my Rosalind.

Enter ROSALIND.

ROSALIND God save you, brother.

OLIVER And you, fair sister. [*Exit.*

ROSALIND O, my dear Orlando, how it grieves me to see thee wear thy heart in a scarf!

ORLANDO It is my arm.

ROSALIND I thought thy heart had been wounded with the claws of a lion.

ORLANDO Wounded it is, but with the eyes of a lady.

ROSALIND Did your brother tell you how I counterfeited to swoon when he show'd me your handkercher.

ORLANDO Ay, and greater wonders than that.

ROSALIND O, I know where you are. Nay, 'tis true. There was never any thing so sudden but the fight of two rams and Caesar's thrasonical brag of 'I came, saw, and overcame'. For your brother and my sister no sooner met but they look'd; no sooner look'd but they lov'd; no sooner lov'd but they sigh'd; no sooner sigh'd but they ask'd one another the reason; no sooner knew the reason but they sought the remedy – and in these degrees have they made a pair of stairs to marriage, which they will climb incontinent, or else be incontinent before marriage. They are in the very wrath of love, and they will together. Clubs cannot part them.

ORLANDO They shall be married to-morrow; and I will bid the Duke to the nuptial. But, O, how bitter a thing it is to look into happiness through another man's eyes! By so much the more shall I to-morrow be at the height of heart-heaviness, by how much I shall think my brother happy in having what he wishes for.

ROSALIND Why, then, to-morrow I cannot serve your turn for Rosalind?

ORLANDO I can live no longer by thinking.

ROSALIND I will weary you, then, no longer with idle talking. Know of me then – for now I speak to some purpose – that I know you are a gentleman of good conceit. I speak not this that you should bear a good opinion of my knowledge, insomuch I say I know you are; neither do I labour for a greater esteem than may in some little measure draw a belief from you, to do yourself good, and not to grace me. Believe then, if you please, that I can do strange things. I have, since I was three year old, convers'd with a magician, most profound in his art and yet not damnable. If you do love Rosalind so near the heart as your gesture cries it out, when your brother marries Aliena shall you marry her. I know into what straits of fortune she is driven; and it is not impossible to me, if it appear not inconvenient to you, to set her before your eyes to-morrow, human as she is, and without any danger.

ORLANDO Speak'st thou in sober meanings?

ROSALIND By my life, I do; which I tender dearly, though I say I am a magician. Therefore put you in your best array, bid your friends; for if you will be married to-morrow, you shall; and to Rosalind, if you will.

Enter SILVIUS and PHEBE.

Look, here comes a lover of mine, and a lover of hers.

PHEBE Youth, you have done me much ungentleness
To show the letter that I writ to you.

ROSALIND I care not if I have. It is my study
To seem despiteful and ungentle to you.
You are there follow'd by a faithful shepherd;
Look upon him, love him, he worships you.

PHEBE Good shepherd, tell this youth what 'tis to love.

SILVIUS It is to be all made of sighs and tears;
And so am I for Phebe.

PHEBE And I for Ganymede.

ORLANDO And I for Rosalind.

ROSALIND And I for no woman.

SILVIUS It is to be all made of faith and service;
And so am I for Phebe.

PHEBE And I for Ganymede.

ORLANDO And I for Rosalind.

ROSALIND And I for no woman.

SILVIUS It is to be all made of fantasy,
All made of passion, and all made of wishes;
All adoration, duty, and observance,
All humbleness, all patience, and impatience,
All purity, all trial, all obedience;
And so am I for Phebe.

PHEBE And so am I for Ganymede.

ORLANDO And so am I for Rosalind.

ROSALIND And so am I for no woman.

PHEBE If this be so, why blame you me to love you?

SILVIUS If this be so, why blame you me to love you?

ORLANDO If this be so, why blame you me to love you?

ROSALIND Why do you speak too 'Why blame you me to love you?'

ORLANDO To her that is not here, nor doth not hear.

ROSALIND Pray you, no more of this; 'tis like the howling of Irish wolves against the moon. [*To Silvius*] I will help you if I can. [*To Phebe*] I would love you if I could. – To-morrow meet me all together. [*To Phebe*] I will marry you if ever I marry woman, and I'll be married to-morrow. [*To Orlando*] I will satisfy you if ever I satisfied man, and you shall be married to-morrow. [*To Silvius*] I will content you if what pleases you contents you, and you shall be married to-morrow. [*To Orlando*] As you love Rosalind, meet. [*To Silvius*] As you love Phebe, meet; – and as I love no woman, I'll meet. So, fare you well; I have left you commands.

SILVIUS I'll not fail, if I live.

PHEBE Nor I.

ORLANDO Nor I. *[Exeunt.*

SCENE III. *The forest.*

Enter TOUCHSTONE and AUDREY.

TOUCHSTONE To-morrow is the joyful day, Audrey; to-morrow will we be married.

AUDREY I do desire it with all my heart; and I hope it is no dishonest desire to desire to be a woman of the world. Here come two of the banish'd Duke's pages.

Enter two Pages.

1 PAGE Well met, honest gentlemen.

TOUCHSTONE By my troth, well met. Come sit, sit, and a song.

2 PAGE We are for you; sit i' th' middle.

1 PAGE Shall we clap into't roundly, without hawking, or spitting, or saying we are hoarse, which are the only prologues to a bad voice?

2 PAGE I'faith, i'faith; and both in a tune, like two gipsies on a horse.

Song.

It was a lover and his lass,
  With a hey, and a ho, and a hey nonino,
That o'er the green corn-field did pass
  In the spring time, the only pretty ring time,
When birds do sing, hey ding a ding, ding.
Sweet lovers love the spring.

Between the acres of the rye,
  With a hey, and a ho, and a hey nonino,
These pretty country folks would lie,
  In the spring time, etc.

This carol they began that hour,
  With a hey, and a ho, and a hey nonino,
How that a life was but a flower,
  In the spring time, etc.

And therefore take the present time,
  With a hey, and a ho, and a hey nonino,
For love is crowned with the prime,
  In the spring time, etc.

TOUCHSTONE Truly, young gentlemen, though there was no great matter in the ditty, yet the note was very untuneable.

1 PAGE You are deceiv'd, sir; we kept time, we lost not our time.

TOUCHSTONE By my troth, yes; I count it but time lost to hear such a foolish song. God buy you; and God mend your voices. Come, Audrey. *[Exeunt.*

SCENE IV. *The forest.*

Enter DUKE SENIOR, AMIENS, JAQUES, ORLANDO, OLIVER, and CELIA.

DUKE SENIOR Dost thou believe, Orlando, that the boy
Can do all this that he hath promised?

ORLANDO I sometimes do believe and sometimes do not;
As those that fear they hope, and know they fear.

Enter ROSALIND, SILVIUS, and PHEBE.

ROSALIND Patience once more, whiles our compact is urg'd:
You say, if I bring in your Rosalind,
You will bestow her on Orlando here?

DUKE SENIOR That would I, had I kingdoms to give with her.

ROSALIND And you say you will have her when I bring her?

ORLANDO That would I, were I of all kingdoms king.

ROSALIND You say you'll marry me, if I be willing?

PHEBE That will I, should I die the hour after.

ROSALIND But if you do refuse to marry me,
You'll give yourself to this most faithful shepherd?

PHEBE So is the bargain.

ROSALIND You say that you'll have Phebe, if she will?

SILVIUS Though to have her and death were both one thing.

ROSALIND I have promis'd to make all this matter even.
Keep you your word, O Duke, to give your daughter;
You yours, Orlando, to receive his daughter;
Keep your word, Phebe, that you'll marry me,
Or else, refusing me, to wed this shepherd;
Keep your word, Silvius, that you'll marry her
If she refuse me; and from hence I go,
To make these doubts all even.
[Exeunt Rosalind and Celia.

DUKE SENIOR I do remember in this shepherd boy
Some lively touches of my daughter's favour.

ORLANDO My lord, the first time that I ever saw him

Methought he was a brother to your daughter.
But, my good lord, this boy is forest-born,
And hath been tutor'd in the rudiments
Of many desperate studies by his uncle,
Whom he reports to be a great magician,
Obscured in the circle of this forest.

Enter TOUCHSTONE and AUDREY.

JAQUES There is, sure, another flood toward, and these couples are coming to the ark. Here comes a pair of very strange beasts which in all tongues are call'd fools.

TOUCHSTONE Salutation and greeting to you all!

JAQUES Good my lord, bid him welcome. This is the motley-minded gentleman that I have so often met in the forest. He hath been a courtier, he swears.

TOUCHSTONE If any man doubt that, let him put me to my purgation. I have trod a measure; I have flatt'red a lady; I have been politic with my friend, smooth with mine enemy; I have undone three tailors; I have had four quarrels, and like to have fought one.

JAQUES And how was that ta'en up?

TOUCHSTONE Faith, we met, and found the quarrel was upon the seventh cause.

JAQUES How seventh cause? Good my lord, like this fellow.

DUKE SENIOR I like him very well.

TOUCHSTONE God 'ild you, sir; I desire you of the like. I press in here, sir, amongst the rest of the country copulatives, to swear and to forswear, according as marriage binds and blood breaks. A poor virgin, sir, an ill-favour'd thing, sir, but mine own; a poor humour of mine, sir, to take that that no man else will. Rich honesty dwells like a miser, sir, in a poor house; as your pearl in your foul oyster.

DUKE SENIOR By my faith, he is very swift and sententious.

TOUCHSTONE According to the fool's bolt, sir, and such dulcet diseases.

JAQUES But, for the seventh cause: how did you find the quarrel on the seventh cause?

TOUCHSTONE Upon a lie seven times removed – bear your body more seeming, Audrey – as thus, sir. I did dislike the cut of a certain courtier's beard; he sent me word, if I said his beard was not cut well, he was in the mind it was. This is call'd the Retort Courteous. If I sent him word again it was not well cut, he would send me word he cut it to please himself. This is call'd the Quip Modest. If again it was not well cut, he disabled my judgment. This is call'd the Reply Churlish. If again it was not well cut, he would answer I spake not true. This is call'd the Reproof Valiant. If again it was not well cut, he would say I lie. This is call'd the Countercheck Quarrelsome. And so to Lie Circumstantial and the Lie Direct.

JAQUES And how oft did you say his beard was not well cut?

TOUCHSTONE I durst go no further than the Lie Circumstantial, nor he durst not give me the Lie Direct; and so we measur'd swords and parted.

JAQUES Can you nominate in order now the degrees of the lie?

TOUCHSTONE O, sir, we quarrel in print by the book, as you have books for good manners. I will name you the degrees. The first, the Retort Courteous; the second, the Quip Modest; the third, the Reply Churlish; the fourth, the Reproof Valiant; the fifth, the Countercheck Quarrelsome; the sixth, the Lie with Circumstance; the seventh, the Lie Direct. All these you may avoid but the Lie Direct; and you may avoid that too with an If. I knew when seven justices could not take up a quarrel; but when the parties were met themselves, one of them thought but of an If, as: 'If you said so, then I said so'. And they shook hands, and swore brothers. Your If is the only peace-maker; much virtue in If.

JAQUES Is not this a rare fellow, my lord? He's as good at any thing, and yet a fool.

DUKE SENIOR He uses his folly like a stalking-horse, and under the presentation of that he shoots his wit.

Enter HYMEN, ROSALIND, and CELIA. Still music.

HYMEN Then is there mirth in heaven,
When earthly things made even
Atone together.
Good Duke, receive thy daughter;
Hymen from heaven brought her,
Yea, brought her hither,
That thou mightst join her hand with his,
Whose heart within his bosom is.

ROSALIND [*To Duke*] To you I give myself, for I am yours.
[*To Orlando*] To you I give myself, for I am yours.

DUKE SENIOR If there be truth in sight, you are my daughter.

ORLANDO If there be truth in sight, you are my Rosalind.

PHEBE If sight and shape be true,
Why then, my love adieu!

ROSALIND I'll have no father, if you be not he;
I'll have no husband, if you be not he;
Nor ne'er wed woman, if you be not she.

HYMEN Peace, ho! I bar confusion;
'Tis I must make conclusion
Of these most strange events.
Here's eight that must take hands
To join in Hymen's bands,
If truth holds true contents.
You and you no cross shall part;
You and you are heart in heart;
You to his love must accord,
Or have a woman to your lord;
You and you are sure together,
As the winter to foul weather.
Whiles a wedlock-hymn we sing,
Feed yourselves with questioning,
That reason wonder may diminish,
How thus we met, and these things finish.

Song.

Wedding is great Juno's crown;
O blessed bond of board and bed!
'Tis Hymen peoples every town;
High wedlock then be honoured.
Honour, high honour, and renown,
To Hymen, god of every town!

DUKE SENIOR O my dear niece, welcome thou art to me!
Even daughter, welcome in no less degree.

PHEBE I will not eat my word, now thou art mine;
Thy faith my fancy to thee doth combine.

Enter JAQUES DE BOYS.

JAQUES DE BOYS Let me have audience for a word or two.
I am the second son of old Sir Rowland,
That bring these tidings to this fair assembly.
Duke Frederick, hearing how that every day
Men of great worth resorted to this forest,
Address'd a mighty power; which were on foot,
In his own conduct, purposely to take
His brother here, and put him to the sword;
And to the skirts of this wild wood he came,
Where, meeting with an old religious man,
After some question with him, was converted
Both from his enterprise and from the world;
His crown bequeathing to his banish'd brother,
And all their lands restor'd to them again
That were with him exil'd. This to be true
I do engage my life.

DUKE SENIOR Welcome, young man.
Thou offer'st fairly to thy brothers' wedding:
To one, his lands withheld; and to the other,
A land itself at large, a potent dukedom.
First, in this forest let us do those ends
That here were well begun and well begot;
And after, every of this happy number,
That have endur'd shrewd days and nights with us,
Shall share the good of our returned fortune,
According to the measure of their states.
Meantime, forget this new-fall'n dignity,
And fall into our rustic revelry.
Play, music; and you brides and bridegrooms all,
With measure heap'd in joy, to th' measures fall.

JAQUES Sir, by your patience. If I heard you rightly,
The Duke hath put on a religious life,
And thrown into neglect the pompous court.

JAQUES DE BOYS He hath.

JAQUES To him will I. Out of these convertites
There is much matter to be heard and learn'd
[*To Duke*] You to your former honour I bequeath;
Your patience and your virtue well deserves it.
[*To Orlando.*] You to a love that your true faith doth merit;
[*To Oliver*] You to your land, and love, and great allies;
[*To Silvius*] You to a long and well-deserved bed;
[*To Touchstone*] And you to wrangling; for thy loving voyage
Is but for two months victuall'd. – So to your pleasures;
I am for other than for dancing measures.

DUKE SENIOR Stay, Jaques, stay.

JAQUES To see no pastime I. What you would have
I'll stay to know at your abandon'd cave. [*Exit.*

DUKE SENIOR Proceed, proceed. We will begin these rites,
As we do trust they'll end, in true delights.
[*A dance. Exeunt.*

EPILOGUE

ROSALIND It is not the fashion to see the lady the epilogue; but it is no more unhandsome than to see the lord the prologue. If it be true that good wine needs no bush, 'tis true that a good play needs no epilogue. Yet to good wine they do use good bushes; and good plays prove the better by the help of good epilogues. What a case am I in then, that am neither a good epilogue, nor cannot insinuate with you in the behalf of a good play! I am not furnish'd like a beggar; therefore to beg will not become me. My way is to conjure you; and I'll begin with the women. I charge you, O women, for the love you bear to men, to like as much of this play as please you; and I charge you, O men, for the love you bear to women – as I perceive by your simp'ring none of you hates them – that between you and the women the play may please. If I were a woman, I would kiss as many of you as had beards that pleas'd me, complexions that lik'd me, and breaths that I defied not; and, I am sure, as many as have good beards, or good faces, or sweet breaths, will, for my kind offer, when I make curtsy, bid me farewell.

The Taming of the Shrew

Introduction by DOROTHY McMILLAN

Michael Bogdanov's modern-dress production of *The Taming of the Shrew* in 1979 was well received in terms of its theatrical competence but a number of critics felt that however well done, it had better not been done at all. Michael Billington in the *Guardian* doubted that there was any reason to revive a play 'that seems totally offensive to our age and our society. My own feeling is that it should be put back firmly and squarely on the shelf'. Suggestions of censorship, as it were, have at least the merit of indicating that the offending object is being taken seriously, nor is Billington the first to find *The Shrew* a peculiarly damning blot on Shakespeare's output: Shaw famously registered shame at 'the lord-of-creation moral implied in the wager and the speech put into the woman's own mouth'. *The Shrew* has generally proved a bit of a facer for those who would claim that Shakespeare is a great universal genius with ideas that transcend the limitations of his time. Hence the tendency of modern readings and productions either to imply that Shakespeare did not really acquiesce in the apparent patriarchal assumptions of the taming plot (nor the reductiveness about female charm implied in Bianca's defection from maidenly modesty), or to suggest that even if he did, the usefulness of the play for the twentieth century is to expose the latent misogyny and brutality that still form the real infrastructure of our *bien pensant*, politically correct culture.

One way of distancing Shakespeare from the implications of the taming plot has been to repair the broken frame of the play, increasing the significance of the Sly plot by importing material from the anonymous *The Taming of a Shrew*, printed in 1594 and possibly a 'memorial reconstruction' of a Shakespearean original. The taming and submission of Katherine can then be made to appear an unattainable and possibly rather vulgar male fantasy of domination, a dream of empowerment not unlike the violent fantasies of Pirate Jenny in Brecht's *Threepenny Opera*. Alternatively, the play can be made to appear more coherent by privileging one or other of its generic modes. On the one hand by ignoring the incipient psychological complexity in the treatment of Katherine in particular (she is after all not the favoured child of her father and Bianca's butter-wouldn't-melt-in-her-mouth demeanour might irritate more than a shrew), and taking the whole as a farcical romp with no power to move or upset. On the other side, the farcical nastinesses can be played down in favour of modern notions of relationship where all is fair between the couple because they really love each other, win through to equality within properly constituted hierarchy, and are even, in the most sentimental versions of such a reading, complicit in Kate's response to the wager.

Certainly H. J. Oliver in his introduction to the New Oxford edition of the play feels that Shakespeare's not having provided a generically consistent play is a consequence of his youthfulness when he devised it – it is 'a young dramatist's attempt to mingle two genres that cannot be combined'. But if generic miscegenation is an effect of youth, then it is surprising to find it again in *All's Well That Ends Well* and *Measure for Measure*. Since in these plays it does much to earn the description 'problem plays', it might be well to consider if this is not also the effect in *The Shrew*. The clash of farcical folk-tale in the taming plot with the legitimate desires of both Petruchio and Katherine for lives that they can live, betrays the inconsistences and half-truths that are daily tolerated and evaded. There seems to me no possible way of doubting that Shakespeare presents Katherine's speech of submission to an idealised hierarchy of gender relationships without irony, but he surely does not do so without thought or without demonstrating the worst that can be said about its potential for physical and psychological tyranny.

The rewards for Katherine's submission in life, as it were, are presumably those 'good days and long' that Petruchio has already stated as his goal. Since it comes as a definitive culmination to the action, the audience is left with no sense of need for its endless repetition, it frames a way of life, while shrewishness is on the contrary a lifetime career, the future of Bianca and the widow. This is not modern but it is not too bad in the circumstances. And the reward in the theatre is the complete stage dominance of Kate. It is possible, of course, to pluck weary disaster out of Katherine's eloquent dignity but it seems not worth the trouble.

The Taming of The Shrew

DRAMATIS PERSONAE

A Lord, CHRISTOPHER SLY *a tinker,*
A Hostess, A Page, Players, Huntsmen, and Servants
Persons in the Induction
BAPTISTA MINOLA
a gentleman of Padua
VINCENTIO
a merchant of Pisa
LUCENTIO
son to Vincentio, in love with Bianca
PETRUCHIO
a gentleman of Verona, a suitor to Katherina
GREMIO, HORTENSIO
suitors to Bianca
TRANIO, BIONDELLO
servants to Lucentio
GRUMIO, CURTIS
servants to Petruchio
A Pedant
KATHERINA, *the shrew,* BIANCA
daughters of Baptista
A Tailor, a Haberdasher, and Servants attending on Baptista and Petruchio

THE SCENE: PADUA, AND PETRUCHIO'S HOUSE IN THE COUNTRY

INDUCTION

SCENE I. *Before an alehouse on a heath.*

Enter Hostess and SLY.

SLY I'll pheeze you, in faith.

HOST A pair of stocks, you rogue!

SLY Y'are a baggage; the Slys are no rogues. Look in the chronicles: we came in with Richard Conqueror. Therefore, paucas pallabris; let the world slide. Sessa!

HOST You will not pay for the glasses you have burst?

SLY No, not a denier. Go by, Saint Jeronimy, go to thy cold bed and warm thee.

HOST I know my remedy; I must go fetch the thirdborough. *[Exit.*

SLY Third, or fourth, or fifth borough, I'll answer him by law. I'll not budge an inch, boy; let him come, and kindly. *[Falls asleep.*

Wind horns. Enter a Lord from hunting, with his Train.

LORD Huntsman, I charge thee, tender well my hounds;
Brach Merriman, the poor cur, is emboss'd;
And couple Clowder with the deep-mouth'd brach.
Saw'st thou not, boy, how Silver made it good
At the hedge corner, in the coldest fault?
I would not lose the dog for twenty pound.

1 HUNTSMAN Why, Belman is as good as he, my lord;
He cried upon it at the merest loss,
And twice to-day pick'd out the dullest scent;
Trust me, I take him for the better dog.

LORD Thou art a fool; if Echo were as fleet,
I would esteem him worth a dozen such.
But sup them well, and look unto them all;
To-morrow I intend to hunt again.

1 HUNTSMAN I will, my lord.

LORD What's here? One dead, or drunk? See, doth he breathe?

2 HUNTSMAN He breathes, my lord. Were he not warm'd with ale,
This were a bed but cold to sleep so soundly.

LORD O monstrous beast, how like a swine he lies!
Grim death, how foul and loathsome is thine image!
Sirs, I will practise on this drunken man.
What think you, if he were convey'd to bed,
Wrapp'd in sweet clothes, rings put upon his fingers,
A most delicious banquet by his bed,
And brave attendants near him when he wakes,
Would not the beggar then forget himself?

1 HUNTSMAN Believe me, lord, I think he cannot choose.

2 HUNTSMAN It would seem strange unto him when he wak'd.

LORD Even as a flatt'ring dream or worthless fancy.
Then take him up, and manage well the jest:
Carry him gently to my fairest chamber,
And hang it round with all my wanton pictures;
Balm his foul head in warm distilled waters,
And burn sweet wood to make the lodging sweet;
Procure me music ready when he wakes,
To make a dulcet and a heavenly sound;

And if he chance to speak, be ready straight,
And with a low submissive reverence
Say 'What is it your honour will command?'
Let one attend him with a silver basin
Full of rose-water and bestrew'd with flowers;
Another bear the ewer, the third a diaper,
And say 'Will't please your lordship cool your hands?'
Some one be ready with a costly suit,
And ask him what apparel he will wear;
Another tell him of his hounds and horse,
And that his lady mourns at his disease;
Persuade him that he hath been lunatic,
And, when he says he is, say that he dreams,
For he is nothing but a mighty lord.
This do, and do it kindly, gentle sirs;
It will be pastime passing excellent,
If it be husbanded with modesty.

1 HUNTSMAN My lord, I warrant you we will play our part
As he shall think by our true diligence
He is no less than what we say he is.

LORD Take him up gently, and to bed with him;
And each one to his office when he wakes.

[Sly is carried out. A trumpet sounds.

Sirrah, go see what trumpet 'tis that sounds –

[Exit Servant.

Belike some noble gentleman that means,
Travelling some journey, to repose him here.

Re-enter a Servant.

How now! who is it?

SERVANT An't please your honour, players
That offer service to your lordship.

LORD Bid them come near.

Enter Players.

Now, fellows, you are welcome.

PLAYERS We thank your honour.

LORD Do you intend to stay with me to-night?

PLAYER So please your lordship to accept our duty.

LORD With all my heart. This fellow I remember
Since once he play'd a farmer's eldest son;
'Twas where you woo'd the gentlewoman so well.
I have forgot your name; but, sure, that part
Was aptly fitted and naturally perform'd.

PLAYER I think 'twas Soto that your honour means.

LORD 'Tis very true; thou didst it excellent.
Well, you are come to me in a happy time,
The rather for I have some sport in hand
Wherein your cunning can assist me much.
There is a lord will hear you play to-night;
But I am doubtful of your modesties,
Lest, over-eying of his odd behaviour,
For yet his honour never heard a play,
You break into some merry passion
And so offend him; for I tell you, sirs,
If you should smile, he grows impatient.

PLAYER Fear not, my lord; we can contain ourselves,
Were he the veriest antic in the world.

LORD Go, sirrah, take them to the buttery,
And give them friendly welcome every one;
Let them want nothing that my house affords.

[Exit one with the Players.

Sirrah, go you to Barthol'mew my page,
And see him dress'd in all suits like a lady;
That done, conduct him to the drunkard's chamber,
And call him 'madam', do him obeisance.
Tell him from me – as he will win my love –
He bear himself with honourable action,
Such as he hath observ'd in noble ladies
Unto their lords, by them accomplished;
Such duty to the drunkard let him do,
With soft low tongue and lowly courtesy,
And say 'What is't your honour will command,
Wherein your lady and your humble wife
May show her duty and make known her love?'
And then with kind embracements, tempting kisses,
And with declining head into his bosom,
Bid him shed tears, as being overjoyed
To see her noble lord restor'd to health,
Who for this seven years hath esteemed him
No better than a poor and loathsome beggar.
And if the boy have not a woman's gift
To rain a shower of commanded tears,
An onion will do well for such a shift,
Which, in a napkin being close convey'd
Shall in despite enforce a watery eye.
See this dispatch'd with all the haste thou canst;
Anon I'll give thee more instructions.

[Exit a Servant.

I know the boy will well usurp the grace,
Voice, gait, and action, of a gentlewoman;
I long to hear him call the drunkard 'husband';
And how my men will stay themselves from laughter
When they do homage to this simple peasant.
I'll in to counsel them; haply my presence
May well abate the over-merry spleen,
Which otherwise would grow into extremes.

[Exeunt.

SCENE II. *A bedchamber in the Lord's house.*

Enter aloft SLY, with Attendants; some with apparel, basin and ewer, and other appurtenances; and Lord.

SLY For God's sake, a pot of small ale.

1 SERVANT Will't please your lordship drink a cup of sack?
2 SERVANT Will't please your honour taste of these conserves?
3 SERVANT What raiment will your honour wear to-day?

SLY I am Christophero Sly; call not me 'honour' nor 'lordship'. I ne'er drank sack in my life; and if you give me any conserves, give me conserves of beef. Ne'er ask me what raiment I'll wear, for I have no more doublets than backs, no more stockings than legs, nor no more shoes than feet – nay, sometime more feet than shoes, or such shoes as my toes look through the overleather.

LORD Heaven cease this idle humour in your honour!
O, that a mighty man of such descent,
Of such possessions, and so high esteem,
Should be infused with so foul a spirit!

SLY What, would you make me mad? Am not I Christopher Sly, old Sly's son of Burton Heath; by birth a pedlar, by education a cardmaker, by transmutation a bearherd, and now by present profession a tinker? Ask Marian Hacket, the fat alewife of Wincot, if she know me not; if she say I am not fourteen pence on the score for sheer ale, score me up for the lying'st knave in Christendom. What! I am not bestraught.
[*Taking a pot of ale*] Here's –

3 SERVANT O, this it is that makes your lady mourn!
2 SERVANT O, this is it that makes your servants droop!
LORD Hence comes it that your kindred shuns your house,
As beaten hence by your strange lunacy.
O noble lord, bethink thee of thy birth!
Call home thy ancient thoughts from banishment,
And banish hence these abject lowly dreams.
Look how thy servants do attend on thee,
Each in his office ready at thy beck.
Wilt thou have music? Hark! Apollo plays, [*Music.*
And twenty caged nightingales do sing.
Or wilt thou sleep? We'll have thee to a couch
Softer and sweeter than the lustful bed
On purpose trimm'd up for Semiramis.
Say thou wilt walk: we will bestrew the ground.
Or wilt thou ride? Thy horses shall be trapp'd,
Their harness studded all with gold and pearl.
Dost thou love hawking? Thou hast hawks will soar
Above the morning lark. Or wilt thou hunt?
Thy hounds shall make the welkin answer them
And fetch shrill echoes from the hollow earth.
1 SERVANT Say thou wilt course; thy grey-hounds are as swift
As breathed stags; ay, fleeter than the roe.
2 SERVANT Dost thou love pictures? We will fetch thee straight
Adonis painted by a running brook,
And Cytherea all in sedges hid,
Which seem to move and wanton with her breath
Even as the waving sedges play wi' th' wind.
LORD We'll show thee Io as she was a maid
And how she was beguiled and surpris'd,
As lively painted as the deed was done.
3 SERVANT Or Daphne roaming through a thorny wood,
Scratching her legs, that one shall swear she bleeds;
And at that sight shall sad Apollo weep,
So workmanly the blood and tears are drawn.
LORD Thou art a lord, and nothing but a lord.
Thou hast a lady far more beautiful
Than any woman in this waning age.
1 SERVANT And, till the tears that she hath shed for thee
Like envious floods o'er-run her lovely face,
She was the fairest creature in the world;
And yet she is inferior to none.
SLY Am I a lord and have I such a lady?
Or do I dream? Or have I dream'd till now?
I do not sleep: I see, I hear, I speak;
I smell sweet savours, and I feel soft things.
Upon my life, I am a lord indeed,
And not a tinker, nor Christopher Sly.
Well, bring our lady hither to our sight;
And once again, a pot o' th' smallest ale.
2 SERVANT Will't please your Mightiness to wash your hands?
O, how we joy to see your wit restor'd!
O, that once more you knew but what you are!
These fifteen years you have been in a dream;
Or, when you wak'd, so wak'd as if you slept.
SLY These fifteen years! by my fay, a goodly nap.
But did I never speak of all that time?
1 SERVANT O, yes, my lord, but very idle words;
For though you lay here in this goodly chamber,
Yet would you say ye were beaten out of door;
And rail upon the hostess of the house,
And say you would present her at the leet,
Because she brought stone jugs and no seal'd quarts.
Sometimes you would call out for Cicely Hacket.
SLY Ay, the woman's maid of the house.
3 SERVANT Why, sir, you know no house nor no such maid,
Nor no such men as you have reckon'd up,

As Stephen Sly, and old John Naps of Greece,
And Peter Turph, and Henry Pimpernell;
And twenty more such names and men as these,
Which never were, nor no man ever saw.

SLY Now, Lord be thanked for my good amends!

ALL Amen.

Enter the Page as a lady, with Attendants.

SLY I thank thee; thou shalt not lose by it.

PAGE How fares my noble lord?

SLY Marry, I fare well; for here is cheer enough.
Where is my wife?

PAGE Here, noble lord; what is thy will with her?

SLY Are you my wife, and will not call me husband?
My men should call me 'lord'; I am your goodman.

PAGE My husband and my lord, my lord and husband;
I am your wife in all obedience.

SLY I know it well. What must I call her?

LORD Madam.

SLY Al'ce madam, or Joan madam?

LORD Madam, and nothing else; so lords call ladies.

SLY Madam wife, they say that I have dream'd
And slept above some fifteen year or more.

PAGE Ay, and the time seems thirty unto me,
Being all this time abandon'd from your bed.

SLY 'Tis much. Servants, leave me and her alone.
[*Exeunt Servants.*
Madam, undress you, and come now to bed.

PAGE Thrice noble lord, let me entreat of you
To pardon me yet for a night or two;
Or, if not so, until the sun be set.
For your physicians have expressly charg'd,
In peril to incur your former malady,
That I should yet absent me from your bed.
I hope this reason stands for my excuse.

SLY Ay, it stands so that I may hardly tarry so long. But I would be loath to fall into my dreams again. I will therefore tarry in despite of the flesh and the blood.

Enter a Messenger.

MESSENGER You honour's players, hearing your amendment,
Are come to play a pleasant comedy;
For so your doctors hold it very meet,
Seeing too much sadness hath congeal'd your blood,
And melancholy is the nurse of frenzy.
Therefore they thought it good you hear a play
And frame your mind to mirth and merriment,
Which bars a thousand harms and lengthens life.

SLY Marry, I will; let them play it. Is not a comonty a Christmas gambold or a tumbling-trick?

PAGE No, my good lord, it is more pleasing stuff.

SLY What, household stuff?

PAGE It is a kind of history.

SLY Well, we'll see't. Come, madam wife, sit by my side and let the world slip; we shall ne'er be younger. [*They sit down.*

A flourish of trumpets announces the play.

ACT ONE

SCENE I. *Padua. A public place.*

Enter LUCENTIO and his man TRANIO.

LUCENTIO Tranio, since for the great desire I had
To see fair Padua, nursery of arts,
I am arriv'd for fruitful Lombardy,
The pleasant garden of great Italy,
And by my father's love and leave am arm'd
With his good will and thy good company,
My trusty servant well approv'd in all,
Here let us breathe, and haply institute
A course of learning and ingenious studies.
Pisa, renowned for grave citizens,
Gave me my being and my father first,
A merchant of great traffic through the world,
Vincentio, come of the Bentivolii;
Vincentio's son, brought up in Florence,
It shall become to serve all hopes conceiv'd,
To deck his fortune with his virtuous deeds.
And therefore, Tranio, for the time I study,
Virtue and that part of philosophy
Will I apply that treats of happiness
By virtue specially to be achiev'd.
Tell me thy mind; for I have Pisa left
And am to Padua come as he that leaves
A shallow plash to plunge him in the deep,
And with satiety seeks to quench his thirst.

TRANIO Mi perdonato, gentle master mine;
I am in all affected as yourself;
Glad that you thus continue your resolve
To suck the sweets of sweet philosophy.
Only, good master, while we do admire
This virtue and this moral discipline,
Let's be no Stoics nor no stocks, I pray,
Or so devote to Aristotle's checks
As Ovid be an outcast quite abjur'd.
Balk logic with acquaintance that you have,
And practise rhetoric in your common talk;
Music and poesy use to quicken you;
The mathematics and the metaphysics,

Fall to them as you find your stomach serves you.
No profit grows where is no pleasure ta'en;
In brief, sir, study what you most affect.
LUCENTIO Gramercies, Tranio, well dost thou advise.
If, Biondello, thou wert come ashore,
We could at once put us in readiness,
And take a lodging fit to entertain
Such friends as time in Padua shall beget.

Enter BAPTISTA with his two daughters, KATHERINA and BIANCA; GREMIO, a pantaloon, HORTENSIO, suitor to Bianca. Lucentio and Tranio stand by.

But stay awhile; what company is this?
TRANIO Master, some show to welcome us to town.
BAPTISTA Gentlemen, importune me no farther,
For how I firmly am resolv'd you know;
That is, not to bestow my youngest daughter
Before I have a husband for the elder.
If either of you both love Katherina,
Because I know you well and love you well,
Leave shall you have to court her at your pleasure.
GREMIO To cart her rather. She's too rough for me.
There, there, Hortensio, will you any wife?
KATHERINA [*To Baptista*] I pray you, sir, is it your will
To make a stale of me amongst these mates?
HORTENSIO Mates, maid! How mean you that? No mates for you,
Unless you were of gentler, milder mould.
KATHERINA I' faith, sir, you shall never need to fear;
Iwis it is not halfway to her heart;
But if it were, doubt not her care should be
To comb your noddle with a three-legg'd stool,
And paint your face, and use you like a fool.
HORTENSIO From all such devils, good Lord deliver us!
GREMIO And me, too, good Lord!
TRANIO Husht, master! Here's some good pastime toward;
That wench is stark mad or wonderful froward.
LUCENTIO But in the other's silence do I see
Maid's mild behaviour and sobriety.
Peace, Tranio!
TRANIO Well said, master; mum! and gaze your fill.
BAPTISTA Gentlemen, that I may soon make good
What I have said – Bianca, get you in;
And let it not displease thee, good Bianca,
For I will love thee ne'er the less, my girl.
KATHERINA A pretty peat! it is best
Put finger in the eye, an she knew why.
BIANCA Sister, content you in my discontent.
Sir, to your pleasure humbly I subscribe;
My books and instruments shall be my company,
On them to look, and practise by myself.
LUCENTIO Hark, Tranio, thou mayst hear Minerva speak!
HORTENSIO Signior Baptista, will you be so strange?
Sorry am I that our good will effects
Bianca's grief.
GREMIO Why will you mew her up,
Signior Baptista, for this fiend of hell,
And make her bear the penance of her tongue?
BAPTISTA Gentlemen, content ye; I am resolv'd.
Go in, Bianca. [*Exit Bianca.*

And for I know she taketh most delight
In music, instruments, and poetry,
Schoolmasters will I keep within my house
Fit to instruct her youth. If you, Hortensio,
Or, Signior Gremio, you, know any such,
Prefer them hither; for to cunning men
I will be very kind, and liberal
To mine own children in good bringing-up;
And so, farewell. Katherina, you may stay;
For I have more to commune with Bianca. [*Exit.*
KATHERINA Why, and I trust I may go too, may I not?
What! shall I be appointed hours, as though, belike,
I knew not what to take and what to leave? Ha! [*Exit.*

GREMIO You may go to the devil's dam; your gifts are so good here's none will hold you. There! Love is not so great, Hortensio, but we may blow our nails together, and fast it fairly out; our cake's dough on both sides. Farewell; yet, for the love I bear my sweet Bianca, if I can by any means light on a fit man to teach her that wherein she delights, I will wish him to her father.

HORTENSIO So will I, Signior Gremio; but a word, I pray. Though the nature of our quarrel yet never brook'd parle, know now, upon advice, it toucheth us both – that we may yet again have access to our fair mistress, and be happy rivals in Bianca's love – to labour and effect one thing specially.

GREMIO What's that, I pray?

HORTENSIO Marry, sir, to get a husband for her sister.

GREMIO A husband? a devil.

HORTENSIO I say a husband.

GREMIO I say a devil. Think'st thou, Hortensio,

though her father be very rich, any man is so very a fool to be married to hell?

HORTENSIO Tush, Gremio! Though it pass your patience and mine to endure her loud alarums, why, man, there be good fellows in the world, an a man could light on them, would take her with all faults, and money enough.

GREMIO I cannot tell; but I had as lief take her dowry with this condition – to be whipp'd at the high cross every morning.

HORTENSIO Faith, as you say, there's small choice in rotten apples. But, come; since this bar in law makes us friends, it shall be so far forth friendly maintain'd till by helping Baptista's eldest daughter to a husband we set his youngest free for a husband, and then have to't afresh. Sweet Bianca! Happy man be his dole! He that runs fastest gets the ring. How say you, Signior Gremio?

GREMIO I am agreed; and would I had given him the best horse in Padua to begin his wooing that would thoroughly woo her, wed her, and bed her, and rid the house of her! Come on.

[Exeunt Gremio and Hortensio.

TRANIO I pray, sir, tell me, is it possible
That love should of a sudden take such hold?

LUCENTIO O Tranio, till I found it to be true,
I never thought it possible or likely.
But see! while idly I stood looking on,
I found the effect of love in idleness;
And now in plainness do confess to thee,
That art to me as secret and as dear
As Anna to the Queen of Carthage was –
Tranio, I burn, I pine, I perish, Tranio,
If I achieve not this young modest girl.
Counsel me, Tranio, for I know thou canst;
Assist me, Tranio, for I know thou wilt.

TRANIO Master, it is no time to chide you now;
Affection is not rated from the heart;
If love have touch'd you, nought remains but so:
'Redime te captum quam queas minimo'.

LUCENTIO Gramercies, lad. Go forward; this contents;
The rest will comfort, for thy counsel's sound.

TRANIO Master, you look'd so longly on the maid,
Perhaps you mark'd not what's the pith of all.

LUCENTIO O, yes, I saw sweet beauty in her face,
Such as the daughter of Agenor had,
That made great Jove to humble him to her hand,
When with his knees he kiss'd the Cretan strand.

TRANIO Saw you no more? Mark'd you not how her sister
Began to scold and raise up such a storm
That mortal ears might hardly endure the din?

LUCENTIO Tranio, I saw her coral lips to move,
And with her breath she did perfume the air;
Sacred and sweet was all I saw in her.

TRANIO Nay, then 'tis time to stir him from his trance.
I pray, awake, sir. If you love the maid,
Bend thoughts and wits to achieve her. Thus it stands:
Her elder sister is so curst and shrewd
That, till the father rid his hands of her,
Master, your love must live a maid at home;
And therefore has he closely mew'd her up,
Because she will not be annoy'd with suitors.

LUCENTIO Ah, Tranio, what a cruel father's he!
But art thou not advis'd he took some care
To get her cunning schoolmasters to instruct her?

TRANIO Ay, marry, am I, sir, and now 'tis plotted.

LUCENTIO I have it, Tranio.

TRANIO Master, for my hand,
Both our inventions meet and jump in one.

LUCENTIO Tell me thine first.

TRANIO You will be schoolmaster,
And undertake the teaching of the maid –
That's your device.

LUCENTIO It is. May it be done?

TRANIO Not possible; for who shall bear your part
And be in Padua here Vincentio's son;
Keep house and ply his book, welcome his friends,
Visit his countrymen, and banquet them?

LUCENTIO Basta, content thee, for I have it full.
We have not yet been seen in any house,
Nor we can be distinguish'd by our faces
For man or master. Then it follows thus:
Thou shalt be master, Tranio, in my stead,
Keep house and port and servants, as I should;
I will some other be – some Florentine,
Some Neapolitan, or meaner man of Pisa.
'Tis hatch'd, and shall be so. Tranio, at once
Uncase thee; take my colour'd hat and cloak.
When Biondello comes, he waits on thee;
But I will charm him first to keep his tongue.

TRANIO So had you need.

[They exchange habits.

In brief, sir, sith it your pleasure is,
And I am tied to be obedient –
For so your father charg'd me at our parting:
'Be serviceable to my son' quoth he,
Although I think 'twas in another sense –
I am content to be Lucentio,
Because so well I love Lucentio.

LUCENTIO Tranio, be so because Lucentio loves;
And let me be a slave t' achieve that maid
Whose sudden sight hath thrall'd my wounded eye.

Enter BIONDELLO.

Here comes the rogue. Sirrah, where have you been?

BIONDELLO Where have I been! Nay, how now! where are you?
Master, has my fellow Tranio stol'n your clothes?
Or you stol'n his? or both? Pray, what's the news?

LUCENTIO Sirrah, come hither; 'tis no time to jest,
And therefore frame your manners to the time.
Your fellow Tranio here, to save my life,
Puts my apparel and my count'nance on,
And I for my escape have put on his;
For in a quarrel since I came ashore
I kill'd a man, and fear I was descried.
Wait you on him, I charge you, as becomes,
While I make way from hence to save my life.
You understand me?

BIONDELLO I, sir? Ne'er a whit.

LUCENTIO And not a jot of Tranio in your mouth:
Tranio is chang'd into Lucentio.

BIONDELLO The better for him; would I were so too!

TRANIO So could I, faith, boy, to have the next wish after,
That Lucentio indeed had Baptista's youngest daughter.
But, sirrah, not for my sake but your master's, I advise
You use your manners discreetly in all kind of companies.
When I am alone, why, then I am Tranio;
But in all places else your master Lucentio.

LUCENTIO Tranio, let's go.
One thing more rests, that thyself execute –
To make one among these wooers. If thou ask me why –
Sufficeth, my reasons are both good and weighty. [*Exeunt.*

The Presenters above speak.

1 SERVANT My lord, you nod; you do not mind the play.

SLY Yes, by Saint Anne do I. A good matter, surely; comes there any more of it?

PAGE My lord, 'tis but begun.

SLY 'Tis a very excellent piece of work, madam lady. Would 'twere done! [*They sit and mark.*

SCENE II. *Padua. Before Hortensio's house.*

Enter PETRUCHIO and his man GRUMIO.

PETRUCHIO Verona, for a while I take my leave,
To see my friends in Padua; but of all
My best beloved and approved friend,
Hortensio; and I trow this is his house.
Here, sirrah Grumio, knock, I say.

GRUMIO Knock, sir! Whom should I knock? Is there any man has rebus'd your worship?

PETRUCHIO Villain, I say, knock me here soundly.

GRUMIO Knock you here, sir? Why, sir, what am I, sir, that I should knock you here, sir?

PETRUCHIO Villain, I say, knock me at this gate,
And rap me well, or I'll knock your knave's pate.

GRUMIO My master is grown quarrelsome. I should knock you first,
And then I know after who comes by the worst.

PETRUCHIO Will it not be?
Faith, sirrah, an you'll not knock I'll ring it;
I'll try how you can sol-fa, and sing it.
[*He wrings him by the ears.*

GRUMIO Help, masters, help! My master is mad.

PETRUCHIO Now knock when I bid you, sirrah villain!

Enter HORTENSIO.

HORTENSIO How now! what's the matter? My old friend Grumio and my good friend Petruchio! How do you all at Verona?

PETRUCHIO Signior Hortensio, come you to part the fray?
'Con tutto il cuore ben trovato' may I say.

HORTENSIO Alla nostra casa ben venuto,
Molto honorato signor mio Petrucio.
Rise, Grumio, rise; we will compound this quarrel.

GRUMIO Nay, 'tis no matter, sir, what he 'leges in Latin. If this be not a lawful cause for me to leave his service – look you, sir: he bid me knock him and rap him soundly, sir. Well, was it fit for a servant to use his master so; being, perhaps, for aught I see, two and thirty, a pip out?
Whom would to God I had well knock'd at first,
Then had not Grumio come by the worst.

PETRUCHIO A senseless villain! Good Hortensio,
I bade the rascal knock upon your gate,
And could not get him for my heart to do it.

GRUMIO Knock at the gate? O heavens! Spake you not these words plain: 'Sirrah knock me here, rap me here, knock me well, and knock me soundly'? And come you now with 'knocking at the gate'?

PETRUCHIO Sirrah, be gone, or talk not, I advise you.

HORTENSIO Petruchio, patience; I am Grumio's pledge;
Why, this's a heavy chance 'twixt him and you,
Your ancient, trusty, pleasant servant Grumio.
And tell me now, sweet friend, what happy gale

Blows you to Padua here from old Verona?
PETRUCHIO Such wind as scatters young men through the world
To seek their fortunes farther than at home,
Where small experience grows. But in a few,
Signior Hortensio, thus it stands with me:
Antonio, my father, is deceas'd,
And I have thrust myself into this maze,
Haply to wive and thrive as best I may;
Crowns in my purse I have, and goods at home,
And so am come abroad to see the world.
HORTENSIO Petruchio, shall I then come roundly to thee
And wish thee to a shrewd ill-favour'd wife?
Thou'dst thank me but a little for my counsel,
And yet I'll promise thee she shall be rich,
And very rich; but th'art too much my friend,
And I'll not wish thee to her.
PETRUCHIO Signior Hortensio, 'twixt such friends as we
Few words suffice; and therefore, if thou know
One rich enough to be Petruchio's wife,
As wealth is burden of my wooing dance,
Be she as foul as was Florentius' love,
As old as Sibyl, and as curst and shrewd
As Socrates' Xanthippe or a worse –
She moves me not, or not removes, at least,
Affection's edge in me, were she as rough
As are the swelling Adriatic seas.
I come to wive it wealthily in Padua;
If wealthily, then happily in Padua.

GRUMIO Nay, look you, sir, he tells you flatly what his mind is. Why, give him gold enough and marry him to a puppet or an aglet-baby, or an old trot with ne'er a tooth in her head, though she have as many diseases as two and fifty horses. Why, nothing comes amiss, so money comes withal.

HORTENSIO Petruchio, since we are stepp'd thus far in,
I will continue that I broach'd in jest.
I can, Petruchio, help thee to a wife
With wealth enough, and young and beauteous;
Brought up as best becomes a gentlewoman;
Her only fault, and that is faults enough,
Is – that she is intolerable curst,
And shrewd and froward so beyond all measure
That, were my state far worser than it is,
I would not wed her for a mine of gold.
PETRUCHIO Hortensio, peace! thou know'st not gold's effect.
Tell me her father's name, and 'tis enough;
For I will board her though she chide as loud
As thunder when the clouds in autumn crack.
HORTENSIO Her father is Baptista Minola,
An affable and courteous gentleman;
Her name is Katherina Minola,
Renown'd in Padua for her scolding tongue.
PETRUCHIO I know her father, though I know not her;
And he knew my deceased father well.
I will not sleep, Hortensio, till I see her;
And therefore let me be thus bold with you
To give you over at this first encounter,
Unless you will accompany me thither.

GRUMIO I pray you, sir, let him go while the humour lasts. O' my word, an she knew him as well as I do, she would think scolding would do little good upon him. She may perhaps call him half a score knaves or so. Why, that's nothing; an he begin once, he'll rail in his rope-tricks. I'll tell you what, sir: an she stand him but a little, he will throw a figure in her face, and so disfigure her with it that she shall have no more eyes to see withal than a cat. You know him not, sir.

HORTENSIO Tarry, Petruchio, I must go with thee,
For in Baptista's keep my treasure is.
He hath the jewel of my life in hold,
His youngest daughter, beautiful Bianca;
And her withholds from me, and other more,
Suitors to her and rivals in my love;
Supposing it a thing impossible –
For those defects I have before rehears'd –
That ever Katherina will be woo'd.
Therefore this order hath Baptista ta'en,
That none shall have access unto Bianca
Till Katherine the curst have got a husband.
GRUMIO Katherine the curst!
A title for a maid of all titles the worst.
HORTENSIO Now shall my friend Petruchio do me grace,
And offer me disguis'd in sober robes
To old Baptista as a schoolmaster
Well seen in music, to instruct Bianca;
That so I may by this device at least
Have leave and leisure to make love to her,
And unsuspected court her by herself.

Enter GREMIO with LUCENTIO disguised as Cambio.

GRUMIO Here's no knavery! See, to beguile the old folks, how the young folks lay their heads together! Master, master, look about you. Who goes there, ha?

HORTENSIO Peace, Grumio! It is the rival of my love. Petruchio, stand by awhile.

GRUMIO A proper stripling, and an amorous!
[*They stand aside.*
GREMIO O, very well; I have perus'd the note.
Hark you, sir; I'll have them very fairly bound –
All books of love, see that at any hand;
And see you read no other lectures to her.
You understand me – over and beside

Signior Baptista's liberality,
I'll mend it with a largess. Take your paper too,
And let me have them very well perfum'd;
For she is sweeter than perfume itself
To whom they go to. What will you read to her?

LUCENTIO Whate'er I read to her, I'll plead for you
As for my patron, stand you so assur'd,
As firmly as yourself were still in place;
Yea, and perhaps with more successful words
Than you, unless you were a scholar, sir.

GREMIO O this learning, what a thing it is!

GRUMIO O this woodcock, what an ass it is!

PETRUCHIO Peace, sirrah!

HORTENSIO Grumio, mum! [*Coming forward*]
God save you, Signior Gremio!

GREMIO And you are well met, Signior Hortensio.
Trow you whither I am going? To Baptista Minola.
I promis'd to enquire carefully
About a schoolmaster for the fair Bianca;
And by good fortune I have lighted well
On this young man; for learning and behaviour
Fit for her turn, well read in poetry
And other books – good ones, I warrant ye.

HORTENSIO 'Tis well; and I have met a gentleman
Hath promis'd me to help me to another,
A fine musician to instruct our mistress;
So shall I no whit be behind in duty
To fair Bianca, so beloved of me.

GREMIO Beloved of me – and that my deeds shall prove.

GRUMIO And that his bags shall prove.

HORTENSIO Gremio, 'tis now no time to vent our love.
Listen to me, and if you speak me fair
I'll tell you news indifferent good for either.
Here is a gentleman whom by chance I met,
Upon agreement from us to his liking,
Will undertake to woo curst Katherine;
Yea, and to marry her, if her dowry please.

GREMIO So said, so done, is well.
Hortensio, have you told him all her faults?

PETRUCHIO I know she is an irksome brawling scold;
If that be all, masters, I hear no harm.

GREMIO No, say'st me so, friend? What countryman?

PETRUCHIO Born in Verona, old Antonio's son.
My father dead, my fortune lives for me;
And I do hope good days and long to see.

GREMIO O sir, such a life with such a wife were strange!
But if you have a stomach, to't a God's name;
You shall have me assisting you in all.
But will you woo this wild-cat?

PETRUCHIO Will I live?

GRUMIO Will he woo her? Ay, or I'll hang her.

PETRUCHIO Why came I hither but to that intent?
Think you a little din can daunt mine ears?
Have I not in my time heard lions roar?
Have I not heard the sea, puff'd up with winds,
Rage like an angry boar chafed with sweat?
Have I not heard great ordnance in the field,
And heaven's artillery thunder in the skies?
Have I not in a pitched battle heard
Loud 'larums, neighing steeds, and trumpets' clang?
And do you tell me of a woman's tongue,
That gives not half so great a blow to hear
As will a chestnut in a farmer's fire?
Tush! tush! fear boys with bugs.

GRUMIO For he fears none.

GREMIO Hortensio, hark:
This gentleman is happily arriv'd
My mind presumes, for his own good and ours.

HORTENSIO I promis'd we would be contributors
And bear his charge of wooing, whatsoe'er.

GREMIO And so we will – provided that he win her.

GRUMIO I would I were as sure of a good dinner.

Enter TRANIO, bravely apparelled as Lucentio, and BIONDELLO.

TRANIO Gentlemen, God save you! If I may be bold,
Tell me, I beseech you, which is the readiest way
To the house of Signior Baptista Minola?

BIONDELLO He that has the two fair daughters; is't he you mean?

TRANIO Even he, Biondello.

GREMIO Hark you, sir, you mean not her to –

TRANIO Perhaps him and her, sir; what have you to do?

PETRUCHIO Not her that chides, sir, at any hand, I pray.

TRANIO I love no chiders, sir. Biondello, let's away.

LUCENTIO [*Aside*] Well begun, Tranio.

HORTENSIO Sir, a word ere you go.
Are you a suitor to the maid you talk of, yea or no?

TRANIO And if I be, sir, is it any offence?

GREMIO No; if without more words you will get you hence.

TRANIO Why, sir, I pray, are not the streets as free
For me as for you?

GREMIO But so is not she.

TRANIO For what reason, I beseech you?

GREMIO For this reason, if you'll know,

That she's the choice love of Signior Gremio.
HORTENSIO That she's the chosen of Signior Hortensio.
TRANIO Softly, my masters! If you be gentlemen,
Do me this right – hear me with patience.
Baptista is a noble gentleman,
To whom my father is not all unknown,
And, were his daughter fairer than she is,
She may more suitors have, and me for one.
Fair Leda's daughter had a thousand wooers;
Then well one more may fair Bianca have;
And so she shall: Lucentio shall make one,
Though Paris came in hope to speed alone.
GREMIO What, this gentleman will out-talk us all!
LUCENTIO Sir, give him head; I know he'll prove a jade.
PETRUCHIO Hortensio, to what end are all these words?
HORTENSIO Sir, let me be so bold as ask you,
Did you yet ever see Baptista's daughter?
TRANIO No, sir, but hear I do that he hath two:
The one as famous for a scolding tongue
As is the other for beauteous modesty.
PETRUCHIO Sir, sir, the first's for me; let her go by.
GREMIO Yea, leave that labour to great Hercules,
And let it be more than Alcides' twelve.
PETRUCHIO Sir, understand you this of me, in sooth:
The youngest daughter, whom you hearken for,
Her father keeps from all access of suitors,
And will not promise her to any man
Until the elder sister first be wed.
The younger then is free, and not before.
TRANIO If it be so, sir, that you are the man
Must stead us all, and me amongst the rest;
And if you break the ice, and do this feat,
Achieve the elder, set the younger free
For our access – whose hap shall be to have her
Will not so graceless be to be ingrate.
HORTENSIO Sir, you say well, and well you do conceive;
And since you do profess to be a suitor,
You must, as we do, gratify this gentleman,
To whom we all rest generally beholding.
TRANIO Sir, I shall not be slack; in sign whereof,
Please ye we may contrive this afternoon,
And quaff carouses to our mistress' health;
And do as adversaries do in law –
Strive mightily, but eat and drink as friends.
GRUMIO, BIONDELLO O excellent motion! Fellows, let's be gone.
HORTENSIO The motion's good indeed, and be it so.
Petruchio, I shall be your ben venuto. [*Exeunt.*

ACT TWO

SCENE I. *Padua. Baptista's house.*

Enter KATHERINA and BIANCA.

BIANCA Good sister, wrong me not, nor wrong yourself,
To make a bondmaid and a slave of me –
That I disdain; but for these other gawds,
Unbind my hands, I'll pull them off myself,
Yea, all my raiment, to my petticoat;
Or what you will command me will I do,
So well I know my duty to my elders.
KATHERINA Of all thy suitors here I charge thee tell
Whom thou lov'st best. See thou dissemble not.
BIANCA Believe me, sister, of all the men alive
I never yet beheld that special face
Which I could fancy more than any other.
KATHERINA Minion, thou liest. Is't not Hortensio?
BIANCA If you affect him, sister, here I swear
I'll plead for you myself but you shall have him.
KATHERINA O then, belike, you fancy riches more:
You will have Gremio to keep you fair.
BIANCA Is it for him you do envy me so?
Nay, then you jest; and now I well perceive
You have but jested with me all this while.
I prithee, sister Kate, untie my hands.
KATHERINA [*Strikes her*] If that be jest, then all the rest was so.

Enter BAPTISTA.

BAPTISTA Why, how now, dame! Whence grows this insolence?
Bianca, stand aside – poor girl! she weeps.
[*He unbinds her.*
Go ply thy needle; meddle not with her.
For shame, thou hilding of a devilish spirit,
Why dost thou wrong her that did ne'er wrong thee?
When did she cross thee with a bitter word?
KATHERINA Her silence flouts me, and I'll be reveng'd. [*Flies after Bianca.*
BAPTISTA What, in my sight? Bianca, get thee in.
[*Exit Bianca.*
KATHERINA What, will you not suffer me? Nay, now I see
She is your treasure, she must have a husband;

I must dance bare-foot on her wedding-day,
And for your love to her lead apes in hell.
Talk not to me; I will go sit and weep,
Till I can find occasion of revenge.
[*Exit Katherina.*

BAPTISTA Was ever gentleman thus griev'd as I?
But who comes here?

Enter GREMIO, with LUCENTIO in the habit of a mean man; PETRUCHIO, with HORTENSIO as a musician; and TRANIO, as Lucentio, with his boy, BIONDELLO, bearing a lute and books.

GREMIO Good morrow, neighbour Baptista.
BAPTISTA Good morrow, neighbour Gremio.
God save you, gentlemen!
PETRUCHIO And you, good sir! Pray, have you not a daughter
Call'd Katherina, fair and virtuous?
BAPTISTA I have a daughter, sir, call'd Katherina.
GREMIO You are too blunt; go to it orderly.
PETRUCHIO You wrong me, Signior Gremio; give me leave.
I am a gentleman of Verona, sir,
That, hearing of her beauty and her wit,
Her affability and bashful modesty,
Her wondrous qualities and mild behaviour,
Am bold to show myself a forward guest
Within your house, to make mine eye the witness
Of that report which I so oft have heard.
And, for an entrance to my entertainment,
I do present you with a man of mine,
[*Presenting Hortensio.*
Cunning in music and the mathematics,
To instruct her fully in those sciences,
Whereof I know she is not ignorant.
Accept of him, or else you do me wrong –
His name is Licio, born in Mantua.
BAPTISTA Y'are welcome, sir, and he for your good sake;
But for my daughter Katherine, this I know,
She is not for your turn, the more my grief.
PETRUCHIO I see you do not mean to part with her;
Or else you like not of my company.
BAPTISTA Mistake me not; I speak but as I find.
Whence are you, sir? What may I call your name?
PETRUCHIO Petruchio is my name, Antonio's son,
A man well known throughout all Italy.
BAPTISTA I know him well; you are welcome for his sake.
GREMIO Saving your tale, Petruchio, I pray,
Let us that are poor petitioners speak too.
Bacare! you are marvellous forward.
PETRUCHIO O, pardon me, Signior Gremio! I would fain be doing.
GREMIO I doubt it not, sir; but you will curse your wooing.
Neighbour, this is a gift very grateful, I am sure of it. To express the like kindness, myself, that have been more kindly beholding to you than any, freely give unto you this young scholar [*presenting Lucentio*] that hath been long studying at Rheims; as cunning in Greek, Latin, and other languages, as the other in music and mathematics. His name is Cambio. Pray accept his service.
BAPTISTA A thousand thanks, Signior Gremio. Welcome, good Cambio. [*To Tranio*] But, gentle sir, methinks you walk like a stranger. May I be so bold to know the cause of your coming?
TRANIO Pardon me, sir, the boldness is mine own
That, being a stranger in this city here,
Do make myself a suitor to your daughter,
Unto Bianca, fair and virtuous.
Nor is your firm resolve unknown to me
In the preferment of the eldest sister.
This liberty is all that I request –
That, upon knowledge of my parentage,
I may have welcome 'mongst the rest that woo,
And free access and favour as the rest.
And toward the education of your daughters
I here bestow a simple instrument,
And this small packet of Greek and Latin books.
If you accept them, then their worth is great.
BAPTISTA Lucentio is your name? Of whence, I pray?
TRANIO Of Pisa, sir; son to Vincentio.
BAPTISTA A mighty man of Pisa. By report
I know him well. You are very welcome, sir.
Take you the lute, and you the set of books;
You shall go see your pupils presently.
Holla, within!

Enter a Servant.

Sirrah, lead these gentlemen
To my daughters; and tell them both
These are their tutors. Bid them use them well.

[*Exit Servant leading Hortensio carrying the lute and Lucentio with the books.*

We will go walk a little in the orchard,
And then to dinner. You are passing welcome,
And so I pray you all to think yourselves.
PETRUCHIO Signior Baptista, my business asketh haste,
And every day I cannot come to woo.
You knew my father well, and in him me,
Left solely heir to all his lands and goods,
Which I have bettered rather than decreas'd.

Then tell me, if I get your daughter's love,
What dowry shall I have with her to wife?

BAPTISTA After my death, the one half of my lands
And, in possession, twenty thousand crowns.

PETRUCHIO And for that dowry, I'll assure her of
Her widowhood, be it that she survive me,
In all my lands and leases whatsoever.
Let specialties be therefore drawn between us,
That covenants may be kept on either hand.

BAPTISTA Ay, when the special thing is well obtain'd,
That is, her love; for that is all in all.

PETRUCHIO Why, that is nothing; for I tell you, father,
I am as peremptory as she proud-minded;
And where two raging fires meet together,
They do consume the thing that feeds their fury.
Though little fire grows great with little wind,
Yet extreme gusts will blow out fire and all.
So I to her, and so she yields to me;
For I am rough, and woo not like a babe.

BAPTISTA Well mayst thou woo, and happy be thy speed!
But be thou arm'd for some unhappy words.

PETRUCHIO Ay, to the proof, as mountains are for winds,
That shake not though they blow perpetually.

Re-enter HORTENSIO, with his head broke.

BAPTISTA How now, my friend! Why dost thou look so pale?

HORTENSIO For fear, I promise you, if I look pale.

BAPTISTA What, will my daughter prove a good musician?

HORTENSIO I think she'll sooner prove a soldier:
Iron may hold with her, but never lutes.

BAPTISTA Why, then thou canst not break her to the lute?

HORTENSIO Why, no; for she hath broke the lute to me.
I did but tell her she mistook her frets,
And bow'd her hand to teach her fingering,
When, with a most impatient devilish spirit,
'Frets, call you these?' quoth she 'I'll fume with them'.
And with that word she struck me on the head,
And through the instrument my pate made way;
And there I stood amazed for a while,
As on a pillory, looking through the lute,
While she did call me rascal fiddler
And twangling Jack, with twenty such vile terms,
As had she studied to misuse me so.

PETRUCHIO Now, by the world, it is a lusty wench;
I love her ten times more than e'er I did.
O, how I long to have some chat with her!

BAPTISTA Well, go with me, and be not so discomfited;
Proceed in practice with my younger daughter;
She's apt to learn, and thankful for good turns.
Signior Petruchio, will you go with us,
Or shall I send my daughter Kate to you?

PETRUCHIO I pray you do.

[*Exeunt all but Petruchio.*

I'll attend her here,
And woo her with some spirit when she comes.
Say that she rail; why, then I'll tell her plain
She sings as sweetly as a nightingale.
Say that she frown; I'll say she looks as clear
As morning roses newly wash'd with dew.
Say she be mute, and will not speak a word;
Then I'll commend her volubility,
And say she uttereth piercing eloquence.
If she do bid me pack, I'll give her thanks,
As though she bid me stay by her a week;
If she deny to wed, I'll crave the day
When I shall ask the banns, and when be married.
But here she comes; and now, Petruchio, speak.

Enter KATHERINA.

Good morrow, Kate – for that's your name, I hear.

KATHERINA Well have you heard, but something hard of hearing:
They call me Katherine that do talk of me.

PETRUCHIO You lie, in faith, for you are call'd plain Kate,
And bonny Kate, and sometimes Kate the curst;
But, Kate, the prettiest Kate in Christendom,
Kate of Kate Hall, my super-dainty Kate,
For dainties are all Kates, and therefore, Kate,
Take this of me, Kate of my consolation –
Hearing thy mildness prais'd in every town,
Thy virtues spoke of, and thy beauty sounded,
Yet not so deeply as to thee belongs,
Myself am mov'd to woo thee for my wife.

KATHERINA Mov'd! in good time! Let him that mov'd you hither
Remove you hence. I knew you at the first
You were a moveable.

PETRUCHIO Why, what's a moveable?

KATHERINA A join'd-stool.

PETRUCHIO Thou hast hit it. Come, sit on me.

KATHERINA Asses are made to bear, and so are you.

PETRUCHIO Women are made to bear, and so are you.

KATHERINA No such jade as you, if me you mean.

PETRUCHIO Alas, good Kate, I will not burden thee!
For, knowing thee to be but young and light –
KATHERINA Too light for such a swain as you to catch;
And yet as heavy as my weight should be.
PETRUCHIO Should be! should – buzz!
KATHERINA Well ta'en, and like a buzzard.
PETRUCHIO O, slow-wing'd turtle, shall a buzzard take thee?
KATHERINA Ay, for a turtle, as he takes a buzzard.
PETRUCHIO Come, come, you wasp; i' faith, you are too angry.
KATHERINA If I be waspish, best beware my sting.
PETRUCHIO My remedy is then to pluck it out.
KATHERINA Ay, if the fool could find it where it lies.
PETRUCHIO Who knows not where a wasp does wear his sting?
In his tail.
KATHERINA In his tongue.
PETRUCHIO Whose tongue?
KATHERINA Yours, if you talk of tales; and so farewell.
PETRUCHIO What, with my tongue in your tail? Nay, come again,
Good Kate; I am a gentleman.
KATHERINA That I'll try.
[She strikes him.
PETRUCHIO I swear I'll cuff you, if you strike again.
KATHERINA So may you lose your arms.
If you strike me, you are no gentleman;
And if no gentleman, why then no arms.
PETRUCHIO A herald, Kate? O, put me in thy books!
KATHERINA What is your crest – a coxcomb?
PETRUCHIO A combless cock, so Kate will be my hen.
KATHERINA No cock of mine: you crow too like a craven.
PETRUCHIO Nay, come, Kate, come; you must not look so sour.
KATHERINA It is my fashion, when I see a crab.
PETRUCHIO Why, here's no crab; and therefore look not sour.
KATHERINA There is, there is.
PETRUCHIO Then show it me.
KATHERINA Had I a glass I would.
PETRUCHIO What, you mean my face?
KATHERINA Well aim'd of such a young one.
PETRUCHIO Now, by Saint George, I am too young for you.
KATHERINA Yet you are wither'd.
PETRUCHIO 'Tis with cares.
KATHERINA I care not.
PETRUCHIO Nay, hear you, Kate – in sooth, you scape not so.
KATHERINA I chafe you, if I tarry; let me go.
PETRUCHIO No, not a whit; I find you passing gentle.
'Twas told me you were rough, and coy, and sullen,
And now I find report a very liar;
For thou art pleasant, gamesome, passing courteous,
But slow in speech, yet sweet as springtime flowers.
Thou canst not frown, thou canst not look askance,
Nor bite the lip, as angry wenches will,
Nor hast thou pleasure to be cross in talk;
But thou with mildness entertain'st thy wooers;
With gentle conference, soft and affable.
Why does the world report that Kate doth limp?
O sland'rous world! Kate like the hazel-twig
Is straight and slender, and as brown in hue
As hazel-nuts, and sweeter than the kernels.
O, let me see thee walk. Thou dost not halt.
KATHERINA Go, fool, and whom thou keep'st command.
PETRUCHIO Did ever Dian so become a grove
As Kate this chamber with her princely gait?
O, be thou Dian, and let her be Kate;
And then let Kate be chaste, and Dian sportful!
KATHERINA Where did you study all this goodly speech?
PETRUCHIO It is extempore, from my mother wit.
KATHERINA A witty mother! witless else her son.
PETRUCHIO Am I not wise?
KATHERINA Yes, keep you warm.
PETRUCHIO Marry, so I mean, sweet Katherine, in thy bed.
And therefore, setting all this chat aside,
Thus in plain terms: your father hath consented
That you shall be my wife; your dowry 'greed on;
And will you, nill you, I will marry you.
Now, Kate, I am a husband for your turn;
For, by this light, whereby I see thy beauty,
Thy beauty that doth make me like thee well,
Thou must be married to no man but me;
For I am he am born to tame you, Kate,
And bring you from a wild Kate to a Kate
Conformable as other household Kates.

Re-enter BAPTISTA, GREMIO, and TRANIO.

Here comes your father. Never make denial;
I must and will have Katherine to my wife.
BAPTISTA Now, Signior Petruchio, how speed you with my daughter?
PETRUCHIO How but well, sir? how but well?

It were impossible I should speed amiss.
BAPTISTA Why, how now, daughter Katherine, in your dumps?
KATHERINA Call you me daughter? Now I promise you
You have show'd a tender fatherly regard
To wish me wed to one half lunatic,
A mad-cap ruffian and a swearing Jack,
That thinks with oaths to face the matter out.
PETRUCHIO Father, 'tis thus: yourself and all the world
That talk'd of her have talk'd amiss of her.
If she be curst, it is for policy,
For she's not froward, but modest as the dove;
She is not hot, but temperate as the morn;
For patience she will prove a second Grissel,
And Roman Lucrece for her chastity.
And, to conclude, we have 'greed so well together
That upon Sunday is the wedding-day.
KATHERINA I'll see thee hang'd on Sunday first.
GREMIO Hark, Petruchio; she says she'll see thee hang'd first.
TRANIO Is this your speeding? Nay, then good-night our part!
PETRUCHIO Be patient, gentlemen. I choose her for myself;
If she and I be pleas'd, what's that to you?
'Tis bargain'd 'twixt us twain, being alone,
That she shall still be curst in company.
I tell you 'tis incredible to believe
How much she loves me – O, the kindest Kate!
She hung about my neck, and kiss on kiss
She vied so fast, protesting oath on oath,
That in a twink she won me to her love.
O, you are novices! 'Tis a world to see
How tame, when men and women are alone,
A meacock wretch can make the curstest shrew.
Give me thy hand, Kate; I will unto Venice,
To buy apparel 'gainst the wedding-day.
Provide the feast, father, and bid the guests;
I will be sure my Katherine shall be fine.
BAPTISTA I know not what to say; but give me your hands.
God send you joy, Petruchio! 'Tis a match.
GREMIO, TRANIO Amen, say we; we will be witnesses.
PETRUCHIO Father, and wife, and gentlemen, adieu.
I will to Venice; Sunday comes apace;
We will have rings and things, and fine array;
And kiss me, Kate; we will be married a Sunday.
[*Exeunt Petruchio and Katherina severally.*
GREMIO Was ever match clapp'd up so suddenly?
BAPTISTA Faith, gentlemen, now I play a merchant's part,
And venture madly on a desperate mart.
TRANIO 'Twas a commodity lay fretting by you;
'Twill bring you gain, or perish on the seas.
BAPTISTA The gain I seek is quiet in the match.
GREMIO No doubt but he hath got a quiet catch.
But now, Baptista, to your younger daughter:
Now is the day we long have looked for;
I am your neighbour, and was suitor first.
TRANIO And I am one that love Bianca more
Than words can witness or your thoughts can guess.
GREMIO Youngling, thou canst not love so dear as I.
TRANIO Greybeard, thy love doth freeze.
GREMIO But thine doth fry.
Skipper, stand back; 'tis age that nourisheth.
TRANIO But youth in ladies' eyes that flourisheth.
BAPTISTA Content you, gentlemen; I will compound this strife.
'Tis deeds must win the prize, and he of both
That can assure my daughter greatest dower
Shall have my Bianca's love.
Say, Signior Gremio, what can you assure her?
GREMIO First, as you know, my house within the city
Is richly furnished with plate and gold,
Basins and ewers to lave her dainty hands;
My hangings all of Tyrian tapestry;
In ivory coffers I have stuff'd my crowns;
In cypress chests my arras counterpoints,
Costly apparel, tents, and canopies,
Fine linen, Turkey cushions boss'd with pearl,
Valance of Venice gold in needle-work;
Pewter and brass, and all things that belongs
To house or housekeeping. Then at my farm
I have a hundred milch-kine to the pail,
Six score fat oxen standing in my stalls,
And all things answerable to this portion.
Myself am struck in years, I must confess;
And if I die to-morrow this is hers,
If whilst I live she will be only mine.
TRANIO That 'only' came well in. Sir, list to me:
I am my father's heir and only son;
If I may have your daughter to my wife,
I'll leave her houses three or four as good
Within rich Pisa's walls as any one
Old Signior Gremio has in Padua;
Besides two thousand ducats by the year
Of fruitful land, all which shall be her jointure.
What, have I pinch'd you, Signior Gremio?
GREMIO Two thousand ducats by the year of land!
[*Aside*] My land amounts not to so much in all. –
That she shall have, besides an argosy
That now is lying in Marseilles road.
What, have I chok'd you with an argosy?

TRANIO Gremio, 'tis known my father hath no less
Than three great argosies, besides two galliasses,
And twelve tight galleys. These I will assure her,
And twice as much whate'er thou off'rest next.
GREMIO Nay, I have off'red all; I have no more;
And she can have no more than all I have;
If you like me, she shall have me and mine.
TRANIO Why, then the maid is mine from all the world
By your firm promise; Gremio is out-vied.
BAPTISTA I must confess your offer is the best;
And let your father make her the assurance,
She is your own. Else, you must pardon me;
If you should die before him, where's her dower?
TRANIO That's but a cavil; he is old, I young.
GREMIO And may not young men die as well as old?
BAPTISTA Well, gentlemen,
I am thus resolv'd: on Sunday next you know
My daughter Katherine is to be married;
Now, on the Sunday following shall Bianca
Be bride to you, if you make this assurance;
If not, to Signior Gremio.
And so I take my leave, and thank you both.
GREMIO Adieu, good neighbour. [*Exit Baptista.*
Now, I fear thee not.
Sirrah young gamester, your father were a fool
To give thee all, and in his waning age
Set foot under thy table. Tut, a toy!
An old Italian fox is not so kind, my boy. [*Exit.*
TRANIO A vengeance on your crafty withered hide!
Yet I have fac'd it with a card of ten.
'Tis in my head to do my master good:
I see no reason but suppos'd Lucentio
Must get a father, call'd suppos'd Vincentio;
And that's a wonder – fathers commonly
Do get their children; but in this case of wooing
A child shall get a sire, if I fail not of my cunning. [*Exit.*

ACT THREE

SCENE I. *Padua. Baptista's house.*

Enter LUCENTIO as Cambio, HORTENSIO as Licio, and BIANCA.

LUCENTIO Fiddler, forbear; you grow too forward, sir.
Have you so soon forgot the entertainment
Her sister Katherine welcom'd you withal?
HORTENSIO But, wrangling pedant, this is
The patroness of heavenly harmony.
Then give me leave to have prerogative;
And when in music we have spent an hour,
Your lecture shall have leisure for as much.
LUCENTIO Preposterous ass, that never read so far
To know the cause why music was ordain'd!
Was it not to refresh the mind of man
After his studies or his usual pain?
Then give me leave to read philosophy,
And while I pause serve in your harmony.
HORTENSIO Sirrah, I will not bear these braves of thine.
BIANCA Why, gentlemen, you do me double wrong
To strive for that which resteth in my choice.
I am no breeching scholar in the schools,
I'll not be tied to hours nor 'pointed times,
But learn my lessons as I please myself.
And to cut off all strife: here sit we down;
Take you your instrument, play you the whiles;
His lecture will be done ere you have tun'd.
HORTENSIO You'll leave his lecture when I am in tune?
LUCENTIO That will be never – tune your instrument.
BIANCA Where left we last?
LUCENTIO Here, madam:
'Hic ibat Simois, hic est Sigeia tellus,
Hic steterat Priami regia celsa senis'.
BIANCA Construe them.
LUCENTIO 'Hic ibat' as I told you before – 'Simois' I am Lucentio – 'hic est' son unto Vincentio of Pisa – 'Sigeia tellus' disguised thus to get your love – 'Hic steterat' and that Lucentio that comes a-wooing – 'Priami' is my man Tranio – 'regia' bearing my port – 'celsa senis' that we might beguile the old pantaloon.
HORTENSIO Madam, my instrument's in tune.
BIANCA Let's hear. O fie! the treble jars.
LUCENTIO Spit in the hole, man, and tune again.
BIANCA Now let me see if I can construe it: 'Hic ibat Simois' I know you not – 'hic est Sigeia tellu' I trust you not – 'Hic steterat Priami' take heed he hear us not – 'regia' presume not – 'celsa senis' despair not.
HORTENSIO Madam, 'tis now in tune.
LUCENTIO All but the bass.
HORTENSIO The bass is right; 'tis the base knave that jars.
[*Aside*] How fiery and forward our pedant is!
Now, for my life, the knave doth court my love.

Pedascule, I'll watch you better yet.
BIANCA In time I may believe, yet I mistrust.
LUCENTIO Mistrust it not – for, sure, AEacides
Was Ajax, call'd so from his grandfather.
BIANCA I must believe my master; else, I promise you,
I should be arguing still upon that doubt;
But let it rest. Now, Licio, to you.
Good master, take it not unkindly, pray,
That I have been thus pleasant with you both.
HORTENSIO [*To Lucentio*] You may go walk and give me leave awhile;
My lessons make no music in three parts.
LUCENTIO Are you so formal, sir? Well, I must wait,
[*Aside*] And watch withal; for, but I be deceiv'd,
Our fine musician groweth amorous.
HORTENSIO Madam, before you touch the instrument
To learn the order of my fingering,
I must begin with rudiments of art,
To teach you gamut in a briefer sort,
More pleasant, pithy, and effectual,
Than hath been taught by any of my trade;
And there it is in writing fairly drawn.
BIANCA Why, I am past my gamut long ago.
HORTENSIO Yet read the gamut of Hortensio.
BIANCA [*Reads*]
'"Gamut" I am, the ground of all accord –
"A re" to plead Hortensio's passion –
"B mi" Bianca, take him for thy lord –
"C fa ut" that loves with all affection –
"D sol re" one clef, two notes have I –
"E la mi" show pity or I die.'
Call you this gamut? Tut, I like it not!
Old fashions please me best; I am not so nice
To change true rules for odd inventions.

Enter a Servant.

SERVANT Mistress, your father prays you leave your books
And help to dress your sister's chamber up.
You know to-morrow is the wedding-day.
BIANCA Farewell, sweet masters, both; I must be gone.
[*Exeunt Bianca and Servant.*
LUCENTIO Faith, mistress, then I have no cause to stay. [*Exit.*
HORTENSIO But I have cause to pry into this pedant;
Methinks he looks as though he were in love.
Yet if thy thoughts, Bianca, be so humble
To cast thy wand'ring eyes on every stale –
Seize thee that list. If once I find thee ranging,
Hortensio will be quit with thee by changing.
[*Exit.*

SCENE II. *Padua. Before Baptista's house.*

Enter BAPTISTA, GREMIO, TRANIO as Lucentio, KATHERINA, BIANCA, LUCENTIO as Cambio, and Attendants.

BAPTISTA [*To Tranio*] Signior Lucentio, this is the 'pointed day
That Katherine and Petruchio should be married,
And yet we hear not of our son-in-law.
What will be said? What mockery will it be
To want the bridegroom when the priest attends
To speak the ceremonial rites of marriage!
What says Lucentio to this shame of ours?
KATHERINA No shame but mine; I must, forsooth, be forc'd
To give my hand, oppos'd against my heart,
Unto a mad-brain rudesby, full of spleen,
Who woo'd in haste and means to wed at leisure.
I told you, I, he was a frantic fool,
Hiding his bitter jests in blunt behaviour;
And, to be noted for a merry man,
He'll woo a thousand, 'point the day of marriage,
Make friends invited, and proclaim the banns;
Yet never means to wed where he hath woo'd.
Now must the world point at poor Katherine,
And say 'Lo, there is mad Petruchio's wife,
If it would please him come and marry her!'
TRANIO Patience, good Katherine, and Baptista too.
Upon my life, Petruchio means but well,
Whatever fortune stays him from his word.
Though he be blunt, I know him passing wise;
Though he be merry, yet withal he's honest.
KATHERINA Would Katherine had never seen him though!
[*Exit, weeping, followed by Bianca and others.*
BAPTISTA Go, girl, I cannot blame thee now to weep,
For such an injury would vex a very saint;
Much more a shrew of thy impatient humour.

Enter BIONDELLO.

BIONDELLO Master, master! News, and such old news as you never heard of!
BAPTISTA Is it new and old too? How may that be?
BIONDELLO Why, is it not news to hear of Petruchio's coming?
BAPTISTA Is he come?
BIONDELLO Why, no, sir.
BAPTISTA What then?
BIONDELLO He is coming.
BAPTISTA When will he be here?
BIONDELLO When he stands where I am and sees you there.
TRANIO But, say, what to thine old news?

BIANCA Why, Petruchio is coming – in a new hat and an old jerkin; a pair of old breeches thrice turn'd; a pair of boots that have been candle-cases, one buckled, another lac'd; an old rusty sword ta'en out of the town armoury, with a broken hilt, and chapeless; with two broken points; his horse hipp'd, with an old mothy saddle and stirrups of no kindred; besides, possess'd with the glanders and like to mose in the chine, troubled with the lampass, infected with the fashions, full of windgalls, sped with spavins, rayed with the yellows, past cure of the fives, stark spoil'd with the staggers, begnawn with the bots, sway'd in the back and shoulder-shotten, near-legg'd before, and with a half-cheek'd bit, and a head-stall of sheep's leather which, being restrain'd to keep him from stumbling, hath been often burst, and now repaired with knots; one girth six times piec'd, and a woman's crupper of velure, which hath two letters for her name fairly set down in studs, and here and there piec'd with pack-thread.

BAPTISTA Who comes with him?

BIONDELLO O, sir, his lackey, for all the world caparison'd like the horse – with a linen stock on one leg and a kersey boot-hose on the other, gart'red with a red and blue list; an old hat, and the humour of forty fancies prick'd in't for a feather; a monster, a very monster in apparel, and not like a Christian footboy or a gentleman's lackey.

TRANIO 'Tis some odd humour pricks him to this fashion;
Yet oftentimes he goes but mean-apparell'd.

BAPTISTA I am glad he's come, howsoe'er he comes.

BIONDELLO Why, sir, he comes not.

BAPTISTA Didst thou not say he comes?

BIONDELLO Who? that Petruchio came?

BAPTISTA Ay, that Petruchio came.

BIONDELLO No, sir; I say his horse comes with him on his back.

BAPTISTA Why, that's all one.

BIONDELLO Nay, by Saint Jamy,
I hold you a penny,
A horse and a man
Is more than one,
And yet not many.

Enter PETRUCHIO and GRUMIO.

PETRUCHIO Come, where be these gallants? Who's at home?

BAPTISTA You are welcome, sir.

PETRUCHIO And yet I come not well.

BAPTISTA And yet you halt not.

TRANIO Not so well apparell'd
As I wish you were.

PETRUCHIO Were it better, I should rush in thus.
But where is Kate? Where is my lovely bride?
How does my father? Gentles, methinks you frown;
And wherefore gaze this goodly company
As if they saw some wondrous monument,
Some comet or unusual prodigy?

BAPTISTA Why, sir, you know this is your wedding-day.
First were we sad, fearing you would not come;
Now sadder, that you come so unprovided.
Fie, doff this habit, shame to your estate,
An eye-sore to our solemn festival!

TRANIO And tell us what occasion of import
Hath all so long detain'd you from your wife,
And sent you hither so unlike yourself?

PETRUCHIO Tedious it were to tell, and harsh to hear;
Sufficeth I am come to keep my word,
Though in some part enforced to digress,
Which at more leisure I will so excuse
As you shall well be satisfied withal.
But where is Kate? I stay too long from her;
The morning wears, 'tis time we were at church.

TRANIO See not your bride in these unreverent robes;
Go to my chamber, put on clothes of mine.

PETRUCHIO Not I, believe me; thus I'll visit her.

BAPTISTA But thus, I trust, you will not marry her.

PETRUCHIO Good sooth, even thus; therefore ha' done with words;
To me she's married, not unto my clothes.
Could I repair what she will wear in me
As I can change these poor accoutrements,
'Twere well for Kate and better for myself.
But what a fool am I to chat with you,
When I should bid good morrow to my bride
And seal the title with a lovely kiss!

[*Exeunt Petruchio and Grumio.*

TRANIO He hath some meaning in his mad attire.
We will persuade him, be it possible,
To put on better ere he go to church.

BAPTISTA I'll after him and see the event of this.

[*Exeunt Baptista, Gremio, Biondello, and Attendants.*

TRANIO But to her love concerneth us to add
Her father's liking; which to bring to pass,
As I before imparted to your worship,
I am to get a man – whate'er he be
It skills not much; we'll fit him to our turn –
And he shall be Vincentio of Pisa,
And make assurance here in Padua
Of greater sums than I have promised.
So shall you quietly enjoy your hope
And marry sweet Bianca with consent.

LUCENTIO Were it not that my fellow school-master
Doth watch Bianca's steps so narrowly,
'Twere good, methinks, to steal our marriage;
Which once perform'd, let all the world say no,
I'll keep mine own despite of all the world.
TRANIO That by degrees we mean to look into
And watch our vantage in this business;
We'll over-reach the greybeard, Gremio,
The narrow-prying father, Minola,
The quaint musician, amorous Licio –
All for my master's sake, Lucentio.

Re-enter GREMIO.

Signior Gremio, came you from the church?
GREMIO As willingly as e'er I came from school.
TRANIO And is the bride and bridegroom coming home?
GREMIO A bridegroom, say you? 'Tis a groom indeed,
A grumbling groom, and that the girl shall find.
TRANIO Curster than she? Why, 'tis impossible.
GREMIO Why, he's a devil, a devil, a very fiend.
TRANIO Why, she's a devil, a devil, the devil's dam.
GREMIO Tut, she's a lamb, a dove, a fool, to him!
I'll tell you, Sir Lucentio: when the priest
Should ask if Katherine should be his wife,
'Ay, by gogs-wouns' quoth he, and swore so loud
That, all amaz'd, the priest let fall the book;
And as he stoop'd again to take it up,
This mad-brain'd bridegroom took him such a cuff
That down fell priest and book, and book and priest.
'Now take them up,' quoth he 'if any list.'
TRANIO What said the wench, when he rose again?
GREMIO Trembled and shook, for why he stamp'd and swore
As if the vicar meant to cozen him.
But after many ceremonies done
He calls for wine: 'A health!' quoth he, as if
He had been abroad, carousing to his mates
After a storm; quaff'd off the muscadel,
And threw the sops all in the sexton's face,
Having no other reason
But that his beard grew thin and hungerly
And seem'd to ask him sops as he was drinking.
This done, he took the bride about the neck,
And kiss'd her lips with such a clamorous smack
That at the parting all the church did echo.
And I, seeing this, came thence for very shame;
And after me, I know, the rout is coming.
Such a mad marriage never was before.
Hark, hark! I hear the minstrels play.
[*Music plays.*

Enter PETRUCHIO, KATHERINA, BIANCA, BAPTISTA, HORTENSIO, GRUMIO, and Train.

PETRUCHIO Gentlemen and friends, I thank you for your pains.
I know you think to dine with me to-day,
And have prepar'd great store of wedding cheer;
But so it is – my haste doth call me hence,
And therefore here I mean to take my leave.
BAPTISTA Is't possible you will away tonight?
PETRUCHIO I must away to-day before night come.
Make it no wonder; if you knew my business,
You would entreat me rather go than stay.
And, honest company, I thank you all
That have beheld me give away myself
To this most patient, sweet, and virtuous wife.
Dine with my father, drink a health to me,
For I must hence; and farewell to you all.
TRANIO Let us entreat you stay till after dinner.
PETRUCHIO It may not be.
GREMIO Let me entreat you.
PETRUCHIO It cannot be.
KATHERINA Let me entreat you.
PETRUCHIO I am content.
KATHERINA Are you content to stay?
PETRUCHIO I am content you shall entreat me stay;
But yet not stay, entreat me how you can.
KATHERINA Now, if you love me, stay.
PETRUCHIO Grumio, my horse.
GRUMIO Ay, sir, they be ready; the oats have eaten the horses.
KATHERINA Nay, then,
Do what thou canst, I will not go to-day;
No, nor to-morrow, not till I please myself.
The door is open, sir; there lies your way;
You may be jogging whiles your boots are green;
For me, I'll not be gone till I please myself.
'Tis like you'll prove a jolly surly groom
That take it on you at the first so roundly.
PETRUCHIO O Kate, content thee; prithee be not angry.
KATHERINA I will be angry; what hast thou to do?
Father, be quiet; he shall stay my leisure.
GREMIO Ay, marry, sir, now it begins to work.
KATHERINA Gentlemen, forward to the bridal dinner.
I see a woman may be made a fool
If she had not a spirit to resist.
PETRUCHIO They shall go forward, Kate, at thy command.
Obey the bride, you that attend on her;
Go to the feast, revel and domineer,
Carouse full measure to her maidenhead;
Be mad and merry, or go hang yourselves.

But for my bonny Kate, she must with me.
Nay, look not big, nor stamp, nor stare, nor fret;
I will be master of what is mine own –
She is my goods, my chattels, she is my house,
My household stuff, my field, my barn,
My horse, my ox, my ass, my any thing,
And here she stands; touch her whoever dare;
I'll bring mine action on the proudest he
That stops my way in Padua. Grumio,
Draw forth thy weapon; we are beset with thieves;
Rescue thy mistress, if thou be a man.
Fear not, sweet wench; they shall not touch thee, Kate;
I'll buckler thee against a million.

[Exeunt Petruchio, Katherina, and Grumio.

BAPTISTA Nay, let them go, a couple of quiet ones.

GREMIO Went they not quickly, I should die with laughing.

TRANIO Of all mad matches, never was the like.

LUCENTIO Mistress, what's your opinion of your sister?

BIANCA That, being mad herself, she's madly mated.

GREMIO I warrant him, Petruchio is Kated.

BAPTISTA Neighbours and friends, though bride and bridegroom wants
For to supply the places at the table,
You know there wants no junkets at the feast.
Lucentio, you shall supply the bridegroom's place;
And let Bianca take her sister's room.

TRANIO Shall sweet Bianca practise how to bride it?

BAPTISTA She shall, Lucentio. Come, gentlemen, let's go. *[Exeunt.*

ACT FOUR

SCENE I. *Petruchio's country house.*

Enter GRUMIO.

GRUMIO Fie, fie on all tired jades, on all mad masters, and all foul ways! Was ever man so beaten? Was ever man so ray'd? Was ever man so weary? I am sent before to make a fire, and they are coming after to warm them. Now were not I a little pot and soon hot, my very lips might freeze to my teeth, my tongue to the roof of my mouth, my heart in my belly, ere I should come by a fire to thaw me. But I with blowing the fire shall warm myself; for, considering the weather, a taller man than I will take cold. Holla, ho! Curtis!

Enter CURTIS.

CURTIS Who is that calls so coldly?

GRUMIO A piece of ice. If thou doubt it, thou mayst slide from my shoulder to my heel with no greater a run but my head and my neck. A fire, good Curtis.

CURTIS Is my master and his wife coming, Grumio?

GRUMIO O, ay, Curtis, ay; and therefore fire, fire; cast on no water.

CURTIS Is she so hot a shrew as she's reported?

GRUMIO She was, good Curtis, before this frost; but thou know'st winter tames man, woman, and beast; for it hath tam'd my old master, and my new mistress, and myself, fellow Curtis.

CURTIS Away, you three-inch fool! I am no beast.

GRUMIO Am I but three inches? Why, thy horn is a foot, and so long am I at the least. But wilt thou make a fire, or shall I complain on thee to our mistress, whose hand – she being now at hand – thou shalt soon feel, to thy cold comfort, for being slow in thy hot office?

CURTIS I prithee, good Grumio, tell me how goes the world?

GRUMIO A cold world, Curtis, in every office but thine; and therefore fire. Do thy duty, and have thy duty, for my master and mistress are almost frozen to death.

CURTIS There's fire ready; and therefore, good Grumio, the news?

GRUMIO Why, 'Jack boy! ho, boy!' and as much news as wilt thou.

CURTIS Come, you are so full of cony-catching!

GRUMIO Why, therefore, fire; for I have caught extreme cold. Where's the cook? Is supper ready, the house trimm'd, rushes strew'd, cobwebs swept, the serving-men in their new fustian, their white stockings, and every officer his wedding-garment on? Be the jacks fair within, the jills fair without, the carpets laid, and everything in order?

CURTIS All ready; and therefore, I pray thee, news.

GRUMIO First know my horse is tired; my master and mistress fall'n out.

CURTIS How?

GRUMIO Out of their saddles into the dirt; and thereby hangs a tale.

CURTIS Let's ha't, good Grumio.

GRUMIO Lend thine ear.

CURTIS Here.

GRUMIO There. *[Striking him.*

CURTIS This 'tis to feel a tale, not to hear a tale.

GRUMIO And therefore 'tis call'd a sensible tale; and this cuff was but to knock at your ear and beseech list'ning. Now I begin: Imprimis, we came down a foul hill, my master riding behind my mistress –

CURTIS Both of one horse?

GRUMIO What's that to thee?

CURTIS Why, a horse.

GRUMIO Tell thou the tale. But hadst thou not cross'd me, thou shouldst have heard how her horse fell and she under her horse; thou shouldst have heard in how miry a place, how she was bemoil'd, how he left her with the horse upon her, how he beat me because her horse stumbled, how she waded through the dirt to pluck him off me, how he swore, how she pray'd that never pray'd before, how I cried, how the horses ran away, how her bridle was burst, how I lost my crupper – with many things of worthy memory, which now shall die in oblivion, and thou return unexperienc'd to thy grave.

CURTIS By this reck'ning he is more shrew than she.

GRUMIO Ay, and that thou and the proudest of you all shall find when he comes home. But what talk I of this? Call forth Nathaniel, Joseph, Nicholas, Philip, Walter, Sugarsop, and the rest; let their heads be sleekly comb'd, their blue coats brush'd and their garters of an indifferent knit; let them curtsy with their left legs, and not presume to touch a hair of my master's horse-tail till they kiss their hands. Are they all ready?

CURTIS They are.

GRUMIO Call them forth.

CURTIS Do you hear, ho? You must meet my master, to countenance my mistress.

GRUMIO Why, she hath a face of her own.

CURTIS Who knows not that?

GRUMIO Thou, it seems, that calls for company to countenance her.

CURTIS I call them forth to credit her.

GRUMIO Why, she comes to borrow nothing of them.

Enter four or five Servants.

NATHANIEL Welcome home, Grumio!

PHILIP How now, Grumio!

JOSEPH What, Grumio!

NICHOLAS Fellow Grumio!

NATHANIEL How now, old lad!

GRUMIO Welcome, you! – how now, you! – what, you! – fellow, you! – and thus much for greeting. Now, my spruce companions, is all ready, and all things neat?

NATHANIEL All things is ready. How near is our master?

GRUMIO E'en at hand, alighted by this; and therefore be not – Cock's passion, silence! I hear my master.

Enter PETRUCHIO and KATHERINA.

PETRUCHIO Where be these knaves? What, no man at door
To hold my stirrup nor to take my horse!
Where is Nathaniel, Gregory, Philip?

ALL SERVANTS Here, here, sir; here, sir.

PETRUCHIO Here, sir! here, sir! here, sir! here, sir!
You logger-headed and unpolish'd grooms!
What, no attendance? no regard? no duty?
Where is the foolish knave I sent before?

GRUMIO Here, sir; as foolish as I was before.

PETRUCHIO You peasant swain! you whoreson malt-horse drudge!
Did I not bid thee meet me in the park
And bring along these rascal knaves with thee?

GRUMIO Nathaniel's coat, sir, was not fully made,
And Gabriel's pumps were all unpink'd i' th' heel;
There was no link to colour Peter's hat,
And Walter's dagger was not come from sheathing;
There were none fine but Adam, Ralph, and Gregory;
The rest were ragged, old, and beggarly;
Yet, as they are, here are they come to meet you.

PETRUCHIO Go, rascals, go and fetch my supper in. *[Exeunt some of the Servants.*
[*Sings*] Where is the life that late I led?
Where are those –
Sit down, Kate, and welcome. Soud, soud, soud, soud!

Re-enter Servants with supper.

Why, when, I say? Nay, good sweet Kate, be merry.
Off with my boots, you rogues! you villains, when?
[*Sings*] It was the friar of orders grey,
As he forth walked on his way –
Out, you rogue! you pluck my foot awry;
Take that, and mend the plucking off the other. *[Strikes him.*
Be merry, Kate. Some water, here, what, ho!

Enter One with water.

Where's my spaniel Troilus? Sirrah, get you hence,
And bid my cousin Ferdinand come hither: *[Exit Servants.*
One, Kate, that you must kiss and be acquainted with.

Where are my slippers? Shall I have some water?
Come, Kate, and wash, and welcome heartily.
You whoreson villain! will you let it fall?
[*Strikes him.*

KATHERINA Patience, I pray you; 'twas a fault unwilling.

PETRUCHIO A whoreson, beetle-headed, flap-ear'd knave!
Come, Kate, sit down; I know you have a stomach.
Will you give thanks, sweet Kate, or else shall I?
What's this? Mutton?

1 SERVANT Ay.

PETRUCHIO Who brought it?

PETER I.

PETRUCHIO 'Tis burnt; and so is all the meat.
What dogs are these? Where is the rascal cook?
How durst you villains bring it from the dresser
And serve it thus to me that love it not?
There, take it to you, trenchers, cups, and all;
[*Throws the meat, etc., at them.*
You heedless joltheads and unmanner'd slaves!
What, do you grumble? I'll be with you straight.
[*Exeunt Servants.*

KATHERINA I pray you, husband, be not so disquiet;
The meat was well, if you were so contented.

PETRUCHIO I tell thee, Kate, 'twas burnt and dried away,
And I expressly am forbid to touch it;
For it engenders choler, planteth anger;
And better 'twere that both of us did fast,
Since, of ourselves, ourselves are choleric,
Than feed it with such over-roasted flesh.
Be patient; to-morrow 't shall be mended,
And for this night we'll fast for company.
Come, I will bring thee to thy bridal chamber.
[*Exeunt.*

Re-enter Servants severally.

NATHANIEL Peter, didst ever see the like?

PETER He kills her in her own humour.

Re-enter Curtis

GRUMIO Where is he?

CURTIS In her chamber. Making a sermon of continency to her,
And rails, and swears, and rates, that she, poor soul,
Knows not which way to stand, to look, to speak,
And sits as one new risen from a dream.
Away, away! for he is coming hither.
[*Exeunt.*

Re-enter PETRUCHIO.

PETRUCHIO Thus have I politicly begun my reign,
And 'tis my hope to end successfully.
My falcon now is sharp and passing empty,
And till she stoop she must not be full-gorg'd,
For then she never looks upon her lure.
Another way I have to man my haggard,
To make her come, and know her keeper's call,
That is, to watch her, as we watch these kites
That bate and beat, and will not be obedient.
She eat no meat to-day, nor none shall eat;
Last night she slept not, nor to-night she shall not;
As with the meat, some undeserved fault
I'll find about the making of the bed;
And here I'll fling the pillow, there the bolster,
This way the coverlet, another way the sheets;
Ay, and amid this hurly I intend
That all is done in reverend care of her –
And, in conclusion, she shall watch all night;
And if she chance to nod I'll rail and brawl
And with the clamour keep her still awake.
This is a way to kill a wife with kindness,
And thus I'll curb her mad and headstrong humour.
He that knows better how to tame a shrew,
Now let him speak; 'tis charity to show.
[*Exit.*

SCENE II. *Padua. Before Baptista's house.*

Enter TRANIO as Lucentio, and HORTENSIO as Licio.

TRANIO Is't possible, friend Licio, that Mistress Bianca
Doth fancy any other but Lucentio?
I tell you, sir, she bears me fair in hand.

HORTENSIO Sir, to satisfy you in what I have said,
Stand by and mark the manner of his teaching.
[*They stand aside.*

Enter BIANCA and LUCENTIO as Cambio.

LUCENTIO Now, mistress, profit you in what you read?

BIANCA What, master, read you? First resolve me that.

LUCENTIO I read that I profess, 'The Art to Love'.

BIANCA And may you prove, sir, master of your art!

LUCENTIO While you, sweet dear, prove mistress of my heart.
[*They retire.*

HORTENSIO Quick proceeders, marry! Now tell me, I pray,
You that durst swear that your Mistress Bianca
Lov'd none in the world so well as Lucentio.

TRANIO O despiteful love! unconstant womankind!

I tell thee, Licio, this is wonderful.
HORTENSIO Mistake no more; I am not Licio,
Nor a musician as I seem to be;
But one that scorn to live in this disguise
For such a one as leaves a gentleman
And makes a god of such a cullion.
Know, sir, that I am call'd Hortensio.
TRANIO Signior Hortensio, I have often heard
Of your entire affection to Bianca;
And since mine eyes are witness of her lightness,
I will with you, if you be so contented,
Forswear Bianca and her love for ever.
HORTENSIO See, how they kiss and court! Signior Lucentio,
Here is my hand, and here I firmly vow
Never to woo her more, but do forswear her,
As one unworthy all the former favours
That I have fondly flatter'd her withal.
TRANIO And here I take the like unfeigned oath,
Never to marry with her though she would entreat;
Fie on her! See how beastly she doth court him!
HORTENSIO Would all the world but he had quite forsworn!
For me, that I may surely keep mine oath,
I will be married to a wealthy widow
Ere three days pass, which hath as long lov'd me
As I have lov'd this proud disdainful haggard.
And so farewell, Signior Lucentio.
Kindness in women, not their beauteous looks,
Shall win my love; and so I take my leave,
In resolution as I swore before.
[*Exit*.
TRANIO Mistress Bianca, bless you with such grace
As 'longeth to a lover's blessed case!
Nay, I have ta'en you napping, gentle love,
And have forsworn you with Hortensio.
BIANCA Tranio, you jest; but have you both forsworn me?
TRANIO Mistress, we have.
LUCENTIO Then we are rid of Licio.
TRANIO I' faith, he'll have a lusty widow now,
That shall be woo'd and wedded in a day.
BIANCA God give him joy!
TRANIO Ay, and he'll tame her.
BIANCA He says so, Tranio.
TRANIO Faith, he is gone unto the taming-school.
BIANCA The taming-school! What, is there such a place?
TRANIO Ay, mistress; and Petruchio is the master,
That teacheth tricks eleven and twenty long,
To tame a shrew and charm her chattering tongue.

Enter BIONDELLO.

BIONDELLO O master, master, I have watch'd so long
That I am dog-weary; but at last I spied
An ancient angel coming down the hill
Will serve the turn.
TRANIO What is he, Biondello?
BIONDELLO Master, a mercatante or a pedant,
I know not what; but formal in apparel,
In gait and countenance surely like a father.
LUCENTIO And what of him, Tranio?
TRANIO If he be credulous and trust my tale,
I'll make him glad to seem Vincentio,
And give assurance to Baptista Minola
As if he were the right Vincentio.
Take in your love, and then let me alone.
[*Exeunt Lucentio and Bianca.*

Enter a Pedant.

PEDANT God save you, sir!
TRANIO And you, sir; you are welcome.
Travel you far on, or are you at the farthest?
PEDANT Sir, at the farthest for a week or two;
But then up farther, and as far as Rome;
And so to Tripoli, if God lend me life.
TRANIO What countryman, I pray?
PEDANT Of Mantua.
TRANIO Of Mantua, sir? Marry, God forbid,
And come to Padua, careless of your life!
PEDANT My life, sir! How, I pray? For that goes hard.
TRANIO 'Tis death for any one in Mantua
To come to Padua. Know you not the cause?
Your ships are stay'd at Venice; and the Duke,
For private quarrel 'twixt your Duke and him,
Hath publish'd and proclaim'd it openly.
'Tis marvel – but that you are but newly come,
You might have heard it else proclaim'd about.
PEDANT Alas, sir, it is worse for me than so!
For I have bills for money by exchange
From Florence, and must here deliver them.
TRANIO Well, sir, to do you courtesy,
This will I do, and this I will advise you –
First, tell me, have you ever been at Pisa?
PEDANT Ay, sir, in Pisa have I often been,
Pisa renowned for grave citizens.
TRANIO Among them know you one Vincentio?
PEDANT I know him not, but I have heard of him,
A merchant of incomparable wealth.
TRANIO He is my father, sir; and, sooth to say,
In count'nance somewhat doth resemble you.
BIONDELLO [*Aside*] As much as an apple doth an oyster, and all one.
TRANIO To save your life in this extremity,
This favour will I do you for his sake;
And think it not the worst of all your fortunes
That you are like to Sir Vincentio.
His name and credit shall you undertake,

And in my house you shall be friendly lodg'd;
Look that you take upon you as you should.
You understand me, sir. So shall you stay
Till you have done your business in the city.
If this be court'sy, sir, accept of it.

PEDANT O, sir, I do; and will repute you ever
The patron of my life and liberty.

TRANIO Then go with me to make the matter good.
This, by the way, I let you understand:
My father is here look'd for every day
To pass assurance of a dow'r in marriage
'Twixt me and one Baptista's daughter here.
In all these circumstances I'll instruct you.
Go with me to clothe you as becomes you.
[Exeunt.

SCENE III. *Petruchio's house.*

Enter KATHERINA and GRUMIO.

GRUMIO No, no, forsooth; I dare not for my life.

KATHERINA The more my wrong, the more his spite appears.
What, did he marry me to famish me?
Beggars that come unto my father's door
Upon entreaty have a present alms;
If not, elsewhere they meet with charity;
But I, who never knew how to entreat,
Nor never needed that I should entreat,
Am starv'd for meat, giddy for lack of sleep;
With oaths kept waking, and with brawling fed;
And that which spites me more than all these wants –
He does it under name of perfect love;
As who should say, if I should sleep or eat,
'Twere deadly sickness or else present death.
I prithee go and get me some repast;
I care not what, so it be wholesome food.

GRUMIO What say you to a neat's foot?

KATHERINA 'Tis passing good; I prithee let me have it.

GRUMIO I fear it is too choleric a meat.
How say you to a fat tripe finely broil'd?

KATHERINA I like it well; good Grumio, fetch it me.

GRUMIO I cannot tell; I fear 'tis choleric.
What say you to a piece of beef and mustard?

KATHERINA A dish that I do love to feed upon.

GRUMIO Ay, but the mustard is too hot a little.

KATHERINA Why then the beef, and let the mustard rest.

GRUMIO Nay, then I will not; you shall have the mustard,
Or else you get no beef of Grumio.

KATHERINA Then both, or one, or anything thou wilt.

GRUMIO Why then the mustard without the beef.

KATHERINA Go, get thee gone, thou false deluding slave, *[Beats him.*
That feed'st me with the very name of meat.
Sorrow on thee and all the pack of you
That triumph thus upon my misery!
Go, get thee gone, I say.

Enter PETRUCHIO, and HORTENSIO with meat.

PETRUCHIO How fares my Kate? What, sweeting, all amort?

HORTENSIO Mistress, what cheer?

KATHERINA Faith, as cold as can be.

PETRUCHIO Pluck up thy spirits, look cheerfully upon me.
Here, love, thou seest how diligent I am,
To dress thy meat myself, and bring it thee.
I am sure, sweet Kate, this kindness merits thanks.
What, not a word? Nay, then thou lov'st it not,
And all my pains is sorted to no proof.
Here, take away this dish.

KATHERINA I pray you, let it stand.

PETRUCHIO The poorest service is repaid with thanks;
And so shall mine, before you touch the meat.

KATHERINA I thank you, sir.

HORTENSIO Signior Petruchio, fie! you are to blame.
Come, Mistress Kate, I'll bear you company.

PETRUCHIO *[Aside]* Eat it up all, Hortensio, if thou lovest me. –
Much good do it unto thy gentle heart!
Kate, eat apace. And now, my honey love,
Will we return unto thy father's house
And revel it as bravely as the best,
With silken coats and caps, and golden rings,
With ruffs and cuffs and farthingales and things,
With scarfs and fans and double change of brav'ry,
With amber bracelets, beads, and all this knav'ry.
What, hast thou din'd? The tailor stays thy leisure,
To deck thy body with his ruffling treasure.

Enter Tailor.

Come, tailor, let us see these ornaments;
Lay forth the gown.

Enter Haberdasher.

What news with you, sir?

HABERDASHER Here is the cap your worship did bespeak.

PETRUCHIO Why, this was moulded on a porringer;
A velvet dish. Fie, fie! 'tis lewd and filthy;
Why, 'tis a cockle or a walnut-shell,
A knack, a toy, a trick, a baby's cap.

Away with it. Come, let me have a bigger.
KATHERINA I'll have no bigger; this doth fit the time,
And gentlewomen wear such caps as these.
PETRUCHIO When you are gentle, you shall have one too,
And not till then.
HORTENSIO [*Aside*] That will not be in haste.
KATHERINA Why, sir, I trust I may have leave to speak;
And speak I will. I am no child, no babe.
Your betters have endur'd me say my mind,
And if you cannot, best you stop your ears.
My tongue will tell the anger of my heart,
Or else my heart, concealing it, will break;
And rather than it shall, I will be free
Even to the uttermost, as I please, in words.
PETRUCHIO Why, thou say'st true; it is a paltry cap,
A custard-coffin, a bauble, a silken pie;
I love thee well in that thou lik'st it not.
KATHERINA Love me or love me not, I like the cap;
And it I will have, or I will have none.

[*Exit Haberdasher.*

PETRUCHIO Thy gown? Why, ay. Come, tailor, let us see't.
O mercy, God! what masquing stuff is here?
What's this? A sleeve? 'Tis like a demi-cannon.
What, up and down, carv'd like an apple-tart?
Here's snip and nip and cut and slish and slash,
Like to a censer in a barber's shop.
Why, what a devil's name, tailor, call'st thou this?
HORTENSIO [*Aside*] I see she's like to have neither cap nor gown.
TAILOR You bid me make it orderly and well,
According to the fashion and the time.
PETRUCHIO Marry, and did; but if you be remememb'red,
I did not bid you mar it to the time.
Go, hop me over every kennel home,
For you shall hop without my custom, sir.
I'll none of it; hence! make your best of it.
KATHERINA I never saw a better fashion'd gown,
More quaint, more pleasing, nor more commendable;
Belike you mean to make a puppet of me.
PETRUCHIO Why, true; he means to make a puppet of thee.
TAILOR She says your worship means to make a puppet of her.
PETRUCHIO O monstrous arrogance! Thou liest, thou thread, thou thimble,
Thou yard, three-quarters, half-yard, quarter, nail,
Thou flea, thou nit, thou winter-cricket thou –
Brav'd in mine own house with a skein of thread!
Away, thou rag, thou quantity, thou remnant;
Or I shall so bemete thee with thy yard
As thou shalt think on prating whilst thou liv'st!
I tell thee, I, that thou hast marr'd her gown.
TAILOR Your worship is deceiv'd; the gown is made
Just as my master had direction.
Grumio gave order how it should be done.
GRUMIO I gave him no order; I gave him the stuff.
TAILOR But how did you desire it should be made?
GRUMIO Marry, sir, with needle and thread.
TAILOR But did you not request to have it cut?
GRUMIO Thou hast fac'd many things.
TAILOR I have.
GRUMIO Face not me. Thou hast brav'd many men; brave not me. I will neither be fac'd nor brav'd. I say unto thee, I bid thy master cut out the gown; but I did not bid him cut it to pieces. Ergo, thou liest.
TAILOR Why, here is the note of the fashion to testify.
PETRUCHIO Read it.
GRUMIO The note lies in's throat, if he say I said so.
TAILOR [*Reads*] 'Imprimis, a loose-bodied gown' –
GRUMIO Master, if ever I said loose-bodied gown, sew me in the skirts of it and beat me to death with a bottom of brown bread; I said a gown.
PETRUCHIO Proceed.
TAILOR [*Reads*] 'With a small compass'd cape' –
GRUMIO I confess the cape.
TAILOR [*Reads*] 'With a trunk sleeve' –
GRUMIO I confess two sleeves.
TAILOR [*Reads*] 'The sleeves curiously cut.'
PETRUCHIO Ay, there's the villainy.
GRUMIO Error i' th' bill, sir; error i' th' bill! I commanded the sleeves should be cut out, and sew'd up again; and that I'll prove upon thee, though thy little finger be armed in a thimble.
TAILOR This is true that I say; an I had thee in place where, thou shouldst know it.
GRUMIO I am for thee straight; take thou the bill, give me thy mete-yard, and spare not me.
HORTENSIO God-a-mercy, Grumio! Then he shall have no odds.
PETRUCHIO Well, sir, in brief, the gown is not for me.
GRUMIO You are i' th' right, sir; 'tis for my mistress.

PETRUCHIO Go, take it up unto thy master's use.
GRUMIO Villain, not for thy life! Take up my mistress' gown for thy master's use!
PETRUCHIO Why, sir, what's your conceit in that?
GRUMIO O, sir, the conceit is deeper than you think for.
Take up my mistress' gown to his master's use!
O fie, fie, fie!
PETRUCHIO [*Aside*] Hortensio, say thou wilt see the tailor paid. –
Go take it hence; be gone, and say no more.
HORTENSIO Tailor, I'll pay thee for thy gown to-morrow;
Take no unkindness of his hasty words.
Away, I say; commend me to thy master.
[*Exit Tailor.*
PETRUCHIO Well, come, my Kate; we will unto your father's
Even in these honest mean habiliments;
Our purses shall be proud, our garments poor;
For 'tis the mind that makes the body rich;
And as the sun breaks through the darkest clouds,
So honour peereth in the meanest habit.
What, is the jay more precious than the lark
Because his feathers are more beautiful?
Or is the adder better than the eel
Because his painted skin contents the eye?
O no, good Kate; neither art thou the worse
For this poor furniture and mean array.
If thou account'st it shame, lay it on me;
And therefore frolic; we will hence forthwith
To feast and sport us at thy father's house.
Go call my men, and let us straight to him;
And bring our horses unto Long-lane end;
There will we mount, and thither walk on foot.
Let's see; I think 'tis now some seven o'clock,
And well we may come there by dinner-time.
KATHERINA I dare assure you, sir, 'tis almost two,
And 'twill be supper-time ere you come there.
PETRUCHIO It shall be seven ere I go to horse.
Look what I speak, or do, or think to do,
You are still crossing it. Sirs, let't alone;
I will not go to-day; and ere I do,
It shall be what o'clock I say it is.
HORTENSIO Why, so this gallant will command the sun.
[*Exeunt.*

SCENE IV. *Padua. Before Baptista's house.*

Enter TRANIO as Lucentio, and the Pedant dress'd like Vincentio.

TRANIO Sir, this is the house; please it you that I call?
PEDANT Ay, what else? And, but I be deceived,
Signior Baptista may remember me
Near twenty years ago in Genoa,
Where we were lodgers at the Pegasus.
TRANIO 'Tis well; and hold your own, in any case,
With such austerity as longeth to a father.

Enter BIONDELLO.

PEDANT I warrant you. But, sir, here comes your boy;
'Twere good he were school'd.
TRANIO Fear you not him. Sirrah Biondello,
Now do your duty throughly, I advise you.
Imagine 'twere the right Vincentio.
BIONDELLO Tut, fear not me.
TRANIO But hast thou done thy errand to Baptista?
BIONDELLO I told him that your father was at Venice,
And that you look'd for him this day in Padua.
TRANIO Th'art a tall fellow; hold thee that to drink.
Here comes Baptista. Set your countenance, sir.

Enter BAPTISTA, and LUCENTIO as Cambio.

Signior Baptista, you are happily met.
[*To the Pedant*] Sir, this is the gentleman I told you of;
I pray you stand good father to me now;
Give me Bianca for my patrimony.
PEDANT Soft, son!
Sir, by your leave: having come to Padua
To gather in some debts, my son Lucentio
Made me acquainted with a weighty cause
Of love between your daughter and himself;
And – for the good report I hear of you,
And for the love he beareth to your daughter,
And she to him – to stay him not too long,
I am content, in a good father's care,
To have him match'd; and, if you please to like
No worse than I, upon some agreement
Me shall you find ready and willing
With one consent to have her so bestow'd;
For curious I cannot be with you,
Signior Baptista, of whom I hear so well.
BAPTISTA Sir, pardon me in what I have to say.
Your plainness and your shortness please me well.
Right true it is your son Lucentio here
Doth love my daughter, and she loveth him,
Or both dissemble deeply their affections;
And therefore, if you say no more than this,
That like a father you will deal with him,
And pass my daughter a sufficient dower,
The match is made, and all is done –
Your son shall have my daughter with consent.
TRANIO I thank you, sir. Where then do you know best

We be affied, and such assurance ta'en
As shall with either part's agreement stand?

BAPTISTA Not in my house, Lucentio, for you know
Pitchers have ears, and I have many servants;
Besides, old Gremio is heark'ning still,
And happily we might be interrupted.

TRANIO Then at my lodging, an it like you.
There doth my father lie; and there this night
We'll pass the business privately and well.
Send for your daughter by your servant here;
My boy shall fetch the scrivener presently.
The worst is this, that at so slender warning
You are like to have a thin and slender pittance.

BAPTISTA It likes me well. Cambio, hie you home,
And bid Bianca make her ready straight;
And, if you will, tell what hath happened –
Lucentio's father is arriv'd in Padua,
And how she's like to be Lucentio's wife.
[Exit Lucentio.

BIONDELLO I pray the gods she may, with all my heart.

TRANIO Dally not with the gods, but get thee gone. *[Exit Biondello.*
Signior Baptista, shall I lead the way?
Welcome! One mess is like to be your cheer;
Come, sir; we will better it in Pisa.

BAPTISTA I follow you. *[Exeunt.*

Re-enter LUCENTIO as Cambio, and BIONDELLO.

BIONDELLO Cambio.

LUCENTIO What say'st thou, Biondello?

BIONDELLO You saw my master wink and laugh upon you?

LUCENTIO Biondello, what of that?

BIONDELLO Faith, nothing; but has left me here behind to expound the meaning or moral of his signs and tokens.

LUCENTIO I pray thee moralize them.

BIONDELLO Then thus: Baptista is safe, talking with the deceiving father of a deceitful son.

LUCENTIO And what of him?

BIONDELLO His daughter is to be brought by you to the supper.

LUCENTIO And then?

BIONDELLO The old priest at Saint Luke's church is at your command at all hours.

LUCENTIO And what of all this?

BIONDELLO I cannot tell, except they are busied about a counterfeit assurance. Take your assurance of her, cum privilegio ad imprimendum solum; to th' church take the priest, clerk, and some sufficient honest witnesses.
If this be not that you look for, I have no more to say,
But bid Bianca farewell for ever and a day.

LUCENTIO Hear'st thou, Biondello?

BIONDELLO I cannot tarry. I knew a wench married in an afternoon as she went to the garden for parsley to stuff a rabbit; and so may you, sir; and so adieu, sir. My master hath appointed me to go to Saint Luke's to bid the priest be ready to come against you come with your appendix. *[Exit.*

LUCENTIO I may and will, if she be so contented.
She will be pleas'd; then wherefore should I doubt?
Hap what hap may, I'll roundly go about her;
It shall go hard if Cambio go without her.
[Exit.

SCENE V. *A public road.*

Enter PETRUCHIO, KATHERINA, HORTENSIO, and Servants.

PETRUCHIO Come on, a God's name; once more toward our father's.
Good Lord, how bright and goodly shines the moon!

KATHERINA The moon? The sun! It is not moonlight now.

PETRUCHIO I say it is the moon that shines so bright.

KATHERINA I know it is the sun that shines so bright.

PETRUCHIO Now by my mother's son, and that's myself,
It shall be moon, or star, or what I list,
Or ere I journey to your father's house.
Go on and fetch our horses back again.
Evermore cross'd and cross'd; nothing but cross'd!

HORTENSIO Say as he says, or we shall never go.

KATHERINA Forward, I pray, since we have come so far,
And be it moon, or sun, or what you please;
And if you please to call it a rush-candle,
Henceforth I vow it shall be so for me.

PETRUCHIO I say it is the moon.

KATHERINA I know it is the moon.

PETRUCHIO Nay, then you lie; it is the blessed sun.

KATHERINA Then, God be bless'd, it is the blessed sun;
But sun it is not, when you say it is not;
And the moon changes even as your mind.
What you will have it nam'd, even that it is,
And so it shall be so for Katherine.

HORTENSIO Petruchio, go thy ways, the field is won.

PETRUCHIO Well, forward, forward! thus the bowl should run,

And not unluckily against the bias.
But, soft! Company is coming here.

Enter VINCENTIO.

[*To Vincentio*] Good-morrow, gentle mistress; where away? –
Tell me, sweet Kate, and tell me truly too,
Hast thou beheld a fresher gentlewoman?
Such war of white and red within her cheeks!
What stars do spangle heaven with such beauty
As those two eyes become that heavenly face?
Fair lovely maid, once more good day to thee.
Sweet Kate, embrace her for her beauty's sake.

HORTENSIO 'A will make the man mad, to make a woman of him.

KATHERINA Young budding virgin, fair and fresh and sweet,
Whither away, or where is thy abode?
Happy the parents of so fair a child;
Happier the man whom favourable stars
Allots thee for his lovely bed-fellow.

PETRUCHIO Why, how now, Kate, I hope thou art not mad!
This is a man, old, wrinkled, faded, withered,
And not a maiden, as thou sayst he is.

KATHERINA Pardon, old father, my mistaking eyes,
That have been so bedazzled with the sun
That everything I look on seemeth green;
Now I perceive thou art a reverend father.
Pardon, I pray thee, for my mad mistaking.

PETRUCHIO Do, good old grandsire, and withal make known
Which way thou travellest – if along with us,
We shall be joyful of thy company.

VINCENTIO Fair sir, and you my merry mistress,
That with your strange encounter much amaz'd me,
My name is call'd Vincentio, my dwelling Pisa,
And bound I am to Padua, there to visit
A son of mine, which long I have not seen.

PETRUCHIO What is his name?

VINCENTIO Lucentio, gentle sir.

PETRUCHIO Happily met; the happier for thy son.
And now by law, as well as reverend age,
I may entitle thee my loving father:
The sister to my wife, this gentlewoman,
Thy son by this hath married. Wonder not,
Nor be not grieved – she is of good esteem,
Her dowry wealthy, and of worthy birth;
Beside, so qualified as may beseem
The spouse of any noble gentleman.
Let me embrace with old Vincentio;
And wander we to see thy honest son,
Who will of thy arrival be full joyous.

VINCENTIO But is this true; or is it else your pleasure,
Like pleasant travellers, to break a jest
Upon the company you overtake?

HORTENSIO I do assure thee, father, so it is.

PETRUCHIO Come, go along, and see the truth hereof;
For our first merriment hath made thee jealous.

[*Exeunt all but Hortensio.*

HORTENSIO Well, Petruchio, this has put me in heart.
Have to my widow; and if she be froward,
Then hast thou taught Hortensio to be untoward. [*Exit.*

ACT FIVE

SCENE I. *Padua. Before Lucentio's house.*

Enter BIONDELLO, LUCENTIO, and BIANCA; GREMIO is out before.

BIONDELLO Softly and swiftly, sir, for the priest is ready.

LUCENTIO I fly, Biondello; but they may chance to need thee at home, therefore leave us.

BIONDELLO Nay, faith, I'll see the church a your back, and then come back to my master's as soon as I can.

[*Exeunt Lucentio, Bianca, and Biondello.*

GREMIO I marvel Cambio comes not all this while.

Enter PETRUCHIO, KATHERINA, VINCENTIO, GRUMIO, and Attendants.

PETRUCHIO Sir, here's the door; this is Lucentio's house;
My father's bears more toward the marketplace;
Thither must I, and here I leave you, sir.

VINCENTIO You shall not choose but drink before you go;
I think I shall command your welcome here,
And by all likelihood some cheer is toward.

[*Knocks.*

GREMIO They're busy within; you were best knock louder.

Pedant looks out of the window.

PEDANT What's he that knocks as he would beat down the gate?

VINCENTIO Is Signior Lucentio within, sir?

PEDANT He's within, sir, but not to be spoken withal.

VINCENTIO What if a man bring him a hundred pound or two to make merry withal?

PEDANT Keep your hundred pounds to yourself; he shall need none so long as I live.

PETRUCHIO Nay, I told you your son was well beloved in Padua. Do you hear, sir? To leave frivolous circumstances, I pray you tell Signior Lucentio that his father is come from Pisa, and is here at the door to speak with him.

PEDANT Thou liest: his father is come from Padua, and here looking out at the window.

VINCENTIO Art thou his father?

PEDANT Ay, sir; so his mother says, if I may believe her.

PETRUCHIO [*To Vincentio*] Why, how now, gentleman! Why, this is flat knavery to take upon you another man's name.

PEDANT Lay hands on the villain; I believe 'a means to cozen somebody in this city under my countenance.

Re-enter BIONDELLO.

BIONDELLO I have seen them in the church together. God send 'em good shipping! But who is here? Mine old master, Vincentio! Now we are undone and brought to nothing.

VINCENTIO [*Seeing Biondello*] Come hither, crack-hemp.

BIONDELLO I hope I may choose, sir.

VINCENTIO Come hither, you rogue. What, have you forgot me?

BIONDELLO Forgot you! No, sir. I could not forget you, for I never saw you before in all my life.

VINCENTIO What, you notorious villain, didst thou never see thy master's father, Vincentio?

BIONDELLO What, my old worshipful old master? Yes, marry, sir; see where he looks out of the window.

VINCENTIO Is't so, indeed? [*He beats Biondello.*

BIONDELLO Help, help, help! Here's a madman will murder me. [*Exit.*

PEDANT Help, son! help, Signior Baptista!

[*Exit from above.*

PETRUCHIO Prithee, Kate, let's stand aside and see the end of this controversy.

[*They stand aside.*

Re-enter Pedant below; BAPTISTA, TRANIO, and Servants.

TRANIO Sir, what are you that offer to beat my servant?

VINCENTIO What am I, sir? Nay, what are you, sir? O immortal gods! O fine villain! A silken doublet, a velvet hose, a scarlet cloak, and a copatain hat! O, I am undone! I am undone! While I play the good husband at home, my son and my servant spend all at the university.

TRANIO How now! what's the matter?

BAPTISTA What, is the man lunatic?

TRANIO Sir, you seem a sober ancient gentleman by your habit, but your words show you a madman. Why, sir, what 'cerns it you if I wear pearl and gold? I thank my good father, I am able to maintain it.

VINCENTIO Thy father! O villain! he is a sailmaker in Bergamo.

BAPTISTA You mistake, sir; you mistake, sir. Pray, what do you think is his name?

VINCENTIO His name! As if I knew not his name! I have brought him up ever since he was three years old, and his name is Tranio.

PEDANT Away, away, mad ass! His name is Lucentio; and he is mine only son, and heir to the lands of me, Signior Vincentio.

VINCENTIO Lucentio! O, he hath murd'red his master! Lay hold on him, I charge you, in the Duke's name. O, my son, my son! Tell me, thou villain, where is my son, Lucentio?

TRANIO Call forth an officer.

Enter One with an Officer.

Carry this mad knave to the gaol. Father Baptista, I charge you see that he be forthcoming.

VINCENTIO Carry me to the gaol!

GREMIO Stay, Officer; he shall not go to prison.

BAPTISTA Talk not, Signior Gremio; I say he shall go to prison.

GREMIO Take heed, Signior Baptista, lest you be cony-catch'd in this business; I dare swear this is the right Vincentio.

PEDANT Swear if thou dar'st.

GREMIO Nay, I dare not swear it.

TRANIO Then thou wert best say that I am not Lucentio.

GREMIO Yes, I know thee to be Signior Lucentio.

BAPTISTA Away with the dotard; to the gaol with him!

VINCENTIO Thus strangers may be hal'd and abus'd. O monstrous villain!

Re-enter BIONDELLO, with LUCENTIO and BIANCA.

BIONDELLO O, we are spoil'd; and yonder he is! Deny him, forswear him, or else we are all undone.

[*Exeunt Biondello, Tranio, and Pedant, as fast as may be.*

LUCENTIO [*Kneeling*] Pardon, sweet father.

VINCENTIO Lives my sweet son?
BIANCA Pardon, dear father.
BAPTISTA How hast thou offended?
Where is Lucentio?
LUCENTIO Here's Lucentio,
Right son to the right Vincentio,
That have by marriage made thy daughter mine,
While counterfeit supposes blear'd thine eyne.

GREMIO Here's packing, with a witness, to deceive us all!

VINCENTIO Where is that damned villain, Tranio,
That fac'd and brav'd me in this matter so?
BAPTISTA Why, tell me, is not this my Cambio?
BIANCA Cambio is chang'd into Lucentio.
LUCENTIO Love wrought these miracles. Bianca's love
Made me exchange my state with Tranio,
While he did bear my countenance in the town;
And happily I have arrived at the last
Unto the wished haven of my bliss.
What Tranio did, myself enforc'd him to;
Then pardon him, sweet father, for my sake.

VINCENTIO I'll slit the villain's nose that would have sent me to the gaol.

BAPTISTA [*To Lucentio*] But do you hear, sir? Have you married my daughter without asking my good will?

VINCENTIO Fear not, Baptista; we will content you, go to; but I will in to be revenged for this villainy. [*Exit.*

BAPTISTA And I to sound the depth of this knavery. [*Exit.*

LUCENTIO Look not pale, Bianca; thy father will not frown. [*Exeunt Lucentio and Bianca.*

GREMIO My cake is dough, but I'll in among the rest;
Out of hope of all but my share of the feast.
[*Exit.*

KATHERINA Husband, let's follow to see the end of this ado.
PETRUCHIO First kiss me, Kate, and we will.
KATHERINA What, in the midst of the street?
PETRUCHIO What, art thou asham'd of me?
KATHERINA No, sir; God forbid; but asham'd to kiss.
PETRUCHIO Why, then, let's home again. Come, sirrah, let's away.
KATHERINA Nay, I will give thee a kiss; now pray thee, love, stay.
PETRUCHIO Is not this well? Come, my sweet Kate:
Better once than never, for never too late.
[*Exeunt.*

SCENE II. *Lucentio's house.*

Enter BAPTISTA, VINCENTIO, GREMIO, the Pedant, LUCENTIO, BIANCA, PETRUCHIO, KATHERINA, HORTENSIO, and Widow. The Servants with TRANIO, BIONDELLO, and GRUMIO, bringing in a banquet.

LUCENTIO At last, though long, our jarring notes agree;
And time it is when raging war is done
To smile at scapes and perils overblown.
My fair Bianca, bid my father welcome,
While I with self-same kindness welcome thine.
Brother Petruchio, sister Katherina,
And thou, Hortensio, with thy loving widow,
Feast with the best, and welcome to my house.
My banquet is to close our stomachs up
After our great good cheer. Pray you, sit down;
For now we sit to chat as well as eat. [*They sit.*
PETRUCHIO Nothing but sit and sit, and eat and eat!
BAPTISTA Padua affords this kindness, son Petruchio.
PETRUCHIO Padua affords nothing but what is kind.
HORTENSIO For both our sakes I would that word were true.
PETRUCHIO Now, for my life, Hortensio fears his widow.
WIDOW Then never trust me if I be afeard.
PETRUCHIO You are very sensible, and yet you miss my sense:
I mean Hortensio is afeard of you.
WIDOW He that is giddy thinks the world turns round.
PETRUCHIO Roundly replied.
KATHERINA Mistress, how mean you that?
WIDOW Thus I conceive by him.
PETRUCHIO Conceives by me! How likes Hortensio that?
HORTENSIO My widow says thus she conceives her tale.
PETRUCHIO Very well mended. Kiss him for that, good widow.
KATHERINA 'He that is giddy thinks the world turns round.'
I pray you tell me what you meant by that.
WIDOW Your husband, being troubled with a shrew,
Measures my husband's sorrow by his woe;
And now you know my meaning.
KATHERINA A very mean meaning.
WIDOW Right, I mean you.
KATHERINA And I am mean, indeed, respecting you.
PETRUCHIO To her, Kate!
HORTENSIO To her, widow!

PETRUCHIO A hundred marks, my Kate does put her down.
HORTENSIO That's my office.
PETRUCHIO Spoke like an officer – ha' to thee, lad. [*Drinks to Hortensio.*
BAPTISTA How likes Gremio these quick-witted folks?
GREMIO Believe me, sir, they butt together well.
BIANCA Head and butt! An hasty-witted body
Would say your head and butt were head and horn.
VINCENTIO Ay, mistress bride, hath that awakened you?
BIANCA Ay, but not frighted me; therefore I'll sleep again.
PETRUCHIO Nay, that you shall not; since you have begun,
Have at you for a bitter jest or two.
BIANCA Am I your bird? I mean to shift my bush,
And then pursue me as you draw your bow.
You are welcome all.
[*Exeunt Bianca, Katherina, and Widow.*
PETRUCHIO She hath prevented me. Here, Signior Tranio,
This bird you aim'd at, though you hit her not;
Therefore a health to all that shot and miss'd.
TRANIO O, sir, Lucentio slipp'd me like his greyhound,
Which runs himself, and catches for his master.
PETRUCHIO A good swift simile, but something currish.
TRANIO 'Tis well, sir, that you hunted for yourself;
'Tis thought your deer does hold you at a bay.
BAPTISTA O, O, Petruchio! Tranio hits you now.
LUCENTIO I thank thee for that gird, good Tranio.
HORTENSIO Confess, confess; hath he not hit you here?
PETRUCHIO 'A has a little gall'd me, I confess;
And, as the jest did glance away from me,
'Tis ten to one it maim'd you two outright.
BAPTISTA Now, in good sadness, son Petruchio,
I think thou hast the veriest shrew of all.
PETRUCHIO Well, I say no; and therefore, for assurance,
Let's each one send unto his wife,
And he whose wife is most obedient,
To come at first when he doth send for her,
Shall win the wager which we will propose.
HORTENSIO Content. What's the wager?
LUCENTIO Twenty crowns.
PETRUCHIO Twenty crowns!
I'll venture so much of my hawk or hound,
But twenty times so much upon my wife.
LUCENTIO A hundred then.
HORTENSIO Content.
PETRUCHIO A match! 'tis done.
HORTENSIO Who shall begin?
LUCENTIO That will I.
Go, Biondello, bid your mistress come to me.
BIONDELLO I go. [*Exit.*
BAPTISTA Son, I'll be your half Bianca comes.
LUCENTIO I'll have no halves; I'll bear it all myself.

Re-enter BIONDELLO.

How now! what news?
BIONDELLO Sir, my mistress sends you word
That she is busy and she cannot come.
PETRUCHIO How! She's busy, and she cannot come!
Is that an answer?
GREMIO Ay, and a kind one too.
Pray God, sir, your wife send you not a worse.
PETRUCHIO I hope better.
HORTENSIO Sirrah Biondello, go and entreat my wife
To come to me forthwith. [*Exit Biondello.*
PETRUCHIO O, ho! entreat her!
Nay, then she must needs come.
HORTENSIO I am afraid, sir,
Do what you can, yours will not be entreated.

Re-enter BIONDELLO.

Now, where's my wife?
BIONDELLO She says you have some goodly jest in hand:
She will not come; she bids you come to her.
PETRUCHIO Worse and worse; she will not come! O vile,
Intolerable, not to be endur'd!
Sirrah Grumio, go to your mistress;
Say I command her come to me. [*Exit Grumio.*
HORTENSIO I know her answer.
PETRUCHIO What?
HORTENSIO She will not.
PETRUCHIO The fouler fortune mine, and there an end.

Re-enter KATHERINA.

BAPTISTA Now, by my holidame, here comes Katherina!
KATHERINA What is your will, sir, that you send for me?
PETRUCHIO Where is your sister, and Hortensio's wife?
KATHERINA They sit conferring by the parlour fire.
PETRUCHIO Go, fetch them hither; if they deny to come,
Swinge me them soundly forth unto their husbands.

Away, I say, and bring them hither straight.
[*Exit Katherina.*

LUCENTIO Here is a wonder, if you talk of a wonder.

HORTENSIO And so it is. I wonder what it bodes.

PETRUCHIO Marry, peace it bodes, and love, and quiet life,
An awful rule, and right supremacy;
And, to be short, what not that's sweet and happy.

BAPTISTA Now fair befall thee, good Petruchio!
The wager thou hast won; and I will add
Unto their losses twenty thousand crowns;
Another dowry to another daughter,
For she is chang'd, as she had never been.

PETRUCHIO Nay, I will win my wager better yet,
And show more sign of her obedience,
Her new-built virtue and obedience.

Re-enter KATHERINA with BIANCA and Widow.

See where she comes, and brings your froward wives
As prisoners to her womanly persuasion.
Katherine, that cap of yours becomes you not:
Off with that bauble, throw it underfoot.
[*Katherina complies.*

WIDOW Lord, let me never have a cause to sigh.
Till I be brought to such a silly pass!

BIANCA Fie! what a foolish duty call you this?

LUCENTIO I would your duty were as foolish too;
The wisdom of your duty, fair Bianca,
Hath cost me a hundred crowns since supper-time!

BIANCA The more fool you for laying on my duty.

PETRUCHIO Katherine, I charge thee, tell these headstrong women
What duty they do owe their lords and husbands.

WIDOW Come, come, you're mocking; we will have no telling.

PETRUCHIO Come on, I say; and first begin with her.

WIDOW She shall not.

PETRUCHIO I say she shall. And first begin with her.

KATHERINA Fie, fie! unknit that threatening unkind brow,
And dart not scornful glances from those eyes
To wound thy lord, thy king, thy governor.
It blots thy beauty as frosts do bite the meads,
Confounds thy fame as whirlwinds shake fair buds,
And in no sense is meet or amiable.
A woman mov'd is like a fountain troubled –
Muddy, ill-seeming, thick, bereft of beauty;
And while it is so, none so dry or thirsty
Will deign to sip or touch one drop of it.
Thy husband is thy lord, thy life, thy keeper,
Thy head, thy sovereign; one that cares for thee,
And for thy maintenance commits his body
To painful labour both by sea and land,
To watch the night in storms, the day in cold,
Whilst thou liest warm at home, secure and safe;
And craves no other tribute at thy hands
But love, fair looks, and true obedience –
Too little payment for so great a debt.
Such duty as the subject owes the prince,
Even such a woman oweth to her husband;
And when she is froward, peevish, sullen, sour,
And not obedient to his honest will,
What is she but a foul contending rebel
And graceless traitor to her loving lord?
I am asham'd that women are so simple
To offer war where they should kneel for peace;
Or seek for rule, supremacy, and sway,
When they are bound to serve, love, and obey.
Why are our bodies soft and weak and smooth,
Unapt to toil and trouble in the world,
But that our soft conditions and our hearts
Should well agree with our external parts?
Come, come, you froward and unable worms!
My mind hath been as big as one of yours,
My heart as great, my reason haply more,
To bandy word for word and frown for frown;
But now I see our lances are but straws,
Our strength as weak, our weakness past compare,
That seeming to be most which we indeed least are.
Then vail your stomachs, for it is no boot,
And place your hands below your husband's foot;
In token of which duty, if he please,
My hand is ready, may it do him ease.

PETRUCHIO Why, there's a wench! Come on, and kiss me, Kate.

LUCENTIO Well, go thy ways, old lad, for thou shalt ha't.

VINCENTIO 'Tis a good hearing when children are toward.

LUCENTIO But a harsh hearing when women are froward.

PETRUCHIO Come, Kate, we'll to bed.
We three are married, but you two are sped.
[*To Lucentio*] 'Twas I won the wager, though you hit the white;
And being a winner, God give you good night!
[*Exeunt Petruchio and Katherina.*

HORTENSIO Now go thy ways; thou hast tam'd a curst shrow.

LUCENTIO 'Tis a wonder, by your leave, she will be tam'd so. [*Exeunt.*

All's Well That Ends Well

Introduction by ALEC YEARLING

Often cited as a 'Problem Play', *All's Well* conforms pretty nearly to Shakespeare's usual comic practice of uniting lovers after disruption and separation. The comic tone is reinforced by a sub-action in which a cowardly braggart is shown in his true colours. But there are asymmetries and questionable matters which have given readers and spectators pause, though in no case is the 'problematic' material without parallel elsewhere in Shakespeare's work. Girl, here, gets Boy, despite his doing everything in his power to evade her (but so had the relationship in *The Taming of the Shrew* misfired until the close). Girl has obtained her title to Boy in a formalised ceremony (but so was Portia won in *The Merchant of Venice*). Girl finally secures Boy by taking another's place in his darkened bed (but thus is Angelo diverted towards a right course of life in *Measure for Measure*). These events belong to folk tales, where characters are manoeuvred until a pattern obtains which satisfies whatever conditions the narrative has set up: a desire fulfilled, a vow performed, falsehood exposed. Neatness and ingenuity prevail in such stories. The people are pawns valued for their ardour or their cunning.

Pawns are conventionally made of wood; and one could say that here Shakespeare's ability to suggest fine shades of personality prevents him from doing the right thing by the folk tale, which would be to suppress 'character' and emphasise narrative processes. Thus whereas we could approve this plot's low-born heroine with amused detachment as she single-mindedly lies and cheats her way towards the nobleman who has spurned her, we feel differently when that heroine is Helena, humble and exalted, repeatedly linked in the play's imagery with sacred values. Bertram, too, is not just an object of pursuit, but an uncomfortably detailed study of a vigorous young aristocrat who will fight to preserve his freedom and pleasures. These characters inhabit an unstable world where merry (and contrived) tricks coexist with autumnal meditations on youth and age, respect and value. The old Countess of Rossillion, dignified, restrained, and peripheral to the plot, hardly exists in the same arena of the imagination as the King of France, whose essentiality in the narrative is supported by no particular individualising touch. The third scene of Act 2 brings the various elements strikingly together. Helena, the King's saviour, is allowed her choice of husband. In virginal simplicity she dedicates herself to 'imperial Love' and the candidates present themselves. The dialogue moves into rhymed couplets. The effect is as mannered and sweetly artificial as anything in *Love's Labour's Lost*. Then when she chooses Bertram, long the object of her heart's desire, the rhyming stops. He rejects her, seeing no necessary connection between the King's restoration to health and his having to take a wife; furthermore, he has never liked Helena. Palpably embarrassed, she seeks to withdraw. The King enforces the marriage, and Bertram flees the country, stating seemingly impossible conditions before he will regard himself as married. One fairytale lies smashed by a participant who refuses to acknowledge how fairytales work; another, this time a quest, straightway rises up in its stead.

It may have been that Shakespeare found a challenge in such disparities and tonal jolts. But what is odder than a healthy interest in stylistic juxtapositions, is that the dramatist did not steer towards a safer haven than is afforded by his final scene, which requires a reformed Bertram. Parolles has been in some sort Bertram's evil genius. An elaborate comic exposure of Parolles' hollowness takes place in the fourth act: what more convenient than to start the hero at this point on his path to reintegration? Free of misguidance, a change in his character promised by the report at the opening of Act 4 Scene 3, Bertram would be ready for Helena's healing love. But Shakespeare refuses. Cornered, Bertram lies, blackens others, does all he can to preserve his grimy selfhood and reputation, until caving in when it is proved that Helena has indeed won him. And was he worth the winning? we may wonder. Consistency in Bertram undercuts the play's scheme. Perhaps its title is ironic. There is no evidence of its having been staged in Shakespeare's day.

All's Well That Ends Well

DRAMATIS PERSONAE

THE KING OF FRANCE

THE DUKE OF FLORENCE

BERTRAM
Count of Rousillon

LAFEU
an old lord

PAROLLES
a follower of Bertram

Two French Lords serving with Bertram

Steward, LAVACHE, a clown, A Page
servants to the Countess of Rousillon

COUNTESS OF ROUSILLON
mother to Bertram

HELENA
a gentlewoman protected by the Countess

A Widow of Florence

DIANA
daughter to the Widow

VIOLENTA, MARIANA
neighbours and friends to the Widow

Lords, Officers, Soldiers, etc., French and Florentine.

THE SCENE: ROUSILLON; PARIS; FLORENCE; MARSEILLES.

ACT ONE

SCENE I. *Rousillon. The Count's palace.*

Enter BERTRAM, the COUNTESS OF ROUSILLON, HELENA, and LAFEU, all in black.

COUNTESS In delivering my son from me, I bury a second husband.

BERTRAM And I in going, madam, weep o'er my father's death anew; but I must attend his Majesty's command, to whom I am now in ward, evermore in subjection.

LAFEU You shall find of the King a husband, madam; you, sir, a father. He that so generally is at all times good must of necessity hold his virtue to you, whose worthiness would stir it up where it wanted, rather than lack it where there is such abundance.

COUNTESS What hope is there of his Majesty's amendment?

LAFEU He hath abandon'd his physicians, madam; under whose practices he hath persecuted time with hope, and finds no other advantage in the process but only the losing of hope by time.

COUNTESS This young gentlewoman had a father – O, that 'had', how sad a passage 'tis! – whose skill was almost as great as his honesty; had it stretch'd so far, would have made nature immortal, and death should have play for lack of work. Would, for the King's sake, he were living! I think it would be the death of the King's disease.

LAFEU How call'd you the man you speak of, madam?

COUNTESS He was famous, sir, in his profession, and it was his great right to be so – Gerard de Narbon.

LAFEU He was excellent indeed, madam; the King very lately spoke of him admiringly and mourningly; he was skilful enough to have liv'd still, if knowledge could be set up against mortality.

BERTRAM What is it, my good lord, the King languishes of?

LAFEU A fistula, my lord.

BERTRAM I heard not of it before.

LAFEU I would it were not notorious. Was this gentlewoman the daughter of Gerard de Narbon?

COUNTESS His sole child, my lord, and bequeathed to my overlooking. I have those hopes of her good that her education promises; her dispositions she inherits, which makes fair gifts fairer; for where an unclean mind carries virtuous qualities, there commendations go with pity – they are virtues and traitors too. In her they are the better for their simpleness; she derives her honesty, and achieves her goodness.

LAFEU Your commendations, madam, get from her tears.

COUNTESS 'Tis the best brine a maiden can season her praise in. The remembrance of her father never approaches her heart but the tyranny of her sorrows takes all livelihood from her cheek. No more of this, Helena; go to, no more, lest it be rather thought you affect a sorrow than to have –

HELENA I do affect a sorrow indeed, but I have it too.

LAFEU Moderate lamentation is the right of the dead: excessive grief the enemy to the living.

COUNTESS If the living be enemy to the grief, the excess makes it soon mortal.

BERTRAM Madam, I desire your holy wishes.

LAFEU How understand we that?

COUNTESS Be thou blest, Bertram, and succeed thy father
In manners, as in shape! Thy blood and virtue
Contend for empire in thee, and thy goodness
Share with thy birthright! Love all, trust a few,
Do wrong to none; be able for thine enemy
Rather in power than use, and keep thy friend
Under thy own life's key; be check'd for silence,
But never tax'd for speech. What heaven more will,
That thee may furnish, and my prayers pluck down,
Fall on thy head! Farewell. My lord,
'Tis an unseason'd courtier; good my lord,
Advise him.

LAFEU He cannot want the best
That shall attend his love.

COUNTESS Heaven bless him! Farewell, Bertram.
[Exit Countess.

BERTRAM The best wishes that can be forg'd in your thoughts be servants to you! *[To Helena]* Be comfortable to my mother, your mistress, and make much of her.

LAFEU Farewell, pretty lady; you must hold the credit of your father.

[Exeunt Bertram and Lafeu.

HELENA O, were that all! I think not on my father;
And these great tears grace his remembrance more
Than those I shed for him. What was he like?
I have forgot him; my imagination
Carries no favour in't but Bertram's.
I am undone; there is no living, none,
If Bertram be away. 'Twere all one
That I should love a bright particular star
And think to wed it, he is so above me.
In his bright radiance and collateral light
Must I be comforted, not in his sphere.
Th' ambition in my love thus plagues itself:
The hind that would be mated by the lion
Must die for love. 'Twas pretty, though a plague,
To see him every hour; to sit and draw
His arched brows, his hawking eye, his curls,
In our heart's table – heart too capable
Of every line and trick of his sweet favour.
But now he's gone, and my idolatrous fancy
Must sanctify his relics. Who comes here?

Enter PAROLLES.

[Aside] One that goes with him. I love him for his sake;
And yet I know him a notorious liar,
Think him a great way fool, solely a coward;
Yet these fix'd evils sit so fit in him
That they take place when virtue's steely bones
Looks bleak i' th' cold wind; withal, full oft we see
Cold wisdom waiting on superfluous folly.

PAROLLES Save you, fair queen!

HELENA And you, monarch!

PAROLLES No.

HELENA And no.

PAROLLES Are you meditating on virginity?

HELENA Ay. You have some stain of soldier in you; let me ask you a question. Man is enemy to virginity; how may we barricado it against him?

PAROLLES Keep him out.

HELENA But he assails; and our virginity, though valiant in the defence, yet is weak. Unfold to us some warlike resistance.

PAROLLES There is none. Man, setting down before you, will undermine you and blow you up.

HELENA Bless our poor virginity from underminers and blowers-up! Is there no military policy how virgins might blow up men?

PAROLLES Virginity being blown down, man will quicklier be blown up; marry, in blowing him down again, with the breach yourselves made, you lose your city. It is not politic in the commonwealth of nature to preserve virginity. Loss of virginity is rational increase; and there was never virgin got till virginity was first lost. That you were made of is metal to make virgins. Virginity by being once lost may be ten times found; by being ever kept, it is ever lost. 'Tis too cold a companion; away with't.

HELENA I will stand for 't a little, though therefore I die a virgin.

PAROLLES There's little can be said in't; 'tis against the rule of nature. To speak on the part of virginity is to accuse your mothers; which is most infallible disobedience. He that hangs himself is a virgin; virginity murders itself, and should be buried in highways, out of all sanctified limit, as a desperate offendress against nature. Virginity breeds mites, much like a cheese; consumes itself to the very paring, and so dies with feeding his own stomach. Besides, virginity is peevish, proud, idle, made of self-love, which is the most inhibited sin in the canon. Keep it not; you cannot choose but lose by't. Out with't. Within ten year it will make itself ten, which is a goodly increase; and the principal itself not much the worse. Away with't.

HELENA How might one do, sir, to lose it to her own liking?

PAROLLES Let me see. Marry, ill to like him that ne'er it likes. 'Tis a commodity will lose the gloss with lying; the longer kept, the less worth. Off with't while 'tis vendible; answer the time of request. Virginity, like an old courtier, wears her cap out of fashion, richly suited but unsuitable; just like the brooch and the toothpick, which wear not now. Your date is better in your pie and your porridge than in your cheek. And your virginity, your old virginity, is like one of our French wither'd pears: it looks ill, it eats drily; marry, 'tis a wither'd pear; it was formerly better; marry, yet 'tis a wither'd pear. Will you anything with it?

HELENA Not my virginity yet.
There shall your master have a thousand loves,
A mother, and a mistress, and a friend,
A phoenix, captain, and an enemy,
A guide, a goddess, and a sovereign,
A counsellor, a traitress, and a dear;
His humble ambition, proud humility,
His jarring concord, and his discord dulcet,
His faith, his sweet disaster; with a world
Of pretty, fond, adoptious christendoms
That blinking Cupid gossips. Now shall he –
I know not what he shall. God send him well!
The court's a learning-place, and he is one –

PAROLLES What one, i' faith?

HELENA That I wish well. 'Tis pity –

PAROLLES What's pity?

HELENA That wishing well had not a body in't
Which might be felt; that we, the poorer born,
Whose baser stars do shut us up in wishes,
Might with effects of them follow our friends
And show what we alone must think, which never
Returns us thanks.

Enter Page.

PAGE Monsieur Parolles, my lord calls for you. [*Exit Page.*

PAROLLES Little Helen, farewell; if I can remember thee, I will think of thee at court.

HELENA Monsieur Parolles, you were born under a charitable star.

PAROLLES Under Mars, I.

HELENA I especially think, under Mars.

PAROLLES Why under Mars?

HELENA The wars hath so kept you under that you must needs be born under Mars.

PAROLLES When he was predominant.

HELENA When he was retrograde, I think, rather.

PAROLLES Why think you so?

HELENA You go so much backward when you fight.

PAROLLES That's for advantage.

HELENA So is running away, when fear proposes the safety; but the composition that your valour and fear makes in you is a virtue of a good wing, and I like the wear well.

PAROLLES I am so full of businesses I cannot answer thee acutely. I will return perfect courtier; in the which my instruction shall serve to naturalize thee, so thou wilt be capable of a courtier's counsel, and understand what advice shall thrust upon thee; else thou diest in thine unthankfulness, and thine ignorance makes thee away. Farewell. When thou hast leisure, say thy prayers; when thou hast none, remember thy friends. Get thee a good husband, and use him as he uses thee. So, farewell. [*Exit.*

HELENA Our remedies oft in ourselves do lie,
Which we ascribe to heaven. The fated sky
Gives us free scope; only doth backward pull
Our slow designs when we ourselves are dull.
What power is it which mounts my love so high,
That makes me see, and cannot feed mine eye?
The mightiest space in fortune nature brings
To join like likes, and kiss like native things.
Impossible be strange attempts to those
That weigh their pains in sense, and do suppose
What hath been cannot be. Who ever strove
To show her merit that did miss her love?
The King's disease – my project may deceive me,
But my intents are fix'd, and will not leave me.
[*Exit.*

SCENE II. *Paris. The King's palace.*

Flourish of cornets. Enter the KING OF FRANCE, with letters, and divers Atendants.

KING The Florentines and Senoys are by th' ears;
Have fought with equal fortune, and continue
A braving war.

1 LORD So 'tis reported, sir.

KING Nay, 'tis most credible. We here receive it,
A certainty, vouch'd from our cousin Austria,
With caution, that the Florentine will move us
For speedy aid; wherein our dearest friend
Prejudicates the business, and would seem
To have us make denial.

1 LORD His love and wisdom,
Approv'd so to your Majesty, may plead
For amplest credence.

KING He hath arm'd our answer,
And Florence is denied before he comes;
Yet, for our gentlemen that mean to see
The Tuscan service, freely have they leave
To stand on either part.

2 LORD It well may serve
A nursery to our gentry, who are sick
For breathing and exploit.

KING What's he comes here?

Enter BERTRAM, LAFEU, and PAROLLES.

1 LORD It is the Count Rousillon, my good lord,
Young Bertram.
KING Youth, thou bear'st thy father's face;
Frank nature, rather curious than in haste,
Hath well compos'd thee. Thy father's moral parts
Mayst thou inherit too! Welcome to Paris.
BERTRAM My thanks and duty are your Majesty's.
KING I would I had that corporal soundness now,
As when thy father and myself in friendship
First tried our soldiership. He did look far
Into the service of the time, and was
Discipled of the bravest. He lasted long;
But on us both did haggish age steal on,
And wore us out of act. It much repairs me
To talk of your good father. In his youth
He had the wit which I can well observe
To-day in our young lords; but they may jest
Till their own scorn return to them unnoted
Ere they can hide their levity in honour.
So like a courtier, contempt nor bitterness
Were in his pride or sharpness; if they were,
His equal had awak'd them; and his honour,
Clock to itself, knew the true minute when
Exception bid him speak, and at this time
His tongue obey'd his hand. Who were below him
He us'd as creatures of another place;
And bow'd his eminent top to their low ranks,
Making them proud of his humility
In their poor praise he humbled. Such a man
Might be a copy to these younger times;
Which, followed well, would demonstrate them now
But goers backward.
BERTRAM His good remembrance, sir,
Lies richer in your thoughts than on his tomb;
So in approof lives not his epitaph
As in your royal speech.
KING Would I were with him! He would always say –
Methinks I hear him now; his plausive words
He scatter'd not in ears, but grafted them
To grow there, and to bear – 'Let me not live' –
This his good melancholy oft began,
On the catastrophe and heel of pastime,
When it was out – 'Let me not live' quoth he
'After my flame lacks oil, to be the snuff
Of younger spirits, whose apprehensive senses
All but new things disdain; whose judgments are
Mere fathers of their garments; whose constancies
Expire before their fashions'. This he wish'd.
I, after him, do after him wish too,
Since I nor wax nor honey can bring home,
I quickly were dissolved from my hive,
To give some labourers room.
2 LORD You're loved, sir;
They that least lend it you shall lack you first.
KING I fill a place, I know't. How long is't, Count,
Since the physician at your father's died?
He was much fam'd.
BERTRAM Some six months since, my lord.
KING If he were living, I would try him yet –
Lend me an arm – the rest have worn me out
With several applications. Nature and sickness
Debate it at their leisure. Welcome, Count;
My son's no dearer.
BERTRAM Thank your Majesty.

[*Exeunt. Flourish.*

SCENE III. *Rousillon. The Count's palace.*

Enter COUNTESS, Steward, and Clown.

COUNTESS I will now hear; what say you of this gentlewoman?

STEWARD Madam, the care I have had to even your content I wish might be found in the calendar of my past endeavours; for then we wound our modesty, and make foul the clearness of our deservings, when of ourselves we publish them.

COUNTESS What does this knave here? Get you gone, sirrah. The complaints I have heard of you I do not all believe; 'tis my slowness that I do not, for I know you lack not folly to commit them and have ability enough to make such knaveries yours.

CLOWN 'Tis not unknown to you, madam, I am a poor fellow.

COUNTESS Well, sir.

CLOWN No, madam, 'tis not so well that I am poor, though many of the rich are damn'd; but if I may have your ladyship's good will to go to the world, Isbel the woman and I will do as we may.

COUNTESS Wilt thou needs be a beggar?

CLOWN I do beg your good will in this case.

COUNTESS In what case?

CLOWN In Isbel's case and mine own. Service is no heritage; and I think I shall never have the blessing of God till I have issue o' my body; for they say barnes are blessings.

COUNTESS Tell me thy reason why thou wilt marry.

CLOWN My poor body, madam, requires it. I am driven on by the flesh; and he must needs go that the devil drives.

COUNTESS Is this all your worship's reason?

CLOWN Faith, madam, I have other holy reasons, such as they are.

COUNTESS May the world know them?

CLOWN I have been, madam, a wicked creature, as you and all flesh and blood are; and, indeed, I do marry that I may repent.

COUNTESS Thy marriage, sooner than thy wickedness.

CLOWN I am out o' friends, madam, and I hope to have friends for my wife's sake.

COUNTESS Such friends are thine enemies, knave.

CLOWN Y'are shallow, madam – in great friends; for the knaves come to do that for me which I am aweary of. He that ears my land spares my team, and gives me leave to in the crop. If I be his cuckold, he's my drudge. He that comforts my wife is the cherisher of my flesh and blood; he that cherishes my flesh and blood loves my flesh and blood; he that loves my flesh and blood is my friend; ergo, he that kisses my wife is my friend. If men could be contented to be what they are, there were no fear in marriage; for young Charbon the puritan and old Poysam the papist, howsome'er their hearts are sever'd in religion, their heads are both one: they may jowl horns together like any deer i' th' herd.

COUNTESS Wilt thou ever be a foul-mouth'd and calumnious knave?

CLOWN A prophet I, madam; and I speak the truth the next way:

For I the ballad will repeat,
  Which men full true shall find:
Your marriage comes by destiny,
Your cuckoo sings by kind.

COUNTESS Get you gone, sir; I'll talk with you more anon.

STEWARD May it please you, madam, that he bid Helen come to you. Of her I am to speak.

COUNTESS Sirrah, tell my gentlewoman I would speak with her; Helen I mean.

CLOWN [*Sings*]

'Was this fair face the cause' quoth she
  'Why the Grecians sacked Troy?
Fond done, done fond,
  Was this King Priam's joy?'
With that she sighed as she stood,
With that she sighed as she stood,
  And gave this sentence then:
'Among nine bad if one be good,
Among nine bad if one be good,
  There's yet one good in ten'.

COUNTESS What, one good in ten? You corrupt the song, sirrah.

CLOWN One good woman in ten, madam, which is a purifying o' th' song. Would God would serve the world so all the year! We'd find no fault with the tithe-woman, if I were the parson. One in ten, quoth 'a! An we might have a good woman born before every blazing star, or at an earthquake, 'twould mend the lottery well: a man may draw his heart out ere 'a pluck one.

COUNTESS You'll be gone, sir knave, and do as I command you.

CLOWN That man should be at woman's command, and yet no hurt done! Though honesty be no puritan, yet it will do no hurt; it will wear the surplice of humility over the black gown of a big heart. I am going, forsooth. The business is for Helen to come hither. [*Exit.*

COUNTESS Well, now.

STEWARD I know, madam, you love your gentlewoman entirely.

COUNTESS Faith, I do. Her father bequeath'd her to me; and she herself, without other advantage, may lawfully make title to as much love as she finds. There is more owing her than is paid; and more shall be paid her than is paid; and more shall be paid her than she'll demand.

STEWARD Madam, I was very late more near her than I think she wish'd me. Alone she was, and did communicate to herself her own words to her own ears; she thought, I dare vow for her, they touch'd not any stranger sense. Her matter was, she loved your son. Fortune, she said, was no goddess, that had put such difference betwixt their two estates; Love no god, that would not extend his might only where qualities were level; Diana no queen of virgins, that would suffer her poor knight surpris'd without rescue in the first assault, or ransom afterward. This she deliver'd in the most bitter touch of sorrow that e'er I heard virgin exclaim in; which I held my duty speedily to acquaint you withal; sithence, in the loss that may happen, it concerns you something to know it.

COUNTESS You have discharg'd this honestly; keep it to yourself. Many likelihoods inform'd me of this before, which hung so tott'ring in the balance that I could neither believe nor misdoubt. Pray you leave me. Stall this in your bosom; and I thank you for your honest care. I will speak with you further anon. [*Exit Steward.*

Enter HELENA.

Even so it was with me when I was young.
If ever we are nature's, these are ours; this thorn
Doth to our rose of youth rightly belong;
Our blood to us, this to our blood is born.
It is the show and seal of nature's truth,
Where love's strong passion is impress'd in youth.
By our remembrances of days foregone,

Such were our faults, or then we thought them
none.
Her eye is sick on't; I observe her now.
HELENA What is your pleasure, madam?
COUNTESS You know, Helen,
I am a mother to you.
HELENA Mine honourable mistress.
COUNTESS Nay, a mother.
Why not a mother? When I said 'a mother',
Methought you saw a serpent. What's in
'mother'
That you start at it? I say I am your mother,
And put you in the catalogue of those
That were enwombed mine. 'Tis often seen
Adoption strives with nature, and choice breeds
A native slip to us from foreign seeds.
You ne'er oppress'd me with a mother's groan,
Yet I express to you a mother's care.
God's mercy, maiden! does it curd thy blood
To say I am thy mother? What's the matter,
That this distempered messenger of wet,
The many-colour'd Iris, rounds thine eye?
Why, that you are my daughter?
HELENA That I am not.
COUNTESS I say I am your mother.
HELENA Pardon, madam.
The Count Rousillon cannot be my brother:
I am from humble, he from honoured name;
No note upon my parents, his all noble.
My master, my dear lord he is; and I
His servant live, and will his vassal die.
He must not be my brother.
COUNTESS Nor I your mother?
HELENA You are my mother, madam; would you
were –
So that my lord your son were not my brother –
Indeed my mother! Or were you both our
mothers,
I care no more for than I do for heaven,
So I were not his sister. Can't no other,
But, I your daughter, he must be my brother?
COUNTESS Yes, Helen, you might be my
daughter-in-law.
God shield you mean it not! 'daughter' and
'mother'
So strive upon your pulse. What! pale again?
My fear hath catch'd your fondness. Now I see
The myst'ry of your loneliness, and find
Your salt tears' head. Now to all sense 'tis gross
You love my son; invention is asham'd,
Against the proclamation of thy passion,
To say thou dost not. Therefore tell me true;
But tell me then, 'tis so; for, look, thy cheeks
Confess it, th' one to th' other; and thine eyes
See it so grossly shown in thy behaviours
That in their kind they speak it; only sin
And hellish obstinacy tie thy tongue,
That truth should be suspected. Speak, is't so?
If it be so, you have wound a goodly clew;
If it be not, forswear't; howe'er, I charge thee,
As heaven shall work in me for thine avail,
To tell me truly.
HELENA Good madam, pardon me.
COUNTESS Do you love my son?
HELENA Your pardon, noble mistress.
COUNTESS Love you my son?
HELENA Do not you love him, madam?
COUNTESS Go not about; my love hath in't a
bond
Whereof the world takes note. Come, come,
disclose
The state of your affection; for your passions
Have to the full appeach'd.
HELENA Then I confess,
Here on my knee, before high heaven and you,
That before you, and next unto high heaven,
I love your son.
My friends were poor, but honest; so's my love.
Be not offended, for it hurts not him
That he is lov'd of me; I follow him not
By any token of presumptuous suit,
Nor would I have him till I do deserve him;
Yet never know how that desert should be.
I know I love in vain, strive against hope;
Yet in this captious and intenible sieve
I still pour in the waters of my love,
And lack not to lose still. Thus, Indian-like,
Religious in mine error, I adore
The sun that looks upon his worshipper
But knows of him no more. My dearest madam,
Let not your hate encounter with my love,
For loving where you do; but if yourself,
Whose aged honour cites a virtuous youth,
Did ever in so true a flame of liking
Wish chastely and love dearly that your Dian
Was both herself and Love; O, then, give pity
To her whose state is such that cannot choose
But lend and give where she is sure to lose;
That seeks not to find that her search implies,
But, riddle-like, lives sweetly where she
dies!
COUNTESS Had you not lately an intent – speak
truly –
To go to Paris?
HELENA Madam, I had.
COUNTESS Wherefore? Tell true.
HELENA I will tell truth; by grace itself I swear.
You know my father left me some prescriptions
Of rare and prov'd effects, such as his reading
And manifest experience had collected
For general sovereignty; and that he will'd me
In heedfull'st reservation to bestow them,
As notes whose faculties inclusive were
More than they were in note. Amongst the rest

There is a remedy, approv'd, set down,
To cure the desperate languishings whereof
The King is render'd lost.
COUNTESS This was your motive
For Paris, was it? Speak.
HELENA My lord your son made me to think of this,
Else Paris, and the medicine, and the King,
Had from the conversation of my thoughts
Haply been absent then.
COUNTESS But think you, Helen,
If you should tender your supposed aid,
He would receive it? He and his physicians
Are of a mind: he, that they cannot help him;
They, that they cannot help. How shall they credit
A poor unlearned virgin, when the schools,
Embowell'd of their doctrine, have left off
The danger to itself?
HELENA There's something in't
More than my father's skill, which was the great'st
Of his profession, that his good receipt
Shall for my legacy be sanctified
By th' luckiest stars in heaven; and, would your honour
But give me leave to try success, I'd venture
The well-lost life of mine on his Grace's cure
By such a day and hour.
COUNTESS Dost thou believe't?
HELENA Ay, madam, knowingly.
COUNTESS Why, Helen, thou shalt have my leave and love,
Means and attendants, and my loving greetings
To those of mine in court. I'll stay at home,
And pray God's blessing into thy attempt.
Be gone to-morrow; and be sure of this,
What I can help thee to thou shalt not miss.
[*Exeunt.*

ACT TWO

SCENE I. *Paris. The King's palace.*

Flourish of cornets. Enter the KING with divers young Lords taking leave for the Florentine war; BERTRAM and PAROLLES; Attendants.

KING Farewell, young lords; these warlike principles
Do not throw from you. And you, my lords, farewell;
Share the advice betwixt you; if both gain all,
The gift doth stretch itself as 'tis receiv'd,
And is enough for both.
1 LORD 'Tis our hope, sir,
After well-ent'red soldiers, to return
And find your Grace in health.
KING No, no, it cannot be; and yet my heart
Will not confess he owes the malady
That doth my life besiege. Farewell, young lords;
Whether I live or die, be you the sons
Of worthy Frenchmen; let higher Italy –
Those bated that inherit but the fall
Of the last monarchy – see that you come
Not to woo honour, but to wed it; when
The bravest questant shrinks, find what you seek,
That fame may cry you loud. I say farewell.
2 LORD Health, at your bidding, serve your Majesty!
KING Those girls of Italy, take heed of them;
They say our French lack language to deny,
If they demand; beware of being captives
Before you serve.
BOTH Our hearts receive your warnings.
KING Farewell. [*To Attendants*] Come hither to me. [*The King retires attended.*
1 LORD O my sweet lord, that you will stay behind us!
PAROLLES 'Tis not his fault, the spark.
2 LORD O, 'tis brave wars!
PAROLLES Most admirable! I have seen those wars.
BERTRAM I am commanded here and kept a coil with
'Too young' and 'The next year' and ''Tis too early'.
PAROLLES An thy mind stand to 't, boy, steal away bravely.
BERTRAM I shall stay here the forehorse to a smock,
Creaking my shoes on the plain masonry,
Till honour be bought up, and no sword worn
But one to dance with. By heaven, I'll steal away.
1 LORD There's honour in the theft.
PAROLLES Commit it, Count.
2 LORD I am your accessary; and so farewell.
BERTRAM I grow to you, and our parting is a tortur'd body.
1 LORD Farewell, Captain.
2 LORD Sweet Monsieur Parolles!
PAROLLES Noble heroes, my sword and yours are kin. Good sparks and lustrous, a word, good metals: you shall find in the regiment of the Spinii one Captain Spurio, with his cicatrice, an emblem of war, here on his sinister cheek; it was

this very sword entrench'd it. Say to him I live; and observe his reports for me.

1 LORD We shall, noble Captain.

PAROLLES Mars dote on you for his novices! [*Exeunt Lords*] What will ye do?

Re-enter the KING.

BERTRAM Stay; the King!

PAROLLES Use a more spacious ceremony to the noble lords; you have restrain'd yourself within the list of too cold an adieu. Be more expressive to them; for they wear themselves in the cap of the time; there do muster true gait; eat, speak, and move, under the influence of the most receiv'd star; and though the devil lead the measure, such are to be followed. After them, and take a more dilated farewell.

BERTRAM And I will do so.

PAROLLES Worthy fellows; and like to prove most sinewy sword-men.

[*Exeunt Bertram and Parolles.*

Enter LAFEU.

LAFEU [*Kneeling*] Pardon, my lord, for me and for my tidings.

KING I'll fee thee to stand up.

LAFEU Then here's a man stands that has brought his pardon.
I would you had kneel'd, my lord, to ask me mercy;
And that at my bidding you could so stand up.

KING I would I had; so I had broke thy pate,
And ask'd thee mercy for't.

LAFEU Good faith, across!
But, my good lord, 'tis thus: will you be cur'd
Of your infirmity?

KING No.

LAFEU O, will you eat
No grapes, my royal fox? Yes, but you will
My noble grapes, an if my royal fox
Could reach them: I have seen a medicine
That's able to breathe life into a stone,
Quicken a rock, and make you dance canary
With spritely fire and motion; whose simple touch
Is powerful to araise King Pepin, nay,
To give great Charlemain a pen in's hand
And write to her a love-line.

KING What her is this?

LAFEU Why, Doctor She! My lord, there's one arriv'd,
If you will see her. Now, by my faith and honour,
If seriously I may convey my thoughts
In this my light deliverance, I have spoke
With one that in her sex, her years, profession,
Wisdom, and constancy, hath amaz'd me more
Than I dare blame my weakness. Will you see her,
For that is her demand, and know her business?
That done, laugh well at me.

KING Now, good Lafeu,
Bring in the admiration, that we with thee
May spend our wonder too, or take off thine
By wond'ring how thou took'st it.

LAFEU Nay, I'll fit you,
And not be all day neither. [*Exit Lafeu.*

KING Thus he his special nothing ever prologues.

Re-enter LAFEU with HELENA.

LAFEU Nay, come your ways.

KING This haste hath wings indeed.

LAFEU Nay, come your ways;
This is his Majesty; say your mind to him.
A traitor you do look like; but such traitors
His Majesty seldom fears. I am Cressid's uncle,
That dare leave two together. Fare you well.
[*Exit.*

KING Now, fair one, does your business follow us?

HELENA Ay, my good lord.
Gerard de Narbon was my father,
In what he did profess, well found.

KING I knew him.

HELENA The rather will I spare my praises towards him;
Knowing him is enough. On's bed of death
Many receipts he gave me; chiefly one,
Which, as the dearest issue of his practice,
And of his old experience th' only darling,
He bade me store up as a triple eye,
Safer than mine own two, more dear. I have so
And, hearing your high Majesty is touch'd
With that malignant cause wherein the honour
Of my dear father's gift stands chief in power,
I come to tender it, and my appliance,
With all bound humbleness.

KING We thank you, maiden;
But may not be so credulous of cure,
When our most learned doctors leave us, and
The congregated college have concluded
That labouring art can never ransom nature
From her inaidable estate – I say we must not
So stain our judgment, or corrupt our hope,
To prostitute our past-cure malady
To empirics; or to dissever so
Our great self and our credit to esteem
A senseless help, when help past sense we deem.

HELENA My duty then shall pay me for my pains.
I will no more enforce mine office on you;
Humbly entreating from your royal thoughts
A modest one to bear me back again.

KING I cannot give thee less, to be call'd grateful.
Thou thought'st to help me; and such thanks I give

As one near death to those that wish him live.
But what at full I know, thou know'st no part;
I knowing all my peril, thou no art.

HELENA What I can do can do no hurt to try,
Since you set up your rest 'gainst remedy.
He that of greatest works is finisher
Oft does them by the weakest minister.
So holy writ in babes hath judgment shown,
When judges have been babes. Great floods have flown
From simple sources, and great seas have dried
When miracles have by the greatest been denied.
Oft expectation fails, and most oft there
Where most it promises; and oft it hits
Where hope is coldest, and despair most fits.

KING I must not hear thee. Fare thee well, kind maid;
Thy pains, not us'd, must by thyself be paid;
Proffers not took reap thanks for their reward.

HELENA Inspired merit so by breath is barr'd.
It is not so with Him that all things knows,
As 'tis with us that square our guess by shows;
But most it is presumption in us when
The help of heaven we count the act of men.
Dear sir, to my endeavours give consent;
Of heaven, not me, make an experiment.
I am not an impostor, that proclaim
Myself against the level of mine aim;
But know I think, and think I know most sure,
My art is not past power nor you past cure.

KING Art thou so confident? Within what space
Hop'st thou my cure?

HELENA The greatest Grace lending grace,
Ere twice the horses of the sun shall bring
Their fiery torcher his diurnal ring,
Ere twice in murk and occidental damp
Moist Hesperus hath quench'd his sleepy lamp,
Or four and twenty times the pilot's glass
Hath told the thievish minutes how they pass,
What is infirm from your sound parts shall fly,
Health shall live free, and sickness freely die.

KING Upon thy certainty and confidence
What dar'st thou venture?

HELENA Tax of impudence,
A strumpet's boldness, a divulged shame,
Traduc'd by odious ballads; my maiden's name
Sear'd otherwise; ne worse of worst – extended
With vilest torture let my life be ended.

KING Methinks in thee some blessed spirit doth speak
His powerful sound within an organ weak;
And what impossibility would slay
In common sense, sense saves another way.
Thy life is dear; for all that life can rate
Worth name of life in thee hath estimate.
Youth, beauty, wisdom, courage, all
That happiness and prime can happy call.
Thou this to hazard needs must intimate
Skill infinite or monstrous desperate.
Sweet practiser, thy physic I will try,
That ministers thine own death if I die.

HELENA If I break time, or flinch in property
Of what I spoke, unpitied let me die;
And well deserv'd. Not helping, death's my fee;
But, if I help, what do you promise me?

KING Make thy demand.

HELENA But will you make it even?

KING Ay, by my sceptre and my hopes of heaven.

HELENA Then shalt thou give me with thy kingly hand
What husband in thy power I will command.
Exempted be from me the arrogance
To choose from forth the royal blood of France,
My low and humble name to propagate
With any branch or image of thy state;
But such a one, thy vassal, whom I know
Is free for me to ask, thee to bestow.

KING Here is my hand; the premises observ'd,
Thy will by my performance shall be serv'd.
So make the choice of thy own time, for I,
Thy resolv'd patient, on thee still rely.
More should I question thee, and more I must,
Though more to know could not be more to trust.
From whence thou cam'st, how tended on. But rest
Unquestion'd welcome and undoubted blest.
Give me some help here, ho! If thou proceed
As high as word, my deed shall match thy deed.

[*Flourish. Exeunt.*

SCENE II. *Rousillon. The Count's palace.*

Enter COUNTESS and Clown.

COUNTESS Come on, sir; I shall now put you to the height of your breeding.

CLOWN I will show myself highly fed and lowly taught. I know my business is but to the court.

COUNTESS To the court! Why, what place make you special, when you put off that with such contempt? But to the court!

CLOWN Truly, madam, if God have lent a man any manners, he may easily put it off at court. He that cannot make a leg, put off's cap, kiss his hand, and say nothing, has neither leg, hands, lip, nor cap; and indeed such a fellow, to say precisely, were not for the court; but for me, I have an answer will serve all men.

COUNTESS Marry, that's a bountiful answer that fits all questions.

CLOWN It is like a barber's chair, that fits all buttocks – the pin buttock, the quatch buttock, the brawn buttock, or any buttock.

COUNTESS Will your answer serve fit to all questions?

CLOWN As fit as ten groats is for the hand of an attorney, as your French crown for your taffety punk, as Tib's rush for Tom's forefinger, as a pancake for Shrove Tuesday, a morris for Mayday, as the nail to his hole, the cuckold to his horn, as a scolding quean to a wrangling knave, as the nun's lip to the friar's mouth; nay, as the pudding to his skin.

COUNTESS Have you, I say, an answer of such fitness for all questions?

CLOWN From below your duke to beneath your constable, it will fit any question.

COUNTESS It must be an answer of most monstrous size that must fit all demands.

CLOWN But a trifle neither, in good faith, if the learned should speak truth of it. Here it is, and all that belongs to't. Ask me if I am a courtier: it shall do you no harm to learn.

COUNTESS To be young again, if we could, I will be a fool in question, hoping to be the wiser by your answer. I pray you, sir, are you a courtier?

CLOWN O Lord, sir! – There's a simple putting off. More, more, a hundred of them.

COUNTESS Sir, I am a poor friend of yours, that loves you.

CLOWN O Lord, sir! – Thick thick; spare not me.

COUNTESS I think, sir, you can eat none of this homely meat.

CLOWN O Lord, sir! – Nay, put me to't, I warrant you.

COUNTESS You were lately whipp'd, sir, as I think.

CLOWN O Lord, sir! – Spare not me.

COUNTESS Do you cry 'O Lord, sir!' at your whipping, and 'spare not me'? Indeed your 'O Lord, sir!' is very sequent to your whipping. You would answer very well to a whipping, if you were but bound to't.

CLOWN I ne'er had worse luck in my life in my 'O Lord, sir!' I see things may serve long, but not serve ever.

COUNTESS I play the noble housewife with the time,
To entertain it so merrily with a fool.

CLOWN O Lord, sir! – Why, there't serves well again.

COUNTESS An end, sir! To your business: give Helen this,
And urge her to a present answer back;
Commend me to my kinsmen and my son.
This is not much.

CLOWN Not much commendation to them?

COUNTESS Not much employment for you. You understand me?

CLOWN Most fruitfully; I am there before my legs.

COUNTESS Haste you again. *[Exeunt.*

SCENE III. *Paris. The King's palace.*

Enter BERTRAM, LAFEU, and PAROLLES.

LAFEU They say miracles are past; and we have our philosophical persons to make modern and familiar things supernatural and causeless. Hence is it that we make trifles of terrors, ensconcing ourselves into seeming knowledge when we should submit ourselves to an unknown fear.

PAROLLES Why, 'tis the rarest argument of wonder that hath shot out in our latter times.

BERTRAM And so 'tis.

LAFEU To be relinquish'd of the artists –

PAROLLES So I say – both of Galen and Paracelsus.

LAFEU Of all the learned and authentic fellows –

PAROLLES Right; so I say.

LAFEU That gave him out incurable –

PAROLLES Why, there 'tis; so say I too.

LAFEU Not to be help'd –

PAROLLES Right; as 'twere a man assur'd of a –

LAFEU Uncertain life and sure death.

PAROLLES Just; you say well; so would I have said.

LAFEU I may truly say it is a novelty to the world.

PAROLLES It is indeed. If you will have it in showing, you shall read it in what-do-ye-call't here.

LAFEU *[Reading the ballad title]* 'A Showing of a Heavenly Effect in an Earthly Actor.'

PAROLLES That's it; I would have said the very same.

LAFEU Why, your dolphin is not lustier. Fore me, I speak in respect –

PAROLLES Nay, 'tis strange, 'tis very strange; that is the brief and the tedious of it; and he's of a most facinerious spirit that will not acknowledge it to be the –

LAFEU Very hand of heaven.

PAROLLES Ay; so I say.

LAFEU In a most weak –

PAROLLES And debile minister, great power, great transcendence; which should, indeed, give us a further use to be made than alone the recov'ry of the King, as to be –

LAFEU Generally thankful.

Enter KING, HELENA, and Attendants.

PAROLLES I would have said it; you say well. Here comes the King.

LAFEU Lustig, as the Dutchman says. I'll like a maid the better, whilst I have a tooth in my head. Why, he's able to lead her a coranto.

PAROLLES Mort du vinaigre! Is not this Helen?
LAFEU Fore God, I think so.
KING Go, call before me all the lords in court.
[*Exit an Attendant.*
Sit, my preserver, by thy patient's side;
And with this healthful hand, whose banish'd sense
Thou hast repeal'd, a second time receive
The confirmation of my promis'd gift,
Which but attends thy naming.
Enter three or four Lords.
Fair maid, send forth thine eye. This youthful parcel
Of noble bachelors stand at my bestowing,
O'er whom both sovereign power and father's voice
I have to use. Thy frank election make;
Thou hast power to choose, and they none to forsake.
HELENA To each of you one fair and virtuous mistress
Fall, when love please. Marry, to each but one!
LAFEU I'd give bay Curtal and his furniture
My mouth no more were broken than these boys',
And writ as little beard.
KING Peruse them well.
Not one of those but had a noble father.
HELENA Gentlemen,
Heaven hath through me restor'd the King to health.
ALL We understand it, and thank heaven for you.
HELENA I am a simple maid, and therein wealthiest
That I protest I simply am a maid.
Please it your Majesty, I have done already.
The blushes in my cheeks thus whisper me:
'We blush that thou shouldst choose; but, be refused,
Let the white death sit on thy cheek for ever,
We'll ne'er come there again'.
KING Make choice and see:
Who shuns thy love shuns all his love in me.
HELENA Now, Dian, from thy altar do I fly,
And to imperial Love, that god most high,
Do my sighs stream. Sir, will you hear my suit?
1 LORD And grant it.
HELENA Thanks, sir; all the rest is mute.
LAFEU I had rather be in this choice than throw ames-ace for my life.
HELENA The honour, sir, that flames in your fair eyes,
Before I speak, too threat'ningly replies.
Love make your fortunes twenty times above
Her that so wishes, and her humble love!
2 LORD No better, if you please.
HELENA My wish receive,
Which great Love grant; and so I take my leave.
LAFEU Do all they deny her? An they were sons of mine I'd have them whipt; or I would send them to th' Turk to make eunuchs of.
HELENA Be not afraid that I your hand should take;
I'll never do you wrong for your own sake.
Blessing upon your vows; and in your bed
Find fairer fortune, if you ever wed!
LAFEU These boys are boys of ice; they'll none have her. Sure, they are bastards to the English; the French ne'er got 'em.
HELENA You are too young, too happy, and too good,
To make yourself a son out of my blood.
4 LORD Fair one, I think not so.
LAFEU There's one grape yet; I am sure thy father drunk wine – but if thou be'st not an ass, I am a youth of fourteen; I have known thee already.
HELENA [*To Bertram*] I dare not say I take you; but I give
Me and my service, ever whilst I live,
Into your guiding power. This is the man.
KING Why, then, young Bertram, take her; she's thy wife.
BERTRAM My wife, my liege! I shall beseech your Highness,
In such a business give me leave to use
The help of mine own eyes.
KING Know'st thou not, Bertram,
What she has done for me?
BERTRAM Yes, my good lord;
But never hope to know why I should marry her.
KING Thou know'st she has rais'd me from my sickly bed.
BERTRAM But follows it, my lord, to bring me down
Must answer for your raising? I know her well:
She had her breeding at my father's charge.
A poor physician's daughter my wife! Disdain
Rather corrupt me ever!
KING 'Tis only title thou disdain'st in her, the which
I can build up. Strange is it that our bloods,
Of colour, weight, and heat, pour'd all together,
Would quite confound distinction, yet stand off
In differences so mighty. If she be
All that is virtuous – save what thou dislik'st,
A poor physician's daughter – thou dislik'st
Of virtue for the name; but do not so.
From lowest place when virtuous things proceed,
The place is dignified by th' doer's deed;
Where great additions swell 's, and virtue none,
It is a dropsied honour. Good alone

Is good without a name. Vileness is so:
The property by what it is should go,
Not by the title. She is young, wise, fair;
In these to nature she's immediate heir;
And these breed honour. That is honour's scorn
Which challenges itself as honour's born
And is not like the sire. Honours thrive
When rather from our acts we them derive
Than our fore-goers. The mere word's a slave,
Debauch'd on every tomb, on every grave
A lying trophy; and as oft is dumb
Where dust and damn'd oblivion is the tomb
Of honour'd bones indeed. What should be said?
If thou canst like this creature as a maid,
I can create the rest. Virtue and she
Is her own dower; honour and wealth from me.

BERTRAM I cannot love her, nor will strive to do't.

KING Thou wrong'st thyself, if thou shouldst strive to choose.

HELENA That you are well restor'd, my lord, I'm glad.
Let the rest go.

KING My honour's at the stake; which to defeat,
I must produce my power. Here, take her hand,
Proud scornful boy, unworthy this good gift,
That dost in vile misprision shackle up
My love and her desert; that canst not dream
We, poising us in her defective scale,
Shall weigh thee to the beam; that wilt not know
It is in us to plant thine honour where
We please to have it grow. Check thy contempt;
Obey our will, which travails in thy good;
Believe not thy disdain, but presently
Do thine own fortunes that obedient right
Which both thy duty owes and our power claims;
Or I will throw thee from my care for ever
Into the staggers and the careless lapse
Of youth and ignorance; both my revenge and hate
Loosing upon thee in the name of justice,
Without all terms of pity. Speak; thine answer.

BERTRAM Pardon, my gracious lord; for I submit
My fancy to your eyes. When I consider
What great creation and what dole of honour
Flies where you bid it, I find that she which late
Was in my nobler thoughts most base is now
The praised of the King; who, so ennobled,
Is as 'twere born so.

KING Take her by the hand,
And tell her she is thine; to whom I promise
A counterpoise, if not to thy estate
A balance more replete.

BERTRAM I take her hand.

KING Good fortune and the favour of the King
Smile upon this contract; whose ceremony
Shall seem expedient on the now-born brief,
And be perform'd to-night. The solemn feast
Shall more attend upon the coming space,
Expecting absent friends. As thou lov'st her,
Thy love's to me religious; else, does err.

[*Exeunt all but Lafeu and Parolles who stay behind, commenting of this wedding.*

LAFEU Do you hear, monsieur? A word with you.

PAROLLES Your pleasure, sir?

LAFEU Your lord and master did well to make his recantation.

PAROLLES Recantation! My Lord! my master!

LAFEU Ay; is it not a language I speak?

PAROLLES A most harsh one, and not to be understood without bloody succeeding. My master!

LAFEU Are you companion to the Count Rousillon?

PAROLLES To any count; to all counts; to what is man.

LAFEU To what is count's man: count's master is of another style.

PAROLLES You are too old, sir; let it satisfy you, you are too old.

LAFEU I must tell thee, sirrah, I write man; to which title age cannot bring thee.

PAROLLES What I dare too well do, I dare not do.

LAFEU I did think thee, for two ordinaries, to be a pretty wise fellow; thou didst make tolerable vent of thy travel; it might pass. Yet the scarfs and the bannerets about thee did manifoldly dissuade me from believing thee a vessel of too great a burden. I have now found thee; when I lose thee again I care not; yet art thou good for nothing but taking up; and that thou'rt scarce worth.

PAROLLES Hadst thou not the privilege of antiquity upon thee –

LAFEU Do not plunge thyself too far in anger, lest thou hasten thy trial; which if – Lord have mercy on thee for a hen! So, my good window of lattice, fare thee well; thy casement I need not open, for I look through thee. Give me thy hand.

PAROLLES My lord, you give me most egregious indignity.

LAFEU Ay, with all my heart; and thou art worthy of it.

PAROLLES I have not, my lord, deserv'd it.

LAFEU Yes, good faith, ev'ry dram of it; and I will not bate thee a scruple.

PAROLLES Well, I shall be wiser.

LAFEU Ev'n as soon as thou canst, for thou hast to pull at a smack o' th' contrary. If ever thou be'st bound in thy scarf and beaten, thou shalt find what it is to be proud of thy bondage. I have a desire to hold my acquaintance with thee, or rather my knowledge, that I may say in the default 'He is a man I know'.

PAROLLES My lord, you do me most insupportable vexation.

LAFEU I would it were hell pains for thy sake, and my poor doing eternal; for doing I am past, as I will by thee, in what motion age will give me leave. [*Exit.*

PAROLLES Well, thou hast a son shall take this disgrace off me; scurvy, old, filthy, scurvy lord! Well, I must be patient; there is no fettering of authority. I'll beat him, by my life, if I can meet him with any convenience, an he were double and double a lord. I'll have no more pity of his age than I would have of – I'll beat him, an if I could but meet him again.

Re-enter LAFEU.

LAFEU Sirrah, your lord and master's married; there's news for you; you have a new mistress.

PAROLLES I most unfeignedly beseech your lordship to make some reservation of your wrongs. He is my good lord: whom I serve above is my master.

LAFEU Who? God?

PAROLLES Ay, sir.

LAFEU The devil it is that's thy master. Why dost thou garter up thy arms o' this fashion? Dost make hose of thy sleeves? Do other servants so? Thou wert best set thy lower part where thy nose stands. By mine honour, if I were but two hours younger, I'd beat thee. Methink'st thou art a general offence, and every man should beat thee. I think thou wast created for men to breathe themselves upon thee.

PAROLLES This is hard and undeserved measure, my lord.

LAFEU Go to, sir; you were beaten in Italy for picking a kernel out of a pomegranate; you are a vagabond, and no true traveller; you are more saucy with lords and honourable personages than the commission of your birth and virtue gives you heraldry. You are not worth another word, else I'd call you knave. I leave you. [*Exit.*

Enter BERTRAM.

PAROLLES Good, very good, it is so then. Good, very good; let it be conceal'd awhile.

BERTRAM Undone, and forfeited to cares for ever!

PAROLLES What's the matter, sweetheart?

BERTRAM Although before the solemn priest I have sworn,
I will not bed her.

PAROLLES What, what, sweetheart?

BERTRAM O my Parolles, they have married me!
I'll to the Tuscan wars, and never bed her.

PAROLLES France is a dog-hole, and it no more merits
The tread of a man's foot. To th' wars!

BERTRAM There's letters from my mother; what th' import is
I know not yet.

PAROLLES Ay, that would be known. To th' wars, my boy, to th' wars!
He wears his honour in a box unseen
That hugs his kicky-wicky here at home,
Spending his manly marrow in her arms,
Which should sustain the bound and high curvet
Of Mars's fiery steed. To other regions!
France is a stable; we that dwell in't jades;
Therefore, to th' war!

BERTRAM It shall be so; I'll send her to my house,
Acquaint my mother with my hate to her,
And wherefore I am fled; write to the King
That which I durst not speak. His present gift
Shall furnish me to those Italian fields
Where noble fellows strike. War is no strife
To the dark house and the detested wife.

PAROLLES Will this capriccio hold in thee, art sure?

BERTRAM Go with me to my chamber and advise me.
I'll send her straight away. To-morrow
I'll to the wars, she to her single sorrow.

PAROLLES Why, these balls bound; there's noise in it. 'Tis hard:
A young man married is a man that's marr'd.
Therefore away, and leave her bravely; go.
The King has done you wrong; but, hush, 'tis so.
[*Exeunt.*

SCENE IV. *Paris. The King's palace.*

Enter HELENA and Clown.

HELENA My mother greets me kindly; is she well?

CLOWN She is not well, but yet she has her health; she's very merry, but yet she is not well. But thanks be given, she's very well, and wants nothing i' th' world; but yet she is not well.

HELENA If she be very well, what does she all that she's not very well?

CLOWN Truly, she's very well indeed, but for two things.

HELENA What two things?

CLOWN One, that she's not in heaven, whither God send her quickly! The other, that she's in earth, from whence God send her quickly!

Enter PAROLLES.

PAROLLES Bless you, my fortunate lady!

HELENA I hope, sir, I have your good will to have

mine own good fortunes.

PAROLLES You had my prayers to lead them on; and to keep them on, have them still. O, my knave, how does my old lady?

CLOWN So that you had her wrinkles and I her money, I would she did as you say.

PAROLLES Why, I say nothing.

CLOWN Marry, you are the wiser man; for many a man's tongue shakes out his master's undoing. To say nothing, to do nothing, to know nothing, and to have nothing, is to be a great part of your title, which is within a very little of nothing.

PAROLLES Away! th'art a knave.

CLOWN You should have said, sir, 'Before a knave th'art a knave'; that's 'Before me th'art a knave'. This had been truth, sir.

PAROLLES Go to, thou art a witty fool; I have found thee.

CLOWN Did you find me in yourself, sir, or were you taught to find me? The search, sir, was profitable; and much fool may you find in you, even to the world's pleasure and the crease of laughter.

PAROLLES A good knave, i' faith, and well fed.
Madam, my lord will go away to-night:
A very serious business calls on him.
The great prerogative and rite of love,
Which, as your due, time claims, he does
 acknowledge;
But puts it off to a compell'd restraint;
Whose want, and whose delay, is strew'd with
 sweets,
Which they distil now in the curbed time,
To make the coming hour o'erflow with joy
And pleasure drown the brim.

HELENA What's his will else?

PAROLLES That you will take your instant leave
 o' th' King,
And make this haste as your own good
 proceeding,
Strength'ned with what apology you think
May make it probable need.

HELENA What more commands he?

PAROLLES That, having this obtain'd, you
 presently
Attend his further pleasure.

HELENA In everything I wait upon his will.

PAROLLES I shall report it so.

HELENA I pray you. [*Exit Parolles*] Come, sirrah.

[*Exeunt.*

SCENE V. *Paris. The King's palace.*

Enter LAFEU and BERTRAM.

LAFEU But I hope your lordship thinks not him a soldier.

BERTRAM Yes, my lord, and of very valiant approof.

LAFEU You have it from his own deliverance.

BERTRAM And by other warranted testimony.

LAFEU Then my dial goes not true; I took this lark for a bunting.

BERTRAM I do assure you, my lord, he is very great in knowledge, and accordingly valiant.

LAFEU I have then sinn'd against his experience and transgress'd against his valour; and my state that way is dangerous, since I cannot yet find in my heart to repent. Here he comes; I pray you make us friends; I will pursue the amity.

Enter PAROLLES.

PAROLLES [*To Bertram*] These things shall be done, sir.

LAFEU Pray you, sir, who's his tailor?

PAROLLES Sir!

LAFEU O, I know him well. Ay, sir; he, sir, 's a good workman, a very good tailor.

BERTRAM [*Aside to Parolles*] Is she gone to the King?

PAROLLES She is.

BERTRAM Will she away to-night?

PAROLLES As you'll have her.

BERTRAM I have writ my letters, casketed my
 treasure,
Given order for our horses; and to-night,
When I should take possession of the bride,
End ere I do begin.

LAFEU A good traveller is something at the latter end of a dinner; but one that lies three-thirds and uses a known truth to pass a thousand nothings with, should be once heard and thrice beaten. God save you, Captain.

BERTRAM Is there any unkindness between my lord and you, monsieur?

PAROLLES I know not how I have deserved to run into my lord's displeasure.

LAFEU You have made shift to run into 't, boots and spurs and all, like him that leapt into the custard; and out of it you'll run again, rather than suffer question for your residence.

BERTRAM It may be you have mistaken him, my lord.

LAFEU And shall do so ever, though I took him at's prayers. Fare you well, my lord; and believe this of me: there can be no kernel in this light nut; the soul of this man is his clothes; trust him not in matter of heavy consequence; I have kept of them tame, and know their natures. Farewell, monsieur; I have spoken better of you than you have or will to deserve at my hand; but we must do good against evil. [*Exit.*

PAROLLES An idle lord, I swear.

BERTRAM I think so.

PAROLLES Why, do you not know him?
BERTRAM Yes, I do know him well; and common speech
Gives him a worthy pass. Here comes my clog.

Enter HELENA.

HELENA I have, sir, as I was commanded from you,
Spoke with the King, and have procur'd his leave
For present parting; only he desires
Some private speech with you.
BERTRAM I shall obey his will.
You must not marvel, Helen, at my course,
Which holds not colour with the time, nor does
The ministration and required office
On my particular. Prepar'd I was not
For such a business; therefore am I found
So much unsettled. This drives me to entreat you
That presently you take your way for home,
And rather muse than ask why I entreat you;
For my respects are better than they seem,
And my appointments have in them a need
Greater than shows itself at the first view
To you that know them not. This to my mother.
[*Giving a letter.*
'Twill be two days ere I shall see you; so
I leave you to your wisdom.
HELENA Sir, I can nothing say
But that I am your most obedient servant.
BERTRAM Come, come, no more of that.
HELENA And ever shall
With true observance seek to eke out that
Wherein toward me my homely stars have fail'd
To equal my great fortune.
BERTRAM Let that go.
My haste is very great. Farewell; hie home.
HELENA Pray, sir, your pardon.
BERTRAM Well, what would you say?
HELENA I am not worthy of the wealth I owe,
Nor dare I say 'tis mine, and yet it is;
But, like a timorous thief, most fain would steal
What law does vouch mine own.
BERTRAM What would you have?
HELENA Something; and scarce so much; nothing, indeed.
I would not tell you what I would, my lord.
Faith, yes:
Strangers and foes do sunder and not kiss.
BERTRAM I pray you, stay not, but in haste to horse.
HELENA I shall not break your bidding, good my lord.
BERTRAM Where are my other men, monsieur?
Farewell! [*Exit Helena.*
Go thou toward home, where I will never come
Whilst I can shake my sword or hear the drum.
Away, and for our flight.
PAROLLES Bravely, coragio!
[*Exeunt.*

ACT THREE

SCENE I. *Florence. The Duke's palace.*

Flourish. Enter the DUKE OF FLORENCE, attended; two French Lords, with a Troop of Soldiers.

DUKE So that, from point to point, now have you heard
The fundamental reasons of this war;
Whose great decision hath much blood let forth
And more thirsts after.
1 LORD Holy seems the quarrel
Upon your Grace's part; black and fearful
On the opposer.
DUKE Therefore we marvel much our cousin France
Would in so just a business shut his bosom
Against our borrowing prayers.
2 LORD Good my lord,
The reasons of our state I cannot yield,
But like a common and an outward man
That the great figure of a council frames
By self-unable motion; therefore dare not
Say what I think of it, since I have found
Myself in my incertain grounds to fail
As often as I guess'd.
DUKE Be it his pleasure.
1 LORD But I am sure the younger of our nature,
That surfeit on their ease, will day by day
Come here for physic.
DUKE Welcome shall they be;
And all the honours that can fly from us
Shall on them settle. You know your places well;
When better fall, for your avails they fell.
To-morrow to th' field. [*Flourish. Exeunt.*

SCENE II. *Rousillon. The Count's palace.*

Enter COUNTESS and Clown.

COUNTESS It hath happen'd all as I would have had it, save that he comes not along with her.

CLOWN By my troth, I take my young lord to be a very melancholy man.

COUNTESS By what observance, I pray you?

CLOWN Why, he will look upon his boot and sing; mend the ruff and sing; ask questions and sing; pick his teeth and sing. I know a man that had this trick of melancholy sold a goodly manor for a song.

COUNTESS Let me see what he writes, and when he means to come. [*Opening a letter.*

CLOWN I have no mind to Isbel since I was at court. Our old ling and our Isbels o' th' country are nothing like your old ling and your Isbels o' th' court. The brains of my Cupid's knock'd out; and I begin to love, as an old man loves money, with no stomach.

COUNTESS What have we here?

CLOWN E'en that you have there. [*Exit.*

COUNTESS [*Reads*] 'I have sent you a daughter-in-law; she hath recovered the King and undone me. I have wedded her, not bedded her; and sworn to make the "not" eternal. You shall hear I am run away; know it before the report come. If there be breadth enough in the world, I will hold a long distance. My duty to you.

Your unfortunate son,

BERTRAM

This is not well, rash and unbridled boy,
To fly the favours of so good a king,
To pluck his indignation on thy head
By the misprizing of a maid too virtuous
For the contempt of empire.

Re-enter Clown.

CLOWN O madam, yonder is heavy news within between two soldiers and my young lady.

COUNTESS What is the matter?

CLOWN Nay, there is some comfort in the news, some comfort; your son will not be kill'd so soon as I thought he would.

COUNTESS Why should he be kill'd?

CLOWN So say I, madam, if he run away, as I hear he does; the danger is in standing to 't; that's the loss of men, though it be the getting of children. Here they come will tell you more. For my part, I only hear your son was run away. [*Exit.*

Enter HELENA and the two French Gentlemen.

2 GENTLEMAN Save you, good madam.

HELENA Madam, my lord is gone, for ever gone.

1 GENTLEMAN Do not say so.

COUNTESS Think upon patience. Pray you, gentlemen –
I have felt so many quirks of joy and grief
That the first face of neither, on the start,
Can woman me unto 't. Where is my son, I pray you.

1 GENTLEMAN Madam, he's gone to serve the Duke of Florence.
We met him thitherward; for thence we came,
And, after some dispatch in hand at court,
Thither we bend again.

HELENA Look on this letter, madam; here's my passport.
[*Reads*] 'When thou canst get the ring upon my finger, which never shall come off, and show me a child begotten of thy body that I am father to, then call me husband; but in such a "then" I write a "never."'
This is a dreadful sentence.

COUNTESS Brought you this letter, gentlemen?

1 GENTLEMAN Ay, madam;
And for the contents' sake are sorry for our pains.

COUNTESS I prithee, lady, have a better cheer;
If thou engrossest all the griefs are thine,
Thou robb'st me of a moiety. He was my son;
But I do wash his name out of my blood,
And thou art all my child. Towards Florence is he?

1 GENTLEMAN Ay, madam.

COUNTESS And to be a soldier?

1 GENTLEMAN Such is his noble purpose; and, believe 't,
The Duke will lay upon him all the honour
That good convenience claims.

COUNTESS Return you thither?

2 GENTLEMAN Ay, madam, with the swiftest wing of speed.

HELENA [*Reads*] 'Till I have no wife, I have nothing in France.'
'Tis bitter.

COUNTESS Find you that there?

HELENA Ay, madam.

2 GENTLEMAN 'Tis but the boldness of his hand haply, which his heart was not consenting to.

COUNTESS Nothing in France until he have no wife!
There's nothing here that is too good for him
But only she; and she deserves a lord
That twenty such rude boys might tend upon,
And call her hourly mistress. Who was with him?

2 GENTLEMAN A servant only, and a gentleman
Which I have sometime known.

COUNTESS Parolles, was it not?

2 GENTLEMAN Ay, my good lady, he.

COUNTESS A very tainted fellow, and full of wickedness.
My son corrupts a well-derived nature
With his inducement.

2 GENTLEMAN Indeed, good lady,
The fellow has a deal of that too much
Which holds him much to have.

COUNTESS Y'are welcome, gentlemen.
I will entreat you, when you see my son,
To tell him that his sword can never win

The honour that he loses. More I'll entreat you
Written to bear along.
I GENTLEMAN We serve you, madam,
In that and all your worthiest affairs.
COUNTESS Not so, but as we change our courtesies.
Will you draw near?
[*Exeunt Countess and Gentlemen.*
HELENA 'Till I have no wife, I have nothing in France.'
Nothing in France until he has no wife!
Thou shalt have none, Rousillon, none in France;
Then hast thou all again. Poor lord! is't I
That chase thee from thy country, and expose
Those tender limbs of thine to the event
Of the none-sparing war? And is it I
That drive thee from the sportive court, where thou
Wast shot at with fair eyes, to be the mark
Of smoky muskets? O you leaden messengers,
That ride upon the violent speed of fire,
Fly with false aim; move the still-piecing air,
That sings with piercing; do not touch my lord.
Whoever shoots at him, I set him there;
Whoever charges on his forward breast,
I am the caitiff that do hold him to't;
And though I kill him not, I am the cause
His death was so effected. Better 'twere
I met the ravin lion when he roar'd
With sharp constraint of hunger; better 'twere
That all the miseries which nature owes
Were mine at once. No; come thou home, Rousillon,
Whence honour but of danger wins a scar,
As oft it loses all. I will be gone.
My being here it is that holds thee hence.
Shall I stay here to do't? No, no, although
The air of paradise did fan the house,
And angels offic'd all. I will be gone,
That pitiful rumour may report my flight
To consolate thine ear. Come, night; end, day.
For with the dark, poor thief, I'll steal away.
[*Exit.*

SCENE III. *Florence. Before the Duke's palace.*

Flourish. Enter the DUKE OF FLORENCE, BERTRAM, PAROLLES, Soldiers, drum and trumpets.

DUKE The General of our Horse thou art; and we,
Great in our hope, lay our best love and credence
Upon thy promising fortune.
BERTRAM Sir, it is
A charge too heavy for my strength; but yet
We'll strive to bear it for your worthy sake
To th' extreme edge of hazard.
DUKE Then go thou forth;
And Fortune play upon thy prosperous helm,
As thy auspicious mistress!
BERTRAM This very day,
Great Mars, I put myself into thy file;
Make me but like my thoughts, and I shall prove
A lover of thy drum, hater of love. [*Exeunt.*

SCENE IV. *Rousillon. The Count's palace.*

Enter COUNTESS and Steward.

COUNTESS Alas! and would you take the letter of her?
Might you not know she would do as she has done
By sending me a letter? Read it again.
STEWARD [*Reads*] 'I am Saint Jaques' pilgrim, thither gone.
Ambitious love hath so in me offended
That barefoot plod I the cold ground upon,
With sainted vow my faults to have amended.
Write, write, that from the bloody course of war
My dearest master, your dear son, may hie.
Bless him at home in peace, whilst I from far
His name with zealous fervour sanctify.
His taken labours bid him me forgive;
I, his despiteful Juno, sent him forth
From courtly friends, with camping foes to live,
Where death and danger dogs the heels of worth.
He is too good and fair for death and me;
Whom I myself embrace to set him free.'
COUNTESS Ah, what sharp stings are in her mildest words!
Rinaldo, you did never lack advice so much
As letting her pass so; had I spoke with her,
I could have well diverted her intents,
Which thus she hath prevented.
STEWARD Pardon me, madam;
If I had given you this at over-night,
She might have been o'erta'en; and yet she writes
Pursuit would be but vain.
COUNTESS What angel shall
Bless this unworthy husband? He cannot thrive,
Unless her prayers, whom heaven delights to hear
And loves to grant, reprieve him from the wrath
Of greatest justice. Write, write, Rinaldo,
To this unworthy husband of his wife;
Let every word weigh heavy of her worth
That he does weigh too light. My greatest grief,
Though little he do feel it, set down sharply.
Dispatch the most convenient messenger.
When haply he shall hear that she is gone

He will return; and hope I may that she,
Hearing so much, will speed her foot again,
Led hither by pure love. Which of them both
Is dearest to me I have no skill in sense
To make distinction. Provide this messenger.
My heart is heavy, and mine age is weak;
Grief would have tears, and sorrow bids me
speak. [*Exeunt.*

SCENE V. *Without the walls of Florence.*

A tucket afar off. Enter an old Widow of Florence, her daughter DIANA, VIOLENTA, and MARIANA, with other Citizens.

WIDOW Nay, come; for if they do approach the city we shall lose all the sight.

DIANA They say the French count has done most honourable service.

WIDOW It is reported that he has taken their great'st commander; and that with his own hand he slew the Duke's brother. [*Tucket*] We have lost our labour; they are gone a contrary way. Hark! you may know by their trumpets.

MARIANA Come, let's return again, and suffice ourselves with the report of it. Well, Diana, take heed of this French earl; the honour of a maid is her name, and no legacy is so rich as honesty.

WIDOW I have told my neighbour how you have been solicited by a gentleman his companion.

MARIANA I know that knave, hang him! one Parolles; a filthy officer he is in those suggestions for the young earl. Beware of them, Diana: their promises, enticements, oaths, tokens, and all these engines of lust, are not the things they go under; many a maid hath been seduced by them; and the misery is, example, that so terrible shows in the wreck of maidenhood, cannot for all that dissuade succession, but that they are limed with the twigs that threatens them. I hope I need not to advise you further; but I hope your own grace will keep you where you are, though there were no further danger known but the modesty which is so lost.

DIANA You shall not need to fear me.

Enter HELENA in the dress of a pilgrim.

WIDOW I hope so. Look, here comes a pilgrim. I know she will lie at my house: thither they send one another. I'll question her. God save you, pilgrim! Whither are bound?

HELENA To Saint Jaques le Grand.
Where do the palmers lodge, I do beseech you?

WIDOW At the Saint Francis here, beside the port.

HELENA Is this the way? [*A march afar.*

WIDOW Ay, marry, is't. Hark you! They come
this way.
If you will tarry, holy pilgrim,
But till the troops come by,
I will conduct you where you shall be lodg'd;
The rather for I think I know your hostess
As ample as myself.

HELENA Is it yourself?

WIDOW If you shall please so, pilgrim.

HELENA I thank you, and will stay upon your
leisure.

WIDOW You came, I think, from France?

HELENA I did so.

WIDOW Here you shall see a countryman of
yours
That has done worthy service.

HELENA His name, I pray you.

DIANA The Count Rousillon. Know you such a
one?

HELENA But by the ear, that hears most nobly of
him;
His face I know not.

DIANA Whatsome'er he is,
He's bravely taken here. He stole from France,
As 'tis reported, for the King had married him
Against his liking. Think you it is so?

HELENA Ay, surely, mere the truth; I know his
lady.

DIANA There is a gentleman that serves the
Count
Reports but coarsely of her.

HELENA What's his name?

DIANA Monsieur Parolles.

HELENA O, I believe with him,
In argument of praise, or to the worth
Of the great Count himself, she is too mean
To have her name repeated; all her deserving
Is a reserved honesty, and that
I have not heard examin'd.

DIANA Alas, poor lady!
'Tis a hard bondage to become the wife
Of a detesting lord.

WIDOW I weet, good creature, wheresoe'er she is
Her heart weighs sadly. This young maid might
do her
A shrewd turn, if she pleas'd.

HELENA How do you mean?
May be the amorous Count solicits her
In the unlawful purpose.

WIDOW He does, indeed;
And brokes with all that can in such a suit
Corrupt the tender honour of a maid;
But she is arm'd for him, and keeps her guard
In honestest defence.

Enter, with drum and colours, BERTRAM, PAROLLES, and the whole Army.

MARIANA The gods forbid else!

WIDOW So, now they come.

That is Antonio, the Duke's eldest son;
That, Escalus.

HELENA Which is the Frenchman?

DIANA He –
That with the plume; 'tis a most gallant fellow.
I would he lov'd his wife; if he were honester
He were much goodlier. Is't not a handsome gentleman?

HELENA I like him well.

DIANA 'Tis pity he is not honest. Yond's that same knave
That leads him to these places; were I his lady
I would poison that vile rascal.

HELENA Which is he?

DIANA That jack-an-apes with scarfs. Why is he melancholy?

HELENA Perchance he's hurt i' th' battle.

PAROLLES Lose our drum! well.

MARIANA He's shrewdly vex'd at something.
Look, he has spied us.

WIDOW Marry, hang you!

MARIANA And your courtesy, for a ring-carrier!

[Exeunt Bertram, Parolles, and army.

WIDOW The troop is past. Come, pilgrim, I will bring you
Where you shall host. Of enjoin'd penitents
There's four or five, to great Saint Jacques bound,
Already at my house.

HELENA I humbly thank you.
Please it this matron and this gentle maid
To eat with us to-night; the charge and thanking
Shall be for me, and, to requite you further,
I will bestow some precepts of this virgin,
Worthy the note.

BOTH We'll take your offer kindly.

[Exeunt.

SCENE VI. *Camp before Florence.*

Enter BERTRAM, and the two French Lords.

2 LORD Nay, good my lord, put him to't; let him have his way.

1 LORD If your lordship find him not a hilding, hold me no more in your respect.

2 LORD On my life, my lord, a bubble.

BERTRAM Do you think I am so far deceived in him?

2 LORD Believe it, my lord, in mine own direct knowledge, without any malice, but to speak of him as my kinsman, he's a most notable coward, an infinite and endless liar, an hourly promise-breaker, the owner of no one good quality worthy your lordship's entertainment.

1 LORD It were fit you knew him; lest, reposing too far in his virtue, which he hath not, he might at some great and trusty business in a main danger fail you.

BERTRAM I would I knew in what particular action to try him.

1 LORD None better than to let him fetch off his drum, which you hear him so confidently undertake to do.

2 LORD I with a troop of Florentines will suddenly surprise him; such I will have whom I am sure he knows not from the enemy. We will bind and hoodwink him so that he shall suppose no other but that he is carried into the leaguer of the adversaries when we bring him to our own tents. Be but your lordship present at his examination; if he do not, for the promise of his life and in the highest compulsion of base fear, offer to betray you and deliver all the intelligence in his power against you, and that with the divine forfeit of his soul upon oath, never trust my judgment in anything.

1 LORD O, for the love of laughter, let him fetch his drum; he says he has a stratagem for't. When your lordship sees the bottom of his success in't, and to what metal this counterfeit lump of ore will be melted, if you give him not John Drum's entertainment, your inclining cannot be removed. Here he comes.

Enter PAROLLES.

2 LORD O, for the love of laughter, hinder not the honour of his design; let him fetch off his drum in any hand.

BERTRAM How now, monsieur! This drum sticks sorely in your disposition.

1 LORD A pox on't; let it go; 'tis but a drum.

PAROLLES But a drum! Is't but a drum? A drum so lost! There was excellent command: to charge in with our horse upon our own wings, and to rend our own soldiers!

1 LORD That was not to be blam'd in the command of the service; it was a disaster of war that Caesar himself could not have prevented, if he had been there to command.

BERTRAM Well, we cannot greatly condemn our success. Some dishonour we had in the loss of that drum; but it is not to be recovered.

PAROLLES It might have been recovered.

BERTRAM It might, but it is not now.

PAROLLES It is to be recovered. But that the merit of service is seldom attributed to the true and exact performer, I would have that drum or another, or 'hic jacet'.

BERTRAM Why, if you have a stomach, to't, monsieur. If you think your mystery in stratagem can bring this instrument of honour again into his native quarter, be magnanimous in the enterprise, and go on; I will grace the attempt for a worthy exploit. If you speed well in it, the Duke shall both speak of it and extend to you what further becomes his greatness, even to the utmost syllable of your worthiness.

PAROLLES By the hand of a soldier, I will undertake it.

BERTRAM But you must not now slumber in it.

PAROLLES I'll about it this evening; and I will presently pen down my dilemmas, encourage myself in my certainty, put myself into my mortal preparation; and by midnight look to hear further from me.

BERTRAM May I be bold to acquaint his Grace you are gone about it?

PAROLLES I know not what the success will be, my lord, but the attempt I vow.

BERTRAM I know th'art valiant; and, to the possibility of thy soldiership, will subscribe for thee. Farewell.

PAROLLES I love not many words. [*Exit.*

2 LORD No more than a fish loves water. Is not this a strange fellow, my lord, that so confidently seems to undertake this business, which he knows is not to be done; damns himself to do, and dares better be damn'd than to do't.

1 LORD You do not know him, my lord, as we do. Certain it is that he will steal himself into a man's favour, and for a week escape a great deal of discoveries; but when you find him out, you have him ever after.

BERTRAM Why, do you think he will make no deed at all of this that so seriously he does address himself unto?

2 LORD None in the world; but return with an invention, and clap upon you two or three probable lies. But we have almost emboss'd him. You shall see his fall tonight; for indeed he is not for your lordship's respect.

1 LORD We'll make you some sport with the fox ere we case him. He was first smok'd by the old Lord Lafeu. When his disguise and he is parted, tell me what a sprat you shall find him; which you shall see this very night.

2 LORD I must go look my twigs; he shall be caught.

BERTRAM Your brother, he shall go along with me.

2 LORD As't please your lordship. I'll leave you. [*Exit.*

BERTRAM Now will I lead you to the house, and show you
The lass I spoke of.

1 LORD But you say she's honest.

BERTRAM That's all the fault. I spoke with her but once,
And found her wondrous cold; but I sent to her,
By this same coxcomb that we have i' th' wind,
Tokens and letters which she did re-send;
And this is all I have done. She's a fair creature;
Will you go see her?

1 LORD With all my heart, my lord.

[*Exeunt.*

SCENE VII. *Florence. The Widow's house.*

Enter HELENA and Widow.

HELENA If you misdoubt me that I am not she,
I know not how I shall assure you further
But I shall lose the grounds I work upon.

WIDOW Though my estate be fall'n, I was well born,
Nothing acquainted with these businesses;
And would not put my reputation now
In any staining act.

HELENA Nor would I wish you.
First give me trust the Count he is my husband,
And what to your sworn counsel I have spoken
Is so from word to word; and then you cannot,
By the good aid that I of you shall borrow,
Err in bestowing it.

WIDOW I should believe you;
For you have show'd me that which well approves
Y'are great in fortune.

HELENA Take this purse of gold,
And let me buy your friendly help thus far,
Which I will over-pay and pay again.
When I have found it. The Count he woos your daughter,
Lays down his wanton siege before her beauty,
Resolv'd to carry her. Let her in fine consent,
As we'll direct her how 'tis best to bear it.
Now his important blood will nought deny
That she'll demand. A ring the County wears
That downward hath succeeded in his house
From son to son some four or five descents
Since the first father wore it. This ring he holds
In most rich choice; yet, in his idle fire,
To buy his will, it would not seem too dear,
Howe'er repented after.

WIDOW Now I see
The bottom of your purpose.

HELENA You see it lawful then. It is no more
But that your daughter, ere she seems as won,
Desires this ring; appoints him an encounter;
In fine, delivers me to fill the time,
Herself most chastely absent. After this,
To marry her, I'll add three thousand crowns
To what is pass'd already.

WIDOW I have yielded.
Instruct my daughter how she shall persever,
That time and place with this deceit so lawful

May prove coherent. Every night he comes
With musics of all sorts, and songs compos'd
To her unworthiness. It nothing steads us
To chide him from our eaves, for he persists
As if his life lay on't.

HELENA Why then to-night
Let us assay our plot; which, if it speed,
Is wicked meaning in a lawful deed,
And lawful meaning in a lawful act;
Where both not sin, and yet a sinful fact.
But let's about it. [*Exeunt.*

ACT FOUR

SCENE I. *Without the Florentine camp.*

Enter Second French Lord with five or six other Soldiers in ambush.

2 LORD He can come no other way but by this hedge-corner. When you sally upon him, speak what terrible language you will; though you understand it not yourselves, no matter; for we must not seem to understand him, unless some one among us, whom we must produce for an interpreter.

1 SOLDIER Good captain, let me be th' interpreter.

2 LORD Art not acquainted with him? Knows he not thy voice?

1 SOLDIER No, sir, I warrant you.

2 LORD But what linsey-woolsey hast thou to speak to us again?

1 SOLDIER E'en such as you speak to me.

2 LORD He must think us some band of strangers i' th' adversary's entertainment. Now he hath a smack of all neighbouring languages, therefore we must every one be a man of his own fancy; not to know what we speak one to another, so we seem to know, is to know straight our purpose: choughs' language, gabble enough, and good enough. As for you, interpreter, you must seem very politic. But couch, ho! here he comes; to beguile two hours in a sleep, and then to return and swear the lies he forges.

Enter PAROLLES.

PAROLLES Ten o'clock. Within these three hours 'twill be time enough to go home. What shall I say I have done? It must be a very plausive invention that carries it. They begin to smoke me; and disgraces have of late knock'd too often at my door. I find my tongue is too foolhardy; but my heart hath the fear of Mars before it, and of his creatures, not daring the reports of my tongue.

2 LORD This is the first truth that e'er thine own tongue was guilty of.

PAROLLES What the devil should move me to undertake the recovery of this drum, being not ignorant of the impossibility, and knowing I had no such purpose? I must give myself some hurts, and say I got them in exploit. Yet slight ones will not carry it. They will say 'Came you off with so little?' And great ones I dare not give. Wherefore, what's the instance? Tongue, I must put you into a butter-woman's mouth, and buy myself another of Bajazet's mule, if you prattle me into these perils.

2 LORD Is it possible he should know what he is, and be that he is?

PAROLLES I would the cutting of my garments would serve the turn, or the breaking of my Spanish sword.

2 LORD We cannot afford you so.

PAROLLES Or the baring of my beard; and to say it was in stratagem.

2 LORD 'Twould not do.

PAROLLES Or to drown my clothes, and say I was stripp'd.

2 LORD Hardly serve.

PAROLLES Though I swore I leap'd from the window of the citadel –

2 LORD How deep?

PAROLLES Thirty fathom.

2 LORD Three great oaths would scarce make that be believed.

PAROLLES I would I had any drum of the enemy's; I would swear I recover'd it.

2 LORD You shall hear one anon. [*Alarum within.*

PAROLLES A drum now of the enemy's!

2 LORD Throca movousus, cargo, cargo, cargo.

ALL Cargo, cargo, cargo, villianda par corbo, cargo.

PAROLLES O, ransom, ransom! Do not hide mine eyes. [*They blindfold him.*

1 SOLDIER Boskos thromuldo boskos.

PAROLLES I know you are the Muskos' regiment,
And I shall lose my life for want of language.
If there be here German, or Dane, Low Dutch,
Italian, or French, let him speak to me;
I'll discover that which shall undo the Florentine.

1 SOLDIER Boskos vauvado. I understand thee, and can speak thy tongue. Kerelybonto, sir, betake thee to thy faith, for seventeen poniards are at thy bosom.

PAROLLES O!

1 SOLDIER O, pray, pray, pray! Manka revania dulche.
2 LORD Oscorbidulchos volivorco.
1 SOLDIER The General is content to spare thee yet;
And, hoodwink'd as thou art, will lead thee on
To gather from thee. Haply thou mayst inform
Something to save thy life.
PAROLLES O, let me live,
And all the secrets of our camp I'll show,
Their force, their purposes. Nay, I'll speak that
Which you will wonder at.
1 SOLDIER But wilt thou faithfully?
PAROLLES If I do not, damn me.
1 SOLDIER Acordo linta.
Come on; thou art granted space.
[*Exit, with Parolles guarded.*

A short alarum within.

2 LORD Go, tell the Count Rousillon and my brother
We have caught the woodcock, and will keep him muffled
Till we do hear from them.
2 SOLDIER Captain, I will.
2 LORD 'A will betray us all unto ourselves –
Inform on that.
2 SOLDIER So I will, sir.
2 LORD Till then I'll keep him dark and safely lock'd. [*Exeunt.*

SCENE II. *Florence. The Widow's house.*

Enter BERTRAM and DIANA.

BERTRAM They told me that your name was Fontibell.
DIANA No, my good lord, Diana.
BERTRAM Titled goddess;
And worth it, with addition! But, fair soul,
In your fine frame hath love no quality?
If the quick fire of youth light not your mind,
You are no maiden, but a monument;
When you are dead, you should be such a one
As you are now, for you are cold and stern;
And now you should be as your mother was
When your sweet self was got.
DIANA She then was honest.
BERTRAM So should you be.
DIANA No.
My mother did but duty; such, my lord,
As you owe to your wife.
BERTRAM No more o' that!
I prithee do not strive against my vows.
I was compell'd to her; but I love thee
By love's own sweet constraint, and will for ever
Do thee all rights of service.
DIANA Ay, so you serve us
Till we serve you; but when you have our roses
You barely leave our thorns to prick ourselves,
And mock us with our bareness.
BERTRAM How have I sworn!
DIANA 'Tis not the many oaths that makes the truth,
But the plain single vow that is vow'd true.
What is not holy, that we swear not by,
But take the High'st to witness. Then, pray you, tell me:
If I should swear by Jove's great attributes
I lov'd you dearly, would you believe my oaths
When I did love you ill? This has no holding,
To swear by him whom I protest to love
That I will work against him. Therefore your oaths
Are words and poor conditions, but unseal'd –
At least in my opinion.
BERTRAM Change it, change it;
Be not so holy-cruel. Love is holy;
And my integrity ne'er knew the crafts
That you do charge men with. Stand no more off,
But give thyself unto my sick desires,
Who then recovers. Say thou art mine, and ever
My love as it begins shall so persever.
DIANA I see that men make ropes in such a scarre
That we'll forsake ourselves. Give me that ring.
BERTRAM I'll lend it thee, my dear, but have no power
To give it from me.
DIANA Will you not, my lord?
BERTRAM It is an honour 'longing to our house,
Bequeathed down from many ancestors;
Which were the greatest obloquy i' th' world
In me to lose.
DIANA Mine honour's such a ring:
My chastity's the jewel of our house,
Bequeathed down from many ancestors;
Which were the greatest obloquy i' th' world
In me to lose. Thus your own proper wisdom
Brings in the champion Honour on my part
Against your vain assault.
BERTRAM Here, take my ring;
My house, mine honour, yea, my life, be thine,
And I'll be bid by thee.
DIANA When midnight comes, knock at my chamber window;
I'll order take my mother shall not hear.
Now will I charge you in the band of truth,
When you have conquer'd my yet maiden bed,
Remain there but an hour, nor speak to me:
My reasons are most strong; and you shall know them
When back again this ring shall be deliver'd.
And on your finger in the night I'll put
Another ring, that what in time proceeds

May token to the future our past deeds.
Adieu till then; then fail not. You have won
A wife of me, though there my hope be done.

BERTRAM A heaven on earth I have won by wooing thee. [*Exit.*

DIANA For which live long to thank both heaven and me!
You may so in the end.
My mother told me just how he would woo,
As if she sat in's heart; she says all men
Have the like oaths. He had sworn to marry me
When his wife's dead; therefore I'll lie with him
When I am buried. Since Frenchmen are so braid,
Marry that will, I live and die a maid.
Only, in this disguise, I think't no sin
To cozen him that would unjustly win. [*Exit.*

SCENE III. *The Florentine camp.*

Enter the two French Lords, and two or three Soldiers.

2 LORD You have not given him his mother's letter?

1 LORD I have deliv'red it an hour since. There is something in't that stings his nature; for on the reading it he chang'd almost into another man.

2 LORD He has much worthy blame laid upon him for shaking off so good a wife and so sweet a lady.

1 LORD Especially he hath incurred the everlasting displeasure of the King, who had even tun'd his bounty to sing happiness to him. I will tell you a thing, but you shall let it dwell darkly with you.

2 LORD When you have spoken it, 'tis dead, and I am the grave of it.

1 LORD He hath perverted a young gentlewoman here in Florence, of a most chaste renown; and this night he fleshes his will in the spoil of her honour. He hath given her his monumental ring, and thinks himself made in the unchaste composition.

2 LORD Now, God delay our rebellion! As we are ourselves, what things are we!

1 LORD Merely our own traitors. And as in the common course of all treasons we still see them reveal themselves till they attain to their abhorr'd ends; so he that in this action contrives against his own nobility, in his proper stream, o'erflows himself.

2 LORD Is it not meant damnable in us to be trumpeters of our unlawful intents? We shall not then have his company to-night?

1 LORD Not till after midnight; for he is dieted to his hour.

2 LORD That approaches apace. I would gladly have him see his company anatomiz'd, that he might take a measure of his own judgments, wherein so curiously he had set this counterfeit.

1 LORD We will not meddle with him till he come; for his presence must be the whip of the other.

2 LORD In the meantime, what hear you of these wars?

1 LORD I hear there is an overture of peace.

2 LORD Nay, I assure you, a peace concluded.

1 LORD What will Count Rousillon do then? Will he travel higher, or return again into France?

2 LORD I perceive, by this demand, you are not altogether of his counsel.

1 LORD Let it be forbid, sir! So should I be a great deal of his act.

2 LORD Sir, his wife, some two months since, fled from his house. Her pretence is a pilgrimage to Saint Jaques le Grand; which holy undertaking with most austere sanctimony she accomplish'd; and, there residing, the tenderness of her nature became as a prey to her grief; in fine, made a groan of her last breath, and now she sings in heaven.

1 LORD How is this justified?

2 LORD The stronger part of it by her own letters, which makes her story true even to the point of her death. Her death itself, which could not be her office to say is come, was faithfully confirm'd by the rector of the place.

1 LORD Hath the Count all this intelligence?

2 LORD Ay, and the particular confirmations, point from point, to the full arming of the verity.

1 LORD I am heartily sorry that he'll be glad of this.

2 LORD How mightily sometimes we make us comforts of our losses!

1 LORD And how mightily some other times we drown our gain in tears! The great dignity that his valour hath here acquir'd for him shall at home be encount'red with a shame as ample.

2 LORD The web of our life is of a mingled yarn, good and ill together. Our virtues would be proud if our faults whipt them not; and our crimes would despair if they were not cherish'd by our virtues.

Enter a Messenger.

How now? Where's your master?

SERVANT He met the Duke in the street, sir; of whom he hath taken a solemn leave. His lordship will next morning for France. The Duke hath offered him letters of commendations to the King.

2 LORD They shall be no more than needful there, if they were more than they can commend.

1 LORD They cannot be too sweet for the King's tartness. Here's his lordship now.

Enter BERTRAM.

How now, my lord, is't not after midnight?

BERTRAM I have to-night dispatch'd sixteen businesses, a month's length apiece; by an abstract of success: I have congied with the Duke, done my adieu with his nearest; buried a wife, mourn'd for her; writ to my lady mother I am returning; entertain'd my convoy; and between these main parcels of dispatch effected many nicer needs. The last was the greatest, but that I have not ended yet.

2 LORD If the business be of any difficulty and this morning your departure hence, it requires haste of your lordship.

BERTRAM I mean the business is not ended, as fearing to hear of it hereafter. But shall we have this dialogue between the Fool and the Soldier? Come, bring forth this counterfeit module has deceiv'd me like a double-meaning prophesier.

2 LORD Bring him forth. [*Exeunt Soldiers*] Has sat i' th' stocks all night, poor gallant knave.

BERTRAM No matter; his heels have deserv'd it, in usurping his spurs so long. How does he carry himself?

2 LORD I have told your lordship already the stocks carry him. But to answer you as you would be understood: he weeps like a wench that had shed her milk; he hath confess'd himself to Morgan, whom he supposes to be a friar, from the time of his remembrance to this very instant disaster of his setting i' th' stocks. And what think you he hath confess'd?

BERTRAM Nothing of me, has 'a?

2 LORD His confession is taken, and it shall be read to his face; if your lordship be in't, as I believe you are, you must have the patience to hear it.

Enter PAROLLES guarded, and First Soldier as interpreter.

BERTRAM A plague upon him! muffled! He can say nothing of me.

2 LORD Hush, hush! Hoodman comes. Portotartarossa.

1 SOLDIER He calls for the tortures. What will you say without 'em?

PAROLLES I will confess what I know without constraint; if ye pinch me like a pasty, I can say no more.

1 SOLDIER Bosko chimurcho.

2 LORD Boblibindo chicurmurco.

1 SOLDIER You are a merciful general. Our General bids you answer to what I shall ask you out of a note.

PAROLLES And truly, as I hope to live.

1 SOLDIER 'First demand of him how many horse the Duke is strong.' What say you to that?

PAROLLES Five or six thousand; but very weak and unserviceable. The troops are all scattered, and the commanders very poor rogues, upon my reputation and credit, and as I hope to live.

1 SOLDIER Shall I set down your answer so?

PAROLLES Do; I'll take the sacrament on't, how and which way you will.

BERTRAM All's one to him. What a past-saving slave is this!

2 LORD Y'are deceiv'd, my lord; this is Monsieur Parolles, the gallant militarist – that was his own phrase – that had the whole theoric of war in the knot of his scarf, and the practice in the chape of his dagger.

1 LORD I will never trust a man again for keeping his sword clean; nor believe he can have everything in him by wearing his apparel neatly.

1 SOLDIER Well, that's set down.

PAROLLES 'Five or six thousand horse' I said – I will say true – 'or thereabouts' set down, for I'll speak truth.

2 LORD He's very near the truth in this.

BERTRAM But I con him no thanks for't in the nature he delivers it.

PAROLLES 'Poor rogues' I pray you say.

1 SOLDIER Well, that's set down.

PAROLLES I humbly thank you, sir. A truth's a truth – the rogues are marvellous poor.

1 SOLDIER 'Demand of him of what strength they are a-foot.' What say you to that?

PAROLLES By my troth, sir, if I were to live this present hour, I will tell true. Let me see: Spurio, a hundred and fifty; Sebastian, so many; Corambus, so many; Jaques, so many; Guiltian, Cosmo, Lodowick, and Gratii, two hundred fifty each; mine own company, Chitopher, Vaumond, Bentii, two hundred fifty each; so that the muster-file, rotten and sound, upon my life, amounts not to fifteen thousand poll; half of the which dare not shake the snow from off their cassocks lest they shake themselves to pieces.

BERTRAM What shall be done to him?

2 LORD Nothing, but let him have thanks. Demand of him my condition, and what credit I have with the Duke.

1 SOLDIER Well, that's set down. 'You shall demand of him whether one Captain Dumain be i' th' camp, a Frenchman; what his reputation is with the Duke, what his valour, honesty, expertness in wars; or whether he thinks it were not possible, with well-weighing sums of gold, to corrupt him to a revolt.' What say you to this? What do you know of it?

PAROLLES I beseech you, let me answer to the

particular of the inter'gatories. Demand them singly.

1 SOLDIER Do you know this Captain Dumain?

PAROLLES I know him: 'a was a botcher's prentice in Paris, from whence he was whipt for getting the shrieve's fool with child – a dumb innocent that could not say him nay.

BERTRAM Nay, by your leave, hold your hands; though I know his brains are forfeit to the next tile that falls.

1 SOLDIER Well, is this captain in the Duke of Florence's camp?

PAROLLES Upon my knowledge, he is, and lousy.

2 LORD Nay, look not so upon me; we shall hear of your lordship anon.

1 SOLDIER What is his reputation with the Duke?

PAROLLES The Duke knows him for no other but a poor officer of mine; and writ to me this other day to turn him out o' th' band. I think I have his letter in my pocket.

1 SOLDIER Marry, we'll search.

PAROLLES In good sadness, I do not know; either it is there or it is upon a file with the Duke's other letters in my tent.

1 SOLDIER Here 'tis; here's a paper. Shall I read it to you?

PAROLLES I do not know if it be it or no.

BERTRAM Our interpreter does it well.

2 LORD Excellently.

1 SOLDIER [*Reads*] 'Dian, the Count's a fool, and full of gold.'

PAROLLES That is not the Duke's letter, sir; that is an advertisement to a proper maid in Florence, one Diana, to take heed of the allurement of one Count Rousillon, a foolish idle boy, but for all that very ruttish. I pray you, sir, put it up again.

1 SOLDIER Nay, I'll read it first by your favour.

PAROLLES My meaning in't, I protest, was very honest in the behalf of the maid; for I knew the young Count to be a dangerous and lascivious boy, who is a whale to virginity, and devours up all the fry it finds.

BERTRAM Damnable both-sides rogue!

1 SOLDIER [*Reads*].

'When he swears oaths, bid him drop gold, and take it;
After he scores, he never pays the score.
Half won is match well made; match, and well make it;
He ne'er pays after-debts, take it before.
And say a soldier, Dian, told thee this:
Men are to mell with, boys are not to kiss;
For count of this, the Count's a fool, I know it,
Who pays before, but not when he does owe it.

Thine, as he vow'd to thee in thine ear,
PAROLLES

BERTRAM He shall be whipt through the army with this rhyme in's forehead.

1 LORD This is your devoted friend, sir, the manifold linguist, and the armipotent soldier.

BERTRAM I could endure anything before but a cat, and now he's a cat to me.

1 SOLDIER I perceive, sir, by our General's looks we shall be fain to hang you.

PAROLLES My life, sir, in any case! Not that I am afraid to die, but that, my offences being many, I would repent out the remainder of nature. Let me live, sir, in a dungeon, i' th' stocks, or anywhere, so I may live.

1 SOLDIER We'll see what may be done, so you confess freely; therefore, once more to this Captain Dumain: you have answer'd to his reputation with the Duke, and to his valour; what is his honesty?

PAROLLES He will steal, sir, an egg out of a cloister; for rapes and ravishments he parallels Nessus. He professes not keeping of oaths; in breaking 'em he is stronger than Hercules. He will lie, sir, with such volubility that you would think truth were a fool. Drunkenness is his best virtue, for he will be swine-drunk; and in his sleep he does little harm, save to his bedclothes about him; but they know his conditions and lay him in straw. I have but little more to say, sir, of his honesty. He has everything that an honest man should not have; what an honest man should have he has nothing.

2 LORD I begin to love him for this.

BERTRAM For this description of thine honesty? A pox upon him! For me, he's more and more a cat.

1 SOLDIER What say you to his expertness in war?

PAROLLES Faith, sir, has led the drum before the English tragedians – to belie him I will not – and more of his soldiership I know not, except in that country he had the honour to be the officer at a place there called Mile-end to instruct for the doubling of files – I would do the man what honour I can – but of this I am not certain.

2 LORD He hath out-villain'd villainy so far that the rarity redeems him.

BERTRAM A pox on him! he's a cat still.

1 SOLDIER His qualities being at this poor price, I need not to ask you if gold will corrupt him to revolt.

PAROLLES Sir, for a cardecue he will sell the fee-simple of his salvation, the inheritance of it; and cut th' entail from all remainders and a perpetual succession for it perpetually.

1 SOLDIER What's his brother, the other Captain Dumain?

1 LORD Why does he ask him of me?

1 SOLDIER What's he?

PAROLLES E'en a crow o' th' same nest; not altogether so great as the first in goodness, but greater a great deal in evil. He excels his brother for a coward; yet his brother is reputed one of the best that is. In a retreat he outruns any lackey: marry, in coming on he has the cramp.

1 SOLDIER If your life be saved, will you undertake to betray the Florentine?

PAROLLES Ay, and the Captain of his Horse, Count Rousillon.

1 SOLDIER I'll whisper with the General, and know his pleasure.

PAROLLES [*Aside*] I'll no more drumming. A plague of all drums! Only to seem to deserve well, and to beguile the supposition of that lascivious young boy the Count, have I run into this danger. Yet who would have suspected an ambush where I was taken?

1 SOLDIER There is no remedy, sir, but you must die. The General says you that have so traitorously discover'd the secrets of your army, and made such pestiferous reports of men very nobly held, can serve the world for no honest use; therefore you must die. Come, headsman, off with his head.

PAROLLES O Lord, sir, let me live, or let me see my death!

1 SOLDIER That shall you, and take your leave of all your friends. [*Unmuffling him.*
So look about you; know you any here?

BERTRAM Good morrow, noble Captain.

1 LORD God bless you, Captain Parolles.

2 LORD God save you, noble Captain.

1 LORD Captain, what greeting will you to my Lord Lafeu? I am for France.

2 LORD Good Captain, will you give me a copy of the sonnet you writ to Diana in behalf of the Count Rousillon? An I were not a very coward I'd compel it of you; but fare you well.

[*Exeunt Bertram and Lords.*

1 SOLDIER You are undone, Captain, all but your scarf; that has a knot on't yet.

PAROLLES Who cannot be crush'd with a plot?

1 SOLDIER If you could find out a country where but women were that had received so much shame, you might begin an impudent nation. Fare ye well, sir; I am for France too; we shall speak of you there. [*Exit with Soldiers.*

PAROLLES Yet am I thankful. If my heart were great,
'Twould burst at this. Captain I'll be no more;
But I will eat, and drink, and sleep as soft
As captain shall. Simply the thing I am
Shall make me live. Who knows himself a braggart,
Let him fear this; for it will come to pass
That every braggart shall be found an ass.
Rust, sword; cool, blushes; and, Parolles, live
Safest in shame. Being fool'd, by fool'ry thrive.
There's place and means for every man alive.
I'll after them. [*Exit.*

SCENE IV. *Florence. The Widow's house.*

Enter HELENA, Widow, and DIANA.

HELENA That you may well perceive I have not wrong'd you,
One of the greatest in the Christian world
Shall be my surety; fore whose throne 'tis needful,
Ere I can perfect mine intents, to kneel.
Time was I did him a desired office,
Dear almost as his life; which gratitude
Through flinty Tartar's bosom would peep forth,
And answer 'Thanks'. I duly am inform'd
His Grace is at Marseilles, to which place
We have convenient convoy. You must know
I am supposed dead. The army breaking,
My husband hies him home; where, heaven aiding,
And by the leave of my good lord the King,
We'll be before our welcome.

WIDOW Gentle madam,
You never had a servant to whose trust
Your business was more welcome.

HELENA Nor you, mistress,
Ever a friend whose thoughts more truly labour
To recompense your love. Doubt not but heaven
Hath brought me up to be your daughter's dower,
As it hath fated her to be my motive
And helper to a husband. But, O strange men!
That can such sweet use make of what they hate,
When saucy trusting of the cozen'd thoughts
Defiles the pitchy night. So lust doth play
With what it loathes, for that which is away.
But more of this hereafter. You, Diana,
Under my poor instructions yet must suffer
Something in my behalf.

DIANA Let death and honesty
Go with your impositions, I am yours
Upon your will to suffer.

HELENA Yet, I pray you:
But with the word the time will bring on summer,
When briers shall have leaves as well as thorns
And be as sweet as sharp. We must away;
Our waggon is prepar'd, and time revives us.
All's Well That Ends Well. Still the fine's the crown.

Whate'er the course, the end is the renown.
[Exeunt.

SCENE V. *Rousillon. The Count's palace.*

Enter COUNTESS, LAFEU, and Clown.

LAFEU No, no, no, your son was misled with a snipt-taffeta fellow there, whose villainous saffron would have made all the unbak'd and doughy youth of a nation in his colour. Your daughter-in-law had been alive at this hour, and your son here at home, more advanc'd by the King than by that red-tail'd humble-bee I speak of.

COUNTESS I would I had not known him. It was the death of the most virtuous gentlewoman that ever nature had praise for creating. If she had partaken of my flesh, and cost me the dearest groans of a mother, I could not have owed her a more rooted love.

LAFEU 'Twas a good lady, 'twas a good lady. We may pick a thousand sallets ere we light on such another herb.

CLOWN Indeed, sir, she was the sweet-marjoram of the sallet, or, rather, the herb of grace.

LAFEU They are not sallet-herbs, you knave; they are nose-herbs.

CLOWN I am no great Nebuchadnezzar, sir; I have not much skill in grass.

LAFEU Whether dost thou profess thyself – a knave or a fool?

CLOWN A fool, sir, at a woman's service, and a knave at a man's.

LAFEU Your distinction?

CLOWN I would cozen the man of his wife, and do his service.

LAFEU So you were a knave at his service, indeed.

CLOWN And I would give his wife my bauble, sir, to do her service.

LAFEU I will subscribe for thee; thou art both knave and fool.

CLOWN At your service.

LAFEU No, no, no.

CLOWN Why, sir, if I cannot serve you, I can serve as great a prince as you are.

LAFEU Who's that? A Frenchman?

CLOWN Faith, sir, 'a has an English name; but his fisnomy is more hotter in France than there.

LAFEU What prince is that?

CLOWN The Black Prince, sir; alias, the Prince of Darkness; alias, the devil.

LAFEU Hold thee, there's my purse. I give thee not this to suggest thee from thy master thou talk'st of; serve him still.

CLOWN I am a woodland fellow, sir, that always loved a great fire; and the master I speak of ever keeps a good fire. But, sure, he is the prince of the world; let his nobility remain in's court. I am for the house with the narrow gate, which I take to be too little for pomp to enter. Some that humble themselves may; but the many will be too chill and tender; and they'll be for the flow'ry way that leads to the broad gate and the great fire.

LAFEU Go thy ways, I begin to be aweary of thee; and I tell thee so before, because I would not fall out with thee. Go thy ways; let my horses be well look'd to, without any tricks.

CLOWN If I put any tricks upon 'em, sir, they shall be jades' tricks, which are their own right by the law of nature. *[Exit.*

LAFEU A shrewd knave, and an unhappy.

COUNTESS So 'a is. My lord that's gone made himself much sport out of him. By his authority he remains here, which he thinks is a patent for his sauciness; and indeed he has no pace, but runs where he will.

LAFEU I like him well; 'tis not amiss. And I was about to tell you, since I heard of the good lady's death, and that my lord your son was upon his return home, I moved the King my master to speak in the behalf of my daughter; which, in the minority of them both, his Majesty out of a self-gracious remembrance did first propose. His Highness hath promis'd me to do it; and, to stop up the displeasure he hath conceived against your son, there is no fitter matter. How does your ladyship like it?

COUNTESS With very much content, my lord; and I wish it happily effected.

LAFEU His Highness comes post from Marseilles, of as able body as when he number'd thirty; 'a will be here to-morrow, or I am deceiv'd by him that in such intelligence hath seldom fail'd.

COUNTESS It rejoices me that I hope I shall see him ere I die. I have letters that my son will be here to-night. I shall beseech your lordship to remain with me till they meet together.

LAFEU Madam, I was thinking with what manners I might safely be admitted.

COUNTESS You need but plead your honourable privilege.

LAFEU Lady, of that I have made a bold charter; but, I thank my God, it holds yet.

Re-enter Clown.

CLOWN O madam, yonder's my lord your son with a patch of velvet on's face; whether there be a scar under 't or no, the velvet knows; but 'tis a goodly patch of velvet. His left cheek is a cheek of two pile and a half, but his right cheek is worn bare.

LAFEU A scar nobly got, or a noble scar, is a good liv'ry of honour; so belike is that.

CLOWN But it is your carbonado'd face.

LAFEU Let us go see your son, I pray you; I long to talk with the young noble soldier.

CLOWN Faith, there's a dozen of 'em, with delicate fine hats, and most courteous feathers, which bow the head and nod at every man.

[*Exeunt.*

ACT FIVE

SCENE I. *Marseilles. A street.*

Enter HELENA, Widow, and DIANA, with two Attendants.

HELENA But this exceeding posting day and night
Must wear your spirits low; we cannot help it.
But since you have made the days and nights as one,
To wear your gentle limbs in my affairs,
Be bold you do so grow in my requital
As nothing can unroot you.

Enter a Gentleman.

In happy time!
This man may help me to his Majesty's ear,
If he would spend his power. God save you, sir.

GENTLEMAN And you.

HELENA Sir, I have seen you in the court of France.

GENTLEMAN I have been sometimes there.

HELENA I do presume, sir, that you are not fall'n
From the report that goes upon your goodness;
And therefore, goaded with most sharp occasions,
Which lay nice manners by, I put you to
The use of your own virtues, for the which
I shall continue thankful.

GENTLEMAN What's your will?

HELENA That it will please you
To give this poor petition to the King;
And aid me with that store of power you have
To come into his presence.

GENTLEMAN The King's not here.

HELENA Not here, sir?

GENTLEMAN Not indeed.
He hence remov'd last night, and with more haste
Than is his use.

WIDOW Lord, how we lose our pains!

HELENA All's Well That Ends Well yet,
Though time seem so adverse and means unfit.
I do beseech you, whither is he gone?

GENTLEMAN Marry, as I take it, to Rousillon;
Whither I am going.

HELENA I do beseech you, sir,
Since you are like to see the King before me,
Commend the paper to his gracious hand;
Which I presume shall render you no blame,
But rather make you thank your pains for it.
I will come after you with what good speed
Our means will make us means.

GENTLEMAN This I'll do for you.

HELENA And you shall find yourself to be well thank'd,
Whate'er falls more. We must to horse again;
Go, go, provide. [*Exeunt.*

SCENE II. *Rousillon. The inner court of the Count's palace.*

Enter Clown and PAROLLES.

PAROLLES Good Monsieur Lavache, give my Lord Lafeu this letter. I have ere now, sir, been better known to you, when I have held familiarity with fresher clothes; but I am now, sir, muddied in Fortune's mood, and smell somewhat strong of her strong displeasure.

CLOWN Truly, Fortune's displeasure is but sluttish, if it smell so strongly as thou speak'st of. I will henceforth eat no fish of Fortune's butt'ring. Prithee, allow the wind.

PAROLLES Nay, you need not to stop your nose, sir; I spake but by a metaphor.

CLOWN Indeed, sir, if your metaphor stink, I will stop my nose; or against any man's metaphor. Prithee, get thee further.

PAROLLES Pray you, sir, deliver me this paper.

CLOWN Foh! prithee stand away. A paper from Fortune's close-stool to give to a nobleman! Look here he comes himself.

Enter LAFEU.

Here is a pur of Fortune's, sir, or of Fortune's cat, but not a musk-cat, that has fall'n into the unclean fishpond of her displeasure, and, as he says, is muddied withal. Pray you, sir, use the carp as you may; for he looks like a poor, decayed, ingenious, foolish, rascally knave. I do pity his distress in my similes of comfort, and leave him to your lordship. [*Exit.*

PAROLLES My lord, I am a man whom Fortune hath cruelly scratch'd.

LAFEU And what would you have me to do? 'Tis too late to pare her nails now. Wherein have you played the knave with Fortune, that she should scratch you, who of herself is a good lady and would not have knaves thrive long under her? There's a cardecue for you. Let the justices make you and Fortune friends; I am for other business.

PAROLLES I beseech your honour to hear me one single word.

LAFEU You beg a single penny more; come, you shall ha't; save your word.

PAROLLES My name, my good lord, is Parolles.

LAFEU You beg more than word then. Cox my passion! give me your hand. How does your drum?

PAROLLES O my good lord, you were the first that found me.

LAFEU Was I, in sooth? And I was the first that lost thee.

PAROLLES It lies in you, my lord, to bring me in some grace, for you did bring me out.

LAFEU Out upon thee, knave! Dost thou put upon me at once both the office of God and the devil? One brings thee in grace, and the other brings thee out. [*Trumpets sound*] The King's coming; I know by his trumpets. Sirrah, inquire further after me; I had talk of you last night. Though you are a fool and a knave, you shall eat. Go to; follow.

PAROLLES I praise God for you. [*Exeunt.*

SCENE III. *Rousillon. The Count's palace.*

Flourish. Enter KING, COUNTESS, LAFEU, the two French Lords, with Attendants.

KING We lost a jewel of her, and our esteem
Was made much poorer by it; but your son,
As mad in folly, lack'd the sense to know
Her estimation home.

COUNTESS 'Tis past, my liege;
And I beseech your Majesty to make it
Natural rebellion, done i' th' blaze of youth,
When oil and fire, too strong for reason's force,
O'erbears it and burns on.

KING My honour'd lady,
I have forgiven and forgotten all;
Though my revenges were high bent upon him
And watch'd the time to shoot.

LAFEU This I must say –
But first, I beg my pardon: the young lord
Did to his Majesty, his mother, and his lady,
Offence of mighty note; but to himself
The greatest wrong of all. He lost a wife
Whose beauty did astonish the survey
Of richest eyes; whose words all ears took captive;
Whose dear perfection hearts that scorn'd to serve
Humbly call'd mistress.

KING Praising what is lost
Makes the remembrance dear. Well, call him hither;
We are reconcil'd, and the first view shall kill
All repetition. Let him not ask our pardon;
The nature of his great offence is dead,
And deeper than oblivion do we bury
Th' incensing relics of it; let him approach,
A stranger, no offender; and inform him
So 'tis our will he should.

GENTLEMAN I shall, my liege.
[*Exit Gentleman.*

KING What says he to your daughter? Have you spoke?

LAFEU All that he is hath reference to your Highness.

KING Then shall we have a match. I have letters sent me
That sets him high in fame.

Enter BERTRAM.

LAFEU He looks well on't.

KING I am not a day of season,
For thou mayst see a sunshine and a hail
In me at once. But to the brightest beams
Distracted clouds give way; so stand thou forth;
The time is fair again.

BERTRAM My high-repented blames,
Dear sovereign, pardon to me.

KING All is whole;
Not one word more of the consumed time.
Let's take the instant by the forward top;
For we are old, and on our quick'st decrees
Th' inaudible and noiseless foot of Time
Steals ere we can effect them. You remember
The daughter of this lord?

BERTRAM Admiringly, my liege. At first
I stuck my choice upon her, ere my heart
Durst make too bold a herald of my tongue;
Where the impression of mine eye infixing,
Contempt his scornful perspective did lend me,
Which warp'd the line of every other favour,
Scorn'd a fair colour or express'd it stol'n,
Extended or contracted all proportions
To a most hideous object. Thence it came
That she whom all men prais'd, and whom myself,
Since I have lost, have lov'd, was in mine eye
The dust that did offend it.

KING Well excus'd.
That thou didst love her, strikes some scores away
From the great compt; but love that comes too late,
Like a remorseful pardon slowly carried,
To the great sender turns a sour offence,
Crying 'That's good that's gone'. Our rash faults
Make trivial price of serious things we have,
Not knowing them until we know their grave.

Oft our displeasures, to ourselves unjust,
Destroy our friends, and after weep their dust;
Our own love waking cries to see what's done,
While shameful hate sleeps out the afternoon.
Be this sweet Helen's knell. And now forget her.
Send forth your amorous token for fair Maudlin.
The main consents are had; and here we'll stay
To see our widower's second marriage-day.

COUNTESS Which better than the first, O dear heaven, bless!
Or, ere they meet, in me, O nature, cesse!

LAFEU Come on, my son, in whom my house's name
Must be digested; give a favour from you,
To sparkle in the spirits of my daughter,
That she may quickly come.

[Bertram gives a ring.

By my old beard,
And ev'ry hair that's on't, Helen, that's dead,
Was a sweet creature; such a ring as this,
The last that e'er I took her leave at court,
I saw upon her finger.

BERTRAM Hers it was not.

KING Now, pray you, let me see it; for mine eye,
While I was speaking, oft was fasten'd to't.
This ring was mine; and when I gave it Helen
I bade her, if her fortunes ever stood
Necessitied to help, that by this token
I would relieve her. Had you that craft to reave her
Of what should stead her most?

BERTRAM My gracious sovereign,
Howe'er it pleases you to take it so,
The ring was never hers.

COUNTESS Son, on my life,
I have seen her wear it; and she reckon'd it
At her life's rate.

LAFEU I am sure I saw her wear it.

BERTRAM You are deceiv'd, my lord; she never saw it.
In Florence was it from a casement thrown me,
Wrapp'd in a paper, which contain'd the name
Of her that threw it. Noble she was, and thought
I stood engag'd; but when I had subscrib'd
To mine own fortune, and inform'd her fully
I could not answer in that course of honour
As she had made the overture, she ceas'd,
In heavy satisfaction, and would never
Receive the ring again.

KING Plutus himself,
That knows the tinct and multiplying med'cine,
Hath not in nature's mystery more science
Than I have in this ring. 'Twas mine, 'twas Helen's,
Whoever gave it you. Then, if you know
That you are well acquainted with yourself,
Confess 'twas hers, and by what rough enforcement
You got it from her. She call'd the saints to surety
That she would never put it from her finger
Unless she gave it to yourself in bed –
Where you have never come – or sent it us
Upon her great disaster.

BERTRAM She never saw it.

KING Thou speak'st it falsely, as I love mine honour;
And mak'st conjectural fears to come into me
Which I would fain shut out. If it should prove
That thou art so inhuman – 'twill not prove so.
And yet I know not – thou didst hate her deadly,
And she is dead; which nothing, but to close
Her eyes myself, could win me to believe
More than to see this ring. Take him away.

[Guards seize Bertram.

My fore-past proofs, howe'er the matter fall,
Shall tax my fears of little vanity,
Having vainly fear'd too little. Away with him.
We'll sift this matter further.

BERTRAM If you shall prove
This ring was ever hers, you shall as easy
Prove that I husbanded her bed in Florence,
Where she yet never was. *[Exit, guarded.*

KING I am wrapp'd in dismal thinkings.

Enter a Gentleman.

GENTLEMAN Gracious sovereign,
Whether I have been to blame or no, I know not:
Here's a petition from a Florentine,
Who hath, for four or five removes, come short
To tender it herself. I undertook it,
Vanquish'd thereto by the fair grace and speech
Of the poor suppliant, who by this, I know,
Is here attending; her business looks in her
With an importing visage; and she told me
In a sweet verbal brief it did concern
Your Highness with herself.

KING *[Reads the letter]* 'Upon his many protestations to marry me when his wife was dead, I blush to say it, he won me. Now is the Count Rousillon a widower; his vows are forfeited to me, and my honour's paid to him. He stole from Florence, taking no leave, and I follow him to his country for justice. Grant it me, O King! in you it best lies; otherwise a seducer flourishes, and a poor maid is undone.
DIANA CAPILET.'

LAFEU I will buy me a son-in-law in a fair, and toll for this. I'll none of him.

KING The heavens have thought well on thee, Lafeu,

To bring forth this discov'ry. Seek these suitors.
Go speedily, and bring again the Count.
[Exeunt Attendants.
I am afeard the life of Helen, lady,
Was foully snatch'd.
COUNTESS Now, justice on the doers!

Enter BERTRAM, guarded.

KING I wonder, sir, sith wives are monsters to you,
And that you fly them as you swear them lordship,
Yet you desire to marry.

Enter Widow and DIANA.

What woman's that?
DIANA I am, my lord, a wretched Florentine,
Derived from the ancient Capilet.
My suit, as I do understand, you know,
And therefore know how far I may be pitied.
WIDOW I am her mother, sir, whose age and honour
Both suffer under this complaint we bring,
And both shall cease, without your remedy.
KING Come hither, Count; do you know these women?
BERTRAM My lord, I neither can nor will deny
But that I know them. Do they charge me further?
DIANA Why do you look so strange upon your wife.
BERTRAM She's none of mine, my lord.
DIANA If you shall marry,
You give away this hand, and that is mine;
You give away heaven's vows, and those are mine;
You give away myself, which is known mine;
For I by vow am so embodied yours
That she which marries you must marry me,
Either both or none.
LAFEU *[To Bertram]* Your reputation comes too short for my daughter; you are no husband for her.
BERTRAM My lord, this is a fond and desp'rate creature
Whom sometime I have laugh'd with. Let your Highness
Lay a more noble thought upon mine honour
Than for to think that I would sink it here.
KING Sir, for my thoughts, you have them ill to friend
Till your deeds gain them. Fairer prove your honour
Than in my thought it lies!
DIANA Good my lord,
Ask him upon his oath if he does think
He had not my virginity.
KING What say'st thou to her?
BERTRAM She's impudent, my lord,
And was a common gamester to the camp.
DIANA He does me wrong, my lord; if I were so
He might have bought me at a common price.
Do not believe him. O, behold this ring,
Whose high respect and rich validity
Did lack a parallel; yet, for all that,
He gave it to a commoner o' th' camp.
If I be one.
COUNTESS He blushes, and 'tis it.
Of six preceding ancestors, that gem
Conferr'd by testament to th' sequent issue,
Hath it been ow'd and worn. This is his wife:
That ring's a thousand proofs.
KING Methought you said
You saw one here in court could witness it.
DIANA I did, my lord, but loath am to produce
So bad an instrument; his name's Parolles.
LAFEU I saw the man to-day, if man he be.
KING Find him, and bring him hither.
[Exit an Attendant.
BERTRAM What of him?
He's quoted for a most perfidious slave,
With all the spots o' th' world tax'd and debauch'd,
Whose nature sickens but to speak a truth.
Am I or that or this for what he'll utter
That will speak anything?
KING She hath that ring of yours.
BERTRAM I think she has. Certain it is I lik'd her,
And boarded her i' th' wanton way of youth.
She knew her distance, and did angle for me,
Madding my eagerness with her restraint,
As all impediments in fancy's course
Are motives of more fancy; and, in fine,
Her infinite cunning with her modern grace
Subdu'd me to her rate. She got the ring;
And I had that which any inferior might
At market-price have bought.
DIANA I must be patient.
You that have turn'd off a first so noble wife
May justly diet me. I pray you yet –
Since you lack virtue, I will lose a husband –
Send for your ring, I will return it home,
And give me mine again.
BERTRAM I have it not.
KING What ring was yours, I pray you?
DIANA Sir, much like
The same upon your finger.
KING Know you this ring? This ring was his of late.
DIANA And this was it I gave him, being abed.
KING The story, then, goes false you threw it him
Out of a casement.
DIANA I have spoke the truth.

Enter PAROLLES.

BERTRAM My lord, I do confess the ring was hers.

KING You boggle shrewdly; every feather starts you.
Is this the man you speak of?
DIANA Ay, my lord.
KING Tell me, sirrah – but tell me true I charge you,
Not fearing the displeasure of your master,
Which, on your just proceeding, I'll keep off –
By him and by this woman here what know you?
PAROLLES So please your Majesty, my master hath been an honourable gentleman; tricks he hath had in him, which gentlemen have.
KING Come, come, to th' purpose. Did he love this woman?
PAROLLES Faith, sir, he did love her; but how?
KING How, I pray you?
PAROLLES He did love her, sir, as a gentleman loves a woman.
KING How is that?
PAROLLES He lov'd her, sir, and lov'd her not.
KING As thou art a knave and no knave. What an equivocal companion is this!
PAROLLES I am a poor man, and at your Majesty's command.
LAFEU He's a good drum, my lord, but a naughty orator.
DIANA Do you know he promis'd me marriage?
PAROLLES Faith, I know more than I'll speak.
KING But wilt thou not speak all thou know'st?
PAROLLES Yes, so please your Majesty. I did go between them, as I said; but more than that, he loved her – for indeed he was mad for her, and talk'd of Satan, and of Limbo, and of Furies, and I know not what. Yet I was in that credit with them at that time that I knew of their going to bed; and of other motions, as promising her marriage, and things which would derive me ill will to speak of; therefore I will not speak what I know.
KING Thou hast spoken all already, unless thou canst say they are married; but thou art too fine in thy evidence; therefore stand aside.
This ring, you say, was yours?
DIANA Ay, my good lord.
KING Where did you buy it? Or who gave it you?
DIANA It was not given me, nor I did not buy it.
KING Who lent it you?
DIANA It was not lent me neither.
KING Where did you find it then?
DIANA I found it not.
KING If it were yours by none of all these ways,
How could you give it him?
DIANA I never gave it him.
LAFEU This woman's an easy glove, my lord; she goes off and on at pleasure.
KING This ring was mine, I gave it his first wife.
DIANA It might be yours or hers, for aught I know.
KING Take her away, I do not like her now;
To prison with her. And away with him.
Unless thou tell'st me where thou hadst this ring,
Thou diest within this hour.
DIANA I'll never tell you.
KING Take her away.
DIANA I'll put in bail, my liege.
KING I think thee now some common customer.
DIANA By Jove, if ever I knew man, 'twas you.
KING Wherefore hast thou accus'd him all this while?
DIANA Because he's guilty, and he is not guilty.
He knows I am no maid, and he'll swear to't:
I'll swear I am a maid, and he knows not.
Great King, I am no strumpet, by my life;
I am either maid, or else this old man's wife.
[*Pointing to Lafeu.*
KING She does abuse our ears; to prison with her.
DIANA Good mother, fetch my bail. Stay, royal sir; [*Exit Widow.*
The jeweller that owes the ring is sent for,
And he shall surety me. But for this lord
Who hath abus'd me as he knows himself,
Though yet he never harm'd me, here I quit him.
He knows himself my bed he hath defil'd;
And at that time he got his wife with child.
Dead though she be, she feels her young one kick;
So there's my riddle: one that's dead is quick –
And now behold the meaning.

Re-enter Widow with HELENA.

KING Is there no exorcist
Beguiles the truer office of mine eyes?
Is't real that I see?
HELENA No, my good lord;
'Tis but the shadow of a wife you see,
The name and not the thing.
BERTRAM Both, both; O, pardon!
HELENA O, my good lord, when I was like this maid,
I found you wondrous kind. There is your ring,
And, look you, here's your letter. This it says:
'When from my finger you can get this ring,
And are by me with child,' etc. This is done.
Will you be mine now you are doubly won?
BERTRAM If she, my liege, can make me know this clearly,
I'll love her dearly, ever, ever dearly.
HELENA If it appear not plain, and prove untrue,
Deadly divorce step between me and you!
O my dear mother, do I see you living?
LAFEU Mine eyes smell onions; I shall weep

anon. [*To Parolles*] Good Tom Drum, lend me a handkercher. So, I thank thee. Wait on me home, I'll make sport with thee; let thy curtsies alone, they are scurvy ones.

KING Let us from point to point this story know,
To make the even truth in pleasure flow.
[*To Diana*] If thou beest yet a fresh uncropped flower,
Choose thou thy husband, and I'll pay thy dower;
For I can guess that by thy honest aid
Thou kept'st a wife herself, thyself a maid. –
Of that and all the progress, more and less,
Resolvedly more leisure shall express.
All yet seems well; and if it end so meet,
The bitter past, more welcome is the sweet.

[*Flourish*.

EPILOGUE

The King's a beggar, now the play is done.
All is well ended if this suit be won,
That you express content; which we will pay
With strife to please you, day exceeding day.
Ours be your patience then, and yours our parts;
Your gentle hands lend us, and take our hearts.

[*Exeunt omnes*.

Twelfth Night

Introduction by DAVID NEWELL

Samuel Pepys grumbled about the irrelevance of the title ('a silly play, and not related at all to the name or day') and King Charles I's Master of the Revels officiously re-christened it 'Malvolio'. But then the rather cavalier subtitle of *Twelfth Night*, 'What You Will', seems cheekily to derail all critical debate from the very start. The play is simply what we want it to be. But exactly what we want – or get – is not clear. Despite comprehending the standard ingredients of Shakespearean comedy – farce, cerebral wit, pathos, romance – *Twelfth Night* stubbornly resists easy analysis.

As Alexander Leggatt has demonstrated (Leggatt, 1974), the comic misunderstandings and false expectations inherent in language are central to title and play. Illyria, itself a word game, is permeated by illness (we meet one supposed madman and a couple of victims of a street brawl), illusion, and lyric poetry. But the first pun is Viola's:

And what should I do in Illyria?
My brother he is in Elysium. [1.2.3–4]

This wistfully oblique attempt to bridge the gulf between the dead and the living prepares us for the other-worldly magic to come. In the touching reunion of brother and sister Illyria, momentarily, *is* Elysium.

Words are constantly changing hands in this linguistically competitive society, where verbal dexterity is essential to survival. The battledore and shuttlecock dialogue between the equally matched Sir Toby and Maria [1.3] echoes the earlier comedies but outstrips them in brevity and functional value, anticipating the play's most plausible marriage.

Where Sir Toby and Maria lead in the national sport, others follow. Feste fields and hoards Malvolio's insults eventually to return them with interest, proving that, as Wilde's Lady Windermere says, 'words are merciless'. Malvolio himself is wedded to a self-centred hermeneutic which can transform Olivia's innocent 'fellow' into a confession of equality, and 'Wilt thou go to bed?' into instant seduction [3.4]. Theirs is the conversation of the mentally deaf, locked in mutual misunderstanding. Sir Andrew, feebly aware that he is no polymath, anxiously and indiscriminately gathers the lexical droppings of others like manna to supply his own deficiency:

Viola: Most excellent accomplish'd lady, the heavens rain odours on you!
Sir Andrew: That youth's a rare courtier – 'Rain odours' well! [3.1.80]

Even Orsino, trapped in his own fantasies, cannot hear 'hart' without thinking 'heart'.

It is Viola, however, who brings warmth to words, freshening up the drab clichés of romantic comedy. The distance between the blatant artificiality of 'Most radiant, exquisite and unmatchable beauty', mocking Orsino's naive platitudes, and the 'willow cabin' speech is that between recycling and rejuvenation.

Indeed, no episode more effectively (and unexpectedly) swings from the banal to the genuine than this first encounter between Olivia and Viola/Cesario [1.5]. Like almost everyone in Illyria, both hide behind roles, Olivia concealing her romantic impulses and Viola her gender. Yet what begins as a light-hearted tournament of wit, each challenging the other's verbal prowess, develops into a love scene simultaneously absurd and poignant because of Viola's disguise. This change is signalled by the shift from prose, the natural medium of banter and jest, to blank verse, the vehicle of tenderness. Even the pronouns in Olivia's speech slip from the formal 'you' to the daringly intimate 'thou'.

If language confuses, so too does plot. *Twelfth Night* draws on earlier plays like *The Comedy of Errors* and *The Two Gentlemen of Verona*, but spices its borrowings with a new irony. Identical twinning separates friends and fertilises romance. Disguise proves self-defeating. Viola's tantalising proximity to Orsino only scuppers any attempts to communicate, while her male clothing embarrassingly demands male heroism. Even the arch-tricksters are tricked. In duping Malvolio, Toby, Andrew and Fabian unwittingly allow him to dominate the stage. While they descend to the level of vegetation ('Get ye all three into the box-tree') the steward rises in imagination to aristocracy ('To be Count Malvolio!'). Further, the gathering malice behind the gulling plot endows its victim with new sympathy and grudging respect for his unshakable sanity ('I say this house is as dark as ignorance'). In a topsy-turvy world Malvolio at least will not be bullied into denying the evidence of his senses.

The comedy which begins with the conventional amatory metaphor of deer-coursing ends with the more disturbing image of bear-baiting. For once, romance fails to get the last word. 'I'll be reveng'd on the whole pack of you', along with Feste's uncomfortable song about age and exposure, lingers in the memory after jests, reunions, and marriages have been forgotten. Perhaps, after all, that Carolean entertainments manager was instinctively right in seeing the enemy of revelry as the awkward centre of *Twelfth Night*.

Twelfth Night

DRAMATIS PERSONAE

ORSINO
Duke of Illyria

SEBASTIAN
brother of Viola

ANTONIO
a sea captain, friend of Sebastian

A Sea Captain friend of Viola

VALENTINE, CURIO
gentlemen attending on the Duke

SIR TOBY BELCH
uncle of Olivia

SIR ANDREW AGUECHEEK

MALVOLIO
steward to Olivia

FABIAN, FESTE, *a clown*
servants to Olivia

OLIVIA
a rich countess

VIOLA
sister of Sebastian

MARIA
Olivia's waiting woman

Lords, Priests, Sailors, Officers, Musicians, and Attendants

THE SCENE: A CITY IN ILLYRIA; AND THE SEA-COAST NEAR IT.

ACT ONE

SCENE I. *The Duke's palace.*

Enter ORSINO, Duke of Illyria, CURIO, and other Lords; Musicians attending.

DUKE If music be the food of love, play on,
Give me excess of it, that, surfeiting,
The appetite may sicken and so die.
That strain again! It had a dying fall;
O, it came o'er my ear like the sweet sound
That breathes upon a bank of violets,
Stealing and giving odour! Enough, no more;
'Tis not so sweet now as it was before.
O spirit of love, how quick and fresh art thou!
That, notwithstanding thy capacity
Receiveth as the sea, nought enters there,
Of what validity and pitch soe'er,
But falls into abatement and low price
Even in a minute. So full of shapes is fancy,
That it alone is high fantastical.

CURIO Will you go hunt, my lord?

DUKE What, Curio?

CURIO The hart.

DUKE Why, so I do, the noblest that I have.
O, when mine eyes did see Olivia first,
Methought she purg'd the air of pestilence!
That instant was I turn'd into a hart,
And my desires, like fell and cruel hounds,
E'er since pursue me.

Enter VALENTINE

How now! what news from her?

VALENTINE So please my lord, I might not be admitted,
But from her handmaid do return this answer
The element itself, till seven years' heat,
Shall not behold her face at ample view;
But like a cloistress she will veiled walk,
And water once a day her chamber round
With eye-offending brine; all this to season
A brother's dead love, which she would keep fresh
And lasting in her sad remembrance.

DUKE O, she that hath a heart of that fine frame
To pay this debt of love but to a brother,
How will she love when the rich golden shaft
Hath kill'd the flock of all affections else
That live in her; when liver, brain, and heart,
These sovereign thrones, are all supplied and fill'd,
Her sweet perfections, with one self king!
Away before me to sweet beds of flow'rs:
Love-thoughts lie rich when canopied with bow'rs.
[*Exeunt.*

SCENE II. *The sea-coast.*

Enter VIOLA, a Captain, and Sailors.

VIOLA What country, friends, is this?

CAPTAIN This is Illyria, lady.

VIOLA And what should I do in Illyria?
My brother he is in Elysium.
Perchance he is not drown'd – what think you, sailors?

CAPTAIN It is perchance that you yourself were saved.

VIOLA O my poor brother! and so perchance may he be.

CAPTAIN True, madam, and, to comfort you with chance,
Assure yourself, after our ship did split,

When you, and those poor number saved with you,
Hung on our driving boat, I saw your brother,
Most provident in peril, bind himself –
Courage and hope both teaching him the practice –
To a strong mast that liv'd upon the sea;
Where, like Arion on the dolphin's back,
I saw him hold acquaintance with the waves
So long as I could see.

VIOLA For saying so, there's gold.
Mine own escape unfoldeth to my hope,
Whereto thy speech serves for authority,
The like of him. Know'st thou this country?

CAPTAIN Ay, madam, well; for I was bred and born
Not three hours' travel from this very place.

VIOLA Who governs here?

CAPTAIN A noble duke, in nature as in name.

VIOLA What is his name?

CAPTAIN Orsino.

VIOLA Orsino! I have heard my father name him.
He was a bachelor then.

CAPTAIN And so is now, or was so very late;
For but a month ago I went from hence,
And then 'twas fresh in murmur – as, you know,
What great ones do the less will prattle of –
That he did seek the love of fair Olivia.

VIOLA What's she?

CAPTAIN A virtuous maid, the daughter of a count
That died some twelvemonth since, then leaving her
In the protection of his son, her brother,
Who shortly also died; for whose dear love,
They say, she hath abjur'd the company
And sight of men.

VIOLA O that I serv'd that lady,
And might not be delivered to the world,
Till I had made mine own occasion mellow,
What my estate is!

CAPTAIN That were hard to compass,
Because she will admit no kind of suit –
No, not the Duke's.

VIOLA There is a fair behaviour in thee, Captain;
And though that nature with a beauteous wall
Doth oft close in pollution, yet of thee
I will believe thou hast a mind that suits
With this thy fair and outward character.
I prithee, and I'll pay thee bounteously,
Conceal me what I am, and be my aid
For such disguise as haply shall become
The form of my intent. I'll serve this duke:
Thou shalt present me as an eunuch to him;
It may be worth thy pains, for I can sing
And speak to him in many sorts of music,
That will allow me very worth his service.
What else may hap to time I will commit;
Only shape thou thy silence to my wit.

CAPTAIN Be you his eunuch and your mute I'll be;
When my tongue blabs, then let mine eyes not see.

VIOLA I thank thee. Lead me on. [*Exeunt.*

SCENE III. *Olivia's house.*

Enter SIR TOBY BELCH and MARIA.

SIR TOBY What a plague means my niece to take the death of her brother thus? I am sure care's an enemy to life.

MARIA By my troth, Sir Toby, you must come in earlier o' nights; your cousin, my lady, takes great exceptions to your ill hours.

SIR TOBY Why, let her except before excepted.

MARIA Ay, but you must confine yourself within the modest limits of order.

SIR TOBY Confine! I'll confine myself no finer than I am. These clothes are good enough to drink in, and so be these boots too; an they be not, let them hang themselves in their own straps.

MARIA That quaffing and drinking will undo you; I heard my lady talk of it yesterday, and of a foolish knight that you brought in one night here to be her wooer.

SIR TOBY Who? Sir Andrew Aguecheek?

MARIA Ay, he.

SIR TOBY He's as tall a man as any's in Illyria.

MARIA What's that to th' purpose?

SIR TOBY Why, he has three thousand ducats a year.

MARIA Ay, but he'll have but a year in all these ducats; he's a very fool and a prodigal.

SIR TOBY Fie that you'll say so! He plays o' th' viol-de-gamboys, and speaks three or four languages word for word without book, and hath all the good gifts of nature.

MARIA He hath indeed, almost natural; for, besides that he's a fool, he's a great quarreller; and but that he hath the gift of a coward to allay the gust he hath in quarrelling, 'tis thought among the prudent he would quickly have the gift of a grave.

SIR TOBY By this hand, they are scoundrels and substractors that say so of him. Who are they?

MARIA They that add, moreover, he's drunk nightly in your company.

SIR TOBY With drinking healths to my niece; I'll drink to her as long as there is a passage in my throat and drink in Illyria. He's a coward and a coystrill that will not drink to my niece till his brains turn o' th' toe like a parish-top. What, wench! Castiliano vulgo! for here comes Sir Andrew Agueface.

Enter SIR ANDREW AGUECHEEK.

SIR ANDREW Sir Toby Belch! How now, Sir Toby Belch!

SIR TOBY Sweet Sir Andrew!

SIR ANDREW Bless you, fair shrew.

MARIA And you too, sir.

SIR TOBY Accost, Sir Andrew, accost.

SIR ANDREW What's that?

SIR TOBY My niece's chambermaid.

SIR ANDREW Good Mistress Accost, I desire better acquaintance.

MARIA My name is Mary, sir.

SIR ANDREW Good Mistress Mary Accost –

SIR TOBY You mistake, knight. 'Accost' is front her, board her, woo her, assail her.

SIR ANDREW By my troth, I would not undertake her in this company. Is that the meaning of 'accost'?

MARIA Fare you well, gentlemen.

SIR TOBY An thou let part so, Sir Andrew, would thou mightst never draw sword again!

SIR ANDREW An you part so, mistress, I would I might never draw sword again. Fair lady, do you think you have fools in hand?

MARIA Sir, I have not you by th' hand.

SIR ANDREW Marry, but you shall have; and here's my hand.

MARIA Now, sir, thought is free. I pray you, bring your hand to th' butt'ry-bar and let it drink.

SIR ANDREW Wherefore, sweetheart? What's your metaphor?

MARIA It's dry, sir.

SIR ANDREW Why, I think so; I am not such an ass but I can keep my hand dry. But what's your jest?

MARIA A dry jest, sir.

SIR ANDREW Are you full of them?

MARIA Ay, sir, I have them at my fingers' ends; marry, now I let go your hand, I am barren.

[*Exit Maria.*

SIR TOBY O knight, thou lack'st a cup of canary! When did I see thee so put down?

SIR ANDREW Never in your life, I think; unless you see canary put me down. Methinks sometimes I have no more wit than a Christian or an ordinary man has; but I am a great eater of beef, and I believe that does harm to my wit.

SIR TOBY No question.

SIR ANDREW An I thought that, I'd forswear it. I'll ride home to-morrow, Sir Toby.

SIR TOBY Pourquoi, my dear knight?

SIR ANDREW What is 'pourquoi' – do or not do? I would I had bestowed that time in the tongues that I have in fencing, dancing, and bear-baiting. O, had I but followed the arts!

SIR TOBY Then hadst thou had an excellent head of hair.

SIR ANDREW Why, would that have mended my hair?

SIR TOBY Past question; for thou seest it will not curl by nature.

SIR ANDREW But it becomes me well enough, does't not?

SIR TOBY Excellent; it hangs like flax on a distaff, and I hope to see a huswife take thee between her legs and spin it off.

SIR ANDREW Faith, I'll home to-morrow, Sir Toby. Your niece will not be seen, or if she be, it's four to one she'll none of me; the Count himself here hard by woos her.

SIR TOBY She'll none o' th' Count; she'll not match above her degree, neither in estate, years, not wit; I have heard her swear't. Tut, there's life in't, man.

SIR ANDREW I'll stay a month longer. I am a fellow o' th' strangest mind i' th' world; I delight in masques and revels sometimes altogether.

SIR TOBY Art thou good at these kick-shawses, knight?

SIR ANDREW As any man in Illyria, whatsoever he be, under the degree of my betters; and yet I will not compare with an old man.

SIR TOBY What is thy excellence in a galliard, knight?

SIR ANDREW Faith, I can cut a caper.

SIR TOBY And I can cut the mutton to't.

SIR ANDREW And I think I have the back-trick simply as strong as any man in Illyria.

SIR TOBY Wherefore are these things hid? Wherefore have these gifts a curtain before 'em? Are they like to take dust, like Mistress Mall's picture? Why dost thou not go to church in a galliard and come home in a coranto? My very walk should be a jig; I would not so much as make water but in a sink-a-pace. What dost thou mean? Is it a world to hide virtues in? I did think, by the excellent constitution of thy leg, it was form'd under the star of a galliard.

SIR ANDREW Ay, 'tis strong, and it does indifferent well in a flame-colour'd stock. Shall we set about some revels?

SIR TOBY What shall we do else? Were we not born under Taurus?

SIR ANDREW Taurus? That's sides and heart.

SIR TOBY No, sir; it is legs and thighs. Let me see thee caper. Ha, higher! Ha, ha, excellent!

[*Exeunt.*

SCENE IV. *The Duke's palace.*

Enter VALENTINE, and VIOLA in a man's attire.

VALENTINE If the Duke continue these favours towards you, Cesario, you are like to be much advanc'd; he hath known you but three days, and already you are no stranger.

VIOLA You either fear his humour or my negligence, that you call in question the continuance of his love. Is he inconstant, sir, in his favours?

VALENTINE No, believe me.

Enter DUKE, CURIO, and Attendants.

VIOLA I thank you. Here comes the Count.

DUKE Who saw Cesario, ho?

VIOLA On your attendance, my lord, here.

DUKE Stand you awhile aloof. Cesario,
Thou know'st no less but all; I have unclasp'd
To thee the book even of my secret soul.
Therefore, good youth, address thy gait unto her;
Be not denied access, stand at her doors,
And tell them there thy fixed foot shall grow
Till thou have audience.

VIOLA Sure, my noble lord,
If she be so abandon'd to her sorrow
As it is spoke, she never will admit me.

DUKE Be clamorous and leap all civil bounds,
Rather than make unprofited return.

VIOLA Say I do speak with her, my lord, what then?

DUKE O, then unfold the passion of my love,
Surprise her with discourse of my dear faith!
It shall become thee well to act my woes:
She will attend it better in thy youth
Than in a nuncio's of more grave aspect.

VIOLA I think not so, my lord.

DUKE Dear lad, believe it,
For they shall yet belie thy happy years
That say thou art a man; Diana's lip
Is not more smooth and rubious; thy small pipe
Is as the maiden's organ, shrill and sound,
And all is semblative a woman's part.
I know thy constellation is right apt
For this affair. Some four or five attend him –
All, if you will, for I myself am best
When least in company. Prosper well in this,
And thou shalt live as freely as thy lord
To call his fortunes thine.

VIOLA I'll do my best
To woo your lady. [*Aside*] Yet, a barful strife!
Whoe'er I woo, myself would be his wife.

SCENE V. *Olivia's house.*

Enter MARIA and Clown.

MARIA Nay, either tell me where thou hast been, or I will not open my lips so wide as a bristle may enter in way of thy excuse; my lady will hang thee for thy absence.

CLOWN Let her hand me. He that is well hang'd in this world needs to fear no colours.

MARIA Make that good.

CLOWN He shall see none to fear.

MARIA A good lenten answer. I can tell thee where that saying was born, of 'I fear no colours.'

CLOWN Where, good Mistress Mary?

MARIA In the wars; and that may you be bold to say in your foolery.

CLOWN Well, God give them wisdom that have it; and those that are fools, let them use their talents.

MARIA Yet you will be hang'd for being so long absent; or to be turn'd away – is not that as good as a hanging to you?

CLOWN Many a good hanging prevents a bad marriage; and for turning away, let summer bear it out.

MARIA You are resolute, then?

CLOWN Not so, neither; but I am resolv'd on two points.

MARIA That if one break, the other will hold; or if both break, your gaskins fall.

CLOWN Apt, in good faith, very apt! Well, go thy way; if Sir Toby would leave drinking, thou wert as witty a piece of Eve's flesh as any in Illyria.

MARIA Peace, you rogue, no more o' that. Here comes my lady. Make your excuse wisely, you were best. [*Exit.*

Enter OLIVIA and MALVOLIO.

CLOWN Wit, an't be thy will, put me into good fooling! Those wits that think they have thee do very oft prove fools; and I that am sure I lack thee may pass for a wise man. For what says Quinapalus? 'Better a witty fool than a foolish wit.' God bless thee, lady!

OLIVIA Take the fool away.

CLOWN Do you not fear, fellows? Take away the lady.

OLIVIA Go to, y'are a dry fool; I'll no more of you. Besides, you grow dishonest.

CLOWN Two faults, madonna, that drink and good counsel will amend; for give the dry fool drink, then is the fool not dry. Bid the dishonest man mend himself; if he mend, he is no longer dishonest; if he cannot, let the botcher mend him. Anything that's mended is but patch'd; virtue that transgresses is but patch'd with sin, and sin that amends is but patch'd with virtue. If that this simple syllogism will serve, so; if it will not, what remedy? As there is no true cuckold but calamity, so beauty's a flower. The lady bade take away the fool; therefore, I say again, take her away.

OLIVIA Sir, I bade them take away you.

CLOWN Misprision in the highest degree! Lady, 'Cucullus non facit monachum'; that's as much to say as I wear not motley in my brain. Good madonna, give me leave to prove you a fool.

OLIVIA Can you do it?

CLOWN Dexteriously, good madonna.

OLIVIA Make your proof.

CLOWN I must catechize you for it, madonna. Good my mouse of virtue, answer me.

OLIVIA Well, sir, for want of other idleness, I'll bide your proof.

CLOWN Good madonna, why mourn'st thou?

OLIVIA Good fool, for my brother's death.

CLOWN I think his soul is in hell, madonna.

OLIVIA I know his soul is in heaven, fool.

CLOWN The more fool, madonna, to mourn for your brother's soul being in heaven. Take away the fool, gentlemen.

OLIVIA What think you of this fool, Malvolio? Doth he not mend?

MALVOLIO Yes, and shall do, till the pangs of death shake him. Infirmity, that decays the wise, doth ever make the better fool.

CLOWN God send you, sir, a speedy infirmity, for the better increasing your folly! Sir Toby will be sworn that I am no fox; but he will not pass his word for twopence that you are no fool.

OLIVIA How say you to that, Malvolio?

MALVOLIO I marvel your ladyship takes delight in such a barren rascal; I saw him put down the other day with an ordinary fool that has no more brain than a stone. Look you now, he's out of his guard already; unless you laugh and minister occasion to him, he is gagg'd. I protest I take these wise men that crow so at these set kind of fools no better than the fools' zanies.

OLIVIA O, you are sick of self-love, Malvolio, and taste with a distemper'd appetite. To be generous, guiltless, and of free disposition, is to take those things for bird-bolts that you deem cannon bullets. There is no slander in an allow'd fool, though he do nothing but rail; nor no railing in a known discreet man, though he do nothing but reprove.

CLOWN Now Mercury endue thee with leasing, for thou speak'st well of fools!

Re-enter MARIA.

MARIA Madam, there is at the gate a young gentleman much desires to speak with you.

OLIVIA From the Count Orsino, is it?

MARIA I know not, madam; 'tis a fair young man, and well attended.

OLIVIA Who of my people hold him in delay?

MARIA Sir Toby, madam, your kinsman.

OLIVIA Fetch him off, I pray you; he speaks nothing but madman. Fie on him! [*Exit Maria*] Go you, Malvolio: if it be a suit from the Count, I am sick, or not at home – what you will to dismiss it. [*Exit Malvolio*] Now you see, sir, how your fooling grows old, and people dislike it.

CLOWN Thou hast spoke for us, madonna, as if thy eldest son should be a fool; whose skull Jove cram with brains! For – here he comes – one of thy kin has a most weak pia mater.

Enter SIR TOBY.

OLIVIA By mine honour, half drunk! What is he at the gate, cousin?

SIR TOBY A gentleman.

OLIVIA A gentleman! What gentleman?

SIR TOBY 'Tis a gentleman here. [*Hiccups*] A plague o' these pickle-herring! How now, sot!

CLOWN Good Sir Toby!

OLIVIA Cousin, cousin, how have you come so early by this lethargy?

SIR TOBY Lechery! I defy lechery. There's one at the gate.

OLIVIA Ay, marry; what is he?

SIR TOBY Let him be the devil an he will, I care not; give me faith, say I. Well, it's all one. [*Exit.*

OLIVIA What's a drunken man like, fool?

CLOWN Like a drown'd man, a fool, and a madman: one draught above heat makes him a fool; the second mads him; and a third drowns him.

OLIVIA Go thou and seek the crowner, and let him sit o' my coz; for he's in the third degree of drink, he's drown'd; go look after him.

CLOWN He is but mad yet, madonna, and the fool shall look to the madman. [*Exit.*

Re-enter MALVOLIO.

MALVOLIO Madam, yond young fellow swears he will speak with you. I told him you were sick; he takes on him to understand so much, and therefore comes to speak with you. I told him you were asleep; he seems to have a foreknowledge of that too, and therefore comes to speak with you. What is to be said to him, lady? He's fortified against any denial.

OLIVIA Tell him he shall not speak with me.

MALVOLIO Has been told so; and he says he'll stand at your door like a sheriff's post, and be the supporter to a bench, but he'll speak with you.

OLIVIA What kind o' man is he?

MALVOLIO Why, of mankind.

OLIVIA What manner of man?

MALVOLIO Of very ill manner; he'll speak with you, will you or no.

OLIVIA Of what personage and years is he?

MALVOLIO Not yet old enough for a man, nor young enough for a boy; as a squash is before 'tis a peascod, or a codling when 'tis almost an apple; 'tis with him in standing water, between boy and man. He is very well-favour'd, and he speaks very shrewishly; one would think his mother's milk were scarce out of him.

OLIVIA Let him approach. Call in my gentlewoman.

MALVOLIO Gentlewoman, my lady calls. [*Exit.*

Re-enter MARIA.

OLIVIA Give me my veil; come, throw it o'er my face;
We'll once more hear Orsino's embassy.

Enter VIOLA.

VIOLA The honourable lady of the house, which is she?

OLIVIA Speak to me; I shall answer for her. Your will?

VIOLA Most radiant, exquisite, and unmatchable beauty – I pray you tell me if this be the lady of the house, for I never saw her. I would be loath to cast away my speech; for, besides that it is excellently well penn'd, I have taken great pains to con it. Good beauties, let me sustain no scorn; I am very comptible, even to the least sinister usage.

OLIVIA Whence came you, sir?

VIOLA I can say little more than I have studied, and that question's out of my part. Good gentle one, give me modest assurance if you be the lady of the house, that I may proceed in my speech.

OLIVIA Are you a comedian?

VIOLA No, my profound heart; and yet, by the very fangs of malice I swear, I am not that I play. Are you the lady of the house?

OLIVIA If I do not usurp myself, I am.

VIOLA Most certain, if you are she, you do usurp yourself; for what is yours to bestow is not yours to reserve. But this is from my commission. I will on with my speech in your praise, and then show you the heart of my message.

OLIVIA Come to what is important in't. I forgive you the praise.

VIOLA Alas, I took great pains to study it, and 'tis poetical.

OLIVIA It is the more like to be feigned; I pray you keep it in. I heard you were saucy at my gates, and allow'd your approach rather to wonder at you than to hear you. If you be not mad, be gone; if you have reason, be brief; 'tis not that time of moon with me to make one in so skipping a dialogue.

MARIA Will you hoist sail, sir? Here lies your way.

VIOLA No, good swabber, I am to hull here a little longer. Some mollification for your giant, sweet lady.

OLIVIA Tell me your mind.

VIOLA I am a messenger.

OLIVIA Sure, you have some hideous matter to deliver, when the courtesy of it is so fearful. Speak your office.

VIOLA It alone concerns your ear. I bring no overture of war, no taxation of homage: I hold the olive in my hand; my words are as full of peace as matter.

OLIVIA Yet you began rudely. What are you? What would you?

VIOLA The rudeness that hath appear'd in me have I learn'd from my entertainment. What I am and what I would are as secret as maidenhead – to your ears, divinity; to any other's, profanation.

OLIVIA Give us the place alone; we will hear this divinity. [*Exeunt Maria and Attendants*] Now, sir, what is your text?

VIOLA Most sweet lady –

OLIVIA A comfortable doctrine, and much may be said of it. Where lies your text?

VIOLA In Orsino's bosom.

OLIVIA In his bosom! In what chapter of his bosom?

VIOLA To answer by the method: in the first of his heart.

OLIVIA O, I have read it; it is heresy. Have you no more to say?

VIOLA Good madam, let me see your face.

OLIVIA Have you any commission from your lord to negotiate with my face? You are now out of your text; but we will draw the curtain and show you the picture. [*Unveiling*] Look you, sir, such a one I was this present. Is't not well done?

VIOLA Excellently done, if God did all.

OLIVIA 'Tis in grain, sir; 'twill endure wind and weather.

VIOLA 'Tis beauty truly blent, whose red and white
Nature's own sweet and cunning hand laid on.
Lady, you are the cruell'st she alive,
If you will lead these graces to the grave,
And leave the world no copy.

OLIVIA O, sir, I will not be so hard-hearted; I will give out divers schedules of my beauty. It shall be inventoried, and every particle and utensil labell'd to my will: as – item, two lips indifferent red; item, two grey eyes with lids to them; item, one neck, one chin, and so forth. Were you sent hither to praise me?

VIOLA I see you what you are: you are too proud;

But, if you were the devil, you are fair.
My lord and master loves you – O, such love
Could be but recompens'd though you were crown'd
The nonpareil of beauty!
OLIVIA How does he love me?
VIOLA With adorations, fertile tears,
With groans that thunder love, with sighs of fire.
OLIVIA Your lord does know my mind; I cannot love him.
Yet I suppose him virtuous, know him noble,
Of great estate, of fresh and stainless youth;
In voices well divulg'd, free, learn'd, and valiant,
And in dimension and the shape of nature
A gracious person; but yet I cannot love him.
He might have took his answer long ago.
VIOLA If I did love you in my master's flame,
With such a suff'ring, such a deadly life,
In your denial I would find no sense;
I would not understand it.
OLIVIA Why, what would you?
VIOLA Make me a willow cabin at your gate,
And call upon my soul within the house;
Write loyal cantons of contemned love
And sing them loud even in the dead of night;
Halloo your name to the reverberate hills,
And make the babbling gossip of the air
Cry out 'Olivia!' O, you should not rest
Between the elements of air and earth
But you should pity me!
OLIVIA You might do much.
What is your parentage?
VIOLA Above my fortunes, yet my state is well:
I am a gentleman.
OLIVIA Get you to your lord.
I cannot love him; let him send no more –
Unless perchance you come to me again
To tell me how he takes it. Fare you well.
I thank you for your pains; spend this for me.
VIOLA I am no fee'd post, lady; keep your purse;
My master, not myself, lacks recompense.
Love make his heart of flint that you shall love;
And let your fervour, like my master's, be
Plac'd in contempt! Farewell, fair cruelty. [*Exit.*

OLIVIA 'What is your parentage?'
'Above my fortunes, yet my state is well:
I am a gentleman.' I'll be sworn thou art;
Thy tongue, thy face, thy limbs, actions, and spirit,
Do give thee five-fold blazon. Not too fast! Soft, soft!
Unless the master were the man. How now!
Even so quickly may one catch the plague?
Methinks I feel this youth's perfections
With an invisible and subtle stealth
To creep in at mine eyes. Well, let it be.
What ho, Malvolio!

Re-enter MALVOLIO.

MALVOLIO Here, madam, at your service.
OLIVIA Run after that same peevish messenger,
The County's man. He left this ring behind him,
Would I or not. Tell him I'll none of it.
Desire him not to flatter with his lord,
Nor hold him up with hopes; I am not for him.
If that the youth will come this way to-morrow,
I'll give him reasons for't. Hie thee, Malvolio.
MALVOLIO Madam, I will. [*Exit.*

OLIVIA I do I know not what, and fear to find
Mine eye too great a flatterer for my mind.
Fate, show thy force: ourselves we do not owe;
What is decreed must be; and be this so! [*Exit.*

ACT TWO

SCENE I. *The sea-coast.*

Enter ANTONIO and SEBASTIAN.

ANTONIO Will you stay no longer; nor will you not that I go with you?

SEBASTIAN By your patience, no. My stars shine darkly over me; the malignancy of my fate might perhaps distemper yours; therefore I shall crave of you your leave that I may bear my evils alone. It were a bad recompense for your love to lay any of them on you.

ANTONIO Let me yet know of you whither you are bound.

SEBASTIAN No, sooth, sir; my determinate voyage is mere extravagancy. But I perceive in you so excellent a touch of modesty that you will not extort from me what I am willing to keep in; therefore it charges me in manners the rather to express myself. You must know of me then, Antonio, my name is Sebastian, which I call'd Roderigo; my father was that Sebastian of Messaline whom I know you have heard of. He left behind him myself and a sister, both born in an hour; if the heavens had been pleas'd, would we had so ended! But you, sir, alter'd that; for some hour before you took me from the breach of the sea was my sister drown'd.

ANTONIO Alas the day!

SEBASTIAN A lady, sir, though it was said she much resembled me, was yet of many accounted beautiful; but though I could not with such estimable wonder overfar believe that, yet thus far I will boldly publish her: she bore a mind that envy could not but call fair. She is drown'd already, sir, with salt water, though I seem to drown her remembrance again with more.

ANTONIO Pardon me, sir, your bad entertainment.

SEBASTIAN O good Antonio, forgive me your trouble.

ANTONIO If you will not murder me for my love, let me be your servant.

SEBASTIAN If you will not undo what you have done – that is, kill him whom you have recover'd – desire it not. Fare ye well at once; my bosom is full of kindness, and I am yet so near the manners of my mother that, upon the least occasion more, mine eyes will tell tales of me. I am bound to the Count Orsino's court. Farewell. [*Exit.*

ANTONIO The gentleness of all the gods go with thee!
I have many enemies in Orsino's court,
Else would I very shortly see thee there.
But come what may, I do adore thee so
That danger shall seem sport, and I will go.
[*Exit.*

SCENE II. *A street.*

Enter VIOLA and MALVOLIO at several doors.

MALVOLIO Were you not ev'n now with the Countess Olivia?

VIOLA Even now, sir; on a moderate pace I have since arriv'd but hither.

MALVOLIO She returns this ring to you, sir; you might have saved me my pains, to have taken it away yourself. She adds, moreover, that you should put your lord into a desperate assurance she will none of him. And one thing more: that you be never so hardy to come again in his affairs, unless it be to report your lord's taking of this. Receive it so.

VIOLA She took the ring of me; I'll none of it.

MALVOLIO Come, sir, you peevishly threw it to her; and her will is it should be so return'd. If it be worth stooping for, there it lies in your eye; if not, be it his that finds it. [*Exit.*

VIOLA I left no ring with her; what means this lady?
Fortune forbid my outside have not charm'd her!
She made good view of me; indeed, so much
That methought her eyes had lost her tongue,
For she did speak in starts distractedly.
She loves me, sure: the cunning of her passion
Invites me in this churlish messenger.
None of my lord's ring! Why, he sent her none.
I am the man. If it be so – as 'tis –
Poor lady, she were better love a dream.
Disguise, I see thou art a wickedness
Wherein the pregnant enemy does much.
How easy is it for the proper-false
In women's waxen hearts to set their forms!
Alas, our frailty is the cause, not we!
For such as we are made of, such we be.
How will this fadge? My master loves her dearly,
And I, poor monster, fond as much on him;
And she, mistaken, seems to dote on me.
What will become of this? As I am man,
My state is desperate for my master's love;
As I am woman – now alas the day! –
What thriftless sighs shall poor Olivia breathe!
O Time, thou must untangle this, not I;
It is too hard a knot for me t' untie! [*Exit.*

SCENE III. *Olivia's house.*

Enter SIR TOBY and SIR ANDREW.

SIR TOBY Approach, Sir Andrew. Not to be abed after midnight is to be up betimes; and 'diluculo surgere' thou know'st –

SIR ANDREW Nay, by my troth, I know not; but I know to be up late is to be up late.

SIR TOBY A false conclusion! I hate it as an unfill'd can. To be up after midnight and to go to bed then is early; so that to go to bed after midnight is to go to bed betimes. Does not our lives consist of the four elements?

SIR ANDREW Faith, so they say; but I think it rather consists of eating and drinking.

SIR TOBY Th'art a scholar; let us therefore eat and drink. Marian, I say! a stoup of wine.

Enter Clown.

SIR ANDREW Here comes the fool, i' faith.

CLOWN How now, my hearts! Did you never see the picture of 'we three'?

SIR TOBY Welcome, ass. Now let's have a catch.

SIR ANDREW By my troth, the fool has an excellent breast. I had rather than forty shillings I had such a leg, and so sweet a breath to sing, as the fool has. In sooth, thou wast in very gracious fooling last night, when thou spok'st of Pigrogromitus, of the Vapians passing the equinoctial of Queubus; 'twas very good, i' faith. I sent thee sixpence for thy leman; hadst it?

CLOWN I did impeticos thy gratillity; for Malvolio's nose is no whipstock. My lady has a white hand, and the Myrmidons are no bottle-ale houses.

SIR ANDREW Excellent! Why, this is the best fooling, when all is done. Now, a song.

SIR TOBY Come on, there is sixpence for you. Let's have a song.

SIR ANDREW There's a testril of me too; if one knight give a –

CLOWN Would you have a love-song, or a song of good life?

SIR TOBY A love-song, a love-song.

SIR ANDREW Ay, ay; I care not for good life.

Clown sings.

O mistress mine, where are you roaming?
O, stay and hear; your true love's coming,
That can sing both high and low.
Trip no further, pretty sweeting;
Journeys end in lovers meeting,
Every wise man's son doth know.

SIR ANDREW Excellent good, i' faith!

SIR TOBY Good, good!

Clown sings.

What is love? 'Tis not hereafter;
Present mirth hath present laughter;
What's to come is still unsure.
In delay there lies no plenty,
Then come kiss me, sweet and twenty;
Youth's a stuff will not endure.

SIR ANDREW A mellifluous voice, as I am true knight.

SIR TOBY A contagious breath.

SIR ANDREW Very sweet and contagious, i' faith.

SIR TOBY To hear by the nose, it is dulcet in contagion. But shall we make the welkin dance indeed? Shall we rouse the night-owl in a catch that will draw three souls out of one weaver? Shall we do that?

SIR ANDREW An you love me, let's do't. I am dog at a catch.

CLOWN By'r lady, sir, and some dogs will catch well.

SIR ANDREW Most certain. Let our catch be 'Thou knave'.

CLOWN 'Hold thy peace, thou knave' knight? I shall be constrain'd in't to call thee knave, knight.

SIR ANDREW 'Tis not the first time I have constrained one to call me knave. Begin, fool: it begins 'Hold thy peace'.

CLOWN I shall never begin if I hold my peace.

SIR ANDREW Good, i' faith! Come, begin. [*Catch sung.*

Enter MARIA.

MARIA What a caterwauling do you keep here! If my lady have not call'd up her steward Malvolio, and bid him turn you out of doors, never trust me.

SIR TOBY My lady's a Cataian, we are politicians, Malvolio's a Peg-a-Ramsey, and [*Sings*]

Three merry men be we.

Am not I consanguineous? Am I not of her blood? Tilly-vally, lady. [*Sings*]

There dwelt a man in Babylon,
Lady, lady.

CLOWN Beshrew me, the knight's in admirable fooling.

SIR ANDREW Ay, he does well enough if he be dispos'd, and so do I too; he does it with a better grace, but I do it more natural.

SIR TOBY [*Sings*] O' the twelfth day of December –

MARIA For the love o' God, peace!

Enter MALVOLIO.

MALVOLIO My masters, are you mad? Or what are you? Have you no wit, manners, nor honesty, but to gabble like tinkers at this time of night? Do ye make an ale-house of my lady's house, that ye squeak out your coziers' catches without any mitigation or remorse of voice? Is there no respect of place, persons, nor time, in you?

SIR TOBY We did keep time, sir, in our catches. Sneck up!

MALVOLIO Sir Toby, I must be round with you. My lady bade me tell you that, though she harbours you as her kinsman, she's nothing allied to your disorders. If you can separate yourself and your misdemeanours, you are welcome to the house; if not, and it would please you to take leave of her, she is very willing to bid you farewell.

SIR TOBY [*Sing*] Farewell, dear heart, since I must needs be gone.

MARIA Nay, good Sir Toby.

CLOWN [*Sings*] His eyes do show his days are almost done.

MARIA Is't even so?

SIR TOBY [*Sings*] But I will never die. [*Falls down.*

CLOWN [*Sings*] Sir Toby, there you lie.

MALVOLIO This is much credit to you.

SIR TOBY [*Sings*] Shall I bid him go?

CLOWN [*Sings*] What an if you do?

SIR TOBY [*Sings*] Shall I bid him go, and spare not?

CLOWN [*Sings*] O, no, no, no, no, you dare not.

SIR TOBY [*Rising*] Out o' tune, sir! Ye lie. Art any more than a steward? Dost thou think, because thou art virtuous, there shall be no more cakes and ale?

CLOWN Yes, by Saint Anne; and ginger shall be hot i' th' mouth too.

SIR TOBY Th'art i' th' right. Go, sir, rub your chain with crumbs. A stoup of wine, Maria!

MALVOLIO Mistress Mary, if you priz'd my lady's favour at anything more than contempt, you would not give means for this uncivil rule; she shall know of it, by this hand. [*Exit.*

MARIA Go shake your ears.

SIR ANDREW 'Twere as good a deed as to drink when a man's ahungry, to challenge him the field, and then to break promise with him and make a fool of him.

SIR TOBY Do't, knight. I'll write thee a challenge; or I'll deliver thy indignation to him by word of mouth.

MARIA Sweet Sir Toby, be patient for tonight; since the youth of the Count's was to-day with my lady, she is much out of quiet. For Monsieur Malvolio, let me alone with him; if I do not gull him into a nay-word, and make him a common recreation, do not think I have wit enough to lie straight in my bed. I know I can do it.

SIR TOBY Possess us, possess us; tell us something of him.

MARIA Marry, sir, sometimes he is a kind of Puritan.

SIR ANDREW O, if I thought that, I'd beat him like a dog.

SIR TOBY What, for being a Puritan? Thy exquisite reason, dear knight?

SIR ANDREW I have no exquisite reason for't, but I have reason good enough.

MARIA The devil a Puritan that he is, or anything constantly but a time-pleaser; an affection'd ass that cons state without book and utters it by great swarths; the best persuaded of himself, so cramm'd, as he thinks, with excellencies that it is his grounds of faith that all that look on him love him; and on that vice in him will my revenge find notable cause to work.

SIR TOBY What wilt thou do?

MARIA I will drop in his way some obscure epistles of love; wherein, by the colour of his beard, the shape of his leg, the manner of his gait, the expressure of his eye, forehead, and complexion, he shall find himself most feelingly personated. I can write very like my lady, your niece; on a forgotten matter we can hardly make distinction of our hands.

SIR TOBY Excellent! I smell a device.

SIR ANDREW I have't in my nose too.

SIR TOBY He shall think, by the letters that thou wilt drop, that they come from my niece, and that she's in love with him.

MARIA My purpose is, indeed, a horse of that colour.

SIR ANDREW And your horse now would make him an ass.

MARIA Ass, I doubt not.

SIR ANDREW O, 'twill be admirable!

MARIA Sport royal, I warrant you. I know my physic will work with him. I will plant you two, and let the fool make a third, where he shall find the letter; observe his construction of it. For this night, to bed, and dream on the event. Farewell. [*Exit.*

SIR TOBY Good night, Penthesilea.

SIR ANDREW Before me, she's a good wench.

SIR TOBY She's a beagle true-bred, and one that adores me. What o' that?

SIR ANDREW I was ador'd once too.

SIR TOBY Let's to bed, knight. Thou hadst need send for more money.

SIR ANDREW If I cannot recover your niece, I am a foul way out.

SIR TOBY Send for money, knight; if thou hast her not i' th' end, call me Cut.

SIR ANDREW If I do not, never trust me; take it how you will.

SIR TOBY Come, come, I'll go burn some sack; 'tis too late to go to bed now. Come, knight; come, knight. [*Exeunt.*

SCENE IV. *The Duke's palace.*

Enter DUKE, VIOLA, CURIO, and Others.

DUKE Give me some music. Now, good morrow, friends.
Now, good Cesario, but that piece of song,
That old and antique song we heard last night;
Methought it did relieve my passion much,
More than light airs and recollected terms
Of these most brisk and giddy-paced times.
Come, but one verse.

CURIO He is not here, so please your lordship, that should sing it.

DUKE Who was it?

CURIO Feste, the jester, my lord; a fool that the Lady Olivia's father took much delight in. He is about the house.

DUKE Seek him out, and play the tune the while.
[*Exit Curio. Music plays.*
Come hither, boy. If ever thou shalt love,
In the sweet pangs of it remember me;
For such as I am all true lovers are,
Unstaid and skittish in all motions else
Save in the constant image of the creature
That is belov'd. How dost thou like this tune?

VIOLA It gives a very echo to the seat
Where Love is thron'd.

DUKE Thou dost speak masterly.
My life upon't, young though thou art, thine eye
Hath stay'd upon some favour that it loves;
Hath it not, boy?

VIOLA A little, by your favour.

DUKE What kind of woman is't?

VIOLA Of your complexion.
DUKE She is not worth thee, then. What years, i' faith?
VIOLA About your years, my lord.
DUKE Too old, by heaven! Let still the woman take
An elder than herself; so wears she to him,
So sways she level in her husband's heart.
For, boy, however we do praise ourselves,
Our fancies are more giddy and unfirm,
More longing, wavering, sooner lost and won,
Than women's are.
VIOLA I think it well, my lord.
DUKE Then let thy love be younger than thyself,
Or thy affection cannot hold the bent;
For women are as roses, whose fair flow'r
Being once display'd doth fall that very hour.
VIOLA And so they are; alas, that they are so!
To die, even when they to perfection grow!

Re-enter CURIO and Clown.

DUKE O, fellow, come, the song we had last night.
Mark it, Cesario; it is old and plain;
The spinsters and the knitters in the sun,
And the free maids that weave their thread with bones,
Do use to chant it; it is silly sooth,
And dallies with the innocence of love,
Like the old age.
CLOWN Are you ready, sir?
DUKE Ay; prithee, sing. [*Music.*

Feste's Song.

Come away, come away, death;
And in sad cypress let me be laid;
Fly away, fly away, breath,
I am slain by a fair cruel maid.
My shroud of white, stuck all with yew,
O, prepare it!
My part of death no one so true
Did share it.

Not a flower, not a flower sweet,
On my black coffin let there be strown;
Not a friend, not a friend greet
My poor corpse where my bones shall be thrown;
A thousand thousand sighs to save,
Lay me, O, where
Sad true lover never find my grave,
To weep there!

DUKE There's for thy pains.
CLOWN No pains, sir; I take pleasure in singing, sir.
DUKE I'll pay thy pleasure, then.
CLOWN Truly, sir, and pleasure will be paid one time or another.
DUKE Give me now leave to leave thee.
CLOWN Now the melancholy god protect thee; and the tailor make thy doublet of changeable taffeta, for thy mind is a very opal. I would have men of such constancy put to sea, that their business might be everything, and their intent everywhere; for that's it that always makes a good voyage of nothing. Farewell. [*Exit Clown.*
DUKE Let all the rest give place.
[*Exeunt Curio and Attendants.*
Once more, Cesario,
Get thee to yond same sovereign cruelty.
Tell her my love, more noble than the world,
Prizes not quantity of dirty lands;
The parts that fortune hath bestow'd upon her,
Tell her I hold as giddily as Fortune;
But 'tis that miracle and queen of gems
That Nature pranks her in attracts my soul.
VIOLA But if she cannot love you, sir?
DUKE I cannot be so answer'd.
VIOLA Sooth, but you must.
Say that some lady, as perhaps there is,
Hath for your love as great a pang of heart
As you have for Olivia. You cannot love her;
You tell her so. Must she not then be answer'd?
DUKE There is no woman's sides
Can bide the beating of so strong a passion
As love doth give my heart; no woman's heart
So big to hold so much; they lack retention.
Alas, their love may be call'd appetite –
No motion of the liver, but the palate –
That suffer surfeit, cloyment, and revolt;
But mine is all as hungry as the sea,
And can digest as much. Make no compare
Between that love a woman can bear me
And that I owe Olivia.
VIOLA Ay, but I know –
DUKE What dost thou know?
VIOLA Too well what love women to men may owe.
In faith, they are as true of heart as we.
My father had a daughter lov'd a man,
As it might be perhaps, were I a woman,
I should your lordship.
DUKE And what's her history?
VIOLA A blank, my lord. She never told her love,
But let concealment, like a worm i' th' bud,
Feed on her damask cheek. She pin'd in thought;
And with a green and yellow melancholy
She sat like Patience on a monument,
Smiling at grief. Was not this love indeed?
We men may say more, swear more, but indeed
Our shows are more than will; for still we prove
Much in our vows, but little in our love.
DUKE But died thy sister of her love, my boy?

VIOLA I am all the daughters of my father's house,
And all the brothers too – and yet I know not.
Sir, shall I to this lady?

DUKE Ay, that's the theme.
To her in haste. Give her this jewel; say
My love can give no place, bide no denay.
[*Exeunt.*

SCENE V. *Olivia's garden.*

Enter SIR TOBY, SIR ANDREW, and FABIAN.

SIR TOBY Come thy ways, Signior Fabian.

FABIAN Nay, I'll come; if I lose a scruple of this sport let me be boil'd to death with melancholy.

SIR TOBY Wouldst thou not be glad to have the niggardly rascally sheep-biter come by some notable shame?

FABIAN I would exult, man; you know he brought me out o' favour with my lady about a bear-baiting here.

SIR TOBY To anger him we'll have the bear again; and we will fool him black and blue – shall we not, Sir Andrew?

SIR ANDREW An we do not, it is pity of our lives.

Enter MARIA.

SIR TOBY Here comes the little villain. How now, my metal of India!

MARIA Get ye all three into the box-tree. Malvolio's coming down this walk. He has been yonder i' the sun practising behaviour to his own shadow this half hour. Observe him, for the love of mockery, for I know this letter will make a contemplative idiot of him. Close, in the name of jesting! [*As the men hide she drops a letter*] Lie thou there; for here comes the trout that must be caught with tickling. [*Exit.*

Enter MALVOLIO.

MALVOLIO 'Tis but fortune; all is fortune. Maria once told me she did affect me; and I have heard herself come thus near, that, should she fancy, it should be one of my complexion. Besides, she uses me with a more exalted respect than any one else that follows her. What should I think on't?

SIR TOBY Here's an overweening rogue!

FABIAN O, peace! Contemplation makes a rare turkey-cock of him; how he jets under his advanc'd plumes!

SIR ANDREW 'Slight, I could so beat the rogue –

SIR TOBY Peace, I say.

MALVOLIO To be Count Malvolio!

SIR TOBY Ah, rogue!

SIR ANDREW Pistol him, pistol him.

SIR TOBY Peace, peace!

MALVOLIO There is example for't: the Lady of the Strachy married the yeoman of the wardrobe.

SIR ANDREW Fie on him, Jezebel!

FABIAN O, peace! Now he's deeply in; look how imagination blows him.

MALVOLIO Having been three months married to her, sitting in my state –

SIR TOBY O, for a stone-bow to hit him in the eye!

MALVOLIO Calling my officers about me, in my branch'd velvet gown, having come from a day-bed – where I have left Olivia sleeping –

SIR TOBY Fire and brimstone!

FABIAN O, peace, peace!

MALVOLIO And then to have the humour of state; and after a demure travel of regard, telling them I know my place as I would they should do theirs, to ask for my kinsman Toby –

SIR TOBY Bolts and shackles!

FABIAN O, peace, peace, peace! Now, now.

MALVOLIO Seven of my people, with an obedient start, make out for him. I frown the while, and perchance wind up my watch, or play with my – some rich jewel. Toby approaches; curtsies there to me –

SIR TOBY Shall this fellow live?

FABIAN Though our silence be drawn from us with cars, yet peace.

MALVOLIO I extend my hand to him thus, quenching my familiar smile with an austere regard of control –

SIR TOBY And does not Toby take you a blow o' the lips then?

MALVOLIO Saying 'Cousin Toby, my fortunes having cast me on your niece give me this prerogative of speech' –

SIR TOBY What, what?

MALVOLIO 'You must amend your drunkenness' –

SIR TOBY Out, scab!

FABIAN Nay, patience, or we break the sinews of our plot.

MALVOLIO 'Besides, you waste the treasure of your time with a foolish knight' –

SIR ANDREW That's me, I warrant you.

MALVOLIO 'One Sir Andrew.'

SIR ANDREW I knew 'twas I; for many do call me fool.

MALVOLIO What employment have we here? [*Taking up the letter.*

FABIAN Now is the woodcock near the gin.

SIR TOBY O, peace! And the spirit of humours intimate reading aloud to him!

MALVOLIO By my life, this is my lady's hand: these be her very C's, her U's, and her T's; and thus makes she her great P's. It is, in contempt of question, her hand.

SIR ANDREW Her C's, her U's, and her T's. Why that?

MALVOLIO [*Reads*] 'To the unknown belov'd, this, and my good wishes.' Her very phrases! By your leave, wax. Soft! And the impressure her Lucrece with which she uses to seal; 'tis my lady. To whom should this be?

FABIAN This wins him, liver and all.

MALVOLIO [*Reads*] 'Jove knows I love,
But who?
Lips, do not move;
No man must know.'

'No man must know.' What follows? The numbers alter'd! 'No man must know.' If this should be thee, Malvolio?

SIR TOBY Marry, hang thee, brock!

MALVOLIO [*Reads*]
'I may command where I adore;
But silence, like a Lucrece knife,
With bloodless stroke my heart doth gore;
M. O. A. I. doth sway my life.'

FABIAN A fustian riddle!

SIR TOBY Excellent wench, say I.

MALVOLIO 'M. O. A. I. doth sway my life.' Nay, but first let me see, let me see, let me see.

FABIAN What dish o' poison has she dress'd him!

SIR TOBY And with what wing the staniel checks at it!

MALVOLIO 'I may command where I adore.' Why, she may command me: I serve her; she is my lady. Why, this is evident to any formal capacity; there is no obstruction in this. And the end – what should that alphabetical position portend? If I could make that resemble something in me. Softly! M. O. A. I. –

SIR TOBY O, ay, make up that! He is now at a cold scent.

FABIAN Sowter will cry upon't for all this, though it be as rank as a fox.

MALVOLIO M – Malvolio; M – why, that begins my name.

FABIAN Did not I say he would work it out? The cur is excellent at faults.

MALVOLIO M – But then there is no consonancy in the sequel; that suffers under probation: A should follow, but O does.

FABIAN And O shall end, I hope.

SIR TOBY Ay, or I'll cudgel him, and make him cry 'O!'

MALVOLIO And then I comes behind.

FABIAN Ay, an you had any eye behind you, you might see more detraction at your heels than fortunes before you.

MALVOLIO M. O. A. I. This simulation is not as the former; and yet, to crush this a little, it would bow to me, for every one of these letters are in my name. Soft! here follows prose.

[*Reads*] 'If this fall into thy hand, revolve. In my stars I am above thee; but be not afraid of greatness. Some are born great, some achieve greatness, and some have greatness thrust upon 'em. Thy Fates open their hands; let thy blood and spirit embrace them; and, to inure thyself to what thou art like to be, cast thy humble slough and appear fresh. Be opposite with a kinsman, surly with servants; let thy tongue tang arguments of state; put thyself into the trick of singularity. She thus advises thee that sighs for thee. Remember who commended thy yellow stockings, and wish'd to see thee ever cross-garter'd. I say, remember. Go to, thou art made, if thou desir'st to be so; if not, let me see thee a steward still, the fellow of servants, and not worthy to touch Fortune's fingers. Farewell. She that would alter services with thee,
THE FORTUNATE-UNHAPPY.'

Daylight and champain discovers not more. This is open. I will be proud, I will read politic authors, I will baffle Sir Toby, I will wash off gross acquaintance, I will be point-devise the very man. I do not now fool myself to let imagination jade me; for every reason excites to this, that my lady loves me. She did commend my yellow stockings of late, she did praise my leg being cross-garter'd; and in this she manifests herself to my love, and with a kind of injunction drives me to these habits of her liking. I thank my stars I am happy. I will be strange, stout, in yellow stockings, and cross-garter'd, even with the swiftness of putting on. Jove and my stars be praised! Here is yet a postscript.

[*Reads*] 'Thou canst not choose but know who I am. If thou entertain'st my love, let it appear in thy smiling; thy smiles become thee well. Therefore in my presence still smile, dear my sweet, I prithee.'

Jove, I thank thee. I will smile; I will do everything that thou wilt have me. [*Exit*.

FABIAN I will not give my part of this sport for a pension of thousands to be paid from the Sophy.

SIR TOBY I could marry this wench for this device.

SIR ANDREW So could I too.

SIR TOBY And ask no other dowry with her but such another jest.

Enter MARIA.

SIR ANDREW Nor I neither.

FABIAN Here comes my noble gull-catcher.

SIR TOBY Wilt thou set thy foot o' my neck?

SIR ANDREW Or o' mine either?

SIR TOBY Shall I play my freedom at tray-trip, and become thy bond-slave?

SIR ANDREW I' faith, or I either?

SIR TOBY Why, thou hast put him in such a dream that when the image of it leaves him he must run mad.

MARIA Nay, but say true; does it work upon him?

SIR TOBY Like aqua-vitae with a midwife.

MARIA If you will then see the fruits of the sport, mark his first approach before my lady. He will come to her in yellow stockings, and 'tis a colour she abhors, and cross-garter'd, a fashion she detests; and he will smile upon her, which will now be so unsuitable to her disposition, being addicted to a melancholy as she is, that it cannot but turn him into a notable contempt. If you will see it, follow me.

SIR TOBY To the gates of Tartar, thou most excellent devil of wit!

SIR ANDREW I'll make one too. [*Exeunt.*

ACT THREE

SCENE I. *Olivia's garden.*

Enter VIOLA, and Clown with a tabor.

VIOLA Save thee, friend, and thy music! Dost thou live by thy tabor?

CLOWN No, sir, I live by the church.

VIOLA Art thou a churchman?

CLOWN No such matter, sir: I do live by the church; for I do live at my house, and my house doth stand by the church.

VIOLA So thou mayst say the king lies by a beggar, if a beggar dwell near him; or the church stands by thy tabor, if thy tabor stand by the church.

CLOWN You have said, sir. To see this age! A sentence is but a chev'ril glove to a good wit. How quickly the wrong side may be turn'd outward!

VIOLA Nay, that's certain; they that dally nicely with words may quickly make them wanton.

CLOWN I would, therefore, my sister had had no name, sir.

VIOLA Why, man?

CLOWN Why, sir, her name's a word; and to dally with that word might make my sister wanton. But indeed words are very rascals since bonds disgrac'd them.

VIOLA Thy reason, man?

CLOWN Troth, sir, I can yield you none without words, and words are grown so false I am loath to prove reason with them.

VIOLA I warrant thou art a merry fellow and car'st for nothing.

CLOWN Not so, sir; I do care for something; but in my conscience, sir, I do not care for you. If that be to care for nothing, sir, I would it would make you invisible.

VIOLA Art not thou the Lady Olivia's fool?

CLOWN No, indeed, sir; the Lady Olivia has no folly; she will keep no fool, sir, till she be married; and fools are as like husbands as pilchers are to herrings – the husband's the bigger. I am indeed not her fool, but her corrupter of words.

VIOLA I saw thee late at the Count Orsino's.

CLOWN Foolery, sir, does walk about the orb like the sun – it shines everywhere. I would be sorry, sir, but the fool should be as oft with your master as with my mistress: I think I saw your wisdom there.

VIOLA Nay, an thou pass upon me, I'll no more with thee. Hold, there's expenses for thee. [*Giving a coin.*

CLOWN Now Jove, in his next commodity of hair, send thee a beard!

VIOLA By my troth, I'll tell thee, I am almost sick for one; [*Aside*] though I would not have it grow on my chin. – Is thy lady within?

CLOWN Would not a pair of these have bred, sir?

VIOLA Yes, being kept together and put to use.

CLOWN I would play Lord Pandarus of Phrygia, sir, to bring a Cressida to this Troilus.

VIOLA I understand you, sir; 'tis well begg'd. [*Giving another coin.*

CLOWN The matter, I hope, is not great, sir, begging but a beggar: Cressida was a beggar. My lady is within, sir. I will construe to them whence you come; who you are and what you would are out of my welkin – I might say 'element' but the word is overworn. [*Exit.*

VIOLA This fellow is wise enough to play the fool;
And to do that well craves a kind of wit.
He must observe their mood on whom he jests,
The quality of persons, and the time;
And, like the haggard, check at every feather
That comes before his eye. This is a practice
As full of labour as a wise man's art;
For folly that he wisely shows is fit;
But wise men, folly-fall'n, quite taint their wit.

Enter SIR TOBY and SIR ANDREW.

SIR TOBY Save you, gentleman!

VIOLA And you, sir.

SIR ANDREW Dieu vous garde, monsieur.

VIOLA Et vous aussi; votre serviteur.

SIR ANDREW I hope, sir, you are; and I am yours.

SIR TOBY Will you encounter the house? My niece is desirous you should enter, if your trade be to her.

VIOLA I am bound to your niece, sir; I mean, she is the list of my voyage.

SIR TOBY Taste your legs, sir; put them to motion.

VIOLA My legs do better understand me, sir, than I understand what you mean by bidding me taste my legs.

SIR TOBY I mean, to go, sir, to enter.

VIOLA I will answer you with gait and entrance.
But we are prevented.

Enter OLIVIA and MARIA.

Most excellent accomplish'd lady, the heavens rain odours on you!

SIR ANDREW That youth's a rare courtier – 'Rain odours' well!

VIOLA My matter hath no voice, lady, but to your own most pregnant and vouchsafed ear.

SIR ANDREW 'Odours', 'pregnant', and 'vouchsafed' – I'll get 'em all three all ready.

OLIVIA Let the garden door be shut, and leave me to my hearing. [*Exeunt all but Olivia and Viola*]
Give me your hand, sir.

VIOLA My duty, madam, and most humble
service.

OLIVIA What is your name?

VIOLA Cesario is your servant's name, fair
Princess.

OLIVIA My servant, sir! 'Twas never merry world
Since lowly feigning was call'd compliment.
Y'are servant to the Count Orsino, youth.

VIOLA And he is yours, and his must needs be
yours:
Your servant's servant is your servant, madam.

OLIVIA For him, I think not on him; for his
thoughts,
Would they were blanks rather than fill'd with
me!

VIOLA Madam, I come to whet your gentle
thoughts.
On his behalf.

OLIVIA O, by your leave, I pray you:
I bade you never speak again of him;
But, would you undertake another suit,
I had rather hear you to solicit that
Than music from the spheres.

VIOLA Dear lady –

OLIVIA Give me leave, beseech you. I did send,
After the last enchantment you did here,
A ring in chase of you; so did I abuse
Myself, my servant, and, I fear me, you.
Under your hard construction must I sit,
To force that on you in a shameful cunning
Which you knew none of yours. What might
you think?
Have you not set mine honour at the stake,
And baited it with all th' unmuzzled thoughts
That tyrannous heart can think? To one of your
receiving
Enough is shown: a cypress, not a bosom,
Hides my heart. So, let me hear you speak.

VIOLA I pity you.

OLIVIA That's a degree to love.

VIOLA No, not a grize; for 'tis a vulgar proof
That very oft we pity enemies.

OLIVIA Why, then, methinks 'tis time to smile
again.
O world, how apt the poor are to be proud!
If one should be a prey, how much the better
To fall before the lion than the wolf!
[*Clock strikes.*
The clock upbraids me with the waste of time.
Be not afraid, good youth; I will not have you;
And yet, when wit and youth is come to
harvest,
Your wife is like to reap a proper man.
There lies your way, due west.

VIOLA Then westward-ho!
Grace and good disposition attend your
ladyship!
You'll nothing, madam, to my lord by me?

OLIVIA Stay.
I prithee tell me what thou think'st of me.

VIOLA That you do think you are not what you
are.

OLIVIA If I think so, I think the same of you.

VIOLA Then think you right: I am not what I am.

OLIVIA I would you were as I would have you be!

VIOLA Would it be better, madam, than I am?
I wish it might, for now I am your fool.

OLIVIA O, what a deal of scorn looks beautiful
In the contempt and anger of his lip!
A murd'rous guilt shows not itself more soon
Than love that would seem hid: love's night is
noon.
Cesario, by the roses of the spring,
By maidhood, honour, truth, and every thing,
I love thee so that, maugre all thy pride,
Nor wit nor reason can my passion hide.
Do not extort thy reasons from this clause,
For that I woo, thou therefore hast no cause;
But rather reason thus with reason fetter:
Love sought is good, but given unsought is
better.

VIOLA By innocence I swear, and by my youth,
I have one heart, one bosom, and one truth,
And that no woman has; nor never none
Shall mistress be of it, save I alone.

And so adieu, good madam; never more
Will I my master's tears to you deplore.
OLIVIA Yet come again; for thou perhaps mayst
160 move
That heart which now abhors to like his love.
[Exeunt.

SCENE II. *Olivia's house.*

Enter SIR TOBY, SIR ANDREW, and FABIAN.

SIR ANDREW No, faith, I'll not stay a jot longer.
SIR TOBY Thy reason, dear venom, give thy reason.
FABIAN You must needs yield your reason, Sir Andrew.
SIR ANDREW Marry, I saw your niece do more favours to the Count's servingman than ever she
6 bestow'd upon me; I saw't i' th' orchard.
SIR TOBY Did she see thee the while, old boy? Tell me that.
9 **SIR ANDREW** As plain as I see you now.
FABIAN This was a great argument of love in her toward you.
SIR ANDREW 'Slight! will you make an ass o' me?
FABIAN I will prove it legitimate, sir, upon the oaths of judgment and reason.
SIR TOBY And they have been grand-jurymen
16 since before Noah was a sailor.
FABIAN She did show favour to the youth in your sight only to exasperate you, to awake your dormouse valour, to put fire in your heart and brimstone in your liver. You should then have accosted her; and with some excellent jests, fire-new from the mint, you should have bang'd the youth into dumbness. This was look'd for at your hand, and this was baulk'd. The double gilt of this opportunity you let time wash off, and you are now sail'd into the north of my lady's opinion; where you will hang like an icicle on a Dutchman's beard, unless you do redeem it by some laudable attempt either of valour or
27 policy.
SIR ANDREW An't be any way, it must be with valour, for policy I hate; I had as lief be a Brownist as a politician.
SIR TOBY Why, then, build me thy fortunes upon the basis of valour. Challenge me the Count's youth to fight with him; hurt him in eleven places. My niece shall take note of it; and assure thyself there is no love-broker in the world can more prevail in man's commendation with
35 woman than report of valour.
FABIAN There is no way but this, Sir Andrew.
SIR ANDREW Will either of you bear me a
38 challenge to him?
SIR TOBY Go, write it in a martial hand; be curst and brief; it is no matter how witty, so it be eloquent and full of invention. Taunt him with the license of ink; if thou thou'st him some thrice, it shall not be amiss; and as many lies as will lie in thy sheet of paper, although the sheet were big enough for the bed of Ware in England, set 'em down; go about it. Let there be gall enough in thy ink, though thou write with a
goose-pen, no matter. About it. 47
SIR ANDREW Where shall I find you?
SIR TOBY We'll call thee at the cubiculo. Go.
[Exit Sir Andrew.
FABIAN This is a dear manakin to you, Sir Toby. 50
SIR TOBY I have been dear to him, lad – some two thousand strong, or so.
FABIAN We shall have a rare letter from him; but
you'll not deliver't? 54
SIR TOBY Never trust me then; and by all means stir on the youth to an answer. I think oxen and wainropes cannot hale them together. For Andrew, if he were open'd and you find so much blood in his liver as will clog the foot of a flea, I'll eat the rest of th' anatomy.
FABIAN And his opposite, the youth, bears in his
visage no great presage of cruelty. 61

Enter MARIA.

SIR TOBY Look where the youngest wren of nine comes.
MARIA If you desire the spleen, and will laugh yourselves into stitches, follow me. Yond gull Malvolio is turned heathen, a very renegado; for there is no Christian that means to be saved by believing rightly can ever believe such impossible passages of grossness. He's in yellow stockings.
SIR TOBY And cross-garter'd? 69
MARIA Most villainously; like a pedant that keeps a school i' th' church. I have dogg'd him like his murderer. He does obey every point of the letter that I dropp'd to betray him. He does smile his face into more lines than is in the new map with the augmentation of the Indies. You have not seen such a thing as 'tis; I can hardly forbear hurling things at him. I know my lady will strike him; if she do, he'll smile and take't for a great
favour. 77
SIR TOBY Come, bring us, bring us where he is.
[Exeunt.

SCENE III. *A street.*

Enter SEBASTIAN and ANTONIO.

SEBASTIAN I would not by my will have troubled
you;
But since you make your pleasure of your pains,
I will no further chide you.
ANTONIO I could not stay behind you: my desire,

More sharp than filed steel, did spur me forth;
And not all love to see you – though so much
As might have drawn one to a longer voyage –
But jealousy what might befall your travel,
Being skilless in these parts; which to a stranger,
Unguided and unfriended, often prove
Rough and unhospitable. My willing love,
The rather by these arguments of fear,
Set forth in your pursuit.

SEBASTIAN My kind Antonio,
I can no other answer make but thanks,
And thanks, and ever thanks; and oft good turns
Are shuffl'd off with such uncurrent pay;
But were my worth as is my conscience firm,
You should find better dealing. What's to do?
Shall we go see the reliques of this town?

ANTONIO To-morrow, sir; best first go see your lodging.

SEBASTIAN I am not weary, and 'tis long to night;
I pray you, let us satisfy our eyes
With the memorials and the things of fame
That do renown this city.

ANTONIO Would you'd pardon me.
I do not without danger walk these streets:
Once in a sea-fight 'gainst the Count his galleys
I did some service; of such note, indeed,
That, were I ta'en here, it would scarce be answer'd.

SEBASTIAN Belike you slew great number of his people.

ANTONIO Th' offence is not of such a bloody nature;
Albeit the quality of the time and quarrel
Might well have given us bloody argument.
It might have since been answer'd in repaying
What we took from them; which, for traffic's sake,
Most of our city did. Only myself stood out;
For which, if I be lapsed in this place,
I shall pay dear.

SEBASTIAN Do not then walk too open.

ANTONIO It doth not fit me. Hold, sir, here's my purse;
In the south suburbs, at the Elephant,
Is best to lodge. I will bespeak our diet,
Whiles you beguile the time and feed your knowledge
With viewing of the town; there shall you have me.

SEBASTIAN Why I your purse?

ANTONIO Haply your eye shall light upon some toy
You have desire to purchase; and your store,
I think, is not for idle markets, sir.

SEBASTIAN I'll be your purse-bearer, and leave you for
An hour.

ANTONIO To th' Elephant.

SEBASTIAN I do remember.

[Exeunt.

SCENE IV. *Olivia's garden.*

Enter OLIVIA and MARIA.

OLIVIA I have sent after him; he says he'll come.
How shall I feast him? What bestow of him?
For youth is bought more oft than begg'd or borrow'd.
I speak too loud.
Where's Malvolio? He is sad and civil,
And suits well for a servant with my fortunes.
Where is Malvolio?

MARIA He's coming, madam; but in very strange manner. He is sure possess'd, madam.

OLIVIA Why, what's the matter? Does he rave?

MARIA No, madam, he does nothing but smile. Your ladyship were best to have some guard about you if he come; for sure the man is tainted in's wits.

OLIVIA Go call him hither. *[Exit Maria.*
I am as mad as he,
If sad and merry madness equal be.

Re-enter MARIA with MALVOLIO.

How now, Malvolio!

MALVOLIO Sweet lady, ho, ho.

OLIVIA Smil'st thou?
I sent for thee upon a sad occasion.

MALVOLIO Sad, lady? I could be sad. This does make some obstruction in the blood, this cross-gartering; but what of that? If it please the eye of one, it is with me as the very true sonnet is: 'Please one and please all'.

OLIVIA Why, how dost thou, man? What is the matter with thee?

MALVOLIO Not black in my mind, though yellow in my legs. It did come to his hands, and commands shall be executed. I think we do know the sweet Roman hand.

OLIVIA Wilt thou go to bed, Malvolio?

MALVOLIO To bed? Ay, sweetheart, and I'll come to thee.

OLIVIA God comfort thee! Why dost thou smile so, and kiss thy hand so oft?

MARIA How do you, Malvolio?

MALVOLIO At your request? Yes, nightingales answer daws!

MARIA Why appear you with this ridiculous boldness before my lady?

MALVOLIO 'Be not afraid of greatness.' 'Twas well writ.

OLIVIA What mean'st thou by that, Malvolio?

MALVOLIO 'Some are born great,' –

OLIVIA Ha?

MALVOLIO 'Some achieve greatness,' –

OLIVIA What say'st thou?

MALVOLIO 'And some have greatness thrust upon them.'

OLIVIA Heaven restore thee!

MALVOLIO 'Remember who commended thy yellow stockings,' –

OLIVIA 'Thy yellow stockings'?

MALVOLIO 'And wish'd to see thee cross-garter'd.'

OLIVIA 'Cross-garter'd'?

MALVOLIO 'Go to, thou art made, if thou desir'st to be so;' –

OLIVIA Am I made?

MALVOLIO 'If not, let me see thee a servant still.'

OLIVIA Why, this is very midsummer madness.

Enter Servant.

SERVANT Madam, the young gentleman of the Count Orsino's is return'd; I could hardly entreat him back; he attends your ladyship's pleasure.

OLIVIA I'll come to him. [*Exit Servant*] Good Maria, let this fellow be look'd to. Where's my cousin Toby? Let some of my people have a special care of him; I would not have him miscarry for the half of my dowry.

[*Exeunt Olivia and Maria.*

MALVOLIO O, ho! do you come near me now? No worse man than Sir Toby to look at me! This concurs directly with the letter: she sends him on purpose, that I may appear stubborn to him; for she incites me to that in the letter. 'Cast thy humble slough' says she. 'Be opposite with a kinsman, surly with servants; let thy tongue tang with arguments of state; put thyself into the trick of singularity' and consequently sets down the manner how, as: a sad face, a reverend carriage, a slow tongue, in the habit of some sir of note, and so forth. I have lim'd her; but it is Jove's doing, and Jove make me thankful! And when she went away now – 'Let this fellow be look'd to'. 'Fellow' not 'Malvolio' nor after my degree, but 'fellow'. Why, everything adheres together, that no dram of a scruple, no scruple of a scruple, no obstacle, no incredulous or unsafe circumstance – What can be said? Nothing that can be can come between me and the full prospect of my hopes. Well, Jove, not I, is the doer of this, and he is to be thanked.

Re-enter MARIA, with SIR TOBY and FABIAN.

SIR TOBY Which way is he, in the name of sanctity? If all the devils of hell be drawn in little, and Legion himself possess'd him, yet I'll speak to him.

FABIAN Here he is, here he is. How is't with you, sir?

SIR TOBY How is't with you, man?

MALVOLIO Go off; I discard you. Let me enjoy my private; go off.

MARIA Lo, how hollow the fiend speaks within him! Did not I tell you? Sir Toby, my lady prays you to have a care of him.

MALVOLIO Ah, ha! does she so?

SIR TOBY Go to, go to; peace, peace; we must deal gently with him. Let me alone. How do you, Malvolio? How is't with you? What, man, defy the devil; consider, he's an enemy to mankind.

MALVOLIO Do you know what you say?

MARIA La you, an you speak ill of the devil, how he takes it at heart! Pray God he be not bewitch'd.

FABIAN Carry his water to th' wise woman.

MARIA Marry, and it shall be done tomorrow morning, if I live. My lady would not lose him for more than I'll say.

MALVOLIO How now, mistress!

MARIA O Lord!

SIR TOBY Prithee hold thy peace; this is not the way. Do you not see you move him? Let me alone with him.

FABIAN No way but gentleness – gently, gently. The fiend is rough, and will not be roughly us'd.

SIR TOBY Why, how now, my bawcock! How dost thou, chuck?

MALVOLIO Sir!

SIR TOBY Ay, Biddy, come with me. What, man, 'tis not for gravity to play at cherry-pit with Satan. Hang him, foul collier!

MARIA Get him to say his prayers, good Sir Toby, get him to pray.

MALVOLIO My prayers, minx!

MARIA No, I warrant you, he will not hear of godliness.

MALVOLIO Go, hang yourselves all! You are idle shallow things; I am not of your element; you shall know more hereafter. [*Exit.*

SIR TOBY Is't possible?

FABIAN If this were play'd upon a stage now, I could condemn it as an improbable fiction.

SIR TOBY His very genius hath taken the infection of the device, man.

MARIA Nay, pursue him now, lest the device take air and taint.

FABIAN Why, we shall make him mad indeed.

MARIA The house will be the quieter.

SIR TOBY Come, we'll have him in a dark room and bound. My niece is already in the belief that he's mad. We may carry it thus, for our pleasure and his penance, till our very pastime, tired out of breath, prompt us to have mercy on him; at which time we will bring the device to the bar and crown thee for a finder of madmen. But see, but see.

Enter SIR ANDREW.

FABIAN More matter for a May morning.

SIR ANDREW Here's the challenge; read it. I warrant there's vinegar and pepper in't.

FABIAN Is't so saucy?

SIR ANDREW Ay, is't, I warrant him; do but read.

SIR TOBY Give me. [*Reads*] 'Youth, whatsoever thou art, thou art but a scurvy fellow.'

FABIAN Good and valiant.

SIR TOBY [*Reads*] 'Wonder not, nor admire not in thy mind, why I do call thee so, for I will show thee no reason for't.'

FABIAN A good note; that keeps you from the blow of the law.

SIR TOBY [*Reads*] 'Thou com'st to the Lady Olivia, and in my sight she uses thee kindly; but thou liest in thy throat; that is not the matter I challenge thee for.'

FABIAN Very brief, and to exceeding good sense – less.

SIR TOBY [*Reads*] 'I will waylay thee going home; where if it be thy chance to kill me' –

FABIAN Good.

SIR TOBY 'Thou kill'st me like a rogue and a villain.'

FABIAN Still you keep o' th' windy side of the law. Good!

SIR TOBY [*Reads*] 'Fare thee well; and God have mercy upon one of our souls! He may have mercy upon mine; but my hope is better, and so look to thyself. Thy friend, as thou usest him, and thy sworn enemy,

ANDREW AGUECHEEK.'

If this letter move him not, his legs cannot. I'll give't him.

MARIA You may have very fit occasion for't; he is now in some commerce with my lady, and will by and by depart.

SIR TOBY Go, Sir Andrew; scout me for him at the corner of the orchard, like a bum-baily; so soon as ever thou seest him, draw; and as thou draw'st, swear horrible; for it comes to pass oft that a terrible oath, with a swaggering accent sharply twang'd off, gives manhood more approbation than ever proof itself would have earn'd him. Away.

SIR ANDREW Nay, let me alone for swearing. [*Exit.*

SIR TOBY Now will not I deliver his letter; for the behaviour of the young gentleman gives him out to be of good capacity and breeding; his employment between his lord and my niece confirms no less. Therefore this letter, being so excellently ignorant, will breed no terror in the youth: he will find it comes from a clodpole. But, sir, I will deliver his challenge by word of mouth, set upon Aguecheek a notable report of valour, and drive the gentleman – as I know his youth will aptly receive it – into a most hideous opinion of his rage, skill, fury, and impetuosity. This will so fright them both that they will kill one another by the look, like cockatrices.

Re-enter OLIVIA, with VIOLA.

FABIAN Here he comes with your niece; give them way till he take leave, and presently after him.

SIR TOBY I will meditate the while upon some horrid message for a challenge.

[*Exeunt Sir Toby, Fabian, and Maria.*

OLIVIA I have said too much unto a heart of stone,
And laid mine honour too unchary out;
There's something in me that reproves my fault;
But such a headstrong potent fault it is
That it but mocks reproof.

VIOLA With the same haviour that your passion bears
Goes on my master's griefs;

OLIVIA Here, wear this jewel for me; 'tis my picture.
Refuse it not; it hath no tongue to vex you.
And I beseech you come again to-morrow.
What shall you ask of me that I'll deny,
That honour sav'd may upon asking give?

VIOLA Nothing but this – your true love for my master.

OLIVIA How with mine honour may I give him that
Which I have given to you?

VIOLA I will acquit you.

OLIVIA Well, come again to-morrow. Fare thee well;
A fiend like thee might bear my soul to hell.

[*Exit.*

Re-enter SIR TOBY and FABIAN.

SIR TOBY Gentleman, God save thee.

VIOLA And you, sir.

SIR TOBY That defence thou hast, betake thee to't. Of what nature the wrongs are thou hast done him, I know not; but thy intercepter, full of despite, bloody as the hunter, attends thee at the orchard end. Dismount thy tuck, be yare in thy preparation, for thy assailant is quick, skilful, and deadly.

VIOLA You mistake, sir; I am sure no man hath any quarrel to me; my remembrance is very free and clear from any image of offence done to any man.

SIR TOBY You'll find it otherwise, I assure you; therefore, if you hold your life at any price, betake you to your guard; for your opposite hath in him what youth, strength, skill, and wrath, can furnish man withal.

VIOLA I pray you, sir, what is he?

SIR TOBY He is knight, dubb'd with unhatch'd rapier and on carpet consideration; but he is a devil in private brawl. Souls and bodies hath he divorc'd three; and his incensement at this moment is so implacable that satisfaction can be none but by pangs of death and sepulchre. Hobnob is his word – give't or take't.

VIOLA I will return again into the house and desire some conduct of the lady. I am no fighter. I have heard of some kind of men that put quarrels purposely on others to taste their valour; belike this is a man of that quirk.

SIR TOBY Sir, no; his indignation derives itself out of a very competent injury; therefore, get you on and give him his desire. Back you shall not to the house, unless you undertake that with me which with as much safety you might answer him; therefore on, or strip your sword stark naked; for meddle you must, that's certain, or forswear to wear iron about you.

VIOLA This is as uncivil as strange. I beseech you do me this courteous office as to know of the knight what my offence to him is: it is something of my negligence, nothing of my purpose.

SIR TOBY I will do so. Signior Fabian, stay you by this gentleman till my return. *[Exit Sir Toby.*

VIOLA Pray you, sir, do you know of this matter?

FABIAN I know the knight is incens'd against you, even to a mortal arbitrement; but nothing of the circumstance more.

VIOLA I beseech you, what manner of man is he?

FABIAN Nothing of that wonderful promise, to read him by his form, as you are like to find him in the proof of his valour. He is indeed, sir, the most skilful, bloody, and fatal opposite that you could possibly have found in any part of Illyria. Will you walk towards him? I will make your peace with him if I can.

VIOLA I shall be much bound to you for't. I am one that would rather go with sir priest than sir knight. I care not who knows so much of my mettle. *[Exeunt.*

Re-enter SIR TOBY with SIR ANDREW.

SIR TOBY Why, man, he's a very devil; I have not seen such a firago. I had a pass with him, rapier, scabbard, and all, and he gives me the stuck in with such a mortal motion that it is inevitable; and on the answer, he pays you as surely as your feet hit the ground they step on. They say he has been fencer to the Sophy.

SIR ANDREW Pox on't, I'll not meddle with him.

SIR TOBY Ay, but he will not now be pacified; Fabian can scarce hold him yonder.

SIR ANDREW Plague on't; an I thought he had been valiant, and so cunning in fence, I'd have seen him damn'd ere I'd have challeng'd him. Let him let the matter slip, and I'll give him my horse, grey Capilet.

SIR TOBY I'll make the motion. Stand here, make a good show on't; this shall end without the perdition of souls. *[Aside]* Marry, I'll ride your horse as well as I ride you.

Re-enter FABIAN and VIOLA.

[To Fabian] I have his horse to take up the quarrel; I have persuaded him the youth's a devil.

FABIAN *[To Sir Toby]* He is as horribly conceited of him; and pants and looks pale, as if a bear were at his heels.

SIR TOBY *[To Viola]* There's no remedy, sir: he will fight with you for's oath sake. Marry, he hath better bethought him of his quarrel, and he finds that now scarce to be worth talking of. Therefore draw for the supportance of his vow; he protests he will not hurt you.

VIOLA *[Aside]* Pray God defend me! A little thing would make me tell them how much I lack of a man.

FABIAN Give ground if you see him furious.

SIR TOBY Come, Sir Andrew, there's no remedy; the gentleman will, for his honour's sake, have one bout with you; he cannot by the duello avoid it; but he has promis'd me, as he is a gentleman and a soldier, he will not hurt you. Come on; to't.

SIR ANDREW Pray God he keep his oath!

[They draw.

Enter ANTONIO.

VIOLA I do assure you 'tis against my will.

ANTONIO Put up your sword. If this young gentleman
Have done offence, I take the fault on me:
If you offend him, I for him defy you.

SIR TOBY You, sir! Why, what are you?

ANTONIO One, sir, that for his love dares yet do more
Than you have heard him brag to you he will.

SIR TOBY Nay, if you be an undertaker, I am for you.

[They draw.

Enter Officers.

FABIAN O good Sir Toby, hold! Here come the officers.

SIR TOBY *[To Antonio]* I'll be with you anon.

VIOLA Pray, sir, put your sword up, if you please.

SIR ANDREW Marry, will I, sir; and for that I

promis'd you, I'll be as good as my word. He will bear you easily and reins well.

1 OFFICER This is the man; do thy office.

2 OFFICER Antonio, I arrest thee at the suit
Of Count Orsino.

ANTONIO You do mistake me, sir.

1 OFFICER No, sir, no jot; I know your favour well,
Though now you have no sea-cap on your head.
Take him away; he knows I know him well.

ANTONIO I must obey. [*To Viola*] This comes with seeking you;
But there's no remedy; I shall answer it.
What will you do, now my necessity
Makes me to ask you for my purse? It grieves me
Much more for what I cannot do for you
Than what befalls myself. You stand amaz'd;
But be of comfort.

2 OFFICER Come, sir, away.

ANTONIO I must entreat of you some of that money.

VIOLA What money, sir?
For the fair kindness you have show'd me here,
And part being prompted by your present trouble,
Out of my lean and low ability
I'll lend you something. My having is not much;
I'll make division of my present with you;
Hold, there's half my coffer.

ANTONIO Will you deny me now?
Is't possible that my deserts to you
Can lack persuasion? Do not tempt my misery,
Lest that it make me so unsound a man
As to upbraid you with those kindnesses
That I have done for you.

VIOLA I know of none,
Nor know I you by voice or any feature.
I hate ingratitude more in a man
Than lying, vainness, babbling drunkenness,
Or any taint of vice whose strong corruption
Inhabits our frail blood.

ANTONIO O heavens themselves!

2 OFFICER Come, sir, I pray you go.

ANTONIO Let me speak a little. This youth that you see here
I snatch'd one half out of the jaws of death,
Reliev'd him with such sanctity of love,
And to his image, which methought did promise
Most venerable worth, did I devotion.

1 OFFICER What's that to us? The time goes by; away.

ANTONIO But, O, how vile an idol proves this god!
Thou hast, Sebastian, done good feature shame.
In nature there's no blemish but the mind:
None can be call'd deform'd but the unkind.
Virtue is beauty; but the beauteous evil
Are empty trunks, o'erflourish'd by the devil.

1 OFFICER The man grows mad. Away with him.
Come, come, sir.

ANTONIO Lead me on. [*Exit with Officers.*

VIOLA Methinks his words do from such passion fly
That he believes himself; so do not I.
Prove true, imagination, O, prove true,
That I, dear brother, be now ta'en for you!

SIR TOBY Come hither, knight; come hither, Fabian; we'll whisper o'er a couplet or two of most sage saws.

VIOLA He nam'd Sebastian. I my brother know
Yet living in my glass; even such and so
In favour was my brother; and he went
Still in this fashion, colour, ornament,
For him I imitate. O, if it prove,
Tempests are kind, and salt waves fresh in love!
[*Exit.*

SIR TOBY A very dishonest paltry boy, and more a coward than a hare. His dishonesty appears in leaving his friend here in necessity and denying him; and for his cowardship, ask Fabian.

FABIAN A coward, a most devout coward, religious in it.

SIR ANDREW 'Slid, I'll after him again and beat him.

SIR TOBY Do; cuff him soundly, but never draw thy sword.

SIR ANDREW An I do not – [*Exit.*

FABIAN Come, let's see the event.

SIR TOBY I dare lay any money 'twill be nothing yet.

[*Exeunt.*

ACT FOUR

SCENE I. *Before Olivia's house.*

Enter SEBASTIAN and Clown.

CLOWN Will you make me believe that I am not sent for you?

SEBASTIAN Go to, go to, thou art a foolish fellow; let me be clear of thee.

CLOWN Well held out, i' faith! No, I do not know you; nor I am not sent to you by my lady, to bid you come speak with her; nor your name is not

Master Cesario; nor this is not my nose neither. Nothing that is so is so.

SEBASTIAN I prithee vent thy folly somewhere else.
Thou know'st not me.

CLOWN Vent my folly! He has heard that word of some great man, and now applies it to a fool. Vent my folly! I am afraid this great lubber, the world, will prove a cockney. I prithee now, ungird thy strangeness, and tell me what I shall vent to my lady. Shall I vent to her that thou art coming?

SEBASTIAN I prithee, foolish Greek, depart from me;
There's money for thee; if you tarry longer
I shall give worse payment.

CLOWN By my troth, thou hast an open hand. These wise men that give fools money get themselves a good report – after fourteen years' purchase.

Enter SIR ANDREW, SIR TOBY, and FABIAN.

SIR ANDREW Now, sir, have I met you again? [*Striking Sebastian*] There's for you.

SEBASTIAN Why, there's for thee, and there, and there.
Are all the people mad?

SIR TOBY Hold, sir, or I'll throw your dagger o'er the house. [*Holding Sebastian.*

CLOWN This will I tell my lady straight. I would not be in some of your coats for two-pence. [*Exit.*

SIR TOBY Come on, sir; hold.

SIR ANDREW Nay, let him alone. I'll go another way to work with him; I'll have an action of battery against him, if there be any law in Illyria; though I struck him first, yet it's no matter for that.

SEBASTIAN Let go thy hand.

SIR TOBY Come, sir, I will not let you go. Come, my young soldier, put up your iron; you are well flesh'd. Come on.

SEBASTIAN I will be free from thee. What wouldst thou now?
If thou dar'st tempt me further, draw thy sword. [*Draws.*

SIR TOBY What, what? Nay, then I must have an ounce or two of this malapert blood from you. [*Draws.*

Enter OLIVIA.

OLIVIA Hold, Toby; on thy life, I charge thee hold.

SIR TOBY Madam!

OLIVIA Will it be ever thus? Ungracious wretch,
Fit for the mountains and the barbarous caves,
Where manners ne'er were preach'd! Out of my sight!
Be not offended, dear Cesario –
Rudesby, be gone!

[*Exeunt Sir Toby, Sir Andrew, and Fabian.*

I prithee, gentle friend,
Let thy fair wisdom, not thy passion, sway
In this uncivil and unjust extent
Against thy peace. Go with me to my house,
And hear thou there how many fruitless pranks
This ruffian hath botch'd up, that thou thereby
Mayst smile at this. Thou shalt not choose but go;
Do not deny. Beshrew his soul for me!
He started one poor heart of mine in thee.

SEBASTIAN What relish is in this? How runs the stream?
Or I am mad, or else this is a dream.
Let fancy still my sense in Lethe steep;
If it be thus to dream, still let me sleep!

OLIVIA Nay, come, I prithee. Would thou'dst be rul'd by me!

SEBASTIAN Madam, I will.

OLIVIA O, say so, and so be!

[*Exeunt.*

SCENE II. *Olivia's house.*

Enter MARIA and Clown.

MARIA Nay, I prithee, put on this gown and this beard; make him believe thou art Sir Topas the curate; do it quickly. I'll call Sir Toby the whilst. [*Exit.*

CLOWN Well, I'll put it on, and I will dissemble myself in't; and I would I were the first that ever dissembled in such a gown. I am not tall enough to become the function well nor lean enough to be thought a good student; but to be said an honest man and a good housekeeper goes as fairly as to say a careful man and a great scholar. The competitors enter.

Enter SIR TOBY and MARIA.

SIR TOBY Jove bless thee, Master Parson.

CLOWN Bonos dies, Sir Toby; for as the old hermit of Prague, that never saw pen and ink, very wittily said to a niece of King Gorboduc 'That that is is'; so I, being Master Parson, am Master Parson; for what is 'that' but that, and 'is' but is?

SIR TOBY To him, Sir Topas.

CLOWN What ho, I say! Peace in this prison!

SIR TOBY The knave counterfeits well; a good knave.

MALVOLIO [*Within*] Who calls there?

CLOWN Sir Topas the curate, who comes to visit Malvolio the lunatic.

MALVOLIO Sir Topas, Sir Topas, good Sir Topas, go to my lady.

CLOWN Out, hyperbolical fiend! How vexest thou this man! Talkest thou nothing but of ladies?

SIR TOBY Well said, Master Parson.

MALVOLIO Sir Topas, never was man thus wronged. Good Sir Topas, do not think I am mad; they have laid me here in hideous darkness.

CLOWN Fie, thou dishonest Satan! I call thee by the most modest terms, for I am one of those gentle ones that will use the devil himself with courtesy. Say'st thou that house is dark?

MALVOLIO As hell, Sir Topas.

CLOWN Why, it hath bay windows transparent as barricadoes, and the clerestories toward the south north are as lustrous as ebony; and yet complainest thou of obstruction?

MALVOLIO I am not mad, Sir Topas. I say to you this house is dark.

CLOWN Madman, thou errest. I say there is no darkness but ignorance; in which thou art more puzzled than the Egyptians in their fog.

MALVOLIO I say this house is as dark as ignorance, though ignorance were as dark as hell; and I say there was never man thus abus'd. I am no more mad than you are; make the trial of it in any constant question.

CLOWN What is the opinion of Pythagoras concerning wild fowl?

MALVOLIO That the soul of our grandam might haply inhabit a bird.

CLOWN What think'st thou of his opinion?

MALVOLIO I think nobly of the soul, and no way approve his opinion.

CLOWN Fare thee well. Remain thou still in darkness: thou shalt hold th' opinion of Pythagoras ere I will allow of thy wits; and fear to kill a woodcock, lest thou dispossess the soul of thy grandam. Fare thee well.

MALVOLIO Sir Topas, Sir Topas!

SIR TOBY My most exquisite Sir Topas!

CLOWN Nay, I am for all waters.

MARIA Thou mightst have done this without thy beard and gown: he sees thee not.

SIR TOBY To him in thine own voice, and bring me word how thou find'st him. I would we were well rid of this knavery. If he may be conveniently deliver'd, I would he were; for I am now so far in offence with my niece that I cannot pursue with any safety this sport to the upshot. Come by and by to my chamber.

[*Exeunt Sir Toby and Maria.*

CLOWN [*Sings*] Hey, Robin, jolly Robin,
Tell me how thy lady does.

MALVOLIO Fool!

CLOWN [*Sings*] My lady is unkind, perdy.

MALVOLIO Fool!

CLOWN [*Sings*] Alas, why is she so?

MALVOLIO Fool I say!

CLOWN [*Sings*] She loves another – Who calls, ha?

MALVOLIO Good fool, as ever thou wilt deserve well at my hand, help me to a candle, and pen, ink, and paper; as I am a gentleman, I will live to be thankful to thee for't.

CLOWN Master Malvolio?

MALVOLIO Ay, good fool.

CLOWN Alas, sir, how fell you besides your five wits?

MALVOLIO Fool, there was never man so notoriously abus'd; I am as well in my wits, fool, as thou art.

CLOWN But as well? Then you are mad indeed, if you be no better in your wits than a fool.

MALVOLIO They have here propertied me; keep me in darkness, send ministers to me, asses, and do all they can to face me out of my wits.

CLOWN Advise you what you say: the minister is here. [*Speaking as Sir Topas*] Malvolio, Malvolio, thy wits the heavens restore! Endeavour thyself to sleep, and leave thy vain bibble-babble.

MALVOLIO Sir Topas!

CLOWN Maintain no words with him, good fellow. – Who, I, sir? Not I, sir. God buy you, good Sir Topas. – Marry, amen. – I will, sir, I will.

MALVOLIO Fool, fool, fool, I say!

CLOWN Alas, sir, be patient. What say you, sir? I am shent for speaking to you.

MALVOLIO Good fool, help me to some light and some paper. I tell thee I am as well in my wits as any man in Illyria.

CLOWN Well-a-day that you were, sir!

MALVOLIO By this hand, I am. Good fool, some ink, paper, and light; and convey what I will set down to my lady. It shall advantage thee more than ever the bearing of letter did.

CLOWN I will help you to't. But tell me true, are you not mad indeed, or do you but counterfeit?

MALVOLIO Believe me, I am not; I tell thee true.

CLOWN Nay, I'll ne'er believe a madman till I see his brains. I will fetch you light and paper and ink.

MALVOLIO Fool, I'll requite it in the highest degree; I prithee be gone.

CLOWN [*Singing*]

I am gone, sir,
And anon, sir,

I'll be with you again,
In a trice,
Like to the old Vice,
Your need to sustain;

Who with dagger of lath,
In his rage and his wrath,
Cries, Ah, ha! to the devil;
Like a mad lad,
Pare thy nails, dad.
Adieu, goodman devil.
[*Exit.*

SCENE III. *Olivia's garden.*

Enter SEBASTIAN.

SEBASTIAN This is the air; that is the glorious sun;
This pearl she gave me, I do feel't and see't;
And though 'tis wonder that enwraps me thus,
Yet 'tis not madness. Where's Antonio, then?
I could not find him at the Elephant;
Yet there he was; and there I found this credit,
That he did range the town to seek me out.
His counsel now might do me golden service;
For though my soul disputes well with my sense
That this may be some error, but no madness,
Yet doth this accident and flood of fortune
So far exceed all instance, all discourse,
That I am ready to distrust mine eyes
And wrangle with my reason, that persuades me
To any other trust but that I am mad,
Or else the lady's mad; yet if 'twere so,
She could not sway her house, command her followers,
Take and give back affairs and their dispatch
With such a smooth, discreet, and stable bearing,
As I perceive she does. There's something in't
That is deceivable. But here the lady comes.

Enter OLIVIA and Priest.

OLIVIA Blame not this haste of mine. If you mean well,
Now go with me and with this holy man
Into the chantry by; there, before him
And underneath that consecrated roof,
Plight me the full assurance of your faith,
That my most jealous and too doubtful soul
May live at peace. He shall conceal it
Whiles you are willing it shall come to note,
What time we will our celebration keep
According to my birth. What do you say?

SEBASTIAN I'll follow this good man, and go with you;
And, having sworn truth, ever will be true.

OLIVIA Then lead the way, good father; and heavens so shine
That they may fairly note this act of mine!
[*Exeunt.*

ACT FIVE

SCENE I. *Before Olivia's house.*

Enter Clown and FABIAN.

FABIAN Now, as thou lov'st me, let me see his letter.

CLOWN Good Master Fabian, grant me another request.

FABIAN Anything.

CLOWN Do not desire to see this letter.

FABIAN This is to give a dog, and in recompense desire my dog again.

Enter DUKE, VIOLA, CURIO and Lords.

DUKE Belong you to the Lady Olivia, friends?

CLOWN Ay, sir, we are some of her trappings.

DUKE I know thee well. How dost thou, my good fellow?

CLOWN Truly, sir, the better for my foes and the worse for my friends.

DUKE Just the contrary: the better for thy friends.

CLOWN No, sir, the worse.

DUKE How can that be?

CLOWN Marry, sir, they praise me and make an ass of me. Now my foes tell me plainly I am an ass; so that by my foes, sir, I profit in the knowledge of myself, and by my friends I am abused; so that, conclusions to be as kisses, if your four negatives make your two affirmatives, why then, the worse for my friends and the better for my foes.

DUKE Why, this is excellent.

CLOWN By my troth, sir, no; though it please you to be one of my friends.

DUKE Thou shalt not be the worse for me. There's gold.

CLOWN But that it would be double-dealing, sir, I would you could make it another.

DUKE O, you give me ill counsel.

CLOWN Put your grace in your pocket, sir, for this once, and let your flesh and blood obey it.

DUKE Well, I will be so much a sinner to be a double-dealer. There's another.

CLOWN Primo, secundo, tertio, is a good play; and the old saying is 'The third pays for all'. The triplex, sir, is a good tripping measure; or the bells of Saint Bennet, sir, may put you in mind – one, two, three.

DUKE You can fool no more money out of me at this throw; if you will let your lady know I am here to speak with her, and bring her along with you, it may awake my bounty further.

CLOWN Marry, sir, lullaby to your bounty till I come again. I go, sir; but I would not have you to think that my desire of having is the sin of covetousness. But, as you say, sir, let your bounty take a nap; I will awake it anon. [*Exit.*

Enter ANTONIO and Officers.

VIOLA Here comes the man, sir, that did rescue me.
DUKE That face of his I do remember well;
Yet when I saw it last it was besmear'd
As black as Vulcan in the smoke of war.
A baubling vessel was he captain of,
For shallow draught and bulk unprizable,
With which such scathful grapple did he make
With the most noble bottom of our fleet
That very envy and the tongue of loss
Cried fame and honour on him. What's the matter?
1 OFFICER Orsino, this is that Antonio
That took the Phoenix and her fraught from Candy;
And this is he that did the Tiger board
When your young nephew Titus lost his leg.
Here in the streets, desperate of shame and state,
In private brabble did we apprehend him.
VIOLA He did me kindness, sir; drew on my side;
But in conclusion put strange speech upon me.
I know not what 'twas but distraction.
DUKE Notable pirate, thou salt-water thief!
What foolish boldness brought thee to their mercies
Whom thou, in terms so bloody and so dear,
Hast made thine enemies?
ANTONIO Orsino, noble sir,
Be pleas'd that I shake off these names you give me:
Antonio never yet was thief or pirate,
Though I confess, on base and ground enough,
Orsino's enemy. A witchcraft drew me hither:
That most ingrateful boy there by your side
From the rude sea's enrag'd and foamy mouth
Did I redeem; a wreck past hope he was.
His life I gave him, and did thereto add
My love without retention or restraint,
All his in dedication; for his sake,
Did I expose myself, pure for his love,
Into the danger of this adverse town;
Drew to defend him when he was beset;
Where being apprehended, his false cunning,
Not meaning to partake with me in danger,
Taught him to face me out of his acquaintance,
And grew a twenty years removed thing
While one would wink; denied me mine own purse,
Which I had recommended to his use
Not half an hour before.
VIOLA How can this be?
DUKE When came he to this town?
ANTONIO To-day, my lord; and for three months before,
No int'rim, not a minute's vacancy,
Both day and night did we keep company.

Enter OLIVIA and Attendants.

DUKE Here comes the Countess; now heaven walks on earth.
But for thee, fellow – fellow, thy words are madness.
Three months this youth hath tended upon me –
But more of that anon. Take him aside.
OLIVIA What would my lord, but that he may not have,
Wherein Olivia may seem serviceable?
Cesario, you do not keep promise with me.
VIOLA Madam?
DUKE Gracious Olivia –
OLIVIA What do you say, Cesario? Good my lord –
VIOLA My lord would speak; my duty hushes me.
OLIVIA If it be aught to the old tune, my lord,
It is as fat and fulsome to mine ear
As howling after music.
DUKE Still so cruel?
OLIVIA Still so constant, lord.
DUKE What, to perverseness? You uncivil lady,
To whose ingrate and unauspicious altars
My soul the faithfull'st off'rings hath breath'd out
That e'er devotion tender'd! What shall I do?
OLIVIA Even what it please my lord, that shall become him.
DUKE Why should I not, had I the heart to do it,
Like to the Egyptian thief at point of death,
Kill what I love? – a savage jealousy
That sometime savours nobly. But hear me this:
Since you to non-regardance cast my faith,
And that I partly know the instrument
That screws me from my true place in your favour,
Live you the marble-breasted tyrant still;
But this your minion, whom I know you love,
And whom, by heaven I swear, I tender dearly,
Him will I tear out of that cruel eye
Where he sits crowned in his master's spite.

Come, boy, with me; my thoughts are ripe in mischief:
I'll sacrifice the lamb that I do love
To spite a raven's heart within a dove.

VIOLA And I, most jocund, apt, and willingly,
To do you rest, a thousand deaths would die.

OLIVIA Where goes Cesario?

VIOLA After him I love
More than I love these eyes, more than my life,
More, by all mores, than e'er I shall love wife.
If I do feign, you witnesses above
Punish my life for tainting of my love!

OLIVIA Ay me, detested! How am I beguil'd!

VIOLA Who does beguile you? Who does do you wrong?

OLIVIA Hast thou forgot thyself? Is it so long?
Call forth the holy father. [*Exit an Attendant.*

DUKE Come, away!

OLIVIA Whither, my lord? Cesario, husband, stay.

DUKE Husband?

OLIVIA Ay, husband; can he that deny?

DUKE Her husband, sirrah?

VIOLA No, my lord, not I.

OLIVIA Alas, it is the baseness of thy fear
That makes thee strangle thy propriety.
Fear not, Cesario, take thy fortunes up;
Be that thou know'st thou art, and then thou art
As great as that thou fear'st.

Enter Priest.

O, welcome, father!
Father, I charge thee, by thy reverence,
Here to unfold – though lately we intended
To keep in darkness what occasion now
Reveals before 'tis ripe – what thou dost know
Hath newly pass'd between this youth and me.

PRIEST A contract of eternal bond of love,
Confirm'd by mutual joinder of your hands,
Attested by the holy close of lips,
Strength'ned by interchangement of your rings;
And all the ceremony of this compact
Seal'd in my function, by my testimony;
Since when, my watch hath told me, toward my grave,
I have travell'd but two hours.

DUKE O thou dissembling cub! What wilt thou be,
When time hath sow'd a grizzle on thy case?
Or will not else thy craft so quickly grow
That thine own trip shall be thine overthrow?
Farewell, and take her; but direct thy feet
Where thou and I henceforth may never meet.

VIOLA My lord, I do protest –

OLIVIA O, do not swear!
Hold little faith, though thou has too much fear.

Enter SIR ANDREW.

SIR ANDREW For the love of God, a surgeon!
Send one presently to Sir Toby.

OLIVIA What's the matter?

SIR ANDREW Has broke my head across, and has given Sir Toby a bloody coxcomb too. For the love of God, your help! I had rather than forty pound I were at home.

OLIVIA Who has done this, Sir Andrew?

SIR ANDREW The Count's gentleman, one Cesario. We took him for a coward, but he's the very devil incardinate.

DUKE My gentleman, Cesario?

SIR ANDREW Od's lifelings, here he is! You broke my head for nothing; and that that I did, I was set on to do't by Sir Toby.

VIOLA Why do you speak to me? I never hurt you.
You drew your sword upon me without cause;
But I bespake you fair and hurt you not.

Enter SIR TOBY and Clown.

SIR ANDREW If a bloody coxcomb be a hurt, you have hurt me; I think you set nothing by a bloody coxcomb. Here comes Sir Toby halting; you shall hear more; but if he had not been in drink, he would have tickl'd you othergates than he did.

DUKE How now, gentleman? How is't with you?

SIR TOBY That's all one; has hurt me, and there's th' end on't. Sot, didst see Dick Surgeon, sot?

CLOWN O, he's drunk, Sir Toby, an hour agone; his eyes were set at eight i' th' morning.

SIR TOBY Then he's a rogue and a passy measures pavin. I hate a drunken rogue.

OLIVIA Away with him. Who hath made this havoc with them?

SIR ANDREW I'll help you, Sir Toby, because we'll be dress'd together.

SIR TOBY Will you help – an ass-head and a coxcomb and a knave, a thin fac'd knave, a gull?

OLIVIA Get him to bed, and let his hurt be look'd to.

[*Exeunt Clown, Fabian, Sir Toby, and Sir Andrew.*

Enter SEBASTIAN.

SEBASTIAN I am sorry, madam, I have hurt your kinsman;
But, had it been the brother of my blood,
I must have done no less with wit and safety.
You throw a strange regard upon me, and by that
I do perceive it hath offended you.
Pardon me, sweet one, even for the vows
We made each other but so late ago.

DUKE One face, one voice, one habit, and two persons!
A natural perspective, that is and is not.

SEBASTIAN Antonio, O my dear Antonio!

How have the hours rack'd and tortur'd me
Since I have lost thee!

ANTONIO Sebastian are you?

SEBASTIAN Fear'st thou that, Antonio?

ANTONIO How have you made division of yourself?
An apple cleft in two is not more twin
Than these two creatures. Which is Sebastian?

OLIVIA Most wonderful!

SEBASTIAN Do I stand there? I never had a brother;
Nor can there be that deity in my nature
Of here and everywhere. I had a sister
Whom the blind waves and surges have devour'd.
Of charity, what kin are you to me?
What countryman, what name, what parentage?

VIOLA Of Messaline; Sebastian was my father.
Such a Sebastian was my brother too;
So went he suited to his watery tomb;
If spirits can assume both form and suit,
You came to fright us.

SEBASTIAN A spirit I am indeed,
But am in that dimension grossly clad
Which from the womb I did participate.
Were you a woman, as the rest goes even,
I should my tears let fall upon your cheek,
And say 'Thrice welcome, drowned Viola!'

VIOLA My father had a mole upon his brow.

SEBASTIAN And so had mine.

VIOLA And died that day when Viola from her birth
Had numb'red thirteen years.

SEBASTIAN O, that record is lively in my soul!
He finished indeed his mortal act
That day that made my sister thirteen years.

VIOLA If nothing lets to make us happy both
But this my masculine usurp'd attire,
Do not embrace me till each circumstance
Of place, time, fortune, do cohere and jump
That I am Viola; which to confirm,
I'll bring you to a captain in this town,
Where lie my maiden weeds; by whose gentle help
I was preserv'd to serve this noble Count.
All the occurrence of my fortune since
Hath been between this lady and this lord.

SEBASTIAN [*To Olivia*] So comes it, lady, you have been mistook;
But nature to her bias drew in that.
You would have been contracted to a maid;
Nor are you therein, by my life, deceiv'd;
You are betroth'd both to a maid and man.

DUKE Be not amaz'd; right noble is his blood.
If this be so, as yet the glass seems true,
I shall have share in this most happy wreck.
[*To Viola*] Boy, thou hast said to me a thousand times
Thou never shouldst love woman like to me.

VIOLA And all those sayings will I overswear;
And all those swearings keep as true in soul
As doth that orbed continent the fire
That severs day from night.

DUKE Give me thy hand;
And let me see thee in thy woman's weeds.

VIOLA The captain that did bring me first on shore
Hath my maid's garments. He, upon some action,
Is now in durance, at Malvolio's suit,
A gentleman and follower of my lady's.

OLIVIA He shall enlarge him. Fetch Malvolio hither;
And yet, alas, now I remember me,
They say, poor gentleman, he's much distract.

Re-enter Clown, with a letter, and FABIAN.

A most extracting frenzy of mine own
From my remembrance clearly banish'd his.
How does he, sirrah?

CLOWN Truly, madam, he holds Belzebub at the stave's end as well as a man in his case may do. Has here writ a letter to you; I should have given 't you to-day morning, but as a madman's epistles are no gospels, so it skills not much when they are deliver'd.

OLIVIA Open't, and read it.

CLOWN Look then to be well edified when the fool delivers the madman. [*Reads madly*] 'By the Lord, madam –'

OLIVIA How now! Art thou mad?

CLOWN No, madam, I do but read madness. An your ladyship will have it as it ought to be, you must allow vox.

OLIVIA Prithee read i' thy right wits.

CLOWN So I do, madonna; but to read his right wits is to read thus; therefore perpend, my Princess, and give ear.

OLIVIA [*To Fabian*] Read it you, sirrah.

FABIAN [*Reads*] 'By the Lord, madam, you wrong me, and the world shall know it. Though you have put me into darkness and given your drunken cousin rule over me, yet have I the benefit of my senses as well as your ladyship. I have your own letter that induced me to the semblance I put on, with the which I doubt not but to do myself much right or you much shame. Think of me as you please. I leave my duty a little unthought of, and speak out of my injury.
THE MADLY-US'D MALVOLIO.'

OLIVIA Did he write this?

CLOWN Ay, Madam.

DUKE This savours not much of distraction.
OLIVIA See him deliver'd, Fabian; bring him hither. [*Exit Fabian.*
My lord, so please you, these things further thought on,
To think me as well a sister as a wife,
One day shall crown th' alliance on't, so please you,
Here at my house, and at my proper cost.
DUKE Madam, I am most apt t' embrace your offer.
[*To Viola*] Your master quits you; and, for your service done him,
So much against the mettle of your sex,
So far beneath your soft and tender breeding,
And since you call'd me master for so long,
Here is my hand; you shall from this time be
Your master's mistress.
OLIVIA A sister! You are she.

Re-enter FABIAN, with MALVOLIO.

DUKE Is this the madman?
OLIVIA Ay, my lord, this same.
How now, Malvolio!
MALVOLIO Madam, you have done me wrong,
Notorious wrong.
OLIVIA Have I, Malvolio? No.
MALVOLIO Lady, you have. Pray you peruse that letter.
You must not now deny it is your hand;
Write from it if you can, in hand or phrase;
Or say 'tis not your seal, not your invention;
You can say none of this. Well, grant it then,
And tell me, in the modesty of honour,
Why you have given me such clear lights of favour,
Bade me come smiling and cross-garter'd to you,
To put on yellow stockings, and to frown
Upon Sir Toby and the lighter people;
And, acting this in an obedient hope,
Why have you suffer'd me to be imprison'd,
Kept in a dark house, visited by the priest,
And made the most notorious geck and gull
That e'er invention play'd on? Tell me why.
OLIVIA Alas, Malvolio, this is not my writing,
Though, I confess, much like the character;
But out of question 'tis Maria's hand.
And now I do bethink me, it was she
First told me thou wast mad; then cam'st in smiling,
And in such forms which here were presuppos'd
Upon thee in the letter. Prithee, be content;
This practice hath most shrewdly pass'd upon thee,
But, when we know the grounds and authors of it,
Thou shalt be both the plaintiff and the judge
Of thine own cause.
FABIAN Good madam, hear me speak,
And let no quarrel nor no brawl to come
Taint the condition of this present hour,
Which I have wond'red at. In hope it shall not,
Most freely I confess myself and Toby
Set this device against Malvolio here,
Upon some stubborn and uncourteous parts
We had conceiv'd against him. Maria writ
The letter, at Sir Toby's great importance,
In recompense whereof he hath married her.
How with a sportful malice it was follow'd
May rather pluck on laughter than revenge,
If that the injuries be justly weigh'd
That have on both sides pass'd.
OLIVIA Alas, poor fool, how have they baffl'd thee!
CLOWN Why, 'Some are born great, some achieve greatness, and some have greatness thrown upon them'. I was one, sir, in this interlude – one Sir Topas, sir; but that's all one. 'By the Lord, fool, I am not mad!' But do you remember – 'Madam, why laugh you at such a barren rascal? An you smile not, he's gagg'd'? And thus the whirligig of time brings in his revenges.
MALVOLIO I'll be reveng'd on the whole pack of you. [*Exit.*
OLIVIA He hath been most notoriously abus'd.
DUKE Pursue him, and entreat him to a peace;
He hath not told us of the captain yet.
When that is known, and golden time convents,
A solemn combination shall be made
Of our dear souls. Meantime, sweet sister,
We will not part from hence. Cesario, come;
For so you shall be while you are a man;
But when in other habits you are seen,
Orsino's mistress, and his fancy's queen.
[*Exeunt all but the Clown.*

Clown sings.

When that I was and a little tiny boy,
With hey, ho, the wind and the rain,
A foolish thing was but a toy,
For the rain it raineth every day.
But when I came to man's estate,
With hey, ho, the wind and the rain,
'Gainst knaves and thieves men shut their gate,
For the rain it raineth every day.

But when I came, alas! to wive,
With hey, ho, the wind and the rain,
By swaggering could I never thrive,
For the rain it raineth every day.

But when I came unto my beds,

With hey, ho, the wind and the rain,
With toss-pots still had drunken heads,
For the rain it raineth every day.
A great while ago the world begun,
With hey, ho, the wind and the rain,
But that's all one, our play is done,
And we'll strive to please you every day.

[*Exit.*

The Winter's Tale

Introduction by PHILIP HOBSBAUM

As a budding playwright, Shakespeare was attacked by an older writer, Robert Greene, for plagiarism: 'an upstart Crow, beautified with our feathers'. Towards the end of his career, for his next-to-last play to be completed, Shakespeare drew upon a story by this same Greene, and so created *The Winter's Tale*.

In Shakespeare's own period, older playgoers, remembering Greene and seeing this work for the first time, must have thought they knew how it ended. The king, consumed by jealousy, repudiates his queen, who dies. He soon after recognises his error, but it is too late. That, at least, is the story of Greene's *Pandosto*. Shakespeare, however, picks up this simple tale and turns it into a myth of resurrection. We all, like the early playgoers, think Hermione to be dead. We see her fall, deadly sick, on stage. News of her death is brought by Paulina, whom we know to be a reliable witness. Sixteen years pass, without any sign of her.

Tragedy lies very close to comedy here. The earlier episodes, the autumn and winter parts of the play, display the imagery of disease and dearth: 'Why then the world and all that's in't is nothing;/The covering sky is nothing; Bohemia nothing;/my wife is nothing; nor nothing have those nothings,/If this be nothing'. But those corrugated rhythms give way to the comedy of Autolycus and his song of spring: 'When daffodils begin to peer,/With heigh! the doxy over the dale'. There is the daughter who was thought lost, Perdita in her harvest scene, also evoking the spring: 'daffodils,/That come before the swallow dares, and take/The winds of March with beauty'. This prefigures the restoration of Hermione, which is the key to the play.

The meeting of Perdita with Leontes, her father, which could have been one of Shakespeare's reconciliation set-pieces, is reported at second hand in order to preserve the grand climax for the restitution of Hermione. There, at the end, is the Statue Scene when Hermione rises, as though from the dead, and joins her repentant husband.

So far from attempting to seem naturalistic, the text drives home the impossibilities: 'That she is living,/Were it but told you, should be hooted at/Like an old tale'. But Shakespeare has paid the 'old tale' of his former enemy, Robert Greene, the supreme compliment of turning it into high drama. Leontes says, 'I saw her,/As I thought, dead; and have, in vain, said many/A prayer upon her grave'. However, the prayers have not been in vain. The whole scene is an acting out of resurrection.

The extravagance of the plot is matched by that of the structure. Such critics as the Italian, Castelvetro, and the Englishman, Sir Philip Sidney, thought that the Greek philosopher, Aristotle, had imposed rules on the drama that decreed restrictions as to the time a play should encompass in its action, the place – only one – it should represent, and the plot – very simple – that it should deploy. These rules were called 'unities', and Shakespeare violated these unities in an exuberant fashion. The action covers sixteen years, and not smoothly: there is a gaping void between Act 3 and Act 4. The scenes swerve between Sicily, the kingdom of Leontes, and Bohemia, the kingdom of his supposed rival, Polixenes. The plot, as we have seen, is far-fetched beyond all decorum. However, the appeal is not to the intricacies of art, but to nature. In the end, what we are shown is nature's own cycle, represented in the death and restoration of Hermione. She is a kind of earth goddess. We see the earth die, every winter. Yet it revives in the spring. It is an idea similar to that of Jesus' parable of the Prodigal Son. He 'was dead, and is alive again; he was lost, and is found' (Luke 15:24).

The Winter's Tale

DRAMATIS PERSONAE

LEONTES
King of Sicilia
MAMILLIUS
his son, the young Prince of Sicilia
CAMILLO, ANTIGONUS, CLEOMENES, DION
lords of Sicilia
POLIXENES
King of Bohemia
FLORIZEL
his son, Prince of Bohemia
ARCHIDAMUS
a lord of Bohemia
Old Shepherd, reputed father of Perdita
Clown, his son
AUTOLYCUS
a rogue
A Mariner
A Gaoler

TIME
as Chorus
HERMIONE
Queen to Leontes
PERDITA
daughter to Leontes and Hermione
PAULINA
wife to Antigonus
EMILIA
a lady attending on the Queen
MOPSA, DORCAS
shepherdesses
Other Lords, Gentlemen, Ladies, Officers, Servants, Shepherds, and Shepherdesses

THE SCENE: SICILIA AND BOHEMIA.

ACT ONE

SCENE I. *Sicilia. The palace of Leontes.*

Enter CAMILLO and ARCHIDAMUS.

ARCHIDAMUS If you shall chance, Camillo, to visit Bohemia, on the like occasion whereon my services are now on foot, you shall see, as I have said, great difference betwixt our Bohemia and your Sicilia.

CAMILLO I think this coming summer the King of Sicilia means to pay Bohemia the visitation which he justly owes him.

ARCHIDAMUS Wherein our entertainment shall shame us we will be justified in our loves; for indeed –

CAMILLO Beseech you –

ARCHIDAMUS Verily, I speak it in the freedom of my knowledge: we cannot with such magnificence, in so rare – I know not what to say. We will give you sleepy drinks, that your senses, unintelligent of our insufficience, may, though they cannot praise us, as little accuse us.

CAMILLO You pay a great deal too dear for what's given freely.

ARCHIDAMUS Believe me, I speak as my understanding instructs me and as mine honesty puts it to utterance.

CAMILLO Sicilia cannot show himself over-kind to Bohemia. They were train'd together in their childhoods; and there rooted betwixt them then such an affection which cannot choose but branch now. Since their more mature dignities and royal necessities made separation of their society, their encounters, though not personal, have been royally attorneyed with interchange of gifts, letters, loving embassies; that they have seem'd to be together, though absent; shook hands, as over a vast; and embrac'd as it were from the ends of opposed winds. The heavens continue their loves!

ARCHIDAMUS I think there is not in the world either malice or matter to alter it. You have an unspeakable comfort of your young Prince Mamillius; it is a gentleman of the greatest promise that ever came into my note.

CAMILLO I very well agree with you in the hopes of him. It is a gallant child; one that indeed physics the subject, makes old hearts fresh; they that went on crutches ere he was born desire yet their life to see him a man.

ARCHIDAMUS Would they else be content to die?

CAMILLO Yes; if there were no other excuse why they should desire to live.

ARCHIDAMUS If the King had no son, they would desire to live on crutches till he had one. [*Exeunt.*

SCENE II. *Sicilia. The palace of Leontes.*

Enter LEONTES, POLIXENES, HERMIONE, MAMILLIUS, CAMILLO, and Attendants.

POLIXENES Nine changes of the wat'ry star hath been
The shepherd's note since we have left our throne
Without a burden. Time as long again

Would be fill'd up, my brother, with our thanks;
And yet we should for perpetuity
Go hence in debt. And therefore, like a cipher,
Yet standing in rich place, I multiply
With one 'We thank you' many thousands moe
That go before it.

LEONTES Stay your thanks a while,
And pay them when you part.

POLIXENES Sir, that's to-morrow.
I am question'd by my fears of what may chance
Or breed upon our absence, that may blow
No sneaping winds at home, to make us say
'This is put forth too truly'. Besides, I have stay'd
To tire your royalty.

LEONTES We are tougher, brother,
Than you can put us to't.

POLIXENES No longer stay.

LEONTES One sev'night longer.

POLIXENES Very sooth, to-morrow.

LEONTES We'll part the time between's then; and in that
I'll no gainsaying.

POLIXENES Press me not, beseech you, so.
There is no tongue that moves, none, none i' th' world,
So soon as yours could win me. So it should now,
Were there necessity in your request, although
'Twere needful I denied it. My affairs
Do even drag me homeward; which to hinder
Were in your love a whip to me; my stay
To you a charge and trouble. To save both,
Farewell, our brother.

LEONTES Tongue-tied, our Queen? Speak you.

HERMIONE I had thought, sir, to have held my peace until
You had drawn oaths from him not to stay. You, sir,
Charge him too coldly. Tell him you are sure
All in Bohemia's well – this satisfaction
The by-gone day proclaim'd. Say this to him,
He's beat from his best ward.

LEONTES Well said, Hermione.

HERMIONE To tell he longs to see his son were strong;
But let him say so then, and let him go;
But let him swear so, and he shall not stay;
We'll thwack him hence with distaffs.
[*To Polixenes*] Yet of your royal presence I'll adventure
The borrow of a week. When at Bohemia
You take my lord, I'll give him my commission
To let him there a month behind the gest
Prefix'd for's parting. – Yet, good deed, Leontes,
I love thee not a jar o' th' clock behind
What lady she her lord. – You'll stay?

POLIXENES No, madam.

HERMIONE Nay, but you will?

POLIXENES I may not, verily.

HERMIONE Verily!
You put me off with limber vows; but I,
Though you would seek t' unsphere the stars with oaths,
Should yet say 'Sir, no going'. Verily,
You shall not go; a lady's 'verily' is
As potent as a lord's. Will you go yet?
Force me to keep you as a prisoner,
Not like a guest; so you shall pay your fees
When you depart, and save your thanks. How say you?
My prisoner or my guest? By your dread 'verily',
One of them you shall be.

POLIXENES Your guest, then, madam:
To be your prisoner should import offending;
Which is for me less easy to commit
Than you to punish.

HERMIONE Not your gaoler then,
But your kind hostess. Come, I'll question you
Of my lord's tricks and yours when you were boys.
You were pretty lordings then!

POLIXENES We were, fair Queen,
Two lads that thought there was no more behind
But such a day to-morrow as to-day,
And to be boy eternal.

HERMIONE Was not my lord
The verier wag o' th' two?

POLIXENES We were as twinn'd lambs that did frisk i' th' sun
And bleat the one at th' other. What we chang'd
Was innocence for innocence; we knew not
The doctrine of ill-doing, nor dream'd
That any did. Had we pursu'd that life,
And our weak spirits ne'er been higher rear'd
With stronger blood, we should have answer'd heaven
Boldly 'Not guilty', the imposition clear'd
Hereditary ours.

HERMIONE By this we gather
You have tripp'd since.

POLIXENES O my most sacred lady,
Temptations have since then been born to 's, for
In those unfledg'd days was my wife a girl;
Your precious self had then not cross'd the eyes
Of my young playfellow.

HERMIONE Grace to boot!
Of this make no conclusion, lest you say
Your queen and I are devils. Yet, go on;
Th' offences we have made you do we'll answer,
If you first sinn'd with us, and that with us
You did continue fault, and that you slipp'd not
With any but with us.

LEONTES Is he won yet?
HERMIONE He'll stay, my lord.
LEONTES At my request he would not.
Hermione, my dearest, thou never spok'st
To better purpose.
HERMIONE Never?
LEONTES Never but once.
HERMIONE What! Have I twice said well? When was't before?
I prithee tell me; cram's with praise, and make's
As fat as tame things. One good deed dying tongueless
Slaughters a thousand waiting upon that.
Our praises are our wages; you may ride's
With one soft kiss a thousand furlongs ere
With spur we heat an acre. But to th' goal:
My last good deed was to entreat his stay;
What was my first? It has an elder sister,
Or I mistake you. O, would her name were Grace!
But once before I spoke to th' purpose – When?
Nay, let me have 't; I long.
LEONTES Why, that was when
Three crabbed months had sour'd themselves to death,
Ere I could make thee open thy white hand
And clap thyself my love; then didst thou utter
'I am yours for ever'.
HERMIONE 'Tis Grace indeed.
Why, lo you now, I have spoke to th' purpose twice:
The one for ever earn'd a royal husband;
Th' other for some while a friend.

[*Giving her hand to Polixenes.*

LEONTES [*Aside*] Too hot, too hot!
To mingle friendship far is mingling bloods.
I have tremor cordis on me; my heart dances,
But not for joy, not joy. This entertainment
May a free face put on; derive a liberty
From heartiness, from bounty, fertile bosom,
And well become the agent. 'T may, I grant;
But to be paddling palms and pinching fingers,
As now they are, and making practis'd smiles
As in a looking-glass; and then to sigh, as 'twere
The mort o' th' deer. O, that is entertainment
My bosom likes not, nor my brows! Mamillius,
Art thou my boy?
MAMILLIUS Ay, my good lord.
LEONTES I' fecks!
Why, that's my bawcock. What! hast smutch'd thy nose?
They say it is a copy out of mine. Come, Captain,
We must be neat – not neat, but cleanly, Captain.
And yet the steer, the heifer, and the calf,
Are all call'd neat. – Still virginalling
Upon his palm? – How now, you wanton calf,
Art thou my calf?
MAMILLIUS Yes, if you will, my lord.
LEONTES Thou want'st a rough pash and the shoots that I have,
To be full like me; yet they say we are
Almost as like as eggs. Women say so,
That will say any thing. But were they false
As o'er-dy'd blacks, as wind, as waters – false
As dice are to be wish'd by one that fixes
No bourn 'twixt his and mine; yet were it true
To say this boy were like me. Come, sir page,
Look on me with your welkin eye. Sweet villain!
Most dear'st! my collop! Can thy dam? – may't be?
Affection! thy intention stabs the centre.
Thou dost make possible things not so held,
Communicat'st with dreams – how can this be? –
With what's unreal thou coactive art,
And fellow'st nothing. Then 'tis very credent
Thou mayst co-join with something; and thou dost –
And that beyond commission; and I find it,
And that to the infection of my brains
And hard'ning of my brows.
POLIXENES What means Sicilia?
HERMIONE He something seems unsettled.
POLIXENES How, my lord!
What cheer? How is't with you, best brother?
HERMIONE You look
As if you held a brow of much distraction.
Are you mov'd, my lord?
LEONTES No, in good earnest.
How sometimes nature will betray its folly,
Its tenderness, and make itself a pastime
To harder bosoms! Looking on the lines
Of my boy's face, methoughts I did recoil
Twenty-three years; and saw myself unbreech'd,
In my green velvet coat; my dagger muzzl'd,
Lest it should bite its master and so prove,
As ornaments oft do, too dangerous.
How like, methought, I then was to this kernel,
This squash, this gentleman. Mine honest friend,
Will you take eggs for money?
MAMILLIUS No, my lord, I'll fight.
LEONTES You will? Why, happy man be's dole! My brother,
Are you so fond of your young prince as we
Do seem to be of ours?
POLIXENES If at home, sir,
He's all my exercise, my mirth, my matter;
Now my sworn friend, and then mine enemy;
My parasite, my soldier, statesman, all.
He makes a July's day short as December,

And with his varying childness cures in me
Thoughts that would thick my blood.
LEONTES So stands this squire
Offic'd with me. We two will walk, my lord,
And leave you to your graver steps. Hermione,
How thou lov'st us show in our brother's welcome;
Let what is dear in Sicily be cheap;
Next to thyself and my young rover, he's
Apparent to my heart.
HERMIONE If you would seek us,
We are yours i' th' garden. Shall's attend you there?
LEONTES To your own bents dispose you; you'll be found,
Be you beneath the sky. [*Aside*] I am angling now,
Though you perceive me not how I give line.
Go to, go to!
How she holds up the neb, the bill to him!
And arms her with the boldness of a wife
To her allowing husband!
[*Exeunt Polixenes, Hermione, and Attendants.*
Gone already!
Inch-thick, knee-deep, o'er head and ears a fork'd one!
Go, play, boy, play; thy mother plays, and I
Play too; but so disgrac'd a part, whose issue
Will hiss me to my grave. Contempt and clamour
Will be my knell. Go, play, boy, play. There have been,
Or I am much deceiv'd, cuckolds ere now;
And many a man there is, even at this present,
Now while I speak this, holds his wife by th' arm
That little thinks she has been sluic'd in's absence,
And his pond fish'd by his next neighbour, by
Sir Smile, his neighbour. Nay, there's comfort in't,
Whiles other men have gates and those gates open'd,
As mine, against their will. Should all despair
That have revolted wives, the tenth of mankind
Would hang themselves. Physic for't there's none;
It is a bawdy planet, that will strike
Where 'tis predominant; and 'tis pow'rful, think it,
From east, west, north, and south. Be it concluded,
No barricado for a belly. Know't,
It will let in and out the enemy
With bag and baggage. Many thousand on's
Have the disease, and feel't not. How now, boy!
MAMILLIUS I am like you, they say.
LEONTES Why, that's some comfort.
What! Camillo there?
CAMILLO Ay, my good lord.
LEONTES Go play, Mamillius; thou'rt an honest man.
[*Exit Mamillius.*
Camillo, this great sir will yet stay longer.
CAMILLO You had much ado to make his anchor hold;
When you cast out, it still came home.
LEONTES Didst note it?
CAMILLO He would not stay at your petitions; made
His business more material.
LEONTES Didst perceive it?
[*Aside*] They're here with me already; whisp'ring, rounding,
'Sicilia is a so-forth'. 'Tis far gone
When I shall gust it last. – How came't, Camillo,
That he did stay?
CAMILLO At the good Queen's entreaty.
LEONTES 'At the Queen's' be't. 'Good' should be pertinent;
But so it is, it is not. Was this taken
By any understanding pate but thine?
For thy conceit is soaking, will draw in
More than the common blocks. Not noted, is't,
But of the finer natures, by some severals
Of head-piece extraordinary? Lower messes
Perchance are to this business purblind? Say.
CAMILLO Business, my lord? I think most understand
Bohemia stays here longer.
LEONTES Ha?
CAMILLO Stays here longer.
LEONTES Ay, but why?
CAMILLO To satisfy your Highness, and the entreaties
Of our most gracious mistress.
LEONTES Satisfy
Th' entreaties of your mistress! Satisfy!
Let that suffice. I have trusted thee, Camillo,
With all the nearest things to my heart, as well
My chamber-councils, wherein, priest-like, thou
Hast cleans'd my bosom – I from thee departed
Thy penitent reform'd; but we have been
Deceiv'd in thy integrity, deceiv'd
In that which seems so.
CAMILLO Be it forbid, my lord!
LEONTES To bide upon't: thou art not honest; or,
If thou inclin'st that way, thou art a coward,
Which hoxes honesty behind, restraining
From course requir'd; or else thou must be counted
A servant grafted in my serious trust,
And therein negligent; or else a fool
That seest a game play'd home, the rich stake drawn,

And tak'st it all for jest.
CAMILLO My gracious lord,
I may be negligent, foolish, and fearful:
In every one of these no man is free
But that his negligence, his folly, fear,
Among the infinite doings of the world,
Sometime puts forth. In your affairs, my lord,
If ever I were wilful-negligent,
It was my folly; if industriously
I play'd the fool, it was my negligence,
Not weighing well the end; if ever fearful
To do a thing where I the issue doubted,
Whereof the execution did cry out
Against the non-performance, 'twas a fear
Which oft infects the wisest. These, my lord,
Are such allow'd infirmities that honesty
Is never free of. But, beseech your Grace,
Be plainer with me; let me know my trespass
By its own visage; if I then deny it,
'Tis none of mine.
LEONTES Ha' not you seen, Camillo –
But that's past doubt; you have, or your eye-glass
Is thicker than a cuckold's horn – or heard –
For to a vision so apparent rumour
Cannot be mute – or thought – for cogitation
Resides not in that man that does not think –
My wife is slippery? If thou wilt confess –
Or else be impudently negative,
To have nor eyes nor ears nor thought – then say
My wife's a hobby-horse, deserves a name
As rank as any flax-wench that puts to
Before her troth-plight. Say't and justify't.
CAMILLO I would not be a stander-by to hear
My sovereign mistress clouded so, without
My present vengeance taken. Shrew my heart!
You never spoke what did become you less
Than this; which to reiterate were sin
As deep as that, though true.
LEONTES Is whispering nothing?
Is leaning cheek to cheek? Is meeting noses?
Kissing with inside lip? Stopping the career
Of laughter with a sigh? – a note infallible
Of breaking honesty. Horsing foot on foot?
Skulking in corners? Wishing clocks more swift;
Hours, minutes; noon, midnight? And all eyes
Blind with the pin and web but theirs, theirs only,
That would unseen be wicked – is this nothing?
Why, then the world and all that's in't is nothing;
The covering sky is nothing; Bohemia nothing;
My wife is nothing; nor nothing have these nothings,
If this be nothing.
CAMILLO Good my lord, be cur'd
Of this diseas'd opinion, and betimes;
For 'tis most dangerous.
LEONTES Say it be, 'tis true.
CAMILLO No, no, my lord.
LEONTES It is; you lie, you lie.
I say thou liest, Camillo, and I hate thee;
Pronounce thee a gross lout, a mindless slave,
Or else a hovering temporizer that
Canst with thine eyes at once see good and evil,
Inclining to them both. Were my wife's liver
Infected as her life, she would not live
The running of one glass.
CAMILLO Who does infect her?
LEONTES Why, he that wears her like her medal, hanging
About his neck, Bohemia; who – if I
Had servants true about me that bare eyes
To see alike mine honour as their profits,
Their own particular thrifts, they would do that
Which should undo more doing. Ay, and thou,
His cupbearer – whom I from meaner form
Have bench'd and rear'd to worship; who mayst see,
Plainly as heaven sees earth and earth sees heaven,
How I am gall'd – mightst bespice a cup
To give mine enemy a lasting wink;
Which draught to me were cordial.
CAMILLO Sir, my lord,
I could do this; and that with no rash potion,
But with a ling'ring dram that should not work
Maliciously like poison. But I cannot
Believe this crack to be in my dread mistress,
So sovereignly being honourable.
I have lov'd thee –
LEONTES Make that thy question, and go rot!
Dost think I am so muddy, so unsettled,
To appoint myself in this vexation; sully
The purity and whiteness of my sheets –
Which to preserve is sleep, which being spotted
Is goads, thorns, nettles, tails of wasps;
Give scandal to the blood o' th' Prince, my son –
Who I do think is mine, and love as mine –
Without ripe moving to 't? Would I do this?
Could man so blench?
CAMILLO I must believe you, sir.
I do; and will fetch off Bohemia for't;
Provided that, when he's remov'd, your Highness
Will take again your queen as yours at first,
Even for your son's sake; and thereby for sealing
The injury of tongues in courts and kingdoms
Known and allied to yours.
LEONTES Thou dost advise me

Even so as I mine own course have set down.
I'll give no blemish to her honour, none.

CAMILLO My lord,
Go then; and with a countenance as clear
As friendship wears at feasts, keep with Bohemia
And with your queen. I am his cupbearer;
If from me he have wholesome beverage,
Account me not your servant.

LEONTES This is all:
Do't, and thou hast the one half of my heart;
Do't not, thou split'st thine own.

CAMILLO I'll do't, my lord.

LEONTES I will seem friendly, as thou hast advis'd me. [*Exit.*

CAMILLO O miserable lady! But, for me,
What case stand I in? I must be the poisoner
Of good Polixenes; and my ground to do't
Is the obedience to a master; one
Who, in rebellion with himself, will have
All that are his so too. To do this deed,
Promotion follows. If I could find example
Of thousands that had struck anointed kings
And flourish'd after, I'd not do't; but since
Nor brass, nor stone, nor parchment, bears not one,
Let villainy itself forswear't. I must
Forsake the court. To do't, or no, is certain
To me a break-neck. Happy star reign now!
Here comes Bohemia.

Enter POLIXENES.

POLIXENES This is strange. Methinks
My favour here begins to warp. Not speak?
Good day, Camillo.

CAMILLO Hail, most royal sir!

POLIXENES What is the news i' th' court?

CAMILLO None rare, my lord.

POLIXENES The King hath on him such a countenance
As he had lost some province, and a region
Lov'd as he loves himself; even now I met him
With customary compliment, when he,
Wafting his eyes to th' contrary and falling
A lip of much contempt, speeds from me; and
So leaves me to consider what is breeding
That changes thus his manners.

CAMILLO I dare not know, my lord.

POLIXENES How, dare not! Do not. Do you know, and dare not
Be intelligent to me? 'Tis thereabouts;
For, to yourself, what you do know, you must,
And cannot say you dare not. Good Camillo,
Your chang'd complexions are to me a mirror
Which shows me mine chang'd too; for I must be
A party in this alteration, finding
Myself thus alter'd with't.

CAMILLO There is a sickness
Which puts some of us in distemper; but
I cannot name the disease; and it is caught
Of you that yet are well.

POLIXENES How! caught of me?
Make me not sighted like the basilisk;
I have look'd on thousands who have sped the better
By my regard, but kill'd none so. Camillo –
As you are certainly a gentleman; thereto
Clerk-like experienc'd, which no less adorns
Our gentry than our parents' noble names,
In whose success we are gentle – I beseech you,
If you know aught which does behove my knowledge
Thereof to be inform'd, imprison't not
In ignorant concealment.

CAMILLO I may not answer.

POLIXENES A sickness caught of me, and yet I well?
I must be answer'd. Dost thou hear, Camillo?
I conjure thee, by all the parts of man
Which honour does acknowledge, whereof the least
Is not this suit of mine, that thou declare
What incidency thou dost guess of harm
Is creeping toward me; how far off, how near;
Which way to be prevented, if to be;
If not, how best to bear it.

CAMILLO Sir, I will tell you;
Since I am charg'd in honour, and by him
That I think honourable. Therefore mark my counsel,
Which must be ev'n as swiftly followed as
I mean to utter it, or both yourself and me
Cry lost, and so goodnight.

POLIXENES On, good Camillo.

CAMILLO I am appointed him to murder you.

POLIXENES By whom, Camillo?

CAMILLO By the King.

POLIXENES For what?

CAMILLO He thinks, nay, with all confidence he swears,
As he had seen 't or been an instrument
To vice you to't, that you have touch'd his queen
Forbiddenly.

POLIXENES O, then my best blood turn
To an infected jelly, and my name
Be yok'd with his that did betray the Best!
Turn then my freshest reputation to
A savour that may strike the dullest nostril
Where I arrive, and my approach be shunn'd,
Nay, hated too, worse than the great'st infection
That e'er was heard or read!

CAMILLO Swear his thought over
By each particular star in heaven and

By all their influences, you may as well
Forbid the sea for to obey the moon
As or by oath remove or counsel shake
The fabric of his folly, whose foundation
Is pil'd upon his faith and will continue
The standing of his body.

POLIXENES How should this grow?

CAMILLO I know not; but I am sure 'tis safer to
Avoid what's grown than question how 'tis born.
If therefore you dare trust my honesty,
That lies enclosed in this trunk which you
Shall bear along impawn'd, away to-night.
Your followers I will whisper to the business;
And will, by twos and threes, at several posterns,
Clear them o' th' city. For myself, I'll put
My fortunes to your service, which are here
By this discovery lost. Be not uncertain,
For, by the honour of my parents, I
Have utt'red truth; which if you seek to prove,
I dare not stand by; nor shall you be safer
Than one condemn'd by the King's own mouth, thereon
His execution sworn.

POLIXENES I do believe thee:
I saw his heart in's face. Give me thy hand;
Be pilot to me, and thy places shall
Still neighbour mine. My ships are ready, and
My people did expect my hence departure
Two days ago. This jealousy
Is for a precious creature; as she's rare,
Must it be great; and, as his person's mighty,
Must it be violent; and as he does conceive
He is dishonour'd by a man which ever
Profess'd to him, why, his revenges must
In that be made more bitter. Fear o'er-shades me.
Good expedition be my friend, and comfort
The gracious Queen, part of his theme, but nothing
Of his ill-ta'en suspicion! Come, Camillo;
I will respect thee as a father, if
Thou bear'st my life off hence. Let us avoid.

CAMILLO It is in mine authority to command
The keys of all the posterns. Please your Highness
To take the urgent hour. Come, sir, away.

[*Exeunt.*

ACT TWO

SCENE I. *Sicilia. The palace of Leontes.*

Enter HERMIONE, MAMILLIUS, and Ladies.

HERMIONE Take the boy to you; he so troubles me,
'Tis past enduring.

1 LADY Come, my gracious lord,
Shall I be your playfellow?

MAMILLIUS No, I'll none of you.

1 LADY Why, my sweet lord?

MAMILLIUS You'll kiss me hard, and speak to me as if
I were a baby still. I love you better.

2 LADY And why so, my lord?

MAMILLIUS Not for because
Your brows are blacker; yet black brows, they say,
Become some women best; so that there be not
Too much hair there, but in a semicircle
Or a half-moon made with a pen.

2 LADY Who taught't this?

MAMILLIUS I learn'd it out of women's faces. Pray now,
What colour are your eyebrows?

1 LADY Blue, my lord.

MAMILLIUS Nay, that's a mock. I have seen a lady's nose
That has been blue, but not her eyebrows.

1 LADY Hark ye:
The Queen your mother rounds apace. We shall
Present our services to a fine new prince
One of these days; and then you'd wanton with us,
If we would have you.

2 LADY She is spread of late
Into a goodly bulk. Good time encounter her!

HERMIONE What wisdom stirs amongst you? Come, sir, now
I am for you again. Pray you sit by us,
And tell's a tale.

MAMILLIUS Merry or sad shall't be?

HERMIONE As merry as you will.

MAMILLIUS A sad tale's best for winter. I have one
Of sprites and goblins.

HERMIONE Let's have that, good sir.
Come on, sit down; come on, and do your best
To fright me with your sprites; you're pow'rful at it.

MAMILLIUS There was a man –

HERMIONE Nay, come, sit down; then on.

MAMILLIUS Dwelt by a churchyard – I will tell it softly;
Yond crickets shall not hear it.

HERMIONE Come on then,
And give't me in mine ear.

Enter LEONTES, ANTIGONUS, Lords and Others.

LEONTES Was he met there? his train? Camillo
with him?
1 LORD Behind the tuft of pines I met them; never
Saw I men scour so on their way. I ey'd them
Even to their ships.
LEONTES How blest am I
In my just censure, in my true opinion!
Alack, for lesser knowledge! How accurs'd
In being so blest! There may be in the cup
A spider steep'd, and one may drink, depart,
And yet partake no venom, for his knowledge
Is not infected; but if one present
Th' abhorr'd ingredient to his eye, make known
How he hath drunk, he cracks his gorge, his
sides,
With violent hefts. I have drunk, and seen the
spider.
Camillo was his help in this, his pander.
There is a plot against my life, my crown;
All's true that is mistrusted. That false villain
Whom I employ'd was pre-employ'd by him;
He has discover'd my design, and I
Remain a pinch'd thing; yea, a very trick
For them to play at will. How came the posterns
So easily open?
1 LORD By his great authority;
Which often hath no less prevail'd than so
On your command.
LEONTES I know't too well.
Give me the boy. I am glad you did not nurse
him;
Though he does bear some signs of me, yet you
Have too much blood in him.
HERMIONE What is this? Sport?
LEONTES Bear the boy hence; he shall not come
about her;
Away with him; and let her sport herself
[*Mamillius is led out.*

With that she's big with – for 'tis Polixenes
Has made thee swell thus.
HERMIONE But I'd say he had not,
And I'll be sworn you would believe my saying,
Howe'er you lean to th' nayward.
LEONTES You, my lords,
Look on her, mark her well; be but about
To say 'She is a goodly lady' and
The justice of your hearts will thereto add
"Tis pity she's not honest – honourable'.
Praise her but for this her without-door form,
Which on my faith deserves high speech, and
straight
The shrug, the hum or ha, these petty brands
That calumny doth use – O, I am out! –
That mercy does, for calumny will sear
Virtue itself – these shrugs, these hum's and
ha's,
When you have said she's goodly, come
between,
Ere you can say she's honest. But be't known,
From him that has most cause to grieve it
should be,
She's an adultress.
HERMIONE Should a villain say so,
The most replenish'd villain in the world,
He were as much more villain: you, my lord,
Do but mistake.
LEONTES You have mistook, my lady,
Polixenes for Leontes. O thou thing!
Which I'll not call a creature of thy place,
Lest barbarism, making me the precedent,
Should a like language use to all degrees
And mannerly distinguishment leave out
Betwixt the prince and beggar. I have said
She's an adultress; I have said with whom.
More, she's a traitor; and Camillo is
A federary with her, and one that knows
What she should shame to know herself
But with her most vile principal – that she's
A bed-swerver, even as bad as those
That vulgars give bold'st titles; ay, and privy
To this their late escape.
HERMIONE No, by my life,
Privy to none of this. How will this grieve you,
When you shall come to clearer knowledge, that
You thus have publish'd me! Gentle my lord,
You scarce can right me throughly then to say
You did mistake.
LEONTES No; if I mistake
In those foundations which I build upon,
The centre is not big enough to bear
A school-boy's top. Away with her to prison.
He who shall speak for her is afar off guilty
But that he speaks.
HERMIONE There's some ill planet reigns.
I must be patient till the heavens look
With an aspect more favourable. Good my
lords,
I am not prone to weeping, as our sex
Commonly are – the want of which vain dew
Perchance shall dry your pities – but I have
That honourable grief lodg'd here which burns
Worse than tears drown. Beseech you all, my
lords,
With thoughts so qualified as your charities
Shall best instruct you, measure me; and so
The King's will be perform'd!
LEONTES [*To the Guard*] Shall I be heard?
HERMIONE Who is't that goes with me?
Beseech your Highness
My women may be with me, for you see
My plight requires it. Do not weep, good fools;
There is no cause; when you shall know your
mistress

Has deserv'd prison, then abound in tears
As I come out: this action I now go on
Is for my better grace. Adieu, my lord.
I never wish'd to see you sorry; now
I trust I shall. My women, come; you have leave.

LEONTES Go, do our bidding; hence!

[*Exeunt Hermione, guarded, and ladies.*

1 LORD Beseech your Highness, call the Queen again.

ANTIGONUS Be certain what you do, sir, lest your justice
Prove violence, in the which three great ones suffer,
Yourself, your queen, your son.

1 LORD For her, my lord,
I dare my life lay down – and will do't, sir,
Please you t' accept it – that the Queen is spotless
I' th' eyes of heaven and to you – I mean
In this which you accuse her.

ANTIGONUS If it prove
She's otherwise, I'll keep my stables where
I lodge my wife; I'll go in couples with her;
Than when I feel and see her no farther trust her;
For every inch of woman in the world,
Ay, every dram of woman's flesh is false,
If she be.

LEONTES Hold your peaces.

1 LORD Good my lord –

ANTIGONUS It is for you we speak, not for ourselves.
You are abus'd, and by some putter-on
That will be damn'd for't. Would I knew the villain!
I would land-damn him. Be she honour-flaw'd –
I have three daughters: the eldest is eleven;
The second and the third, nine and some five;
If this prove true, they'll pay for't. By mine honour,
I'll geld 'em all; fourteen they shall not see
To bring false generations. They are co-heirs;
And I had rather glib myself than they
Should not produce fair issue.

LEONTES Cease; no more.
You smell this business with a sense as cold
As is a dead man's nose; but I do see't and feel't
As you feel doing thus; and see withal
The instruments that feel.

ANTIGONUS If it be so,
We need no grave to bury honesty;
There's not a grain of it the face to sweeten
Of the whole dungy earth.

LEONTES What! Lack I credit?

1 LORD I had rather you did lack than I, my lord,
Upon this ground; and more it would content me
To have her honour true than your suspicion,
Be blam'd for't how you might.

LEONTES Why, what need we
Commune with you of this, but rather follow
Our forceful instigation? Our prerogative
Calls not your counsels; but our natural goodness
Imparts this; which, if you – or stupified
Or seeming so in skill – cannot or will not
Relish a truth like us, inform yourselves
We need no more of your advice. The matter,
The loss, the gain, the ord'ring on't, is all
Properly ours.

ANTIGONUS And I wish, my liege,
You had only in your silent judgment tried it,
Without more overture.

LEONTES How could that be?
Either thou art most ignorant by age,
Or thou wert born a fool. Camillo's flight,
Added to their familiarity –
Which was as gross as ever touch'd conjecture,
That lack'd sight only, nought for approbation
But only seeing, all other circumstances
Made up to th' deed – doth push on this proceeding.
Yet, for a greater confirmation –
For, in an act of this importance, 'twere
Most piteous to be wild – I have dispatch'd in post
To sacred Delphos, to Apollo's temple,
Cleomenes and Dion, whom you know
Of stuff'd sufficiency. Now, from the oracle
They will bring all, whose spiritual counsel had,
Shall stop or spur me. Have I done well?

1 LORD Well done, my lord.

LEONTES Though I am satisfied, and need no more
Than what I know, yet shall the oracle
Give rest to th' minds of others such as he
Whose ignorant credulity will not
Come up to th' truth. So have we thought it good
From our free person she should be confin'd,
Lest that the treachery of the two fled hence
Be left her to perform. Come, follow us;
We are to speak in public; for this business
Will raise us all.

ANTIGONUS [*Aside*] To laughter, as I take it,
If the good truth were known. [*Exeunt.*

SCENE II. *Sicilia. A prison.*

Enter PAULINA, a Gentleman, and Attendants.

PAULINA The keeper of the prison – call to him;

Let him have knowledge who I am.
[Exit Gentleman.
Good lady!
No court in Europe is too good for thee;
What dost thou then in prison?
Re-enter Gentleman with the Gaoler.
Now, good sir,
You know me, do you not?

GAOLER For a worthy lady,
And one who much I honour.

PAULINA Pray you, then,
Conduct me to the Queen.

GAOLER I may not, madam;
To the contrary I have express commandment.

PAULINA Here's ado, to lock up honesty and honour from
Th' access of gentle visitors! Is't lawful, pray you,
To see her women – any of them? Emilia?

GAOLER So please you, madam,
To put apart these your attendants, I
Shall bring Emilia forth.

PAULINA I pray now, call her.
Withdraw yourselves. *[Exeunt Attendants.*

GAOLER And, madam,
I must be present at your conference.

PAULINA Well, be't so, prithee. *[Exit Gaoler.*
Here's such ado to make no stain a stain
As passes colouring.
Re-enter Gaoler, with EMILIA.
Dear gentlewoman,
How fares our gracious lady?

EMILIA As well as one so great and so forlorn
May hold together. On her frights and griefs,
Which never tender lady hath borne greater,
She is, something before her time, deliver'd.

PAULINA A boy?

EMILIA A daughter, and a goodly babe,
Lusty, and like to live. The Queen receives
Much comfort in't; says 'My poor prisoner,
I am as innocent as you'.

PAULINA I dare be sworn.
These dangerous unsafe lunes i' th' King, beshrew them!
He must be told on't, and he shall. The office
Becomes a woman best; I'll take't upon me;
If I prove honey-mouth'd, let my tongue blister,
And never to my red-look'd anger be
The trumpet any more. Pray you, Emilia,
Commend my best obedience to the Queen;
If she dares trust me with her little babe,
I'll show't the King, and undertake to be
Her advocate to th' loud'st. We do not know
How he may soften at the sight o' th' child:
The silence often of pure innocence
Persuades when speaking fails.

EMILIA Most worthy madam,
Your honour and your goodness is so evident
That your free undertaking cannot miss
A thriving issue; there is no lady living
So meet for this great errand. Please your ladyship
To visit the next room, I'll presently
Acquaint the Queen of your most noble offer;
Who but to-day hammer'd of this design,
But durst not tempt a minister of honour,
Lest she should be denied.

PAULINA Tell her, Emilia,
I'll use that tongue I have; if wit flow from't
As boldness from my bosom, let't not be doubted
I shall do good.

EMILIA Now be you blest for it!
I'll to the Queen. Please you come something nearer.

GAOLER Madam, if't please the Queen to send the babe,
I know not what I shall incur to pass it,
Having no warrant.

PAULINA You need not fear it, sir.
This child was prisoner to the womb, and is
By law and process of great Nature thence
Freed and enfranchis'd – not a party to
The anger of the King, nor guilty of,
If any be, the trespass of the Queen.

GAOLER I do believe it.

PAULINA Do not you fear. Upon mine honour, I
Will stand betwixt you and danger. *[Exeunt.*

SCENE III. *Sicilia. The palace of Leontes.*

Enter LEONTES, ANTIGONUS, Lords, and Servants.

LEONTES Nor night nor day no rest! It is but weakness
To bear the matter thus – mere weakness. If
The cause were not in being – part o' th' cause,
She, th' adultress; for the harlot king
Is quite beyond mine arm, out of the blank
And level of my brain, plot-proof; but she
I can hook to me – say that she were gone,
Given to the fire, a moiety of my rest
Might come to me again. Who's there?

1 SERVANT My lord?

LEONTES How does the boy?

1 SERVANT He took good rest to-night;
'Tis hop'd his sickness is discharg'd.

LEONTES To see his nobleness!
Conceiving the dishonour of his mother,
He straight declin'd, droop'd, took it deeply,
Fasten'd and fix'd the shame on't in himself,
Threw off his spirit, his appetite, his sleep,
And downright languish'd. Leave me solely. Go,
See how he fares. *[Exit Servant]* Fie, fie! no

thought of him!'
The very thought of my revenges that way
Recoil upon me – in himself too mighty,
And in his parties, his alliance. Let him be,
Until a time may serve; for present vengeance,
Take it on her. Camillo and Polixenes
Laugh at me, make their pastime at my sorrow.
They should not laugh if I could reach them; nor
Shall she, within my pow'r.

Enter PAULINA, with a Child.

1 LORD You must not enter.
PAULINA Nay, rather, good my lords, be second to me.
Fear you his tyrannous passion more, alas,
Than the Queen's life? A gracious innocent soul,
More free than he is jealous.
ANTIGONUS That's enough.
2 SERVANT Madam, he hath not slept tonight; commanded
None should come at him.
PAULINA Not so hot, good sir;
I come to bring him sleep. 'Tis such as you,
That creep like shadows by him, and do sigh
At each his needless heavings – such as you
Nourish the cause of his awaking: I
Do come with words as medicinal as true,
Honest as either, to purge him of that humour
That presses him from sleep.
LEONTES What noise there, ho?
PAULINA No noise, my lord; but needful conference
About some gossips for your Highness.
LEONTES How!
Away with that audacious lady! Antigonus,
I charg'd thee that she should not come about me;
I knew she would.
ANTIGONUS I told her so, my lord,
On your displeasure's peril, and on mine,
She should not visit you.
LEONTES What, canst not rule her?
PAULINA From all dishonesty he can: in this,
Unless he take the course that you have done –
Commit me for committing honour – trust it,
He shall not rule me.
ANTIGONUS La you now, you hear!
When she will take the rein, I let her run;
But she'll not stumble.
PAULINA Good my liege, I come –
And I beseech you hear me, who professes
Myself your loyal servant, your physician,
Your most obedient counsellor; yet that dares
Less appear so, in comforting your evils,
Than such as most seem yours – I say I come
From your good Queen.
LEONTES Good Queen!
PAULINA Good Queen, my lord, good Queen – I say good Queen;
And would by combat make her good, so were I
A man, the worst about you.
LEONTES Force her hence.
PAULINA Let him that makes but trifles of his eyes.
First hand me. On mine own accord I'll off;
But first I'll do my errand. The good Queen,
For she is good, hath brought you forth a daughter;
Here 'tis; commends it to your blessing.
[Laying down the child.
LEONTES Out!
A mankind witch! Hence with her, out o' door!
A most intelligencing bawd!
PAULINA Not so.
I am as ignorant in that as you
In so entitling me; and no less honest
Than you are mad; which is enough, I'll warrant,
As this world goes, to pass for honest.
LEONTES Traitors!
Will you not push her out? Give her the bastard.
[*To Antigonus*] Thou dotard, thou art woman-tir'd, unroosted
By thy Dame Partlet here. Take up the bastard;
Take't up, I say; give't to thy crone.
PAULINA For ever
Unvenerable be thy hands, if thou
Tak'st up the Princess by that forced baseness
Which he has put upon't!
LEONTES He dreads his wife.
PAULINA So I would you did; then 'twere past all doubt
You'd call your children yours.
LEONTES A nest of traitors!
ANTIGONUS I am none, by this good light.
PAULINA Nor I; nor any
But one that's here; and that's himself; for he
The sacred honour of himself, his Queen's,
His hopeful son's, his babe's, betrays to slander,
Whose sting is sharper than the sword's; and will not –
For, as the case now stands, it is a curse
He cannot be compell'd to 't – once remove
The root of his opinion, which is rotten
As ever oak or stone was sound.
LEONTES A callat
Of boundless tongue, who late hath beat her husband,
And now baits me! This brat is none of mine;
It is the issue of Polixenes.
Hence with it, and together with the dam
Commit them to the fire.

PAULINA It is yours.
And, might we lay th' old proverb to your charge,
So like you 'tis the worse. Behold, my lords,
Although the print be little, the whole matter
And copy of the father – eye, nose, lip,
The trick of's frown, his forehead; nay, the valley,
The pretty dimples of his chin and cheek; his smiles;
The very mould and frame of hand, nail, finger.
And thou, good goddess Nature, which hast made it
So like to him that got it, if thou hast
The ordering of the mind too, 'mongst all colours
No yellow in't, lest she suspect, as he does,
Her children not her husband's!

LEONTES A gross hag!
And, lozel, thou art worthy to be hang'd
That wilt not stay her tongue.

ANTIGONUS Hang all the husbands
That cannot do that feat, you'll leave yourself
Hardly one subject.

LEONTES Once more, take her hence.

PAULINA A most unworthy and unnatural lord
Can do no more.

LEONTES I'll ha' thee burnt.

PAULINA I care not.
It is an heretic that makes the fire,
Not she which burns in't. I'll not call you tyrant;
But this most cruel usage of your Queen –
Not able to produce more accusation
Than your own weak-hing'd fancy – something savours
Of tyranny, and will ignoble make you,
Yea, scandalous to the world.

LEONTES On your allegiance,
Out of the chamber with her! Were I a tyrant,
Where were her life? She durst not call me so,
If she did know me one. Away with her!

PAULINA I pray you, do not push me; I'll be gone.
Look to your babe, my lord; 'tis yours. Jove send her
A better guiding spirit! What needs these hands?
You that are thus so tender o'er his follies
Will never do him good, not one of you.
So, so. Farewell; we are gone. [*Exit.*

LEONTES Thou, traitor, hast set on thy wife to this.
My child! Away with't. Even thou, that hast
A heart so tender o'er it, take it hence,
And see it instantly consum'd with fire;
Even thou, and none but thou. Take it up straight.
Within this hour bring me word 'tis done,
And by good testimony, or I'll seize thy life,
With what thou else call'st thine. If thou refuse,
And wilt encounter with my wrath, say so;
The bastard brains with these my proper hands
Shall I dash out. Go, take it to the fire;
For thou set'st on thy wife.

ANTIGONUS I did not, sir.
These lords, my noble fellows, if they please,
Can clear me in't.

LORDS We can. My royal liege,
He is not guilty of her coming hither.

LEONTES You're liars all.

1 LORD Beseech your Highness, give us better credit.
We have always truly serv'd you; and beseech
So to esteem of us; and on our knees we beg,
As recompense of our dear services
Past and to come, that you do change this purpose,
Which being so horrible, so bloody, must
Lead on to some foul issue. We all kneel.

LEONTES I am a feather for each wind that blows.
Shall I live on to see this bastard kneel
And call me father? Better burn it now
Than curse it then. But be it; let it live.
It shall not neither. [*To Antigonus*] You, sir, come you hither.
You that have been so tenderly officious
With Lady Margery, your midwife there,
To save this bastard's life – for 'tis a bastard,
So sure as this beard's grey – what will you adventure
To save this brat's life?

ANTIGONUS Anything, my lord,
That my ability may undergo,
And nobleness impose. At least, thus much:
I'll pawn the little blood which I have left
To save the innocent – anything possible.

LEONTES It shall be possible. Swear by this sword
Thou wilt perform my bidding.

ANTIGONUS I will, my lord.

LEONTES Mark, and perform it – seest thou? For the fail
Of any point in't shall not only be
Death to thyself, but to thy lewd-tongu'd wife,
Whom for this time we pardon. We enjoin thee,
As thou art liegeman to us, that thou carry
This female bastard hence; and that thou bear it
To some remote and desert place, quite out
Of our dominions; and that there thou leave it,
Without more mercy, to it own protection
And favour of the climate. As by strange fortune
It came to us, I do in justice charge thee,
On thy soul's peril and thy body's torture,
That thou commend it strangely to some place
Where chance may nurse or end it. Take it up.

ANTIGONUS I swear to do this, though a present death
Had been more merciful. Come on, poor babe.
Some powerful spirit instruct the kites and ravens
To be thy nurses! Wolves and bears, they say,
Casting their savageness aside, have done
Like offices of pity. Sir, be prosperous
In more than this deed does require! And blessing
Against this cruelty fight on thy side,
Poor thing, condemn'd to loss!
[*Exit with the child.*

LEONTES No, I'll not rear
Another's issue.

Enter a Servant.

SERVANT Please your Highness, posts
From those you sent to th' oracle are come
An hour since. Cleomenes and Dion,
Being well arriv'd from Delphos, are both landed,
Hasting to th' court.

1 LORD So please you, sir, their speed
Hath been beyond account.

LEONTES Twenty-three days
They have been absent; 'tis good speed; foretells
The great Apollo suddenly will have
The truth of this appear. Prepare you, lords;
Summon a session, that we may arraign
Our most disloyal lady; for, as she hath
Been publicly accus'd, so shall she have
A just and open trial. While she lives,
My heart will be a burden to me. Leave me;
And think upon my bidding. [*Exeunt.*

ACT THREE

SCENE I. *Sicilia. On the road to the Capital.*

Enter CLEOMENES and DION.

CLEOMENES The climate's delicate, the air most sweet,
Fertile the isle, the temple much surpassing
The common praise it bears.

DION I shall report,
For most it caught me, the celestial habits –
Methinks I so should term them – and the reverence
Of the grave wearers. O, the sacrifice!
How ceremonious, solemn, and unearthly,
It was i' th' off'ring!

CLEOMENES But of all, the burst
And the ear-deaf'ning voice o' th' oracle,
Kin to Jove's thunder, so surpris'd my sense
That I was nothing.

DION If th' event o' th' journey
Prove as successful to the Queen – O, be't so! –
As it hath been to us rare, pleasant, speedy,
The time is worth the use on't.

CLEOMENES Great Apollo
Turn all to th' best! These proclamations,
So forcing faults upon Hermione,
I little like.

DION The violent carriage of it
Will clear or end the business. When the oracle –
Thus by Apollo's great divine seal'd up –
Shall the contents discover, something rare
Even then will rush to knowledge. Go; fresh horses.
And gracious be the issue! [*Exeunt.*

SCENE II. *Sicilia. A court of justice.*

Enter LEONTES, Lords, and Officers.

LEONTES This sessions, to our great grief we pronounce,
Even pushes 'gainst our heart – the party tried,
The daughter of a king, our wife, and one
Of us too much belov'd. Let us be clear'd
Of being tyrannous, since we so openly
Proceed in justice, which shall have due course,
Even to the guilt or the purgation.
Produce the prisoner.

OFFICER It is his Highness' pleasure that the Queen
Appear in person here in court.

Enter HERMIONE, as to her trial, PAULINA, and Ladies.

Silence!

LEONTES Read the indictment.

OFFICER [*Reads*] 'Hermione, Queen to the worthy Leontes, King of Sicilia, thou art here accused and arraigned of high treason, in committing adultery with Polixenes, King of Bohemia; and conspiring with Camillo to take away the life of our sovereign lord the King, thy royal husband: the pretence whereof being by circumstances partly laid open, thou, Hermione, contrary to the faith and allegiance of a true subject, didst counsel and aid them, for their better safety, to fly away by night.'

HERMIONE Since what I am to say must be but that
Which contradicts my accusation, and
The testimony on my part no other

But what comes from myself, it shall scarce boot me
To say 'Not guilty'. Mine integrity
Being counted falsehood shall, as I express it,
Be so receiv'd. But thus – if pow'rs divine
Behold our human actions, as they do,
I doubt not then but innocence shall make
False accusation blush, and tyranny
Tremble at patience. You, my lord, best know –
Who least will seem to do so – my past life
Hath been as continent, as chaste, as true,
As I am now unhappy; which is more
Than history can pattern, though devis'd
And play'd to take spectators; for behold me –
A fellow of the royal bed, which owe
A moiety of the throne, a great king's daughter,
The mother to a hopeful prince – here standing
To prate and talk for life and honour fore
Who please to come and hear. For life, I prize it
As I weigh grief, which I would spare; for honour,
'Tis a derivative from me to mine,
And only that I stand for. I appeal
To your own conscience, sir, before Polixenes
Came to your court, how I was in your grace,
How merited to be so; since he came,
With what encounter so uncurrent I
Have strain'd t' appear thus; if one jot beyond
The bound of honour, or in act or will
That way inclining, hard'ned be the hearts
Of all that hear me, and my near'st of kin
Cry fie upon my grave!

LEONTES I ne'er heard yet
That any of these bolder vices wanted
Less impudence to gainsay what they did
Than to perform it first.

HERMIONE That's true enough;
Though 'tis a saying, sir, not due to me.

LEONTES You will not own it.

HERMIONE More than mistress of
Which comes to me in name of fault, I must not
At all acknowledge. For Polixenes,
With whom I am accus'd, I do confess
I lov'd him as in honour he requir'd;
With such a kind of love as might become
A lady like me; with a love even such,
So and no other, as yourself commanded;
Which not to have done, I think had been in me
Both disobedience and ingratitude
To you and toward your friend; whose love had spoke,
Even since it could speak, from an infant, freely,
That it was yours. Now for conspiracy:
I know not how it tastes, though it be dish'd
For me to try how; all I know of it
Is that Camillo was an honest man;
And why he left your court, the gods themselves,
Wotting no more than I, are ignorant.

LEONTES You knew of his departure, as you know
What you have underta'en to do in's absence.

HERMIONE Sir,
You speak a language that I understand not.
My life stands in the level of your dreams,
Which I'll lay down.

LEONTES Your actions are my dreams.
You had a bastard by Polixenes,
And I but dream'd it. As you were past all shame –
Those of your fact are so – so past all truth;
Which to deny concerns more than avails; for as
Thy brat hath been cast out, like to itself,
No father owning it – which is indeed
More criminal in thee than it – so thou
Shalt feel our justice; in whose easiest passage
Look for no less than death.

HERMIONE Sir, spare your threats.
The bug which you would fright me with I seek.
To me can life be no commodity.
The crown and comfort of my life, your favour,
I do give lost, for I do feel it gone,
But know not how it went; my second joy
And first fruits of my body, from his presence
I am barr'd, like one infectious; my third comfort,
Starr'd most unluckily, is from my breast –
The innocent milk in it most innocent mouth –
Hal'd out to murder; myself on every post
Proclaim'd a strumpet; with immodest hatred
The child-bed privilege denied, which 'longs
To women of all fashion; lastly, hurried
Here to this place, i' th' open air, before
I have got strength of limit. Now, my liege,
Tell me what blessings I have here alive
That I should fear to die. Therefore proceed.
But yet hear this – mistake me not: no life,
I prize it not a straw, but for mine honour
Which I would free – if I shall be condemn'd
Upon surmises, all proofs sleeping else
But what your jealousies awake, I tell you
'Tis rigour, and not law. Your honours all,
I do refer me to the oracle:
Apollo be my judge!

LORD This your request
Is altogether just. Therefore, bring forth,
And in Apollo's name, his oracle.

[*Exeunt certain Officers.*

HERMIONE The Emperor of Russia was my father;
O that he were alive, and here beholding
His daughter's trial! that he did but see
The flatness of my misery; yet with eyes
Of pity, not revenge!

Re-enter Officers, with CLEOMENES and DION.

OFFICER You here shall swear upon this sword of justice
That you, Cleomenes and Dion, have
Been both at Delphos, and from thence have brought
This seal'd-up oracle, by the hand deliver'd
Of great Apollo's priest; and that since then
You have not dar'd to break the holy seal
Nor read the secrets in't.

CLEOMENES, DION All this we swear.

LEONTES Break up the seals and read.

OFFICER [*Reads*] 'Hermione is chaste; Polixenes blameless; Camillo a true subject; Leontes a jealous tyrant; his innocent babe truly begotten; and the King shall live without an heir, if that which is lost be not found.'

LORDS Now blessed be the great Apollo!

HERMIONE Praised!

LEONTES Hast thou read truth?

OFFICER Ay, my lord; even so
As it is here set down.

LEONTES There is no truth at all i' th' oracle.
The sessions shall proceed. This is mere falsehood.

Enter a Servant.

SERVANT My lord the King, the King!

LEONTES What is the business?

SERVANT O sir, I shall be hated to report it:
The Prince your son, with mere conceit and fear
Of the Queen's speed, is gone.

LEONTES How! Gone?

SERVANT Is dead.

LEONTES Apollo's angry; and the heavens themselves
Do strike at my injustice [*Hermione swoons.*
How now, there!

PAULINA This news is mortal to the Queen. Look down
And see what death is doing.

LEONTES Take her hence.
Her heart is but o'ercharg'd; she will recover.
I have too much believ'd mine own suspicion.
Beseech you tenderly apply to her
Some remedies for life.

[*Exeunt Paulina and Ladies with Hermione.*

Apollo, pardon
My great profaneness 'gainst thine oracle.
I'll reconcile me to Polixenes,
New woo my queen, recall the good Camillo –
Whom I proclaim a man of truth, of mercy.
For, being transported by my jealousies
To bloody thoughts and to revenge, I chose
Camillo for the minister to poison
My friend Polixenes; which had been done
But that the good mind of Camillo tardied
My swift command, though I with death and with
Reward did threaten and encourage him,
Not doing it and being done. He, most humane
And fill'd with honour, to my kingly guest
Unclasp'd my practice, quit his fortunes here,
Which you knew great, and to the certain hazard
Of all incertainties himself commended,
No richer than his honour. How he glisters
Thorough my rust! And how his piety
Does my deeds make the blacker!

Re-enter PAULINA.

PAULINA Woe the while!
O, cut my lace, lest my heart, cracking it,
Break too!

1 LORD What fit is this, good lady?

PAULINA What studied torments, tyrant, hast for me?
What wheels, racks, fires? what flaying, boiling
In leads or oils? What old or newer torture
Must I receive, whose every word deserves
To taste of thy most worst? Thy tyranny
Together working with thy jealousies,
Fancies too weak for boys, too green and idle
For girls of nine – O, think what they have done,
And then run mad indeed, stark mad; for all
Thy by-gone fooleries were but spices of it.
That thou betray'dst Polixenes, 'twas nothing;
That did but show thee, of a fool, inconstant,
And damnable ingrateful. Nor was't much
Thou wouldst have poison'd good Camillo's honour,
To have him kill a king – poor trespasses,
More monstrous standing by; whereof I reckon
The casting forth to crows thy baby daughter
To be or none or little, though a devil
Would have shed water out of fire ere done't;
Nor is't directly laid to thee, the death
Of the young Prince, whose honourable thoughts –
Thoughts high for one so tender – cleft the heart
That could conceive a gross and foolish sire
Blemish'd his gracious dam. This is not, no,
Laid to thy answer; but the last – O lords,
When I have said, cry 'Woe!' – the Queen, the Queen,
The sweet'st, dear'st creature's dead; and vengeance for't
Not dropp'd down yet.

LORD The higher pow'rs forbid!

PAULINA I say she's dead; I'll swear't. If word nor oath
Prevail not, go and see. If you can bring

Tincture or lustre in her lip, her eye,
Heat outwardly or breath within, I'll serve you
As I would do the gods. But, O thou tyrant!
Do not repent these things, for they are heavier
Than all thy woes can stir; therefore betake thee
To nothing but despair. A thousand knees
Ten thousand years together, naked, fasting,
Upon a barren mountain, and still winter
In storm perpetual, could not move the gods
To look that way thou wert.

LEONTES Go on, go on.
Thou canst not speak too much; I have deserv'd
All tongues to talk their bitt'rest.

1 LORD Say no more;
Howe'er the business goes, you have made fault
I' th' boldness of your speech.

PAULINA I am sorry for't.
All faults I make, when I shall come to know
them,
I do repent. Alas, I have show'd too much
The rashness of a woman! He is touch'd
To th' noble heart. What's gone and what's past
help
Should be past grief. Do not receive affliction
At my petition; I beseech you, rather
Let me be punish'd that have minded you
Of what you should forget. Now, good my liege,
Sir, royal sir, forgive a foolish woman.
The love I bore your queen – lo, fool again!
I'll speak of her no more, nor of your children;
I'll not remember you of my own lord,
Who is lost too. Take your patience to you,
And I'll say nothing.

LEONTES Thou didst speak but well
When most the truth; which I receive much
better
Than to be pitied of thee. Prithee, bring me
To the dead bodies of my queen and son.
One grave shall be for both. Upon them shall
The causes of their death appear, unto
Our shame perpetual. Once a day I'll visit
The chapel where they lie; and tears shed there
Shall be my recreation. So long as nature
Will bear up with this exercise, so long
I daily vow to use it. Come, and lead me
To these sorrows. [*Exeunt.*

SCENE III. *Bohemia. The sea-coast.*

Enter ANTIGONUS with the Child, and a Mariner.

ANTIGONUS Thou art perfect then our ship hath
touch'd upon
The deserts of Bohemia?

MARINER Ay, my lord, and fear
We have landed in ill time; the skies look grimly
And threaten present blusters. In my
conscience,
The heavens with that we have in hand are
angry
And frown upon 's.

ANTIGONUS Their sacred wills be done! Go, get
aboard;
Look to thy bark. I'll not be long before
I call upon thee.

MARINER Make your best haste; and go not
Too far i' th' land; 'tis like to be loud weather;
Besides, this place is famous for the creatures
Of prey that keep upon't.

ANTIGONUS Go thou away;
I'll follow instantly.

MARINER I am glad at heart
To be so rid o' th' business. [*Exit.*

ANTIGONUS Come, poor babe.
I have heard, but not believ'd, the spirits o' th'
dead
May walk again. If such thing be, thy mother
Appear'd to me last night; for ne'er was dream
So like a waking. To me comes a creature,
Sometimes her head on one side some another –
I never saw a vessel of like sorrow,
So fill'd and so becoming; in pure white robes,
Like very sanctity, she did approach
My cabin where I lay; thrice bow'd before me;
And, gasping to begin some speech, her eyes
Became two spouts; the fury spent, anon
Did this break from her: 'Good Antigonus,
Since fate, against thy better disposition,
Hath made thy person for the thrower-out
Of my poor babe, according to thine oath,
Places remote enough are in Bohemia,
There weep, and leave it crying; and, for the
babe
Is counted lost for ever, Perdita
I prithee call't. For this ungentle business,
Put on thee by my lord, thou ne'er shalt see
Thy wife Paulina more'. And so, with shrieks,
She melted into air. Affrighted much,
I did in time collect myself, and thought
This was so and no slumber. Dreams are toys;
Yet, for this once, yea, superstitiously,
I will be squar'd by this. I do believe
Hermione hath suffer'd death, and that
Apollo would, this being indeed the issue
Of King Polixenes, it should here be laid,
Either for life or death, upon the earth
Of its right father. Blossom, speed thee well!
[*Laying down the child.*
There lie, and there thy character; there these
[*Laying down a bundle.*
Which may, if fortune please, both breed thee,
pretty,
And still rest thine. The storm begins. Poor
wretch,

That for thy mother's fault art thus expos'd
To loss and what may follow! Weep I cannot,
But my heart bleeds; and most accurs'd am I
To be by oath enjoin'd to this. Farewell!
The day frowns more and more. Thou'rt like to have
A lullaby too rough; I never saw
The heavens so dim by day. [*Noise of hunt within*] A savage clamour!
Well may I get aboard! This is the chase;
I am gone for ever. [*Exit, pursued by a bear.*

Enter an old Shepherd.

SHEPHERD I would there were no age between ten and three and twenty, or that youth would sleep out the rest; for there is nothing in the between but getting wenches with child, wronging the ancientry, stealing, fighting – [*Horns*] Hark you now! Would any but these boil'd brains of nineteen and two and twenty hunt this weather? They have scar'd away two of my best sheep, which I fear the wolf will sooner find than the master. If any where I have them, 'tis by the sea-side, browsing of ivy. Good luck, an't be thy will! What have we here? [*Taking up the child*] Mercy on's, a barne! A very pretty barne. A boy or a child, I wonder? A pretty one; a very pretty one – sure, some scape. Though I am not bookish, yet I can read waiting-gentle-woman in the scape. This has been some stair-work, some trunk-work, some behind-door-work; they were warmer that got this than the poor thing is here. I'll take it up for pity; yet I'll tarry till my son come; he halloo'd but even now. Whoa-ho-hoa!

Enter Clown.

CLOWN Hilloa, loa!

SHEPHERD What, art so near? If thou'lt see a thing to talk on when thou art dead and rotten, come hither. What ail'st thou, man?

CLOWN I have seen two such sights, by sea and by land! But I am not to say it is a sea, for it is now the sky; betwixt the firmament and it you cannot thrust a bodkin's point.

SHEPHERD Why, boy, how is it?

CLOWN I would you did but see how it chafes, how it rages, how it takes up the shore! But that's not to the point. O, the most piteous cry of the poor souls! Sometimes to see 'em, and not to see 'em; now the ship boring the moon with her mainmast, and anon swallowed with yeast and froth, as you'd thrust a cork into a hogs-head. And then for the land service – to see how the bear tore out his shoulder-bone; how he cried to me for help, and said his name was Antigonus, a nobleman! But to make an end of the ship – to see how the sea flap-dragon'd it; but first, how the poor souls roared, and the sea mock'd them; and how the poor gentleman roared, and the bear mock'd him, both roaring louder than the sea or weather.

SHEPHERD Name of mercy, when was this, boy?

CLOWN Now, now; I have not wink'd since I saw these sights; the men are not yet cold under water, nor the bear half din'd on the gentleman; he's at it now.

SHEPHERD Would I had been by to have help'd the old man!

CLOWN I would you had been by the ship-side, to have help'd her; there your charity would have lack'd footing.

SHEPHERD Heavy matters, heavy matters! But look thee here, boy. Now bless thyself; thou met'st with things dying, I with things new-born. Here's a sight for thee; look thee, a bearing-cloth for a squire's child! Look thee here; take up, take up, boy; open't. So, let's see – it was told me I should be rich by the fairies. This is some changeling. Open't. What's within, boy?

CLOWN You're a made old man; if the sins of your youth are forgiven you, you're well to live. Gold! all gold!

SHEPHERD This is fairy gold, boy, and 'twill prove so. Up with't, keep it close. Home, home, the next way! We are lucky, boy; and to be so still requires nothing but secrecy. Let my sheep go. Come, good boy, the next way home.

CLOWN Go you the next way with your findings. I'll go see if the bear be gone from the gentleman, and how much he hath eaten. They are never curst but when they are hungry. If there be any of him left, I'll bury it.

SHEPHERD That's a good deed. If thou mayest discern by that which is left of him what he is, fetch me to th' sight of him.

CLOWN Marry, will I; and you shall help to put him i' th' ground.

SHEPHERD 'Tis a lucky day, boy; and we'll do good deeds on't. [*Exeunt.*

ACT FOUR

SCENE I. *Enter TIME, the Chorus.*

TIME I, that please some, try all, both joy and terror
Of good and bad, that makes and unfolds error,
Now take upon me, in the name of Time,
To use my wings. Impute it not a crime
To me or my swift passage that I slide
O'er sixteen years, and leave the growth untried
Of that wide gap, since it is in my pow'r
To o'erthrow law, and in one self-born hour
To plant and o'erwhelm custom. Let me pass
The same I am, ere ancient'st order was
Or what is now receiv'd. I witness to
The times that brought them in; so shall I do
To th' freshest things now reigning, and make stale
The glistering of this present, as my tale
Now seems to it. Your patience this allowing,
I turn my glass, and give my scene such growing
As you had slept between. Leontes leaving –
Th' effects of his fond jealousies so grieving
That he shuts up himself – imagine me,
Gentle spectators, that I now may be
In fair Bohemia; and remember well
I mention'd a son o' th' King's, which Florizel
I now name to you; and with speed so pace
To speak of Perdita, now grown in grace
Equal with wond'ring. What of her ensues
I list not prophesy; but let Time's news
Be known when 'tis brought forth. A shepherd's daughter,
And what to her adheres, which follows after,
Is th' argument of Time. Of this allow,
If ever you have spent time worse ere now;
If never, yet that Time himself doth say
He wishes earnestly you never may. [*Exit.*

SCENE II. *Bohemia. The palace of Polixenes.*

Enter POLIXENES and CAMILLO.

POLIXENES I pray thee, good Camillo, be no more importunate: 'tis a sickness denying thee anything; a death to grant this.

CAMILLO It is fifteen years since I saw my country; though I have for the most part been aired abroad, I desire to lay my bones there. Besides, the penitent King, my master, hath sent for me; to whose feeling sorrows I might be some allay, or I o'erween to think so, which is another spur to my departure.

POLIXENES As thou lov'st me, Camillo, wipe not out the rest of thy services by leaving me now. The need I have of thee thine own goodness hath made. Better not to have had thee than thus to want thee; thou, having made me businesses which none without thee can sufficiently manage, must either stay to execute them thyself, or take away with thee the very services thou hast done; which if I have not enough considered – as too much I cannot – to be more thankful to thee shall be my study; and my profit therein the heaping friendships. Of that fatal country Sicilia, prithee, speak no more; whose very naming punishes me with the remembrance of that penitent, as thou call'st him, and reconciled king, my brother; whose loss of his most precious queen and children are even now to be afresh lamented. Say to me, when saw'st thou the Prince Florizel, my son? Kings are no less unhappy, their issue not being gracious, than they are in losing them when they have approved their virtues.

CAMILLO Sir, it is three days since I saw the Prince. What his happier affairs may be are to me unknown; but I have missingly noted he is of late much retired from court, and is less frequent to his princely exercises than formerly he hath appeared.

POLIXENES I have considered so much, Camillo, and with some care, so far that I have eyes under my service which look upon his removedness; from whom I have this intelligence, that he is seldom from the house of a most homely shepherd – a man, they say, that from very nothing, and beyond the imagination of his neighbours, is grown into an unspeakable estate.

CAMILLO I have heard, sir, of such a man, who hath a daughter of most rare note. The report of her is extended more than can be thought to begin from such a cottage.

POLIXENES That's likewise part of my intelligence; but, I fear, the angle that plucks our son thither. Thou shalt accompany us to the place; where we will, not appearing what we are, have some question with the shepherd; from whose simplicity I think it not uneasy to get the cause of my son's resort thither. Prithee be my present partner in this business, and lay aside the thoughts of Sicilia.

CAMILLO I willingly obey your command.

POLIXENES My best Camillo! We must disguise ourselves. [*Exeunt.*

SCENE III. *Bohemia. A road near the shepherd's cottage.*

Enter AUTOLYCUS, singing.

When daffodils begin to peer,
  With heigh! the doxy over the dale,
Why, then comes in the sweet o' the year,
  For the red blood reigns in the winter's pale.
The white sheet bleaching on the hedge,
  With heigh! the sweet birds, O, how they sing!
Doth set my pugging tooth on edge,
  For a quart of ale is a dish for a king.

The lark, that tirra-lirra chants,
  With heigh! with heigh! the thrush and the jay,
Are summer songs for me and my aunts,
  While we lie tumbling in the hay.

I have serv'd Prince Florizel, and in my time wore three-pile; but now I am out of service.

But shall I go mourn for that, my dear?
  The pale moon shines by night;
And when I wander here and there,
  I then do most go right.
If tinkers may have leave to live,
  And bear the sow-skin budget,
Then my account I well may give
  And in the stocks avouch it.

My traffic is sheets; when the kite builds, look to lesser linen. My father nam'd me Autolycus; who, being, as I am, litter'd under Mercury, was likewise a snapper-up of unconsidered trifles. With die and drab I purchas'd this caparison; and my revenue is the silly-cheat. Gallows and knock are too powerful on the highway; beating and hanging are terrors to me; for the life to come, I sleep out the thought of it. A prize! a prize!

Enter Clown.

CLOWN Let me see: every 'leven wether tods; every tod yields pound and odd shilling; fifteen hundred shorn, what comes the wool to?

AUTOLYCUS [*Aside*] If the springe hold, the cock's mine.

CLOWN I cannot do 't without counters. Let me see: what am I to buy for our sheep-shearing feast? Three pound of sugar, five pound of currants, rice – what will this sister of mine do with rice? But my father hath made her mistress of the feast, and she lays it on. She hath made me four and twenty nosegays for the shearers – three-man song-men all, and very good ones; but they are most of them means and bases; but one Puritan amongst them, and he sings psalms to hornpipes. I must have saffron to colour the warden pies; mace; dates – none, that's out of my note; nutmegs, seven; a race or two of ginger, but that I may beg; four pound of prunes, and as many of raisins o' th' sun.

AUTOLYCUS [*Grovelling on the ground*] O that ever I was born!

CLOWN I' th' name of me!

AUTOLYCUS O, help me, help me! Pluck but off these rags; and then, death, death!

CLOWN Alack, poor soul! thou hast need of more rags to lay on thee, rather than have these off.

AUTOLYCUS O sir, the loathsomeness of them offend me more than the stripes I have received, which are mighty ones and millions.

CLOWN Alas, poor man! a million of beating may come to a great matter.

AUTOLYCUS I am robb'd, sir, and beaten; my money and apparel ta'en from me, and these detestable things put upon me.

CLOWN What, by a horseman or a footman?

AUTOLYCUS A footman, sweet sir, a footman.

CLOWN Indeed, he should be a footman, by the garments he has left with thee; if this be a horseman's coat, it hath seen very hot service. Lend me thy hand, I'll help thee. Come, lend me thy hand. [*Helping him up.*

AUTOLYCUS O, good sir, tenderly, O!

CLOWN Alas, poor soul!

AUTOLYCUS O, good sir, softly, good sir; I fear, sir, my shoulder blade is out.

CLOWN How now! Canst stand?

AUTOLYCUS Softly, dear sir [*Picks his pocket*]; good sir, softly. You ha' done me a charitable office.

CLOWN Dost lack any money? I have a little money for thee.

AUTOLYCUS No, good sweet sir; no, I beseech you, sir. I have a kinsman not past three quarters of a mile hence, unto whom I was going; I shall there have money or anything I want. Offer me no money, I pray you; that kills my heart.

CLOWN What manner of fellow was he that robb'd you?

AUTOLYCUS A fellow, sir, that I have known to go about with troll-my-dames; I knew him once a servant of the Prince. I cannot tell, good sir, for which of his virtues it was, but he was certainly whipt out of the court.

CLOWN His vices, you would say; there's no virtue whipt out of the court. They cherish it to make it stay there; and yet it will no more but abide.

AUTOLYCUS Vices, I would say, sir. I know this man well; he hath been since an ape-bearer; then a process-server, a bailiff; then he compass'd a motion of the Prodigal Son, and married a tinker's wife within a mile where my land and living lies; and, having flown over many knavish professions, he settled only in rogue. Some call him Autolycus.

CLOWN Out upon him! prig, for my life, prig! He haunts wakes, fairs, and bear-baitings.

AUTOLYCUS Very true, sir; he, sir, he; that's the rogue that put me into this apparel.

CLOWN Not a more cowardly rogue in all Bohemia; if you had but look'd big and spit at him, he'd have run.

AUTOLYCUS I must confess to you, sir, I am no fighter; I am false of heart that way; and that he knew, I warrant him.

CLOWN How do you now?

AUTOLYCUS Sweet sir, much better than I was; I can stand and walk. I will even take my leave of you and pace softly towards my kinsman's.

CLOWN Shall I bring thee on the way?

AUTOLYCUS No, good-fac'd sir; no, sweet sir.

CLOWN Then fare thee well. I must go buy spices for our sheep-shearing.

AUTOLYCUS Prosper you, sweet sir! [*Exit Clown.* Your purse is not hot enough to purchase your spice. I'll be with you at your sheep-shearing too. If I make not this cheat bring out another, and the shearers prove sheep, let me be unroll'd, and my name put in the book of virtue! [*Sings.*

Jog on, jog on, the footpath way,
And merrily hent the stile-a;
A merry heart goes all the day,
Your sad tires in a mile-a. [*Exit.*

SCENE IV. *Bohemia. The shepherd's cottage.*

Enter FLORIZEL and PERDITA.

FLORIZEL These your unusual weeds to each part of you
Do give a life – no shepherdess, but Flora
Peering in April's front. This your sheep-shearing
Is as a meeting of the petty gods,
And you the Queen on't.

PERDITA Sir, my gracious lord,
To chide at your extremes it not becomes me –
O, pardon that I name them! Your high self,
The gracious mark o' th' land, you have obscur'd
With a swain's wearing; and me, poor lowly maid,
Most goddess-like prank'd up. But that our feasts
In every mess have folly, and the feeders
Digest it with a custom, I should blush
To see you so attir'd; swoon, I think,
To show myself a glass.

FLORIZEL I bless the time
When my good falcon made her flight across
Thy father's ground.

PERDITA Now Jove afford you cause!
To me the difference forges dread; your greatness
Hath not been us'd to fear. Even now I tremble
To think your father, by some accident,
Should pass this way, as you did. O, the Fates!
How would he look to see his work, so noble,
Vilely bound up? What would he say? Or how
Should I, in these my borrowed flaunts, behold
The sternness of his presence?

FLORIZEL Apprehend
Nothing but jollity. The gods themselves,
Humbling their deities to love, have taken
The shapes of beasts upon them: Jupiter
Became a bull and bellow'd; the green Neptune
A ram and bleated; and the fire-rob'd god,
Golden Apollo, a poor humble swain,
As I seem now. Their transformations
Were never for a piece of beauty rarer,
Nor in a way so chaste, since my desires
Run not before mine honour, nor my lusts
Burn hotter than my faith.

PERDITA O, but, sir,
Your resolution cannot hold when 'tis
Oppos'd, as it must be, by th' pow'r of the King.
One of these two must be necessities,
Which then will speak, that you must change this purpose,
Or I my life.

FLORIZEL Thou dearest Perdita,
With these forc'd thoughts, I prithee, darken not
The mirth o' th' feast. Or I'll be thine, my fair,
Or not my father's; for I cannot be
Mine own, nor anything to any, if
I be not thine. To this I am most constant,
Though destiny say no. Be merry, gentle;
Strangle such thoughts as these with any thing
That you behold the while. Your guests are coming.
Lift up your countenance, as it were the day
Of celebration of that nuptial which
We two have sworn shall come.

PERDITA O Lady Fortune,
Stand you auspicious!

FLORIZEL See, your guests approach.
Address yourself to entertain them sprightly,
And let's be red with mirth.

Enter Shepherd, with POLIXENES and CAMILLO, disguised; Clown, MOPSA, DORCAS, with Others.

SHEPHERD Fie, daughter! When my old wife liv'd, upon
This day she was both pantler, butler, cook;
Both dame and servant; welcom'd all; serv'd all;
Would sing her song and dance her turn; now here

At upper end o' th' table, now i' th' middle;
On his shoulder, and his; her face o' fire
With labour, and the thing she took to quench it
She would to each one sip. You are retired,
As if you were a feasted one, and not
The hostess of the meeting. Pray you bid
These unknown friends to's welcome, for it is
A way to make us better friends, more known.
Come, quench your blushes, and present yourself
That which you are, Mistress o' th' Feast. Come on,
And bid us welcome to your sheep-shearing,
As your good flock shall prosper.

PERDITA [*To Polixenes*] Sir, welcome.
It is my father's will I should take on me
The hostess-ship o' th' day. [*To Camillo*] You're welcome, sir.
Give me those flow'rs there, Dorcas. Reverend sirs,
For you there's rosemary and rue; these keep
Seeming and savour all the winter long.
Grace and remembrance be to you both!
And welcome to our shearing.

POLIXENES Shepherdess –
A fair one are you – well you fit our ages
With flow'rs of winter.

PERDITA Sir, the year growing ancient,
Not yet on summer's death nor on the birth
Of trembling winter, the fairest flow'rs o' th' season
Are our carnations and streak'd gillyvors,
Which some call nature's bastards. Of that kind
Our rustic garden's barren; and I care not
To get slips of them.

POLIXENES Wherefore, gentle maiden,
Do you neglect them?

PERDITA For I have heard it said
There is an art which in their piedness shares
With great creating nature.

POLIXENES Say there be;
Yet nature is made better by no mean
But nature makes that mean; so over that art,
Which you say adds to nature, is an art
That nature makes. You see, sweet maid, we marry
A gentler scion to the wildest stock,
And make conceive a bark of baser kind
By bud of nobler race. This is an art
Which does mend nature – change it rather; but
The art itself is nature.

PERDITA So it is.

POLIXENES Then make your garden rich in gillyvors,
And do not call them bastards.

PERDITA I'll not put
The dibble in earth to set one slip of them;
No more than were I painted I would wish
This youth should say 'twere well, and only therefore
Desire to breed by me. Here's flow'rs for you:
Hot lavender, mints, savory, marjoram;
The marigold, that goes to bed wi' th' sun,
And with him rises weeping; these are flow'rs
Of middle summer, and I think they are given
To men of middle age. Y'are very welcome.

CAMILLO I should leave grazing, were I of your flock,
And only live by gazing.

PERDITA Out, alas!
You'd be so lean that blasts of January
Would blow you through and through. Now, my fair'st friend,
I would I had some flow'rs o' th' spring that might
Become your time of day – and yours, and yours,
That wear upon your virgin branches yet
Your maidenheads growing. O Proserpina,
For the flowers now that, frighted, thou let'st fall
From Dis's waggon! – daffodils,
That come before the swallow dares, and take
The winds of March with beauty; violets, dim
But sweeter than the lids of Juno's eyes
Or Cytherea's breath; pale primroses,
That die unmarried ere they can behold
Bright Phoebus in his strength – a malady
Most incident to maids; bold oxlips, and
The crown-imperial; lilies of all kinds,
The flow'r-de-luce being one. O, these I lack
To make you garlands of, and my sweet friend
To strew him o'er and o'er!

FLORIZEL What, like a corse?

PERDITA No; like a bank for love to lie and play on;
Not like a corse; or if – not to be buried,
But quick, and in mine arms. Come, take your flow'rs.
Methinks I play as I have seen them do
In Whitsun pastorals. Sure, this robe of mine
Does change my disposition.

FLORIZEL What you do
Still betters what is done. When you speak, sweet,
I'd have you do it ever. When you sing,
I'd have you buy and sell so; so give alms;
Pray so; and, for the ord'ring your affairs,
To sing them too. When you do dance, I wish you
A wave o' th' sea, that you might ever do
Nothing but that; move still, still so,

And own no other function. Each your doing,
So singular in each particular,
Crowns what you are doing in the present deeds,
That all your acts are queens.

PERDITA O Doricles,
Your praises are too large. But that your youth,
And the true blood which peeps fairly through't,
Do plainly give you out an unstain'd shepherd,
With wisdom I might fear, my Doricles,
You woo'd me the false way.

FLORIZEL I think you have
As little skill to fear as I have purpose
To put you to't. But, come; our dance, I pray.
Your hand, my Perdita; so turtles pair
That never mean to part.

PERDITA I'll swear for 'em.

POLIXENES This is the prettiest low-born lass that ever
Ran on the green-sward; nothing she does or seems
But smacks of something greater than herself,
Too noble for this place.

CAMILLO He tells her something
That makes her blood look out. Good sooth, she is
The queen of curds and cream.

CLOWN Come on, strike up.

DORCAS Mopsa must be your mistress; marry, garlic,
To mend her kissing with!

MOPSA Now, in good time!

CLOWN Not a word, a word; we stand upon our manners.
Come, strike up. [*Music.*

Here a dance of Shepherds and Shepherdesses.

POLIXENES Pray, good shepherd, what fair swain is this
Which dances with your daughter?

SHEPHERD They call him Doricles, and boasts himself
To have a worthy feeding; but I have it
Upon his own report, and I believe it:
He looks like sooth. He says he loves my daughter;
I think so too; for never gaz'd the moon
Upon the water as he'll stand and read,
As 'twere, my daughter's eyes; and, to be plain,
I think there is not half a kiss to choose
Who loves another best.

POLIXENES She dances featly.

SHEPHERD So she does any thing; though I report it
That should be silent. If young Doricles
Do light upon her, she shall bring him that
Which he not dreams of.

Enter a Servant.

SERVANT O master, if you did but hear the pedlar at the door, you would never dance again after a tabor and pipe; no, the bagpipe could not move you. He sings several tunes faster than you'll tell money; he utters them as he had eaten ballads, and all men's ears grew to his tunes.

CLOWN He could never come better; he shall come in. I love a ballad but even too well, if it be doleful matter merrily set down, or a very pleasant thing indeed and sung lamentably.

SERVANT He hath songs for man or woman of all sizes; no milliner can so fit his customers with gloves. He has the prettiest love-songs for maids; so without bawdry, which is strange; with such delicate burdens of dildos and fadings, 'jump her and thump her'; and where some stretch-mouth'd rascal would, as it were, mean mischief, and break a foul gap into the matter, he makes the maid to answer 'Whoop, do me no harm, good man' – puts him off, slights him, with 'Whoop, do me no harm, good man'.

POLIXENES This is a brave fellow.

CLOWN Believe me, thou talkest of an admirable conceited fellow. Has he any unbraided wares?

SERVANT He hath ribbons of all the colours i' th' rainbow; points, more than all the lawyers in Bohemia can learnedly handle, though they come to him by th' gross; inkles, caddisses, cambrics, lawns. Why he sings 'em over as they were gods or goddesses; you would think a smock were a she-angel, he so chants to the sleevehand and the work about the square on't.

CLOWN Prithee bring him in; and let him approach singing.

PERDITA Forewarn him that he use no scurrilous words in's tunes. [*Exit Servant.*

CLOWN You have of these pedlars that have more in them than you'd think, sister.

PERDITA Ay, good brother, or go about to think.

Enter AUTOLYCUS, singing:

Lawn as white as driven snow;
Cypress black as e'er was crow;
Gloves as sweet as damask roses;
Masks for faces and for noses;
Bugle bracelet, necklace amber,
Perfume for a lady's chamber;
Golden quoifs and stomachers,
For my lads to give their dears;
Pins and poking-sticks of steel –
What maids lack from head to heel.
Come, buy of me, come; come buy, come buy;
Buy, lads, or else your lasses cry.
Come, buy.

CLOWN If I were not in love with Mopsa, thou shouldst take no money of me; but being enthrall'd as I am, it will also be the bondage of certain ribbons and gloves.

MOPSA I was promis'd them against the feast; but they come not too late now.

DORCAS He hath promis'd you more than that, or there be liars.

MOPSA He hath paid you all he promis'd you. May be he has paid you more, which will shame you to give him again.

CLOWN Is there no manners left among maids? Will they wear their plackets where they should bear their faces? Is there not milking-time, when you are going to bed, or kiln-hole, to whistle off these secrets, but you must be tittle-tattling before all our our guests? 'Tis well they are whisp'ring. Clammer your tongues, and not a word more.

MOPSA I have done. Come, you promis'd me a tawdry-lace, and a pair of sweet gloves.

CLOWN Have I not told thee how I was cozen'd by the way, and lost all my money?

AUTOLYCUS And indeed, sir, there are cozeners abroad; therefore it behoves men to be wary.

CLOWN Fear not thou, man; thou shalt lose nothing here.

AUTOLYCUS I hope so, sir; for I have about me many parcels of charge.

CLOWN What hast here? Ballads?

MOPSA Pray now, buy some. I love a ballad in print a-life, for then we are sure they are true.

AUTOLYCUS Here's one to a very doleful tune: how a usurer's wife was brought to bed of twenty money-bags at a burden, and how she long'd to eat adders' heads and toads carbonado'd.

MOPSA Is it true, think you?

AUTOLYCUS Very true, and but a month old.

DORCAS Bless me from marrying a usurer!

AUTOLYCUS Here's the midwife's name to't, one Mistress Taleporter, and five or six honest wives that were present. Why should I carry lies abroad?

MOPSA Pray you now, buy it.

CLOWN Come on, lay it by; and let's first see moe ballads; we'll buy the other things anon.

AUTOLYCUS Here's another ballad, of a fish that appeared upon the coast on Wednesday the fourscore of April, forty thousand fathom above water, and sung this ballad against the hard hearts of maids. It was thought she was a woman, and was turn'd into a cold fish for she would not exchange flesh with one that lov'd her. The ballad is very pitiful, and as true.

DORCAS Is it true too, think you?

AUTOLYCUS Five justices' hands at it; and witnesses more than my pack will hold.

CLOWN Lay it by too. Another.

AUTOLYCUS This is a merry ballad, but a very pretty one.

MOPSA Let's have some merry ones.

AUTOLYCUS Why, this is a passing merry one, and goes to the tune of 'Two maids wooing a man.' There's scarce a maid westward but she sings it; 'tis in request, I can tell you.

MOPSA We can both sing it. If thou'lt bear a part, thou shalt hear; 'tis in three parts.

DORCAS We had the tune on't a month ago.

AUTOLYCUS I can bear my part; you must know 'tis my occupation. Have at it with you.

Song.

AUTOLYCUS Get you hence, for I must go
Where it fits not you to know.
DORCAS Whither?
MOPSA O, whither?
DORCAS Whither?
MOPSA It becomes thy oath full well
Thou to me thy secrets tell.
DORCAS Me too! Let me go thither.
MOPSA Or thou goest to th' grange or mill.
DORCAS If to either, thou dost ill.
AUTOLYCUS Neither.
DORCAS What, neither?
AUTOLYCUS Neither.
DORCAS Thou hast sworn my love to be.
MOPSA Thou hast sworn it more to me.
Then whither goest? Say, whither?

CLOWN We'll have this song out anon by ourselves; my father and the gentlemen are in sad talk, and we'll not trouble them. Come, bring away thy pack after me. Wenches, I'll buy for you both. Pedlar, let's have the first choice. Follow me, girls. [*Exit with Dorcas and Mopsa.*

AUTOLYCUS And you shall pay well for 'em.

[*Exit Autolycus, singing:*

Will you buy any tape,
Or lace for your cape,
My dainty duck, my dear-a?
Any silk, any thread,
Any toys for your head,
Of the new'st and fin'st, fin'st
wear-a?
Come to the pedlar;
Money's a meddler
That doth utter all men's ware-a.

Re-enter Servant.

SERVANT Master, there is three carters, three shepherds, three neat-herds, three swine-herds, that have made themselves all men of hair; they call themselves Saltiers, and they have a dance which the wenches say is a gallimaufry of gambols, because they are not in't; but they themselves are o' th' mind, if it be not too rough for some that know little but bowling, it will please plentifully.

SHEPHERD Away! We'll none on't; here has been too much homely foolery already. I know, sir, we weary you.

POLIXENES You weary those that refresh us. Pray, let's see these four threes of herdsmen.

SERVANT One three of them, by their own report, sir, hath danc'd before the King; and not the worst of the three but jumps twelve foot and a half by th' squier.

SHEPHERD Leave your prating; since these good men are pleas'd, let them come in; but quickly now.

SERVANT Why, they stay at door, sir. *[Exit.*

Here a Dance of twelve Satyrs.

POLIXENES *[To Shepherd]* O, father, you'll know more of that hereafter.
[To Camillo] Is it not too far gone? 'Tis time to part them.
He's simple and tells much. *[To Florizel]* How now, fair shepherd!
Your heart is full of something that does take
Your mind from feasting. Sooth, when I was young
And handed love as you do, I was wont
To load my she with knacks; I would have ransack'd
The pedlar's silken treasury and have pour'd it
To her acceptance: you have let him go
And nothing marted with him. If your lass
Interpretation should abuse and call this
Your lack of love or bounty, you were straited
For a reply, at least if you make a care
Of happy holding her.

FLORIZEL Old sir, I know
She prizes not such trifles as these are.
The gifts she looks from me are pack'd and lock'd
Up in my heart, which I have given already,
But not deliver'd. O, hear me breathe my life
Before this ancient sir, whom, it should seem,
Hath sometime lov'd. I take thy hand – this hand,
As soft as dove's down and as white as it,
Or Ethiopian's tooth, or the fann'd snow that's bolted
By th' northern blasts twice o'er.

POLIXENES What follows this?
How prettily the young swain seems to wash
The hand was fair before! I have put you out.
But to your protestation; let me hear
What you profess.

FLORIZEL Do, and be witness to't.

POLIXENES And this my neighbour too?

FLORIZEL And he, and more
Than he, and men – the earth, the heavens, and all:
That, were I crown'd the most imperial monarch,
Thereof most worthy, were I the fairest youth
That ever made eye swerve, had force and knowledge
More than was ever man's, I would not prize them
Without her love; for her employ them all;
Commend them and condemn them to her service
Or to their own perdition.

POLIXENES Fairly offer'd.

CAMILLO This shows a sound affection.

SHEPHERD But, my daughter,
Say you the like to him?

PERDITA I cannot speak
So well, nothing so well; no, nor mean better.
By th' pattern of mine own thoughts I cut out
The purity of his.

SHEPHERD Take hands, a bargain!
And, friends unknown, you shall bear witness to't:
I give my daughter to him, and will make
Her portion equal his.

FLORIZEL O, that must be
I' th' virtue of your daughter. One being dead,
I shall have more than you can dream of yet;
Enough then for your wonder. But come on,
Contract us fore these witnesses.

SHEPHERD Come, your hand;
And, daughter, yours.

POLIXENES Soft, swain, awhile, beseech you;
Have you a father?

FLORIZEL I have, but what of him?

POLIXENES Knows he of this?

FLORIZEL He neither does nor shall.

POLIXENES Methinks a father
Is at the nuptial of his son a guest
That best becomes the table. Pray you, once more,
Is not your father grown incapable
Of reasonable affairs? Is he not stupid
With age and alt'ring rheums? Can he speak, hear,
Know man from man, dispute his own estate?
Lies he not bed-rid, and again does nothing
But what he did being childish?

FLORIZEL No, good sir;
He has his health, and ampler strength indeed
Than most have of his age.

POLIXENES By my white beard,
You offer him, if this be so, a wrong
Something unfilial. Reason my son
Should choose himself a wife; but as good reason
The father – all whose joy is nothing else
But fair posterity – should hold some counsel
In such a business.

FLORIZEL I yield all this;
But, for some other reasons, my grave sir,
Which 'tis not fit you know, I not acquaint
My father of this business.

POLIXENES Let him know't.

FLORIZEL He shall not.

POLIXENES Prithee let him.

FLORIZEL No, he must not.

SHEPHERD Let him, my son; he shall not need to grieve
At knowing of thy choice.

FLORIZEL Come, come, he must not.
Mark our contract.

POLIXENES [*Discovering himself*] Mark your divorce, young sir,
Whom son I dare not call; thou art too base
To be acknowledg'd – thou a sceptre's heir,
That thus affects a sheep-hook! Thou, old traitor,
I am sorry that by hanging thee I can but
Shorten thy life one week. And thou, fresh piece
Of excellent witchcraft, who of force must know
The royal fool thou cop'st with –

SHEPHERD O, my heart!

POLIXENES I'll have thy beauty scratch'd with briers and made
More homely than thy state. For thee, fond boy,
If I may ever know thou dost but sigh
That thou no more shalt see this knack – as never
I mean thou shalt – we'll bar thee from succession;
Not hold thee of our blood, no, not our kin,
Farre than Deucalion off. Mark thou my words.
Follow us to the court. Thou churl, for this time,
Though full of our displeasure, yet we free thee
From the dead blow of it. And you, enchantment,
Worthy enough a herdsman – yea, him too
That makes himself, but for our honour therein,
Unworthy thee – if ever henceforth thou
These rural latches to his entrance open,
Or hoop his body more with thy embraces,
I will devise a death as cruel for thee
As thou art tender to't. [*Exit.*

PERDITA Even here undone!
I was not much afeard; for once or twice
I was about to speak and tell him plainly
The self-same sun that shines upon his court
Hides not his visage from our cottage, but
Looks on alike. [*To Florizel*] Will't please you, sir, be gone?
I told you what would come of this. Beseech you,
Of your own state take care. This dream of mine –
Being now awake, I'll queen it no inch farther,
But milk my ewes and weep.

CAMILLO Why, how now, father!
Speak ere thou diest.

SHEPHERD I cannot speak nor think,
Nor dare to know that which I know. [*To Florizel*] O sir,
You have undone a man of fourscore-three
That thought to fill his grave in quiet, yea,
To die upon the bed my father died,
To lie close by his honest bones; but now
Some hangman must put on my shroud and lay me
Where no priest shovels in dust. [*To Perdita*] O cursed wretch,
That knew'st this was the Prince, and wouldst adventure
To mingle faith with him! – Undone, undone!
If I might die within this hour, I have liv'd
To die when I desire. [*Exit.*

FLORIZEL Why look you so upon me?
I am but sorry, not afeard; delay'd,
But nothing alt'red. What I was, I am:
More straining on for plucking back; not following
My leash unwillingly.

CAMILLO Gracious, my lord,
You know your father's temper. At this time
He will allow no speech – which I do guess
You do not purpose to him – and as hardly
Will he endure your sight as yet, I fear;
Then, till the fury of his Highness settle,
Come not before him.

FLORIZEL I not purpose it.
I think Camillo?

CAMILLO Even he, my lord.

PERDITA How often have I told you 'twould be thus!
How often said my dignity would last
But till 'twere known!

FLORIZEL It cannot fail but by
The violation of my faith; and then
Let nature crush the sides o' th' earth together
And mar the seeds within! Lift up thy looks.
From my succession wipe me, father; I
Am heir to my affection.

CAMILLO Be advis'd.

FLORIZEL I am – and by my fancy; if my reason
Will thereto be obedient, I have reason;
If not, my senses, better pleas'd with madness,
Do bid it welcome.
CAMILLO This is desperate, sir.
FLORIZEL So call it; but it does fulfil my vow:
I needs must think it honesty. Camillo,
Not for Bohemia, nor the pomp that may
Be thereat glean'd, for all the sun sees or
The close earth wombs, or the profound seas hides
In unknown fathoms, will I break my oath
To this my fair belov'd. Therefore, I pray you,
As you have ever been my father's honour'd friend,
When he shall miss me – as, in faith, I mean not
To see him any more – cast your good counsels
Upon his passion. Let myself and Fortune
Tug for the time to come. This you may know,
And so deliver: I am put to sea
With her who here I cannot hold on shore.
And most opportune to her need I have
A vessel rides fast by, but not prepar'd
For this design. What course I mean to hold
Shall nothing benefit your knowledge, nor
Concern me the reporting.
CAMILLO O my lord,
I would your spirit were easier for advice,
Or stronger for your need.
FLORIZEL Hark, Perdita.
[*Takes her aside.*
[*To Camillo*] I'll hear you by and by.
CAMILLO He's irremovable,
Resolv'd for flight. Now were I happy if
His going I could frame to serve my turn,
Save him from danger, do him love and honour,
Purchase the sight again of dear Sicilia
And that unhappy king, my master, whom
I so much thirst to see.
FLORIZEL Now, good Camillo,
I am so fraught with curious business that
I leave out ceremony.
CAMILLO Sir, I think
You have heard of my poor services i' th' love
That I have borne your father?
FLORIZEL Very nobly
Have you deserv'd. It is my father's music
To speak your deeds; not little of his care
To have them recompens'd as thought on.
CAMILLO Well, my lord,
If you may please to think I love the King,
And through him what's nearest to him, which is
Your gracious self, embrace but my direction.
If your more ponderous and settled project
May suffer alteration, on mine honour,
I'll point you where you shall have such receiving
As shall become your Highness; where you may
Enjoy your mistress, from the whom, I see,
There's no disjunction to be made but by,
As heavens forfend! your ruin – marry her;
And with my best endeavours in your absence
Your discontenting father strive to qualify,
And bring him up to liking.
FLORIZEL How, Camillo,
May this, almost a miracle, be done?
That I may call thee something more than man,
And after that trust to thee.
CAMILLO Have you thought on
A place whereto you'll go?
FLORIZEL Not any yet;
But as th' unthought-on accident is guilty
To what we wildly do, so we profess
Ourselves to be the slaves of chance and flies
Of every wind that blows.
CAMILLO Then list to me.
This follows, if you will not change your purpose
But undergo this flight: make for Sicilia,
And there present yourself and your fair princess –
For so, I see, she must be – fore Leontes.
She shall be habited as it becomes
The partner of your bed. Methinks I see
Leontes opening his free arms and weeping
His welcomes forth; asks thee there 'Son, forgiveness!'
As 'twere i' th' father's person; kisses the hands
Of your fresh princess; o'er and o'er divides him
'Twixt his unkindness and his kindness – th'one
He chides to hell, and bids the other grow
Faster than thought or time.
FLORIZEL Worthy Camillo,
What colour for my visitation shall I
Hold up before him?
CAMILLO Sent by the King your father
To greet him and to give him comforts. Sir,
The manner of your bearing towards him, with
What you as from your father shall deliver,
Things known betwixt us three, I'll write you down;
The which shall point you forth at every sitting
What you must say, that he shall not perceive
But that you have your father's bosom there
And speak his very heart.
FLORIZEL I am bound to you.
There is some sap in this.
CAMILLO A course more promising
Than a wild dedication of yourselves
To unpath'd waters, undream'd shores, most certain
To miseries enough; no hope to help you,

But as you shake off one to take another;
Nothing so certain as your anchors, who
Do their best office if they can but stay you
Where you'll be loath to be. Besides, you know
Prosperity's the very bond of love,
Whose fresh complexion and whose heart together
Affliction alters.

PERDITA One of these is true:
I think affliction may subdue the cheek,
But not take in the mind.

CAMILLO Yea, say you so?
There shall not at your father's house these seven years
Be born another such.

FLORIZEL My good Camillo,
She is as forward of her breeding as
She is i' th' rear o' our birth.

CAMILLO I cannot say 'tis pity
She lacks instructions, for she seems a mistress
To most that teach.

PERDITA Your pardon, sir; for this
I'll blush you thanks.

FLORIZEL My prettiest Perdita!
But, O, the thorns we stand upon! Camillo –
Preserver of my father, now of me;
The medicine of our house – how shall we do?
We are not furnish'd like Bohemia's son;
Nor shall appear in Sicilia.

CAMILLO My lord,
Fear none of this. I think you know my fortunes
Do all lie there. It shall be so my care
To have you royally appointed as if
The scene you play were mine. For instance, sir,
That you may know you shall not want – one word.
[They talk aside.

Re-enter AUTOLYCUS.

AUTOLYCUS Ha, ha! what a fool Honesty is! and Trust, his sworn brother, a very simple gentleman! I have sold all my trumpery; not a counterfeit stone, not a ribbon, glass, pomander, brooch, table-book, ballad, knife, tape, glove, shoe-tie, bracelet, horn-ring, to keep my pack from fasting. They throng who should buy first, as if my trinkets had been hallowed and brought a benediction to the buyer; by which means I saw whose purse was best in picture; and what I saw, to my good use I rememb'red. My clown, who wants but something to be a reasonable man, grew so in love with the wenches' song that he would not stir his pettitoes till he had both tune and words, which so drew the rest of the herd to me that all their other senses stuck in ears. You might have pinch'd a placket, it was senseless; 'twas nothing to geld a codpiece of a purse; I would have fil'd keys off that hung in chains. No hearing, no feeling, but my sir's song, and admiring the nothing of it. So that in this time of lethargy I pick'd and cut most of their festival purses; and had not the old man come in with a whoobub against his daughter and the King's son and scar'd my choughs from the chaff, I had not left a purse alive in the whole army.

[Camillo, Florizel, and Perdita, come forward.

CAMILLO Nay, but my letters, by this means being there
So soon as you arrive, shall clear that doubt.

FLORIZEL And those that you'll procure from King Leontes?

CAMILLO Shall satisfy your father.

PERDITA Happy be you!
All that you speak shows fair.

CAMILLO *[Seeing Autolycus]* Who have we here?
We'll make an instrument of this; omit
Nothing may give us aid.

AUTOLYCUS *[Aside]* If they have overheard me now – why, hanging.

CAMILLO How now, good fellow! Why shak'st thou so? Fear not, man; here's no harm intended to thee.

AUTOLYCUS I am a poor fellow, sir.

CAMILLO Why, be so still; here's nobody will steal that from thee. Yet for the outside of thy poverty we must make an exchange; therefore discase thee instantly – thou must think there's a necessity in't – and change garments with this gentleman. Though the pennyworth on his side be the worst, yet hold thee, there's some boot.
[Giving money.

AUTOLYCUS I am a poor fellow, sir. *[Aside]* I know ye well enough.

CAMILLO Nay, prithee dispatch. The gentleman is half flay'd already.

AUTOLYCUS Are you in earnest, sir? *[Aside]* I smell the trick on't.

FLORIZEL Dispatch, I prithee.

AUTOLYCUS Indeed, I have had earnest; but I cannot with conscience take it.

CAMILLO Unbuckle, unbuckle.

[Florizel and Autolycus exchange garments.

Fortunate mistress – let my prophecy
Come home to ye! – you must retire yourself
Into some covert; take your sweetheart's hat
And pluck it o'er your brows, muffle your face,
Dismantle you, and, as you can, disliken
The truth of your own seeming, that you may –
For I do fear eyes over – to shipboard
Get undescried.

PERDITA I see the play so lies
That I must bear a part.

CAMILLO No remedy.
Have you done there?
FLORIZEL Should I now meet my father,
He would not call me son.
CAMILLO Nay, you shall have no hat.
[Giving it to Perdita.
Come, lady, come. Farewell, my friend.
AUTOLYCUS Adieu, sir.
FLORIZEL O Perdita, what have we twain forgot!
Pray you a word. *[They converse apart.*

CAMILLO *[Aside]* What I do next shall be to tell the King
Of this escape, and whither they are bound;
Wherein my hope is I shall so prevail
To force him after; in whose company
I shall re-view Sicilia, for whose sight
I have a woman's longing.
FLORIZEL Fortune speed us!
Thus we set on, Camillo, to th' sea-side.
CAMILLO The swifter speed the better.
[Exeunt Florizel, Perdita, and Camillo.

AUTOLYCUS I understand the business, I hear it. To have an open ear, a quick eye, and a nimble hand, is necessary for a cut-purse; a good nose is requisite also, to smell out work for th' other senses. I see this is the time that the unjust man doth thrive. What an exchange had this been without boot! What a boot is here with this exchange! Sure, the gods do this year connive at us, and we may do anything extempore. The Prince himself is about a piece of iniquity – stealing away from his father with his clog at his heels. If I thought it were a piece of honesty to acquaint the King withal, I would not do't. I hold it the more knavery to conceal it; and therein am I constant to my profession.

Re-enter Clown and Shepherd.

Aside, aside – here is more matter for a hot brain. Every lane's end, every shop, church, session, hanging, yields a careful man work.

CLOWN See, see; what a man you are now! There is no other way but to tell the King she's a changeling and none of your flesh and blood.
SHEPHERD Nay, but hear me.
CLOWN Nay – but hear me.
SHEPHERD Go to, then.
CLOWN She being none of your flesh and blood, your flesh and blood has not offended the King; and so your flesh and blood is not to be punish'd by him. Show those things you found about her, those secret things – all but what she has with her. This being done, let the law go whistle; I warrant you.
SHEPHERD I will tell the King all, every word – yea, and his son's pranks too; who, I may say, is no honest man, neither to his father nor to me, to go about to make me the King's brother-in-law.
CLOWN Indeed, brother-in-law was the farthest off you could have been to him; and then your blood had been the dearer by I know how much an ounce.
AUTOLYCUS *[Aside]* Very wisely, puppies!
SHEPHERD Well, let us to the King. There is that in this fardel will make him scratch his beard.
AUTOLYCUS *[Aside]* I know not what impediment this complaint may be to the flight of my master.
CLOWN Pray heartily he be at palace.
AUTOLYCUS *[Aside]* Though I am not naturally honest, I am so sometimes by chance. Let me pocket up my pedlar's excrement. *[Takes off his false beard]* How now, rustics! Whither are you bound?
SHEPHERD To th' palace, an it like your worship.
AUTOLYCUS Your affairs there, what, with whom, the condition of that fardel, the place of your dwelling, your names, your ages, of what having, breeding, and anything that is fitting to be known – discover.
CLOWN We are but plain fellows, sir.
AUTOLYCUS A lie: you are rough and hairy. Let me have no lying; it becomes none but tradesmen, and they often give us soldiers the lie; but we pay them for it with stamped coin, not stabbing steel; therefore they do not give us the lie.
CLOWN Your worship had like to have given us one, if you had not taken yourself with the manner.
SHEPHERD Are you a courtier, an't like you, sir?
AUTOLYCUS Whether it like me or no, I am a courtier. Seest thou not the air of the court in these enfoldings? Hath not my gait in it the measure of the court? Receives not thy nose court-odour from me? Reflect I not on thy baseness court-contempt? Think'st thou, for that I insinuate, that toaze from thee thy business, I am therefore no courtier? I am courtier cap-a-pe, and one that will either push on or pluck back thy business there; whereupon I command thee to open thy affair.
SHEPHERD My business, sir, is to the King.
AUTOLYCUS What advocate hast thou to him?
SHEPHERD I know not, an't like you.
CLOWN Advocate's the court-word for a pheasant; say you have none.
SHEPHERD None, sir; I have no pheasant, cock nor hen.
AUTOLYCUS How blessed are we that are not simple men!
Yet nature might have made me as these are,

Therefore I will not disdain.

CLOWN This cannot be but a great courtier.

SHEPHERD His garments are rich, but he wears them not handsomely.

CLOWN He seems to be the more noble in being fantastical. A great man, I'll warrant; I know by the picking on's teeth.

AUTOLYCUS The fardel there? What's i' th' fardel? Wherefore that box?

SHEPHERD Sir, there lies such secrets in this fardel and box which none must know but the King; and which he shall know within this hour, if I may come to th' speech of him.

AUTOLYCUS Age, thou hast lost thy labour.

SHEPHERD Why, sir?

AUTOLYCUS The King is not at the palace; he is gone aboard a new ship to purge melancholy and air himself; for, if thou be'st capable of things serious, thou must know the King is full of grief.

SHEPHERD So 'tis said, sir – about his son, that should have married a shepherd's daughter.

AUTOLYCUS If that shepherd be not in handfast, let him fly; the curses he shall have, the tortures he shall feel, will break the back of man, the heart of monster.

CLOWN Think you so, sir?

AUTOLYCUS Not he alone shall suffer what wit can make heavy and vengeance bitter; but those that are germane to him, though remov'd fifty times, shall all come under the hangman – which, though it be great pity, yet it is necessary. An old sheep-whistling rogue, a ram-tender, to offer to have his daughter come into grace! Some say he shall be ston'd; but that death is too soft for him, say I. Draw our throne into a sheep-cote ! – all deaths are too few, the sharpest too easy.

CLOWN Has the old man e'er a son, sir, do you hear, an't like you, sir?

AUTOLYCUS He has a son – who shall be flay'd alive; then 'nointed over with honey, set on the head of a wasp's nest; then stand till he be three quarters and a dram dead; then recover'd again with aqua-vitae or some other hot infusion; then, raw as he is, and in the hottest day prognostication proclaims, shall he be set against a brick wall, the sun looking with a southward eye upon him, where he is to behold him with flies blown to death. But what talk we of these traitorly rascals, whose miseries are to be smil'd at, their offences being so capital? Tell me, for you seem to be honest plain men, what you have to the King. Being something gently consider'd, I'll bring you where he is aboard, tender your persons to his presence, whisper him in your behalfs; and if it be in man besides the King to effect your suits, here is man shall do it.

CLOWN He seems to be of great authority. Close with him, give him gold; and though authority be a stubborn bear, yet he is oft led by the nose with gold. Show the inside of your purse to the outside of his hand, and no more ado. Remember – ston'd and flay'd alive.

SHEPHERD An't please you, sir, to undertake the business for us, here is that gold I have. I'll make it as much more, and leave this young man in pawn till I bring it you.

AUTOLYCUS After I have done what I promised?

SHEPHERD Ay, sir.

AUTOLYCUS Well, give me the moiety. Are you a party in this business?

CLOWN In some sort, sir; but though my case be a pitiful one, I hope I shall not be flay'd out of it.

AUTOLYCUS O, that's the case of the shepherd's son! Hang him, he'll be made an example.

CLOWN Comfort, good comfort! We must to the King and show our strange sights. He must know 'tis none of your daughter nor my sister; we are gone else. Sir, I will give you as much as this old man does, when the business is performed; and remain, as he says, your pawn till it be brought you.

AUTOLYCUS I will trust you. Walk before toward the sea-side; go on the right-hand; I will but look upon the hedge, and follow you.

CLOWN We are blest in this man, as I may say, even blest.

SHEPHERD Let's before, as he bids us. He was provided to do us good.

[Exeunt Shepherd and Clown.

AUTOLYCUS If I had a mind to be honest, I see Fortune would not suffer me: she drops booties in my mouth. I am courted now with a double occasion – gold, and a means to do the Prince my master good; which who knows how that may turn back to my advancement? I will bring these two moles, these blind ones, aboard him. If he think it fit to shore them again, and that the complaint they have to the King concerns him nothing, let him call me rogue for being so far officious; for I am proof against that title, and what shame else belongs to't. To him will I present them. There may be matter in it. *[Exit.*

ACT FIVE

SCENE I. *Sicilia. The palace of Leontes.*

Enter LEONTES, CLEOMENES, DION, PAULINA, and Others.

CLEOMENES Sir, you have done enough, and have perform'd
A saint-like sorrow. No fault could you make
Which you have not redeem'd; indeed, paid down,
More penitence than done trespass. At the last,
Do as the heavens have done: forget your evil;
With them forgive yourself.
LEONTES Whilst I remember
Her and her virtues, I cannot forget
My blemishes in them, and so still think of
The wrong I did myself; which was so much
That heirless it hath made my kingdom, and
Destroy'd the sweet'st companion that e'er man
Bred his hopes out of.
PAULINA True, too true, my lord.
If, one by one, you wedded all the world,
Or from the all that are took something good
To make a perfect woman, she you kill'd
Would be unparallel'd.
LEONTES I think so. Kill'd!
She I kill'd! I did so; but thou strik'st me
Sorely, to say I did. It is as bitter
Upon thy tongue as in my thought. Now, good now,
Say so but seldom.
CLEOMENES Not at all, good lady.
You might have spoken a thousand things that would
Have done the time more benefit, and grac'd
Your kindness better.
PAULINA You are one of those
Would have him wed again.
DION If you would not so,
You pity not the state, nor the remembrance
Of his most sovereign name; consider little
What dangers, by his Highness' fail of issue,
May drop upon his kingdom and devour
Incertain lookers-on. What were more holy
Than to rejoice the former queen is well?
What holier than, for royalty's repair,
For present comfort, and for future good,
To bless the bed of majesty again
With a sweet fellow to't?
PAULINA There is none worthy,
Respecting her that's gone. Besides, the gods
Will have fulfill'd their secret purposes;
For has not the divine Apollo said,
Is't not the tenour of his oracle,
That King Leontes shall not have an heir
Till his lost child be found? Which that it shall,
Is all as monstrous to our human reason
As my Antigonus to break his grave
And come again to me; who, on my life,
Did perish with the infant. 'Tis your counsel
My lord should to the heavens be contrary,
Oppose against their wills. [*To Leontes*] Care not for issue;
The crown will find an heir. Great Alexander
Left his to th' worthiest; so his successor
Was like to be the best.
LEONTES Good Paulina,
Who hast the memory of Hermione,
I know, in honour, O that ever I
Had squar'd me to thy counsel! Then, even now,
I might have look'd upon my queen's full eyes,
Have taken treasure from her lips –
PAULINA And left them
More rich for what they yielded.
LEONTES Thou speak'st truth.
No more such wives; therefore, no wife. One worse,
And better us'd, would make her sainted spirit
Again possess her corpse, and on this stage,
Where we offend her now, appear soul-vex'd,
And begin 'Why to me' –
PAULINA Had she such power,
She had just cause.
LEONTES She had; and would incense me
To murder her I married.
PAULINA I should so.
Were I the ghost that walk'd, I'd bid you mark
Her eye, and tell me for what dull part in't
You chose her; then I'd shriek, that even your ears
Should rift to hear me; and the words that follow'd
Should be 'Remember mine'.
LEONTES Stars, stars,
And all eyes else dead coals! Fear thou no wife;
I'll have no wife, Paulina.
PAULINA Will you swear
Never to marry but by my free leave?
LEONTES Never, Paulina; so be blest my spirit!
PAULINA Then, good my lords, bear witness to his oath.
CLEOMENES You tempt him over-much.
PAULINA Unless another,
As like Hermione as is her picture,
Affront his eye.
CLEOMENES Good madam –
PAULINA I have done.
Yet, if my lord will marry – if you will, sir,
No remedy but you will – give me the office
To choose you a queen. She shall not be so young

As was your former; but she shall be such
As, walk'd your first queen's ghost, it should take joy
To see her in your arms.

LEONTES My true Paulina,
We shall not marry till thou bid'st us.

PAULINA That
Shall be when your first queen's again in breath;
Never till then.

Enter a Gentleman.

GENTLEMAN One that gives out himself Prince Florizel,
Son of Polixenes, with his princess – she
The fairest I have yet beheld – desires access
To your high presence.

LEONTES What with him? He comes not
Like to his father's greatness. His approach,
So out of circumstance and sudden, tells us
'Tis not a visitation fram'd, but forc'd
By need and accident. What train?

GENTLEMAN But few,
And those but mean.

LEONTES His princess, say you, with him?

GENTLEMAN Ay; the most peerless piece of earth, I think,
That e'er the sun shone bright on.

PAULINA O Hermione,
As every present time doth boast itself
Above a better gone, so must thy grave
Give way to what's seen now! Sir, you yourself
Have said and writ so, but your writing now
Is colder than that theme: 'She had not been,
Nor was not to be equall'd'. Thus your verse
Flow'd with her beauty once; 'tis shrewdly ebb'd,
To say you have seen a better.

GENTLEMAN Pardon, madam.
The one I have almost forgot – your pardon;
The other, when she has obtain'd your eye,
Will have your tongue too. This is a creature,
Would she begin a sect, might quench the zeal
Of all professors else, make proselytes
Of who she but bid follow.

PAULINA How! not women?

GENTLEMAN Women will love her that she is a woman
More worth than any man; men, that she is
The rarest of all women.

LEONTES Go, Cleomenes;
Yourself, assisted with your honour'd friends,
Bring them to our embracement. [*Exeunt*] Still, 'tis strange
He thus should steal upon us.

PAULINA Had our prince,
Jewel of children, seen this hour, he had pair'd
Well with this lord; there was not full a month
Between their births.

LEONTES Prithee no more; cease. Thou know'st
He dies to me again when talk'd of. Sure,
When I shall see this gentleman, thy speeches
Will bring me to consider that which may
Unfurnish me of reason.

Re-enter CLEOMENES, with FLORIZEL, PERDITA, and Attendants.

They are come.
Your mother was most true to wedlock, Prince;
For she did print your royal father off,
Conceiving you. Were I but twenty-one,
Your father's image is so hit in you,
His very air, that I should call you brother,
As I did him, and speak of something wildly
By us perform'd before. Most dearly welcome!
And your fair princess – goddess! O, alas!
I lost a couple that 'twixt heaven and earth
Might thus have stood begetting wonder as
You, gracious couple, do. And then I lost –
All mine own folly – the society,
Amity too, of your brave father, whom,
Though bearing misery, I desire my life
Once more to look on him.

FLORIZEL By his command
Have I here touch'd Sicilia, and from him
Give you all greetings that a king, at friend,
Can send his brother; and, but infirmity,
Which waits upon worn times, hath something seiz'd
His wish'd ability, he had himself
The lands and waters 'twixt your throne and his
Measur'd, to look upon you; whom he loves,
He bade me say so, more than all the sceptres
And those that bear them living.

LEONTES O my brother –
Good gentleman! – the wrongs I have done thee stir
Afresh within me; and these thy offices,
So rarely kind, are as interpreters
Of my behind-hand slackness! Welcome hither,
As is the spring to th' earth. And hath he too
Expos'd this paragon to th' fearful usage,
At least ungentle, of the dreadful Neptune,
To greet a man not worth her pains, much less
Th' adventure of her person?

FLORIZEL Good, my lord,
She came from Libya.

LEONTES Where the warlike Smalus,
That noble honour'd lord, is fear'd and lov'd?

FLORIZEL Most royal sir, from thence; from him whose daughter
His tears proclaim'd his, parting with her; thence,
A prosperous south-wind friendly, we have cross'd,

To execute the charge my father gave me
For visiting your Highness. My best train
I have from your Sicilian shores dismiss'd;
Who for Bohemia bend, to signify
Not only my success in Libya, sir,
But my arrival and my wife's in safety
Here where we are.

LEONTES The blessed gods
Purge all infection from our air whilst you
Do climate here! You have a holy father,
A graceful gentleman, against whose person,
So sacred as it is, I have done sin,
For which the heavens, taking angry note,
Have left me issueless; and your father's blest,
As he from heaven merits it, with you,
Worthy his goodness. What might I have been,
Might I a son and daughter now have look'd on,
Such goodly things as you!

Enter a Lord.

LORD Most noble sir,
That which I shall report will bear no credit,
Were not the proof so nigh. Please you, great
sir,
Bohemia greets you from himself by me;
Desires you to attach his son, who has –
His dignity and duty both cast off –
Fled from his father, from his hopes, and with
A shepherd's daughter.

LEONTES Where's Bohemia? Speak.

LORD Here in your city; I now came from him.
I speak amazedly; and it becomes
My marvel and my message. To your court
Whiles he was hast'ning – in the chase, it seems,
Of this fair couple – meets he on the way
The father of this seeming lady and
Her brother, having both their country quitted
With this young prince.

FLORIZEL Camillo has betray'd me;
Whose honour and whose honesty till now
Endur'd all weathers.

LORD Lay't so to his charge;
He's with the King your father.

LEONTES Who? Camillo?

LORD Camillo, sir; I spake with him; who now
Has these poor men in question. Never saw I
Wretches so quake. They kneel, they kiss the
earth;
Forswear themselves as often as they speak.
Bohemia stops his ears, and threatens them
With divers deaths in death.

PERDITA O my poor father!
The heaven sets spies upon us, will not have
Our contract celebrated.

LEONTES You are married?

FLORIZEL We are not, sir, nor are we like to be;
The stars, I see, will kiss the valleys first.
The odds for high and low's alike.

LEONTES My lord,
Is this the daughter of a king?

FLORIZEL She is,
When once she is my wife.

LEONTES That 'once', I see by your good father's
speed,
Will come on very slowly. I am sorry,
Most sorry, you have broken from his liking
Where you were tied in duty; and as sorry
Your choice is not so rich in worth as beauty,
That you might well enjoy her.

FLORIZEL Dear, look up.
Though Fortune, visible an enemy,
Should chase us with my father, pow'r no jot
Hath she to change our loves. Beseech you, sir,
Remember since you ow'd no more to time
Than I do now. With thought of such affections,
Step forth mine advocate; at your request
My father will grant precious things as trifles.

LEONTES Would he do so, I'd beg your precious
mistress,
Which he counts but a trifle.

PAULINA Sir, my liege,
Your eye hath too much youth in't. Not a month
Fore your queen died, she was more worth such
gazes
Than what you look on now.

LEONTES I thought of her
Even in these looks I made. [*To Florizel*] But
your petition
Is yet unanswer'd. I will to your father.
Your honour not o'erthrown by your desires,
I am friend to them and you. Upon which
errand
I now go toward him; therefore, follow me,
And mark what way I make. Come, good my
lord. [*Exeunt.*

SCENE II. *Sicilia. Before the palace of Leontes.*

Enter AUTOLYCUS and a Gentleman.

AUTOLYCUS Beseech you, sir, were you present at this relation?

1 GENTLEMAN I was by the opening of the fardel, heard the old shepherd deliver the manner how he found it; whereupon, after a little amazedness, we were all commanded out of the chamber; only this, methought I heard the shepherd say he found the child.

AUTOLYCUS I would most gladly know the issue of it.

1 GENTLEMAN I make a broken delivery of the business; but the changes I perceived in the King and Camillo were very notes of

admiration. They seem'd almost, with staring on one another, to tear the cases of their eyes; there was speech in their dumbness, language in their very gesture; they look'd as they had heard of a world ransom'd, or one destroyed. A notable passion of wonder appeared in them; but the wisest beholder that knew no more but seeing could not say if th' importance were joy or sorrow – but in the extremity of the one it must needs be.

Enter another Gentleman.

Here comes a gentleman that happily knows more. The news, Rogero?

2 GENTLEMAN Nothing but bonfires. The oracle is fulfill'd: the King's daughter is found. Such a deal of wonder is broken out within this hour that ballad-makers cannot be able to express it.

Enter another Gentleman.

Here comes the Lady Paulina's steward; he can deliver you more. How goes it now, sir? This news, which is call'd true, is so like an old tale that the verity of it is in strong suspicion. Has the King found his heir?

3 GENTLEMAN Most true, if ever truth were pregnant by circumstance. That which you hear you'll swear you see, there is such unity in the proofs. The mantle of Queen Hermione's; her jewel about the neck of it; the letters of Antigonus found with it, which they know to be his character; the majesty of the creature in resemblance of the mother; the affection of nobleness which nature shows above her breeding; and many other evidences – proclaim her with all certainty to be the King's daughter. Did you see the meeting of the two kings?

2 GENTLEMAN No.

3 GENTLEMAN Then have you lost a sight which was to be seen, cannot be spoken of. There might you have beheld one joy crown another, so and in such manner that it seem'd sorrow wept to take leave of them; for their joy waded in tears. There was casting up of eyes, holding up of hands, with countenance of such distraction that they were to be known by garment, not by favour. Our king, being ready to leap out of himself for joy of his found daughter, as if that joy were now become a loss, cries 'O, thy mother, thy mother!' then asks Bohemia forgiveness; then embraces his son-in-law; then again worries he his daughter with clipping her. Now he thanks the old shepherd, which stands by like a weather-bitten conduit of many kings' reigns. I never heard of such another encounter, which lames report to follow it and undoes description to do it.

2 GENTLEMAN What, pray you, became of Antigonus, that carried hence the child?

3 GENTLEMAN Like an old tale still, which will have matter to rehearse, though credit be asleep and not an ear open: he was torn to pieces with a bear. This avouches the shepherd's son, who has not only his innocence, which seems much, to justify him, but a handkerchief and rings of his that Paulina knows.

1 GENTLEMAN What became of his bark and his followers?

3 GENTLEMAN Wreck'd the same instant of their master's death, and in the view of the shepherd; so that all the instruments which aided to expose the child were even then lost when it was found. But, O, the noble combat that 'twixt joy and sorrow was fought in Paulina! She had one eye declin'd for the loss of her husband, another elevated that the oracle was fulfill'd. She lifted the Princess from the earth, and so locks her in embracing as if she would pin her to her heart, that she might no more be in danger of losing.

1 GENTLEMAN The dignity of this act was worth the audience of kings and princes; for by such was it acted.

3 GENTLEMAN One of the prettiest touches of all, and that which angl'd for mine eyes – caught the water, though not the fish – was, when at the relation of the Queen's death, with the manner how she came to't bravely confess'd and lamented by the King, how attentiveness wounded his daughter; till, from one sign of dolour to another, she did with an 'Alas!' – I would fain say – bleed tears; for I am sure my heart wept blood. Who was most marble there changed colour; some swooned, all sorrowed. If all the world could have seen't, the woe had been universal.

1 GENTLEMAN Are they returned to the court?

3 GENTLEMAN No. The Princess hearing of her mother's statue, which is in the keeping of Paulina – a piece many years in doing and now newly perform'd by that rare Italian master, Julio Romano, who, had he himself eternity and could put breath into his work, would beguile nature of her custom, so perfectly he is her ape. He so near to Hermione hath done Hermione that they say one would speak to her and stand in hope of answer – thither with all greediness of affection are they gone, and there they intend to sup.

2 GENTLEMAN I thought she had some great matter there in hand; for she hath privately twice or thrice a day, ever since the death of Hermione, visited that removed house. Shall we thither, and with our company piece the rejoicing?

I GENTLEMAN Who would be thence that has the benefit of access? Every wink of an eye some new grace will be born. Our absence makes us unthrifty to our knowledge. Let's along.

[*Exeunt Gentlemen.*

AUTOLYCUS Now, had I not the dash of my former life in me, would preferment drop on my head. I brought the old man and his son aboard the Prince; told him I heard them talk of a fardel and I know not what; but he at that time over-fond of the shepherd's daughter – so he then took her to be – who began to be much sea-sick, and himself little better, extremity of weather continuing, this mystery remained undiscover'd. But 'tis all one to me; for had I been the finder-out of this secret, it would not have relish'd among my other discredits.

Enter Shepherd and Clown.

Here come those I have done good to against my will, and already appearing in the blossoms of their fortune.

SHEPHERD Come, boy; I am past moe children, but thy sons and daughters will be all gentlemen born.

CLOWN You are well met, sir. You denied to fight with me this other day, because I was no gentleman born. See you these clothes? Say you see them not and think me still no gentleman born. You were best say these robes are not gentlemen born. Give me the lie, do; and try whether I am not now a gentleman born.

AUTOLYCUS I know you are now, sir, a gentleman born.

CLOWN Ay, and have been so any time these four hours.

SHEPHERD And so have I, boy.

CLOWN So you have; but I was a gentleman born before my father; for the King's son took me by the hand and call'd me brother; and then the two kings call'd my father brother; and then the Prince, my brother, and the Princess, my sister, call'd my father father. And so we wept; and there was the first gentleman-like tears that ever we shed.

SHEPHERD We may live, son, to shed many more.

CLOWN Ay; or else 'twere hard luck, being in so preposterous estate as we are.

AUTOLYCUS I humbly beseech you, sir, to pardon me all the faults I have committed to your worship, and to give me your good report to the Prince my master.

SHEPHERD Prithee, son, do; for we must be gentle, now we are gentlemen.

CLOWN Thou wilt amend thy life?

AUTOLYCUS Ay, an it like your good worship.

CLOWN Give me thy hand. I will swear to the Prince thou art as honest a true fellow as any is in Bohemia.

SHEPHERD You may say it, but not swear it.

CLOWN Not swear it, now I am a gentleman? Let boors and franklins say it: I'll swear it.

SHEPHERD How if it be false, son?

CLOWN If it be ne'er so false, a true gentleman may swear it in the behalf of his friend. And I'll swear to the Prince thou art a tall fellow of thy hands and that thou wilt not be drunk; but I know thou art no tall fellow of thy hands and that thou wilt be drunk. But I'll swear it; and I would thou wouldst be a tall fellow of thy hands.

AUTOLYCUS I will prove so, sir, to my power.

CLOWN Ay, by any means, prove a tall fellow. If I do not wonder how thou dar'st venture to be drunk not being a tall fellow, trust me not. Hark! the kings and the princes, our kindred, are going to see the Queen's picture. Come, follow us; we'll be thy good masters.

[*Exeunt.*

SCENE III. *Sicilia. A chapel in Paulina's house.*

Enter LEONTES, POLIXENES, FLORIZEL, PERDITA, CAMILLO, PAULINA, Lords, and Attendants.

LEONTES O grave and good Paulina, the great comfort
That I have had of thee!
PAULINA What, sovereign sir,
I did not well, I meant well. All my services
You have paid home; but that you have vouchsaf'd
With your crown'd brother and these your contracted
Heirs of your kingdoms, my poor house to visit,
It is a surplus of your grace, which never
My life may last to answer.
LEONTES O Paulina,
We honour you with trouble; but we came
To see the statue of our queen. Your gallery
Have we pass'd through, not without much content
In many singularities; but we saw not
That which my daughter came to look upon,
The statue of her mother.
PAULINA As she liv'd peerless,
So her dead likeness, I do well believe,
Excels whatever yet you look'd upon
Or hand of man hath done; therefore I keep it
Lonely, apart. But here it is. Prepare
To see the life as lively mock'd as ever
Still sleep mock'd death. Behold; and say 'tis well.
[*Pauline draws a curtain, and discovers Hermione standing like a statue.*

I like your silence; it the more shows off
Your wonder; but yet speak. First, you, my liege.
Comes it not something near?

LEONTES Her natural posture!
Chide me, dear stone, that I may say indeed
Thou art Hermione; or rather, thou art she
In thy not chiding; for she was as tender
As infancy and grace. But yet, Paulina,
Hermione was not so much wrinkled, nothing
So aged as this seems.

POLIXENES O, not by much!

PAULINA So much the more our carver's excellence,
Which lets go by some sixteen years and makes her
As she liv'd now.

LEONTES As now she might have done,
So much to my good comfort as it is
Now piercing to my soul. O, thus she stood,
Even with such life of majesty – warm life,
As now it coldly stands – when first I woo'd her!
I am asham'd. Does not the stone rebuke me
For being more stone than it? O royal piece,
There's magic in thy majesty, which has
My evils conjur'd to remembrance, and
From thy admiring daughter took the spirits,
Standing like stone with thee!

PERDITA And give me leave,
And do not say 'tis superstition that
I kneel, and then implore her blessing. Lady,
Dear queen, that ended when I but began,
Give me that hand of yours to kiss.

PAULINA O, patience!
The statue is but newly fix'd, the colour's
Not dry.

CAMILLO My lord, your sorrow was too sore laid on,
Which sixteen winters cannot blow away,
So many summers dry. Scarce any joy
Did ever so long live; no sorrow
But kill'd itself much sooner.

POLIXENES Dear my brother,
Let him that was the cause of this have pow'r
To take off so much grief from you as he
Will piece up in himself.

PAULINA Indeed, my lord,
If I had thought the sight of my poor image
Would thus have wrought you – for the stone is mine –
I'd not have show'd it.

LEONTES Do not draw the curtain.

PAULINA No longer shall you gaze on't, lest your fancy
May think anon it moves.

LEONTES Let be, let be.
Would I were dead, but that methinks already –
What was he that did make it? See, my lord,
Would you not deem it breath'd, and that those veins
Did verily bear blood?

POLIXENES Masterly done!
The very life seems warm upon her lip.

LEONTES The fixure of her eye has motion in't,
As we are mock'd with art.

PAULINA I'll draw the curtain.
My lord's almost so far transported that
He'll think anon it lives.

LEONTES O sweet Paulina,
Make me to think so twenty years together!
No settled senses of the world can match
The pleasure of that madness. Let't alone.

PAULINA I am sorry, sir, I have thus far stirr'd you; but
I could afflict you farther.

LEONTES Do, Paulina;
For this affliction has a taste as sweet
As any cordial comfort. Still, methinks,
There is an air comes from her. What fine chisel
Could ever yet cut breath? Let no man mock me,
For I will kiss her.

PAULINA Good my lord, forbear.
The ruddiness upon her lip is wet;
You'll mar it if you kiss it; stain your own
With oily painting. Shall I draw the curtain?

LEONTES No, not these twenty years.

PERDITA So long could I
Stand by, a looker-on.

PAULINA Either forbear,
Quit presently the chapel, or resolve you
For more amazement. If you can behold it,
I'll make the statue move indeed, descend,
And take you by the hand, but then you'll think –
Which I protest against – I am assisted
By wicked powers.

LEONTES What you can make her do
I am content to look on; what to speak
I am content to hear; for 'tis as easy
To make her speak as move.

PAULINA It is requir'd
You do awake your faith. Then all stand still;
Or those that think it is unlawful business
I am about, let them depart.

LEONTES Proceed.
No foot shall stir.

PAULINA Music, awake her: strike. [*Music.*
'Tis time; descend; be stone no more; approach;
Strike all that look upon with marvel. Come;
I'll fill your grave up. Stir; nay, come away.
Bequeath to death your numbness, for from him
Dear life redeems you. You perceive she stirs.

[*Hermione comes down from the pedestal.*

Start not; her actions shall be holy as
You hear my spell is lawful. Do not shun her
Until you see her die again; for then
You kill her double. Nay, present your hand.
When she was young you woo'd her; now in age
Is she become the suitor?

LEONTES O, she's warm!
If this be magic, let it be an art
Lawful as eating.

POLIXENES She embraces him.

CAMILLO She hangs about his neck.
If she pertain to life, let her speak too.

POLIXENES Ay, and make it manifest where she has liv'd,
Or how stol'n from the dead.

PAULINA That she is living,
Were it but told you, should be hooted at
Like an old tale; but it appears she lives
Though yet she speak not. Mark a little while.
Please you to interpose, fair madam. Kneel,
And pray your mother's blessing. Turn, good lady;
Our Perdita is found.

HERMIONE You gods, look down,
And from your sacred vials pour your graces
Upon my daughter's head! Tell me, mine own,
Where hast thou been preserv'd? Where liv'd? How found
Thy father's court? For thou shalt hear that I,
Knowing by Paulina that the oracle
Gave hope thou wast in being, have preserv'd
Myself to see the issue.

PAULINA There's time enough for that,
Lest they desire upon this push to trouble
Your joys with like relation. Go together,
You precious winners all; your exultation
Partake to every one. I, an old turtle,
Will wing me to some wither'd bough, and there
My mate, that's never to be found again,
Lament till I am lost.

LEONTES O peace, Paulina!
Thou shouldst a husband take by my consent,
As I by thine a wife. This is a match,
And made between's by vows. Thou hast found mine;
But how, is to be question'd; for I saw her,
As I thought, dead; and have, in vain, said many
A prayer upon her grave. I'll not seek far –
For him, I partly know his mind – to find thee
An honourable husband. Come, Camillo,
And take her by the hand whose worth and honesty
Is richly noted, and here justified
By us, a pair of kings. Let's from this place.
What! look upon my brother. Both your pardons,
That e'er I put between your holy looks
My ill suspicion. This your son-in-law,
And son unto the King, whom heavens directing,
Is troth-plight to your daughter. Good Paulina,
Lead us from hence where we may leisurely
Each one demand and answer to his part
Perform'd in this wide gap of time since first
We were dissever'd. Hastily lead away. [*Exeunt.*

King John

Introduction by STUART GILLESPIE

Most commentators suppose *King John* to have been composed at some point between Shakespeare's first and second historical tetralogies, which is to say in the mid 1590s. Though not, on this dating, an especially early work, it does not match most of Shakespeare's other history plays in polish or in clarity of design. Its mixture of tragic and sardonically comic textures, the absence of any clear hero or even winner from the action, and the comparatively inconclusive ending are among the features that puzzle audiences and critics alike. Some have found it an artistic failure while others discern unity through an analysis of themes: a clash between 'honour' and 'commodity', or between candidates for kingship.

King John is perhaps best seen as a capacious vehicle for experiment of various kinds. Its shortcomings, both artistic and purely formal, are certainly legion. Shakespeare fails to explain why in Act 4 Scene 2 the king requires a second coronation, and a motive for his later poisoning is never established. There is inconsistency between John's express instruction to Hubert to kill Arthur [3.3], and Act 4 Scene 1 in which we find Hubert intending, and empowered to carry out, only Arthur's blinding. These problems are attributable to haste, probably during Shakespeare's rapid revision of an earlier play (*The Troublesome Raigne of Iohn*, author unknown, printed 1591). Failings of other kinds involve consistency of characters, management of dialogue (including much hyperbolic pother), and control of tempo. But for all this, the play has been regularly performed, and performances have brought out its most interesting and attractive features.

First there is the Bastard, Falconbridge, whose strong personality clearly interested Shakespeare. The playwright was to remould some aspects of it – Falconbridge's bluff and witty cynicism, for example – into the more expansive form of Sir John Falstaff in *Henry IV*. In *King John* one feels, indeed, that the Bastard's full possibilities are incompletely explored, and his sardonic comedy is circumscribed in Acts 4–5 when he adopts a more serious role. Still, he is the only character in this play to be given prolonged soliloquies, often in the form of asides to the audience; and with the exception of Arthur he is the only character we find to be consistently honest.

Falconbridge is on stage almost exclusively during the public, official business of courts and kings, but other scenes in this play are of a very different type: intimate, private episodes in which individuals have to deal with the consequences of their decisions and those of their rulers. Queen Constance is much more impressive in such scenes, developing into a figure of some pathos. But the most memorable such episode is Hubert's attempt to blind Arthur at a pivotal point in the play, Act 4 Scene 1. The interlude is dramatically very effective, and its intensity, developed out of the contrast between Arthur's 'innocent prate' and Hubert's agonised taciturnity, seems to give renewed impetus to what remains of the play. Arthur's death is the turning-point in King John's fortunes, ushering in the series of disasters which commence with the revolt of his barons and end with his own abrupt demise. In some sense, we are meant to conclude that John's decline is the result of his barbarity (commissioned, if not actually enacted) towards the young prince.

In these last acts, as before, our attention is concentrated less on historical or political events than on the effect these have on individuals: the development of the stories of Salisbury and Pembroke is one example. King John, too, is seen more in the round in these later acts, his vacillation and self-deception over his instructions to Hubert [4.2], and his weakness in compounding with Pandulph, confirming him as a flawed, though hardly, in the context of this play, an especially unpleasant personality. These acts hum with invention, with rapid sequences of scenes of martial action and quiet contemplation, political machinations and deathbeds. Shakespeare is opportunistic in manipulating his material, and the play may still seem to lack a unitary drive or subject; but there is energy aplenty here.

King John

DRAMATIS PERSONAE

KING JOHN
PRINCE HENRY
his son
ARTHUR, DUKE OF BRITAINE
son of Geffrey, late Duke of Britaine, the elder brother of King John
Earl of PEMBROKE
Earl of ESSEX
Earl of SALISBURY
Lord BIGOT
HUBERT DE BURGH
ROBERT FAULCONBRIDGE
son to Sir Robert Faulconbridge
PHILIP THE BASTARD
his half-brother
JAMES GURNEY
servant to Lady Faulconbridge
PETER of Pomfret
a prophet
KING PHILIP OF FRANCE
LEWIS
the Dauphin
LYMOGES
Duke of Austria
CARDINAL PANDULPH
the Pope's legate
MELUN
a French lord
CHATILLON
ambassador from France to King John
QUEEN ELINOR
widow of King Henry II and mother to King John
CONSTANCE
mother to Arthur
BLANCH of Spain
daughter to the King of Castile and niece to King John
LADY FAULCONBRIDGE
widow of Sir Robert Faulconbridge
Lords, Citizens of Angiers, a Sheriff, Heralds, Officers, Soldiers, Executioners, Messengers, and Attendants.

THE SCENE: ENGLAND AND FRANCE.

ACT ONE

SCENE I. *King John's palace.*

Enter KING JOHN, QUEEN ELINOR, PEMBROKE, ESSEX, SALISBURY, and Others, with CHATILLON.

KING JOHN Now, say, Chatillon, what would France with us?
CHATILLON Thus, after greeting, speaks the King of France
In my behaviour to the majesty,
The borrowed majesty, of England here.
ELINOR A strange beginning – 'borrowed majesty'!
KING JOHN Silence, good mother; hear the embassy.
CHATILLON Philip of France, in right and true behalf
Of thy deceased brother Geffrey's son,
Arthur Plantagenet, lays most lawful claim
To this fair island and the territories,
To Ireland, Poictiers, Anjou, Touraine, Maine,
Desiring thee to lay aside the sword
Which sways usurpingly these several titles,
And put the same into young Arthur's hand,
Thy nephew and right royal sovereign.
KING JOHN What follows if we disallow of this?
CHATILLON The proud control of fierce and bloody war,
To enforce these rights so forcibly withheld.
KING JOHN Here have we war for war, and blood for blood,
Controlment for controlment – so answer France.
CHATILLON Then take my king's defiance from my mouth –
The farthest limit of my embassy.
KING JOHN Bear mine to him, and so depart in peace;
Be thou as lightning in the eyes of France;
For ere thou canst report I will be there,
The thunder of my cannon shall be heard.
So hence! Be thou the trumpet of our wrath
And sullen presage of your own decay.
An honourable conduct let him have –
Pembroke, look to't. Farewell, Chatillon.

[Exeunt Chatillon and Pembroke.

ELINOR What now, my son! Have I not ever said
How that ambitious Constance would not cease
Till she had kindled France and all the world
Upon the right and party of her son?

This might have been prevented and made whole
With very easy arguments of love,
Which now the manage of two kingdoms must
With fearful bloody issue arbitrate.

KING JOHN Our strong possession and our right for us!

ELINOR Your strong possession much more than your right,
Or else it must go wrong with you and me;
So much my conscience whispers in your ear,
Which none but heaven and you and I shall hear.

Enter a Sheriff.

ESSEX My liege, here is the strangest controversy
Come from the country to be judg'd by you
That e'er I heard. Shall I produce the men?

KING JOHN Let them approach. *[Exit Sheriff.*
Our abbeys and our priories shall pay
This expedition's charge.

Enter ROBERT FAULCONBRIDGE and PHILIP, his bastard brother.

What men are you?

BASTARD Your faithful subject I, a gentleman
Born in Northamptonshire, and eldest son,
As I suppose, to Robert Faulconbridge –
A soldier by the honour-giving hand
Of Coeur-de-lion knighted in the field.

KING JOHN What art thou?

ROBERT The son and heir to that same Faulconbridge.

KING JOHN Is that the elder, and art thou the heir?
You came not of one mother then, it seems.

BASTARD Most certain of one mother, mighty king –
That is well known – and, as I think, one father;
But for the certain knowledge of that truth
I put you o'er to heaven and to my mother.
Of that I doubt, as all men's children may.

ELINOR Out on thee, rude man! Thou dost shame thy mother,
And wound her honour with this diffidence.

BASTARD I, madam? No, I have no reason for it –
That is my brother's plea, and none of mine;
The which if he can prove, 'a pops me out
At least from fair five hundred pound a year.
Heaven guard my mother's honour and my land!

KING JOHN A good blunt fellow. Why, being younger born,
Doth he lay claim to thine inheritance?

BASTARD I know not why, except to get the land.
But once he slander'd me with bastardy;
But whe'er I be as true begot or no,
That still I lay upon my mother's head;
But that I am as well begot, my liege –
Fair fall the bones that took the pains for me! –
Compare our faces and be judge yourself.
If old Sir Robert did beget us both
And were our father, and this son like him –
O old Sir Robert, father, on my knee
I give heaven thanks I was not like to thee!

KING JOHN Why, what a madcap hath heaven lent us here!

ELINOR He hath a trick of Coeur-de-lion's face;
The accent of his tongue affecteth him.
Do you not read some tokens of my son
In the large composition of this man?

KING JOHN Mine eye hath well examined his parts
And finds them perfect Richard. Sirrah, speak,
What doth move you to claim your brother's land?

BASTARD Because he hath a half-face, like my father.
With half that face would he have all my land:
A half-fac'd groat five hundred pound a year!

ROBERT My gracious liege, when that my father liv'd,
Your brother did employ my father much –

BASTARD Well, sir, by this you cannot get my land:
Your tale must be how he employ'd my mother.

ROBERT And once dispatch'd him in an embassy
To Germany, there with the Emperor
To treat of high affairs touching that time.
Th'advantage of his absence took the King,
And in the meantime sojourn'd at my father's;
Where how he did prevail I shame to speak –
But truth is truth: large lengths of seas and shores
Between my father and my mother lay,
As I have heard my father speak himself,
When this same lusty gentleman was got.
Upon his death-bed he by will bequeath'd
His lands to me, and took it on his death
That this my mother's son was none of his;
And if he were, he came into the world
Full fourteen weeks before the course of time.
Then, good my liege, let me have what is mine,
My father's land, as was my father's will.

KING JOHN Sirrah, your brother is legitimate:
Your father's wife did after wedlock bear him,
And if she did play false, the fault was hers;
Which fault lies on the hazards of all husbands
That marry wives. Tell me, how if my brother,
Who, as you say, took pains to get this son,
Had of your father claim'd this son for his?
In sooth, good friend, your father might have kept

This calf, bred from his cow, from all the world;
In sooth, he might; then, if he were my brother's,
My brother might not claim him; nor your father,
Being none of his, refuse him. This concludes:
My mother's son did get your father's heir;
Your father's heir must have your father's land.
ROBERT Shall then my father's will be of no force
To dispossess that child which is not his?
BASTARD Of no more force to dispossess me, sir,
Than was his will to get me, as I think.
ELINOR Whether hadst thou rather be a Faulconbridge,
And like thy brother, to enjoy thy land,
Or the reputed son of Coeur-de-lion,
Lord of thy presence and no land beside?
BASTARD Madam, an if my brother had my shape
And I had his, Sir Robert's his, like him;
And if my legs were two such riding-rods,
My arms such eel-skins stuff'd, my face so thin
That in mine ear I durst not stick a rose
Lest men should say 'Look where three-farthings goes!'
And, to his shape, were heir to all this land –
Would I might never stir from off this place,
I would give it every foot to have this face!
I would not be Sir Nob in any case.
ELINOR I like thee well. Wilt thou forsake thy fortune,
Bequeath thy land to him and follow me?
I am a soldier and now bound to France.
BASTARD Brother, take you my land, I'll take my chance.
Your face hath got five hundred pound a year,
Yet sell your face for fivepence and 'tis dear.
Madam, I'll follow you unto the death.
ELINOR Nay, I would have you go before me thither.
BASTARD Our country manners give our betters way.
KING JOHN What is thy name?
BASTARD Philip, my liege, so is my name begun:
Philip, good old Sir Robert's wife's eldest son.
KING JOHN From henceforth bear his name whose form thou bearest:
Kneel thou down Philip, but rise more great –
Arise Sir Richard and Plantagenet.
BASTARD Brother by th' mother's side, give me your hand;
My father gave me honour, yours gave land.
Now blessed be the hour, by night or day,
When I was got, Sir Robert was away!
ELINOR The very spirit of Plantagenet!
I am thy grandam, Richard: call me so.
BASTARD Madam, by chance, but not by truth; what though?
Something about, a little from the right,
In at the window, or else o'er the hatch;
Who dares not stir by day must walk by night;
And have is have, however men do catch.
Near or far off, well won is still well shot;
And I am I, howe'er I was begot.
KING JOHN Go, Faulconbridge; now hast thou thy desire:
A landless knight makes thee a landed squire.
Come, madam, and come, Richard, we must speed
For France, for France, for it is more than need.
BASTARD Brother, adieu. Good fortune come to thee!
For thou wast got i' th' way of honesty.
[Exeunt all but the Bastard.
A foot of honour better than I was;
But many a many foot of land the worse.
Well, now can I make any Joan a lady.
'Good den, Sir Richard!' – 'God-a-mercy, fellow!'
And if his name be George, I'll call him Peter;
For new-made honour doth forget men's names:
'Tis too respective and too sociable
For your conversion. Now your traveller,
He and his toothpick at my worship's mess –
And when my knightly stomach is suffic'd,
Why then I suck my teeth and catechize
My picked man of countries: 'My dear sir,'
Thus leaning on mine elbow I begin
'I shall beseech you' – That is question now;
And then comes answer like an Absey book:
'O sir,' says answer 'at your best command,
At your employment, at your service, sir!'
'No, sir,' says question 'I, sweet sir, at yours.'
And so, ere answer knows what question would,
Saving in dialogue of compliment,
And talking of the Alps and Apennines,
The Pyrenean and the river Po –
It draws toward supper in conclusion so.
But this is worshipful society,
And fits the mounting spirit like myself;
For he is but a bastard to the time
That doth not smack of observation –
And so am I, whether I smack or no;
And not alone in habit and device,
Exterior form, outward accoutrement,
But from the inward motion to deliver
Sweet, sweet, sweet poison for the age's tooth;
Which, though I will not practise to deceive,
Yet, to avoid deceit, I mean to learn;
For it shall strew the footsteps of my rising.
But who comes in such haste in riding-robes?
What woman-post is this? Hath she no husband.

That will take pains to blow a horn before her?

Enter LADY FAULCONBRIDGE, and JAMES GURNEY.

O me, 'tis my mother! How now, good lady!
What brings you here to court so hastily?

LADY FAULCONBRIDGE Where is that slave, thy brother? Where is he
That holds in chase mine honour up and down?

BASTARD My brother Robert, old Sir Robert's son?
Colbrand the giant, that same mighty man?
Is it Sir Robert's son that you seek so?

LADY FAULCONBRIDGE Sir Robert's son! Ay, thou unreverend boy,
Sir Robert's son! Why scorn'st thou at Sir Robert?
He is Sir Robert's son, and so art thou.

BASTARD James Gurney, wilt thou give us leave awhile?

GURNEY Good leave, good Philip.

BASTARD Philip – Sparrow! James,
There's toys abroad – anon I'll tell thee more.
[*Exit Gurney.*
Madam, I was not old Sir Robert's son;
Sir Robert might have eat his part in me
Upon Good Friday, and ne'er broke his fast.
Sir Robert could do: well – marry, to confess –
Could he get me? Sir Robert could not do it:
We know his handiwork. Therefore, good mother,
To whom am I beholding for these limbs?
Sir Robert never holp to make this leg.

LADY FAULCONBRIDGE Hast thou conspired with thy brother too,
That for thine own gain shouldst defend mine honour?
What means this scorn, thou most untoward knave?

BASTARD Knight, knight, good mother, Basilisco-like.
What! I am dubb'd; I have it on my shoulder.
But, mother, I am not Sir Robert's son:
I have disclaim'd Sir Robert and my land;
Legitimation, name, and all is gone.
Then, good my mother, let me know my father –
Some proper man, I hope. Who was it, mother?

LADY FAULCONBRIDGE Hast thou denied thyself a Faulconbridge?

BASTARD As faithfully as I deny the devil.

LADY FAULCONBRIDGE King Richard Coeur-de-lion was thy father.
By long and vehement suit I was seduc'd
To make room for him in my husband's bed.
Heaven lay not my transgression to my charge!
Thou art the issue of my dear offence,
Which was so strongly urg'd past my defence.

BASTARD Now, by this light, were I to get again,
Madam, I would not wish a better father.
Some sins do bear their privilege on earth,
And so doth yours: your fault was not your folly;
Needs must you lay your heart at his dispose,
Subjected tribute to commanding love,
Against whose fury and unmatched force
The aweless lion could not wage the fight
Nor keep his princely heart from Richard's hand.
He that perforce robs lions of their hearts
May easily win a woman's. Ay, my mother,
With all my heart I thank thee for my father!
Who lives and dares but say thou didst not well
When I was got, I'll send his soul to hell.
Come, lady, I will show thee to my kin;
And they shall say when Richard me begot,
If thou hadst said him nay, it had been sin.
Who says it was, he lies; I say 'twas not.
[*Exeunt.*

ACT TWO

SCENE I. *France. Before Angiers.*

Enter, on one side, AUSTRIA and Forces; on the other, KING PHILIP OF FRANCE, LEWIS the Dauphin, CONSTANCE, ARTHUR, and Forces.

KING PHILIP Before Angiers well met, brave Austria.
Arthur, that great forerunner of thy blood,
Richard, that robb'd the lion of his heart
And fought the holy wars in Palestine,
By this brave duke came early to his grave;
And for amends to his posterity,
At our importance hither is he come
To spread his colours, boy, in thy behalf;
And to rebuke the usurpation
Of thy unnatural uncle, English John.
Embrace him, love him, give him welcome hither.

ARTHUR God shall forgive you Coeur-de-lion's death
The rather that you give his offspring life,
Shadowing their right under your wings of war.
I give you welcome with a powerless hand,
But with a heart full of unstained love;
Welcome before the gates of Angiers, Duke.

KING PHILIP A noble boy! Who would not do thee right?

AUSTRIA Upon thy cheek lay I this zealous kiss
As seal to this indenture of my love:
That to my home I will no more return
Till Angiers and the right thou hast in France,
Together with that pale, that white-fac'd shore,
Whose foot spurns back the ocean's roaring tides
And coops from other lands her islanders –
Even till that England, hedg'd in with the main,
That water-walled bulwark, still secure
And confident from foreign purposes –
Even till that utmost corner of the west
Salute thee for her king. Till then, fair boy,
Will I not think of home, but follow arms.
CONSTANCE O, take his mother's thanks, a widow's thanks,
Till your strong hand shall help to give him strength
To make a more requital to your love!
AUSTRIA The peace of heaven is theirs that lift their swords
In such a just and charitable war.
KING PHILIP Well then, to work! Our cannon shall be bent
Against the brows of this resisting town;
Call for our chiefest men of discipline,
To cull the plots of best advantages.
We'll lay before this town our royal bones,
Wade to the market-place in Frenchmen's blood,
But we will make it subject to this boy.
CONSTANCE Stay for an answer to your embassy,
Lest unadvis'd you stain your swords with blood;
My Lord Chatillon may from England bring
That right in peace which here we urge in war,
And then we shall repent each drop of blood
That hot rash haste so indirectly shed.

Enter CHATILLON.

KING PHILIP A wonder, lady! Lo, upon thy wish,
Our messenger Chatillon is arriv'd.
What England says, say briefly, gentle lord;
We coldly pause for thee. Chatillon, speak.
CHATILLON Then turn your forces from this paltry siege
And stir them up against a mightier task.
England, impatient of your just demands,
Hath put himself in arms. The adverse winds,
Whose leisure I have stay'd, have given him time
To land his legions all as soon as I;
His marches are expedient to this town,
His forces strong, his soldiers confident.
With him along is come the mother-queen,
An Ate, stirring him to blood and strife;
With her her niece, the Lady Blanch of Spain;
With them a bastard of the king's deceas'd;
And all th' unsettled humours of the land –
Rash, inconsiderate, fiery voluntaries,
With ladies' faces and fierce dragons' spleens –
Have sold their fortunes at their native homes,
Bearing their birthrights proudly on their backs,
To make a hazard of new fortunes here.
In brief, a braver choice of dauntless spirits
Than now the English bottoms have waft o'er
Did never float upon the swelling tide
To do offence and scathe in Christendom.
[*Drum beats.*
The interruption of their churlish drums
Cuts off more circumstance: they are at hand;
To parley or to fight, therefore prepare.
KING PHILIP How much unlook'd for is this expedition!
AUSTRIA By how much unexpected, by so much
We must awake endeavour for defence,
For courage mounteth with occasion.
Let them be welcome then; we are prepar'd.

Enter KING JOHN, ELINOR, BLANCH, the BASTARD, PEMBROKE, and Others.

KING JOHN Peace be to France, if France in peace permit
Our just and lineal entrance to our own!
If not, bleed France, and peace ascend to heaven,
Whiles we, God's wrathful agent, do correct
Their proud contempt that beats His peace to heaven!
KING PHILIP Peace be to England, if that war return
From France to England, there to live in peace!
England we love, and for that England's sake
With burden of our armour here we sweat.
This toil of ours should be a work of thine;
But thou from loving England art so far
That thou hast under-wrought his lawful king,
Cut off the sequence of posterity,
Outfaced infant state, and done a rape
Upon the maiden virtue of the crown.
Look here upon thy brother Geffrey's face:
These eyes, these brows, were moulded out of his;
This little abstract doth contain that large
Which died in Geffrey, and the hand of time
Shall draw this brief into as huge a volume.
That Geffrey was thy elder brother born,
And this his son; England was Geffrey's right,
And this is Geffrey's. In the name of God,
How comes it then that thou art call'd a king,
When living blood doth in these temples beat
Which owe the crown that thou o'er-masterest?
KING JOHN From whom hast thou this great commission, France,

To draw my answer from thy articles?
KING PHILIP From that supernal judge that stirs good thoughts
In any breast of strong authority
To look into the blots and stains of right.
That judge hath made me guardian to this boy,
Under whose warrant I impeach thy wrong,
And by whose help I mean to chastise it.
KING JOHN Alack, thou dost usurp authority.
KING PHILIP Excuse it is to beat usurping down.
ELINOR Who is it thou dost call usurper, France?
CONSTANCE Let me make answer: thy usurping son.
ELINOR Out, insolent! Thy bastard shall be king,
That thou mayst be a queen and check the world!
CONSTANCE My bed was ever to thy son as true
As thine was to thy husband; and this boy
Liker in feature to his father Geffrey
Than thou and John in manners – being as like
As rain to water, or devil to his dam.
My boy a bastard! By my soul, I think
His father never was so true begot;
It cannot be, an if thou wert his mother.
ELINOR There's a good mother, boy, that blots thy father.
CONSTANCE There's a good grandam, boy, that would blot thee.
AUSTRIA Peace!
BASTARD Hear the crier.
AUSTRIA What the devil art thou?
BASTARD One that will play the devil, sir, with you
An 'a may catch your hide and you alone.
You are the hare of whom the proverb goes,
Whose valour plucks dead lions by the beard;
I'll smoke your skin-coat an I catch you right;
Sirrah, look to 't; i' faith I will, i' faith.
BLANCH O, well did he become that lion's robe
That did disrobe the lion of that robe!
BASTARD It lies as sightly on the back of him
As great Alcides' shows upon an ass;
But, ass, I'll take that burden from your back,
Or lay on that shall make your shoulders crack.
AUSTRIA What cracker is this same that deafs our ears
With this abundance of superfluous breath?
King Philip, determine what we shall do straight.
KING PHILIP Women and fools, break off your conference.
King John, this is the very sum of all:
England and Ireland, Anjou, Touraine, Maine,
In right of Arthur, do I claim of thee;
Wilt thou resign them and lay down thy arms?
KING JOHN My life as soon. I do defy thee, France.
Arthur of Britaine, yield thee to my hand,
And out of my dear love I'll give thee more
Than e'er the coward hand of France can win.
Submit thee, boy.
ELINOR Come to thy grandam, child.
CONSTANCE Do, child, go to it grandam, child;
Give grandam kingdom, and it grandam will
Give it a plum, a cherry, and a fig.
There's a good grandam!
ARTHUR Good my mother, peace!
I would that I were low laid in my grave:
I am not worth this coil that's made for me.
ELINOR His mother shames him so, poor boy, he weeps.
CONSTANCE Now shame upon you, whe'er she does or no!
His grandam's wrongs, and not his mother's shames,
Draws those heaven-moving pearls from his poor eyes,
Which heaven shall take in nature of a fee;
Ay, with these crystal beads heaven shall be brib'd
To do him justice and revenge on you.
ELINOR Thou monstrous slanderer of heaven and earth!
CONSTANCE Thou monstrous injurer of heaven and earth,
Call not me slanderer! Thou and thine usurp
The dominations, royalties, and rights,
Of this oppressed boy; this is thy eldest son's son,
Infortunate in nothing but in thee.
Thy sins are visited in this poor child;
The canon of the law is laid on him,
Being but the second generation
Removed from thy sin-conceiving womb.
KING JOHN Bedlam, have done.
CONSTANCE I have but this to say –
That he is not only plagued for her sin,
But God hath made her sin and her the plague
On this removed issue, plagued for her
And with her plague; her sin his injury,
Her injury the beadle to her sin;
All punish'd in the person of this child,
And all for her – a plague upon her!
ELINOR Thou unadvised scold, I can produce
A will that bars the title of thy son.
CONSTANCE Ay, who doubts that? A will, a wicked will;
A woman's will; a cank'red grandam's will!
KING PHILIP Peace, lady! pause, or be more temperate.
It ill beseems this presence to cry aim
To these ill-tuned repetitions.
Some trumpet summon hither to the walls
These men of Angiers; let us hear them speak

Whose title they admit, Arthur's or John's.

Trumpet sounds. Enter Citizens upon the walls.

CITIZENS Who is it that hath warn'd us to the walls?

KING PHILIP 'Tis France, for England.

KING JOHN England for itself.
You men of Angiers, and my loving subjects –

KING PHILIP You loving men of Angiers, Arthur's subjects,
Our trumpet call'd you to this gentle parle –

KING JOHN For our advantage; therefore hear us first.
These flags of France, that are advanced here
Before the eye and prospect of your town,
Have hither march'd to your endamagement;
The cannons have their bowels full of wrath,
And ready mounted are they to spit forth
Their iron indignation 'gainst your walls;
All preparation for a bloody siege
And merciless proceeding by these French
Confront your city's eyes, your winking gates;
And but for our approach those sleeping stones
That as a waist doth girdle you about
By the compulsion of their ordinance
By this time from their fixed beds of lime
Had been dishabited, and wide havoc made
For bloody power to rush upon your peace.
But on the sight of us your lawful king,
Who painfully with much expedient march
Have brought a countercheck before your gates,
To save unscratch'd your city's threat'ned cheeks –
Behold, the French amaz'd vouchsafe a parle;
And now, instead of bullets wrapp'd in fire,
To make a shaking fever in your walls,
They shoot but calm words folded up in smoke,
To make a faithless error in your ears;
Which trust accordingly, kind citizens,
And let us in – your King, whose labour'd spirits,
Forwearied in this action of swift speed,
Craves harbourage within your city walls.

KING PHILIP When I have said, make answer to us both.
Lo, in this right hand, whose protection
Is most divinely vow'd upon the right
Of him it holds, stands young Plantagenet,
Son to the elder brother of this man,
And king o'er him and all that he enjoys;
For this down-trodden equity we tread
In warlike march these greens before your town,
Being no further enemy to you
Than the constraint of hospitable zeal
In the relief of this oppressed child
Religiously provokes. Be pleased then
To pay that duty which you truly owe
To him that owes it, namely, this young prince;
And then our arms, like to a muzzled bear,
Save in aspect, hath all offence seal'd up;
Our cannons' malice vainly shall be spent
Against th' invulnerable clouds of heaven;
And with a blessed and unvex'd retire,
With unhack'd swords and helmets all unbruis'd,
We will bear home that lusty blood again
Which here we came to spout against your town,
And leave your children, wives, and you, in peace.
But if you fondly pass our proffer'd offer,
'Tis not the roundure of your old-fac'd walls
Can hide you from our messengers of war,
Though all these English and their discipline
Were harbour'd in their rude circumference.
Then tell us, shall your city call us lord
In that behalf which we have challeng'd it;
Or shall we give the signal to our rage,
And stalk in blood to our possession?

CITIZENS In brief: we are the King of England's subjects;
For him, and in his right, we hold this town.

KING JOHN Acknowledge then the King, and let me in.

CITIZENS That can we not; but he that proves the King,
To him will we prove loyal. Till that time
Have we ramm'd up our gates against the world.

KING JOHN Doth not the crown of England prove the King?
And if not that, I bring you witnesses:
Twice fifteen thousand hearts of England's breed –

BASTARD Bastards and else.

KING JOHN To verify our title with their lives.

KING PHILIP As many and as well-born bloods as those –

BASTARD Some bastards too.

KING PHILIP Stand in his face to contradict his claim.

CITIZENS Till you compound whose right is worthiest,
We for the worthiest hold the right from both.

KING JOHN Then God forgive the sin of all those souls
That to their everlasting residence,
Before the dew of evening fall, shall fleet
In dreadful trial of our kingdom's king!

KING PHILIP Amen, Amen! Mount, chevaliers; to arms!

BASTARD Saint George, that swing'd the dragon, and e'er since
Sits on's horse back at mine hostess' door,

Teach us some fence! [*To Austria*] Sirrah, were I at home,
At your den, sirrah, with your lioness,
I would set an ox-head to your lion's hide,
And make a monster of you.

AUSTRIA Peace! no more.

BASTARD O, tremble, for you hear the lion roar!

KING JOHN Up higher to the plain, where we'll set forth
In best appointment all our regiments.

BASTARD Speed then to take advantage of the field.

KING PHILIP It shall be so; and at the other hill
Command the rest to stand. God and our right!

[*Exeunt.*

Here, after excursions, enter the Herald of France, with trumpets, to the gates.

FRENCH HERALD You men of Angiers, open wide your gates
And let young Arthur, Duke of Britaine, in,
Who by the hand of France this day hath made
Much work for tears in many an English mother,
Whose sons lie scattered on the bleeding ground;
Many a widow's husband grovelling lies,
Coldly embracing the discoloured earth;
And victory with little loss doth play
Upon the dancing banners of the French,
Who are at hand, triumphantly displayed,
To enter conquerors, and to proclaim
Arthur of Britaine England's King and yours.

Enter English Herald, with trumpet.

ENGLISH HERALD Rejoice, you men of Angiers, ring your bells:
King John, your king and England's, doth approach,
Commander of this hot malicious day.
Their armours that march'd hence so silver bright
Hither return all gilt with Frenchmen's blood.
There stuck no plume in any English crest
That is removed by a staff of France;
Our colours do return in those same hands
That did display them when we first march'd forth;
And like a jolly troop of huntsmen come
Our lusty English, all with purpled hands,
Dy'd in the dying slaughter of their foes.
Open your gates and give the victors way.

CITIZENS Heralds, from off our tow'rs we might behold
From first to last the onset and retire
Of both your armies, whose equality
By our best eyes cannot be censured.
Blood hath bought blood, and blows have answer'd blows;
Strength match'd with strength, and power confronted power;
Both are alike, and both alike we like.
One must prove greatest. While they weigh so even,
We hold our town for neither, yet for both.

Enter the two KINGS, with their Powers, at several doors.

KING JOHN France, hast thou yet more blood to cast away?
Say, shall the current of our right run on?
Whose passage, vex'd with thy impediment,
Shall leave his native channel and o'erswell
With course disturb'd even thy confining shores,
Unless thou let his silver water keep
A peaceful progress to the ocean.

KING PHILIP England, thou hast not sav'd one drop of blood
In this hot trial more than we of France;
Rather, lost more. And by this hand I swear,
That sways the earth this climate overlooks,
Before we will lay down our just-borne arms,
We'll put thee down, 'gainst whom these arms we bear,
Or add a royal number to the dead,
Gracing the scroll that tells of this war's loss
With slaughter coupled to the name of kings.

BASTARD Ha, Majesty! how high thy glory tow'rs
When the rich blood of kings is set on fire!
O, now doth Death line his dead chaps with steel;
The swords of soldiers are his teeth, his fangs;
And now he feasts, mousing the flesh of men,
In undetermin'd differences of kings.
Why stand these royal fronts amazed thus?
Cry 'havoc!' kings; back to the stained field,
You equal potents, fiery kindled spirits!
Then let confusion of one part confirm
The other's peace. Till then, blows, blood, and death!

KING JOHN Whose party do the townsmen yet admit?

KING PHILIP Speak, citizens, for England; who's your king?

CITIZENS The King of England, when we know the King.

KING PHILIP Know him in us that here hold up his right.

KING JOHN In us that are our own great deputy
And bear possession of our person here,
Lord of our presence, Angiers, and of you.

CITIZENS A greater pow'r than we denies all this;
And till it be undoubted, we do lock
Our former scruple in our strong-barr'd gates;

King'd of our fears, until our fears, resolv'd,
Be by some certain king purg'd and depos'd.

BASTARD By heaven, these scroyles of Angiers flout you, kings,
And stand securely on their battlements
As in a theatre, whence they gape and point
At your industrious scenes and acts of death.
Your royal presences be rul'd by me:
Do like the mutines of Jerusalem,
Be friends awhile, and both conjointly bend
Your sharpest deeds of malice on this town.
By east and west let France and England mount
Their battering cannon, charged to the mouths,
Till their soul-fearing clamours have brawl'd down
The flinty ribs of this contemptuous city.
I'd play incessantly upon these jades,
Even till unfenced desolation
Leave them as naked as the vulgar air.
That done, dissever your united strengths
And part your mingled colours once again,
Turn face to face and bloody point to point;
Then in a moment Fortune shall cull forth
Out of one side her happy minion,
To whom in favour she shall give the day,
And kiss him with a glorious victory.
How like you this wild counsel, mighty states?
Smacks it not something of the policy?

KING JOHN Now, by the sky that hangs above our heads,
I like it well. France, shall we knit our pow'rs
And lay this Angiers even with the ground;
Then after fight who shall be king of it?

BASTARD An if thou hast the mettle of a king,
Being wrong'd as we are by this peevish town,
Turn thou the mouth of thy artillery,
As we will ours, against these saucy walls;
And when that we have dash'd them to the ground,
Why then defy each other, and pell-mell
Make work upon ourselves, for heaven or hell.

KING PHILIP Let it be so. Say, where will you assault?

KING JOHN We from the west will send destruction
Into this city's bosom.

AUSTRIA I from the north.

KING PHILIP Our thunder from the south
Shall rain their drift of bullets on this town.

BASTARD [*Aside*] O prudent discipline! From north to south,
Austria and France shoot in each other's mouth.
I'll stir them to it. – Come, away, away!

CITIZENS Hear us, great kings: vouchsafe awhile to stay,
And I shall show you peace and fair-fac'd league;
Win you this city without stroke or wound;
Rescue those breathing lives to die in beds
That here come sacrifices for the field.
Persever not, but hear me, mighty kings.

KING JOHN Speak on with favour; we are bent to hear.

CITIZENS That daughter there of Spain, the Lady Blanch,
Is niece to England; look upon the years
Of Lewis the Dauphin and that lovely maid.
If lusty love should go in quest of beauty,
Where should he find it fairer than in Blanch?
If zealous love should go in search of virtue,
Where should he find it purer than in Blanch?
If love ambitious sought a match of birth,
Whose veins bound richer blood than Lady Blanch?
Such as she is, in beauty, virtue, birth,
Is the young Dauphin every way complete –
If not complete of, say he is not she;
And she again wants nothing, to name want,
If want it be not that she is not he.
He is the half part of a blessed man,
Left to be finished by such as she;
And she a fair divided excellence,
Whose fulness of perfection lies in him.
O, two such silver currents, when they join,
Do glorify the banks that bound them in;
And two such shores to two such streams made one,
Two such controlling bounds, shall you be, Kings,
To these two princes, if you marry them.
This union shall do more than battery can
To our fast-closed gates; for at this match
With swifter spleen than powder can enforce,
The mouth of passage shall we fling wide ope
And give you entrance; but without this match,
The sea enraged is not half so deaf,
Lions more confident, mountains and rocks
More free from motion – no, not Death himself
In mortal fury half so peremptory
As we to keep this city.

BASTARD Here's a stay
That shakes the rotten carcass of old Death
Out of his rags! Here's a large mouth, indeed,
That spits forth death and mountains, rocks and seas;
Talks as familiarly of roaring lions
As maids of thirteen do of puppy-dogs!
What cannoneer begot this lusty blood?
He speaks plain cannon-fire, and smoke and bounce;
He gives the bastinado with his tongue;
Our ears are cudgell'd; not a word of his
But buffets better than a fist of France.
Zounds! I was never so bethump'd with words

Since I first call'd my brother's father dad.
ELINOR Son, list to this conjunction, make this match;
Give with our niece a dowry large enough;
For by this knot thou shalt so surely tie
Thy now unsur'd assurance to the crown
That yon green boy shall have no sun to ripe
The bloom that promiseth a mighty fruit.
I see a yielding in the looks of France;
Mark how they whisper. Urge them while their souls
Are capable of this ambition,
Lest zeal, now melted by the windy breath
Of soft petitions, pity, and remorse,
Cool and congeal again to what it was.
CITIZENS Why answer not the double majesties
This friendly treaty of our threat'ned town?
KING PHILIP Speak England first, that hath been forward first
To speak unto this city: what say you?
KING JOHN If that the Dauphin there, thy princely son,
Can in this book of beauty read 'I love',
Her dowry shall weigh equal with a queen;
For Anjou, and fair Touraine, Maine, Poictiers,
And all that we upon this side the sea –
Except this city now by us besieg'd –
Find liable to our crown and dignity,
Shall gild her bridal bed, and make her rich
In titles, honours, and promotions,
As she in beauty, education, blood,
Holds hand with any princess of the world.
KING PHILIP What say'st thou, boy? Look in the lady's face.
LEWIS I do, my lord, and in her eye I find
A wonder, or a wondrous miracle,
The shadow of myself form'd in her eye;
Which, being but the shadow of your son,
Becomes a sun, and makes your son a shadow.
I do protest I never lov'd myself
Till now infixed I beheld myself
Drawn in the flattering table of her eye.
[Whispers with Blanch.
BASTARD *[Aside]* Drawn in the flattering table of her eye,
Hang'd in the frowning wrinkle of her brow,
And quarter'd in her heart – he doth espy
Himself love's traitor. This is pity now,
That hang'd and drawn and quarter'd there should be
In such a love so vile a lout as he.
BLANCH My uncle's will in this respect is mine.
If he see aught in you that makes him like,
That any thing he sees which moves his liking
I can with ease translate it to my will;
Or if you will, to speak more properly,
I will enforce it eas'ly to my love.
Further I will not flatter you, my lord,
That all I see in you is worthy love,
Than this: that nothing do I see in you –
Though churlish thoughts themselves should be your judge –
That I can find should merit any hate.
KING JOHN What say these young ones? What say you, my niece?
BLANCH That she is bound in honour still to do
What you in wisdom still vouchsafe to say.
KING JOHN Speak then, Prince Dauphin; can you love this lady?
LEWIS Nay, ask me if I can refrain from love;
For I do love her most unfeignedly.
KING JOHN Then do I give Volquessen, Touraine, Maine,
Poictiers, and Anjou, these five provinces,
With her to thee; and this addition more,
Full thirty thousand marks of English coin.
Philip of France, if thou be pleas'd withal,
Command thy son and daughter to join hands.
KING PHILIP It likes us well; young princes, close your hands.
AUSTRIA And your lips too; for I am well assur'd
That I did so when I was first assur'd.
KING PHILIP Now, citizens of Angiers, ope your gates,
Let in that amity which you have made;
For at Saint Mary's chapel presently
The rites of marriage shall be solemniz'd.
Is not the Lady Constance in this troop?
I know she is not; for this match made up
Her presence would have interrupted much.
Where is she and her son? Tell me, who knows.
LEWIS She is sad and passionate at your Highness' tent.
KING PHILIP And, by my faith, this league that we have made
Will give her sadness very little cure.
Brother of England, how may we content
This widow lady? In her right we came;
Which we, God knows, have turn'd another way,
To our own vantage.
KING JOHN We will heal up all,
For we'll create young Arthur Duke of Britaine,
And Earl of Richmond; and this rich fair town
We make him lord of. Call the Lady Constance;
Some speedy messenger bid her repair
To our solemnity. I trust we shall,
If not fill up the measure of her will,
Yet in some measure satisfy her so
That we shall stop her exclamation.
Go we as well as haste will suffer us
To this unlook'd-for, unprepared pomp.

[*Exeunt all but the Bastard.*

BASTARD Mad world! mad kings! mad composition!
John, to stop Arthur's title in the whole,
Hath willingly departed with a part;
And France, whose armour conscience buckled on,
Whom zeal and charity brought to the field
As God's own soldier, rounded in the ear
With that same purpose-changer, that sly devil
That broker that still breaks the pate of faith,
That daily break-vow, he that wins of all,
Of kings, of beggars, old men, young men, maids,
Who having no external thing to lose
But the word 'maid', cheats the poor maid of that;
That smooth-fac'd gentleman, tickling commodity,
Commodity, the bias of the world –
The world, who of itself is peised well,
Made to run even upon even ground,
Till this advantage, this vile-drawing bias,
This sway of motion, this commodity,
Makes it take head from all indifferency,
From all direction, purpose, course, intent –
And this same bias, this commodity,
This bawd, this broker, this all-changing word,
Clapp'd on the outward eye of fickle France,
Hath drawn him from his own determin'd aid,
From a resolv'd and honourable war,
To a most base and vile-concluded peace.
And why rail I on this commodity?
But for because he hath not woo'd me yet;
Not that I have the power to clutch my hand
When his fair angels would salute my palm,
But for my hand, as unattempted yet,
Like a poor beggar raileth on the rich.
Well, whiles I am a beggar, I will rail
And say there is no sin but to be rich;
And being rich, my virtue then shall be
To say there is no vice but beggary.
Since kings break faith upon commodity,
Gain, be my lord, for I will worship thee. [*Exit.*

ACT THREE

SCENE I. *France. The French King's camp.*

Enter CONSTANCE, ARTHUR, and SALISBURY.

CONSTANCE Gone to be married! Gone to swear a peace!
False blood to false blood join'd! Gone to be friends!
Shall Lewis have Blanch, and Blanch those provinces?
It is not so; thou hast misspoke, misheard;
Be well advis'd, tell o'er thy tale again.
It cannot be; thou dost but say 'tis so;
I trust I may not trust thee, for thy word
Is but the vain breath of a common man:
Believe me I do not believe thee, man;
I have a king's oath to the contrary.
Thou shalt be punish'd for thus frighting me,
For I am sick and capable of fears,
Oppress'd with wrongs, and therefore full of fears;
A widow, husbandless, subject to fears;
A woman, naturally born to fears;
And though thou now confess thou didst but jest,
With my vex'd spirits I cannot take a truce,
But they will quake and tremble all this day.
What dost thou mean by shaking of thy head?
Why dost thou look so sadly on my son?
What means that hand upon that breast of thine?
Why holds thine eye that lamentable rheum,
Like a proud river peering o'er his bounds?
Be these sad signs confirmers of thy words?
Then speak again – not all thy former tale,
But this one word, whether thy tale be true.

SALISBURY As true as I believe you think them false
That give you cause to prove my saying true.

CONSTANCE O, if thou teach me to believe this sorrow,
Teach thou this sorrow how to make me die;
And let belief and life encounter so
As doth the fury of two desperate men
Which in the very meeting fall and die!
Lewis marry Blanch! O boy, then where art thou?
France friend with England; what becomes of me?
Fellow, be gone: I cannot brook thy sight;
This news hath made thee a most ugly man.

SALISBURY What other harm have I, good lady, done
But spoke the harm that is by others done?

CONSTANCE Which harm within itself so heinous is
As it makes harmful all that speak of it.

ARTHUR I do beseech you, madam, be content.

CONSTANCE If thou that bid'st me be content wert grim,
Ugly, and sland'rous to thy mother's womb,
Full of unpleasing blots and sightless stains,

Lame, foolish, crooked, swart, prodigious,
Patch'd with foul moles and eye-offending marks,
I would not care, I then would be content;
For then I should not love thee; no, nor thou
Become thy great birth, nor deserve a crown.
But thou art fair, and at thy birth, dear boy,
Nature and Fortune join'd to make thee great:
Of Nature's gifts thou mayst with lilies boast,
And with the half-blown rose; but Fortune, O!
She is corrupted, chang'd, and won from thee;
Sh' adulterates hourly with thine uncle John,
And with her golden hand hath pluck'd on France
To tread down fair respect of sovereignty,
And made his majesty the bawd to theirs.
France is a bawd to Fortune and King John –
That strumpet Fortune, that usurping John!
Tell me, thou fellow, is not France forsworn?
Envenom him with words, or get thee gone
And leave those woes alone which I alone
Am bound to under-bear.

SALISBURY Pardon me, madam,
I may not go without you to the kings.

CONSTANCE Thou mayst, thou shalt; I will not go with thee;
I will instruct my sorrows to be proud,
For grief is proud, and makes his owner stoop.
To me, and to the state of my great grief,
Let kings assemble; for my grief's so great
That no supporter but the huge firm earth
Can hold it up. [*Seats herself on the ground.*
Here I and sorrows sit;
Here is my throne, bid kings come bow to it.

Enter KING JOHN, KING PHILIP, LEWIS, BLANCH, ELINOR, the BASTARD, AUSTRIA, and Attendants.

KING PHILIP 'Tis true, fair daughter, and this blessed day
Ever in France shall be kept festival.
To solemnize this day the glorious sun
Stays in his course and plays the alchemist,
Turning with splendour of his precious eye
The meagre cloddy earth to glittering gold.
The yearly course that brings this day about
Shall never see it but a holiday.

CONSTANCE [*Rising*] A wicked day, and not a holy day!
What hath this day deserv'd? what hath it done
That it in golden letters should be set
Among the high tides in the calendar?
Nay, rather turn this day out of the week,
This day of shame, oppression, perjury;
Or, if it must stand still, let wives with child
Pray that their burdens may not fall this day,
Lest that their hopes prodigiously be cross'd;
But on this day let seamen fear no wreck;
No bargains break that are not this day made;
This day, all things begun come to ill end,
Yea, faith itself to hollow falsehood change!

KING PHILIP By heaven, lady, you shall have no cause
To curse the fair proceedings of this day.
Have I not pawn'd to you my majesty?

CONSTANCE You have beguil'd me with a counterfeit
Resembling majesty, which, being touch'd and tried,
Proves valueless; you are forsworn, forsworn;
You came in arms to spill mine enemies' blood,
But now in arms you strengthen it with yours.
The grappling vigour and rough frown of war
Is cold in amity and painted peace,
And our oppression hath made up this league.
Arm, arm, you heavens, against these perjur'd kings!
A widow cries: Be husband to me, heavens!
Let not the hours of this ungodly day
Wear out the day in peace; but, ere sunset,
Set armed discord 'twixt these perjur'd kings!
Hear me, O, hear me!

AUSTRIA Lady Constance, peace!

CONSTANCE War! war! no peace! Peace is to me a war.
O Lymoges! O Austria! thou dost shame
That bloody spoil. Thou slave, thou wretch, thou coward!
Thou little valiant, great in villainy!
Thou ever strong upon the stronger side!
Thou Fortune's champion that dost never fight
But when her humorous ladyship is by
To teach thee safety! Thou art perjur'd too,
And sooth'st up greatness. What a fool art thou,
A ramping fool, to brag and stamp and swear
Upon my party! Thou cold-blooded slave,
Hast thou not spoke like thunder on my side,
Been sworn my soldier, bidding me depend
Upon thy stars, thy fortune, and thy strength,
And dost thou now fall over to my foes?
Thou wear a lion's hide! Doff it for shame,
And hang a calf's-skin on those recreant limbs.

AUSTRIA O that a man should speak those words to me!

BASTARD And hang a calf's-skin on those recreant limbs.

AUSTRIA Thou dar'st not say so, villain, for thy life.

BASTARD And hang a calf's-skin on those recreant limbs.

KING JOHN We like not this: thou dost forget thyself.

Enter PANDULPH.

KING PHILIP Here comes the holy legate of the Pope.

PANDULPH Hail, you anointed deputies of heaven!
To thee, King John, my holy errand is.
I Pandulph, of fair Milan cardinal,
And from Pope Innocent the legate here,
Do in his name religiously demand
Why thou against the church, our holy mother,
So wilfully dost spurn; and force perforce
Keep Stephen Langton, chosen Archbishop
Of Canterbury, from that holy see?
This, in our foresaid holy father's name,
Pope Innocent, I do demand of thee.

KING JOHN What earthly name to interrogatories
Can task the free breath of a sacred king?
Thou canst not, Cardinal, devise a name
So slight, unworthy, and ridiculous,
To charge me to an answer, as the Pope.
Tell him this tale, and from the mouth of England
Add thus much more, that no Italian priest
Shall tithe or toll in our dominions;
But as we under heaven are supreme head,
So, under Him that great supremacy,
Where we do reign we will alone uphold,
Without th' assistance of a mortal hand.
So tell the Pope, all reverence set apart
To him and his usurp'd authority.

KING PHILIP Brother of England, you blaspheme in this.

KING JOHN Though you and all the kings of Christendom
Are led so grossly by this meddling priest,
Dreading the curse that money may buy out,
And by the merit of vile gold, dross, dust,
Purchase corrupted pardon of a man,
Who in that sale sells pardon from himself –
Though you and all the rest, so grossly led,
This juggling witchcraft with revenue cherish;
Yet I alone, alone do me oppose
Against the Pope, and count his friends my foes.

PANDULPH Then by the lawful power that I have
Thou shalt stand curs'd and excommunicate;
And blessed shall he be that doth revolt
From his allegiance to an heretic;
And meritorious shall that hand be call'd,
Canonized, and worshipp'd as a saint,
That takes away by any secret course
Thy hateful life.

CONSTANCE O, lawful let it be
That I have room with Rome to curse awhile!
Good father Cardinal, cry thou 'amen'
To my keen curses; for without my wrong
There is no tongue hath power to curse him right.

PANDULPH There's law and warrant, lady, for my curse.

CONSTANCE And for mine too: when law can do no right,
Let it be lawful that law bar no wrong;
Law cannot give my child his kingdom here,
For he that holds his kingdom holds the law;
Therefore, since law itself is perfect wrong,
How can the law forbid my tongue to curse?

PANDULPH Philip of France, on peril of a curse,
Let go the hand of that arch-heretic,
And raise the power of France upon his head,
Unless he do submit himself to Rome.

ELINOR Look'st thou pale, France? Do not let go thy hand.

CONSTANCE Look to that, devil, lest that France repent
And by disjoining hands hell lose a soul.

AUSTRIA King Philip, listen to the Cardinal.

BASTARD And hang a calf's-skin on his recreant limbs.

AUSTRIA Well, ruffian, I must pocket up these wrongs,
Because –

BASTARD Your breeches best may carry them.

KING JOHN Philip, what say'st thou to the Cardinal?

CONSTANCE What should he say, but as the Cardinal?

LEWIS Bethink you, father; for the difference
Is purchase of a heavy curse from Rome
Or the light loss of England for a friend.
Forgo the easier.

BLANCH That's the curse of Rome.

CONSTANCE O Lewis, stand fast! The devil tempts thee here
In likeness of a new untrimmed bride.

BLANCH The Lady Constance speaks not from her faith,
But from her need.

CONSTANCE O, if thou grant my need,
Which only lives but by the death of faith,
That need must needs infer this principle –
That faith would live again by death of need.
O then, tread down my need, and faith mounts up:
Keep my need up, and faith is trodden down!

KING JOHN The King is mov'd, and answers not to this.

CONSTANCE O, be remov'd from him, and answer well!

AUSTRIA Do so, King Philip; hang no more in doubt.

BASTARD Hang nothing but a calf's-skin, most sweet lout.

KING PHILIP I am perplex'd and know not what to say.

PANDULPH What canst thou say but will perplex thee more,

If thou stand excommunicate and curs'd?
KING PHILIP Good reverend father, make my person yours,
And tell me how you would bestow yourself.
This royal hand and mine are newly knit,
And the conjunction of our inward souls
Married in league, coupled and link'd together
With all religious strength of sacred vows;
The latest breath that gave the sound of words
Was deep-sworn faith, peace, amity, true love,
Between our kingdoms and our royal selves;
And even before this truce, but new before,
No longer than we well could wash our hands,
To clap this royal bargain up of peace,
Heaven knows, they were besmear'd and overstain'd
With slaughter's pencil, where revenge did paint
The fearful difference of incensed kings.
And shall these hands, so lately purg'd of blood,
So newly join'd in love, so strong in both,
Unyoke this seizure and this kind regreet?
Play fast and loose with faith? so jest with heaven,
Make such unconstant children of ourselves,
As now again to snatch our palm from palm,
Unswear faith sworn, and on the marriage-bed
Of smiling peace to march a bloody host,
And make a riot on the gentle brow
Of true sincerity? O, holy sir,
My reverend father, let it not be so!
Out of your grace, devise, ordain, impose,
Some gentle order; and then we shall be blest
To do your pleasure, and continue friends.
PANDULPH All form is formless, order orderless,
Save what is opposite to England's love.
Therefore, to arms! be champion of our church,
Or let the church, our mother, breathe her curse –
A mother's curse – on her revolting son.
France, thou mayst hold a serpent by the tongue,
A chafed lion by the mortal paw,
A fasting tiger safer by the tooth,
Than keep in peace that hand which thou dost hold.
KING PHILIP I may disjoin my hand, but not my faith.
PANDULPH So mak'st thou faith an enemy to faith;
And like a civil war set'st oath to oath,
Thy tongue against thy tongue. O, let thy vow
First made to heaven, first be to heaven perform'd,
That is, to be the champion of our church.
What since thou swor'st is sworn against thyself
And may not be performed by thyself,
For that which thou hast sworn to do amiss
Is not amiss when it is truly done;
And being not done, where doing tends to ill,
The truth is then most done not doing it;
The better act of purposes mistook
Is to mistake again; though indirect,
Yet indirection thereby grows direct,
And falsehood falsehood cures, as fire cools fire
Within the scorched veins of one newburn'd.
It is religion that doth make vows kept;
But thou hast sworn against religion
By what thou swear'st against the thing thou swear'st,
And mak'st an oath the surety for thy truth
Against an oath; the truth thou art unsure
To swear swears only not to be forsworn;
Else what a mockery should it be to swear!
But thou dost swear only to be forsworn;
And most forsworn to keep what thou dost swear.
Therefore thy later vows against thy first
Is in thyself rebellion to thyself;
And better conquest never canst thou make
Than arm thy constant and thy nobler parts
Against these giddy loose suggestions;
Upon which better part our pray'rs come in,
If thou vouchsafe them. But if not, then know
The peril of our curses light on thee
So heavy as thou shalt not shake them off,
But in despair die under their black weight.
AUSTRIA Rebellion, flat rebellion!
BASTARD Will't not be?
Will not a calf's-skin stop that mouth of thine?
LEWIS Father, to arms!
BLANCH Upon thy wedding-day?
Against the blood that thou hast married?
What, shall our feast be kept with slaughtered men?
Shall braying trumpets and loud churlish drums,
Clamours of hell, be measures to our pomp?
O husband, hear me! ay, alack, how new
Is 'husband' in my mouth! – even for that name,
Which till this time my tongue did ne'er pronounce,
Upon my knee I beg, go not to arms
Against mine uncle.
CONSTANCE O, upon my knee,
Made hard with kneeling, I do pray to thee,
Thou virtuous Dauphin, alter not the doom
Forethought by heaven!
BLANCH Now shall I see thy love. What motive may
Be stronger with thee than the name of wife?
CONSTANCE That which upholdeth him that thee upholds,
His honour. O, thine honour, Lewis, thine honour!

LEWIS I muse your Majesty doth seem so cold,
When such profound respects do pull you on.
PANDULPH I will denounce a curse upon his head.
KING PHILIP Thou shalt not need. England, I will fall from thee.
CONSTANCE O fair return of banish'd majesty!
ELINOR O foul revolt of French inconstancy!
KING JOHN France, thou shalt rue this hour within this hour.
BASTARD Old Time the clock-setter, that bald sexton Time,
Is it as he will? Well then, France shall rue.
BLANCH The sun's o'ercast with blood. Fair day, adieu!
Which is the side that I must go withal?
I am with both: each army hath a hand;
And in their rage, I having hold of both,
They whirl asunder and dismember me.
Husband, I cannot pray that thou mayst win;
Uncle, I needs must pray that thou mayst lose;
Father, I may not wish the fortune thine;
Grandam, I will not wish thy wishes thrive.
Whoever wins, on that side shall I lose:
Assured loss before the match be play'd.
LEWIS Lady, with me, with me thy fortune lies.
BLANCH There where my fortune lives, there my life dies.
KING JOHN Cousin, go draw our puissance together. [*Exit Bastard.*
France, I am burn'd up with inflaming wrath,
A rage whose heat hath this condition
That nothing can allay, nothing but blood,
The blood, and dearest-valu'd blood, of France.
KING PHILIP Thy rage shall burn thee up, and thou shalt turn
To ashes, ere our blood shall quench that fire.
Look to thyself, thou art in jeopardy.
KING JOHN No more than he that threats.
To arms let's hie! [*Exeunt severally.*

SCENE II. *France. Plains near Angiers.*

Alarums, excursions. Enter the BASTARD with Austria's head.

BASTARD Now, by my life, this day grows wondrous hot;
Some airy devil hovers in the sky
And pours down mischief. Austria's head lie there,
While Philip breathes.

Enter KING JOHN, ARTHUR, and HUBERT.

KING JOHN Hubert, keep this boy. Philip, make up:
My mother is assailed in our tent,
And ta'en, I fear.
BASTARD My lord, I rescued her;
Her Highness is in safety, fear you not;
But on, my liege, for very little pains
Will bring this labour to an happy end. [*Exeunt.*

SCENE III. *France. Plains near Angiers.*

Alarums, excursions, retreat. Enter KING JOHN, ELINOR, ARTHUR, the BASTARD, HUBERT, and Lords.

KING JOHN [*To Elinor*] So shall it be; your Grace shall stay behind,
So strongly guarded. [*To Arthur*] Cousin, look not sad;
Thy grandam loves thee, and thy uncle will
As dear be to thee as thy father was.
ARTHUR O, this will make my mother die with grief!
KING JOHN [*To the Bastard*] Cousin, away for England! haste before,
And, ere our coming, see thou shake the bags
Of hoarding abbots; imprisoned angels
Set at liberty; the fat ribs of peace
Must by the hungry now be fed upon.
Use our commission in his utmost force.
BASTARD Bell, book, and candle, shall not drive me back,
When gold and silver becks me to come on.
I leave your Highness. Grandam, I will pray,
If ever I remember to be holy,
For your fair safety. So, I kiss your hand.
ELINOR Farewell, gentle cousin.
KING JOHN Coz, farewell. [*Exit Bastard.*
ELINOR Come hither, little kinsman; hark, a word.
KING JOHN Come hither, Hubert. O my gentle Hubert,
We owe thee much! Within this wall of flesh
There is a soul counts thee her creditor,
And with advantage means to pay thy love;
And, my good friend, thy voluntary oath
Lives in this bosom, dearly cherished.
Give me thy hand. I had a thing to say –
But I will fit it with some better time.
By heaven, Hubert, I am almost asham'd
To say what good respect I have of thee.
HUBERT I am much bounden to your Majesty.
KING JOHN Good friend, thou hast no cause to say so yet,
But thou shalt have; and creep time ne'er so slow,
Yet it shall come for me to do thee good.
I had a thing to say – but let it go:
The sun is in the heaven, and the proud day,
Attended with the pleasures of the world,
Is all too wanton and too full of gawds

To give me audience. If the midnight bell
Did with his iron tongue and brazen mouth
Sound on into the drowsy race of night;
If this same were a churchyard where we stand,
And thou possessed with a thousand wrongs;
Or if that surly spirit, melancholy,
Had bak'd thy blood and made it heavy-thick,
Which else runs tickling up and down the veins,
Making that idiot, laughter, keep men's eyes
And strain their cheeks to idle merriment,
A passion hateful to my purposes;
Or if that thou couldst see me without eyes,
Hear me without thine ears, and make reply
Without a tongue, using conceit alone,
Without eyes, ears, and harmful sound of
words –
Then, in despite of brooded watchful day,
I would into thy bosom pour my thoughts.
But, ah, I will not! Yet I love thee well;
And, by my troth, I think thou lov'st me well.
HUBERT So well that what you bid me undertake,
Though that my death were adjunct to my act,
By heaven, I would do it.
KING JOHN Do not I know thou wouldst?
Good Hubert, Hubert, Hubert, throw thine eye
On yon young boy. I'll tell thee what, my friend,
He is a very serpent in my way;
And wheresoe'er this foot of mine doth tread,
He lies before me. Dost thou understand me?
Thou art his keeper.
HUBERT And I'll keep him so
That he shall not offend your Majesty.
KING JOHN Death.
HUBERT My lord?
KING JOHN A grave.
HUBERT He shall not live.
KING JOHN Enough!
I could be merry now. Hubert, I love thee.
Well, I'll not say what I intend for thee.
Remember. Madam, fare you well;
I'll send those powers o'er to your Majesty.
ELINOR My blessing go with thee!
KING JOHN [*To Arthur*] For England, cousin, go;
Hubert shall be your man, attend on you
With all true duty. On toward Calais, ho!
[*Exeunt.*

SCENE IV. *France. The French King's camp.*

Enter KING PHILIP, LEWIS, PANDULPH, and Attendants.

KING PHILIP So by a roaring tempest on the flood
A whole armado of convicted sail
Is scattered and disjoin'd from fellowship.
PANDULPH Courage and comfort! All shall yet go
well.
KING PHILIP What can go well, when we have
run so ill.
Are we not beaten? Is not Angiers lost?
Arthur ta'en prisoner? Divers dear friends slain?
And bloody England into England gone,
O'erbearing interruption, spite of France?
LEWIS What he hath won, that hath he fortified;
So hot a speed with such advice dispos'd,
Such temperate order in so fierce a cause,
Doth want example; who hath read or heard
Of any kindred action like to this?
KING PHILIP Well could I bear that England had
this praise,
So we could find some pattern of our shame.

Enter CONSTANCE.

Look who comes here! a grave unto a soul;
Holding th' eternal spirit, against her will,
In the vile prison of afflicted breath.
I prithee, lady, go away with me.
CONSTANCE Lo now! now see the issue of your
peace!
KING PHILIP Patience, good lady! Comfort, gentle
Constance!
CONSTANCE No, I defy all counsel, all redress,
But that which ends all counsel, true redress –
Death, death; O amiable lovely death!
Thou odoriferous stench! sound rottenness!
Arise forth from the couch of lasting night,
Thou hate and terror to prosperity,
And I will kiss thy detestable bones,
And put my eyeballs in thy vaulty brows,
And ring these fingers with thy household
worms,
And stop this gap of breath with fulsome dust,
And be a carrion monster like thyself.
Come, grin on me, and I will think thou smil'st,
And buss thee as thy wife. Misery's love,
O, come to me!
KING PHILIP O fair affliction, peace!
CONSTANCE No, no, I will not, having breath to
cry.
O that my tongue were in the thunder's mouth!
Then with a passion would I shake the world,
And rouse from sleep that fell anatomy
Which cannot hear a lady's feeble voice,
Which scorns a modern invocation.
PANDULPH Lady, you utter madness and not
sorrow.
CONSTANCE Thou art not holy to belie me so.
I am not mad: this hair I tear is mine;
My name is Constance; I was Geffrey's wife;
Young Arthur is my son, and he is lost.
I am not mad – I would to heaven I were!
For then 'tis like I should forget myself.
O, if I could, what grief should I forget!
Preach some philosophy to make me mad,

And thou shalt be canoniz'd, Cardinal;
For, being not mad, but sensible of grief,
My reasonable part produces reason
How I may be deliver'd of these woes,
And teaches me to kill or hang myself.
If I were mad I should forget my son,
Or madly think a babe of clouts were he.
I am not mad; too well, too well I feel
The different plague of each calamity.

KING PHILIP Bind up those tresses. O, what love I note
In the fair multitude of those her hairs!
Where but by a chance a silver drop hath fall'n,
Even to that drop ten thousand wiry friends
Do glue themselves in sociable grief,
Like true, inseparable, faithful loves,
Sticking together in calamity.

CONSTANCE To England, if you will.

KING PHILIP Bind up your hairs.

CONSTANCE Yes, that I will; and wherefore will I do it?
I tore them from their bonds, and cried aloud
'O that these hands could so redeem my son,
As they have given these hairs their liberty!'
But now I envy at their liberty,
And will again commit them to their bonds,
Because my poor child is a prisoner.
And, father Cardinal, I have heard you say
That we shall see and know our friends in heaven;
If that be true, I shall see my boy again;
For since the birth of Cain, the first male child,
To him that did but yesterday suspire,
There was not such a gracious creature born.
But now will canker sorrow eat my bud
And chase the native beauty from his cheek,
And he will look as hollow as a ghost,
As dim and meagre as an ague's fit;
And so he'll die; and, rising so again,
When I shall meet him in the court of heaven
I shall not know him. Therefore never, never
Must I behold my pretty Arthur more.

PANDULPH You hold too heinous a respect of grief.

CONSTANCE He talks to me that never had a son.

KING PHILIP You are as fond of grief as of your child.

CONSTANCE Grief fills the room up of my absent child,
Lies in his bed, walks up and down with me,
Puts on his pretty looks, repeats his words,
Remembers me of all his gracious parts,
Stuffs out his vacant garments with his form;
Then have I reason to be fond of grief.
Fare you well; had you such a loss as I,
I could give better comfort than you do.
I will not keep this form upon my head,

[*Tearing her hair.*

When there is such disorder in my wit.
O Lord! my boy, my Arthur, my fair son!
My life, my joy, my food, my all the world!
My widow-comfort, and my sorrows' cure!

[*Exit.*

KING PHILIP I fear some outrage, and I'll follow her.

[*Exit.*

LEWIS There's nothing in this world can make me joy.
Life is as tedious as a twice-told tale
Vexing the dull ear of a drowsy man;
And bitter shame hath spoil'd the sweet world's taste,
That it yields nought but shame and bitterness.

PANDULPH Before the curing of a strong disease,
Even in the instant of repair and health,
The fit is strongest; evils that take leave
On their departure most of all show evil;
What have you lost by losing of this day?

LEWIS All days of glory, joy, and happiness.

PANDULPH If you had won it, certainly you had.
No, no; when Fortune means to men most good,
She looks upon them with a threat'ning eye.
'Tis strange to think how much King John hath lost
In this which he accounts so clearly won.
Are not you griev'd that Arthur is his prisoner?

LEWIS As heartily as he is glad he hath him.

PANDULPH Your mind is all as youthful as your blood.
Now hear me speak with a prophetic spirit;
For even the breath of what I mean to speak
Shall blow each dust, each straw, each little rub,
Out of the path which shall directly lead
Thy foot to England's throne. And therefore mark:
John hath seiz'd Arthur; and it cannot be
That, whiles warm life plays in that infant's veins,
The misplac'd John should entertain an hour,
One minute, nay, one quiet breath of rest.
A sceptre snatch'd with an unruly hand
Must be as boisterously maintain'd as gain'd,
And he that stands upon a slipp'ry place
Makes nice of no vile hold to stay him up;
That John may stand then, Arthur needs must fall;
So be it, for it cannot be but so.

LEWIS But what shall I gain by young Arthur's fall?

PANDULPH You, in the right of Lady Blanch your wife,
May then make all the claim that Arthur did.

LEWIS And lose it, life and all, as Arthur did.

PANDULPH How green you are and fresh in this

old world!
John lays you plots; the times conspire with you;
For he that steeps his safety in true blood
Shall find but bloody safety and untrue.
This act, so evilly borne, shall cool the hearts
Of all his people and freeze up their zeal,
That none so small advantage shall step forth
To check his reign but they will cherish it;
No natural exhalation in the sky,
No scope of nature, no distemper'd day,
No common wind, no customed event,
But they will pluck away his natural cause
And call them meteors, prodigies, and signs,
Abortives, presages, and tongues of heaven,
Plainly denouncing vengeance upon John.

LEWIS May be he will not touch young Arthur's life,
But hold himself safe in his prisonment.

PANDULPH O, sir, when he shall hear of your approach,
If that young Arthur be not gone already,
Even at that news he dies; and then the hearts
Of all his people shall revolt from him,
And kiss the lips of unacquainted change,
And pick strong matter of revolt and wrath
Out of the bloody fingers' ends of John.
Methinks I see this hurly all on foot;
And, O, what better matter breeds for you
Than I have nam'd! The bastard Faulconbridge
Is now in England ransacking the Church,
Offending charity; if but a dozen French
Were there in arms, they would be as a call
To train ten thousand English to their side;
Or as a little snow, tumbled about,
Anon becomes a mountain. O noble Dauphin,
Go with me to the King. 'Tis wonderful
What may be wrought out of their discontent,
Now that their souls are topful of offence.
For England go; I will whet on the King.

LEWIS Strong reasons makes strong actions. Let us go;
If you say ay, the King will not say no. *[Exeunt.*

ACT FOUR

SCENE I. *England. A castle.*

Enter HUBERT and Executioners.

HUBERT Heat me these irons hot; and look thou stand
Within the arras. When I strike my foot
Upon the bosom of the ground, rush forth
And bind the boy which you shall find with me
Fast to the chair. Be heedful; hence, and watch.

1 EXECUTIONER I hope your warrant will bear out the deed.

HUBERT Uncleanly scruples! Fear not you. Look to't. *[Exeunt Executioners.*
Young lad, come forth; I have to say with you.

Enter ARTHUR.

ARTHUR Good morrow, Hubert.

HUBERT Good morrow, little Prince.

ARTHUR As little prince, having so great a title
To be more prince, as may be. You are sad.

HUBERT Indeed, I have been merrier.

ARTHUR Mercy on me!
Methinks no body should be sad but I;
Yet, I remember, when I was in France,
Young gentlemen would be as sad as night,
Only for wantonness. By my christendom,
So I were out of prison and kept sheep,
I should be as merry as the day is long;
And so I would be here but that I doubt
My uncle practises more harm to me;
He is afraid of me, and I of him.
Is it my fault that I was Geffrey's son?
No, indeed, is't not; and I would to heaven
I were your son, so you would love me, Hubert.

HUBERT *[Aside]* If I talk to him, with his innocent prate
He will awake my mercy, which lies dead;
Therefore I will be sudden and dispatch.

ARTHUR Are you sick, Hubert? You look pale to-day;
In sooth, I would you were a little sick,
That I might sit all night and watch with you.
I warrant I love you more than you do me.

HUBERT *[Aside]* His words do take possession of my bosom. –
Read here, young Arthur. *[Showing a paper.*
[Aside] How now, foolish rheum!
Turning dispiteous torture out of door!
I must be brief, lest resolution drop
Out at mine eyes in tender womanish tears. –
Can you not read it? Is it not fair writ?

ARTHUR Too fairly, Hubert, for so foul effect.
Must you with hot irons burn out both mine eyes?

HUBERT Young boy, I must.

ARTHUR And will you?

HUBERT And I will.

ARTHUR Have you the heart? When your head did but ache,
I knit my handkerchief about your brows –
The best I had, a princess wrought it me –

And I did never ask it you again;
And with my hand at midnight held your head;
And, like the watchful minutes to the hour,
Still and anon cheer'd up the heavy time,
Saying 'What lack you?' and 'Where lies your grief?'
Or 'What good love may I perform for you?'
Many a poor man's son would have lyen still,
And ne'er have spoke a loving word to you;
But you at your sick service had a prince.
Nay, you may think my love was crafty love,
And call it cunning. Do, an if you will.
If heaven be pleas'd that you must use me ill,
Why, then you must. Will you put out mine eyes,
These eyes that never did nor never shall
So much as frown on you?

HUBERT I have sworn to do it;
And with hot irons must I burn them out.

ARTHUR Ah, none but in this iron age would do it!
The iron of itself, though heat red-hot,
Approaching near these eyes would drink my tears,
And quench his fiery indignation
Even in the matter of mine innocence;
Nay, after that, consume away in rust
But for containing fire to harm mine eye.
Are you more stubborn-hard than hammer'd iron?
An if an angel should have come to me
And told me Hubert should put out mine eyes,
I would not have believ'd him – no tongue but Hubert's.

HUBERT [*Stamps*] Come forth.

Re-enter Executioners, with cord, irons, etc.

Do as I bid you do.

ARTHUR O, save me, Hubert, save me! My eyes are out
Even with the fierce looks of these bloody men.

HUBERT Give me the iron, I say, and bind him here.

ARTHUR Alas, what need you be so boist'rous rough?
I will not struggle, I will stand stone-still.
For heaven sake, Hubert, let me not be bound!
Nay, hear me, Hubert! Drive these men away,
And I will sit as quiet as a lamb;
I will not stir, nor wince, nor speak a word,
Nor look upon the iron angrily;
Thrust but these men away, and I'll forgive you,
Whatever torment you do put me to.

HUBERT Go, stand within; let me alone with him.

I EXECUTIONER I am best pleas'd to be from such a deed. [*Exeunt Executioners.*

ARTHUR Alas, I then have chid away my friend!
He hath a stern look but a gentle heart.
Let him come back, that his compassion may
Give life to yours.

HUBERT Come, boy, prepare yourself.

ARTHUR Is there no remedy?

HUBERT None, but to lose your eyes.

ARTHUR O heaven, that there were but a mote in yours,
A grain, a dust, a gnat, a wandering hair,
Any annoyance in that precious sense!
Then, feeling what small things are boisterous there,
Your vile intent must needs seem horrible.

HUBERT Is this your promise? Go to, hold your tongue.

ARTHUR Hubert, the utterance of a brace of tongues
Must needs want pleading for a pair of eyes.
Let me not hold my tongue, let me not, Hubert;
Or, Hubert, if you will, cut out my tongue,
So I may keep mine eyes. O, spare mine eyes,
Though to no use but still to look on you!
Lo, by my troth, the instrument is cold
And would not harm me.

HUBERT I can heat it, boy.

ARTHUR No, in good sooth; the fire is dead with grief,
Being create for comfort, to be us'd
In undeserved extremes. See else yourself:
There is no malice in this burning coal;
The breath of heaven hath blown his spirit out,
And strew'd repentant ashes on his head.

HUBERT But with my breath I can revive it, boy.

ARTHUR An if you do, you will but make it blush
And glow with shame of your proceedings, Hubert.
Nay, it perchance will sparkle in your eyes,
And, like a dog that is compell'd to fight,
Snatch at his master that doth tarre him on.
All things that you should use to do me wrong
Deny their office; only you do lack
That mercy which fierce fire and iron extends,
Creatures of note for mercy-lacking uses.

HUBERT Well, see to live; I will not touch thine eye
For all the treasure that thine uncle owes.
Yet am I sworn, and I did purpose, boy,
With this same very iron to burn them out.

ARTHUR O, now you look like Hubert! All this while
You were disguis'd.

HUBERT Peace; no more. Adieu.
Your uncle must not know but you are dead:
I'll fill these dogged spies with false reports;
And, pretty child, sleep doubtless and secure
That Hubert, for the wealth of all the world,
Will not offend thee.

ARTHUR O heaven! I thank you, Hubert.
HUBERT Silence; no more. Go closely in with me.
Much danger do I undergo for thee. [*Exeunt.*

SCENE II. *England. King John's palace.*

Enter KING JOHN, PEMBROKE, SALISBURY, and other Lords.

KING JOHN Here once again we sit, once again crown'd,
And look'd upon, I hope, with cheerful eyes.
PEMBROKE This once again, but that your Highness pleas'd,
Was once superfluous: you were crown'd before,
And that high royalty was ne'er pluck'd off,
The faiths of men ne'er stained with revolt;
Fresh expectation troubled not the land
With any long'd-for change or better state.
SALISBURY Therefore, to be possess'd with double pomp,
To guard a title that was rich before,
To gild refined gold, to paint the lily,
To throw a perfume on the violet,
To smooth the ice, or add another hue
Unto the rainbow, or with taper-light
To seek the beauteous eye of heaven to garnish,
Is wasteful and ridiculous excess.
PEMBROKE But that your royal pleasure must be done,
This act is as an ancient tale new told
And, in the last repeating, troublesome,
Being urged at a time unseasonable.
SALISBURY In this the antique and well-noted face
Of plain old form is much disfigured;
And like a shifted wind unto a sail
It makes the course of thoughts to fetch about,
Startles and frights consideration,
Makes sound opinion sick, and truth suspected,
For putting on so new a fashion'd robe.
PEMBROKE When workmen strive to do better than well,
They do confound their skill in covetousness;
And oftentimes excusing of a fault
Doth make the fault the worse by th' excuse,
As patches set upon a little breach
Discredit more in hiding of the fault
Than did the fault before it was so patch'd.
SALISBURY To this effect, before you were new-crown'd,
We breath'd our counsel; but it pleas'd your Highness
To overbear it; and we are all well pleas'd,
Since all and every part of what we would
Doth make a stand at what your Highness will.
KING JOHN Some reasons of this double coronation
I have possess'd you with, and think them strong;
And more, more strong, when lesser is my fear,
I shall indue you with. Meantime but ask
What you would have reform'd that is not well,
And well shall you perceive how willingly
I will both hear and grant you your requests.
PEMBROKE Then I, as one that am the tongue of these,
To sound the purposes of all their hearts,
Both for myself and them – but, chief of all,
Your safety, for the which myself and them
Bend their best studies – heartily request
Th' enfranchisement of Arthur, whose restraint
Doth move the murmuring lips of discontent
To break into this dangerous argument:
If what in rest you have in right you hold,
Why then your fears – which, as they say, attend
The steps of wrong – should move you to mew up
Your tender kinsman, and to choke his days
With barbarous ignorance, and deny his youth
The rich advantage of good exercise?
That the time's enemies may not have this
To grace occasions, let it be our suit
That you have bid us ask his liberty;
Which for our goods we do no further ask
Than whereupon our weal, on you depending,
Counts it your weal he have his liberty.
KING JOHN Let it be so. I do commit his youth
To your direction.

Enter HUBERT.

[*Aside*] Hubert, what news with you?
PEMBROKE This is the man should do the bloody deed:
He show'd his warrant to a friend of mine;
The image of a wicked heinous fault
Lives in his eye; that close aspect of his
Doth show the mood of a much troubled breast,
And I do fearfully believe 'tis done
What we so fear'd he had a charge to do.
SALISBURY The colour of the King doth come and go
Between his purpose and his conscience,
Like heralds 'twixt two dreadful battles set.
His passion is so ripe it needs must break.
PEMBROKE And when it breaks, I fear will issue thence
The foul corruption of a sweet child's death.
KING JOHN We cannot hold mortality's strong hand.
Good lords, although my will to give is living,
The suit which you demand is gone and dead:
He tells us Arthur is deceas'd to-night.
SALISBURY Indeed, we fear'd his sickness was past cure.

PEMBROKE Indeed, we heard how near his death he was,
Before the child himself felt he was sick.
This must be answer'd either here or hence.

KING JOHN Why do you bend such solemn brows on me?
Think you I bear the shears of destiny?
Have I commandment on the pulse of life?

SALISBURY It is apparent foul-play; and 'tis shame
That greatness should so grossly offer it.
So thrive it in your game! and so, farewell.

PEMBROKE Stay yet, Lord Salisbury, I'll go with thee
And find th' inheritance of this poor child,
His little kingdom of a forced grave.
That blood which ow'd the breadth of all this isle
Three foot of it doth hold – bad world the while!
This must not be thus borne: this will break out
To all our sorrows, and ere long I doubt.

[*Exeunt Lords.*

KING JOHN They burn in indignation. I repent.
There is no sure foundation set on blood,
No certain life achiev'd by others' death.

Enter a Messenger.

A fearful eye thou hast; where is that blood
That I have seen inhabit in those cheeks?
So foul a sky clears not without a storm.
Pour down thy weather – how goes all in France?

MESSENGER From France to England. Never such a pow'r
For any foreign preparation
Was levied in the body of a land.
The copy of your speed is learn'd by them,
For when you should be told they do prepare,
The tidings comes that they are all arriv'd.

KING JOHN O, where hath our intelligence been drunk?
Where hath it slept? Where is my mother's care,
That such an army could be drawn in France,
And she not hear of it?

MESSENGER My liege, her ear
Is stopp'd with dust: the first of April died
Your noble mother; and as I hear, my lord,
The Lady Constance in a frenzy died
Three days before; but this from rumour's tongue
I idly heard – if true or false I know not.

KING JOHN Withhold thy speed, dreadful occasion!
O, make a league with me, till I have pleas'd
My discontented peers! What! mother dead!
How wildly then walks my estate in France!
Under whose conduct came those pow'rs of France
That thou for truth giv'st out are landed here?

MESSENGER Under the Dauphin.

KING JOHN Thou hast made me giddy
With these ill tidings.

Enter the BASTARD and PETER of Pomfret.

Now! What says the world
To your proceedings? Do not seek to stuff
My head with more ill news, for it is full.

BASTARD But if you be afear'd to hear the worst,
Then let the worst, unheard, fall on your head.

KING JOHN Bear with me, cousin, for I was amaz'd
Under the tide; but now I breathe again
Aloft the flood, and can give audience
To any tongue, speak it of what it will.

BASTARD How I have sped among the clergymen
The sums I have collected shall express.
But as I travell'd hither through the land,
I find the people strangely fantasied;
Possess'd with rumours, full of idle dreams,
Not knowing what they fear, but full of fear;
And here's a prophet that I brought with me
From forth the streets of Pomfret, whom I found
With many hundreds treading on his heels;
To whom he sung, in rude harsh-sounding rhymes,
That, ere the next Ascension-day at noon,
Your Highness should deliver up your crown.

KING JOHN Thou idle dreamer, wherefore didst thou so?

PETER Foreknowing that the truth will fall out so.

KING JOHN Hubert, away with him; imprison him;
And on that day at noon whereon he says
I shall yield up my crown let him be hang'd.
Deliver him to safety; and return,
For I must use thee.

[*Exit Hubert with Peter.*

O my gentle cousin,
Hear'st thou the news abroad, who are arriv'd?

BASTARD The French, my lord; men's mouths are full of it;
Besides, I met Lord Bigot and Lord Salisbury,
With eyes as red as new-enkindled fire,
And others more, going to seek the grave
Of Arthur, whom they say is kill'd to-night
On your suggestion.

KING JOHN Gentle kinsman, go
And thrust thyself into their companies.
I have a way to win their loves again;
Bring them before me.

BASTARD I will seek them out.

KING JOHN Nay, but make haste; the better foot before.

O, let me have no subject enemies
When adverse foreigners affright my towns
With dreadful pomp of stout invasion!
Be Mercury, set feathers to thy heels,
And fly like thought from them to me again.

BASTARD The spirit of the time shall teach me speed.

KING JOHN Spoke like a sprightful noble gentleman. [*Exit Bastard.*
Go after him; for he perhaps shall need
Some messenger betwixt me and the peers;
And be thou he.

MESSENGER With all my heart, my liege. [*Exit.*

KING JOHN My mother dead!

Re-enter HUBERT.

HUBERT My lord, they say five moons were seen to-night;
Four fixed, and the fifth did whirl about
The other four in wondrous motion.

KING JOHN Five moons!

HUBERT Old men and beldams in the streets
Do prophesy upon it dangerously;
Young Arthur's death is common in their mouths;
And when they talk of him, they shake their heads,
And whisper one another in the ear;
And he that speaks doth gripe the hearer's wrist,
Whilst he that hears makes fearful action
With wrinkled brows, with nods, with rolling eyes.
I saw a smith stand with his hammer, thus,
The whilst his iron did on the anvil cool,
With open mouth swallowing a tailor's news;
Who, with his shears and measure in his hand,
Standing on slippers, which his nimble haste
Had falsely thrust upon contrary feet,
Told of a many thousand warlike French
That were embattailed and rank'd in Kent.
Another lean unwash'd artificer
Cuts off his tale, and talks of Arthur's death.

KING JOHN Why seek'st thou to possess me with these fears?
Why urgest thou so oft young Arthur's death?
Thy hand hath murd'red him. I had a mighty cause
To wish him dead, but thou hadst none to kill him.

HUBERT No had, my lord! Why, did you not provoke me?

KING JOHN It is the curse of kings to be attended
By slaves that take their humours for a warrant
To break within the bloody house of life,
And on the winking of authority
To understand a law; to know the meaning
Of dangerous majesty, when perchance it frowns
More upon humour than advis'd respect.

HUBERT Here is your hand and seal for what I did.

KING JOHN O, when the last account 'twixt heaven and earth
Is to be made, then shall this hand and seal
Witness against us to damnation!
How oft the sight of means to do ill deeds
Make deeds ill done! Hadst not thou been by,
A fellow by the hand of nature mark'd,
Quoted and sign'd to do a deed of shame,
This murder had not come into my mind;
But, taking note of thy abhorr'd aspect,
Finding thee fit for bloody villainy,
Apt, liable to be employ'd in danger,
I faintly broke with thee of Arthur's death;
And thou, to be endeared to a king,
Made it no conscience to destroy a prince.

HUBERT My lord –

KING JOHN Hadst thou but shook thy head or made a pause,
When I spake darkly what I purposed,
Or turn'd an eye of doubt upon my face,
As bid me tell my tale in express words,
Deep shame had struck me dumb, made me break off,
And those thy fears might have wrought fears in me.
But thou didst understand me by my signs,
And didst in signs again parley with sin;
Yea, without stop, didst let thy heart consent,
And consequently thy rude hand to act
The deed which both our tongues held vile to name.
Out of my sight, and never see me more!
My nobles leave me; and my state is braved,
Even at my gates, with ranks of foreign pow'rs;
Nay, in the body of this fleshly land,
This kingdom, this confine of blood and breath,
Hostility and civil tumult reigns
Between my conscience and my cousin's death.

HUBERT Arm you against your other enemies,
I'll make a peace between your soul and you.
Young Arthur is alive. This hand of mine
Is yet a maiden and an innocent hand,
Not painted with the crimson spots of blood.
Within this bosom never ent'red yet
The dreadful motion of a murderous thought;
And you have slander'd nature in my form,
Which, howsoever rude exteriorly,
Is yet the cover of a fairer mind
Than to be butcher of an innocent child.

KING JOHN Doth Arthur live? O, haste thee to the peers,
Throw this report on their incensed rage

And make them tame to their obedience!
Forgive the comment that my passion made
Upon thy feature; for my rage was blind,
And foul imaginary eyes of blood
Presented thee more hideous than thou art.
O, answer not; but to my closet bring
The angry lords with all expedient haste.
I conjure thee but slowly; run more fast. [*Exeunt.*

SCENE III. *England. Before the castle.*

Enter ARTHUR, on the walls.

ARTHUR The wall is high, and yet will I leap down.
Good ground, be pitiful and hurt me not!
There's few or none do know me; if they did,
This ship-boy's semblance hath disguis'd me quite.
I am afraid; and yet I'll venture it.
If I get down and do not break my limbs,
I'll find a thousand shifts to get away.
As good to die and go, as die and stay.
[*Leaps down.*
O me! my uncle's spirit is in these stones.
Heaven take my soul, and England keep my bones! [*Dies.*

Enter PEMBROKE, SALISBURY, and BIGOT.

SALISBURY Lords, I will meet him at Saint Edmundsbury;
It is our safety, and we must embrace
This gentle offer of the perilous time.
PEMBROKE Who brought that letter from the Cardinal?
SALISBURY The Count Melun, a noble lord of France,
Whose private with me of the Dauphin's love
Is much more general than these lines import.
BIGOT To-morrow morning let us meet him then.
SALISBURY Or rather then set forward; for 'twill be
Two long days' journey, lords, or ere we meet.

Enter the BASTARD.

BASTARD Once more to-day well met, distemper'd lords!
The King by me requests your presence straight.
SALISBURY The King hath dispossess'd himself of us.
We will not line his thin bestained cloak
With our pure honours, nor attend the foot
That leaves the print of blood where'er it walks.
Return and tell him so. We know the worst.
BASTARD Whate'er you think, good words, I think, were best.
SALISBURY Our griefs, and not our manners, reason now.
BASTARD But there is little reason in your grief;
Therefore 'twere reason you had manners now.
PEMBROKE Sir, sir, impatience hath his privilege.
BASTARD 'Tis true – to hurt his master, no man else.
SALISBURY This is the prison. What is he lies here?
PEMBROKE O death, made proud with pure and princely beauty!
The earth had not a hole to hide this deed.
SALISBURY Murder, as hating what himself hath done,
Doth lay it open to urge on revenge.
BIGOT Or, when he doom'd this beauty to a grave,
Found it too precious-princely for a grave.
SALISBURY Sir Richard, what think you? Have you beheld,
Or have you read or heard, or could you think?
Or do you almost think, although you see,
That you do see? Could thought, without this object,
Form such another? This is the very top,
The height, the crest, or crest unto the crest,
Of murder's arms; this is the bloodiest shame,
The wildest savagery, the vilest stroke,
That ever wall-ey'd wrath or staring rage
Presented to the tears of soft remorse.
PEMBROKE All murders past do stand excus'd in this;
And this, so sole and so unmatchable,
Shall give a holiness, a purity,
To the yet unbegotten sin of times,
And prove a deadly bloodshed but a jest,
Exampled by this heinous spectacle.
BASTARD It is a damned and a bloody work;
The graceless action of a heavy hand,
If that it be the work of any hand.
SALISBURY If that it be the work of any hand!
We had a kind of light what would ensue.
It is the shameful work of Hubert's hand;
The practice and the purpose of the King;
From whose obedience I forbid my soul,
Kneeling before this ruin of sweet life,
And breathing to his breathless excellence
The incense of a vow, a holy vow,
Never to taste the pleasures of the world,
Never to be infected with delight,
Nor conversant with ease and idleness,
Till I have set a glory to this hand
By giving it the worship of revenge.
PEMBROKE, BIGOT Our souls religiously confirm thy words.

Enter HUBERT.

HUBERT Lords, I am hot with haste in seeking you.

Arthur doth live; the King hath sent for you.
SALISBURY O, he is bold, and blushes not at death!
Avaunt, thou hateful villain, get thee gone!
HUBERT I am no villain.
SALISBURY Must I rob the law?
[Drawing his sword.
BASTARD Your sword is bright, sir; put it up again.
SALISBURY Not till I sheathe it in a murderer's skin.
HUBERT Stand back, Lord Salisbury, stand back, I say;
By heaven, I think my sword's as sharp as yours.
I would not have you, lord, forget yourself,
Nor tempt the danger of my true defence;
Lest I, by marking of your rage, forget
Your worth, your greatness, and nobility.
BIGOT Out, dunghill! Dar'st thou brave a nobleman?
HUBERT Not for my life; but yet I dare defend
My innocent life against an emperor.
SALISBURY Thou art a murderer.
HUBERT Do not prove me so.
Yet I am none. Whose tongue soe'er speaks false,
Not truly speaks; who speaks not truly, lies.
PEMBROKE Cut him to pieces.
BASTARD Keep the peace, I say.
SALISBURY Stand by, or I shall gall you, Faulconbridge.
BASTARD Thou wert better gall the devil, Salisbury.
If thou but frown on me, or stir thy foot,
Or teach thy hasty spleen to do me shame,
I'll strike thee dead. Put up thy sword betime;
Or I'll so maul you and your toasting-iron
That you shall think the devil is come from hell.
BIGOT What wilt thou do, renowned Faulconbridge?
Second a villain and a murderer?
HUBERT Lord Bigot, I am none.
BIGOT Who kill'd this prince?
HUBERT 'Tis not an hour since I left him well.
I honour'd him, I lov'd him, and will weep
My date of life out for his sweet life's loss.
SALISBURY Trust not those cunning waters of his eyes,
For villainy is not without such rheum;
And he, long traded in it, makes it seem
Like rivers of remorse and innocency.
Away with me, all you whose souls abhor
Th' uncleanly savours of a slaughter-house;
For I am stifled with this smell of sin.
BIGOT Away toward Bury, to the Dauphin there!
PEMBROKE There tell the King he may inquire us out. *[Exeunt Lords.*
BASTARD Here's a good world! Knew you of this fair work?
Beyond the infinite and boundless reach
Of mercy, if thou didst this deed of death,
Art thou damn'd, Hubert.
HUBERT Do but hear me, sir.
BASTARD Ha! I'll tell thee what:
Thou'rt damn'd as black – nay, nothing is so black –
Thou art more deep damn'd than Prince Lucifer;
There is not yet so ugly a fiend of hell
As thou shalt be, if thou didst kill this child.
HUBERT Upon my soul –
BASTARD If thou didst but consent
To this most cruel act, do but despair;
And if thou want'st a cord, the smallest thread
That ever spider twisted from her womb
Will serve to strangle thee; a rush will be a beam
To hang thee on; or wouldst thou drown thyself,
Put but a little water in a spoon
And it shall be as all the ocean,
Enough to stifle such a villain up.
I do suspect thee very grievously.
HUBERT If I in act, consent, or sin of thought,
Be guilty of the stealing that sweet breath
Which was embounded in this beauteous clay,
Let hell want pains enough to torture me!
I left him well.
BASTARD Go, bear him in thine arms.
I am amaz'd, methinks, and lose my way
Among the thorns and dangers of this world.
How easy dost thou take all England up!
From forth this morsel of dead royalty
The life, the right, and truth of all this realm
Is fled to heaven; and England now is left
To tug and scamble, and to part by th' teeth
The unowed interest of proud-swelling state.
Now for the bare-pick'd bone of majesty
Doth dogged war bristle his angry crest
And snarleth in the gentle eyes of peace;
Now powers from home and discontents at home
Meet in one line; and vast confusion waits,
As doth a raven on a sick-fall'n beast,
The imminent decay of wrested pomp.
Now happy he whose cloak and cincture can
Hold out this tempest. Bear away that child,
And follow me with speed. I'll to the King;
A thousand businesses are brief in hand,
And heaven itself doth frown upon the land.
[Exeunt.

ACT FIVE

SCENE I. *England. King John's palace.*

Enter KING JOHN, PANDULPH, and Attendants.

KING JOHN Thus have I yielded up into your hand
The circle of my glory.
PANDULPH [*Gives back the crown*] Take again
From this my hand, as holding of the Pope,
Your sovereign greatness and authority.
KING JOHN Now keep your holy word; go meet the French;
And from his Holiness use all your power
To stop their marches fore we are inflam'd.
Our discontented counties do revolt;
Our people quarrel with obedience,
Swearing allegiance and the love of soul
To stranger blood, to foreign royalty.
This inundation of mistemp'red humour
Rests by you only to be qualified.
Then pause not; for the present time's so sick
That present med'cine must be minist'red
Or overthrow incurable ensues.
PANDULPH It was my breath that blew this tempest up,
Upon your stubborn usage of the Pope;
But since you are a gentle convertite,
My tongue shall hush again this storm of war
And make fair weather in your blust'ring land.
On this Ascension-day, remember well,
Upon your oath of service to the Pope,
Go I to make the French lay down their arms.
[*Exit.*
KING JOHN Is this Ascension-day? Did not the prophet
Say that before Ascension-day at noon
My crown I should give off? Even so I have.
I did suppose it should be on constraint;
But, heaven be thank'd, it is but voluntary.

Enter the BASTARD.

BASTARD All Kent hath yielded; nothing there holds out
But Dover Castle. London hath receiv'd,
Like a kind host, the Dauphin and his powers.
Your nobles will not hear you, but are gone
To offer service to your enemy;
And wild amazement hurries up and down
The little number of your doubtful friends.
KING JOHN Would not my lords return to me again
After they heard young Arthur was alive?
BASTARD They found him dead, and cast into the streets,
An empty casket, where the jewel of life
By some damn'd hand was robb'd and ta'en away.
KING JOHN That villain Hubert told me he did live.
BASTARD So, on my soul, he did, for aught he knew.
But wherefore do you droop? Why look you sad?
But great in act, as you have been in thought;
Let not the world see fear and sad distrust
Govern the motion of a kingly eye.
Be stirring as the time; be fire with fire;
Threaten the threat'ner, and outface the brow
Of bragging horror; so shall inferior eyes,
That borrow their behaviours from the great,
Grow great by your example and put on
The dauntless spirit of resolution.
Away, and glister like the god of war
When he intendeth to become the field;
Show boldness and aspiring confidence.
What, shall they seek the lion in his den,
And fright him there, and make him tremble there?
O, let it not be said! Forage, and run
To meet displeasure farther from the doors
And grapple with him ere he come so nigh.
KING JOHN The legate of the Pope hath been with me,
And I have made a happy peace with him;
And he hath promis'd to dismiss the powers
Led by the Dauphin.
BASTARD O inglorious league!
Shall we, upon the footing of our land,
Send fair-play orders, and make compromise,
Insinuation, parley, and base truce,
To arms invasive? Shall a beardless boy,
A cock'red silken wanton, brave our fields
And flesh his spirit in a warlike soil,
Mocking the air with colours idly spread,
And find no check? Let us, my liege, to arms.
Perchance the Cardinal cannot make your peace;
Or, if he do, let it at least be said
They saw we had a purpose of defence.
KING JOHN Have thou the ordering of this present time.
BASTARD Away, then, with good courage! Yet, I know
Our party may well meet a prouder foe. [*Exeunt.*

SCENE II. *England. The Dauphin's camp at Saint Edmundsbury.*

Enter, in arms, LEWIS, SALISBURY, MELUN, PEMBROKE, BIGOT, and Soldiers.

LEWIS My Lord Melun, let this be copied out

And keep it safe for our remembrance;
Return the precedent to these lords again,
That, having our fair order written down,
Both they and we, perusing o'er these notes,
May know wherefore we took the sacrament,
And keep our faiths firm and inviolable.

SALISBURY Upon our sides it never shall be broken.
And, noble Dauphin, albeit we swear
A voluntary zeal and an unurg'd faith
To your proceedings; yet, believe me, Prince,
I am not glad that such a sore of time
Should seek a plaster by contemn'd revolt,
And heal the inveterate canker of one wound
By making many. O, it grieves my soul
That I must draw this metal from my side
To be a widow-maker! O, and there
Where honourable rescue and defence
Cries out upon the name of Salisbury!
But such is the infection of the time
That, for the health and physic of our right,
We cannot deal but with the very hand
Of stern injustice and confused wrong.
And is't not pity, O my grieved friends!
That we, the sons and children of this isle,
Were born to see so sad an hour as this;
Wherein we step after a stranger-march
Upon her gentle bosom, and fill up
Her enemies' ranks – I must withdraw and weep
Upon the spot of this enforced cause –
To grace the gentry of a land remote
And follow unacquainted colours here?
What, here? O nation, that thou couldst remove!
That Neptune's arms, who clippeth thee about,
Would bear thee from the knowledge of thyself
And grapple thee unto a pagan shore,
Where these two Christian armies might combine
The blood of malice in a vein of league,
And not to spend it so unneighbourly!

LEWIS A noble temper dost thou show in this;
And great affections wrestling in thy bosom
Doth make an earthquake of nobility.
O, what a noble combat hast thou fought
Between compulsion and a brave respect!
Let me wipe off this honourable dew
That silverly doth progress on thy cheeks.
My heart hath melted at a lady's tears,
Being an ordinary inundation;
But this effusion of such manly drops,
This show'r, blown up by tempest of the soul,
Startles mine eyes and makes me more amaz'd
Than had I seen the vaulty top of heaven
Figur'd quite o'er with burning meteors.
Lift up thy brow, renowned Salisbury,
And with a great heart heave away this storm;
Commend these waters to those baby eyes
That never saw the giant world enrag'd,
Nor met with fortune other than at feasts,
Full of warm blood, of mirth, of gossiping.
Come, come; for thou shalt thrust thy hand as deep
Into the purse of rich prosperity
As Lewis himself. So, nobles, shall you all,
That knit your sinews to the strength of mine.

Enter PANDULPH.

And even there, methinks, an angel spake:
Look where the holy legate comes apace,
To give us warrant from the hand of heaven
And on our actions set the name of right
With holy breath.

PANDULPH Hail, noble prince of France!
The next is this: King John hath reconcil'd
Himself to Rome; his spirit is come in,
That so stood out against the holy church,
The great metropolis and see of Rome.
Therefore thy threat'ning colours now wind up
And tame the savage spirit of wild war,
That, like a lion fostered up at hand,
It may lie gently at the foot of peace
And be no further harmful than in show.

LEWIS Your Grace shall pardon me, I will not back:
I am too high-born to be propertied,
To be a secondary at control,
Or useful serving-man and instrument
To any sovereign state throughout the world.
Your breath first kindled the dead coal of wars
Between this chastis'd kingdom and myself
And brought in matter that should feed this fire;
And now 'tis far too huge to be blown out
With that same weak wind which enkindled it.
You taught me how to know the face of right,
Acquainted me with interest to this land,
Yea, thrust this enterprise into my heart;
And come ye now to tell me John hath made
His peace with Rome? What is that peace to me?
I, by the honour of my marriage-bed,
After young Arthur, claim this land for mine;
And, now it is half-conquer'd, must I back
Because that John hath made his peace with Rome?
Am I Rome's slave? What penny hath Rome borne,
What men provided, what munition sent,
To underprop this action? Is't not I
That undergo this charge? Who else but I,
And such as to my claim are liable,
Sweat in this business and maintain this war?
Have I not heard these islanders shout out
'Vive le roi!' as I have bank'd their towns?
Have I not here the best cards for the game

To win this easy match, play'd for a crown?
And shall I now give o'er the yielded set?
No, no, on my soul, it never shall be said.
PANDULPH You look but on the outside of this work.
LEWIS Outside or inside, I will not return
Till my attempt so much be glorified
As to my ample hope was promised
Before I drew this gallant head of war,
And cull'd these fiery spirits from the world
To outlook conquest, and to win renown
Even in the jaws of danger and of death.
[*Trumpet sounds.*
What lusty trumpet thus doth summon us?

Enter the BASTARD, attended.

BASTARD According to the fair play of the world,
Let me have audience: I am sent to speak.
My holy lord of Milan, from the King
I come, to learn how you have dealt for him;
And, as you answer, I do know the scope
And warrant limited unto my tongue.
PANDULPH The Dauphin is too wilful-opposite,
And will not temporize with my entreaties;
He flatly says he'll not lay down his arms.
BASTARD By all the blood that ever fury breath'd,
The youth says well. Now hear our English King;
For thus his royalty doth speak in me.
He is prepar'd, and reason too he should.
This apish and unmannerly approach,
This harness'd masque and unadvised revel,
This unhair'd sauciness and boyish troops,
The King doth smile at; and is well prepar'd
To whip this dwarfish war, these pigmy arms,
From out the circle of his territories.
That hand which had the strength, even at your door,
To cudgel you and make you take the hatch,
To dive like buckets in concealed wells,
To crouch in litter of your stable planks,
To lie like pawns lock'd up in chests and trunks,
To hug with swine, to seek sweet safety out
In vaults and prisons, and to thrill and shake
Even at the crying of your nation's crow,
Thinking this voice an armed Englishman –
Shall that victorious hand be feebled here
That in your chambers gave you chastisement?
No. Know the gallant monarch is in arms
And like an eagle o'er his aery tow'rs
To souse annoyance that comes near his nest.
And you degenerate, you ingrate revolts,
You bloody Neroes, ripping up the womb
Of your dear mother England, blush for shame;
For your own ladies and pale-visag'd maids,
Like Amazons, come tripping after drums,
Their thimbles into armed gauntlets change,
Their needles to lances, and their gentle hearts
To fierce and bloody inclination.
LEWIS There end thy brave, and turn thy face in peace;
We grant thou canst outscold us. Fare thee well;
We hold our time too precious to be spent
With such a brabbler.
PANDULPH Give me leave to speak.
BASTARD No, I will speak.
LEWIS We will attend to neither.
Strike up the drums; and let the tongue of war,
Plead for our interest and our being here.
BASTARD Indeed, your drums, being beaten, will cry out;
And so shall you, being beaten. Do but start
An echo with the clamour of thy drum,
And even at hand a drum is ready brac'd
That shall reverberate all as loud as thine:
Sound but another, and another shall,
As loud as thine, rattle the welkin's ear
And mock the deep-mouth'd thunder; for at hand –
Not trusting to this halting legate here,
Whom he hath us'd rather for sport than need –
Is warlike John; and in his forehead sits
A bare-ribb'd death, whose office is this day
To feast upon whole thousands of the French.
LEWIS Strike up our drums to find this danger out.
BASTARD And thou shalt find it, Dauphin, do not doubt. [*Exeunt.*

SCENE III. *England. The field of battle.*

Alarums. Enter KING JOHN and HUBERT.

KING JOHN How goes the day with us? O, tell he, Hubert.
HUBERT Badly, I fear. How fares your Majesty?
KING JOHN This fever that hath troubled me so long
Lies heavy on me. O, my heart is sick!

Enter a Messenger.

MESSENGER My lord, your valiant kinsman, Faulconbridge,
Desires your Majesty to leave the field
And send him word by me which way you go.
KING JOHN Tell him, toward Swinstead, to the abbey there.
MESSENGER Be of good comfort; for the great supply
That was expected by the Dauphin here
Are wreck'd three nights ago on Goodwin Sands;
This news was brought to Richard but even now.
The French fight coldly, and retire themselves.
KING JOHN Ay me, this tyrant fever burns me up

And will not let me welcome this good news.
Set on toward Swinstead; to my litter straight;
Weakness possesseth me, and I am faint. [*Exeunt.*

SCENE IV. *England. Another part of the battlefield.*

Enter SALISBURY, PEMBROKE, and BIGOT.

SALISBURY I did not think the King so stor'd with friends.
PEMBROKE Up once again; put spirit in the French;
If they miscarry, we miscarry too.
SALISBURY That misbegotten devil, Faulconbridge,
In spite of spite, alone upholds the day.
PEMBROKE They say King John, sore sick, hath left the field.

Enter MELUN wounded.

MELUN Lead me to the revolts of England here.
SALISBURY When we were happy we had other names.
PEMBROKE It is the Count Melun.
SALISBURY Wounded to death.
MELUN Fly, noble English, you are bought and sold;
Unthread the rude eye of rebellion,
And welcome home again discarded faith.
Seek out King John, and fall before his feet;
For if the French be lords of this loud day,
He means to recompense the pains you take
By cutting off your heads. Thus hath he sworn,
And I with him, and many moe with me,
Upon the altar at Saint Edmundsbury;
Even on that altar where we swore to you
Dear amity and everlasting love.
SALISBURY May this be possible? May this be true?
MELUN Have I not hideous death within my view,
Retaining but a quantity of life,
Which bleeds away even as a form of wax
Resolveth from his figure 'gainst the fire?
What in the world should make me now deceive,
Since I must lose the use of all deceit?
Why should I then be false, since it is true
That I must die here, and live hence by truth?
I say again, if Lewis do win the day,
He is forsworn if e'er those eyes of yours
Behold another day break in the east;
But even this night, whose black contagious breath
Already smokes about the burning crest
Of the old, feeble, and day-wearied sun,
Even this ill night, your breathing shall expire,
Paying the fine of rated treachery
Even with a treacherous fine of all your lives,
If Lewis by your assistance win the day.
Commend me to one Hubert, with your king;
The love of him – and this respect besides,
For that my grandsire was an Englishman –
Awakes my conscience to confess all this.
In lieu whereof, I pray you, bear me hence
From forth the noise and rumour of the field,
Where I may think the remnant of my thoughts
In peace, and part this body and my soul
With contemplation and devout desires.
SALISBURY We do believe thee; and beshrew my soul
But I do love the favour and the form
Of this most fair occasion, by the which
We will untread the steps of damned flight,
And like a bated and retired flood,
Leaving our rankness and irregular course,
Stoop low within those bounds we have o'erlook'd,
And calmly run on in obedience
Even to our ocean, to our great King John.
My arm shall give thee help to bear thee hence;
For I do see the cruel pangs of death
Right in thine eye. Away, my friends! New flight,
And happy newness, that intends old right.
[*Exeunt, leading off Melun.*

SCENE V. *England. The French camp.*

Enter LEWIS and his Train.

LEWIS The sun of heaven, methought, was loath to set,
But stay'd and made the western welkin blush,
When English measure backward their own ground
In faint retire. O, bravely came we off,
When with a volley of our needless shot,
After such bloody toil, we bid good night;
And wound our tott'ring colours clearly up,
Last in the field and almost lords of it!

Enter a Messenger.

MESSENGER Where is my prince, the Dauphin?
LEWIS Here; what news?
MESSENGER The Count Melun is slain; the English lords
By his persuasion are again fall'n off,
And your supply, which you have wish'd so long,
Are cast away and sunk on Goodwin Sands.
LEWIS Ah, foul shrewd news! Beshrew thy very heart!
I did not think to be so sad to-night
As this hath made me. Who was he that said

King John did fly an hour or two before
The stumbling night did part our weary pow'rs?
MESSENGER Whoever spoke it, it is true, my lord.
LEWIS Well; keep good quarter and good care to-night;
The day shall not be up so soon as I
To try the fair adventure of to-morrow. [*Exeunt.*

SCENE VI. *An open place near Swinstead Abbey.*

Enter the BASTARD and HUBERT, severally.

HUBERT Who's there? Speak, ho! speak quickly, or I shoot.
BASTARD A friend. What art thou?
HUBERT Of the part of England.
BASTARD Whither dost thou go?
HUBERT What's that to thee? Why may I not demand
Of thine affairs as well as thou of mine?
BASTARD Hubert, I think.
HUBERT Thou hast a perfect thought.
I will upon all hazards well believe
Thou art my friend that know'st my tongue so well.
Who art thou?
BASTARD Who thou wilt. And if thou please,
Thou mayst befriend me so much as to think
I come one way of the Plantagenets.
HUBERT Unkind remembrance! thou and eyeless night
Have done me shame. Brave soldier, pardon me
That any accent breaking from thy tongue
Should scape the true acquaintance of mine ear.
BASTARD Come, come; sans compliment, what news abroad?
HUBERT Why, here walk I in the black brow of night
To find you out.
BASTARD Brief, then; and what's the news?
HUBERT O, my sweet sir, news fitting to the night,
Black, fearful, comfortless, and horrible.
BASTARD Show me the very wound of this ill news;
I am no woman, I'll not swoon at it.
HUBERT The King, I fear, is poison'd by a monk;
I left him almost speechless and broke out
To acquaint you with this evil, that you might
The better arm you to the sudden time
Than if you had at leisure known of this.
BASTARD How did he take it; who did taste to him?
HUBERT A monk, I tell you; a resolved villain,
Whose bowels suddenly burst out. The King
Yet speaks, and peradventure may recover.
BASTARD Who didst thou leave to tend his Majesty?
HUBERT Why, know you not? The lords are all come back,
And brought Prince Henry in their company;
At whose request the King hath pardon'd them,
And they are all about his Majesty.
BASTARD Withhold thine indignation, mighty heaven,
And tempt us not to bear above our power!
I'll tell thee, Hubert, half my power this night,
Passing these flats, are taken by the tide –
These Lincoln Washes have devoured them;
Myself, well-mounted, hardly have escap'd.
Away, before! conduct me to the King;
I doubt he will be dead or ere I come. [*Exeunt.*

SCENE VII. *The orchard at Swinstead Abbey.*

Enter PRINCE HENRY, SALISBURY, and BIGOT.

PRINCE HENRY It is too late; the life of all his blood
Is touch'd corruptibly, and his pure brain,
Which some suppose the soul's frail dwelling-house,
Doth by the idle comments that it makes
Foretell the ending of mortality.

Enter PEMBROKE.

PEMBROKE His Highness yet doth speak, and holds belief
That, being brought into the open air,
It would allay the burning quality
Of that fell poison which assaileth him.
PRINCE HENRY Let him be brought into the orchard here.
Doth he still rage? [*Exit Bigot.*
PEMBROKE He is more patient
Than when you left him; even now he sung.
PRINCE HENRY O vanity of sickness! Fierce extremes
In their continuance will not feel themselves.
Death, having prey'd upon the outward parts,
Leaves them invisible, and his siege is now
Against the mind, the which he pricks and wounds
With many legions of strange fantasies,
Which, in their throng and press to that last hold,
Confound themselves. 'Tis strange that death should sing.
I am the cygnet to this pale faint swan
Who chants a doleful hymn to his own death,
And from the organ-pipe of frailty sings
His soul and body to their lasting rest.
SALISBURY Be of good comfort, Prince; for you are born

To set a form upon that indigest
Which he hath left so shapeless and so rude.

Re-enter BIGOT and Attendants, who bring in KING JOHN in a chair.

KING JOHN Ay, marry, now my soul hath elbow-room;
It would not out at windows nor at doors.
There is so hot a summer in my bosom
That all my bowels crumble up to dust.
I am a scribbled form drawn with a pen
Upon a parchment, and against this fire
Do I shrink up.
PRINCE HENRY How fares your Majesty?
KING JOHN Poison'd – ill-fare! Dead, forsook, cast off;
And none of you will bid the winter come
To thrust his icy fingers in my maw,
Nor let my kingdom's rivers take their course
Through my burn'd bosom, nor entreat the north
To make his bleak winds kiss my parched lips
And comfort me with cold. I do not ask you much;
I beg cold comfort; and you are so strait
And so ingrateful you deny me that.
PRINCE HENRY O that there were some virtue in my tears,
That might relieve you!
KING JOHN The salt in them is hot.
Within me is a hell; and there the poison
Is as a fiend confin'd to tyrannize
On unreprievable condemned blood.

Enter the BASTARD.

BASTARD O, I am scalded with my violent motion
And spleen of speed to see your Majesty!
KING JOHN O cousin, thou art come to set mine eye!
The tackle of my heart is crack'd and burnt,
And all the shrouds wherewith my life should sail
And turned to one thread, one little hair;
My heart hath one poor string to stay it by,
Which holds but till thy news be uttered;
And then all this thou seest is but a clod
And module of confounded royalty.
BASTARD The Dauphin is preparing hitherward,
Where God He knows how we shall answer him;
For in a night the best part of my pow'r,
As I upon advantage did remove,
Were in the Washes all unwarily
Devoured by the unexpected flood.
[*The King dies.*
SALISBURY You breathe these dead news in as dead an ear.
My liege! my lord! But now a king – now thus.
PRINCE HENRY Even so must I run on, and even so stop.
What surety of the world, what hope, what stay,
When this was now a king, and now is clay?
BASTARD Art thou gone so? I do but stay behind
To do the office for thee of revenge,
And then my soul shall wait on thee to heaven,
As it on earth hath been thy servant still.
Now, now, you stars that move in your right spheres,
Where be your pow'rs? Show now your mended faiths,
And instantly return with me again
To push destruction and perpetual shame
Out of the weak door of our fainting land.
Straight let us seek, or straight we shall be sought;
The Dauphin rages at our very heels.
SALISBURY It seems you know not, then, so much as we:
The Cardinal Pandulph is within at rest,
Who half an hour since came from the Dauphin,
And brings from him such offers of our peace
As we with honour and respect may take,
With purpose presently to leave this war.
BASTARD He will the rather do it when he sees
Ourselves well sinewed to our defence.
SALISBURY Nay, 'tis in a manner done already;
For many carriages he hath dispatch'd
To the sea-side, and put his cause and quarrel
To the disposing of the Cardinal;
With whom yourself, myself, and other lords,
If you think meet, this afternoon will post
To consummate this business happily.
BASTARD Let it be so. And you, my noble Prince,
With other princes that may best be spar'd,
Shall wait upon your father's funeral.
PRINCE HENRY At Worcester must his body be interr'd;
For so he will'd it.
BASTARD Thither shall it, then;
And happily may your sweet self put on
The lineal state and glory of the land!
To whom, with all submission, on my knee
I do bequeath my faithful services
And true subjection everlastingly.
SALISBURY And the like tender of our love we make,
To rest without a spot for evermore.
PRINCE HENRY I have a kind soul that would give you thanks,
And knows not how to do it but with tears.
BASTARD O, let us pay the time but needful woe,
Since it hath been beforehand with our griefs.
This England never did, nor never shall,
Lie at the proud foot of a conqueror,

But when it first did help to wound itself.
Now these her princes are come home again,
Come the three corners of the world in arms,
And we shall shock them. Nought shall make us rue,
If England to itself do rest but true. [*Exeunt.*

King Richard the Second

Introduction by ROBERT GRANT

To use an operatic analogy, *Richard II* stands to its sequels *Henry IV* and *Henry V* as a kind of overture, in which all the major themes are deployed and their development and resolution anticipated. Economical, lucid and open-textured, yet also coolly ironical, *Richard II* is to its young author's so-called second tetralogy what the mature Wagner's *Rhinegold* was to *The Ring*. As in *Rhinegold*, the protagonists are mostly rather unsympathetic. This might be thought *Richard II*'s only serious dramatic weakness. But we may surely discount that as simply the price of the play's great virtues: its matchlessly acute observation and its wholly unsentimental realism concerning the crucial political questions of power, legitimacy and authority.

The play focuses with unusual intentness on the hereditary monarch's supposed divine right to unconditional obedience, irrespective of his actual fitness to rule. As a self-conscious theory, this seemingly ultra-traditionalist doctrine was in fact fairly new, and was far more vigorously promoted by the modernising and centralising Tudors and Stuarts than by their feudal predecessors. For traditionally, as Lord Chief Justice Coke pointed out to an unamused James I, the king was subject not only to God, but also to the laws and customs of his people, whose figurehead and representative he was.

Shakespeare seems sympathetic to this older view, which now seems more modern than its rival. Unlike Richard, a wise ruler, if he wants his laws to be obeyed, will surely try to be seen observing them himself. Richard's downfall is due partly to chance (he and his army are in Ireland when Bolingbroke invades), but mostly to his own childlike defects of character, his vanity and frivolity. These lead him first into extravagance and bankruptcy, thence to extortion, and finally to his barefaced seizure of Bolingbroke's inheritance. He almost wilfully alienates the jealous feudal nobility, helping himself to their goods, entrusting his offices to upstarts and parasites, and compromising the majesty of state (whence the nobility derives its lustre) by selling Crown revenues as if they were his alone to dispose of.

His fecklessness and arrogance, his manic oscillation between vainglory and self-pity, his invariable propensity to strike fantastic theatrical poses rather than face up to reality; above all, his obsessive, near-magical conviction that his divine right automatically guarantees him God's protection from the inevitable consequences of his folly and incompetence; all ensure that he learns nothing from experience until everything is irrevocably lost. Only when, tragically and far too late, he awakens to the truth about himself are we finally moved to sympathy and, struck by his unexpected courage in confronting his assassins, even to admiration.

By contrast with Richard, Henry Bolingbroke has everything a ruler needs except a title (though as his henchman Northumberland stresses, he is Richard's near kinsman). Popular and robustly patriotic, as the effete Richard is not, he is equally not short of the requisite deviousness, hypocrisy and ruthlessness. Never fully admitting, even to himself, the real reason for his return from banishment, though he has set sail for England even before learning of his dispossession, he more or less sleepwalks to the throne. Indeed, as both he and Richard recognise, the throne is effectively his from the instant that the helpless king is forced to acquiesce in his initial disobedience.

At least in the short run, and as Marvell later pointed out in his *Horatian Ode*, power won by force can only be maintained by force. The second tetralogy consistently demonstrates how true civil peace can be the product of neither force, nor virtue, nor law, nor myth taken singly, but only of all four together, and that when a successful usurper flouts one myth (hereditary right, say), he is constrained, if he hopes ever to rule by consent, to manufacture another.

The simplest alternative myth, hit upon independently by both Bolingbroke and the conscience-stricken defector York, is that success might in itself be evidence of God's approval and assistance. Unfortunately many of Henry's supporters, especially the self-seeking, deeply unattractive Northumberland, rather ascribe his victory to their own efforts, and accordingly, in *Henry IV*, reckon themselves hard done by in the division of the spoils. It is left to Bolingbroke's son, Henry V, to secure national unity by the most drastic and Machiavellian of expedients, viz. declaring unprovoked war on a neighbour, twisting the Church's arm to get it declared a crusade, leading it in person, and (perhaps most important of all) coming within an ace of defeat.

In such a world of disingenuousness, the deep chivalric pieties of John of Gaunt and the unfortunate Mowbray, already reduced to irrelevance by Richard's shamelessly cynical dismissal or exploitation of them, seem like mere fragrant memories of a vanished innocence. The honour which triumphs at Agincourt alongside a new populist and pragmatic conception of legitimacy is an altogether less rarefied affair.

King Richard The Second

DRAMATIS PERSONAE

KING RICHARD THE SECOND
JOHN OF GAUNT, *Duke of Lancaster,* EDMUND OF LANGLEY, *Duke of York*
uncles to the King
HENRY *surnamed* BOLINGBROKE
Duke of Hereford, son of John of Gaunt, afterwards King Henry IV
DUKE OF AUMERLE
son of the Duke of York
THOMAS MOWBRAY
Duke of Norfolk
DUKE OF SURREY
EARL OF SALISBURY
EARL BERKELEY
BUSHY, BAGOT, GREEN
favourites of King Richard
EARL OF NORTHUMBERLAND
HENRY PERCY *surnamed* HOTSPUR
his son
LORD ROSS
LORD WILLOUGHBY
LORD FITZWATER
BISHOP OF CARLISLE
ABBOT OF WESTMINSTER
LORD MARSHAL
SIR STEPHEN SCROOP
SIR PIERCE OF EXTON
Captain of a band of Welshmen
Two Gardeners
QUEEN
to King Richard
DUCHESS OF YORK
DUCHESS OF GLOUCESTER
widow of Thomas of Woodstock, Duke of Gloucester
Lady attending on the Queen
Lords, Heralds, Officers, Soldiers, a Keeper, a Messenger, a Groom, and other Attendants

THE SCENE: ENGLAND AND WALES.

ACT ONE

SCENE I. *London. The palace.*

Enter KING RICHARD, JOHN OF GAUNT, with other Nobles and Attendants.

KING RICHARD Old John of Gaunt, time-honoured Lancaster,
Hast thou, according to thy oath and band,
Brought hither Henry Hereford, thy bold son,
Here to make good the boist'rous late appeal,
Which then our leisure would not let us hear,
Against the Duke of Norfolk, Thomas Mowbray?
GAUNT I have, my liege.
KING RICHARD Tell me, moreover, hast thou sounded him
If he appeal the Duke on ancient malice,
Or worthily, as a good subject should,
On some known ground of treachery in him?
GAUNT As near as I could sift him on that argument,
On some apparent danger seen in him
Aim'd at your Highness – no inveterate malice.
KING RICHARD Then call them to our presence: face to face
And frowning brow to brow, ourselves will hear
The accuser and the accused freely speak.
High-stomach'd are they both and full of ire,
In rage, deaf as the sea, hasty as fire.

Enter BOLINGBROKE and MOWBRAY.

BOLINGBROKE Many years of happy days befall
My gracious sovereign, my most loving liege!
MOWBRAY Each day still better other's happiness
Until the heavens, envying earth's good hap,
Add an immortal title to your crown!
KING RICHARD We thank you both; yet one but flatters us,
As well appeareth by the cause you come;
Namely, to appeal each other of high treason.
Cousin of Hereford, what dost thou object
Against the Duke of Norfolk, Thomas Mowbray?
BOLINGBROKE First – heaven be the record to my speech!
In the devotion of a subject's love,
Tend'ring the precious safety of my prince,
And free from other misbegotten hate,
Come I appellant to this princely presence.
Now, Thomas Mowbray, do I turn to thee,
And mark my greeting well; for what I speak
My body shall make good upon this earth,
Or my divine soul answer it in heaven –
Thou art a traitor and a miscreant,
Too good to be so, and too bad to live,
Since the more fair and crystal is the sky,
The uglier seem the clouds that in it fly.
Once more, the more to aggravate the note,

With a foul traitor's name stuff I thy throat;
And wish – so please my sovereign – ere I move,
What my tongue speaks, my right drawn sword may prove.

MOWBRAY Let not my cold words here accuse my zeal.
'Tis not the trial of a woman's war,
The bitter clamour of two eager tongues,
Can arbitrate this cause betwixt us twain;
The blood is hot that must be cool'd for this.
Yet can I not of such tame patience boast
As to be hush'd and nought at all to say.
First, the fair reverence of your Highness curbs me
From giving reins and spurs to my free speech;
Which else would post until it had return'd
These terms of treason doubled down his throat.
Setting aside his blood's royalty,
And let him be no kinsman to my liege,
I do defy him, and I spit at him,
Call him a slanderous coward and a villain;
Which to maintain, I would allow him odds
And meet him, were I tied to run afoot
Even to the frozen ridges of the Alps,
Or any other ground inhabitable
Where ever Englishman durst set his foot.
Meantime let this defend my loyalty –
By all my hopes, most falsely doth he lie.

BOLINGBROKE Pale trembling coward, there I throw my gage,
Disclaiming here the kindred of the King;
And lay aside my high blood's royalty,
Which fear, not reverence, makes thee to except.
If guilty dread have left thee so much strength
As to take up mine honour's pawn, then stoop.
By that and all the rites of knighthood else
Will I make good against thee, arm to arm,
What I have spoke or thou canst worse devise.

MOWBRAY I take it up; and by that sword I swear
Which gently laid my knighthood on my shoulder
I'll answer thee in any fair degree
Or chivalrous design of knightly trial;
And when I mount, alive may I not light
If I be traitor or unjustly fight!

KING RICHARD What doth our cousin lay to Mowbray's charge?
It must be great that can inherit us
So much as of a thought of ill in him.

BOLINGBROKE Look what I speak, my life shall prove it true –
That Mowbray hath receiv'd eight thousand nobles
In name of lendings for your Highness' soldiers,
The which he hath detain'd for lewd employments
Like a false traitor and injurious villain.
Besides, I say and will in battle prove –
Or here, or elsewhere to the furthest verge
That ever was survey'd by English eye –
That all the treasons for these eighteen years
Complotted and contrived in this land
Fetch from false Mowbray their first head and spring.
Further I say, and further will maintain
Upon his bad life to make all this good,
That he did plot the Duke of Gloucester's death,
Suggest his soon-believing adversaries,
And consequently, like a traitor coward,
Sluic'd out his innocent soul through streams of blood;
Which blood, like sacrificing Abel's, cries,
Even from the tongueless caverns of the earth,
To me for justice and rough chastisement;
And, by the glorious worth of my descent,
This arm shall do it, or this life be spent.

KING RICHARD How high a pitch his resolution soars!
Thomas of Norfolk, what say'st thou to this?

MOWBRAY O, let my sovereign turn away his face
And bid his ears a little while be deaf,
Till I have told this slander of his blood
How God and good men hate so foul a liar.

KING RICHARD Mowbray, impartial are our eyes and ears.
Were he my brother, nay, my kingdom's heir,
As he is but my father's brother's son,
Now by my sceptre's awe I make a vow,
Such neighbour nearness to our sacred blood
Should nothing privilege him nor partialize
The unstooping firmness of my upright soul.
He is our subject, Mowbray; so art thou:
Free speech and fearless I to thee allow.

MOWBRAY Then, Bolingbroke, as low as to thy heart,
Through the false passage of thy throat, thou liest.
Three parts of that receipt I had for Calais
Disburs'd I duly to his Highness' soldiers;
The other part reserv'd I by consent,
For that my sovereign liege was in my debt
Upon remainder of a dear account
Since last I went to France to fetch his queen:
Now swallow down that lie. For Gloucester's death –
I slew him not, but to my own disgrace
Neglected my sworn duty in that case.
For you, my noble Lord of Lancaster,
The honourable father to my foe,
Once did I lay an ambush for your life,
A trespass that doth vex my grieved soul;
But ere I last receiv'd the sacrament
I did confess it, and exactly begg'd

Your Grace's pardon; and I hope I had it.
This is my fault. As for the rest appeal'd,
It issues from the rancour of a villain,
A recreant and most degenerate traitor;
Which in myself I boldly will defend,
And interchangeably hurl down my gage
Upon this overweening traitor's foot
To prove myself a loyal gentleman
Even in the best blood chamber'd in his bosom.
In haste whereof, most heartily I pray
Your Highness to assign our trial day.

KING RICHARD Wrath-kindled gentlemen, be rul'd by me;
Let's purge this choler without letting blood –
This we prescribe, though no physician;
Deep malice makes too deep incision.
Forget, forgive; conclude and be agreed:
Our doctors say this is no month to bleed.
Good uncle, let this end where it begun;
We'll calm the Duke of Norfolk, you your son.

GAUNT To be a make-peace shall become my age.
Throw down, my son, the Duke of Norfolk's gage.

KING RICHARD And, Norfolk, throw down his.

GAUNT When, Harry, when?
Obedience bids I should not bid again.

KING RICHARD Norfolk, throw down; we bid. There is no boot.

MOWBRAY Myself I throw, dread sovereign, at thy foot;
My life thou shalt command, but not my shame:
The one my duty owes; but my fair name,
Despite of death, that lives upon my grave
To dark dishonour's use thou shalt not have.
I am disgrac'd, impeach'd, and baffl'd here;
Pierc'd to the soul with slander's venom'd spear,
The which no balm can cure but his heartblood
Which breath'd this poison.

KING RICHARD Rage must be withstood:
Give me his gage – lions make leopards tame.

MOWBRAY Yea, but not change his spots. Take but my shame,
And I resign my gage. My dear dear lord,
The purest treasure mortal times afford
Is spotless reputation; that away,
Men are but gilded loam or painted clay.
A jewel in a ten-times barr'd-up chest
Is a bold spirit in a loyal breast.
Mine honour is my life; both grow in one;
Take honour from me, and my life is done:
Then, dear my liege, mine honour let me try;
In that I live, and for that will I die.

KING RICHARD Cousin, throw up your gage; do you begin.

BOLINGBROKE O, God defend my soul from such deep sin!
Shall I seem crest-fallen in my father's sight?
Or with pale beggar-fear impeach my height
Before this outdar'd dastard? Ere my tongue
Shall wound my honour with such feeble wrong
Or sound so base a parle, my teeth shall tear
The slavish motive of recanting fear,
And spit it bleeding in his high disgrace,
Where shame doth harbour, even in Mowbray's face. [*Exit Gaunt.*

KING RICHARD We were not born to sue, but to command;
Which since we cannot do to make you friends,
Be ready, as your lives shall answer it,
At Coventry, upon Saint Lambert's day.
There shall your swords and lances arbitrate
The swelling difference of your settled hate;
Since we can not atone you, we shall see
Justice design the victor's chivalry.
Lord Marshal, command our officers-at-arms
Be ready to direct these home alarms. [*Exeunt.*

SCENE II. *London. The Duke of Lancaster's palace.*

Enter JOHN OF GAUNT with the DUCHESS OF GLOUCESTER.

GAUNT Alas, the part I had in Woodstock's blood
Doth more solicit me than your exclaims
To stir against the butchers of his life!
But since correction lieth in those hands
Which made the fault that we cannot correct,
Put we our quarrel to the will of heaven;
Who, when they see the hours ripe on earth,
Will rain hot vengeance on offenders' heads.

DUCHESS Finds brotherhood in thee no sharper spur?
Hath love in thy old blood no living fire?
Edward's seven sons, whereof thyself art one,
Were as seven vials of his sacred blood,
Or seven fair branches springing from one root.
Some of those seven are dried by nature's course,
Some of those branches by the Destinies cut;
But Thomas, my dear lord, my life, my Gloucester,
One vial full of Edward's sacred blood,
One flourishing branch of his most royal root,
Is crack'd, and all the precious liquor spilt;
Is hack'd down, and his summer leaves all faded,
By envy's hand and murder's bloody axe.
Ah, Gaunt, his blood was thine! That bed, that womb,
That mettle, that self mould, that fashion'd thee,
Made him a man; and though thou livest and breathest,
Yet art thou slain in him. Thou dost consent
In some large measure to thy father's death

In that thou seest thy wretched brother die,
Who was the model of thy father's life.
Call it not patience, Gaunt – it is despair;
In suff'ring thus thy brother to be slaught'red,
Thou showest the naked pathway to thy life,
Teaching stern murder how to butcher thee.
That which in mean men we entitle patience
Is pale cold cowardice in noble breasts.
What shall I say? To safeguard thine own life
The best way is to venge my Gloucester's death.

GAUNT God's is the quarrel; for God's substitute,
His deputy anointed in His sight,
Hath caus'd his death; the which if wrongfully,
Let heaven revenge; for I may never lift
An angry arm against His minister.

DUCHESS Where then, alas, may I complain myself?

GAUNT To God, the widow's champion and defence.

DUCHESS Why then I will. Farewell, old Gaunt.
Thou goest to Coventry, there to behold
Our cousin Hereford and fell Mowbray fight.
O, sit my husband's wrongs on Hereford's spear,
That it may enter butcher Mowbray's breast!
Or, if misfortune miss the first career,
Be Mowbray's sins so heavy in his bosom
That they may break his foaming courser's back
And throw the rider headlong in the lists,
A caitiff recreant to my cousin Hereford!
Farewell, old Gaunt; thy sometimes brother's wife,
With her companion, Grief, must end her life.

GAUNT Sister, farewell; I must to Coventry.
As much good stay with thee as go with me!

DUCHESS Yet one word more – grief boundeth where it falls,
Not with the empty hollowness, but weight.
I take my leave before I have begun,
For sorrow ends not when it seemeth done.
Commend me to thy brother, Edmund York.
Lo, this is all – nay, yet depart not so;
Though this be all, do not so quickly go;
I shall remember more. Bid him – ah, what? –
With all good speed at Plashy visit me.
Alack, and what shall good old York there see
But empty lodgings and unfurnish'd walls,
Unpeopled offices, untrodden stones?
And what hear there for welcome but my groans?
Therefore commend me; let him not come there
To seek out sorrow that dwells every where.
Desolate, desolate, will I hence and die;
The last leave of thee takes my weeping eye.

[Exeunt.

SCENE III. *The lists at Coventry.*

Enter the LORD MARSHAL and the DUKE OF AUMERLE.

MARSHAL My Lord Aumerle, is Harry Hereford arm'd?

AUMERLE Yea, at all points; and longs to enter in.

MARSHAL The Duke of Norfolk, sprightfully and bold,
Stays but the summons of the appellant's trumpet.

AUMERLE Why then, the champions are prepar'd, and stay
For nothing but his Majesty's approach.

The trumpets sound, and the KING enters with his nobles, GAUNT, BUSHY, BAGOT, GREEN, and Others. When they are set, enter MOWBRAY, DUKE OF NORFOLK, in arms, defendant, and a Herald.

KING RICHARD Marshal, demand of yonder champion
The cause of his arrival here in arms;
Ask him his name; and orderly proceed
To swear him in the justice of his cause.

MARSHAL In God's name and the King's, say who thou art,
And why thou comest thus knightly clad in arms;
Against what man thou com'st, and what thy quarrel.
Speak truly on thy knighthood and thy oath;
As so defend thee heaven and thy valour!

MOWBRAY My name is Thomas Mowbray, Duke of Norfolk;
Who hither come engaged by my oath –
Which God defend a knight should violate! –
Both to defend my loyalty and truth
To God, my King, and my succeeding issue,
Against the Duke of Hereford that appeals me;
And, by the grace of God and this mine arm,
To prove him, in defending of myself,
A traitor to my God, my King, and me.
And as I truly fight, defend me heaven!

The trumpets sound. Enter BOLINGBROKE, DUKE OF HEREFORD, appellant, in armour, and a Herald.

KING RICHARD Marshal, ask yonder knight in arms,
Both who he is and why he cometh hither
Thus plated in habiliments of war;
And formally, according to our law,
Depose him in the justice of his cause.

MARSHAL What is thy name? and wherefore com'st thou hither
Before King Richard in his royal lists?
Against whom comest thou? and what's thy quarrel?
Speak like a true knight, so defend thee heaven!

BOLINGBROKE Harry of Hereford, Lancaster, and Derby,
Am I; who ready here do stand in arms
To prove, by God's grace and my body's valour,
In lists on Thomas Mowbray, Duke of Norfolk,
That he is a traitor, foul and dangerous,
To God of heaven, King Richard, and to me.
And as I truly fight, defend me heaven!
MARSHAL On pain of death, no person be so bold
Or daring-hardy as to touch the lists,
Except the Marshal and such officers
Appointed to direct these fair designs.
BOLINGBROKE Lord Marshal, let me kiss my sovereign's hand,
And bow my knee before his Majesty;
For Mowbray and myself are like two men
That vow a long and weary pilgrimage.
Then let us take a ceremonious leave
And loving farewell of our several friends.
MARSHAL The appellant in all duty greets your Highness,
And craves to kiss your hand and take his leave.
KING RICHARD We will descend and fold him in our arms.
Cousin of Hereford, as thy cause is right,
So be thy fortune in this royal fight!
Farewell, my blood; which if to-day thou shed,
Lament we may, but not revenge thee dead.
BOLINGBROKE O, let no noble eye profane a tear
For me, if I be gor'd with Mowbray's spear.
As confident as is the falcon's flight
Against a bird, do I with Mowbray fight.
My loving lord, I take my leave of you:
Of you, my noble cousin, Lord Aumerle;
Not sick, although I have to do with death,
But lusty, young, and cheerly drawing breath.
Lo, as at English feasts, so I regreet
The daintiest last, to make the end most sweet.
O thou, the earthly author of my blood,
Whose youthful spirit, in me regenerate,
Doth with a twofold vigour lift me up
To reach at victory above my head,
Add proof unto mine armour with thy prayers,
And with thy blessings steel my lance's point,
That it may enter Mowbray's waxen coat
And furbish new the name of John o' Gaunt,
Even in the lusty haviour of his son.
GAUNT God in thy good cause make thee prosperous!
Be swift like lightning in the execution,
And let thy blows, doubly redoubled,
Fall like amazing thunder on the casque
Of thy adverse pernicious enemy.
Rouse up thy youthful blood, be valiant, and live.
BOLINGBROKE Mine innocence and Saint George to thrive!
MOWBRAY However God or fortune cast my lot,
There lives or dies, true to King Richard's throne,
A loyal, just, and upright gentleman.
Never did captive with a freer heart
Cast off his chains of bondage, and embrace
His golden uncontroll'd enfranchisement,
More than my dancing soul doth celebrate
This feast of battle with mine adversary.
Most mighty liege, and my companion peers,
Take from my mouth the wish of happy years.
As gentle and as jocund as to jest
Go I to fight: truth hath a quiet breast.
KING RICHARD Farewell, my lord, securely I espy
Virtue with valour couched in thine eye.
Order the trial, Marshal, and begin.
MARSHAL Harry of Hereford, Lancaster, and Derby,
Receive thy lance; and God defend the right!
BOLINGBROKE Strong as a tower in hope, I cry amen.
MARSHAL [*To an Officer*] Go bear this lance to Thomas, Duke of Norfolk.
1 HERALD Harry of Hereford, Lancaster, and Derby,
Stands here for God, his sovereign, and himself,
On pain to be found false and recreant,
To prove the Duke of Norfolk, Thomas Mowbray,
A traitor to his God, his King, and him;
And dares him to set forward to the fight.
2 HERALD Here standeth Thomas Mowbray, Duke of Norfolk,
On pain to be found false and recreant,
Both to defend himself, and to approve
Henry of Hereford, Lancaster, and Derby,
To God, his sovereign, and to him disloyal,
Courageously and with a free desire
Attending but the signal to begin.
MARSHAL Sound trumpets; and set forward, combatants. [*A charge sounded.*
Stay, the King hath thrown his warder down.
KING RICHARD Let them lay by their helmets and their spears,
And both return back to their chairs again.
Withdraw with us; and let the trumpets sound
While we return these dukes what we decree.

A long flourish, while the King consults his Council.

Draw near,
And list what with our council we have done.
For that our kingdom's earth should not be soil'd
With that dear blood which it hath fostered;
And for our eyes do hate the dire aspect
Of civil wounds plough'd up with neighbours' sword;

And for we think the eagle-winged pride
Of sky-aspiring and ambitious thoughts,
With rival-hating envy, set on you
To wake our peace, which in our country's cradle
Draws the sweet infant breath of gentle sleep;
Which so rous'd up with boist'rous untun'd drums,
With harsh-resounding trumpets' dreadful bray,
And grating shock of wrathful iron arms,
Might from our quiet confines fright fair peace
And make us wade even in our kindred's blood –
Therefore we banish you our territories.
You, cousin Hereford, upon pain of life,
Till twice five summers have enrich'd our fields
Shall not regreet our fair dominions,
But tread the stranger paths of banishment.

BOLINGBROKE Your will be done. This must my comfort be –
That sun that warms you here shall shine on me,
And those his golden beams to you here lent
Shall point on me and gild my banishment.

KING RICHARD Norfolk, for thee remains a heavier doom,
Which I with some unwillingness pronounce:
The sly slow hours shall not determinate
The dateless limit of thy dear exile;
The hopeless word of 'never to return'
Breathe I against thee, upon pain of life.

MOWBRAY A heavy sentence, my most sovereign liege,
And all unlook'd for from your Highness' mouth.
A dearer merit, not so deep a maim
As to be cast forth in the common air,
Have I deserved at your Highness' hands.
The language I have learnt these forty years,
My native English, now I must forgo;
And now my tongue's use is to me no more
Than an unstringed viol or a harp;
Or like a cunning instrument cas'd up
Or, being open, put into his hands
That knows no touch to tune the harmony.
Within my mouth you have engaol'd my tongue,
Doubly portcullis'd with my teeth and lips;
And dull, unfeeling, barren ignorance
Is made my gaoler to attend on me.
I am too old to fawn upon a nurse,
Too far in years to be a pupil now.
What is thy sentence, then, but speechless death,
Which robs my tongue from breathing native breath?

KING RICHARD It boots thee not to be compassionate;
After our sentence plaining comes too late.

MOWBRAY Then thus I turn me from my country's light,
To dwell in solemn shades of endless night.

KING RICHARD Return again, and take an oath with thee.
Lay on our royal sword your banish'd hands;
Swear by the duty that you owe to God,
Our part therein we banish with yourselves,
To keep the oath that we administer:
You never shall, so help you truth and God,
Embrace each other's love in banishment;
Nor never look upon each other's face;
Nor never write, regreet, nor reconcile
This louring tempest of your home-bred hate;
Nor never by advised purpose meet
To plot, contrive, or complot any ill,
'Gainst us, our state, our subjects, or our land.

BOLINGBROKE I swear.

MOWBRAY And I, to keep all this.

BOLINGBROKE Norfolk, so far as to mine enemy:
By this time, had the King permitted us,
One of our souls had wand'red in the air,
Banish'd this frail sepulchre of our flesh,
As now our flesh is banish'd from this land –
Confess thy treasons ere thou fly the realm;
Since thou hast far to go, bear not along
The clogging burden of a guilty soul.

MOWBRAY No, Bolingbroke; if ever I were traitor,
My name be blotted from the book of life,
And I from heaven banish'd as from hence!
But what thou art, God, thou, and I, do know;
And all too soon, I fear, the King shall rue.
Farewell, my liege. Now no way can I stray:
Save back to England, all the world's my way.

[*Exit*.

KING RICHARD Uncle, even in the glasses of thine eyes
I see thy grieved heart. Thy sad aspect
Hath from the number of his banish'd years
Pluck'd four away. [*To Bolingbroke*] Six frozen winters spent,
Return with welcome home from banishment.

BOLINGBROKE How long a time lies in one little word!
Four lagging winters and four wanton springs
End in a word: such is the breath of Kings.

GAUNT I thank my liege that in regard of me
He shortens four years of my son's exile;
But little vantage shall I reap thereby,
For ere the six years that he hath to spend
Can change their moons and bring their times about,
My oil-dried lamp and time-bewasted light
Shall be extinct with age and endless night;
My inch of taper will be burnt and done,

And blindfold death not let me see my son.
KING RICHARD Why, uncle, thou hast many years to live.
GAUNT But not a minute, King, that thou canst give:
Shorten my days thou canst with sullen sorrow
And pluck nights from me, but not lend a morrow;
Thou canst help time to furrow me with age,
But stop no wrinkle in his pilgrimage;
Thy word is current with him for my death,
But dead, thy kingdom cannot buy my breath.
KING RICHARD Thy son is banish'd upon good advice,
Whereto thy tongue a party-verdict gave.
Why at our justice seem'st thou then to lour?
GAUNT Things sweet to taste prove in digestion sour.
You urg'd me as a judge; but I had rather
You would have bid me argue like a father.
O, had it been a stranger, not my child,
To smooth his fault I should have been more mild.
A partial slander sought I to avoid,
And in the sentence my own life destroy'd.
Alas, I look'd when some of you should say
I was too strict to make mine own away;
But you gave leave to my unwilling tongue
Against my will to do myself this wrong.
KING RICHARD Cousin, farewell; and, uncle, bid him so.
Six years we banish him, and he shall go.
[*Flourish. Exit King with train.*
AUMERLE Cousin, farewell; what presence must not know,
From where you do remain let paper show.
MARSHAL My lord, no leave take I, for I will ride
As far as land will let me by your side.
GAUNT O, to what purpose dost thou hoard thy words,
That thou returnest no greeting to thy friends?
BOLINGBROKE I have too few to take my leave of you,
When the tongue's office should be prodigal
To breathe the abundant dolour of the heart.
GAUNT Thy grief is but thy absence for a time.
BOLINGBROKE Joy absent, grief is present for that time.
GAUNT What is six winters? They are quickly gone.
BOLINGBROKE To men in joy; but grief makes one hour ten.
GAUNT Call it a travel that thou tak'st for pleasure.
BOLINGBROKE My heart will sigh when I miscall it so,
Which finds it an enforced pilgrimage.
GAUNT The sullen passage of thy weary steps
Esteem as foil wherein thou art to set
The precious jewel of thy home return.
BOLINGBROKE Nay, rather, every tedious stride I make
Will but remember me what a deal of world
I wander from the jewels that I love.
Must I not serve a long apprenticehood
To foreign passages; and in the end,
Having my freedom, boast of nothing else
But that I was a journeyman to grief?
GAUNT All places that the eye of heaven visits
Are to a wise man ports and happy havens.
Teach thy necessity to reason thus:
There is no virtue like necessity.
Think not the King did banish thee,
But thou the King. Woe doth the heavier sit
Where it perceives it is but faintly borne.
Go, say I sent thee forth to purchase honour,
And not the King exil'd thee; or suppose
Devouring pestilence hangs in our air
And thou art flying to a fresher clime.
Look what thy soul holds dear, imagine it
To lie that way thou goest, not whence thou com'st.
Suppose the singing birds musicians,
The grass whereon thou tread'st the presence strew'd,
The flowers fair ladies, and thy steps no more
Than a delightful measure or a dance;
For gnarling sorrow hath less power to bite
The man that mocks at it and sets it light.
BOLINGBROKE O, who can hold a fire in his hand
By thinking on the frosty Caucasus?
Or cloy the hungry edge of appetite
By bare imagination of a feast?
Or wallow naked in December snow
By thinking on fantastic summer's heat?
O, no! the apprehension of the good
Gives but the greater feeling to the worse.
Fell sorrow's tooth doth never rankle more
Than when he bites, but lanceth not the sore.
GAUNT Come, come, my son, I'll bring thee on thy way.
Had I thy youth and cause, I would not stay.
BOLINGBROKE Then, England's ground, farewell; sweet soil, adieu;
My mother, and my nurse, that bears me yet!
Where'er I wander, boast of this I can:
Though banish'd, yet a trueborn English man.
[*Exeunt.*

SCENE IV. *London. The court.*

Enter the KING, with BAGOT and GREEN, at one door; and the DUKE OF AUMERLE at another.

KING RICHARD We did observe. Cousin Aumerle,
How far brought you high Hereford on his way?
AUMERLE I brought high Hereford, if you call him so,
But to the next high way, and there I left him.
KING RICHARD And say, what store of parting tears were shed?
AUMERLE Faith, none for me; except the north-east wind,
Which then blew bitterly against our faces,
Awak'd the sleeping rheum, and so by chance
Did grace our hollow parting with a tear.
KING RICHARD What said our cousin when you parted with him?
AUMERLE 'Farewell.'
And, for my heart disdained that my tongue
Should so profane the word, that taught me craft
To counterfeit oppression of such grief
That words seem'd buried in my sorrow's grave.
Marry, would the word 'farewell' have length'ned hours
And added years to his short banishment,
He should have had a volume of farewells;
But since it would not, he had none of me.
KING RICHARD He is our cousin, cousin; but 'tis doubt,
When time shall call him home from banishment,
Whether our kinsman come to see his friends.
Ourself, and Bushy, Bagot here, and Green,
Observ'd his courtship to the common people;
How he did seem to dive into their hearts
With humble and familiar courtesy;
What reverence he did throw away on slaves,
Wooing poor craftsmen with the craft of smiles
And patient underbearing of his fortune,
As 'twere to banish their affects with him.
Off goes his bonnet to an oyster-wench;
A brace of draymen bid God speed him well
And had the tribute of his supple knee,
With 'Thanks, my countrymen, my loving friends';
As were our England in reversion his,
And he our subjects' next degree in hope.
GREEN Well, he is gone; and with him go these thoughts!
Now for the rebels which stand out in Ireland,
Expedient manage must be made, my liege,
Ere further leisure yield them further means
For their advantage and your Highness' loss.
KING RICHARD We will ourself in person to this war;
And, for our coffers, with too great a court
And liberal largess, are grown somewhat light,
We are enforc'd to farm our royal realm;
The revenue whereof shall furnish us
For our affairs in hand. If that come short,
Our substitutes at home shall have blank charters;
Whereto, when they shall know what men are rich,
They shall subscribe them for large sums of gold,
And send them after to supply our wants;
For we will make for Ireland presently.

Enter BUSHY.

Bushy, what news?
BUSHY Old John of Gaunt is grievous sick, my lord,
Suddenly taken; and hath sent post-haste
To entreat your Majesty to visit him.
KING RICHARD Where lies he?
BUSHY At Ely House.
KING RICHARD Now put it, God, in the physician's mind
To help him to his grave immediately!
The lining of his coffers shall make coats
To deck our soldiers for these Irish wars.
Come, gentlemen, let's all go visit him.
Pray God we may make haste, and come too late!
ALL Amen. [*Exeunt.*

ACT TWO

SCENE I. *London. Ely House.*

Enter JOHN OF GAUNT, sick, with the DUKE OF YORK, etc.

GAUNT Will the King come, that I may breathe my last
In wholesome counsel to his unstaid youth?
YORK Vex not yourself, nor strive not with your breath;
For all in vain comes counsel to his ear.
GAUNT O, but they say the tongues of dying men
Enforce attention like deep harmony.
Where words are scarce, they are seldom spent in vain;
For they breathe truth that breathe their words in pain.
He that no more must say is listen'd more
Than they whom youth and ease have taught to

glose;
More are men's ends mark'd than their lives before.
The setting sun, and music at the close,
As the last taste of sweets, is sweetest last,
Writ in remembrance more than things long past.
Though Richard my life's counsel would not hear,
My death's sad tale may yet undeaf his ear.

YORK No; it is stopp'd with other flattering sounds,
As praises, of whose taste the wise are fond,
Lascivious metres, to whose venom sound
The open ear of youth doth always listen;
Report of fashions in proud Italy,
Whose manners still our tardy apish nation
Limps after in base imitation.
Where doth the world thrust forth a vanity –
So it be new, there's no respect how vile –
That is not quickly buzz'd into his ears?
Then all too late comes counsel to be heard
Where will doth mutiny with wit's regard.
Direct not him whose way himself will choose.
'Tis breath thou lack'st, and that breath wilt thou lose.

GAUNT Methinks I am a prophet new inspir'd,
And thus expiring do foretell of him:
His rash fierce blaze of riot cannot last,
For violent fires soon burn out themselves;
Small showers last long, but sudden storms are short;
He tires betimes that spurs too fast betimes;
With eager feeding food doth choke the feeder;
Light vanity, insatiate cormorant,
Consuming means, soon preys upon itself.
This royal throne of kings, this scept'red isle,
This earth of majesty, this seat of Mars,
This other Eden, demi-paradise,
This fortress built by Nature for herself
Against infection and the hand of war,
This happy breed of men, this little world,
This precious stone set in the silver sea,
Which serves it in the office of a wall,
Or as a moat defensive to a house,
Against the envy of less happier lands;
This blessed plot, this earth, this realm, this England,
This nurse, this teeming womb of royal kings,
Fear'd by their breed, and famous by their birth,
Renowned for their deeds as far from home,
For Christian service and true chivalry,
As is the sepulchre in stubborn Jewry
Of the world's ransom, blessed Mary's Son;
This land of such dear souls, this dear dear land,
Dear for her reputation through the world,
Is now leas'd out – I die pronouncing it –
Like to a tenement or pelting farm.
England, bound in with the triumphant sea,
Whose rocky shore beats back the envious siege
Of wat'ry Neptune, is now bound in with shame,
With inky blots and rotten parchment bonds;
That England, that was wont to conquer others,
Hath made a shameful conquest of itself.
Ah, would the scandal vanish with my life,
How happy then were my ensuing death!

Enter KING and QUEEN, AUMERLE, BUSHY, GREEN, BAGOT, ROSS, and WILLOUGHBY.

YORK The King is come; deal mildly with his youth,
For young hot colts being rag'd do rage the more.

QUEEN How fares our noble uncle Lancaster?

KING RICHARD What comfort, man? How is't with aged Gaunt?

GAUNT O, how that name befits my composition!
Old Gaunt, indeed; and gaunt in being old.
Within me grief hath kept a tedious fast;
And who abstains from meat that is not gaunt?
For sleeping England long time have I watch'd;
Watching breeds leanness, leanness is all gaunt.
The pleasure that some fathers feeds upon
Is my strict fast – I mean my children's looks;
And therein fasting, hast thou made me gaunt.
Gaunt am I for the grave, gaunt as a grave,
Whose hollow womb inherits nought but bones.

KING RICHARD Can sick men play so nicely with their names?

GAUNT No, misery makes sport to mock itself:
Since thou dost seek to kill my name in me,
I mock my name, great king, to flatter thee.

KING RICHARD Should dying men flatter with those that live?

GAUNT No, no; men living flatter those that die.

KING RICHARD Thou, now a-dying, sayest thou flatterest me.

GAUNT O, no! thou diest, though I the sicker be.

KING RICHARD I am in health, I breathe, and see thee ill.

GAUNT Now He that made me knows I see thee ill;
Ill in myself to see, and in thee seeing ill.
Thy death-bed is no lesser than thy land
Wherein thou liest in reputation sick;
And thou, too careless patient as thou art,
Commit'st thy anointed body to the cure
Of those physicians that first wounded thee:
A thousand flatterers sit within thy crown,
Whose compass is no bigger than thy head;
And yet, incaged in so small a verge,
The waste is no whit lesser than thy land.

O, had thy grandsire with a prophet's eye
Seen how his son's son should destroy his sons,
From forth thy reach he would have laid thy shame,
Deposing thee before thou wert possess'd,
Which art possess'd now to depose thyself.
Why, cousin, wert thou regent of the world,
It were a shame to let this land by lease;
But for thy world enjoying but this land,
Is it not more than shame to shame it so?
Landlord of England art thou now, not King.
Thy state of law is bondslave to the law;
And thou –

KING RICHARD A lunatic lean-witted fool,
Presuming on an ague's privilege,
Darest with thy frozen admonition
Make pale our cheek, chasing the royal blood
With fury from his native residence.
Now by my seat's right royal majesty,
Wert thou not brother to great Edward's son,
This tongue that runs so roundly in thy head
Should run thy head from thy unreverent shoulders.

GAUNT O, spare me not, my brother Edward's son,
For that I was his father Edward's son;
That blood already, like the pelican,
Hast thou tapp'd out, and drunkenly carous'd.
My brother Gloucester, plain well-meaning soul –
Whom fair befall in heaven 'mongst happy souls! –
May be a precedent and witness good
That thou respect'st not spilling Edward's blood.
Join with the present sickness that I have;
And thy unkindness be like crooked age,
To crop at once a too long withered flower.
Live in thy shame, but die not shame with thee!
These words hereafter thy tormentors be!
Convey me to my bed, then to my grave.
Love they to live that love and honour have.

[*Exit, borne out by his Attendants*.

KING RICHARD And let them die that age and sullens have;
For both hast thou, and both become the grave.

YORK I do beseech your Majesty impute his words
To wayward sickliness and age in him.
He loves you, on my life, and holds you dear
As Harry Duke of Hereford, were he here.

KING RICHARD Right, you say true: as Hereford's love, so his;
As theirs, so mine; and all be as it is.

Enter NORTHUMBERLAND.

NORTHUMBERLAND My liege, old Gaunt commends him to your Majesty.

KING RICHARD What says he?

NORTHUMBERLAND Nay, nothing; all is said.
His tongue is now a stringless instrument;
Words, life, and all, old Lancaster hath spent.

YORK Be York the next that must be bankrupt so!
Though death be poor, it ends a mortal woe.

KING RICHARD The ripest fruit first falls, and so doth he;
His time is spent, our pilgrimage must be.
So much for that. Now for our Irish wars.
We must supplant those rough rug-headed kerns,
Which live like venom where no venom else
But only they have privilege to live.
And for these great affairs do ask some charge,
Towards our assistance we do seize to us
The plate, coin, revenues, and moveables,
Whereof our uncle Gaunt did stand possess'd.

YORK How long shall I be patient? Ah, how long
Shall tender duty make me suffer wrong?
Not Gloucester's death, nor Hereford's banishment,
Nor Gaunt's rebukes, nor England's private wrongs,
Nor the prevention of poor Bolingbroke
About his marriage, nor my own disgrace,
Have ever made me sour my patient cheek
Or bend one wrinkle on my sovereign's face.
I am the last of noble Edward's sons,
Of whom thy father, Prince of Wales, was first.
In war was never lion rag'd more fierce,
In peace was never gentle lamb more mild,
Than was that young and princely gentleman.
His face thou hast, for even so look'd he,
Accomplish'd with the number of thy hours;
But when he frown'd, it was against the French
And not against his friends. His noble hand
Did win what he did spend, and spent not that
Which his triumphant father's hand had won.
His hands were guilty of no kindred blood,
But bloody with the enemies of his kin.
O Richard! York is too far gone with grief,
Or else he never would compare between –

KING RICHARD Why, uncle, what's the matter?

YORK O my liege,
Pardon me, if you please; if not, I, pleas'd
Not to be pardoned, am content withal.
Seek you to seize and gripe into your hands
The royalties and rights of banish'd Hereford?
Is not Gaunt dead? and doth not Hereford live?
Was not Gaunt just? and is not Harry true?
Did not the one deserve to have an heir?
Is not his heir a well-deserving son?
Take Hereford's rights away, and take from Time
His charters and his customary rights;
Let not to-morrow then ensue to-day;

Be not thyself – for how art thou a king
But by fair sequence and succession?
Now, afore God – God forbid I say true! –
If you do wrongfully seize Hereford's rights,
Call in the letters patents that he hath
By his attorneys-general to sue
His livery, and deny his off'red homage,
You pluck a thousand dangers on your head,
You lose a thousand well-disposed hearts,
And prick my tender patience to those thoughts
Which honour and allegiance cannot think.
KING RICHARD Think what you will, we seize into our hands
His plate, his goods, his money, and his lands.
YORK I'll not be by the while. My liege, farewell.
What will ensue hereof there's none can tell;
But by bad courses may be understood
That their events can never fall out good. *[Exit.*

KING RICHARD Go, Bushy, to the Earl of Wiltshire straight;
Bid him repair to us to Ely House
To see this business. To-morrow next
We will for Ireland; and 'tis time, I trow.
And we create, in absence of ourself,
Our Uncle York Lord Governor of England;
For he is just, and always lov'd us well.
Come on, our queen; to-morrow must we part;
Be merry, for our time of stay is short.

[Flourish. Exeunt King, Queen, Bushy, Aumerle, Green, and Bagot.

NORTHUMBERLAND Well, lords, the Duke of Lancaster is dead.
ROSS And living too; for now his son is Duke.
WILLOUGHBY Barely in title, not in revenues.
NORTHUMBERLAND Richly in both, if justice had her right.
ROSS My heart is great; but it must break with silence,
Ere't be disburdened with a liberal tongue.
NORTHUMBERLAND Nay, speak thy mind; and let him ne'er speak more
That speaks thy words again to do thee harm!
WILLOUGHBY Tends that thou wouldst speak to the Duke of Hereford?
If it be so, out with it boldly, man;
Quick is mine ear to hear of good towards him.
ROSS No good at all that I can do for him;
Unless you call it good to pity him,
Bereft and gelded of his patrimony.
NORTHUMBERLAND Now, afore God, 'tis shame such wrongs are borne
In him, a royal prince, and many moe
Of noble blood in this declining land.
The King is not himself, but basely led
By flatterers; and what they will inform,
Merely in hate, 'gainst any of us all,
That will the King severely prosecute
'Gainst us, our lives, our children, and our heirs.
ROSS The commons hath he pill'd with grievous taxes;
And quite lost their hearts; the nobles hath he fin'd
For ancient quarrels and quite lost their hearts.
WILLOUGHBY And daily new exactions are devis'd,
As blanks, benevolences, and I wot not what;
But what, a God's name, doth become of this?
NORTHUMBERLAND Wars hath not wasted it, for warr'd he hath not,
But basely yielded upon compromise
That which his noble ancestors achiev'd with blows.
More hath he spent in peace than they in wars.
ROSS The Earl of Wiltshire hath the realm in farm.
WILLOUGHBY The King's grown bankrupt like a broken man.
NORTHUMBERLAND Reproach and dissolution hangeth over him.
ROSS He hath not money for these Irish wars,
His burdenous taxations notwithstanding,
But by the robbing of the banish'd Duke.
NORTHUMBERLAND His noble kinsman – most degenerate king!
But, lords, we hear this fearful tempest sing,
Yet seek no shelter to avoid the storm;
We see the wind sit sore upon our sails,
And yet we strike not, but securely perish.
ROSS We see the very wreck that we must suffer;
And unavoided is the danger now
For suffering so the causes of our wreck.
NORTHUMBERLAND Not so; even through the hollow eyes of death
I spy life peering; but I dare not say
How near the tidings of our comfort is.
WILLOUGHBY Nay, let us share thy thoughts as thou dost ours.
ROSS Be confident to speak, Northumberland.
We three are but thyself, and, speaking so,
Thy words are but as thoughts; therefore be bold.
NORTHUMBERLAND Then thus: I have from Le Port Blanc, a bay
In Brittany, receiv'd intelligence
That Harry Duke of Hereford, Rainold Lord Cobham,
That late broke from the Duke of Exeter,
His brother, Archbishop late of Canterbury,
Sir Thomas Erpingham, Sir John Ramston,
Sir John Norbery, Sir Robert Waterton, and Francis Quoint –
All these, well furnish'd by the Duke of Britaine,

With eight tall ships, three thousand men of war,
Are making hither with all due expedience,
And shortly mean to touch our northern shore.
Perhaps they had ere this, but that they stay
The first departing of the King for Ireland.
If then we shall shake off our slavish yoke,
Imp out our drooping country's broken wing,
Redeem from broking pawn the blemish'd crown,
Wipe off the dust that hides our sceptre's gilt,
And make high majesty look like itself,
Away with me in post to Ravenspurgh;
But if you faint, as fearing to do so,
Stay and be secret, and myself will go.

ROSS To horse, to horse! Urge doubts to them that fear.

WILLOUGHBY Hold out my horse, and I will first be there. *[Exeunt.*

SCENE II. *Windsor Castle.*

Enter QUEEN, BUSHY, and BAGOT.

BUSHY Madam, your Majesty is too much sad.
You promis'd, when you parted with the King,
To lay aside life-harming heaviness
And entertain a cheerful disposition.

QUEEN To please the King, I did; to please myself
I cannot do it; yet I know no cause
Why I should welcome such a guest as grief,
Save bidding farewell to so sweet a guest
As my sweet Richard. Yet again methinks
Some unborn sorrow, ripe in fortune's womb,
Is coming towards me, and my inward soul
With nothing trembles. At some thing it grieves
More than with parting from my lord the King.

BUSHY Each substance of a grief hath twenty shadows,
Which shows like grief itself, but is not so;
For sorrow's eye, glazed with blinding tears,
Divides one thing entire to many objects,
Like perspectives which, rightly gaz'd upon,
Show nothing but confusion – ey'd awry,
Distinguish form. So your sweet Majesty,
Looking awry upon your lord's departure,
Find shapes of grief more than himself to wail;
Which, look'd on as it is, is nought but shadows
Of what it is not. Then, thrice-gracious Queen,
More than your lord's departure weep not – more is not seen;
Or if it be, 'tis with false sorrow's eye,
Which for things true weeps things imaginary.

QUEEN It may be so; but yet my inward soul
Persuades me it is otherwise. Howe'er it be,
I cannot but be sad; so heavy sad
As – though, on thinking, on no thought I think –
Makes me with heavy nothing faint and shrink.

BUSHY 'Tis nothing but conceit, my gracious lady.

QUEEN 'Tis nothing less: conceit is still deriv'd
From some forefather grief; mine is not so,
For nothing hath begot my something grief,
Or something hath the nothing that I grieve;
'Tis in reversion that I do possess –
But what it is that is not yet known what,
I cannot name; 'tis nameless woe, I wot.

Enter GREEN.

GREEN God save your Majesty! and well met, gentlemen.
I hope the King is not yet shipp'd for Ireland.

QUEEN Why hopest thou so? 'Tis better hope he is;
For his designs crave haste, his haste good hope.
Then wherefore dost thou hope he is not shipp'd?

GREEN That he, our hope, might have retir'd his power
And driven into despair an enemy's hope
Who strongly hath set footing in this land.
The banish'd Bolingbroke repeals himself,
And with uplifted arms is safe arriv'd
At Ravenspurgh.

QUEEN Now God in heaven forbid!

GREEN Ah, madam, 'tis too true; and that is worse,
The Lord Northumberland, his son young Henry Percy,
The Lords of Ross, Beaumond, and Willoughby,
With all their powerful friends, are fled to him.

BUSHY Why have you not proclaim'd Northumberland
And all the rest revolted faction traitors?

GREEN We have; whereupon the Earl of Worcester
Hath broken his staff, resign'd his stewardship,
And all the household servants fled with him
To Bolingbroke.

QUEEN So, Green, thou art the midwife to my woe,
And Bolingbroke my sorrow's dismal heir.
Now hath my soul brought forth her prodigy;
And I, a gasping new-deliver'd mother,
Have woe to woe, sorrow to sorrow join'd.

BUSHY Despair not, madam.

QUEEN Who shall hinder me?
I will despair, and be at enmity
With cozening hope – he is a flatterer,
A parasite, a keeper-back of death,
Who gently would dissolve the bands of life,
Which false hope lingers in extremity.

Enter YORK.

GREEN Here comes the Duke of York.

QUEEN With signs of war about his aged neck.
O, full of careful business are his looks!
Uncle, for God's sake, speak comfortable words.
YORK Should I do so, I should belie my thoughts.
Comfort's in heaven; and we are on the earth,
Where nothing lives but crosses, cares, and grief.
Your husband, he is gone to save far off,
Whilst others come to make him lose at home.
Here am I left to underprop his land,
Who, weak with age, cannot support myself.
Now comes the sick hour that his surfeit made;
Now shall he try his friends that flatter'd him.

Enter a Servant.

SERVANT My lord, your son was gone before I came.
YORK He was – why so go all which way it will!
The nobles they are fled, the commons they are cold
And will, I fear, revolt on Hereford's side.
Sirrah, get thee to Plashy, to my sister Gloucester;
Bid her send me presently a thousand pound.
Hold, take my ring.
SERVANT My lord, I had forgot to tell your lordship,
To-day, as I came by, I called there –
But I shall grieve you to report the rest.
YORK What is't, knave?
SERVANT An hour before I came, the Duchess died.
YORK God for his mercy! what a tide of woes
Comes rushing on this woeful land at once!
I know not what to do. I would to God,
So my untruth had not provok'd him to it,
The King had cut off my head with my brother's.
What, are there no posts dispatch'd for Ireland?
How shall we do for money for these wars?
Come, sister – cousin, I would say – pray, pardon me.
Go, fellow, get thee home, provide some carts,
And bring away the armour that is there.
[*Exit Servant.*
Gentlemen, will you go muster men?
If I know how or which way to order these affairs
Thus disorderly thrust into my hands,
Never believe me. Both are my kinsmen.
T'one is my sovereign, whom both my oath
And duty bids defend; t'other again
Is my kinsman, whom the King hath wrong'd,
Whom conscience and my kindred bids to right.
Well, somewhat we must do. – Come, cousin,
I'll dispose of you. Gentlemen, go muster up your men,
And meet me presently at Berkeley.
I should to Plashy too,
But time will not permit. All is uneven,
And everything is left at six and seven.
[*Exeunt York and Queen.*
BUSHY The wind sits fair for news to go to Ireland.
But none returns. For us to levy power
Proportionable to the enemy
Is all unpossible.
GREEN Besides, our nearness to the King in love
Is near the hate of those love not the King.
BAGOT And that is the wavering commons; for their love
Lies in their purses; and whoso empties them,
By so much fills their hearts with deadly hate.
BUSHY Wherein the King stands generally condemn'd.
BAGOT If judgment lie in them, then so do we,
Because we ever have been near the King.
GREEN Well, I will for refuge straight to Bristow Castle.
The Earl of Wiltshire is already there.
BUSHY Thither will I with you; for little office
Will the hateful commons perform for us,
Except like curs to tear us all to pieces.
Will you go along with us?
BAGOT No; I will to Ireland to his Majesty.
Farewell. If heart's presages be not vain,
We three here part that ne'er shall meet again.
BUSHY That's as York thrives to beat back Bolingbroke.
GREEN Alas, poor Duke! the task he undertakes
Is numb'ring sands and drinking oceans dry.
Where one on his side fights, thousands will fly.
Farewell at once – for once, for all, and ever.
BUSHY Well, we may meet again.
BAGOT I fear me, never. [*Exeunt.*

SCENE III. *Gloucestershire.*

Enter BOLINGBROKE and NORTHUMBERLAND, with Forces.

BOLINGBROKE How far is it, my lord, to Berkeley now?
NORTHUMBERLAND Believe me, noble lord,
I am a stranger here in Gloucestershire.
These high wild hills and rough uneven ways
Draws out our miles, and makes them wearisome;
And yet your fair discourse hath been as sugar,
Making the hard way sweet and delectable.
But I bethink me what a weary way
From Ravenspurgh to Cotswold will be found
In Ross and Willoughby, wanting your company,

Which, I protest, hath very much beguil'd
The tediousness and process of my travel.
But theirs is sweet'ned with the hope to have
The present benefit which I possess;
And hope to joy is little less in joy
Than hope enjoy'd. By this the weary lords
Shall make their way seem short, as mine hath done
By sight of what I have, your noble company.

BOLINGBROKE Of much less value is my company
Than your good words. But who comes here?

Enter HARRY PERCY.

NORTHUMBERLAND It is my son, young Harry Percy,
Sent from my brother Worcester, whencesoever.
Harry, how fares your uncle?

PERCY I had thought, my lord, to have learn'd his health of you.

NORTHUMBERLAND Why, is he not with the Queen?

PERCY No, my good lord; he hath forsook the court,
Broken his staff of office, and dispers'd
The household of the King.

NORTHUMBERLAND What was his reason?
He was not so resolv'd when last we spake together.

PERCY Because your lordship was proclaimed traitor.
But he, my lord, is gone to Ravenspurgh,
To offer service to the Duke of Hereford;
And sent me over by Berkeley, to discover
What power the Duke of York had levied there;
Then with directions to repair to Ravenspurgh.

NORTHUMBERLAND Have you forgot the Duke of Hereford, boy?

PERCY No, my good lord; for that is not forgot
Which ne'er I did remember; to my knowledge,
I never in my life did look on him.

NORTHUMBERLAND Then learn to know him now; this is the Duke.

PERCY My gracious lord, I tender you my service,
Such as it is, being tender, raw, and young;
Which elder days shall ripen, and confirm
To more approved service and desert.

BOLINGBROKE I thank thee, gentle Percy; and be sure
I count myself in nothing else so happy
As in a soul rememb'ring my good friends;
And as my fortune ripens with thy love,
It shall be still thy true love's recompense.
My heart this covenant makes, my hand thus seals it.

NORTHUMBERLAND How far is it to Berkeley? And what stir
Keeps good old York there with his men of war?

PERCY There stands the castle, by yon tuft of trees,
Mann'd with three hundred men, as I have heard;
And in it are the Lords of York, Berkeley, and Seymour –
None else of name and noble estimate.

Enter ROSS and WILLOUGHBY.

NORTHUMBERLAND Here come the Lords of Ross and Willoughby,
Bloody with spurring, fiery-red with haste.

BOLINGBROKE Welcome, my lords. I wot your love pursues
A banish'd traitor. All my treasury
Is yet but unfelt thanks, which, more enrich'd,
Shall be your love and labour's recompense.

ROSS Your presence makes us rich, most noble lord.

WILLOUGHBY And far surmounts our labour to attain it.

BOLINGBROKE Evermore thanks, the exchequer of the poor;
Which, till my infant fortune comes to years,
Stands for my bounty. But who comes here?

Enter BERKELEY.

NORTHUMBERLAND It is my Lord of Berkeley, as I guess.

BERKELEY My Lord of Hereford, my message is to you.

BOLINGBROKE My lord, my answer is – 'to Lancaster';
And I am come to seek that name in England;
And I must find that title in your tongue
Before I make reply to aught you say.

BERKELEY Mistake me not, my lord; 'tis not my meaning
To raze one title of your honour out.
To you, my lord, I come – what lord you will –
From the most gracious regent of this land,
The Duke of York, to know what pricks you on
To take advantage of the absent time,
And fright our native peace with self-borne arms.

Enter YORK, attended.

BOLINGBROKE I shall not need transport my words by you;
Here comes his Grace in person. My noble uncle! [*Kneels.*

YORK Show me thy humble heart, and not thy knee,
Whose duty is deceivable and false.

BOLINGBROKE My gracious uncle! –

YORK Tut, tut!
Grace me no grace, nor uncle me no uncle.

I am no traitor's uncle; and that word 'grace'
In an ungracious mouth is but profane.
Why have those banish'd and forbidden legs
Dar'd once to touch a dust of England's ground?
But then more 'why?' – why have they dar'd to march
So many miles upon her peaceful bosom,
Frighting her pale-fac'd villages with war
And ostentation of despised arms?
Com'st thou because the anointed King is hence?
Why, foolish boy, the King is left behind,
And in my loyal bosom lies his power.
Were I but now lord of such hot youth
As when brave Gaunt, thy father, and myself
Rescued the Black Prince, that young Mars of men,
From forth the ranks of many thousand French,
O, then how quickly should this arm of mine,
Now prisoner to the palsy, chastise thee
And minister correction to thy fault!

BOLINGBROKE My gracious uncle, let me know my fault;
On what condition stands it and wherein?

YORK Even in condition of the worst degree –
In gross rebellion and detested treason.
Thou art a banish'd man, and here art come
Before the expiration of thy time,
In braving arms against thy sovereign.

BOLINGBROKE As I was banish'd, I was banish'd Hereford;
But as I come, I come for Lancaster.
And, noble uncle, I beseech your Grace
Look on my wrongs with an indifferent eye.
You are my father, for methinks in you
I see old Gaunt alive. O, then, my father,
Will you permit that I shall stand condemn'd
A wandering vagabond; my rights and royalties
Pluck'd from my arms perforce, and given away
To upstart unthrifts? Wherefore was I born?
If that my cousin king be King in England,
It must be granted I am Duke of Lancaster.
You have a son, Aumerle, my noble cousin;
Had you first died, and he been thus trod down,
He should have found his uncle Gaunt a father
To rouse his wrongs and chase them to the bay.
I am denied to sue my livery here,
And yet my letters patents give me leave.
My father's goods are all distrain'd and sold;
And these and all are all amiss employ'd.
What would you have me do? I am a subject,
And I challenge law – attorneys are denied me;
And therefore personally I lay my claim
To my inheritance of free descent.

NORTHUMBERLAND The noble Duke hath been too much abused.

ROSS It stands your Grace upon to do him right.

WILLOUGHBY Base men by his endowments are made great.

YORK My lords of England, let me tell you this:
I have had feeling of my cousin's wrongs,
And labour'd all I could to do him right;
But in this kind to come, in braving arms,
Be his own carver and cut out his way,
To find out right with wrong – it may not be;
And you that do abet him in this kind
Cherish rebellion, and are rebels all.

NORTHUMBERLAND The noble Duke hath sworn his coming is
But for his own; and for the right of that
We all have strongly sworn to give him aid;
And let him never see joy that breaks that oath!

YORK Well, well, I see the issue of these arms.
I cannot mend it, I must needs confess,
Because my power is weak and all ill left;
But if I could, by Him that gave me life,
I would attach you all and make you stoop
Unto the sovereign mercy of the King;
But since I cannot, be it known unto you
I do remain as neuter. So, fare you well;
Unless you please to enter in the castle,
And there repose you for this night.

BOLINGBROKE An offer, uncle, that we will accept.
But we must win your Grace to go with us
To Bristow Castle, which they say is held
By Bushy, Bagot, and their complices,
The caterpillars of the commonwealth,
Which I have sworn to weed and pluck away.

YORK It may be I will go with you; but yet I'll pause,
For I am loath to break our country's laws.
Nor friends nor foes, to me welcome you are.
Things past redress are now with me past care.

[*Exeunt*.

SCENE IV. *A camp in Wales.*

Enter EARL OF SALISBURY and a Welsh Captain.

CAPTAIN My Lord of Salisbury, we have stay'd ten days
And hardly kept our countrymen together,
And yet we hear no tidings from the King;
Therefore we will disperse ourselves. Farewell.

SALISBURY Stay yet another day, thou trusty Welshman;
The king reposeth all his confidence in thee.

CAPTAIN 'Tis thought the King is dead; we will not stay.
The bay trees in our country are all wither'd,
And meteors fright the fixed stars of heaven;
The pale-fac'd moon looks bloody on the earth,
And lean-look'd prophets whisper fearful change;

Rich men look sad, and ruffians dance and leap –
The one in fear to lose what they enjoy,
The other to enjoy by rage and war.
These signs forerun the death or fall of kings.
Farewell. Our countrymen are gone and fled,
As well assur'd Richard their King is dead.
[*Exit.*

SALISBURY Ah, Richard, with the eyes of heavy mind,
I see thy glory like a shooting star
Fall to the base earth from the firmament!
The sun sets weeping in the lowly west,
Witnessing storms to come, woe, and unrest;
Thy friends are fled, to wait upon thy foes;
And crossly to thy good all fortune goes. [*Exit.*

ACT THREE

SCENE I. *Bolingbroke's camp at Bristol.*

Enter BOLINGBROKE, YORK, NORTHUMBERLAND, PERCY, ROSS, WILLOUGHBY, with BUSHY and GREEN, prisoners.

BOLINGBROKE Bring forth these men.
Bushy and Green, I will not vex your souls –
Since presently your souls must part your bodies –
With too much urging your pernicious lives,
For 'twere no charity; yet, to wash your blood
From off my hands, here in the view of men
I will unfold some causes of your deaths:
You have misled a prince, a royal king,
A happy gentleman in blood and lineaments,
By you unhappied and disfigured clean;
You have in manner with your sinful hours
Made a divorce betwixt his queen and him;
Broke the possession of a royal bed,
And stain'd the beauty of a fair queen's cheeks
With tears drawn from her eyes by your foul wrongs;
Myself – a prince by fortune of my birth,
Near to the King in blood, and near in love
Till you did make him misinterpret me –
Have stoop'd my neck under your injuries
And sigh'd my English breath in foreign clouds,
Eating the bitter bread of banishment,
Whilst you have fed upon my signories,
Dispark'd my parks and fell'd my forest woods,
From my own windows torn my household coat,
Raz'd out my imprese, leaving me no sign
Save men's opinions and my living blood
To show the world I am a gentleman.
This and much more, much more than twice all this,
Condemns you to the death. See them delivered over
To execution and the hand of death.

BUSHY More welcome is the stroke of death to me
Than Bolingbroke to England. Lords, farewell.

GREEN My comfort is that heaven will take our souls,
And plague injustice with the pains of hell.

BOLINGBROKE My Lord Northumberland, see them dispatch'd.

[*Exeunt Northumberland, and others, with the prisoners.*

Uncle, you say the Queen is at your house;
For God's sake, fairly let her be entreated.
Tell her I send to her my kind commends;
Take special care my greetings be delivered.

YORK A gentleman of mine I have dispatch'd
With letters of your love to her at large.

BOLINGBROKE Thanks, gentle uncle. Come, lords, away,
To fight with Glendower and his complices.
Awhile to work, and after holiday. [*Exeunt.*

SCENE II. *The coast of Wales. A castle in view.*

Drums. Flourish and colours. Enter the KING, the BISHOP OF CARLISLE, AUMERLE and Soldiers.

KING RICHARD Barkloughly Castle call they this at hand?

AUMERLE Yea, my lord. How brooks your Grace the air
After your late tossing on the breaking seas?

KING RICHARD Needs must I like it well. I weep for joy
To stand upon my kingdom once again.
Dear earth, I do salute thee with my hand,
Though rebels wound thee with their horses' hoofs.
As a long-parted mother with her child
Plays fondly with her tears and smiles in meeting,
So weeping-smiling greet I thee, my earth,
And do thee favours with my royal hands.
Feed not thy sovereign's foe, my gentle earth,
Nor with thy sweets comfort his ravenous sense;
But let thy spiders, that suck up thy venom,
And heavy-gaited toads, lie in their way,

Doing annoyance to the treacherous feet
Which with usurping steps do trample thee;
Yield stinging nettles to mine enemies;
And when they from thy bosom pluck a flower,
Guard it, I pray thee, with a lurking adder,
Whose double tongue may with a mortal touch
Throw death upon thy sovereign's enemies.
Mock not my senseless conjuration, lords.
This earth shall have a feeling, and these stones
Prove armed soldiers, ere her native King
Shall falter under foul rebellion's arms.

CARLISLE Fear not, my lord; that Power that made you king
Hath power to keep you king in spite of all.
The means that heaven yields must be embrac'd
And not neglected; else, if heaven would,
And we will not, heaven's offer we refuse,
The proffered means of succour and redress.

AUMERLE He means, my lord, that we are too remiss;
Whilst Bolingbroke, through our security,
Grows strong and great in substance and in power.

KING RICHARD Discomfortable cousin! know'st thou not
That when the searching eye of heaven is hid,
Behind the globe, that lights the lower world,
Then thieves and robbers range abroad unseen
In murders and in outrage boldly here;
But when from under this terrestrial ball
He fires the proud tops of the eastern pines
And darts his light through every guilty hole,
Then murders, treasons, and detested sins,
The cloak of night being pluck'd from off their backs,
Stand bare and naked, trembling at themselves?
So when this thief, this traitor, Bolingbroke,
Who all this while hath revell'd in the night,
Whilst we were wand'ring with the Antipodes,
Shall see us rising in our throne, the east,
His treasons will sit blushing in his face,
Not able to endure the sight of day,
But self-affrighted tremble at his sin.
Not all the water in the rough rude sea
Can wash the balm off from an anointed king;
The breath of worldly men cannot despose
The deputy elected by the Lord.
For every man that Bolingbroke hath press'd
To lift shrewd steel against our golden crown,
God for his Richard hath in heavenly pay
A glorious angel. Then, if angels fight,
Weak men must fall; for heaven still guards the right.

Enter SALISBURY.

Welcome, my lord. How far off lies your power?

SALISBURY Nor near nor farther off, my gracious lord,
Than this weak arm. Discomfort guides my tongue,
And bids me speak of nothing but despair.
One day too late, I fear me, noble lord,
Hath clouded all thy happy days on earth.
O, call back yesterday, bid time return,
And thou shalt have twelve thousand fighting men!
To-day, to-day, unhappy day, too late,
O'erthrows thy joys, friends, fortune, and thy state;
For all the Welshmen, hearing thou wert dead,
Are gone to Bolingbroke, dispers'd, and fled.

AUMERLE Comfort, my liege, why looks your Grace so pale?

KING RICHARD But now the blood of twenty thousand men
Did triumph in my face, and they are fled;
And, till so much blood thither come again,
Have I not reason to look pale and dead?
All souls that will be safe, fly from my side;
For time hath set a blot upon my pride.

AUMERLE Comfort, my liege; remember who you are.

KING RICHARD I had forgot myself; am I not King?
Awake, thou coward majesty! thou sleepest.
Is not the King's name twenty thousand names?
Arm, arm, my name! a puny subject strikes
At thy great glory. Look not to the ground,
Ye favourites of a king; are we not high?
High be our thoughts. I know my uncle York
Hath power enough to serve our turn. But who comes here?

Enter SCROOP.

SCROOP More health and happiness betide my liege
Than can my care-tun'd tongue deliver him.

KING RICHARD Mine ear is open and my heart prepar'd.
The worst is worldly loss thou canst unfold.
Say, is my kingdom lost? Why, 'twas my care;
And what loss is it to be rid of care?
Strives Bolingbroke to be as great as we?
Greater he shall not be; if he serve God,
We'll serve him too, and be his fellow so.
Revolt our subjects? That we cannot mend;
They break their faith to God as well as us.
Cry woe, destruction, ruin, and decay –
The worst is death, and death will have his day.

SCROOP Glad am I that your Highness is so arm'd
To bear the tidings of calamity.
Like an unseasonable stormy day
Which makes the silver rivers drown their

shores,
As if the world were all dissolv'd to tears,
So high above his limits swells the rage
Of Bolingbroke, covering your fearful land
With hard bright steel and hearts harder than steel.
White-beards have arm'd their thin and hairless scalps
Against thy majesty; boys, with women's voices,
Strive to speak big, and clap their female joints
In stiff unwieldly arms against thy crown;
Thy very beadsmen learn to bend their bows
Of double-fatal yew against thy state;
Yea, distaff-women manage rusty bills
Against thy seat: both young and old rebel,
And all goes worse than I have power to tell.

KING RICHARD Too well, too well thou tell'st a tale so ill.
Where is the Earl of Wiltshire? Where is Bagot?
What is become of Bushy? Where is Green?
That they have let the dangerous enemy
Measure our confines with such peaceful steps?
If we prevail, their heads shall pay for it.
I warrant they have made peace with Bolingbroke.

SCROOP Peace have they made with him indeed, my lord.

KING RICHARD O villains, vipers, damn'd without redemption!
Dogs, easily won to fawn on any man!
Snakes, in my heart-blood warm'd, that sting my heart!
Three Judases, each one thrice worse than Judas!
Would they make peace? Terrible hell make war
Upon their spotted souls for this offence!

SCROOP Sweet love, I see, changing his property,
Turns to the sourest and most deadly hate.
Again uncurse their souls; their peace is made
With heads, and not with hands; those whom you curse
Have felt the worst of death's destroying wound
And lie full low, grav'd in the hollow ground.

AUMERLE Is Bushy, Green, and the Earl of Wiltshire dead?

SCROOP Ay, all of them at Bristow lost their heads.

AUMERLE Where is the Duke my father with his power?

KING RICHARD No matter where – of comfort no man speak.
Let's talk of graves, of worms, and epitaphs;
Make dust our paper, and with rainy eyes
Write sorrow on the bosom of the earth.
Let's choose executors and talk of wills;
And yet not so – for what can we bequeath
Save our deposed bodies to the ground?
Our lands, our lives, and all, are Bolingbroke's.
And nothing can we call our own but death
And that small model of the barren earth
Which serves as paste and cover to our bones.
For God's sake let us sit upon the ground
And tell sad stories of the death of kings:
How some have been depos'd, some slain in war,
Some haunted by the ghosts they have depos'd,
Some poison'd by their wives, some sleeping kill'd,
All murder'd – for within the hollow crown
That rounds the mortal temples of a king
Keeps Death his court; and there the antic sits,
Scoffing his state and grinning at his pomp;
Allowing him a breath, a little scene,
To monarchize, be fear'd, and kill with looks;
Infusing him with self and vain conceit,
As if this flesh which walls about our life
Were brass impregnable; and, humour'd thus,
Comes at the last, and with a little pin
Bores through his castle wall, and farewell, king!
Cover your heads, and mock not flesh and blood
With solemn reverence; throw away respect,
Tradition, form, and ceremonious duty;
For you have but mistook me all this while.
I live with bread like you, feel want,
Taste grief, need friends; subjected thus,
How can you say to me I am a king?

CARLISLE My lord, wise men ne'er sit and wail their woes,
But presently prevent the ways to wail.
To fear the foe, since fear oppresseth strength,
Gives, in your weakness, strength unto your foe,
And so your follies fight against yourself.
Fear and be slain – no worse can come to fight;
And fight and die is death destroying death,
Where fearing dying pays death servile breath.

AUMERLE My father hath a power; inquire of him,
And learn to make a body of a limb.

KING RICHARD Thou chid'st me well. Proud Bolingbroke, I come
To change blows with thee for our day of doom.
This ague fit of fear is over-blown;
An easy task it is to win our own.
Say, Scroop, where lies our uncle with his power?

Speak sweetly, man, although thy looks be sour.
SCROOP Men judge by the complexion of the sky
The state and inclination of the day;
So may you by my dull and heavy eye,
My tongue hath but a heavier tale to say.
I play the torturer, by small and small
To lengthen out the worst that must be spoken:
Your uncle York is join'd with Bolingbroke;
And all your northern castles yielded up,
And all your southern gentlemen in arms
Upon his party.
KING RICHARD Thou hast said enough.
[*To Aumerle*] Beshrew thee, cousin, which didst lead me forth
Of that sweet way I was in to despair!
What say you now? What comfort have we now?
By heaven, I'll hate him everlastingly
That bids me be of comfort any more.
Go to Flint Castle; there I'll pine away;
A king, woe's slave, shall kingly woe obey.
That power I have, discharge; and let them go
To ear the land that hath some hope to grow,
For I have none. Let no man speak again
To alter this, for counsel is but vain.
AUMERLE My liege, one word.
KING RICHARD He does me double wrong
That wounds me with the flatteries of his tongue.
Discharge my followers; let them hence away,
From Richard's night to Bolingbroke's fair day.
[*Exeunt.*

SCENE III. *Wales. Before Flint Castle.*

Enter, with drum and colours, BOLINGBROKE, YORK, NORTHUMBERLAND, and Forces.

BOLINGBROKE So that by this intelligence we learn
The Welshmen are dispers'd; and Salisbury
Is gone to meet the King, who lately landed
With some few private friends upon this coast.
NORTHUMBERLAND The news is very fair and good, my lord.
Richard not far from hence hath hid his head.
YORK It would beseem the Lord Northumberland
To say 'King Richard'. Alack the heavy day
When such a sacred king should hide his head!
NORTHUMBERLAND Your Grace mistakes; only to be brief,
Left I his title out.
YORK The time hath been,
Would you have been so brief with him, he would
Have been so brief with you to shorten you,
For taking so the head, your whole head's length.
BOLINGBROKE Mistake not, uncle, further than you should.
YORK Take not, good cousin, further than you should,
Lest you mistake. The heavens are over our heads.
BOLINGBROKE I know it, uncle; and oppose not myself
Against their will. But who comes here?

Enter PERCY.

Welcome, Harry. What, will not this castle yield?
PERCY The castle royally is mann'd, my lord,
Against thy entrance.
BOLINGBROKE Royally!
Why, it contains no king?
PERCY Yes, my good lord,
It doth contain a king; King Richard lies
Within the limits of yon lime and stone;
And with him are the Lord Aumerle, Lord Salisbury,
Sir Stephen Scroop, besides a clergyman
Of holy reverence; who, I cannot learn.
NORTHUMBERLAND O, belike it is the Bishop of Carlisle.
BOLINGBROKE [*To Northumberland*] Noble lord,
Go to the rude ribs of that ancient castle;
Through brazen trumpet send the breath of parley
Into his ruin'd ears, and thus deliver:
Henry Bolingbroke
On both his knees doth kiss King Richard's hand,
And sends allegiance and true faith of heart
To his most royal person; hither come
Even at his feet to lay my arms and power,
Provided that my banishment repeal'd
And lands restor'd again be freely granted;
If not, I'll use the advantage of my power
And lay the summer's dust with showers of blood
Rain'd from the wounds of slaughtered Englishmen;
The which how far off from the mind of Bolingbroke
It is such crimson tempest should bedrench
The fresh green lap of fair King Richard's land,
My stooping duty tenderly shall show.
Go, signify as much, while here we march
Upon the grassy carpet of this plain.
[*Northumberland advances to the Castle, with a trumpet.*
Let's march without the noise of threat'ning drum,

That from this castle's tottered battlements
Our fair appointments may be well perus'd.
Methinks King Richard and myself should meet
With no less terror than the elements
Of fire and water, when their thund'ring shock
At meeting tears the cloudy cheeks of heaven.
Be he the fire, I'll be the yielding water;
The rage be his, whilst on the earth I rain
My waters – on the earth, and not on him.
March on, and mark King Richard how he looks.

Parle without, and answer within; then a flourish. Enter on the walls, the KING, the BISHOP OF CARLISLE, AUMERLE, SCROOP and SALISBURY.

See, see, King Richard doth himself appear,
As doth the blushing discontented sun
From out the fiery portal of the east,
When he perceives the envious clouds are bent
To dim his glory and to stain the track
Of his bright passage to the occident.

YORK Yet looks he like a king. Behold, his eye,
As bright as is the eagle's, lightens forth
Controlling majesty. Alack, alack, for woe,
That any harm should stain so fair a show!

KING RICHARD [*To Northumberland*] We are amaz'd; and thus long have we stood
To watch the fearful bending of thy knee,
Because we thought ourself thy lawful king;
And if we be, how dare thy joints forget
To pay their awful duty to our presence?
If we be not, show us the hand of God
That hath dismiss'd us from our stewardship;
For well we know no hand of blood and bone
Can gripe the sacred handle of our sceptre,
Unless he do profane, steal, or usurp.
And though you think that all, as you have done,
Have torn their souls by turning them from us,
And we are barren and bereft of friends,
Yet know – my master, God omnipotent,
Is mustering in his clouds on our behalf
Armies of pestilence; and they shall strike
Your children yet unborn and unbegot,
That lift your vassal hands against my head
And threat the glory of my precious crown.
Tell Bolingbroke, for yon methinks he stands,
That every stride he makes upon my land
Is dangerous treason; he is come to open
The purple testament of bleeding war;
But ere the crown he looks for live in peace,
Ten thousand bloody crowns of mothers' sons
Shall ill become the flower of England's face,
Change the complexion of her maid-pale peace
To scarlet indignation, and bedew
Her pastures' grass with faithful English blood.

NORTHUMBERLAND The King of Heaven forbid our lord the King
Should so with civil and uncivil arms
Be rush'd upon! Thy thrice noble cousin,
Harry Bolingbroke, doth humbly kiss thy hand;
And by the honourable tomb he swears
That stands upon your royal grandsire's bones,
And by the royalties of both your bloods,
Currents that spring from one most gracious head,
And by the buried hand of warlike Gaunt,
And by the worth and honour of himself,
Comprising all that may be sworn or said,
His coming hither hath no further scope
Than for his lineal royalties, and to beg
Enfranchisement immediate on his knees;
Which on thy royal party granted once,
His glittering arms he will commend to rust,
His barbed steeds to stables, and his heart
To faithful service of your Majesty.
This swears he, as he is a prince, is just;
And as I am a gentleman I credit him.

KING RICHARD Northumberland, say thus the King returns:
His noble cousin is right welcome hither;
And all the number of his fair demands
Shall be accomplish'd without contradiction.
With all the gracious utterance thou hast
Speak to his gentle hearing kind commends.
[*To Aumerle*] We do debase ourselves, cousin, do we not,
To look so poorly and to speak so fair?
Shall we call back Northumberland, and send
Defiance to the traitor, and so die?

AUMERLE No, good my lord; let's fight with gentle words
Till time lend friends, and friends their helpful swords.

KING RICHARD O God, O God! that e'er this tongue of mine
That laid the sentence of dread banishment
On yon proud man should take it off again
With words of sooth! O that I were as great
As is my grief, or lesser than my name!
Or that I could forget what I have been!
Or not remember what I must be now!
Swell'st thou, proud heart? I'll give thee scope to beat,
Since foes have scope to beat both thee and me.

AUMERLE Northumberland comes back from Bolingbroke.

KING RICHARD What must the King do now? Must he submit?
The King shall do it. Must he be depos'd?
The King shall be contented. Must he lose
The name of king? A God's name, let it go.
I'll give my jewels for a set of beads,

My gorgeous palace for a hermitage,
My gay apparel for an almsman's gown,
My figur'd goblets for a dish of wood,
My sceptre for a palmer's walking staff,
My subjects for a pair of carved saints,
And my large kingdom for a little grave,
A little little grave, an obscure grave –
Or I'll be buried in the king's high way,
Some way of common trade, where subjects' feet
May hourly trample on their sovereign's head;
For on my heart they tread now whilst I live,
And buried once, why not upon my head?
Aumerle, thou weep'st, my tender-hearted cousin!
We'll make foul weather with despised tears;
Our sighs and they shall lodge the summer corn
And make a dearth in this revolting land.
Or shall we play the wantons with our woes
And make some pretty match with shedding tears?
As thus: to drop them still upon one place
Till they have fretted us a pair of graves
Within the earth; and, therein laid – there lies
Two kinsmen digg'd their graves with weeping eyes.
Would not this ill do well? Well, well, I see
I talk but idly, and you laugh at me.
Most mighty prince, my Lord Northumberland,
What says King Bolingbroke? Will his Majesty
Give Richard leave to live till Richard die?
You make a leg, and Bolingbroke says ay.

NORTHUMBERLAND My lord, in the base court he doth attend
To speak with you; may it please you to come down?

KING RICHARD Down, down I come, like glist'ring Phaethon,
Wanting the manage of unruly jades.
In the base court? Base court, where kings grow base,
To come at traitors' calls, and do them grace.
In the base court? Come down? Down, court! down, king!
For night-owls shriek where mounting larks should sing. [*Exeunt from above.*

BOLINGBROKE What says his Majesty?

NORTHUMBERLAND Sorrow and grief of heart
Makes him speak fondly, like a frantic man;
Yet he is come.

Enter the KING, and his Attendants, below.

BOLINGBROKE Stand all apart,
And show fair duty to his Majesty.
[*He kneels down.*
My gracious lord –

KING RICHARD Fair cousin, you debase your princely knee
To make the base earth proud with kissing it.
Me rather had my heart might feel your love
Than my unpleas'd eye see your courtesy.
Up, cousin, up; your heart is up, I know,
[*Touching his own head*] Thus high at least, although your knee be low.

BOLINGBROKE My gracious lord, I come but for mine own.

KING RICHARD Your own is yours, and I am yours, and all.

BOLINGBROKE So far be mine, my most redoubted lord,
As my true service shall deserve your love.

KING RICHARD Well you deserve. They well deserve to have
That know the strong'st and surest way to get.
Uncle, give me your hands; nay, dry your eyes:
Tears show their love, but want their remedies.
Cousin, I am too young to be your father,
Though you are old enough to be my heir.
What you will have, I'll give, and willing too;
For do we must what force will have us do.
Set on towards London. Cousin, is it so?

BOLINGBROKE Yea, my good lord.

KING RICHARD Then I must not say no.
[*Flourish. Exeunt.*

SCENE IV. *The Duke of York's garden.*

Enter the QUEEN and two Ladies.

QUEEN What sport shall we devise here in this garden
To drive away the heavy thought of care?

LADY Madam, we'll play at bowls.

QUEEN 'Twill make me think the world is full of rubs
And that my fortune runs against the bias.

LADY Madam, we'll dance.

QUEEN My legs can keep no measure in delight,
When my poor heart no measure keeps in grief;
Therefore no dancing, girl; some other sport.

LADY Madam, we'll tell tales.

QUEEN Of sorrow or of joy?

LADY Of either, madam.

QUEEN Of neither, girl;
For if of joy, being altogether wanting,
It doth remember me the more of sorrow;
Or if of grief, being altogether had,
It adds more sorrow to my want of joy;
For what I have I need not to repeat,
And what I want it boots not to complain.

LADY Madam, I'll sing.

QUEEN 'Tis well that thou hast cause;
But thou shouldst please me better wouldst thou weep.

LADY I could weep, madam, would it do you good.
QUEEN And I could sing, would weeping do me good,
And never borrow any tear of thee.

Enter a Gardener and two Servants.

But stay, here come the gardeners.
Let's step into the shadow of these trees.
My wretchedness unto a row of pins,
They will talk of state, for every one doth so
Against a change: woe is forerun with woe.

[*Queen and Ladies retire.*

GARDENER Go, bind thou up yon dangling apricocks,
Which, like unruly children, make their sire
Stoop with oppression of their prodigal weight;
Give some supportance to the bending twigs.
Go thou, and like an executioner
Cut off the heads of too fast growing sprays
That look too lofty in our commonwealth:
All must be even in our government.
You thus employ'd, I will go root away
The noisome weeds which without profit suck
The soil's fertility from wholesome flowers.
SERVANT Why should we, in the compass of a pale,
Keep law and form and due proportion,
Showing, as in a model, our firm estate,
When our sea-walled garden, the whole land,
Is full of weeds; her fairest flowers chok'd up,
Her fruit trees all unprun'd, her hedges ruin'd,
Her knots disordered, and her wholesome herbs
Swarming with caterpillars?
GARDENER Hold thy peace.
He that hath suffer'd this disorder'd spring
Hath now himself met with the fall of leaf;
The weeds which his broad-spreading leaves did shelter,
That seem'd in eating him to hold him up,
Are pluck'd up root and all by Boling-broke –
I mean the Earl of Wiltshire, Bushy, Green.
SERVANT What, are they dead?
GARDENER They are; and Bolingbroke
Hath seiz'd the wasteful king. O, what pity is it
That he had not so trimm'd and dress'd his land
As we this garden! We at time of year
Do wound the bark, the skin of our fruit trees,
Lest, being over-proud in sap and blood,
With too much riches it confound itself;
Had he done so to great and growing men,
They might have liv'd to bear, and he to taste
Their fruits of duty. Superfluous branches
We lop away, that bearing boughs may live;
Had he done so, himself had borne the crown,
Which waste of idle hours hath quite thrown down.
SERVANT What, think you the King shall be deposed?
GARDENER Depress'd he is already, and depos'd
'Tis doubt he will be. Letters came last night
To a dear friend of the good Duke of York's
That tell black tidings.
QUEEN O, I am press'd to death through want of speaking! [*Coming forward.*
Thou, old Adam's likeness, set to dress this garden,
How dares thy harsh rude tongue sound this unpleasing news?
What Eve, what serpent, hath suggested thee
To make a second fall of cursed man?
Why dost thou say King Richard is depos'd?
Dar'st thou, thou little better thing than earth,
Divine his downfall? Say, where, when, and how,
Cam'st thou by this ill tidings? Speak, thou wretch.
GARDENER Pardon me, madam; little joy have I
To breathe this news; yet what I say is true.
King Richard, he is in the mighty hold
Of Bolingbroke. Their fortunes both are weigh'd.
In your lord's scale is nothing but himself,
And some few vanities that make him light;
But in the balance of great Bolingbroke,
Besides himself, are all the English peers,
And with that odds he weighs King Richard down.
Post you to London, and you will find it so;
I speak no more than every one doth know.
QUEEN Nimble mischance, that art so light of foot,
Doth not thy embassage belong to me,
And am I last that knows it? O, thou thinkest
To serve me last, that I may longest keep
Thy sorrow in my breast. Come, ladies, go
To meet at London London's king in woe.
What, was I born to this, that my sad look
Should grace the triumph of great Bolingbroke?
Gard'ner, for telling me these news of woe,
Pray God the plants thou graft'st may never grow! [*Exeunt Queen and Ladies.*
GARDENER Poor Queen, so that thy state might be no worse,
I would my skill were subject to thy curse.
Here did she fall a tear; here in this place
I'll set a bank of rue, sour herb of grace.
Rue, even for ruth, here shortly shall be seen,
In the remembrance of a weeping queen.

[*Exeunt.*

ACT FOUR

SCENE I. *Westminster Hall.*

Enter, as to the Parliament, BOLINGBROKE, AUMERLE, NORTHUMBERLAND, PERCY, FITZWATER, SURREY, the BISHOP OF CARLISLE, the ABBOT OF WESTMINSTER, and Others; Herald, Officers, and BAGOT.

BOLINGBROKE Call forth Bagot.
Now, Bagot, freely speak thy mind –
What thou dost know of noble Gloucester's death;
Who wrought it with the King, and who perform'd
The bloody office of his timeless end.

BAGOT Then set before my face the Lord Aumerle.

BOLINGBROKE Cousin, stand forth, and look upon that man.

BAGOT My Lord Aumerle, I know your daring tongue
Scorns to unsay what once it hath deliver'd.
In that dead time when Gloucester's death was plotted
I heard you say 'Is not my arm of length,
That reacheth from the restful English Court
As far as Calais, to mine uncle's head?'
Amongst much other talk that very time
I heard you say that you had rather refuse
The offer of an hundred thousand crowns
Than Bolingbroke's return to England;
Adding withal, how blest this land would be
In this your cousin's death.

AUMERLE Princes, and noble lords,
What answer shall I make to this base man?
Shall I so much dishonour my fair stars
On equal terms to give him chastisement?
Either I must, or have mine honour soil'd
With the attainder of his slanderous lips.
There is my gage, the manual seal of death
That marks thee out for hell. I say thou liest,
And will maintain what thou hast said is false
In thy heart-blood, though being all too base
To stain the temper of my knightly sword.

BOLINGBROKE Bagot, forbear; thou shalt not take it up.

AUMERLE Excepting one, I would he were the best
In all this presence that hath mov'd me so.

FITZWATER If that thy valour stand on sympathy,
There is my gage, Aumerle, in gage to thine.
By that fair sun which shows me where thou stand'st,
I heard thee say, and vauntingly thou spak'st it,
That thou wert cause of noble Gloucester's death.
If thou deniest it twenty times, thou liest;
And I will turn thy falsehood to thy heart,
Where it was forged, with my rapier's point.

AUMERLE Thou dar'st not, coward, live to see that day.

FITZWATER Now, by my soul, I would it were this hour.

AUMERLE Fitzwater, thou art damn'd to hell for this.

PERCY Aumerle, thou liest; his honour is as true
In this appeal as thou art all unjust;
And that thou art so, there I throw my gage,
To prove it on thee to the extremest point
Of mortal breathing. Seize it, if thou dar'st.

AUMERLE An if I do not, may my hands rot off
And never brandish more revengeful steel
Over the glittering helmet of my foe!

ANOTHER LORD I task the earth to the like, forsworn Aumerle;
And spur thee on with full as many lies
As may be holloa'd in thy treacherous ear
From sun to sun. There is my honour's pawn;
Engage it to the trial, if thou darest.

AUMERLE Who sets me else? By heaven, I'll throw at all!
I have a thousand spirits in one breast
To answer twenty thousand such as you.

SURREY My Lord Fitzwater, I do remember well
The very time Aumerle and you did talk.

FITZWATER 'Tis very true; you were in presence then,
And you can witness with me this is true.

SURREY As false, by heaven, as heaven itself is true.

FITZWATER Surrey, thou liest.

SURREY Dishonourable boy!
That lie shall lie so heavy on my sword
That it shall render vengeance and revenge
Till thou the lie-giver and that lie do lie
In earth as quiet as thy father's skull.
In proof whereof, there is my honour's pawn;
Engage it to the trial, if thou dar'st.

FITZWATER How fondly dost thou spur a forward horse!
If I dare eat, or drink, or breathe, or live,
I dare meet Surrey in a wilderness,
And spit upon him whilst I say he lies,
And lies, and lies. There is my bond of faith,
To tie thee to my strong correction.
As I intend to thrive in this new world,
Aumerle is guilty of my true appeal.
Besides, I heard the banish'd Norfolk say
That thou, Aumerle, didst send two of thy men
To execute the noble Duke at Calais.

AUMERLE Some honest Christian trust me with a gage
That Norfolk lies. Here do I throw down this,
If he may be repeal'd to try his honour.

BOLINGBROKE These differences shall all rest under gage
Till Norfolk be repeal'd – repeal'd he shall be
And, though mine enemy, restor'd again
To all his lands and signories. When he is return'd,
Against Aumerle we will enforce his trial.

CARLISLE That honourable day shall never be seen.
Many a time hath banish'd Norfolk fought
For Jesu Christ in glorious Christian field,
Streaming the ensign of the Christian cross
Against black pagans, Turks, and Saracens;
And, toil'd with works of war, retir'd himself
To Italy; and there, at Venice, gave
His body to that pleasant country's earth,
And his pure soul unto his captain, Christ,
Under whose colours he had fought so long.

BOLINGBROKE Why, Bishop, is Norfolk dead?

CARLISLE As surely as I live, my lord.

BOLINGBROKE Sweet peace conduct his sweet soul to the bosom
Of good old Abraham! Lords appellants,
Your differences shall all rest under gage
Till we assign you to your days of trial.

Enter YORK, attended.

YORK Great Duke of Lancaster, I come to thee
From plume-pluck'd Richard, who with willing soul
Adopts thee heir, and his high sceptre yields
To the possession of thy royal hand.
Ascend his throne, descending now from him –
And long live Henry, fourth of that name!

BOLINGBROKE In God's name, I'll ascend the regal throne.

CARLISLE Marry, God forbid!
Worst in this royal presence may I speak,
Yet best beseeming me to speak the truth.
Would God that any in this noble presence
Were enough noble to be upright judge
Of noble Richard! Then true noblesse would
Learn him forbearance from so foul a wrong.
What subject can give sentence on his king?
And who sits here that is not Richard's subject?
Thieves are not judg'd but they are by to hear,
Although apparent guilt be seen in them;
And shall the figure of God's majesty,
His captain, steward, deputy elect,
Anointed, crowned, planted many years,
Be judg'd by subject and inferior breath,
And he himself not present? O, forfend it, God,
That in a Christian climate souls refin'd
Should show so heinous, black, obscene a deed!
I speak to subjects, and a subject speaks,
Stirr'd up by God, thus boldly for his king.
My Lord of Hereford here, whom you call king,
Is a foul traitor to proud Hereford's king;
And if you crown him, let me prophesy –
The blood of English shall manure the ground,
And future ages groan for this foul act;
Peace shall go sleep with Turks and infidels,
And in this seat of peace tumultuous wars
Shall kin with kin and kind with kind confound;
Disorder, horror, fear, and mutiny,
Shall here inhabit, and this land be call'd
The field of Golgotha and dead men's skulls.
O, if you raise this house against this house,
It will the woefullest division prove
That ever fell upon this cursed earth.
Prevent it, resist it, let it not be so,
Lest child, child's children, cry against you woe.

NORTHUMBERLAND Well have you argued, sir; and, for your pains,
Of capital treason we arrest you here.
My Lord of Westminster, be it your charge
To keep him safely till his day of trial.
May it please you, lords, to grant the commons' suit?

BOLINGBROKE Fetch hither Richard, that in common view
He may surrender; so we shall proceed
Without suspicion.

YORK I will be his conduct. [*Exit.*

BOLINGBROKE Lords, you that here are under our arrest,
Procure your sureties for your days of answer.
Little are we beholding to your love,
And little look'd for at your helping hands.

Re-enter YORK, with KING RICHARD, and Officers bearing the regalia.

KING RICHARD Alack, why am I sent for to a king,
Before I have shook off the regal thoughts
Wherewith I reign'd? I hardly yet have learn'd
To insinuate, flatter, bow, and bend my knee.
Give sorrow leave awhile to tutor me
To this submission. Yet I well remember
The favours of these men. Were they not mine?
Did they not sometime cry 'All hail!' to me?
So Judas did to Christ; but he, in twelve,
Found truth in all but one; I, in twelve thousand, none.
God save the King! Will no man say amen?
Am I both priest and clerk? Well then, amen.
God save the King! although I be not he;
And yet, amen, if heaven do think him me.
To do what service am I sent for hither?

YORK To do that office of thine own good will

Which tired majesty did make thee offer –
The resignation of thy state and crown
To Henry Bolingbroke.

KING RICHARD Give me the crown. Here, cousin, seize the crown.
Here, cousin,
On this side my hand, and on that side thine.
Now is this golden crown like a deep well
That owes two buckets, filling one another;
The emptier ever dancing in the air,
The other down, unseen, and full of water.
That bucket down, and full of tears am I,
Drinking my griefs, whilst you mount up on high.

BOLINGBROKE I thought you had been willing to resign.

KING RICHARD My crown I am; but still my griefs are mine.
You may my glories and my state depose,
But not my griefs; still am I king of those.

BOLINGBROKE Part of your cares you give me with your crown.

KING RICHARD Your cares set up do not pluck my cares down.
My care is loss of care, by old care done;
Your care is gain of care, by new care won.
The cares I give I have, though given away;
They tend the crown, yet still with me they stay.

BOLINGBROKE Are you contented to resign the crown?

KING RICHARD Ay, no; no, ay; for I must nothing be;
Therefore no no, for I resign to thee.
Now mark me how I will undo myself:
I give this heavy weight from off my head,
And this unwieldy sceptre from my hand,
The pride of kingly sway from out my heart;
With mine own tears I wash away my balm,
With mine own hands I give away my crown,
With mine own tongue deny my sacred state,
With mine own breath release all duteous oaths;
All pomp and majesty I do forswear;
My manors, rents, revenues, I forgo;
My acts, decrees, and statutes, I deny.
God pardon all oaths that are broke to me!
God keep all vows unbroke are made to thee!
Make me, that nothing have, with nothing griev'd,
And thou with all pleas'd, that hast all achiev'd.
Long mayst thou live in Richard's seat to sit,
And soon lie Richard in an earthy pit.
God save King Henry, unking'd Richard says,
And send him many years of sunshine days!
What more remains?

NORTHUMBERLAND No more; but that you read
These accusations, and these grievous crimes
Committed by your person and your followers
Against the state and profit of this land;
That, by confessing them, the souls of men
May deem that you are worthily depos'd.

KING RICHARD Must I do so? And must I ravel out
My weav'd-up follies? Gentle Northumberland,
If thy offences were upon record,
Would it not shame thee in so fair a troop
To read a lecture of them? If thou wouldst,
There shouldst thou find one heinous article,
Containing the deposing of a king
And cracking the strong warrant of an oath,
Mark'd with a blot, damn'd in the book of heaven.
Nay, all of you that stand and look upon me
Whilst that my wretchedness doth bait myself,
Though some of you, with Pilate, wash your hands,
Showing an outward pity – yet you Pilates
Have here deliver'd me to my sour cross,
And water cannot wash away your sin.

NORTHUMBERLAND My lord, dispatch; read o'er these articles.

KING RICHARD Mine eyes are full of tears; I cannot see.
And yet salt water blinds them not so much
But they can see a sort of traitors here.
Nay, if I turn mine eyes upon myself,
I find myself a traitor with the rest;
For I have given here my soul's consent
T' undeck the pompous body of a king;
Made glory base, and sovereignty a slave,
Proud majesty a subject, state a peasant.

NORTHUMBERLAND My lord –

KING RICHARD No lord of thine, thou haught insulting man,
Nor no man's lord; I have no name, no title –
No, not that name was given me at the font –
But 'tis usurp'd. Alack the heavy day,
That I have worn so many winters out,
And know not now what name to call myself!
O that I were a mockery king of snow,
Standing before the sun of Bolingbroke
To melt myself away in water drops!
Good king, great king, and yet not greatly good,
An if my word be sterling yet in England,
Let it command a mirror hither straight,
That it may show me what a face I have
Since it is bankrupt of his majesty.

BOLINGBROKE Go some of you and fetch a looking-glass. [*Exit an Attendant.*

NORTHUMBERLAND Read o'er this paper while the glass doth come.

KING RICHARD Fiend, thou torments me ere I come to hell.

BOLINGBROKE Urge it no more, my Lord Northumberland.

NORTHUMBERLAND The commons will not, then, be satisfied.
KING RICHARD They shall be satisfied. I'll read enough,
When I do see the very book indeed
Where all my sins are writ, and that's myself.

Re-enter Attendant with a glass.

Give me that glass, and therein will I read.
No deeper wrinkles yet? Hath sorrow struck
So many blows upon this face of mine
And made no deeper wounds? O flatt'ring glass,
Like to my followers in prosperity,
Thou dost beguile me! Was this face the face
That every day under his household roof
Did keep ten thousand men? Was this the face
That like the sun did make beholders wink?
Is this the face which fac'd so many follies
That was at last out-fac'd by Bolingbroke?
A brittle glory shineth in this face;
As brittle as the glory is the face;
[*Dashes the glass against the ground.*

For there it is, crack'd in a hundred shivers.
Mark, silent king, the moral of this sport –
How soon my sorrow hath destroy'd my face.
BOLINGBROKE The shadow of your sorrow hath destroy'd
The shadow of your face.
KING RICHARD Say that again.
The shadow of my sorrow? Ha! let's see.
'Tis very true: my grief lies all within;
And these external manner of laments
Are merely shadows to the unseen grief
That swells with silence in the tortur'd soul.
There lies the substance; and I thank thee, king,
For thy great bounty, that not only giv'st
Me cause to wail, but teachest me the way
How to lament the cause. I'll beg one boon,
And then be gone and trouble you no more.
Shall I obtain it?
BOLINGBROKE Name it, fair cousin.
KING RICHARD Fair cousin! I am greater than a king;
For when I was a king, my flatterers
Were then but subjects; being now a subject,
I have a king here to my flatterer.
Being so great, I have no need to beg.
BOLINGBROKE Yet ask.
KING RICHARD And shall I have?
BOLINGBROKE You shall.
KING RICHARD Then give me leave to go.
BOLINGBROKE Whither?
KING RICHARD Whither you will, so I were from your sights.
BOLINGBROKE Go, some of you convey him to the Tower.
KING RICHARD O, good! Convey! Conveyers are you all,
That rise thus nimbly by a true king's fall.

[*Exeunt King Richard, some Lords, and a Guard.*

BOLINGBROKE On Wednesday next we solemnly set down
Our coronation. Lords, prepare yourselves.

[*Exeunt all but the Abbot of Westminster, the Bishop of Carlisle, and Aumerle.*

ABBOT A woeful pageant have we here beheld.
CARLISLE The woe's to come; the children yet unborn
Shall feel this day as sharp to them as thorn.
AUMERLE You holy clergymen, is there no plot
To rid the realm of this pernicious blot?
ABBOT My lord,
Before I freely speak my mind herein,
You shall not only take the sacrament
To bury mine intents, but also to effect
Whatever I shall happen to devise.
I see your brows are full of discontent,
Your hearts of sorrow, and your eyes of tears.
Come home with me to supper; I will lay
A plot shall show us all a merry day. [*Exeunt.*

ACT FIVE

SCENE I. *London. A street leading to the Tower.*

Enter the QUEEN, with her Attendants.

QUEEN This way the King will come; this is the way
To Julius Caesar's ill-erected tower,
To whose flint bosom my condemned lord
Is doom'd a prisoner by proud Bolingbroke.
Here let us rest, if this rebellious earth
Have any resting for her true king's queen.

Enter KING RICHARD and Guard.

But soft, but see, or rather do not see,
My fair rose wither. Yet look up, behold,
That you in pity may dissolve to dew,
And wash him fresh again with true-love tears.
Ah, thou, the model where old Troy did stand;
Thou map of honour, thou King Richard's tomb,
And not King Richard; thou most beauteous inn,

Why should hard-favour'd grief be lodg'd in thee,
When triumph is become an alehouse guest?

KING RICHARD Join not with grief, fair woman, do not so,
To make my end too sudden. Learn, good soul,
To think our former state a happy dream;
From which awak'd, the truth of what we are
Shows us but this: I am sworn brother, sweet,
To grim Necessity; and he and I
Will keep a league till death. Hie thee to France,
And cloister thee in some religious house.
Our holy lives must win a new world's crown,
Which our profane hours here have thrown down.

QUEEN What, is my Richard both in shape and mind
Transform'd and weak'ned? Hath Bolingbroke depos'd
Thine intellect? Hath he been in thy heart?
The lion dying thrusteth forth his paw
And wounds the earth, if nothing else, with rage
To be o'erpow'r'd; and wilt thou, pupil-like,
Take the correction mildly, kiss the rod,
And fawn on rage with base humility,
Which art a lion and the king of beasts?

KING RICHARD A king of beasts, indeed! If aught but beasts,
I had been still a happy king of men.
Good sometimes queen, prepare thee hence for France.
Think I am dead, and that even here thou takest,
As from my death-bed, thy last living leave.
In winter's tedious nights sit by the fire
With good old folks, and let them tell thee tales
Of woeful ages long ago betid;
And ere thou bid good night, to quit their griefs
Tell thou the lamentable tale of me,
And send the hearers weeping to their beds;
For why the senseless brands will sympathize
The heavy accent of thy moving tongue,
And in compassion weep the fire out;
And some will mourn in ashes, some coal-black,
For the deposing of a rightful king.

Enter NORTHUMBERLAND attended.

NORTHUMBERLAND My lord, the mind of Bolingbroke is chang'd;
You must to Pomfret, not unto the Tower.
And, madam, there is order ta'en for you:
With all swift speed you must away to France.

KING RICHARD Northumberland, thou ladder wherewithal
The mounting Bolingbroke ascends my throne,
The time shall not be many hours of age
More than it is, ere foul sin gathering head
Shall break into corruption. Thou shalt think
Though he divide the realm and give thee half
It is too little, helping him to all;
And he shall think that thou, which knowest the way
To plant unrightful kings, wilt know again,
Being ne'er so little urg'd, another way
To pluck him headlong from the usurped throne.
The love of wicked men converts to fear;
That fear to hate; and hate turns one or both
To worthy danger and deserved death.

NORTHUMBERLAND My guilt be on my head, and there an end.
Take leave, and part; for you must part forthwith.

KING RICHARD Doubly divorc'd! Bad men, you violate
A twofold marriage – 'twixt my crown and me,
And then betwixt me and my married wife.
Let me unkiss the oath 'twixt thee and me;
And yet not so, for with a kiss 'twas made.
Part us, Northumberland; I towards the north,
Where shivering cold and sickness pines the clime;
My wife to France, from whence set forth in pomp,
She came adorned hither like sweet May,
Sent back like Hallowmas or short'st of day.

QUEEN And must we be divided? Must we part?

KING RICHARD Ay, hand from hand, my love, and heart from heart.

QUEEN Banish us both, and send the King with me.

NORTHUMBERLAND That were some love, but little policy.

QUEEN Then whither he goes thither let me go.

KING RICHARD So two, together weeping, make one woe.
Weep thou for me in France, I for thee here;
Better far off than near, be ne'er the near.
Go, count thy way with sighs; I mine with groans.

QUEEN So longest way shall have the longest moans.

KING RICHARD Twice for one step I'll groan, the way being short,
And piece the way out with a heavy heart.
Come, come, in wooing sorrow let's be brief,
Since, wedding it, there is such length in grief.
One kiss shall stop our mouths, and dumbly part;
Thus give I mine, and thus take I thy heart.

QUEEN Give me mine own again; 'twere no good part
To take on me to keep and kill thy heart.
So, now I have mine own again, be gone,
That I may strive to kill it with a groan.

KING RICHARD We make woe wanton with this fond delay.
Once more, adieu; the rest let sorrow say.
[*Exeunt.*

SCENE II. *The Duke of York's palace.*

Enter the DUKE OF YORK and the DUCHESS.

DUCHESS My lord, you told me you would tell the rest,
When weeping made you break the story off,
Of our two cousins' coming into London.
YORK Where did I leave?
DUCHESS At that sad stop, my lord,
Where rude misgoverned hands from windows' tops
Threw dust and rubbish on King Richard's head.
YORK Then, as I said, the Duke, great Bolingbroke,
Mounted upon a hot and fiery steed
Which his aspiring rider seem'd to know,
With slow but stately pace kept on his course,
Whilst all tongues cried 'God save thee, Bolingbroke!'
You would have thought the very windows spake,
So many greedy looks of young and old
Through casements darted their desiring eyes
Upon his visage; and that all the walls
With painted imagery had said at once
'Jesu preserve thee! Welcome, Bolingbroke!'
Whilst he, from the one side to the other turning,
Bareheaded, lower than his proud steed's neck,
Bespake them thus, 'I thank you, countrymen'.
And thus still doing, thus he pass'd along.
DUCHESS Alack, poor Richard! where rode he the whilst?
YORK As in a theatre the eyes of men
After a well-grac'd actor leaves the stage
Are idly bent on him that enters next,
Thinking his prattle to be tedious;
Even so, or with much more contempt, men's eyes
Did scowl on gentle Richard; no man cried 'God save him!'
No joyful tongue gave him his welcome home;
But dust was thrown upon his sacred head;
Which with such gentle sorrow he shook off,
His face still combating with tears and smiles,
The badges of his grief and patience,
That had not God, for some strong purpose, steel'd
The hearts of men, they must perforce have melted,
And barbarism itself have pitied him.
But heaven hath a hand in these events,
To whose high will we bound our calm contents.
To Bolingbroke are we sworn subjects now,
Whose state and honour I for aye allow.
DUCHESS Here comes my son Aumerle.
YORK Aumerle that was;
But that is lost for being Richard's friend,
And, madam, you must call him Rutland now.
I am in Parliament pledge for his truth
And lasting fealty to the new-made king.

Enter AUMERLE.

DUCHESS Welcome, my son. Who are the violets now
That strew the green lap of the new come spring?
AUMERLE Madam, I know not, nor I greatly care not.
God knows I had as lief be none as one.
YORK Well, bear you well in this new spring of time,
Lest you be cropp'd before you come to prime.
What news from Oxford? Do these justs and triumphs hold?
AUMERLE For aught I know, my lord, they do.
YORK You will be there, I know.
AUMERLE If God prevent not, I purpose so.
YORK What seal is that that hangs without thy bosom?
Yea, look'st thou pale? Let me see the writing.
AUMERLE My lord, 'tis nothing.
YORK No matter, then, who see it.
I will be satisfied; let me see the writing.
AUMERLE I do beseech your Grace to pardon me;
It is a matter of small consequence
Which for some reasons I would not have seen.
YORK Which for some reasons, sir, I mean to see.
I fear, I fear –
DUCHESS What should you fear?
'Tis nothing but some bond that he is ent'red into
For gay apparel 'gainst the triumph-day.
YORK Bound to himself! What doth he with a bond
That he is bound to? Wife, thou art a fool.
Boy, let me see the writing.
AUMERLE I do beseech you, pardon me; I may not show it.
YORK I will be satisfied; let me see it, I say.
[*He plucks it out of his bosom, and reads it.*
Treason, foul treason! Villain! traitor! slave!
DUCHESS What is the matter, my lord?
YORK Ho! who is within there?

Enter a Servant.

Saddle my horse.
God for his mercy, what treachery is here!
DUCHESS Why, what is it, my lord?

YORK Give me my boots, I say; saddle my horse.
[Exit Servant.
Now, by mine honour, by my life, my troth,
I will appeach the villain.
DUCHESS What is the matter?
YORK Peace, foolish woman.
DUCHESS I will not peace. What is the matter, Aumerle?
AUMERLE Good mother, be content; it is no more
Than my poor life must answer.
DUCHESS Thy life answer!
YORK Bring me my boots. I will unto the King.

His Man enters with his boots.

DUCHESS Strike him, Aumerle. Poor boy, thou art amaz'd.
Hence, villain! never more come in my sight.
YORK Give me my boots, I say.
DUCHESS Why, York, what wilt thou do?
Wilt thou not hide the trespass of thine own?
Have we more sons? or are we like to have?
Is not my teeming date drunk up with time?
And wilt thou pluck my fair son from mine age
And rob me of a happy mother's name?
Is he not like thee? Is he not thine own?
YORK Thou fond mad woman,
Wilt thou conceal this dark conspiracy?
A dozen of them here have ta'en the sacrament,
And interchangeably set down their hands
To kill the King at Oxford.
DUCHESS He shall be none;
We'll keep him here. Then what is that to him?
YORK Away fond woman! were he twenty times my son
I would appeach him.
DUCHESS Hadst thou groan'd for him
As I have done, thou wouldst be more pitiful.
But now I know thy mind: thou dost suspect
That I have been disloyal to thy bed
And that he is a bastard, not thy son.
Sweet York, sweet husband, be not of that mind.
He is as like thee as a man may be,
Not like to me, or any of my kin,
And yet I love him.
YORK Make way, unruly woman!
[Exit.

DUCHESS After, Aumerle! Mount thee upon his horse;
Spur post, and get before him to the King,
And beg thy pardon ere he do accuse thee.
I'll not be long behind; though I be old,
I doubt not but to ride as fast as York;
And never will I rise up from the ground
Till Bolingbroke have pardon'd thee. Away, be gone.
[Exeunt.

SCENE III. *Windsor Castle.*

Enter BOLINGBROKE as King, PERCY, and other Lords.

BOLINGBROKE Can no man tell me of my unthrifty son?
'Tis full three months since I did see him last.
If any plague hang over us, 'tis he.
I would to God, my lords, he might be found.
Inquire at London, 'mongst the taverns there,
For there, they say, he daily doth frequent
With unrestrained loose companions,
Even such, they say, as stand in narrow lanes
And beat our watch and rob our passengers,
Which he, young wanton and effeminate boy,
Takes on the point of honour to support
So dissolute a crew.
PERCY My lord, some two days since I saw the Prince,
And told him of those triumphs held at Oxford.
BOLINGBROKE And what said the gallant?
PERCY His answer was, he would unto the stews,
And from the common'st creature pluck a glove
And wear it as a favour; and with that
He would unhorse the lustiest challenger.
BOLINGBROKE As dissolute as desperate; yet through both
I see some sparks of better hope, which elder years
May happily bring forth. But who comes here?

Enter AUMERLE amazed.

AUMERLE Where is the King?
BOLINGBROKE What means our cousin that he stares and looks
So wildly?
AUMERLE God save your Grace! I do beseech your Majesty,
To have some conference with your Grace alone.
BOLINGBROKE Withdraw yourselves, and leave us here alone.
[Exeunt Percy and Lords.

What is the matter with our cousin now?
AUMERLE For ever may my knees grow to the earth, *[Kneels.*
My tongue cleave to my roof within my mouth,
Unless a pardon ere I rise or speak.
BOLINGBROKE Intended or committed was this fault?
If on the first, how heinous e'er it be,
To win thy after-love I pardon thee.
AUMERLE Then give me leave that I may turn the key,
That no man enter till my tale be done.
BOLINGBROKE Have thy desire.
[The Duke of York knocks at the door and crieth.

YORK [*Within*] My liege, beware; look to thyself;
Thou hast a traitor in thy presence there.
BOLINGBROKE [*Drawing*] Villain, I'll make thee safe.
AUMERLE Stay thy revengeful hand; thou hast no cause to fear.
YORK [*Within*] Open the door, secure, foolhardy King.
Shall I, for love, speak treason to thy face?
Open the door, or I will break it open.

Enter YORK.

BOLINGBROKE What is the matter, uncle? Speak;
Recover breath; tell us how near is danger,
That we may arm us to encounter it.
YORK Peruse this writing here, and thou shalt know
The treason that my haste forbids me show.
AUMERLE Remember, as thou read'st, thy promise pass'd.
I do repent me; read not my name there;
My heart is not confederate with my hand.
YORK It was, villain, ere thy hand did set it down.
I tore it from the traitor's bosom, King;
Fear, and not love, begets his penitence.
Forget to pity him, lest thy pity prove
A serpent that will sting thee to the heart.
BOLINGBROKE O heinous, strong, and bold conspiracy!
O loyal father of a treacherous son!
Thou sheer, immaculate, and silver fountain,
From whence this stream through muddy passages
Hath held his current and defil'd himself!
Thy overflow of good converts to bad;
And thy abundant goodness shall excuse
This deadly blot in thy digressing son.
YORK So shall my virtue be his vice's bawd;
And he shall spend mine honour with his shame,
As thriftless sons their scraping fathers' gold.
Mine honour lives when his dishonour dies,
Or my sham'd life in his dishonour lies.
Thou kill'st me in his life; giving him breath,
The traitor lives, the true man's put to death.
DUCHESS [*Within*] What ho, my liege, for God's sake, let me in.
BOLINGBROKE What shrill-voic'd suppliant makes this eager cry?
DUCHESS [*Within*] A woman, and thine aunt, great King; 'tis I.
Speak with me, pity me, open the door.
A beggar begs that never begg'd before.
BOLINGBROKE Our scene is alt'red from a serious thing,
And now chang'd to 'The Beggar and the King'.
My dangerous cousin, let your mother in.
I know she is come to pray for your foul sin.
YORK If thou do pardon whosoever pray,
More sins for this forgiveness prosper may.
This fest'red joint cut off, the rest rest sound;
This let alone will all the rest confound.

Enter DUCHESS.

DUCHESS O King, believe not this hard-hearted man!
Love loving not itself, none other can.
YORK Thou frantic woman, what dost thou make here?
Shall thy old dugs once more a traitor rear?
DUCHESS Sweet York, be patient. Hear me, gentle liege. [*Kneels.*
BOLINGBROKE Rise up, good aunt.
DUCHESS Not yet, I thee beseech.
For ever will I walk upon my knees,
And never see day that the happy sees
Till thou give joy; until thou bid me joy
By pardoning Rutland, my transgressing boy.
AUMERLE Unto my mother's prayers I bend my knee. [*Kneels.*
YORK Against them both, my true joints bended be. [*Kneels.*
Ill mayst thou thrive, if thou grant any grace!
DUCHESS Pleads he in earnest? Look upon his face;
His eyes do drop no tears, his prayers are in jest;
His words come from his mouth, ours from our breast.
He prays but faintly and would be denied;
We pray with heart and soul, and all beside.
His weary joints would gladly rise, I know;
Our knees still kneel till to the ground they grow.
His prayers are full of false hypocrisy;
Ours of true zeal and deep integrity.
Our prayers do out-pray his; then let them have
That mercy which true prayer ought to have.
BOLINGBROKE Good aunt, stand up.
DUCHESS Nay, do not say 'stand up';
Say 'pardon' first, and afterwards 'stand up'.
An if I were thy nurse, thy tongue to teach,
'Pardon' should be the first word of thy speech.
I never long'd to hear a word till now;
Say 'pardon' King; let pity teach thee how.
The word is short, but not so short as sweet;
No word like 'pardon' for kings' mouths so meet.
YORK Speak it in French, King, say 'pardonne moy'.
DUCHESS Dost thou teach pardon pardon to destroy?
Ah, my sour husband, my hard-hearted lord,
That sets the word itself against the word!
Speak 'pardon' as 'tis current in our land;

The chopping French we do not understand.
Thine eye begins to speak, set thy tongue there;
Or in thy piteous heart plant thou thine ear,
That hearing how our plaints and prayers do pierce,
Pity may move thee 'pardon' to rehearse.

BOLINGBROKE Good aunt, stand up.

DUCHESS I do not sue to stand;
Pardon is all the suit I have in hand.

BOLINGBROKE I pardon him, as God shall pardon me.

DUCHESS O happy vantage of a kneeling knee!
Yet am I sick for fear. Speak it again.
Twice saying 'pardon' doth not pardon twain,
But makes one pardon strong.

BOLINGBROKE With all my heart
I pardon him.

DUCHESS A god on earth thou art.

BOLINGBROKE But for our trusty brother-in-law and the Abbot,
With all the rest of that consorted crew,
Destruction straight shall dog them at the heels.
Good uncle, help to order several powers
To Oxford, or where'er these traitors are.
They shall not live within this world, I swear,
But I will have them, if I once know where.
Uncle, farewell; and, cousin, adieu;
Your mother well hath pray'd, and prove you true.

DUCHESS Come, my old son; I pray God make thee new. [*Exeunt*.

SCENE IV. *Windsor Castle.*

Enter SIR PIERCE OF EXTON and a Servant.

EXTON Didst thou not mark the King, what words he spake?
'Have I no friend will rid me of this living fear?'
Was it not so?

SERVANT These were his very words.

EXTON 'Have I no friend?' quoth he. He spake it twice,
And urg'd it twice together, did he not?

SERVANT He did.

EXTON And, speaking it, he wishtly look'd on me,
As who should say 'I would thou wert the man
That would divorce this terror from my heart';
Meaning the king at Pomfret. Come, let's go.
I am the King's friend, and will rid his foe. [*Exeunt*.

SCENE V. *Pomfret Castle. The dungeon of the Castle.*

Enter KING RICHARD.

KING RICHARD I have been studying how I may compare
This prison where I live unto the world;
And, for because the world is populous
And here is not a creature but myself,
I cannot do it. Yet I'll hammer it out.
My brain I'll prove the female to my soul,
My soul the father; and these two beget
A generation of still-breeding thoughts,
And these same thoughts people this little world,
In humours like the people of this world,
For no thought is contented. The better sort,
As thoughts of things divine, are inter-mix'd
With scruples, and do set the word itself
Against the word,
As thus: 'Come, little ones'; and then again,
'It is as hard to come as for a camel
To thread the postern of a small needle's eye'.
Thoughts tending to ambition, they do plot
Unlikely wonders: how these vain weak nails
May tear a passage through the flinty ribs
Of this hard world, my ragged prison walls;
And, for they cannot, die in their own pride.
Thoughts tending to content flatter themselves
That they are not the first of fortune's slaves,
Nor shall not be the last; like silly beggars
Who, sitting in the stocks, refuge their shame,
That many have and others must sit there;
And in this thought they find a kind of ease,
Bearing their own misfortunes on the back
Of such as have before endur'd the like.
Thus play I in one person many people,
And none contented. Sometimes am I king;
Then treasons make me wish myself a beggar,
And so I am. Then crushing penury
Persuades me I was better when a king;
Then am I king'd again; and by and by
Think that I am unking'd by Bolingbroke,
And straight am nothing. But whate'er I be,
Nor I, nor any man that but man is,
With nothing shall be pleas'd till he be eas'd
With being nothing.

The music plays.

Music do I hear?
Ha, ha! keep time. How sour sweet music is
When time is broke and no proportion kept!
So is it in the music of men's lives.
And here have I the daintiness of ear
To check time broke in a disorder'd string;
But, for the concord of my state and time,
Had not an ear to hear my true time broke.
I wasted time, and now doth time waste me;
For now hath time made me his numb'ring clock:
My thoughts are minutes; and with sighs they jar
Their watches on unto mine eyes, the outward watch.

Whereto my finger, like a dial's point,
Is pointing still, in cleansing them from tears.
Now, sir, the sound that tells what hour it is
Are clamorous groans which strike upon my heart,
Which is the bell. So sighs, and tears, and groans,
Show minutes, times, and hours; but my time
Runs posting on in Bolingbroke's proud joy,
While I stand fooling here, his Jack of the clock.
This music mads me. Let it sound no more;
For though it have holp madmen to their wits,
In me it seems it will make wise men mad.
Yet blessing on his heart that gives it me!
For 'tis a sign of love; and love to Richard
Is a strange brooch in this all-hating world.

Enter a Groom of the stable.

GROOM Hail, royal Prince!
KING RICHARD Thanks, noble peer!
The cheapest of us is ten groats too dear.
What art thou? and how comest thou hither,
Where no man never comes but that sad dog
That brings me food to make misfortune live?
GROOM I was a poor groom of thy stable, King,
When thou wert king; who, travelling towards York,
With much ado at length have gotten leave
To look upon my sometimes royal master's face.
O, how it ern'd my heart, when I beheld,
In London streets, that coronation-day,
When Bolingbroke rode on roan Barbary –
That horse that thou so often hast bestrid,
That horse that I so carefully have dress'd!
KING RICHARD Rode he on Barbary? Tell me, gentle friend,
How went he under him?
GROOM So proudly as if he disdain'd the ground.
KING RICHARD So proud that Bolingbroke was on his back!
That jade hath eat bread from my royal hand;
This hand hath made him proud with clapping him.
Would he not stumble? would he not fall down,
Since pride must have a fall, and break the neck
Of that proud man that did usurp his back?
Forgiveness, horse! Why do I rail on thee,
Since thou, created to be aw'd by man,
Wast born to bear? I was not made a horse;
And yet I bear a burden like an ass,
Spurr'd, gall'd, and tir'd, by jauncing Bolingbroke.

Enter Keeper with meat.

KEEPER Fellow, give place; here is no longer stay.
KING RICHARD If thou love me, 'tis time thou wert away.
GROOM What my tongue dares not, that my heart shall say. [*Exit.*

KEEPER My lord, will't please you to fall to?
KING RICHARD Taste of it first as thou art wont to do.
KEEPER My lord, I dare not. Sir Pierce of Exton,
Who lately came from the King, commands the contrary.
KING RICHARD The devil take Henry of Lancaster and thee!
Patience is stale, and I am weary of it.
[*Beats the Keeper.*

KEEPER Help, help, help!

The murderers, EXTON and Servants, rush in, armed.

KING RICHARD How now! What means death in this rude assault?
Villain, thy own hand yields thy death's instrument.
[*Snatching a weapon and killing one.*
Go thou and fill another room in hell.
[*He kills another, then Exton strikes him down.*
That hand shall burn in never-quenching fire
That staggers thus my person. Exton, thy fierce hand
Hath with the King's blood stain'd the King's own land.
Mount, mount, my soul! thy seat is up on high;
Whilst my gross flesh sinks downward, here to die. [*Dies.*

EXTON As full of valour as of royal blood.
Both have I spill'd. O, would the deed were good!
For now the devil, that told me I did well,
Says that this deed is chronicled in hell.
This dead king to the living king I'll bear.
Take hence the rest, and give them burial here.
[*Exeunt.*

SCENE VI. *Windsor Castle.*

Flourish. Enter BOLINGBROKE, the DUKE OF YORK, with other Lords and Attendants.

BOLINGBROKE Kind uncle York, the latest news we hear
Is that the rebels have consum'd with fire
Our town of Ciceter in Gloucestershire;
But whether they be ta'en or slain we hear not.

Enter NORTHUMBERLAND.

Welcome, my lord. What is the news?
NORTHUMBERLAND First, to thy sacred state wish I all happiness.

The next news is, I have to London sent
The heads of Salisbury, Spencer, Blunt, and
Kent.
The manner of their taking may appear
At large discoursed in this paper here.

BOLINGBROKE We thank thee, gentle Percy, for thy pains;
And to thy worth will add right worthy gains.

Enter FITZWATER.

FITZWATER My lord, I have from Oxford sent to London
The heads of Brocas and Sir Bennet Seely;
Two of the dangerous consorted traitors
That sought at Oxford thy dire overthrow.

BOLINGBROKE Thy pains, Fitzwater, shall not be forgot;
Right noble is thy merit, well I wot.

Enter PERCY, with the BISHOP OF CARLISLE.

PERCY The grand conspirator, Abbot of Westminster,
With clog of conscience and sour melancholy,
Hath yielded up his body to the grave;
But here is Carlisle living, to abide
Thy kingly doom, and sentence of his pride.

BOLINGBROKE Carlisle, this is your doom:
Choose out some secret place, some reverend room,
More than thou hast, and with it joy thy life;
So as thou liv'st in peace, die free from strife;
For though mine enemy thou hast ever been,
High sparks of honour in thee have I seen.

Enter EXTON, with Attendants, bearing a coffin.

EXTON Great King, within this coffin I present
Thy buried fear. Herein all breathless lies
The mightiest of thy greatest enemies,
Richard of Bordeaux, by me hither brought.

BOLINGBROKE Exton, I thank thee not; for thou hast wrought
A deed of slander with thy fatal hand
Upon my head and all this famous land.

EXTON From your own mouth, my lord, did I this deed.

BOLINGBROKE They love not poison that do poison need,
Nor do I thee. Though I did wish him dead,
I hate the murderer, love him murdered.
The guilt of conscience take thou for thy labour,
But neither my good word nor princely favour;
With Cain go wander thorough shades of night,
And never show thy head by day nor light.
Lords, I protest my soul is full of woe
That blood should sprinkle me to make me grow.
Come, mourn with me for what I do lament,
And put on sullen black incontinent.
I'll make a voyage to the Holy Land,
To wash this blood off from my guilty hand.
March sadly after; grace my mournings here
In weeping after this untimely bier. [*Exeunt.*

The First Part of King Henry the Fourth

Introduction by ALEC YEARLING

This play differs notably from its predecessor *Richard II* (apparently written several years before), which had been lyrical in manner and largely single-minded in chronicling its protagonist's downfall. Events in the later play largely stem from that traumatic deposition; but here the approach is prismatic and disjunct. We see manoeuvres of statecraft and rebellion, glimpse common life, hear idealistic and cynical voices; and centrally, we contemplate the prince who will be Henry V and his association with Sir John Falstaff.

The result is the first of those dramas in which Shakespeare perfects the art of fruitful confusion. We are beset by contrarieties in a continually self-modifying text where no statement can be taken as absolute. 'Thus ever did rebellion find rebuke' says the finally victorious monarch who gained his position by successful revolt against his anointed liege.

It is magnificent to be a king; also a barely tolerable burden, as Henry's opening words indicate. Shakespeare's interest is in how, by what codes, rulers rule. The rebel allies are doomed to failure because they are factious, with traits either ridiculous (Glendower's sorcery) or unrealistic (Hotspur's pursuit of honour). None of them has any idea of what it means to unite a kingdom. Their shallowness is far from the spiritual dimension – manifest in guilt – which is a marked feature of King Henry's part, and it is into this deeper awareness that Prince Hal must be initiated. Shakespeare was bold with the details of his source-chronicles, but he followed their insistence that God's providential scheme required atonement for the overthrow and murder of King Richard: Hal will eventually accept his burden (in *Part Two*) and glorify it (in *Henry V*), but for the moment father and son are caught in a primal tragic situation. We see Hal finding his way, accessible to our gaze as the king rarely is. He is repeatedly paralleled with Hotspur, and given contrasting father-figures in Falstaff and the king. Schematically, his role is to learn through observation and experience so as finally to perfectly blend humanity and royalty. A difficulty arises in that this is not quite what the play delivers. In Act 1 Scene 2 the prince reveals himself only superficially involved in the Eastcheap world which, epitomised in Falstaff, signifies the pleasures and miseries of carnal frailty. He pretends to be errant so as to impress his people with an eventual appearance of reform. (His father in Act 3 Scene 2 is similarly dedicated to the manipulation of public opinion.) This is the world of *Realpolitik*; the danger is that it will render Hal unsympathetic and cripple the dramatic potential of his relationship with Falstaff. In popular tradition Hal was genuinely errant: Shakespeare sanitises him. He becomes a virtuous trickster in the Gadshill robbery, with potentially anarchic moments like the assault on the Lord Chief Justice confined to passing reported references.

Whereas Hal is thematically central, with the climactic battle at Shrewsbury showing his maturity in vanquishing Hotspur and his magnanimity in condoning Falstaff's outrageous lies, Falstaff himself is at the human heart of the drama. Essentially his is a simple character-type: the Braggart Soldier, with limitless entertainment-potential in the chasm between words and actualities. Some see him as a version of the traditional Vice, a gleeful tempter to sin. But a rich vitality overruns the stereotypes. Falstaff is a Vice only as Shylock, a contemporary creation, is a Wicked Jew. Unlike the Vice, he neither delights in wickedness for its own sake, nor rejoices in misleading youth. Compounded of the seven sins, he will eventually be cast out and punished: but as with Shylock, we need to consider causes and effects, and the human complexity that blurs moral judgements. Shylock the humanised monster fits indifferently into his conventional plot; Falstaff gains from being featured rather in a series of incidents, and is the superior creation because a degree of irony is suggested in his portrayal. So keen on citing scriptural and moral tags, so blatant at denying the truth about himself, and yet so clearly not an idiot, he comes across as self-constructed. A role-playing Falstaff confronts a Hal locked in a public-relations exercise:

– Banish plump Jack, and banish all the world.
– I do, I will. [2.4.462–464]

And if we find ourselves deeply uneasy at the implications of that, then we are attuned to this disturbing, equivocal play.

The First Part of King Henry the Fourth

DRAMATIS PERSONAE

KING HENRY THE FOURTH
HENRY, PRINCE OF WALES, PRINCE JOHN OF LANCASTER
sons of Henry IV
EARL OF WESTMORELAND, SIR WALTER BLUNT
friends of the King
THOMAS PERCY, EARL OF WORCESTER
HENRY PERCY, EARL OF NORTHUMBERLAND
HENRY PERCY, *surnamed* HOTSPUR
his son
EDMUND MORTIMER, EARL OF MARCH
ARCHIBALD, EARL OF DOUGLAS
SCROOP, ARCHBISHOP OF YORK
SIR MICHAEL
friend of the Archbishop
OWEN GLENDOWER
SIR RICHARD VERNON
SIR JOHN FALSTAFF, POINS, BARDOLPH, PETO, GADSHILL
irregular humorists
FRANCIS
a drawer
LADY PERCY
wife of Hotspur and sister of Mortimer
LADY MORTIMER
wife of Mortimer and daughter of Glendower
HOSTESS QUICKLY
of the Boar's Head, Eastcheap
Lords, Officers, Attendants, an Ostler, a Servant, a Messenger, a Sheriff, a Vintner, a Chamberlain, Drawers, Carriers, and Travellers.

THE SCENE: ENGLAND AND WALES.

ACT ONE

SCENE I. *London. The palace.*

Enter the KING, LORD JOHN OF LANCASTER, EARL OF WESTMORELAND, SIR WALTER BLUNT, and Others.

KING So shaken as we are, so wan with care,
Find we a time for frighted peace to pant
And breathe short-winded accents of new broils
To be commenc'd in strands afar remote.
No more the thirsty entrance of this soil
Shall daub her lips with her own children's blood;
No more shall trenching war channel her fields,
Nor bruise her flow'rets with the armed hoofs
Of hostile paces. Those opposed eyes
Which, like the meteors of a troubled heaven,
All of one nature, of one substance bred,
Did lately meet in the intestine shock
And furious close of civil butchery,
Shall now in mutual well-beseeming ranks
March all one way, and be no more oppos'd
Against acquaintance, kindred, and allies.
The edge of war, like an ill-sheathed knife,
No more shall cut his master. Therefore, friends,
As far as to the sepulchre of Christ –
Whose soldier now, under whose blessed cross
We are impressed and engag'd to fight –
Forthwith a power of English shall we levy,
Whose arms were moulded in their mothers' womb
To chase these pagans in those holy fields
Over whose acres walk'd those blessed feet
Which fourteen hundred years ago were nail'd
For our advantage on the bitter cross.
But this our purpose now is twelvemonth old,
And bootless 'tis to tell you we will go;
Therefore we meet not now. Then let me hear
Of you, my gentle cousin Westmoreland,
What yesternight our Council did decree
In forwarding this dear expedience.

WESTMORELAND My liege, this haste was hot in question
And many limits of the charge set down
But yesternight, when all athwart there came
A post from Wales loaden with heavy news;
Whose worst was that the noble Mortimer,
Leading the men of Herefordshire to fight
Against the irregular and wild Glendower,
Was by the rude hands of that Welshman taken,
A thousand of his people butchered;
Upon whose dead corpse there was such misuse,
Such beastly shameless transformation,
By those Welshwomen done, as may not be
Without much shame re-told or spoken of.

KING It seems then that the tidings of this broil

Brake off our business for the Holy Land.
WESTMORELAND This match'd with other did, my gracious Lord;
For more uneven and unwelcome news
Came from the north, and thus it did import:
On Holy-rood day, the gallant Hotspur there,
Young Harry Percy, and brave Archibald,
That ever-valiant and approved Scot,
At Holmedon met,
Where they did spend a sad and bloody hour;
As by discharge of their artillery
And shape of likelihood the news was told;
For he that brought them, in the very heat
And pride of their contention did take horse,
Uncertain of the issue any way.
KING Here is a dear, a true industrious friend,
Sir Walter Blunt, new lighted from his horse,
Stain'd with the variation of each soil
Betwixt that Holmedon and this seat of ours;
And he hath brought us smooth and welcome news.
The Earl of Douglas is discomfited:
Ten thousand bold Scots, two and twenty knights,
Balk'd in their own blood, did Sir Walter see
On Holmedon's plains; of prisoners, Hotspur took
Mordake, Earl of Fife and eldest son
To beaten Douglas; and the Earl of Athol,
Of Murray, Angus, and Menteith.
And is not this an honourable spoil?
A gallant prize? Ha, cousin, is it not?
WESTMORELAND In faith,
It is a conquest for a prince to boast of.
KING Yea, there thou mak'st me sad and mak'st me sin
In envy that my Lord Northumberland
Should be the father to so blest a son –
A son who is the theme of honour's tongue;
Amongst a grove, the very straightest plant;
Who is sweet Fortune's minion and her pride;
Whilst I, by looking on the praise of him,
See riot and dishonour stain the brow
Of my young Harry. O that it could be prov'd
That some night-tripping fairy had exchang'd
In cradle-clothes our children where they lay,
And call'd mine Percy, his Plantagenet!
Then would I have his Harry, and he mine.
But let him from my thoughts. What think you, coz,
Of this young Percy's pride? The prisoners
Which he in this adventure hath surpris'd
To his own use he keeps; and sends me word,
I shall have none but Mordake Earl of Fife.
WESTMORELAND This is his uncle's teaching, this is Worcester,
Malevolent to you in all aspects;
Which makes him prune himself, and bristle up
The crest of youth against your dignity.
KING But I have sent for him to answer this;
And for this cause awhile we must neglect
Our holy purpose to Jerusalem.
Cousin, on Wednesday next our council we
Will hold at Windsor – so inform the lords;
But come yourself with speed to us again,
For more is to be said and to be done
Than out of anger can be uttered.
WESTMORELAND I will, my liege. [*Exeunt.*

SCENE II. *London. The Prince's lodging.*

Enter the PRINCE OF WALES and SIR JOHN FALSTAFF.

FALSTAFF Now, Hal, what time of day is it, lad?

PRINCE Thou art so fat-witted with drinking of old sack, and unbuttoning thee after supper, and sleeping upon benches after noon, that thou hast forgotten to demand that truly which thou wouldest truly know. What a devil hast thou to do with the time of the day? Unless hours were cups of sack, and minutes capons, and clocks the tongues of bawds, and dials the signs of leaping-houses, and the blessed sun himself a fair hot wench in flame-coloured taffeta, I see no reason why thou shouldst be so superfluous to demand the time of the day. 11

FALSTAFF Indeed, you come near me now, Hal; for we that take purses go by the moon and the seven stars, and not by Phœbus, he 'that wand'ring knight so fair'. And, I prithee, sweet wag, when thou art a king, as, God save thy Grace – Majesty, I should say; for grace thou wilt have none – 17

PRINCE What, none?

FALSTAFF No, by my troth; not so much as will serve to be prologue to an egg and butter. 20

PRINCE Well, how then? Come, roundly, roundly.

FALSTAFF Marry, then, sweet wag, when thou art king, let not us that are squires of the night's body be called thieves of the day's beauty; let us be Diana's foresters, gentlemen of the shade, minions of the moon; and let men say we be men of good government, being governed, as the sea is, by our noble and chaste mistress the moon, under whose Countenance we steal. 28

PRINCE Thou sayest well, and it holds well too; for the fortune of us that are the moon's men doth ebb and flow like the sea, being governed, as the sea is, by the moon. As, for proof, now: a purse of gold most resolutely snatch'd on Monday night, and most dissolutely spent on Tuesday morning; got with swearing 'Lay by' and spent with crying 'Bring in'; now in as low an ebb as the foot of the ladder, and by and by in as high a flow as the ridge of the gallows.

FALSTAFF By the Lord, thou say'st true, lad. And is not my hostess of the tavern a most sweet wench?

PRINCE As the honey of Hybla, my old lad of the castle. And is not a buff jerkin a most sweet robe of durance?

FALSTAFF How now, how now, mad wag! What, in thy quips and thy quiddities? What a plague have I to do with a buff jerkin?

PRINCE Why, what a pox have I to do with my hostess of the tavern?

FALSTAFF Well, thou hast call'd her to a reckoning many a time and oft.

PRINCE Did I ever call for thee to pay thy part?

FALSTAFF No; I'll give thee thy due, thou hast paid all there.

PRINCE Yea, and elsewhere, so far as my coin would stretch; and where it would not, I have used my credit.

FALSTAFF Yea, and so us'd it that, were it not here apparent that thou art heir apparent – but, I prithee, sweet wag, shall there be gallows standing in England when thou art king, and resolution thus fubb'd as it is with the rusty curb of old father antic the law? Do not thou, when thou art king, hang a thief.

PRINCE No; thou shalt.

FALSTAFF Shall I? O rare! By the Lord, I'll be a brave judge!

PRINCE Thou judgest false already: I mean thou shalt have the hanging of the thieves, and so become a rare hangman.

FALSTAFF Well, Hal, well; and in some sort it jumps with my humour as well as waiting in the court, I can tell you.

PRINCE For obtaining of suits?

FALSTAFF Yea, for obtaining of suits, whereof the hangman hath no lean wardrobe. 'Sblood, I am as melancholy as a gib cat or a lugg'd bear.

PRINCE Or an old lion, or a lover's lute.

FALSTAFF Yea, or the drone of a Lincolnshire bagpipe.

PRINCE What sayest thou to a hare, or the melancholy of Moor Ditch?

FALSTAFF Thou hast the most unsavoury similes, and art indeed the most comparative, rascalliest, sweet young prince. But, Hal, I prithee, trouble me no more with vanity. I would to God thou and I knew where a commodity of good names were to be bought. An old lord of the Council rated me the other day in the street about you, sir, but I mark'd him not; and yet he talk'd very wisely, but I regarded him not; and yet he talk'd wisely, and in the street too.

PRINCE Thou didst well; for wisdom cries out in the streets, and no man regards it.

FALSTAFF O, thou hast damnable iteration, and art indeed able to corrupt a saint. Thou hast done much harm upon me, Hal – God forgive thee for it! Before I knew thee, Hal, I knew nothing; and now am I, if a man should speak truly, little better than one of the wicked. I must give over this life, and I will give it over. By the Lord, an I do not I am a villain! I'll be damn'd for never a king's son in Christendom.

PRINCE Where shall we take a purse to-morrow, Jack?

FALSTAFF Zounds, where thou wilt, lad: I'll make one. An I do not, call me villain and baffle me.

PRINCE I see a good amendment of life in thee – from praying to purse-taking.

FALSTAFF Why, Hal, 'tis my vocation, Hal; 'tis no sin for a man to labour in his vocation.

Enter POINS.

Poins! – Now shall we know if Gadshill have set a match. O, if men were to be saved by merit, what hole in hell were hot enough for him? This is the most omnipotent villain that ever cried 'Stand' to a true man.

PRINCE Good morrow, Ned.

POINS Good morrow, sweet Hal. What says Monsieur Remorse? What says Sir John Sack and Sugar? Jack, how agrees the devil and thee about thy soul, that thou soldest him on Good Friday last for a cup of Madeira and a cold capon's leg?

PRINCE Sir John stands to his word – the devil shall have his bargain; for he was never yet a breaker of proverbs; he will give the devil his due.

POINS Then art thou damn'd for keeping thy word with the devil.

PRINCE Else he had been damn'd for cozening the devil.

POINS But, my lads, my lads, to-morrow morning, by four o'clock early, at Gadshill! There are pilgrims going to Canterbury with rich offerings, and traders riding to London with fat purses. I have vizards for you all; you have horses for yourselves. Gadshill lies to-night in Rochester; I have bespoke supper to-morrow night in Eastcheap. We may do it as secure as sleep. If you will go, I will stuff your purses full of crowns; if you will not, tarry at home and be hang'd.

FALSTAFF Hear ye, Yedward: if I tarry at home and go not, I'll hang you for going.

POINS You will, chops?

FALSTAFF Hal, wilt thou make one?

PRINCE Who? – I rob, I a thief? Not I, by my faith.

FALSTAFF There's neither honesty, manhood, nor good fellowship in thee, nor thou cam'st not of the blood royal, if thou darest not stand for ten shillings.

PRINCE Well then, once in my days I'll be a madcap.

FALSTAFF Why, that's well said.

PRINCE Well, come what will, I'll tarry at home.

FALSTAFF By the lord, I'll be a traitor then, when thou art king.

PRINCE I care not.

POINS Sir John, I prithee, leave the Prince and me alone: I will lay him down such reasons for this adventure that he shall go.

FALSTAFF Well, God give thee the spirit of persuasion, and him the ears of profiting, that what thou speakest may move, and what he hears may be believed; that the true prince may, for recreation sake, prove a false thief; for the poor abuses of the time want countenance. Farewell; you shall find me in Eastcheap.

PRINCE Farewell, thou latter spring! Farewell, All-hallown summer! *[Exit Falstaff.*

POINS Now, my good sweet honey lord, ride with us to-morrow. I have a jest to execute that I cannot manage alone. Falstaff, Bardolph, Peto, and Gadshill, shall rob those men that we have already waylaid; yourself and I will not be there; and when they have the booty, if you and I do not rob them, cut this head off from my shoulders.

PRINCE How shall we part with them in setting forth?

POINS Why, we will set forth before or after them, and appoint them a place of meeting, wherein it is at our pleasure to fail; and then will they adventure upon the exploit themselves; which they shall have no sooner achieved but we'll set upon them.

PRINCE Yea, but 'tis like that they will know us by our horses, by our habits, and by every other appointment, to be ourselves.

POINS Tut! our horses they shall not see – I'll tie them in the wood; our vizards we will change after we leave them; and, sirrah, I have cases of buckram for the nonce, to immask our noted outward garments.

PRINCE Yea, but I doubt they will be too hard for us.

POINS Well, for two of them, I know them to be as true-bred cowards as ever turn'd back; and for the third, if he fight longer than he sees reason, I'll forswear arms. The virtue of this jest will be the incomprehensible lies that this same fat rogue will tell us when we meet at supper: how thirty, at least, he fought with; what wards, what blows, what extremities he endured; and in the reproof of this lives the jest.

PRINCE Well, I'll go with thee. Provide us all things necessary, and meet me to-morrow night in Eastcheap; there I'll sup. Farewell.

POINS Farewell, my lord. *[Exit Poins.*

PRINCE I know you all, and will awhile uphold
The unyok'd humour of your idleness;
Yet herein will I imitate the sun,
Who doth permit the base contagious clouds
To smother up his beauty from the world,
That, when he please again to be himself,
Being wanted, he may be more wond'red at
By breaking through the foul and ugly mists
Of vapours that did seem to strangle him.
If all the year were playing holidays,
To sport would be as tedious as to work;
But when they seldom come, they wish'd-for come,
And nothing pleaseth but rare accidents.
So, when this loose behaviour I throw off
And pay the debt I never promised,
By how much better than my word I am,
By so much shall I falsify men's hopes;
And, like bright metal on a sullen ground,
My reformation, glitt'ring o'er my fault,
Shall show more goodly and attract more eyes
Than that which hath no foil to set it off.
I'll so offend to make offence a skill,
Redeeming time when men think least I will.
[Exit.

SCENE III. *London. The palace.*

Enter the KING, NORTHUMBERLAND, WORCESTER, HOTSPUR, SIR WALTER BLUNT, with Others.

KING My blood hath been too cold and temperate,
Unapt to stir at these indignities,
And you have found me; for accordingly
You tread upon my patience. But be sure
I will from henceforth rather be myself,
Mighty and to be fear'd, than my condition,
Which hath been smooth as oil, soft as young down,
And therefore lost that title of respect
Which the proud soul ne'er pays but to the proud.

WORCESTER Our house, my sovereign liege, little deserves
The scourge of greatness to be us'd on it –
And that same greatness too which our own hands

Have holp to make so portly.
NORTHUMBERLAND My lord –
KING Worcester, get thee gone; for I do see
Danger and disobedience in thine eye.
O, sir, your presence is too bold and
peremptory,
And majesty might never yet endure
The moody frontier of a servant brow.
You have good leave to leave us; when we need
Your use and counsel, we shall send for you.
[*Exit Worcester.*
You were about to speak.
NORTHUMBERLAND Yea, my good lord.
Those prisoners in your Highness' name
demanded,
Which Harry Percy here at Holmedon took,
Were, as he says, not with such strength denied
As is delivered to your Majesty.
Either envy, therefore, or misprision
Is guilty of this fault, and not my son.
HOTSPUR My liege, I did deny no prisoners.
But I remember when the fight was done,
When I was dry with rage and extreme toil,
Breathless and faint, leaning upon my sword,
Came there a certain lord, neat, and trimly
dress'd,
Fresh as a bridegroom, and his chin new reap'd
Show'd like a stubble-land at harvest-home.
He was perfumed like a milliner,
And 'twixt his finger and his thumb he held
A pouncet-box, which ever and anon
He gave his nose and took't away again;
Who therewith angry, when it next came there,
Took it in snuff – and still he smil'd and talk'd –
And as the soldiers bore dead bodies by,
He call'd them untaught knaves, unmannerly,
To bring a slovenly unhandsome corse
Betwixt the wind and his nobility.
With many holiday and lady terms
He questioned me: amongst the rest, demanded
My prisoners in your Majesty's behalf.
I then, all smarting with my wounds being cold,
To be so pest'red with a popinjay,
Out of my grief and my impatience
Answer'd neglectingly I know not what –
He should, or he should not – for he made me
mad
To see him shine so brisk, and smell so sweet,
And talk so like a waiting-gentlewoman
Of guns, and drums, and wounds – God save the
mark! –
And telling me the sovereignest thing on earth
Was parmaceti for an inward bruise;
And that it was great pity, so it was,
This villainous saltpetre should be digg'd
Out of the bowels of the harmless earth,
Which many a good tall fellow had destroy'd
So cowardly; and but for these vile guns
He would himself have been a soldier.
This bald unjointed chat of his, my lord,
I answered indirectly, as I said;
And I beseech you, let not his report
Come current for an accusation
Betwixt my love and your high Majesty.
BLUNT The circumstance considered, good my
lord,
Whate'er Lord Harry Percy then had said
To such a person, and in such a place,
At such a time, with all the rest re-told,
May reasonably die, and never rise
To do him wrong, or any way impeach
What then he said, so he unsay it now.
KING Why, yet he doth deny his prisoners,
But with proviso and exception –
That we at our own charge shall ransom straight
His brother-in-law, the foolish Mortimer;
Who, on my soul, hath wilfully betray'd
The lives of those that he did lead to fight
Against that great magician, damn'd Glendower,
Whose daughter, as we hear, that Earl of March
Hath lately married. Shall our coffers, then,
Be emptied to redeem a traitor home?
Shall we buy treason, and indent with fears,
When they have lost and forfeited themselves?
No, on the barren mountains let him starve;
For I shall never hold that man my friend
Whose tongue shall ask me for one penny cost
To ransom home revolted Mortimer.
HOTSPUR Revolted Mortimer!
He never did fall off, my sovereign liege,
But by the chance of war; to prove that true,
Needs no more but one tongue for all those
wounds,
Those mouthed wounds, which valiantly he
took
When on the gentle Severn's sedgy bank,
In single opposition hand to hand,
He did confound the best part of an hour
In changing hardiment with great Glendower.
Three times they breath'd, and three times did
they drink,
Upon agreement, of swift Severn's flood;
Who then, affrighted with their bloody looks,
Ran fearfully among the trembling reeds
And hid his crisp head in the hollow bank
Bloodstained with these valiant combatants.
Never did base and rotten policy
Colour her working with such deadly wounds;
Nor never could the noble Mortimer
Receive so many, and all willingly.
Then let him not be slandered with revolt.
KING Thou dost belie him, Percy, thou dost belie
him;

He never did encounter with Glendower.
I tell thee
He durst as well have met the devil alone
As Owen Glendower for an enemy.
Art thou not asham'd? But, sirrah, henceforth
Let me not hear you speak of Mortimer;
Send me your prisoners with the speediest means,
Or you shall hear in such a kind from me
As will displease you. My Lord Northumberland,
We license your departure with your son.
Send us your prisoners, or you will hear of it.

[Exeunt King Henry, Blunt, and Train.

HOTSPUR An if the devil come and roar for them,
I will not send them. I will after straight
And tell him so; for I will ease my heart,
Albeit I make a hazard of my head.

NORTHUMBERLAND What, drunk with choler? Stay and pause awhile.
Here comes your uncle.

Re-enter WORCESTER.

HOTSPUR Speak of Mortimer!
Zounds, I will speak of him; and let my soul
Want mercy if I do not join with him.
Yea, on his part I'll empty all these veins
And shed my dear blood drop by drop in the dust,
But I will lift the down-trod Mortimer
As high in the air as this unthankful king,
As this ingrate and cank'red Bolingbroke.

NORTHUMBERLAND Brother, the King hath made your nephew mad.

WORCESTER Who struck this heat up after I was gone?

HOTSPUR He will, forsooth, have all my prisoners;
And when I urg'd the ransom once again
Of my wife's brother, then his cheek look'd pale,
And on my face he turn'd an eye of death,
Trembling even at the name of Mortimer.

WORCESTER I cannot blame him: was not he proclaim'd
By Richard that dead is the next of blood?

NORTHUMBERLAND He was: I heard the proclamation;
And then it was when the unhappy King –
Whose wrongs in us God pardon! – did set forth
Upon his Irish expedition;
From whence he intercepted did return
To be depos'd, and shortly murdered.

WORCESTER And for whose death we in the world's wide mouth
Live scandaliz'd and foully spoken of.

HOTSPUR But soft, I pray you: did King Richard then
Proclaim my brother, Edmund Mortimer,
Heir to the crown?

NORTHUMBERLAND He did: myself did hear it.

HOTSPUR Nay, then I cannot blame his cousin king,
That wish'd him on the barren mountains starve.
But shall it be that you that set the crown
Upon the head of this forgetful man,
And for his sake wear the detested blot
Of murderous subornation – shall it be
That you a world of curses undergo,
Being the agents or base second means,
The cords, the ladder, or the hangman rather?
O, pardon me that I descend so low
To show the line and the predicament
Wherein you range under this subtle king!
Shall it, for shame, be spoken in these days
Or fill up chronicles in time to come,
That men of your nobility and power
Did gage them both in an unjust behalf –
As both of you, God pardon it! have done –
To put down Richard, that sweet lovely rose,
And plant this thorn, this canker, Bolingbroke?
And shall it, in more shame, be further spoken
That you are fool'd, discarded, and shook off,
By him for whom these shames ye underwent?
No; yet time serves wherein you may redeem
Your banish'd honours, and restore yourselves
Into the good thoughts of the world again;
Revenge the jeering and disdain'd contempt
Of this proud king, who studies day and night
To answer all the debt he owes to you
Even with the bloody payment of your deaths.
Therefore I say –

WORCESTER Peace, cousin, say no more.
And now I will unclasp a secret book,
And to your quick-conceiving discontents
I'll read you matter deep and dangerous,
As full of peril and adventurous spirit
As to o'er-walk a current roaring loud
On the unsteadfast footing of a spear.

HOTSPUR If he fall in, good night, or sink or swim.
Send danger from the east unto the west,
So honour cross it from the north to south,
And let them grapple. O, the blood more stirs
To rouse a lion than to start a hare!

NORTHUMBERLAND Imagination of some great exploit
Drives him beyond the bounds of patience.

HOTSPUR By heaven, methinks it were an easy leap
To pluck bright honour from the pale-fac'd moon;
Or dive into the bottom of the deep,
Where fathom-line could never touch the ground,

And pluck up drowned honour by the locks;
So he that doth redeem her thence might wear
Without corrival all her dignities.
But out upon this half-fac'd fellowship!

WORCESTER He apprehends a world of figures here,
But not the form of what he should attend.
Good cousin, give me audience for a while.

HOTSPUR I cry you mercy.

WORCESTER Those same noble Scots
That are your prisoners –

HOTSPUR I'll keep them all;
By God, he shall not have a Scot of them;
No, if a Scot would save his soul, he shall not.
I'll keep them, by this hand.

WORCESTER You start away,
And lend no ear unto my purposes.
Those prisoners you shall keep.

HOTSPUR Nay, I will; that's flat.
He said he would not ransom Mortimer;
Forbad my tongue to speak of Mortimer;
But I will find him when he lies asleep,
And in his ear I'll holla 'Mortimer!'
Nay,
I'll have a starling shall be taught to speak
Nothing but 'Mortimer', and give it him
To keep his anger still in motion.

WORCESTER Hear you, cousin; a word.

HOTSPUR All studies here I solemnly defy,
Save how to gall and pinch this Bolingbroke.
And that same sword-and-buckler Prince of Wales –
But that I think his father loves him not
And would be glad he met with some mischance –
I would have him poison'd with a pot of ale.

WORCESTER Farewell, kinsman: I'll talk to you
When you are better temper'd to attend.

NORTHUMBERLAND Why, what a wasp-stung and impatient fool
Art thou to break into this woman's mood,
Tying thine ear to no tongue but thine own!

HOTSPUR Why, look you, I am whipt and scourg'd with rods,
Nettled, and stung with pismires, when I hear
Of this vile politician, Bolingbroke.
In Richard's time – what do you call the place? –
A plague upon it, it is in Gloucestershire –
'Twas where the madcap duke his uncle kept –
His uncle York – where I first bow'd my knee
Unto this king of smiles, this Bolingbroke –
'Sblood!
When you and he came back from Ravenspurgh –

NORTHUMBERLAND At Berkeley Castle.

HOTSPUR You say true.
Why, what a candy deal of courtesy
This fawning greyhound then did proffer me!
'Look when his infant fortune came to age'
And 'gentle Harry Percy' and 'kind cousin' –
O, the devil take such cozeners! God forgive me!
Good uncle, tell your tale – I have done.

WORCESTER Nay, if you have not, to it again;
We will stay your leisure.

HOTSPUR I have done, i' faith.

WORCESTER Then once more to your Scottish prisoners:
Deliver them up without their ransom straight,
And make the Douglas' son your only mean
For powers in Scotland; which, for divers reasons
Which I shall send you written, be assur'd
Will easily be granted. [*To Northumberland*] You, my lord,
Your son in Scotland being thus employ'd,
Shall secretly into the bosom creep
Of that same noble prelate, well belov'd,
The Archbishop.

HOTSPUR Of York, is it not?

WORCESTER True; who bears hard
His brother's death at Bristow, the Lord Scroop.
I speak not this in estimation,
As what I think might be, but what I know
Is ruminated, plotted, and set down,
And only stays but to behold the face
Of that occasion that shall bring it on.

HOTSPUR I smell it. Upon my life, it will do well.

NORTHUMBERLAND Before the game is afoot thou still let'st slip.

HOTSPUR Why, it cannot choose but be a noble plot.
And then the power of Scotland and of York
To join with Mortimer, ha?

WORCESTER And so they shall.

HOTSPUR In faith, it is exceedingly well aim'd.

WORCESTER And 'tis no little reason bids us speed,
To save our heads by raising of a head;
For, bear ourselves as even as we can,
The King will always think him in our debt,
And think we think ourselves unsatisfied,
Till he hath found a time to pay us home.
And see already how he doth begin
To make us strangers to his looks of love.

HOTSPUR He does, he does. We'll be reveng'd on him.

WORCESTER Cousin, farewell. No further go in this
Than I by letters shall direct your course.
When time is ripe, which will be suddenly,
I'll steal to Glendower and Lord Mortimer;
Where you and Douglas and our pow'rs at once,

As I will fashion it, shall happily meet,
To bear our fortunes in our own strong arms,
Which now we hold at much uncertainty.

NORTHUMBERLAND Farewell, good brother. We shall thrive, I trust.

HOTSPUR Uncle, adieu. O, let the hours be short
Till fields and blows and groans applaud our sport! *[Exeunt.*

ACT TWO

SCENE I. *Rochester. An inn yard.*

Enter a Carrier with a lantern in his hand.

FIRST CARRIER Heigh-ho! an it be not four by the day, I'll be hang'd; Charles' wain is over the new chimney, and yet our horse not pack'd. What, ostler!

OSTLER *[Within]* Anon, anon.

FIRST CARRIER I prithee, Tom, beat Cut's saddle; put a few flocks in the point; poor jade is wrung in the withers out of all cess.

Enter another Carrier.

SECOND CARRIER Peas and beans are as dank here as a dog, and that is the next way to give poor jades the bots; this house is turned upside down since Robin Ostler died.

FIRST CARRIER Poor fellow never joyed since the price of oats rose; it was the death of him.

SECOND CARRIER I think this be the most villainous house in all London road for fleas; I am stung like a tench.

FIRST CARRIER Like a tench! By the mass, there is ne'er a king christen could be better bit than I have been since the first cock.

SECOND CARRIER Why, they will allow us ne'er a jordan; and then we leak in your chimney; and your chamber-lye breeds fleas like a loach.

FIRST CARRIER What, ostler! come away, and be hang'd; come away.

SECOND CARRIER I have a gammon of bacon and two razes of ginger, to be delivered as far as Charing Cross.

FIRST CARRIER God's body! the turkeys in my pannier are quite starved. What, ostler! A plague on thee! hast thou never an eye in thy head? Canst not hear? An 'twere not as good deed as drink to break the pate on thee, I am a very villain. Come, and be hang'd! Hast no faith in thee?

Enter GADSHILL.

GADSHILL Good morrow, carries. What's o'clock?

FIRST CARRIER I think it be two o'clock.

GADSHILL I prithee lend me thy lantern to see my gelding in the stable.

FIRST CARRIER Nay, by God! Soft! I know a trick worth two of that, i' faith.

GADSHILL I pray thee lend me thine.

SECOND CARRIER Ay, when, canst tell? Lend me thy lantern, quoth 'a? Marry, I'll see thee hang'd first.

GADSHILL Sirrah carrier, what time do you mean to come to London?

SECOND CARRIER Time enough to go to bed with a candle, I warrant thee. Come, neighbour Mugs, we'll call up the gentlemen; they will along with company, for they have great charge. *[Exeunt Carriers.*

GADSHILL What, ho! chamberlain!

CHAMBERLAIN *[Within]* At hand, quoth pick-purse.

GADSHILL That's even as fair as – at hand, quoth the chamberlain; for thou variest no more from picking of purses than giving direction doth from labouring; thou layest the plot how.

Enter Chamberlain.

CHAMBERLAIN Good morrow, Master Gadshill. It holds current that I told you yesternight: there's a franklin in the Wild of Kent hath brought three hundred marks with him in gold; I heard him tell it to one of his company last night at supper, a kind of auditor; one that hath abundance of charge too – God knows what. They are up already and call for eggs and butter; they will away presently.

GADSHILL Sirrah, if they meet not with Saint Nicholas' clerks, I'll give thee this neck.

CHAMBERLAIN No, I'll none of it; I pray thee keep that for the hangman; for I know thou worshippest Saint Nicholas as truly as a man of falsehood may.

GADSHILL What talkest thou to me of the hangman? If I hang, I'll make a fat pair of gallows; for if I hang, old Sir John hangs with me; and thou knowest he is no starveling. Tut! there are other Troyans that thou dream'st not of, the which for sport sake are content to do the profession some grace; that would, if matters should be look'd into, for their own credit sake, make all whole. I am joined with no foot landrakers, no long-staff six-penny strikers, none of these mad mustachio purple-hu'd malt-worms; but with nobility and tranquility, burgomasters and great oneyers, such as can hold in, such as will strike sooner than speak, and speak sooner than drink, and drink sooner than pray. And yet, zounds, I lie; for they pray continually to their saint, the commonwealth; or, rather, not pray to her, but prey on her; for they ride up and down on her, and make her their boots.

CHAMBERLAIN What, the commonwealth their boots? Will she hold out water in foul way?

GADSHILL She will, she will; justice hath liquor'd her. We steal as in a castle, cocksure; we have the receipt of fern-seed, we walk invisible.

CHAMBERLAIN Nay, by my faith, I think you are more beholding to the night than to fern-seed for your walking invisible.

GADSHILL Give me thy hand: thou shalt have a share in our purchase, as I am a true man.

CHAMBERLAIN Nay, rather let me have it, as you are a false thief.

GADSHILL Go to; 'homo' is a common name to all men. Bid the ostler bring my gelding out of the stable. Farewell, you muddy knave. [*Exeunt.*

SCENE II. *The highway, near Gadshill.*

Enter the PRINCE OF WALES and POINS.

POINS Come, shelter, shelter; I have remov'd Falstaff's horse, and he frets like a gumm'd velvet.

PRINCE Stand close.

Enter FALSTAFF.

FALSTAFF Poins! Poins! And be hang'd! Poins!

PRINCE Peace, ye fat-kidney'd rascal; what a brawling dost thou keep!

FALSTAFF Where's Poins, Hal?

PRINCE He is walk'd up to the top of the hill; I'll go seek him.

FALSTAFF I am accurs'd to rob in that thief's company; the rascal hath removed my horse, and tied him I know not where. If I travel but four foot by the squier further afoot, I shall break my wind. Well, I doubt not but to die a fair death for all this, if I scape hanging for killing that rogue. I have forsworn his company hourly any time this two and twenty years, and yet I am bewitch'd with the rogue's company. If the rascal have not given me medicines to make me love him, I'll be hang'd. It could not be else: I have drunk medicines. Poins! Hal! A plague upon you both! Bardolph! Peto! I'll starve ere I'll rob a foot further. An 'twere not as good a deed as drink to turn true man, and to leave these rogues, I am the veriest varlet that ever chewed with a tooth. Eight yards of uneven ground is three-score and ten miles afoot with me; and the stony-hearted villains know it well enough. A plague upon it, when thieves cannot be true one to another! [*They whistle*] Whew! A plague upon you all! Give me my horse, you rogues; give me my horse, and be hang'd.

PRINCE Peace, ye fat-guts! lie down; lay thine ear close to the ground, and list if thou canst hear the tread of travellers.

FALSTAFF Have you any levers to lift me up again, being down? 'Sblood, I'll not bear mine own flesh so far afoot again for all the coin in thy father's exchequer. What a plague mean ye to colt me thus?

PRINCE Thou liest: thou art not colted, thou art uncolted.

FALSTAFF I prithee, good Prince Hal, help me to my horse, good king's son.

PRINCE Out, ye rogue! shall I be your ostler?

FALSTAFF Hang thyself in thine own heir-apparent garters. If I be ta'en, I'll peach for this. An I have not ballads made on you all, and sung to filthy tunes, let a cup of sack be my poison. When a jest is so forward, and afoot too! – I hate it.

Enter GADSHILL, BARDOLPH and PETO with him.

GADSHILL Stand!

FALSTAFF So I do, against my will.

POINS O, 'tis our setter: I know his voice. Bardolph, what news?

BARDOLPH Case ye, case ye; on with your vizards: there's money of the King's coming down the hill; 'tis going to the King's exchequer.

FALSTAFF You lie, ye rogue; 'tis going to the King's tavern.

GADSHILL There's enough to make us all.

FALSTAFF To be hang'd.

PRINCE Sirs, you four shall front them in the narrow lane; Ned Poins and I will walk lower; if they scape from your encounter, then they light on us.

PETO How many be there of them?

GADSHILL Some eight or ten.

FALSTAFF Zounds, will they not rob us?

PRINCE What, a coward, Sir John Paunch?

FALSTAFF Indeed, I am not John of Gaunt, your grandfather; but yet no coward, Hal.

PRINCE Well, we leave that to the proof.

POINS Sirrah Jack, thy horse stands behind the hedge: when thou need'st him, there thou shalt find him. Farewell, and stand fast.

FALSTAFF Now cannot I strike him, if I should be hang'd.

PRINCE [*Aside to Poins*] Ned, where are our disguises?

POINS [*Aside*] Here, hard by; stand close.

Exeunt the Prince and Poins.

FALSTAFF Now, my masters, happy man be his dole, say I; every man to his business.

Enter the Travellers.

FIRST TRAVELLER Come, neighbour; the boy shall lead our horses down the hill; we'll walk afoot awhile, and ease our legs.

THIEVES Stand!

TRAVELLERS Jesus bless us!

FALSTAFF Strike; down with them; cut the villains' throats. Ah, whoreson caterpillars! bacon-fed knaves! They hate us youth. Down with them; fleece them.

TRAVELLER O, we are undone, both we and ours for ever!

FALSTAFF Hang ye, gorbellied knaves, are ye undone? No, ye fat chuffs; I would your store were here. On, bacons, on! What, ye knaves! young men must live. You are grand-jurors, are ye? we'll jure ye, faith.

[*Here they rob them and bind them. Exeunt.*

Re-enter the PRINCE and POINS in buckram.

PRINCE The thieves have bound the true men. Now, could thou and I rob the thieves and go merrily to London, it would be argument for a week, laughter for a month, and a good jest for ever.

POINS Stand close; I hear them coming.

Enter the Thieves again.

FALSTAFF Come, my masters, let us share, and then to horse before day. An the Prince and Poins be not two arrant cowards, there's no equity stirring. There's no more valour in that Poins than in a wild duck.

[*As they are sharing, the Prince and Poins set upon them.*

PRINCE Your money!

POINS Villains!

[*They all run away, and Falstaff, after a blow or two, runs away too, leaving the booty behind them.*

PRINCE Got with much ease. Now merrily to horse.
The thieves are all scattered, and possess'd with fear
So strongly that they dare not meet each other;
Each takes his fellow for an officer.
Away, good Ned. Falstaff sweats to death
And lards the lean earth as he walks along.
Were't not for laughing, I should pity him.

POINS How the fat rogue roar'd! [*Exeunt.*

SCENE III. *Warkworth Castle.*

Enter HOTSPUR solus, reading a letter.

HOTSPUR 'But, for mine own part, my lord, I could be well contented to be there, in respect of the love I bear your house.' He could be contented – why is he not, then? In respect of the love he bears our house – he shows in this he loves his own barn better than he loves our house. Let me see some more. 'The purpose you undertake is dangerous' – why, that's certain: 'tis dangerous to take a cold, to sleep, to drink; but I tell you, my lord fool, out of this nettle, danger, we pluck this flower, safety. 'The purpose you undertake is dangerous; the friends you have named uncertain; the time itself unsorted; and your whole plot too light for the counterpoise of so great an opposition.' Say you so, say you so? I say unto you again, you are a shallow, cowardly hind, and you lie. What a lack-brain is this! By the Lord, our plot is a good plot as ever was laid; our friends true and constant – a good plot, good friends, and full of expectation; an excellent plot, very good friends. What a frosty-spirited rogue is this! Why, my Lord of York commends the plot and the general course of the action. Zounds, an I were now by this rascal, I could brain him with his lady's fan. Is there not my father, my uncle, and myself; Lord Edmund Mortimer, my Lord of York, and Owen Glendower? Is there not, besides, the Douglas? Have I not all their letters to meet me in arms by the ninth of the next month, and are they not some of them set forward already? What a pagan rascal is this! an infidel! Ha! you shall see now, in very sincerity of fear and cold heart, will he to the King and lay open all our proceedings. O, I could divide myself and go to buffets for moving such a dish of skim milk with so honourable an action! Hang him; let him tell the King: we are prepared. I will set forward to-night.

Enter LADY PERCY.

How now, Kate! I must leave you within these two hours.

LADY PERCY O my good lord, why are you thus alone?
For what offence have I this fortnight been
A banish'd woman from my Harry's bed?
Tell me, sweet lord, what is't that takes from thee
Thy stomach, pleasure, and thy golden sleep?
Why dost thou bend thine eyes upon the earth,
And start so often when thou sit'st alone?
Why hast thou lost the fresh blood in thy cheeks,
And given my treasures and my rights of thee

To thick-ey'd musing and curs'd melancholy?
In thy faint slumbers I by thee have watch'd,
And heard thee murmur tales of iron wars;
Speak terms of manage to thy bounding steed;
Cry 'Courage! To the field!' And thou hast talk'd
Of sallies and retires, of trenches, tents,
Of palisadoes, frontiers, parapets,
Of basilisks, of cannon, culverin,
Of prisoners' ransom, and of soldiers slain,
And all the currents of a heady fight.
Thy spirit within thee hath been so at war,
And thus hath so bestirr'd thee in thy sleep,
That beads of sweat have stood upon thy brow
Like bubbles in a late disturbed stream;
And in thy face strange motions have appear'd,
Such as we see when men restrain their breath
On some great sudden hest. O, what portents are these?
Some heavy business hath my lord in hand,
And I must know it, else he loves me not.

HOTSPUR What, ho!

Enter a Servant.

Is Gilliams with the packet gone?

SERVANT He is, my lord, an hour ago.

HOTSPUR Hath Butler brought those horses from the sheriff?

SERVANT One horse, my lord, he brought even now.

HOTSPUR What horse? A roan, a crop-ear, is it not?

SERVANT It is, my lord.

HOTSPUR That roan shall be my throne.
Well, I will back him straight. O esperance!
Bid Butler lead him forth into the park.

[Exit Servant.

LADY PERCY But hear you, my lord.

HOTSPUR What say'st thou, my lady?

LADY PERCY What is it carries you away?

HOTSPUR Why, my horse, my love, my horse.

LADY PERCY Out, you mad-headed ape!
A weasel hath not such a deal of spleen
As you are toss'd with. In faith,
I'll know your business, Harry, that I will.
I fear my brother Mortimer doth stir
About his title and hath sent for you
To line his enterprise; but if you go –

HOTSPUR So far afoot, I shall be weary, love.

LADY PERCY Come, come, you paraquito, answer me
Directly unto this question that I ask.
In faith, I'll break thy little finger, Harry,
An if thou wilt not tell me all things true.

HOTSPUR Away.
Away, you trifler! Love, I love thee not,
I care not for thee, Kate; this is no world
To play with mammets and to tilt with lips:
We must have bloody noses and crack'd crowns,
And pass them current too. God's me, my horse!
What say'st thou, Kate? what wouldst thou have with me?

LADY PERCY Do you not love me? Do you not, indeed?
Well, do not, then; for since you love me not,
I will not love myself. Do you not love me?
Nay, tell me if you speak in jest or no.

HOTSPUR Come, wilt thou see me ride?
And when I am o' horseback, I will swear
I love thee infinitely. But hark you, Kate:
I must not have you henceforth question me
Whither I go, nor reason whereabout.
Whither I must, I must; and, to conclude,
This evening must I leave you, gentle Kate.
I know you wise, but yet no farther wise
Than Harry Percy's wife; constant you are,
But yet a woman; and for secrecy,
No lady closer; for I well believe
Thou wilt not utter what thou dost not know,
And so far will I trust thee, gentle Kate.

LADY PERCY How, so far?

HOTSPUR Not an inch further. But hark you, Kate:
Whither I go, thither shall you go too;
To-day will I set forth, to-morrow you.
Will this content you, Kate?

LADY PERCY It must, of force. *[Exeunt.*

SCENE IV. *Eastcheap. The Boar's Head Tavern.*

Enter the PRINCE, and POINS.

PRINCE Ned, prithee, come out of that fat room and lend me thy hand to laugh a little.

POINS Where hast been, Hal?

PRINCE With three or four loggerheads amongst three or fourscore hogsheads. I have sounded the very base-string of humility. Sirrah, I am sworn brother to a leash of drawers and can call them all by their christen names, as Tom, Dick, and Francis. They take it already upon their salvation that though I be but Prince of Wales yet I am the king of courtesy; and tell me flatly I am no proud Jack, like Falstaff, but a Corinthian, a lad of mettle, a good boy – by the Lord, so they call me – and when I am King of England I shall command all the good lads in Eastcheap. They call drinking deep, dyeing scarlet; and when you breathe in your watering, they cry 'hem!' and bid you play it off. To conclude, I am so good a proficient in one quarter of an hour that I can drink with any tinker in his own language during my life. I tell thee, Ned, thou hast lost much honour that thou wert not with me in this action. But, sweet Ned – to sweeten which name of Ned, I give thee this pennyworth of sugar, clapp'd even now into my hand by an under-skinker, one that never spake other English in his life than 'Eight shillings and sixpence' and 'You are welcome' with this shrill addition, 'Anon, anon, sir! Score a pint of bastard in the Half-moon' or so. But, Ned, to drive away the time till Falstaff come, I prithee, do thou stand in some by-room, while I question my puny drawer to what end he gave me the sugar; and do thou never leave calling 'Francis!' that his tale to me may be nothing but 'Anon'. Step aside, and I'll show thee a precedent.

[*Exit Poins.*

POINS [*Within*] Francis!

PRINCE Thou are perfect.

POINS [*Within*] Francis!

Enter FRANCIS.

FRANCIS Anon, anon, sir. Look down into the Pomgarnet, Ralph.

PRINCE Come hither, Francis.

FRANCIS My lord?

PRINCE How long has thou to serve, Francis?

FRANCIS Forsooth, five years, and as much as to –

POINS [*Within*] Francis!

FRANCIS Anon, anon, sir.

PRINCE Five year! by'r lady, a long lease for the clinking of pewter. But, Francis, darest thou be so valiant as to play the coward with thy indenture and show it a fair pair of heels and run from it?

FRANCIS O Lord, sir, I'll be sworn upon all the books in England, I could find in my heart –

POINS [*Within*] Francis!

FRANCIS Anon, sir.

PRINCE How old art thou, Francis?

FRANCIS Let me see, about Michaelmas next I shall be –

POINS [*Within*] Francis!

FRANCIS Anon, sir. Pray stay a little, my lord.

PRINCE Nay, but hark you, Francis: for the sugar thou gavest me – 'twas a penny-worth, was't not?

FRANCIS O Lord, I would it had been two!

PRINCE I will give thee for it a thousand pound; ask me when thou wilt, and thou shalt have it.

POINS [*Within*] Francis!

FRANCIS Anon, anon.

PRINCE Anon, Francis? No, Francis; but to-morrow, Francis; or, Francis, o' Thursday; or indeed, Francis, when thou wilt. But, Francis –

FRANCIS My lord?

PRINCE Wilt thou rob this leathern jerkin, crystal-button, knot-pated, agatering, puke stocking, caddis-garter, smooth-tongue, Spanish-pouch –

FRANCIS O Lord, sir, who do you mean?

PRINCE Why, then, your brown bastard is your only drink; for, look you, Francis, your white canvas doublet will sully. In Barbary, sir, it cannot come to so much.

FRANCIS What, sir?

POINS [*Within*] Francis!

PRINCE Away, you rogue! Dost thou not hear them call?

[*Here they both call him; Francis stands amazed, not knowing which way to go.*

Enter VINTNER.

VINTNER What, stand'st thou still, and hear'st such a calling? Look to the guests within. [*Exit Francis*] My lord, old Sir John, with half-a-dozen more, are at the door. Shall I let them in?

PRINCE Let them alone awhile, and then open the door. [*Exit Vintner*] Poins!

Re-enter POINS.

POINS Anon, anon, sir.

PRINCE Sirrah, Falstaff and the rest of the thieves are at the door. Shall we be merry?

POINS As merry as crickets, my lad. But hark ye: what cunning match have you made with this jest of the drawer? Come, what's the issue?

PRINCE I am now of all humours that have showed themselves humours since the old days of goodman Adam to the pupil-age of this present twelve o'clock at midnight.

Re-enter FRANCIS.

What's o'clock, Francis?

FRANCIS Anon, anon, sir. [*Exit.*

PRINCE That ever this fellow should have fewer words than a parrot, and yet the son of a woman! His industry is upstairs and downstairs; his eloquence the parcel of a reckoning. I am not yet of Percy's mind, the Hotspur of the north; he that kills me some six or seven dozen of Scots at a breakfast, washes his hands, and says to his wife 'Fie upon this quiet life! I want work'. 'O my sweet Harry,' says she 'how many hast thou kill'd to-day?' 'Give my roan horse a drench' says he; and answers 'Some fourteen,' an hour after, 'a trifle, a trifle'. 'I prithee call in Falstaff; I'll play Percy, and that damn'd brawn shall play Dame Mortimer his wife. 'Rivo!' says the drunkard. Call in ribs, call in tallow.

Enter FALSTAFF, GADSHILL, BARDOLPH, and PETO; followed by FRANCIS with wine.

POINS Welcome, Jack. Where hast thou been?

FALSTAFF A plague of all cowards, I say, and a vengeance too! Marry and amen! Give me a cup of sack, boy. Ere I lead this life long, I'll sew nether-stocks, and mend them and foot them too. A plague of all cowards! Give me a cup of sack, rogue. Is there no virtue extant?

[*He drinks*.

PRINCE Didst thou never see Titan kiss a dish of butter, pitiful-hearted Titan, that melted at the sweet tale of the sun's? If thou didst, then behold that compound.

FALSTAFF You rogue, here's lime in this sack too! There is nothing but roguery to be found in villainous man; yet a coward is worse than a cup of sack with lime in it. A villainous coward! Go thy ways, old Jack; die when thou wilt; if manhood, good manhood, be not forgot upon the face of the earth, then am I a shotten herring. There lives not three good men unhang'd in England, and one of them is fat and grows old. God help the while! A bad world, I say. I would I were a weaver; I could sing psalms or anything. A plague of all cowards, I say still.

PRINCE How now, woolsack! What mutter you?

FALSTAFF A king's son! If I do not beat thee out of thy kingdom with a dagger of lath, and drive all thy subjects afore thee like a flock of wild geese, I'll never wear hair on my face more. You Prince of Wales!

PRINCE Why, you whoreson round man, what's the matter?

FALSTAFF Are not you a coward? Answer me to that – and Poins there?

POINS Zounds, ye fat paunch, an ye call me coward, by the Lord, I'll stab thee.

FALSTAFF I call thee coward! I'll see thee damn'd ere I call thee coward; but I would give a thousand pound I could run as fast as thou canst. You are straight enough in the shoulders – you care not who sees your back. Call you that backing of your friends? A plague upon such backing! Give me them that will face me. Give me a cup of sack; I am a rogue if I drunk to-day.

PRINCE O villain! thy lips are scarce wip'd since thou drunk'st last.

FALSTAFF All is one for that. [*He drinks*] A plague of all cowards, still say I.

PRINCE What's the matter?

FALSTAFF What's the matter! There be four of us here have ta'en a thousand pound this day morning.

PRINCE Where is it, Jack? Where is it?

FALSTAFF Where is it! taken from us it is: a hundred upon poor four of us.

PRINCE What, a hundred, man?

FALSTAFF I am a rogue if I were not at halfsword with a dozen of them two hours together. I have scap'd by miracle. I am eight times thrust through the doublet, four through the hose; my buckler cut through and through; my sword hack'd like a hand-saw – ecce signum! I never dealt better since I was a man – all would not do. A plague of all cowards! Let them speak; if they speak more or less than truth, they are villains and the sons of darkness.

PRINCE Speak, sirs; how was it?

GADSHILL We four set upon some dozen –

FALSTAFF Sixteen at least, my lord.

GADSHILL And bound them.

PETO No, no, they were not bound.

FALSTAFF You rogue, they were bound, every man of them; or I am a Jew else, an Ebrew Jew.

GADSHILL As we were sharing, some six or seven fresh men set upon us –

FALSTAFF And unbound the rest, and then come in the other.

PRINCE What, fought you with them all?

FALSTAFF All! I know not what you call all, but if I fought not with fifty of them, I am a bunch of radish. If there were not two or three and fifty upon poor old Jack, then am I no two-legg'd creature.

PRINCE Pray God you have not murd'red some of them.

FALSTAFF Nay, that's past praying for: I have pepper'd two of them; two I am sure I have paid – two rogues in buckram suits. I tell thee what, Hal, if I tell thee a lie, spit in my face, call me horse. Thou knowest my old ward: here I lay, and thus I bore my point. Four rogues in buckram let drive at me –

PRINCE What, four? Thou saidst but two even now.

FALSTAFF Four, Hal; I told thee four.

POINS Ay, ay, he said four.

FALSTAFF These four came all afront, and mainly thrust at me. I made me no more ado but took all their seven points in my target, thus.

PRINCE Seven? Why, there were but four even now.

FALSTAFF In buckram.

POINS Ay, four, in buckram suits.

FALSTAFF Seven, by these hilts, or I am a villain else.

PRINCE [*Aside to Poins*] Prithee, let him alone; we shall have more anon.

FALSTAFF Dost thou hear me, Hal?

PRINCE Ay, and mark thee too, Jack.

FALSTAFF Do so, for it is worth the list'ning to. These nine in buckram that I told thee of –

PRINCE So, two more already.

FALSTAFF Their points being broken –

POINS Down fell their hose.

FALSTAFF Began to give me ground; but I followed me close, came in foot and hand, and with a thought seven of the eleven I paid.

PRINCE O monstrous! eleven buckram men grown out of two!

FALSTAFF But, as the devil would have it, three misbegotten knaves in Kendal green came at my back and let drive at me – for it was so dark, Hal, that thou couldest not see thy hand.

PRINCE These lies are like their father that begets them – gross as a mountain, open, palpable. Why, thou clay-brain'd guts, thou knotty-pated fool, thou whoreson, obscene, greasy tallow-catch –

FALSTAFF What, art thou mad? art thou mad? Is not the truth the truth?

PRINCE Why, how couldst thou know these men in Kendal green, when it was so dark thou couldst not see thy hand? Come, tell us your reason; what sayest thou to this?

POINS Come, your reason, Jack, your reason.

FALSTAFF What, upon compulsion? Zounds, an I were at the strappado, or all the racks in the world, I would not tell you on compulsion. Give you a reason on compulsion! If reasons were as plentiful as blackberries, I would give no man a reason upon compulsion, I.

PRINCE I'll be no longer guilty of this sin; this sanguine coward, this bed-presser, this horse-back-breaker, this huge hill of flesh –

FALSTAFF 'Sblood, you starveling, you eel-skin, you dried neat's-tongue, you bull's pizzle, you stock-fish – O for breath to utter what is like thee! – you tailor's yard, you sheath, you bow-case, you vile standing tuck!

PRINCE Well, breathe awhile, and then to it again; and when thou hast tired thyself in base comparisons, hear me speak but this.

POINS Mark, Jack.

PRINCE We two saw you four set on four, and bound them and were masters of their wealth. Mark now, how a plain tale shall put you down. Then did we two set on you four; and, with a word, out-fac'd you from your prize, and have it; yea, and can show it you here in the house. And, Falstaff, you carried your guts away as nimbly, with as quick dexterity, and roar'd for mercy, and still run and roar'd, as ever I heard bull-calf. What a slave art thou to hack thy sword as thou hast done, and then say it was in fight! What trick, what device, what starting-hole, canst thou now find out to hide thee from this open and apparent shame?

POINS Come, let's hear, Jack; what trick hast thou now?

FALSTAFF By the Lord, I knew ye as well as he that made ye. Why, hear you, my masters: was it for me to kill the heir-apparent? Should I turn upon the true prince? Why, thou knowest I am as valiant as Hercules; but beware instinct – the lion will not touch the true prince. Instinct is a great matter: I was now a coward on instinct. I shall think the better of myself and thee during my life – I for a valiant lion, and thou for a true prince. But, by the Lord, lads, I am glad you have the money. Hostess, clap to the doors. Watch to-night, pray to-morrow. Gallants, lads, boys, hearts of gold, all the titles of good fellowship come to you! What, shall we be merry? Shall we have a play extempore?

PRINCE Content – and the argument shall be thy running away.

FALSTAFF Ah, no more of that, Hal, an thou lovest me!

Enter Hostess.

HOSTESS O Jesu, my lord the Prince!

PRINCE How now, my lady the hostess! What say'st thou to me?

HOSTESS Marry, my lord, there is a nobleman of the court at door would speak with you; he says he comes from your father.

PRINCE Give him as much as will make him a royal man, and send him back again to my mother.

FALSTAFF What manner of man is he?

HOSTESS An old man.

FALSTAFF What doth gravity out of his bed at midnight? Shall I give him his answer?

PRINCE Prithee do, Jack.

FALSTAFF Faith, and I'll send him packing. [*Exit.*

PRINCE Now, sirs: by'r lady, you fought fair; so did you, Peto; so did you, Bardolph. You are lions too: you ran away upon instinct; you will not touch the true prince; no, fie!

BARDOLPH Faith, I ran when I saw others run.

PRINCE Faith, tell me now in earnest, how came Falstaff's sword so hack'd?

PETO Why, he hack'd it with his dagger, and said he would swear truth out of England but he would make you believe it was done in fight; and persuaded us to do the like.

BARDOLPH Yea, and to tickle our noses with spear-grass to make them bleed, and then to beslubber our garments with it, and swear it was the blood of true men. I did that I did not this seven year before – I blush'd to hear his monstrous devices.

PRINCE O villain! Thou stolest a cup of sack eighteen years ago, and wert taken with the manner, and ever since thou hast blush'd extempore. Thou hadst fire and sword on thy side, and yet thou ran'st away; what instinct hadst thou for it?

BARDOLPH My lord, do you see these meteors? do you behold these exhalations?

PRINCE I do.

BARDOLPH What think you they portend?

PRINCE Hot livers and cold purses.

BARDOLPH Choler, my lord, if rightly taken.

PRINCE No, if rightly taken, halter.

Re-enter FALSTAFF.

Here comes lean Jack, here comes barebone. How now, my sweet creature of bombast! How long is't ago, Jack, since thou sawest thine own knee?

FALSTAFF My own knee! When I was about thy years, Hal, I was not an eagle's talon in the waist: I could have crept into any alderman's thumb-ring. A plague of sighing and grief! it blows a man up like a bladder. There's villainous news abroad. Here was Sir John Bracy from your father: you must to the court in the morning. That same mad fellow of the north, Percy, and he of Wales that gave Amaimon the bastinado, and made Lucifer cuckold, and swore the devil his true liegeman upon the cross of a Welsh hook – what a plague call you him?

POINS O, Glendower.

FALSTAFF Owen, Owen – the same; and his son-in-law Mortimer, and old Northumberland, and that sprightly Scot of Scots, Douglas, that runs o' horseback up a hill perpendicular –

PRINCE He that rides at high speed and with his pistol kills a sparrow flying?

FALSTAFF You have hit it.

PRINCE So did he never the sparrow.

FALSTAFF Well, that rascal hath good mettle in him; he will not run.

PRINCE Why, what a rascal art thou, then, to praise him so for running!

FALSTAFF O' horseback, ye cuckoo; but afoot he will not budge a foot.

PRINCE Yes, Jack, upon instinct.

FALSTAFF I grant ye, upon instinct. Well, he is there too, and one Mordake, and a thousand blue-caps more. Worcester is stol'n away to-night; thy father's beard is turn'd white with the news; you may buy land now as cheap as stinking mack'rel.

PRINCE Why, then, it is like, if there come a hot June, and this civil buffeting hold, we shall buy maidenheads as they buy hob-nails, by the hundreds.

FALSTAFF By the mass, lad, thou sayest true: it is like we shall have good trading that way. But tell me, Hal, art not thou horrible afeard. Thou being heir-apparent, could the world pick thee out three such enemies again as that fiend Douglas, that spirit Percy, and that devil Glendower? Art thou not horribly afraid? Doth not thy blood thrill at it?

PRINCE Not a whit, i' faith; I lack some of thy instinct.

FALSTAFF Well, thou wilt be horribly chid tomorrow when thou comest to thy father. If thou love me, practise an answer.

PRINCE Do thou stand for my father, and examine me upon the particulars of my life.

FALSTAFF Shall I? Content! This chair shall be my state, this dagger my sceptre, and this cushion my crown.

PRINCE Thy state is taken for a join'd-stool, thy golden sceptre for a leaden dagger, and thy precious rich crown for a pitiful bald crown!

FALSTAFF Well, an the fire of grace be not quite out of thee, now shalt thou be moved. Give me a cup of sack to make my eyes look red, that it may be thought I have wept; for I must speak in passion, and I will do it in King Cambyses' vein.

PRINCE Well, here is my leg.

FALSTAFF And here is my speech. Stand aside, nobility.

HOSTESS O Jesu, this is excellent sport, i' faith!

FALSTAFF Weep not, sweet queen, for trickling
tears are vain.

HOSTESS O, the father, how he holds his countenance!

FALSTAFF For God's sake, lords, convey my
tristful queen;
For tears do stop the floodgates of her eyes.

HOSTESS O Jesu, he doth it as like one of these harlotry players as ever I see!

FALSTAFF Peace, good pint-pot; peace, good tickle-brain. – Harry, I do not only marvel where thou spendest thy time, but also how thou art accompanied; for though the camomile, the more it is trodden on the faster it grows, yet youth, the more it is wasted the sooner it wears. That thou art my son I have partly thy mother's word, partly my own opinion, but chiefly a villainous trick of thine eye, and a foolish hanging of thy nether lip, that doth warrant me. If then thou be son to me, here lies the point: why, being son to me, art thou so pointed at? Shall the blessed sun of heaven prove a micher and eat blackberries? A question not to be ask'd. Shall the son of England prove a thief and take purses? A question to be ask'd. There is a thing, Harry, which thou hast often heard of, and it is known to many in our land by the name of pitch. This pitch, as ancient writers do report, doth defile; so doth the company thou keepest; for, Harry, now I do not speak to thee in drink, but in tears; not in pleasure, but in passion; not in words only, but in woes also. And yet there is

a virtuous man whom I have often noted in thy
406 company, but I know not his name.
PRINCE What manner of man, an it like your
Majesty?
FALSTAFF A goodly portly man, i' faith, and a
corpulent; of a cheerful look, a pleasing eye, and
a most noble carriage; and, as I think, his age
some fifty, or, by'r lady, inclining to three-score.
And now I remember me, his name is Falstaff. If
that man should be lewdly given, he deceiveth
me; for, Harry, I see virtue in his looks. If then
the tree may be known by the fruit, as the fruit
by the tree, then peremptorily I speak it, there is
virtue in that Falstaff: him keep with, the rest
banish. And tell me now, thou naughty varlet,
417 tell me, where hast thou been this month?
PRINCE Dost thou speak like a king? Do thou
stand for me, and I'll play my father.
FALSTAFF Depose me? If thou dost it half so
gravely, so majestically, both in word and
matter, hang me up by the heels for a
rabbit-sucker or a poulter's hare.
422 PRINCE Well, here I am set.
FALSTAFF And here I stand. Judge, my masters.
PRINCE Now, Harry, whence come you?
FALSTAFF My noble lord, from Eastcheap.
PRINCE The complaints I hear of thee are
grievous.
FALSTAFF 'Sblood, my lord, they are false. Nay,
429 I'll tickle ye for a young prince, i' faith.
PRINCE Swearest thou, ungracious boy?
Henceforth ne'er look on me. Thou art violently
carried away from grace; there is a devil haunts
thee in the likeness of an old fat man; a tun of
man is thy companion. Why dost thou converse
with that trunk of humours, that bolting-hutch
of beastliness, that swoll'n parcel of dropsies,
that huge bombard of sack, that stuff'd
cloak-bag of guts, that roasted Manningtree ox
with the pudding in his belly, that reverend
vice, that grey iniquity, that father ruffian, that
vanity in years? Wherein is he good, but to taste
sack and drink it? wherein neat and cleanly, but
to carve a capon and eat it? wherein cunning,
but in craft? wherein crafty, but in villainy?
wherein villainous, but in all things? wherein
worthy, but in nothing?
FALSTAFF I would your Grace would take me
445 with you; whom means your Grace?
PRINCE That villainous abominable misleader of
youth, Falstaff, that old white-bearded Satan.
FALSTAFF My lord, the man I know.
449 PRINCE I know thou dost.
FALSTAFF But to say I know more harm in him
than in myself were to say more than I know.
That he is old – the more the pity – his white
hairs do witness it; but that he is – saving your
reverence – a whoremaster, that I utterly deny.
If sack and sugar be a fault, God help the
wicked! If to be old and merry be a sin, then
many an old host that I know is damn'd; if to be
fat be to be hated, then Pharaoh's lean kine are
to be loved. No, my good lord: banish Peto,
banish Bardolph, banish Poins; but, for sweet
Jack Falstaff, kind Jack Falstaff, true Jack
Falstaff, valiant Jack Falstaff – and therefore
more valiant, being, as he is, old Jack Falstaff –
banish not him thy Harry's company, banish not
him thy Harry's company. Banish plump Jack,
and banish all the world. 463
PRINCE I do, I will. [*A knocking heard.*

[*Exeunt Hostess, Francis, and Bardolph.*

Re-enter BARDOLPH, running.

BARDOLPH O, my lord, my lord! the sheriff with
a most monstrous watch is at the door.
FALSTAFF Out, ye rogue! Play out the play: I
have much to say in the behalf of that Falstaff.

Re-enter the Hostess.

HOSTESS O Jesu, my lord, my lord! 469
PRINCE Heigh, heigh! the devil rides upon a
fiddle-stick; what's the matter?
HOSTESS The sheriff and all the watch are at the
door; they are come to search the house. Shall I
let them in?
FALSTAFF Dost thou hear, Hal? Never call a true
piece of gold a counterfeit. Thou art essentially
made, without seeming so. 476
PRINCE And thou a natural coward, without
instinct.
FALSTAFF I deny your major. If you will deny the
sheriff, so; if not, let him enter. If I become not a
cart as well as another man, a plague on my
bringing up! I hope I shall as soon be strangled
with a halter as another. 481
PRINCE Go, hide thee behind the arras; the rest
walk up above. Now, my masters, for a true face
and good conscience.
FALSTAFF Both which I have had; but their date
is out, and therefore I'll hide me. 486

[*Exeunt all but the Prince and Peto.*

PRINCE Call in the sheriff.

Enter Sheriff and the Carrier.

Now, master sheriff, what is your will with
me?
SHERIFF First, pardon me, my lord. A hue and
cry
Hath followed certain men unto this house.
PRINCE What men? 491
SHERIFF One of them is well known, my gracious
lord –
A gross fat man.

CARRIER As fat as butter.
PRINCE The man, I do assure you, is not here,
For I myself at this time have employ'd him.
And, sheriff, I will engage my word to thee
That I will, by to-morrow dinner-time,
Send him to answer thee, or any man,
For any thing he shall be charg'd withal;
And so let me entreat you leave the house.
SHERIFF I will, my lord. There are two gentlemen
Have in this robbery lost three hundred marks.
PRINCE It may be so; if he have robb'd these men
He shall be answerable; and so, farewell.
SHERIFF Good night, my noble lord.
PRINCE I think it is good morrow, is it not?
SHERIFF Indeed, my lord, I think it be two o'clock. *[Exeunt Sheriff and Carrier.*
PRINCE This oily rascal is known as well as Paul's. Go, call him forth.

PETO Falstaff! Fast asleep behind the arras, and snorting like a horse.

PRINCE Hark how hard he fetches breath. Search his pockets. *[He searcheth his pocket, and findeth certain papers]* What hast thou found?

PETO Nothing but papers, my lord.

PRINCE Let's see what they be: read them.

PETO *[Reads]*

Item, A capon - - - - - - - - - - - - - - - -	2s. 2d.
Item, Sauce - - - - - - - - - - - - - - - - - -	4d.
Item, Sack, two gallons - - - - - - - - - - -	5s. 8d.
Item, Anchovies and sack after supper	2s. 6d.
Item, Bread - - - - - - - - - - - - - - - - - -	ob.

PRINCE O monstrous! but one halfpenny-worth of bread to this intolerable deal of sack! What there is else, keep close; we'll read it at more advantage. There let him sleep till day. I'll to the court in the morning. We must all to the wars, and thy place shall be honourable. I'll procure this fat rogue a charge of foot; and I know his death will be a march of twelve-score. The money shall be paid back again with advantage. Be with me betimes in the morning; and so, good morrow, Peto.

PETO Good morrow, good my lord. *[Exeunt.*

ACT THREE

SCENE I. *Wales. Glendower's castle.*

Enter HOTSPUR, WORCESTER, MORTIMER, and GLENDOWER.

MORTIMER These promises are fair, the parties sure,
And our induction full of prosperous hope.
HOTSPUR Lord Mortimer, and cousin Glendower,
Will you sit down?
And uncle Worcester – a plague upon it!
I have forgot the map.
GLENDOWER No, here it is.
Sit, cousin Percy; sit, good cousin Hotspur,
For by that name as oft as Lancaster
Doth speak of you, his cheek looks pale, and with
A rising sigh he wisheth you in heaven.
HOTSPUR And you in hell, as oft as he hears
Owen Glendower spoke of.
GLENDOWER I cannot blame him: at my nativity
The front of heaven was full of fiery shapes,
Of burning cressets; and at my birth
The frame and huge foundation of the earth
Shaked like a coward.

HOTSPUR Why, so it would have done at the same season if your mother's cat had but kitten'd, though yourself had never been born.

GLENDOWER I say the earth did shake when I was born.
HOTSPUR And I say the earth was not of my mind,
If you suppose as fearing you it shook.
GLENDOWER The heavens were all on fire, the earth did tremble.
HOTSPUR O, then the earth shook to see the heavens on fire,
And not in fear of your nativity.
Diseased nature oftentimes breaks forth
In strange eruptions; oft the teeming earth
Is with a kind of colic pinch'd and vex'd
By the imprisoning of unruly wind
Within her womb; which, for enlargement striving,
Shakes the old beldam earth, and topples down
Steeples and moss-grown towers. At your birth,
Our grandam earth, having this distemp'rature,
In passion shook.
GLENDOWER Cousin, of many men
I do not bear these crossings. Give me leave
To tell you once again that at my birth
The front of heaven was full of fiery shapes,
The goats ran from the mountains, and the herds
Were strangely clamorous to the frighted fields.
These signs have mark'd me extraordinary;

And all the courses of my life do show
I am not in the roll of common men.
Where is he living, clipp'd in with the sea
That chides the banks of England, Scotland, Wales,
Which calls me pupil or hath read to me?
And bring him out that is but woman's son
Can trace me in the tedious ways of art
And hold me pace in deep experiments.

HOTSPUR I think there's no man speaks better Welsh. I'll to dinner.

MORTIMER Peace, cousin Percy; you will make him mad.

GLENDOWER I can call spirits from the vasty deep.

HOTSPUR Why, so can I, or so can any man;
But will they come when you do call for them?

GLENDOWER Why, I can teach you, cousin, to command
The devil.

HOTSPUR And I can teach thee, coz, to shame the devil
By telling truth: tell truth, and shame the devil.
If thou have power to raise him, bring him hither,
And I'll be sworn I have power to shame him hence.
O, while you live, tell truth, and shame the devil!

MORTIMER Come, come, no more of this unprofitable chat.

GLENDOWER Three times hath Henry Bolingbroke made head
Against my power; thrice from the banks of Wye
And sandy-bottom'd Severn have I sent him
Bootless home and weather-beaten back.

HOTSPUR Home without boots, and in foul weather too!
How scapes he agues, in the devil's name?

GLENDOWER Come, here is the map; shall we divide our right
According to our threefold order ta'en?

MORTIMER The Archdeacon hath divided it
Into three limits very equally:
England, from Trent and Severn hitherto,
By south and east is to my part assign'd;
All westward, Wales beyond the Severn shore,
And all the fertile land within that bound,
To Owen Glendower; and, dear coz, to you
The remnant northward lying off from Trent.
And our indentures tripartite are drawn;
Which being sealed interchangeably,
A business that this night may execute,
To-morrow, cousin Percy, you and I
And my good Lord of Worcester will set forth
To meet your father and the Scottish power,
As is appointed us, at Shrewsbury.
My father Glendower is not ready yet,
Nor shall we need his help these fourteen days.
[*To Glendower*] Within that space you may have drawn together
Your tenants, friends, and neighbouring gentlemen.

GLENDOWER A shorter time shall send me to you, lords;
And in my conduct shall your ladies come,
From whom you now must steal and take no leave;
For there will be a world of water shed
Upon the parting of your wives and you.

HOTSPUR Methinks my moiety, north from Burton here,
In quantity equals not one of yours.
See how this river comes me cranking in,
And cuts me from the best of all my land
A huge half-moon, a monstrous cantle out.
I'll have the current in this place damm'd up,
And here the smug and silver Trent shall run
In a new channel, fair and evenly;
It shall not wind with such a deep indent
To rob me of so rich a bottom here.

GLENDOWER Not wind! It shall, it must; you see it doth.

MORTIMER Yea, but
Mark how he bears his course and runs me up
With like advantage on the other side,
Gelding the opposed continent as much
As on the other side it takes from you.

WORCESTER Yea, but a little charge will trench him here,
And on this north side win this cape of land,
And then he runs straight and even.

HOTSPUR I'll have it so; a little charge will do it.

GLENDOWER I'll not have it alt'red.

HOTSPUR Will not you?

GLENDOWER No, nor you shall not.

HOTSPUR Who shall say me nay?

GLENDOWER Why, that will I.

HOTSPUR Let me not understand you, then; speak it in Welsh.

GLENDOWER I can speak English, lord, as well as you,
For I was train'd up in the English court;
Where, being but young, I framed to the harp
Many an English ditty lovely well,
And gave the tongue a helpful ornament –
A virtue that was never seen in you.

HOTSPUR Marry,
And I am glad of it with all my heart!
I had rather be a kitten and cry mew
Than one of these same metre ballad-mongers;
I had rather hear a brazen canstick turn'd,
Or a dry wheel grate on the axle-tree;
And that would set my teeth nothing on edge,

Nothing so much as mincing poetry.
'Tis like the forc'd gait of a shuffling nag.

GLENDOWER Come, you shall have Trent turn'd.

HOTSPUR I do not care; I'll give thrice so much land
To any well-deserving friend;
But in the way of bargain, mark ye me,
I'll cavil on the ninth part of a hair.
Are the indentures drawn? Shall we be gone?

GLENDOWER The moon shines fair; you may away by night;
I'll haste the writer, and withal
Break with your wives of your departure hence.
I am afraid my daughter will run mad,
So much she doteth on her Mortimer. [*Exit.*

MORTIMER Fie, cousin Percy! how you cross my father!

HOTSPUR I cannot choose. Sometime he angers me
With telling me of the moldwarp and the ant,
Of the dreamer Merlin and his prophecies,
And of a dragon and a finless fish,
A clip-wing'd griffin and a moulten raven,
A couching lion and a ramping cat,
And such a deal of skimble-skamble stuff
As puts me from my faith. I tell you what:
He held me last night at least nine hours
In reckoning up the several devils' names
That were his lackeys. I cried 'hum' and 'well, go to'
But mark'd him not a word. O, he is as tedious
As a tired horse, a railing wife;
Worse than a smoky house; I had rather live
With cheese and garlic in a windmill, far,
Than feed on cates and have him talk to me
In any summer house in Christendom.

MORTIMER In faith, he is a worthy gentleman,
Exceedingly well read, and profited
In strange concealments; valiant as a lion,
And wondrous affable; and as bountiful
As mines of India. Shall I tell you, cousin?
He holds your temper in a high respect,
And curbs himself even of his natural scope
When you come 'cross his humour; faith, he does.
I warrant you that man is not alive
Might so have tempted him as you have done
Without the taste of danger and reproof;
But do not use it oft, let me entreat you.

WORCESTER In faith, my lord, you are too wilfulblame;
And since your coming hither have done enough
To put him quite besides his patience.
You must needs learn, lord, to amend this fault;
Though sometimes it show greatness, courage, blood –
And that's the dearest grace it renders you –
Yet oftentimes it doth present harsh rage,
Defect of manners, want of government,
Pride, haughtiness, opinion, and disdain;
The least of which, haunting a nobleman,
Loseth men's hearts, and leaves behind a stain
Upon the beauty of all parts besides,
Beguiling them of commendation.

HOTSPUR Well, I am school'd: good manners be your speed!
Here come our wives, and let us take our leave.

Re-enter GLENDOWER, with LADY MORTIMER and LADY PERCY.

MORTIMER This is the deadly spite that angers me:
My wife can speak no English, I no Welsh.

GLENDOWER My daughter weeps: she'll not part with you;
She'll be a soldier too, she'll to the wars.

MORTIMER Good father, tell her that she and my aunt Percy
Shall follow in your conduct speedily.

[*Glendower speaks to her in Welsh, and she answers him in the same.*

GLENDOWER She is desperate here; a peevish, self-will'd harlotry, one that no persuasion can do good upon. [*The Lady speaks in Welsh.*

MORTIMER I understand thy looks: that pretty Welsh
Which thou pourest down from these swelling heavens
I am too perfect in; and, but for shame,
In such a parley should I answer thee.
[*The Lady speaks again in Welsh.*
I understand thy kisses, and thou mine,
And that's a feeling disputation;
But I will never be a truant, love,
Till I have learnt thy language; for thy tongue
Makes Welsh as sweet as ditties highly penn'd,
Sung by a fair queen in a summer's bow'r,
With ravishing division, to her lute.

GLENDOWER Nay, if you melt, then will she run mad. [*The Lady speaks again in Welsh.*

MORTIMER O, I am ignorance itself in this!

GLENDOWER She bids you on the wanton rushes lay you down,
And rest your gentle head upon her lap,
And she will sing the song that pleaseth you,
And on your eyelids crown the god of sleep,
Charming your blood with pleasing heaviness,
Making such difference 'twixt wake and sleep
As is the difference betwixt day and night

The hour before the heavenly-harness'd team
Begins his golden progress in the east.

MORTIMER With all my heart I'll sit and hear her sing;
By that time will our book, I think, be drawn.

GLENDOWER Do so;
And those musicians that shall play to you
Hang in the air a thousand leagues from hence,
And straight they shall be here; sit, and attend.

HOTSPUR Come, Kate, thou art perfect in lying down. Come, quick, quick, that I may lay my head in thy lap.

LADY PERCY Go, ye giddy goose. [*The music plays.*

HOTSPUR Now I perceive the devil understands Welsh;
And 'tis no marvel he is so humorous.
By'r lady, he is a good musician.

LADY PERCY Then should you be nothing but musical, for you are altogether govern'd by humours. Lie still, ye thief, and hear the lady sing in Welsh.

HOTSPUR I had rather hear Lady, my brach, howl in Irish.

LADY PERCY Wouldst thou have thy head broken?

HOTSPUR No.

LADY PERCY Then be still.

HOTSPUR Neither; 'tis a woman's fault.

LADY PERCY Now God help thee!

HOTSPUR To the Welsh lady's bed.

LADY PERCY What's that?

HOTSPUR Peace! she sings.

[*Here, the Lady sings a Welsh song.*

HOTSPUR Come, Kate, I'll have your song too.

LADY PERCY Not mine, in good sooth.

HOTSPUR Not yours, in good sooth! Heart! you swear like a comfit-maker's wife. 'Not you, in good sooth' and 'As true as I live' and 'As God shall mend me' and 'As sure as day'.
And givest such sarcenet surety for thy oaths
As if thou never walk'st further than Finsbury.
Swear me, Kate, like a lady as thou art,
A good mouth-filling oath; and leave 'in sooth'
And such protest of pepper-gingerbread
To velvet-guards and Sunday-citizens.
Come, sing.

LADY PERCY I will not sing.

HOTSPUR 'Tis the next way to turn tailor, or be redbreast teacher. An the indentures be drawn, I'll away within these two hours; and so come in when ye will. [*Exit*

GLENDOWER Come, come, Lord Mortimer; you are as slow
As hot Lord Percy is on fire to go.
By this our book is drawn; we'll but seal,
And then to horse immediately.

MORTIMER With all my heart. [*Exeunt.*

SCENE II. *London. The palace.*

Enter the KING, the PRINCE OF WALES, and Lords.

KING Lords, give us leave; the Prince of Wales and I
Must have some private conference; but be near at hand,
For we shall presently have need of you.
[*Exeunt Lords.*
I know not whether God will have it so,
For some displeasing service I have done,
That, in his secret doom, out of my blood
He'll breed revengement and a scourge for me;
But thou dost in thy passages of life
Make me believe that thou art only mark'd
For the hot vengeance and the rod of heaven
To punish my mistreadings. Tell me else,
Could such inordinate and low desires,
Such poor, such bare, such lewd, such mean attempts,
Such barren pleasures, rude society,
As thou art match'd withal and grafted to,
Accompany the greatness of thy blood
And hold their level with thy princely heart?

PRINCE So please your Majesty, I would I could
Quit all offences with as clear excuse,
As well as I am doubtless I can purge
Myself of many I am charg'd withal;
Yet such extenuation let me beg,
As, in reproof of many tales devis'd,
Which oft the ear of greatness needs must hear,
By smiling pick-thanks and base news-mongers,
I may, for some things true, wherein my youth
Hath faulty wand'red and irregular,
Find pardon on my true submission.

KING God pardon thee! Yet let me wonder, Harry,
At thy affections, which do hold a wing
Quite from the flight of all thy ancestors.
Thy place in council thou hast rudely lost,
Which by thy younger brother is supplied,
And art almost an alien to the hearts
Of all the court and princes of my blood.
The hope and expectation of thy time
Is ruin'd, and the soul of every man
Prophetically do forethink thy fall.
Had I so lavish of my presence been,
So common-hackney'd in the eyes of men,
So stale and cheap to vulgar company,
Opinion, that did help me to the crown,

Had still kept loyal to possession
And left me in reputeless banishment
A fellow of no mark nor likelihood.
By being seldom seen, I could not stir
But, like a comet, I was wond'red at;
That men would tell their children 'This is he';
Others would say 'Where, which is Bolingbroke?'
And then I stole all courtesy from heaven,
And dress'd myself in such humility
That I did pluck allegiance from men's hearts,
Loud shouts and salutations from their mouths,
Even in the presence of the crowned King.
Thus did I keep my person fresh and new,
My presence, like a robe pontifical,
Ne'er seen but wond'red at, and so my state,
Seldom but sumptuous, show'd like a feast
And won by rareness such solemnity.
The skipping King, he ambled up and down
With shallow jesters and rash bavin wits,
Soon kindled and soon burnt; carded his state,
Mingled his royalty with cap'ring fools;
Had his great name profaned with their scorns,
And gave his countenance, against his name,
To laugh at gibing boys and stand the push
Of every beardless vain comparative;
Grew a companion to the common streets,
Enfeoff'd himself to popularity;
That, being daily swallowed by men's eyes,
They surfeited with honey and began
To loathe the taste of sweetness, whereof a little
More than a little is by much too much.
So, when he had occasion to be seen,
He was but as the cuckoo is in June,
Heard, not regarded, seen, but with such eyes
As, sick and blunted with community,
Afford no extraordinary gaze,
Such as is bent on sun-like majesty
When it shines seldom in admiring eyes;
But rather drowz'd and hung their eyelids down,
Slept in his face, and rend'red such aspect
As cloudy men use to their adversaries,
Being with his presence glutted, gorg'd, and full.
And in that very line, Harry, standest thou;
For thou hast lost thy princely privilege
With vile participation. Not an eye
But is aweary of thy common sight,
Save mine, which hath desir'd to see thee more;
Which now doth that I would not have it do –
Make blind itself with foolish tenderness.

PRINCE I shall hereafter, my thrice-gracious lord,
Be more myself.

KING For all the world
As thou art to this hour was Richard then
When I from France set foot at Ravenspurgh;
And even as I was then is Percy now.
Now, by my sceptre and my soul to boot,
He hath more worthy interest to the state
Than thou the shadow of succession;
For of no right, nor colour like to right,
He doth fill fields with harness in the realm;
Turns head against the lion's armed jaws;
And, being no more in debt to years than thou,
Leads ancient lords and reverend bishops on
To bloody battles and to bruising arms.
What never-dying honour hath he got
Against renowned Douglas! whose high deeds,
Whose hot incursions, and great name in arms,
Holds from all soldiers chief majority
And military title capital
Through all the kingdoms that acknowledge Christ.
Thrice hath this Hotspur, Mars in swathling clothes,
This infant warrior, in his enterprises
Discomfited great Douglas; ta'en him once,
Enlarged him and made a friend of him,
To fill the mouth of deep defiance up
And shake the peace and safety of our throne.
And what say you to this? Percy, Northumberland,
The Archbishop's Grace of York, Douglas, Mortimer,
Capitulate against us and are up.
But wherefore do I tell these news to thee?
Why, Harry, do I tell thee of my foes,
Which art my nearest and dearest enemy?
Thou that art like enough, through vassal fear,
Base inclination, and the start of spleen,
To fight against me under Percy's pay,
To dog his heels, and curtsy at his frowns,
To show how much thou art degenerate.

PRINCE Do not think so; you shall not find it so;
And God forgive them that so much have sway'd
Your Majesty's good thoughts away from me!
I will redeem all this on Percy's head,
And in the closing of some glorious day
Be bold to tell you that I am your son,
When I will wear a garment all of blood,
And stain my favours in a bloody mask,
Which, wash'd away, shall scour my shame with it;
And that shall be the day, whene'er it lights,
That this same child of honour and renown,
This gallant Hotspur, this all-praised knight,
And your unthought-of Harry chance to meet.
For every honour sitting on his helm,
Would they were multitudes, and on my head
My shames redoubled! For the time will come
That I shall make this northern youth exchange
His glorious deeds for my indignities.

Percy is but my factor, good my lord,
To engross up glorious deeds on my behalf;
And I will call him to so strict account
That he shall render every glory up,
Yea, even the slightest worship of his time,
Or I will tear the reckoning from his heart.
This, in the name of God, I promise here;
The which if He be pleas'd I shall perform,
I do beseech your Majesty may salve
The long-grown wounds of my intemperature.
If not, the end of life cancels all bands;
And I will die a hundred thousand deaths
Ere break the smallest parcel of this vow.

KING A hundred thousand rebels die in this:
Thou shalt have charge and sovereign trust herein.

Enter SIR WALTER BLUNT.

How now, good Blunt! Thy looks are full of speed.

BLUNT So hath the business that I come to speak of.
Lord Mortimer of Scotland hath sent word
That Douglas and the English rebels met
The eleventh of this month at Shrewsbury.
A mighty and a fearful head they are,
If promises be kept on every hand,
As ever off'red foul play in a state.

KING The Earl of Westmoreland set forth to-day,
With him my son, Lord John of Lancaster;
For this advertisement is five days old.
On Wednesday next, Harry, you shall set forward;
On Thursday we ourselves will march. Our meeting
Is Bridgenorth. And, Harry, you shall march
Through Gloucestershire; by which account,
Our business valued, some twelve days hence
Our general forces at Bridgenorth shall meet.
Our hands are full of business. Let's away.
Advantage feeds him fat while men delay.

[*Exeunt.*

SCENE III. *Eastcheap. The Boar's Head Tavern.*

Enter FALSTAFF and BARDOLPH.

FALSTAFF Bardolph, am I not fall'n away vilely since this last action? Do I not bate? Do I not dwindle? Why, my skin hangs about me like an old lady's loose gown; I am withered like an old applejohn. Well, I'll repent, and that suddenly, while I am in some liking; I shall be out of heart shortly, and then I shall have no strength to repent. An I have not forgotten what the inside of a church is made of, I am a peppercorn, a brewer's horse. The inside of a church! Company, villainous company, hath been the spoil of me.

BARDOLPH Sir John, you are so fretful you cannot live long.

FALSTAFF Why, there is it; come, sing me a bawdy song, make me merry. I was as virtuously given as a gentleman need to be; virtuous enough: swore little, dic'd not above seven times a week, went to a bawdy-house not above once in a quarter – of an hour, paid money that I borrowed – three or four times, lived well, and in good compass; and now I live out of all order, out of all compass.

BARDOLPH Why, you are so fat, Sir John, that you must needs be out of all compass – out of all reasonable compass, Sir John.

FALSTAFF Do thou amend thy face, and I'll amend my life. Thou art our admiral, thou bearest the lantern in the poop, but 'tis in the nose of thee; thou art the Knight of the Burning Lamp.

BARDOLPH Why, Sir John, my face does you no harm.

FALSTAFF No, I'll be sworn; I make as good use of it as many a man doth of a death's head or a memento mori: I never see thy face but I think upon hell-fire, and Dives that lived in purple; for there he is in his robes, burning, burning. If thou wert any way given to virtue, I would swear by thy face: my oath should be 'By this fire, that's God's angel'. But thou art altogether given over, and wert indeed, but for the light in thy face, the son of utter darkness. When thou ran'st up Gadshill in the night to catch my horse, if I did not think thou hadst been an ignis fatuus or a ball of wildfire, there's no purchase in money. O, thou art a perpetual triumph, an everlasting bonfire light! Thou hast saved me a thousand marks in links and torches, walking with thee in the night betwixt tavern and tavern; but the sack that thou hast drunk me would have bought me lights as good cheap at the dearest chandler's in Europe. I have maintained that salamander of yours with fire any time this two and thirty years; God reward me for it!

BARDOLPH 'Sblood, I would my face were in your belly!

FALSTAFF God-a-mercy! so should I be sure to be heart-burnt.

Enter Hostess.

How now, Dame Partlet the hen! Have you inquir'd yet who pick'd my pocket?

HOSTESS Why, Sir John, what do you think, Sir John? Do you think I keep thieves in my house? I have search'd, I have inquired, so has my husband, man by man, boy by boy, servant by servant. The tithe of a hair was never lost in my house before.

FALSTAFF Ye lie, hostess: Bardolph was shav'd and lost many a hair, and I'll be sworn my pocket was pick'd. Go to, you are a woman, go.

HOSTESS Who, I? No, I defy thee. God's light, I was never call'd so in mine own house before.

FALSTAFF Go to, I know you well enough.

HOSTESS No, Sir John, you do not know me, Sir John. I know you, Sir John: you owe me money, Sir John; and now you pick a quarrel to beguile me of it. I bought you a dozen of shirts to your back.

FALSTAFF Dowlas, filthy dowlas! I have given them away to bakers' wives; they have made bolters of them.

HOSTESS Now, as I am a true woman, holland of eight shillings an ell. You owe money here besides, Sir John, for your diet and by-drinkings, and money lent you, four and twenty pound.

FALSTAFF He had his part of it; let him pay.

HOSTESS He? Alas, he is poor; he hath nothing.

FALSTAFF How! poor? Look upon his face: what call you rich? Let them coin his nose, let them coin his cheeks. I'll not pay a denier. What, will you make a younker of me? Shall I not take mine ease in mine inn but I shall have my pocket pick'd? I have lost a seal-ring of my grandfather's worth forty mark.

HOSTESS O Jesu, I have heard the Prince tell him, I know not how oft, that that ring was copper!

FALSTAFF How! the Prince is a Jack, a sneakcup. 'Sblood, an he were here, I would cudgel him like a dog if he would say so.'

Enter the PRINCE marching, with PETO; and Falstaff meets him, playing upon his truncheon like a fife.

FALSTAFF How now, lad! Is the wind in that door, i' faith? Must we all march?

BARDOLPH Yea, two and two, Newgate fashion.

HOSTESS My lord, I pray you hear me.

PRINCE What say'st thou, Mistress Quickly? How doth thy husband? I love him well; he is an honest man.

HOSTESS Good my lord, hear me.

FALSTAFF Prithee, let her alone, and list to me.

PRINCE What say'st thou, Jack?

FALSTAFF The other night I fell asleep here behind the arras and had my pocket pick'd; this house is turn'd bawdy-house; they pick pockets.

PRINCE What didst thou lose, Jack?

FALSTAFF Wilt thou believe me, Hal? Three or four bonds of forty pound a-piece and a seal-ring of my grandfather's.

PRINCE A trifle, some eight-penny matter.

HOSTESS So I told him, my lord; and I said I heard your Grace say so; and, my lord, he speaks most vilely of you, like a foulmouth'd man as he is, and said he would cudgel you.

PRINCE What! he did not?

HOSTESS There's neither faith, truth, nor womanhood, in me else.

FALSTAFF There's no more faith in thee than in a stewed prune; nor no more truth in thee than in a drawn fox; and for womanhood, Maid Marian may be the deputy's wife of the ward to thee. Go, you thing, go.

HOSTESS Say, what thing? what thing?

FALSTAFF What thing! Why, a thing to thank God on.

HOSTESS I am no thing to thank God on, I would thou shouldst know it; I am an honest man's wife; and setting thy knighthood aside, thou art a knave to call me so.

FALSTAFF Setting thy womanhood aside, thou art a beast to say otherwise.

HOSTESS Say, what beast, thou knave, thou?

FALSTAFF What beast! Why, an otter.

PRINCE An otter, Sir John! Why an otter?

FALSTAFF Why, she's neither fish nor flesh: a man knows not where to have her.

HOSTESS Thou art an unjust man in saying so: thou or any man knows where to have me, thou knave, thou!

PRINCE Thou say'st true, hostess; and he slanders thee most grossly.

HOSTESS So he doth you, my lord; and said this other day you ought him a thousand pound.

PRINCE Sirrah, do I owe you a thousand pound?

FALSTAFF A thousand pound, Hal! A million. Thy love is worth a million: thou owest me thy love.

HOSTESS Nay, my lord, he call'd you Jack, and said he would cudgel you.

FALSTAFF Did I, Bardolph?

BARDOLPH Indeed, Sir John, you said so.

FALSTAFF Yea, if he said my ring was copper.

PRINCE I say 'tis copper. Darest thou be as good as thy word now?

FALSTAFF Why, Hal, thou knowest, as thou art but man, I dare; but as thou art prince, I fear thee as I fear the roaring of the lion's whelp.

PRINCE And why not as the lion?

FALSTAFF The King himself is to be feared as the lion. Dost thou think I'll fear thee as I fear thy father? Nay, an I do, I pray God my girdle break.

PRINCE O, if it should, how would thy guts fall about thy knees! But, sirrah, there's no room for faith, truth, nor honesty, in this bosom of thine – it is all fill'd up with guts and midriff. Charge an honest woman with picking thy pocket! Why, thou whoreson, impudent, emboss'd rascal, if there were anything in thy pocket but tavern-reckonings, memorandums of bawdy-houses, and one poor penny-worth of sugar-candy to make thee long-winded – if thy pocket were enrich'd with any other injuries but these, I am a villain. And yet you will stand to it, you will not pocket-up wrong. Art thou not ashamed?

FALSTAFF Dost thou hear, Hal? Thou knowest in the state of innocency Adam fell; and what should poor Jack Falstaff do in the days of villainy? Thou seest I have more flesh than another man, and therefore more frailty. You confess, then, you pick'd my pocket?

PRINCE It appears so by the story.

FALSTAFF Hostess, I forgive thee. Go make ready breakfast, love thy husband, look to thy servants, cherish thy guests. Thou shalt find me tractable to any honest reason. Thou seest I am pacified still. Nay, prithee, be gone. [*Exit Hostess*] Now, Hal, to the news at court: for the robbery, lad, how is that answered?

PRINCE O, my sweet beef, I must still be good angel to thee: the money is paid back again.

FALSTAFF O, I do not like that paying back; 'tis a double labour.

PRINCE I am good friends with my father, and may do anything.

FALSTAFF Rob me the exchequer the first thing thou doest, and do it with unwash'd hands too.

BARDOLPH Do, my lord.

PRINCE I have procured thee, Jack, a charge of foot.

FALSTAFF I would it had been of horse. Where shall I find one that can steal well? O for a fine thief, of the age of two and twenty or thereabouts! I am heinously unprovided. Well, God be thanked for these rebels – they offend none but the virtuous; I laud them, I praise them.

PRINCE Bardolph!

BARDOLPH My lord?

PRINCE Go bear this letter to Lord John of Lancaster,
To my brother John; this to my Lord of Westmoreland. [*Exit Bardolph.*

Go, Peto, to horse, to horse; for thou and I
Have thirty miles to ride yet ere dinnertime. [*Exit Peto.*

Jack, meet me to-morrow in the Temple Hall
At two o'clock in the afternoon;
There shalt thou know thy charge, and there receive
Money and order for their furniture.
The land is burning; Percy stands on high;
And either we or they must lower lie. [*Exit.*

FALSTAFF Rare words! brave world! Hostess, my breakfast, come!
O, I could wish this tavern were my drum! [*Exit.*

ACT FOUR

SCENE I. *The rebel camp near Shrewsbury.*

Enter HOTSPUR, WORCESTER, and DOUGLAS.

HOTSPUR Well said, my noble Scot. If speaking truth
In this fine age were not thought flattery,
Such attribution should the Douglas have
As not a soldier of this season's stamp
Should go so general current through the world.
By God, I cannot flatter; I do defy
The tongues of soothers; but a braver place
In my heart's love hath no man than yourself.
Nay, task me to my word; approve me, lord.

DOUGLAS Thou art the king of honour:
No man so potent breathes upon the ground
But I will beard him.

HOTSPUR Do so, and 'tis well.

Enter a Messenger with letters.

What letters hast thou there? – I can but thank you.

MESSENGER These letters come from your father.

HOTSPUR Letters from him! Why comes he not himself?

MESSENGER He cannot come, my lord, he is grievous sick.

HOTSPUR Zounds! how has he the leisure to be sick
In such a justling time? Who leads his power?
Under whose government come they along?

MESSENGER His letters bears his mind, not I, my lord.

WORCESTER I prithee tell me, doth he keep his bed?

MESSENGER He did, my lord, four days ere I set forth;
And at the time of my departure thence
He was much fear'd by his physicians.

WORCESTER I would the state of time had first been whole
Ere he by sickness had been visited:
His health was never better worth than now.

HOTSPUR Sick now! droop now! This sickness doth infect
The very life-blood of our enterprise;
'Tis catching hither, even to our camp.
He writes me here that inward sickness –
And that his friends by deputation could not
So soon be drawn; nor did he think it meet
To lay so dangerous and dear a trust
On any soul remov'd, but on his own.
Yet doth he give us bold advertisement
That with our small conjunction we should on,
To see how fortune is dispos'd to us;
For, as he writes, there is no quailing now,
Because the King is certainly possess'd
Of all our purposes. What say you to it?
WORCESTER Your father's sickness is a maim to us.
HOTSPUR A perilous gash, a very limb lopp'd off.
And yet, in faith, it is not. His present want
Seems more than we shall find it. Were it good
To set the exact wealth of all our states
All at one cast? To set so rich a main
On the nice hazard of one doubtful hour?
It were not good; for therein should we read
The very bottom and the soul of hope,
The very list, the very utmost bound
Of all our fortunes.
DOUGLAS Faith, and so we should;
Where now remains a sweet reversion.
We may boldly spend upon the hope of what
Is to come in.
A comfort of retirement lives in this.
HOTSPUR A rendezvous, a home to fly unto,
If that the devil and mischance look big
Upon the maidenhead of our affairs.
WORCESTER But yet I would your father had been here.
The quality and hair of our attempt
Brooks no division. It will be thought
By some, that know not why he is away,
That wisdom, loyalty, and mere dislike
Of our proceedings, kept the earl from hence;
And think how such an apprehension
May turn the tide of fearful faction
And breed a kind of question in our cause;
For well you know we of the off'ring side
Must keep aloof from strict arbitrement,
And stop all sight-holes, every loop from whence
The eye of reason may pry upon us.
This absence of your father's draws a curtain
That shows the ignorant a kind of fear
Before not dreamt of.
HOTSPUR You strain too far.
I rather of his absence make this use:
It lends a lustre and more great opinion,
A larger dare to our great enterprise,
Than if the earl were here; for men must think,
If we, without his help, can make a head
To push against a kingdom, with his help
We shall o'erturn it topsy-turvy down.
Yet all goes well, yet all our joints are whole.
DOUGLAS As heart can think; there is not such a word
Spoke of in Scotland as this term of fear.

Enter SIR RICHARD VERNON.

HOTSPUR My cousin Vernon! welcome, by my soul.
VERNON Pray God my news be worth a welcome, lord.
The Earl of Westmoreland, seven thousand strong,
Is marching hitherwards; with him Prince John.
HOTSPUR No harm; what more?
VERNON And further, I have learn'd
The King himself in person is set forth,
Or hitherwards intended speedily,
With strong and mighty preparation.
HOTSPUR He shall be welcome too. Where is his son,
The nimble-footed madcap Prince of Wales,
And his comrades that daff'd the world aside
And bid it pass?
VERNON All furnish'd, all in arms;
All plum'd like estridges, that with the wind
Bated like eagles having lately bath'd;
Glittering in golden coats, like images;
As full of spirit as the month of May
And gorgeous as the sun at midsummer;
Wanton as youthful goats, wild as young bulls.
I saw young Harry with his beaver on,
His cushes on his thighs, gallantly arm'd,
Rise from the ground like feathered Mercury,
And vaulted with such ease into his seat
As if an angel dropp'd down from the clouds
To turn and wind a fiery Pegasus,
And witch the world with noble horsemanship.
HOTSPUR No more, no more; worse than the sun in March,
This praise doth nourish agues. Let them come.
They come like sacrifices in their trim,
And to the fire-ey'd maid of smoky war
All hot and bleeding will we offer them.
The mailed Mars shall on his altar sit
Up to the ears in blood. I am on fire
To hear this rich reprisal is so nigh
And yet not ours. Come, let me taste my horse,
Who is to bear me like a thunderbolt
Against the bosom of the Prince of Wales.
Harry to Harry shall, hot horse to horse,
Meet, and ne'er part till one drop down a corse.
O that Glendower were come!
VERNON There is more news.
I learn'd in Worcester, as I rode along,

He cannot draw his power this fourteen days.

DOUGLAS That's the worst tidings that I hear of yet.

WORCESTER Ay, by my faith, that bears a frosty sound.

HOTSPUR What may the King's whole battle reach unto?

VERNON To thirty thousand.

HOTSPUR Forty let it be:
My father and Glendower being both away,
The powers of us may serve so great a day.
Come, let us take a muster speedily.
Doomsday is near; die all, die merrily.

DOUGLAS Talk not of dying; I am out of fear
Of death or death's hand for this one half year.
[*Exeunt.*

SCENE II. *A public road near Coventry.*

Enter FALSTAFF and BARDOLPH.

FALSTAFF Bardolph, get thee before to Coventry; fill me a bottle of sack. Our soldiers shall march through; we'll to Sutton Co'fil' to-night.

BARDOLPH Will you give me money, Captain?

FALSTAFF Lay out, lay out.

BARDOLPH This bottle makes an angel.

FALSTAFF An if it do, take it for thy labour; and if it make twenty, take them all; I'll answer the coinage. Bid my lieutenant Peto meet me at town's end.

BARDOLPH I will, Captain; farewell. [*Exit.*

FALSTAFF If I be not ashamed of my soldiers, I am a sous'd gurnet. I have misused the King's press damnably. I have got, in exchange of a hundred and fifty soldiers, three hundred and odd pounds. I press me none but good householders, yeomen's sons; inquire me out contracted bachelors, such as had been ask'd twice on the banns; such a commodity of warm slaves as had as lief hear the devil as a drum; such as fear the report of a caliver worse than a struck fowl or a hurt wild-duck. I press'd me none but such toasts-and-butter, with hearts in their bellies no bigger than pins' heads, and they have bought out their services; and now my whole charge consists of ancients, corporals, lieutenants, gentlemen of companies – slaves as ragged as Lazarus in the painted cloth, where the Glutton's dogs licked his sores; and such as indeed were never soldiers, but discarded unjust serving-men, younger sons to younger brothers, revolted tapsters, and ostlers trade-fall'n; the cankers of a calm world and a long peace; ten times more dishonourable ragged than an old-fac'd ancient. And such have I, to fill up the rooms of them as have bought out their services, that you would think that I had a hundred and fifty tattered Prodigals lately come from swine-keeping, from eating draff and husks. A mad fellow met me on the way, and told me I had unloaded all the gibbets and press'd the dead bodies. No eye hath seen such scarecrows. I'll not march through Coventry with them, that's flat. Nay, and the villains march wide betwixt the legs, as if they had gyves on; for indeed I had the most of them out of prison. There's not a shirt and a half in all my company; and the half shirt is two napkins tack'd together and thrown over the shoulders like a herald's coat without sleeves; and the shirt, to say the truth, stol'n from my host at Saint Albans, or the red-nose innkeeper of Daventry. But that's all one; they'll find linen enough on every hedge.

Enter the PRINCE OF WALES and WESTMORELAND.

PRINCE How now, blown Jack! how now, quilt!

FALSTAFF What, Hal! how now, mad wag! What a devil dost thou in Warwickshire? My good Lord of Westmoreland, I cry you mercy; I thought your honour had already been at Shrewsbury.

WESTMORELAND Faith, Sir John, 'tis more than time that I were there, and you too; but my powers are there already. The King, I can tell you, looks for us all; we must away all night.

FALSTAFF Tut, never fear me; I am as vigilant as a cat to steal cream.

PRINCE I think, to steal cream indeed; for thy theft hath already made thee butter. But tell me, Jack, whose fellows are these that come after?

FALSTAFF Mine, Hal, mine.

PRINCE I did never see such pitiful rascals.

FALSTAFF Tut, tut; good enough to toss; food for powder, food for powder; they'll fill a pit as well as better: tush, man, mortal men, mortal men.

WESTMORELAND Ay, but, Sir John, methinks they are exceeding poor and bare – too beggarly.

FALSTAFF Faith, for their poverty, I know not where they had that; and for their bareness, I am sure they never learn'd that of me.

PRINCE No, I'll be sworn; unless you call three fingers in the ribs bare. But, sirrah, make haste; Percy is already in the field. [*Exit.*

FALSTAFF What, is the King encamp'd?

WESTMORELAND He is, Sir John: I fear we shall stay too long. [*Exit.*

FALSTAFF Well,
To the latter end of a fray and the beginning of a feast
Fits a dull fighter and a keen guest. [*Exit.*

SCENE III. *The rebel camp near Shrewsbury.*

Enter HOTSPUR, WORCESTER, DOUGLAS, and VERNON.

HOTSPUR We'll fight with him to-night.
WORCESTER It may not be.
DOUGLAS You give him, then, advantage.
VERNON Not a whit.
HOTSPUR Why say you so? looks he not for supply?
VERNON So do we.
HOTSPUR His is certain, ours is doubtful.
WORCESTER Good cousin, be advis'd, stir not to-night.
VERNON Do not, my lord.
DOUGLAS You do not counsel well;
You speak it out of fear and cold heart.
VERNON Do me no slander, Douglas; by my life,
And I dare well maintain it with my life,
If well-respected honour bid me on,
I hold as little counsel with weak fear
As you, my lord, or any Scot that this day lives;
Let it be seen to-morrow in the battle
Which of us fears.
DOUGLAS Yea, or to-night.
VERNON Content.
HOTSPUR To-night, say I.
VERNON Come, come, it may not be. I wonder much,
Being men of such great leading as you are,
That you foresee not what impediments
Drag back our expedition: certain horse
Of my cousin Vernon's are not yet come up;
Your uncle Worcester's horse came but today;
And now their pride and mettle is asleep,
Their courage with hard labour tame and dull,
That not a horse is half the half of himself.
HOTSPUR So are the horses of the enemy
In general, journey-bated and brought low;
The better part of ours are full of rest.
WORCESTER The number of the King exceedeth ours.
For God's sake, cousin, stay till all come in.
[*The trumpet sounds a parley.*

Enter SIR WALTER BLUNT.

BLUNT I come with gracious offers from the King,
If you vouchsafe me hearing and respect.
HOTSPUR Welcome, Sir Walter Blunt; and would to God
You were of our determination!
Some of us love you well; and even those some
Envy your great deservings and good name,
Because you are not of our quality,
But stand against us like an enemy.
BLUNT And God defend but still I should stand so,
So long as out of limit and true rule
You stand against anointed majesty!
But, to my charge. The King hath sent to know
The nature of your griefs; and whereupon
You conjure from the breast of civil peace
Such bold hostility, teaching his duteous land
Audacious cruelty. If that the King
Have any way your good deserts forgot,
Which he confesseth to be manifold,
He bids you name your griefs, and with all speed
You shall have your desires with interest,
And pardon absolute for yourself and these
Herein misled by your suggestion.
HOTSPUR The King is kind; and well we know the King
Knows at what time to promise, when to pay.
My father and my uncle and myself
Did give him that same royalty he wears;
And when he was not six and twenty strong,
Sick in the world's regard, wretched and low,
A poor unminded outlaw sneaking home,
My father gave him welcome to the shore;
And when he heard him swear and vow to God
He came but to be Duke of Lancaster,
To sue his livery and beg his peace,
With tears of innocency and terms of zeal,
My father, in kind heart and pity mov'd,
Swore him assistance, and perform'd it too.
Now when the lords and barons of the realm
Perceiv'd Northumberland did lean to him,
The more and less came in with cap and knee;
Met him in boroughs, cities, villages;
Attended him on bridges, stood in lanes,
Laid gifts before him, proffer'd him their oaths,
Gave him their heirs as pages, followed him
Even at the heels in golden multitudes.
He presently – as greatness knows itself –
Steps me a little higher than his vow
Made to my father, while his blood was poor,
Upon the naked shore at Ravenspurgh;
And now, forsooth, takes on him to reform
Some certain edicts, and some strait decrees
That lie too heavy on the commonwealth;
Cries out upon abuses, seems to weep
Over his country's wrongs; and by this face,
This seeming brow of justice, did he win
The hearts of all that he did angle for;
Proceeded further: cut me off the heads
Of all the favourites that the absent King
In deputation left behind him here,
When he was personal in the Irish war.
BLUNT Tut, I came not to hear this.
HOTSPUR Then to the point.
In short time after, he depos'd the King;
Soon after that depriv'd him of his life;
And in the neck of that, task'd the whole state;

To make that worse, suff'red his kinsman March –
Who is, if every owner were well plac'd,
Indeed his king – to be engag'd in Wales,
There without ransom to lie forfeited;
Disgrac'd me in my happy victories;
Sought to entrap me by intelligence;
Rated mine uncle from the council-board;
In rage dismiss'd my father from the court;
Broke oath on oath, committed wrong on wrong;
And in conclusion drove us to seek out
This head of safety, and withal to pry
Into his title, the which we find
Too indirect for long continuance.

BLUNT Shall I return this answer to the King?

HOTSPUR Not so, Sir Walter; we'll withdraw awhile.
Go to the King; and let there be impawn'd
Some surety for a safe return again,
And in the morning early shall mine uncle
Bring him our purposes. And so, farewell.

BLUNT I would you would accept of grace and love.

HOTSPUR And may be so we shall.

BLUNT Pray God you do. [*Exeunt.*

SCENE IV. *York. The Archbishop's palace.*

Enter the ARCHBISHOP OF YORK, and SIR MICHAEL.

ARCHBISHOP Hie, good Sir Michael; bear this sealed brief
With winged haste to the Lord Marshall;
This to my cousin Scroop; and all the rest
To whom they are directed. If you knew
How much they do import, you would make haste.

SIR MICHAEL My good lord,
I guess their tenour.

ARCHBISHOP Like enough you do.
To-morrow, good Sir Michael, is a day
Wherein the fortune of ten thousand men
Must bide the touch; for, sir, at Shrewsbury,
As I am truly given to understand,
The King with mighty and quick-raised power
Meets with Lord Harry; and I fear, Sir Michael,
What with the sickness of Northumberland,
Whose power was in the first proportion,
And what with Owen Glendower's absence thence,
Who with them was a rated sinew too
And comes not in, o'errul'd by prophecies,
I fear the power of Percy is too weak
To wage an instant trial with the King.

SIR MICHAEL Why, my good lord, you need not fear;
There is Douglas and Lord Mortimer.

ARCHBISHOP No, Mortimer is not there.

SIR MICHAEL But there is Mordake, Vernon, Lord Harry Percy,
And there is my Lord of Worcester, and a head
Of gallant warriors, noble gentlemen.

ARCHBISHOP And so there is; but yet the King hath drawn
The special head of all the land together:
The Prince of Wales, Lord John of Lancaster,
The noble Westmoreland, and warlike Blunt;
And many moe corrivals and dear men
Of estimation and command in arms.

SIR MICHAEL Doubt not, my lord, they shall be well oppos'd.

ARCHBISHOP I hope no less, yet needful 'tis to fear;
And, to prevent the worst, Sir Michael, speed;
For if Lord Percy thrive not, ere the King
Dismiss his power, he means to visit us –
For he hath heard of our confederacy –
And 'tis but wisdom to make strong against him;
Therefore make haste. I must go write again
To other friends; and so farewell, Sir Michael.
[*Exeunt severally.*

ACT FIVE

SCENE I. *The King's camp near Shrewsbury.*

Enter the KING, the PRINCE OF WALES, PRINCE JOHN OF LANCASTER, SIR WALTER BLUNT, and SIR JOHN FALSTAFF.

KING How bloodily the sun begins to peer
Above yon busky hill! The day looks pale
At his distemp'rature.

PRINCE The southern wind
Doth play the trumpet to his purposes,
And by his hollow whistling in the leaves
Foretells a tempest and a blust'ring day.

KING Then with the losers let it sympathize,
For nothing can seem foul to those that win.
[*The trumpet sounds.*

Enter WORCESTER and VERNON.

How now, my Lord of Worcester! 'Tis not well
That you and I should meet upon such terms
As now we meet. You have deceiv'd our trust,
And made us doff our easy robes of peace
To crush our old limbs in ungentle steel;
This is not well, my lord, this is not well.

What say you to it? Will you again unknit
This churlish knot of all-abhorred war,
And move in that obedient orb again
Where you did give a fair and natural light,
And be no more an exhal'd meteor,
A prodigy of fear, and a portent
Of broached mischief to the unborn times?

WORCESTER Hear me, my liege:
For mine own part, I could be well content
To entertain the lag-end of my life
With quiet hours; for I protest
I have not sought the day of this dislike.

KING You have not sought it! How comes it then?

FALSTAFF Rebellion lay in his way, and he found it.

PRINCE Peace, chewet, peace!

WORCESTER It pleas'd your Majesty to turn your looks
Of favour from myself and all our house;
And yet I must remember you, my lord,
We were the first and dearest of your friends.
For you my staff of office did I break
In Richard's time, and posted day and night
To meet you on the way and kiss your hand,
When yet you were in place and in account
Nothing so strong and fortunate as I.
It was myself, my brother, and his son,
That brought you home, and boldly did outdare
The dangers of the time. You swore to us –
And you did swear that oath at Doncaster –
That you did nothing purpose 'gainst the state,
Nor claim no further than your new-fall'n right,
The seat of Gaunt, dukedom of Lancaster;
To this we swore our aid. But in short space
It rain'd down fortune show'ring on your head;
And such a flood of greatness fell on you,
What with our help, what with the absent King,
What with the injuries of a wanton time,
The seeming sufferances that you had borne,
And the contrarious winds that held the King
So long in his unlucky Irish wars
That all in England did repute him dead;
And from this swarm of fair advantages
You took occasion to be quickly woo'd
To gripe the general sway into your hand;
Forgot your oath to us at Doncaster;
And being fed by us you us'd us so
As that ungentle gull, the cuckoo's bird,
Useth the sparrow – did oppress our nest,
Grew by our feeding to so great a bulk
That even our love durst not come near your sight
For fear of swallowing; but with nimble wing
We were enforc'd, for safety sake, to fly
Out of your sight, and raise this present head;
Whereby we stand opposed by such means
As you yourself have forg'd against yourself,
By unkind usage, dangerous countenance,
And violation of all faith and troth
Sworn to us in your younger enterprise.

KING These things, indeed, you have articulate,
Proclaim'd at market-crosses, read in churches,
To face the garment of rebellion
With some fine colour that may please the eye
Of fickle changelings and poor discontents,
Which gape and rub the elbow at the news
Of hurlyburly innovation;
And never yet did insurrection want
Such water-colours to impaint his cause,
Nor moody beggars, starving for a time
Of pellmell havoc and confusion.

PRINCE In both your armies there is many a soul
Shall pay full dearly for this encounter,
If once they join in trial. Tell your nephew
The Prince of Wales doth join with all the world
In praise of Henry Percy. By my hopes,
This present enterprise set off his head,
I do not think a braver gentleman,
More active-valiant or more valiant-young,
More daring or more bold, is now alive
To grace this latter age with noble deeds.
For my part, I may speak it to my shame,
I have a truant been to chivalry;
And so I hear he doth account me too.
Yet this before my father's majesty –
I am content that he shall take the odds
Of his great name and estimation,
And will, to save the blood on either side,
Try fortune with him in a single fight.

KING And, Prince of Wales, so dare we venture thee,
Albeit considerations infinite
Do make against it. No, good Worcester, no,
We love our people well; even those we love
That are misled upon your cousin's part;
And will they take the offer of our grace,
Both he and they and you, yea, every man
Shall be my friend again, and I'll be his.
So tell your cousin, and bring me word
What he will do. But if he will not yield,
Rebuke and dread correction wait on us,
And they shall do their office. So, be gone;
We will not now be troubled with reply.
We offer fair; take it advisedly.

[*Exeunt Worcester and Vernon.*

PRINCE It will not be accepted, on my life:
The Douglas and the Hotspur both together
Are confident against the world in arms.

KING Hence, therefore, every leader to his charge;
For, on their answer, will we set on them;

And God befriend us, as our cause is just!
[Exeunt all but the Prince and Falstaff.

FALSTAFF Hal, if thou see me down in the battle, and bestride me, so; 'tis a point of friendship.

PRINCE Nothing but a colossus can do thee that friendship. Say thy prayers, and farewell.

FALSTAFF I would 'twere bed-time, Hal, and all well.

PRINCE Why, thou owest God a death. *[Exit.*

FALSTAFF 'Tis not due yet; I would be loath to pay him before his day. What need I be so forward with him that calls not on me? Well, 'tis no matter; honour pricks me on. Yea, but how if honour prick me off when I come on? How then? Can honour set to a leg? No. Or an arm? No. Or take away the grief of a wound? No. Honour hath no skill in surgery, then? No. What is honour? A word. What is in that word? Honour. What is that honour? Air. A trim reckoning! Who hath it? He that died o' Wednesday. Doth he feel it? No. Doth he hear it? No. 'Tis insensible, then? Yea, to the dead. But will it not live with the living? No. Why? Detraction will not suffer it. Therefore I'll none of it. Honour is a mere scutcheon. And so ends my catechism. *[Exit.*

SCENE II. *The rebel camp.*

Enter WORCESTER and VERNON.

WORCESTER O, no, my nephew must not know, Sir Richard,
The liberal and kind offer of the King.
VERNON 'Twere best he did.
WORCESTER Then are we all undone.
It is not possible, it cannot be,
The King should keep his word in loving us;
He will suspect us still, and find a time
To punish this offence in other faults;
Supposition all our lives shall be stuck full of eyes,
For treason is but trusted like the fox,
Who, never so tame, so cherish'd, and lock'd up,
Will have a wild trick of his ancestors.
Look how we can, or sad or merrily,
Interpretation will misquote our looks,
And we shall feed like oxen at a stall,
The better cherish'd still the nearer death.
My nephew's trespass may be well forgot;
It hath the excuse of youth and heat of blood,
And an adopted name of privilege –
A hare-brain'd Hotspur, govern'd by a spleen.
All his offences live upon my head
And on his father's: we did train him on;
And, his corruption being ta'en from us,
We, as the spring of all, shall pay for all.
Therefore, good cousin, let not Harry know,
In any case, the offer of the King.
VERNON Deliver what you will, I'll say 'tis so.
Here comes your cousin.

Enter HOTSPUR and DOUGLAS.

HOTSPUR My uncle is return'd:
Deliver up my Lord of Westmoreland.
Uncle, what news?
WORCESTER The King will bid you battle presently.
DOUGLAS Defy him by the Lord of Westmoreland.
HOTSPUR Lord Douglas, go you and tell him so.
DOUGLAS Marry, and shall, and very willingly.
[Exit.

WORCESTER There is no seeming mercy in the King.
HOTSPUR Did you beg any? God forbid!
WORCESTER I told him gently of our grievances,
Of his oath-breaking; which he mended thus,
By now forswearing that he is forsworn.
He calls us rebels, traitors, and will scourge
With haughty arms this hateful name in us.

Re-enter DOUGLAS.

DOUGLAS Arm, gentlemen, to arms! for I have thrown
A brave defiance in King Henry's teeth –
And Westmoreland, that was engag'd, did bear it –
Which cannot choose but bring him quickly on.
WORCESTER The Prince of Wales stepp'd forth before the King,
And, nephew, challeng'd you to single fight.
HOTSPUR O, would the quarrel lay upon our heads;
And that no man might draw short breath to-day
But I and Harry Monmouth! Tell me, tell me,
How show'd his tasking? Seem'd it in contempt?
VERNON No, by my soul, I never in my life
Did hear a challenge urg'd more modestly,
Unless a brother should a brother dare
To gentle exercise and proof of arms.
He gave you all the duties of a man;
Trimm'd up your praises with a princely tongue;
Spoke your deservings like a chronicle;
Making you ever better than his praise,
By still dispraising praise valued with you;
And, which became him like a prince indeed,
He made a blushing cital of himself,
And chid his truant youth with such a grace
As if he mast'red there a double spirit,
Of teaching and of learning instantly.
There did he pause; but let me tell the world –

If he outlive the envy of this day,
England did never owe so sweet a hope,
So much misconstrued in his wantonness.

HOTSPUR Cousin, I think thou art enamoured
On his follies. Never did I hear
Of any prince so wild a liberty.
But be he as he will, yet once ere night
I will embrace him with a soldier's arm,
That he shall shrink under my courtesy.
Arm, arm with speed! and, fellows, soldiers, friends,
Better consider what you have to do
Than I, that have not well the gift of tongue,
Can lift your blood up with persuasion.

Enter a Messenger.

MESSENGER My lord, here are letters for you.

HOTSPUR I cannot read them now.
O gentlemen, the time of life is short!
To spend that shortness basely were too long,
If life did ride upon a dial's point,
Still ending at the arrival of an hour.
And if we live, we live to tread on kings;
If die, brave death, when princes die with us!
Now, for our consciences, the arms are fair,
When the intent of bearing them is just.

Enter another Messenger.

MESSENGER My lord, prepare; the King comes on apace.

HOTSPUR I thank him that he cuts me from my tale,
For I profess not talking; only this –
Let each man do his best. And here draw I
A sword, whose temper I intend to stain
With the best blood that I can meet withal
In the adventure of this perilous day.
Now, Esperance! Percy! and set on.
Sound all the lofty instruments of war,
And by that music let us all embrace;
For, heaven to earth, some of us never shall
A second time do such a courtesy.

[*They embrace. The trumpets sound. Exeunt.*

SCENE III. *A plain between the camps.*

The KING passes across with his power. Alarum to the battle. Then enter DOUGLAS and SIR WALTER BLUNT.

BLUNT What is thy name, that in battle thus
Thou crossest me? What honour dost thou seek
Upon my head?

DOUGLAS Know, then, my name is Douglas;
And I do haunt thee in the battle thus
Because some tell me that thou art a king.

BLUNT They tell thee true.

DOUGLAS The Lord of Stafford dear to-day hath bought
Thy likeness; for instead of thee, King Harry,
This sword hath ended him. So shall it thee,
Unless thou yield thee as my prisoner.

BLUNT I was not born a yielder, thou proud Scot;
And thou shalt find a king that will revenge
Lord Stafford's death.

[*They fight. Douglas kills Blunt.*

Enter HOTSPUR.

HOTSPUR O Douglas, hadst thou fought at Holmedon thus,
I never had triumph'd upon a Scot.

DOUGLAS All's done, all's won; here breathless lies the King.

HOTSPUR Where?

DOUGLAS Here.

HOTSPUR This, Douglas? No: I know this face full well;
A gallant knight he was, his name was Blunt;
Semblably furnish'd like the King himself.

DOUGLAS A fool go with thy soul whither it goes!
A borrowed title hast thou bought too dear;
Why didst thou tell me that thou wert a king?

HOTSPUR The King hath many marching in his coats.

DOUGLAS Now, by my sword, I will kill all his coats;
I'll murder all his wardrobe, piece by piece,
Until I meet the King.

HOTSPUR Up, and away!
Our soldiers stand full fairly for the day.

[*Exeunt.*

Alarum. Enter FALSTAFF, solus.

FALSTAFF Though I could scape shot-free at London, I fear the shot here: here's no scoring but upon the pate. Soft! who are you? Sir Walter Blunt. There's honour for you! Here's no vanity! I am as hot as molten lead, and as heavy too. God keep lead out of me! I need no more weight than mine own bowels. I have led my ragamuffins where they are pepper'd; there's not three of my hundred and fifty left alive, and they are for the town's end, to beg during life. But who comes here?

Enter the PRINCE OF WALES.

PRINCE What, stand'st thou idle here? Lend me thy sword.
Many a nobleman lies stark and stiff
Under the hoofs of vaunting enemies,
Whose deaths are yet unreveng'd. I prithee lend me thy sword.

FALSTAFF O Hal, I prithee give me leave to breathe awhile. Turk Gregory never did such deeds in arms as I have done this day. I have paid Percy, I have made him sure.

PRINCE He is, indeed, and living to kill thee. I prithee lend me thy sword.

FALSTAFF Nay, before God, Hal, if Percy be alive, thou get'st not my sword; but take my pistol, if thou wilt.

PRINCE Give it me. What, is it in the case?

FALSTAFF Ay, Hal; 'tis hot, 'tis hot; there's that will sack a city. [*The Prince draws it out, and finds it to be a bottle of sack.*

PRINCE What, is it a time to jest and dally now?
[*He throws the bottle at him. Exit.*

FALSTAFF Well, if Percy be alive, I'll pierce him. If he do come in my way, so; if he do not, if I come in his willingly, let him make a carbonado of me. I like not such grinning honour as Sir Walter hath. Give me life, which if I can save, so; if not, honour comes unlook'd for, and there's an end. [*Exit.*

SCENE IV. *Another part of the field.*

Alarums. Excursions. Enter the KING, the PRINCE OF WALES, PRINCE JOHN OF LANCASTER, and WESTMORELAND.

KING I prithee,
Harry, withdraw thyself; thou bleedest too much;
Lord John of Lancaster, go you with him.

PRINCE JOHN Not I, my lord, unless I did bleed too.

PRINCE I beseech your Majesty, make up,
Lest your retirement do amaze your friends.

KING I will do so.
My Lord of Westmoreland, lead him to his tent.

WESTMORELAND Come, my lord, I'll lead you to your tent.

PRINCE Lead me, my lord? I do not need your help;
And God forbid a shallow scratch should drive
The Prince of Wales from such a field as this,
Where stain'd nobility lies trodden on,
And rebels' arms triumph in massacres!

PRINCE JOHN We breathe too long. Come, cousin Westmoreland,
Our duty this way lies; for God's sake, come.
[*Exeunt Prince John and Westmoreland.*

PRINCE By God, thou hast deceiv'd me, Lancaster!
I did not think thee lord of such a spirit;
Before, I lov'd thee as a brother, John,
But now I do respect thee as my soul.

KING I saw him hold Lord Percy at the point
With lustier maintenance than I did look for
Of such an ungrown warrior.

PRINCE O, this boy
Lends mettle to us all! [*Exit.*

Enter DOUGLAS.

DOUGLAS Another king! They grow like Hydra's heads.
I am the Douglas, fatal to all those
That wear those colours on them. What art thou,
That counterfeit'st the person of a king?

KING The King himself, who, Douglas, grieves at heart
So many of his shadows thou hast met,
And not the very King. I have two boys
Seek Percy and thyself about the field;
But, seeing thou fall'st on me so luckily,
I will assay thee; so, defend thyself.

DOUGLAS I fear thou art another counterfeit;
And yet, in faith, thou bearest thee like a king;
But mine I am sure thou art, who'er thou be,
And thus I win thee.
[*They fight, the King being in danger.*

Re-enter the PRINCE.

PRINCE Hold up thy head, vile Scot, or thou art like
Never to hold it up again. The spirits
Of valiant Shirley, Stafford, Blunt, are in my arms;
It is the Prince of Wales that threatens thee,
Who never promiseth but he means to pay.
[*They fight; Douglas flies.*
Cheerly, my lord: how fares your Grace?
Sir Nicholas Gawsey hath for succour sent,
And so hath Clifton. I'll to Clifton straight.

KING Stay, and breathe awhile.
Thou hast redeem'd thy lost opinion;
And show'd thou mak'st some tender of my life,
In this fair rescue thou hast brought to me.

PRINCE O God, they did me too much injury
That ever said I heark'ned for your death!
If it were so, I might have let alone
The insulting hand of Douglas over you,
Which would have been as speedy in your end
As all the poisonous potions in the world,
And sav'd the treacherous labour of your son.

KING Make up to Clifton, I'll to Sir Nicholas Gawsey. [*Exit.*

Enter HOTSPUR.

HOTSPUR If I mistake not, thou art Harry Monmouth.

PRINCE Thou speak'st as if I would deny my name.

HOTSPUR My name is Harry Percy.

PRINCE Why, then I see
A very valiant rebel of the name.
I am the Prince of Wales; and think not, Percy,

To share with me in glory any more.
Two stars keep not their motion in one sphere,
Nor can one England brook a double reign
Of Harry Percy and the Prince of Wales.

HOTSPUR Nor shall it, Harry, for the hour is come
To end the one of us; and would to God
Thy name in arms were now as great as mine!

PRINCE I'll make it greater ere I part from thee,
And all the budding honours on thy crest
I'll crop to make a garland for my head.

HOTSPUR I can no longer brook thy vanities.

[*They fight.*

Enter FALSTAFF.

FALSTAFF Well said, Hal! to it, Hal! Nay, you shall find no boy's play here, I can tell you.

Re-enter DOUGLAS; he fights with Falstaff, who falls down as if he were dead; Douglas withdraws. Hotspur is wounded, and falls.

HOTSPUR O, Harry, thou hast robb'd me of my youth!
I better brook the loss of brittle life
Than those proud titles thou hast won of me:
They wound my thoughts worse than thy sword my flesh;
But thoughts, the slaves of life, and life, time's fool,
And time, that takes survey of all the world,
Must have a stop. O, I could prophesy,
But that the earthy and cold hand of death
Lies on my tongue. No, Percy, thou art dust
And food for – [*Dies.*

PRINCE For worms, brave Percy. Fare thee well, great heart!
Ill-weav'd ambition, how much art thou shrunk!
When that this body did contain a spirit,
A kingdom for it was too small a bound;
But now two paces of the vilest earth
Is room enough. This earth that bears thee dead
Bears not alive so stout a gentleman.
If thou wert sensible of courtesy,
I should not make so dear a show of zeal;
But let my favours hide thy mangled face,
And, even in thy behalf, I'll thank myself
For doing these fair rites of tenderness.
Adieu, and take thy praise with thee to heaven!
Thy ignominy sleep with thee in the grave,
But not remember'd in thy epitaph!

[*He spieth Falstaff on the ground.*

What, old acquaintance! Could not all this flesh
Keep in a little life? Poor Jack, farewell!
I could have better spar'd a better man.
O, I should have a heavy miss of thee,
If I were much in love with vanity!
Death hath not struck so fat a deer to-day,
Though many dearer, in this bloody fray.
Embowell'd will I see thee by and by;
Till then in blood by noble Percy lie. [*Exit.*

FALSTAFF [*Rising up*] Embowell'd! If thou embowel me to-day, I'll give you leave to powder me and eat me too to-morrow. 'Sblood, 'twas time to counterfeit, or that hot termagant Scot had paid me scot and lot too. Counterfeit? I lie, I am no counterfeit: to die is to be a counterfeit; for he is but the counterfeit of a man who hath not the life of a man; but to counterfeit dying, when a man thereby liveth, is to be no counterfeit, but the true and perfect image of life indeed. The better part of valour is discretion; in the which better part I have saved my life. Zounds, I am afraid of this gunpowder Percy, though he be dead; how if he should counterfeit too, and rise? By my faith, I am afraid he would prove the better counterfeit. Therefore I'll make him sure; yea, and I'll swear I kill'd him. Why may not he rise as well as I? Nothing confutes me but eyes, and nobody sees me. Therefore, sirrah [*stabbing him*], with a new wound in your thigh, come you along with me.

[*He takes up Hotspur on his back.*

Re-enter the PRINCE OF WALES and PRINCE JOHN OF LANCASTER.

PRINCE Come, brother John, full bravely hast thou flesh'd
Thy maiden sword.

PRINCE JOHN But, soft! whom have we here?
Did you not tell me this fat man was dead?

PRINCE I did; I saw him dead,
Breathless and bleeding on the ground. Art thou alive?
Or is it fantasy that plays upon our eyesight?
I prithee speak; we will not trust our eyes
Without our ears: thou art not what thou seem'st.

FALSTAFF No, that's certain: I am not a double man; but if I be not Jack Falstaff, then am I a Jack. There is Percy [*throwing the body down*]; if your father will do me any honour, so; if not, let him kill the next Percy himself. I look to be either earl or duke, I can assure you.

PRINCE Why, Percy I kill'd myself, and saw thee dead.

FALSTAFF Didst thou? Lord, Lord, how this world is given to lying! I grant you I was down and out of breath, and so was he; but we rose both at an instant, and fought a long hour by Shrewsbury clock. If I may be believ'd, so; if not, let them that should reward valour bear the sin upon their own heads. I'll take it upon my death, I gave him this wound in the thigh; if the man were alive, and would deny it, zounds, I would make him eat a piece of my sword.

PRINCE JOHN This is the strangest tale that ever I heard.

PRINCE This is the strangest fellow, brother John.
Come, bring your luggage nobly on your back.
For my part, if a lie may do thee grace,
I'll gild it with the happiest terms I have.
[*A retreat is sounded.*
The trumpet sounds retreat; the day is ours.
Come, brother, let us to the highest of the field,
To see what friends are living, who are dead.
[*Exeunt the Prince and Prince John of Lancaster.*

FALSTAFF I'll follow, as they say, for reward. He that rewards me, God reward him! If I do grow great, I'll grow less; for I'll purge, and leave sack, and live cleanly, as a nobleman should do.
[*Exit.*

SCENE V. *Another part of the field.*

The Trumpets sound. Enter the KING, the PRINCE OF WALES, PRINCE JOHN OF LANCASTER, WESTMORELAND, with WORCESTER and VERNON prisoners.

KING Thus ever did rebellion find rebuke.
Ill-spirited Worcester! did not we send grace,
Pardon and terms of love to all of you?
And wouldst thou turn our offers contrary?
Misuse the tenour of thy kinsman's trust?
Three knights upon our party slain to-day,
A noble earl, and many a creature else,
Had been alive this hour,
If like a Christian thou hadst truly borne
Betwixt our armies true intelligence.

WORCESTER What I have done my safety urg'd me to;
And I embrace this fortune patiently,
Since not to be avoided it falls on me.

KING Bear Worcester to the death, and Vernon too;
Other offenders we will pause upon.
[*Exeunt Worcester and Vernon guarded.*
How goes the field?

PRINCE The noble Scot, Lord Douglas, when he saw
The fortune of the day quite turn'd from him,
The noble Percy slain, and all his men
Upon the foot of fear, fled with the rest;
And falling from a hill, he was so bruis'd
That the pursuers took him. At my tent
The Douglas is; and I beseech your Grace
I may dispose of him.

KING With all my heart.

PRINCE Then, brother John of Lancaster, to you
This honourable bounty shall belong:
Go to the Douglas, and deliver him
Up to his pleasure, ransomless and free;
His valours shown upon our crests to-day
Have taught us how to cherish such high deeds
Even in the bosom of our adversaries.

PRINCE JOHN I thank your Grace for this high courtesy,
Which I shall give away immediately.

KING Then this remains – that we divide our power.
You, son John, and my cousin Westmoreland,
Towards York shall bend you with your dearest speed
To meet Northumberland and the prelate Scroop,
Who, as we hear, are busily in arms.
Myself, and you, son Harry, will towards Wales
To fight with Glendower and the Earl of March.
Rebellion in this land shall lose his sway,
Meeting the check of such another day;
And since this business so fair is done,
Let us not leave till all our own be won. [*Exeunt.*

The Second Part of King Henry the Fourth

Introduction by DONALD MACKENZIE

Sequels are always risky and the sequel to a play as packed and brilliant as *1 Henry IV* not least. It would be a plausible guess that *2 Henry IV* has always been the less enjoyed and esteemed of the two. And one can readily argue for that response. The political action is only the mopping up of a rebellion decisively broken by the end of Part One; plus the (too?) long-drawn-out deathbed of Henry IV and succession of Hal. The Eastcheap scenes lack the brio of those in Part One and their satiric dance with high politics. Falstaff himself, diseased, aged (as distinct from old), something of a predator, has lost his comic verve and fertility. The recruiting scene, like his taking of Colville, can seem a mere ripple from the previous play. Above all do we need or want – indeed how seriously can we take? – a Hal who returns to Eastcheap and has to reconcile himself all over again to his father? Has Shakespeare not been defeated – as a playwright dramatising history is apt to be – by his material: too much, in this case, for five acts and not enough for ten? (cf Jenkins in Armstrong, 1972).

The case is strong; and yet – at the very least – *2 Henry IV* scores its own distinctive successes. Repetition can prove creatively varied. The slackening of the action allows the play space to probe and brood. This can be focussed in a single figure: the sleepless, memory-haunted king of Act 3 Scene 1; the frustrated heir-apparent Hal of Act 2 Scene 2. Or it can expand diversely as in the great central triptych of *temps perdu* [2.4, 3.1, 3.2]. In Act 3 Scene 1 the reversals and betrayals of politics pass into a sombre vision of unresting cosmic change. This is flanked by two Falstaff scenes, steeped in memory and intimations of mortality. The first – the one meeting of Hal and Falstaff in this play before the final rejection – is (purposefully) sleazy as none of the Eastcheap scenes in *Part One* had been. But its sleaziness can muster a Hogarthian vigour or be transfixed by a sudden bleak pathos. Counterpointing all of these are the scenes with Shallow which blend the mellow, the muddled and a haunting prose lyricism in ways that have no parallel till Chekov (cf Nuttall, 1989). Memory in them is also *mis*rembering and, as such, one form of the confusion that permeates the play from the Prologue of Rumour to Mistress Quickly's verbal straggle to Hal's confounding of expectation at the climax. Confusion darkens into a vision of the body politic as diseased, of history as insuperably tangled (the latter voiced by the rebel archbishop as a ground of hope just before, in the most acrid of the play's reversals, his rebellion is quenched by the casuistic treachery of Prince John).

The succession of Hal as Henry V makes a strong bid to knit confusion into order. He succeeds his usurping father as legitimate heir. He rejects the disordered surrogate father Falstaff, choosing in his place the Lord Chief Justice who embodies the authority of impersonal law [5.2.72–121]. The sea imagery of violence and instability now, channelled, celebrates monarchic power [cf 5.2.129–32 with 1.1.153f or 3.1.45f].

Yet what cuts deepest in those final scenes may be, first, the rejection of Falstaff with what it tells of the cost – necessary, even justified – of political success; and second the irony and poignancy of the deathbed itself. There is irony in the fulfilment of Henry's prophesied death in Jerusalem; poignancy in that even in this full reconciliation neither father nor son can speak quite the whole truth (Henry 'met' – he did not take – the crown; the devoted and ambitious Hal gives a slightly but significantly misleading account of his own taking of it in turn).

Henry IV Part One is sinewed by the primal tragic motifs of inherited guilt and family conflict. Recycling the alienation and reconciling of father and son Shakespeare (at the cost of some implausibility) gives those motifs not a resolution but a refocussing that can pluck disorientatingly at the edge of the mind: 'My father is gone wild into his grave,/For in his tomb lie my affections;/And with his spirits sadly I survive'. The conflict and transposing of parent and child end *Henry IV Part Two* where *Lear* begins. Its sense of the burden of the past and of the ironic fulfilments that corrode human action key it to *Hamlet*, as its deployment of mood and memory key it to *Antony and Cleopatra*. The history plays (far more than the diploma-piece melodrama of *Titus Andronicus* or the inverted Shakespearean comedy of *Romeo and Juliet*) are the matrix and predecessors of Shakespearean tragedy; and the final case to be made for *Henry IV Part Two* is that it offers the fullest gateway to the latter.

The Second Part of King Henry the Fourth

DRAMATIS PERSONAE

RUMOUR
the Presenter
KING HENRY THE FOURTH
HENRY, PRINCE OF WALES, *afterwards Henry V*, PRINCE JOHN OF LANCASTER, PRINCE HUMPHREY OF GLOUCESTER, THOMAS, DUKE OF CLARENCE
sons of Henry IV
EARL OF NORTHUMBERLAND, SCROOP, ARCHBISHOP OF YORK, LORD MOWBRAY, LORD HASTINGS, LORD BARDOLPH, SIR JOHN COLVILLE,
TRAVERS, MORTON
retainers of Northumberland
opposites against King Henry IV
EARL OF WARWICK, EARL OF WESTMORELAND, EARL OF SURREY, EARL OF KENT, GOWER, HARCOURT, BLUNT
of the King's party
LORD CHIEF JUSTICE
Servant, to Lord Chief Justice
SIR JOHN FALSTAFF, EDWARD POINS, BARDOLPH, PISTOL, PETO
irregular humorists
Page, to Falstaff
ROBERT SHALLOW, SILENCE
country Justices
DAVY
servant to Shallow
FANG, SNARE
Sheriff's officers
RALPH MOULDY, SIMON SHADOW, THOMAS WART, FRANCIS FEEBLE, PETER BULLCALF
country soldiers
FRANCIS
a drawer
LADY NORTHUMBERLAND
LADY PERCY
Percy's widow
HOSTESS QUICKLY
of the Boar's Head, Eastcheap
DOLL TEARSHEET
Lords, Attendants, a Porter, a Messenger, Drawers, Beadles, Grooms and Servants.

THE SCENE: ENGLAND.

INDUCTION

Warkworth. Before Northumberland's castle.

Enter RUMOUR, painted full of tongues.

RUMOUR Open your ears; for which of you will stop
The vent of hearing when loud Rumour speaks?
I, from the orient to the drooping west,
Making the wind my post-horse, still unfold
The acts commenced on this ball of earth.
Upon my tongues continual slanders ride,
The which in every language I pronounce,
Stuffing the ears of men with false reports.
I speak of peace while covert enmity,
Under the smile of safety, wounds the world;
And who but Rumour, who but only I,
Make fearful musters and prepar'd defence,
Whiles the big year, swoln with some other grief,
Is thought with child by the stern tyrant war,
And no such matter? Rumour is a pipe
Blown by surmises, jealousies, conjectures,
And of so easy and so plain a stop
That the blunt monster with uncounted heads,
The still-discordant wav'ring multitude,
Can play upon it. But what need I thus
My well-known body to anatomize
Among my household? Why is Rumour here?
I run before King Harry's victory,
Who, in a bloody field by Shrewsbury,
Hath beaten down young Hotspur and his troops,
Quenching the flame of bold rebellion
Even with the rebels' blood. But what mean I
To speak so true at first? My office is
To noise abroad that Harry Monmouth fell
Under the wrath of noble Hotspur's sword,
And that the King before the Douglas' rage
Stoop'd his anointed head as low as death.
This have I rumour'd through the peasant towns
Between that royal field of Shrewsbury
And this worm-eaten hold of ragged stone,
Where Hotspur's father, old Northumberland,
Lies crafty-sick. The posts come tiring on,
And not a man of them brings other news

Than they have learnt of me. From Rumour's tongues
They bring smooth comforts false, worse than true wrongs. [*Exit.*

ACT ONE

SCENE I. *Warkworth. Before Northumberland's castle.*

Enter LORD BARDOLPH.

LORD BARDOLPH Who keeps the gate here, ho?

The Porter opens the gate.

Where is the Earl?

PORTER What shall I say you are?

LORD BARDOLPH Tell thou the Earl
That the Lord Bardolph doth attend him here.

PORTER His lordship is walk'd forth into the orchard.
Please it your honour knock but at the gate,
And he himself will answer.

Enter NORTHUMBERLAND.

LORD BARDOLPH Here comes the Earl. [*Exit Porter.*

NORTHUMBERLAND What news, Lord Bardolph? Every minute now
Should be the father of some stratagem.
The times are wild; contention, like a horse
Full of high feeding, madly hath broke loose
And bears down all before him.

LORD BARDOLPH Noble Earl,
I bring you certain news from Shrewsbury.

NORTHUMBERLAND Good, an God will!

LORD BARDOLPH As good as heart can wish.
The King is almost wounded to the death;
And, in the fortune of my lord your son,
Prince Harry slain outright; and both the Blunts
Kill'd by the hand of Douglas; young Prince John,
And Westmoreland, and Stafford, fled the field;
And Harry Monmouth's brawn, the hulk Sir John,
Is prisoner to your son. O, such a day,
So fought, so followed, and so fairly won,
Came not till now to dignify the times,
Since Caesar's fortunes!

NORTHUMBERLAND How is this deriv'd?
Saw you the field? Came you from Shrewsbury?

LORD BARDOLPH I spake with one, my lord, that came from thence;
A gentleman well bred and of good name,
That freely rend'red me these news for true.

Enter TRAVERS.

NORTHUMBERLAND Here comes my servant Travers, whom I sent
On Tuesday last to listen after news.

LORD BARDOLPH My lord, I over-rode him on the way;
And he is furnish'd with no certainties
More than he haply may retail from me.

NORTHUMBERLAND Now, Travers, what good tidings comes with you?

TRAVERS My lord, Sir John Umfrevile turn'd me back
With joyful tidings; and, being better hors'd,
Out-rode me. After him came spurring hard
A gentleman, almost forspent with speed,
That stopp'd by me to breathe his bloodied horse.
He ask'd the way to Chester; and of him
I did demand what news from Shrewsbury.
He told me that rebellion had bad luck,
And that young Harry Percy's spur was cold.
With that he gave his able horse the head
And, bending forward, struck his armed heels
Against the panting sides of his poor jade
Up to the rowel-head; and starting so,
He seem'd in running to devour the way,
Staying no longer question.

NORTHUMBERLAND Ha! Again:
Said he young Harry Percy's spur was cold?
Of Hotspur, Coldspur? that rebellion
Had met ill luck?

LORD BARDOLPH My lord, I'll tell you what:
If my young lord your son have not the day,
Upon mine honour, for a silken point
I'll give my barony. Never talk of it.

NORTHUMBERLAND Why should that gentleman that rode by Travers
Give then such instances of loss?

LORD BARDOLPH Who – he?
He was some hilding fellow that had stol'n
The horse he rode on and, upon my life,
Spoke at a venture. Look, here comes more news.

Enter MORTON.

NORTHUMBERLAND Yea, this man's brow, like to a title-leaf,
Foretells the nature of a tragic volume.
So looks the strand whereon the imperious flood
Hath left a witness'd usurpation.
Say, Morton, didst thou come from Shrewsbury?

MORTON I ran from Shrewsbury, my noble lord;
Where hateful death put on his ugliest mask

To fright our party.
NORTHUMBERLAND How doth my son and brother?
Thou tremblest; and the whiteness in thy cheek
Is apter than thy tongue to tell thy errand.
Even such a man, so faint, so spiritless,
So dull, so dead in look, so woe-begone,
Drew Priam's curtain in the dead of night
And would have told him half his Troy was burnt;
But Priam found the fire ere he his tongue,
And I my Percy's death ere thou report'st it.
This thou wouldst say: 'Your son did thus and thus;
Your brother thus; so fought the noble Douglas' –
Stopping my greedy ear with their bold deeds;
But in the end, to stop my ear indeed,
Thou hast a sigh to blow away this praise,
Ending with 'Brother, son, and all, are dead'.
MORTON Douglas is living, and your brother, yet;
But for my lord your son –
NORTHUMBERLAND Why, he is dead.
See what a ready tongue suspicion hath!
He that but fears the thing he would not know
Hath by instinct knowledge from others' eyes
That what he fear'd is chanced. Yet speak, Morton;
Tell thou an earl his divination lies,
And I will take it as a sweet disgrace
And make thee rich for doing me such wrong.
MORTON You are too great to be by me gainsaid;
Your spirit is too true, your fears too certain.
NORTHUMBERLAND Yet, for all this, say not that Percy's dead.
I see a strange confession in thine eye;
Thou shak'st thy head, and hold'st it fear or sin
To speak a truth. If he be slain, say so:
The tongue offends not that reports his death;
And he doth sin that doth belie the dead,
Not he which says the dead is not alive. –
Yet the first bringer of unwelcome news
Hath but a losing office, and his tongue
Sounds ever after as a sullen bell,
Rememb'red tolling a departing friend.
LORD BARDOLPH I cannot think, my lord, your son is dead.
MORTON I am sorry I should force you to believe
That which I would to God I had not seen;
But these mine eyes saw him in bloody state,
Rend'ring faint quittance, wearied and outbreath'd,
To Harry Monmouth, whose swift wrath beat down
The never-daunted Percy to the earth,
From whence with life he never more sprung up.
In few, his death – whose spirit lent a fire
Even to the dullest peasant in his camp –
Being bruited once, took fire and heat away
From the best-temper'd courage in his troops;
For from his metal was his party steeled;
Which once in him abated, all the rest
Turn'd on themselves, like dull and heavy lead.
And as the thing that's heavy in itself
Upon enforcement flies with greatest speed,
So did our men, heavy in Hotspur's loss,
Lend to this weight such lightness with their fear
That arrows fled not swifter toward their aim
Than did our soldiers, aiming at their safety,
Fly from the field. Then was that noble Worcester
Too soon ta'en prisoner; and that furious Scot,
The bloody Douglas, whose well-labouring sword
Had three times slain th' appearance of the King,
Gan vail his stomach and did grace the shame
Of those that turn'd their backs, and in his flight,
Stumbling in fear, was took. The sum of all
Is that the King hath won, and hath sent out
A speedy power to encounter you, my lord,
Under the conduct of young Lancaster
And Westmoreland. This is the news at full.
NORTHUMBERLAND For this I shall have time enough to mourn.
In poison there is physic; and these news,
Having been well, that would have made me sick,
Being sick, have in some measure made me well;
And as the wretch whose ever-weak'ned joints,
Like strengthless hinges, buckle under life,
Impatient of his fit, breaks like a fire
Out of his keeper's arms, even so my limbs,
Weak'ned with grief, being now enrag'd with grief,
Are thrice themselves. Hence, therefore, thou nice crutch!
A scaly gauntlet now with joints of steel
Must glove this hand; and hence, thou sickly coif!
Thou art a guard too wanton for the head
Which princes, flesh'd with conquest, aim to hit.
Now bind my brows with iron; and approach
The ragged'st hour that time and spite dare bring
To frown upon th' enrag'd Northumberland!
Let heaven kiss earth! Now let not Nature's hand
Keep the wild flood confin'd! Let order die!
And let this world no longer be a stage
To feed contention in a ling'ring act;

But let one spirit of the first-born Cain
Reign in all bosoms, that, each heart being set
On bloody courses, the rude scene may end
And darkness be the burier of the dead!

LORD BARDOLPH This strained passion doth you wrong, my lord.

MORTON Sweet Earl, divorce not wisdom from your honour.
The lives of all your loving complices
Lean on your health; the which, if you give o'er
To stormy passion, must perforce decay.
You cast th' event of war, my noble lord,
And summ'd the account of chance before you said
'Let us make head'. It was your presurmise
That in the dole of blows your son might drop.
You knew he walk'd o'er perils on an edge,
More likely to fall in than to get o'er;
You were advis'd his flesh was capable
Of wounds and scars, and that his forward spirit
Would lift him where most trade of danger rang'd;
Yet did you say 'Go forth'; and none of this,
Though strongly apprehended, could restrain
The stiff-borne action. What hath then befall'n,
Or what hath this bold enterprise brought forth
More than that being which was like to be?

LORD BARDOLPH We all that are engaged to this loss
Knew that we ventured on such dangerous seas
That if we wrought out life 'twas ten to one;
And yet we ventur'd, for the gain propos'd
Chok'd the respect of likely peril fear'd;
And since we are o'erset, venture again.
Come, we will all put forth, body and goods.

MORTON 'Tis more than time. And, my most noble lord,
I hear for certain, and dare speak the truth:
The gentle Archbishop of York is up
With well-appointed pow'rs. He is a man
Who with a double surety binds his followers.
My lord your son had only but the corpse,
But shadows and the shows of men, to fight;
For that same word 'rebellion' did divide
The action of their bodies from their souls;
And they did fight with queasiness, constrain'd,
As men drink potions; that their weapons only
Seem'd on our side, but for their spirits and souls
This word 'rebellion' – it had froze them up,
As fish are in a pond. But now the Bishop
Turns insurrection to religion.
Suppos'd sincere and holy in his thoughts,
He's follow'd both with body and with mind;
And doth enlarge his rising with the blood
Of fair King Richard, scrap'd from Pomfret stones;
Derives from heaven his quarrel and his cause;
Tells them he doth bestride a bleeding land,
Gasping for life under great Bolingbroke;
And more and less do flock to follow him.

NORTHUMBERLAND I knew of this before; but, to speak truth,
This present grief had wip'd it from my mind.
Go in with me; and counsel every man
The aptest way for safety and revenge.
Get posts and letters, and make friends with speed –
Never so few, and never yet more need. [*Exeunt.*

SCENE II. *London. A street.*

Enter SIR JOHN FALSTAFF, with his Page bearing his sword and buckler.

FALSTAFF Sirrah, you giant, what says the doctor to my water?

PAGE He said, sir, the water itself was a good healthy water; but for the party that owed it, he might have moe diseases than he knew for.

FALSTAFF Men of all sorts take a pride to gird at me. The brain of this foolish-compounded clay, man, is not able to invent anything that intends to laughter, more than I invent or is invented on me. I am not only witty in myself, but the cause that wit is in other men. I do here walk before thee like a sow that hath overwhelm'd all her litter but one. If the Prince put thee into my service for any other reason than to set me off, why then I have no judgment. Thou whoreson mandrake, thou art fitter to be worn in my cap than to wait at my heels. I was never mann'd with an agate till now; but I will inset you neither in gold nor silver, but in vile apparel, and send you back again to your master, for a jewel – the juvenal, the Prince your master, whose chin is not yet fledge. I will sooner have a beard grow in the palm of my hand than he shall get one off his cheek; and yet he will not stick to say his face is a face-royal. God may finish it when he will, 'tis not a hair amiss yet. He may keep it still at a face-royal, for a barber shall never earn sixpence out of it; and yet he'll be crowing as if he had writ man ever since his father was a bachelor. He may keep his own grace, but he's almost out of mine, I can assure him. What said Master Dommelton about the satin for my short cloak and my slops?

PAGE He said, sir, you should procure him better assurance than Bardolph. He would not take his band and yours; he liked not the security.

FALSTAFF Let him be damn'd, like the Glutton; pray God his tongue be hotter! A whoreson Achitophel! A rascal-yea-forsooth knave, to bear a gentleman in hand, and then stand upon security! The whoreson smooth-pates do now wear nothing but high shoes, and bunches of keys at their girdles; and if a man is through with them in honest taking-up, then they must stand upon security. I had as lief they would put ratsbane in my mouth as offer to stop it with security. I look'd 'a should have sent me two and twenty yards of satin, as I am a true knight, and he sends me security. Well, he may sleep in security; for he hath the horn of abundance, and the lightness of his wife shines through it; and yet cannot he see, though he have his own lanthorn to light him. Where's Bardolph?

PAGE He's gone into Smithfield to buy your worship a horse.

FALSTAFF I bought him in Paul's, and he'll buy me a horse in Smithfield. An I could get me but a wife in the stews, I were mann'd, hors'd, and wiv'd.

Enter the LORD CHIEF JUSTICE and Servant.

PAGE Sir, here comes the nobleman that committed the Prince for striking him about Bardolph.

FALSTAFF Wait close; I will not see him.

CHIEF JUSTICE What's he that goes there?

SERVANT Falstaff, an't please your lordship.

CHIEF JUSTICE He that was in question for the robb'ry?

SERVANT He, my lord; but he hath since done good service at Shrewsbury, and, as I hear, is now going with some charge to the Lord John of Lancaster.

CHIEF JUSTICE What, to York? Call him back again.

SERVANT Sir John Falstaff!

FALSTAFF Boy, tell him I am deaf.

PAGE You must speak louder; my master is deaf.

CHIEF JUSTICE I am sure he is, to the hearing of anything good. Go, pluck him by the elbow; I must speak with him.

SERVANT Sir John!

FALSTAFF What! a young knave, and begging! Is there not wars? Is there not employment? Doth not the King lack subjects? Do not the rebels need soldiers? Though it be a shame to be on any side but one, it is worse shame to beg than to be on the worst side, were it worse than the name of rebellion can tell how to make it.

SERVANT You mistake me, sir.

FALSTAFF Why, sir, did I say you were an honest man? Setting my knighthood and my soldiership aside, I had lied in my throat if I had said so.

SERVANT I pray you, sir, then set your knighthood and your soldiership aside; and give me leave to tell you you lie in your throat, if you say I am any other than an honest man.

FALSTAFF I give thee leave to tell me so! I lay aside that which grows to me! If thou get'st any leave of me, hang me; if thou tak'st leave, thou wert better be hang'd. You hunt counter. Hence! Avaunt!

SERVANT Sir, my lord would speak with you.

CHIEF JUSTICE Sir John Falstaff, a word with you.

FALSTAFF My good lord! God give your lordship good time of day. I am glad to see your lordship abroad. I heard say your lordship was sick; I hope your lordship goes abroad by advice. Your lordship, though not clean past your youth, hath yet some smack of age in you, some relish of the saltness of time; and I most humbly beseech your lordship to have a reverend care of your health.

CHIEF JUSTICE Sir John, I sent for you before your expedition to Shrewsbury.

FALSTAFF An't please your lordship, I hear his Majesty is return'd with some discomfort from Wales.

CHIEF JUSTICE I talk not of his Majesty. You would not come when I sent for you.

FALSTAFF And I hear, moreover, his Highness is fall'n into this same whoreson apoplexy.

CHIEF JUSTICE Well, God mend him! I pray you let me speak with you.

FALSTAFF This apoplexy, as I take it, is a kind of lethargy, an't please your lordship, a kind of sleeping in the blood, a whoreson tingling.

CHIEF JUSTICE What tell you me of it? Be it as it is.

FALSTAFF It hath it original from much grief, from study, and perturbation of the brain. I have read the cause of his effects in Galen; it is a kind of deafness.

CHIEF JUSTICE I think you are fall'n into the disease, for you hear not what I say to you.

FALSTAFF Very well, my lord, very well. Rather an't please you, it is the disease of not listening, the malady of not marking, that I am troubled withal.

CHIEF JUSTICE To punish you by the heels would amend the attention of your ears; and I care not if I do become your physician.

FALSTAFF I am as poor as Job, my lord, but not so patient. Your lordship may minister the potion of imprisonment to me in respect of poverty; but how I should be your patient to follow your prescriptions, the wise may make some dram of a scruple, or indeed a scruple itself.

CHIEF JUSTICE I sent for you, when there were matters against you for your life, to come speak with me.

FALSTAFF As I was then advis'd by my learned counsel in the laws of this land-service, I did not come.

CHIEF JUSTICE Well, the truth is, Sir John, you live in great infamy.

FALSTAFF He that buckles himself in my belt cannot live in less.

CHIEF JUSTICE Your means are very slender, and your waste is great.

FALSTAFF I would it were otherwise; I would my means were greater and my waist slenderer.

CHIEF JUSTICE You have misled the youthful Prince.

FALSTAFF The young Prince hath misled me. I am the fellow with the great belly, and he my dog.

CHIEF JUSTICE Well, I am loath to gall a newheal'd wound. Your day's service at Shrewsbury hath a little gilded over your night's exploit on Gadshill. You may thank th' unquiet time for your quiet o'erposting that action.

FALSTAFF My lord –

CHIEF JUSTICE But since all is well, keep it so: wake not a sleeping wolf.

FALSTAFF To wake a wolf is as bad as smell a fox.

CHIEF JUSTICE What! you are as a candle, the better part burnt out.

FALSTAFF A wassail candle, my lord – all tallow; if I did say of wax, my growth would approve the truth.

CHIEF JUSTICE There is not a white hair in your face but should have his effect of gravity.

FALSTAFF His effect of gravy, gravy, gravy.

CHIEF JUSTICE You follow the young Prince up and down, like his ill angel.

FALSTAFF Not so, my lord. Your ill angel is light; but I hope he that looks upon me will take me without weighing. And yet in some respects, I grant, I cannot go – I cannot tell. Virtue is of so little regard in these costermongers' times that true valour is turn'd berod; pregnancy is made a tapster, and his quick wit wasted in giving reckonings; all the other gifts appertinent to man, as the malice of this age shapes them, are not worth a gooseberry. You that are old consider not the capacities of us that are young; you do measure the heat of our livers with the bitterness of your galls; and we that are in the vaward of our youth, I must confess, are wags too.

CHIEF JUSTICE Do you set down your name in the scroll of youth, that are written down old with all the characters of age? Have you not a moist eye, a dry hand, a yellow cheek, a white beard, a decreasing leg, an increasing belly? Is not your voice broken, your wind short, your chin double, your wit single, and every part about you blasted with antiquity? And will you yet call yourself young? Fie, fie, fie, Sir John!

FALSTAFF My lord, I was born about three of the clock in the afternoon, with a white head and something a round belly. For my voice – I have lost it with hallooing and singing of anthems. To approve my youth further, I will not. The truth is, I am only old in judgement and understanding; and he that will caper with me for a thousand marks, let him lend me the money, and have at him. For the box of the ear that the Prince gave you – he gave it like a rude prince, and you took it like a sensible lord. I have check'd him for it; and the young lion repents – marry, not in ashes and sackcloth, but in new silk and old sack.

CHIEF JUSTICE Well, God send the Prince a better companion!

FALSTAFF God send the companion a better prince! I cannot rid my hands of him.

CHIEF JUSTICE Well, the King hath sever'd you. I hear you are going with Lord John of Lancaster against the Archbishop and the Earl of Northumberland.

FALSTAFF Yea; I thank your pretty sweet wit for it. But look you pray, all you that kiss my Lady Peace at home, that our armies join not in a hot day; for, by the Lord, I take but two shirts out with me, and I mean not to sweat extraordinarily. If it be a hot day, and I brandish anything but a bottle, I would I might never spit white again. There is not a dangerous action can peep out his head but I am thrust upon it. Well, I cannot last ever; but it was alway yet the trick of our English nation, if they have a good thing, to make it too common. If ye will needs say I am an old man, you should give me rest. I would to God my name were not so terrible to the enemy as it is. I were better to be eaten to death with a rust than to be scoured to nothing with perpetual motion.

CHIEF JUSTICE Well, be honest, be honest; and God bless your expedition!

FALSTAFF Will your lordship lend me a thousand pound to furnish me forth?

CHIEF JUSTICE Not a penny, not a penny; you are too impatient to bear crosses. Fare you well. Commend me to my cousin Westmoreland.

[*Exeunt Chief Justice and Servant.*

FALSTAFF If I do, fillip me with a three-man beetle. A man can no more separate age and covetousness than 'a can part young limbs and lechery; but the gout galls the one, and the pox pinches the other; and so both the degrees prevent my curses. Boy!

PAGE Sir?

FALSTAFF What money is in my purse?
PAGE Seven groats and two pence.
FALSTAFF I can get no remedy against this consumption of the purse; borrowing only lingers and lingers it out, but the disease is incurable. Go bear this letter to my Lord of Lancaster; this to the Prince; this to the Earl of Westmoreland; and this to old Mistress Ursula, whom I have weekly sworn to marry since I perceiv'd the first white hair of my chin. About it; you know where to find me. [*Exit Page*] A pox of this gout! or, a gout of this pox! for the one or the other plays the rogue with my great toe. 'Tis no matter if I do halt; I have the wars for my colour, and my pension shall seem the more reasonable. A good wit will make use of anything. I will turn diseases to commodity.
[*Exit.*

SCENE III. *York. The Archbishop's palace.*

Enter the ARCHBISHOP, THOMAS MOWBRAY the Earl Marshal, LORD HASTINGS and LORD BARDOLPH.

ARCHBISHOP Thus have you heard our cause and known our means;
And, my most noble friends, I pray you all
Speak plainly your opinions of our hopes –
And first, Lord Marshal, what say you to it?
MOWBRAY I well allow the occasion of our arms;
But gladly would be better satisfied
How, in our means, we should advance ourselves
To look with forehead bold and big enough
Upon the power and puissance of the King.
HASTINGS Our present musters grow upon the file
To five and twenty thousand men of choice;
And our supplies live largely in the hope
Of great Northumberland, whose bosom burns
With an incensed fire of injuries.
LORD BARDOLPH The question then, Lord Hastings, standeth thus:
Whether our present five and twenty thousand
May hold up head without Northumberland?
HASTINGS With him, we may.
LORD BARDOLPH Yea, marry, there's the point;
But if without him we be thought too feeble,
My judgment is we should not step too far
Till we had his assistance by the hand;
For, in a theme so bloody-fac'd as this,
Conjecture, expectation, and surmise
Of aids incertain, should not be admitted.
ARCHBISHOP 'Tis very true, Lord Bardolph; for indeed
It was young Hotspur's case at Shrewsbury.
LORD BARDOLPH It was, my lord; who lin'd himself with hope,
Eating the air and promise of supply,
Flatt'ring himself in project of a power
Much smaller than the smallest of his thoughts;
And so, with great imagination
Proper to madmen, led his powers to death,
And, winking, leapt into destruction.
HASTINGS But, by your leave, it never yet did hurt
To lay down likelihoods and forms of hope.
LORD BARDOLPH Yes, if this present quality of war –
Indeed the instant action, a cause on foot –
Lives so in hope, as in an early spring
We see th' appearing buds; which to prove fruit
Hope gives not so much warrant, as despair
That frosts will bite them. When we mean to build,
We first survey the plot, then draw the model;
And when we see the figure of the house,
Then must we rate the cost of the erection;
Which if we find outweighs ability,
What do we then but draw anew the model
In fewer offices, or at least desist
To build at all? Much more, in this great work –
Which is almost to pluck a kingdom down
And set another up – should we survey
The plot of situation and the model,
Consent upon a sure foundation,
Question surveyors, know our own estate
How able such a work to undergo –
To weigh against his opposite; or else
We fortify in paper and in figures,
Using the names of men instead of men;
Like one that draws the model of a house
Beyond his power to build it; who, half through,
Gives o'er and leaves his part-created cost
A naked subject to the weeping clouds
And waste for churlish winter's tyranny.
HASTINGS Grant that our hopes – yet likely of fair birth –
Should be still-born, and that we now possess'd
The utmost man of expectation,
I think we are so a body strong enough,
Even as we are, to equal with the King.
LORD BARDOLPH What, is the King but five and twenty thousand?
HASTINGS To us no more; nay, not so much, Lord Bardolph;
For his divisions, as the times do brawl,
Are in three heads: one power against the French,
And one against Glendower; perforce a third
Must take up us. So is the unfirm King
In three divided; and his coffers sound
With hollow poverty and emptiness.
ARCHBISHOP That he should draw his several strengths together

And come against us in full puissance
Need not be dreaded.
HASTINGS If he should do so,
He leaves his back unarm'd, the French and Welsh
Baying him at the heels. Never fear that.
LORD BARDOLPH Who is it like should lead his forces hither?
HASTINGS The Duke of Lancaster and Westmoreland;
Against the Welsh, himself and Harry Monmouth;
But who is substituted against the French
I have no certain notice.
ARCHBISHOP Let us on,
And publish the occasion of our arms.
The commonwealth is sick of their own choice;
Their over-greedy love hath surfeited.
An habitation giddy and unsure
Hath he that buildeth on the vulgar heart.
O thou fond many, with what loud applause
Didst thou beat heaven with blessing Bolingbroke
Before he was what thou wouldst have him be!
And being now trimm'd in thine own desires,
Thou, beastly feeder, art so full of him
That thou provok'st thyself to cast him up.
So, so, thou common dog, didst thou disgorge
Thy glutton bosom of the royal Richard;
And now thou wouldst eat thy dead vomit up,
And howl'st to find it. What trust is in these times?
They that, when Richard liv'd, would have him die
Are now become enamour'd on his grave.
Thou that threw'st dust upon his goodly head,
When through proud London he came sighing on
After th' admired heels of Bolingbroke,
Criest now 'O earth, yield us that king again,
And take thou this!' O thoughts of men accurs'd!
Past and to come seems best; things present, worst.
MOWBRAY Shall we go draw our numbers, and set on?
HASTINGS We are time's subjects, and time bids be gone.
[*Exeunt*.

ACT TWO

SCENE I. *London. A street.*

Enter Hostess with two officers, FANG and SNARE.

HOSTESS Master Fang, have you ent'red the action?

FANG It is ent'red.

HOSTESS Where's your yeoman? Is't a lusty yeoman? Will 'a stand to't?

FANG Sirrah, where's Snare?

HOSTESS O Lord, ay! good Master Snare.

SNARE Here, here.

FANG Snare, we must arrest Sir John Falstaff.

HOSTESS Yea, good Master Snare; I have ent'red him and all.

SNARE It may chance cost some of us our lives, for he will stab.

HOSTESS Alas the day! take heed of him; he stabb'd me in mine own house, and that most beastly. In good faith, 'a cares not what mischief he does, if his weapon be out; he will foin like any devil; he will spare neither man, woman, nor child.

FANG If I can close with him, I care not for his thrust.

HOSTESS No, nor I neither; I'll be at your elbow.

FANG An I but fist him once; an 'a come but within my vice!

HOSTESS I am undone by his going; I warrant you, he's an infinitive thing upon my score. Good Master Fang, hold him sure. Good Master Snare, let him not scape. 'A comes continuantly to Piecorner – saving your manhoods – to buy a saddle; and he is indited to dinner to the Lubber's Head in Lumbert Street, to Master Smooth's the silkman. I pray you, since my exion is ent'red, and my case so openly known to the world, let him be brought in to his answer. A hundred mark is a long one for a poor lone woman to bear; and I have borne, and borne, and borne; and have been fubb'd off, and fubb'd off, and fubb'd off, from this day to that day, that it is a shame to be thought on. There is no honesty in such dealing; unless a woman should be made an ass and a beast, to bear every knave's wrong.

Enter SIR JOHN FALSTAFF, Page, and BARDOLPH.

Yonder he comes; and that arrant malmsey-nose knave, Bardolph, with him. Do your offices, do your offices, Master Fang and Master Snare; do me, do me, do me your offices.

FALSTAFF How now! whose mare's dead? What's the matter?

FANG Sir John, I arrest you at the suit of Mistress Quickly.

FALSTAFF Away, varlets! Draw, Bardolph. Cut me off the villain's head. Throw the quean in the channel.

HOSTESS Throw me in the channel! I'll throw thee in the channel. Wilt thou? wilt thou? thou bastardly rogue! Murder, murder! Ah, thou honeysuckle villain! wilt thou kill God's officers and the King's? Ah, thou honey-seed rogue! thou art a honey-seed; a man-queller and a woman-queller.

FALSTAFF Keep them off, Bardolph.

FANG A rescue! a rescue!

HOSTESS Good people, bring a rescue or two. Thou wot, wot thou! thou wot, wot ta? Do, do, thou rogue! do, thou hemp-seed!

PAGE Away, you scullion! you rampallian! you fustilarian! I'll tickle your catastrophe.

Enter the LORD CHIEF JUSTICE and his Men.

CHIEF JUSTICE What is the matter? Keep the peace here, ho!

HOSTESS Good my lord, be good to me. I beseech you, stand to me.

CHIEF JUSTICE How now, Sir John! what, are you brawling here?
Doth this become your place, your time, and business?
You should have been well on your way to York.
Stand from him, fellow; wherefore hang'st thou upon him?

HOSTESS O my most worshipful lord, an't please your Grace, I am a poor widow of Eastcheap, and he is arrested at my suit.

CHIEF JUSTICE For what sum?

HOSTESS It is more than for some, my lord; it is for all – all I have. He hath eaten me out of house and home; he hath put all my substance into that fat belly of his. But I will have some of it out again, or I will ride thee a nights like the mare.

FALSTAFF I think I am as like to ride the mare, if I have any vantage of ground to get up.

CHIEF JUSTICE How comes this, Sir John? Fie! What man of good temper would endure this tempest of exclamation? Are you not ashamed to enforce a poor widow to so rough a course to come by her own?

FALSTAFF What is the gross sum that I owe thee?

HOSTESS Marry, if thou wert an honest man, thyself and the money too. Thou didst swear to me upon a parcel-gilt goblet, sitting in my Dolphin chamber, at the round table, by a sea-coal fire, upon Wednesday in Wheeson week, when the Prince broke thy head for liking his father to a singing-man of Windsor – thou didst swear to me then, as I was washing thy wound, to marry me and make me my lady thy wife. Canst thou deny it? Did not goodwife Keech, the butcher's wife, come in then and call me gossip Quickly? Coming in to borrow a mess of vinegar, telling us she had a good dish of prawns, whereby thou didst desire to eat some, whereby I told thee they were ill for a green wound? And didst thou not, when she was gone down stairs, desire me to be no more so familiarity with such poor people, saying that ere long they should call me madam? And didst thou not kiss me, and bid me fetch thee thirty shillings? I put thee now to thy book-oath. Deny it, if thou canst.

FALSTAFF My lord, this is a poor mad soul, and she says up and down the town that her eldest son is like you. She hath been in good case, and, the truth is, poverty hath distracted her. But for these foolish officers, I beseech you I may have redress against them.

CHIEF JUSTICE Sir John, Sir John, I am well acquainted with your manner of wrenching the true cause the false way. It is not a confident brow, nor the throng of words that come with such more than impudent sauciness from you, can thrust me from a level consideration. You have, as it appears to me, practis'd upon the easy yielding spirit of this woman, and made her serve your uses both in purse and in person.

HOSTESS Yea, in truth, my lord.

CHIEF JUSTICE Pray thee, peace. Pay her the debt you owe her, and unpay the villainy you have done with her; the one you may do with sterling money, and the other with current repentance.

FALSTAFF My lord, I will not undergo this sneap without reply. You call honourable boldness impudent sauciness; if a man will make curtsy and say nothing, he is virtuous. No, my lord, my humble duty remembr'red, I will not be your suitor. I say to you I do desire deliverance from these officers, being upon hasty employment in the King's affairs.

CHIEF JUSTICE You speak as having power to do wrong; but answer in th' effect of your reputation, and satisfy the poor woman.

FALSTAFF Come hither hostess.

Enter GOWER

CHIEF JUSTICE Now, Master Gower, what news?

GOWER The King, my lord, and Harry Prince of Wales
Are near at hand. The rest the paper tells.
[*Gives a letter.*

FALSTAFF As I am a gentleman!

HOSTESS Faith, you said so before.

FALSTAFF As I am a gentleman! Come, no more words of it.

HOSTESS By this heavenly ground I tread on, I must be fain to pawn both my plate and the tapestry of my dining-chambers.

FALSTAFF Glasses, glasses, is the only drinking; and for thy walls, a pretty slight drollery, or the story of the Prodigal, or the German hunting, in water-work, is worth a thousand of these bed-hangers and these fly-bitten tapestries. Let it be ten pound, if thou canst. Come, an 'twere not for thy humours, there's not a better wench in England. Go, wash thy face, and draw the action. Come, thou must not be in this humour with me; dost not know me? Come, come, I know thou wast set on to this.

HOSTESS Pray thee, Sir John, let it be but twenty nobles; i' faith, I am loath to pawn my plate, so God save me, la!

FALSTAFF Let it alone; I'll make other shift. You'll be a fool still.

HOSTESS Well, you shall have it, though I pawn my gown. I hope you'll come to supper. You'll pay me all together?

FALSTAFF Will I live? [*To Bardolph*] Go, with her, with her; hook on, hook on.

HOSTESS Will you have Doll Tearsheet meet you at supper?

FALSTAFF No more words; let's have her.

[*Exeunt Hostess, Bardolph, and Officers.*

CHIEF JUSTICE I have heard better news.

FALSTAFF What's the news, my lord?

CHIEF JUSTICE Where lay the King to-night?

GOWER At Basingstoke, my lord.

FALSTAFF I hope, my lord, all's well. What is the news, my lord?

CHIEF JUSTICE Come all his forces back?

GOWER No; fifteen hundred foot, five hundred horse,
Are march'd up to my Lord of Lancaster,
Against Northumberland and the Archbishop.

FALSTAFF Comes the King back from Wales, my noble lord?

CHIEF JUSTICE You shall have letters of me presently.
Come, go along with me, good Master Gower.

FALSTAFF My lord!

CHIEF JUSTICE What's the matter?

FALSTAFF Master Gower, shall I entreat you with me to dinner?

GOWER I must wait upon my good lord here, I thank you, good Sir John.

CHIEF JUSTICE Sir John, you loiter here too long, being you are to take soldiers up in counties as you go.

FALSTAFF Will you sup with me, Master Gower?

CHIEF JUSTICE What foolish master taught you these manners, Sir John?

FALSTAFF Master Gower, if they become me not, he was a fool that taught them me. This is the right fencing grace, my lord: tap for tap, and so part fair.

CHIEF JUSTICE Now, the Lord lighten thee!
Thou art a great fool. [*Exeunt.*

SCENE II. *London. Another street.*

Enter PRINCE HENRY and POINS.

PRINCE Before God, I am exceeding weary.

POINS Is't come to that? I had thought weariness durst not have attach'd one of so high blood.

PRINCE Faith, it does me; though it discolours the complexion of my greatness to acknowledge it. Doth it not show vilely in me to desire small beer?

POINS Why, a prince should not be so loosely studied as to remember so weak a composition.

PRINCE Belike then my appetite was not princely got; for, by my troth, I do now remember the poor creature, small beer. But indeed these humble considerations make me out of love with my greatness. What a disgrace is it to me to remember thy name, or to know thy face to-morrow, or to take note how many pair of silk stockings thou hast – viz., these, and those that were thy peach-colour'd ones – or to bear the inventory of thy shirts – as, one for superfluity, and another for use! But that the tennis-court-keeper knows better than I; for it is a low ebb of linen with thee when thou keepest not racket there; as thou hast not done a great while, because the rest of thy low countries have made a shift to eat up thy holland. And God knows whether those that bawl out the ruins of thy linen shall inherit his kingdom; but the midwives say the children are not in the fault; whereupon the world increases, and kindreds are mightily strengthened.

POINS How ill it follows, after you have laboured so hard, you should talk so idly! Tell me, how many good young princes would do so, their fathers being so sick as yours at this time is?

PRINCE Shall I tell thee one thing, Poins?

POINS Yes, faith; and let it be an excellent good thing.

PRINCE It shall serve among wits of no higher breeding than thine.

POINS Go to; I stand the push of your one thing that you will tell.

PRINCE Marry, I tell thee it is not meet that I should be sad, now my father is sick; albeit I could tell to thee – as to one it pleases me, for fault of a better, to call my friend – I could be sad and sad indeed too.

POINS Very hardly upon such a subject.

PRINCE By this hand, thou thinkest me as far in the devil's book as thou and Falstaff for obduracy and persistency: let the end try the man. But I tell thee my heart bleeds inwardly that my father is so sick; and keeping such vile company as thou art hath in reason taken from me all ostentation of sorrow.

POINS The reason?

PRINCE What wouldst thou think of me if I should weep?

POINS I would think thee a most princely hypocrite.

PRINCE It would be every man's thought; and thou art a blessed fellow to think as every man thinks. Never a man's thought in the world keeps the road-way better than thine. Every man would think me an hypocrite indeed. And what accites your most worshipful thought to think so?

POINS Why, because you have been so lewd and so much engraffed to Falstaff.

PRINCE And to thee.

POINS By this light, I am well spoke on; I can hear it with mine own ears. The worst that they can say of me is that I am a second brother and that I am a proper fellow of my hands; and those two things, I confess, I cannot help. By the mass, here comes Bardolph.

Enter BARDOLPH and Page.

PRINCE And the boy that I gave Falstaff. 'A had him from me Christian; and look if the fat villain have not transform'd him ape.

BARDOLPH God save your Grace!

PRINCE And yours, most noble Bardolph!

POINS Come, you virtuous ass, you bashful fool, must you be blushing? Wherefore blush you now? What a maidenly man-at-arms are you become! Is't such a matter to get a pottle-pot's maidenhead?

PAGE 'A calls me e'en now, my lord, through a red lattice, and I could discern no part of his face from the window. At last I spied his eyes; and methought he had made two holes in the alewife's new petticoat, and so peep'd through.

PRINCE Has not the boy profited?

BARDOLPH Away, you whoreson upright rabbit, away!

PAGE Away, you rascally Althaea's dream, away!

PRINCE Instruct us, boy; what dream, boy?

PAGE Marry, my lord, Althaea dreamt she was delivered of a fire-brand; and therefore I call him her dream.

PRINCE A crown's worth of good interpretation. There 'tis, boy. [*Giving a crown.*

POINS O that this blossom could be kept from cankers! Well, there is sixpence to preserve thee.

BARDOLPH An you do not make him be hang'd among you, the gallows shall have wrong.

PRINCE And how doth thy master, Bardolph?

BARDOLPH Well, my lord. He heard of your Grace's coming to town. There's a letter for you.

POINS Deliver'd with good respect. And how doth the martlemas, your master?

BARDOLPH In bodily health, sir.

POINS Marry, the immortal part needs a physician; but that moves not him. Though that be sick, it dies not.

PRINCE I do allow this wen to be as familiar with me as my dog; and he holds his place, for look you how he writes.

POINS [*Reads*] 'John Falstaff, knight' – Every man must know that as oft as he has occasion to name himself, even like those that are kin to the King; for they never prick their finger but they say 'There's some of the King's blood spilt'. 'How comes that?' says he that takes upon him not to conceive. The answer is as ready as a borrower's cap: 'I am the King's poor cousin, sir'.

PRINCE Nay, they will be kin to us, or they will fetch it from Japhet. But the letter: [*Reads*] 'Sir John Falstaff, knight, to the son of the King nearest his father, Harry Prince of Wales, greeting'.

POINS Why, this is a certificate.

PRINCE Peace! [*Reads*] 'I will imitate the honourable Romans in brevity.' –

POINS He sure means brevity in breath, short-winded.

PRINCE [*Reads*] 'I commend me to thee, I commend thee, and I leave thee. Be not too familiar with Poins; for he misuses thy favours so much that he swears thou art to marry his sister Nell. Repent at idle times as thou mayst, and so farewell.

Thine, by yea and no – which is as much as to say as thou usest him – JACK FALSTAFF with my familiars, JOHN with my brothers and sisters, and SIR JOHN with all Europe.'

POINS My lord, I'll steep this letter in sack and make him eat it.

PRINCE That's to make him eat twenty o his words. But do you use me thus, Ned? Must I marry your sister?

POINS God send the wench no worse fortune. But I never said so.

PRINCE Well, thus we play the fools with the time, and the spirits of the wise sit in the clouds and mock us. Is your master here in London?

BARDOLPH Yea, my lord.

PRINCE Where sups he? Doth the old boar feed in the old frank?

BARDOLPH At the old place, my lord, in Eastcheap.

PRINCE What company?

PAGE Ephesians, my lord, of the old church.

PRINCE Sup any women with him?

PAGE None, my lord, but old Mistress Quickly and Mistress Doll Tearsheet.

PRINCE What pagan may that be?

PAGE A proper gentlewoman, sir, and a kinswoman of my master's.

PRINCE Even such kin as the parish heifers are to the town bull. Shall we steal upon them, Ned, at supper?

POINS I am your shadow, my lord; I'll follow you.

PRINCE Sirrah, you boy, and Bardolph, no word to your master that I am yet come to town. There's for your silence.

BARDOLPH I have no tongue, sir.

PAGE And for mine, sir, I will govern it.

PRINCE Fare you well; go. [*Exeunt Bardolph and Page*] This Doll Tearsheet should be some road.

POINS I warrant you, as common as the way between Saint Albans and London.

PRINCE How might we see Falstaff bestow himself to-night in his true colours, and not ourselves be seen?

POINS Put on two leathern jerkins and aprons, and wait upon him at his table as drawers.

PRINCE From a god to a bull? A heavy descension! It was Jove's case. From a prince to a prentice? A low transformation! That shall be mine; for in everything the purpose must weigh with the folly. Follow me, Ned. [*Exeunt.*

SCENE III. *Warkworth. Before the castle.*

Enter NORTHUMBERLAND, LADY NORTHUMBERLAND, and LADY PERCY.

NORTHUMBERLAND I pray thee, loving wife, and gentle daughter,
Give even way unto my rough affairs;
Put not you on the visage of the times
And be, like them, to Percy troublesome.

LADY NORTHUMBERLAND I have given over, I will speak no more.
Do what you will; your wisdom be your guide.

NORTHUMBERLAND Alas, sweet wife, my honour is at pawn;
And but my going nothing can redeem it.

LADY PERCY O, yet, for God's sake, go not to these wars!
The time was, father, that you broke your word,
When you were more endear'd to it than now;
When your own Percy, when my heart's dear Harry,
Threw many a northward look to see his father
Bring up his powers; but he did long in vain.
Who then persuaded you to stay at home?
There were two honours lost, yours and your son's.
For yours, the God of heaven brighten it!
For his, it stuck upon him as the sun
In the grey vault of heaven; and by his light
Did all the chivalry of England move
To do brave acts. He was indeed the glass
Wherein the noble youth did dress themselves.
He had no legs that practis'd not his gait;
And speaking thick, which nature made his blemish,
Became the accents of the valiant;
For those that could speak low and tardily
Would turn their own perfection to abuse
To seem like him: so that in speech, in gait,
In diet, in affections of delight,
In military rules, humours of blood,
He was the mark and glass, copy and book,
That fashion'd others. And him – O wondrous him!
O miracle of men! – him did you leave –
Second to none, unseconded by you –
To look upon the hideous god of war
In disadvantage, to abide a field
Where nothing but the sound of Hotspur's name
Did seem defensible. So you left him.
Never, O never, do his ghost the wrong
To hold your honour more precise and nice
With others than with him! Let them alone.
The Marshal and the Archbishop are strong.
Had my sweet Harry had but half their numbers,
To-day might I, hanging on Hotspur's neck,
Have talk'd of Monmouth's grave.

NORTHUMBERLAND Beshrew your heart,
Fair daughter, you do draw my spirits from me
With new lamenting ancient oversights.
But I must go and meet with danger there,
Or it will seek me in another place,
And find me worse provided.

LADY NORTHUMBERLAND O, fly to Scotland
Till that the nobles and the armed commons
Have of their puissance made a little taste.

LADY PERCY If they get ground and vantage of the King,
Then join you with them, like a rib of steel,
To make strength stronger; but, for all our loves,
First let them try themselves. So did your son;
He was so suff'red; so came I a widow;
And never shall have length of life enough
To rain upon remembrance with mine eyes,
That it may grow and sprout as high as heaven,

For recordation to my noble husband.

NORTHUMBERLAND Come, come, go in with me.
'Tis with my mind
As with the tide swell'd up unto his height,
That makes a still-stand, running neither way.
Fain would I go to meet the Archbishop,
But many thousand reasons hold me back.
I will resolve for Scotland. There am I,
Till time and vantage crave my company.

[*Exeunt.*

SCENE IV. *London. The Boar's Head Tavern in Eastcheap.*

Enter FRANCIS and another Drawer.

FRANCIS What the devil hast thou brought there – apple-johns? Thou knowest Sir John cannot endure an apple-john.

2 DRAWER Mass, thou say'st true. The Prince once set a dish of apple-johns before him, and told him there were five more Sir Johns; and, putting off his hat, said 'I will now take my leave of these six dry, round, old, withered knights'. It ang'red him to the heart; but he hath forgot that.

FRANCIS Why, then, cover and set them down; and see if thou canst find out Sneak's noise; Mistress Tearsheet would fain hear some music.

Enter third Drawer.

3 DRAWER Dispatch! The room where they supp'd is too hot; they'll come in straight.

FRANCIS Sirrah, here will be the Prince and Master Poins anon; and they will put on two of our jerkins and aprons; and Sir John must not know of it. Bardolph hath brought word.

3 DRAWER By the mass, here will be old utis; it will be an excellent stratagem.

2 DRAWER I'll see if I can find out Sneak.

[*Exeunt second and third Drawers.*

Enter Hostess and DOLL TEARSHEET.

HOSTESS I' faith, sweetheart, methinks now you are in an excellent good temperality. Your pulsidge beats as extraordinarily as heart would desire; and your colour, I warrant you, is as red as any rose, in good truth, la! But, i' faith, you have drunk too much canaries; and that's a marvellous searching wine, and it perfumes the blood ere one can say 'What's this?' How do you now?

DOLL Better than I was – hem.

HOSTESS Why, that's well said; a good heart's worth gold. Lo, here comes Sir John.

Enter FALSTAFF.

FALSTAFF [*Singing*] 'When Arthur first in court' – Empty the jordan. [*Exit Francis*] – [*Singing*] 'And was a worthy king' – How now, Mistress Doll!

HOSTESS Sick of a calm; yea, good faith.

FALSTAFF So is all her sect; an they be once in a calm, they are sick.

DOLL A pox damn you, you muddy rascal! Is that all the comfort you give me?

FALSTAFF You make fat rascals, Mistress Doll.

DOLL I make them! Gluttony and diseases make them: I make them not.

FALSTAFF If the cook help to make the gluttony, you help to make the diseases, Doll. We catch of you, Doll, we catch of you; grant that, my poor virtue, grant that.

DOLL Yea, joy, our chains and our jewels.

FALSTAFF 'Your brooches, pearls, and ouches.' For to serve bravely is to come halting off; you know, to come off the breach with his pike bent bravely, and to surgery bravely; to venture upon the charg'd chambers bravely –

DOLL Hang yourself, you muddy conger, hang yourself!

HOSTESS By my troth, this is the old fashion; you two never meet but you fall to some discord. You are both, i' good truth, as rheumatic as two dry toasts; you cannot one bear with another's confirmities. What the good-year! one must bear, and that must be you. You are the weaker vessel, as they say, the emptier vessel.

DOLL Can a weak empty vessel bear such a huge full hogshead? There's a whole merchant's venture of Bourdeaux stuff in him; you have not seen a hulk better stuff'd in the hold. Come, I'll be friends with thee, Jack. Thou art going to the wars; and whether I shall ever see thee again or no, there is nobody cares.

Re-enter FRANCIS.

FRANCIS Sir, Ancient Pistol's below and would speak with you.

DOLL Hang him, swaggering rascal! Let him not come hither; it is the foulmouth'dst rogue in England.

HOSTESS If he swagger, let him not come here. No, by my faith! I must live among my neighbours; I'll no swaggerers. I am in good name and fame with the very best. Shut the door. There comes no swaggerers here; I have not liv'd all this while to have swaggering now. Shut the door, I pray you.

FALSTAFF Dost thou hear, hostess?

HOSTESS Pray ye, pacify yourself, Sir John; there comes no swaggerers here.

FALSTAFF Dost thou hear? It is mine ancient.

HOSTESS Tilly-fally, Sir John, ne'er tell me; and your ancient swagg'rer comes not in my doors. I was before Master Tisick, the debuty, t' other day; and, as he said to me – 'twas no longer ago than Wednesday last i' good faith! – 'Neighbour Quickly,' says he – Master Dumbe, our minister, was by then – 'Neighbour Quickly,' says he 'receive those that are civil, for' said he 'you are in an ill name.' Now 'a said so, I can tell whereupon. 'For' says he 'you are an honest woman and well thought on, therefore take heed what guests you receive. Receive' says he 'no swaggering companions.' There comes none here. You would bless you to hear what he said. No, I'll no swagg'rers.

FALSTAFF He's no swagg'rer, hostess; a tame cheater, i' faith; you may stroke him as gently as a puppy greyhound. He'll not swagger with a Barbary hen, if her feathers turn back in any show of resistance. Call him up, drawer.

[Exit Francis.

HOSTESS Cheater, call you him? I will bar no honest man my house, nor no cheater; but I do not love swaggering, by my troth. I am the worse when one says 'swagger'. Feel, masters, how I shake; look you, I warrant you.

DOLL So you do, hostess.

HOSTESS Do I? Yea, in very truth, do I, an 'twere an aspen leaf. I cannot abide swagg'rers.

Enter PISTOL, BARDOLPH, and PAGE.

PISTOL God save you, Sir John!

FALSTAFF Welcome, Ancient Pistol. Here, Pistol, I charge you with a cup of sack; do you discharge upon mine hostess.

PISTOL I will discharge upon her, Sir John, with two bullets.

FALSTAFF She is pistol-proof, sir; you shall not hardly offend her.

HOSTESS Come, I'll drink no proofs nor no bullets. I'll drink no more than will do me good, for no man's pleasure, I.

PISTOL Then to you, Mistress Dorothy; I will charge you.

DOLL Charge me! I scorn you, scurvy companion. What! you poor, base, rascally, cheating, lack-linen mate! Away, you mouldy rogue, away! I am meat for your master.

PISTOL I know you, Mistress Dorothy.

DOLL Away, you cut-purse rascal! you filthy bung, away! By this wine, I'll thrust my knife in your mouldy chaps, an you play the saucy cuttle with me. Away, you bottle-ale rascal! you basket-hilt stale juggler, you! Since when, I pray you, sir? God's light, with two points on your shoulder? Much!

PISTOL God let me not live but I will murder your ruff for this.

FALSTAFF No more, Pistol; I would not have you go off here. Discharge yourself of our company, Pistol.

HOSTESS No, good Captain Pistol; not here, sweet captain.

DOLL Captain! Thou abominable damn'd cheater, art thou not ashamed to be called captain? An captains were of my mind, they would truncheon you out, for taking their names upon you before you have earn'd them. You a captain! you slave, for what? For tearing a poor whore's ruff in a bawdy-house? He a captain! hang him, rouge! He lives upon mouldy stew'd prunes and dried cakes. A captain! God's light, these villains will make the word as odious as the word 'occupy'; which was an excellent good word before it was ill sorted. Therefore captains had need look to't.

BARDOLPH Pray thee go down, good ancient.

FALSTAFF Hark thee hither, Mistress Doll.

PISTOL Not I! I tell thee what, Corporal Bardolph, I could tear her; I'll be reveng'd of her.

PAGE Pray thee go down.

PISTOL I'll see her damn'd first; to Pluto's damn'd lake, by this hand, to th' infernal deep, with Erebus and tortures vile also. Hold hook and line, say I. Down, down, dogs! down, faitors! Have we not Hiren here?

HOSTESS Good Captain Peesel, be quiet; 'tis very late, i' faith; I beseek you now, aggravate your choler.

PISTOL These be good humours, indeed! Shall packhorses,
And hollow pamper'd jades of Asia,
Which cannot go but thirty mile a day,
Compare with Caesars, and with Cannibals,
And Troiant Greeks? Nay, rather damn them with
King Cerberus; and let the welkin roar.
Shall we fall foul for toys?

HOSTESS By my troth, Captain, these are very bitter words.

BARDOLPH Be gone, good ancient; this will grow to a brawl anon.

PISTOL Die men like dogs! Give crowns like pins! Have we not Hiren here?

HOSTESS O' my word, Captain, there's none such here. What the good-year! do you think I would deny her? For God's sake, be quiet.

PISTOL Then feed and be fat, my fair Calipolis.
Come, give some sack.
'Si fortune me tormente sperato me contento.'
Fear we broadsides? No, let the fiend give fire.
Give me some sack; and, sweetheart, lie thou there. *[Laying down his sword.*
Come we to full points here, and are etceteras nothings?

FALSTAFF Pistol, I would be quiet.

PISTOL Sweet knight, I kiss thy neaf. What! we have seen the seven stars.

DOLL For God's sake thrust him down stairs; I cannot endure such a fustian rascal.

PISTOL Thrust him down stairs! Know we not Galloway nags?

FALSTAFF Quoit him down, Bardolph, like a shove-groat shilling. Nay, an 'a do nothing but speak nothing, 'a shall be nothing here.

BARDOLPH Come, get you down stairs.

PISTOL What! shall we have incision? Shall we imbrue? [*Snatching up his sword.*
Then death rock me asleep, abridge my doleful days!
Why, then, let grievous, ghastly, gaping wounds
Untwine the Sisters Three! Come, Atropos, I say!

HOSTESS Here's goodly stuff toward!

FALSTAFF Give me my rapier, boy.

DOLL I pray thee, Jack, I pray thee, do not draw.

FALSTAFF Get you down stairs.

[*Drawing and driving Pistol out.*

HOST Here's a goodly tumult! I'll forswear keeping house afore I'll be in these tirrits and frights. So; murder, I warrant now. Alas, alas! put up your naked weapons, put up your naked weapons. [*Exeunt Pistol and Bardolph.*

DOLL I pray thee, Jack, be quiet; the rascal's gone. Ah, you whoreson little valiant villain, you!

HOSTESS Are you not hurt i' th' groin? Methought 'a made a shrewd thrust at your belly.

Re-enter BARDOLPH.

FALSTAFF Have you turn'd him out a doors?

BARDOLPH Yea, sir. The rascal's drunk. You have hurt him, sir, i' th' shoulder.

FALSTAFF A rascal! to brave me!

DOLL Ah, you sweet little rogue, you! Alas, poor ape, how thou sweat'st! Come, let me wipe thy face. Come on, you whoreson chops. Ah, rogue! i' faith, I love thee. Thou art as valorous as Hector of Troy, worth five of Agamemnon, and ten times better than the Nine Worthies. Ah, villain!

FALSTAFF A rascally slave! I will toss the rogue in a blanket.

DOLL Do, an thou dar'st for thy heart. An thou dost, I'll canvass thee between a pair of sheets.

Enter Musicians.

PAGE The music is come, sir.

FALSTAFF Let them play. Play, sirs. Sit on my knee, Doll. A rascal bragging slave! The rogue fled from me like quicksilver.

DOLL I' faith, and thou follow'dst him like a church. Thou whoreson little tidy Bartholomew boar-pig, when wilt thou leave fighting a days and foining a nights, and begin to patch up thine old body for heaven?

Enter, behind, PRINCE HENRY and POINS disguised as drawers.

FALSTAFF Peace, good Doll! Do not speak like a death's-head; do not bid me remember mine end.

DOLL Sirrah, what humour's the Prince of?

FALSTAFF A good shallow young fellow. 'A would have made a good pantler; 'a would ha' chipp'd bread well.

DOLL They say Poins has a good wit.

FALSTAFF He a good wit! hang him, baboon! His wit's as thick as Tewksbury mustard; there's no more conceit in him than is in a mallet.

DOLL Why does the Prince love him so, then?

FALSTAFF Because their legs are both of a bigness, and 'a plays at quoits well, and eats conger and fennel, and drinks off candles' ends for flap-dragons, and rides the wild mare with the boys, and jumps upon join'd-stools, and swears with a good grace, and wears his boots very smooth, like unto the sign of the Leg, and breeds no bate with telling of discreet stories; and such other gambol faculties 'a has, that show a weak mind and an able body, for the which the Prince admits him. For the Prince himself is such another; the weight of a hair will turn the scales between their avoirdupois.

PRINCE Would not this nave of a wheel have his ears cut off?

POINS Let's beat him before his whore.

PRINCE Look whe'er the wither'd elder hath not his poll claw'd like a parrot.

POINS Is it not strange that desire should so many years outlive performance?

FALSTAFF Kiss me, Doll.

PRINCE Saturn and Venus this year in conjunction! What says th' almanac to that?

POINS And look whether the fiery Trigon, his man, be not lisping to his master's old tables, his note-book, his counsel-keeper.

FALSTAFF Thou dost give me flattering busses.

DOLL By my troth, I kiss thee with a most constant heart.

FALSTAFF I am old, I am old.

DOLL I love thee better than I love e'er a scurvy young boy of them all.

FALSTAFF What stuff wilt have a kirtle of? I shall receive money a Thursday. Shalt have a cap to-morrow. A merry song, come. 'A grows late; we'll to bed. Thou't forget me when I am gone.

DOLL By my troth, thou't set me a-weeping, an thou say'st so. Prove that ever I dress myself handsome till thy return. Well, hearken a' th' end.

FALSTAFF Some sack, Francis.

PRINCE, POINS Anon, anon, sir. [*Advancing*

FALSTAFF Ha! a bastard son of the King's? And art thou not Poins his brother?

PRINCE Why, thou globe of sinful continents, what a life dost thou lead!

FALSTAFF A better than thou. I am a gentleman: thou art a drawer.

PRINCE Very true, sir, and I come to draw you out by the ears.

HOSTESS O, the Lord preserve thy Grace! By my troth, welcome to London. How the Lord bless that sweet face of thine! O Jesu, are you come from Wales?

FALSTAFF Thou whoreson mad compound of majesty, by this light flesh and corrupt blood, thou art welcome. [*Leaning his hand upon Doll.*

DOLL How, you fat fool! I scorn you.

POINS My lord, he will drive you out of your revenge and turn all to a merriment, if you take not the heat.

PRINCE You whoreson candle-mine, you, how vilely did you speak of me even now before this honest, virtuous, civil gentlewoman!

HOSTESS God's blessing of your good heart! and so she is, by my troth.

FALSTAFF Didst thou hear me?

PRINCE Yea; and you knew me, as you did when you ran away by Gadshill. You knew I was at your back, and spoke it on purpose to try my patience.

FALSTAFF No, no, no; not so; I did not think thou wast within hearing.

PRINCE I shall drive you then to confess the wilful abuse, and then I know how to handle you.

FALSTAFF No abuse, Hal, o' mine honour; no abuse.

PRINCE Not – to dispraise me, and call me pantler, and bread-chipper, and I know not what!

FALSTAFF No abuse, Hal.

POINS No abuse!

FALSTAFF No abuse Ned, i' th' world; honest Ned, none. I disprais'd him before the wicked – that the wicked might not fall in love with thee; in which doing, I have done the part of a careful friend and a true subject; and thy father is to give me thanks for it. No abuse, Hal; none, Ned, none; no, faith, boys, none.

PRINCE See now, whether pure fear and entire cowardice doth not make thee wrong this virtuous gentlewoman to close with us? Is she of the wicked? Is thine hostess here of the wicked? Or is thy boy of the wicked? Or honest Bardolph, whose zeal burns in his nose, of the wicked?

POINS Answer, thou dead elm, answer.

FALSTAFF The fiend hath prick'd down Bardolph irrecoverable; and his face is Lucifer's privy-kitchen, where he doth nothing but roast malt-worms. For the boy – there is a good angel about him; but the devil outbids him too.

PRINCE For the women?

FALSTAFF For one of them – she's in hell already, and burns poor souls. For th' other – I owe her money; and whether she be damn'd for that, I know not.

HOSTESS No, I warrant you.

FALSTAFF No, I think thou art not; I think thou are quit for that. Marry, there is another indictment upon thee for suffering flesh to be eaten in thy house, contrary to the law; for the which I think thou wilt howl.

HOSTESS All vict'lers do so. What's a joint of mutton or two in a whole Lent?

PRINCE You, gentlewoman –

DOLL What says your Grace?

FALSTAFF His Grace says that which his flesh rebels against. [*Knocking within.*

HOSTESS Who knocks so loud at door? Look to th' door there, Francis.

Enter PETO.

PRINCE Peto, how now! What news?

PETO The King your father is at Westminster;
And there are twenty weak and wearied posts
Come from the north; and as I came along
I met and overtook a dozen captains,
Bare-headed, sweating, knocking at the taverns,
And asking every one for Sir John Falstaff.

PRINCE By heaven, Poins, I feel me much to blame
So idly to profane the precious time,
When tempest of commotion, like the south,
Borne with black vapour, doth begin to melt
And drop upon our bare unarmed heads.
Give me my sword and cloak. Falstaff, good night.

[*Exeunt Prince, Poins, Peto, and Bardolph.*

FALSTAFF Now comes in the sweetest morsel of the night, and we must hence, and leave it unpick'd. [*Knocking within*] More knocking at the door!

Re-enter BARDOLPH.

How now! What's the matter?

BARDOLPH You must away to court, sir, presently;
A dozen captains stay at door for you.

FALSTAFF [*To the Page*] Pay the musicians,

sirrah. – Farewell, hostess; farewell, Doll. You see, my good wenches, how men of merit are sought after; the underserver may sleep, when the man of action is call'd on. Farewell, good wenches. If I be not sent away post, I will see you again ere I go.

DOLL I cannot speak. If my heart be not be ready to burst! Well, sweet Jack, have a care of thyself.

FALSTAFF Farewell, farewell.

[Exeunt Falstaff and Bardolph.

HOSTESS Well, fare thee well. I have known thee these twenty-nine years, come peascodtime; but an honester and truer-hearted man – well, fare thee well.

BARDOLPH *[Within]* Mistress Tearsheet!

HOSTESS What's the matter?

BARDOLPH *[Within]* Bid Mistress Tearsheet come to my master.

HOSTESS O, run Doll, run, run, good Doll. Come. *[To Bardolph]* She comes blubber'd. – Yea, will you come, Doll? *[Exeunt.*

ACT THREE

SCENE I. *Westminster. The palace.*

Enter the KING in his nightgown, with a Page.

KING Go call the Earls of Surrey and of Warwick;
But, ere they come, bid them o'er-read these letters
And well consider of them. Make good speed.

[Exit Page.

How many thousand of my poorest subjects
Are at this hour asleep! O sleep, O gentle sleep,
Nature's soft nurse, how have I frighted thee,
That thou no more wilt weigh my eyelids down,
And steep my senses in forgetfulness?
Why rather, sleep, liest thou in smoky cribs,
Upon uneasy pallets stretching thee,
And hush'd with buzzing night-flies to thy slumber,
Than in the perfum'd chambers of the great,
Under the canopies of costly state,
And lull'd with sound of sweetest melody?
O thou dull god, why liest thou with the vile
In loathsome beds, and leav'st the kingly couch
A watch-case or a common 'larum-bell?
Wilt thou upon the high and giddy mast
Seal up the ship-boy's eyes, and rock his brains
In cradle of the rude imperious surge,
And in the visitation of the winds,
Who take the ruffian billows by the top,
Curling their monstrous heads, and hanging them
With deafing clamour in the slippery clouds,
That with the hurly death itself awakes?
Canst thou, O partial sleep, give thy repose
To the wet sea-boy in an hour so rude;
And in the calmest and most stillest night,
With all appliances and means to boot,
Deny it to a king? Then, happy low, lie down!
Uneasy lies the head that wears a crown.

Enter WARWICK and SURREY.

WARWICK Many good morrows to your Majesty!

KING Is it good morrow, lords?

WARWICK 'Tis one o'clock, and past.

KING Why then, good morrow to you all, my lords.
Have you read o'er the letters that I sent you?

WARWICK We have, my liege.

KING Then you perceive the body of our kingdom
How foul it is; what rank diseases grow,
And with what danger, near the heart of it.

WARWICK It is but as a body yet distempered;
Which to his former strength may be restored
With good advice and little medicine.
My Lord Northumberland will soon be cool'd.

KING O God! that one might read the book of fate,
And see the revolution of the times
Make mountains level, and the continent,
Weary of solid firmness, melt itself
Into the sea; and other times to see
The beachy girdle of the ocean
Too wide for Neptune's hips; how chances mock,
And changes fill the cup of alteration
With divers liquors! O, if this were seen,
The happiest youth, viewing his progress through,
What perils past, what crosses to ensue,
Would shut the book and sit him down and die.
'Tis not ten years gone
Since Richard and Northumberland, great friends,
Did feast together, and in two years after
Were they at wars. It is but eight years since
This Percy was the man nearest my soul;
Who like a brother toil'd in my affairs
And laid his love and life under my foot;
Yea, for my sake, even to the eyes of Richard
Gave him defiance. But which of you was by –
[To Warwick] You, cousin Nevil, as I may remember –
When Richard, with his eye brim full of tears,

Then check'd and rated by Northumberland,
Did speak these words, now prov'd a prophecy?
'Northumberland, thou ladder by the which
My cousin Bolingbroke ascends my throne' –
Though then, God knows, I had no such intent
But that necessity so bow'd the state
That I and greatness were compell'd to kiss –
'The time shall come' – thus did he follow it –
'The time will come that foul sin, gathering head,
Shall break into corruption' so went on,
Foretelling this same time's condition
And the division of our amity.

WARWICK There is a history in all men's lives,
Figuring the natures of the times deceas'd;
The which observ'd, a man may prophesy,
With a near aim, of the main chance of things
As yet not come to life, who in their seeds
And weak beginning lie intreasured.
Such things become the hatch and brood of time;
And, by the necessary form of this,
King Richard might create a perfect guess
That great Northumberland, then false to him,
Would of that seed grow to a greater falseness;
Which should not find a ground to root upon
Unless on you.

KING Are these things then necessities?
Then let us meet them like necessities;
And that same word even now cries out on us.
They say the Bishop and Northumberland
Are fifty thousand strong.

WARWICK It cannot be, my lord.
Rumour doth double, like the voice and echo,
The numbers of the feared. Please it your Grace
To go to bed. Upon my soul, my lord,
The powers that you already have sent forth
Shall bring this prize in very easily.
To comfort you the more, I have receiv'd
A certain instance that Glendower is dead.
Your Majesty hath been this fortnight ill;
And these unseasoned hours perforce must add
Unto your sickness.

KING I will take your counsel.
And, were these inward wars once out of hand,
We would, dear lords, unto the Holy Land.

[*Exeunt.*

SCENE II. *Gloucestershire. Before Justice Shallow's house.*

Enter SHALLOW and SILENCE, meeting; MOULDY, SHADOW, WART, FEEBLE, BULLCALF, and Servants, behind.

SHALLOW Come on, come on, come on; give me your hand, sir; give me your hand, sir. An early stirrer, by the rood! And how doth my good cousin Silence?

SILENCE Good morrow, good cousin Shallow.

SHALLOW And how doth my cousin, your bedfellow? and your fairest daughter and mine, my god-daughter Ellen?

SILENCE Alas, a black ousel, cousin Shallow!

SHALLOW By yea and no, sir. I dare say my cousin William is become a good scholar; he is at Oxford still, is he not?

SILENCE Indeed, sir, to my cost.

SHALLOW 'A must, then, to the Inns o' Court shortly. I was once of Clement's Inn; where I think they will talk of mad Shallow yet.

SILENCE You were call'd 'lusty Shallow' then, cousin.

SHALLOW By the mass, I was call'd anything; and I would have done anything indeed too, and roundly too. There was I, and little John Doit of Staffordshire, and black George Barnes, and Francis Pickbone, and Will Squele a Cotsole man – you had not four such swinge-bucklers in all the Inns o' Court again. And I may say to you we knew where the bona-robas were, and had the best of them all at commandment. Then was Jack Falstaff, now Sir John, a boy, and page to Thomas Mowbray, Duke of Norfolk.

SILENCE This Sir John, cousin, that comes hither anon about soldiers?

SHALLOW The same Sir John, the very same. I see him break Scoggin's head at the court gate, when 'a was a crack not thus high; and the very same day did I fight with one Sampson Stockfish, a fruiterer, behind Gray's Inn. Jesu, Jesu, the mad days that I have spent! and to see how many of my old acquaintance are dead!

SILENCE We shall all follow, cousin.

SHALLOW Certain, 'tis certain; very sure, very sure. Death, as the Psalmist saith, is certain to all; all shall die. How a good yoke of bullocks at Stamford fair?

SILENCE By my troth, I was not there.

SHALLOW Death is certain. Is old Double of your town living yet?

SILENCE Dead, sir.

SHALLOW Jesu, Jesu, dead! 'A drew a good bow; and dead! 'A shot a fine shoot. John a Gaunt loved him well, and betted much money on his head. Dead! 'A would have clapp'd i' th' clout at twelve score, and carried you a forehand shaft a fourteen and fourteen and a half, that it would have done a man's heart good to see. How a score of ewes now?

SILENCE Thereafter as they be – a score of good ewes may be worth ten pounds.

SHALLOW And is old Double dead?

Enter BARDOLPH and One with him.

SILENCE Here come two of Sir John Falstaff's men, as I think.

SHALLOW Good morrow, honest gentlemen.

BARDOLPH I beseech you, which is Justice Shallow?

SHALLOW I am Robert Shallow, sir, a poor esquire of this county, and one of the King's justices of the peace. What is your good pleasure with me?

BARDOLPH My captain, sir, commends him to you; my captain, Sir John Falstaff – a tall gentleman, by heaven, and a most gallant leader.

SHALLOW He greets me well, sir; I knew him a good backsword man. How doth the good knight? May I ask how my lady his wife doth?

BARDOLPH Sir, pardon; a solider is better accommodated than with a wife.

SHALLOW It is well said, in faith, sir; and it is well said indeed, too. 'Better accommodated'! It is good; yea, indeed, is it. Good phrases are surely, and ever were, very commendable. 'Accommodated'! It comes of accommodo. Very good; a good phrase.

BARDOLPH Pardon, sir; I have heard the word. 'Phrase' call you it? By this day, I know not the phrase; but I will maintain the word with my sword to be a soldier-like word, and a word of exceeding good command, by heaven. Accommodated: that is, when a man is, as they say, accommodated; or when a man is being – whereby 'a may be thought to be accommodated; which is an excellent thing.

Enter FALSTAFF.

SHALLOW It is very just. Look, here comes good Sir John. Give me your good hand, give me your worship's good hand. By my troth, you like well and bear your years very well. Welcome, good Sir John.

FALSTAFF I am glad to see you well, good Master Robert Shallow. Master Surecard, as I think?

SHALLOW No, Sir John; it is my cousin Silence, in commission with me.

FALSTAFF Good Master Silence, it well befits you should be of the peace.

SILENCE Your good worship is welcome.

FALSTAFF Fie! this is hot weather. Gentlemen, have you provided me here half a dozen sufficient men?

SHALLOW Marry, have we, sir. Will you sit?

FALSTAFF Let me see them, I beseech you.

SHALLOW Where's the roll? Where's the roll? Where's the roll? Let me see, let me see, let me see. So, so, so, so, so – so, so – yea, marry, sir. Rafe Mouldy! Let them appear as I call; let them do so, let them do so. Let me see; where is Mouldy?

MOULDY Here, an't please you.

SHALLOW What think you, Sir John? A good limb'd fellow; young, strong, and of good friends.

FALSTAFF Is thy name Mouldy?

MOULDY Yea, an't please you.

FALSTAFF 'Tis the more time thou wert us'd.

SHALLOW Ha, ha, ha! most excellent, i' faith! Things that are mouldy lack use. Very singular good! In faith, well said, Sir John; very well said.

FALSTAFF Prick him.

MOULDY I was prick'd well enough before, an you could have let me alone. My old dame will be undone now for one to do her husbandry and her drudgery. You need not to have prick'd me; there are other men fitter to go out than I.

FALSTAFF Go to; peace, Mouldy; you shall go. Mouldy, it is time you were spent.

MOULDY Spent!

SHALLOW Peace, fellow, peace; stand aside; know you where you are? For th' other, Sir John – let me see. Simon Shadow!

FALSTAFF Yea, marry, let me have him to sit under. He's like to be a cold soldier.

SHALLOW Where's Shadow?

SHADOW Here, sir.

FALSTAFF Shadow, whose son art thou?

SHADOW My mother's son, sir.

FALSTAFF Thy mother's son! Like enough; and thy father's shadow. So the son of the female is the shadow of the male. It is often so indeed; but much of the father's substance!

SHALLOW Do you like him, Sir John?

FALSTAFF Shadow will serve for summer. Prick him; for we have a number of shadows fill up the muster-book.

SHALLOW Thomas Wart!

FALSTAFF Where's he?

WART Here, sir.

FALSTAFF Is thy name Wart?

WART Yea, sir.

FALSTAFF Thou art a very ragged wart.

SHALLOW Shall I prick him, Sir John?

FALSTAFF It were superfluous; for his apparel is built upon his back, and the whole frame stands upon pins. Prick him no more.

SHALLOW Ha, ha, ha! You can do it, sir; you can do it. I commend you well. Francis Feeble!

FEEBLE Here, Sir.

FALSTAFF What trade art thou, Feeble?

FEEBLE A woman's tailor, sir.

SHALLOW Shall I prick him, sir?

FALSTAFF You may; but if he had been a man's tailor, he'd ha' prick'd you. Wilt thou make as many holes in an enemy's battle as thou hast done in a woman's petticoat?

FEEBLE I will do my good will, sir; you can have no more.

FALSTAFF Well said, good woman's tailor! well said, courageous Feeble! Thou wilt be as valiant as the wrathful dove or most magnanimous mouse. Prick the woman's tailor – well, Master Shallow, deep, Master Shallow.

FEEBLE I would Wart might have gone, sir.

FALSTAFF I would thou wert a man's tailor, that thou mightst mend him and make him fit to go. I cannot put him to a private soldier, that is the leader of so many thousands. Let that suffice, most forcible Feeble.

FEEBLE It shall suffice, sir.

FALSTAFF I am bound to thee, reverend Feeble. Who is next?

SHALLOW Peter Bullcalf o' th' green!

FALSTAFF Yea, marry, let's see Bullcalf.

BULLCALF Here, sir.

FALSTAFF Fore God, a likely fellow! Come, prick me Bullcalf till he roar again.

BULLCALF O Lord! good my lord captain –

FALSTAFF What, dost thou roar before thou art prick'd?

BULLCALF O Lord, sir! I am a diseased man.

FALSTAFF What disease hast thou?

BULLCALF A whoreson cold, sir, a cough, sir, which I caught with ringing in the King's affairs upon his coronation day, sir.

FALSTAFF Come, thou shalt go to the wars in a gown. We will have away thy cold; and I will take such order that thy friends shall ring for thee. Is here all?

SHALLOW Here is two more call'd than your number. You must have but four here, sir; and so, I pray you, go in with me to dinner.

FALSTAFF Come, I will go drink with you, but I cannot tarry dinner. I am glad to see you, by my troth, Master Shallow.

SHALLOW O, Sir John, do you remember since we lay all night in the windmill in Saint George's Field?

FALSTAFF No more of that, Master Shallow, no more of that.

SHALLOW Ha, 'twas a merry night. And is Jane Nightwork alive?

FALSTAFF She lives, Master Shallow.

SHALLOW She never could away with me.

FALSTAFF Never, never; she would always say she could not abide Master Shallow.

SHALLOW By the mass, I could anger her to th' heart. She was then a bona-roba. Doth she hold her own well?

FALSTAFF Old, old, Master Shallow.

SHALLOW Nay, she must be old; she cannot choose but be old; certain she's old; and had Robin Nightwork, by old Nightwork, before I came to Clement's Inn.

SILENCE That's fifty-five year ago.

SHALLOW Ha, cousin Silence, that thou hadst seen that that this knight and I have seen! Ha, Sir John, said I well?

FALSTAFF We have heard the chimes at midnight, Master Shallow.

SHALLOW That we have, that we have, that we have; in faith, Sir John, we have. Our watchword was 'Hem, boys!' Come, let's to dinner; come, let's to dinner. Jesus, the days that we have seen! Come, come.

[*Exeunt Falstaff and the Justices.*

BULLCALF Good Master Corporate Bardolph, stand my friend; and here's four Harry ten shillings in French crowns for you. In very truth, sir, I had as lief be hang'd, sir, as go. And yet, for mine own part, sir, I do not care; but rather because I am unwilling and, for mine own part, have a desire to stay with my friends; else, sir, I did not care for mine own part so much.

BARDOLPH Go to; stand aside.

MOULDY And, good Master Corporal Captain, for my old dame's sake, stand my friend. She has nobody to do anything about her when I am gone; and she is old, and cannot help herself. You shall have forty, sir.

BARDOLPH Go to; stand aside.

FEEBLE By my troth, I care not; a man can die but once; we owe God a death. I'll ne'er bear a base mind. An't be my destiny, so; an't be not, so. No man's too good to serve's Prince; and, let it go which way it will, he that dies this year is quit for the next.

BARDOLPH Well said; th'art a good fellow.

FEEBLE Faith, I'll bear no base mind.

Re-enter FALSTAFF and the Justices.

FALSTAFF Come, sir, which men shall I have?

SHALLOW Four of which you please.

BARDOLPH Sir, a word with you. I have three pound to free Mouldy and Bullcalf.

FALSTAFF Go to; well.

SHALLOW Come, Sir John, which four will you have?

FALSTAFF Do you choose for me.

SHALLOW Marry, then – Mouldy, Bullcalf, Feeble, and Shadow.

FALSTAFF Mouldy and Bullcalf: for you, Mouldy, stay at home till you are past service; and for your part, Bullcalf, grow till you come unto it. I will none of you.

SHALLOW Sir John, Sir John, do not yourself wrong. They are your likeliest men, and I would have you serv'd with the best.

FALSTAFF Will you tell me, Master Shallow, how to choose a man? Care I for the limb, the thews, the stature, bulk, and big assemblance of a man! Give me the spirit, Master Shallow. Here's Wart; you see what a ragged appearance it is. 'A shall charge you and discharge you with the motion of a pewterer's hammer, come off and on swifter than he that gibbets on the brewer's bucket. And this same half-fac'd fellow, Shadow – give me this man. He presents no mark to the enemy; the foeman may with as great aim level at the edge of a penknife. And, for a retreat – how swiftly will this Feeble, the woman's tailor, run off! O, give me the spare men, and spare me the great ones. Put me a caliver into Wart's hand, Bardolph.

BARDOLPH Hold, Wart. Traverse – thus, thus, thus.

FALSTAFF Come, manage me your caliver. So – very well. Go to; very good; exceeding good. O, give me always a little, lean, old, chopt, bald shot. Well said, i' faith, Wart; th'art a good scab. Hold, there's a tester for thee.

SHALLOW He is not his craft's master, he doth not do it right. I remember at Mile-end Green, when I lay at Clement's Inn – I was then Sir Dagonet in Arthur's show – there was a little quiver fellow, and 'a would manage you his piece thus; and 'a would about and about, and come you in and come you in. 'Rah, tah, tah!' would 'a say; 'Bounce!' would 'a say; and away again would 'a go, and again would 'a come. I shall ne'er see such a fellow.

FALSTAFF These fellows will do well. Master Shallow, God keep you! Master Silence, I will not use many words with you: Fare you well! Gentlemen both, I thank you. I must a dozen mile to-night. Bardolph, give the soldiers coats.

SHALLOW Sir John, the Lord bless you; God prosper your affairs; God send us peace! At your return, visit our house; let our old acquaintance be renewed. Peradventure I will with ye to the court.

FALSTAFF Fore God, would you would.

SHALLOW Go to; I have spoke at a word. God keep you.

FALSTAFF Fare you well, gentle gentlemen. [*Exeunt Justices*] On, Bardolph; lead the men away. [*Exeunt all but Falstaff*] As I return, I will fetch off these justices. I do see the bottom of Justice Shallow. Lord, Lord, how subject we old men are to this vice of lying! This same starv'd justice hath done nothing but prate to me of the wildness of his youth and the feats he hath done about Turnbull Street; and every third word a lie, duer paid to the hearer that the Turk's tribute. I do remember him at Clement's Inn, like a man made after supper of a cheese-paring. When 'a was naked, he was for all the world like a fork'd radish, with a head fantastically carved upon it with a knife. 'A was so forlorn that his dimensions to any thick sight were invisible. 'A was the very genius of famine; yet lecherous as a monkey, and the whores call'd him mandrake. 'A came ever in the rearward of the fashion, and sung those tunes to the overscutch'd huswifes that he heard the carmen whistle, and sware they were his fancies or his good-nights. And now is this Vice's dagger become a squire, and talks as familiarly of John a Gaunt as if he had been sworn brother to him; and I'll be sworn 'a ne'er saw him but once in the Tiltyard; and then he burst his head for crowding among the marshal's men. I saw it, and told John a Gaunt he beat his own name; for you might have thrust him and all his apparel into an eel-skin; the case of a treble hautboy was a mansion for him, a court – and now has he land and beeves. Well, I'll be acquainted with him if I return; and't shall go hard but I'll make him a philosopher's two stones to me. If the young dace be a bait for the old pike, I see no reason in the law of nature but I may snap at him. Let time shape, and there an end. [*Exit.*

ACT FOUR

SCENE I. *Yorkshire. Within the Forest of Gaultree.*

Enter the ARCHBISHOP OF YORK, MOWBRAY, HASTINGS, and Others.

ARCHBISHOP What is this forest call'd?

HASTINGS 'Tis Gaultree Forest, an't shall please your Grace.

ARCHBISHOP Here stand, my lords, and send discoverers forth
To know the numbers of our enemies.

HASTINGS We have sent forth already.

ARCHBISHOP 'Tis well done.
My friends and brethren in these great affairs,
I must acquaint you that I have receiv'd
New-dated letters from Northumberland;
Their cold intent, tenour, and substance, thus:
Here doth he wish his person, with such powers
As might hold sortance with his quality,
The which he could not levy; whereupon
He is retir'd, to ripe his growing fortunes,

To Scotland; and concludes in hearty prayers
That your attempts may overlive the hazard
And fearful meeting of their opposite.

MOWBRAY Thus do the hopes we have in him touch ground
And dash themselves to pieces.

Enter a Messenger.

HASTINGS Now, what news?

MESSENGER West of this forest, scarcely off a mile,
In goodly form comes on the enemy;
And, by the ground they hide, I judge their number
Upon or near the rate of thirty thousand.

MOWBRAY The just proportion that we gave them out.
Let us sway on and face them in the field.

Enter WESTMORELAND.

ARCHBISHOP What well-appointed leader fronts us here?

MOWBRAY I think it is my Lord of Westmoreland.

WESTMORELAND Health and fair greeting from our general,
The Prince, Lord John and Duke of Lancaster.

ARCHBISHOP Say on, my Lord of Westmoreland, in peace,
What doth concern your coming.

WESTMORELAND Then, my lord,
Unto your Grace do I in chief address
The substance of my speech. If that rebellion
Came like itself, in base and abject routs,
Led on by bloody youth, guarded with rags,
And countenanc'd by boys and beggary –
I say, if damn'd commotion so appear'd
In his true, native, and most proper shape,
You, reverend father, and these noble lords,
Had not been here to dress the ugly form
Of base and bloody insurrection
With your fair honours. You, Lord Archbishop,
Whose see is by a civil peace maintain'd,
Whose beard the silver hand of peace hath touch'd,
Whose learning and good letters peace hath tutor'd,
Whose white investments figure innocence,
The dove, and very blessed spirit of peace –
Wherefore do you so ill translate yourself
Out of the speech of peace, that bears such grace,
Into the harsh and boist'rous tongue of war;
Turning your books to graves, your ink to blood,
Your pens to lances, and your tongue divine
To a loud trumpet and a point of war?

ARCHBISHOP Wherefore do I this? So the question stands.
Briefly to this end: we are all diseas'd
And with our surfeiting and wanton hours
Have brought ourselves into a burning fever,
And we must bleed for it; of which disease
Our late King, Richard, being infected, died.
But, my most noble Lord of Westmoreland,
I take not on me here as a physician;
Nor do I as an enemy to peace
Troop in the throngs of military men;
But rather show awhile like fearful war
To diet rank minds sick of happiness,
And purge th' obstructions which begin to stop
Our very veins of life. Hear me more plainly.
I have in equal balance justly weigh'd
What wrongs our arms may do, what wrongs we suffer,
And find our griefs heavier than our offences.
We see which way the stream of time doth run
And are enforc'd from our most quiet there
By the rough torrent of occasion;
And have the summary of all our griefs,
When time shall serve, to show in articles;
Which long ere this we offer'd to the King,
And might by no suit gain our audience:
When we are wrong'd, and would unfold our griefs,
We are denied access unto his person,
Even by those men that most have done us wrong.
The dangers of the days but newly gone,
Whose memory is written on the earth
With yet appearing blood, and the examples
Of every minute's instance, present now,
Hath put us in these ill-beseeming arms;
Not to break peace, or any branch of it,
But to establish here a peace indeed,
Concurring both in name and quality.

WESTMORELAND When ever yet was your appeal denied;
Wherein have you been galled by the King;
What peer hath been suborn'd to grate on you
That you should seal this lawless bloody book
Of forg'd rebellion with a seal divine,
And consecrate commotion's bitter edge?

ARCHBISHOP My brother general, the commonwealth,
To brother born an household cruelty,
I make my quarrel in particular.

WESTMORELAND There is no need of any such redress;
Or if there were, it not belongs to you.

MOWBRAY Why not to him in part, and to us all
That feel the bruises of the days before,
And suffer the condition of these times
To lay a heavy and unequal hand
Upon our honours?

WESTMORELAND O my good Lord Mowbary,
Construe the times to their necessities,
And you shall say, indeed, it is the time,
And not the King, that doth you injuries.
Yet, for your part, it not appears to me,
Either from the King or in the present time,
That you should have an inch of any ground
To build a grief on. Were you not restor'd
To all the Duke of Norfolk's signiories,
Your noble and right well-rememb'red father's?

MOWBRAY What thing, in honour, had my father lost
That need to be reviv'd and breath'd in me?
The King that lov'd him, as the state stood then,
Was force perforce compell'd to banish him,
And then that Henry Bolingbroke and he,
Being mounted and both roused in their seats,
Their neighing coursers daring of the spur,
Their armed staves in charge, their beavers down,
Their eyes of fire sparkling through sights of steel,
And the loud trumpet blowing them together –
Then, then, when there was nothing could have stay'd
My father from the breast of Bolingbroke,
O, when the King did throw his warder down –
His own life hung upon the staff he threw –
Then threw he down himself, and all their lives
That by indictment and by dint of sword
Have since miscarried under Bolingbroke.

WESTMORELAND You speak, Lord Mowbray, now you know not what.
The Earl of Hereford was reputed then
In England the most valiant gentleman.
Who knows on whom fortune would then have smil'd?
But if your father had been victor there,
He ne'er had borne it out of Coventry;
For all the country, in a general voice,
Cried hate upon him; and all their prayers and love
Were set on Hereford, whom they doted on,
And bless'd and grac'd indeed more than the King.
But this is mere digression from my purpose.
Here come I from our princely general
To know your griefs; to tell you from his Grace
That he will give you audience; and wherein
It shall appear that your demands are just,
You shall enjoy them, everything set off
That might so much as think you enemies.

MOWBRAY But he hath forc'd us to compel this offer;
And it proceeds from policy, not love.

WESTMORELAND Mowbray, you overween to take it so.
This offer comes from mercy, not from fear;
For, lo! within a ken our army lies –
Upon mine honour, all too confident
To give admittance to a thought of fear.
Our battle is more full of names than yours,
Our men more perfect in the use of arms,
Our armour all as strong, our cause the best;
Then reason will our hearts should be as good.
Say you not, then, our offer is compell'd.

MOWBRAY Well, by my will we shall admit no parley.

WESTMORELAND That argues but the shame of your offence:
A rotten case abides no handling.

HASTINGS Hath the Prince John a full commission,
In very ample virtue of his father,
To hear and absolutely to determine
Of what conditions we shall stand upon?

WESTMORELAND That is intended in the general's name.
I muse you make so slight a question.

ARCHBISHOP Then take, my Lord of Westmoreland, this schedule,
For this contains our general grievances.
Each several article herein redress'd,
All members of our cause, both here and hence,
That are insinewed to this action,
Acquitted by a true substantial form,
And present execution of our wills
To us and to our purposes confin'd –
We come within our awful banks again,
And knit our powers to the arm of peace.

WESTMORELAND This will I show the general. Please you, lords,
In sight of both our battles we may meet;
And either end in peace – which God so frame! –
Or to the place of diff'rence call the swords
Which must decide it.

ARCHBISHOP My lord, we will do so.

[Exit Westmoreland.

MOWBRAY There is a thing within my bosom tells me
That no conditions of our peace can stand.

HASTINGS Fear you not that: if we can make our peace
Upon such large terms and so absolute
As our conditions shall consist upon,
Our peace shall stand as firm as rocky mountains.

MOWBRAY Yea, but our valuation shall be such
That every slight and false-derived cause,
Yea, every idle, nice, and wanton reason,
Shall to the King taste of this action;
That, were our royal faiths martyrs in love,

We shall be winnow'd with so rough a wind
That even our corn shall seem as light as chaff,
And good from bad find no partition.

ARCHBISHOP No, no, my lord. Note this: the King is weary
Of dainty and such picking grievances;
For he hath found to end one doubt by death
Revives two greater in the heirs of life;
And therefore will he wipe his tables clean,
And keep no tell-tale to his memory
That may repeat and history his loss
To new remembrance. For full well he knows
He cannot so precisely weed this land
As his misdoubts present occasion:
His foes are so enrooted with his friends
That, plucking to unfix an enemy,
He doth unfasten so and shake a friend.
So that this land, like an offensive wife
That hath enrag'd him on to offer strokes,
As he is striking, holds his infant up,
And hangs resolv'd correction in the arm
That was uprear'd to execution.

HASTINGS Besides, the King hath wasted all his rods
On late offenders, that he now doth lack
The very instruments of chastisement;
So that his power, like to a fangless lion,
May offer, but not hold.

ARCHBISHOP 'Tis very true;
And therefore be assur'd, my good Lord Marshal,
If we do now make our atonement well,
Our peace will, like a broken limb united,
Grow stronger for the breaking.

MOWBRAY Be it so.
Here is return'd my Lord of Westmoreland.

Re-enter WESTMORELAND.

WESTMORELAND The Prince is here at hand. Pleaseth your lordship
To meet his Grace just distance 'tween our armies?

MOWBRAY Your Grace of York, in God's name then, set forward.

ARCHBISHOP Before, and greet his Grace. My lord, we come. [*Exeunt.*

SCENE II. *Another part of the forest.*

Enter, from one side, MOWBRAY, attended; afterwards, the ARCHBISHOP, HASTINGS, and Others: from the other side, PRINCE JOHN OF LANCASTER, WESTMORELAND, Officers and Others.

PRINCE JOHN You are well encount'red here, my cousin Mowbray.
Good day to you, gentle Lord Archbishop;
And so to you, Lord Hastings, and to all.
My Lord of York, it better show'd with you
When that your flock, assembled by the bell,
Encircled you to hear with reverence
Your exposition on the holy text
Than now to see you here an iron man,
Cheering a rout of rebels with your drum,
Turning the word to sword, and life to death.
That man that sits within a monarch's heart
And ripens in the sunshine of his favour,
Would he abuse the countenance of the king,
Alack, what mischiefs might be set abroach
In shadow of such greatness! With you, Lord Bishop,
It is even so. Who hath not heard it spoken
How deep you were within the books of God?
To us the speaker in His parliament,
To us th' imagin'd voice of God himself,
The very opener and intellingencer
Between the grace, the sanctities of heaven,
And our dull workings. O, who shall believe
But you misuse the reverence of your place,
Employ the countenance and grace of heav'n
As a false favourite doth his prince's name,
In deeds dishonourable? You have ta'en up,
Under the counterfeited zeal of God,
The subjects of His substitute, my father,
And both against the peace of heaven and him
Have here up-swarm'd them.

ARCHBISHOP Good my Lord of Lancaster,
I am not here against your father's peace;
But, as I told my Lord of Westmoreland,
The time misord'red doth, in common sense,
Crowd us and crush us to this monstrous form
To hold our safety up. I sent your Grace
The parcels and particulars of our grief,
The which hath been with scorn shov'd from the court,
Whereon this hydra son of war is born;
Whose dangerous eyes may well be charm'd asleep
With grant of our most just and right desires;
And true obedience, of this madness cur'd,
Stoop tamely to the foot of majesty.

MOWBRAY If not, we ready are to try our fortunes
To the last man.

HASTINGS And though we here fall down,
We have supplies to second our attempt.
If they miscarry, theirs shall second them;
And so success of mischief shall be born,
And heir from heir shall hold this quarrel up
Whiles England shall have generation.

PRINCE JOHN You are too shallow, Hastings, much too shallow,
To sound the bottom of the after-times.

WESTMORELAND Pleaseth your Grace to answer them directly
How far forth you do like their articles.

PRINCE JOHN I like them all and do allow them well;
And swear here, by the honour of my blood,
My father's purposes have been mistook;
And some about him have too lavishly
Wrested his meaning and authority.
My lord, these griefs shall be with speed redress'd;
Upon my soul, they shall. If this may please you,
Discharge your powers unto their several counties,
As we will ours; and here, between the armies,
Let's drink together friendly and embrace,
That all their eyes may bear those tokens home
Of our restored love and amity.
ARCHBISHOP I take your princely word for these redresses.
PRINCE JOHN I give it you, and will maintain my word;
And thereupon I drink unto your Grace.
HASTINGS Go, Captain, and deliver to the army
This news of peace. Let them have pay, and part.
I know it will well please them. Hie thee, Captain. [*Exit Officer.*

ARCHBISHOP To you, my noble Lord of Westmoreland.
WESTMORELAND I pledge your Grace; and if you knew what pains
I have bestow'd to breed this present peace,
You would drink freely; but my love to ye
Shall show itself more openly hereafter.
ARCHBISHOP I do not doubt you.
WESTMORELAND I am glad of it.
Health to my lord and gentle cousin, Mowbray.
MOWBRAY You wish me health in very happy season,
For I am on the sudden something ill.
ARCHBISHOP Against ill chances men are ever merry;
But heaviness foreruns the good event.
WESTMORELAND Therefore be merry, coz; since sudden sorrow
Serves to say thus; 'Some good thing comes to-morrow'.
ARCHBISHOP Believe me, I am passing light in spirit.
MOWBRAY So much the worse, if your own rule be true. [*Shouts within.*

PRINCE JOHN The word of peace is rend'red.
Hark, how they shout!
MOWBRAY This had been cheerful after victory.
ARCHBISHOP A peace is of the nature of a conquest;
For then both parties nobly are subdu'd,
And neither party loser.
PRINCE JOHN Go, my lord,
And let our army be discharged too. [*Exit Westmoreland.*

And, good my lord, so please you let our trains
March by us, that we may peruse the men
We should have cop'd withal.
ARCHBISHOP Go, good Lord Hastings,
And, ere they be dismiss'd, let them march by. [*Exit Hastings.*

PRINCE JOHN I trust, lords, we shall lie tonight together.

Re-enter WESTMORELAND.

Now, cousin, wherefore stands our army still?
WESTMORELAND The leaders, having charge from you to stand,
Will not go off until they hear you speak.
PRINCE JOHN They know their duties.

Re-enter HASTINGS.

HASTINGS My lord, our army is dispers'd already.
Like youthful steers unyok'd, they take their courses
East, west, north, south; or like a school broke up,
Each hurries toward his home and sporting-place.
WESTMORELAND Good tidings, my Lord Hastings; for the which
I do arrest thee, traitor, of high treason;
And you, Lord Archbishop, and you, Lord Mowbray,
Of capital treason I attach you both.
MOWBRAY Is this proceeding just and honourable?
WESTMORELAND Is your assembly so?
ARCHBISHOP Will you thus break your faith?
PRINCE JOHN I pawn'd thee none:
I promis'd you redress of these same grievances
Whereof you did complain; which, by mine honour,
I will perform with a most Christian care.
But for you, rebels – look to taste the due
Meet for rebellion and such acts as yours.
Most shallowly did you these arms commence,
Fondly brought here, and foolishly sent hence.
Strike up our drums, pursue the scatt'red stray.
God, and not we, hath safely fought to-day.
Some guard these traitors to the block of death,
Treason's true bed and yielder-up of breath. [*Exeunt.*

SCENE III. *Another part of the forest.*

Alarum; excursions. Enter FALSTAFF and COLVILLE, meeting.

FALSTAFF What's your name, sir? Of what

condition are you, and of what place, I pray?

COLVILLE I am a knight sir; and my name is Colville of the Dale.

FALSTAFF Well then, Colville is your name, a knight is your degree, and your place the Dale. Colville shall be still your name, a traitor your degree, and the dungeon your place – a place deep enough; so shall you be still Colville of the Dale.

COLVILLE Are not you Sir John Falstaff?

FALSTAFF As good a man as he, sir, whoe'er I am. Do ye yield, sir, or shall I sweat for you? If I do sweat, they are the drops of thy lovers, and they weep for thy death; therefore rouse up fear and trembling, and do observance to my mercy.

COLVILLE I think you are Sir John Falstaff, and in that thought yield me.

FALSTAFF I have a whole school of tongues in this belly of mine; and not a tongue of them all speaks any other word but my name. An I had but a belly of any indifferency, I were simply the most active fellow in Europe. My womb, my womb, my womb undoes me. Here comes our general.

Enter PRINCE JOHN OF LANCASTER, WESTMORELAND, BLUNT, and Others.

PRINCE JOHN The heat is past; follow no further now.
Call in the powers, good cousin Westmoreland.
[*Exit Westmoreland.*
Now, Falstaff, where have you been all this while?
When everything is ended, then you come.
These tardy tricks of yours will, on my life,
One time or other break some gallows' back.

FALSTAFF I would be sorry, my lord, but it should be thus: I never knew yet but rebuke and check was the reward of valour. Do you think me a swallow, an arrow, or a bullet? Have I, in my poor and old motion, the expedition of thought? I have speeded hither with the very extremest inch of possibility; I have found'red nine score and odd posts; and here, travel tainted as I am, have, in my pure and immaculate valour, taken Sir John Colville of the Dale, a most furious knight and valorous enemy. But what of that? He saw me, and yielded; that I may justly say with the hook-nos'd fellow of Rome – I came, saw, and overcame.

PRINCE JOHN It was more of his courtesy than your deserving.

FALSTAFF I know not. Here he is, and here I yield him; and I beseech your Grace, let it be book'd with the rest of this day's deeds; or, by the Lord, I will have it in a particular ballad else, with mine own picture on the top on't, Colville kissing my foot; to the which course if I be enforc'd, if you do not all show like gilt twopences to me, and I, in the clear sky of fame, o'ershine you as much as the full moon doth the cinders of the element, which show like pins' heads to her, believe not the word of the noble. Therefore let me have right, and let desert mount.

PRINCE JOHN Thine's too heavy to mount.

FALSTAFF Let it shine, then.

PRINCE JOHN Thine's too thick to shine.

FALSTAFF Let it do something, my good lord, that may do me good, and call it what you will.

PRINCE JOHN Is thy name Colville?

COLVILLE It is, my lord.

PRINCE JOHN A famous rebel art thou, Colville.

FALSTAFF And a famous true subject took him.

COLVILLE I am, my lord, but as my betters are
That led me hither. Had they been rul'd by me,
You should have won them dearer than you have.

FALSTAFF I know not how they sold themselves; but thou, like a kind fellow, gavest thyself away gratis; and I thank thee for thee.

Re-enter WESTMORELAND.

PRINCE JOHN Now, have you left pursuit?

WESTMORELAND Retreat is made, and execution stay'd.

PRINCE JOHN Send Colville, with his confederates,
To York, to present execution.
Blunt, lead him hence; and see you guard him sure.
[*Exeunt Blunt and others.*
And now dispatch we toward the court, my lords.
I hear the King my father is sore sick.
Our news shall go before us to his Majesty,
Which, cousin, you shall bear to comfort him;
And we with sober speed will follow you.

FALSTAFF My lord, I beseech you, give me leave to go through Gloucestershire; and, when you come to court, stand my good lord, pray, in your good report.

PRINCE JOHN Fare you well, Falstaff. I, in my condition,
Shall better speak of you than you deserve.
[*Exeunt all but Falstaff.*

FALSTAFF I would you had but the wit; 'twere better than your dukedom. Good faith, this same young sober-blooded boy doth not love me; nor a man cannot make him laugh – but that's no marvel; he drinks no wine. There's never none of these demure boys come to any proof; for thin drink doth so over-cool their blood, and making many fish-meals, that they fall into a kind of male green-sickness; and then, when they marry, they get wenches. They are generally fools and cowards – which some of us should be too, but for inflammation. A good sherris-sack hath a twofold operation in it. It ascends me into the brain; dries me there all the foolish and dull and crudy vapours which environ it; makes it apprehensive, quick, forgetive, full of nimble, fiery, and delectable shapes; which delivered o'er to the voice, the tongue, which is the birth, becomes excellent wit. The second property of your excellent sherris is the warming of the blood; which before, cold and settled, left the liver white and pale, which is the badge of pusillanimity and cowardice; but the sherris warms it, and makes it course from the inwards to the parts extremes. It illumineth the face, which, as a beacon, gives warning to all the rest of this little kingdom, man, to arm; and then the vital commoners and inland petty spirits muster me all to their captain, the heart, who, great and puff'd up with this retinue, doth any deed of courage – and this valour comes of sherris. So that skill in the weapon is nothing without sack, for that sets it a-work; and learning, a mere hoard of gold kept by a devil till sack commences it and sets it in act and use. Hereof comes it that Prince Harry is valiant; for the cold blood he did naturally inherit of his father, he hath, like lean, sterile, and bare land, manured, husbanded, and till'd, with excellent endeavour of drinking good and good store of fertile sherris, that he is become very hot and valiant. If I had a thousand sons, the first humane principle I would teach them should be to forswear thin potations, and to addict themselves to sack.

Enter BARDOLPH.

How now, Bardolph!

BARDOLPH The army is discharged all and gone.

FALSTAFF Let them go. I'll through Gloucestershire, and there will I visit Master Robert Shallow, Esquire. I have him already temp'ring between my finger and my thumb, and shortly will I seal with him. Come away.

[*Exeunt*.

SCENE IV. *Westminster. The Jerusalem Chamber.*

Enter the KING, PRINCE THOMAS OF CLARENCE, PRINCE HUMPHREY OF GLOUCESTER, WARWICK, *and Others*.

KING Now, lords, if God doth give successful end
To this debate that bleedeth at our doors,
We will our youth lead on to higher fields,
And draw no swords but what are sanctified.
Our navy is address'd, our power collected,
Our substitutes in absence well invested,
And everything lies level to our wish.
Only we want a little personal strength;
And pause us till these rebels, now afoot,
Come underneath the yoke of government.

WARWICK Both which we doubt not but your Majesty
Shall soon enjoy.

KING Humphrey, my son of Gloucester,
Where is the Prince your brother?

GLOUCESTER I think he's gone to hunt, my lord, at Windsor.

KING And how accompanied?

GLOUCESTER I do not know, my lord.

KING Is not his brother, Thomas of Clarence, with him?

GLOUCESTER No, my good lord, he is in presence here.

CLARENCE What would my lord and father?

KING Nothing but well to thee, Thomas of Clarence.
How chance thou art not with the Prince thy brother?
He loves thee, and thou dost neglect him, Thomas.
Thou hast a better place in his affection
Than all thy brothers; cherish it, my boy,
And noble offices thou mayst effect
Of mediation, after I am dead,
Between his greatness and thy other brethren.
Therefore omit him not; blunt not his love,
Nor lose the good advantage of his grace
By seeming cold or careless of his will;
For he is gracious if he be observ'd.
He hath a tear for pity and a hand
Open as day for melting charity;
Yet notwithstanding, being incens'd, he is flint;
As humorous as winter, and as sudden
As flaws congealed in the spring of day.
His temper, therefore, must be well observ'd.
Chide him for faults, and do it reverently,
When you perceive his blood inclin'd to mirth;
But, being moody, give him line and scope
Till that his passions, like a whale on ground,
Confound themselves with working. Learn this, Thomas,
And thou shalt prove a shelter to thy friends,
A hoop of gold to bind thy brothers in,
That the united vessel of their blood,
Mingled with venom of suggestion –
As, force perforce, the age will pour it in –
Shall never leak, though it do work as strong
As aconitum or rash gunpowder.

CLARENCE I shall observe him with all care and love.

KING Why art thou not at Windsor with him, Thomas?
CLARENCE He is not there to-day; he dines in London.
KING And how accompanied? Canst thou tell that?
CLARENCE With Poins, and other his continual followers.
KING Most subject is the fattest soil to weeds;
And he, the noble image of my youth,
Is overspread with them; therefore my grief
Stretches itself beyond the hour of death.
The blood weeps from my heart when I do shape,
In forms imaginary, th' unguided days
And rotten times that you shall look upon
When I am sleeping with my ancestors.
For when his headstrong riot hath no curb,
When rage and hot blood are his counsellors,
When means and lavish manners meet together,
O, with what wings shall his affections fly
Towards fronting peril and oppos'd decay!
WARWICK My gracious lord, you look beyond him quite.
The Prince but studies his companions
Like a strange tongue, wherein, to gain the language,
'Tis needful that the most immodest word
Be look'd upon and learnt; which once attain'd,
Your Highness knows, comes to no further use
But to be known and hated. So, like gross terms,
The Prince will, in the perfectness of time,
Cast off his followers; and their memory
Shall as a pattern or a measure live
By which his Grace must mete the lives of other,
Turning past evils to advantages.
KING 'Tis seldom when the bee doth leave her comb
In the dead carrion.

Enter WESTMORELAND.

Who's here? Westmoreland?
WESTMORELAND Health to my sovereign, and new happiness
Added to that that I am to deliver!
Prince John, your son, doth kiss your Grace's hand.
Mowbray, the Bishop Scroop, Hastings, and all,
Are brought to the correction of your law.
There is not now a rebel's sword unsheath'd,
But Peace puts forth her olive everywhere.
The manner how this action hath been borne
Here at more leisure may your Highness read,
With every course in his particular.
KING O Westmoreland, thou art a summer bird,
Which ever in the haunch of winter sings
The lifting up of day.

Enter HARCOURT.

Look here's more news.
HARCOURT From enemies heaven keep your Majesty;
And, when they stand against you, may they fall
As those that I am come to tell you of!
The Earl Northumberland and the Lord Bardolph,
With a great power of English and of Scots,
Are by the shrieve of Yorkshire overthrown.
The manner and true order of the fight
This packet, please it you, contains at large.
KING And wherefore should these good news make me sick?
Will Fortune never come with both hands full,
But write her fair words still in foulest letters?
She either gives a stomach and no food –
Such are the poor, in health – or else a feast,
And takes away the stomach – such are the rich
That have abundance and enjoy it not.
I should rejoice now at this happy news;
And now my sight fails, and my brain is giddy.
O me! come near me now I am much ill.
GLOUCESTER Comfort, your Majesty!
CLARENCE O my royal father!
WESTMORELAND My sovereign lord, cheer up yourself, look up.
WARWICK Be patient, Princes; you do know these fits
Are with his Highness very ordinary.
Stand from him, give him air; he'll straight be well.
CLARENCE No, no; he cannot long hold out these pangs.
Th' incessant care and labour of his mind
Hath wrought the mure that should confine it in
So thin that life looks through, and will break out.
GLOUCESTER The people fear me; for they do observe
Unfather'd heirs and loathly births of nature.
The seasons change their manners, as the year
Had found some months asleep, and leapt them over.
CLARENCE The river hath thrice flow'd, no ebb between;
And the old folk, Time's doting chronicles,
Say it did so a little time before
That our great grandsire, Edward, sick'd and died.
WARWICK Speak lower, Princes, for the King recovers.
GLOUCESTER This apoplexy will certain be his end.
KING I pray you take me up, and bear me hence
Into some other chamber. Softly, pray.

SCENE V. *Westminster. Another chamber.*

The KING lying on a bed; CLARENCE, GLOUCESTER, WARWICK, and Others in attendance.

KING Let there be no noise made, my gentle friends;
Unless some dull and favourable hand
Will whisper music to my weary spirit.

WARWICK Call for the music in the other room.

KING Set me the crown upon my pillow here.

CLARENCE His eye is hollow, and he changes much.

WARWICK Less noise, less noise!

Enter PRINCE HENRY.

PRINCE Who saw the Duke of Clarence?

CLARENCE I am here, brother, full of heaviness.

PRINCE How now! Rain within doors, and none abroad!
How doth the King?

GLOUCESTER Exceeding ill.

PRINCE Heard he the good news yet? Tell it him.

GLOUCESTER He alt'red much upon the hearing it.

PRINCE If he be sick with joy, he'll recover without physic.

WARWICK Not so much noise, my lords. Sweet Prince, speak low;
The King your father is dispos'd to sleep.

CLARENCE Let us withdraw into the other room.

WARWICK Will't please your Grace to go along with us?

PRINCE No; I will sit and watch here by the King.

[*Exeunt all but the Prince.*

Why doth the crown lie there upon his pillow,
Being so troublesome a bedfellow?
O polish'd perturbation! golden care!
That keep'st the ports of slumber open wide
To many a watchful night! Sleep with it now!
Yet not so sound and half so deeply sweet
As he whose brow with homely biggen bound
Snores out the watch of night. O majesty!
When thou dost pinch thy bearer, thou dost sit
Like a rich armour worn in heat of day
That scald'st with safety. By his gates of breath
There lies a downy feather which stirs not.
Did he suspire, that light and weightless down
Perforce must move. My gracious lord! my father!
This sleep is sound indeed; this is a sleep
That from this golden rigol hath divorc'd
So many English kings. Thy due from me
Is tears and heavy sorrows of the blood
Which nature, love, and filial tenderness,
Shall, O dear father, pay thee plenteously.
My due from thee is this imperial crown,
Which, as immediate from thy place and blood,
Derives itself to me. [*Putting on the crown*] Lo where it sits –
Which God shall guard; and put the world's whole strength
Into one giant arm, it shall not force
This lineal honour from me. This from thee
Will I to mine leave as 'tis left to me. [*Exit.*

KING Warwick! Gloucester! Clarence!

Re-enter WARWICK, GLOUCESTER, CLARENCE.

CLARENCE Doth the King call?

WARWICK What would your Majesty? How fares your Grace?

KING Why did you leave me here alone, my lords?

CLARENCE We left the Prince my brother here, my liege,
Who undertook to sit and watch by you.

KING The Prince of Wales! Where is he? Let me see him.
He is not here.

WARWICK This door is open; he is gone this way.

GLOUCESTER He came not through the chamber where we stay'd.

KING Where is the crown? Who took it from my pillow?

WARWICK When we withdrew, my liege, we left it here.

KING The Prince hath ta'en it hence. Go, seek him out.
Is he so hasty that he doth suppose
My sleep my death?
Find him, my Lord of Warwick; chide him hither. [*Exit Warwick.*
This part of his conjoins with my disease
And helps to end me. See, sons, what things you are!
How quickly nature falls into revolt
When gold becomes her object!
For this the foolish over-careful fathers
Have broke their sleep with thoughts,
Their brains with care, their bones with industry;
For this they have engrossed and pil'd up
The cank'red heaps of strange-achieved gold;
For this they have been thoughtful to invest
Their sons with arts and martial exercises;
When, like the bee, tolling from every flower
The virtuous sweets,
Our thighs with wax, our mouths with honey pack'd,
We bring it to the hive, and, like the bees,
Are murd'red for our pains. This bitter taste
Yields his engrossments to the ending father.

Re-enter WARWICK.

Now where is he that will not stay so long

Till his friend sickness hath determin'd me?

WARWICK My lord, I found the Prince in the next room,
Washing with kindly tears his gentle cheeks,
With such a deep demeanour in great sorrow,
That tyranny, which never quaff'd but blood,
Would, by beholding him, have wash'd his knife
With gentle eye-drops. He is coming hither.

KING But wherefore did he take away the crown?

Re-enter PRINCE HENRY.

Lo where he comes. Come hither to me, Harry.
Depart the chamber, leave us here alone.

[Exeunt all but the King and the Prince.

PRINCE I never thought to hear you speak again.

KING Thy wish was father, Harry, to that thought.
I stay too long by thee, I weary thee.
Dost thou so hunger for mine empty chair
That thou wilt needs invest thee with my honours
Before thy hour be ripe? O foolish youth!
Thou seek'st the greatness that will overwhelm thee.
Stay but a little, for my cloud of dignity
Is held from falling with so weak a wind
That it will quickly drop; my day is dim.
Thou hast stol'n that which, after some few hours,
Were thine without offence; and at my death
Thou hast seal'd up my expectation.
Thy life did manifest thou lov'dst me not,
And thou wilt have me die assur'd of it.
Thou hid'st a thousand daggers in thy thoughts,
Which thou hast whetted on thy stony heart,
To stab at half an hour of my life.
What, canst thou not forbear me half an hour?
Then get thee gone, and dig my grave thyself;
And bid the merry bells ring to thine ear
That thou art crowned, not that I am dead.
Let all the tears that should bedew my hearse
Be drops of balm to sanctify thy head;
Only compound me with forgotten dust;
Give that which gave thee life unto the worms.
Pluck down my officers, break my decrees;
For now a time is come to mock at form –
Harry the Fifth is crown'd. Up, vanity:
Down, royal state. All you sage counsellors, hence.
And to the English court assemble now,
From every region, apes of idleness.
Now, neighbour confines, purge you of your scum.
Have you a ruffian that will swear, drink, dance,
Revel the night, rob, murder, and commit
The oldest sins the newest kind of ways?
Be happy, he will trouble you no more.
England shall double gild his treble guilt;
England shall give him office, honour, might;
For the fifth Harry from curb'd license plucks
The muzzle of restraint, and the wild dog
Shall flesh his tooth on every innocent.
O my poor kingdom, sick with civil blows!
When that my care could not withhold thy riots,
What wilt thou do when riot is thy care?
O, thou wilt be a wilderness again,
Peopled with wolves, thy old inhabitants!

PRINCE O, pardon me, my liege! But for my tears,
The moist impediments unto my speech,
I had forestall'd this dear and deep rebuke
Ere you with grief had spoke and I had heard
The course of it so far. There is your crown,
And He that wears the crown immortally
Long guard it yours! *[Kneeling]* If I affect it more
Than as your honour and as your renown,
Let me no more from this obedience rise,
Which my most inward true and duteous spirit
Teacheth this prostrate and exterior bending!
God witness with me, when I here came in
And found no course of breath within your Majesty,
How cold it struck my heart! If I do feign,
O, let me in my present wildness die,
And never live to show th' incredulous world
The noble change that I have purposed!
Coming to look on you, thinking you dead –
And dead almost, my liege, to think you were –
I spake unto this crown as having sense,
And thus upbraided it: 'The care on thee depending
Hath fed upon the body of my father;
Therefore thou best of gold art worst of gold.
Other, less fine in carat, is more precious,
Preserving life in med'cine potable;
But thou, most fine, most honour'd, most renown'd,
Hast eat thy bearer up'. Thus, my most royal liege,
Accusing it, I put it on my head,
To try with it – as with an enemy
That had before my face murd'red my father –
The quarrel of a true inheritor.
But if it did infect my blood with joy,
Or swell my thoughts to any strain of pride;
If any rebel or vain spirit of mine
Did with the least affection of a welcome
Give entertainment to the might of it,
Let God for ever keep it from my head,
And make me as the poorest vassal is,
That doth with awe and terror kneel to it!

KING O my son,
God put it in thy mind to take it hence,

That thou mightst win the more thy father's love,
Pleading so wisely in excuse of it!
Come hither, Harry; sit thou by my bed,
And hear, I think, the very latest counsel
That ever I shall breathe. God knows, my son,
By what by-paths and indirect crook'd ways
I met this crown; and I myself know well
How troublesome it sat upon my head:
To thee it shall descend with better quiet,
Better opinion, better confirmation;
For all the soil of the achievement goes
With me into the earth. It seem'd in me
But as an honour snatch'd with boist'rous hand;
And I had many living to upbraid
My gain of it by their assistances;
Which daily grew to quarrel and to bloodshed,
Wounding supposed peace. All these bold fears
Thou seest with peril I have answered;
For all my reign hath been but as a scene
Acting that argument. And now my death
Changes the mood; for what in me was purchas'd
Falls upon thee in a more fairer sort;
So thou the garland wear'st successively.
Yet, though thou stand'st more sure than I could do,
Thou art not firm enough, since griefs are green;
And all my friends, which thou must make thy friends,
Have but their stings and teeth newly ta'en out;
By whose fell working I was first advanc'd,
And by whose power I well might lodge a fear
To be again displac'd; which to avoid,
I cut them off; and had a purpose now
To lead out many to the Holy Land,
Lest rest and lying still might make them look
Too near unto my state. Therefore, my Harry,
Be it thy course to busy giddy minds
With foreign quarrels, that action, hence borne out,
May waste the memory of the former days.
More would I, but my lungs are wasted so
That strength of speech is utterly denied me.
How I came by the crown, O God, forgive;
And grant it may with thee in true peace live!

PRINCE My gracious liege,
You won it, wore it, kept it, gave it me;
Then plain and right must my possession be;
Which I with more than with a common pain
'Gainst all the world will rightfully maintain.

Enter PRINCE JOHN OF LANCASTER, WARWICK, Lords, and Others.

KING Look, look, here comes my John of Lancaster.

PRINCE JOHN Health, peace, and happiness, to my royal father!

KING Thou bring'st me happiness and peace, son John;
But health, alack, with youthful wings is flown
From this bare wither'd trunk. Upon thy sight
My worldly business makes a period.
Where is my Lord of Warwick?

PRINCE My Lord of Warwick!

KING Doth any name particular belong
Unto the lodging where I first did swoon?

WARWICK 'Tis call'd Jerusalem, my noble lord.

KING Laud be to God! Even there my life must end.
It hath been prophesied to me many years,
I should not die but in Jerusalem;
Which vainly I suppos'd the Holy Land.
But bear me to that chamber; there I'll lie;
In that Jerusalem shall Harry die. [*Exeunt.*

ACT FIVE

SCENE I. *Gloucestershire. Shallow's house.*

Enter SHALLOW, FALSTAFF, BARDOLPH, and Page.

SHALLOW By cock and pie, sir, you shall not away to-night. What, Davy, I say!

FALSTAFF You must excuse me, Master Robert Shallow.

SHALLOW I will not excuse you; you shall not be excus'd; excuses shall not be admitted; there is no excuse shall serve; you shall not be excus'd. Why, Davy!

Enter DAVY.

DAVY Here, sir.

SHALLOW Davy, Davy, Davy, Davy; let me see, Davy; let me see, Davy; let me see – yea, marry, William cook, bid him come hither. Sir John, you shall not be excus'd.

DAVY Marry, sir, thus: those precepts cannot be served; and, again, sir – shall we sow the headland with wheat?

SHALLOW With red wheat, Davy. But for William cook – are there no young pigeons?

DAVY Yes, sir. Here is now the smith's note for shoeing and plough-irons.

SHALLOW Let it be cast, and paid. Sir John, you shall not be excused.

DAVY Now, sir, a new link to the bucket must needs be had; and, sir, do you mean to stop any of William's wages about the sack he lost the other day at Hinckley fair?

SHALLOW 'A shall answer it. Some pigeons, Davy, a couple of short-legg'd hens, a joint of mutton, and any pretty little tiny kickshaws, tell William cook.

DAVY Doth the man of war stay all night, sir?

SHALLOW Yea, Davy; I will use him well. A friend i' th' court is better than a penny in purse. Use his men well, Davy; for they are arrant knaves and will backbite.

DAVY No worse than they are backbitten, sir; for they have marvellous foul linen.

SHALLOW Well conceited, Davy – about thy business, Davy.

DAVY I beseech you, sir, to countenance William Visor of Woncot against Clement Perkes o' th' hill.

SHALLOW There is many complaints, Davy, against that Visor. That Visor is an arrant knave, on my knowledge.

DAVY I grant your worship that he is a knave, sir; but yet God forbid, sir, but a knave should have some countenance at his friend's request. An honest man, sir, is able to speak for himself, when a knave is not. I have serv'd your worship truly, sir, this eight years; an I cannot once or twice in a quarter bear out a knave against an honest man, I have but a very little credit with your worship. The knave is mine honest friend, sir; therefore, I beseech you, let him be countenanc'd.

SHALLOW Go to; I say he shall have no wrong. Look about, Davy. [*Exit Davy*] Where are you, Sir John? Come, come, come, off with your boots. Give me your hand, Master Bardolph.

BARDOLPH I am glad to see your worship.

SHALLOW I thank thee with all my heart, kind Master Bardolph. [*To the Page*] And welcome, my tall fellow. Come, Sir John.

FALSTAFF I'll follow you, good Master Robert Shallow. [*Exit Shallow*] Bardolph, look to our horses. [*Exeunt Bardolph and Page*] If I were sawed into quantities, I should make four dozen of such bearded hermits' staves as Master Shallow. It is a wonderful thing to see the semblable coherence of his men's spirits and his. They, by observing of him, do bear themselves like foolish justices: he, by conversing with them, is turned into a justice-like serving-man. Their spirits are so married in conjunction with the participation of society that they flock together in consent, like so many wild geese. If I had a suit to Master Shallow, I would humour his men with the imputation of being near their master; if to his men, I would curry with Master Shallow that no man could better command his servants. It is certain that either wise bearing or ignorant carriage is caught, as men take diseases, one of another; therefore let men take heed of their company. I will devise matter enough out of this Shallow to keep Prince Harry in continual laughter the wearing out of six fashions, which is four terms, or two actions; and 'a shall laugh without intervallums. O, it is much that a lie with a slight oath, and a jest with a sad brow, will do with a fellow that never had the ache in his shoulders! O, you shall see him laugh till his face be like a wet cloak ill laid up!

SHALLOW [*Within*] Sir John!

FALSTAFF I come, Master Shallow; I come, Master Shallow. [*Exit.*

SCENE II. *Westminster. The palace.*

Enter, severally, WARWICK and the LORD CHIEF JUSTICE.

WARWICK How now, my Lord Chief Justice; whither away?
CHIEF JUSTICE How doth the King?
WARWICK Exceeding well; his cares are now all ended.
CHIEF JUSTICE I hope, not dead.
WARWICK He's walk'd the way of nature;
And to our purposes he lives no more.
CHIEF JUSTICE I would his Majesty had call'd me with him.
The service that I truly did his life
Hath left me open to all injuries.
WARWICK Indeed I think the young King loves you not.
CHIEF JUSTICE I know he doth not, and do arm myself
To welcome the condition of the time,
Which cannot look more hideously upon me
Than I have drawn it in my fantasy.

Enter LANCASTER, CLARENCE, GLOUCESTER, WESTMORELAND, and Others.

WARWICK Here come the heavy issue of dead Harry.
O that the living Harry had the temper
Of he, the worst of these three gentlemen!
How many nobles then should hold their places
That must strike sail to spirits of vile sort!
CHIEF JUSTICE O God, I fear all will be overturn'd.
PRINCE JOHN Good morrow, cousin Warwick, good morrow.
GLOUCESTER, CLARENCE Good morrow, cousin.
PRINCE JOHN We meet like men that had forgot to speak.
WARWICK We do remember; but our argument
Is all too heavy to admit much talk.
PRINCE JOHN Well, peace be with him that hath made us heavy!

CHIEF JUSTICE Peace be with us, lest we be heavier!
GLOUCESTER O, good my lord, you have lost a friend indeed;
And I dare swear you borrow not that face
Of seeming sorrow – it is sure your own.
PRINCE JOHN Though no man be assur'd what grace to find,
You stand in coldest expectation.
I am the sorrier; would 'twere otherwise.
CLARENCE Well, you must now speak Sir John Falstaff fair;
Which swims against your stream of quality.
CHIEF JUSTICE Sweet Princes, what I did, I did in
honour,
Led by th' impartial conduct of my soul;
And never shall you see that I will beg
A ragged and forestall'd remission.
If truth and upright innocency fail me,
I'll to the King my master that is dead,
And tell him who hath sent me after him.
WARWICK Here comes the Prince.

Enter KING HENRY THE FIFTH, attended.

CHIEF JUSTICE Good morrow, and God save your
Majesty!
KING This new and gorgeous garment, majesty,
Sits not so easy on me as you think.
Brothers, you mix your sadness with some fear.
This is the English, not the Turkish court;
Not Amurath an Amurath succeeds,
But Harry Harry. Yet be sad, good brothers,
For, by my faith, it very well becomes you.
Sorrow so royally in you appears
That I will deeply put the fashion on,
And wear it in my heart. Why, then, be sad;
But entertain no more of it, good brothers,
Than a joint burden laid upon us all.
For me, by heaven, I bid you be assur'd,
I'll be your father and your brother too;
Let me but bear your love, I'll bear your cares.
Yet weep that Harry's dead, and so will I;
But Harry lives that shall convert those tears
By number into hours of happiness.
BROTHERS We hope no otherwise from your Majesty.
KING You all look strangely on me; and you most.
You are, I think, assur'd I love you not.
CHIEF JUSTICE I am assur'd, if I be measur'd rightly,
Your Majesty hath no just cause to hate me.
KING No?
How might a prince of my great hopes forget
So great indignities you laid upon me?
What, rate, rebuke, and roughly send to prison,
Th' immediate heir of England! Was this easy?
May this be wash'd in Lethe and forgotten?
CHIEF JUSTICE I then did use the person of your father;
The image of his power lay then in me;
And in th' administration of his law,
Whiles I was busy for the commonwealth,
Your Highness pleased to forget my place,
The majesty and power of law and justice,
The image of the King whom I presented,
And struck me in my very seat of judgment;
Whereon, as an offender to your father,
I gave bold way to my authority
And did commit you. If the deed were ill,
Be you contented, wearing now the garland,
To have a son set your decrees at nought,
To pluck down justice from your awful bench,
To trip the course of law, and blunt the sword
That guards the peace and safety of your person;
Nay, more, to spurn at your most royal image,
And mock your workings in a second body.
Question your royal thoughts, make the case yours;
Be now the father, and propose a son;
Hear your own dignity so much profan'd,
See your most dreadful laws so loosely slighted,
Behold yourself so by a son disdain'd;
And then imagine me taking your part
And, in your power, soft silencing your son.
After this cold considerance, sentence me;
And, as you are a king, speak in your state
What I have done that misbecame my place,
My person, or my liege's sovereignty.
KING You are right, Justice, and you weigh this well;
Therefore still bear the balance and the sword;
And I do wish your honours may increase
Till you do live to see a son of mine
Offend you, and obey you, as I did.
So shall I live to speak my father's words:
'Happy am I that have a man so bold
That dares do justice on my proper son;
And not less happy, having such a son
That would deliver up his greatness so
Into the hands of justice'. You did commit me;
For which I do commit into your hand
Th' unstained sword that you have us'd to bear;
With this remembrance – that you use the same
With the like bold, just, and impartial spirit
As you have done 'gainst me. There is my hand.
You shall be as a father to my youth;
My voice shall sound as you do prompt mine ear;
And I will stoop and humble my intents
To your well-practis'd wise directions.
And, Princes all, believe me, I beseech you,

My father is gone wild into his grave,
For in his tomb lie my affections;
And with his spirits sadly I survive,
To mock the expectation of the world,
To frustrate prophecies, and to raze out
Rotten opinion, who hath writ me down
After my seeming. The tide of blood in me
Hath proudly flow'd in vanity till now.
Now doth it turn and ebb back to the sea,
Where it shall mingle with the state of floods,
And flow henceforth in formal majesty.
Now call we our high court of parliament;
And let us choose such limbs of noble counsel,
That the great body of our state may go
In equal rank with the best govern'd nation;
That war, or peace, or both at once, may be
As things acquainted and familiar to us;
In which you, father, shall have foremost hand.
Our coronation done, we will accite,
As I before remember'd, all our state;
And – God consigning to my good intents –
No prince nor peer shall have just cause to say,
God shorten Harry's happy life one day. [*Exeunt*.

SCENE III. *Gloucestershire. Shallow's orchard.*

Enter FALSTAFF, SHALLOW, SILENCE, BARDOLPH, the Page, and DAVY.

SHALLOW Nay, you shall see my orchard, where, in an arbour, we will eat a last year's pippin of mine own graffing, with a dish of caraways, and so forth. Come, cousin Silence. And then to bed.

FALSTAFF Fore God, you have here a goodly dwelling and rich.

SHALLOW Barren, barren, barren; beggars all, beggars all, Sir John – marry, good air. Spread, Davy, spread, Davy; well said, Davy.

FALSTAFF This Davy serves you for good uses; he is your serving-man and your husband.

SHALLOW A good varlet, a good varlet, a very good varlet, Sir John. By the mass, I have drunk too much sack at supper. A good varlet. Now sit down, now sit down; come, cousin.

SILENCE Ah, sirrah! quoth-a – we shall [*Singing*.
Do nothing but eat and make good cheer,
And praise God for the merry year;
When flesh is cheap and females dear,
And lusty lads roam here and there,
So merrily,
And ever among so merrily.

FALSTAFF There's a merry heart! Good Master Silence, I'll give you a health for that anon.

SHALLOW Give Master Bardolph some wine, Davy.

DAVY Sweet sir, sit; I'll be with you anon; most sweet sir, sit. Master Page, good Master Page, sit. Proface! What you want in meat, we'll have in drink. But you must bear; the heart's all. [*Exit*.

SHALLOW Be merry, Master Bardolph; and, my little soldier there, be merry.

SILENCE [*Singing*]
Be merry, be merry, my wife has all;
For women are shrews, both short and tall;
'Tis merry in hall when beards wag all;
And welcome merry Shrove-tide.
Be merry, be merry.

FALSTAFF I did not think Master Silence had been a man of this mettle.

SILENCE Who, I? I have been merry twice and once ere now.

Re-enter DAVY.

DAVY [*To Bardolph*] There's a dish of leather-coats for you.

SHALLOW Davy!

DAVY Your workship! I'll be with you straight. [*To Bardolph*] A cup of wine, sir?

SILENCE [*Singing*]
A cup of wine that's brisk and fine,
And drink unto the leman mine;
And a merry heart lives long-a.

FALSTAFF Well said, Master Silence.

SILENCE An we shall be merry, now comes in the sweet o' th' night.

FALSTAFF Health and long life to you, Master Silence!

SILENCE [*Singing*]
Fill the cup, and let it come,
I'll pledge you a mile to th' bottom.

SHALLOW Honest Bardolph, welcome; if thou want'st anything and wilt not call, beshrew thy heart. Welcome, my little tiny thief and welcome indeed too. I'll drink to Master Bardolph, and to all the cabileros about London.

DAVY I hope to see London once ere I die.

BARDOLPH An I might see you there, Davy!

SHALLOW By the mass, you'll crack a quart together – ha! will you not, Master Bardolph?

BARDOLPH Yea, sir, in a pottle-pot.

SHALLOW By God's liggens, I thank thee. The knave will stick by thee, I can assure thee that. 'A will not out, 'a; 'tis true bred.

BARDOLPH And I'll stick by him, sir.

SHALLOW Why, there spoke a king. Lack nothing; be merry. [*One knocks at door*] Look who's at door there, ho! Who knocks? [*Exit Davy*.

FALSTAFF [*To Silence, who has drunk a bumper*] Why, now you have done me right.

SILENCE [*Singing*] Do me right,
And dub me knight.
Samingo.
Is't not so?

FALSTAFF 'Tis so.

SILENCE Is't so? Why then, say an old man can do somewhat.

Re-enter DAVY.

DAVY An't please your worship, there's one Pistol come from the court with news.

FALSTAFF From the court? Let him come in.

Enter PISTOL.

How now, Pistol?

PISTOL Sir John, God save you!

FALSTAFF What wind blew you hither, Pistol?

PISTOL Not the ill wind which blows no man to good. Sweet knight, thou art now one of the greatest men in this realm.

SILENCE By'r lady, I think 'a be, but goodman Puff of Barson.

PISTOL Puff!
Puff in thy teeth, most recreant coward base!
Sir John, I am thy Pistol and thy friend,
And helter-skelter have I rode to thee;
And tidings do I bring, and lucky joys,
And golden times, and happy news of price.

FALSTAFF I pray thee now, deliver them like a man of this world.

PISTOL A foutra for the world and worldlings base!
I speak of Africa and golden joys.

FALSTAFF O base Assyrian knight, what is thy news?
Let King Cophetua know the truth thereof.

SILENCE [*Singing*] And Robin Hood, Scarlet, and John.

PISTOL Shall dunghill curs confront the Helicons?
And shall good news be baffled?
Then, Pistol, lay thy head in Furies' lap.

SHALLOW Honest gentleman, I know not your breeding.

PISTOL Why, then, lament therefore.

SHALLOW Give me pardon, sir. If, sir, you come with news from the court, I take it there's but two ways – either to utter them or conceal them. I am, sir, under the King, in some authority.

PISTOL Under which king, Bezonian? Speak, or die.

SHALLOW Under King Harry.

PISTOL Harry the Fourth – or Fifth?

SHALLOW Harry the Fourth.

PISTOL A foutra for thine office!
Sir John, thy tender lambkin now is King;
Harry the Fifth's the man. I speak the truth.
When Pistol lies, do this; and fig me, like
The bragging Spaniard.

FALSTAFF What, is the old king dead?

PISTOL As nail in door. The things I speak are just.

FALSTAFF Away, Bardolph! saddle my horse. Master Robert Shallow, choose what office thou wilt in the land, 'tis thine. Pistol, I will double-charge thee with dignities.

BARDOLPH O joyful day!
I would not take a knighthood for my fortune.

PISTOL What, I do bring good news?

FALSTAFF Carry Master Silence to bed. Master Shallow, my Lord Shallow, be what thou wilt – I am Fortune's steward. Get on thy boots; we'll ride all night. O sweet Pistol! Away, Bardolph! [*Exit Bardolph*] Come, Pistol, utter more to me; and withal devise something to do thyself good. Boot, boot, Master Shallow! I know the young King is sick for me. Let us take any man's horses: the laws of England are at my commandment. Blessed are they that have been my friends; and woe to my Lord Chief Justice!

PISTOL Let vultures vile seize on his lungs also!
'Where is the life that late I led?' say they.
Why, here it is. Welcome these pleasant days!

[*Exeunt*

SCENE IV. *London. A street.*

Enter Beadles, dragging in HOSTESS QUICKLY and DOLL TEARSHEET.

HOSTESS No, thou arrant knave; I would to God that I might die, that I might have thee hang'd. Thou hast drawn my shoulder out of joint.

1 BEADLE The constables have delivered her over to me; and she shall have whipping-cheer enough, I warrant her. There hath been a man or two lately kill'd about her.

DOLL Nut-hook, nut-hook, you lie. Come on; I'll tell thee what, thou damn'd tripe-visag'd rascal, an the child I now go with do miscarry, thou wert better thou hadst struck thy mother, thou paper-fac'd villain.

HOSTESS O the Lord, that Sir John were come! He would make this a bloody day to somebody. But I pray God the fruit of her womb miscarry!

1 BEADLE If it do, you shall have a dozen of cushions again; you have but eleven now. Come, I charge you both go with me; for the man is dead that you and Pistol beat amongst you.

DOLL I'll tell you what, you thin man in a censer, I will have you as soundly swing'd for this – you due-bottle rogue, you filthy famish'd correctioner, if you be not swing'd, I'll forswear half-kirtles.

1 BEADLE Come, come, you she knight-errant, come.

HOSTESS O God, that right should thus overcome might! Well, of sufferance comes ease.

DOLL Come, you rogue, come; bring me to a justice.

HOSTESS Ay, come, you starv'd bloodhound.

DOLL Goodman death, goodman bones!

HOSTESS Thou atomy, thou!

DOLL Come, you thin thing! come, you rascal!

1 BEADLE Very well. [*Exeunt.*

SCENE V. *Westminster. Near the Abbey.*

Enter Grooms, strewing rushes.

1 GROOM More rushes, more rushes!

2 GROOM The trumpets have sounded twice.

3 GROOM 'Twill be two o'clock ere they come from the coronation. Dispatch, dispatch. [*Exeunt.*

Trumpets sound, and the KING and his Train pass over the stage. After them enter FALSTAFF, SHALLOW, PISTOL, BARDOLPH, and Page.

FALSTAFF Stand here by me, Master Robert Shallow; I will make the King do you grace. I will leer upon him, as 'a comes by; and do but mark the countenance that he will give me.

PISTOL God bless thy lungs, good knight!

FALSTAFF Come here, Pistol; stand behind me. [*To Shallow*] O, if I had had time to have made new liveries, I would have bestowed the thousand pound I borrowed of you. But 'tis no matter; this poor show doth better; this doth infer the zeal I had to see him.

SHALLOW It doth so.

FALSTAFF It shows my earnestness of affection –

SHALLOW It doth so.

FALSTAFF My devotion –

SHALLOW It doth, it doth, it doth.

FALSTAFF As it were, to ride day and night; and not to deliberate, not to remember, not to have patience to shift me –

SHALLOW It is best, certain.

FALSTAFF But to stand stained with travel, and sweating with desire to see him; thinking of nothing else, putting all affairs else in oblivion, as if there were nothing else to be done but to see him.

PISTOL 'Tis 'semper idem' for 'obsque hoc nihil est'. 'Tis all in every part.

SHALLOW 'Tis so, indeed.

PISTOL My knight, I will inflame thy noble liver
And make thee rage.
Thy Doll, and Helen of thy noble thoughts,
Is in base durance and contagious prison;
Hal'd thither
By most mechanical and dirty hand.
Rouse up revenge from ebon den with fell Alecto's snake,
For Doll is in. Pistol speaks nought but truth.

FALSTAFF I will deliver her.

[*Shouts within, and the trumpets sound.*

PISTOL There roar'd the sea, and trumpet-clangor sounds.

Enter the KING and his Train, the LORD CHIEF JUSTICE among them.

FALSTAFF God save thy Grace, King Hal; my royal Hal!

PISTOL The heavens thee guard and keep, most royal imp of fame!

FALSTAFF God save thee, my sweet boy!

KING My Lord Chief Justice, speak to that vain man.

CHIEF JUSTICE Have you your wits? Know you what 'tis you speak?

FALSTAFF My king! my Jove! I speak to thee, my heart!

KING I know thee not, old man. Fall to thy prayers.
How ill white hairs become a fool and jester!
I have long dreamt of such a kind of man,
So surfeit-swell'd, so old, and so profane;
But, being awak'd, I do despise my dream.
Make less thy body hence, and more thy grace;
Leave gormandizing; know the grave doth gape
For thee thrice wider than for other men –
Reply not to me with a fool-born jest;
Presume not that I am the thing I was,
For God doth know, so shall the world perceive,
That I have turn'd away my former self;
So will I those that kept me company.
When thou dost hear I am as I have been,
Approach me, and thou shalt be as thou wast,
The tutor and the feeder of my riots.
Till then I banish thee, on pain of death,
As I have done the rest of my misleaders,
Not to come near our person by ten mile.
For competence of life I will allow you,
That lack of means enforce you not to evils;
And, as we hear you do reform yourselves,
We will, according to your strengths and qualities,
Give you advancement. Be it your charge, my lord,
To see perform'd the tenour of our word.
Set on. [*Exeunt the King and his train.*

FALSTAFF Master Shallow, I owe you a thousand pound.

SHALLOW Yea, marry, Sir John; which I beseech you to let me have home with me.

FALSTAFF That can hardly be, Master Shallow. Do not you grieve at this; I shall be sent for in private to him. Look you, he must seem thus to the world. Fear not your advancements; I will be the man yet that shall make you great.

SHALLOW I cannot perceive how, unless you give me your doublet, and stuff me out with straw. I beseech you, good Sir John, let me have five hundred of my thousand.

FALSTAFF Sir, I will be as good as my word. This that you heard was but a colour.

SHALLOW A colour that I fear you will die in, Sir John.

FALSTAFF Fear no colours; go with me to dinner. Come, Lieutenant Pistol; come, Bardolph. I shall be sent for soon at night.

Re-enter PRINCE JOHN, the LORD CHIEF JUSTICE, with Officers.

CHIEF JUSTICE Go, carry Sir John Falstaff to the Fleet;
Take all his company along with him.

FALSTAFF My lord, my lord –

CHIEF JUSTICE I cannot now speak. I will hear you soon.
Take them away.

PISTOL Si fortuna me tormenta, spero me contenta.

[Exeunt all but Prince John and the Lord Chief Justice.

PRINCE JOHN I like this fair proceeding of the King's.
He hath intent his wonted followers
Shall all be very well provided for;
But all are banish'd till their conversations
Appear more wise and modest to the world.

CHIEF JUSTICE And so they are.

PRINCE JOHN The King hath call'd his parliament, my lord.

CHIEF JUSTICE He hath.

PRINCE JOHN I will lay odds that, ere this year expire,
We bear our civil swords and native fire
As far as France. I heard a bird so sing,
Whose music, to my thinking, pleas'd the King.
Come, will you hence? *[Exeunt.*

EPILOGUE

First my fear, then my curtsy, last my speech. My fear, is your displeasure; my curtsy, my duty; and my speech, to beg your pardons. If you look for a good speech now, you undo me; for what I have to say is of mine own making; and what, indeed, I should say will, I doubt, prove mine own marring. But to the purpose, and so to the venture. Be it known to you, as it is very well, I was lately here in the end of a displeasing play, to pray your patience for it and to promise you a better. I meant indeed, to pay you with this; which if like an ill venture it come unluckily home, I break, and you, my gentle creditors, lose. Here I promis'd you I would be, and here I commit my body to your mercies. Bate me some, and I will pay you some, and, as most debtors do, promise you infinitely; and so I kneel down before you – but, indeed, to pray for the Queen. If my tongue cannot entreat you to acquit me, will you command me to use my legs? And yet that were but light payment – to dance out of your debt. But a good conscience will make any possible satisfaction, and so would I. All the gentlewomen here have forgiven me. If the gentlemen will not, then the gentlemen do not agree with the gentlewomen, which was never seen before in such an assembly.

One word more, I beseech you. If you be not too much cloy'd with fat meat, ou· humble author will continue the story, with Sir John in it, and make you merry with fair Katherine of France; where, for anything I know, Falstaff shall die of a sweat, unless already 'a be kill'd with your hard opinions; for Oldcastle died a martyr and this is not the man. My tongue is weary; when my legs are too, I will bid you good night.

King Henry the Fifth

Introduction by DONALD MACKENZIE

Shakespearean history prefigures Shakespearean tragedy, not least in the innovative dramaturgy it demands. Shakespearean comedy is formulaic, recycling stock figures and conventional patterns. Turning chronicle history into drama Shakespeare has no such formulae to mobilise. Hence the varied (*and* varyingly successful) dramaturgy of the history plays which flowers in the astonishing inventiveness of the tragedies that follow. In the second tetralogy we move from the operatic elegance of *Richard II* through the carnival fertility (combined with taut pattern) of *Henry IV Part 1* to the open texture of *Henry IV Part 2* which can unravel into the empty or the haunting. After these *Henry V* seems a reversion to mere chronicle; at best a Tudor patriotic pageant with the limitations – chauvinism, simplistic celebration – that implies (cf. e.g. Edwards, 1979).

More limited than its predecessors – yes; but *Henry V* is more ambitious, more commanding of its audience than this allows. If chronicle, it is chronicle that aspires to the weight and surge of epic (cf. e.g. Taylor, 1982, Introduction). In voicing that aspiration the Chorus clashes it insistently against the confines of theatre and summons the audience to transcend the clash in a strenuous imaginative participation. Participation flows into our engagement by the play's oratory which generates a forward-thrusting energy that recurrently threatens to explode in violence. We experience this as early as Act 1 Scene 2 with the crescendo of urging from Henry's counsellors followed by the Dauphin's taunting gift and the accelerating vehemence of the king's response. Energy and vehemence are repeatedly reined in (as with Henry's second speech at Harfleur) or frustrated (as by Mountjoy's entry in Act 4 Scene 3 when the audience are keyed up for the charge to battle). The powerful tensions thus set up find release in the complex orchestration of Agincourt. Violence has run as a disturbing undertow or counter-tug to the play's epic heroism of war. In Henry's speeches of Act 1 Scene 2 or Act 3 it is present as rhetorical threat. In the apocalyptic fantasia of Williams's argument with the king [4.1.129–40] it twines with the question of the justice of the war to remind us that even a just war cannot be fought without injustice. The staging of Agincourt gives this a forceful twist when the plangency of the deaths of York and Suffolk is punctuated by the cold military imperative of Henry's command to have the prisoners' throats cut.

None of this, however, (and more could be cited) warrants a reading of the play as ironic (e.g. Gould in Quinn, 1969). For better or worse *Henry V* celebrates patriotic heroism. But its celebration is flexible: the king's going incognito among his troops leads to the challenging encounter with Williams and the comedy of its sequel, as well as to his soliloquy on the burden of kingship and the final desperate prayer for victory. And the triumph of Agincourt modulates down into the humility of Henry's thanksgiving.

All this shapes us for the coda of Act 5 where the destructiveness of war is unrolled in the speech of Burgundy and the drive of Henry's oratory wheels into the dancing energy of the speeches in which he woos Catherine. Military heroism and its cost yields to comedy; the play's action is crowned by marriage and peace – to be followed immediately by the final Chorus, decanting epic achievement into the hour-glass compression of the Epilogue sonnet which not only presents the ironical coda of history to the aspirations of the play's actors at the end but returns us (through the recall of Shakespeare's own first tetralogy) to history as staged.

Henry V is, overridingly, a public play, its private scenes or episodes interpenetrated by the public world and its necessities. Hence the scope it gives to oratory. This may mark an affinity with epic; it certainly meshes with the changing nature of kingship as Shakespeare has tracked that through his second tetralogy. As against Richard II, the legitimate, sacred *ruler* who is also incompetent and unjust and Henry IV, an effective ruler but also a conscience-haunted usurper, Henry V is the charismatic *leader* whose kingship is defined by his power to inspire.

The central role of oratory carries over into the first of the major tragedies, *Julius Caesar*, written immediately afterwards. In *Henry V* oratory calls out a style at once athletic and burnished which the conversation of the French nobles before Agincourt (3.7) spins into parody as Pistol's bombast provides a distant kettle-banging counterpoint. The style gives its own distinctive pleasures (Goldman, 1972) and is the principal means by which the play lifts chronicle into epic. It works on us most potently in Henry's Crispin speech where epic motifs (the passion for honour, the stand against overwhelming odds, the loyalties of the warrior band) are swept up into a supreme display of charismatic leadership which is also the creation of a patriotic myth. Against it stands the style of that other supreme moment, Falstaff's death, which interrupts the flow of chronicle or epic with an elegaic finality, bringing home irresistibly what political success and epic heroism can cost and must bypass.

King Henry the Fifth

DRAMATIS PERSONAE

CHORUS

KING HENRY THE FIFTH

DUKE OF GLOUCESTER, DUKE OF BEDFORD
brothers to the King

DUKE OF EXETER
uncle to the King

DUKE OF YORK
cousin to the King

EARL OF SALISBURY

EARL OF WESTMORELAND

EARL OF WARWICK

ARCHBISHOP OF CANTERBURY

BISHOP OF ELY

EARL OF CAMBRIDGE, LORD SCROOP, SIR THOMAS GREY
conspirators against the King

SIR THOMAS ERPINGHAM, GOWER, FLUELLEN, MACMORRIS, JAMY
officers in the King's army

BATES, COURT, WILLIAMS, NYM, BARDOLPH, PISTOL
soldiers in the King's army

Boy
A Herald

CHARLES THE SIXTH
King of France

LEWIS
the Dauphin

DUKE OF BURGUNDY

DUKE OF ORLEANS

DUKE OF BRITAINE

DUKE OF BOURBON

DUKE OF BERRI
The Constable of France

RAMBURES, GRANDPRÉ
French lords
Governor of Harfleur

MONTJOY
a French herald
Ambassadors to the King of England

ISABEL
Queen of France

KATHERINE
daughter to Charles and Isabel

ALICE
a lady attending her

HOSTESS
of the Boar's Head, Eastcheap; formerly Mrs. Quickly, now married to Pistol
Lords, Ladies, Officers, Soldiers, Messengers, and Attendants.

THE SCENE: ENGLAND AND FRANCE.

PROLOGUE

Enter CHORUS.

CHORUS O for a Muse of fire, that would ascend
The brightest heaven of invention,
A kingdom for a stage, princes to act,
And monarchs to behold the swelling scene!
Then should the warlike Harry, like himself,
Assume the port of Mars; and at his heels,
Leash'd in like hounds, should famine, sword, and fire,
Crouch for employment. But pardon, gentles all,
The flat unraised spirits that hath dar'd
On this unworthy scaffold to bring forth
So great an object. Can this cockpit hold
The vasty fields of France? Or may we cram
Within this wooden O the very casques
That did affright the air at Agincourt?
O, pardon! since a crooked figure may
Attest in little place a million;
And let us, ciphers to this great accompt,
On your imaginary forces work.
Suppose within the girdle of these walls
Are now confin'd two mighty monarchies,
Whose high upreared and abutting fronts
The perilous narrow ocean parts asunder.
Piece out our imperfections with your thoughts:
Into a thousand parts divide one man,
And make imaginary puissance;
Think, when we talk of horses, that you see them
Printing their proud hoofs i' th' receiving earth;
For 'tis your thoughts that now must deck our kings,
Carry them here and there, jumping o'er times,
Turning th' accomplishment of many years
Into an hour-glass; for the which supply,
Admit me Chorus to this history;
Who, prologue-like, your humble patience
pray Gently to hear, kindly to judge, our play.

[*Exit.*

ACT ONE

SCENE I. *London. An ante-chamber in the King's palace.*

Enter the ARCHBISHOP OF CANTERBURY and the BISHOP OF ELY.

CANTERBURY My lord, I'll tell you: that self bill is urg'd
Which in th' eleventh year of the last king's reign
Was like, and had indeed against us pass'd
But that the scambling and unquiet time
Did push it out of farther question.

ELY But how, my lord, shall we resist it now?

CANTERBURY It must be thought on. If it pass against us,
We lose the better half of our possession;
For all the temporal lands which men devout
By testament have given to the church
Would they strip from us; being valu'd thus –
As much as would maintain, to the King's honour,
Full fifteen earls and fifteen hundred knights,
Six thousand and two hundred good esquires;
And, to relief of lazars and weak age,
Of indigent faint souls, past corporal toil,
A hundred alms-houses right well supplied;
And to the coffers of the King, beside,
A thousand pounds by th' year: thus runs the bill.

ELY This would drink deep.

CANTERBURY 'Twould drink the cup and all.

ELY But what prevention?

CANTERBURY The King is full of grace and fair regard.

ELY And a true lover of the holy Church.

CANTERBURY The courses of his youth promis'd it not.
The breath no sooner left his father's body
But that his wildness, mortified in him,
Seem'd to die too; yea, at that very moment,
Consideration like an angel came
And whipp'd th' offending Adam out of him,
Leaving his body as a paradise
T' envelop and contain celestial spirits.
Never was such a sudden scholar made;
Never came reformation in a flood,
With such a heady currance, scouring faults;
Nor never Hydra-headed wilfulness
So soon did lose his seat, and all at once,
As in this king.

ELY We are blessed in the change.

CANTERBURY Hear him but reason in divinity,
And, all-admiring, with an inward wish
You would desire the King were made a prelate;
Hear him debate of commonwealth affairs,
You would say it hath been all in all his study;
List his discourse of war, and you shall hear
A fearful battle rend'red you in music.
Turn him to any cause of policy,
The Gordian knot of it he will unloose,
Familiar as his garter; that, when he speaks,
The air, a charter'd libertine, is still,
And the mute wonder lurketh in men's ears
To steal his sweet and honey'd sentences;
So that the art and practic part of life
Must be the mistress to this theoric;
Which is a wonder how his Grace should glean it,
Since his addiction was to courses vain,
His companies unletter'd, rude, and shallow,
His hours fill'd up with riots, banquets, sports;
And never noted in him and study,
Any retirement, any sequestration
From open haunts and popularity.

ELY The strawberry grows underneath the nettle,
And wholesome berries thrive and ripen best
Neighbour'd by fruit of baser quality;
And so the Prince obscur'd his contemplation
Under the veil of wildness; which, no doubt,
Grew like the summer grass, fastest by night,
Unseen, yet crescive in his faculty.

CANTERBURY It must be so; for miracles are ceas'd;
And therefore we must needs admit the means
How things are perfected.

ELY But, my good lord,
How now for mitigation of this bill
Urg'd by the Commons? Doth his Majesty
Incline to it, or no?

CANTERBURY He seems indifferent;
Or rather swaying more upon our part
Than cherishing th' exhibiters against us;
For I have made an offer to his Majesty –
Upon our spiritual convocation
And in regard of causes now in hand,
Which I have open'd to his Grace at large,
As touching France – to give a greater sum
Than ever at one time the clergy yet
Did to his predecessors part withal.

ELY How did this offer seem receiv'd, my lord?

CANTERBURY With good acceptance of his Majesty;
Save that there was not time enough to hear,
As I perceiv'd his Grace would fain have done,
The severals and unhidden passages
Of his true titles to some certain dukedoms,
And generally to the crown and seat of France,
Deriv'd from Edward, his great-grand-father.

ELY What was th' impediment that broke this off?
CANTERBURY The French ambassador upon that instant
Crav'd audience; and the hour, I think, is come
To give him hearing: is it four o'clock?
ELY It is.
CANTERBURY Then go we in, to know his embassy;
Which I could with a ready guess declare,
Before the Frenchman speak a word of it.
ELY I'll wait upon you, and I long to hear it.
[*Exeunt.*

SCENE II. *London. The Presence Chamber in the King's palace.*

Enter the KING, GLOUCESTER, BEDFORD, EXETER, WARWICK, WESTMORELAND, and Attendants.

KING Where is my gracious Lord of Canterbury?
EXETER Not here in presence.
KING Send for him, good uncle.
WESTMORELAND Shall we call in th' ambassador, my liege?
KING Not yet, my cousin; we would be resolv'd,
Before we hear him, of some things of weight
That task our thoughts, concerning us and France.

Enter the ARCHBISHOP OF CANTERBURY and the BISHOP OF ELY.

CANTERBURY God and his angels guard your sacred throne,
And make you long become it!
KING Sure, we thank you.
My learned lord, we pray you to proceed,
And justly and religiously unfold
Why the law Salique, that they have in France,
Or should or should not bar us in our claim;
And God forbid, my dear and faithful lord,
That you should fashion, wrest, or bow your reading,
Or nicely charge your understanding soul
With opening titles miscreate whose right
Suits not in native colours with the truth;
For God doth know how many, now in health,
Shall drop their blood in approbation
Of what your reverence shall incite us to.
Therefore take heed how you impawn our person,
How you awake our sleeping sword of war –
We charge you, in the name of God, take heed;
For never two such kingdoms did contend
Without much fall of blood; whose guiltless drops
Are every one a woe, a sore complaint,
'Gainst him whose wrongs gives edge unto the swords
That makes such waste in brief mortality.
Under this conjuration speak, my lord;
For we will hear, note, and believe in heart,
That what you speak is in your conscience wash'd
As pure as sin with baptism.
CANTERBURY Then hear me, gracious sovereign, and you peers,
That owe yourselves, your lives, and services,
To this imperial throne. There is no bar
To make against your Highness' claim to France
But this, which they produce from Pharamond:
'In terram Salicam mulieres ne succedant' –
'No woman shall succeed in Salique land';
Which Salique land the French unjustly gloze
To be the realm of France, and Pharamond
The founder of this law and female bar.
Yet their own authors faithfully affirm
That the land Salique is in Germany,
Between the floods of Sala and of Elbe;
Where Charles the Great, having subdu'd the Saxons,
There left behind and settled certain French;
Who, holding in disdain the German women
For some dishonest manners of their life,
Establish'd then this law: to wit, no female
Should be inheritrix in Salique land;
Which Salique, as I said, 'twixt Elbe and Sala,
Is at this day in Germany call'd Meisen.
Then doth it well appear the Salique law
Was not devised for the realm of France;
Nor did the French possess the Salique land
Until four hundred one and twenty years
After defunction of King Pharamond,
Idly suppos'd the founder of this law;
Who died within the year of our redemption
Four hundred twenty-six; and Charles the Great
Subdu'd the Saxons, and did seat the French
Beyond the river Sala, in the year
Eight hundred five. Besides, their writers say,
King Pepin, which deposed Childeric,
Did, as heir general, being descended
Of Blithild, which was daughter to King Clothair,
Make claim and title to the crown of France.
Hugh Capet also, who usurp'd the crown
Of Charles the Duke of Lorraine, sole heir male
Of the true line and stock of Charles the Great,
To find his title with some shows of truth –
Though in pure truth it was corrupt and naught –
Convey'd himself as th' heir to th' Lady Lingare,
Daughter to Charlemain, who was the son
To Lewis the Emperor, and Lewis the son
Of Charles the Great. Also King Lewis the Tenth,

Who was sole heir to the usurper Capet,
Could not keep quiet in his conscience,
Wearing the crown of France, till satisfied
That fair Queen Isabel, his grandmother,
Was lineal of the Lady Ermengare,
Daughter to Charles the foresaid Duke of Lorraine;
By the which marriage the line of Charles the Great
Was re-united to the Crown of France.
So that, as clear as is the summer's sun,
King Pepin's title, and Hugh Capet's claim,
King Lewis his satisfaction, all appear
To hold in right and title of the female;
So do the kings of France unto this day,
Howbeit they would hold up this Salique law
To bar your Highness claiming from the female;
And rather choose to hide them in a net
Than amply to imbar their crooked titles
Usurp'd from you and your progenitors.

KING May I with right and conscience make this claim?

CANTERBURY The sin upon my head, dread sovereign!
For in the book of Numbers is it writ,
When the man dies, let the inheritance
Descend unto the daughter. Gracious lord,
Stand for your own, unwind your bloody flag,
Look back into your mighty ancestors.
Go, my dread lord, to your great-grand-sire's tomb,
From whom you claim; invoke his warlike spirit,
And your great-uncle's, Edward the Black Prince,
Who on the French ground play'd a tragedy,
Making defeat on the full power of France,
Whiles his most mighty father on a hill
Stood smiling to behold his lion's whelp
Forage in blood of French nobility.
O noble English, that could entertain
With half their forces the full pride of France,
And let another half stand laughing by,
All out of work and cold for action!

ELY Awake remembrance of these valiant dead,
And with your puissant arm renew their feats.
You are their heir; you sit upon their throne;
The blood and courage that renowned them
Runs in your veins; and my thrice-puissant liege
Is in the very May-morn of his youth,
Ripe for exploits and mighty enterprises.

EXETER Your brother kings and monarchs of the earth
Do all expect that you should rouse yourself,
As did the former lions of your blood.

WESTMORELAND They know your Grace hath cause and means and might –
So hath your Highness; never King of England
Had nobles richer and more loyal subjects,
Whose hearts have left their bodies here in England
And lie pavilion'd in the fields of France.

CANTERBURY O, let their bodies follow, my dear liege,
With blood and sword and fire to win your right!
In aid whereof we of the spiritualty
Will raise your Highness such a mighty sum
As never did the clergy at one time
Bring in to any of your ancestors.

KING We must not only arm t' invade the French,
But lay down our proportions to defend
Against the Scot, who will make road upon us
With all advantages.

CANTERBURY They of those marches, gracious sovereign,
Shall be a wall sufficient to defend
Our inland from the pilfering borderers.

KING We do not mean the coursing snatchers only,
But fear the main intendment of the Scot,
Who hath been still a giddy neighbour to us;
For you shall read that my great-grandfather
Never went with his forces into France
But that the Scot on his unfurnish'd kingdom
Came pouring, like the tide into a breach,
With ample and brim fulness of his force,
Galling the gleaned land with hot assays,
Girding with grievous siege castles and towns;
That England, being empty of defence,
Hath shook and trembled at th' ill neighbourhood.

CANTERBURY She hath been then more fear'd than harm'd, my liege;
For hear her but exampled by herself:
When all her chivalry hath been in France,
And she a mourning widow of her nobles,
She hath herself not only well defended
But taken and impounded as a stray
The King of Scots; whom she did send to France,
To fill King Edward's fame with prisoner kings,
And make her chronicle as rich with praise
As is the ooze and bottom of the sea
With sunken wreck and sumless treasuries.

WESTMORELAND But there's a saying, very old and true:
'If that you will France win,
Then with Scotland first begin'.
For once the eagle England being in prey,
To her unguarded nest the weasel Scot
Comes sneaking, and so sucks her princely eggs,
Playing the mouse in absence of the cat,

To tear and havoc more than she can eat.
EXETER It follows, then, the cat must stay at home;
Yet that is but a crush'd necessity,
Since we have locks to safeguard necessaries
And pretty traps to catch the petty thieves.
While that the armed hand doth fight abroad,
Th' advised head defends itself at home;
For government, though high, and low, and lower,
Put into parts, doth keep in one consent,
Congreeing in a full and natural close,
Like music.
CANTERBURY Therefore doth heaven divide
The state of man in divers functions,
Setting endeavour in continual motion;
To which is fixed as an aim or butt
Obedience; for so work the honey bees,
Creatures that by a rule in nature teach
The act of order to a peopled kingdom.
They have a king, and officers of sorts,
Where some like magistrates correct at home;
Others like merchants venture trade abroad;
Others like soldiers, armed in their stings,
Make boot upon the summer's velvet buds,
Which pillage they with merry march bring home
To the tent-royal of their emperor;
Who, busied in his majesty, surveys
The singing masons building roofs of gold,
The civil citizens kneading up the honey,
The poor mechanic porters crowding in
Their heavy burdens at his narrow gate,
The sad-ey'd justice, with his surly hum,
Delivering o'er to executors pale
The lazy yawning drone. I this infer,
That many things, having full reference
To one consent, may work contrariously;
As many arrows loosed several ways
Come to one mark, as many ways meet in one town,
As many fresh streams meet in one salt sea,
As many lines close in the dial's centre;
So many a thousand actions, once afoot,
End in one purpose, and be all well borne
Without defeat. Therefore to France, my liege.
Divide your happy England into four;
Whereof take you one quarter into France,
And you withal shall make all Gallia shake.
If we, with thrice such powers left at home,
Cannot defend our own doors from the dog,
Let us be worried, and our nation lose
The name of hardiness and policy.
KING Call in the messengers sent from the Dauphin. *[Exeunt some Attendants.*
Now are we well resolv'd; and, by God's help
And yours, the noble sinews of our power,
France being ours, we'll bend it to our awe,
Or break it all to pieces; or there we'll sit,
Ruling in large and ample empery
O'er France and all her almost kingly dukedoms,
Or lay these bones in an unworthy urn,
Tombless, with no remembrance over them.
Either our history shall with full mouth
Speak freely of our acts, or else our grave,
Like Turkish mute, shall have a tongueless mouth,
Not worshipp'd with a waxen epitaph.

Enter Ambassadors of France.

Now are we well prepar'd to know the pleasure
Of our fair cousin Dauphin; for we hear
Your greeting is from him, not from the King.
1 AMBASSADOR May't please your Majesty to give us leave
Freely to render what we have in charge;
Or shall we sparingly show you far off
The Dauphin's meaning and our embassy?
KING We are no tyrant, but a Christian king,
Unto whose grace our passion is as subject
As are our wretches fett'red in our prisons;
Therefore with frank and with uncurbed plainness
Tell us the Dauphin's mind.
1 AMBASSADOR Thus then, in few.
Your Highness, lately sending into France,
Did claim some certain dukedoms in the right
Of your great predecessor, King Edward the Third.
In answer of which claim, the Prince our master
Says that you savour too much of your youth,
And bids you be advis'd there's nought in France
That can be with a nimble galliard won;
You cannot revel into dukedoms there.
He therefore sends you, meeter for your spirit,
This tun of treasure; and, in lieu of this,
Desires you let the dukedoms that you claim
Hear no more of you. This the Dauphin speaks.
KING What treasure, uncle?
EXETER Tennis-balls, my liege.
KING We are glad the Dauphin is so pleasant with us;
His present and your pains we thank you for.
When we have match'd our rackets to these balls,
We will in France, by God's grace, play a set
Shall strike his father's crown into the hazard.
Tell him he hath made a match with such a wrangler
That all the courts of France will be disturb'd
With chaces. And we understand him well,
How he comes o'er us with our wilder days,

Not measuring what use we made of them.
We never valu'd this poor seat of England;
And therefore, living hence, did give ourself
To barbarous licence; as 'tis ever common
That men are merriest when they are from home.
But tell the Dauphin I will keep my state,
Be like a king, and show my sail of greatness,
When I do rouse me in my throne of France;
For that I have laid by my majesty
And plodded like a man for working-days;
But I will rise there with so full a glory
That I will dazzle all the eyes of France,
Yea, strike the Dauphin blind to look on us.
And tell the pleasant Prince this mock of his
Hath turn'd his balls to gun-stones, and his soul
Shall stand sore charged for the wasteful vengeance
That shall fly with them; for many a thousand widows
Shall this his mock mock out of their dear husbands;
Mock mothers from their sons, mock castles down;
And some are yet ungotten and unborn
That shall have cause to curse the Dauphin's scorn.
But this lies all within the will of God,
To whom I do appeal; and in whose name,
Tell you the Dauphin, I am coming on,
To venge me as I may and to put forth
My rightful hand in a well-hallow'd cause.
So get you hence in peace; and tell the Dauphin
His jest will savour but of shallow wit,
When thousands weep more than did laugh at it.
Convey them with safe conduct. Fare you well.
[Exeunt Ambassadors.

EXETER This was a merry message.
KING We hope to make the sender blush at it.
Therefore, my lords, omit no happy hour
That may give furth'rance to our expedition;
For we have now no thought in us but France,
Save those to God, that run before our business.
Therefore let our proportions for these wars
Be soon collected, and all things thought upon
That may with reasonable swiftness add
More feathers to our wings; for, God before,
We'll chide this Dauphin at his father's door.
Therefore let every man now task his thought
That this fair action may on foot be brought.
[Exeunt.

ACT TWO

PROLOGUE *Flourish. Enter CHORUS.*

CHORUS Now all the youth of England are on fire,
And silken dalliance in the wardrobe lies;
Now thrive the armourers, and honour's thought
Reigns solely in the breast of every man;
They sell the pasture now to buy the horse,
Following the mirror of all Christian kings
With winged heels, as English Mercuries.
For now sits Expectation in the air,
And hides a sword from hilts unto the point
With crowns imperial, crowns, and coronets,
Promis'd to Harry and his followers.
The French, advis'd by good intelligence
Of this most dreadful preparation,
Shake in their fear and with pale policy
Seek to divert the English purposes.
O England! model to thy inward greatness,
Like little body with a mighty heart,
What mightst thou do that honour would thee do,
Were all thy children kind and natural!
But see thy fault! France hath in thee found out
A nest of hollow bosoms, which he fills
With treacherous crowns; and three corrupted men –
One, Richard Earl of Cambridge, and the second,
Henry Lord Scroop of Masham, and the third,
Sir Thomas Grey, knight, of Northumberland,
Have, for the gilt of France – O guilt indeed! –
Confirm'd conspiracy with fearful France;
And by their hands this grace of kings must die –
If hell and treason hold their promises,
Ere he take ship for France – and in Southampton.
Linger your patience on, and we'll digest
Th' abuse of distance, force a play.
The sum is paid, the traitors are agreed,
The King is set from London, and the scene
Is now transported, gentles, to Southampton;
There is the play-house now, there must you sit,
And thence to France shall we convey you safe
And bring you back, charming the narrow seas
To give you gentle pass; for, if we may,
We'll not offend one stomach with our play.
But, till the King come forth, and not till then,
Unto Southampton do we shift our scene. *[Exit.*

SCENE I. *London. Before the Boar's Head Tavern, Eastcheap.*

Enter Corporal NYM and Lieutenant BARDOLPH.

BARDOLPH Well met, Corporal Nym.

NYM Good morrow, Lieutenant Bardolph.

BARDOLPH What, are Ancient Pistol and you friends yet?

NYM For my part, I care not; I say little, but when time shall serve, there shall be smiles – but that shall be as it may. I dare not fight; but I will wink and hold out mine iron. It is a simple one; but what though? It will toast cheese, and it will endure cold as another man's sword will; and there's an end.

BARDOLPH I will bestow a breakfast to make you friends; and we'll be all three sworn brothers to France. Let't be so, good Corporal Nym.

NYM Faith, I will live so long as I may, that's the certain of it; and when I cannot live any longer, I will do as I may. That is my rest, that is the rendezvous of it.

BARDOLPH It is certain, Corporal, that he is married to Nell Quickly; and certainly she did you wrong, for you were troth-plight to her.

NYM I cannot tell; things must be as they may. Men may sleep, and they may have their throats about them at that time; and some say knives have edges. It must be as it may; though patience be a tired mare, yet she will plod. There must be conclusions. Well, I cannot tell.

Enter PISTOL and Hostess.

BARDOLPH Here comes Ancient Pistol and his wife. Good Corporal, be patient here.

NYM How now, mine host Pistol!

PISTOL Base tike, call'st thou me host?
Now, by this hand, I swear I scorn the term;
Nor shall my Nell keep lodgers.

HOSTESS No, by my troth, not long; for we cannot lodge and board a dozen or fourteen gentlewomen that live honestly by the prick of their needles, but it will be thought we keep a bawdy-house straight. [*Nym draws*] O well-a-day, Lady, if he be not drawn! Now we shall see wilful adultery and murder committed.

BARDOLPH Good Lieutenant, good Corporal, offer nothing here.

NYM Pish!

PISTOL Pish for thee, Iceland dog! Thou prick-ear'd cur of Iceland!

HOSTESS Good Corporal Nym, show thy valour, and put up your sword.

NYM Will you shog off? I would have you solus.

PISTOL 'Solus' egregious dog? O viper vile!
The 'solus' in thy most mervailous face;
The 'solus' in thy teeth, and in thy throat,
And in thy hateful lungs, yea, in thy maw, perdy;
And, which is worse, within thy nasty mouth!
I do retort the 'solus' in thy bowels;
For I can take, and Pistol's cock is up,
And flashing fire will follow.

NYM I am not Barbason: you cannot conjure me. I have an humour to knock you indifferently well. If you grow foul with me, Pistol, I will scour you with my rapier, as I may, in fair terms; if you would walk off I would prick your guts a little, in good terms, as I may, and that's the humour of it.

PISTOL O braggart vile and damned furious wight!
The grave doth gape and doting death is near;
Therefore exhale. [*Pistol draws.*

BARDOLPH Hear me, hear me what I say: he that strikes the first stroke I'll run him up to the hilts, as I am a soldier. [*Draws.*

PISTOL An oath of mickle might; and fury shall abate. [*Pistol and Nym sheathe their swords.*
Give me thy fist, thy fore-foot to me give;
Thy spirits are most tall.

NYM I will cut thy throat one time or other, in fair terms; that is the humour of it.

PISTOL 'Couple a gorge!'
That is the word. I thee defy again.
O hound of Crete, think'st thou my spouse to get?
No; to the spital go,
And from the powd'ring tub of infamy
Fetch forth the lazar kite of Cressid's kind,
Doll Tearsheet she by name, and her espouse.
I have, and I will hold, the quondam Quickly
For the only she; and – pauca, there's enough.
Go to.

Enter the Boy.

BOY Mine host Pistol, you must come to my master; and your hostess – he is very sick, and would to bed. Good Bardolph, put thy face between his sheets, and do the office of a warming-pan. Faith, he's very ill.

BARDOLPH Away, you rogue.

HOSTESS By my troth, he'll yield the crow a pudding one of these days: the King has kill'd his heart. Good husband, come home presently.

[*Exeunt Hostess and Boy.*

BARDOLPH Come, shall I make you two friends? We must to France together; why the devil should we keep knives to cut one another's throats?

PISTOL Let floods o'erswell, and fiends for food howl on!

NYM You'll pay me the eight shillings I won of you at betting?

PISTOL Base is the slave that pays.

NYM That now I will have; that's the humour of it.

PISTOL As manhood shall compound: push home. *[Pistol and Nym draw.*

BARDOLPH By this sword, he that makes the first thrust I'll kill him; by this sword, I will.

PISTOL Sword is an oath, and oaths must have their course. *[Sheathes his sword.*

BARDOLPH Corporal Nym, an thou wilt be friends, be friends; an thou wilt not, why then be enemies with me too. Prithee put up.

NYM I shall have my eight shillings I won of you at betting?

PISTOL A noble shalt thou have, and present pay;
And liquor likewise will I give to thee,
And friendship shall combine, and brotherhood.
I'll live by Nym and Nym shall live by me.
Is not this just? For I shall sutler be
Unto the camp, and profits will accrue.
Give me thy hand.

NYM *[Sheathing his sword]* I shall have my noble?

PISTOL In cash most justly paid.

NYM *[Shaking hands]* Well, then, that's the humour of't.

Re-enter Hostess.

HOSTESS As ever you come of women, come in quickly to Sir John. Ah, poor heart! he is so shak'd of a burning quotidian tertian that it is most lamentable to behold. Sweet men, come to him.

NYM The King hath run bad humours on the knight; that's the even of it.

PISTOL Nym, thou hast spoke the right;
His heart is fracted and corroborate.

NYM The King is a good king, but it must be as it may; he passes some humours and careers.

PISTOL Let us condole the knight; for, lambkins, we will live. *[Exeunt.*

SCENE II. *Southampton. A council-chamber.*

Enter EXETER, BEDFORD, and WESTMORELAND.

BEDFORD Fore God, his Grace is bold, to trust these traitors.

EXETER They shall be apprehended by and by.

WESTMORELAND How smooth and even they do bear themselves,
As if allegiance in their bosoms sat,
Crowned with faith and constant loyalty!

BEDFORD The King hath note of all that they intend,
By interception which they dream not of.

EXETER Nay, but the man that was his bedfellow,
Whom he hath dull'd and cloy'd with gracious favours –
That he should, for a foreign purse, so sell
His sovereign's life to death and treachery!

Trumpets sound. Enter the KING, SCROOP, CAMBRIDGE, GREY, and Attendants.

KING Now sits the wind fair, and we will aboard.
My Lord of Cambridge, and my kind Lord of Masham,
And you, my gentle knight, give me your thoughts.
Think you not that the pow'rs we bear with us
Will cut their passage through the force of France,
Doing the execution and the act
For which we have in head assembled them?

SCROOP No doubt, my liege, if each man do his best.

KING I doubt not that, since we are well persuaded
We carry not a heart with us from hence
That grows not in a fair consent with ours;
Nor leave not one behind that doth not wish
Success and conquest to attend on us.

CAMBRIDGE Never was monarch better fear'd and lov'd
Than is your Majesty. There's not, I think, a subject
That sits in heart-grief and uneasiness
Under the sweet shade of your government.

GREY True: those that were your father's enemies
Have steep'd their galls in honey, and do serve you
With hearts create of duty and of zeal.

KING We therefore have great cause of thankfulness,
And shall forget the office of our hand
Sooner than quittance of desert and merit
According to the weight and worthiness.

SCROOP So service shall with steeled sinews toil,
And labour shall refresh itself with hope,
To do your Grace incessant services.

KING We judge no less. Uncle of Exeter,
Enlarge the man committed yesterday
That rail'd against our person. We consider
It was excess of wine that set him on;
And on his more advice we pardon him.

SCROOP That's mercy, but too much security.
Let him be punish'd, sovereign, lest example
Breed, by his sufferance, more of such a kind.

KING O, let us yet be merciful!

CAMBRIDGE So may your Highness, and yet punish too.
GREY Sir,
You show great mercy if you give him life,
After the taste of much correction.
KING Alas, your too much love and care of me
Are heavy orisons 'gainst this poor wretch!
If little faults proceeding on distemper
Shall not be wink'd at, how shall we stretch our eye
When capital crimes, chew'd, swallow'd, and digested,
Appear before us? We'll yet enlarge that man,
Though Cambridge, Scroop, and Grey, in their dear care
And tender preservation of our person,
Would have him punish'd. And now to our French causes:
Who are the late commissioners?
CAMBRIDGE I one, my lord.
Your Highness bade me ask for it to-day.
SCROOP So did you me, my liege.
GREY And I, my royal sovereign.
KING Then, Richard Earl of Cambridge, there is yours;
There yours, Lord Scroop of Masham; and, Sir Knight,
Grey of Northumberland, this same is yours.
Read them, and know I know your worthiness.
My Lord of Westmoreland, and uncle Exeter,
We will aboard to-night. Why, how now, gentlemen?
What see you in those papers, that you lose
So much complexion? Look ye how they change!
Their cheeks are paper. Why, what read you there
That have so cowarded and chas'd your blood
Out of appearance?
CAMBRIDGE I do confess my fault,
And do submit me to your Highness' mercy.
GREY, SCROOP To which we all appeal.
KING The mercy that was quick in us but late
By your own counsel is suppress'd and kill'd.
You must not dare, for shame, to talk of mercy;
For your own reasons turn into your bosoms
As dogs upon their masters, worrying you.
See you, my princes and my noble peers,
These English monsters! My Lord of Cambridge here –
You know how apt our love was to accord
To furnish him with all appertinents
Belonging to his honour; and this man
Hath, for a few light crowns, lightly conspir'd,
And sworn unto the practices of France
To kill us here in Hampton; to the which
This knight, no less for bounty bound to us
Than Cambridge is, hath likewise sworn.
But, O,
What shall I say to thee, Lord Scroop, thou cruel,
Ingrateful, savage, and inhuman creature?
Thou that didst bear the key of all my counsels,
That knew'st the very bottom of my soul,
That almost mightst have coin'd me into gold,
Wouldst thou have practis'd on me for thy use –
May it be possible that foreign hire
Could out of thee extract one spark of evil
That might annoy my finger? 'Tis so strange
That, though the truth of it stands off as gross
As black and white, my eye will scarcely see it.
Treason and murder ever kept together,
As two yoke-devils sworn to either's purpose,
Working so grossly in a natural cause
That admiration did not whoop at them;
But thou, 'gainst all proportion, didst bring in
Wonder to wait on treason and on murder;
And whatsoever cunning fiend it was
That wrought upon thee so preposterously
Hath got the voice in hell for excellence;
And other devils that suggest by treasons
Do botch and bungle up damnation
With patches, colours, and with forms, being fetch'd
From glist'ring semblances of piety;
But he that temper'd thee bade thee stand up,
Gave thee no instance why thou shouldst do treason,
Unless to dub thee with the name of traitor.
If that same demon that hath gull'd thee thus
Should with his lion gait walk the whole world,
He might return to vasty Tartar back,
And tell the legions 'I can never win
A soul so easy as that Englishman's'.
O, how hast thou with jealousy infected
The sweetness of affiance! Show men dutiful?
Why, so didst thou. Seem they grave and learned?
Why, so didst thou. Come they of noble family?
Why, so didst thou. Seem they religious?
Why, so didst thou. Or are they spare in diet,
Free from gross passion or of mirth or anger,
Constant in spirit, not swerving with the blood,
Garnish'd and deck'd in modest complement,
Not working with the eye without the ear,
And but in purged judgment trusting neither?
Such and so finely bolted didst thou seem;
And thus thy fall hath left a kind of blot
To mark the full-fraught man and best indued
With some suspicion. I will weep for thee;
For this revolt of thine, methinks, is like
Another fall of man. Their faults are open.
Arrest them to the answer of the law;
And God acquit them of their practices!

EXETER I arrest thee of high treason, by the name
of Richard Earl of Cambridge.
I arrest thee of high treason, by the name of
Henry Lord Scroop of Masham.
I arrest thee of high treason, by the name of
Thomas Grey, knight, of Northumberland.

SCROOP Our purposes God justly hath discover'd,
And I repent my fault more than my death;
Which I beseech your Highness to forgive,
Although my body pay the price of it.

CAMBRIDGE For me, the gold of France did not seduce,
Although I did admit it as a motive
The sooner to effect what I intended;
But God be thanked for prevention,
Which I in sufferance heartily will rejoice,
Beseeching God and you to pardon me.

GREY Never did faithful subject more rejoice
At the discovery of most dangerous treason
Than I do at this hour joy o'er myself,
Prevented from a damned enterprise.
My fault, but not my body, pardon, sovereign.

KING God quit you in his mercy! Hear your sentence.
You have conspir'd against our royal person,
Join'd with an enemy proclaim'd, and from his coffers
Receiv'd the golden earnest of our death;
Wherein you would have sold your king to slaughter,
His princes and his peers to servitude,
His subjects to oppression and contempt,
And his whole kingdom into desolation.
Touching our person seek we no revenge;
But we our kingdom's safety must so tender,
Whose ruin you have sought, that to her laws
We do deliver you. Get you therefore hence,
Poor miserable wretches, to your death;
The taste whereof God of his mercy give
You patience to endure, and true repentance
Of all your dear offences. Bear them hence.

[Exeunt Cambridge, Scroop, and Grey, guarded.

Now, lords, for France; the enterprise whereof
Shall be to you as us like glorious.
We doubt not of a fair and lucky war,
Since God so graciously hath brought to light
This dangerous treason, lurking in our way
To hinder our beginnings; we doubt not now
But every rub is smoothed on our way.
Then, forth, dear countrymen; let us deliver
Our puissance into the hand of God,
Putting it straight in expedition.
Cheerly to sea; the signs of war advance;
No king of England, if not king of France!

[Flourish. Exeunt.

SCENE III. *Eastcheap. Before the Boar's Head tavern.*

Enter PISTOL, Hostess, NYM, BARDOLPH, and Boy.

HOSTESS Prithee, honey-sweet husband, let me bring thee to Staines.

PISTOL No; for my manly heart doth earn.
Bardolph, be blithe; Nym, rouse thy vaunting veins;
Boy, bristle thy courage up. For Falstaff he is dead,
And we must earn therefore.

BARDOLPH Would I were with him, wheresome'er he is, either in heaven or in hell!

HOSTESS Nay, sure, he's not in hell: he's in Arthur's bosom, if ever man went to Arthur's bosom. 'A made a finer end, and went away an it had been any christom child; 'a parted ev'n just between twelve and one, ev'n at the turning o' th' tide; for after I saw him fumble with the sheets, and play with flowers, and smile upon his fingers' end, I knew there was but one way; for his nose was as sharp as a pen, and 'a babbl'd of green fields. 'How now, Sir John!' quoth I 'What, man, be o' good cheer.' So 'a cried out 'God, God, God!' three or four times. Now I, to comfort him, bid him 'a should not think of God; I hop'd there was no need to trouble himself with any such thoughts yet. So 'a bade me lay more clothes on his feet; I put my hand into the bed and felt them, and they were as cold as any stone; then I felt to his knees, and so upward and upward, and all was as cold as any stone.

NYM They say he cried out of sack.

HOSTESS Ay, that'a did.

BARDOLPH And of women.

HOSTESS Nay, that'a did not.

BOY Yes, that 'a did, and said they were devils incarnate.

HOSTESS 'A could never abide carnation; 'twas a colour he never lik'd.

BOY 'A said once the devil would have him about women.

HOSTESS 'A did in some sort, indeed, handle women; but then he was rheumatic, and talk'd of the Whore of Babylon.

BOY Do you not remember 'a saw a flea stick upon Bardolph's nose, and 'a said it was a black soul burning in hell?

BARDOLPH Well, the fuel is gone that maintain'd that fire: that's all the riches I got in his service.

NYM Shall we shog? The King will be gone from Southampton.

PISTOL Come, let's away. My love, give me thy lips.
Look to my chattels and my moveables;

Let senses rule. The word is 'Pitch and Pay'.
Trust none;
For oaths are straws, men's faiths are wafer-cakes,
And Holdfast is the only dog, my duck.
Therefore, Caveto be thy counsellor.
Go, clear thy crystals. Yoke-fellows in arms,
Let us to France, like horse-leeches, my boys,
To suck, to suck, the very blood to suck.

BOY And that's but unwholesome food, they say.

PISTOL Touch her soft mouth and march.

BARDOLPH Farewell, hostess. *[Kissing her.*

NYM I cannot kiss, that is the humour of it; but, adieu.

PISTOL Let housewifery appear; keep close, I thee command.

HOSTESS Farewell; adieu. *[Exeunt.*

SCENE IV. *France. The King's palace.*

Flourish. Enter the FRENCH KING, the DAUPHIN, the DUKES OF BERRI and BRITAINE, the CONSTABLE, and Others.

KING OF FRANCE Thus comes the English with full power upon us;
And more than carefully it us concerns
To answer royally in our defences.
Therefore the Dukes of Berri and of Britaine,
Of Brabant and of Orleans, shall make forth,
And you, Prince Dauphin, with all swift dispatch,
To line and new repair our towns of war
With men of courage and with means defendant;
For England his approaches makes as fierce
As waters to the sucking of a gulf.
It fits us, then, to be as provident
As fear may teach us, out of late examples
Left by the fatal and neglected English
Upon our fields.

DAUPHIN My most redoubted father,
It is most meet we arm us 'gainst the foe;
For peace itself should not so dull a kingdom,
Though war nor no known quarrel were in question,
But that defences, musters, preparations,
Should be maintain'd, assembled, and collected,
As were a war in expectation.
Therefore, I say, 'tis meet we all go forth
To view the sick and feeble parts of France;
And let us do it with no show of fear –
No, with no more than if we heard that England
Were busied with a Whitsun morris-dance;
For, my good liege, she is so idly king'd,
Her sceptre so fantastically borne
By a vain, giddy, shallow, humorous youth,
That fear attends her not.

CONSTABLE O peace, Prince Dauphin!
You are too much mistaken in this king.
Question your Grace the late ambassadors
With what great state he heard their embassy,
How well supplied with noble counsellors,
How modest in exception, and withal
How terrible in constant resolution,
And you shall find his vanities forespent
Were but the outside of the Roman Brutus,
Covering discretion with a coat of folly;
As gardeners do with ordure hide those roots
That shall first spring and be most delicate.

DAUPHIN Well, 'tis not so, my Lord High Constable;
But though we think it so, it is no matter.
In cases of defence 'tis best to weigh
The enemy more mighty than he seems;
So the proportions of defence are fill'd;
Which of a weak and niggardly projection
Doth like a miser spoil his coat with scanting
A little cloth.

KING OF FRANCE Think we King Harry strong;
And, Princes, look you strongly arm to meet him.
The kindred of him hath been flesh'd upon us;
And he is bred out of that bloody strain
That haunted us in our familiar paths.
Witness our too much memorable shame
When Cressy battle fatally was struck,
And all our princes captiv'd by the hand
Of that black name, Edward, Black Prince of Wales;
Whiles that his mountain sire – on mountain standing,
Up in the air, crown'd with the golden sun –
Saw his heroical seed, and smil'd to see him,
Mangle the work of nature, and deface
The patterns that by God and by French fathers
Had twenty years been made. This is a stem
Of that victorious stock; and let us fear
The native mightiness and fate of him.

Enter a Messenger.

MESSENGER Ambassadors from Harry King of England
Do crave admittance to your Majesty.

KING OF FRANCE We'll give them present audience. Go and bring them.
[Exeunt Messenger and certain Lords.
You see this chase is hotly followed, friends.

DAUPHIN Turn head and stop pursuit; for coward dogs
Most spend their mouths when what they seem to threaten
Runs far before them. Good my sovereign,
Take up the English short, and let them know
Of what a monarchy you are the head.

Self-love, my liege, is not so vile a sin
As self-neglecting.

Re-enter Lords, with EXETER and Train.

KING OF FRANCE From our brother of England?

EXETER From him, and thus he greets your Majesty:
He wills you, in the name of God Almighty,
That you divest yourself, and lay apart
The borrowed glories that by gift of heaven,
By law of nature and of nations, 'longs
To him and to his heirs – namely, the crown,
And all wide-stretched honours that pertain,
By custom and the ordinance of times,
Unto the crown of France. That you may know
'Tis no sinister nor no awkward claim,
Pick'd from the worm-holes of long vanish'd days,
Nor from the dust of old oblivion rak'd,
He sends you this most memorable line,
[*Gives a paper.*
In every branch truly demonstrative;
Willing you overlook this pedigree.
And when you find him evenly deriv'd
From his most fam'd of famous ancestors,
Edward the Third, he bids you then resign
Your crown and kingdom, indirectly held
From him, the native and true challenger.

KING OF FRANCE Or else what follows?

EXETER Bloody constraint; for if you hide the crown
Even in your hearts, there will he rake for it.
Therefore in fierce tempest is he coming,
In thunder and in earthquake, like a Jove,
That if requiring fail, he will compel;
And bids you, in the bowels of the Lord,
Deliver up the crown; and to take mercy
On the poor souls for whom this hungry war
Opens his vasty jaws; and on your head
Turning the widows' tears, the orphans' cries,
The dead men's blood, the privy maidens' groans,
For husbands, fathers, and betrothed lovers,
That shall be swallowed in this controversy.
This is his claim, his threat'ning, and my message;
Unless the Dauphin be in presence here,
To whom expressly I bring greeting too.

KING OF FRANCE For us, we will consider of this further;
To-morrow shall you bear our full intent
Back to our brother of England.

DAUPHIN For the Dauphin:
I stand here for him. What to him from England?

EXETER Scorn and defiance, slight regard, contempt,
And anything that may not misbecome
The mighty sender, doth he prize you at.
Thus says my king: an if your father's Highness
Do not, in grant of all demands at large,
Sweeten the bitter mock you sent his Majesty,
He'll call you to so hot an answer of it
That caves and womby vaultages of France
Shall chide your trespass and return your mock
In second accent of his ordinance.

DAUPHIN Say, if my father render fair return,
It is against my will; for I desire
Nothing but odds with England. To that end,
As matching to his youth and vanity,
I did present him with the Paris balls.

EXETER He'll make your Paris Louvre shake for it,
Were it the mistress court of mighty Europe;
And be assur'd you'll find a difference,
As we his subjects have in wonder found,
Between the promise of his greener days
And these he masters now. Now he weighs time
Even to the utmost grain; that you shall read
In your own losses, if he stay in France.

KING OF FRANCE To-morrow shall you know our mind at full.

EXETER Dispatch us with all speed, lest that our king
Come here himself to question our delay;
For he is footed in this land already.

KING OF FRANCE You shall be soon dispatch'd with fair conditions.
A night is but small breath and little pause
To answer matters of this consequence.
[*Flourish. Exeunt.*

ACT THREE

PROLOGUE *Flourish. Enter CHORUS.*

CHORUS Thus with imagin'd wing our swift scene flies,
In motion of no less celerity
Than that of thought. Suppose that you have seen
The well-appointed King at Hampton pier
Embark his royalty; and his brave fleet
With silken streamers the young Phoebus fanning.
Play with your fancies; and in them behold
Upon the hempen tackle ship-boys climbing;

Hear the shrill whistle which doth order give
To sounds confus'd; behold the threaden sails,
Borne with th' invisible and creeping wind,
Draw the huge bottoms through the furrowed sea,
Breasting the lofty surge. O, do but think
You stand upon the rivage and behold
A city on th' inconstant billows dancing;
For so appears this fleet majestical,
Holding due course to Harfleur. Follow, follow!
Grapple your minds to sternage of this navy
And leave your England as dead midnight still,
Guarded with grandsires, babies, and old women,
Either past or not arriv'd to pith and puissance;
For who is he whose chin is but enrich'd
With one appearing hair that will not follow
These cull'd and choice-drawn cavaliers to France?
Work, work your thoughts, and therein see a siege;
Behold the ordnance on their carriages,
With fatal mouths gaping on girded Harfleur.
Suppose th' ambassador from the French comes back;
Tells Harry that the King doth offer him
Katharine his daughter, and with her to dowry
Some petty and unprofitable dukedoms.
The offer likes not; and the nimble gunner
With linstock now the devilish cannon touches,

[Alarum, and chambers go off.

And down goes all before them. Still be kind,
And eke out our performance with your mind.

[Exit.

SCENE I. *France. Before Harfleur.*

Alarum. Enter the KING, EXETER, BEDFORD, GLOUCESTER, and Soldiers with scaling-ladders.

KING Once more unto the breach, dear friends, once more;
Or close the wall up with our English dead.
In peace there's nothing so becomes a man
As modest stillness and humility;
But when the blast of war blows in our ears,
Then imitate the action of the tiger:
Stiffen the sinews, summon up the blood,
Disguise fair nature with hard-favour'd rage;
Then lend the eye a terrible aspect;
Let it pry through the portage of the head
Like the brass cannon; let the brow o'erwhelm it
As fearfully as doth a galled rock
O'erhang and jutty his confounded base,
Swill'd with the wild and wasteful ocean.
Now set the teeth and stretch the nostril wide;
Hold hard the breath, and bend up every spirit
To his full height. On, on, you noblest English,
Whose blood is fet from fathers of war-proof –
Fathers that like so many Alexanders
Have in these parts from morn till even fought,
And sheath'd their swords for lack of argument.
Dishonour not your mothers; now attest
That those whom you call'd fathers did beget you.
Be copy now to men of grosser blood,
And teach them how to war. And you, good yeomen,
Whose limbs were made in England, show us here
The mettle of your pasture; let us swear
That you are worth your breeding – which I doubt not;
For there is none of you so mean and base
That hath not noble lustre in your eyes.
I see you stand like greyhounds in the slips,
Straining upon the start. The game's afoot;
Follow your spirit; and upon this charge
Cry 'God for Harry, England, and Saint George!'

[Exeunt. Alarum, and chambers go off.

SCENE II. *Before Harfleur.*

Enter NYM, BARDOLPH, PISTOL, and Boy.

BARDOLPH On, on, on, on, on! to the breach, to the breach!

NYM Pray thee, Corporal, stay; the knocks are too hot, and for mine own part I have not a case of lives. The humour of it is too hot; that is the very plain-song of it.

PISTOL The plain-song is most just; for humours do abound.
Knocks go and come; God's vassals drop and die;
And sword and shield
In bloody field
Doth win immortal fame.

BOY Would I were in an alehouse in London! I would give all my fame for a pot of ale and safety.

PISTOL And I:
If wishes would prevail with me,
My purpose should not fail with me,
But thither would I hie.

BOY As duly, but not as truly,
As bird doth sing on bough.

Enter FLUELLEN.

FLUELLEN Up to the breach, you dogs!
Avaunt, you cullions!

[Driving them forward.

PISTOL Be merciful, great duke, to men of mould.
Abate thy rage, abate thy manly rage;
Abate thy rage, great duke.
Good bawcock, bate thy rage. Use lenity, sweet
chuck.

NYM These be good humours. Your honour wins bad humours. [*Exeunt all but Boy.*

BOY As young as I am, I have observ'd these three swashers. I am boy to them all three; but all they three, though they would serve me, could not be man to me; for indeed three such antics do not amount to a man. For Bardolph, he is white-liver'd and red-fac'd; by the means whereof 'a faces it out, but fights not. For Pistol, he hath a killing tongue and a quiet sword; by the means whereof 'a breaks words and keeps whole weapons. For Nym, he hath heard that men of few words are the best men, and therefore he scorns to say his prayers lest 'a should be thought a coward; but his few bad words are match'd with as few good deeds; for 'a never broke any man's head but his own, and that was against a post when he was drunk. They will steal anything, and call it purchase. Bardolph stole a lute-case, bore it twelve leagues, and sold it for three halfpence. Nym and Bardolph are sworn brothers in filching, and in Calais they stole a fire-shovel; I knew by that piece of service the men would carry coals. They would have me as familiar with men's pockets as their gloves or their handkerchers; which makes much against my manhood, if I should take from another's pocket to put into mine; for it is plain pocketing up of wrongs. I must leave them and seek some better service; their villainy goes against my weak stomach, and therefore I must cast it up. [*Exit.*

Re-enter FLUELLEN, GOWER following.

GOWER Captain Fluellen, you must come presently to the mines; the Duke of Gloucester would speak with you.

FLUELLEN To the mines! Tell you the Duke it is not so good to come to the mines; for, look you, the mines is not according to the disciplines of the war; the concavities of it is not sufficient. For, look you, th' athversary – you may discuss unto the Duke, look you – is digt himself four yard under the countermines; by Cheshu, I think 'a will plow up all, if there is not better directions.

GOWER The Duke of Gloucester, to whom the order of the siege is given, is altogether directed by an Irishman – a very valiant gentleman, i' faith.

FLUELLEN It is Captain Macmorris, is it not?

GOWER I think it be.

FLUELLEN By Cheshu, he is an ass, as in the world: I will verify as much in his beard; he has no more directions in the true disciplines of the wars, look you, of the Roman disciplines, than is a puppy-dog.

Enter MACMORRIS and Captain JAMY.

GOWER Here 'a comes; and the Scots captain, Captain Jamy, with him.

FLUELLEN Captain Jamy is a marvellous falorous gentleman, that is certain, and of great expedition and knowledge in th' aunchiant wars, upon my particular knowledge of his directions. By Cheshu, he will maintain his argument as well as any military man in the world, in the disciplines of the pristine wars of the Romans.

JAMY I say gud day, Captain Fluellen.

FLUELLEN God-den to your worship, good Captain James.

GOWER How now, Captain Macmorris! Have you quit the mines? Have the pioneers given o'er?

MACMORRIS By Chrish, la, tish ill done! The work ish give over, the trompet sound the retreat. By my hand, I swear, and my father's soul, the work ish ill done; it ish give over; I would have blowed up the town, so Chrish save me, la, in an hour. O, tish ill done, tish ill done; by my hand, tish ill done!

FLUELLEN Captain Macmorris, I beseech you now, will you voutsafe me, look you, a few disputations with you, as partly touching or concerning the disciplines of the war, the Roman wars, in the way of argument, look you, and friendly communication; partly to satisfy my opinion, and partly for the satisfaction, look you, of my mind, as touching the direction of the military discipline, that is the point.

JAMY It sall be very gud, gud feith, gud captains bath; and I sall quit you with gud leve, as I may pick occasion; that sall I, marry.

MACMORRIS It is no time to discourse, so Chrish save me. The day is hot, and the weather, and the wars, and the King, and the Dukes; it is no time to discourse. The town is beseech'd, and the trumpet call us to the breach; and we talk and, be Chrish, do nothing. 'Tis shame for us all, so God sa' me, 'tis shame to stand still; it is shame, by my hand; and there is throats to be cut, and works to be done; and there ish nothing done, so Chrish sa' me, la.

JAMY By the mess, ere theise eyes of mine take themselves to slomber, ay'll de gud service, or I'll lig i' th' grund for it; ay, or go to death. And I'll pay't as valorously as I may, that sall I suerly do, that is the breff and the long. Marry, I wad full fain heard some question 'tween you tway.

FLUELLEN Captain Macmorris, I think, look you, under your correction, there is not many of your nation –

MACMORRIS Of my nation? What ish my nation? Ish a villain, and a bastard, and a knave, and a rascal. What ish my nation? Who talks of my nation?

FLUELLEN Look you, if you take the matter otherwise than is meant, Captain Macmorris, peradventure I shall think you do not use me with that affability as in discretion you ought to use me, look you; being as good a man as yourself, both in the disciplines of war and in the derivation of my birth, and in other particularities.

MACMORRIS I do not know you so good a man as myself; so Chrish save me, I will cut off your head.

GOWER Gentlemen both, you will mistake each other.

JAMY Ah! that's a foul fault. [*A parley sounded.*

GOWER The town sounds a parley.

FLUELLEN Captain Macmorris, when there is more better opportunity to be required, look you, I will be so bold as to tell you I know the disciplines of war; and there is an end. [*Exeunt.*

SCENE III. *Before the gates of Harfleur.*

Enter the Governor and some Citizens on the walls. Enter the KING and all his Train before the gates.

KING How yet resolves the Governor of the town?
This is the latest parle we will admit;
Therefore to our best mercy give yourselves
Or, like to men proud of destruction,
Defy us to our worst; for, as I am a soldier,
A name that in my thoughts becomes me best,
If I begin the batt'ry once again,
I will not leave the half-achieved Harfleur
Till in her ashes she lie buried.
The gates of mercy shall be all shut up,
And the flesh'd soldier, rough and hard of heart,
In liberty of bloody hand shall range
With conscience wide as hell, mowing like grass
Your fresh fair virgins and your flow'ring infants.
What is it then to me if impious war,
Array'd in flames, like to the prince of fiends,
Do, with his smirch'd complexion, all fell feats
Enlink'd to waste and desolation?
What is't to me when you yourselves are cause,
If your pure maidens fall into the hand
Of hot and forcing violation?
What rein can hold licentious wickedness
When down the hill he holds his fierce career?
We may as bootless spend our vain command
Upon th' enraged soldiers in their spoil,
As send precepts to the Leviathan
To come ashore. Therefore, you men of Harfleur,
Take pity of your town and of your people
Whiles yet my soldiers are in my command;
Whiles yet the cool and temperate wind of grace
O'erblows the filthy and contagious clouds
Of heady murder, spoil, and villainy.
If not – why, in a moment look to see
The blind and bloody soldier with foul hand
Defile the locks of your shrill-shrieking daughters;
Your fathers taken by the silver beards,
And their most reverend heads dash'd to the walls;
Your naked infants spitted upon pikes,
Whiles the mad mothers with their howls confus'd
Do break the clouds, as did the wives of Jewry
At Herod's bloody-hunting slaughtermen.
What say you? Will you yield, and this avoid?
Or, guilty in defence, be thus destroy'd?

GOVERNOR Our expectation hath this day an end:
The Dauphin, whom of succours we entreated,
Returns us that his powers are yet not ready
To raise so great a siege. Therefore, great King,
We yield our town and lives to thy soft mercy.
Enter our gates; dispose of us and ours;
For we no longer are defensible.

KING Open your gates. [*Exit Governor.*] Come, uncle Exeter,
Go you and enter Harfleur; there remain,
And fortify it strongly 'gainst the French;
Use mercy to them all. For us, dear uncle,
The winter coming on, and sickness growing
Upon our soldiers, we will retire to Calais.
To-night in Harfleur will we be your guest;
To-morrow for the march are we addrest.

[*Flourish. The King and his train enter the town.*

SCENE IV. *Rouen. The French King's palace.*

Enter KATHERINE and ALICE.

KATHERINE Alice, tu as été en Angleterre, et tu parles bien le langage.

ALICE Un peu, madame.

KATHERINE Je te prie, m'enseignez; il faut que j'apprenne à parler. Comment appelez-vous la main en Anglais?

ALICE La main? Elle est appelée de hand.

KATHERINE De hand. Et les doigts?

ALICE Les doigts? Ma foi, j'oublie les doigts; mais je me souviendrai. Les doigts? Je pense qu'ils sont appelés de fingres; oui, de fingres.

KATHERINE La main, de hand; les doigts, de fingres. Je pense que je suis le bon écolier; j'ai gagné deux mots d'Anglais vîtement. Comment appelez-vous les ongles?

ALICE Les ongles? Nous les appelons de nails.

KATHERINE De nails. Ecoutez; dites-moi si je parle bien: de hand, de fingres, et de nails.

ALICE C'est bien dit, madame; il est fort bon Anglais.

KATHERINE Dites-moi l'Anglais pour le bras.

ALICE De arm, madame.

KATHERINE Et le coude?

ALICE D'elbow.

KATHERINE D'elbow. Je m'en fais la répétition de tous les mots que vous m'avez appris dès à présent.

ALICE Il est trop difficile, madame, comme je pense.

KATHERINE Excusez-moi, Alice; écoutez: d'hand, de fingre, de nails, d'arma, de bilbow.

ALICE D'elbow, madame.

KATHERINE O Seigneur Dieu, je m'en oublie! D'elbow. Comment appelez-vous le col?

ALICE De nick, madame.

KATHERINE De nick. Et le menton?

ALICE De chin.

KATHERINE De sin. Le col, de nick; le menton, de sin.

ALICE Oui. Sauf votre honneur, en vérité, vous prononcez les mots aussi droit que les natifs d'Angleterre.

KATHERINE Je ne doute point d'apprendre, par la grace de Dieu, et en peu de temps.

ALICE N'avez-vous pas déjà oublié ce que je vous ai ensigné?

KATHERINE Non, je reciterai à vous promptement: d'hand, de fingre, de mails –

ALICE De nails, madame.

KATHERINE De nails, de arm, de ilbow.

ALICE Sauf votre honneur, d'elbow.

KATHERINE Ainsi dis-je; d'elbow, de nick, et de sin. Comment appelez-vous le pied et la robe?

ALICE Le foot, madame; et le count.

KATHERINE Le foot et le count. O Seigneur Dieu! ils sont mots de son mauvais, corruptible, gros, et impudique, et non pour les dames d'honneur d'user: je ne voudrais prononcer ces mots devant les seigneurs de France pour tout le monde. Foh! le foot et le count! Néanmoins, je reciterai une autre fois ma lecon ensemble: d'hand, de fingre, de nails, d'arm, d'elbow, de nick, de sin, de foot, le count.

ALICE Excellent, madame!

KATHERINE C'est assez pour une fois: allons-nous à diner. [*Exeunt.*

SCENE V. *The French King's palace.*

Enter the KING OF FRANCE, the DAUPHIN, DUKE OF BRITAINE, the CONSTABLE OF FRANCE, and Others.

KING OF FRANCE 'Tis certain he hath pass'd the river Somme.

CONSTABLE And if he be not fought withal, my lord,
Let us not live in France; let us quit all,
And give our vineyards to a barbarous people.

DAUPHIN O Dieu vivant! Shall a few sprays of us,
The emptying of our fathers' luxury,
Our scions, put in wild and savage stock,
Spirt up so suddenly into the clouds,
And overlook their grafters?

BRITAINE Normans, but bastard Normans, Norman bastards!
Mort Dieu, ma vie! if they march along
Unfought withal, but I will sell my dukedom
To buy a slobb'ry and a dirty farm
In that nook-shotten isle of Albion.

CONSTABLE Dieu de batailles! where have they this mettle?
Is not their climate foggy, raw, and dull;
On whom, as in despite, the sun looks pale,
Killing their fruit with frowns? Can sodden water,
A drench for sur-rein'd jades, their barley-broth,
Decoct their cold blood to such valiant heat?
And shall our quick blood, spirited with wine,
Seem frosty? O, for honour of our land,
Let us not hang like roping icicles
Upon our houses' thatch, whiles a more frosty people
Sweat drops of gallant youth in our rich fields –
Poor we call them in their native lords!

DAUPHIN By faith and honour,
Our madams mock at us and plainly say
Our mettle is bred out, and they will give
Their bodies to the lust of English youth
To new-store France with bastard warriors.

BRITAINE They bid us to the English dancing-schools
And teach lavoltas high and swift corantos,
Saying our grace is only in our heels
And that we are most lofty runaways.

KING OF FRANCE Where is Montjoy the herald? Speed him hence;
Let him greet England with our sharp defiance.
Up, Princes, and, with spirit of honour edged
More sharper than your swords, hie to the field:
Charles Delabreth, High Constable of France;
You Dukes of Orleans, Bourbon, and of Berri,

Alençon, Brabant, Bar, and Burgundy;
Jaques Chatillon, Rambures, Vaudemont,
Beaumont, Grandpré, Roussi, and Faucon-bridge,
Foix, Lestrake, Bouciqualt, and Charolois;
High dukes, great princes, barons, lords, and knights,
For your great seats now quit you of great shames.
Bar Harry England, that sweeps through our land
With pennons painted in the blood of Harfleur.
Rush on his host as doth the melted snow
Upon the valleys, whose low vassal seat
The Alps doth spit and void his rheum upon;
Go down upon him, you have power enough,
And in a captive chariot into Rouen
Bring him our prisoner.

CONSTABLE This becomes the great.
Sorry am I his numbers are so few,
His soldiers sick and famish'd in their march;
For I am sure, when he shall see our army,
He'll drop his heart into the sink of fear,
And for achievement offer us his ransom.

KING OF FRANCE Therefore, Lord Constable, haste on Montjoy,
And let him say to England that we send
To know what willing ransom he will give.
Prince Dauphin, you shall stay with us in Rouen.

DAUPHIN Not so, I do beseech your Majesty.

KING OF FRANCE Be patient, for you shall remain with us.
Now forth, Lord Constable and Prince all,
And quickly bring us word of England's fall.

[*Exeunt.*

SCENE VI. *The English camp in Picardy.*

Enter Captains, English and Welsh, GOWER and FLUELLEN.

GOWER How now, Captain Fluellen! Come you from the bridge?

FLUELLEN I assure you there is very excellent services committed at the bridge.

GOWER Is the Duke of Exeter safe?

FLUELLEN The Duke of Exeter is as magnanimous as Agamemnon; and a man that I love and honour with my soul, and my heart, and my duty, and my live, and my living, and my uttermost power. He is not – God be praised and blessed! – any hurt in the world, but keeps the bridge most valiantly, with excellent discipline. There is an aunchient Lieutenant there at the bridge – I think in my very conscience he is as valiant a man as Mark Antony; and he is a man of no estimation in the world; but I did see him do as gallant service.

GOWER What do you call him?

FLUELLEN He is call'd Aunchient Pistol.

GOWER I know him not.

Enter PISTOL.

FLUELLEN Here is the man.

PISTOL Captain, I thee beseech to do me favours.
The Duke of Exeter doth love thee well.

FLUELLEN Ay, I praise God; and I have merited some love at his hands.

PISTOL Bardolph, a soldier, firm and sound of heart,
And of buxom valour, hath by cruel fate
And giddy Fortune's furious fickle wheel,
That goddess blind,
That stands upon the rolling restless stone –

FLUELLEN By your patience, Aunchient Pistol. Fortune is painted blind, with a muffler afore her eyes, to signify to you that Fortune is blind; and she is painted also with a wheel, to signify to you, which is the moral of it, that she is turning, and inconstant, and mutability, and variation; and her foot, look you, is fixed upon a spherical stone, which rolls, and rolls, and rolls. In good truth, the poet makes a most excellent description of it: Fortune is an excellent moral.

PISTOL Fortune is Bardolph's foe, and frowns on him;
For he hath stol'n a pax, and hanged must 'a be –
A damned death!
Let gallows gape for dog; let man go free,
And let not hemp his windpipe suffocate.
But Exeter hath given the doom of death
For pax of little price.
Therefore, go speak – the Duke will hear thy voice;
And let not Bardolph's vital thread be cut
With edge of penny cord and vile reproach.
Speak, Captain, for his life, and I will thee requite.

FLUELLEN Aunchient Pistol, I do partly understand your meaning.

PISTOL Why then, rejoice therefore.

FLUELLEN Certainly, Aunchient, it is not a thing to rejoice at; for if, look you, he were my brother, I would desire the Duke to use his good pleasure, and put him to execution; for discipline ought to be used.

PISTOL Die and be damn'd! and figo for thy friendship!

FLUELLEN It is well.

PISTOL The fig of Spain!

[*Exit.*

FLUELLEN Very good.

GOWER Why, this is an arrant counterfeit rascal; I remember him now – a bawd, a cutpurse.

FLUELLEN I'll assure you, 'a utt'red as prave words at the pridge as you shall see in a summer's day. But it is very well; what he has spoke to me, that is well, I warrant you, when time is serve.

GOWER Why, 'tis a gull, a fool, a rogue, that now and then goes to the wars to grace himself, at his return into London, under the form of a soldier. And such fellows are perfect in the great commanders' names; and they will learn you by rote where services were done – at such and such a sconce, at such a breach, at such a convoy; who came off bravely, who was shot, who disgrac'd, what terms the enemy stood on; and this they con perfectly in the phrase of war, which they trick up with new-tuned oaths; and what a beard of the General's cut and a horrid suit of the camp will do among foaming bottles and ale-wash'd wits is wonderful to be thought on. But you must learn to know such slanders of the age, or else you may be marvellously mistook.

FLUELLEN I tell you what, Captain Gower, I do perceive he is not the man that he would gladly make show to the world he is; if I find a hole in his coat I will tell him my mind. [*Drum within*] Hark you, the King is coming; and I must speak with him from the pridge.

Drum and colours. Enter the KING and his poor Soldiers, and GLOUCESTER.

God pless your Majesty!

KING How now, Fluellen! Cam'st thou from the bridge?

FLUELLEN Ay, so please your Majesty. The Duke of Exeter has very gallantly maintain'd the pridge; the French is gone off, look you, and there is gallant and most prave passages. Marry, th' athversary was have possession of the pridge; but he is enforced to retire, and the Duke of Exeter is master of the pridge; I can tell your Majesty the Duke is a prave man.

KING What men have you lost, Fluellen?

FLUELLEN The perdition of th' athversary hath been very great, reasonable great; marry, for my part, I think the Duke hath lost never a man, but one that is like to be executed for robbing a church – one Bardolph, if your Majesty know the man; his face is all bubukles, and whelks, and knobs, and flames o' fire; and his lips blows at his nose, and it is like a coal of fire, sometimes plue and sometimes red; but his nose is executed and his fire's out.

KING We would have all such offenders so cut off. And we give express charge that in our marches through the country there be nothing compell'd from the villages, nothing taken but paid for, none of the French upbraided or abused in disdainful language; for when lenity and cruelty play for a kingdom the gentler gamester is the soonest winner.

Tucket. Enter MONTJOY.

MONTJOY You know me by my habit.

KING Well then, I know thee; what shall I know of thee?

MONTJOY My master's mind.

KING Unfold it.

MONTJOY Thus says my king. Say thou to Harry of England: Though we seem'd dead we did but sleep; advantage is a better soldier than rashness. Tell him we could have rebuk'd him at Harfleur, but that we thought not good to bruise an injury till it were full ripe. Now we speak upon our cue, and our voice is imperial: England shall repent his folly, see his weakness, and admire our sufferance. Bid him therefore consider of his ransom, which must proportion the losses we have borne, the subjects we have lost, the disgrace we have digested; which, in weight to re-answer, his pettiness would bow under. For our losses his exchequer is too poor; for th' effusion of our blood, the muster of his kingdom too faint a number; and for our disgrace, his own person kneeling at our feet but a weak and worthless satisfaction. To this add defiance; and tell him, for conclusion, he hath betrayed his followers, whose condemnation is pronounc'd. So far my king and master; so much my office.

KING What is thy name? I know thy quality.

MONTJOY Montjoy.

KING Thou dost thy office fairly. Turn thee back,
And tell thy king I do not seek him now,
But could be willing to march on to Calais
Without impeachment; for, to say the sooth –
Though 'tis no wisdom to confess so much
Unto an enemy of craft and vantage –
My people are with sickness much enfeebled;
My numbers lessen'd; and those few I have
Almost no better than so many French;
Who when they were in health, I tell thee, herald,
I thought upon one pair of English legs
Did march three Frenchmen. Yet forgive me, God,
That I do brag thus; this your air of France
Hath blown that vice in me; I must repent.
Go, therefore, tell thy master here I am;
My ransom is this frail and worthless trunk;
My army but a weak and sickly guard;
Yet, God before, tell him we will come on,
Though France himself and such another neighbour

Stand in our way. There's for thy labour, Montjoy.
Go, bid thy master well advise himself.
If we may pass, we will; if we be hind'red,
We shall your tawny ground with your red blood
Discolour; and so, Montjoy, fare you well.
The sum of all our answer is but this:
We would not seek a battle as we are;
Nor as we are, we say, we will not shun it.
So tell your master.

MONTJOY I shall deliver so. Thanks to your Highness. [*Exit.*

GLOUCESTER I hope they will not come upon us now.

KING We are in God's hand, brother, not in theirs.
March to the bridge, it now draws toward night;
Beyond the river we'll encamp ourselves,
And on to-morrow bid them march away. [*Exeunt.*

SCENE VII. *The French camp near Agincourt.*

Enter the CONSTABLE OF FRANCE, the LORD RAMBURES, the DUKE OF ORLEANS, the DAUPHIN, with Others.

CONSTABLE Tut! I have the best armour of the world. Would it were day!

ORLEANS You have an excellent armour; but let my horse have his due.

CONSTABLE It is the best horse of Europe.

ORLEANS Will it never be morning?

DAUPHIN My Lord of Orleans and my Lord High Constable, you talk of horse and armour?

ORLEANS You are as well provided of both as any prince in the world.

DAUPHIN What a long night is this! I will not change my horse with any that treads but on four pasterns. Ça, ha! he bounds from the earth as if his entrails were hairs; le cheval volant, the Pegasus, chez les narines de feu! When I bestride him I soar, I am a hawk. He trots the air; the earth sings when he touches it; the basest horn of his hoof is more musical than the pipe of Hermes.

ORLEANS He's of the colour of the nutmeg.

DAUPHIN And of the heat of the ginger. It is a beast for Perseus: he is pure air and fire; and the dull elements of earth and water never appear in him, but only in patient stillness while his rider mounts him; he is indeed a horse, and all other jades you may call beasts.

CONSTABLE Indeed, my lord, it is a most absolute and excellent horse.

DAUPHIN It is the prince of palfreys; his neigh is like the bidding of a monarch, and his countenance enforces homage.

ORLEANS No more, cousin.

DAUPHIN Nay, the man hath no wit that cannot, from the rising of the lark to the lodging of the lamb, vary deserved praise on my palfrey. It is a theme as fluent as the sea: turn the sands into eloquent tongues, and my horse is argument for them all; 'tis a subject for a sovereign to reason on, and for a sovereign's sovereign to ride on; and for the world – familiar to us and unknown – to lay apart their particular functions and wonder at him. I once writ a sonnet in his praise and began thus: 'Wonder of nature' –

ORLEANS I have heard a sonnet begin so to one's mistress.

DAUPHIN Then did they imitate that which I compos'd to my courser; for my horse is my mistress.

ORLEANS Your mistress bears well.

DAUPHIN Me well; which is the prescript praise and perfection of a good and particular mistress.

CONSTABLE Nay, for methought yesterday your mistress shrewdly shook your back.

DAUPHIN So perhaps did yours.

CONSTABLE Mine was not bridled.

DAUPHIN O, then belike she was old and gentle; and you rode like a kern of Ireland, your French hose off and in your strait strossers.

CONSTABLE You have good judgment in horsemanship.

DAUPHIN Be warn'd by me, then: they that ride so, and ride not warily, fall into foul bogs. I had rather have my horse to my mistress.

CONSTABLE I had as lief have my mistress a jade.

DAUPHIN I tell thee, Constable, my mistress wears his own hair.

CONSTABLE I could make as true a boast as that, if I had a sow to my mistress.

DAUPHIN 'Le chien est retourné à son propre vomissement, et la truie lavée au bourbier.' Thou mak'st use of anything.

CONSTABLE Yet do I not use my horse for my mistress, or any such proverb so little kin to the purpose.

RAMBURES My Lord Constable, the armour that I saw in your tent to-night – are those stars or suns upon it?

CONSTABLE Stars, my lord.

DAUPHIN Some of them will fall to-morrow, I hope.

CONSTABLE And yet my sky shall not want.

DAUPHIN That may be, for you bear a many superfluously, and 'twere more honour some were away.

CONSTABLE Ev'n as your horse bears your praises, who would trot as well were some of your brags dismounted.

DAUPHIN Would I were able to load him with his desert! Will it never be day? I will trot to-morrow a mile, and my way shall be paved with English faces.

CONSTABLE I will not say so, for fear I should be fac'd out of my way; but I would it were morning, for I would fain be about the ears of the English.

RAMBURES Who will go to hazard with me for twenty prisoners?

CONSTABLE You must first go yourself to hazard ere you have them.

DAUPHIN 'Tis midnight; I'll go arm myself. [*Exit.*

ORLEANS The Dauphin longs for morning.

RAMBURES He longs to eat the English.

CONSTABLE I think he will eat all he kills.

ORLEANS By the white hand of my lady, he's a gallant prince.

CONSTABLE Swear by her foot, that she may tread out the oath.

ORLEANS He is simply the most active gentleman of France.

CONSTABLE Doing is activity, and he will still be doing.

ORLEANS He never did harm that I heard of.

CONSTABLE Nor will do none to-morrow: he will keep that good name still.

ORLEANS I know him to be valiant.

CONSTABLE I was told that by one that knows him better than you.

ORLEANS What's he?

CONSTABLE Marry, he told me so himself; and he said he car'd not who knew it.

ORLEANS He needs not; it is no hidden virtue in him.

CONSTABLE By my faith, sir, but it is; never anybody saw it but his lackey. 'Tis a hooded valour, and when it appears it will bate.

ORLEANS Ill-will never said well.

CONSTABLE I will cap that proverb with 'There is flattery in friendship'.

ORLEANS And I will take up that with 'Give the devil his due'.

CONSTABLE Well plac'd! There stands your friend for the devil; have at the very eye of that proverb with 'A pox of the devil!'

ORLEANS You are the better at proverbs by how much 'A fool's bolt is soon shot'.

CONSTABLE You have shot over.

ORLEANS 'Tis not the first time you were overshot.

Enter a Messenger.

MESSENGER My Lord High Constable, the English lie within fifteen hundred paces of your tents.

CONSTABLE Who hath measur'd the ground?

MESSENGER The Lord Grandpré.

CONSTABLE A valiant and most expert gentleman. Would it were day! Alas, poor Harry of England! he longs not for the dawning as we do.

ORLEANS What a wretched and peevish fellow is this King of England, to mope with his fat-brain'd followers so far out of his knowledge!

CONSTABLE If the English had any apprehension, they would run away.

ORLEANS That they lack; for if their heads had any intellectual armour, they could never wear such heavy head-pieces.

RAMBURES That island of England breeds very valiant creatures; their mastiffs are of unmatchable courage.

ORLEANS Foolish curs, that run winking into the mouth of a Russian bear, and have their heads crush'd like rotten apples! You may as well say that's a valiant flea that dare eat his breakfast on the lip of a lion.

CONSTABLE Just, just! and the men do sympathise with the mastiffs in robustious and rough coming on, leaving their wits with their wives; and then give them great meals of beef and iron and steel; they will eat like wolves and fight like devils.

ORLEANS Ay, but these English are shrewdly out of beef.

CONSTABLE Then shall we find to-morrow they have only stomachs to eat, and none to fight. Now is it time to arm. Come, shall we about it?

ORLEANS It is now two o'clock; but let me see – by ten
We shall have each a hundred Englishmen.

[*Exeunt.*

ACT FOUR

PROLOGUE *Enter CHORUS.*

CHORUS Now entertain conjecture of a time
When creeping murmur and the poring dark
Fills the wide vessel of the universe.
From camp to camp, through the foul womb of night,
The hum of either army stilly sounds,
That the fix'd sentinels almost receive
The secret whispers of each other's watch.
Fire answers fire, and through their paly flames
Each battle sees the other's umber'd face;
Steed threatens steed, in high and boastful neighs
Piercing the night's dull ear; and from the tents
The armourers accomplishing the knights,
With busy hammers closing rivets up,
Give dreadful note of preparation.
The country cocks do crow, the clocks do toll,
And the third hour of drowsy morning name.
Proud of their numbers and secure in soul,
The confident and over-lusty French
Do the low-rated English play at dice;
And chide the cripple tardy-gaited night
Who like a foul and ugly witch doth limp
So tediously away. The poor condemned English,
Like sacrifices, by their watchful fires
Sit patiently and inly ruminate
The morning's danger; and their gesture sad
Investing lank-lean cheeks and war-worn coats
Presenteth them unto the gazing moon
So many horrid ghosts. O, now, who will behold
The royal captain of this ruin'd band
Walking from watch to watch, from tent to tent,
Let him cry 'Praise and glory on his head!'
For forth he goes and visits all his host;
Bids them good morrow with a modest smile,
And calls them brothers, friends, and countrymen.
Upon his royal face there is no note
How dread an army hath enrounded him;
Nor doth he dedicate one jot of colour
Unto the weary and all-watched night;
But freshly looks, and over-bears attaint
With cheerful semblance and sweet majesty;
That every wretch, pining and pale before,
Beholding him, plucks comfort from his looks;
A largess universal, like the sun,
His liberal eye doth give to every one,
Thawing cold fear, that mean and gentle all
Behold, as may unworthiness define,
A little touch of Harry in the night.
And so our scene must to the battle fly;
Where – O for pity! – we shall much disgrace
With four or five most vile and ragged foils,
Right ill-dispos'd in brawl ridiculous,
The name of Agincourt. Yet sit and see,
Minding true things by what their mock'ries be.
[*Exit.*

SCENE I. *France. The English camp at Agincourt.*

Enter the KING, BEDFORD, and GLOUCESTER.

KING Gloucester, 'tis true that we are in great danger;
The greater therefore should our courage be.
Good morrow, brother Bedford. God Almighty!
There is some soul of goodness in things evil,
Would men observingly distil it out;
For our bad neighbour makes us early stirrers,
Which is both healthful and good husbandry.
Besides, they are our outward consciences
And preachers to us all, admonishing
That we should dress us fairly for our end.
Thus may we gather honey from the weed,
And make a moral of the devil himself.

Enter ERPINGHAM.

Good morrow, old Sir Thomas Erpingham:
A good soft pillow for that good white head
Were better than a churlish turf of France.

ERPINGHAM Not so, my liege; this lodging likes me better,
Since I may say 'Now lie I like a king'.

KING 'Tis good for men to love their present pains
Upon example; so the spirit is eased;
And when the mind is quick'ned, out of doubt
The organs, though defunct and dead before,
Break up their drowsy grave and newly move
With casted slough and fresh legerity.
Lend me thy cloak, Sir Thomas. Brothers both,
Commend me to the princes in our camp;
Do my good morrow to them, and anon
Desire them all to my pavilion.

GLOUCESTER We shall, my liege.

ERPINGHAM Shall I attend your Grace?

KING No, my good knight:
Go with my brothers to my lords of England;
I and my bosom must debate awhile,
And then I would no other company.

ERPINGHAM The Lord in heaven bless thee, noble Harry! [*Exeunt all but the King.*

KING God-a-mercy, old heart! thou speak'st cheerfully.

Enter PISTOL.

PISTOL Qui va là?

KING A friend.

PISTOL Discuss unto me: art thou officer,
Or art thou base, common, and popular?

KING I am a gentleman of a company.

PISTOL Trail'st thou the puissant pike?

KING Even so. What are you?

PISTOL As good a gentleman as the Emperor.

KING Then you are a better than the King.

PISTOL The King's a bawcock and a heart of gold,
A lad of life, an imp of fame;
Of parents good, of fist most valiant.
I kiss his dirty shoe, and from heart-string
I love the lovely bully. What is thy name?

KING Harry le Roy.

PISTOL Le Roy! a Cornish name; art thou of
Cornish crew?

KING No, I am a Welshman.

PISTOL Know'st thou Fluellen?

KING Yes.

PISTOL Tell him I'll knock his leek about his pate
Upon Saint Davy's day.

KING Do not you wear your dagger in your cap that day, lest he knock that about yours.

PISTOL Art thou his friend?

KING And his kinsman too.

PISTOL The figo for thee, then!

KING I thank you; God be with you!

PISTOL My name is Pistol call'd.

[*Exit.*

KING It sorts well with your fierceness.

Enter FLUELLEN and GOWER.

GOWER Captain Fluellen!

FLUELLEN So! in the name of Jesu Christ, speak fewer. It is the greatest admiration in the universal world, when the true and aunchient prerogatifes and laws of the wars is not kept; if you would take the pains but to examine the wars of Pompey the Great, you shall find, I warrant you, that there is no tiddle-taddle nor pibble-pabble in Pompey's camp; I warrant you, you shall find the ceremonies of the wars, and the cares of it, and the forms of it, and the sobriety of it, and the modesty of it, to be otherwise.

GOWER Why, the enemy is loud; you hear him all night.

FLUELLEN If the enemy is an ass, and a fool, and a prating coxcomb, is it meet, think you, that we should also, look you, be an ass, and a fool, and a prating coxcomb? In your own conscience, now?

GOWER I will speak lower.

FLUELLEN I pray you and beseech you that you will.

[*Exeunt Gower and Fluellen.*

KING Though it appear a little out of fashion,
There is much care and valour in this
Welshman.

Enter three soldiers: JOHN BATES, ALEXANDER COURT, and MICHAEL WILLIAMS.

COURT Brother John Bates, is not that the morning which breaks yonder?

BATES I think it be; but we have no great cause to desire the approach of day.

WILLIAMS We see yonder the beginning of the day, but I think we shall never see the end of it. Who goes there?

KING A friend.

WILLIAMS Under what captain serve you?

KING Under Sir Thomas Erpingham.

WILLIAMS A good old commander and a most kind gentleman. I pray you, what thinks he of our estate?

KING Even as men wreck'd upon a sand, that look to be wash'd off the next tide.

BATES He hath not told his thought to the King?

KING No; nor it is not meet he should. For though I speak it to you, I think the King is but a man as I am: the violet smells to him as it doth to me; the element shows to him as it doth to me; all his senses have but human conditions; his ceremonies laid by, in his nakedness he appears but a man; and though his affections are higher mounted than ours, yet, when they stoop, they stoop with the like wing. Therefore, when he sees reason of fears, as we do, his fears, out of doubt, be of the same relish as ours are; yet, in reason, no man should possess him with any appearance of fear, lest he, by showing it, should dishearten his army.

BATES He may show what outward courage he will; but I believe, as cold a night as 'tis, he could wish himself in Thames up to the neck; and so I would he were, and I by him, at all adventures, so we were quit here.

KING By my troth, I will speak my conscience of the King: I think he would not wish himself anywhere but where he is.

BATES Then I would he were here alone; so should he be sure to be ransomed, and a many poor men's lives saved.

KING I dare say you love him not so ill to wish him here alone, howsoever you speak this, to feel other men's minds; methinks I could not die anywhere so contented as in the King's company, his cause being just and his quarrel honourable.

WILLIAMS That's more than we know.

BATES Ay, or more than we should seek after; for we know enough if we know we are the King's subjects. If his cause be wrong, our obedience to the King wipes the crime of it out of us.

WILLIAMS But if the cause be not good, the King himself hath a heavy reckoning to make when all those legs and arms and heads, chopp'd off in a battle, shall join together at the latter day and cry all 'We died at such a place' – some swearing, some crying for a surgeon, some upon their wives left poor behind them, some upon the debts they owe, some upon their children rawly left. I am afeard there are few die well that die in a battle; for how can they charitably dispose of anything when blood is their argument? Now, if these men do not die well, it will be a black matter for the King that led them to it; who to disobey were against all proportion of subjection.

KING So, if a son that is by his father sent about merchandise do sinfully miscarry upon the sea, the imputation of his wickedness, by your rule, should be imposed upon his father that sent him; or if a servant, under his master's command transporting a sum of money, be assailed by robbers and die in many irreconcil'd iniquities, you may call the business of the master the author of the servant's damnation. But this is not so: the King is not bound to answer the particular endings of his soldiers, the father of his son, nor the master of his servant; for they purpose not their death when they purpose their services. Besides, there is no king, be his cause never so spotless, if it come to the arbitrement of swords, can try it out with all unspotted soldiers: some peradventure have on them the guilt of premeditated and contrived murder; some, of beguiling virgins with the broken seals of perjury; some, making the wars their bulwark, that have before gored the gentle bosom of peace with pillage and robbery. Now, if these men have defeated the law and outrun native punishment, though they can outstrip men they have no wings to fly from God: war is His beadle, war is His vengeance; so that here men are punish'd for before-breach of the King's laws in now the King's quarrel. Where they feared the death they have borne life away; and where they would be safe they perish. Then if they die unprovided, no more is the King guilty of their damnation than he was before guilty of those impieties for the which they are now visited. Every subject's duty is the King's; but every subject's soul is his own. Therefore should every soldier in the wars do as every sick man in his bed – wash every mote out of his conscience; and dying so, death is to him advantage; or not dying, the time was blessedly lost wherein such preparation was gained; and in him that escapes it were not sin to think that, making God so free an offer, He let him outlive that day to see His greatness, and to teach others how they should prepare.

WILLIAMS 'Tis certain, every man that dies ill, the ill upon his own head – the King is not to answer for it.

BATES I do not desire he should answer for me, and yet I determine to fight lustily for him.

KING I myself heard the King say he would not be ransom'd.

WILLIAMS Ay, he said so, to make us fight cheerfully; but when our throats are cut he may be ransom'd, and we ne'er the wiser.

KING If I live to see it, I will never trust his word after.

WILLIAMS You pay him then! That's a perilous shot out of an elder-gun, that a poor and a private displeasure can do against a monarch! You may as well go about to turn the sun to ice with fanning in his face with a peacock's feather. You'll never trust his word after! Come, 'tis a foolish saying.

KING Your reproof is something too round; I should be angry with you, if the time were convenient.

WILLIAMS Let it be a quarrel between us if you live.

KING I embrace it.

WILLIAMS How shall I know thee again?

KING Give me any gage of thine, and I will wear it in my bonnet; then if ever thou dar'st acknowledge it, I will make it my quarrel.

WILLIAMS Here's my glove; give me another of thine.

KING There.

WILLIAMS This will I also wear in my cap; if ever thou come to me and say, after tomorrow, 'This is my glove', by this hand I will take thee a box on the ear.

KING If ever I live to see it, I will challenge it.

WILLIAMS Thou dar'st as well be hang'd.

KING Well, I will do it, though I take thee in the King's company.

WILLIAMS Keep thy word. Fare thee well.

BATES Be friends, you English fools, be friends; we have French quarrels enow, if you could tell how to reckon.

KING Indeed, the French may lay twenty French crowns to one they will beat us, for they bear them on their shoulders; but it is no English treason to cut French crowns, and to-morrow the King himself will be a clipper.

[*Exeunt Soldiers.*

Upon the King! Let us our lives, our souls,
Our debts, our careful wives,
Our children, and our sins, lay on the King!
We must bear all. O hard condition,

Twin-born with greatness, subject to the breath
Of every fool, whose sense no more can feel
But his own wringing! What infinite heart's ease
Must kings neglect that private men enjoy!
And what have kings that privates have not too,
Save ceremony – save general ceremony?
And what art thou, thou idol Ceremony?
What kind of god art thou, that suffer'st more
Of mortal griefs than do thy worshippers?
What are thy rents? What are they comings-in?
O Ceremony, show me but thy worth!
What is thy soul of adoration?
Art thou aught else but place, degree, and form,
Creating awe and fear in other men?
Wherein thou art less happy being fear'd
Than they in fearing.
What drink'st thou oft, instead of homage sweet,
But poison'd flattery? O, be sick, great greatness,
And bid thy ceremony give thee cure!
Thinks thou the fiery fever will go out
With titles blown from adulation?
Will it give place to flexure and low bending?
Canst thou, when thou command'st the beggar's knee,
Command the health of it? No, thou proud dream,
That play'st so subtly with a king's repose.
I am a king that find thee; and I know
'Tis not the balm, the sceptre, and the ball,
The sword, the mace, the crown imperial,
The intertissued robe of gold and pearl,
The farced title running fore the king,
The throne he sits on, nor the tide of pomp
That beats upon the high shore of this world –
No, not all these, thrice gorgeous ceremony,
Not all these, laid in bed majestical,
Can sleep so soundly as the wretched slave
Who, with a body fill'd and vacant mind,
Gets him to rest, cramm'd with distressful bread;
Never sees horrid night, the child of hell;
But, like a lackey, from the rise to set
Sweats in the eye of Phoebus, and all night
Sleeps in Elysium; next day, after dawn,
Doth rise and help Hyperion to his horse;
And follows so the ever-running year
With profitable labour, to his grave.
And but for ceremony, such a wretch,
Winding up days with toil and nights with sleep,
Had the fore-hand and vantage of a king.
The slave, a member of the country's peace,
Enjoys it; but in gross brain little wots
What watch the king keeps to maintain the peace
Whose hours the peasant best advantages.

Enter ERPINGHAM.

ERPINGHAM My lord, your nobles, jealous of your absence,
Seek through your camp to find you.

KING Good old knight,
Collect them all together at my tent;
I'll be there before thee.

ERPINGHAM I shall do't, my lord. [*Exit.*

KING O God of battles, steel my soldiers' hearts,
Possess them not with fear! Take from them now
The sense of reck'ning, if th' opposed numbers
Pluck their hearts from them! Not to-day, O Lord,
O, not to-day, think not upon the fault
My father made in compassing the crown!
I Richard's body have interred new,
And on it have bestowed more contrite tears
Than from it issued forced drops of blood;
Five hundred poor I have in yearly pay,
Who twice a day their wither'd hands hold up
Toward heaven, to pardon blood; and I have built
Two chantries, where the sad and solemn priests
Sing still for Richard's soul. More will I do;
Though all that I can do is nothing worth,
Since that my penitence comes after all,
Imploring pardon.

Enter GLOUCESTER.

GLOUCESTER My liege!

KING My brother Gloucester's voice? Ay;
I know thy errand, I will go with thee;
The day, my friends, and all things, stay for me. [*Exeunt.*

SCENE II. *The French camp.*

Enter the DAUPHIN, ORLEANS, RAMBURES, and Others.

ORLEANS The sun doth gild our armour; up, my lords!

DAUPHIN Montez á cheval! My horse! Varlet, laquais! Ha!

ORLEANS O brave spirit!

DAUPHIN Via! Les eaux et la terre –

ORLEANS Rien puis? L'air et le feu.

DAUPHIN Ciel! cousin Orleans.

Enter CONSTABLE.

Now, my Lord Constable!

CONSTABLE Hark how our steeds for present service neigh!
DAUPHIN Mount them, and make incision in their hides,
That their hot blood may spin in English eyes,
And dout them with superfluous courage, ha!
RAMBURES What, will you have them weep our horses' blood?
How shall we then behold their natural tears?

Enter a Messenger.

MESSENGER The English are embattl'd, you French peers.
CONSTABLE To horse, you gallant Princes! straight to horse!
Do but behold yon poor and starved band,
And your fair show shall suck away their souls,
Leaving them but the shales and husks of men.
There is not work enough for all our hands;
Scarce blood enough in all their sickly veins
To give each naked curtle-axe a stain
That our French gallants shall to-day draw out,
And sheathe for lack of sport. Let us but blow on them,
The vapour of our valour will o'erturn them.
'Tis positive 'gainst all exceptions, lords,
That our superfluous lackeys and our peasants –
Who in unnecessary action swarm
About our squares of battle – were enow
To purge this field of such a hilding foe;
Though we upon this mountain's basis by
Took stand for idle speculation –
But that our honours must not. What's to say?
A very little little let us do,
And all is done. Then let the trumpets sound
The tucket sonance and the note to mount;
For our approach shall so much dare the field
That England shall couch down in fear and yield.

Enter GRANDPRÉ.

GRANDPRÉ Why do you stay so long, my lords of France?
Yond island carrions, desperate of their bones,
Ill-favouredly become the morning field;
Their ragged curtains poorly are let loose,
And our air shakes them passing scornfully;
Big Mars seems bankrupt in their beggar'd host,
And faintly through a rusty beaver peeps.
The horsemen sit like fixed candlesticks
With torch-staves in their hand; and their poor jades
Lob down their heads, dropping the hides and hips,
The gum down-roping from their pale-dead eyes,
And in their pale dull mouths the gimmal'd bit
Lies foul with chaw'd grass, still and motionless;
And their executors, the knavish crows,
Fly o'er them, all impatient for their hour.
Description cannot suit itself in words
To demonstrate the life of such a battle
In life so lifeless as it shows itself.
CONSTABLE They have said their prayers and they stay for death.
DAUPHIN Shall we go send them dinners and fresh suits,
And give their fasting horses provender,
And after fight with them?
CONSTABLE I stay but for my guidon. To the field!
I will the banner from a trumpet take,
And use it for my haste. Come, come, away!
The sun is high, and we outwear the day.

[*Exeunt.*

SCENE III. *The English camp.*

Enter GLOUCESTER, BEDFORD, EXETER, ERPINGHAM, with all his Host; SALISBURY, and WESTMORELAND.

GLOUCESTER Where is the King?
BEDFORD The King himself is rode to view their battle.
WESTMORELAND Of fighting men they have full three-score thousand.
EXETER There's five to one; besides, they all are fresh.
SALISBURY God's arm strike with us! 'tis a fearful odds.
God bye you, Princes all; I'll to my charge.
If we no more meet till we meet in heaven,
Then joyfully, my noble Lord of Bedford,
My dear Lord Gloucester, and my good Lord Exeter,
And my kind kinsman – warriors all, adieu!
BEDFORD Farewell, good Salisbury; and good luck go with thee!
EXETER Farewell, kind lord. Fight valiantly to-day;
And yet I do thee wrong to mind thee of it,
For thou art fram'd of the firm truth of valour.

[*Exit Salisbury.*

BEDFORD He is as full of valour as of kindness;
Princely in both.

Enter the KING.

WESTMORELAND O that we now had here
But one ten thousand of those men in England
That do no work to-day!
KING What's he that wishes so?
My cousin Westmoreland? No, my fair cousin;
If we are mark'd to die, we are enow
To do our country loss; and if to live,
The fewer men, the greater share of honour.

God's will! I pray thee, wish not one man more.
By Jove, I am not covetous for gold,
Nor care I who doth feed upon my cost;
It yearns me not if men my garments wear;
Such outward things dwell not in my desires.
But if it be a sin to covet honour,
I am the most offending soul alive.
No, faith, my coz, wish not a man from England.
God's peace! I would not lose so great an honour
As one man more methinks would share from me
For the best hope I have. O, do not wish one more!
Rather proclaim it, Westmoreland, through my host,
That he which hath no stomach to this fight,
Let him depart; his passport shall be made,
And crowns for convoy put into his purse;
We would not die in that man's company
That fears his fellowship to die with us.
This day is call'd the feast of Crispian.
He that outlives this day, and comes safe home,
Will stand a tip-toe when this day is nam'd,
And rouse him at the name of Crispian.
He that shall live this day, and see old age,
Will yearly on the vigil feast his neighbours,
And say 'To-morrow is Saint Crispian'.
Then will he strip his sleeve and show his scars,
And say 'These wounds I had on Crispian's day'.
Old men forget; yet all shall be forgot,
But he'll remember, with advantages,
What feats he did that day. Then shall our names,
Familiar in his mouth as household words –
Harry the King, Bedford and Exeter,
Warwick and Talbot, Salisbury and Gloucester –
Be in their flowing cups freshly rememb'red.
This story shall the good man teach his son;
And Crispin Crispian shall ne'er go by,
From this day to the ending of the world,
But we in it shall be remembered –
We few, we happy few, we band of brothers;
For he to-day that sheds his blood with me
Shall be my brother; be he ne'er so vile,
This day shall gentle his condition;
And gentlemen in England now a-bed
Shall think themselves accurs'd they were not here,
And hold their manhoods cheap whiles any speaks
That fought with us upon Saint Crispin's day.

Re-enter SALISBURY.

SALISBURY My sovereign lord, bestow yourself with speed:
The French are bravely in their battles set,
And will with all expedience charge on us.

KING All things are ready, if our minds be so.

WESTMORELAND Perish the man whose mind is backward now!

KING Thou dost not wish more help from England, coz?

WESTMORELAND God's will, my liege! would you and I alone,
Without more help, could fight this royal battle!

KING Why, now thou hast unwish'd five thousand men;
Which likes me better than to wish us one.
You know your places. God be with you all!

Tucket. Enter MONTJOY.

MONTJOY Once more I come to know of thee, King Harry,
If for thy ransom thou wilt now compound,
Before thy most assured overthrow;
For certainly thou art so near the gulf
Thou needs must be englutted. Besides, in mercy,
The Constable desires thee thou wilt mind
Thy followers of repentance, that their souls
May make a peaceful and a sweet retire
From off these fields, where, wretches, their poor bodies
Must lie and fester.

KING Who hath sent thee now?

MONTJOY The Constable of France.

KING I pray thee bear my former answer back:
Bid them achieve me, and then sell my bones.
Good God! why should they mock poor fellows thus?
The man that once did sell the lion's skin
While the beast liv'd was kill'd with hunting him.
A many of our bodies shall no doubt
Find native graves; upon the which, I trust,
Shall witness live in brass of this day's work.
And those that leave their valiant bones in France,
Dying like men, though buried in your dunghills,
They shall be fam'd; for there the sun shall greet them
And draw their honours reeking up to heaven,
Leaving their earthly parts to choke your clime,
The smell whereof shall breed a plague in France.
Mark then abounding valour in our English,
That, being dead, like to the bullet's grazing
Break out into a second course of mischief,
Killing in relapse of mortality.
Let me speak proudly: tell the Constable
We are but warriors for the working-day;

Our gayness and our gilt are all besmirch'd
With rainy marching in the painful field;
There's not a piece of feather in our host –
Good argument, I hope, we will not fly –
And time hath worn us into slovenry.
But, by the mass, our hearts are in the trim;
And my poor soldiers tell me yet ere night
They'll be in fresher robes, or they will pluck
The gay new coats o'er the French soldiers' heads
And turn them out of service. If they do this –
As, if God please, they shall – my ransom then
Will soon be levied. Herald, save thou thy labour;
Come thou no more for ransom, gentle herald;
They shall have none, I swear, but these my joints;
Which if they have, as I will leave 'em them,
Shall yield them little, tell the Constable.

MONTJOY I shall, King Harry. And so fare thee well:
Thou never shalt hear herald any more. [*Exit.*

KING I fear thou wilt once more come again for a ransom.

Enter the DUKE OF YORK.

YORK My lord, most humbly on my knee I beg
The leading of the vaward.

KING Take it, brave York. Now, soldiers, march away;
And how thou pleasest, God, dispose the day! [*Exeunt.*

SCENE IV. *The field of battle.*

Alarum. Excursions. Enter French Soldier, PISTOL, and Boy.

PISTOL Yield, cur!

FRENCH SOLDIER Je pense que vous êtes le gentil-homme de bonne qualité.

PISTOL Cality! Calen o custure me! Art thou a gentleman? What is thy name? Discuss.

FRENCH SOLDIER O Seigneur Dieu!

PISTOL O, Signieur Dew should be a gentleman.
Perpend my words, O Signieur Dew, and mark:
O Signieur Dew, thou diest on point of fox,
Except, O Signieur, thou do give to me
Egregious ransom.

FRENCH SOLDIER O, prennez miséricorde; ayez pitié de moi!

PISTOL Moy shall not serve; I will have forty moys;
Or I will fetch thy rim out at thy throat
In drops of crimson blood.

FRENCH SOLDIER Est-il impossible d'échapper la force de ton bras?

PISTOL Brass, cur!
Thou damned and luxurious mountain-goat,
Offer'st me brass?

FRENCH SOLDIER O, pardonnez-moi!

PISTOL Say'st thou me so? Is that a ton of moys?
Come hither, boy; ask me this slave in French
What is his name.

BOY Ecoutez: comment êtes-vous appelé?

FRENCH SOLDIER Monsieur le Fer.

BOY He says his name is Master Fer.

PISTOL Master Fer! I'll fer him, and firk him, and ferret him – discuss the same in French unto him.

BOY I do not know, the French for fer, and ferret, and firk.

PISTOL Bid him prepare; for I will cut his throat.

FRENCH SOLDIER Que dit-il, monsieur?

BOY Il me commande à vous dire que vous faites vous prêt; car ce soldat ici est disposé tout à cette heure de couper votre gorge.

PISTOL Owy, cuppele gorge, permafoy!
Peasant, unless thou give me crowns, brave crowns;
Or mangled shalt thou be by this my sword.

FRENCH SOLDIER O, je vous supplie, pour l'amour de Dieu, me pardonner! Je suis gentilhomme de bonne maison. Gardez ma vie, et je vous donnerai deux cents écus.

PISTOL What are his words?

BOY He prays you to save his life; he is a gentleman of a good house, and for his ransom he will give you two hundred crowns.

PISTOL Tell him my fury shall abate, and I
The crowns will take.

FRENCH SOLDIER Petit monsieur, que dit-il?

BOY Encore qu'il est contre son jurement de pardonner aucun prisonnier, néanmoins, pour les écus que vous l'avez promis, il est content à vous donner la liberté, le franchisement.

FRENCH SOLDIER Sur mes genoux je vous donne mille remercîmens; et je m'estime heureux que je suis tombé entre les mains d'un chevalier, je pense, le plus brave, vaillant, et très distingué seigneur d'Angleterre.

PISTOL Expound unto me, boy.

BOY He gives you, upon his knees, a thousand thanks; and he esteems himself happy that he hath fall'n into the hands of one – as he thinks – the most brave, valorous, and thrice-worthy signieur of England.

PISTOL As I suck blood, I will some mercy show.
Follow me. [*Exit.*

BOY Suivez-vous le grand capitaine. [*Exit French Soldier*] I did never know so full a voice issue from so empty a heart; but the saying is true – the empty vessel makes the greatest sound. Bardolph and Nym had ten times more valour than this roaring devil i' th' old play, that every one may pare his nails with a wooden dagger; and they are both hang'd; and so would this be, if he durst steal anything adventurously. I must stay with the lackeys, with the luggage of our camp. The French might have a good prey of us, if he knew of it; for there is none to guard it but boys. [*Exit.*

SCENE V. *Another part of the field of battle.*

Enter CONSTABLE, ORLEANS, BOURBON, DAUPHIN, and RAMBURES.

CONSTABLE O diable!

ORLEANS O Seigneur! le jour est perdu, tout est perdu!

DAUPHIN Mort Dieu, ma vie! all is confounded, all!
Reproach and everlasting shame
Sits mocking in our plumes. [*A short alarum.*
O méchante fortune! Do not run away.

CONSTABLE Why, all our ranks are broke.

DAUPHIN O perdurable shame! Let's stab ourselves.
Be these the wretches that we play'd at dice for?

ORLEANS Is this the king we sent to for his ransom?

BOURBON Shame, and eternal shame, nothing but shame!
Let us die in honour: once more back again;
And he that will not follow Bourbon now,
Let him go hence and, with his cap in hand
Like a base pander, hold the chamber-door
Whilst by a slave, no gentler than my dog,
His fairest daughter is contaminated.

CONSTABLE Disorder, that hath spoil'd us, friend us now!
Let us on heaps go offer up our lives.

ORLEANS We are enow yet living in the field
To smother up the English in our throngs,
If any order might be thought upon.

BOURBON The devil take order now! I'll to the throng.
Let life be short, else shame will be too long.
[*Exeunt.*

SCENE VI. *Another part of the field.*

Alarum. Enter the KING and his Train, with Prisoners; EXETER, and Others.

KING Well have we done, thrice-valiant countrymen;
But all's not done – yet keep the French the field.

EXETER The Duke of York commends him to your Majesty.

KING Lives he, good uncle? Thrice within this hour
I saw him down; thrice up again, and fighting;
From helmet to the spur all blood he was.

EXETER In which array, brave soldier, doth he lie
Larding the plain; and by his bloody side,
Yoke-fellow to his honour-owing wounds,
The noble Earl of Suffolk also lies.
Suffolk first died; and York, all haggled over,
Comes to him, where in gore he lay in-steeped,
And takes him by the beard, kisses the gashes
That bloodily did yawn upon his face,
He cries aloud 'Tarry, my cousin Suffolk.
My soul shall thine keep company to heaven;
Tarry, sweet soul, for mine, then fly a-breast;
As in this glorious and well-foughten field
We kept together in our chivalry'.
Upon these words I came and cheer'd him up;
He smil'd me in the face, raught me his hand,
And, with a feeble grip, says 'Dear my lord,
Commend my service to my sovereign'.
So did he turn, and over Suffolk's neck
He threw his wounded arm and kiss'd his lips;
And so, espous'd to death, with blood he seal'd
A testament of noble-ending love.
The pretty and sweet manner of it forc'd
Those waters from me which I would have stopp'd;
But I had not so much of man in me,
And all my mother came into mine eyes
And gave me up to tears.

KING I blame you not;
For, hearing this, I must perforce compound
With mistful eyes, or they will issue too.
[*Alarum.*
But, hark! what new alarum is this same?
The French have reinforc'd their scatter'd men.
Then every soldier kill his prisoners;
Give the word through.
[*Exeunt.*

SCENE VII. *Another part of the field.*

Enter FLUELLEN and GOWER.

FLUELLEN Kill the poys and the luggage! 'Tis expressly against the law of arms; 'tis as arrant a piece of knavery, mark you now, as can be offert; in your conscience, now, is it not? 4

GOWER 'Tis certain there's not a boy left alive; and the cowardly rascals that ran from the battle ha' done this slaughter; besides, they have burned and carried away all that was in the King's tent; wherefore the King most worthily hath caus'd every soldier to cut his prisoner's throat. O, 'tis a gallant King!

FLUELLEN Ay, he was porn at Monmouth, Captain Gower. What call you the town's name where Alexander the Pig was born?

GOWER Alexander the Great.

FLUELLEN Why, I pray you, is not 'pig' great? The pig, or the great, or the mighty, or the huge, or the magnanimous, are all one reckonings, save the phrase is a little variations.

GOWER I think Alexander the Great was born in Macedon; his father was called Philip of Macedon, as I take it.

FLUELLEN I think it is in Macedon where Alexander is porn. I tell you, Captain, if you look in the maps of the 'orld, I warrant you sall find, in the comparisons between Macedon and Monmouth, that the situations, look you, is both alike. There is a river in Macedon; and there is also moreover a river at Monmouth; it is call'd Wye at Monmouth, but it is out of my prains what is the name of the other river; but 'tis all one, 'tis alike as my fingers is to my fingers, and there is salmons in both. If you mark Alexander's life well, Harry of Monmouth's life is come after it indifferent well; for there is figures in all things. Alexander – God knows, and you know – in his rages, and his furies, and his wraths, and his cholers, and his moods, and his displeasures, and his indignations, and also being a little intoxicates in his prains, did, in his ales and his angers, look you, kill his best friend, Cleitus.

GOWER Our king is not like him in that: he never kill'd any of his friends.

FLUELLEN It is not well done, mark you now, to take the tales out of my mouth ere it is made and finished. I speak but in the figures and comparisons of it; as Alexander kill'd his friend Cleitus, being in his ales and his cups, so also Harry Monmouth, being in his right wits and his good judgments, turn'd away the fat knight with the great belly doublet; he was full of jests, and gipes, and knaveries, and mocks; I have forgot his name.

GOWER Sir John Falstaff.

FLUELLEN That is he. I'll tell you there is good men porn at Monmouth.

GOWER Here comes his Majesty.

Alarum. Enter the KING, WARWICK, GLOUCESTER, EXETER, and Others, with Prisoners. Flourish.

KING I was not angry since I came to France
Until this instant. Take a trumpet, herald;
Ride thou into the horsemen on yond hill;
If they will fight with us, bid them come down
Or void the field; they do offend our sight.
If they'll do neither, we will come to them
And make them skirr away as swift as stones
Enforced from the old Assyrian slings;
Besides, we'll cut the throats of those we have,
And not a man of them that we shall take
Shall taste our mercy. Go and tell them so.

Enter MONTJOY.

EXETER Here comes the herald of the French, my liege.

GLOUCESTER His eyes are humbler than they us'd to be.

KING How now! What means this, herald? know'st thou not
That I have fin'd these bones of mine for ransom?
Com'st thou again for ransom?

MONTJOY No, great King;
I come to thee for charitable licence,
That we may wander o'er this bloody field
To book our dead, and then to bury them;
To sort our nobles from our common men;
For many of our princes – woe the while! –
Lie drown'd and soak'd in mercenary blood;
So do our vulgar drench their peasant limbs
In blood of princes; and their wounded steeds
Fret fetlock deep in gore, and with wild rage
Yerk out their armed heels at their dead masters,
Killing them twice. O, give us leave, great King,
To view the field in safety, and dispose
Of their dead bodies!

KING I tell thee truly, herald,
I know not if the day be ours or no;
For yet a many of your horsemen peer
And gallop o'er the field.

MONTJOY The day is yours.

KING Praised be God, and not our strength, for it!
What is this castle call'd that stands hard by?

MONTJOY They call it Agincourt.

KING Then call we this the field of Agincourt,
Fought on the day of Crispin Crispianus.

FLUELLEN Your grandfather of famous memory, an't please your Majesty, and your great-uncle Edward the Plack Prince of Wales, as I have read in the chronicles, fought a most prave pattle here in France.

KING They did, Fluellen.

FLUELLEN Your Majesty says very true; if your Majesties is rememb'red of it, the Welshmen did good service in a garden where leeks did grow, wearing leeks in their Monmouth caps; which your Majesty know to this hour is an honourable badge of the service; and I do believe your Majesty takes no scorn to wear the leek upon Saint Tavy's day.

KING I wear it for a memorable honour;
For I am Welsh, you know, good countryman.

FLUELLEN All the water in Wye cannot wash your Majesty's Welsh plood out of your pody, I can tell you that. Got pless it and preserve it as long as it pleases his Grace and his Majesty too!

KING Thanks, good my countryman.

FLUELLEN By Jeshu, I am your Majesty's countryman, I care not who know it; I will confess it to all the 'orld: I need not be asham'd of your Majesty, praised be Got, so long as your Majesty is an honest man.

Enter WILLIAMS.

KING God keep me so! Our heralds go with him:
Bring me just notice of the numbers dead
On both our parts. Call yonder fellow hither.
[*Exeunt Heralds with Montjoy.*

EXETER Soldier, you must come to the King.

KING Soldier, why wear'st thou that glove in thy cap?

WILLIAMS An't please your Majesty, 'tis the gage of one that I should fight withal, if he be alive.

KING An Englishman?

WILLIAMS An't please your Majesty, a rascal that swagger'd with me last night; who, if 'a live and ever dare to challenge this glove, I have sworn to take him a box o' th' ear; or if I can see my glove in his cap – which he swore, as he was a soldier, he would wear if alive – I will strike it out soundly.

KING What think you, Captain Fluellen, is it fit this soldier keep his oath?

FLUELLEN He is a craven and a villain else, an't please your Majesty, in my conscience.

KING It may be his enemy is a gentleman of great sort, quite from the answer of his degree.

FLUELLEN Though he be as good a gentleman as the Devil is, as Lucifer and Belzebub himself, it is necessary, look your Grace, that he keep his vow and his oath; if he be perjur'd, see you now, his reputation is as arrant a villain and a Jacksauce as ever his black shoe trod upon God's ground and his earth, in my conscience, la.

KING Then keep thy vow, sirrah, when thou meet'st the fellow.

WILLIAMS So I will, my liege, as I live.

KING Who serv'st thou under?

WILLIAMS Under Captain Gower, my liege.

FLUELLEN Gower is a good captain, and is good knowledge and literatured in the wars.

KING Call him hither to me, soldier.

WILLIAMS I will, my liege. [*Exit.*

KING Here, Fluellen; wear thou this favour for me, and stick it in thy cap; when Alençon and myself were down together, I pluck'd this glove from his helm. If any man challenge this, he is a friend to Alencon and an enemy to our person; if thou encounter any such, apprehend him, an thou dost me love.

FLUELLEN Your Grace does me as great honours as can be desir'd in the hearts of his subjects. I would fain see the man that has but two legs that shall find himself aggrief'd at this glove, that is all; but I would fain see it once, an please God of his grace that I might see.

KING Know'st thou Gower?

FLUELLEN He is my dear friend, an please you.

KING Pray thee, go seek him, and bring him to my tent.

FLUELLEN I will fetch him. [*Exit.*

KING My Lord of Warwick and my brother Gloucester,
Follow Fluellen closely at the heels;
The glove which I have given him for a favour
May haply purchase him a box o' th' ear.
It is the soldier's: I, by bargain, should
Wear it myself. Follow, good cousin Warwick;
If that the soldier strike him, as I judge
By his blunt bearing he will keep his word,
Some sudden mischief may arise of it;
For I do know Fluellen valiant,
And touch'd with choler, hot as gunpowder,
And quickly will return an injury;
Follow, and see there be no harm between them.
Go you with me, uncle of Exeter. [*Exeunt.*

SCENE VIII. *Before King Henry's pavilion.*

Enter GOWER and WILLIAMS.

WILLIAMS I warrant it is to knight you, Captain.

Enter FLUELLEN.

FLUELLEN God's will and his pleasure, Captain, I beseech you now, come apace to the King: there is more good toward you peradventure than is in your knowledge to dream of.

WILLIAMS Sir, know you this glove?

FLUELLEN Know the glove? I know the glove is a glove.

WILLIAMS I know this; and thus I challenge it. [*Strikes him.*

FLUELLEN 'Sblood, an arrant traitor as any's in the universal world, or in France, or in England.

GOWER How now, sir! you villain!

WILLIAMS Do you think I'll be forsworn?

FLUELLEN Stand away, Captain Gower; I will give treason his payment into plows, I warrant you.

WILLIAMS I am not traitor.

FLUELLEN That's a lie in thy throat. I charge you in his Majesty's name, apprehend him: he's a friend of the Duke Alençon's.

Enter WARWICK and GLOUCESTER.

WARWICK How now, how now! what's the matter?

FLUELLEN My Lord of Warwick, here is – praised be God for it! – a most contagious treason come to light, look you, as you shall desire in a summer's day. Here is his Majesty.

Enter the KING and EXETER.

KING How now! what's the matter?

FLUELLEN My liege, here is a villain and a traitor, that, look your Grace, has struck the glove which your Majesty is take out of the helmet of Alençon.

WILLIAMS My liege, this was my glove: here is the fellow of it; and he that I gave it to in change promis'd to wear it in his cap; I promis'd to strike him if he did; I met this man with my glove in his cap, and I have been as good as my word.

FLUELLEN Your Majesty hear now, saving your Majesty's manhood, what an arrant, rascally, beggarly, lousy knave it is; I hope your Majesty is pear me testimony and witness, and will avouchment, that this is the glove of Alençon that your Majesty is give me; in your conscience, now.

KING Give me thy glove, soldier; look here is the fellow of it.
'Twas I, indeed, thou promised'st to strike,
And thou hast given me most bitter terms.

FLUELLEN An please your Majesty, let his neck answer for it, if there is any martial law in the world.

KING How canst thou make me satisfaction?

WILLIAMS All offences, my lord, come from the heart: never came any from mine that might offend your Majesty.

KING It was ourself thou didst abuse.

WILLIAMS Your Majesty came not like yourself: you appear'd to me but as a common man; witness the night, your garments, your lowliness; and what your Highness suffer'd under that shape I beseech you take it for your own fault, and not mine; for had you been as I took you for, I made no offence; therefore, I beseech your Highness pardon me.

KING Here, uncle Exeter, fill this glove with crowns,
And give it to this fellow. Keep it, fellow;
And wear it for an honour in thy cap
Till I do challenge it. Give him the crowns;
And, Captain, you must needs be friends with him.

FLUELLEN By this day and this light, the fellow has mettle enough in his belly: hold, there is twelve pence for you; and I pray you to serve God, and keep you out of prawls, and prabbles, and quarrels, and dissensions, and, I warrant you, it is the better for you.

WILLIAMS I will none of your money.

FLUELLEN It is with a good will; I can tell you it will serve you to mend your shoes. Come, wherefore should you be so pashful? your shoes is not so good, 'tis a good silling, I warrant you, or I will change it.

Enter an English Herald.

KING Now, herald, are the dead numb'red?

HERALD Here is the number of the slaught'red French. [*Gives a paper.*

KING What prisoners of good sort are taken, uncle?

EXETER Charles Duke of Orleans, nephew to the King;
John Duke of Bourbon, and Lord Bouciqualt;
Of other lords and barons, knights and squires,
Full fifteen hundred, besides common men.

KING This note doth tell me of ten thousand French
That in the field lie slain; of princes, in this number,
And nobles bearing banners, there lie dead
One hundred twenty-six; added to these,
Of knights, esquires, and gallant gentlemen,
Eight thousand and four hundred; of the which
Five hundred were but yesterday dubb'd knights.
So that, in these ten thousand they have lost,
There are but sixteen hundred mercenaries;
The rest are princes, barons, lords, knights, squires,
And gentlemen of blood and quality.
The names of those their nobles that lie dead:
Charles Delabreth, High Constable of France;
Jaques of Chatillon, Admiral of France;
The master of the cross-bows, Lord Rambures;
Great Master of France, the brave Sir Guichard Dolphin;
John Duke of Alençon; Antony Duke of Brabant,
The brother to the Duke of Burgundy;
And Edward Duke of Bar. Of lusty earls,
Grandpré and Roussi, Fauconbridge and Foix,
Beaumont and Marle, Vaudemont and Lestrake.
Here was a royal fellowship of death!
Where is the number of our English dead?
[*Herald presents another paper.*
Edward the Duke of York, the Earl of Suffolk,
Sir Richard Kikely, Davy Gam, Esquire;
None else of name; and of all other men
But five and twenty. O God, thy arm was here!
And not to us, but to thy arm alone,
Ascribe we all. When, without stratagem,

But in plain shock and even play of battle,
Was ever known so great and little loss
On one part and on th' other? Take it, God,
For it is none but thine.

EXETER 'Tis wonderful!

KING Come, go we in procession to the village;
And be it death proclaimed through our host
To boast of this or take that praise from God
Which is his only.

FLUELLEN Is it not lawful, an please your Majesty, to tell how many is kill'd?

KING Yes. Captain; but with this acknowledgement,
That God fought for us.

FLUELLEN Yes, my conscience, he did us great good.

KING Do we all holy rites:
Let there be sung 'Non nobis' and 'Te Deum';
The dead with charity enclos'd in clay –
And then to Calais; and to England then;
Where ne'er from France arriv'd more happy men. [*Exeunt.*

ACT FIVE

PROLOGUE *Enter CHORUS.*

CHORUS Vouchsafe to those that have not read the story
That I may prompt them; and of such as have,
I humbly pray them to admit th' excuse
Of time, of numbers, and due course of things,
Which cannot in their huge and proper life
Be here presented. Now we bear the King
Toward Calais. Grant him there. There seen,
Heave him away upon your winged thoughts
Athwart the sea. Behold, the English beach
Pales in the flood with men, with wives, and boys,
Whose shouts and claps out-voice the deep-mouth'd sea,
Which, like a mighty whiffler, fore the King
Seems to prepare his way. So let him land,
And solemnly see him set on to London.
So swift a pace hath thought that even now
You may imagine him upon Blackheath;
Where that his lords desire him to have borne
His bruised helmet and his bended sword
Before him through the city. He forbids it,
Being free from vainness and self-glorious pride;
Giving full trophy, signal, and ostent,
Quite from himself to God. But now behold
In the quick forge and working-house of thought,
How London doth pour out her citizens!
The mayor and all his brethren in best sort –
Like to the senators of th' antique Rome,
With the plebeians swarming at their heels –
Go forth and fetch their conqu'ring Caesar in;
As, by a lower but loving likelihood,
Were now the General of our gracious Empress –
As in good time he may – from Ireland coming,
Bringing rebellion broached on his sword,
How many would the peaceful city quit
To welcome him! Much more, and much more cause,
Did they this Harry. Now in London place him –
As yet the lamentation of the French
Invites the King of England's stay at home;
The Emperor's coming in behalf of France
To order peace between them; and omit
All the occurrences, whatever chanc'd,
Till Harry's back-return again to France.
There must we bring him; and myself have play'd
The interim, by rememb'ring you 'tis past.
Then brook abridgment; and your eyes advance,
After your thoughts, straight back again to France. [*Exit.*

SCENE I. *France. The English camp.*

Enter FLUELLEN and GOWER.

GOWER Nay, that's right; but why wear you your leek to-day? Saint Davy's day is past.

FLUELLEN There is occasions and causes why and wherefore in all things. I will tell you, ass my friend, Captain Gower: the rascally, scald, beggarly, lousy, pragging knave, Pistol – which you and yourself and all the world know to be no petter than a fellow, look you now, of no merits – he is come to me, and prings me pread and salt yesterday, look you, and bid me eat my leek; it was in a place where I could not breed no contention with him; but I will be so bold as to wear it in my cap till I see him once again, and then I will tell him a little piece of my desires.

Enter PISTOL.

GOWER Why, here he comes, swelling like a turkey-cock.

FLUELLEN 'Tis no matter for his swellings nor his turkey-cocks. God pless you, Aunchient Pistol! you scurvy, lousy knave, God pless you!

PISTOL Ha! art thou bedlam? Dost thou thirst, base Troyan,

To have me fold up Parca's fatal web?
Hence! I am qualmish at the smell of leek.

FLUELLEN I peseech you heartily, scurvy, lousy knave, at my desires, and my requests, and my petitions, to eat, look you, this leek; because, look you, you do not love it, nor your affections, and your appetites, and your digestions, does not agree with it, I would desire you to eat it.

PISTOL Not for Cadwallader and all his goats.

FLUELLEN There is one goat for you. [*Strikes him*] Will you be so good, scald knave, as eat it?

PISTOL Base Troyan, thou shalt die.

FLUELLEN You say very true, scald knave – when God's will is. I will desire you to live in the meantime, and eat your victuals; come, there is sauce for it. [*Striking him again*] You call'd me yesterday mountain-squire; but I will make you to-day a squire of low degree. I pray you fall to; if you can mock a leek, you can eat a leek.

GOWER Enough, Captain, you have astonish'd him.

FLUELLEN I say I will make him eat some part of my leek, or I will peat his pate four days. Bite, I pray you, it is good for your green wound and your ploody coxcomb.

PISTOL Must I bite?

FLUELLEN Yes, certainly, and out of doubt, and out of question too, and ambiguities.

PISTOL By this leek, I will most horribly revenge – I eat and eat, I swear –

FLUELLEN Eat, I pray you; will you have some more sauce to your leek? There is not enough leek to swear by.

PISTOL Quiet thy cudgel: thou dost see I eat.

FLUELLEN Much good do you, scald knave, heartily. Nay, pray you throw none away; the skin is good for your broken coxcomb. When you take occasions to see leeks hereafter, I pray you mock at 'em; that is all.

PISTOL Good.

FLUELLEN Ay, leeks is good. Hold you, there is a groat to heal your pate.

PISTOL Me a groat!

FLUELLEN Yes, verily and in truth, you shall take it; or I have another leek in my pocket which you shall eat.

PISTOL I take thy groat in earnest of revenge.

FLUELLEN If I owe you anything I will pay you in cudgels; you shall be a woodmonger, and buy nothing of me but cudgels. God bye you, and keep you, and heal your pate. [*Exit.*

PISTOL All hell shall stir for this.

GOWER Go, go; you are a counterfeit cowardly knave. Will you mock at an ancient tradition, begun upon an honourable respect, and worn as a memorable trophy of predeceased valour, and dare not avouch in your deeds any of your words? I have seen you gleeking and galling at this gentleman twice or thrice. You thought, because he could not speak English in the native garb, he could not therefore handle an English cudgel; you find it otherwise, and henceforth let a Welsh correction teach you a good English condition. Fare ye well. [*Exit.*

PISTOL Doth Fortune play the huswife with me now?
News have I that my Nell is dead i' th' spital
Of malady of France;
And there my rendezvous is quite cut off.
Old I do wax; and from my weary limbs
Honour is cudgell'd. Well, bawd I'll turn,
And something lean to cutpurse of quick hand.
To England will I steal, and there I'll steal;
And patches will I get unto these cudgell'd scars,
And swear I got them in the Gallia wars. [*Exit.*

SCENE II. *France. The French King's palace.*

Enter at one door, KING HENRY, EXETER, BEDFORD, GLOUCESTER, WARWICK, WESTMORELAND, and other Lords; at another, the FRENCH KING, QUEEN ISABEL, the PRINCESS KATHERINE, ALICE, and other Ladies; the DUKE OF BURGUNDY, and his Train.

KING Peace to this meeting, wherefore we are met!
Unto our brother France, and to our sister,
Health and fair time of day; joy and good wishes
To our most fair and princely cousin Katherine.
And, as a branch and member of this royalty,
By whom this great assembly is contriv'd,
We do salute you, Duke of Burgundy.
And, princes French, and peers, health to you all!

KING OF FRANCE Right joyous are we to behold your face,
Most worthy brother England; fairly met!
So are you, princes English, every one.

QUEEN ISABEL So happy be the issue, brother England,
Of this good day and of this gracious meeting
As we are now glad to behold your eyes –
Your eyes, which hitherto have borne in them,
Against the French that met them in their bent,
The fatal balls of murdering basilisks;
The venom of such looks, we fairly hope,
Have lost their quality; and that this day
Shall change all griefs and quarrels into love.

KING To cry amen to that, thus we appear.

QUEEN ISABEL You English princes all, I do salute you.

BURGUNDY My duty to you both, on equal love,
Great Kings of France and England! That I have labour'd
With all my wits, my pains, and strong endeavours,
To bring your most imperial Majesties
Unto this bar and royal interview,
Your mightiness on both parts best can witness.
Since then my office hath so far prevail'd
That face to face and royal eye to eye
You have congreeted, let it not disgrace me
If I demand, before this royal view,
What rub or what impediment there is
Why that the naked, poor, and mangled Peace,
Dear nurse of arts, plenties, and joyful births,
Should not in this best garden of the world,
Our fertile France, put up her lovely visage?
Alas, she hath from France too long been chas'd!
And all her husbandry doth lie on heaps,
Corrupting in it own fertility.
Her vine, the merry cheerer of the heart,
Unpruned dies; her hedges even-pleach'd,
Like prisoners wildly overgrown with hair,
Put forth disorder'd twigs; her fallow leas
The darnel, hemlock, and rank fumitory,
Doth root upon, while that the coulter rusts
That should deracinate such savagery;
The even mead, that erst brought sweetly forth
The freckled cowslip, burnet, and green clover,
Wanting the scythe, all uncorrected, rank,
Conceives by idleness, and nothing teems
But hateful docks, rough thistles, kecksies, burs,
Losing both beauty and utility.
And as our vineyards, fallows, meads, and hedges,
Defective in their natures, grow to wildness;
Even so our houses and ourselves and children
Have lost, or do not learn for want of time,
The sciences that should become our country;
But grow, like savages – as soldiers will,
That nothing do but meditate on blood –
To swearing and stern looks, diffus'd attire,
And everything that seems unnatural.
Which to reduce into our former favour
You are assembled; and my speech entreats
That I may know the let why gentle Peace
Should not expel these inconveniences
And bless us with her former qualities.

KING If, Duke of Burgundy, you would the peace
Whose want gives growth to th' imperfections
Which you have cited, you must buy that peace
With full accord to all our just demands;
Whose tenours and particular effects
You have, enschedul'd briefly, in your hands.

BURGUNDY The King hath heard them; to the which as yet
There is no answer made.

KING Well then, the peace,
Which you before so urg'd, lies in his answer.

KING OF FRANCE I have but with a cursorary eye
O'erglanced the articles; pleaseth your Grace
To appoint some of your council presently
To sit with us once more, with better heed
To re-survey them, we will suddenly
Pass our accept and peremptory answer.

KING Brother, we shall. Go, uncle Exeter,
And brother Clarence, and you, brother Gloucester,
Warwick, and Huntington, go with the King;
And take with you free power to ratify,
Augment, or alter, as your wisdoms best
Shall see advantageable for our dignity,
Any thing in or out of our demands;
And we'll consign thereto. Will you, fair sister,
Go with the princes or stay here with us?

QUEEN ISABEL Our gracious brother, I will go with them;
Haply a woman's voice may do some good,
When articles too nicely urg'd be stood on.

KING Yet leave our cousin Katherine, here with us;
She is our capital demand, compris'd
Within the fore-rank of our articles.

QUEEN ISABEL She hath good leave.

[Exeunt all but the King, Katherine, and Alice.

KING Fair Katherine, and most fair,
Will you vouchsafe to teach a soldier terms
Such as will enter at a lady's ear,
And plead his love-suit to her gentle heart?

KATHERINE Your Majesty shall mock at me;
I cannot speak your England.

KING O fair Katherine, if you will love me soundly with your French heart, I will be glad to hear you confess it brokenly with your English tongue. Do you like me, Kate?

KATHERINE Pardonnez-moi, I cannot tell vat is like me.

KING An angel is like you, Kate, and you are like an angel.

KATHERINE Que dit-il? que je suis semblable à les anges?

ALICE Oui, vraiment, sauf votre grace, ainsi dit-il.

KING I said so, dear Katherine, and I must not blush to affirm it.

KATHERINE O bon Dieu! les langues des hommes sont pleines de tromperies.

KING What says she, fair one? that the tongues of men are full of deceits?

ALICE Oui, dat de tongues of de mans is be full of deceits – dat is de Princess.

KING The Princess is the better English-woman.

I' faith, Kate, my wooing is fit for thy understanding: I am glad thou canst speak no better English; for if thou couldst, thou wouldst find me such a plain king that thou wouldst think I had sold my farm to buy my crown. I know no ways to mince it in love, but directly to say 'I love you'. Then, if you urge me farther than to say 'Do you in faith?' I wear out my suit. Give me your answer; i' faith, do; and so clap hands and a bargain. How say you, lady?

KATHERINE Sauf votre honneur, me understand well.

KING Marry, if you would put me to verses or to dance for your sake, Kate, why you undid me; for the one I have neither words nor measure, and for the other I have no strength in measure, yet a reasonable measure in strength. If I could win a lady at leap-frog, or by vaulting into my saddle with my armour on my back, under the correction of bragging be it spoken, I should quickly leap into a wife. Or if I might buffet for my love, or bound my horse for her favours, I could lay on like a butcher, and sit like a jack-an-apes, never off. But, before God, Kate, I cannot look greenly, nor gasp out my eloquence, nor I have no cunning in protestation; only downright oaths, which I never use till urg'd, nor never break for urging. If thou canst love a fellow of this temper, Kate, whose face is not worth sun-burning, that never looks in his glass for love of anything he sees there, let thine eye be thy cook. I speak to thee plain soldier. If thou canst love me for this, take me; if not, to say to thee that I shall die is true – but for thy love, by the Lord, no; yet I love thee too. And while thou liv'st, dear Kate, take a fellow of plain and uncoined constancy; for he perforce must do thee right, because he hath not the gift to woo in other places; for these fellows of infinite tongue, that can rhyme themselves into ladies' favours, they do always reason themselves out again. What! a speaker is but a prater: a rhyme is but a ballad. A good leg will fall; a straight back will stoop; a black beard will turn white; a curl'd pate will grow bald; a fair face will wither; a full eye will wax hollow. But a good heart, Kate, is the sun and the moon; or, rather, the sun, and not the moon – for it shines bright and never changes, but keeps his course truly. If thou would have such a one, take me; and take me, take a soldier; take a soldier, take a king. And what say'st thou, then, to my love? Speak, my fair, and fairly, I pray thee.

KATHERINE Is it possible dat I sould love de enemy of France?

KING No, it is not possible you should love the enemy of France, Kate, but in loving me you should love the friend of France; for I love France so well that I will not part with a village of it; I will have it all mine. And, Kate, when France is mine and I am yours, then yours is France and you are mine.

KATHERINE I cannot tell vat is dat.

KING No, Kate? I will tell thee in French, which I am sure will hang upon my tongue like a new-married wife about her husband's neck, hardly to be shook off. Je quand sur le possession de France, et quand vous avez le possession de moi – let me see, what then? Saint Denis be my speed! – donc votre est France et vous êtes mienne. It is as easy for me, Kate, to conquer the kingdom as to speak so much more French: I shall never move thee in French, unless it be to laugh at me.

KATHERINE Sauf votre honneur, le Français que vous parlez, il est meilleur que l'Anglais lequel je parle.

KING No, faith, is't not, Kate; but thy speaking of my tongue, and I thine, most truly falsely, must needs be granted to be much at one. But, Kate, dost thou understand thus much English – Canst thou love me?

KATHERINE I cannot tell.

KING Can any of your neighbours tell, Kate? I'll ask them. Come, I know thou lovest me; and at night, when you come into your closet, you'll question this gentle-woman about me; and I know, Kate, you will to her dispraise those parts in me that you love with your heart. But, good Kate, mock me mercifully; the rather, gentle Princess, because I love thee cruelly. If ever thou beest mine, Kate, as I have a saving faith within me tells me thou shalt, I get thee with scambling, and thou must therefore needs prove a good soldier-breeder. Shall not thou and I, between Saint Denis and Saint George, compound a boy, half French, half English, that shall go to Constantinople and take the Turk by the beard? Shall we not? What say'st thou, my fair flower-de-luce?

KATHERINE I do not know dat.

KING No: 'tis hereafter to know, but now to promise; do but now promise, Kate, you will endeavour for your French part of such a boy; and for my English moiety take the word of a king and a bachelor. How answer you, la plus belle Katherine du monde, mon tres chèr et divin déesse?

KATHERINE Your Majestee ave fausse French enough to deceive de most sage damoiselle dat is en France.

KING Now, fie upon my false French! By mine honour, in true English, I love thee, Kate; by which honour I dare not swear thou lovest me;

yet my blood begins to flatter me that thou dost, notwithstanding the poor and untempering effect of my visage. Now beshrew my father's ambition! He was thinking of civil wars when he got me; therefore was I created with a stubborn outside, with an aspect of iron, that when I come to woo ladies I fright them. But, in faith, Kate, the elder I wax, the better I shall appear: my comfort is, that old age, that ill layer-up of beauty, can do no more spoil upon my face; thou hast me, if thou hast me, at the worst; and thou shalt wear me, if thou wear me, better and better. And therefore tell me, most fair Katherine, will you have me? Put off your maiden blushes; avouch the thoughts of your heart with the looks of an empress; take me by the hand and say 'Harry of England, I am thine'. Which word thou shalt no sooner bless mine ear withal but I will tell thee aloud 'England is thine, Ireland is thine, France is thine, and Henry Plantagenet is thine'; who, though I speak it before his face, if he be not fellow with the best king, thou shalt find the best king of good fellows. Come, your answer in broken music – for thy voice is music and thy English broken; therefore, Queen of all, Katherine, break thy mind to me in broken English, wilt thou have me?

KATHERINE Dat is as it shall please de roi mon père.

KING Nay, it will please him well, Kate – it shall please him, Kate.

KATHERINE Den it sall also content me.

KING Upon that I kiss your hand, and I call you my queen.

KATHERINE Laissez, mon seigneur, laissez, laissez! Ma foi, je ne veux point que vous abaissiez votre grandeur en baisant la main d'une, notre seigneur, indigne serviteur; excusez-moi, je vous supplie, mon très puissant seigneur.

KING Then I will kiss your lips, Kate.

KATHERINE Les dames et les demoiselles pour être baisées devant leur noces, il n'est pas la coutume de France.

KING Madam my interpreter, what says she?

ALICE Dat it is not be de fashion pour le ladies of France – I cannot tell vat is baiser en Anglish.

KING To kiss.

ALICE Your Majestee entendre bettre que moi.

KING It is not a fashion for the maids in France to kiss before they are married, would she say?

ALICE Oui, vraiment.

KING O Kate, nice customs curtsy to great kings. Dear Kate, you and I cannot be confin'd within the weak list of a country's fashion: we are the makers of the manners, Kate; and the liberty that follows our places stops the mouth of all find-faults – as I will do yours for upholding the nice fashion of your country in denying me a kiss; therefore, patiently and yielding. [*Kissing her*] You have witchcraft in your lips, Kate: there is more eloquence in a sugar touch of them than in the tongues of the French council; and they should sooner persuade Henry of England than a general petition of monarchs. Here comes your father.

Enter the FRENCH POWER and the ENGLISH LORDS.

BURGUNDY God save your Majesty! My royal cousin,
Teach you our princess English?

KING I would have her learn, my fair cousin, how perfectly I love her; and that is good English.

BURGUNDY Is she not apt?

KING Our tongue is rough, coz, and my condition is not smooth; so that, having neither the voice nor the heart of flattery about me, I cannot so conjure up the spirit of love in her that he will appear in his true likeness.

BURGUNDY Pardon the frankness of my mirth, if I answer you for that. If you would conjure in her, you must make a circle; if conjure up love in her in his true likeness, he must appear naked and blind. Can you blame her, then, being a maid yet ros'd over with the virgin crimson of modesty, if she deny the appearance of a naked blind boy in her naked seeing self? It were, my lord, a hard condition for a maid to consign to.

KING Yet they do wink and yield, as love is blind and enforces.

BURGUNDY They are then excus'd, my lord, when they see not what they do.

KING Then, good my lord, teach your cousin to consent winking.

BURGUNDY I will wink on her to consent, my lord, if you will teach her to know my meaning; for maids well summer'd and warm kept are like flies at Bartholomew-tide, blind, though they have their eyes; and then they will endure handling, which before would not abide looking on.

KING This moral ties me over to time and a hot summer; and so I shall catch the fly, your cousin, in the latter end, and she must be blind too.

BURGUNDY As love is, my lord, before it loves.

KING It is so; and you may, some of you, thank love for my blindness, who cannot see many a fair French city for one fair French maid that stands in my way.

KING OF FRANCE Yes, my lord, you see them perspectively, the cities turned into a maid; for they are all girdled with maiden walls that war hath never ent'red.

KING Shall Kate be my wife?

KING OF FRANCE So please you.

KING I am content, so the maiden cities you talk of may wait on her; so the maid that stood in the way for my wish shall show me the way to my will.

KING OF FRANCE We have consented to all terms of reason.

KING Is't so, my lords of England?

WESTMORELAND The king hath granted every article:
His daughter first; and then in sequel, all,
According to their firm proposed natures.

EXETER Only he hath not yet subscribed this: Where your Majesty demands that the King of France, having any occasion to write for matter of grant, shall name your Highness in this form and with this addition, in French, Notre très cher fils Henri, Roi d'Angleterre, Héritier de France; and thus in Latin, Praeclarissimus filius noster Henricus, Rex Angliae et Haeres Franciae.

KING OF FRANCE Nor this I have not, brother, so denied
But your request shall make me let it pass.

KING I pray you, then, in love and dear alliance,
Let that one article rank with the rest;
And thereupon give me your daughter.

KING OF FRANCE Take her, fair son, and from her blood raise up
Issue to me; that the contending kingdoms
Of France and England, whose very shores look pale
With envy of each other's happiness,
May cease their hatred; and this dear conjunction
Plant neighbourhood and Christian-like accord
In their sweet bosoms, that never war advance
His bleeding sword 'twixt England and fair France.

LORDS Amen!

KING Now, welcome, Kate; and bear me witness all,
That here I kiss her as my sovereign queen.
[*Flourish.*

QUEEN ISABEL God, the best maker of all marriages,
Combine your hearts in one, your realms in one!
As man and wife, being two, are one in love,
So be there 'twixt your kingdoms such a spousal
That never may ill office or fell jealousy,
Which troubles oft the bed of blessed marriage,
Thrust in between the paction of these kingdoms,
To make divorce of their incorporate league;
That English may as French, French Englishmen,
Receive each other. God speak this Amen!

ALL Amen!

KING Prepare we for our marriage; on which day,
My Lord of Burgundy, we'll take your oath,
And all the peers', for surety of our leagues.
Then shall I swear to Kate, and you to me,
And may our oaths well kept and prosp'rous be!
[*Sennet. Exeunt.*

Enter CHORUS.

CHORUS Thus far, with rough and all-unable pen,
Our bending author hath pursu'd the story,
In little room confining mighty men,
Mangling by starts the full course of their glory.
Small time, but, in that small, most greatly lived
This star of England. Fortune made his sword;
By which the world's best garden he achieved,
And of it left his son imperial lord.
Henry the Sixth, in infant bands crown'd king
Of France and England, did this king succeed;
Whose state so many had the managing
That they lost France and made his England bleed;
Which oft our stage hath shown; and, for their sake,
In your fair minds let this acceptance take.
[*Exit*

The First Part of King Henry the Sixth

Introduction by ROBERT MASLEN

The three plays that have come to be known as *Henry VI Parts 1, 2 and 3* were Shakespeare's ambitious first attempts to dramatize English history. Recent scholarship inclines to the belief that *The First Part of Henry VI* was written after the second and third parts but whatever the order of their composition, the three plays form an impressively tightly organised narrative, which redistributes the complex material of the chronicles so as to focus on recurring issues and to generate suspense. The choice of subject was bold: this particular period of English history was a touchy subject for the Tudors, focussing attention on their somewhat tenuous claim to the throne and reminding the audience of rival claims. But the risk paid off. In 1592, what was probably the first performance of Shakespeare's *Henry VI Part 1* attracted the largest audiences of the season, and was acted fifteen more times over the next ten months. Clearly the political events of the previous century remained of intense interest to an Elizabethan audience.

The play opens with the funeral of Henry V, who is celebrated as the epitome of regal power: 'England ne'er had a king until his time' [1.1.8]. With his death, the political unity he managed to preserve begins to fall apart. The funeral obsequies quickly degenerate into bickering between Duke Humphrey of Gloucester and the ambitious bishop of Winchester: a quarrel which resurfaces throughout the play, and reaches its bloody climax in *Part 2*. For a time the shreds of English unity are tenuously held together by the heroic Lord Talbot, commander of the English forces in the wars against France. At one point, in an interpolated episode which owes something to the legends of Robin Hood, Talbot finds himself trapped in the castle of a French Countess, who expresses disappointment that a man with such a fearsome reputation should have such a puny body [2.3]. Talbot replies that the bulk of his body is made up of English men-at-arms, and when he blows his horn they confirm the point by rescuing him. Shakespeare stresses the integrity and masculinity of the front-line English troops at the expense of the French, whom he depicts as cowardly turncoats dominated by women. The French commanders put their trust in Joan La Pucelle (Joan of Arc), one of a number of strong women in the early history plays who seize every opportunity to involve themselves in the power-struggles which the men regard as their exclusive province. Like the other women – the Duchess of Gloucester in *Part* 2 and Queen Margaret in *Part* 3 – Joan finds herself mocked and vilified for her efforts, and her body is repeatedly subjected to attack, first by bawdy innuendo, later by fire. Joan responds to the male attitude to her interference in their affairs by making more and more daring use of the sole power permitted her, that of forging sexual alliances: she has affairs first with the French king Charles and then with spirits, and all her lovers betray her. The French alliance with Joan sets them in stark opposition to the saintly and virginal English king Henry VI, to whom Talbot gives his undivided loyalty.

But this crude opposition of English and French, godly and satanic, is gradually supplanted in the course of the play by the more insidious political divisions breaking out in England, above all the split between the houses of York and Lancaster. Shakespeare cleverly weaves the story of this growing domestic antagonism into the history of the war with France, until at the climax of the play the death of Talbot is brought about (unhistorically) by a dispute between York and his chief Lancastrian rival Somerset over which of them should send him reinforcements. The burning of Joan La Pucelle in the fifth act only heralds the commencement of an equally savage war within England itself.

The folly of the ensuing 'War of the Roses' is brilliantly evoked in a scene set in the Temple garden [2.4], where a squabble breaks out between the followers of York and Somerset. At the height of the quarrel the followers of either party pluck red or white roses to signal their allegiances; but the arbitrariness of the choice becomes obvious when each faction begins to play with words, warning their opponents that in time the colour of their roses will change: the red rose will turn pale with fear, the white rose will be dyed with blood. The stage is set for the insanity of civil war, where every oath of allegiance can be reversed at a moment's notice. In this scene alone, Shakespeare established his credentials as a sardonic commentator on the shiftiness of politicians both in the previous century and in his own.

The First Part of King Henry the Sixth

DRAMATIS PERSONAE

KING HENRY THE SIXTH
DUKE OF GLOUCESTER
uncle to the King, and Protector
DUKE OF BEDFORD
uncle to the King, and Regent of France
THOMAS BEAUFORT
Duke of Exeter, great-uncle to the King
HENRY BEAUFORT
great-uncle to the King, Bishop of Winchester, and afterwards Cardinal
JOHN BEAUFORT
Earl of Somerset, afterwards Duke
RICHARD PLANTAGENET
son of Richard late Earl of Cambridge, afterwards Duke of York
EARL OF WARWICK
EARL OF SALISBURY
EARL OF SUFFOLK
LORD TALBOT
afterwards Earl of Shrewsbury
JOHN TALBOT
his son
EDMUND MORTIMER
Earl of March
SIR JOHN FASTOLFE
SIR WILLIAM LUCY
SIR WILLIAM GLANSDALE
SIR THOMAS GARGRAVE
Mayor of London
WOODVILLE
Lieutenant of the Tower
VERNON
of the White Rose or York faction
BASSET
of the Red Rose or Lancaster faction
A Lawyer
Gaolers to Mortimer
CHARLES
Dauphin, and afterwards King of France
REIGNIER
Duke of Anjou, and titular King of Naples
DUKE OF BURGUNDY
DUKE OF ALENÇON
BASTARD OF ORLEANS
Governor of Paris
Master-Gunner of Orleans and his Son
General of the French Forces in Bordeaux
A French Sergeant
A Porter
An old Shepherd father to Joan la Pucelle
MARGARET
daughter to Reignier, afterwards married to King Henry
COUNTESS OF AUVERGNE
JOAN LA PUCELLE
commonly called Joan of Arc
Lords, Warders of the Tower, Heralds, Officers, Soldiers, Messengers, English and French Attendants
Fiends appearing to La Pucelle

THE SCENE: ENGLAND AND FRANCE.

ACT ONE

SCENE I. *Westminster Abbey.*

Dead March. Enter the funeral of King Henry the Fifth, attended on by the DUKE OF BEDFORD, Regent of France, the DUKE OF GLOUCESTER, Protector, the DUKE OF EXETER, the EARL OF WARWICK, the BISHOP OF WINCHESTER.

BEDFORD Hung be the heavens with black, yield day to night!
Comets, importing change of times and states,
Brandish your crystal tresses in the sky
And with them scourge the bad revolting stars
That have consented unto Henry's death!
King Henry the Fifth, too famous to live long!
England ne'er lost a king of so much worth.

GLOUCESTER England ne'er had a king until his time.
Virtue he had, deserving to command;
His brandish'd sword did blind men with his beams;
His arms spread wider than a dragon's wings;
His sparkling eyes, replete with wrathful fire,
More dazzled and drove back his enemies
Than mid-day sun fierce bent against their faces.
What should I say? His deeds exceed all speech:
He ne'er lift up his hand but conquered.

EXETER We mourn in black; why mourn we not in blood?
Henry is dead and never shall revive.

Upon a wooden coffin we attend;
And death's dishonourable victory
We with our stately presence glorify,
Like captives bound to a triumphant car.
What! shall we curse the planets of mishap
That plotted thus our glory's overthrow?
Or shall we think the subtle-witted French
Conjurers and sorcerers, that, afraid of him,
By magic verses have contriv'd his end?

WINCHESTER He was a king bless'd of the King of kings;
Unto the French the dreadful judgment-day
So dreadful will not be as was his sight.
The battles of the Lord of Hosts he fought;
The Church's prayers made him so prosperous.

GLOUCESTER The Church! Where is it? Had not churchmen pray'd,
His thread of life had not so soon decay'd.
None do you like but an effeminate prince,
Whom like a school-boy you may overawe.

WINCHESTER Gloucester, whate'er we like, thou art Protector
And lookest to command the Prince and realm.
Thy wife is proud; she holdeth thee in awe
More than God or religious churchmen may.

GLOUCESTER Name not religion, for thou lov'st the flesh;
And ne'er throughout the year to church thou go'st,
Except it be to pray against thy foes.

BEDFORD Cease, cease these jars and rest your minds in peace;
Let's to the altar. Heralds, wait on us.
Instead of gold, we'll offer up our arms,
Since arms avail not, now that Henry's dead.
Posterity, await for wretched years,
When at their mother's moist'ned eyes babes shall suck,
Our isle be made a nourish of salt tears,
And none but women left to wail the dead.
Henry the Fifth, thy ghost I invocate:
Prosper this realm, keep it from civil broils,
Combat with adverse planets in the heavens.
A far more glorious star thy soul will make
Than Julius Caesar or bright –

Enter a Messenger.

MESSENGER My honourable lords, health to you all!
Sad tidings bring I to you out of France,
Of loss, of slaughter, and discomfiture:
Guienne, Champagne, Rheims, Orleans,
Paris, Guysors, Poictiers, are all quite lost.

BEDFORD What say'st thou, man, before dead Henry's corse?
Speak softly, or the loss of those great towns
Will make him burst his lead and rise from death.

GLOUCESTER In Paris lost? Is Rouen yielded up?
If Henry were recall'd to life again,
These news would cause him once more yield the ghost.

EXETER How were they lost? What treachery was us'd?

MESSENGER No treachery, but want of men and money.
Amongst the soldiers this is muttered –
That here you maintain several factions;
And whilst a field should be dispatch'd and fought,
You are disputing of your generals:
One would have ling'ring wars, with little cost;
Another would fly swift, but wanteth wings;
A third thinks, without expense at all,
By guileful fair words peace may be obtain'd.
Awake, awake, English nobility!
Let not sloth dim your honours, new-begot.
Cropp'd are the flower-de-luces in your arms;
Of England's coat one half is cut away.

EXETER Were our tears wanting to this funeral,
These tidings would call forth their flowing tides.

BEDFORD Me they concern; Regent I am of France.
Give me my steeled coat; I'll fight for France.
Away with these disgraceful wailing robes!
Wounds will I lend the French instead of eyes,
To weep their intermissive miseries.

Enter a second Messenger.

2 MESSENGER Lords, view these letters full of bad mischance.
France is revolted from the English quite,
Except some petty towns of no import.
The Dauphin Charles is crowned king in Rheims;
The Bastard of Orleans with him is join'd;
Reignier, Duke of Anjou, doth take his part;
The Duke of Alençon flieth to his side.

EXETER The Dauphin crowned king! all fly to him!
O, whither shall we fly from this reproach?

GLOUCESTER We will not fly but to our enemies' throats.
Bedford, if thou be slack I'll fight it out.

BEDFORD Gloucester, why doubt'st thou of my forwardness?
An army have I muster'd in my thoughts,
Wherewith already France is overrun.

Enter a third Messenger.

3 MESSENGER My gracious lords, to add to your laments,
Wherewith you now bedew King Henry's hearse,

I must inform you of a dismal fight
Betwixt the stout Lord Talbot and the French.
WINCHESTER What! Wherein Talbot overcame? Is't so?
3 MESSENGER O, no; wherein Lord Talbot was o'erthrown.
The circumstances I'll tell you more at large.
The tenth of August last this dreadful lord,
Retiring from the siege of Orleans,
Having full scarce six thousand in his troop,
By three and twenty thousand of the French
Was round encompassed and set upon.
No leisure had he to enrank his men;
He wanted pikes to set before his archers;
Instead whereof sharp stakes pluck'd out of hedges
They pitched in the ground confusedly
To keep the horsemen off from breaking in.
More than three hours the fight continued;
Where valiant Talbot, above human thought,
Enacted wonders with his sword and lance:
Hundreds he sent to hell, and none durst stand him;
Here, there, and everywhere, enrag'd he slew –
The French exclaim'd the devil was in arms;
All the whole army stood agaz'd on him.
His soldiers, spying his undaunted spirit,
'A Talbot! a Talbot!' cried out amain,
And rush'd into the bowels of the battle.
Here had the conquest fully been seal'd up
If Sir John Fastolfe had not play'd the coward.
He, being in the vaward – plac'd behind
With purpose to relieve and follow them –
Cowardly fled, not having struck one stroke;
Hence grew the general wreck and massacre.
Enclosed were they with their enemies.
A base Walloon, to win the Dauphin's grace,
Thrust Talbot with a spear into the back;
Whom all France, with their chief assembled strength,
Durst not presume to look once in the face.
BEDFORD Is Talbot slain? Then I will slay myself,
For living idly here in pomp and ease,
Whilst such a worthy leader, wanting aid,
Unto his dastard foemen is betray'd.
3 MESSENGER O no, he lives, but is took prisoner,
And Lord Scales with him, and Lord Hungerford;
Most of the rest slaughter'd or took likewise.
BEDFORD His ransom there is none but I shall pay.
I'll hale the Dauphin headlong from his throne;
His crown shall be the ransom of my friend;
Four of their lords I'll change for one of ours.
Farewell, my masters; to my task will I;
Bonfires in France forthwith I am to make
To keep our great Saint George's feast withal.
Ten thousand soldiers with me I will take,
Whose bloody deeds shall make all Europe quake.
3 MESSENGER So you had need; for Orleans is besieg'd;
The English army is grown weak and faint;
The Earl of Salisbury craveth supply
And hardly keeps his men from mutiny,
Since they, so few, watch such a multitude.
EXETER Remember, lords, your oaths to Henry sworn,
Either to quell the Dauphin utterly,
Or bring him in obedience to your yoke.
BEDFORD I do remember it, and here take my leave
To go about my preparation. [*Exit.*
GLOUCESTER I'll to the Tower with all the haste I can
To view th' artillery and munition;
And then I will proclaim young Henry king. [*Exit.*
EXETER To Eltham will I, where the young King is,
Being ordain'd his special governor;
And for his safety there I'll best devise. [*Exit.*
WINCHESTER [*Aside*] Each hath his place and function to attend:
I am left out; for me nothing remains.
But long I will not be Jack out of office.
The King from Eltham I intend to steal,
And sit at chiefest stern of public weal. [*Exeunt.*

SCENE II. *France. Before Orleans.*

Sound a flourish. Enter CHARLES THE DAUPHIN, ALENÇON, and REIGNIER, marching with drum and Soldiers.

CHARLES Mars his true moving, even as in the heavens
So in the earth, to this day is not known.
Late did he shine upon the English side;
Now we are victors, upon us he smiles.
What towns of any moment but we have?
At pleasure here we lie near Orleans;
Otherwhiles the famish'd English, like pale ghosts,
Faintly besiege us one hour in a month.
ALENCON They want their porridge and their fat bull-beeves.
Either they must be dieted like mules
And have their provender tied to their mouths,
Or piteous they will look, like drowned mice.

REIGNIER Let's raise the siege. Why live we idly here?
Talbot is taken, whom we wont to fear;
Remaineth none but mad-brain'd Salisbury,
And he may well in fretting spend his gall –
Nor men nor money hath he to make war.
CHARLES Sound, sound alarum; we will rush on them.
Now for the honour of the forlorn French!
Him I forgive my death that killeth me,
When he sees me go back one foot or flee.
[Exeunt.

Here alarum. They are beaten back by the English, with great loss. Re-enter CHARLES, ALENÇON, and REIGNIER.

CHARLES Who ever saw the like? What men have I!
Dogs! cowards! dastards! I would ne'er have fled
But that they left me midst my enemies.
REIGNIER Salisbury is a desperate homicide;
He fighteth as one weary of his life.
The other lords, like lions wanting food,
Do rush upon us as their hungry prey.
ALENÇON Froissart, a countryman of ours, records
England all Olivers and Rowlands bred
During the time Edward the Third did reign.
More truly now may this be verified;
For none but Samsons and Goliases
It sendeth forth to skirmish. One to ten!
Lean raw-bon'd rascals! Who would e'er suppose
They had such courage and audacity?
CHARLES Let's leave this town; for they are hare-brain'd slaves,
And hunger will enforce them to be more eager.
Of old I know them; rather with their teeth
The walls they'll tear down than forsake the siege.
REIGNIER I think by some odd gimmers or device
Their arms are set, like clocks, still to strike on;
Else ne'er could they hold out so as they do.
By my consent, we'll even let them alone.
ALENÇON Be it so.

Enter the BASTARD OF ORLEANS.

BASTARD Where's the Prince Dauphin? I have news for him.
CHARLES Bastard of Orleans, thrice welcome to us.
BASTARD Methinks your looks are sad, your cheer appall'd.
Hath the late overthrow wrought this offence?
Be not dismay'd, for succour is at hand.
A holy maid hither with me I bring,
Which, by a vision sent to her from heaven,
Ordained is to raise this tedious siege
And drive the English forth the bounds of France.
The spirit of deep prophecy she hath,
Exceeding the nine sibyls of old Rome:
What's past and what's to come she can descry.
Speak, shall I call her in? Believe my words,
For they are certain and unfallible.
CHARLES Go, call her in. *[Exit Bastard]* But first, to try her skill,
Reignier, stand thou as Dauphin in my place;
Question her proudly; let thy looks be stern;
By this means shall we sound what skill she hath.

Re-enter the BASTARD OF ORLEANS, with JOAN LA PUCELLE.

REIGNIER Fair maid, is 't thou wilt do these wondrous feats?
LA PUCELLE Reignier, is 't thou that thinkest to beguile me?
Where is the Dauphin? Come, come from behind;
I know thee well, though never seen before.
Be not amaz'd, there's nothing hid from me.
In private will I talk with thee apart.
Stand back, you lords, and give us leave awhile.
REIGNIER She takes upon her bravely at first dash.
LA PUCELLE Dauphin, I am by birth a shepherd's daughter,
My wit untrain'd in any kind of art.
Heaven and our Lady gracious hath it pleas'd
To shine on my contemptible estate.
Lo, whilst I waited on my tender lambs
And to sun's parching heat display'd my cheeks,
God's Mother deigned to appear to me,
And in a vision full of majesty
Will'd me to leave my base vocation
And free my country from calamity –
Her aid she promis'd and assur'd success.
In complete glory she reveal'd herself;
And whereas I was black and swart before,
With those clear rays which she infus'd on me
That beauty am I bless'd with which you may see.
Ask me what question thou canst possible,
And I will answer unpremeditated.
My courage try by combat if thou dar'st,
And thou shalt find that I exceed my sex.
Resolve on this: thou shalt be fortunate
If thou receive me for thy warlike mate.
CHARLES Thou hast astonish'd me with thy high terms.
Only this proof I'll of thy valour make –
In single combat thou shalt buckle with me;
And if thou vanquishest, thy words are true;

Otherwise I renounce all confidence.

LA PUCELLE I am prepar'd; here is my keen-edg'd sword,
Deck'd with five flower-de-luces on each side,
The which at Touraine, in Saint Katherine's churchyard,
Out of a great deal of old iron I chose forth.

CHARLES Then come, o' God's name; I fear no woman.

LA PUCELLE And while I live I'll ne'er fly from a man. [*Here they fight and Joan la Pucelle overcomes.*

CHARLES Stay, stay thy hands; thou art an Amazon,
And fightest with the sword of Deborah.

LA PUCELLE Christ's Mother helps me, else I were too weak.

CHARLES Whoe'er helps thee, 'tis thou that must help me.
Impatiently I burn with thy desire;
My heart and hands thou hast at once subdu'd.
Excellent Pucelle, if thy name be so,
Let me thy servant and not sovereign be.
'Tis the French Dauphin sueth to thee thus.

LA PUCELLE I must not yield to any rites of love,
For my profession's sacred from above.
When I have chased all thy foes from hence,
Then will I think upon a recompense.

CHARLES Meantime look gracious on thy prostrate thrall.

REIGNIER My lord, methinks, is very long in talk.

ALENÇON Doubtless he shrives this woman to her smock;
Else ne'er could he so long protract his speech.

REIGNIER Shall we disturb him, since he keeps no mean?

ALENÇON He may mean more than we poor men do know;
These women are shrewd tempters with their tongues.

REIGNIER My lord, where are you? What devise you on?
Shall we give o'er Orleans, or no?

LA PUCELLE Why, no, I say; distrustful recreants!
Fight till the last gasp; I will be your guard.

CHARLES What she says I'll confirm; we'll fight it out.

LA PUCELLE Assign'd am I to be the English scourge.
This night the siege assuredly I'll raise.
Expect Saint Martin's summer, halcyon days,
Since I have entered into these wars.
Glory is like a circle in the water,
Which never ceaseth to enlarge itself
Till by broad spreading it disperse to nought.
With Henry's death the English circle ends;
Dispersed are the glories it included.
Now am I like that proud insulting ship
Which Caesar and his fortune bare at once.

CHARLES Was Mahomet inspired with a dove?
Thou with an eagle art inspired then.
Helen, the mother of great Constantine,
Nor yet Saint Philip's daughters were like thee.
Bright star of Venus, fall'n down on the earth,
How may I reverently worship thee enough?

ALENÇON Leave off delays, and let us raise the siege.

REIGNIER Woman, do what thou canst to save our honours;
Drive them from Orleans, and be immortaliz'd.

CHARLES Presently we'll try. Come, let's away about it.
No prophet will I trust if she prove false. [*Exeunt.*

SCENE III. *London. Before the Tower gates.*

Enter the DUKE OF GLOUCESTER, *with his Servants in blue coats.*

GLOUCESTER I am come to survey the Tower this day;
Since Henry's death, I fear, there is conveyance.
Where be these warders that they wait not here?
Open the gates; 'tis Gloucester that calls.

1 WARD [*Within*] Who's there that knocks so imperiously?

1 SERVANT It is the noble Duke of Gloucester.

2 WARD [*Within*] Whoe'er he be, you may not be let in.

1 SERVANT Villains, answer you so the Lord Protector?

1 WARD [*Within*] The Lord protect him! so we answer him.
We do no otherwise than we are will'd.

GLOUCESTER Who willed you, or whose will stands but mine?
There's none Protector of the realm but I.
Break up the gates, I'll be your warrantize.
Shall I be flouted thus by dunghill grooms?

[*Gloucester's men rush at the Tower gates, and Woodville the Lieutenant speaks within.*

WOODVILLE [*Within*] What noise is this?
What traitors have we here?

GLOUCESTER Lieutenant, is it you whose voice I hear?
Open the gates; here's Gloucester that would enter.

WOODVILLE [*Within*] Have patience, noble Duke, I may not open;
The Cardinal of Winchester forbids.
From him I have express commandment
That thou nor none of thine shall be let in.

GLOUCESTER Faint-hearted Woodville, prizest him fore me?
Arrogant Winchester, that haughty prelate
Whom Henry, our late sovereign, ne'er could brook!
Thou art no friend to God or to the King.
Open the gates, or I'll shut thee out shortly.

SERVANTS Open the gates unto the Lord Protector,
Or we'll burst them open, if that you come not quickly.

Enter to the Protector at the Tower gates WINCHESTER and his Men in tawny coats.

WINCHESTER How now, ambitious Humphry! What means this?

GLOUCESTER Peel'd priest, dost thou command me to be shut out?

WINCHESTER I do, thou most usurping proditor,
And not Protector of the King or realm.

GLOUCESTER Stand back, thou manifest conspirator,
Thou that contrived'st to murder our dead lord;
Thou that giv'st whores indulgences to sin.
I'll canvass thee in thy broad cardinal's hat,
If thou proceed in this thy insolence.

WINCHESTER Nay, stand thou back; I will not budge a foot.
This be Damascus; be thou cursed Cain,
To slay thy brother Abel, if thou wilt.

GLOUCESTER I will not slay thee, but I'll drive thee back.
Thy scarlet robes as a child's bearing-cloth
I'll use to carry thee out of this place.

WINCHESTER Do what thou dar'st; I beard thee to thy face.

GLOUCESTER What! am I dar'd and bearded to my face?
Draw, men, for all this privileged place –
Blue-coats to tawny-coats. Priest, beware your beard;
I mean to tug it, and to cuff you soundly;
Under my feet I stamp thy cardinal's hat;
In spite of Pope or dignities of church,
Here by the cheeks I'll drag thee up and down.

WINCHESTER Gloucester, thou wilt answer this before the Pope.

GLOUCESTER Winchester goose! I cry 'A rope, a rope!'
Now beat them hence; why do you let them stay?
Thee I'll chase hence, thou wolf in sheep's array.
Out, tawny-coats! Out, scarlet hypocrite!

Here Gloucester's men beat out the Cardinal's men; and enter in the hurly-burly the MAYOR of London, and his Officers.

MAYOR Fie, lords! that you, being supreme magistrates,
Thus contumeliously should break the peace!

GLOUCESTER Peace, Mayor! thou know'st little of my wrongs:
Here's Beaufort, that regards nor God nor King,
Hath here distrain'd the Tower to his use.

WINCHESTER Here's Gloucester, a foe to citizens;
One that still motions war and never peace,
O'ercharging your free purses with large fines;
That seeks to overthrow religion,
Because he is Protector of the realm,
And would have armour here out of the Tower,
To crown himself King and suppress the Prince.

GLOUCESTER I will not answer thee with words, but blows. [*Here they skirmish again.*

MAYOR Nought rests for me in this tumultuous strife
But to make open proclamation.
Come, officer, as loud as e'er thou canst,
Cry.

OFFICER [*Cries*] All manner of men assembled here in arms this day against God's peace and the King's, we charge and command you, in his Highness' name, to repair to your several dwelling-places; and not to wear, handle, or use, any sword, weapon, or dagger, henceforward, upon pain of death.

GLOUCESTER Cardinal, I'll be no breaker of the law;
But we shall meet and break our minds at large.

WINCHESTER Gloucester, we'll meet to thy cost, be sure;
Thy heart-blood I will have for this day's work.

MAYOR I'll call for clubs if you will not away.
This Cardinal's more haughty than the devil.

GLOUCESTER Mayor, farewell; thou dost but what thou mayst.

WINCHESTER Abominable Gloucester, guard thy head,
For I intend to have it ere long.

[*Exeunt, severally, Gloucester and Winchester with their Servants.*

MAYOR See the coast clear'd, and then we will depart.
Good God, these nobles should such stomachs bear!
I myself fight not once in forty year. [*Exeunt.*

SCENE IV. *France. Before Orleans.*

Enter, on the walls, the Master-Gunner of Orleans and his Boy.

MASTER-GUNNER Sirrah, thou know'st how Orleans is besieg'd,
And how the English have the suburbs won.

BOY Father, I know; and oft have shot at them,
Howe'er unfortunate I miss'd my aim.
MASTER-GUNNER But now thou shalt not. Be thou rul'd by me.
Chief master-gunner am I of this town;
Something I must do to procure me grace.
The Prince's espials have informed me
How the English, in the suburbs close intrench'd,
Wont, through a secret grate of iron bars
In yonder tower, to overpeer the city,
And thence discover how with most advantage
They may vex us with shot or with assault.
To intercept this inconvenience,
A piece of ordnance 'gainst it I have plac'd;
And even these three days have I watch'd
If I could see them. Now do thou watch,
For I can stay no longer.
If thou spy'st any, run and bring me word;
And thou shalt find me at the Governor's. [*Exit.*
BOY Father, I warrant you; take you no care;
I'll never trouble you, if I may spy them. [*Exit.*

Enter SALISBURY and TALBOT on the turrets, with SIR WILLIAM GLANSDALE, SIR THOMAS GARGRAVE, and Others.

SALISBURY Talbot, my life, my joy, again return'd!
How wert thou handled being prisoner?
Or by what means got'st thou to be releas'd?
Discourse, I prithee, on this turret's top.
TALBOT The Earl of Bedford had a prisoner
Call'd the brave Lord Ponton de Santrailles;
For him was I exchang'd and ransomed.
But with a baser man of arms by far
Once, in contempt, they would have barter'd me;
Which I disdaining scorn'd, and craved death
Rather than I would be so vile esteem'd.
In fine, redeem'd I was as I desir'd.
But, O! the treacherous Fastolfe wounds my heart;
Whom with my bare fists I would execute,
If I now had him brought into my power.
SALISBURY Yet tell'st thou not how thou wert entertain'd.
TALBOT With scoffs, and scorns, and contumelious taunts.
In open market-place produc'd they me
To be a public spectacle to all;
Here, said they, is the terror of the French,
The scarecrow that affrights our children so.
Then broke I from the officers that led me,
And with my nails digg'd stones out of the ground
To hurl at the beholders of my shame;
My grisly countenance made others fly;
None durst come near for fear of sudden death.
In iron walls they deem'd me not secure;
So great fear of my name 'mongst them was spread
That they suppos'd I could rend bars of steel
And spurn in pieces posts of adamant;
Wherefore a guard of chosen shot I had
That walk'd about me every minute-while;
And if I did but stir out of my bed,
Ready they were to shoot me to the heart.

Enter the Boy with a linstock.

SALISBURY I grieve to hear what torments you endur'd;
But we will be reveng'd sufficiently.
Now it is supper-time in Orleans:
Here, through this grate, I count each one
And view the Frenchmen how they fortify.
Let us look in; the sight will much delight thee.
Sir Thomas Gargrave and Sir William Glansdale,
Let me have your express opinions
Where is best place to make our batt'ry next.
GARGRAVE I think at the North Gate; for there stand lords.
GLANSDALE And I here, at the bulwark of the bridge.
TALBOT For aught I see, this city must be famish'd,
Or with light skirmishes enfeebled.
[*Here they shoot and Salisbury and Gargrave fall down.*
SALISBURY O Lord, have mercy on us, wretched sinners!
GARGRAVE O Lord, have mercy on me, woeful man!
TALBOT What chance is this that suddenly hath cross'd us?
Speak, Salisbury; at least, if thou canst speak.
How far'st thou, mirror of all martial men?
One of thy eyes and thy cheek's side struck off!
Accursed tower! accursed fatal hand
That hath contriv'd this woeful tragedy!
In thirteen battles Salisbury o'ercame;
Henry the Fifth he first train'd to the wars;
Whilst any trump did sound or drum struck up,
His sword did ne'er leave striking in the field.
Yet liv'st thou, Salisbury? Though thy speech doth fail,
One eye thou hast to look to heaven for grace;
The sun with one eye vieweth all the world.
Heaven, be thou gracious to none alive
If Salisbury wants mercy at thy hands!
Bear hence his body; I will help to bury it.
Sir Thomas Gargrave, hast thou any life?

Speak unto Talbot; nay, look up to him.
Salisbury, cheer thy spirit with this comfort,
Thou shalt not die whiles –
He beckons with his hand and smiles on me,
As who should say 'When I am dead and gone,
Remember to avenge me on the French'.
Plantagenet, I will; and like thee, Nero,
Play on the lute, beholding the towns burn.
Wretched shall France be only in my name.

[*Here an alarum, and it thunders and lightens.*

What stir is this? What tumult's in the heavens?
Whence cometh this alarum and the noise?

Enter a Messenger.

MESSENGER My lord, my lord, the French have gather'd head.
The Dauphin, with one Joan la Pucelle join'd,
A holy prophetess new risen up,
Is come with a great power to raise the siege.

[*Here Salisbury lifteth himself up and groans.*

TALBOT Hear, hear how dying Salisbury doth groan.
It irks his heart he cannot be reveng'd.
Frenchmen, I'll be a Salisbury to you.
Pucelle or puzzel, dolphin or dogfish,
Your hearts I'll stamp out with my horse's heels
And make a quagmire of your mingled brains.
Convey me Salisbury into his tent,
And then we'll try what these dastard
Frenchmen dare. [*Alarum.* [*Exeunt.*

SCENE V. *Before Orleans.*

Here an alarum again, and TALBOT pursueth the DAUPHIN and driveth him. Then enter JOAN LA PUCELLE driving Englishmen before her. Then enter TALBOT.

TALBOT Where is my strength, my valour, and my force?
Our English troops retire, I cannot stay them;
A woman clad in armour chaseth them.

Enter LA PUCELLE.

Here, here she comes. I'll have a bout with thee.
Devil or devil's dam, I'll conjure thee;
Blood will I draw on thee – thou art a witch –
And straightway give thy soul to him thou serv'st.

LA PUCELLE Come, come, 'tis only I that must disgrace thee. [*Here they fight.*

TALBOT Heavens, can you suffer hell so to prevail?
My breast I'll burst with straining of my courage,
And from my shoulders crack my arms asunder,
But I will chastise this high-minded strumpet.

[*They fight again.*

LA PUCELLE Talbot, farewell; thy hour is not yet come.
I must go victual Orleans forthwith.

[*A short alarum; then enter the town with soldiers.*

O'ertake me if thou canst; I scorn thy strength.
Go, go, cheer up thy hungry starved men;
Help Salisbury to make his testament.
This day is ours, as many more shall be. [*Exit.*

TALBOT My thoughts are whirled like a potter's wheel;
I know not where I am nor what I do.
A witch by fear, not force, like Hannibal,
Drives back our troops and conquers as she lists.
So bees with smoke and doves with noisome stench
Are from their hives and houses driven away.
They call'd us, for our fierceness, English dogs;
Now like to whelps we crying run away.

[*A short alarum.*

Hark, countrymen! Either renew the fight
Or tear the lions out of England's coat;
Renounce your soil, give sheep in lions' stead:
Sheep run not half so treacherous from the wolf,
Or horse or oxen from the leopard,
As you fly from your oft-subdued slaves.

[*Alarum. Here another skirmish.*

It will not be – retire into your trenches.
You all consented unto Salisbury's death,
For none would strike a stroke in his revenge.
Pucelle is ent'red into Orleans
In spite of us or aught that we could do.
O, would I were to die with Salisbury!
The shame hereof will make me hide my head.

[*Exit Talbot. Alarum; retreat.*

SCENE VI. *Orleans.*

Flourish. Enter on the walls, LA PUCELLE, CHARLES, REIGNIER, ALENÇON, and Soldiers.

LA PUCELLE Advance our waving colours on the walls;
Rescu'd is Orleans from the English.
Thus Joan la Pucelle hath perform'd her word.

CHARLES Divinest creature, Astraea's daughter,
How shall I honour thee for this success?
Thy promises are like Adonis' gardens,
That one day bloom'd and fruitful were the next.
France, triumph in thy glorious prophetess.

Recover'd is the town of Orleans.
More blessed hap did ne'er befall our state.

REIGNIER Why ring not out the bells aloud throughout the town?
Dauphin, command the citizens make bonfires
And feast and banquet in the open streets
To celebrate the joy that God hath given us.

ALENÇON All France will be replete with mirth and joy
When they shall hear how we have play'd the men.

CHARLES 'Tis Joan, not we, by whom the day is won;
For which I will divide my crown with her;
And all the priests and friars in my realm
Shall in procession sing her endless praise.
A statelier pyramis to her I'll rear
Than Rhodope's of Memphis ever was.
In memory of her, when she is dead,
Her ashes, in an urn more precious
Than the rich jewell'd coffer of Darius,
Transported shall be at high festivals
Before the kings and queens of France.
No longer on Saint Denis will we cry,
But Joan la Pucelle shall be France's saint.
Come in, and let us banquet royally
After this golden day of victory.

[Flourish. Exeunt.

ACT TWO

SCENE I. *Before Orleans.*

Enter a French Sergeant and two Sentinels.

SERGEANT Sirs, take your places and be vigilant.
If any noise or soldier you perceive
Near to the walls, by some apparent sign
Let us have knowledge at the court of guard.

1 SENTINEL Sergeant, you shall. *[Exit Sergeant]*
Thus are poor servitors,
When others sleep upon their quiet beds,
Constrain'd to watch in darkness, rain, and cold.

Enter TALBOT, BEDFORD, BURGUNDY, and Forces, with scaling-ladders; their drums beating a dead march.

TALBOT Lord Regent, and redoubted Burgundy,
By whose approach the regions of Artois,
Wallon, and Picardy, are friends to us,
This happy night the Frenchmen are secure,
Having all day carous'd and banqueted;
Embrace we then this opportunity,
As fitting best to quittance their deceit,
Contriv'd by art and baleful sorcery.

BEDFORD Coward of France, how much he wrongs his fame,
Despairing of his own arm's fortitude,
To join with witches and the help of hell!

BURGUNDY Traitors have never other company.
But what's that Pucelle whom they term so pure?

TALBOT A maid, they say.

BEDFORD A maid! and be so martial!

BURGUNDY Pray God she prove not masculine ere long,
If underneath the standard of the French
She carry armour as she hath begun.

TALBOT Well, let them practise and converse with spirits:
God is our fortress, in whose conquering name
Let us resolve to scale their flinty bulwarks.

BEDFORD Ascend, brave Talbot; we will follow thee.

TALBOT Not all together; better far, I guess,
That we do make our entrance several ways;
That if it chance the one of us do fail
The other yet may rise against their force.

BEDFORD Agreed; I'll to yond corner.

BURGUNDY And I to this.

TALBOT And here will Talbot mount or make his grave.
Now, Salisbury, for thee, and for the right
Of English Henry, shall this night appear
How much in duty I am bound to both.

[The English scale the walls and cry 'Saint George! a Talbot!'

SENTINEL Arm! arm! The enemy doth make assault.

The French leap o'er the walls in their shirts. Enter, several ways, BASTARD, ALENÇON, REIGNIER, half ready and half unready.

ALENÇON How now, my lords? What, all unready so?

BASTARD Unready! Ay, and glad we 'scap'd so well.

REIGNIER 'Twas time, I trow, to wake and leave our beds,
Hearing alarums at our chamber doors.

ALENÇON Of all exploits since first I follow'd arms
Ne'er heard I of a warlike enterprise
More venturous or desperate than this.

BASTARD I think this Talbot be a fiend of hell.

REIGNIER If not of hell, the heavens, sure, favour him.

ALENÇON Here cometh Charles; I marvel how he sped.

Enter CHARLES and LA PUCELLE

BASTARD Tut! holy Joan was his defensive guard.
CHARLES Is this thy cunning, thou deceitful dame?
Didst thou at first, to flatter us withal,
Make us partakers of a little gain
That now our loss might be ten times so much?
LA PUCELLE Wherefore is Charles impatient with his friend?
At all times will you have my power alike?
Sleeping or waking, must I still prevail,
Or will you blame and lay the fault on me?
Improvident soldiers! Had your watch been good
This sudden mischief never could have fall'n.
CHARLES Duke Alençon, this was your default
That, being captain of the watch to-night,
Did look no better to that weighty charge.
ALENÇON Had all your quarters been as safely kept
As that whereof I had the government,
We had not been thus shamefully surpris'd.
BASTARD Mine was secure.
REIGNIER And so was mine, my lord.
CHARLES And, for myself, most part of all this night,
Within her quarter and mine own precinct
I was employ'd in passing to and fro
About relieving of the sentinels.
Then how or which way should they first break in?
LA PUCELLE Question, my lords, no further of the case,
How or which way; 'tis sure they found some place
But weakly guarded, where the breach was made.
And now there rests no other shift but this –
To gather our soldiers, scatter'd and dispers'd
And lay new platforms to endamage them.

Alarum. Enter an English Soldier, crying 'A Talbot! A Talbot!' They fly, leaving their clothes behind.

SOLDIER I'll be so bold to take what they have left.
The cry of Talbot serves me for a sword;
For I have loaden me with many spoils,
Using no other weapon but his name. [*Exit.*

SCENE II. *Orleans. Within the town.*

Enter TALBOT, BEDFORD, BURGUNDY, a Captain and Others.

BEDFORD The day begins to break, and night is fled
Whose pitchy mantle over-veil'd the earth.
Here sound retreat and cease our hot pursuit.
[*Retreat sounded.*
TALBOT Bring forth the body of old Salisbury
And here advance it in the market-place,
The middle centre of this cursed town.
Now have I paid my vow unto his soul;
For every drop of blood was drawn from him
There hath at least five Frenchmen died to-night.
And that hereafter ages may behold
What ruin happened in revenge of him,
Within their chiefest temple I'll erect
A tomb, wherein his corpse shall be interr'd;
Upon the which, that every one may read,
Shall be engrav'd the sack of Orleans,
The treacherous manner of his mournful death,
And what a terror he had been to France.
But, lords, in all our bloody massacre,
I muse we met not with the Dauphin's grace,
His new-come champion, virtuous Joan of Arc,
Nor any of his false confederates.
BEDFORD 'Tis thought, Lord Talbot, when the fight began,
Rous'd on the sudden from their drowsy beds
They did amongst the troops of armed men
Leap o'er the walls for refuge in the field.
BURGUNDY Myself, as far as I could well discern
For smoke and dusky vapours of the night,
Am sure I scar'd the Dauphin and his trull,
When arm in arm they both came swiftly running,
Like to a pair of loving turtle-doves
That could not live asunder day or night.
After that things are set in order here,
We'll follow them with all the power we have.

Enter a Messenger.

MESSENGER All hail, my lords! Which of this princely train
Call ye the warlike Talbot, for his acts
So much applauded through the realm of France?
TALBOT Here is the Talbot; who would speak with him?
MESSENGER The virtuous lady, Countess of Auvergne,
With modesty admiring thy renown,
By me entreats, great lord, thou wouldst vouchsafe
To visit her poor castle where she lies,
That she may boast she hath beheld the man
Whose glory fills the world with loud report.
BURGUNDY Is it even so? Nay, then I see our wars
Will turn unto a peaceful comic sport,
When ladies crave to be encount'red with.
You may not, my lord, despise her gentle suit.

TALBOT Ne'er trust me then; for when a world of men
Could not prevail with all their oratory,
Yet hath a woman's kindness overrul'd;
And therefore tell her I return great thanks
And in submission will attend on her.
Will not your honours bear me company?

BEDFORD No, truly; 'tis more than manners will;
And I have heard it said unbidden guests
Are often welcomest when they are gone.

TALBOT Well then, alone, since there's no remedy,
I mean to prove this lady's courtesy.
Come hither, Captain. [*Whispers*] You perceive my mind?

CAPTAIN I do, my lord, and mean accordingly. [*Exeunt.*

SCENE III. *Auvergne. The castle.*

Enter the COUNTESS and her Porter.

COUNTESS Porter, remember what I gave in charge;
And when you have done so, bring the keys to me.

PORTER Madam, I will. [*Exit.*

COUNTESS The plot is laid; if all things fall out right,
I shall as famous be by this exploit
As Scythian Tomyris by Cyrus' death.
Great is the rumour of this dreadful knight,
And his achievements of no less account.
Fain would mine eyes be witness with mine ears
To give their censure of these rare reports.

Enter Messenger and TALBOT.

MESSENGER Madam, according as you ladyship desir'd,
By message crav'd, so is Lord Talbot come.

COUNTESS And he is welcome. What! is this the man?

MESSENGER Madam, it is.

COUNTESS Is this the scourge of France?
Is this the Talbot, so much fear'd abroad
That with his name the mothers still their babes?
I see report is fabulous and false.
I thought I should have seen some Hercules,
A second Hector, for his grim aspect
And large proportion of his strong-knit limbs.
Alas, this is a child, a silly dwarf!
It cannot be this weak and writhled shrimp
Should strike such terror to his enemies.

TALBOT Madam, I have been bold to trouble you;
But since your ladyship is not at leisure,
I'll sort some other time to visit you. [*Going.*

COUNTESS What means he now? Go ask him whither he goes.

MESSENGER Stay, my Lord Talbot; for my lady craves
To know the cause of your abrupt departure.

TALBOT Marry, for that she's in a wrong belief,
I go to certify her Talbot's here.

Re-enter Porter with keys.

COUNTESS If thou be he, then art thou prisoner.

TALBOT Prisoner! To whom?

COUNTESS To me, blood-thirsty lord;
And for that cause I train'd thee to my house.
Long time thy shadow hath been thrall to me,
For in my gallery thy picture hangs;
But now the substance shall endure the like
And I will chain these legs and arms of thine
That hast by tyranny these many years
Wasted our country, slain our citizens,
And sent our sons and husbands captivate.

TALBOT Ha, ha, ha!

COUNTESS Laughest thou, wretch? Thy mirth shall turn to moan.

TALBOT I laugh to see your ladyship so fond
To think that you have aught but Talbot's shadow
Whereon to practise your severity.

COUNTESS Why, art not thou the man?

TALBOT I am indeed.

COUNTESS Then have I substance too.

TALBOT No, no, I am but shadow of myself.
You are deceiv'd, my substance is not here;
For what you see is but the smallest part
And least proportion of humanity.
I tell you, madam, were the whole frame here,
It is of such a spacious lofty pitch
Your roof were not sufficient to contain't

COUNTESS This is a riddling merchant for the nonce;
He will be here, and yet he is not here.
How can these contrarieties agree?

TALBOT That will I show you presently.

Winds his horn; drums strike up; a peal of ordnance. Enter Soldiers.

How say you, madam? Are you now persuaded
That Talbot is but shadow of himself?
These are his substance, sinews, arms, and strength,
With which he yoketh your rebellious necks,
Razeth your cities, and subverts your towns,
And in a moment makes them desolate.

COUNTESS Victorious Talbot! pardon my abuse.
I find thou art no less than fame hath bruited,
And more than may be gathered by thy shape.
Let my presumption not provoke thy wrath,
For I am sorry that with reverence
I did not entertain thee as thou art.

TALBOT Be not dismay'd, fair lady; nor misconster
The mind of Talbot as you did mistake
The outward composition of his body.
What you have done hath not offended me.
Nor other satisfaction do I crave
But only, with your patience, that we may
Taste of your wine and see what cates you have,
For soldiers' stomachs always serve them well.
COUNTESS With all my heart, and think me honoured
To feast so great a warrior in my house.
[Exeunt.

SCENE IV. *London. The Temple garden.*

Enter the EARLS OF SOMERSET, SUFFOLK, and WARWICK; RICHARD PLANTAGENET, VERNON, and another Lawyer.

PLANTAGENET Great lords and gentlemen, what means this silence?
Dare no man answer in a case of truth?
SUFFOLK Within the Temple Hall we were too loud;
The garden here is more convenient.
PLANTAGENET Then say at once if I maintain'd the truth;
Or else was wrangling Somerset in th' error?
SUFFOLK Faith, I have been a truant in the law
And never yet could frame my will to it;
And therefore frame the law unto my will.
SOMERSET Judge you, my Lord of Warwick, then, between us.
WARWICK Between two hawks, which flies the higher pitch;
Between two dogs, which hath the deeper mouth;
Between two blades, which bears the better temper;
Between two horses, which doth bear him best;
Between two girls, which hath the merriest eye –
I have perhaps some shallow spirit of judgment;
But in these nice sharp quillets of the law,
Good faith, I am no wiser than a daw.
PLANTAGENET Tut, tut, here is a mannerly forbearance:
The truth appears so naked on my side
That any purblind eye may find it out.
SOMERSET And on my side it is so well apparell'd,
So clear, so shining, and so evident,
That it will glimmer through a blind man's eye.
PLANTAGENET Since you are tongue-tied and so loath to speak,
In dumb significants proclaim your thoughts.
Let him that is a true-born gentleman
And stands upon the honour of his birth,
If he suppose that I have pleaded truth,
From off this brier pluck a white rose with me.
SOMERSET Let him that is no coward nor no flatterer,
But dare maintain the party of the truth,
Pluck a red rose from off this thorn with me.
WARWICK I love no colours; and, without all colour
Of base insinuating flattery,
I pluck this white rose with Plantagenet.
SUFFOLK I pluck this red rose with young Somerset,
And say withal I think he held the right.
VERNON Stay, lords and gentlemen, and pluck no more
Till you conclude that he upon whose side
The fewest roses are cropp'd from the tree
Shall yield the other in the right opinion.
SOMERSET Good Master Vernon, it is well objected;
If I have fewest, I subscribe in silence.
PLANTAGENET And I.
VERNON Then, for the truth and plainness of the case,
I pluck this pale and maiden blossom here,
Giving my verdict on the white rose side.
SOMERSET Prick not your finger as you pluck it off,
Lest, bleeding, you do paint the white rose red,
And fall on my side so, against your will.
VERNON If I, my lord, for my opinion bleed,
Opinion shall be surgeon to my hurt
And keep me on the side where still I am.
SOMERSET Well, well, come on; who else?
LAWYER *[To Somerset]* Unless my study and my books be false,
The argument you held was wrong in you;
In sign whereof I pluck a white rose too.
PLANTAGENET Now, Somerset, where is your argument?
SOMERSET Here in my scabbard, meditating that
Shall dye your white rose in a bloody red.
PLANTAGENET Meantime your cheeks do counterfeit our roses;
For pale they look with fear, as witnessing
The truth on our side.
SOMERSET No, Plantagenet,
'Tis not for fear but anger that thy cheeks
Blush for pure shame to counterfeit our roses,
And yet thy tongue will not confess thy error.
PLANTAGENET Hath not thy rose a canker, Somerset?
SOMERSET Hath not thy rose a thorn Plantagenet?
PLANTAGENET Ay, sharp and piercing, to maintain his truth;
Whiles thy consuming canker eats his falsehood.

SOMERSET Well, I'll find friends to wear my bleeding roses,
That shall maintain what I have said is true,
Where false Plantagenet dare not be seen.
PLANTAGENET Now, by this maiden blossom in my hand,
I scorn thee and thy fashion, peevish boy.
SUFFOLK Turn not thy scorns this way, Plantagenet.
PLANTAGENET Proud Pole, I will, and scorn both him and thee.
SUFFOLK I'll turn my part thereof into thy throat.
SOMERSET Away, away, good William de la Pole!
We grace the yeoman by conversing with him.
WARWICK Now, by God's will, thou wrong'st him, Somerset;
His grandfather was Lionel Duke of Clarence,
Third son to the third Edward, King of England.
Spring crestless yeoman from so deep a root?
PLANTAGENET He bears him on the place's privilege,
Or durst not for his craven heart say thus.
SOMERSET By Him that made me, I'll maintain my words
On any plot of ground in Christendom.
Was not thy father, Richard Earl of Cambridge,
For treason executed in our late king's days?
And by his treason stand'st not thou attainted,
Corrupted, and exempt from ancient gentry?
His trespass yet lives guilty in thy blood;
And till thou be restor'd thou art a yeoman.
PLANTAGENET My father was attached, not attainted;
Condemn'd to die for treason, but no traitor;
And that I'll prove on better men than Somerset,
Were growing time once ripened to my will.
For your partaker Pole, and you yourself,
I'll note you in my book of memory
To scourge you for this apprehension.
Look to it well, and say you are well warn'd.
SOMERSET Ay, thou shalt find us ready for thee still;
And know us by these colours for thy foes –
For these my friends in spite of thee shall wear.
PLANTAGENET And, by my soul, this pale and angry rose,
As cognizance of my blood-drinking hate,
Will I for ever, and my faction, wear,
Until it wither with me to my grave,
Or flourish to the height of my degree.
SUFFOLK Go forward, and be chok'd with thy ambition!
And so farewell until I meet thee next. *[Exit.*
SOMERSET Have with thee, Pole. Farewell, ambitious Richard. *[Exit.*
PLANTAGENET How I am brav'd, and must perforce endure it!
WARWICK This blot that they object against your house
Shall be wip'd out in the next Parliament,
Call'd for the truce of Winchester and Gloucester;
And if thou be not then created York,
I will not live to be accounted Warwick.
Meantime, in signal of my love to thee,
Against proud Somerset and William Pole,
Will I upon thy party wear this rose;
And here I prophesy: this brawl to-day,
Grown to this faction in the Temple Garden,
Shall send between the Red Rose and the White
A thousand souls to death and deadly night.
PLANTAGENET Good Master Vernon, I am bound to you
That you on my behalf would pluck a flower.
VERNON In your behalf still will I wear the same.
LAWYER And so will I.
PLANTAGENET Thanks, gentle sir.
Come, let us four to dinner. I dare say
This quarrel will drink blood another day.
[Exeunt.

SCENE V. *The Tower of London.*

Enter MORTIMER, brought in a chair, and Gaolers.

MORTIMER Kind keepers of my weak decaying age,
Let dying Mortimer here rest himself.
Even like a man new haled from the rack,
So fare my limbs with long imprisonment;
And these grey locks, the pursuivants of death,
Nestor-like aged in an age of care,
Argue the end of Edmund Mortimer.
These eyes, like lamps whose wasting oil is spent,
Wax dim, as drawing to their exigent;
Weak shoulders, overborne with burdening grief,
And pithless arms, like to a withered vine
That droops his sapless branches to the ground.
Yet are these feet, whose strengthless stay is numb,
Unable to support this lump of clay,
Swift-winged with desire to get a grave,
As witting I no other comfort have.
But tell me, keeper, will my nephew come?
1 KEEP Richard Plantagenet, my lord, will come.
We sent unto the Temple, unto his chamber;
And answer was return'd that he will come.
MORTIMER Enough; my soul shall then be satisfied.
Poor gentleman! his wrong doth equal mine.
Since Henry Monmouth first began to reign,

Before whose glory I was great in arms,
This loathsome sequestration have I had;
And even since then hath Richard been obscur'd,
Depriv'd of honour and inheritance.
But now the arbitrator of despairs,
Just Death, kind umpire of men's miseries,
With sweet enlargement doth dismiss me hence.
I would his troubles likewise were expir'd,
That so he might recover what was lost.

Enter RICHARD PLANTAGENET.

1 KEEP My lord, your loving nephew now is come.

MORTIMER Richard Plantagenet, my friend, is he come?

PLANTAGENET Ay, noble uncle, thus ignobly us'd,
Your nephew, late despised Richard, comes.

MORTIMER Direct mine arms I may embrace his neck
And in his bosom spend my latter gasp.
O, tell me when my lips do touch his cheeks,
That I may kindly give one fainting kiss.
And now declare, sweet stem from York's great stock,
Why didst thou say of late thou wert despis'd?

PLANTAGENET First, lean thine aged back against mine arm;
And, in that ease, I'll tell thee my disease.
This day, in argument upon a case,
Some words there grew 'twixt Somerset and me;
Among which terms he us'd his lavish tongue
And did upbraid me with my father's death;
Which obloquy set bars before my tongue,
Else with the like I had requited him.
Therefore, good uncle, for my father's sake,
In honour of a true Plantagenet,
And for alliance sake, declare the cause
My father, Earl of Cambridge, lost his head.

MORTIMER That cause, fair nephew, that imprison'd me
And hath detain'd me all my flow'ring youth
Within a loathsome dungeon, there to pine,
Was cursed instrument of his decease.

PLANTAGENET Discover more at large what cause that was,
For I am ignorant and cannot guess.

MORTIMER I will, if that my fading breath permit
And death approach not ere my tale be done.
Henry the Fourth, grandfather to this king,
Depos'd his nephew Richard, Edward's son,
The first-begotten and the lawful heir
Of Edward king, the third of that descent;
During whose reign the Percies of the north,
Finding his usurpation most unjust,
Endeavour'd my advancement to the throne.
The reason mov'd these warlike lords to this
Was, for that – young Richard thus remov'd,
Leaving no heir begotten of his body –
I was the next by birth and parentage;
For by my mother I derived am
From Lionel Duke of Clarence, third son
To King Edward the Third; whereas he
From John of Gaunt doth bring his pedigree,
Being but fourth of that heroic line.
But mark: as in this haughty great attempt
They laboured to plant the rightful heir,
I lost my liberty, and they their lives.
Long after this, when Henry the Fifth,
Succeeding his father Bolingbroke, did reign,
Thy father, Earl of Cambridge, then deriv'd
From famous Edmund Langley, Duke of York,
Marrying my sister, that thy mother was,
Again, in pity of my hard distress,
Levied an army, weening to redeem
And have install'd me in the diadem;
But, as the rest, so fell that noble earl,
And was beheaded. Thus the Mortimers,
In whom the title rested, were suppress'd.

PLANTAGENET Of which, my lord, your honour is the last.

MORTIMER True; and thou seest that I no issue have,
And that my fainting words do warrant death.
Thou art my heir; the rest I wish thee gather;
But yet be wary in thy studious care.

PLANTAGENET Thy grave admonishments prevail with me.
But yet methinks my father's execution
Was nothing less than bloody tyranny.

MORTIMER With silence, nephew, be thou politic;
Strong fixed is the house of Lancaster
And like a mountain not to be remov'd.
But now thy uncle is removing hence,
As princes do their courts when they are cloy'd
With long continuance in a settled place.

PLANTAGENET O uncle, would some part of my young years
Might but redeem the passage of your age!

MORTIMER Thou dost then wrong me, as that slaughterer doth
Which giveth many wounds when one will kill.
Mourn not, except thou sorrow for my good;
Only give order for my funeral.
And so, farewell; and fair be all thy hopes,
And prosperous be thy life in peace and war!

[*Dies.*

PLANTAGENET And peace, no war, befall thy parting soul!
In prison hast thou spent a pilgrimage,
And like a hermit overpass'd thy days.

Well, I will lock his counsel in my breast;
And what I do imagine, let that rest.
Keepers, convey him hence; and I myself
Will see his burial better than his life.
[Exeunt Gaolers, bearing out the body of Mortimer.
Here dies the dusky torch of Mortimer,
Chok'd with ambition of the meaner sort;
And for those wrongs, those bitter injuries,
Which Somerset hath offer'd to my house,
I doubt not but with honour to redress;
And therefore haste I to the Parliament,
Either to be restored to my blood,
Or make my ill th' advantage of my good. *[Exit.*

ACT THREE

SCENE I. *London. The Parliament House.*

Flourish. Enter the KING, EXETER, GLOUCESTER, WARWICK, SOMERSET, and SUFFOLK; the BISHOP OF WINCHESTER, RICHARD PLANTAGENET, and Others. Gloucester offers to put up a bill; Winchester snatches it, and tears it.

WINCHESTER Com'st thou with deep premeditated lines,
With written pamphlets studiously devis'd?
Humphrey of Gloucester, if thou canst accuse
Or aught intend'st to lay unto my charge,
Do it without invention, suddenly;
As I with sudden and extemporal speech
Purpose to answer what thou canst object.
GLOUCESTER Presumptuous priest, this place commands my patience,
Or thou shouldst find thou hast dishonour'd me.
Think not, although in writing I preferr'd
The manner of thy vile outrageous crimes,
That therefore I have forg'd, or am not able
Verbatim to rehearse the method of my pen.
No, prelate; such is thy audacious wickedness,
Thy lewd, pestiferous, and dissentious pranks,
As very infants prattle of thy pride.
Thou art a most pernicious usurer;
Froward by nature, enemy to peace;
Lascivious, wanton, more than well beseems
A man of thy profession and degree;
And for thy treachery, what's more manifest –
In that thou laid'st a trap to take my life,
As well at London Bridge as at the Tower?
Beside, I fear me, if thy thoughts were sifted,
The King, thy sovereign, is not quite exempt
From envious malice of thy swelling heart.
WINCHESTER Gloucester, I do defy thee. Lords, vouchsafe
To give me hearing what I shall reply.
If I were covetous, ambitious, or perverse,
As he will have me, how am I so poor?
Or how haps it I seek not to advance
Or raise myself, but keep my wonted calling?
And for dissension, who preferreth peace
More than I do, except I be provok'd?
No, my good lords, it is not that offends;
It is not that that hath incens'd the Duke:
It is because no one should sway but he;
No one but he should be about the King;
And that engenders thunder in his breast
And makes him roar these accusations forth.
But he shall know I am as good –
GLOUCESTER As good!
Thou bastard of my grandfather!
WINCHESTER Ay, lordly sir; for what are you, I pray,
But one imperious in another's throne?
GLOUCESTER Am I not Protector, saucy priest?
WINCHESTER And am not I a prelate of the church?
GLOUCESTER Yes, as an outlaw in a castle keeps,
And useth it to patronage his theft.
WINCHESTER Unreverent Gloucester!
GLOUCESTER Thou art reverend
Touching thy spiritual function, not thy life.
WINCHESTER Rome shall remedy this.
WARWICK Roam thither then.
SOMERSET My lord, it were your duty to forbear.
WARWICK Ay, see the bishop be not overborne.
SOMERSET Methinks my lord should be religious,
And know the office that belongs to such.
WARWICK Methinks his lordship should be humbler;
It fitteth not a prelate so to plead.
SOMERSET Yes, when his holy state is touch'd so near.
WARWICK State holy or unhallow'd, what of that?
Is not his Grace Protector to the King?
PLANTAGENET *[Aside]* Plantagenet, I see, must hold his tongue,
Lest it be said 'Speak, sirrah, when you should;
Must your bold verdict enter talk with lords?'
Else would I have a fling at Winchester.
KING Uncles of Gloucester and of Winchester,
The special watchmen of our English weal,
I would prevail, if prayers might prevail,
To join your hearts in love and amity.
O, what a scandal is it to our crown
That two such noble peers as ye should jar!

Believe me, lords, my tender years can tell
Civil dissension is a viperous worm
That gnaws the bowels of the commonwealth.

[*A noise within:* Down with the tawny coats.
What tumult's this?

WARWICK An uproar, I dare warrant,
Begun through malice of the Bishop's men.

[*A noise again:* Stones! Stones!

Enter the MAYOR of London attended.

MAYOR O, my good lords, and virtuous Henry,
Pity the city of London, pity us!
The Bishop and the Duke of Gloucester's men,
Forbidden late to carry any weapon,
Have fill'd their pockets full of pebble stones
And, banding themselves in contrary parts,
Do pelt so fast at one another's pate
That many have their giddy brains knock'd out.
Our windows are broke down in every street,
And we for fear compell'd to shut our shops.

Enter in skirmish, the Retainers of Gloucester and Winchester, with bloody pates.

KING We charge you, on allegiance to ourself,
To hold your slaught'ring hands and keep the peace.
Pray, uncle Gloucester, mitigate this strife.

1 SERVANT Nay, if we be forbidden stones, we'll fall to it with our teeth.

2 SERVANT Do what ye dare, we are as resolute.

[*Skirmish again.*

GLOUCESTER You of my household, leave this peevish broil,
And set this unaccustom'd fight aside.

3 SERVANT My lord, we know your Grace to be a man
Just and upright, and for your royal birth
Inferior to none but to his Majesty;
And ere that we will suffer such a prince,
So kind a father of the commonweal,
To be disgraced by an inkhorn mate,
We and our wives and children all will fight
And have our bodies slaught'red by thy foes.

1 SERVANT Ay, and the very parings of our nails
Shall pitch a field when we are dead.

[*Begin again.*

GLOUCESTER Stay, stay, I say!
And if you love me, as you say you do,
Let me persuade you to forbear awhile.

KING O, how this discord doth afflict my soul!
Can you, my Lord of Winchester, behold
My sighs and tears and will not once relent?
Who should be pitiful, if you be not?
Or who should study to prefer a peace,
If holy churchmen take delight in broils?

WARWICK Yield, my Lord Protector; yield, Winchester;
Except you mean with obstinate repulse
To slay your sovereign and destroy the realm.
You see what mischief, and what murder too,
Hath been enacted through your enmity;
Then be at peace, except ye thirst for blood.

WINCHESTER He shall submit, or I will never yield.

GLOUCESTER Compassion on the King commands me stoop,
Or I would see his heart out ere the priest
Should ever get that privilege of me.

WARWICK Behold, my Lord of Winchester, the Duke
Hath banish'd moody discontented fury,
As by his smoothed brows it doth appear;
Why look you still so stern and tragical?

GLOUCESTER Here, Winchester, I offer thee my hand.

KING Fie, uncle Beaufort! I have heard you preach
That malice was a great and grievous sin;
And will not you maintain the thing you teach,
But prove a chief offender in the same?

WARWICK Sweet King! The Bishop hath a kindly gird.
For shame, my Lord of Winchester, relent;
What, shall a child instruct you what to do?

WINCHESTER Well, Duke of Gloucester, I will yield to thee;
Love for thy love and hand for hand I give.

GLOUCESTER [*Aside*] Ay, but, I fear me, with a hollow heart. –
See here, my friends and loving countrymen:
This token serveth for a flag of truce
Betwixt ourselves and all our followers.
So help me God, as I dissemble not!

WINCHESTER [*Aside*] So help me God, as I intend it not!

KING O loving uncle, kind Duke of Gloucester,
How joyful am I made by this contract!
Away, my masters! trouble us no more;
But join in friendship, as your lords have done.

1 SERVANT Content: I'll to the surgeon's.

2 SERVANT And so will I.

3 SERVANT And I will see what physic the tavern affords.

[*Exeunt Servants, Mayor, etc.*

WARWICK Accept this scroll, most gracious sovereign;
Which in the right of Richard Plantagenet
We do exhibit to your Majesty.

GLOUCESTER Well urg'd, my Lord of Warwick; for, sweet prince,
And if your Grace mark every circumstance,

You have great reason to do Richard right;
Especially for those occasions
At Eltham Place I told your Majesty.

KING And those occasions, uncle, were of force;
Therefore, my loving lords, our pleasure is
That Richard be restored to his blood.

WARWICK Let Richard be restored to his blood;
So shall his father's wrongs be recompens'd.

WINCHESTER As will the rest, so willeth Winchester.

KING If Richard will be true, not that alone
But all the whole inheritance I give
That doth belong unto the house of York,
From whence you spring by lineal descent.

PLANTAGENET Thy humble servant vows obedience
And humble service till the point of death.

KING Stoop then and set your knee against my foot;
And in reguerdon of that duty done
I grit thee with the valiant sword of York.
Rise, Richard, like a true Plantagenet,
And rise created princely Duke of York.

PLANTAGENET And so thrive Richard as thy foes may fall!
And as my duty springs, so perish they
That grudge one thought against your Majesty!

ALL Welcome, high Prince, the mighty Duke of York!

SOMERSET [*Aside*] Perish, base Prince, ignoble Duke of York!

GLOUCESTER Now will it best avail your Majesty
To cross the seas and to be crown'd in France:
The presence of a king engenders love
Amongst his subjects and his loyal friends,
As it disanimates his enemies.

KING When Gloucester says the word, King Henry goes;
For friendly counsel cuts off many foes.

GLOUCESTER Your ships already are in readiness.

[*Sennet. Flourish. Exeunt all but Exeter.*

EXETER Ay, we may march in England or in France,
Not seeing what is likely to ensue.
This late dissension grown betwixt the peers
Burns under feigned ashes of forg'd love
And will at last break out into a flame;
As fest'red members rot but by degree
Till bones and flesh and sinews fall away,
So will this base and envious discord breed.
And now I fear that fatal prophecy
Which in the time of Henry nam'd the Fifth
Was in the mouth of every sucking babe:
That Henry born at Monmouth should win all,
And Henry born at Windsor should lose all.
Which is so plain that Exeter doth wish
His days may finish ere that hapless time. [*Exit.*

SCENE II. *France. Before Rouen.*

Enter LA PUCELLE disguis'd, with four Soldiers dressed like Countrymen, with sacks upon their backs.

LA PUCELLE These are the city gates, the gates of Rouen,
Through which our policy must make a breach.
Take heed, be wary how you place your words;
Talk like the vulgar sort of market-men
That come to gather money for their corn.
If we have entrance, as I hope we shall,
And that we find the slothful watch but weak,
I'll by a sign give notice to our friends,
That Charles the Daulpin may encounter them.

1 SOLDIER Our sacks shall be a mean to sack the city,
And we be lords and rulers over Rouen;
Therefore we'll knock. [*Knocks.*

WATCH [*Within*] Qui est là?

LA PUCELLE Paysans, pauvres gens de France –
Poor market-folks that come to sell their corn.

WATCH Enter, go in; the market-bell is rung.

LA PUCELLE Now, Rouen, I'll shake thy bulwarks to the ground. [*La Pucelle, etc., enter the town.*

Enter CHARLES, BASTARD, ALENÇON, REIGNIER, and Forces.

CHARLES Saint Denis bless this happy stratagem!
And once again we'll sleep secure in Rouen.

BASTARD Here ent'red Pucelle and her practisants;
Now she is there, how will she specify
Here is the best and safest passage in?

ALENÇON By thrusting out a torch from yonder tower;
Which once discern'd shows that her meaning is –
No way to that, for weakness, which she ent'red.

Enter LA PUCELLE, on the top, thrusting out a torch burning.

LA PUCELLE Behold, this is the happy wedding torch
That joineth Rouen unto her countrymen,
But burning fatal to the Talbotites. [*Exit.*

BASTARD See, noble Charles, the beacon of our friend;
The burning torch in yonder turret stands.

CHARLES Now shine it like a comet of revenge,
A prophet to the fall of all our foes!

ALENÇON Defer no time, delays have dangerous ends;
Enter, and cry 'The Dauphin!' presently,
And then do execution on the watch.

[*Alarum. Exeunt.*

An alarum. Enter TALBOT in an excursion.

TALBOT France, thou shalt rue this treason with thy tears,
If Talbot but survive thy treachery.
Pucelle, that witch, that damned sorceress,
Hath wrought this hellish mischief unawares,
That hardly we escap'd the pride of France.
[Exit.

An alarum; excursions. BEDFORD brought in sick in a chair. Enter TALBOT and BURGUNDY without; within, LA PUCELLE, CHARLES, BASTARD, ALENÇON, and REIGNIER, on the walls.

LA PUCELLE Good morrow, gallants! Want ye corn for bread?
I think the Duke of Burgundy will fast
Before he'll buy again at such a rate.
'Twas full of darnel – do you like the taste?

BURGUNDY Scoff on, vile fiend and shameless courtezan.
I trust ere long to choke thee with thine own,
And make thee curse the harvest of that corn.

CHARLES Your Grace may starve, perhaps, before that time.

BEDFORD O, let no words, but deeds, revenge this treason!

LA PUCELLE What will you do, good grey-beard? Break a lance,
And run a tilt at death within a chair?

TALBOT Foul fiend of France and hag of all despite,
Encompass'd with thy lustful paramours,
Becomes it thee to taunt his valiant age
And twit with cowardice a man half dead?
Damsel, I'll have a bout with you again,
Or else let Talbot perish with this shame.

LA PUCELLE Are ye so hot, sir? Yet, Pucelle, hold thy peace;
If Talbot do but thunder, rain will follow.
[The English party whisper together in council.
God speed the parliament! Who shall be the Speaker?

TALBOT Dare ye come forth and meet us in the field?

LA PUCELLE Belike your lordship takes us then for fools,
To try if that our own be ours or no.

TALBOT I speak not to that railing Hecate,
But unto thee, Alençon, and the rest.
Will ye, like soldiers, come and fight it out?

ALENÇON Signior, no.

TALBOT Signior, hang! Base muleteers of France!
Like peasant foot-boys do they keep the walls,
And dare not take up arms like gentlemen.

LA PUCELLE Away, captains! Let's get us from the walls
For Talbot means no goodness by his looks.
God b'uy, my lord; we came but to tell you
That we are here. *[Exeunt from the walls.*

TALBOT And there will we be too, ere it be long,
Or else reproach be Talbot's greatest fame!
Vow, Burgundy, by honour of thy house,
Prick'd on by public wrongs sustain'd in France,
Either to get the town again or die;
And I, as sure as English Henry lives
And as his father here was conqueror,
As sure as in this late-betrayed town
Great Coeur-de-lion's heart was buried –
So sure I swear to get the town or die.

BURGUNDY My vows are equal partners with thy vows.

TALBOT But ere we go, regard this dying prince,
The valiant Duke of Bedford. Come, my lord,
We will bestow you in some better place,
Fitter for sickness and for crazy age.

BEDFORD Lord Talbot, do not so dishonour me;
Here will I sit before the walls of Rouen,
And will be partner of your weal or woe.

BURGUNDY Courageous Bedford, let us now persuade you.

BEDFORD Not to be gone from hence; for once I read
That stout Pendragon in his litter sick
Came to the field, and vanquished his foes.
Methinks I should revive the soldiers' hearts,
Because I ever found them as myself.

TALBOT Undaunted spirit in a dying breast!
Then be it so. Heavens keep old Bedford safe!
And now no more ado, brave Burgundy,
But gather we our forces out of hand
And set upon our boasting enemy.

[Exeunt against the town all but Bedford and attendants.

An alarum; excursions. Enter SIR JOHN FASTOLFE, and a Captain.

CAPTAIN Whither away, Sir John Fastolfe, in such haste?

FASTOLFE Whither away? To save myself by flight:
We are like to have the overthrow again.

CAPTAIN What! Will you fly, and leave Lord Talbot?

FASTOLFE Ay.
All the Talbots in the world, to save my life.
[Exit.

CAPTAIN Cowardly knight! ill fortune follow thee! *[Exit into the town.*

Retreat; excursions. LA PUCELLE, ALENÇON, and CHARLES fly.

BEDFORD Now, quiet soul, depart when heaven please.

For I have seen our enemies' overthrow.
What is the trust or strength of foolish man?
They that of late were daring with their scoffs
Are glad and fain by flight to save themselves.
[*Bedford dies and is carried in by two in his chair.*

An alarum. Re-enter TALBOT, BURGUNDY and the Rest.

TALBOT Lost and recovered in a day again!
This is a double honour, Burgundy.
Yet heavens have glory for this victory!
BURGUNDY Warlike and martial Talbot, Burgundy
Enshrines thee in his heart, and there erects
Thy noble deeds as valour's monuments.
TALBOT Thanks, gentle Duke. But where is Pucelle now?
I think her old familiar is asleep.
Now where's the Bastard's braves, and Charles his gleeks?
What, all amort? Rouen hangs her head for grief
That such a valiant company are fled.
Now will we take some order in the town,
Placing therein some expert officers;
And then depart to Paris to the King,
For there young Henry with his nobles lie.
BURGUNDY What wills Lord Talbot pleaseth Burgundy.
TALBOT But yet, before we go, let's not forget
The noble Duke of Bedford, late deceas'd,
But see his exequies fulfill'd in Rouen.
A braver soldier never couched lance,
A gentler heart did never sway in court;
But kings and mightiest potentates must die,
For that's the end of human misery. [*Exeunt.*

SCENE III. *The plains near Rouen.*

Enter CHARLES, the BASTARD, ALENÇON, LA PUCELLE, and Forces.

LA PUCELLE Dismay not, Princes, at this accident,
Nor grieve that Rouen is so recovered.
Care is no cure, but rather corrosive,
For things that are not to be remedied.
Let frantic Talbot triumph for a while
And like a peacock sweep along his tail;
We'll pull his plumes and take away his train,
If Dauphin and the rest will be but rul'd.
CHARLES We have been guided by thee hitherto,
And of thy cunning had no diffidence;
One sudden foil shall never breed distrust.
BASTARD Search out thy wit for secret policies,
And we will make thee famous through the world.
ALENCON We'll set thy statue in some holy place,
And have thee reverenc'd like a blessed saint.
Employ thee, then, sweet virgin, for our good.
LA PUCELLE Then thus it must be; this doth Joan devise:
By fair persuasions, mix'd with sug'red words,
We will entice the Duke of Burgundy
To leave the Talbot and to follow us.
CHARLES Ay, marry, sweeting, if we could do that,
France were no place for Henry's warriors;
Nor should that nation boast it so with us,
But be extirped from our provinces.
ALENCON For ever should they be expuls'd from France,
And not have title of an earldom here.
LA PUCELLE Your honours shall perceive how I will work
To bring this matter to the wished end.
[*Drum sounds afar off.*
Hark! by the sound of drum you may perceive
Their powers are marching unto Parisward.

Here sound an English march. Enter, and pass over at a distance, TALBOT and his Forces.

There goes the Talbot, with his colours spread,
And all the troops of English after him.

French march. Enter the DUKE OF BURGUNDY and his Forces.

Now in the rearward comes the Duke and his.
Fortune in favour makes him lag behind.
Summon a parley; we will talk with him.
[*Trumpets sound a parley.*
CHARLES A parley with the Duke of Burgundy!
BURGUNDY Who craves a parley with the Burgundy?
LA PUCELLE The princely Charles of France, thy countryman.
BURGUNDY What say'st thou, Charles? for I am marching hence.
CHARLES Speak, Pucelle, and enchant him with thy words.
LA PUCELLE Brave Burgundy, undoubted hope of France!
Stay, let thy humble handmaid speak to thee.
BURGUNDY Speak on; but be not over-tedious.
LA PUCELLE Look on thy country, look on fertile France,
And see the cities and the towns defac'd
By wasting ruin of the cruel foe;
As looks the mother on her lowly babe
When death doth close his tender dying eyes,
See, see the pining malady of France

Behold the wounds, the most unnatural wounds,
Which thou thyself hast given her woeful breast.
O, turn thy edged sword another way;
Strike those that hurt, and hurt not those that help!
One drop of blood drawn from thy country's bosom
Should grieve thee more than streams of foreign gore.
Return thee therefore with a flood of tears,
And wash away thy country's stained spots.

BURGUNDY Either she hath bewitch'd me with her words,
Or nature makes me suddenly relent.

LA PUCELLE Besides, all French and France exclaims on thee,
Doubting thy birth and lawful progeny.
Who join'st thou with but with a lordly nation
That will not trust thee but for profit's sake?
When Talbot hath set footing once in France,
And fashion'd thee that instrument of ill,
Who then but English Henry will be lord,
And thou be thrust out like a fugitive?
Call we to mind – and mark but this for proof:
Was not the Duke of Orleans thy foe?
And was he not in England prisoner?
But when they heard he was thine enemy
They set him free without his ransom paid,
In spite of Burgundy and all his friends.
See then, thou fight'st against thy countrymen,
And join'st with them will be thy slaughtermen.
Come, come, return; return, thou wandering lord;
Charles and the rest will take thee in their arms.

BURGUNDY I am vanquished; these haughty words of hers
Have batt'red me like roaring cannon-shot
And made me almost yield upon my knees.
Forgive me, country, and sweet countrymen!
And, lords, accept this hearty kind embrace.
My forces and my power of men are yours;
So, farewell, Talbot; I'll no longer trust thee.

LA PUCELLE Done like a Frenchman – [*Aside*] turn and turn again.

CHARLES Welcome, brave Duke! Thy friendship makes us fresh.

BASTARD And doth beget new courage in our breasts.

ALENCON Pucelle hath bravely play'd her part in this,
And doth deserve a coronet of gold.

CHARLES Now let us on, my lords, and join our powers,
And seek how we may prejudice the foe.

[*Exeunt.*

SCENE IV. *Paris. The palace.*

Enter the KING, GLOUCESTER, WINCHESTER, YORK, SUFFOLK, SOMERSET, WARWICK, EXETER, VERNON, BASSET, *and Others. To them, with his Soldiers,* TALBOT.

TALBOT My gracious Prince, and honourable peers,
Hearing of your arrival in this realm,
I have awhile given truce unto my wars
To do my duty to my sovereign;
In sign whereof, this arm that hath reclaim'd
To your obedience fifty fortresses,
Twelve cities, and seven walled towns of strength,
Beside five hundred prisoners of esteem,
Lets fall his sword before your Highness' feet,
And with submissive loyalty of heart
Ascribes the glory of his conquest got
First to my God and next unto your Grace.

[*Kneels.*

KING Is this the Lord Talbot, uncle Gloucester,
That hath so long been resident in France?

GLOUCESTER Yes, if it please your Majesty, my liege.

KING Welcome, brave captain and victorious lord!
When I was young, as yet I am not old,
I do remember how my father said
A stouter champion never handled sword.
Long since we were resolved of your truth,
Your faithful service, and your toil in war;
Yet never have you tasted our reward,
Or been reguerdon'd with so much as thanks,
Because till now we never saw your face.
Therefore stand up; and for these good deserts
We here create you Earl of Shrewsbury;
And in our coronation take your place.

[*Sennet. Flourish. Exeunt all but Vernon and Basset.*

VERNON Now, sir, to you, that were so hot at sea,
Disgracing of these colours that I wear
In honour of my noble Lord of York –
Dar'st thou maintain the former words thou spak'st?

BASSET Yes, sir; as well as you dare patronage
The envious barking of your saucy tongue
Against my lord the Duke of Somerset.

VERNON Sirrah, thy lord I honour as he is.

BASSET Why, what is he? As good a man as York!

VERNON Hark ye: not so. In witness, take ye that.

[*Strikes him*

BASSET Villian, thou knowest the law of arms is such
That whoso draws a sword 'tis present death,
Or else this blow should broach thy dearest blood.

But I'll unto his Majesty and crave
I may have liberty to venge this wrong;
When thou shalt see I'll meet thee to thy cost.

VERNON Well, miscreant, I'll be there as soon as you;
And, after, meet you sooner than you would.
[*Exeunt.*

ACT FOUR

SCENE I. *Paris. The palace.*

Enter the KING, GLOUCESTER, WINCHESTER, YORK, SUFFOLK, SOMERSET, WARWICK, TALBOT, EXETER, the GOVERNOR of Paris, and Others.

GLOUCESTER Lord Bishop, set the crown upon his head.

WINCHESTER God save King Henry, of that name the Sixth!

GLOUCESTER Now, Governor of Paris, take your oath – [*Governor kneels.*
That you elect no other king but him,
Esteem none friends but such as are his friends,
And none your foes but such as shall pretend
Malicious practices against his state.
This shall ye do, so help you righteous God!
[*Exeunt Governor and his Train.*

Enter SIR JOHN FASTOLFE.

FASTOLFE My gracious sovereign, as I rode from Calais,
To haste unto your coronation,
A letter was deliver'd to my hands,
Writ to your Grace from th' Duke of Burgundy.

TALBOT Shame to the Duke of Burgundy and thee!
I vow'd, base knight, when I did meet thee next
To tear the Garter from thy craven's leg,
[*Plucking it off.*
Which I have done, because unworthily
Thou was installed in that high degree.
Pardon me, princely Henry, and the rest:
This dastard, at the battle of Patay,
When but in all I was six thousand strong,
And that the French were almost ten to one,
Before we met or that a stroke was given,
Like to a trusty squire did run away;
In which assault we lost twelve hundred men;
Myself and divers gentlemen beside
Were there surpris'd and taken prisoners.
Then judge, great lords, if I have done amiss,
Or whether that such cowards ought to wear
This ornament of knighthood – yea or no.

GLOUCESTER To say the truth, this fact was infamous
And ill beseeming any common man,
Much more a knight, a captain, and a leader.

TALBOT When first this order was ordain'd, my lords,
Knights of the Garter were of noble birth,
Valiant and virtuous, full of haughty courage,
Such as were grown to credit by the wars;
Not fearing death nor shrinking for distress,
But always resolute in most extremes.
He then that is not furnish'd in this sort
Doth but usurp the sacred name of knight,
Profaning this most honourable order,
And should, if I were worthy to be judge,
Be quite degraded, like a hedge-born swain
That doth presume to boast of gentle blood.

KING Stain to thy countrymen, thou hear'st thy doom.
Be packing, therefore, thou that wast a knight;
Henceforth we banish thee on pain of death.
[*Exit Fastolfe.*
And now, my Lord Protector, view the letter
Sent from our uncle Duke of Burgundy.

GLOUCESTER [*Viewing the superscription*] What means his Grace, that he hath chang'd his style?
No more but plain and bluntly 'To the King!'
Hath he forgot he is his sovereign?
Or doth this churlish superscription
Pretend some alteration in good-will?
What's here? [*Reads*] 'I have, upon especial cause,
Mov'd with compassion of my country's wreck,
Together with the pitiful complaints
Of such as your oppression feeds upon,
Forsaken your pernicious faction,
And join'd with Charles, the rightful King of France.'
O monstrous treachery! Can this be so –
That in alliance, amity, and oaths,
There should be found such false dissembling, guile?

KING What! Doth my uncle Burgundy revolt?

GLOUCESTER He doth, my lord, and is become your foe.

KING Is that the worst this letter doth contain?

GLOUCESTER It is the worst, and all, my lord, he writes.

KING Why then Lord Talbot there shall talk with him
And give him chastisement for this abuse.

How say you, my lord, are you not content?
TALBOT Content, my liege! Yes; but that I am prevented,
I should have begg'd I might have been employ'd.
KING Then gather strength and march unto him straight;
Let him perceive how ill we brook his treason,
And what offence it is to flout his friends.
TALBOT I go, my lord, in heart desiring still
You may behold confusion of your foes.
[*Exit.*

Enter VERNON and BASSET.

VERNON Grant me the combat, gracious sovereign.
BASSET And me, my lord, grant me the combat too.
YORK This is my servant: hear him, noble Prince.
SOMERSET And this is mine: sweet Henry, favour him.
KING Be patient, lords, and give them leave to speak.
Say, gentlemen, what makes you thus exclaim,
And wherefore crave you combat, or with whom?
VERNON With him, my lord; for he hath done me wrong.
BASSET And I with him; for he hath done me wrong.
KING What is that wrong whereof you both complain?
First let me know, and then I'll answer you.
BASSET Crossing the sea from England into France,
This fellow here, with envious carping tongue,
Upbraided me about the rose I wear,
Saying the sanguine colour of the leaves
Did represent my master's blushing cheeks
When stubbornly he did repugn the truth
About a certain question in the law
Argu'd betwixt the Duke of York and him;
With other vile and ignominious terms –
In confutation of which rude reproach
And in defence of my lord's worthiness,
I crave the benefit of law of arms.
VERNON And that is my petition, noble lord;
For though he seem with forged quaint conceit
To set a gloss upon his bold intent,
Yet know, my lord, I was provok'd by him,
And he first took exceptions at this badge,
Pronouncing that the paleness of this flower
Bewray'd the faintness of my master's heart.
YORK Will not this malice, Somerset, be left?
SOMERSET Your private grudge, my Lord of York, will out,
Though ne'er so cunningly you smother it.
KING Good Lord, what madness rules in brainsick men,
When for so slight and frivolous a cause
Such factious emulations shall arise!
Good cousins both, of York and Somerset,
Quiet yourselves, I pray, and be at peace.
YORK Let this dissension first be tried by fight,
And then your Highness shall command a peace.
SOMERSET The quarrel toucheth none but us alone;
Betwixt ourselves let us decide it then.
YORK There is my pledge; accept it, Somerset.
VERNON Nay, let it rest where it began at first.
BASSET Confirm it so, mine honourable lord.
GLOUCESTER Confirm it so? Confounded be your strife;
And perish ye, with your audacious prate!
Presumptuous vassals, are you not asham'd
With this immodest clamorous outrage
To trouble and disturb the King and us?
And you, my lords – methinks you do not well
To bear with their perverse objections,
Much less to take occasion from their mouths
To raise a mutiny betwixt yourselves.
Let me persuade you take a better course.
EXETER It grieves his Highness. Good my lords, be friends.
KING Come hither, you that would be combatants:
Henceforth I charge you, as you love our favour,
Quite to forget this quarrel and the cause.
And you, my lords, remember where we are:
In France, amongst a fickle wavering nation;
If they perceive dissension in our looks
And that within ourselves we disagree,
How will their grudging stomachs be provok'd
To wilful disobedience, and rebel!
Beside, what infamy will there arise
When foreign princes shall be certified
That for a toy, a thing of no regard,
King Henry's peers and chief nobility
Destroy'd themselves and lost the realm of France!
O, think upon the conquest of my father,
My tender years; and let us not forgo
That for a trifle that was bought with blood!
Let me be umpire in this doubtful strife.
I see no reason, if I wear this rose,
[*Putting on a red rose.*
That any one should therefore be suspicious
I more incline to Somerset than York:
Both are my kinsmen, and I love them both.
As well they may upbraid me with my crown,
Because, forsooth, the King of Scots is crown'd.
But your discretions better can persuade

Than I am able to instruct or teach;
And, therefore, as we hither came in peace,
So let us still continue peace and love.
Cousin of York, we institute your Grace
To be our Regent in these parts of France.
And, good my Lord of Somerset, unite
Your troops of horsemen with his bands of
foot;
And like true subjects, sons of your
progenitors,
Go cheerfully together and digest
Your angry choler on your enemies.
Ourself, my Lord Protector, and the rest,
After some respite will return to Calais;
From thence to England, where I hope ere long
To be presented by your victories
With Charles, Alençon, and that traitorous
rout.

[*Flourish. Exeunt all but York, Warwick, Exeter, Vernon.*

WARWICK My Lord of York, I promise you, the
King
Prettily, methought, did play the orator.

YORK And so he did; but yet I like it not,
In that he wears the badge of Somerset.

WARWICK Tush, that was but his fancy; blame
him not;
I dare presume, sweet prince, he thought no
harm.

YORK An if I wist he did – but let it rest;
Other affairs must now be managed.

[*Exeunt all but Exeter.*

EXETER Well didst thou, Richard, to suppress thy
voice;
For had the passions of thy heart burst out,
I fear we should have seen decipher'd there
More rancorous spite, more furious raging
broils,
Than yet can be imagin'd or suppos'd.
But howsoe'er, no simple man that sees
This jarring discord of nobility,
This shouldering of each other in the court,
This factious bandying of their favourites,
But that it doth presage some ill event.
'Tis much when sceptres are in children's hands;
But more when envy breeds unkind division:
There comes the ruin, there begins confusion.

[*Exit.*

SCENE II. *France. Before Bordeaux.*

Enter TALBOT, with trump and drum.

TALBOT Go to the gates of Bordeaux, trumpeter;
Summon their general unto the wall.

Trumpet sounds a parley. Enter, aloft, the General of the French, and Others.

English John Talbot, Captains, calls you forth,
Servant in arms to Harry King of England;
And thus he would – Open your city gates,
Be humble to us, call my sovereign yours
And do him homage as obedient subjects,
And I'll withdraw me and my bloody power;
But if you frown upon this proffer'd peace,
You tempt the fury of my three attendants,
Lean famine, quartering steel, and climbing fire;
Who in a moment even with the earth
Shall lay your stately and air-braving towers,
If you forsake the offer of their love.

GENERAL Thou ominous and fearful owl of
death,
Our nation's terror and their bloody scourge!
The period of thy tyranny approacheth.
On us thou canst not enter but by death;
For, I protest, we are well fortified,
And strong enough to issue out and fight.
If thou retire, the Dauphin, well appointed,
Stands with the snares of war to tangle thee.
On either hand thee there are squadrons pitch'd
To wall thee from the liberty of flight,
And no way canst thou turn thee for redress
But death doth front thee with apparent spoil
And pale destruction meets thee in the face.
Ten thousand French have ta'en the sacrament
To rive their dangerous artillery
Upon no Christian soul but English Talbot.
Lo, there thou stand'st, a breathing valiant man,
Of an invincible unconquer'd spirit!
This is the latest glory of thy praise
That I, thy enemy, due thee withal;
For ere the glass that now begins to run
Finish the process of his sandy hour,
These eyes that see thee now well coloured
Shall see thee withered, bloody, pale, and dead.

[*Drum afar off.*

Hark! hark! The Dauphin's drum, a warning
bell,
Sings heavy music to thy timorous soul;
And mine shall ring thy dire departure out.

[*Exit General.*

TALBOT He fables not; I hear the enemy.
Out, some light horsemen, and peruse their
wings.
O, negligent and heedless discipline!
How are we park'd and bounded in a pale –
A little herd of England's timorous deer,
Maz'd with a yelping kennel of French curs!
If we be English deer, be then in blood;
Not rascal-like to fall down with a pinch,
But rather, moody-mad and desperate stags,
Turn on the bloody hounds with heads of steel

And make the cowards stand aloof at bay.
Sell every man his life as dear as mine,
And they shall find dear deer of us, my friends.
God and Saint George, Talbot and England's right,
Prosper our colours in this dangerous fight!
[*Exeunt.*

SCENE III. *Plains in Gascony.*

Enter YORK, with trumpet and many Soldiers. A Messenger meets him.

YORK Are not the speedy scouts return'd again
That dogg'd the mighty army of the Dauphin?
MESSENGER They are return'd, my lord, and give it out
That he is march'd to Bordeaux with his power
To fight with Talbot; as he march'd along,
By your espials were discovered
Two mightier troops than that the Dauphin led,
Which join'd with him and made their march for Bordeaux.
YORK A plague upon that villain Somerset
That thus delays my promised supply
Of horsemen that were levied for this siege!
Renowned Talbot doth expect my aid,
And I am louted by a traitor villain
And cannot help the noble chevalier.
God comfort him in this necessity!
If he miscarry, farewell wars in France.

Enter SIR WILLIAM LUCY.

LUCY Thou princely leader of our English strength,
Never so needful on the earth of France,
Spur to the rescue of the noble Talbot,
Who now is girdled with a waist of iron
And hemm'd about with grim destruction.
To Bordeaux, warlike Duke! to Bordeaux, York!
Else, farewell Talbot, France, and England's honour.
YORK O God, that Somerset, who in proud heart
Doth stop my cornets, were in Talbot's place!
So should we save a valiant gentleman
By forfeiting a traitor and a coward.
Mad ire and wrathful fury makes me weep
That thus we die while remiss traitors sleep.
LUCY O, send some succour to the distress'd lord!
YORK He dies; we lose; I break my warlike word.
We mourn: France smiles. We lose: they daily get –
All long of this vile traitor Somerset.
LUCY Then God take mercy on brave Talbot's soul,
And on his son, young John, who two hours since
I met in travel toward his warlike father.
This seven years did not Talbot see his son;
And now they meet where both their lives are done.
YORK Alas, what joy shall noble Talbot have
To bid his young son welcome to his grave?
Away! vexation almost stops my breath,
That sund'red friends greet in the hour of death.
Lucy, farewell; no more my fortune can
But curse the cause I cannot aid the man.
Maine, Blois, Poictiers, and Tours, are won away
Long all of Somerset and his delay.
[*Exit with Forces.*
LUCY Thus, while the vulture of sedition
Feeds in the bosom of such great commanders,
Sleeping neglection doth betray to loss
The conquest of our scarce-cold conqueror,
That ever-living man of memory,
Henry the Fifth. Whiles they each other cross,
Lives, honours, lands, and all, hurry to loss.
[*Exit.*

SCENE IV. *Other plains of Gascony.*

Enter SOMERSET, with his Forces; an Officer of Talbot's with him.

SOMERSET It is too late; I cannot send them now.
This expedition was by York and Talbot
Too rashly plotted; all our general force
Might with a sally of the very town
Be buckled with. The over-daring Talbot
Hath sullied all his gloss of former honour
By this unheedful, desperate, wild adventure.
York set him on to fight and die in shame
That, Talbot dead, great York might bear the name.
OFFICER Here is Sir William Lucy, who with me
Set from our o'er-match'd forces forth for aid.

Enter SIR WILLIAM LUCY

SOMERSET How now, Sir William! Whither were you sent?
LUCY Whither, my lord! From bought and sold Lord Talbot,
Who, ring'd about with bold adversity,
Cries out for noble York and Somerset
To beat assailing death from his weak legions;
And whiles the honourable captain there
Drops bloody sweat from his war-wearied limbs
And, in advantage ling'ring, looks for rescue,
You, his false hopes, the trust of England's honour,
Keep off aloof with worthless emulation.
Let not your private discord keep away
The levied succours that should lend him aid,
While he, renowned noble gentleman,
Yield up his life unto a world of odds.

Orleans the Bastard, Charles, Burgundy,
Alençon, Reignier, compass him about,
And Talbot perisheth by your default.
SOMERSET York set him on; York should have sent him aid.
LUCY And York as fast upon your Grace exclaims,
Swearing that you withhold his levied host,
Collected for this expedition.
SOMERSET York lies; he might have sent and had the horse.
I owe him little duty and less love,
And take foul scorn of fawn on him by sending.
LUCY The fraud of England, not the force of France,
Hath now entrapp'd the noble-minded Talbot.
Never to England shall he bear his life,
But dies betray'd to fortune by your strife.
SOMERSET Come, go; I will dispatch the horsemen straight;
Within six hours they will be at his aid.
LUCY Too late comes rescue; he is ta'en or slain,
For fly he could not if he would have fled;
And fly would Talbot never, though he might.
SOMERSET If he be dead, brave Talbot, then, adieu!
LUCY His fame lives in the world, his shame in you. [*Exeunt.*

SCENE V. *The English camp near Bordeaux.*

Enter TALBOT and JOHN his son.

TALBOT O young John Talbot! I did send for thee
To tutor thee in stratagems of war,
That Talbot's name might be in thee reviv'd
When sapless age and weak unable limbs
Should bring thy father to his drooping chair.
But – O malignant and ill-boding stars! –
Now thou art come unto a feast of death,
A terrible and unavoided danger;
Therefore, dear boy, mount on my swiftest horse,
And I'll direct thee how thou shalt escape
By sudden flight. Come, dally not, be gone.
JOHN Is my name Talbot, and am I your son?
And shall I fly? O, if you love my mother,
Dishonour not her honourable name,
To make a bastard and a slave of me!
The world will say he is not Talbot's blood
That basely fled when noble Talbot stood.
TALBOT Fly to revenge my death, if I be slain.
JOHN He that flies so will ne'er return again.
TALBOT If we both stay, we both are sure to die.
JOHN Then let me stay; and, father, do you fly.
Your loss is great, so your regard should be;
My worth unknown, no loss is known in me;
Upon my death the French can little boast;
In yours they will, in you all hopes are lost.
Flight cannot stain the honour you have won;
But mine it will, that no exploit have done;
You fled for vantage, every one will swear;
But if I bow, they'll say it was for fear.
There is no hope that ever I will stay
If the first hour I shrink and run away.
Here, on my knee, I beg mortality,
Rather than life preserv'd with infamy.
TALBOT Shall all thy mother's hopes lie in one tomb?
JOHN Ay, rather than I'll shame my mother's womb.
TALBOT Upon my blessing I command thee go.
JOHN To fight I will, but not to fly the foe.
TALBOT Part of thy father may be sav'd in thee.
JOHN No part of him but will be shame in me.
TALBOT Thou never hadst renown, nor canst not lose it.
JOHN Yes, your renowned name; shall flight abuse it?
TALBOT Thy father's charge shall clear thee from that stain.
JOHN You cannot witness for me, being slain.
If death be so apparent, then both fly.
TALBOT And leave my followers here to fight and die?
My age was never tainted with such shame.
JOHN And shall my youth be guilty of such blame?
No more can I be severed from your side
Than can yourself yourself in twain divide.
Stay, go, do what you will, the like do I;
For live I will not if my father die.
TALBOT Then here I take my leave of thee, fair son,
Born to eclipse thy life this afternoon.
Come, side by side together live and die;
And soul with soul from France to heaven fly. [*Exeunt.*

SCENE VI. *A field of battle.*

Alarum: excursions wherein JOHN TALBOT is hemm'd about, and TALBOT rescues him.

TALBOT Saint George and victory! Fight, soldiers, fight.
The Regent hath with Talbot broke his word
And left us to the rage of France his sword.
Where is John Talbot? Pause and take thy breath;
I gave thee life and rescu'd thee from death.
JOHN O, twice my father, twice am I thy son!
The life thou gav'st me first was lost and done
Till with thy warlike sword, despite of fate,
To my determin'd time thou gav'st new date.
TALBOT When from the Dauphin's crest thy

sword struck fire,
It warm'd thy father's heart with proud desire
Of bold-fac'd victory. Then leaden age,
Quicken'd with youthful spleen and warlike rage,
Beat down Alençon, Orleans, Burgundy,
And from the pride of Gallia rescued thee.
The ireful bastard Orleans, that drew blood
From thee, my boy, and had the maidenhood
Of thy first fight, I soon encountered
And, interchanging blows, I quickly shed
Some of his bastard blood; and in disgrace
Bespoke him thus: 'Contaminated, base,
And misbegotten blood I spill of thine,
Mean and right poor, for that pure blood of mine
Which thou didst force from Talbot, my brave boy'.
Here purposing the Bastard to destroy,
Came in strong rescue. Speak, thy father's care;
Art thou not weary, John? How dost thou fare?
Wilt thou yet leave the battle, boy, and fly,
Now thou art seal'd the son of chivalry?
Fly, to revenge my death when I am dead:
The help of one stands me in little stead.
O, too much folly is it, well I wot,
To hazard all our lives in one small boat!
If I to-day die not with Frenchmen's rage,
To-morrow I shall die with mickle age.
By me they nothing gain an if I stay:
'Tis but the short'ning of my life one day.
In thee thy mother dies, our household's name,
My death's revenge, thy youth, and England's fame.
All these and more we hazard by thy stay;
All these are sav'd if thou wilt fly away.

JOHN The sword of Orleans hath not made me smart;
These words of yours draw life-blood from my heart.
On that advantage, bought with such a shame,
To save a paltry life and slay bright fame,
Before young Talbot from old Talbot fly,
The coward horse that bears me fall and die!
And like me to the peasant boys of France,
To be shame's scorn and subject of mischance!
Surely, by all the glory you have won,
An if I fly, I am not Talbot's son;
Then talk no more of flight, it is no boot.
If son to Talbot, die at Talbot's foot.

TALBOT Then follow thou thy desp'rate sire of Crete,
Thou Icarus; thy life to me is sweet.
If thou wilt fight, fight by thy father's side;
And, commendable prov'd, let's die in pride.
[*Exeunt.*

SCENE VII. *Another part of the field.*

Alarum; excursions. Enter old TALBOT led by a Servant.

TALBOT Where is my other life? Mine own is gone.
O, where's young Talbot? Where is valiant John?
Triumphant death, smear'd with captivity,
Young Talbot's valour makes me smile at thee.
When he perceiv'd me shrink and on my knee,
His bloody sword he brandish'd over me,
And like a hungry lion did commence
Rough deeds of rage and stern impatience;
But when my angry guardant stood alone,
Tend'ring my ruin and assail'd of none,
Dizzy-ey'd fury and great rage of heart
Suddenly made him from my side to start
Into the clust'ring battle of the French;
And in that sea of blood my boy did drench
His overmounting spirit; and there died,
My Icarus, my blossom, in his pride.

Enter Soldiers, bearing the body of John Talbot.

SERVANT O my dear lord, lo where your son is borne!

TALBOT Thou antic Death, which laugh'st us here to scorn,
Anon, from thy insulting tyranny,
Coupled in bonds of perpetuity,
Two Talbots, winged through the lither sky,
In thy despite shall scape mortality.
O thou whose wounds become hard-favoured Death,
Speak to thy father ere thou yield thy breath!
Brave Death by speaking, whether he will or no;
Imagine him a Frenchman and thy foe.
Poor boy! he smiles, methinks, as who should say,
Had Death been French, then Death had died to-day.
Come, come, and lay him in his father's arms.
My spirit can no longer bear these harms.
Soldiers, adieu! I have what I would have,
Now my old arms are young John Talbot's grave. [*Dies.*

Enter CHARLES, ALENÇON, BURGUNDY, BASTARD, LA PUCELLE, and Forces.

CHARLES Had York and Somerset brought rescue in,
We should have found a bloody day of this.

BASTARD How the young whelp of Talbot's, raging wood,
Did flesh his puny sword in Frenchmen's blood!

LA PUCELLE Once I encount'red him, and thus I said:
'Thou maiden youth, be vanquish'd by a maid'.

But with a proud majestical high scorn
He answer'd thus: 'Young Talbot was not born
To be the pillage of a giglot wench'.
So, rushing in the bowels of the French,
He left me proudly, as unworthy fight.

BURGUNDY Doubtless he would have made a noble knight.
See where he lies inhearsed in the arms
Of the most bloody nurser of his harms!

BASTARD Hew them to pieces, hack their bones asunder,
Whose life was England's glory, Gallia's wonder.

CHARLES O, no; forbear! For that which we have fled
During the life, let us not wrong it dead.

Enter SIR WILLIAM LUCY attended; a French Herald preceding.

LUCY Herald, conduct me to the Dauphin's tent,
To know who hath obtain'd the glory of the day.

CHARLES On what submissive message art thou sent?

LUCY Submission, Dauphin! 'Tis a mere French word:
We English warriors wot not what it means.
I come to know what prisoners thou hast ta'en,
And to survey the bodies of the dead.

CHARLES For prisoners ask'st thou? Hell our prison is.
But tell me whom thou seek'st.

LUCY But where's the great Alcides of the field,
Valiant Lord Talbot, Earl of Shrewsbury,
Created for his rare success in arms
Great Earl of Washford, Waterford, and Valence,
Lord Talbot of Goodrig and Urchinfield,
Lord Strange of Blackmere, Lord Verdun of Alton,
Lord Cromwell of Wingfield, Lord Furnival of Sheffield,
The thrice victorious Lord of Falconbridge,
Knight of the noble order of Saint George,
Worthy Saint Michael, and the Golden Fleece,
Great Marshal to Henry the Sixth
Of all his wars within the realm of France?

LA PUCELLE Here's a silly-stately style indeed!
The Turk, that two and fifty kingdoms hath,
Writes not so tedious a style as this.
Him that thou magnifi'st with all these titles,
Stinking and fly-blown lies here at our feet.

LUCY Is Talbot slain – the Frenchmen's only scourge,
Your kingdom's terror and black Nemesis?
O, were mine eye-balls into bullets turn'd,
That I in rage might shoot them at your faces!
O that I could but call these dead to life!
It were enough to fright the realm of France.
Were but his picture left amongst you here,
It would amaze the proudest of you all.
Give me their bodies, that I may bear them hence
And give them burial as beseems their worth.

LA PUCELLE I think this upstart is old Talbot's ghost,
He speaks with such a proud commanding spirit.
For God's sake, let him have them; to keep them here,
They would but stink, and putrefy the air.

CHARLES Go, take their bodies hence.

LUCY I'll bear them hence; but from their ashes shall be rear'd
A phoenix that shall make all France afeard.

CHARLES So we be rid of them, do with them what thou wilt.
And now to Paris in this conquering vein!
All will be ours, now bloody Talbot's slain.

[*Exeunt.*

ACT FIVE

SCENE I. *London. The Palace.*

Sennet. Enter the KING, GLOUCESTER, and EXETER.

KING Have you perus'd the letters from the Pope,
The Emperor, and the Earl of Armagnac?

GLOUCESTER I have, my lord; and their intent is this:
They humbly sue unto your Excellence
To have a godly peace concluded of
Between the realms of England and of France.

KING How doth your Grace affect their motion?

GLOUCESTER Well, my good lord, and as the only means
To stop effusion of our Christian blood
And stablish quietness on every side.

KING Ay, marry, uncle; for I always thought
It was both impious and unnatural
That such immanity and bloody strife
Should reign among professors of one faith.

GLOUCESTER Beside, my lord, the sooner to effect
And surer bind this knot of amity,
The Earl of Armagnac, near knit to Charles,
A man of great authority in France,

Proffers his only daughter to your Grace
In marriage, with a large and sumptuous dowry.
KING Marriage, uncle! Alas, my years are young!
And fitter is my study and my books
Than wanton dalliance with a paramour.
Yet call th' ambassadors, and, as you please,
So let them have their answers every one.
I shall be well content with any choice
Tends to God's glory and my country's weal.

Enter WINCHESTER in Cardinal's habit as CARDINAL BEAUFORT, the Papal Legate, and two Ambassadors.

EXETER What! Is my Lord of Winchester install'd
And call'd unto a cardinal's degree?
Then I perceive that will be verified
Henry the Fifth did sometime prophesy:
'If once he come to be a cardinal,
He'll make his cap co-equal with the crown'.
KING My Lords Ambassadors, your several suits
Have been consider'd and debated on.
Your purpose is both good and reasonable,
And therefore are we certainly resolv'd
To draw conditions of a friendly peace,
Which by my Lord of Winchester we mean
Shall be transported presently to France.
GLOUCESTER And for the proffer of my lord your master,
I have inform'd his Highness so at large,
As, liking of the lady's virtuous gifts,
Her beauty, and the value of her dower,
He doth intend she shall be England's Queen.
KING [*To Ambassador*] In argument and proof of which contract,
Bear her this jewel, pledge of my affection.
And so, my Lord Protector, see them guarded
And safely brought to Dover; where, inshipp'd,
Commit them to the fortune of the sea.

[*Exeunt all but Winchester and the Legate.*

WINCHESTER Stay, my Lord Legate; you shall first receive
The sum of money which I promised
Should be delivered to his Holiness
For clothing me in these grave ornaments.
LEGATE I will attend upon your lordship's leisure.
WINCHESTER [*Aside*] Now Winchester will not submit, I trow,
Or be inferior to the proudest peer.
Humphrey of Gloucester, thou shalt well perceive
That neither in birth or for authority
The Bishop will be overborne by thee.
I'll either make thee stoop and bend thy knee,
Or sack this country with a mutiny. [*Exeunt.*

SCENE II. *France. Plains in Anjou.*

Enter CHARLES, BURGUNDY, LA PUCELLE and Forces.

CHARLES These news, my lords, may cheer our drooping spirits:
'Tis said the stout Parisians do revolt
And turn again unto the warlike French.
ALENÇON Then march to Paris, royal Charles of France,
And keep not back your powers in dalliance.
LA PUCELLE Peace be amongst them, if they turn to us;
Else ruin combat with their palaces!

Enter a Scout.

SCOUT Success unto our valiant general,
And happiness to his accomplices!
CHARLES What tidings send our scouts? I prithee speak.
SCOUT The English army, that divided was
Into two parties, is now conjoin'd in one,
And means to give you battle presently.
CHARLES Somewhat too sudden, sirs, the warning is;
But we will presently provide for them.
BURGUNDY I trust the ghost of Talbot is not there.
Now he is gone, my lord, you need not fear.
LA PUCELLE Of all base passions fear is most accurs'd.
Command the conquest, Charles, it shall be thine,
Let Henry fret and all the world repine.
CHARLES Then on, my lords; and France be fortunate! [*Exeunt.*

SCENE III. *Before Angiers.*

Alarum; excursions. Enter LA PUCELLE.

LA PUCELLE The Regent conquers and the Frenchmen fly.
Now help, ye charming spells and periapts;
And ye choice spirits that admonish me
And give me signs of future accidents;

[*Thunder.*

You speedy helpers that are substitutes
Under the lordly monarch of the north,
Appear and aid me in this enterprise!

Enter Fiends.

This speedy and quick appearance argues proof
Of your accustom'd diligence to me.
Now, ye familiar spirits that are cull'd
Out of the powerful regions under earth,
Help me this once, that France may get the field.

[*They walk and speak not.*
O, hold me not with silence over-long!
Where I was wont to feed you with my blood,
I'll lop a member off and give it you
In earnest of a further benefit,
So you do condescend to help me now.
[*They hang their heads.*
No hope to have redress? My body shall
Pay recompense, if you will grant my suit.
[*They shake their heads.*
Cannot my body nor blood sacrifice
Entreat you to your wonted furtherance?
Then take my soul – my body, soul, and all,
Before that England give the French the foil.
[*They depart.*
See! they forsake me. Now the time is come
That France must vail her lofty-plumed crest
And let her head fall into England's lap.
My ancient incantations are too weak,
And hell too strong for me to buckle with.
Now, France, thy glory droopeth to the dust.
[*Exit.*

Excursions. Enter French and English, fighting. LA PUCELLE and YORK fight hand to hand; La Pucelle is taken. The French fly.

YORK Damsel of France, I think I have you fast.
Unchain your spirits now with spelling charms,
And try if they can gain your liberty.
A goodly prize, fit for the devil's grace!
See how the ugly witch doth bend her brows
As if, with Circe, she would change my shape!

LA PUCELLE Chang'd to a worser shape thou canst not be.

YORK O, Charles the Dauphin is a proper man:
No shape but his can please your dainty eye.

LA PUCELLE A plaguing mischief light on Charles and thee!
And may ye both be suddenly surpris'd
By bloody hands, in sleeping on your beds!

YORK Fell banning hag; enchantress, hold thy tongue.

LA PUCELLE I prithee give me leave to curse awhile.

YORK Curse, miscreant, when thou comest to the stake. [*Exeunt.*

Alarum. Enter SUFFOLK, with MARGARET in his hand.

SUFFOLK Be what thou wilt, thou art my prisoner. [*Gazes on her.*
O fairest beauty, do not fear nor fly!
For I will touch thee but with reverent hands;
I kiss these fingers for eternal peace,
And lay them gently on thy tender side.
Who art thou? Say, that I may honour thee.

MARGARET Margaret my name, and daughter to a king,
The King of Naples – whosoe'er thou art.

SUFFOLK An earl I am, and Suffolk am I call'd.
Be not offended, nature's miracle,
Thou art allotted to be ta'en by me.
So doth the swan her downy cygnets save,
Keeping them prisoner underneath her wings.
Yet, if this servile usage once offend,
Go and be free again as Suffolk's friend.
[*She is going.*
O, stay! [*Aside*] I have no power to let her pass;
My hand would free her, but my heart says no.
As plays the sun upon the glassy streams,
Twinkling another counterfeited beam,
So seems this gorgeous beauty to mine eyes.
Fain would I woo her, yet I dare not speak.
I'll call for pen and ink, and write my mind.
Fie, de la Pole! disable not thyself;
Hast not a tongue? Is she not here thy prisoner?
Wilt thou be daunted at a woman's sight?
Ay, beauty's princely majesty is such
Confounds the tongue and makes the senses rough.

MARGARET Say, Earl of Suffolk, if thy name be so,
What ransom must I pay before I pass?
For I perceive I am thy prisoner.

SUFFOLK [*Aside*] How canst thou tell she will deny thy suit,
Before thou make a trial of her love?

MARGARET Why speak'st thou not? What ransom must I pay?

SUFFOLK [*Aside*] She's beautiful, and therefore to be woo'd;
She is a woman, therefore to be won.

MARGARET Wilt thou accept of ransom – yea or no?

SUFFOLK [*Aside*] Fond man, remember that thou hast a wife;
Then how can Margaret be thy paramour?

MARGARET I were best leave him, for he will not hear.

SUFFOLK [*Aside*] There all is marr'd; there lies a cooling card.

MARGARET He talks at random; sure, the man is mad.

SUFFOLK [*Aside*] And yet a dispensation may be had.

MARGARET And yet I would that you would answer me.

SUFFOLK [*Aside*] I'll win this Lady Margaret. For whom?
Why, for my king! Tush, that's a wooden thing!
MARGARET He talks of wood. It is some carpenter.
SUFFOLK [*Aside*] Yet so my fancy may be satisfied,
And peace established between these realms.
But there remains a scruple in that too;
For though her father be the King of Naples,
Duke of Anjou and Maine, yet is he poor,
And our nobility will scorn the match.
MARGARET Hear ye, Captain – are you not at leisure?
SUFFOLK [*Aside*] It shall be so, disdain they ne'er so much.
Henry is youthful, and will quickly yield. –
Madam, I have a secret to reveal.
MARGARET [*Aside*] What though I be enthrall'd? He seems a knight,
And will not any way dishonour me.
SUFFOLK Lady, vouchsafe to listen what I say.
MARGARET [*Aside*] Perhaps I shall be rescu'd by the French;
And then I need not crave his courtesy.
SUFFOLK Sweet madam, give me hearing in a cause –
MARGARET [*Aside*] Tush! women have been captivate ere now.
SUFFOLK Lady, wherefore talk you so?
MARGARET I cry you mercy, 'tis but quid for quo.
SUFFOLK Say, gentle Princess, would you not suppose
Your bondage happy, to be made a queen?
MARGARET To be a queen in bondage is more vile
Than is a slave in base servility;
For princes should be free.
SUFFOLK And so shall you,
If happy England's royal king be free.
MARGARET Why, what concerns his freedom unto me?
SUFFOLK I'll undertake to make thee Henry's queen,
To put a golden sceptre in thy hand
And set a precious crown upon thy head,
If thou wilt condescend to be my –
MARGARET What?
SUFFOLK His love.
MARGARET I am unworthy to be Henry's wife.
SUFFOLK No, gentle madam; I unworthy am
To woo so fair a dame to be his wife
And have no portion in the choice myself.
How say you, madam? Are you so content?
MARGARET An if my father please, I am content.
SUFFOLK Then call our captains and our colours forth!
And, madam, at your father's castle walls
We'll crave a parley to confer with him.

Sound a parley. Enter REIGNIER on the walls.

See, Reignier see, thy daughter prisoner!
REIGNIER To whom?
SUFFOLK To me.
REIGNIER Suffolk, what remedy?
I am a soldier and unapt to weep
Or to exclaim on fortune's fickleness.
SUFFOLK Yes, there is remedy enough, my lord.
Consent, and for thy honour give consent,
They daughter shall be wedded to my king,
Whom I with pain have woo'd and won thereto;
And this her easy-held imprisonment
Hath gain'd thy daughter princely liberty.
REIGNIER Speaks Suffolk as he thinks?
SUFFOLK Fair Margaret knows
That Suffolk doth not flatter, face, or feign.
REIGNIER Upon thy princely warrant I descend
To give thee answer of thy just demand.
[*Exit Reignier from the walls.*
SUFFOLK And here I will expect thy coming.

Trumpets sound. Enter REIGNIER below.

REIGNIER Welcome, brave Earl, into our territories;
Command in Anjou what your Honour pleases.
SUFFOLK Thanks, Reignier, happy for so sweet a child,
Fit to be made companion with a king.
What answer makes your Grace unto my suit?
REIGNIER Since thou dost deign to woo her little worth
To be the princely bride of such a lord,
Upon condition I may quietly
Enjoy mine own, the country Maine and Anjou,
Free from oppression or the stroke of war,
My daughter shall be Henry's, if he please.
SUFFOLK That is her ransom; I deliver her.
And those two counties I will undertake
Your Grace shall well and quietly enjoy.
REIGNIER And I again, in Henry's royal name,
As deputy unto that gracious king,
Give thee her hand for sign of plighted faith.
SUFFOLK Reignier of France, I give thee kingly thanks,
Because this is in traffic of a king.
[*Aside*] And yet, methinks, I could be well content
To be mine own attorney in this case. –
I'll over then to England with this news,
And make this marriage to be solemniz'd.
So, farewell, Reignier. Set this diamond safe
In golden palaces, as it becomes.
REIGNIER I do embrace thee as I would embrace
The Christian prince, King Henry, were he here.

MARGARET Farewell, my lord. Good wishes, praise, and prayers,
Shall Suffolk ever have of Margaret. *[She is going.*
SUFFOLK Farewell, sweet madam. But hark you, Margaret –
No princely commendations to my king?
MARGARET Such commendations as becomes a maid,
A virgin, and his servant, say to him.
SUFFOLK Words sweetly plac'd and modestly directed.
But, madam, I must trouble you again –
No loving token to his Majesty?
MARGARET Yes, my good lord: a pure unspotted heart,
Never yet taint with love, I send the King.
SUFFOLK And this withal. *[Kisses her.*
MARGARET That for thyself – I will not so presume
To send such peevish tokens to a king.
[Exeunt Reignier and Margaret.
SUFFOLK O, wert thou for myself! But, Suffolk, stay;
Thou mayst not wander in that labyrinth:
There Minotaurs and ugly treasons lurk.
Solicit Henry with her wondrous praise.
Bethink thee on her virtues that surmount,
And natural graces that extinguish art;
Repeat their semblance often on the seas,
That, when thou com'st to kneel at Henry's feet,
Thou mayst bereave him of his wits with wonder. *[Exit.*

SCENE IV. *Camp of the Duke of York in Anjou.*

Enter YORK, WARWICK, and Others.

YORK Bring forth that sorceress, condemn'd to burn.

Enter LA PUCELLE, guarded, and a Shepherd.

SHEPHERD Ah, Joan, this kills thy father's heart outright!
Have I sought every country far and near,
And, now it is my chance to find thee out,
Must I behold thy timeless cruel death?
Ah, Joan, sweet daughter Joan, I'll die with thee!
LA PUCELLE Decrepit miser! base ignoble wretch!
I am descended of a gentler blood;
Thou art no father nor no friend of mine.
SHEPHERD Out, out! My lords, an please you, 'tis not so;
I did beget her, all the parish knows.
Her mother liveth yet, can testify
She was the first fruit of my bach'lorship.
WARWICK Graceless, wilt thou deny thy parentage?
YORK This argues what her kind of life hath been –
Wicked and vile; and so her death concludes.
SHEPHERD Fie, Joan, that thou wilt be so obstacle!
God knows thou art a collop of my flesh;
And for thy sake have I shed many a tear.
Deny me not, I prithee, gentle Joan.
LA PUCELLE Peasant, avaunt! You have suborn'd this man
Of purpose to obscure my noble birth.
SHEPHERD 'Tis true, I gave a noble to the priest
The morn that I was wedded to her mother.
Kneel down and take my blessing, good my girl.
Wilt thou not stoop? Now cursed be the time
Of thy nativity. I would the milk
Thy mother gave thee when thou suck'dst her breast
Had been a little ratsbane for thy sake.
Or else, when thou didst keep my lambs a-field,
I wish some ravenous wolf had eaten thee.
Dost thou deny thy father, cursed drab?
O, burn her, burn her! Hanging is too good. *[Exit.*
YORK Take her away; for she hath liv'd too long,
To fill the world with vicious qualities.
LA PUCELLE First let me tell you whom you have condemn'd:
Not me begotten of a shepherd swain,
But issued from the progeny of kings;
Virtuous and holy, chosen from above
By inspiration of celestial grace,
To work exceeding miracles on earth.
I never had to do with wicked spirits.
But you, that are polluted with your lusts,
Stain'd with the guiltless blood of innocents,
Corrupt and tainted with a thousand vices,
Because you want the grace that others have,
You judge it straight a thing impossible
To compass wonders but by help of devils.
No, misconceived! Joan of Arc hath been
A virgin from her tender infancy,
Chaste and immaculate in very thought;
Whose maiden blood, thus rigorously effus'd,
Will cry for vengeance at the gates of heaven.
YORK Ay, ay. Away with her to execution!
WARWICK And hark ye, sirs; because she is a maid,
Spare for no fagots, let there be enow.
Place barrels of pitch upon the fatal stake,
That so her torture may be shortened.
LA PUCELLE Will nothing turn your unrelenting hearts?
Then, Joan, discover thine infirmity

That warranteth by law to be thy privilege:
I am with child, ye bloody homicides;
Murder not then the fruit within my womb,
Although ye hale me to a violent death.

YORK Now heaven forfend! The holy maid with child!

WARWICK The greatest miracle that e'er ye wrought:
Is all your strict preciseness come to this?

YORK She and the Dauphin have been juggling.
I did imagine what would be her refuge.

WARWICK Well, go to; we'll have no bastards live;
Especially since Charles must father it.

LA PUCELLE You are deceiv'd; my child is none of his:
It was Alençon that enjoy'd my love.

YORK Alençon, that notorious Machiavel!
It dies, an if it had a thousand lives.

LA PUCELLE O, give me leave, I have deluded you.
'Twas neither Charles nor yet the Duke I nam'd,
But Reignier, King of Naples, that prevail'd.

WARWICK A married man! That's most intolerable.

YORK Why, here's a girl! I think she knows not well –
There were so many – whom she may accuse.

WARWICK It's sign she hath been liberal and free.

YORK And yet, forsooth, she is a virgin pure.
Strumpet, thy words condemn thy brat and thee
Use no entreaty, for it is in vain.

LA PUCELLE Then lead me hence – with whom I leave my curse:
May never glorious sun reflex his beams
Upon the country where you make abode;
But darkness and the gloomy shade of death
Environ you, till mischief and despair
Drive you to break your necks or hang yourselves! *[Exit, guarded.*

YORK Break thou in pieces and consume to ashes,
Thou foul accursed minister of hell!

Enter CARDINAL BEAUFORT, attended.

CARDINAL Lord Regent, I do greet your Excellence
With letters of commission from the King.
For know, my lords, the states of Christendom,
Mov'd with remorse of these outrageous broils,
Have earnestly implor'd a general peace
Betwixt our nation and the aspiring French;
And here at hand the Dauphin and his train
Approacheth, to confer about some matter.

YORK Is all our travail turn'd to this effect?
After the slaughter of so many peers,
So many captains, gentlemen, and soldiers,
That in this quarrel have been overthrown
And sold their bodies for their country's benefit,
Shall we at last conclude effeminate peace?
Have we not lost most part of all the towns,
By treason, falsehood, and by treachery,
Our great progenitors had conquered?
O Warwick, Warwick! I foresee with grief
The utter loss of all the realm of France.

WARWICK Be patient, York. If we conclude a peace,
It shall be with such strict and severe covenants
As little shall the Frenchmen gain thereby.

Enter CHARLES, ALENÇON, BASTARD, REIGNIER, and Others.

CHARLES Since, lords of England, it is thus agreed
That peaceful truce shall be proclaim'd in France,
We come to be informed by yourselves
What the conditions of that league must be.

YORK Speak, Winchester; for boiling choler chokes
The hollow passage of my poison'd voice,
By sight of these our baleful enemies.

CARDINAL Charles, and the rest, it is enacted thus:
That, in regard King Henry gives consent,
Of mere compassion and of lenity,
To ease your country of distressful war,
And suffer you to breathe in fruitful peace,
You shall become true liegemen to his crown;
And, Charles, upon condition thou wilt swear
To pay him tribute and submit thyself,
Thou shalt be plac'd as viceroy under him,
And still enjoy thy regal dignity.

ALENÇON Must he be then as shadow of himself?
Adorn his temples with a coronet
And yet, in substance and authority,
Retain but privilege of a private man?
This proffer is absurd and reasonless.

CHARLES 'Tis known already that I am possess'd
With more than half the Gallian territories,
And therein reverenc'd for their lawful king.
Shall I, for lucre of the rest unvanquish'd,
Detract so much from that prerogative
As to be call'd but viceroy of the whole?
No, Lord Ambassador; I'll rather keep
That which I have than, coveting for more,
Be cast from possibility of all.

YORK Insulting Charles! Hast thou by secret means
Us'd intercession to obtain a league,
And now the matter grows to compromise
Stand'st thou aloof upon comparison?
Either accept the title thou usurp'st,
Of benefit proceeding from our king
And not of any challenge of desert,

Or we will plague thee with incessant wars.
REIGNIER [*To Charles*] My lord, you do not well in obstinacy
To cavil in the course of this contract.
If once it be neglected, ten to one
We shall not find like opportunity.
ALENCON [*To Charles*] To say the truth, it is your policy
To save your subjects from such massacre
And ruthless slaughters as are daily seen
By our proceeding in hostility;
And therefore take this compact of a truce,
Although you break it when your pleasure serves.
WARWICK How say'st thou, Charles? Shall our condition stand?
CHARLES It shall;
Only reserv'd, you claim no interest
In any of our towns of garrison.
YORK Then swear allegiance to his Majesty:
As thou art knight, never to disobey
Nor be rebellious to the crown of England –
Thou, nor thy nobles, to the crown of England.

[*Charles and the rest give tokens of fealty.*

So, now dismiss your army when ye please;
Hang up your ensigns, let your drums be still,
For here we entertain a solemn peace. [*Exeunt.*

SCENE V. *London. The palace.*

Enter SUFFOLK, in conference with the KING, GLOUCESTER and EXETER.

KING Your wondrous rare description, noble Earl,
Of beauteous Margaret hath astonish'd me.
Her virtues, graced with external gifts,
Do breed love's settled passions in my heart;
And like as rigour of tempestuous gusts
Provokes the mightiest hulk against the tide,
So am I driven by breath of her renown
Either to suffer shipwreck or arrive
Where I may have fruition of her love.
SUFFOLK Tush, my good lord! This superficial tale
Is but a preface of her worthy praise.
The chief perfections of that lovely dame,
Had I sufficient skill to utter them,
Would make a volume of enticing lines,
Able to ravish any dull conceit;
And, which is more, she is not so divine,
So full-replete with choice of all delights,
But with as humble lowliness of mind
She is content to be at your command –
Command, I mean, of virtuous chaste intents,
To love and honour Henry as her lord.
KING And otherwise will Henry ne'er presume.
Therefore, my Lord Protector, give consent
That Marg'ret may be England's royal Queen.
GLOUCESTER So should I give consent to flatter sin.
You know, my lord, your Highness is betroth'd
Unto another lady of esteem.
How shall we then dispense with that contract,
And not deface your honour with reproach?
SUFFOLK As doth a ruler with unlawful oaths;
Or one that at a triumph, having vow'd
To try his strength, forsaketh yet the lists
By reason of his adversary's odds:
A poor earl's daughter is unequal odds,
And therefore may be broke without offence.
GLOUCESTER Why, what, I pray, is Margaret more than that?
Her father is no better than an earl,
Although in glorious titles he excel.
SUFFOLK Yes, my lord, her father is a king,
The King of Naples and Jerusalem;
And of such great authority in France
As his alliance will confirm our peace,
And keep the Frenchmen in allegiance.
GLOUCESTER And so the Earl of Armagnac may do,
Because he is near kinsman unto Charles.
EXETER Beside, his wealth doth warrant a liberal dower;
Where Reignier sooner will receive than give.
SUFFOLK A dow'r, my lords! Disgrace not so your king,
That he should be so abject, base, and poor,
To choose for wealth and not for perfect love.
Henry is able to enrich his queen,
And not to seek a queen to make him rich.
So worthless peasants bargain for their wives,
As market-men for oxen, sheep, or horse.
Marriage is a matter of more worth
Than to be dealt in by attorneyship;
Not whom we will, but whom his Grace affects,
Must be companion of his nuptial bed.
And therefore, lords, since he affects her most,
It most of all these reasons bindeth us,
In our opinions she should be preferr'd;
For what is wedlock forced but a hell,
An age of discord and continual strife?
Whereas the contrary bringeth bliss,
And is a pattern of celestial peace.
Whom should we match with Henry, being a king,
But Margaret, that is daughter to a king?
Her peerless feature, joined with her birth,
Approves her fit for none but for a king;
Her valiant courage and undaunted spirit,
More than in women commonly is seen,
Will answer our hope in issue of a king;
For Henry, son unto a conqueror,
Is likely to beget more conquerors,

If with a lady of so high resolve
As is fair Margaret he be link'd in love.
Then yield, my lords; and here conclude with me
That Margaret shall be Queen, and none but she.

KING Whether it be through force of your report,
My noble Lord of Suffolk, or for that
My tender youth was never yet attaint
With any passion of inflaming love,
I cannot tell; but this I am assur'd,
I feel such sharp dissension in my breast,
Such fierce alarums both of hope and fear,
As I am sick with working of my thoughts.
Take therefore shipping; post, my lord, to France;
Agree to any covenants; and procure
That Lady Margaret do vouchsafe to come
To cross the seas to England, and be crown'd
King Henry's faithful and anointed queen.
For your expenses and sufficient charge,
Among the people gather up a tenth.
Be gone, I say; for till you do return
I rest perplexed with a thousand cares.
And you, good uncle, banish all offence:
If you do censure me by what you were,
Not what you are, I know it will excuse
This sudden execution of my will.
And so conduct me where, from company,
I may revolve and ruminate my grief. [*Exit.*

GLOUCESTER Ay, grief, I fear me, both at first and last. [*Exeunt Gloucester and Exeter.*

SUFFOLK Thus Suffolk hath prevail'd; and thus he goes,
As did the youthful Paris once to Greece,
With hope to find the like event in love
But prosper better than the Troyan did.
Margaret shall now be Queen, and rule the King;
But I will rule both her, the King, and realm.
[*Exit.*

The Second Part of King Henry the Sixth

Introduction by ROBERT MASLEN

The Second Part of King Henry the Sixth may well have been Shakespeare's first play to deal with the controversial topic of English history. If it was written before *Henry VI Part One*, as scholars have argued, then it was a courageous debut. The play was first published in 1594 with the title *The First Part of the Contention of the Two Famous Houses of York and Lancaster with the Death of the Good Duke Humphrey*, and this accurately reflects its subject, which is a state in turmoil where rival factions struggle for possession of the English crown. The Elizabethan authorities could be expected to scrutinise any play dealing with such a subject with special care, and there is evidence that at least one speech was suppressed for political reasons before the publication of the 1623 Folio. But despite the controversial nature of the events it relates, this play contains some of the period's sharpest political satire.

Shakespeare compresses into five acts the events of a decade, 1445–55. The play opens with a succession of scenes in which contending factions range themselves in opposition to one another: The Duke of Suffolk and Margaret, King Henry's queen, who hope to rule England through Margaret's influence with Henry; Cardinal Beaufort the Bishop of Winchester, who hopes to supplant Duke Humphrey of Gloucester as Protector of the Realm; Duke Humphrey's ambitious wife Eleanor, who plots to depose the king by magic; and Richard Plantagenet the Duke of York, who bides his time until he can seize the crown he regards as rightfully his. The impression is that the crown of England is public property, freely available to whichever member of the ruling classes proves trickiest and most unscrupulous. Gradually as the action unfolds the weaker factions fall away, until by the end of the third act there are only two opposing parties left. The supporters of the house of Lancaster gather about the king, and York prepares to seize the crown with the help of the Irish army. As the antagonism between Yorkists and Lancastrians grows, Shakespeare signals the approach of war with metaphors that invoke a rising storm. York warns that 'I will stir up in England some black storm/Shall blow ten thousand souls to heaven or hell' [3.1.349–50], Margaret relates how her approach to England was beset with stormy weather [3.2.73–121], and the corpse of the murdered Duke Humphrey is likened to 'the summer's corn by tempest lodged' [3.2.176]. The storm breaks in Act 4, when Jack Cade's rebellion erupts in Kent, stirred up by supporters of the Yorkist cause.

Shakespeare makes use of Cade's rebellion to satirise the claims of the rival factions. In Act 4 Scene 2 Cade invents his own spurious genealogy to support his claim to the throne, parodying York's earlier account of his descent [2.2]. In Cade's projected commonwealth 'all things shall be in common' [4.7.17] and the trappings that exclude working people from power shall be forbidden, from Latin and reading to lordships and fine clothes. Cade's incoherent dreams serve to stress the fact that the power-games of the aristocracy have nothing to do with the living conditions of the English public: that they are founded, in fact, on little more than grandiose words, of which the ruling classes have a monopoly. The point is driven home when Clifford disperses the rebellion with a rousing speech, in which he invokes the memory of Henry V to persuade the rebels that it would be better to fight the French than to involve themselves in political action at home.

By the end of Act 4 the rebel leader is left abandoned and starving, so that when a local squire succeeds in wounding him mortally Cade insists that 'Famine and no other hath slain me' [4.10.59]; he seems to believe that heroism contributes less towards the outcome of a battle than the condition of the common soldiers. The combat between York and Lancaster which follows in Act 5 is heralded with more grandiose words and punctuated with celebrations of the participants' heroism. But it is also fought with unprecedented savagery: the Lancastrian Clifford declares: 'York not our old men spares; No more will I their babes' [5.2.51–2]. This savagery is rendered the more dreadful by Cade's exposure of its irrelevance to most of its victims. Shakespeare's version of history in this play is not so much heroic as horribly farcical.

The Second Part of King Henry the Sixth

DRAMATIS PERSONAE

KING HENRY THE SIXTH

HUMPHREY, *Duke of Gloucester*
his uncle

CARDINAL BEAUFORT, *Bishop of Winchester, great-uncle to the King*

RICHARD PLANTAGENET
Duke of York

EDWARD and RICHARD
his sons

DUKE OF SOMERSET

DUKE OF SUFFOLK

DUKE OF BUCKINGHAM

LORD CLIFFORD

YOUNG CLIFFORD
his son

EARL OF SALISBURY

EARL OF WARWICK

LORD SCALES

LORD SAY

SIR HUMPHREY STAFFORD

WILLIAM STAFFORD
his brother

SIR JOHN STANLEY

VAUX

MATTHEW GOFFE

A Lieutenant, a Shipmaster, a Master's Mate and WALTER WHITMORE

Two Gentlemen, and prisoners with Suffolk

JOHN HUME and JOHN SOUTHWELL
two priests

ROGER BOLINGBROKE
a conjurer

A Spirit raised by him

THOMAS HORNER
an armourer

PETER
his man

Clerk of Chatham

Mayor of Saint Albans

SAUNDER SIMPCOX
an impostor

ALEXANDER IDEN
a Kentish gentleman

JACK CADE
a rebel

GEORGE BEVIS, JOHN HOLLAND, DICK *the butcher,* SMITH *the weaver,* MICHAEL, *etc. followers of Cade*

Two Murderers

MARGARET
Queen to King Henry

ELEANOR
Duchess of Gloucester

MARGERY JOURDAIN
a witch

Wife to Simpcox

Lords, Ladies, and Attendants; Petitioners, Aldermen, a Herald, a Beadle, a Sheriff, Officers, Citizens, Prentices, Falconers, Guards, Soldiers, and Messengers etc.

THE SCENE: ENGLAND.

ACT ONE

SCENE I. *London. The palace.*

Flourish of trumpets; then hautboys. Enter the KING, DUKE HUMPHREY OF GLOUCESTER, SALISBURY, WARWICK, and CARDINAL BEAUFORT, on the one side; the QUEEN, SUFFOLK, YORK, SOMERSET, and BUCKINGHAM, on the other.

SUFFOLK As by your high imperial Majesty
I had in charge at my depart for France,
As procurator to your Excellence,
To marry Princess Margaret for your Grace;
So, in the famous ancient city Tours,
In presence of the Kings of France and Sicil,
The Dukes of Orleans, Calaber, Bretagne, and Alencon,
Seven earls, twelve barons, and twenty reverend bishops,
I have perform'd my task, and was espous'd;
And humbly now upon my bended knee,
In sight of England and her lordly peers,
Deliver up my title in the Queen
To your most gracious hands, that are the substance

Of that great shadow I did represent:
The happiest gift that ever marquis gave,
The fairest queen that ever king receiv'd.

KING Suffolk, arise. Welcome, Queen Margaret:
I can express no kinder sign of love
Than this kind kiss. O Lord, that lends me life,
Lend me a heart replete with thankfulness!
For thou hast given me in this beauteous face
A world of earthly blessings to my soul,
If sympathy of love unite our thoughts.

QUEEN Great King of England, and my gracious lord,
The mutual conference that my mind hath had,
By day, by night, waking and in my dreams,
In courtly company or at my beads,
With you, mine alder-liefest sovereign,
Makes me the bolder to salute my king
With ruder terms, such as my wit affords
And over-joy of heart doth minister.

KING Her sight did ravish, but her grace in speech,
Her words y-clad with wisdom's majesty,
Makes me from wond'ring fall to weeping joys,
Such is the fulness of my heart's content.
Lords, with one cheerful voice welcome my love.

ALL [*Kneeling*] Long live Queen Margaret, England's happiness!

QUEEN We thank you all. [*Flourish.*

SUFFOLK My Lord Protector, so it please your Grace,
Here are the articles of contracted peace
Between our sovereign and the French King Charles,
For eighteen months concluded by consent.

GLOUCESTER [*Reads*] 'Imprimis: It is agreed between the French King Charles and William de la Pole, Marquess of Suffolk, ambassador for Henry King of England, that the said Henry shall espouse the Lady Margaret, daughter unto Reignier King of Naples, Sicilia, and Jerusalem, and crown her Queen of England ere the thirtieth of May next ensuing.
Item: That the duchy of Anjou and the county of Maine shall be released and delivered to the King her father' – [*Lets the paper fall.*

KING Uncle, how now!

GLOUCESTER Pardon me, gracious lord;
Some sudden qualm hath struck me at the heart,
And dimm'd mine eyes, that I can read no further.

KING Uncle of Winchester, I pray read on.

CARDINAL [*Reads*] 'Item: It is further agreed between them that the duchies of Anjou and Maine shall be released and delivered over to the King her father, and she sent over to the King of England's own proper cost and charges, without having any dowry.'

KING They please us well. Lord Marquess, kneel down:
We here create thee the first Duke of Suffolk,
And girt thee with the sword. Cousin of York,
We here discharge your Grace from being Regent
I' th' parts of France, till term of eighteen months
Be full expir'd. Thanks, uncle Winchester,
Gloucester, York, Buckingham, Somerset,
Salisbury, and Warwick;
We thank you all for this great favour done
In entertainment to my princely queen.
Come, let us in, and with all speed provide
To see her coronation be perform'd.

[*Exeunt King, Queen, and Suffolk.*

GLOUCESTER Brave peers of England, pillars of the state,
To you Duke Humphrey must unload his grief –
Your grief, the common grief of all the land.
What! did my brother Henry spend his youth,
His valour, coin, and people, in the wars?
Did he so often lodge in open field,
In winter's cold and summer's parching heat,
To conquer France, his true inheritance?
And did my brother Bedford toil his wits
To keep by policy what Henry got?
Have you yourselves, Somerset, Buckingham,
Brave York, Salisbury, and victorious Warwick,
Receiv'd deep scars in France and Normandy?
Or hath mine uncle Beaufort and myself,
With all the learned Council of the realm,
Studied so long, sat in the Council House
Early and late, debating to and fro
How France and Frenchmen might be kept in awe?
And had his Highness in his infancy
Crowned in Paris, in despite of foes?
And shall these labours and these honours die?
Shall Henry's conquest, Bedford's vigilance,
Your deeds of war, and all our counsel die?
O peers of England, shameful is this league!
Fatal this marriage, cancelling your fame,
Blotting your names from books of memory,
Razing the characters of your renown,
Defacing monuments of conquer'd France,
Undoing all, as all had never been!

CARDINAL Nephew, what means this passionate discourse,
This peroration with such circumstance?
For France, 'tis ours; and we will keep it still.

GLOUCESTER Ay, uncle, we will keep it if we can;
But now it is impossible we should.

Suffolk, the new-made duke that rules the roast,
Hath given the duchy of Anjou and Maine
Unto the poor King Reignier, whose large style
Agrees not with the leanness of his purse.

SALISBURY Now, by the death of Him that died for all,
These counties were the keys of Normandy!
But wherefore weeps Warwick, my valiant son?

WARWICK For grief that they are past recovery;
For were there hope to conquer them again
My sword should shed hot blood, mine eyes no tears.
Anjou and Maine! myself did win them both;
Those provinces these arms of mine did conquer;
And are the cities that I got with wounds
Deliver'd up again with peaceful words?
Mort Dieu!

YORK For Suffolk's duke, may he be suffocate,
That dims the honour of this warlike isle!
France should have torn and rent my very heart
Before I would have yielded to this league.
I never read but England's kings have had
Large sums of gold and dowries with their wives;
And our King Henry gives away his own
To match with her that brings no vantages.

GLOUCESTER A proper jest, and never heard before,
That Suffolk should demand a whole fifteenth
For costs and charges in transporting her!
She should have stay'd in France, and starv'd in France,
Before –

CARDINAL My Lord of Gloucester, now ye grow too hot:
It was the pleasure of my lord the King.

GLOUCESTER My Lord of Winchester, I know your mind;
'Tis not my speeches that you do mislike,
But 'tis my presence that doth trouble ye.
Rancour will out: proud prelate, in thy face
I see thy fury; if I longer stay
We shall begin our ancient bickerings.
Lordings, farewell; and say, when I am gone,
I prophesied France will be lost ere long. [*Exit.*

CARDINAL So, there goes our Protector in a rage.
'Tis known to you he is mine enemy;
Nay, more, an enemy unto you all,
And no great friend, I fear me, to the King.
Consider, lords, he is the next of blood
And heir apparent to the English crown.
Had Henry got an empire by his marriage
And all the wealthy kingdoms of the west,
There's reason he should be displease'd at it.
Look to it, lords; let not his smoothing words
Bewitch your hearts; be wise and circumspect.
What though the common people favour him,
Calling him 'Humphrey, the good Duke of Gloucester',
Clapping their hands, and crying with loud voice
'Jesu maintain your royal excellence!'
With 'God preserve the good Duke Humphrey!'
I fear me, lords, for all this flattering gloss,
He will be found a dangerous Protector.

BUCKINGHAM Why should he then protect our sovereign,
He being of age to govern of himself?
Cousin of Somerset, join you with me,
And all together, with the Duke of Suffolk,
We'll quickly hoise Duke Humphrey from his seat.

CARDINAL This weighty business will not brook delay;
I'll to the Duke of Suffolk presently. [*Exit.*

SOMERSET Cousin of Buckingham, though Humphrey's pride
And greatness of his place be grief to us,
Yet let us watch the haughty cardinal;
His insolence is more intolerable
Than all the princes in the land beside;
If Gloucester be displac'd, he'll be Protector.

BUCKINGHAM Or thou or I, Somerset, will be Protector,
Despite Duke Humphrey or the Cardinal.
[*Exeunt Buckingham and Somerset.*

SALISBURY Pride went before, ambition follows him.
While these do labour for their own preferement,
Behoves it us to labour for the realm.
I never saw but Humphrey Duke of Gloucester
Did bear him like a noble gentleman.
Oft have I seen the haughty Cardinal –
More like a soldier than a man o' th' church,
As stout and proud as he were lord of all –
Swear like a ruffian and demean himself
Unlike the ruler of a commonweal.
Warwick my son, the comfort of my age,
Thy deeds, thy plainness, and thy housekeeping,
Hath won the greatest favour of the commons,
Excepting none but good Duke Humphrey.
And, brother York, thy acts in Ireland,
In bringing them to civil discipline,
Thy late exploits done in the heart of France
When thou wert Regent for our sovereign,
Have made thee fear'd and honour'd of the people:

Join we together for the public good,
In what we can, to bridle and suppress
The pride of Suffolk and the Cardinal,
With Somerset's and Buckingham's ambition;
And, as we may, cherish Duke Humphrey's deeds
While they do tend the profit of the land.

WARWICK So God help Warwick, as he loves the land
And common profit of his country!

YORK And so says York – [*Aside*] for he hath greatest cause.

SALISBURY Then let's make haste away and look unto the main.

WARWICK Unto the main! O father, Maine is lost –
That Maine which by main force Warwick did win,
And would have kept so long as breath did last.
Main chance, father, you meant; but I meant Maine,
Which I will win from France, or else be slain.

[*Exeunt Warwick and Salisbury.*

YORK Anjou and Maine are given to the French;
Paris is lost; the state of Normandy
Stands on a tickle point now they are gone.
Suffolk concluded on the articles;
The peers agreed; and Henry was well pleas'd
To change two dukedoms for a duke's fair daughter.
I cannot blame them all: what is't to them?
'Tis thine they give away, and not their own.
Pirates may make cheap pennyworths of their pillage,
And purchase friends, and give to courtezans,
Still revelling like lords till all be gone;
While as the silly owner of the goods
Weeps over them and wrings his hapless hands
And shakes his head and trembling stands aloof,
While all is shar'd and all is borne away,
Ready to starve and dare not touch his own.
So York must sit and fret and bite his tongue,
While his own lands are bargain'd for and sold.
Methinks the realms of England, France, and Ireland,
Bear that proportion to my flesh and blood
As did the fatal brand Althaea burnt
Unto the prince's heart of Calydon.
Anjou and Maine both given unto the French!
Cold news for me, for I had hope of France,
Even as I have of fertile England's soil.
A day will come when York shall claim his own;
And therefore I will take the Nevil's parts,
And make a show of love to proud Duke Humphrey,
And when I spy advantage, claim the crown,
For that's the golden mark I seek to hit.
Nor shall proud Lancaster usurp my right,
Nor hold the sceptre in his childish fist,
Nor wear the diadem upon his head,
Whose church-like humours fits not for a crown.
Then, York, be still awhile, till time do serve;
Watch thou and wake, when others be asleep,
To pry into the secrets of the state;
Till Henry, surfeiting in joys of love
With his new bride and England's dear-bought queen,
And Humphrey with the peers be fall'n at jars;
Then will I raise aloft the milk-white rose,
With whose sweet smell the air shall be perfum'd,
And in my standard bear the arms of York,
To grapple with the house of Lancaster;
And force perforce I'll make him yield the crown,
Whose bookish rule hath pull'd fair England down. [*Exit.*

SCENE II. *The Duke of Gloucester's house.*

Enter DUKE HUMPHREY and his wife ELEANOR.

DUCHESS Why droops my lord, like over-ripen'd corn
Hanging the head at Ceres' plenteous load?
Why doth the great Duke Humphrey knit his brows,
As frowning at the favours of the world?
Why are thine eyes fix'd to the sullen earth,
Gazing on that which seems to dim thy sight?
What see'st thou there? King Henry's diadem,
Enchas'd with all the honours of the world?
If so, gaze on, and grovel on thy face
Until thy head be circled with the same.
Put forth thy hand, reach at the glorious gold.
What, is't too short? I'll lengthen it with mine;
And having both together heav'd it up,
We'll both together lift our heads to heaven,
And never more abase our sight so low
As to vouchsafe one glance unto the ground.

GLOUCESTER O Nell, sweet Nell, if thou dost love thy lord,
Banish the canker of ambitious thoughts!
And may that thought, when I imagine ill
Against my king and nephew, virtuous Henry,
Be my last breathing in this mortal world!
My troublous dreams this night doth make me sad.

DUCHESS What dream'd my lord? Tell me, and I'll requite it
With sweet rehearsal of my morning's dream.

GLOUCESTER Methought this staff, mine office badge in court,

Was broke in twain; by whom I have forgot,
But, as I think, it was by th' Cardinal;
And on the pieces of the broken wand
Were plac'd the heads of Edmund Duke of Somerset
And William de la Pole, first Duke of Suffolk.
This was my dream; what it doth bode God knows.

DUCHESS Tut, this was nothing but an argument
That he that breaks a stick of Gloucester's grove
Shall lose his head for his presumption.
But list to me, my Humphrey, my sweet Duke:
Methought I sat in seat of majesty
In the cathedral church of Westminster,
And in that chair where kings and queens were crown'd;
Where Henry and Dame Margaret kneel'd to me,
And on my head did set the diadem.

GLOUCESTER Nay, Eleanor, then must I chide outright.
Presumptuous dame, ill-nurtur'd Eleanor!
Art thou not second woman in the realm,
And the Protector's wife, belov'd of him?
Hast thou not worldly pleasure at command
Above the reach or compass of thy thought?
And wilt thou still be hammering treachery
To tumble down thy husband and thyself
From top of honour to disgrace's feet?
Away from me, and let me hear no more!

DUCHESS What, what, my lord! Are you so choleric
With Eleanor for telling but her dream?
Next time I'll keep my dreams unto myself
And not be check'd.

GLOUCESTER Nay, be not angry; I am pleas'd again.

Enter a Messenger.

MESSENGER My Lord Protector, 'tis his Highness' pleasure
You do prepare to ride unto Saint Albans,
Where as the King and Queen do mean to hawk.

GLOUCESTER I go. Come, Nell, thou wilt ride with us?

DUCHESS Yes, my good lord, I'll follow presently.

[*Exeunt Gloucester and Messenger.*

Follow I must; I cannot go before,
While Gloucester bears this base and humble mind.
Were I a man, a duke, and next of blood,
I would remove these tedious stumbling-blocks
And smooth my way upon their headless necks;
And, being a woman, I will not be slack
To play my part in Fortune's pageant.
Where are you there, Sir John? Nay, fear not, man,
We are alone; here's none but thee and I.

Enter HUME.

HUME Jesus preserve your royal Majesty!

DUCHESS What say'st thou? Majesty! I am but Grace.

HUME But, by the grace of God and Hume's advice,
Your Grace's title shall be multiplied.

DUCHESS What say'st thou, man? Hast thou as yet conferr'd
With Margery Jourdain, the cunning witch of Eie,
With Roger Bolingbroke, the conjurer?
And will they undertake to do me good?

HUME This they have promised, to show your Highness
A spirit rais'd from depth of underground
That shall make answer to such questions
As by your Grace shall be propounded him.

DUCHESS It is enough; I'll think upon the questions;
When from Saint Albans we do make return
We'll see these things effected to the full.
Here, Hume, take this reward; make merry, man,
With thy confederates in this weighty cause.

[*Exit.*

HUME Hume must make merry with the Duchess' gold;
Marry, and shall. But, how now, Sir John Hume!
Seal up your lips and give no words but mum:
The business asketh silent secrecy.
Dame Eleanor gives gold to bring the witch:
Gold cannot come amiss were she a devil.
Yet have I gold flies from another coast –
I dare not say from the rich Cardinal,
And from the great and new-made Duke of Suffolk;
Yet I do find it so; for, to be plain,
They, knowing Dame Eleanor's aspiring humour,
Have hired me to undermine the Duchess,
And buzz these conjurations in her brain.
They say 'A crafty knave does need no broker';
Yet am I Suffolk and the Cardinal's broker.
Hume, if you take not heed, you shall go near
To call them both a pair of crafty knaves.
Well, so it stands; and thus, I fear, at last
Hume's knavery will be the Duchess' wreck,
And her attainture will be Humphrey's fall.
Sort how it will, I shall have gold for all. [*Exit.*

SCENE III. *London. The palace.*

Enter three or four Petitioners, PETER, the Armourer's man, being one.

1 PETITIONER My masters, let's stand close; my

Lord Protector will come this way by and by, and then we may deliver our supplications in the quill.

2 PETITIONER Marry, the Lord protect him, for he's a good man, Jesu bless him!

Enter SUFFOLK and QUEEN.

1 PETITIONER Here 'a comes, methinks, and the Queen with him. I'll be the first, sure.

2 PETITIONER Come back, fool; this is the Duke of Suffolk and not my Lord Protector.

SUFFOLK How now, fellow! Wouldst anything with me?

1 PETITIONER I pray, my lord, pardon me; I took ye for my Lord Protector.

QUEEN [*Reads*] 'To my Lord Protector!' Are your supplications to his lordship? Let me see them. What is thine?

1 PETITIONER Mine is, an't please your Grace, against John Goodman, my Lord Cardinal's man, for keeping my house and lands, and wife and all, from me.

SUFFOLK Thy wife too! That's some wrong indeed. What's yours? What's here! [*Reads*] 'Against the Duke of Suffolk, for enclosing the commons of Melford.' How now, sir knave!

2 PETITIONER Alas, sir, I am but a poor petitioner of our whole township.

PETER [*Presenting his petition*] Against my master, Thomas Horner, for saying that the Duke of York was rightful heir to the crown.

QUEEN What say'st thou? Did the Duke of York say he was rightful heir to the crown?

PETER That my master was? No, forsooth. My master said that he was, and that the King was an usurper.

SUFFOLK Who is there? [*Enter Servant.*
Take this fellow in, and send for his master with a pursuivant presently. We'll hear more of your matter before the King.

[*Exit Servant with Peter.*

QUEEN And as for you, that love to be protected
Under the wings of our Protector's grace,
Begin your suits anew, and sue to him.
[*Tears the supplications.*
Away, base cullions! Suffolk, let them go.

ALL Come, let's be gone. [*Exeunt.*

QUEEN My Lord of Suffolk, say, is this the guise,
Is this the fashions in the court of England?
Is this the government of Britain's isle,
And this the royalty of Albion's king?
What, shall King Henry be a pupil still,
Under the surly Gloucester's governance?
Am I a queen in title and in style,
And must be made a subject to a duke?
I tell thee, Pole, when in the city Tours
Thou ran'st a tilt in honour of my love
And stol'st away the ladies' hearts of France,
I thought King Henry had resembled thee
In courage, courtship, and proportion;
But all his mind is bent to holiness,
To number Ave-Maries on his beads;
His champions are the prophets and apostles;
His weapons, holy saws of sacred writ;
His study is his tilt-yard, and his loves
Are brazen images of canonized saints.
I would the college of the Cardinals
Would choose him Pope, and carry him to Rome,
And set the triple crown upon his head;
That were a state fit for his holiness.

SUFFOLK Madam, be patient. As I was cause
Your Highness came to England, so will I
In England work your Grace's full content.

QUEEN Beside the haughty Protector, have we Beaufort
The imperious churchman; Somerset, Buckingham,
And grumbling York; and not the least of these
But can do more in England than the King.

SUFFOLK And he of these that can do most of all
Cannot do more in England than the Nevils;
Salisbury and Warwick are no simple peers.

QUEEN Not all these lords do vex me half so much
As that proud dame, the Lord Protector's wife.
She sweeps it through the court with troops of ladies,
More like an empress than Duke Humphrey's wife.
Strangers in court do take her for the Queen.
She bears a duke's revenues on her back,
And in her heart she scorns our poverty;
Shall I not live to be aveng'd on her?
Contemptuous base-born callet as she is,
She vaunted 'mongst her minions t' other day
The very train of her worst wearing gown
Was better worth than all my father's lands,
Till Suffolk gave two dukedoms for his daughter.

SUFFOLK Madam, myself have lim'd a bush for her,
And plac'd a quire of such enticing birds
That she will light to listen to the lays,
And never mount to trouble you again.
So, let her rest. And, madam, list to me,
For I am bold to counsel you in this:
Although we fancy not the Cardinal,
Yet must we join with him and with the lords,
Till we have brought Duke Humphrey in disgrace.

As for the Duke of York, this late complaint
Will make but little for his benefit.
So one by one we'll weed them all at last,
And you yourself shall steer the happy helm.

Sound a sennet. Enter the KING, DUKE HUMPHREY, CARDINAL BEAUFORT, BUCKINGHAM, YORK, SOMERSET, SALISBURY, WARWICK, and the DUCHESS OF GLOUCESTER.

KING For my part, noble lords, I care not which:
Or Somerset or York, all's one to me.
YORK If York have ill demean'd himself in France,
Then let him be denay'd the regentship.
SOMERSET If Somerset be unworthy of the place,
Let York be Regent; I will yield to him.
WARWICK Whether your Grace be worthy, yea or no,
Dispute not that; York is the worthier.
CARDINAL Ambitious Warwick, let thy betters speak.
WARWICK The Cardinal's not my better in the field.
BUCKINGHAM All in this presence are thy betters, Warwick.
WARWICK Warwick may live to be the best of all.
SALISBURY Peace, son! And show some reason, Buckingham,
Why Somerset should be preferr'd in this.
QUEEN Because the King, forsooth, will have it so.
GLOUCESTER Madam, the King is old enough himself
To give his censure. These are no women's matters.
QUEEN If he be old enough, what needs your Grace
To be Protector of his Excellence?
GLOUCESTER Madam, I am Protector of the realm;
And at his pleasure will resign my place.
SUFFOLK Resign it then, and leave thine insolence.
Since thou wert king – as who is king but thou? –
The commonwealth hath daily run to wrack,
The Dauphin hath prevail'd beyond the seas,
And all the peers and nobles of the realm
Have been as bondmen to thy sovereignty.
CARDINAL The commons hast thou rack'd; the clergy's bags
Are lank and lean with thy extortions.
SOMERSET Thy sumptuous buildings and thy wife's attire
Have cost a mass of public treasury.
BUCKINGHAM Thy cruelty in execution
Upon offenders hath exceeded law,
And left thee to the mercy of the law.
QUEEN Thy sale of offices and towns in France,
If they were known, as the suspect is great,
Would make thee quickly hop without thy head.

[Exit Gloucester. The Queen drops her fan.

Give me my fan. What, minion, can ye not?

[She gives the Duchess a box on the ear.

I cry your mercy, madam; was it you?
DUCHESS Was't I? Yea, I it was, proud Frenchwoman.
Could I come near your beauty with my nails,
I could set my ten commandments in your face.
KING Sweet aunt, be quiet; 'twas against her will.
DUCHESS Against her will, good King? Look to 't in time;
She'll hamper thee and dandle thee like a baby.
Though in this place most master wear no breeches,
She shall not strike Dame Eleanor unreveng'd.

[Exit.

BUCKINGHAM Lord Cardinal, I will follow Eleanor,
And listen after Humphrey, how he proceeds.
She's tickled now; her fume needs no spurs,
She'll gallop far enough to her destruction.

[Exit.

Re-enter GLOUCESTER.

GLOUCESTER Now, lords, my choler being overblown
With walking once about the quadrangle,
I come to talk of commonwealth affairs.
As for your spiteful false objections,
Prove them, and I lie open to the law;
But God in mercy so deal with my soul
As I in duty love my king and country!
But to the matter that we have in hand:
I say, my sovereign, York is meetest man
To be your Regent in the realm of France.
SUFFOLK Before we make election, give me leave
To show some reason, of no little force,
That York is most unmeet of any man.
YORK I'll tell thee, Suffolk, why I am unmeet:
First, for I cannot flatter thee in pride;
Next, if I be appointed for the place,
My Lord of Somerset will keep me here
Without discharge, money, or furniture,
Till France be won into the Dauphin's hands.
Last time I danc'd attendance on his will
Till Paris was besieg'd, famish'd, and lost.
WARWICK That can I witness; and a fouler fact
Did never traitor in the land commit.
SUFFOLK Peace, headstrong Warwick!
WARWICK Image of pride, why should I hold my peace?

Enter HORNER, the Armourer, and his man PETER, guarded.

SUFFOLK Because here is a man accus'd of treason:
Pray God the Duke of York excuse himself!

YORK Doth any one accuse York for a traitor?

KING What mean'st thou, Suffolk? Tell me, what are these?

SUFFOLK Please it your Majesty, this is the man
That doth accuse his master of high treason;
His words were these: that Richard Duke of York
Was rightful heir unto the English crown,
And that your Majesty was an usurper.

KING Say, man, were these thy words?

HORNER An't shall please your Majesty, I never said nor thought any such matter. God is my witness, I am falsely accus'd by the villain.

PETER [*Holding up his hands*] By these ten bones, my lords, he did speak them to me in the garret one night, as we were scouring my Lord of York's armour.

YORK Base dunghill villain and mechanical,
I'll have thy head for this thy traitor's speech.
I do beseech your royal Majesty,
Let him have all the rigour of the law.

HORNER Alas, my lord, hang me if ever I spake the words. My accuser is my prentice; and when I did correct him for his fault the other day, he did vow upon his knees he would be even with me. I have good witness of this; therefore I beseech your Majesty, do not cast away an honest man for a villain's accusation.

KING Uncle, what shall we say to this in law?

GLOUCESTER This doom, my lord, if I may judge:
Let Somerset be Regent o'er the French,
Because in York this breeds suspicion;
And let these have a day appointed them
For single combat in convenient place,
For he hath witness of his servant's malice.
This is the law, and this Duke Humphrey's doom.

SOMERSET I humbly thank your royal Majesty.

HORNER And I accept the combat willingly.

PETER Alas, my lord, I cannot fight; for God's sake, pity my case! The spite of man prevaileth against me. O Lord, have mercy upon me, I shall never be able to fight a blow! O Lord, my heart!

GLOUCESTER Sirrah, or you must fight or else be hang'd.

KING Away with them to prison; and the day of combat shall be the last of the next month.
Come, Somerset, we'll see thee sent away.

[*Flourish. Exeunt.*

SCENE IV. *London. The Duke of Gloucester's garden.*

Enter MARGERY JOURDAIN, the witch; the two priests, HUME and SOUTHWELL; and BOLINGBROKE.

HUME Come, my masters; the Duchess, I tell you, expects performance of your promises.

BOLINGBROKE Master Hume, we are therefore provided; will her ladyship behold and hear our exorcisms?

HUME Ay, what else? Fear you not her courage.

BOLINGBROKE I have heard her reported to be a woman of an invincible spirit; but it shall be convenient, Master Hume, that you be by her aloft while we be busy below; and so I pray you go, in God's name, and leave us. [*Exit Hume*] Mother Jourdain, be you prostrate and grovel on the earth; John Southwell, read you; and let us to our work.

Enter DUCHESS aloft, followed by HUME.

DUCHESS Well said, my masters; and welcome all. To this gear, the sooner the better.

BOLINGBROKE Patience, good lady; wizards know their times:
Deep night, dark night, the silent of the night,
The time of night when Troy was set on fire;
The time when screech-owls cry and bandogs howl,
And spirits walk and ghosts break up their graves –
That time best fits the work we have in hand.
Madam, sit you, and fear not: whom we raise
We will make fast within a hallow'd verge.

[*Here they do the ceremonies belonging, and make the circle; Bolingbroke or Southwell reads:* 'Conjuro te,' etc. *It thunders and lightens terribly; then the Spirit riseth.*

SPIRIT Adsum.

MARGERY JOURDAIN Asmath,
By the eternal God, whose name and power
Thou tremblest at, answer that I shall ask;
For till thou speak thou shalt not pass from hence.

SPIRIT Ask what thou wilt; that I had said and done.

BOLINGBROKE [*Reads*] 'First of the King: what shall of him become?'

SPIRIT The Duke yet lives that Henry shall depose;
But him outlive, and die a violent death.

[*As the Spirit speaks, Southwell writes the answer.*

BOLINGBROKE 'What fates await the Duke of Suffolk?'

SPIRIT By water shall he die and take his end.'

BOLINGBROKE 'What shall befall the Duke of Somerset?'

SPIRIT Let him shun castles:
Safer shall he be upon the sandy plains
Than where castles mounted stand.
Have done, for more I hardly can endure.

BOLINGBROKE Descend to darkness and the burning lake;
False fiend, avoid!

[Thunder and lightning. Exit Spirit.

Enter the DUKE OF YORK and the DUKE OF BUCKINGHAM with their Guard, and break in.

YORK Lay hands upon these traitors and their trash.
Beldam, I think we watch'd you at an inch.
What, madam, are you there? The King and commonweal
Are deeply indebted for this piece of pains;
My Lord Protector will, I doubt it not,
See you well guerdon'd for these good deserts.

DUCHESS Not half so bad as thine to England's king,
Injurious Duke, that threatest where's no cause.

BUCKINGHAM True, madam, none at all. What call you this?
Away with them! let them be clapp'd up close,
And kept asunder. You, madam, shall with us.
Stafford, take her to thee.
We'll see your trinkets here all forthcoming.
All, away!

[Exeunt, above, Duchess and Hume, guarded; below, Witch, Southwell and Bolingbroke, guarded.

YORK Lord Buckingham, methinks you watch'd her well.
A pretty plot, well chosen to build upon!
Now, pray, my lord, let's see the devil's writ.
What have we here? *[Reads.*
'The duke yet lives that Henry shall depose;
But him outlive, and die a violent death.'
Why, this is just
'Aio te, Aeacida, Romanos vincere posse'.
Well, to the rest:
'Tell me what fate awaits the Duke of Suffolk?
'By water shall he die and take his end.'
'What shall betide the Duke of Somerset?'
'Let him shun castles;
Safer shall he be upon the sandy plains
Than where castles mounted stand.
Come, come, my lords;
These oracles are hardly attain'd,
And hardly understood.
The King is now in progress towards Saint Albans,
With him the husband of this lovely lady;
Thither go these news as fast as horse can carry them –
A sorry breakfast for my Lord Protector.

BUCKINGHAM Your Grace shall give me leave, my Lord of York,
To be the post, in hope of his reward.

YORK At your pleasure, my good lord.
Who's within there, ho?

Enter a Servant.

Invite my Lords of Salisbury and Warwick
To sup with me to-morrow night. Away!

[Exeunt.

ACT TWO

SCENE I. *Saint Albans.*

Enter the KING, QUEEN, GLOUCESTER, CARDINAL, and SUFFOLK, with Falconers halloing.

QUEEN Believe me, lords, for flying at the brook,
I saw not better sport these seven years' day;
Yet, by your leave, the wind was very high,
And ten to one old Joan had not gone out.

KING But what a point, my lord, your falcon made,
And what a pitch she flew above the rest!
To see how God in all His creatures works!
Yea, man and birds are fain of climbing high.

SUFFOLK No marvel, an it like your Majesty,
My Lord Protector's hawks do tow'r so well;
They know their master loves to be aloft,
And bears his thoughts above his falcon's pitch.

GLOUCESTER My lord, 'tis but a base ignoble mind
That mounts no higher than a bird can soar.

CARDINAL I thought as much; he would be above the clouds.

GLOUCESTER Ay, my lord Cardinal, how think you by that?
Were it not good your Grace could fly to heaven?

KING The treasury of everlasting joy!

CARDINAL Thy heaven is on earth; thine eyes and thoughts
Beat on a crown, the treasure of thy heart;
Pernicious Protector, dangerous peer,
That smooth'st it so with King and commonweal.

GLOUCESTER What, Cardinal, is your priesthood grown peremptory?

Tantaene animis coelestibus irae?
Churchmen so hot? Good uncle, hide such malice;
With such holiness can you do it?
SUFFOLK No malice, sir; no more than well becomes
So good a quarrel and so bad a peer.
GLOUCESTER As who, my lord?
SUFFOLK Why, as you, my lord,
An't like your lordly Lord's Protectorship.
GLOUCESTER Why, Suffolk, England knows thine insolence.
QUEEN And thy ambition, Gloucester.
KING I prithee, peace,
Good Queen, and whet not on these furious peers;
For blessed are the peacemakers on earth.
CARDINAL Let me be blessed for the peace I make
Against this proud Protector with my sword!
GLOUCESTER *[Aside to Cardinal]* Faith, holy uncle, would 'twere come to that!
CARDINAL *[Aside to Gloucester]* Marry, when thou dar'st.
GLOUCESTER *[Aside to Cardinal]* Make up no factious numbers for the matter;
In thine own person answer thy abuse.
CARDINAL *[Aside to Gloucester]* Ay, where thou dar'st not peep; an if thou dar'st,
This evening on the east side of the grove.
KING How now, my lords!
CARDINAL Believe me, cousin Gloucester,
Had not your man put up the fowl so suddenly,
We had had more sport. *[Aside to Gloucester]*
Come with thy two-hand sword.
GLOUCESTER True, uncle.
CARDINAL *[Aside to Gloucester]* Are ye advis'd? The east side of the grove?
GLOUCESTER *[Aside to Cardinal]* Cardinal, I am with you.
KING Why, how now, uncle Gloucester!
GLOUCESTER Talking of hawking; nothing else, my lord.
[Aside to Cardinal] Now, by God's Mother, priest,
I'll shave your crown for this,
Or all my fence shall fail.
CARDINAL *[Aside to Gloucester]* Medice, teipsum;
Protector, see to't well; protect yourself.
KING The winds grow high; so do your stomachs, lords.
How irksome is this music to my heart!
When such strings jar, what hope of harmony?
I pray, my lords, let me compound this strife.

Enter a Townsman of Saint Albans, crying 'A miracle! '

GLOUCESTER What means this noise?
Fellow, what miracle dost thou proclaim?
TOWNSMAN A miracle! a miracle!
SUFFOLK Come to the King, and tell him what miracle.
TOWNSMAN Forsooth, a blind man at Saint Albans shrine
Within this half hour hath receiv'd his sight;
A man that ne'er saw in his life before.
KING Now God be prais'd that to believing souls
Gives light in darkness, comfort in despair!

Enter the Mayor of Saint Albans and his Brethren, bearing SIMPCOX between two in a chair; his Wife and a multitude following.

CARDINAL Here comes the townsmen on procession
To present your Highness with the man.
KING Great is his comfort in this earthly vale,
Although by his sight his sin be multiplied.
GLOUCESTER Stand by, my masters; bring him near the King;
His Highness' pleasure is to talk with him.
KING Good fellow, tell us here the circumstance,
That we for thee may glorify the Lord.
What, hast thou been long blind and now restor'd?
SIMPCOX Born blind, an't please your Grace.
WIFE Ay indeed was he.
SUFFOLK What woman is this?
WIFE His wife, an't like your worship.
GLOUCESTER Hadst thou been his mother, thou couldst have better told.
KING Where wert thou born?
SIMPCOX At Berwick in the north, an't like your Grace.
KING Poor soul, God's goodness hath been great to thee.
Let never day nor night unhallowed pass,
But still remember what the Lord hath done.
QUEEN Tell me, good fellow, cam'st thou here by chance,
Or of devotion, to this holy shrine?
SIMPCOX God knows, of pure devotion; being call'd
A hundred times and oft'ner, in my sleep,
By good Saint Alban, who said 'Simpcox, come,
Come, offer at my shrine, and I will help thee'.
WIFE Most true, forsooth; and many time and oft
Myself have heard a voice to call him so.
CARDINAL What, art thou lame?
SIMPCOX Ay, God Almighty help me!
SUFFOLK How cam'st thou so?
SIMPCOX A fall off of a tree.
WIFE A plum tree, master.
GLOUCESTER How long hast thou been blind?
SIMPCOX O, born so, master!

GLOUCESTER What, and wouldst climb a tree?

SIMPCOX But that in all my life, when I was a youth.

WIFE Too true; and bought his climbing very dear.

GLOUCESTER Mass, thou lov'dst plums well, that wouldst venture so.

SIMPCOX Alas, good master, my wife desir'd some damsons
And made me climb, with danger of my life.

GLOUCESTER A subtle knave! But yet it shall not serve:
Let me see thine eyes; wink now; now open them;
In my opinion yet thou seest not well.

SIMPCOX Yes, master, clear as day, I thank God and Saint Alban.

GLOUCESTER Say'st thou me so? What colour is this cloak of?

SIMPCOX Red, master; red as blood.

GLOUCESTER Why, that's well said. What colour is my gown of?

SIMPCOX Black, forsooth; coal-black as jet.

KING Why, then, thou know'st what colour jet is of?

SUFFOLK And yet, I think, jet did he never see.

GLOUCESTER But cloaks and gowns before this day a many.

WIFE Never before this day in all his life.

GLOUCESTER Tell me, sirrah, what's my name?

SIMPCOX Alas, master, I know not.

GLOUCESTER What's his name?

SIMPCOX I know not.

GLOUCESTER Nor his?

SIMPCOX No, indeed, master.

GLOUCESTER What's thine own name?

SIMPCOX Saunder Simpcox, an if it please you, master.

GLOUCESTER Then, Saunder, sit there, the lying'st knave in Christendom. If thou hadst been born blind, thou mightst as well have known all our names as thus to name the several colours we do wear. Sight may distinguish of colours; but suddenly to nominate them all, it is impossible. My lords, Saint Alban here hath done a miracle; and would ye not think it cunning to be great that could restore this cripple to his legs again?

SIMPCOX O master, that you could!

GLOUCESTER My master, of Saint Albans, have you not beadles in your town, and things call'd whips?

MAYOR Yes, my lord, if it please your Grace.

GLOUCESTER Then send for one presently.

MAYOR Sirrah, go fetch the beadle hither straight.
[Exit an Attendant.

GLOUCESTER Now fetch me a stool hither by and by. *[A stool brought]* Now, sirrah, if you mean to save yourself from whipping, leap me over this stool and run away.

SIMPCOX Alas, master, I am not able to stand alone!
You go about to torture me in vain.

Enter a Beadle with whips.

GLOUCESTER Well, sir, we must have you find your legs. Sirrah beadle, whip him till he leap over that same stool.

BEADLE I will, my lord. Come on, sirrah; off with your doublet quickly.

SIMPCOX Alas, master, what shall I do? I am not able to stand.

[After the Beadle hath hit him once, he leaps over the stool and runs away; and they follow and cry 'A miracle!'

KING O God, seest Thou this, and bearest so long?

QUEEN It made me laugh to see the villain run.

GLOUCESTER Follow the knave, and take this drab away.

WIFE Alas, sir, we did it for pure need!

GLOUCESTER Let them be whipp'd through every market town till they come to Berwick, from whence they came.
[Exeunt Mayor, Beadle, Wife, etc.

CARDINAL Duke Humphrey has done a miracle to-day.

SUFFOLK True; made the lame to leap and fly away.

GLOUCESTER But you have done more miracles than I:
You made in a day, my lord, whole towns to fly.

Enter BUCKINGHAM.

KING What tidings with our cousin Buckingham?

BUCKINGHAM Such as my heart doth tremble to unfold:
A sort of naughty persons, lewdly bent,
Under the countenance and confederacy
Of Lady Eleanor, the Protector's wife,
The ringleader and head of all this rout,
Have practis'd dangerously against your state,
Dealing with witches and with conjurers,
Whom we have apprehended in the fact,
Raising up wicked spirits from under ground,
Demanding of King Henry's life and death
And other of your Highness' Privy Council,
As more at large your Grace shall understand.

CARDINAL And so, my Lord Protector, by this means
Your lady is forthcoming yet at London.
This news, I think, hath turn'd your weapon's edge;

'Tis like, my lord, you will not keep your hour.
GLOUCESTER Ambitious churchman, leave to afflict my heart.
Sorrow and grief have vanquish'd all my powers;
And, vanquish'd as I am, I yield to thee
Or to the meanest groom.
KING O God, what mischiefs work the wicked ones,
Heaping confusion on their own heads thereby!
QUEEN Gloucester, see here the tainture of thy nest;
And look thyself be faultless, thou wert best.
GLOUCESTER Madam, for myself, to heaven I do appeal
How I have lov'd my King and commonweal;
And for my wife I know not how it stands.
Sorry I am to hear what I have heard.
Noble she is; but if she have forgot
Honour and virtue, and convers'd with such
As, like to pitch, defile nobility,
I banish her my bed and company
And give her as a prey to law and shame,
That hath dishonoured Gloucester's honest name.
KING Well, for this night we will repose us here.
To-morrow toward London back again
To look into this business thoroughly
And call these foul offenders to their answers,
And poise the cause in justice' equal scales,
Whose beam stands sure, whose rightful cause prevails. *[Flourish. Exeunt.*

SCENE II. *London. The Duke of York's garden.*

Enter YORK, SALISBURY, and WARWICK.

YORK Now, my good Lords of Salisbury and Warwick,
Our simple supper ended, give me leave
In this close walk to satisfy myself
In craving your opinion of my title,
Which is infallible, to England's crown.
SALISBURY My lord, I long to hear it at full.
WARWICK Sweet York, begin; and if thy claim be good,
The Nevils are thy subjects to command.
YORK Then thus:
Edward the Third, my lords, had seven sons;
The first, Edward the Black Prince, Prince of Wales;
The second, William of Hatfield; and the third,
Lionel Duke of Clarence; next to whom
Was John of Gaunt, the Duke of Lancaster;
The fifth was Edmund Langley, Duke of York;
The sixth was Thomas of Woodstock, Duke of Gloucester;
William of Windsor was the seventh and last.
Edward the Black Prince died before his father
And left behind him Richard, his only son,
Who, after Edward the Third's death, reign'd as king
Till Henry Bolingbroke, Duke of Lancaster,
The eldest son and heir of John of Gaunt,
Crown'd by the name of Henry the Fourth,
Seiz'd on the realm, depos'd the rightful king,
Sent his poor queen to France, from whence she came,
And him to Pomfret, where, as all you know,
Harmless Richard was murdered traitorously.
WARWICK Father, the Duke hath told the truth;
Thus got the house of Lancaster the crown.
YORK Which now they hold by force, and not by right;
For Richard, the first son's heir, being dead,
The issue of the next son should have reign'd.
SALISBURY But William of Hatfield died without an heir.
YORK The third son, Duke of Clarence, from whose line
I claim the crown, had issue Philippe, a daughter,
Who married Edmund Mortimer, Earl of March;
Edmund had issue, Roger Earl of March;
Roger had issue, Edmund, Anne, and Eleanor.
SALISBURY This Edmund, in the reign of Bolingbroke,
As I have read, laid claim unto the crown;
And, but for Owen Glendower, had been king,
Who kept him in captivity till he died.
But, to the rest.
YORK His eldest sister, Anne,
My mother, being heir unto the crown,
Married Richard Earl of Cambridge, who was son
To Edmund Langley, Edward the Third's fifth son.
By her I claim the kingdom: she was heir
To Roger Earl of March, who was the son
Of Edmund Mortimer, who married Philippe,
Sole daughter unto Lionel Duke of Clarence;
So, if the issue of the elder son
Succeed before the younger, I am King.
WARWICK What plain proceedings is more plain than this?
Henry doth claim the crown from John of Gaunt,
The fourth son: York claims it from the third.
Till Lionel's issue fails, his should not reign.
It fails not yet, but flourishes in thee
And in thy sons, fair slips of such a stock.
Then, father Salisbury, kneel we together,
And in this private plot be we the first
That shall salute our rightful sovereign
With honour of his birthright to the crown.

BOTH Long live our sovereign Richard, England's King!
YORK We thank you, lords. But I am not your king
Till I be crown'd, and that my sword be stain'd
With heart-blood of the house of Lancaster;
And that's not suddenly to be perform'd,
But with advice and silent secrecy.
Do you as I do in these dangerous days:
Wink at the Duke of Suffolk's insolence,
At Beaufort's pride, at Somerset's ambition,
At Buckingham, and all the crew of them,
Till they have snar'd the shepherd of the flock,
That virtuous prince, the good Duke Humphrey;
'Tis that they seek; and they, in seeking that,
Shall find their deaths, if York can prophesy.
SALISBURY My lord, break we off; we know your mind at full.
WARWICK My heart assures me that the Earl of Warwick
Shall one day make the Duke of York a king.
YORK And, Nevil, this I do assure myself,
Richard shall live to make the Earl of Warwick
The greatest man in England but the King.
[*Exeunt.*

SCENE III. *London. A hall of justice.*

Sound trumpets. Enter the KING and State: the QUEEN, GLOUCESTER, YORK, SUFFOLK, and SALISBURY, with Guard, to banish the Duchess. Enter, guarded, the DUCHESS OF GLOUCESTER, MARGERY JOURDAIN, HUME, SOUTHWELL, and BOLINGBROKE.

KING Stand forth, Dame Eleanor Cobham, Gloucester's wife:
In sight of God and us, your guilt is great;
Receive the sentence of the law for sins
Such as by God's book are adjudg'd to death.
You four, from hence to prison back again;
From thence unto the place of execution:
The witch in Smithfield shall be burnt to ashes,
And you three shall be strangled on the gallows.
You, madam, for you are more nobly born,
Despoiled of your honour in your life,
Shall, after three days' open penance done,
Live in your country here in banishment
With Sir John Stanley in the Isle of Man.
DUCHESS Welcome is banishment; welcome were my death.
GLOUCESTER Eleanor, the law, thou seest, hath judged thee.
I cannot justify whom the law condemns.
[*Exeunt the Duchess and the other prisoners, guarded.*
Mine eyes are full of tears, my heart of grief.
Ah, Humphrey, this dishonour in thine age
Will bring thy head with sorrow to the ground!
I beseech your Majesty give me leave to go;
Sorrow would solace, and mine age would ease.
KING Stay, Humphrey Duke of Gloucester; ere thou go,
Give up thy staff; Henry will to himself
Protector be; and God shall be my hope,
My stay, my guide, and lantern to my feet.
And go in peace, Humphrey, no less belov'd
Than when thou wert Protector to thy King.
QUEEN I see no reason why a king of years
Should be to be protected like a child.
God and King Henry govern England's realm!
Give up your staff, sir, and the King his realm.
GLOUCESTER My staff! Here, noble Henry, is my staff.
As willingly do I the same resign
As ere thy father Henry made it mine;
And even as willingly at thy feet I leave it
As others would ambitiously receive it.
Farewell, good King; when I am dead and gone,
May honourable peace attend thy throne! [*Exit.*
QUEEN Why, now is Henry King, and Margaret Queen,
And Humphrey Duke of Gloucester scarce himself,
That bears so shrewd a maim: two pulls at once –
His lady banish'd and a limb lopp'd off.
This staff of honour raught, there let it stand
Where it best fits to be, in Henry's hand.
SUFFOLK Thus droops this lofty pine and hangs his sprays;
Thus Eleanor's pride dies in her youngest days.
YORK Lords, let him go. Please it your Majesty,
This is the day appointed for the combat;
And ready are the appellant and defendant,
The armourer and his man, to enter the lists,
So please your Highness to behold the fight.
QUEEN Ay, good my lord; for purposely therefore
Left I the court, to see this quarrel tried.
KING A God's name, see the lists and all things fit;
Here let them end it, and God defend the right!
YORK I never saw a fellow worse bested,
Or more afraid to fight, than is the appellant,
The servant of this armourer, my lords.

Enter at one door, HORNER, the Armourer, and his Neighbours, drinking to him so much that he is drunk; and he enters with a drum before him and his staff with a sand-bag fastened to it; and at the other door PETER, his man, with a drum and sand-bag, and Prentices drinking to him.

1 NEIGHBOUR Here, neighbour Horner, I drink to you in a cup of sack; and fear not, neighbour, you shall do well enough.

2 NEIGHBOUR And here, neighbour, here's a cup of charneco.

3 NEIGHBOUR And here's a pot of good double beer, neighbour; drink, and fear not your man.

HORNER Let it come, i' faith, and I'll pledge you all; and a fig for Peter!

1 PRENTICE Here, Peter, I drink to thee; and be not afraid.

2 PRENTICE Be merry, Peter, and fear not thy master: fight for credit of the prentices.

PETER I thank you all. Drink, and pray for me, I pray you; for I think I have taken my last draught in this world. Here, Robin, an if I die, I give thee my apron; and, Will, thou shalt have my hammer; and here, Tom, take all the money that I have. O Lord bless me, I pray God! for I am never able to deal with my master, he hath learnt so much fence already.

SALISBURY Come, leave your drinking and fall to blows. Sirrah, what's thy name?

PETER Peter, forsooth.

SALISBURY Peter? What more?

PETER Thump.

SALISBURY Thump? Then see thou thump thy master well.

HORNER Masters, I am come hither, as it were, upon my man's instigation, to prove him a knave and myself an honest man; and touching the Duke of York, I will take my death I never meant him any ill, nor the King, nor the Queen; and therefore, Peter, have at thee with a downright blow!

YORK Dispatch – this knave's tongue begins to double.
Sounds, trumpets, alarum to the combatants!

[Alarum. They fight, and Peter strikes him down.

HORNER Hold, Peter, hold! I confess, I confess treason. *[Dies.*

YORK Take away his weapon. Fellow, thank God, and the good wine in thy master's way.

PETER O God, have I overcome mine enemies in this presence? O Peter, thou hast prevail'd in right!

KING Go, take hence that traitor from our sight,
For by his death we do perceive his guilt;
And God in justice hath reveal'd to us
The truth and innocence of this poor fellow,
Which he had thought to have murder'd wrongfully.
Come, fellow, follow us for thy reward.

[Sound a flourish. Exeunt.

SCENE IV. *London. A street.*

Enter DUKE HUMPHREY and his Men, in mourning cloaks.

GLOUCESTER Thus sometimes hath the brightest day a cloud,
And after summer evermore succeeds
Barren winter, with his wrathful nipping cold;
So cares and joys abound, as seasons fleet.
Sirs, what's o'clock?

SERVANT Ten, my lord.

GLOUCESTER Ten is the hour that was appointed me
To watch the coming of my punish'd duchess.
Uneath may she endure the flinty streets
To tread them with her tender-feeling feet.
Sweet Nell, ill can thy noble mind abrook
The abject people gazing on thy face,
With envious looks, laughing at thy shame,
That erst did follow thy proud chariot wheels
When thou didst ride in triumph through the streets.
But, soft! I think she comes, and I'll prepare
My tear-stain'd eyes to see her miseries.

Enter the DUCHESS OF GLOUCESTER in a white sheet, and a taper burning in her hand, with SIR JOHN STANLEY, the Sheriff, and Officers.

SERVANT So please your Grace, we'll take her from the sheriff.

GLOUCESTER No, stir not for your lives; let her pass by.

DUCHESS Come you, my lord, to see my open shame?
Now thou dost penance too. Look how they gaze!
See how the giddy multitude do point
And nod their heads and throw their eyes on thee!
Ah, Gloucester, hide thee from their hateful looks,
And, in thy closet pent up, rue my shame
And ban thine enemies, both mine and thine!

GLOUCESTER Be patient, gentle Nell; forget this grief.

DUCHESS Ah, Gloucester, teach me to forget myself!
For whilst I think I am thy married wife
And thou a prince, Protector of this land,
Methinks I should not thus be led along,
Mail'd up in shame, with papers on my back,
And follow'd with a rabble that rejoice
To see my tears and hear my deep-fet groans.
The ruthless flint doth cut my tender feet,
And when I start, the envious people laugh
And bid me be advised how I tread.
Ah, Humphrey, can I bear this shameful yoke?
Trowest thou that e'er I'll look upon the world

Or count them happy that enjoy the sun?
No; dark shall be my light and night my day;
To think upon my pomp shall be my hell.
Sometimes I'll say I am Duke Humphrey's wife,
And he a prince, and ruler of the land;
Yet so he rul'd, and such a prince he was,
As he stood by whilst I, his forlorn duchess,
Was made a wonder and a pointing-stock
To every idle rascal follower.
But be thou mild, and blush not at my shame,
Nor stir at nothing till the axe of death
Hang over thee, as sure it shortly will.
For Suffolk – he that can do all in all
With her that hateth thee and hates us all –
And York, and impious Beaufort, that false priest,
Have all lim'd bushes to betray thy wings,
And, fly thou how thou canst, they'll tangle thee.
But fear not thou until thy foot be snar'd,
Nor never seek prevention of thy foes.

GLOUCESTER Ah, Nell, forbear! Thou aimest all awry.
I must offend before I be attainted;
And had I twenty times so many foes,
And each of them had twenty times their power,
All these could not procure me any scathe
So long as I am loyal, true, and crimeless.
Wouldst have me rescue thee from this reproach?
Why, yet thy scandal were not wip'd away,
But I in danger for the breach of law.
Thy greatest help is quiet, gentle Nell.
I pray thee sort thy heart to patience;
These few days' wonder will be quickly worn.

Enter a Herald.

HERALD I summon your Grace to his Majesty's Parliament,
Holden at Bury the first of this next month.

GLOUCESTER And my consent ne'er ask'd herein before!
This is close dealing. Well, I will be there.
[*Exit Herald.*
My Nell, I take my leave – and, master sheriff,
Let not her penance exceed the King's commission.

SHERIFF An't please your Grace, here my commission stays;
And Sir John Stanley is appointed now
To take her with him to the Isle of Man.

GLOUCESTER Must you, Sir John, protect my lady here?

STANLEY So am I given in charge, may't please your Grace.

GLOUCESTER Entreat her not the worse in that I pray
You use her well; the world may laugh again,
And I may live to do you kindness if
You do it her. And so, Sir John, farewell.

DUCHESS What, gone, my lord, and bid me not farewell!

GLOUCESTER Witness my tears, I cannot stay to speak. [*Exeunt Gloucester and Servants.*

DUCHESS Art thou gone too? All comfort go with thee!
For none abides with me. My joy is death –
Death, at whose name I oft have been afeard,
Because I wish'd this world's eternity.
Stanley, I prithee go, and take me hence;
I care not whither, for I beg no favour,
Only convey me where thou art commanded.

STANLEY Why, madam, that is to the Isle of Man,
There to be us'd according to your state.

DUCHESS That's bad enough, for I am but reproach –
And shall I then be us'd reproachfully?

STANLEY Like to a duchess and Duke Humphrey's lady;
According to that state you shall be us'd.

DUCHESS Sheriff, farewell, and better than I fare,
Although thou hast been conduct of my shame.

SHERIFF It is my office; and, madam, pardon me.

DUCHESS Ay, ay, farewell; thy office is discharg'd.
Come, Stanley, shall we go?

STANLEY Madam, your penance done, throw off this sheet,
And go we to attire you for our journey.

DUCHESS My shame will not be shifted with my sheet.
No, it will hang upon my richest robes
And show itself, attire me how I can.
Go, lead the way; I long to see my prison.
[*Exeunt.*

ACT THREE

SCENE I. *The Abbey at Bury St. Edmunds.*

Sound a sennet. Enter the KING, the QUEEN, CARDINAL, SUFFOLK, YORK, BUCKINGHAM, SALISBURY, and WARWICK, to the Parliament.

KING I muse my Lord of Gloucester is not come.
'Tis not his wont to be the hindmost man,
Whate'er occasion keeps him from us now.

QUEEN Can you not see, or will ye not observe
The strangeness of his alter'd countenance?
With what a majesty he bears himself;
How insolent of late he is become,
How proud, how peremptory, and unlike himself?
We know the time since he was mild and affable,
And if we did but glance a far-off look
Immediately he was upon his knee,
That all the court admir'd him for submission.
But meet him now and be it in the morn,
When every one will give the time of day,
He knits his brow and shows an angry eye
And passeth by with stiff unbowed knee,
Disdaining duty that to us belongs.
Small curs are not regarded when they grin,
But great men tremble when the lion roars,
And Humphrey is no little man in England.
First note that he is near you in descent,
And should you fall he is the next will mount;
Me seemeth, then, it is no policy –
Respecting what a rancorous mind he bears,
And his advantage following your decease –
That he should come about your royal person
Or be admitted to your Highness' Council.
By flattery hath he won the commons' hearts;
And when he please to make commotion,
'Tis to be fear'd they all will follow him.
Now 'tis the spring, and weeds are shallow-rooted;
Suffer them now, and they'll o'ergrow the garden
And choke the herbs for want of husbandry.
The reverent care I bear unto my lord
Made me collect these dangers in the Duke.
If it be fond, call it a woman's fear;
Which fear if better reasons can supplant,
I will subscribe, and say I wrong'd the Duke.
My Lord of Suffolk, Buckingham, and York,
Reprove my allegation if you can,
Or else conclude my words effectual.

SUFFOLK Well hath your Highness seen into this duke;
And had I first been put to speak my mind,
I think I should have told your Grace's tale.
The Duchess, by his subornation,
Upon my life, began her devilish practices;
Or if he were not privy to those faults,
Yet by reputing of his high descent –
As next the King he was successive heir –
And such high vaunts of his nobility,
Did instigate the bedlam brainsick Duchess
By wicked means to frame our sovereign's fall.
Smooth runs the water where the brook is deep,
And in his simple show he harbours treason.
The fox barks not when he would steal the lamb.
No, no, my sovereign, Gloucester is a man
Unsounded yet, and full of deep deceit.

CARDINAL Did he not, contrary to form of law,
Devise strange deaths for small offences done?

YORK And did he not, in his protectorship,
Levy great sums of money through the realm
For soldiers' pay in France, and never sent it?
By means whereof the towns each day revolted.

BUCKINGHAM Tut, these are pretty faults to faults unknown
Which time will bring to light in smooth Duke Humphrey.

KING My lords, at once: the care you have of us,
To mow down thorns that would annoy our foot,
Is worthy praise; but shall I speak my conscience?
Our kinsman Gloucester is as innocent
From meaning treason to our royal person
As is the sucking lamb or harmless dove:
The Duke is virtuous, mild, and too well given
To dream on evil or to work my downfall.

QUEEN Ah, what's more dangerous than this fond affiance?
Seems he a dove? His feathers are but borrow'd.
For he's disposed as the hateful raven.
Is he a lamb? His skin is surely lent him,
For he's inclin'd as is the ravenous wolf.
Who cannot steal a shape that means deceit?
Take heed, my lord; the welfare of us all
Hangs on the cutting short that fraudful man.

Enter SOMERSET.

SOMERSET All health unto my gracious sovereign!

KING Welcome, Lord Somerset. What news from France?

SOMERSET That all your interest in those territories
Is utterly bereft you; all is lost.

KING Cold news, Lord Somerset; but God's will be done!

YORK [*Aside*] Cold news for me; for I had hope of France

As firmly as I hope for fertile England.
Thus are my blossoms blasted in the bud,
And caterpillars eat my leaves away;
But I will remedy this gear ere long,
Or sell my title for a glorious grave.

Enter GLOUCESTER.

GLOUCESTER All happiness unto my lord the King!
Pardon, my liege, that I have stay'd so long.

SUFFOLK Nay, Gloucester, know that thou art come too soon,
Unless thou wert more loyal than thou art.
I do arrest thee of high treason here.

GLOUCESTER Well, Suffolk, thou shalt not see me blush
Nor change my countenance for this arrest:
A heart unspotted is not easily daunted.
The purest spring is not so free from mud
As I am clear from treason to my sovereign.
Who can accuse me? Wherein am I guilty?

YORK 'Tis thought, my lord, that you took bribes of France
And, being Protector, stay'd the soldiers' pay;
By means whereof his Highness hath lost France.

GLOUCESTER Is it but thought so? What are they that think it?
I never robb'd the soldiers of their pay
Nor ever had one penny bribe from France.
So help me God, as I have watch'd the night –
Ay, night by night – in studying good for England!
That doit that e'er I wrested from the King,
Or any groat I hoarded to my use,
Be brought against me at my trial-day!
No; many a pound of mine own proper store,
Because I would not tax the needy commons,
Have I dispursed to the garrisons,
And never ask'd for restitution.

CARDINAL It serves you well, my lord, to say so much.

GLOUCESTER I say no more than truth, so help me God!

YORK In your protectorship you did devise
Strange tortures for offenders, never heard of,
That England was defam'd by tyranny.

GLOUCESTER Why, 'tis well known that whiles I was Protector
Pity was all the fault that was in me;
For I should melt at an offender's tears,
And lowly words were ransom for their fault.
Unless it were a bloody murderer,
Or foul felonious thief that fleec'd poor passengers,
I never gave them condign punishment.
Murder indeed, that bloody sin, I tortur'd
Above the felon or what trespass else.

SUFFOLK My lord, these faults are easy, quickly answer'd;
But mightier crimes are laid unto your charge,
Whereof you cannot easily purge yourself.
I do arrest you in his Highness' name,
And here commit you to my Lord Cardinal
To keep until your further time of trial.

KING My Lord of Gloucester, 'tis my special hope
That you will clear yourself from all suspence.
My conscience tells me you are innocent.

GLOUCESTER Ah, gracious lord, these days are dangerous!
Virtue is chok'd with foul ambition,
And charity chas'd hence by rancour's hand;
Foul subornation is predominant,
And equity exil'd your Highness' land.
I know their complot is to have my life;
And if my death might make this island happy
And prove the period of their tyranny,
I would expend it with all willingness.
But mine is made the prologue to their play;
For thousands more that yet suspect no peril
Will not conclude their plotted tragedy.
Beaufort's red sparkling eyes blab his heart's malice,
And Suffolk's cloudy brow his stormy hate;
Sharp Buckingham unburdens with his tongue
The envious load that lies upon his heart;
And dogged York, that reaches at the moon,
Whose overweening arm I have pluck'd back,
By false accuse doth level at my life.
And you, my sovereign lady, with the rest,
Causeless have laid disgraces on my head,
And with your best endeavour have stirr'd up
My liefest liege to be mine enemy;
Ay, all of you have laid your heads together –
Myself had notice of your conventicles –
And all to make away my guiltless life.
I shall not want false witness to condemn me
Nor store of treasons to augment my guilt.
The ancient proverb will be well effected:
'A staff is quickly found to beat a dog'.

CARDINAL My liege, his railing is intolerable.
If those that care to keep your royal person
From treason's secret knife and traitor's rage
Be thus upbraided, chid, and rated at,
And the offender granted scope of speech,
'Twill make them cool in zeal unto your Grace.

SUFFOLK Hath he not twit our sovereign lady here
With ignominious words, though clerkly couch'd,
As if she had suborned some to swear
False allegations to o'erthrow his state?

QUEEN But I can give the loser leave to chide.

GLOUCESTER Far truer spoke than meant: I lose indeed.
Beshrew the winners, for they play'd me false!
And well such losers may have leave to speak.
BUCKINGHAM He'll wrest the sense, and hold us here all day.
Lord Cardinal, he is your prisoner.
CARDINAL Sirs, take away the Duke, and guard him sure.
GLOUCESTER Ah, thus King Henry throws away his crutch
Before his legs be firm to bear his body!
Thus is the shepherd beaten from thy side,
And wolves are gnarling who shall gnaw thee first.
Ah, that my fear were false! ah, that it were!
For, good King Henry, thy decay I fear.
[*Exit, guarded.*
KING My lords, what to your wisdoms seemeth best
Do or undo, as if ourself were here.
QUEEN What, will your Highness leave the Parliament?
KING Ay, Margaret; my heart is drown'd with grief,
Whose flood begins to flow within mine eyes;
My body round engirt with misery –
For what's more miserable than discontent?
Ah, uncle Humphrey, in thy face I see
The map of honour, truth, and loyalty!
And yet, good Humphrey, is the hour to come
That e'er I prov'd thee false or fear'd thy faith.
What louring star now envies thy estate
That these great lords, and Margaret our Queen,
Do seek subversion of thy harmless life?
Thou never didst them wrong, nor no man wrong;
And as the butcher takes away the calf,
And binds the wretch, and beats it when it strays,
Bearing it to the bloody slaughter-house,
Even so, remorseless, have they borne him hence;
And as the dam runs lowing up and down,
Looking the way her harmless young one went,
And can do nought but wail her darling's loss,
Even so myself bewails good Gloucester's case
With sad unhelpful tears, and with dimm'd eyes
Look after him, and cannot do him good,
So mighty are his vowed enemies.
His fortunes I will weep, and 'twixt each groan
Say 'Who's a traitor? Gloucester he is none'.
[*Exit.*
QUEEN Free lords, cold snow melts with the sun's hot beams:
Henry my lord is cold in great affairs,
Too full of foolish pity; and Gloucester's show
Beguiles him as the mournful crocodile
With sorrow snares relenting passengers;
Or as the snake, roll'd in a flow'ring bank,
With shining checker'd slough, doth sting a child
That for the beauty thinks it excellent.
Believe me, lords, were none more wise than I –
And yet herein I judge mine own wit good –
This Gloucester should be quickly rid the world
To rid us from the fear we have of him.
CARDINAL That he should die is worthy policy;
But yet we want a colour for his death.
'Tis meet he be condemn'd by course of law.
SUFFOLK But, in my mind, that were no policy:
The King will labour still to save his life;
The commons haply rise to save his life;
And yet we have but trivial argument,
More than mistrust, that shows him worthy death.
YORK So that, by this, you would not have him die.
SUFFOLK Ah, York, no man alive so fain as I!
YORK 'Tis York that hath more reason for his death.
But, my Lord Cardinal, and you, my Lord of Suffolk,
Say as you think, and speak it from your souls:
Were't not all one an empty eagle were set
To guard the chicken from a hungry kite
As place Duke Humphrey for the King's Protector?
QUEEN So the poor chicken should be sure of death.
SUFFOLK Madam, 'tis true; and were't not madness then
To make the fox surveyor of the fold?
Who being accus'd a crafty murderer,
His guilt should be but idly posted over,
Because his purpose is not executed.
No; let him die, in that he is a fox,
By nature prov'd an enemy to the flock,
Before his chaps be stain'd with crimson blood,
As Humphrey, prov'd by reasons, to my liege.
And do not stand on quillets how to slay him;
Be it by gins, by snares, by subtlety,
Sleeping or waking, 'tis no matter how,
So he be dead; for that is good deceit
Which mates him first that first intends deceit.
QUEEN Thrice-noble Suffolk, 'tis resolutely spoke.
SUFFOLK Not resolute, except so much were done,
For things are often spoke and seldom meant;
But that my heart accordeth with my tongue,
Seeing the deed is meritorious,
And to preserve my sovereign from his foe,
Say but the word, and I will be his priest.

CARDINAL But I would have him dead, my Lord of Suffolk,
Ere you can take due orders for a priest;
Say you consent and censure well the deed,
And I'll provide his executioner –
I tender so the safety of my liege.

SUFFOLK Here is my hand the deed is worthy doing.

QUEEN And so say I.

YORK And I. And now we three have spoke it,
It skills not greatly who impugns our doom.

Enter a Post.

POST Great lords, from Ireland am I come amain
To signify that rebels there are up
And put the Englishmen unto the sword.
Send succours, lords, and stop the rage betime,
Before the wound do grow uncurable;
For, being green, there is great hope of help.

CARDINAL A breach that craves a quick expedient stop!
What counsel give you in this weighty cause?

YORK That Somerset be sent as Regent thither;
'Tis meet that lucky ruler be employ'd,
Witness the fortune he hath had in France.

SOMERSET If York, with all his far-fet policy,
Had been the Regent there instead of me,
He never would have stay'd in France so long.

YORK No, not to lose it all as thou hast done.
I rather would have lost my life betimes
Than bring a burden of dishonour home
By staying there so long till all were lost.
Show me one scar character'd on thy skin:
Men's flesh preserv'd so whole do seldom win.

QUEEN Nay then, this spark will prove a raging fire,
If wind and fuel be brought to feed it with;
No more, good York; sweet Somerset, be still.
Thy fortune, York, hadst thou been Regent there,
Might happily have prov'd far worse than his.

YORK What, worse than nought? Nay, then a shame take all!

SOMERSET And in the number, thee that wishest shame!

CARDINAL My Lord of York, try what your fortune is.
Th' uncivil kerns of Ireland are in arms
And temper clay with blood of Englishmen;
To Ireland will you lead a band of men,
Collected choicely, from each county some,
And try your hap against the Irishmen?

YORK I will, my lord, so please his Majesty.

SUFFOLK Why, our authority is his consent,
And what we do establish he confirms;
Then, noble York, take thou this task in hand.

YORK I am content; provide me soldiers, lords,
Whiles I take order for mine own affairs.

SUFFOLK A charge, Lord York, that I will see perform'd.
But now return we to the false Duke Humphrey.

CARDINAL No more of him; for I will deal with him
That henceforth he shall trouble us no more.
And so break off; the day is almost spent.
Lord Suffolk, you and I must talk of that event.

YORK My Lord of Suffolk, within fourteen days
At Bristol I expect my soldiers;
For there I'll ship them all for Ireland.

SUFFOLK I'll see it truly done, my Lord of York.

[*Exeunt all but York.*

YORK Now, York, or never, steel thy fearful thoughts
And change misdoubt to resolution;
Be that thou hop'st to be; or what thou art
Resign to death – it is not worth th' enjoying.
Let pale-fac'd fear keep with the mean-born man
And find no harbour in a royal heart.
Faster than spring-time show'rs comes thought on thought,
And not a thought but thinks on dignity.
My brain, more busy than the labouring spider,
Weaves tedious snares to trap mine enemies.
Well, nobles, well, 'tis politicly done
To send me packing with an host of men.
I fear me you but warm the starved snake,
Who, cherish'd in your breasts, will sting your hearts.
'Twas men I lack'd, and you will give them me;
I take it kindly. Yet be well assur'd
You put sharp weapons in a madman's hands.
Whiles I in Ireland nourish a mighty band,
I will stir up in England some black storm
Shall blow ten thousand souls to heaven or hell;
And this fell tempest shall not cease to rage
Until the golden circuit on my head,
Like to the glorious sun's transparent beams,
Do calm the fury of this mad-bred flaw.
And for a minister of my intent
I have seduc'd a headstrong Kentishman,
John Cade of Ashford,
To make commotion, as full well he can,
Under the title of John Mortimer.
In Ireland have I seen this stubborn Cade
Oppose himself against a troop of kerns,
And fought so long till that his thighs with darts
Were almost like a sharp-quill'd porpentine;
And in the end being rescu'd, I have seen
Him caper upright like a wild Morisco,
Shaking the bloody darts as he his bells.
Full often, like a shag-hair'd crafty kern,
Hath he conversed with the enemy,
And undiscover'd come to me again

And given me notice of their villainies.
This devil here shall be my substitute;
For that John Mortimer, which now is dead,
In face, in gait, in speech, he doth resemble.
By this I shall perceive the commons' mind,
How they affect the house and claim of York.
Say he be taken, rack'd, and tortured;
I know no pain they can inflict upon him
Will make him say I mov'd him to those arms.
Say that he thrive, as 'tis great like he will,
Why, then from Ireland come I with my strength,
And reap the harvest which that rascal sow'd;
For Humphrey being dead, as he shall be,
And Henry put apart, the next for me. *[Exit.*

SCENE II. *Bury St. Edmunds. A room of state.*

Enter two or three Murderers running over the stage, from the murder of Duke Humphrey.

1 MURDERER Run to my Lord of Suffolk; let him know
We have dispatch'd the Duke, as he commanded.
2 MURDERER O that it were to do! What have we done?
Didst ever hear a man so penitent?

Enter SUFFOLK.

1 MURDERER Here comes my lord.
SUFFOLK Now, sirs, have you dispatch'd this thing?
1 MURDERER Ay, my good lord, he's dead.
SUFFOLK Why, that's well said. Go, get you to my house;
I will reward you for this venturous deed.
The King and all the peers are here at hand.
Have you laid fair the bed? Is all things well,
According as I gave directions?
1 MURDERER 'Tis, my good lord.
SUFFOLK Away! be gone. *[Exeunt Murderers.*

Sound trumpets. Enter the KING, the QUEEN, CARDINAL, SOMERSET, with Attendants.

KING Go call our uncle to our presence straight;
Say we intend to try his Grace to-day,
If he be guilty, as 'tis published.
SUFFOLK I'll call him presently, my noble lord. *[Exit.*
KING Lords, take your places; and, I pray you all,
Proceed no straiter 'gainst our uncle Gloucester
Than from true evidence, of good esteem,
He be approv'd in practice culpable.
QUEEN God forbid any malice should prevail
That faultless may condemn a nobleman!
Pray God he may acquit him of suspicion!
KING I thank thee, Meg; these words content me much.

Re-enter SUFFOLK.

How now! Why look'st thou pale?
Why tremblest thou?
Where is our uncle? What's the matter, Suffolk?
SUFFOLK Dead in his bed, my lord; Gloucester is dead.
QUEEN Marry, God forfend!
CARDINAL God's secret judgment! I did dream to-night
The Duke was dumb and could not speak a word. *[The King swoons.*
QUEEN How fares my lord? Help, lords! The King is dead.
SOMERSET Rear up his body; wring him by the nose.
QUEEN Run, go, help, help! O Henry, ope thine eyes!
SUFFOLK He doth revive again; madam, be patient.
KING O heavenly God!
QUEEN How fares my gracious lord?
SUFFOLK Comfort, my sovereign! Gracious Henry, comfort!
KING What, doth my Lord of Suffolk comfort me?
Came he right now to sing a raven's note,
Whose dismal tune bereft my vital pow'rs;
And thinks he that the chirping of a wren,
By crying comfort from a hollow breast,
Can chase away the first conceived sound?
Hide not thy poison with such sug'red words;
Lay not thy hands on me; forbear, I say,
Their touch affrights me as a serpent's sting.
Thou baleful messenger, out of my sight!
Upon thy eye-balls murderous tyranny
Sits in grim majesty to fright the world.
Look not upon me, for thine eyes are wounding;
Yet do not go away; come, basilisk,
And kill the innocent gazer with thy sight;
For in the shade of death I shall find joy –
In life but double death, now Gloucester's dead.
QUEEN Why do you rate my Lord of Suffolk thus?
Although the Duke was enemy to him,
Yet he most Christian-like laments his death;
And for myself – foe as he was to me –
Might liquid tears, or heart-offending groans,
Or blood-consuming sighs, recall his life,
I would be blind with weeping, sick with groans,
Look pale as primrose with blood-drinking sighs,
And all to have the noble Duke alive.

What know I how the world may deem of me?
For it is known we were but hollow friends:
It may be judg'd I made the Duke away;
So shall my name with slander's tongue be wounded,
And princes' courts be fill'd with my reproach.
This get I by his death. Ay me, unhappy!
To be a queen and crown'd with infamy!

KING Ah, woe is me for Gloucester, wretched man!

QUEEN Be woe for me, more wretched than he is.
What, dost thou turn away, and hide thy face?
I am no loathsome leper – look on me.
What, art thou like the adder waxen deaf?
Be poisonous too, and kill thy forlorn Queen.
Is all thy comfort shut in Gloucester's tomb?
Why, then Dame Margaret was ne'er thy joy.
Erect his statue and worship it,
And make my image but an alehouse sign.
Was I for this nigh wreck'd upon the sea,
And twice by awkward wind from England's bank
Drove back again unto my native clime?
What boded this but well-forewarning wind
Did seem to say 'Seek not a scorpion's nest,
Nor set no footing on this unkind shore'?
What did I then but curs'd the gentle gusts,
And he that loos'd them forth their brazen caves;
And bid them blow towards England's blessed shore,
Or turn our stern upon a dreadful rock?
Yet Aeolus would not be a murderer,
But left that hateful office unto thee.
The pretty-vaulting sea refus'd to drown me,
Knowing that thou wouldst have me drown'd on shore
With tears as salt as sea through thy unkindness;
The splitting rocks cow'r'd in the sinking sands
And would not dash me with their ragged sides,
Because thy flinty heart, more hard than they,
Might in thy palace perish Margaret.
As far as I could ken thy chalky cliffs,
When from thy shore the tempest beat us back,
I stood upon the hatches in the storm;
And when the dusky sky began to rob
My earnest-gaping sight of thy land's view,
I took a costly jewel from my neck –
A heart it was, bound in with diamonds –
And threw it towards thy land. The sea receiv'd it;
And so I wish'd thy body might my heart.
And even with this I lost fair England's view,
And bid mine eyes be packing with my heart,
And call'd them blind and dusky spectacles
For losing ken of Albion's wished coast.
How often have I tempted Suffolk's tongue –
The agent of thy foul inconstancy –
To sit and witch me, as Ascanius did
When he to madding Dido would unfold
His father's acts commenc'd in burning Troy!
Am I not witch'd like her? Or thou not false like him?
Ay me, I can no more! Die, Margaret,
For Henry weeps that thou dost live so long.

Noise within. Enter WARWICK, SALISBURY, and many Commons.

WARWICK It is reported, mighty sovereign,
That good Duke Humphrey traitorously is murd'red
By Suffolk and the Cardinal Beaufort's means.
The commons, like an angry hive of bees
That want their leader, scatter up and down
And care not who they sting in his revenge.
Myself have calm'd their spleenful mutiny
Until they hear the order of his death.

KING That he is dead, good Warwick, 'tis too true;
But how he died God knows, not Henry.
Enter his chamber, view his breathless corpse,
And comment then upon his sudden death.

WARWICK That shall I do, my liege. Stay, Salisbury,
With the rude multitude till I return. [*Exit.*
[*Exit Salisbury with the Commons.*

KING O Thou that judgest all things, stay my thoughts –
My thoughts that labour to persuade my soul
Some violent hands were laid on Humphrey's life!
If my suspect be false, forgive me, God;
For judgment only doth belong to Thee.
Fain would I go to chafe his paly lips
With twenty thousand kisses and to drain
Upon his face an ocean of salt tears
To tell my love unto his dumb deaf trunk;
And with my fingers feel his hand unfeeling;
But all in vain are these mean obsequies;
And to survey his dead and earthy image,
What were it but to make my sorrow greater?

Bed put forth with the body. Enter WARWICK.

WARWICK Come hither, gracious sovereign, view this body.

KING That is to see how deep my grave is made;
For with his soul fled all my worldly solace,
For, seeing him, I see my life in death.

WARWICK As surely as my soul intends to live
With that dread King that took our state upon Him
To free us from his Father's wrathful curse,
I do believe that violent hands were laid
Upon the life of this thrice-famed Duke.

SUFFOLK A dreadful oath, sworn with a solemn tongue!
What instance gives Lord Warwick for his vow?
WARWICK See how the blood is settled in his face.
Oft have I seen a timely-parted ghost,
Of ashy semblance, meagre, pale, and bloodless,
Being all descended to the labouring heart,
Who, in the conflict that it holds with death,
Attracts the same for aidance 'gainst the enemy,
Which with the heart there cools, and ne'er returneth
To blush and beautify the cheek again.
But see, his face is black and full of blood;
His eye-balls further out than when he liv'd,
Staring full ghastly like a strangled man;
His hair uprear'd, his nostrils stretch'd with struggling;
His hands abroad display'd, as one that grasp'd
And tugg'd for life, and was by strength subdu'd.
Look, on the sheets his hair, you see, is sticking;
His well-proportion'd beard made rough and rugged,
Like to the summer's corn by tempest lodged.
It cannot be but he was murd'red here:
The least of all these signs were probable.
SUFFOLK Why, Warwick, who should do the Duke to death?
Myself and Beaufort had him in protection;
And we, I hope, sir, are no murderers.
WARWICK But both of you were vow'd Duke Humphrey's foes;
And you, forsooth, had the good Duke to keep.
'Tis like you would not feast him like a friend;
And 'tis well seen he found an enemy.
QUEEN Then you, belike, suspect these noblemen
As guilty of Duke Humphrey's timeless death.
WARWICK Who finds the heifer dead and bleeding fresh,
And sees fast by a butcher with an axe,
But will suspect 'twas he that made the slaughter?
Who finds the partridge in the puttock's nest
But may imagine how the bird was dead,
Although the kite soar with unbloodied beak?
Even so suspicious is this tragedy.
QUEEN Are you the butcher, Suffolk? Where's your knife?
Is Beaufort term'd a kite? Where are his talons?
SUFFOLK I wear no knife to slaughter sleeping men;
But here's a vengeful sword, rusted with ease,
That shall be scoured in his rancorous heart
That slanders me with murder's crimson badge.
Say, if thou dar'st, proud Lord of Warwickshire,
That I am faulty in Duke Humphrey's death.
[*Exeunt Cardinal, Somerset, and others.*
WARWICK What dares not Warwick, if false Suffolk dare him?
QUEEN He dares not calm his contumelious spirit,
Nor cease to be an arrogant controller,
Though Suffolk dare him twenty thousand times.
WARWICK Madam, be still – with reverence may I say;
For every word you speak in his behalf
Is slander to your royal dignity.
SUFFOLK Blunt-witted lord, ignoble in demeanour,
If ever lady wrong'd her lord so much,
Thy mother took into her blameful bed
Some stern untutor'd churl, and noble stock
Was graft with crab-tree slip, whose fruit thou art,
And never of the Nevils' noble race.
WARWICK But that the guilt of murder bucklers thee,
And I should rob the deathsman of his fee,
Quitting thee thereby of ten thousand shames,
And that my sovereign's presence makes me mild,
I would, false murd'rous coward, on thy knee
Make thee beg pardon for thy passed speech
And say it was thy mother that thou meant'st,
That thou thyself wast born in bastardy;
And, after all this fearful homage done,
Give thee thy hire and send thy soul to hell,
Pernicious blood-sucker of sleeping men.
SUFFOLK Thou shalt be waking while I shed thy blood,
If from this presence thou dar'st go with me.
WARWICK Away even now, or I will drag thee hence.
Unworthy though thou art, I'll cope with thee,
And do some service to Duke Humphrey's ghost.
[*Exeunt Suffolk and Warwick.*
KING What stronger breastplate than a heart untainted?
Thrice is he arm'd that hath his quarrel just;
And he but naked, though lock'd up in steel,
Whose conscience with injustice is corrupted.
[*A noise within.*
QUEEN What noise is this?

Re-enter SUFFOLK and WARWICK, with their weapons drawn.

KING Why, how now, lords, your wrathful weapons drawn
Here in our presence! Dare you be so bold?
Why, what tumultuous clamour have we here?

SUFFOLK The trait'rous Warwick, with the men of Bury,
Set all upon me, mighty sovereign.

Re-enter SALISBURY.

SALISBURY [*To the Commons within*] Sirs, stand apart, the King shall know your mind.
Dread lord, the commons send you word by me
Unless Lord Suffolk straight be done to death,
Or banished fair England's territories,
They will by violence tear him from your palace
And torture him with grievous ling'ring death.
They say by him the good Duke Humphrey died;
They say in him they fear your Highness' death;
And mere instinct of love and loyalty,
Free from a stubborn opposite intent,
As being thought to contradict your liking,
Makes them thus forward in his banishment
They say, in care of your most royal person,
That if your Highness should intend to sleep
And charge that no man should disturb your rest,
In pain of your dislike or pain of death,
Yet, notwithstanding such a strait edict,
Were there a serpent seen with forked tongue
That slily glided towards your Majesty,
It were but necessary you were wak'd,
Lest, being suffer'd in that harmful slumber,
The mortal worm might make the sleep eternal.
And therefore do they cry, though you forbid,
That they will guard you, whe'er you will or no,
From such fell serpents as false Suffolk is;
With whose envenomed and fatal sting
Your loving uncle, twenty times his worth,
They say, is shamefully bereft of life.

COMMONS [*Within*] An answer from the King, my Lord of Salisbury!

SUFFOLK 'Tis like the commons, rude unpolish'd hinds,
Could send such message to their sovereign;
But you, my lord, were glad to be employ'd,
To show how quaint an orator you are.
But all the honour Salisbury hath won
Is that he was the lord ambassador
Sent from a sort of tinkers to the King.

COMMONS [*Within*] An answer from the King, or we will all break in!

KING Go, Salisbury, and tell them all from me
I thank them for their tender loving care;
And had I not been cited so by them,
Yet did I purpose as they do entreat;
For sure my thoughts do hourly prophesy
Mischance unto my state by Suffolk's means.
And therefore by His Majesty I swear,
Whose far unworthy deputy I am,
He shall not breathe infection in this air
But three days longer, on the pain of death.
[*Exit Salisbury.*

QUEEN O Henry, let me plead for gentle Suffolk!

KING Ungentle Queen, to call him gentle Suffolk!
No more, I say; if thou dost plead for him,
Thou wilt but add increase unto my wrath.
Had I but said, I would have kept my word;
But when I swear, it is irrevocable.
If after three days' space thou here be'st found
On any ground that I am ruler of,
The world shall not be ransom for thy life.
Come, Warwick, come, good Warwick, go with me;
I have great matters to impart to thee.
[*Exeunt all but Queen and Suffolk.*

QUEEN Mischance and sorrow go along with you!
Heart's discontent and sour affliction
Be playfellows to keep you company!
There's two of you; the devil make a third,
And threefold vengeance tend upon your steps!

SUFFOLK Cease, gentle Queen, these execrations,
And let thy Suffolk take his heavy leave.

QUEEN Fie, coward woman and soft-hearted wretch,
Hast thou not spirit to curse thine enemy?

SUFFOLK A plague upon them! Wherefore should I curse them?
Would curses kill as doth the mandrake's groan,
I would invent as bitter searching terms,
As curst, as harsh, and horrible to hear,
Deliver'd strongly through my fixed teeth,
With full as many signs of deadly hate,
As lean-fac'd Envy in her loathsome cave.
My tongue should stumble in mine earnest words,
Mine eyes should sparkle like the beaten flint,
Mine hair be fix'd an end, as one distract;
Ay, every joint should seem to curse and ban;
And even now my burden'd heart would break,
Should I not curse them. Poison be their drink!
Gall, worse than gall, the daintiest that they taste!
Their sweetest shade a grove of cypress trees!
Their chiefest prospect murd'ring basilisks!
Their softest touch as smart as lizards' stings!
Their music frightful as the serpent's hiss,
And boding screech-owls make the consort full!
All the foul terrors in dark-seated hell –

QUEEN Enough, sweet Suffolk, thou torment'st thyself;
And these dread curses, like the sun 'gainst glass,
Or like an overcharged gun, recoil,
And turns the force of them upon thyself.

SUFFOLK You bade me ban, and will you bid me leave?

Now, by the ground that I am banish'd from,
Well could I curse away a winter's night,
Though standing naked on a mountain top
Where biting cold would never let grass grow,
And think it but a minute spent in sport.

QUEEN O, let me entreat thee cease! Give me thy hand,
That I may dew it with my mournful tears;
Nor let the rain of heaven wet this place
To wash away my woeful monuments.
O, could this kiss be printed in thy hand,
That thou might'st think upon these by the seal,
Through whom a thousand sighs are breath'd for thee!
So, get thee gone, that I may know my grief;
'Tis but surmis'd whiles thou art standing by,
As one that surfeits thinking on a want.
I will repeal thee or, be well assur'd,
Adventure to be banished myself;
And banished I am, if but from thee.
Go, speak not to me; even now be gone.
O, go not yet! Even thus two friends condemn'd
Embrace, and kiss, and take ten thousand leaves,
Loather a hundred times to part than die.
Yet now, farewell; and farewell life with thee!

SUFFOLK Thus is poor Suffolk ten times banished,
Once by the King and three times thrice by thee.
'Tis not the land I care for, wert thou thence;
A wilderness is populous enough,
So Suffolk had thy heavenly company;
For where thou art, there is the world itself,
With every several pleasure in the world;
And where thou art not, desolation.
I can no more: Live thou to joy thy life;
Myself no joy in nought but that thou liv'st.

Enter VAUX.

QUEEN Whither goes Vaux so fast? What news, I prithee?

VAUX To signify unto his Majesty
That Cardinal Beaufort is at point of death;
For suddenly a grievous sickness took him
That makes him gasp, and stare, and catch the air,
Blaspheming God, and cursing men on earth.
Sometime he talks as if Duke Humphrey's ghost
Were by his side; sometime he calls the King
And whispers to his pillow, as to him,
The secrets of his overcharged soul;
And I am sent to tell his Majesty
That even now he cries aloud for him.

QUEEN Go tell this heavy message to the King. [*Exit Vaux.*
Ay me! What is this world! What news are these!
But wherefore grieve I at an hour's poor loss,
Omitting Suffolk's exile, my soul's treasure?
Why only, Suffolk, mourn I not for thee,
And with the southern clouds contend in tears –
Theirs for the earth's increase, mine for my sorrows?
Now get thee hence: the King, thou know'st, is coming;
If thou be found by me, thou art but dead.

SUFFOLK If I depart from thee I cannot live;
And in thy sight to die, what were it else
But like a pleasant slumber in thy lap?
Here could I breathe my soul into the air,
As mild and gentle as the cradle-babe
Dying with mother's dug between its lips;
Where, from thy sight, I should be raging mad
And cry out for thee to close up mine eyes,
To have thee with thy lips to stop my mouth;
So shouldst thou either turn my flying soul,
Or I should breathe it so into thy body,
And then it liv'd in sweet Elysium.
To die by thee were but to die in jest:
From thee to die were torture more than death.
O, let me stay, befall what may befall!

QUEEN Away! Though parting be a fretful corrosive,
It is applied to a deathful wound.
To France, sweet Suffolk. Let me hear from thee;
For whereso'er thou art in this world's globe
I'll have an Iris that shall find thee out.

SUFFOLK I go.

QUEEN And take my heart with thee.
[*She kisses him.*

SUFFOLK A jewel, lock'd into the woefull'st cask
That ever did contain a thing of worth.
Even as a splitted bark, so sunder we:
This way fall I to death.

QUEEN This way for me. [*Exeunt severally.*

SCENE III. *London. Cardinal Beaufort's bedchamber.*

Enter the KING, SALISBURY, and WARWICK, to the CARDINAL in bed.

KING How fares my lord? Speak, Beaufort, to thy sovereign.

CARDINAL If thou be'st Death I'll give thee England's treasure,
Enough to purchase such another island,
So thou wilt let me live and feel no pain.

KING Ah, what a sign it is of evil life
Where death's approach is seen so terrible!

WARWICK Beaufort, it is thy sovereign speaks to thee.

CARDINAL Bring me unto my trial when you will.
Died he not in his bed? Where should he die?
Can I make men live, whe'er they will or no?
O, torture me no more! I will confess.
Alive again? Then show me where he is;
I'll give a thousand pound to look upon him.
He hath no eyes, the dust hath blinded them.
Comb down his hair; look, look! it stands upright,
Like lime-twigs set to catch my winged soul!
Give me some drink; and bid the apothecary
Bring the strong poison that I bought of him.

KING O Thou eternal Mover of the heavens,
Look with a gentle eye upon this wretch!
O, beat away the busy meddling fiend
That lays strong siege unto this wretch's soul,
And from his bosom purge this black despair!

WARWICK See how the pangs of death do make him grin.

SALISBURY Disturb him not, let him pass peaceably.

KING Peace to his soul, if God's good pleasure be!
Lord Card'nal, if thou think'st on heaven's bliss,
Hold up thy hand, make signal of thy hope.
He dies, and makes no sign: O God, forgive him!

WARWICK So bad a death argues a monstrous life.

KING Forbear to judge, for we are sinners all.
Close up his eyes, and draw the curtain close;
And let us all to meditation. [*Exeunt.*

ACT FOUR

SCENE I. *The coast of Kent.*

Alarum. Fight at sea. Ordnance goes off.

Enter a Lieutenant, a Shipmaster and his Mate, and WALTER WHITMORE, with Sailors; SUFFOLK and other Gentlemen, as prisoners.

LIEUTENANT The gaudy, blabbing, and remorseful day
Is crept into the bosom of the sea;
And now loud-howling wolves arouse the jades
That drag the tragic melancholy night;
Who with their drowsy, slow, and flagging wings
Clip dead men's graves, and from their misty jaws
Breathe foul contagious darkness in the air.
Therefore bring forth the soldiers of our prize;
For, whilst our pinnace anchors in the Downs,
Here shall they make their ransom on the sand,
Or with their blood stain this discoloured shore.
Master, this prisoner freely give I thee;
And thou that art his mate make boot of this;
The other, Walter Whitmore, is thy share.

1 GENTLEMAN What is my ransom, master, let me know?

MASTER A thousand crowns, or else lay down your head.

MATE And so much shall you give, or off goes yours.

LIEUTENANT What, think you much to pay two thousand crowns,
And bear the name and port of gentlemen?
Cut both the villains' throats – for die you shall;
The lives of those which we have lot in fight
Be counterpois'd with such a petty sum!

1 GENTLEMAN I'll give it, sir; and therefore spare my life.

2 GENTLEMAN And so will I, and write home for it straight.

WHITMORE I lost mine eye in laying the prize aboard,
[*To Suffolk*] And therefore, to revenge it, shalt thou die;
And so should these, if I might have my will.

LIEUTENANT Be not so rash; take ransom, let him live.

SUFFOLK Look on my George, I am a gentleman:
Rate me at what thou wilt, thou shalt be paid.

WHITMORE And so am I: my name is Walter Whitmore.
How now! Why start'st thou? What, doth death affright?

SUFFOLK Thy name affrights me, in whose sound is death.
A cunning man did calculate my birth
And told me that by water I should die;
Yet let not this make thee be bloody-minded;
Thy name is Gualtier, being rightly sounded.

WHITMORE Gualtier or Walter, which it is I care not:
Never yet did base dishonour blur our name
But with our sword we wip'd away the blot;
Therefore, when merchant-like I sell revenge,
Broke be my sword, my arms torn and defac'd,
And I proclaim'd a coward through the world.

SUFFOLK Stay, Whitmore, for thy prisoner is a prince,
The Duke of Suffolk, William de la Pole.

WHITMORE The Duke of Suffolk muffled up in rags?

SUFFOLK Ay, but these rags are no part of the Duke:
Jove sometime went disguis'd, and why not I?
LIEUTENANT But Jove was never slain, as thou shalt be.
SUFFOLK Obscure and lowly swain, King Henry's blood,
The honourable blood of Lancaster,
Must not be shed by such a jaded groom.
Hast thou not kiss'd thy hand and held my stirrup,
Bareheaded plodded by my foot-cloth mule,
And thought thee happy when I shook my head?
How often hast thou waited at my cup,
Fed from my trencher, kneel'd down at the board,
When I have feasted with Queen Margaret?
Remember it, and let it make thee crest-fall'n,
Ay, and allay thus thy abortive pride,
How in our voiding-lobby hast thou stood
And duly waited for my coming forth.
This hand of mine hath writ in thy behalf,
And therefore shall it charm thy riotous tongue.
WHITMORE Speak, Captain, shall I stab the forlorn swain?
LIEUTENANT First let my words stab him, as he hath me.
SUFFOLK Base slave, thy words are blunt, and so art thou.
LIEUTENANT Convey him hence, and on our longboat's side
Strike off his head.
SUFFOLK Thou dar'st not, for thy own.
LIEUTENANT Poole!
SUFFOLK Poole?
LIEUTENANT Ay, kennel, puddle, sink, whose filth and dirt
Troubles the silver spring where England drinks;
Now will I dam up this thy yawning mouth
For swallowing the treasure of the realm.
Thy lips, that kiss'd the Queen, shall sweep the ground;
And thou that smil'dst at good Duke Humphrey's death
Against the senseless winds shalt grin in vain,
Who in contempt shall hiss at thee again;
And wedded be thou to the hags of hell
For daring to affy a mighty lord
Unto the daughter of a worthless king,
Having neither subject, wealth, nor diadem.
By devilish policy art thou grown great,
And, like ambitious Sylla, overgorg'd
With gobbets of thy mother's bleeding heart.
By thee Anjou and Maine were sold to France;
The false revolting Normans thorough thee
Disdain to call us lord; and Picardy
Hath slain their governors, surpris'd our forts,
And sent the ragged soldiers wounded home.
The princely Warwick, and the Nevils all,
Whose dreadful swords were never drawn in vain,
As hating thee, are rising up in arms;
And now the house of York – thrust from the crown
By shameful murder of a guiltless king
And lofty proud encroaching tyranny –
Burns with revenging fire, whose hopeful colours
Advance our half-fac'd sun, striving to shine,
Under the which is writ 'Invitis nubibus'.
The commons here in Kent are up in arms;
And to conclude, reproach and beggary
Is crept into the palace of our King,
And all by thee. Away! convey him hence.
SUFFOLK O that I were a god, to shoot forth thunder
Upon these paltry, servile, abject drudges!
Small things make base men proud: this villain here,
Being captain of a pinnace, threatens more
Than Bargulus, the strong Illyrian pirate.
Drones suck not eagles' blood but rob bee-hives.
It is impossible that I should die
By such a lowly vassal as thyself.
Thy words move rage and not remorse in me.
I go of message from the Queen to France:
I charge thee waft me safely cross the Channel.
LIEUTENANT Walter –
WHITMORE Come, Suffolk, I must waft thee to thy death.
SUFFOLK Gelidus timor occupat artus: it is thee I fear.
WHITMORE Thou shalt have cause to fear before I leave thee.
What, are ye daunted now? Now will ye stoop?
1 GENTLEMAN My gracious lord, entreat him, speak him fair.
SUFFOLK Suffolk's imperial tongue is stern and rough,
Us'd to command, untaught to plead for favour.
Far be it we should honour such as these
With humble suit: no, rather let my head
Stoop to the block than these knees bow to any
Save to the God of heaven and to my king;
And sooner dance upon a bloody pole
Than stand uncover'd to the vulgar groom.
True nobility is exempt from fear:
More can I bear than you dare execute.
LIEUTENANT Hale him away, and let him talk no more.
SUFFOLK Come, soldiers, show what cruelty ye can,
That this my death may never be forgot –

Great men oft die by vile bezonians:
A Roman sworder and banditto slave
Murder'd sweet Tully; Brutus' bastard hand
Stabb'd Julius Caesar; savage islanders
Pompey the Great; and Suffolk dies by pirates.
[Exit Whitmore with Suffolk.

LIEUTENANT And as for these, whose ransom we have set,
It is our pleasure one of them depart;
Therefore come you with us, and let him go.
[Exeunt all but the first Gentleman.

Re-enter WHITMORE with Suffolk's body.

WHITMORE There let his head and lifeless body lie,
Until the Queen his mistress bury it. *[Exit.*

1 GENTLEMAN O barbarous and bloody spectacle!
His body will I bear unto the King.
If he revenge it not, yet will his friends;
So will the Queen, that living held him dear.
[Exit with the body.

SCENE II. *Blackheath.*

Enter GEORGE BEVIS and JOHN HOLLAND.

GEORGE Come and get thee a sword, though made of a lath; they have been up these two days.

JOHN They have the more need to sleep now, then.

GEORGE I tell thee Jack Cade the clothier means to dress the commonwealth, and turn it, and set a new nap upon it.

JOHN So he had need, for 'tis threadbare. Well, I say it was never merry world in England since gentlemen came up.

GEORGE O miserable age! Virtue is not regarded in handicraftsmen.

JOHN The nobility think scorn to go in leather aprons.

GEORGE Nay, more, the King's Council are no good workmen.

JOHN True; and yet it is said 'Labour in thy vocation'; which is as much to say as 'Let the magistrates be labouring men'; and therefore should we be magistrates.

GEORGE Thou hast hit it; for there's no better sign of a brave mind than a hard hand.

JOHN I see them! I see them! There's Best's son, the tanner of Wingham –

GEORGE He shall have the skins of our enemies to make dog's leather of.

JOHN And Dick the butcher –

GEORGE Then is sin struck down, like an ox, and iniquity's throat cut like a calf.

JOHN And Smith the weaver –

GEORGE Argo, their thread of life is spun.

JOHN Come, come, let's fall in with them.

Drum. Enter CADE, DICK the Butcher, SMITH the Weaver, and a Sawyer, with infinite numbers.

CADE We John Cade, so term'd of our supposed father –

DICK *[Aside]* Or rather, of stealing a cade of herrings.

CADE For our enemies shall fall before us, inspired with the spirit of putting down kings and princes – command silence.

DICK Silence!

CADE My father was a Mortimer –

DICK *[Aside]* He was an honest man and a good bricklayer.

CADE My mother a Plantagenet –

DICK *[Aside]* I knew her well; she was a midwife.

CADE My wife descended of the Lacies –

DICK *[Aside]* She was, indeed, a pedlar's daughter, and sold many laces.

SMITH *[Aside]* But now of late, not able to travel with her furr'd pack, she washes bucks here at home.

CADE Therefore am I of an honourable house.

DICK *[Aside]* Ay, by my faith, the field is honourable, and there was he born, under a hedge, for his father had never a house but the cage.

CADE Valiant I am.

SMITH *[Aside]* 'A must needs; for beggary is valiant.

CADE I am able to endure much.

DICK *[Aside]* No question of that; for I have seen him whipt three market days together.

CADE I fear neither sword nor fire.

SMITH *[Aside]* He need not fear the sword, for his coat is of proof.

DICK *[Aside]* But methinks he should stand in fear of fire, being burnt i' th' hand for stealing of sheep.

CADE Be brave, then, for your captain is brave, and vows reformation. There shall be in England seven halfpenny loaves sold for a penny; the three-hoop'd pot shall have ten hoops; and I will make it felony to drink small beer. All the realm shall be in common, and in Cheapside shall my palfrey go to grass. And when I am king – as king I will be –

ALL God save your Majesty!

CADE I thank you, good people – there shall be no money; all shall eat and drink on my score, and I will apparel them all in one livery, that they may agree like brothers and worship me their lord.

DICK The first thing we do, let's kill all the lawyers.

CADE Nay, that I mean to do. Is not this a lamentable thing, that of the skin of an innocent lamb should be made parchment? That parchment, being scribbl'd o'er, should undo a man? Some say the bee stings; but I say 'tis the bee's wax; for I did but seal once to a thing, and I was never mine own man since. How now! Who's there?

Enter some, bringing in the Clerk of Chatham.

SMITH The clerk of Chatham. He can write and read and cast accompt.

CADE O monstrous!

SMITH We took him setting of boys' copies.

CADE Here's a villain!

SMITH Has a book in his pocket with red letters in't.

CADE Nay, then he is a conjurer.

DICK Nay, he can make obligations and write court-hand.

CADE I am sorry for't; the man is a proper man, of mine honour; unless I find him guilty, he shall not die. Come hither, sirrah, I must examine thee. What is thy name?

CLERK Emmanuel.

DICK They use to write it on the top of letters; 'twill go hard with you.

CADE Let me alone. Dost thou use to write thy name, or hast thou a mark to thyself, like a honest plain-dealing man?

CLERK Sir, I thank God, I have been so well brought up that I can write my name.

ALL He hath confess'd. Away with him! He's a villain and a traitor.

CADE Away with him, I say! Hang him with his pen and inkhorn about his neck.

[Exit one with the Clerk.

Enter MICHAEL.

MICHAEL Where's our General?

CADE Here I am, thou particular fellow.

MICHAEL Fly, fly, fly! Sir Humphrey Stafford and his brother are hard by, with the King's forces.

CADE Stand, villain, stand, or I'll fell thee down. He shall be encount'red with a man as good as himself. He is but a knight, is 'a?

MICHAEL No.

CADE To equal him, I will make myself a knight presently. *[Kneels]* Rise up, Sir John Mortimer. *[Rises]* Now have at him!

Enter SIR HUMPHREY STAFFORD and WILLIAM his brother, with drum and Soldiers.

STAFFORD Rebellious hinds, the filth and scum of Kent,
Mark'd for the gallows, lay your weapons down;
Home to your cottages, forsake this groom;
The King is merciful if you revolt.

WILLIAM STAFFORD But angry, wrathful, and inclin'd to blood,
If you go forward; therefore yield or die.

CADE As for these silken-coated slaves, I pass not;
It is to you, good people, that I speak,
O'er whom, in time to come, I hope to reign;
For I am rightful heir unto the crown.

STAFFORD Villain, thy father was a plasterer;
And thou thyself a shearman, art thou not?

CADE And Adam was a gardener.

WILLIAM STAFFORD And what of that?

CADE Marry, this: Edmund Mortimer, Earl of March,
Married the Duke of Clarence' daughter, did he not?

STAFFORD Ay, sir.

CADE By her he had two children at one birth.

WILLIAM STAFFORD That's false.

CADE Ay, there's the question; but I say 'tis true.
The elder of them being put to nurse,
Was by a beggar-woman stol'n away,
And, ignorant of his birth and parentage,
Became a bricklayer when he came to age.
His son am I; deny it if you can.

DICK Nay, 'tis too true; therefore he shall be king.

SMITH Sir, he made a chimney in my father's house, and the bricks are alive at this day to testify it; therefore deny it not.

STAFFORD And will you credit this base drudge's words
That speaks he knows not what?

ALL Ay, marry, will we; therefore get ye gone.

WILLIAM STAFFORD Jack Cade, the Duke of York hath taught you this.

CADE *[Aside]* He lies, for I invented it myself – Go to, sirrah, tell the King from me that for his father's sake, Henry the Fifth, in whose time boys went to span-counter for French crowns, I am content he shall reign; but I'll be Protector over him.

DICK And furthermore, we'll have the Lord Say's head for selling the dukedom of Maine.

CADE And good reason; for thereby is England main'd and fain to go with a staff, but that my puissance holds it up. Fellow kings, I tell you that that Lord Say hath gelded the commonwealth and made it an eunuch; and more than that, he can speak French, and therefore he is a traitor.

STAFFORD O gross and miserable ignorance!

CADE Nay, answer if you can; the Frenchmen are our enemies. Go to, then, I ask but this: can he that speaks with the tongue of an enemy be a good counsellor, or no?

ALL No, no; and therefore we'll have his head.
WILLIAM STAFFORD Well, seeing gentle words will not prevail,
Assail them with the army of the King.
STAFFORD Herald, away; and throughout every town
Proclaim them traitors that are up with Cade;
That those which fly before the battle ends
May, even in their wives' and children's sight,
Be hang'd up for example at their doors.
And you that be the King's friends, follow me.
[*Exeunt the two Staffords and Soldiers.*
CADE And you that love the commons follow me.
Now show yourselves men; 'tis for liberty.
We will not leave one lord, one gentleman;
Spare none but such as go in clouted shoon,
For they are thrifty honest men and such
As would – but that they dare not – take our parts.
DICK They are all in order, and march toward us.
CADE But then are we in order when we are most out of order. Come, march forward. [*Exeunt.*

SCENE III. *Another part of Blackheath.*

Alarums to the fight, wherein both the Staffords are slain. Enter CADE and the rest.

CADE Where's Dick, the butcher of Ashford?
DICK Here, sir.
CADE They fell before thee like sheep and oxen, and thou behavedst thyself as if thou hadst been in thine own slaughter-house; therefore thus will I reward thee – the Lent shall be as long again as it is, and thou shalt have a licence to kill for a hundred lacking one.
DICK I desire no more.
CADE And, to speak truth, thou deserv'st no less. [*Putting on Sir Humphrey's brigandine*] This monument of the victory will I bear, and the bodies shall be dragged at my horse heels till I do come to London, where we will have the mayor's sword borne before us.
DICK If we mean to thrive and do good, break open the goals and let out the prisoners.
CADE Fear not that, I warrant thee. Come, let's march towards London. [*Exeunt.*

SCENE IV. *London. The palace.*

Enter the KING with a supplication, and the QUEEN with Suffolk's head; the DUKE OF BUCKINGHAM, and the LORD SAY.

QUEEN Oft have I heard that grief softens the mind
And makes it fearful and degenerate;
Think therefore on revenge and cease to weep.
But who can cease to weep, and look on this?
Here may his head lie on my throbbing breast;
But where's the body that I should embrace?
BUCKINGHAM What answer makes your Grace to the rebels' supplication?
KING I'll send some holy bishop to entreat;
For God forbid so many simple souls
Should perish by the sword! And I myself,
Rather than bloody war shall cut them short,
Will parley with Jack Cade their general.
But stay, I'll read it over once again.
QUEEN Ah, barbarous villains! Hath this lovely face
Rul'd like a wandering planet over me,
And could it not enforce them to relent
That were unworthy to behold the same?
KING Lord Say, Jack Cade hath sworn to have thy head.
SAY Ay, but I hope your Highness shall have his.
KING How now, madam!
Still lamenting and mourning for Suffolk's death?
I fear me, love, if that I had been dead,
Thou wouldst not have mourn'd so much for me.
QUEEN No, my love, I should not mourn, but die for thee.

Enter a Messenger.

KING How now! What news? Why com'st thou in such haste?
MESSENGER The rebels are in Southwark; fly, my lord!
Jack Cade proclaims himself Lord Mortimer,
Descended from the Duke of Clarence' house,
And calls your Grace usurper, openly,
And vows to crown himself in Westminster.
His army is a ragged multitude
Of hinds and peasants, rude and merciless;
Sir Humphrey Stafford and his brother's death
Hath given them heart and courage to proceed.
All scholars, lawyers, courtiers, gentlemen,
They call false caterpillars and intend their death.
KING O graceless men! they know not what they do.
BUCKINGHAM My gracious lord, retire to Killingworth
Until a power be rais'd to put them down.
QUEEN Ah, were the Duke of Suffolk now alive,
These Kentish rebels would be soon appeas'd!
KING Lord Say, the traitors hate thee;
Therefore away with us to Killingworth.
SAY So might your Grace's person be in danger.
The sight of me is odious in their eyes;
And therefore in this city will I stay
And live alone as secret as I may.

Enter another Messenger.

2 MESSENGER Jack Cade hath gotten London Bridge.
The citizens fly and forsake their houses;
The rascal people, thirsting after prey,
Join with the traitor; and they jointly swear
To spoil the city and your royal court.

BUCKINGHAM Then linger not, my lord; away, take horse.

KING Come, Margaret; God. our hope, will succour us.

QUEEN My hope is gone, now Suffolk is deceas'd.

KING [*To Lord Say*] Farewell, my lord, trust not the Kentish rebels.

BUCKINGHAM Trust nobody, for fear you be betray'd.

SAY The trust I have is in mine innocence,
And therefore am I bold and resolute. [*Exeunt.*

SCENE V. *London. The Tower.*

Enter LORD SCALES upon the Tower, walking. Then enter two or three Citizens, below.

SCALES How now! Is Jack Cade slain?

1 CITIZEN No, my lord, nor likely to be slain; for they have won the bridge, killing all those that withstand them. The Lord Mayor craves aid of your honour from the Tower, to defend the city from the rebels.

SCALES Such aid as I can spare you shall command,
But I am troubled here with them myself;
The rebels have assay'd to win the Tower.
But get you to Smithfield, and gather head,
And thither I will send you Matthew Goffe.
Fight for your King, your country, and your lives;
And so, farewell, for I must hence again.
[*Exeunt.*

SCENE VI. *London. Cannon street.*

Enter JACK CADE and the rest, and strikes his staff on London stone.

CADE Now is Mortimer lord of this city. And here, sitting upon London Stone, I charge and command that, of the city's cost, the pissing-conduit run nothing but claret wine this first year of our reign. And now henceforward it shall be treason for any that calls me other than Lord Mortimer.

Enter a Soldier, running.

SOLDIER Jack Cade! Jack Cade!

CADE Knock him down there. [*They kill him.*

SMITH If this fellow be wise, he'll never call ye Jack Cade more; I think he hath a very fair warning.

DICK My lord, there's an army gathered together in Smithfield.

CADE Come then, let's go fight with them. But first go and set London Bridge on fire; and, if you can, burn down the Tower too. Come, let's away. [*Exeunt.*

SCENE VII. *London. Smithfield.*

Alarums. MATTHEW GOFFE is slain, and all the rest. Then enter JACK CADE, with his company.

CADE So, sirs. Now go some and pull down the Savoy; others to th' Inns of Court; down with them all.

DICK I have a suit unto your lordship.

CADE Be it a lordship, thou shalt have it for that word.

DICK Only that the laws of England may come out of your mouth.

JOHN [*Aside*] Mass, 'twill be sore law then; for he was thrust in the mouth with a spear, and 'tis not whole yet.

SMITH [*Aside*] Nay, John, it will be stinking law; for his breath stinks with eating toasted cheese.

CADE I have thought upon it; it shall be so. Away, burn all the records of the realm. My mouth shall be the Parliament of England.

JOHN [*Aside*] Then we are like to have biting statutes, unless his teeth be pull'd out.

CADE And henceforward all things shall be in common.

Enter a Messenger.

MESSENGER My lord, a prize, a prize! Here's the Lord Say, which sold the towns in France; he that made us pay one and twenty fifteens, and one shilling to the pound, the last subsidy.

Enter GEORGE BEVIS, with the LORD SAY.

CADE Well, he shall be beheaded for it ten times. Ah, thou say, thou serge, nay, thou buckram lord! Now art thou within point blank of our jurisdiction regal. What canst thou answer to my Majesty for giving up of Normandy unto Mounsieur Basimecu the Dauphin of France? Be it known unto thee by these presence, even the presence of Lord Mortimer, that I am the besom that must sweep the court clean of such filth as thou art. Thou hast most traitorously corrupted the youth of the realm in erecting a grammar school; and whereas, before, our forefathers had no other books but the score and the tally, thou hast caused printing to be us'd, and, contrary to the King, his crown, and dignity, thou hast built a paper-mill. It will be proved to thy face that thou hast men about thee that usually talk of a noun and a verb, and such abominable words as no Christian ear can endure to hear. Thou hast appointed justices of peace, to call poor men before them about matters they were not able to answer. Moreover, thou hast put them in prison, and because they could not read, thou hast hang'd them, when, indeed, only for that cause they have been most worthy to live. Thou dost ride in a foot-cloth, dost thou not?

SAY What of that?

CADE Marry, thou ought'st not to let thy horse wear a cloak, when honester men than thou go in their hose and doublets.

DICK And work in their shirt too, as myself, for example, that am a butcher.

SAY You men of Kent –

DICK What say you of Kent?

SAY Nothing but this: 'tis 'bona terra, mala gens'.

CADE Away with him, away with him! He speaks Latin.

SAY Hear me but speak, and bear me where you will.
Kent, in the Commentaries Caesar writ,
Is term'd the civil'st place of all this isle.
Sweet is the country, because full of riches;
The people liberal, valiant, active, wealthy;
Which makes me hope you are not void of pity.
I sold not Maine, I lost not Normandy;
Yet, to recover them, would lose my life.
Justice with favour have I always done;
Pray'rs and tears have mov'd me, gifts could never.
When have I aught exacted at your hands,
But to maintain the King, the realm, and you?
Large gifts have I bestow'd on learned clerks,
Because my book preferr'd me to the King,
And seeing ignorance is the curse of God,
Knowledge the wing wherewith we fly to heaven,
Unless you be possess'd with devilish spirits
You cannot but forbear to murder me.
This tongue hath parley'd unto foreign kings
For your behoof.

CADE Tut, when struck'st thou one blow in the field?

SAY Great men have reaching hands. Oft have I struck
Those that I never saw, and struck them dead.

GEORGE O monstrous coward! What, to come behind folks?

SAY These cheeks are pale for watching for your good.

CADE Give him a box o' th' ear, and that will make 'em red again.

SAY Long sitting to determine poor men's causes
Hath made me full of sickness and diseases.

CADE Ye shall have a hempen caudle then, and the help of hatchet.

DICK Why dost thou quiver, man?

SAY The palsy, and not fear, provokes me.

CADE Nay, he nods at us, as who should say 'I'll be even with you'; I'll see if his head will stand steadier on a pole, or no. Take him away, and behead him.

SAY Tell me: wherein have I offended most?
Have I affected wealth or honour? Speak.
Are my chests fill'd up with extorted gold?
Is my apparel sumptuous to behold?
Whom have I injur'd, that ye seek my death?
These hands are free from guiltless blood-shedding,
This breast from harbouring foul deceitful thoughts.
O, let me live!

CADE [*Aside*] I feel remorse in myself with his words; but I'll bridle it. He shall die, an it be but for pleading so well for his life. – Away with him! He has a familiar under his tongue; he speaks not o' God's name. Go, take him away, I say, and strike off his head presently, and then break into his son-in-law's house, Sir James Cromer, and strike off his head, and bring them both upon two poles hither.

ALL It shall be done.

SAY Ah, countrymen! if when you make your pray'rs,
God should be so obdurate as yourselves,
How would it fare with your departed souls?
And therefore yet relent, and save my life.

CADE Away with him, and do as I command ye. [*Exeunt some with Lord Say*] The proudest peer in the realm shall not wear a head on his shoulders, unless he pay me tribute; there shall not a maid be married, but she shall pay to me her maidenhead ere they have it. Men shall hold of me in capite; and we charge and command that their wives be as free as heart can wish or tongue can tell.

DICK My lord, when shall we go to Cheapside, and take up commodities upon our bills?

CADE Marry, presently.

ALL O, brave!

Re-enter one with the heads.

CADE But is not this braver? Let them kiss one another, for they lov'd well when they were alive. Now part them again, lest they consult about the giving up of some more towns in France. Soldiers, defer the spoil of the city until night; for with these borne before us instead of maces will we ride through the streets, and at every corner have them kiss. Away! [*Exeunt.*

SCENE VIII. *Southwark.*

Alarum and retreat. Enter again CADE and all his Rabblement.

CADE Up Fish Street! down Saint Magnus' Corner! Kill and knock down! Throw them into Thames! [*Sound a parley*] What noise is this I hear? Dare any be so bold to sound retreat or parley when I command them kill?

Enter BUCKINGHAM and old CLIFFORD, attended.

BUCKINGHAM Ay, here they be that dare and will disturb thee.
Know, Cade, we come ambassadors from the King
Unto the commons whom thou hast misled;
And here pronounce free pardon to them all
That will forsake thee and go home in peace.

CLIFFORD What say ye, countrymen? Will ye relent
And yield to mercy whilst 'tis offer'd you,
Or let a rebel lead you to your deaths?
Who loves the King, and will embrace his pardon,
Fling up his cap and say 'God save his Majesty!'
Who hateth him and honours not his father,
Henry the Fifth, that made all France to quake,
Shake he his weapon at us and pass by.

ALL God save the King! God save the King!

CADE What, Buckingham and Clifford, are ye so brave? And you, base peasants, do ye believe him? Will you needs be hang'd with your pardons about your necks? Hath my sword therefore broke through London gates, that you should leave me at the White Hart in Southwark? I thought ye would never have given out these arms till you had recovered your ancient freedom. But you are all recreants and dastards, and delight to live in slavery to the nobility. Let them break your backs with burdens, take your houses over your heads, ravish your wives and daughters before your faces. For me, I will make shift for one; and so God's curse light upon you all!

ALL We'll follow Cade, we'll follow Cade!

CLIFFORD Is Cade the son of Henry the Fifth,
That thus you do exclaim you'll go with him?
Will he conduct you through the heart of France,
And make the meanest of you earls and dukes?
Alas, he hath no home, no place to fly to;
Nor knows he how to live but by the spoil,
Unless by robbing of your friends and us.
Were't not a shame that whilst you live at jar
The fearful French, whom you late vanquished,
Should make a start o'er seas and vanquish you?
Methinks already in this civil broil
I see them lording it in London streets,
Crying 'Villiago!' unto all they meet.
Better ten thousand base-born Cades miscarry
Than you should stoop unto a Frenchman's mercy.
To France, to France, and get what you have lost;
Spare England, for it is your native coast.
Henry hath money; you are strong and manly.
God on our side, doubt not of victory.

ALL A Clifford! a Clifford! We'll follow the King and Clifford.

CADE Was ever feather so lightly blown to and fro as this multitude? The name of Henry the Fifth hales them to an hundred mischiefs, and makes them leave me desolate. I see them lay their heads together to surprise me. My sword make way for me for here is no staying. In despite of the devils and hell, have through the very middest of you! and heavens and honour be witness that no want of resolution in me, but only my followers' base and ignominious treasons, makes me betake me to my heels. [*Exit.*

BUCKINGHAM What, is he fled? Go some, and follow him;
And he that brings his head unto the King
Shall have a thousand crowns for his reward.
[*Exeunt some of them.*
Follow me, soldiers; we'll devise a mean
To reconcile you all unto the King. [*Exeunt.*

SCENE IX. *Killingworth Castle.*

Sound trumpets. Enter KING, QUEEN, and SOMERSET, on the terrace.

KING Was ever king that joy'd an earthly throne
And could command no more content than I?
No sooner was I crept out of my cradle
But I was made a king, at nine months old.
Was never subject long'd to be a king
As I do long and wish to be a subject.

Enter BUCKINGHAM and old CLIFFORD.

BUCKINGHAM Health and glad tidings to your Majesty!

KING Why, Buckingham, is the traitor Cade surpris'd?
Or is he but retir'd to make him strong?

Enter, below, Multitudes, with halters about their necks.

CLIFFORD He is fled, my lord, and all his powers do yield,
And humbly thus, with halters on their necks,
Expect your Highness' doom of life or death.

KING Then, heaven, set ope thy everlasting gates,
To entertain my vows of thanks and praise!

Soldiers, this day have you redeem'd your lives,
And show'd how well you love your Prince and country.
Continue still in this so good a mind,
And Henry, though he be infortunate,
Assure yourselves, will never be unkind.
And so, with thanks and pardon to you all,
I do dismiss you to your several countries.

ALL God save the King! God save the King!

Enter a Messenger.

MESSENGER Please it your Grace to be advertised
The Duke of York is newly come from Ireland
And with a puissant and a mighty power
Of gallowglasses and stout kerns
Is marching hitherward in proud array,
And still proclaimeth, as he comes along,
His arms are only to remove from thee
The Duke of Somerset, whom he terms a traitor.

KING Thus stands my state, 'twixt Cade and York distress'd;
Like to a ship that, having scap'd a tempest,
Is straightway calm'd, and boarded with a pirate;
But now is Cade driven back, his men dispers'd,
And now is York in arms to second him.
I pray thee, Buckingham, go and meet him
And ask him what's the reason of these arms.
Tell him I'll send Duke Edmund to the Tower –
And, Somerset, we will commit thee thither
Until his army be dismiss'd from him.

SOMERSET My lord,
I'll yield myself to prison willingly,
Or unto death, to do my country good.

KING In any case be not too rough in terms,
For he is fierce and cannot brook hard language.

BUCKINGHAM I will, my lord, and doubt not so to deal
As all things shall redound unto your good.

KING Come, wife, let's in, and learn to govern better;
For yet may England curse my wretched reign.

[*Flourish. Exeunt.*

SCENE X. *Kent. Iden's garden.*

Enter CADE.

CADE Fie on ambitions! Fie on myself, that have a sword and yet am ready to famish! These five days have I hid me in these woods and durst not peep out, for all the country is laid for me; but now am I so hungry that, if I might have a lease of my life for a thousand years, I could stay no longer. Wherefore, on a brick wall have I climb'd into this garden, to see if I can eat grass or pick a sallet another while, which is not amiss to cool a man's stomach this hot weather. And I think this word 'sallet' was born to do me good; for many a time, but for a sallet, my brain-pan had been cleft with a brown bill; and many a time, when I have been dry, and bravely marching, it hath serv'd me instead of a quart-pot to drink in; and now the word 'sallet' must serve me to feed on.

Enter IDEN.

IDEN Lord, who would live turmoiled in the court
And may enjoy such quiet walks as these?
This small inheritance my father left me
Contenteth me, and worth a monarchy.
I seek not to wax great by others' waning
Or gather wealth I care not with what envy;
Sufficeth that I have maintains my state,
And sends the poor well pleased from my gate.

CADE Here's the lord of the soil come to seize me for a stray, for entering his fee-simple without leave. Ah, villain, thou wilt betray me, and get a thousand crowns of the King by carrying my head to him; but I'll make thee eat iron like an ostrich and swallow my sword like a great pin ere thou and I part.

IDEN Why, rude companion, whatsoe'er thou be,
I know thee not; why then should I betray thee?
Is't not enough to break into my garden
And like a thief to come to rob my grounds,
Climbing my walls in spite of me the owner,
But thou wilt brave me with these saucy terms?

CADE Brave thee? Ay, by the best blood that ever was broach'd, and beard thee too. Look on me well: I have eat no meat these five days, yet come thou and thy five men and if I do not leave you all as dead as a door-nail, I pray God I may never eat grass more.

IDEN Nay, it shall ne'er be said, while England stands,
That Alexander Iden, an esquire of Kent,
Took odds to combat a poor famish'd man.
Oppose thy steadfast-gazing eyes to mine;
See if thou canst outface me with thy looks;
Set limb to limb, and thou art far the lesser;
Thy hand is but a finger to my fist,
Thy leg a stick compared with this truncheon;
My foot shall fight with all the strength thou hast,
And if mine arm be heaved in the air,
Thy grave is digg'd already in the earth.
As for words, whose greatness answers words,
Let this my sword report what speech forbears.

CADE By my valour, the most complete champion that ever I heard! Steel, if thou turn the edge, or cut not out the burly-bon'd clown in chines of beef ere thou sleep in thy sheath, I beseech God on my knees thou mayst be turn'd to hobnails. [*Here they fight; Cade falls*] O, I am slain! famine and no other hath slain me. Let ten thousand devils come against me, and give me but the ten meals I have lost, and I'd defy them all. Wither, garden, and be henceforth a burying place to all that do dwell in this house, because the unconquered soul of Cade is fled.

IDEN Is't Cade that I have slain, that monstrous traitor?
Sword, I will hallow thee for this thy deed
And hang thee o'er my tomb when I am dead.
Ne'er shall this blood be wiped from thy point,
But thou shalt wear it as a herald's coat
To emblaze the honour that thy master got.

CADE Iden, farewell; and be proud of thy victory. Tell Kent from me she hath lost her best man, and exhort all the world to be cowards; for I, that never feared any, am vanquished by famine, not by valour. [*Dies.*

IDEN How much thou wrong'st me, heaven be my judge.
Die, damned wretch, the curse of her that bare thee!
And as I thrust thy body in with my sword,
So wish I I might thrust thy soul to hell.
Hence will I drag thee headlong by the heels
Unto a dunghill, which shall be thy grave,
And there cut off thy most ungracious head,
Which I will bear in triumph to the King,
Leaving thy trunk for crows to feed upon.
[*Exit.*

ACT FIVE

SCENE I. *Fields between Dartford and Blackheath.*

Enter YORK, and his army of Irish, with drum and colours.

YORK From Ireland thus comes York to claim his right
And pluck the crown from feeble Henry's head:
Ring bells aloud, burn bonfires clear and bright,
To entertain great England's lawful king.
Ah, sancta majestas! who would not buy thee dear?
Let them obey that knows not how to rule;
This hand was made to handle nought but gold.
I cannot give due action to my words
Except a sword or sceptre balance it.
A sceptre shall it have, have I a soul,
On which I'll toss the flower-de-luce of France.

Enter BUCKINGHAM.

[*Aside*] Whom have we here? Buckingham, to disturb me?
The King hath sent him, sure: I must dissemble.

BUCKINGHAM York, if thou meanest well, I greet thee well.

YORK Humphrey of Buckingham, I accept thy greeting.
Art thou a messenger, or come of pleasure?

BUCKINGHAM A messenger from Henry, our dread liege,
To know the reason of these arms in peace;
Or why thou, being a subject as I am,
Against thy oath and true allegiance sworn,
Should raise so great a power without his leave,
Or dare to bring thy force so near the court.

YORK [*Aside*] Scarce can I speak, my choler is so great.
O, I could hew up rocks and fight with flint,
I am so angry at these abject terms;
And now, like Ajax Telamonius,
On sheep or oxen could I spend my fury.
I am far better born than is the King,
More like a king, more kingly in my thoughts;
But I must make fair weather yet awhile,
Till Henry be more weak and I more strong. –
Buckingham, I prithee, pardon me
That I have given no answer all this while;
My mind was troubled with deep melancholy.
The cause why I have brought this army hither
Is to remove proud Somerset from the King,
Seditious to his Grace and to the state.

BUCKINGHAM That is too much presumption on thy part;
But if thy arms be to no other end,
The King hath yielded unto thy demand:
The Duke of Somerset is in the Tower.

YORK Upon thine honour, is he prisoner?

BUCKINGHAM Upon mine honour, he is prisoner.

YORK Then, Buckingham, I do dismiss my pow'rs.
Soldiers, I thank you all; disperse yourselves;
Meet me to-morrow in Saint George's field,
You shall have pay and everything you wish.
And let my sovereign, virtuous Henry,
Command my eldest son, nay, all my sons,
As pledges of my fealty and love.
I'll send them all as willing as I live:
Lands, goods, horse, armour, anything I have,
Is his to use, so Somerset may die.

BUCKINGHAM York, I commend this kind submission.

We twain will go into his Highness' tent.

Enter the KING, and Attendants.

KING Buckingham, doth York intend no harm to us,
That thus he marcheth with thee arm in arm?
YORK In all submission and humility
York doth present himself unto your Highness.
KING Then what intends these forces thou dost bring?
YORK To heave the traitor Somerset from hence,
And fight against that monstrous rebel Cade,
Who since I heard to be discomfited.

Enter IDEN, with Cade's head.

IDEN If one so rude and of so mean condition
May pass into the presence of a king,
Lo, I present your Grace a traitor's head,
The head of Cade, whom I in combat slew.
KING The head of Cade! Great God, how just art Thou!
O, let me view his visage, being dead,
That living wrought me such exceeding trouble.
Tell me, my friend, art thou the man that slew him?
IDEN I was, an't like your Majesty.
KING How art thou call'd? And what is thy degree?
IDEN Alexander Iden, that's my name;
A poor esquire of Kent that loves his king.
BUCKINGHAM So please it you, my lord, 'twere not amiss
He were created knight for his good service.
KING Iden, kneel down. [*He kneels*] Rise up a knight.
We give thee for reward a thousand marks,
And will that thou thenceforth attend on us.
IDEN May Iden live to merit such a bounty,
And never live but true unto his liege!

Enter the QUEEN and SOMERSET.

KING See, Buckingham! Somerset comes with th' Queen:
Go, bid her hide him quickly from the Duke.
QUEEN For thousand Yorks he shall not hide his head,
But boldly stand and front him to his face.
YORK How now! Is Somerset at liberty?
Then, York, unloose thy long-imprisoned thoughts
And let thy tongue be equal with thy heart.
Shall I endure the sight of Somerset?
False king, why hast thou broken faith with me,
Knowing how hardly I can brook abuse?
King did I call thee? No, thou art not king;
Not fit to govern and rule multitudes,
Which dar'st not, no, nor canst not rule a traitor.
That head of thine doth not become a crown;
Thy hand is made to grasp a palmer's staff,
And not to grace an awful princely sceptre.
That gold must round engirt these brows of mine,
Whose smile and frown, like to Achilles' spear,
Is able with the change to kill and cure.
Here is a hand to hold a sceptre up,
And with the same to act controlling laws.
Give place. By heaven, thou shalt rule no more
O'er him whom heaven created for thy ruler.
SOMERSET O monstrous traitor! I arrest thee, York,
Of capital treason 'gainst the King and crown.
Obey, audacious traitor; kneel for grace.
YORK Wouldst have me kneel? First let me ask of these,
If they can brook I bow a knee to man.
Sirrah, call in my sons to be my bail:
[*Exit Attendant.*
I know, ere they will have me go to ward,
They'll pawn their swords for my enfranchisement.
QUEEN Call hither Clifford; bid him come amain,
To say if that the bastard boys of York
Shall be the surety for their traitor father.
[*Exit Buckingham.*
YORK O blood-bespotted Neapolitan,
Outcast of Naples, England's bloody scourge!
The sons of York, thy betters in their birth,
Shall be their father's bail; and bane to those
That for my surety will refuse the boys!

Enter EDWARD and RICHARD PLANTAGENET.

See where they come: I'll warrant they'll make it good.

Enter CLIFFORD and his Son.

QUEEN And here comes Clifford to deny their bail.
CLIFFORD Health and all happiness to my lord the King! [*Kneels.*
YORK I thank thee, Clifford. Say, what news with thee?
Nay, do not fright us with an angry look.
We are thy sovereign, Clifford, kneel again;
For thy mistaking so, we pardon thee.
CLIFFORD This is my King, York, I do not mistake;
But thou mistakes me much to think I do.
To Bedlam with him! Is the man grown mad?
KING Ay, Clifford; a bedlam and ambitious humour
Makes him oppose himself against his king.
CLIFFORD He is a traitor; let him to the Tower,

And chop away that factious pate of his.
QUEEN He is arrested, but will not obey;
His sons, he says, shall give their words for him.
YORK Will you not, sons?
EDWARD Ay, noble father, if our words will serve.
RICHARD And if words will not, then our weapons shall.
CLIFFORD Why, what a brood of traitors have we here!
YORK Look in a glass, and call thy image so:
I am thy king, and thou a false-heart traitor.
Call hither to the stake my two brave bears,
That with the very shaking of their chains
They may astonish these fell-lurking curs.
Bid Salisbury and Warwick come to me.

Enter the EARLS OF WARWICK and SALISBURY.

CLIFFORD Are these thy bears? We'll bait thy bears to death,
And manacle the berard in their chains,
If thou dar'st bring them to the baiting-place.
RICHARD Oft have I seen a hot o'erweening cur
Run back and bite, because he was withheld;
Who, being suffer'd, with the bear's fell paw,
Hath clapp'd his tail between his legs and cried;
And such a piece of service will you do,
If you oppose yourselves to match Lord Warwick.
CLIFFORD Hence, heap of wrath, foul indigested lump,
As crooked in thy manners as thy shape!
YORK Nay, we shall heat you thoroughly anon.
CLIFFORD Take heed, lest by your heat you burn yourselves.
KING Why, Warwick, hath thy knee forgot to bow?
Old Salisbury, shame to thy silver hair,
Thou mad misleader of thy brainsick son!
What, wilt thou on thy death-bed play the ruffian
And seek for sorrow with thy spectacles?
O, where is faith? O, where is loyalty?
If it be banish'd from the frosty head,
Where shall it find a harbour in the earth?
Wilt thou go dig a grave to find out war
And shame thine honourable age with blood?
Why art thou old, and want'st experience?
Or wherefore dost abuse it, if thou hast it?
For shame! In duty bend thy knee to me,
That bows unto the grave with mickle age.
SALISBURY My lord, I have considered with myself
The title of this most renowned duke,
And in my conscience do repute his Grace
The rightful heir to England's royal seat.
KING Hast thou not sworn allegiance unto me?
SALISBURY I have.
KING Canst thou dispense with heaven for such an oath?
SALISBURY It is great sin to swear unto a sin;
But greater sin to keep a sinful oath.
Who can be bound by any solemn vow
To do a murd'rous deed, to rob a man,
To force a spotless virgin's chastity,
To reave the orphan of his patrimony,
To wring the widow from her custom'd right,
And have no other reason for this wrong
But that he was bound by a solemn oath?
QUEEN A subtle traitor needs no sophister.
KING Call Buckingham, and bid him arm himself.
YORK Call Buckingham, and all the friends thou hast,
I am resolv'd for death or dignity.
CLIFFORD The first I warrant thee, if dreams prove true.
WARWICK You were best to go to bed and dream again
To keep thee from the tempest of the field.
CLIFFORD I am resolv'd to bear a greater storm
Than any thou canst conjure up to-day;
And that I'll write upon thy burgonet,
Might I but know thee by thy household badge.
WARWICK Now, by my father's badge, old Nevil's crest,
The rampant bear chain'd to the ragged staff,
This day I'll wear aloft my burgonet,
As on a mountain-top the cedar shows,
That keeps his leaves in spite of any storm,
Even to affright thee with the view thereof.
CLIFFORD And from thy burgonet I'll rend thy bear
And tread it under foot with all contempt,
Despite the berard that protects the bear.
YOUNG CLIFFORD And so to arms, victorious father,
To quell the rebels and their complices.
RICHARD Fie! charity, for shame! Speak not in spite,
For you shall sup with Jesu Christ to-night.
YOUNG CLIFFORD Foul stigmatic, that's more than thou canst tell.
RICHARD If not in heaven, you'll surely sup in hell. [*Exeunt severally.*

SCENE II. *Saint Albans.*

Alarums to the battle. Enter WARWICK.

WARWICK Clifford of Cumberland, 'tis Warwick calls;
And if thou dost not hide thee from the bear,
Now, when the angry trumpet sounds alarum
And dead men's cries do fill the empty air,
Clifford, I say, come forth and fight with me.

Proud northern lord, Clifford of Cumberland,
Warwick is hoarse with calling thee to arms.

Enter YORK.

How now, my noble lord! what, all a-foot?

YORK The deadly-handed Clifford slew my steed;
But match to match I have encount'red him,
And made a prey for carrion kites and crows
Even of the bonny beast he lov'd so well.

Enter old CLIFFORD.

WARWICK Of one or both of us the time is come.

YORK Hold, Warwick, seek thee out some other chase,
For I myself must hunt this deer to death.

WARWICK Then, nobly, York; 'tis for a crown thou fight'st.
As I intend, Clifford, to thrive to-day,
It grieves my soul to leave thee unassail'd. [*Exit.*

CLIFFORD What seest thou in me, York? Why dost thou pause?

YORK With thy brave bearing should I be in love
But that thou art so fast mine enemy.

CLIFFORD Nor should thy prowess want praise and esteem
But that 'tis shown ignobly and in treason.

YORK So let it help me now against thy sword,
As I in justice and true right express it!

CLIFFORD My soul and body on the action both!

YORK A dreadful lay! Address thee instantly.

[*They fight and Clifford falls.*

CLIFFORD La fin couronne les oeuvres. [*Dies.*

YORK Thus war hath given thee peace, for thou art still.
Peace with his soul, heaven, if it be thy will!

[*Exit.*

Enter young CLIFFORD.

YOUNG CLIFFORD Shame and confusion! All is on the rout;
Fear frames disorder, and disorder wounds
Where it should guard. O war, thou son of hell,
Whom angry heavens do make their minister,
Throw in the frozen bosoms of our part
Hot coals of vengeance! Let no soldier fly.
He that is truly dedicate to war
Hath no self-love; nor he that loves himself
Hath not essentially, but by circumstance,
The name of valour. [*Sees his father's body.*
O, let the vile world end
And the premised flames of the last day
Knit earth and heaven together!
Now let the general trumpet blow his blast,
Particularities and petty sounds
To cease! Wast thou ordain'd, dear father,
To lose thy youth in peace and to achieve
The silver livery of advised age,
And in thy reverence and thy chair-days thus
To die in ruffian battle? Even at this sight
My heart is turn'd to stone; and while 'tis mine
It shall be stony. York not our old men spares;
No more will I their babes. Tears virginal
Shall be to me even as the dew to fire;
And beauty, that the tyrant oft reclaims,
Shall to my flaming wrath be oil and flax.
Henceforth I will not have to do with pity:
Meet I an infant of the house of York,
Into as many gobbets will I cut it
As wild Medea young Absyrtus did;
In cruelty will I seek out my fame.
Come, thou new ruin of old Clifford's house;
As did Aeneas old Anchises bear,
So bear I thee upon my manly shoulders;
But then Aeneas bare a living load,
Nothing so heavy as these woes of mine.

[*Exit with the body.*

Enter RICHARD and SOMERSET to fight. Somerset is killed.

RICHARD So, lie thou there;
For underneath an alehouse' paltry sign,
The Castle in Saint Albans, Somerset
Hath made the wizard famous in his death.
Sword, hold thy temper; heart, be wrathful still:
Priests pray for enemies, but princes kill. [*Exit.*

Fight. Excursions. Enter KING, QUEEN, and Others.

QUEEN Away, my lord! You are slow; for shame, away!

KING Can we outrun the heavens? Good Margaret, stay.

QUEEN What are you made of? You'll nor fight nor fly.
Now is it manhood, wisdom, and defence,
To give the enemy way, and to secure us
By what we can, which can no more but fly.

[*Alarum afar off.*

If you be ta'en, we then should see the bottom
Of all our fortunes; but if we haply scape –
As well we may, if not through your neglect –
We shall to London get, where you are lov'd,
And where this breach now in our fortunes made
May readily be stopp'd.

Re-enter young CLIFFORD.

YOUNG CLIFFORD But that my heart's on future mischief set,
I would speak blasphemy ere bid you fly;
But fly you must; uncurable discomfit
Reigns in the hearts of all our present parts.
Away, for your relief! and we will live
To see their day and them our fortune give.

Away, my lord, away! [*Exeunt.*

SCENE III. *Fields near Saint Albans.*

Alarum. Retreat. Enter YORK, RICHARD, WARWICK, and Soldiers, with drum and colours.

YORK Of Salisbury, who can report of him,
That winter lion, who in rage forgets
Aged contusions and all brush of time
And, like a gallant in the brow of youth,
Repairs him with occasion? This happy day
Is not itself, nor have we won one foot,
If Salisbury be lost.

RICHARD My noble father,
Three times to-day I holp him to his horse,
Three times bestrid him, thrice I led him off,
Persuaded him from any further act;
But still where danger was, still there I met him;
And like rich hangings in a homely house,
So was his will in his old feeble body.
But, noble as he is, look where he comes.

Enter SALISBURY.

SALISBURY Now, by my sword, well hast thou fought to-day!
By th' mass, so did we all. I thank you, Richard:
God knows how long it is I have to live,
And it hath pleas'd Him that three times to-day
You have defended me from imminent death.
Well, lords, we have not got that which we have;
'Tis not enough our foes are this time fled,
Being opposites of such repairing nature

YORK I know our safety is to follow them;
For, as I hear, the King is fled to London
To call a present court of Parliament.
Let us pursue him ere the writs go forth.
What says Lord Warwick? Shall we after them?

WARWICK After them? Nay, before them, if we can.
Now, by my faith, lords, 'twas a glorious day:
Saint Albans' battle, won by famous York,
Shall be eterniz'd in all age to come.
Sound drum and trumpets and to London all;
And more such days as these to us befall!

[*Exeunt.*

The Third Part of King Henry the Sixth

Introduction by ROBERT MASLEN

The Third Part of King Henry the Sixth is the most mournfully contemplative of Shakespeare's dramatic studies of fifteenth-century politics. In 1595 an unauthorized edition of the play appeared with the title *The True Tragedy of Richard, Duke of York, and the Death of Good King Henry the Sixth*. This reflects the two-part structure of the narrative: the tragedy begins and ends with the deaths of two sets of fathers and sons, caught in a vicious cycle of murder and retaliation from which many of the play's characters can see no escape. In the first act the Lancastrian Clifford captures and murders the Duke of York's young son, thus exacting a savage revenge for the death of his own father in the previous play. Soon afterwards Margaret, King Henry's aggressive wife, captures and murders York himself, after subjecting him to the grim parody of a royal coronation which is one of the most powerful scenes in Shakespeare's early plays [1.4]. In the last act the tragedy afflicts the Lancastrians in their turn, as first Henry's young son and then Henry himself are murdered by Richard of Gloucester, the future King Richard III. In between these two sets of murders, a succession of alliances and betrayals, successes and defeats follow one another with bewildering rapidity, as combatants struggle – and invariably fail – to reconcile familial ties with political expediency.

The play is dominated by the struggle of either faction over the proprietorship of the concept of 'right'. In the first scene York insists that the 'right' belongs to him: 'I mean to take possession of my right' [1.1.44], but later in the scene his enemy Clifford announces his intention to support Henry's cause 'be thy title right or wrong' [1.1.159]. From this point on, both sides lay claim to sole possession of the 'right', and die (as the young Prince Edward does [5.5.36–7]) with the word on their lips, as if it had not been rendered meaningless by its constant shifts in meaning.

In the same way the emblems of the two contending houses, Lancaster and York, the red rose and the white, gradually lose all significance in the course of the play. From the beginning the roses seem to have grown so entangled that they can hardly be distinguished. King Henry VI, who adopts the role of a resigned commentator on the action, watches a father who has accidentally killed his son in battle and observes that 'The red rose and the white are on his face, / The fatal colours of our striving houses' [2.5.97–8]. Elsewhere the red and white roses seem to have grown into a wood of thorns which embraces all the combatants. The Yorkist King Edward refers to the Lancastrians as a 'thorny wood' which 'Must by the roots be hewn up yet ere night' [5.4.67–9]. But for Edward's ambitious brother Richard of Gloucester the metaphor of the wood applies equally to both factions. In a soliloquy that anticipates the savagery of his future career he wishes Edward may prove impotent, 'That from his loins no hopeful branch may spring' [3.2.126], and mourns the number of other branches sprung from York's 'root' that stand between him and the throne:

And I – like one lost in a thorny wood

That rents the thorns and is rent with the thorns,
Seeking a way, and straying from the way; [...]
Torment myself to catch the English crown;
And from that torment I will free myself
Or hew my way out with a bloody axe. [3.2.174–81]

Richard identifies himself with neither faction: 'I am myself alone', he announces after he has murdered King Henry [5.6.83]. Ironically his refusal of all ties either of family or of political party offers a means of escape from the cycle of violence which is the civil war – a cycle which is perpetuated by rivalry between families – even if the escape must be made through the horrors of his reign as king. The other escape-route offered by the play is a more hopeful one. In Act 4 Scene 6 Henry meets the future King Henry VII, and prophesies as Tudor propaganda demanded that this is the child whose accession to the throne will end all civil strife. In depicting the instability of fifteenth-century England, Shakespeare was careful to imply that all the issues raised by the political crises of the previous century would be satisfactorily resolved in his own – while leaving his more sceptical spectators room to doubt it.

The Third Part of King Henry the Sixth

DRAMATIS PERSONAE

KING HENRY THE SIXTH
EDWARD
Prince of Wales
his son
LOUIS XI
King of France
DUKE OF SOMERSET
DUKE OF EXETER
EARL OF OXFORD
EARL OF NORTHUMBERLAND
EARL OF WESTMORELAND
LORD CLIFFORD
RICHARD PLANTAGENET
Duke of York
EDWARD *Earl of March, afterwards King Edward IV, EDMUND, Earl of Rutland, GEORGE, afterwards Duke of Clarence, RICHARD, afterwards Duke of Gloucester*
his sons
DUKE OF NORFOLK
MARQUIS OF MONTAGUE
EARL OF WARWICK
EARL OF PEMBROKE
LORD HASTINGS
LORD STAFFORD
SIR JOHN MORTIMER, SIR HUGH MORTIMER
uncles to the Duke of York
HENRY
Earl of Richard, a youth
LORD RIVERS
brother to Lady Grey
SIR WILLIAM STANLEY
SIR JOHN MONTGOMERY
SIR JOHN SOMERVILLE
TUTOR
to Rutland
Mayor of York
Lieutenant of the Tower
A Nobleman
Two Keepers
A Huntsman
A Son that has killed his father
A Father that has killed his son
QUEEN MARGARET
LADY GREY
afterwards Queen to Edward IV
BONA
sister to the French Queen
Soldiers, Attendants, Messengers, and Watchmen etc.

THE SCENE: ENGLAND AND FRANCE.

ACT ONE

SCENE I. *London. The Parliament House.*

Alarum. Enter DUKE OF YORK, EDWARD, RICHARD, NORFOLK, MONTAGUE, WARWICK, and Soldiers, with white roses in their hats.

WARWICK I wonder how the King escap'd our hands.
YORK While we pursu'd the horsemen of the north,
He slily stole away and left his men;
Whereat the great Lord of Northumberland,
Whose warlike ears could never brook retreat,
Cheer'd up the drooping army, and himself,
Lord Clifford, and Lord Stafford, all abreast,
Charg'd our main battle's front, and, breaking in,
Were by the swords of common soldiers slain.
EDWARD Lord Stafford's father, Duke of Buckingham,
Is either slain or wounded dangerous;
I cleft his beaver with a downright blow.
That this is true, father, behold his blood.
MONTAGUE And, brother, here's the Earl of Wiltshire's blood,
Whom I encount'red as the battles join'd.
RICHARD Speak thou for me, and tell them what I did. [*Throwing down Somerset's head.*
YORK Richard hath best deserv'd of all my sons.
But is your Grace dead, my Lord of Somerset?
NORFOLK Such hope have all the line of John of Gaunt!
RICHARD Thus do I hope to shake King Henry's head.
WARWICK And so do I. Victorious Prince of York,

Before I see thee seated in that throne
Which now the house of Lancaster usurps,
I vow by heaven these eyes shall never close.
This is the palace of the fearful King,
And this the regal seat. Possess it, York;
For this is thine, and not King Henry's heirs'.

YORK Assist me then, sweet Warwick, and I will;
For hither we have broken in by force.

NORFOLK We'll all assist you; he that flies shall die.

YORK Thanks, gentle Norfolk. Stay by me, my lords;
And, soldiers, stay and lodge by me this night.

[They go up.

WARWICK And when the King comes, offer him no violence,
Unless he seek to thrust you out perforce.

YORK The Queen this day here holds her parliament,
But little thinks we shall be of her council.
By words or blows here let us win our right.

RICHARD Arm'd as we are, let's stay within this house.

WARWICK The bloody parliament shall this be call'd,
Unless Plantagenet, Duke of York, be King,
And bashful Henry depos'd, whose cowardice
Hath made us by-words to our enemies.

YORK Then leave me not, my lords; be resolute:
I mean to take possession of my right.

WARWICK Neither the King, nor he that loves him best,
The proudest he that holds up Lancaster,
Dares stir a wing if Warwick shake his bells.
I'll plant Plantagenet, root him up who dares.
Resolve thee, Richard; claim the English crown.

[York occupies the throne.

Flourish. Enter KING HENRY, CLIFFORD, NORTHUMBERLAND, WESTMORELAND, EXETER, and Others, with red roses in their hats.

KING HENRY My lords, look where the sturdy rebel sits,
Even in the chair of state! Belike he means,
Back'd by the power of Warwick, that false peer,
To aspire unto the crown and reign as king.
Earl of Northumberland, he slew thy father;
And thine, Lord Clifford; and you both have vow'd revenge
On him, his sons, his favourites, and his friends.

NORTHUMBERLAND If I be not, heavens be reveng'd on me!

CLIFFORD The hope thereof makes Clifford mourn in steel.

WESTMORELAND What, shall we suffer this? Let's pluck him down;
My heart for anger burns; I cannot brook it.

KING HENRY Be patient, gentle Earl of Westmoreland.

CLIFFORD Patience is for poltroons such as he;
He durst not sit there had your father liv'd.
My gracious lord, here in the parliament
Let us assail the family of York.

NORTHUMBERLAND Well hast thou spoken, cousin; be it so.

KING HENRY Ah, know you not the city favours them,
And they have troops of soldiers at their beck?

EXETER But when the Duke is slain they'll quickly fly.

KING HENRY Far be the thought of this from Henry's heart,
To make a shambles of the parliament house!
Cousin of Exeter, frowns, words, and threats,
Shall be the war that Henry means to use.
Thou factious Duke of York, descend my throne
And kneel for grace and mercy at my feet;
I am thy sovereign.

YORK I am thine.

EXETER For shame, come down; he made thee Duke of York.

YORK 'Twas my inheritance, as the earldom was.

EXETER Thy father was a traitor to the crown.

WARWICK Exeter, thou art a traitor to the crown
In following this usurping Henry.

CLIFFORD Whom should he follow but his natural king?

WARWICK True, Clifford; and that's Richard Duke of York.

KING HENRY And shall I stand, and thou sit in my throne?

YORK It must and shall be so; content thyself.

WARWICK Be Duke of Lancaster; let him be King.

WESTMORELAND He is both King and Duke of Lancaster;
And that the Lord of Westmoreland shall maintain.

WARWICK And Warwick shall disprove it. You forget
That we are those which chas'd you from the field,
And slew your fathers, and with colours spread
March'd through the city to the palace gates.

NORTHUMBERLAND Yes, Warwick, I remember it to my grief;
And, by his soul, thou and thy house shall rue it.

WESTMORELAND Plantagenet, of thee, and these thy sons,
Thy kinsmen, and thy friends, I'll have more lives
Than drops of blood were in my father's veins.

CLIFFORD Urge it no more; less that instead of words

I send thee, Warwick, such a messenger
As shall revenge his death before I stir.

WARWICK Poor Clifford, how I scorn his worthless threats!

YORK Will you we show our title to the crown?
If not, our swords shall plead it in the field.

KING HENRY What title hast thou, traitor, to the crown?
Thy father was, as thou art, Duke of York;
Thy grandfather, Roger Mortimer, Earl of March:
I am the son of Henry the Fifth,
Who made the Dauphin and the French to stoop,
And seiz'd upon their towns and provinces.

WARWICK Talk not of France, sith thou hast lost it all.

KING HENRY The Lord Protector lost it, and not I:
When I was crown'd, I was but nine months old.

RICHARD You are old enough now, and yet methinks you lose.
Father, tear the crown from the usurper's head.

EDWARD Sweet father, do so; set it on your head.

MONTAGUE Good brother, as thou lov'st and honourest arms,
Let's fight it out and not stand cavilling thus.

RICHARD Sound drums and trumpets, and the King will fly.

YORK Sons, peace!

KING HENRY Peace thou! and give King Henry leave to speak.

WARWICK Plantagenet shall speak first. Hear him, lords;
And be you silent and attentive too,
For he that interrupts him shall not live.

KING HENRY Think'st thou that I will leave my kingly throne,
Wherein my grandsire and my father sat?
No; first shall war unpeople this my realm;
Ay, and their colours, often borne in France,
And now in England to our heart's great sorrow,
Shall be my winding-sheet. Why faint you, lords?
My title's good, and better far than his.

WARWICK Prove it, Henry, and thou shalt be King.

KING HENRY Henry the Fourth by conquest got the crown.

YORK 'Twas by rebellion against his king.

KING HENRY [*Aside*] I know not what to say; my title's weak.—
Tell me, may not a king adopt an heir?

YORK What then?

KING HENRY An if he may, then am I lawful King;
For Richard, in the view of many lords,
Resign'd the crown to Henry the Fourth,
Whose heir my father was, and I am his.

YORK He rose against him, being his sovereign,
And made him to resign his crown perforce.

WARWICK Suppose, my lords, he did it unconstrain'd,
Think you 'twere prejudicial to his crown?

EXETER No; for he could not so resign his crown
But that the next heir should succeed and reign.

KING HENRY Art thou against us, Duke of Exeter?

EXETER His is the right, and therefore pardon me.

YORK Why whisper you, my lords, and answer not?

EXETER My conscience tells me he is lawful King.

KING HENRY [*Aside*] All will revolt from me, and turn to him.

NORTHUMBERLAND Plantagenet, for all the claim thou lay'st,
Think not that Henry shall be so depos'd.

WARWICK Depos'd he shall be, in despite of all.

NORTHUMBERLAND Thou art deceiv'd. 'Tis not thy southern power
Of Essex, Norfolk, Suffolk, nor of Kent,
Which makes thee thus presumptuous and proud,
Can set the Duke up in despite of me.

CLIFFORD King Henry, be thy title right or wrong,
Lord Clifford vows to fight in thy defence.
May that ground gape, and swallow me alive,
Where I shall kneel to him that slew my father!

KING HENRY O Clifford, how thy words revive my heart!

YORK Henry of Lancaster, resign thy crown.
What mutter you, or what conspire you, lords?

WARWICK Do right unto this princely Duke of York;
Or I will fill the house with armed men,
And over the chair of state, where now he sits,
Write up his title with usurping blood.

[*He stamps with his foot and the Soldiers show themselves*

KING HENRY My Lord of Warwick, hear but one word:
Let me for this my life-time reign as king.

YORK Confirm the crown to me and to mine heirs,
And thou shalt reign in quiet while thou liv'st.

KING HENRY I am content. Richard Plantagenet,
Enjoy the kingdom after my decease.

CLIFFORD What wrong is this unto the Prince your son!

WARWICK What good is this to England and himself!

WESTMORELAND Base, fearful, and despairing Henry!

CLIFFORD How hast thou injur'd both thyself and us!

WESTMORELAND I cannot stay to hear these articles.
NORTHUMBERLAND Nor I.
CLIFFORD Come, cousin, let us tell the Queen these news.
WESTMORELAND Farewell, faint-hearted and degenerate king,
In whose cold blood no spark of honour bides.
NORTHUMBERLAND Be thou a prey unto the house of York
And die in bands for this unmanly deed!
CLIFFORD In dreadful war mayst thou be overcome,
Or live in peace abandon'd and despis'd!
[Exeunt Northumberland, Clifford and Westmoreland.

WARWICK Turn this way, Henry, and regard them not.
EXETER They seek revenge, and therefore will not yield.
KING HENRY Ah, Exeter!
WARWICK Why should you sigh, my lord?
KING HENRY Not for myself, Lord Warwick, but my son,
Whom I unnaturally shall disinherit.
But be it as it may. *[To York]* I here entail
The crown to thee and to thine heirs for ever;
Conditionally, that here thou take an oath
To cease this civil war, and, whilst I live,
To honour me as thy king and sovereign,
And neither by treason nor hostility
To seek to put me down and reign thyself.
YORK This oath I willingly take, and will perform.
[Coming from the throne.

WARWICK Long live King Henry! Plantagenet, embrace him.
KING HENRY And long live thou, and these thy forward sons!
YORK Now York and Lancaster are reconcil'd.
EXETER Accurs'd be he that seeks to make them foes! *[Sennet. Here they come down.*

YORK Farewell, my gracious lord; I'll to my castle.
WARWICK And I'll keep London with my soldiers.
NORFOLK And I to Norfolk with my followers.
MONTAGUE And I unto the sea, from whence I came. *[Exeunt the Yorkists.*

KING HENRY And I, with grief and sorrow, to the court.

Enter QUEEN MARGARET and the PRINCE OF WALES.

EXETER Here comes the Queen, whose looks brewray her anger.
I'll steal away.
KING HENRY Exeter, so will I.
QUEEN MARGARET Nay, go not from me; I will follow thee.
KING HENRY Be patient, gentle queen, and I will stay.
QUEEN MARGARET Who can be patient in such extremes?
Ah, wretched man! Would I had died a maid,
And never seen thee, never borne thee son,
Seeing thou hast prov'd so unnatural a father!
Hath he deserv'd to lose his birthright thus?
Hadst thou but lov'd him half so well as I,
Or felt that pain which I did for him once,
Or nourish'd him as I did with my blood,
Thou wouldst have left thy dearest heartblood there
Rather than have made that savage duke thine heir,
And disinherited thine only son.
PRINCE Father, you cannot disinherit me.
If you be King, why should not I succeed?
KING HENRY Pardon me, Margaret; pardon me, sweet son.
The Earl of Warwick and the Duke enforc'd me.
QUEEN MARGARET Enforc'd thee! Art thou King and wilt be forc'd?
I shame to hear thee speak. Ah, timorous wretch!
Thou hast undone thyself, thy son, and me;
And giv'n unto the house of York such head
As thou shalt reign but by their sufferance.
To entail him and his heirs unto the crown,
What is it but to make thy sepulchre
And creep into it far before thy time?
Warwick is Chancellor and the lord of Calais;
Stern Falconbridge commands the narrow seas;
The Duke is made Protector of the realm;
And yet shalt thou be safe? Such safety finds
The trembling lamb environed with wolves.
Had I been there, which am a silly woman,
The soldiers should have toss'd me on their pikes
Before I would have granted to that act.
But thou prefer'st thy life before thine honour;
And seeing thou dost, I here divorce myself
Both from thy table, Henry, and thy bed,
Until that act of parliament be repeal'd
Whereby my son is disinherited.
The northern lords that have forsworn thy colours
Will follow mine, if once they see them spread;
And spread they shall be, to thy foul disgrace
And utter ruin of the house of York.
Thus do I leave thee. Come, son, let's away;
Our army is ready; come, we'll after them.
KING HENRY Stay, gentle Margaret, and hear me speak.

QUEEN MARGARET Thou hast spoke too much already; get thee gone.
KING HENRY Gentle son Edward, thou wilt stay with me?
QUEEN MARGARET Ay, to be murder'd by his enemies.
PRINCE When I return with victory from the field
I'll see your Grace; till then I'll follow her.
QUEEN MARGARET Come, son, away; we may not linger thus. [*Exeunt Queen Margaret and the Prince.*
KING HENRY Poor queen! How love to me and to her son
Hath made her break out into terms of rage!
Reveng'd may she be on that hateful Duke,
Whose haughty spirit, winged with desire,
Will cost my crown, and like an empty eagle
Tire on the flesh of me and of my son!
The loss of those three lords torments my heart.
I'll write unto them, and entreat them fair;
Come, cousin, you shall be the messenger.
EXETER And I, I hope, shall reconcile them all.
[*Exeunt.*

SCENE II. *Sandal Castle, near Wakefield, in Yorkshire.*

Flourish. Enter EDWARD, RICHARD, and MONTAGUE.

RICHARD Brother, though I be youngest, give me leave.
EDWARD No, I can better play the orator.
MONTAGUE But I have reasons strong and forcible.

Enter the DUKE OF YORK.

YORK Why, how now, sons and brother! at a strife?
What is your quarrel? How began it first?
EDWARD No quarrel, but a slight contention.
YORK About what?
RICHARD About that which concerns your Grace and us –
The crown of England, father, which is yours.
YORK Mine, boy? Not till King Henry be dead.
RICHARD Your right depends not on his life or death.
EDWARD Now you are heir, therefore enjoy it now.
By giving the house of Lancaster leave to breathe,
It will outrun you, father, in the end.
YORK I took an oath that he should quietly reign.
EDWARD But for a kingdom any oath may be broken:
I would break a thousand oaths to reign one year.
RICHARD No; God forbid your Grace should be forsworn.
YORK I shall be, if I claim by open war.
RICHARD I'll prove the contrary, if you'll hear me speak.
YORK Thou canst not, son; it is impossible.
RICHARD An oath is of no moment, being not took
Before a true and lawful magistrate
That hath authority over him that swears.
Henry had none, but did usurp the place;
Then, seeing 'twas he that made you to depose,
Your oath, my lord, is vain and frivolous.
Therefore, to arms. And, father, do but think
How sweet a thing it is to wear a crown,
Within whose circuit is Elysium
And all that poets feign of bliss and joy.
Why do we linger thus? I cannot rest
Until the white rose that I wear be dy'd
Even in the lukewarm blood of Henry's heart.
YORK Richard, enough; I will be King, or die.
Brother, thou shalt to London presently
And whet on Warwick to this enterprise.
Thou, Richard, shalt to the Duke of Norfolk
And tell him privily of our intent.
You, Edward, shall unto my Lord Cobham,
With whom the Kentishmen will willingly rise;
In them I trust, for they are soldiers,
Witty, courteous, liberal, full of spirit.
While you are thus employ'd, what resteth more
But that I seek occasion how to rise,
And yet the King not privy to my drift,
Nor any of the house of Lancaster?

Enter a Messenger.

But, stay. What news? Why com'st thou in such post?
MESSENGER The Queen with all the northern earls and lords
Intend here to besiege you in your castle.
She is hard by with twenty thousand men;
And therefore fortify your hold, my lord.
YORK Ay, with my sword. What! think'st thou that we fear them?
Edward and Richard, you shall stay with me;
My brother Montague shall post to London.
Let noble Warwick, Cobham, and the rest,
Whom we have left protectors of the King,
With pow'rful policy strengthen themselves
And trust not simple Henry nor his oaths.
MONTAGUE Brother, I go; I'll win them, fear it not.
And thus most humbly I do take my leave.
[*Exit.*

Enter SIR JOHN and SIR HUGH MORTIMER.

YORK Sir John and Sir Hugh Mortimer, mine uncles!

You are come to Sandal in a happy hour;
The army of the Queen mean to besiege us.
SIR JOHN She shall not need; we'll meet her in the field.
YORK What, with five thousand men?
RICHARD Ay, with five hundred, father, for a need.
A woman's general; what should we fear?

[A march afar off.

EDWARD I hear their drums. Let's set our men in order,
And issue forth and bid them battle straight.
YORK Five men to twenty! Though the odds be great,
I doubt not, uncle, of our victory.
Many a battle have I won in France,
When as the enemy hath been ten to one;
Why should I not now have the like success?

[Exeunt.

SCENE III. *Field of battle between Sandal Castle and Wakefield*

Alarum. Enter RUTLAND and his Tutor.

RUTLAND Ah, whither shall I fly to scape their hands?
Ah, tutor, look where bloody Clifford comes!

Enter CLIFFORD and Soldiers.

CLIFFORD Chaplain, away! Thy priesthood saves thy life.
As for the brat of this accursed duke,
Whose father slew my father, he shall die.
TUTOR And I, my lord, will bear him company.
CLIFFORD Soldiers, away with him!
TUTOR Ah, Clifford, murder not this innocent child,
Lest thou be hated both of God and man.

[Exit, forced off by Soldiers.

CLIFFORD How now, is he dead already? Or is it fear
That makes him close his eyes? I'll open them.
RUTLAND So looks the pent-up lion o'er the wretch
That trembles under his devouring paws;
And so he walks, insulting o'er his prey,
And so he comes, to rend his limbs asunder.
Ah, gentle Clifford, kill me with thy sword,
And not with such a cruel threat'ning look!
Sweet Clifford, hear me speak before I die.
I am too mean a subject for thy wrath;
Be thou reveng'd on men, and let me live.
CLIFFORD In vain thou speak'st, poor boy; my father's blood
Hath stopp'd the passage where thy words should enter.
RUTLAND Then let my father's blood open it again:
He is a man, and, Clifford, cope with him.
CLIFFORD Had I thy brethren here, their lives and thine
Were not revenge sufficient for me;
No, if I digg'd up thy forefathers' graves
And hung their rotten coffins up in chains,
It could not slake mine ire nor ease my heart.
The sight of any of the house of York
Is as a fury to torment my soul;
And till I root out their accursed line
And leave not one alive, I live in hell.
Therefore –
RUTLAND O, let me pray before I take my death!
To thee I pray: sweet Clifford, pity me.
CLIFFORD Such pity as my rapier's point affords.
RUTLAND I never did thee harm; why wilt thou slay me?
CLIFFORD Thy father hath.
RUTLAND But 'twas ere I was born.
Thou hast one son; for his sake pity me,
Lest in revenge thereof, sith God is just,
He be as miserably slain as I.
Ah, let me live in prison all my days;
And when I give occasion of offence
Then let me die, for now thou hast no cause.
CLIFFORD No cause!
Thy father slew my father; therefore, die.

[Stabs him.

RUTLAND Di faciant laudis summa sit ista tuae!

[Dies.

CLIFFORD Plantagenet, I come, Plantagenet;
And this thy son's blood cleaving to my blade
Shall rust upon my weapon, till thy blood,
Congeal'd with this, do make me wipe off both.

[Exit.

SCENE IV. *Another part of the field.*

Alarum. Enter the DUKE OF YORK.

YORK The army of the Queen hath got the field.
My uncles both are slain in rescuing me;
And all my followers to the eager foe
Turn back and fly, like ships before the wind,
Or lambs pursu'd by hunger-starved wolves.
My sons – God knows what hath bechanced them;
But this I know – they have demean'd themselves
Like men born to renown by life or death.
Three times did Richard make a lane to me,
And thrice cried 'Courage, father! fight it out'.
And full as oft came Edward to my side
With purple falchion, painted to the hilt
In blood of those that had encount'red him.

And when the hardiest warriors did retire,
Richard cried 'Charge, and give no foot of
ground'.
And cried 'A crown, or else a glorious tomb!
A sceptre, or an earthly sepulchre!'
With this we charg'd again; but out alas!
We bodg'd again; as I have seen a swan
With bootless labour swim against the tide
And spend her strength with over-matching
waves. [*A short alarum within.*

Ah, hark! The fatal followers do pursue,
And I am faint and cannot fly their fury;
And were I strong, I would not shun their fury
The sands are numb'red that make up my life;
Here must I stay, and here my life must end.

Enter QUEEN MARGARET, CLIFFORD, NORTHUMBERLAND, *the* PRINCE OF WALES, *and Soldiers.*

Come, bloody Clifford, rough
Northumberland,
I dare your quenchless fury to more rage;
I am your butt, and I abide your shot.

NORTHUMBERLAND Yield to our mercy, proud
Plantagenet.

CLIFFORD Ay, to such mercy as his ruthless arm
With downright payment show'd unto my
father.
Now Phaethon hath tumbled from his car,
And made an evening at the noontide prick.

YORK My ashes, as the phoenix, may bring forth
A bird that will revenge upon you all;
And in that hope I throw mine eyes to heaven,
Scorning whate'er you can afflict me with.
Why come you not? What! multitudes, and
fear?

CLIFFORD So cowards fight when they can fly no
further;
So doves do peck the falcon's piercing talons;
So desperate thieves, all hopeless of their lives,
Breathe out invectives 'gainst the officers.

YORK O Clifford, but bethink thee once again,
And in thy thought o'errun my former time;
And, if thou canst for blushing, view this face,
And bite thy tongue that slanders him with
cowardice
Whose frown hath made thee faint and fly ere
this!

CLIFFORD I will not bandy with thee word for
word,
But buckler with thee blows, twice two for one.

QUEEN MARGARET Hold, valiant Clifford; for a
thousand causes
I would prolong awhile the traitor's life.
Wrath makes him deaf; speak thou,
Northumberland.

NORTHUMBERLAND Hold, Clifford! do not
honour him so much
To prick thy finger, though to wound his heart.
What valour were it, when a cur doth grin,
For one to thrust his hand between his teeth,
When he might spurn him with his foot away?
It is war's prize to take all vantages;
And ten to one is no impeach of valour.

[*They lay hands on York, who struggles.*

CLIFFORD Ay, ay, so strives the woodcock with
the gin.

NORTHUMBERLAND So doth the cony struggle in
the net.

YORK So triumph thieves upon their conquer'd
booty;
So true men yield, with robbers so o'er-match'd.

NORTHUMBERLAND What would your Grace
have done unto him now?

QUEEN MARGARET Brave warriors, Clifford and
Northumberland,
Come, make him stand upon this molehill here
That raught at mountains with outstretched
arms,
Yet parted but the shadow with his hand.
What, was it you that would be England's king?
Was't you that revell'd in our parliament
And made a preachment of your high descent?
Where are your mess of sons to back you now?
The wanton Edward and the lusty George?
And where's that valiant crook-back prodigy,
Dicky your boy, that with his grumbling voice
Was wont to cheer his dad in mutinies?
Or, with the rest, where is your darling
Rutland?
Look, York: I stain'd this napkin with the blood
That valiant Clifford with his rapier's point
Made issue from the bosom of the boy;
And if thine eyes can water for his death,
I give thee this to dry thy cheeks withal.
Alas, poor York! but that I hate thee deadly,
I should lament thy miserable state.
I prithee grieve to make me merry, York.
What, hath thy fiery heart so parch'd thine
entrails
That not a tear can fall for Rutland's death?
Why art thou patient, man? Thou shouldst be
mad;
And I to make thee mad do mock thee thus.
Stamp, rave, and fret, that I may sing and dance.
Thou wouldst be fee'd, I see, to make me sport;
York cannot speak unless he wear a crown.
A crown for York! – and, lords, bow low to him.
Hold you his hands whilst I do set it on.

[*Putting a paper crown on his head.*

Ay, marry, sir, now looks he like a king!
Ay, this is he that took King Henry's chair,
And this is he was his adopted heir.

But how is it that great Plantagenet
Is crown'd so soon and broke his solemn oath?
As I bethink me, you should not be King
Till our King Henry had shook hands with death.
And will you pale your head in Henry's glory,
And rob his temples of the diadem,
Now in his life, against your holy oath?
O, 'tis a fault too too unpardonable!
Off with the crown and with the crown his head;
And, whilst we breathe, take time to do him dead.

CLIFFORD That is my office, for my father's sake.

QUEEN MARGARET Nay, stay; let's hear the orisons he makes.

YORK She-wolf of France, but worse than wolves of France,
Whose tongue more poisons than the adder's tooth!
How ill-beseeming is it in thy sex
To triumph like an Amazonian trull
Upon their woes whom fortune captivates!
But that thy face is visard-like, unchanging,
Made impudent with use of evil deeds,
I would assay, proud queen, to make thee blush.
To tell thee whence thou cam'st, of whom deriv'd,
Were shame enough to shame thee, wert thou not shameless.
Thy father bears the type of King of Naples,
Of both the Sicils and Jerusalem,
Yet not so wealthy as an English yeoman.
Hath that poor monarch taught thee to insult?
It needs not, nor it boots thee not, proud queen;
Unless the adage must be verified,
That beggars mounted run their horse to death.
'Tis beauty that doth oft make women proud;
But, God He knows, thy share thereof is small.
'Tis virtue that doth make them most admir'd;
The contrary doth make thee wond'red at.
'Tis government that makes them seem divine;
The want thereof makes thee abominable.
Thou art as opposite to every good
As the Antipodes are unto us,
Or as the south to the septentrion.
O tiger's heart wrapp'd in a woman's hide!
How couldst thou drain the life-blood of the child,
To bid the father wipe his eyes withal,
And yet be seen to bear a woman's face?
Women are soft, mild, pitiful, and flexible:
Thou stern, obdurate, flinty, rough, remorseless.
Bid'st thou me rage? Why, now thou hast thy wish;
Wouldst have me weep? Why, now thou hast thy will;
For raging wind blows up incessant showers,
And when the rage allays, the rain begins.
These tears are my sweet Rutland's obsequies;
And every drop cries vengeance for his death
'Gainst thee, fell Clifford, and thee, false Frenchwoman.

NORTHUMBERLAND Beshrew me, but his passions move me so
That hardly can I check my eyes from tears.

YORK That face of his the hungry cannibals
Would not have touch'd, would not have stain'd with blood;
But you are more inhuman, more inexorable –
O, ten times more – than tigers of Hyrcania.
See, ruthless queen, a hapless father's tears.
This cloth thou dipp'dst in blood of my sweet boy,
And I with tears do wash the blood away.
Keep thou the napkin, and go boast of this;
And if thou tell'st the heavy story right,
Upon my soul, the hearers will shed tears;
Yea, even my foes will shed fast-falling tears
And say 'Alas, it was a piteous deed!'
There, take the crown, and with the crown my curse;
And in thy need such comfort come to thee
As now I reap at thy too cruel hand!
Hard-hearted Clifford, take me from the world;
My soul to heaven, my blood upon your heads!

NORTHUMBERLAND Had he been slaughter-man to all my kin,
I should not for my life but weep with him,
To see how inly sorrow gripes his soul.

QUEEN MARGARET What, weeping-ripe, my Lord Northumberland?
Think but upon the wrong he did us all,
And that will quickly dry thy melting tears.

CLIFFORD Here's for my oath, here's for my father's death. *[Stabbing him.*

QUEEN MARGARET And here's to right our gentle-hearted king. *[Stabbing him.*

YORK Open Thy gate of mercy, gracious God!
My soul flies through these wounds to seek out Thee. *[Dies.*

QUEEN MARGARET Off with his head, and set it on York gates;
So York may overlook the town of York.

[Flourish. Exeunt.

ACT TWO

SCENE I. *A plain near Mortimer's Cross in Herefordshire.*

A march. Enter EDWARD, RICHARD, and their Power.

EDWARD I wonder how our princely father scap'd,
Or whether he be scap'd away or no
From Clifford's and Northumberland's pursuit.
Had he been ta'en, we should have heard the news;
Had he been slain, we should have heard the news;
Or had he scap'd, methinks we should have heard
The happy tidings of his good escape.
How fares my brother? Why is he so sad?

RICHARD I cannot joy until I be resolv'd
Where our right valiant father is become.
I saw him in the battle range about,
And watch'd him how he singled Clifford forth.
Methought he bore him in the thickest troop
As doth a lion in a heard of neat;
Or as a bear, encompass'd round with dogs,
Who having pinch'd a few and made them cry,
The rest stand all aloof and bark at him.
So far'd our father with his enemies;
So fled his enemies my warlike father.
Methinks 'tis prize enough to be his son.
See how the morning opes her golden gates
And takes her farewell of the glorious sun.
How well resembles it the prime of youth,
Trimm'd like a younker prancing to his love!

EDWARD Dazzle mine eyes, or do I see three suns?

RICHARD Three glorious suns, each one a perfect sun;
Not separated with the racking clouds,
But sever'd in a pale clear-shining sky.
See, see! they join, embrace, and seem to kiss,
As if they vow'd some league inviolable.
Now are they but one lamp, one light, one sun.
In this the heaven figures some event.

EDWARD 'Tis wondrous strange, the like yet never heard of.
I think it cites us, brother, to the field,
That we, the sons of brave Plantagenet,
Each one already blazing by our meeds,
Should notwithstanding join our lights together
And overshine the earth, as this the world.
Whate'er it bodes, henceforward will I bear
Upon my target three fair shining suns.

RICHARD Nay, bear three daughters – by your leave I speak it,
You love the breeder better than the male.

Enter a Messenger, blowing.

But what art thou, whose heavy looks foretell
Some dreadful story hanging on thy tongue?

MESSENGER Ah, one that was a woeful looker-on
When as the noble Duke of York was slain,
Your princely father and my loving lord!

EDWARD O, speak no more! for I have heard too much.

RICHARD Say how he died, for I will hear it all.

MESSENGER Environed he was with many foes,
And stood against them as the hope of Troy
Against the Greeks that would have ent'red Troy.
But Hercules himself must yield to odds;
And many strokes, though with a little axe,
Hews down and fells the hardest-timber'd oak.
By many hands your father was subdu'd;
But only slaught'red by the ireful arm
Of unrelenting Clifford and the Queen,
Who crown'd the gracious Duke in high despite,
Laugh'd in his face; and when with grief he wept,
The ruthless Queen gave him to dry his cheeks
A napkin steeped in the harmless blood
Of sweet young Rutland, by rough Clifford slain;
And after many scorns, many foul taunts,
They took his head, and on the gates of York
They set the same; and there it doth remain,
The saddest spectacle that e'er I view'd.

EDWARD Sweet Duke of York, our prop to lean upon,
Now thou art gone, we have no staff, no stay.
O Clifford, boist'rous Clifford, thou hast slain
The flow'r of Europe for his chivalry;
And treacherously hast thou vanquish'd him,
For hand to hand he would have vanquish'd thee.
Now my soul's palace is become a prison.
Ah, would she break from hence, that this my body
Might in the ground be closed up in rest!
For never henceforth shall I joy again;
Never, O never, shall I see more joy.

RICHARD I cannot weep, for all my body's moisture
Scarce serves to quench my furnace-burning heart;
Nor can my tongue unload my heart's great burden,
For self-same wind that I should speak withal
Is kindling coals that fires all my breast,
And burns me up with flames that tears would quench.

To weep is to make less the depth of grief.
Tears then for babes; blows and revenge for me!
Richard, I bear thy name; I'll venge thy death,
Or die renowned by attempting it.

EDWARD His name that valiant duke hath left with thee;
His dukedom and his chair with me is left.

RICHARD Nay, if thou be that princely eagle's bird,
Show thy descent by gazing 'gainst the sun;
For chair and dukedom, throne and kingdom, say:
Either that is thine, or else thou wert not his.

March. Enter WARWICK, MONTAGUE, and their Army.

WARWICK How now, fair lords! What fare? What news abroad?

RICHARD Great Lord of Warwick, if we should recount
Our baleful news and at each word's deliverance
Stab poinards in our flesh till all were told,
The words would add more anguish than the wounds.
O valiant lord, the Duke of York is slain!

EDWARD O Warwick, Warwick! that Plantagenet
Which held thee dearly as his soul's redemption
Is by the stern Lord Clifford done to death.

WARWICK Ten days ago I drown'd these news in tears;
And now, to add more measure to your woes,
I come to tell you things sith then befall'n.
After the bloody fray at Wakefield fought,
Where your brave father breath'd his latest gasp,
Tidings, as swiftly as the posts could run,
Were brought me of your loss and his depart.
I, then in London, keeper of the King,
Muster'd my soldiers, gathered flocks of friends,
And very well appointed, as I thought,
March'd toward Saint Albans to intercept the Queen,
Bearing the King in my behalf along;
For by my scouts I was advertised
That she was coming with a full intent
To dash our late decree in parliament
Touching King Henry's oath and your succession.
Short tale to make – we at St. Albans met,
Our battles join'd, and both sides fiercely fought;
But whether 'twas the coldness of the King,
Who look'd full gently on his warlike queen,
That robb'd my soldiers of their heated spleen,
Or whether 'twas report of her success,
Or more than common fear of Clifford's rigour,
Who thunders to his captives blood and death,
I cannot judge; but, to conclude with truth,
Their weapons like to lightning came and went:
Our soldiers', like the night-owl's lazy flight
Or like an idle thresher with a flail,
Fell gently down, as if they struck their friends.
I cheer'd them up with justice of our cause,
With promise of high pay and great rewards,
But all in vain; they had no heart to fight,
And we in them no hope to win the day;
So that we fled: the King unto the Queen;
Lord George your brother, Norfolk, and myself,
In haste post-haste are come to join with you;
For in the marches here we heard you were
Making another head to fight again.

EDWARD Where is the Duke of Norfolk, gentle Warwick?
And when came George from Burgundy to England?

WARWICK Some six miles off the Duke is with the soldiers;
And for your brother, he was lately sent
From your kind aunt, Duchess of Burgundy,
With aid of soldiers to this needful war.

RICHARD 'Twas odds, belike, when valiant Warwick fled.
Oft have I heard his praises in pursuit,
But ne'er till now his scandal of retire.

WARWICK Nor now my scandal, Richard, dost thou hear;
For thou shalt know this strong right hand of mine
Can pluck the diadem from faint Henry's head
And wring the awful sceptre from his fist,
Were he as famous and as bold in war
As he is fam'd for mildness, peace, and prayer.

RICHARD I know it well, Lord Warwick; blame me not.
'Tis love I bear thy glories makes me speak.
But in this troublous time what's to be done?
Shall we go throw away our coats of steel
And wrap our bodies in black mourning-gowns,
Numbering our Ave-Maries with our beads?
Or shall we on the helmets of our foes
Tell our devotion with revengeful arms?
If for the last, say 'Ay', and to it, lords.

WARWICK Why, therefore Warwick came to seek you out;
And therefore comes my brother Montague.
Attend me, lords. The proud insulting Queen,
With Clifford and the haught Northumberland,
And of their feather many moe proud birds,
Have wrought the easy-melting King like wax.
He swore consent to your succession,
His oath enrolled in the parliament;
And now to London all the crew are gone
To frustrate both his oath and what beside
May make against the house of Lancaster.
Their power, I think, is thirty thousand strong.

Now if the help of Norfolk and myself,
With all the friends that thou, brave Earl of March,
Amongst the loving Welshmen canst procure,
Will but amount to five and twenty thousand,
Why, Via! to London will we march amain,
And once again bestride our foaming steeds,
And once again cry 'Charge upon our foes!'
But never once again turn back and fly.

RICHARD Ay, now methinks I hear great Warwick speak.
Ne'er may he live to see a sunshine day
That cries 'Retire!' if Warwick bid him stay.

EDWARD Lord Warwick, on thy shoulder will I lean;
And when thou fail'st – as God forbid the hour! –
Must Edward fall, which peril heaven forfend.

WARWICK No longer Earl of March, but Duke of York;
The next degree is England's royal throne,
For King of England shalt thou be proclaim'd
In every borough as we pass along;
And he that throws not up his cap for joy
Shall for the fault make forfeit of his head.
King Edward, valiant Richard, Montague,
Stay we no longer, dreaming of renown,
But sound the trumpets and about our task.

RICHARD Then, Clifford, were thy heart as hard as steel,
As thou hast shown it flinty by thy deeds,
I come to pierce it or to give thee mine.

EDWARD Then strike up drums. God and Saint George for us!

Enter a Messenger.

WARWICK How now! what news?

MESSENGER The Duke of Norfolk sends you word by me
The Queen is coming with a puissant host,
And craves your company for speedy counsel.

WARWICK Why, then it sorts; brave warriors, let's away. [*Exeunt.*

SCENE II. *Before York.*

Flourish. Enter KING HENRY, QUEEN MARGARET, the PRINCE OF WALES, CLIFFORD, NORTHUMBERLAND, with drum and trumpets.

QUEEN MARGARET Welcome, my lord, to this brave town of York.
Yonder's the head of that arch-enemy
That sought to be encompass'd with your crown.
Doth not the object cheer your heart, my lord?

KING HENRY Ay, as the rocks cheer them that fear their wreck –
To see this sight, it irks my very soul.
Withhold revenge, dear God; 'tis not my fault,
Nor wittingly have I infring'd my vow.

CLIFFORD My gracious liege, this too much lenity
And harmful pity must be laid aside.
To whom do lions cast their gentle looks?
Not to the beast that would usurp their den.
Whose hand is that the forest bear doth lick?
Not his that spoils her young before her face.
Who scapes the lurking serpent's mortal sting?
Not he that sets his foot upon her back.
The smallest worm will turn, being trodden on,
And doves will peck in safeguard of their brood.
Ambitious York did level at thy crown,
Thou smiling while he knit his angry brows.
He, but a Duke, would have his son a king,
And raise his issue like a loving sire:
Thou, being a king, bless'd with a goodly son,
Didst yield consent to disinherit him,
Which argued thee a most unloving father.
Unreasonable creatures feed their young;
And though man's face be fearful to their eyes,
Yet, in protection of their tender ones,
Who hath not seen them – even with those wings
Which sometime they have us'd with fearful flight –
Make war with him that climb'd unto their nest,
Offering their own lives in their young's defence?
For shame, my liege, make them your precedent!
Were it not pity that this goodly boy
Should lose his birthright by his father's fault,
And long hereafter say unto his child
'What my great-grandfather and grandsire got
My careless father fondly gave away'?
Ah, what a shame were this! Look on the boy;
And let his manly face, which promiseth
Successful fortune, steel thy melting heart
To hold thine own and leave thine own with him.

KING HENRY Full well hath Clifford play'd the orator,
Inferring arguments of mighty force.
But, Clifford, tell me, didst thou never hear
That things ill got had ever bad success?
And happy always was it for that son
Whose father for his hoarding went to hell?
I'll leave my son my virtuous deeds behind;
And would my father had left me no more!
For all the rest is held at such a rate
As brings a thousand-fold more care to keep
Than in possession any jot of pleasure.
Ah, cousin York! would thy best friends did know
How it doth grieve me that thy head is here!

QUEEN MARGARET My lord, cheer up your spirits; our foes are nigh,
And this soft courage makes your followers faint.
You promis'd knighthood to our forward son:
Unsheathe your sword and dub him presently.
Edward, kneel down.

KING HENRY Edward Plantagent, arise a knight;
And learn this lesson: Draw thy sword in right.

PRINCE My gracious father, by your kingly leave,
I'll draw it as apparent to the crown,
And in that quarrel use it to the death.

CLIFFORD Why, that is spoken like a toward prince.

Enter a Messenger.

MESSENGER Royal commanders, be in readiness;
For with a band of thirty thousand men
Comes Warwick, backing of the Duke of York,
And in the towns, as they do march along,
Proclaims him king, and many fly to him.
Darraign your battle, for they are at hand.

CLIFFORD I would your Highness would depart the field:
The Queen hath best success when you are absent.

QUEEN MARGARET Ay, good my lord, and leave us to our fortune.

KING HENRY Why, that's my fortune too; therefore I'll stay.

NORTHUMBERLAND Be it with resolution, then, to fight.

PRINCE My royal father, cheer, these noble lords,
And hearten those that fight in your defence.
Unsheathe your sword, good father; cry 'Saint George!'

March. Enter EDWARD, GEORGE, RICHARD, WARWICK, NORFOLK, MONTAGUE, and Soldiers.

EDWARD Now, perjur'd Henry, wilt thou kneel for grace
And set thy diadem upon my head,
Or bide the mortal fortune of the field?

QUEEN MARGARET Go rate thy minions, proud insulting boy.
Becomes it thee to be thus bold in terms
Before thy sovereign and thy lawful king?

EDWARD I am his king, and he should bow his knee.
I was adopted heir by his consent:
Since when, his oath is broke; for, as I hear,
You that are King, though he do wear the crown,
Have caus'd him by new act of parliament
To blot out me and put his own son in.

CLIFFORD And reason too:
Who should succeed the father but the son?

RICHARD Are you there, butcher? O, I cannot speak!

CLIFFORD Ay, crook-back, here I stand to answer thee,
Or any he, the proudest of thy sort.

RICHARD 'Twas you that kill'd young Rutland, was it not?

CLIFFORD Ay, and old York, and yet not satisfied.

RICHARD For God's sake, lords, give signal to the fight.

WARWICK What say'st thou, Henry? Wilt thou yield the crown?

QUEEN MARGARET Why, how now, long-tongu'd Warwick! Dare you speak?
When you and I met at Saint Albans last
Your legs did better service than your hands.

WARWICK Then 'twas my turn to fly, and now 'tis thine.

CLIFFORD You said so much before, and yet you fled.

WARWICK 'Twas not your valour, Clifford, drove me thence.

NORTHUMBERLAND No, nor your manhood that durst make you stay.

RICHARD Northumberland, I hold thee reverently.
Break off the parley; for scarce I can refrain
The execution of my big-swol'n heart
Upon that Clifford, that cruel child-killer.

CLIFFORD I slew thy father; call'st thou him a child?

RICHARD Ay, like a dastard and a treacherous coward,
As thou didst kill our tender brother Rutland;
But ere sunset I'll make thee curse the deed.

KING HENRY Have done with words, my lords, and hear me speak.

QUEEN MARGARET Defy them then, or else hold close thy lips.

KING HENRY I prithee give no limits to my tongue:
I am a king, and privileg'd to speak.

CLIFFORD My liege, the wound that bred this meeting here
Cannot be cur'd by words; therefore be still.

RICHARD Then, executioner, unsheathe thy sword.
By Him that made us all, I am resolv'd
That Clifford's manhood lies upon his tongue.

EDWARD Say, Henry, shall I have my right, or no?
A thousand men have broke their fasts to-day
That ne'er shall dine unless thou yield the crown.

WARWICK If thou deny, their blood upon thy head;
For York in justice puts his armour on.

PRINCE If that be right which Warwick says is right,
There is no wrong, but every thing is right.
RICHARD Whoever got thee, there thy mother stands;
For well I wot thou hast thy mother's tongue.
QUEEN MARGARET But thou art neither like thy sire nor dam;
But like a foul misshapen stigmatic,
Mark'd by the destinies to be avoided,
As venom toads or lizards' dreadful stings.
RICHARD Iron of Naples hid with English gilt,
Whose father bears the title of a king –
As if a channel should be call'd the sea –
Sham'st thou not, knowing whence thou art extraught,
To let thy tongue detect thy base-born heart?
EDWARD A wisp of straw were worth a thousand crowns
To make this shameless callet know herself.
Helen of Greece was fairer far than thou,
Although thy husband may be Menelaus;
And ne'er was Agamemnon's brother wrong'd
By that false woman as this king by thee.
His father revell'd in the heart of France,
And tam'd the King, and made the Dauphin stoop;
And had he match'd according to his state,
He might have kept that glory to this day;
But when he took a beggar to his bed
And grac'd thy poor sire with his bridal day,
Even then that sunshine brew'd a show'r for him
That wash'd his father's fortunes forth of France
And heap'd sedition on his crown at home.
For what hath broach'd this tumult but thy pride?
Hadst thou been meek, our title still had slept;
And we, in pity of the gentle King,
Had slipp'd our claim until another age.
GEORGE But when we saw our sunshine made thy spring,
And that thy summer bred us no increase,
We set the axe to thy usurping root;
And though the edge hath something hit ourselves,
Yet know thou, since we have begun to strike,
We'll never leave till we have hewn thee down,
Or bath'd thy growing with our heated bloods.
EDWARD And in this resolution I defy thee;
Not willing any longer conference,
Since thou deniest the gentle King to speak.
Sound trumpets; let our bloody colours wave,
And either victory or else a grave!
QUEEN MARGARET Stay, Edward.
EDWARD No, wrangling woman, we'll no longer stay;
These words will cost ten thousand lives this day. [*Exeunt.*

SCENE III. *A field of battle between Towton and Saxton, in Yorkshire.*

Alarum; excursions. Enter WARWICK.

WARWICK Forspent with toil, as runners with a race,
I lay me down a little while to breathe;
For strokes receiv'd and many blows repaid
Have robb'd my strong-knit sinews of their strength,
And spite of spite needs must I rest awhile.

Enter EDWARD, running.

EDWARD Smile, gentle heaven, or strike, ungentle death;
For this world frowns, and Edward's sun is clouded.
WARWICK How now, my lord! What hap? What hope of good?

Enter GEORGE.

GEORGE Our hap is lost, our hope but sad despair;
Our ranks are broke, and ruin follows us.
What counsel give you? Whither shall we fly?
EDWARD Bootless is flight: they follow us with wings;
And weak we are, and cannot shun pursuit.

Enter RICHARD.

RICHARD Ah, Warwick, why hast thou withdrawn thyself?
Thy brother's blood the thirsty earth hath drunk,
Broach'd with the steely point of Clifford's lance;
And in the very pangs of death he cried,
Like to a dismal clangor heard from far,
'Warwick, revenge! Brother, revenge my death'.
So, underneath the belly of their steeds,
That stain'd their fetlocks in his smoking blood,
The noble gentleman gave up the ghost.
WARWICK Then let the earth be drunken with our blood,
I'll kill my horse, because I will not fly.
Why stand we like soft-hearted women here,
Wailing our losses, whiles the foe doth rage,
And look upon, as if the tragedy
Were play'd in jest by counterfeiting actors?
Here on my knee I vow to God above
I'll never pause again, never stand still,
Till either death hath clos'd these eyes of mine
Or fortune given me measure of revenge.
EDWARD O Warwick, I do bend my knee with thine,
And in this vow do chain my soul to thine!
And ere my knee rise from the earth's cold face
I throw my hands, mine eyes, my heart to Thee,
Thou setter-up and plucker-down of kings,

Beseeching Thee, if with Thy will it stands
That to my foes this body must be prey,
Yet that Thy brazen gates of heaven may ope
And give sweet passage to my sinful soul.
Now, lords, take leave until we meet again,
Where'er it be, in heaven or in earth.

RICHARD Brother, give me thy hand; and, gentle Warwick,
Let me embrace thee in my weary arms.
I that did never weep now melt with woe
That winter should cut off our spring-time so.

WARWICK Away, away! Once more, sweet lords, farewell.

GEORGE Yet let us all together to our troops,
And give them leave to fly that will not stay,
And call them pillars that will stand to us;
And if we thrive, promise them such rewards
As victors wear at the Olympian games.
This may plant courage in their quailing breasts,
For yet is hope of life and victory.
Forslow no longer; make we hence amain.
[Exeunt.

SCENE IV. *Another part of the field.*

Excursions. Enter RICHARD and CLIFFORD.

RICHARD Now, Clifford, I have singled thee alone.
Suppose this arm is for the Duke of York,
And this for Rutland; both bound to revenge,
Wert thou environ'd with a brazen wall.

CLIFFORD Now, Richard, I am with thee here alone.
This is the hand that stabb'd thy father York;
And this the hand that slew thy brother Rutland;
And here's the heart that triumphs in their death
And cheers these hands that slew thy sire and brother
To execute the like upon thyself;
And so, have at thee! *[They fight.*

Enter WARWICK; Clifford flies.

RICHARD Nay, Warwick, single out some other chase;
For I myself will hunt this wolf to death.
[Exeunt.

SCENE V. *Another part of the field.*

Alarum. Enter KING HENRY alone.

KING HENRY This battle fares like to the morning's war,
When dying clouds contend with growing light,
What time the shepherd, blowing of his nails,
Can neither call it perfect day nor night.
Now sways it this way, like a mighty sea
Forc'd by the tide to combat with the wind;
Now sways it that way, like the selfsame sea
Forc'd to retire by fury of the wind.
Sometime the flood prevails, and then the wind;
Now one the better, then another best;
Both tugging to be victors, breast to breast,
Yet neither conqueror nor conquered.
So is the equal poise of this fell war.
Here on this molehill will I sit me down.
To whom God will, there be the victory!
For Margaret my queen, and Clifford too,
Have chid me from the battle, swearing both
They prosper best of all when I am thence.
Would I were dead, if God's good will were so!
For what is in this world but grief and woe?
O God! methinks it were a happy life
To be no better than a homely swain;
To sit upon a hill, as I do now,
To carve out dials quaintly, point by point,
Thereby to see the minutes how they run –
How many makes the hour full complete,
How many hours brings about the day,
How many days will finish up the year,
How many years a mortal man may live.
When this is known, then to divide the times –
So many hours must I tend my flock;
So many hours must I take my rest;
So many hours must I contemplate;
So many hours must I sport myself;
So many days my ewes have been with young;
So many weeks ere the poor fools will ean;
So many years ere I shall shear the fleece:
So minutes, hours, days, months, and years,
Pass'd over to the end they were created,
Would bring white hairs unto a quiet grave.
Ah, what a life were this! how sweet! how lovely!
Gives not the hawthorn bush a sweeter shade
To shepherds looking on their silly sheep,
Than doth a rich embroider'd canopy
To kings that fear their subjects' treachery?
O yes, it doth; a thousand-fold it doth.
And to conclude: the shepherd's homely curds,
His cold thin drink out of his leather bottle,
His wonted sleep under a fresh tree's shade,
All which secure and sweetly he enjoys,
Is far beyond a prince's delicates –
His viands sparkling in a golden cup,
His body couched in a curious bed,
When care, mistrust, and treason waits on him.

Alarum. Enter a Son that hath kill'd his Father, at one door; and a Father that hath kill'd his Son, at another door.

SON Ill blows the wind that profits nobody.
This man whom hand to hand I slew in fight

May be possessed with some store of crowns;
And I, that haply take them from him now,
May yet ere night yield both my life and them
To some man else, as this dead man doth me.
Who's this? O God! It is my father's face,
Whom in this conflict I unwares have kill'd.
O heavy times, begetting such events!
From London by the King was I press'd forth;
My father, being the Earl of Warwick's man,
Came on the part of York, press'd by his master;
And I, who at his hands receiv'd my life,
Have by my hands of life bereaved him.
Pardon me, God, I knew not what I did.
And pardon, father, for I knew not thee.
My tears shall wipe away these bloody marks;
And no more words till they have flow'd their fill.

KING HENRY O piteous spectacle! O bloody times!
Whiles lions war and battle for their dens,
Poor harmless lambs abide their enmity.
Weep, wretched man; I'll aid thee tear for tear;
And let our hearts and eyes, like civil war,
Be blind with tears and break o'ercharg'd with grief.

Enter Father, bearing of his Son.

FATHER Thou that so stoutly hath resisted me,
Give me thy gold, if thou hast any gold;
For I have bought it with an hundred blows.
But let me see. Is this our foeman's face?
Ah, no, no, no, it is mine only son!
Ah, boy, if any life be left in thee,
Throw up thine eye! See, see what show'rs arise,
Blown with the windy tempest of my heart
Upon thy wounds, that kills mine eye and heart!
O, pity. God, this miserable age!
What stratagems, how fell, how butcherly,
Erroneous, mutinous, and unnatural,
This deadly quarrel daily doth beget!
O boy, thy father gave thee life too soon,
And hath bereft thee of thy life too late!

KING HENRY Woe above woe! grief more than common grief!
O that my death would stay these ruthful deeds!
O pity, pity, gentle heaven, pity!
The red rose and the white are on his face,
The fatal colours of our striving houses:
The one his purple blood right well resembles;
The other his pale cheeks, methinks, presenteth.
Wither one rose, and let the other flourish!
If you contend, a thousand lives must perish.

SON How will my mother for a father's death
Take on with me, and ne'er be satisfied!

FATHER How will my wife for slaughter of my son
Shed seas of tears, and ne'er be satisfied!

KING HENRY How will the country for these woeful chances
Misthink the King, and not be satisfied!

SON Was ever son so rued a father's death?

FATHER Was ever father so bemoan'd his son?

KING HENRY Was ever king so griev'd for subjects' woe?
Much is your sorrow; mine ten times so much.

SON I'll bear thee hence, where I may weep my fill. [*Exit with the body.*

FATHER These arms of mine shall be thy winding-sheet;
My heart, sweet boy, shall be thy sepulchre,
For from my heart thine image ne'er shall go;
My sighing breast shall be thy funeral bell;
And so obsequious will thy father be,
Even for the loss of thee, having no more,
As Priam was for all his valiant sons.
I'll bear thee hence; and let them fight that will,
For I have murdered where I should not kill.
[*Exit with the body.*

KING HENRY Sad-hearted men, much overgone with care,
Here sits a king more woeful than you are.

Alarums; excursions. Enter QUEEN MARGARET, PRINCE OF WALES, and EXETER.

PRINCE Fly, father, fly; for all your friends are fled,
And Warwick rages like a chafed bull.
Away! for death doth hold us in pursuit.

QUEEN MARGARET Mount you, my lord; towards Berwick post amain.
Edward and Richard, like a brace of greyhounds
Having the fearful flying hare in sight,
With fiery eyes sparkling for very wrath,
And bloody steel grasp'd in their ireful hands,
Are at our backs; and therefore hence amain.

EXETER Away! for vengeance comes along with them.
Nay, stay not to expostulate; make speed;
Or else come after. I'll away before.

KING HENRY Nay, take me with thee, good sweet Exeter.
Not that I fear to stay, but love to go
Whither the Queen intends. Forward; away!
[*Exeunt.*

SCENE VI. *Another part of the field.*

A loud alarum. Enter CLIFFORD, wounded.

CLIFFORD Here burns my candle out; ay, here it dies,
Which, whiles it lasted, gave King Henry light.
O Lancaster, I fear thy overthrow

More than my body's parting with my soul!
My love and fear glu'd many friends to thee;
And, now I fall, thy tough commixture melts,
Impairing Henry, strength'ning misproud York.
The common people swarm like summer flies;
And whither fly the gnats but to the sun?
And who shines now but Henry's enemies?
O Phoebus, hadst thou never given consent
That Phaethon should check thy fiery steeds,
Thy burning car never had scorch'd the earth!
And, Henry, hadst thou sway'd as kings should do,
Or as thy father and his father did,
Giving no ground unto the house of York,
They never then had sprung like summer flies;
I and ten thousand in this luckless realm
Had left no mourning widows for our death;
And thou this day hadst kept thy chair in peace.
For what doth cherish weeds but gentle air?
And what makes robbers bold but too much lenity?
Bootless are plaints, and cureless are my wounds.
No way to fly, nor strength to hold out flight.
The foe is merciless and will not pity;
For at their hands I have deserv'd no pity.
The air hath got into my deadly wounds,
And much effuse of blood doth make me faint.
Come, York and Richard, Warwick and the rest;
I stabb'd your fathers' bosoms: split my breast.
[*He faints.*

Alarum and retreat. Enter EDWARD, GEORGE, RICHARD, MONTAGUE, WARWICK, and Soldiers.

EDWARD Now breathe we, lords. Good fortune bids us pause
And smooth the frowns of war with peaceful looks.
Some troops pursue the bloody-minded Queen
That led calm Henry, though he were a king,
As doth a sail, fill'd with a fretting gust,
Command an argosy to stem the waves.
But think you, lords, that Clifford fled with them?
WARWICK No, 'tis impossible he should escape;
For, though before his face I speak the words,
Your brother Richard mark'd him for the grave;
And, wheresoe'er he is, he's surely dead.
[*Clifford groans, and dies.*

RICHARD Whose soul is that which takes her heavy leave?
A deadly groan, like life and death's departing.
See who it is.
EDWARD And now the battle's ended,
If friend or foe, let him be gently used.
RICHARD Revoke that doom of mercy, for 'tis Clifford;
Who not contented that he lopp'd the branch
In hewing Rutland when his leaves put forth,
But set his murd'ring knife unto the root
From whence that tender spray did sweetly spring –
I mean our princely father, Duke of York.
WARWICK From off the gates of York fetch down the head,
Your father's head, which Clifford placed there;
Instead whereof let this supply the room.
Measure for measure must be answered.
EDWARD Bring forth that fatal screech-owl to our house,
That nothing sung but death to us and ours.
Now death shall stop his dismal threat'ning sound,
And his ill-boding tongue no more shall speak.
WARWICK I think his understanding is bereft.
Speak, Clifford, dost thou know who speaks to thee?
Dark cloudy death o'ershades his beams of life,
And he nor sees nor hears us what we say.
RICHARD O, would he did! and so, perhaps, he doth.
'Tis but his policy to counterfeit,
Because he would avoid such bitter taunts
Which in the time of death he gave our father.
GEORGE If so thou think'st, vex him with eager words.
RICHARD Clifford, ask mercy and obtain no grace.
EDWARD Clifford, repent in bootless penitence.
WARWICK Clifford, devise excuses for thy faults.
GEORGE While we devise fell tortures for thy faults.
RICHARD Thou didst love York, and I am son to York.
EDWARD Thou pitied'st Rutland, I will pity thee.
GEORGE Where's Captain Margaret, to fence you now?
WARWICK They mock thee, Clifford; swear as thou wast wont.
RICHARD What, not an oath? Nay, then the world goes hard
When Clifford cannot spare his friends an oath.
I know by that he's dead; and by my soul,
If this right hand would buy two hours' life,
That I in all despite might rail at him,
This hand should chop it off, and with the issuing blood
Stifle the villain whose unstanched thirst
York and young Rutland could not satisfy.
WARWICK Ay, but he's dead. Off with the traitor's head,
And rear it in the place your father's stands.

And now to London with triumphant march,
There to be crowned England's royal King;
From whence shall Warwick cut the sea to France,
And ask the Lady Bona for thy queen.
So shalt thou sinew both these lands together;
And, having France thy friend, thou shalt not dread
The scatt'red foe that hopes to rise again;
For though they cannot greatly sting to hurt,
Yet look to have them buzz to offend thine ears.
First will I see the coronation;
And then to Brittany I'll cross the sea
To effect this marriage, so it please my lord.

EDWARD Even as thou wilt, sweet Warwick, let it be;
For in thy shoulder do I build my seat,
And never will I undertake the thing
Wherein thy counsel and consent is wanting.
Richard, I will create thee Duke of Gloucester;
And George, of Clarence; Warwick, as ourself,
Shall do and undo as him pleaseth best.

RICHARD Let me be Duke of Clarence, George of Gloucester;
For Gloucester's dukedom is too ominous.

WARWICK Tut, that's a foolish observation.
Richard, be Duke of Gloucester. Now to London
To see these honours in possession. [*Exeunt.*

ACT THREE

SCENE I. *A chase in the north of England.*

Enter two Keepers, with cross-bows in their hands.

1 KEEPER Under this thick-grown brake we'll shroud ourselves,
For through this laund anon the deer will come;
And in this covert will we make our stand,
Culling the principal of all the deer.

2 KEEPER I'll stay above the hill, so both may shoot.

1 KEEPER That cannot be; the noise of thy cross-bow
Will scare the herd, and so my shoot is lost.
Here stand we both, and aim we at the best;
And, for the time shall not seem tedious,
I'll tell thee what befell me on a day
In this self-place where now we mean to stand.

2 KEEPER Here comes a man; let's stay till he be past.

Enter KING HENRY, disguised, with a prayer-book.

KING HENRY From Scotland am I stol'n, even of pure love,
To greet mine own land with my wishful sight.
No, Harry, Harry, 'tis no land of thine;
Thy place is fill'd, thy sceptre wrung from thee,
Thy balm wash'd off wherewith thou wast anointed.
No bending knee will call thee Caesar now,
No humble suitors press to speak for right,
No, not a man comes for redress of thee;
For how can I help them and not myself?

1 KEEPER Ay, here's a deer whose skin's a keeper's fee.
This is the quondam king; let's seize upon him.

KING HENRY Let me embrace thee, sour adversity,
For wise men say it is the wisest course.

2 KEEPER Why linger we? let us lay hands upon him.

1 KEEPER Forbear awhile; we'll hear a little more.

KING HENRY My Queen and son are gone to France for aid;
And, as I hear, the great commanding Warwick
Is thither gone to crave the French King's sister
To wife for Edward. If this news be true,
Poor queen and son, your labour is but lost;
For Warwick is a subtle orator,
And Lewis a prince soon won with moving words.
By this account, then, Margaret may win him;
For she's a woman to be pitied much.
Her sighs will make a batt'ry in his breast;
Her tears will pierce into a marble heart;
The tiger will be mild whiles she doth mourn;
And Nero will be tainted with remorse
To hear and see her plaints, her brinish tears.
Ay, but she's come to beg: Warwick, to give.
She, on his left side, craving aid for Henry:
He, on his right, asking a wife for Edward.
She weeps, and says her Henry is depos'd:
He smiles, and says his Edward is install'd;
That she, poor wretch, for grief can speak no more;
Whiles Warwick tells his title, smooths the wrong,
Inferreth arguments of mighty strength,
And in conclusion wins the King from her
With promise of his sister, and what else,
To strengthen and support King Edward's place.
O Margaret, thus 'twill be; and thou, poor soul,
Art then forsaken, as thou went'st forlorn!

2 KEEPER Say, what art thou that talk'st of kings and queens?

KING HENRY More than I seem, and less than I was born to:
A man at least, for less I should not be;
And men may talk of kings, and why not I?
2 KEEPER Ay, but thou talk'st as if thou wert a king.
KING HENRY Why, so I am – in mind; and that's enough.
2 KEEPER But, if thou be a king, where is thy crown?
KING HENRY My crown is in my heart, not on my head;
Not deck'd with diamonds and Indian stones,
Nor to be seen. My crown is call'd content;
A crown it is that seldom kings enjoy.
2 KEEPER Well, if you be a king crown'd with content,
Your crown content and you must be contented
To go along with us; for, as we think,
You are the king King Edward hath depos'd;
And we his subjects, sworn in all allegiance,
Will apprehend you as his enemy.
KING HENRY But did you never swear, and break an oath?
2 KEEPER No, never such an oath; nor will not now.
KING HENRY Where did you dwell when I was King of England?
2 KEEPER Here in this country, where we now remain.
KING HENRY I was anointed king at nine months old;
My father and my grandfather were kings;
And you were sworn true subjects unto me;
And tell me, then, have you not broke your oaths?
1 KEEPER No;
For we were subjects but while you were king.
KING HENRY Why, am I dead? Do I not breathe a man?
Ah, simple men, you know not what you swear!
Look, as I blow this feather from my face,
And as the air blows it to me again,
Obeying with my wind when I do blow,
And yielding to another when it blows,
Commanded always by the greater gust,
Such is the lightness of you common men.
But do not break your oaths; for of that sin
My mild entreaty shall not make you guilty.
Go where you will, the King shall be commanded;
And be you kings: command, and I'll obey.
1 KEEPER We are true subjects to the King, King Edward.
KING HENRY So would you be again to Henry,
If he were seated as King Edward is.
1 KEEPER We charge you, in God's name and the King's,
To go with us unto the officers.
KING HENRY In God's name, lead; your King's name be obey'd;
And what God will, that let your King perform;
And what he will, I humbly yield unto. [*Exeunt.*

SCENE II. *London. The palace.*

Enter KING EDWARD, GLOUCESTER, CLARENCE, and LADY GREY.

KING EDWARD Brother of Gloucester, at Saint Albans' field
This lady's husband, Sir Richard Grey, was slain,
His land then seiz'd on by the conqueror.
Her suit is now to repossess those lands;
Which we in justice cannot well deny,
Because in quarrel of the house of York
The worthy gentleman did lose his life.
GLOUCESTER Your Highness shall do well to grant her suit;
It were dishonour to deny it her.
KING EDWARD It were no less; but yet I'll make a pause.
GLOUCESTER [*Aside to Clarence*] Yea, is it so?
I see the lady hath a thing to grant,
Before the King will grant her humble suit.
CLARENCE [*Aside to Gloucester*] He knows the game; how true he keeps the wind!
GLOUCESTER [*Aside to Clarence*] Silence!
KING EDWARD Widow, we will consider of your suit;
And come some other time to know our mind.
LADY GREY Right gracious lord, I cannot brook delay.
May it please your Highness to resolve me now;
And what your pleasure is shall satisfy me.
GLOUCESTER [*Aside*] Ay, widow? Then I'll warrant you all your lands,
An if what pleases him shall pleasure you.
Fight closer or, good faith, you'll catch a blow.
CLARENCE [*Aside to Gloucester*] I fear her not, unless she chance to fall.
GLOUCESTER [*Aside to Clarence*] God forbid that, for he'll take vantages.
KING EDWARD How many children hast thou, widow, tell me.
CLARENCE [*Aside to Gloucester*] I think he means to beg a child of her.
GLOUCESTER [*Aside to Clarence*] Nay, then whip me; he'll rather give her two.
LADY GREY Three, my most gracious lord.
GLOUCESTER [*Aside*] You shall have four if you'll be rul'd by him.
KING EDWARD 'Twere pity they should lose their father's lands.

LADY GREY Be pitiful, dread lord, and grant it, then.
KING EDWARD Lords, give us leave; I'll try this widow's wit.
GLOUCESTER [*Aside*] Ay, good leave have you; for you will have leave
Till youth take leave and leave you to the crutch. [*Gloucester and Clarence withdraw.*
KING EDWARD Now tell me, madam, do you love your children?
LADY GREY Ay, full as dearly as I love myself.
KING EDWARD And would you not do much to do them good?
LADY GREY To do them good I would sustain some harm.
KING EDWARD Then get your husband's lands, to do them good.
LADY GREY Therefore I came unto your Majesty.
KING EDWARD I'll tell you how these lands are to be got.
LADY GREY So shall you bind me to your Highness' service.
KING EDWARD What service wilt thou do me if I give them?
LADY GREY What you command that rests in me to do.
KING EDWARD But you will take exceptions to my boon.
LADY GREY No, gracious lord, except I cannot do it.
KING EDWARD Ay, but thou canst do what I mean to ask.
LADY GREY Why, then I will do what your Grace commands.
GLOUCESTER He plies her hard; and much rain wears the marble.
CLARENCE As red as fire! Nay, then her wax must melt.
LADY GREY Why stops my lord? Shall I not hear my task?
KING EDWARD An easy task; 'tis but to love a king.
LADY GREY That's soon perform'd, because I am a subject.
KING EDWARD Why, then, thy husband's lands I freely give thee.
LADY GREY I take my leave with many thousand thanks.
GLOUCESTER The match is made; she seals it with a curtsy.
KING EDWARD But stay thee – 'tis the fruits of love I mean.
LADY GREY The fruits of love I mean, my loving liege.
KING EDWARD Ay, but, I fear me, in another sense.
What love, thinkst thou, I sue so much to get?
LADY GREY My love till death, my humble thanks, my prayers;
That love which virtue begs and virtue grants.
KING EDWARD No, by my troth, I did not mean such love.
LADY GREY Why, then you mean not as I thought you did.
KING EDWARD But now you partly may perceive my mind.
LADY GREY My mind will never grant what I perceive
Your Highness aims at, if I aim aright.
KING EDWARD To tell thee plain, I aim to lie with thee.
LADY GREY To tell you plain, I had rather lie in prison.
KING EDWARD Why, then thou shalt not have thy husband's lands.
LADY GREY Why, then mine honesty shall be my dower;
For by that loss I will not purchase them.
KING EDWARD Therein thou wrong'st thy children mightily.
LADY GREY Herein your Highness wrongs both them and me.
But, mighty lord, this merry inclination
Accords not with the sadness of my suit.
Please you dismiss me, either with ay or no.
KING EDWARD Ay, if thou wilt say ay to my request;
No, if thou dost say no to my demand.
LADY GREY Then, no, my lord. My suit is at an end.
GLOUCESTER The widow likes him not; she knits her brows.
CLARENCE He is the bluntest wooer in Christendom.
KING EDWARD [*Aside*] Her looks doth argue her replete with modesty;
Her words doth show her wit incomparable;
All her perfections challenge sovereignty.
One way or other, she is for a king;
And she shall be my love, or else my queen.
Say that King Edward take thee for his queen?
LADY GREY 'Tis better said than done, my gracious lord.
I am a subject fit to jest withal,
But far unfit to be a sovereign.
KING EDWARD Sweet widow, by my state I swear to thee
I speak no more than what my soul intends;
And that is to enjoy thee for my love.
LADY GREY And that is more than I will yield unto.
I know I am too mean to be your queen,
And yet too good to be your concubine.

KING EDWARD You cavil, widow; I did mean my queen.
LADY GREY 'Twill grieve your Grace my sons should call you father.
KING EDWARD No more than when my daughters call thee mother.
Thou art a widow, and thou hast some children;
And, by God's Mother, I, being but a bachelor,
Have other some. Why, 'tis a happy thing
To be the father unto many sons.
Answer no more, for thou shalt be my queen.
GLOUCESTER The ghostly father now hath done his shrift.
CLARENCE When he was made a shriver, 'twas for shift.
KING EDWARD Brothers, you muse what chat we two have had.
GLOUCESTER The widow likes it not, for she looks very sad.
KING EDWARD You'd think it strange if I should marry her.
CLARENCE To who, my lord?
KING EDWARD Why, Clarence, to myself.
GLOUCESTER That would be ten days' wonder at the least.
CLARENCE That's a day longer than a wonder lasts.
GLOUCESTER By so much is the wonder in extremes.
KING EDWARD Well, jest on, brothers; I can tell you both
Her suit is granted for her husband's lands.

Enter a Nobleman.

NOBLEMAN My gracious lord, Henry your foe is taken
And brought your prisoner to your palace gate.
KING EDWARD See that he be convey'd unto the Tower.
And go we, brothers, to the man that took him
To question of his apprehension.
Widow, go you along. Lords, use her honourably. [*Exeunt all but Gloucester.*

GLOUCESTER Ay, Edward will use women honourably.
Would he were wasted, marrow, bones, and all,
That from his loins no hopeful branch may spring
To cross me from the golden time I look for!
And yet, between my soul's desire and me –
The lustful Edward's title buried –
Is Clarence, Henry, and his son young Edward,
And all the unlook'd for issue of their bodies,
To take their rooms ere I can place myself.
A cold premeditation for my purpose!
Why, then I do but dream on sovereignty;
Like one that stands upon a promontory
And spies a far-off shore where he would tread,
Wishing his foot were equal with his eye;
And chides the sea that sunders him from thence,
Saying he'll lade it dry to have his way –
So do I wish the crown, being so far off;
And so I chide the means that keeps me from it;
And so I say I'll cut the causes off,
Flattering me with impossibilities.
My eye's too quick, my heart o'erweens too much,
Unless my hand and strength could equal them.
Well, say there is no kingdom then for Richard;
What other pleasure can the world afford?
I'll make my heaven in a lady's lap,
And deck my body in gay ornaments,
And witch sweet ladies with my words and looks.
O miserable thought! and more unlikely
Than to accomplish twenty golden crowns.
Why, love forswore me in my mother's womb;
And, for I should not deal in her soft laws,
She did corrupt frail nature with some bribe
To shrink mine arm up like a wither'd shrub;
To make an envious mountain on my back,
Where sits deformity to mock my body;
To shape my legs of an unequal size;
To disproportion me in every part,
Like to a chaos, or an unlick'd bear-whelp
That carries no impression like the dam.
And am I, then, a man to be belov'd?
O monstrous fault to harbour such a thought!
Then, since this earth affords no joy to me
But to command, to check, to o'erbear such
As are of better person than myself,
I'll make my heaven to dream upon the crown,
And whiles I live t' account this world but hell,
Until my misshap'd trunk that bears this head
Be round impaled with a glorious crown.
And yet I know not how to get the crown,
For many lives stand between me and home;
And I – like one lost in a thorny wood
That rents the thorns and is rent with the thorns,
Seeking a way and straying from the way;
Not knowing how to find the open air,
But toiling desperately to find it out –
Torment myself to catch the English crown;
And from that torment I will free myself
Or hew my way out with a bloody axe.
Why, I can smile, and murder whiles I smile,
And cry 'Content!' to that which grieves my heart,
And wet my cheeks with artificial tears,
And frame my face to all occasions.
I'll drown more sailors than the mermaid shall;
I'll slay more gazers than the basilisk;

I'll play the orator as well as Nestor,
Deceive more slily than Ulysses could,
And, like a Sinon, take another Troy.
I can add colours to the chameleon,
Change shapes with Protheus for advantages,
And set the murderous Machiavel to school.
Can I do this, and cannot get a crown?
Tut, were it farther off, I'll pluck it down. [*Exit*.

SCENE III. *France. The King's palace.*

Flourish. Enter LEWIS the French King, his sister BONA, his Admiral call'd BOURBON; PRINCE EDWARD, QUEEN MARGARET, and the EARL OF OXFORD. Lewis sits, and riseth up again.

LOUIS Fair Queen of England, worthy Margaret,
Sit down with us. It ill befits thy state
And birth that thou shouldst stand while Lewis doth sit.

QUEEN MARGARET No, mighty King of France. Now Margaret
Must strike her sail and learn a while to serve
Where kings command. I was, I must confess,
Great Albion's Queen in former golden days;
But now mischance hath trod my title down
And with dishonour laid me on the ground,
Where I must take like seat unto my fortune,
And to my humble seat conform myself.

LOUIS Why, say, fair Queen, whence springs this deep despair?

QUEEN MARGARET From such a cause as fills mine eyes with tears
And stops my tongue, while heart is drown'd in cares.

LOUIS Whate'er it be, be thou still like thyself,
And sit thee by our side. [*Seats her by him*] Yield not thy neck
To fortune's yoke, but let thy dauntless mind
Still ride in triumph over all mischance.
Be plain, Queen Margaret, and tell thy grief;
It shall be eas'd, if France can yield relief.

QUEEN MARGARET Those gracious words revive my drooping thoughts
And give my tongue-tied sorrows leave to speak.
Now therefore be it known to noble Lewis
That Henry, sole possessor of my love,
Is, of a king, become a banish'd man,
And forc'd to live in Scotland a forlorn;
While proud ambitious Edward Duke of York
Usurps the regal title and the seat
Of England's true-anointed lawful King.
This is the cause that I, poor Margaret,
With this my son, Prince Edward, Henry's heir,
Am come to crave thy just and lawful aid;
And if thou fail us, all our hope is done.
Scotland hath will to help, but cannot help;
Our people and our peers are both misled,
Our treasure seiz'd, our soldiers put to flight,
And, as thou seest, ourselves in heavy plight.

LOUIS Renowned Queen, with patience calm the storm,
While we bethink a means to break it off.

QUEEN MARGARET The more we stay, the stronger grows our foe.

LOUIS The more I stay, the more I'll succour thee.

QUEEN MARGARET O, but impatience waiteth on true sorrow.
And see where comes the breeder of my sorrow!

Enter WARWICK.

LOUIS What's he approacheth boldly to our presence?

QUEEN MARGARET Our Earl of Warwick, Edward's greatest friend.

LOUIS Welcome, brave Warwick! What brings thee to France? [*He descends. She ariseth.*

QUEEN MARGARET Ay, now begins a second storm to rise;
For this is he that moves both wind and tide.

WARWICK From worthy Edward, King of Albion,
My lord and sovereign, and thy vowed friend,
I come, in kindness and unfeigned love,
First to do greetings to thy royal person,
And then to crave a league of amity,
And lastly to confirm that amity
With nuptial knot, if thou vouchsafe to grant
That virtuous Lady Bona, thy fair sister,
To England's King in lawful marriage.

QUEEN MARGARET [*Aside*] If that go forward, Henry's hope is done.

WARWICK [*To Bona*] And, gracious madam, in our king's behalf,
I am commanded, with your leave and favour,
Humbly to kiss your hand, and with my tongue
To tell the passion of my sovereign's heart;
Where fame, late ent'ring at his heedful ears,
Hath plac'd thy beauty's image and thy virtue.

QUEEN MARGARET King Lewis and Lady Bona, hear me speak
Before you answer Warwick. His demand
Springs not from Edward's well-meant honest love,
But from deceit bred by necessity;
For how can tyrants safely govern home
Unless abroad they purchase great alliance?
To prove him tyrant this reason may suffice,
That Henry liveth still; but were he dead,
Yet here Prince Edward stands, King Henry's son.
Look therefore, Lewis, that by this league and marriage
Thou draw not on thy danger and dishonour;
For though usurpers sway the rule a while

Yet heav'ns are just, and time suppresseth wrongs.
WARWICK Injurious Margaret!
PRINCE And why not Queen?
WARWICK Because thy father Henry did usurp;
And thou no more art prince than she is queen.
OXFORD Then Warwick disannuls great John of Gaunt,
Which did subdue the greatest part of Spain;
And, after John of Gaunt, Henry the Fourth,
Whose wisdom was a mirror to the wisest;
And, after that wise prince, Henry the Fifth,
Who by his prowess conquered all France.
From these our Henry lineally descends.
WARWICK Oxford, how haps it in this smooth discourse
You told not how Henry the Sixth hath lost
All that which Henry the Fifth had gotten?
Methinks these peers of France should smile at that.
But for the rest: you tell a pedigree
Of threescore and two years – a silly time
To make prescription for a kingdom's worth.
OXFORD Why, Warwick, canst thou speak against thy liege,
Whom thou obeyed'st thirty and six years,
And not bewray thy treason with a blush?
WARWICK Can Oxford that did ever fence the right
Now buckler falsehood with a pedigree?
For shame! Leave Henry, and call Edward king.
OXFORD Call him my king by whose injurious doom
My elder brother, the Lord Aubrey Vere,
Was done to death; and more than so, my father,
Even in the downfall of his mellow'd years,
When nature brought him to the door of death?
No, Warwick, no; while life upholds this arm,
This arm upholds the house of Lancaster.
WARWICK And I the house of York.
LOUIS Queen Margaret, Prince Edward, and Oxford,
Vouchsafe at our request to stand aside
While I use further conference with Warwick.
[*They stand aloof.*
QUEEN MARGARET Heavens grant that Warwick's words bewitch him not!
LOUIS Now, Warwick, tell me, even upon thy conscience,
Is Edward your true king? for I were loath
To link with him that were not lawful chosen.
WARWICK Thereon I pawn my credit and mine honour.
LOUIS But is he gracious in the people's eye?
WARWICK The more that Henry was unfortunate.
LOUIS Then further: all dissembling set aside,
Tell me for truth the measure of his love
Unto our sister Bona.
WARWICK Such it seems
As may beseem a monarch like himself.
Myself have often heard him say and swear
That this his love was an eternal plant
Whereof the root was fix'd in virtue's ground,
The leaves and fruit maintain'd with beauty's sun,
Exempt from envy, but not from disdain,
Unless the Lady Bona quit his pain.
LOUIS Now, sister, let us hear your firm resolve.
BONA Your grant or your denial shall be mine.
[*To Warwick*] Yet I confess that often ere this day,
When I have heard your king's desert recounted,
Mine ear hath tempted judgment to desire.
LOUIS Then, Warwick, thus: our sister shall be Edward's.
And now forthwith shall articles be drawn
Touching the jointure that your king must make,
Which with her dowry shall be counter-pois'd.
Draw near, Queen Margaret, and be a witness
That Bona shall be wife to the English king.
PRINCE To Edward, but not to the English king.
QUEEN MARGARET Deceitful Warwick, it was thy device
By this alliance to make void my suit.
Before thy coming, Lewis was Henry's friend.
LOUIS And still is friend to him and Margaret.
But if your title to the crown be weak,
As may appear by Edward's good success,
Then 'tis but reason that I be releas'd
From giving aid which late I promised.
Yet shall you have all kindness at my hand
That your estate requires and mine can yield.
WARWICK Henry now lives in Scotland at his ease,
Where having nothing, nothing can he lose.
And as for you yourself, our quondam queen,
You have a father able to maintain you,
And better 'twere you troubled him than France.
QUEEN MARGARET Peace, impudent and shameless Warwick,
Proud setter up and puller down of kings!
I will not hence till with my talk and tears,
Both full of truth, I make King Lewis behold
Thy sly conveyance and thy lord's false love;
For both of you are birds of self-same feather.
[*Post blowing a horn within.*
LOUIS Warwick, this is some post to us or thee.

Enter the Post.

POST My lord ambassador, these letters are for you,
Sent from your brother, Marquis Montague.
These from our King unto your Majesty.
And, madam, these for you; from whom I know not. [*They all read their letters.*
OXFORD I like it well that our fair Queen and mistress
Smiles at her news, while Warwick frowns at his.
PRINCE Nay, mark how Lewis stamps as he were nettled.
I hope all's for the best.
LOUIS Warwick, what are thy news? And yours, fair Queen?
QUEEN MARGARET Mine such as fill my heart with unhop'd joys.
WARWICK Mine full of sorrow and heart's discontent.
LOUIS What, has your king married the Lady Grey?
And now, to soothe your forgery and his,
Sends me a paper to persuade me patience?
Is this th' alliance that he seeks with France?
Dare he presume to scorn us in this manner?
QUEEN MARGARET I told your Majesty as much before.
This proveth Edward's love and Warwick's honesty.
WARWICK King Lewis, I here protest in sight of heaven,
And by the hope I have of heavenly bliss,
That I am clear from this misdeed of Edward's –
No more my king, for he dishonours me,
But most himself, if he could see his shame.
Did I forget that by the house of York
My father came untimely to his death?
Did I let pass th' abuse done to my niece?
Did I impale him with the regal crown?
Did I put Henry from his native right?
And am I guerdon'd at the last with shame?
Shame on himself! for my desert is honour;
And to repair my honour lost for him
I here renounce him and return to Henry.
My noble Queen, let former grudges pass,
And henceforth I am thy true servitor.
I will revenge his wrong to Lady Bona,
And replant Henry in his former state.
QUEEN MARGARET Warwick, these words have turn'd my hate to love;
And I forgive and quite forget old faults,
And joy that thou becom'st King Henry's friend.
WARWICK So much his friend, ay, his unfeigned friend,
That if King Lewis vouchsafe to furnish us
With some few bands of chosen soldiers,
I'll undertake to land them on our coast
And force the tyrant from his seat by war.
'Tis not his new-made bride shall succour him;
And as for Clarence, as my letters tell me,
He's very likely now to fall from him
For matching more for wanton lust than honour
Or than for strength and safety of our country.
BONA Dear brother, how shall Bona be reveng'd
But by thy help to this distressed queen?
QUEEN MARGARET Renowned Prince, how shall poor Henry live
Unless thou rescue him from foul despair?
BONA My quarrel and this English queen's are one.
WARWICK And mine, fair Lady Bona, joins with yours.
LOUIS And mine with hers, and thine, and Margaret's.
Therefore, at last, I firmly am resolv'd
You shall have aid.
QUEEN MARGARET Let me give humble thanks for all at once.
LOUIS Then, England's messenger, return in post
And tell false Edward, thy supposed king,
That Lewis of France is sending over masquers
To revel it with him and his new bride.
Thou seest what's past; go fear thy king withal.
BONA Tell him, in hope he'll prove a widower shortly,
I'll wear the willow-garland for his sake.
QUEEN MARGARET Tell him my mourning weeds are laid aside,
And I am ready to put armour on.
WARWICK Tell him from me that he hath done me wrong,
And therefore I'll uncrown him ere't be long.
There's thy reward; be gone. [*Exit Post.*
LOUIS But, Warwick,
Thou and Oxford, with five thousand men,
Shall cross the seas and bid false Edward battle;
And, as occasion serves, this noble Queen
And Prince shall follow with a fresh supply.
Yet, ere thou go, but answer me one doubt:
What pledge have we of thy firm loyalty?
WARWICK This shall assure my constant loyalty:
That if our Queen and this young Prince agree,
I'll join mine eldest daughter and my joy
To him forthwith in holy wedlock bands.
QUEEN MARGARET Yes, I agree, and thank you for your motion.
Son Edward, she is fair and virtuous,
Therefore delay not – give thy hand to Warwick;
And with thy hand thy faith irrevocable
That only Warwick's daughter shall be thine.
PRINCE Yes, I accept her, for she well deserves it;
And here, to pledge my vow, I give my hand.

[*He gives his hand to Warwick.*

LOUIS Why stay we now? These soldiers shall be levied;
And thou, Lord Bourbon, our High Admiral,
Shall waft them over with our royal fleet.
I long till Edward fall by war's mischance
For mocking marriage with a dame of France.

[*Exeunt all but Warwick.*

WARWICK I came from Edward as ambassador,
But I return his sworn and mortal foe.
Matter of marriage was the charge he gave me,
But dreadful war shall answer his demand.
Had he none else to make a stale but me?
Then none but I shall turn his jest to sorrow.
I was the chief that rais'd him to the crown,
And I'll be chief to bring him down again;
Not that I pity Henry's misery,
But seek revenge on Edward's mockery. [*Exit.*

ACT FOUR

SCENE I. *London. The Palace.*

Enter GLOUCESTER, CLARENCE, SOMERSET, and MONTAGUE.

GLOUCESTER Now tell me, brother Clarence, what think you
Of this new marriage with the Lady Grey?
Hath not our brother made a worthy choice?

CLARENCE Alas, you know 'tis far from hence to France!
How could he stay till Warwick made return?

SOMERSET My lords, forbear this talk; here comes the King.

Flourish. Enter KING EDWARD, attended; LADY GREY, as Queen; PEMBROKE, STAFFORD, HASTINGS, and Others. Four stand on one side, and four on the other.

GLOUCESTER And his well-chosen bride.

CLARENCE I mind to tell him plainly what I think.

KING EDWARD Now, brother of Clarence, how like you our choice
That you stand pensive as half malcontent?

CLARENCE As well as Lewis of France or the Earl of Warwick,
Which are so weak of courage and in judgment
That they'll take no offence at our abuse.

KING EDWARD Suppose they take offence without a cause;
They are but Lewis and Warwick: I am Edward,
Your King and Warwick's, and must have my will.

GLOUCESTER And shall have your will, because our King.
Yet hasty marriage seldom proveth well.

KING EDWARD Yea, brother Richard, are you offended too?

GLOUCESTER Not I.
No, God forbid that I should wish them sever'd
Whom God hath join'd together; ay, and 'twere pity
To sunder them that yoke so well together.

KING EDWARD Setting your scorns and your mislike aside,
Tell me some reason why the Lady Grey
Should not become my wife and England's Queen.
And you too, Somerset and Montague,
Speak freely what you think.

CLARENCE Then this is mine opinion: that King Lewis
Becomes your enemy for mocking him
About the marriage of the Lady Bona.

GLOUCESTER And Warwick, doing what you gave in charge,
Is now dishonoured by this new marriage.

KING EDWARD What if both Lewis and Warwick be appeas'd
By such invention as I can devise?

MONTAGUE Yet to have join'd with France in such alliance
Would more have strength'ned this our commonwealth
'Gainst foreign storms than any home-bred marriage.

HASTINGS Why, knows not Montague that of itself
England is safe, if true within itself?

MONTAGUE But the safer when 'tis back'd with France.

HASTINGS 'Tis better using France than trusting France.
Let us be back'd with God, and with the seas
Which He hath giv'n for fence impregnable,
And with their helps only defend ourselves.
In them and in ourselves our safety lies.

CLARENCE For this one speech Lord Hastings well deserves
To have the heir of the Lord Hungerford.

KING EDWARD Ay, what of that? it was my will and grant;
And for this once my will shall stand for law.

GLOUCESTER And yet methinks your Grace hath not done well
To give the heir and daughter of Lord Scales
Unto the brother of your loving bride.

She better would have fitted me or Clarence;
But in your bride you bury brotherhood.
CLARENCE Or else you would not have bestow'd the heir
Of the Lord Bonville on your new wife's son,
And leave your brothers to go speed elsewhere.
KING EDWARD Alas, poor Clarence! Is it for a wife
That thou art malcontent? I will provide thee.
CLARENCE In choosing for yourself you show'd your judgment,
Which being shallow, you shall give me leave
To play the broker in mine own behalf;
And to that end I shortly mind to leave you.
KING EDWARD Leave me or tarry, Edward will be King,
And not be tied unto his brother's will.
QUEEN ELIZABETH My lords, before it pleas'd his Majesty
To raise my state to title of a queen,
Do me but right, and you must all confess
That I was not ignoble of descent;
And meaner than myself have had like fortune.
But as this title honours me and mine,
So your dislikes, to whom I would be pleasing,
Doth cloud my joys with danger and with sorrow.
KING EDWARD My love, forbear to fawn upon their frowns.
What danger or what sorrow can befall thee,
So long as Edward is thy constant friend
And their true sovereign whom they must obey?
Nay, whom they shall obey, and love thee too,
Unless they seek for hatred at my hands;
Which if they do, yet will I keep thee safe,
And they shall feel the vengeance of my wrath.
GLOUCESTER [*Aside*] I hear, yet say not much, but think the more.

Enter a Post.

KING EDWARD Now, messenger, what letters or what news
From France?
MESSENGER My sovereign liege, no letters, and few words,
But such as I, without your special pardon,
Dare not relate.
KING EDWARD Go to, we pardon thee; therefore, in brief,
Tell me their words as near as thou canst guess them.
What answer makes King Lewis unto our letters?
MESSENGER At my depart, these were his very words:
'Go tell false Edward, the supposed king,
That Lewis of France is sending over masquers
To revel it with him and his new bride'.
KING EDWARD Is Lewis so brave? Belike he thinks me Henry.
But what said Lady Bona to my marriage?
MESSENGER These were her words, utt'red with mild disdain:
'Tell him, in hope he'll prove a widower shortly,
I'll wear the willow-garland for his sake'.
KING EDWARD I blame not her: she could say little less;
She had the wrong. But what said Henry's queen?
For I have heard that she was there in place.
MESSENGER 'Tell him' quoth she 'my mourning weeds are done,
And I am ready to put armour on.'
KING EDWARD Belike she minds to play the Amazon.
But what said Warwick to these injuries?
MESSENGER He, more incens'd against your Majesty
Than all the rest, discharg'd me with these words:
'Tell him from me that he hath done me wrong;
And therefore I'll uncrown him ere't be long'.
KING EDWARD Ha! durst the traitor breathe out so proud words?
Well, I will arm me, being thus forewarn'd.
They shall have wars and pay for their presumption.
But say, is Warwick friends with Margaret?
MESSENGER Ay, gracious sovereign; they are so link'd in friendship
That young Prince Edward marries Warwick's daughter.
CLARENCE Belike the elder; Clarence will have the younger.
Now, brother king, farewell, and sit you fast,
For I will hence to Warwick's other daughter;
That, though I want a kingdom, yet in marriage
I may not prove inferior to yourself.
You that love me and Warwick, follow me.

[*Exit, and Somerset follows.*

GLOUCESTER [*Aside*] Not I.
My thoughts aim at a further matter; I
Stay not for the love of Edward but the crown.
KING EDWARD Clarence and Somerset both gone to Warwick!
Yet am I arm'd against the worst can happen;
And haste is needful in this desp'rate case.
Pembroke and Stafford, you in our behalf
Go levy men and make prepare for war;
They are already, or quickly will be landed.
Myself in person will straight follow you.

[*Exeunt Pembroke and Stafford.*

But ere I go, Hastings and Montague,

Resolve my doubt. You twain, of all the rest,
Are near to Warwick by blood and by alliance.
Tell me if you love Warwick more than me?
If it be so, then both depart to him:
I rather wish you foes than hollow friends.
But if you mind to hold your true obedience,
Give me assurance with some friendly vow,
That I may never have you in suspect.

MONTAGUE So God help Montague as he proves true!

HASTINGS And Hastings as he favours Edward's cause!

KING EDWARD Now, brother Richard, will you stand by us?

GLOUCESTER Ay, in despite of all that shall withstand you.

KING EDWARD Why, so! then am I sure of victory.
Now therefore let us hence, and lose no hour
Till we meet Warwick with his foreign pow'r.
[*Exeunt.*

SCENE II. *A plain in Warwickshire.*

Enter WARWICK and OXFORD, with French Soldiers.

WARWICK Trust me, my lord, all hitherto goes well;
The common people by numbers swarm to us.

Enter CLARENCE and SOMERSET.

But see where Somerset and Clarence comes.
Speak suddenly, my lords – are we all friends?

CLARENCE Fear not that, my lord.

WARWICK Then, gentle Clarence, welcome unto Warwick;
And welcome, Somerset. I hold it cowardice
To rest mistrustful where a noble heart
Hath pawn'd an open hand in sign of love;
Else might I think that Clarence, Edward's brother,
Were but a feigned friend to our proceedings.
But welcome, sweet Clarence; my daughter shall be thine.
And now what rests but, in night's coverture,
Thy brother being carelessly encamp'd,
His soldiers lurking in the towns about,
And but attended by a simple guard,
We may surprise and take him at our pleasure?
Our scouts have found the adventure very easy;
That as Ulysses and stout Diomede
With sleight and manhood stole to Rhesus' tents,
And brought from thence the Thracian fatal steeds,
So we, well cover'd with the night's black mantle,
At unawares may beat down Edward's guard
And seize himself – I say not 'slaughter him',
For I intend but only to surprise him.
You that will follow me to this attempt,
Applaud the name of Henry with your leader.
[*They all cry* 'Henry!'
Why then, let's on our way in silent sort.
For Warwick and his friends, God and Saint George!
[*Exeunt.*

SCENE III. *Edward's camp, near Warwick.*

Enter three Watchmen, to guard the King's tent.

1 WATCH Come on, my masters, each man take his stand;
The King by this is set him down to sleep.

2 WATCH What, will he not to bed?

1 WATCH Why, no; for he hath made a solemn vow
Never to lie and take his natural rest
Till Warwick or himself be quite suppress'd.

2 WATCH To-morrow then, belike, shall be the day,
If Warwick be so near as men report.

3 WATCH But say, I pray, what nobleman is that
That with the King here resteth in his tent?

1 WATCH 'Tis the Lord Hastings, the King's chiefest friend.

3 WATCH O, is it so? But why commands the King
That his chief followers lodge in towns about him,
While he himself keeps in the cold field?

2 WATCH 'Tis the more honour, because more dangerous.

3 WATCH Ay, but give me worship and quietness;
I like it better than a dangerous honour.
If Warwick knew in what estate he stands,
'Tis to be doubted he would waken him.

1 WATCH Unless our halberds did shut up his passage.

2 WATCH Ay, wherefore else guard we his royal tent
But to defend his person from night-foes?

Enter WARWICK, CLARENCE, OXFORD, SOMERSET, and French Soldiers, silent all.

WARWICK This is his tent; and see where stand his guard.
Courage, my masters! Honour now or never!
But follow me, and Edward shall be ours.

1 WATCH Who goes there?

2 WATCH Stay, or thou diest.

Warwick and the rest cry all 'Warwick! Warwick!' *and set upon the Guard, who fly, crying* 'Arm! Arm!' *Warwick and the rest following them.*

The drum playing and trumpet sounding, re-enter WARWICK and the rest, bringing the KING out in his gown, sitting in a chair. GLOUCESTER and HASTINGS fly over the stage.

SOMERSET What are they that fly there?
WARWICK Richard and Hastings. Let them go; here is the Duke.
KING EDWARD The Duke! Why, Warwick, when we parted,
Thou call'dst me King?
WARWICK Ay, but the case is alter'd.
When you disgrac'd me in my embassade,
Then I degraded you from being King,
And come now to create you Duke of York.
Alas, how should you govern any kingdom
That know not how to use ambassadors,
Nor how to be contented with one wife,
Nor how to use your brothers brotherly,
Nor how to study for the people's welfare,
Nor how to shroud yourself from enemies?
KING EDWARD Yea, brother of Clarence, art thou here too?
Nay, then I see that Edward needs must down.
Yet, Warwick, in despite of all mischance,
Of thee thyself and all thy complices,
Edward will always bear himself as King.
Though fortune's malice overthrow my state,
My mind exceeds the compass of her wheel.
WARWICK Then, for his mind, be Edward England's king;

[*Takes off his crown.*

But Henry now shall wear the English crown
And be true King indeed; thou but the shadow.
My Lord of Somerset, at my request,
See that forthwith Duke Edward be convey'd
Unto my brother, Archbishop of York.
When I have fought with Pembroke and his fellows,
I'll follow you and tell what answer
Lewis and the Lady Bona send to him.
Now for a while farewell, good Duke of York.

KING EDWARD What fates impose, that men must needs abide;
It boots not to resist both wind and tide.

[*They lead him out forcibly.*

OXFORD What now remains, my lords, for us to do
But march to London with our soldiers?
WARWICK Ay, that's the first thing that we have to do;
To free King Henry from imprisonment,
And see him seated in the regal throne.

[*Exeunt.*

SCENE IV. *London. The palace.*

Enter QUEEN ELIZABETH and RIVERS.

RIVERS Madam, what makes you in this sudden change?
QUEEN ELIZABETH Why, brother Rivers, are you yet to learn
What late misfortune is befall'n King Edward?
RIVERS What, loss of some pitch'd battle against Warwick?
QUEEN ELIZABETH No, but the loss of his own royal person.
RIVERS Then is my sovereign slain?
QUEEN ELIZABETH Ay, almost slain, for he is taken prisoner;
Either betray'd by falsehood of his guard
Or by his foe surpris'd at unawares;
And, as I further have to understand,
Is new committed to the Bishop of York,
Fell Warwick's brother, and by that our foe.
RIVERS These news, I must confess, are full of grief;
Yet, gracious madam, bear it as you may:
Warwick may lose that now hath won the day.
QUEEN ELIZABETH Till then, fair hope must hinder life's decay.
And I the rather wean me from despair
For love of Edward's offspring in my womb.
This is it that makes me bridle passion
And bear with mildness my misfortune's cross;
Ay, ay, for this I draw in many a tear
And stop the rising of blood-sucking sighs,
Lest with my sighs or tears I blast or drown
King Edward's fruit, true heir to th' English crown.
RIVERS But, madam, where is Warwick then become?
QUEEN ELIZABETH I am inform'd that he comes towards London
To set the crown once more on Henry's head.
Guess thou the rest: King Edward's friends must down.
But to prevent the tyrant's violence –
For trust not him that hath once broken faith –
I'll hence forthwith unto the sanctuary
To save at least the heir of Edward's right.
There shall I rest secure from force and fraud.
Come, therefore, let us fly while we may fly:
If Warwick take us, we are sure to die. [*Exeunt.*

SCENE V. *A park near Middleham Castle in Yorkshire.*

Enter GLOUCESTER, LORD HASTINGS, SIR WILLIAM STANLEY, and Others.

GLOUCESTER Now, my Lord Hastings and Sir William Stanley,
Leave off to wonder why I drew you hither

Into this chiefest thicket of the park.
Thus stands the case: you know our King, my brother,
Is prisoner to the Bishop here, at whose hands
He hath good usage and great liberty;
And often but attended with weak guard
Comes hunting this way to disport himself.
I have advertis'd him by secret means
That if about this hour he make this way,
Under the colour of his usual game,
He shall here find his friends, with horse and men,
To set him free from his captivity.

Enter KING EDWARD and a Huntsman with him.

HUNTSMAN This way, my lord; for this way lies the game.
KING EDWARD Nay, this way, man. See where the huntsmen stand.
Now, brother of Gloucester, Lord Hastings, and the rest,
Stand you thus close to steal the Bishop's deer?
GLOUCESTER Brother, the time and case requireth haste;
Your horse stands ready at the park corner.
KING EDWARD But whither shall we then?
HASTINGS To Lynn, my lord; and shipt from thence to Flanders.
GLOUCESTER Well guess'd, believe me; for that was my meaning.
KING EDWARD Stanley, I will requite thy forwardness.
GLOUCESTER But wherefore stay we? 'Tis no time to talk.
KING EDWARD Huntsmen, what say'st thou? Wilt thou go along?
HUNTSMAN Better do so than tarry and be hang'd.
GLOUCESTER Come then, away; let's ha' no more ado.
KING EDWARD Bishop, farewell. Shield thee from Warwick's frown,
And pray that I may repossess the crown.
[*Exeunt.*

SCENE VI. *London. The Tower.*

Flourish. Enter KING HENRY, CLARENCE, WARWICK, SOMERSET, young HENRY EARL OF RICHMOND, OXFORD, MONTAGUE, Lieutenant of the Tower, and Attendants.

KING HENRY Master Lieutenant, now that God and friends
Have shaken Edward from the regal seat
And turn'd my captive state to liberty,
My fear to hope, my sorrows unto joys,
At our enlargement what are thy due fees?
LIEUTENANT Subjects may challenge nothing of their sov'reigns;
But if an humble prayer may prevail,
I then crave pardon of your Majesty.
KING HENRY For what, Lieutenant? For well using me?
Nay, be thou sure I'll well requite thy kindness,
For that it made my imprisonment a pleasure;
Ay, such a pleasure as incaged birds
Conceive when, after many moody thoughts,
At last by notes of household harmony
They quite forget their loss of liberty.
But, Warwick, after God, thou set'st me free,
And chiefly therefore I thank God and thee;
He was the author, thou the instrument.
Therefore, that I may conquer fortune's spite
By living low where fortune cannot hurt me,
And that the people of this blessed land
May not be punish'd with my thwarting stars,
Warwick, although my head still wear the crown,
I here resign my government to thee,
For thou art fortunate in all thy deeds.
WARWICK Your Grace hath still been fam'd for virtuous,
And now may seem as wise as virtuous
By spying and avoiding fortune's malice,
For few men rightly temper with the stars;
Yet in this one thing let me blame your Grace,
For choosing me when Clarence is in place.
CLARENCE No, Warwick, thou art worthy of the sway,
To whom the heav'ns in thy nativity
Adjudg'd an olive branch and laurel crown,
As likely to be blest in peace and war;
And therefore I yield thee my free consent.
WARWICK And I choose Clarence only for Protector.
KING HENRY Warwick and Clarence, give me both your hands.
Now join your hands, and with your hands your hearts,
That no dissension hinder government.
I make you both Protectors of this land,
While I myself will lead a private life
And in devotion spend my latter days,
To sin's rebuke and my Creator's praise.
WARWICK What answers Clarence to his sovereign's will?
CLARENCE That he consents, if Warwick yield consent,
For on thy fortune I repose myself.
WARWICK Why, then, though loath, yet must I be content.
We'll yoke together, like a double shadow
To Henry's body, and supply his place;
I mean, in bearing weight of government,

While he enjoys the honour and his ease.
And, Clarence, now then it is more than needful
Forthwith that Edward be pronounc'd a traitor,
And all his lands and goods confiscated.

CLARENCE What else? And that succession be determin'd.

WARWICK Ay, therein Clarence shall not want his part.

KING HENRY But, with the first of all your chief affairs,
Let me entreat – for I command no more –
That Margaret your Queen and my son Edward
Be sent for to return from France with speed;
For till I see them here, by doubtful fear
My joy of liberty is half eclips'd.

CLARENCE It shall be done, my sovereign, with all speed.

KING HENRY My Lord of Somerset, what youth is that,
Of whom you seem to have so tender care?

SOMERSET My liege, it is young Henry, Earl of Richmond.

KING HENRY Come hither, England's hope.
[*Lays his hand on his head.*
If secret powers
Suggest but truth to my divining thoughts,
This pretty lad will prove our country's bliss.
His looks are full of peaceful majesty;
His head by nature fram'd to wear a crown,
His hand to wield a sceptre; and himself
Likely in time to bless a regal throne.
Make much of him, my lords; for this is he
Must help you more than you are hurt by me.

Enter a Post.

WARWICK What news, my friend?

POST That Edward is escaped from your brother
And fled, as he hears since, to Burgundy.

WARWICK Unsavoury news! But how made he escape?

POST He was convey'd by Richard Duke of Gloucester
And the Lord Hastings, who attended him
In secret ambush on the forest side
And from the Bishop's huntsmen rescu'd him;
For hunting was his daily exercise.

WARWICK My brother was too careless of his charge.
But let us hence, my sovereign, to provide
A salve for any sore that may betide.
[*Exeunt all but Somerset, Richmond, and Oxford.*

SOMERSET My lord, I like not of this flight of Edward's;
For doubtless Burgundy will yield him help,
And we shall have more wars before't be long.
As Henry's late presaging prophecy
Did glad my heart with hope of this young Richmond,
So doth my heart misgive me, in these conflicts,
What may befall him to his harm and ours.
Therefore, Lord Oxford, to prevent the worst,
Forthwith we'll send him hence to Brittany,
Till storms be past of civil enmity.

OXFORD Ay, for if Edward repossess the crown,
'Tis like that Richmond with the rest shall down.

SOMERSET It shall be so; he shall to Brittany.
Come therefore, let's about it speedily. [*Exeunt.*

SCENE VII. *Before York.*

Flourish. Enter KING EDWARD, GLOUCESTER, HASTINGS, and Soldiers.

KING EDWARD Now, brother Richard, Lord Hastings, and the rest,
Yet thus far fortune maketh us amends,
And says that once more I shall interchange
My waned state for Henry's regal crown.
Well have we pass'd and now repass'd the seas,
And brought desired help from Burgundy;
What then remains, we being thus arriv'd
From Ravenspurgh haven before the gates of York,
But that we enter, as into our dukedom?

GLOUCESTER The gates made fast! Brother, I like not this;
For many men that stumble at the threshold
Are well foretold that danger lurks within.

KING EDWARD Tush, man, abodements must not now affright us.
By fair or foul means we must enter in,
For hither will our friends repair to us.

HASTINGS My liege, I'll knock once more to summon them.

Enter, on the walls, the Mayor of York and his Brethren.

MAYOR My lords, we were forewarned of your coming
And shut the gates for safety of ourselves,
For now we owe allegiance unto Henry.

KING EDWARD But, Master Mayor, if Henry be your King,
Yet Edward at the least is Duke of York.

MAYOR True, my good lord; I know you for no less.

KING EDWARD Why, and I challenge nothing but my dukedom,
As being well content with that alone.

GLOUCESTER [*Aside*] But when the fox hath once got in his nose,
He'll soon find means to make the body follow.

HASTINGS Why, Master Mayor, why stand you in a doubt?

Open the gates; we are King Henry's friends.
MAYOR Ay, say you so? The gates shall then be open'd. *[He descends.*
GLOUCESTER A wise stout captain, and soon persuaded!
HASTINGS The good old man would fain that all were well,
So 'twere not long of him; but being ent'red,
I doubt not, I, but we shall soon persuade
Both him and all his brothers unto reason.
Enter, below, the Mayor and two Aldermen.
KING EDWARD So, Master Mayor. These gates must not be shut
But in the night or in the time of war.
What! fear not, man, but yield me up the keys; *[Takes his keys.*
For Edward will defend the town and thee,
And all those friends that deign to follow me.

March. Enter MONTGOMERY with drum and Soldiers.

GLOUCESTER Brother, this is Sir John Montgomery,
Our trusty friend, unless I be deceiv'd.
KING EDWARD Welcome, Sir John! But why come you in arms?
MONTAGUE To help King Edward in his time of storm,
As every loyal subject ought to do.
KING EDWARD Thanks, good Montgomery; but we now forget
Our title to the crown, and only claim
Our dukedom till God please to send the rest.
MONTAGUE Then fare you well, for I will hence again.
I came to serve a king and not a duke.
Drummer, strike up, and let us march away.
[The Drum begins to march.
KING EDWARD Nay, stay, Sir John, a while, and we'll debate
By what safe means the crown may be recover'd.
MONTAGUE What talk you of debating? In few words:
If you'll not here proclaim yourself our King,
I'll leave you to your fortune and be gone
To keep them back that come to succour you.
Why shall we fight, if you pretend no title?
GLOUCESTER Why, brother, wherefore stand you on nice points?
KING EDWARD When we grow stronger, then we'll make our claim;
Till then 'tis wisdom to conceal our meaning.
HASTINGS Away with scrupulous wit! Now arms must rule.
GLOUCESTER And fearless minds climb soonest unto crowns.
Brother, we will proclaim you out of hand;
The bruit thereof will bring you many friends.
KING EDWARD Then be it as you will; for 'tis my right,
And Henry but usurps the diadem.
MONTAGUE Ay, now my sovereign speaketh like himself;
And now will I be Edward's champion.
HASTINGS Sound trumpet; Edward shall be here proclaim'd.
Come, fellow soldier, make thou proclamation.
[Gives him a paper. Flourish.
SOLDIER *[Reads]* 'Edward the Fourth, by the grace of God, King of England and France, and Lord of Ireland, etc.'
MONTAGUE And whoso'er gainsays King Edward's right,
By this I challenge him to single fight. *[Throws down his gauntlet.*
ALL Long live Edward the Fourth!
KING EDWARD Thanks, brave Montgomery, and thanks unto you all;
If fortune serve me, I'll requite this kindness.
Now for this night let's harbour here in York;
And when the morning sun shall raise his car
Above the border of this horizon,
We'll forward towards Warwick and his mates;
For well I wot that Henry is no soldier.
Ah, forward Clarence, how evil it beseems thee
To flatter Henry and forsake thy brother!
Yet, as we may, we'll meet both thee and Warwick.
Come on, brave soldiers; doubt not of the day,
And, that once gotten, doubt not of large pay.
[Exeunt.

SCENE VIII. *London. The palace.*

Flourish. Enter KING HENRY, WARWICK, MONTAGUE, CLARENCE, OXFORD, and EXETER.

WARWICK What counsel, lords? Edward from Belgia,
With hasty Germans and blunt Hollanders,
Hath pass'd in safety through the narrow seas
And with his troops doth march amain to London;
And many giddy people flock to him.
KING HENRY Let's levy men and beat him back again.
CLARENCE A little fire is quickly trodden out,
Which, being suffer'd, rivers cannot quench.
WARWICK In Warwickshire I have truehearted friends,
Not mutinous in peace, yet bold in war;

Those will I muster up, and thou, son Clarence,
Shalt stir up in Suffolk, Norfolk, and in Kent,
The knights and gentlemen to come with thee.
Thou, brother Montague, in Buckingham,
Northampton, and in Leicestershire, shalt find
Men well inclin'd to hear what thou command'st.
And thou, brave Oxford, wondrous well belov'd,
In Oxfordshire shalt muster up thy friends.
My sovereign, with the loving citizens,
Like to his island girt in with the ocean
Or modest Dian circled with her nymphs,
Shall rest in London till we come to him.
Fair lords, take leave and stand not to reply.
Farewell, my sovereign.

KING HENRY Farewell, my Hector and my Troy's true hope.

CLARENCE In sign of truth, I kiss your Highness' hand.

KING HENRY Well-minded Clarence, be thou fortunate!

MONTAGUE Comfort, my lord; and so I take my leave.

OXFORD [*Kissing the King's hand*] And thus I seal my truth and bid adieu.

KING HENRY Sweet Oxford, and my loving Montague,
And all at once, once more a happy farewell.

WARWICK Farewell, sweet lords; let's meet at Coventry. [*Exeunt all but the King and Exeter*.

KING HENRY Here at the palace will I rest a while.
Cousin of Exeter, what thinks your lordship?
Methinks the power that Edward hath in field
Should not be able to encounter mine.

EXETER The doubt is that he will seduce the rest.

KING HENRY That's not my fear; my meed hath got me fame:
I have not stopp'd mine ears to their demands,
Nor posted off their suits with slow delays;
My pity hath been balm to heal their wounds,
My mildness hath allay'd their swelling griefs,
My mercy dried their water-flowing tears;
I have not been desirous of their wealth,
Nor much oppress'd them with great subsidies,
Nor forward of revenge, though they much err'd.
Then why should they love Edward more than me?
No, Exeter, these graces challenge grace;
And, when the lion fawns upon the lamb,
The lamb will never cease to follow him.

[*Shout within* 'A Lancaster! A Lancaster!'

EXETER Hark, hark, my lord! What shouts are these?

Enter KING EDWARD, GLOUCESTER, and Soldiers.

KING EDWARD Seize on the shame-fac'd Henry, bear him hence;
And once again proclaim us King of England.
You are the fount that makes small brooks to flow.
Now stops thy spring; my sea shall suck them dry,
And swell so much the higher by their ebb.
Hence with him to the Tower: let him not speak.

[*Exeunt some with King Henry.*

And, lords, towards Coventry bend we our course,
Where peremptory Warwick now remains.
The sun shines hot; and, if we use delay,
Cold biting winter mars our hop'd-for hay.

GLOUCESTER Away betimes, before his forces join,
And take the great-grown traitor unawares.
Brave warriors, march amain towards Coventry.

[*Exeunt.*

ACT FIVE

SCENE I. *Coventry.*

Enter WARWICK, the Mayor of Coventry, two Messengers, and Others upon the walls.

WARWICK Where is the post that came from valiant Oxford?
How far hence is thy lord, mine honest fellow?

1 MESSENGER By this at Dunsmore, marching hitherward.

WARWICK How far off is our brother Montague?
Where is the post that came from Montague?

2 MESSENGER By this at Daintry, with a puissant troop.

Enter SIR JOHN SOMERVILLE.

WARWICK Say, Somerville, what says my loving son?
And by thy guess how nigh is Clarence now?

SOMERVILLE At Southam I did leave him with his forces,
And do expect him with here some two hours hence. [*Drum heard.*

WARWICK Then Clarence is at hand; I hear his drum.

SOMERVILLE It is not his, my lord; here Southam lies.

The drum your Honour hears marcheth from Warwick.
WARWICK Who should that be? Belike unlook'd for friends.
SOMERVILLE They are at hand, and you shall quickly know.

March. Flourish. Enter KING EDWARD, GLOUCESTER, and Soldiers.

KING EDWARD Go, trumpet, to the walls, and sound a parle.
GLOUCESTER See how the surly Warwick mans the wall.
WARWICK O unbid spite! Is sportful Edward come?
Where slept our scouts or how are they seduc'd
That we could hear no news of his repair?
KING EDWARD Now, Warwick, wilt thou ope the city gates,
Speak gentle words, and humbly bend thy knee,
Call Edward King, and at his hands beg mercy?
And he shall pardon thee these outrages.
WARWICK Nay, rather wilt thou draw thy forces hence,
Confess who set thee up and pluck'd thee down,
Call Warwick patron, and be penitent?
And thou shalt still remain the Duke of York.
GLOUCESTER I thought, at least, he would have said the King;
Or did he make the jest against his will?
WARWICK Is not a dukedom, sir, a goodly gift?
GLOUCESTER Ay, by my faith, for a poor earl to give.
I'll do thee service for so good a gift.
WARWICK 'Twas I that gave the kingdom to thy brother.
KING EDWARD Why then 'tis mine, if but by Warwick's gift.
WARWICK Thou art no Atlas for so great a weight;
And, weakling, Warwick takes his gift again;
And Henry is my King, Warwick his subject.
KING EDWARD But Warwick's king is Edward's prisoner.
And, gallant Warwick, do but answer this:
What is the body when the head is off?
GLOUCESTER Alas, that Warwick had no more forecast,
But, whiles he thought to steal the single ten,
The king was slily finger'd from the deck!
You left poor Henry at the Bishop's palace,
And ten to one you'll meet him in the Tower.
KING EDWARD 'Tis even so; yet you are Warwick still.
GLOUCESTER Come, Warwick, take the time; kneel down, kneel down.
Nay, when? Strike now, or else the iron cools.
WARWICK I had rather chop this hand off at a blow,
And with the other fling it at thy face,
Than bear so low a sail to strike to thee.
KING EDWARD Sail how thou canst, have wind and tide thy friend,
This hand, fast wound about thy coal-black hair,
Shall, whiles thy head is warm and new cut off,
Write in the dust this sentence with thy blood:
'Wind-changing Warwick now can change no more'.

Enter OXFORD, with drum and colours.

WARWICK O cheerful colours! See where Oxford comes.
OXFORD Oxford, Oxford, for Lancaster!
[He and his forces enter the city.
GLOUCESTER The gates are open, let us enter too.
KING EDWARD So other foes may set upon our backs.
Stand we in good array, for they no doubt
Will issue out again and bid us battle;
If not, the city being but of small defence,
We'll quickly rouse the traitors in the same.
WARWICK O, welcome, Oxford! for we want thy help.

Enter MONTAGUE, with drum and colours.

MONTAGUE Montague, Montague, for Lancaster!
[He and his forces enter the city.
GLOUCESTER Thou and thy brother both shall buy this treason
Even with the dearest blood your bodies bear.
KING EDWARD The harder match'd, the greater victory.
My mind presageth happy gain and conquest.

Enter SOMERSET, with drum and colours.

SOMERSET Somerset, Somerset, for Lancaster!
[He and his forces enter the city.
GLOUCESTER Two of thy name, both Dukes of Somerset,
Have sold their lives unto the house of York;
And thou shalt be the third, if this sword hold.

Enter CLARENCE, with drum and colours.

WARWICK And lo where George of Clarence sweeps along,
Of force enough to bid his brother battle;
With whom an upright zeal to right prevails
More than the nature of a brother's love.
CLARENCE Clarence, Clarence, for Lancaster!
KING EDWARD Et tu Brute – wilt thou stab Caesar too?
A parley, sirrah, to George of Clarence.
[Sound a parley. Richard and Clarence whisper.

WARWICK Come, Clarence, come. Thou wilt if Warwick call.
CLARENCE [*Taking the red rose from his hat and throwing it at Warwick*] Father of Warwick, know you what this means?
Look here, I throw my infamy at thee.
I will not ruinate my father's house,
Who gave his blood to lime the stones together,
And set up Lancaster. Why, trowest thou, Warwick,
That Clarence is so harsh, so blunt, unnatural,
To bend the fatal instruments of war
Against his brother and his lawful King?
Perhaps thou wilt object my holy oath.
To keep that oath were more impiety
Than Jephtha when he sacrific'd his daughter.
I am so sorry for my trespass made
That, to deserve well at my brother's hands,
I here proclaim myself thy mortal foe;
With resolution whereso'er I meet thee –
As I will meet thee, if thou stir abroad –
To plague thee for thy foul misleading me.
And so, proud-hearted Warwick, I defy thee,
And to my brother turn my blushing cheeks.
Pardon me, Edward, I will make amends;
And, Richard, do not frown upon my faults,
For I will henceforth be no more unconstant.
KING EDWARD Now welcome more, and ten times more belov'd,
Than if thou never hadst deserv'd our hate.
GLOUCESTER Welcome, good Clarence; this is brother-like.
WARWICK O passing traitor, perjur'd and unjust!
KING EDWARD What, Warwick, wilt thou leave the town and fight?
Or shall we beat the stones about thine ears?
WARWICK Alas, I am not coop'd here for defence!
I will away towards Barnet presently
And bid thee battle, Edward, if thou dar'st.
KING EDWARD Yes, Warwick, Edward dares and leads the way.
Lords, to the field; Saint George and victory!
[*Exeunt Yorkists. March. Warwick and his company follow.*

SCENE II. *A field of battle near Barnet.*

Alarum and excursions. Enter KING EDWARD, bringing forth WARWICK wounded.

KING EDWARD So, lie thou there. Die thou, and die our fear;
For Warwick was a bug that fear'd us all.
Now, Montague, sit fast; I seek for thee,
That Warwick's bones may keep thine company. [*Exit.*
WARWICK Ah, who is nigh? Come to me, friend or foe,
And tell me who is victor, York or Warwick?
Why ask I that? My mangled body shows,
My blood, my want of strength, my sick heart shows,
That I must yield my body to the earth
And, by my fall, the conquest to my foe.
Thus yields the cedar to the axe's edge,
Whose arms gave shelter to the princely eagle,
Under whose shade the ramping lion slept,
Whose top-branch overpeer'd Jove's spreading tree
And kept low shrubs from winter's pow'rful wind.
These eyes, that now are dimm'd with death's black veil,
Have been as piercing as the mid-day sun
To search the secret treasons of the world;
The wrinkles in my brows, now fill'd with blood,
Were lik'ned oft to kingly sepulchres;
For who liv'd King, but I could dig his grave?
And who durst smile when Warwick bent his brow?
Lo now my glory smear'd in dust and blood!
My parks, my walks, my manors, that I had,
Even now forsake me; and of all my lands
Is nothing left me but my body's length.
Why, what is pomp, rule, reign, but earth and dust?
And live we how we can, yet die we must.

Enter OXFORD and SOMERSET.

SOMERSET Ah, Warwick, Warwick! wert thou as we are,
We might recover all our loss again.
The Queen from France hath brought a puissant power;
Even now we heard the news. Ah, couldst thou fly!
WARWICK Why then, I would not fly. Ah, Montague,
If thou be there, sweet brother, take my hand,
And with thy lips keep in my soul a while!
Thou lov'st me not; for, brother, if thou didst,
Thy tears would wash this cold congealed blood
That glues my lips and will not let me speak.
Come quickly, Montague, or I am dead.
SOMERSET Ah, Warwick! Montague hath breath'd his last;
And to the latest gasp cried out for Warwick,
And said 'Commend me to my valiant brother'.
And more he would have said; and more he spoke,
Which sounded like a clamour in a vault,
That mought not be distinguish'd; but at last,
I well might hear, delivered with a groan,
'O farewell, Warwick!'

WARWICK Sweet rest his soul! Fly, lords, and save yourselves;
For Warwick bids you all farewell, to meet in heaven. *[Dies.*
OXFORD Away, away, to meet the Queen's great power! *[Here they bear away his body.*

SCENE III. *Another part of the field.*

Flourish. Enter KING EWARD in triumph; with GLOUCESTER, CLARENCE, and the rest.

KING EDWARD Thus far our fortune keeps an upward course,
And we are grac'd with wreaths of victory.
But in the midst of this bright-shining day
I spy a black, suspicious, threat'ning cloud
That will encounter with our glorious sun
Ere he attain his easeful western bed –
I mean, my lords, those powers that the Queen
Hath rais'd in Gallia have arriv'd our coast
And, as we hear, march on to fight with us.
CLARENCE A little gale will soon disperse that cloud
And blow it to the source from whence it came;
Thy very beams will dry those vapours up,
For every cloud engenders not a storm.
GLOUCESTER The Queen is valued thirty thousand strong,
And Somerset, with Oxford, fled to her.
If she have time to breathe, be well assur'd
Her faction will be full as strong as ours.
KING EDWARD We are advertis'd by our loving friends
That they do hold their course toward Tewksbury;
We, having now the best at Barnet field,
Will thither straight, for willingness rids way;
And as we march our strength will be augmented
In every county as we go along.
Strike up the drum; cry 'Courage!' and away.
[Exeunt.

SCENE IV. *Plains near Tewksbury.*

Flourish. March. Enter QUEEN MARGARET, PRINCE EDWARD, SOMERSET, OXFORD, and Soldiers.

QUEEN MARGARET Great lords, wise men ne'er sit and wail their loss,
But cheerly seek how to redress their harms.
What though the mast be now blown overboard,
The cable broke, the holding-anchor lost,
And half our sailors swallow'd in the flood;
Yet lives our pilot still. Is't meet that he
Should leave the helm and, like a fearful lad,
With tearful eyes add water to the sea
And give more strength to that which hath too much;
Whiles, in his moan, the ship splits on the rock,
Which industry and courage might have sav'd?
Ah, what a shame! ah, what a fault were this!
Say Warwick was our anchor; what of that?
And Montague our top-mast; what of him?
Our slaught'red friends the tackles; what of these?
Why, is not Oxford here another anchor?
And Somerset another goodly mast?
The friends of France our shrouds and tacklings?
And, though unskilful, why not Ned and I
For once allow'd the skilful pilot's charge?
We will not from the helm to sit and weep,
But keep our course, though the rough wind say no,
From shelves and rocks that threaten us with wreck.
As good to chide the waves as speak them fair.
And what is Edward but a ruthless sea?
What Clarence but a quicksand of deceit?
And Richard but a ragged fatal rock?
All these the enemies to our poor bark.
Say you can swim; alas, 'tis but a while!
Tread on the sand; why, there you quickly sink.
Bestride the rock; the tide will wash you off,
Or else you famish – that's a threefold death.
This speak I, lords, to let you understand,
If case some one of you would fly from us,
That there's no hop'd-for mercy with the brothers
More than with ruthless waves, with sands, and rocks.
Why, courage then! What cannot be avoided
'Twere childish weakness to lament or fear.
PRINCE Methinks a woman of this valiant spirit
Should, if a coward heard her speak these words,
Infuse his breast with magnanimity
And make him naked foil a man-at-arms.
I speak not this as doubting any here;
For did I but suspect a fearful man,
He should have leave to go away betimes,
Lest in our need he might infect another
And make him of like spirit to himself.
If any such be here – as God forbid! –
Let him depart before we need his help.
OXFORD Women and children of so high a courage,
And warriors faint! Why, 'twere perpetual shame.
O brave young Prince! thy famous grandfather
Doth live again in thee. Long mayst thou live
To bear his image and renew his glories!

SOMERSET And he that will not fight for such a hope,
Go home to bed and, like the owl by day,
If he arise, be mock'd and wond'red at.

QUEEN MARGARET Thanks, gentle Somerset; sweet Oxford, thanks.

PRINCE And take his thanks that yet hath nothing else.

Enter a Messenger.

MESSENGER Prepare you, lords, for Edward is at hand
Ready to fight; therefore be resolute.

OXFORD I thought no less. It is his policy
To haste thus fast, to find us unprovided.

SOMERSET But he's deceiv'd; we are in readiness.

QUEEN MARGARET This cheers my heart, to see your forwardness.

OXFORD Here pitch our battle; hence we will not budge.

Flourish and march. Enter, at a distance, KING EDWARD, GLOUCESTER, CLARENCE and Soldiers.

KING EDWARD Brave followers, yonder stands the thorny wood
Which, by the heavens' assistance and your strength,
Must by the roots be hewn up yet ere night.
I need not add more fuel to your fire,
For well I wot ye blaze to burn them out.
Give signal to the fight, and to it, lords.

QUEEN MARGARET Lords, knights, and gentlemen, what I should say
My tears gainsay; for every word I speak,
Ye see, I drink the water of my eye.
Therefore, no more but this: Henry, your sovereign,
Is prisoner to the foe; his state usurp'd,
His realm a slaughter-house, his subjects slain,
His statutes cancell'd, and his treasure spent;
And yonder is the wolf that makes this spoil.
You fight in justice. Then, in God's name, lords,
Be valiant, and give signal to the fight.

[*Alarum, retreat, excursions. Exeunt.*

SCENE V. *Another part of the field.*

Flourish. Enter KING EDWARD, CLARENCE, GLOUCESTER, and Forces, with QUEEN MARGARET, OXFORD, and SOMERSET, prisoners.

KING EDWARD Now here a period of tumultuous broils.
Away with Oxford to Hames Castle straight;
For Somerset, off with his guilty head.
Go, bear them hence; I will not hear them speak.

OXFORD For my part, I'll not trouble thee with words.

SOMERSET Nor I, but stoop with patience to my fortune.

[*Exeunt Oxford and Somerset, guarded.*

QUEEN MARGARET So part we sadly in this troublous world,
To meet with joy in sweet Jerusalem.

KING EDWARD Is proclamation made that who finds Edward
Shall have a high reward, and he his life?

GLOUCESTER It is; and lo where youthful Edward comes.

Enter Soldiers, with PRINCE EDWARD.

KING EDWARD Bring forth the gallant; let us hear him speak.
What, can so young a man begin to prick?
Edward, what satisfaction canst thou make
For bearing arms, for stirring up my subjects,
And all the trouble thou hast turn'd me to?

PRINCE Speak like a subject, proud ambitious York.
Suppose that I am now my father's mouth;
Resign thy chair, and where I stand kneel thou,
Whilst I propose the self-same words to thee
Which, traitor, thou wouldst have me answer to.

QUEEN MARGARET Ah, that thy father had been so resolv'd!

GLOUCESTER That you might still have worn the petticoat
And ne'er have stol'n the breech from Lancaster.

PRINCE Let Aesop fable in a winter's night;
His currish riddles sorts not with this place.

GLOUCESTER By heaven, brat, I'll plague ye for that word.

QUEEN MARGARET Ay, thou wast born to be a plague to men.

GLOUCESTER For God's sake, take away this captive scold.

PRINCE Nay, take away this scolding crookback rather.

KING EDWARD Peace, wilful boy, or I will charm your tongue.

CLARENCE Untutor'd lad, thou art too malapert.

PRINCE I know my duty; you are all undutiful.
Lascivious Edward, and thou perjur'd George,
And thou misshapen Dick, I tell ye all
I am your better, traitors as ye are;
And thou usurp'st my father's right and mine.

KING EDWARD Take that, the likeness of this railer here. [*Stabs him.*

GLOUCESTER Sprawl'st thou? Take that, to end the agony. [*Stabs him.*

CLARENCE And there's for twitting me with perjury. [*Stabs him.*

QUEEN MARGARET O, kill me too!

GLOUCESTER Marry, and shall. [*Offers to kill her*.
KING EDWARD Hold, Richard, hold; for we have done too much.
GLOUCESTER Why should she live to fill the world with words?
KING EDWARD What, doth she swoon? Use means for her recovery.
GLOUCESTER Clarence, excuse me to the King my brother.
I'll hence to London on a serious matter;
Ere ye come there, be sure to hear some news.
CLARENCE What? what?
GLOUCESTER The Tower! the Tower! [*Exit*.
QUEEN MARGARET O Ned, sweet Ned, speak to thy mother, boy!
Canst thou not speak? O traitors! murderers!
They that stabb'd Caesar shed no blood at all,
Did not offend, nor were not worthy blame,
If this foul deed were by to equal it.
He was a man: this, in respect, a child;
And men ne'er spend their fury on a child.
What's worse than murderer, that I may name it?
No, no, my heart will burst, an if I speak –
And I will speak, that so my heart may burst.
Butchers and villains! bloody cannibals!
How sweet a plant have you untimely cropp'd!
You have no children, butchers; if you had,
The thought of them would have stirr'd up remorse.
But if you ever chance to have a child,
Look in his youth to have him so cut off
As, deathsmen, you have rid this sweet young prince!
KING EDWARD Away with her; go, bear her hence perforce.
QUEEN MARGARET Nay, never bear me hence; dispatch me here.
Here sheathe thy sword; I'll pardon thee my death.
What, wilt thou not? Then, Clarence, do it thou.
CLARENCE By heaven, I will not do thee so much ease.
QUEEN MARGARET Good Clarence, do; sweet Clarence, do thou do it.
CLARENCE Didst thou not hear me swear I would not do it?
QUEEN MARGARET Ay, but thou usest to forswear thyself.
'Twas sin before, but now 'tis charity.
What! wilt thou not? Where is that devil's butcher,
Hard-favour'd Richard? Richard, where art thou?
Thou art not here. Murder is thy almsdeed;
Petitioners for blood thou ne'er put'st back.
KING EDWARD Away, I say; I charge ye bear her hence.
QUEEN MARGARET So come to you and yours as to this prince! [*Exit, led out forcibly*.
KING EDWARD Where's Richard gone?
CLARENCE To London, all in post; and, as I guess,
To make a bloody supper in the Tower.
KING EDWARD He's sudden, if a thing comes in his head.
Now march we hence. Discharge the common sort
With pay and thanks; and let's away to London
And see our gentle queen how well she fares.
By this, I hope, she hath a son for me. [*Exeunt*.

SCENE VI. *London. The Tower.*

Enter KING HENRY and GLOUCESTER with the Lieutenant, on the walls.

GLOUCESTER Good day, my lord. What, at your book so hard?
KING HENRY Ay, my good lord – my lord, I should say rather.
'Tis sin to flatter; 'good' was little better.
'Good Gloucester' and 'good devil' were alike,
And both preposterous; therefore, not 'good lord'.
GLOUCESTER Sirrah, leave us to ourselves; we must confer. [*Exit Lieutenant*.
KING HENRY So flies the reckless shepherd from the wolf;
So first the harmless sheep doth yield his fleece,
And next his throat unto the butcher's knife.
What scene of death hath Roscius now to act?
GLOUCESTER Suspicion always haunts the guilty mind:
The thief doth fear each bush an officer.
KING HENRY The bird that hath been limed in a bush
With trembling wings misdoubteth every bush;
And I, the hapless male to one sweet bird,
Have now the fatal object in my eye
Where my poor young was lim'd, was caught, and kill'd.
GLOUCESTER Why, what a peevish fool was that of Crete
That taught his son the office of a fowl!
And yet, for all his wings, the fool was drown'd.
KING HENRY I, Daedalus; my poor boy, Icarus;
Thy father, Minos, that denied our course;
The sun that sear'd the wings of my sweet boy,
Thy brother Edward; and thyself, the sea
Whose envious gulf did swallow up his life.
Ah, kill me with thy weapon, not with words!
My breast can better brook thy dagger's point

Than can my ears that tragic history.
But wherefore dost thou come? Is't for my life?

GLOUCESTER Think'st thou I am an executioner?

KING HENRY A persecutor I am sure thou art.
If murdering innocents be executing,
Why, then thou art an executioner.

GLOUCESTER Thy son I kill'd for his presumption.

KING HENRY Hadst thou been kill'd when first thou didst presume,
Thou hadst not liv'd to kill a son of mine.
And thus I prophesy, that many a thousand
Which now mistrust no parcel of my fear,
And many an old man's sigh, and many a widow's,
And many an orphan's water-standing eye –
Men for their sons, wives for their husbands,
Orphans for their parents' timeless death –
Shall rue the hour that ever thou wast born.
The owl shriek'd at thy birth – an evil sign;
The night-crow cried, aboding luckless time;
Dogs howl'd, and hideous tempest shook down trees;
The raven rook'd her on the chimney's top,
And chatt'ring pies in dismal discords sung;
Thy mother felt more than a mother's pain,
And yet brought forth less than a mother's hope,
To wit, an indigest deformed lump,
Not like the fruit of such a goodly tree.
Teeth hadst thou in thy head when thou wast born,
To signify thou cam'st to bite the world;
And if the rest be true which I have heard,
Thou cam'st –

GLOUCESTER I'll hear no more. Die, prophet, in thy speech. [*Stabs him.*
For this, amongst the rest, was I ordain'd.

KING HENRY Ay, and for much more slaughter after this.
O, God forgive my sins and pardon thee! [*Dies.*

GLOUCESTER What, will the aspiring blood of Lancaster
Sink in the ground? I thought it would have mounted.
See how my sword weeps for the poor King's death.
O, may such purple tears be always shed
From those that wish the downfall of our house!
If any spark of life be yet remaining,
Down, down to hell; and say I sent thee thither – [*Stabs him again.*
I, that have neither pity, love, nor fear.
Indeed, 'tis true that Henry told me of;
For I have often heard my mother say
I came into the world with my legs forward.
Had I not reason, think ye, to make haste
And seek their ruin that usurp'd our right?
The midwife wonder'd; and the women cried
'O, Jesus bless us, he is born with teeth!'
And so I was, which plainly signified
That I should snarl, and bite, and play the dog.
Then, since the heavens have shap'd my body so,
Let hell make crook'd my mind to answer it.
I have no brother, I am like no brother;
And this word 'love', which greybeards call divine,
Be resident in men like one another,
And not in me! I am myself alone.
Clarence, beware; thou keep'st me from the light,
But I will sort a pitchy day for thee;
For I will buzz abroad such prophecies
That Edward shall be fearful of his life;
And then to purge his fear, I'll be thy death.
King Henry and the Prince his son are gone.
Clarence, thy turn is next, and then the rest;
Counting myself but bad till I be best.
I'll throw thy body in another room,
And triumph, Henry, in thy day of doom.
[*Exit with the body.*

SCENE VII. *London. The palace.*

Flourish. Enter KING EDWARD, QUEEN ELIZABETH, CLARENCE, GLOUCESTER, HASTINGS, Nurse with the young PRINCE, and Attendants.

KING EDWARD Once more we sit in England's royal throne,
Repurchas'd with the blood of enemies.
What valiant foemen, like to autumn's corn,
Have we mow'd down in tops of all their pride!
Three Dukes of Somerset, threefold renown'd
For hardy and undoubted champions;
Two Cliffords, as the father and the son;
And two Northumberlands – two braver men
Ne'er spurr'd their coursers at the trumpet's sound;
With them the two brave bears, Warwick and Montague,
That in their chains fetter'd the kingly lion
And made the forest tremble when they roar'd.
Thus have we swept suspicion from our seat
And made our footstool of security.
Come hither, Bess, and let me kiss my boy.
Young Ned, for thee thine uncles and myself
Have in our armours watch'd the winter's night,
Went all afoot in summer's scalding heat,
That thou might'st repossess the crown in peace;
And of our labours thou shalt reap the gain.

GLOUCESTER [*Aside*] I'll blast his harvest if your head were laid;
For yet I am not look'd on in the world.
This shoulder was ordain'd so thick to heave;
And heave it shall some weight or break my back.
Work thou the way – and that shall execute.

KING EDWARD Clarence and Gloucester, love my lovely queen;
And kiss your princely nephew, brothers both.

CLARENCE The duty that I owe unto your Majesty
I seal upon the lips of this sweet babe.

KING EDWARD Thanks, noble Clarence; worthy brother, thanks.

GLOUCESTER And that I love the tree from whence thou sprang'st,
Witness the loving kiss I give the fruit.
[*Aside*] To say the truth, so Judas kiss'd his master
And cried 'All hail!' when as he meant all harm.

KING EDWARD Now am I seated as my soul delights,
Having my country's peace and brothers' loves.

CLARENCE What will your Grace have done with Margaret?
Reignier, her father, to the King of France
Hath pawn'd the Sicils and Jerusalem,
And hither have they sent it for her ransom.

KING EDWARD Away with her, and waft her hence to France.
And now what rests but that we spend the time
With stately triumphs, mirthful comic shows,
Such as befits the pleasure of the court?
Sound drums and trumpets. Farewell, sour annoy!
For here, I hope, begins our lasting joy.

[*Exeunt*.

King Richard the Third

Introduction by ROBERT MASLEN

Richard III is Shakespeare's most exuberantly self-promoting villain. The charm and skill with which he perpetrates his atrocities has made the story of his rise and fall one of Shakespeare's biggest successes on page, stage and screen. There is no record of the play's reception on its first performance (in about 1592–3), but it was frequently reprinted and often alluded to. Its popularity was confirmed when Colley Cibber produced his bowdlerized version, which held the stage from 1700 until Laurence Olivier adopted parts of it for his film of 1955. Acting as vengeful commentators on Richard's career, the women of the play dub him by turns a 'lump of foul deformity' [1.2.57], a toad, a hedgehog, and an 'elvish-mark'd, abortive, rooting hog' [1.3.228], but his reign in the theatre has proved anything but abortive.

It seems appropriate that the play should have been known for so long in a rewritten version, because much of Richard's appeal derives from the skill with which he rewrites history. In the three parts of *Henry VI* the warring factions of the aristocracy arranged themselves along familial lines, brother joining with brother to avenge wrongs done to fathers and sons. Richard is the monstrous product of this blood-letting among relatives, a child born and raised in a time of violence and hypocrisy, whose physical difference sets him apart from the loyalties of his contemporaries. Nature, he claims at the beginning of *Richard III*, sent him into the world 'scarce half made up' [1.1.21], and he spends the remainder of the play imaginatively 'making up' the rest of himself in a variety of different roles. One by one he takes on every role that figured prominently in the conflicts of Henry's reign: the innocent child, the lover making a daring political match, the churchman, the warrior; and as he does so he revises the history of the 'Wars of the Roses'. With breathtaking dexterity he rearranges the contours of the feuding families to suit his purposes, first by wooing the widow of the prince he has murdered, then by killing his own brother and branding his nephews as bastards. On the eve of his defeat at Bosworth he is in the process of engineering his most outrageous revision yet: he plans to transform King Edward's daughter, whose two young brothers he has recently murdered, from his enemy into his wife. His suit consists of narrating to the girl's mother a potted history of the future – a future in which the audience knows he will have no share:

> Again shall you be mother to a king,
> And all the ruins of distressful times
> Repair'd with double riches of content [4.4.317–9].

Even as death approaches, Richard has the gall to manipulate future history to give himself centre stage.

For Richard, time itself is a malleable entity. He tells us he was 'sent before my time/ Into this breathing world' [1.1.20–1], and he delights in disrupting other people's conceptions of time. In the first scene he dismisses the 'piping time of peace' that follows the coronation of Edward IV, and he hurries to transform it into the 'distressful times' of his own reign: what Lord Hastings calls 'the fearfull'st time . . . That ever wretched aged hath look'd upon' [3.4.106–7]. Hastings has good reason to be bitter, since he is the victim of Richard's most daring manipulation of chronology. We learn from a scrivener that the 'indictment of the good Lord Hastings' was begun on Richard's orders six hours before the unsuspecting lord was arrested for treason [3.6]. Richard loves to spring surprises like this on his colleagues; in Act Two he gleefully startles King Edward with the news of his brother's death. And his manipulations do not end with the characters on stage. He plays just as cunningly with the theatre audience, who find themselves drawn into complicity with his barbaric practical jokes whenever he lets them in on his secrets in soliloquies and asides.

Richard's mocking revision of history ends the power-struggle between the noble families of England which had been the driving force of the three parts of *Henry VI*. The deaths of the little princes in the Tower unite the houses of Lancaster and York in self-righteous horror; the murderer Tyrrell describes the children as combining the colours of the two houses in death, with their 'alabaster innocent arms' and their lips like 'four red roses on a stalk' [4.3.11–2]. With Richard's death at the end of the play the kingdom purges itself of its own guilt, and clears the way for the reign of the Tudors to 'Enrich the time to come' [5.5.33]. but like the victims of those he has murdered, the ghost of the man who was destroyed by the Tudors refuses, and still refuses, to be laid.

King Richard the Third

DRAMATIS PERSONAE

KING EDWARD THE FOURTH
EDWARD, *Prince of Wales, afterwards King Edward V*, RICHARD, *Duke of York*
sons to the King
GEORGE, *Duke of Clarence*, RICHARD, *Duke of Gloucester, afterwards King Richard III*,
brothers to the King
A Young Son of Clarence [Edward, Earl of Warwick]
HENRY
Earl of Richmond, afterwards King Henry VII
CARDINAL BOURCHIER
Archbishop of Canterbury
THOMAS ROTHERHAM
Archbishop of York
JOHN MORTON
Bishop of Ely
DUKE OF BUCKINGHAM
DUKE OF NORFOLK
EARL OF SURREY
his son
EARL RIVERS
brother to King Edward's Queen
MARQUIS OF DORSET and LORD GREY
her sons
EARL OF OXFORD
LORD HASTINGS
LORD STANLEY
called also Earl of Derby
LORD LOVELL
SIR THOMAS VAUGHAN
SIR RICHARD RATCLIFF
SIR WILLIAM CATESBY
SIR JAMES TYRREL
SIR JAMES BLUNT
SIR WALTER HERBERT
SIR ROBERT BRAKENBURY
Lieutenant of the Tower
SIR WILLIAM BRANDON
CHRISTOPHER URSWICK
a priest
LORD MAYOR OF LONDON
Sheriff of Wiltshire
HASTINGS
a pursuivant
TRESSEL and BERKELEY
gentlemen attending on the Lady Anne
ELIZABETH
Queen to King Edward IV
MARGARET
widow of King Henry VI
DUCHESS OF YORK
mother to King Edward IV, Clarence, and Gloucester
LADY ANNE
widow of Edward Prince of Wales, son to King Henry VI; afterwards married to the Duke of Gloucester
A Young Daughter of Clarence [Margaret Plantagenet, Countess of Salisbury]
Ghosts of Richard's victims
Lords, Gentlemen, and Attendants; a Priest, a Scrivener, a Page, Bishops, Aldermen, Citizens, Soldiers, Messengers, Murderers, and a Keeper.

THE SCENE: ENGLAND.

ACT ONE

SCENE I. *London. A street.*

Enter RICHARD, DUKE OF GLOUCESTER, solus.

GLOUCESTER Now is the winter of our discontent
Made glorious summer by this sun of York;
And all the clouds that lour'd upon our house
In the deep bosom of the ocean buried.
Now are our brows bound with victorious wreaths;
Our bruised arms hung up for monuments;
Our stern alarums chang'd to merry meetings,
Our dreadful marches to delightful measures.
Grim-visag'd war hath smooth'd his wrinkled front,
And now, instead of mounting barbed steeds
To fright the souls of fearful adversaries,
He capers nimbly in a lady's chamber
To the lascivious pleasing of a lute.
But I – that am not shap'd for sportive tricks,
Nor made to court an amorous looking-glass –
I – that am rudely stamp'd, and want love's majesty
To strut before a wanton ambling nymph –
I – that am curtail'd of this fair proportion,
Cheated of feature by dissembling nature,
Deform'd, unfinish'd, sent before my time
Into this breathing world scarce half made up,
And that so lamely and unfashionable

That dogs bark at me as I halt by them –
Why, I, in this weak piping time of peace,
Have no delight to pass away the time,
Unless to spy my shadow in the sun
And descant on mine own deformity.
And therefore, since I cannot prove a lover
To entertain these fair well-spoken days,
I am determined to prove a villain
And hate the idle pleasures of these days.
Plots have I laid, inductions dangerous,
By drunken prophecies, libels, and dreams,
To set my brother Clarence and the King
In deadly hate the one against the other;
And if King Edward be as true and just
As I am subtle, false, and treacherous,
This day should Clarence closely be mew'd up –
About a prophecy which says that G
Of Edward's heirs the murderer shall be.
Dive, thoughts, down to my soul. Here Clarence comes.

Enter CLARENCE, guarded, and BRAKENBURY.

Brother, good day. What means this armed guard
That waits upon your Grace?

CLARENCE His Majesty,
Tend'ring my person's safety, hath appointed
This conduct to convey me to th' Tower.

GLOUCESTER Upon what cause?

CLARENCE Because my name is George.

GLOUCESTER Alack, my lord, that fault is none of yours:
He should, for that, commit your godfathers.
O, belike his Majesty hath some intent
That you should be new-christ'ned in the Tower.
But what's the matter, Clarence? May I know?

CLARENCE Yea, Richard, when I know; for I protest
As yet I do not; but as I can learn,
He hearkens after prophecies and dreams,
And from the cross-row plucks the letter G,
And says a wizard told him that by G
His issue disinherited should be;
And, for my name of George begins with G,
It follows in his thought that I am he.
These, as I learn, and such like toys as these.
Hath mov'd his Highness to commit me now.

GLOUCESTER Why, this it is when men are rul'd by women:
'Tis not the King that sends you to the Tower;
My Lady Grey his wife, Clarence, 'tis she
That tempers him to this extremity.
Was it not she and that good man of worship,
Antony Woodville, her brother there,
That made him send Lord Hastings to the Tower,
From whence this present day he is delivered?
We are not safe, Clarence; we are not safe.

CLARENCE By heaven, I think there is no man is secure
But the Queen's kindred, and night-walking heralds
That trudge betwixt the King and Mistress Shore.
Heard you not what an humble suppliant
Lord Hastings was, for her delivery?

GLOUCESTER Humbly complaining to her deity
Got my Lord Chamberlain his liberty.
I'll tell you what – I think it is our way,
If we will keep in favour with the King,
To be her men and wear her livery:
The jealous o'er-worn widow and herself,
Since that our brother dubb'd them gentlewomen,
Are mighty gossips in our monarchy.

BRAKENBURY I beseech your Graces both to pardon me:
His Majesty hath straitly given in charge
That no man shall have private conference,
Of what degree soever, with your brother.

GLOUCESTER Even so; an't please your worship, Brakenbury,
You may partake of any thing we say:
We speak no treason, man; we say the King
Is wise and virtuous, and his noble queen
Well struck in years, fair, and not jealous;
We say that Shore's wife hath a pretty foot,
A cherry lip, a bonny eye, a passing pleasing tongue;
And that the Queen's kindred are made gentlefolks.
How say you, sir? Can you deny all this?

BRAKENBURY With this, my lord, myself have nought to do.

GLOUCESTER Nought to do with Mistress Shore! I tell thee, fellow,
He that doth naught with her, excepting one,
Were best to do it secretly alone.

BRAKENBURY What one, my lord?

GLOUCESTER Her husband, knave! Wouldst thou betray me?

BRAKENBURY I do beseech your Grace to pardon me, and withal
Forebear your conference with the noble Duke.

CLARENCE We know thy charge, Brakenbury, and will obey.

GLOUCESTER We are the Queen's abjects and must obey.
Brother, farewell; I will unto the King;
And whatsoe'er you will employ me in –
Were it to call King Edward's widow sister –
I will perform it to enfranchise you.
Meantime, this deep disgrace in brotherhood

Touches me deeper than you can imagine.
CLARENCE I know it pleaseth neither of us well.
GLOUCESTER Well, your imprisonment shall not be long;
I will deliver you, or else lie for you.
Meantime, have patience.
CLARENCE I must perforce. Farewell.
[Exeunt Clarence, Brakenbury, and Guard.
GLOUCESTER Go tread the path that thou shalt ne'er return.
Simple, plain Clarence, I do love thee so
That I will shortly send thy soul to heaven,
If heaven will take the present at our hands.
But who comes here? The new-delivered Hastings?

Enter LORD HASTINGS.

HASTINGS Good time of day unto my gracious lord!
GLOUCESTER As much unto my good Lord Chamberlain!
Well are you welcome to the open air.
How hath your lordship brook'd imprisonment?
HASTINGS With patience, noble lord, as prisoners must;
But I shall live, my lord, to give them thanks
That were the cause of my imprisonment.
GLOUCESTER No doubt, no doubt; and so shall Clarence too;
For they that were your enemies are his,
And have prevail'd as much on him as you.
HASTINGS More pity that the eagles should be mew'd
Whiles kites and buzzards prey at liberty.
GLOUCESTER What news abroad?
HASTINGS No news so bad abroad as this at home:
The King is sickly, weak, and melancholy,
And his physicians fear him mightily.
GLOUCESTER Now, by Saint John, that news is bad indeed.
O, he hath kept an evil diet long
And overmuch consum'd his royal person!
'Tis very grievous to be thought upon.
Where is he? In his bed?
HASTINGS He is.
GLOUCESTER Go you before, and I will follow you. *[Exit Hastings.*
He cannot live, I hope, and must not die
Till George be pack'd with posthorse up to heaven.
I'll in to urge his hatred more to Clarence
With lies well steel'd with weighty arguments;
And, if I fail not in my deep intent,
Clarence hath not another day to live;
Which done, God take King Edward to his mercy,
And leave the world for me to bustle in!
For then I'll marry Warwick's youngest daughter.
What though I kill'd her husband and her father?
The readiest way to make the wench amends
Is to become her husband and her father;
The which will I – not all so much for love
As for another secret close intent
By marrying her which I must reach unto.
But yet I run before my horse to market.
Clarence still breathes; Edward still lives and reigns;
When they are gone, then must I count my gains. *[Exit.*

SCENE II. *London. Another street.*

Enter the corpse of King Henry the Sixth, with Halberds to guard it; LADY ANNE being the mourner, attended by TRESSEL and BERKELEY.

ANNE Set down, set down your honourable load –
If honour may be shrouded in a hearse;
Whilst I awhile obsequiously lament
Th' untimely fall of virtuous Lancaster.
Poor key-cold figure of a holy king!
Pale ashes of the house of Lancaster!
Thou bloodless remnant of that royal blood!
Be it lawful that I invocate thy ghost
To hear the lamentations of poor Anne,
Wife to thy Edward, to thy slaughtered son,
Stabb'd by the self-same hand that made these wounds.
Lo, in these windows that let forth thy life
I pour the helpless balm of my poor eyes.
Curs'd be the hand that made these fatal holes!
Cursed the heart that had the heart to do it!
Cursed the blood that let this blood from hence!
More direful hap betide that hated wretch
That makes us wretched by the death of thee
Than I can wish to adders, spiders, toads,
Or any creeping venom'd thing that lives!
If ever he have child, abortive be it,
Prodigious, and untimely brought to light,
Whose ugly and unnatural aspect
May fright the hopeful mother at the view,
And that be heir to his unhappiness!
If ever he have wife, let her be made
More miserable by the death of him
Than I am made by my young lord and thee!
Come, now towards Chertsey with your holy load,
Taken from Paul's to be interred there;
And still as you are weary of this weight

Rest you, whiles I lament King Henry's corse.
[*The bearers take up the coffin.*

Enter GLOUCESTER.

GLOUCESTER Stay, you that bear the corse, and set it down.
ANNE What black magician conjures up this fiend
To stop devoted charitable deeds?
GLOUCESTER Villains, set down the corse; or, by Saint Paul,
I'll make a corse of him that disobeys!
1 GENTLEMAN My lord, stand back, and let the coffin pass.
GLOUCESTER Unmanner'd dog! Stand thou, when I command.
Advance thy halberd higher than my breast,
Or, by Saint Paul, I'll strike thee to my foot
And spurn upon thee, beggar, for thy boldness.
[*The Bearers set down the coffin.*
ANNE What, do you tremble? Are you all afraid?
Alas, I blame you not, for you are mortal,
And mortal eyes cannot endure the devil.
Avaunt, thou dreadful minister of hell!
Thou hadst but power over his mortal body,
His soul thou canst not have; therefore, be gone.
GLOUCESTER Sweet saint, for charity, be not so curst.
ANNE Foul devil, for God's sake, hence and trouble us not;
For thou hast made the happy earth thy hell,
Fill'd it with cursing cries and deep exclaims.
If thou delight to view thy heinous deeds,
Behold this pattern of thy butcheries.
O, gentlemen, see, see! Dead Henry's wounds
Open their congeal'd mouths and bleed afresh.
Blush, blush, thou lump of foul deformity,
For 'tis thy presence that exhales this blood
From cold and empty veins where no blood dwells;
Thy deeds inhuman and unnatural
Provokes this deluge most unnatural.
O God, which this blood made'st, revenge his death!
O earth, which this blood drink'st, revenge his death!
Either, heav'n, with lightning strike the murd'rer dead;
Or, earth, gape open wide and eat him quick,
As thou dost swallow up this good king's blood,
Which his hell-govern'd arm hath butchered.
GLOUCESTER Lady, you know no rules of charity,
Which renders good for bad, blessings for curses.
ANNE Villain, thou knowest nor law of God nor man:
No beast so fierce but knows some touch of pity.
GLOUCESTER But I know none, and therefore am no beast.
ANNE O wonderful, when devils tell the truth!
GLOUCESTER More wonderful when angels are so angry.
Vouchsafe, divine perfection of a woman,
Of these supposed crimes to give me leave
By circumstance but to acquit myself.
ANNE Vouchsafe, deffus'd infection of a man,
For these known evils but to give me leave
By circumstance to curse thy cursed self.
GLOUCESTER Fairer than tongue can name thee, let me have
Some patient leisure to excuse myself.
ANNE Fouler than heart can think thee, thou canst make
No excuse current but to hang thyself.
GLOUCESTER By such despair I should accuse myself.
ANNE And by despairing shalt thou stand excused
For doing worthy vengeance on thyself
That didst unworthy slaughter upon others.
GLOUCESTER Say that I slew them not?
ANNE Then say they were not slain.
But dead they are, and, devilish slave, by thee.
GLOUCESTER I did not kill your husband.
ANNE Why, then he is alive.
GLOUCESTER Nay, he is dead, and slain by Edward's hands.
ANNE In thy foul throat thou liest: Queen Margaret saw
Thy murd'rous falchion smoking in his blood;
The which thou once didst bend against her breast,
But that thy brothers beat aside the point.
GLOUCESTER I was provoked by her sland'rous tongue
That laid their guilt upon my guiltless shoulders.
ANNE Thou wast provoked by thy bloody mind,
That never dream'st on aught but butcheries.
Didst thou not kill this king?
GLOUCESTER I grant ye.
ANNE Dost grant me, hedgehog? Then, God grant me too
Thou mayst be damned for that wicked deed!
O, he was gentle, mild, and virtuous!
GLOUCESTER The better for the King of Heaven, that hath him.
ANNE He is in heaven, where thou shalt never come.
GLOUCESTER Let him thank me that holp to send him thither,

For he was fitter for that place than earth.
ANNE And thou unfit for any place but hell.
GLOUCESTER Yes, one place else, if you will hear me name it.
ANNE Some dungeon.
GLOUCESTER Your bed-chamber.
ANNE Ill rest betide the chamber where thou liest!
GLOUCESTER So will it, madam, till I lie with you.
ANNE I hope so.
GLOUCESTER I know so. But, gentle Lady Anne,
To leave this keen encounter of our wits,
And fall something into a slower method –
Is not the causer of the timeless deaths
Of these Plantagenets, Henry and Edward,
As blameful as the executioner?
ANNE Thou wast the cause and most accurs'd effect.
GLOUCESTER Your beauty was the cause of that effect –
Your beauty that did haunt me in my sleep
To undertake the death of all the world
So I might live one hour in your sweet bosom.
ANNE If I thought that, I tell thee, homicide,
These nails should rend that beauty from my cheeks.
GLOUCESTER These eyes could not endure that beauty's wreck;
You should not blemish it if I stood by.
As all the world is cheered by the sun,
So I by that; it is my day, my life.
ANNE Black night o'ershade thy day, and death thy life!
GLOUCESTER Curse not thyself, fair creature; thou art both.
ANNE I would I were, to be reveng'd on thee.
GLOUCESTER It is a quarrel most unnatural,
To be reveng'd on him that loveth thee.
ANNE It is a quarrel just and reasonable,
To be reveng'd on him that kill'd my husband.
GLOUCESTER He that bereft thee, lady, of thy husband
Did it to help thee to a better husband.
ANNE His better doth not breathe upon the earth.
GLOUCESTER He lives that loves thee better than he could.
ANNE Name him.
GLOUCESTER Plantagenet.
ANNE Why, that was he.
GLOUCESTER The self-same name, but one of better nature.
ANNE Where is he?
GLOUCESTER Here. [*She spits at him*] Why dost thou spit at me?
ANNE Would it were mortal poison, for thy sake!
GLOUCESTER Never came poison from so sweet a place.
ANNE Never hung poison on a fouler toad.
Out of my sight! Thou dost infect mine eyes.
GLOUCESTER Thine eyes, sweet lady, have infected mine.
ANNE Would they were basilisks to strike thee dead!
GLOUCESTER I would they were, that I might die at once;
For now they kill me with a living death.
Those eyes of thine from mine have drawn salt tears,
Sham'd their aspects with store of childish drops –
These eyes, which never shed remorseful tear,
No, when my father York and Edward wept
To hear the piteous moan that Rutland made
When black-fac'd Clifford shook his sword at him;
Nor when thy warlike father, like a child,
Told the sad story of my father's death,
And twenty times made pause to sob and weep
That all the standers-by had wet their cheeks
Like trees bedash'd with rain – in that sad time
My manly eyes did scorn an humble tear;
And what these sorrows could not thence exhale
Thy beauty hath, and made them blind with weeping.
I never sued to friend nor enemy;
My tongue could never learn sweet smoothing word;
But, now thy beauty is propos'd my fee,
My proud heart sues, and prompts my tongue to speak. [*She looks scornfully at him.*
Teach not thy lip such scorn; for it was made
For kissing, lady, not for such contempt.
If thy revengeful heart cannot forgive,
Lo here I lend thee this sharp-pointed sword;
Which if thou please to hide in this true breast
And let the soul forth that adoreth thee,
I lay it naked to the deadly stroke,
And humbly beg the death upon my knee.
[*He lays his breast open; she offers at it with his sword.*
Nay, do not pause; for I did kill King Henry –
But 'twas thy beauty that provoked me.
Nay, now dispatch; 'twas I that stabb'd young Edward –
But 'twas thy heavenly face that set me on.
[*She falls the sword.*
Take up the sword again, or take up me.
ANNE Arise, dissembler; though I wish thy death,
I will not be thy executioner.

GLOUCESTER Then bid me kill myself, and I will do it.
ANNE I have already.
GLOUCESTER That was in thy rage.
Speak it again, and even with the word
This hand, which for thy love did kill thy love,
Shall for thy love kill a far truer love;
To both their deaths shalt thou be accessary.
ANNE I would I knew thy heart.
GLOUCESTER 'Tis figur'd in my tongue.
ANNE I fear me both are false.
GLOUCESTER Then never was man true.
ANNE Well, well, put up your sword.
GLOUCESTER Say, then, my peace is made.
ANNE That shalt thou know hereafter.
GLOUCESTER But shall I live in hope?
ANNE All men, I hope, live so.
GLOUCESTER Vouchsafes to wear this ring.
ANNE To take is not to give. *[Puts on the ring.*
GLOUCESTER Look how my ring encompasseth thy finger,
Even so thy breast encloseth my poor heart;
Wear both of them, for both of them are thine.
And if thy poor devoted servant may
But beg one favour at thy gracious hand,
Thou dost confirm his happiness for ever.
ANNE What is it?
GLOUCESTER That it may please you leave these sad designs
To him that hath most cause to be a mourner,
And presently repair to Crosby House;
Where – after I have solemnly interr'd
At Chertsey monast'ry this noble king,
And wet his grave with my repentant tears –
I will with all expedient duty see you.
For divers unknown reasons, I beseech you,
Grant me this boon.
ANNE With all my heart; and much it joys me too
To see you are become so penitent.
Tressel and Berkeley, go along with me.
GLOUCESTER Bid me farewell.
ANNE 'Tis more than you deserve;
But since you teach me how to flatter you,
Imagine I have said farewell already.
[Exeunt two gentlemen with Lady Anne.
GLOUCESTER Sirs, take up the corse.
GENTLEMAN Towards Chertesy, noble lord?
GLOUCESTER No, to White Friars; there attend my coming. *[Exeunt all but Gloucester.*
Was ever woman in this humour woo'd?
Was ever woman in this humour won?
I'll have her; but I will not keep her long.
What! I that kill'd her husband and his father –
To take her in her heart's extremest hate,
With curses in her mouth, tears in her eyes,
The bleeding witness of my hatred by;
Having God, her conscience, and these bars against me,
And I no friends to back my suit at all
But the plain devil and dissembling looks,
And yet to win her, all the world to nothing!
Ha!
Hath she forgot already that brave prince,
Edward, her lord, whom I, some three months since,
Stabb'd in my angry mood at Tewksbury?
A sweeter and a lovelier gentleman –
Fram'd in the prodigality of nature,
Young, valiant, wise, and no doubt right royal –
The spacious world cannot again afford;
And will she yet abase her eyes on me,
That cropp'd the golden prime of this sweet prince
And made her widow to a woeful bed?
On me, whose all not equals Edward's moiety?
On me, that halts and am misshapen thus?
My dukedom to a beggarly denier,
I do mistake my person all this while.
Upon my life, she finds, although I cannot,
Myself to be a marv'llous proper man.
I'll be at charges for a looking-glass,
And entertain a score or two of tailors
To study fashions to adorn my body,
Since I am crept in favour with myself,
I will maintain it with some little cost.
But first I'll turn yon fellow in his grave,
And then return lamenting to my love.
Shine out, fair sun, till I have bought a glass,
That I may see my shadow as I pass. *[Exit.*

SCENE III. *London. The palace.*

Enter QUEEN ELIZABETH, LORD RIVERS, and LORD GREY.

RIVERS Have patience, madam; there's no doubt his Majesty
Will soon recover his accustom'd health.
GREY In that you brook it ill, it makes him worse;
Therefore, for God's sake, entertain good comfort,
And cheer his Grace with quick and merry eyes.
QUEEN ELIZABETH If he were dead, what would betide on me?
GREY No other harm but loss of such a lord.
QUEEN ELIZABETH The loss of such a lord includes all harms.
GREY The heavens have bless'd you with a goodly son
To be your comforter when he is gone.
QUEEN ELIZABETH Ah, he is young; and his minority
Is put unto the trust of Richard Gloucester,

A man that loves not me, nor none of you.
RIVERS Is it concluded he shall be Protector?
QUEEN ELIZABETH It is determin'd, not concluded yet;
But so it must be, if the King miscarry.

Enter BUCKINGHAM and DERBY.

GREY Here come the Lords of Buckingham and Derby.
BUCKINGHAM Good time of day unto your royal Grace!
DERBY God make your Majesty joyful as you have been.
QUEEN ELIZABETH The Countess Richmond, good my Lord of Derby,
To your good prayer will scarcely say amen.
Yet, Derby, notwithstanding she's your wife
And loves not me, be you, good lord, assur'd
I hate not you for her proud arrogance.
DERBY I do beseech you, either not believe
The envious slanders of her false accusers;
Or, if she be accus'd on true report,
Bear with her weakness, which I think proceeds
From wayward sickness and no grounded malice.
QUEEN ELIZABETH Saw you the King to-day, my Lord of Derby?
DERBY But now he Duke of Buckingham and I
Are come from visiting his Majesty.
QUEEN ELIZABETH What likelihood of his amendment, lords?
BUCKINGHAM Madam, good hope; his Grace speaks cheerfully.
QUEEN ELIZABETH God grant him health! Did you confer with him?
BUCKINGHAM Ay, madam; he desires to make atonement
Between the Duke of Gloucester and your brothers,
And between them and my Lord Chamberlain;
And sent to warn them to his royal presence.
QUEEN ELIZABETH Would all were well! But that will never be.
I fear our happiness is at the height.

Enter GLOUCESTER, HASTINGS, and DORSET.

GLOUCESTER They do me wrong, and I will not endure it.
Who is it that complains unto the King
That I, forsooth, am stern and love them not?
By holy Paul, they love his Grace but lightly
That fill his ears with such dissentious rumours.
Because I cannot flatter and look fair,
Smile in men's faces, smooth, deceive, and cog,
Duck with French nods and apish courtesy,
I must be held a rancorous enemy.
Cannot a plain man live and think no harm
But thus his simple truth must be abus'd
With silken, sly, insinuating Jacks?
GREY To who in all this presence speaks your Grace?
GLOUCESTER To thee, that hast nor honesty nor grace.
When have I injur'd thee? when done thee wrong,
Or thee, or thee, or any of your faction?
A plague upon you all! His royal Grace –
Whom God preserve better than you would wish! –
Cannot be quiet scarce a breathing while
But you must trouble him with lewd complaints.
QUEEN ELIZABETH Brother of Gloucester, you mistake the matter.
The King, on his own royal disposition
And not provok'd by any suitor else –
Aiming, belike, at your interior hatred
That in your outward action shows itself
Against my children, brothers, and myself –
Makes him to send that he may learn the ground.
GLOUCESTER I cannot tell; the world is grown so bad
That wrens make prey where eagles dare not perch.
Since every Jack became a gentleman,
There's many a gentle person made a Jack.
QUEEN ELIZABETH Come, come, we know your meaning, brother Gloucester:
You envy my advancement and my friends';
God grant we never may have need of you!
GLOUCESTER Meantime, God grants that I have need of you.
Our brother is imprison'd by your means,
Myself disgrac'd, and the nobility
Held in contempt; while great promotions
Are daily given to ennoble those
That scarce some two days since were worth a noble.
QUEEN ELIZABETH By Him that rais'd me to this careful height
From that contented hap which I enjoy'd,
I never did incense his Majesty
Against the Duke of Clarence, but have been
An earnest advocate to plead for him.
My lord, you do me shameful injury
Falsely to draw me in these vile suspects.
GLOUCESTER You may deny that you were not the mean
Of my Lord Hastings' late imprisonment.
RIVERS She may, my lord; for –
GLOUCESTER She may, Lord Rivers? Why, who knows not so?
She may do more, sir, than denying that:
She may help you to many fair preferments

And then deny her aiding hand therein,
And lay those honours on your high desert.
What may she not? She may – ay, marry, may she –

RIVERS What, marry, may she?

GLOUCESTER What, marry, may she? Marry with a king,
A bachelor, and a handsome stripling too.
Iwis your grandam had a worser match.

QUEEN ELIZABETH My Lord of Gloucester, I have too long borne
Your blunt upbraidings and your bitter scoffs.
By heaven, I will acquaint his Majesty
Of those gross taunts that oft I have endur'd.
I had rather be a country servant-maid
Than a great queen with this condition –
To be so baited, scorn'd, and stormed at.

Enter old QUEEN MARGARET, behind.

Small joy have I in being England's Queen.

QUEEN MARGARET And less'ned be that small, God, I beseech Him!
Thy honour, state, and seat, is due to me.

GLOUCESTER What! Threat you me with telling of the King?
Tell him and spare not. Look what I have said
I will avouch't in presence of the King.
I dare adventure to be sent to th' Tow'r.
'Tis time to speak – my pains are quite forgot.

QUEEN MARGARET Out, devil! I do remember them too well:
Thou kill'dst my husband Henry in the Tower,
And Edward, my poor son, at Tewksbury.

GLOUCESTER Ere you were queen, ay, or your husband king,
I was a pack-horse in his great affairs,
A weeder-out of his proud adversaries,
A liberal rewarder of his friends;
To royalize his blood I spent mine own.

QUEEN MARGARET Ay, and much better blood than his or thine.

GLOUCESTER In all which time you and your husband Grey
Were factious for the house of Lancaster;
And, Rivers, so were you. Was not your husband
In Margaret's battle at Saint Albans slain?
Let me put in your minds, if you forget,
What you have been ere this, and what you are;
Withal, what I have been, and what I am.

QUEEN MARGARET A murd'rous villain, and so still thou art.

GLOUCESTER Poor Clarence did forsake his father, Warwick,
Ay, and forswore himself – which Jesu pardon! –

QUEEN MARGARET Which God revenge!

GLOUCESTER To fight on Edward's party for the crown;
And for his meed, poor lord, he is mewed up.
I would to God my heart were flint like Edward's,
Or Edward's soft and pitiful like mine.
I am too childish-foolish for this world.

QUEEN MARGARET Hie thee to hell for shame and leave this world,
Thou cacodemon; there thy kingdom is.

RIVERS My Lord of Gloucester, in those busy days
Which here you urge to prove us enemies,
We follow'd then our lord, our sovereign king.
So should we you, if you should be our king.

GLOUCESTER If I should be! I had rather be a pedlar.
Far be it from my heart, the thought thereof!

QUEEN ELIZABETH As little joy, my lord, as you suppose
You should enjoy were you this country's king,
As little joy you may suppose in me
That I enjoy, being the Queen thereof.

QUEEN MARGARET A little joy enjoys the Queen thereof;
For I am she, and altogether joyless.
I can no longer hold me patient. [*Advancing.*
Hear me, you wrangling pirates, that fall out
In sharing that which you have pill'd from me.
Which of you trembles not that looks on me?
If not that, I am Queen, you bow like subjects,
Yet that, by you depos'd, you quake like rebels?
Ah, gentle villain, do not turn away!

GLOUCESTER Foul wrinkled witch, what mak'st thou in my sight?

QUEEN MARGARET But repetition of what thou hast marr'd,
That will I make before I let thee go.

GLOUCESTER Wert thou not banished on pain of death?

QUEEN MARGARET I was; but I do find more pain in banishment
Than death can yield me here by my abode.
A husband and a son thou ow'st to me;
And thou a kingdom; all of you allegiance.
This sorrow that I have by right is yours;
And all the pleasures you usurp are mine.

GLOUCESTER The curse my noble father laid on thee,
When thou didst crown his warlike brows with paper
And with thy scorns drew'st rivers from his eyes,
And then to dry them gav'st the Duke a clout
Steep'd in the faultless blood of pretty Rutland –

His curses then from bitterness of soul
Denounc'd against thee are all fall'n upon thee;
And God, not we, hath plagu'd thy bloody deed.

QUEEN ELIZABETH So just is God to right the innocent.

HASTINGS O, 'twas the foulest deed to slay that babe,
And the most merciless that e'er was heard of!

RIVERS Tyrants themselves wept when it was reported.

DORSET No man but prophesied revenge for it.

BUCKINGHAM Northumberland, then present, wept to see it.

QUEEN MARGARET What, were you snarling all before I came,
Ready to catch each other by the throat,
And turn you all your hatred now on me?
Did York's dread curse prevail so much with heaven
That Henry's death, my lovely Edward's death,
Their kingdom's loss, my woeful banishment,
Should all but answer for that peevish brat?
Can curses pierce the clouds and enter heaven?
Why then, give way, dull clouds, to my quick curses!
Though not by war, by surfeit die your king,
As ours by murder, to make him a king!
Edward thy son, that now is Prince of Wales,
For Edward our son, that was Prince of Wales,
Die in his youth by like untimely violence!
Thyself a queen, for me that was a queen,
Outlive thy glory, like my wretched self!
Long mayest thou live to wail thy children's death,
And see another, as I see thee now,
Deck'd in thy rights, as thou art stall'd in mine!
Long die thy happy days before thy death;
And, after many length'ned hours of grief,
Die neither mother, wife, nor England's Queen!
Rivers and Dorset, you were standers by,
And so wast thou, Lord Hastings, when my son
Was stabb'd with bloody daggers. God, I pray him,
That none of you may live his natural age,
But by some unlook'd accident cut off!

GLOUCESTER Have done thy charm, thou hateful wither'd hag.

QUEEN MARGARET And leave out thee? Stay, dog, for thou shalt hear me.
If heaven have any grievous plague in store
Exceeding those that I can wish upon thee,
O, let them keep it till thy sins be ripe,
And then hurl down their indignation
On thee, the troubler of the poor world's peace!
The worm of conscience still be-gnaw thy soul!
Thy friends suspect for traitors while thou liv'st,
And take deep traitors for thy dearest friends!
No sleep close up that deadly eye of thine,
Unless it be while some tormenting dream
Affrights thee with a hell of ugly devils!
Thou elvish-mark'd, abortive, rooting hog,
Thou that wast seal'd in thy nativity
The slave of nature and the son of hell,
Thou slander of thy heavy mother's womb,
Thou loathed issue of thy father's loins,
Thou rag of honour, thou detested –

GLOUCESTER Margaret!

QUEEN MARGARET Richard!

GLOUCESTER Ha?

QUEEN MARGARET I call thee not.

GLOUCESTER I cry thee mercy then, for I did think
That thou hadst call'd me all these bitter names.

QUEEN MARGARET Why, so I did, but look'd for no reply.
O, let me make the period to my curse!

GLOUCESTER 'Tis done by me, and ends in – Margaret.

QUEEN ELIZABETH Thus have you breath'd your curse against yourself.

QUEEN MARGARET Poor painted queen, vain flourish of my fortune!
Why strew'st thou sugar on that bottled spider
Whose deadly web ensnareth thee about?
Fool, fool! thou whet'st a knife to kill thyself.
The day will come that thou shalt wish for me
To help thee curse this poisonous bunch-back'd toad.

HASTINGS False-boding woman, end thy frantic curse,
Lest to thy harm thou move our patience.

QUEEN MARGARET Foul shame upon you! you have all mov'd mine.

RIVERS Were you well serv'd, you would be taught your duty.

QUEEN MARGARET To serve me well you all should do me duty,
Teach me to be your queen and you my subjects.
O, serve me well, and teach yourselves that duty!

DORSET Dispute not with her; she is lunatic.

QUEEN MARGARET Peace, Master Marquis, you are malapert;
Your fire-new stamp of honour is scarce current.
O, that your young nobility could judge
What 'twere to lose it and be miserable!
They that stand high have many blasts to shake them,
And if they fall they dash themselves to pieces.

GLOUCESTER Good counsel, marry; learn it, learn it, Marquis.

DORSET It touches you, my lord, as much as me.

GLOUCESTER Ay, and much more; but I was born so high,
Our aery buildeth in the cedar's top,
And dallies with the wind, and scorns the sun.
QUEEN MARGARET And turns the sun to shade – alas! alas!
Witness my son, now in the shade of death,
Whose bright out-shining beams thy cloudy wrath
Hath in eternal darkness folded up.
Your aery buildeth in our aery's nest.
O God that seest it, do not suffer it;
As it is won with blood, lost be it so!
BUCKINGHAM Peace, peace, for shame, if not for charity!
QUEEN MARGARET Urge neither charity nor shame to me.
Uncharitably with me have you dealt,
And shamefully my hopes by you are butcher'd.
My charity is outrage, life my shame;
And in that shame still live my sorrow's rage!
BUCKINGHAM Have done, have done.
QUEEN MARGARET O princely Buckingham, I'll kiss thy hand
In sign of league and amity with thee.
Now fair befall thee and thy noble house!
Thy garments are not spotted with our blood,
Nor thou within the compass of my curse.
BUCKINGHAM Nor no one here; for curses never pass
The lips of those that breathe them in the air.
QUEEN MARGARET I will not think but they ascend the sky
And there awake God's gentle-sleeping peace.
O Buckingham, take heed of yonder dog!
Look when he fawns, he bites; and when he bites,
His venom tooth will rankle to the death:
Have not to do with him, beware of him;
Sin, death, and hell, have set their marks on him,
And all their ministers attend on him.
GLOUCESTER What doth she say, my Lord of Buckingham?
BUCKINGHAM Nothing that I respect, my gracious lord.
QUEEN MARGARET What, dost thou scorn me for my gentle counsel,
And soothe the devil that I warn thee from?
O, but remember this another day,
When he shall split thy very heart with sorrow,
And say poor Margaret was a prophetess!
Live each of you the subjects to his hate,
And he to yours, and all of you to God's! [*Exit.*
BUCKINGHAM My hair doth stand an end to hear her curses.
RIVERS And so doth mine. I muse why she's at liberty.
GLOUCESTER I cannot blame her; by God's holy Mother,
She hath had too much wrong; and I repent
My part thereof that I have done to her.
QUEEN ELIZABETH I never did her any to my knowledge.
GLOUCESTER Yet you have all the vantage of her wrong.
I was too hot to do somebody good
That is too cold in thinking of it now.
Marry, as for Clarence, he is well repaid;
He is frank'd up to fatting for his pains;
God pardon them that are the cause thereof!
RIVERS A virtuous and a Christian-like conclusion,
To pray for them that have done scathe to us!
GLOUCESTER So do I ever – [*Aside*] being well advis'd;
For had I curs'd now, I had curs'd myself.

Enter CATESBY.

CATESBY Madam, his Majesty doth call for you,
And for your Grace, and you, my gracious lords.
QUEEN ELIZABETH Catesby, I come. Lords, will you go with me?
RIVERS We wait upon your Grace.
[*Exeunt all but Gloucester.*
GLOUCESTER I do the wrong, and first begin to brawl.
The secret mischiefs that I set abroach
I lay unto the grievous charge of others.
Clarence, who I indeed have cast in darkness,
I do beweep to many simple gulls;
Namely, to Derby, Hastings, Buckingham;
And tell them 'tis the Queen and her allies
That stir the King against the Duke my brother.
Now they believe it, and withal whet me
To be reveng'd on Rivers, Dorset, Grey;
But then I sigh and, with a piece of Scripture,
Tell them that God bids us do good for evil.
And thus I clothe my naked villainy
With odd old ends stol'n forth of holy writ,
And seem a saint when most I play the devil.

Enter two Murderers.

But, soft, here come my executioners.
How now, my hardy stout resolved mates!
Are you now going to dispatch this thing?
1 MURDERER We are, my lord, and come to have the warrant,
That we may be admitted where he is.
GLOUCESTER Well thought upon; I have it here about me. [*Gives the warrant.*
When you have done, repair to Crosby Place.
But, sirs, be sudden in the execution,
Withal obdurate, do not hear him plead;

For Clarence is well-spoken, and perhaps
May move your hearts to pity, if you mark him.
1 MURDERER Tut, tut, my lord, we will not stand
to prate;
Talkers are no good doers. Be assur'd
We go to use our hands and not our tongues.
GLOUCESTER Your eyes drop millstones when fools' eyes fall tears.
I like you, lads; about your business straight;
Go, go, dispatch.
1 MURDERER We will, my noble lord.
[*Exeunt.*

SCENE IV. *London. The Tower.*

Enter CLARENCE and Keeper.

KEEPER Why looks your Grace so heavily to-day?
CLARENCE O, I have pass'd a miserable night,
So full of fearful dreams, of ugly sights,
That, as I am a Christian faithful man,
I would not spend another such a night
Though 'twere to buy a world of happy days –
So full of dismal terror was the time!
KEEPER What was your dream, my lord? I pray you tell me.
CLARENCE Methoughts that I had broken from the Tower
And was embark'd to cross to Burgundy;
And in my company my brother Gloucester,
Who from my cabin tempted me to walk
Upon the hatches. Thence we look'd toward England,
And cited up a thousand heavy times,
During the wars of York and Lancaster,
That had befall'n us. As we pac'd along
Upon the giddy footing of the hatches,
Methought that Gloucester stumbled, and in falling
Struck me, that thought to stay him, overboard
Into the tumbling billows of the main.
O Lord, methought what pain it was to drown,
What dreadful noise of waters in my ears,
What sights of ugly death within my eyes!
Methoughts I saw a thousand fearful wrecks,
A thousand men that fishes gnaw'd upon,
Wedges of gold, great anchors, heaps of pearl,
Inestimable stones, unvalued jewels,
All scatt'red in the bottom of the sea;
Some lay in dead men's skulls, and in the holes
Where eyes did once inhabit there were crept,
As 'twere in scorn of eyes, reflecting gems,
That woo'd the slimy bottom of the deep
And mock'd the dead bones that lay scatt'red by.
KEEPER Had you such leisure in the time of death
To gaze upon these secrets of the deep?
CLARENCE Methought I had; and often did I strive
To yield the ghost, but still the envious flood
Stopp'd in my soul and would not let it forth
To find the empty, vast, and wand'ring air;
But smother'd it within my panting bulk,
Who almost burst to belch it in the sea.
KEEPER Awak'd you not in this sore agony?
CLARENCE No, no, my dream was lengthen'd after life.
O, then began the tempest to my soul!
I pass'd, methought, the melancholy flood
With that sour ferryman which poets write of,
Unto the kingdom of perpetual night.
The first that there did greet my stranger soul
Was my great father-in-law, renowned Warwick,
Who spake aloud 'What scourge for perjury
Can this dark monarchy afford false Clarence?'
And so he vanish'd. Then came wand'ring by
A shadow like an angel, with bright hair
Dabbled in blood, and he shriek'd out aloud
'Clarence is come – false, fleeting, perjur'd Clarence,
That stabb'd me in the field by Tewksbury.
Seize on him, Furies, take him unto torment!'
With that, methoughts, a legion of fouls fiends
Environ'd me, and howled in mine ears
Such hideous cries that, with the very noise,
I trembling wak'd, and for a season after
Could not believe but that I was in hell,
Such terrible impression made my dream.
KEEPER No marvel, lord, though it affrighted you;
I am afraid, methinks, to hear you tell it.
CLARENCE Ah, Keeper, Keeper, I have done these things
That now give evidence against my soul
For Edward's sake, and see how he requites me!
O God! If my deep prayers cannot appease Thee,
But Thou wilt be aveng'd on my misdeeds,
Yet execute Thy wrath in me alone;
O, spare my guiltless wife and my poor children!
Keeper, I prithee sit by me awhile;
My soul is heavy, and I fain would sleep.
KEEPER I will, my lord. God give your Grace good rest. [*Clarence sleeps.*

Enter BRAKENBURY the Lieutenant.

BRAKENBURY Sorrow breaks seasons and reposing hours,
Makes the night morning and the noontide night.
Princes have but their titles for their glories,
An outward honour for an inward toil;
And for unfelt imaginations
They often feel a world of restless cares,

So that between their titles and low name
There's nothing differs but the outward fame.

Enter the two Murderers.

1 MURDERER Ho! who's here?

BRAKENBURY What wouldst thou, fellow, and how cam'st thou hither?

1 MURDERER I would speak with Clarence, and I came hither on my legs.

BRAKENBURY What, so brief?

2 MURDERER 'Tis better, sir, than to be tedious.
Let him see our commission and talk no more.

[Brakenbury reads it.

BRAKENBURY I am, in this, commanded to deliver
The noble Duke of Clarence to your hands.
I will not reason what is meant hereby,
Because I will be guiltless from the meaning.
There lies the Duke asleep; and there the keys.
I'll to the King and signify to him
That thus I have resign'd to you my charge.

1 MURDERER You may, sir; 'tis a point of wisdom.
Fare you well. *[Exeunt Brakenbury and Keeper.*

2 MURDERER What, shall I stab him as he sleeps?

1 MURDERER No; he'll say 'twas done cowardly, when he wakes.

2 MURDERER Why, he shall never wake until the great judgment-day.

1 MURDERER Why, then he'll say we stabb'd him sleeping.

2 MURDERER The urging of that word judgment hath bred a kind of remorse in me.

1 MURDERER What, art thou afraid?

2 MURDERER Not to kill him, having a warrant; but to be damn'd for killing him, from the which no warrant can defend me.

1 MURDERER I thought thou hadst been resolute.

2 MURDERER So I am, to let him live.

1 MURDERER I'll back to the Duke of Gloucester and tell him so.

2 MURDERER Nay, I prithee, stay a little. I hope this passionate humour of mine will change; it was wont to hold me but while one tells twenty.

1 MURDERER How dost thou feel thyself now?

2 MURDERER Faith, some certain dregs of conscience are yet within me.

1 MURDERER Remember our reward, when the deed's done.

2 MURDERER Zounds, he dies; I had forgot the reward.

1 MURDERER Where's thy conscience now?

2 MURDERER O, in the Duke of Gloucester's purse!

1 MURDERER When he opens his purse to give us our reward, thy conscience flies out.

2 MURDERER 'Tis no matter; let it go; there's few or none will entertain it.

1 MURDERER What if it come to thee again?

2 MURDERER I'll not meddle with it – it makes a man a coward: a man cannot steal, but it accuseth him; a man cannot swear, but it checks him; a man cannot lie with his neighbour's wife, but it detects him. 'Tis a blushing shamefac'd spirit that mutinies in a man's bosom; it fills a man full of obstacles: it made me once restore a purse of gold that – by chance I found. It beggars any man that keeps it. It is turn'd out of towns and cities for a dangerous thing; and every man that means to live well endeavours to trust to himself and live without it.

1 MURDERER Zounds, 'tis even now at my elbow, persuading me not to kill the Duke.

2 MURDERER Take the devil in thy mind and believe him not; he would insinuate with thee but to make thee sigh.

1 MURDERER I am strong-fram'd; he cannot prevail with me.

2 MURDERER Spoke like a tall man that respects thy reputation. Come, shall we fall to work?

1 MURDERER Take him on the costard with the hilts of thy sword, and then chop him in the malmsey-butt in the next room.

2 MURDERER O excellent device! and make a sop of him.

1 MURDERER Soft! he wakes.

2 MURDERER Strike!

1 MURDERER No, we'll reason with him.

CLARENCE Where art thou, Keeper? Give me a cup of wine.

2 MURDERER You shall have wine enough, my lord, anon.

CLARENCE In God's name, what art thou?

1 MURDERER A man, as you are.

CLARENCE But not as I am, royal.

2 MURDERER Nor you as we are, loyal.

CLARENCE Thy voice is thunder, but thy looks are humble.

1 MURDERER My voice is now the King's, my looks mine own.

CLARENCE How darkly and how deadly dost thou speak!
Your eyes do menace me. Why look you pale?
Who sent you hither? Wherefore do you come?

2 MURDERER To, to, to –

CLARENCE To murder me?

BOTH MURDERERS Ay, ay.

CLARENCE You scarcely have the hearts to tell me so,
And therefore cannot have the hearts to do it.
Wherein, my friends, have I offended you?

1 MURDERER Offended us you have not, but the King.

CLARENCE I shall be reconcil'd to him again.
2 MURDERER Never, my lord; therefore prepare to die.
CLARENCE Are you drawn forth among a world of men
To slay the innocent? What is my offence?
Where is the evidence that doth accuse me?
What lawful quest have given their verdict up
Unto the frowning judge, or who pronounc'd
The bitter sentence of poor Clarence' death?
Before I be convict by course of law,
To threaten me with death is most unlawful.
I charge you, as you hope to have redemption
By Christ's dear blood shed for our grievous sins,
That you depart and lay no hands on me.
The deed you undertake is damnable.
1 MURDERER What we will do, we do upon command.
2 MURDERER And he that hath commanded is our king.
CLARENCE Erroneous vassals! the great King of kings
Hath in the tables of his law commanded
That thou shalt do no murder. Will you then
Spurn at his edict and fulfil a man's?
Take heed; for he holds vengeance in his hand
To hurl upon their heads that break his law.
2 MURDERER And that same vengeance doth he hurl on thee
For false forswearing, and for murder too;
Thou didst receive the sacrament to fight
In quarrel of the house of Lancaster.
1 MURDERER And like a traitor to the name of God
Didst break that vow; and with thy treacherous blade
Unripp'dst the bowels of thy sov'reign's son.
2 MURDERER Whom thou wast sworn to cherish and defend.
1 MURDERER How canst thou urge God's dreadful law to us,
When thou hast broke it in such dear degree?
CLARENCE Alas! for whose sake did I that ill deed?
For Edward, for my brother, for his sake.
He sends you not to murder me for this,
For in that sin he is as deep as I.
If God will be avenged for the deed,
O, know you yet He doth it publicly.
Take not the quarrel from His pow'rful arm;
He needs no indirect or lawless course
To cut off those that have offended Him.
1 MURDERER Who made thee then a bloody minister
When gallant-springing brave Plantagenet,
That princely novice, was struck dead by thee?
CLARENCE My brother's love, the devil, and my rage.
1 MURDERER Thy brother's love, our duty, and thy faults,
Provoke us hither now to slaughter thee.
CLARENCE If you do love my brother, hate not me;
I am his brother, and I love him well.
If you are hir'd for meed, go back again,
And I will send you to my brother Gloucester,
Who shall reward you better for my life
Than Edward will for tidings of my death.
2 MURDERER You are deceiv'd: your brother Gloucester hates you.
CLARENCE O, no, he loves me, and he holds me dear.
Go you to him from me.
1 MURDERER Ay, so we will.
CLARENCE Tell him when that our princely father York
Bless'd his three sons with his victorious arm
And charg'd us from his soul to love each other,
He little thought of this divided friendship.
Bid Gloucester think of this, and he will weep.
1 MURDERER Ay, millstones; as he lesson'd us to weep.
CLARENCE O, do not slander him, for he is kind.
1 MURDERER Right, as snow in harvest. Come, you deceive yourself:
'Tis he that sends us to destroy you here.
CLARENCE It cannot be; for he bewept my fortune
And hugg'd me in his arms, and swore with sobs
That he would labour my delivery.
1 MURDERER Why, so he doth, when he delivers you
From this earth's thraldom to the joys of heaven.
2 MURDERER Make peace with God, for you must die, my lord.
CLARENCE Have you that holy feeling in your souls
To counsel me to make my peace with God,
And are you yet to your own souls so blind
That you will war with God by murd'ring me?
O, sirs, consider: they that set you on
To do this deed will hate you for the deed.
2 MURDERER What shall we do?
CLARENCE Relent, and save your souls.
1 MURDERER Relent! No, 'tis cowardly and womanish.
CLARENCE Not to relent is beastly, savage, devilish.
Which of you, if you were a prince's son,
Being pent from liberty as I am now,
If two such murderers as yourselves came to you,

Would not entreat for life?
My friend, I spy some pity in thy looks;
O, if thine eye be not a flatterer,
Come thou on my side and entreat for me –
As you would beg were you in my distress.
A begging prince what beggar pities not?

2 MURDERER Look behind you, my lord.

1 MURDERER [*Stabbing him*] Take that, and that. If all this will not do,
I'll drown you in the malmsey-butt within.
[*Exit with the body.*

2 MURDERER A bloody deed, and desperately dispatch'd!
How fain, like Pilate, would I wash my hands
Of this most grievous murder!

Re-enter First Murderer.

1 MURDERER How now, what mean'st thou that thou help'st me not?
By heavens, the Duke shall know how slack you have been!

2 MURDERER I would he knew that I had sav'd his brother!
Take thou the fee, and tell him what I say;
For I repent me that the Duke is slain. [*Exit.*

1 MURDERER So do not I. Go, coward as thou art.
Well, I'll go hide the body in some hole,
Till that the Duke give order for his burial;
And when I have my meed, I will away;
For this will out, and then I must not stay.
[*Exit.*

ACT TWO

SCENE I. *London. The palace.*

Flourish. Enter KING EDWARD sick, QUEEN ELIZABETH, DORSET, RIVERS, HASTINGS, BUCKINGHAM, GREY, and Others.

KING EDWARD Why, so. Now have I done a good day's work.
You peers, continue this united league.
I every day expect an embassage
From my Redeemer to redeem me hence;
And more at peace my soul shall part to heaven,
Since I have made my friends at peace on earth.
Hastings and Rivers, take each other's hand;
Dissemble not your hatred, swear your love.

RIVERS By heaven, my soul is purg'd from grudging hate;
And with my hand I seal my true heart's love.

HASTINGS So thrive I, as I truly swear the like!

KING EDWARD Take heed you dally not before your king;
Lest He that is the supreme King of kings
Confound your hidden falsehood and award
Either of you to be the other's end.

HASTINGS So prosper I, as I swear perfect love!

RIVERS And I, as I love Hastings with my heart!

KING EDWARD Madam, yourself is not exempt from this;
Nor you, son Dorset; Buckingham, nor you:
You have been factious one against the other.
Wife, love Lord Hastings, let him kiss your hand;
And what you do, do it unfeignedly.

QUEEN ELIZABETH There, Hastings; I will never more remember
Our former hatred, so thrive I and mine!

KING EDWARD Dorset, embrace him; Hastings, love Lord Marquis.

DORSET This interchange of love, I here protest,
Upon my part shall be inviolable.

HASTINGS And so swear I. [*They embrace.*

KING EDWARD Now, princely Buckingham, seal thou this league
With thy embracements to my wife's allies,
And make me happy in your unity.

BUCKINGHAM [*To the Queen*] Whenever Buckingham doth turn his hate
Upon your Grace, but with all duteous love
Doth cherish you and yours, God punish me
With hate in those where I expect most love!
When I have most need to employ a friend
And most assured that he is a friend,
Deep, hollow, treacherous and full of guile,
Be he unto me! This do I beg of God
When I am cold in love to you or yours.
[*They embrace.*

KING EDWARD A pleasing cordial, princely Buckingham,
Is this thy vow unto my sickly heart.
There wanteth now our brother Gloucester here
To make the blessed period of this peace.

BUCKINGHAM And, in good time,
Here comes Sir Richard Ratcliff and the Duke.

Enter GLOUCESTER, and RATCLIFF.

GLOUCESTER Good morrow to my sovereign king and queen;
And, princely peers, a happy time of day!

KING EDWARD Happy, indeed, as we have spent the day.
Gloucester, we have done deeds of charity,
Made peace of enmity, fair love of hate,
Between these swelling wrong-incensed peers.

GLOUCESTER A blessed labour, my most sovereign lord.

Among this princely heap, if any here,
By false intelligence or wrong surmise,
Hold me a foe –
If I unwittingly, or in my rage,
Have aught committed that is hardly borne
To any in this presence, I desire
To reconcile me to his friendly peace:
'Tis death to me to be at enmity;
I hate it, and desire all good men's love.
First, madam, I entreat true peace of you,
Which I will purchase with my duteous service;
Of you, my noble cousin Buckingham,
If ever any grudge were lodg'd between us;
Of you, and you, Lord Rivers, and of Dorset,
That all without desert have frown'd on me;
Of you, Lord Woodville, and, Lord Scales, of you;
Dukes, earls, lords, gentlemen – indeed, of all.
I do not know that Englishman alive
With whom my soul is any jot at odds
More than the infant that is born to-night.
I thank my God for my humility.

QUEEN ELIZABETH A holy day shall this be kept hereafter.
I would to God all strifes were well compounded.
My sovereign lord, I do beseech your Highness
To take our brother Clarence to your grace.

GLOUCESTER Why, madam, have I off'red love for this,
To be so flouted in this royal presence?
Who knows not that the gentle Duke is dead?

[*They all start.*

You do him injury to scorn his corse.

KING EDWARD Who knows not he is dead! Who knows he is?

QUEEN ELIZABETH All-seeing heaven, what a world is this!

BUCKINGHAM Look I so pale, Lord Dorset, as the rest?

DORSET Ay, my good lord; and no man in the presence
But his red colour hath forsook his cheeks.

KING EDWARD Is Clarence dead? The order was revers'd.

GLOUCESTER But he, poor man, by your first order died,
And that a winged Mercury did bear;
Some tardy cripple bare the countermand
That came too lag to see him buried.
God grant that some, less noble and less loyal,
Nearer in bloody thoughts, an not in blood,
Deserve not worse than wretched Clarence did,
And yet go current from suspicion!

Enter DERBY.

DERBY A boon, my sovereign, for my service done!

KING EDWARD I prithee, peace; my soul is full of sorrow.

DERBY I will not rise unless your Highness hear me.

KING EDWARD Then say at once what is it thou requests.

DERBY The forfeit, sovereign, of my servant's life;
Who slew to-day a riotous gentleman
Lately attendant on the Duke of Norfolk.

KING EDWARD Have I a tongue to doom my brother's death,
And shall that tongue give pardon to a slave?
My brother kill'd no man – his fault was thought,
And yet his punishment was bitter death.
Who sued to me for him? Who, in my wrath,
Kneel'd at my feet, and bid me be advis'd?
Who spoke of brotherhood? Who spoke of love?
Who told me how the poor soul did forsake
The mighty Warwick and did fight for me?
Who told me, in the field at Tewksbury
When Oxford had me down, he rescued me
And said 'Dear Brother, live, and be a king'?
Who told me, when we both lay in the field
Frozen almost to death, how he did lap me
Even in his garments, and did give himself,
All thin and naked, to the numb cold night?
All this from my remembrance brutish wrath
Sinfully pluck'd, and not a man of you
Had so much grace to put it in my mind.
But when your carters or your waiting-vassals
Have done a drunken slaughter and defac'd
The precious image of our dear Redeemer,
You straight are on your knees for pardon, pardon;
And I, unjustly too, must grant it you.

[*Derby rises.*

But for my brother not a man would speak;
Nor I, ungracious, speak unto myself
For him, poor soul. The proudest of you all
Have been beholding to him in his life;
Yet none of you would once beg for his life.
O God, I fear thy justice will take hold
On me, and you, and mine, and yours, for this!
Come, Hastings, help me to my closet. Ah, poor Clarence!

[*Exeunt some with King and Queen.*

GLOUCESTER This is the fruits of rashness. Mark'd you not
How that the guilty kindred of the Queen
Look'd pale when they did hear of Clarence' death?
O, they did urge it still unto the King!

God will revenge it. Come, lords, will you go
To comfort Edward with our company?
BUCKINGHAM We wait upon your Grace.
[Exeunt.

SCENE II. *London. The palace.*

Enter the old DUCHESS OF YORK, with the Son and Daughter of Clarence.

SON Good grandam, tell us, is our father dead?
DUCHESS No, boy.
DAUGHTER Why do you weep so oft, and beat your breast,
And cry 'O Clarence, my unhappy son!'?
SON Why do you look on us, and shake your head,
And call us orphans, wretches, castaways,
If that our noble father were alive?
DUCHESS My pretty cousins, you mistake me both;
I do lament the sickness of the King,
As loath to lose him, not your father's death;
It were lost sorrow to wail one that's lost.
SON Then you conclude, my grandam, he is dead.
The King mine uncle is to blame for it.
God will revenge it; whom I will importune
With earnest prayers all to that effect.
DAUGHTER And so will I.
DUCHESS Peace, children, peace! The King doth love you well.
Incapable and shallow innocents,
You cannot guess who caus'd your father's death.
SON Grandam, we can; for my good uncle Gloucester
Told me the King, provok'd to it by the Queen,
Devis'd impeachments to imprison him.
And when my uncle told me so, he wept,
And pitied me, and kindly kiss'd my cheek;
Bade me rely on him as on my father,
And he would love me dearly as a child.
DUCHESS Ah, that deceit should steal such gentle shape,
And with a virtuous vizor hide deep vice!
He is my son; ay, and therein my shame;
Yet from my dugs he drew not this deceit.
SON Think you my uncle did dissemble, grandam?
DUCHESS Ay, boy.
SON I cannot think it. Hark! what noise is this?

Enter QUEEN ELIZABETH, with her hair about her ears; RIVERS and DORSET after her.

QUEEN ELIZABETH Ah, who shall hinder me to wail and weep,
To chide my fortune, and torment myself?
I'll join with black despair against my soul
And to myself become an enemy.
DUCHESS What means this scene of rude impatience?
QUEEN ELIZABETH To make an act of tragic violence.
Edward, my lord, thy son, our king, is dead.
Why grow the branches when the root is gone?
Why wither not the leaves that want their sap?
If you will live, lament; if die, be brief,
That our swift-winged souls may catch the King's,
Or like obedient subjects follow him
To his new kingdom of ne'er-changing night.
DUCHESS Ah, so much interest have I in thy sorrow
As I had title in thy noble husband!
I have bewept a worthy husband's death,
And liv'd with looking on his images;
But now two mirrors of his princely semblance
Are crack'd in pieces by malignant death,
And I for comfort have but one false glass,
That grieves me when I see my shame in him.
Thou art a widow, yet thou art a mother
And hast the comfort of thy children left;
But death hath snatch'd my husband from mine arms
And pluck'd two crutches from my feeble hands –
Clarence and Edward. O, what cause have I –
Thine being but a moiety of my moan –
To overgo thy woes and drown thy cries?
SON Ah, aunt, you wept not for our father's death!
How can we aid you with our kindred tears?
DAUGHTER Our fatherless distress was left unmoan'd;
Your widow-dolour likewise be unwept!
QUEEN ELIZABETH Give me no help in lamentation;
I am not barren to bring forth complaints.
All springs reduce their currents to mine eyes
That I, being govern'd by the watery moon,
May send forth plenteous tears to drown the world!
Ah for my husband, for my dear Lord Edward!
CHILDREN Ah for our father, for our dear Lord Clarence!
DUCHESS Alas for both, both mine, Edward and Clarence!
QUEEN ELIZABETH What stay had I but Edward? and he's gone.
CHILDREN What stay had we but Clarence? and he's gone.
DUCHESS What stays had I but they? and they are gone.
QUEEN ELIZABETH Was never widow had so dear a loss.

CHILDREN Were never orphans had so dear a loss.
DUCHESS Was never mother had so dear a loss.
Alas, I am the mother of these griefs!
Their woes are parcell'd, mine is general.
She for an Edward weeps, and so do I:
I for a Clarence weep, so doth not she.
These babes for Clarence weep, and so do I:
I for an Edward weep, so do not they.
Alas, you three on me, threefold distress'd
Pour all your tears! I am your sorrow's nurse,
And I will pamper it with lamentation.
DORSET Comfort, dear mother. God is much displeas'd
That you take with unthankfulness his doing.
In common worldly things 'tis call'd ungrateful
With dull unwillingness to repay a debt
Which with a bounteous hand was kindly lent;
Much more to be thus opposite with heaven,
For it requires the royal debt it lent you.
RIVERS Madam, bethink you, like a careful mother,
Of the young prince your son. Send straight for him;
Let him be crown'd; in him your comfort lives.
Drown desperate sorrow in dead Edward's grave,
And plant your joys in living Edward's throne.

Enter GLOUCESTER, BUCKINGHAM, DERBY, HASTINGS, and RATCLIFF.

GLOUCESTER Sister, have comfort. All of us have cause
To wail the dimming of our shining star;
But none can help our harms by wailing them.
Madam, my mother, I do cry you mercy;
I did not see your Grace. Humbly on my knee
I crave your blessing.
DUCHESS God bless thee; and put meekness in thy breast,
Love, charity, obedience, and true duty!
GLOUCESTER Amen! [*Aside*] And make me die a good old man!
That is the butt end of a mother's blessing;
I marvel that her Grace did leave it out.
BUCKINGHAM You cloudly princes and heart-sorrowing peers,
That bear this heavy mutual load of moan,
Now cheer each other in each other's love.
Though we have spent our harvest of this king,
We are to reap the harvest of his son.
The broken rancour of your high-swol'n hearts,
But lately splinter'd, knit, and join'd together,
Must gently be preserv'd, cherish'd, and kept.
Me seemeth good that, with some little train,
Forthwith from Ludlow the young prince be fet
Hither to London, to be crown'd our King.
RIVERS Why with some little train, my Lord of Buckingham?
BUCKINGHAM Marry, my lord, lest by a multitude
The new-heal'd wound of malice should break out,
Which would be so much the more dangerous
By how much the estate is green and yet ungovern'd;
Where every horse bears his commanding rein
And may direct his course as please himself,
As well the fear of harm as harm apparent,
In my opinion, ought to be prevented.
GLOUCESTER I hope the King made peace with all of us;
And the compact is firm and true in me.
RIVERS And so in me; and so, I think, in all.
Yet, since it is but green, it should be put
To no apparent likelihood of breach,
Which haply by much company might be urg'd;
Therefore I say with noble Buckingham
That it is meet so few should fetch the Prince.
HASTINGS And so say I.
GLOUCESTER Then be it so; and go we to determine
Who they shall be that straight shall post to Ludlow.
Madam, and you, my sister, will you go
To give your censures in this business?
[*Exeunt all but Buckingham and Gloucester.*
BUCKINGHAM My lord, whoever journeys to the Prince,
For God sake, let not us two stay at home;
For by the way I'll sort occasion,
As index to the story we late talk'd of,
To part the Queen's proud kindred from the Prince.
GLOUCESTER My other self, my counsel's consistory,
My oracle, my prophet, my dear cousin,
I, as a child, will go by thy direction.
Toward Ludlow then, for we'll not stay behind.
[*Exeunt.*

SCENE III. *London. A street.*

Enter one Citizen at one door, and another at the other.

1 CITIZEN Good morrow, neighbour. Whither away so fast?
2 CITIZEN I promise you, I scarcely know myself.
Hear you the news abroad?
1 CITIZEN Yes, that the King is dead.
2 CITIZEN Ill news, by'r lady; seldom comes the better.
I fear, I fear 'twill prove a giddy world.

Enter another Citizen.

3 CITIZEN Neighbours, God speed!
1 CITIZEN Give you good morrow, sir.
3 CITIZEN Doth the news hold of good King Edward's death?
2 CITIZEN Ay, sir, it is too true; God help, the while!
3 CITIZEN Then, masters, look to see a troublous world.
1 CITIZEN No, no; by God's good grace, his son shall reign.
3 CITIZEN Woe to that land that's govern'd by a child.
2 CITIZEN In him there is a hope of government,
Which, in his nonage, council under him,
And, in his full and ripened years, himself,
No doubt, shall then, and till then, govern well.
1 CITIZEN So stood the state when Henry the Sixth
Was crown'd in Paris but at nine months old.
3 CITIZEN Stood the state so? No, no, good friends, God wot;
For then this land was famously enrich'd
With politic grave counsel; then the King
Had virtuous uncles to protect his Grace.
1 CITIZEN Why, so hath this, both by his father and mother.
3 CITIZEN Better it were they all came by his father,
Or by his father there were none at all;
For emulation who shall now be nearest
Will touch us all too near, if God prevent not.
O, full of danger is the Duke of Gloucester!
And the Queen's sons and brothers haught and proud;
And were they to be rul'd, and not to rule,
This sickly land might solace as before.
1 CITIZEN Come, come, we fear the worst; all will be well.
3 CITIZEN When clouds are seen, wise men put on their cloaks;
When great leaves fall, then winter is at hand;
When the sun sets, who doth not look for night?
Untimely storms make men expect a dearth.
All may be well; but, if God sort it so,
'Tis more than we deserve or I expect.
2 CITIZEN Truly, the hearts of men are full of fear.
You cannot reason almost with a man
That looks not heavily and full of dread.
3 CITIZEN Before the days of change, still is it so;
By a divine instinct men's minds mistrust
Ensuing danger; as by proof we see
The water swell before a boist'rous storm.
But leave it all to God. Whither away?
2 CITIZEN Marry, we were sent for to the justices.
3 CITIZEN And so was I; I'll bear you company.
[*Exeunt.*

SCENE IV. *London. The palace.*

Enter the ARCHBISHOP OF YORK, the young DUKE OF YORK, QUEEN ELIZABETH, and the DUCHESS OF YORK.

ARCHBISHOP Last night, I hear, they lay at Stony Stratford,
And at Northampton they do rest to-night;
To-morrow or next day they will be here.
DUCHESS I long with all my heart to see the Prince.
I hope he is much grown since last I saw him.
QUEEN ELIZABETH But I hear no; they say my son of York
Has almost overta'en him in his growth.
YORK Ay, mother; but I would not have it so.
DUCHESS Why, my good cousin, it is good to grow.
YORK Grandam, one night as we did sit at supper,
My uncle Rivers talk'd how I did grow
More than my brother. 'Ay,' quoth my uncle Gloucester
'Small herbs have grace: great weeds do grow apace.'
And since, methinks, I would not grow so fast,
Because sweet flow'rs are slow and weeds make haste.
DUCHESS Good faith, good faith, the saying did not hold
In him that did object the same to thee.
He was the wretched'st thing when he was young,
So long a-growing and so leisurely
That, if his rule were true, he should be gracious.
ARCHBISHOP And so no doubt he is, my gracious madam.
DUCHESS I hope he is; but yet let mothers doubt.
YORK Now, by my troth, if I had been remember'd,
I could have given my uncle's Grace a flout
To touch his growth nearer than he touch'd mine.
DUCHESS How, my young York? I prithee let me hear it.
YORK Marry, they say my uncle grew so fast
That he could gnaw a crust at two hours old.
'Twas full two years ere I could get a tooth.
Grandam, this would have been a biting jest.
DUCHESS I prithee, pretty York, who told thee this?
YORK Grandam, his nurse.
DUCHESS His nurse! Why she was dead ere thou wast born.
YORK If 'twere not she, I cannot tell who told me.
QUEEN ELIZABETH A parlous boy! Go to, you are too shrewd.

ARCHBISHOP Good madam, be not angry with the child.
QUEEN ELIZABETH Pitchers have ears.

Enter a Messenger.

ARCHBISHOP Here comes a messenger. What news?
MESSENGER Such news, my lord, as grieves me to report.
QUEEN ELIZABETH How doth the Prince?
MESSENGER Well, madam, and in health.
DUCHESS What is thy news?
MESSENGER Lord Rivers and Lord Grey
Are sent to Pomfret, and with them
Sir Thomas Vaughan, prisoners.
DUCHESS Who hath committed them?
MESSENGER The mighty Dukes,
Gloucester and Buckingham.
ARCHBISHOP For what offence?
MESSENGER The sum of all I can, I have disclos'd.
Why or for what the nobles were committed
Is all unknown to me, my gracious lord.
QUEEN ELIZABETH Ay me, I see the ruin of my house!
The tiger now hath seiz'd the gentle hind;
Insulting tyranny begins to jet
Upon the innocent and aweless throne.
Welcome, destruction, blood, and massacre!
I see, as in a map, the end of all.
DUCHESS Accursed and unquiet wrangling days,
How many of you have mine eyes beheld!
My husband lost his life to get the crown;
And often up and down my sons were toss'd
For me to joy and weep their gain and loss;
And being seated, and domestic broils
Clean over-blown, themselves the conquerors
Make war upon themselves – brother to brother,
Blood to blood, self against self. O, preposterous
And frantic outrage, end thy damned spleen,
Or let me die, to look on death no more!
QUEEN ELIZABETH Come, come, my boy; we will to sanctuary.
Madam, farewell.
DUCHESS Stay, I will go with you.
QUEEN ELIZABETH You have no cause.
ARCHBISHOP [*To the Queen*] My gracious lady, go.
And thither bear your treasure and your goods.
For my part, I'll resign unto your Grace
The seal I keep; and so betide to me
As well I tender you and all of yours!
Go, I'll conduct you to the sanctuary. [*Exeunt.*

ACT THREE

SCENE I. *London. A street.*

The trumpets sound. Enter the PRINCE OF WALES, GLOUCESTER, BUCKINGHAM, CATESBY, CARDINAL BOURCHIER, and Others.

BUCKINGHAM Welcome, sweet Prince, to London, to your chamber.
GLOUCESTER Welcome, dear cousin, my thoughts' sovereign.
The weary way hath made you melancholy.
PRINCE No, uncle; but our crosses on the way
Have made it tedious, wearisome, and heavy.
I want more uncles here to welcome me.
GLOUCESTER Sweet Prince, the untainted virtue of your years
Hath not yet div'd into the world's deceit;
Nor more can you distinguish of a man
Than of his outward show; which, God He knows,
Seldom or never jumpeth with the heart.
Those uncles which you want were dangerous;
Your Grace attended to their sug'red words
But look'd not on the poison of their hearts.
God keep you from them and from such false friends!
PRINCE God keep me from false friends! but they were none.
GLOUCESTER My lord, the Mayor of London comes to greet you.

Enter the Lord Mayor and his Train.

MAYOR God bless your Grace with health and happy days!
PRINCE I thank you, good my lord, and thank you all.
I thought my mother and my brother York
Would long ere this have met us on the way.
Fie, what a slug is Hastings, that he comes not
To tell us whether they will come or no!

Enter LORD HASTINGS.

BUCKINGHAM And, in good time, here comes the sweating lord.
PRINCE Welcome, my lord. What, will our mother come?
HASTINGS On what occasion, God He knows, not I,
The Queen your mother and your brother York
Have taken sanctuary. The tender Prince
Would fain have come with me to meet your Grace,
But by his mother was perforce withheld.

BUCKINGHAM Fie, what an indirect and peevish course
Is this of hers? Lord Cardinal, will your Grace
Persuade the Queen to send the Duke of York
Unto his princely brother presently?
If she deny, Lord Hastings, go with him
And from her jealous arms pluck him perforce.
CARDINAL My Lord of Buckingham, if my weak oratory
Can from his mother win the Duke of York,
Anon expect him here; but if she be obdurate
To mild entreaties, God in heaven forbid
We should infringe the holy privilege
Of blessed sanctuary! Not for all this land
Would I be guilty of so deep a sin.
BUCKINGHAM You are too senseless-obstinate, my lord,
Too ceremonious and traditional.
Weigh it but with the grossness of this age,
You break not sanctuary in seizing him.
The benefit thereof is always granted
To those whose dealings have deserv'd the place
And those who have the wit to claim the place.
This Prince hath neither claim'd it nor deserv'd it,
And therefore, in mine opinion, cannot have it.
Then, taking him from thence that is not there,
You break no privilege nor charter there.
Oft have I heard of sanctuary men;
But sanctuary children never till now.
CARDINAL My lord, you shall overrule my mind for once.
Come on, Lord Hastings, will you go with me?
HASTINGS I go, my lord.
PRINCE Good lords, make all the speedy haste you may. [*Exeunt Cardinal and Hastings.*
Say, uncle Gloucester, if our brother come,
Where shall we sojourn till our coronation?
GLOUCESTER Where it seems best unto your royal self.
If I may counsel you, some day or two
Your Highness shall repose you at the Tower,
Then where you please and shall be thought most fit
For your best health and recreation.
PRINCE I do not like the Tower, of any place.
Did Julius Caesar build that place, my lord?
GLOUCESTER He did, my gracious lord, begin that place,
Which, since, succeeding ages have reedified.
PRINCE Is it upon record, or else reported
Successively from age to age, he built it?
BUCKINGHAM Upon record, my gracious lord.
PRINCE But say, my lord, it were not regist'red,
Methinks the truth should live from age to age,
As 'twere retail'd to all posterity,
Even to the general all-ending day.
GLOUCESTER [*Aside*] So wise so young, they say, do never live long.
PRINCE What say you, uncle?
GLOUCESTER I say, without characters, fame lives long.
[*Aside*] Thus, like the formal vice, Iniquity,
I moralize two meanings in one word.
PRINCE That Julius Caesar was a famous man;
With what his valour did enrich his wit,
His wit set down to make his valour live.
Death makes no conquest of this conqueror;
For now he lives in fame, though not in life.
I'll tell you what, my cousin Buckingham –
BUCKINGHAM What, my gracious lord?
PRINCE An if I live until I be a man,
I'll win our ancient right in France again,
Or die a soldier as I liv'd a king.
GLOUCESTER [*Aside*] Short summers lightly have a forward spring.

Enter young YORK, HASTINGS, and the CARDINAL.

BUCKINGHAM Now, in good time, here comes the Duke of York.
PRINCE Richard of York, how fares our loving brother?
YORK Well my dread lord; so must I call you now.
PRINCE Ay brother, to our grief, as it is yours.
Too late he died that might have kept that title,
Which by his death hath lost much majesty.
GLOUCESTER How fares our cousin, noble Lord of York?
YORK I thank you, gentle uncle. O, my lord,
You said that idle weeds are fast in growth.
The Prince my brother hath outgrown me far.
GLOUCESTER He hath, my lord.
YORK And therefore is he idle?
GLOUCESTER O, my fair cousin, I must not say so.
YORK Then he is more beholding to you than I.
GLOUCESTER He may command me as my sovereign;
But you have power in me as in a kinsman.
YORK I pray you, uncle, give me this dagger.
GLOUCESTER My dagger, little cousin? With all my heart!
PRINCE A beggar, brother?
YORK Of my kind uncle, that I know will give,
And being but a toy, which is no grief to give.
GLOUCESTER A greater gift than that I'll give my cousin.
YORK A greater gift! O, that's the sword to it!
GLOUCESTER Ay, gentle cousin, were it light enough.

YORK O, then, I see you will part but with light gifts:
In weightier things you'll say a beggar nay.
GLOUCESTER It is too heavy for your Grace to wear.
YORK I weigh it lightly, were it heavier.
GLOUCESTER What, would you have my weapon, little lord?
YORK I would, that I might thank you as you call me.
GLOUCESTER How?
YORK Little.
PRINCE My Lord of York will still be cross in talk.
Uncle, your Grace knows how to bear with him.
YORK You mean, to bear me, not to bear with me.
Uncle, my brother mocks both you and me;
Because that I am little, like an ape,
He thinks that you should bear me on your shoulders.
BUCKINGHAM With what a sharp-provided wit he reasons!
To mitigate the scorn he gives his uncle
He prettily and aptly taunts himself.
So cunning and so young is wonderful.
GLOUCESTER My lord, will't please you pass along?
Myself and my good cousin Buckingham
Will to your mother, to entreat of her
To meet you at the Tower and welcome you.
YORK What, will you go unto the Tower, my lord?
PRINCE My Lord Protector needs will have it so.
YORK I shall not sleep in quiet at the Tower.
GLOUCESTER Why, what should you fear?
YORK Marry, my uncle Clarence' angry ghost.
My grandam told me he was murder'd there.
PRINCE I fear no uncles dead.
GLOUCESTER Nor none that live, I hope.
PRINCE An if they live, I hope I need not fear.
But come, my lord; with a heavy heart,
Thinking on them, go I unto the Tower.
[*A sennet. Exeunt all but Gloucester, Buckingham, and Catesby.*

BUCKINGHAM Think you, my lord, this little prating York
Was not incensed by his subtle mother
To taunt and scorn you thus opprobriously?
GLOUCESTER No doubt, no doubt. O, 'tis a perilous boy;
Bold, quick, ingenious, forward, capable.
He is all the mother's, from the top to toe.
BUCKINGHAM Well, let them rest. Come hither, Catesby.
Thou art sworn as deeply to effect what we intend
As closely to conceal what we impart.
Thou know'st our reasons urg'd upon the way.
What think'st thou? Is it not an easy matter
To make William Lord Hastings of our mind,
For the instalment of this noble Duke
In the seat royal of this famous isle?
CATESBY He for his father's sake so loves the Prince
That he will not be won to aught against him.
BUCKINGHAM What think'st thou then of Stanley? Will not he?
CATESBY He will do all in all as Hastings doth.
BUCKINGHAM Well then, no more but this: go, gentle Catesby,
And, as it were far off, sound thou Lord Hastings
How he doth stand affected to our purpose;
And summon him to-morrow to the Tower,
To sit about the coronation.
If thou dost find him tractable to us,
Encourage him, and tell him all our reasons;
If he be leaden, icy, cold, unwilling,
Be thou so too, and so break off the talk,
And give us notice of his inclination;
For we to-morrow hold divided councils,
Wherein thyself shalt highly be employ'd.
GLOUCESTER Commend me to Lord William. Tell him, Catesby,
His ancient knot of dangerous adversaries
To-morrow are let blood at Pomfret Castle;
And bid my lord, for joy of this good news,
Give Mistress Shore one gentle kiss the more.
BUCKINGHAM Good Catesby, go effect this business soundly.
CATESBY My good lords both, with all the heed I can.
GLOUCESTER Shall we hear from you, Catesby, ere we sleep?
CATESBY You shall, my lord.
GLOUCESTER At Crosby House, there shall you find us both. [*Exit Catesby.*
BUCKINGHAM Now, my lord, what shall we do it we perceive
Lord Hastings will not yield to our complots?
GLOUCESTER Chop off his head – something we will determine.
And, look when I am King, claim thou of me
The earldom of Hereford and all the movables
Whereof the King my brother was possess'd.
BUCKINGHAM I'll claim that promise at your Grace's hand.
GLOUCESTER And look to have it yielded with all kindness.
Come, let us sup betimes, that afterwards
We may digest our complots in some form.
[*Exeunt.*

SCENE II. *Before Lord Hastings' house.*

Enter a Messenger to the door of Hastings.

MESSENGER My lord, my lord! [*Knocking.*
HASTINGS [*Within*] Who knocks?
MESSENGER One from the Lord Stanley.
HASTINGS [*Within*] What is't o'clock?
MESSENGER Upon the stroke of four.

Enter LORD HASTINGS.

HASTINGS Cannot my Lord Stanley sleep these tedious nights?
MESSENGER So it appears by that I have to say.
First, he commends him to your noble self.
HASTINGS What then?
MESSENGER Then certifies your lordship that this night
He dreamt the boar had razed off his helm.
Besides, he says there are two councils kept,
And that may be determin'd at the one
Which may make you and him to rue at th' other.
Therefore he sends to know your lordship's pleasure –
If you will presently take horse with him
And with all speed post with him toward the north
To shun the danger that his soul divines.
HASTINGS Go, fellow, go, return unto thy lord;
Bid him not fear the separated council:
His honour and myself are at the one,
And at the other is my good friend Catesby;
Where nothing can proceed that toucheth us
Whereof I shall not have intelligence.
Tell him his fears are shallow, without instance;
And for his dreams, I wonder he's so simple
To trust the mock'ry of unquiet slumbers.
To fly the boar before the boar pursues
Were to incense the boar to follow us
And make pursuit where he did mean no chase.
Go, bid thy master rise and come to me;
And we will both together to the Tower,
Where, he shall see, the boar will use us kindly.
MESSENGER I'll go, my lord, and tell him what you say. [*Exit.*

Enter CATESBY.

CATESBY Many good morrows to my noble lord!
HASTINGS Good morrow, Catesby; you are early stirring.
What news, what news, in this our tott'ring state?
CATESBY It is a reeling world indeed, my lord;
And I believe will never stand upright
Till Richard wear the garland of the realm.
HASTINGS How, wear the garland! Dost thou mean the crown?
CATESBY Ay, my good lord.
HASTINGS I'll have this crown of mine cut from my shoulders
Before I'll see the crown so foul misplac'd.
But canst thou guess that he doth aim at it?
CATESBY Ay, on my life; and hopes to find you forward
Upon his party for the gain thereof;
And thereupon he sends you this good news,
That this same very day your enemies,
The kindred of the Queen, must die at Pomfret.
HASTINGS Indeed, I am no mourner for that news,
Because they have been still my adversaries;
But that I'll give my voice on Richard's side
To bar my master's heirs in true descent,
God knows I will not do it to the death.
CATESBY God keep your lordship in that gracious mind!
HASTINGS But I shall laugh at this a twelve month hence,
That they which brought me in my master's hate,
I live to look upon their tragedy.
Well, Catesby, ere a fortnight make me older,
I'll send some packing that yet think not on't.
CATESBY 'Tis a vile thing to die, my gracious lord,
When men are unprepar'd and look not for it.
HASTINGS O monstrous, monstrous! And so falls it out
With Rivers, Vaughan, Grey; and so 'twill do
With some men else that think themselves as safe
As thou and I, who, as thou knowest, are dear
To princely Richard and to Buckingham.
CATESBY The Princes both make high account of you –
[*Aside*] For they account his head upon the bridge.
HASTINGS I know they do, and I have well deserv'd it.

Enter LORD STANLEY.

Come on, come on; where is your boar-spear, man?
Fear you the boar, and go so unprovided?
STANLEY My lord, good morrow; good morrow, Catesby.
You may jest on, but, by the holy rood,
I do not like these several councils, I.
HASTINGS My lord, I hold my life as dear as yours,
And never in my days, I do protest,
Was it so precious to me as 'tis now.
Think you, but that I know our state secure,
I would be so triumphant as I am?
STANLEY The lords at Pomfret, when they rode from London,

Were jocund and suppos'd their states were sure,
And they indeed had no cause to mistrust;
But yet you see how soon the day o'ercast.
This sudden stab of rancour I misdoubt;
Pray God, I say, I prove a needless coward.
What, shall we toward the Tower? The day is spent.

HASTINGS Come, come, have with you. Wot you what, my lord?
To-day the lords you talk'd of are beheaded.

STANLEY They, for their truth, might better wear their heads
Than some that have accus'd them wear their hats.
But come, my lord, let's away.

Enter HASTINGS, a poursuivant.

HASTINGS Go on before; I'll talk with this good fellow. [*Exeunt Stanley and Catesby.*
How now, Hastings! How goes the world with thee?

PURSUIVANT The better that your lordship please to ask.

HASTINGS I tell thee, man, 'tis better with me now
Than when thou met'st me last where now we meet:
Then was I going prisoner to the Tower
By the suggestion of the Queen's allies;
But now, I tell thee – keep it to thyself –
This day those enemies are put to death,
And I in better state than e'er I was.

PURSUIVANT God hold it, to your honour's good content!

HASTINGS Gramercy, Hastings; there, drink that for me. [*Throws him his purse.*

PURSUIVANT I thank your honour. [*Exit.*

Enter a Priest.

PRIEST Well met, my lord; I am glad to see your honour.

HASTINGS I thank thee, good Sir John, with all my heart.
I am in your debt for your last exercise;
Come the next Sabbath, and I will content you.
[*He whispers in his ear.*

PRIEST I'll wait upon your lordship.

Enter BUCKINGHAM.

BUCKINGHAM What, talking with a priest, Lord Chamberlain!
Your friends at Pomfret, they do need the priest:
Your honour hath no shriving work in hand.

HASTINGS Good faith, and when I met this holy man,
The men you talk of came into my mind.
What, go you toward the Tower?

BUCKINGHAM I do, my lord, but long I cannot stay there;
I shall return before your lordship thence.

HASTINGS Nay, like enough, for I stay dinner there.

BUCKINGHAM [*Aside*] And supper too, although thou knowest it not. –
Come, will you go?

HASTINGS I'll wait upon your lordship.
[*Exeunt.*

SCENE III. *Pomfret Castle.*

Enter SIR RICHARD RATCLIFF, with Halberds, carrying the Nobles, RIVERS, GREY, and VAUGHAN, to death.

RIVERS Sir Richard Ratcliff, let me tell thee this:
To-day shalt thou behold a subject die
For truth, for duty, and for loyalty.

GREY God bless the Prince from all the pack of you!
A knot you are of damned blood-suckers.

VAUGHAN You live that shall cry woe for this hereafter.

RATCLIFF Dispatch; the limit of your lives is out.

RIVERS O Pomfret, Pomfret! O thou bloody prison,
Fatal and ominous to noble peers!
Within the guilty closure of thy walls
Richard the Second here was hack'd to death;
And, for more slander to thy dismal seat,
We give to thee our guiltless blood to drink.

GREY Now Margaret's curse is fall'n upon our heads,
When she exclaim'd on Hastings, you, and I,
For standing by when Richard stabb'd her son.

RIVERS Then curs'd she Richard, then curs'd she Buckingham,
Then curs'd she Hastings. O, remember, God,
To hear her prayer for them, as now for us!
And for my sister, and her princely sons,
Be satisfied, dear God, with our true blood,
Which, as thou know'st, unjustly must be spilt.

RATCLIFF Make haste; the hour of death is expiate.

RIVERS Come, Grey; come, Vaughan; let us here embrace.
Farewell, until we meet again in heaven.
[*Exeunt.*

SCENE IV. *London. The Tower.*

Enter BUCKINGHAM, DERBY, HASTINGS, the BISHOP OF ELY, RATCLIFF, LOVELL, with Others and seat themselves at a table.

HASTINGS Now, noble peers, the cause why we are met
Is to determine of the coronation.

In God's name speak – when is the royal day?

BUCKINGHAM Is all things ready for the royal time?

DERBY It is, and wants but nomination.

ELY To-morrow then I judge a happy day.

BUCKINGHAM Who knows the Lord Protector's mind herein?
Who is most inward with the noble Duke?

ELY Your Grace, we think, should soonest know his mind.

BUCKINGHAM We know each other's faces; for our hearts,
He knows no more of mine than I of yours;
Or I of his, my lord, than you of mine.
Lord Hastings, you and he are near in love.

HASTINGS I thank his Grace, I know he loves me well;
But for his purpose in the coronation
I have not sounded him, nor he deliver'd
His gracious pleasure any way therein.
But you, my honourable lords, may name the time;
And in the Duke's behalf I'll give my voice,
Which, I presume, he'll take in gentle part.

Enter GLOUCESTER.

ELY In happy time, here comes the Duke himself.

GLOUCESTER My noble lords and cousins all, good morrow.
I have been long a sleeper, but I trust
My absence doth neglect no great design
Which by my presence might have been concluded.

BUCKINGHAM Had you not come upon your cue, my lord,
William Lord Hastings had pronounc'd your part –
I mean, your voice for crowning of the King.

GLOUCESTER Than my Lord Hastings no man might be bolder;
His lordship knows me well and loves me well.
My lord of Ely, when I was last in Holborn
I saw good strawberries in your garden there.
I do beseech you send for some of them.

ELY Marry and will, my lord, with all my heart. *[Exit.*

GLOUCESTER Cousin of Buckingham, a word with you. *[Takes him aside.*
Catesby hath sounded Hastings in our business,
And finds the testy gentleman so hot
That he will lose his head ere give consent
His master's child, as worshipfully he terms it,
Shall lose the royalty of England's throne.

BUCKINGHAM Withdraw yourself awhile; I'll go with you.

[Exeunt Gloucester and Buckingham.

DERBY We have not yet set down this day of triumph.
To-morrow, in my judgment, is too sudden;
For I myself am not so well provided
As else I would be, were the day prolong'd.

Re-enter the BISHOP OF ELY.

ELY Where is my lord the Duke of Gloucester?
I have sent for these strawberries.

HASTINGS His Grace looks cheerfully and smooth this morning;
There's some conceit or other likes him well
When that he bids good morrow with such spirit.
I think there's never a man in Christendom
Can lesser hide his love or hate than he;
For by his face straight shall you know his heart.

DERBY What of his heart perceive you in his face.
By any livelihood he show'd to-day?

HASTINGS Marry, that with no man here he is offended;
For, were he, he had shown it in his looks.

Re-enter GLOUCESTER and BUCKINGHAM.

GLOUCESTER I pray you all, tell me what they deserve
That do conspire my death with devilish plots
Of damned witchcraft, and that have prevail'd
Upon my body with their hellish charms?

HASTINGS The tender love I bear your Grace, my lord,
Makes me most forward in this princely presence
To doom th' offenders, whosoe'er they be.
I say, my lord, they have deserved death.

GLOUCESTER Then be your eyes the witness of their evil.
Look how I am bewitch'd; behold, mine arm
Is like a blasted sapling wither'd up.
And this is Edward's wife, that monstrous witch,
Consorted with that harlot strumpet Shore,
That by their witchcraft thus have marked me.

HASTINGS If they have done this deed, my noble lord –

GLOUCESTER If? – thou protector of this damned strumpet,
Talk'st thou to me of ifs? Thou art a traitor.
Off with his head! Now by Saint Paul I swear
I will not dine until I see the same.
Lovel and Ratcliff, look that it be done.
The rest that love me, rise and follow me.

[Exeunt all but Hastings, Lovell, and Ratcliff.

HASTINGS Woe, woe, for England! not a whit for me;
For I, too fond, might have prevented this.
Stanley did dream the boar did raze our helms,

And I did scorn it and disdain to fly.
Three times to-day my foot-cloth horse did stumble,
And started when he look'd upon the Tower,
As loath to bear me to the slaughter-house.
O, now I need the priest that spake to me!
I now repent I told the pursuivant,
As too triumphing, how mine enemies
To-day at Pomfret bloodily were butcher'd,
And I myself secure in grace and favour.
O Margaret, Margaret, now thy heavy curse
Is lighted on poor Hastings' wretched head!

RATCLIFF Come, come, dispatch; the Duke would be at dinner.
Make a short shrift; he longs to see your head.

HASTINGS O momentary grace of mortal men,
Which we more hunt for than the grace of God!
Who builds his hope in air of your good looks
Lives like a drunken sailor on a mast,
Ready with every nod to tumble down
Into the fatal bowels of the deep.

LOVELL Come, come, dispatch; 'tis bootless to exclaim.

HASTINGS O bloody Richard! Miserable England!
I prophesy the fearfull'st time to thee
That ever wretched age hath look'd upon.
Come, lead me to the block; bear him my head.
They smile at me who shortly shall be dead.

[Exeunt.

SCENE V. *London. The Tower-walls.*

Enter GLOUCESTER and BUCKINGHAM in rotten armour, marvellous ill-favoured.

GLOUCESTER Come, cousin, canst thou quake and change thy colour,
Murder thy breath in middle of a word,
And then again begin, and stop again,
As if thou were distraught and mad with terror?

BUCKINGHAM Tut, I can counterfeit the deep tragedian;
Speak and look back, and pry on every side,
Tremble and start at wagging of a straw,
Intending deep suspicion. Ghastly looks
Are at my service, like enforced smiles;
And both are ready in their offices
At any time to grace my stratagems.
But what, is Catesby gone?

GLOUCESTER He is; and, see, he brings the mayor along.

Enter the Lord Mayor and CATESBY.

BUCKINGHAM Lord Mayor –

GLOUCESTER Look to the drawbridge there!

BUCKINGHAM Hark! a drum.

GLOUCESTER Catesby, o'erlook the walls.

BUCKINGHAM Lord Mayor, the reason we have sent –

GLOUCESTER Look back, defend thee; here are enemies.

BUCKINGHAM God and our innocence defend and guard us!

Enter LOVELL and RATCLIFF, with Hastings' head.

GLOUCESTER Be patient; they are friends – Ratcliff and Lovel.

LOVELL Here is the head of that ignoble traitor,
The dangerous and unsuspected Hastings.

GLOUCESTER So dear I lov'd the man that I must weep.
I took him for the plainest harmless creature
That breath'd upon the earth a Christian;
Made him my book, wherein my soul recorded
The history of all her secret thoughts.
So smooth he daub'd his vice with show of virtue
That, his apparent open guilt omitted,
I mean his conversation with Shore's wife –
He liv'd from all attainder of suspects.

BUCKINGHAM Well, well, he was the covert'st shelt'red traitor
That ever liv'd.
Would you imagine, or almost believe –
Were't not that by great preservation
We live to tell it – that the subtle traitor
This day had plotted, in the council-house,
To murder me and my good Lord of Gloucester.

MAYOR Had he done so?

GLOUCESTER What! think you we are Turks or Infidels?
Or that we would, against the form of law,
Proceed thus rashly in the villain's death
But that the extreme peril of the case,
The peace of England and our persons' safety,
Enforc'd us to this execution?

MAYOR Now, fair befall you! He deserv'd his death;
And your good Graces both have well proceeded
To warn false traitors from the like attempts.
I never look'd for better at his hands
After he once fell in with Mistress Shore.

BUCKINGHAM Yet had we not determin'd he should die
Until your lordship came to see his end –
Which now the loving haste of these our friends,
Something against our meanings, have prevented –
Because, my lord, I would have had you heard
The traitor speak, and timorously confess
The manner and the purpose of his treasons;
That you might well have signified the same

Unto the citizens, who haply may
Misconster us in him and wail his death.

MAYOR But, my good lord, your Grace's word shall serve
As well as I had seen and heard him speak;
And do not doubt, right noble Princes both,
But I'll acquaint our duteous citizens
With all your just proceedings in this cause.

GLOUCESTER And to that end we wish'd your lordship here,
T' avoid the censures of the carping world.

BUCKINGHAM Which since you come too late of our intent,
Yet witness what you hear we did intend.
And so, my good Lord Mayor, we bid farewell.

[*Exit Lord Mayor.*

GLOUCESTER Go, after, after, cousin Buckingham.
The Mayor towards Guildhall hies him in all post.
There, at your meet'st advantage of the time,
Infer the bastardy of Edward's children.
Tell them how Edward put to death a citizen
Only for saying he would make his son
Heir to the crown – meaning indeed his house,
Which by the sign thereof was termed so.
Moreover, urge his hateful luxury
And bestial appetite in change of lust,
Which stretch'd unto their servants, daughters, wives,
Even where his raging eye or savage heart
Without control lusted to make a prey.
Nay, for a need, thus far come near my person:
Tell them, when that my mother went with child
Of that insatiate Edward, noble York
My princely father then had wars in France
And, by true computation of the time,
Found that the issue was not his begot;
Which well appeared in his lineaments,
Being nothing like the noble Duke my father.
Yet touch this sparingly, as 'twere far off;
Because, my lord, you know my mother lives.

BUCKINGHAM Doubt not, my lord, I'll play the orator
As if the golden plea for which I plead
Were for myself; and so, my lord, adieu.

GLOUCESTER If you thrive well, bring them to Baynard's Castle;
Where you shall find me well accompanied
With reverend fathers and well learned bishops.

BUCKINGHAM I go; and towards three or four o'clock
Look for the news that the Guildhall affords.

[*Exit.*

GLOUCESTER Go, Lovel, with all speed to Doctor Shaw.
[*To Catesby*] Go thou to Friar Penker. Bid them both
Meet me within this hour at Baynard's Castle.

[*Exeunt all but Gloucester.*

Now will I go to take some privy order
To draw the brats of Clarence out of sight,
And to give order that no manner of person
Have any time recourse unto the Princes. [*Exit.*

SCENE VI. *London. A street.*

Enter a Scrivener.

SCRIVENER Here is the indictment of the good Lord Hastings;
Which in a set hand fairly is engross'd
That it may be to-day read o'er in Paul's.
And mark how well the sequel hangs together:
Eleven hours I have spent to write it over,
For yesternight by Catesby was it sent me;
The precedent was full as long a-doing;
And yet within these five hours Hastings liv'd,
Untainted, unexamin'd, free, at liberty.
Here's a good world the while! Who is so gross
That cannot see this palpable device?
Yet who so bold but says he sees it not?
Bad is the world; and all will come to nought,
When such ill dealing must be seen in thought.

[*Exit.*

SCENE VII. *London. Baynard's Castle.*

Enter GLOUCESTER and BUCKINGHAM, at several doors.

GLOUCESTER How now, how now! What say the citizens?

BUCKINGHAM Now, but the holy Mother of our Lord,
The citizens are mum, say not a word.

GLOUCESTER Touch'd you the bastardy of Edward's children?

BUCKINGHAM I did; with his contract with Lady Lucy,
And his contract by deputy in France;
Th' insatiate greediness of his desire,
And his enforcement of the city wives;
His tyranny for trifles; his own bastardy,
As being got, your father then in France,
And his resemblance, being not like the Duke.
Withal I did infer your lineaments,
Being the right idea of your father,
Both in your form and nobleness of mind;
Laid open all your victories in Scotland,
Your discipline in war, wisdom in peace,
Your bounty, virtue, fair humility;
Indeed, left nothing fitter for your purpose

Untouch'd or slightly handled in discourse.
And when mine oratory drew toward end
I bid them that did love their country's good
Cry 'God save Richard, England's royal King!'

GLOUCESTER And did they so?

BUCKINGHAM No, so God help me, they spake not a word;
But, like dumb statues or breathing stones,
Star'd each on other, and look'd deadly pale.
Which when I saw, I reprehended them,
And ask'd the Mayor what meant this wilful silence.
His answer was, the people were not used
To be spoke to but by the Recorder.
Then he was urg'd to tell my tale again.
'Thus saith the Duke, thus hath the Duke inferr'd' –
But nothing spoke in warrant from himself.
When he had done, some followers of mine own
At lower end of the hall hurl'd up their caps,
And some ten voices cried 'God save King Richard!'
And thus I took the vantage of those few –
'Thanks, gentle citizens and friends,' quoth I
'This general applause and cheerful shout
Argues your wisdoms and your love to Richard'.
And even here brake off and came away.

GLOUCESTER What, tongueless blocks were they? Would they not speak?
Will not the Mayor then and his brethren come?

BUCKINGHAM The Mayor is here at hand. Intend some fear;
Be not you spoke with but by mighty suit;
And look you get a prayer-book in your hand,
And stand between two churchmen, good my lord;
For on that ground I'll make a holy descant;
And be not easily won to our requests.
Play the maid's part: still answer nay, and take it.

GLOUCESTER I go; and if you plead as well for them
As I can say nay to thee for myself,
No doubt we bring it to a happy issue.

BUCKINGHAM Go, go, up to the leads; the Lord Mayor knocks. [*Exit Gloucester.*

Enter the Lord Mayor, Aldermen, and Citizens.

Welcome, my lord. I dance attendance here;
I think the Duke will not be spoke withal.

Enter CATESBY.

Now, Catesby, what says your lord to my request?

CATESBY He doth entreat your Grace, my noble lord,
To visit him to-morrow or next day.
He is within, with two right reverend fathers,
Divinely bent to meditation;
And in no worldly suits would he be mov'd,
To draw him from his holy exercise.

BUCKINGHAM Return, good Catesby, to the gracious Duke;
Tell him, myself, the Mayor and Aldermen,
In deep designs, in matter of great moment,
No less importing than our general good,
Are come to have some conference with his Grace.

CATESBY I'll signify so much unto him straight. [*Exit.*

BUCKINGHAM Ah ha, my lord, this prince is not an Edward!
He is not lolling on a lewd love-bed,
But on his knees at meditation;
Not dallying with a brace of courtezans,
But meditating with two deep divines;
Not sleeping, to engross his idle body,
But praying, to enrich his watchful soul.
Happy were England would this virtuous prince
Take on his Grace the sovereignty thereof;
But, sure, I fear we shall not win him to it.

MAYOR Marry, God defend his Grace should say us nay!

BUCKINGHAM I fear he will. Here Catesby comes again.

Re-enter CATESBY.

Now, Catesby, what says his Grace?

CATESBY My lord,
He wonders to what end you have assembled
Such troops of citizens to come to him.
His Grace not being warn'd thereof before,
He fears, my lord, you mean no good to him.

BUCKINGHAM Sorry I am my noble cousin should
Suspect me that I mean no good to him.
By heaven, we come to him in perfect love;
And so once more return and tell his Grace. [*Exit Catesby.*
When holy and devout religious men
Are at their beads, 'tis much to draw them thence,
So sweet is zealous contemplation.

Enter GLOUCESTER aloft, between two Bishops. CATESBY returns.

MAYOR See where his Grace stands 'tween two clergymen!

BUCKINGHAM Two props of virtue for a Christian prince,
To stay him from the fall of vanity;
And, see, a book of prayer in his hand,
True ornaments to know a holy man.

Famous Plantagenet, most gracious Prince,
Lend favourable ear to our requests,
And pardon us the interruption
Of thy devotion and right Christian zeal.

GLOUCESTER My lord, there needs no such apology:
I do beseech your Grace to pardon me,
Who, earnest in the service of my God,
Deferr'd the visitation of my friends.
But, leaving this, what is your Grace's pleasure?

BUCKINGHAM Even that, I hope, which pleaseth God above,
And all good men of this ungovern'd isle.

GLOUCESTER I do suspect I have done some offence
That seems disgracious in the city's eye,
And that you come to reprehend my ignorance.

BUCKINGHAM You have, my lord. Would it might please your Grace,
On our entreaties, to amend your fault!

GLOUCESTER Else wherefore breathe I in a Christian land?

BUCKINGHAM Know then, it is your fault that you resign
The supreme seat, the throne majestical,
The scept'red office of your ancestors,
Your state of fortune and your due of birth,
The lineal glory of your royal house,
To the corruption of a blemish'd stock;
Whiles in the mildness of your sleepy thoughts,
Which here we waken to our country's good,
The noble isle doth want her proper limbs;
Her face defac'd with scars of infamy,
Her royal stock graft with ignoble plants,
And almost should'red in the swallowing gulf
Of dark forgetfulness and deep oblivion.
Which to recure, we heartily solicit
Your gracious self to take on you the charge
And kingly government of this your land –
Not as protector, steward, substitute,
Or lowly factor for another's gain;
But as successively, from blood to blood,
Your right of birth, your empery, your own.
For this, consorted with the citizens,
Your very worshipful and loving friends,
And by their vehement instigation,
In this just cause come I to move your Grace.

GLOUCESTER I cannot tell if to depart in silence
Or bitterly to speak in your reproof
Best fitteth my degree or your condition.
If not to answer, you might haply think
Tongue-tied ambition, not replying, yielded
To bear the golden yoke of sovereignty,
Which fondly you would here impose on me;
If to reprove you for this suit of yours,
So season'd with your faithful love to me,
Then, on the other side, I check'd my friends.
Therefore – to speak, and to avoid the first,
And then, in speaking, not to incur the last –
Definitively thus I answer you:
Your love deserves my thanks, but my desert
Unmeritable shuns your high request.
First, if all obstacles were cut away,
And that my path were even to the crown,
As the ripe revenue and due of birth,
Yet so much is my poverty of spirit,
So mighty and so many my defects,
That I would rather hide me from my greatness –
Being a bark to brook no mighty sea –
Than in my greatness covet to be hid,
And in the vapour of my glory smother'd.
But, God be thank'd, there is no need of me –
And much I need to help you, were there need.
The royal tree hath left us royal fruit
Which, mellow'd by the stealing hours of time,
Will well become the seat of majesty
And make, no doubt, us happy by his reign.
On him I lay that you would lay on me –
The right and fortune of his happy stars,
Which God defend that I should wring from him.

BUCKINGHAM My lord, this argues conscience in your Grace;
But the respects thereof are nice and trivial,
All circumstances well considered.
You say that Edward is your brother's son.
So say we too, but not by Edward's wife;
For first was he contract to Lady Lucy –
Your mother lives a witness to his vow –
And afterward by substitute betroth'd
To Bona, sister to the King of France.
These both put off, a poor petitioner,
A care-craz'd mother to a many sons,
A beauty-waning and distressed widow,
Even in the afternoon of her best days,
Made prize and purchase of his wanton eye,
Seduc'd the pitch and height of his degree
To base declension and loath'd bigamy.
By her, in his unlawful bed, he got
This Edward, whom our manners call the Prince.
More bitterly could I expostulate,
Save that, for reverence to some alive,
I give a sparing limit to my tongue.
Then, good my lord, take to your royal self
This proffer'd benefit of dignity;
If not to bless us and the land withal,
Yet to draw forth your noble ancestry
From the corruption of abusing times
Unto a lineal true-derived course.

MAYOR Do, good my lord; your citizens entreat you.

BUCKINGHAM Refuse not, mighty lord, this proffer'd love.

CATESBY O, make them joyful, grant their lawful suit!
GLOUCESTER Alas, why would you heap this care on me?
I am unfit for state and majesty.
I do beseech you, take it not amiss:
I cannot nor I will not yield to you.
BUCKINGHAM If you refuse it – as, in love and zeal,
Loath to depose the child, your brother's son;
As well we know your tenderness of heart
And gentle, kind, effeminate remorse,
Which we have noted in you to your kindred
And egally indeed to all estates –
Yet know, whe'er you accept our suit or no,
Your brother's son shall never reign our king;
But we will plant some other in the throne
To the disgrace and downfall of your house;
And in this resolution here we leave you.
Come, citizens. Zounds, I'll entreat no more.
GLOUCESTER O, do not swear, my lord of Buckingham. *[Exeunt Buckingham, Mayor, and Citizens.*
CATESBY Call him again, sweet Prince, accept their suit.
If you deny them, all the land will rue it.
GLOUCESTER Will you enforce me to a world of cares?
Call them again. I am not made of stones,
But penetrable to your kind entreaties,
Albeit against my conscience and my soul.

Re-enter BUCKINGHAM and the rest.

Cousin of Buckingham, and sage grave men,
Since you will buckle fortune on my back,
To bear her burden, whe'er I will or no,
I must have patience to endure the load;
But if black scandal or foul-fac'd reproach
Attend the sequel of your imposition,
Your mere enforcement shall acquittance me
From all the impure blots and stains thereof;
For God doth know, and you may partly see,
How far I am from the desire of this.
MAYOR God bless your Grace! We see it, and will say it.
GLOUCESTER In saying so, you shall but say the truth.
BUCKINGHAM Then I salute you with this royal title –
Long live King Richard, England's worthy King!
ALL Amen.
BUCKINGHAM To-morrow may it please you to be crown'd?
GLOUCESTER Even when you please, for you will have it so.
BUCKINGHAM To-morrow, then, we will attend your Grace;
And so, most joyfully, we take our leave.
GLOUCESTER *[To the Bishops]* Come, let us to our holy work again.
Farewell, my cousin; farewell, gentle friends.
[Exeunt.

ACT FOUR

SCENE I. *London. Before the Tower.*

Enter QUEEN ELIZABETH, DUCHESS OF YORK, and MARQUIS OF DORSET, at one door; ANNE DUCHESS OF GLOUCESTER, leading LADY MARGARET PLANTAGENET, Clarence's young daughter, at another door.

DUCHESS Who meets us here? My niece Plantagenet,
Led in the hand of her kind aunt of Gloucester?
Now, for my life, she's wand'ring to the Tower,
On pure heart's love, to greet the tender Princes.
Daughter, well met.
ANNE God give your Graces both
A happy and a joyful time of day!
QUEEN ELIZABETH As much to you, good sister! Whither away?
ANNE No farther than the Tower; and, as I guess,
Upon the like devotion as yourselves,
To gratulate the gentle Princes there.
QUEEN ELIZABETH Kind sister, thanks; we'll enter all together.

Enter BRAKENBURY.

And in good time, here the lieutenant comes.
Master Lieutenant, pray you, by your leave,
How doth the Prince, and my young son of York?
BRAKENBURY Right well, dear madam. By your patience,
I may not suffer you to visit them.
The King hath strictly charg'd the contrary.
QUEEN ELIZABETH The King! Who's that?
BRAKENBURY I mean the Lord Protector
QUEEN ELIZABETH The Lord protect him from that kingly title!
Hath he set bounds between their love and me?
I am their mother; who shall bar me from them?
DUCHESS I am their father's mother; I will see them.
ANNE Their aunt I am in law, in love their mother.

Then bring me to their sights; I'll bear thy blame,
And take thy office from thee on my peril.

BRAKENBURY No, madam, no. I may not leave it so;
I am bound by oath, and therefore pardon me.
[*Exit.*

Enter STANLEY.

STANLEY Let me but meet you, ladies, one hour hence,
And I'll salute your Grace of York as mother
And reverend looker-on of two fair queens.
[*To Anne*] Come, madam, you must straight to Westminster,
There to be crowned Richard's royal queen.

QUEEN ELIZABETH Ah, cut my lace asunder
That my pent heart may have some scope to beat,
Or else I swoon with this dead-killing news!

ANNE Despiteful tidings! O unpleasing news!

DORSET Be of good cheer; mother, how fares your Grace?

QUEEN ELIZABETH O Dorset, speak not to me, get thee gone!
Death and destruction dogs thee at thy heels;
Thy mother's name is ominous to children.
If thou wilt outstrip death, go cross the seas,
And live with Richmond, from the reach of hell.
Go, hie thee, hie thee from this slaughter-house,
Lest thou increase the number of the dead,
And make me die the thrall of Margaret's curse,
Nor mother, wife, nor England's counted queen.

STANLEY Full of wise care is this your counsel, madam.
Take all the swift advantage of the hours;
You shall have letters from me to my son
In your behalf, to meet you on the way.
Be not ta'en tardy by unwise delay.

DUCHESS O ill-dispersing wind of misery!
O my accursed womb, the bed of death!
A cockatrice hast thou hatch'd to the world,
Whose unavoided eye is murderous.

STANLEY Come, madam, come; I in all haste was sent.

ANNE And I with all unwillingness will go.
O, would to God that the inclusive verge
Of golden metal that must round my brow
Were red-hot steel, to sear me to the brains!
Anointed let me be with deadly venom,
And die ere men can say 'God save the Queen!'

QUEEN ELIZABETH Go, go, poor soul; I envy not thy glory.
To feed my humour, wish thyself no harm.

ANNE No, why? When he that is my husband now
Came to me, as I follow'd Henry's corse;
When scarce the blood was well wash'd from his hands
Which issued from my other angel husband,
And that dear saint which then I weeping follow'd –
O, when, I say, I look'd on Richard's face,
This was my wish: 'Be thou' quoth I accurs'd
For making me, so young, so old a widow;
And when thou wed'st, let sorrow haunt thy bed;
And be thy wife, if any be so mad,
More miserable by the life of thee
Than thou hast made me by my dear lord's death'.
Lo, ere I can repeat this curse again,
Within so small a time, my woman's heart
Grossly grew captive to his honey words
And prov'd the subject of mine own soul's curse,
Which hitherto hath held my eyes from rest;
For never yet one hour in his bed
Did I enjoy the golden dew of sleep,
But with his timorous dreams was still awak'd.
Besides, he hates me for my father Warwick;
And will, no doubt, shortly be rid of me.

QUEEN ELIZABETH Poor heart, adieu! I pity thy complaining.

ANNE No more than with my soul I mourn for yours.

DORSET Farewell, thou woeful welcomer of glory!

ANNE Adieu, poor soul, that tak'st thy leave of it!

DUCHESS [*To Dorset*] Go thou to Richmond, and good fortune guide thee!
[*To Anne*] Go thou to Richard, and good angels tend thee!
[*To Queen Elizabeth*] Go thou to sanctuary, and good thoughts possess thee!
I to my grave, where peace and rest lie with me!
Eighty odd years of sorrow have I seen,
And each hour's joy wreck'd with a week of teen.

QUEEN ELIZABETH Stay, yet look back with me unto the Tower.
Pity, you ancient stones, those tender babes
Whom envy hath immur'd within your walls,
Rough cradle for such little pretty ones.
Rude ragged nurse, old sullen playfellow
For tender princes, use my babies well.
So foolish sorrows bids your stones farewell.
[*Exeunt.*

SCENE II. *London. The palace.*

Sound a sennet. Enter RICHARD, in pomp, as King; BUCKINGHAM, CATESBY, RATCLIFF, LOVELL, a Page, and Others.

KING RICHARD Stand all apart. Cousin of Buckingham!

BUCKINGHAM My gracious sovereign?
KING RICHARD Give me thy hand.
[*Here he ascendeth the throne. Sound*.
Thus high, by thy advice
And thy assistance, is King Richard seated.
But shall we wear these glories for a day;
Or shall they last, and we rejoice in them?

BUCKINGHAM Still live they, and for ever let them last!

KING RICHARD Ah, Buckingham, now do I play the touch,
To try if thou be current gold indeed.
Young Edward lives – think now what I would speak.

BUCKINGHAM Say on, my loving lord.

KING RICHARD Why, Buckingham, I say I would be King.

BUCKINGHAM Why, so you are, my thrice-renowned lord.

KING RICHARD Ha! am I King? 'Tis so; but Edward lives.

BUCKINGHAM True, noble Prince.

KING RICHARD O bitter consequence:
That Edward still should live – true noble Prince!
Cousin, thou wast not wont to be so dull.
Shall I be plain? I wish the bastards dead.
And I would have it suddenly perform'd.
What say'st thou now? Speak suddenly, be brief.

BUCKINGHAM Your Grace may do your pleasure.

KING RICHARD Tut, tut, thou art all ice; thy kindness freezes.
Say, have I thy consent that they shall die?

BUCKINGHAM Give me some little breath, some pause, dear lord,
Before I positively speak in this.
I will resolve you herein presently. [*Exit*.

CATESBY [*Aside to another*] The King is angry; see, he gnaws his lip.

KING RICHARD I will converse with iron-witted fools. [*Descends from the throne*.
And unrespective boys; none are for me
That look into me with considerate eyes.
High-reaching Buckingham grows circumspect.
Boy!

PAGE My lord?

KING RICHARD Know'st thou not any whom corrupting gold
Will tempt unto a close exploit of death?

PAGE I know a discontented gentleman
Whose humble means match not his haughty spirit.
Gold were as good as twenty orators,
And will, no doubt, tempt him to anything.

KING RICHARD What is his name?

PAGE His name, my lord, is Tyrrel.

KING RICHARD I partly know the man. Go, call him hither, boy. [*Exit Page*.
The deep-revolving witty Buckingham
No more shall be the neighbour to my counsels.
Hath he so long held out with me, untir'd,
And stops he now for breath? Well, be it so.

Enter STANLEY.

How now, Lord Stanley! What's the news?

STANLEY Know, my loving lord,
The Marquis Dorset, as I hear, is fled
To Richmond, in the parts where he abides.
[*Stands apart*.

KING RICHARD Come hither, Catesby. Rumour it abroad
That Anne, my wife, is very grievous sick;
I will take order for her keeping close.
Inquire me out some mean poor gentleman,
Whom I will marry straight to Clarence' daughter –
The boy is foolish, and I fear not him.
Look how thou dream'st! I say again, give out
That Anne, my queen, is sick and like to die.
About it; for it stands me much upon
To stop all hopes whose growth may damage me. [*Exit Catesby*.
I must be married to my brother's daughter,
Or else my kingdom stands on brittle glass.
Murder her brothers, and then marry her!
Uncertain way of gain! But I am in
So far in blood that sin will pluck on sin.
Tear-falling pity dwells not in this eye.

Re-enter Page, with TYRREL.

Is thy name Tyrrel?

TYRREL James Tyrrel, and your most obedient subject.

KING RICHARD Art thou, indeed?

TYRREL Prove me, my gracious lord.

KING RICHARD Dar'st thou resolve to kill a friend of mine?

TYRREL Please you;
But I had rather kill two enemies.

KING RICHARD Why, then thou hast it. Two deep enemies,
Foes to my rest, and my sweet sleep's disturbers,
Are they that I would have thee deal upon.
Tyrrel, I mean those bastards in the Tower.

TYRREL Let me have open means to come to them,
And soon I'll rid you from the fear of them.

KING RICHARD Thou sing'st sweet music. Hark, come hither, Tyrrel.
Go, by this token. Rise, and lend thine ear.
[*Whispers*.

There is no more but so: say it is done,
And I will love thee and prefer thee for it.

TYRREL I will dispatch it straight. [*Exit*.

Re-enter BUCKINGHAM.

BUCKINGHAM My lord, I have consider'd in my mind
The late request that you did sound me in.

KING RICHARD Well, let that rest. Dorset is fled to Richmond.

BUCKINGHAM I hear the news, my lord.

KING RICHARD Stanley, he is your wife's son: well, look unto it.

BUCKINGHAM My lord, I claim the gift, my due by promise,
For which your honour and your faith is pawn'd:
Th' earldom of Hereford and the movables
Which you have promised I shall possess.

KING RICHARD Stanley, look to your wife; if she convey
Letters to Richmond, you shall answer it.

BUCKINGHAM What says your Highness to my just request?

KING RICHARD I do remember me: Henry the Sixth
Did prophesy that Richmond should be King,
When Richmond was a little peevish boy.
A king! – perhaps –

BUCKINGHAM My lord –

KING RICHARD How chance the prophet could not at that time
Have told me, I being by, that I should kill him?

BUCKINGHAM My lord, your promise for the earldom –

KING RICHARD Richmond! When last I was at Exeter,
The mayor in courtesy show'd me the castle
And call'd it Rugemount, at which name I started,
Because a bard of Ireland told me once
I should not live long after I saw Richmond.

BUCKINGHAM My lord –

KING RICHARD Ay, what's o'clock?

BUCKINGHAM I am thus bold to put your Grace in mind
Of what you promis'd me.

KING RICHARD Well, but what's o'clock?

BUCKINGHAM Upon the stroke of ten.

KING RICHARD Well, let it strike.

BUCKINGHAM Why let it strike?

KING RICHARD Because that like a Jack thou keep'st the stroke
Betwixt thy begging and my meditation.
I am not in the giving vein to-day.

BUCKINGHAM May it please you to resolve me in my suit.

KING RICHARD Thou troublest me; I am not in the vein. [*Exeunt all but Buckingham*.

BUCKINGHAM And is it thus? Repays he my deep service
With such contempt? Made I him King for this?
O, let me think on Hastings, and be gone
To Brecknock while my fearful head is on! [*Exit*.

SCENE III. *London. The palace.*

Enter TYRREL.

TYRREL The tyrannous and bloody act is done,
The most arch deed of piteous massacre
That ever yet this land was guilty of.
Dighton and Forrest, who I did suborn
To do this piece of ruthful butchery,
Albeit they were flesh'd villains, bloody dogs,
Melted with tenderness and mild compassion,
Wept like two children in their deaths' sad story.
'O, thus' quoth Dighton 'lay the gentle babes' –
'Thus, thus,' quoth Forrest 'girdling one another
Within their alabaster innocent arms.
Their lips were four red roses on a stalk,
And in their summer beauty kiss'd each other.
A book of prayers on their pillow lay;
Which once,' quoth Forrest 'almost chang'd my mind;
But, O, the devil' – there the villain stopp'd;
When Dighton thus told on: 'We smothered
The most replenished sweet work of nature
That from the prime creation e'er she framed'.
Hence both are gone with conscience and remorse
They could not speak; and so I left them both,
To bear this tidings to the bloody King.

Enter KING RICHARD.

And here he comes. All health, my sovereign lord!

KING RICHARD Kind Tyrrel, am I happy in thy news?

TYRREL If to have done the thing you gave in charge
Beget your happiness, be happy then,
For it is done.

KING RICHARD But didst thou see them dead?

TYRREL I did, my lord.

KING RICHARD And buried, gentle Tyrrel?

TYRREL The chaplain of the Tower hath buried them;
But where, to say the truth, I do not know.

KING RICHARD Come to me, Tyrrel, soon at after supper,

When thou shalt tell the process of their death.
Meantime, but think how I may do thee good
And be inheritor of thy desire.
Farewell till then.

TYRREL I humbly take my leave. [*Exit.*

KING RICHARD The son of Clarence have I pent up close;
His daughter meanly have I match'd in marriage;
The sons of Edward sleep in Abraham's bosom,
And Anne my wife hath bid this world good night.
Now, for I know the Britaine Richmond aims
At young Elizabeth, my brother's daughter,
And by that knot looks proudly on the crown,
To her go I, a jolly thriving wooer.

Enter RATCLIFF.

RATCLIFF My lord!

KING RICHARD Good or bad news, that thou com'st in so bluntly?

RATCLIFF Bad news, my lord: Morton is fled to Richmond;
And Buckingham, back'd with the hardy Welshmen,
Is in the field, and still his power increaseth.

KING RICHARD Ely with Richmond troubles me more near
Than Buckingham and his rash-levied strength.
Come, I have learn'd that fearful commenting
Is leaden servitor to dull delay;
Delay leads impotent and snail-pac'd beggary.
Then fiery expedition be my wing,
Jove's Mercury, and herald for a king!
Go, muster men. My counsel is my shield.
We must be brief when traitors brave the field.
[*Exeunt.*

SCENE IV. *London. Before the palace.*

Enter old QUEEN MARGARET.

QUEEN MARGARET So now prosperity begins to mellow
And drop into the rotten mouth of death.
Here in these confines slily have I lurk'd
To watch the waning of mine enemies.
A dire induction am I witness to,
And will to France, hoping the consequence
Will prove as bitter, black, and tragical.
Withdraw thee, wretched Margaret. Who comes here? [*Retires.*

Enter QUEEN ELIZABETH and the DUCHESS OF YORK.

QUEEN ELIZABETH Ah, my poor princes! ah, my tender babes!
My unblown flowers, new-appearing sweets!
If yet your gentle souls fly in the air
And be not fix'd in doom perpetual,
Hover about me with your airy wings
And hear your mother's lamentation.

QUEEN MARGARET Hover about her; say that right for right
Hath dimm'd your infant morn to aged night.

DUCHESS So many miseries have craz'd my voice
That my woe-wearied tongue is still and mute.
Edward Plantagenet, why art thou dead?

QUEEN MARGARET Plantagenet doth quit Plantagenet,
Edward for Edward pays a dying debt.

QUEEN ELIZABETH Wilt thou, O God, fly from such gentle lambs
And throw them in the entrails of the wolf?
When didst thou sleep when such a deed was done?

QUEEN MARGARET When holy Harry died, and my sweet son.

DUCHESS Dead life, blind sight, poor mortal living ghost,
Woe's scene, world's shame, grave's due by life usurp'd,
Brief abstract and record of tedious days,
Rest thy unrest on England's lawful earth, [*Sitting down.*
Unlawfully made drunk with innocent blood.

QUEEN ELIZABETH Ah, that thou wouldst as soon afford a grave
As thou canst yield a melancholy seat!
Then would I hide my bones, not rest them here.
Ah, who hath any cause to mourn but we?
[*Sitting down by her.*

QUEEN MARGARET [*Coming forward*] If ancient sorrow be most reverend,
Give mine the benefit of seniory,
And let my griefs frown on the upper hand.
If sorrow can admit society,
[*Sitting down with them.*
Tell o'er your woes again by viewing mine.
I had an Edward, till a Richard kill'd him;
I had a husband, till a Richard kill'd him:
Thou hadst an Edward, till a Richard kill'd him;
Thou hadst a Richard, till a Richard kill'd him.

DUCHESS I had a Richard too, and thou didst kill him;
I had a Rutland too, thou holp'st to kill him.

QUEEN MARGARET Thou hadst a Clarence too, and Richard kill'd him.
From forth the kennel of thy womb hath crept
A hell-hound that doth hunt us all to death.
That dog, that had his teeth before his eyes

To worry lambs and lap their gentle blood,
That foul defacer of God's handiwork,
That excellent grand tyrant of the earth
That reigns in galled eyes of weeping souls,
Thy womb let loose to chase us to our graves.
O upright, just, and true-disposing God,
How do I thank thee that this carnal cur
Preys on the issue of his mother's body
And makes her pew-fellow with others' moan!

DUCHESS O Harry's wife, triumph not in my woes!
God witness with me, I have wept for thine.

QUEEN MARGARET Bear with me; I am hungry for revenge,
And now I cloy me with beholding it.
Thy Edward he is dead, that kill'd my Edward;
The other Edward dead, to quit my Edward;
Young York he is but boot, because both they
Match'd not the high perfection of my loss.
Thy Clarence he is dead that stabb'd my Edward;
And the beholders of this frantic play,
Th' adulterate Hastings, Rivers, Vaughan, Grey,
Untimely smother'd in their dusky graves.
Richard yet lives, hell's black intelligencer;
Only reserv'd their factor to buy souls
And send them thither. But at hand, at hand,
Ensues his piteous and unpitied end.
Earth gapes, hell burns, fiends roar, saints pray,
To have him suddenly convey'd from hence.
Cancel his bond of life, dear God, I pray,
That I may live and say 'The dog is dead'.

QUEEN ELIZABETH O, thou didst prophesy the time would come
That I should wish for thee to help me curse
That bottled spider, that foul bunch-back'd toad!

QUEEN MARGARET I call'd thee then vain flourish of my fortune;
I call'd thee then poor shadow, painted queen,
The presentation of but what I was,
The flattering index of a direful pageant,
One heav'd a-high to be hurl'd down below,
A mother only mock'd with two fair babes,
A dream of what thou wast, a garish flag
To be the aim of every dangerous shot,
A sign of dignity, a breath, a bubble,
A queen in jest, only to fill the scene.
Where is thy husband now? Where be thy brothers?
Where be thy two sons? Wherein dost thou joy?
Who sues, and kneels, and says 'God save the Queen'?
Where be the bending peers that flattered thee?
Where be the thronging troops that followed thee?
Decline all this, and see what now thou art:
For happy wife, a most distressed widow;
For joyful mother, one that wails the name;
For one being su'd to, one that humbly sues;
For Queen, a very caitiff crown'd with care;
For she that scorn'd at me, now scorn'd of me;
For she being fear'd of all, now fearing one;
For she commanding all, obey'd of none.
Thus hath the course of justice whirl'd about
And left thee but a very prey to time,
Having no more but thought of what thou wast
To torture thee the more, being what thou art.
Thou didst usurp my place, and dost thou not
Usurp the just proportion of my sorrow?
Now thy proud neck bears half my burden'd yoke,
From which even here I slip my weary head
And leave the burden of it all on thee.
Farewell, York's wife, and queen of sad mischance;
These English woes shall make me smile in France.

QUEEN ELIZABETH O thou well skill'd in curses, stay awhile
And teach me how to curse mine enemies!

QUEEN MARGARET Forbear to sleep the nights, and fast the days;
Compare dead happiness with living woe;
Think that thy babes were sweeter than they were,
And he that slew them fouler than he is.
Bett'ring thy loss makes the bad-causer worse;
Revolving this will teach thee how to curse.

QUEEN ELIZABETH My words are dull; O, quicken them with thine!

QUEEN MARGARET Thy woes will make them sharp and pierce like mine. *[Exit.*

DUCHESS Why should calamity be full of words?

QUEEN ELIZABETH Windy attorneys to their client woes,
Airy succeeders of intestate joys,
Poor breathing orators of miseries,
Let them have scope; though what they will impart
Help nothing else, yet do they ease the heart.

DUCHESS If so, then be not tongue-tied. Go with me,
And in the breath of bitter words let's smother
My damned son that thy two sweet sons smother'd.
The trumpet sounds; be copious in exclaims.

Enter KING RICHARD and his Train, marching with drums and trumpets.

KING RICHARD Who intercepts me in my expedition?

DUCHESS O, she that might have intercepted thee,

By strangling thee in her accursed womb,
From all the slaughters, wretch, that thou hast done!

QUEEN ELIZABETH Hidest thou that forehead with a golden crown
Where should be branded, if that right were right,
The slaughter of the Prince that ow'd that crown,
And the dire death of my poor sons and brothers?
Tell me, thou villain slave, where are my children?

DUCHESS Thou toad, thou toad, where is thy brother Clarence?
And little Ned Plantagenet, his son?

QUEEN ELIZABETH Where is the gentle Rivers, Vaughan, Grey?

DUCHESS Where is kind Hastings?

KING RICHARD A flourish, trumpets! Strike alarum, drums!
Let not the heavens hear these tell-tale women
Rail on the Lord's anointed. Strike, I say!
[*Flourish. Alarums.*
Either be patient and entreat me fair,
Or with the clamorous report of war
Thus will I drown your exclamations.

DUCHESS Art thou my son?

KING RICHARD Ay, I thank God, my father, and yourself.

DUCHESS Then patiently hear my impatience.

KING RICHARD Madam, I have a touch of your condition
That cannot brook the accent of reproof.

DUCHESS O, let me speak!

KING RICHARD Do, then; but I'll not hear.

DUCHESS I will be mild and gentle in my words.

KING RICHARD And brief, good mother; for I am in haste.

DUCHESS Art thou so hasty? I have stay'd for thee,
God knows, in torment and in agony.

KING RICHARD And came I not at last to comfort you?

DUCHESS No, by the holy rood, thou know'st it well
Thou cam'st on earth to make the earth my hell.
A grievous burden was thy birth to me;
Tetchy and wayward was thy infancy;
Thy school-days frightful, desp'rate, wild, and furious;
Thy prime of manhood daring, bold, and venturous;
Thy age confirm'd, proud, subtle, sly, and bloody,
More mild, but yet more harmful-kind in hatred.
What comfortable hour canst thou name
That ever grac'd me with thy company?

KING RICHARD Faith, none but Humphrey Hour, that call'd your Grace
To breakfast once forth of my company.
If I be so disgracious in your eye,
Let me march on and not offend you, madam.
Strike up the drum.

DUCHESS I prithee hear me speak.

KING RICHARD You speak too bitterly.

DUCHESS Hear me a word;
For I shall never speak to thee again.

KING RICHARD So.

DUCHESS Either thou wilt die by God's just ordinance
Ere from this war thou turn a conqueror;
Or I with grief and extreme age shall perish
And never more behold thy face again.
Therefore take with thee my most grievous curse,
Which in the day of battle tire thee more
Than all the complete armour that thou wear'st!
My prayers on the adverse party fight;
And there the little souls of Edward's children
Whisper the spirits of thine enemies
And promise them success and victory.
Bloody thou art; bloody will be thy end.
Shame serves thy life and doth thy death attend.
[*Exit.*

QUEEN ELIZABETH Though far more cause, yet much less spirit to curse
Abides in me; I say amen to her.

KING RICHARD Stay, madam, I must talk a word with you.

QUEEN ELIZABETH I have no moe sons of the royal blood
For thee to slaughter. For my daughters, Richard,
They shall be praying nuns, not weeping queens;
And therefore level not to hit their lives.

KING RICHARD You have a daughter call'd Elizabeth,
Virtuous and fair, royal and gracious.

QUEEN ELIZABETH And must she die for this? O, let her live,
And I'll corrupt her manners, stain her beauty,
Slander myself as false to Edward's bed,
Throw over her the veil of infamy;
So she may live unscarr'd of bleeding slaughter,
I will confess she was not Edward's daughter.

KING RICHARD Wrong not her birth; she is a royal Princess.

QUEEN ELIZABETH To save her life I'll say she is not so.

KING RICHARD Her life is safest only in her birth.
QUEEN ELIZABETH And only in that safety died her brothers.
KING RICHARD Lo, at their birth good stars were opposite.
QUEEN ELIZABETH No, to their lives ill friends were contrary.
KING RICHARD All unavoided is the doom of destiny.
QUEEN ELIZABETH True, when avoided grace makes destiny.
My babes were destin'd to a fairer death,
If grace had bless'd thee with a fairer life.
KING RICHARD You speak as if that I had slain my cousins.
QUEEN ELIZABETH Cousins, indeed; and by their uncle cozen'd
Of comfort, kingdom, kindred, freedom, life.
Whose hand soever lanc'd their tender hearts,
Thy head, all indirectly, gave direction.
No doubt the murd'rous knife was dull and blunt
Till it was whetted on thy stone-hard heart
To revel in the entrails of my lambs.
But that still use of grief makes wild grief tame,
My tongue should to thy ears not name my boys
Till that my nails were anchor'd in thine eyes;
And I, in such a desp'rate bay of death,
Like a poor bark, of sails and tackling reft,
Rush all to pieces on thy rocky bosom.
KING RICHARD Madam, so thrive I in my enterprise
And dangerous success of bloody wars,
As I intend more good to you or yours
Than ever you or yours by me were harm'd!
QUEEN ELIZABETH What good is cover'd with the face of heaven,
To be discover'd, that can do me good?
KING RICHARD Th' advancement of your children, gentle lady.
QUEEN ELIZABETH Up to some scaffold, there to lose their heads?
KING RICHARD Unto the dignity and height of Fortune,
The high imperial type of this earth's glory.
QUEEN ELIZABETH Flatter my sorrow with report of it;
Tell me what state, what dignity, what honour,
Canst thou demise to any child of mine?
KING RICHARD Even all I have – ay, and myself and all
Will I withal endow a child of thine;
So in the Lethe of thy angry soul
Thou drown the sad remembrance of those wrongs
Which thou supposest I have done to thee.
QUEEN ELIZABETH Be brief, lest that the process of thy kindness
Last longer telling than thy kindness' date.
KING RICHARD Then know, that from my soul I love thy daughter.
QUEEN ELIZABETH My daughter's mother thinks it with her soul.
KING RICHARD What do you think?
QUEEN ELIZABETH That thou dost love my daughter from thy soul.
So from thy soul's love didst thou love her brothers,
And from my heart's love I do thank thee for it.
KING RICHARD Be not so hasty to confound my meaning.
I mean that with my soul I love thy daughter
And do intend to make her Queen of England.
QUEEN ELIZABETH Well, then, who dost thou mean shall be her king?
KING RICHARD Even he that makes her Queen. Who else should be?
QUEEN ELIZABETH What, thou?
KING RICHARD Even so. How think you of it?
QUEEN ELIZABETH How canst thou woo her?
KING RICHARD That would I learn of you,
As one being best acquainted with her humour.
QUEEN ELIZABETH And wilt thou learn of me?
KING RICHARD Madam, with all my heart.
QUEEN ELIZABETH Send to her, by the man that slew her brothers,
A pair of bleeding hearts; thereon engrave
'Edward' and 'York'. Then haply will she weep;
Therefore present to her – as sometimes Margaret
Did to thy father, steep'd in Rutland's blood –
A handkerchief; which, say to her, did drain
The purple sap from her sweet brother's body,
And bid her wipe her weeping eyes withal.
If this inducement move her not to love,
Send her a letter of thy noble deeds;
Tell her thou made'st away her uncle Clarence,
Her uncle Rivers; ay, and for her sake
Mad'st quick conveyance with her good aunt Anne.
KING RICHARD You mock me, madam; this is not the way
To win your daughter.
QUEEN ELIZABETH There is no other way;
Unless thou couldst put on some other shape
And not be Richard that hath done all this.
KING RICHARD Say that I did all this for love of her.
QUEEN ELIZABETH Nay, then indeed she cannot choose but hate thee,
Having bought love with such a bloody spoil.
KING RICHARD Look what is done cannot be now amended.
Men shall deal unadvisedly sometimes,

Which after-hours gives leisure to repent.
If I did take the kingdom from your sons,
To make amends I'll give it to your daughter.
If I have kill'd the issue of your womb,
To quicken your increase I will beget
Mine issue of your blood upon your daughter.
A grandam's name is little less in love
Than is the doating title of a mother;
They are as children but one step below,
Even of your metal, of your very blood;
Of all one pain, save for a night of groans
Endur'd of her, for whom you bid like sorrow.
Your children were vexation to your youth;
But mine shall be a comfort to your age.
The loss you have is but a son being King,
And by that loss your daughter is made Queen.
I cannot make you what amends I would,
Therefore accept such kindness as I can.
Dorset your son, that with a fearful soul
Leads discontented steps in foreign soil,
This fair alliance quickly shall call home
To high promotions and great dignity.
The King, that calls your beauteous daughter wife,
Familiarly shall call thy Dorset brother;
Again shall you be mother to a king,
And all the ruins of distressful times
Repair'd with double riches of content.
What! we have many goodly days to see.
The liquid drops of tears that you have shed
Shall come again, transform'd to orient pearl,
Advantaging their loan with interest
Of ten times double gain of happiness.
Go, then, my mother, to thy daughter go;
Make bold her bashful years with your experience;
Prepare her ears to hear a wooer's tale;
Put in her tender heart th' aspiring flame
Of golden sovereignty; acquaint the Princess
With the sweet silent hours of marriage joys.
And when this arm of mine hath chastised
The petty rebel, dull-brain'd Buckingham,
Bound with triumphant garlands will I come,
And lead thy daughter to a conqueror's bed;
To whom I will retail my conquest won,
And she shall be sole victoress, Caesar's Caesar.

QUEEN ELIZABETH What were I best to say? Her father's brother
Would be her lord? Or shall I say her uncle?
Or he that slew her brothers and her uncles?
Under what title shall I woo for thee
That God, the law, my honour, and her love
Can make seem pleasing to her tender years?

KING RICHARD Infer fair England's peace by this alliance.

QUEEN ELIZABETH Which she shall purchase with still-lasting war.

KING RICHARD Tell her the King, that may command, entreats.

QUEEN ELIZABETH That at her hands which the King's King forbids.

KING RICHARD Say she shall be a high and mighty queen.

QUEEN ELIZABETH To wail the title, as her mother doth.

KING RICHARD Say I will love her everlastingly.

QUEEN ELIZABETH But how long shall that title 'ever' last?

KING RICHARD Sweetly in force unto her fair life's end.

QUEEN ELIZABETH But how long fairly shall her sweet life last?

KING RICHARD As long as heaven and nature lengthens it.

QUEEN ELIZABETH As long as hell and Richard likes of it.

KING RICHARD Say I, her sovereign, am her subject low.

QUEEN ELIZABETH But she, your subject, loathes such sovereignty.

KING RICHARD Be eloquent in my behalf to her.

QUEEN ELIZABETH An honest tale speeds best being plainly told.

KING RICHARD Then plainly to her tell my loving tale.

QUEEN ELIZABETH Plain and not honest is too harsh a style.

KING RICHARD Your reasons are too shallow and too quick.

QUEEN ELIZABETH O, no, my reasons are too deep and dead –
Too deep and dead, poor infants, in their graves.

KING RICHARD Harp not on that string, madam; that is past.

QUEEN ELIZABETH Harp on it still shall I till heartstrings break.

KING RICHARD Now, by my George, my garter, and my crown –

QUEEN ELIZABETH Profan'd, dishonour'd, and the third usurp'd.

KING RICHARD I swear –

QUEEN ELIZABETH By nothing; for this is no oath:
Thy George, profan'd, hath lost his lordly honour;
Thy garter, blemish'd, pawn'd his knightly virtue;
Thy crown, usurp'd, disgrac'd his kingly glory.
If something thou wouldst swear to be believ'd,
Swear then by something that thou hast not wrong'd.

KING RICHARD Then, by my self –

QUEEN ELIZABETH Thy self is self-misus'd.

KING RICHARD Now, by the world –
QUEEN ELIZABETH 'Tis full of thy foul wrongs.
KING RICHARD My father's death –
QUEEN ELIZABETH Thy life hath it dishonour'd.
KING RICHARD Why, then, by God –
QUEEN ELIZABETH God's wrong is most of all.
If thou didst fear to break an oath with Him,
The unity the King my husband made
Thou hadst not broken, nor my brothers died.
If thou hadst fear'd to break an oath by Him,
Th' imperial metal, circling now thy head,
Had grac'd the tender temples of my child;
And both the Princes had been breathing here,
Which now, two tender bedfellows for dust,
Thy broken faith hath made the prey for worms.
What canst thou swear by now?
KING RICHARD The time to come.
QUEEN ELIZABETH That thou hast wronged in the time o'erpast;
For I myself have many tears to wash
Hereafter time, for time past wrong'd by thee.
The children live whose fathers thou hast slaughter'd,
Ungovern'd youth, to wail it in their age;
The parents live whose children thou hast butcher'd,
Old barren plants, to wail it with their age.
Swear not by time to come; for that thou hast
Misus'd ere us'd, by times ill-us'd o'erpast.
KING RICHARD As I intend to prosper and repent,
So thrive I in my dangerous affairs
Of hostile arms! Myself myself confound!
Heaven and fortune bar me happy hours!
Day, yield me not thy light; nor, night, thy rest!
Be opposite all planets of good luck
To my proceeding! – if, with dear heart's love,
Immaculate devotion, holy thoughts,
I tender not thy beauteous princely daughter.
In her consists my happiness and thine;
Without her, follows to myself and thee,
Herself, the land, and many a Christian soul,
Death, desolation, ruin, and decay.
It cannot be avoided but by this;
It will not be avoided but by this.
Therefore, dear mother – I must call you so –
Be the attorney of my love to her;
Plead what I will be, not what I have been;
Not my deserts, but what I will deserve.
Urge the necessity and state of times,
And be not peevish-fond in great designs.
QUEEN ELIZABETH Shall I be tempted of the devil thus?
KING RICHARD Ay, if the devil tempt you to do good.
QUEEN ELIZABETH Shall I forget myself to be myself?
KING RICHARD Ay, if your self's remembrance wrong yourself.
QUEEN ELIZABETH Yet thou didst kill my children.
KING RICHARD But in your daughter's womb I bury them;
Where, in that nest of spicery, they will breed
Selves of themselves, to your recomforture.
QUEEN ELIZABETH Shall I go win my daughter to thy will?
KING RICHARD And be a happy mother by the deed.
QUEEN ELIZABETH I go. Write to me very shortly,
And you shall understand from me her mind.
KING RICHARD Bear her my true love's kiss; and so, farewell.
[*Kissing her. Exit Queen Elizabeth.*
Relenting fool, and shallow, changing woman!

Enter RATCLIFF; CATESBY following.

How now! what news?
RATCLIFF Most mighty sovereign, on the western coast
Rideth a puissant navy; to our shores
Throng many doubtful hollow-hearted friends,
Unarm'd, and unresolv'd to beat them back.
'Tis thought that Richmond is their admiral;
And there they hull, expecting but the aid
Of Buckingham to welcome them ashore.
KING RICHARD Some light-foot friend post to the Duke of Norfolk.
Ratcliff, thyself – or Catesby; where is he?
CATESBY Here, my good lord.
KING RICHARD Catesby, fly to the Duke.
CATESBY I will, my lord, with all convenient haste.
KING RICHARD Ratcliff, come hither. Post to Salisbury;
When thou com'st thither – [*To Catesby*] Dull, unmindful villain,
Why stay'st thou here, and go'st not to the Duke?
CATESBY First, mighty liege, tell me your Highness' pleasure,
What from your Grace I shall deliver to him.
KING RICHARD O, true, good Catesby. Bid him levy straight
The greatest strength and power that he can make
And meet me suddenly at Salisbury.
CATESBY I go. [*Exit.*
RATCLIFF What, may it please you, shall I do at Salisbury?
KING RICHARD Why, what wouldst thou do there before I go?
RATCLIFF Your Highness told me I should post before.

KING RICHARD My mind is chang'd.
Enter LORD STANLEY.
Stanley, what news with you.
STANLEY None good, my liege, to please you with the hearing;
Nor none so bad but well may be reported.
KING RICHARD Hoyday, a riddle! neither good nor bad!
What need'st thou run so many miles about,
When thou mayest tell thy tale the nearest way?
Once more, what news?
STANLEY Richmond is on the seas.
KING RICHARD There let him sink, and be the seas on him!
White-liver'd runagate, what doth he there?
STANLEY I know not, mighty sovereign, but by guess.
KING RICHARD Well, as you guess?
STANLEY Stirr'd up by Dorset, Buckingham, and Morton,
He makes for England here to claim the crown.
KING RICHARD Is the chair empty? Is the sword unsway'd?
Is the King dead, the empire unpossess'd?
What heir of York is there alive but we?
And who is England's King but great York's heir?
Then tell me what makes he upon the seas.
STANLEY Unless for that, my liege, I cannot guess.
KING RICHARD Unless for that he comes to be your liege,
You cannot guess wherefore the Welshman comes.
Thou wilt revolt and fly to him, I fear.
STANLEY No, my good lord; therefore mistrust me not.
KING RICHARD Where is thy power then, to beat him back?
Where be thy tenants and thy followers?
Are they not now upon the western shore,
Safe-conducting the rebels from their ships?
STANLEY No, my good lord, my friends are in the north.
KING RICHARD Cold friends to me. What do they in the north,
When they should serve their sovereign in the west?
STANLEY They have not been commanded, mighty King.
Pleaseth your Majesty to give me leave,
I'll muster up my friends and meet your Grace
Where and what time your Majesty shall please.
KING RICHARD Ay, ay, thou wouldst be gone to join with Richmond;
But I'll not trust thee.
STANLEY Most mighty sovereign,
You have no cause to hold my friendship doubtful.
I never was nor never will be false.
KING RICHARD Go, then, and muster men. But leave behind
Your son, George Stanley. Look your heart be firm,
Or else his head's assurance is but frail.
STANLEY So deal with him as I prove true to you.
[*Exit.*

Enter a Messenger.

MESSENGER My gracious sovereign, now in Devonshire,
As I by friends am well advertised,
Sir Edward Courtney and the haughty prelate,
Bishop of Exeter, his elder brother,
With many moe confederates, are in arms.

Enter another Messenger.

2 MESSENGER In Kent, my liege, the Guilfords are in arms;
And every hour more competitors
Flock to the rebels, and their power grows strong.

Enter another Messenger.

3 MESSENGER My lord, the army of great Buckingham –
KING RICHARD Out on you, owls! Nothing but songs of death? [*He strikes him.*
There, take thou that till thou bring better news.
3 MESSENGER The news I have to tell your Majesty
Is that by sudden floods and fall of waters
Buckingham's army is dispers'd and scatter'd;
And he himself wand'red away alone,
No man knows whither.
KING RICHARD I cry thee mercy.
There is my purse to cure that blow of thine.
Hath any well-advised friend proclaim'd
Reward to him that brings the traitor in?
3 MESSENGER Such proclamation hath been made, my lord.

Enter another Messenger.

4 MESSENGER Sir Thomas Lovel and Lord Marquis Dorset,
'Tis said, my liege, in Yorkshire are in arms.
But this good comfort bring I to your Highness –
The Britaine navy is dispers'd by tempest.
Richmond in Dorsetshire sent out a boat
Unto the shore, to ask those on the banks
If they were his assistants, yea or no;
Who answer'd him they came from Buckingham

Upon his party. He, mistrusting them,
Hois'd sail, and made his course again for Britaine.

KING RICHARD March on, march on, since we are up in arms;
If not to fight with foreign enemies,
Yet to beat down these rebels here at home.

Re-enter CATESBY.

CATESBY My liege, the Duke of Buckingham is taken –
That is the best news. That the Earl of Richmond
Is with a mighty power landed at Milford
Is colder tidings, but yet they must be told.

KING RICHARD Away towards Salisbury! While we reason here
A royal battle might be won and lost.
Some one take order Buckingham be brought
To Salisbury; the rest march on with me.
[Flourish. Exeunt.

SCENE V. *Lord Derby's house.*

Enter STANLEY and SIR CHRISTOPHER URSWICK.

STANLEY Sir Christopher, tell Richmond this from me:
That in the sty of the most deadly boar
My son George Stanley is frank'd up in hold;
If I revolt, off goes young George's head;
The fear of that holds off my present aid.
So, get thee gone; commend me to thy lord.
Withal say that the Queen hath heartily consented
He should espouse Elizabeth her daughter.
But tell me, where is princely Richmond now?

CHRISTOPHER At Pembroke, or at Ha'rford west in Wales.

STANLEY What men of name resort to him?

CHRISTOPHER Sir Walter Herbert, a renowned soldier;
Sir Gilbert Talbot, Sir William Stanley,
Oxford, redoubted Pembroke, Sir James Blunt,
And Rice ap Thomas, with a valiant crew;
And many other of great name and worth;
And towards London do they bend their power,
If by the way they be not fought withal.

STANLEY Well, hie thee to thy lord; I kiss his hand;
My letter will resolve him of my mind.
Farewell. *[Exeunt.*

ACT FIVE

SCENE I. *Salisbury. An open place.*

Enter the Sheriff and Guard, with BUCKINGHAM, led to execution.

BUCKINGHAM Will not King Richard let me speak with him?

SHERIFF No, my good lord; therefore be patient.

BUCKINGHAM Hastings, and Edward's children, Grey, and Rivers,
Holy King Henry, and thy fair son Edward,
Vaughan, and all that have miscarried
By underhand corrupted foul injustice,
If that your moody discontented souls
Do through the clouds behold this present hour,
Even for revenge mock my destruction!
This is All-Souls' day, fellow, is it not?

SHERIFF It is, my lord.

BUCKINGHAM Why, then All-Souls' day is my body's doomsday.
This is the day which in King Edward's time
I wish'd might fall on me when I was found
False to his children and his wife's allies;
This is the day wherein I wish'd to fall
By the false faith of him whom most I trusted;
This, this All-Souls' day to my fearful soul
Is the determin'd respite of my wrongs;
That high All-Seer which I dallied with
Hath turn'd my feigned prayer on my head
And given in earnest what I begg'd in jest.
Thus doth He force the swords of wicked men
To turn their own points in their masters' bosoms.
Thus Margaret's curse falls heavy on my neck.
'When he' quoth she 'shall split thy heart with sorrow,
Remember Margaret was a prophetess.'
Come lead me, officers, to the block of shame;
Wrong hath but wrong, and blame the due of blame.
[Exeunt.

SCENE II. *Camp near Tamworth.*

Enter RICHMOND, OXFORD, SIR JAMES BLUNT, SIR WALTER HERBERT, and Others, with drum and colours.

RICHMOND Fellows in arms, and my most loving friends,
Bruis'd underneath the yoke of tyranny,
Thus far into the bowels of the land
Have we march'd on without impediment;
And here receive we from our father Stanley
Lines of fair comfort and encouragement.
The wretched, bloody, and usurping boar,

That spoil'd your summer fields and fruitful vines,
Swills your warm blood like wash, and makes his trough
In your embowell'd bosoms – this foul swine
Is now even in the centre of this isle,
Near to the town of Leicester, as we learn.
From Tamworth thither is but one day's march.
In God's name cheerly on, courageous friends,
To reap the harvest of perpetual peace
By this one bloody trial of sharp war.

OXFORD Every man's conscience is a thousand men,
To fight against this guilty homicide.

HERBERT I doubt not but his friends will turn to us.

BLUNT He hath no friends but what are friends for fear,
Which in his dearest need will fly from him.

RICHMOND All for our vantage. Then in God's name march.
True hope is swift and flies with swallow's wings;
Kings it makes gods, and meaner creatures kings. *[Exeunt.*

SCENE III. *Bosworth Field.*

Enter KING RICHARD in arms, with NORFOLK, RATCLIFF, the EARL OF SURREY, and Others.

KING RICHARD Here pitch our tent, even here in Bosworth field.
My Lord of Surrey, why look you so sad?

SURREY My heart is ten times lighter than my looks.

KING RICHARD My Lord of Norfolk!

NORFOLK Here, most gracious liege.

KING RICHARD Norfolk, we must have knocks; ha! must we not?

NORFOLK We must both give and take, my loving lord.

KING RICHARD Up with my tent! Here will I lie to-night;
[Soldiers begin to set up the King's tent.
But where to-morrow? Well, all's one for that.
Who hath descried the number of the traitors?

NORFOLK Six or seven thousand is their utmost power.

KING RICHARD Why, our battalia trebles that account;
Besides, the King's name is a tower of strength,
Which they upon the adverse faction want.
Up with the tent! Come, noble gentlemen,
Let us survey the vantage of the ground.
Call for some men of sound direction.
Let's lack no discipline, make no delay;
For, lords, to-morrow is a busy day. *[Exeunt.*

Enter, on the other side of the Field, RICHMOND, SIR WILLIAM BRANDON, OXFORD, DORSET, and Others. Some pitch Richmond's tent.

RICHMOND The weary sun hath made a golden set,
And by the bright tract of his fiery car
Gives token of a goodly day to-morrow.
Sir William Brandon, you shall bear my standard.
Give me some ink and paper in my tent.
I'll draw the form and model of our battle,
Limit each leader to his several charge,
And part in just proportion our small power.
My Lord of Oxford – you, Sir William Brandon –
And you, Sir Walter Herbert – stay with me.
The Earl of Pembroke keeps his regiment;
Good Captain Blunt, bear my good night to him,
And by the second hour in the morning
Desire the Earl to see me in my tent.
Yet one thing more, good Captain, do for me –
Where is Lord Stanley quarter'd, do you know?

BLUNT Unless I have mista'en his colours much –
Which well I am assur'd I have not done –
His regiment lies half a mile at least
South from the mighty power of the King.

RICHMOND If without peril it be possible,
Sweet Blunt, make some good means to speak with him
And give him from me this most needful note.

BLUNT Upon my life, my lord, I'll undertake it;
And so, God give you quiet rest to-night!

RICHMOND Good night, good Captain Blunt. Come, gentlemen,
Let us consult upon to-morrow's business.
In to my tent; the dew is raw and cold.
[They withdraw into the tent.

Enter, to his tent, KING RICHARD, NORFOLK, RATCLIFF, and CATESBY.

KING RICHARD What is't o'clock?

CATESBY It's supper-time, my lord;
It's nine o'clock.

KING RICHARD I will not sup to-night.
Give me some ink and paper.
What, is my beaver easier than it was?
And all my armour laid into my tent?

CATESBY It is, my liege; and all things are in readiness.

KING RICHARD Good Norfolk, hie thee to thy charge;
Use careful watch, choose trusty sentinels.

NORFOLK I go, my lord.

KING RICHARD Stir with the lark to-morrow, gentle Norfolk.

NORFOLK I warrant you, my lord. *[Exit.*

KING RICHARD Catesby!

CATESBY My lord?

KING RICHARD Send out a pursuivant-at-arms
To Stanley's regiment; bid him bring his power
Before sunrising, lest his son George fall
Into the blind cave of eternal night.
[Exit Catesby.
Fill me a bowl of wine. Give me a watch.
Saddle white Surrey for the field to-morrow.
Look that my staves be sound, and not too heavy.
Ratcliff!

RATCLIFF My lord?

KING RICHARD Saw'st thou the melancholy Lord Northumberland?

RATCLIFF Thomas the Earl of Surrey and himself,
Much about cock-shut time, from troop to troop
Went through the army, cheering up the soldiers.

KING RICHARD So, I am satisfied. Give me a bowl of wine.
I have not that alacrity of spirit
Nor cheer of mind that I was wont to have.
Set it down. Is ink and paper ready?

RATCLIFF It is, my lord.

KING RICHARD Bid my guard watch; leave me.
Ratcliff, about the mid of night come to my tent
And help to arm me. Leave me, I say.
[Exit Ratcliff. Richard sleeps.

Enter DERBY to RICHMOND in his tent; LORDS attending.

DERBY Fortune and victory sit on thy helm!

RICHMOND All comfort that the dark night can afford
Be to thy person, noble father-in-law!
Tell me, how fares our loving mother?

DERBY I, by attorney, bless thee from thy mother,
Who prays continually for Richmond's good.
So much for that. The silent hours steal on,
And flaky darkness breaks within the east.
In brief, for so the season bids us be,
Prepare thy battle early in the morning,
And put thy fortune to the arbitrement
Of bloody strokes and mortal-staring war.
I, as I may – that which I would I cannot –
With best advantage will deceive the time
And aid thee in this doubtful shock of arms;
But on thy side I may not be too forward,
Lest, being seen, thy brother, tender George,
Be executed in his father's sight.
Farewell; the leisure and the fearful time
Cuts off the ceremonious vows of love
And ample interchange of sweet discourse
Which so-long-sund'red friends should dwell upon.
God give us leisure for these rites of love!
Once more, adieu; be valiant, and speed well!

RICHMOND Good lords, conduct him to his regiment.
I'll strive with troubled thoughts to take a nap,
Lest leaden slumber peise me down to-morrow
When I should mount with wings of victory.
Once more, good night, kind lords and gentlemen. *[Exeunt all but Richmond.*
O Thou, whose captain I account myself,
Look on my forces with a gracious eye;
Put in their hands Thy bruising irons of wrath,
That they may crush down with a heavy fall
The usurping helmets of our adversaries!
Make us Thy ministers of chastisement,
That we may praise Thee in the victory!
To Thee I do commend my watchful soul
Ere I let fall the windows of mine eyes.
Sleeping and waking, O, defend me still!
[Sleeps.

Enter the Ghost of young PRINCE EDWARD, son to Henry the Sixth.

GHOST *[To Richard]* Let me sit heavy on thy soul to-morrow!
Think how thou stabb'dst me in my prime of youth
At Tewksbury; despair, therefore, and die!
[To Richmond] Be cheerful, Richmond; for the wronged souls
Of butcher'd princes fight in thy behalf.
King Henry's issue, Richmond, comforts thee.

Enter the Ghost of HENRY THE SIXTH.

GHOST *[To Richard]* When I was mortal, my anointed body
By thee was punched full of deadly holes.
Think on the Tower and me. Despair, and die.
Harry the Sixth bids thee despair and die.
[To Richmond] Virtuous and holy, be thou conqueror!
Harry, that prophesied thou shouldst be King,
Doth comfort thee in thy sleep. Live and flourish!

Enter the Ghost of CLARENCE.

GHOST *[To Richard]* Let me sit heavy in thy soul to-morrow!
I that was wash'd to death with fulsome wine,
Poor Clarence, by thy guile betray'd to death!
To-morrow in the battle think on me,
And fall thy edgeless sword. Despair and die!
[To Richmond] Thou offspring of the house of Lancaster,
The wronged heirs of York do pray for thee.
Good angels guard thy battle! Live and flourish!

Enter the Ghosts of RIVERS, GREY, and VAUGHAN.

RIVERS [*To Richard*] Let me sit heavy in thy soul to-morrow,
Rivers that died at Pomfret! Despair and die!

GREY [*To Richard*] Think upon Grey, and let thy soul despair!

VAUGHAN [*To Richard*] Think upon Vaughan, and with guilty fear
Let fall thy lance. Despair and die!

ALL [*To Richmond*] Awake, and think our wrongs in Richard's bosom
Will conquer him. Awake and win the day.

Enter the Ghost of HASTINGS.

GHOST [*To Richard*] Bloody and guilty, guiltily awake,
And in a bloody battle end thy days!
Think on Lord Hastings. Despair and die.
[*To Richmond*] Quiet untroubled soul, awake, awake!
Arm, fight, and conquer, for fair England's sake!

Enter the Ghosts of the two young Princes.

GHOSTS [*To Richard*] Dream on thy cousins smothered in the Tower.
Let us be lead within thy bosom, Richard,
And weigh thee down to ruin, shame, and death!
Thy nephews' souls bid thee despair and die.
[*To Richmond*] Sleep, Richmond, sleep in peace, and wake in joy;
Good angels guard thee from the boar's annoy!
Live, and beget a happy race of kings!
Edward's unhappy sons do bid thee flourish.

Enter the Ghost of LADY ANNE, his wife.

GHOST [*To Richard*] Richard, thy wife, that wretched Anne thy wife
That never slept a quiet hour with thee
Now fills thy sleep with perturbations.
To-morrow in the battle think on me,
And fall thy edgeless sword. Despair and die.
[*To Richmond*] Thou quiet soul, sleep thou a quiet sleep;
Dream of success and happy victory.
Thy adversary's wife doth pray for thee.

Enter the Ghost of BUCKINGHAM.

GHOST [*To Richard*] The first was I that help'd thee to the crown;
The last was I that felt thy tyranny.
O, in the battle think on Buckingham,
And die in terror of thy guiltiness!
Dream on, dream on of bloody deeds and death;
Fainting, despair; despairing, yield thy breath!
[*To Richmond*] I died for hope ere I could lend thee aid;
But cheer thy heart and be thou not dismay'd:
God and good angels fight on Richmond's side;
And Richard falls in height of all his pride.

[*The Ghosts vanish. Richard starts out of his dream.*

KING RICHARD Give me another horse. Bind up my wounds.
Have mercy, Jesu! Soft! I did but dream.
O coward conscience, how dost thou afflict me!
The lights burn blue. It is now dead midnight.
Cold fearful drops stand on my trembling flesh.
What do I fear? Myself? There's none else by.
Richard loves Richard; that is, I am I.
Is there a murderer here? No – yes, I am.
Then fly. What, from myself? Great reason why –
Lest I revenge. What, myself upon myself!
Alack, I love myself. Wherefore? For any good.
That I myself have done unto myself?
O, no! Alas, I rather hate myself
For hateful deeds committed by myself!
I am a villain; yet I lie, I am not.
Fool, of thyself speak well. Fool, do not flatter.
My conscience hath a thousand several tongues,
And every tongue brings in a several tale,
And every tale condemns me for a villain.
Perjury, perjury, in the high'st degree;
Murder, stern murder, in the dir'st degree;
All several sins, all us'd in each degree,
Throng to the bar, crying all 'Guilty! guilty!'
I shall despair. There is no creature loves me;
And if I die no soul will pity me:
And wherefore should they, since that I myself
Find myself no pity to myself?
Methought the souls of all that I had murder'd
Came to my tent, and every one did threat
To-morrow's vengeance on the head of Richard.

Enter RATCLIFF.

RATCLIFF My lord!

KING RICHARD Zounds, who is there?

RATCLIFF Ratcliff, my lord; 'tis I. The early village-cock
Hath twice done salutation to the morn;
Your friends are up and buckle on their armour.

KING RICHARD O Ratcliff, I have dream'd a fearful dream!
What think'st thou – will our friends prove all true?

RATCLIFF No doubt, my lord.

KING RICHARD O Ratcliff, I fear, I fear.

RATCLIFF Nay, good my lord, be not afraid of shadows.

KING RICHARD By the apostle Paul, shadows to-night
Have struck more terror to the soul of Richard
Than can the substance of ten thousand soldiers
Armed in proof and led by shallow Richmond.
'Tis not yet near day. Come, go with me;
Under our tents I'll play the eaves-dropper,

To see if any mean to shrink from me. [*Exeunt.*

Enter the Lords to RICHMOND sitting in his tent.

LORDS Good morrow, Richmond!
RICHMOND Cry mercy, lords and watchful gentlemen,
That you have ta'en a tardy sluggard here.
LORDS How have you slept, my lord?
RICHMOND The sweetest sleep and fairest-boding dreams.
That ever ent'red in a drowsy head
Have I since your departure had, my lords.
Methought their souls whose bodies Richard murder'd
Came to my tent and cried on victory.
I promise you my soul is very jocund
In the remembrance of so fair a dream.
How far into the morning is it, lords?
LORDS Upon the stroke of four.
RICHMOND Why, then 'tis time to arm and give direction.
His Oration to his Soldiers.
More than I have said, loving countrymen,
The leisure and enforcement of the time
Forbids to dwell upon; yet remember this:
God and our good cause fight upon our side;
The prayers of holy saints and wronged souls,
Like high-rear'd bulwarks, stand before our faces;
Richard except, those whom we fight against
Had rather have us win than him they follow.
For what is he they follow? Truly, gentlemen,
A bloody tyrant and a homicide;
One rais'd in blood, and one in blood establish'd;
One that made means to come by what he hath,
And slaughtered those that were the means to help him;
A base foul stone, made precious by the foil
Of England's chair, where he is falsely set;
One that hath ever been God's enemy.
Then if you fight against God's enemy,
God will in justice ward you as his soldiers;
If you do sweat to put a tyrant down,
You sleep in peace, the tyrant being slain;
If you do fight against your country's foes,
Your country's fat shall pay your pains the hire;
If you do fight in safeguard of your wives,
Your wives shall welcome home the conquerors;
If you do free your children from the sword,
Your children's children quits it in your age.
Then, in the name of God and all these rights,
Advance your standards, draw your willing swords.
For me, the ransom of my bold attempt
Shall be this cold corpse on the earth's cold face;
But if I thrive, the gain of my attempt
The least of you shall share his part thereof.
Sound drums and trumpets boldly and cheerfully;
God and Saint and George! Richmond and victory! [*Exeunt.*

Re-enter KING RICHARD, RATCLIFF, Attendants, and Forces.

KING RICHARD What said Northumberland as touching Richmond?
RATCLIFF That he was never trained up in arms.
KING RICHARD He said the truth; and what said Surrey then?
RATCLIFF He smil'd, and said 'The better for our purpose.'
KING RICHARD He was in the right; and so indeed it is. [*Clock strikes.*
Tell the clock there. Give me a calendar.
Who saw the sun to-day?
RATCLIFF Not I, my lord.
KING RICHARD Then he disdains to shine; for by the book
He should have brav'd the east an hour ago.
A black day will it be to somebody.
Ratcliff!
RATCLIFF My lord?
KING RICHARD The sun will not be seen to-day;
The sky doth frown and lour upon our army.
I would these dewy tears were from the ground.
Not shine to-day! Why, what is that to me
More than to Richmond? For the selfsame heaven
That frowns on me looks sadly upon him.

Enter NORFOLK.

NORFOLK Arm, arm, my lord; the foe vaunts in the field.
KING RICHARD Come, bustle, bustle; caparison my horse;
Call up Lord Stanley, bid him bring his power.
I will lead forth my soldiers to the plain,
And thus my battle shall be ordered:
My foreward shall be drawn out all in length,
Consisting equally of horse and foot;
Our archers shall be placed in the midst.
John Duke of Norfolk, Thomas Earl of Surrey,
Shall have the leading of this foot and horse.
They thus directed, we will follow
In the main battle, whose puissance on either side
Shall be well winged with our chiefest horse.
This, and Saint George to boot! What think'st thou, Norfolk?
NORFOLK A good direction, warlike sovereign.
This found I on my tent this morning.
[*He sheweth him a paper.*

KING RICHARD [*Reads*]
'Jockey to Norfolk, be not so bold,
For Dickon thy master is bought and sold.'
A thing devised by the enemy.
Go, gentlemen, every man unto his charge.
Let not our babbling dreams affright our souls;
Conscience is but a word that cowards use,
Devis'd at first to keep the strong in awe.
Our strong arms be our conscience, swords our law.
March on, join bravely, let us to it pell-mell;
If not to heaven, then hand in hand to hell.

His Oration to his Army.

What shall I say more than I have inferr'd?
Remember whom you are to cope withal –
A sort of vagabonds, rascals, and runaways,
A scum of Britaines, and base lackey peasants,
Whom their o'er-cloyed country vomits forth
To desperate adventures and assur'd destruction.
You sleeping safe, they bring to you unrest;
You having lands, and bless'd with beauteous wives,
They would restrain the one, distain the other.
And who doth lead them but a paltry fellow,
Long kept in Britaine at our mother's cost?
A milk-sop, one that never in his life
Felt so much cold as over shoes in snow?
Let's whip these stragglers o'er the seas again;
Lash hence these over-weening rags of France,
These famish'd beggars, weary of their lives;
Who, but for dreaming on this fond exploit,
For want of means, poor rats, had hang'd themselves.
If we be conquered, let men conquer us,
And not these bastard Britaines, whom our fathers
Have in their own land beaten, bobb'd, and thump'd,
And, in record, left them the heirs of shame.
Shall these enjoy our lands? lie with our wives,
Ravish our daughters? [*Drum afar off*] Hark! I hear their drum.
Fight, gentlemen of England! Fight, bold yeomen!
Draw, archers, draw your arrows to the head!
Spur your proud horses hard, and ride in blood;
Amaze the welkin with your broken staves!

Enter a Messenger

What says Lord Stanley? Will he bring his power?

MESSENGER My lord, he doth deny to come.

KING RICHARD Off with his son George's head!

NORFOLK My lord, the enemy is pass'd the marsh.
After the battle let George Stanley die.

KING RICHARD A thousand hearts are great within my bosom.
Advance our standards, set upon our foes;
Our ancient word of courage, fair Saint George,
Inspire us with the spleen of fiery dragons!
Upon them! Victory sits on our helms. [*Exeunt.*

SCENE IV. *Another part of the field.*

Alarum; excursions. Enter NORFOLK and Forces; to him CATESBY.

CATESBY Rescue, my Lord of Norfolk, rescue, rescue!
The King enacts more wonders than a man,
Daring an opposite to every danger.
His horse is slain, and all on foot he fights,
Seeking for Richmond in the throat of death.
Rescue, fair lord, or else the day is lost.

Alarums. Enter KING RICHARD.

KING RICHARD A horse! a horse! my kingdom for a horse!

CATESBY Withdraw, my lord; I'll help you to a horse.

KING RICHARD Slave, I have set my life upon a cast
And I will stand the hazard of the die.
I think there be six Richmonds in the field;
Five have I slain to-day instead of him.
A horse! a horse! my kingdom for a horse!

[*Exeunt.*

SCENE V. *Another part of the field.*

Alarum. Enter RICHARD and RICHMOND; they fight; Richard is slain. Retreat and Flourish. Enter RICHMOND, DERBY bearing the crown, with other Lords.

RICHMOND God and your arms be prais'd, victorious friends;
The day is ours, the bloody dog is dead.

DERBY Courageous Richmond, well hast thou acquit thee!
Lo, here, this long-usurped royalty
From the dead temples of this bloody wretch
Have I pluck'd off, to grace thy brows withal.
Wear it, enjoy it, and make much of it.

RICHMOND Great God of heaven, say Amen to all!
But, tell me is young George Stanley living.

DERBY He is, my lord, and safe in Leicester town,

Whither, if it please you, we may now withdraw us.

RICHMOND What men of name are slain on either side?

DERBY John Duke of Norfolk, Walter Lord Ferrers,
Sir Robert Brakenbury, and Sir William Brandon.

RICHMOND Inter their bodies as becomes their births.
Proclaim a pardon to the soldiers fled
That in submission will return to us.
And then, as we have ta'en the sacrament,
We will unite the white rose and the red.
Smile heaven upon this fair conjunction,
That long have frown'd upon their enmity!
What traitor hears me, and says not amen?
England hath long been mad, and scarr'd herself;
The brother blindly shed the brother's blood,
The father rashly slaughter'd his own son,
The son, compell'd, been butcher to the sire;
All this divided York and Lancaster,
Divided in their dire division,
O, now let Richmond and Elizabeth,
The true succeeders of each royal house,
By God's fair ordinance conjoin together!
And let their heirs, God, if thy will be so,
Enrich the time to come with smooth-fac'd peace,
With smiling plenty, and fair prosperous days!
Abate the edge of traitors, gracious Lord,
That would reduce these bloody days again
And make poor England weep in streams of blood!
Let them not live to taste this land's increase
That would with treason wound this fair land's peace!
Now civil wounds are stopp'd, peace lives again –
That she may long live here, God say amen!

[*Exeunt.*

King Henry the Eighth

Introduction by STUART GILLESPIE

Henry VIII is known to have been performed in 1613, much later than Shakespeare's other histories (none of which are thought to fall within the seventeenth century), and so late, in fact, as to imply that it is the last work of his dramatic career. The play has been consistently successful in the theatre since this date, and latterly as a television production. But the dominant feature of its historical reception, and still a topic of debate today, is the question of its authorship. Despite its appearance in the First Folio, the earliest printed text of Shakespeare's plays, questions about its authenticity were raised in the eighteenth century, and in 1850 James Spedding published an article entitled 'Who wrote Shakespeare's *Henry VIII*?' Spedding voiced his dissatisfaction with the play's handling of the King and the Reformation, and combined this with stylistic arguments to suggest that some scenes were written by John Fletcher, Shakespeare's successor as regular playwright for his theatre company and perhaps his collaborator on *The Two Noble Kinsmen* at about the same date.

Peter Alexander was one of those who defended the play as wholly Shakespeare's, and drew attention, as others have done since, to the connections between it and other late Shakespearean works, notably its 'compassionate outlook' (Alexander, 1931). But it remains unusual to think of *Henry VIII* as 'the only fitting culmination of Shakespeare's work' (Wilson Knight, 1947). Whatever the truth about its authorship, most readers find problematic its episodic structure; the absence of a fully fledged central character; the inconclusive treatment of Henry VIII himself; and the apparent discontinuity of Act 5 (often omitted in performance) with the rest. For Samuel Johnson, in fact, Shakespeare had only one real interest in the play: 'the genius of Shakespeare', he wrote, 'comes in and goes out with Catherine' (Johnson, 1765).

Against these complaints it can be argued, first, that the play's structure, with the clearly marked sequence of four trials (of Buckingham, Katharine, Wolsey and Cranmer), strongly conveys the continuous movement of historical time. The unpredictable but unending progress of history is kept in the audience's minds from the first: the play opens with references to events before it begins (in particular, the Field of the Cloth of Gold), and ends with Cranmer's prophesies for the future that lies beyond it. The sequence of trials, and attendant falls from or ascents to pre-eminence, as well as offering opportunities for much powerful writing on the dichotomy between worldly status and quiet of mind, creates a strong impression of the remorselessness of historical change. This is not to say that the play presents us with any 'philosophy of history', merely that its apparent structural discontinuities may be deliberate.

The King, who of course remains secure through the trials of others, can be seen in various ways. His relative indistinctness, or ambiguity, as a character has been accounted for in terms of supposed restraints on Shakespeare's ability to write freely about the father of Queen Elizabeth and the founder of the Church of England. Others have argued that Henry is intended to grow in moral stature in the course of the play, from his domination by Wolsey to his beneficent and protective treatment of Cranmer.

But Shakespeare's audience must have recognised that Cranmer, as well as Anne Boleyn, was doomed to fall as royal favour changed course again – Cranmer was burned at the stake (under Mary Tudor), Anne Boleyn executed. Perhaps Shakespeare's (or Fletcher's) problem is only a refusal to simplify, to tidy up the contradictions of human personality for a neat and easily digested effect. On this reading, the play is neither an idealised account of a model king's education, nor a failed attempt at close-up treatment of individual psychology. The play was also known originally as '*All is True*': arguably, the character of Henry is problematic simply because it is so 'true to life'.

It is, however, the characters of Wolsey and of Katharine that remain ultimately most compelling. The final scenes of both are marked by intense poetry in set-piece forms. Wolsey's [3.2] overturns our previous conception of his character with his repentance; Katharine's [4.2] – which Johnson called 'perhaps above any scene of any other poet, tender and pathetic' (Johnson, 1765) – contains a charitable, rehabilitatory view of Wolsey together with a damning one. Once again, in Wolsey's case, we end with ambiguity, with two versions of his story where other dramatists might supply only one. The satisfaction a unitary resolution might provide is not necessarily to be preferred above the more unusual, and perhaps here more suggestive effect of divergent perspectives.

King Henry the Eighth

DRAMATIS PERSONAE

KING HENRY THE EIGHTH
CARDINAL WOLSEY
CARDINAL CAMPEIUS
CAPUCIUS
Ambassador from the Emperor Charles V
CRANMER
Archbishop of Canterbury
DUKE OF NORFOLK
DUKE OF BUCKINGHAM
DUKE OF SUFFOLK
EARL OF SURREY
Lord Chamberlain
Lord Chancellor
GARDINER
Bishop of Winchester
Bishop of Lincoln
LORD ABERGAVENNY
LORD SANDYS
SIR HENRY GUILDFORD
SIR THOMAS LOVELL
SIR ANTHONY DENNY
SIR NICHOLAS VAUX
Secretaries to Wolsey
CROMWELL
servant to Wolsey
GRIFFITH
gentleman-usher to Queen Katharine
Three Gentlemen
DR. BUTTS
physician to the King
Garter King-at-Arms
Surveyor to the Duke of Buckingham
BRANDON, *and a Sergeant-at-Arms*
Doorkeeper of the Council Chamber
Porter and his Man
Page to Gardiner
A Crier
QUEEN KATHARINE
wife to King Henry, afterwards divorced
ANNE BULLEN
her Maid of Honour, afterwards Queen
An old Lady friend to Anne Bullen
PATIENCE
woman to Queen Katharine
Lord Mayor, Aldermen, Lords and Ladies in the Dumb Shows; Women attending upon the Queen; Scribes, Officers, Guards, other Attendants; and Spirits.

THE SCENE: LONDON; WESTMINSTER; KIMBOLTON.

THE PROLOGUE

I come no more to make you laugh; things now
That bear a weighty and a serious brow,
Sad, high, and working, full of state and woe,
Such noble scenes as draw the eye to flow,
We now present. Those that can pity here
May, if they think it well, let fall a tear:
The subject will deserve it. Such as give
Their money out of hope they may believe
May here find truth too. Those that come to see
Only a show or two, and so agree
The play may pass, if they be still and willing,
I'll undertake may see away their shilling
Richly in two short hours. Only they
That come to hear a merry bawdy play,
A noise of targets, or to see a fellow
In a long motley coat guarded with yellow,
Will be deciev'd; for, gentle hearers, know,
To rank our chosen truth with such a show
As fool and fight is, beside forfeiting
Our own brains, and the opinion that we bring
To make that only true we now intend,
Will leave us never an understanding friend.
Therefore, for goodness sake, and as you are known
The first and happiest hearers of the town,
Be sad, as we would make ye. Think ye see
The very persons of our noble story
As they were living; think you see them great,
And follow'd with the general throng and sweat
Of thousand friends; then, in a moment, see
How soon this mightiness meets misery.
And if you can be merry then, I'll say
A man may weep upon his wedding-day.

ACT ONE

SCENE I. *London. The palace.*

Enter the DUKE OF NORFOLK at one door; at the other, the DUKE OF BUCKINGHAM and the LORD ABERGAVENNY.

BUCKINGHAM Good morrow, and well met. How have ye done
Since last we saw in France?

NORFOLK I thank your Grace,
Healthful; and ever since a fresh admirer
Of what I saw there.

BUCKINGHAM An untimely ague
Stay'd me a prisoner in my chamber when
Those suns of glory, those two lights of men,
Met in the vale of Andren.

NORFOLK 'Twixt Guynes and Arde –
I was then present, saw them salute on horseback;
Beheld them, when they lighted, how they clung
In their embracement, as they grew together;
Which had they, what four thron'd ones could have weigh'd
Such a compounded one?

BUCKINGHAM All the whole time
I was my chamber's prisoner.

NORFOLK Then you lost
The view of earthly glory; men might say,
Till this time pomp was single, but now married
To one above itself. Each following day
Became the next day's master, till the last
Made former wonders its. To-day the French,
All clinquant, all in gold, like heathen gods,
Shone down the English; and to-morrow they
Made Britain India: every man that stood
Show'd like a mine. Their dwarfish pages were
As cherubins, all gilt; the madams too,
Not us'd to toil, did almost sweat to bear
The pride upon them, that their very labour
Was to them as a painting. Now this masque
Was cried incomparable; and th' ensuing night
Made it a fool and beggar. The two kings,
Equal in lustre, were now best, now worst,
As presence did present them: him in eye
Still him in praise; and being present both,
'Twas said they saw but one, and no discerner
Durst wag his tongue in censure. When these suns –
For so they phrase 'em – by their heralds challeng'd
The noble spirits to arms, they did perform
Beyond thought's compass, that former fabulous story,
Being now seen possible enough, got credit,
That Bevis was believ'd.

BUCKINGHAM O, you go far!

NORFOLK As I belong to worship, and affect
In honour honesty, the tract of ev'rything
Would by a good discourser lose some life
Which action's self was tongue to. All was royal:
To the disposing of it nought rebell'd;
Order gave each thing view. The office did
Distinctly his full function.

BUCKINGHAM Who did guide –
I mean, who set the body and the limbs
Of this great sport together, as you guess?

NORFOLK One, certes, that promises no element
In such a business.

BUCKINGHAM I pray you, who, my lord?

NORFOLK All this was ord'red by the good discretion
Of the right reverend Cardinal of York.

BUCKINGHAM The devil speed him! No man's pie is freed
From his ambitious finger. What had he
To do in these fierce vanities? I wonder
That such a keech can with his very bulk
Take up the rays o' th' beneficial sun,
And keep it from the earth.

NORFOLK Surely, sir,
There's in him stuff that puts him to these ends;
For, being not propp'd by ancestry, whose grace
Chalks successors their way, nor call'd upon
For high feats done to th' crown, neither allied
To eminent assistants, but spider-like,
Out of his self-drawing web, 'a gives us note
The force of his own merit makes his way –
A gift that heaven gives for him, which buys
A place next to the King.

ABERGAVENNY I cannot tell
What heaven hath given him – let some graver eye
Pierce into that; but I can see his pride
Peep through each part of him. Whence has he that?
If not from hell, the devil is a niggard
Or has given all before, and he begins
A new hell in himself.

BUCKINGHAM Why the devil,
Upon this French going out, took he upon him –
Without the privity o' th' King – t' appoint
Who should attend on him? He makes up the file
Of all the gentry; for the most part such
To whom as great a charge as little honour
He meant to lay upon; and his own letter,
The honourable board of council out,
Must fetch him in he papers.

ABERGAVENNY I do know
Kinsmen of mine, three at the least, that have
By this so sicken'd their estates that never
They shall abound as formerly.
BUCKINGHAM O, many
Have broke their backs with laying manors on 'em
For this great journey. What did this vanity
But minister communication of
A most poor issue?
NORFOLK Grievingly I think
The peace between the French and us not values
The cost that did conclude it.
BUCKINGHAM Every man,
After the hideous storm that follow'd, was
A thing inspir'd, and, not consulting, broke
Into a general prophecy – that this tempest,
Dashing the garment of this peace, aboded
The sudden breach on't.
NORFOLK Which is budded out;
For France hath flaw'd the league, and hath attach'd
Our merchants' goods at Bordeaux.
ABERGAVENNY Is it therefore
Th' ambassador is silenc'd?
NORFOLK Marry, is't.
ABERGAVENNY A proper title of a peace, and purchas'd
At a superfluous rate!
BUCKINGHAM Why, all this business
Our reverend Cardinal carried.
NORFOLK Like it your Grace,
The state takes notice of the private difference
Betwixt you and the Cardinal. I advise you –
And take it from a heart that wishes towards you
Honour and plenteous safety – that you read
The Cardinal's malice and his potency
Together; to consider further, that
What his high hatred would effect wants not
A minister in his power. You know his nature,
That he's revengeful; and I know his sword
Hath a sharp edge – it's long and't may be said
It reaches far, and where 'twill not extend,
Thither he darts it. Bosom up my counsel,
You'll find it wholesome. Lo, where comes that rock
That I advise your shunning.

Enter CARDINAL WOLSEY, the purse borne before him, certain of the Guard, and two Secretaries with papers. The Cardinal in his passage fixeth his eye on Buckingham, and Buckingham on him, both full of disdain.

WOLSEY The Duke of Buckingham's surveyor? Ha!
Where's his examination?
1 SECRETARY Here, so please you.
WOLSEY Is he in person ready?
1 SECRETARY Ay, please your Grace.
WOLSEY Well, we shall then know more, and Buckingham
Shall lessen this big look.

[Exeunt Wolsey and his Train.

BUCKINGHAM This butcher's cur is venom-mouth'd, and I
Have not the power to muzzle him; therefore best
Not wake him in his slumber. A beggar's book
Outworths a noble's blood.
NORFOLK What, are you chaf'd?
Ask God for temp'rance; that's th' appliance only
Which your disease requires.
BUCKINGHAM I read in's looks
Matter against me, and his eye revil'd
Me as his abject object. At this instant
He bores me with some trick. He's gone to th' King;
I'll follow, and outstare him.
NORFOLK Stay, my lord,
And let your reason with your choler question
What 'tis you go about. To climb steep hills
Requires slow pace at first. Anger is like
A full hot horse, who being allow'd his way,
Self-mettle tires him. Not a man in England
Can advise me like you; be to yourself
As you would to your friend.
BUCKINGHAM I'll to the King,
And from a mouth of honour quite cry down
This Ipswich fellow's insolence; or proclaim
There's difference in no persons.
NORFOLK Be advis'd:
Heat not a furnace for your foe so hot
That it do singe yourself. We may outrun
By violent swiftness that which we run at,
And lose by over-running. Know you not
The fire that mounts the liquor till't run o'er
In seeming to augment it wastes it? Be advis'd.
I say again there is no English soul
More stronger to direct you than yourself,
If with the sap of reason you would quench
Or but allay the fire of passion.
BUCKINGHAM Sir,
I am thankful to you, and I'll go along
By your prescription; but this top-proud fellow –
Whom from the flow of gall I name not, but
From sincere motions, by intelligence,
And proofs as clear as founts in July when
We see each grain of gravel – I do know
To be corrupt and treasonous.
NORFOLK Say not treasonous.
BUCKINGHAM To th' King I'll say't, and make my

vouch as strong
As shore of rock. Attend: this holy fox,
Or wolf, or both – for he is equal rav'nous
As he is subtle, and as prone to mischief
As able to perform't, his mind and place
Infecting one another, yea, reciprocally –
Only to show his pomp as well in France
As here at home, suggests the King our master
To this last costly treaty, th' interview
That swallowed so much treasure and like a glass
Did break i' th' wrenching.

NORFOLK Faith, and so it did.

BUCKINGHAM Pray, give me favour, sir: this cunning cardinal
The articles o' th' combination drew
As himself pleas'd; and they were ratified
As he cried 'Thus let be' to as much end
As give a crutch to th' dead. But our Count-Cardinal
Has done this, and 'tis well; for worthy Wolsey,
Who cannot err, he did it. Now this follows,
Which, as I take it, is a kind of puppy
To th' old dam treason: Charles the Emperor,
Under pretence to see the Queen his aunt –
For 'twas indeed his colour, but he came
To whisper Wolsey – here makes visitation –
His fears were that the interview betwixt
England and France might through their amity
Breed him some prejudice; for from this league
Peep'd harms that menac'd him – privily
Deals with our Cardinal; and, as I trow –
Which I do well, for I am sure the Emperor
Paid ere he promis'd; whereby his suit was granted
Ere it was ask'd – but when the way was made,
And pav'd with gold, the Emperor thus desir'd,
That he would please to alter the King's course,
And break the foresaid peace. Let the King know,
As soon he shall by me, that thus the Cardinal
Does buy and sell his honour as he pleases,
And for his own advantage.

NORFOLK I am sorry
To hear this of him, and could wish he were
Something mistaken in't.

BUCKINGHAM No, not a syllable:
I do pronounce him in that very shape
He shall appear in proof.

Enter BRANDON, a Sergeant-at-Arms before him, and two or three of the Guard.

BRANDON Your office, sergeant: execute it.

SERGEANT Sir,
My lord the Duke of Buckingham, and Earl
Of Hereford, Stafford, and Northampton, I
Arrest thee of high treason, in the name
Of our most sovereign King.

BUCKINGHAM Lo you, my lord,
The net has fall'n upon me! I shall perish
Under device and practice.

BRANDON I am sorry
To see you ta'en from liberty, to look on
The business present; 'tis his Highness' pleasure
You shall to th' Tower.

BUCKINGHAM It will help me nothing
To plead mine innocence; for that dye is on me
Which makes my whit'st part black. The will of heav'n
Be done in this and all things! I obey.
O my Lord Aberga'ny, fare you well!

BRANDON Nay, he must bear you company.
[*To Abergavenny*] The King
Is pleas'd you shall to th' Tower, till you know
How he determines further.

ABERGAVENNY As the Duke said,
The will of heaven be done, and the King's pleasure
By me obey'd.

BRANDON Here is warrant from
The King t' attach Lord Montacute and the bodies
Of the Duke's confessor, John de la Car,
One Gilbert Peck, his chancellor –

BUCKINGHAM So, so!
These are the limbs o' th' plot; no more, I hope.

BRANDON A monk o' th' Chartreux.

BUCKINGHAM O, Nicholas Hopkins?

BRANDON He.

BUCKINGHAM My surveyor is false. The o'er great Cardinal
Hath show'd him gold; my life is spann'd already.
I am the shadow of poor Buckingham,
Whose figure even this instant cloud puts on
By dark'ning my clear sun. My lord, farewell.

[*Exeunt.*

SCENE II. *London. The Council Chamber.*

Cornets. Enter KING HENRY, leaning on the CARDINAL'S shoulder, the Nobles, and SIR THOMAS LOVELL, with Others. The Cardinal places himself under the King's feet on his right side.

KING My life itself, and the best heart of it,
Thanks you for this great care; I stood i' th' level
Of a full-charg'd confederacy, and give thanks
To you that chok'd it. Let be call'd before us
That gentleman of Buckingham's. In person
I'll hear him his confessions justify;
And point by point the treasons of his master
He shall again relate.

A noise within, crying 'Room for the Queen!' Enter the QUEEN, usher'd by the DUKES OF NORFOLK and SUFFOLK; she kneels. The King riseth from his state, takes her up, kisses and placeth her by him.

QUEEN KATHARINE Nay, we must longer kneel: I am a suitor.
KING Arise, and take place by us. Half your suit
Never name to us: you have half our power.
The other moiety ere you ask is given;
Repeat your will, and take it.
QUEEN KATHARINE Thank your Majesty.
That you would love yourself, and in that love
Not unconsidered leave your honour nor
The dignity of your office, is the point
Of my petition.
KING Lady mine, proceed.
QUEEN KATHARINE I am solicited, not by a few,
And those of true condition, that your subjects
Are in great grievance: there have been commissions
Sent down among 'em which hath flaw'd the heart
Of all their loyalties; wherein, although,
My good Lord Cardinal, they vent reproaches
Most bitterly on you as putter-on
Of these exactions, yet the King our master –
Whose honour Heaven shield from soil! – even he escapes not
Language unmannerly; yea, such which breaks
The sides of loyalty, and almost appears
In loud rebellion.
NORFOLK Not almost appears –
It doth appear; for, upon these taxations,
The clothiers all, not able to maintain
The many to them 'longing, have put off
The spinsters, carders, fullers, weavers, who,
Unfit for other life, compell'd by hunger
And lack of other means, in desperate manner
Daring th' event to th' teeth, are all in uproar,
And danger serves among them.
KING Taxation!
Wherein? and what taxation? My Lord Cardinal,
You that are blam'd for it alike with us,
Know you of this taxation?
WOLSEY Please you, sir,
I know but of a single part in aught
Pertains to th' state, and front but in that file
Where others tell steps with me.
QUEEN KATHARINE No, my lord!
You know no more than others! But you frame
Things that are known alike, which are not wholesome
To those which would not know them, and yet must
Perforce be their acquaintance. These exactions,
Whereof my sovereign would have note, they are
Most pestilent to th' hearing; and to bear 'em
The back is sacrifice to th' load. They say
They are devis'd by you, or else you suffer
Too hard an exclamation.
KING Still exaction!
The nature of it? In what kind, let's know,
Is this exaction?
QUEEN KATHARINE I am much too venturous
In tempting of your patience, but am bold'ned
Under your promis'd pardon. The subjects' grief
Comes through commissions, which compels from each
The sixth part of his substance, to be levied
Without delay; and the pretence for this
Is nam'd your wars in France. This makes bold mouths;
Tongues spit their duties out, and cold hearts freeze
Allegiance in them; their curses now
Live where their prayers did; and it's come to pass
This tractable obedience is a slave
To each incensed will. I would your Highness
Would give it quick consideration, for
There is no primer business.
KING By my life,
This is against our pleasure.
WOLSEY And for me,
I have no further gone in this than by
A single voice; and that not pass'd me but
By learned approbation of the judges. If I am
Traduc'd by ignorant tongues, which neither know
My faculties nor person, yet will be
The chronicles of my doing, let me say
'Tis but the fate of place, and the rough brake
That virtue must go through. We must not stint
Our necessary actions in the fear
To cope malicious censurers, which ever
As rav'nous fishes do a vessel follow
That is new-trimm'd, but benefit no further
Than vainly longing. What we oft do best,
By sick interpreters, once weak ones, is
Not ours, or not allow'd; what worst, as oft
Hitting a grosser quality, is cried up
For our best act. If we shall stand still,
In fear our motion will be mock'd or carp'd at,
We should take root here where we sit, or sit
State-statues only.
KING Things done well
And with a care exempt themselves from fear:
Things done without example, in their issue
Are to be fear'd. Have you a precedent
Of this commission? I believe, not any.

We must not rend our subjects from our laws,
And stick them in our will. Sixth part of each?
A trembling contribution! Why, we take
From every tree lop, bark, and part o' th' timber;
And though we leave it with a root, thus hack'd,
The air will drink the sap. To every county
Where this is question'd send our letters with
Free pardon to each man that has denied
The force of this commission. Pray, look to't;
I put it to your care.
WOLSEY [*Aside to the Secretary*]
A word with you.
Let there be letters writ to every shire
Of the King's grace and pardon. The grieved
commons
Hardly conceive of me – let it be nois'd
That through our intercession this revokement
And pardon comes. I shall anon advise you
Further in the proceeding. [*Exit Secretary.*

Enter Surveyor.

QUEEN KATHARINE I am sorry that the Duke of
Buckingham
Is run in your displeasure.
KING It grieves many.
The gentleman is learn'd and a most rare
speaker;
To nature none more bound; his training such
That he may furnish and instruct great teachers
And never seek for aid out of himself. Yet see,
When these so noble benefits shall prove
Not well dispos'd, the mind growing once
corrupt,
They turn to vicious forms, ten times more ugly
Than ever they were fair. This man so complete,
Who was enroll'd 'mongst wonders, and when
we,
Almost with ravish'd list'ning, could not find
His hour of speech a minute – he, my lady,
Hath into monstrous habits put the graces
That once were his, and is become as black
As if besmear'd in hell. Sit by us; you shall
hear –
This was his gentleman in trust – of him
Things to strike honour sad. Bid him recount
The fore-recited practices, whereof
We cannot feel too little, hear too much.
WOLSEY Stand forth, and with bold spirit relate
what you,
Most like a careful subject, have collected
Out of the Duke of Buckingham.
KING Speak freely.
SURVEYOR First, it was usual with him – every
day
It would infect his speech – that if the King
Should without issue die, he'll carry it so
To make the sceptre his. These very words
I've heard him utter to his son-in-law,
Lord Aberga'ny, to whom by oath he menac'd
Revenge upon the Cardinal.
WOLSEY Please your Highness, note
This dangerous conception in this point:
Not friended by his wish, to your high person
His will is most malignant, and it stretches
Beyond you to your friends.
QUEEN KATHARINE My learn'd Lord Cardinal,
Deliver all with charity.
KING Speak on.
How grounded he his title to the crown
Upon our fail? To this point hast thou heard
him
At any time speak aught?
SURVEYOR He was brought to this
By a vain prophecy of Nicholas Henton.
KING What was that Henton?
SURVEYOR Sir, a Chartreux friar,
His confessor, who fed him every minute
With words of sovereignty.
KING How know'st thou this?
SURVEYOR Not long before your Highness sped
to France,
The Duke being at the Rose, within the parish
Saint Lawrence Poultney, did of me demand
What was the speech among the Londoners
Concerning the French journey. I replied
Men fear'd the French would prove perfidious,
To the King's danger. Presently the Duke
Said 'twas the fear indeed and that he doubted
'Twould prove the verity of certain words
Spoke by a holy monk 'that oft' says he
'Hath sent to me, wishing me to permit
John de la Car, my chaplain, a choice hour
To hear from him a matter of some moment;
Whom after under the confession's seal
He solemnly had sworn that what he spoke
My chaplain to no creature living but
To me should utter, with demure confidence
This pausingly ensu'd: 'Neither the King nor's
heirs,
Tell you the Duke, shall prosper; bid him strive
To gain the love o' th' commonalty; the Duke
Shall govern England' '.
QUEEN KATHARINE If I know you well,
You were the Duke's surveyor, and lost your
office
On the complaint o' th' tenants. Take good heed
You charge not in your spleen a noble person
And spoil your nobler soul. I say, take heed;
Yes, heartily beseech you.
KING Let him on.
Go forward.
SURVEYOR On my soul, I'll speak but truth.
I told my lord the Duke, by th' devil's illusions
The monk might be deceiv'd, and that 'twas

dangerous for him
To ruminate on this so far, until
It forg'd him some design, which, being believ'd,
It was much like to do. He answer'd 'Tush,
It can do me no damage'; adding further
That, had the King in his last sickness fail'd,
The Cardinal's and Sir Thomas Lovell's heads
Should have gone off.
KING Ha! what, so rank? Ah ha!
There's mischief in this man. Canst thou say
further?
SURVEYOR I can, my liege.
KING Proceed.
SURVEYOR Being at Greenwich,
After your Highness had reprov'd the Duke
About Sir William Bulmer –
KING I remember
Of such a time: being my sworn servant,
The Duke retain'd him his. But on: what hence?
SURVEYOR 'If' quoth he 'I for this had been
committed –
As to the Tower I thought – I would have play'd
The part my father meant to act upon
Th' usurper Richard; who, being at Salisbury,
Made suit to come in's presence, which if
granted,
As he made semblance of his duty, would
Have put his knife into him.'
KING A giant traitor!
WOLSEY Now, madam, may his Highness live in
freedom,
And this man out of prison?
QUEEN KATHARINE God mend all!
KING There's something more would out of thee:
what say'st?
SURVEYOR After 'the Duke his father' with the
'knife',
He stretch'd him, and, with one hand on his
dagger,
Another spread on's breast, mounting his eyes,
He did discharge a horrible oath, whose tenour
Was, were he evil us'd, he would outgo
His father by as much as a performance
Does an irresolute purpose.
KING There's his period,
To sheath his knife in us. He is attach'd;
Call him to present trial. If he may
Find mercy in the law, 'tis his; if none,
Let him not seek't of us. By day and night!
He's traitor to th' height. [*Exeunt.*

SCENE III. *London. The palace.*

Enter the Lord Chamberlain and LORD SANDYS.

CHAMBERLAIN Is't possible the spells of France
should juggle
Men into such strange mysteries?
SANDYS New customs,
Though they be never so ridiculous,
Nay, let 'em be unmanly, yet are follow'd.
CHAMBERLAIN As far as I see, all the good our
English
Have got by the late voyage is but merely
A fit or two o' th' face; but they are shrewd ones;
For when they hold 'em, you would swear
directly
Their very noses had been counsellors
To Pepin or Clotharius, they keep state so.
SANDYS They have all new legs, and lame ones.
One would take it,
That never saw 'em pace before, the spavin
Or springhalt reign'd among 'em.
CHAMBERLAIN Death! my lord,
Their clothes are after such a pagan cut to't,
That sure th' have worn out Christendom.

Enter SIR THOMAS LOVELL.

How now?
What news, Sir Thomas Lovell?
LOVELL Faith, my lord,
I hear of none but the new proclamation
That's clapp'd upon the court gate.
CHAMBERLAIN What is't for?
LOVELL The reformation of our travell'd gallants,
That fill the court with quarrels, talk, and
tailors.
CHAMBERLAIN I am glad 'tis there. Now I would
pray our monsieurs
To think an English courtier may be wise,
And never see the Louvre.
LOVELL They must either,
For so run the conditions, leave those remnants
Of fool and feather that they got in France,
With all their honourable points of ignorance
Pertaining thereunto – as fights and fireworks;
Abusing better men than they can be,
Out of a foreign wisdom – renouncing clean
The faith they have in tennis, and tall stockings,
Short blist'red breeches, and those types of
travel,
And understand again like honest men,
Or pack to their old playfellows. There, I take it,
They may, cum privilegio, wear away
The lag end of their lewdness and be laugh'd at.
SANDYS 'Tis time to give 'em physic, their
diseases
Are grown so catching.
CHAMBERLAIN What a loss our ladies
Will have of these trim vanities!
LOVELL Ay, marry,
There will be woe indeed, lords: the sly
whoresons
Have got a speeding trick to lay down ladies.
A French song and a fiddle has no fellow.

SANDYS The devil fiddle 'em! I am glad they are going,
For sure there's no converting of 'em. Now
An honest country lord, as I am, beaten
A long time out of play, may bring his plainsong
And have an hour of hearing; and, by'r Lady,
Held current music too.

CHAMBERLAIN Well said, Lord Sandys;
Your colt's tooth is not cast yet.

SANDYS No, my lord,
Nor shall not while I have a stump.

CHAMBERLAIN Sir Thomas,
Whither were you a-going?

LOVELL To the Cardinal's;
Your lordship is a guest too.

CHAMBERLAIN O, 'tis true;
This night he makes a supper, and a great one,
To many lords and ladies; there will be
The beauty of this kingdom, I'll assure you.

LOVELL That churchman bears a bounteous mind indeed,
A hand as fruitful as the land that feeds us;
His dews fall everywhere.

CHAMBERLAIN No doubt he's noble;
He had a black mouth that said other of him.

SANDYS He may, my lord; has wherewithal. In him
Sparing would show a worse sin than ill doctrine:
Men of his way should be most liberal,
They are set here for examples.

CHAMBERLAIN True, they are so;
But few now give so great ones. My barge stays;
Your lordship shall along. Come, good Sir Thomas,
We shall be late else; which I would not be,
For I was spoke to, with Sir Henry Guildford,
This night to be comptrollers.

SANDYS I am your lordship's.
[*Exeunt.*

SCENE IV. *London. The Presence Chamber in York Place.*

Hautboys. A small table under a state for the Cardinal, a longer table for the guests. Then enter ANNE BULLEN, and divers other Ladies and Gentlemen, as guests, at one door; at another door enter SIR HENRY GUILDFORD.

GUILDFORD Ladies, a general welcome from his Grace
Salutes ye all; this night he dedicates
To fair content and you. None here, he hopes,
In all this noble bevy, has brought with her
One care abroad; he would have all as merry
As, first, good company, good wine, good welcome,
Can make good people.

Enter Lord Chamberlain, LORD SANDYS, and SIR THOMAS LOVELL.

O, my lord, y'are tardy,
The very thought of this fair company
Clapp'd wings to me.

CHAMBERLAIN You are young, Sir Harry Guildford.

SANDYS Sir Thomas Lovell, had the Cardinal
But half my lay thoughts in him, some of these
Should find a running banquet ere they rested
I think would better please 'em. By my life,
They are a sweet society of fair ones.

LOVELL O that your lordship were but now confessor
To one or two of these!

SANDYS I would I were;
They should find easy penance.

LOVELL Faith, how easy?

SANDYS As easy as a down bed would afford it.

CHAMBERLAIN Sweet ladies, will it please you sit? Sir Harry,
Place you that side; I'll take the charge of this.
His Grace is ent'ring. Nay, you must not freeze:
Two women plac'd together makes cold weather.
My Lord Sandys, you are one will keep 'em waking:
Pray sit between these ladies.

SANDYS By my faith,
And thank your lordship. By your leave, sweet ladies. [*Seats himself between Anne Bullen and another lady.*
If I chance to talk a little wild, forgive me;
I had it from my father.

ANNE Was he mad, sir?

SANDYS O, very mad, exceeding mad, in love too.
But he would bite none; just as I do now,
He would kiss you twenty with a breath.
[*Kisses her.*

CHAMBERLAIN Well said, my lord.
So, now y'are fairly seated. Gentlemen,
The penance lies on you if these fair ladies
Pass away frowning.

SANDYS For my little cure,
Let me alone.

Hautboys. Enter CARDINAL WOLSEY, attended; and takes his state.

WOLSEY Y'are welcome, my fair guests. That noble lady
Or gentleman that is not freely merry
Is not my friend. This, to confirm my welcome –
And to you all, good health! [*Drinks.*

SANDYS Your Grace is noble.
Let me have such a bowl may hold my thanks

And save me so much talking.
WOLSEY My Lord Sandys,
I am beholding to you. Cheer your neighbours.
Ladies, you are not merry. Gentlemen,
Whose fault is this?
SANDYS The red wine first must rise
In their fair cheeks, my lord; then we shall have 'em
Talk us to silence.
ANNE You are a merry gamester,
My Lord Sandys.
SANDYS Yes, if I make my play.
Here's to your ladyship; and pledge it, madam,
For 'tis to such a thing –
ANNE You cannot show me.
SANDYS I told your Grace they would talk anon.
[Drum and trumpet. Chambers discharg'd.
WOLSEY What's that?
CHAMBERLAIN Look out there, some of ye.
[Exit a Servant.
WOLSEY What warlike voice,
And to what end, is this? Nay, ladies, fear not:
By all the laws of war y'are privileg'd.
Re-enter Servant.
CHAMBERLAIN How now! what is't?
SERVANT A noble troop of strangers –
For so they seem. Th' have left their barge and landed,
And hither make, as great ambassadors
From foreign princes.
WOLSEY Good Lord Chamberlain,
Go, give 'em welcome; you can speak the French tongue;
And pray receive 'em nobly and conduct 'em
Into our presence, where this heaven of beauty
Shall shine at full upon them. Some attend him.
[Exit Chamberlain attended. All rise, and tables remov'd.
You have now a broken banquet, but we'll mend it.
A good digestion to you all; and once more
I show'r a welcome on ye: welcome all.
Hautboys. Enter the KING, and Others, as maskers, habited like shepherds, usher'd by the Lord Chamberlain. They pass directly before the Cardinal, and gracefully salute him.
A noble company! What are their pleasures?
CHAMBERLAIN Because they speak no English, thus they pray'd
To tell your Grace, that, having heard by fame
Of this so noble and so fair assembly
This night to meet here, they could do no less,
Out of the great respect they bear to beauty,
But leave their flocks and, under your fair conduct,
Crave leave to view these ladies and entreat
An hour of revels with 'em.
WOLSEY Say, Lord Chamberlain,
They have done my poor house grace; for which I pay 'em
A thousand thanks, and pray 'em take their pleasures. *[They choose ladies. The King chooses Anne Bullen.*
KING The fairest hand I ever touch'd! O beauty,
Till now I never knew thee! *[Music. Dance.*
WOLSEY My lord!
CHAMBERLAIN Your Grace?
WOLSEY Pray tell 'em thus much from me:
There should be one amongst 'em, by his person,
More worthy this place than myself; to whom,
If I but knew him, with my love and duty
I would surrender it.
CHAMBERLAIN I will, my lord.
[He whispers to the Maskers.
WOLSEY What say they?
CHAMBERLAIN Such a one, they all confess,
There is indeed; which they would have your Grace
Find out, and he will take it.
WOLSEY Let me see, then.
[Comes from his state.
By all your good leaves, gentlemen, here I'll make
My royal choice.
KING *[Unmasking]* Ye have found him, Cardinal.
You hold a fair assembly; you do well, lord.
You are a churchman, or, I'll tell you, Cardinal,
I should judge now unhappily.
WOLSEY I am glad
Your Grace is grown so pleasant.
KING My Lord Chamberlain,
Prithee come hither: what fair lady's that?
CHAMBERLAIN An't please your Grace, Sir Thomas Bullen's daughter –
The Viscount Rochford – one of her Highness' women.
KING By heaven, she is a dainty one. Sweet heart,
I were unmannerly to take you out
And not to kiss you. A health, gentlemen!
Let it go round.
WOLSEY Sir Thomas Lovell, is the banquet ready
I' th' privy chamber?
LOVELL Yes, my lord.
WOLSEY Your Grace,
I fear, with dancing is a little heated.
KING I fear, too much.
WOLSEY There's fresher air, my lord,
In the next chamber.
KING Lead in your ladies, ev'ry one. Sweet

partner,
I must not yet forsake you. Let's be merry:
Good my Lord Cardinal, I have half a dozen
healths
To drink to these fair ladies, and a measure
To lead 'em once again; and then let's dream
Who's best in favour. Let the music knock it.
[Exeunt, with trumpets.

ACT TWO

SCENE I. *Westminster. A street.*

Enter two Gentlemen, at several doors.

1 GENTLEMAN Whither away so fast?
2 GENTLEMAN O, God save ye!
Ev'n to the Hall, to hear what shall become
Of the great Duke of Buckingham.
1 GENTLEMAN I'll save you
That labour, sir. All's now done but the
ceremony
Of bringing back the prisoner.
2 GENTLEMAN Were you there?
1 GENTLEMAN Yes, indeed, was I.
2 GENTLEMAN Pray, speak what has happen'd.
1 GENTLEMAN You may guess quickly what.
2 GENTLEMAN Is he found guilty?
1 GENTLEMAN Yes, truly is he, and condemn'd
upon't.
2 GENTLEMAN I am sorry for't.
1 GENTLEMAN So are a number more.
2 GENTLEMAN But, pray, how pass'd it?
1 GENTLEMAN I'll tell you in a little. The great
Duke
Came to the bar; where to his accusations
He pleaded still not guilty, and alleged
Many sharp reasons to defeat the law.
The King's attorney, on the contrary,
Urg'd on the examinations, proofs, confessions,
Of divers witnesses; which the Duke desir'd
To have brought, viva voce, to his face;
At which appear'd against him his surveyor,
Sir Gilbert Peck his chancellor, and John Car,
Confessor to him, with that devil-monk,
Hopkins, that made this mischief.
2 GENTLEMAN That was he
That fed him with his prophecies?
1 GENTLEMAN The same.
All these accus'd him strongly, which he fain
Would have flung from him; but indeed he
could not;
And so his peers, upon this evidence,
Have found him guilty of high treason. Much
He spoke, and learnedly, for life; but all
Was either pitied in him or forgotten.
2 GENTLEMAN After all this, how did he bear
himself?
1 GENTLEMAN When he was brought again to th'
bar to hear
His knell rung out, his judgment, he was stirr'd
With such an agony he sweat extremely,
And something spoke in choler, ill and hasty;
But he fell to himself again, and sweetly
In all the rest show'd a most noble patience.
2 GENTLEMAN I do not think he fears death.
1 GENTLEMAN Sure, he does not;
He never was so womanish; the cause
He may a little grieve at.
2 GENTLEMAN Certainly
The Cardinal is the end of this.
1 GENTLEMAN 'Tis likely,
By all conjectures: first, Kildare's attainder,
Then deputy of Ireland, who remov'd,
Earl Surrey was sent thither, and in haste too,
Lest he should help his father.
2 GENTLEMAN That trick of state
Was a deep envious one.
1 GENTLEMAN At his return
No doubt he will requite it. This is noted,
And generally: whoever the King favours
The Cardinal instantly will find employment,
And far enough from court too.
2 GENTLEMAN All the commons
Hate him perniciously, and, o' my conscience,
Wish him ten fathom deep: this Duke as much
They love and dote on; call him bounteous
Buckingham,
The mirror of all courtesy –

Enter BUCKINGHAM from his arraignment; Tipstaves before him; the axe with the edge towards him; halberds on each side; accompanied with SIR THOMAS LOVELL, SIR NICHOLAS VAUX, SIR WILLIAM SANDYS, and common people, etc.

1 GENTLEMAN Stay there, sir,
And see the noble ruin'd man you speak of.
2 GENTLEMAN Let's stand close, and behold him.
BUCKINGHAM All good people,
You that thus far have come to pity me,
Hear what I say, and then go home and lose me.
I have this day receiv'd a traitor's judgment,
And by that name must die; yet, heaven bear
witness,
And if I have a conscience, let it sink me
Even as the axe falls, if I be not faithful!
The law I bear no malice for my death:
'T has done, upon the premises, but justice.
But those that sought it I could wish more
Christians.

Be what they will, I heartily forgive 'em;
Yet let 'em look they glory not in mischief
Nor build their evils on the graves of great men,
For then my guiltless blood must cry against 'em.
For further life in this world I ne'er hope
Nor will I sue, although the King have mercies
More than I dare make faults. You few that lov'd me
And dare be bold to weep for Buckingham,
His noble friends and fellows, whom to leave
Is only bitter to him, only dying,
Go with me like good angels to my end;
And as the long divorce of steel falls on me
Make of your prayers one sweet sacrifice,
And lift my soul to heaven. Lead on, a God's name.

LOVELL I do beseech your Grace, for charity,
If ever any malice in your heart
Were hid against me, now to forgive me frankly.

BUCKINGHAM Sir Thomas Lovell, I as free forgive you
As I would be forgiven. I forgive all.
There cannot be those numberless offences
'Gainst me that I cannot take peace with. No black envy
Shall mark my grave. Commend me to his Grace;
And if he speak of Buckingham, pray tell him
You met him half in heaven. My vows and prayers
Yet are the King's, and, till my soul forsake,
Shall cry for blessings on him. May he live
Longer than I have time to tell his years;
Ever belov'd and loving may his rule be;
And when old time shall lead him to his end,
Goodness and he fill up one monument!

LOVELL To th' water side I must conduct your Grace;
Then give my charge up to Sir Nicholas Vaux,
Who undertakes you to your end.

VAUX Prepare there;
The Duke is coming; see the barge be ready;
And fit it with such furniture as suits
The greatness of his person.

BUCKINGHAM Nay, Sir Nicholas,
Let it alone; my state now will but mock me.
When I came hither I was Lord High Constable
And Duke of Buckingham; now, poor Edward Bohun.
Yet I am richer than my base accusers
That never knew what truth meant; I now seal it;
And with that blood will make 'em one day groan for't.
My noble father, Henry of Buckingham,
Who first rais'd head against usurping Richard,
Flying for succour to his servant Banister,
Being distress'd, was by that wretch betray'd
And without trial fell; God's peace be with him!
Henry the Seventh succeeding, truly pitying
My father's loss, like a most royal prince,
Restor'd me to my honours, and out of ruins
Made my name once more noble. Now his son,
Henry the Eighth, life, honour, name, and all
That made me happy, at one stroke has taken
For ever from the world. I had my trial,
And must needs say a noble one; which makes me
A little happier than my wretched father;
Yet thus far we are one in fortunes: both
Fell by our servants, by those men we lov'd most –
A most unnatural and faithless service.
Heaven has an end in all. Yet, you that hear me,
This from a dying man receive as certain:
Where you are liberal of your loves and counsels,
Be sure you be not loose; for those you make friends
And give your hearts to, when they once perceive
The least rub in your fortunes, fall away
Like water from ye, never found again
But where they mean to sink ye. All good people,
Pray for me! I must now forsake ye; the last hour
Of my long weary life is come upon me.
Farewell;
And when you would say something that is sad,
Speak how I fell. I have done; and God forgive me! *[Exeunt Buckingham and Train.*

1 GENTLEMAN O, this is full of pity! Sir, it calls,
I fear, too many curses on their heads
That were the authors.

2 GENTLEMAN If the Duke be guiltless,
'Tis full of woe; yet I can give you inkling
Of an ensuing evil, if it fall,
Greater than this.

1 GENTLEMAN Good angels keep it from us!
What may it be? You do not doubt my faith, sir?

2 GENTLEMAN This secret is so weighty, 'twill require
A strong faith to conceal it.

1 GENTLEMAN Let me have it;
I do not talk much.

2 GENTLEMAN I am confident.
You shall, sir. Did you not of late days hear
A buzzing of a separation
Between the King and Katharine?

1 GENTLEMAN Yes, but it held not;
For when the King once heard it, out of anger

He sent command to the Lord Mayor straight
To stop the rumour and allay those tongues
That durst disperse it.
2 GENTLEMAN But that slander, sir,
Is found a truth now; for it grows again
Fresher than e'er it was, and held for certain
The King will venture at it. Either the Cardinal
Or some about him near have, out of malice
To the good Queen, possess'd him with a
scruple
That will undo her. To confirm this too,
Cardinal Campeius is arriv'd and lately;
As all think, for this business.
1 GENTLEMAN 'Tis the Cardinal;
And merely to revenge him on the Emperor
For not bestowing on him at his asking
The archbishopric of Toledo, this is purpos'd.
2 GENTLEMAN I think you have hit the mark; but
is't not cruel
That she should feel the smart of this? The
Cardinal
Will have his will, and she must fall.
1 GENTLEMAN 'Tis woeful.
We are too open here to argue this;
Let's think in private more. [*Exeunt.*

SCENE II. *London. The palace.*

Enter the Lord Chamberlain reading this letter.

CHAMBERLAIN 'My lord,
The horses your lordship sent for, with all the care I had, I saw well chosen, ridden, and furnish'd. They were young and handsome, and of the best breed in the north. When they were ready to set out for London, a man of my Lord Cardinal's, by commission, and main power, took 'em from me, with this reason: his master would be serv'd before a subject, if not before the King; which stopp'd our mouths, sir.'
I fear he will indeed. Well, let him have them.
He will have all, I think.

Enter to the Lord Chamberlain the DUKES OF NORFOLK and SUFFOLK.

NORFOLK Well met, my Lord Chamberlain.
CHAMBERLAIN Good day to both your Graces.
SUFFOLK How is the King employ'd?
CHAMBERLAIN I left him private,
Full of sad thoughts and troubles.
NORFOLK What's the cause?
CHAMBERLAIN It seems the marriage with his
brother's wife
Has crept too near his conscience.
SUFFOLK No, his conscience
Has crept too near another lady.
NORFOLK 'Tis so;
This is the Cardinal's doing; the King-Cardinal,
That blind priest, like the eldest son of fortune,
Turns what he list. The King will know him one
day.
SUFFOLK Pray God he do! He'll never know
himself else.
NORFOLK How holily he works in all his
business!
And with what zeal! For, now he has crack'd the
league
Between us and the Emperor, the Queen's great
nephew,
He dives into the King's soul and there scatters
Dangers, doubts, wringing of the conscience,
Fears, and despairs – and all these for his
marriage;
And out of all these to restore the King,
He counsels a divorce, a loss of her
That like a jewel has hung twenty years
About his neck, yet never lost her lustre;
Of her that loves him with that excellence
That angels love good men with; even of her
That, when the greatest stroke of fortune falls,
Will bless the King – and is not this course
pious?
CHAMBERLAIN Heaven keep me from such
counsel! 'Tis most true
These news are everywhere; every tongue
speaks 'em,
And every true heart weeps for't. All that dare
Look into these affairs see this main end –
The French King's sister. Heaven will one day
open
The King's eyes, that so long have slept upon
This bold bad man.
SUFFOLK And free us from his slavery.
NORFOLK We had need pray, and heartily, for
our deliverance;
Or this imperious man will work us all
From princes into pages. All men's honours
Lie like one lump before him, to be fashion'd
Into what pitch he please.
SUFFOLK For me, my lords,
I love him not, nor fear him – there's my creed;
As I am made without him, so I'll stand,
If the King please; his curses and his blessings
Touch me alike; th'are breath I not believe in.
I knew him, and I know him; so I leave him
To him that made him proud – the Pope.
NORFOLK Let's in;
And with some other business put the King
From these sad thoughts that work too much
upon him.
My lord, you'll bear us company?
CHAMBERLAIN Excuse me,
The King has sent me otherwhere; besides,
You'll find a most unfit time to disturb him.
Health to your lordships!
NORFOLK Thanks, my good Lord Chamberlain.

[*Exit Lord Chamberlain; and the King draws the curtain and sits reading pensively.*

SUFFOLK How sad he looks; sure, he is much afflicted.
KING Who's there, ha?
NORFOLK Pray God he be not angry.
KING Who's there, I say? How dare you thrust yourselves
Into my private meditations?
Who am I, ha?
NORFOLK A gracious king that pardons all offences
Malice ne'er meant. Our breach of duty this way
Is business of estate, in which we come
To know your royal pleasure.
KING Ye are too bold.
Go to; I'll make ye know your times of business.
Is this an hour for temporal affairs, ha?

Enter WOLSEY and CAMPEIUS with a commission.

Who's there? My good Lord Cardinal? O my Wolsey,
The quiet of my wounded conscience,
Thou art a cure fit for a King. [*To Campeius*] You're welcome,
Most learned reverend sir, into our kingdom.
Use us and it. [*To Wolsey*] My good lord, have great care
I be not found a talker.
WOLSEY Sir, you cannot.
I would your Grace would give us but an hour
Of private conference.
KING [*To Norfolk and Suffolk*] We are busy; go.
NORFOLK [*Aside to Suffolk*] This priest has no pride in him!
SUFFOLK [*Aside to Norfolk*] Not to speak of!
I would not be so sick though for his place.
But this cannot continue.
NORFOLK [*Aside to Suffolk*] If it do,
I'll venture one have-at-him.
SUFFOLK [*Aside to Norfolk*] I another.
[*Exeunt Norfolk and Suffolk.*

WOLSEY Your Grace has given a precedent of wisdom
Above all princes, in committing freely
Your scruple to the voice of Christendom.
Who can be angry now? What envy reach you?
The Spaniard, tied by blood and favour to her,
Must now confess, if they have any goodness,
The trial just and noble. All the clerks,
I mean the learned ones, in Christian kingdoms
Have their free voices. Rome the nurse of judgment,
Invited by your noble self, hath sent
One general tongue unto us, this good man,
This just and learned priest, Cardinal Campeius,
Whom once more I present unto your Highness.
KING And once more in mine arms I bid him welcome,
And thank the holy conclave for their loves.
They have sent me such a man I would have wish'd for.
CAMPEIUS Your Grace must needs deserve all strangers' loves,
You are so noble. To your Highness' hand
I tender my commission; by whose virtue –
The court of Rome commanding – you, my Lord
Cardinal of York, are join'd with me their servant
In the unpartial judging of this business.
KING Two equal men. The Queen shall be acquainted
Forthwith for what you come. Where's Gardiner?
WOLSEY I know your Majesty has always lov'd her
So dear in heart not to deny her that
A woman of less place might ask by law –
Scholars allow'd freely to argue for her.
KING Ay, and the best she shall have; and my favour
To him that does best. God forbid else. Cardinal,
Prithee call Gardiner to me, my new secretary;
I find him a fit fellow. [*Exit Wolsey.*

Re-enter WOLSEY with GARDINER.

WOLSEY [*Aside to Gardiner*] Give me your hand: much joy and favour to you;
You are the King's now.
GARDINER [*Aside to Wolsey*] But to be commanded
For ever by your Grace, whose hand has rais'd me.
KING Come hither, Gardiner. [*Walks and whispers.*
CAMPEIUS My Lord of York, was not one Doctor Pace
In this man's place before him?
WOLSEY Yes, he was.
CAMPEIUS Was he not held a learned man?
WOLSEY Yes, surely.
CAMPEIUS Believe me, there's an ill opinion spread then,
Even of yourself, Lord Cardinal.
WOLSEY How! Of me?
CAMPEIUS They will not stick to say you envied him
And, fearing he would rise, he was so virtuous,
Kept him a foreign man still; which so griev'd him
That he ran mad and died.
WOLSEY Heav'n's peace be with him!

That's Christian care enough. For living murmurers
There's places of rebuke. He was a fool,
For he would needs be virtuous: that good fellow,
If I command him, follows my appointment.
I will have none so near else. Learn this, brother,
We live not to be grip'd by meaner persons.

KING Deliver this with modesty to th' Queen.
[*Exit Gardiner.*
The most convenient place that I can think of
For such receipt of learning is Blackfriars;
There ye shall meet about this weighty business –
My Wolsey, see it furnish'd. O, my lord,
Would it not grieve an able man to leave
So sweet a bedfellow? But, conscience, conscience!
O, 'tis a tender place! and I must leave her.
[*Exeunt.*

SCENE III. *London. The palace.*

Enter ANNE BULLEN and an old Lady.

ANNE Not for that neither. Here's the pang that pinches:
His Highness having liv'd so long with her, and she
So good a lady that no tongue could ever
Pronounce dishonour of her – by my life,
She never knew harm-doing – O, now, after
So many courses of the sun enthroned,
Still growing in a majesty and pomp, the which
To leave a thousand-fold more bitter than
'Tis sweet at first t' acquire – after this process,
To give her the avaunt, it is a pity
Would move a monster.

OLD LADY Hearts of most hard temper
Melt and lament for her.

ANNE O, God's will! much better
She ne'er had known pomp; though't be temporal,
Yet, if that quarrel, fortune, do divorce
It from the bearer, 'tis a sufferance panging
As soul and body's severing.

OLD LADY Alas, poor lady!
She's a stranger now again.

ANNE So much the more
Must pity drop upon her. Verily,
I swear 'tis better to be lowly born
And range with humble livers in content
Than to be perk'd up in a glist'ring grief
And wear a golden sorrow.

OLD LADY Our content
Is our best having.

ANNE By my troth and maidenhead,
I would not be a queen.

OLD LADY Beshrew me, I would,
And venture maidenhead for't; and so would you,
For all this spice of your hypocrisy.
You that have so fair parts of woman on you
Have too a woman's heart, which ever yet
Affected eminence, wealth, sovereignty;
Which, to say sooth, are blessings; and which gifts,
Saving your mincing, the capacity
Of your soft cheveril conscience would receive
If you might please to stretch it.

ANNE Nay, good troth.

OLD LADY Yes, troth and troth. You would not be a queen!

ANNE No, not for all the riches under heaven.

OLD LADY 'Tis strange: a threepence bow'd would hire me,
Old as I am, to queen it. But, I pray you,
What think you of a duchess? Have you limbs
To bear that load of title?

ANNE No, in truth.

OLD LADY Then you are weakly made. Pluck off a little;
I would not be a young count in your way
For more than blushing comes to. If your back
Cannot vouchsafe this burden, 'tis too weak
Ever to get a boy.

ANNE How you do talk!
I swear again I would not be a queen
For all the world.

OLD LADY In faith, for little England
You'd venture an emballing. I myself
Would for Carnarvonshire, although there long'd
No more to th' crown but that. Lo, who comes here?

Enter the Lord Chamberlain.

CHAMBERLAIN Good morrow, ladies. What were't worth to know
The secret of your conference?

ANNE My good lord,
Not your demand; it values not your asking.
Our mistress' sorrows we were pitying.

CHAMBERLAIN It was a gentle business and becoming
The action of good women; there is hope
All will be well.

ANNE Now, I pray God, amen!

CHAMBERLAIN You bear a gentle mind, and heav'nly blessings
Follow such creatures. That you may, fair lady,
Perceive I speak sincerely and high note's
Ta'en of your many virtues, the King's Majesty
Commends his good opinion of you to you, and

Does purpose honour to you no less flowing
Than Marchioness of Pembroke; to which title
A thousand pounds a year, annual support,
Out of his grace he adds.

ANNE I do not know
What kind of my obedience I should tender;
More than my all is nothing, nor my prayers
Are not words duly hallowed, nor my wishes
More worth than empty vanities; yet prayers and wishes
Are all I can return. Beseech your lordship,
Vouchsafe to speak my thanks and my obedience,
As from a blushing handmaid, to his Highness;
Whose health and royalty I pray for.

CHAMBERLAIN Lady,
I shall not fail t'approve the fair conceit
The King hath of you. [*Aside*] I have perus'd her well:
Beauty and honour in her are so mingled
That they have caught the King; and who knows yet
But from this lady may proceed a gem
To lighten all this isle? – I'll to the King
And say I spoke with you.

ANNE My honour'd lord!

[*Exit Lord Chamberlain.*

OLD LADY Why, this it is: see, see!
I have been begging sixteen years in court –
Am yet a courtier beggarly – nor could
Come pat betwixt too early and too late
For any suit of pounds; and you, O fate!
A very fresh-fish here – fie, fie, fie upon
This compell'd fortune! – have your mouth fill'd up
Before you open it.

ANNE This is strange to me.

OLD LADY How tastes it? Is it bitter? Forty pence, no.
There was a lady once – 'tis an old story –
That would not be a queen, that would she not,
For all the mud in Egypt. Have you heard it?

ANNE Come, you are pleasant.

OLD LADY With your theme I could
O'ermount the lark. The Marchioness of Pembroke!
A thousand pounds a year for pure respect!
No other obligation! By my life,
That promises moe thousands: honour's train
Is longer than his foreskirt. By this time
I know your back will bear a duchess. Say,
Are you not stronger than you were?

ANNE Good lady,
Make yourself mirth with your particular fancy,
And leave me out on't. Would I had no being,
If this salute my blood a jot; it faints me
To think what follows.
The Queen is comfortless, and we forgetful
In our long absence. Pray, do not deliver
What here y' have heard to her.

OLD LADY What do you think me?

[*Exeunt.*

SCENE IV. *London. A hall in Blackfriars.*

Trumpets, sennet, and cornets. Enter two Vergers, with short silver wands; next them, two Scribes, in the habit of doctors; after them, the ARCHBISHOP OF CANTERBURY alone; after him, the BISHOPS OF LINCOLN, ELY, ROCHESTER, and SAINT ASAPH; next them, with some small distance, follows a Gentleman bearing the purse, with the great seal, and a Cardinal's hat; then two Priests, bearing each a silver cross; then a Gentleman Usher bareheaded, accompanied with a Sergeant-at-Arms bearing a silver mace; then two Gentlemen bearing two great silver pillars; after them, side by side, the two Cardinals, WOLSEY and CAMPEIUS; two Noblemen with the sword and mace. Then enter the KING and QUEEN and their Trains. The King takes place under the cloth of state; the two Cardinals sit under him as judges. The Queen takes place some distance from the King. The Bishops place themselves on each side the court, in manner of a consistory; below them the Scribes. The Lords sit next the Bishops. The rest of the Attendants stand in convenient order about the stage.

WOLSEY Whilst our commission from Rome is read,
Let silence be commanded.

KING What's the need?
It hath already publicly been read,
And on all sides th' authority allow'd;
You may then spare that time.

WOLSEY Be't so; proceed.

SCRIBE Say 'Henry King of England, come into the court'.

CRIER Henry King of England, etc.

KING Here.

SCRIBE Say 'Katharine Queen of England, come into the court'.

CRIER Katharine Queen of England, etc.

[*The Queen makes no answer, rises out of her chair, goes about the court, comes to the King, and kneels at his feet; then speaks.*

QUEEN KATHARINE Sir, I desire you do me right and justice,
And to bestow your pity on me; for
I am a most poor woman and a stranger,
Born out of your dominions, having here
No judge indifferent, nor no more assurance

Of equal friendship and proceeding. Alas, sir,
In what have I offended you? What cause
Hath my behaviour given to your displeasure
That thus you should proceed to put me off
And take your good grace from me? Heaven witness,
I have been to you a true and humble wife,
At all times to your will conformable,
Ever in fear to kindle your dislike,
Yea, subject to your countenance – glad or sorry
As I saw it inclin'd. When was the hour
I ever contradicted your desire
Or made it not mine too? Or which of your friends
Have I not strove to love, although I knew
He were mine enemy? What friend of mine
That had to him deriv'd your anger did I
Continue in my liking? Nay, gave notice
He was from thence discharg'd? Sir, call to mind
That I have been your wife in this obedience
Upward of twenty years, and have been blest
With many children by you. If, in the course
And process of this time, you can report,
And prove it too against mine honour, aught,
My bond to wedlock or my love and duty,
Against your sacred person, in God's name,
Turn me away and let the foul'st contempt
Shut door upon me, and so give me up
To the sharp'st kind of justice. Please you, sir,
The King, your father, was reputed for
A prince most prudent, of an excellent
And unmatch'd wit and judgment; Ferdinand,
My father, King of Spain, was reckon'd one
The wisest prince that there had reign'd by many
A year before. It is not to be question'd
That they had gather'd a wise council to them
Of every realm, that did debate this business,
Who deem'd our marriage lawful. Wherefore I humbly
Beseech you, sir, to spare me till I may
Be by my friends in Spain advis'd, whose counsel
I will implore. If not, i' th' name of God,
Your pleasure be fulfill'd!

WOLSEY You have here, lady,
And of your choice, these reverend fathers – men
Of singular integrity and learning,
Yea, the elect o' th' land, who are assembled
To plead your cause. It shall be therefore bootless
That longer you desire the court, as well
For your own quiet as to rectify
What is unsettled in the King.

CAMPEIUS His Grace
Hath spoken well and justly; therefore, madam,
It's fit this royal session do proceed
And that, without delay, their arguments
Be now produc'd and heard.

QUEEN KATHARINE Lord Cardinal,
To you I speak.

WOLSEY Your pleasure, madam?

QUEEN KATHARINE Sir,
I am about to weep; but, thinking that
We are a queen, or long have dream'd so, certain
The daughter of a king, my drops of tears
I'll turn to sparks of fire.

WOLSEY Be patient yet.

QUEEN KATHARINE I will, when you are humble; nay, before,
Or God will punish me. I do believe,
Induc'd by potent circumstances, that
You are mine enemy, and make my challenge
You shall not be my judge; for it is you
Have blown this coal betwixt my lord and me –
Which God's dew quench! Therefore I say again,
I utterly abhor, yea, from my soul
Refuse you for my judge, whom yet once more
I hold my most malicious foe and think not
At all a friend to truth.

WOLSEY I do profess
You speak not like yourself, who ever yet
Have stood to charity and display'd th' effects
Of disposition gentle and of wisdom
O'ertopping woman's pow'r. Madam, you do me wrong:
I have no spleen against you, nor injustice
For you or any; how far I have proceeded,
Or how far further shall, is warranted
By a commission from the Consistory,
Yea, the whole Consistory of Rome. You charge me
That I have blown this coal: I do deny it.
The King is present; if it be known to him
That I gainsay my deed, how may he wound,
And worthily, my falsehood! Yea, as much
As you have done my truth. If he know
That I am free of your report, he knows
I am not of your wrong. Therefore in him
It lies to cure me, and the cure is to
Remove these thoughts from you; the which before
His Highness shall speak in, I do beseech
You, gracious madam, to unthink your speaking
And to say so no more.

QUEEN KATHARINE My lord, my lord,
I am a simple woman, much too weak
T' oppose your cunning. Y'are meek and humble-mouth'd;
You sign your place and calling, in full seeming,
With meekness and humility; but your heart
Is cramm'd with arrogancy, spleen, and pride.

You have, by fortune and his Highness' favours,
Gone slightly o'er low steps, and now are mounted
Where pow'rs are your retainers, and your words,
Domestics to you, serve your will as't please
Yourself pronounce their office. I must tell you
You tender more your person's honour than
Your high profession spiritual; that again
I do refuse you for my judge and here,
Before you all, appeal unto the Pope,
To bring my whole cause 'fore his Holiness
And to be judg'd by him. [*She curtsies to the King, and offers to depart.*

CAMPEIUS The Queen is obstinate,
Stubborn to justice, apt to accuse it, and
Disdainful to be tried by't; 'tis not well.
She's going away.

KING Call her again.

CRIER Katharine Queen of England, come into the court.

GRIFFITH Madam, you are call'd back.

QUEEN KATHARINE What need you note it? Pray you keep your way;
When you are call'd, return. Now the Lord help!
They vex me past my patience. Pray you pass on.
I will not tarry; no, nor ever more
Upon this business my appearance make
In any of their courts. [*Exeunt Queen and her Attendants.*

KING Go thy ways, Kate.
That man i' th' world who shall report he has
A better wife, let him in nought be trusted
For speaking false in that. Thou art, alone –
If thy rare qualities, sweet gentleness,
Thy meekness saint-like, wife-like government,
Obeying in commanding, and thy parts
Sovereign and pious else, could speak thee out –
The queen of earthly queens. She's noble born;
And like her true nobility she has
Carried herself toward me.

WOLSEY Most gracious sir,
In humblest manner I require your Highness
That it shall please you to declare in hearing
Of all these ears – for where I am robb'd and bound,
There must I be unloos'd, although not there
At once and fully satisfied – whether ever I
Did broach this business to your Highness, or
Laid any scruple in your way which might
Induce you to the question on't, or ever
Have to you, but with thanks to God for such
A royal lady, spake one the least word that might
Be to the prejudice of her present state,
Or touch of her good person?

KING My Lord Cardinal,
I do excuse you; yea, upon mine honour,
I free you from't. You are not to be taught
That you have many enemies that know not
Why they are so, but, like to village curs,
Bark when their fellows do. By some of these
The Queen is put in anger. Y'are excus'd.
But will you be more justified? You ever
Have wish'd the sleeping of this business; never desir'd
It to be stirr'd; but oft have hind'red, oft,
The passages made toward it. On my honour,
I speak my good Lord Cardinal to this point,
And thus far clear him. Now, what mov'd me to't,
I will be bold with time and your attention.
Then mark th' inducement. Thus it came – give heed to't:
My conscience first receiv'd a tenderness,
Scruple, and prick, on certain speeches utter'd
By th' Bishop of Bayonne, then French ambassador,
Who had been hither sent on the debating
A marriage 'twixt the Duke of Orleans and
Our daughter Mary. I' th' progress of this business,
Ere a determinate resolution, he –
I mean the Bishop – did require a respite
Wherein he might the King his lord advertise
Whether our daughter were legitimate,
Respecting this our marriage with the dowager,
Sometimes our brother's wife. This respite shook
The bosom of my conscience, enter'd me,
Yea, with a splitting power, and made to tremble
The region of my breast, which forc'd such way
That many maz'd considerings did throng
And press'd in with this caution. First, methought
I stood not in the smile of heaven, who had
Commanded nature that my lady's womb,
If it conceiv'd a male child by me, should
Do no more offices of life to't than
The grave does to the dead; for her male issue
Or died where they were made, or shortly after
This world had air'd them. Hence I took a thought
This was a judgment on me, that my kingdom,
Well worthy the best heir o' th' world, should not
Be gladded in't by me. Then follows that
I weigh'd the danger which my realms stood in
By this my issue's fail, and that gave to me
Many a groaning throe. Thus hulling in
The wild sea of my conscience, I did steer
Toward this remedy, whereupon we are
Now present here together; that's to say

I meant to rectify my conscience, which
I then did feel full sick, and yet not well,
By all the reverend fathers of the land
And doctors learn'd. First, I began in private
With you, my Lord of Lincoln; you remember
How under my oppression I did reek,
When I first mov'd you.

LINCOLN Very well, my liege.

KING I have spoke long; be pleas'd yourself to say
How far you satisfied me.

LINCOLN So please your Highness,
The question did at first so stagger me –
Bearing a state of mighty moment in't
And consequence of dread – that I committed
The daring'st counsel which I had to doubt,
And did entreat your Highness to this course
Which you are running here.

KING I then mov'd you,
My Lord of Canterbury, and got your leave
To make this present summons. Unsolicited
I left no reverend person in this court,
But by particular consent proceeded
Under your hands and seals; therefore, go on,
For no dislike i' th' world against the person
Of the good Queen, but the sharp thorny points
Of my alleged reasons, drives this forward.
Prove but our marriage lawful, by my life
And kingly dignity, we are contented
To wear our mortal state to come with her,
Katharine our queen, before the primest creature
That's paragon'd o' th' world.

CAMPEIUS So please your Highness,
The Queen being absent, 'tis a needful fitness
That we adjourn this court till further day;
Meanwhile must be an earnest motion
Made to the Queen to call back her appeal
She intends unto his Holiness.

KING [*Aside*] I may perceive
These cardinals trifle with me. I abhor
This dilatory sloth and tricks of Rome.
My learn'd and well-beloved servant, Cranmer,
Prithee return. With thy approach I know
My comfort comes along. – Break up the court;
I say, set on. [*Exeunt in manner as they enter'd.*

ACT THREE

SCENE I. *London. The Queen's apartments.*

Enter the QUEEN and her Women, as at work.

QUEEN KATHARINE Take thy lute, wench. My soul grows sad with troubles;
Sing and disperse 'em, if thou canst. Leave working.

SONG

Orpheus with his lute made trees,
And the mountain tops that freeze,
Bow themselves when he did sing;
To his music plants and flowers
Ever sprung, as sun and showers
There had made a lasting spring.
Every thing that heard him play,
Even the billows of the sea,
Hung their heads and then lay by.
In sweet music is such art,
Killing care and grief of heart
Fall asleep or hearing die.

Enter a Gentleman.

QUEEN KATHARINE How now?

GENTLEMAN An't please your Grace, the two great Cardinals
Wait in the presence.

QUEEN KATHARINE Would they speak with me?

GENTLEMAN They will'd me say so, madam.

QUEEN KATHARINE Pray their Graces
To come near. [*Exit Gentleman*] What can be their business
With me, a poor weak woman, fall'n from favour?
I do not like their coming. Now I think on't,
They should be good men, their affairs as righteous;
But all hoods make not monks.

Enter the two Cardinals, WOLSEY and CAMPEIUS.

WOLSEY Peace to your Highness!

QUEEN KATHARINE Your Graces find me here part of a housewife;
I would be all, against the worst may happen.
What are your pleasures with me, reverend lords?

WOLSEY May it please you, noble madam, to withdraw
Into your private chamber, we shall give you
The full cause of our coming.

QUEEN KATHARINE Speak it here;
There's nothing I have done yet, o' my conscience,
Deserves a corner. Would all other women
Could speak this with as free a soul as I do!
My lords, I care not – so much I am happy
Above a number – if my actions
Were tried by ev'ry tongue, ev'ry eye saw 'em,
Envy and base opinion set against 'em,
I know my life so even. If your business
Seek me out, and that way I am wife in,

Out with it boldly; truth loves open dealing.
WOLSEY Tanta est erga te mentis integritas, regina serenissima –
QUEEN KATHARINE O, good my lord, no Latin!
I am not such a truant since my coming,
As not to know the language I have liv'd in;
A strange tongue makes my cause more strange, suspicious;
Pray speak in English. Here are some will thank you,
If you speak truth, for their poor mistress' sake;
Believe me, she has had much wrong. Lord Cardinal,
The willing'st sin I ever yet committed
May be absolv'd in English.
WOLSEY Noble lady,
I am sorry my integrity should breed,
And service to his Majesty and you,
So deep suspicion, where all faith was meant.
We come not by the way of accusation
To taint that honour every good tongue blesses,
Nor to betray you any way to sorrow –
You have too much, good lady; but to know
How you stand minded in the weighty difference
Between the King and you, and to deliver,
Like free and honest men, our just opinions
And comforts to your cause.
CAMPEIUS Most honour'd madam,
My Lord of York, out of his noble nature,
Zeal and obedience he still bore your Grace,
Forgetting, like a good man, your late censure
Both of his truth and him – which was too far –
Offers, as I do, in a sign of peace,
His service and his counsel.
QUEEN KATHARINE [*Aside*] To betray me. –
My lords, I thank you both for your good wills;
Ye speak like honest men – pray God ye prove so!
But how to make ye suddenly an answer,
In such a point of weight, so near mine honour,
More near my life, I fear, with my weak wit,
And to such men of gravity and learning,
In truth I know not. I was set at work
Among my maids, full little, God knows, looking
Either for such men or such business.
For her sake that I have been – for I feel
The last fit of my greatness – good your Graces,
Let me have time and counsel for my cause.
Alas, I am a woman, friendless, hopeless!
WOLSEY Madam, you wrong the King's love with these fears;
Your hopes and friends are infinite.
QUEEN KATHARINE In England
But little for my profit; can you think, lords,
That any Englishman dare give me counsel?
Or be a known friend, 'gainst his Highness' pleasure –
Though he be grown so desperate to be honest –
And live a subject? Nay, forsooth, my friends,
They that must weigh out my afflictions,
They that my trust must grow to, live not here;
They are, as all my other comforts, far hence,
In mine own country, lords.
CAMPEIUS I would your Grace
Would leave your griefs, and take my counsel.
QUEEN KATHARINE How, sir?
CAMPEIUS Put your main cause into the King's protection;
He's loving and most gracious. 'Twill be much
Both for your honour better and your cause;
For if the trial of the law o'ertake ye
You'll part away disgrac'd.
WOLSEY He tells you rightly.
QUEEN KATHARINE Ye tell me what ye wish for both – my ruin.
Is this your Christian counsel? Out upon ye!
Heaven is above all yet: there sits a Judge
That no king can corrupt.
CAMPEIUS Your rage mistakes us.
QUEEN KATHARINE The more shame for ye; holy men I thought ye,
Upon my soul, two reverend cardinal virtues;
But cardinal sins and hollow hearts I fear ye.
Mend 'em, for shame, my lords. Is this your comfort?
The cordial that ye bring a wretched lady –
A woman lost among ye, laugh'd at, scorn'd?
I will not wish ye half my miseries:
I have more charity; but say I warn'd ye.
Take heed, for heaven's sake take heed, lest at once
The burden of my sorrows fall upon ye.
WOLSEY Madam, this is a mere distraction;
You turn the good we offer into envy.
QUEEN KATHARINE Ye turn me into nothing. Woe upon ye,
And all such false professors! Would you have me –
If you have any justice, any pity,
If ye be any thing but churchmen's habits –
Put my sick cause into his hands that hates me?
Alas! has banish'd me his bed already,
His love too long ago! I am old, my lords,
And all the fellowship I hold now with him
Is only my obedience. What can happen
To me above this wretchedness? All your studies
Make me a curse like this.
CAMPEIUS Your fears are worse.
QUEEN KATHARINE Have I liv'd thus long – let me speak myself,
Since virtue finds no friends – a wife, a true one?

A woman, I dare say without vain-glory,
Never yet branded with suspicion?
Have I with all my full affections
Still met the King, lov'd him next heav'n, obey'd him,
Been, out of fondness, superstitious to him,
Almost forgot my prayers to content him,
And am I thus rewarded? 'Tis not well, lords.
Bring me a constant woman to her husband,
One that ne'er dream'd a joy beyond his pleasure,
And to that woman, when she has done most,
Yet will I add an honour – a great patience.

WOLSEY Madam, you wander from the good we aim at.

QUEEN KATHARINE My lord, I dare not make myself so guilty,
To give up willingly that noble title
Your master wed me to: nothing but death
Shall e'er divorce my dignities.

WOLSEY Pray hear me.

QUEEN KATHARINE Would I had never trod this English earth,
Or felt the flatteries that grow upon it!
Ye have angels' faces, but heaven knows your hearts.
What will become of me now, wretched lady?
I am the most unhappy woman living.
[*To her Women*] Alas, poor wenches, where are now your fortunes?
Shipwreck'd upon a kingdom, where no pity,
No friends, no hope; no kindred weep for me;
Almost no grave allow'd me. Like the lily,
That once was mistress of the field, and flourish'd,
I'll hang my head and perish.

WOLSEY If your Grace
Could but be brought to know our ends are honest,
You'd feel more comfort. Why should we, good lady,
Upon what cause, wrong you? Alas, our places,
The way of our profession is against it;
We are to cure such sorrows, not to sow 'em.
For goodness' sake, consider what you do;
How you may hurt yourself, ay, utterly
Grow from the King's acquaintance, by this carriage.
The hearts of princes kiss obedience,
So much they love it; but to stubborn spirits
They swell and grow as terrible as storms.
I know you have a gentle, noble temper,
A soul as even as a calm. Pray think us
Those we profess, peace-makers, friends, and servants.

CAMPEIUS Madam, you'll find it so. You wrong your virtues
With these weak women's fears. A noble spirit,
As yours was put into you, ever casts
Such doubts as false coin from it. The King loves you;
Beware you lose it not. For us, if you please
To trust us in your business, we are ready
To use our utmost studies in your service.

QUEEN KATHARINE Do what ye will, my lords; and pray forgive me
If I have us'd myself unmannerly;
You know I am a woman, lacking wit
To make a seemly answer to such persons.
Pray do my service to his Majesty;
He has my heart yet, and shall have my prayers
While I shall have my life. Come, reverend fathers,
Bestow your counsels on me; she now begs
That little thought, when she set footing here,
She should have bought her dignities so dear.
[*Exeunt.*

SCENE II. *London. The palace.*

Enter the DUKE OF NORFOLK, the DUKE OF SUFFOLK, the EARL OF SURREY, and the Lord Chamberlain.

NORFOLK If you will now unite in your complaints
And force them with a constancy, the Cardinal
Cannot stand under them; if you omit
The offer of this time, I cannot promise
But that you shall sustain moe new disgraces
With these you bear already.

SURREY I am joyful
To meet the least occasion that may give me
Remembrance of my father-in-law, the Duke,
To be reveng'd on him.

SUFFOLK Which of the peers
Have uncontemn'd gone by him, or at least
Strangely neglected? When did he regard
The stamp of nobleness in any person
Out of himself?

CHAMBERLAIN My lords, you speak your pleasures.
What he deserves of you and me I know;
What we can do to him – though now the time
Gives way to us – I much fear. If you cannot
Bar his access to th' King, never attempt
Anything on him; for he hath a witchcraft
Over the King in's tongue.

NORFOLK O, fear him not!
His spell in that is out; the King hath found
Matter against him that for ever mars
The honey of his language. No, he's settled,
Not to come off, in his displeasure.

SURREY Sir,
I should be glad to hear such news as this

Once every hour.
NORFOLK Believe it, this is true:
In the divorce his contrary proceedings
Are all unfolded; wherein he appears
As I would wish mine enemy.
SURREY How came
His practices to light?
SUFFOLK Most strangely.
SURREY O, how, how?
SUFFOLK The Cardinal's letters to the Pope miscarried,
And came to th' eye o' th' King; wherein was read
How that the Cardinal did entreat his Holiness
To stay the judgment o' th' divorce; for if
It did take place, 'I do' quoth he 'perceive
My king is tangled in affection to
A creature of the Queen's, Lady Anne Bullen'.
SURREY Has the King this?
SUFFOLK Believe it.
SURREY Will this work?
CHAMBERLAIN The King in this perceives him how he coasts
And hedges his own way. But in this point
All his tricks founder, and he brings his physic
After his patient's death: the King already
Hath married the fair lady.
SURREY Would he had!
SUFFOLK May you be happy in your wish, my lord!
For, I profess, you have it.
SURREY Now, all my joy
Trace the conjunction!
SUFFOLK My amen to't!
NORFOLK All men's!
SUFFOLK There's order given for her coronation;
Marry, this is yet but young, and may be left
To some ears unrecounted. But, my lords,
She is a gallant creature, and complete
In mind and feature. I persuade me from her
Will fall some blessing to this land, which shall
In it be memoriz'd.
SURREY But will the King
Digest this letter of the Cardinal's?
The Lord forbid!
NORFOLK Marry, amen!
SUFFOLK No, no;
There be moe wasps that buzz about his nose
Will make this sting the sooner. Cardinal Campeius
Is stol'n away to Rome; hath ta'en no leave;
Has left the cause o' th' King unhandled, and
Is posted, as the agent of our Cardinal,
To second all his plot. I do assure you
The King cried 'Ha!' at this.
CHAMBERLAIN Now, God incense him,
And let him cry 'Ha!' louder!
NORFOLK But, my lord,
When returns Cranmer?
SUFFOLK He is return'd, in his opinions; which
Have satisfied the King for his divorce,
Together with all famous colleges
Almost in Christendom. Shortly, I believe,
His second marriage shall be publish'd, and
Her coronation. Katharine no more
Shall be call'd queen, but princess dowager
And widow to Prince Arthur.
NORFOLK This same Cranmer's
A worthy fellow, and hath ta'en much pain
In the King's business.
SUFFOLK He has; and we shall see him
For it an archbishop.
NORFOLK So I hear.
SUFFOLK 'Tis so.

Enter WOLSEY and CROMWELL.

The Cardinal!
NORFOLK Observe, observe, he's moody.
WOLSEY The packet, Cromwell,
Gave't you the King?
CROMWELL To his own hand, in's bedchamber.
WOLSEY Look'd he o' th' inside of the paper?
CROMWELL Presently
He did unseal them; and the first he view'd,
He did it with a serious mind; a heed
Was in his countenance. You he bade
Attend him here this morning.
WOLSEY Is he ready
To come abroad?
CROMWELL I think by this he is.
WOLSEY Leave me awhile. [*Exit Cromwell.*
[*Aside*] It shall be to the Duchess of Alençon,
The French King's sister; he shall marry her.
Anne Bullen! No, I'll no Anne Bullens for him;
There's more in't than fair visage. Bullen!
No, we'll no Bullens. Speedily I wish
To hear from Rome. The Marchioness of Pembroke!
NORFOLK He's discontented.
SUFFOLK May be he hears the King
Does whet his anger to him.
SURREY Sharp enough,
Lord, for thy justice!
WOLSEY [*Aside*] The late Queen's gentlewoman, a knight's daughter,
To be her mistress' mistress! The Queen's queen!
This candle burns not clear. 'Tis I must snuff it;
Then out it goes. What though I know her virtuous
And well deserving? Yet I know her for
A spleeny Lutheran; and not wholesome to
Our cause that she should lie i' th' bosom of
Our hard-rul'd King. Again, there is sprung up

An heretic, an arch one, Cranmer; one
Hath crawl'd into the favour of the King,
And is his oracle.

NORFOLK He is vex'd at something.

Enter the KING, reading of a schedule, and LOVELL.

SURREY I would 'twere something that would fret the string,
The master-cord on's heart!

SUFFOLK The King, the King!

KING What piles of wealth hath he accumulated
To his own portion! And what expense by th' hour
Seems to flow from him! How, i' th' name of thrift,
Does he rake this together? – Now, my lords,
Saw you the Cardinal?

NORFOLK My lord, we have
Stood here observing him. Some strange commotion
Is in his brain: he bites his lip and starts,
Stops on a sudden, looks upon the ground,
Then lays his finger on his temple; straight
Springs out into fast gait; then stops again,
Strikes his breast hard; and anon he casts
His eye against the moon. In most strange postures
We have seen him set himself.

KING It may well be
There is a mutiny in's mind. This morning
Papers of state he sent me to peruse,
As I requir'd; and wot you what I found
There – on my conscience, put unwittingly?
Forsooth, an inventory, thus importing
The several parcels of his plate, his treasure,
Rich stuffs, and ornaments of household; which
I find at such proud rate that it outspeaks
Possession of a subject.

NORFOLK It's heaven's will;
Some spirit put this paper in the packet
To bless your eye withal.

KING If we did think
His contemplation were above the earth
And fix'd on spiritual object, he should still
Dwell in his musings; but I am afraid
His thinkings are below the moon, not worth
His serious considering.

[*The King takes his seat and whispers Lovell, who goes to the Cardinal.*

WOLSEY Heaven forgive me!
Ever God bless your Highness!

KING Good, my lord,
You are full of heavenly stuff, and bear the inventory
Of your best graces in your mind; the which
You were now running o'er. You have scarce time
To steal from spiritual leisure a brief span
To keep your earthly audit; sure, in that
I deem you an ill husband, and am glad
To have you therein my companion.

WOLSEY Sir,
For holy offices I have a time; a time
To think upon the part of business which
I bear i' th' state; and nature does require
Her times of preservation, which perforce
I, her frail son, amongst my brethren mortal,
Must give my tendance to.

KING You have said well.

WOLSEY And ever may your Highness yoke together,
As I will lend you cause, my doing well
With my well saying!

KING 'Tis well said again;
And 'tis a kind of good deed to say well;
And yet words are no deeds. My father lov'd you:
He said he did; and with his deed did crown
His word upon you. Since I had my office
I have kept you next my heart; have not alone
Employ'd you where high profits might come home,
But par'd my present havings to bestow
My bounties upon you.

WOLSEY [*Aside*] What should this mean?

SURREY [*Aside*] The Lord increase this business!

KING Have I not made you
The prime man of the state? I pray you tell me
If what I now pronounce you have found true;
And, if you may confess it, say withal
If you are bound to us or no. What say you?

WOLSEY My sovereign, I confess your royal graces,
Show'r'd on me daily, have been more than could
My studied purposes requite; which went
Beyond all man's endeavours. My endeavours,
Have ever come too short of my desires,
Yet fil'd with my abilities; mine own ends
Have been mine so that evermore they pointed
To th' good of your most sacred person and
The profit of the state. For your great graces
Heap'd upon me, poor undeserver, I
Can nothing render but allegiant thanks;
My pray'rs to heaven for you; my loyalty,
Which ever has and ever shall be growing,
Till death, that winter, kill it.

KING Fairly answer'd!
A loyal and obedient subject is
Therein illustrated; the honour of it
Does pay the act of it, as, i' th' contrary,
The foulness is the punishment. I presume
That, as my hand has open'd bounty to you,

My heart dropp'd love, my pow'r rain'd honour, more
On you than any, so your hand and heart,
Your brain, and every function of your power,
Should, notwithstanding that your bond of duty,
As 'twere in love's particular, be more
To me, your friend, than any.

WOLSEY I do profess
That for your Highness' good I ever labour'd
More than mine own; that am, have, and will be –
Though all the world should crack their duty to you,
And throw it from their soul; though perils did
Abound as thick as thought could make 'em, and
Appear in forms more horrid – yet my duty,
As doth a rock against the chiding flood,
Should the approach of this wild river break,
And stand unshaken yours.

KING 'Tis nobly spoken.
Take notice, lords, he has a loyal breast,
For you have seen him open 't. Read o'er this;
[*Giving him papers.*
And after, this; and then to breakfast with
What appetite you have. [*Exit the King, frowning upon the Cardinal; the Nobles throng after him, smiling and whispering.*

WOLSEY What should this mean?
What sudden anger's this? How have I reap'd it?
He parted frowning from me, as if ruin
Leap'd from his eyes; so looks the chafed lion
Upon the daring huntsman that has gall'd him –
Then makes him nothing. I must read this paper;
I fear, the story of his anger. 'Tis so;
This paper has undone me. 'Tis th' account
Of all that world of wealth I have drawn together
For mine own ends; indeed, to gain the popedom,
And fee my friends in Rome. O negligence,
Fit for a fool to fall by! What cross devil
Made me put this main secret in the packet
I sent the King? Is there no way to cure this?
No new device to beat this from his brains?
I know 'twill stir him strongly; yet I know
A way, if it take right, in spite of fortune,
Will bring me off again. What's this? 'To th' Pope.'
The letter, as I live, with all the business
I writ to's Holiness. Nay then, farewell!
I have touch'd the highest point of all my greatness,
And from that full meridian of my glory
I haste now to my setting. I shall fall
Like a bright exhalation in the evening,
And no man see me more.

Re-enter to Wolsey the DUKES OF NORFOLK and SUFFOLK, the EARL OF SURREY and the Lord Chamberlain.

NORFOLK Hear the King's pleasure, Cardinal, who commands you
To render up the great seal presently
Into our hands, and to confine yourself
To Asher House, my Lord of Winchester's,
Till you hear further from his Highness.

WOLSEY Stay:
Where's your commission, lords? Words cannot carry
Authority so weighty.

SUFFOLK Who dare cross 'em,
Bearing the King's will from his mouth expressly?

WOLSEY Till I find more than will or words to do it –
I mean your malice – know, officious lords,
I dare and must deny it. Now I feel
Of what coarse metal ye are moulded – envy;
How eagerly ye follow my disgraces,
As if it fed ye; and how sleek and wanton
Ye appear in every thing may bring my ruin!
Follow your envious courses, men of malice;
You have Christian warrant for 'em, and no doubt
In time will find their fit rewards. That seal
You ask with such a violence, the King –
Mine and your master – with his own hand gave me;
Bade me enjoy it, with the place and honours,
During my life; and, to confirm his goodness,
Tied it by letters-patents. Now, who'll take it?

SURREY The King, that gave it.

WOLSEY It must be himself then.

SURREY Thou art a proud traitor, priest.

WOLSEY Proud lord, thou liest.
Within these forty hours Surrey durst better
Have burnt that tongue than said so.

SURREY Thy ambition,
Thou scarlet sin, robb'd this bewailing land
Of noble Buckingham, my father-in-law.
The heads of all thy brother cardinals,
With thee and all thy best parts bound together,
Weigh'd not a hair of his. Plague of your policy!
You sent me deputy for Ireland;
Far from his succour, from the King, from all
That might have mercy on the fault thou gav'st him;
Whilst your great goodness, out of holy pity,
Absolv'd him with an axe.

WOLSEY This, and all else

This talking lord can lay upon my credit,
I answer is most false. The Duke by law
Found his deserts; how innocent I was
From any private malice in his end,
His noble jury and foul cause can witness.
If I lov'd many words, lord, I should tell you
You have as little honesty as honour,
That in the way of loyalty and truth
Toward the King, my ever royal master,
Dare mate a sounder man than Surrey can be
And all that love his follies.

SURREY By my soul,
Your long coat, priest, protects you; thou shouldst feel
My sword i' th' life-blood of thee else. My lords,
Can ye endure to hear this arrogance?
And from this fellow? If we live thus tamely,
To be thus jaded by a piece of scarlet,
Farewell nobility! Let his Grace go forward
And dare us with his cap like larks.

WOLSEY All goodness
Is poison to thy stomach.

SURREY Yes, that goodness
Of gleaning all the land's wealth into one,
Into your own hands, Cardinal, by extortion;
The goodness of your intercepted packets
You writ to th' Pope against the King; your goodness,
Since you provoke me, shall be most notorious.
My Lord of Norfolk, as you are truly noble,
As you respect the common good, the state
Of our despis'd nobility, our issues,
Whom, if he live, will scarce be gentlemen –
Produce the grand sum of his sins, the articles
Collected from his life. I'll startle you
Worse than the sacring bell, when the brown wench
Lay kissing in your arms, Lord Cardinal.

WOLSEY How much, methinks, I could despise this man,
But that I am bound in charity against it!

NORFOLK Those articles, my lord, are in the King's hand;
But, thus much, they are foul ones.

WOLSEY So much fairer
And spotless shall mine innocence arise,
When the King knows my truth.

SURREY This cannot save you.
I thank my memory I yet remember
Some of these articles; and out they shall.
Now, if you can blush and cry guilty, Cardinal,
You'll show a little honesty.

WOLSEY Speak on, sir;
I dare your worst objections. If I blush,
It is to see a nobleman want manners.

SURREY I had rather want those than my head. Have at you!
First, that without the King's assent or knowledge
You wrought to be a legate; by which power
You maim'd the jurisdiction of all bishops.

NORFOLK Then, that in all you writ to Rome, or else
To foreign princes, 'Ego et Rex meus'
Was still inscrib'd; in which you brought the King
To be your servant.

SUFFOLK Then, that without the knowledge
Either of King or Council, when you went
Ambassador to the Emperor, you made bold
To carry into Flanders the great seal.

SURREY Item, you sent a large commission
To Gregory de Cassado, to conclude,
Without the King's will or the state's allowance,
A league between his Highness and Ferrara.

SUFFOLK That out of mere ambition you have caus'd
Your holy hat to be stamp'd on the King's coin.

SURREY Then, that you have sent innumerable substance,
By what means got I leave to your own conscience,
To furnish Rome and to prepare the ways
You have for dignities, to the mere undoing
Of all the kingdom. Many more there are,
Which, since they are of you, and odious,
I will not taint my mouth with.

CHAMBERLAIN O my lord,
Press not a falling man too far! 'Tis virtue.
His faults lie open to the laws; let them,
Not you, correct him. My heart weeps to see him
So little of his great self.

SURREY I forgive him.

SUFFOLK Lord Cardinal, the King's further pleasure is –
Because all those things you have done of late,
By your power legatine within this kingdom,
Fall into th' compass of a praemunire –
That therefore such a writ be sued against you:
To forfeit all your goods, lands, tenements,
Chattels, and whatsoever, and to be
Out of the King's protection. This is my charge.

NORFOLK And so we'll leave you to your meditations
How to live better. For your stubborn answer
About the giving back the great seal to us,
The King shall know it, and, no doubt, shall thank you.
So fare you well, my little good Lord Cardinal.

[*Exeunt all but Wolsey.*

WOLSEY So farewell to the little good you bear me.

Farewell, a long farewell, to all my greatness!
This is the state of man: to-day he puts forth
The tender leaves of hopes; to-morrow blossoms
And bears his blushing honours thick upon him;
The third day comes a frost, a killing frost,
And when he thinks, good easy man, full surely
His greatness is a-ripening, nips his root,
And then he falls, as I do. I have ventur'd,
Like little wanton boys that swim on bladders,
This many summers in a sea of glory;
But far beyond my depth. My high-blown pride
At length broke under me, and now has left me,
Weary and old with service, to the mercy
Of a rude stream, that must for ever hide me.
Vain pomp and glory of this world, I hate ye;
I feel my heart new open'd. O, how wretched
Is that poor man that hangs on princes' favours!
There is betwixt that smile we would aspire to,
That sweet aspect of princes, and their ruin
More pangs and fears than wars or women have;
And when he falls, he falls like Lucifer,
Never to hope again.

Enter CROMWELL, standing amazed.

Why, how now, Cromwell!

CROMWELL I have no power to speak, sir.

WOLSEY What, amaz'd
At my misfortunes? Can thy spirit wonder
A great man should decline? Nay, an you weep,
I am fall'n indeed.

CROMWELL How does your Grace?

WOLSEY Why, well;
Never so truly happy, my good Cromwell.
I know myself now, and I feel within me
A peace above all earthly dignities,
A still and quiet conscience. The King has cur'd me,
I humbly thank his Grace; and from these shoulders,
These ruin'd pillars, out of pity, taken
A load would sink a navy – too much honour.
O, 'tis a burden, Cromwell, 'tis a burden
Too heavy for a man that hopes for heaven!

CROMWELL I am glad your Grace has made that right use of it.

WOLSEY I hope I have. I am able now, methinks,
Out of a fortitude of soul I feel,
To endure more miseries and greater far
Than my weak-hearted enemies dare offer.
What news abroad?

CROMWELL The heaviest and the worst
Is your displeasure with the King.

WOLSEY God bless him!

CROMWELL The next is that Sir Thomas More is chosen
Lord Chancellor in your place.

WOLSEY That's somewhat sudden.
But he's a learned man. May he continue
Long in his Highness' favour, and do justice
For truth's sake and his conscience; that his bones,
When he has run his course and sleeps in blessings,
May have a tomb of orphans' tears wept on him!
What more?

CROMWELL That Cranmer is return'd with welcome,
Install'd Lord Archbishop of Canterbury.

WOLSEY That's news indeed.

CROMWELL Last, that the Lady Anne,
Whom the King hath in secrecy long married,
This day was view'd in open as his queen,
Going to chapel; and the voice is now
Only about her coronation.

WOLSEY There was the weight that pull'd me down. O Cromwell,
The King has gone beyond me. All my glories
In that one woman I have lost for ever.
No sun shall ever usher forth mine honours,
Or gild again the noble troops that waited
Upon my smiles. Go get thee from me, Cromwell;
I am a poor fall'n man, unworthy now
To be thy lord and master. Seek the King;
That sun, I pray, may never set! I have told him
What and how true thou art. He will advance thee;
Some little memory of me will stir him –
I know his noble nature – not to let
Thy hopeful service perish too. Good Cromwell,
Neglect him not; make use now, and provide
For thine own future safety.

CROMWELL O my lord,
Must I then leave you? Must I needs forgo
So good, so noble, and so true a master?
Bear witness, all that have not hearts of iron,
With what a sorrow Cromwell leaves his lord.
The King shall have my service; but my prayers
For ever and for ever shall be yours.

WOLSEY Cromwell, I did not think to shed a tear
In all my miseries; but thou hast forc'd me,
Out of thy honest truth, to play the woman.
Let's dry our eyes; and thus far hear me, Cromwell,
And when I am forgotten, as I shall be,
And sleep in dull cold marble, where no mention
Of me more must be heard of, say I taught thee –
Say Wolsey, that once trod the ways of glory,
And sounded all the depths and shoals of honour,

Found thee a way, out of his wreck, to rise in –
A sure and safe one, though thy master miss'd it.
Mark but my fall and that that ruin'd me.
Cromwell, I charge thee, fling away ambition:
By that sin fell the angels. How can man then,
The image of his Maker, hope to win by it?
Love thyself last; cherish those hearts that hate thee;
Corruption wins not more than honesty.
Still in thy right hand carry gentle peace
To silence envious tongues. Be just, and fear not;
Let all the ends thou aim'st at be thy country's,
Thy God's, and truth's; then, if thou fall'st, O Cromwell,
Thou fall'st a blessed martyr!
Serve the King, and – prithee lead me in.
There take an inventory of all I have
To the last penny; 'tis the King's. My robe,
And my integrity to heaven, is all
I dare now call mine own. O Cromwell, Cromwell!
Had I but serv'd my God with half the zeal
I serv'd my King, he would not in mine age
Have left me naked to mine enemies.

CROMWELL Good sir, have patience.

WOLSEY So I have. Farewell
The hopes of court! My hopes in heaven do dwell. [*Exeunt.*

ACT FOUR

SCENE I. *A street in Westminster.*

Enter two Gentlemen, meeting one another.

1 GENTLEMAN Y'are well met once again.

2 GENTLEMAN So are you.

1 GENTLEMAN You come to take your stand here, and behold
The Lady Anne pass from her coronation?

2 GENTLEMAN 'Tis all my business. At our last encounter
The Duke of Buckingham came from his trial.

1 GENTLEMAN 'Tis very true. But that time offer'd sorrow;
This, general joy.

2 GENTLEMAN 'Tis well. The citizens,
I am sure, have shown at full their royal minds –
As, let 'em have their rights, they are ever forward –
In celebration of this day with shows,
Pageants, and sights of honour.

1 GENTLEMAN Never greater,
Nor, I'll assure you, better taken, sir.

2 GENTLEMAN May I be bold to ask what that contains,
That paper in your hand?

1 GENTLEMAN Yes; 'tis the list
Of those that claim their offices this day,
By custom of the coronation.
The Duke of Suffolk is the first, and claims
To be High Steward; next, the Duke of Norfolk,
He to be Earl Marshal. You may read the rest.

2 GENTLEMAN I thank you, sir; had I not known those customs,
I should have been beholding to your paper.
But, I beseech you, what's become of Katharine,
The Princess Dowager? How goes her business?

1 GENTLEMAN That I can tell you too. The Archbishop
Of Canterbury, accompanied with other
Learned and reverend fathers of his order,
Held a late court at Dunstable, six miles off
From Ampthill, where the Princess lay; to which
She was often cited by them, but appear'd not.
And, to be short, for not appearance and
The King's late scruple, by the main assent
Of all these learned men, she was divorc'd,
And the late marriage made of none effect;
Since which she was removed to Kimbolton,
Where she remains now sick.

2 GENTLEMAN Alas, good lady!
[*Trumpets.*
The trumpets sound. Stand close, the Queen is coming. [*Hautboys.*

THE ORDER OF THE CORONATION.

1. *A lively flourish of trumpets.*
2. *Then two Judges.*
3. *Lord Chancellor, with purse and mace before him.*
4. *Choristers singing* [*Music.*
5. *Mayor of London, bearing the mace. Then Garter, in his coat of arms, and on his head he wore a gilt copper crown.*
6. *MARQUIS DORSET, bearing a sceptre of gold, on his head a demi-coronal of gold. With him, the EARL OF SURREY, bearing the rod of silver with the dove, crowned with an earl's coronet. Collars of Esses.*
7. *DUKE OF SUFFOLK, in his robe of estate, his coronet on his head, bearing a long white wand, as High Steward. With him, the DUKE OF NORFOLK, with the rod of marshalship, a*

coronet on his head. Collars of Esses.

8. *A canopy borne by four of the CINQUEPORTS; under it the QUEEN in her robe; in her hair richly adorned with pearl, crowned. On each side her, the Bishops of London and Winchester.*

9. *The old DUCHESS OF NORFOLK, in a coronal of gold, wrought with flowers, bearing the Queen's train.*

10. *Certain Ladies or Countesses, with plain circlets of gold without flowers.*

[*Exeunt, first passing over the stage in order and state, and then a great flourish of trumpets.*

2 GENTLEMAN A royal train, believe me. These I know.
Who's that that bears the sceptre?
1 GENTLEMAN Marquis Dorset;
And that the Earl of Surrey, with the rod.
2 GENTLEMAN A bold brave gentleman. That should be
The Duke of Suffolk?
1 GENTLEMAN 'Tis the same – High Steward.
2 GENTLEMAN And that my Lord of Norfolk?
1 GENTLEMAN Yes.
2 GENTLEMAN [*Looking on the Queen*] Heaven bless thee!
Thou hast the sweetest face I ever look'd on.
Sir, as I have a soul! she is an angel;
Our king has all the Indies in his arms,
And more and richer, when he strains that lady;
I cannot blame his conscience.
1 GENTLEMAN They that bear
The cloth of honour over her are four barons
Of the Cinque-ports.
2 GENTLEMAN Those men are happy; and so are all are near her.
I take it she that carries up the train
Is that old noble lady, Duchess of Norfolk.
1 GENTLEMAN It is; and all the rest are countesses.
2 GENTLEMAN Their coronets say so. These are stars indeed,
And sometimes falling ones.
1 GENTLEMAN No more of that.

[*Exit Procession, with a great flourish of trumpets.*

Enter a third Gentleman.

God save you, sir! Where have you been broiling?
3 GENTLEMAN Among the crowd i' th' Abbey, where a finger
Could not be wedg'd in more; I am stifled
With the mere rankness of their joy.
2 GENTLEMAN You saw
The ceremony?
3 GENTLEMAN That I did.
1 GENTLEMAN How was it?
3 GENTLEMAN Well worth the seeing.
2 GENTLEMAN Good sir, speak it to us.
3 GENTLEMAN As well as I am able. The rich stream
Of lords and ladies, having brought the Queen
To a prepar'd place in the choir, fell off
A distance from her, while her Grace sat down
To rest awhile, some half an hour or so,
In a rich chair of state, opposing freely
The beauty of her person to the people.
Believe me, sir, she is the goodliest woman
That ever lay by man; which when the people
Had the full view of, such a noise arose
As the shrouds make at sea in a stiff tempest,
As loud, and to as many tunes; hats, cloaks –
Doublets, I think – flew up, and had their faces
Been loose, this day they had been lost. Such joy
I never saw before. Great-bellied women,
That had not half a week to go, like rams
In the old time of war, would shake the press,
And make 'em reel before 'em. No man living
Could say 'This is my wife' there, all were woven
So strangely in one piece.
2 GENTLEMAN But what follow'd?
3 GENTLEMAN At length her Grace rose, and with modest paces
Came to the altar, where she kneel'd, and saintlike
Cast her fair eyes to heaven, and pray'd devoutly.
Then rose again, and bow'd her to the people;
When by the Archbishop of Canterbury
She had all the royal makings of a queen:
As holy oil, Edward Confessor's crown,
The rod, and bird of peace, and all such emblems
Laid nobly on her; which perform'd, the choir,
With all the choicest music of the kingdom,
Together sung 'Te Deumn'. So she parted,
And with the same full state pac'd back again
To York Place, where the feast is held.
1 GENTLEMAN Sir,
You must no more call it York Place: that's past;
For since the Cardinal fell that title's lost.
'Tis now the King's, and call'd Whitehall.
3 GENTLEMAN I know it;
But 'tis so lately alter'd that the old name
Is fresh about me.
2 GENTLEMAN What two reverend bishops
Were those that went on each side of the Queen?
3 GENTLEMAN Stokesly and Gardiner: the one of Winchester,
Newly preferr'd from the King's secretary;
The other, London.
2 GENTLEMAN He of Winchester

Is held no great good lover of the Archbishop's,
The virtuous Cranmer.
3 GENTLEMAN All the land knows that;
However, yet there is no great breach. When it comes,
Cranmer will find a friend will not shrink from him.
2 GENTLEMAN Who may that be, I pray you?
3 GENTLEMAN Thomas Cromwell,
A man in much esteem with th' King, and truly
A worthy friend. The King has made him Master
O' th' Jewel House,
And one, already, of the Privy Council.
2 GENTLEMAN He will deserve more.
3 GENTLEMAN Yes, without all doubt.
Come, gentlemen, ye shall go my way, which
Is to th' court, and there ye shall be my guests:
Something I can command. As I walk thither,
I'll tell ye more.
BOTH You may command us, sir.
[*Exeunt.*

SCENE II. *Kimbolton.*

Enter KATHARINE, Dowager, sick; led between GRIFFITH, her Gentleman Usher, and PATIENCE, her woman.

GRIFFITH How does your Grace?
KATHARINE O Griffith, sick to death!
My legs like loaden branches bow to th' earth,
Willing to leave their burden. Reach a chair.
So – now, methinks, I feel a little ease.
Didst thou not tell me, Griffith, as thou led'st me,
That the great child of honour, Cardinal Wolsey,
Was dead?
GRIFFITH Yes, madam; but I think your Grace,
Out of the pain you suffer'd, gave no ear to't.
KATHARINE Prithee, good Griffith, tell me how he died.
If well, he stepp'd before me, happily,
For my example.
GRIFFITH Well, the voice goes, madam;
For after the stout Earl Northumberland
Arrested him at York and brought him forward,
As a man sorely tainted, to his answer,
He fell sick suddenly, and grew so ill
He could not sit his mule.
KATHARINE Alas, poor man!
GRIFFITH At last, with easy roads, he came to Leicester,
Lodg'd in the abbey; where the reverend abbot,
With all his convent, honourably receiv'd him;
To whom he gave these words: 'O father Abbot,
An old man, broken with the storms of state,
Is come to lay his weary bones among ye;
Give him a little earth for charity!'
So went to bed; where eagerly his sickness
Pursu'd him still. And three nights after this,
About the hour of eight – which he himself
Foretold should be his last – full of repentance,
Continual meditations, tears, and sorrows,
He gave his honours to the world again,
His blessed part to heaven, and slept in peace.
KATHARINE So may he rest; his faults lie gently on him!
Yet thus far, Griffith, give me leave to speak him,
And yet with charity. He was a man
Of an unbounded stomach, ever ranking
Himself with princes; one that, by suggestion,
Tied all the kingdom. Simony was fair play;
His own opinion was his law. I' th' presence
He would say untruths, and be ever double
Both in his words and meaning. He was never,
But where he meant to ruin, pitiful.
His promises were, as he then was, mighty;
But his performance, as he is now, nothing.
Of his own body he was ill, and gave
The clergy ill example.
GRIFFITH Noble madam,
Men's evil manners live in brass: their virtues
We write in water. May it please your Highness
To hear me speak his good now?
KATHARINE Yes, good Griffith;
I were malicious else.
GRIFFITH This Cardinal,
Though from an humble stock, undoubtedly
Was fashion'd to much honour from his cradle.
He was a scholar, and a ripe and good one;
Exceeding wise, fair-spoken, and persuading;
Lofty and sour to them that lov'd him not,
But to those men that sought him sweet as summer.
And though he were unsatisfied in getting –
Which was a sin – yet in bestowing, madam,
He was most princely: ever witness for him
Those twins of learning that he rais'd in you,
Ipswich and Oxford! One of which fell with him,
Unwilling to outlive the good that did it;
The other, thought unfinish'd, yet so famous,
So excellent in art, and still so rising,
That Christendom shall ever speak his virtue.
His overthrow heap'd happiness upon him;
For then, and not till then, he felt himself,
And found the blessedness of being little.
And, to add greater honours to his age
Than man could give him, he died fearing God.
KATHARINE After my death I wish no other herald,
No other speaker of my living actions,
To keep mine honour from corruption,

But such an honest chronicler as Griffith.
Whom I most hated living, thou hast made me,
With thy religious truth and modesty,
Now in his ashes honour. Peace be with him!
Patience, be near me still, and set me lower:
I have not long to trouble thee. Good Griffith,
Cause the musicians play me that sad note
I nam'd my knell, whilst I sit meditating
On that celestial harmony I go to.
[Sad and solemn music.

GRIFFITH She is asleep. Good wench, let's sit down quiet,
For fear we wake her. Softly, gentle Patience.

THE VISION

Enter, solemnly tripping one after another, six Personages clad in white robes, wearing on their heads garlands of bays, and golden vizards on their faces; branches of bays or palm in their hands. They first congee unto her, then dance; and, at certain changes, the first two hold a spare garland over her head, at which the other four make reverent curtsies. Then the two that held the garland deliver the same to the other next two, who observe the same order in their changes, and holding the garland over her head; which done, they deliver the same garland to the last two, who likewise observe the same order; at which, as it were by inspiration, she makes in her sleep signs of rejoicing, and holdeth up her hands to heaven. And so in their dancing vanish, carrying the garland with them. The music continues.

KATHARINE Spirits of peace, where are ye? Are ye all gone?
And leave me here in wretchedness behind ye?
GRIFFITH Madam, we are here.
KATHARINE It is not you I call for.
Saw ye none enter since I slept?
GRIFFITH None, madam.
KATHARINE No? Saw you not, even now, a blessed troop
Invite me to a banquet; whose bright faces
Cast thousand beams upon me, like the sun?
They promis'd me eternal happiness,
And brought me garlands, Griffith, which I feel
I am not worthy yet to wear. I shall, assuredly.
GRIFFITH I am most joyful, madam, such good dreams
Possess your fancy.
KATHARINE Bid the music leave,
They are harsh and heavy to me. *[Music ceases.*
PATIENCE Do you note
How much her Grace is alter'd on the sudden?
How long her face is drawn! How pale she looks,
And of an earthy cold! Mark her eyes.
GRIFFITH She is going, wench. Pray, pray.
PATIENCE Heaven comfort her!

Enter a Messenger.

MESSENGER An't like your Grace –
KATHARINE You are a saucy fellow.
Deserve we no more reverence?
GRIFFITH You are to blame,
Knowing she will not lose her wonted greatness,
To use so rude behaviour. Go to, kneel.
MESSENGER I humbly do entreat your Highness' pardon;
My haste made me unmannerly. There is staying
A gentleman, sent from the King, to see you.
KATHARINE Admit him entrance, Griffith; but this fellow
Let me ne'er see again. *[Exit Messenger.*

Enter LORD CAPUCIUS.

If my sight fail not,
You should be Lord Ambassador from the Emperor,
My royal nephew, and your name Capucius.
CAPUCIUS Madam, the same – your servant.
KATHARINE O, my Lord,
The times and titles now are alter'd strangely
With me since first you knew me. But, I pray you,
What is your pleasure with me?
CAPUCIUS Noble lady,
First, mine own service to your Grace; the next,
The King's request that I would visit you,
Who grieves much for your weakness, and by me
Sends you his princely commendations
And heartily entreats you take good comfort.
KATHARINE O my good lord, that comfort comes too late,
'Tis like a pardon after execution:
That gentle physic, given in time, had cur'd me;
But now I am past all comforts here, but prayers.
How does his Highness?
CAPUCIUS Madam, in good health.
KATHARINE So may he ever do! and ever flourish
When I shall dwell with worms, and my poor name
Banish'd the kingdom! Patience, is that letter
I caus'd you write yet sent away?
PATIENCE No, madam.
[Giving it to Katharine.
KATHARINE Sir, I most humbly pray you to deliver
This to my lord the King.
CAPUCIUS Most willing, madam.
KATHARINE In which I have commended to his goodness

The model of our chaste loves, his young daughter –
The dews of heaven fall thick in blessings on her! –
Beseeching him to give her virtuous breeding –
She is young, and of a noble modest nature;
I hope she will deserve well – and a little
To love her for her mother's sake, that lov'd him,
Heaven knows how dearly. My next poor petition
Is that his noble Grace would have some pity
Upon my wretched women that so long
Have follow'd both my fortunes faithfully;
Of which there is not one, I dare avow –
And now I should not lie – but will deserve,
For virtue and true beauty of the soul,
For honesty and decent carriage,
A right good husband, let him be a noble;
And sure those men are happy that shall have 'em.
The last is for my men – they are the poorest,
But poverty could never draw 'em from me –
That they may have their wages duly paid 'em,
And something over to remember me by.
If heaven had pleas'd to have given me longer life
And able means, we had not parted thus.
These are the whole contents; and, good my lord,
By that you love the dearest in this world,
As you wish Christian peace to souls departed,
Stand these poor people's friend, and urge the King
To do me this last right.

CAPUCIUS By heaven, I will,
Or let me lose the fashion of a man!

KATHARINE I thank you, honest lord. Remember me
In all humility unto his Highness;
Say his long trouble now is passing
Out of this world. Tell him in death I bless'd him,
For so I will. Mine eyes grow dim. Farewell,
My lord. Griffith, farewell. Nay, Patience,
You must not leave me yet. I must to bed;
Call in more women. When I am dead good wench,
Let me be us'd with honour; strew me over
With maiden flowers, that all the world may know
I was a chaste wife to my grave. Embalm me,
Then lay me forth; although unqueen'd, yet like
A queen, and daughter to a king, inter me.
I can no more. [*Exeunt, leading Katharine.*

ACT FIVE

SCENE I. *London. A gallery in the palace.*

Enter GARDINER, BISHOP OF WINCHESTER, a Page with a torch before him, met by SIR THOMAS LOVELL.

GARDINER It's one o'clock, boy, is't not?

BOY It hath struck.

GARDINER These should be hours for necessities,
Not for delights; times to repair our nature
With comforting repose, and not for us
To waste these times. Good hour of night, Sir Thomas!
Whither so late?

LOVELL Came you from the King, my lord?

GARDINER I did, Sir Thomas, and left him at primero
With the Duke of Suffolk.

LOVELL I must to him too,
Before he go to bed. I'll take my leave.

GARDINER Not yet, Sir Thomas Lovell. What's the matter?
It seems you are in haste. An if there be
No great offence belongs to't, give your friend
Some touch of your late business. Affairs that walk –
As they say spirits do – at midnight, have
In them a wilder nature than the business
That seeks despatch by day.

LOVELL My lord, I love you;
And durst commend a secret to your ear
Much weightier than this work. The Queen's in labour,
They say in great extremity, and fear'd
She'll with the labour end.

GARDINER The fruit she goes with
I pray for heartily, that it may find
Good time, and live; but for the stock, Sir Thomas,
I wish it grubb'd up now.

LOVELL Methinks I could
Cry thee amen; and yet my conscience says
She's a good creature, and, sweet lady, does
Deserve our better wishes.

GARDINER But, sir, sir –
Hear me, Sir Thomas. Y'are a gentleman
Of mine own way; I know you wise, religious;
And, let me tell you, it will ne'er be well –
'Twill not, Sir Thomas Lovell, take't of me –
Till Cranmer, Cromwell, her two hands, and she,

Sleep in their graves.
LOVELL Now, sir, you speak of two
The most remark'd i' th' kingdom. As for Cromwell,
Beside that of the Jewel House, is made Master
O' th' Rolls, and the King's secretary; further, sir,
Stands in the gap and trade of moe preferments,
With which the time will load him. Th' Archbishop
Is the King's hand and tongue, and who dare speak
One syllable against him?
GARDINER Yes, yes, Sir Thomas,
There are that dare; and I myself have ventur'd
To speak my mind of him; and indeed this day,
Sir – I may tell it you – I think I have
Incens'd the lords o' th' Council, that he is –
For so I know he is, they know he is –
A most arch heretic, a pestilence
That does infect the land; with which they moved
Have broken with the King, who hath so far
Given ear to our complaint – of his great grace
And princely care, foreseeing those fell mischiefs
Our reasons laid before him – hath commanded
To-morrow morning to the Council board
He be convented. He's a rank weed, Sir Thomas,
And we must root him out. From your affairs
I hinder you too long – good night, Sir Thomas.
LOVELL Many good nights, my lord; I rest your servant. *[Exeunt Gardiner and Page.*

Enter the KING and the DUKE OF SUFFOLK.

KING Charles, I will play no more to-night;
My mind's not on't; you are too hard for me.
SUFFOLK Sir, I did never win of you before.
KING But little, Charles;
Nor shall not, when my fancy's on my play.
Now, Lovell, from the Queen what is the news?
LOVELL I could not personally deliver to her
What you commanded me, but by her woman
I sent your message; who return'd her thanks
In the great'st humbleness, and desir'd your Highness
Most heartily to pray for her.
KING What say'st thou, ha?
To pray for her? What, is she crying out?
LOVELL So said her woman; and that her suff'rance made
Almost each pang a death.
KING Alas, good lady!
SUFFOLK God safely quit her of her burden, and
With gentle travail, to the gladding of
Your Highness with an heir!
KING 'Tis midnight, Charles;
Prithee to bed; and in thy pray'rs remember
Th' estate of my poor queen. Leave me alone,
For I must think of that which company
Will not be friendly to.
SUFFOLK I wish your Highness
A quiet night, and my good mistress will
Remember in my prayers.
KING Charles, good night.
[Exit Suffolk.

Enter SIR ANTHONY DENNY.

Well, sir, what follows?
DENNY Sir, I have brought my lord the Archbishop,
As you commanded me.
KING Ha! Canterbury?
DENNY Ay, my good lord.
KING 'Tis true. Where is he, Denny?
DENNY He attends your Highness' pleasure.
KING Bring him to us.
[Exit Denny.

LOVELL *[Aside]* This is about that which the bishop spake.
I am happily come hither.

Re-enter DENNY, with CRANMER.

KING Avoid the gallery. *[Lovell seems to stay.*
Ha! I have said. Be gone.
What! *[Exeunt Lovell and Denny.*

CRANMER *[Aside]* I am fearful – wherefore frowns he thus?
'Tis his aspect of terror. All's not well.
KING How now, my lord? You do desire to know
Wherefore I sent for you.
CRANMER *[Kneeling]* It is my duty
T' attend your Highness' pleasure.
KING Pray you, arise,
My good and gracious Lord of Canterbury.
Come, you and I must walk a turn together;
I have news to tell you; come, come, give me your hand.
Ah, my good lord, I grieve at what I speak,
And am right sorry to repeat what follows.
I have, and most unwillingly, of late
Heard many grievous – I do say, my lord,
Grievous – complaints of you; which, being consider'd,
Have mov'd us and our Council that you shall
This morning come before us; where I know
You cannot with such freedom purge yourself
But that, till further trial in those charges
Which will require your answer, you must take
Your patience to you and be well contented

To make your house our Tow'r. You a brother of us,
It fits we thus proceed, or else no witness
Would come against you.

CRANMER I humbly thank your Highness,
And am right glad to catch this good occasion
Most throughly to be winnowed where my chaff
And corn shall fly asunder; for I know
There's none stands under more calumnious tongues
Than I myself, poor man.

KING Stand up, good Canterbury;
Thy truth and thy integrity is rooted
In us, thy friend. Give me thy hand, stand up;
Prithee let's walk. Now, by my holidame,
What manner of man are you? My lord, I look'd
You would have given me your petition that
I should have ta'en some pains to bring together
Yourself and your accusers, and to have heard you
Without indurance further.

CRANMER Most dread liege,
The good I stand on is my truth and honesty;
If they shall fail, I with mine enemies
Will triumph o'er my person; which I weigh not,
Being of those virtues vacant. I fear nothing
What can be said against me.

KING Know you not
How your state stands i' th' world, with the whole world?
Your enemies are many, and not small; their practices
Must bear the same proportion; and not ever
The justice and the truth o' th' question carries
The due o' th' verdict with it; at what ease
Might corrupt minds procure knaves as corrupt
To swear against you? Such things have been done.
You are potently oppos'd, and with a malice
Of as great size. Ween you of better luck,
I mean in perjur'd witness, than your Master,
Whose minister you are, whiles here He liv'd
Upon this naughty earth? Go to, go to;
You take a precipice for no leap of danger,
And woo your own destruction.

CRANMER God and your Majesty
Protect mine innocence, or I fall into
The trap is laid for me!

KING Be of good cheer;
They shall no more prevail than we give way to.
Keep comfort to you, and this morning see
You do appear before them; if they shall chance,
In charging you with matters, to commit you,
The best persuasions to the contrary
Fail not to use, and with what vehemency
Th' occasion shall instruct you. If entreaties
Will render you no remedy, this ring
Deliver them, and your appeal to us
There make before them. Look, the good man weeps!
He's honest, on mine honour. God's blest Mother!
I swear he is true-hearted, and a soul
None better in my kingdom. Get you gone,
And do as I have bid you. [*Exit Cranmer.*
He has strangled his language in his tears.

Enter Old Lady.

GENTLEMAN [*Within*] Come back; what mean you?

OLD LADY I'll not come back; the tidings that I bring
Will make my boldness manners. Now, good angels
Fly o'er thy royal head, and shade thy person
Under their blessed wings!

KING Now, by thy looks
I guess thy message. Is the Queen deliver'd?
Say ay, and of a boy.

OLD LADY Ay, ay, my liege;
And of a lovely boy. The God of Heaven
Both now and ever bless her! 'Tis a girl,
Promises boys hereafter. Sir, your queen
Desires your visitation, and to be
Acquainted with this stranger; 'tis as like you
As cherry is to cherry.

KING Lovell!

Enter LOVELL.

LOVELL Sir?

KING Give her an hundred marks. I'll to the Queen. [*Exit.*

OLD LADY An hundred marks? By this light, I'll ha' more!
An ordinary groom is for such payment.
I will have more, or scold it out of him.
Said I for this the girl was like to him? I'll
Have more, or else unsay't; and now, while 'tis hot,
I'll put it to the issue. [*Exeunt.*

SCENE II. *Lobby before the Council Chamber.*

Enter CRANMER, ARCHBISHOP OF CANTERBURY.

CRANMER I hope I am not too late; and yet the gentleman
That was sent to me from the Council pray'd me
To make great haste. All fast? What means this? Ho!
Who waits there? Sure you know me?

Enter Keeper.

KEEPER Yes, my lord;
But yet I cannot help you.

CRANMER Why?

KEEPER Your Grace must wait till you be call'd
for.

Enter DOCTOR BUTTS.

CRANMER So.
BUTTS [*Aside*] This is a piece of malice. I am glad
I came this way so happily; the King
Shall understand it presently. [*Exit.*
CRANMER [*Aside*] 'Tis Butts,
The King's physician; as he pass'd along,
How earnestly he cast his eyes upon me!
Pray heaven he sound not my disgrace! For
certain,
This is of purpose laid by some that hate me –
God turn their hearts! I never sought their
malice –
To quench mine honour; they would shame to
make me
Wait else at door, a fellow councillor,
'Mong boys, grooms, and lackeys. But their
pleasures
Must be fulfill'd, and I attend with patience.

Enter the KING and BUTTS at a window above.

BUTTS I'll show your Grace the strangest sight –
KING What's that, Butts?
BUTTS I think your Highness saw this many a
day.
KING Body a me, where is it?
BUTTS There my lord:
The high promotion of his Grace of Canterbury;
Who holds his state at door, 'mongst
pursuivants,
Pages, and footboys.
KING Ha, 'tis he indeed.
Is this the honour they do one another?
'Tis well there's one above 'em yet. I had
thought
They had parted so much honesty among 'em –
At least good manners – as not thus to suffer
A man of his place, and so near our favour,
To dance attendance on their lordships'
pleasures,
And at the door too, like a post with packets.
By holy Mary, Butts, there's knavery!
Let 'em alone, and draw the curtain close;
We shall hear more anon. [*Exeunt.*

SCENE III. *The Council Chamber.*

A Council table brought in, with chairs and stools, and placed under the state. Enter Lord Chancellor, places himself at the upper end of the table on the left hand, a seat being left void above him, as for Canterbury's seat. DUKE OF SUFFOLK, DUKE OF NORFOLK, SURREY, LORD CHAMBERLAIN, GARDINER, seat themselves in order on each side; CROMWELL at lower end, as secretary. Keeper at the door.

CHANCELLOR Speak to the business, master
secretary;
Why are we met in council?
CROMWELL Please your honours,
The chief cause concerns his Grace of
Canterbury.
GARDINER Has he had knowledge of it?
CROMWELL Yes.
NORFOLK Who waits there?
KEEPER Without, my noble lords?
GARDINER Yes.
KEEPER My Lord Archbishop;
And has done half an hour, to know your
pleasures.
CHANCELLOR Let him come in.
KEEPER Your Grace may enter now.

CRANMER approaches the Council table.

CHANCELLOR My good Lord Archbishop, I am
very sorry
To sit here at this present, and behold
That chair stand empty; but we all are men,
In our own natures frail and capable
Of our flesh; few are angels; out of which frailty
And want of wisdom, you, that best should
teach us,
Have misdemean'd yourself, and not a little,
Toward the King first, then his laws, in filling
The whole realm by your teaching and your
chaplains –
For so we are inform'd – with new opinions,
Divers and dangerous; which are heresies,
And, not reform'd, may prove pernicious.
GARDINER Which reformation must be sudden
too,
My noble lords; for those that tame wild horses
Pace 'em not in their hands to make 'em gentle,
But stop their mouths with stubborn bits and
spur 'em
Till they obey the manage. If we suffer,
Out of our easiness and childish pity
To one man's honour, this contagious sickness,
Farewell all physic; and what follows then?
Commotions, uproars, with a general taint
Of the whole state; as of late days our
neighbours,
The upper Germany, can dearly witness,
Yet freshly pitied in our memories.
CRANMER My good lords, hitherto in all the
progress
Both of my life and office, I have labour'd,
And with no little study, that my teaching
And the strong course of my authority
Might go one way, and safely; and the end
Was ever to do well. Nor is there living –
I speak it with a single heart, my lords –
A man that more detests, more stirs against,
Both in his private conscience and his place,

Defacers of a public peace than I do.
Pray heaven the King may never find a heart
With less allegiance in it! Men that make
Envy and crooked malice nourishment
Dare bite the best. I do beseech your lordships
That, in this case of justice, my accusers,
Be what they will, may stand forth face to face
And freely urge against me.

SUFFOLK Nay, my lord,
That cannot be; you are a councillor,
And by that virtue no man dare accuse you.

GARDINER My lord, because we have business of more moment,
We will be short with you. 'Tis his Highness' pleasure
And our consent, for better trial of you,
From hence you be committed to the Tower;
Where, being but a private man again,
You shall know many dare accuse you boldly,
More than, I fear, you are provided for.

CRANMER Ah, my good Lord of Winchester, I thank you;
You are always my good friend; if your will pass,
I shall both find your lordship judge and juror,
You are so merciful. I see your end –
'Tis my undoing. Love and meekness, lord,
Become a churchman better than ambition;
Win straying souls with modesty again,
Cast none away. That I shall clear myself,
Lay all the weight ye can upon my patience,
I make as little doubt as you do conscience
In doing daily wrongs. I could say more,
But reverence to your calling makes me modest.

GARDINER My lord, my lord, you are a sectary;
That's the plain truth. Your painted gloss discovers,
To men that understand you, words and weakness.

CROMWELL My lord of Winchester, y'are a little,
By your good favour, too sharp; men so noble,
However faulty, yet should find respect
For what they have been; 'tis a cruelty
To load a falling man.

GARDINER Good Master Secretary,
I cry your honour mercy; you may, worst
Of all this table, say so.

CROMWELL Why, my lord?

GARDINER Do not I know you for a favourer
Of this new sect? Ye are not sound.

CROMWELL Not sound?

GARDINER Not sound, I say.

CROMWELL Would you were half so honest!
Men's prayers then would seek you, not their fears.

GARDINER I shall remember this bold language.

CROMWELL Do.
Remember your bold life too.

CHANCELLOR This is too much;
Forbear, for shame, my lords.

GARDINER I have done.

CROMWELL And I.

CRANMER Then thus for you, my lord: it stands agreed,
I take it, by all voices, that forthwith
You be convey'd to th' Tower a prisoner;
There to remain till the King's further pleasure
Be known unto us. Are you all agreed, lords?

ALL We are.

CRANMER Is there no other way of mercy,
But I must needs to th' Tower, my lords?

GARDINER What other
Would you expect? You are strangely troublesome.
Let some o' th' guard be ready there.

Enter the Guard.

CRANMER For me?
Must I go like a traitor thither?

GARDINER Receive him,
And see him safe i' th' Tower.

CRANMER Stay, good my lords,
I have a little yet to say. Look there, my lords;
By virtue of that ring I take my cause
Out of the gripes of cruel men and give it
To a most noble judge, the King my master.

CHAMBERLAIN This is the King's ring.

SURREY 'Tis no counterfeit.

SUFFOLK 'Tis the right ring, by heav'n. I told ye all,
When we first put this dangerous stone a-rolling,
'Twould fall upon ourselves.

NORFOLK Do you think, my lords,
The King will suffer but the little finger
Of this man to be vex'd?

CHAMBERLAIN 'Tis now too certain;
How much more is his life in value with him!
Would I were fairly out on't!

CROMWELL My mind gave me,
In seeking tales and informations
Against this man – whose honesty the devil
And his disciples only envy at –
Ye blew the fire that burns ye. Now have at ye!

Enter the KING frowning on them; he takes his seat.

GARDINER Dread sovereign, how much are we bound to heaven
In daily thanks, that gave us such a prince;
Not only good and wise but most religious;
One that in all obedience makes the church
The chief aim of his honour and, to strengthen
That holy duty, out of dear respect,
His royal self in judgment comes to hear
The cause betwixt her and this great offender.

KING You were ever good at sudden commendations,
Bishop of Winchester. But know I come not
To hear such flattery now, and in my presence
They are too thin and bare to hide offences.
To me you cannot reach you play the spaniel,
And think with wagging of your tongue to win me;
But whatsoe'er thou tak'st me for, I'm sure
Thou hast a cruel nature and a bloody.
[*To Cranmer*] Good man, sit down. Now let me see the proudest
He that dares most but wag his finger at thee.
By all that's holy, he had better starve
Than but once think this place becomes thee not.

SURREY May it please your Grace –

KING No, sir, it does not please me.
I had thought I had had men of some understanding
And wisdom of my Council; but I find none.
Was it discretion, lords, to let this man,
This good man – few of you deserve that title –
This honest man, wait like a lousy footboy
At chamber door? and one as great as you are?
Why, what a shame was this! Did my commission
Bid ye so far forget yourselves? I gave ye
Power as he was a councillor to try him,
Not as a groom. There's some of ye, I see,
More out of malice than integrity,
Would try him to the utmost, had ye mean;
Which ye shall never have while I live.

CHANCELLOR Thus far,
My most dread sovereign, may it like your Grace
To let my tongue excuse all. What was purpos'd
Concerning his imprisonment was rather –
If there be faith in men – meant for his trial
And fair purgation to the world, than malice,
I'm sure, in me.

KING Well, well, my lords, respect him;
Take him, and use him well, he's worthy of it.
I will say thus much for him: if a prince
May be beholding to a subject, I
Am for his love and service so to him.
Make me no more ado, but all embrace him;
Be friends, for shame, my lords! My Lord of Canterbury,
I have a suit which you must not deny me:
That is, a fair young maid that yet wants baptism;
You must be godfather, and answer for her.

CRANMER The greatest monarch now alive may glory
In such an honour; how may I deserve it,
That am a poor and humble subject to you?

KING Come, come, my lord, you'd spare your spoons. You shall have
Two noble partners with you: the old Duchess of Norfolk
And Lady Marquis Dorset. Will these please you?
Once more, my Lord of Winchester, I charge you,
Embrace and love this man.

GARDINER With a true heart
And brother-love I do it.

CRANMER And let heaven
Witness how dear I hold this confirmation.

KING Good man, those joyful tears show thy true heart.
The common voice, I see, is verified
Of thee, which says thus: 'Do my Lord of Canterbury
A shrewd turn and he's your friend for ever'.
Come, lords, we trifle time away; I long
To have this young one made a Christian.
As I have made ye one, lords, one remain;
So I grow stronger, you more honour gain.
[*Exeunt.*

SCENE IV. *The palace yard.*

Noise and tumult within. Enter Porter and his Man.

PORTER You'll leave your noise anon, ye rascals. Do you take the court for Paris garden? Ye rude slaves, leave your gaping.

[*Within*: Good master porter, I belong to th' larder.

PORTER Belong to th' gallows, and be hang'd, ye rogue! Is this a place to roar in? Fetch me a dozen crab-tree staves, and strong ones: these are but switches to 'em. I'll scratch your heads. You must be seeing christenings? Do you look for ale and cakes here, you rude rascals?

MAN Pray, sir, be patient; 'tis as much impossible,
Unless we sweep 'em from the door with cannons,
To scatter 'em as 'tis to make 'em sleep
On May-day morning; which will never be.
We may as well push against Paul's as stir 'em.

PORTER How got they in, and be hang'd?

MAN Alas, I know not: how gets the tide in?
As much as one sound cudgel of four foot –
You see the poor remainder – could distribute,
I made no spare, sir.

PORTER You did nothing, sir.

MAN I am not Samson, nor Sir Guy, nor Colbrand,
To mow 'em down before me; but if I spar'd any
That had a head to hit, either young or old,
He or she, cuckold or cuckold-maker,
Let me ne'er hope to see a chine again;
And that I would not for a cow, God save her!

[*Within*: Do you hear, master porter?

PORTER I shall be with you presently, good master puppy. Keep the door close, sirrah.

MAN What would you have me do?

PORTER What should you do, but knock 'em down by th' dozens? Is this Moorfields to muster in? Or have we some strange Indian with the great tool come to court, the women so besiege us? Bless me, what a fry of fornication is at door! On my Christian conscience, this one christening will beget a thousand: here will be father, godfather, and all together.

MAN The spoons will be the bigger, sir. There is a fellow somewhat near the door, he should be a brazier by his face, for, o' my conscience, twenty of the dog-days now reign in's nose; all that stand about him are under the line, they need no other penance. That fire-drake did I hit three times on the head, and three times was his nose discharged against me; he stands there like a mortar-piece, to blow us. There was a haberdasher's wife of small wit near him, that rail'd upon me till her pink'd porringer fell off her head, for kindling such a combustion in the state. I miss'd the meteor once, and hit that woman, who cried out 'Clubs!' when I might see from far some forty truncheoners draw to her succour, which were the hope o' th' Strand, where she was quartered. They fell on; I made good my place. At length they came to th' broomstaff to me; I defied 'em still; when suddenly a file of boys behind 'em loose shot, deliver'd such a show'r of pebbles that I was fain to draw mine honour in and let 'em win the work: the devil was amongst 'em, I think surely.

PORTER These are the youths that thunder at a playhouse and fight for bitten apples; that no audience but the tribulation of Tower-hill or the limbs of Limehouse, their dear brothers, are able to endure. I have some of 'em in Limbo Patrum, and there they are like to dance these three days; besides the running banquet of two beadles that is to come.

Enter the Lord Chamberlain.

CHAMBERLAIN Mercy o' me, what a multitude are here!
They grow still too; from all parts they are coming,
As if we kept a fair here! Where are these porters,
These lazy knaves? Y' have made a fine hand, fellows.
There's a trim rabble let in: are all these
Your faithful friends o' th' suburbs? We shall have
Great store of room, no doubt, left for the ladies,
When they pass back from the christening.

PORTER An't please your honour,
We are but men; and what so many may do,
Not being torn a pieces, we have done.
An army cannot rule 'em.

CHAMBERLAIN As I live,
If the King blame me for't, I'll lay ye all
By th' heels, and suddenly; and on your heads
Clap round fines for neglect. Y'are lazy knaves;
And here ye lie baiting of bombards, when
Ye should do service. Hark! the trumpets sound;
Th'are come already from the christening.
Go break among the press and find a way out
To let the troop pass fairly, or I'll find
A Marshalsea shall hold ye play these two months.

PORTER Make way there for the Princess.

MAN You great fellow,
Stand close up, or I'll make your head ache.

PORTER You i' th' camlet, get up o' th' rail;
I'll peck you o'er the pales else. [*Exeunt.*

SCENE V. *The palace.*

Enter Trumpets, sounding; then two Aldermen, Lord Mayor, Garter, CRANMER, DUKE OF NORFOLK, with his marshal's staff, DUKE OF SUFFOLK, two Noblemen bearing great standing-bowls for the christening gifts; then four Noblemen bearing a canopy, under which the DUCHESS OF NORFOLK, godmother, bearing the child richly habited in a mantle, etc., train borne by a Lady; then follows the MARCHIONESS DORSET, the other godmother, and Ladies. The troop pass once about the stage, and Garter speaks.

GARTER Heaven, from thy endless goodness, send prosperous life, long and ever-happy, to the high and mighty Princess of England, Elizabeth!

Flourish. Enter KING and Guard.

CRANMER [*Kneeling*] And to your royal Grace and the good Queen!
My noble partners and myself thus pray:
All comfort, joy, in this most gracious lady,
Heaven ever laid up to make parents happy,
May hourly fall upon ye!

KING Thank you, good Lord Archbishop.
What is her name?

CRANMER Elizabeth.

KING Stand up, lord.
[*The King kisses the child.*
With this kiss take my blessing: God protect thee!
Into whose hand I give thy life.

CRANMER Amen.

KING My noble gossips, y'have been too prodigal;

I thank ye heartily. So shall this lady,
When she has so much English.

CRANMER Let me speak, sir,
For heaven now bids me; and the words I utter
let Let none think flattery, for they'll find 'em truth.
This royal infant – heaven still move about her! –
Though in her cradle, yet now promises
Upon this land a thousand thousand blessings,
Which time shall bring to ripeness. She shall be –
But few now living can behold that goodness –
A pattern to all princes living with her,
And all that shall succeed. Saba was never
More covetous of wisdom and fair virtue
Than this pure soul shall be. All princely graces
That mould up such a mighty piece as this is,
With all the virtues that attend the good,
Shall still be doubled on her. Truth shall nurse her,
Holy and heavenly thoughts still counsel her;
She shall be lov'd and fear'd. Her own shall bless her:
Her foes shake like a field of beaten corn,
And hang their heads with sorrow. Good grows with her;
In her days every man shall eat in safety
Under his own vine what he plants, and sing
The merry songs of peace to all his neighbours.
God shall be truly known; and those about her
From her shall read the perfect ways of honour,
And by those claim their greatness not by blood.
Nor shall this peace sleep with her; but as when
The bird of wonder dies, the maiden phoenix,
Her ashes new create another heir
As great in admiration as herself,
So shall she leave her blessedness to one –
When heaven shall call her from this cloud of darkness –
Who from the sacred ashes of her honour
Shall star-like rise, as great in fame as she was,
And so stand fix'd. Peace, plenty, love, truth, terror,
That were the servants to this chosen infant,
Shall then be his, and like a vine grow to him;
Wherever the bright sun of heaven shall shine,
His honour and the greatness, of his name
Shall be, and make new nations; he shall flourish,
And like a mountain cedar reach his branches
To all the plains about him; our children's children
Shall see this and bless heaven.

KING Thou speakest wonders.

CRANMER She shall be, to the happiness of England,
An aged princess; many days shall see her,
And yet no day without a deed to crown it.
Would I had known no more! But she must die –
She must, the saints must have her – yet a virgin;
A most unspotted lily shall she pass
To th' ground, and all the world shall mourn her.

KING O Lord Archbishop,
Thou hast made me now a man; never before
This happy child did I get anything.
This oracle of comfort has so pleas'd me
That when I am in heaven I shall desire
To see what this child does, and praise my Maker.
I thank ye all. To you, my good Lord Mayor,
And you, good brethren, I am much beholding;
I have receiv'd much honour by your presence,
And ye shall find me thankful. Lead the way, lords;
Ye must all see the Queen, and she must thank ye,
She will be sick else. This day, no man think
Has business at his house; for all shall stay.
This little one shall make it holiday. [*Exeunt.*

THE EPILOGUE

'Tis ten to one this play can never please
All that are here. Some come to take their ease
And sleep an act or two; but those, we fear,
W'have frighted with our trumpets; so, 'tis clear,
They'll say 'tis nought; others to hear the city
Abus'd extremely, and to cry 'That's witty!'
Which we have not done neither; that, I fear,
All the expected good w'are like to hear
For this play at this time is only in
The merciful construction of good women;
For such a one we show'd 'em. If they smile
And say 'twill do, I know within a while
All the best men are ours; for 'tis ill hap
If they hold when their ladies bid 'em clap.

Troilus and Cressida

Introduction by ROBERT CUMMINGS

Derived from Chaucer's *Troilus and Criseyde*, certainly the most complete achievement of English poetry available to Shakespeare, and written in the shadow of the newly rediscovered *Iliad*, Shakespeare's play enjoys a more ambiguous reputation than either. When Dowden came to write his *Critical Study* of Shakespeare's mind and art in 1874 he omitted it from his account altogether. Even if we do not find *Troilus and Cressida* disgusting (once a common opinion), we are likely to find it unamenable to our ways of talking about Shakespeare in particular or the drama in general. Published first in Quarto in 1609 it is advertised on the title page as a history, and then described as a comedy in the Epistle to the reader; worse, it is set as the first of the tragedies in the First Folio of 1623. Coleridge calls it the most difficult to characterise of all Shakespeare's plays. Shakespeare's contemporaries were unsure what kind of play *Troilus and Cressida* was; and the options that have since multiplied into something like Polonius's parodic list of dramatic kinds: various compound genres – tragical satire, comical satire, problem play, heroic farce and the like – are regularly invoked.

The critics' indecisions may reflect Shakespeare's own. The differences between the Quarto and Folio texts (mainly trivial in themselves) betray a history of tinkering with a play which was promised for publication as early as 1603, and suggest that Shakespeare struggled not only with details of phrasing but with the play's whole tendency. This is characteristically literary rather than dramatic. Its first authenticated English staging was in 1907 (and its stage history since exposes its problematical dramatic character). Though described in 1603 as a play recently acted by the Lord Chamberlain's Men, and in a cancelled title page of the 1609 Quarto as a play acted at the Globe, it is recommended by the writer of the 1609 Epistle as a play 'never clapper clawed with the palms of the vulgar' – which means either that it was never acted publicly or never acted at all. The same writer imagines that the play wants a commentary in the manner of those on classical comedy. Peter Alexander has influentially imagined for it a private and elite audience of lawyers appreciative of its mannered style.

The mannerism is most obvious in the language, which veers between a Latinate sublime (Troilus casting himself as a hurricane 'constringed in mass', Ulysses arguing that the heavens observe 'insisture') and a boisterous colloquialism largely inspired by Nashe's pamphleteering prose. It shows also in such set piece pseudo-debates as those in the Greek and Trojan councils (1.3 and 2.2), the rhetorically self-conscious betrothal scene between Troilus and Cressida (3.2), or the farcically set-up but bewilderingly moving interplay of perspectives on Diomedes's wooing of Cressida (5.2). It shows in the determined undercutting of expectation: heroic pageant dissolves into chat (1.2), anticipated combat peters out in pieties (4.5), heroic confrontation is translated into murder (5.8). The celebrated and ambitious declarations of philosophies of order or value are undone by 'one touch of nature', memory and aspiration crumbled into 'the formless ruin of oblivion'. Characters disintegrate into incoherence: 'This is and is not Cressid', says Troilus, and we are bound to agree. To call these affronts to dramatic or moral expectation a manifestation of literary realism or a manifesto for moral realism will not do, for they depend almost uniformly on ostentatiously artificial procedures, and the behaviour of the characters is almost consistently incredible.

The play survived on stage in Dryden's adaptation of 1679, a version which claimed to rescue its inchoate excellencies from under a 'heap of rubbish'. But in reforming the style, remodelling the plot, developing the characterisation in a morally coherent way, Dryden ironed out precisely those features of incompleteness and disjunction for which the play now tends to be valued. Coleridge talks of Shakespeare's projecting the outlines of Homeric epic into the more 'featurely' world of romantic drama, incongruously writing a grand history piece in the style of Dürer. The analogy with Dürer is suggestive but unstable. Shakespeare has projected his heroes into a world governed by disappointments, the New Troy precisely as it seemed in the dotage of Elizabeth and after the failure of Essex. This projection is not realistic, but almost surreally messy. Its messiness is only doubtfully supposed to have appeal in our century. But Shakespeare's self-consciousness about his play's necessary inadequacies may indeed have such appeal. One recent critic calls the play's refusal to resolve its own problems seminal for succeeding Jacobean tragedy; another calls its waywardness with its own originals paradigmatic for everything in the period. If we do indeed prefer problems to solutions and waywardness to submission, *Troilus and Cressida* is our play. But we should be haunted too by Dr Johnson's unececentric judgment that it is a play 'more correctly written than most of Shakespeare's compositions'.

Troilus and Cressida

DRAMATIS PERSONAE

PRIAM
King of Troy
HECTOR, TROILUS, PARIS, DEIPHOBUS, HELENUS
his sons
MARGARELON
a bastard son of Priam
AENEAS, ANTENOR
Trojan commanders
CALCHAS
a Trojan priest, taking part with the Greeks
PANDARUS
uncle to Cressida
AGAMEMNON
the Greek general
MENELAUS
his brother
ACHILLES, AJAX
Greek commanders
ULYSSES, NESTOR, DIOMEDES, PATROCLUS
Greek commanders
THERSITES
a deformed and scurrilous Greek
ALEXANDER
servant to Cressida
Servant to Troilus
Servant to Paris
Servant to Diomedes
HELEN
wife to Menelaus
ANDROMACHE
wife to Hector
CASSANDRA
daughter to Priam, a prophetess
CRESSIDA
daughter to Calchas
Trojan and Greek Soldiers, and Attendants

THE SCENE: TROY AND THE GREEK CAMP BEFORE IT.

PROLOGUE

In Troy, there lies the scene. From isles of Greece
The princes orgillous, their high blood chaf'd,
Have to the port of Athens sent their ships
Fraught with the ministers and instruments
Of cruel war. Sixty and nine that wore
Their crownets regal from th' Athenian bay
Put forth toward Phrygia; and their vow is made
To ransack Troy, within whose strong immures
The ravish'd Helen, Menelaus' queen,
With wanton Paris sleeps – and that's the quarrel.
To Tenedos they come,
And the deep-drawing barks do there disgorge
Their war-like fraughtage. Now on Dardan plains
The fresh and yet unbruised Greeks do pitch
Their brave pavilions: Priam's six-gated city,
Dardan, and Tymbria, Helias, Chetas, Troien,
And Antenorides, with massy staples
And corresponsive and fulfilling bolts,
Sperr up the sons of Troy.
Now expectation, tickling skittish spirits
On one and other side, Troyan and Greek,
Sets all on hazard – and hither am I come
A Prologue arm'd, but not in confidence
Of author's pen or actor's voice, but suited
In like conditions as our argument,
To tell you, fair beholders, that our play
Leaps o'er the vaunt and firstlings of those broils,
Beginning in the middle; starting thence away
To what may be digested in a play.
Like or find fault; do as your pleasures are;
Now good or bad, 'tis but the chance of war.

ACT ONE

SCENE I. *Troy. Before Priam's palace.*

Enter TROILUS armed, and PANDARUS.

TROILUS Call here my varlet; I'll unarm again.
Why should I war without the walls of Troy
That find such cruel battle here within?
Each Troyan that is master of his heart,
Let him to field; Troilus, alas, hath none!
PANDARUS Will this gear ne'er be mended?
TROILUS The Greeks are strong, and skilful to their strength,

Fierce to their skill, and to their fierceness valiant;
But I am weaker than a woman's tear,
Tamer than sleep, fonder than ignorance,
Less valiant than the virgin in the night,
And skilless as unpractis'd infancy.

PANDARUS Well, I have told you enough of this; for my part, I'll not meddle nor make no farther. He that will have a cake out of the wheat must needs tarry the grinding.

TROILUS Have I not tarried?

PANDARUS Ay, the grinding; but you must tarry the bolting.

TROILUS Have I not tarried?

PANDARUS Ay, the bolting; but you must tarry the leavening.

TROILUS Still have I tarried.

PANDARUS Ay, to the leavening; but here's yet in the word 'hereafter' the kneading, the making of the cake, the heating of the oven, and the baking; nay, you must stay the cooling too, or you may chance to burn your lips.

TROILUS Patience herself, what goddess e'er she be,
Doth lesser blench at suff'rance than I do.
At Priam's royal table do I sit;
And when fair Cressid comes into my thoughts –
So, traitor, then she comes when she is thence.

PANDARUS Well, she look'd yesternight fairer than ever I saw her look, or any woman else.

TROILUS I was about to tell thee: when my heart,
As wedged with a sigh, would rive in twain,
Lest Hector or my father should perceive me,
I have, as when the sun doth light a storm,
Buried this sigh in wrinkle of a smile.
But sorrow that is couch'd in seeming gladness
Is like that mirth fate turns to sudden sadness.

PANDARUS An her hair were not somewhat darker than Helen's – well, go to – there were no more comparison between the women. But, for my part, she is my kinswoman; I would not, as they term it, praise her, but I would somebody had heard her talk yesterday, as I did. I will not dispraise your sister Cassandra's wit; but –

TROILUS O Pandarus! I tell thee, Pandarus –
When I do tell thee there my hopes lie drown'd,
Reply not in how many fathoms deep
They lie indrench'd. I tell thee I am mad
In Cressid's love. Thou answer'st 'She is fair' –
Pourest in the open ulcer of my heart –
Her eyes, her hair, her cheek, her gait, her voice,
Handlest in thy discourse. O, that her hand,
In whose comparison all whites are ink
Writing their own reproach; to whose soft seizure
The cygnet's down is harsh, and spirit of sense
Hard as the palm of ploughman! This thou tell'st me,
As true thou tell'st me, when I say I love her;
But, saying thus, instead of oil and balm,
Thou lay'st in every gash that love hath given me
The knife that made it.

PANDARUS I speak no more than truth.

TROILUS Thou dost not speak so much.

PANDARUS Faith, I'll not meddle in it. Let her be as she is: if she be fair, 'tis the better for her; an she be not, she has the mends in her own hands.

TROILUS Good Pandarus! How now, Pandarus!

PANDARUS I have had my labour for my travail, ill thought on of her and ill thought on of you; gone between and between, but small thanks for my labour.

TROILUS What, art thou angry, Pandarus? What, with me?

PANDARUS Because she's kin to me, therefore she's not so fair as Helen. An she were not kin to me, she would be as fair a Friday as Helen is on Sunday. But what care I? I care not an she were a blackamoor; 'tis all one to me.

TROILUS Say I she is not fair?

PANDARUS I do not care whether you do or no. She's a fool to stay behind her father. Let her to the Greeks; and so I'll tell her the next time I see her. For my part, I'll meddle nor make no more i' th' matter.

TROILUS Pandarus!

PANDARUS Not I.

TROILUS Sweet Pandarus!

PANDARUS Pray you, speak no more to me: I will leave all as I found it, and there an end.

[*Exit. Sound alarum.*

TROILUS Peace, you ungracious clamours! Peace, rude sounds!
Fools on both sides! Helen must needs be fair,
When with your blood you daily paint her thus.
I cannot fight upon this argument;
It is too starv'd a subject for my sword.
But Pandarus – O gods, how do you plague me!
I cannot come to Cressid but by Pandar;
And he's as tetchy to be woo'd to woo
As she is stubborn-chaste against all suit.
Tell me, Apollo, for thy Daphne's love,
What Cressid is, what Pandar, and what we?
Her bed is India; there she lies, a pearl;
Between our Ilium and where she resides
Let it be call'd the wild and wand'ring flood;
Ourself the merchant, and this sailing Pandar
Our doubtful hope, our convoy, and our bark.

Alarum. Enter AENEAS.

AENEAS How now, Prince Troilus! Wherefore not afield?

TROILUS Because not there. This woman's answer sorts,
For womanish it is to be from thence.
What news, Aeneas, from the field to-day?

AENEAS That Paris is returned home, and hurt.

TROILUS By whom, Aeneas?

AENEAS Troilus, by Menelaus.

TROILUS Let Paris bleed: 'tis but a scar to scorn;
Paris is gor'd with Menelaus' horn. [*Alarum.*

AENEAS Hark what good sport is out of town to-day!

TROILUS Better at home, if 'would I might' were 'may'.
But to the sport abroad. Are you bound thither?

AENEAS In all swift haste.

TROILUS Come, go we then together.
[*Exeunt.*

SCENE II. *Troy. A street.*

Enter CRESSIDA and her man ALEXANDER.

CRESSIDA Who were those went by?

ALEXANDER Queen Hecuba and Helen.

CRESSIDA And whither go they?

ALEXANDER Up to the eastern tower,
Whose height commands as subject all the vale,
To see the battle. Hector, whose patience
Is as a virtue fix'd, to-day was mov'd.
He chid Andromache, and struck his armourer;
And, like as there were husbandry in war,
Before the sun rose he was harness'd light,
And to the field goes he; where every flower
Did as a prophet weep what it foresaw
In Hector's wrath.

CRESSIDA What was his cause of anger?

ALEXANDER The noise goes, this: there is among the Greeks
A lord of Troyan blood, nephew to Hector;
They call him Ajax.

CRESSIDA Good; and what of him?

ALEXANDER They say he is a very man per se
And stands alone.

CRESSIDA So do all men, unless they are drunk, sick, or have no legs.

ALEXANDER This man, lady, hath robb'd many beasts of their particular additions: he is as valiant as the lion, churlish as the bear, slow as the elephant – a man into whom nature hath so crowded humours that his valour is crush'd into folly, his folly sauced with discretion. There is no man hath a virtue that he hath not a glimpse of, nor any man an attaint but he carries some stain of it; he is melancholy without cause and merry against the hair; he hath the joints of every thing; but everything so out of joint that he is a gouty Briareus, many hands and no use, or purblind Argus, all eyes and no sight.

CRESSIDA But how should this man, that makes me smile, make Hector angry?

ALEXANDER They say he yesterday cop'd Hector in the battle and struck him down, the disdain and shame whereof hath ever since kept Hector fasting and waking.

Enter PANDARUS.

CRESSIDA Who comes here?

ALEXANDER Madam, your uncle Pandarus.

CRESSIDA Hector's a gallant man.

ALEXANDER As may be in the world, lady.

PANDARUS What's that? What's that?

CRESSIDA Good morrow, uncle Pandarus.

PANDARUS Good morrow, cousin Cressid. What do you talk of? – Good morrow, Alexander. – How do you, cousin? When were you at Ilium?

CRESSIDA This morning, uncle.

PANDARUS What were you talking of when I came? Was Hector arm'd and gone ere you came to Ilium? Helen was not up, was she?

CRESSIDA Hector was gone; but Helen was not up.

PANDARUS E'en so. Hector was stirring early.

CRESSIDA That were we talking of, and of his anger.

PANDARUS Was he angry?

CRESSIDA So he says here.

PANDARUS True, he was so; I know the cause too; he'll lay about him to-day, I can tell them that. And there's Troilus will not come far behind him; let them take heed of Troilus, I can tell them that too.

CRESSIDA What, is he angry too?

PANDARUS Who, Troilus? Troilus is the better man of the two.

CRESSIDA O Jupiter! there's no comparison.

PANDARUS What, not between Troilus and Hector? Do you know a man if you see him?

CRESSIDA Ay, if I ever saw him before and knew him.

PANDARUS Well, I say Troilus is Troilus.

CRESSIDA Then you say as I say, for I am sure he is not Hector.

PANDARUS No, nor Hector is not Troilus in some degrees.

CRESSIDA 'Tis just to each of them: he is himself.

PANDARUS Himself! Alas, poor Troilus! I would he were!

CRESSIDA So he is.

PANDARUS Condition I had gone barefoot to India.

CRESSIDA He is not Hector.

PANDARUS Himself! no, he's not himself. Would 'a were himself! Well, the gods are above; time must friend or end. Well, Troilus, well! I would my heart were in her body! No, Hector is not a better man than Troilus.

CRESSIDA Excuse me.

PANDARUS He is elder.

CRESSIDA Pardon me, pardon me.

PANDARUS Th' other's not come to't; you shall tell me another tale when th' other's come to't. Hector shall not have his wit this year.

CRESSIDA He shall not need it if he have his own.

PANDARUS Nor his qualities.

CRESSIDA No matter.

PANDARUS Nor his beauty.

CRESSIDA 'Twould not become him: his own's better.

PANDARUS You have no judgment, niece. Helen herself swore th' other day that Troilus, for a brown favour, for so 'tis, I must confess – not brown neither –

CRESSIDA No, but brown.

PANDARUS Faith, to say truth, brown and not brown.

CRESSIDA To say the truth, true and not true.

PANDARUS She prais'd his complexion above Paris.

CRESSIDA Why, Paris hath colour enough.

PANDARUS So he has.

CRESSIDA Then Troilus should have too much. If she prais'd him above, his complexion is higher than his; he having colour enough, and the other higher, is too flaming a praise for a good complexion. I had as lief Helen's golden tongue had commended Troilus for a copper nose.

PANDARUS I swear to you I think Helen loves him better than Paris.

CRESSIDA Then she's a merry Greek indeed.

PANDARUS Nay, I am sure she does. She came to him th' other day into the compass'd window – and you know he has not past three or four hairs on his chin –

CRESSIDA Indeed a tapster's arithmetic may soon bring his particulars therein to a total.

PANDARUS Why, he is very young, and yet will he within three pound lift as much as his brother Hector.

CRESSIDA Is he so young a man and so old a lifter?

PANDARUS But to prove to you that Helen loves him: she came and puts me her white hand to his cloven chin –

CRESSIDA Juno have mercy! How came it cloven?

PANDARUS Why, you know, 'tis dimpled. I think his smiling becomes him better than any man in all Phrygia.

CRESSIDA O, he smiles valiantly!

PANDARUS Does he not?

CRESSIDA O yes, an 'twere a cloud in autumn!

PANDARUS Why, go to, then! But to prove to you that Helen loves Troilus –

CRESSIDA Troilus will stand to the proof, if you'll prove it so.

PANDARUS Troilus! Why, he esteems her no more than I esteem an addle egg.

CRESSIDA If you love an addle egg as well as you love an idle head, you would eat chickens i' th' shell.

PANDARUS I cannot choose but laugh to think how she tickled his chin. Indeed, she has a marvell's white hand, I must needs confess.

CRESSIDA Without the rack.

PANDARUS And she takes upon her to spy a white hair on his chin.

CRESSIDA Alas, poor chin! Many a wart is richer.

PANDARUS But there was such laughing! Queen Hecuba laugh'd that her eyes ran o'er.

CRESSIDA With millstones.

PANDARUS And Cassandra laugh'd.

CRESSIDA But there was a more temperate fire under the pot of her eyes. Did her eyes run o'er too?

PANDARUS And Hector laugh'd.

CRESSIDA At what was all this laughing?

PANDARUS Marry, at the white hair that Helen spied on Troilus' chin.

CRESSIDA An't had been a green hair I should have laugh'd too.

PANDARUS They laugh'd not so much at the hair as at his pretty answer.

CRESSIDA What was his answer?

PANDARUS Quoth she 'Here's but two and fifty hairs on your chin, and one of them is white'.

CRESSIDA This is her question.

PANDARUS That's true; make no question of that. 'Two and fifty hairs,' quoth he 'and one white. That white hair is my father, and all the rest are his sons.' 'Jupiter!' quoth she 'which of these hairs is Paris my husband?' 'The forked one,' quoth he 'pluck't out and give it him.' But there was such laughing! and Helen so blush'd, and Paris so chaf'd; and all the rest so laugh'd that it pass'd.

CRESSIDA So let it now; for it has been a great while going by.

PANDARUS Well, cousin, I told you a thing yesterday; think on't.

CRESSIDA So I do.

PANDARUS I'll be sworn 'tis true; he will weep you, an 'twere a man born in April.

CRESSIDA And I'll spring up in his tears, an 'twere a nettle against May. [*Sound a retreat.*

PANDARUS Hark! they are coming from the field. Shall we stand up here and see them as they pass toward Ilium? Good niece, do, sweet niece Cressida.

174 CRESSIDA At your pleasure.
PANDARUS Here, here, here's an excellent place;
here we may see most bravely. I'll tell you them
all by their names as they pass by; but mark
Troilus above the rest.

AENEAS passes.

178 CRESSIDA Speak not so loud.
PANDARUS That's Aeneas. Is not that a brave
man? He's one of the flowers of Troy, I can tell
181 you. But mark Troilus; you shall see anon.

ANTENOR passes.

CRESSIDA Who's that?
PANDARUS That's Antenor. He has a shrewd wit,
I can tell you; and he's a man good enough; he's
one o' th' soundest judgments in Troy,
whosoever, and a proper man of person. When
comes Troilus? I'll show you Troilus anon. If he
187 see me, you shall see him nod at me.
CRESSIDA Will he give you the nod?
PANDARUS You shall see.
CRESSIDA If he do, the rich shall have more.

HECTOR passes.

PANDARUS That's Hector, that, that, look you,
that; there's a fellow! Go thy way, Hector!
There's a brave man, niece. O brave Hector!
Look how he looks. There's a countenance! Is't
not a brave man?
195 CRESSIDA O, a brave man!
PANDARUS Is 'a not? It does a man's heart good.
Look you what hacks are on his helmet! Look
you yonder, do you see? Look you there. There's
no jesting; there's laying on; take't off who will,
200 as they say. There be hacks.
CRESSIDA Be those with swords?
PANDARUS Swords! anything, he cares not; an
the devil come to him, it's all one. By God's lid,
it does one's heart good. Yonder comes Paris,
204 yonder comes Paris.

PARIS passes.

Look ye yonder, niece; is't not a gallant man too,
is't not? Why, this is brave now. Who said he
came hurt home to-day? He's not hurt. Why,
this will do Helen's heart good now, ha! Would
I could see Troilus now! You shall see Troilus
anon.

HELENUS passes.

210 CRESSIDA Who's that?
PANDARUS That's Helenus. I marvel where
Troilus is. That's Helenus. I think he went not
forth to-day. That's Helenus.
214 CRESSIDA Can Helenus fight, uncle?
PANDARUS Helenus! no. Yes, he'll fight
indifferent well. I marvel where Troilus is.
Hark! do you not hear the people cry 'Troilus'?
Helenus is a priest.
CRESSIDA What sneaking fellow comes yonder? 218

TROILUS passes.

PANDARUS Where? yonder? That's Deiphobus.
'Tis Troilus. There's a man, niece. Hem!
Brave Troilus, the prince of chivalry! 221
CRESSIDA Peace, for shame, peace!
PANDARUS Mark him; note him. O brave Troilus!
Look well upon him, niece; look you how his
sword is bloodied, and his helm more hack'd
than Hector's; and how he looks, and how he
goes! O admirable youth! he never saw three
and twenty. Go thy way, Troilus, go thy way.
Had I a sister were a grace or a daughter a
goddess, he should take his choice. O admirable
man! Paris? Paris is dirt to him; and, I warrant,
Helen, to change, would give an eye to boot. 231
CRESSIDA Here comes more.

Common Soldiers pass.

PANDARUS Asses, fools, dolts! chaff and bran,
chaff and bran! porridge after meat! I could live
and die in the eyes of Troilus. Ne'er look, ne'er
look; the eagles are gone. Crows and daws,
crows and daws! I had rather be such a man as
Troilus than Agamemnon and all Greece.
CRESSIDA There is amongst the Greeks Achilles,
a better man than Troilus. 240
PANDARUS Achilles? A drayman, a porter, a very
camel!
CRESSIDA Well, well.
PANDARUS Well, well! Why, have you any
discretion? Have you any eyes? Do you know
what a man is? Is not birth, beauty, good shape,
discourse, manhood, learning, gentleness,
virtue, youth, liberality, and such like, the spice
and salt that season a man? 247
CRESSIDA Ay, a minc'd man; and then to be bak'd
with no date in the pie, for then the man's date
is out.
PANDARUS You are such a woman! A man knows
not at what ward you lie. 251
CRESSIDA Upon my back, to defend my belly;
upon my wit, to defend my wiles; upon my
secrecy, to defend mine honesty; my mask, to
defend my beauty; and you, to defend all these;
and at all these wards I lie at, at a thousand
watches. 256
PANDARUS Say one of your watches.
CRESSIDA Nay, I'll watch you for that; and that's
one of the chiefest of them too. If I cannot ward
what I would not have hit, I can watch you for
telling how I took the blow; unless it swell past
hiding, and then it's past watching. 262
PANDARUS You are such another!

Enter Troilus' Boy.

BOY Sir, my lord would instantly speak with you.
PANDARUS Where?
BOY At your own house; there he unarms him.
PANDARUS Good boy, tell him I come. [*Exit Boy.*
I doubt he be hurt. Fare ye well, good niece.
CRESSIDA Adieu, uncle.
PANDARUS I will be with you, niece, by and by.
CRESSIDA To bring, uncle.
PANDARUS Ay, a token from Troilus.
CRESSIDA By the same token, you are a bawd.
[*Exit Pandarus.*
Words, vows, gifts, tears, and love's full sacrifice,
He offers in another's enterprise;
But more in Troilus thousand-fold I see
Than in the glass of Pandar's praise may be,
Yet hold I off. Women are angels, wooing:
Things won are done; joy's soul lies in the doing.
That she belov'd knows nought that knows not this:
Men prize the thing ungain'd more than it is.
That she was never yet that ever knew
Love got so sweet as when desire did sue;
Therefore this maxim out of love I teach:
Achievement is command; ungain'd, beseech.
Then though my heart's content firm love doth bear,
Nothing of that shall from mine eyes appear.
[*Exit.*

SCENE III. *The Grecian camp. Before Agamemnon's tent.*

Sennet. Enter AGAMEMNON, NESTOR, ULYSSES, DIOMEDES, MENELAUS, and Others.

AGAMEMNON Princes,
What grief hath set these jaundies o'er your cheeks?
The ample proposition that hope makes
In all designs begun on earth below
Fails in the promis'd largeness; checks and disasters
Grow in the veins of actions highest rear'd,
As knots, by the conflux of meeting sap,
Infects the sound pine, and diverts his grain
Tortive and errant from his course of growth.
Nor, princes, is it matter new to us
That we come short of our suppose so far
That after seven years' siege yet Troy walls stand;
Sith every action that hath gone before,
Whereof we have record, trial did draw
Bias and thwart, not answering the aim,
And that unbodied figure of the thought
That gave't surmised shape. Why then, you princes,
Do you with cheeks abash'd behold our works
And call them shames, which are, indeed, nought else
But the protractive trials of great Jove
To find persistive constancy in men;
The fineness of which metal is not found
In fortune's love? For then the bold and coward,
The wise and fool, the artist and unread,
The hard and soft, seem all affin'd and kin.
But in the wind and tempest of her frown
Distinction, with a broad and powerful fan,
Puffing at all, winnows the light away;
And what hath mass or matter by itself
Lies rich in virtue and unmingled.
NESTOR With due observance of thy godlike seat,
Great Agamemnon, Nestor shall apply
Thy latest words. In the reproof of chance
Lies the true proof of men. The sea being smooth,
How many shallow bauble boats dare sail
Upon her patient breast, making their way
With those of nobler bulk!
But let the ruffian Boreas once enrage
The gentle Thetis, and anon behold
The strong-ribb'd bark through liquid mountains cut,
Bounding between the two moist elements
Like Perseus' horse. Where's then the saucy boat,
Whose weak untimber'd sides but even now
Co-rivall'd greatness? Either to harbour fled
Or made a toast for Neptune. Even so
Doth valour's show and valour's worth divide
In storms of fortune; for in her ray and brightness
The herd hath more annoyance by the breese
Than by the tiger; but when the splitting wind
Makes flexible the knees of knotted oaks,
And flies fled under shade – why, then the thing of courage,
As rous'd with rage, with rage doth sympathise,
And with an accent tun'd in self-same key
Retorts to chiding fortune.
ULYSSES Agamemnon,
Thou great commander, nerve and bone of Greece,
Heart of our numbers, soul and only spirit
In whom the tempers and the minds of all
Should be shut up – hear what Ulysses speaks.
Besides the applause and approbation
The which, [*To Agamemnon*] most mighty, for thy place and sway,
[*To Nestor*] And, thou most reverend, for thy stretch'd-out life,
I give to both your speeches – which were such
As Agamemnon and the hand of Greece
Should hold up high in brass; and such again

As venerable Nestor, hatch'd in silver,
Should with a bond of air, strong as the axle-tree
On which heaven rides, knit all the Greekish ears
To his experienc'd tongue – yet let it please both,
Thou great, and wise, to hear Ulysses speak.

AGAMEMNON Speak, Prince of Ithaca; and be't of less expect
That matter needless, of importless burden,
Divide thy lips than we are confident,
When rank Thersites opes his mastic jaws,
We shall hear music, wit, and oracle.

ULYSSES Troy, yet upon his basis, had been down,
And the great Hector's sword had lack'd a master,
But for these instances:
The specialty of rule hath been neglected;
And look how many Grecian tents do stand
Hollow upon this plain, so many hollow factions.
When that the general is not like the hive,
To whom the foragers shall all repair,
What honey is expected? Degree being vizarded,
Th' unworthiest shows as fairly in the mask.
The heavens themselves, the planets, and this centre,
Observe degree, priority, and place,
Insisture, course, proportion, season, form,
Office, and custom, in all line of order;
And therefore is the glorious planet Sol
In noble eminence enthron'd and spher'd
Amidst the other, whose med'cinable eye
Corrects the ill aspects of planets evil,
And posts, like the commandment of a king,
Sans check, to good and bad. But when the planets
In evil mixture to disorder wander,
What plagues and what portents, what mutiny,
What raging of the sea, shaking of earth,
Commotion in the winds! Frights, changes, horrors,
Divert and crack, rend and deracinate,
The unity and married calm of states
Quite from their fixture! O, when degree is shak'd,
Which is the ladder of all high designs,
The enterprise is sick! How could communities,
Degrees in schools, and brotherhoods in cities,
Peaceful commerce from dividable shores,
The primogenity and due of birth,
Prerogative of age, crowns, sceptres, laurels,
But by degree, stand in authentic place?
Take but degree away, untune that string,
And hark what discord follows! Each thing melts
In mere oppugnancy: the bounded waters
Should lift their bosoms higher than the shores,
And make a sop of all this solid globe;
Strength should be lord of imbecility,
And the rude son should strike his father dead;
Force should be right; or, rather, right and wrong –
Between whose endless jar justice resides –
Should lose their names, and so should justice too.
Then everything includes itself in power,
Power into will, will into appetite;
And appetite, an universal wolf,
So doubly seconded with will and power,
Must make perforce an universal prey,
And last eat up himself. Great Agamemnon,
This chaos, when degree is suffocate,
Follows the choking.
And this neglection of degree it is
That by a pace goes backward, with a purpose
It hath to climb. The general's disdain'd
By him one step below, he by the next,
That next by him beneath; so every step,
Exampl'd by the first pace that is sick
Of his superior, grows to an envious fever
Of pale and bloodless emulation.
And 'tis this fever that keeps Troy on foot,
Not her own sinews. To end a tale of length,
Troy in our weakness stands, not in her strength.

NESTOR Most wisely hath Ulysses here discover'd
The fever whereof all our power is sick.

AGAMEMNON The nature of the sickness found, Ulysses,
What is the remedy?

ULYSSES The great Achilles, whom opinion crowns
The sinew and the forehand of our host,
Having his ear full of his airy fame,
Grows dainty of his worth, and in his tent
Lies mocking our designs; with him Patroclus
Upon a lazy bed the livelong day
Breaks scurril jests;
And with ridiculous and awkward action –
Which, slanderer, he imitation calls –
He pageants us. Sometime, great Agamemnon,
Thy topless deputation he puts on;
And like a strutting player whose conceit
Lies in his hamstring, and doth think it rich
To hear the wooden dialogue and sound
'Twixt his stretch'd footing and the scaffoldage –
Such to-be-pitied and o'er-wrested seeming
He acts thy greatness in; and when he speaks
'Tis like a chime a-mending; with terms unsquar'd,
Which, from the tongue of roaring Typhon dropp'd,

Would seem hyperboles. At this fusty stuff
The large Achilles, on his press'd bed lolling,
From his deep chest laughs out a loud applause;
Cries 'Excellent! 'tis Agamemnon just.
Now play me Nestor; hem, and stroke thy beard,
As he being drest to some oration'.
That's done – as near as the extremest ends
Of parallels, as like as Vulcan and his wife;
Yet good Achilles still cries 'Excellent!
'Tis Nestor right. Now play him me, Patroclus,
Arming to answer in a night alarm'.
And then, forsooth, the faint defects of age
Must be the scene of mirth: to cough and spit
And, with a palsy-fumbling on his gorget,
Shake in and out the rivet. And at this sport
Sir Valour dies; cries 'O, enough, Patroclus;
Or give me ribs of steel! I shall split all
In pleasure of my spleen'. And in this fashion
All our abilities, gifts, natures, shapes,
Severals and generals of grace exact,
Achievements, plots, orders, preventions,
Excitements to the field or speech for truce,
Success or loss, what is or is not, serves
As stuff for these two to make paradoxes.

NESTOR And in the imitation of these twain –
Who, as Ulysses says, opinion crowns
With an imperial voice – many are infect.
Ajax is grown self-will'd and bears his head
In such a rein, in full as proud a place
As broad Achilles; keeps his tent like him;
Makes factious feasts; rails on our state of war
Bold as an oracle, and sets Thersites,
A slave whose gall coins slanders like a mint,
To match us in comparisons with dirt,
To weaken and discredit our exposure,
How rank soever rounded in with danger.

ULYSSES They tax our policy and call it cowardice,
Count wisdom as no member of the war,
Forestall prescience, and esteem no act
But that of hand. The still and mental parts
That do contrive how many hands shall strike
When fitness calls them on, and know, by measure
Of their observant toil, the enemies' weight –
Why, this hath not a finger's dignity:
They call this bed-work, mapp'ry, closet-war;
So that the ram that batters down the wall,
For the great swinge and rudeness of his poise,
They place before his hand that made the engine,
Or those that with the fineness of their souls
By reason guide his execution.

NESTOR Let this be granted, and Achilles' horse
Makes many Thetis' sons. [*Tucket*.

AGAMEMNON What trumpet? Look, Menelaus.

MENELAUS From Troy.

Enter AENEAS.

AGAMEMNON What would you fore our tent?

AENEAS Is this great Agamemnon's tent, I pray you?

AGAMEMNON Even this.

AENEAS May one that is a herald and a prince
Do a fair message to his kingly eyes?

AGAMEMNON With surety stronger than Achilles' arm
Fore all the Greekish heads, which with one voice
Call Agamemnon head and general.

AENEAS Fair leave and large security. How may
A stranger to those most imperial looks
Know them from eyes of other mortals?

AGAMEMNON How?

AENEAS Ay;
I ask, that I might waken reverence,
And bid the cheek be ready with a blush
Modest as Morning when she coldly eyes
The youthful Phoebus.
Which is that god in office, guiding men?
Which is the high and mighty Agamemnon?

AGAMEMNON This Troyan scorns us, or the men of Troy
Are ceremonious courtiers.

AENEAS Courtiers as free, as debonair, unarm'd,
As bending angels; that's their fame in peace.
But when they would seem soldiers, they have galls,
Good arms, strong joints, true swords; and, Jove's accord,
Nothing so full of heart. But peace, Aeneas,
Peace, Troyan; lay thy finger on thy lips.
The worthiness of praise distains his worth,
If that the prais'd himself bring the praise forth;
But what the repining enemy commends,
That breath fame blows; that praise, sole pure, transcends.

AGAMEMNON Sir, you of Troy, call you yourself Aeneas?

AENEAS Ay, Greek, that is my name.

AGAMEMNON What's your affair, I pray you?

AENEAS Sir, pardon; 'tis for Agamemnon's ears.

AGAMEMNON He hears nought privately that comes from Troy.

AENEAS Nor I from Troy come not to whisper with him;
I bring a trumpet to awake his ear,
To set his sense on the attentive bent,
And then to speak.

AGAMEMNON Speak frankly as the wind;
It is not Agamemnon's sleeping hour.
That thou shalt know, Troyan, he is awake,
He tells thee so himself.

AENEAS Trumpet, blow loud,

Send thy brass voice through all these lazy tents;
And every Greek of mettle, let him know
What Troy means fairly shall be spoke aloud.

[Sound trumpet.

We have, great Agamemnon, here in Troy
A prince called Hector – Priam is his father –
Who in this dull and long-continued truce
Is resty grown; he bade me take a trumpet
And to this purpose speak: Kings, princes, lords!
If there be one among the fair'st of Greece
That holds his honour higher than his ease,
That seeks his praise more than he fears his peril,
That knows his valour and knows not his fear,
That loves his mistress more than in confession
With truant vows to her own lips he loves,
And dare avow her beauty and her worth
In other arms than hers – to him this challenge.
Hector, in view of Troyans and of Greeks,
Shall make it good or do his best to do it:
He hath a lady wiser, fairer, truer,
Than ever Greek did couple in his arms;
And will to-morrow with his trumpet call
Mid-way between your tents and walls of Troy
To rouse a Grecian that is true in love.
If any come, Hector shall honour him;
If none, he'll say in Troy, when he retires,
The Grecian dames are sunburnt and not worth
The splinter of a lance. Even so much.

AGAMEMNON This shall be told our lovers, Lord Aeneas.
If none of them have soul in such a kind,
We left them all at home. But we are soldiers;
And may that soldier a mere recreant prove
That means not, hath not, or is not in love.
If then one is, or hath, or means to be,
That one meets Hector; if none else, I am he.

NESTOR Tell him of Nestor, one that was a man
When Hector's grandsire suck'd. He is old now;
But if there be not in our Grecian mould
One noble man that hath one spark of fire
To answer for his love, tell him from me
I'll hide my silver beard in a gold beaver,
And in my vantbrace put this wither'd brawn,
And, meeting him, will tell him that my lady
Was fairer than his grandame, and as chaste
As may be in the world. His youth in flood,
I'll prove this truth with my three drops of blood.

AENEAS Now heavens forfend such scarcity of youth!

ULYSSES Amen.

AGAMEMNON Fair Lord Aeneas, let me touch your hand;
To our pavilion shall I lead you, first.
Achilles shall have word of this intent;
So shall each lord of Greece, from tent to tent.
Yourself shall feast with us before you go,
And find the welcome of a noble foe.

[Exeunt all but Ulysses and Nestor.

ULYSSES Nestor!

NESTOR What says Ulysses?

ULYSSES I have a young conception in my brain;
Be you my time to bring it to some shape.

NESTOR What is't?

ULYSSES This 'tis:
Blunt wedges rive hard knots. The seeded pride
That hath to this maturity blown up
In rank Achilles must or now be cropp'd
Or, shedding, breed a nursery of like evil
To overbulk us all.

NESTOR Well, and how?

ULYSSES This challenge that the gallant Hector sends,
However it is spread in general name,
Relates in purpose only to Achilles.

NESTOR True. The purpose is perspicuous even as substance
Whose grossness little characters sum up;
And, in the publication, make no strain
But that Achilles, were his brain as barren
As banks of Libya – though, Apollo knows,
'Tis dry enough – will with great speed of judgment,
Ay, with celerity, find Hector's purpose
Pointing on him.

ULYSSES And wake him to the answer, think you?

NESTOR Why, 'tis most meet. Who may you else oppose
That can from Hector bring those honours off,
If not Achilles? Though't be a sportful combat,
Yet in this trial much opinion dwells;
For here the Troyans taste our dear'st repute
With their fin'st palate; and trust to me, Ulysses,
Our imputation shall be oddly pois'd
In this vile action; for the success,
Although particular, shall give a scantling
Of good or bad unto the general;
And in such indexes, although small pricks
To their subsequent volumes, there is seen
The baby figure of the giant mass
Of things to come at large. It is suppos'd
He that meets Hector issues from our choice;
And choice, being mutual act of all our souls,
Makes merit her election, and doth boil,
As 'twere from forth us all, a man distill'd
Out of our virtues; who miscarrying,
What heart receives from hence a conquering part,
To steal a strong opinion to themselves?

Which entertain'd, limbs are his instruments,
In no less working than are swords and bows
Directive by the limbs.

ULYSSES Give pardon to my speech.
Therefore 'tis meet Achilles meet not Hector.
Let us, like merchants, show our foulest wares
And think perchance they'll sell; if not, the lustre
Of the better yet to show shall show the better,
By showing the worst first. Do not consent
That ever Hector and Achilles meet;
For both our honour and our shame in this
Are dogg'd with two strange followers.

NESTOR I see them not with my old eyes. What are they?

ULYSSES What glory our Achilles shares from Hector,
Were he not proud, we all should wear with him;
But he already is too insolent;
And it were better parch in Afric sun
Than in the pride and salt scorn of his eyes,
Should he scape Hector fair. If he were foil'd,
Why, then we do our main opinion crush
In taint of our best man. No, make a lott'ry;
And, by device, let blockish Ajax draw
The sort to fight with Hector. Among ourselves
Give him allowance for the better man;
For that will physic the great Myrmidon,
Who broils in loud applause, and make him fall
His crest, that prouder than blue Iris bends.
If the dull brainless Ajax come safe off,
[We'll dress him up in voices; if he fail,
Yet go we under our opinion still
That we have better men. But, hit or miss,
Our project's life this shape of sense assumes –
Ajax employ'd plucks down Achilles' plumes.

NESTOR Now, Ulysses, I begin to relish thy advice;
And I will give a taste thereof forthwith
To Agamemnon. Go we to him straight.
Two curs shall tame each other: pride alone
Must tarre the mastiffs on, as 'twere their bone.

[*Exeunt.*

ACT TWO

SCENE I. *The Grecian camp.*

Enter AJAX and THERSITES.

AJAX Thersites!

THERSITES Agamemnon – how if he had boils full, all over, generally?

AJAX Thersites!

THERSITES And those boils did run – say so. Did not the general run then? Were not that a botchy core?

AJAX Dog!

THERSITES Then there would come some matter from him; I see none now.

AJAX Thou bitch-wolf's son, canst thou not hear? Feel, then. [*Strikes him.*

THERSITES The plague of Greece upon thee, thou mongrel beef-witted lord!

AJAX Speak, then, thou whinid'st leaven, speak. I will beat thee into handsomeness.

THERSITES I shall sooner rail thee into wit and holiness; but I think thy horse will sooner con an oration than thou learn a prayer without book. Thou canst strike, canst thou? A red murrain o' thy jade's tricks!

AJAX Toadstool, learn me the proclamation.

THERSITES Dost thou think I have no sense, thou strikest me thus?

AJAX The proclamation!

THERSITES Thou art proclaim'd a fool, I think.

AJAX Do not, porpentine, do not; my fingers itch.

THERSITES I would thou didst itch from head to foot and I had the scratching of thee; I would make thee the loathsomest scab in Greece. When thou art forth in the incursions, thou strikest as slow as another.

AJAX I say, the proclamation.

THERSITES Thou grumblest and railest every hour on Achilles; and thou art as full of envy at his greatness as Cerberus is at Prosperpina's beauty – ay, that thou bark'st at him.

AJAX Mistress Thersites!

THERSITES Thou shouldst strike him.

AJAX Cobloaf!

THERSITES he would pun thee into shivers with his fist, as a sailor breaks a biscuit.

AJAX You whoreson cur! [*Strikes him.*

THERSITES Do, do.

AJAX Thou stool for a witch!

THERSITES Ay, do, do; thou sodden-witted lord! Thou hast no more brain than I have in mine elbows; an assinico may tutor thee. You scurvy valiant ass! Thou art here but to thrash Troyans, and thou art bought and sold among those of any wit like a barbarian slave. If thou use to beat me, I will begin at thy heel and tell what thou art by inches, thou thing of no bowels, thou!

AJAX You dog!

THERSITES You scurvy lord!

AJAX You cur! [*Strikes him.*

THERSITES Mars his idiot! Do, rudeness; do, camel; do, do.

Enter ACHILLES and PATROCLUS.

ACHILLES Why, how now, Ajax! Wherefore do you thus?
How now, Thersites! What's the matter, man?

THERSITES You see him there, do you?

ACHILLES Ay; what's the matter?

THERSITES Nay, look upon him.

ACHILLES So I do. What's the matter?

THERSITES Nay, but regard him well.

ACHILLES Well! why, so I do.

THERSITES But yet you look not well upon him; for who some ever you take him to be, he is Ajax.

ACHILLES I know that, fool.

THERSITES Ay, but that fool knows not himself.

AJAX Therefore I beat thee.

THERSITES Lo, lo, lo, lo, what modicums of wit he utters! His evasions have ears thus long. I have bobb'd his brain more than he has beat my bones. I will buy nine sparrows for a penny, and his pia mater is not worth the ninth part of a sparrow. This lord, Achilles, Ajax – who wears his wit in his belly and his guts in his head – I'll tell you what I say of him.

ACHILLES What?

THERSITES I say this Ajax – [*Ajax offers to strike him.*

ACHILLES Nay, good Ajax.

THERSITES Has not so much wit –

ACHILLES Nay, I must hold you.

THERSITES As will stop the eye of Helen's needle, for whom he comes to fight.

ACHILLES Peace, fool!

THERSITES I would have peace and quietness, but the fool will not – he there; that he; look you there.

AJAX O thou damned cur! I shall –

ACHILLES Will you set your wit to a fool's?

THERSITES No, I warrant you; the fool's will shame it.

PATROCLUS Good words, Thersites.

ACHILLES What's the quarrel?

AJAX I bade the vile owl go learn me the tenour of the proclamation, and he rails upon me.

THERSITES I serve thee not.

AJAX Well, go to, go to.

THERSITES I serve here voluntary.

ACHILLES Your last service was suff'rance; 'twas not voluntary. No man is beaten voluntary. Ajax was here the voluntary, and you as under an impress.

THERSITES E'en so; a great deal of your wit too lies in your sinews, or else there be liars. Hector shall have a great catch an he knock out either of your brains: 'a were as good crack a fusty nut with no kernel.

ACHILLES What, with me too, Thersites?

THERSITES There's Ulysses and old Nestor – whose wit was mouldy ere your grandsires had nails on their toes – yoke you like draught oxen, and make you plough up the wars.

ACHILLES What, what?

THERSITES Yes, good sooth. To Achilles, to Ajax, to –

AJAX I shall cut out your tongue.

THERSITES 'Tis no matter; I shall speak as much as thou afterwards.

PATROCLUS No more words, Thersites; peace!

THERSITES I will hold my peace when Achilles' brach bids me, shall I?

ACHILLES There's for you, Patroclus.

THERSITES I will see you hang'd like clotpoles ere I come any more to your tents. I will keep where there is wit stirring, and leave the faction of fools. [*Exit.*

PATROCLUS A good riddance.

ACHILLES Marry, this, sir, is proclaim'd through all our host,
That Hector, by the fifth hour of the sun,
Will with a trumpet 'twixt our tents and Troy,
To-morrow morning, call some knight to arms
That hath a stomach; and such a one that dare
Maintain I know not what; 'tis trash. Farewell.

AJAX Farewell. Who shall answer him?

ACHILLES I know not; 'tis put to lott'ry. Otherwise
He knew his man.

AJAX O, meaning you! I will go learn more of it.
[*Exeunt.*

SCENE II. *Troy. Priam's palace.*

Enter PRIAM, HECTOR, TROILUS, PARIS and HELENUS.

PRIAM After so many hours, lives, speeches, spent,
Thus once again says Nestor from the Greeks:
'Deliver Helen, and all damage else –
As honour, loss of time, travail, expense,
Wounds, friends, and what else dear that is consum'd
In hot digestion of this cormorant war –
Shall be struck off'. Hector, what say you to't?

HECTOR Though no man lesser fears the Greeks than I,
As far as toucheth my particular,
Yet, dread Priam,
There is no lady of more softer bowels,
More spongy to suck in the sense of fear,
More ready to cry out 'Who knows what follows?'
Than Hector is. The wound of peace is surety,
Surety secure; but modest doubt is call'd

The beacon of the wise, the tent that searches
To th' bottom of the worst. Let Helen go.
Since the first sword was drawn about this question,
Every tithe soul 'mongst many thousand dismes
Hath been as dear as Helen – I mean, of ours.
If we have lost so many tenths of ours
To guard a thing not ours, nor worth to us,
Had it our name, the value of one ten,
What merit's in that reason which denies
The yielding of her up?

TROILUS Fie, fie, my brother!
Weigh you the worth and honour of a king,
So great as our dread father's, in a scale
Of common ounces? Will you with counters sum
The past-proportion of his infinite,
And buckle in a waist most fathomless
With spans and inches so diminutive
As fears and reasons? Fie, for godly shame!

HELENUS No marvel though you bite so sharp at reasons,
You are so empty of them. Should not our father
Bear the great sway of his affairs with reasons,
Because your speech hath none that tells him so?

TROILUS You are for dreams and slumbers, brother priest;
You fur your gloves with reason. Here are your reasons:
You know an enemy intends you harm;
You know a sword employ'd is perilous,
And reason flies the object of all harm.
Who marvels, then, when Helenus beholds
A Grecian and his sword, if he do set
The very wings of reason to his heels
And fly like chidden Mercury from Jove,
Or like a star disorb'd? Nay, if we talk of reason,
Let's shut our gates and sleep. Manhood and honour
Should have hare hearts, would they but fat their thoughts
With this cramm'd reason. Reason and respect
Make livers pale and lustihood deject.

HECTOR Brother, she is not worth what she doth cost
The keeping.

TROILUS What's aught but as 'tis valued?

HECTOR But value dwells not in particular will:
It holds his estimate and dignity
As well wherein 'tis precious of itself
As in the prizer. 'Tis mad idolatry
To make the service greater than the god;
And the will dotes that is attributive
To what infectiously itself affects,
Without some image of th' affected merit.

TROILUS I take to-day a wife, and my election
Is led on in the conduct of my will;
My will enkindled by mine eyes and ears,
Two traded pilots 'twixt the dangerous shores
Of will and judgement: how may I avoid,
Although my will distaste what it elected,
The wife I chose? There can be no evasion
To blench from this and to stand firm by honour.
We turn not back the silks upon the merchant
When we have soil'd them; nor the remainder viands
We do not throw in unrespective sieve,
Because we now are full. It was thought meet
Paris should do some vengeance on the Greeks;
Your breath with full consent bellied his sails;
The seas and winds, old wranglers, took a truce,
And did him service. He touch'd the ports desir'd;
And for an old aunt whom the Greeks held captive
He brought a Grecian queen, whose youth and freshness
Wrinkles Apollo's, and makes stale the morning.
Why keep we her? The Grecians keep our aunt.
Is she worth keeping? Why, she is a pearl
Whose price hath launch'd above a thousand ships,
And turn'd crown'd kings to merchants.
If you'll avouch 'twas wisdom Paris went –
As you must needs, for you all cried 'Go, go' –
If you'll confess he brought home worthy prize –
As you must needs, for you all clapp'd your hands,
And cried 'Inestimable!' – why do you now
The issue of your proper wisdoms rate,
And do a deed that never fortune did –
Beggar the estimation which you priz'd
Richer than sea and land? O theft most base,
That we have stol'n what we do fear to keep!
But thieves unworthy of a thing so stol'n
That in their country did them that disgrace
We fear to warrant in our native place!

CASSANDRA [*Within*] Cry, Troyans, cry.

PRIAM What noise, what shriek is this?

TROILUS 'Tis our mad sister; I do know her voice.

CASSANDRA [*Within*] Cry, Troyans.

HECTOR It is Cassandra.

Enter CASSANDRA raving.

CASSANDRA Cry, Troyans, cry. Lend me ten thousand eyes,
And I will fill them with prophetic tears.

HECTOR Peace, sister, peace.

CASSANDRA Virgins and boys, mid-age and wrinkled eld,

Soft infancy, that nothing canst but cry,
Add to my clamours. Let us pay betimes
A moiety of that mass of moan to come.
Cry, Troyans, cry. Practise your eyes with tears.
Troy must not be, nor goodly Ilion stand;
Our firebrand brother, Paris, burns us all.
Cry, Troyans, cry, A Helen and a woe!
Cry, cry. Troy burns, or else let Helen go.
[*Exit.*

HECTOR Now, youthful Troilus, do not these high strains
Of divination in our sister work
Some touches of remorse, or is your blood
So madly hot that no discourse of reason,
Nor fear of bad success in a bad cause,
Can qualify the same?

TROILUS Why, brother Hector,
We may not think the justness of each act
Such and no other than event doth form it;
Nor once deject the courage of our minds
Because Cassandra's mad. Her brain-sick raptures
Cannot distaste the goodness of a quarrel
Which hath our several honours all engag'd
To make it gracious. For my private part,
I am no more touch'd than all Priam's sons;
And Jove forbid there should be done amongst us
Such things as might offend the weakest spleen
To fight for and maintain.

PARIS Else might the world convince of levity
As well my undertakings as your counsels;
But I attest the gods, your full consent
Gave wings to my propension, and cut off
All fears attending on so dire a project.
For what, alas, can these my single arms?
What propugnation is in one man's valour
To stand the push and enmity of those
This quarrel would excite? Yet, I protest,
Were I alone to pass the difficulties,
And had as ample power as I have will,
Paris should ne'er retract what he hath done
Nor faint in the pursuit.

PRIAM Paris, you speak
Like one besotted on your sweet delights.
You have the honey still, but these the gall;
So to be valiant is no praise at all.

PARIS Sir, I propose not merely to myself
The pleasures such a beauty brings with it;
But I would have the soil of her fair rape
Wip'd off in honourable keeping her.
What treason were it to the ransack'd queen,
Disgrace to your great worths, and shame to me,
Now to deliver her possession up
On terms of base compulsion! Can it be
That so degenerate a strain as this
Should once set footing in your generous bosoms?
There's not the meanest spirit on our party
Without a heart to dare or sword to draw
When Helen is defended; nor none so noble
Whose life were ill bestow'd or death unfam'd
Where Helen is the subject. Then, I say,
Well may we fight for her whom we know well
The world's large spaces cannot parallel.

HECTOR Paris and Troilus, you have both said well;
And on the cause and question now in hand
Have gloz'd, but superficially; not much
Unlike young men, whom Aristotle thought
Unfit to hear moral philosophy.
The reasons you allege do more conduce
To the hot passion of distemp'red blood
Than to make up a free determination
'Twixt right and wrong; for pleasure and revenge
Have ears more deaf than adders to the voice
Of any true decision. Nature craves
All dues be rend'red to their owners. Now,
What nearer debt in all humanity
Than wife is to the husband? If this law
Of nature be corrupted through affection;
And that great minds, of partial indulgence
To their benumbed wills, resist the same;
There is a law in each well-order'd nation
To curb those raging appetites that are
Most disobedient and refractory.
If Helen, then, be wife to Sparta's king –
As it is known she is – these moral laws
Of nature and of nations speak aloud
To have her back return'd. Thus to persist
In doing wrong extenuates not wrong,
But makes it much more heavy. Hector's opinion
Is this, in way of truth. Yet, ne'er the less,
My spritely brethren, I propend to you
In resolution to keep Helen still;
For 'tis a cause that hath no mean dependence
Upon our joint and several dignities.

TROILUS Why, there you touch'd the life of our design.
Were it not glory that we more affected
Than the performance of our heaving spleens,
I would not wish a drop of Troyan blood
Spent more in her defence. But, worthy Hector,
She is a theme of honour and renown,
A spur to valiant and magnanimous deeds,
Whose present courage may beat down our foes,
And fame in time to come canonize us;
For I presume brave Hector would not lose
So rich advantage of a promis'd glory
As smiles upon the forehead of this action

For the wide world's revenue.

HECTOR I am yours,
You valiant offspring of great Priamus.
I have a roisting challenge sent amongst
The dull and factious nobles of the Greeks
Will strike amazement to their drowsy spirits.
I was advertis'd their great general slept,
Whilst emulation in the army crept.
This, I presume, will wake him. [*Exeunt.*

SCENE III. *The Grecian camp. Before the tent of Achilles.*

Enter THERSITES, solus.

THERSITES How now, Thersites! What, lost in the labyrinth of thy fury? Shall the elephant Ajax carry it thus? He beats me, and I rail at him. O worthy satisfaction! Would it were otherwise: that I could beat him, whilst he rail'd at me! 'Sfoot, I'll learn to conjure and raise devils, but I'll see some issue of my spiteful execrations. Then there's Achilles, a rare engineer! If Troy be not taken till these two undermine it, the walls will stand till they fall of themselves. O thou great thunder-darter of Olympus, forget that thou art Jove, the king of gods, and, Mercury, lose all the serpentine craft of thy caduceus, if ye take not that little little less-than-little wit from them that they have! which short-arm'd ignorance itself knows is so abundant scarce, it will not in circumvention deliver a fly from a spider without drawing their massy irons and cutting the web. After this, the vengeance on the whole camp! or, rather, the Neapolitan bone-ache! for that, methinks, is the curse depending on those that war for a placket. I have said my prayers; and devil Envy say 'Amen'. What ho! my Lord Achilles!

Enter PATROCLUS.

PATROCLUS Who's there? Thersites! Good Thersites, come in and rail.

THERSITES If I could 'a rememb'red a gilt counterfeit, thou wouldst not have slipp'd out of my contemplation; but it is no matter; thyself upon thyself! The common curse of mankind, folly and ignorance, be thine in great revenue! Heaven bless thee from a tutor, and discipline come not near thee! Let thy blood be thy direction till thy death. Then if she that lays thee out says thou art a fair corse, I'll be sworn and sworn upon't she never shrouded any but lazars. Amen. Where's Achilles?

PATROCLUS What, art thou devout? Wast thou in prayer?

THERSITES Ay, the heavens hear me!

PATROCLUS Amen.

Enter ACHILLES.

ACHILLES Who's there?

PATROCLUS Thersites, my lord.

ACHILLES Where, where? O, where? Art thou come? Why, my cheese, my digestion, why hast thou not served thyself in to my table so many meals? Come, what's Agamemnon?

THERSITES Thy commander, Achilles. Then tell me, Patroclus, what's Achilles?

PATROCLUS Thy lord, Thersites. Then tell me, I pray thee, what's Thersites?

THERSITES Thy knower, Patroclus. Then tell me, Patroclus, what art thou?

PATROCLUS Thou must tell that knowest.

ACHILLES O, tell, tell!

THERSITES I'll decline the whole question. Agamemnon commands Achilles; Achilles is my lord; I am Patroclus' knower; and Patroclus is a fool.

PATROCLUS You rascal!

THERSITES Peace, fool! I have not done.

ACHILLES He is a privileg'd man. Proceed, Thersites.

THERSITES Agamemnon is a fool; Achilles is a fool; Thersites is a fool; and, as aforesaid, Patroclus is a fool.

ACHILLES Derive this; come.

THERSITES Agamemnon is a fool to offer to command Achilles; Achilles is a fool to be commanded of Agamemnon; Thersites is a fool to serve such a fool; and this Patroclus is a fool positive.

PATROCLUS Why am I a fool?

THERSITES Make that demand of the Creator. It suffices me thou art. Look you, who comes here?

ACHILLES Come, Patroclus, I'll speak with nobody. Come in with me, Thersites. [*Exit.*

THERSITES Here is such patchery, such juggling, and such knavery. All the argument is a whore and a cuckold – a good quarrel to draw emulous factions and bleed to death upon. Now the dry serpigo on the subject, and war and lechery confound all! [*Exit.*

Enter AGAMEMNON, ULYSSES, NESTOR, DIOMEDES, AJAX and CALCAS

AGAMEMNON Where is Achilles?

PATROCLUS Within his tent; but ill-dispos'd, my lord.

AGAMEMNON Let it be known to him that we are here.
He shent our messengers; and we lay by
Our appertainings, visiting of him.
Let him be told so; lest, perchance, he think

We dare not move the question of our place
Or know not what we are.
PATROCLUS I shall say so to him. [*Exit.*
ULYSSES We saw him at the opening of his tent.
He is not sick.
AJAX Yes, lion-sick, sick of proud heart. You may call it melancholy, if you will favour the man; but, by my head, 'tis pride. But why, why? let him show us a cause. A word, my lord.
[*Takes Agamemnon aside.*
NESTOR What moves Ajax thus to bay at him?
ULYSSES Achilles hath inveigled his fool from him.
NESTOR Who, Thersites?
ULYSSES He.
NESTOR Then will Ajax lack matter, if he have lost his argument.
ULYSSES No; you see he is his argument that has his argument – Achilles.
NESTOR All the better; their fraction is more our wish than their fraction. But it was a strong composure a fool could disunite!
ULYSSES The amity that wisdom knits not, folly may easily untie.

Re-enter PATROCLUS.

Here comes Patroclus.
NESTOR No Achilles with him.
ULYSSES The elephant hath joints, but none for courtesy; his legs are legs for necessity, not for flexure.
PATROCLUS Achilles bids me say he is much sorry
If any thing more than your sport and pleasure
Did move your greatness and this noble state
To call upon him; he hopes it is no other
But for your health and your digestion sake,
An after-dinner's breath.
AGAMEMNON Hear you, Patroclus.
We are too well acquainted with these answers;
But his evasion, wing'd thus swift with scorn,
Cannot outfly our apprehensions.
Much attribute he hath, and much the reason
Why we ascribe it to him. Yet all his virtues,
Not virtuously on his own part beheld,
Do in our eyes begin to lose their gloss;
Yea, like fair fruit in an unwholesome dish,
Are like to rot untasted. Go and tell him
We come to speak with him; and you shall not sin
If you do say we think him over-proud
And under-honest, in self-assumption greater
Than in the note of judgment; and worthier than himself
Here tend the savage strangeness he puts on,
Disguise the holy strength of their command,
And underwrite in an observing kind
His humorous predominance; yea, watch
His pettish lunes, his ebbs, his flows, as if
The passage and whole carriage of this action
Rode on his tide. Go tell him this, and add
That if he overhold his price so much
We'll none of him, but let him, like an engine
Not portable, lie under this report:
Bring action hither; this cannot go to war.
A stirring dwarf we do allowance give
Before a sleeping giant. Tell him so.
PATROCLUS I shall, and bring his answer presently. [*Exit.*
AGAMEMNON In second voice we'll not be satisfied;
We come to speak with him. Ulysses, enter you.
[*Exit Ulysses.*
AJAX What is he more than another?
AGAMEMNON No more than what he thinks he is.
AJAX Is he so much? Do you not think he thinks himself a better man than I am?
AGAMEMNON No question.
AJAX Will you subscribe his thought and say he is?
AGAMEMNON No, noble Ajax; you are as strong, as valiant, as wise, no less noble, much more gentle, and altogether more tractable.
AJAX Why should a man be proud? How doth pride grow? I know not what pride is.
AGAMEMNON Your mind is the clearer, Ajax, and your virtues the fairer. He that is proud eats up himself. Pride is his own glass, his own trumpet, his own chronicle; and whatever praises itself but in the deed devours the deed in the praise.

Re-enter ULYSSES.

AJAX I do hate a proud man as I do hate the engend'ring of toads.
NESTOR [*Aside*] And yet he loves himself: is't not strange?
ULYSSES Achilles will not to the field to-morrow.
AGAMEMNON What's his excuse?
ULYSSES He doth rely on none;
But carries on the stream of his dispose,
Without observance or respect of any,
In will peculiar and in self-admission.
AGAMEMNON Why will he not, upon our fair request,
Untent his person and share the air with us?
ULYSSES Things small as nothing, for request's sake only,
He makes important; possess'd he is with greatness,
And speaks not to himself but with a pride
That quarrels at self-breath. Imagin'd worth
Holds in his blood such swol'n and hot discourse

That 'twixt his mental and his active parts
Kingdom'd Achilles in commotion rages,
And batters down himself. What should I say?
He is so plaguy proud that the death tokens of it
Cry 'No recovery'.

AGAMEMNON Let Ajax go to him.
Dear lord, go you and greet him in his tent.
'Tis said he holds you well; and will be led
At your request a little from himself.

ULYSSES O Agamemnon, let it not be so!
We'll consecrate the steps that Ajax makes
When they go from Achilles. Shall the proud lord
That bastes his arrogance with his own seam
And never suffers matter of the world
Enter his thoughts, save such as doth revolve
And ruminate himself – shall he be worshipp'd
Of that we hold an idol more than he?
No, this thrice-worthy and right valiant lord
Shall not so stale his palm, nobly acquir'd,
Nor, by my will, assubjugate his merit,
As amply titled as Achilles is,
By going to Achilles.
That were to enlard his fat-already pride,
And add more coals to Cancer when he burns
With entertaining great Hyperion.
This lord go to him! Jupiter forbid,
And say in thunder 'Achilles go to him'.

NESTOR [*Aside*] O, this is well! He rubs the vein of him.

DIOMEDES [*Aside*] And how his silence drinks up this applause!

AJAX If I go to him, with my armed fist I'll pash him o'er the face.

AGAMEMNON O, no, you shall not go.

AJAX An 'a be proud with me I'll pheeze his pride.
Let me go to him.

ULYSSES Not for the worth that hangs upon our quarrel.

AJAX A paltry, insolent fellow!

NESTOR [*Aside*] How he describes himself!

AJAX Can he not be sociable?

ULYSSES [*Aside*] The raven chides blackness.

AJAX I'll let his humours blood.

AGAMEMNON [*Aside*] He will be the physician that should be the patient.

AJAX An all men were a my mind –

ULYSSES [*Aside*] Wit would be out of fashion.

AJAX 'A should not bear it so, 'a should eat's words first. Shall pride carry it?

NESTOR [*Aside*] An 'twould, you'd carry half.

ULYSSES [*Aside*] 'A would have ten shares.

AJAX I will knead him, I'll make him supple.

NESTOR [*Aside*] He's not yet through warm.
Force him with praises; pour in, pour in; his ambition is dry.

ULYSSES [*To Agamemnon*] My lord, you feed too much on this dislike.

NESTOR Our noble general, do not do so.

DIOMEDES You must prepare to fight without Achilles.

ULYSSES Why 'tis this naming of him does him harm.
Here is a man – but 'tis before his face;
I will be silent.

NESTOR Wherefore should you so?
He is not emulous, as Achilles is.

ULYSSES Know the whole world, he is as valiant.

AJAX A whoreson dog, that shall palter with us thus! Would he were a Troyan!

NESTOR What a vice were it in Ajax now –

ULYSSES If he were proud.

DIOMEDES Or covetous of praise.

ULYSSES Ay, or surly borne.

DIOMEDES Or strange, or self-affected.

ULYSSES Thank the heavens, lord, thou art of sweet composure;
Praise him that gat thee, she that gave thee suck;
Fam'd be thy tutor, and thy parts of nature
Thrice-fam'd beyond, beyond all erudition;
But he that disciplin'd thine arms to fight –
Let Mars divide eternity in twain
And give him half; and, for thy vigour,
Bull-bearing Milo his addition yield
To sinewy Ajax. I will not praise thy wisdom,
Which, like a bourn, a pale, a shore, confines
Thy spacious and dilated parts. Here's Nestor,
Instructed by the antiquary times –
He must, he is, he cannot but be wise;
But pardon, father Nestor, were your days
As green as Ajax' and your brain so temper'd,
You should not have the eminence of him,
But be as Ajax.

AJAX Shall I call you father?

NESTOR Ay, my good son.

DIOMEDES Be rul'd by him, Lord Ajax.

ULYSSES There is no tarrying here; the hart Achilles
Keeps thicket. Please it our great general
To call together all his state of war;
Fresh kings are come to Troy. To-morrow
We must with all our main of power stand fast;
And here's a lord – come knights from east to west
And cull their flower, Ajax shall cope the best.

AGAMEMNON Go we to council. Let Achilles sleep.
Light boats sail swift, though greater hulks draw deep. [*Exeunt.*

ACT THREE

SCENE I. *Troy. Priam's palace.*

Music sounds within. Enter PANDARUS and a Servant.

PANDARUS Friend, you – pray you, a word. Do you not follow the young Lord Paris?

SERVANT Ay, sir, when he goes before me.

PANDARUS You depend upon him, I mean?

SERVANT Sir, I do depend upon the lord.

PANDARUS You depend upon a notable gentleman; I must needs praise him.

SERVANT The lord be praised!

PANDARUS You know me, do you not?

SERVANT Faith, sir, superficially.

PANDARUS Friend, know me better: I am the Lord Pandarus.

SERVANT I hope I shall know your honour better.

PANDARUS I do desire it.

SERVANT You are in the state of grace.

PANDARUS Grace! Not so, friend; honour and lordship are my titles. What music is this?

SERVANT I do but partly know, sir; it is music in parts.

PANDARUS Know you the musicians?

SERVANT Wholly, sir.

PANDARUS Who play they to?

SERVANT To the hearers, sir.

PANDARUS At whose pleasure, friend?

SERVANT At mine, sir, and theirs that love music.

PANDARUS Command, I mean, friend.

SERVANT Who shall I command, sir?

PANDARUS Friend, we understand not one another: I am too courtly, and thou art too cunning. At whose request do these men play?

SERVANT That's to't, indeed, sir. Marry, sir, at the request of Paris my lord, who is there in person; with him the mortal Venus, the heart-blood of beauty, love's invisible soul –

PANDARUS Who, my cousin, Cressida?

SERVANT No, sir, Helen. Could not you find out that by her attributes?

PANDARUS It should seem, fellow, that thou hast not seen the Lady Cressida. I come to speak with Paris from the Prince Troilus; I will make a complimental assault upon him, for my business seethes.

SERVANT Sodden business! There's a stew'd phrase indeed!

Enter PARIS and HELEN, attended.

PANDARUS Fair be to you, my lord, and to all this fair company! Fair desires, in all fair measure, fairly guide them – especially to you, fair queen! Fair thoughts be your fair pillow.

HELEN Dear lord, you are full of fair words.

PANDARUS You speak your fair pleasure, sweet queen. Fair prince, here is good broken music.

PARIS You have broke it, cousin; and by my life, you shall make it whole again; you shall piece it out with a piece of your performance.

HELEN He is full of harmony.

PANDARUS Truly, lady, no.

HELEN O, sir –

PANDARUS Rude, in sooth; in good sooth, very rude.

PARIS Well said, my lord. Well, you say so in fits.

PANDARUS I have business to my lord, dear queen. My lord, will you vouchsafe me a word?

HELEN Nay, this shall not hedge us out. We'll hear you sing, certainly.

PANDARUS Well, sweet queen, you are pleasant with me. But, marry, thus, my lord: my dear lord and most esteemed friend, your brother Troilus –

HELEN My Lord Pandarus, honey-sweet lord –

PANDARUS Go to, sweet queen, go to – commends himself most affectionately to you –

HELEN You shall not bob us out of our melody. If you do, our melancholy upon your head!

PANDARUS Sweet queen, sweet queen; that's a sweet queen, i' faith.

HELEN And to make a sweet lady sad is a sour offence.

PANDARUS Nay, that shall not serve your turn; that shall it not, in truth, la. Nay, I care not for such words; no, no. – And, my lord, he desires you that, if the King call for him at supper, you will make his excuse.

HELEN My Lord Pandarus!

PANDARUS What says my sweet queen, my very very sweet queen?

PARIS What exploit's in hand? Where sups he to-night?

HELEN Nay, but, my lord –

PANDARUS What says my sweet queen? – My cousin will fall out with you.

HELEN You must not know where he sups.

PARIS I'll lay my life, with my disposer Cressida.

PANDARUS No, no, no such matter; you are wide. Come, your disposer is sick.

PARIS Well, I'll make's excuse.

PANDARUS Ay, good my lord. Why should you say Cressida? No, your poor disposer's sick.

PARIS I spy.

PANDARUS You spy! What do you spy? – Come, give me an instrument. Now, sweet queen.

HELEN Why, this is kindly done.

PANDARUS My niece is horribly in love with a thing you have, sweet queen.

HELEN She shall have it, my lord, if it be not my Lord Paris.

PANDARUS He! No, she'll none of him; they two are twain.

HELEN Falling in, after falling out, may make them three.

PANDARUS Come, come. I'll hear no more of this; I'll sing you a song now.

HELEN Ay, ay, prithee now. By my troth, sweet lord, thou hast a fine forehead.

PANDARUS Ay, you may, you may.

HELEN Let thy song be love. This love will undo us all. O Cupid, Cupid, Cupid!

PANDARUS Love! Ay, that it shall, i' faith.

PARIS Ay, good now, love, love, nothing but love.

PANDARUS In good troth, it begins so. [*Sings*]

Love, love, nothing but love, still love, still more!
For, oh, love's bow
Shoots buck and doe;
The shaft confounds
Not that it wounds,
But tickles still the sore.
These lovers cry, O ho, they die!
Yet that which seems the wound to kill
Doth turn O ho! to ha! ha! he!
So dying love lives still.
O ho! a while, but ha! ha! ha!
O ho! groans out for ha! ha! ha! – hey ho!

HELEN In love, i' faith, to the very tip of the nose.

PARIS He eats nothing but doves, love; and that breeds hot blood, and hot blood begets hot thoughts, and hot thoughts beget hot deeds, and hot deeds is love.

PANDARUS Is this the generation of love: hot blood, hot thoughts, and hot deeds? Why, they are vipers. Is love a generation of vipers? Sweet lord, who's a-field today?

PARIS Hector, Deiphobus, Helenus, Antenor, and all the gallantry of Troy. I would fain have arm'd to-day, but my Nell would not have it so. How chance my brother Troilus went not?

HELEN He hangs the lip at something. You know all, Lord Pandarus.

PANDARUS Not I, honey-sweet queen. I long to hear how they sped to-day. You'll remember your brother's excuse?

PARIS To a hair.

PANDARUS Farewell, sweet queen.

HELEN Commend me to your niece.

PANDARUS I will, sweet queen. [*Exit*.

[*Sound a retreat*.

PARIS They're come from the field. Let us to Priam's hall
To greet the warriors. Sweet Helen, I must woo you
To help unarm our Hector. His stubborn buckles,
With these your white enchanting fingers touch'd,
Shall more obey than to the edge of steel
Or force of Greekish sinews; you shall do more
Than all the island kings – disarm great Hector.

HELEN 'Twill make us proud to be his servant, Paris;
Yea, what he shall receive of us in duty
Gives us more palm in beauty than we have,
Yea, overshines ourself.

PARIS Sweet, above thought I love thee. [*Exeunt*.

SCENE II. *Troy. Pandarus' orchard.*

Enter PANDARUS and Troilus' Boy, meeting.

PANDARUS How now! Where's thy master? At my cousin Cressida's?

BOY No, sir; he stays for you to conduct him thither.

Enter TROILUS.

PANDARUS O, here he comes. How now, how now!

TROILUS Sirrah, walk off. [*Exit Boy*.

PANDARUS Have you seen my cousin?

TROILUS No, Pandarus. I stalk about her door
Like a strange soul upon the Stygian banks
Staying for waftage. O, be thou my Charon,
And give me swift transportance to these fields
Where I may wallow in the lily beds
Propos'd for the deserver! O gentle Pandar,
From Cupid's shoulder pluck his painted wings,
And fly with me to Cressid!

PANDARUS Walk here i' th' orchard, I'll bring her straight. [*Exit*.

TROILUS I am giddy; expectation whirls me round.
Th' imaginary relish is so sweet
That it enchants my sense; what will it be
When that the wat'ry palate tastes indeed
Love's thrice-repured nectar? Death, I fear me;
Swooning destruction; or some joy too fine,
Too subtle-potent, tun'd too sharp in sweetness,
For the capacity of my ruder powers.
I fear it much; and I do fear besides
That I shall lose distinction in my joys;
As doth a battle, when they charge on heaps
The enemy flying.

Re-enter PANDARUS.

PANDARUS She's making her ready, she'll come straight; you must be witty now. She does so blush, and fetches her wind so short, as if she were fray'd with a sprite. I'll fetch her. It is the prettiest villain; she fetches her breath as short as a new ta'en sparrow. [*Exit.*

TROILUS Even such a passion doth embrace my bosom.
My heart beats thicker than a feverous pulse,
And all my powers do their bestowing lose,
Like vassalage at unawares encount'ring
The eye of majesty.

Re-enter PANDARUS with CRESSIDA.

PANDARUS Come, come, what need you blush? Shame's a baby. – Here she is now; swear the oaths now to her that you have sworn to me. – What, are you gone again? You must be watch'd ere you be made tame, must you? Come your ways, come your ways; an you draw backward, we'll put you i' th' fills. – Why do you not speak to her? – Come, draw this curtain and let's see your picture. Alas the day, how loath you are to offend daylight! An 'twere dark, you'd close sooner. So, so; rub on, and kiss the mistress. How now, a kiss in fee-farm! Build there, carpenter; the air is sweet. Nay, you shall fight your hearts out ere I part you. The falcon as the tercel, for all the ducks i' th' river. Go to, go to.

TROILUS You have bereft me of all words, lady.

PANDARUS Words pay no debts, give her deeds; but she'll bereave you o' th' deeds too, if she call your activity in question. What, billing again? Here's 'In witness whereof the parties interchangeably'. Come in, come in; I'll go get a fire. [*Exit.*

CRESSIDA Will you walk in, my lord?

TROILUS O Cressid, how often have I wish'd me thus!

CRESSIDA Wish'd, my lord! The gods grant – O my lord!

TROILUS What should they grant? What makes this pretty abruption? What too curious dreg espies my sweet lady in the fountain of our love?

CRESSIDA More dregs than water, if my fears have eyes.

TROILUS Fears make devils of cherubins; they never see truly.

CRESSIDA Blind fear, that seeing reason leads, finds safer footing than blind reason stumbling without fear. To fear the worst oft cures the worse.

TROILUS O, let my lady apprehend no fear! In all Cupid's pageant there is presented no monster.

CRESSIDA Nor nothing monstrous neither?

TROILUS Nothing, but our undertakings when we vow to weep seas, live in fire, eat rocks, tame tigers; thinking it harder for our mistress to devise imposition enough than for us to undergo any difficulty imposed. This is the monstruosity in love, lady, that the will is infinite, and the execution confin'd; that the desire is boundless, and the act a slave to limit.

CRESSIDA They say all lovers swear more performance than they are able, and yet reserve an ability that they never perform; vowing more than the perfection of ten, and discharging less than the tenth part of one. They that have the voice of lions and the act of hares, are they not monsters?

TROILUS Are there such? Such are not we. Praise us as we are tasted, allow us as we prove; our head shall go bare till merit crown it. No perfection in reversion shall have a praise in present. We will not name desert before his birth; and, being born, his addition shall be humble. Few words to fair faith: Troilus shall be such to Cressid as what envy can say worst shall be a mock for his truth; and what truth can speak truest not truer than Troilus.

CRESSIDA Will you walk in, my lord?

Re-enter PANDARUS.

PANDARUS What, blushing still? Have you not done talking yet?

CRESSIDA Well, uncle, what folly I commit, I dedicate to you.

PANDARUS I thank you for that; if my lord get a boy of you, you'll give him me. Be true to my lord; if he flinch, chide me for it.

TROILUS You know now your hostages: your uncle's word and my firm faith.

PANDARUS Nay, I'll give my word for her too: our kindred, though they be long ere they are wooed, they are constant being won; they are burs, I can tell you; they'll stick where they are thrown.

CRESSIDA Boldness comes to me now and brings me heart.
Prince Troilus, I have lov'd you night and day
For many weary months.

TROILUS Why was my Cressid then so hard to win?

CRESSIDA Hard to seem won; but I was won, my lord,
With the first glance that ever – pardon me.
If I confess much, you will play the tyrant.
I love you now; but till now not so much
But I might master it. In faith, I lie;
My thoughts were like unbridled children, grown
Too headstrong for their mother. See, we fools!
Why have I blabb'd? Who shall be true to us,
When we are so unsecret to ourselves?
But, though I lov'd you well, I woo'd you not;
And yet, good faith, I wish'd myself a man,
Or that we women had men's privilege

Of speaking first. Sweet, bid me hold my
tongue,
For in this rapture I shall surely speak
The thing I shall repent. See, see, your silence,
Cunning in dumbness, from my weakness
draws
My very soul of counsel. Stop my mouth.

TROILUS And shall, albeit sweet music issues
thence.

PANDARUS Pretty, i' faith.

CRESSIDA My lord, I do beseech you, pardon me;
'Twas not my purpose thus to beg a kiss.
I am asham'd. O heavens! what have I done?
For this time will I take my leave, my lord.

TROILUS Your leave, sweet Cressid!

PANDARUS Leave! An you take leave till
to-morrow morning –

CRESSIDA Pray you, content you.

TROILUS What offends you, lady?

CRESSIDA Sir, mine own company.

TROILUS You cannot shun yourself.

CRESSIDA Let me go and try.
I have a kind of self resides with you;
But an unkind self, that it self will leave
To be another's fool. I would be gone.
Where is my wit? I know not what I speak.

TROILUS Well know they what they speak that
speak so wisely.

CRESSIDA Perchance, my lord, I show more craft
than love;
And fell so roundly to a large confession
To angle for your thoughts; but you are wise –
Or else you love not; for to be wise and love
Exceeds man's might; that dwells with gods
above.

TROILUS O that I thought it could be in a
woman –
As, if it can, I will presume in you –
To feed for aye her lamp and flames of love;
To keep her constancy in plight and youth,
Outliving beauty's outward, with a mind
That doth renew swifter than blood decays!
Or that persuasion could but thus convince me
That my integrity and truth to you
Might be affronted with the match and weight
Of such a winnowed purity in love.
How were I then uplifted! but, alas,
I am as true as truth's simplicity,
And simpler than the infancy of truth.

CRESSIDA In that I'll war with you.

TROILUS O virtuous fight,
When right with right wars who shall be most
right!
True swains in love shall in the world to come
Approve their truth by Troilus, when their
rhymes,
Full of protest, of oath, and big compare,
Want similes, truth tir'd with iteration –
As true as steel, as plantage to the moon,
As sun to day, as turtle to her mate,
As iron to adamant, as earth to th' centre –
Yet, after all comparisons of truth,
As truth's authentic author to be cited,
'As true as Troilus' shall crown up the verse
And sanctify the numbers.

CRESSIDA Prophet may you be!
If I be false, or swerve a hair from truth,
When time is old and hath forgot itself,
When waterdrops have worn the stones of Troy,
And blind oblivion swallow'd cities up,
And mighty states characterless are grated
To dusty nothing – yet let memory
From false to false, among false maids in love,
Upbraid my falsehood when th' have said 'As
false
As air, as water, wind, or sandy earth,
As fox to lamb, or wolf to heifer's calf,
Pard to the hind, or stepdame to her son' –
Yea, let them say, to stick the heart of falsehood,
'As false as Cressid'.

PANDARUS Go to, a bargain made; seal it, seal it; I'll be the witness. Here I hold your hand; here my cousin's. If ever you prove false one to another, since I have taken such pains to bring you together, let all pitiful goers-between be call'd to the world's end after my name – call them all Pandars; let all constant men be Troiluses, all false women Cressids, and all brokers between Pandars. Say 'Amen'.

TROILUS Amen.

CRESSIDA Amen.

PANDARUS Amen. Whereupon I will show you a chamber and a bed; which bed, because it shall not speak of your pretty encounters, press it to death. Away!
And Cupid grant all tongue-tied maidens here,
Bed, chamber, pander, to provide this gear!

[*Exeunt.*

SCENE III. *The Greek camp.*

Flourish. Enter AGAMEMNON, ULYSSES, DIOMEDES, NESTOR, AJAX, MENELAUS, and CALCHAS.

CALCHAS Now, Princes, for the service I have
done,
Th' advantage of the time prompts me aloud
To call for recompense. Appear it to your mind
That, through the sight I bear in things to come,
I have abandon'd Troy, left my possession,
Incurr'd a traitor's name, expos'd myself
From certain and possess'd conveniences
To doubtful fortunes, sequest'ring from me all

That time, acquaintance, custom, and condition,
Made tame and most familiar to my nature;
And here, to do you service, am become
As new into the world, strange, unacquainted –
I do beseech you, as in way of taste,
To give me now a little benefit
Out of those many regist'red in promise,
Which you say live to come in my behalf.

AGAMEMNON What wouldst thou of us, Troyan? Make demand.

CALCHAS You have a Troyan prisoner call'd Antenor,
Yesterday took; Troy holds him very dear.
Oft have you – often have you thanks therefore –
Desir'd my Cressid in right great exchange,
Whom Troy hath still denied; but this Antenor,
I know, is such a wrest in their affairs
That their negotiations all must slack
Wanting his manage; and they will almost
Give us a prince of blood, a son of Priam,
In change of him. Let him be sent, great Princes,
And he shall buy my daughter; and her presence
Shall quite strike off all service I have done
In most accepted pain.

AGAMEMNON Let Diomedes bear him,
And bring us Cressid hither. Calchas shall have
What he requests of us. Good Diomed,
Furnish you fairly for this interchange;
Withal, bring word if Hector will to-morrow
Be answer'd in his challenge. Ajax is ready.

DIOMEDES This shall I undertake; and 'tis a burden
Which I am proud to bear.
[*Exeunt Diomedes and Calchas.*

ACHILLES and PATROCLUS stand in their tent.

ULYSSES Achilles stands i' th' entrance of his tent.
Please it our general pass strangely by him,
As if he were forgot; and, Princes all,
Lay negligent and loose regard upon him.
I will come last. 'Tis like he'll question me
Why such unplausive eyes are bent, why turn'd on him?
If so, I have derision med'cinable
To use between your strangeness and his pride,
Which his own will shall have desire to drink.
It may do good. Pride hath no other glass
To show itself but pride; for supple knees
Feed arrogance and are the proud man's fees.

AGAMEMNON We'll execute your purpose, and put on
A form of strangeness as we pass along.
So do each lord; and either greet him not,
Or else disdainfully, which shall shake him more
Than if not look'd on. I will lead the way.

ACHILLES What comes the general to speak with me?
You know my mind, I'll fight no more 'gainst Troy.

AGAMEMNON What says Achilles? Would he aught with us?

NESTOR Would you, my lord, aught with the general?

ACHILLES No.

NESTOR Nothing, my lord.

AGAMEMNON The better.
[*Exeunt Agamemnon and Nestor.*

ACHILLES Good day, good day.

MENELAUS How do you? How do you? [*Exit.*

ACHILLES What, does the cuckold scorn me?

AJAX How now, Patroclus?

ACHILLES Good morrow, Ajax.

AJAX Ha?

ACHILLES Good morrow.

AJAX Ay, and good next day too. [*Exit.*

ACHILLES What mean these fellows? Know they not Achilles?

PATROCLUS They pass by strangely. They were us'd to bend,
To send their smiles before them to Achilles,
To come as humbly as they us'd to creep
To holy altars.

ACHILLES What, am I poor of late?
'Tis certain, greatness, once fall'n out with fortune,
Must fall out with men too. What the declin'd is,
He shall as soon read in the eyes of others
As feel in his own fall; for men, like butterflies,
Show not their mealy wings but to the summer;
And not a man for being simply man
Hath any honour, but honour for those honours
That are without him, as place, riches, and favour,
Prizes of accident, as oft as merit;
Which when they fall, as being slippery standers,
The love that lean'd on them as slippery too,
Doth one pluck down another, and together
Die in the fall. But 'tis not so with me:
Fortune and I are friends; I do enjoy
At ample point all that I did possess
Save these men's looks; who do, methinks, find out
Something not worth in me such rich beholding
As they have often given. Here is Ulysses.
I'll interrupt his reading.
How now, Ulysses!

ULYSSES Now, great Thetis' son!

ACHILLES What are you reading?

ULYSSES A strange fellow here
Writes me that man – how dearly ever parted,

How much in having, or without or in –
Cannot make boast to have that which he hath,
Nor feels not what he owes, but by reflection;
As when his virtues shining upon others
Heat them, and they retort that heat again
To the first giver.

ACHILLES This is not strange, Ulysses.
The beauty that is borne here in the face
The bearer knows not, but commends itself
To others' eyes; nor doth the eye itself –
That most pure spirit of sense – behold itself,
Not going from itself; but eye to eye opposed
Salutes each other with each other's form;
For speculation turns not to itself
Till it hath travell'd, and is mirror'd there
Where it may see itself. This is not strange at all.

ULYSSES I do not strain at the position –
It is familiar – but at the author's drift;
Who, in his circumstance, expressly proves
That no man is the lord of anything,
Though in and of him there be much consisting,
Till he communicate his parts to others;
Nor doth he of himself know them for aught
Till he behold them formed in th' applause
Where th' are extended; who, like an arch, reverb'rate
The voice again; or, like a gate of steel
Fronting the sun, receives and renders back
His figure and his heat. I was much rapt in this;
And apprehended here immediately
Th' unknown Ajax. Heavens, what a man is there!
A very horse that has he knows not what!
Nature, what things there are
Most abject in regard and dear in use!
What things again most dear in the esteem
And poor in worth! Now shall we see to-morrow –
An act that very chance doth throw upon him –
Ajax renown'd. O heavens, what some men do,
While some men leave to do!
How some men creep in skittish Fortune's hall,
Whiles others play the idiots in her eyes!
How one man eats into another's pride,
While pride is fasting in his wantonness!
To see these Grecian lords! – why, even already
They clap the lubber Ajax on the shoulder,
As if his foot were on brave Hector's breast,
And great Troy shrinking.

ACHILLES I do believe it; for they pass'd by me
As misers do by beggars – neither gave to me
Good word nor look. What, are my deeds forgot?

ULYSSES Time hath, my lord, a wallet at his back,
Wherein he puts alms for oblivion,
A great-siz'd monster of ingratitudes.
Those scraps are good deeds past, which are devour'd
As fast as they are made, forgot as soon
As done. Perseverance, dear my lord,
Keeps honour bright. To have done is to hang
Quite out of fashion, like a rusty mail
In monumental mock'ry. Take the instant way;
For honour travels in a strait so narrow
Where one but goes abreast. Keep then the path,
For emulation hath a thousand sons
That one by one pursue; if you give way,
Or hedge aside from the direct forthright,
Like to an ent'red tide they all rush by
And leave you hindmost;
Or, like a gallant horse fall'n in first rank,
Lie there for pavement to the abject rear,
O'er-run and trampled on. Then what they do in present,
Though less than yours in past, must o'ertop yours;
For Time is like a fashionable host,
That slightly shakes his parting guest by th' hand;
And with his arms out-stretch'd, as he would fly,
Grasps in the comer. The welcome ever smiles,
And farewell goes out sighing. O, let not virtue seek
Remuneration for the thing it was;
For beauty, wit,
High birth, vigour of bone, desert in service,
Love, friendship, charity, are subjects all
To envious and calumniating Time.
One touch of nature makes the whole world kin –
That all with one consent praise new-born gawds,
Though they are made and moulded of things past,
And give to dust that is a little gilt
More laud than gilt o'er-dusted.
The present eye praises the present object.
Then marvel not, thou great and complete man,
That all the Greeks begin to worship Ajax,
Since things in motion sooner catch the eye
Than what stirs not. The cry went once on thee,
And still it might, and yet it may again,
If thou wouldst not entomb thyself alive
And case thy reputation in thy tent,
Whose glorious deeds but in these fields of late
Made emulous missions 'mongst the gods themselves,
And drave great Mars to faction.

ACHILLES Of this my privacy
I have strong reasons.

ULYSSES But 'gainst your privacy
The reasons are more potent and heroical.

'Tis known, Achilles, that you are in love
With one of Priam's daughters.
ACHILLES Ha! known!
ULYSSES Is that a wonder?
The providence that's in a watchful state
Knows almost every grain of Plutus' gold;
Finds bottom in th' uncomprehensive deeps;
Keeps place with thought, and almost, like the gods,
Do thoughts unveil in their dumb cradles.
There is a mystery – with whom relation
Durst never meddle – in the soul of state,
Which hath an operation more divine
Than breath or pen can give expressure to.
All the commerce that you have had with Troy
As perfectly is ours as yours, my lord;
And better would it fit Achilles much
To throw down Hector than Polyxena.
But it must grieve young Pyrrhus now at home,
When fame shall in our island, sound her trump,
And all the Greekish girls shall tripping sing
'Great Hector's sister did Achilles win;
But our great Ajax bravely beat down him'.
Farewell, my lord. I as your lover speak.
The fool slides o'er the ice that you should break. [*Exit.*
PATROCLUS To this effect, Achilles, have I mov'd you.
A woman impudent and mannish grown
Is not more loath'd than an effeminate man
In time of action. I stand condemn'd for this;
They think my little stomach to the war
And your great love to me restrains you thus.
Sweet, rouse yourself; and the weak wanton Cupid
Shall from your neck unloose his amorous fold,
And, like a dew-drop from the lion's mane,
Be shook to airy air.
ACHILLES Shall Ajax fight with Hector?
PATROCLUS Ay, and perhaps receive much honour by him.
ACHILLES I see my reputation is at stake;
My fame is shrewdly gor'd.
PATROCLUS O, then, beware:
Those wounds heal ill that men do give themselves;
Omission to do what is necessary
Seals a commission to a blank of danger;
And danger, like an ague, subtly taints
Even then when they sit idly in the sun.
ACHILLES Go call Thersites hither, sweet Patroclus.
I'll send the fool to Ajax, and desire him
T' invite the Troyan lords, after the combat,
To see us here unarm'd. I have a woman's longing,
An appetite that I am sick withal,
To see great Hector in his weeds of peace;
To talk with him, and to behold his visage,
Even to my full of view.

Enter THERSITES.

A labour sav'd!
THERSITES A wonder!
ACHILLES What?
THERSITES Ajax goes up and down the field asking for himself.
ACHILLES How so?
THERSITES He must fight singly to-morrow with Hector, and is so prophetically proud of an heroical cudgelling that he raves in saying nothing.
ACHILLES How can that be?
THERSITES Why, 'a stalks up and down like a peacock – a stride and a stand; ruminates like an hostess that hath no arithmetic but her brain to set down her reckoning, bites his lip with a politic regard, as who should say 'There were wit in this head, an 'twould out'; and so there is; but it lies as coldly in him as fire in a flint, which will not show without knocking. The man's undone for ever; for if Hector break not his neck i' th' combat, he'll break't himself in vainglory. He knows not me. I said 'Good morrow, Ajax'; and he replies 'Thanks, Agamemnon'. What think you of this man that takes me for the general? He's grown a very land fish, languageless, a monster. A plague of opinion! A man may wear it on both sides, like a leather jerkin.
ACHILLES Thou must be my ambassador to him, Thersites.
THERSITES Who, I? Why, he'll answer nobody; he professes not answering. Speaking is for beggars: he wears his tongue in's arms. I will put on his presence. Let Patroclus make his demands to me, you shall see the pageant of Ajax.
ACHILLES To him, Patroclus. Tell him I humbly desire the valiant Ajax to invite the most valorous Hector to come unarm'd to my tent; and to procure safe conduct for his person of the magnanimous and most illustrious six-or-seven-times-honour'd Captain General of the Grecian army, et cetera, Agamemnon. Do this.
PATROCLUS Jove bless great Ajax!
THERSITES Hum!
PATROCLUS I come from the worthy Achilles –
THERSITES Ha!
PATROCLUS Who most humbly desires you to invite Hector to his tent –
THERSITES Hum!

PATROCLUS And to procure safe conduct from Agamemnon.
THERSITES Agamemnon!
PATROCLUS Ay, my lord.
THERSITES Ha!
PATROCLUS What say you to't?
THERSITES God buy you, with all my heart.
PATROCLUS Your answer, sir.
THERSITES If to-morrow be a fair day, by eleven of the clock it will go one way or other. Howsoever, he shall pay for me ere he has me.
PATROCLUS Your answer, sir.
THERSITES Fare ye well, with all my heart.
ACHILLES Why, but he is not in this tune, is he?
THERSITES No, but he's out a tune thus. What music will be in him when Hector has knock'd out his brains I know not; but, I am sure, none; unless the fiddler Apollo get his sinews to make catlings on.
ACHILLES Come, thou shalt bear a letter to him straight.
THERSITES Let me carry another to his horse; for that's the more capable creature.
ACHILLES My mind is troubled, like a fountain stirr'd;
And I myself see not the bottom of it.
[*Exeunt Achilles and Patroclus.*

THERSITES Would the fountain of your mind were clear again, that I might water an ass at it. I had rather be a tick in a sheep than such a valiant ignorance. [*Exit.*

ACT FOUR

SCENE I. *Troy. A street.*

Enter, at one side, AENEAS, and Servant with a torch; at another, PARIS, DEIPHOBUS, ANTENOR, DIOMEDES the Grecian, and Others, with torches.

PARIS See ho! Who is that there?
DEIPHOBUS It is the Lord Aeneas.
AENEAS Is the Prince there in person?
Had I so good occasion to lie long
As you, Prince Paris, nothing but heavenly business
Should rob my bed-mate of my company.
DIOMEDES That's my mind too. Good morrow, Lord Aeneas.
PARIS A valiant Greek, Aeneas – take his hand:
Witness the process of your speech, wherein
You told how Diomed, a whole week by days,
Did haunt you in the field.
AENEAS Health to you, valiant sir,
During all question of the gentle truce;
But when I meet you arm'd, as black defiance
As heart can think or courage execute.
DIOMEDES The one and other Diomed embraces.
Our bloods are now in calm; and so long health!
But when contention and occasion meet,
By Jove, I'll play the hunter for thy life
With all my force, pursuit, and policy.
AENEAS And thou shalt hunt a lion, that will fly
With his face backward. In humane gentleness,
Welcome to Troy! now, by Anchises' life,
Welcome indeed! By Venus' hand I swear
No man alive can love in such a sort
The thing he means to kill, more excellently.
DIOMEDES We sympathise. Jove let Aeneas live,
If to my sword his fate be not the glory,
A thousand complete courses of the sun!
But in mine emulous honour let him die
With every joint a wound, and that to-morrow!
AENEAS We know each other well.
DIOMEDES We do; and long to know each other worse.
PARIS This is the most despiteful'st gentle greeting,
The noblest hateful love, that e'er I heard of.
What business, lord, so early?
AENEAS I was sent for to the King; but why, I know not.
PARIS His purpose meets you: 'twas to bring this Greek
To Calchas' house, and there to render him,
For the enfreed Antenor, the fair Cressid.
Let's have your company; or, if you please,
Haste there before us. I constantly believe –
Or rather call my thought a certain knowledge –
My brother Troilus lodges there to-night.
Rouse him and give him note of our approach,
With the whole quality wherefore; I fear
We shall be much unwelcome.
AENEAS That I assure you:
Troilus had rather Troy were borne to Greece
Than Cressid borne from Troy.
PARIS There is no help;
The bitter disposition of the time
Will have it so. On, lord; we'll follow you.
AENEAS Good morrow, all. [*Exit with servant.*

PARIS And tell me, noble Diomed – faith, tell me true,
Even in the soul of sound good-fellowship –
Who in your thoughts deserves fair Helen best,
Myself or Menelaus?
DIOMEDES Both alike:

He merits well to have her that doth seek her,
Not making any scruple of her soilure,
With such a hell of pain and world of charge;
And you as well to keep her that defend her,
Not palating the taste of her dishonour,
With such a costly loss of wealth and friends.
He like a puling cuckold would drink up
The lees and dregs of a flat tamed piece;
You, like a lecher, out of whorish lions
Are pleas'd to breed out your inheritors.
Both merits pois'd, each weighs nor less nor more;
But he as he, the heavier for a whore.

PARIS You are too bitter to your country-woman.

DIOMEDES She's bitter to her country. Hear me, Paris:
For every false drop in her bawdy veins
A Grecian's life hath sunk; for every scruple
Of her contaminated carrion weight
A Troyan hath been slain; since she could speak,
She hath not given so many good words breath
As for her Greeks and Troyans suff'red death.

PARIS Fair Diomed, you do as chapmen do,
Dispraise the thing that you desire to buy;
But we in silence hold this virtue well:
We'll not commend what we intend to sell.
Here lies our way. [*Exeunt.*

SCENE II. *Troy. The court of Pandarus' house.*

Enter TROILUS and CRESSIDA.

TROILUS Dear, trouble not yourself; the morn is cold.

CRESSIDA Then, sweet my lord, I'll call mine uncle down;
He shall unbolt the gates.

TROILUS Trouble him not;
To bed, to bed! Sleep kill those pretty eyes,
And give as soft attachment to thy senses
As infants' empty of all thought!

CRESSIDA Good morrow, then.

TROILUS I prithee now, to bed.

CRESSIDA Are you aweary of me?

TROILUS O Cressida! but that the busy day,
Wak'd by the lark, hath rous'd the ribald crows,
And dreaming night will hide our joys no longer,
I would not from thee.

CRESSIDA Night hath been too brief.

TROILUS Beshrew the witch! with venomous wights she stays
As tediously as hell, but flies the grasps of love
With wings more momentary-swift than thought.
You will catch cold, and curse me.

CRESSIDA Prithee tarry.
You men will never tarry.
O foolish Cressid! I might have still held off,
And then you would have tarried. Hark! there's one up.

PANDARUS [*Within*] What's all the doors open here?

TROILUS It is your uncle.

Enter PANDARUS.

CRESSIDA A pestilence on him! Now will he be mocking.
I shall have such a life!

PANDARUS How now, how now! How go maidenheads? Here, you maid! Where's my cousin Cressid?

CRESSIDA Go hang yourself, you naughty mocking uncle.
You bring me to do, and then you flout me too.

PANDARUS To do what? to do what? Let her say what. What have I brought you to do?

CRESSIDA Come, come, beshrew your heart! You'll ne'er be good,
Nor suffer others.

PANDARUS Ha, ha! Alas, poor wretch! a poor capocchia! hast not slept to-night? Would he not, a naughty man, let it sleep? A bugbear take him!

CRESSIDA Did not I tell you? Would he were knock'd i' th' head! [*One knocks.*]
Who's that at door? Good uncle, go and see.
My lord, come you again into my chamber.
You smile and mock me, as if I meant naughtily.

TROILUS Ha! ha!

CRESSIDA Come, you are deceiv'd, I think of no such thing. [*Knock.*
How earnestly they knock! Pray you come in:
I would not for half Troy have you seen here.
[*Exeunt Troilus and Cressida.*

PANDARUS Who's there? What's the matter?
Will you beat down the door? How now?
What's the matter?

Enter AENEAS.

AENEAS Good morrow, lord, good morrow.

PANDARUS Who's there? My lord Aeneas? By my troth,
I knew you not. What news with you so early?

AENEAS Is not Prince Troilus here?

PANDARUS Here! What should he do here?

AENEAS Come, he is here, my lord; do not deny him.
It doth import him much to speak with me.

PANDARUS Is he here, say you? It's more than I know, I'll be sworn. For my own part, I came in late. What should he do here?

AENEAS Who! – nay, then. Come, come, you'll do him wrong ere you are ware; you'll be so true to him to be false to him. Do not you know of him, but yet go fetch him hither; go.

Re-enter TROILUS.

TROILUS How now! What's the matter?
AENEAS My lord, I scarce have leisure to salute you,
My matter is so rash. There is at hand
Paris your brother, and Deiphobus,
The Grecian Diomed, and our Antenor
Deliver'd to us; and for him forthwith,
Ere the first sacrifice, within this hour,
We must give up to Diomedes' hand
The Lady Cressida.
TROILUS Is it so concluded?
AENEAS By Priam, and the general state of Troy.
They are at hand and ready to effect it.
TROILUS How my achievements mock me!
I will go meet them; and, my lord Aeneas,
We met by chance; you did not find me here.
AENEAS Good, good, my lord, the secrets of neighbour Pandar
Have not more gift in taciturnity.
[*Exeunt Troilus and Aeneas.*

PANDARUS Is't possible? No sooner got but lost? The devil take Antenor! The young prince will go mad. A plague upon Antenor! I would they had broke's neck.

Re-enter CRESSIDA.

CRESSIDA How now! What's the matter? Who was here?
PANDARUS Ah, ah!
CRESSIDA Why sigh you so profoundly? Where's my lord? Gone? Tell me, sweet uncle, what's the matter?
PANDARUS Would I were as deep under the earth as I am above!
CRESSIDA O the gods! What's the matter?
PANDARUS Pray thee, get thee in. Would thou hadst ne'er been born! I knew thou wouldst be his death! O, poor gentleman! A plague upon Antenor!
CRESSIDA Good uncle, I beseech you, on my knees I beseech you, what's the matter?
PANDARUS Thou must be gone, wench, thou must be gone; thou art chang'd for Antenor; thou must to thy father, and be gone from Troilus. 'Twill be his death; 'twill be his bane; he cannot bear it.
CRESSIDA O you immortal gods! I will not go.
PANDARUS Thou must.
CRESSIDA I will not, uncle. I have forgot my father;
I know no touch of consanguinity,
No kin, no love, no blood, no soul so near me
As the sweet Troilus. O you gods divine,
Make Cressid's name the very crown of falsehood,
If ever she leave Troilus! Time, force, and death,
Do to this body what extremes you can,
But the strong base and building of my love
Is as the very centre of the earth,
Drawing all things to it. I'll go in and weep –
PANDARUS Do, do.
CRESSIDA Tear my bright hair, and scratch my praised cheeks,
Crack my clear voice with sobs and break my heart,
With sounding 'Troilus'. I will not go from Troy.
[*Exeunt.*

SCENE III. *Troy. A street before Pandarus' house.*

Enter PARIS, TROILUS, AENEAS, DEIPHOBUS, ANTENOR, and DIOMEDES.

PARIS It is great morning; and the hour prefix'd
For her delivery to this valiant Greek
Comes fast upon. Good my brother Troilus,
Tell you the lady what she is to do,
And haste her to the purpose.
TROILUS Walk into her house.
I'll bring her to the Grecian presently;
And to his hand when I deliver her,
Think it an altar, and thy brother Troilus
A priest, there off'ring to it his own heart.
[*Exit.*
PARIS I know what 'tis to love
And would, as I shall pity, I could help!
Please you walk in, my lords. [*Exeunt.*

SCENE IV. *Troy. Pandarus' house.*

Enter PANDARUS and CRESSIDA.

PANDARUS Be moderate, be moderate.
CRESSIDA Why tell you me of moderation?
The grief is fine, full, perfect, that I taste,
And violenteth in a sense as strong
As that which causeth it. How can I moderate it?
If I could temporize with my affections
Or brew it to a weak and colder palate,
The like allayment could I give my grief.
My love admits no qualifying dross;
No more my grief, in such a precious loss.

Enter TROILUS.

PANDARUS Here, here, here he comes. Ah, sweet ducks!
CRESSIDA O Troilus! Troilus! [*Embracing him.*
PANDARUS What a pair of spectacles is here!

Let me embrace too. 'O heart,' as the goodly saying is,

> O heart, heavy heart,
> Why sigh'st thou without breaking?

where he answers again

> Because thou canst not ease thy smart
> By friendship nor by speaking.

There was never a truer rhyme. Let us cast away nothing, for we may live to have need of such a verse. We see it, we see it. How now, lambs!

TROILUS Cressid, I love thee in so strain'd a purity
That the bless'd gods, as angry with my fancy,
More bright in zeal than the devotion which
Cold lips blow to their deities, take thee from me.

CRESSIDA Have the gods envy?

PANDARUS Ay, ay, ay, ay; 'tis too plain a case.

CRESSIDA And is it true that I must go from Troy?

TROILUS A hateful truth.

CRESSIDA What, and from Troilus too?

TROILUS From Troy and Troilus.

CRESSIDA Is't possible?

TROILUS And suddenly; where injury of chance
Puts back leave-taking, justles roughly by
All time of pause, rudely beguiles our lips
Of all rejoindure, forcibly prevents
Our lock'd embrasures, strangles our dear vows
Even in the birth of our own labouring breath.
We two, that with so many thousand sighs
Did buy each other, must poorly sell ourselves
With the rude brevity and discharge of one.
Injurious time now with a robber's haste
Crams his rich thievery up, he knows not how.
As many farewells as be stars in heaven,
With distinct breath and consign'd kisses to them,
He fumbles up into a loose adieu,
And scants us with a single famish'd kiss,
Distasted with the salt of broken tears.

AENEAS [*Within*] My lord, is the lady ready?

TROILUS Hark! you are call'd. Some say the Genius so
Cries 'Come' to him that instantly must die.
Bid them have patience; she shall come anon.

PANDARUS Where are my tears? Rain, to lay this wind, or my heart will be blown up by th' root?

[*Exit.*

CRESSIDA I must then to the Grecians?

TROILUS No remedy.

CRESSIDA A woeful Cressid 'mongst the merry Greeks!
When shall we see again?

TROILUS Hear me, my love. Be thou but true of heart –

CRESSIDA I true! how now! What wicked deem is this?

TROILUS Nay, we must use expostulation kindly,
For it is parting from us.
I speak not 'Be thou true' as fearing thee,
For I will throw my glove to Death himself
That there's no maculation in thy heart;
But 'Be thou true' say I to fashion in
My sequent protestation: be thou true,
And I will see thee.

CRESSIDA O, you shall be expos'd, my lord, to dangers
As infinite as imminent! But I'll be true.

TROILUS And I'll grow friend with danger. Wear this sleeve.

CRESSIDA And you this glove. When shall I see you?

TROILUS I will corrupt the Grecian sentinels
To give thee nightly visitation.
But yet be true.

CRESSIDA O heavens! 'Be true' again!

TROILUS Hear why I speak it, love.
The Grecian youths are full of quality;
They're loving, well compos'd with gifts of nature,
And flowing o'er with arts and exercise.
How novelties may move, and parts with person,
Alas, a kind of godly jealousy,
Which I beseech you call a virtuous sin,
Makes me afeard.

CRESSIDA O heavens! you love me not.

TROILUS Die I a villain, then!
In this I do not call your faith in question
So mainly as my merit. I cannot sing,
Nor heel the high lavolt, nor sweeten talk,
Nor play at subtle games – fair virtues all,
To which the Grecians are most prompt and pregnant;
But I can tell that in each grace of these
There lurks a still and dumb-discoursive devil
That tempts most cunningly. But be not tempted.

CRESSIDA Do you think I will?

TROILUS No.
But something may be done that we will not;
And sometimes we are devils to ourselves,
When we will tempt the frailty of our powers,
Presuming on their changeful potency.

AENEAS [*Within*] Nay, good my lord!

TROILUS Come, kiss; and let us part.

PARIS [*Within*] Brother Troilus!

TROILUS Good brother, come you hither;
And bring Aeneas and the Grecian with you.

CRESSIDA My lord, will you be true?

TROILUS Who, I? Alas, it is my vice, my fault!
Whiles others fish with craft for great opinion,

I with great truth catch mere simplicity;
Whilst some with cunning gild their copper crowns,
With truth and plainness I do wear mine bare.

Enter AENEAS, PARIS, ANTENOR, DEIPHOBUS, and DIOMEDES.

Fear not my truth: the moral of my wit
Is 'plain and true'; there's all the reach of it.
Welcome, Sir Diomed! Here is the lady
Which for Antenor we deliver you;
At the port, lord, I'll give her to thy hand,
And by the way possess thee what she is.
Entreat her fair; and, by my soul, fair Greek,
If e'er thou stand at mercy of my sword,
Name Cressid, and thy life shall be as safe
As Priam is in Ilion.

DIOMEDES Fair Lady Cressid,
So please you, save the thanks this prince expects.
The lustre in your eye, heaven in your cheek,
Pleads your fair usage; and to Diomed
You shall be mistress, and command him wholly.

TROILUS Grecian, thou dost not use me courteously
To shame the zeal of my petition to thee
In praising her. I tell thee, lord of Greece,
She is as far high-soaring o'er thy praises
As thou unworthy to be call'd her servant.
I charge thee use her well, even for my charge;
For, by the dreadful Pluto, if thou dost not,
Though the great bulk Achilles be thy guard,
I'll cut thy throat.

DIOMEDES O, be not mov'd, Prince Troilus.
Let me be privileg'd by my place and message
To be a speaker free: when I am hence
I'll answer to my lust. And know you, lord,
I'll nothing do on charge: to her own worth
She shall be priz'd. But that you say 'Be't so',
I speak it in my spirit and honour, 'No'.

TROILUS Come, to the port. I'll tell thee, Diomed,
This brave shall oft make thee to hide thy head.
Lady, give me your hand; and, as we walk,
To our own selves bend we our needful talk.

[Exeunt Troilus, Cressida, and Diomedes.

[Sound trumpet.

PARIS Hark! Hector's trumpet.

AENEAS How have we spent this morning!
The Prince must think me tardy and remiss,
That swore to ride before him to the field.

PARIS 'Tis Troilus' fault. Come, come to field with him.

DEIPHOBUS Let us make ready straight.

AENEAS Yea, with a bridegroom's fresh alacrity
Let us address to tend on Hector's heels.
The glory of our Troy doth this day lie
On his fair worth and single chivalry. *[Exeunt.*

SCENE V. *The Grecian Camp. Lists set out.*

Enter AJAX, armed; AGAMEMNON, ACHILLES, PATROCLUS, MENELAUS, ULYSSES, NESTOR, and Others.

AGAMEMNON Here art thou in appointment fresh and fair,
Anticipating time with starting courage.
Give with thy trumpet a loud note to Troy,
Thou dreadful Ajax, that the appalled air
May pierce the head of the great combatant,
And hale him hither.

AJAX Thou, trumpet, there's my purse.
Now crack thy lungs and split thy brazen pipe;
Blow, villain, till thy sphered bias cheek
Out-swell the colic of puff'd Aquilon.
Come, stretch thy chest, and let thy eyes spout blood:
Thou blowest for Hector. *[Trumpet sounds.*

ULYSSES No trumpet answers.

ACHILLES 'Tis but early days.

Enter DIOMEDES, with CRESSIDA.

AGAMEMNON Is not yond Diomed, with Calchas' daughter?

ULYSSES 'Tis he, I ken the manner of his gait:
He rises on the toe. That spirit of his
In aspiration lifts him from the earth.

AGAMEMNON Is this the lady Cressid?

DIOMEDES Even she.

AGAMEMNON Most dearly welcome to the Greeks, sweet lady.

NESTOR Our general doth salute you with a kiss.

ULYSSES Yet is the kindness but particular;
'Twere better she were kiss'd in general.

NESTOR And very courtly counsel: I'll begin.
So much for Nestor.

ACHILLES I'll take that winter from your lips, fair lady.
Achilles bids you welcome.

MENELAUS I had good argument for kissing once.

PATROCLUS But that's no argument for kissing now;
For thus popp'd Paris in his hardiment,
And parted thus you and your argument.

ULYSSES O deadly gall, and theme of all our scorns!
For which we lose our heads to gild his horns.

PATROCLUS The first was Menelaus' kiss; this, mine – *[Kisses her again.*
Patroclus kisses you.

MENELAUS O, this is trim!

PATROCLUS Paris and I kiss evermore for him.

MENELAUS I'll have my kiss, sir. Lady, by your leave.
CRESSIDA In kissing, do you render or receive?
PATROCLUS Both take and give.
CRESSIDA I'll make my match to live,
The kiss you take is better than you give;
Therefore no kiss.
MENELAUS I'll give you boot; I'll give you three for one.
CRESSIDA You are an odd man; give even or give none.
MENELAUS An odd man, lady? Every man is odd.
CRESSIDA No, Paris is not; for you know 'tis true
That you are odd, and he is even with you.
MENELAUS You fillip me o' th' head.
CRESSIDA No, I'll be sworn.
ULYSSES It were no match, your nail against his horn.
May I, sweet lady, beg a kiss of you?
CRESSIDA You may.
ULYSSES I do desire it.
CRESSIDA Why, beg then.
ULYSSES Why then, for Venus' sake give me a kiss
When Helen is a maid again, and his.
CRESSIDA I am your debtor; claim it when 'tis due.
ULYSSES Never's my day, and then a kiss of you.
DIOMEDES Lady, a word. I'll bring you to your father. *[Exit with Cressida.*
NESTOR A woman of quick sense.
ULYSSES Fie, fie upon her!
There's language in her eye, her cheek, her lip,
Nay, her foot speaks; her wanton spirits look out
At every joint and motive of her body.
O these encounterers so glib of tongue
That give a coasting welcome ere it comes,
And wide unclasp the tables of their thoughts
To every ticklish reader! Set them down
For sluttish spoils of opportunity,
And daughters of the game. *[Trumpet within.*
ALL The Troyans' trumpet.

Enter HECTOR, armed; AENEAS, TROILUS, PARIS, HELENUS, and other Trojans, with Attendants.

AGAMEMNON Yonder comes the troop.
AENEAS Hail, all the state of Greece! What shall be done
To him that victory commands? Or do you purpose
A victor shall be known? Will you the knights
Shall to the edge of all extremity
Pursue each other, or shall they be divided
By any voice or order of the field?
Hector bade ask.
AGAMEMNON Which way would Hector have it?
AENEAS He cares not; he'll obey conditions.
ACHILLES 'Tis done like Hector; but securely done,
A little proudly, and great deal misprizing
The knight oppos'd.
AENEAS If not Achilles, sir,
What is your name?
ACHILLES If not Achilles, nothing.
AENEAS Therefore Achilles. But whate'er, know this:
In the extremity of great and little
Valour and pride excel themselves in Hector;
The one almost as infinite as all,
The other blank as nothing. Weigh him well,
And that which looks like pride is courtesy.
This Ajax is half made of Hector's blood;
In love whereof half Hector stays at home;
Half heart, half hand, half Hector comes to seek
This blended knight, half Troyan and half Greek.
ACHILLES A maiden battle then? O, I perceive you!

Re-enter DIOMEDES.

AGAMEMNON Here is Sir Diomed. Go, gentle knight,
Stand by our Ajax. As you and Lord Aeneas
Consent upon the order of their fight,
So be it; either to the uttermost,
Or else a breath. The combatants being kin
Half stints their strife before their strokes begin.
[Ajax and Hector enter the lists.

ULYSSES They are oppos'd already.
AGAMEMNON What Troyan is that same that looks so heavy?
ULYSSES The youngest son of Priam, a true knight;
Not yet mature, yet matchless; firm of word;
Speaking in deeds and deedless in his tongue;
Not soon provok'd, nor being provok'd soon calm'd;
His heart and hand both open and both free;
For what he has he gives, what thinks he shows,
Yet gives he not till judgment guide his bounty,
Nor dignifies an impair thought with breath;
Manly as Hector, but more dangerous;
For Hector in his blaze of wrath subscribes
To tender objects, but he in heat of action
Is more vindicative than jealous love.
They call him Troilus, and on him erect
A second hope as fairly built as Hector.
Thus says Aeneas, one that knows the youth
Even to his inches, and, with private soul,
Did in great Ilion thus translate him to me.
[Alarum. Hector and Ajax fight.
AGAMEMNON They are in action.

NESTOR Now, Ajax, hold thine own!
TROILUS Hector, thou sleep'st;
Awake thee.
AGAMEMNON His blows are well dispos'd. There, Ajax! *[Trumpets cease.*
DIOMEDES You must no more.
AENEAS Princes, enough, so please you.
AJAX I am not warm yet; let us fight again.
DIOMEDES As Hector pleases.
HECTOR Why, then will I no more.
Thou art, great lord, my father's sister's son,
A cousin-german to great Priam's seed;
The obligation of our blood forbids
A gory emulation 'twixt us twain:
Were thy commixtion Greek and Troyan so
That thou could'st say 'This hand is Grecian all,
And this is Troyan; the sinews of this leg
All Greek, and this all Troy; my mother's blood
Runs on the dexter cheek, and this sinister
Bounds in my father's'; by Jove multipotent,
Thou shouldst not bear from me a Greekish member
Wherein my sword had not impressure made
Of our rank feud; but the just gods gainsay
That any drop thou borrow'dst from thy mother,
My sacred aunt, should by my mortal sword
Be drained! Let me embrace thee, Ajax.
By him that thunders, thou hast lusty arms;
Hector would have them fall upon him thus.
Cousin, all honour to thee!
AJAX I thank thee, Hector.
Thou art too gentle and too free a man.
I came to kill thee, cousin, and bear hence
A great addition earned in thy death.
HECTOR Not Neoptolemus so mirable,
On whose bright crest Fame with her loud'st Oyes
Cries 'This is he' could promise to himself
A thought of added honour torn from Hector.
AENEAS There is expectance here from both the sides
What further you will do.
HECTOR We'll answer it:
The issue is embracement. Ajax, farewell.
AJAX If I might in entreaties find success,
As seld I have the chance, I would desire
My famous cousin to our Grecian tents.
DIOMEDES 'Tis Agamemnon's wish; and great Achilles
Doth long to see unarm'd the valiant Hector.
HECTOR Aeneas, call my brother Troilus to me,
And signify this loving interview
To the expecters of our Troyan part;
Desire them home. Give me thy hand, my cousin;
I will go eat with thee, and see your knights.

Agamemnon and the rest of the Greeks come forward.

AJAX Great Agamemnon comes to meet us here.
HECTOR The worthiest of them tell me name by name;
But for Achilles, my own searching eyes
Shall find him by his large and portly size.
AGAMEMNON Worthy all arms! as welcome as to one
That would be rid of such an enemy.
But that's no welcome. Understand more clear,
What's past and what's to come is strew'd with husks
And formless ruin of oblivion;
But in this extant moment, faith and troth,
Strain'd purely from all hollow bias-drawing,
Bids thee with most divine integrity,
From heart of very heart, great Hector, welcome.
HECTOR I thank thee, most imperious Agamemnon.
AGAMEMNON *[To Troilus]* My well-fam'd lord of Troy, no less to you.
MENELAUS Let me confirm my princely brother's greeting.
You brace of warlike brothers, welcome hither.
HECTOR Who must we answer?
AENEAS The noble Menelaus.
HECTOR O you, my lord? By Mars his gauntlet, thanks!
Mock not that I affect the untraded oath;
Your quondam wife swears still by Venus' glove.
She's well, but bade me not commend her to you.
MENELAUS Name her not now, sir; she's a deadly theme.
HECTOR O, pardon; I offend.
NESTOR I have, thou gallant Troyan, seen thee oft,
Labouring for destiny, make cruel way
Through ranks of Greekish youth; and I have seen thee,
As hot as Perseus, spur thy Phrygian steed,
Despising many forfeits and subduements,
When thou hast hung thy advanced sword i' th' air,
Not letting it decline on the declined;
That I have said to some my standers-by
'Lo, Jupiter is yonder, dealing life!'
And I have seen thee pause and take thy breath,
When that a ring of Greeks have hemm'd thee in,
Like an Olympian wrestling. This have I seen;
But this thy countenance, still lock'd in steel,
I never saw till now. I knew thy grandsire,

And once fought with him. He was a soldier good,
But, by great Mars, the captain of us all,
Never like thee. O, let an old man embrace thee;
And, worthy warrior, welcome to our tents.

AENEAS 'Tis the old Nestor.

HECTOR Let me embrace thee, good old chronicle,
That hast so long walk'd hand in hand with time.
Most reverend Nestor, I am glad to clasp thee.

NESTOR I would my arms could match thee in contention
As they contend with thee in courtesy.

HECTOR I would they could.

NESTOR Ha!
By this white beard, I'd fight with thee to-morrow.
Well, welcome, welcome! I have seen the time.

ULYSSES I wonder now how yonder city stands,
When we have here her base and pillar by us.

HECTOR I know your favour, Lord Ulysses, well.
Ah, sir, there's many a Greek and Troyan dead,
Since first I saw yourself and Diomed
In Ilion on your Greekish embassy.

ULYSSES Sir, I foretold you then what would ensue.
My prophecy is but half his journey yet;
For yonder walls, that pertly front your town,
Yond towers, whose wanton tops do buss the clouds,
Must kiss their own feet.

HECTOR I must not believe you.
There they stand yet; and modestly I think
The fall of every Phrygian stone will cost
A drop of Grecian blood. The end crowns all;
And that old common arbitrator, Time,
Will one day end it.

ULYSSES So to him we leave it.
Most gentle and most valiant Hector, welcome.
After the General, I beseech you next
To feast with me and see me at my tent.

ACHILLES I shall forestall thee, Lord Ulysses, thou!
Now, Hector, I have fed mine eyes on thee;
I have with exact view perus'd thee, Hector,
And quoted joint by joint.

HECTOR Is this Achilles?

ACHILLES I am Achilles.

HECTOR Stand fair, I pray thee; let me look on thee.

ACHILLES Behold thy fill.

HECTOR Nay, I have done already.

ACHILLES Thou art too brief. I will the second time,
As I would buy thee, view thee limb by limb.

HECTOR O, like a book of sport thou'lt read me o'er;
But there's more in me than thou understand'st.
Why dost thou so oppress me with thine eye?

ACHILLES Tell me, you heavens, in which part of his body
Shall I destroy him? Whether there, or there, or there?
That I may give the local wound a name,
And make distinct the very breach whereout
Hector's great spirit flew. Answer me, heavens.

HECTOR It would discredit the blest gods, proud man,
To answer such a question. Stand again.
Think'st thou to catch my life so pleasantly
As to prenominate in nice conjecture
Where thou wilt hit me dead?

ACHILLES I tell thee yea.

HECTOR Wert thou an oracle to tell me so,
I'd not believe thee. Henceforth guard thee well;
For I'll not kill thee there, nor there, nor there;
But, by the forge that stithied Mars his helm,
I'll kill thee everywhere, yea, o'er and o'er.
You wisest Grecians, pardon me this brag.
His insolence draws folly from my lips;
But I'll endeavour deeds to match these words,
Or may I never –

AJAX Do not chafe thee, cousin;
And you, Achilles, let these threats alone
Till accident or purpose bring you to't.
You may have every day enough of Hector,
If you have stomach. The general state, I fear,
Can scarce entreat you to be odd with him.

HECTOR I pray you let us see you in the field;
We have had pelting wars since you refus'd
The Grecians' cause.

ACHILLES Dost thou entreat me, Hector?
To-morrow do I meet thee, fell as death;
To-night all friends.

HECTOR Thy hand upon that match.

AGAMEMNON First, all you peers of Greece, go to my tent;
There in the full convive we; afterwards,
As Hector's leisure and your bounties shall
Concur together, severally entreat him.
Beat loud the tabourines, let the trumpets blow,
That this great soldier may his welcome know.

[Exeunt all but Troilus and Ulysses.

TROILUS My Lord Ulysses, tell me, I beseech you,
In what place of the field doth Calchas keep?

ULYSSES At Menelaus' tent, most princely Troilus.
There Diomed doth feast with him to-night,
Who neither looks upon the heaven nor earth,
But gives all gaze and bent of amorous view
On the fair Cressid.

TROILUS Shall I, sweet lord, be bound to you so much,
After we part from Agamemnon's tent,
To bring me thither?
ULYSSES You shall command me, sir.
As gentle tell me of what honour was
This Cressida in Troy? Had she no lover there
That wails her absence?
TROILUS O, sir, to such as boasting show their scars
A mock is due. Will you walk on, my lord?
She was belov'd, she lov'd; she is, and doth;
But still sweet love is food for fortune's tooth.
[Exeunt.

ACT FIVE

SCENE I. *The Grecian camp. Before the tent of Achilles.*

Enter ACHILLES and PATROCLUS.

ACHILLES I'll heat his blood with Greekish wine to-night,
Which with my scimitar I'll coll to-morrow.
Patroclus, let us feast him to the height.
PATROCLUS Here comes Thersites.

Enter THERSITES.

ACHILLES How now, thou core of envy!
Thou crusty batch of nature, what's the news?

THERSITES Why, thou picture of what thou seemest, and idol of idiot worshippers, here's a letter for thee.

ACHILLES From whence, fragment?

THERSITES Why, thou full dish of fool, from Troy.

PATROCLUS Who keeps the tent now?

THERSITES The surgeon's box or the patient's wound.

PATROCLUS Well said Adversity! and what needs these tricks?

THERSITES Prithee, be silent, boy; I profit not by thy talk; thou art said to be Achilles' male varlet.

PATROCLUS Male varlet, you rogue! What's that?

THERSITES Why, his masculine whore. Now, the rotten diseases of the south, the guts-gripping ruptures, catarrhs, loads o' gravel in the back, lethargies, cold palsies, raw eyes, dirt-rotten livers, wheezing lungs, bladders full of imposthume, sciaticas, limekilns i' th' palm, incurable bone-ache, and the rivelled fee-simple of the tetter, take and take again such preposterous discoveries!

PATROCLUS Why, thou damnable box of envy, thou, what meanest thou to curse thus?

THERSITES Do I curse thee?

PATROCLUS Why, no, you ruinous butt; you whoreson indistinguishable cur, no.

THERSITES No! Why art thou, then, exasperate, thou idle immaterial skein of sleid silk, thou green sarcenet flap for a sore eye, thou tassel of a prodigal's purse, thou? Ah, how the poor world is pest'red with such water-flies – diminutives of nature!

PATROCLUS Out, gall!

THERSITES Finch egg!

ACHILLES My sweet Patroclus, I am thwarted quite
From my great purpose in to-morrow's battle.
Here is a letter from Queen Hecuba,
A token from her daughter, my fair love,
Both taxing me and gaging me to keep
An oath that I have sworn. I will not break it.
Fall Greeks; fail fame; honour or go or stay;
My major vow lies here, this I'll obey.
Come, come, Thersites, help to trim my tent;
This night in banqueting must all be spent.
Away, Patroclus! *[Exit with Patroclus.*

THERSITES With too much blood and too little brain these two may run mad; but, if with too much brain and too little blood they do, I'll be a curer of madmen. Here's Agamemnon, an honest fellow enough, and one that loves quails, but he has not so much brain as ear-wax; and the goodly transformation of Jupiter there, his brother, the bull, the primitive statue and oblique memorial of cuckolds, a thrifty shoeing-horn in a chain, hanging at his brother's leg – to what form but that he is, should wit larded with malice, and malice forced with wit, turn him to? To an ass, were nothing: he is both ass and ox. To an ox, were nothing: he is both ox and ass. To be a dog, a mule, a cat, a fitchew, a toad, a lizard, an owl, a puttock, or a herring without a roe, I would not care; but to be Menelaus, I would conspire against destiny. Ask me not what I would be, if I were not Thersites; for I care not to be the louse of a lazar, so I were not Menelaus. Hey-day! sprites and fires!

Enter HECTOR, TROILUS, AJAX, AGAMEMNON, ULYSSES, NESTOR, MENELAUS, and DIOMEDES, with lights.

AGAMEMNON We go wrong, we go wrong.
AJAX No, yonder 'tis;
There, where we see the lights.
HECTOR I trouble you.

AJAX No, not a whit.

Re-enter ACHILLES.

ULYSSES Here comes himself to guide you.

ACHILLES Welcome, brave Hector; welcome Princes all.

AGAMEMNON So now, fair Prince of Troy, I bid good night;
Ajax commands the guard to tend on you.

HECTOR Thanks, and good night to the Greeks' general.

MENELAUS Good night, my lord.

HECTOR Good night, sweet Lord Menelaus.

THERSITES Sweet draught! 'Sweet' quoth 'a?
Sweet sink, sweet sewer!

ACHILLES Good night and welcome, both at once, to those
That go or tarry.

AGAMEMNON Good night.

[Exeunt Agamemnon and Menelaus.

ACHILLES Old Nestor tarries; and you too, Diomed,
Keep Hector company an hour or two.

DIOMEDES I cannot, lord; I have important business,
The tide whereof is now. Good night, great Hector.

HECTOR Give me your hand.

ULYSSES *[Aside to Troilus]* Follow his torch; he goes to Calchas' tent;
I'll keep you company.

TROILUS Sweet sir, you honour me.

HECTOR And so, good night.

[Exit Diomedes; Ulysses and Troilus following.

ACHILLES Come, come, enter my tent.

[Exeunt all but Thersites.

THERSITES That same Diomed's a false-hearted rogue, a most unjust knave; I will no more trust him when he leers than I will a serpent when he hisses. He will spend his mouth and promise, like Brabbler the hound; but when he performs, astronomers foretell it: it is prodigious, there will come some change; the sun borrows of the moon when Diomed keeps his word. I will rather leave to see Hector than not to dog him. They say he keeps a Troyan drab, and uses the traitor Calchas' tent. I'll after. Nothing but lechery! All incontinent varlets! *[Exit.*

SCENE II. *The Grecian camp. Before Calchas' tent.*

Enter DIOMEDES.

DIOMEDES What, are you up here, ho? Speak.

CALCHAS *[Within]* Who calls?

DIOMEDES Diomed. Calchas, I think. Where's your daughter?

CALCHAS *[Within]* She comes to you.

Enter TROILUS and ULYSSES, at a distance; after them THERSITES.

ULYSSES Stand where the torch may not discover us.

Enter CRESSIDA.

TROILUS Cressid comes forth to him.

DIOMEDES How now, my charge!

CRESSIDA Now, my sweet guardian! Hark, a word with you. *[Whispers.*

TROILUS Yea, so familiar!

ULYSSES She will sing any man at first sight.

THERSITES And any man may sing her, if he can take her cliff; she's noted.

DIOMEDES Will you remember?

CRESSIDA Remember? Yes.

DIOMEDES Nay, but do, then;
And let your mind be coupled with your words.

TROILUS What shall she remember?

ULYSSES List!

CRESSIDA Sweet honey Greek, tempt me no more to folly.

THERSITES Roguery!

DIOMEDES Nay, then –

CRESSIDA I'll tell you what –

DIOMEDES Fo, fo! come, tell a pin; you are a forsworn –

CRESSIDA In faith, I cannot. What would you have me do?

THERSITES A juggling trick, to be secretly open.

DIOMEDES What did you swear you would bestow on me?

CRESSIDA I prithee, do not hold me to mine oath;
Bid me do anything but that, sweet Greek.

DIOMEDES Good night.

TROILUS Hold, patience!

ULYSSES How now, Troyan!

CRESSIDA Diomed!

DIOMEDES No, no, good night; I'll be your fool no more.

TROILUS Thy better must.

CRESSIDA Hark! a word in your ear.

TROILUS O plague and madness!

ULYSSES You are moved, Prince; let us depart, I pray,
Lest your displeasure should enlarge itself
To wrathful terms. This place is dangerous;
The time right deadly; I beseech you, go.

TROILUS Behold, I pray you.

ULYSSES Nay, good my lord, go off;
You flow to great distraction; come, my lord.

TROILUS I prithee stay.

ULYSSES You have not patience; come.

TROILUS I pray you, stay; by hell and all hell's torments,

I will not speak a word.
DIOMEDES And so, good night.
CRESSIDA Nay, but you part in anger.
TROILUS Doth that grieve thee? O withered truth!
ULYSSES How now, my lord?
TROILUS By Jove, I will be patient.
CRESSIDA Guardian! Why, Greek!
DIOMEDES Fo, fo! adieu! you palter.
CRESSIDA In faith, I do not. Come hither once again.
ULYSSES You shake, my lord, at something; will you go?
You will break out.
TROILUS She strokes his cheek.
ULYSSES Come, come.
TROILUS Nay, stay; by Jove, I will not speak a word:
There is between my will and all offences
A guard of patience. Stay a little while.
THERSITES How the devil luxury, with his fat rump and potato finger, tickles these together! Fry, lechery, fry!
DIOMEDES But will you, then?
CRESSIDA In faith, I will, lo; never trust me else.
DIOMEDES Give me some token for the surety of it.
CRESSIDA I'll fetch you one. [*Exit.*
ULYSSES You have sworn patience.
TROILUS Fear me not, my lord;
I will not be myself, nor have cognition
Of what I feel. I am all patience.

Re-enter CRESSIDA.

THERSITES Now the pledge; now, now, now!
CRESSIDA Here, Diomed, keep this sleeve.
TROILUS O beauty! where is thy faith?
ULYSSES My lord!
TROILUS I will be patient; outwardly I will.
CRESSIDA You look upon that sleeve; behold it well.
He lov'd me – O false wench! – Give't me again.
DIOMEDES Whose was't?
CRESSIDA It is no matter, now I ha't again.
I will not meet with you to-morrow night.
I prithee, Diomed, visit me no more.
THERSITES Now she sharpens. Well said, whetstone.
DIOMEDES I shall have it.
CRESSIDA What, this?
DIOMEDES Ay, that.
CRESSIDA O all you gods! O pretty, pretty pledge!
Thy master now lies thinking on his bed
Of thee and me, and sighs, and takes my glove,
And gives memorial dainty kisses to it,
As I kiss thee. Nay, do not snatch it from me;
He that takes that doth take my heart withal.
DIOMEDES I had your heart before; this follows it.
TROILUS I did swear patience.
CRESSIDA You shall not have it, Diomed; faith, you shall not;
I'll give you something else.
DIOMEDES I will have this. Whose was it?
CRESSIDA It is no matter.
DIOMEDES Come, tell me whose it was.
CRESSIDA 'Twas one's that lov'd me better than you will.
But, now you have it, take it.
DIOMEDES Whose was it?
CRESSIDA By all Diana's waiting women yond,
And by herself, I will not tell you whose.
DIOMEDES To-morrow will I wear it on my helm,
And grieve his spirit that dares not challenge it.
TROILUS Wert thou the devil and wor'st it on thy horn,
It should be challeng'd.
CRESSIDA Well, well, 'tis done, 'tis past; and yet it is not;
I will not keep my word.
DIOMEDES Why, then farewell;
Thou never shalt mock Diomed again.
CRESSIDA You shalt not go. One cannot speak a word
But it straight starts you.
DIOMEDES I do not like this fooling.
THERSITES Nor I, by Pluto; but that that likes not you
Pleases me best.
DIOMEDES What, shall I come? The hour –
CRESSIDA Ay, come – O Jove! Do come. I shall be plagu'd.
DIOMEDES Farewell till then.
CRESSIDA Good night. I prithee come.
[*Exit Diomedes.*
Troilus, farewell! One eye yet looks on thee;
But with my heart the other eye doth see.
Ah, poor our sex! this fault in us I find,
The error of our eye directs our mind.
What error leads must err; O, then conclude,
Minds sway'd by eyes are full of turpitude.
[*Exit.*
THERSITES A proof of strength she could not publish more,
Unless she said 'My mind is now turn'd whore'.
ULYSSES All's done, my lord.
TROILUS It is.
ULYSSES Why stay we, then?
TROILUS To make a recordation to my soul
Of every syllable that here was spoke.
But if I tell how these two did coact,
Shall I not lie in publishing a truth?

Sith yet there is a credence in my heart,
An esperance so obstinately strong,
That doth invert th' attest of eyes and ears;
As if those organs had deceptious functions
Created only to calumniate.
Was Cressid here?

ULYSSES I cannot conjure, Troyan.

TROILUS She was not, sure.

ULYSSES Most sure she was.

TROILUS Why, my negation hath no taste of madness.

ULYSSES Nor mine, my lord. Cressid was here but now.

TROILUS Let it not be believ'd for womanhood.
Think, we had mothers; do not give advantage
To stubborn critics, apt, without a theme,
For depravation, to square the general sex
By Cressid's rule. Rather think this not Cressid.

ULYSSES What hath she done, Prince, that can soil our mothers?

TROILUS Nothing at all, unless that this were she.

THERSITES Will 'a swagger himself out on's own eyes?

TROILUS This she? No; this is Diomed's Cressida.
If beauty have a soul, this is not she;
If souls guide vows, if vows be sanctimonies,
If sanctimony be the gods' delight,
If there be rule in unity itself,
This was not she. O madness of discourse,
That cause sets up with and against itself!
Bifold authority! where reason can revolt
Without perdition, and loss assume all reason
Without revolt: this is, and is not, Cressid.
Within my soul there doth conduce a fight
Of this strange nature, that a thing inseparate
Divides more wider than the sky and earth;
And yet the spacious breadth of this division
Admits no orifex for a point as subtle
As Ariachne's broken woof to enter.
Instance, O instance! strong as Pluto's gates:
Cressid is mine, tied with the bonds of heaven.
Instance, O instance! strong as heaven itself:
The bonds of heaven are slipp'd, dissolv'd, and loos'd;
And with another knot, five-finger-tied,
The fractions of her faith, orts of her love,
The fragments, scraps, the bits, and greasy relics
Of her o'er-eaten faith, are bound to Diomed.

ULYSSES May worthy Troilus be half-attach'd
With that which here his passion doth express?

TROILUS Ay, Greek; and that shall be divulged well
In characters as red as Mars his heart
Inflam'd with Venus. Never did young man fancy
With so eternal and so fix'd a soul.
Hark, Greek: as much as I do Cressid love,
So much by weight hate I her Diomed.
That sleeve is mine that he'll bear on his helm;
Were it a casque compos'd by Vulcan's skill
My sword should bite it. Not the dreadful spout
Which shipmen do the hurricano call,
Constring'd in mass by the almighty sun,
Shall dizzy with more clamour Neptune's ear
In his descent than shall my prompted sword
Falling on Diomed.

THERSITES He'll tickle it for his concupy.

TROILUS O Cressid! O false Cressid! false, false, false!
Let all untruths stand by thy stained name,
And they'll seem glorious.

ULYSSES O, contain yourself;
Your passion draws ears hither.

Enter AENEAS.

AENEAS I have been seeking you this hour, my lord.
Hector, by this, is arming him in Troy;
Ajax, your guard, stays to conduct you home.

TROILUS Have with you, Prince. My courteous lord, adieu.
Farewell, revolted fair! – and, Diomed,
Stand fast and wear a castle on thy head.

ULYSSES I'll bring you to the gates.

TROILUS Accept distracted thanks.

[*Exeunt Troilus, AEneas, and Ulysses.*

THERSITES Would I could meet that rogue Diomed! I would croak like a raven; I would bode, I would bode. Patroclus will give me anything for the intelligence of this whore; the parrot will not do more for an almond than he for a commodious drab. Lechery, lechery! Still wars and lechery! Nothing else holds fashion. A burning devil take them! [*Exit.*

SCENE III. *Troy. Before Priam's palace.*

Enter HECTOR and ANDROMACHE.

ANDROMACHE When was my lord so much ungently temper'd
To stop his ears against admonishment?
Unarm, unarm, and do not fight to-day.

HECTOR You train me to offend you; get you in.
By all the everlasting gods, I'll go.

ANDROMACHE My dreams will, sure, prove ominous to the day.

HECTOR No more, I say.

Enter CASSANDRA.

CASSANDRA Where is my brother Hector?

ANDROMACHE Here, sister, arm'd, and bloody in intent.
Consort with me in loud and dear petition,
Pursue we him on knees; for I have dreamt

Of bloody turbulence, and this whole night
Hath nothing been but shapes and forms of
slaughter.

CASSANDRA O, 'tis true!

HECTOR Ho! bid my trumpet sound.

CASSANDRA No notes of sally, for the heavens, sweet brother!

HECTOR Be gone, I say. The gods have heard me swear.

CASSANDRA The gods are deaf to hot and peevish vows;
They are polluted off'rings, more abhorr'd
Than spotted livers in the sacrifice.

ANDROMACHE O, be persuaded! Do not count it holy
To hurt by being just. It is as lawful,
For we would give much, to use violent thefts
And rob in the behalf of charity.

CASSANDRA It is the purpose that makes strong the vow;
But vows to every purpose must not hold.
Unarm, sweet Hector.

HECTOR Hold you still, I say.
Mine honour keeps the weather of my fate.
Life every man holds dear; but the dear man
Holds honour far more precious dear than life.

Enter TROILUS.

How now, young man! Mean'st thou to fight to-day?

ANDROMACHE Cassandra, call my father to persuade. [*Exit Cassandra.*

HECTOR No, faith, young Troilus; doff thy harness, youth;
I am to-day i' th' vein of chivalry.
Let grow thy sinews till their knots be strong,
And tempt not yet the brushes of the war.
Unarm thee, go; and doubt thou not, brave boy,
I'll stand to-day for thee and me and Troy.

TROILUS Brother, you have a vice of mercy in you
Which better fits a lion than a man.

HECTOR What vice is that, good Troilus? Chide me for it.

TROILUS When many times the captive Grecian falls,
Even in the fan and wind of your fair sword,
You bid them rise and live.

HECTOR O, 'tis fair play!

TROILUS Fool's play, by heaven, Hector.

HECTOR How now! how now!

TROILUS For th' love of all the gods,
Let's leave the hermit Pity with our mother;
And when we have our armours buckled on,
The venom'd vengeance ride upon our swords,
Spur them to ruthful work, rein them from ruth!

HECTOR Fie, savage, fie!

TROILUS Hector, then 'tis wars.

HECTOR Troilus, I would not have you fight to-day.

TROILUS Who should withhold me?
Not fate, obedience, nor the hand of Mars
Beck'ning with fiery truncheon my retire;
Not Priamus and Hecuba on knees,
Their eyes o'ergalled with recourse of tears;
Nor you, my brother, with your true sword drawn,
Oppos'd to hinder me, should stop my way,
But by my ruin.

Re-enter CASSANDRA, with PRIAM.

CASSANDRA Lay hold upon him, Priam, hold him fast;
He is thy crutch; now if thou lose thy stay,
Thou on him leaning, and all Troy on thee,
Fall all together.

PRIAM Come, Hector, come, go back.
Thy wife hath dreamt; thy mother hath had visions;
Cassandra doth foresee; and I myself
Am like a prophet suddenly enrapt
To tell thee that this day is ominous.
Therefore, come back.

HECTOR Aeneas is a-field;
And I do stand engag'd to many Greeks,
Even in the faith of valour, to appear
This morning to them.

PRIAM Ay, but thou shalt not go.

HECTOR I must not break my faith.
You know me dutiful; therefore, dear sir,
Let me not shame respect; but give me leave
To take that course by your consent and voice
Which you do here forbid me, royal Priam.

CASSANDRA O Priam, yield not to him!

ANDROMACHE Do not, dear father.

HECTOR Andromache, I am offended with you.
Upon the love you bear me, get you in.
[*Exit Andromache.*

TROILUS This foolish, dreaming, superstitious girl
Makes all these bodements.

CASSANDRA O, farewell, dear Hector!
Look how thou diest. Look how thy eye turns pale.
Look how thy wounds do bleed at many vents.
Hark how Troy roars; how Hecuba cries out;
How poor Andromache shrills her dolours forth;
Behold distraction, frenzy, and amazement,
Like witless antics, one another meet,
And all cry, Hector! Hector's dead! O Hector!

TROILUS Away, away!

CASSANDRA Farewell! – yet, soft! Hector I take my leave.
Thou dost thyself and all our Troy deceive.
[Exit.

HECTOR You are amaz'd, my liege, at her exclaim.
Go in, and cheer the town; we'll forth, and fight,
Do deeds worth praise and tell you them at night.

PRIAM Farewell. The gods with safety stand about thee!

[Exeunt severally Priam and Hector. Alarums.

TROILUS They are at it, hark! Proud Diomed, believe,
I come to lose my arm or win my sleeve.

Enter PANDARUS.

PANDARUS Do you hear, my lord? Do you hear?

TROILUS What now?

PANDARUS Here's a letter come from yond poor girl.

TROILUS Let me read.

PANDARUS A whoreson tisick, a whoreson rascally tisick so troubles me, and the foolish fortune of this girl, and what one thing, what another, that I shall leave you one o' th's days; and I have a rheum in mine eyes too, and such an ache in my bones that unless a man were curs'd I cannot tell what to think on't. What says she there?

TROILUS Words, words, mere words, no matter from the heart;
Th' effect doth operate another way.
[Tearing the letter.
Go, wind, to wind, there turn and change together.
My love with words and errors still she feeds,
But edifies another with her deeds.

PANDARUS Why but heare you.

TROILUS Hence broker-lackey. Ignominy and shame
Pursue thy life and live aye with thy name!
[Exeunt severally.

SCENE IV. *The plain between Troy and the Grecian camp.*

Enter THERSITES. Excursions.

THERSITES Now they are clapper-clawing one another; I'll go look on. That dissembling abominable varlet, Diomed, has got that same scurvy doting foolish young knave's sleeve of Troy there in his helm. I would fain see them meet, that that same young Troyan ass that loves the whore there might send that Greekish whoremasterly villain with the sleeve back to the dissembling luxurious drab of a sleeve-less errand. A th' t'other side, the policy of those crafty swearing rascals – that stale old mouse-eaten dry cheese, Nestor, and that same dog-fox, Ulysses – is not prov'd worth a blackberry. They set me up, in policy, that mongrel cur, Ajax, against that dog of as bad a kind, Achilles; and now is the cur Ajax prouder than the cur Achilles, and will not arm to-day; whereupon the Grecians begin to proclaim barbarism, and policy grows into an ill opinion.

Enter DIOMEDES, TROILUS following.

Soft! here comes sleeve, and t'other.

TROILUS Fly not; for shouldst thou take the river Styx
I would swim after.

DIOMEDES Thou dost miscall retire.
I do not fly; but advantageous care
Withdrew me from the odds of multitude.
Have at thee.

THERSITES Hold thy whore, Grecian; now for thy whore, Troyan – now the sleeve, now the sleeve!

[Exeunt Troilus and Diomedes fighting.

Enter HECTOR.

HECTOR What art thou, Greek? Art thou for Hector's match?
Art thou of blood and honour?

THERSITES No, no – I am a rascal; a scurvy railing knave; a very filthy rogue.

HECTOR I do believe thee. Live. *[Exit.*

THERSITES God-a-mercy, that thou wilt believe me; but a plague break thy neck for frighting me! What's become of the wenching rogues? I think they have swallowed one another. I would laugh at that miracle. Yet, in a sort, lechery eats itself. I'll seek them. *[Exit.*

SCENE V *Another part of the plain.*

Enter DIOMEDES and a Servant.

DIOMEDES Go, go, my servant, take thou Troilus' horse;
Present the fair steed to my lady Cressid.
Fellow, commend my service to her beauty;
Tell her I have chastis'd the amorous Troyan,
And am her knight by proof.

SERVANT I go, my lord. *[Exit.*

Enter AGAMEMNON.

AGAMEMNON Renew, renew! The fierce Polydamus
Hath beat down Menon; bastard Margarelon
Hath Doreus prisoner,

And stands colossus-wise, waving his beam,
Upon the pashed corses of the kings
Epistrophus and Cedius. Polixenes is slain;
Amphimacus and Thoas deadly hurt;
Patroclus ta'en, or slain; and Palamedes
Sore hurt and bruis'd. The dreadful Sagittary
Appals our numbers. Haste we, Diomed,
To reinforcement, or we perish all.

Enter NESTOR.

NESTOR Go, bear Patroclus' body to Achilles,
And bid the snail-pac'd Ajax arm for shame.
There is a thousand Hectors in the field;
Now here he fights on Galathe his horse,
And there lacks work; anon he's there afoot,
And there they fly or die, like scaled sculls
Before the belching whale; then is he yonder,
And there the strawy Greeks, ripe for his edge,
Fall down before him like the mower's swath.
Here, there, and everywhere, he leaves and takes;
Dexterity so obeying appetite
That what he will he does, and does so much
That proof is call'd impossibility.

Enter ULYSSES.

ULYSSES O, courage, courage, Princes! Great Achilles
Is arming, weeping, cursing, vowing vengeance.
Patroclus' wounds have rous'd his drowsy blood,
Together with his mangled Myrmidons,
That noseless, handless, hack'd and chipp'd, come to him,
Crying on Hector. Ajax hath lost a friend
And foams at mouth, and he is arm'd and at it,
Roaring for Troilus; who hath done to-day
Mad and fantastic execution,
Engaging and redeeming of himself
With such a careless force and forceless care
As if that luck, in very spite of cunning,
Bade him win all.

Enter AJAX.

AJAX Troilus! thou coward Troilus! *[Exit.*

DIOMEDES Ay, there, there.

NESTOR So, so, we draw together. *[Exit.*

Enter ACHILLES.

ACHILLES Where is this Hector?
Come, come, thou boy-queller, show thy face;
Know what it is to meet Achilles angry.
Hector! where's Hector? I will none but Hector. *[Exeunt.*

SCENE VI. *Another part of the plain.*

Enter AJAX.

AJAX Troilus, thou coward Troilus, show thy head.

Enter DIOMEDES.

DIOMEDES Troilus, I say! Where's Troilus?

AJAX What wouldst thou?

DIOMEDES I would correct him.

AJAX Were I the general, thou shouldst have my office
Ere that correction. Troilus, I say! What, Troilus!

Enter TROILUS.

TROILUS O traitor Diomed! Turn thy false face, thou traitor,
And pay thy life thou owest me for my horse.

DIOMEDES Ha! art thou there?

AJAX I'll fight with him alone. Stand, Diomed.

DIOMEDES He is my prize. I will not look upon.

TROILUS Come, both, you cogging Greeks; have at you both. *[Exeunt fighting.*

Enter HECTOR.

HECTOR Yea, Troilus? O, well fought, my youngest brother!

Enter ACHILLES.

ACHILLES Now do I see thee, ha! Have at thee, Hector!

HECTOR Pause, if thou wilt.

ACHILLES I do disdain thy courtesy, proud Troyan.
Be happy that my arms are out of use;
My rest and negligence befriends thee now,
But thou anon shalt hear of me again;
Till when, go seek thy fortune. *[Exit.*

HECTOR Fare thee well.
I would have been much more a fresher man,
Had I expected thee.

Re-enter TROILUS.

How now, my brother!

TROILUS Ajax hath ta'en Aeneas. Shall it be?
No, by the flame of yonder glorious heaven,
He shall not carry him; I'll be ta'en too,
Or bring him off. Fate, hear me what I say:
I reck not though thou end my life to-day. *[Exit.*

Enter One in armour.

HECTOR Stand, stand, thou Greek; thou art a goodly mark.
No? wilt thou not? I like thy armour well;
I'll frush it and unlock the rivets all
But I'll be master of it. Wilt thou not, beast, abide?
Why then, fly on; I'll hunt thee for thy hide. *[Exeunt.*

SCENE VII. *Another part of the plain.*

Enter ACHILLES, with Myrmidons.

ACHILLES Come here about me, you my Myrmidons;
Mark what I say. Attend me where I wheel;
Strike not a stroke, but keep yourselves in breath;
And when I have the bloody Hector found,
Empale him with your weapons round about;
In fellest manner execute your arms.
Follow me, sirs, and my proceedings eye.
It is decreed Hector the great must die.
[*Exeunt.*

Enter MENELAUS and PARIS, fighting; then THERSITES.

THERSITES The cuckold and the cuckold-maker are at it. Now, bull! now, dog! 'Loo, Paris, 'loo! now my double-horn'd Spartan! 'loo, Paris, 'loo! The bull has the game. Ware horns, ho!
[*Exeunt Paris and Menelaus.*

Enter MARGARELON.

MARGARELON Turn, slave, and fight.
THERSITES What art thou?
MARGARELON A bastard son of Priam's.
THERSITES I am a bastard too; I love bastards. I am a bastard begot, bastard instructed, bastard in mind, bastard in valour, in everything illegitimate. One bear will not bite another, and wherefore should one bastard? Take heed, the quarrel's most ominous to us: if the son of a whore fight for a whore, he tempts judgment. Farewell, bastard. [*Exit.*
MARGARELON The devil take thee, coward!
[*Exit.*

SCENE VIII. *Another part of the plain.*

Enter HECTOR.

HECTOR Most putrified core so fair without,
Thy goodly armour thus hath cost thy life.
Now is my day's work done; I'll take good breath:
Rest, sword; thou hast thy fill of blood and death!
[*Disarms.*

Enter ACHILLES and his Myrmidons.

ACHILLES Look, Hector, how the sun begins to set;
How ugly night comes breathing at his heels;
Even with the vail and dark'ning of the sun,
To close the day up, Hector's life is done.
HECTOR I am unarm'd; forego this vantage, Greek.
ACHILLES Strike, fellows, strike; this is the man I seek. [*Hector falls.*
So, Ilion, fall thou next! Come, Troy, sink down;
Here lies thy heart, thy sinews, and thy bone.
On, Myrmidons, and cry you all amain
'Achilles hath the mighty Hector slain'.
[*A retreat sounded.*
Hark! a retire upon our Grecian part.
MYRMIDONS The Troyan trumpets sound the like, my lord.
ACHILLES The dragon wing of night o'er-spreads the earth
And, stickler-like, the armies separates.
My half-supp'd sword, that frankly would have fed,
Pleas'd with this dainty bait, thus goes to bed.
[*Sheathes his sword.*
Come, tie his body to my horse's tail;
Along the field I will the Troyan trail. [*Exeunt.*

SCENE IX. *Another part of the plain.*

Sound retreat. Shout. Enter AGAMEMNON, AJAX, MENELAUS, NESTOR, DIOMEDES, and the rest, marching.

AGAMEMNON Hark! hark! what shout is this?
NESTOR Peace, drums!
SOLDIERS [*Within*] Achilles! Achilles!
Hector's slain. Achilles!
DIOMEDES The bruit is Hector's slain, and by Achilles.
AJAX If it be so, yet bragless let it be;
Great Hector was as good a man as he.
AGAMEMNON March patiently along. Let one be sent
To pray Achilles see us at our tent.
If in his death the gods have us befriended;
Great Troy is ours, and our sharp wars are ended. [*Exeunt.*

SCENE X. *Another part of the plain.*

Enter AENEAS, PARIS, ANTENOR, and DEIPHOBUS.

AENEAS Stand, ho! yet are we masters of the field.
Never go home; here starve we out the night.

Enter TROILUS.

TROILUS Hector is slain
ALL Hector! The gods forbid!
TROILUS He's dead, and at the murderer's horse's tail,
In beastly sort, dragg'd through the shameful field.

Frown on, you heavens, effect your rage with speed.
Sit, gods, upon your thrones, and smile at Troy.
I say at once let your brief plagues be mercy,
And linger not our sure destructions on.

AENEAS My lord, you do discomfort all the host.

TROILUS You understand me not that tell me so.
I do not speak of flight, of fear of death,
But dare all imminence that gods and men
Address their dangers in. Hector is gone.
Who shall tell Priam so, or Hecuba?
Let him that will a screech-owl aye be call'd
Go in to Troy, and say there 'Hector's dead'.
There is a word will Priam turn to stone;
Make wells and Niobes of the maids and wives,
Cold statues of the youth; and, in a word,
Scare Troy out of itself. But, march away;
Hector is dead; there is no more to say.
Stay yet. You vile abominable tents,
Thus proudly pight upon our Phrygian plains,
Let Titan rise as early as he dare,
I'll through and through you. And, thou great-siz'd coward,
No space of earth shall sunder our two hates;
I'll haunt thee like a wicked conscience still,
That mouldeth goblins swift as frenzy's thoughts.
Strike a free march to Troy. With comfort go;
Hope of revenge shall hide our inward woe.

Enter PANDARUS.

PANDARUS But hear you, hear you!

TROILUS Hence, broker-lackey. Ignominy and shame
Pursue thy life and live aye with thy name!

[*Exeunt all but Pandarus.*

PANDARUS A goodly medicine for my aching bones! O world! world! world! thus is the poor agent despis'd! O traitors and bawds, how earnestly are you set a work, and how ill requited! Why should our endeavour be so lov'd, and the performance so loathed? What verse for it? What instance for it? Let me see –

Full merrily the humble-bee doth sing
Till he hath lost his honey and his sting;
And being once subdu'd in armed tail,
Sweet honey and sweet notes together fail.

Good traders in the flesh, set this in your painted cloths.
As many as be here of pander's hall,
Your eyes, half out, weep out at Pandar's fall;
Or, if you cannot weep, yet give some groans,
Though not for me, yet for your aching bones.
Brethren and sisters of the hold-door trade,
Some two months hence my will shall here be made.
It should be now, but that my fear is this,
Some galled goose of Winchester would hiss.
Till then I'll sweat and seek about for eases,
And at that time bequeath you my diseases.

[*Exit.*

Coriolanus

Introduction by CATHERINE E. DURIE

This is a political play about a man who cannot play politics. The last of the tragedies and the last of the Roman plays, it recapitulates on earlier probings of the relationship of the troubled state and the exceptional individual, this time through a series of oppositions: noise and silence, blood and milk, words and blows, action and acting, class warfare and social interdependence. If conflict is the stuff of drama, this is the most dramatic of works, for there is barely a scene that does not hinge upon physical fighting, clash of wills, fierce debate or power struggles. The very title suggests contested territory, an identity forged in destruction, but unstable, only bestowed in Act 1 and repudiated by Act 5.

It remains a stark play, spare and hard, even in the verse; at its centre stands a hero who is compelling and unlikable. Caius Martius Coriolanus is the single focus of the play; he dominates the stage whenever he is on it, and is discussed endlessly in his absence. He is seen as a god, a beast of prey, and a 'boy', mother-dominated and petulant. All these contradictions contain some truths and even the tragic pattern does not reconcile them; at the play's end Coriolanus remains as torn and self-divided as Rome.

One action defines him; he fights alone within the gates of Corioles, and so understands aloneness as strength. It is only so in military exploit, if there; isolation does not make a great leader. Compare Coriolanus with some of Shakespeare's other studies in leadership; Antony's generalship has fallen into dotage, but hard-bitten soldiers would literally die for him. No-one would die alongside Coriolanus, much less for him. Before Agincourt Henry V, disguised, prowls through the camp to absorb the sufferings of his men. Coriolanus curses his men, shaming and scolding them. In a moment of exaltation he offers himself to them, not as a brother or a friend, but as a sword, 'make you a sword of me', and an impersonal engine of destruction is what he is most fitted to be.

The same aloneness disables him in the body politic. Inflexible and haughty, he sees the people as less than human, as scabs, curs, geese. He has no grasp of the interdependence preached by Menenius (although no-one else in the play believes this either); one citizen tells him the price of support for the consulship is 'to ask it kindly'. Coriolanus offends against kindness, that network of acknowledged relationship in humanity; the people reject and banish him. He is one who could burn a city but not live peaceably within it.

Yet no-one measures up to him. The tribunes are unscrupulous, the crowd vacillating and easily manipulated, Aufidius envious and Menenius ineffectual. Always over the son falls the shadow of the mother; Volumnia has made him what he is and can still chide him into action inimical to his nature.

Coriolanus is destroyed by his inability to recognise his own need, of Rome, of the identity it gives him, of family and kinship. He is broken not by the aggression of enemies but the tenderness of women, of Virgilia, his almost silent wife, and

Volumnia's pleading. She challenges him to new-mint his identity with Volscian kin; hitherto he has believed he can author himself, but now the full reality of exile and estrangement comes home. Invariably defeated by words, he responds in a way both telling and moving. In silence he takes her hand, acknowledging vulnerability and connectedness. For once we see him aware and mature, with the tragic hero's acceptance of inevitable death. He dies as he has lived, contemptuous, his last word 'sword', alone in the enemy camp, with the Rome without which he cannot live distant, safe and almost forgotten.

Coriolanus

DRAMATIS PERSONAE

CAIUS MARCIUS
afterwards Caius Marcius Coriolanus
TITUS LARTIUS, COMINIUS
Generals against the Volscians
MENENIUS AGRIPPA
friend to Coriolanus
SICINIUS VELUTUS, JUNIUS BRUTUS
Tribunes of the people
YOUNG MARCIUS
son to Coriolanus
A Roman Herald
NICANOR
a Roman
TULLUS AUFIDIUS
General of the Volscians
Lieutenant to Aufidius
Conspirators with Aufidius
ADRIAN
a Volscian
A Citizen of Antium
Two Volscian Guards
VOLUMNIA
mother to Coriolanus
VIRGILIA
wife to Coriolanus
VALERIA
friend to Virgilia
Gentlewoman attending on Virgilia
Roman and Volscian Senators, Patricians, Aediles, Lictors, Soldiers, Citizens, Messengers, Servants to Aufidius, and other Attendants.

THE SCENE: ROME AND THE NEIGHBOURHOOD; CORIOLI AND THE NEIGHBOURHOOD; ANTIUM.

ACT ONE

SCENE I. *Rome. A street.*

Enter a company of mutinous Citizens, with staves, clubs, and other weapons.

1 CITIZEN Before we proceed any further, hear me speak.

ALL Speak, speak.

1 CITIZEN You are all resolv'd rather to die than to famish?

ALL Resolv'd, resolv'd.

1 CITIZEN First, you know Caius Marcius is chief enemy to the people.

ALL We know't, we know't.

1 CITIZEN Let us kill him, and we'll have corn at our own price. Is't a verdict?

ALL No more talking on't; let it be done. Away, away!

2 CITIZEN One word, good citizens.

1 CITIZEN We are accounted poor citizens, the patricians good. What authority surfeits on would relieve us; if they would yield us but the superfluity while it were wholesome, we might guess they relieved us humanely; but they think we are too dear. The leanness that afflicts us, the object of our misery, is as an inventory to particularize their abundance; our sufferance is a gain to them. Let us revenge this with our pikes ere we become rakes; for the gods know I speak this in hunger for bread, not in thirst for revenge.

2 CITIZEN Would you proceed especially against Caius Marcius?

1 CITIZEN Against him first; he's a very dog to the commonalty.

2 CITIZEN Consider you what services he has done for his country?

1 CITIZEN Very well, and could be content to give him good report for't but that he pays himself with being proud.

2 CITIZEN Nay, but speak not maliciously.

1 CITIZEN I say unto you, what he hath done famously he did it to that end; though soft-conscienc'd men can be content to say it was for his country, he did it to please his mother and to be partly proud, which he is, even to the altitude of his virtue.

2 CITIZEN What he cannot help in his nature you account a vice in him. You must in no way say he is covetous.

1 CITIZEN If I must not, I need not be barren of accusations; he hath faults, with surplus, to tire in repetition. [*Shouts within*] What shouts are these? The other side o' th' city is risen. Why stay we prating here? To th' Capitol!

ALL Come, come.

1 CITIZEN Soft! who comes here?

Enter MENENIUS AGRIPPA.

2 CITIZEN Worthy Menenius Agrippa; one that hath always lov'd the people.

1 CITIZEN He's one honest enough; would all the rest were so!

MENENIUS What work's, my countrymen, in hand? Where go you
With bats and clubs? The matter? Speak, I pray you.

1 CITIZEN Our business is not unknown to th' Senate; they have had inkling this fortnight what we intend to do, which now we'll show 'em in deeds. They say poor suitors have strong breaths; they shall know we have strong arms too.

MENENIUS Why, masters, my good friends, mine honest neighbours,
Will you undo yourselves?

1 CITIZEN We cannot, sir; we are undone already.

MENENIUS I tell you, friends, most charitable care
Have the patricians of you. For your wants,
Your suffering in this dearth, you may as well
Strike at the heaven with your staves as lift them
Against the Roman state; whose course will on
The way it takes, cracking ten thousand curbs
Of more strong link asunder than can ever
Appear in your impediment. For the dearth,
The gods, not the patricians, make it, and
Your knees to them, not arms, must help. Alack,
You are transported by calamity
Thither where more attends you; and you slander
The helms o' th' state, who care for you like fathers,
When you curse them as enemies.

1 CITIZEN Care for us! True, indeed! They ne'er car'd for us yet. Suffer us to famish, and their storehouses cramm'd with grain; make edicts for usury, to support usurers; repeal daily any wholesome act established against the rich, and provide more piercing statutes daily to chain up and restrain the poor. If the wars eat us not up, they will; and there's all the love they bear us.

MENENIUS Either you must
Confess yourselves wondrous malicious,
Or be accus'd of folly. I shall tell you
A pretty tale. It may be you have heard it;
But, since it serves my purpose, I will venture
To stale't a little more.

1 CITIZEN Well, I'll hear it, sir; yet you must not think to fob off our disgrace with a tale. But, an't please you, deliver.

MENENIUS There was a time when all the body's members
Rebell'd against the belly; thus accus'd it:
That only like a gulf it did remain
I' th' midst o' th' body, idle and unactive,
Still cupboarding the viand, never bearing
Like labour with the rest; where th' other instruments
Did see and hear, devise, instruct, walk, feel,
And, mutually participate, did minister
Unto the appetite and affection common
Of the whole body. The belly answer'd –

1 CITIZEN Well, sir, what answer made the belly?

MENENIUS Sir, I shall tell you. With a kind of smile,
Which ne'er came from the lungs, but even thus –
For look you, I may make the belly smile
As well as speak – it tauntingly replied
To th' discontented members, the mutinous parts
That envied his receipt; even so most fitly
As you malign our senators for that
They are not such as you.

1 CITIZEN Your belly's answer – What?
The kingly crowned head, the vigilant eye,
The counsellor heart, the arm our soldier,
Our steed the leg, the tongue our trumpeter,
With other muniments and petty helps
Is this our fabric, if that they –

MENENIUS What then?
Fore me, this fellow speaks! What then? What then?

1 CITIZEN Should by the cormorant belly be restrain'd,
Who is the sink o' th' body –

MENENIUS Well, what then?

1 CITIZEN The former agents, if they did complain,
What could the belly answer?

MENENIUS I will tell you;
If you'll bestow a small – of what you have little –
Patience awhile, you'st hear the belly's answer.

1 CITIZEN Y'are long about it.

MENENIUS Note me this, good friend:
Your most grave belly was deliberate,
Not rash like his accusers, and thus answered.
'True is it, my incorporate friends,' quoth he
'That I receive the general food at first
Which you do live upon; and fit it is,
Because I am the storehouse and the shop
Of the whole body. But, if you do remember,
I send it through the rivers of your blood,
Even to the court, the heart, to th' seat o' th' brain;
And, through the cranks and offices of man,
The strongest nerves and small inferior veins
From me receive that natural competency
Whereby they live. And though that all at once
You, my good friends' – this says the belly; mark me.

1 CITIZEN Ay, sir; well, well.

MENENIUS 'Though all at once cannot
See what I do deliver out to each,
Yet I can make my audit up, that all

From me do back receive the flour of all,
And leave me but the bran.' What say you to't?

1 CITIZEN It was an answer. How apply you this?

MENENIUS The senators of Rome are this good belly,
And you the mutinous members; for, examine
Their counsels and their cares, digest things rightly
Touching the weal o' th' common, you shall find
No public benefit which you receive
But it proceeds or comes from them to you,
And no way from yourselves. What do you think,
You, the great toe of this assembly?

1 CITIZEN I the great toe? Why the great toe?

MENENIUS For that, being one o' th' lowest, basest, poorest,
Of this most wise rebellion, thou goest foremost.
Thou rascal, that art worst in blood to run,
Lead'st first to win some vantage.
But make you ready your stiff bats and clubs.
Rome and her rats are at the point of battle;
The one side must have bale.

Enter CAIUS MARCIUS.

Hail, noble Marcius!

MARCIUS Thanks. What's the matter, you dissentious rogues
That, rubbing the poor itch of your opinion,
Make yourselves scabs?

1 CITIZEN We have ever your good word.

MARCIUS He that will give good words to thee will flatter
Beneath abhorring. What would you have, you curs,
That like nor peace nor war? The one affrights you,
The other makes you proud. He that trusts to you,
Where he should find you lions, finds you hares;
Where foxes, geese; you are no surer, no,
Than is the coal of fire upon the ice
Or hailstone in the sun. Your virtue is
To make him worthy whose offence subdues him,
And curse that justice did it. Who deserves greatness
Deserves your hate; and your affections are
A sick man's appetite, who desires most that
Which would increase his evil. He that depends
Upon your favours swims with fins of lead,
And hews down oaks with rushes. Hang ye! Trust ye?
With every minute you do change a mind
And call him noble that was now your hate,
Him vile that was your garland. What's the matter
That in these several places of the city
You cry against the noble Senate, who,
Under the gods, keep you in awe, which else
Would feed on one another? What's their seeking?

MENENIUS For corn at their own rates, whereof they say
The city is well stor'd.

MARCIUS Hang 'em! They say!
They'll sit by th' fire and presume to know
What's done i' th' Capitol, who's like to rise,
Who thrives and who declines; side factions, and give out
Conjectural marriages, making parties strong,
And feebling such as stand not in their liking
Below their cobbled shoes. They say there's grain enough!
Would the nobility lay aside their ruth
And let me use my sword, I'd make a quarry
With thousands of these quarter'd slaves, as high
As I could pick my lance.

MENENIUS Nay, these are almost thoroughly persuaded;
For though abundantly they lack discretion,
Yet are they passing cowardly. But, I beseech you,
What says the other troop?

MARCIUS They are dissolv'd. Hang 'em!
They said they were an-hungry; sigh'd forth proverbs –
That hunger broke stone walls, that dogs must eat,
That meat was made for mouths, that the gods sent not
Corn for the rich men only. With these shreds
They vented their complainings; which being answer'd,
And a petition granted them – a strange one,
To break the heart of generosity
And make bold power look pale – they threw their caps
As they would hang them on the horns o' th' moon,
Shouting their emulation.

MENENIUS What is granted them?

MARCIUS Five tribunes, to defend their vulgar wisdoms,
Of their own choice. One's Junius Brutus –
Sicinius Velutus, and I know not. 'Sdeath!
The rabble should have first unroof'd the city
Ere so prevail'd with me; it will in time
Win upon power and throw forth greater themes
For insurrection's arguing.

MENENIUS This is strange.
MARCIUS Go get you home, you fragments.

Enter a Messenger, hastily.

MESSENGER Where's Caius Marcius?
MARCIUS Here. What's the matter?
MESSENGER The news is, sir, the Volsces are in arms.
MARCIUS I am glad on't; then we shall ha' means to vent
Our musty superfluity. See, our best elders.

Enter COMINIUS, TITUS LARTIUS, with other Senators; JUNIUS BRUTUS and SICINIUS VELUTUS.

1 SENATOR Marcius, 'tis true that you have lately told us:
The Volsces are in arms.
MARCIUS They have a leader,
Tullus Aufidius, that will put you to't.
I sin in envying his nobility;
And were I anything but what I am,
I would wish me only he.
COMINIUS You have fought together?
MARCIUS Were half to half the world by th' ears, and he
Upon my party, I'd revolt, to make
Only my wars with him. He is a lion
That I am proud to hunt.
1 SENATOR Then, worthy Marcius,
Attend upon Cominius to these wars.
COMINIUS It is your former promise.
MARCIUS Sir, it is;
And I am constant. Titus Lartius, thou
Shalt see me once more strike at Tullus' face.
What, art thou stiff? Stand'st out?
LARTIUS No, Caius, Marcius;
I'll lean upon one crutch and fight with t'other
Ere stay behind this business.
MENENIUS O, true bred!
1 SENATOR Your company to th' Capitol; where, I know,
Our greatest friends attend us.
LARTIUS [*To Cominius*] Lead you on.
[*To Marcius*] Follow Cominius; we must follow you;
Right worthy you priority.
COMINIUS Noble Marcius!
1 SENATOR [*To the Citizens*] Hence to your homes; be gone.
MARCIUS Nay, let them follow.
The Volsces have much corn: take these rats thither
To gnaw their garners. Worshipful mutineers,
Your valour puts well forth; pray follow.

[*Citizens steal away. Exeunt all but Sicinius and Brutus.*

SICINIUS Was ever man so proud as is this Marcius?
BRUTUS He has no equal.
SICINIUS When we were chosen tribunes for the people –
BRUTUS Mark'd you his lip and eyes?
SICINIUS Nay, but his taunts!
BRUTUS Being mov'd, he will not spare to gird the gods.
SICINIUS Bemock the modest moon.
BRUTUS The present wars devour him! He is grown
Too proud to be so valiant.
SICINIUS Such a nature,
Tickled with good success, disdains the shadow
Which he treads on at noon. But I do wonder
His insolence can brook to be commanded
Under Cominius.
BRUTUS Fame, at the which he aims –
In whom already he is well grac'd – cannot
Better be held nor more attain'd than by
A place below the first; for what miscarries
Shall be the general's fault, though he perform
To th' utmost of a man, and giddy censure
Will then cry out of Marcius 'O, if he
Had borne the business!'
SICINIUS Besides, if things go well,
Opinion, that so sticks on Marcius, shall
Of his demerits rob Cominius.
BRUTUS Come.
Half all Cominius' honours are to Marcius,
Though Marcius earn'd them not; and all his faults
To Marcius shall be honours, though indeed
In aught he merit not.
SICINIUS Let's hence and hear
How the dispatch is made, and in what fashion,
More than his singularity, he goes
Upon this present action.
BRUTUS Let's along. [*Exeunt.*

SCENE II. *Corioli. The Senate House.*

Enter TULLUS AUFIDIUS with Senators of Corioli.

1 SENATOR So, your opinion is, Aufidius,
That they of Rome are ent'red in our counsels
And know how we proceed.
AUFIDIUS Is it not yours?
What ever have been thought on in this state
That could be brought to bodily act ere Rome
Had circumvention? 'Tis not four days gone
Since I heard thence; these are the words – I think
I have the letter here; yes, here it is:
[*Reads*] 'They have press'd a power, but it is not known
Whether for east or west. The dearth is great;
The people mutinous; and it is rumour'd,

Cominius, Marcius your old enemy,
Who is of Rome worse hated than of you,
And Titus Lartius, a most valiant Roman,
These three lead on this preparation
Whither 'tis bent. Most likely 'tis for you;
Consider of it.'

1 SENATOR Our army's in the field;
We never yet made doubt but Rome was ready
To answer us.

AUFIDIUS Nor did you think it folly
To keep your great pretences veil'd till when
They needs must show themselves; which in the hatching,
It seem'd, appear'd to Rome. By the discovery
We shall be short'ned in our aim, which was
To take in many towns ere almost Rome
Should know we were afoot.

2 SENATOR Noble Aufidius,
Take your commission; hie you to your bands;
Let us alone to guard Corioli.
If they set down before's, for the remove
Bring up your army; but I think you'll find
Th'have not prepar'd for us.

AUFIDIUS O, doubt not that!
I speak from certainties. Nay more,
Some parcels of their power are forth already,
And only hitherward. I leave your honours.
If we and Caius Marcius chance to meet,
'Tis sworn between us we shall ever strike
Till one can do no more.

ALL The gods assist you!

AUFIDIUS And keep your honours safe!

1 SENATOR Farewell.

2 SENATOR Farewell.

ALL Farewell. [*Exeunt.*

SCENE III. *Rome. Marcius' house.*

Enter VOLUMNIA, and VIRGILIA, mother and wife to Marcius; they set them down on two low stools and sew.

VOLUMNIA I pray you, daughter, sing, or express yourself in a more comfortable sort. If my son were my husband, I should freelier rejoice in that absence wherein he won honour than in the embracements of his bed where he would show most love. When yet he was but tender-bodied, and the only son of my womb; when youth with comeliness pluck'd all gaze his way; when, for a day of kings' entreaties, a mother should not sell him an hour from her beholding; I, considering how honour would become such a person – that it was no better than picture-like to hang by th' wall, if renown made it not stir – was pleas'd to let him seek danger where he was like to find fame. To a cruel war I sent him, from whence he return'd his brows bound with oak. I tell thee, daughter, I sprang not more in joy at first hearing he was a man-child than now in first seeing he had proved himself a man.

VIRGILIA But had he died in the business, madam, how then?

VOLUMNIA Then his good report should have been my son; I therein would have found issue. Hear me profess sincerely: had I a dozen sons, each in my love alike, and none less dear than thine and my good Marcius, I had rather had eleven die nobly for their country than one voluptuously surfeit out of action.

Enter a Gentlewoman.

GENTLEWOMAN Madam, the Lady Valeria is come to visit you.

VIRGILIA Beseech you give me leave to retire myself.

VOLUMNIA Indeed you shall not.
Methinks I hear hither your husband's drum;
See him pluck Aufidius down by th' hair;
As children from a bear, the Volsces shunning him.
Methinks I see him stamp thus, and call thus:
'Come on, you cowards! You were got in fear,
Though you were born in Rome'. His bloody brow
With his mail'd hand then wiping, forth he goes,
Like to a harvest-man that's task'd to mow
Or all or lose his hire.

VIRGILIA His bloody brow? O Jupiter, no blood!

VOLUMNIA Away, you fool! It more becomes a man
Than gilt his trophy. The breasts of Hecuba,
When she did suckle Hector, look'd not lovelier
Than Hector's forehead when it spit forth blood
At Grecian sword, contemning. Tell Valeria
We are fit to bid her welcome. [*Exit Gentlewoman.*

VIRGILIA Heavens bless my lord from fell Aufidius!

VOLUMNIA He'll beat Aufidius' head below his knee
And tread upon his neck.

Re-enter Gentlewoman, with VALERIA and an Usher.

VALERIA My ladies both, good day to you.

VOLUMNIA Sweet madam!

VIRGILIA I am glad to see your ladyship.

VALERIA How do you both? You are manifest housekeepers. What are you sewing here? A fine spot, in good faith. How does your little son?

VIRGILIA I thank your ladyship; well, good madam.

VOLUMNIA He had rather see the swords and hear a drum than look upon his schoolmaster.

VALERIA O' my word, the father's son! I'll swear 'tis a very pretty boy. O' my troth, I look'd upon him a Wednesday half an hour together; has such a confirm'd countenance! I saw him run after a gilded butterfly; and when he caught it he let it go again, and after it again, and over and over he comes, and up again, catch'd it again; or whether his fall enrag'd him, or how 'twas, he did so set his teeth and tear it. O, I warrant, how he mammock'd it!

VOLUMNIA One on's father's moods.

VALERIA Indeed, la, 'tis a noble child.

VIRGILIA A crack, madam.

VALERIA Come, lay aside your stitchery; I must have you play the idle huswife with me this afternoon.

VIRGILIA No, good madam; I will not out of doors.

VALERIA Not out of doors!

VOLUMNIA She shall, she shall.

VIRGILIA Indeed, no, by your patience; I'll not over the threshold till my lord return from the wars.

VALERIA Fie, you confine yourself most unreasonably; come, you must go visit the good lady that lies in.

VIRGILIA I will wish her speedy strength, and visit her with my prayers; but I cannot go thither.

VOLUMNIA Why, I pray you?

VIRGILIA 'Tis not to save labour, nor that I want love.

VALERIA You would be another Penelope; yet they say all the yarn she spun in Ulysses' absence did but fill Ithaca full of moths. Come, I would your cambric were sensible as your finger, that you might leave pricking it for pity. Come, you shall go with us.

VIRGILIA No, good madam, pardon me; indeed I will not forth.

VALERIA In truth, la, go with me; and I'll tell you excellent news of your husband.

VIRGILIA O, good madam, there can be none yet.

VALERIA Verily, I do not jest with you; there came news from him last night.

VIRGILIA Indeed, madam?

VALERIA In earnest, it's true; I heard a senator speak it. Thus it is: the Volsces have an army forth; against whom Cominius the general is gone, with one part of our Roman power. Your lord and Titus Lartius are set down before their city Corioli; they nothing doubt prevailing, and to make it brief wars. This is true, on mine honour; and so, I pray, go with us.

VIRGILIA Give me excuse, good madam; I will obey you in everything hereafter.

VOLUMNIA Let her alone, lady; as she is now, she will but disease our better mirth.

VALERIA In troth, I think she would. Fare you well, then. Come, good sweet lady. Prithee, Virgilia, turn thy solemness out o' door and go along with us.

VIRGILIA No, at a word, madam; indeed I must not. I wish you much mirth.

VALERIA Well then, farewell. *[Exeunt.*

SCENE IV. *Before Corioli.*

Enter MARCIUS, TITUS LARTIUS, with drum and colours, with Captains and Soldiers. To them a Messenger.

MARCIUS Yonder comes news; a wager – they have met.
LARTIUS My horse to yours – no.
MARCIUS 'Tis done.
LARTIUS Agreed.
MARCIUS Say, has our general met the enemy?
MESSENGER They lie in view, but have not spoke as yet.
LARTIUS So, the good horse is mine.
MARCIUS I'll buy him of you.
LARTIUS No, I'll nor sell nor give him; lend you him I will
For half a hundred years. Summon the town.
MARCIUS How far off lie these armies?
MESSENGER Within this mile and half.
MARCIUS Then shall we hear their 'larum, and they ours.
Now, Mars, I prithee, make us quick in work,
That we with smoking swords may march from hence
To help our fielded friends! Come, blow thy blast.

They sound a parley. Enter two Senators with Others, on the walls of Corioli.

Tullus Aufidius, is he within your walls?
1 SENATOR No, nor a man that fears you less than he:
That's lesser than a little. *[Drum afar off]* Hark, our drums
Are bringing forth our youth. We'll break our walls
Rather than they shall pound us up; our gates,
Which yet seem shut, we have but pinn'd with rushes;
They'll open of themselves. *[Alarum far off]* Hark you far off!
There is Aufidius. List what work he makes
Amongst your cloven army.
MARCIUS O, they are at it!
LARTIUS Their noise be our instruction. Ladders, ho!

Enter the army of the Volsces.

MARCIUS They fear us not, but issue forth their city.
Now put your shields before your hearts, and fight
With hearts more proof than shields. Advance, brave Titus.
They do disdain us much beyond our thoughts,
Which makes me sweat with wrath. Come on, my fellows.
He that retires, I'll take him for a Volsce,
And he shall feel mine edge.

Alarum. The Romans are beat back to their trenches. Re-enter MARCIUS, cursing.

MARCIUS All the contagion of the south light on you,
You shames of Rome! you herd of – Boils and plagues
Plaster you o'er, that you may be abhorr'd
Farther than seen, and one infect another
Against the wind a mile! You souls of geese
That bear the shapes of men, how have you run
From slaves that apes would beat! Pluto and hell!
All hurt behind! Backs red, and faces pale
With flight and agued fear! Mend and charge home,
Or, by the fires of heaven, I'll leave the foe
And make my wars on you. Look to't. Come on;
If you'll stand fast we'll beat them to their wives,
As they us to our trenches. Follow me.

Another alarum. The Volsces fly, and Marcius follows them to the gates.

So, now the gates are ope; now prove good seconds;
'Tis for the followers fortune widens them,
Not for the fliers. Mark me, and do the like.
[*Marcius enters the gates.*

1 SOLDIER Fool-hardiness; not I.
2 SOLDIER Not I. [*Marcius is shut in.*
1 SOLDIER See, they have shut him in.
ALL To th' pot, I warrant him.
[*Alarum continues.*

Re-enter TITUS LARTIUS.

LARTIUS What is become of Marcius?
ALL Slain, sir, doubtless.
1 SOLDIER Following the fliers at the very heels,
With them he enters; who, upon the sudden,
Clapp'd to their gates. He is himself alone,
To answer all the city.
LARTIUS O noble fellow!
Who sensibly outdares his senseless sword,
And when it bows stand'st up. Thou art left, Marcius;
A carbuncle entire, as big as thou art,
Were not so rich a jewel. Thou wast a soldier
Even to Cato's wish, not fierce and terrible
Only in strokes; but with thy grim looks and
The thunder-like percussion of thy sounds
Thou mad'st thine enemies shake, as if the world
Were feverous and did tremble.

Re-enter MARCIUS, bleeding, assaulted by the Enemy.

1 SOLDIER Look, sir.
LARTIUS O, 'tis Marcius!
Let's fetch him off, or make remain alike.
[*They fight, and all enter the city.*

SCENE V. *Within Corioli. A street.*

Enter certain Romans, with spoils.

1 ROMAN This will I carry to Rome.
2 ROMAN And I this.
3 ROMAN A murrain on't! I took this for silver.
[*Alarum continues still afar off.*

Enter MARCIUS and TITUS LARTIUS with a trumpetor.

MARCIUS See here these movers that do prize their hours
At a crack'd drachma! Cushions, leaden spoons,
Irons of a doit, doublets that hangmen would
Bury with those that wore them, these base slaves,
Ere yet the fight be done, pack up. Down with them! [*Exeunt pillagers.*
And hark, what noise the general makes! To him!
There is the man of my soul's hate, Aufidius,
Piercing our Romans; then, valiant Titus, take
Convenient numbers to make good the city;
Whilst I, with those that have the spirit, will haste
To help Cominius.
LARTIUS Worthy sir, thou bleed'st;
Thy exercise hath been too violent
For a second course of fight.
MARCIUS Sir, praise me not;
My work hath yet not warm'd me. Fare you well;
The blood I drop is rather physical
Than dangerous to me. To Aufidius thus
I will appear, and fight.
LARTIUS Now the fair goddess, Fortune,
Fall deep in love with thee, and her great charms
Misguide thy opposers' swords! Bold gentleman,
Prosperity be thy page!

MARCIUS Thy friend no less
Than those she placeth highest! So farewell.
LARTIUS Thou worthiest Marcius!
[*Exit Marcius*.
Go sound thy trumpet in the market-place;
Call thither all the officers o' th' town,
Where they shall know our mind. Away!
[*Exeunt*.

SCENE VI. *Near the camp of Cominius.*

Enter COMINIUS, as it were in retire, with Soldiers.

COMINIUS Breathe you, my friends. Well fought; we are come off
Like Romans, neither foolish in our stands
Nor cowardly in retire. Believe me, sirs,
We shall be charg'd again. Whiles we have struck,
By interims and conveying gusts we have heard
The charges of our friends. The Roman gods,
Lead their successes as we wish our own,
That both our powers, with smiling fronts encount'ring,
May give you thankful sacrifice!

Enter a Messenger.

Thy news?
MESSENGER The citizens of Corioli have issued
And given to Lartius and to Marcius battle;
I saw our party to their trenches driven,
And then I came away.
COMINIUS Though thou speak'st truth,
Methinks thou speak'st not well. How long is't since?
MESSENGER Above an hour, my lord.
COMINIUS 'Tis not a mile; briefly we heard their drums.
How couldst thou in a mile confound an hour,
And bring thy news so late?
MESSENGER Spies of the Volsces
Held me in chase, that I was forc'd to wheel
Three or four miles about; else had I, sir,
Half an hour since brought my report.

Enter MARCIUS.

COMINIUS Who's yonder
That does appear as he were flay'd? O gods!
He has the stamp of Marcius, and I have
Before-time seen him thus.
MARCIUS Come I too late?
COMINIUS The shepherd knows not thunder from a tabor
More than I know the sound of Marcius' tongue
From every meaner man.
MARCIUS Come I too late?
COMINIUS Ay, if you come not in the blood of others,
But mantled in your own.
MARCIUS O! let me clip ye
In arms as sound as when I woo'd, in heart
As merry as when our nuptial day was done,
And tapers burn'd to bedward.
COMINIUS Flower of warriors,
How is't with Titus Lartius?
MARCIUS As with a man busied about decrees:
Condemning some to death and some to exile;
Ransoming him or pitying, threat'ning th' other;
Holding Corioli in the name of Rome
Even like a fawning greyhound in the leash,
To let him slip at will.
COMINIUS Where is that slave
Which told me they had beat you to your trenches?
Where is he? Call him hither.
MARCIUS Let him alone;
He did inform the truth. But for our gentlemen,
The common file – a plague! tribunes for them!
The mouse ne'er shunn'd the cat as they did budge
From rascals worse than they.
COMINIUS But how prevail'd you?
MARCIUS Will the time serve to tell? I do not think.
Where is the enemy? Are you lords o' th' field?
If not, why cease you till you are so?
COMINIUS Marcius,
We have at disadvantage fought, and did
Retire to win our purpose.
MARCIUS How lies their battle? Know you on which side
They have plac'd their men of trust?
COMINIUS As I guess, Marcius,
Their bands i' th' vaward are the Antiates,
Of their best trust; o'er them Aufidius,
Their very heart of hope.
MARCIUS I do beseech you,
By all the battles wherein we have fought,
By th' blood we have shed together, by th' vows
We have made to endure friends, that you directly
Set me against Aufidius and his Antiates;
And that you not delay the present, but,
Filling the air with swords advanc'd and darts,
We prove this very hour.
COMINIUS Though I could wish
You were conducted to a gentle bath
And balms applied to you, yet dare I never
Deny your asking: take your choice of those
That best can aid your action.
MARCIUS Those are they
That most are willing. If any such be here –
As it were sin to doubt – that love this painting
Wherein you see me smear'd; if any fear
Lesser his person than an ill report;

If any think brave death outweighs bad life
And that his country's dearer than himself;
Let him alone, or so many so minded,
Wave thus to express his disposition,
And follow Marcius.

[They all shout and wave their swords, take him up in their arms and cast up their caps.

O, me alone! Make you a sword of me?
If these shows be not outward, which of you
But is four Volsces? None of you but is
Able to bear against the great Aufidius
A shield as hard as his. A certain number,
Though thanks to all, must I select from all; the rest
Shall bear the business in some other fight,
As cause will be obey'd. Please you to march;
And four shall quickly draw out my command,
Which men are best inclin'd.

COMINIUS March on, my fellows;
Make good this ostentation, and you shall
Divide in all with us. *[Exeunt.*

SCENE VII. *The gates of Corioli.*

TITUS LARTIUS, having set a guard upon Corioli, going with drum and trumpet toward Cominius and Caius Marcius, enters with a Lieutenant, other Soldiers, and a Scout.

LARTIUS So, let the ports be guarded; keep your duties
As I have set them down. If I do send, dispatch
Those centuries to our aid; the rest will serve
For a short holding. If we lose the field
We cannot keep the town.

LIEUTENANT Fear not our care, sir.

LARTIUS Hence, and shut your gates upon's.
Our guider, come; to th' Roman camp conduct us. *[Exeunt.*

SCENE VIII. *A field of battle between the Roman and the Volscian camps.*

Alarum, as in battle. Enter MARCIUS and AUFIDIUS at several doors.

MARCIUS I'll fight with none but thee, for I do hate thee
Worse than a promise-breaker.

AUFIDIUS We hate alike:
Not Afric owns a serpent I abhor
More than thy fame and envy. Fix thy foot.

MARCIUS Let the first budger die the other's slave,
And the gods doom him after!

AUFIDIUS If I fly, Marcius,
Halloa me like a hare.

MARCIUS Within these three hours, Tullus,
Alone I fought in your Corioli walls,
And made what work I pleas'd. 'Tis not my blood
Wherein thou seest me mask'd. For thy revenge
Wrench up thy power to th' highest.

AUFIDIUS Wert thou the Hector
That was the whip of your bragg'd progeny,
Thou shouldst not scape me here.

[Here they fight, and certain Volsces come in the aid of Aufidius. Marcius fights till they be driven in breathless.

Officious, and not valiant, you have sham'd me
In your condemned seconds. *[Exeunt.*

SCENE IX. *The Roman camp.*

Flourish. Alarum. A retreat is sounded. Enter, at one door, COMINIUS with the Romans; at another door, MARCIUS, with his arm in a scarf.

COMINIUS If I should tell thee o'er this thy day's work,
Thou't not believe thy deeds; but I'll report it
Where senators shall mingle tears with smiles;
Where great patricians shall attend, and shrug,
I' th' end admire; where ladies shall be frighted
And, gladly quak'd, hear more; where the dull tribunes,
That with the fusty plebeians hate thine honours,
Shall say against their hearts 'We thank the gods
Our Rome hath such a soldier'.
Yet cam'st thou to a morsel of this feast,
Having fully din'd before.

Enter TITUS LARTIUS, with his Power, from the pursuit.

LARTIUS O General,
Here is the steed, we the caparison.
Hadst thou beheld –

MARCIUS Pray now, no more; my mother,
Who has a charter to extol her blood,
When she does praise me grieves me. I have done
As you have done – that's what I can; induc'd
As you have been – that's for my country.
He that has but effected his good will
Hath overta'en mine act.

COMINIUS You shall not be
The grave of your deserving; Rome must know
The value of her own. 'Twere a concealment
Worse than a theft, no less than a traducement,
To hide your doings and to silence that
Which, to the spire and top of praises vouch'd,
Would seem but modest. Therefore, I beseech you,

In sign of what you are, not to reward
What you have done, before our army hear me.
MARCIUS I have some wounds upon me, and they smart
To hear themselves rememb'red.
COMINIUS Should they not,
Well might they fester 'gainst ingratitude
And tent themselves with death. Of all the horses –
Whereof we have ta'en good, and good store – of all
The treasure in this field achiev'd and city,
We render you the tenth; to be ta'en forth
Before the common distribution at
Your only choice.
MARCIUS I thank you, General,
But cannot make my heart consent to take
A bribe to pay my sword. I do refuse it,
And stand upon my common part with those
That have beheld the doing.
[A long flourish. They all cry 'Marcius, Marcius!' cast up their caps and lances. Cominius and Lartius stand bare.
May these same instruments which you profane
Never sound more! When drums and trumpets shall
I' th' field prove flatterers, let courts and cities be
Made all of false-fac'd soothing. When steel grows
Soft as the parasite's silk, let him be made
An overture for th' wars. No more, I say.
For that I have not wash'd my nose that bled,
Or foil'd some debile wretch, which without note
Here's many else have done, you shout me forth
In acclamations hyperbolical,
As if I lov'd my little should be dieted
In praises sauc'd with lies.
COMINIUS Too modest are you;
More cruel to your good report than grateful
To us that give you truly. By your patience,
If 'gainst yourself you be incens'd, we'll put you –
Like one that means his proper harm – in manacles,
Then reason safely with you. Therefore be it known,
As to us, to all the world, that Caius Marcius
Wears this war's garland; in token of the which,
My noble steed, known to the camp, I give him,
With all his trim belonging; and from this time,
For what he did before Corioli, call him
With all th' applause and clamour of the host,
Caius Marcius Coriolanus.
Bear th' addition nobly ever!
[Flourish. Trumpets sound, and drums.
ALL Caius Marcius Coriolanus!
CORIOLANUS I will go wash;
And when my face is fair you shall perceive
Whether I blush or no. Howbeit, I thank you;
I mean to stride your steed, and at all times
To undercrest your good addition
To th' fairness of my power.
COMINIUS So, to our tent;
Where, ere we do repose us, we will write
To Rome of our success. You, Titus Lartius,
Must to Corioli back. Send us to Rome
The best, with whom we may articulate
For their own good and ours.
LARTIUS I shall, my lord.
CORIOLANUS The gods begin to mock me. I, that now
Refus'd most princely gifts, am bound to beg
Of my Lord General.
COMINIUS Take't – 'tis yours; what is't?
CORIOLANUS I sometime lay here in Corioli
At a poor man's house; he us'd me kindly.
He cried to me; I saw him prisoner;
But then Aufidius was within my view,
And wrath o'erwhelm'd my pity. I request you
To give my poor host freedom.
COMINIUS O, well begg'd!
Were he the butcher of my son, he should
Be free as is the wind. Deliver him, Titus.
LARTIUS Marcius, his name?
CORIOLANUS By Jupiter, forgot!
I am weary; yea, my memory is tir'd.
Have we no wine here?
COMINIUS Go we to our tent.
The blood upon your visage dries; 'tis time
It should be look'd to. Come. *[Exeunt.*

SCENE X. *The camp of the Volsces.*

A flourish. Cornets. Enter TULLUS AUFIDIUS bloody, with two or three Soldiers.

AUFIDIUS The town is ta'en.
1 SOLDIER 'Twill be deliver'd back on good condition.
AUFIDIUS Condition!
I would I were a Roman; for I cannot,
Being a Volsce, be that I am. Condition?
What good condition can a treaty find
I' th' part that is at mercy? Five times, Marcius,
I have fought with thee; so often hast thou beat me;
And wouldst do so, I think, should we encounter
As often as we eat. By th' elements,
If e'er again I meet him beard to beard,

He's mine or I am his. Mine emulation
Hath not that honour in't it had; for where
I thought to crush him in an equal force,
True sword to sword, I'll potch at him some
way,
Or wrath or craft may get him.

1 SOLDIER He's the devil.

AUFIDIUS Bolder, though not so subtle. My
valour's poison'd
With only suff'ring stain by him; for him
Shall fly out of itself. Nor sleep nor sanctuary,
Being naked, sick, nor fane nor Capitol,
The prayers of priests nor times of sacrifice,
Embarquements all of fury, shall lift up
Their rotten privilege and custom 'gainst
My hate to Marcius. Where I find him, were it
At home, upon my brother's guard, even there,
Against the hospitable canon, would I
Wash my fierce hand in's heart. Go you to th'
city;
Learn how 'tis held, and what they are that must
Be hostages for Rome.

1 SOLDIER Will not you go?

AUFIDIUS I am attended at the cypress grove; I
pray you –
'Tis south the city mills – bring me word thither
How the world goes, that to the pace of it
I may spur on my journey.

1 SOLDIER I shall, sir.

[Exeunt.

ACT TWO

SCENE I. *Rome. A public place.*

Enter MENENIUS, with the two Tribunes of the people, SICINIUS and BRUTUS.

MENENIUS The augurer tells me we shall have news to-night.

BRUTUS Good or bad?

MENENIUS Not according to the prayer of the people, for they love not Marcius.

SICINIUS Nature teaches beasts to know their friends.

MENENIUS Pray you, who does the wolf love?

SICINIUS The lamb.

MENENIUS Ay, to devour him, as the hungry plebeians would the noble Marcius.

BRUTUS He's a lamb indeed, that baes like a bear.

MENENIUS He's a bear indeed, that lives like a lamb. You two are old men; tell me one thing that I shall ask you.

BOTH TRIBUNES Well, sir.

MENENIUS In what enormity is Marcius poor in that you two have not in abundance?

BRUTUS He's poor in no one fault, but stor'd with all.

SICINIUS Especially in pride.

BRUTUS And topping all others in boasting.

MENENIUS This is strange now. Do you two know how you are censured here in the city – I mean of us o' th' right-hand file? Do you?

BOTH TRIBUNES Why, how are we censur'd?

MENENIUS Because you talk of pride now – will you not be angry?

BOTH TRIBUNES Well, well, sir, well.

MENENIUS Why, 'tis no great matter; for a very little thief of occasion will rob you of a great deal of patience. Give your dispositions the reins, and be angry at your pleasures – at the least, if you take it as a pleasure to you in being so. You blame Marcius for being proud?

BRUTUS We do it not alone, sir.

MENENIUS I know you can do very little alone; for your helps are many, or else your actions would grow wondrous single: your abilities are too infant-like for doing much alone. You talk of pride. O that you could turn your eyes toward the napes of your necks, and make but an interior survey of your good selves! O that you could!

BOTH What then, sir?

MENENIUS Why, then you should discover a brace of unmeriting, proud, violent, testy magistrates – alias fools – as any in Rome.

SICINIUS Menenius, you are known well enough too.

MENENIUS I am known to be a humorous patrician, and one that loves a cup of hot wine with not a drop of allaying Tiber in't; said to be something imperfect in favouring the first complaint, hasty and tinder-like upon too trivial motion; one that converses more with the buttock of the night than with the forehead of the morning. What I think I utter, and spend my malice in my breath. Meeting two such wealsmen as you are – I cannot call you Lycurguses – if the drink you give me touch my palate adversely, I make a crooked face at it. I cannot say your worships have deliver'd the matter well, when I find the ass in compound with the major part of your syllables; and though I must be content to bear with those that say you are reverend grave men, yet they lie deadly that tell you you have good faces. If you see this in the map of my microcosm, follows it that I am known well enough too? What harm can your bisson conspectuities glean out of this character, if I be known well enough too?

BRUTUS Come, sir, come, we know you well enough.

MENENIUS You know neither me, yourselves, nor any thing. You are ambitious for poor knaves' caps and legs; you wear out a good wholesome forenoon in hearing a cause between an orange-wife and a fosset-seller, and then rejourn the controversy of threepence to a second day of audience. When you are hearing a matter between party and party, if you chance to be pinch'd with the colic, you make faces like mummers, set up the bloody flag against all patience, and, in roaring for a chamber-pot, dismiss the controversy bleeding, the more entangled by your hearing. All the peace you make in their cause is calling both the parties knaves. You are a pair of strange ones.

BRUTUS Come, come, you are well understood to be a perfecter giber for the table than a necessary bencher in the Capitol.

MENENIUS Our very priests must become mockers, if they shall encounter such ridiculous subjects as you are. When you speak best unto the purpose, it is not worth the wagging of your beards; and your beards deserve not so honourable a grave as to stuff a botcher's cushion or to be entomb'd in an ass's pack-saddle. Yet you must be saying Marcius is proud; who, in a cheap estimation, is worth all your predecessors since Deucalion; though peradventure some of the best of 'em were hereditary hangmen. God-den to your worships. More of your conversation would infect my brain, being the herdsmen of the beastly plebeians. I will be bold to take my leave of you.

[*Brutus and Sicinius go aside.*

Enter VOLUMNIA, VIRGILIA, and VALERIA.

How now, my as fair as noble ladies – and the moon, were she earthly, no nobler – whither do you follow your eyes so fast?

VOLUMNIA Honourable Menenius, my boy Marcius approaches; for the love of Juno let's go.

MENENIUS Ha! Marcius coming home?

VOLUMNIA Ay, worthy Menenius, and with most prosperous approbation.

MENENIUS Take my cap, Jupiter, and I thank thee. Hoo! Marcius coming home!

VOLUMNIA, VIRGILIA Nay, 'tis true.

VOLUMNIA Look, here's a letter from him; the state hath another, his wife another; and I think there's one at home for you.

MENENIUS I will make my very house reel to-night. A letter for me?

VIRGILIA Yes, certain, there's a letter for you; I saw't.

MENENIUS A letter for me! It gives me an estate of seven years' health; in which time I will make a lip at the physician. The most sovereign prescription in Galen is but empiricutic and, to this preservative, of no better report than a horse-drench. Is he not wounded? He was wont to come home wounded.

VIRGILIA O, no, no, no.

VOLUMNIA O, he is wounded, I thank the gods for't.

MENENIUS So do I too, if it be not too much. Brings 'a victory in his pocket? The wounds become him.

VOLUMNIA On's brows, Menenius, he comes the third time home with the oaken garland.

MENENIUS Has he disciplin'd Aufidius soundly?

VOLUMNIA Titus Lartius writes they fought together, but Aufidius got off.

MENENIUS And 'twas time for him too, I'll warrant him that; an he had stay'd by him, I would not have been so fidius'd for all the chests in Corioli and the gold that's in them. Is the Senate possess'd of this?

VOLUMNIA Good ladies, let's go. Yes, yes, yes: the Senate has letters from the General, wherein he gives my son the whole name of the war; he hath in this action outdone his former deeds doubly.

VALERIA In troth, there's wondrous things spoke of him.

MENENIUS Wondrous! Ay, I warrant you, and not without his true purchasing.

VIRGILIA The gods grant them true!

VOLUMNIA True! pow, waw.

MENENIUS True! I'll be sworn they are true. Where is he wounded? [*To the Tribunes*] God save your good worships! Marcius is coming home; he has more cause to be proud. Where is he wounded?

VOLUMNIA I' th' shoulder and i' th' left arm; there will be large cicatrices to show the people when he shall stand for his place. He received in the repulse of Tarquin seven hurts i' th' body.

MENENIUS One i' th' neck and two i' th' thigh – there's nine that I know.

VOLUMNIA He had before this last expedition twenty-five wounds upon him.

MENENIUS Now it's twenty-seven; every gash was an enemy's grave. [*A shout and flourish*] Hark! the trumpets.

VOLUMNIA These are the ushers of Marcius.
Before him he carries noise, and behind him he
leaves tears;
Death, that dark spirit, in's nervy arm doth
lie,

Which, being advanc'd, declines, and then men
die.

A sennet. Trumpets sound. Enter COMINIUS the General, and TITUS LARTIUS; between them, CORIOLANUS, crown'd with an oaken garland; with Captains and Soldiers and a Herald.

HERALD Know, Rome, that all alone Marcius did
fight
Within Corioli gates, where he hath won,
With fame, a name to Caius Marcius; these
In honour follows Coriolanus.
Welcome to Rome, renowned Coriolanus!
[*Flourish.*

ALL Welcome to Rome, renowned Coriolanus!

CORIOLANUS No more of this, it does offend my
heart.
Pray now, no more.

COMINIUS Look, sir, your mother!

CORIOLANUS O,
You have, I know, petition'd all the gods
For my prosperity! [*Kneels.*

VOLUMNIA Nay, my good soldier, up;
My gentle Marcius, worthy Caius, and
By deed-achieving honour newly nam'd –
What is it? Coriolanus must I call thee?
But, O, thy wife!

CORIOLANUS My gracious silence, hail!
Wouldst thou have laugh'd had I come coffin'd
home,
That weep'st to see me triumph? Ah, my dear,
Such eyes the widows in Corioli wear,
And mothers that lack sons.

MENENIUS Now the gods crown thee!

CORIOLANUS And live you yet? [*To Valeria*] O
my sweet lady, pardon.

VOLUMNIA I know not where to turn.
O, welcome home! And welcome, General.
And y'are welcome all.

MENENIUS A hundred thousand welcomes. I
could weep
And I could laugh; I am light and heavy.
Welcome!
A curse begin at very root on's heart
That is not glad to see thee! You are three
That Rome should dote on; yet, by the faith of
men,
We have some old crab trees here at home that
will not
Be grafted to your relish. Yet welcome, warriors.
We call a nettle but a nettle, and
The faults of fools but folly.

COMINIUS Ever right.

CORIOLANUS Menenius ever, ever.

HERALD Give way there, and go on.

CORIOLANUS [*To his wife and mother*] Your
hand, and yours.
Ere in our own house I do shade my head,
The good patricians must be visited;
From whom I have receiv'd not only greetings,
But with them change of honours.

VOLUMNIA I have lived
To see inherited my very wishes,
And the buildings of my fancy; only
There's one thing wanting, which I doubt not
but
Our Rome will cast upon thee.

CORIOLANUS Know, good mother,
I had rather be their servant in my way
Than sway with them in theirs.

COMINIUS On, to the Capitol.

[*Flourish. Cornets. Exeunt in state, as before. Brutus and Sicinius come forward.*

BRUTUS All tongues speak of him and the bleared
sights
Are spectacled to see him. Your prattling nurse
Into a rapture lets her baby cry
While she chats him; the kitchen malkin pins
Her richest lockram 'bout her reechy neck,
Clamb'ring the walls to eye him; stalls, bulks,
windows,
Are smother'd up, leads fill'd and ridges hors'd
With variable complexions, all agreeing
In earnestness to see him. Seld-shown flamens
Do press among the popular throngs and puff
To win a vulgar station; our veil'd dames
Commit the war of white and damask in
Their nicely gawded cheeks to th' wanton spoil
Of Phoebus' burning kisses. Such a pother,
As if that whatsoever god who leads him
Were slily crept into his human powers,
And gave him graceful posture.

SICINIUS On the sudden
I warrant him consul.

BRUTUS Then our office may
During his power go sleep.

SICINIUS He cannot temp'rately transport his
honours
From where he should begin and end, but will
Lose those he hath won.

BRUTUS In that there's comfort.

SICINIUS Doubt not
The commoners, for whom we stand, but they
Upon their ancient malice will forget
With the least cause these his new honours;
which
That he will give them make I as little question
As he is proud to do't.

BRUTUS I heard him swear,
Were he to stand for consul, never would he
Appear i' th' market-place, nor on him put
The napless vesture of humility;
Nor, showing, as the manner is, his wounds

To th' people, beg their stinking breaths.

SICINIUS 'Tis right.

BRUTUS It was his word. O, he would miss it rather
Than carry it but by the suit of the gentry to him
And the desire of the nobles.

SICINIUS I wish no better
Than have him hold that purpose, and to put it
In execution.

BRUTUS 'Tis most like he will.

SICINIUS It shall be to him then as our good wills:
A sure destruction.

BRUTUS So it must fall out
To him or our authorities. For an end,
We must suggest the people in what hatred
He still hath held them; that to's power he would
Have made them mules, silenc'd their pleaders, and
Dispropertied their freedoms; holding them
In human action and capacity
Of no more soul nor fitness for the world
Than camels in their war, who have their provand
Only for bearing burdens, and sore blows
For sinking under them.

SICINIUS This, as you say, suggested
At some time when his soaring insolence
Shall touch the people – which time shall not want,
If he be put upon't, and that's as easy
As to set dogs on sheep – will be his fire
To kindle their dry stubble; and their blaze
Shall darken him for ever.

Enter a Messenger.

BRUTUS What's the matter?

MESSENGER You are sent for to the Capitol. 'Tis thought
That Marcius shall be consul.
I have seen the dumb men throng to see him and
The blind to hear him speak; matrons flung gloves,
Ladies and maids their scarfs and handkerchers,
Upon him as he pass'd; the nobles bended
As to Jove's statue, and the commons made
A shower and thunder with their caps and shouts.
I never saw the like.

BRUTUS Let's to the Capitol,
And carry with us ears and eyes for th' time,
But hearts for the event.

SICINIUS Have with you. [*Exeunt.*

SCENE II. *Rome. The Capitol.*

Enter two Officers, to lay cushions, as it were in the Capitol.

1 OFFICER Come, come, they are almost here. How many stand for consulships?

2 OFFICER Three, they say; but 'tis thought of every one Coriolanus will carry it.

1 OFFICER That's a brave fellow; but he's vengeance proud and loves not the common people.

2 OFFICER Faith, there have been many great men that have flatter'd the people, who ne'er loved them; and there be many that they have loved, they know not wherefore; so that, if they love they know not why, they hate upon no better a ground. Therefore, for Coriolanus neither to care whether they love or hate him manifests the true knowledge he has in their disposition, and out of his noble carelessness lets them plainly see't.

1 OFFICER If he did not care whether he had their love or no, he waved indifferently 'twixt doing them neither good nor harm; but he seeks their hate with greater devotion than they can render it him, and leaves nothing undone that may fully discover him their opposite. Now to seem to affect the malice and displeasure of the people is as bad as that which he dislikes – to flatter them for their love.

2 OFFICER He hath deserved worthily of his country; and his ascent is not by such easy degrees as those who, having been supple and courteous to the people, bonneted, without any further deed to have them at all, into their estimation and report; but he hath so planted his honours in their eyes and his actions in their hearts that for their tongues to be silent and not confess so much were a kind of ingrateful injury; to report otherwise were a malice that, giving itself the lie, would pluck reproof and rebuke from every ear that heard it.

1 OFFICER No more of him; he's a worthy man. Make way, they are coming.

A Sennet. Enter the Patricians and the Tribunes of the People, Lictors before them; CORIOLANUS, MENENIUS, COMINIUS the Consul. Sicinius and Brutus take their places by themselves. Coriolanus stands.

MENENIUS Having determin'd of the Volsces, and
To send for Titus Lartius, it remains,
As the main point of this our after-meeting,
To gratify his noble service that
Hath thus stood for his country. Therefore please you,
Most reverend and grave elders, to desire
The present consul and last general

In our well-found successes to report
A little of that worthy work perform'd
By Caius Marcius Coriolanus; whom
We met here both to thank and to remember
With honours like himself. [*Coriolanus sits.*

1 SENATOR Speak, good Cominius.
Leave nothing out for length, and make us think
Rather our state's defective for requital
Than we to stretch it out. Masters o' th' people,
We do request your kindest ears and, after,
Your loving motion toward the common body,
To yield what passes here.

SICINIUS We are convented
Upon a pleasing treaty, and have hearts
Inclinable to honour and advance
The theme of our assembly.

BRUTUS Which the rather
We shall be bless'd to do, if he remember
A kinder value of the people than
He hath hereto priz'd them at.

MENENIUS That's off, that's off;
I would you rather had been silent. Please you
To hear Cominius speak?

BRUTUS Most willingly.
But yet my caution was more pertinent
Than the rebuke you give it.

MENENIUS He loves your people;
But tie him not to be their bedfellow.
Worthy Cominius, speak.
[*Coriolanus rises, and offers to go away.*
Nay, keep your place.

1 SENATOR Sit, Coriolanus, never shame to hear
What you have nobly done.

CORIOLANUS Your Honours' pardon.
I had rather have my wounds to heal again
Than hear say how I got them.

BRUTUS Sir, I hope
My words disbench'd you not.

CORIOLANUS No, sir; yet oft,
When blows have made me stay, I fled from words.
You sooth'd not, therefore hurt not. But your people,
I love them as they weigh –

MENENIUS Pray now, sit down.

CORIOLANUS I had rather have one scratch my head i' th' sun
When the alarum were struck than idly sit
To hear my nothings monster'd. [*Exit.*

MENENIUS Masters of the people,
Your multiplying spawn how can he flatter –
That's thousand to one good one – when you now see
He had rather venture all his limbs for honour
Than one on's ears to hear it? Proceed, Cominius.

COMINIUS I shall lack voice; the deeds of Coriolanus
Should not be utter'd feebly. It is held
That valour is the chiefest virtue and
Most dignifies the haver. If it be,
The man I speak of cannot in the world
Be singly counterpois'd. At sixteen years,
When Tarquin made a head for Rome, he fought
Beyond the mark of others; our then Dictator,
Whom with all praise I point at, saw him fight
When with his Amazonian chin he drove
The bristled lips before him; he bestrid
An o'erpress'd Roman and i' th' consul's view
Slew three opposers; Tarquin's self he met,
And struck him on his knee. In that day's feats,
When he might act the woman in the scene,
He prov'd best man i' th' field, and for his meed
Was brow-bound with the oak. His pupil age
Man-ent'red thus, he waxed like a sea,
And in the brunt of seventeen battles since
He lurch'd all swords of the garland. For this last,
Before and in Corioli, let me say
I cannot speak him home. He stopp'd the fliers,
And by his rare example made the coward
Turn terror into sport; as weeds before
A vessel under sail, so men obey'd
And fell below his stem. His sword, death's stamp,
Where it did mark, it took; from face to foot
He was a thing of blood, whose every motion
Was tim'd with dying cries. Alone he ent'red
The mortal gate of th' city, which he painted
With shunless destiny; aidless came off,
And with a sudden re-enforcement struck
Corioli like a planet. Now all's his.
When by and by the din of war 'gan pierce
His ready sense, then straight his doubled spirit
Re-quick'ned what in flesh was fatigate,
And to the battle came he; where he did
Run reeking o'er the lives of men, as if
'Twere a perpetual spoil; and till we call'd
Both field and city ours he never stood
To ease his breast with panting.

MENENIUS Worthy man!

1 SENATOR He cannot but with measure fit the honours
Which we devise him.

COMINIUS Our spoils he kick'd at,
And look'd upon things precious as they were
The common muck of the world. He covets less
Than misery itself would give, rewards
His deeds with doing them, and is content
To spend the time to end it.

MENENIUS He's right noble;
Let him be call'd for.

1 SENATOR Call Coriolanus.

OFFICER He doth appear.

Re-enter CORIOLANUS.

MENENIUS The Senate, Coriolanus, are well
pleas'd
To make thee consul.

CORIOLANUS I do owe them still
My life and services.

MENENIUS It then remains
That you do speak to the people.

CORIOLANUS I do beseech you
Let me o'erleap that custom; for I cannot
Put on the gown, stand naked, and entreat them
For my wounds' sake to give their suffrage.
Please you
That I may pass this doing.

SICINIUS Sir, the people
Must have their voices; neither will they bate
One jot of ceremony.

MENENIUS Put them not to't.
Pray you go fit you to the custom, and
Take to you, as your predecessors have,
Your honour with your form.

CORIOLANUS It is a part
That I shall blush in acting, and might well
Be taken from the people.

BRUTUS Mark you that?

CORIOLANUS To brag unto them 'Thus I did, and
thus!'
Show them th' unaching scars which I should
hide,
As if I had receiv'd them for the hire
Of their breath only!

MENENIUS Do not stand upon't.
We recommend to you, Tribunes of the People,
Our purpose to them; and to our noble consul
Wish we all joy and honour.

SENATORS To Coriolanus come all joy and
honour!

[*Flourish. Cornets. Then exeunt all but Sicinius and Brutus.*

BRUTUS You see how he intends to use the
people.

SICINIUS May they perceive's intent! He will
require them
As if he did contemn what he requested
Should be in them to give.

BRUTUS Come, we'll inform them
Of our proceedings here. On th' marketplace
I know they do attend us. [*Exeunt.*

SCENE III. *Rome. The Forum.*

Enter seven or eight Citizens.

1 CITIZEN Once, if he do require our voices, we ought not to deny him.

2 CITIZEN We may, sir, if we will.

3 CITIZEN We have power in ourselves to do it, but it is a power that we have no power to do; for if he show us his wounds and tell us his deeds, we are to put our tongues into those wounds and speak for them; so, if he tell us his noble deeds, we must also tell him our noble acceptance of them. Ingratitude is monstrous, and for the multitude to be ingrateful were to make a monster of the multitude; of the which we being members should bring ourselves to be monstrous members.

1 CITIZEN And to make us no better thought of, a little help will serve; for once we stood up about the corn, he himself stuck not to call us the many-headed multitude.

3 CITIZEN We have been call'd so of many; not that our heads are some brown, some black, some abram, some bald, but that our wits are so diversely colour'd; and truly I think if all our wits were to issue out of one skull, they would fly east, west, north, south, and their consent of one direct way should be at once to all the points o' th' compass.

2 CITIZEN Think you so? Which way do you judge my wit would fly?

3 CITIZEN Nay, your wit will not so soon out as another man's will – 'tis strongly wedg'd up in a block-head; but if it were at liberty 'twould sure southward.

2 CITIZEN Why that way?

3 CITIZEN To lose itself in a fog; where being three parts melted away with rotten dews, the fourth would return for conscience' sake, to help to get thee a wife.

2 CITIZEN You are never without your tricks; you may, you may.

3 CITIZEN Are you all resolv'd to give your voices? But that's no matter, the greater part carries it. I say, if he would incline to the people, there was never a worthier man.

Enter CORIOLANUS, in a gown of humility, with MENENIUS.

Here he comes, and in the gown of humility. Mark his behaviour. We are not to stay all together, but to come by him where he stands, by ones, by twos, and by threes. He's to make his requests by particulars, wherein every one of us has a single honour, in giving him our own voices with our own tongues; therefore follow me, and I'll direct you how you shall go by him.

ALL Content, content. [*Exeunt Citizens.*

MENENIUS O sir, you are not right; have you not
known
The worthiest men have done't?

CORIOLANUS What must I say?

'I pray, sir' – Plague upon't! I cannot bring
My tongue to such a pace. 'Look, sir, my wounds!
I got them in my country's service, when
Some certain of your brethren roar'd, and ran
From th' noise of our own drums.'

MENENIUS O me, the gods!
You must not speak of that. You must desire them
To think upon you.

CORIOLANUS Think upon me? Hang 'em!
I would they would forget me, like the virtues
Which our divines lose by 'em.

MENENIUS You'll mar all.
I'll leave you. Pray you speak to 'em, I pray you,
In wholesome manner. [*Exit.*

Re-enter three of the Citizens.

CORIOLANUS Bid them wash their faces
And keep their teeth clean. So, here comes a brace.
You know the cause, sir, of my standing here.

3 CITIZEN We do, sir; tell us what hath brought you to't.

CORIOLANUS Mine own desert.

2 CITIZEN Your own desert?

CORIOLANUS Ay, not mine own desire.

3 CITIZEN How, not your own desire?

CORIOLANUS No, sir, 'twas never my desire yet to trouble the poor with begging.

3 CITIZEN You must think, if we give you anything, we hope to gain by you.

CORIOLANUS Well then, I pray, your price o' th' consulship?

1 CITIZEN The price is to ask it kindly.

CORIOLANUS Kindly, sir, I pray let me ha't. I have wounds to show you, which shall be yours in private. Your good voice, sir; what say you?

2 CITIZEN You shall ha' it, worthy sir.

CORIOLANUS A match, sir. There's in all two worthy voices begg'd. I have your alms. Adieu.

3 CITIZEN But this is something odd.

2 CITIZEN An 'twere to give again – but 'tis no matter. [*Exeunt the three Citizens.*

Re-enter two other Citizens.

CORIOLANUS Pray you now, if it may stand with the tune of your voices that I may be consul, I have here the customary gown.

4 CITIZEN You have deserved nobly of your country, and you have not deserved nobly.

CORIOLANUS Your enigma?

4 CITIZEN You have been a scourge to her enemies; you have been a rod to her friends. You have not indeed loved the common people.

CORIOLANUS You should account me the more virtuous, that I have not been common in my love. I will, sir, flatter my sworn brother, the people, to earn a dearer estimation of them; 'tis a condition they account gentle; and since the wisdom of their choice is rather to have my hat than my heart, I will practise the insinuating nod and be off to them most counterfeitly. That is, sir, I will counterfeit the bewitchment of some popular man and give it bountiful to the desirers. Therefore, beseech you I may be consul.

5 CITIZEN We hope to find you our friend; and therefore give you our voices heartily.

4 CITIZEN You have received many wounds for your country.

CORIOLANUS I will not seal your knowledge with showing them. I will make much of your voices, and so trouble you no farther.

BOTH CITIZENS The gods give you joy, sir, heartily! [*Exeunt Citizens.*

CORIOLANUS Most sweet voices!
Better it is to die, better to starve,
Than crave the hire which first we do deserve.
Why in this wolvish toge should I stand here
To beg of Hob and Dick that do appear
Their needless vouches? Custom calls me to't.
What custom wills, in all things should we do't,
The dust on antique time would lie unswept,
And mountainous error be too highly heap'd
For truth to o'erpeer. Rather than fool it so,
Let the high office and the honour go
To one that would do thus. I am half through:
The one part suffered, the other will I do.

Re-enter three Citizens more.

Here come moe voices.
Your voices. For your voices I have fought;
Watch'd for your voices; for your voices bear
Of wounds two dozen odd; battles thrice six
I have seen and heard of; for your voices have
Done many things, some less, some more. Your voices?
Indeed, I would be consul.

6 CITIZEN He has done nobly, and cannot go without any honest man's voice.

7 CITIZEN Therefore let him be consul. The gods give him joy, and make him good friend to the people!

ALL Amen, amen. God save thee, noble consul! [*Exeunt Citizens.*

CORIOLANUS Worthy voices!

Re-enter MENENIUS with BRUTUS and SICINIUS.

MENENIUS You have stood your limitation, and the tribunes
Endue you with the people's voice. Remains
That, in th' official marks invested, you
Anon do meet the Senate.

CORIOLANUS Is this done?
SICINIUS The custom of request you have discharg'd.
The people do admit you, and are summon'd
To meet anon, upon your approbation.
CORIOLANUS Where? At the Senate house?
SICINIUS There, Coriolanus.
CORIOLANUS May I change these garments?
SICINIUS You may, sir.
CORIOLANUS That I'll straight do, and, knowing myself again,
Repair to th' Senate House.
MENENIUS I'll keep you company. Will you along?
BRUTUS We stay here for the people.
SICINIUS Fare you well.
[*Exeunt Coriolanus and Menenius.*
He has it now; and by his looks methinks
'Tis warm at's heart.
BRUTUS With a proud heart he wore
His humble weeds. Will you dismiss the people?

Re-enter Citizens.

SICINIUS How now, my masters! Have you chose this man?
1 CITIZEN He has our voices, sir.
BRUTUS We pray the gods he may deserve your loves.
2 CITIZEN Amen, sir. To my poor unworthy notice,
He mock'd us when he begg'd our voices.
3 CITIZEN Certainly;
He flouted us downright.
1 CITIZEN No, 'tis his kind of speech – he did not mock us.
2 CITIZEN Not one amongst us, save yourself, but says
He us'd us scornfully. He should have show'd us
His marks of merit, wounds receiv'd for's country.
SICINIUS Why, so he did, I am sure.
ALL No, no; no man saw 'em.
3 CITIZEN He said he had wounds which he could show in private,
And with his hat, thus waving it in scorn,
'I would be consul,' says he 'aged custom
But by your voices will not so permit me;
Your voices therefore'. When we granted that,
Here was 'I thank you for your voices. Thank you,
Your most sweet voices. Now you have left your voices,
I have no further with you'. Was not this mockery?
SICINIUS Why either were you ignorant to see't,
Or, seeing it, of such childish friendliness
To yield your voices?
BRUTUS Could you not have told him –
As you were lesson'd – when he had no power
But was a petty servant to the state,
He was your enemy; even spake against
Your liberties and the charters that you bear
I' th' body of the weal; and now, arriving
A place of potency and sway o' th' state,
If he should still malignantly remain
Fast foe to th' plebeii, your voices might
Be curses to yourselves? You should have said
That as his worthy deeds did claim no less
Than what he stood for so his gracious nature
Would think upon you for your voices, and
Translate his malice towards you into love,
Standing your friendly lord.
SICINIUS Thus to have said,
As you were fore-advis'd, had touch'd his spirit
And tried his inclination; from him pluck'd
Either his gracious promise, which you might,
As cause had call'd you up, have held him to;
Or else it would have gall'd his surly nature,
Which easily endures not article
Tying him to aught. So, putting him to rage,
You should have ta'en th' advantage of his choler
And pass'd him unelected.
BRUTUS Did you perceive
He did solicit you in free contempt
When he did need your loves; and do you think
That his contempt shall not be bruising to you
When he hath power to crush? Why, had your bodies
No heart among you? Or had you tongues to cry
Against the rectorship of judgment?
SICINIUS Have you
Ere now denied the asker, and now again,
Of him that did not ask but mock, bestow
Your su'd-for tongues?
3 CITIZEN He's not confirm'd: we may deny him yet.
2 CITIZEN And will deny him;
I'll have five hundred voices of that sound.
1 CITIZEN I twice five hundred, and their friends to piece 'em.
BRUTUS Get you hence instantly, and tell those friends
They have chose a consul that will from them take
Their liberties, make them of no more voice
Than dogs, that are often beat for barking
As therefore kept to do so.
SICINIUS Let them assemble;
And, on a safer judgment, all revoke
Your ignorant election. Enforce his pride
And his old hate unto you; besides, forget not
With what contempt he wore the humble weed;
How in his suit he scorn'd you; but your loves,

Thinking upon his services, took from you
Th' apprehension of his present portance,
Which, most gibingly, ungravely, he did fashion
After the inveterate hate he bears you.

BRUTUS Lay
A fault on us, your tribunes, that we labour'd,
No impediment between, but that you must
Cast your election on him.

SICINIUS Say you chose him
More after our commandment than as guided
By your own true affections; and that your minds,
Pre-occupied with what you rather must do
Than what you should, made you against the grain
To voice him consul. Lay the fault on us.

BRUTUS Ay, spare us not. Say we read lectures to you,
How youngly he began to serve his country,
How long continued; and what stock he springs of –
The noble house o' th' Marcians; from whence came
That Ancus Marcius, Numa's daughter's son,
Who, after great Hostilius, here was king;
Of the same house Publius and Quintus were,
That our best water brought by conduits hither;
And Censorinus, nobly named so,
Twice being by the people chosen censor,
Was his great ancestor.

SICINIUS One thus descended,
That hath beside well in his person wrought
To be set high in place, we did commend
To your remembrances; but you have found,
Scaling his present bearing with his past,
That he's your fixed enemy, and revoke
Your sudden approbation.

BRUTUS Say you ne'er had done't –
Harp on that still – but by our putting on;
And presently, when you have drawn your number
Repair to th' Capitol.

CITIZENS We will so; almost all
Repent in their election.

[Exeunt Plebeians.

BRUTUS Let them go on;
This mutiny were better put in hazard
Than stay, past doubt, for greater.
If, as his nature is, he fall in rage
With their refusal, both observe and answer
The vantage of his anger.

SICINIUS To th' Capitol, come.
We will be there before the stream o' th' people;
And this shall seem, as partly 'tis, their own,
Which we have goaded onward.

[Exeunt.

ACT THREE

SCENE I. *Rome. A street.*

Cornets. Enter CORIOLANUS, MENENIUS, all the Gentry, COMINIUS, TITUS LARTIUS, and other Senators.

CORIOLANUS Tullus Aufidius, then, had made new head?

LARTIUS He had, my lord; and that it was which caus'd
Our swifter composition.

CORIOLANUS So then the Volsces stand but as at first,
Ready, when time shall prompt them, to make road
Upon's again.

COMINIUS They are worn, Lord Consul, so
That we shall hardly in our ages see
Their banners wave again.

CORIOLANUS Saw you Aufidius?

LARTIUS On safeguard he came to me, and did curse
Against the Volsces, for they had so vilely
Yielded the town. He is retir'd to Antium.

CORIOLANUS Spoke he of me?

LARTIUS He did, my lord.

CORIOLANUS How? What?

LARTIUS How often he had met you, sword to sword;
That of all things upon the earth he hated
Your person most; that he would pawn his fortunes
To hopeless restitution, so he might
Be call'd your vanquisher.

CORIOLANUS At Antium lives he?

LARTIUS At Antium.

CORIOLANUS I wish I had a cause to seek him there,
To oppose his hatred fully. Welcome home.

Enter SICINIUS and BRUTUS.

Behold, these are the tribunes of the people,
The tongues o' th' common mouth. I do despise them,
For they do prank them in authority,
Against all noble sufferance.

SICINIUS Pass no further.

CORIOLANUS Ha! What is that?

BRUTUS It will be dangerous to go on – no further.
CORIOLANUS What makes this change?
MENENIUS The matter?
COMINIUS Hath he not pass'd the noble and the common?
BRUTUS Cominius, no.
CORIOLANUS Have I had children's voices?
1 SENATOR Tribunes, give way: he shall to th' market-place.
BRUTUS The people are incens'd against him.
SICINIUS Stop,
Or all will fall in broil.
CORIOLANUS Are these your herd?
Must these have voices, that can yield them now
And straight disclaim their tongues? What are your offices?
You being their mouths, why rule you not their teeth?
Have you not set them on?
MENENIUS Be calm, be calm.
CORIOLANUS It is a purpos'd thing, and grows by plot,
To curb the will of the nobility;
Suffer't, and live with such as cannot rule
Nor ever will be rul'd.
BRUTUS Call't not a plot.
The people cry you mock'd them; and of late,
When corn was given them gratis, you repin'd;
Scandal'd the suppliants for the people, call'd them
Time-pleasers, flatterers, foes to nobleness.
CORIOLANUS Why, this was known before.
BRUTUS Not to them all.
CORIOLANUS Have you inform'd them sithence?
BRUTUS How? I inform them!
COMINIUS You are like to do such business.
BRUTUS Not unlike
Each way to better yours.
CORIOLANUS Why then should I be consul? By yond clouds,
Let me deserve so ill as you, and make me
Your fellow tribune.
SICINIUS You show too much of that
For which the people stir; if you will pass
To where you are bound, you must enquire your way,
Which you are out of, with a gentler spirit,
Or never be so noble as a consul,
Nor yoke with him for tribune.
MENENIUS Let's be calm.
COMINIUS The people are abus'd; set on. This palt-ring
Becomes not Rome; nor has Coriolanus
Deserv'd this so dishonour'd rub, laid falsely
I' th' plain way of his merit.
CORIOLANUS Tell me of corn!
This was my speech, and I will speak't again –
MENENIUS Not now, not now.
1 SENATOR Not in this heat, sir, now.
CORIOLANUS Now, as I live, I will.
My nobler friends, I crave their pardons.
For the mutable, rank-scented meiny, let them
Regard me as I do not flatter, and
Therein behold themselves. I say again,
In soothing them we nourish 'gainst our Senate
The cockle of rebellion, insolence, sedition,
Which we ourselves have plough'd for, sow'd, and scatter'd,
By mingling them with us, the honour'd number,
Who lack not virtue, no, nor power, but that
Which they have given to beggars.
MENENIUS Well, no more.
1 SENATOR No more words, we beseech you.
CORIOLANUS How? no more!
As for my country I have shed my blood,
Not fearing outward force, so shall my lungs
Coin words till their decay against those measles
Which we disdain should tetter us, yet sought
The very way to catch them.
BRUTUS You speak o' th' people
As if you were a god, to punish; not
A man of their infirmity.
SICINIUS 'Twere well
We let the people know't.
MENENIUS What, what? his choler?
CORIOLANUS Choler!
Were I as patient as the midnight sleep,
By Jove, 'twould be my mind!
SICINIUS It is a mind!
That shall remain a poison where it is,
Not poison any further.
CORIOLANUS Shall remain!
Hear you this Triton of the minnows? Mark you
His absolute 'shall'?
COMINIUS 'Twas from the canon.
CORIOLANUS 'Shall'!
O good but most unwise patricians! Why,
You grave but reckless senators, have you thus
Given Hydra here to chose an officer
That with his peremptory 'shall', being but
The horn and noise o' th' monster's, wants not spirit
To say he'll turn your current in a ditch,
And make your channel his? If he have power,
Then vail your ignorance; if none, awake
Your dangerous lenity. If you are learn'd,
Be not as common fools; if you are not,
Let them have cushions by you. You are plebeians,
If they be senators; and they are no less,
When, both your voices blended, the great'st taste

Most palates theirs. They choose their magistrate;
And such a one as he, who puts his 'shall',
His popular 'shall', against a graver bench
Than ever frown'd in Greece. By Jove himself,
It makes the consuls base; and my soul aches
To know, when two authorities are up,
Neither supreme, how soon confusion
May enter 'twixt the gap of both and take
The one by th' other.

COMINIUS Well, on to th' market-place.

CORIOLANUS Whoever gave that counsel to give forth
The corn o' th' storehouse gratis, as 'twas us'd
Sometime in Greece –

MENENIUS Well, well, no more of that.

CORIOLANUS Though there the people had more absolute pow'r –
I say they nourish'd disobedience, fed
The ruin of the state.

BRUTUS Why shall the people give
One that speaks thus their voice?

CORIOLANUS I'll give my reasons,
More worthier than their voices. They know the corn
Was not our recompense, resting well assur'd
They ne'er did service for't; being press'd to th' war
Even when the navel of the state was touch'd,
They would not thread the gates. This kind of service
Did not deserve corn gratis. Being i' th' war,
Their mutinies and revolts, wherein they show'd
Most valour, spoke not for them. Th' accusation
Which they have often made against the Senate,
All cause unborn, could never be the native
Of our so frank donation. Well, what then?
How shall this bosom multiplied digest
The Senate's courtesy? Let deeds express
What's like to be their words: 'We did request it;
We are the greater poll, and in true fear
They gave us our demands'. Thus we debase
The nature of our seats, and make the rabble
Call our cares fears; which will in time
Break ope the locks o' th' Senate and bring in
The crows to peck the eagles.

MENENIUS Come, enough.

BRUTUS Enough, with over measure.

CORIOLANUS No, take more.
What may be sworn by, both divine and human,
Seal what I end withal! This double worship,
Where one part does disdain with cause, the other
Insult without all reason; where gentry, title, wisdom,
Cannot conclude but by the yea and no
Of general ignorance – it must omit
Real necessities, and give way the while
To unstable slightness. Purpose so barr'd, it follows
Nothing is done to purpose. Therefore, beseech you –
You that will be less fearful than discreet;
That love the fundamental part of state
More than you doubt the change on't; that prefer
A noble life before a long, and wish
To jump a body with a dangerous physic
That's sure of death without it – at once pluck out
The multitudinous tongue; let them not lick
The sweet which is their poison. Your dishonour
Mangles true judgment, and bereaves the state
Of that integrity which should become't,
Not having the power to do the good it would,
For th' ill which doth control't.

BRUTUS Has said enough.

SICINIUS Has spoken like a traitor and shall answer
As traitors do.

CORIOLANUS Thou wretch, despite o'erwhelm thee!
What should the people do with these bald tribunes,
On whom depending, their obedience fails
To the greater bench? In a rebellion,
When what's not meet, but what must be, was law,
Then were they chosen; in a better hour
Let what is meet be said it must be meet,
And throw their power i' th' dust.

BRUTUS Manifest treason!

SICINIUS This a consul? No.

BRUTUS The aediles, ho!

Enter an Aedile.

Let him be apprehended.

SICINIUS Go call the people, [*Exit Aedile*] in whose name myself
Attach thee as a traitorous innovator,
A foe to th' public weal. Obey, I charge thee,
And follow to thine answer.

CORIOLANUS Hence, old goat!

PATRICIANS We'll surety him.

COMINIUS Ag'd sir, hands off.

CORIOLANUS Hence, rotten thing! or I shall shake thy bones
Out of thy garments.

SICINIUS Help, ye citizens!

Enter a rabble of Plebeians, with the Aediles.

MENENIUS On both sides more respect.

SICINIUS Here's he that would take from you all your power.

BRUTUS Seize him, aediles.
PLEBEIANS Down with him! down with him!
2 SENATOR Weapons, weapons, weapons!
[They all bustle about Coriolanus.
ALL Tribunes! patricians! citizens! What, ho!
Sicinius! Brutus! Coriolanus! Citizens!
PATRICIANS Peace, peace, peace; stay, hold, peace!
MENENIUS What is about to be? I am out of breath;
Confusion's near; I cannot speak. You Tribunes
To th' people – Coriolanus, patience!
Speak, good Sicinius.
SICINIUS Hear me, people; peace!
PLEBEIANS Let's hear our tribune. Peace!
Speak, speak, speak.
SICINIUS You are at point to lose your liberties.
Marcius would have all from you; Marcius,
Whom late you have nam'd for consul.
MENENIUS Fie, fie, fie!
This is the way to kindle, not to quench.
1 SENATOR To unbuild the city, and to lay all flat.
SICINIUS What is the city but the people?
PLEBEIANS True,
The people are the city.
BRUTUS By the consent of all we were establish'd
The people's magistrates.
PLEBEIANS You so remain.
MENENIUS And so are like to do.
COMINIUS That is the way to lay the city flat,
To bring the roof to the foundation,
And bury all which yet distinctly ranges
In heaps and piles of ruin.
SICINIUS This deserves death.
BRUTUS Or let us stand to our authority
Or let us lose it. We do here pronounce,
Upon the part o' th' people, in whose power
We were elected theirs: Marcius is worthy
Of present death.
SICINIUS Therefore lay hold of him;
Bear him to th' rock Tarpeian, and from thence
Into destruction cast him.
BRUTUS Aediles, seize him.
PLEBEIANS Yield, Marcius, yield.
MENENIUS Hear me one word; beseech you, Tribunes,
Hear me but a word.
AEDILES Peace, peace!
MENENIUS Be that you seem, truly your country's friend,
And temp'rately proceed to what you would
Thus violently redress.
BRUTUS Sir, those cold ways,
That seem like prudent helps, are very poisonous
Where the disease is violent. Lay hands upon him
And bear him to the rock.
[Coriolanus draws his sword.
CORIOLANUS No: I'll die here.
There's some among you have beheld me fighting;
Come, try upon yourselves what you have seen me.
MENENIUS Down with that sword! Tribunes, withdraw awhile.
BRUTUS Lay hands upon him.
MENENIUS Help Marcius, help,
You that be noble; help him, young and old.
PLEBEIANS Down with him, down with him!
[In this mutiny the Tribunes, the Aediles, and the People are beat in.
MENENIUS Go, get you to your house; be gone, away.
All will be nought else.
2 SENATOR Get you gone.
CORIOLANUS Stand fast;
We have as many friends as enemies.
MENENIUS Shall it be put to that?
1 SENATOR The gods forbid!
I prithee, noble friend, home to thy house;
Leave us to cure this cause.
MENENIUS For 'tis a sore upon us
You cannot tent yourself; be gone, beseech you.
COMINIUS Come, sir, along with us.
CORIOLANUS I would they were barbarians, as they are,
Though in Rome litter'd not Romans, as they are not,
Though calved i' th' porch o' th' Capitol.
MENENIUS Be gone.
Put not your worthy rage into your tongue;
One time will owe another.
CORIOLANUS On fair ground
I could beat forty of them.
MENENIUS I could myself
Take up a brace o' th' best of them; yea, the two tribunes.
COMINIUS But now 'tis odds beyond arithmetic,
And manhood is call'd foolery when it stands
Against a falling fabric. Will you hence,
Before the tag return? whose rage doth rend
Like interrupted waters, and o'erbear
What they are us'd to bear.
MENENIUS Pray you be gone.
I'll try whether my old wit be in request
With those that have but little; this must be patch'd
With cloth of any colour.
COMINIUS Nay, come away.
[Exeunt Coriolanus and Cominius, with others.

PATRICIAN This man has marr'd his fortune.
MENENIUS His nature is too noble for the world:
He would not flatter Neptune for his trident,
Or Jove for's power to thunder. His heart's his mouth;
What his breast forges, that his tongue must vent;
And, being angry, does forget that ever
He heard the name of death.
[*A noise within.*
Here's goodly work!
PATRICIAN I would they were a-bed.
MENENIUS I would they were in Tiber.
What the vengeance, could he not speak 'em fair?

Re-enter BRUTUS and SICINIUS with the Rabble again.

SICINIUS Where is this viper
That would depopulate the city and
Be every man himself?
MENENIUS You worthy Tribunes –
SICINIUS He shall be thrown down the Tarpeian rock
With rigorous hands; he hath resisted law,
And therefore law shall scorn him further trial
Than the severity of the public power,
Which he so sets at nought.
1 CITIZEN He shall well know
The noble tribunes are the people's mouths,
And we their hands.
PLEBEIANS He shall, sure on't.
MENENIUS Sir, sir –
SICINIUS Peace!
MENENIUS Do not cry havoc, where you should but hunt
With modest warrant.
SICINIUS Sir, how comes't that you
Have holp to make this rescue?
MENENIUS Hear me speak.
As I do know the consul's worthiness,
So can I name his faults.
SICINIUS Consul! What consul?
MENENIUS The consul Coriolanus.
BRUTUS He consul!
PLEBEIANS No, no, no, no, no.
MENENIUS If, by the tribune's leave, and yours, good people,
I may be heard, I would crave a word or two;
The which shall turn you to no further harm
Than so much loss of time.
SICINIUS Speak briefly, then,
For we are peremptory to dispatch
This viperous traitor; to eject him hence
Were but one danger, and to keep him here
Our certain death; therefore it is decreed
He dies to-night.
MENENIUS Now the good gods forbid
That our renowned Rome, whose gratitude
Towards her deserved children is enroll'd
In Jove's own book, like an unnatural dam
Should now eat up her own!
SICINIUS He's a disease that must be cut away.
MENENIUS O, he's a limb that has but a disease –
Mortal, to cut it off: to cure it, easy.
What has he done to Rome that's worthy death?
Killing our enemies, the blood he hath lost –
Which I dare vouch is more than that he hath
By many an ounce – he dropt it for his country;
And what is left, to lose it by his country
Were to us all that do't and suffer it
A brand to th' end o' th' world.
SICINIUS This is clean kam.
BRUTUS Merely awry. When he did love his country,
It honour'd him.
SICINIUS The service of the foot,
Being once gangren'd, is not then respected
For what before it was.
BRUTUS We'll hear no more.
Pursue him to his house and pluck him thence,
Lest his infection, being of catching nature,
Spread further.
MENENIUS One word more, one word!
This tiger-footed rage, when it shall find
The harm of unscann'd swiftness, will, too late,
Tie leaden pounds to's heels. Proceed by process,
Lest parties – as he is belov'd – break out,
And sack great Rome with Romans.
BRUTUS If it were so –
SICINIUS What do ye talk?
Have we not had a taste of his obedience –
Our aediles smote, ourselves resisted? Come!
MENENIUS Consider this: he has been bred i' th' wars
Since 'a could draw a sword, and is ill school'd
In bolted language; meal and bran together
He throws without distinction. Give me leave,
I'll go to him and undertake to bring him
Where he shall answer by a lawful form,
In peace, to his utmost peril.
1 SENATOR Noble Tribunes,
It is the humane way; the other course
Will prove too bloody, and the end of it
Unknown to the beginning.
SICINIUS Noble Menenius,
Be you then as the people's officer.
Masters, lay down your weapons.
BRUTUS Go not home.
SICINIUS Meet on the market-place. We'll attend you there;
Where, if you bring not Marcius, we'll proceed
In our first way.

MENENIUS I'll bring him to you.
[*To the Senators*] Let me desire your company; he must come,
Or what is worst will follow.
1 SENATOR Pray you let's to him.
[*Exeunt.*

SCENE II. *Rome. The house of Coriolanus.*

Enter CORIOLANUS with Nobles.

CORIOLANUS Let them pull all about mine ears, present me
Death on the wheel or at wild horses' heels;
Or pile ten hills on the Tarpeian rock,
That the precipitation might down stretch
Below the beam of sight; yet will I still
Be thus to them.
1 PATRICIAN You do the nobler.
CORIOLANUS I muse my mother
Does not approve me further, who was wont
To call them woollen vassals, things created
To buy and sell with groats; to show bare heads
In congregations, to yawn, be still, and wonder,
When one but of my ordinance stood up
To speak of peace or war.

Enter VOLUMNIA.

I talk of you:
Why did you wish me milder? Would you have me
False to my nature? Rather say I play
The man I am.
VOLUMNIA O, sir, sir, sir,
I would have had you put your power well on
Before you had worn it out.
CORIOLANUS Let go.
VOLUMNIA You might have been enough the man you are
With striving less to be so; lesser had been
The thwartings of your dispositions, if
You had not show'd them how ye were dispos'd,
Ere they lack'd power to cross you.
CORIOLANUS Let them hang.
VOLUMNIA Ay, and burn too.

Enter MENENIUS with the Senators.

MENENIUS Come, come, you have been too rough, something too rough;
You must return and mend it.
1 SENATOR There's no remedy,
Unless, by not so doing, our good city
Cleave in the midst and perish.
VOLUMNIA Pray be counsell'd;
I have a heart as little apt as yours,
But yet a brain that leads my use of anger
To better vantage.
MENENIUS Well said, noble woman!
Before he should thus stoop to th' herd, but that
The violent fit o' th' time craves it as physic
For the whole state, I would put mine armour on,
Which I can scarcely bear.
CORIOLANUS What must I do?
MENENIUS Return to th' tribunes.
CORIOLANUS Well, what then, what then?
MENENIUS Repent what you have spoke.
CORIOLANUS For them! I cannot do it to the gods;
Must I then do't to them?
VOLUMNIA You are too absolute;
Though therein you can never be too noble
But when extremities speak. I have heard you say
Honour and policy, like unsever'd friends,
I' th' war do grow together; grant that, and tell me
In peace what each of them by th' other lose
That they combine not there.
CORIOLANUS Tush, tush!
MENENIUS A good demand.
VOLUMNIA If it be honour in your wars to seem
The same you are not, which for your best ends
You adopt your policy, how is it less or worse
That it shall hold companionship in peace
With honour as in war; since that to both
It stands in like request?
CORIOLANUS Why force you this?
VOLUMNIA Because that now it lies you on to speak
To th' people, not by your own instruction,
Nor by th' matter which your heart prompts you,
But with such words that are but roted in
Your tongue, though but bastards and syllables
Of no allowance to your bosom's truth.
Now, this no more dishonours you at all
Than to take in a town with gentle words,
Which else would put you to your fortune and
The hazard of much blood.
I would dissemble with my nature where
My fortunes and my friends at stake requir'd
I should do so in honour. I am in this
Your wife, your son, these senators, the nobles;
And you will rather show our general louts
How you can frown, than spend a fawn upon 'em
For the inheritance of their loves and safeguard
Of what that want might ruin.
MENENIUS Noble lady!
Come, go with us, speak fair; you may salve so,
Not what is dangerous present, but the loss
Of what is past.
VOLUMNIA I prithee now, my son,
Go to them with this bonnet in thy hand;

And thus far having stretch'd it – here be with them –
Thy knee bussing the stones – for in such business
Action is eloquence, and the eyes of th' ignorant
More learned than the ears – waving thy head,
Which often thus correcting thy stout heart,
Now humble as the ripest mulberry
That will not hold the handling. Or say to them
Thou art their soldier and, being bred in broils,
Hast not the soft way which, thou dost confess,
Were fit for thee to use, as they to claim,
In asking their good loves; but thou wilt frame
Thyself, forsooth, hereafter theirs, so far
As thou hast power and person.

MENENIUS This but done
Even as she speaks, why, their hearts were yours;
For they have pardons, being ask'd, as free
As words to little purpose.

VOLUMNIA Prithee now,
Go, and be rul'd; although I know thou hadst rather
Follow thine enemy in a fiery gulf
Than flatter him in a bower.

Enter COMINIUS.

Here is Cominius.

COMINIUS I have been i' th' market-place; and, sir, 'tis fit
You make strong party, or defend yourself
By calmness or by absence; all's in anger.

MENENIUS Only fair speech.

COMINIUS I think 'twill serve, if he
Can thereto frame his spirit.

VOLUMNIA He must and will.
Prithee now, say you will, and go about it.

CORIOLANUS Must I go show them my unbarb'd sconce? Must I
With my base tongue give to my noble heart
A lie that it must bear? Well, I will do't;
Yet, were there but this single plot to lose,
This mould of Marcius, they to dust should grind it,
And throw't against the wind. To th' market-place!
You have put me now to such a part which never
I shall discharge to th' life.

COMINIUS Come, come, we'll prompt you.

VOLUMNIA I prithee now, sweet son, as thou hast said
My praises made thee first a soldier, so,
To have my praise for this, perform a part
Thou hast not done before.

CORIOLANUS Well, I must do't.
Away, my disposition, and possess me
Some harlot's spirit! My throat of war be turn'd,
Which quier'd with my drum, into a pipe
Small as an eunuch or the virgin voice
That babies lulls asleep! The smiles of knaves
Tent in my cheeks, and schoolboys' tears take up
The glasses of my sight! A beggar's tongue
Make motion through my lips, and my arm'd knees,
Who bow'd but in my stirrup, bend like his
That hath receiv'd an alms! I will not do't,
Lest I surcease to honour mine own truth,
And by my body's action teach my mind
A most inherent baseness.

VOLUMNIA At thy choice, then.
To beg of thee, it is my more dishonour
Than thou of them. Come all to ruin. Let
Thy mother rather feel thy pride than fear
Thy dangerous stoutness; for I mock at death
With as big heart as thou. Do as thou list.
Thy valiantness was mine, thou suck'dst it from me;
But owe thy pride thyself.

CORIOLANUS Pray be content.
Mother, I am going to the market-place;
Chide me no more. I'll mountebank their loves,
Cog their hearts from them, and come home belov'd
Of all the trades in Rome. Look, I am going.
Commend me to my wife. I'll return consul,
Or never trust to what my tongue can do
I' th' way of flattery further.

VOLUMNIA Do your will. [*Exit.*

COMINIUS Away! The tribunes do attend you. Arm yourself
To answer mildly; for they are prepar'd
With accusations, as I hear, more strong
Than are upon you yet.

CORIOLANUS The word is 'mildly'. Pray you let us go.
Let them accuse me by invention; I
Will answer in mine honour.

MENENIUS Ay, but mildly.

CORIOLANUS Well, mildly be it then – mildly.

[*Exeunt.*

SCENE III. *Rome. The Forum.*

Enter SICINIUS and BRUTUS.

BRUTUS In this point charge him home, that he affects
Tyrannical power. If he evade us there,
Enforce him with his envy to the people,
And that the spoil got on the Antiates
Was ne'er distributed.

Enter an Aedile.

What, will he come?

AEDILE He's coming
BRUTUS How accompanied?
AEDILE With old Menenius, and those senators
That always favour'd him.
SICINIUS Have you a catalogue
Of all the voices that we have procur'd,
Set down by th' poll?
AEDILE I have; 'tis ready.
SICINIUS Have you collected them by tribes?
AEDILE I have.
SICINIUS Assemble presently the people hither;
And when they hear me say 'It shall be so
I' th' right and strength o' th' commons' be it either
For death, for fine, or banishment, then let them,
If I say fine, cry 'Fine!' – if death, cry 'Death!'
Insisting on the old prerogative
And power i' th' truth o' th' cause.
AEDILE I shall inform them.
BRUTUS And when such time they have begun to cry,
Let them not cease, but with a din confus'd
Enforce the present execution
Of what we chance to sentence.
AEDILE Very well.
SICINIUS Make them be strong, and ready for this hint,
When we shall hap to give't them.
BRUTUS Go about it.
[*Exit Aedile.*
Put him to choler straight. He hath been us'd
Ever to conquer, and to have his worth
Of contradiction; being once chaf'd, he cannot
Be rein'd again to temperance; then he speaks
What's in his heart, and that is there which looks
With us to break his neck.

Enter CORIOLANUS, MENENIUS, and COMINIUS, with Others.

SICINIUS Well, here he comes.
MENENIUS Calmly, I do beseech you.
CORIOLANUS Ay, as an ostler, that for th' poorest piece
Will bear the knave by th' volume. Th' honour'd gods
Keep Rome in safety, and the chairs of justice
Supplied with worthy men! plant love among's!
Throng our large temples with the shows of peace,
And not our streets with war!
1 SENATOR Amen, amen!
MENENIUS A noble wish.

Re-enter the Aedile, with the Plebeians.

SICINIUS Draw near, ye people.
AEDILE List to your tribunes. Audience! peace, I say!
CORIOLANUS First, hear me speak.
BOTH TRIBUNES Well, say. Peace, ho!
CORIOLANUS Shall I be charg'd no further than this present?
Must all determine here?
SICINIUS I do demand,
If you submit you to the people's voices,
Allow their officers, and are content
To suffer lawful censure for such faults
As shall be prov'd upon you.
CORIOLANUS I am content.
MENENIUS Lo, citizens, he says he is content.
The warlike service he has done, consider; think
Upon the wounds his body bears, which show
Like graves i' th' holy churchyard.
CORIOLANUS Scratches with briers,
Scars to move laughter only.
MENENIUS Consider further,
That when he speaks not like a citizen,
You find him like a soldier; do not take
His rougher accents for malicious sounds,
But, as I say, such as become a soldier
Rather than envy you.
COMINIUS Well, well! No more.
CORIOLANUS What is the matter,
That being pass'd for consul with full voice,
I am so dishonour'd that the very hour
You take it off again?
SICINIUS Answer to us.
CORIOLANUS Say then; 'tis true, I ought so.
SICINIUS We charge you that you have contriv'd to take
From Rome all season'd office, and to wind
Yourself into a power tyrannical;
For which you are a traitor to the people.
CORIOLANUS How – traitor?
MENENIUS Nay, temperately! Your promise.
CORIOLANUS The fires i' th' lowest hell fold in the people!
Call me their traitor! Thou injurious tribune!
Within thine eyes sat twenty thousand deaths
In thy hands clutch'd as many millions, in
Thy lying tongue both numbers, I would say
'Thou liest' unto thee with a voice as free
As I do pray the gods.
SICINIUS Mark you this, people?
PLEBEIANS To th' rock, to th' rock, with him!
SICINIUS Peace!
We need not put new matter to his charge.
What you have seen him do and heard him speak,
Beating your officers, cursing yourselves,
Opposing laws with strokes, and here defying
Those whose great power must try him – even this,

So criminal and in such capital kind,
Deserves th' extremest death.

BRUTUS But since he hath
Serv'd well for Rome –

CORIOLANUS What do you prate of service?

BRUTUS I talk of that that know it.

CORIOLANUS You!

MENENIUS Is this the promise that you made your mother?

COMINIUS Know, I pray you –

CORIOLANUS I'll know no further.
Let them pronounce the steep Tarpeian death,
Vagabond exile, flaying, pent to linger
But with a grain a day, I would not buy
Their mercy at the price of one fair word,
Nor check my courage for what they can give,
To have't with saying 'Good morrow'.

SICINIUS For that he has –
As much as in him lies – from time to time
Envied against the people, seeking means
To pluck away their power; as now at last
Given hostile strokes, and that not in the presence
Of dreaded justice, but on the ministers
That do distribute it – in the name o' th' people,
And in the power of us the tribunes, we,
Ev'n from this instant, banish him our city,
In peril of precipitation
From off the rock Tarpeian, never more
To enter our Rome gates. I' th' people's name,
I say it shall be so.

PLEBEIANS It shall be so, it shall be so! Let him away!
He's banish'd, and it shall be so.

COMINIUS Hear me, my masters and my common friends –

SICINIUS He's sentenc'd; no more hearing.

COMINIUS Let me speak.
I have been consul, and can show for Rome
Her enemies' marks upon me. I do love
My country's good with a respect more tender,
More holy and profound, than mine own life,
My dear wife's estimate, her womb's increase
And treasure of my loins. Then if I would
Speak that –

SICINIUS We know your drift. Speak what?

BRUTUS There's no more to be said, but he is banish'd,
As enemy to the people and his country.
It shall be so.

PLEBEIANS It shall be so, it shall be so.

CORIOLANUS You common cry of curs, whose breath I hate
As reek o' th' rotten fens, whose loves I prize
As the dead carcasses of unburied men
That do corrupt my air – I banish you.
And here remain with your uncertainty!
Let every feeble rumour shake your hearts;
Your enemies, with nodding of their plumes,
Fan you into despair! Have the power still
To banish your defenders, till at length
Your ignorance – which finds not till it feels,
Making but reservation of yourselves
Still your own foes – deliver you
As most abated captives to some nation
That won you without blows! Despising
For you the city, thus I turn my back;
There is a world elsewhere.

[*Exeunt Coriolanus, Cominius, Menenius, with the other Patricians.*

AEDILE The people's enemy is gone, is gone!

[*They all shout and throw up their caps.*

PLEBEIANS Our enemy is banish'd, he is gone! Hoo-oo!

SICINIUS Go see him out at gates, and follow him,
As he hath follow'd you, with all despite;
Give him deserv'd vexation. Let a guard
Attend us through the city.

PLEBEIANS Come, come, let's see him out at gates; come!
The gods preserve our noble tribunes! Come.

[*Exeunt.*

ACT FOUR

SCENE I. *Rome. Before a gate of the city.*

Enter CORIOLANUS, VOLUMNIA, VIRGILIA, MENENIUS, COMINIUS, with the young Nobility of Rome.

CORIOLANUS Come, leave your tears; a brief farewell. The beast
With many heads butts me away. Nay, mother,
Where is your ancient courage? You were us'd
To say extremities was the trier of spirits;
That common chances common men could bear;
That when the sea was calm all boats alike
Show'd mastership in floating; fortune's blows,
When most struck home, being gentle wounded craves
A noble cunning. You were us'd to load me
With precepts that would make invincible
The heart that conn'd them.

VIRGILIA O heavens! O heavens!

CORIOLANUS Nay, I prithee, woman –
VOLUMNIA Now the red pestilence strike all trades in Rome,
And occupations perish!
CORIOLANUS What, what, what!
I shall be lov'd when I am lack'd. Nay, mother,
Resume that spirit when you were wont to say,
If you had been the wife of Hercules,
Six of his labours you'd have done, and sav'd
Your husband so much sweat. Cominius,
Droop not; adieu. Farewell, my wife, my, mother.
I'll do well yet. Thou old and true Menenius,
Thy tears are salter than a younger man's
And venomous to thine eyes. My sometime General,
I have seen thee stern, and thou hast oft beheld
Heart-hard'ning spectacles; tell these sad women
'Tis fond to wail inevitable strokes,
As 'tis to laugh at 'em. My mother, you wot well
My hazards still have been your solace; and
Believe't not lightly – though I go alone,
Like to a lonely dragon, that his fen
Makes fear'd and talk'd of more than seen – your son
Will or exceed the common or be caught
With cautelous baits and practice.
VOLUMNIA My first son,
Whither wilt thou go? Take good Cominius
With thee awhile; determine on some course
More than a wild exposture to each chance
That starts i' th' way before thee.
VIRGILIA O the gods!
COMINIUS I'll follow thee a month, devise with thee
Where thou shalt rest, that thou mayst hear of us,
And we of thee; so, if the time thrust forth
A cause for thy repeal, we shall not send
O'er the vast world to seek a single man,
And lose advantage, which doth ever cool
I' th' absence of the needer.
CORIOLANUS Fare ye well;
Thou hast years upon thee, and thou art too full
Of the wars' surfeits to go rove with one
That's yet unbruis'd; bring me but out at gate.
Come, my sweet wife, my dearest mother, and
My friends of noble touch; when I am forth,
Bid me farewell, and smile. I pray you come.
While I remain above the ground you shall
Hear from me still, and never of me aught
But what is like me formerly.
MENENIUS That's worthily
As any ear can hear. Come, let's not weep.
If I could shake off but one seven years
From these old arms and legs, by the good gods,
I'd with thee every foot.
CORIOLANUS Give me thy hand.
Come. *[Exeunt.*

SCENE II. *Rome. A street near the gate.*

Enter the two Tribunes, SICINIUS and BRUTUS, with the Aedile.

SICINIUS Bid them all home; he's gone, and we'll no further.
The nobility are vex'd, whom we see have sided
In his behalf.
BRUTUS Now we have shown our power,
Let us seem humbler after it is done
Than when it was a-doing.
SICINIUS Bid them home.
Say their great enemy is gone, and they
Stand in their ancient strength.
BRUTUS Dismiss them home.
[Exit Aedile.
Here comes his mother.

Enter VOLUMNIA, VIRGILIA, and MENENIUS.

SICINIUS Let's not meet her.
BRUTUS Why?
SICINIUS They say she's mad.
BRUTUS They have ta'en note of us; keep on your way.
VOLUMNIA O, y'are well met; th' hoarded plague o' th' gods
Requite your love!
MENENIUS Peace, peace, be not so loud.
VOLUMNIA If that I could for weeping, you should hear –
Nay, and you shall hear some. *[To Brutus]* Will you be gone?
VIRGILIA *[To Sicinius]* You shall stay too. I would I had the power
To say so to my husband.
SICINIUS Are you mankind?
VOLUMNIA Ay, fool; is that a shame? Note but this, fool:
Was not a man my father? Hadst thou foxship
To banish him that struck more blows for Rome
Than thou hast spoken words?
SICINIUS O blessed heavens!
VOLUMNIA Moe noble blows than ever thou wise words;
And for Rome's good. I'll tell thee what – yet go!
Nay, but thou shalt stay too. I would my son
Were in Arabia, and thy tribe before him,
His good sword in his hand.
SICINIUS What then?
VIRGILIA What then!
He'd make an end of thy posterity.
VOLUMNIA Bastards and all.
Good man, the wounds that he does bear for Rome!

MENENIUS Come, come, peace.
SICINIUS I would he had continued to his country
As he began, and not unknit himself
The noble knot he made.
BRUTUS I would he had.
VOLUMNIA 'I would he had'! 'Twas you incens'd the rabble –
Cats that can judge as fitly of his worth
As I can of those mysteries which heaven
Will not have earth to know.
BRUTUS Pray, let's go.
VOLUMNIA Now, pray, sir, get you gone;
You have done a brave deed. Ere you go, hear this:
As far as doth the Capitol exceed
The meanest house in Rome, so far my son –
This lady's husband here, this, do you see? –
Whom you have banish'd does exceed you all.
BRUTUS Well, well, we'll leave you.
SICINIUS Why stay we to be baited
With one that wants her wits?

[Exeunt Tribunes.

VOLUMNIA Take my prayers with you.
I would the gods had nothing else to do
But to confirm my curses. Could I meet 'em
But once a day, it would unclog my heart
Of what lies heavy to't.
MENENIUS You have told them home,
And, by my troth, you have cause. You'll sup with me?
VOLUMNIA Anger's my meat; I sup upon myself,
And so shall starve with feeding. Come, let's go.
Leave this faint puling and lament as I do,
In anger, Juno-like. Come, come, come.

[Exeunt Volumnia and Virgilia.

MENENIUS Fie, fie, fie! *[Exit.*

SCENE III. *A highway between Rome and Antium.*

Enter a Roman and a Volsce, meeting.

ROMAN I know you well, sir, and you know me; your name, I think, is Adrian.

VOLSCE It is so, sir. Truly, I have forgot you.

ROMAN I am a Roman; and my services are, as you are, against 'em. Know you me yet?

VOLSCE Nicanor? No!

ROMAN The same, sir.

VOLSCE You had more beard when I last saw you, but your favour is well appear'd by your tongue. What's the news in Rome? I have a note from the Volscian state, to find you out there. You have well saved me a day's journey.

ROMAN There hath been in Rome strange insurrections: the people against the senators, patricians, and nobles.

VOLSCE Hath been! Is it ended, then? Our state thinks not so; they are in a most warlike preparation, and hope to come upon them in the heat of their division.

ROMAN The main blaze of it is past, but a small thing would make it flame again; for the nobles receive so to heart the banishment of that worthy Coriolanus that they are in a ripe aptness to take all power from the people, and to pluck from them their tribunes for ever. This lies glowing, I can tell you, and is almost mature for the violent breaking out.

VOLSCE Coriolanus banish'd!

ROMAN Banish'd, sir.

VOLSCE You will be welcome with this intelligence, Nicanor.

ROMAN The day serves well for them now. I have heard it said the fittest time to corrupt a man's wife is when she's fall'n out with her husband. Your noble Tullus Aufidius will appear well in these wars, his great opposer, Coriolanus, being now in no request of his country.

VOLSCE He cannot choose. I am most fortunate thus accidentally to encounter you; you have ended my business, and I will merrily accompany you home.

ROMAN I shall between this and supper tell you most strange things from Rome, all tending to the good of their adversaries. Have you an army ready, say you?

VOLSCE A most royal one: the centurions and their charges, distinctly billeted, already in th' entertainment, and to be on foot at an hour's warning.

ROMAN I am joyful to hear of their readiness, and am the man, I think, that shall set them in present action. So, sir, heartily well met, and most glad of your company.

VOLSCE You take my part from me, sir. I have the most cause to be glad of yours.

ROMAN Well, let us go together. *[Exeunt.*

SCENE IV. *Antium. Before Aufidius's house.*

Enter CORIOLANUS in mean apparel, disguis'd and muffled.

CORIOLANUS A goodly city is this Antium. City,
'Tis I that made thy widows; many an heir
Of these fair edifices fore my wars
Have I heard groan and drop. Then know me not,
Lest that thy wives with spits and boys with stones,
In puny battle slay me.

Enter a Citizen.

Save you, sir.

CITIZEN And you.
CORIOLANUS Direct me, if it be your will,
Where great Aufidius lies. Is he in Antium?
CITIZEN He is, and feasts the nobles of the state
At his house this night.
CORIOLANUS Which is his house, beseech you?
CITIZEN This here before you.
CORIOLANUS Thank you, sir; farewell.
[*Exit Citizen.*

O world, thy slippery turns! Friends now fast sworn,
Whose double bosoms seems to wear one heart,
Whose hours, whose bed, whose meal and exercise
Are still together, who twin, as 'twere, in love
Unseparable, shall within this hour,
On a dissension of a doit, break out
To bitterest enmity; so fellest foes,
Whose passions and whose plots have broke their sleep
To take the one the other, by some chance,
Some trick not worth an egg, shall grow dear friends
And interjoin their issues. So with me:
My birthplace hate I, and my love's upon
This enemy town. I'll enter. If he slay me,
He does fair justice; if he give me way,
I'll do his country service. [*Exit.*

SCENE V. *Antium. Aufidius's house.*

Music plays. Enter a Servant.

1 SERVANT Wine, wine, wine! What service is here! I think our fellows are asleep. [*Exit.*

Enter another Servant.

2 SERVANT Where's Cotus? My master calls for him. Cotus! [*Exit.*

Enter CORIOLANUS.

CORIOLANUS A goodly house. The feast smells well, but I
Appear not like a guest.

Re-enter the first Servant.

1 SERVANT What would you have, friend? Whence are you? Here's no place for you: pray go to the door. [*Exit.*

CORIOLANUS I have deserv'd no better entertainment
In being Coriolanus.

Re-enter second Servant.

2 SERVANT Whence are you, sir? Has the porter his eyes in his head that he gives entrance to such companions? Pray get you out.

CORIOLANUS Away!
2 SERVANT Away? Get you away.
CORIOLANUS Now th' art troublesome.
2 SERVANT Are you so brave? I'll have you talk'd with anon.

Enter a third Servant. The first meets him.

3 SERVANT What fellow's this?
1 SERVANT A strange one as ever I look'd on. I cannot get him out o' th' house. Prithee call my master to him.
3 SERVANT What have you to do here, fellow? Pray you avoid the house.
CORIOLANUS Let me but stand – I will not hurt your hearth.
3 SERVANT What are you?
CORIOLANUS A gentleman.
3 SERVANT A marv'llous poor one.
CORIOLANUS True, so I am.
3 SERVANT Pray you, poor gentleman, take up some other station; here's no place for you. Pray you avoid. Come.
CORIOLANUS Follow your function, go and batten on cold bits. [*Pushes him away from him.*
3 SERVANT What, you will not? Prithee tell my master what a strange guest he has here.
2 SERVANT And I shall. [*Exit.*
3 SERVANT Where dwell'st thou?
CORIOLANUS Under the canopy.
3 SERVANT Under the canopy?
CORIOLANUS Ay.
3 SERVANT Where's that?
CORIOLANUS I' th' city of kites and crows.
3 SERVANT I' th' city of kites and crows! What an ass it is! Then thou dwell'st with daws too?
CORIOLANUS No, I serve not thy master.
3 SERVANT How, sir! Do you meddle with my master?
CORIOLANUS Ay; 'tis an honester service than to meddle with thy mistress. Thou prat'st and prat'st; serve with thy trencher; hence!
[*Beats him away.*

Enter AUFIDIUS with the second Servant.

AUFIDIUS Where is this fellow?
2 SERVANT Here, sir; I'd have beaten him like a dog, but for disturbing the lords within.
AUFIDIUS Whence com'st thou? What wouldst thou? Thy name?
Why speak'st not? Speak, man. What's thy name?
CORIOLANUS [*Unmuffling*] If, Tullus,
Not yet thou know'st me, and, seeing me, dost not
Think me for the man I am, necessity
Commands me name myself.
AUFIDIUS What is thy name?

CORIOLANUS A name unmusical to the Volscians' ears,
And harsh in sound to thine.
AUFIDIUS Say, what's thy name?
Thou hast a grim appearance, and thy face
Bears a command in't; though thy tackle's torn,
Thou show'st a noble vessel. What's thy name?
CORIOLANUS Prepare thy brow to frown – know'st thou me yet?
AUFIDIUS I know thee not. Thy name?
CORIOLANUS My name is Caius Marcius, who hath done
To thee particularly, and to all the Volsces,
Great hurt and mischief; thereto witness may
My surname, Coriolanus. The painful service,
The extreme dangers, and the drops of blood
Shed for my thankless country, are requited
But with that surname – a good memory
And witness of the malice and displeasure
Which thou shouldst bear me. Only that name remains;
The cruelty and envy of the people,
Permitted by our dastard nobles, who
Have all forsook me, hath devour'd the rest,
And suffer'd me by th' voice of slaves to be
Whoop'd out of Rome. Now this extremity
Hath brought me to thy hearth; not out of hope,
Mistake me not, to save my life; for if
I had fear'd death, of all the men i' th' world
I would have 'voided thee; but in mere spite,
To be full quit of those my banishers,
Stand I before thee here. Then if thou hast
A heart of wreak in thee, that wilt revenge
Thine own particular wrongs and stop those maims
Of shame seen through thy country, speed thee straight
And make my misery serve thy turn. So use it
That my revengeful services may prove
As benefits to thee; for I will fight
Against my cank'red country with the spleen
Of all the under fiends. But if so be
Thou dar'st not this, and that to prove more fortunes
Th'art tir'd, then, in a word, I also am
Longer to live most weary, and present
My throat to thee and to thy ancient malice;
Which not to cut would show thee but a fool,
Since I have ever followed thee with hate,
Drawn tuns of blood out of thy country's breast,
And cannot live but to thy shame, unless
It be to do thee service.
AUFIDIUS O Marcius, Marcius!
Each word thou hast spoke hath weeded from my heart
A root of ancient envy. If Jupiter
Should from yond cloud speak divine things,
And say ''Tis true', I'd not believe them more
Than thee, all noble Marcius. Let me twine
Mine arms about that body, where against
My grained ash an hundred times hath broke
And scarr'd the moon with splinters; here I clip
The anvil of my sword, and do contest
As hotly and as nobly with thy love
As ever in ambitious strength I did
Contend against thy valour. Know thou first,
I lov'd the maid I married; never man
Sigh'd truer breath; but that I see thee here,
Thou noble thing, more dances my rapt heart
Than when I first my wedded mistress saw
Bestride my threshold. Why, thou Mars, I tell thee
We have a power on foot, and I had purpose
Once more to hew thy target from thy brawn,
Or lose mine arm for't. Thou hast beat me out
Twelve several times, and I have nightly since
Dreamt of encounters 'twixt thyself and me –
We have been down together in my sleep,
Unbuckling helms, fisting each other's throat –
And wak'd half dead with nothing. Worthy Marcius,
Had we no other quarrel else to Rome but that
Thou art thence banish'd, we would muster all
From twelve to seventy, and, pouring war
Into the bowels of ungrateful Rome,
Like a bold flood o'erbea. O, come, go in,
And take our friendly senators by th' hands,
Who now are here, taking their leaves of me
Who am prepar'd against your territories,
Though not for Rome itself.
CORIOLANUS You bless me, gods!
AUFIDIUS Therefore, most absolute sir, if thou wilt have
The leading of thine own revenges, take
Th' one half of my commission, and set down –
As best thou art experienc'd, since thou know'st
Thy country's strength and weakness – thine own ways,
Whether to knock against the gates of Rome,
Or rudely visit them in parts remote
To fright them ere destroy. But come in;
Let me commend thee first to those that shall
Say yea to thy desires. A thousand welcomes!
And more a friend than e'er an enemy;
Yet, Marcius, that was much. Your hand; most welcome! [*Exeunt Coriolanus and Aufidius.*

The two Servants come forward.

1 SERVANT Here's a strange alteration!

2 SERVANT By my hand, I had thought to have strucken him with a cudgel; and yet my mind gave me his clothes made a false report of him.

1 SERVANT What an arm he has! He turn'd me about with his finger and his thumb, as one

would set up a top.

2 SERVANT Nay, I knew by his face that there was something in him; he had, sir, a kind of face, methought – I cannot tell how to term it.

1 SERVANT He had so, looking as it were – Would I were hang'd, but I thought there was more in him than I could think.

2 SERVANT So did I, I'll be sworn. He is simply the rarest man i' th' world.

1 SERVANT I think he is; but a greater soldier than he you wot one.

2 SERVANT Who, my master?

1 SERVANT Nay, it's no matter for that.

2 SERVANT Worth six on him.

1 SERVANT Nay, not so neither; but I take him to be the greater soldier.

2 SERVANT Faith, look you, one cannot tell how to say that; for the defence of a town our general is excellent.

1 SERVANT Ay, and for an assault too.

Re-enter the third Servant.

3 SERVANT O slaves, I can tell you news – news, you rascals!

BOTH What, what, what? Let's partake.

3 SERVANT I would not be a Roman, of all nations; I had as lief be a condemn'd man.

BOTH Wherefore? wherefore?

3 SERVANT Why, here's he that was wont to thwack our general – Caius Marcius.

1 SERVANT Why do you say 'thwack our general'?

3 SERVANT I do not say 'thwack our general', but he was always good enough for him.

2 SERVANT Come, we are fellows and friends. He was ever too hard for him, I have heard him say so himself.

1 SERVANT He was too hard for him directly, to say the troth on't; before Corioli he scotch'd him and notch'd him like a carbonado.

2 SERVANT An he had been cannibally given, he might have broil'd and eaten him too.

1 SERVANT But more of thy news!

3 SERVANT Why, he is so made on here within as if he were son and heir to Mars; set at upper end o' th' table; no question asked him by any of the senators but they stand bald before him. Our general himself makes a mistress of him, sanctifies himself with's hand, and turns up the white o' th' eye to his discourse. But the bottom of the news is, our general is cut i' th' middle and but one half of what he was yesterday, for the other has half by the entreaty and grant of the whole table. He'll go, he says, and sowl the porter of Rome gates by th' ears; he will mow all down before him, and leave his passage poll'd.

2 SERVANT And he's as like to do't as any man I can imagine.

3 SERVANT Do't! He will do't; for look you, sir, he has as many friends as enemies; which friends, sir, as it were, durst not – look you, sir – show themselves, as we term it, his friends, whilest he's in directitude.

1 SERVANT Directitude? What's that?

3 SERVANT But when they shall see, sir, his crest up again and the man in blood, they will out of their burrows, like conies after rain, and revel all with him.

1 SERVANT But when goes this forward?

3 SERVANT To-morrow, to-day, presently. You shall have the drum struck up this afternoon; 'tis as it were a parcel of their feast, and to be executed ere they wipe their lips.

2 SERVANT Why, then we shall have a stirring world again. This peace is nothing but to rust iron, increase tailors, and breed balladmakers.

1 SERVANT Let me have war, say I; it exceeds peace as far as day does night; it's spritely, waking, audible, and full of vent. Peace is a very apoplexy, lethargy; mull'd, deaf, sleepy, insensible; a getter of more bastard children than war's a destroyer of men.

2 SERVANT 'Tis so; and as war in some sort may be said to be a ravisher, so it cannot be denied but peace is a great maker of cuckolds.

1 SERVANT Ay, and it makes men hate one another.

3 SERVANT Reason: because they then less need one another. The wars for my money. I hope to see Romans as cheap as Volscians. They are rising, they are rising.

BOTH In, in, in, in! [*Exeunt.*

SCENE VI. *Rome. A public place.*

Enter the two Tribunes, SICINIUS and BRUTUS.

SICINIUS We hear not of him, neither need we fear him.
His remedies are tame. The present peace
And quietness of the people, which before
Were in wild hurry, here do make his friends
Blush that the world goes well; who rather had,
Though they themselves did suffer by't, behold
Dissentious numbers pest'ring streets than see
Our tradesmen singing in their shops, and going
About their functions friendly.

Enter MENENIUS.

BRUTUS We stood to't in good time. Is this Menenius?

SICINIUS 'Tis he, 'tis he. O, he is grown most kind
Of late. Hail, sir!

MENENIUS Hail to you both!

SICINIUS Your Coriolanus is not much miss'd
But with his friends. The commonwealth doth stand,

And so would do, were he more angry at it.
MENENIUS All's well, and might have been much better if
He could have temporiz'd.
SICINIUS Where is he, hear you?
MENENIUS Nay, I hear nothing; his mother and his wife
Hear nothing from him.

Enter three or four Citizens.

CITIZENS The gods preserve you both!
SICINIUS God-den, our neighbours.
BRUTUS God-den to you all, god-den to you all.
1 CITIZEN Ourselves, our wives, and children, on our knees
Are bound to pray for you both.
SICINIUS Live and thrive!
BRUTUS Farewell, kind neighbours; we wish'd Coriolanus
Had lov'd you as we did.
CITIZENS Now the gods keep you!
BOTH TRIBUNES Farewell, farewell.

[*Exeunt Citizens.*

SICINIUS This is a happier and more comely time
Than when these fellows ran about the streets
Crying confusion.
BRUTUS Caius Marcius was
A worthy officer i' th' war, but insolent,
O'ercome with pride, ambitious past all thinking,
Self-loving –
SICINIUS And affecting one sole throne,
Without assistance.
MENENIUS I think not so.
SICINIUS We should by this, to all our lamentation,
If he had gone forth consul, found it so.
BRUTUS The gods have well prevented it, and Rome
Sits safe and still without him.

Enter an Aedile.

AEDILE Worthy tribunes,
There is a slave, whom we have put in prison,
Reports the Volsces with two several powers
Are ent'red in the Roman territories,
And with the deepest malice of the war
Destroy what lies before 'em.
MENENIUS 'Tis Aufidius,
Who, hearing of our Marcius' banishment,
Thrusts forth his horns again into the world,
Which were inshell'd when Marcius stood for Rome,
And durst not once peep out.
SICINIUS Come, what talk you of Marcius?
BRUTUS Go see this rumourer whipp'd. It cannot be
The Volsces dare break with us.
MENENIUS Cannot be!
We have record that very well it can;
And three examples of the like hath been
Within my age. But reason with the fellow
Before you punish him, where he heard this,
Lest you shall chance to whip your information
And beat the messenger who bids beware
Of what is to be dreaded.
SICINIUS Tell not me.
I know this cannot be.
BRUTUS Not possible.

Enter a Messenger.

MESSENGER The nobles in great earnestness are going
All to the Senate House some news is come
That turns their countenances.
SICINIUS 'Tis this slave –
Go whip him fore the people's eyes – his raising,
Nothing but his report.
MESSENGER Yes, worthy sir,
The slave's report is seconded, and more,
More fearful, is deliver'd.
SICINIUS What more fearful?
MESSENGER It is spoke freely out of many mouths –
How probable I do not know – that Marcius,
Join'd with Aufidius, leads a power 'gainst Rome,
And vows revenge as spacious as between
The young'st and oldest thing.
SICINIUS This is most likely!
BRUTUS Rais'd only that the weaker sort may wish
Good Marcius home again.
SICINIUS The very trick on't.
MENENIUS This is unlikely.
He and Aufidius can no more atone
Than violent'st contrariety.

Enter a second Messenger.

2 MESSENGER You are sent for to the Senate.
A fearful army, led by Caius Marcius
Associated with Aufidius, rages
Upon our territories, and have already
O'erborne their way, consum'd with fire and took
What lay before them.

Enter COMINIUS.

COMINIUS O, you have made good work!
MENENIUS What news? what news?
COMINIUS You have holp to ravish your own daughters and
To melt the city leads upon your pates,
To see your wives dishonour'd to your noses –
MENENIUS What's the news? What's the news?
COMINIUS Your temples burned in their cement, and

Your franchises, whereon you stood, confin'd
Into an auger's bore.

MENENIUS Pray now, your news?
You have made fair work, I fear me. Pray, your news.
If Marcius should be join'd wi' th' Volscians –

COMINIUS If!
He is their god; he leads them like a thing
Made by some other deity than Nature,
That shapes man better; and they follow him
Against us brats with no less confidence
Than boys pursuing summer butterflies,
Or butchers killing flies.

MENENIUS You have made good work,
You and your apron men; you that stood so much
Upon the voice of occupation and
The breath of garlic-eaters!

COMINIUS He'll shake
Your Rome about your ears.

MENENIUS As Hercules
Did shake down mellow fruit. You have made fair work!

BRUTUS But is this true, sir?

COMINIUS Ay; and you'll look pale
Before you find it other. All the regions
Do smilingly revolt, and who resists
Are mock'd for valiant ignorance,
And perish constant fools. Who is't can blame him?
Your enemies and his find something in him.

MENENIUS We are all undone unless
The noble man have mercy.

COMINIUS Who shall ask it?
The tribunes cannot do't for shame; the people
Deserve such pity of him as the wolf
Does of the shepherds; for his best friends, if they
Should say 'Be good to Rome' – they charg'd him even
As those should do that had deserv'd his hate,
And therein show'd like enemies.

MENENIUS 'Tis true;
If he were putting to my house the brand
That should consume it, I have not the face
To say 'Beseech you, cease'. You have made fair hands,
You and your crafts! You have crafted fair!

COMINIUS You have brought
A trembling upon Rome, such as was never
S' incapable of help.

BOTH TRIBUNES Say not we brought it.

MENENIUS How! Was't we? We lov'd him, but, like beasts
And cowardly nobles, gave way unto your clusters,
Who did hoot him out o' th' city.

COMINIUS But I fear
They'll roar him in again. Tullus Aufidius,
The second name of men, obeys his points
As if he were his officer. Desperation
Is all the policy, strength, and defence,
That Rome can make against them.

Enter a troop of Citizens.

MENENIUS Here comes the clusters.
And is Aufidius with him? You are they
That made the air unwholesome when you cast
Your stinking greasy caps in hooting at
Coriolanus' exile. Now he's coming,
And not a hair upon a soldier's head
Which will not prove a whip; as many coxcombs
As you threw caps up will he tumble down,
And pay you for your voices. 'Tis no matter;
If he could burn us all into one coal,
We have deserv'd it.

PLEBEIANS Faith, we hear fearful news.

1 CITIZEN For mine own part,
When I said banish him, I said 'twas pity.

2 CITIZEN And so did I.

3 CITIZEN And so did I; and, to say the truth, so did very many of us. That we did, we did for the best; and though we willingly consented to his banishment, yet it was against our will.

COMINIUS Y'are goodly things, you voices!

MENENIUS You have made
Good work, you and your cry! Shall's to the Capitol?

COMINIUS O, ay, what else?

[Exeunt Cominius and Menenius.

SICINIUS Go masters, get you home; be not dismay'd;
These are a side that would be glad to have
This true which they so seem to fear. Go home,
And show no sign of fear.

1 CITIZEN The gods be good to us! Come, masters, let's home. I ever said we were i' th' wrong when we banish'd him.

2 CITIZEN So did we all. But come, let's home.

[Exeunt Citizens.

BRUTUS I do not like this news.

SICINIUS Nor I.

BRUTUS Let's to the Capitol. Would half my wealth
Would buy this for a lie!

SICINIUS Pray let's go. *[Exeunt.*

SCENE VII. *A camp at a short distance from Rome.*

Enter AUFIDIUS with his Lieutenant.

AUFIDIUS Do they still fly to th' Roman?

LIEUTENANT I do not know what witchcraft's in him, but

Your soldiers use him as the grace fore meat,
Their talk at table, and their thanks at end;
And you are dark'ned in this action, sir,
Even by your own.

AUFIDIUS I cannot help it now,
Unless by using means I lame the foot
Of our design. He bears himself more proudlier,
Even to my person, than I thought he would
When first I did embrace him; yet his nature
In that's no changeling, and I must excuse
What cannot be amended.

LIEUTENANT Yet I wish, sir –
I mean, for your particular – you had not
Join'd in commission with him, but either
Had borne the action of yourself, or else
To him had left it solely.

AUFIDIUS I understand thee well; and be thou sure,
When he shall come to his account, he knows not
What I can urge against him. Although it seems,
And so he thinks, and is no less apparent
To th' vulgar eye, that he bears all things fairly
And shows good husbandry for the Volscian state,
Fights dragon-like, and does achieve as soon
As draw his sword; yet he hath left undone
That which shall break his neck or hazard mine
Whene'er we come to our account.

LIEUTENANT Sir, I beseech you, think you he'll carry Rome?

AUFIDIUS All places yield to him ere he sits down,
And the nobility of Rome are his;
The senators and patricians love him too.
The tribunes are no soldiers, and their people
Will be as rash in the repeal as hasty
To expel him thence. I think he'll be to Rome
As is the osprey to the fish, who takes it
By sovereignty of nature. First he was
A noble servant to them, but he could not
Carry his honours even. Whether 'twas pride,
Which out of daily fortune ever taints
The happy man; whether defect of judgment,
To fail in the disposing of those chances
Which he was lord of; or whether nature,
Not to be other than one thing, not moving
From th' casque to th' cushion, but commanding peace
Even with the same austerity and garb
As he controll'd the war; but one of these –
As he hath spices of them all – not all,
For I dare so far free him – made him fear'd,
So hated, and so banish'd. But he has a merit
To choke it in the utt'rance. So our virtues
Lie in th' interpretation of the time;
And power, unto itself most commendable,
Hath not a tomb so evident as a chair
T' extol what it hath done.
One fire drives out one fire; one nail, one nail;
Rights by rights falter, strengths by strengths do fail.
Come, let's away. When, Caius, Rome is thine,
Thou art poor'st of all; then shortly art thou mine.

[*Exeunt.*

ACT FIVE

SCENE I. *Rome. A public place.*

Enter MENENIUS, COMINIUS, SICINIUS and BRUTUS the two Tribunes, with Others.

MENENIUS No, I'll not go. You hear what he hath said
Which was sometime his general, who lov'd him
In a most dear particular. He call'd me father;
But what o' that? Go, you that banish'd him:
A mile before his tent fall down, and knee
The way into his mercy. Nay, if he coy'd
To hear Cominius speak, I'll keep at home.

COMINIUS He would not seem to know me.

MENENIUS Do you hear?

COMINIUS Yet one time he did call me by my name.
I urg'd our old acquaintance, and the drops
That we have bled together. 'Coriolanus'
He would not answer to; forbad all names;
He was a kind of nothing, titleless,
Till he had forg'd himself a name i' th' fire
Of burning Rome.

MENENIUS Why, so! You have made good work.
A pair of tribunes that have wrack'd for Rome
To make coals cheap – a noble memory!

COMINIUS I minded him how royal 'twas to pardon
When it was less expected; he replied,
It was a bare petition of a state
To one whom they had punish'd.

MENENIUS Very well.
Could he say less?

COMINIUS I offer'd to awaken his regard
For's private friends; his answer to me was,
He could not stay to pick them in a pile
Of noisome musty chaff. He said 'twas folly,
For one poor grain or two, to leave unburnt

And still to nose th' offence.
MENENIUS For one poor grain or two!
I am one of those. His mother, wife, his child,
And this brave fellow too – we are the grains:
You are the musty chaff, and you are smelt
Above the moon. We must be burnt for you.
SICINIUS Nay, pray be patient; if you refuse your aid
In this so never-needed help, yet do not
Upbraid's with our distress. But sure, if you
Would be your country's pleader, your good tongue,
More than the instant army we can make,
Might stop our countryman.
MENENIUS No; I'll not meddle.
SICINIUS Pray you go to him.
MENENIUS What should I do?
BRUTUS Only make trial what your love can do
For Rome, towards Marcius.
MENENIUS Well, and say that Marcius
Return me, as Cominius is return'd,
Unheard – what then?
But as a discontented friend, grief-shot
With his unkindness? Say't be so?
SICINIUS Yet your good will
Must have that thanks from Rome after the measure
As you intended well.
MENENIUS I'll undertake't;
I think he'll hear me. Yet to bite his lip
And hum at good Cominius much unhearts me.
He was not taken well; he had not din'd;
The veins unfill'd, our blood is cold, and then
We pout upon the morning, are unapt
To give or to forgive; but when we have stuff'd
These pipes and these conveyances of our blood
With wine and feeding, we have suppler souls
Than in our priest-like fasts. Therefore I'll watch him
Till he be dieted to my request,
And then I'll set upon him.
BRUTUS You know the very road into his kindness
And cannot lose your way.
MENENIUS Good faith, I'll prove him,
Speed how it will. I shall ere long have knowledge
Of my success. *[Exit.*
COMINIUS He'll never hear him.
SICINIUS Not?
COMINIUS I tell you he does sit in gold, his eye
Red as 'twould burn Rome, and his injury
The gaoler to his pity. I kneel'd before him;
'Twas very faintly he said 'Rise'; dismiss'd me
Thus with his speechless hand. What he would do,
He sent in writing after me; what he would not,
Bound with an oath to yield to his conditions;
So that all hope is vain,
Unless his noble mother and his wife,
Who, as I hear, mean to solicit him
For mercy to his country. Therefore let's hence,
And with our fair entreaties haste them on.
[Exeunt.

SCENE II. *The Volscian camp before Rome.*

Enter MENENIUS to the Watch on guard.

1 WATCH Stay. Whence are you?
2 WATCH Stand, and go back.
MENENIUS You guard like men, 'tis well; but, by your leave,
I am an officer of state and come
To speak with Coriolanus.
1 WATCH From whence?
MENENIUS From Rome.
1 WATCH You may not pass; you must return. Our general
Will no more hear from thence.
2 WATCH You'll see your Rome embrac'd with fire before
You'll speak with Coriolanus.
MENENIUS Good my friends,
If you have heard your general talk of Rome
And of his friends there, it is lots to blanks
My name hath touch'd your ears: it is Menenius.
1 WATCH Be it so; go back. The virtue of your name
Is not here passable.
MENENIUS I tell thee, fellow,
Thy general is my lover. I have been
The book of his good acts whence men have read
His fame unparallel'd haply amplified;
For I have ever verified my friends –
Of whom he's chief – with all the size that verity
Would without lapsing suffer. Nay, sometimes,
Like to a bowl upon a subtle ground,
I have tumbled past the throw, and in his praise
Have almost stamp'd the leasing; therefore, fellow,
I must have leave to pass.
1 WATCH Faith, sir, if you had told as many lies in his behalf as you have uttered words in your own, you should not pass here; no, though it were as virtuous to lie as to live chastely. Therefore go back.
MENENIUS Prithee, fellow, remember my name is Menenius, always factionary on the party of your general.
2 WATCH Howsoever you have been his liar, as you say you have, I am one that, telling true

under him, must say you cannot pass. Therefore go back.

MENENIUS Has he din'd, canst thou tell? For I would not speak with him till after dinner.

1 WATCH You are a Roman, are you?

MENENIUS I am as thy general is.

1 WATCH Then you should hate Rome, as he does. Can you, when you have push'd out your gates the very defender of them, and in a violent popular ignorance given your enemy your shield, think to front his revenges with the easy groans of old women, the virginal palms of your daughters, or with the palsied intercession of such a decay'd dotant as you seem to be? Can you think to blow out the intended fire your city is ready to flame in with such weak breath as this? No, you are deceiv'd; therefore back to Rome and prepare for your execution. You are condemn'd; our general has sworn you out of reprieve and pardon.

MENENIUS Sirrah, if thy captain knew I were here, he would use me with estimation.

1 WATCH Come, my captain knows you not.

MENENIUS I mean thy general.

1 WATCH My general cares not for you. Back, I say; go, lest I let forth your half pint of blood. Back – that's the utmost of your having. Back.

MENENIUS Nay, but fellow, fellow –

Enter CORIOLANUS with AUFIDIUS.

CORIOLANUS What's the matter?

MENENIUS Now, you companion, I'll say an errand for you; you shall know now that I am in estimation; you shall perceive that a Jack guardant cannot office me from my son Coriolanus. Guess but by my entertainment with him if thou stand'st not i' th' state of hanging, or of some death more long in spectatorship and crueller in suffering; behold now presently, and swoon for what's to come upon thee. The glorious gods sit in hourly synod about thy particular prosperity, and love thee no worse than thy old father Menenius does! O my son! my son! thou art preparing fire for us; look thee, here's water to quench it. I was hardly moved to come to thee; but being assured none but myself could move thee, I have been blown out of your gates with sighs, and conjure thee to pardon Rome and thy petitionary countrymen. The good gods assuage thy wrath, and turn the dregs of it upon this varlet here; this, who, like a block, hath denied my access to thee.

CORIOLANUS Away!

MENENIUS How! away!

CORIOLANUS Wife, mother, child, I know not.
My affairs
Are servanted to others. Though I owe
My revenge properly, my remission lies
In Volscian breasts. That we have been familiar,
Ingrate forgetfulness shall poison rather
Than pity note how much. Therefore be gone.
Mine ears against your suits are stronger than
Your gates against my force. Yet, for I lov'd thee,
Take this along; I writ it for thy sake
[*Gives a letter.*
And would have sent it. Another word,
Menenius,
I will not hear thee speak. This man, Aufidius,
Was my belov'd in Rome; yet thou behold'st.

AUFIDIUS You keep a constant temper.

[*Exeunt Coriolanus and Aufidius.*

1 WATCH Now, sir, is your name Menenius?

2 WATCH 'Tis a spell, you see, of much power! You know the way home again.

1 WATCH Do you hear how we are shent for keeping your greatness back?

2 WATCH What cause, do you think, I have to swoon?

MENENIUS I neither care for th' world nor your general; for such things as you, I can scarce think there's any, y'are so slight. He that hath a will to die by himself fears it not from another. Let your general do his worst. For you, be that you are, long; and your misery increase with your age! I say to you, as I was said to: Away!

[*Exit.*

1 WATCH A noble fellow, I warrant him.

2 WATCH The worthy fellow is our general; he's the rock, the oak not to be windshaken.

[*Exeunt.*

SCENE III. *The tent of Coriolanus.*

Enter CORIOLANUS, AUFIDIUS, and Others.

CORIOLANUS We will before the walls of Rome
to-morrow
Set down our host. My partner in this action,
You must report to th' Volscian lords how
plainly
I have borne this business.

AUFIDIUS Only their ends
You have respected; stopp'd your ears against
The general suit of Rome; never admitted
A private whisper – no, not with such friends
That though them sure of you.

CORIOLANUS This last old man,
Whom with a crack'd heart I have sent to Rome,
Lov'd me above the measure of a father;
Nay, godded me indeed. Their latest refuge
Was to send him; for whose old love I have –
Though I show'd sourly to him – once more
offer'd

The first conditions, which they did refuse
And cannot now accept. To grace him only,
That thought he could do more, a very little
I have yielded to; fresh embassies and suits,
Nor from the state nor private friends, hereafter
Will I lend ear to. [*Shout within*] Ha! what shout is this?
Shall I be tempted to infringe my vow
In the same time 'tis made? I will not.

Enter, in mourning habits, VIRGILIA, VOLUMNIA, VALERIA, young MARCIUS, with Attendants.

My wife comes foremost, then the honour'd mould
Wherein this trunk was fram'd, and in her hand
The grandchild to her blood. But out, affection!
All bond and privilege of nature, break!
Let it be virtuous to be obstinate.
What is that curtsy worth? or those doves' eyes,
Which can make gods forsworn? I melt, and am not
Of stronger earth than others. My mother bows,
As if Olympus to a molehill should
In supplication nod; and my young boy
Hath an aspect of intercession which
Great nature cries 'Deny not'. Let the Volsces
Plough Rome and harrow Italy; I'll never
Be such a gosling to obey instinct, but stand
As if a man were author of himself
And knew no other kin.

VIRGILIA My lord and husband!

CORIOLANUS These eyes are not the same I wore in Rome.

VIRGILIA The sorrow that delivers us thus chang'd
Makes you think so.

CORIOLANUS Like a dull actor now
I have forgot my part and I am out,
Even to a full disgrace. Best of my flesh,
Forgive my tyranny; but do not say,
For that, 'Forgive our Romans'. O, a kiss
Long as my exile, sweet as my revenge!
Now, by the jealous queen of heaven, that kiss
I carried from thee, dear, and my true lip
Hath virgin'd it e'er since. You gods! I prate,
And the most noble mother of the world
Leave unsaluted. Sink, my knee, i' th' earth; [*Kneels.*
Of thy deep duty more impression show
Than that of common sons.

VOLUMNIA O, stand up blest!
Whilst with no softer cushion than the flint
I kneel before thee, and unproperly
Show duty, as mistaken all this while
Between the child and parent. [*Kneels.*

CORIOLANUS What's this?
Your knees to me, to your corrected son?
Then let the pebbles on the hungry beach
Fillip the stars; then let the mutinous winds
Strike the proud cedars 'gainst the fiery sun,
Murd'ring impossibility, to make
What cannot be slight work.

VOLUMNIA Thou art my warrior;
I holp to frame thee. Do you know this lady?

CORIOLANUS The noble sister of Publicola,
The moon of Rome, chaste as the icicle
That's curdied by the frost from purest snow,
And hangs on Dian's temple – dear Valeria!

VOLUMNIA This is a poor epitome of yours,
Which by th' interpretation of full time
May show like all yourself.

CORIOLANUS The god of soldiers,
With the consent of supreme Jove, inform
Thy thoughts with nobleness, that thou mayst prove
To shame unvulnerable, and stick i' th' wars
Like a great sea-mark, standing every flaw,
And saving those that eye thee!

VOLUMNIA Your knee, sirrah.

CORIOLANUS That's my brave boy.

VOLUMNIA Even he, your wife, this lady, and myself,
Are suitors to you.

CORIOLANUS I beseech you, peace!
Or, if you'd ask, remember this before:
The thing I have forsworn to grant may never
Be held by you denials. Do not bid me
Dismiss my soldiers, or capitulate
Again with Rome's mechanics. Tell me not
Wherein I seem unnatural; desire not
T'allay my rages and revenges with
Your colder reasons.

VOLUMNIA O, no more, no more!
You have said you will not grant us any thing –
For we have nothing else to ask but that
Which you deny already; yet we will ask,
That, if you fail in our request, the blame
May hang upon your hardness; therefore hear us.

CORIOLANUS Aufidius, and you Volsces, mark; for we'll
Hear nought from Rome in private. Your request?

VOLUMNIA Should we be silent and not speak, our raiment
And state of bodies would bewray what life
We have led since thy exile. Think with thyself
How more unfortunate than all living women

Are we come hither; since that thy sight, which should
Make our eyes flow with joy, hearts dance with comforts,
Constrains them weep and shake with fear and sorrow,
Making the mother, wife, and child, to see
The son, the husband, and the father, tearing
His country's bowels out. And to poor we
Thine enmity's most capital: thou bar'st us
Our prayers to the gods, which is a comfort
That all but we enjoy. For how can we,
Alas, how can we for our country pray,
Whereto we are bound, together with thy victory,
Whereto we are bound? Alack, or we must lose
The country, our dear nurse, or else thy person,
Our comfort in the country. We must find
An evident calamity, though we had
Our wish, which side should win; for either thou
Must as a foreign recreant be led
With manacles through our streets, or else
Triumphantly tread on thy country's ruin,
And bear the palm for having bravely shed
Thy wife and children's blood. For myself, son,
I purpose not to wait on fortune till
These wars determine; if I can not persuade thee
Rather to show a noble grace to both parts
Than seek the end of one, thou shalt no sooner
March to assault thy country than to tread –
Trust to't, thou shalt not – on thy mother's womb
That brought thee to this world.

VIRGILIA Ay, and mine,
That brought you forth this boy to keep your name
Living to time.

BOY 'A shall not tread on me!
I'll run away till I am bigger, but then I'll fight.

CORIOLANUS Not of a woman's tenderness to be
Requires nor child nor woman's face to see.
I have sat too long. *[Rising.*

VOLUMNIA Nay, go not from us thus.
If it were so that our request did tend
To save the Romans, thereby to destroy
The Volsces whom you serve, you might condemn us
As poisonous of your honour. No, our suit
Is that you reconcile them: while the Volsces
May say 'This mercy we have show'd', the Romans
'This we receiv'd', and each in either side
Give the all-hail to thee, and cry 'Be blest
For making up this peace!' Thou know'st, great son,
The end of war's uncertain; but this certain
That, if thou conquer Rome, the benefit
Which thou shalt thereby reap is such a name
Whose repetition will be dogg'd with curses;
Whose chronicle thus writ: 'The man was noble,
But with his last attempt he wip'd it out,
Destroy'd his country, and his name remains
To th' ensuing age abhorr'd'. Speak to me, son.
Thou hast affected the fine strains of honour,
To imitate the graces of the gods,
To tear with thunder the wide cheeks o' th' air,
And yet to charge thy sulphur with a bolt
That should but rive an oak. Why dost not speak?
Think'st thou it honourable for a noble man
Still to remember wrongs? Daughter, speak you:
He cares not for your weeping. Speak thou, boy;
Perhaps thy childishness will move him more
Than can our reasons. There's no man in the world
More bound to's mother, yet here he lets me prate
Like one i' th' stocks. Thou hast never in thy life
Show'd thy dear mother any courtesy,
When she, poor hen, fond of no second brood,
Has cluck'd thee to the wars, and safely home
Loaden with honour. Say my request's unjust,
And spurn me back; but if it be not so,
Thou art not honest, and the gods will plague thee,
That thou restrain'st from me the duty which
To a mother's part belongs. He turns away.
Down, ladies; let us shame him with our knees.
To his surname Coriolanus 'longs more pride
Than pity to our prayers. Down. An end;
This is the last. So we will home to Rome,
And die among our neighbours. Nay, behold's!
This boy, that cannot tell what he would have
But kneels and holds up hands for fellowship,
Does reason our petition with more strength
Than thou hast to deny't. Come, let us go.
This fellow had a Volscian to his mother;
His wife is in Corioli, and his child
Like him by chance. Yet give us our dispatch.
I am hush'd until our city be afire,
And then I'll speak a little.
[He holds her by the hand, silent.

CORIOLANUS O mother, mother!
What have you done? Behold, the heavens do ope,
The gods look down, and this unnatural scene
They laugh at. O my mother, mother! O!
You have won a happy victory to Rome;
But for your son – believe it, O, believe it! –
Most dangerously you have with him prevail'd,
If not most mortal to him. But let it come.
Aufidius, though I cannot make true wars,

I'll frame convenient peace. Now, good Aufidius,
Were you in my stead, would you have heard
A mother less, or granted less, Aufidius?

AUFIDIUS I was mov'd withal.

CORIOLANUS I dare be sworn you were!
And, sir, it is no little thing to make
Mine eyes to sweat compassion. But, good sir,
What peace you'll make, advise me. For my part,
I'll not to Rome, I'll back with you; and pray you
Stand to me in this cause. O mother! wife!

AUFIDIUS [*Aside*] I am glad thou hast set thy mercy and thy honour
At difference in thee. Out of that I'll work
Myself a former fortune.

CORIOLANUS [*To the ladies*] Ay, by and by;
But we will drink together; and you shall bear
A better witness back than words, which we,
On like conditions, will have counter-seal'd.
Come, enter with us. Ladies, you deserve
To have a temple built you. All the swords
In Italy, and her confederate arms,
Could not have made this peace. [*Exeunt.*

SCENE IV. *Rome. A public place.*

Enter MENENIUS and SICINIUS.

MENENIUS See you yond coign o' th' Capitol, yond corner-stone?

SICINIUS Why, what of that?

MENENIUS If it be possible for you to displace it with your little finger, there is some hope the ladies of Rome, especially his mother, may prevail with him. But I say there is no hope in't; our throats are sentenc'd, and stay upon execution. SICINIUS Is't possible that so short a time can alter the condition of a man?

MENENIUS There is differency between a grub and a butterfly; yet your butterfly was a grub. This Marcius is grown from man to dragon; he has wings, he's more than a creeping thing.

SICINIUS He lov'd his mother dearly.

MENENIUS So did he me; and he no more remembers his mother now than an eight-year-old horse. The tartness of his face sours ripe grapes; when he walks, he moves like an engine and the ground shrinks before his treading. He is able to pierce a corslet with his eye, talks like a knell, and his hum is a battery. He sits in his state as a thing made for Alexander. What he bids be done is finish'd with his bidding. He wants nothing of a god but eternity, and a heaven to throne in.

SICINIUS Yes – mercy, if you report him truly.

MENENIUS I paint him in the character. Mark what mercy his mother shall bring from him. There is no more mercy in him than there is milk in a male tiger; that shall our poor city find. And all this is 'long of you.

SICINIUS The gods be good unto us!

MENENIUS No, in such a case the gods will not be good unto us. When we banish'd him we respected not them; and, he returning to break our necks, they respect not us.

Enter a Messenger.

MESSENGER Sir, if you'd save your life, fly to your house.
The plebeians have got your fellow tribune
And hale him up and down; all swearing if
The Roman ladies bring not comfort home
They'll give him death by inches.

Enter another Messenger.

SICINIUS What's the news?

2 MESSENGER Good news, good news! The ladies have prevail'd,
The Volscians are dislodg'd, and Marcius gone.
A merrier day did never yet greet Rome,
No, not th' expulsion of the Tarquins.

SICINIUS Friend,
Art thou certain this is true? Is't most certain?

2 MESSENGER As certain as I know the sun is fire.
Where have you lurk'd, that you make doubt of it?
Ne'er through an arch so hurried the blown tide
As the recomforted through th' gates.
Why, hark you! [*Trumpets, hautboys, drums beat, all together.*
The trumpets, sackbuts, psalteries, and fifes,
Tabors and cymbals, and the shouting Romans,
Make the sun dance. Hark you! [*A shout within.*

MENENIUS This is good news.
I will go meet the ladies. This Volumnia
Is worth of consuls, senators, patricians,
A city full; of tribunes such as you,
A sea and land full. You have pray'd well to-day:
This morning for ten thousand of your throats
I'd not have given a doit. Hark, how they joy!

[*Sound still with the shouts.*

SICINIUS First, the gods bless you for your tidings; next,
Accept my thankfulness.

2 MESSENGER Sir, we have all
Great cause to give great thanks.

SICINIUS They are near the city?

MESSENGER Almost at point to enter.

SICINIUS We'll meet them,
And help the joy. [*Exeunt.*

SCENE V. *Rome. A street near the gate.*

Enter two Senators with VOLUMNIA, VIRGILIA, VALERIA, passing over the stage, with other Lords.

1 SENATOR Behold our patroness, the life of Rome!
Call all your tribes together, praise the gods,
And make triumphant fires; strew flowers before them.
Unshout the noise that banish'd Marcius,
Repeal him with the welcome of his mother;
Cry 'Welcome, ladies, welcome!'

ALL Welcome, ladies, Welcome!

[*A flourish with drums and trumpets. Exeunt.*

SCENE VI. *Corioli. A public place.*

Enter TULLUS AUFIDIUS, with Attendants.

AUFIDIUS Go tell the lords o' th' city I am here;
Deliver them this paper; having read it,
Bid them repair to th' market-place, where I,
Even in theirs and in the commons' ears,
Will vouch the truth of it. Him I accuse
The city ports by this hath enter'd and
Intends t' appear before the people, hoping
To purge himself with words. Dispatch.

[*Exeunt Attendants.*

Enter three or four Conspirators of Aufidius' faction.

Most welcome!

1 CONSPIRATOR How is it with our general?

AUFIDIUS Even so
As with a man by his own alms empoison'd,
And with his charity slain.

2 CONSPIRATOR Most noble sir,
If you do hold the same intent wherein
You wish'd us parties, we'll deliver you
Of your great danger.

AUFIDIUS Sir, I cannot tell;
We must proceed as we do find the people.

3 CONSPIRATOR The people will remain uncertain whilst
'Twixt you there's difference; but the fall of either
Makes the survivor heir of all.

AUFIDIUS I know it;
And my pretext to strike at him admits
A good construction. I rais'd him, and I pawn'd
Mine honour for his truth; who being so heighten'd,
He watered his new plants with dews of flattery,
Seducing so my friends; and to this end
He bow'd his nature, never known before
But to be rough, unswayable, and free.

3 CONSPIRATOR Sir, his stoutness
When he did stand for consul, which he lost
By lack of stooping –

AUFIDIUS That I would have spoke of.
Being banish'd for't, he came unto my hearth,
Presented to my knife his throat. I took him;
Made him joint-servant with me; gave him way
In all his own desires; nay, let him choose
Out of my files, his projects to accomplish,
My best and freshest men; serv'd his designments
In mine own person; holp to reap the fame
Which he did end all his, and took some pride
To do myself this wrong. Till, at the last,
I seem'd his follower, not partner; and
He wag'd me with his countenance as if
I had been mercenary.

1 CONSPIRATOR So he did, my lord.
The army marvell'd at it; and, in the last,
When he had carried Rome and that we look'd
For no less spoil than glory –

AUFIDIUS There was it;
For which my sinews shall be stretch'd upon him.
At a few drops of women's rheum, which are
As cheap as lies, he sold the blood and labour
Of our great action; therefore shall he die,
And I'll renew me in his fall. But, hark!

[*Drums and trumpets sound, with great shouts of the people.*

1 CONSPIRATOR Your native town you enter'd like a post,
And had no welcomes home; but he returns
Splitting the air with noise.

2 CONSPIRATOR And patient fools,
Whose children he hath slain, their base throats tear
With giving him glory.

3 CONSPIRATOR Therefore, at your vantage,
Ere he express himself or move the people
With what he would say, let him feel your sword,
Which we will second. When he lies along,
After your way his tale pronounc'd shall bury
His reasons with his body.

AUFIDIUS Say no more:
Here come the lords.

Enter the Lords of the city.

LORDS You are most welcome home.

AUFIDIUS I have not deserv'd it.
But, worthy lords, have you with heed perused
What I have written to you?

LORDS We have.

1 LORD And grieve to hear't.
What faults he made before the last, I think
Might have found easy fines; but there to end
Where he was to begin, and give away
The benefit of our levies, answering us
With our own charge, making a treaty where
There was a yielding – this admits no excuse.

AUFIDIUS He approaches; you shall hear him.

Enter CORIOLANUS, marching with drum and colours: the Commoners being with him.

CORIOLANUS Hail, lords! I am return'd your soldier;
No more infected with my country's love
Than when I parted hence, but still subsisting
Under your great command. You are to know
That prosperously I have attempted, and
With bloody passage led your wars even to
The gates of Rome. Our spoils we have brought home
Doth more than counterpoise a full third part
The charges of the action. We have made peace
With no less honour to the Antiates
Than shame to th' Romans; and we here deliver,
Subscrib'd by th' consuls and patricians,
Together with the seal o' th' Senate, what
We have compounded on.
AUFIDIUS Read it not, noble lords;
But tell the traitor in the highest degree
He hath abus'd your powers.
CORIOLANUS Traitor! How now?
AUFIDIUS Ay, traitor, Marcius.
CORIOLANUS Marcius!
AUFIDIUS Ay, Marcius, Caius Marcius! Dost thou think
I'll grace thee with that robbery, thy stol'n name
Coriolanus, in Corioli?
You lords and heads o' th' state, perfidiously
He has betray'd your business and given up,
For certain drops of salt, your city Rome –
I say your city – to his wife and mother;
Breaking his oath and resolution like
A twist of rotten silk; never admitting
Counsel o' th' war; but at his nurse's tears
He whin'd and roar'd away your victory,
That pages blush'd at him, and men of heart
Look'd wond'ring each at others.
CORIOLANUS Hear'st thou, Mars?
AUFIDIUS Name not the god, thou boy of tears –
CORIOLANUS Ha!
AUFIDIUS – no more.
CORIOLANUS Measureless liar, thou hast made my heart
Too great for what contains it. 'Boy'! O slave!
Pardon me, lords, 'tis the first time that ever
I was forc'd to scold. Your judgments, my grave lords,
Must give this cur the lie; and his own notion –
Who wears my stripes impress'd upon him, that
Must bear my beating to his grave – shall join
To thrust the lie unto him.
1 LORD Peace, both, and hear me speak.
CORIOLANUS Cut me to pieces, Volsces; men and lads,
Stain all your edges on me. 'Boy'! False hound!
If you have writ your annals true, 'tis there
That, like an eagle in a dove-cote, I
Flutter'd your Volscians in Corioli.
Alone I did it. 'Boy'!
AUFIDIUS Why, noble lords,
Will you be put in mind of his blind fortune,
Which was your shame, by this unholy braggart,
Fore your own eyes and ears?
CONSPIRATORS Let him die for't.
ALL THE PEOPLE Tear him to pieces. Do it presently. He kill'd my son. My daughter. He kill'd my cousin Marcus. He kill'd my father.
2 LORD Peace, ho! No outrage – peace!
The man is noble, and his fame folds in
This orb o' th' earth. His last offences to us
Shall have judicious hearing. Stand, Aufidius,
And trouble not the peace.
CORIOLANUS O that I had him,
With six Aufidiuses, or more – his tribe,
To use my lawful sword!
AUFIDIUS Insolent villain!
CONSPIRATORS Kill, kill, kill, kill, kill him!

[*The Conspirators draw and kill Coriolanus, who falls. Aufidius stands on him.*

LORDS Hold, hold, hold, hold!
AUFIDIUS My noble masters, hear me speak.
1 LORD O Tullus!
2 LORD Thou hast done a deed whereat valour will weep.
3 LORD Tread not upon him. Masters all, be quiet;
Put up your swords.
AUFIDIUS My lords, when you shall know – as in this rage,
Provok'd by him, you cannot – the great danger
Which this man's life did owe you, you'll rejoice
That he is thus cut off. Please it your honours
To call me to your Senate, I'll deliver
Myself your loyal servant, or endure
Your heaviest censure.
1 LORD Bear from hence his body,
And mourn you for him. Let him be regarded
As the most noble corse that ever herald
Did follow to his urn.
2 LORD His own impatience
Takes from Aufidius a great part of blame.
Let's make the best of it.
AUFIDIUS My rage is gone,
And I am struck with sorrow. Take him up.
Help, three o' th' chiefest soldiers; I'll be one.
Beat thou the drum, that it speak mournfully;
Trail your steel pikes. Though in this city he
Hath widowed and unchilded many a one,
Which to this hour bewail the injury,
Yet he shall have a noble memory.
Assist.

[*Exeunt, bearing the body of Coriolanus. A dead march sounded.*

Titus Andronicus

Introduction by ROBERT MASLEN

Titus Andronicus is the earliest, the bloodiest and the most under-rated of Shakespeare's tragedies. It is also a daring experiment in political fiction. The first recorded performance took place in 1594, but most scholars agree that the play was written much earlier, perhaps in 1590. It seems to have been popular at the time, but since the late seventeenth century it has often been dismissed as too tasteless to be admitted into the Shakespeare canon. *Titus Andronicus* retains its power to shock, and since Peter Brook's celebrated production in 1955 has proved itself time and again to be a brilliant and unnerving spectacle on stage.

The tragedy takes as its setting an unspecified moment in late Roman history when Rome is under threat of invasion by the Goths; contemporary audiences might have seen a resemblance to England's volatile relations with Spain. It opens with another political situation that would have been familiar to the Elizabethans, a quarrel over the succession. The brothers Saturninus and Bassianus both claim the right to succeed their father as Emperor: Saturninus bases his claim on his hereditary right as the eldest son, while Bassianus appeals to the Roman people to recognise his superior qualities as a leader. But the people have confidence in neither brother, and instead elect Titus Andronicus, an ageing general who has spent his life defending Rome against the Goths. Titus refuses the imperial crown on grounds of old age (Rome deserves a 'better head . . . Than his that shakes for age and feebleness' [1.1.187–8]), and gives his support to the autocratic Saturninus. In doing so he unwittingly transforms Rome into a 'wilderness of tigers' [3.1.54], a hell on earth in which the will of a small governing elite overthrows the systems of both law and language in the irresponsible pursuit of its own interests.

The power of the play derives in part from its relentless use of the body as the space, in which tyranny operates. The chief emblem of the agony of the Roman people is Titus' daughter Lavinia, whose name associates her with the wife of Aeneas, the founder of Rome. she is first rejected as wife by Saturninus, then raped by his stepsons, who cut out her tongue and lop off her hands as a graphic illustration of the silencing of opposition and protest under tyranny. The rest of the Andronici suffer different mutilations: the sons of Titus lose their heads for a crime they did not commit, while Titus, finding his verbal appeals for mercy ignored, is tricked into cutting off his own hand in the belief that this will persuade the judges to spare the condemned men. Meanwhile, Saturninus marries Titus' old enemy, Tamora queen of the Goths. Together with her black lover Aaron, Tamora sets about demonstrating what a fine line separates Roman from Goth, 'civilisation' from 'barbarism'.

Aaron is the first of Shakespeare's great villians, a ruthless master of ceremonies who masterminds the destruction of Titus' family. In a succession of the most inventive speeches in the play he transforms himself into Rome's avenging demon:

> What signifies by deadly-standing eye, [...]
> My fleece of woolly hair that now uncurls

Even as an adder when she doth unroll
To do some fatal execution?
No, madam, these are no venereal signs.
Blood and revenge are hammering in my head [2.3.32–39]

Aaron is so successful in setting the tone of the play that it is only by adopting a similar style of grotesquely inventive violence that Titus can restore Rome to the control of the Romans. In the last act he abandons tears and lamentations for a more vigorous form of self-expression, chopping up Tamora's sons and serving them to her for dinner, baked in a pie. In this way he writes his own conclusion to the tale of Philomela from Ovid's *Metamorphoses* on which the play is based. The tragedy ends with a general massacre of the major characters, and with the election of Titus' last surviving son Lucius as emperor.

Like his father, Lucius is a favourite with the Roman people, and his election serves to 'knit again' the 'broken limbs' of Rome into 'one body' [5.369–71]. One might suspect that Shakespeare was warning his contemporaries in this play about the dangers of absolute monarchy and the suppression of the popular voice. In the process he produced a wonderfully nasty piece of entertainment.

Titus Andronicus

DRAMATIS PERSONAE

SATURNINUS
son to the late Emperor of Rome, afterwards Emperor
BASSIANUS
brother to Saturninus
TITUS ANDRONICUS
a noble Roman
MARCUS ANDRONICUS
Tribune of the People, and brother to Titus
LUCIUS, QUINTUS, MARTIUS, MUTIUS
sons to Titus Andronicus
YOUNG LUCIUS
a boy, son to Lucius
PUBLIUS
son to Marcus Andronicus
SEMPRONIUS, CAIUS, VALENTINE
kinsmen to Titus

AEMILIUS
a noble Roman
ALARBUS, DEMETRIUS, CHIRON
sons to Tamora
AARON
a Moor, beloved by Tamora
A Captain
A Messenger
A Clown
TAMORA
Queen of the Goths
LAVINIA
daughter to Titus Andronicus
A Nurse and a black Child
Romans and Goths, Senators, Tribunes, Officers, Soldiers and Attendants.

THE SCENE: ROME AND THE NEIGHBOURHOOD.

ACT ONE

SCENE I. *Rome. Before the Capitol.*

Flourish. Enter the Tribunes and Senators aloft; and then enter below SATURNINUS and his Followers at one door, and BASSIANUS and his Followers at the other, with drums and trumpets.

SATURNINUS Noble patricians, patrons of my right,
Defend the justice of my cause with arms;
And, countrymen, my loving followers,
Plead my successive title with your swords.
I am his first-born son that was the last
That ware the imperial diadem of Rome;
Then let my father's honours live in me,
Nor wrong mine age with this indignity.

BASSIANUS Romans, friends, followers, favourers of my right,
If ever Bassianus, Caesar's son,
Were gracious in the eyes of royal Rome,
Keep then this passage to the Capitol;
And suffer not dishonour to approach
The imperial seat, to virtue consecrate,
To justice, continence, and nobility;
But let desert in pure election shine;
And, Romans, fight for freedom in your choice.

Enter MARCUS ANDRONICUS aloft, with the crown.

MARCUS Princes, that strive by factions and by friends
Ambitiously for rule and empery,
Know that the people of Rome, for whom we stand
A special party, have by common voice
In election for the Roman empery
Chosen Andronicus, surnamed Pius
For many good and great deserts to Rome.
A nobler man, a braver warrior,
Lives not this day within the city walls.
He by the Senate is accited home,
From weary wars against the barbarous Goths,
That with his sons, a terror to our foes,
Hath yok'd a nation strong, train'd up in arms.
Ten years are spent since first he undertook
This cause of Rome, and chastised with arms
Our enemies' pride; five times he hath return'd
Bleeding to Rome, bearing his valiant sons
In coffins from the field; *and at this day*
To the monument of that Andronici
Done sacrifice of expiation,
And slain the noblest prisoner of the Goths.
And now at last, laden with honour's spoils,
Returns the good Andronicus to Rome,
Renowned Titus, flourishing in arms.
Let us entreat, by honour of his name
Whom worthily you would have now succeed,
And in the Capitol and Senate's right,
Whom you pretend to honour and adore,
That you withdraw you and abate your strength,
Dismiss your followers, and, as suitors should,
Plead your deserts in peace and humbleness.

SATURNINUS How fair the Tribune speaks to calm my thoughts!

BASSIANUS Marcus Andronicus, so I do affy

In thy uprightness and integrity,
And so I love and honour thee and thine,
Thy noble brother Titus and his sons,
And her to whom my thoughts are humbled all,
Gracious Lavinia, Rome's rich ornament,
That I will here dismiss my loving friends,
And to my fortunes and the people's favour
Commit my cause in balance to be weigh'd.

[Exeunt the soldiers of Bassianus.

SATURNINUS Friends, that have been thus forward in my right,
I thank you all and here dismiss you all,
And to the love and favour of my country
Commit myself, my person, and the cause.

[Exeunt the soldiers of Saturninus.

Rome, be as just and gracious unto me
As I am confident and kind to thee.
Open the gates and let me in.

BASSIANUS Tribunes, and me, a poor competitor.

[Flourish. They go up into the Senate House.

Enter a Captain.

CAPTAIN Romans, make way. The good Andronicus,
Patron of virtue, Rome's best champion,
Successful in the battles that he fights,
With honour and with fortune is return'd
From where he circumscribed with his sword
And brought to yoke the enemies of Rome.

Sound drums and trumpets, and then enter MARTIUS and MUTIUS, two of Titus' sons; and then two Men bearing a coffin covered with black; then LUCIUS and QUINTUS, two other sons; then TITUS ANDRONICUS; and then TAMORA the Queen of Goths, with her three sons, ALARBUS, DEMETRIUS and CHIRON, with AARON the Moor, and Others, as many as can be. Then set down the coffin and Titus speaks.

TITUS Hail, Rome, victorious in thy mourning weeds!
Lo, as the bark that hath discharg'd her fraught
Returns with precious lading to the bay
From whence at first she weigh'd her anchorage,
Cometh Andronicus, bound with laurel boughs,
To re-salute his country with his tears,
Tears of true joy for his return to Rome.
Thou great defender of this Capitol,
Stand gracious to the rites that we intend!
Romans, of five and twenty valiant sons,
Half of the number that King Priam had,
Behold the poor remains, alive and dead!
These that survive let Rome reward with love;
These that I bring unto their latest home,
With burial amongst their ancestors.
Here Goths have given me leave to sheathe my sword.
Titus, unkind, and careless of thine own,
Why suffer'st thou thy sons, unburied yet,
To hover on the dreadful shore of Styx?
Make way to lay them by their brethren.

[They open the tomb.

There greet in silence, as the dead are wont,
And sleep in peace, slain in your country's wars.
O sacred receptacle of my joys,
Sweet cell of virtue and nobility,
How many sons hast thou of mine in store
That thou wilt never render to me more!

LUCIUS Give us the proudest prisoner of the Goths,
That we may hew his limbs, and on a pile
Ad manes fratrum sacrifice his flesh
Before this earthy prison of their bones,
That so the shadows be not unappeas'd,
Nor we disturb'd with prodigies on earth.

TITUS I give him you – the noblest that survives,
The eldest son of this distressed queen.

TAMORA Stay, Roman brethren! Gracious conqueror,
Victorious Titus, rue the tears I shed,
A mother's tears in passion for her son;
And if thy sons were ever dear to thee,
O, think my son to be as dear to me!
Sufficeth not that we are brought to Rome
To beautify thy triumphs, and return
Captive to thee and to thy Roman yoke;
But must my sons be slaughtered in the streets
For valiant doings in their country's cause?
O, if to fight for king and commonweal
Were piety in thine, it is in these.
Andronicus, stain not thy tomb with blood.
Wilt thou draw near the nature of the gods?
Draw near them then in being merciful.
Sweet mercy is nobility's true badge.
Thrice-noble Titus, spare my first-born son.

TITUS Patient yourself, madam, and pardon me.
These are their brethren, whom your Goths beheld
Alive and dead; and for their brethren slain
Religiously they ask a sacrifice.
To this your son is mark'd, and die he must
T' appease their groaning shadows that are gone.

LUCIUS Away with him, and make a fire straight;
And with our swords, upon a pile of wood,
Let's hew his limbs till they be clean consum'd.

[Exeunt Titus' sons, with Alarbus.

TAMORA O cruel, irreligious piety!

CHIRON Was never Scythia half so barbarous!

DEMETRIUS Oppose not Scythia to ambitious Rome.

Alarbus goes to rest, and we survive
To tremble under Titus' threat'ning look.
Then, madam, stand resolv'd, but hope withal
The self-same gods that arm'd the Queen of Troy
With opportunity of sharp revenge
Upon the Thracian tyrant in his tent
May favour Tamora, the queen of Goths –
When Goths were Goths and Tamora was queen –
To quit the bloody wrongs upon her foes.

Re-enter LUCIUS, QUINTUS, MARTIUS, and MUTIUS the sons of Andronicus, with their swords bloody.

LUCIUS See, lord and father, how we have perform'd
Our Roman rites: Alarbus' limbs are lopp'd,
And entrails feed the sacrificing fire,
Whose smoke like incense doth perfume the sky.
Remaineth nought but to inter our brethren,
And with loud 'larums welcome them to Rome.

TITUS Let it be so, and let Andronicus
Make this his latest farewell to their souls.

Sound trumpets and lay the coffin in the tomb.

In peace and honour rest you here, my sons;
Rome's readiest champions, repose you here in rest,
Secure from worldly chances and mishaps!
Here lurks no treason, here no envy swells,
Here grow no damned drugs, here are no storms,
No noise, but silence and eternal sleep.
In peace and honour rest you here, my sons!

Enter LAVINIA.

LAVINIA In peace and honour live Lord Titus long;
My noble lord and father, live in fame!
Lo, at this tomb my tributary tears
I render for my brethren's obsequies;
And at thy feet I kneel, with tears of joy
Shed on this earth for thy return to Rome.
O, bless me here with thy victorious hand,
Whose fortunes Rome's best citizens applaud!

TITUS Kind Rome, that hast thus lovingly reserv'd
The cordial of mine age to glad my heart!
Lavinia, live; outlive thy father's days,
And fame's eternal date, for virtue's praise!

Enter, above, MARCUS ANDRONICUS and Tribunes; re-enter SATURNINUS, BASSIANUS, and Attendants.

MARCUS Long live Lord Titus, my beloved brother,
Gracious triumpher in the eyes of Rome!

TITUS Thanks, gentle Tribune, noble brother Marcus.

MARCUS And welcome, nephews, from successful wars,
You that survive and you that sleep in fame.
Fair lords, your fortunes are alike in all
That in your country's service drew your swords;
But safer triumph is this funeral pomp
That hath aspir'd to Solon's happiness
And triumphs over chance in honour's bed.
Titus Andronicus, the people of Rome,
Whose friend in justice thou hast ever been,
Send thee by me, their Tribune and their trust,
This palliament of white and spotless hue;
And name thee in election for the empire
With these our late-deceased Emperor's sons:
Be candidatus then, and put it on,
And help to set a head on headless Rome.

TITUS A better head her glorious body fits
Than his that shakes for age and feebleness.
What should I don this robe and trouble you?
Be chosen with proclamations to-day,
To-morrow yield up rule, resign my life,
And set abroad new business for you all?
Rome, I have been thy soldier forty years,
And led my country's strength successfully,
And buried one and twenty valiant sons,
Knighted in field, slain manfully in arms,
In right and service of their noble country.
Give me a staff of honour for mine age,
But not a sceptre to control the world.
Upright he held it, lords, that held it last.

MARCUS Titus, thou shalt obtain and ask the empery.

SATURNINUS Proud and ambitious Tribune, canst thou tell?

TITUS Patience, Prince Saturninus.

SATURNINUS Romans, do me right.
Patricians, draw your swords, and sheathe them not
Till Saturninus be Rome's Emperor.
Andronicus, would thou were shipp'd to hell
Rather than rob me of the people's hearts!

LUCIUS Proud Saturnine, interrupter of the good
That noble-minded Titus means to thee!

TITUS Content thee, Prince; I will restore to thee
The people's hearts, and wean them from themselves.

BASSIANUS Andronicus, I do not flatter thee,
But honour thee, and will do till I die.
My faction if thou strengthen with thy friends,
I will most thankful be; and thanks to men
Of noble minds is honourable meed.

TITUS People of Rome, and people's Tribunes here,

I ask your voices and your suffrages:
Will ye bestow them friendly on Andronicus?
TRIBUNES To gratify the good Andronicus,
And gratulate his safe return to Rome,
The people will accept whom he admits.
TITUS Tribunes, I thank you; and this suit I make,
That you create our Emperor's eldest son,
Lord Saturnine; whose virtues will, I hope,
Reflect on Rome as Titan's rays on earth,
And ripen justice in this commonweal.
Then, if you will elect by my advice,
Crown him, and say 'Long live our Emperor!'
MARCUS With voices and applause of every sort,
Patricians and plebeians, we create
Lord Saturninus Rome's great Emperor,
And say 'Long live our Emperor Saturnine!'
[A long flourish till they come down.
SATURNINUS Titus Andronicus, for thy favours done
To us in our election this day
I give thee thanks in part of thy deserts,
And will with deeds requite thy gentleness;
And for an onset, Titus, to advance
Thy name and honourable family,
Lavinia will I make my empress,
Rome's royal mistress, mistress of my heart,
And in the sacred Pantheon her espouse.
Tell me, Andronicus, doth this motion please thee?
TITUS It doth, my worthy lord, and in this match
I hold me highly honoured of your Grace,
And here in sight of Rome, to Saturnine,
King and commander of our commonweal,
The wide world's Emperor, do I consecrate
My sword, my chariot, and my prisoners,
Presents well worthy Rome's imperious lord;
Receive them then, the tribute that I owe,
Mine honour's ensigns humbled at thy feet.
SATURNINUS Thanks, noble Titus, father of my life.
How proud I am of thee and of thy gifts
Rome shall record; and when I do forget
The least of these unspeakable deserts,
Romans, forget your fealty to me.
TITUS *[To Tamora]* Now, madam, are you prisoner to an emperor;
To him that for your honour and your state
Will use you nobly and your followers.
SATURNINUS *[Aside]* A goodly lady, trust me; of the hue
That I would choose, were I to choose anew. –
Clear up, fair Queen, that cloudy countenance;
Though chance of war hath wrought this change of cheer,
Thou com'st not to be made a scorn in Rome –
Princely shall be thy usage every way.
Rest on my word, and let not discontent
Daunt all your hopes. Madam, he comforts you
Can make you greater than the Queen of Goths.
Lavinia, you are not displeas'd with this?
LAVINIA Not I, my lord, sith true nobility
Warrants these words in princely courtesy.
SATURNINUS Thanks, sweet Lavinia. Romans, let us go.
Ransomless here we set our prisoners free.
Proclaim our honours, lords, with trump and drum. *[Flourish.*
BASSIANUS Lord Titus, by your leave, this maid is mine. *[Seizing Lavinia.*
TITUS How, sir! Are you in earnest then, my lord?
BASSIANUS Ay, noble Titus, and resolv'd withal
To do myself this reason and this right.
MARCUS Suum cuique is our Roman justice:
This prince in justice seizeth but his own.
LUCIUS And that he will and shall, if Lucius live.
TITUS Traitors, avaunt! Where is the Emperor's guard?
Treason, my lord – Lavinia is surpris'd!
SATURNINUS Surpris'd! By whom?
BASSIANUS By him that justly may
Bear his betroth'd from all the world away.
[Exeunt Bassianus and Marcus with Lavinia.
MUTIUS Brothers, help to convey her hence away.
And with my sword I'll keep this door safe.
[Exeunt Lucius, Quintus, and Martius.
TITUS Follow, my lord, and I'll soon bring her back.
MUTIUS My lord, you pass not here.
TITUS What, villain boy!
Bar'st me my way in Rome?
MUTIUS Help, Lucius, help!
[Titus kills him. During the fray, exeunt Saturninus, Tamora, Demetrius, Chiron, and Aaron.

Re-enter LUCIUS.

LUCIUS My lord, you are unjust, and more than so:
In wrongful quarrel you have slain your son.
TITUS Nor thou nor he are any sons of mine;
My sons would never so dishonour me.

Re-enter aloft the EMPEROR *with* TAMORA *and her two Sons, and* AARON *the Moor.*

Traitor, restore Lavinia to the Emperor.
LUCIUS Dead, if you will; but not to be his wife,
That is another's lawful promis'd love. *[Exit.*
SATURNINUS No, Titus, no; the Emperor needs her not,

Nor her, nor thee, nor any of thy stock.
I'll trust by leisure him that mocks me once;
Thee never, nor thy traitorous haughty sons,
Confederates all thus to dishonour me.
Was there none else in Rome to make a stale
But Saturnine? Full well, Andronicus,
Agree these deeds with that proud brag of thine
That saidst I begg'd the empire at thy hands.

TITUS O monstrous! What reproachful words are these?

SATURNINUS But go thy ways; go, give that changing piece
To him that flourish'd for her with his sword.
A valiant son-in-law thou shalt enjoy;
One fit to bandy with thy lawless sons,
To ruffle in the commonwealth of Rome.

TITUS These words are razors to my wounded heart.

SATURNINUS And therefore, lovely Tamora, Queen of Goths,
That, like the stately Phoebe 'mongst her nymphs,
Dost overshine the gallant'st dames of Rome,
If thou be pleas'd with this my sudden choice,
Behold, I choose thee, Tamora, for my bride
And will create thee Emperess of Rome.
Speak, Queen of Goths, dost thou applaud my choice?
And here I swear by all the Roman gods –
Sith priest and holy water are so near,
And tapers burn so bright, and everything
In readiness for Hymenaeus stand –
I will not re-salute the streets of Rome,
Or climb my palace, till from forth this place
I lead espous'd my bride along with me.

TAMORA And here in sight of heaven to Rome I swear,
If Saturnine advance the Queen of Goths,
She will a handmaid be to his desires,
A loving nurse, a mother to his youth.

SATURNINUS Ascend, fair queen, Pantheon. Lords, accompany
Your noble Emperor and his lovely bride,
Sent by the heavens for Prince Saturnine,
Whose wisdom hath her fortune conquered;
There shall we consummate our spousal rites.

[*Exeunt all but Titus.*

TITUS I am not bid to wait upon this bride.
Titus, when wert thou wont to walk alone,
Dishonoured thus, and challenged of wrongs?

Re-enter MARCUS, and Titus' sons, LUCIUS, QUINTUS, and MARTIUS.

MARCUS O Titus, see, O, see what thou hast done!
In a bad quarrel slain a virtuous son.

TITUS No, foolish Tribune, no; no son of mine –
Nor thou, nor these, confederates in the deed
That hath dishonoured all our family;
Unworthy brother and unworthy sons!

LUCIUS But let us give him burial, as becomes;
Give Mutius burial with our bretheren.

TITUS Traitors, away! He rests not in this tomb.
This monument five hundred years hath stood,
Which I have sumptuously re-edified;
Here none but soldiers and Rome's servitors
Repose in fame; none basely slain in brawls.
Bury him where you can, he comes not here.

MARCUS My lord, this is impiety in you.
My nephew Mutius' deeds do plead for him;
He must be buried with his bretheren.

QUINTUS, MARTIUS And shall, or him we will accompany.

TITUS 'And shall'! What villain was it spake that word?

QUINTUS He that would vouch it in any place but here.

TITUS What, would you bury him in my despite?

MARCUS No, noble Titus, but entreat of thee
To pardon Mutius and to bury him.

TITUS Marcus, even thou hast struck upon my crest,
And with these boys mine honour thou hast wounded.
My foes I do repute you every one;
So trouble me no more, but get you gone.

MARTIUS He is not with himself; let us withdraw.

QUINTUS Not I, till Mutius' bones be buried.

[*The brother and the sons kneel.*

MARCUS Brother, for in that name doth nature plead –

QUINTUS Father, and in that name doth nature speak –

TITUS Speak thou no more, if all the rest will speed.

MARCUS Renowned Titus, more than half my soul –

LUCIUS Dear father, soul and substance of us all –

MARCUS Suffer thy brother Marcus to inter
His noble nephew here in virtue's nest,
That died in honour and Lavinia's cause.
Thou art a Roman – be not barbarous.
The Greeks upon advice did bury Ajax,
That slew himself; and wise Laertes' son
Did graciously plead for his funerals.
Let not young Mutius, then, that was thy joy,
Be barr'd his entrance here.

TITUS Rise, Marcus, rise;
The dismal'st day is this that e'er I saw,
To be dishonoured by my sons in Rome!
Well, bury him, and bury me the next.

[*They put Mutius in the tomb.*

LUCIUS There lie thy bones, sweet Mutius, with thy friends,
Till we with trophies do adorn thy tomb.
ALL [*Kneeling*] No man shed tears for noble Mutius;
He lives in fame that died in virtue's cause.
MARCUS My lord – to step out of these dreary dumps –
How comes it that the subtle Queen of Goths
Is of a sudden thus advanc'd in Rome?
TITUS I know not, Marcus, but I know it is –
Whether by device or no, the heavens can tell.
Is she not, then, beholding to the man
That brought her for this high good turn so far?
MARCUS Yes, and will nobly him remunerate.

Flourish. Re-enter the EMPEROR, TAMORA and her two Sons, with the Moor, at one door; at the other door, BASSIANUS and LAVINIA, with Others.

SATURNINUS So, Bassianus, you have play'd your prize:
God give you joy, sir, of your gallant bride!
BASSIANUS And you of yours, my lord! I say no more,
Nor wish no less; and so I take my leave.
SATURNINUS Traitor, if Rome have law or we have power,
Thou and thy faction shall repent this rape.
BASSIANUS Rape, call you it, my lord, to seize my own,
My true betrothed love, and now my wife?
But let the laws of Rome determine all;
Meanwhile am I possess'd of that is mine.
SATURNINUS 'Tis good, sir. You are very short with us;
But if we live we'll be as sharp with you.
BASSIANUS My lord, what I have done, as best I may,
Answer I must, and shall do with my life.
Only thus much I give your Grace to know:
By all the duties that I owe to Rome,
This noble gentleman, Lord Titus here,
Is in opinion and in honour wrong'd,
That, in the rescue of Lavinia,
With his own hand did slay his youngest son,
In zeal to you, and highly mov'd to wrath
To be controll'd in that he frankly gave.
Receive him then to favour, Saturnine,
That hath express'd himself in all his deeds
A father and a friend to thee and Rome.
TITUS Prince Bassianus, leave to plead my deeds.
'Tis thou and those that have dishonoured me.
Rome and the righteous heavens be my judge
How I have lov'd and honoured Saturnine!
TAMORA My worthy lord, if ever Tamora
Were gracious in those princely eyes of thine,
Then hear me speak indifferently for all;
And at my suit, sweet, pardon what is past.
SATURNINUS What, madam! be dishonoured openly,
And basely put it up without revenge?
TAMORA Not so, my lord; the gods of Rome forfend
I should be author to dishonour you!
But on mine honour dare I undertake
For good Lord Titus' innocence in all,
Whose fury not dissembled speaks his griefs.
Then at my suit look graciously on him;
Lose not so noble a friend on vain suppose,
Nor with sour looks afflict his gentle heart.
[*Aside to Saturninus*] My lord, be rul'd by me, be won at last;
Dissemble all your griefs and discontents.
You are but newly planted in your throne;
Lest, then, the people, and patricians too,
Upon a just survey take Titus' part,
And so supplant you for ingratitude,
Which Rome reputes to be a heinous sin,
Yield at entreats, and then let me alone:
I'll find a day to massacre them all,
And raze their faction and their family,
The cruel father and his traitorous sons,
To whom I sued for my dear son's life;
And make them know what 'tis to let a queen
Kneel in the streets and beg for grace in vain. –
Come, come, sweet Emperor; come, Andronicus.
Take up this good old man, and cheer the heart
That dies in tempest of thy angry frown.
SATURNINUS Rise, Titus, rise; my Empress hath prevail'd.
TITUS I thank your Majesty and her, my lord;
These words, these looks, infuse new life in me.
TAMORA Titus, I am incorporate in Rome,
A Roman now adopted happily,
And must advise the Emperor for his good.
This day all quarrels die, Andronicus;
And let it be mine honour, good my lord,
That I have reconcil'd your friends and you.
For you, Prince Bassianus, I have pass'd
My word and promise to the Emperor
That you will be more mild and tractable.
And fear not, lords – and you, Lavinia.
By my advice, all humbled on your knees,
You shall ask pardon of his Majesty.
LUCIUS We do, and vow to heaven and to his Highness
That what we did was mildly as we might,
Tend'ring our sister's honour and our own.
MARCUS That on mine honour here do I protest.
SATURNINUS Away, and talk not; trouble us no more.
TAMORA Nay, nay, sweet Emperor, we must all be friends.
The Tribune and his nephews kneel for grace.

I will not be denied. Sweet heart, look back.
SATURNINUS Marcus, for thy sake, and thy brother's here,
And at my lovely Tamora's entreats,
I do remit these young men's heinous faults.
Stand up.
Lavinia, though you left me like a churl,
I found a friend; and sure as death I swore
I would not part a bachelor from the priest.
Come, if the Emperor's court can feast two brides,
You are my guest, Lavinia, and your friends.
This day shall be a love-day, Tamora.
TITUS To-morrow, an it please your Majesty
To hunt the panther and the hart with me,
With horn and hound we'll give your Grace bonjour.
SATURNINUS Be it so, Titus, and gramercy too.
[*Exeunt. Sound trumpets.*

ACT TWO

SCENE I. *Rome. Before the palace.*

Enter AARON.

AARON Now climbeth Tamora Olympus' top,
Safe out of Fortune's shot, and sits aloft,
Secure of thunder's crack or lightning flash,
Advanc'd above pale envy's threat'ning reach.
As when the golden sun salutes the morn,
And, having gilt the ocean with his beams,
Gallops the zodiac in his glistering coach
And overlooks the highest-peering hills,
So Tamora.
Upon her wit doth earthly honour wait,
And virtue stoops and trembles at her frown.
Then, Aaron, arm thy heart and fit thy thoughts
To mount aloft with thy imperial mistress,
And mount her pitch whom thou in triumph long
Hast prisoner held, fett'red in amorous chains,
And faster bound to Aaron's charming eyes
Than is Prometheus tied to Caucasus.
Away with slavish weeds and servile thoughts!
I will be bright and shine in pearl and gold,
To wait upon this new-made emperess.
To wait, said I? To wanton with this queen,
This goddess, this Semiramis, this nymph,
This siren that will charm Rome's Saturnine,
And see his shipwreck and his commonweal's.
Hullo! what storm is this?

Enter CHIRON and DEMETRIUS, braving.

DEMETRIUS Chiron, thy years wants wit, thy wits wants edge
And manners, to intrude where I am grac'd,
And may, for aught thou knowest, affected be.
CHIRON Demetrius, thou dost over-ween in all;
And so in this, to bear me down with braves.
'Tis not the difference of a year or two
Makes me less gracious or thee more fortunate:
I am as able and as fit as thou
To serve and to deserve my mistress' grace;
And that my sword upon thee shall approve,
And plead my passions for Lavinia's love.
AARON [*Aside*] Clubs, clubs! These lovers will not keep the peace.
DEMETRIUS Why, boy, although our mother, unadvis'd,
Gave you a dancing-rapier by your side,
Are you so desperate grown to threat your friends?
Go to; have your lath glued within your sheath
Till you know better how to handle it.
CHIRON Meanwhile, sir, with the little skill I have,
Full well shalt thou perceive how much I dare.
DEMETRIUS Ay, boy, grow ye so brave?
[*They draw.*
AARON [*Coming forward*] Why, how now, lords!
So near the Emperor's palace dare ye draw
And maintain such a quarrel openly?
Full well I wot the ground of all this grudge:
I would not for a million of gold
The cause were known to them it most concerns;
Nor would your noble mother for much more
Be so dishonoured in the court of Rome.
For shame, put up.
DEMETRIUS Not I, till I have sheath'd
My rapier in his bosom, and withal
Thrust those reproachful speeches down his throat
That he hath breath'd in my dishonour here.
CHIRON For that I am prepar'd and full resolv'd,
Foul-spoken coward, that thund'rest with thy tongue,
And with thy weapon nothing dar'st perform.
AARON Away, I say!
Now, by the gods that warlike Goths adore,
This petty brabble will undo us all.
Why, lords, and think you not how dangerous
It is to jet upon a prince's right?
What, is Lavinia then become so loose,
Or Bassianus so degenerate,

That for her love such quarrels may be broach'd
Without controlment, justice, or revenge?
Young lords, beware; an should the Empress know
This discord's ground, the music would not please.

CHIRON I care not, I, knew she and all the world:
I love Lavinia more than all the world.

DEMETRIUS Youngling, learn thou to make some meaner choice:
Lavinia is thine elder brother's hope.

AARON Why, are ye mad, or know ye not in Rome
How furious and impatient they be,
And cannot brook competitors in love?
I tell you, lords, you do but plot your deaths
By this device.

CHIRON Aaron, a thousand deaths
Would I propose to achieve her whom I love.

AARON To achieve her – How?

DEMETRIUS Why mak'st thou it so strange?
She is a woman, therefore may be woo'd;
She is a woman, therefore may be won;
She is Lavinia, therefore must be lov'd.
What, man! more water glideth by the mill
Than wots the miller of; and easy it is
Of a cut loaf to steal a shive, we know.
Though Bassianus be the Emperor's brother,
Better than he have worn Vulcan's badge.

AARON [*Aside*] Ay, and as good as Saturninus may.

DEMETRIUS Then why should he despair that knows to court it
With words, fair looks, and liberality?
What, hast not thou full often struck a doe,
And borne her cleanly by the keeper's nose?

AARON Why, then, it seems some certain snatch or so
Would serve your turns.

CHIRON Ay, so the turn were served.

DEMETRIUS Aaron, thou hast hit it.

AARON Would you had hit it too!
Then should not we be tir'd with this ado.
Why, hark ye, hark ye! and are you such fools
To square for this? Would it offend you, then,
That both should speed?

CHIRON Faith, not me.

DEMETRIUS Nor me, so I were one.

AARON For shame, be friends, and join for that you jar.
'Tis policy and stratagem must do
That you affect; and so must you resolve
That what you cannot as you would achieve,
You must perforce accomplish as you may.
Take this of me: Lucrece was not more chaste
Than this Lavinia, Bassianus' love.
A speedier course than ling'ring languishment
Must we pursue, and I have found the path.
My lords, a solemn hunting is in hand;
There will the lovely Roman ladies troop;
The forest walks are wide and spacious,
And many unfrequented plots there are
Fitted by kind for rape and villainy.
Single you thither then this dainty doe,
And strike her home by force if not by words.
This way, or not at all, stand you in hope.
Come, come, our Empress, with her sacred wit
To villainy and vengeance consecrate,
Will we acquaint with all what we intend;
And she shall file our engines with advice
That will not suffer you to square yourselves,
But to your wishes' height advance you both.
The Emperor's court is like the house of Fame,
The palace full of tongues, of eyes, and ears;
The woods are ruthless, dreadful, deaf, and dull.
There speak and strike, brave boys, and take your turns;
There serve your lust, shadowed from heaven's eye,
And revel in Lavinia's treasury.

CHIRON Thy counsel, lad, smells of no cowardice.

DEMETRIUS Sit fas aut nefas, till I find the stream
To cool this heat, a charm to calm these fits,
Per Styga, per manes vehor. [*Exeunt.*

SCENE II. *A forest near Rome.*

Enter TITUS ANDRONICUS, and his three sons, LUCIUS, QUINTUS, MARTIUS, making a noise with hounds and horns; and MARCUS.

TITUS The hunt is up, the morn is bright and grey,
The fields are fragrant, and the woods are green.
Uncouple here, and let us make a bay,
And wake the Emperor and his lovely bride,
And rouse the Prince, and ring a hunter's peal,
That all the court may echo with the noise.
Sons, let it be your charge, as it is ours,
To attend the Emperor's person carefully.
I have been troubled in my sleep this night,
But dawning day new comfort hath inspir'd.

Here a cry of hounds, and wind horns in a peal. Then enter SATURNINUS, TAMORA, BASSIANS, LAVINIA, CHIRON, DEMETRIUS, and their Attendants.

Many good morrows to your Majesty!
Madam, to you as many and as good!
I promised your Grace a hunter's peal.

SATURNINUS And you have rung it lustily, my lords –
Somewhat too early for new-married ladies.

BASSIANUS Lavinia, how say you?

LAVINIA I say no;
I have been broad awake two hours and more.
SATURNINUS Come on then, horse and chariots let us have,
And to our sport. [*To Tamora*] Madam, now shall ye see
Our Roman hunting.
MARCUS I have dogs, my lord,
Will rouse the proudest panther in the chase,
And climb the highest promontory top.
TITUS And I have horse will follow where the game
Makes way, and run like swallows o'er the plain.
DEMETRIUS Chiron, we hunt not, we, with horse nor hound,
But hope to pluck a dainty doe to ground.
[*Exeunt*.

SCENE III. *A lonely part of the forest.*

Enter AARON alone, with a bag of gold.

AARON He that had wit would think that I had none,
To bury so much gold under a tree
And never after to inherit it.
Let him that thinks of me so abjectly
Know that this gold must coin a stratagem,
Which, cunningly effected, will beget
A very excellent piece of villainy.
And so repose, sweet gold, for their unrest
[*Hides the gold*.
That have their alms out of the Empress' chest.

Enter TAMORA alone, to the Moor.

TAMORA My lovely Aaron, wherefore look'st thou sad
When everything doth make a gleeful boast?
The birds chant melody on every bush;
The snakes lie rolled in the cheerful sun;
The green leaves quiver with the cooling wind
And make a chequer'd shadow on the ground;
Under their sweet shade, Aaron, let us sit,
And whilst the babbling echo mocks the hounds,
Replying shrilly to the well-tun'd horns,
As if a double hunt were heard at once,
Let us sit down and mark their yellowing noise;
And – after conflict such as was suppos'd
The wand'ring prince and Dido once enjoyed,
When with a happy storm they were surpris'd,
And curtain'd with a counsel-keeping cave –
We may, each wreathed in the other's arms,
Our pastimes done, possess a golden slumber,
Whiles hounds and horns and sweet melodious birds
Be unto us as is a nurse's song
Of lullaby to bring her babe asleep.
AARON Madam, though Venus govern your desires,
Saturn is dominator over mine.
What signifies my deadly-standing eye,
My silence and my cloudy melancholy,
My fleece of woolly hair that now uncurls
Even as an adder when she doth unroll
To do some fatal execution?
No, madam, these are no venereal signs.
Vengeance is in my heart, death in my hand,
Blood and revenge are hammering in my head.
Hark, Tamora, the empress of my soul,
Which never hopes more heaven than rests in thee –
This is the day of doom for Bassianus;
His Philomel must lose her tongue to-day,
Thy sons make pillage of her chastity,
And wash their hands in Bassianus' blood.
Seest thou this letter? Take it up, I pray thee,
And give the king this fatal-plotted scroll.
Now question me no more; we are espied.
Here comes a parcel of our hopeful booty,
Which dreads not yet their lives' destruction.

Enter BASSIANUS and LAVINIA.

TAMORA Ah, my sweet Moor, sweeter to me than life!
AARON No more, great Empress: Bassianus comes.
Be cross with him; and I'll go fetch thy sons
To back thy quarrels, whatsoe'er they be.
[*Exit*.
BASSIANUS Who have we here? Rome's royal Emperess,
Unfurnish'd of her well-beseeming troop?
Or is it Dian, habited like her,
Who hath abandoned her holy groves
To see the general hunting in this forest?
TAMORA Saucy controller of my private steps!
Had I the pow'r that some say Dian had,
Thy temples should be planted presently
With horns, as was Actaeon's; and the hounds
Should drive upon thy new-transformed limbs,
Unmannerly intruder as thou art!
LAVINIA Under your patience, gentle Empress,
'Tis thought you have a goodly gift in horning,
And to be doubted that your Moor and you
Are singled forth to try thy experiments.
Jove shield your husband from his hounds to-day!
'Tis pity they should take him for a stag.
BASSIANUS Believe me, Queen, your swarth Cimmerian
Doth make your honour of his body's hue,
Spotted, detested, and abominable.
Why are you sequest'red from all your train,
Dismounted from your snow-white goodly steed,

And wand'red hither to an obscure plot,
Accompanied but with a barbarous Moor,
If foul desire had not conducted you?

LAVINIA And, being intercepted in your sport,
Great reason that my noble lord be rated
For sauciness. I pray you let us hence,
And let her joy her raven-coloured love;
This valley fits the purpose passing well.

BASSIANUS The King my brother shall have notice of this.

LAVINIA Ay, for these slips have made him noted long.
Good king, to be so mightily abused!

TAMORA Why, I have patience to endure all this.

Enter CHIRON and DEMETRIUS.

DEMETRIUS How now, dear sovereign, and our gracious mother!
Why doth your Highness look so pale and wan?

TAMORA Have I not reason, think you, to look pale?
These two have 'ticed me hither to this place.
A barren detested vale you see it is:
The trees, though summer, yet forlorn and lean,
Overcome with moss and baleful mistletoe;
Here never shines the sun; here nothing breeds,
Unless the nightly owl or fatal raven.
And when they show'd me this abhorred pit,
They told me, here, at dead time of the night,
A thousand fiends, a thousand hissing snakes,
Ten thousand swelling toads, as many urchins,
Would make such fearful and confused cries
As any mortal body hearing it
Should straight fall mad or else die suddenly.
No sooner had they told this hellish tale
But straight they told me they would bind me here
Unto the body of a dismal yew,
And leave me to this miserable death.
And then they call'd me foul adulteress,
Lascivious Goth, and all the bitterest terms
That ever ear did hear to such effect;
And had you not by wondrous fortune come,
This vengeance on me had they executed.
Revenge it, as you love your mother's life,
Or be ye not henceforth call'd my children.

DEMETRIUS This is a witness that I am thy son.
[*Stabs Bassianus.*

CHIRON And this for me, struck home to show my strength. [*Also stabs.*

LAVINIA Ay, come, Semiramis – nay, barbarous Tamora,
For no name fits thy nature but thy own!

TAMORA Give me the poniard; you shall know, my boys,
Your mother's hand shall right your mother's wrong.

DEMETRIUS Stay, madam, here is more belongs to her;
First thrash the corn, then after burn the straw.
This minion stood upon her chastity,
Upon her nuptial vow, her loyalty,
And with that painted hope braves your mightiness;
And shall she carry this unto her grave?

CHIRON An if she do, I would I were an eunuch.
Drag hence her husband to some secret hole,
And make his dead trunk pillow to our lust.

TAMORA But when ye have the honey we desire,
Let not this wasp outlive, us both to sting.

CHIRON I warrant you, madam, we will make that sure.
Come, mistress, now perforce we will enjoy
That nice-preserved honesty of yours.

LAVINIA O Tamora! thou bearest a woman's face –

TAMORA I will not hear her speak; away with her!

LAVINIA Sweet lords, entreat her hear me but a word.

DEMETRIUS Listen, fair madam: let it be your glory
To see her tears; but be your heart to them
As unrelenting flint to drops of rain.

LAVINIA When did the tiger's young ones teach the dam?
O, do not learn her wrath – she taught it thee;
The milk thou suck'dst from her did turn to marble,
Even at thy teat thou hadst thy tyranny.
Yet every mother breeds not sons alike:
[*To Chiron*] Do thou entreat her show a woman's pity.

CHIRON What, wouldst thou have me prove myself a bastard?

LAVINIA 'Tis true, the raven doth not hatch a lark.
Yet have I heard – O, could I find it now! –
The lion, mov'd with pity, did endure
To have his princely paws par'd all away.
Some say that ravens foster forlorn children,
The whilst their own birds famish in their nests;
O, be to me, though thy hard heart say no,
Nothing so kind, but something pitiful!

TAMORA I know not what it means; away with her!

LAVINIA O, let me teach thee! For my father's sake,
That gave thee life when well he might have slain thee,
Be not obdurate, open thy deaf ears.

TAMORA Hadst thou in person ne'er offended me,

Even for his sake am I pitiless.
Remember, boys, I pour'd forth tears in vain
To save your brother from the sacrifice;
But fierce Andronicus would not relent.
Therefore away with her, and use her as you will;
The worse to her the better lov'd of me.

LAVINIA O Tamora, be call'd a gentle queen,
And with thine own hands kill me in this place!
For 'tis not life that I have begg'd so long;
Poor I was slain when Bassianus died.

TAMORA What beg'st thou, then? Fond woman, let me go.

LAVINIA 'Tis present death I beg; and one thing more,
That womanhood denies my tongue to tell:
O keep me from their worse than killing lust,
And tumble me into some loathsome pit,
Where never man's eye may behold my body;
Do this, and be a charitable murderer.

TAMORA So should I rob my sweet sons of their fee;
No, let them satisfy their lust on thee.

DEMETRIUS Away! for thou hast stay'd us here too long.

LAVINIA No grace? no womanhood? Ah, beastly creature,
The blot and enemy to our general name!
Confusion fall –

CHIRON Nay, then I'll stop your mouth. Bring thou her husband.
This is the hole where Aaron bid us hide him.

[*Demetrius throws the body of Bassianus into the pit; then exeunt Demetrius and Chiron, dragging off Lavinia.*

TAMORA Farewell, my sons; see that you make her sure.
Ne'er let my heart know merry cheer indeed
Till all the Andronici be made away.
Now will I hence to seek my lovely Moor,
And let my spleenful sons this trull deflower.
[*Exit*

Re-enter AARON, with two of Titus' sons, QUINTUS and MARTIUS.

AARON Come on, my lords, the better foot before;
Straight will I bring you to the loathsome pit
Where I espied the panther fast asleep.

QUINTUS My sight is very dull, whate'er it bodes.

MARTIUS And mine, I promise you; were it not for shame,
Well could I leave our sport to sleep awhile.
[*Falls into the pit.*

QUINTUS What, art thou fallen? What subtle hole is this,
Whose mouth is covered with rude-growing briers,
Upon whose leaves are drops of new-shed blood
As fresh as morning dew distill'd on flowers?
A very fatal place it seems to me.
Speak, brother, hast thou hurt thee with the fall?

MARTIUS O brother, with the dismal'st object hurt
That ever eye with sight made heart lament!

AARON [*Aside*] Now will I fetch the King to find them here,
That he thereby may have a likely guess
How these were they that made away his brother.
[*Exit.*

MARTIUS Why dost not comfort me, and help me out
From this unhallow'd and blood-stained hole?

QUINTUS I am surprised with an uncouth fear;
A chilling sweat o'er-runs my trembling joints;
My heart suspects more than mine eye can see.

MARTIUS To prove thou hast a true divining heart,
Aaron and thou look down into this den,
And see a fearful sight of blood and death.

QUINTUS Aaron is gone, and my compassionate heart
Will not permit mine eyes once to behold
The thing whereat it trembles by surmise;
O, tell me who it is, for ne'er till now
Was I a child to fear I know not what.

MARTIUS Lord Bassianus lies beray'd in blood,
All on a heap, like to a slaughtered lamb,
In this detested, dark, blood-drinking pit.

QUINTUS If it be dark, how dost thou know 'tis he?

MARTIUS Upon his bloody finger he doth wear
A precious ring that lightens all this hole,
Which, like a taper in some monument,
Doth shine upon the dead man's earthy cheeks,
And shows the ragged entrails of this pit;
So pale did shine the moon on Pyramus
When he by night lay bath'd in maiden blood.
O brother, help me with thy fainting hand –
If fear hath made thee faint, as me it hath –
Out of this fell devouring receptacle,
As hateful as Cocytus' misty mouth.

QUINTUS Reach me thy hand, that I may help thee out,
Or, wanting strength to do thee so much good,
I may be pluck'd into the swallowing womb
Of this deep pit, poor Bassianus' grave.
I have no strength to pluck thee to the brink.

MARTIUS Nor I no strength to climb without thy help.

QUINTUS Thy hand once more; I will not loose again,

Till thou art here aloft, or I below.
Thou canst not come to me – I come to thee.
[*Falls in.*

Enter the EMPEROR and AARON the Moor.

SATURNINUS Along with me! I'll see what hole is here,
And what he is that now is leapt into it.
Say, who art thou that lately didst descend
Into this gaping hollow of the earth?

MARTIUS The unhappy sons of old Andronicus,
Brought hither in a most unlucky hour,
To find thy brother Bassianus dead.

SATURNINUS My brother dead! I know thou dost but jest:
He and his lady both are at the lodge
Upon the north side of this pleasant chase;
'Tis not an hour since I left them there.

MARTIUS We know not where you left them all alive;
But, out alas! here have we found him dead.

Re-enter TAMORA, with Attendants; TITUS ANDRONICUS and LUCIUS.

TAMORA Where is my lord the King?

SATURNINUS Here, Tamora; though griev'd with killing grief.

TAMORA Where is thy brother Bassianus?

SATURNINUS Now to the bottom dost thou search my wound;
Poor Bassianus here lies murdered.

TAMORA Then all too late I bring this fatal writ,
The complot of this timeless tragedy;
And wonder greatly that man's face can fold
In pleasing smiles such murderous tyranny.
[*She giveth Saturnine a letter.*

SATURNINUS [*Reads*] 'An if we miss to meet him handsomely,
Sweet huntsman – Bassianus 'tis we mean –
Do thou so much as dig the grave for him.
Thou know'st our meaning. Look for thy reward
Among the nettles at the elder-tree
Which overshades the mouth of that same pit
Where we decreed to bury Bassianus.
Do this, and purchase us thy lasting friends.'
O Tamora! was ever heard the like?
This is the pit and this the elder-tree.
Look, sirs, if you can find the huntsman out
That should have murdered Bassianus here.

AARON My gracious lord, here is the bag of gold.

SATURNINUS [*To Titus*] Two of thy whelps, fell curs of bloody kind,
Have here bereft my brother of his life.
Sirs, drag them from the pit unto the prison;
There let them bide until we have devis'd
Some never-heard-of torturing pain for them.

TAMORA What, are they in this pit? O wondrous thing!
How easily murder is discovered!

TITUS High Emperor, upon my feeble knee
I beg this boon, with tears not lightly shed,
That this fell fault of my accursed sons –
Accursed if the fault be prov'd in them –

SATURNINUS If it be prov'd! You see it is apparent.
Who found this letter? Tamora, was it you?

TAMORA Andronicus himself did take it up.

TITUS I did, my lord, yet let me be their bail;
For, by my fathers' reverend tomb, I vow
They shall be ready at your Highness' will
To answer their suspicion with their lives.

SATURNINUS Thou shalt not bail them; see thou follow me.
Some bring the murdered body, some the murderers;
Let them not speak a word – the guilt is plain;
For, by my soul, were there worse end than death,
That end upon them should be executed.

TAMORA Andronicus, I will entreat the King.
Fear not thy sons; they shall do well enough.

TITUS Come, Lucius, come; stay not to talk with them.
[*Exeunt.*

SCENE IV. *Another part of the forest.*

Enter the Empress' sons, DEMETRIUS and CHIRON, with LAVINIA, her hands cut off, and her tongue cut out, and ravish'd.

DEMETRIUS So, now go tell, an if thy tongue can speak,
Who 'twas that cut thy tongue and ravish'd thee.

CHIRON Write down thy mind, bewray thy meaning so,
An if thy stumps will let thee play the scribe.

DEMETRIUS See how with signs and tokens she can scrowl.

CHIRON Go home, call for sweet water, wash thy hands.

DEMETRIUS She hath no tongue to call, nor hands to wash;
And so let's leave her to her silent walks.

CHIRON An 'twere my cause, I should go hang myself.

DEMETRIUS If thou hadst hands to help thee knit the cord.
[*Exeunt Demetrius and Chiron.*

Wind horns. Enter MARCUS, from hunting.

MARCUS Who is this? – my niece, that flies away so fast?
Cousin, a word: where is your husband?
If I do dream, would all my wealth would wake me!
If I do wake, some planet strike me down,

That I may slumber an eternal sleep!
Speak, gentle niece. What stern ungentle hands
Hath lopp'd, and hew'd, and made thy body bare
Of her two branches – those sweet ornaments
Whose circling shadows kings have sought to sleep in,
And might not gain so great a happiness
As half thy love? Why dost not speak to me?
Alas, a crimson river of warm blood,
Like to a bubbling fountain stirr'd with wind,
Doth rise and fall between thy rosed lips,
Coming and going with thy honey breath.
But sure some Tereus hath deflowered thee,
And, lest thou shouldst detect him, cut thy tongue.
Ah, now thou turn'st away thy face for shame!
And notwithstanding all this loss of blood –
As from a conduit with three issuing spouts –
Yet do thy cheeks look red as Titan's face
Blushing to be encount'red with a cloud.
Shall I speak for thee? Shall I say 'tis so?
O, that I knew thy heart, and knew the beast,
That I might rail at him to ease my mind!
Sorrow concealed, like an oven stopp'd,
Doth burn the heart to cinders where it is.
Fair Philomel, why she but lost her tongue,
And in a tedious sampler sew'd her mind;
But, lovely niece, that mean is cut from thee.
A craftier Tereus, cousin, hast thou met,
And he hath cut those pretty fingers off
That could have better sew'd than Philomel.
O, had the monster seen those lily hands
Tremble like aspen leaves upon a lute
And make the silken strings delight to kiss them,
He would not then have touch'd them for his life!
Or had he heard the heavenly harmony
Which that sweet tongue hath made,
He would have dropp'd his knife, and fell asleep,
As Cerberus at the Thracian poet's feet.
Come, let us go, and make thy father blind,
For such a sight will blind a father's eye;
One hour's storm will drown the fragrant meads,
What will whole months of tears thy father's eyes?
Do not draw back, for we will mourn with thee;
O, could our mourning ease thy misery!

[Exeunt.

ACT THREE

SCENE I. *Rome. A street.*

Enter the Judges, Tribunes, and Senators, with Titus' two sons MARTIUS and QUINTUS bound, passing on the stage to the place of execution, and TITUS going before, pleading.

TITUS Hear me, grave fathers; noble Tribunes, stay!
For pity of mine age, whose youth was spent
In dangerous wars whilst you securely slept;
For all my blood in Rome's great quarrel shed,
For all the frosty nights that I have watch'd,
And for these bitter tears, which now you see
Filling the aged wrinkles in my cheeks,
Be pitiful to my condemned sons,
Whose souls are not corrupted as 'tis thought.
For two and twenty sons I never wept,
Because they died in honour's lofty bed.

[Andronicus lieth down, and the Judges pass by him with the prisoners, and exeunt.

For these, Tribunes, in the dust I write
My heart's deep languor and my soul's sad tears.
Let my tears stanch the earth's dry appetite;
My sons' sweet blood will make it shame and blush.
O earth, I will befriend thee more with rain
That shall distil from these two ancient urns,
Than youthful April shall with all his show'rs.
In summer's drought I'll drop upon thee still;
In winter with warm tears I'll melt the snow
And keep eternal spring-time on thy face,
So thou refuse to drink my dear sons' blood.

Enter LUCIUS with his weapon drawn.

O reverend Tribunes! O gentle aged men!
Unbind my sons, reverse the doom of death,
And let me say, that never wept before,
My tears are now prevailing orators.

LUCIUS O noble father, you lament in vain;
The Tribunes hear you not, no man is by,
And you recount your sorrows to a stone.

TITUS Ah, Lucius, for thy brothers let me plead!
Grave Tribunes, once more I entreat of you.

LUCIUS My gracious lord, no tribune hears you speak.

TITUS Why, 'tis no matter, man: if they did hear,
They would not mark me; if they did mark,
They would not pity me; yet plead I must,
And bootless unto them.
Therefore I tell my sorrows to the stones;
Who though they cannot answer my distress,

Yet in some sort they are better than the Tribunes,
For that they will not intercept my tale.
When I do weep, they humbly at my feet
Receive my tears, and seem to weep with me;
And were they but attired in grave weeds,
Rome could afford no tribunes like to these.
A stone is soft as wax: tribunes more hard than stones.
A stone is silent and offendeth not,
And tribunes with their tongues doom men to death. *[Rises.*
But wherefore stand'st thou with thy weapon drawn?

LUCIUS To rescue my two brothers from their death;
For which attempt the judges have pronounc'd
My everlasting doom of banishment.

TITUS O happy man! they have befriended thee.
Why, foolish Lucius, dost thou not perceive
That Rome is but a wilderness of tigers?
Tigers must prey, and Rome affords no prey
But me and mine; how happy art thou then
From these devourers to be banished!
But who comes with our brother Marcus here?

Enter MARCUS with LAVINIA.

MARCUS Titus, prepare thy aged eyes to weep,
Or if not so, thy noble heart to break.
I bring consuming sorrow to thine age.

TITUS Will it consume me? Let me see it then.

MARCUS This was thy daughter.

TITUS Why, Marcus, so she is.

LUCIUS Ay me! this object kills me.

TITUS Faint-hearted boy, arise, and look upon her.
Speak, Lavinia, what accursed hand
Hath made thee handless in thy father's sight?
What fool hath added water to the sea,
Or brought a fagot to bright-burning Troy?
My grief was at the height before thou cam'st,
And now like Nilus it disdaineth bounds.
Give me a sword, I'll chop off my hands too,
For they have fought for Rome, and all in vain;
And they have nurs'd this woe in feeding life;
In bootless prayer have they been held up,
And they have serv'd me to effectless use.
Now all the service I require of them
Is that the one will help to cut the other.
'Tis well, Lavinia, that thou hast no hands;
For hands to do Rome service is but vain.

LUCIUS Speak, gentle sister, who hath martyr'd thee?

MARCUS O, that delightful engine of her thoughts
That blabb'd them with such pleasing eloquence
Is torn from forth that pretty hollow cage,
Where like a sweet melodious bird it sung
Sweet varied notes, enchanting every ear!

LUCIUS O, say thou for her, who hath done this deed?

MARCUS O, thus I found her straying in the park,
Seeking to hide herself as doth the deer
That hath receiv'd some unrecuring wound.

TITUS It was my dear, and he that wounded her
Hath hurt me more than had he kill'd me dead;
For now I stand as one upon a rock,
Environ'd with a wilderness of sea,
Who marks the waxing tide grow wave by wave,
Expecting ever when some envious surge
Will in his brinish bowels swallow him.
This way to death my wretched sons are gone;
Here stands my other son, a banish'd man,
And here my brother, weeping at my woes.
But that which gives my soul the greatest spurn
Is dear Lavinia, dearer than my soul.
Had I but seen thy picture in this plight,
It would have madded me; what shall I do
Now I behold thy lively body so?
Thou hast no hands to wipe away thy tears,
Nor tongue to tell me who hath martyr'd thee;
Thy husband he is dead, and for his death
Thy brothers are condemn'd, and dead by this.
Look, Marcus! Ah, son Lucius, look on her!
When I did name her brothers, then fresh tears
Stood on her cheeks, as doth the honey dew
Upon a gath'red lily almost withered.

MARCUS Perchance she weeps because they kill'd her husband;
Perchance because she knows them innocent.

TITUS If they did kill thy husband, then be joyful,
Because the law hath ta'en revenge on them.
No, no, they would not do so foul a deed;
Witness the sorrow that their sister makes.
Gentle Lavinia, let me kiss thy lips,
Or make some sign how I may do thee ease.
Shall thy good uncle and thy brother Lucius
And thou and I sit round about some fountain,
Looking all downwards to behold our cheeks
How they are stain'd, like meadows yet not dry
With miry slime left on them by a flood?
And in the fountain shall we gaze so long,
Till the fresh taste be taken from that clearness,
And made a brine-pit with our bitter tears?
Or shall we cut away our hands like thine?
Or shall we bite our tongues, and in dumb shows
Pass the remainder of our hateful days?
What shall we do? Let us that have our tongues
Plot some device of further misery
To make us wonder'd at in time to come.

LUCIUS Sweet father, cease your tears; for at your grief
See how my wretched sister sobs and weeps.

MARCUS Patience, dear niece. Good Titus, dry thine eyes.
TITUS Ah, Marcus, Marcus! Brother, well I wot
Thy napkin cannot drink a tear of mine,
For thou, poor man, hast drown'd it with thine own.
LUCIUS Ah, my Lavinia, I will wipe thy cheeks.
TITUS Mark, Marcus, mark! I understand her signs.
Had she a tongue to speak, now would she say
That to her brother which I said to thee:
His napkin, with his true tears all bewet,
Can do no service on her sorrowful cheeks.
O, what a sympathy of woe is this –
As far from help as Limbo is from bliss!

Enter AARON the Moor.

AARON Titus Andronicus, my lord the Emperor
Sends thee this word, that, if thou love thy sons,
Let Marcus, Lucius, or thyself, old Titus,
Or any one of you, chop off your hand
And send it to the King: he for the same
Will send thee hither both thy sons alive,
And that shall be the ransom for their fault.
TITUS O gracious Emperor! O gentle Aaron!
Did ever raven sing so like a lark
That gives sweet tidings of the sun's uprise?
With all my heart I'll send the Emperor my hand.
Good Aaron, wilt thou help to chop it off?
LUCIUS Stay, father! for that noble hand of thine,
That hath thrown down so many enemies,
Shall not be sent. My hand will serve the turn,
My youth can better spare my blood than you,
And therefore mine shall save my brothers' lives.
MARCUS Which of your hands hath not defended Rome
And rear'd aloft the bloody battle-axe,
Writing destruction on the enemy's castle?
O, none of both but are of high desert!
My hand hath been but idle; let it serve
To ransom my two nephews from their death;
Then have I kept it to a worthy end.
AARON Nay, come, agree whose hand shall go along,
For fear they die before their pardon come.
MARCUS My hand shall go.
LUCIUS By heaven, it shall not go!
TITUS Sirs, strive no more; such with'red herbs as these
Are meet for plucking up, and therefore mine.
LUCIUS Sweet father, if I shall be thought thy son,
Let me redeem my brothers both from death.
MARCUS And for our father's sake and mother's care,
Now let me show a brother's love to thee.
TITUS Agree between you; I will spare my hand.
LUCIUS Then I'll go fetch an axe.
MARCUS But I will use the axe.

[*Exeunt Lucius and Marcus.*

TITUS Come hither, Aaron, I'll deceive them both;
Lend me thy hand, and I will give thee mine.
AARON [*Aside*] If that be call'd deceit, I will be honest,
And never whilst I live deceive men so;
But I'll deceive you in another sort,
And that you'll say ere half an hour pass.

[*He cuts off Titus' hand.*

Re-enter LUCIUS and MARCUS.

TITUS Now stay your strife. What shall be is dispatch'd.
Good Aaron, give his Majesty my hand;
Tell him it was a hand that warded him
From thousand dangers; bid him bury it.
More hath it merited – that let it have.
As for my sons, say I account of them
As jewels purchas'd at an easy price;
And yet dear too, because I bought mine own.
AARON I go, Andronicus; and for thy hand
Look by and by to have thy sons with thee.
[*Aside*] Their heads I mean. O, how this villainy
Doth fat me with the very thoughts of it!
Let fools do good, and fair men call for grace:
Aaron will have his soul black like his face.

[*Exit.*

TITUS O, here I lift this one hand up to heaven,
And bow this feeble ruin to the earth;
If any power pities wretched tears,
To that I call! [*To Lavinia*] What, would'st thou kneel with me?
Do, then, dear heart; for heaven shall hear our prayers,
Or with our sighs we'll breathe the welkin dim
And stain the sun with fog, as sometime clouds
When they do hug him in their melting bosoms.
MARCUS O brother, speak with possibility,
And do not break into these deep extremes.
TITUS Is not my sorrow deep, having no bottom?
Then be my passions bottomless with them.
MARCUS But yet let reason govern thy lament.
TITUS If there were reason for these miseries,
Then into limits could I bind my woes.
When heaven doth weep, doth not the earth o'erflow?
If the winds rage, doth not the sea wax mad,
Threat'ning the welkin with his big-swol'n face?
And wilt thou have a reason for this coil?
I am the sea; hark how her sighs do blow.
She is the weeping welkin, I the earth;

Then must my sea be moved with her sighs;
Then must my earth with her continual tears
Become a deluge, overflow'd and drown'd;
For why my bowels cannot hide her woes,
But like a drunkard must I vomit them.
Then give me leave; for losers will have leave
To ease their stomachs with their bitter tongues.

Enter a Messenger, with two heads and a hand.

MESSENGER Worthy Andronicus, ill art thou repaid
For that good hand thou sent'st the Emperor.
Here are the heads of thy two noble sons;
And here's thy hand, in scorn to thee sent back –
Thy grief their sports, thy resolution mock'd,
That woe is me to think upon thy woes,
More than remembrance of my father's death.
[*Exit.*

MARCUS Now let hot Aetna cool in Sicily,
And be my heart an ever-burning hell!
These miseries are more than may be borne.
To weep with them that weep doth ease some deal,
But sorrow flouted at is double death.

LUCIUS Ah, that this sight should make so deep a wound,
And yet detested life not shrink thereat!
That ever death should let life bear his name,
Where life hath no more interest but to breathe!
[*Lavinia kisses Titus.*

MARCUS Alas, poor heart, that kiss is comfortless
As frozen water to a starved snake.

TITUS When will this fearful slumber have an end?

MARCUS Now farewell, flatt'ry; die, Andronicus.
Thou dost not slumber: see thy two sons' heads,
Thy warlike hand, thy mangled daughter here;
Thy other banish'd son with this dear sight
Struck pale and bloodless; and thy brother, I,
Even like a stony image, cold and numb.
Ah! now no more will I control thy griefs.
Rent off thy silver hair, thy other hand
Gnawing with thy teeth; and be this dismal sight
The closing up of our most wretched eyes.
Now is a time to storm; why art thou still?

TITUS Ha, ha, ha!

MARCUS Why dost thou laugh? It fits not with this hour.

TITUS Why, I have not another tear to shed;
Besides, this sorrow is an enemy,
And would usurp upon my wat'ry eyes
And make them blind with tributary tears.
Then which way shall I find Revenge's cave?
For these two heads do seem to speak to me,
And threat me I shall never come to bliss
Till all these mischiefs be return'd again
Even in their throats that have committed them.
Come, let me see what task I have to do.
You heavy people, circle me about,
That I may turn me to each one of you
And swear unto my soul to right your wrongs.
The vow is made. Come, brother, take a head,
And in this hand the other will I bear.
And, Lavinia, thou shalt be employ'd in this;
Bear thou my hand, sweet wench, between thy teeth.
As for thee, boy, go, get thee from my sight;
Thou art an exile, and thou must not stay.
Hie to the Goths and raise an army there;
And if ye love me, as I think you do,
Let's kiss and part, for we have much to do.
[*Exeunt all but Lucius.*

LUCIUS Farewell, Andronicus, my noble father,
The woefull'st man that ever liv'd in Rome.
Farewell, proud Rome; till Lucius come again,
He leaves his pledges dearer than his life.
Farewell, Lavinia, my noble sister;
O, would thou wert as thou tofore hast been!
But now nor Lucius nor Lavinia lives
But in oblivion and hateful griefs.
If Lucius live, he will requite your wrongs
And make proud Saturnine and his empress
Beg at the gates like Tarquin and his queen.
Now will I go to the Goths, and raise a pow'r
To be reveng'd on Rome and Saturnine. [*Exit.*

SCENE II. *Rome. Titus' house.*

A banquet. Enter TITUS, MARCUS, LAVINIA, and the boy YOUNG LUCIUS.

TITUS So so, now sit; and look you eat no more
Than will preserve just so much strength in us
As will revenge these bitter woes of ours.
Marcus, unknit that sorrow-wreathen knot;
Thy niece and I, poor creatures, want our hands,
And cannot passionate our tenfold grief
With folded arms. This poor right hand of mine
Is left to tyrannize upon my breast;
Who, when my heart, all mad with misery,
Beats in this hollow prison of my flesh,
Then thus I thump it down.
[*To Lavinia*] Thou map of woe, that thus dost talk in signs!
When thy poor heart beats with outrageous beating,
Thou canst not strike it thus to make it still.
Wound it with sighing, girl, kill it with groans;
Or get some little knife between thy teeth
And just against thy heart make thou a hole,
That all the tears that thy poor eyes let fall
May run into that sink and, soaking in,
Drown the lamenting fool, in sea-salt tears.

MARCUS Fie, brother, fie! Teach her not thus to lay
Such violent hands upon her tender life.
TITUS How now! Has sorrow made thee dote already?
Why, Marcus, no man should be mad but I.
What violent hands can she lay on her life?
Ah, wherefore dost thou urge the name of hands?
To bid Aeneas tell the tale twice o'er
How Troy was burnt and he made miserable?
O, handle not the theme, to talk of hands,
Lest we remember still that we have none.
Fie, fie, how franticly I square my talk,
As if we should forget we had no hands,
If Marcus did not name the word of hands!
Come, let's fall to; and, gentle girl, eat this:
Here is no drink. Hark, Marcus, what she says –
I can interpret all her martyr'd signs;
She says she drinks no other drink but tears,
Brew'd with her sorrow, mesh'd upon her cheeks.
Speechless complainer, I will learn thy thought;
In thy dumb action will I be as perfect
As begging hermits in their holy prayers.
Thou shalt not sigh, nor hold thy stumps to heaven,
Nor wink, nor nod, nor kneel, nor make a sign,
But I of these will wrest an alphabet,
And by still practice learn to know thy meaning.
BOY Good grandsire, leave these bitter deep laments;
Make my aunt merry with some pleasing tale.
MARCUS Alas, the tender boy, in passion mov'd,
Doth weep to see his grandsire's heaviness.
TITUS Peace, tender sapling; thou art made of tears,
And tears will quickly melt thy life away.
[*Marcus strikes the dish with a knife.*
What dost thou strike at, Marcus, with thy knife?
MARCUS At that that I have kill'd, my lord – a fly.
TITUS Out on thee, murderer, thou kill'st my heart!
Mine eyes are cloy'd with view of tyranny;
A deed of death done on the innocent
Becomes not Titus' brother. Get thee gone;
I see thou art not for my company.
MARCUS Alas, my lord, I have but kill'd a fly.
TITUS 'But'! How if that fly had a father and mother?
How would he hang his slender gilded wings
And buzz lamenting doings in the air!
Poor harmless fly,
That with his pretty buzzing melody
Came here to make us merry! And thou hast kill'd him.
MARCUS Pardon me, sir; it was a black ill-favour'd fly,
Like to the Empress' Moor; therefore I kill'd him.
TITUS O, O, O!
Then pardon me for reprehending thee,
For thou hast done a charitable deed.
Give me thy knife, I will insult on him,
Flattering myself as if it were the Moor
Come hither purposely to poison me.
There's for thyself, and that's for Tamora.
Ah, sirrah!
Yet, I think, we are not brought so low
But that between us we can kill a fly
That comes in likeness of a coal-black Moor.
MARCUS Alas, poor man! grief has so wrought on him,
He takes false shadows for true substances.
TITUS Come, take away. Lavinia, go with me;
I'll to thy closet, and go read with thee
Sad stories chanced in the times of old.
Come, boy, and go with me; thy sight is young,
And thou shalt read when mine begin to dazzle.
[*Exeunt.*

ACT FOUR

SCENE I. *Rome. Titus' garden.*

Enter YOUNG LUCIUS and LAVINIA running after him, and the boy flies from her with his books under his arm. Enter TITUS and MARCUS.

BOY Help, grandsire, help! my aunt Lavinia
Follows me everywhere, I know not why.
Good uncle Marcus, see how swift she comes!
Alas, sweet aunt, I know not what you mean.
MARCUS Stand by me, Lucius; do not fear thine aunt.
TITUS She loves thee, boy, too well to do thee harm.
BOY Ay, when my father was in Rome she did.
MARCUS What means my niece Lavinia by these signs?
TITUS Fear her not, Lucius; somewhat doth she mean.
See, Lucius, see how much she makes of thee.
Somewhither would she have thee go with her.
Ah, boy, Cornelia never with more care

Read to her sons than she hath read to thee
Sweet poetry and Tully's Orator.
MARCUS Canst thou not guess wherefore she plies thee thus?
BOY My lord, I know not, I, nor can I guess,
Unless some fit or frenzy do possess her;
For I have heard my grandsire say full oft
Extremity of griefs would make men mad;
And I have read that Hecuba of Troy
Ran mad for sorrow. That made me to fear;
Although, my lord, I know my noble aunt
Loves me as dear as e'er my mother did,
And would not, but in fury, fright my youth;
Which made me down to throw my books, and fly –
Causeless, perhaps. But pardon me, sweet aunt;
And, madam, if my uncle Marcus go,
I will most willingly attend your ladyship.
MARCUS Lucius, I will. [*Lavinia turns over with her stumps the books which Lucius has let fall.*
TITUS How now, Lavinia! Marcus, what means this?
Some book there is that she desires to see.
Which is it, girl, of these? – Open them, boy. –
But thou art deeper read and better skill'd;
Come and take choice of all my library,
And so beguile thy sorrow, till the heavens
Reveal the damn'd contriver of this deed.
Why lifts she up her arms in sequence thus?
MARCUS I think she means that there were more than one
Confederate in the fact; ay, more there was,
Or else to heaven she heaves them for revenge.
TITUS Lucius, what book is that she tosseth so?
BOY Grandsire, 'tis Ovid's Metamorphoses;
My mother gave it me.
MARCUS For love of her that's gone,
Perhaps she cull'd it from among the rest.
TITUS Soft! So busily she turns the leaves! Help her.
What would she find? Lavinia, shall I read?
This is the tragic tale of Philomel
And treats of Tereus' treason and his rape;
And rape, I fear, was root of thy annoy.
MARCUS See, brother, see! Note how she quotes the leaves.
TITUS Lavinia, wert thou thus surpris'd, sweet girl,
Ravish'd and wrong'd as Philomela was,
Forc'd in the ruthless, vast, and gloomy woods?
See, see!
Ay, such a place there is where we did hunt –
O, had we never, never hunted there! –
Pattern'd by that the poet here describes,
By nature made for murders and for rapes.
MARCUS O, why should nature build so foul a den,
Unless the gods delight in tragedies?
TITUS Give signs, sweet girl, for here are none but friends,
What Roman lord it was durst do the deed.
Or slunk not Saturnine, as Tarquin erst,
That left the camp to sin in Lucrece' bed?
MARCUS Sit down, sweet niece; brother, sit down by me.
Apollo, Pallas, Jove, or Mercury,
Inspire, me, that I may this treason find!
My lord, look here! Look here, Lavinia!
[*He writes his name with his staff, and guides it with feet and mouth.*

This sandy plot is plain; guide, if thou canst,
This after me. I have writ my name
Without the help of any hand at all.
Curs'd be that heart that forc'd us to this shift!
Write thou, good niece, and here display at last
What God will have discovered for revenge.
Heaven guide thy pen to print thy sorrows plain,
That we may know the traitors and the truth!
[*She takes the staff in her mouth and guides it with her stumps, and writes.*

O, do ye read, my lord, what she hath writ?
TITUS 'Stuprum – Chiron – Demetrius.'
MARCUS What, what! the lustful sons of Tamora
Performers of this heinous bloody deed?
TITUS Magni Dominator poli,
Tam lentus audis scelera? tam lentus vides?
MARCUS O, calm thee, gentle lord! although I know
There is enough written upon this earth
To stir a mutiny in the mildest thoughts,
And arm the minds of infants to exclaims.
My lord, kneel down with me; Lavinia, kneel;
And kneel, sweet boy, the Roman Hector's hope;
And swear with me – as, with the woeful fere
And father of that chaste dishonoured dame,
Lord Junius Brutus sware for Lucrece rape –
That we will prosecute, by good advice,
Mortal revenge upon these traitorous Goths,
And see their blood or die with this reproach.
TITUS 'Tis sure enough, an you knew how;
But if you hunt these bear-whelps, then beware:
The dam will wake; and if she wind ye once,
She's with the lion deeply still in league,
And lulls him whilst she playeth on her back,
And when he sleeps will she do what she list.
You are a young huntsman, Marcus; let alone;
And come, I will go get a leaf of brass,
And with a gad of steel will write these words,
And lay it by. The angry northern wind
Will blow these sands like Sibyl's leaves abroad,
And where's our lesson, then? Boy, what say you?

BOY I say, my lord, that if I were a man
Their mother's bedchamber should not be safe
For these base bondmen to the yoke of Rome.
MARCUS Ay, that's my boy! Thy father hath full oft
For his ungrateful country done the like.
BOY And, uncle, so will I, an if I live.
TITUS Come, go with me into mine armoury.
Lucius, I'll fit thee; and withal my boy
Shall carry from me to the Empress' sons
Presents that I intend to send them both.
Come, come; thou'lt do my message, wilt thou not?
BOY Ay, with my dagger in their bosoms, grandsire.
TITUS No, boy, not so; I'll teach thee another course.
Lavinia, come. Marcus, look to my house.
Lucius and I'll go brave it at the court;
Ay, marry, will we, sir! and we'll be waited on.

[Exeunt Titus, Lavinia, and Young Lucius.

MARCUS O, heavens, can you hear a good man groan
And not relent, or not compassion him?
Marcus, attend him in his ecstasy,
That hath more scars of sorrow in his heart
Than foemen's marks upon his batt'red shield,
But yet so just that he will not revenge.
Revenge the heavens for old Andronicus!

[Exit.

SCENE II. *Rome. The palace.*

Enter AARON, DEMETRIUS and CHIRON, at one door; and at the other door, YOUNG LUCIUS and another with a bundle of weapons, and verses writ upon them.

CHIRON Demetrius, here's the son of Lucius;
He hath some message to deliver us.
AARON Ay, some mad message from his mad grandfather.
BOY My lords, with all the humbleness I may,
I greet your honours from Andronicus –
[*Aside*] And pray the Roman gods confound you both!
DEMETRIUS Gramercy, lovely Lucius. What's the news?
BOY [*Aside*] That you are both decipher'd, that's the news,
For villains mark'd with rape. – May it please you,
My grandsire, well-advis'd, hath sent by me
The goodliest weapons of his armoury
To gratify your honourable youth,
The hope of Rome; for so he bid me say;
And so I do, and with his gifts present
Your lordships, that, whenever you have need,
You may be armed and appointed well.
And so I leave you both – [*Aside*] like bloody villains.

[Exeunt Young Lucius and Attendant.

DEMETRIUS What's here? A scroll, and written round about.
Let's see:
[*Reads*] 'Integer vitae, scelerisque purus,
Non eget Mauri iaculis, nec arcu.
CHIRON O, 'tis a verse in Horace, I know it well;
I read it in the grammar long ago.
AARON Ay, just – a verse in Horace. Right, you have it.
[*Aside*] Now, what a thing it is to be an ass!
Here's no sound jest! The old man hath found their guilt,
And sends them weapons wrapp'd about with lines
That wound, beyond their feeling, to the quick.
But were our witty Empress well afoot,
She would applaud Andronicus' conceit.
But let her rest in her unrest awhile –
And now, young lords, was't not a happy star
Led us to Rome, strangers, and more than so,
Captives, to be advanced to this height?
It did me good before the palace gate
To brave the Tribune in his brother's hearing.
DEMETRIUS But me more good to see so great a lord
Basely insinuate and send us gifts.
AARON Had he not reason, Lord Demetrius?
Did you not use his daughter very friendly?
DEMETRIUS I would we had a thousand Roman dames
At such a bay, by turn to serve our lust.
CHIRON A charitable wish and full of love.
AARON Here lacks but your mother for to say amen.
CHIRON And that would she for twenty thousand more.
DEMETRIUS Come, let us go and pray to all the gods
For our beloved mother in her pains.
AARON [*Aside*] Pray to the devils; the gods have given us over. *[Trumpets sound.*
DEMETRIUS Why do the Emperor's trumpets flourish thus?
CHIRON Belike, for joy the Emperor hath a son.
DEMETRIUS Soft! who comes here?

Enter Nurse, with a blackamoor Child.

NURSE Good morrow, lords.
O, tell me, did you see Aaron the Moor?
AARON Well, more or less, or ne'er a whit at all,
Here Aaron is; and what with Aaron now?
NURSE O gentle Aaron, we are all undone!

Now help, or woe betide thee evermore!
AARON Why, what a caterwauling dost thou keep!
What dost thou wrap and fumble in thy arms?
NURSE O, that which I would hide from heaven's eye:
Our Empress' shame and stately Rome's disgrace!
She is delivered, lords; she is delivered.
AARON To whom?
NURSE I mean she is brought a-bed.
AARON Well, God give her good rest! What hath he sent her?
NURSE A devil.
AARON Why, then she is the devil's dam;
A joyful issue.
NURSE A joyless, dismal, black, and sorrowful issue!
Here is the babe, as loathsome as a toad
Amongst the fair-fac'd breeders of our clime;
The Empress sends it thee, thy stamp, thy seal,
And bids thee christen it with thy dagger's point.
AARON Zounds, ye whore! Is black so base a hue?
Sweet blowse, you are a beauteous blossom sure.
DEMETRIUS Villain, what hast thou done?
AARON That which thou canst not undo.
CHIRON Thou hast undone our mother.
AARON Villain, I have done thy mother.
DEMETRIUS And therein, hellish dog, thou hast undone her.
Woe to her chance, and damn'd her loathed choice!
Accurs'd the offspring of so foul a fiend!
CHIRON It shall not live.
AARON It shall not die.
NURSE Aaron, it must; the mother wills it so.
AARON What, must it, nurse? Then let no man but I
Do execution on my flesh and blood.
DEMETRIUS I'll broach the tadpole on my rapier's point.
Nurse, give it me; my sword shall soon dispatch it.
AARON Sooner this sword shall plough thy bowels up.
[*Takes the Child from the Nurse, and draws.*
Stay, murderous villains, will you kill your brother!
Now, by the burning tapers of the sky
That shone so brightly when this boy was got,
He dies upon my scimitar's sharp point
That touches this my first-born son and heir.
I tell you, younglings, not Enceladus,
With all his threat'ning band of Typhon's brood,
Nor great Alcides, nor the god of war,
Shall seize this prey out of his father's hands.
What, what, ye sanguine, shallow-hearted boys!
Ye white-lim'd walls! ye alehouse painted signs!
Coal-black is better than another hue
In that it scorns to bear another hue;
For all the water in the ocean
Can never turn the swan's black legs to white.
Although she lave them hourly in the flood.
Tell the Empress from me I am of age
To keep mine own – excuse it how she can.
DEMETRIUS Wilt thou betray thy noble mistress thus?
AARON My mistress is my mistress: this my self,
The vigour and the picture of my youth.
This before all the world do I prefer;
This maugre all the world will I keep safe,
Or some of you shall smoke for it in Rome.
DEMETRIUS By this our mother is for ever sham'd.
CHIRON Rome will despise her for this foul escape.
NURSE The Emperor in his rage will doom her death.
CHIRON I blush to think upon this ignomy.
AARON Why, there's the privilege your beauty bears:
Fie, treacherous hue, that will betray with blushing
The close enacts and counsels of thy heart!
Here's a young lad fram'd of another leer.
Look how the black slave smiles upon the father,
As who should say 'Old lad, I am thine own'.
He is your brother, lords, sensibly fed
Of that self-blood that first gave life to you;
And from your womb where you imprisoned were
He is enfranchised and come to light.
Nay, he is your brother by the surer side,
Although my seal be stamped in his face.
NURSE Aaron, what shall I say unto the Empress?
DEMETRIUS Advise thee, Aaron, what is to be done,
And we will all subscribe to thy advice.
Save thou the child, so we may all be safe.
AARON Then sit we down and let us all consult.
My son and I will have the wind of you:
Keep there; now talk at pleasure of your safety.
[*They sit.*
DEMETRIUS How many women saw this child of his?
AARON Why, so, brave lords! When we join in league

I am a lamb; but if you brave the Moor,
The chafed boar, the mountain lioness,
The ocean swells not so as Aaron storms.
But say, again, how many saw the child?

NURSE Cornelia the midwife and myself;
And no one else but the delivered Empress.

AARON The Empress, the midwife, and yourself.
Two may keep counsel when the third's away:
Go to the Empress, tell her this I said.
[He kills her.
Weeke weeke!
So cries a pig prepared to the spit.

DEMETRIUS What mean'st thou, Aaron?
Wherefore didst thou this?

AARON O Lord, sir, 'tis a deed of policy.
Shall she live to betray this guilt of ours –
A long-tongu'd babbling gossip? No, lords, no.
And now be it known to you my full intent:
Not far, one Muliteus, my countryman –
His wife but yesternight was brought to bed;
His child is like to her, fair as you are.
Go pack with him, and give the mother gold,
And tell them both the circumstance of all,
And how by this their child shall be advanc'd,
And be received for the Emperor's heir
And substituted in the place of mine,
To calm this tempest whirling in the court;
And let the Emperor dandle him for his own.
Hark ye, lords. You see I have given her physic,
[Pointing to the Nurse.
And you must needs bestow her funeral;
The fields are near, and you are gallant grooms.
This done, see that you take no longer days,
But send the midwife presently to me.
The midwife and the nurse well made away,
Then let the ladies tattle what they please.

CHIRON Aaron, I see thou wilt not trust the air
With secrets.

DEMETRIUS For this care of Tamora,
Herself and hers are highly bound to thee.

[Exeunt Demetrius and Chiron, bearing off the dead Nurse.

AARON Now to the Goths, as swift as swallow flies,
There to dispose this treasure in mine arms,
And secretly to greet the Empress' friends.
Come on, you thick-lipp'd slave, I'll bear you hence;
For it is you that puts us to our shifts.
I'll make you feed on berries and on roots,
And feed on curds and whey, and suck the goat,
And cabin in a cave, and bring you up
To be a warrior and command a camp.
[Exit with the child.

SCENE III. *Rome. A public place.*

Enter TITUS, bearing arrows with letters on the ends of them; with him MARCUS, YOUNG LUCIUS, and other gentlemen, PUBLIUS, SEMPRONIUS, and CAIUS, with bows.

TITUS Come, Marcus, come; kinsmen, this is the way.
Sir boy, let me see your archery;
Look ye draw home enough, and 'tis there straight.
Terras Astraea reliquit,
Be you remember'd, Marcus; she's gone, she's fled.
Sirs, take you to your tools. You, cousins, shall
Go sound the ocean and cast your nets;
Happily you may catch her in the sea;
Yet there's as little justice as at land.
No; Publius and Sempronius, you must do it;
'Tis you must dig with mattock and with spade,
And pierce the inmost centre of the earth;
Then, when you come to Pluto's region,
I pray you deliver him this petition.
Tell him it is for justice and for aid,
And that it comes from old Andronicus,
Shaken with sorrows in ungrateful Rome.
Ah, Rome! Well, well, I made thee miserable
What time I threw the people's suffrages
On him that thus doth tyrannize o'er me.
Go get you gone; and pray be careful all,
And leave you not a man-of-war unsearch'd.
This wicked Emperor may have shipp'd her hence;
And, kinsmen, then we may go pipe for justice.

MARCUS O Publius, is not this a heavy case,
To see thy noble uncle thus distract?

PUBLIUS Therefore, my lords, it highly us concerns
By day and night t'attend him carefully,
And feed his humour kindly as we may
Till time beget some careful remedy.

MARCUS Kinsmen, his sorrows, are past remedy.
Join with the Goths, and with revengeful war
Take wreak on Rome for this ingratitude,
And vengeance on the traitor Saturnine.

TITUS Publius, how now? How now, my masters?
What, have you met with her?

PUBLIUS No, my good lord; but Pluto sends you word,
If you will have Revenge from hell, you shall.
Marry, for Justice, she is so employ'd
He thinks, with Jove in heaven, or somewhere else,
So that perforce you must needs stay a time.

TITUS He doth me wrong to feed me with delays.
I'll dive into the burning lake below

And pull her out of Acheron by the heels.
Marcus, we are but shrubs, no cedars we,
No big-bon'd men fram'd of the Cyclops' size;
But metal, Marcus, steel to the very back,
Yet wrung with wrongs more than our backs can bear;
And, sith there's no justice in earth nor hell,
We will solicit heaven, and move the gods
To send down Justice for to wreak our wrongs.
Come, to this gear. You are a good archer, Marcus. [*He gives them the arrows.*
'Ad Jovem' that's for you; here 'Ad Apollinem'.
'Ad Martem' that's for myself.
Here, boy, 'To Pallas'; here 'To Mercury'.
'To Saturn' Caius – not to Saturnine:
You were as good to shoot against the wind.
To it, boy. Marcus, loose when I bid.
Of my word, I have written to effect;
There's not a god left unsolicited.

MARCUS Kinsmen, shoot all your shafts into the court;
We will afflict the Emperor in his pride.

TITUS Now, masters, draw. [*They shoot*] O, well said, Lucius!
Good boy, in Virgo's lap! Give it Pallas.

MARCUS My lord, I aim a mile beyond the moon;
Your letter is with Jupiter by this.

TITUS Ha! ha!
Publius, Publius, what hast thou done?
See, see, thou hast shot off one of Taurus' horns.

MARCUS This was the sport, my lord: when Publius shot,
The Bull, being gall'd, gave Aries such a knock
That down fell both the Ram's horns in the court;
And who should find them but the Empress' villain?
She laugh'd, and told the Moor he should not choose
But give them to his master for a present.

TITUS Why, there it goes! God give his lordship joy!

Enter the Clown, with a basket and two pigeons in it.

News, news from heaven! Marcus, the post is come.
Sirrah, what tidings? Have you any letters?
Shall I have justice? What says Jupiter?

CLOWN Ho, the gibbet-maker? He says that he hath taken them down again, for the man must not be hang'd till the next week.

TITUS But what says Jupiter, I ask thee?

CLOWN Alas, sir, I know not Jupiter; I never drank with him in all my life.

TITUS Why, villain, art not thou the carrier?

CLOWN Ay, of my pigeons, sir; nothing else.

TITUS Why, didst thou not come from heaven?

CLOWN From heaven! Alas, sir, I never came there. God forbid I should be so bold to press to heaven in my young days. Why, I am going with my pigeons to the Tribunal Plebs, to take up a matter of brawl betwixt my uncle and one of the Emperal's men.

MARCUS Why, sir, that is as fit as can be to serve for your oration; and let him deliver the pigeons to the Emperor from you.

TITUS Tell me, can you deliver an oration to the Emperor with a grace?

CLOWN Nay, truly, sir, I could never say grace in all my life.

TITUS Sirrah, come hither. Make no more ado,
But give your pigeons to the Emperor;
By me thou shalt have justice at his hands.
Hold, hold! Meanwhile here's money for thy charges.
Give me pen and ink. Sirrah, can you with a grace deliver up a supplication?

CLOWN Ay, sir.

TITUS Then here is a supplication for you. And when you come to him, at the first approach you must kneel; then kiss his foot; then deliver up your pigeons; and then look for your reward. I'll be at hand, sir; see you do it bravely.

CLOWN I warrant you, sir; let me alone.

TITUS Sirrah, hast thou a knife? Come, let me see it.
Here, Marcus, fold it in the oration;
For thou hast made it like an humble suppliant.
And when thou hast given it to the Emperor,
Knock at my door, and tell me what he says.

CLOWN God be with you, sir; I will.

TITUS Come, Marcus, let us go. Publius, follow me. [*Exeunt.*

SCENE IV. *Rome. Before the palace.*

Enter the EMPEROR, and the EMPRESS and her two sons, DEMETRIUS and CHIRON; Lords and Others. The Emperor brings the arrows in his hand that Titus shot at him.

SATURNINUS Why, lords, what wrongs are these! Was ever seen
An emperor in Rome thus overborne,
Troubled, confronted thus; and, for the extent
Of egal justice, us'd in such contempt?
My lords, you know, as know the mightful gods,
However these disturbers of our peace
Buzz in the people's ears, there nought hath pass'd
But even with law against the wilful sons
Of old Andronicus. And what an if
His sorrows have so overwhelm'd his wits,

Shall we be thus afflicted in his wreaks,
His fits, his frenzy, and his bitterness?
And now he writes to heaven for his redress.
See, here's 'To Jove' and this 'To Mercury';
This 'To Apollo'; this 'To the God of War' –
Sweet scrolls to fly about the streets of Rome!
What's this but libelling against the Senate,
And blazoning our unjustice every where?
A goodly humour, is it not, my lords?
As who would say in Rome no justice were.
But if I live, his feigned ecstasies
Shall be no shelter to these outrages;
But he and his shall know that justice lives.
In Saturninus' health; whom, if she sleep,
He'll so awake as he in fury shall
Cut off the proud'st conspirator that lives

TAMORA My gracious lord, my lovely Saturnine,
Lord of my life, commander of my thoughts,
Calm thee, and bear the faults of Titus' age,
Th' effects of sorrow for his valiant sons,
Whose loss hath pierc'd him deep and scarr'd his heart;
And rather comfort his distressed plight
Than prosecute the meanest or the best
For these contempts. [*Aside*] Why, thus it shall become
High-witted Tamora to gloze with all.
But, Titus, I have touch'd thee to the quick,
Thy life-blood out; if Aaron now be wise,
Then is all safe, the anchor in the port.

Enter Clown.

How now, good fellow! Wouldst thou speak with us?

CLOWN Yes, forsooth, an your mistriship be Emperial.

TAMORA Empress I am, but yonder sits the Emperor.

CLOWN 'Tis he. – God and Saint Stephen give you godden. I have brought you a letter and a couple of pigeons here.

[*Saturninus reads the letter.*

SATURNINUS Go take him away, and hang him presently.

CLOWN How much money must I have?

TAMORA Come, sirrah, you must be hang'd.

CLOWN Hang'd! by'r lady, then I have brought up a neck to a fair end.

[*Exit guarded.*

SATURNINUS Despiteful and intolerable wrongs!
Shall I endure this monstrous villainy?
I know from whence this same device proceeds.
May this be borne – as if his traitorous sons
That died by law for murder of our brother
Have by my means been butchered wrongfully?
Go drag the villain hither by the hair;
Nor age nor honour shall shape privilege.
For this proud mock I'll be thy slaughter-man,
Sly frantic wretch, that holp'st to make me great,
In hope thyself should govern Rome and me.

Enter Nuntius AEMILIUS.

What news with thee, Aemilius?

AEMILIUS Arm, my lords! Rome never had more cause.
The Goths have gathered head; and with a power
Of high resolved men, bent to the spoil,
They hither march amain, under conduct
Of Lucius, son to old Andronicus;
Who threats in course of this revenge to do
As much as ever Coriolanus did.

SATURNINUS Is warlike Lucius general of the Goths?
These tidings nip me, and I hang the head
As flowers with frost, or grass beat down with storms.
Ay, now begins our sorrows to approach.
'Tis he the common people love so much;
Myself hath often heard them say –
When I have walked like a private man –
That Lucius' banishment was wrongfully,
And they have wish'd that Lucius were their emperor.

TAMORA Why should you fear? Is not your city strong?

SATURNINUS Ay, but the citizens favour Lucius,
And will revolt from me to succour him.

TAMORA King, be thy thoughts imperious like thy name!
Is the sun dimm'd, that gnats do fly in it?
The eagle suffers little birds to sing,
And is not careful what they mean thereby,
Knowing that with the shadow of his wings
He can at pleasure stint their melody;
Even so mayest thou the giddy men of Rome.
Then cheer thy spirit; for know thou, Emperor,
I will enchant the old Andronicus
With words more sweet, and yet more dangerous,
Than baits to fish or honey-stalks to sheep,
When as the one is wounded with the bait,
The other rotted with delicious feed.

SATURNINUS But he will not entreat his son for us.

TAMORA If Tamora entreat him, then he will;
For I can smooth and fill his aged ears
With golden promises, that, were his heart
Almost impregnable, his old ears deaf,
Yet should both ear and heart obey my tongue.
[*To Aemilius*] Go thou before to be our ambassador;
Say that the Emperor requests a parley

Of warlike Lucius, and appoint the meeting
Even at his father's house, the old Andronicus.
SATURNINUS Aemilius, do this message honourably;
And if he stand on hostage for his safety,
Bid him demand what pledge will please him best.
AEMILIUS Your bidding shall I do effectually. [*Exit.*
TAMORA Now will I to that old Andronicus,
And temper him with all the art I have,
To pluck proud Lucius from the warlike Goths.
And now, sweet Emperor, be blithe again,
And bury all thy fear in my devices.
SATURNINUS Then go successantly, and plead to him. [*Exeunt.*

ACT FIVE

SCENE I. *Plains near Rome.*

Enter LUCIUS with an army of Goths with drums and colours.

LUCIUS Approved warriors and my faithful friends,
I have received letters from great Rome
Which signifies what hate they bear their Emperor
And how desirous of our sight they are.
Therefore, great lords, be, as your titles witness,
Imperious and impatient of your wrongs;
And wherein Rome hath done you any scath,
Let him make treble satisfaction.
1 GOTH Brave slip, sprung from the great Andronicus,
Whose name was once our terror, now our comfort,
Whose high exploits and honourable deeds
Ingrateful Rome requites with foul contempt,
Be bold in us: we'll follow where thou lead'st,
Like stinging bees in hottest summer's day,
Led by their master to the flow'red fields,
And be aveng'd on cursed Tamora.
ALL THE GOTHS And as he saith, so say we all with him.
LUCIUS I humbly thank him, and I thank you all.
But who comes here, led by a lusty Goth?

Enter a Goth, leading AARON with his Child in his arms

2 GOTH Renowned Lucius, from our troops I stray'd
To gaze upon a ruinous monastery;
And as I earnestly did fix mine eye
Upon the wasted building, suddenly
I heard a child cry underneath a wall.
I made unto the noise, when soon I heard
The crying babe controll'd with this discourse:
'Peace, tawny slave, half me and half thy dam!
Did not thy hue bewray whose brat thou art,
Had nature lent thee but thy mother's look,
Villain, thou mightst have been an emperor;
But where the bull and cow are both milk-white,
They never do beget a coal-black calf.
Peace, villain, peace!' – even thus he rates the babe –
'For I must bear thee to a trusty Goth,
Who, when he knows thou art the Empress' babe,
Will hold thee dearly for thy mother's sake'.
With this, my weapon drawn, I rush'd upon him,
Surpris'd him suddenly, and brought him hither
To use as you think needful of the man.
LUCIUS O worthy Goth, this is the incarnate devil
That robb'd Andronicus of his good hand;
This is the pearl that pleas'd your Empress' eye;
And here's the base fruit of her burning lust.
Say, wall-ey'd slave, whither wouldst thou convey
This growing image of thy fiend-like face?
Why dost not speak? What, deaf? Not a word?
A halter, soldiers! Hang him on this tree,
And by his side his fruit of bastardy.
AARON Touch not the boy, he is of royal blood.
LUCIUS Too like the sire for ever being good.
First hang the child, that he may see it sprawl –
A sight to vex the father's soul withal.
Get me a ladder. [*A ladder brought, which Aaron is made to climb.*
AARON Lucius, save the child,
And bear it from me to the Empress.
If thou do this, I'll show thee wondrous things
That highly may advantage thee to hear;
If thou wilt not, befall what may befall,
I'll speak no more but 'Vengeance rot you all!'
LUCIUS Say on; an if it please me which thou speak'st,
Thy child shall live, and I will see it nourish'd.
AARON An if it please thee! Why, assure thee, Lucius,
'Twill vex thy soul to hear what I shall speak;
For I must talk of murders, rapes, and massacres,
Acts of black night, abominable deeds,
Complots of mischief, treason, villainies,
Ruthful to hear, yet piteously perform'd;
And this shall all be buried in my death,

Unless thou swear to me my child shall live.
LUCIUS Tell on thy mind; I say thy child shall live.
AARON Swear that he shall, and then I will begin.
LUCIUS Who should I swear by? Thou believest no god;
That granted, how canst thou believe an oath?
AARON What if I do not? – as indeed I do not;
Yet, for I know thou art religious
And hast a thing within thee called conscience,
With twenty popish tricks and ceremonies
Which I have seen thee careful to observe,
Therefore I urge thy oath. For that I know
An idiot holds his bauble for a god,
And keeps the oath which by that god he swears,
To that I'll urge him. Therefore thou shalt vow
By that same god – what god soe'er it be
That thou adorest and hast in reverence –
To save my boy, to nourish and bring him up;
Or else I will discover nought to thee.
LUCIUS Even by my god I swear to thee I will.
AARON First know thou, I begot him on the Empress.
LUCIUS O most insatiate and luxurious woman!
AARON Tut, Lucius, this was but a deed of charity
To that which thou shalt hear of me anon.
'Twas her two sons that murdered Bassianus;
They cut thy sister's tongue, and ravish'd her,
And cut her hands, and trimm'd her as thou sawest.
LUCIUS O detestable villain! Call'st thou that trimming?
AARON Why, she was wash'd, and cut, and trimm'd, and 'twas
Trim sport for them which had the doing of it.
LUCIUS O barbarous beastly villains like thyself!
AARON Indeed, I was their tutor to instruct them.
That codding spirit had they from their mother,
As sure a card as ever won the set;
That bloody mind, I think, they learn'd of me,
As true a dog as ever fought at head.
Well, let my deeds be witness of my worth.
I train'd thy brethren to that guileful hole
Where the dead corpse of Bassianus lay;
I wrote the letter that thy father found,
And hid the gold within that letter mention'd,
Confederate with the queen and her two sons;
And what not done, that thou hast cause to rue,
Wherein I had no stroke of mischief in it?
I play'd the cheater for thy father's hand,
And, when I had it, drew myself apart
And almost broke my heart with extreme laughter.
I pried me through the crevice of a wall,
When, for his hand, he had his two sons' heads;
Beheld his tears, and laugh'd so heartily
That both mine eyes were rainy like to his;
And when I told the Empress of this sport,
She swooned almost at my pleasing tale,
And for my tidings gave me twenty kisses.
GOTH What, canst thou say all this and never blush?
AARON Ay, like a black dog, as the saying is.
LUCIUS Art thou not sorry for these heinous deeds?
AARON Ay, that I had not done a thousand more.
Even now I curse the day – and yet, I think,
Few come within the compass of my curse –
Wherein I did not some notorious ill:
As kill a man, or else devise his death;
Ravish a maid, or plot the way to do it;
Accuse some innocent, and forswear myself;
Set deadly enmity between two friends;
Make poor men's cattle break their necks;
Set fire on barns and hay-stacks in the night,
And bid the owners quench them with their tears.
Oft have I digg'd up dead men from their graves,
And set them upright at their dear friends' door
Even when their sorrows almost was forgot,
And on their skins, as on the bark of trees,
Have with my knife carved in Roman letters
'Let not your sorrow die, though I am dead'.
Tut, I have done a thousand dreadful things
As willingly as one would kill a fly;
And nothing grieves me heartily indeed
But that I cannot do ten thousand more.
LUCIUS Bring down the devil, for he must not die
So sweet a death as hanging presently.
AARON If there be devils, would I were a devil,
To live and burn in everlasting fire,
So I might have your company in hell
But to torment you with my bitter tongue!
LUCIUS Sirs, stop his mouth, and let him speak no more.

Enter AEMILIUS.

GOTH My lord, there is a messenger from Rome
Desires to be admitted to your presence.
LUCIUS Let him come near.
Welcome, Aemilius. What's the news from Rome?
AEMILIUS Lord Lucius, and you Princes of the Goths,
The Roman Emperor greets you all by me;
And, for he understands you are in arms,
He craves a parley at your father's house,
Willing you to demand your hostages,
And they shall be immediately deliver'd.
1 GOTH What says our general?
LUCIUS Aemilius, let the Emperor give his pledges
Unto my father and my uncle Marcus.

And we will come. March away. [*Exeunt.*

SCENE II. *Rome. Before Titus' house.*

Enter TAMORA, and her two sons, DEMETRIUS and CHIRON, disguised.

TAMORA Thus, in this strange and sad habiliment,
I will encounter with Andronicus,
And say I am Revenge, sent from below
To join with him and right his heinous wrongs.
Knock at his study, where they say he keeps
To ruminate strange plots of dire revenge;
Tell him Revenge is come to join with him,
And work confusion on his enemies.

They knock, and TITUS opens his study door, above.

TITUS Who doth molest my contemplation?
Is it your trick to make me ope the door,
That so my sad decrees may fly away
And all my study be to no effect?
You are deceiv'd; for what I mean to do
See here in bloody lines I have set down;
And what is written shall be executed.

TAMORA Titus, I am come to talk with thee.

TITUS No, not a word. How can I grace my talk,
Wanting a hand to give it that accord?
Thou hast the odds of me; therefore no more.

TAMORA If thou didst know me, thou wouldst talk with me.

TITUS I am not mad, I know thee well enough:
Witness this wretched stump, witness these crimson lines;
Witness these trenches made by grief and care;
Witness the tiring day and heavy night;
Witness all sorrow that I know thee well
For our proud Empress, mighty Tamora.
Is not thy coming for my other hand?

TAMORA Know thou, sad man, I am not Tamora:
She is thy enemy and I thy friend.
I am Revenge, sent from th' infernal kingdom
To ease the gnawing vulture of thy mind
By working wreakful vengeance on thy foes.
Come down and welcome me to this world's light;
Confer with me of murder and of death;
There's not a hollow cave or lurking-place,
No vast obscurity or misty vale,
Where bloody murder or detested rape
Can couch for fear but I will find them out;
And in their ears tell them my dreadful name –
Revenge, which makes the foul offender quake.

TITUS Art thou Revenge? and art thou sent to me
To be a torment to mine enemies?

TAMORA I am; therefore come down and welcome me.

TITUS Do me some service ere I come to thee.
Lo, by thy side where Rape and Murder stands;
Now give some surance that thou art Revenge –
Stab them, or tear them on thy chariot wheels;
And then I'll come and be thy waggoner
And whirl along with thee about the globes.
Provide thee two proper palfreys, black as jet,
To hale thy vengeful waggon swift away,
And find out murderers in their guilty caves;
And when thy car is loaden with their heads,
I will dismount, and by thy waggon wheel
Trot, like a servile footman, all day long,
Even from Hyperion's rising in the east
Until his very downfall in the sea.
And day by day I'll do this heavy task,
So thou destroy Rapine and Murder there.

TAMORA These are my ministers, and come with me.

TITUS Are they thy ministers? What are they call'd?

TAMORA Rape and Murder; therefore called so
'Cause they take vengeance of such kind of men.

TITUS Good Lord, how like the Empress' sons they are!
And you the Empress! But we worldly men
Have miserable, mad, mistaking eyes.
O sweet Revenge, now do I come to thee;
And, if one arm's embracement will content thee,
I will embrace thee in it by and by. [*Exit above.*

TAMORA This closing with him fits his lunacy.
Whate'er I forge to feed his brain-sick humours,
Do you uphold and maintain in your speeches,
For now he firmly takes me for Revenge;
And, being credulous in this mad thought,
I'll make him send for Lucius his son,
And whilst I at a banquet hold him sure,
I'll find some cunning practice out of hand
To scatter and disperse the giddy Goths,
Or, at the least, make them his enemies.
See, here he comes, and I must ply my theme.

Enter TITUS, below.

TITUS Long have I been forlorn, and all for thee.
Welcome, dread Fury, to my woeful house.
Rapine and Murder, you are welcome too.
How like the Empress and her sons you are!
Well are you fitted, had you but a Moor.
Could not all hell afford you such a devil?
For well I wot the Empress never wags
But in her company there is a Moor;
And, would you represent our queen aright,
It were convenient you had such a devil.
But welcome as you are. What shall we do?

TAMORA What wouldst thou have us do, Andronicus?

DEMETRIUS Show me a murderer, I'll deal with him.

CHIRON Show me a villain that hath done a rape,
And I am sent to be reveng'd on him.
TAMORA Show me a thousand that hath done thee wrong,
And I will be revenged on them all.
TITUS Look round about the wicked streets of Rome,
And when thou find'st a man that's like thyself,
Good Murder, stab him; he's a murderer.
Go thou with him, and when it is thy hap
To find another that is like to thee,
Good Rapine, stab him; he is a ravisher.
Go thou with them; and in the Emperor's court
There is a queen, attended by a Moor;
Well shalt thou know her by thine own proportion,
For up and down she doth resemble thee.
I pray thee, do on them some violent death;
They have been violent to me and mine.
TAMORA Well hast thou lesson'd us; this shall we do.
But would it please thee, good Andronicus,
To send for Lucius, thy thrice-valiant son,
Who leads towards Rome a band of warlike Goths,
And bid him come and banquet at thy house;
When he is here, even at thy solemn feast,
I will bring in the Empress and her sons,
The Emperor himself, and all thy foes;
And at thy mercy shall they stoop and kneel,
And on them shalt thou ease thy angry heart.
What says Andronicus to this device?
TITUS Marcus, my brother! 'Tis sad Titus calls.

Enter MARCUS.

Go, gentle Marcus, to thy nephew Lucius;
Thou shalt inquire him out among the Goths.
Bid him repair to me, and bring with him
Some of the chiefest princes of the Goths;
Bid him encamp his soldiers where they are.
Tell him the Emperor and the Empress too
Feast at my house, and he shall feast with them.
This do thou for my love; and so let him,
As he regards his aged father's life.
MARCUS This will I do, and soon return again. [*Exit.*
TAMORA Now will I hence about thy business,
And take my ministers along with me.
TITUS Nay, nay, let Rape and Murder stay with me,
Or else I'll call my brother back again,
And cleave to no revenge but Lucius.
TAMORA [*Aside to her sons*] What say you, boys? Will you abide with him,
Whiles I go tell my lord the Emperor
How I have govern'd our determin'd jest?
Yield to his humour, smooth and speak him fair,
And tarry with him till I turn again.
TITUS [*Aside*] I knew them all, though they suppos'd me mad,
And will o'er-reach them in their own devices,
A pair of cursed hell-hounds and their dam.
DEMETRIUS Madam, depart at pleasure; leave us here.
TAMORA Farewell, Andronicus, Revenge now goes
To lay a complot to betray thy foes.
TITUS I know thou dost: and, sweet Revenge, farewell. [*Exit Tamora.*
CHIRON Tell us, old man, how shall we be employ'd?
TITUS Tut, I have work enough for you to do.
Publius, come hither, Caius, and Valentine.

Enter PUBLIUS, CAIUS, and VALENTINE.

PUBLIUS What is your will?
TITUS Know you these two?
PUBLIUS The Empress' sons, I take them: Chiron, Demetrius.
TITUS Fie, Publius, fie! thou art too much deceiv'd.
The one is Murder, and Rape is the other's name;
And therefore bind them, gentle Publius –
Caius and Valentine, lay hands on them.
Oft have you heard me wish for such an hour,
And now I find it; therefore bind them sure,
And stop their mouths if they begin to cry.

[*Exit. They lay hold on Chiron and Demetrius.*

CHIRON Villains, forbear! we are the Empress' sons.
PUBLIUS And therefore do we what we are commanded.
Stop close their mouths, let them not speak a word.
Is he sure bound? Look that you bind them fast.

Re-enter TITUS ANDRONICUS with a knife, and LAVINIA with a basin.

TITUS Come, come, Lavinia; look, thy foes are bound.
Sirs, stop their mouths, let them not speak to me;
But let them hear what fearful words I utter.
O villains, Chiron and Demetrius!
Here stands the spring whom you have stain'd with mud;
This goodly summer with your winter mix'd.
You kill'd her husband; and for that vile fault
Two of her brothers were condemn'd to death,
My hand cut off and made a merry jest;
Both her sweet hands, her tongue, and that more dear

Than hands or tongue, her spotless chastity,
Inhuman traitors, you constrain'd and forc'd.
What would you say, if I should let you speak?
Villains, for shame you could not beg for grace.
Hark, wretches! how I mean to martyr you.
This one hand yet is left to cut your throats,
Whiles that Lavinia 'tween her stumps doth hold
The basin that receives your guilty blood.
You know your mother means to feast with me,
And calls herself Revenge, and thinks me mad.
Hark, villains! I will grind your bones to dust,
And with your blood and it I'll make a paste;
And of the paste a coffin I will rear,
And make two pasties of your shameful heads;
And bid that strumpet, your unhallowed dam,
Like to the earth, swallow her own increase.
This is the feast that I have bid her to,
And this the banquet she shall surfeit on;
For worse than Philomel you us'd my daughter,
And worse than Progne I will be reveng'd.
And now prepare your throats. Lavinia, come,
Receive the blood; and when that they are dead,
Let me go grind their bones to powder small,
And with this hateful liquor temper it;
And in that paste let their vile heads be bak'd.
Come, come, be every one officious
To make this banquet, which I wish may prove
More stern and bloody than the Centaurs' feast.

[*He cuts their throats.*

So.
Now bring them in, for I will play the cook,
And see them ready against their mother comes.

[*Exeunt, bearing the dead bodies.*

SCENE III. *The court of Titus' house.*

Enter LUCIUS, MARCUS, and the Goths, with AARON prisoner, and his Child in the arms of an Attendant.

LUCIUS Uncle Marcus, since 'tis my father's mind
That I repair to Rome, I am content.
1 GOTH And ours with thine, befall what fortune will.
LUCIUS Good uncle, take you in this barbarous Moor,
This ravenous tiger, this accursed devil;
Let him receive no sust'nance, fetter him,
Till he be brought unto the Empress' face
For testimony of her foul proceedings.
And see the ambush of our friends be strong;
I fear the Emperor means no good to us.
AARON Some devil whisper curses in my ear,
And prompt me that my tongue may utter forth
The venomous malice of my swelling heart!
LUCIUS Away, inhuman dog, unhallowed slave!
Sirs, help our uncle to convey him in.

[*Exeunt Goths with Aaron. Flourish within.*

The trumpets show the Emperor is at hand.

Sound trumpets. Enter SATURNINUS and TAMORA, with AEMILIUS, Tribunes, Senators, and Others.

SATURNINUS What, hath the firmament moe suns than one?
LUCIUS What boots it thee to call thyself a sun?
MARCUS Rome's Emperor, and nephew, break the parle;
These quarrels must be quietly debated.
The feast is ready which the careful Titus
Hath ordain'd to an honourable end,
For peace, for love, for league, and good to Rome.
Please you, therefore, draw nigh and take your places.
SATURNINUS Marcus, we will. [*A table brought in. The company sit down.*

Trumpets sounding, enter TITUS like a cook, placing the dishes, and LAVINIA with a veil over her face; also YOUNG LUCIUS, and Others.

TITUS Welcome, my lord; welcome, dread Queen;
Welcome, ye warlike Goths; welcome, Lucius;
And welcome all. Although the cheer be poor,
'Twill fill your stomachs; please you eat of it.
SATURNINUS Why art thou thus attir'd, Andronicus?
TITUS Because I would be sure to have all well
To entertain your Highness and your Empress.
TAMORA We are beholding to you, good Andronicus.
TITUS An if your Highness knew my heart, you were.
My lord the Emperor, resolve me this:
Was it well done of rash Virginius
To slay his daughter with his own right hand,
Because she was enforc'd, stain'd, and deflower'd?
SATURNINUS It was, Andronicus.
TITUS Your reason, mighty lord.
SATURNINUS Because the girl should not survive her shame,
And by her presence still renew his sorrows.
TITUS A reason mighty, strong, and effectual;
A pattern, precedent, and lively warrant
For me, most wretched, to perform the like.
Die, die, Lavinia, and thy shame with thee;

[*He kills her.*

And with thy shame thy father's sorrow die!
SATURNINUS What hast thou done, unnatural and unkind?

TITUS Kill'd her for whom my tears have made me blind.
I am as woeful as Virginius was,
And have a thousand times more cause than he
To do this outrage; and it now is done.
SATURNINUS What, was she ravish'd? Tell who did the deed.
TITUS Will't please you eat? Will't please your Highness feed?
TAMORA Why hast thou slain thine only daughter thus?
TITUS Not I; 'twas Chiron and Demetrius.
They ravish'd her, and cut away her tongue;
And they, 'twas they, that did her all this wrong.
SATURNINUS Go, fetch them hither to us presently.
TITUS Why, there they are, both baked in this pie,
Whereof their mother daintily hath fed,
Eating the flesh that she herself hath bred.
'Tis true, 'tis true: witness my knife's sharp point. *[He stabs the Empress.*
SATURNINUS Die, frantic wretch, for this accursed deed! *[He stabs Titus.*

LUCIUS Can the son's eye behold his father bleed?
There's meed for meed, death for a deadly deed.
[He stabs Saturninus. A great tumult. Lucius, Marcus, and their friends go up into the balcony.
MARCUS You sad-fac'd men, people and sons of Rome,
By uproars sever'd, as a flight of fowl
Scatter'd by winds and high tempestuous gusts,
O, let me teach you how to knit again
This scattered corn into one mutual sheaf,
These broken limbs again into one body;
Lest Rome herself be bane unto herself,
And she whom mighty kingdoms curtsy to,
Like a forlorn and desperate castaway,
Do shameful execution on herself.
But if my frosty signs and chaps of age,
Grave witnesses of true experience,
Cannot induce you to attend my words,
[*To Lucius*] Speak, Rome's dear friend, as erst our ancestor,
When with his solemn tongue he did discourse
To love-sick Dido's sad attending ear
The story of that baleful burning night,
When subtle Greeks surpris'd King Priam's Troy.
Tell us what Sinon hath bewitch'd our ears,
Or who hath brought the fatal engine in
That gives our Troy, our Rome, the civil wound.
My heart is not compact of flint nor steel;
Nor can I utter all our bitter grief,
But floods of tears will drown my oratory
And break my utt'rance, even in the time
When it should move ye to attend me most,
And force you to commiseration.
Here's Rome's young Captain, let him tell the tale;
While I stand by and weep to hear him speak.
LUCIUS Then, gracious auditory, be it known to you
That Chiron and the damn'd Demetrius
Were they that murd'red our Emperor's brother;
And they it were that ravished our sister.
For their fell faults our brothers were beheaded,
Our father's tears despis'd, and basely cozen'd
Of that true hand that fought Rome's quarrel out
And sent her enemies unto the grave.
Lastly, myself unkindly banished,
The gates shut on me, and turn'd weeping out,
To beg relief among Rome's enemies;
Who drown'd their enmity in my true tears,
And op'd their arms to embrace me as a friend.
I am the turned forth, be it known to you,
That have preserv'd her welfare in my blood
And from her bosom took the enemy's point,
Sheathing the steel in my advent'rous body.
Alas! you know I am no vaunter, I;
My scars can witness, dumb although they are,
That my report is just and full of truth.
But, soft! methinks I do digress too much,
Citing my worthless praise. O, pardon me!
For when no friends are by, men praise themselves.
MARCUS Now is my turn to speak. Behold the child.
[Pointing to the child in an Attendant's arms.

Of this was Tamora delivered,
The issue of an irreligious Moor,
Chief architect and plotter of these woes.
The villain is alive in Titus' house,
Damn'd as he is, to witness this is true.
Now judge what cause had Titus to revenge
These wrongs unspeakable, past patience,
Or more than any living man could bear.
Now have you heard the truth: what say you, Romans?
Have we done aught amiss, show us wherein,
And, from the place where you behold us pleading,
The poor remainder of Andronici
Will hand in hand all headlong hurl ourselves,
And on the ragged stones beat forth our souls,
And make a mutual closure of our house.
Speak, Romans, speak; and if you say we shall,
Lo, hand in hand, Lucius and I will fall.

AEMILIUS Come, come, thou reverend man of Rome,
And bring our Emperor gently in thy hand,

Lucius our Emperor; for well I know
The common voice do cry it shall be so.

ALL Lucius, all hail, Rome's royal Emperor!

MARCUS Go, go into old Titus' sorrowful house,
And hither hale that misbelieving Moor
To be adjudg'd some direful slaught'ring death,
As punishment for his most wicked life.

[Exeunt some Attendants. Lucius, Marcus, and the others descend.

ALL Lucius, all hail, Rome's gracious governor!

LUCIUS Thanks, gentle Romans! May I govern so
To heal Rome's harms and wipe away her woe!
But, gentle people, give me aim awhile,
For nature puts me to a heavy task.
Stand all aloof; but, uncle, draw you near
To shed obsequious tears upon this trunk.
O, take this warm kiss on thy pale cold lips,

[Kisses Titus.

These sorrowful drops upon thy blood-stain'd face,
The last true duties of thy noble son!

MARCUS Tear for tear and loving kiss for kiss
Thy brother Marcus tenders on thy lips.
O, were the sum of these that I should pay
Countless and infinite, yet would I pay them!

LUCIUS Come hither, boy; come, come, and learn of us
To melt in showers. Thy grandsire lov'd thee well;
Many a time he danc'd thee on his knee,
Sung thee asleep, his loving breast thy pillow;
Many a story hath he told to thee,
And bid thee bear his pretty tales in mind
And talk of them when he was dead and gone.

MARCUS How many thousand times hath these poor lips,
When they were living, warm'd themselves on thine!
O, now, sweet boy, give them their latest kiss!
Bid him farewell; commit him to the grave;
Do them that kindness, and take leave of them.

BOY O grandsire, grandsire! ev'n with all my heart
Would I were dead, so you did live again!
O Lord, I cannot speak to him for weeping;
My tears will choke me, if I ope my mouth.

Re-enter Attendants with AARON.

A ROMAN You sad Andronici, have done with woes;
Give sentence on this execrable wretch
That hath been breeder of these dire events.

LUCIUS Set him breast-deep in earth, and famish him;
There let him stand and rave and cry for food.
If any one relieves or pities him,
For the offence he dies. This is our doom.
Some stay to see him fast'ned in the earth.

AARON Ah, why should wrath be mute and fury dumb?
I am no baby, I, that with base prayers
I should repent the evils I have done;
Ten thousand worse than ever yet I did
Would I perform, if I might have my will.
If one good deed in all my life I did,
I do repent it from my very soul.

LUCIUS Some loving friends convey the Emperor hence,
And give him burial in his father's grave.
My father and Lavinia shall forthwith
Be closed in our household's monument.
As for that ravenous tiger, Tamora,
No funeral rite, nor man in mourning weed,
No mournful bell shall ring her burial;
But throw her forth to beasts and birds to prey.
Her life was beastly and devoid of pity,
And being dead, let birds on her take pity.

[Exeunt.

Romeo and Juliet

Introduction by STUART GILLESPIE

Romeo and Juliet is usually dated to the mid 1590s, well before any of Shakespeare's major tragedies of the 1600s. The question of the play's relation to these later works is worth raising first.

Modern readers are inclined to equate tragic power with large quotients of bleakness and pessimism: this is one reason why, in the late twentieth century, *King Lear* is often felt to represent the apogee of Shakespeare's tragic work. But the absence of such qualities from *Romeo and Juliet* is not a sufficient reason to relegate it to a lower status as a tragedy. Nor is the presence in it of remarkably effective comic scenes, which can easily be paralleled from the later tragedies. But in the two respects in which the play can most readily be seen as operating within the tragic pattern, limitations are in evidence. First, the 'supernatural' elements in the situation, though frequently referred to by the characters, seem not to create the effect of tragic forces in play. The Prologue famously refers to 'star-cross'd lovers', and Romeo begins by describing his fear of 'some consequence yet hanging in the stars' that will 'expire the term' of his life [1.4]. But these references to fate and fortune never build up to a coherent explanation for the play's catastrophe. Romeo's death scene itself offers no suggestion of 'cosmic forces' at work, and the chain of events which led to it is described by Friar Lawrence in his final résumé [5.3]as a mere sequence of accidents. Secondly, the two points in Act 5 offering scope for climactic tragic intensity, containing the deaths of Romeo and Juliet, fifty lines apart in Act 5 Scene 3, are both emotionally frigid. Neither character 'looks death in the face as it really is'; death is to them 'a relief', almost a mere 'figure of speech' (Mason, 1970).

None of this is to deny that the play can boast wonderful qualities and incomparable moments; it is merely to say that we should not imagine its appeal to lie principally in its tragicality or associate it too strongly with Shakespeare's later tragedies. In other ways, in fact, the play gains by comparison with later Shakespearean works. Not a few of Shakespeare's later young lovers seem insipid and half-hearted creations when we recall the robust and vibrant energy with which Romeo and Juliet are invested. Shakespeare's achievement here does not lie in giving the lovers 'truth to life' in any direct sense. The extreme youth of Juliet, for example, seems to have more to do with romance than with contemporary reality. In the balcony scene [2.2], which T. S. Eliot called 'a kind of image of the perfection of verse drama' (Eliot, 1951), what matters is not a realistic effect but an atmosphere of wonder and delight. Here as so often in the play, the most striking impression is of the poetry – a poetry of exhilarated surges, magically swift, light, and intense. Here are the transports of an imagination which is recklessly quick and headlong, but also accurate and subtle.

Nor will any audience forget the two characters Shakespeare added to those found in the story as he knew it from his source, Arthur Brooke's poem *The Tragicall Historye of Romeus and Iuliet*: the Nurse and Mercutio. The former's comic verbosity certainly suggests she is 'one of the characters in which the Author delighted' (Johnson, 1765), and no actor who is capable of speaking her lines can really fail with the part. Hers is 'perhaps Shakespeare's first greatly human verse speech' (Everett, 1989), its rhythms so supple that some early editions erroneously printed parts of it as prose. 'The phrases are hers and hers alone, character unfolds with each phrase' (Granville-Barker, 1930). But she is more than a detached personality, a 'character-sketch', in the play. The Nurse's discourse operates within the region of the 'painfully funny', and ultimately has similarities with that of Lear's fool: like him she is 'licensed to speak profound nonsense' (Everett, 1989).

But Mercutio is, perhaps, this play's greatest single invention. His 'exquisite ebullience and overflow of youthful life' (Coleridge, 1818) issues out in his wit, in which arena he is the only match for Romeo. It was once said that Shakespeare 'was obliged to kill *Mercutio* in the third act, lest he be killed by him' (Johnson, 1765) – that Mercutio's appeal risks overbalancing the play and distracting us from the lovers. Mercutio's death is, at any rate, something of a show-stopper. It involves a serious sense of loss, more serious in many ways than those we experience with the lovers. 'They have made worms meat of me./I have it, and soundly too' [3.1] are Mercutio's last words: he has no regrets, nor any hypocrisy of resignation, but dies with his teeth set, impenitently himself to the last.

Romeo and Juliet

DRAMATIS PERSONAE

CHORUS
ESCALUS
Prince of Verona
PARIS
a young nobleman, kinsman to the Prince
MONTAGUE, CAPULET
heads of two houses at variance with each other
An Old Man of the Capulet family
ROMEO
son to Montague
MERCUTIO
kinsman to the Prince, and friend to Romeo
BENVOLIO
nephew to Montague, and friend to Romeo
TYBALT
nephew to Lady Capulet
FRIAR LAWRENCE, FRIAR JOHN
Franciscans
BALTHASAR
servant to Romeo
SAMPSON, GREGORY
servants to Capulet
PETER
servant to Juliet's nurse
ABRAHAM
servant to Montague
An Apothecary
Three Musicians
An Officer
LADY MONTAGUE
wife to Montague
LADY CAPULET
wife to Capulet
JULIET
daughter to Capulet
Nurse to Juliet
Citizens of Verona; Gentlemen and Gentlewomen of both houses; Maskers, Torchbearers, Pages, Guards, Watchmen, Servants, and Attendants

THE SCENE: VERONA AND MANTUA.

THE PROLOGUE

Enter CHORUS.

Two households, both alike in dignity,
In fair Verona, where we lay our scene,
From ancient grudge break to new mutiny,
Where civil blood makes civil hands unclean.
From forth the fatal loins of these two foes
A pair of star-cross'd lovers take their life;
Whose misadventur'd piteous overthrows
Doth with their death bury their parents' strife.
The fearful passage of their death-mark'd love,
And the continuance of their parents' rage,
Which, but their children's end, nought could remove,
Is now the two hours' traffic of our stage;
The which if you with patient ears attend,
What here shall miss, our toil shall strive to mend. [*Exit.*

ACT ONE

SCENE I. *Verona. A public place.*

Enter SAMPSON and GREGORY, of the house of Capulet, with swords and bucklers on.

SAMPSON Gregory, on my word, we'll not carry coals.

GREGORY No, for then we should be colliers.

SAMPSON I mean, an we be in choler, we'll draw.

GREGORY Ay, while you live, draw your neck out of collar.

SAMPSON I strike quickly, being moved.

GREGORY But thou art not quickly moved to strike.

SAMPSON A dog of the house of Montague moves me.

GREGORY To move is to stir, and to be valiant is to stand; therefore, if thou art moved, thou run'st away.

SAMPSON A dog of that house shall move me to stand. I will take the wall of any man or maid of Montague's.

GREGORY That shows thee a weak slave; for the weakest goes to the wall.

SAMPSON 'Tis true; and therefore women, being the weaker vessels, are ever thrust to the wall; therefore I will push Montague's men from the wall and thrust his maids to the wall.

GREGORY The quarrel is between our masters and us their men.

SAMPSON 'Tis all one; I will show myself a tyrant. When I have fought with the men, I will be civil with the maids – I will cut off their heads.

GREGORY The heads of the maids?

SAMPSON Ay, the heads of the maids, or their maidenheads; take it in what sense thou wilt.

GREGORY They must take it in sense that feel it.

SAMPSON Me they shall feel while I am able to stand; and 'tis known I am a pretty piece of flesh.

GREGORY 'Tis well thou art not fish; if thou hadst, thou hadst been poor-John. Draw thy tool; here comes two of the house of Montagues.

Enter two other Servants, ABRAHAM and BALTHASAR.

SAMPSON My naked weapon is out; quarrel, I will back thee.

GREGORY How? turn thy back and run?

SAMPSON Fear me not.

GREGORY No, marry; I fear thee!

SAMPSON Let us take the law of our sides; let them begin.

GREGORY I will frown as I pass by, and let them take it as they list.

SAMPSON Nay, as they dare. I will bite my thumb at them, which is disgrace to them if they bear it.

ABRAHAM Do you bite your thumb at us, sir?

SAMPSON I do bite my thumb, sir.

ABRAHAM Do you bite your thumb at us, sir?

SAMPSON [*Aside to Gregory*] Is the law of our side, if I say ay?

GREGORY [*Aside to Sampson*] No.

SAMPSON No, sir, I do not bite my thumb at you, sir; but I bite my thumb, sir.

GREGORY Do you quarrel, sir?

ABRAHAM Quarrel, sir! No, sir.

SAMPSON But if you do, sir, I am for you. I serve as good a man as you.

ABRAHAM No better?

SAMPSON Well, sir.

Enter BENVOLIO.

GREGORY [*Aside to Sampson*] Say 'better'; here comes one of my master's kinsmen.

SAMPSON Yes, better, sir.

ABRAHAM You lie.

SAMPSON Draw, if you be men. Gregory, remember thy swashing blow. [*They fight.*

BENVOLIO Part, fools! [*Beats down their swords.*
Put up your swords; you know not what you do.

Enter TYBALT.

TYBALT What, art thou drawn among these heartless hinds?
Turn thee, Benvolio; look upon thy death.

BENVOLIO I do but keep the peace; put up thy sword,
Or manage it to part these men with me.

TYBALT What, drawn, and talk of peace! I hate the word,
As I hate hell, all Montagues, and thee.
Have at thee, coward! [*They fight.*

Enter an Officer, and three or four Citizens with clubs or partisans.

OFFICER Clubs, bills, and partisans! Strike; beat them down.

CITIZENS Down with the Capulets! Down with the Montagues!

Enter Old CAPULET in his gown, and his Wife.

CAPULET What noise is this? Give me my long sword, ho!

LADY CAPULET A crutch, a crutch! Why call you for a sword?

CAPULET My sword, I say! Old Montague is come,
And flourishes his blade in spite of me.

Enter Old MONTAGUE and his Wife.

MONTAGUE Thou villain Capulet! – Hold me not, let me go.

LADY MONTAGUE Thou shalt not stir one foot to seek a foe.

Enter PRINCE ESCALUS, with his Train.

PRINCE Rebellious subjects, enemies to peace,
Profaners of this neighbour-stained steel –
Will they not hear? What, ho! you men, you beasts,
That quench the fire of your pernicious rage
With purple fountains issuing from your veins!
On pain of torture, from those bloody hands
Throw your mistempered weapons to the ground,
And hear the sentence of your moved prince.
Three civil brawls, bred of an airy word,
By thee, old Capulet, and Montague,
Have thrice disturb'd the quiet of our streets
And made Verona's ancient citizens
Cast by their grave beseeming ornaments
To wield old partisans, in hands as old,
Cank'red with peace, to part your cank'red hate.
If ever you disturb our streets again,
Your lives shall pay the forfeit of the peace.
For this time all the rest depart away.
You, Capulet, shall go along with me;
And, Montague, come you this afternoon,
To know our farther pleasure in this case,
To old Free-town, our common judgment-place.
Once more, on pain of death, all men depart.
[*Exeunt all but Montague, his Wife, and Benvolio.*

MONTAGUE Who set this ancient quarrel new abroach?
Speak, nephew; were you by when it began?

BENVOLIO Here were the servants of your adversary
And yours, close fighting ere I did approach.
I drew to part them; in the instant came
The fiery Tybalt, with his sword prepar'd;
Which, as he breath'd defiance to my ears,
He swung about his head and cut the winds,
Who, nothing hurt withal, hiss'd him in scorn.
While we were interchanging thrusts and blows,
Came more and more, and fought on part and part,
Till the Prince came, who parted either part.

LADY MONTAGUE O, where is Romeo? Saw you him to-day?
Right glad I am he was not at this fray.

BENVOLIO Madam, an hour before the worshipp'd sun
Peer'd forth the golden window of the east,
A troubled mind drew me to walk abroad;
Where, underneath the grove of sycamore
That westward rooteth from this city side,
So early walking did I see your son.
Towards him I made; but he was ware of me
And stole into the covert of the wood.
I, measuring his affections by my own,
Which then most sought where most might not be found,
Being one too many by my weary self,
Pursu'd my humour, not pursuing his,
And gladly shunn'd who gladly fled from me.

MONTAGUE Many a morning hath he there been seen,
With tears augmenting the fresh morning's dew,
Adding to clouds more clouds with his deep sighs;
But all so soon as the all-cheering sun
Should in the farthest east begin to draw
The shady curtains from Aurora's bed,
Away from light steals home my heavy son,
And private in his chamber pens himself,
Shuts up his windows, locks fair daylight out,
And makes himself an artificial night.
Black and portentous must this humour prove,
Unless good counsel may the cause remove.

BENVOLIO My noble uncle, do you know the cause?

MONTAGUE I neither know it nor can learn of him.

BENVOLIO Have you importun'd him by any means?

MONTAGUE Both by myself and many other friends.
But he, his own affections' counsellor,
Is to himself – I will not say how true;
But to himself so secret and so close,
So far from sounding and discovery,
As is the bud bit with an envious worm,
Ere he can spread his sweet leaves to the air,
Or dedicate his beauty to the sun.
Could we but learn from whence his sorrows grow,
We would as willingly give cure as know.

Enter ROMEO.

BENVOLIO See where he comes. So please you step aside;
I'll know his grievance or be much denied.

MONTAGUE I would thou wert so happy by thy stay
To hear true shrift. Come, madam, let's away.

[*Exeunt Montague and his Wife.*

BENVOLIO Good morrow, cousin.

ROMEO Is the day so young?

BENVOLIO But new struck nine.

ROMEO Ay me! sad hours seem long.
Was that my father that went hence so fast?

BENVOLIO It was. What sadness lengthens Romeo's hours?

ROMEO Not having that which having makes them short.

BENVOLIO In love?

ROMEO Out –

BENVOLIO Of love?

ROMEO Out of her favour where I am in love.

BENVOLIO Alas that love, so gentle in his view,
Should be so tyrannous and rough in proof!

ROMEO Alas that love, whose view is muffled still,
Should without eyes see pathways to his will!
Where shall we dine? O me! What fray was here?
Yet tell me not, for I have heard it all.
Here's much to do with hate, but more with love.
Why then, O brawling love! O loving hate!
O anything, of nothing first create!
O heavy lightness! serious vanity!
Mis-shapen chaos of well-seeming forms!
Feather of lead, bright smoke, cold fire, sick health!
Still-waking sleep, that is not what it is!
This love feel I, that feel no love in this.
Dost thou not laugh?

BENVOLIO No, coz, I rather weep.

ROMEO Good heart, at what?

BENVOLIO At thy good heart's oppression.

ROMEO Why, such is love's transgression.
Griefs of mine own lie heavy in my breast,
Which thou wilt propagate, to have it prest
With more of thine. This love that thou hast shown

Doth add more grief to too much of mine own.
Love is a smoke rais'd with the fume of sighs;
Being purg'd, a fire sparkling in lovers' eyes;
Being vex'd, a sea nourish'd with loving tears.
What is it else? A madness most discreet,
A choking gall, and a preserving sweet.
Farewell, my coz.

BENVOLIO Soft! I will go along;
An if you leave me so, you do me wrong.

ROMEO Tut, I have lost myself; I am not here:
This is not Romeo, he's some other where.

BENVOLIO Tell me in sadness who is that you love.

ROMEO What, shall I groan and tell thee?

BENVOLIO Groan! Why, no;
But sadly tell me who.

ROMEO Bid a sick man in sadness make his will.
Ah, word ill urg'd to one that is so ill!
In sadness, cousin, I do love a woman.

BENVOLIO I aim'd so near when I suppos'd you lov'd.

ROMEO A right good markman! And she's fair I love.

BENVOLIO A right fair mark, fair coz, is soonest hit.

ROMEO Well, in that hit you miss: she'll not be hit
With Cupid's arrow. She hath Dian's wit,
And in strong proof of chastity well arm'd,
From Love's weak childish bow she lives unharm'd.
She will not stay the siege of loving terms,
Nor bide th' encounter of assailing eyes,
Nor ope her lap to saint-seducing gold.
O, she is rich in beauty; only poor
That, when she dies, with beauty dies her store.

BENVOLIO Then she hath sworn that she will still live chaste?

ROMEO She hath, and in that sparing makes huge waste;
For beauty, starv'd with her severity,
Cuts beauty off from all posterity.
She is too fair, too wise, wisely too fair,
To merit bliss by making me despair.
She hath forsworn to love, and in that vow
Do I live dead that live to tell it now.

BENVOLIO Be rul'd by me: forget to think of her.

ROMEO O, teach me how I should forget to think!

BENVOLIO By giving liberty unto thine eyes.
Examine other beauties.

ROMEO 'Tis the way
To call hers, exquisite, in question more.
These happy masks that kiss fair ladies' brows,
Being black, puts us in mind they hide the fair.
He that is strucken blind cannot forget
The precious treasure of his eyesight lost.
Show me a mistress that is passing fair,
What doth her beauty serve but as a note
Where I may read who pass'd that passing fair?
Farewell; thou canst not teach me to forget.

BENVOLIO I'll pay that doctrine or else die in debt. *[Exeunt.*

SCENE II. *A street.*

Enter CAPULET, COUNTY PARIS, and the Clown, his servant.

CAPULET But Montague is bound as well as I,
In penalty alike; and 'tis not hard, I think,
For men so old as we to keep the peace.

PARIS Of honourable reckoning are you both,
And pity 'tis you liv'd at odds so long.
But now, my lord, what say you to my suit?

CAPULET But saying o'er what I have said before:
My child is yet a stranger in the world,
She hath not seen the change of fourteen years;
Let two more summers wither in their pride
Ere we may think her ripe to be a bride.

PARIS Younger than she are happy mothers made.

CAPULET And too soon marr'd are those so early made.
Earth hath swallowed all my hopes but she;
She is the hopeful lady of my earth.
But woo her, gentle Paris, get her heart;
My will to her consent is but a part.
And, she agreed, within her scope of choice
Lies my consent and fair according voice.
This night I hold an old accustom'd feast,
Whereto I have invited many a guest,
Such as I love; and you among the store,
One more, most welcome, makes my number more.
At my poor house look to behold this night
Earth-treading stars that make dark heaven light.
Such comfort as do lusty young men feel
When well-apparell'd April on the heel
Of limping winter treads, even such delight
Among fresh female buds shall you this night
Inherit at my house. Hear all, all see,
And like her most whose merit most shall be;
Which on more view of many, mine, being one,
May stand in number, though in reck'ning none.
Come, go with me. *[To Servant, giving him a paper]* Go, sirrah, trudge about
Through fair Verona; find those persons out
Whose names are written there, and to them say
My house and welcome on their pleasure stay.
[Exeunt Capulet and Paris.

SERVANT Find them out whose names are written here! It is written that the shoemaker should meddle with his yard and the tailor with his last, the fisher with his pencil and the painter with his nets; but I am sent to find those persons whose names are here writ, and can never find what names the writing person hath here writ. I must to the learned. In good time!

Enter BENVOLIO and ROMEO.

BENVOLIO Tut, man, one fire burns out another's burning,
One pain is less'ned by another's anguish;
Turn giddy, and be holp by backward turning;
One desperate grief cures with another's languish.
Take thou some new infection to thy eye,
And the rank poison of the old will die.

ROMEO Your plantain leaf is excellent for that.

BENVOLIO For what, I pray thee?

ROMEO For your broken shin.

BENVOLIO Why, Romeo, art thou mad?

ROMEO Not mad, but bound more than a madman is;
Shut up in prison, kept without my food,
Whipt and tormented, and – God-den, good fellow.

SERVANT God gi' go'den. I pray, sir, can you read?

ROMEO Ay, mine own fortune in my misery.

SERVANT Perhaps you have learned it without book. But I pray, can you read anything you see?

ROMEO Ay, if I know the letters and the language.

SERVANT Ye say honestly; rest you merry!

ROMEO Stay, fellow; I can read.
[*He reads the list*] 'Signior Martino and his wife and daughters; County Anselme and his beauteous sisters; the lady widow of Vitruvio; Signior Placentio and his lovely nieces; Mercutio and his brother Valentine; mine uncle Capulet, his wife, and daughters; my fair niece Rosaline and Livia; Signior Valentio and his cousin Tybalt; Lucio and the lively Helena.'
A fair assembly. [*Gives back the paper*] Whither should they come?

SERVANT Up.

ROMEO Whither?

SERVANT To supper. To our house.

ROMEO Whose house?

SERVANT My master's.

ROMEO Indeed, I should have ask'd you that before.

SERVANT Now I'll tell you without asking: my master is the great rich Capulet; and if you be not of the house of Montagues, I pray come and crush a cup of wine. Rest you merry! [*Exit.*

BENVOLIO At this same ancient feast of Capulet's
Sups the fair Rosaline whom thou so loves,
With all the admired beauties of Verona.
Go thither, and with unattainted eye
Compare her face with some that I shall show,
And I will make thee think thy swan a crow.

ROMEO When the devout religion of mine eye
Maintains such falsehood, then turn tears to fires;
And these, who, often drown'd, could never die,
Transparent heretics, be burnt for liars!
One fairer than my love! The all-seeing sun
Ne'er saw her match since first the world begun.

BENVOLIO Tut, you saw her fair, none else being by,
Herself pois'd with herself in either eye;
But in that crystal scales let there be weigh'd
Your lady's love against some other maid
That I will show you shining at this feast,
And she shall scant show well that now seems best.

ROMEO I'll go along, no such sight to be shown,
But to rejoice in splendour of mine own.

[*Exeunt.*

SCENE III. *Capulet's house.*

Enter LADY CAPULET and Nurse.

LADY CAPULET Nurse, where's my daughter? Call her forth to me.

NURSE Now, by my maidenhead at twelve year old,
I bade her come. What, lamb! what, lady-bird!
God forbid! Where's this girl? What, Juliet!

Enter JULIET.

JULIET How now, who calls?

NURSE Your mother.

JULIET Madam, I am here. What is your will?

LADY CAPULET This is the matter. Nurse, give leave awhile,
We must talk in secret. Nurse, come back again;
I have rememb'red me, thou's hear our counsel.
Thou knowest my daughter's of a pretty age.

NURSE Faith, I can tell her age unto an hour.

LADY CAPULET She's not fourteen.

NURSE I'll lay fourteen of my teeth –
And yet, to my teen be it spoken, I have but four –
She's not fourteen. How long is it now
To Lammas-tide?

LADY CAPULET A fortnight and odd days.

NURSE Even or odd, of all days in the year,
Come Lammas Eve at night shall she be fourteen.
Susan and she – God rest all Christian souls! –
Were of an age. Well, Susan is with God;
She was too good for me. But, as I said,
On Lammas Eve at night shall she be fourteen;

That shall she, marry; I remember it well.
'Tis since the earthquake now eleven years;
And she was wean'd – I never shall forget it –
Of all the days of the year, upon that day;
For I had then laid wormwood to my dug,
Sitting in the sun under the dove-house wall;
My lord and you were then at Mantua.
Nay, I do bear a brain. But, as I said,
When it did taste the wormwood on the nipple
Of my dug, and felt it bitter, pretty fool,
To see it tetchy, and fall out with the dug!
Shake, quoth the dove-house. 'Twas no need, I trow,
To bid me trudge.
And since that time it is eleven years;
For then she could stand high-lone; nay, by th' rood,
She could have run and waddled all about;
For even the day before, she broke her brow;
And then my husband – God be with his soul!
'A was a merry man – took up the child.
'Yea,' quoth he 'dost thou fall upon thy face?
Thou wilt fall backward when thou hast more wit,
Wilt thou not, Jule?' And, by my holidam,
The pretty wretch left crying, and said 'Ay'.
To see, now, how a jest shall come about!
I warrant, an I should live a thousand years,
I never should forget it: 'Wilt thou not, Jule?' quoth he;
And, pretty fool, it stinted, and said 'Ay'.

LADY CAPULET Enough of this; I pray thee hold thy peace.

NURSE Yes, madam. Yet I cannot choose but laugh
To think it should leave crying and say 'Ay'.
And yet, I warrant, it had upon it brow
A bump as big as a young cock'rel's stone –
A perilous knock; and it cried bitterly.
'Yea,' quoth my husband 'fall'st upon thy face?
Thou wilt fall backward when thou comest to age;
Wilt thou not, Jule?' It stinted, and said 'Ay'.

JULIET And stint thou too, I pray thee, nurse, say I.

NURSE Peace, I have done. God mark thee to his grace!
Thou wast the prettiest babe that e'er I nurs'd;
An I might live to see thee married once,
I have my wish.

LADY CAPULET Marry, that 'marry' is the very theme
I came to talk of. Tell me, daughter Juliet,
How stands your dispositions to be married?

JULIET It is an honour that I dream not of.

NURSE An honour! Were not I thine only nurse,
I would say thou hadst suck'd wisdom from thy teat.

LADY CAPULET Well, think of marriage now.
Younger than you,
Here in Verona, ladies of esteem,
Are made already mothers. By my count,
I was your mother much upon these years
That you are now a maid. Thus, then, in brief:
The valiant Paris seeks you for his love.

NURSE A man, young lady! lady, such a man
As all the world – why, he's a man of wax.

LADY CAPULET Verona's summer hath not such a flower.

NURSE Nay, he's a flower; in faith, a very flower.

LADY CAPULET What say you? Can you love the gentleman?
This night you shall behold him at our feast;
Read o'er the volume of young Paris' face,
And find delight writ there with beauty's pen;
Examine every married lineament,
And see how one another lends content;
And what obscur'd in this fair volume lies
Find written in the margent of his eyes.
This precious book of love, this unbound lover,
To beautify him, only lacks a cover.
The fish lives in the sea, and 'tis much pride
For fair without the fair within to hide.
That book in many's eyes doth share the glory
That in gold clasps locks in the golden story;
So shall you share all that he doth possess,
By having him making yourself no less.

NURSE No less! Nay, bigger; women grow by men.

LADY CAPULET Speak briefly, can you like of Paris' love?

JULIET I'll look to like, if looking liking move;
But no more deep will I endart mine eye
Than your consent gives strength to make it fly.

Enter a Servant.

SERVANT Madam, the guests are come, supper serv'd up, you call'd, my young lady ask'd for, the nurse curs'd in the pantry, and everything in extremity. I must hence to wait; I beseech you, follow straight.

LADY CAPULET We follow thee. [*Exit Servant*]
Juliet, the County stays.

NURSE Go, girl, seek happy nights to happy days.

[*Exeunt.*

SCENE IV. *A street.*

Enter ROMEO, MERCUTIO, BENVOLIO, with five or six other Maskers; Torch-bearers.

ROMEO What, shall this speech be spoke for our excuse?
Or shall we on without apology?

BENVOLIO The date is out of such prolixity.

We'll have no Cupid hoodwink'd with a scarf,
Bearing a Tartar's painted bow of lath,
Scaring the ladies like a crow-keeper;
Nor no without-book prologue, faintly spoke
After the prompter, for our entrance;
But, let them measure us by what they will,
We'll measure them a measure, and be gone.

ROMEO Give me a torch; I am not for this ambling;
Being but heavy, I will bear the light.

MERCUTIO Nay, gentle Romeo, we must have you dance.

ROMEO Not I, believe me. You have dancing shoes
With nimble soles: I have a soul of lead
So stakes me to the ground I cannot move.

MERCUTIO You are a lover; borrow Cupid's wings
And soar with them above a common bound.

ROMEO I am too sore enpierced with his shaft
To soar with his light feathers; and so bound
I cannot bound a pitch above dull woe.
Under love's heavy burden do I sink.

MERCUTIO And to sink in it should you burden love;
Too great oppression for a tender thing.

ROMEO Is love a tender thing? It is too rough,
Too rude, too boist'rous, and it pricks like thorn.

MERCUTIO If love be rough with you, be rough with love;
Prick love for pricking, and you beat love down.
Give me a case to put my visage in.
[*Putting on a mask.*
A visor for a visor! What care I
What curious eye doth quote deformities?
Here are the beetle brows shall blush for me.

BENVOLIO Come, knock and enter; and no sooner in
But every man betake him to his legs.

ROMEO A torch for me. Let wantons, light of heart,
Tickle the senseless rushes with their heels;
For I am proverb'd with a grandsire phrase;
I'll be a candle-holder and look on;
The game was ne'er so fair, and I am done.

MERCUTIO Tut, dun's the mouse, the constable's own word;
If thou art Dun, we'll draw thee from the mire
Of this sir-reverence love, wherein thou stickest
Up to the ears. Come, we burn daylight, ho!

ROMEO Nay, that's not so.

MERCUTIO I mean, sir, in delay
We waste our lights in vain – like lights by day.
Take our good meaning, for our judgment sits
Five times in that ere once in our five wits.

ROMEO And we mean well in going to this mask;
But 'tis no wit to go.

MERCUTIO Why, may one ask?

ROMEO I dreamt a dream to-night.

MERCUTIO And so did I.

ROMEO Well, what was yours?

MERCUTIO That dreamers often lie.

ROMEO In bed asleep, while they do dream things true.

MERCUTIO O, then I see Queen Mab hath been with you.
She is the fairies' midwife, and she comes
In shape no bigger than an agate stone
On the fore-finger of an alderman,
Drawn with a team of little atomies
Athwart men's noses as they lie asleep;
Her waggon-spokes made of long spinners' legs;
The cover, of the wings of grasshoppers;
Her traces, of the smallest spider's web;
Her collars, of the moonshine's wat'ry beams;
Her whip, of cricket's bone; the lash, of film;
Her waggoner, a small grey-coated gnat,
Not half so big as a round little worm
Prick'd from the lazy finger of a maid.
Her chariot is an empty hazel-nut,
Made by the joiner squirrel or old grub,
Time out o' mind the fairies' coachmakers.
And in this state she gallops night by night
Through lovers' brains, and then they dream of love;
O'er courtiers' knees, that dream on curtsies straight;
O'er lawyers' fingers, who straight dream on fees;
O'er ladies' lips, who straight on kisses dream,
Which oft the angry Mab with blisters plagues,
Because their breaths with sweetmeats tainted are.
Sometime she gallops o'er a courtier's nose,
And then dreams he of smelling out a suit;
And sometime comes she with a tithe-pig's tail,
Tickling a parson's nose as 'a lies asleep,
Then dreams he of another benefice.
Sometime she driveth o'er a soldier's neck,
And then dreams he of cutting foreign throats,
Of breaches, ambuscadoes, Spanish blades,
Of healths five fathom deep; and then anon
Drums in his ear, at which he starts and wakes,
And, being thus frighted, swears a prayer or two,
And sleeps again. This is that very Mab
That plats the manes of horses in the night;
And bakes the elf-locks in foul sluttish hairs,
Which once untangled much misfortune bodes.
This is the hag, when maids lie on their backs,
That presses them and learns them first to bear,
Making them women of good carriage.

This is she –
ROMEO Peace, peace, Mercutio, peace!
Thou talk'st of nothing.
MERCUTIO True, I talk of dreams,
Which are the children of an idle brain,
Begot of nothing but vain fantasy;
Which is as thin of substance as the air,
And more inconstant than the wind, who woos
Even now the frozen bosom of the north,
And, being anger'd, puffs away from thence,
Turning his side to the dew-dropping south.
BENVOLIO This wind you talk of blows us from ourselves:
Supper is done, and we shall come too late.
ROMEO I fear, too early; for my mind misgives
Some consequence, yet hanging in the stars,
Shall bitterly begin his fearful date
With this night's revels and expire the term
Of a despised life clos'd in my breast,
By some vile forfeit of untimely death.
But He that hath the steerage of my course
Direct my sail! On, lusty gentlemen.
BENVOLIO Strike, drum.

[*They march about the stage. Exeunt.*

SCENE V. *Capulet's house.*

Enter the Maskers. Servants come forth with napkins.

SERVANT Where's Potpan, that he helps not to take away? He shift a trencher! He scrape a trencher!

2 SERVANT When good manners shall lie all in one or two men's hands, and they unwash'd too, 'tis a foul thing.

SERVANT Away with the join-stools, remove the court-cubbert, look to the plate. Good thou, save me a piece of marchpane; and as thou loves me let the porter let in Susan Grindstone and Nell. Antony, and Potpan!

2 SERVANT Ay, boy, ready.

SERVANT You are look'd for and call'd for, ask'd for and sought for, in the great chamber.

3 SERVANT We cannot be here and there too. Cheerly, boys! Be brisk a while, and the longer liver take all! [*Servants retire.*

Enter CAPULET, with all the Guests and Gentlewomen to the Maskers.

CAPULET Welcome, gentlemen! Ladies that have their toes
Unplagu'd with corns will have a bout with you.
Ah ha, my mistresses! which of you all
Will now deny to dance? She that makes dainty,
She I'll swear hath corns; am I come near ye now?
Welcome, gentlemen! I have seen the day
That I have worn a visor and could tell
A whispering tale in a fair lady's ear,
Such as would please. 'Tis gone, 'tis gone, 'tis gone!
You are welcome, gentlemen. Come, musicians, play.
A hall, a hall! give room; and foot it, girls.

[*Music plays, and they dance.*

More light, you knaves; and turn the tables up,
And quench the fire, the room is grown too hot.
Ah, sirrah, this unlook'd-for sport comes well.
Nay, sit, nay, sit, good cousin Capulet,
For you and I are past our dancing days.
How long is't now since last yourself and I
Were in a mask?
2 CAPULET By'r Lady, thirty years.
CAPULET What, man? 'tis not so much, 'tis not so much.
'Tis since the nuptial of Lucentio,
Come Pentecost as quickly as it will,
Some five and twenty years; and then we mask'd.
2 CAPULET 'Tis more, 'tis more: his son is elder, sir;
His son is thirty.
CAPULET Will you tell me that?
His son was but a ward two years ago.
ROMEO [*To a servant*] What lady's that which doth enrich the hand
Of yonder knight?
SERVANT I know not, sir.
ROMEO O, she doth teach the torches to burn bright!
It seems she hangs upon the cheek of night
As a rich jewel in an Ethiop's ear –
Beauty too rich for use, for earth too dear!
So shows a snowy dove trooping with crows
As yonder lady o'er her fellows shows.
The measure done, I'll watch her place of stand,
And, touching hers, make blessed my rude hand.
Did my heart love till now? Forswear it, sight;
For I ne'er saw true beauty till this night.
TYBALT This, by his voice, should be a Montague.
Fetch me my rapier, boy. What, dares the slave
Come hither, cover'd with an antic face,
To fleer and scorn at our solemnity?
Now, by the stock and honour of my kin,
To strike him dead I hold it not a sin.
CAPULET Why, how now, kinsman! Wherefore storm you so?
TYBALT Uncle, this is a Montague, our foe;
A villain, that is hither come in spite
To scorn at our solemnity this night.
CAPULET Young Romeo, is it?

TYBALT 'Tis he, that villain Romeo.
CAPULET Content thee, gentle coz, let him alone.
'A bears him like a portly gentleman;
And, to say truth, Verona brags of him
To be a virtuous and well-govern'd youth.
I would not for the wealth of all this town
Here in my house do him disparagement.
Therefore be patient, take no note of him;
It is my will; the which if thou respect,
Show a fair presence and put off these frowns,
An ill-beseeming semblance for a feast.
TYBALT It fits, when such a villain is a guest.
I'll not endure him.
CAPULET He shall be endur'd.
What, goodman boy! I say he shall. Go to;
Am I the master here or you? Go to.
You'll not endure him! God shall mend my soul!
You'll make a mutiny among my guests!
You will set cock-a-hoop! You'll be the man!
TYBALT Why, uncle, 'tis a shame.
CAPULET Go to, go to;
You are a saucy boy. Is't so, indeed?
This trick may chance to scathe you. I know what:
You must contrary me. Marry, 'tis time. –
Well said, my hearts! – You are a princox; go.
Be quiet, or – More light, more light! – For shame!
I'll make you quiet. What! – Cheerly, my hearts!
TYBALT Patience perforce with wilful choler meeting
Makes my flesh tremble in their different greeting.
I will withdraw; but this intrusion shall,
Now seeming sweet, convert to bitt'rest gall.
[Exit.
ROMEO *[To Juliet]* If I profane with my unworthiest hand
This holy shrine, the gentle fine is this:
My lips, two blushing pilgrims, ready stand
To smooth that rough touch with a tender kiss.
JULIET Good pilgrim, you do wrong your hand too much,
Which mannerly devotion shows in this;
For saints have hands that pilgrims' hands do touch,
And palm to palm is holy palmers' kiss.
ROMEO Have not saints lips, and holy palmers too?
JULIET Ay, pilgrim, lips that they must use in pray'r.
ROMEO O, then, dear saint, let lips do what hands do!
They pray; grant thou, lest faith turn to despair.
JULIET Saints do not move, though grant for prayers' sake.
ROMEO Then move not while my prayer's effect I take
Thus from my lips by thine my sin is purg'd.
[Kissing her.
JULIET Then have my lips the sin that they have took.
ROMEO Sin from my lips? O trespass sweetly urg'd!
Give me my sin again. *[Kissing her.*
JULIET You kiss by th' book.
NURSE Madam, your mother craves a word with you.
ROMEO What is her mother?
NURSE Marry, bachelor,
Her mother is the lady of the house,
And a good lady, and a wise and virtuous.
I nurs'd her daughter that you talk'd withal.
I tell you, he that can lay hold of her
Shall have the chinks.
ROMEO Is she a Capulet?
O dear account! my life is my foe's debt.
BENVOLIO Away, be gone; the sport is at the best.
ROMEO Ay, so I fear; the more is my unrest.
CAPULET Nay, gentlemen, prepare not to be gone;
We have a trifling foolish banquet towards.
Is it e'en so? Why, then I thank you all;
I thank you, honest gentlemen; good night.
More torches here! *[Exeunt Maskers]* Come on then, let's to bed.
Ah, sirrah, by my fay, it waxes late;
I'll to my rest.
[Exeunt all but Juliet and Nurse.
JULIET Come hither, nurse. What is yond gentleman?
NURSE The son and heir of old Tiberio.
JULIET What's he that now is going out of door?
NURSE Marry, that I think be young Petruchio.
JULIET What's he that follows there, that would not dance?
NURSE I know not.
JULIET Go ask his name. – If he be married,
My grave is like to be my wedding bed.
NURSE His name is Romeo, and a Montague;
The only son of your great enemy.
JULIET My only love sprung from my only hate!
Too early seen unknown, and known too late!
Prodigious birth of love it is to me,
That I must love a loathed enemy.
NURSE What's this? What's this?
JULIET A rhyme I learnt even now
Of one I danc'd withal.
[One calls within 'Juliet'.
NURSE Anon, anon!
Come, let's away; the strangers all are gone.
[Exeunt.

ACT TWO

PROLOGUE *Enter CHORUS.*

Now old desire doth in his death-bed lie,
And young affection gapes to be his heir;
That fair for which love groan'd for and would die,
With tender Juliet match'd, is now not fair.
Now Romeo is belov'd, and loves again,
Alike bewitched by the charm of looks;
But to his foe suppos'd he must complain,
And she steal love's sweet bait from fearful hooks.
Being held a foe, he may not have access
To breathe such vows as lovers use to swear;
And she as much in love, her means much less
To meet her new beloved any where.
But passion lends them power, time means, to meet,
Temp'ring extremities with extreme sweet.

[*Exit.*

SCENE I. *A lane by the wall of Capulet's orchard.*

Enter ROMEO.

ROMEO Can I go forward when my heart is here?
Turn back, dull earth, and find thy centre out.

[*He climbs the wall and leaps down within it.*

Enter BENVOLIO with MERCUTIO.

BENVOLIO Romeo! my cousin, Romeo! Romeo!
MERCUTIO He is wise,
And, on my life, hath stol'n him home to bed.
BENVOLIO He ran this way, and leapt this orchard wall.
Call, good Mercutio.
MERCUTIO Nay, I'll conjure too.
Romeo! humours! madman! passion! lover!
Appear thou in the likeness of a sigh;
Speak but one rhyme and I am satisfied;
Cry but 'Ay me!' pronounce but 'love' and 'dove';
Speak to my gossip Venus one fair word,
One nickname for her purblind son and heir,
Young Adam Cupid, he that shot so trim
When King Cophetua lov'd the beggar-maid!
He heareth not, he stirreth not, he moveth not;
The ape is dead, and I must conjure him.
I conjure thee by Rosaline's bright eyes,
By her high forehead and her scarlet lip,
By her fine foot, straight leg, and quivering thigh,
And the demesnes that there adjacent lie,
That in thy likeness thou appear to us.
BENVOLIO An if he hear thee, thou wilt anger him.
MERCUTIO This cannot anger him: 'twould anger him
To raise a spirit in his mistress' circle
Of some strange nature, letting it there stand
Till she had laid it and conjur'd it down;
That were some spite. My invocation
Is fair and honest: in his mistress' name,
I conjure only but to raise up him.
BENVOLIO Come, he hath hid himself among these trees
To be consorted with the humorous night:
Blind is his love, and best befits the dark.
MERCUTIO If love be blind, love cannot hit the mark.
Now will he sit under a medlar tree,
And wish his mistress were that kind of fruit
As maids call medlars when they laugh alone.
O Romeo, that she were, O that she were
An open et cetera, thou a pop'rin pear!
Romeo, good night. I'll to my truckle bed;
This field-bed is too cold for me to sleep.
Come, shall we go?
BENVOLIO Go, then; for 'tis in vain
To seek him here that means not to be found.

[*Exeunt.*

SCENE II. *Capulet's orchard.*

Enter ROMEO.

ROMEO He jests at scars that never felt a wound.

Enter JULIET above at a window.

But, soft! What light through yonder window breaks?
It is the east, and Juliet is the sun.
Arise, fair sun, and kill the envious moon,
Who is already sick and pale with grief
That thou her maid art far more fair than she.
Be not her maid, since she is envious;
Her vestal livery is but sick and green,
And none but fools do wear it; cast it off.
It is my lady; O, it is my love!
O that she knew she were!
She speaks, yet she says nothing. What of that?
Her eye discourses; I will answer it.
I am too bold, 'tis not to me she speaks;
Two of the fairest stars in all the heaven,
Having some business, do entreat her eyes
To twinkle in their spheres till they return.
What if her eyes were there, they in her head?
The brightness of her cheek would shame those stars,
As daylight doth a lamp; her eyes in heaven
Would through the airy region stream so bright

That birds would sing, and think it were not night.
See how she leans her cheek upon her hand!
O that I were a glove upon that hand,
That I might touch that cheek!

JULIET Ay me!

ROMEO She speaks.
O, speak again, bright angel, for thou art
As glorious to this night, being o'er my head,
As is a winged messenger of heaven
Unto the white-upturned wond'ring eyes
Of mortals that fall back to gaze on him,
When he bestrides the lazy-pacing clouds
And sails upon the bosom of the air.

JULIET O Romeo, Romeo! wherefore art thou Romeo?
Deny thy father and refuse thy name;
Or, if thou wilt not, be but sworn my love,
And I'll no longer be a Capulet.

ROMEO [*Aside*] Shall I hear more, or shall I speak at this?

JULIET 'Tis but thy name that is my enemy;
Thou art thyself, though not a Montague.
What's Montague? It is nor hand, nor foot,
Nor arm, nor face, nor any other part
Belonging to a man. O, be some other name!
What's in a name? That which we call a rose
By any other name would smell as sweet;
So Romeo would, were he not Romeo call'd,
Retain that dear perfection which he owes
Without that title. Romeo, doff thy name;
And for thy name, which is no part of thee,
Take all myself.

ROMEO I take thee at thy word:
Call me but love, and I'll be new baptiz'd;
Henceforth I never will be Romeo.

JULIET What man art thou, that, thus bescreen'd in night,
So stumblest on my counsel?

ROMEO By a name
I know not how to tell thee who I am:
My name, dear saint, is hateful to myself,
Because it is an enemy to thee;
Had I it written, I would tear the word.

JULIET My ears have yet not drunk a hundred words
Of thy tongue's uttering, yet I know the sound:
Art thou not Romeo, and a Montague?

ROMEO Neither, fair maid, if either thee dislike.

JULIET How cam'st thou hither, tell me, and wherefore?
The orchard walls are high and hard to climb;
And the place death, considering who thou art,
If any of my kinsmen find thee here.

ROMEO With love's light wings did I o'er-perch these walls,
For stony limits cannot hold love out;
And what love can do, that dares love attempt.
Therefore thy kinsmen are no stop to me.

JULIET If they do see thee, they will murder thee.

ROMEO Alack, there lies more peril in thine eye
Than twenty of their swords; look thou but sweet,
And I am proof against their enmity.

JULIET I would not for the world they saw thee here.

ROMEO I have night's cloak to hide me from their eyes;
And but thou love me, let them find me here.
My life were better ended by their hate
Than death prorogued wanting of thy love.

JULIET By whose direction found'st thou out this place?

ROMEO By love, that first did prompt me to enquire;
He lent me counsel, and I lent him eyes.
I am no pilot; yet, wert thou as far
As that vast shore wash'd with the farthest sea,
I should adventure for such merchandise.

JULIET Thou knowest the mask of night is on my face,
Else would a maiden blush bepaint my cheek
For that which thou hast heard me speak to-night.
Fain would I dwell on form, fain, fain deny
What I have spoke; but farewell compliment!
Dost thou love me? I know thou wilt say ay,
And I will take thy word; yet, if thou swear'st,
Thou mayst prove false; at lovers' perjuries
They say Jove laughs. O gentle Romeo,
If thou dost love, pronounce it faithfully.
Or, if thou think'st I am too quickly won,
I'll frown, and be perverse, and say thee nay,
So thou wilt woo; but else, not for the world.
In truth, fair Montague, I am too fond;
And therefore thou mayst think my haviour light;
But trust me, gentleman, I'll prove more true
Than those that have more cunning to be strange.
I should have been more strange, I must confess,
But that thou overheard'st, ere I was ware,
My true love's passion. Therefore pardon me,
And not impute this yielding to light love,
Which the dark night hath so discovered.

ROMEO Lady, by yonder blessed moon I vow,
That tips with silver all these fruit-tree tops –

JULIET O, swear not by the moon, th' inconstant moon,
That monthly changes in her circled orb,
Lest that thy love prove likewise variable.

ROMEO What shall I swear by?
JULIET Do not swear at all;
Or, if thou wilt, swear by thy gracious self,
Which is the god of my idolatry,
And I'll believe thee.
ROMEO If my heart's dear love –
JULIET Well, do not swear. Although I joy in thee,
I have no joy of this contract to-night:
It is too rash, too unadvis'd, too sudden;
Too like the lightning, which doth cease to be
Ere one can say 'It lightens'. Sweet, good night!
This bud of love, by summer's ripening breath,
May prove a beauteous flow'r when next we meet.
Good night, good night! As sweet repose and rest
Come to thy heart as that within my breast!
ROMEO O, wilt thou leave me so unsatisfied?
JULIET What satisfaction canst thou have to-night?
ROMEO Th' exchange of thy love's faithful vow for mine.
JULIET I gave thee mine before thou didst request it;
And yet I would it were to give again.
ROMEO Wouldst thou withdraw it? For what purpose, love?
JULIET But to be frank, and give it thee again.
And yet I wish but for the thing I have.
My bounty is as boundless as the sea,
My love as deep: the more I give to thee,
The more I have, for both are infinite.

[Nurse calls within.

I hear some noise within. Dear love, adieu! –
Anon, good nurse! – Sweet Montague, be true.
Stay but a little, I will come again. *[Exit.*

ROMEO O blessed, blessed night! I am afeard,
Being in night, all this is but a dream,
Too flattering-sweet to be substantial.

Re-enter JULIET above.

JULIET Three words, dear Romeo, and good night indeed.
If that thy bent of love be honourable,
Thy purpose marriage, send me word tomorrow,
By one that I'll procure to come to thee,
Where and what time thou wilt perform the rite;
And all my fortunes at thy foot I'll lay,
And follow thee, my lord, throughout the world.
NURSE *[Within]* Madam!
JULIET I come anon. – But if thou meanest not well,
I do beseech thee –
NURSE *[Within]* Madam!
JULIET By and by, I come –
To cease thy suit, and leave me to my grief.
To-morrow will I send.
ROMEO So thrive my soul –
JULIET A thousand times good night! *[Exit.*
ROMEO A thousand times the worse, to want thy light.
Love goes toward love as school-boys from their books;
But love from love, toward school with heavy looks.

Re-enter JULIET above.

JULIET Hist! Romeo, hist! – O for a falc'ner's voice,
To lure this tassel-gentle back again!
Bondage is hoarse, and may not speak aloud;
Else would I tear the cave where Echo lies,
And make her airy tongue more hoarse than mine
With repetition of my Romeo's name.
Romeo!
ROMEO It is my soul that calls upon my name.
How silver-sweet sound lovers' tongues by night,
Like softest music to attending ears!
JULIET Romeo!
ROMEO My dear?
JULIET At what o'clock to-morrow
Shall I send to thee?
ROMEO By the hour of nine.
JULIET I will not fail. 'Tis twenty years till then.
I have forgot why I did call thee back.
ROMEO Let me stand here till thou remember it.
JULIET I shall forget, to have thee still stand there,
Rememb'ring how I love thy company.
ROMEO And I'll still stay, to have thee still forget,
Forgetting any other home but this.
JULIET 'Tis almost morning. I would have thee gone;
And yet no farther than a wanton's bird,
That lets it hop a little from her hand,
Like a poor prisoner in his twisted gyves,
And with a silk thread plucks it back again,
So loving-jealous of his liberty.
ROMEO I would I were thy bird.
JULIET Sweet, so would I.
Yet I should kill thee with much cherishing.
Good night, good night! Parting is such sweet sorrow
That I shall say good night till it be morrow.

[Exit.

ROMEO Sleep dwell upon thine eyes, peace in thy breast!
Would I were sleep and peace, so sweet to rest!

Hence will I to my ghostly father's cell,
His help to crave and my dear hap to tell.
[*Exit*.

SCENE III. *Friar Lawrence's cell.*

Enter FRIAR LAWRENCE with a basket.

FRIAR LAWRENCE The gray-ey'd morn smiles on the frowning night,
Check'ring the eastern clouds with streaks of light;
And fleckel'd darkness like a drunkard reels
From forth day's path and Titan's fiery wheels.
Now, ere the sun advance his burning eye
The day to cheer and night's dank dew to dry,
I must up-fill this osier cage of ours
With baleful weeds and precious-juiced flowers.
The earth that's nature's mother is her tomb;
What is her burying grave, that is her womb.
And from her womb children of divers kind
We sucking on her natural bosom find;
Many for many virtues excellent,
None but for some, and yet all different.
O, mickle is the powerful grace that lies
In plants, herbs, stones, and their true qualities;
For nought so vile that on the earth doth live
But to the earth some special good doth give;
Nor aught so good but, strain'd from that fair use,
Revolts from true birth, stumbling on abuse:
Virtue itself turns vice, being misapplied,
And vice sometime's by action dignified.
Within the infant rind of this weak flower
Poison hath residence, and medicine power;
For this, being smelt, with that part cheers each part;
Being tasted, slays all senses with the heart.
Two such opposed kings encamp them still
In man as well as herbs – grace and rude will;
And where the worser is predominant,
Full soon the canker death eats up that plant.

Enter ROMEO.

ROMEO Good morrow, father!
FRIAR LAWRENCE Benedicite!
What early tongue so sweet saluteth me?
Young son, it argues a distempered head
So soon to bid good morrow to thy bed.
Care keeps his watch in every old man's eye,
And where care lodges sleep will never lie;
But where unbruised youth with unstuff'd brain
Doth couch his limbs, there golden sleep doth reign.
Therefore thy earliness doth me assure
Thou art uprous'd with some distemp'rature;
Or if not so, then here I hit it right –
Our Romeo hath not been in bed to-night.

ROMEO That last is true; the sweeter rest was mine.
FRIAR LAWRENCE God pardon sin! Wast thou with Rosaline?
ROMEO With Rosaline, my ghostly father? No;
I have forgot that name, and that name's woe.
FRIAR LAWRENCE That's my good son; but where hast thou been then?
ROMEO I'll tell thee ere thou ask it me again.
I have been feasting with mine enemy;
Where, on a sudden, one hath wounded me
That's by me wounded; both our remedies
Within thy help and holy physic lies.
I bear no hatred, blessed man, for, lo,
My intercession likewise steads my foe.
FRIAR LAWRENCE Be plain, good son, and homely in thy drift;
Riddling confession finds but riddling shrift.
ROMEO Then plainly know my heart's dear love is set
On the fair daughter of rich Capulet.
As mine on hers, so hers is set on mine;
And all combin'd, save what thou must combine
By holy marriage. When, and where, and how,
We met, we woo'd, and made exchange of vow,
I'll tell thee as we pass; but this I pray,
That thou consent to marry us to-day.
FRIAR LAWRENCE Holy Saint Francis! What a change is here!
Is Rosaline, that thou didst love so dear,
So soon forsaken? Young men's love, then, lies
Not truly in their hearts, but in their eyes.
Jesu Maria, what a deal of brine
Hath wash'd thy sallow cheeks for Rosaline!
How much salt water thrown away in waste,
To season love, that of it doth not taste!
The sun not yet thy sighs from heaven clears,
Thy old groans yet ring in mine ancient ears;
Lo, here upon thy cheek the stain doth sit
Of an old tear that is not wash'd off yet.
If e'er thou wast thyself, and these woes thine,
Thou and these woes were all for Rosaline.
And art thou chang'd? Pronounce this sentence, then:
Women may fall, when there's no strength in men.
ROMEO Thou chid'st me oft for loving Rosaline.
FRIAR LAWRENCE For doting, not for loving, pupil mine.
ROMEO And bad'st me bury love.
FRIAR LAWRENCE Not in a grave
To lay one in, another out to have.
ROMEO I pray thee chide me not; her I love now
Doth grace for grace and love for love allow;
The other did not so.
FRIAR LAWRENCE O, she knew well
Thy love did read by rote that could not spell.

But come, young waverer, come, go with me,
In one respect I'll thy assistant be;
For this alliance may so happy prove
To turn your households' rancour to pure love.

ROMEO O, let us hence; I stand on sudden haste.

FRIAR LAWRENCE Wisely and slow; they stumble that run fast. [*Exeunt.*

SCENE IV. *A street.*

Enter BENVOLIO and MERCUTIO.

MERCUTIO Where the devil should this Romeo be?
Came he not home to-night?

BENVOLIO Not to his father's; I spoke with his man.

MERCUTIO Why, that same pale hard-hearted wench, that Rosaline,
Torments him so that he will sure run mad.

BENVOLIO Tybalt, the kinsman to old Capulet,
Hath sent a letter to his father's house.

MERCUTIO A challenge, on my life.

BENVOLIO Romeo will answer it.

MERCUTIO Any man that can write may answer a letter.

BENVOLIO Nay, he will answer the letter's master, how he dares, being dared.

MERCUTIO Alas, poor Romeo, he is already dead: stabb'd with a white wench's black eye; run through the ear with a love-song; the very pin of his heart cleft with the blind bow-boy's butt-shaft. And is he a man to encounter Tybalt?

BENVOLIO Why, what is Tybalt?

MERCUTIO More than Prince of Cats. O, he's the courageous captain of compliments. He fights as you sing prick-song; keeps time, distance, and proportion; he rests his minim rests, one, two, and the third in your bosom; the very butcher of a silk button, a duellist, a duellist; a gentleman of the very first house, of the first and second cause. Ah, the immortal passado! the punto reverso! the hay! –

BENVOLIO The what?

MERCUTIO The pox of such antic, lisping, affecting fantasticoes; these new tuners of accent! – 'By Jesu, a very good blade! a very tall man! a very good whore!' Why, is not this a lamentable thing, grandsire, that we should be thus afflicted with these strange flies, these fashion-mongers, these pardon me's, who stand so much on the new form that they cannot sit at ease on the old bench? O, their bones, their bones!

Enter ROMEO.

BENVOLIO Here comes Romeo, here comes Romeo.

MERCUTIO Without his roe, like a dried herring. O flesh, flesh, how art thou fishified! Now is he for the numbers that Petrarch flow'd in; Laura, to his lady, was a kitchen-wench – marry, she had a better love to berhyme her; Dido, a dowdy; Cleopatra, a gipsy; Helen and Hero, hildings and harlots; Thisbe, a gray eye or so, but not to the purpose – Signior Romeo, bon jour! There's a French salutation to your French slop. You gave us the counterfeit fairly last night.

ROMEO Good morrow to you both. What counterfeit did I give you?

MERCUTIO The slip, sir, the slip; can you not conceive?

ROMEO Pardon, good Mercutio; my business was great, and in such a case as mine a man may strain courtesy.

MERCUTIO That's as much as to say, such a case as yours constrains a man to bow in the hams.

ROMEO Meaning, to curtsy.

MERCUTIO Thou hast most kindly hit it.

ROMEO A most courteous exposition.

MERCUTIO Nay, I am the very pink of courtesy.

ROMEO Pink for flower.

MERCUTIO Right.

ROMEO Why, then is my pump well flower'd.

MERCUTIO Sure wit! Follow me this jest now till thou hast worn out thy pump, that, when the single sole of it is worn, the jest may remain, after the wearing, solely singular.

ROMEO O single-sol'd jest, solely singular for the singleness!

MERCUTIO Come between us, good Benvolio; my wits faints.

ROMEO Swits and spurs, swits and spurs; or I'll cry a match.

MERCUTIO Nay, if our wits run the wild-goose chase, I am done; for thou hast more of the wild goose in one of thy wits than, I am sure, I have in my whole five. Was I with you there for the goose?

ROMEO Thou wast never with me for anything when thou wast not there for the goose.

MERCUTIO I will bite thee by the ear for that jest.

ROMEO Nay, good goose, bite not.

MERCUTIO Thy wit is a very bitter sweeting; it is a most sharp sauce.

ROMEO And is it not then well serv'd in to a sweet goose?

MERCUTIO O, here's a wit of cheveril, that stretches from an inch narrow to an ell broad!

ROMEO I stretch it out for that word 'broad', which, added to the goose, proves thee far and wide a broad goose.

MERCUTIO Why, is not this better now than groaning for love? Now art thou sociable, now art thou Romeo; now art thou what thou art by art as well as by nature; for this drivelling love is like a great natural that runs lolling up and down to hide his bauble in a hole.

BENVOLIO Stop there, stop there.

MERCUTIO Thou desirest me to stop in my tale against the hair.

BENVOLIO Thou wouldst else have made thy tale large.

MERCUTIO O, thou art deceiv'd: I would have made it short; for I was come to the whole depth of my tale, and meant, indeed, to occupy the argument no longer.

ROMEO Here's goodly gear!

Enter Nurse and her man, PETER.

MERCUTIO A sail, a sail!

BENVOLIO Two, two; a shirt and a smock.

NURSE Peter!

PETER Anon.

NURSE My fan, Peter.

MERCUTIO Good Peter, to hide her face; for her fan's the fairer face.

NURSE God ye good morrow, gentlemen.

MERCUTIO God ye good den, fair gentlewoman.

NURSE Is it good den?

MERCUTIO 'Tis no less, I tell ye; for the bawdy hand of the dial is now upon the prick of noon.

NURSE Out upon you! What a man are you?

ROMEO One, gentlewoman, that God hath made himself to mar.

NURSE By my troth, it is well said. 'For himself to mar' quoth 'a! Gentlemen, can any of you tell me where I may find the young Romeo?

ROMEO I can tell you; but young Romeo will be older when you have found him than he was when you sought him. I am the youngest of that name, for fault of a worse.

NURSE You say well.

MERCUTIO Yea, is the worst well? Very well took, i' faith; wisely, wisely.

NURSE If you be he, sir, I desire some confidence with you.

BENVOLIO She will indite him to some supper.

MERCUTIO A bawd, a bawd, a bawd! So ho!

ROMEO What hast thou found?

MERCUTIO No hare, sir; unless a hare, sir, in a lenten pie, that is something stale and hoar ere it be spent. [*He walks by them and sings.*

An old hare hoar,
And an old hare hoar,
Is very good meat in Lent;
But a hare that is hoar
Is too much for a score,
When it hoars ere it be spent.

Romeo, will you come to your father's? We'll to dinner thither.

ROMEO I will follow you.

MERCUTIO Farewell, ancient lady; farewell, [*Sings*] lady, lady, lady.

[*Exeunt Mercutio and Benvolio.*

NURSE I pray you, sir, what saucy merchant was this that was so full of his ropery?

ROMEO A gentleman, nurse, that loves to hear himself talk, and will speak more in a minute than he will stand to in a month.

NURSE An 'a speak anything against me, I'll take him down, an 'a were lustier than he is, and twenty such Jacks; and if I cannot, I'll find those that shall. Scurvy knave! I am none of his flirt-gills; I am none of his skains-mates. And thou must stand by too, and suffer every knave to use me at his pleasure?

PETER I saw no man use you at his pleasure; if I had, my weapon should quickly have been out, I warrant you. I dare draw as soon as another man, if I see occasion in a good quarrel, and the law on my side.

NURSE Now, afore God, I am so vex'd that every part about me quivers. Scurvy knave! – Pray you, sir, a word; and as I told you, my young lady bid me enquire you out; what she bid me say I will keep to myself. But first let me tell ye, if ye should lead her in a fool's paradise, as they say, it were a very gross kind of behaviour, as they say; for the gentlewoman is young; and, therefore, if you should deal double with her, truly it were an ill thing to be off'red to any gentlewoman, and very weak dealing.

ROMEO Nurse, commend me to thy lady and mistress. I protest unto thee –

NURSE Good heart, and, i' faith, I will tell her as much. Lord, Lord! she will be a joyful woman.

ROMEO What wilt thou tell her, nurse? Thou dost not mark me.

NURSE I will tell her, sir, that you do protest; which, as I take it, is a gentleman-like offer.

ROMEO Bid her devise
Some means to come to shrift this afternoon;
And there she shall at Friar Lawrence' cell
Be shriv'd and married. Here is for thy pains.

NURSE No, truly, sir; not a penny.

ROMEO Go to; I say you shall.

NURSE This afternoon, sir? Well, she shall be there.

ROMEO And stay, good nurse – behind the abbey wall
Within this hour my man shall be with thee,
And bring thee cords made like a tackled stair;
Which to the high top-gallant of my joy
Must be my convoy in the secret night.
Farewell; be trusty, and I'll quit thy pains.
Farewell; commend me to thy mistress.

NURSE Now God in heaven bless thee! –
Hark you, sir.

ROMEO What say'st thou, my dear nurse?
NURSE Is your man secret? Did you ne'er hear say
Two may keep counsel, putting one away?
ROMEO I warrant thee my man's as true as steel.

NURSE Well, sir. My mistress is the sweetest lady – Lord, Lord! when 'twas a little prating thing! O, there is a nobleman in town, one Paris, that would fain lay knife aboard; but she, good soul, had as lief see a toad, a very toad, as see him. I anger her sometimes, and tell her that Paris is the properer man; but, I'll warrant you, when I say so she looks as pale as any clout in the versal world. Doth not rosemary and Romeo begin both with a letter?

ROMEO Ay, nurse; what of that? Both with an R.

NURSE Ah, mocker! that's the dog's name. R is for the – no, I know it begins with some other letter. And she hath the prettiest sententious of it, of you and rosemary, that it would do you good to hear it.

ROMEO Commend me to thy lady.
NURSE Ay, a thousand times. – Peter!
PETER Anon.
NURSE [*Handing him her fan*] Before and apace.
[*Exeunt.*

SCENE V. *Capulet's orchard.*

Enter JULIET.

JULIET The clock struck nine when I did send the nurse;
In half an hour she promis'd to return.
Perchance she cannot meet him – that's not so.
O, she is lame! Love's heralds should be thoughts,
Which ten times faster glide than the sun's beams
Driving back shadows over louring hills;
Therefore do nimble-pinion'd doves draw Love,
And therefore hath the wind-swift Cupid wings.
Now is the sun upon the highmost hill
Of this day's journey; and from nine till twelve
Is three long hours, yet she is not come.
Had she affections and warm youthful blood,
She would be as swift in motion as a ball;
My words would bandy her to my sweet love,
And his to me.
But old folks – many feign as they were dead;
Unwieldy, slow, heavy, and pale as lead.

Enter Nurse and PETER.

O God, she comes! O honey nurse, what news?
Hast thou met with him? Send thy man away.
NURSE Peter, stay at the gate. [*Exit Peter.*
JULIET Now, good sweet nurse – O Lord, why look'st thou sad?
Though news be sad, yet tell them merrily;
If good, thou shamest the music of sweet news
By playing it to me with so sour a face.
NURSE I am aweary, give me leave a while;
Fie, how my bones ache! What a jaunce have I had!
JULIET I would thou hadst my bones and I thy news.
Nay, come, I pray thee speak; good, good nurse, speak.
NURSE Jesu, what haste? Can you not stay a while?
Do you not see that I am out of breath?
JULIET How art thou out of breath, when thou hast breath
To say to me that thou art out of breath?
The excuse that thou dost make in this delay
Is longer than the tale thou dost excuse.
Is thy news good or bad? Answer to that;
Say either, and I'll stay the circumstance.
Let me be satisfied, is't good or bad?

NURSE Well, you have made a simple choice; you know not how to choose a man. Romeo! no, not he; though his face be better than any man's, yet his leg excels all men's; and for a hand, and a foot, and a body, though they be not to be talk'd on, yet they are past compare. He is not the flower of courtesy, but I'll warrant him as gentle as a lamb. Go thy ways, wench; serve God. What, have you din'd at home?

JULIET No, no. But all this did I know before.
What says he of our marriage? What of that?
NURSE Lord, how my head aches! What a head have I!
It beats as it would fall in twenty pieces.
My back a t' other side – ah, my back, my back!
Beshrew your heart for sending me about
To catch my death with jauncing up and down!
JULIET I' faith, I am sorry that thou art not well.
Sweet, sweet, sweet nurse, tell me, what says my love?
NURSE Your love says like an honest gentleman,
and a courteous, and a kind, and a handsome,
and, I warrant, a virtuous – Where is your mother?
JULIET Where is my mother! Why, she is within;
Where should she be? How oddly thou repliest!
'Your love says like an honest gentleman,
Where is your mother?'
NURSE O God's lady dear!
Are you so hot? Marry, come up, I trow;
Is this the poultice for my aching bones?
Henceforward, do your messages yourself.
JULIET Here's such a coil! Come, what says Romeo?
NURSE Have you got leave to go to shrift to-day?
JULIET I have.

NURSE Then hie you hence to Friar Lawrence' cell;
There stays a husband to make you a wife.
Now comes the wanton blood up in your cheeks;
They'll be in scarlet straight at any news.
Hie you to church; I must another way,
To fetch a ladder, by the which your love
Must climb a bird's nest soon when it is dark.
I am the drudge, and toil in your delight;
But you shall bear the burden soon at night.
Go; I'll to dinner; hie you to the cell.

JULIET Hie to high fortune! Honest nurse, farewell. *[Exeunt.*

SCENE VI. *Friar Lawrence's cell.*

Enter FRIAR LAWRENCE and ROMEO.

FRIAR LAWRENCE So smile the heavens upon this holy act
That after-hours with sorrow chide us not!

ROMEO Amen, amen! But come what sorrow can,
It cannot countervail the exchange of joy
That one short minute gives me in her sight.
Do thou but close our hands with holy words,
Then love-devouring death do what he dare;
It is enough I may but call her mine.

FRIAR LAWRENCE These violent delights have violent ends,
And in their triumph die; like fire and powder,
Which, as thy kiss, consume. The sweetest honey
Is loathsome in his own deliciousness,
And in the taste confounds the appetite.
Therefore love moderately: long love doth so;
Too swift arrives as tardy as too slow.

Enter JULIET.

Here comes the lady. O, so light a foot
Will ne'er wear out the everlasting flint.
A lover may bestride the gossamer
That idles in the wanton summer air
And yet not fall, so light is vanity.

JULIET Good even to my ghostly confessor.

FRIAR LAWRENCE Romeo shall thank thee, daughter, for us both.

JULIET As much to him, else is his thanks too much.

ROMEO Ah, Juliet, if the measure of thy joy
Be heap'd like mine, and that thy skill be more
To blazon it, then sweeten with thy breath
This neighbour air, and let rich music's tongue
Unfold the imagin'd happiness that both
Receive in either by this dear encounter.

JULIET Conceit, more rich in matter than in words,
Brags of his substance, not of ornament.
They are but beggars that can count their worth;
But my true love is grown to such excess
I cannot sum up sum of half my wealth.

FRIAR LAWRENCE Come, come with me, and we will make short work;
For, by your leaves, you shall not stay alone
Till holy church incorporate two in one. *[Exeunt.*

ACT THREE

SCENE I. *A public place.*

Enter MERCUTIO, BENVOLIO, Page, and Servants.

BENVOLIO I pray thee, good Mercutio, let's retire.
The day is hot, the Capulets abroad,
And if we meet we shall not scape a brawl;
For now, these hot days, is the mad blood stirring.

MERCUTIO Thou art like one of these fellows that, when he enters the confines of a tavern, claps me his sword upon the table, and says 'God send me no need of thee!' and by the operation of the second cup draws him on the drawer, when, indeed, there is no need.

BENVOLIO Am I like such a fellow?

MERCUTIO Come, come, thou art as hot a Jack in thy mood as any in Italy; and as soon moved to be moody, and as soon moody to be moved.

BENVOLIO And what to?

MERCUTIO Nay, an there were two such, we should have none shortly, for one would kill the other. Thou! why, thou wilt quarrel with a man that hath a hair more or a hair less in his beard than thou hast. Thou wilt quarrel with a man for cracking nuts, having no other reason but because thou hast hazel eyes. What eye but such an eye would spy out such a quarrel? Thy head is as full of quarrels as an egg is full of meat; and yet thy head hath been beaten as addle as an egg for quarrelling. Thou hast quarrell'd with a man for coughing in the street, because he hath wakened thy dog that hath lain asleep in the sun. Didst thou not fall out with a tailor for wearing his new doublet before Easter? With another for tying his new shoes with old riband? And yet thou wilt tutor me from quarrelling!

BENVOLIO An I were so apt to quarrel as thou art, any man should buy the fee simple of my life for an hour and a quarter.

MERCUTIO The fee simple! O simple!

Enter TYBALT and Others.

BENVOLIO By my head, here comes the Capulets.

MERCUTIO By my heel, I care not.

TYBALT Follow me close, for I will speak to them.
Gentlemen, good den; a word with one of you.

MERCUTIO And but one word with one of us? Couple it with something; make it a word and a blow.

TYBALT You shall find me apt enough to that, sir, an you will give me occasion.

MERCUTIO Could you not take some occasion without giving?

TYBALT Mercutio, thou consortest with Romeo.

MERCUTIO Consort! What, dost thou make us minstrels? An thou make minstrels of us, look to hear nothing but discords. Here's my fiddlestick; here's that shall make you dance. Zounds, consort!

BENVOLIO We talk here in the public haunt of men;
Either withdraw unto some private place,
Or reason coldly of your grievances,
Or else depart; here all eyes gaze on us.

MERCUTIO Men's eyes were made to look, and let them gaze;
I will not budge for no man's pleasure, I.

Enter ROMEO.

TYBALT Well, peace be with you, sir. Here comes my man.

MERCUTIO But I'll be hang'd, sir, if he wear your livery.
Marry, go before to field, he'll be your follower;
Your worship in that sense may call him man.

TYBALT Romeo, the love I bear thee can afford
No better term than this: thou art a villain.

ROMEO Tybalt, the reason that I have to love thee
Doth much excuse the appertaining rage
To such a greeting. Villain am I none;
Therefore, farewell; I see thou knowest me not.

TYBALT Boy, this shall not excuse the injuries
That thou hast done me; therefore turn and draw.

ROMEO I do protest I never injur'd thee,
But love thee better than thou canst devise
Till thou shalt know the reason of my love;
And so, good Capulet – which name I tender
As dearly as mine own – be satisfied.

MERCUTIO O calm, dishonourable, vile submission!
Alla stoccata carries it away. [*Draws.*
Tybalt, you rat-catcher, will you walk?

TYBALT What wouldst thou have with me?

MERCUTIO Good King of Cats, nothing but one of your nine lives; that I mean to make bold withal, and, as you shall use me hereafter, dry-beat the rest of the eight. Will you pluck your sword out of his pilcher by the ears? Make haste, lest mine be about your ears ere it be out.

TYBALT I am for you. [*Draws.*

ROMEO Gentle Mercutio, put thy rapier up.

MERCUTIO Come, sir, your passado. [*They fight.*

ROMEO Draw, Benvolio; beat down their weapons.
Gentlemen, for shame, forbear this outrage!
Tybalt! Mercutio! the Prince expressly hath
Forbid this bandying in Verona streets.
Hold, Tybalt! Good Mercutio!

[*Tybalt under Romeo's arm thrusts Mercutio in, and flies with his friends.*

MERCUTIO I am hurt.
A plague a both your houses! I am sped.
Is he gone and hath nothing?

BENVOLIO What, art thou hurt?

MERCUTIO Ay, ay, a scratch, a scratch; marry, 'tis enough.
Where is my page? Go, villain, fetch a surgeon.

[*Exit Page.*

ROMEO Courage, man; the hurt cannot be much.

MERCUTIO No, 'tis not so deep as a well, nor so wide as a church door, but 'tis enough, 'twill serve. Ask for me to-morrow, and you shall find me a grave man. I am peppered, I warrant, for this world. A plague a both your houses! Zounds, a dog, a rat, a mouse, a cat, to scratch a man to death! A braggart, a rogue, a villain, that fights by the book of arithmetic! Why the devil came you between us? I was hurt under your arm.

ROMEO I thought all for the best.

MERCUTIO Help me into some house, Benvolio, or I shall faint.
A plague a both your houses!
They have made worms' meat of me.
I have it, and soundly too – Your houses!

[*Exeunt Mercutio and Benvolio.*

ROMEO This gentleman, the Prince's near ally,
My very friend, hath got this mortal hurt
In my behalf; my reputation stain'd
With Tybalt's slander – Tybalt, that an hour
Hath been my cousin. O sweet Juliet,
Thy beauty hath made me effeminate,
And in my temper soft'ned valour's steel!

Re-enter BENVOLIO.

BENVOLIO O Romeo, Romeo, brave Mercutio is dead!
That gallant spirit hath aspir'd the clouds,
Which too untimely here did scorn the earth.

ROMEO This day's black fate on moe days doth depend;

This but begins the woe others must end.

Re-enter TYBALT.

BENVOLIO Here comes the furious Tybalt back again.
ROMEO Alive in triumph and Mercutio slain!
Away to heaven respective lenity,
And fire-ey'd fury be my conduct now!
Now, Tybalt, take the 'villain' back again
That late thou gav'st me; for Mercutio's soul
Is but a little way above our heads,
Staying for thine to keep him company.
Either thou or I, or both, must go with him.
TYBALT Thou, wretched boy, that didst consort him here,
Shalt with him hence.
ROMEO This shall determine that.

[*They fight; Tybalt falls.*

BENVOLIO Romeo, away, be gone.
The citizens are up, and Tybalt slain.
Stand not amaz'd. The Prince will doom thee death
If thou art taken. Hence, be gone, away!
ROMEO O, I am fortune's fool!
BENVOLIO Why dost thou stay?

[*Exit Romeo.*

Enter Citizens.

1 CITIZEN Which way ran he that kill'd Mercutio?
Tybalt, that murderer, which way ran he?
BENVOLIO There lies that Tybalt.
1 CITIZEN Up, sir, go with me;
I charge thee in the Prince's name, obey.

Enter PRINCE, attended; MONTAGUE, CAPULET, their Wives, and All.

PRINCE Where are the vile beginners of this fray?
BENVOLIO O noble Prince, I can discover all
The unlucky manage of this fatal brawl:
There lies the man, slain by young Romeo,
That slew thy kinsman, brave Mercutio.
LADY CAPULET Tybalt, my cousin! O my brother's child!
O Prince! O husband! O, the blood is spill'd
Of my dear kinsman! Prince, as thou art true,
For blood of ours shed blood of Montague.
O cousin, cousin!
PRINCE Benvolio, who began this bloody fray?
BENVOLIO Tybalt, here slain, whom Romeo's hand did slay;
Romeo that spoke him fair, bid him bethink
How nice the quarrel was, and urg'd withal
Your high displeasure. All this, uttered
With gentle breath, calm look, knees humbly bow'd,
Could not take truce with the unruly spleen
Of Tybalt, deaf to peace, but that he tilts
With piercing steel at bold Mercutio's breast;
Who, all as hot, turns deadly point to point,
And, with a martial scorn, with one hand beats
Cold death aside, and with the other sends
It back to Tybalt, whose dexterity
Retorts it. Romeo he cries aloud
'Hold, friends! friends, part!' and, swifter than his tongue,
His agile arm beats down their fatal points,
And 'twixt them rushes; underneath whose arm
An envious thrust from Tybalt hit the life
Of stout Mercutio; and then Tybalt fled;
But by and by comes back to Romeo,
Who had but newly entertain'd revenge,
And to't they go like lightning; for ere I
Could draw to part them was stout Tybalt slain;
And as he fell did Romeo turn and fly.
This is the truth, or let Benvolio die.
LADY CAPULET He is a kinsman to the Montague,
Affection makes him false, he speaks not true;
Some twenty of them fought in this black strife,
And all those twenty could but kill one life.
I beg for justice, which thou, Prince, must give:
Romeo slew Tybalt, Romeo must not live.
PRINCE Romeo slew him; he slew Mercutio.
Who now the price of his dear blood doth owe?
MONTAGUE Not Romeo, Prince; he was Mercutio's friend;
His fault concludes but what the law should end,
The life of Tybalt.
PRINCE And for that offence,
Immediately we do exile him hence.
I have an interest in your hate's proceeding,
My blood for your rude brawls doth lie a-bleeding;
But I'll amerce you with so strong a fine
That you shall all repent the loss of mine.
I will be deaf to pleading and excuses,
Nor tears nor prayers shall purchase out abuses;
Therefore use none. Let Romeo hence in haste,
Else when he is found that hour is his last.
Bear hence this body, and attend our will:
Mercy but murders, pardoning those that kill.

[*Exeunt.*

SCENE II. *Capulet's orchard.*

Enter JULIET.

JULIET Gallop apace, you fiery-footed steeds
Towards Phoebus' lodging; such a waggoner
As Phaethon would whip you to the west,
And bring in cloudy night immediately.
Spread thy close curtain, love-performing night,
That runaways' eyes may wink, and Romeo
Leap to these arms, untalk'd of and unseen.

Lovers can see to do their amorous rites
By their own beauties; or if love be blind,
It best agrees with night. Come, civil night,
Thou sober-suited matron, all in black,
And learn me how to lose a winning match,
Play'd for a pair of stainless maidenhoods;
Hood my unmann'd blood, bating in my cheeks,
With thy black mantle, till strange love, grown bold,
Think true love acted simple modesty.
Come, night; come, Romeo; come, thou day in night;
For thou wilt lie upon the wings of night
Whiter than new snow on a raven's back.
Come, gentle night, come, loving black-brow'd night,
Give me my Romeo; and, when he shall die,
Take him and cut him out in little stars,
And he will make the face of heaven so fine
That all the world will be in love with night,
And pay no worship to the garish sun.
O, I have bought the mansion of a love,
But not possess'd it; and though I am sold,
Not yet enjoy'd. So tedious is this day
As is the night before some festival
To an impatient child that hath new robes,
And may not wear them. O, here comes my nurse,

Enter Nurse with cords.

And she brings news; and every tongue that speaks
But Romeo's name speaks heavenly eloquence.
Now, nurse, what news? What hast thou there? The cords
That Romeo bid thee fetch?

NURSE Ay, ay, the cords.

[*Throws them down.*

JULIET Ay, me! what news? Why dost thou wring thy hands?

NURSE Ah, well-a-day! he's dead, he's dead, he's dead.
We are undone, lady, we are undone.
Alack the day! he's gone, he's kill'd, he's dead.

JULIET Can heaven be so envious?

NURSE Romeo can,
Though heaven cannot. O Romeo, Romeo!
Who ever would have thought it? Romeo!

JULIET What devil art thou that dost torment me thus?
This torture should be roar'd in dismal hell.
Hath Romeo slain himself? Say thou but 'I',
And that bare vowel I shall poison more
Than the death-darting eye of cockatrice.
I am not I if there be such an 'I';
Or those eyes shut that makes thee answer 'I'.
If he be slain, say 'I'; or if not, 'No';
Brief sounds determine of my weal or woe.

NURSE I saw the wound, I saw it with mine eyes –
God save the mark! – here on his manly breast.
A piteous corse, a bloody piteous corse;
Pale, pale as ashes, all bedaub'd in blood,
All in gore-blood. I swounded at the sight.

JULIET O, break, my heart! poor bankrupt, break at once!
To prison, eyes; ne'er look on liberty.
Vile earth, to earth resign; end motion here;
And thou and Romeo press one heavy bier!

NURSE O Tybalt, Tybalt, the best friend I had!
O courteous Tybalt! honest gentleman!
That ever I should live to see thee dead!

JULIET What storm is this that blows so contrary?
Is Romeo slaught'red, and is Tybalt dead?
My dearest cousin and my dearer lord?
Then, dreadful trumpet, sound the general doom;
For who is living if those two are gone?

NURSE Tybalt is gone, and Romeo banished;
Romeo that kill'd him, he is banished.

JULIET O God! Did Romeo's hand shed Tybalt's blood?

NURSE It did, it did; alas the day, it did!

JULIET O serpent heart, hid with a flow'ring face!
Did ever dragon keep so fair a cave?
Beautiful tyrant! fiend angelical!
Dove-feather'd raven! wolfish-ravening lamb!
Despised substance of divinest show!
Just opposite to what thou justly seem'st,
A damned saint, an honourable villain!
O nature, what hadst thou to do in hell,
When thou didst bower the spirit of a fiend
In mortal paradise of such sweet flesh?
Was ever book containing such vile matter
So fairly bound? O, that deceit should dwell
In such a gorgeous palace!

NURSE There's no trust,
No faith, no honesty in men; all perjur'd,
All forsworn, all naught, all dissemblers.
Ah, where's my man? Give me some aqua vitae.
These griefs, these woes, these sorrows, make me old.
Shame come to Romeo!

JULIET Blister'd be thy tongue
For such a wish! He was not born to shame:
Upon his brow shame is asham'd to sit;
For 'tis a throne where honour may be crown'd
Sole monarch of the universal earth.
O, what a beast was I to chide at him!

NURSE Will you speak well of him that kill'd your cousin?

JULIET Shall I speak ill of him that is my husband?
Ah, poor my lord, what tongue shall smooth thy name,

When I, thy three-hours wife, have mangled it?
But wherefore, villain, didst thou kill my cousin?
That villain cousin would have kill'd my husband.
Back, foolish tears, back to your native spring;
-Your tributary drops belong to woe,
Which you, mistaking, offer up to joy.
My husband lives that Tybalt would have slain,
And Tybalt's dead that would have slain my husband.
All this is comfort; wherefore weep I then?
Some word there was, worser than Tybalt's death,
That murd'red me; I would forget it fain,
But, O, it presses to my memory
Like damned guilty deeds to sinners' minds:
'Tybalt is dead, and Romeo banished'.
That 'banished', that one word 'banished'
Hath slain ten thousand Tybalts. Tybalt's death
Was woe enough, if it had ended there;
Or if sour woe delights in fellowship
And needly will be rank'd with other griefs,
Why followed not, when she said 'Tybalt's dead',
Thy father or thy mother, nay, or both,
Which modern lamentation might have mov'd?
But, with a rear-ward following Tybalt's death,
'Romeo is banished' – to speak that word
Is father, mother, Tybalt, Romeo, Juliet,
All slain, all dead. 'Romeo is banished' –
There is no end, no limit, measure, bound,
In that word's death; no words can that woe sound.
Where is my father and my mother, nurse?

NURSE Weeping and wailing over Tybalt's corse.
Will you go to them? I will bring you thither.

JULIET Wash they his wounds with tears!
Mine shall be spent,
When theirs are dry, for Romeo's banishment.
Take up those cords. Poor ropes, you are beguil'd,
Both you and I, for Romeo is exil'd;
He made you for a highway to my bed,
But I, a maid, die maiden-widowed.
Come, cords; come, nurse; I'll to my wedding-bed;
And death, not Romeo, take my maiden-head!

NURSE Hie to your chamber; I'll find Romeo
To comfort you. I wot well where he is.
Hark ye, your Romeo will be here at night.
I'll to him; he is hid at Lawrence' cell.

JULIET O, find him! give this ring to my true knight,
And bid him come to take his last farewell.

[*Exeunt.*

SCENE III. *Friar Lawrence's cell.*

Enter FRIAR LAWRENCE.

FRIAR LAWRENCE Romeo, come forth; come forth, thou fearful man;
Affliction is enamour'd of thy parts,
And thou art wedded to calamity.

Enter ROMEO.

ROMEO Father, what news? What is the Prince's doom?
What sorrow craves acquaintance at my hand
That I yet know not?

FRIAR LAWRENCE Too familiar
Is my dear son with such sour company;
I bring thee tidings of the Prince's doom.

ROMEO What less than doomsday is the Prince's doom?

FRIAR LAWRENCE A gentler judgment vanish'd from his lips –
Not body's death, but body's banishment.

ROMEO Ha, banishment! Be merciful, say 'death';
For exile hath more terror in his look,
Much more than death. Do not say 'banishment'.

FRIAR LAWRENCE Here from Verona art thou banished.
Be patient, for the world is broad and wide.

ROMEO There is no world without Verona walls,
But purgatory, torture, hell itself.
Hence banished is banish'd from the world,
And world's exile is death. Then 'banished'
Is death mis-term'd; calling death 'banished',
Thou cut'st my head off with a golden axe,
And smilest upon the stroke that murders me.

FRIAR LAWRENCE O deadly sin! O rude unthankfulness!
Thy fault our law calls death; but the kind Prince,
Taking thy part, hath rush'd aside the law,
And turn'd that black word death to banishment.
This is dear mercy, and thou seest it not.

ROMEO 'Tis torture, and not mercy; heaven is here
Where Juliet lives, and every cat, and dog,
And little mouse, every unworthy thing,
Live here in heaven and may look on her;
But Romeo may not. More validity,
More honourable state, more courtship lives
In carrion flies than Romeo. They may seize
On the white wonder of dear Juliet's hand,
And steal immortal blessing from her lips;
Who, even in pure and vestal modesty,
Still blush, as thinking their own kisses sin;
But Romeo may not – he is banished.
This may flies do, when I from this must fly;
They are free men, but I am banished.

And sayest thou yet that exile is not death?
Hadst thou no poison mix'd, no sharp-ground knife,
No sudden mean of death, though ne'er so mean,
But 'banished' to kill me – 'banished'?
O friar, the damned use that word in hell;
Howling attends it; how hast thou the heart,
Being a divine, a ghostly confessor,
A sin-absolver, and my friend profess'd,
To mangle me with that word 'banished'?

FRIAR LAWRENCE Thou fond mad man, hear me a little speak.

ROMEO O, thou wilt speak again of banishment.

FRIAR LAWRENCE I'll give thee armour to keep off that word;
Adversity's sweet milk, philosophy,
To comfort thee, though thou art banished.

ROMEO Yet 'banished'? Hang up philosophy;
Unless philosophy can make a Juliet,
Displant a town, reverse a prince's doom,
It helps not, it prevails not. Talk no more.

FRIAR LAWRENCE O, then I see that madmen have no ears.

ROMEO How should they, when that wise men have no eyes?

FRIAR LAWRENCE Let me dispute with thee of thy estate.

ROMEO Thou canst not speak of that thou dost not feel.
Wert thou as young as I, Juliet thy love,
An hour but married, Tybalt murdered,
Doting like me, and like me banished,
Then mightst thou speak, then mightst thou tear thy hair,
And fall upon the ground, as I do now,
Taking the measure of an unmade grave.
[*Knocking within*.

FRIAR LAWRENCE Arise; one knocks. Good Romeo, hide thyself.

ROMEO Not I; unless the breath of heart-sick groans,
Mist-like, enfold me from the search of eyes.
[*Knocking*.

FRIAR LAWRENCE Hark how they knock! Who's there? Romeo, arise;
Thou wilt be taken. – Stay awhile. – Stand up;
[*Knocking*. Run to my study. – By and by. – God's will,
What simpleness is this! – I come, I come.
[*Knocking*.
Who knocks so hard? Whence come you? What's your will?

NURSE [*Within*] Let me come in and you shall know my errand;
I come from Lady Juliet.

FRIAR LAWRENCE Welcome, then.

Enter Nurse.

NURSE O holy friar, O, tell me, holy friar,
Where's my lady's lord, where's Romeo?

FRIAR LAWRENCE There on the ground, with his own tears made drunk.

NURSE O, he is even in my mistress' case,
Just in her case!

FRIAR LAWRENCE O woeful sympathy!
Piteous predicament!

NURSE Even so lies she,
Blubb'ring and weeping, weeping and blubb'ring.
Stand up, stand up; stand, an you be a man;
For Juliet's sake, for her sake, rise and stand;
Why should you fall into so deep an O?

ROMEO Nurse!

NURSE Ah, sir! ah, sir! Well, death's the end of all.

ROMEO Spakest thou of Juliet? How is it with her?
Doth not she think me an old murderer,
Now I have stain'd the childhood of our joy
With blood remov'd but little from her own?
Where is she? and how doth she? and what says
My conceal'd lady to our cancell'd love?

NURSE O, she says nothing, sir, but weeps and weeps;
And now falls on her bed, and then starts up,
And Tybalt calls; and then on Romeo cries,
And then down falls again.

ROMEO As if that name,
Shot from the deadly level of a gun,
Did murder her; as that name's cursed hand
Murder'd her kinsman. O, tell me, friar, tell me,
In what vile part of this anatomy
Doth my name lodge? Tell me that I may sack
The hateful mansion. [*Drawing his sword*.

FRIAR LAWRENCE Hold thy desperate hand.
Art thou a man? Thy form cries out thou art:
Thy tears are womanish; thy wild acts denote
The unreasonable fury of a beast.
Unseemly woman in a seeming man!
And ill-beseeming beast in seeming both!
Thou hast amaz'd me. By my holy order,
I thought thy disposition better temper'd.
Hast thou slain Tybalt? Wilt thou slay thyself?
And slay thy lady that in thy life lives,
By doing damned hate upon thyself?
Why railest thou on thy birth, the heaven, and earth?
Since birth, and heaven, and earth, all three do meet
In thee at once; which thou at once wouldst lose.

Fie, fie! thou shamest thy shape, thy love, thy wit;
Which, like a usurer, abound'st in all,
And usest none in that true use indeed
Which should bedeck thy shape, thy love, thy wit.
Thy noble shape is but a form of wax,
Digressing from the valour of a man;
Thy dear love sworn but hollow perjury,
Killing that love which thou hast vow'd to cherish;
Thy wit, that ornament to shape and love,
Misshapen in the conduct of them both,
Like powder in a skilless soldier's flask,
Is set afire by thine own ignorance,
And thou dismemb'red with thine own defence.
What, rouse thee, man! Thy Juliet is alive,
For whose dear sake thou wast but lately dead;
There art thou happy. Tybalt would kill thee,
But thou slewest Tybalt; there art thou happy too.
The law, that threat'ned death, becomes thy friend,
And turns it to exile; there art thou happy.
A pack of blessings lights upon thy back;
Happiness courts thee in her best array;
But, like a misbehav'd and sullen wench,
Thou pout'st upon thy fortune and thy love.
Take heed, take heed, for such die miserable.
Go, get thee to thy love, as was decreed,
Ascend her chamber, hence and comfort her.
But look thou stay not till the watch be set,
For then thou canst not pass to Mantua,
Where thou shalt live till we can find a time
To blaze your marriage, reconcile your friends,
Beg pardon of the Prince, and call thee back
With twenty hundred thousand times more joy
Than thou went'st forth in lamentation.
Go before, nurse; commend me to thy lady;
And bid her hasten all the house to bed,
Which heavy sorrow makes them apt unto;
Romeo is coming.

NURSE O Lord, I could have stay'd here all the night
To hear good counsel; O, what learning is!
My lord, I'll tell my lady you will come.

ROMEO Do so, and bid my sweet prepare to chide.

NURSE Here, sir, a ring she bid me give you, sir.
Hie you, make haste, for it grows very late.
[*Exit.*

ROMEO How well my comfort is reviv'd by this!

FRIAR LAWRENCE Go hence; good night; and here stands all your state:
Either be gone before the watch be set,
Or by the break of day disguis'd from hence.
Sojourn in Mantua; I'll find out your man,
And he shall signify from time to time
Every good hap to you that chances here.
Give me thy hand. 'Tis late; farewell; good night.

ROMEO But that a joy past joy calls out on me,
It were a grief so brief to part with thee.
Farewell. [*Exeunt.*

SCENE IV. *Capulet's house.*

Enter CAPULET, LADY CAPULET, and PARIS.

CAPULET Things have fall'n out, sir, so unluckily
That we have had no time to move our daughter.
Look you, she lov'd her kinsman Tybalt dearly,
And so did I. Well, we were born to die.
'Tis very late; she'll not come down tonight.
I promise you, but for your company,
I would have been abed an hour ago.

PARIS These times of woe afford no time to woo.
Madam, good night; commend me to your daughter.

LADY CAPULET I will, and know her mind early to-morrow;
To-night she's mew'd up to her heaviness.

CAPULET Sir Paris, I will make a desperate tender
Of my child's love. I think she will be rul'd
In all respects by me; nay, more, I doubt it not.
Wife, go you to her ere you go to bed;
Acquaint her here of my son Paris' love
And bid her, mark you me, on Wednesda next –
But, soft! what day is this?

PARIS Monday, my lord.

CAPULET Monday! ha, ha! Well, Wednesday is too soon.
A Thursday let it be; a Thursday, tell her,
She shall be married to this noble earl.
Will you be ready? Do you like this haste?
We'll keep no great ado – a friend or two;
For, hark you, Tybalt being slain so late,
It may be thought we held him carelessly,
Being our kinsman, if we revel much;
Therefore we'll have some half a dozen friends,
And there an end. But what say you to Thursday?

PARIS My lord, I would that Thursday were to-morrow.

CAPULET Well, get you gone; a Thursday be it then.
Go you to Juliet ere you go to bed;
Prepare her, wife, against this wedding-day.
Farewell, my lord. Light to my chamber, ho!
Afore me, it is so very very late
That we may call it early by and by.
Good night. [*Exeunt.*

SCENE V. *Capulet's orchard.*

Enter ROMEO and JULIET, aloft.

JULIET Wilt thou be gone? It is not yet near day;
It was the nightingale, and not the lark,
That pierc'd the fearful hollow of thine ear;
Nightly she sings on yond pomegranate tree.
Believe me, love, it was the nightingale.

ROMEO It was the lark, the herald of the morn,
No nightingale. Look, love, what envious streaks
Do lace the severing clouds in yonder east;
Night's candles are burnt out, and jocund day
Stands tiptoe on the misty mountain tops.
I must be gone and live, or stay and die.

JULIET Yond light is not daylight; I know it, I:
It is some meteor that the sun exhales
To be to thee this night a torch-bearer,
And light thee on thy way to Mantua;
Therefore stay yet; thou need'st not to be gone.

ROMEO Let me be ta'en, let me be put to death;
I am content, so thou wilt have it so.
I'll say yon grey is not the morning's eye,
'Tis but the pale reflex of Cynthia's brow;
Nor that is not the lark whose notes do beat
The vaulty heaven so high above our heads.
I have more care to stay than will to go.
Come death, and welcome! Juliet wills it so.
How is't, my soul? Let's talk – it is not day.

JULIET It is, it is; hie hence, be gone, away!
It is the lark that sings so out of tune,
Straining harsh discords and unpleasing sharps.
Some say the lark makes sweet division;
This doth not so, for she divideth us.
Some say the lark and loathed toad change eyes;
O, now I would they had chang'd voices too!
Since arm from arm that voice doth us affray,
Hunting thee hence with hunts-up to the day.
O, now be gone! More light and light it grows.

ROMEO More light and light – more dark and dark our woes!

Enter Nurse.

NURSE Madam!

JULIET Nurse?

NURSE Your lady mother is coming to your chamber.
The day is broke; be wary, look about. [*Exit.*

JULIET Then, window, let day in and let life out.

ROMEO Farewell, farewell! One kiss, and I'll descend. [*He goeth down.*

JULIET Art thou gone so, love – lord, ay, husband, friend!
I must hear from thee every day in the hour,
For in a minute there are many days;
O, by this count I shall be much in years
Ere I again behold my Romeo!

ROMEO Farewell!
I will omit no opportunity
That may convey my greetings, love, to thee.

JULIET O, think'st thou we shall ever meet again?

ROMEO I doubt it not; and all these woes shall serve
For sweet discourses in our times to come.

JULIET O, God, I have an ill-divining soul!
Methinks I see thee, now thou art below,
As one dead in the bottom of a tomb;
Either my eyesight fails or thou look'st pale.

ROMEO And trust me, love, in my eye so do you;
Dry sorrow drinks our blood. Adieu, adieu!
[*Exit below.*

JULIET O Fortune. Fortune! all men call thee fickle.
If thou art fickle, what dost thou with him
That is renown'd for faith? Be fickle, Fortune;
For then, I hope, thou wilt not keep him long,
But send him back.

LADY CAPULET [*Within*] Ho, daughter! are you up?

JULIET Who is't that calls? It is my lady mother.
Is she not down so late, or up so early?
What unaccustom'd cause procures her hither?

Enter LADY CAPULET.

LADY CAPULET Why, how now, Juliet!

JULIET Madam, I am not well.

LADY CAPULET Evermore weeping for your cousin's death?
What, wilt thou wash him from his grave with tears?
An if thou couldst, thou couldst not make him live;
Therefore have done. Some grief shows much of love;
But much of grief shows still some want of wit.

JULIET Yet let me weep for such a feeling loss.

LADY CAPULET So shall you feel the loss, but not the friend
Which you weep for.

JULIET Feeling so the loss,
I cannot choose but ever weep the friend.

LADY CAPULET Well, girl, thou weep'st not so much for his death
As that the villain lives which slaughter'd him.

JULIET What villain, madam?

LADY CAPULET That same villain, Romeo.

JULIET [*Aside*] Villain and he be many miles asunder! –
God pardon him! I do, with all my heart;
And yet no man like he doth grieve my heart.

LADY CAPULET That is because the traitor murderer lives.

JULIET Ay, madam, from the reach of these my hands.
Would none but I might venge my cousin's death

LADY CAPULET We will have vengeance for it, fear thou not;
Then weep no more. I'll send to one in Mantua –
Where that same banish'd runagate doth live –
Shall give him such an unaccustom'd dram
That he shall soon keep Tybalt company;
And then I hope thou wilt be satisfied.
JULIET Indeed I never shall be satisfied
With Romeo till I behold him – dead –
Is my poor heart so for a kinsman vex'd.
Madam, if you could find out but a man
To bear a poison, I would temper it,
That Romeo should, upon receipt thereof,
Soon sleep in quiet. O, how my heart abhors
To hear him nam'd, and cannot come to him,
To wreak the love I bore my cousin Tybalt
Upon his body that hath slaughter'd him!
LADY CAPULET Find thou the means, and I'll find such a man.
But now I'll tell thee joyful tidings, girl.
JULIET And joy comes well in such a needy time.
What are they, beseech your ladyship?
LADY CAPULET Well, well, thou hast a careful father, child;
One who, to put thee from thy heaviness,
Hath sorted out a sudden day of joy
That thou expects not, nor I look'd not for.
JULIET Madam, in happy time, what day is that?
LADY CAPULET Marry, my child, early next Thursday morn
The gallant, young, and noble gentleman,
The County Paris, at Saint Peter's Church,
Shall happily make thee there a joyful bride.
JULIET Now, by Saint Peter's Church, and Peter too,
He shall not make me there a joyful bride.
I wonder at this haste, that I must wed
Ere he that should be husband comes to woo.
I pray you tell my lord and father, madam,
I will not marry yet; and when I do, I swear
It shall be Romeo, whom you know I hate,
Rather than Paris. These are news indeed!
LADY CAPULET Here comes your father; tell him so yourself,
And see how he will take it at your hands.

Enter CAPULET and Nurse.

CAPULET When the sun sets, the air doth drizzle dew;
But for the sunset of my brother's son
It rains downright.
How now! a conduit, girl? What, still in tears?
Evermore show'ring? In one little body
Thou counterfeit'st a bark, a sea, a wind;
For still thy eyes, which I may call the sea,
Do ebb and flow with tears. The bark thy body is,
Sailing in this salt flood; the winds thy sighs,
Who, raging with thy tears, and they with them,
Without a sudden calm will overset
Thy tempest-tossed body. How now, wife!
Have you delivered to her our decree?
LADY CAPULET Ay, sir; but she will none, she gives you thanks.
I would the fool were married to her grave!
CAPULET Soft! take me with you, take me with you, wife.
How will she none? Doth she not give us thanks?
Is she not proud? Doth she not count her blest,
Unworthy as she is, that we have wrought
So worthy a gentleman to be her bride-groom?
JULIET Not proud you have, but thankful that you have.
Proud can I never be of what I hate,
But thankful even for hate that is meant love.
CAPULET How how, how how, chopt logic! What is this?
'Proud' – and 'I thank you' – and 'I thank you not' –
And yet 'not proud'? Mistress minion, you,
Thank me no thankings, nor proud me no prouds,
But fettle your fine joints 'gainst Thursday next,
To go with Paris to Saint Peter's Church,
Or I will drag thee on a hurdle thither.
Out, you green-sickness carrion! Out, you baggage!
You tallow-face!
LADY CAPULET Fie, fie! what, are you mad?
JULIET Good father, I beseech you on my knees,
Hear me with patience but to speak a word.
CAPULET Hang thee, young baggage! disobedient wretch!
I tell thee what – get thee to church a Thursday,
Or never after look me in the face.
Speak not, reply not, do not answer me;
My fingers itch. Wife, we scarce thought us blest
That God had lent us but this only child;
But now I see this one is one too much,
And that we have a curse in having her.
Out on her, hilding!
NURSE God in heaven bless her!
You are to blame, my lord, to rate her so.
CAPULET And why, my Lady Wisdom? Hold your tongue,
Good Prudence; smatter with your gossips, go.
NURSE I speak no treason.
CAPULET O, God-i-goden!
NURSE May not one speak?
CAPULET Peace, you mumbling fool!
Utter your gravity o'er a gossip's bowl,
For here we need it not.

LADY CAPULET You are too hot.
CAPULET God's bread! it makes me mad:
Day, night, hour, tide, time, work, play,
Alone, in company, still my care hath been
To have her match'd; and having now provided
A gentleman of noble parentage,
Of fair demesnes, youthful, and nobly train'd,
Stuff'd, as they say, with honourable parts,
Proportion'd as one's thought would wish a
man –
And then to have a wretched puling fool,
A whining mammet, in her fortune's tender,
To answer 'I'll not wed, I cannot love,
I am too young, I pray you pardon me'!
But, an you will not wed, I'll pardon you.
Graze where you will, you shall not house with
me.
Look to 't, think on't; I do not use to jest.
Thursday is near; lay hand on heart, advise:
An you be mine, I'll give you to my friend;
An you be not, hang, beg, starve, die in the
streets,
For, by my soul, I'll ne'er acknowledge thee,
Nor what is mine shall never do thee good.
Trust to't, bethink you, I'll not be forsworn.
[*Exit.*
JULIET Is there no pity sitting in the clouds
That sees into the bottom of my grief?
O, sweet my mother, cast me not away!
Delay this marriage for a month, a week;
Or, if you do not, make the bridal bed
In that dim monument where Tybalt lies.
LADY CAPULET Talk not to me, for I'll not speak
a word;
Do as thou wilt, for I have done with thee.
[*Exit.*
JULIET O God! – O nurse! how shall this be
prevented?
My husband is on earth, my faith in heaven;
How shall that faith return again to earth,
Unless that husband send it me from heaven
By leaving earth? Comfort me, counsel me.
Alack, alack, that heaven should practise
stratagems
Upon so soft a subject as myself!
What say'st thou! Hast thou not a word of joy?
Some comfort, nurse.
NURSE Faith, here it is:
Romeo is banished; and all the world to nothing
That he dares ne'er come back to challenge you;
Or, if he do, it needs must be by stealth.
Then, since the case so stands as now it doth,
I think it best you married with the County.
O, he's a lovely gentleman!
Romeo's a dishclout to him; an eagle, madam,
Hath not so green, so quick, so fair an eye
As Paris hath. Beshrew my very heart,
I think you are happy in this second match,
For it excels your first; or, if it did not,
Your first is dead, or 'twere as good he were
As living here and you no use of him.
JULIET Speak'st thou from thy heart?
NURSE And from my soul too, else beshrew them
both.
JULIET Amen!
NURSE What?
JULIET Well, thou hast comforted me marvellous
much.
Go in; and tell my lady I am gone,
Having displeas'd my father, to Lawrence' cell
To make confession, and to be absolv'd.
NURSE Marry, I will; and this is wisely done.
[*Exit.*
JULIET Ancient damnation! O most wicked fiend!
Is it more sin to wish me thus forsworn,
Or to dispraise my lord with that same tongue
Which she hath prais'd him with above compare
So many thousand times? Go, counsellor;
Thou and my bosom henceforth shall be twain.
I'll to the friar to know his remedy;
If all else fail, myself have power to die. [*Exit.*

ACT FOUR

SCENE I. *Friar Lawrence's cell.*

Enter FRIAR LAWRENCE and COUNTY PARIS.

FRIAR LAWRENCE On Thursday, sir? The time is
very short.
PARIS My father Capulet will have it so,
And I am nothing slow to slack his haste.
FRIAR LAWRENCE You say you do not know the
lady's mind;
Uneven is the course; I like it not.
PARIS Immoderately she weeps for Tybalt's
death,
And therefore have I little talk'd of love;
For Venus smiles not in a house of tears.
Now, sir, her father counts it dangerous
That she do give her sorrow so much sway,
And in his wisdom hastes our marriage,
To stop the inundation of her tears;
Which, too much minded by herself alone,
May be put from her by society.
Now do you know the reason of this haste.

FRIAR LAWRENCE [*Aside*] I would I knew not why it should be slow'd. –
Look, sir, here comes the lady toward my cell.

Enter JULIET.

PARIS Happily met, my lady and my wife!
JULIET That may be, sir, when I may be a wife.
PARIS That may be must be, love, on Thursday next.
JULIET What must be shall be.
FRIAR LAWRENCE That's a certain text.
PARIS Come you to make confession to this father?
JULIET To answer that, I should confess to you.
PARIS Do not deny to him that you love me.
JULIET I will confess to you that I love him.
PARIS So will ye, I am sure, that you love me.
JULIET If I do so, it will be of more price
Being spoke behind your back than to your face.
PARIS Poor soul, thy face is much abus'd with tears.
JULIET The tears have got small victory by that,
For it was bad enough before their spite.
PARIS Thou wrong'st it more than tears with that report.
JULIET That is no slander, sir, which is a truth;
And what I spake, I spake it to my face.
PARIS Thy face is mine, and thou hast sland'red it.
JULIET It may be so, for it is not mine own.
Are you at leisure, holy father, now,
Or shall I come to you at evening mass?
FRIAR LAWRENCE My leisure serves me, pensive daughter, now.
My lord, we must entreat the time alone.
PARIS God shield I should disturb devotion!
Juliet, on Thursday early will I rouse ye;
Till then, adieu, and keep this holy kiss. [*Exit.*
JULIET O, shut the door, and when thou hast done so,
Come weep with me – past hope, past cure, past help.
FRIAR LAWRENCE O, Juliet, I already know thy grief;
It strains me past the compass of my wits.
I hear thou must, and nothing may prorogue it,
On Thursday next be married to this County.
JULIET Tell me not, friar, that thou hear'st of this,
Unless thou tell me how I may prevent it;
If, in thy wisdom, thou canst give no help,
Do thou but call my resolution wise,
And with this knife I'll help it presently.
God join'd my heart and Romeo's, thou our hands;
And ere this hand, by thee to Romeo's seal'd,
Shall be the label to another deed,
Or my true heart with treacherous revolt
Turn to another, this shall slay them both.
Therefore, out of thy long-experienc'd time,
Give me some present counsel; or, behold,
'Twixt my extremes and me this bloody knife
Shall play the umpire, arbitrating that
Which the commission of thy years and art
Could to no issue of true honour bring.
Be not so long to speak; I long to die,
If what thou speak'st speak not of remedy.
FRIAR LAWRENCE Hold, daughter; I do spy a kind of hope,
Which craves as desperate an execution
As that is desperate which we would prevent.
If, rather than to marry County Paris,
Thou hast the strength of will to slay thyself,
Then is it likely thou wilt undertake
A thing like death to chide away this shame,
That cop'st with death himself to scape from it;
And, if thou dar'st, I'll give thee remedy.
JULIET O, bid me leap, rather than marry Paris,
From off the battlements of any tower,
Or walk in thievish ways, or bid me lurk
Where serpents are; chain me with roaring bears,
Or hide me nightly in a charnel house,
O'er-cover'd quite with dead men's rattling bones,
With reeky shanks and yellow chapless skulls;
Or bid me go into a new-made grave,
And hide me with a dead man in his shroud –
Things that, to hear them told, have made me tremble –
And I will do it without fear or doubt,
To live an unstain'd wife to my sweet love.
FRIAR LAWRENCE Hold, then; go home, be merry, give consent
To marry Paris. Wednesday is to-morrow;
To-morrow night look that thou lie alone,
Let not the nurse lie with thee in thy chamber.
Take thou this vial, being then in bed,
And this distilled liquor drink thou off;
When presently through all thy veins shall run
A cold and drowsy humour; for no pulse
Shall keep his native progress, but surcease;
No warmth, no breath, shall testify thou livest;
The roses in thy lips and cheeks shall fade
To paly ashes, thy eyes' windows fall,
Like death when he shuts up the day of life;
Each part, depriv'd of supple government,
Shall, stiff and stark and cold, appear like death;
And in this borrow'd likeness of shrunk death
Thou shalt continue two and forty hours,
And then awake as from a pleasant sleep.
Now, when the bridegroom in the morning comes
To rouse thee from thy bed, there art thou dead.
Then, as the manner of our country is,

In thy best robes, uncovered on the bier,
Thou shalt be borne to that same ancient vault
Where all the kindred of the Capulets lie.
In the meantime, against thou shalt awake,
Shall Romeo by my letters know our drift,
And hither shall he come; and he and I
Will watch thy waking, and that very night
Shall Romeo bear thee hence to Mantua.
And this shall free thee from this present shame,
If no inconstant toy nor womanish fear
Abate thy valour in the acting it.

JULIET Give me, give me! O, tell not me of fear!

FRIAR LAWRENCE Hold; get you gone, be strong and prosperous
In this resolve. I'll send a friar with speed
To Mantua, with my letters to thy lord.

JULIET Love give me strength! and strength shall help afford.
Farewell, dear father! *[Exeunt.*

SCENE II. *Capulet's house.*

Enter CAPULET, LADY CAPULET, Nurse, and two or three Servingmen.

CAPULET So many guests invite as here are writ. *[Exit a Servingmen.*
Sirrah, go hire me twenty cunning cooks.

SERVANT You shall have none ill, sir; for I'll try if they can lick their fingers.

CAPULET How canst thou try them so?

SERVANT Marry, sir, 'tis an ill cook that cannot lick his own fingers; therefore he that cannot lick his fingers goes not with me.

CAPULET Go, be gone. *[Exit second Servant.*
We shall be much unfurnish'd for this time.
What, is my daughter gone to Friar Lawrence?

NURSE Ay, forsooth.

CAPULET Well, he may chance to do some good on her:
A peevish self-will'd harlotry it is.

Enter JULIET.

NURSE See where she comes from shrift with merry look.

CAPULET How now, my headstrong! Where have you been gadding?

JULIET Where I have learnt me to repent the sin
Of disobedient opposition
To you and your behests; and am enjoin'd
By holy Lawrence to fall prostrate here,
To beg your pardon. Pardon, I beseech you.
Henceforward I am ever rul'd by you.

CAPULET Send for the County; go tell him of this.
I'll have this knot knit up to-morrow morning.

JULIET I met the youthful lord at Lawrence' cell,
And gave him what becomed love I might,
Not stepping o'er the bounds of modesty.

CAPULET Why, I am glad on't; this is well – stand up –
This is as't should be. Let me see the County;
Ay, marry, go, I say, and fetch him hither.
Now, afore God, this reverend holy friar,
All our whole city is much bound to him.

JULIET Nurse, will you go with me into my closet
To help me sort such needful ornaments
As you think fit to furnish me to-morrow?

LADY CAPULET No, not till Thursday; there is time enough.

CAPULET Go, nurse, go with her. We'll to church to-morrow. *[Exeunt Juliet and Nurse.*

LADY CAPULET We shall be short in our provision;
'Tis now near night.

CAPULET Tush, I will stir about,
And all things shall be well, I warrant thee, wife.
Go thou to Juliet, help to deck up her;
I'll not to bed to-night; let me alone.
I'll play the huswife for this once. What, ho!
They are all forth; well, I will walk myself
To County Paris, to prepare up him
Against to-morrow. My heart is wondrous light
Since this same wayward girl is so reclaim'd.
[Exeunt.

SCENE III. *Juliet's chamber.*

Enter JULIET and Nurse.

JULIET Ay, those attires are best; but, gentle nurse,
I pray thee, leave me to myself to-night,
For I have need of many orisons
To move the heavens to smile upon my state,
Which well thou knowest is cross and full of sin.

Enter LADY CAPULET.

LADY CAPULET What, are you busy, ho? Need you my help?

JULIET No, madam; we have cull'd such necessaries
As are behoveful for our state to-morrow.
So please you, let me now be left alone,
And let the nurse this night sit up with you;
For I am sure you have your hands full all
In this so sudden business.

LADY CAPULET Good night.
Get thee to bed, and rest; for thou hast need.
[Exeunt Lady Capulet and Nurse.

JULIET Farewell! God knows when we shall meet again.
I have a faint cold fear thrills through my veins,
That almost freezes up the heat of life;

I'll call them back again to comfort me.
Nurse! – What should she do here?
My dismal scene I needs must act alone.
Come, vial.
What if this mixture do not work at all?
Shall I be married, then, to-morrow morning?
No, no; this shall forbid it. Lie thou there.
[Laying down her dagger.
What if it be a poison which the friar
Subtly hath minist'red to have me dead,
Lest in this marriage he should be dishonour'd,
Because he married me before to Romeo?
I fear it is; and yet methinks it should not,
For he hath still been tried a holy man.
How if, when I am laid into the tomb,
I wake before the time that Romeo
Come to redeem me? There's a fearful point.
Shall I not then be stifled in the vault,
To whose foul mouth no healthsome air breathes in,
And there die strangled ere my Romeo comes?
Or, if I live, is it not very like
The horrible conceit of death and night,
Together with the terror of the place –
As in a vault, an ancient receptacle
Where for this many hundred years the bones
Of all my buried ancestors are pack'd;
Where bloody Tybalt, yet but green in earth,
Lies fest'ring in his shroud; where, as they say,
At some hours in the night spirits resort –
Alack, alack, is it not like that I,
So early waking – what with loathsome smells,
And shrieks like mandrakes' torn out of the earth,
That living mortals, hearing them, run mad –
O, if I wake, shall I not be distraught,
Environed with all these hideous fears,
And madly play with my forefathers' joints,
And pluck the mangled Tybalt from his shroud,
And, in this rage, with some great kinsman's bone,
As with a club, dash out my desp'rate brains?
O, look! methinks I see my cousin's ghost
Seeking out Romeo, that did spit his body
Upon a rapier's point. Stay, Tybalt, stay.
Romeo, I come. This do I drink to thee.
[She drinks and falls upon her bed within the curtains

SCENE IV. *Capulet's house.*

Enter LADY CAPULET and Nurse.

LADY CAPULET Hold, take these keys, and fetch more spices, nurse.

NURSE They call for dates and quinces in the pastry.

Enter CAPULET.

CAPULET Come, stir, stir, stir! The second cock hath crow'd,
The curfew bell hath rung, 'tis three o'clock.
Look to the bak'd meats, good Angelica;
Spare not for cost.

NURSE Go, you cot-quean, go,
Get you to bed; faith, you'll be sick to-morrow
For this night's watching.

CAPULET No, not a whit; what! I have watch'd ere now
All night for lesser cause, and ne'er been sick.

LADY CAPULET Ay, you have been a mouse-hunt in your time;
But I will watch you from such watching now.
[Exeunt Lady Capulet and Nurse.

CAPULET A jealous-hood, a jealous-hood!

Enter three or four Servants with spits and logs and baskets.

Now, fellow,
What is there?

1 FELLOW Things for the cook, sir; but I know not what.

CAPULET Make haste, make haste. *[Exit 1 Fellow*
Sirrah, fetch drier logs;
Call Peter; he will show thee where they are.

2 FELLOW I have a head, sir, that will find out logs,
And never trouble Peter for the matter.

CAPULET Mass, and well said; a merry whoreson, ha!
Thou shalt be logger-head. *[Exit 2 Fellow*
Good faith, 'tis day;
The County will be here with music straight,
For so he said he would. *[Play music]* I hear him near.
Nurse! Wife! What, ho! What, nurse, I say!

Re-enter Nurse.

Go waken Juliet, go and trim her up;
I'll go and chat with Paris. Hie, make haste,
Make haste. The bridegroom he is come already.
Make haste, I say. *[Exeunt.*

SCENE V. *Juliet's chamber.*

Enter Nurse.

NURSE Mistress! What, mistress! Juliet! Fast, I warrant her, she.
Why, lamb! Why, lady! Fie, you slug-a-bed!
Why, love, I say! madam! sweetheart! Why, bride!
What, not a word? You take your penny-worths now

Sleep for a week; for the next night, I warrant,
The County Paris hath set up his rest
That you shall rest but little. God forgive me!
Marry, and amen. How sound is she asleep!
I needs must wake her. Madam, madam, madam!
Ay, let the County take you in your bed;
He'll fright you up, i' faith. Will it not be?

[Draws the curtains.

What, dress'd, and in your clothes, and down again!
I must needs wake you. Lady! lady! lady!
Alas, alas! Help, help! my lady's dead!
O well-a-day that ever I was born!
Some aqua-vitae, ho! My lord! My lady!

Enter LADY CAPULET.

LADY CAPULET What noise is here?
NURSE O lamentable day!
LADY CAPULET What is the matter?
NURSE Look, look! O heavy day!
LADY CAPULET O me, O me! My child, my only life,
Revive, look up, or I will die with thee!
Help, help! Call help.

Enter CAPULET.

CAPULET For shame, bring Juliet forth; her lord is come.
NURSE She's dead, deceas'd, she's dead; alack the day!
LADY CAPULET Alack the day, she's dead, she's dead, she's dead!
CAPULET Ha! let me see her. Out, alas! she's cold;
Her blood is settled, and her joints are stiff.
Life and these lips have long been separated.
Death lies on her like an untimely frost
Upon the sweetest flower of all the field.
NURSE O lamentable day!
LADY CAPULET O woeful time!
CAPULET Death, that hath ta'en her hence to make me wail,
Ties up my tongue and will not let me speak.

Enter FRIAR LAWRENCE and COUNTY PARIS, with Musicians.

FRIAR LAWRENCE Come, is the bride ready to go to church?
CAPULET Ready to go, but never to return.
O son, the night before thy wedding day
Hath Death lain with thy wife. There she lies,
Flower as she was, deflowered by him.
Death is my son-in-law, Death is my heir;
My daughter he hath wedded; I will die,
And leave him all; life, living, all is Death's.
PARIS Have I thought long to see this morning's face,
And doth it give me such a sight as this?
LADY CAPULET Accurs'd, unhappy, wretched, hateful day!
Most miserable hour that e'er time saw
In lasting labour of his pilgrimage!
But one, poor one, one poor and loving child,
But one thing to rejoice and solace in,
And cruel Death hath catch'd it from my sight!
NURSE O woe! O woeful, woeful, woeful day!
Most lamentable day, most woeful day
That ever, ever, I did yet behold!
O day! O day! O day! O hateful day!
Never was seen so black a day as this.
O woeful day, O woeful day!
PARIS Beguil'd, divorced, wronged, spited, slain!
Most detestable Death, by thee beguil'd,
By cruel cruel thee quite overthrown!
O love! O life! – not life, but love in death!
CAPULET Despis'd, distressed, hated, martyr'd, kill'd! –
Uncomfortable time, why cam'st thou now
To murder, murder our solemnity?
O child! O child! my soul, and not my child!
Dead art thou; alack, my child is dead,
And with my child my joys are buried.
FRIAR LAWRENCE Peace, ho, for shame! Confusion's cure lives not
In these confusions. Heaven and yourself
Had part in this fair maid; now heaven hath all,
And all the better is it for the maid.
Your part in her you could not keep from death,
But heaven keeps his part in eternal life.
The most you sought was her promotion,
For 'twas your heaven she should be advanc'd;
And weep ye now, seeing she is advanc'd
Above the clouds, as high as heaven itself?
O, in this love, you love your child so ill
That you run mad, seeing that she is well.
She's not well married that lives married long,
But she's best married that dies married young.
Dry up your tears, and stick your rosemary
On this fair corse, and, as the custom is,
In all her best array bear her to church;
For though fond nature bids us all lament,
Yet nature's tears are reason's merriment.
CAPULET All things that we ordained festival
Turn from their office to black funeral:
Our instruments to melancholy bells,
Our wedding cheer to a sad burial feast,
Our solemn hymns to sullen dirges change;
Our bridal flowers serve for a buried corse;
And all things change them to the contrary.
FRIAR LAWRENCE Sir, go you in; and, madam, go with him;
And go, Sir Paris. Every one prepare
To follow this fair corse unto her grave.
The heavens do lour upon you for some ill;

Move them no more by crossing their high will.
[*Exeunt all but Nurse and Musicians.*

1 MUSICIAN Faith, we may put up our pipes and be gone.

NURSE Honest good fellows, ah, put up, put up;
For well you know this is a pitiful case. [*Exit*

1 MUSICIAN Ay, by my troth, the case may be amended.

Enter PETER.

PETER Musicians, O, musicians, 'Heart's ease', 'Heart's ease'! O, an you will have me live, play 'Heart's ease'.

1 MUSICIAN Why 'Heart's ease'?

PETER O, musicians, because my heart itself plays 'My heart is full of woe'. O, play me some merry dump to comfort me.

1 MUSICIAN Not a dump we! 'Tis no time to play now.

PETER You will not, then?

1 MUSICIAN No.

PETER I will then give it you soundly.

1 MUSICIAN What will you give us?

PETER No money, on my faith, but the gleek. I will give you the minstrel.

1 MUSICIAN Then will I give you the serving-creature.

PETER Then will I lay the serving-creature's dagger on your pate. I will carry no crotchets: I'll re you, I'll fa you; do you note me?

1 MUSICIAN An you re us and fa us, you note us.

2 MUSICIAN Pray you put up your dagger, and put out your wit.

PETER Then have at you with my wit! I will dry-beat you with an iron wit, and put up my iron dagger. Answer me like men.
'When griping grief the heart doth wound
And doleful dumps the mind oppress,
Then music with her silver sound' –

Why 'silver sound'? Why 'music with her silver sound'? What say you, Simon Catling?

1 MUSICIAN Marry, sir, because silver hath a sweet sound.

PETER Pretty! What say you, Hugh Rebeck?

2 MUSICIAN I say 'silver sound' because musicians sound for silver.

PETER Pretty too! What say you, James Soundpost?

3 MUSICIAN Faith, I know not what to say.

PETER O, I cry you mercy, you are the singer; I will say for you. It is 'music with her silver sound' because musicians have no gold for sounding.

'Then music with her silver sound
With speedy help doth lend redress.'

[*Exit.*

1 MUSICIAN What a pestilent knave is this same!

2 MUSICIAN Hang him, Jack! Come, we'll in here; tarry for the mourners, and stay dinner.

[*Exeunt.*

ACT FIVE

SCENE I. *Mantua. A street.*

Enter ROMEO.

ROMEO If I may trust the flattering truth of sleep,
My dreams presage some joyful news at hand.
My bosom's lord sits lightly in his throne,
And all this day an unaccustom'd spirit
Lifts me above the ground with cheerful thoughts.
I dreamt my lady came and found me dead –
Strange dream, that gives a dead man leave to think! –
And breath'd such life with kisses in my lips
That I reviv'd, and was an emperor.
Ah me! how sweet is love itself possess'd,
When but love's shadows are so rich in joy!

Enter BALTHASAR, Romeo's man.

News from Verona! How now, Balthasar!
Dost thou not bring me letters from the friar?
How doth my lady? Is my father well?
How fares my Juliet? That I ask again,
For nothing can be ill if she be well.

BALTHASAR Then she is well, and nothing can be ill.
Her body sleeps in Capels' monument,
And her immortal part with angels lives.
I saw her laid low in her kindred's vault,
And presently took post to tell it you.
O, pardon me for bringing these ill news,
Since you did leave it for my office, sir.

ROMEO Is it e'en so? Then I defy you, stars.
Thou knowest my lodging: get me ink and paper,
And hire post-horses; I will hence to-night.

BALTHASAR I do beseech you, sir, have patience;
Your looks are pale and wild, and do import
Some misadventure.

ROMEO Tush, thou art deceiv'd;
Leave me, and do the thing I bid thee do.
Hast thou no letters to me from the friar?

BALTHASAR No, my good lord.

ROMEO No matter; get thee gone,

And hire those horses; I'll be with thee straight.
[*Exit Balthasar.*
Well, Juliet, I will lie with thee to-night.
Let's see for means. O mischief, thou art swift
To enter in the thoughts of desperate men!
I do remember an apothecary,
And hereabouts 'a dwells, which late I noted
In tatt'red weeds, with overwhelming brows,
Culling of simples. Meagre were his looks;
Sharp misery had worn him to the bones;
And in his needy shop a tortoise hung,
An alligator stuff'd, and other skins
Of ill-shap'd fishes; and about his shelves
A beggarly account of empty boxes,
Green earthen pots, bladders, and musty seeds,
Remnants of packthread, and old cakes of roses,
Were thinly scattered, to make up a show.
Noting this penury, to myself I said
'An if a man did need a poison now,
Whose sale is present death in Mantua,
Here lives a caitiff wretch would sell it him'.
O, this same thought did but forerun my need;
And this same needy man must sell it me.
As I remember, this should be the house.
Being holiday, the beggar's shop is shut.
What, ho! Apothecary!

Enter Apothecary.

APOTHECARY Who calls so loud?

ROMEO Come hither, man. I see that thou art poor.
Hold, there is forty ducats; let me have
A dram of poison, such soon-speeding gear
As will disperse itself through all the veins
That the life-weary taker may fall dead,
And that the trunk may be discharg'd of breath
As violently as hasty powder fir'd
Doth hurry from the fatal cannon's womb.

APOTHECARY Such mortal drugs I have; but Mantua's law
Is death to any he that utters them.

ROMEO Art thou so bare and full of wretchedness
And fearest to die? Famine is in thy cheeks,
Need and oppression starveth in thy eyes,
Contempt and beggary hangs upon thy back,
The world is not thy friend, nor the world's law;
The world affords no law to make thee rich;
Then be not poor, but break it and take this.

APOTHECARY My poverty but not my will consents.

ROMEO I pay thy poverty and not thy will.

APOTHECARY Put this in any liquid thing you will
And drink it off; and if you had the strength
Of twenty men, it would dispatch you straight.

ROMEO There is thy gold – worse poison to men's souls,
Doing more murder in this loathsome world
Than these poor compounds that thou mayst not sell.
I sell thee poison: thou hast sold me none.
Farewell; buy food, and get thyself in flesh.
Come, cordial and not poison, go with me
To Juliet's grave; for there must I use thee.
[*Exeunt*

SCENE II. *Friar Lawrence's cell.*

Enter FRIAR JOHN.

FRIAR JOHN Holy Franciscan friar! Brother, ho!

Enter FRIAR LAWRENCE.

FRIAR LAWRENCE This same should be the voice of Friar John.
Welcome from Mantua! What says Romeo?
Or, if his mind be writ, give me his letter.

FRIAR JOHN Going to find a barefoot brother out,
One of our order, to associate me,
Here in this city visiting the sick,
And finding him, the searchers of the town,
Suspecting that we both were in a house
Where the infectious pestilence did reign,
Seal'd up the doors, and would not let us forth,
So that my speed to Mantua there was stay'd.

FRIAR LAWRENCE Who bare my letter, then, to Romeo?

FRIAR JOHN I could not send it – here it is again –
Nor get a messenger to bring it thee,
So fearful were they of infection.

FRIAR LAWRENCE Unhappy fortune! By my brotherhood,
The letter was not nice, but full of charge
Of dear import; and the neglecting it
May do much danger. Friar John, go hence;
Get me an iron crow, and bring it straight
Unto my cell.

FRIAR JOHN Brother, I'll go and bring it thee.
[*Exit.*

FRIAR LAWRENCE Now must I to the monument alone.
Within this three hours will fair Juliet wake;
She will beshrew me much that Romeo
Hath had no notice of these accidents.
But I will write again to Mantua,
And keep her at my cell till Romeo come –
Poor living corse, clos'd in a dead man's tomb!
[*Exit*

SCENE III. *Verona. A churchyard; in it the tomb of the Capulets.*

Enter PARIS, and his Page bearing flowers and a torch.

PARIS Give me thy torch, boy; hence, and stand aloof;

Yet put it out, for I would not be seen.
Under yond yew trees lay thee all along,
Holding thy ear close to the hollow ground;
So shall no foot upon the churchyard tread –
Being loose, unfirm, with digging up of graves –
But thou shalt hear it. Whistle then to me,
As signal that thou hearest something approach.
Give me those flowers. Do as I bid thee, go.

PAGE [*Aside*] I am almost afraid to stand alone
Here in the churchyard; yet I will adventure.
[*Retires.*

PARIS Sweet flower, with flowers thy bridal bed I strew –
O woe, thy canopy is dust and stones! –
Which with sweet water nightly I will dew;
Or, wanting that, with tears distill'd by moans.
The obsequies that I for thee will keep,
Nightly shall be to strew thy grave and weep.
[*The Page whistles.*
The boy gives warning something doth approach.
What cursed foot wanders this way to-night
To cross my obsequies and true love's rite?
What, with a torch! Muffle me, night, awhile.
[*Retires.*

Enter ROMEO and BALTHASAR, with a torch, a mattock, and a crow of iron.

ROMEO Give me that mattock and the wrenching iron.
Hold, take this letter; early in the morning
See thou deliver it to my lord and father.
Give me the light; upon thy life I charge thee,
Whate'er thou hearest or seest, stand all aloof
And do not interrupt me in my course.
Why I descend into this bed of death
Is partly to behold my lady's face,
But chiefly to take thence from her dead finger
A precious ring – a ring that I must use
In dear employment; therefore hence, be gone.
But if thou, jealous, dost return to pry
In what I farther shall intend to do,
By heaven, I will tear thee joint by joint,
And strew this hungry churchyard with thy limbs.
The time and my intents are savage-wild,
More fierce and more inexorable far
Than empty tigers or the roaring sea.

BALTHASAR I will be gone, sir, and not trouble ye.

ROMEO So shalt thou show me friendship. Take thou that;
Live and be prosperous; and farewell, good fellow.

BALTHASAR [*Aside*] For all this same, I'll hide me hereabout;
His looks I fear, and his intents I doubt.
[*Retires.*

ROMEO Thou detestable maw, thou womb of death,
Gorg'd with the dearest morsel of the earth,
Thus I enforce thy rotten jaws to open,
[*Breaking open the tomb.*
And, in despite, I'll cram thee with more food.

PARIS This is that banish'd haughty Montague
That murd'red my love's cousin – with which grief
It is supposed the fair creature died –
And here is come to do some villainous shame
To the dead bodies. I will apprehend him.
Stop thy unhallowed toil, vile Montague.
Can vengeance be pursued further than death?
Condemned villain, I do apprehend thee.
Obey, and go with me; for thou must die.

ROMEO I must indeed; and therefore came I hither.
Good gentle youth, tempt not a desp'rate man;
Fly hence, and leave me. Think upon these gone;
Let them affright thee. I beseech thee, youth,
Put not another sin upon my head
By urging me to fury; O, be gone!
By heaven, I love thee better than myself,
For I come hither arm'd against myself.
Stay not, be gone; live, and hereafter say
A madman's mercy bid thee run away.

PARIS I do defy thy conjuration,
And apprehend thee for a felon here.

ROMEO Wilt thou provoke me? Then have at thee, boy! [*They fight.*

PAGE O lord, they fight! I will go call the watch.
[*Exit. Paris falls.*

PARIS O, I am slain! If thou be merciful,
Open the tomb, lay me with Juliet. [*Dies.*

ROMEO In faith, I will. Let me peruse this face.
Mercutio's kinsman, noble County Paris!
What said my man, when my betossed soul
Did not attend him as we rode? I think
He told me Paris should have married Juliet.
Said he not so, or did I dream it so?
Or am I mad, hearing him talk of Juliet,
To think it was so? O, give me thy hand,
One writ with me in sour misfortune's book!
I'll bury thee in a triumphant grave.
A grave? O no! A lantern, slaught'red youth;
For here lies Juliet, and her beauty makes
This vault a feasting presence full of light.
Death, lie thou there, by a dead man interr'd.
[*Laying Paris in the tomb.*

How oft when men are at the point of death
Have they been merry! Which their keepers
call
A lightning before death. O, how may I
Call this a lightning? O my love! my wife!
Death, that hath suck'd the honey of thy
breath,
Hath had no power yet upon thy beauty.
Thou art not conquer'd; beauty's ensign yet
Is crimson in thy lips and in thy cheeks,
And death's pale flag is not advanced there.
Tybalt, liest thou there in thy bloody sheet?
O, what more favour can I do to thee
Than with that hand that cut thy youth in
twain
To sunder his that was thine enemy?
Forgive me, cousin. Ah, dear Juliet,
Why art thou yet so fair? Shall I believe
That unsubstantial Death is amorous,
And that the lean abhorred monster keeps
Thee here in dark to be his paramour?
For fear of that I still will stay with thee,
And never from this palace of dim night
Depart again. Here, here will I remain
With worms that are thy chambermaids. O,
here
Will I set up my everlasting rest,
And shake the yoke of inauspicious stars
From this world-wearied flesh. Eyes, look your
last.
Arms, take your last embrace. And, lips, O you
The doors of breath, seal with a righteous kiss
A dateless bargain to engrossing death!
Come, bitter conduct, come, unsavoury guide.
Thou desperate pilot, now at once run on
The dashing rocks thy sea-sick weary bark.
Here's to my love! [*Drinks*] O true apothecary!
Thy drugs are quick. Thus with a kiss I die.
[*Falls.*

Enter FRIAR LAWRENCE, with lantern, crow, and spade.

FRIAR LAWRENCE Saint Francis be my speed!
How oft to-night
Have my old feet stumbled at graves!
Who's there?

BALTHASAR Here's one, a friend, and one that
knows you well.

FRIAR LAWRENCE Bliss be upon you! Tell me,
good my friend,
What torch is yond that vainly lends his light
To grubs and eyeless skulls? As I discern,
It burneth in the Capels' monument.

BALTHASAR It doth so, holy sir; and there's my
master,
One that you love.

FRIAR LAWRENCE Who is it?

BALTHASAR Romeo.

FRIAR LAWRENCE How long hath he been there?

BALTHASAR Full half an hour.

FRIAR LAWRENCE Go with me to the vault.

BALTHASAR I dare not, sir.
My master knows not but I am gone hence,
And fearfully did menace me with death,
If I did stay to look on his intents.

FRIAR LAWRENCE Stay, then, I'll go alone; fear
comes upon me;
O, much I fear some ill unthrifty thing.

BALTHASAR As I did sleep under this yew tree
here,
I dreamt my master and another fought,
And that my master slew him.

FRIAR LAWRENCE Romeo!
Alack, alack, what blood is this which stains
The stony entrance of this sepulchre?
What mean these masterless and gory swords
To lie discolour'd by this place of peace?
[*Enters the tomb.*
Romeo! O, pale! Who else? What, Paris too?
And steep'd in blood? Ah, what an unkind
hour
Is guilty of this lamentable chance!
The lady stirs. [*Juliet wakes.*

JULIET O comfortable friar! Where is my lord?
I do remember well where I should be,
And there I am. Where is my Romeo?
[*Noise within.*

FRIAR LAWRENCE I hear some noise. Lady, come
from that nest
Of death, contagion, and unnatural sleep;
A greater power than we can contradict
Hath thwarted our intents. Come, come away;
Thy husband in thy bosom there lies dead;
And Paris too. Come, I'll dispose of thee
Among a sisterhood of holy nuns.
Stay not to question, for the watch is coming;
Come, go, good Juliet. I dare no longer stay.

JULIET Go, get thee hence, for I will not away.
[*Exit Friar Lawrence.*
What's here? A cup, clos'd in my true love's
hand?
Poison, I see, hath been his timeless end.
O churl! drunk all, and left no friendly drop
To help me after? I will kiss thy lips;
Haply some poison yet doth hang on them,
To make me die with a restorative.
[*Kisses him*
Thy lips are warm.

1 WATCH [*Within*] Lead, boy. Which way?

JULIET Yea, noise? Then I'll be brief. O happy
dagger!
[*Snatching Romeo's dagger.*

This is thy sheath; there rust, and let me die.
[She stabs herself and falls on Romeo's body.

Enter Watch, with Paris's Page.

PAGE This is the place; there, where the torch doth burn.
1 WATCH The ground is bloody; search about the churchyard.
Go, some of you, whoe'er you find attach.
[Exeunt some of the Watch.
Pitiful sight! here lies the County slain;
And Juliet bleeding, warm, and newly dead,
Who here hath lain this two days buried.
Go, tell the Prince; run to the Capulets;
Raise up the Montagues; some others search.
[Exeunt others of the Watch.
We see the ground whereon these woes do lie;
But the true ground of all these piteous woes
We cannot without circumstance descry.

Re-enter some of the Watch with BALTHASAR.

2 WATCH Here's Romeo's man; we found him in the churchyard.
1 WATCH Hold him in safety till the Prince come hither.

Re-enter FRIAR LAWRENCE and another Watchman.

3 WATCH Here is a friar that trembles, sighs, and weeps;
We took this mattock and this spade from him,
As he was coming from this churchyard's side.
1 WATCH A great suspicion; stay the friar too.

Enter the PRINCE and Attendants.

PRINCE What misadventure is so early up,
That calls our person from our morning rest?

Enter CAPULET, LADY CAPULET, and Others.

CAPULET What should it be that is so shriek'd abroad?
LADY CAPULET The people in the street cry 'Romeo',
Some 'Juliet' and some 'Paris'; and all run,
With open outcry, toward our monument.
PRINCE What fear is this which startles in our ears?
1 WATCH Sovereign, here lies the County Paris slain;
And Romeo dead; and Juliet, dead before,
Warm and new kill'd.
PRINCE Search, seek, and know how this foul murder comes.
1 WATCH Here is a friar, and slaughter'd Romeo's man,
With instruments upon them fit to open
These dead men's tombs.
CAPULET O heavens! O wife, look how our daughter bleeds!
This dagger hath mista'en, for, lo, his house
Is empty on the back of Montague,
And it mis-sheathed in my daughter's bosom.
LADY CAPULET O me! this sight of death is as a bell
That warns my old age to a sepulchre.

Enter MONTAGUE and Others.

PRINCE Come, Montague, for thou art early up
To see thy son and heir more early down.
MONTAGUE Alas, my liege, my wife is dead to-night;
Grief of my son's exile hath stopp'd her breath.
What further woe conspires against mine age?
PRINCE Look, and thou shalt see.
MONTAGUE O thou untaught! what manners is in this,
To press before thy father to a grave?
PRINCE Seal up the mouth of outrage for a while,
Till we can clear these ambiguities,
And know their spring, their head, their true descent;
And then will I be general of your woes,
And lead you even to death. Meantime forbear,
And let mischance be slave to patience.
Bring forth the parties of suspicion.
FRIAR LAWRENCE I am the greatest, able to do least,
Yet most suspected, as the time and place
Doth make against me, of this direful murder;
And here I stand, both to impeach and purge
Myself condemned and myself excus'd.
PRINCE Then say at once what thou dost know in this.
FRIAR LAWRENCE I will be brief, for my short date of breath
Is not so long as is a tedious tale.
Romeo, there dead, was husband to that Juliet;
And she, there dead, that Romeo's faithful wife.
I married them; and their stol'n marriage day
Was Tybalt's doomsday, whose untimely death
Banish'd the new-made bridegroom from this city;
For whom, and not for Tybalt, Juliet pin'd.
You, to remove that siege of grief from her,
Betroth'd, and would have married her perforce,
To County Paris. Then comes she to me,
And with wild looks bid me devise some mean
To rid her from this second marriage,
Or in my cell there would she kill herself.
Then gave I her, so tutor'd by my art,
A sleeping potion; which so took effect
As I intended, for it wrought on her
The form of death. Meantime I writ to Romeo
That he should hither come as this dire night

To help to take her from her borrowed grave,
Being the time the potion's force should cease.
But he which bore my letter, Friar John,
Was stay'd by accident, and yesternight
Return'd my letter back. Then all alone
At the prefixed hour of her waking
Came I to take her from her kindred's vault;
Meaning to keep her closely at my cell
Till I conveniently could send to Romeo.
But when I came, some minute ere the time
Of her awakening, here untimely lay
The noble Paris and true Romeo dead.
She wakes; and I entreated her come forth,
And bear this work of heaven with patience.
But then a noise did scare me from the tomb,
And she, too desperate, would not go with me,
But, as it seems, did violence on herself.
All this I know, and to the marriage
Her nurse is privy; and if ought in this
Miscarried by my fault, let my old life
Be sacrific'd, some hour before his time,
Unto the rigour of severest law.

PRINCE We still have known thee for a holy man.
Where's Romeo's man? What can he say to this?

BALTHASAR I brought my master news of Juliet's death;
And then in post he came from Mantua
To this same place, to this same monument.
This letter he early bid me give his father;
And threat'ned me with death, going in the vault,
If I departed not and left him there.

PRINCE Give me the letter, I will look on it.
Where is the County's page that rais'd the watch?
Sirrah, what made your master in this place?

PAGE He came with flowers to strew his lady's grave;
And bid me stand aloof, and so I did.
Anon comes one with light to ope the tomb;
And by and by my master drew on him;
And then I ran away to call the watch.

PRINCE This letter doth make good the friar's words,
Their course of love, the tidings of her death;
And here he writes that he did buy a poison
Of a poor pothecary, and therewithal
Came to this vault to die, and lie with Juliet.
Where be these enemies? Capulet, Montague,
See what a scourge is laid upon your hate,
That heaven finds means to kill your joys with love!
And I, for winking at your discords too,
Have lost a brace of kinsmen. All are punish'd.

CAPULET O brother Montague, give me thy hand.
This is my daughter's jointure, for no more
Can I demand.

MONTAGUE But I can give thee more;
For I will raise her statue in pure gold,
That whiles Verona by that name is known,
There shall no figure at such rate be set
As that of true and faithful Juliet.

CAPULET As rich shall Romeo's by his lady's lie –
Poor sacrifices of our enmity!

PRINCE A glooming peace this morning with it brings;
The sun for sorrow will not show his head.
Go hence, to have more talk of these sad things;
Some shall be pardon'd and some punished;
For never was a story of more woe
Than this of Juliet and her Romeo. [*Exeunt.*

Timon of Athens

Introduction by DONALD MACKENZIE

Timon is the Ugly Duckling of Shakespearean tragedy and no critic, not even Wilson Knight (1949, 1964), has advanced a reading which persuasively reveals it as, in the end, a swan. Some features – the sketchiness of Alcibiades as foil or counterweight to Timon, the possible muddle over epitaphs in Act 5 Scene 4, the writing that in places seems only to have had its first blocking in as against its wrought brilliance in others strongly suggest a play left unfinished. On any view *Timon* is an extreme and isolated work, marginal to the other tragedies, if not eccentric. It lacks the family bonding and rending that beats at the heart of so much Shakespearean tragedy – never more fiercely than in *Lear*, with which *Timon* has sometimes been misleadingly paired. Its protagonist has no wife, no family, no ancestors. In the first half of the play he moves in a social world projected by satire as an x-ray skeleton print; in the second the world of nature provides a cosmic amphitheatre to reverberate his denunciations of mankind. If the primary human relationships are those of family, friendship and service, it might be claimed that this play centres the second (and to a much lesser degree the third) at the expense of the first, and that Timon's is a tragedy of friendship betrayed. But this would overlook the ironies which question his bounty from the start, and not only in its recklessness [e.g. 1.2.1881] or the sentimentality that tinges it [1.2.84f]. Absolute generosity has its own ambivalence. When Timon on his first entry declares he will ransom Ventidius who is imprisoned for debt, the latter's messenger responds: 'Your lordship ever binds him' [1.1.107]. The half-obsequious gratitude concentrates an irony adumbrated in the preceding dialogue of Poet and Painter [1.1.45f] on Timon's munificence. (But if we recall Shakespeare's probing of generosity and its bonds in that earlier money-dominated play, *The Merchant of Venice*, we register how schematic, how much a morality play of ideas, *Timon* is).

Irony distends itself into the satiric inversions of feasting as an image of fellowship (mounting from the comments of Apemantus in 1.2.38f and the First Stranger in 3.2.63f, with their suggestions of a eucharist monstrously parodied, to the climax of Timon's mock-banquet in 3.6). Satire in the first half of the play can be swift, and intimate with its targets (Bayley, 1981); in the second it plates itself in the magnificence of Timon's static invectives. Its dominating presence gives the play a closer kinship with the drama of Middleton (now widely held to have collaborated on it) or Jonson than with anything in Shakespeare.

Yet *Timon*'s very extremism can crystallise out key elements of Shakespearean tragedy at large, most notably in the pivotal scene of rejection [3,4] and in the (non-) staging of the protagonist's death. In the first, a recurrent tragic paradigm is reduced to blade-edged intensity. The paradigm is that in which the hero absorbs the forces which assail him, intensifies and projects, and, in so doing, masters them, but with a mastery that points to his ultimate destruction. This is what we have in Lear's flinging out into the storm or in Macbeth's waking out of his half-tranced horror at the end of the banquet scene ('I am in blood/Stepp'd in so far that, should I wade no more,/Returning were as tedious as go o'er') to resolve on hardening himself in evil. In *Timon* the effect is of a naked, sacrificial savagery. But through this there flickers the sense of a histrionic violence in Timon himself. Either could be linked with other aspects of the play; the problem of integrating them may point up an uncertainty at its core in the conception of its protagonist.

A second paradigm is that of the tragic protagonists' self-defining in death. They concentrate what they have been and are in a speech (Othello, Cleopatra) or an image (Coriolanus as an 'eagle in a dove-cote') or an action (Lear looking for the feather to stir on the lips of the dead Cordelia). Timon dies off-stage, his self-defining only a last snarl of rejection. This is relayed to us through the soldier's wax impression (which – a nice small touch – would reverse the original carving of the epitaph). Alcibiades who reads it lifts it into his own valediction: 'rich conceit/Taught thee to make vast Neptune weep for aye/On thy low grave, on faults forgiven'. This consummates that imagination of the liquid and free-moving that wells up intermittently in this angular, metallic play: in its opening characterisations of poetry [1.1.22–7 and 48–53], in the break-up [4.2] of Timon's household, and most hauntingly in Timon's proclamation [5.1.213–5] of his own coming burial 'Upon the beached verge of the salt flood,/Who once a day with his embossed froth/The turbulent surge shall cover.' This sea-music is one of several features in *Timon* that anticipate the romances; but it evokes no such intimations of renewal as a like music does in *Pericles* or *The Tempest* Instead Alcibiades, dovetailing it into the cyclic patterns of nature invoked by Timon's invectives, gives this most nihilistic, least palpable of tragic heroes the grandest epitaph in Shakespeare. It makes an appropriate ending for a play that continues to impress and dissatisfy in about equal measure.

Timon of Athens

DRAMATIS PERSONAE

TIMON
of Athens
LUCIUS, LUCULLUS, SEMPRONIUS
flattering lords
VENTIDIUS
one of Timon's false friends
ALCIBIADES
an Athenian captain
APEMANTUS
a churlish philosopher
FLAVIUS
steward to Timon
FLAMINIUS, LUCILIUS, SERVILIUS
Timon's servants
CAPHIS, PHILOTUS, TITUS, HORTENSIUS
servants to Timon's creditors
Poet
Painter
Jeweller
Merchant
Mercer
An Old Athenian
Three Strangers
A Page
A Fool
PHRYNIA, TIMANDRA
mistresses to Alcibiades
CUPID, AMAZONS
in the Mask
Lords, Senators, Officers, Soldiers, Servants, Thieves and Attendants.

THE SCENE: ATHENS AND THE NEIGHBOURING WOODS.

ACT ONE

SCENE I. *Athens. Timon's house.*

Enter Poet, Painter, Jeweller, Merchant, and Mercer at several doors.

POET Good day, sir.
PAINTER I am glad y'are well.
POET I have not seen you long; how goes the world?
PAINTER It wears, sir, as it grows.
POET Ay, that's well known.
But what particular rarity? What strange,
Which manifold record not matches? See,
Magic of bounty, all these spirits thy power
Hath conjur'd to attend! I know the merchant.
PAINTER I know them both; th' other's a jeweller.
MERCHANT O, 'tis a worthy lord!
JEWELLER Nay, that's most fix'd.
MERCHANT A most incomparable man; breath'd, as it were,
To an untirable and continuate goodness.
He passes.
JEWELLER I have a jewel here –
MERCHANT O, pray let's see't. For the Lord Timon, sir?
JEWELLER If he will touch the estimate. But for that –
POET When we for recompense have prais'd the vile,
It stains the glory in that happy verse
Which aptly sings the good.
MERCHANT [*Looking at the jewel*] 'Tis a good form.
JEWELLER And rich. Here is a water, look ye.
PAINTER You are rapt, sir, in some work, some dedication
To the great lord.
POET A thing slipp'd idly from me.
Our poesy is as a gum, which oozes
From whence 'tis nourish'd. The fire i' th' flint
Shows not till it be struck: our gentle flame
Provokes itself, and like the current flies
Each bound it chafes. What have you there?
PAINTER A picture, sir. When comes your book forth?
POET Upon the heels of my presentment, sir.
Let's see your piece.
PAINTER 'Tis a good piece.
POET So 'tis; this comes off well and excellent.
PAINTER Indifferent.
POET Admirable. How this grace
Speaks his own standing! What a mental power
This eye shoots forth! How big imagination
Moves in this lip! To th' dumbness of the gesture
One might interpret.
PAINTER It is a pretty mocking of the life.
Here is a touch; is't good?
POET I will say of it
It tutors nature. Artificial strife
Lives in these touches, livelier than life.

Enter certain Senators, and pass over.

PAINTER How this lord is followed!
POET The senators of Athens – happy man!

PAINTER Look, moe!
POET You see this confluence, this great flood of visitors.
I have in this rough work shap'd out a man
Whom this beneath world doth embrace and hug
With amplest entertainment. My free drift
Halts not particularly, but moves itself
In a wide sea of tax. No levell'd malice
Infects one comma in the course I hold,
But flies an eagle flight, bold and forth on,
Leaving no tract behind.
PAINTER How shall I understand you?
POET I will unbolt to you.
You see how all conditions, how all minds –
As well of glib and slipp'ry creatures as
Of grave and austere quality, tender down
Their services to Lord Timon. His large fortune,
Upon his good and gracious nature hanging,
Subdues and properties to his love and tendance
All sorts of hearts; yea, from the glass-fac'd flatterer
To Apemantus, that few things loves better
Than to abhor himself; even he drops down
The knee before him, and returns in peace
Most rich in Timon's nod.
PAINTER I saw them speak together.
POET Sir, I have upon a high and pleasant hill
Feign'd Fortune to be thron'd. The base o' th' mount
Is rank'd with all deserts, all kind of natures
That labour on the bosom of this sphere
To propagate their states. Amongst them all
Whose eyes are on this sovereign lady fix'd
One do I personate of Lord Timon's frame,
Whom Fortune with her ivory hand wafts to her;
Whose present grace to present slaves and servants
Translates his rivals.
PAINTER 'Tis conceiv'd to scope.
This throne, this Fortune, and this hill, methinks,
With one man beckon'd from the rest below,
Bowing his head against the steepy mount
To climb his happiness, would be well express'd
In our condition.
POET Nay, sir, but hear me on.
All those which were his fellows but of late –
Some better than his value – on the moment
Follow his strides, his lobbies fill with tendance,
Rain sacrificial whisperings in his ear,
Make sacred even his stirrup, and through him
Drink the free air.
PAINTER Ay, marry, what of these?
POET When Fortune in her shift and change of mood
Spurns down her late beloved, all his dependants,
Which labour'd after him to the mountain's top
Even on their knees and hands, let him slip down,
Not one accompanying his declining foot.
PAINTER 'Tis common.
A thousand moral paintings I can show
That shall demonstrate these quick blows of Fortune's
More pregnantly than words. Yet you do well
To show Lord Timon that mean eyes have seen
The foot above the head.

Trumpets sound. Enter TIMON, addressing himself courteously to every suitor, a Messenger from Ventidius talking with him; LUCILIUS and other Servants following.

TIMON Imprison'd is he, say you?
MESSENGER Ay, my good lord. Five talents is his debt;
His means most short, his creditors most strait.
Your honourable letter he desires
To those have shut him up; which failing,
Periods his comfort.
TIMON Noble Ventidius! Well.
I am not of that feather to shake off
My friend when he must need me. I do know him
A gentlemen that well deserves a help,
Which he shall have. I'll pay the debt, and free him.
MESSENGER Your lordship ever binds him.
TIMON Commend me to him; I will send his ransom;
And being enfranchis'd, bid him come to me.
'Tis not enough to help the feeble up,
But to support him after. Fare you well.
MESSENGER All happiness to your honour! [*Exit.*

Enter an Old Athenian.

OLD ATHENIAN Lord Timon, hear me speak.
TIMON Freely, good father.
OLD ATHENIAN Thou hast a servant nam'd Lucilius.
TIMON I have so; what of him?
OLD ATHENIAN Most noble Timon, call the man before thee.
TIMON Attends he here, or no? Lucilius!
LUCILIUS Here, at your lordship's service.
OLD ATHENIAN This fellow here, Lord Timon, this thy creature,
By night frequents my house. I am a man
That from my first have been inclin'd to thrift,
And my estate deserves an heir more rais'd
Than one which holds a trencher.

TIMON Well; what further?
OLD ATHENIAN One only daughter have I, no kin else,
On whom I may confer what I have got.
The maid is fair, o' th' youngest for a bride,
And I have bred her at my dearest cost
In qualities of the best. This man of thine
Attempts her love; I prithee, noble lord,
Join with me to forbid him her resort;
Myself have spoke in vain.
TIMON The man is honest.
OLD ATHENIAN Therefore he will be, Timon.
His honesty rewards him in itself;
It must not bear my daughter.
TIMON Does she love him?
OLD ATHENIAN She is young and apt:
Our own precedent passions do instruct us
What levity's in youth.
TIMON Love you the maid?
LUCILIUS Ay, my good lord, and she accepts of it.
OLD ATHENIAN If in her marriage my consent be missing,
I call the gods to witness I will choose
Mine heir from forth the beggars of the world,
And dispossess her all.
TIMON How shall she be endow'd,
If she be mated with an equal husband?
OLD ATHENIAN Three talents on the present; in future, all.
TIMON This gentleman of mine hath serv'd me long;
To build his fortune I will strain a little,
For 'tis a bond in men. Give him thy daughter:
What you bestow, in him I'll counterpoise,
And make him weigh with her.
OLD ATHENIAN Most noble lord,
Pawn me to this your honour, she is his.
TIMON My hand to thee; mine honour on my promise.
LUCILIUS Humbly I thank your lordship. Never may
That state or fortune fall into my keeping
Which is not owed to you!
[*Exeunt Lucilius and Old Athenian.*
POET [*Presenting his poem*] Vouchsafe my labour, and long live your lordship!
TIMON I thank you; you shall hear from me anon;
Go not away. What have you there, my friend?
PAINTER A piece of painting, which I do beseech
Your lordship to accept.
TIMON Painting is welcome.
The painting is almost the natural man;
For since dishonour traffics with man's nature,
He is but outside; these pencill'd figures are
Even such as they give out. I like your work,
And you shall find I like it; wait attendance
Till you hear further from me.
PAINTER The gods preserve ye!
TIMON Well fare you, gentleman. Give me your hand;
We must needs dine together. Sir, your jewel
Hath suffered under praise.
JEWELLER What, my lord! Dispraise?
TIMON A mere satiety of commendations;
If I should pay you for't as 'tis extoll'd,
It would unclew me quite.
JEWELLER My lord, 'tis rated
As those which sell would give; but you well know
Things of like value, differing in the owners,
Are prized by their masters. Believe't, dear lord,
You mend the jewel by the wearing it.
TIMON Well mock'd.

Enter APEMANTUS.

MERCHANT No, my good lord; he speaks the common tongue,
Which all men speak with him.
TIMON Look who comes here; will you be chid?
JEWELLER We'll bear, with your lordship.
MERCHANT He'll spare none.
TIMON Good morrow to thee, gentle Apemantus!
APEMANTUS Till I be gentle, stay thou for thy good morrow;
When thou art Timon's dog, and these knaves honest.
TIMON Why dost thou call them knaves?
Thou know'st them not.
APEMANTUS Are they not Athenians?
TIMON Yes.
APEMANTUS Then I repent not.
JEWELLER You know me, Apemantus?
APEMANTUS Thou know'st I do; I call'd thee by thy name.
TIMON Thou art proud, Apemantus.
APEMANTUS Of nothing so much as that I am not like Timon.
TIMON Whither art going?
APEMANTUS To knock out an honest Athenian's brains.
TIMON That's a deed thou't die for.
APEMANTUS Right, if doing nothing be death by th' law.
TIMON How lik'st thou this picture, Apemantus?
APEMANTUS The best, for the innocence.
TIMON Wrought he not well that painted it?
APEMANTUS He wrought better that made the painter; and yet he's but a filthy piece of work.
PAINTER Y'are a dog.
APEMANTUS Thy mother's of my generation; what's she, if I be a dog?
TIMON Wilt dine with me, Apemantus?
APEMANTUS No; I eat not lords.

TIMON An thou shouldst, thou'dst anger ladies.

APEMANTUS O, they eat lords; so they come by great bellies.

TIMON That's a lascivious apprehension.

APEMANTUS So thou apprehend'st it take it for thy labour.

TIMON How dost thou like this jewel, Apemantus?

APEMANTUS Not so well as plain dealing, which will not cost a man a doit.

TIMON What dost thou think 'tis worth?

APEMANTUS Not worth my thinking. How now, poet!

POET How now, philosopher!

APEMANTUS Thou liest.

POET Art not one?

APEMANTUS Yes.

POET Then I lie not.

APEMANTUS Art not a poet?

POET Yes.

APEMANTUS Then thou liest. Look in thy last work, where thou hast feign'd him a worthy fellow.

POET That's not feign'd – he is so.

APEMANTUS Yes, he is worthy of thee, and to pay thee for thy labour. He that loves to be flattered is worthy o' th' flatterer. Heavens, that I were a lord!

TIMON What wouldst do then, Apemantus?

APEMANTUS E'en as Apemantus does now: hate a lord with my heart.

TIMON What, thyself?

APEMANTUS Ay.

TIMON Wherefore?

APEMANTUS That I had no angry wit to be a lord. – Art not thou a merchant?

MERCHANT Ay, Apemantus.

APEMANTUS Traffic confound thee, if the gods will not!

MERCHANT If traffic do it, the gods do it.

APEMANTUS Traffic's thy god, and thy god confound thee!

Trumpet sounds. Enter a Messenger.

TIMON What trumpet's that?

MESSENGER 'Tis Alcibiades, and some twenty horse,
All of companionship.

TIMON Pray entertain them; give them guide to us. [*Exeunt some Attendants.*
You must needs dine with me. Go not you hence
Till I have thank'd you. When dinner's done
Show me this piece. I am joyful of your sights.

Enter ALCIBIADES, with the rest.

Most welcome, sir! [*They salute*

APEMANTUS So, so, there!
Aches contract and starve your supple joints!
That there should be small love amongst these sweet knaves,
And all this courtesy! The strain of man's bred out
Into baboon and monkey.

ALCIBIADES Sir, you have sav'd my longing, and I feed
Most hungerly on your sight.

TIMON Right welcome, sir!
Ere we depart we'll share a bounteous time
In different pleasures. Pray you, let us in.
[*Exeunt all but Apemantus.*

Enter two Lords.

1 LORD What time o' day is't, Apemantus?

APEMANTUS Time to be honest.

1 LORD That time serves still.

APEMANTUS The more accursed thou that still omit'st it.

2 LORD Thou art going to Lord Timon's feast.

APEMANTUS Ay; to see meat fill knaves and wine heat fools.

2 LORD Fare thee well, fare thee well.

APEMANTUS Thou art a fool to bid me farewell twice.

2 LORD Why, Apemantus?

APEMANTUS Shouldst have kept one to thyself, for I mean to give thee none.

1 LORD Hang thyself.

APEMANTUS No, I will do nothing at thy bidding; make thy requests to thy friend.

2 LORD Away, unpeaceable dog, or I'll spurn thee hence.

APEMANTUS I will fly, like a dog, the heels o' th' ass. [*Exit.*

1 LORD He's opposite to humanity. Come, shall we in
And taste Lord Timon's bounty? He outgoes
The very heart of kindness.

2 LORD He pours it out: Plutus, the god of gold,
Is but his steward; no meed but he repays
Sevenfold above itself; no gift to him
But breeds the giver a return exceeding
All use of quittance.

1 LORD The noblest mind he carries
That ever govern'd man.

2 LORD Long may he live in fortunes!
Shall we in?

1 LORD I'll keep you company. [*Exeunt.*

SCENE II. *A room of state in Timon's house.*

Hautboys playing loud music. A great banquet serv'd in; FLAVIUS and Others attending; and then enter LORD TIMON, the States, the Athenian Lords, VENTIDIUS, which Timon redeem'd from prison. Then comes, dropping after all, APEMANTUS, discontentedly, like himself.

VENTIDIUS Most honoured Timon,
It hath pleas'd the gods to remember my father's age,
And call him to long peace.
He is gone happy, and has left me rich.
Then, as in grateful virtue I am bound
To your free heart, I do return those talents,
Doubled with thanks and service, from whose help
I deriv'd liberty.

TIMON O, by no means,
Honest Ventidius! You mistake my love;
I gave it freely ever; and there's none
Can truly say he gives, if he receives.
If our betters play at that game, we must not dare
To imitate them: faults that are rich are fair.

VENTIDIUS A noble spirit!

TIMON Nay, my lords, ceremony was but devis'd at first
To set a gloss on faint deeds, hollow welcomes,
Recanting goodness, sorry ere 'tis shown;
But where there is true friendship there needs none.
Pray, sit; more welcome are ye to my fortunes
Than my fortunes to me. [*They sit.*

1 LORD My lord, we always have confess'd it.

APEMANTUS Ho, ho, confess'd it! Hang'd it, have you not?

TIMON O, Apemantus, you are welcome.

APEMANTUS No;
You shall not make me welcome.
I come to have thee thrust me out of doors.

TIMON Fie, th'art a churl; ye have got a humour there
Does not become a man; 'tis much to blame.
They say, my lords, Ira furor brevis est; but yond man is ever angry. Go, let him have a table by himself; for he does neither affect company nor is he fit for't indeed.

APEMANTUS Let me stay at thine apperil, Timon. I come to observe; I give thee warning on't.

TIMON I take no heed of thee. Th'art an Athenian, therefore welcome. I myself would have no power; prithee let my meat make thee silent.

APEMANTUS I scorn thy meat; 'twould choke me, for I should ne'er flatter thee. O you gods, what a number of men eats Timon, and he sees 'em not! It grieves me to see so many dip their meat in one man's blood; and all the madness is, he cheers them up too.
I wonder men dare trust themselves with men.
Methinks they should invite them without knives:
Good for their meat and safer for their lives.
There's much example for't; the fellow that sits next him now, parts bread with him, pledges the breath of him in a divided draught, is the readiest man to kill him. 'T has been proved. If I were a huge man I should fear to drink at meals,
Lest they should spy my windpipe's dangerous notes.
Great men should drink with harness on their throats.

TIMON My lord, in heart! and let the health go round.

2 LORD Let it flow this way, my good lord.

APEMANTUS Flow this way! A brave fellow! He keeps his tides well. Those healths will make thee and thy state look ill, Timon. Here's that which is too weak to be a sinner, honest water, which ne'er left man i' th' mire.
This and my food are equals; there's no odds.
Feasts are too proud to give thanks to the gods.

Apemantus' Grace.

Immortal gods, I crave no pelf;
I pray for no man but myself.
Grant I may never prove so fond
To trust man on his oath or bond,
Or a harlot for her weeping,
Or a dog that seems a-sleeping,
Or a keeper with my freedom,
Or my friends, if I should need 'em.
Amen. So fall to't.
Rich men sin, and I eat root.
[*Eats and drinks.*

Much good dich thy good heart, Apemantus!

TIMON Captain Alcibiades, your heart's in the field now.

ALCIBIADES My heart is ever at your service, my lord.

TIMON You had rather be at a breakfast of enemies than a dinner of friends.

ALCIBIADES So they were bleeding new, my lord, there's no meat like 'em; I could wish my best friend at such a feast.

APEMANTUS Would all those flatterers were thine enemies then, that then thou mightst kill 'em, and bid me to 'em.

1 LORD Might we but have that happiness, my lord, that you would once use our hearts, whereby we might express some part of our zeals, we should think ourselves for ever perfect.

TIMON O, no doubt, my good friends, but the gods themselves have provided that I shall have much help from you. How had you been my friends else? Why have you that charitable title from thousands, did not you chiefly belong to my heart? I have told more of you to myself than you can with modesty speak in your own behalf; and thus far I confirm you. O you gods, think I, what need we have any friends if we should ne'er have need of 'em? They were the most needless creatures living, should we ne'er have use for 'em; and would most resemble sweet instruments hung up in cases, that keep their sounds to themselves. Why, I have often wish'd myself poorer, that I might come nearer to you. We are born to do benefits; and what better or properer can we call our own than the riches of our friends? O, what a precious comfort 'tis to have so many like brothers commanding one another's fortunes! O, joy's e'en made away ere't can be born! Mine eyes cannot hold out water, methinks. To forget their faults, I drink to you.

APEMANTUS Thou weep'st to make them drink, Timon.

2 LORD Joy had the like conception in our eyes,
And at that instant like a babe sprung up.

APEMANTUS Ho, ho! I laugh to think that babe a bastard.

3 LORD I promise you, my lord, you mov'd me much.

APEMANTUS Much! *[Sound tucket.*

TIMON What means that trump?

Enter a Servant.

How now?

SERVANT Please you, my lord, there are certain ladies most desirous of admittance.

TIMON Ladies! What are their wills?

SERVANT There comes with them a forerunner, my lord, which bears that office to signify their pleasures.

TIMON I pray let them be admitted.

Enter CUPID.

CUPID Hail to thee, worthy Timon, and to all
That of his bounties taste! The five best Senses
Acknowledge thee their patron, and come freely
To gratulate thy plenteous bosom. Th' Ear,
Taste, Touch, Smell, pleas'd from thy table rise;
They only now come but to feast thine eyes.

TIMON They're welcome all; let 'em have kind admittance.
Music, make their welcome. *[Exit Cupid.*

1 LORD You see, my lord, how ample y'are belov'd.

Music. Re-enter CUPID, with a Masque of Ladies as Amazons, with lutes in their hands, dancing and playing.

APEMANTUS Hoy-day, what a sweep of vanity comes this way!
They dance? They are mad women.
Like madness is the glory of this life,
As this pomp shows to a little oil and root.
We make ourselves fools to disport ourselves,
And spend our flatteries to drink those men
Upon whose age we void it up again
With poisonous spite and envy.
Who lives that's not depraved or depraves?
Who dies that bears not one spurn to their graves
Of their friends' gift?
I should fear those that dance before me now
Would one day stamp upon me. 'T has been done:
Men shut their doors against a setting sun.

The Lords rise from table, with much adoring of Timon; and to show their loves, each single out an Amazon, and all dance, men with women, a lofty strain or two to the hautboys, and cease.

TIMON You have done our pleasures much grace, fair ladies,
Set a fair fashion on our entertainment,
Which was not half so beautiful and kind;
You have added worth unto't and lustre,
And entertain'd me with mine own device;
I am to thank you for't.

1 LADY My lord, you take us even at the best.

APEMANTUS Faith, for the worst is filthy, and would not hold taking, I doubt me.

TIMON Ladies, there is an idle banquet attends you;
Please you to dispose yourselves.

ALL LADIES Most thankfully, my lord.
[Exeunt Cupid and Ladies.

TIMON Flavius!

FLAVIUS My lord?

TIMON The little casket bring me hither.

FLAVIUS Yes, my lord. *[Aside]* More jewels yet!
There is no crossing him in's humour,
Else I should tell him – well i' faith, I should –
When all's spent, he'd be cross'd then, an he could.
'Tis pity bounty had not eyes behind,
That man might ne'er be wretched for his mind.
[Exit.

1 LORD Where be our men?

SERVANT Here, my lord, in readiness.

2 LORD Our horses!

Re-enter FLAVIUS, with the casket.

TIMON O my friends,

I have one word to say to you. Look you, my good lord,
I must entreat you honour me so much
As to advance this jewel; accept it and wear it,
Kind my lord.

1 LORD I am so far already in your gifts –

ALL So are we all.

Enter a Servant.

SERVANT My lord, there are certain nobles of the Senate newly alighted and come to visit you.

TIMON They are fairly welcome. [*Exit Servant.*

FLAVIUS I beseech your honour, vouchsafe me a word; it does concern you near.

TIMON Near! Why then, another time I'll hear thee. I prithee let's be provided to show them entertainment.

FLAVIUS [*Aside*] I scarce know how.

Enter another Servant.

2 SERVANT May it please your honour, Lord Lucius, out of his free love, hath presented to you four milk-white horses, trapp'd in silver.

TIMON I shall accept them fairly. Let the presents
Be worthily entertain'd. [*Exit Servant.*

Enter a third Servant.

How now! What news?

3 SERVANT Please you, my lord, that honourable gentleman, Lord Lucullus, entreats your company to-morrow to hunt with him and has sent your honour two brace of greyhounds.

TIMON I'll hunt with him; and let them be receiv'd,
Not without fair reward. [*Exit Servant.*

FLAVIUS [*Aside*] What will this come to?
He commands us to provide and give great gifts,
And all out of an empty coffer;
Nor will he know his purse, or yield me this,
To show him what a beggar his heart is,
Being of no power to make his wishes good.
His promises fly so beyond his state
That what he speaks is all in debt; he owes
For ev'ry word. He is so kind that he now
Pays interest for't; his land's put to their books.
Well, would I were gently put out of office
Before I were forc'd out!
Happier is he that has no friend to feed
Than such that do e'en enemies exceed.
I bleed inwardly for my lord. [*Exit.*

TIMON You do yourselves much wrong;
You bate too much of your own merits.
Here, my lord, a trifle of our love.

2 LORD With more than common thanks I will receive it.

3 LORD O, he's the very soul of bounty!

TIMON And now I remember, my lord, you gave good words the other day of a bay courser I rode on. 'Tis yours because you lik'd it.

3 LORD O, I beseech you pardon me, my lord, in that.

TIMON You may take my word, my lord: I know no man
Can justly praise but what he does affect.
I weigh my friend's affection with mine own.
I'll tell you true; I'll call to you.

ALL LORDS O, none so welcome!

TIMON I take all and your several visitations
So kind to heart 'tis not enough to give;
Methinks I could deal kingdoms to my friends.
And ne'er be weary. Alcibiades,
Thou art a soldier, therefore seldom rich.
It comes in charity to thee; for all thy living
Is 'mongst the dead, and all the lands thou hast
Lie in a pitch'd field.

ALCIBIADES Ay, defil'd land, my lord.

1 LORD We are so virtuously bound –

TIMON And so am I to you.

2 LORD So infinitely endear'd –

TIMON All to you. Lights, more lights!

1 LORD The best of happiness, honour, and fortunes, keep with you, Lord Timon!

TIMON Ready for his friends.

[*Exeunt all but Apemantus and Timon.*

APEMANTUS What a coil's here!
Serving of becks and jutting-out of bums!
I doubt whether their legs be worth the sums
That are given for 'em. Friendship's full of dregs:
Methinks false hearts should never have sound legs.
Thus honest fools lay out their wealth on curtsies.

TIMON Now, Apemantus, if thou wert not sullen
I would be good to thee.

APEMANTUS No, I'll nothing; for if I should be brib'd too, there would be none left to rail upon thee, and then thou wouldst sin the faster. Thou giv'st so long, Timon, I fear me thou wilt give away thyself in paper shortly. What needs these feasts, pomps, and vainglories?

TIMON Nay, an you begin to rail on society once, I am sworn not to give regard to you. Farewell; and come with better music. [*Exit.*

APEMANTUS So. Thou wilt not hear me now: thou shalt not then. I'll lock thy heaven from thee.
O that men's ears should be To counsel deaf, but not to flattery! [*Exit.*

ACT TWO

SCENE I. *A Senator's house.*

Enter a Senator, with papers in his hand.

SENATOR And late, five thousand. To Varro and to Isidore
He owes nine thousand; besides my former sum,
Which makes it five and twenty. Still in motion
Of raging waste? It cannot hold; it will not.
If I want gold, steal but a beggar's dog
And give it Timon, why, the dog coins gold.
If I would sell my horse and buy twenty moe
Better than he, why, give my horse to Timon,
Ask nothing, give it him, it foals me straight,
And able horses. No porter at his gate,
But rather one that smiles and still invites
All that pass by. It cannot hold; no reason
Can sound his state in safety. Caphis, ho!
Caphis, I say!

Enter CAPHIS.

CAPHIS Here, sir; what is your pleasure?

SENATOR Get on your cloak and haste you to Lord Timon;
Importune him for my moneys; be not ceas'd
With slight denial, nor then silenc'd when
'Commend me to your master' and the cap
Plays in the right hand, thus; but tell him
My uses cry to me, I must serve my turn
Out of mine own; his days and times are past,
And my reliances on his fracted dates
Have smit my credit. I love and honour him,
But must not break my back to heal his finger.
Immediate are my needs, and my relief
Must not be toss'd and turn'd to me in words,
But find supply immediate. Get you gone;
Put on a most importunate aspect,
A visage of demand; for I do fear,
When every feather sticks in his own wing,
Lord Timon will be left a naked gull,
Which flashes now a phoenix. Get you gone.

CAPHIS I go, sir.

SENATOR Take the bonds along with you,
And have the dates in compt.

CAPHIS I will, sir.

SENATOR Go.

[*Exeunt.*

SCENE II. *Before Timon's house.*

Enter FLAVIUS, Timon's steward, with many bills in his hand.

FLAVIUS No care, no stop! So senseless of expense
That he will neither know how to maintain it
Nor cease his flow of riot; takes no account
How things go from him, nor resumes no care
Of what is to continue. Never mind
Was to be so unwise to be so kind.
What shall be done? He will not hear till feel.
I must be round with him. Now he comes from hunting.
Fie, fie, fie, fie!

Enter CAPHIS, and the Servants of Isidore and Varro.

CAPHIS Good even, Varro. What, you come for money?

VARRO'S SERVANT Is't not your business too?

CAPHIS It is. And yours business too, Isidore?

ISIDORE'S SERVANT It is so.

CAPHIS Would we were all discharg'd!

VARRO'S SERVANT I fear it.

CAPHIS Here comes the lord.

Enter TIMON and his Train, with ALCIBIADES.

TIMON So soon as dinner's done we'll forth again,
My Alcibiades. – With me? What is your will?

CAPHIS My lord, here is a note of certain dues.

TIMON Dues! Whence are you?

CAPHIS Of Athens here, my lord.

TIMON Go to my steward.

CAPHIS Please it your lordship, he hath put me off
To the succession of new days this month.
My master is awak'd by great occasion
To call upon his own, and humbly prays you
That with your other noble parts you'll suit
In giving him his right.

TIMON Mine honest friend,
I prithee but repair to me next morning.

CAPHIS Nay, good my lord –

TIMON Contain thyself, good friend.

VARRO'S SERVANT One Varro's servant, my good lord –

ISIDORE'S SERVANT From Isidore: he humbly prays your speedy payment –

CAPHIS If you did know, my lord, my master's wants –

VARRO'S SERVANT 'Twas due on forfeiture, my lord, six weeks and past.

ISIDORE'S SERVANT Your steward puts me off, my lord; and I am sent expressly to your lordship.

TIMON Give me breath.

I do beseech you, good my lords, keep on; I'll wait upon you instantly.

[*Exeunt Alcibiades and Lords.*

[*To Flavius*] Come hither. Pray you,
How goes the world that I am thus encount'red
With clamorous demands of date-broke bonds
And the detention of long-since-due debts,
Against my honour?

FLAVIUS Please you, gentlemen,
The time is unagreeable to this business.
Your importunacy cease till after dinner,
That I may make his lordship understand
Wherefore you are not paid.

TIMON Do so, my friends.
See them well entertain'd [*Exit*

FLAVIUS Pray draw near. [*Exit.*

Enter APEMANTUS and Fool.

CAPHIS Stay, stay, here comes the fool with Apemantus. Let's ha' some sport with 'em.

VARRO'S SERVANT Hang him, he'll abuse us!

ISIDORE'S SERVANT A plague upon him, dog!

VARRO'S SERVANT How dost, fool?

APEMANTUS Dost dialogue with thy shadow?

VARRO'S SERVANT I speak not to thee.

APEMANTUS No, 'tis to thyself. [*To the Fool*] Come away.

ISIDORE'S SERVANT [*To Varro's Servant.*] There's the fool hangs on your back already.

APEMANTUS No, thou stand'st single; th'art not on him yet.

CAPHIS Where's the fool now?

APEMANTUS He last ask'd the question. Poor rogues and usurers' men! Bawds between gold and want!

ALL SERVANTS What are we, Apemantus?

APEMANTUS Asses.

ALL SERVANTS Why?

APEMANTUS That you ask me what you are, and do not know yourselves. Speak to 'em, fool.

FOOL How do you, gentlemen?

ALL SERVANTS Gramercies, good fool. How does your mistress?

FOOL She's e'en setting on water to scald such chickens as you are. Would we could see you at Corinth!

APEMANTUS Good! gramercy.

Enter Page.

FOOL Look you, here comes my mistress' page.

PAGE [*To the Fool*] Why, how now, Captain? What do you in this wise company? How dost thou, Apemantus?

APEMANTUS Would I had a rod in my mouth, that I might answer thee profitably!

PAGE Prithee, Apemantus, read me the superscription of these letters; I know not which is which.

APEMANTUS Canst not read?

PAGE No.

APEMANTUS There will little learning die, then, that day thou art hang'd. This is to Lord Timon; this to Alcibiades. Go; thou wast born a bastard, and thou't die a bawd.

PAGE Thou wast whelp'd a dog, and thou shalt famish a dog's death. Answer not: I am gone.

[*Exit Page.*

APEMANTUS E'en so thou outrun'st grace. Fool, I will go with you to Lord Timon's.

FOOL Will you leave me there?

APEMANTUS If Timon stay at home. You three serve three usurers?

ALL SERVANTS Ay; would they serv'd us!

APEMANTUS So would I – as good a trick as ever hangman serv'd thief.

FOOL Are you three usurers' men?

ALL SERVANTS Ay, fool.

FOOL I think no usurer but has a fool to his servant. My mistress is one, and I am her fool. When men come to borrow of your masters, they approach sadly and go away merry; but they enter my mistress' house merrily and go away sadly. The reason of this?

VARRO'S SERVANT I could render one.

APEMANTUS Do it then, that we may account thee a whoremaster and a knave; which notwithstanding, thou shalt be no less esteemed.

VARRO'S SERVANT What is a whoremaster, fool?

FOOL A fool in good clothes, and something like thee. 'Tis a spirit. Sometime't appears like a lord; sometime like a lawyer; sometime like a philosopher, with two stones moe than's artificial one. He is very often like a knight; and, generally, in all shapes that man goes up and down in from fourscore to thirteen, this spirit walks in.

VARRO'S SERVANT Thou art not altogether a fool.

FOOL Nor thou altogether is a wise man.
As much foolery as I have, so much wit thou lack'st.

APEMANTUS That answer might have become Apemantus.

VARRO'S SERVANT Aside, aside; here comes Lord Timon.

Re-enter TIMON and FLAVIUS.

APEMANTUS Come with me, fool, come.

FOOL I do not always follow lover, elder brother, and woman; sometime the philosopher.

[*Exeunt Apemantus and Fool.*

FLAVIUS Pray you walk near; I'll speak with you anon. [*Exeunt Servants.*

TIMON You make me marvel wherefore ere this time
Had you not fully laid my state before me,
That I might so have rated my expense
As I had leave of means.

FLAVIUS You would not hear me
At many leisures I propos'd.

TIMON Go to;
Perchance some single vantages you took
When my indisposition put you back,
And that unaptness made your minister
Thus to excuse yourself.

FLAVIUS O my good lord,
At many times I brought in my accounts,
Laid them before you; you would throw them off
And say you found them in mine honesty.
When, for some trifling present, you have bid me
Return so much, I have shook my head and wept;
Yea,'gainst th' authority of manners, pray'd you
To hold your hand more close. I did endure
Not seldom, nor no slight checks, when I have
Prompted you in the ebb of your estate
And your great flow of debts. My lov'd lord,
Though you hear now – too late! – yet now's a time:
The greatest of your having lacks a half
To pay your present debts.

TIMON Let all my land be sold.

FLAVIUS 'Tis all engag'd, some forfeited and gone;
And what remains will hardly stop the mouth
Of present dues. The future comes apace;
What shall defend the interim? And at length
How goes our reck'ning?

TIMON To Lacedaemon did my land extend.

FLAVIUS O my good lord, the world is but a word;
Were it all yours to give it in a breath,
How quickly were it gone!

TIMON You tell me true.

FLAVIUS If you suspect my husbandry or falsehood,
Call me before th' exactest auditors
And set me on the proof. So the gods bless me,
When all our offices have been oppress'd
With riotous feeders, when our vaults have wept
With drunken spilth of wine, when every room
Hath blaz'd with lights and bray'd with minstrelsy,
I have retir'd me to a wasteful cock
And set mine eyes at flow.

TIMON Prithee no more.

FLAVIUS 'Heavens,' have I said 'the bounty of this lord!
How many prodigal bits have slaves and peasants
This night englutted! Who is not Lord Timon's?
What heart, head, sword, force, means, but is Lord Timon's?
Great Timon, noble, worthy, royal Timon!'
Ah! when the means are gone that buy this praise,
The breath is gone whereof this praise is made.
Feast-won, fast-lost; one cloud of winter show'rs,
These flies are couch'd.

TIMON Come, sermon me no further.
No villainous bounty yet hath pass'd my heart;
Unwisely, not ignobly, have I given.
Why dost thou weep? Canst thou the conscience lack
To think I shall lack friends? Secure thy heart:
If I would broach the vessels of my love,
And try the argument of hearts by borrowing,
Men and men's fortunes could I frankly use
As I can bid thee speak.

FLAVIUS Assurance bless your thoughts!

TIMON And, in some sort, these wants of mine are crown'd
That I account them blessings; for by these
Shall I try friends. You shall perceive how you
Mistake my fortunes; I am wealthy in my friends.
Within there! Flaminius! Servilius!

Enter FLAMINIUS, SERVILIUS, and another Servant.

SERVANTS My lord! my lord!

TIMON I will dispatch you severally – you to Lord Lucius; to Lord Lucullus you; I hunted with his honour to-day. You to Sempronius. Commend me to their loves; and I am proud, say, that my occasions have found time to use 'em toward a supply of money. Let the request be fifty talents.

FLAMINIUS As you have said, my lord.

[Exeunt Servants.

FLAVIUS *[Aside]* Lord Lucius and Lucullus? Humh!

TIMON Go you, sir, to the senators,
Of whom, even to the state's best health, I have
Deserv'd this hearing. Bid 'em send o' th' instant
A thousand talents to me.

FLAVIUS I have been bold,
For that I knew it the most general way,
To them to use your signet and your name;
But they do shake their heads, and I am here
No richer in return.

TIMON Is't true? Can't be?

FLAVIUS They answer, in a joint and corporate voice,
That now they are at fall, want treasure, cannot

Do what they would, are sorry – you are honourable –
But yet they could have wish'd – they know not –
Something hath been amiss – a noble nature
May catch a wrench – would all were well! – 'tis pity –
And so, intending other serious matters,
After distasteful looks, and these hard fractions,
With certain half-caps and cold-moving nods,
They froze me into silence.

TIMON You gods, reward them!
Prithee, man, look cheerly. These old fellows
Have their ingratitude in them hereditary.
Their blood is cak'd, 'tis cold, it seldom flows;
'Tis lack of kindly warmth they are not kind;
And nature, as it grows again toward earth,
Is fashion'd for the journey dull and heavy.
Go to Ventidius. Prithee be not sad,
Thou art true and honest; ingeniously I speak,
No blame belongs to thee. Ventidius lately
Buried his father, by whose death he's stepp'd
Into a great estate. When he was poor,
Imprison'd, and in scarcity of friends,
I clear'd him with five talents. Greet him from me,
Bid him suppose some good necessity
Touches his friend, which craves to be remember'd
With those five talents. That had, give't these fellows
To whom 'tis instant due. Nev'r speak or think
That Timon's fortunes 'mong his friends can sink.

FLAVIUS I would I could not think it.
That thought is bounty's foe;
Being free itself, it thinks all others so. [*Exeunt.*

ACT THREE

SCENE I. *Lucullus' house.*

FLAMINIUS waiting to speak with Lucullus. Enter a Servant to him.

SERVANT I have told my lord of you; he is coming down to you.

FLAMINIUS I thank you, sir.

Enter LUCULLUS.

SERVANT Here's my lord.

LUCULLUS [*Aside*] One of Lord Timon's men? A gift, I warrant. Why, this hits right; I dreamt of a silver basin and ewer to-night – Flaminius, honest Flaminius, you are very respectively welcome, sir. Fill me some wine. [*Exit Servant*]. And how does that honourable, complete, free-hearted gentleman of Athens, thy very bountiful good lord and master?

FLAMINIUS His health is well, sir.

LUCULLUS I am right glad that his health is well, sir. And what hast thou there under thy cloak, pretty Flaminius?

FLAMINIUS Faith, nothing but an empty box, sir, which in my lord's behalf I come to entreat your honour to supply; who, having great and instant occasion to use fifty talents, hath sent to your lordship to furnish him, nothing doubting your present assistance therein.

LUCULLUS La, la, la, la! 'Nothing doubting' says he? Alas, good lord! a noble gentleman 'tis, if he would not keep so good a house. Many a time and often I ha' din'd with him and told him on't; and come again to supper to him of purpose to have him spend less; and yet he would embrace no counsel, take no warning by my coming. Every man has his fault, and honesty is his. I ha' told him on't, but I could ne'er get him from't.

Re-enter Servant, with wine.

SERVANT Please your lordship, here is the wine.

LUCULLUS Flaminius, I have noted thee always wise. Here's to thee.

FLAMINIUS Your lordship speaks your pleasure.

LUCULLUS I have observed thee always for a towardly prompt spirit, give thee thy due, and one that knows what belongs to reason, and canst use the time well, if the time use thee well. Good parts in thee. [*To Servant*] Get you gone, sirrah. [*Exit Servant*] Draw nearer, honest Flaminius. Thy lord's a bountiful gentleman; but thou art wise, and thou know'st well enough, although thou com'st to me, that this is no time to lend money, especially upon bare friendship without security. Here's three solidares for thee. Good boy, wink at me, and say thou saw'st me not. Fare thee well.

FLAMINIUS Is't possible the world should so much differ,
And we alive that liv'd? Fly, damned baseness,
To him that worships thee.
[*Throwing the money back.*

LUCULLUS Ha! Now I see thou art a fool, and fit for thy master. [*Exit.*

FLAMINIUS May these add to the number that may scald thee!
Let molten coin be thy damnation,
Thou disease of a friend and not himself!

Has friendship such a faint and milky heart
It turns in less than two nights? O you gods,
I feel my master's passion! This slave
Unto his honour has my lord's meat in him;
Why should it thrive and turn to nutriment
When he is turn'd to poison?
O, may diseases only work upon't!
And when he's sick to death, let not that part of nature
Which my lord paid for be of any power
To expel sickness, but prolong his hour!

[*Exit.*

SCENE II. *A public place.*

Enter LUCIUS, with three Strangers.

LUCIUS Who, the Lord Timon? He is my very good friend, and an honourable gentleman.

1 STRANGER We know him for no less, though we are but strangers to him. But I can tell you one thing, my lord, and which I hear from common rumours: now Lord Timon's happy hours are done and past, and his estate shrinks from him.

LUCIUS Fie, no: do not believe it; he cannot want for money.

2 STRANGER But believe you this, my lord, that not long ago one of his men was with the Lord Lucullus to borrow so many talents; nay, urg'd extremely for't, and showed what necessity belong'd to't, and yet was denied.

LUCIUS How?

2 STRANGER I tell you, denied, my lord.

LUCIUS What a strange case was that! Now, before the gods, I am asham'd on't. Denied that honourable man! There was very little honour show'd in't. For my own part, I must needs confess I have received some small kindnesses from him, as money, plate, jewels, and such-like trifles, nothing comparing to his; yet, had he mistook him and sent to me, I should ne'er have denied his occasion so many talents.

Enter SERVILIUS.

SERVILIUS See, by good hap, yonder's my lord; I have sweat to see his honour. – My honour'd lord!

LUCIUS Servilius? You are kindly met, sir. Fare thee well; commend me to thy honourable virtuous lord, my very exquisite friend.

SERVILIUS May it please your honour, my lord hath sent –

LUCIUS Ha! What has he sent? I am so much endeared to that lord; he's ever sending. How shall I thank him, think'st thou? And what has he sent now?

SERVILIUS Has only sent his present occasion now, my lord, requesting your lordship to supply his instant use with so many talents.

LUCIUS I know his lordship is but merry with me;
He cannot want fifty-five hundred talents.

SERVILIUS But in the mean time he wants less, my lord.
If his occasion were not virtuous
I should not urge it half so faithfully.

LUCIUS Dost thou speak seriously, Servilius?

SERVILIUS Upon my soul, 'tis true, sir.

LUCIUS What a wicked beast was I to disfurnish myself against such a good time, when I might ha' shown myself honourable! How unluckily it happ'ned that I should purchase the day before for a little part and undo a great deal of honour! Servilius, now before the gods, I am not able to do – the more beast, I say! I was sending to use Lord Timon myself, these gentlemen can witness; but I would not for the wealth of Athens I had done't now. Commend me bountifully to his good lordship, and I hope his honour will conceive the fairest of me, because I have no power to be kind. And tell him this from me: I count it one of my greatest afflictions, say, that I cannot pleasure such an honourable gentleman. Good Servilius, will you befriend me so far as to use mine own words to him?

SERVILIUS Yes, sir, I shall.

LUCIUS I'll look you out a good turn, Servilius.

[*Exit Servilius.*

True, as you said, Timon is shrunk indeed;
And he that's once denied will hardly speed.

[*Exit.*

1 STRANGER Do you observe this, Hostilius?

2 STRANGER Ay, too well.

1 STRANGER Why, this is the world's soul; and just of the same piece
Is every flatterer's spirit. Who can call him his friend
That dips in the same dish? For, in my knowing,
Timon has been this lord's father,
And kept his credit with his purse;
Supported his estate; nay, Timon's money
Has paid his men their wages. He ne'er drinks
But Timon's silver treads upon his lip;
And yet – O, see the monstrousness of man
When he looks out in an ungrateful shape! –
He does deny him, in respect of his,
What charitable men afford to beggars.

3 STRANGER Religion groans at it.

1 STRANGER For mine own part,
I never tasted Timon in my life,
Nor came any of his bounties over me
To mark me for his friend; yet I protest,

For his right noble mind, illustrious virtue,
And honourable carriage,
Had his necessity made use of me,
I would have put my wealth into donation,
And the best half should have return'd to him,
So much I love his heart. But I perceive
Men must learn now with pity to dispense;
For policy sits above conscience. [*Exeunt.*

SCENE III. *Sempronius' house.*

Enter SEMPRONIUS and a Servant of Timon's.

SEMPRONIUS Must he needs trouble me in't? Hum! 'Bove all others?
He might have tried Lord Lucius or Lucullus;
And now Ventidius is wealthy too,
Whom he redeem'd from prison. All these
Owe their estates unto him.

SERVANT My lord,
They have all been touch'd and found base metal, for
They have all denied him.

SEMPRONIUS How! Have they denied him?
Has Ventidius and Lucullus denied him?
And does he send to me? Three? Humh!
It shows but little love or judgment in him.
Must I be his last refuge? His friends, like physicians,
Thrice give him over. Must I take th' cure upon me?
Has much disgrac'd me in't; I'm angry at him,
That might have known my place. I see no sense for't,
But his occasions might have woo'd me first;
For, in my conscience, I was the first man
That e'er received gift from him.
And does he think so backwardly of me now
That I'll requite it last? No;
So it may prove an argument of laughter
To th' rest, and I 'mongst lords be thought a fool.
I'd rather than the worth of thrice the sum
Had sent to me first, but for my mind's sake;
I'd such a courage to do him good. But now return,
And with their faint reply this answer join:
Who bates mine honour shall not know my coin. [*Exit.*

SERVANT Excellent! Your lordship's a goodly villain. The devil knew not what he did when he made man politic – he cross'd himself by't; and I cannot think but, in the end, the villainies of man will set him clear. How fairly this lord strives to appear foul! Takes virtuous copies to be wicked, like those that under hot ardent zeal would set whole realms on fire.
Of such a nature is his politic love.
This was my lord's best hope; now all are fled,
Save only the gods. Now his friends are dead,
Doors that were ne'er acquainted with their wards
Many a bounteous year must be employ'd
Now to guard sure their master.
And this is all a liberal course allows:
Who cannot keep his wealth must keep his house. [*Exit.*

SCENE IV. *A hall in Timon's house.*

Enter two of Varro's Men, meeting Lucius' Servant, and Others, all being servants of Timon's creditors, to wait for his coming out. Then enter TITUS and HORTENSIUS.

1 VARRO'S SERVANT Well met; good morrow, Titus and Hortensius.

TITUS The like to you, kind Varro.

HORTENSIUS Lucius! What, do we meet together?

LUCIUS' SERVANT Ay, and I think one business does command us all; for mine is money.

TITUS So is theirs and ours.

Enter PHILOTUS.

LUCIUS' SERVANT And Sir Philotus too!

PHILOTUS Good day at once.

LUCIUS' SERVANT Welcome, good brother, what do you think the hour?

PHILOTUS Labouring for nine.

LUCIUS' SERVANT So much?

PHILOTUS Is not my lord seen yet?

LUCIUS' SERVANT Not yet.

PHILOTUS I wonder on't; he was wont to shine at seven.

LUCIUS' SERVANT Ay, but the days are wax'd shorter with him;
You must consider that a prodigal course
Is like the sun's, but not like his recoverable.
I fear
'Tis deepest winter in Lord Timon's purse;
That is, one may reach deep enough and yet
Find little.

PHILOTUS I am of your fear for that.

TITUS I'll show you how t' observe a strange event.
Your lord sends now for money.

HORTENSIUS Most true, he does.

TITUS And he wears jewels now of Timon's gift,
For which I wait for money.

HORTENSIUS It is against my heart.

LUCIUS' SERVANT Mark how strange it shows
Timon in this should pay more than he owes;
And e'en as if your lord should wear rich jewels
And send for money for 'em.

HORTENSIUS I'm weary of this charge, the gods can witness;

I know my lord hath spent of Timon's wealth,
And now ingratitude makes it worse than stealth.

1 VARRO'S SERVANT Yes, mine's three thousand crowns; what's yours?

LUCIUS' SERVANT Five thousand mine.

1 VARRO'S SERVANT 'Tis much deep; and it should seem by th' sum
Your master's confidence was above mine,
Else surely his had equall'd.

Enter FLAMINIUS.

TITUS One of Lord Timon's men.

LUCIUS' SERVANT Flaminius! Sir, a word. Pray, is my lord ready to come forth?

FLAMINIUS No, indeed, he is not.

TITUS We attend his lordship; pray signify so much.

FLAMINIUS I need not tell him that; he knows you are too diligent. [*Exit.*

Enter FLAVIUS, in a cloak, muffled.

LUCIUS' SERVANT Ha! Is not that his steward muffled so? He goes away in a cloud. Call him, call him.

TITUS Do you hear, sir?

2 VARRO'S SERVANT By your leave, sir.

FLAVIUS What do ye ask of me, my friend?

TITUS We wait for certain money here, sir.

FLAVIUS Ay,
If money were as certain as your waiting,
'Twere sure enough.
Why then preferr'd you not your sums and bills
When your false masters eat of my lord's meat?
Then they could smile, and fawn upon his debts,
And take down th' int'rest into their glutt'nous maws.
You do yourselves but wrong to stir me up;
Let me pass quietly.
Believe't, my lord and I have made an end:
I have no more to reckon, he to spend.

LUCIUS' SERVANT Ay, but this answer will not serve.

FLAVIUS If 'twill not serve, 'tis not so base as you,
For you serve knaves. [*Exit.*

1 VARRO'S SERVANT How! What does his cashier'd worship mutter?

2 VARRO'S SERVANT No matter what; he's poor, and that's revenge enough. Who can speak broader than he that has no house to put his head in? Such may rail against great buildings.

Enter SERVILIUS.

TITUS O, here's Servilius; now we shall know some answer.

SERVILIUS If I might beseech you, gentlemen, to repair some other hour, I should derive much from't; for take't of my soul, my lord leans wondrously to discontent. His comfortable temper has forsook him; he's much out of health and keeps his chamber.

LUCIUS' SERVANT Many do keep their chambers are not sick;
And if it be so far beyond his health,
Methinks he should the sooner pay his debts,
And make a clear way to the gods.

SERVILIUS Good gods!

TITUS We cannot take this for answer, sir.

FLAMINIUS [*Within*] Servilius, help! My lord! my lord!

Enter TIMON, in a rage, FLAMINIUS following.

TIMON What, are my doors oppos'd against my passage?
Have I been ever free, and must my house
Be my retentive enemy, my gaol?
The place which I have feasted, does it now,
Like all mankind, show me an iron heart?

LUCIUS' SERVANT Put in now, Titus.

TITUS My lord, here is my bill.

LUCIUS SERVANT Here's mine.

HORTENSIUS And mine, my lord.

BOTH VARRO'S SERVANTS And ours, my lord

PHILOTUS All our bills.

TIMON Knock me down with 'em; cleave me to the girdle.

LUCIUS' SERVANT Alas, my lord –

TIMON Cut my heart in sums.

TITUS Mine, fifty talents.

TIMON Tell out my blood.

LUCIUS' SERVANT Five thousand crowns, my lord.

TIMON Five thousand drops pays that.
What yours? and yours?

1 VARRO'S SERVANT My lord –

2 VARRO'S SERVANT My lord –

TIMON Tear me, take me, and the gods fall upon you! [*Exit.*

HORTENSIUS Faith, I perceive our masters may throw their caps at their money. These debts may well be call'd desperate ones, for a madman owes 'em. [*Exeunt.*

Re-enter TIMON and FLAVIUS.

TIMON They have e'en put my breath from me, the slaves.
Creditors? Devils!

FLAVIUS My dear lord –

TIMON What if it should be so?

FLAMINIUS My lord. –

TIMON I'll have it so. My steward!

FLAVIUS Here, my lord.

TIMON So fitly? Go, bid all my friends again:

Lucius, Lucullus, and Sempronius – all.
I'll once more feast the rascals.

FLAVIUS O my lord,
You only speak from your distracted soul;
There is not so much left to furnish out
A moderate table.

TIMON Be it not in thy care.
Go, I charge thee, invite them all; let in the tide
Of knaves once more; my cook and I'll provide.

[Exeunt.

SCENE V. *The Senate House.*

Enter three Senators at one door, ALCIBIADES meeting them, with Attendants.

1 SENATOR My, lord, you have my voice to't: the fault's bloody.
'Tis necessary he should die:
Nothing emboldens sin so much as mercy.

2 SENATOR Most true; the law shall bruise him.

ALCIBIADES Honour, health, and compassion, to the Senate!

1 SENATOR Now, Captain?

ALCIBIADES I am an humble suitor to your virtues;
For pity is the virtue of the law,
And none but tyrants use it cruelly.
It pleases time and fortune to lie heavy
Upon a friend of mine, who in hot blood
Hath stepp'd into the law, which is past depth
To those that without heed do plunge into't.
He is a man, setting his fate aside,
Of comely virtues;
Nor did he soil the fact with cowardice –
An honour in him which buys out his fault –
But with a noble fury and fair spirit,
Seeing his reputation touch'd to death,
He did oppose his foe;
And with such sober and unnoted passion
He did behove his anger ere 'twas spent,
As if he had but prov'd an argument.

1 SENATOR You undergo too strict a paradox,
Striving to make an ugly deed look fair;
Your words have took such pains as if they labour'd
To bring manslaughter into form and set
Quarrelling upon the head of valour; which, indeed,
Is valour misbegot, and came into the world
When sects and factions were newly born.
He's truly valiant that can wisely suffer
The worst that man can breathe,
And make his wrongs his outsides,
To wear them like his raiment, carelessly,
And ne'er prefer his injuries to his heart,
To bring it into danger.
If wrongs be evils, and enforce us kill,
What folly 'tis to hazard life for ill!

ALCIBIADES My lord –

1 SENATOR You cannot make gross sins look clear:
To revenge is no valour, but to bear.

ALCIBIADES My lords, then, under favour, pardon me
If I speak like a captain:
Why do fond men expose themselves to battle,
And not endure all threats? Sleep upon't,
And let the foes quietly cut their throats,
Without repugnancy? If there be
Such valour in the bearing, what make we
Abroad? Why, then, women are more valiant,
That stay at home, if bearing carry it;
And the ass more captain than the lion; the fellow
Loaden with irons wiser than the judge,
If wisdom be in suffering. O my lords,
As you are great, be pitifully good.
Who cannot condemn rashness in cold blood?
To kill, I grant, is sin's extremest gust;
But, in defence, by mercy, 'tis most just.
To be in anger is impiety;
But who is man that is not angry?
Weigh but the crime with this.

2 SENATOR You breathe in vain.

ALCIBIADES In vain! His service done
At Lacedaemon and Byzantium
Were a sufficient briber for his life.

1 SENATOR What's that?

ALCIBIADES Why, I say, my lords, has done fair service,
And slain in fight many of your enemies;
How full of valour did he bear himself
In the last conflict, and made plenteous wounds!

2 SENATOR He has made too much plenty with 'em.
He's a sworn rioter; he has a sin that often
Drowns him and takes his valour prisoner.
If there were no foes, that were enough
To overcome him. In that beastly fury
He has been known to commit outrages
And cherish factions. 'Tis inferr'd to us
His days are foul and his drink dangerous.

1 SENATOR He dies.

ALCIBIADES Hard fate! He might have died in war.
My lords, if not for any parts in him –
Though his right arm might purchase his own time,
And be in debt to none – yet, more to move you,
Take my deserts to his, and join 'em both;
And, for I know your reverend ages love
Security, I'll pawn my victories, all
My honours to you, upon his good returns.

If by this crime he owes the law his life,
Why, let the war receive't in valiant gore;
For law is strict, and war is nothing more.

1 SENATOR We are for law: he dies. Urge it no more
On height of our displeasure. Friend or brother,
He forfeits his own blood that spills another.

ALCIBIADES Must it be so? It must not be. My lords,
I do beseech you, know me.

2 SENATOR How!

ALCIBIADES Call me to your remembrances.

3 SENATOR What!

ALCIBIADES I cannot think but your age has forgot me;
It could not else be I should prove so base
To sue, and be denied such common grace.
My wounds ache at you.

1 SENATOR Do you dare our anger?
'Tis in few words, but spacious in effect:
We banish thee for ever.

ALCIBIADES Banish me!
Banish your dotage! Banish usury
That makes the Senate ugly.

1 SENATOR If after two days' shine Athens contain thee,
Attend our weightier judgment. And, not to swell our spirit,
He shall be executed presently.

[Exeunt Senators.

ALCIBIADES Now the gods keep you old enough that you may live
Only in bone, that none may look on you!
I'm worse than mad; I have kept back their foes,
While they have told their money and let out
Their coin upon large interest, I myself
Rich only in large hurts. All those for this?
Is this the balsam that the usuring Senate
Pours into captains' wounds? Banishment!
It comes not ill; I hate not to be banish'd;
It is a cause worthy my spleen and fury,
That I may strike at Athens. I'll cheer up
My discontented troops, and lay for hearts.
'Tis honour with most lands to be at odds;
Soldiers should brook as little wrongs as gods.

[Exit.

SCENE VI. *A banqueting hall in Timon's house.*

Music. Tables set out; Servants attending. Enter divers Lords, friends of Timon, at several doors.

1 LORD The good time of day to you, sir.

2 LORD I also wish it to you. I think this honourable lord did but try us this other day.

1 LORD Upon that were my thoughts tiring when we encount'red. I hope it is not so low with him as he made it seem in the trial of his several friends.

2 LORD It should not be, by the persuasion of his new feasting.

1 LORD I should think so. He hath sent me an earnest inviting, which many my near occasions did urge me to put off; but he hath conjur'd me beyond them, and I must needs appear.

2 LORD In like manner was I in debt to my importunate business, but he would not hear my excuse. I am sorry, when he sent to borrow of me, that my provision was out.

1 LORD I am sick of that grief too, as I understand how all things go.

2 LORD Every man here's so. What would he have borrowed of you?

1 LORD A thousand pieces.

2 LORD A thousand pieces!

1 LORD What of you?

2 LORD He sent to me, sir – here he comes.

Enter TIMON and Attendants.

TIMON With all my heart, gentlemen both! And how fare you?

1 LORD Ever at the best, hearing well of your lordship.

2 LORD The swallow follows not summer more willing than we your lordship.

TIMON *[Aside]* Nor more willingly leaves winter; such summer-birds are men – Gentlemen, our dinner will not recompense this long stay; feast your ears with the music awhile, if they will fare so harshly 'o th' trumpet's sound; we shall to't presently.

1 LORD I hope it remains not unkindly with your lordship that I return'd you an empty messenger.

TIMON O sir, let it not trouble you.

2 LORD My noble lord –

TIMON Ah, my good friend, what cheer?

2 LORD My most honourable lord, I am e'en sick of shame that, when your lordship this other day sent to me, I was so unfortunate a beggar.

TIMON Think not on't, sir.

2 LORD If you had sent but two hours before –

TIMON Let it not cumber your better remembrance. *[The banquet brought in.*
Come, bring in all together.

2 LORD All cover'd dishes!

1 LORD Royal cheer, I warrant you.

3 LORD Doubt not that, if money and the season can yield it.

1 LORD How do you? What's the news?

3 LORD Alcibiades is banish'd. Hear you of it?

1 AND 2 LORDS Alcibiades banish'd!

3 LORD 'Tis so, be sure of it.
1 LORD How? how?
2 LORD I pray you, upon what?
TIMON My worthy friends, will you draw near?
3 LORD I'll tell you more anon Here's a noble feast toward.
2 LORD This is the old man still.
3 LORD Will't hold? Will't hold?
2 LORD It does; but time will – and so –
3 LORD I do conceive.

TIMON Each man to his stool with that spur as he would to the lip of his mistress; your diet shall be in all places alike. Make not a city feast of it, to let the meat cool ere we can agree upon the first place. Sit, sit. The gods require our thanks: You great benefactors, sprinkle our society with thankfulness. For your own gifts make yourselves prais'd; but reserve still to give, lest your deities be despised. Lend to each man enough, that one need not lend to another; for were your god-heads to borrow of men, men would forsake the gods. Make the meat be beloved more than the man that gives it. Let no assembly of twenty be without a score of villains. If there sit twelve women at the table, let a dozen of them be – as they are. The rest of your foes, O gods, the Senators of Athens, together with the common lag of people, what is amiss in them, you gods, make suitable for destruction. For these my present friends, as they are to me nothing, so in nothing bless them, and to nothing are they welcome.

Uncover, dogs, and lap.

[*The dishes are uncovered and seen to be full of warm water.*

SOME SPEAK What does his lordship mean?
SOME OTHER I know not.
TIMON May you a better feast never behold,
You knot of mouth-friends! Smoke and lukewarm water
Is your perfection. This is Timon's last;
Who, stuck and spangled with your flatteries,
Washes it off, and sprinkles in your faces
[*Throwing the water in their faces.*
Your reeking villainy. Live loath'd and long,
Most smiling, smooth, detested parasites,
Courteous destroyers, affable wolves, meek bears,
You fools of fortune, trencher friends, time's flies,
Cap and knee slaves, vapours, and minute-jacks!
Of man and beast the infinite malady
Crust you quite o'er! What, dost thou go?
Soft, take thy physic first; thou too, and thou.
Stay, I will lend thee money, borrow none.

[*Throws the dishes at them, and drives them out.*

What, all in motion? Henceforth be no feast
Whereat a villain's not a welcome guest.
Burn house ! Sink Athens! Henceforth hated be
Of Timon man and all humanity! [*Exit.*

Re-enter the Lords.

1 LORD How now, my lords!
2 LORD Know you the quality of Lord Timon's fury?
3 LORD Push! Did you see my cap?
4 LORD I have lost my gown.
1 LORD He's but a mad lord, and nought but humours sways him. He gave me a jewel th' other day, and now he has beat it out of my hat. Did you see my jewel?
3 LORD Did you see my cap?
2 LORD Here 'tis.
4 LORD Here lies my gown.
1 LORD Let's make no stay.
2 LORD Lord Timon's mad.
3 LORD I feel't upon my bones.
4 LORD One day he gives us diamonds, next day stones. [*Exeunt.*

ACT FOUR

SCENE I. *Without the walls of Athens.*

Enter TIMON.

TIMON Let me look back upon thee. O thou wall
That girdles in those wolves, dive in the earth
And fence not Athens! Matrons, turn incontinent.
Obedience, fail in children! Slaves and fools,
Pluck the grave wrinkled Senate from the bench
And minister in their steads. To general filths
Convert, o' th' instant, green virginity.
Do't in your parents' eyes. Bankrupts, hold fast;
Rather than render back, out with your knives
And cut your trusters' throats. Bound servants, steal:
Large-handed robbers your grave masters are,
And pill by law. Maid, to thy master's bed:
Thy mistress is o' th' brothel. Son of sixteen,
Pluck the lin'd crutch from thy old limping sire,

With it beat out his brains. Piety and fear,
Religion to the gods, peace, justice, truth,
Domestic awe, night-rest, and neighbourhood,
Instruction, manners, mysteries, and trades,
Degrees, observances, customs and laws,
Decline to your confounding contraries
And let confusion live. Plagues incident to men,
Your potent and infectious fevers heap
On Athens, ripe for stroke. Thou cold sciatica,
Cripple our senators, that their limbs may halt
As lamely as their manners. Lust and liberty,
Creep in the minds and marrows of our youth;
That 'gainst the stream of virtue they may strive
And drown themselves in riot. Itches, blains,
Sow all th' Athenian bosoms, and their crop
Be general leprosy! Breath infect breath,
That their society, as their friendship, may
Be merely poison! Nothing I'll bear from thee
But nakedness, thou detestable town!
Take thou that too, with multiplying bans.
Timon will to the woods, where he shall find
Th' unkindest beast more kinder than mankind.
The gods confound – hear me, you good gods all –
The Athenians both within and out that wall!
And grant, as Timon grows, his hate may grow
To the whole race of mankind, high and low!
Amen. *[Exit.*

SCENE II. *Athens. Timon's house.*

Enter FLAVIUS, with two or three Servants.

1 SERVANT Hear you, Master Steward, where's our master?
Are we undone, cast off, nothing remaining?

FLAVIUS Alack, my fellows, what should I say to you?
Let me be recorded by the righteous gods,
I am as poor as you.

1 SERVANT Such a house broke!
So noble a master fall'n! All gone, and not
One friend to take his fortune by the arm
And go along with him?

2 SERVANT As we do turn our backs
From our companion, thrown into his grave,
So his familiars to his buried fortunes
Slink all away; leave their false vows with him,
Like empty purses pick'd; and his poor self,
A dedicated beggar to the air,
With his disease of all-shunn'd poverty,
Walks, like contempt, alone. More of our fellows.

Enter other Servants.

FLAVIUS All broken implements of a ruin'd house.

3 SERVANT Yet do our hearts wear Timon's livery;
That see I by our faces. We are fellows still,
Serving alike in sorrow. Leak'd is our bark;
And we, poor mates, stand on the dying deck,
Hearing the surges threat. We must all part
Into this sea of air.

FLAVIUS Good fellows all,
The latest of my wealth I'll share amongst you.
Wherever we shall meet, for Timon's sake,
Let's yet be fellows; let's shake our heads and say,
As 'twere a knell unto our master's fortune,
'We have seen better days'. Let each take some.
[Giving them money.
Nay, put out all your hands. Not one word more!
Thus part we rich in sorrow, parting poor.
[Embrace, and part several ways.
O the fierce wretchedness that glory brings us!
Who would not wish to be from wealth exempt,
Since riches point to misery and contempt?
Who would be so mock'd with glory, or to live
But in a dream of friendship,
To have his pomp, and all what state compounds,
But only painted, like his varnish'd friends?
Poor honest lord, brought low by his own heart,
Undone by goodness! Strange, unusual blood,
When man's worst sin is he does too much good!
Who then dares to be half so kind again?
For bounty, that makes gods, does still mar men.
My dearest lord – blest to be most accurst,
Rich only to be wretched – thy great fortunes
Are made thy chief afflictions. Alas, kind lord!
He's flung in rage from this ingrateful seat
Of monstrous friends; nor has he with him to
Supply his life, or that which can command it.
I'll follow and enquire him out.
I'll ever serve his mind with my best will;
Whilst I have gold, I'll be his steward still.
[Exit.

SCENE III. *The woods near the sea-shore. Before Timon's cave.*

Enter TIMON in the woods.

TIMON O blessed breeding sun, draw from the earth
Rotten humidity; below thy sister's orb
Infect the air! Twinn'd brothers of one womb –
Whose procreation, residence, and birth,
Scarce is dividant – touch them with several fortunes:
The greater scorns the lesser. Not nature,
To whom all sores lay siege, can bear great fortune

But by contempt of nature.
Raise me this beggar and deny't that lord:
The senator shall bear contempt hereditary,
The beggar native honour.
It is the pasture lards the rother's sides,
The want that makes him lean. Who dares, who dares,
In purity of manhood stand upright,
And say 'This man's a flatterer'? If one be,
So are they all; for every grise of fortune
Is smooth'd by that below. The learned pate
Ducks to the golden fool. All's oblique;
There's nothing level in our cursed natures
But direct villainy. Therefore be abhorr'd
All feasts, societies, and throngs of men!
His semblable, yea, himself, Timon disdains.
Destruction fang mankind! Earth, yield me roots. [*Digging.*
Who seeks for better of thee, sauce his palate
With thy most operant poison. What is here?
Gold? Yellow, glittering, precious gold? No, gods,
I am no idle votarist. Roots, you clear heavens!
Thus much of this will make black white, foul fair,
Wrong right, base noble, old young, coward valiant.
Ha, you gods! why this? What, this, you gods?
Why, this
Will lug your priests and servants from your sides,
Pluck stout men's pillows from below their heads –
This yellow slave
Will knit and break religious, bless th' accurs'd,
Make the hoar leprosy ador'd, place thieves
And give them title, knee, and approbation,
With senators on the bench. This is it
That makes the wappen'd widow wed again –
She whom the spital-house and ulcerous sores
Would cast the gorge at this embalms and spices
To th' April day again. Come, damn'd earth,
Thou common whore of mankind, that puts odds
Among the rout of nations, I will make thee
Do thy right nature. [*March afar off.*
Ha! a drum? Th'art quick,
But yet I'll bury thee. Thou't go, strong thief,
When gouty keepers of thee cannot stand.
Nay, stay thou out for earnest.

[*Keeping some gold.*

Enter ALCIBIADES, with drum and fife, in warlike manner; and PHRYNIA and TIMANDRA.

ALCIBIADES What art thou there? Speak.

TIMON A beast, as thou art. The canker gnaw thy heart
For showing me again the eyes of man!

ALCIBIADES What is thy name? Is man so hateful to thee
That art thyself a man?

TIMON I am Misanthropos, and hate mankind.
For thy part, I do wish thou wert a dog,
That I might love thee something.

ALCIBIADES I know thee well;
But in thy fortunes am unlearn'd and strange.

TIMON I know thee too; and more than that I know thee
I not desire to know. Follow thy drum;
With man's blood paint the ground, gules, gules.
Religious canons, civil laws, are cruel;
Then what should war be? This fell whore of thine
Hath in her more destruction than thy sword
For all her cherubin look.

PHRYNIA Thy lips rot off!

TIMON I will not kiss thee; then the rot returns
To thine own lips again.

ALCIBIADES How came the noble Timon to this change?

TIMON As the moon does, by wanting light to give.
But then renew I could not, like the moon;
There were no suns to borrow of.

ALCIBIADES Noble Timon,
What friendship may I do thee?

TIMON None, but to
Maintain my opinion.

ALCIBIADES What is it, Timon?

TIMON Promise me friendship, but perform none. If thou wilt not promise, the gods plague thee, for thou art a man! If thou dost perform, confound thee, for thou art a man!

ALCIBIADES I have heard in some sort of thy miseries.

TIMON Thou saw'st them when I had prosperity.

ALCIBIADES I see them now; then was a blessed time.

TIMON As thine is now, held with a brace of harlots.

TIMANDRA Is this th' Athenian minion whom the world
Voic'd so regardfully?

TIMON Art thou Timandra?

TIMANDRA Yes.

TIMON Be a whore still; they love thee not that use thee.
Give them disease, leaving with thee their lust.
Make use of thy salt hours. Season the slaves
For tubs and baths; bring down rose-cheek'd youth

To the tub-fast and the diet.
TIMANDRA Hang thee, monster!
ALCIBIADES Pardon him, sweet Timandra, for his wits
Are drown'd and lost in his calamities.
I have but little gold of late, brave Timon,
The want whereof doth daily make revolt
In my penurious band. I have heard, and griev'd,
How cursed Athens, mindless of thy worth,
Forgetting thy great deeds, when neighbour states,
But for thy sword and fortune, trod upon them –
TIMON I prithee beat thy drum and get thee gone.
ALCIBIADES I am thy friend, and pity thee, dear Timon.
TIMON How dost thou pity him whom thou dost trouble?
I had rather be alone.
ALCIBIADES Why, fare thee well;
Here is some gold for thee.
TIMON Keep it: I cannot eat it.
ALCIBIADES When I have laid proud Athens on a heap –
TIMON War'st thou 'gainst Athens?
ALCIBIADES Ay, Timon, and have cause.
TIMON The gods confound them all in thy conquest;
And thee after, when thou hast conquer'd!
ALCIBIADES Why me, Timon?
TIMON That by killing of villains
Thou wast born to conquer my country.
Put up thy gold. Go on. Here's gold. Go on.
Be as a planetary plague, when Jove
Will o'er some high-vic'd city hang his poison
In the sick air; let not thy sword skip one.
Pity not honour'd age for his white beard:
He is an usurer. Strike me the counterfeit matron:
It is her habit only that is honest,
Herself's a bawd. Let not the virgin's cheek
Make soft thy trenchant sword; for those milk paps
That through the window bars bore at men's eyes
Are not within the leaf of pity writ,
But set them down horrible traitors. Spare not the babe
Whose dimpled smiles from fools exhaust their mercy;
Think it a bastard whom the oracle
Hath doubtfully pronounc'd thy throat shall cut,
And mince it sans remorse. Swear against abjects;
Put armour on thine ears and on thine eyes,
Whose proof nor yells of mothers, maids, nor babes,
Nor sight of priests in holy vestments bleeding,
Shall pierce a jot. There's gold to pay thy soldiers.
Make large confusion; and, thy fury spent,
Confounded be thyself! Speak not, be gone.
ALCIBIADES Hast thou gold yet? I'll take the gold thou givest me,
Not all thy counsel.
TIMON Dost thou, or dost thou not, heaven's curse upon thee!
PHRYNIA AND TIMANDRA Give us some gold, good Timon. Hast thou more?
TIMON Enough to make a whore forswear her trade,
And to make whores a bawd. Hold up, you sluts,
Your aprons mountant; you are not oathable,
Although I know you'll swear, terribly swear,
Into strong shudders and to heavenly agues,
Th' immortal gods that hear you. Spare your oaths;
I'll trust to your conditions. Be whores still;
And he whose pious breath seeks to convert you –
Be strong in whore, allure him, burn him up;
Let your close fire predominate his smoke,
And be no turncoats. Yet may your pains six months
Be quite contrary! And thatch your poor thin roofs
With burdens of the dead – some that were hang'd,
No matter. Wear them, betray with them. Whore still;
Paint till a horse may mire upon your face.
A pox of wrinkles!
PHRYNIA AND TIMANDRA Well, more gold. What then?
Believe't that we'll do anything for gold.
TIMON Consumptions sow
In hollow bones of man; strike their sharp shins,
And mar men's spurring. Crack the lawyer's voice,
That he may never more false title plead,
Nor sound his quillets shrilly. Hoar the flamen,
That scolds against the quality of flesh
And not believes himself. Down with the nose,
Down with it flat, take the bridge quite away
Of him that, his particular to foresee,
Smells from the general weal. Make curl'd pate ruffians bald,
And let the unscarr'd braggarts of the war
Derive some pain from you. Plague all,
That your activity may defeat and quell
The source of all erection. There's more gold.
Do you damn others, and let this damn you,
And ditches grave you all!
PHRYNIA AND TIMANDRA More counsel

with more money, bounteous Timon.
TIMON More whore, more mischief first; I have given you earnest.
ALCIBIADES Strike up the drum towards Athens. Farewell, Timon;
If I thrive well, I'll visit thee again.
TIMON If I hope well, I'll never see thee more.
ALCIBIADES I never did thee harm.
TIMON Yes, thou spok'st well of me.
ALCIBIADES Call'st thou that harm?
TIMON Men daily find it. Get thee away, and take
Thy beagles with thee.
ALCIBIADES We but offend him.
Strike.
[Drum beats. Exeunt all but Timon.
TIMON That nature, being sick of man's unkindness,
Should yet be hungry! Common mother, thou, *[Digging.*
Whose womb unmeasurable and infinite breast
Teems and feeds all; whose self-same mettle,
Whereof thy proud child, arrogant man, is puff'd,
Engenders the black toad and adder blue,
The gilded newt and eyeless venom'd worm,
With all th' abhorred births below crisp heaven
Whereon Hyperion's quick'ning fire doth shine –
Yield him, who all thy human sons doth hate,
From forth thy plenteous bosom, one poor root!
Ensear thy fertile and conceptious womb,
Let it no more bring out ingrateful man!
Go great with tigers, dragons, wolves, and bears;
Teem with new monsters whom thy upward face
Hath to the marbled mansion all above
Never presented! – O, a root! Dear thanks! –
Dry up thy marrows, vines, and ploughtorn leas,
Whereof ingrateful man, with liquorish draughts
And morsels unctuous, greases his pure mind,
That from it all consideration slips –
Enter APEMANTUS.
More man? Plague, plague!
APEMANTUS I was directed hither. Men report
Thou dost affect my manners and dost use them.
TIMON 'Tis, then, because thou dost not keep a dog,
Whom I would imitate. Consumption catch thee!
APEMANTUS This is in thee a nature but infected,
A poor unmanly melancholy sprung
From change of fortune. Why this spade, this place?
This slave-like habit and these looks of care?
Thy flatterers yet wear silk, drink wine, lie soft,
Hug their diseas'd perfumes, and have forgot
That ever Timon was. Shame not these woods
By putting on the cunning of a carper.
Be thou a flatterer now, and seek to thrive
By that which has undone thee: hinge thy knee,
And let his very breath whom thou'lt observe
Blow off thy cap; praise his most vicious strain,
And call it excellent. Thou wast told thus;
Thou gav'st thine ears, like tapsters that bade welcome,
To knaves and all approachers. 'Tis most just
That thou turn rascal; hadst thou wealth again
Rascals should have't. Do not assume my likeness.
TIMON Were I like thee, I'd throw away myself.
APEMANTUS Thou hast cast away thyself, being like thyself;
A madman so long, now a fool. What, think'st
That the bleak air, thy boisterous chamberlain,
Will put thy shirt on warm? Will these moist trees,
That have outliv'd the eagle, page thy heels
And skip when thou point'st out? Will the cold brook,
Candied with ice, caudle thy morning taste
To cure thy o'ernight's surfeit? Call the creatures
Whose naked natures live in all the spite
Of wreakful heaven, whose bare unhoused trunks,
To the conflicting elements expos'd,
Answer mere nature – bid them flatter thee.
O, thou shalt find –
TIMON A fool of thee. Depart.
APEMANTUS I love thee better now than e'er I did.
TIMON I hate thee worse.
APEMANTUS Why?
TIMON Thou flatter'st misery.
APEMANTUS I flatter not, but say thou art a caitiff.
TIMON Why dost thou seek me out?
APEMANTUS To vex thee.
TIMON Always a villain's office or a fool's.
Dost please thyself in't?
APEMANTUS Ay.
TIMON What, a knave too?
APEMANTUS If thou didst put this sour-cold habit on
To castigate thy pride, 'twere well; but thou
Dost it enforcedly. Thou'dst courtier be again
Wert thou not beggar. Willing misery

Outlives incertain pomp, is crown'd before.
The one is filling still, never complete;
The other, at high wish. Best state, contentless,
Hath a distracted and most wretched being,
Worse than the worst, content.
Thou should'st desire to die, being miserable.

TIMON Not by his breath that is more miserable.
Thou art a slave whom Fortune's tender arm
With favour never clasp'd, but bred a dog.
Hadst thou, like us from our first swath, proceeded
The sweet degrees that this brief world affords
To such as may the passive drugs of it
Freely command, thou wouldst have plung'd thyself
In general riot, melted down thy youth
In different beds of lust, and never learn'd
The icy precepts of respect, but followed
The sug'red game before thee. But myself,
Who had the world as my confectionary;
The mouths, the tongues, the eyes, and hearts of men
At duty, more than I could frame employment;
That numberless upon me stuck, as leaves
Do on the oak, have with one winter's brush
Fell from their boughs, and left me open, bare
For every storm that blows – I to bear this,
That never knew but better, is some burden.
Thy nature did commence in sufferance; time
Hath made thee hard in't. Why shouldst thou hate men?
They never flatter'd thee. What hast thou given?
If thou wilt curse, thy father, that poor rag,
Must be thy subject; who, in spite, put stuff
To some she-beggar and compounded thee
Poor rogue hereditary. Hence, be gone.
If thou hadst not been born the worst of men,
Thou hadst been a knave and flatterer.

APEMANTUS Art thou proud yet?

TIMON Ay, that I am not thee.

APEMANTUS I, that I was
No prodigal.

TIMON I, that I am one now.
Were all the wealth I have shut up in thee,
I'd give thee leave to hang it. Get thee gone.
That the whole life of Athens were in this!
Thus would I eat it. [*Eating a root.*

APEMANTUS Here! I will mend thy feast.
[*Offering him food.*

TIMON First mend my company: take away thyself.

APEMANTUS So I shall mend mine own by th' lack of thine.

TIMON 'Tis not well mended so; it is but botch'd.
If not, I would it were.

APEMANTUS What wouldst thou have to Athens?

TIMON Thee thither in a whirlwind. If thou wilt,
Tell them there I have gold; look, so I have.

APEMANTUS Here is no use for gold.

TIMON The best and truest;
For here it sleeps and does no hired harm.

APEMANTUS Where liest a nights, Timon?

TIMON Under that's above me.
Where feed'st thou a days, Apemantus?

APEMANTUS Where my stomach finds meat; or rather, where I eat it.

TIMON Would poison were obedient, and knew my mind!

APEMANTUS Where wouldst thou send it?

TIMON To sauce thy dishes.

APEMANTUS The middle of humanity thou never knewest, but the extremity of both ends. When thou wast in thy gilt and thy perfume, they mock'd thee for too much curiosity; in thy rags thou know'st none, but art despis'd for the contrary. There's a medlar for thee; eat it.

TIMON On what I hate I feed not.

APEMANTUS Dost hate a medlar?

TIMON Ay, though it look like thee.

APEMANTUS An th'hadst hated medlars sooner, thou shouldst have loved thyself better now. What man didst thou ever know unthrift that was beloved after his means?

TIMON Who, without those means thou talk'st of, didst thou ever know belov'd?

APEMANTUS Myself.

TIMON I understand thee: thou hadst some means to keep a dog.

APEMANTUS What things in the world canst thou nearest compare to thy flatterers?

TIMON Women nearest; but men, men are the things themselves. What wouldst thou do with the world, Apemantus, if it lay in thy power?

APEMANTUS Give it the beasts, to be rid of the men.

TIMON Would'st thou have thyself fall in the confusion of men, and remain a beast with the beasts?

APEMANTUS Ay, Timon.

TIMON A beastly ambition, which the gods grant thee t' attain to! If thou wert the lion, the fox would beguile thee; if thou wert the lamb, the fox would eat thee; if thou wert the fox, the lion would suspect thee, when, peradventure, thou wert accus'd by the ass. If thou wert the ass, thy dulness would torment thee; and still thou liv'dst but as a breakfast to the wolf. If thou wert the wolf, thy greediness would afflict thee, and oft thou shouldst hazard thy life for thy dinner. Wert thou the unicorn, pride and wrath would confound thee, and make thine own self the conquest of thy fury. Wert thou a bear, thou wouldst be kill'd by the horse; wert thou a horse, thou wouldst be seiz'd by the leopard; wert thou a leopard, thou wert german to the lion, and the spots of thy kindred were jurors on thy life. All thy safety were remotion, and thy defence absence. What beast couldst thou be that were not subject to a beast? And what a beast art thou already, that seest not thy loss in transformation!

APEMANTUS If thou couldst please me with speaking to me, thou mightst have hit upon it here. The commonwealth of Athens is become a forest of beasts.

TIMON How has the ass broke the wall, that thou art out of the city?

APEMANTUS Yonder comes a poet and a painter. The plague of company light upon thee! I will fear to catch it, and give way. When I know not what else to do, I'll see thee again.

TIMON When there is nothing living but thee, thou shalt be welcome. I had rather be a beggar's dog than Apemantus.

APEMANTUS Thou art the cap of all the fools
alive.

TIMON Would thou wert clean enough to spit
upon!

APEMANTUS A plague on thee! thou art too bad
to curse.

TIMON All villains that do stand by thee are pure.

APEMANTUS There is no leprosy but what thou
speak'st.

TIMON If I name thee.
I'll beat thee – but I should infect my hands.

APEMANTUS I would my tongue could rot them
off!

TIMON Away, thou issue of a mangy dog!
Choler does kill me that thou art alive;
I swoon to see thee.

APEMANTUS Would thou wouldst burst!

TIMON Away,
Thou tedious rogue! I am sorry I shall lose
A stone by thee. [*Throws a stone at him.*

APEMANTUS Beast!

TIMON Slave!

APEMANTUS Toad!

TIMON Rogue, rogue, rogue!
I am sick of this false world, and will love
nought
But even the mere necessities upon't.
Then, Timon, presently prepare thy grave;
Lie where the light foam of the sea may beat
Thy gravestone daily; make thine epitaph,
That death in me at others' lives may laugh.
[*Looks at the gold*] O thou sweet king-killer,
and dear divorce
'Twixt natural son and sire! thou bright defiler
Of Hymen's purest bed! thou valiant Mars!
Thou ever young, fresh, lov'd, and delicate
wooer,
Whose blush doth thaw the consecrated snow
That lies on Dian's lap! thou visible god,
That sold'rest close impossibilities,
And mak'st them kiss! that speak'st with every
tongue
To every purpose! O thou touch of hearts!
Think thy slave man rebels, and by thy virtue
Set them into confounding odds, that beasts
May have the world in empire!

APEMANTUS Would 'twere so!
But not till I am dead. I'll say th' hast gold.
Thou wilt be throng'd to shortly.

TIMON Throng'd to?

APEMANTUS Ay.

TIMON Thy back, I prithee.

APEMANTUS Live, and love thy misery!

TIMON Long live so, and so die! [*Exit Apemantus*]
I am quit.
Moe things like men? Eat, Timon, and abhor
them.

Enter the Banditti.

1 BANDIT Where should he have this gold? It is some poor fragment, some slender ort of his remainder. The mere want of gold and the falling-from of his friends drove him into this melancholy.

2 BANDIT It is nois'd he hath a mass of treasure.

3 BANDIT Let us make the assay upon him; if he care not for't, he will supply us easily; if he covetously reserve it, how shall's get it?

2 BANDIT True; for he bears it not about him. 'Tis hid.

1 BANDIT Is not this he?

1 BANDIT Where?

2 BANDIT 'Tis his description.

3 BANDIT He; I know him.

1 BANDIT Save thee, Timon!

TIMON Now, thieves?

1 BANDIT Soldiers, not thieves.

TIMON Both too, and women's sons.

1 BANDIT We are not thieves, but men that much
do want.

TIMON Your greatest want is, you want much of
meat.
Why should you want? Behold, the earth hath
roots;
Within this mile break forth a hundred springs;
The oaks bear mast, the briars scarlet hips;
The bounteous housewife Nature on each bush
Lays her full mess before you. Want! Why
want?

1 BANDIT We cannot live on grass, on berries,
water,
As beasts and birds and fishes.

TIMON Nor on the beasts themselves, the birds, and fishes;
You must eat men. Yet thanks I must you con
That you are thieves profess'd, that you work not
In holier shapes; for there is boundless theft
In limited professions. Rascal thieves,
Here's gold. Go, suck the subtle blood o' th' grape
Till the high fever seethe your blood to froth,
And so scape hanging. Trust not the physician;
His antidotes are poison, and he slays
Moe than you rob. Take wealth and lives together;
Do villainy, do, since you protest to do't,
Like workmen. I'll example you with thievery:
The sun's a thief, and with his great attraction
Robs the vast sea; the moon's an arrant thief,
And her pale fire she snatches from the sun;
The sea's a thief, whose liquid surge resolves
The moon into salt tears; the earth's a thief,
That feeds and breeds by a composture stol'n
From gen'ral excrement – each thing's a thief.
The laws, your curb and whip, in their rough power
Has uncheck'd theft. Love not yourselves; away,
Rob one another. There's more gold. Cut throats;
All that you meet are thieves. To Athens go,
Break open shops; nothing can you steal
But thieves do lose it. Steal not less for this
I give you; and gold confound you howsoe'er!
Amen.

3 BANDIT Has almost charm'd me from my profession by persuading me to it.

1 BANDIT 'Tis in the malice of mankind that he thus advises us; not to have us thrive in our mystery.

2 BANDIT I'll believe him as an enemy, and give over my trade.

1 BANDIT Let us first see peace in Athens. There is no time so miserable but a man may be true. [*Exeunt Thieves.*

Enter FLAVIUS, to Timon.

FLAVIUS O you gods!
Is yond despis'd and ruinous man my lord?
Full of decay and failing? O monument
And wonder of good deeds evilly bestow'd!
What an alteration of honour
Has desp'rate want made!
What viler thing upon the earth than friends,
Who can bring noblest minds to basest ends!
How rarely does it meet with this time's guise,
When man was wish'd to love his enemies!
Grant I may ever love, and rather woo
Those that would mischief me than those that do!
Has caught me in his eye; I will present
My honest grief unto him, and as my lord
Still serve him with my life. My dearest master!

TIMON Away! What art thou?

FLAVIUS Have you forgot me, sir?

TIMON Why dost ask that? I have forgot all men;
Then, if thou grant'st th'art a man, I have forgot thee.

FLAVIUS An honest poor servant of yours.

TIMON Then I know thee not.
I never had honest man about me, I.
All I kept were knaves, to serve in meat to villains.

FLAVIUS The gods are witness,
Nev'r did poor steward wear a truer grief
For his undone lord than mine eyes for you.

TIMON What, dost thou weep? Come nearer. Then I love thee
Because thou art a woman and disclaim'st
Flinty mankind, whose eyes do never give
But thorough lust and laughter. Pity's sleeping.
Strange times, that weep with laughing, not with weeping!

FLAVIUS I beg of you to know me, good my lord,
T' accept my grief, and whilst this poor wealth lasts
To entertain me as your steward still.

TIMON Had I a steward
So true, so just, and now so comfortable?
It almost turns my dangerous nature mild.
Let me behold thy face. Surely, this man
Was born of woman.
Forgive my general and exceptless rashness,
You perpetual-sober gods! I do proclaim
One honest man – mistake me not, but one;
No more, I pray – and he's a steward.
How fain would I have hated all mankind!
And thou redeem'st thyself. But all, save thee,
I fell with curses.
Methinks thou art more honest now than wise;
For by oppressing and betraying me
Thou mightst have sooner got another service;
For many so arrive at second masters
Upon their first lord's neck. But tell me true,
For I must ever doubt though ne'er so sure,
Is not thy kindness subtle, covetous,
If not a usuring kindness, and as rich men deal gifts,
Expecting in return twenty for one?

FLAVIUS No, my most worthy master, in whose breast
Doubt and suspect, alas, are plac'd too late!
You should have fear'd false times when you did feast:
Suspect still comes where an estate is least.
That which I show, heaven knows, is merely love,

Duty, and zeal, to your unmatched mind,
Care of your food and living; and believe it,
My most honour'd lord,
For any benefit that points to me,
Either in hope or present, I'd exchange
For this one wish, that you had power and wealth
To requite me by making rich yourself.

TIMON Look thee, 'tis so! Thou singly honest man,
Here, take. The gods, out of my misery,
Have sent thee treasure. Go, live rich and happy,
But thus condition'd: thou shalt build from men;
Hate all, curse all, show charity to none,
But let the famish'd flesh slide from the bone
Ere thou relieve the beggar. Give to dogs
What thou deniest to men; let prisons swallow 'em,
Debts wither 'em to nothing. Be men like blasted woods,
And may diseases lick up their false bloods!
And so, farewell and thrive.

FLAVIUS O, let me stay
And comfort you, my master.

TIMON If thou hat'st curses,
Stay not; fly whilst thou art blest and free.
Ne'er see thou man, and let me ne'er see thee.

[Exeunt severally.

ACT FIVE

SCENE I. *The woods. Before Timon's cave.*

Enter Poet and Painter.

PAINTER As I took note of the place, it cannot be far where he abides.

POET What's to be thought of him? Does the rumour hold for true that he's so full of gold?

PAINTER Certain. Alcibiades reports it; Phrynia and Timandra had gold of him. He likewise enrich'd poor straggling soldiers with great quantity. 'Tis said he gave unto his steward a mighty sum.

POET Then this breaking of his has been but a try for his friends?

PAINTER Nothing else. You shall see him a palm in Athens again, and flourish with the highest. Therefore 'tis not amiss we tender our loves to him in this suppos'd distress of his; it will show honestly in us, and is very likely to load our purposes with what they travail for, if it be a just and true report that goes of his having.

POET What have you now to present unto him?

PAINTER Nothing at this time but my visitation; only I will promise him an excellent piece.

POET I must serve him so too, tell him of an intent that's coming toward him.

PAINTER Good as the best. Promising is the very air o' th' time; it opens the eyes of expectation. Performance is ever the duller for his act, and but in the plainer and simpler kind of people the deed of saying is quite out of use. To promise is most courtly and fashionable; performance is a kind of will or testament which argues a great sickness in his judgment that makes it.

Enter TIMON from his cave.

TIMON [Aside] Excellent workman! Thou canst not paint a man so bad as is thyself.

POET I am thinking what I shall say I have provided for him. It must be a personating of himself; a satire against the softness of prosperity, with a discovery of the infinite flatteries that follow youth and opulency.

TIMON [*Aside*] Must thou needs stand for a villain in thine own work? Wilt thou whip thine own faults in other men? Do so, I have gold for thee.

POET Nay, let's seek him;
Then do we sin against our own estate
When we may profit meet and come too late.

PAINTER True;
When the day serves, before black-corner'd night,
Find what thou want'st by free and offer'd light.
Come.

TIMON [*Aside*] I'll meet you at the turn. What a god's gold,
That he is worshipp'd in a baser temple
Than where swine feed!
'Tis thou that rig'st the bark and plough'st the foam,
Settlest admired reverence in a slave.
To thee be worship! and thy saints for aye
Be crown'd with plagues, that thee alone obey!
Fit I meet them. *[Advancing from his cave.*

POET Hail, worthy Timon!

PAINTER Our late noble master!

TIMON Have I once liv'd to see two honest men?

POET Sir,
Having often of your open bounty tasted,
Hearing you were retir'd, your friends fall'n off,
Whose thankless natures – O abhorred spirits! –
Not all the whips of heaven are large enough –

What! to you,
Whose star-like nobleness gave life and influence
To their whole being! I am rapt, and cannot cover
The monstrous bulk of this ingratitude
With any size of words.

TIMON Let it go naked: men may see't the better.
You that are honest, by being what you are,
Make them best seen and known.

PAINTER He and myself
Have travail'd in the great show'r of your gifts,
And sweetly felt it.

TIMON Ay, you are honest men.

PAINTER We are hither come to offer you our service.

TIMON Most honest men! Why, how shall I requite you?
Can you eat roots, and drink cold water – No?

BOTH What we can do, we'll do, to do you service.

TIMON Y'are honest men. Y'have heard that I have gold;
I am sure you have. Speak truth; y'are honest men.

PAINTER So it is said, my noble lord; but therefore
Came not my friend nor I.

TIMON Good honest men! Thou draw'st a counterfeit
Best in all Athens. Th'art indeed the best;
Thou counterfeit'st most lively.

PAINTER So, so, my lord.

TIMON E'en so, sir, as I say. [*To the Poet*] And for thy fiction,
Why, thy verse swells with stuff so fine and smooth
That thou art even natural in thine art.
But for all this, my honest-natur'd friends,
I must needs say you have a little fault.
Marry, 'tis not monstrous in you; neither wish I
You take much pains to mend.

BOTH Beseech your honour
To make it known to us.

TIMON You'll take it ill.

BOTH Most thankfully, my lord.

TIMON Will you indeed?

BOTH Doubt it not, worthy lord.

TIMON There's never a one of you but trusts a knave
That mightily deceives you.

BOTH Do we, my lord?

TIMON Ay, and you hear him cog, see him dissemble,
Know his gross patchery, love him, feed him,
Keep in your bosom; yet remain assur'd
That he's a made-up villain.

PAINTER I know not such, my lord.

POET Nor I.

TIMON Look you, I love you well; I'll give you gold,
Rid me these villains from your companies.
Hang them or stab them, drown them in a draught,
Confound them by some course, and come to me,
I'll give you gold enough.

BOTH Name them, my lord; let's know them.

TIMON You that way, and you this – but two in company;
Each man apart, all single and alone,
Yet an arch-villain keeps him company.
[*To the Painter*] If, where thou art, two villains shall not be,
Come not near him. [*To the Poet*] If thou wouldst not reside
But where one villain is, then him abandon. –
Hence, pack! there's gold; you came for gold, ye slaves.
[*To the Painter*] You have work for me; there's payment; hence!
[*To the Poet*] You are an alchemist; make gold of that. –
Out, rascal dogs! [*Beats and drives them out.*

Enter FLAVIUS and two Senators.

FLAVIUS It is vain that you would speak with Timon;
For he is set so only to himself
That nothing but himself which looks like man
Is friendly with him.

1 SENATOR Bring us to his cave.
It is our part and promise to th' Athenians
To speak with Timon.

2 SENATOR At all times alike
Men are not still the same; 'twas time and griefs
That fram'd him thus. Time, with his fairer hand,
Offering the fortunes of his former days,
The former man may make him. Bring us to him,
And chance it as it may.

FLAVIUS Here is his cave.
Peace and content be here! Lord Timon! Timon!
Look out, and speak to friends. Th' Athenians
By two of their most reverend Senate greet thee.
Speak to them, noble Timon.

Enter TIMON out of his cave.

TIMON Thou sun that comforts, burn. Speak and be hang'd!
For each true word a blister, and each false
Be as a cauterizing to the root o' th' tongue,
Consuming it with speaking!

1 SENATOR Worthy Timon –
TIMON Of none but such as you, and you of Timon.
1 SENATOR The senators of Athens greet thee, Timon.
TIMON I thank them; and would send them back the plague,
Could I but catch it for them.
1 SENATOR O, forget
What we are sorry for ourselves in thee.
The senators with one consent of love
Entreat thee back to Athens, who have thought
On special dignities, which vacant lie
For thy best use and wearing.
2 SENATOR They confess
Toward thee forgetfulness too general, gross;
Which now the public body, which doth seldom
Play the recanter, feeling in itself
A lack of Timon's aid, hath sense withal
Of it own fail, restraining aid to Timon,
And send forth us to make their sorrowed render,
Together with a recompense more fruitful
Than their offence can weigh down by the dram;
Ay, even such heaps and sums of love and wealth
As shall to thee blot out what wrongs were theirs
And write in thee the figures of their love,
Ever to read them thine.
TIMON You witch me in it;
Surprise me to the very brink of tears.
Lend me a fool's heart and a woman's eyes,
And I'll beweep these comforts, worthy senators.
1 SENATOR Therefore so please thee to return with us,
And of our Athens, thine and ours, to take
The captainship, thou shalt be met with thanks,
Allow'd with absolute power, and thy good name
Live with authority. So soon we shall drive back
Of Alcibiades th' approaches wild,
Who, like a boar too savage, doth root up
His country's peace.
2 SENATOR And shakes his threat'ning sword
Against the walls of Athens.
1 SENATOR Therefore, Timon –
TIMON Well, sir, I will. Therefore I will, sir, thus:
If Alcibiades kill my countrymen,
Let Alcibiades know this of Timon,
That Timon cares not. But if he sack fair Athens,
And take our goodly aged men by th' beards,
Giving our holy virgins to the stain
Of contumelious, beastly, mad-brain'd war,
Then let him know – and tell him Timon speaks it
In pity of our aged and our youth –
I cannot choose by tell him that I care not,
And let him take't at worst; for their knives care not,
While you have throats to answer. For myself,
There's not a whittle in th' unruly camp
But I do prize it at my love before
The reverend'st throat in Athens. So I leave you
To the protection of the prosperous gods,
As thieves to keepers.
FLAVIUS Stay not, all's in vain.
TIMON Why, I was writing of my epitaph;
It will be seen to-morrow. My long sickness
Of health and living now begins to mend,
And nothing brings me all things. Go, live still;
Be Alcibiades your plague, you his,
And last so long enough!
1 SENATOR We speak in vain.
TIMON But yet I love my country, and am not
One that rejoices in the common wreck,
As common bruit doth put it.
1 SENATOR That's well spoke.
TIMON Commend me to my loving country-men –
1 SENATOR These words become your lips as they pass thorough them.
2 SENATOR And enter in our ears like great triumphers
In their applauding gates.
TIMON Commend me to them,
And tell them that, to ease them of their griefs,
Their fears of hostile strokes, their aches, losses,
Their pangs of love, with other incident throes
That nature's fragile vessel doth sustain
In life's uncertain voyage, I will some kindness do them –
I'll teach them to prevent wild Alcibiades' wrath.
1 SENATOR I like this well; he will return again.
TIMON I have a tree, which grows here in my close,
That mine own use invites me to cut down,
And shortly must I fell it. Tell my friends,
Tell Athens, in the sequence of degree
From high to low throughout, that whoso please
To stop affliction, let him take his haste,
Come hither, ere my tree hath felt the axe,
And hang himself. I pray you do my greeting.
FLAVIUS Trouble him no further; thus you still shall find him.
TIMON Come not to me again; but say to Athens
Timon hath made his everlasting mansion
Upon the beached verge of the salt flood,
Who once a day with his embossed froth
The turbulent surge shall cover. Thither come,
And let my gravestone be your oracle.
Lips, let sour words go by and language end:

What is amiss, plague and infection mend!
Graves only be men's works and death their gain!
Sun, hide thy beams. Timon hath done his reign. [*Exit Timon into his cave.*

1 SENATOR His discontents are unremovably
Coupled to nature.

2 SENATOR Our hope in him is dead. Let us return.
And strain what other means is left unto us
In our dear peril.

1 SENATOR It requires swift foot. [*Exeunt.*

SCENE II. *Before the walls of Athens.*

Enter two other Senators with a Messenger.

1 SENATOR Thou hast painfully discover'd; are his files
As full as thy report?

MESSENGER I have spoke the least.
Besides, his expedition promises
Present approach

2 SENATOR We stand much hazard if they bring not Timon.

MESSENGER I met a courier, one mine ancient friend,
Whom, though in general part we were oppos'd,
Yet our old love had a particular force,
And made us speak like friends. This man was riding
From Alcibiades to Timon's cave
With letters of entreaty, which imported
His fellowship i' th' cause against your city,
In part for his sake mov'd.

Enter the other Senators, from Timon.

1 SENATOR Here come our brothers.

3 SENATOR No talk of Timon, nothing of him expect.
The enemies' drum is heard, and fearful scouring
Doth choke the air with dust. In, and prepare.
Ours is the fall, I fear; our foes the snare.

[*Exeunt.*

SCENE III. *The woods. Timon's cave, and a rude tomb seen.*

Enter a Soldier in the woods, seeking Timon.

SOLDIER By all description this should be the place.
Who's here? Speak, ho! No answer? What is this?
Timon is dead, who hath outstretch'd his span.
Some beast rear'd this; here does not live a man.
Dead, sure; and this his grave. What's on this tomb
I cannot read; the character I'll take with wax.
Our captain hath in every figure skill,
An ag'd interpreter, though young in days;
Before proud Athens he's set down by this,
Whose fall the mark of his ambition is. [*Exit.*

SCENE IV. *Before the walls of Athens.*

Trumpets sound. Enter ALCIBIADES with his Powers before Athens.

ALCIBIADES Sound to this coward and lascivious town
Our terrible approach.

Sound a parley. The Senators appear upon the walls.

Till now you have gone on and fill'd the time
With all licentious measure, making your wills
The scope of justice; till now, myself, and such
As slept within the shadow of your power,
Have wander'd with our travers'd arms, and breath'd
Our sufferance vainly. Now the time is flush,
When crouching marrow, in the bearer strong,
Cries of itself 'No more!' Now breathless wrong
Shall sit and pant in your great chairs of ease,
And pursy insolence shall break his wind.
With fear and horrid flight.

1 SENATOR Noble and young,
When thy first griefs were but a mere conceit,
Ere thou hadst power or we had cause of fear,
We sent to thee, to give thy rages balm,
To wipe out our ingratitude with loves
Above their quantity.

2 SENATOR So did we woo
Transformed Timon to our city's love
By humble message and by promis'd means.
We were not all unkind, nor all deserve
The common stroke of war.

1 SENATOR These walls of ours
Were not erected by their hands from whom
You have receiv'd your griefs; nor are they such
That these great tow'rs, trophies, and schools, should fall
For private faults in them.

2 SENATOR Nor are they living
Who were the motives that you first went out;
Shame, that they wanted cunning, in excess
Hath broke their hearts. March, noble lord,
Into our city with thy banners spread.
By decimation and a tithed death –
If thy revenges hunger for that food
Which nature loathes – take thou the destin'd tenth,
And by the hazard of the spotted die
Let die the spotted.

1 SENATOR All have not offended;

For those that were, it is not square to take,
On those that are, revenge: crimes, like lands,
Are not inherited. Then, dear countryman,
Bring in thy ranks, but leave without thy rage;
Spare thy Athenian cradle, and those kin
Which, in the bluster of thy wrath, must fall
With those that have offended. Like a shepherd
Approach the fold and cull th' infected forth,
But kill not all together.

2 SENATOR What thou wilt,
Thou rather shalt enforce it with thy smile
Then hew to't with thy sword.

1 SENATOR Set but thy foot
Against our rampir'd gates and they shall ope,
So thou wilt send thy gentle heart before
To say thou't enter friendly.

2 SENATOR Throw thy glove,
Or any token of thine honour else,
That thou wilt use the wars as thy redress
And not as our confusion, all thy powers
Shall make their harbour in our town till we
Have seal'd thy full desire.

ALCIBIADES Then there's my glove;
Descend, and open your uncharged ports.
Those enemies of Timon's and mine own,
Whom you yourselves shall set out for reproof,
Fall, and no more. And, to atone your fears
With my more noble meaning, not a man
Shall pass his quarter or offend the stream
Of regular justice in your city's bounds,
But shall be render'd to your public laws
At heaviest answer.

BOTH 'Tis most nobly spoken.

ALCIBIADES Descend, and keep your words.

[*The Senators descend and open the gates.*

Enter a Soldier as a Messenger.

SOLDIER My noble General, Timon is dead;
Entomb'd upon the very hem o' th' sea;
And on his grave-stone this insculpture, which
With wax I brought away, whose soft impression
Interprets for my poor ignorance.

Alcibiades reads the Epitaph.

'Here lies a wretched corse, of wretched soul bereft;
Seek not my name. A plague consume you wicked caitiffs left!
Here lie I, Timon, who alive all living men did hate.
Pass by, and curse thy fill; but pass, and stay not here thy gait.'
These well express in thee thy latter spirits.
Though thou abhorr'dst in us our human griefs,
Scorn'dst our brain's flow, and those our droplets which
From niggard nature fall, yet rich conceit
Taught thee to make vast Neptune weep for aye
On thy low grave, on faults forgiven. Dead
Is noble Timon, of whose memory
Hereafter more. Bring me into your city,
And I will use the olive, with my sword;
Make war breed peace, make peace stint war, make each
Prescribe to other, as each other's leech.
Let our drums strike. [*Exeunt.*

Julius Caesar

Introduction by PATRICK REILLY

Julius Caesar is a study of division in the state and in the self: a divided city, a divided hero, a divided response from the reader to the key characters and central action of the play – is Caesar demigod or braggart, is Brutus noble or foolish, what is the morality of the pre-emptive strike, the ethics of political assassination? The civil war, which is the basic subject-matter, permeates every aspect of the play.

In the opening scene is a joke that touches the core of the play's meaning. Flavius, supporter of the side in the civil war just vanquished by Caesar, indignantly asks a workman why he is so inappropriately making holiday by leading his men through the streets. The man, a cobbler, pertly replies: 'Truly, sir, to wear out their shoes to get myself into more work', before supplying the 'real' reason – to celebrate Caesar's triumph. The jocosely divided motives of the cobbler are a comic anticipation of the tragic dilemma of the central character. In addition, the answer opens a door upon the key question of the play: the nature of politics and the motives of those who participate therein. Cassius and Brutus are also leading men about the streets in a conspiracy that will end in Caesar's assassination. Are they doing it from self-interest or higher motives?

Cassius is easy to understand because there is no division in him. He is simply envy masquerading as principle, resentful of Caesar because he himself would be Caesar, an up-market version of the self-interested cobbler, leading his men for his own advantage. Antony and Octavius are also all too easily comprehensible as they coldbloodedly carve up the spoils, cynically bartering the lives of their closest kinsmen, each concerned only with clawing as much power for himself as he can. These are the single-minded people in the play who so uncomplicatedly, unagonisingly know what they want.

Brutus, by contrast, solicits our interest because he is double, the divided man par excellence, cruelly torn between competing obligations – affection for Caesar (his 'best lover') and concern for the good of Rome, split between friendship and patriotism. The civil war in Rome is also waged within Brutus himself, as he reluctantly consents to Caesar's death (Cassius is avid for it); if only, he laments, they could destroy Caesarism without harming Caesar himself. Unlike Cassius, Brutus acts from principle; he does what he thinks is right and it turns out to be disastrously wrong. The republican era is over – 'our day is gone', says Titinius at Philippi, but this is true from the outset: Rome is destined for Caesarism – the only thing doubtful is the identity of the Caesar. This is made ironically manifest in the acclamation of the crowd at the close of Brutus's speech justifying his enforced killing of Caesar: 'let him be Caesar'. The people want to reward him for what he has done by making him the very thing he loathes most of all – he is to become the man he killed; he has killed for nothing.

Brutus is yesterday's man; the killing of Caesar is revealed as a political blunder of the first magnitude. The man Caesar, arrogant, deaf, so easily swayed, is dead, but the spirit of Caesar lives on. Brutus tries to resist history, stand up against Caesarism, and is ruthlessly swept aside. Hence the justification of the play's title, named for a character who departs the scene with two acts still to go. Caesar, dead, continues to control the action:

> O Julius Caesar, thou art mighty yet!
> Thy spirit walks abroad, and turns our swords
> In our own proper entrails [5.3.94–96].

Brutus has blundered and he pays the ultimate forfeit.

But, Dante notwithstanding, Shakespeare presents him as a good if mistaken man. At the beginning, Cassius, speaking in soliloquy, calls him noble and tells us that, were the positions reversed, i.e. if Caesar favoured Cassius as he so clearly does Brutus, then he, Cassius, would never have been tempted to join the conspiracy. This candid admission confirms the envious, malcontent character of Cassius, while simultaneously vindicating the integrity of Brutus; whatever else, he did not become a conspirator for the cobbler's reason, private gain. Casca, too, tells us that the conspiracy needs Brutus as the one irreproachable man, respected by everyone, whose participation will indemnify the assassins and present their action in the most favourable light. And, at the close, the victory won and the need for propaganda, i.e. lies, removed, Antony, Brutus's foremost enemy, says the same thing over the corpse:

> This was the noblest Roman of them all.
> All the conspirators save only he
> Did what they did in envy of great Caesar. [5.5.68–70]

Dante consigns him to the lowest pit in hell; Shakespeare, it is clear, holds a very different view.

Julius Caesar

DRAMATIS PERSONAE

JULIUS CAESAR

OCTAVIUS CAESAR, MARCUS ANTONIUS, M. AEMIL. LEPIDUS
Triumvirs after the death of Julius Caesar

CICERO, PUBLIUS, POPILIUS LENA
senators

MARCUS BRUTUS, CASSIUS, CASCA, TREBONIUS, LIGARIUS, DECIUS BRUTUS, METELLUS CIMBER, CINNA
conspirators against Julius Caesar

FLAVIUS and MARULLUS
tribunes

ARTEMIDORUS
a sophist of Cnidos

A Soothsayer

CINNA
a poet

Another Poet

LUCILIUS, TITINIUS, MESSALA, YOUNG CATO, VOLUMNIUS
friends to Brutus and Cassius

VARRO, CLITUS, CLAUDIUS, STRATO, LUCIUS, DARDANIUS
servants to Brutus

PINDARUS
servant to Cassius

CALPHURNIA
wife to Caesar

PORTIA
wife to Brutus

Senators, Citizens, Guards, and Attendants etc.

THE SCENE: ROME; NEAR SARDIS; NEAR PHILIPPI.

ACT ONE

SCENE I. *Rome. A street.*

Enter FLAVIUS, MARULLUS, and certain Commoners over the stage.

FLAVIUS Hence! home, you idle creatures, get you home.
Is this a holiday? What! know you not,
Being mechanical, you ought not walk
Upon a labouring day without the sign
Of your profession? Speak, what trade art thou?

1 CITIZEN Why, sir, a carpenter.

MARULLUS Where is thy leather apron and thy rule?
What dost thou with thy best apparel on?
You, sir, what trade are you?

2 CITIZEN Truly, sir, in respect of a fine workman, I am but, as you would say, a cobbler.

MARULLUS But what trade art thou? Answer me directly.

2 CITIZEN A trade, sir, that I hope I may use with a safe conscience, which is indeed, sir, a mender of bad soles.

MARULLUS What trade, thou knave? Thou naughty knave, what trade?

2 CITIZEN Nay, I beseech you, sir, be not out with me; yet, if you be out, sir, I can mend you.

MARULLUS What mean'st thou by that? Mend me, thou saucy fellow!

2 CITIZEN Why, sir, cobble you.

FLAVIUS Thou art a cobbler, art thou?

2 CITIZEN Truly, sir, all that I live by is with the awl. I meddle with no tradesman's matters nor women's matters, but with awl. I am indeed, sir, a surgeon to old shoes. When they are in great danger, I re-cover them. As proper men as ever trod upon neat's leather have gone upon my handiwork.

FLAVIUS But wherefore art not in thy shop today?
Why dost thou lead these men about the streets?

2 CITIZEN Truly, sir, to wear out their shoes, to get myself into more work. But indeed, sir, we make holiday to see Caesar, and to rejoice in his triumph.

MARULLUS Wherefore rejoice? What conquest brings he home?
What tributaries follow him to Rome,
To grace in captive bonds his chariot wheels?
You blocks, you stones, you worse than senseless things!
O you hard hearts, you cruel men of Rome,
Knew you not Pompey? Many a time and oft
Have you climb'd up to walls and battlements,
To tow'rs and windows, yea, to chimney-tops,
Your infants in your arms, and there have sat
The livelong day, with patient expectation,
To see great Pompey pass the streets of Rome.
And when you saw his chariot but appear,

Have you not made an universal shout,
That Tiber trembled underneath her banks,
To hear the replication of your sounds
Made in her concave shores?
And do you now put on your best attire?
And do you now cull out a holiday?
And do you now strew flowers in his way
That comes in triumph over Pompey's blood?
Be gone!
Run to your houses, fall upon your knees,
Pray to the gods to intermit the plague
That needs must light on this ingratitude.

FLAVIUS Go, go, good countrymen, and for this fault
Assemble all the poor men of your sort;
Draw them to Tiber banks, and weep your tears
Into the channel, till the lowest stream
Do kiss the most exalted shores of all.

[*Exeunt all the Commoners.*

See whe'r their basest metal be not mov'd;
They vanish tongue-tied in their guiltiness.
Go you down that way towards the Capitol;
This way will I. Disrobe the images
If you do find them deck'd with ceremonies.

MARULLUS May we do so?
You know it is the feast of Lupercal.

FLAVIUS It is no matter; let no images
Be hung with Caesar's trophies. I'll about,
And drive away the vulgar from the streets;
So do you too, where you perceive them thick.
These growing feathers pluck'd from Caesar's wing
Will make him fly an ordinary pitch,
Who else would soar above the view of men,
And keep us all in servile fearfulness. [*Exeunt.*

SCENE II. *Rome. A public place.*

Music. Enter CAESAR; ANTHONY, for the course; CALPHURNIA, PORTIA, DECIUS, CICERO, BRUTUS, CASSIUS, and CASCA; a great crowd following, among them a Soothsayer; after them, MARULLUS and FLAVIUS.

CAESAR Calphurnia.

CASCA Peace, ho! Caesar speaks.

[*Music ceases.*

CAESAR Calphurnia.

CALPHURNIA Here, my lord.

CAESAR Stand you directly in Antonius' way
When he doth run his course. Antonius!

ANTONY Caesar, my lord.

CAESAR Forget not in your speed, Antonius,
To touch Calphurnia; for our elders say,
The barren, touched in this holy chase,
Shake off their sterile curse.

ANTONY I shall remember.
When Caesar says 'Do this', it is perform'd.

CAESAR Set on, and leave no ceremony out.

[*Music.*

SOOTHSAYER Caesar!

CAESAR Ha! Who calls?

CASCA Bid every noise be still. Peace yet again.

[*Music ceases.*

CAESAR Who is it in the press that calls on me?
I hear a tongue, shriller than all the music,
Cry 'Caesar!' Speak. Caesar is turn'd to hear.

SOOTHSAYER Beware the ides of March.

CAESAR What man is that?

BRUTUS A soothsayer bids you beware the ides of March.

CAESAR Set him before me; let me see his face.

CASSIUS Fellow, come from the throng; look upon Caesar.

CAESAR What say'st thou to me now? Speak once again.

SOOTHSAYER Beware the ides of March.

CAESAR He is a dreamer; let us leave him. Pass.

[*Sennet. Exeunt all but Brutus and Cassius.*

CASSIUS Will you go see the order of the course?

BRUTUS Not I.

CASSIUS I pray you do.

BRUTUS I am not gamesome: I do lack some part
Of that quick spirit that is in Antony.
Let me not hinder, Cassius, your desires;
I'll leave you.

CASSIUS Brutus, I do observe you now of late;
I have not from your eyes that gentleness
And show of love as I was wont to have.
You bear too stubborn and too strange a hand
Over your friend that loves you.

BRUTUS Cassius,
Be not deceiv'd. If I have veil'd my look,
I turn the trouble of my countenance
Merely upon myself. Vexed I am
Of late with passions of some difference,
Conceptions only proper to myself,
Which give some soil, perhaps, to my behaviours;
But let not therefore my good friends be griev'd –
Among which number, Cassius, be you one –
Nor construe any further my neglect
Than that poor Brutus, with himself at war,
Forgets the shows of love to other men.

CASSIUS Then, Brutus, I have much mistook your passion,
By means whereof this breast of mine hath buried
Thoughts of great value, worthy cogitations.
Tell me, good Brutus, can you see your face?

BRUTUS No, Cassius; for the eye sees not itself
But by reflection, by some other things.
CASSIUS 'Tis just;
And it is very much lamented, Brutus,
That you have no such mirrors as will turn
Your hidden worthiness into your eye,
That you might see your shadow. I have heard,
Where many of the best respect in Rome –
Except immortal Caesar – speaking of Brutus,
And groaning underneath this age's yoke,
Have wish'd that noble Brutus had his eyes.
BRUTUS Into what dangers would you lead me, Cassius,
That you would have me seek into myself
For that which is not in me?
CASSIUS Therefore, good Brutus, be prepar'd to hear;
And since you know you cannot see yourself
So well as by reflection, I, your glass,
Will modestly discover to yourself
That of yourself which you yet know not of.
And be not jealous on me, gentle Brutus:
Were I a common laughter, or did use
To stale with ordinary oaths my love
To every new protester; if you know
That I do fawn on men and hug them hard,
And after scandal them; or if you know
That I profess myself in banqueting
To all the rout, then hold me dangerous.
[Flourish and shout.
BRUTUS What means this shouting? I do fear the people
Choose Caesar for their king.
CASSIUS Ay, do you fear it?
Then must I think you would not have it so.
BRUTUS I would not, Cassius; yet I love him well.
But wherefore do you hold me here so long?
What is it that you would impart to me?
If it be aught toward the general good,
Set honour in one eye and death i' th' other,
And I will look on both indifferently;
For let the gods so speed me as I love
The name of honour more than I fear death.
CASSIUS I know that virtue to be in you, Brutus,
As well as I do know your outward favour.
Well, honour is the subject of my story.
I cannot tell what you and other men
Think of this life; but, for my single self,
I had as lief not be as live to be
In awe of such a thing as I myself.
I was born free as Caesar; so were you.
We both have fed as well, and we can both
Endure the winter's cold as well as he.
For once, upon a raw and gusty day,
The troubled Tiber chafing with her shores,
Caesar said to me 'Dar'st thou, Cassius, now
Leap in with me into this angry flood,
And swim to yonder point?' Upon the word,
Accoutred as I was, I plunged in
And bade him follow. So indeed he did.
The torrent roar'd, and we did buffet it
With lusty sinews, throwing it aside
And stemming it with hearts of controversy;
But ere we could arrive the point propos'd,
Caesar cried 'Help me, Cassius, or I sink!'
I, as AEneas, our great ancestor,
Did from the flames of Troy upon his shoulder
The old Anchises bear, so from the waves of Tiber
Did I the tired Caesar. And this man
Is now become a god; and Cassius is
A wretched creature, and must bend his body
If Caesar carelessly but nod on him.
He had a fever when he was in Spain,
And when the fit was on him I did mark
How he did shake. 'Tis true, this god did shake.
His coward lips did from their colour fly,
And that same eye, whose bend doth awe the world,
Did lose his lustre. I did hear him groan.
Ay, and that tongue of his, that bade the Romans
Mark him, and write his speeches in their books,
Alas! it cried 'Give me some drink, Titinius'
As a sick girl. Ye gods! it doth amaze me
A man of such a feeble temper should
So get the start of the majestic world,
And bear the palm alone. *[Shout. Flourish.*
BRUTUS Another general shout!
I do believe that these applauses are
For some new honours that are heap'd on Caesar.
CASSIUS Why, man, he doth bestride the narrow world
Like a Colossus, and we petty men
Walk under his huge legs, and peep about
To find ourselves dishonourable graves.
Men at some time are masters of their fates:
The fault, dear Brutus, is not in our stars,
But in ourselves, that we are underlings.
'Brutus' and 'Caesar'. What should be in that 'Caesar'?
Why should that name be sounded more than yours?
Write them together: yours is as fair a name.
Sound them: it doth become the mouth as well.
Weigh them: it as heavy. Conjure with 'em:
'Brutus' will start a spirit as soon as 'Caesar'.
Now, in the names of all the gods at once,
Upon what meat doth this our Caesar feed,
That he is grown so great? Age, thou art sham'd!

Rome, thou has lost the breed of noble bloods!
When went there by an age, since the great flood,
But it was fam'd with more than with one man?
When could they say, till now, that talk'd of Rome,
That her wide walls encompass'd but one man?
Now is it Rome indeed, and room enough,
When there is in it but one only man.
O! you and I have heard our fathers say
There was a Brutus once that would have brook'd
Th' eternal devil to keep his state in Rome
As easily as a king.

BRUTUS That you do love me, I am nothing jealous;
What you would work me to, I have some aim;
How I have thought of this, and of these times,
I shall recount hereafter. For this present,
I would not, so with love I might entreat you,
Be any further mov'd. What you have said
I will consider; what you have to say
I will with patience hear; and find a time
Both meet to hear and answer such high things.
Till then, my noble friend, chew upon this:
Brutus had rather be a villager
Than to repute himself a son of Rome
Under these hard conditions as this time
Is like to lay upon us.

CASSIUS I am glad that my weak words
Have struck but thus much show of fire from Brutus.

Re-enter CAESAR and his Train.

BRUTUS The games are done, and Caesar is returning.

CASSIUS As they pass by, pluck Casca by the sleeve,
And he will, after his sour fashion, tell you
What hath proceeded worthy note to-day.

BRUTUS I will do so. But, look you, Cassius,
The angry spot doth glow on Caesar's brow,
And all the rest look like a chidden train;
Calphurnia's cheek is pale, and Cicero
Looks with such ferret and such fiery eyes
As we have seen him in the Capitol,
Being cross'd in conference by some senators.

CASSIUS Casca will tell us what the matter is.

CAESAR Antonius!

ANTONY Caesar?

CAESAR Let me have men about me that are fat;
Sleek-headed men, and such as sleep o' nights.
Yond Cassius has a lean and hungry look;
He thinks too much. Such men are dangerous.

ANTONY Fear him not, Caesar, he's not dangerous;
He is a noble Roman, and well given.

CAESAR Would he were fatter! But I fear him not.
Yet if my name were liable to fear,
I do not know the man I should avoid
So soon as that spare Cassius. He reads much,
He is a great observer, and he looks
Quite through the deeds of men. He loves no plays,
As thou dost, Antony; he hears no music.
Seldom he smiles, and smiles in such a sort
As if he mock'd himself, and scorn'd his spirit
That could be mov'd to smile at anything.
Such men as he be never at heart's ease
Whiles they behold a greater than themselves,
And therefore are they very dangerous.
I rather tell thee what is to be fear'd
Than what I fear; for always I am Caesar.
Come on my right hand, for this ear is deaf,
And tell me truly what thou think'st of him.

[Sennet. Exeunt Caesar and his Train.

CASCA You pull'd me by the cloak. Would you speak with me?

BRUTUS Ay, Casca; tell us what hath chanc'd to-day,
That Caesar looks so sad?

CASCA Why, you were with him, were you not?

BRUTUS I should not then ask Casca what had chanc'd.

CASCA Why, there was a crown offer'd him; and being offer'd him, he put it by with the back of his hand, thus; and then the people fell a-shouting.

BRUTUS What was the second noise for?

CASCA Why, for that too.

CASSIUS They shouted thrice; what was the last cry for?

CASCA Why, for that too.

BRUTUS Was the crown offer'd him thrice?

CASCA Ay, marry, was't, and he put it by thrice, every time gentler than other; and at every putting by mine honest neighbours shouted.

CASSIUS Who offer'd him the crown?

CASCA Why, Antony.

BRUTUS Tell us the manner of it, gentle Casca.

CASCA I can as well be hang'd as tell the manner of it: it was mere foolery; I did not mark it. I saw Mark Antony offer him a crown – yet 'twas not a crown neither, 'twas one of these coronets – and, as I told you, he put it by once; but for all that, to my thinking, he would fain have had it. Then he offered it to him again; then he put it by again; but to my thinking, he was very loath to lay his fingers off it. And then he offered it the third time; he put it the third time by; and still as he refus'd it, the rabblement hooted, and clapp'd their chopt hands, and threw up their sweaty night-caps, and uttered such a deal of stinking breath because Caesar refus'd the crown, that it had almost choked Caesar; for he swooned and fell down at it. And for mine own part I durst not laugh, for fear of opening my lips and receiving the bad air.

CASSIUS But soft, I pray you. What, did Caesar
swoon?

CASCA He fell down in the market-place, and foam'd at mouth, and was speechless.

BRUTUS 'Tis very like. He hath the falling
sickness.

CASSIUS No, Caesar hath it not; but you, and I,
And honest Casca, we have the falling sickness.

CASCA I know not what you mean by that, but I am sure Caesar fell down. If the tag-rag people did not clap him and hiss him, according as he pleas'd and displeas'd them, as they use to do the players in the theatre, I am no true man.

BRUTUS What said he when he came unto
himself?

CASCA Marry, before he fell down, when he perceiv'd the common herd was glad he refus'd the crown, he pluckt me ope his doublet, and offer'd them his throat to cut. An I had been a man of any occupation, if I would not have taken him at a word, I would I might go to hell among the rogues. And so he fell. When he came to himself again, he said, if he had done or said anything amiss, he desir'd their worships to think it was his infirmity. Three or four wenches, where I stood, cried 'Alas, good soul!' and forgave him with all their hearts. But there's no heed to be taken of them; if Caesar had stabb'd their mothers, they would have done no less.

BRUTUS And after that, he came thus sad away?

CASCA Ay.

CASSIUS Did Cicero say anything?

CASCA Ay, he spoke Greek.

CASSIUS To what effect?

CASCA Nay, an I tell you that, I'll ne'er look you i' th' face again. But those that understood him smil'd at one another, and shook their heads; but for mine own part, it was Greek to me. I could tell you more news too: Marullus and Flavius, for pulling scarfs off Caesar's images, are put to silence. Fare you well. There was more foolery yet, if I could remember it.

CASSIUS Will you sup with me to-night, Casca?

CASCA No, I am promis'd forth.

CASSIUS Will you dine with me to-morrow?

CASCA Ay, if I be alive, and your mind hold, and your dinner worth the eating.

CASSIUS Good; I will expect you.

CASCA Do so. Farewell, both. *[Exit.*

BRUTUS What a blunt fellow is this grown to be!
He was quick mettle when he went to school.

CASSIUS So is he now, in execution
Of any bold or noble enterprise,
However he puts on this tardy form.
This rudeness is a sauce to his good wit,
Which gives men stomach to digest his words
With better appetite.

BRUTUS And so it is. For this time I will leave
you.
To-morrow, if you please to speak with me,
I will come home to you; or, if you will,
Come home to me, and I will wait for you.

CASSIUS I will do so. Till then, think of the
world. *[Exit Brutus.*
Well, Brutus, thou art noble; yet, I see,
Thy honourable metal may be wrought
From that it is dispos'd. Therefore it is meet
That noble minds keep ever with their likes;
For who so firm that cannot be seduc'd?
Caesar doth bear me hard; but he loves Brutus.
If I were Brutus now and he were Cassius,
He should not humour me. I will this night,
In several hands, in at his windows throw,
As if they came from several citizens,
Writings, all tending to the great opinion
That Rome holds of his name; wherein
obscurely
Caesar's ambition shall be glanced at.
And, after this, let Caesar seat him sure;
For we will shake him, or worse days endure.
[Exit.

SCENE III. *Rome. A street.*

Thunder and lightning. Enter, from opposite sides, CASCA, with his sword drawn, and CICERO.

CICERO Good even, Casca. Brought you Caesar
home?
Why are you breathless? and why stare you so?

CASCA Are not you mov'd, when all the sway of
earth
Shakes like a thing unfirm? O Cicero,
I have seen tempests when the scolding winds
Have riv'd the knotty oaks, and I have seen
Th' ambitious ocean swell, and rage, and foam,
To be exalted with the threat'ning clouds;
But never till to-night, never till now,
Did I go through a tempest dropping fire.
Either there is a civil strife in heaven,
Or else the world, too saucy with the gods,
Incenses them to send destruction.

CICERO Why, saw you any thing more
wonderful?

CASCA A common slave – you know him well by
sight –
Held up his left hand, which did flame and burn
Like twenty torches join'd; and yet his hand,

Not sensible of fire, remain'd unscorch'd.
Besides – I ha' not since put up my sword –
Against the Capitol I met a lion,
Who glaz'd upon me, and went surly by
Without annoying me; and there were drawn
Upon a heap a hundred ghastly women,
Transformed with their fear, who swore they saw
Men, all in fire, walk up and down the streets.
And yesterday the bird of night did sit,
Even at noon-day, upon the market-place,
Hooting and shrieking. When these prodigies
Do so conjointly meet, let not men say
'These are their reasons – they are natural',
For I believe they are portentous things
Unto the climate that they point upon.

CICERO Indeed, it is a strange-disposed time;
But men may construe things after their fashion,
Clean from the purpose of the things themselves.
Comes Caesar to the Capitol to-morrow?

CASCA He doth; for he did bid Antonius
Send word to you he would be there to-morrow.

CICERO Good night, then, Casca; this disturbed sky
Is not to walk in.

CASCA Farewell, Cicero. [*Exit Cicero.*

Enter CASSIUS.

CASSIUS Who's there?

CASCA A Roman.

CASSIUS Casca, by your voice.

CASCA Your ear is good. Cassius, what night is this!

CASSIUS A very pleasing night to honest men.

CASCA Who ever knew the heavens menace so?

CASSIUS Those that have known the earth so full of faults.
For my part, I have walk'd about the streets,
Submitting me unto the perilous night,
And, thus unbraced, Casca, as you see,
Have bar'd my bosom to the thunder-stone;
And when the cross blue lighting seem'd to open
The breast of heaven, I did present myself
Even in the aim and very flash of it.

CASCA But wherefore did you so much tempt the heavens?
It is the part of men to fear and tremble
When the most mighty gods by tokens send
Such dreadful heralds to astonish us.

CASSIUS You are dull, Casca, and those sparks of life
That should be in a Roman you do want,
Or else you use not. You look pale, and gaze,
And put on fear, and cast yourself in wonder,
To see the strange impatience of the heavens;
But if you would consider the true cause –
Why all these fires, why all these gliding ghosts,
Why birds and beasts, from quality and kind;
Why old men, fools, and children calculate;
Why all these things change from their ordinance,
Their natures and preformed faculties,
To monstrous quality – why, you shall find
That heaven hath infus'd them with these spirits,
To make them instruments of fear and warning
Unto some monstrous state.
Now could I, Casca, name to thee a man
Most like this dreadful night
That thunders, lightens, opens graves, and roars
As doth the lion in the Capitol;
A man no mightier than thyself or me
In personal action, yet prodigious grown,
And fearful, as these strange eruptions are.

CASCA 'Tis Caesar that you mean, is it not, Cassius?

CASSIUS Let it be who it is; for Romans now
Have thews and limbs like to their ancestors.
But woe the while! our fathers' minds are dead,
And we are govern'd with our mothers' spirits;
Our yoke and sufferance show us womanish.

CASCA Indeed they say the senators to-morrow
Mean to establish Caesar as a king;
And he shall wear his crown by sea and land,
In every place save here in Italy.

CASSIUS I know where I will wear this dagger then;
Cassius from bondage will deliver Cassius.
Therein, ye gods, you make the weak most strong;
Therein, ye gods, you tyrants do defeat.
Nor stony tower, nor walls of beaten brass,
Nor airless dungeon, nor strong links of iron,
Can be retentive to the strength of spirit;
But life, being weary of these worldly bars,
Never lacks power to dismiss itself.
If I know this, know all the world besides,
That part of tyranny that I do bear,
I can shake off at pleasure. [*Thunder still.*

CASCA So can I;
So every bondman in his own hand bears
The power to cancel his captivity.

CASSIUS And why should Caesar be a tyrant, then?
Poor man! I know he would not be a wolf
But that he sees the Romans are but sheep;
He were no lion, were not Romans hinds.
Those that with haste will make a mighty fire
Begin it with weak straws. What trash is Rome,
What rubbish, and what offal, when it serves
For the base matter to illuminate

So vile a thing as Caesar! But, O grief,
Where hast thou led me? I perhaps speak this
Before a willing bondman; then I know
My answer must be made. But I am arm'd,
And dangers are to me indifferent.
CASCA You speak to Casca, and to such a man
That is no fleering tell-tale. Hold, my hand.
Be factious for redress of all these griefs,
And I will set this foot of mine as far
As who goes farthest.
CASSIUS There's a bargain made.
Now know you, Casca, I have mov'd already
Some certain of the noblest-minded Romans
To undergo with me an enterprise
Of honourable-dangerous consequence;
And I do know by this they stay for me
In Pompey's porch; for now, this fearful night,
There is no stir or walking in the streets,
And the complexion of the element
In favour's like the work we have in hand,
Most bloody, fiery, and most terrible.

Enter CINNA.

CASCA Stand close awhile, for here comes one in haste.
CASSIUS 'Tis Cinna, I do know him by his gait;
He is a friend. Cinna, where haste you so?
CINNA To find out you. Who's that? Metellus Cimber?
CASSIUS No, it is Casca, one incorporate
To our attempts. Am I not stay'd for, Cinna?
CINNA I am glad on't. What a fearful night is this!
There's two or three of us have seen strange sights.
CASSIUS Am I not stay'd for? Tell me.
CINNA Yes, you are. O Cassius, if you could
But win the noble Brutus to our party –
CASSIUS Be you content. Good Cinna, take this paper,
And look you lay it in the praetor's chair,
Where Brutus may but find it; and throw this
In at his window; set this up with wax
Upon old Brutus' statue. All this done,
Repair to Pompey's porch, where you shall find us.
Is Decius Brutus and Trebonius there?
CINNA All but Metellus Cimber, and he's gone
To seek you at your house. Well, I will hie,
And so bestow these papers as you bade me.
CASSIUS That done, repair to Pompey's theatre.
[*Exit Cinna.*
Come, Casca, you and I will yet ere day
See Brutus at his house. Three parts of him
Is ours already, and the man entire
Upon the next encounter yields him ours.
CASCA O, he sits high in all the people's hearts;
And that which would appear offence in us
His countenance, like richest alchemy,
Will change to virtue and to worthiness.
CASSIUS Him and his worth and our great need of him
You have right well conceited. Let us go,
For it is after midnight; and ere day
We will awake him and be sure of him.
[*Exeunt.*

ACT TWO

SCENE I. *Rome.*

Enter BRUTUS in his orchard.

BRUTUS What, Lucius, ho!
I cannot by the progress of the stars
Give guess how near to day. Lucius, I say!
I would it were my fault to sleep so soundly.
When, Lucius, when? Awake, I say! What, Lucius!

Enter LUCIUS.

LUCIUS Call'd you, my lord?
BRUTUS Get me a taper in my study, Lucius;
When it is lighted, come and call me here.
LUCIUS I will, my lord. [*Exit.*
BRUTUS It must be by his death; and for my part,
I know no personal cause to spurn at him,
But for the general: he would be crown'd.
How that might change his nature, there's the question.
It is the bright day that brings forth the adder,
And that craves wary walking. Crown him – that!
And then, I grant, we put a sting in him
That at his will he may do danger with.
Th' abuse of greatness is, when it disjoins
Remorse from power; and to speak truth of Caesar,
I have not known when his affections sway'd
More than his reason. But 'tis a common proof
That lowliness is young ambition's ladder,
Whereto the climber-upward turns his face;
But when he once attains the upmost round,
He then unto the ladder turns his back,
Looks in the clouds, scorning the base degrees
By which he did ascend. So Caesar may.
Then, lest he may, prevent. And since the quarrel
Will bear no colour for the thing he is,
Fashion it thus – that what he is, augmented,

Would run to these and these extremities;
And therefore think him as a serpent's egg,
Which, hatch'd, would as his kind grow mischievous,
And kill him in the shell.

Re-enter LUCIUS.

LUCIUS The taper burneth in your closet, sir.
Searching the window for a flint, I found
This paper, thus seal'd up; and I am sure
It did not lie there when I went to bed.
[*Giving him a letter.*

BRUTUS Get you to bed again, it is not day.
Is not to-morrow, boy, the ides of March?

LUCIUS I know not, sir.

BRUTUS Look in the calender, and bring me word.

LUCIUS I will, sir. [*Exit.*

BRUTUS The exhalations, whizzing in the air,
Give so much light that I may read by them.
[*Opens the letter and reads.*
'Brutus, thou sleep'st. Awake, and see thyself.
Shall Rome, etc. Speak, strike, redress!
Brutus, thou sleep'st; awake.'
Such instigations have been often dropp'd
Where I have took them up.
'Shall Rome, etc.' Thus must I piece it out:
Shall Rome stand under one man's awe? What, Rome?
My ancestors did from the streets of Rome
The Tarquin drive, when he was call'd a king.
'Speak, strike, redress!' Am I entreated
To speak and strike? O Rome, I make thee promise,
If the redress will follow, thou receivest
Thy full petition at the hand of Brutus!

Re-enter LUCIUS.

LUCIUS Sir, March is wasted fifteen days.
[*Knocking within.*

BRUTUS 'Tis good. Go to the gate; somebody knocks. [*Exit Lucius.*
Since Cassius first did whet me against Caesar,
I have not slept.
Between the acting of a dreadful thing
And the first motion, all the interim is
Like a phantasma or a hideous dream.
The Genius and the mortal instruments
Are then in council; and the state of man,
Like to a little kingdom, suffers then
The nature of an insurrection.

Re-enter LUCIUS.

LUCIUS Sir, 'tis your brother Cassius at the door
Who doth desire to see you.

BRUTUS Is he alone?

LUCIUS No, sir, there are moe with him.

BRUTUS Do you know them?

LUCIUS No, sir; their hats are pluck'd about their ears
And half their faces buried in their cloaks,
That by no means I may discover them
By any mark of favour.

BRUTUS Let 'em enter.
[*Exit Lucius.*
They are the faction. O conspiracy,
Sham'st thou to show thy dang'rous brow by night,
When evils are most free? O, then by day
Where wilt thou find a cavern dark enough
To mask thy monstrous visage? Seek none, conspiracy;
Hide it in smiles and affability!
For if thou path, thy native semblance on,
Not Erebus itself were dim enough
To hide thee from prevention.

Enter the conspirators, CASSIUS, CASCA, DECIUS, CINNA, METELLUS CIMBER, and TREBONIUS.

CASSIUS I think we are too bold upon your rest.
Good morrow, Brutus. Do we trouble you?

BRUTUS I have been up this hour, awake all night.
Know I these men that come along with you?

CASSIUS Yes, every man of them; and no man here
But honours you; and every one doth wish
You had but that opinion of yourself
Which every noble Roman bears of you.
This is Trebonius.

BRUTUS He is welcome hither.

CASSIUS This, Decius Brutus.

BRUTUS He is welcome too.

CASSIUS This, Casca; this, Cinna;
And this, Metellus Cimber.

BRUTUS They are all welcome.
What watchful cares do interpose themselves
Betwixt your eyes and night?

CASSIUS Shall I entreat a word? [*They whisper.*

DECIUS Here lies the east. Doth not the day break here?

CASCA No.

CINNA O, pardon, sir, it doth; and yon grey lines
That fret the clouds are messengers of day.

CASCA You shall confess that you are both deceiv'd.
Here, as I point my sword, the sun arises;
Which is a great way growing on the south,
Weighing the youthful season of the year.
Some two months hence up higher toward the north
He first presents his fire; and the high east
Stands as the Capitol, directly here.

BRUTUS Give me your hands all over, one by one.
CASSIUS And let us swear our resolution.
BRUTUS No, not an oath. If not the face of men,
The sufferance of our souls, the time's abuse,
If these be motives weak, break off betimes,
And every man hence to his idle bed.
So let high-sighted tyranny range on,
Till each man drop by lottery. But if these,
As I am sure they do, bear fire enough
To kindle cowards, and to steel with valour
The melting spirits of women, then, countrymen,
What need we any spur but our own cause
To prick us to redress? What other bond
Than secret Romans that have spoke the word
And will not palter? And what other oath
Than honesty to honesty engag'd
That this shall be or we will fall for it?
Swear priests and cowards and men cautelous,
Old feeble carrions and such suffering souls
That welcome wrongs; unto bad causes swear
Such creatures as men doubt; but do not stain
The even virtue of our enterprise,
Nor th' insuppressive mettle of our spirits,
To think that or our cause or our performance
Did need an oath; when every drop of blood
That every Roman bears, and nobly bears,
Is guilty of a several bastardy,
If he do break the smallest particle
Of any promise that hath pass'd from him.
CASSIUS But what of Cicero? Shall we sound him?
I think he will stand very strong with us.
CASCA Let us not leave him out.
CINNA No, by no means.
METELLUS O, let us have him; for his silver hairs
Will purchase us a good opinion,
And buy men's voices to commend our deeds.
It shall be said his judgment rul'd our hands;
Our youths and wildness shall no whit appear,
But all be buried in his gravity.
BRUTUS O, name him not! Let us not break with him;
For he will never follow any thing
That other men begin.
CASSIUS Then leave him out.
CASCA Indeed he is not fit.
DECIUS Shall no man else be touch'd but only Caesar?
CASSIUS Decius, well urg'd. I think it is not meet
Mark Antony, so well belov'd of Caesar,
Should outlive Caesar. We shall find of him
A shrewd contriver; and you know his means,
If he improve them, may well stretch so far
As to annoy us all; which to prevent,
Let Antony and Caesar fall together.
BRUTUS Our course will seem too bloody, Caius Cassius,
To cut the head off and then hack the limbs –
Like wrath in death and envy afterwards;
For Antony is but a limb of Caesar.
Let's be sacrificers, but not butchers, Caius.
We all stand up against the spirit of Caesar,
And in the spirit of men there is no blood.
O that we then could come by Caesar's spirit,
And not dismember Caesar! But, alas,
Caesar must bleed for it! And, gentle friends,
Let's kill him boldly, but not wrathfully;
Let's carve him as a dish fit for the gods,
Not hew him as a carcase fit for hounds;
And let our hearts, as subtle masters do,
Stir up their servants to an act of rage,
And after seem to chide 'em. This shall make
Our purpose necessary, and not envious;
Which so appearing to the common eyes,
We shall be call'd purgers, not murderers.
And for Mark Antony, think not of him;
For he can do no more than Caesar's arm
When Caesar's head is off.
CASSIUS Yet I fear him;
For in the engrafted love he bears to Caesar –
BRUTUS Alas, good Cassius, do not think of him!
If he love Caesar, all that he can do
Is to himself take thought and die for Caesar;
And that were much he should, for he is given
To sports, to wildness, and much company.
TREBONIUS There is no fear in him. Let him not die;
For he will live, and laugh at this hereafter.
[*Clock strikes.*
BRUTUS Peace! Count the clock.
CASSIUS The clock hath stricken three.
TREBONIUS 'Tis time to part.
CASSIUS But it is doubtful yet
Whether Caesar will come forth to-day or no;
For he is superstitious grown of late,
Quite from the main opinion he held once
Of fantasy, of dreams, and ceremonies.
It may be these apparent prodigies,
The unaccustom'd terror of this night,
And the persuasion of his augurers,
May hold him from the Capitol to-day.
DECIUS Never fear that. If he be so resolv'd,
I can o'ersway him; for he loves to hear
That unicorns may be betray'd with trees,
And bears with glasses, elephants with holes,
Lions with toils, and men with flatterers;
But when I tell him he hates flatterers,
He says he does, being then most flattered.
Let me work;
For I can give his humour the true bent,
And I will bring him to the Capitol.
CASSIUS Nay, we will all of us be there to fetch

him.
BRUTUS By the eighth hour. Is that the uttermost?
CINNA Be that the uttermost, and fail not then.
METELLUS Caius Ligarius doth bear Caesar hard,
Who rated him for speaking well of Pompey.
I wonder none of you have thought of him.
BRUTUS Now, good Metellus, go along by him.
He loves me well, and I have given him reasons;
Send him but hither, and I'll fashion him.
CASSIUS The morning comes upon's. We'll leave you, Brutus.
And, friends, disperse yourselves; but all remember
What you have said, and show yourselves true Romans.
BRUTUS Good gentlemen, look fresh and merrily;
Let not our looks put on our purposes,
But bear it as our Roman actors do,
With untir'd spirits and formal constancy.
And so good morrow to you every one.
[*Exeunt all but Brutus.*

Boy! Lucius! Fast asleep? It is no matter;
Enjoy the honey-heavy dew of slumber.
Thou hast no figures nor no fantasies
Which busy care draws in the brains of men;
Therefore thou sleep'st so sound.

Enter PORTIA.

PORTIA Brutus, my lord!
BRUTUS Portia, what mean you? Wherefore rise you now?
It is not for your health thus to commit
Your weak condition to the raw cold morning.
PORTIA Nor for yours neither. Y'have ungently, Brutus,
Stole from my bed; and yesternight at supper
You suddenly arose and walk'd about,
Musing and sighing, with your arms across;
And when I ask'd you what the matter was,
You star'd upon me with ungentle looks.
I urg'd you further; then you scratch'd your head
And too impatiently stamp'd with your foot.
Yet I insisted; yet you answer'd not,
But with an angry wafture of your hand
Gave sign for me to leave you. So I did,
Fearing to strengthen that impatience
Which seem'd too much enkindled; and withal
Hoping it was but an effect of humour,
Which sometimes hath his hour with every man.
It will not let you eat, nor talk, nor sleep;
And, could it work so much upon your shape
As it hath much prevail'd on your condition,
I should not know you Brutus. Dear my lord,
Make me acquainted with your cause of grief.
BRUTUS I am not well in health, and that is all.
PORTIA Brutus is wise, and, were he not in health,
He would embrace the means to come by it.
BRUTUS Why, so I do. Good Portia, go to bed.
PORTIA Is Brutus sick, and is it physical
To walk unbraced and suck up the humours
Of the dank morning? What, is Brutus sick,
And will he steal out of his wholesome bed,
To dare the vile contagion of the night,
And tempt the rheumy and unpurged air
To add unto his sickness? No, my Brutus;
You have some sick offence within your mind,
Which by the right and virtue of my place
I ought to know of; and upon my knees
I charm you, by my once-commended beauty,
By all your vows of love, and that great vow
Which did incorporate and make us one,
That you unfold to me, your self, your half,
Why you are heavy – and what men to-night
Have had resort to you; for here have been
Some six or seven, who did hide their faces
Even from darkness.
BRUTUS Kneel not, gentle Portia.
PORTIA I should not need, if you were gentle Brutus.
Within the bond of marriage, tell me, Brutus,
Is it excepted I should know no secrets
That appertain to you? Am I your self
But, as it were, in sort or limitation?
To keep with you at meals, comfort your bed,
And talk to you sometimes? Dwell I but in the suburbs
Of your good pleasure? If it be no more,
Portia is Brutus' harlot, not his wife.
BRUTUS You are my true and honourable wife,
As dear to me as are the ruddy drops
That visit my sad heart.
PORTIA If this were true, then should I know this secret.
I grant I am a woman; but withal
A woman that Lord Brutus took to wife.
I grant I am a woman; but withal
A woman well reputed, Cato's daughter.
Think you I am no stronger than my sex,
Being so father'd and so husbanded?
Tell me your counsels, I will not disclose 'em.
I have made strong proof of my constancy,
Giving myself a voluntary wound
Here, in the thigh. Can I bear that with patience,
And not my husband's secrets?
BRUTUS O ye gods,
Render me worthy of this noble wife!
[*Knocking within.*

Hark, hark! one knocks. Portia, go in awhile,
And by and by thy bosom shall partake

The secrets of my heart.
All my engagements I will construe to thee,
All the charactery of my sad brows.
Leave me with haste. [*Exit Portia.*
Lucius, who's that knocks?

Enter LUCIUS and LIGARIUS.

LUCIUS Here is a sick man that would speak with you.

BRUTUS Caius Ligarius, that Metellus spake of.
Boy, stand aside. Caius Ligarius, how?

LIGARIUS Vouchsafe good morrow from a feeble tongue.

BRUTUS O, what a time have you chose out, brave Caius,
To wear a kerchief! Would you were not sick!

LIGARIUS I am not sick, if Brutus have in hand
Any exploit worthy the name of honour.

BRUTUS Such an exploit have I in hand, Ligarius,
Had you a healthful ear to hear of it.

LIGARIUS By all the gods that Romans bow before,
I here discard my sickness. [*Pulls off his kerchief*] Soul of Rome!
Brave son, deriv'd from honourable loins!
Thou, like an exorcist, hast conjur'd up
My mortified spirit. Now bid me run,
And I will strive with things impossible;
Yea, get the better of them. What's to do?

BRUTUS A piece of work that will make sick men whole.

LIGARIUS But are not some whole that we must make sick?

BRUTUS That must we also. What it is, my Caius,
I shall unfold to thee, as we are going
To whom it must be done.

LIGARIUS Set on your foot,
And with a heart new-fir'd I follow you
To do I know not what; but it sufficeth
That Brutus leads me on. [*Thunder.*

BRUTUS Follow me, then.
[*Exeunt.*

SCENE II. *Rome. Caesar's house.*

Thunder and lightning. Enter JULIUS CAESAR in his night-gown.

CAESAR Nor heaven nor earth have been at peace to-night.
Thrice hath Calphurnia in her sleep cried out
'Help, ho! They murder Caesar!' Who's within?

Enter a Servant.

SERVANT My lord?

CAESAR Go bid the priests do present sacrifice,
And bring me their opinions of success.

SERVANT I will, my lord. [*Exit.*

Enter CALPHURNIA.

CALPHURNIA At mean you, Caesar? Think you to walk forth?
You shall not stir out of your house to-day.

CAESAR Caesar shall forth; the things that threaten'd me
Ne'er look'd but on my back. When they shall see
The face of Caesar, they are vanished.

CALPHURNIA Caesar, I never stood on ceremonies,
Yet now they fright me. There is one within,
Besides the things that we have heard and seen,
Recounts most horrid sights seen by the watch.
A lioness hath whelped in the streets,
And graves have yawn'd and yielded up their dead;
Fierce fiery warriors fight upon the clouds,
In ranks and squadrons and right form of war,
Which drizzled blood upon the Capitol;
The noise of battle hurtled in the air;
Horses did neigh, and dying men did groan,
And ghosts did shriek and squeal about the streets.
O Caesar, these things are beyond all use,
And I do fear them!

CAESAR What can be avoided,
Whose end is purpos'd by the mighty gods?
Yet Caesar shall go forth; for these predictions
Are to the world in general as to Caesar.

CALPHURNIA When beggars die there are no comets seen:
The heavens themselves blaze forth the death of princes.

CAESAR Cowards die many times before their deaths:
The valiant never taste of death but once.
Of all the wonders that I yet have heard,
It seems to me most strange that men should fear,
Seeing that death, a necessary end,
Will come when it will come.

Re-enter Servant.

What say the augurers?

SERVANT They would not have you to stir forth to-day.
Plucking the entrails of an offering forth,
They could not find a heart within the beast.

CAESAR The gods do this in shame of cowardice.
Caesar should be a beast without a heart,
If he should stay at home to-day for fear.
No, Caesar shall not. Danger knows full well

That Caesar is more dangerous than he:
We are two lions litter'd in one day,
And I the elder and more terrible;
And Caesar shall go forth.

CALPHURNIA Alas, my lord,
Your wisdom is consum'd in confidence.
Do not go forth to-day. Call it my fear
That keeps you in the house, and not your own.
We'll send Mark Antony to the Senate House,
And he shall say you are not well to-day.
Let me, upon my knee, prevail in this.

CAESAR Mark Antony shall say I am not well;
And for thy humour I will stay at home.

Enter DECIUS.

Here's Decius Brutus, he shall tell them so.

DECIUS Caesar, all hail! Good morrow, worthy Caesar.
I come to fetch you to the Senate House.

CAESAR And you are come in very happy time,
To bear my greeting to the senators
And tell them that I will not come to-day.
Cannot, is false; and that I dare not, falser;
I will not come to-day. Tell them so, Decius.

CALPHURNIA Say he is sick.

CAESAR Shall Caesar send a lie?
Have I in conquest stretch'd mine arm so far,
To be afeard to tell greybeards the truth?
Decius, go tell them, Caesar will not come.

DECIUS Most mighty Caesar, let me know some cause,
Lest I be laugh'd at when I tell them so.

CAESAR The cause is in my will: I will not come.
That is enough to satisfy the Senate.
But for your private satisfaction,
Because I love you, I will let you know:
Calphurnia here, my wife, stays me at home.
She dreamt to-night she saw my statua,
Which, like a fountain with an hundred spouts,
Did run pure blood; and many lusty Romans
Came smiling and did bathe their hands in it.
And these does she apply for warnings and portents
And evils imminent, and on her knee
Hath begg'd that I will stay at home to-day.

DECIUS This dream is all amiss interpreted;
It was a vision fair and fortunate.
Your statue spouting blood in many pipes,
In which so many smiling Romans bath'd,
Signifies that from you great Rome shall suck
Reviving blood, and that great men shall press
For tinctures, stains, relics, and cognizance.
This by Calphurnia's dream is signified.

CAESAR And this way have you well expounded it.

DECIUS I have, when you have heard what I can say –
And know it now: the Senate have concluded
To give this day a crown to mighty Caesar.
If you shall send them word you will not come,
Their minds may change. Besides, it were a mock
Apt to be render'd, for some one to say
'Break up the Senate till another time,
When Caesar's wife shall meet with better dreams'.
If Caesar hide himself, shall they not whisper
'Lo, Caesar is afraid'?
Pardon me, Caesar; for my dear dear love
To your proceeding bids me tell you this,
And reason to my love is liable.

CAESAR How foolish do your fears seem now, Calphurnia!
I am ashamed I did yield to them.
Give me my robe, for I will go.

Enter BRUTUS, LIGARIUS, METELLUS, CASCA, TREBONIUS, CINNA, and PUBLIUS.

And look where Publius is come to fetch me.

PUBLIUS Good morrow, Caesar.

CAESAR Welcome, Publius.
What, Brutus, are you stirr'd so early too?
Good morrow, Casca. Caius Ligarius,
Caesar was ne'er so much your enemy
As that same ague which hath made you lean.
What is't o'clock?

BRUTUS Caesar, 'tis strucken eight.

CAESAR I thank you for your pains and courtesy.

Enter ANTONY.

See! Antony, that revels long o' nights,
Is notwithstanding up. Good morrow, Antony.

ANTONY So to most noble Caesar.

CAESAR Bid them prepare within.
I am to blame to be thus waited for.
Now, Cinna. Now, Metellus. What, Trebonius!
I have an hour's talk in store for you.
Remember that you call on me to-day;
Be near me, that I may remember you.

TREBONIUS Caesar, I will. [*Aside*] And so near will I be,
That your best friends shall wish I had been further.

CAESAR Good friends, go in and taste some wine with me;
And we, like friends, will straightway go together.

BRUTUS [*Aside*] That every like is not the same, O Caesar,
The heart of Brutus earns to think upon!

[*Exeunt.*

SCENE III. *Rome. A street near the Capitol.*

Enter ARTEMIDORUS reading a paper.

ARTEMIDORUS 'Caesar, beware of Brutus; take heed of Cassius; come not near Casca; have an eye to Cinna; trust not Trebonius; mark well Metellus Cimber; Decius Brutus loves thee not; thou hast wrong'd Caius Ligarius. There is but one mind in all these men, and it is bent against Caesar. If thou beest not immortal, look about you. Security gives way to conspiracy. The mighty gods defend thee!

Thy lover,
ARTEMIDORUS.'

Here will I stand till Caesar pass along,
And as a suitor will I give him this.
My heart laments that virtue cannot live
Out of the teeth of emulation.
If thou read this, O, Caesar, thou mayest live;
If not, the fates with traitors do contrive.
[*Exit.*

SCENE IV. *Rome. Before the house of Brutus.*

Enter PORTIA and LUCIUS.

PORTIA I prithee, boy, run to the Senate House.
Stay not to answer me, but get thee gone.
Why dost thou stay?
LUCIUS To know my errand, madam.
PORTIA I would have had thee there and here again,
Ere I can tell thee what thou shouldst do there.
[*Aside*] O constancy, be strong upon my side!
Set a huge mountain 'tween my heart and tongue!
I have a man's mind, but a woman's might.
How hard it is for women to keep counsel! –
Art thou here yet?
LUCIUS Madam, what should I do?
Run to the Capitol, and nothing else?
And so return to you, and nothing else?
PORTIA Yes, bring me word, boy, if thy lord look well,
For he went sickly forth; and take good note
What Caesar doth, what suitors press to him.
Hark, boy! What noise is that?
LUCIUS I hear none, madam.
PORTIA Prithee listen well.
I heard a bustling rumour, like a fray,
And the wind brings it from the Capitol.
LUCIUS Sooth, madam, I hear nothing.

Enter the Soothsayer.

PORTIA Come hither, fellow.
Which way hast thou been?
SOOTHSAYER At mine own house, good lady.
PORTIA What is't o'clock?
SOOTHSAYER About the ninth hour, lady.
PORTIA Is Caesar yet gone to the Capitol?
SOOTHSAYER Madam, not yet. I go to take my stand,
To see him pass on to the Capitol.
PORTIA Thou hast some suit to Caesar, hast thou not?
SOOTHSAYER That I have, lady. If it will please him Caesar
To be so good to Caesar as to hear me,
I shall beseech him to befriend himself.
PORTIA Why, know'st thou any harm's intended towards him?
SOOTHSAYER None that I know will be, much that I fear may chance.
Good morrow to you. Here the street is narrow;
The throng that follows Caesar at the heels,
Of senators, of praetors, common suitors,
Will crowd a feeble man almost to death.
I'll get me to a place more void, and there
Speak to great Caesar as he comes along.
[*Exit.*
PORTIA I must go in. [Aside] Ay me, how weak a thing
The heart of woman is! O Brutus,
The heavens speed thee in thine enterprise!
Sure the boy heard me. – Brutus hath a suit
That Caesar will not grant. – O, I grow faint. –
Run, Lucius, and commend me to my lord;
Say I am merry. Come to me again,
And bring me word what he doth say to thee.
[*Exeunt severally.*

ACT THREE

SCENE I. *Rome. A street before the Capitol.*

Flourish. Enter CAESAR, BRUTUS, CASSIUS, CASCA, DECIUS, METELLUS, TREBONIUS, CINNA, ANTONY, LEPIDUS, ARTEMIDORUS, POPILIUS, PUBLIUS, and the Soothsayer.

CAESAR The ides of March are come.
SOOTHSAYER Ay, Caesar, but not gone.
ARTEMIDORUS Hail, Caesar! Read this schedule.
DECIUS Trebonius doth desire you to o'er-read,
At your best leisure, this his humble suit.
ARTEMIDORUS O Caesar, read mine first; for mine's a suit
That touches Caesar nearer. Read it, great Caesar.
CAESAR What touches us ourself shall be last serv'd.
ARTEMIDORUS Delay not, Caesar; read it instantly.

CAESAR What, is the fellow mad?
PUBLIUS Sirrah, give place.
CASSIUS What, urge you your petitions in the street?
Come to the Capitol.

Caesar enters the Capitol, the rest following.

POPILIUS I wish your enterprise to-day may thrive.
CASSIUS What enterprise, Popilius?
POPILIUS Fare you well.
[*Advances to Caesar.*
BRUTUS What said Popilius Lena?
CASSIUS He wish'd to-day our enterprise might thrive.
I fear our purpose is discovered.
BRUTUS Look how he makes to Caesar. Mark him.
CASSIUS Casca, be sudden, for we fear prevention.
Brutus, what shall be done? If this be known,
Cassius or Caesar never shall turn back,
For I will slay myself.
BRUTUS Cassius, be constant.
Popilius Lena speaks not of our purposes;
For look, he smiles, and Caesar doth not change.
CASSIUS Trebonius knows his time; for look you, Brutus,
He draws Mark Antony out of the way.
[*Exeunt Antony and Trebonius.*
DECIUS Where is Metellus Cimber? Let him go
And presently prefer his suit to Caesar.
BRUTUS He is address'd; press near and second him.
CINNA Casca, you are the first that rears your hand.
CAESAR Are we all ready? What is now amiss
That Caesar and his Senate must redress?
METELLUS Most high, most mighty, and most puissant Caesar,
Metellus Cimber throws before thy seat
An humble heart. [*Kneeling.*
CAESAR I must prevent thee, Cimber.
These couchings and these lowly courtesies
Might fire the blood of ordinary men,
And turn pre-ordinance and first decree
Into the law of children. Be not fond
To think that Caesar bears such rebel blood
That will be thaw'd from the true quality
With that which melteth fools – I mean, sweet words,
Low-crooked curtsies, and base spaniel fawning.
Thy brother by decree is banished;
If thou dost bend, and pray, and fawn for him,
I spurn thee like a cur out of my way.
Know, Caesar doth not wrong; nor without cause
Will he be satisfied.
METELLUS Is there no voice more worthy than my own
To sound more sweetly in great Caesar's ear
For the repealing of my banish'd brother?
BRUTUS I kiss thy hand, but not in flattery, Caesar,
Desiring thee that Publius Cimber may
Have an immediate freedom of repeal.
CAESAR What, Brutus!
CASSIUS Pardon, Caesar! Caesar, pardon!
As low as to thy foot doth Cassius fall,
To beg enfranchisement for Publius Cimber.
CAESAR I could be well mov'd, if I were as you;
If I could pray to move, prayers would move me;
But I am constant as the northern star,
Of whose true-fix'd and resting quality
There is no fellow in the firmament.
The skies are painted with unnumb'red sparks,
They are all fire, and every one doth shine;
But there's but one in all doth hold his place.
So in the world: 'tis furnish'd well with men,
And men are flesh and blood, and apprehensive;
Yet in the number I do know but one
That unassailable holds on his rank,
Unshak'd of motion; and that I am he,
Let me a little show it, even in this –
That I was constant Cimber should be banish'd,
And constant do remain to keep him so.
CINNA O Caesar!
CAESAR Hence! Wilt thou lift up Olympus?
DECIUS Great Caesar!
CAESAR Doth not Brutus bootless kneel?
CASCA Speak, hands, for me!
[*They stab Caesar. Casca strikes the first, Brutus the last blow.*
CAESAR Et tu, Brute? – Then fall, Caesar!
[*Dies.*
CINNA Liberty! Freedom! Tyranny is dead!
Run hence, proclaim, cry it about the streets.
CASSIUS Some to the common pulpits, and cry out
'Liberty, freedom, and enfranchisement!'
BRUTUS People and Senators, be not affrighted.
Fly not; stand still. Ambition's debt is paid.
CASCA Go to the pulpit, Brutus.
DECIUS And Cassius too.
BRUTUS Where's Publius?
CINNA Here, quite confounded with this mutiny.
METELLUS Stand fast together, lest some friend of Caesar's
Should chance –
BRUTUS Talk not of standing. Publius, good cheer!

There is no harm intended to your person,
Nor to no Roman else. So tell them, Publius.
CASSIUS And leave us, Publius, lest that the people,
Rushing on us, should do your age some mischief.
BRUTUS Do so; and let no man abide this deed
But we the doers.

Re-enter TREBONIUS.

CASSIUS Where is Antony?
TREBONIUS Fled to his house amaz'd.
Men, wives, and children, stare, cry out, and run,
As it were doomsday.
BRUTUS Fates, we will know your pleasures.
That we shall die, we know; 'tis but the time,
And drawing days out, that men stand upon.
CASSIUS Why, he that cuts off twenty years of life
Cuts off so many years of fearing death.
BRUTUS Grant that, and then is death a benefit.
So are we Caesar's friends, that have abridg'd
His time of fearing death. Stoop, Romans, stoop,
And let us bathe our hands in Caesar's blood
Up to the elbows, and besmear our swords.
Then walk we forth, even to the marketplace,
And waving our red weapons o'er our heads,
Let's all cry 'Peace, freedom, and liberty!'
CASSIUS Stoop then, and wash. How many ages hence
Shall this our lofty scene be acted over
In states unborn and accents yet unknown!
BRUTUS How many times shall Caesar bleed in sport,
That now on Pompey's basis lies along
No worthier than the dust!
CASSIUS So oft as that shall be,
So often shall the knot of us be call'd
The men that gave their country liberty.
DECIUS What, shall we forth?
CASSIUS Ay, every man away.
Brutus shall lead, and we will grace his heels
With the most boldest and best hearts of Rome.

Enter a Servant.

BRUTUS Soft, who comes here? A friend of Antony's.
SERVANT Thus, Brutus, did my master bid me kneel;
Thus did Mark Antony bid me fall down;
And, being prostrate, thus he bade me say:
Brutus is noble, wise, valiant, and honest;
Caesar was mighty, bold, royal, and loving.
Say I love Brutus, and I honour him;
Say I fear'd Caesar, honour'd him, and lov'd him.
If Brutus will vouchsafe that Antony
May safely come to him, and be resolv'd
How Caesar hath deserv'd to lie in death,
Mark Antony shall not love Caesar dead
So well as Brutus living; but will follow
The fortunes and affairs of noble Brutus
Thorough the hazards of this untrod state
With all true faith. So says my master Antony.
BRUTUS Thy master is a wise and valiant Roman;
I never thought him worse.
Tell him, so please him come unto this place,
He shall be satisfied and, by my honour,
Depart untouch'd.
SERVANT I'll fetch him presently.
[*Exit.*

BRUTUS I know that we shall have him well to friend.
CASSIUS I wish we may. But yet have I a mind
That fears him much; and my misgiving still
Falls shrewdly to the purpose.

Re-enter ANTONY.

BRUTUS But here comes Antony. Welcome, Mark Antony.
ANTONY O mighty Caesar! dost thou lie so low?
Are all thy conquests, glories, triumphs, spoils,
Shrunk to this little measure? Fare thee well.
I know not, gentlemen, what you intend,
Who else must be let blood, who else is rank.
If I myself, there is no hour so fit
As Caesar's death's hour; nor no instrument
Of half that worth as those your swords, made rich
With the most noble blood of all this world.
I do beseech ye, if you bear me hard,
Now, whilst your purpled hands do reek and smoke,
Fulfil your pleasure. Live a thousand years,
I shall not find myself so apt to die.
No place will please me so, no mean of death,
As here by Caesar, and by you cut off,
The choice and master spirits of this age.
BRUTUS O Antony! beg not your death of us.
Though now we must appear bloody and cruel,
As by our hands and this our present act
You see we do; yet see you but our hands,
And this the bleeding business they have done.
Our hearts you see not; they are pitiful;
And pity to the general wrong of Rome,
As fire drives out fire, so pity pity,
Hath done this deed on Caesar. For your part,
To you our swords have leaden points, Mark Antony;
Our arms in strength of malice, and our hearts
Of brothers' temper, do receive you in
With all kind love, good thoughts, and reverence.
CASSIUS Your voice shall be as strong as any man's
In the disposing of new dignities.

BRUTUS Only be patient till we have appeas'd
The multitude, beside themselves with fear,
And then we will deliver you the cause
Why I, that did love Caesar when I struck him,
Have thus proceeded.
ANTONY I doubt not of your wisdom.
Let each man render me his bloody hand.
First, Marcus Brutus, will I shake with you;
Next, Caius Cassius, do I take your hand;
Now, Decius Brutus, yours; now yours, Metellus;
Yours, Cinna; and, my valiant Casca, yours.
Though last, not least in love, yours, good Trebonius.
Gentlemen all – alas, what shall I say?
My credit now stands on such slippery ground
That one of two bad ways you must conceit me,
Either a coward or a flatterer.
That I did love thee, Caesar, O, 'tis true!
If then thy spirit look upon us now,
Shall it not grieve thee dearer than thy death
To see thy Antony making his peace,
Shaking the bloody fingers of thy foes,
Most noble! in the presence of thy corse?
Had I as many eyes as thou hast wounds,
Weeping as fast as they stream forth thy blood,
It would become me better than to close
In terms of friendship with thine enemies.
Pardon me, Julius! Here wast thou bay'd, brave hart;
Here didst thou fall; and here thy hunters stand,
Sign'd in thy spoil, and crimson'd in thy lethe.
O world, thou wast the forest to this hart;
And this indeed, O world, the heart of thee!
How like a deer strucken by many princes
Dost thou here lie!
CASSIUS Mark Antony –
ANTONY Pardon me, Caius Cassius.
The enemies of Caesar shall say this;
Then, in a friend, it is cold modesty.
CASSIUS I blame you not for praising Caesar so;
But what compact mean you to have with us?
Will you be prick'd in number of our friends,
Or shall we on, and not depend on you?
ANTONY Therefore I took your hands; but was indeed
Sway'd from the point by looking down on Caesar.
Friends am I with you all, and love you all,
Upon this hope, that you shall give me reasons
Why and wherein Caesar was dangerous.
BRUTUS Or else were this a savage spectacle.
Our reasons are so full of good regard
That were you, Antony, the son of Caesar,
You should be satisfied.
ANTONY That's all I seek;
And am moreover suitor that I may
Produce his body to the market-place
And, in the pulpit, as becomes a friend,
Speak in the order of his funeral.
BRUTUS You shall, Mark Antony.
CASSIUS Brutus, a word with you.
[*Aside to Brutus*] You know not what you do. Do not consent
That Antony speak in his funeral.
Know you how much the people may be mov'd
By that which he will utter?
BRUTUS [*Aside to Cassius*] By your pardon –
I will myself into the pulpit first,
And show the reason of our Caesar's death.
What Antony shall speak, I will protest
He speaks by leave and by permission;
And that we are contented Caesar shall
Have all true rites and lawful ceremonies.
It shall advantage more than do us wrong.
CASSIUS I know not what may fall. I like it not.
BRUTUS Mark Antony, here, take you Caesar's body.
You shall not in your funeral speech blame us,
But speak all good you can devise of Caesar;
And say you do't by our permission;
Else shall you not have any hand at all
About his funeral. And you shall speak
In the same pulpit whereto I am going,
After my speech is ended.
ANTONY Be it so;
I do desire no more.
BRUTUS Prepare the body then, and follow us.

[*Exeunt all but Antony.*

ANTONY O, pardon me, thou bleeding piece of earth,
That I am meek and gentle with these butchers!
Thou art the ruins of the noblest man
That ever lived in the tide of times.
Woe to the hand that shed this costly blood!
Over thy wounds now do I prophesy –
Which like dumb mouths do ope their ruby lips
To beg the voice and utterance of my tongue –
A curse shall light upon the limbs of men;
Domestic fury and fierce civil strife
Shall cumber all the parts of Italy;
Blood and destruction shall be so in use,
And dreadful objects so familiar,
That mothers shall but smile when they behold
Their infants quartered with the hands of war,
All pity chok'd with custom of fell deeds;
And Caesar's spirit, ranging for revenge,
With Até by his side come hot from hell,
Shall in these confines with a monarch's voice
Cry 'Havoc!' and let slip the dogs of war,
That this foul deed shall smell above the earth
With carrion men, groaning for burial.

Enter Octavius' Servant.

You serve Octavius Caesar, do you not?
SERVANT I do, Mark Antony.
ANTONY Caesar did write for him to come to Rome.
SERVANT He did receive his letters, and is coming,
And bid me say to you by word of mouth –
O Caesar! *[Seeing the body.*
ANTONY Thy heart is big, get thee apart and weep.
Passion, I see, is catching; for mine eyes,
Seeing those beads of sorrow stand in thine,
Began to water. Is thy master coming?
SERVANT He lies to-night within seven leagues of Rome.
ANTONY Post back with speed, and tell him what hath chanc'd.
Here is a mourning Rome, a dangerous Rome,
No Rome of safety for Octavius yet;
Hie hence and tell him so. Yet stay awhile;
Thou shalt not back till I have borne this corse
Into the market-place. There shall I try,
In my oration, how the people take
The cruel issue of these bloody men;
According to the which thou shalt discourse
To young Octavius of the state of things.
Lend me your hand.
[Exeunt with Caesar's body.

SCENE II. *Rome. The Forum.*

Enter BRUTUS and CASSIUS, with the Plebeians.

CITIZENS We will be satisfied! Let us be satisfied!
BRUTUS Then follow me, and give me audience, friends.
Cassius, go you into the other street,
And part the numbers.
Those that will hear me speak, let 'em stay here;
Those that will follow Cassius, go with him;
And public reasons shall be rendered
Of Caesar's death.
1 PLEBEIAN I will hear Brutus speak.
2 PLEBEIAN I will hear Cassius, and compare their reasons,
When severally we hear them rendered.
[Exit Cassius, with some of the Plebeians. Brutus goes into the pulpit.
3 PLEBEIAN The noble Brutus is ascended. Silence!
BRUTUS Be patient till the last.

Romans, countrymen, and lovers! hear me for my cause, and be silent, that you may hear. Believe me for mine honour, and have respect to mine honour, that you may believe. Censure me in your wisdom, and awake your senses, that you may the better judge. If there be any in this assembly, any dear friend of Caesar's, to him I say that Brutus' love to Caesar was no less than his. If then that friend demand why Brutus rose against Caesar, this is my answer: Not that I lov'd Caesar less, but that I lov'd Rome more. Had you rather Caesar were living, and die all slaves, than that Caesar were dead, to live all free men? As Caesar lov'd me, I weep for him; as he was fortunate, I rejoice at it; as he was valiant, I honour him; but – as he was ambitious, I slew him. There is tears for his love; joy for his fortune; honour for his valour; and death for his ambition. Who is here so base that would be a bondman? If any, speak; for him have I offended. Who is here so rude that would not be a Roman? If any, speak; for him have I offended. Who is here so vile that will not love his country? If any, speak; for him have I offended. I pause for a reply.

ALL None, Brutus, none.

BRUTUS Then none have I offended. I have done no more to Caesar than you shall do to Brutus. The question of his death is enroll'd in the Capitol; his glory not extenuated, wherein he was worthy; nor his offences enforc'd, for which he suffered death.

Enter ANTONY and Others with Caesar's body.

Here comes his body, mourn'd by Mark Antony, who, though he had no hand in his death, shall receive the benefit of his dying, a place in the commonwealth, as which of you shall not? With this I depart, that, as I slew my best lover for the good of Rome, I have the same dagger for myself, when it shall please my country to need my death.

ALL Live, Brutus! live, live!
1 PLEBEIAN Bring him with triumph home unto his house.
2 PLEBEIAN Give him a statue with his ancestors.
3 PLEBEIAN Let him be Caesar.
4 PLEBEIAN Caesar's better parts
Shall be crown'd in Brutus.
1 PLEBEIAN We'll bring him to his house with shouts and clamours.
BRUTUS My countrymen –
2 PLEBEIAN Peace, silence! Brutus speaks.
1 PLEBEIAN Peace, ho!
BRUTUS Good countrymen, let me depart alone,
And for my sake stay here with Antony.
Do grace to Caesar's corpse, and grace his speech
Tending to Caesar's glories, which Mark Antony,
By our permission, is allow'd to make.
I do entreat you, not a man depart
Save I alone, till Antony have spoke. *[Exit.*

1 PLEBEIAN Stay, ho! and let us hear Mark Antony.
3 PLEBEIAN Let him go up into the public chair.
We'll hear him. Noble Antony, go up.
ANTONY For Brutus' sake I am beholding to you.
[*Goes up.*
4 PLEBEIAN What does he say of Brutus?
3 PLEBEIAN He says, for Brutus' sake
He finds himself beholding to us all.
4 PLEBEIAN 'Twere best he speak no harm of Brutus here.
1 PLEBEIAN This Caesar was a tyrant.
3 PLEBEIAN Nay, that's certain.
We are blest that Rome is rid of him.
2 PLEBEIAN Peace! let us hear what Antony can say.
ANTONY You gentle Romans –
ALL Peace, ho! let us hear him.
ANTONY Friends, Romans, countrymen, lend me your ears;
I come to bury Caesar, not to praise him.
The evil that men do lives after them;
The good is oft interred with their bones;
So let it be with Caesar. The noble Brutus
Hath told you Caesar was ambitious.
If it were so, it was a grievous fault;
And grievously hath Caesar answer'd it.
Here, under leave of Brutus and the rest –
For Brutus is an honourable man;
So are they all, all honourable men –
Come I to speak in Caesar's funeral.
He was my friend, faithful and just to me;
But Brutus says he was ambitious,
And Brutus is an honourable man.
He hath brought many captives home to Rome,
Whose ransoms did the general coffers fill;
Did this in Caesar seem ambitious?
When that the poor have cried, Caesar hath wept;
Ambition should be made of sterner stuff.
Yet Brutus says he was ambitious;
And Brutus is an honourable man.
You all did see that on the Lupercal
I thrice presented him a kingly crown,
Which he did thrice refuse. Was this ambition?
Yet Brutus says he was ambitious;
And sure he is an honourable man.
I speak not to disprove what Brutus spoke,
But here I am to speak what I do know.
You all did love him once, not without cause;
What cause withholds you, then, to mourn for him?
O judgment, thou art fled to brutish beasts,
And men have lost their reason! Bear with me;
My heart is in the coffin there with Caesar,
And I must pause till it come back to me.
1 PLEBEIAN Methinks there is much reason in his sayings.
2 PLEBEIAN If thou consider rightly of the matter,
Caesar has had great wrong.
3 PLEBEIAN Has he, masters!
I fear there will a worse come in his place.
4 PLEBEIAN Mark'd ye his words? He would not take the crown;
Therefore 'tis certain he was not ambitious.
1 PLEBEIAN If it be found so, some will dear abide it.
2 PLEBEIAN Poor soul! his eyes are red as fire with weeping.
3 PLEBEIAN There's not a nobler man in Rome than Antony.
4 PLEBEIAN Now mark him, he begins again to speak.
ANTONY But yesterday the word of Caesar might
Have stood against the world: now lies he there,
And none so poor to do him reverence.
O masters, if I were dispos'd to stir
Your hearts and minds to mutiny and rage,
I should do Brutus wrong, and Cassius wrong,
Who, you all know, are honourable men.
I will not do them wrong; I rather choose
To wrong the dead, to wrong myself and you,
Than I will wrong such honourable men.
But here's a parchment with the seal of Caesar;
I found it in his closet – 'tis his will.
Let but the commons hear this testament,
Which, pardon me, I do not mean to read,
And they would go and kiss dead Caesar's wounds
And dip their napkins in his sacred blood;
Yea, beg a hair of him for memory
And, dying, mention it within their wills,
Bequeathing it as a rich legacy
Unto their issue.
4 PLEBEIAN We'll hear the will. Read it, Mark Antony.
ALL The will, the will! We will hear Caesar's will.
ANTONY Have patience, gentle friends, I must not read it;
It is not meet you know how Caesar lov'd you.
You are not wood, you are not stones, but men;
And being men, hearing the will of Caesar,
It will inflame you, it will make you mad.
'Tis good you know not that you are his heirs;
For if you should, O, what would come of it?
4 PLEBEIAN Read the will; we'll hear it, Antony!
You shall read us the will – Caesar's will.
ANTONY Will you be patient? Will you stay awhile?
I have o'ershot myself to tell you of it.
I fear I wrong the honourable men
Whose daggers have stabb'd Caesar; I do fear it.
4 PLEBEIAN They were traitors. Honourable men!

ALL The will! the testament!
2 PLEBEIAN They were villains, murderers. The will! Read the will.
ANTONY You will compel me, then, to read the will?
Then make a ring about the corpse of Caesar,
And let me show you him that made the will.
Shall I descend? and will you give me leave?
ALL Come down.
2 PLEBEIAN Descend. [*Antony comes down.*
3 PLEBEIAN You shall have leave.
4 PLEBEIAN A ring! Stand round.
1 PLEBEIAN Stand from the hearse, stand from the body.
2 PLEBEIAN Room for Antony, most noble Antony!
ANTONY Nay, press not so upon me; stand far off.
ALL Stand back. Room! Bear back.
ANTONY If you have tears, prepare to shed them now.
You all do know this mantle. I remember
The first time ever Caesar put it on;
'Twas on a summer's evening, in his tent,
That day he overcame the Nervii.
Look! in this place ran Cassius' dagger through;
See what a rent the envious Casca made;
Through this the well-beloved Brutus stabb'd,
And as he pluck'd his cursed steel away,
Mark how the blood of Caesar follow'd it,
As rushing out of doors, to be resolv'd
If Brutus so unkindly knock'd or no;
For Brutus, as you know, was Caesar's angel.
Judge, O you gods, how dearly Caesar lov'd him!
This was the most unkindest cut of all;
For when the noble Caesar saw him stab,
Ingratitude, more strong than traitors' arms,
Quite vanquish'd him. Then burst his mighty heart;
And in his mantle muffling up his face,
Even at the base of Pompey's statua,
Which all the while ran blood, great Caesar fell.
O, what a fall was there, my countrymen!
Then I, and you, and all of us fell down,
Whilst bloody treason flourish'd over us.
O, now you weep, and I perceive you feel
The dint of pity. These are gracious drops.
Kind souls, what weep you when you but behold
Our Caesar's vesture wounded? Look you here,
Here is himself, marr'd as you see with traitors.
1 PLEBEIAN O piteous spectacle!
2 PLEBEIAN O noble Caesar!
3 PLEBEIAN O woeful day!
4 PLEBEIAN O traitors, villains!
1 PLEBEIAN O most bloody sight!
2 PLEBEIAN We will be reveng'd.
ALL Revenge! About! Seek! Burn! Fire! Kill! Slay! Let not a traitor live!
ANTONY Stay, countrymen.
1 PLEBEIAN Peace there! Hear the noble Antony.
2 PLEBEIAN We'll hear him, we'll follow him, we'll die with him.
ANTONY Good friends, sweet friends, let me not stir you up
To such a sudden flood of mutiny.
They that have done this deed are honourable.
What private griefs they have, alas, I know not,
That made them do it; they are wise and honourable,
And will, no doubt, with reasons answer you.
I come not, friends, to steal away your hearts;
I am no orator, as Brutus is,
But, as you know me all, a plain blunt man,
That love my friend; and that they know full well
That gave me public leave to speak of him.
For I have neither wit, nor words, nor worth,
Action, nor utterance, nor the power of speech,
To stir men's blood; I only speak right on.
I tell you that which you yourselves do know;
Show you sweet Caesar's wounds, poor poor dumb mouths,
And bid them speak for me. But were I Brutus,
And Brutus Antony, there were an Antony
Would ruffle up your spirits, and put a tongue
In every wound of Caesar, that should move
The stones of Rome to rise and mutiny.
ALL We'll mutiny.
1 PLEBEIAN We'll burn the house of Brutus.
3 PLEBEIAN Away, then! Come seek the conspirators.
ANTONY Yet hear me, countrymen; yet hear me speak.
ALL Peace, ho! Hear Antony, most noble Antony.
ANTONY Why, friends, you go to do you know not what.
Wherein hath Caesar thus deserv'd your loves?
Alas, you know not! I must tell you, then:
You have forgot the will I told you of.
ALL Most true. The will! Let's stay and hear the will.
ANTONY Here is the will, and under Caesar's seal:
To every Roman citizen he gives,
To every several man, seventy-five drachmas.
2 PLEBEIAN Most noble Caesar! We'll revenge his death.
3 PLEBEIAN O royal Caesar!
ANTONY Hear me with patience.
ALL Peace, ho!
ANTONY Moreover, he hath left you all his walks,
His private arbours, and new-planted orchards,
On this side Tiber; he hath left them you,
And to your heirs for ever – common pleasures,

To walk abroad and recreate yourselves.
Here was a Caesar! When comes such another?
1 PLEBEIAN Never, never! Come away, away!
We'll burn his body in the holy place,
And with the brands fire the traitors' houses.
Take up the body.
2 PLEBEIAN Go, fetch fire.
3 PLEBEIAN Pluck down benches.
4 PLEBEIAN Pluck down forms, windows, any thing. *[Exeunt Plebeians with the body.*
ANTONY Now let it work. Mischief, thou art afoot,
Take thou what course thou wilt.

Enter a Servant.

How now, fellow!
SERVANT Sir, Octavius is already come to Rome.
ANTONY Where is he?
SERVANT He and Lepidus are at Caesar's house.
ANTONY And thither will I straight to visit him.
He comes upon a wish. Fortune is merry,
And in this mood will give us any thing.
SERVANT I heard him say Brutus and Cassius
Are rid like madmen through the gates of Rome.
ANTONY Belike they had some notice of the people,
How I had mov'd them. Bring me to Octavius.
[Exeunt.

SCENE III. *Rome. A street.*

Enter CINNA the Poet, and after him the Plebeians.

CINNA I dreamt to-night that I did feast with Caesar,
And things unluckily charge my fantasy.
I have no will to wander forth of doors,
Yet something leads me forth.
1 PLEBEIAN What is your name?
2 PLEBEIAN Whither are you going?
3 PLEBEIAN Where do you dwell?
4 PLEBEIAN Are you a married man or a bachelor?
2 PLEBEIAN Answer every man directly.
1 PLEBEIAN Ay, and briefly.
4 PLEBEIAN Ay, and wisely.
3 PLEBEIAN Ay, and truly, you were best.

CINNA What is my name? Whither am I going? Where do I dwell? Am I a married man or a bachelor? Then to answer every man directly and briefly, wisely and truly: wisely, I say I am a bachelor.

2 PLEBEIAN That's as much as to say they are fools that marry. You'll bear me a bang for that, I fear. Proceed directly.

CINNA Directly, I am going to Caesar's funeral.
1 PLEBEIAN As a friend or an enemy?
CINNA As a friend.
2 PLEBEIAN That matter is answered directly.
4 PLEBEIAN For your dwelling – briefly.
CINNA Briefly, I dwell by the Capitol.
3 PLEBEIAN Your name, sir, truly.
CINNA Truly, my name is Cinna.

1 PLEBEIAN Tear him to pieces; he's a conspirator!

CINNA I am Cinna the poet, I am Cinna the poet.

4 PLEBEIAN Tear him for his bad verses, tear him for his bad verses!

CINNA I am not Cinna the conspirator.

4 PLEBEIAN It is no matter, his name's Cinna; pluck but his name out of his heart, and turn him going.

3 PLEBEIAN Tear him, tear him! Come, brands, ho! fire-brands! To Brutus', to Cassius'! Burn all! Some to Decius' house, and some to Casca's; some to Ligarius'. Away, go!

[Exeunt all the Plebeians with Cinna.

ACT FOUR

SCENE I. *Rome. Antony's house.*

Enter ANTONY, OCTAVIUS, and LEPIDUS.

ANTONY These many, then, shall die; their names are prick'd.
OCTAVIUS Your brother too must die. Consent you, Lepidus?
LEPIDUS I do consent.
OCTAVIUS Prick him down, Antony.
LEPIDUS Upon condition Publius shall not live,
Who is your sister's son, Mark Antony.
ANTONY He shall not live; look, with a spot I damn him.
But, Lepidus, go you to Caesar's house;
Fetch the will hither, and we shall determine
How to cut off some charge in legacies.
LEPIDUS What, shall I find you here?
OCTAVIUS Or here or at the Capitol.
[Exit Lepidus.
ANTONY This is a slight unmeritable man,
Meet to be sent on errands. Is it fit,
The threefold world divided, he should stand
One of the three to share it?
OCTAVIUS So you thought him,
And took his voice who should be prick'd to die
In our black sentence and proscription.
ANTONY Octavius, I have seen more days than you;
And though we lay these honours on this man,

To ease ourselves of divers sland'rous loads,
He shall but bear them as the ass bears gold,
The groan and sweat under the business,
Either led or driven as we point the way;
And having brought our treasure where we will,
Then take we down his load, and turn him off,
Like to the empty ass, to shake his ears
And graze in commons.

OCTAVIUS You may do your will;
But he's a tried and valiant soldier.

ANTONY So is my horse, Octavius, and for that
I do appoint him store of provender.
It is a creature that I teach to fight,
To wind, to stop, to run directly on,
His corporal motion govern'd by my spirit.
And, in some taste, is Lepidus but so:
He must be taught, and train'd, and bid go forth;
A barren-spirited fellow; one that feeds
On abjects, orts, and imitations,
Which, out of use and stal'd by other men,
Begin his fashion. Do not talk of him
But as a property. And now, Octavius,
Listen great things: Brutus and Cassius
Are levying powers; we must straight make head;
Therefore let our alliance be combin'd,
Our best friends made, our means stretch'd;
And let us presently go sit in council
How covert matters may be best disclos'd,
And open perils surest answered.

OCTAVIUS Let us do so; for we are at the stake,
And bay'd about with many enemies;
And some that smile have in their hearts, I fear,
Millions of mischiefs. *[Exeunt.*

SCENE II. *The Camp near Sardis. Before the tent of Brutus.*

Drum. Enter BRUTUS, LUCILIUS, LUCIUS, and the Army. TITINIUS and PINDARUS meet them.

BRUTUS Stand, ho!

LUCILIUS Give the word, ho! and stand.

BRUTUS What now, Lucilius? Is Cassius near?

LUCILIUS He is at hand, and Pindarus is come
To do you salutation from his master.

BRUTUS He greets me well. Your master, Pindarus,
In his own change, or by ill officers,
Hath given me some worthy cause to wish
Things done undone; but if he be at hand
I shall be satisfied.

PINDARUS I do not doubt
But that my noble master will appear
Such as he is, full of regard and honour.

BRUTUS He is not doubted. A word, Lucilius,
How he receiv'd you; let me be resolv'd.

LUCILIUS With courtesy and with respect enough,
But not with such familiar instances
Nor with such free and friendly conference
As he hath us'd of old.

BRUTUS Thou hast describ'd
A hot friend cooling. Ever note, Lucillius,
When love begins to sicken and decay,
It useth an enforced ceremony.
There are no tricks in plain and simple faith;
But hollow men, like horses hot at hand,
Make gallant show and promise of their mettle;
But when they should endure the bloody spur,
They fall their crests, and like deceitful jades
Sink in the trial. Comes his army on?

LUCILIUS They mean this night in Sardis to be quarter'd.
The greater part, the horse in general,
Are come with Cassius. *[Low march within.*

BRUTUS Hark! he is arriv'd:
March gently on to meet him.

Enter CASSIUS and his Powers.

CASSIUS Stand, ho!

BRUTUS Stand, ho! Speak the word along.

1 SOLDIER Stand!

2 SOLDIER Stand!

3 SOLDIER Stand!

CASSIUS Most noble brother, you have done me wrong.

BRUTUS Judge me, you gods! wrong I mine enemies?
And, if not so, how should I wrong a brother?

CASSIUS Brutus, this sober form of yours hides wrongs;
And when you do them –

BRUTUS Cassius, be content;
Speak your griefs softly; I do know you well.
Before the eyes of both our armies here,
Which should perceive nothing but love from us,
Let us not wrangle. Bid them move away;
Then in my tent, Cassius, enlarge your griefs,
And I will give you audience.

CASSIUS Pindarus,
Bid our commanders lead their charges off
A little from this ground.

BRUTUS Lucilius, do you the like; and let no man
Come to our tent till we have done our conference.
Let Lucius and Titinius guard our door.
[Exeunt.

SCENE III. *The Camp near Sardis. Within the tent of Brutus.*

Enter BRUTUS and CASSIUS.

CASSIUS That you have wrong'd me doth appear in this:

You have condemn'd and noted Lucius Pella
For taking bribes here of the Sardians;
Wherein my letters, praying on his side,
Because I knew the man, were slighted off.

BRUTUS You wrong'd yourself to write in such a case.

CASSIUS In such a time as this it is not meet
That every nice offence should bear his comment.

BRUTUS Let me tell you, Cassius, you yourself
Are much condemn'd to have an itching palm,
To sell and mart your offices for gold
To undeservers.

CASSIUS I an itching palm!
You know that you are Brutus that speaks this,
Or, by the gods, this speech were else your last.

BRUTUS The name of Cassius honours this corruption,
And chastisement doth therefore hide his head.

CASSIUS Chastisement!

BRUTUS Remember March, the ides of March remember:
Did not great Julius bleed for justice sake?
What villian touch'd his body, that did stab,
And not for justice? What, shall one of us,
That struck the foremost man of all this world
But for supporting robbers, shall we now
Contaminate our fingers with base bribes,
And sell the mighty space of our large honours
For so much trash as may be grasped thus?
I had rather be a dog and bay the moon
Than such a Roman.

CASSIUS Brutus, bait not me!
I'll not endure it. You forget yourself,
To hedge me in. I am a soldier, I,
Older in practice, abler than yourself
To make conditions.

BRUTUS Go to; you are not, Cassius.

CASSIUS I am.

BRUTUS I say you are not.

CASSIUS Urge me no more, I shall forget myself;
Have mind upon your health, tempt me no farther.

BRUTUS Away, slight man!

CASSIUS Is't possible?

BRUTUS Hear me, for I will speak.
Must I give way and room to your rash choler?
Shall I be frighted when a madman stares?

CASSIUS O ye gods, ye gods! must I endure all this?

BRUTUS All this? Ay, more! Fret till your proud heart break.
Go show your slaves how choleric you are,
And make your bondmen tremble. Must I budge?
Must I observe you? Must I stand and crouch
Under your testy humour? By the gods,
You shall digest the venom of your spleen
Though it do split you; for from this day forth
I'll use you for my mirth, yea, for my laughter,
When you are waspish.

CASSIUS Is it come to this?

BRUTUS You say you are a better soldier.
Let it appear so; make your vaunting true,
And it shall please me well. For mine own part,
I shall be glad to learn of noble men.

CASSIUS You wrong me every way; you wrong me, Brutus;
I said an elder soldier, not a better.
Did I say 'better'?

BRUTUS If you did, I care not.

CASSIUS When Caesar liv'd, he durst not thus have mov'd me.

BRUTUS Peace, peace! You durst not so have tempted him.

CASSIUS I durst not?

BRUTUS No.

CASSIUS What, durst not tempt him?

BRUTUS For your life you durst not.

CASSIUS Do not presume too much upon my love;
I may do that I shall be sorry for.

BRUTUS You have done that you should be sorry for.
There is no terror, Cassius, in your threats;
For I am arm'd so strong in honesty
That they pass by me as the idle wind,
Which I respect not. I did send to you
For certain sums of gold, which you denied me;
For I can raise no money by vile means.
By heaven, I had rather coin my heart,
And drop my blood for drachmas, than to wring
From the hard hands of peasants their vile trash
By any indirection. I did send
To you for gold to pay my legions,
Which you denied me; was that done like Cassius?
Should I have answer'd Caius Cassius so?
When Marcus Brutus grows so covetous,
To lock such rascal counters from his friends,
Be ready, gods, with all your thunderbolts,
Dash him to pieces!

CASSIUS I denied you not.

BRUTUS You did.

CASSIUS I did not. He was but a fool
That brought my answer back.
Brutus hath riv'd my heart.
A friend should bear his friend's infirmities,
But Brutus makes mine greater than they are.

BRUTUS I do not, till you practise them on me.

CASSIUS You love me not.

BRUTUS I do not like your faults.

CASSIUS A friendly eye could never see such faults.

BRUTUS A flatterer's would not, though they do appear
As huge as high Olympus.
CASSIUS Come, Antony, and young Octavius, come,
Revenge yourselves alone on Cassius,
For Cassius is aweary of the world:
Hated by one he loves; brav'd by his brother;
Check'd like a bondman; all his faults observ'd,
Set in a notebook, learn'd, and conn'd by rote,
To cast into my teeth. O, I could weep
My spirit from mine eyes! There is my dagger,
And here my naked breast; within, a heart
Dearer than Plutus' mine, richer than gold;
If that thou be'st a Roman, take it forth.
I, that denied thee gold, will give my heart.
Strike as thou didst at Caesar; for I know,
When thou didst hate him worst, thou lov'dst him better
Than ever thou lov'dst Cassius.
BRUTUS Sheathe your dagger.
Be angry when you will, it shall have scope;
Do what you will, dishonour shall be humour.
O Cassius, you are yoked with a lamb,
That carries anger as the flint bears fire;
Who, much enforced, shows a hasty spark,
And straight is cold again.
CASSIUS Hath Cassius liv'd
To be but mirth and laughter to his Brutus,
When grief and blood ill-temper'd vexeth him?
BRUTUS When I spoke that I was ill-temper'd too.
CASSIUS Do you confess so much? Give me your hand.
BRUTUS And my heart too.
CASSIUS O Brutus!
BRUTUS What's the matter?
CASSIUS Have not you love enough to bear with me,
When that rash humour which my mother gave me
Makes me forgetful?
BRUTUS Yes, Cassius; and from henceforth,
When you are over-earnest with your Brutus,
He'll think your mother chides, and leave you so.

Enter a Poet, followed by LUCILIUS, TITINIUS, and LUCIUS.

POET Let me go in to see the generals.
There is some grudge between 'em; 'tis not meet
They be alone.
LUCILIUS You shall not come to them.
POET Nothing but death shall stay me.
CASSIUS How now! What's the matter?
POET For shame, you generals! What do you mean?
Love, and be friends, as two such men should be;
For I have seen more years, I'm sure, than ye.
CASSIUS Ha, ha! How vilely doth this cynic rhyme!
BRUTUS Get you hence, sirrah; saucy fellow, hence!
CASSIUS Bear with him, Brutus: 'tis his fashion.
BRUTUS I'll know his humour when he knows his time.
What should the wars do with these jigging fools?
Companion, hence!
CASSIUS Away, away, be gone!
[*Exit Poet.*

BRUTUS Lucilius and Titinius, bid the commanders
Prepare to lodge their companies to-night.
CASSIUS And come yourselves, and bring Messala with you
Immediately to us.
[*Exeunt Lucilius and Titinius.*

BRUTUS Lucius, a bowl of wine!
[*Exit Lucius.*

CASSIUS I did not think you could have been so angry.
BRUTUS O Cassius, I am sick of many griefs!
CASSIUS Of your philosophy you make no use,
If you give place to accidental evils.
BRUTUS No man bears sorrow better. Portia is dead.
CASSIUS Ha! Portia?
BRUTUS She is dead.
CASSIUS How scap'd I killing when I cross'd you so?
O insupportable and touching loss!
Upon what sickness?
BRUTUS Impatient of my absence,
And grief that young Octavius with Mark Antony
Have made themselves so strong; for with her death
That tidings came. With this she fell distract,
And, her attendants absent, swallow'd fire.
CASSIUS And died so?
BRUTUS Even so?
CASSIUS O ye immortal gods!
Enter LUCIUS with wine and tapers.
BRUTUS Speak no more of her. Give me a bowl of wine.
In this I bury all unkindness, Cassius. [*Drinks.*
CASSIUS My heart is thirsty for that noble pledge.
Fill, Lucius, till the wine o'erswell the cup;
I cannot drink too much of Brutus' love.
[*Drinks. Exit Lucius.*

Re-enter TITINIUS, with MESSALA.

BRUTUS Come in, Titinius! Welcome, good Messala!
Now sit we close about this taper here,
And call in question our necessities.
CASSIUS Portia, art thou gone?
BRUTUS No more, I pray you.
Messala, I have here received letters,
That young Octavius and Mark Antony
Come down upon us with a mighty power,
Bending their expedition toward Philippi.
MESSALA Myself have letters of the self-same tenour.
BRUTUS With what addition?
MESSALA That, by proscription and bills of outlawry,
Octavius, Antony, and Lepidus,
Have put to death an hundred senators.
BRUTUS Therein our letters do not well agree;
Mine speak of seventy senators that died
By their proscriptions, Cicero being one.
CASSIUS Cicero one!
MESSALA Cicero is dead,
And by that order of proscription.
Had you your letters from your wife, my lord?
BRUTUS No, Messala.
MESSALA Nor nothing in your letters writ of her?
BRUTUS Nothing, Messala.
MESSALA That, methinks is strange.
BRUTUS Why ask you? Hear you aught of her in yours?
MESSALA No, my lord.
BRUTUS Now, as you are a Roman, tell me true.
MESSALA Then like a Roman bear the truth I tell:
For certain she is dead, and by strange manner.
BRUTUS Why, farewell, Portia. We must die, Messala.
With meditating that she must die once,
I have the patience to endure it now.
MESSALA Even so great men great losses should endure.
CASSIUS I have as much of this in art as you,
But yet my nature could not bear it so.
BRUTUS Well, to our work alive. What do you think
Of marching to Philippi presently?
CASSIUS I do not think it good.
BRUTUS Your reason?
CASSIUS This it is:
'Tis better that the enemy seek us;
So shall he waste his means, weary his soldiers,
Doing himself offence, whilst we, lying still,
Are full of rest, defence, and nimbleness.
BRUTUS Good reasons must, of force, give place to better.
The people 'twixt Philippi and this ground
Do stand but in a forc'd affection;
For they have grudg'd us contribution.
The enemy, marching along by them,
By them shall make a fuller number up,
Come on refresh'd, new-added, and encourag'd;
From which advantage shall we cut him off,
If at Philippi we do face him there,
These people at our back.
CASSIUS Hear me, good brother.
BRUTUS Under your pardon. You must note beside
That we have tried the utmost of our friends,
Our legions are brim full, our cause is ripe.
The enemy increaseth every day:
We, at the height, are ready to decline.
There is a tide in the affairs of men
Which, taken at the flood, leads on to fortune;
Omitted, all the voyage of their life
Is bound in shallows and in miseries.
On such a full sea are we now afloat,
And we must take the current when it serves,
Or lose our ventures.
CASSIUS Then, with your will, go on;
We'll along ourselves and meet them at Philippi.
BRUTUS The deep of night is crept upon our talk,
And nature must obey necessity,
Which we will niggard with a little rest.
There is no more to say?
CASSIUS No more. Good night:
Early to-morrow will we rise, and hence.
BRUTUS Lucius! [*Enter LUCIUS*] My gown.
[*Exit Lucius*] Farewell, good Messala.
Good night, Titinius. Noble, noble Cassius,
Good night, and good repose!
CASSIUS O my dear brother,
This was an ill beginning of the night!
Never come such division 'tween our souls!
Let it not, Brutus.
BRUTUS Everything is well.
CASSIUS Good night, my lord.
BRUTUS Good night, good brother.
TITINIUS AND MESSALA Good night, Lord Brutus.
BRUTUS Farewell, every one.

[*Exeunt Cassius, Titinius, and Messala.*

Re-enter LUCIUS with the gown.

Give me the gown. Where is thy instrument?
LUCIUS Here in the tent.
BRUTUS What, thou speak'st drowsily?
Poor knave, I blame thee not; thou art o'erwatch'd.
Call Claudius and some other of my men;

I'll have them sleep on cushions in my tent.
LUCIUS Varro and Claudius!

Enter VARRO and CLAUDIUS.

VARRO Calls my lord?
BRUTUS I pray you, sirs, lie in my tent and sleep;
It may be I shall raise you by and by
On business to my brother Cassius.
VARRO So please you we will stand and watch your pleasure.
BRUTUS I will not have it so. Lie down, good sirs;
It may be I shall otherwise bethink me.
Look, Lucius, here's the book I sought for so;
I put it in the pocket of my gown.

[Varro and Claudius lie down.

LUCIUS I was sure your lordship did not give it me.
BRUTUS Bear with me, good boy, I am much forgetful.
Canst thou hold up thy heavy eyes awhile,
And touch thy instrument a strain or two?
LUCIUS Ay, my lord, an't please you.
BRUTUS It does, my boy.
I trouble thee too much, but thou art willing.
LUCIUS It is my duty, sir.
BRUTUS I should not urge thy duty past thy might;
I know young bloods look for a time of rest.
LUCIUS I have slept, my lord, already.
BRUTUS It was well done; and thou shalt sleep again;
I will not hold thee long. If I do live,
I will be good to thee.

[Music and a song. Lucius falls asleep.

This is a sleepy tune. O murd'rous slumber!
Layest thou thy leaden mace upon my boy,
That plays thee music? Gentle knave, good night.
I will not do thee so much wrong to wake thee.
If thou dost nod, thou break'st thy instrument;
I'll take it from thee; and, good boy, good night.
Let me see, let me see; is not the leaf turn'd down
Where I left reading? Here it is, I think.

[Sits down.

Enter the Ghost of CAESAR.

How ill this taper burns! Ha! who comes here?
I think it is the weakness of mine eyes
That shapes this monstrous apparition.
It comes upon me. Art thou any thing?
Art thou some god, some angel, or some devil,
That mak'st my blood cold and my hair to stare?
Speak to me what thou art.
GHOST Thy evil spirit, Brutus.
BRUTUS Why com'st thou?
GHOST To tell thee thou shalt see me at Philippi.
BRUTUS Well; then I shall see thee again?
GHOST Ay, at Philippi.
BRUTUS Why, I will see thee at Philippi, then.

[Exit Ghost.

Now I have taken heart thou vanishest.
Ill spirit, I would hold more talk with thee.
Boy! Lucius! Varro! Claudius! Sirs, awake!
Claudius!
LUCIUS The strings, my lord, are false.
BRUTUS He thinks he still is at his instrument.
Lucius, awake!
LUCIUS My lord!
BRUTUS Didst thou dream, Lucius, that thou so criedst out?
LUCIUS My lord, I do not know that I did cry.
BRUTUS Yes, that thou didst. Didst thou see any thing?
LUCIUS Nothing, my lord.
BRUTUS Sleep again, Lucius. Sirrah Claudius!
[To Varro] Fellow thou, awake!
VARRO My lord?
CLAUDIUS My lord?
BRUTUS Why did you so cry out, sirs, in your sleep?
BOTH Did we, my lord?
BRUTUS Ay. Saw you any thing?
VARRO No, my lord, I saw nothing.
CLAUDIUS Nor I, my lord.
BRUTUS Go and commend me to my brother Cassius;
Bid him set on his pow'rs betimes before,
And we will follow.
VARRO AND CLAUDIUS It shall be done, my lord.

[Exeunt.

ACT FIVE

SCENE I. *Near Philippi.*

Enter OCTAVIUS, ANTONY, and their Army.

OCTAVIUS Now, Antony, our hopes are answered.
You said the enemy would not come down,
But keep the hills and upper regions;
It proves not so. Their battles are at hand;
They mean to warn us at Philippi here,
Answering before we do demand of them.

ANTONY Tut, I am in their bosoms, and I know
Wherefore they do it. They could be content
To visit other places, and come down
With fearful bravery, thinking by this face
To fasten in our thoughts that they have courage;
But 'tis not so.

Enter a Messenger.

MESSENGER Prepare you, generals:
The enemy comes on in gallant show;
Their bloody sign of battle is hung out,
And something to be done immediately.

ANTONY Octavius, lead your battle softly on,
Upon the left hand of the even field.

OCTAVIUS Upon the right hand I: keep thou the left.

ANTONY Why do you cross me in this exigent?

OCTAVIUS I do not cross you; but I will do so. *[March.*

Drum. Enter BRUTUS, CASSIUS, and their Army; LUCILIUS, TITINIUS, MESSALA, and Others.

BRUTUS They stand, and would have parley.

CASSIUS Stand fast, Titinius; we must out and talk.

OCTAVIUS Mark Antony, shall we give sign of battle?

ANTONY No, Caesar, we will answer on their charge.
Make forth; the generals would have some words.

OCTAVIUS Stir not until the signal.

BRUTUS Words before blows. Is it so, countrymen?

OCTAVIUS Not that we love words better, as you do.

BRUTUS Good words are better than bad strokes, Octavius.

ANTONY In your bad strokes, Brutus, you give good words;
Witness the hole you made in Caesar's heart,
Crying 'Long live! Hail, Caesar!

CASSIUS Antony,
The posture of your blows are yet unknown;
But for your words, they rob the Hybla bees,
And leave them honeyless.

ANTONY Not stingless too?

BRUTUS O yes, and soundless too;
For you have stol'n their buzzing, Antony,
And very wisely threat before you sting.

ANTONY Villains, you did not so when your vile daggers
Hack'd one another in the sides of Caesar.
You show'd your teeth like apes, and fawn'd like hounds,
And bow'd like bondmen, kissing Caesar's feet;
Whilst damned Casca, like a cur, behind
Struck Caesar on the neck. O you flatterers!

CASSIUS Flatterers! Now, Brutus, thank yourself:
This tongue had not offended so to-day
If Cassius might have rul'd.

OCTAVIUS Come, come, the cause. If arguing make us sweat,
The proof of it will turn to redder drops.
Look,
I draw a sword against conspirators;
When think you that the sword goes up again?
Never till Caesar's three and thirty wounds
Be well aveng'd, or till another Caesar
Have added slaughter to the sword of traitors.

BRUTUS Caesar, thou canst not die by traitors' hands,
Unless thou bring'st them with thee.

OCTAVIUS So I hope.
I was not born to die on Brutus' sword.

BRUTUS O, if thou wert the noblest of thy strain,
Young man, thou couldst not die more honourable.

CASSIUS A peevish schoolboy, worthless of such honour,
Join'd with a masker and a reveller!

ANTONY Old Cassius still!

OCTAVIUS Come, Antony; away!
Defiance, traitors, hurl we in your teeth.
If you dare fight to-day, come to the field;
If not, when you have stomachs. *[Exeunt Octavius, Antony, and their Army.*

CASSIUS Why, now, blow wind, swell billow, and swim bark!
The storm is up, and all is on the hazard.

BRUTUS Ho, Lucilius! hark, a word with you.

LUCILIUS My lord. *[Brutus and Lucilius converse apart.*

CASSIUS Messala.

MESSALA What says my general?

CASSIUS Messala,
This is my birth-day; as this very day
Was Cassius born. Give me thy hand Messala.
Be thou my witness that against my will,
As Pompey was, am I compell'd to set
Upon one battle all our liberties.
You know that I held Epicurus strong,
And his opinion; now I change my mind,
And partly credit things that do presage.
Coming from Sardis, on our former ensign
Two mighty eagles fell; and there they perch'd,
Gorging and feeding from our soldiers' hands,
Who to Philippi here consorted us.
This morning are they fled away and gone,
And in their steads do ravens, crows, and kites,
Fly o'er our heads and downward look on us
As we were sickly prey. Their shadows seem

A canopy most fatal, under which
Our army lies, ready to give up the ghost.
MESSALA Believe not so.
CASSIUS I but believe it partly;
For I am fresh of spirit and resolv'd
To meet all perils very constantly.
BRUTUS Even so, Lucilius.
CASSIUS Now, most noble Brutus,
The gods to-day stand friendly, that we may,
Lovers in peace, lead on our days to age!
But, since the affairs of men rest still in-certain,
Let's reason with the worst that may befall.
If we do lose this battle, then is this
The very last time we shall speak together.
What are you then determined to do?
BRUTUS Even by the rule of that philosophy
By which I did blame Cato for the death
Which he did give himself – I know not how,
But I do find it cowardly and vile,
For fear of what might fall, so to prevent
The time of life – arming myself with patience
To stay the providence of some high powers
That govern us below.
CASSIUS Then, if we lose this battle,
You are contented to be led in triumph
Thorough the streets of Rome?
BRUTUS No, Cassius, no. Think not, thou noble
Roman,
That ever Brutus will go bound to Rome;
He bears too great a mind. But this same day
Must end that work the ides of March begun,
And whether we shall meet again I know not.
Therefore our everlasting farewell take:
For ever and for ever farewell, Cassius!
If we do meet again, why, we shall smile;
If not, why then this parting was well made.
CASSIUS For ever and for ever farewell, Brutus!
If we do meet again, we'll smile indeed;
If not, 'tis true this parting was well made.
BRUTUS Why then, lead on. O that a man might
know
The end of this day's business ere it come!
But it sufficeth that the day will end,
And then the end is known. Come, ho! away!
[*Exeunt.*

SCENE II. *Near Philippi. The field of battle.*

Alarum. Enter BRUTUS and MESSALA.

BRUTUS Ride, ride, Messala, ride, and give these
bills
Unto the legions on the other side.
[*Loud alarum.*

Let them set on at once; for I perceive
But cold demeanour in Octavius' wing,
And sudden push gives them the overthrow.
Ride, ride, Messala; let them all come down.
[*Exeunt.*

SCENE III. *Another part of the field.*

Alarums. Enter CASSIUS and TITINIUS.

CASSIUS O, look, Titinius, look, the villains fly!
Myself have to mine own turn'd enemy.
This ensign here of mine was turning back;
I slew the coward, and did take it from him.
TITINIUS O Cassius, Brutus gave the word too
early,
Who, having some advantage on Octavius,
Took it too eagerly. His soldiers fell to spoil,
Whilst we by Antony are all enclos'd.

Enter PINDARUS.

PINDARUS Fly further off, my lord, fly further off;
Mark Antony is in your tents, my lord;
Fly, therefore, noble Cassius, fly far off.
CASSIUS This hill is far enough. Look, look,
Titinius.
Are those my tents where I perceive the fire?
TITINIUS They are, my lord.
CASSIUS Titinius, if thou lovest me,
Mount thou my horse and hide thy spurs in
him,
Till he have brought thee up to yonder troops
And here again, that I may rest assur'd
Whether yond troops are friend or enemy.
TITINIUS I will be here again even with a
thought.
[*Exit.*
CASSIUS Go, Pindarus, get higher on that hill;
My sight was ever thick; regard Titinius,
And tell me what thou not'st about the field.
[*Pindarus goes up.*

This day I breathed first. Time is come round,
And where I did begin there shall I end;
My life is run his compass. Sirrah, what news?
PINDARUS [*Above*] O my lord!
CASSIUS What news?
PINDARUS Titinius is enclosed round about
With horsemen that make to him on the spur;
Yet he spurs on. Now they are almost on him.
Now Titinius! Now some light. O, he lights too!
He's ta'en.
[*Shout.*
And hark! They shout for joy.
CASSIUS Come down; behold no more.
O, coward that I am to live so long
To see my best friend ta'en before my face!

Enter PINDARUS.

Come hither, sirrah.
In Parthia did I take thee prisoner;
And then I swore thee, saving of thy life,
That whatsoever I did bid thee do

Thou shouldst attempt it. Come now, keep thine oath;
Now be a freeman, and with this good sword,
That ran through Caesar's bowels, search this bosom.
Stand not to answer; here, take thou the hilts;
And when my face is cover'd, as 'tis now,
Guide thou the sword. [*Pindarus stabs him.*
Caesar, thou art reveng'd,
Even with the sword that kill'd thee. [*Dies.*

PINDARUS So, I am free; yet would not so have been,
Durst I have done my will. O Cassius!
Far from this country Pindarus shall run,
Where never Roman shall take note of him. [*Exit.*

Re-enter TITINIUS, with MESSALA.

MESSALA It is but change, Titinius; for Octavius
Is overthrown by noble Brutus' power,
As Cassius' legions are by Antony.

TITINIUS These tidings will well comfort Cassius.

MESSALA Where did you leave him?

TITINIUS All disconsolate,
With Pindarus, his bondman, on this hill.

MESSALA Is not that he that lies upon the ground?

TITINIUS He lies not like the living. O my heart!

MESSALA Is not that he?

TITINIUS No, this was he, Messala;
But Cassius is no more. O setting sun,
As in thy red rays thou dost sink to night,
So in his red blood Cassius' day is set!
The sun of Rome is set. Our day is gone;
Clouds, dews, and dangers come; our deeds are done.
Mistrust of my success hath done this deed.

MESSALA Mistrust of good success hath done this deed.
O hateful error, melancholy's child,
Why dost thou show to the apt thoughts of men
The things that are not? O error, soon conceiv'd,
Thou never com'st unto a happy birth,
But kill'st the mother that engend'red thee!

TITINIUS What, Pindarus! Where art thou, Pindarus?

MESSALA Seek him, Titinius, whilst I go to meet
The noble Brutus, thrusting this report
Into his ears. I may say 'thrusting' it;
For piercing steel and darts envenomed
Shall be as welcome to the ears of Brutus
As tidings of this sight.

TITINIUS Hie you, Messala,
And I will seek for Pindarus the while. [*Exit Messala.*
Why didst thou send me forth, brave Cassius?
Did I not meet they friends, and did not they
Put on my brows this wreath of victory,
And bid me give it thee? Didst thou not hear their shouts?
Alas, thou hast misconstrued every thing!
But hold thee, take this garland on thy brow;
Thy Brutus bid me give it thee, and I
Will do his bidding. Brutus, come apace,
And see how I regarded Caius Cassius.
By your leave, gods. This is a Roman's part.
Come, Cassius' sword, and find Titinius' heart. [*Dies.*

Alarum. Re-enter MESSALA, with BRUTUS, YOUNG CATO, STRATO, VOLUMNIUS, and LUCILIUS.

BRUTUS Where, where, Messala, doth his body lie?

MESSALA Lo yonder, and Titinius mourning it.

BRUTUS Titinius' face is upward.

CATO He is slain.

BRUTUS O Julius Caesar, thou art mighty yet!
Thy spirit walks abroad and turns our swords
In our own proper entrails. [*Low alarums.*

CATO Brave Titinius!
Look whe'r he have not crown'd dead Cassius!

BRUTUS Are yet two Romans living such as these?
The last of all the Romans, fare thee well!
It is impossible that ever Rome
Should breed they fellow. Friends, I owe moe tears
To this dead man than you shall see me pay.
I shall find time, Cassius, I shall find time.
Come, therefore, and to Thasos send his body.
His funerals shall not be in our camp,
Lest it discomfort us. Lucilius, come;
And come, young Cato; let us to the field.
Labeo and Flavius set our battles on.
'Tis three o'clock; and, Romans, yet ere night
We shall try fortune in a second fight. [*Exeunt.*

SCENE IV. *Another part of the field.*

Alarum. Enter BRUTUS, MESSALA, YOUNG CATO, LUCILIUS, and FLAVIUS.

BRUTUS Yet, countrymen, O, yet hold up your heads!

CATO What bastard doth not? Who will go with me?
I will proclaim my name about the field:
I am the son of Marcus Cato, ho!
A foe to tyrants, and my country's friend.
I am the son of Marcus Cato, ho!

Enter Soldiers and fight.

BRUTUS And I am Brutus, Marcus Brutus, I!
Brutus, my country's friend! Know me for

Brutus! [*Exit. Young Cato falls.*

LUCILIUS O young and noble Cato, art thou down?
Why, now thou diest as bravely as Titinius,
And mayst be honour'd, being Cato's son.

1 SOLDIER Yield, or thou diest.

LUCILIUS Only I yield to die.
[*Offering money*] There is so much that thou wilt kill me straight.
Kill Brutus, and be honour'd in his death.

1 SOLDIER We must not. A noble prisoner!

Enter ANTONY.

2 SOLDIER Room, ho! Tell Antony Brutus is ta'en.

1 SOLDIER I'll tell the news. Here comes the general.
Brutus is ta'en! Brutus is ta'en, my lord!

ANTONY Where is he?

LUCILIUS Safe, Antony; Brutus is safe enough.
I dare assure thee that no enemy
Shall ever take alive the noble Brutus.
The gods defend him from so great a shame!
When you do find him, or alive or dead,
He will be found like Brutus, like himself.

ANTONY This is not Brutus, friend; but, I assure you,
A prize no less in worth. Keep this man safe;
Give him all kindness. I had rather have
Such men my friends than enemies. Go on,
And see whe'r Brutus be alive or dead;
And bring us word unto Octavius' tent
How everything is chanc'd. [*Exeunt.*

SCENE V. *Another part of the field.*

Enter BRUTUS, DARDANIUS, CLITUS, STRATO, and VOLUMNIUS.

BRUTUS Come, poor remains of friends, rest on this rock.

CLITUS Statilius show'd the torch-light; but, my lord,
He came not back. He is or ta'en or slain.

BRUTUS Sit thee down, Clitus. Slaying is the word;
It is a deed in fashion. Hark thee, Clitus. [*Whispering.*

CLITUS What, I, my lord? No, not for all the world.

BRUTUS Peace, then, no words.

CLITUS I'll rather kill myself.

BRUTUS Hark thee, Dardanius!

DARDANIUS Shall I do such a deed?

CLITUS O Dardanius!

DARDANIUS O Clitus!

CLITUS What ill request did Brutus make to thee?

DARDANIUS To kill him, Clitus. Look, he meditates.

CLITUS Now is that noble vessel full of grief,
That it runs over even at his eyes.

BRUTUS Come hither, good Volumnius; list a word.

VOLUMNIUS What says my lord?

BRUTUS Why, this, Volumnius:
The ghost of Caesar hath appear'd to me
Two several times by night – at Sardis once,
And this last night here in Philippi fields.
I know my hour is come.

VOLUMNIUS Not so, my lord.

BRUTUS Nay, I am sure it is, Volumnius.
Thou seest the world, Volumnius, how it goes:
Our enemies have beat us to the pit; [*Low alarums.*
It is more worthy to leap in ourselves
Than tarry till they push us. Good Volumnius,
Thou know'st that we two went to school together;
Even for that our love of old, I prithee,
Hold thou my sword-hilts whilst I run on it.

VOLUMNIUS That's not an office for a friend, my lord. [*Alarum still.*

CLITUS Fly, fly, my lord; there is no tarrying here.

BRUTUS Farewell to you; and you; and you, Volumnius.
Strato, thou hast been all this while asleep;
Farewell to thee too, Strato. Countrymen,
My heart doth joy that yet in all my life
I found no man but he was true to me.
I shall have glory by this losing day,
More than Octavius and Mark Antony
By this vile conquest shall attain unto.
So fare you well at once; for Brutus' tongue
Hath almost ended his life's history.
Night hangs upon mine eyes; my bones would rest,
That have but labour'd to attain this hour.
[*Alarum. Cry within* 'Fly, fly, fly!'

CLITUS Fly, my lord, fly.

BRUTUS Hence! I will follow.
[*Exeunt Clitus, Dardanius, and Volumnius.*
I prithee, Strato, stay thou by thy lord;
Thou art a fellow of a good respect;
Thy life hath had some smatch of honour in it.
Hold then my sword, and turn away thy face,
While I do run upon it. Wilt thou, Strato?

STRATO Give me your hand first. Fare you well, my lord.

BRUTUS Farewell, good Strato. Caesar, now be still.

I kill'd not thee with half so good a will.
[*He runs on his sword, and dies.*

Alarum. Retreat. Enter OCTAVIUS, ANTONY, MESSALA, LUCILIUS, and the Army.

OCTAVIUS What man is that?

MESSALA My master's man. Strato, where is thy master?

STRATO Free from the bondage you are in, Messala.
The conquerors can but make a fire of him;
For Brutus only overcame himself,
And no man else hath honour by his death.

LUCILIUS So Brutus should be found. I thank thee, Brutus,
That thou hast prov'd Lucilius' saying true.

OCTAVIUS All that serv'd Brutus, I will entertain them.
Fellow, wilt thou bestow thy time with me?

STRATO Ay, if Messala will prefer me to you.

OCTAVIUS Do so, good Messala.

MESSALA How died my master, Strato?

STRATO I held the sword, and he did run on it.

MESSALA Octavius, then take him to follow thee,
That did the latest service to my master.

ANTONY This was the noblest Roman of them all.
All the conspirators save only he
Did that they did in envy of great Caesar;
He only in a general honest thought
And common good to all made one of them.
His life was gentle; and the elements
So mix'd in him that Nature might stand up
And say to all the world 'This was a man!'

OCTAVIUS According to his virtue let us use him,
With all respect and rites of burial.
Within my tent his bones to-night shall lie,
Most like a soldier, ordered honourably.
So call the field to rest, and let's away
To part the glories of this happy day. [*Exeunt.*

Macbeth

Introduction by DOROTHY McMILLAN

Macbeth, famously short and concentrated (for whatever reason), has imprinted itself as a play of evil, human and supernatural, darkness, blood and battle, issuing it would seem, out of the imitation of a culture, stark and primitive even to Shakespeare. Its deployment of witches, air-drawn dagger, apparitions and walking woods, its tight focus on Macbeth and his Lady may seem to provoke excited wonderment which, nevertheless, does not trouble audiences into introspection. What, after all, has Dunsinane to do with most of us?

Yet the most celebrated question asked about the play remains, I think, the much mocked enquiry of A. C. Bradley, 'How many children had Lady Macbeth?' L. C. Knights, in the essay which takes its title from the question, rebukes this curiosity, claiming *Macbeth* as a text which may be examined like a self-sufficient poem. Had Shakespeare wanted his audience to know how many children Lady Macbeth had he would, Knights believes, have included the information in the play. But then, if he had wanted the audience to worry about it, he might have left it out. Bradley's is a question that cannot be asked without attention being directed to Macbeth's dissatisfaction with the 'barren sceptre' in his 'gripe' and to all the other children in picture and in the flesh that inhabit the play's spaces. It may well turn out that an emphasis on 'babes' is as fruitful a key to the production of meaning in *Macbeth* as is fixing on beldam, blood and battle.

Lady Macbeth needs to invoke an unnatural desexing as a preparation for murder and expresses her murderous commitment in terms of the destruction of 'the babe that milks me', yet it is her memory of her own father that shakes her violent resolve and it is as a disordered girl that she sleepwalks and dies, overwhelmed by a deed that 'the eye of childhood' could have foreseen as murder as much of the self as of the other. Macbeth, more prescient, imagines the pity that Duncan's murder will give rise to 'like a naked, newborn babe,/Striding the blast', powerful in its very gentleness. After the murder he finds that he has given birth to a new and intolerable self, dislocated from his former life. He must be this self until his final mutilation which is merely the physical fulfilment of his psychic disfigurement. But if Macbeth's former self becomes for him an enemy to be obliterated, so too does his country. With the escape of Fleance the barrenness of his sceptre is confirmed and his act is exposed in its naked lack of meaning; all values of stability and continuity are subsumed into the animal need for immediate security.

The consequences for Scotland are equally pictured in terms of children, specifically of Macduff's family. Macduff is, of course, himself the 'bloody child' of the witches' apparations who becomes Macbeth's nemesis, but the play does not absolve him of blame for the death of his family. His failure to protect them is, however, a demonstration of the appalling difficulty of remaining true to domestic pieties in a polity which is founded on their violation. The death of Macduff's son, like the later death of Young Siward, is as awful as it is affecting, yet in the courage and faithfulness of these children lies Scotland's hope. And in the fragile, threatened sweetness of Lady Macduff's relationship with her son lies the key to the proper meaning of kingship as public guarantor of the private space within which human life finds its fulfilment. Macbeth is made tolerable in the end because he recognises this, longs for the 'honour, love, obedience, troops of friends' that his deed has denied to himself and to his subjects. Malcolm's promise to perform what is needful 'in measure, time, and place' celebrates the restoration of the ceremony of innocence the violation and power of which are signalled equally by the bloody babes of *Macbeth*.

It has been suggested that *Macbeth* was performed at Hampton Court around 1606 as a compliment to King James, thought to have been descended from Banquo, keen on the Divine Right of Kings and unquestionably interested in witches. There is no record of such a performance but imagining one, one cannot feel that it would have been an unmixed compliment. Admittedly it is not necessary to be a very good king to be better than Macbeth, yet the play's persistent reminders of the duties of kings to protect the weak and the innocent might well seem presumptuous. Nor could the witches' show of Kings have been taken only as compliment, for missing from the line is the mother, Mary Queen of Scots, without whose beheading James could scarcely have been where he was. It is at least awkward for a king to have had his mother the victim of a public executioner. The absence of a mother's children and the absence of a child's mother may help to account for the special character of *Macbeth*.

Macbeth

DRAMATIS PERSONAE

DUNCAN
King of Scotland
MALCOLM, DONALBAIN
his sons
MACBETH, BANQUO
Generals of the King's army
MACDUFF, LENNOX, ROSS, MENTEITH, ANGUS, CAITHNESS
Noblemen of Scotland
FLEANCE
son to Banquo
SIWARD
Earl of Northumberland, General of the English forces
YOUNG SIWARD
his son
SEYTON
an officer attending on Macbeth
BOY
son to Macduff
A Sergeant
A Porter
An Old Man
An English Doctor
A Scots Doctor
LADY MACBETH
LADY MACDUFF
Gentlewoman attending on Lady Macbeth
THE WEIRD SISTERS
HECATE
The Ghost of Banquo
Apparitions
Lords, Gentlemen, Officers, Soldiers, Murderers, Attendants, and Messengers

THE SCENE: SCOTLAND AND ENGLAND

ACT ONE

SCENE I. *An open place.*

Thunder and lightning. Enter three Witches.

1 WITCH When shall we three meet again?
In thunder, lightning, or in rain?
2 WITCH When the hurlyburly's done,
When the battle's lost and won.
3 WITCH That will be ere the set of sun.
1 WITCH Where the place?
2 WITCH Upon the heath.
3 WITCH There to meet with Macbeth.
1 WITCH I come, Graymalkin.
2 WITCH Paddock calls.
3 WITCH Anon!
ALL Fair is foul, and foul is fair:
Hover through the fog and filthy air.
[Witches vanish.

SCENE II. *A camp near Forres.*

Alarum within. Enter KING DUNCAN, MALCOLM, DONALBAIN, LENNOX, with Attendants, meeting a bleeding Sergeant.

DUNCAN What bloody man is that? He can report,
As seemeth by his plight, of the revolt
The newest state.
MALCOLM This is the sergeant
Who like a good and hardy soldier fought
'Gainst my captivity. Hail, brave friend!
Say to the King the knowledge of the broil
As thou didst leave it.
SERGEANT Doubtful it stood,
As two spent swimmers that do cling together
And choke their art. The merciless Macdonwald –
Worthy to be a rebel, for to that
The multiplying villainies of nature
Do swarm upon him – from the Western Isles
Of kerns and gallowglasses is supplied;
And Fortune, on his damned quarrel smiling,
Show'd like a rebel's whore. But all's too weak;
For brave Macbeth – well he deserves that name –
Disdaining Fortune, with his brandish'd steel
Which smok'd with bloody execution,
Like valour's minion, carv'd out his passage
Till he fac'd the slave;
Which ne'er shook hands, nor bade farewell to him,
Till he unseam'd him from the nave to th' chaps,
And fix'd his head upon our battlements.
DUNCAN O valiant cousin! worthy gentleman!
SERGEANT As whence the sun gins his reflection
Shipwrecking storms and direful thunders break,
So from that spring whence comfort seem'd to come
Discomfort swells. Mark, King of Scotland, mark:
No sooner justice had, with valour arm'd,

Compell'd these skipping kerns to trust their
heels,
But the Norweyan lord, surveying vantage,
With furbish'd arms and new supplies of men,
Began a fresh assault.

DUNCAN Dismay'd not this
Our captains, Macbeth and Banquo?

SERGEANT Yes;
As sparrows eagles, or the hare the lion.
If I say sooth, I must report they were
As cannons overcharg'd with double cracks;
So they doubly redoubled strokes upon the foe.
Except they meant to bathe in reeking wounds,
Or memorize another Golgotha,
I cannot tell –
But I am faint; my gashes cry for help.

DUNCAN So well thy words become thee as thy
wounds;
They smack of honour both. – Go get him
surgeons. *[Exit Sergeant, attended.*

Enter ROSS.

Who comes here?

MALCOLM The worthy Thane of Ross.

LENNOX What a haste looks through his eyes!
So should he look that seems to speak things
strange.

ROSS God save the King!

DUNCAN Whence cam'st thou, worthy thane?

ROSS From Fife, great King,
Where the Norweyan banners flout the sky
And fan our people cold.
Norway himself, with terrible numbers,
Assisted by that most disloyal traitor
The Thane of Cawdor, began a dismal conflict,
Till that Bellona's bridegroom, lapp'd in proof,
Confronted him with self-comparisons,
Point against point rebellious, arm 'gainst arm,
Curbing his lavish spirit; and to conclude,
The victory fell on us.

DUNCAN Great happiness!

ROSS That now
Sweno, the Norways' king, craves composition;
Nor would we deign him burial of his men
Till he disbursed, at Saint Colme's Inch,
Ten thousand dollars to our general use.

DUNCAN No more that Thane of Cawdor shall
deceive
Our bosom interest. Go pronounce his present
death,
And with his former title greet Macbeth.

ROSS I'll see it done.

DUNCAN What he hath lost, noble Macbeth hath
won. *[Exeunt.*

SCENE III. *A blasted heath.*

Thunder. Enter the three Witches.

1 WITCH Where hast thou been, sister?

2 WITCH Killing swine.

3 WITCH Sister, where thou?

1 WITCH A sailor's wife had chestnuts in her lap,
And mounch'd, and mounch'd, and mounch'd.
'Give me' quoth I.
'Aroint thee, witch!' the rump-fed ronyon cries.
Her husband's to Aleppo gone, master o' th'
Tiger;
But in a sieve I'll thither sail
And, like a rat without a tail,
I'll do, I'll do, and I'll do.

2 WITCH I'll give thee a wind.

1 WITCH Th'art kind.

3 WITCH And I another.

1 WITCH I myself have all the other;
And the very ports they blow,
All the quarters that they know
I' th' shipman's card.
I'll drain him dry as hay:
Sleep shall neither night nor day
Hang upon his pent-house lid;
He shall live a man forbid;
Weary sev'nights, nine times nine,
Shall he dwindle, peak, and pine.
Though his bark cannot be lost,
Yet it shall be tempest-tost.
Look what I have.

2 WITCH Show me, show me.

1 WITCH Here I have a pilot's thumb,
Wreck'd as homeward he did come.
[Drum within.

3 WITCH A drum, a drum!
Macbeth doth come.

ALL The Weird Sisters, hand in hand,
Posters of the sea and land,
Thus do go about, about;
Thrice to thine, and thrice to mine,
And thrice again, to make up nine.
Peace! The charm's wound up.

Enter MACBETH and BANQUO.

MACBETH So foul and fair a day I have not seen.

BANQUO How far is't call'd to Forres? What are
these,
So wither'd, and so wild in their attire,
That look not like th' inhabitants o' th' earth,
And yet are on't? Live you, or are you aught
That man may question? You seem to
understand me,
By each at once her choppy finger laying
Upon her skinny lips. You should be women,
And yet your beards forbid me to interpret
That you are so.

MACBETH Speak, if you can. What are you?
1 WITCH All hail, Macbeth! Hail to thee, Thane of Glamis!
2 WITCH All hail, Macbeth! Hail to thee, Thane of Cawdor!
3 WITCH All hail, Macbeth, that shalt be King hereafter!
BANQUO Good sir, why do you start, and seem to fear
Things that do sound so fair? I' th' name of truth,
Are ye fantastical, or that indeed
Which outwardly ye show? My noble partner
You greet with present grace and great prediction
Of noble having and of royal hope,
That he seems rapt withal. To me you speak not.
If you can look into the seeds of time
And say which grain will grow and which will not,
Speak then to me, who neither beg nor fear
Your favours nor your hate.
1 WITCH Hail!
2 WITCH Hail!
3 WITCH Hail!
1 WITCH Lesser than Macbeth, and greater.
2 WITCH Not so happy, yet much happier.
3 WITCH Thou shalt get kings, though thou be none.
So, all hail, Macbeth and Banquo!
1 WITCH Banquo and Macbeth, all hail!
MACBETH Stay, you imperfect speakers, tell me more.
By Sinel's death I know I am Thane of Glamis;
But how of Cawdor? The Thane of Cawdor lives,
A prosperous gentleman; and to be King
Stands not within the prospect of belief,
No more than to be Cawdor. Say from whence
You owe this strange intelligence, or why
Upon this blasted heath you stop our way
With such prophetic greeting? Speak, I charge you.
[*Witches vanish.*
BANQUO The earth hath bubbles, as the water has,
And these are of them. Whither are they vanish'd?
MACBETH Into the air; and what seem'd corporal melted
As breath into the wind. Would they had stay'd!
BANQUO Were such things here as we do speak about?
Or have we eaten on the insane root
That takes the reason prisoner?
MACBETH Your children shall be kings.
BANQUO You shall be King.
MACBETH And Thane of Cawdor too; went it not so?
BANQUO To th' self-same tune and words. Who's here?

Enter ROSS and ANGUS.

ROSS The King hath happily receiv'd, Macbeth,
The news of thy success; and when he reads
Thy personal venture in the rebels' fight,
His wonders and his praises do contend
Which should be thine or his. Silenc'd with that,
In viewing o'er the rest o' th' self-same day,
He finds thee in the stout Norweyan ranks,
Nothing afeard of what thyself didst make,
Strange images of death. As thick as tale
Came post with post, and every one did bear
Thy praises in his kingdom's great defence,
And pour'd them down before him.
ANGUS We are sent
To give thee, from our royal master, thanks;
Only to herald thee into his sight,
Not pay thee.
ROSS And, for an earnest of a greater honour,
He bade me, from him, call thee Thane of Cawdor;
In which addition, hail, most worthy Thane!
For it is thine.
BANQUO What, can the devil speak true?
MACBETH The Thane of Cawdor lives; why do you dress me
In borrowed robes?
ANGUS Who was the Thane lives yet;
But under heavy judgment bears that life
Which he deserves to lose. Whether he was combin'd
With those of Norway, or did line the rebel
With hidden help and vantage, or that with both
He labour'd in his country's wreck, I know not;
But treasons capital, confess'd and prov'd,
Have overthrown him.
MACBETH [*Aside*] Glamis, and Thane of Cawdor!
The greatest is behind. – Thanks for your pains.
[*Aside to Banquo*] Do you not hope your children shall be kings,
When those that gave the Thane of Cawdor to me
Promis'd no less to them?
BANQUO [*Aside to Macbeth*] That, trusted home,
Might yet enkindle you unto the crown,
Besides the Thane of Cawdor. But 'tis strange;
And oftentimes to win us to our harm,
The instruments of darkness tell us truths,
Win us with honest trifles, to betray's
In deepest consequence. –
Cousins, a word, I pray you.

MACBETH [*Aside*] Two truths are told,
As happy prologues to the swelling act
Of the imperial theme. – I thank you,
gentlemen.
[*Aside*] This supernatural soliciting
Cannot be ill; cannot be good. If ill,
Why hath it given me earnest of success,
Commencing in a truth? I am Thane of Cawdor.
If good, why do I yield to that suggestion
Whose horrid image doth unfix my hair
And make my seated heart knock at my ribs
Against the use of nature? Present fears
Are less than horrible imaginings.
My thought, whose murder yet is but
fantastical,
Shakes so my single state of man
That function is smother'd in surmise,
And nothing is but what is not.

BANQUO Look how our partner's rapt.

MACBETH [*Aside*] If chance will have me King,
why, chance may crown me,
Without my stir.

BANQUO New honours come upon him,
Like our strange garments, cleave not to their
mould
But with the aid of use.

MACBETH [*Aside*] Come what come may,
Time and the hour runs through the roughest
day.

BANQUO Worthy Macbeth, we stay upon your
leisure.

MACBETH Give me your favour. My dull brain
was wrought
With things forgotten. Kind gentlemen, your
pains
Are regist'red where every day I turn
The leaf to read them. Let us toward the King.
[*Aside to Banquo*] Think upon what hath
chanc'd; and, at more time,
The interim having weigh'd it, let us speak
Our free hearts each to other.

BANQUO [*Aside to Macbeth*] Very gladly.

MACBETH [*Aside to Banquo*] Till then, enough. –
Come, friends. [*Exeunt.*

SCENE IV. *Forres. The palace.*

Flourish. Enter DUNCAN, MALCOLM, DONALBAIN, LENNOX and Attendants.

DUNCAN Is execution done on Cawdor? Are not
Those in commission yet return'd?

MALCOLM My liege,
They are not yet come back. But I have spoke
With one that saw him die; who did report
That very frankly he confess'd his treasons,
Implor'd your Highness' pardon, and set forth
A deep repentance. Nothing in his life
Became him like the leaving it: he died
As one that had been studied in his death
To throw away the dearest thing he ow'd
As 'twere a careless trifle.

DUNCAN There's no art
To find the mind's construction in the face.
He was a gentleman on whom I built
An absolute trust.

Enter MACBETH, BANQUO, ROSS, and ANGUS.

O worthiest cousin!
The sin of my ingratitude even now
Was heavy on me. Thou art so far before
That swiftest wing of recompense is slow
To overtake thee. Would thou hadst less
deserv'd,
That the proportion both of thanks and
payment
Might have been mine! Only I have left to say,
More is thy due than more than all can pay.

MACBETH The service and the loyalty I owe,
In doing it, pays itself. Your Highness' part
Is to receive our duties; and our duties
Are to your throne and state children and
servants,
Which do but what they should by doing
everything
Safe toward your love and honour.

DUNCAN Welcome hither.
I have begun to plant thee, and will labour
To make thee full of growing. Noble Banquo,
That hast no less deserv'd, nor must be known
No less to have done so, let me infold thee
And hold thee to my heart.

BANQUO There if I grow,
The harvest is your own.

DUNCAN My plenteous joys,
Wanton in fulness, seek to hide themselves
In drops of sorrow. Sons, kinsmen, thanes,
And you whose places are the nearest, know
We will establish our estate upon
Our eldest, Malcolm, whom we name here-after
The Prince of Cumberland; which honour must
Not unaccompanied invest him only,
But signs of nobleness, like stars, shall shine
On all deservers. From hence to Inverness,
And bind us further to you.

MACBETH The rest is labour, which is not us'd for
you.
I'll be myself the harbinger, and make joyful
The hearing of my wife with your approach;
So, humbly take my leave.

DUNCAN My worthy Cawdor!

MACBETH [*Aside*] The Prince of Cumberland!
That is a step,
On which I must fall down, or else o'er-leap,
For in my way it lies. Stars, hide your fires;

Let not light see my black and deep desires.
The eye wink at the hand; yet let that be
Which the eye fears, when it is done, to see.
[*Exit.*

DUNCAN True, worthy Banquo: he is full so valiant;
And in his commendations I am fed;
It is a banquet to me. Let's after him,
Whose care is gone before to bid us welcome.
It is a peerless kinsman. [*Flourish. Exeunt.*

SCENE V. *Inverness. Macbeth's castle.*

Enter LADY MACBETH, reading a letter.

LADY MACBETH 'They met me in the day of success; and I have learn'd by the perfect'st report they have more in them than mortal knowledge. When I burn'd in desire to question them further, they made themselves air, into which they vanish'd. Whiles I stood rapt in the wonder of it, came missives from the King, who all-hail'd me "Thane of Cawdor"; by which title, before, these weird sisters saluted me, and referr'd me to the coming on of time, with "Hail, king that shalt be!" This have I thought good to deliver thee, my dearest partner of greatness, that thou mightst not lose the dues of rejoicing by being ignorant of what greatness is promis'd thee. Lay it to thy heart, and farewell.'

Glamis thou art, and Cawdor; and shalt be
What thou art promis'd. Yet do I fear thy nature;
It is too full o' th' milk of human kindness
To catch the nearest way. Thou wouldst be great;
Art not without ambition, but without
The illness should attend it. What thou wouldst highly,
That wouldst thou holily; wouldst not play false,
And yet wouldst wrongly win.
Thou'dst have, great Glamis, that which cries
'Thus thou must do' if thou have it;
And that which rather thou dost fear to do
Than wishest should be undone. Hie thee hither,
That I may pour my spirits in thine ear,
And chastise with the valour of my tongue
All that impedes thee from the golden round
Which fate and metaphysical aid doth seem
To have thee crown'd withal.

Enter a Messenger.

What is your tidings?

MESSENGER The King comes here to-night.

LADY MACBETH Thou'rt mad to say it.
Is not thy master with him? who, were't so,
Would have inform'd for preparation.

MESSENGER So please you, it is true. Our Thane is coming.
One of my fellows had the speed of him,
Who, almost dead for breath, had scarcely more
Than would make up his message.

LADY MACBETH Give him tending:
He brings great news. [*Exit Messenger.*
The raven himself is hoarse
That croaks the fatal entrance of Duncan
Under my battlements. Come, you spirits
That tend on mortal thoughts, unsex me here;
And fill me, from the crown to the toe, top-full
Of direst cruelty. Make thick my blood,
Stop up th' access and passage to remorse,
That no compunctious visitings of nature
Shake my fell purpose nor keep peace between
Th' effect and it. Come to my woman's breasts,
And take my milk for gall, you murd'ring ministers,
Wherever in your sightless substances
You wait on nature's mischief. Come, thick night,
And pall thee in the dunnest smoke of hell,
That my keen knife see not the wound it makes,
Nor heaven peep through the blanket of the dark
To cry 'Hold, hold'.

Enter MACBETH.

Great Glamis! Worthy Cawdor!
Greater than both, by the all-hail hereafter!
Thy letters have transported me beyond
This ignorant present, and I feel now
The future in the instant.

MACBETH My dearest love,
Duncan comes here to-night.

LADY MACBETH And when goes hence?

MACBETH To-morrow – as he purposes.

LADY MACBETH O, never
Shall sun that morrow see!
Your face, my thane, is as a book where men
May read strange matters. To beguile the time,
Look like the time; bear welcome in your eye,
Your hand, your tongue; look like th' innocent flower,
But be the serpent under't. He that's coming
Must be provided for; and you shall put
This night's great business into my dispatch;
Which shall to all our nights and days to come
Give solely sovereign sway and masterdom.

MACBETH We will speak further.

LADY MACBETH Only look up clear.
To alter favour ever is to fear.
Leave all the rest to me. [*Exeunt.*

SCENE VI. *Inverness. Before Macbeth's castle.*

Hautboys and torches. Enter DUNCAN, MALCOLM, DONALBAIN, BANQUO, LENNOX, MACDUFF, ROSS, ANGUS, and Attendants.

DUNCAN This castle hath a pleasant seat; the air
Nimbly and sweetly recommends itself
Unto our gentle senses.

BANQUO This guest of summer,
The temple-haunting martlet, does approve
By his lov'd mansionry that the heaven's breath
Smells wooingly here; no jutty, frieze,
Buttress, nor coign of vantage, but this bird
Hath made her pendent bed and procreant cradle.
Where they most breed and haunt, I have observ'd
The air is delicate.

Enter LADY MACBETH.

DUNCAN See, see, our honour'd hostess!
The love that follows us sometime is our trouble,
Which still we thank as love. Herein I teach you
How you shall bid God 'ield us for your pains,
And thank us for your trouble.

LADY MACBETH All our service
In every point twice done, and then done double,
Were poor and single business to contend
Against those honours deep and broad wherewith
Your Majesty loads our house; for those of old,
And the late dignities heap'd up to them,
We rest your hermits.

DUNCAN Where's the Thane of Cawdor?
We cours'd him at the heels and had a purpose
To be his purveyor; but he rides well,
And his great love, sharp as his spur, hath holp him
To his home before us. Fair and noble hostess,
We are your guest to-night.

LADY MACBETH Your servants ever
Have theirs, themselves, and what is theirs, in compt,
To make their audit at your Highness' pleasure,
Still to return your own.

DUNCAN Give me your hand;
Conduct me to mine host. We love him highly,
And shall continue our graces towards him.
By your leave, hostess. [*Exeunt.*

SCENE VII. *Inverness. Macbeth's castle.*

Hautboys, torches. Enter a Sewer, and divers Servants with dishes and service over the stage. Then enter MACBETH.

MACBETH If it were done when 'tis done, then 'twere well
It were done quickly. If th' assassination
Could trammel up the consequence, and catch,
With his surcease, success; that but this blow
Might be the be-all and the end-all here –
But here upon this bank and shoal of time –
We'd jump the life to come. But in these cases
We still have judgment here, that we but teach
Bloody instructions, which being taught return
To plague th' inventor. This even-handed justice
Commends th' ingredience of our poison'd chalice
To our own lips. He's here in double trust:
First, as I am his kinsman and his subject –
Strong both against the deed; then, as his host,
Who should against his murderer shut the door,
Not bear the knife myself. Besides, this Duncan
Hath borne his faculties so meek, hath been
So clear in his great office, that his virtues
Will plead like angels, trumpet-tongu'd, against
The deep damnation of his taking-off;
And pity, like a naked new-born babe,
Striding the blast, or heaven's cherubin hors'd
Upon the sightless couriers of the air,
Shall blow the horrid deed in every eye,
That tears shall drown the wind. I have no spur
To prick the sides of my intent, but only
Vaulting ambition, which o'er-leaps itself,
And falls on th' other.

Enter LADY MACBETH.

How now! What news?

LADY MACBETH He has almost supp'd. Why have you left the chamber?

MACBETH Hath he ask'd for me?

LADY MACBETH Know you not he has?

MACBETH We will proceed no further in this business.
He hath honour'd me of late; and I have bought
Golden opinions from all sorts of people,
Which would be worn now in their newest gloss,
Not cast aside so soon.

LADY MACBETH Was the hope drunk
Wherein you dress'd yourself? Hath it slept since,
And wakes it now to look so green and pale
At what it did so freely? From this time
Such I account thy love. Art thou afeard
To be the same in thine own act and valour
As thou art in desire? Wouldst thou have that
Which thou esteem'st the ornament of life,
And live a coward in thine own esteem,
Letting 'I dare not' wait upon 'I would',
Like the poor cat i' th' adage?

MACBETH Prithee, peace;
I dare do all that may become a man;

Who dares do more is none.
LADY MACBETH What beast was't then
That made you break this enterprise to me?
When you durst do it, then you were a man;
And to be more than what you were, you would
Be so much more the man. Nor time nor place
Did then adhere, and yet you would make both;
They have made themselves, and that their fitness now
Does unmake you. I have given suck, and know
How tender 'tis to love the babe that milks me –
I would, while it was smiling in my face,
Have pluck'd my nipple from his boneless gums,
And dash'd the brains out, had I so sworn
As you have done to this.
MACBETH If we should fail?
LADY MACBETH We fail!
But screw your courage to the sticking place,
And we'll not fail. When Duncan is asleep –
Whereto the rather shall his day's hard journey
Soundly invite him – his two chamberlains
Will I with wine and wassail so convince
That memory, the warder of the brain,
Shall be a fume, and the receipt of reason
A limbec only. When in swinish sleep
Their drenched natures lie as in a death,
What cannot you and I perform upon
Th' unguarded Duncan? What not put upon
His spongy officers, who shall bear the guilt
Of our great quell?
MACBETH Bring forth men-children only;
For thy undaunted mettle should compose
Nothing but males. Will it not be receiv'd,
When we have mark'd with blood those sleepy two
Of his own chamber, and us'd their very daggers,
That they have done 't?
LADY MACBETH Who dares receive it other,
As we shall make our griefs and clamour roar
Upon his death?
MACBETH I am settled, and bend up
Each corporal agent to this terrible feat.
Away, and mock the time with fairest show;
False face must hide what the false heart doth know.
[*Exeunt.*

ACT TWO

SCENE I. *Inverness. Court of Macbeth's castle.*

Enter BANQUO, and FLEANCE with a torch before him.

BANQUO How goes the night, boy?
FLEANCE The moon is down; I have not heard the clock.
BANQUO And she goes down at twelve.
FLEANCE I take 't, 'tis later, sir.
BANQUO Hold, take my sword. There's husbandry in heaven;
Their candles are all out. Take thee that too.
A heavy summons lies like lead upon me,
And yet I would not sleep. Merciful powers
Restrain in me the cursed thoughts that nature
Gives way to in repose!

Enter MACBETH and a Servant with a torch.

Give me my sword.
Who's there?
MACBETH A friend.
BANQUO What, sir, not yet at rest? The king's a-bed.
He hath been in unusual pleasure, and
Sent forth great largess to your offices.
This diamond he greets your wife withal,
By the name of most kind hostess; and shut up
In measureless content.
MACBETH Being unprepar'd,
Our will became the servant to defect;
Which else should free have wrought.
BANQUO All's well.
I dreamt last night of the three Weird Sisters.
To you they have show'd some truth.
MACBETH I think not of them;
Yet, when we can entreat an hour to serve,
We would spend it in some words upon that business,
If you would grant the time.
BANQUO At your kind'st leisure.
MACBETH If you shall cleave to my consent, when 'tis,
It shall make honour for you.
BANQUO So I lose none
In seeking to augment it, but still keep
My bosom franchis'd and allegiance clear,
I shall be counsell'd.
MACBETH Good repose the while!
BANQUO Thanks, sir; the like to you!
[*Exeunt Banquo and Fleance.*
MACBETH Go bid thy mistress, when my drink is ready,
She strike upon the bell. Get thee to bed.
[*Exit Servant.*
Is this a dagger which I see before me,
The handle toward my hand? Come, let me clutch thee.

I have thee not, and yet I see thee still.
Art thou not, fatal vision, sensible
To feeling as to sight? or art thou but
A dagger of the mind, a false creation,
Proceeding from the heat-oppressed brain?
I see thee yet, in form as palpable
As this which now I draw.
Thou marshall'st me the way that I was going;
And such an instrument I was to use.
Mine eyes are made the fools o' th' other senses,
Or else worth all the rest. I see thee still;
And on thy blade and dudgeon gouts of blood,
Which was not so before. There's no such thing:
It is the bloody business which informs
Thus to mine eyes. Now o'er the one half-world
Nature seems dead, and wicked dreams abuse
The curtain'd sleep; now witchcraft celebrates
Pale Hecate's offerings; and wither'd murder,
Alarum'd by his sentinel, the wolf,
Whose howl's his watch, thus with his stealthy pace,
With Tarquin's ravishing strides, towards his design
Moves like a ghost. Thou sure and firm-set earth,
Hear not my steps which way they walk, for fear
Thy very stones prate of my whereabout
And take the present horror from the time,
Which now suits with it. Whiles I threat, he lives;
Words to the heat of deeds too cold breath gives. [*A bell rings.*
I go, and it is done; the bell invites me.
Hear it not, Duncan, for it is a knell
That summons thee to heaven or to hell.
[*Exit.*

SCENE II. *Inverness. Macbeth's castle.*

Enter LADY MACBETH.

LADY MACBETH That which hath made them drunk hath made me bold;
What hath quench'd them hath given me fire. Hark! Peace!
It was the owl that shriek'd, the fatal bell-man,
Which gives the stern'st good-night. He is about it.
The doors are open; and the surfeited grooms
Do mock their charge with snores. I have drugg'd their possets,
That death and nature do contend about them,
Whether they live or die.

MACBETH [*Within*] Who's there! What, ho!

LADY MACBETH Alack! I am afraid they have awak'd,
And 'tis not done. Th' attempt, and not the deed,
Confounds us. Hark! I laid their daggers ready;
He could not miss 'em. Had he not resembled
My father as he slept, I had done't.

Enter MACBETH.

My husband!

MACBETH I have done the deed. Didst thou not hear a noise?

LADY MACBETH I heard the owl scream and the crickets cry.
Did not you speak?

MACBETH When?

LADY MACBETH Now.

MACBETH As I descended?

LADY MACBETH Ay.

MACBETH Hark!
Who lies i' th' second chamber?

LADY MACBETH Donalbain.

MACBETH This is a sorry sight. [*Looking on his hands.*

LADY MACBETH A foolish thought to say a sorry sight.

MACBETH There's one did laugh in's sleep, and one cried 'Murder!'
That they did wake each other. I stood and heard them;
But they did say their prayers, and address'd them
Again to sleep.

LADY MACBETH There are two lodg'd together.

MACBETH One cried 'God bless us', and 'Amen' the other,
As they had seen me with these hangman's hands.
List'ning their fear, I could not say 'Amen'
When they did say 'God bless us!'

LADY MACBETH Consider it not so deeply.

MACBETH But wherefore could not I pronounce 'Amen'?
I had most need of blessing, and 'Amen'
Stuck in my throat.

LADY MACBETH These deeds must not be thought
After these ways: so, it will make us mad.

MACBETH Methought I heard a voice cry 'Sleep no more;
Macbeth does murder sleep' – the innocent sleep,
Sleep that knits up the ravell'd sleave of care,
The death of each day's life, sore labour's bath,
Balm of hurt minds, great nature's second course,
Chief nourisher in life's feast.

LADY MACBETH What do you mean?

MACBETH Still it cried 'Sleep no more' to all the house;
'Glamis hath murder'd sleep; and therefore Cawdor
Shall sleep no more – Macbeth shall sleep no more'.

LADY MACBETH Who was it that thus cried? Why, worthy Thane,
You do unbend your noble strength to think
So brainsickly of things. Go get some water
And wash this filthy witness from your hand.
Why did you bring these daggers from the place?
They must lie there. Go carry them, and smear
The sleepy grooms with blood.

MACBETH I'll go no more:
I am afraid to think what I have done;
Look on't again I dare not.

LADY MACBETH Infirm of purpose!
Give me the daggers. The sleeping and the dead
Are but as pictures; 'tis the eye of childhood
That fears a painted devil. If he do bleed,
I'll gild the faces of the grooms withal,
For it must seem their guilt.

[*Exit. Knocking within.*

MACBETH Whence is that knocking?
How is't with me, when every noise appals me?
What hands are here? Ha! they pluck out mine eyes.
Will all great Neptune's ocean wash this blood
Clean from my hand? No; this my hand will rather
The multitudinous seas incarnadine,
Making the green one red.

Re-enter LADY MACBETH.

LADY MACBETH My hands are of your colour; but I shame
To wear a heart so white. [*Knock*] I hear a knocking
At the south entry; retire we to our chamber.
A little water clears us of this deed.
How easy is it then! Your constancy
Hath left you unattended. [*Knock*] Hark! more knocking.
Get on your nightgown, lest occasion call us
And show us to be watchers. Be not lost
So poorly in your thoughts.

MACBETH To know my deed, 'twere best not know myself. [*Knock.*
Wake Duncan with thy knocking! I would thou couldst! [*Exeunt.*

SCENE III. *Inverness. Macbeth's castle.*

Knocking within. Enter a Porter.

PORTER Here's a knocking indeed! If a man were porter of hell-gate, he should have old turning the key. [*Knock*] Knock, knock, knock! Who's there, i' th' name of Beelzebub? Here's a farmer that hang'd himself on th' expectation of plenty. Come in time; have napkins enow about you; here you'll sweat for't. [*Knock*] Knock, knock! Who's there, i' th' other devil's name? Faith, here's an equivocator, that could swear in both the scales against either scale; who committed treason enough for God's sake, yet could not equivocate to heaven. O, come in, equivocator. [*Knock*] Knock, knock, knock! Who's there? Faith, here's an English tailor come hither for stealing out of a French hose. Come in, tailor, here you may roast your goose. [*Knock*] Knock, knock; never at quiet! What are you? But this place is too cold for hell. I'll devil-porter it no further. I had thought to have let in some of all professions that go the primrose way to th' everlasting bonfire. [*Knock*] Anon, anon! [*Opens the gate*] I pray you remember the porter.

Enter MACDUFF and LENNOX.

MACDUFF Was it so late, friend, ere you went to bed, that you do lie so late?

PORTER Faith, sir, we were carousing till the second cock; and drink, sir, is a great provoker of three things.

MACDUFF What three things does drink especially provoke?

PORTER Marry, sir, nose-painting, sleep, and urine. Lechery, sir, it provokes and unprovokes: it provokes the desire, but it takes away the performance. Therefore much drink may be said to be an equivocator with lechery: it makes him, and it mars him; it sets him on, and it takes him off; it persuades him, and disheartens him; makes him stand to, and not stand to; in conclusion, equivocates him in a sleep, and, giving him the lie, leaves him.

MACDUFF I believe drink gave thee the lie last night.

PORTER That it did, sir, i' the very throat on me; but I requited him for his lie; and, I think, being too strong for him, though he took up my legs sometime, yet I made a shift to cast him.

MACDUFF Is thy master stirring?

Enter MACBETH.

Our knocking has awak'd him; here he comes.

LENNOX Good morrow, noble sir!

MACBETH Good morrow, both!

MACDUFF Is the King stirring, worthy Thane?

MACBETH Not yet.

MACDUFF He did command me to call timely on him;
I have almost slipp'd the hour.

MACBETH I'll bring you to him.

MACDUFF I know this is a joyful trouble to you;
But yet 'tis one.

MACBETH The labour we delight in physics pain.
This is the door.

MACDUFF I'll make so bold to call,
For 'tis my limited service. [*Exit Macduff.*

LENNOX Goes the King hence to-day?

MACBETH He does: he did appoint so.

LENNOX The night has been unruly. Where we lay,
Our chimneys were blown down; and, as they say,
Lamentings heard i' th' air, strange screams of death,
And prophesying, with accents terrible,
Of dire combustion and confus'd events
New hatch'd to th' woeful time; the obscure bird
Clamour'd the livelong night. Some say the earth
Was feverous and did shake.

MACBETH 'Twas a rough night.

LENNOX My young remembrance cannot parallel
A fellow to it.

Re-enter MACDUFF.

MACDUFF O horror, horror, horror! Tongue nor heart
Cannot conceive nor name thee.

MACBETH, LENNOX, What's the matter?

MACDUFF Confusion now hath made his masterpiece.
Most sacrilegious murder hath broke ope
The Lord's anointed temple, and stole thence
The life o' th' building.

MACBETH What is't you say – the life?

LENNOX Mean you his Majesty?

MACDUFF Approach the chamber, and destroy your sight
With a new Gorgon. Do not bid me speak;
See, and then speak yourselves.

[*Exeunt Macbeth and Lennox.*

Awake, awake!
Ring the alarum bell. Murder and treason!
Banquo and Donalbain! Malcolm! awake!
Shake off this downy sleep, death's counterfeit,
And look on death itself. Up, up, and see
The great doom's image! Malcolm! Banquo!
As from your graves rise up and walk like sprites
To countenance this horror! Ring the bell.

[*Bell rings.*

Enter LADY MACBETH.

LADY MACBETH What's the business,
That such a hideous trumpet calls to parley
The sleepers of the house? Speak, speak!

MACDUFF O gentle lady,
'Tis not for you to hear what I can speak!
The repetition in a woman's ear
Would murder as it fell.

Enter BANQUO.

O Banquo, Banquo,
Our royal master's murder'd!

LADY MACBETH Woe, alas!
What, in our house?

BANQUO Too cruel any where.
Dear Duff, I prithee contradict thyself,
And say it is not so.

Re-enter MACBETH, LENNOX, with ROSS.

MACBETH Had I but died an hour before this chance,
I had liv'd a blessed time; for, from this instant,
There's nothing serious in mortality –
All is but toys; renown and grace is dead;
The wine of life is drawn, and the mere lees
Is left this vault to brag of.

Enter MALCOLM and DONALBAIN.

DONALBAIN What is amiss?

MACBETH You are, and do not know't.
The spring, the head, the fountain of your blood,
Is stopp'd; the very source of it is stopp'd.

MACDUFF Your royal father's murder'd.

MALCOLM O, by whom?

LENNOX Those of his chamber, as it seem'd, had done't.
Their hands and faces were all badg'd with blood;
So were their daggers, which unwip'd we found
Upon their pillows. They star'd and were distracted;
No man's life was to be trusted with them.

MACBETH O, yet I do repent me of my fury
That I did kill them.

MACDUFF Wherefore did you so?

MACBETH Who can be wise, amaz'd, temp'rate, and furious,
Loyal and neutral, in a moment? No man.
The expedition of my violent love
Outrun the pauser reason. Here lay Duncan,
His silver skin lac'd with his golden blood;
And his gash'd stabs look'd like a breach in nature
For ruin's wasteful entrance: there, the murderers,
Steep'd in the colours of their trade, their daggers
Unmannerly breech'd with gore. Who could refrain,
That had a heart to love, and in that heart
Courage to make's love known?

LADY MACBETH Help me hence, ho!
MACDUFF Look to the lady.
MALCOLM [*Aside to Donalbain*] Why do we hold our tongues that most may claim
This argument for ours?
DONALBAIN [*Aside to Malcolm*] What should be spoken
Here, where our fate, hid in an auger-hole,
May rush and seize us? Let's away.
Our tears are not yet brew'd.
MALCOLM [*Aside to Donalbain*] Nor our strong sorrow
Upon the foot of motion.
BANQUO Look to the lady.
[*Lady Macbeth is carried out.*
And when we have our naked frailties hid,
That suffer in exposure, let us meet,
And question this most bloody piece of work,
To know it further. Fears and scruples shake us.
In the great hand of God I stand, and thence
Against the undivulg'd pretence I fight
Of treasonous malice.
MACDUFF And so do I.
ALL So all.
MACBETH Let's briefly put on manly readiness
And meet i' th' hall together.
ALL Well contented.
[*Exeunt all but Malcolm and Donalbain.*
MALCOLM What will you do? Let's not consort with them.
To show an unfelt sorrow is an office
Which the false man does easy. I'll to England.
DONALBAIN To Ireland I; our separated fortune
Shall keep us both the safer. Where we are,
There's daggers in men's smiles; the near in blood,
The nearer bloody.
MALCOLM This murderous shaft that's shot
Hath not yet lighted; and our safest way
Is to avoid the aim. Therefore to horse;
And let us not be dainty of leave-taking,
But shift away. There's warrant in that theft
Which steals itself, when there's no mercy left.
[*Exeunt.*

SCENE IV. *Inverness. Without Macbeth's castle.*

Enter ROSS with an Old Man.

OLD MAN Threescore and ten I can remember well;
Within the volume of which time I have seen
Hours dreadful and things strange; but this sore night
Hath trifled former knowings.
ROSS Ah, good father,
Thou seest, the heavens, as troubled with man's act,
Threatens his bloody stage. By th' clock 'tis day,
And yet dark night strangles the travelling lamp.
Is't night's predominance, or the day's shame,
That darkness does the face of earth entomb,
When living light should kiss it?
OLD MAN 'Tis unnatural,
Even like the deed that's done. On Tuesday last,
A falcon, tow'ring in her pride of place,
Was by a mousing owl hawk'd at and kill'd.
ROSS And Duncan's horses – a thing most strange and certain –
Beautous and swift, the minions of their race,
Turn'd wild in nature, broke their stalls, flung out,
Contending 'gainst obedience, as they would make
War with mankind.
OLD MAN 'Tis said they eat each other.
ROSS They did so; to the amazement of mine eyes,
That look'd upon't.

Enter MACDUFF.

Here comes the good Macduff.
How goes the world, sir, now?
MACDUFF Why, see you not?
ROSS Is't known who did this more than bloody deed?
MACDUFF Those that Macbeth hath slain.
ROSS Alas, the day!
What good could they pretend?
MACDUFF They were suborn'd.
Malcolm and Donalbain, the King's two sons,
Are stol'n away and fled; which puts upon them
Suspicion of the deed.
ROSS 'Gainst nature still.
Thriftless ambition, that wilt ravin up
Thine own life's means! Then 'tis most like
The sovereignty will fall upon Macbeth.
MACDUFF He is already nam'd, and gone to Scone
To be invested.
ROSS Where is Duncan's body?
MACDUFF Carried to Colmekill,
The sacred storehouse of his predecessors
And guardian of their bones.
ROSS Will you to Scone?
MACDUFF No, cousin, I'll to Fife.
ROSS Well, I will thither.
MACDUFF Well, may you see things well done there! Adieu,
Lest our old robes sit easier than our new.
ROSS Farewell, father.

OLD MAN God's benison go with you, and with those
That would make good of bad, and friends of foes. [*Exeunt.*

ACT THREE

SCENE I. *Forres. The palace.*

Enter BANQUO.

BANQUO Thou hast it now – King, Cawdor, Glamis, all
As the weird women promis'd; and I fear
Thou play'dst most foully for't; yet it was said
It should not stand in thy posterity;
But that myself should be the root and father
Of many kings. If there come truth from them –
As upon thee, Macbeth, their speeches shine –
Why, by the verities on thee made good,
May they not be my oracles as well
And set me up in hope? But, hush, no more.

Sennet sounded. Enter MACBETH as King, LADY MACBETH as Queen; LENNOX, ROSS, Lords, Ladies, and Attendants.

MACBETH Here's our chief guest.
LADY MACBETH If he had been forgotten,
It had been as a gap in our great feast,
And all-thing unbecoming.
MACBETH To-night we hold a solemn supper, sir,
And I'll request your presence.
BANQUO Let your Highness
Command upon me; to the which my duties
Are with a most indissoluble tie
For ever knit.
MACBETH Ride you this afternoon?
BANQUO Ay, my good lord.
MACBETH We should have else desir'd your good advice –
Which still hath been both grave and prosperous –
In this day's council; but we'll take to-morrow.
Is't far you ride?
BANQUO As far, my lord, as will fill up the time
'Twixt this and supper. Go not my horse the better,
I must become a borrower of the night
For a dark hour or twain.
MACBETH Fail not our feast.
BANQUO My lord, I will not.
MACBETH We hear our bloody cousins are bestow'd
In England and in Ireland, not confessing
Their cruel parricide, filling their hearers
With strange invention; but of that to-morrow,
When therewithal we shall have cause of state
Craving us jointly. Hie you to horse; adieu,
Till you return at night. Goes Fleance with you?
BANQUO Ay, my good lord; our time does call upon's.
MACBETH I wish your horses swift and sure of foot,
And so I do commend you to their backs.
Farewell. [*Exit Banquo.*
Let every man be master of his time
Till seven at night; to make society
The sweeter welcome, we will keep ourself
Till supper-time alone. While then, God be with you!
[*Exeunt all but Macbeth and a Servant.*
Sirrah, a word with you. Attend those men our pleasure?
SERVANT They are, my lord, without the palace gate.
MACBETH Bring them before us.
[*Exit Servant.*
To be thus is nothing,
But to be safely thus. Our fears in Banquo,
Stick deep; and in his royalty of nature
Reigns that which would be fear'd. 'Tis much he dares,
And to that dauntless temper of his mind
He hath a wisdom that doth guide his valour
To act in safety. There is none but he
Whose being I do fear; and under him
My Genius is rebuk'd, as it is said
Mark Antony's was by Caesar. He chid the Sisters
When first they put the name of King upon me,
And bade them speak to him; then, prophet-like,
They hail'd him father to a line of kings.
Upon my head they plac'd a fruitless crown
And put a barren sceptre in my gripe,
Thence to be wrench'd with an unlineal hand,
No son of mine succeeding. If't be so,
For Banquo's issue have I fil'd my mind;
For them the gracious Duncan have I murder'd;
Put rancours in the vessel of my peace
Only for them, and mine eternal jewel
Given to the common enemy of man
To make them kings – the seeds of Banquo kings!
Rather than so, come, Fate, into the list,
And champion me to th' utterance! Who's there?

Re-enter Servant and two Murderers.

Now go to the door and stay there till we call
[Exit Servant.

Was it not yesterday we spoke together?

1 MURDERER It was, so please your Highness.

MACBETH Well then, now
Have you consider'd of my speeches? Know
That it was he, in the times past, which held you
So under fortune; which you thought had been
Our innocent self. This I made good to you
In our last conference, pass'd in probation with you,
How you were borne in hand, how cross'd, the instruments,
Who wrought with them, and all things else that might
To half a soul and to a notion craz'd Say 'Thus did Banquo'.

1 MURDERER You made it known to us.

MACBETH I did so; and went further, which is now
Our point of second meeting. Do you find
Your patience so predominant in your nature
That you can let this go? Are you so gospell'd,
To pray for this good man and for his issue,
Whose heavy hand hath bow'd you to the grave
And beggar'd yours for ever?

1 MURDERER We are men, my liege.

MACBETH Ay, in the catalogue ye go for men;
As hounds, and greyhounds, mongrels, spaniels, curs,
Shoughs, water-rugs, and demi-wolves, are clept
All by the name of dogs. The valued file
Distinguishes the swift, the slow, the subtle,
The house-keeper, the hunter, every one
According to the gift which bounteous nature
Hath in him clos'd; whereby he does receive
Particular addition, from the bill
That writes them all alike; and so of men.
Now, if you have a station in the file,
Not i' th' worst rank of manhood, say't;
And I will put that business in your bosoms
Whose execution takes your enemy off,
Grapples you to the heart and love of us,
Who wear our health but sickly in his life,
Which in his death were perfect.

2 MURDERER I am one, my liege,
Whom the vile blows and buffets of the world
Hath so incens'd that I am reckless what
I do to spite the world.

1 MURDERER And I another,
So weary with disasters, tugg'd with fortune,
That I would set my life on any chance,
To mend it or be rid on't.

MACBETH Both of you
Know Banquo was your enemy.

BOTH MURDERERS True, my lord.

MACBETH So is he mine; and in such bloody distance
That every minute of his being thrusts
Against my near'st of life; and though I could
With bare-fac'd power sweep him from my sight,
And bid my will avouch it, yet I must not,
For certain friends that are both his and mine,
Whose loves I may not drop, but wail his fall
Who I myself struck down. And thence it is
That I to your assistance do make love,
Masking the business from the common eye
For sundry weighty reasons.

2 MURDERER We shall, my lord,
Perform what you command us.

1 MURDERER Though our lives –

MACBETH Your spirits shine through you. Within this hour at most,
I will advise you where to plant yourselves,
Acquaint you with the perfect spy o' th' time,
The moment on't; for 't must be done to-night,
And something from the palace; always thought
That I require a clearness; and with him,
To leave no rubs nor botches in the work,
Fleance his son, that keeps him company,
Whose absence is no less material to me
Than is his father's, must embrace the fate
Of that dark hour. Resolve yourselves apart;
I'll come to you anon.

BOTH MURDERERS We are resolv'd, my lord.

MACBETH I'll call upon you straight; abide within.
[Exeunt Murderers.

It is concluded: Banquo, thy soul's flight
If it find heaven must find it out to-night.
[Exit.

SCENE II. *Forres. The palace.*

Enter LADY MACBETH and a Servant.

LADY MACBETH Is Banquo gone from court?

SERVANT Ay, madam, but returns again to-night.

LADY MACBETH Say to the King I would attend his leisure
For a few words.

SERVANT Madam, I will.
[Exit.

LADY MACBETH Nought's had, all's spent,
Where our desire is got without content.
'Tis safer to be that which we destroy,
Than by destruction dwell in doubtful joy.

Enter MACBETH.

How now, my lord! Why do you keep alone,
Of sorriest fancies your companions making,
Using those thoughts which should indeed have died

With them they think on? Things without all remedy
Should be without regard. What's done is done.

MACBETH We have scotch'd the snake, not kill'd it;
She'll close, and be herself, whilst our poor malice
Remains in danger of her former tooth.
But let the frame of things disjoint, both the worlds suffer,
Ere we will eat our meal in fear and sleep
In the affliction of these terrible dreams
That shake us nightly. Better be with the dead,
Whom we, to gain our peace, have sent to peace,
Than on the torture of the mind to lie
In restless ecstasy. Duncan is in his grave;
After life's fitful fever he sleeps well;
Treason has done his worst; nor steel, nor poison,
Malice domestic, foreign levy, nothing,
Can touch him further.

LADY MACBETH Come on.
Gentle my lord, sleek o'er your rugged looks;
Be bright and jovial among your guests to-night.

MACBETH So shall I, love; and so, I pray, be you.
Let your remembrance apply to Banquo;
Present him eminence, both with eye and tongue –
Unsafe the while, that we
Must lave our honours in these flattering streams,
And make our faces vizards to our hearts,
Disguising what they are.

LADY MACBETH You must leave this.

MACBETH O, full of scorpions is my mind, dear wife!
Thou know'st that Banquo, and his Fleance, lives.

LADY MACBETH But in them nature's copy's not eterne.

MACBETH There's comfort yet; they are assailable.
Then be thou jocund. Ere the bat hath flown
His cloister'd flight; ere to black Hecate's summons
The shard-borne beetle with his drowsy hums
Hath rung night's yawning peal, there shall be done
A deed of dreadful note.

LADY MACBETH What's to be done?

MACBETH Be innocent of the knowledge, dearest chuck,
Till thou applaud the deed. Come, seeling night,
Scarf up the tender eye of pitiful day,
And with thy bloody and invisible hand
Cancel and tear to pieces that great bond
Which keeps me pale. Light thickens, and the crow
Makes wing to th' rooky wood;
Good things of day begin to droop and drowse,
Whiles night's black agents to their preys do rouse.
Thou marvell'st at my words; but hold thee still:
Things bad begun make strong themselves by ill.
So, prithee go with me. *[Exeunt.*

SCENE III. *Forres. The approaches to the palace.*

Enter three Murderers.

1 MURDERER But who did bid thee join with us?

3 MURDERER Macbeth.

2 MURDERER He needs not our mistrust, since he delivers
Our offices, and what we have to do,
To the direction just.

1 MURDERER Then stand with us.
The west yet glimmers with some streaks of day;
Now spurs the lated traveller apace
To gain the timely inn, and near approaches
The subject of our watch.

3 MURDERER Hark! I hear horses.

BANQUO *[Within]* Give us a light there, ho!

2 MURDERER Then 'tis he; the rest
That are within the note of expectation
Already are i' th' court.

1 MURDERER His horses go about.

3 MURDERER Almost a mile; but he does usually,
So all men do, from hence to th' palace gate
Make it their walk.

Enter BANQUO, and FLEANCE with a torch.

2 MURDERER A light, a light!

3 MURDERER 'Tis he.

1 MURDERER Stand to 't.

BANQUO It will be rain to-night.

1 MURDERER Let it come down. *[Stabs Banquo.*

BANQUO O, treachery! Fly, good Fleance, fly, fly, fly.
Thou mayst revenge. O slave!
[Dies. Fleance escapes.

3 MURDERER Who did strike out the light?

1 MURDERER Was't not the way?

3 MURDERER There's but one down; the son is fled.

2 MURDERER We have lost
Best half of our affair.

1 MURDERER Well, let's away,
And say how much is done. *[Exeunt.*

SCENE IV. *Forres. The palace.*

Banquet prepar'd. Enter MACBETH, LADY MACBETH, ROSS, LENNOX, Lords, and Attendants.

MACBETH You know your own degrees, sit down.
At first and last the hearty welcome.
LORDS Thanks to your Majesty.
MACBETH Our self will mingle with society
And play the humble host.
Our hostess keeps her state; but in best time
We will require her welcome.
LADY MACBETH Pronounce it for me, sir, to all our friends;
For my heart speaks they are welcome.

Enter First Murderer to the door.

MACBETH See, they encounter thee with their hearts' thanks.
Both sides are even; here I'll sit i' th' midst.
Be large in mirth; anon we'll drink a measure
The table round. [*Going to the door.*
There's blood upon thy face.
MURDERER 'Tis Banquo's then.
MACBETH 'Tis better thee without than he within.
Is he despatch'd?
MURDERER My lord, his throat is cut;
That I did for him.
MACBETH Thou art the best o' th' cut-throats;
Yet he's good that did the like for Fleance.
If thou didst it, thou art the nonpareil.
MURDERER Most royal sir – Fleance is 'scap'd.
MACBETH Then comes my fit again. I had else been perfect,
Whole as the marble, founded as the rock,
As broad and general as the casing air,
But now I am cabin'd, cribb'd, confin'd, bound in
To saucy doubts and fears. But Banquo's safe?
MURDERER Ay, my good lord. Safe in a ditch he bides,
With twenty trenched gashes on his head,
The least a death to nature.
MACBETH Thanks for that.
There the grown serpent lies; the worm that's fled
Hath nature that in time will venom breed,
No teeth for th' present. Get thee gone; to-morrow
We'll hear, ourselves, again. [*Exit Murderer.*
LADY MACBETH My royal lord,
You do not give the cheer; the feast is sold
That is not often vouch'd, while 'tis a-making,
'Tis given with welcome. To feed were best at home:
From thence the sauce to meat is ceremony;
Meeting were bare without it.

Enter the Ghost of BANQUO and sits in Macbeth's place.

MACBETH Sweet remembrancer!
Now good digestion wait on appetite,
And health on both!
LENNOX May't please your Highness sit?
MACBETH Here had we now our country's honour roof'd,
Were the grac'd person of our Banquo present;
Who may I rather challenge for unkindness
Than pity for mischance.
ROSS His absence, sir,
Lays blame upon his promise. Please 't your Highness
To grace us with your royal company.
MACBETH The table's full.
LENNOX Here is a place reserv'd, sir.
MACBETH Where?
LENNOX Here, my good lord.
What is't that moves your Highness?
MACBETH Which of you have done this?
LORDS What, my good lord?
MACBETH Thou canst not say I did it; never shake
Thy gory locks at me.
ROSS Gentlemen, rise; his Highness is not well.
LADY MACBETH Sit, worthy friends. My lord is often thus,
And hath been from his youth. Pray you, keep seat.
The fit is momentary; upon a thought
He will again be well. If much you note him,
You shall offend him and extend his passion.
Feed, and regard him not. – Are you a man?
MACBETH Ay, and a bold one that dare look on that
Which might appal the devil.
LADY MACBETH O proper stuff!
This is the very painting of your fear;
This is the air-drawn dagger which you said
Led you to Duncan. O, these flaws and starts –
Impostors to true fear – would well become
A woman's story at a winter's fire,
Authoriz'd by her grandam. Shame itself!
Why do you make such faces? When all's done,
You look but on a stool.
MACBETH Prithee see there.
Behold! look! lo! how say you?
Why, what care I? If thou canst nod, speak too.
If charnel-houses and our graves must send
Those that we bury back, our monuments
Shall be the maws of kites. [*Exit Ghost.*
LADY MACBETH What, quite unmann'd in folly?
MACBETH If I stand here, I saw him.
LADY MACBETH Fie, for shame!

MACBETH Blood hath been shed ere now, i' th' olden time,
Ere humane statute purg'd the gentle weal;
Ay, and since too, murders have been perform'd
Too terrible for the ear. The time has been
That when the brains were out the man would die,
And there an end; but now they rise again,
With twenty mortal murders on their crowns,
And push us from our stools. This is more strange
Than such a murder is.

LADY MACBETH My worthy lord,
Your noble friends do lack you.

MACBETH I do forget.
Do not muse at me, my most worthy friends;
I have a strange infirmity, which is nothing
To those that know me. Come, love and health to all;
Then I'll sit down. Give me some wine, fill full.

Enter Ghost.

I drink to the general joy o' th' whole table,
And to our dear friend Banquo, whom we miss.
Would he were here! To all, and him, we thirst,
And all to all.

LORDS Our duties, and the pledge.

MACBETH Avaunt, and quit my sight. Let the earth hide thee.
Thy bones are marrowless, thy blood is cold;
Thou hast no speculation in those eyes
Which thou dost glare with!

LADY MACBETH Think of this, good peers,
But as a thing of custom. 'Tis no other;
Only it spoils the pleasure of the time.

MACBETH What man dare, I dare.
Approach thou like the rugged Russian bear,
The arm'd rhinoceros, or th' Hyrcan tiger;
Take any shape but that, and my firm nerves
Shall never tremble. Or be alive again,
And dare me to the desert with thy sword;
If trembling I inhabit, then protest me
The baby of a girl. Hence, horrible shadow!
Unreal mock'ry, hence! [*Exit Ghost.*
Why, so; being gone,
I am a man again. Pray you, sit still.

LADY MACBETH You have displac'd the mirth, broke the good meeting,
With most admir'd disorder.

MACBETH Can such things be,
And overcome us like a summer's cloud,
Without our special wonder? You make me strange
Even to the disposition that I owe,
When now I think you can behold such sights
And keep the natural ruby of your cheeks,
When mine is blanch'd with fear.

ROSS What sights, my lord?

LADY MACBETH I pray you speak not; he grows worse and worse;
Question enrages him. At once, good night.
Stand not upon the order of your going,
But go at once.

LENNOX Good night; and better health
Attend his Majesty!

LADY MACBETH A kind good night to all!
[*Exeunt Lords and Attendants.*

MACBETH It will have blood; they say blood will have blood.
Stones have been known to move, and trees to speak;
Augurs and understood relations have
By maggot-pies and choughs and rooks brought forth
The secret'st man of blood. What is the night?

LADY MACBETH Almost at odds with morning, which is which.

MACBETH How say'st thou that Macduff denies his person
At our great bidding?

LADY MACBETH Did you send to him, sir?

MACBETH I hear it by the way; but I will send –
There's not a one of them but in this house
I keep a servant fee'd – I will to-morrow.
And betimes I will to the Weird Sisters:
More shall they speak; for now I am bent to know
By the worst means the worst. For mine own good
All causes shall give way. I am in blood
Stepp'd in so far that, should I wade no more,
Returning were as tedious as go o'er.
Strange things I have in head that will to hand,
Which must be acted ere they may be scann'd.

LADY MACBETH You lack the season of all natures, sleep.

MACBETH Come, we'll to sleep. My strange and self-abuse
Is the initiate fear that wants hard use.
We are yet but young in deed. [*Exeunt.*

SCENE V. *A heath.*

Thunder. Enter the three Witches, meeting HECATE.

1 WITCH Why, how now, Hecat! You look angerly.

HECATE Have I not reason, beldams as you are,
Saucy and overbold? How did you dare
To trade and traffic with Macbeth
In riddles and affairs of death;
And I, the mistress of your charms,
The close contriver of all harms,
Was never call'd to bear my part,

Or show the glory of our art?
And, which is worse, all you have done
Hath been but for a wayward son,
Spiteful and wrathful; who, as others do,
Loves for his own ends, not for you.
But make amends now. Get you gone,
And at the pit of Acheron
Meet me i' th' morning; thither he
Will come to know his destiny.
Your vessels and your spells provide,
Your charms, and everything beside.
I am for th' air; this night I'll spend
Unto a dismal and a fatal end.
Great business must be wrought ere noon.
Upon the corner of the moon
There hangs a vap'rous drop profound;
I'll catch it ere it come to ground;
And that, distill'd by magic sleights,
Shall raise such artificial sprites
As, by the strength of their illusion,
Shall draw him on to his confusion.
He shall spurn fate, scorn death, and bear
His hopes 'bove wisdom, grace, and fear;
And you all know security
Is mortals' chiefest enemy.

[*Music and a song within:*
'Come away, come away, etc.'

Hark! I am call'd; my little spirit, see,
Sits in a foggy cloud, and stays for me. [*Exit.*

1 WITCH Come, let's make haste; she'll soon be back again. [*Exeunt.*

SCENE VI. *Forres. The palace.*

Enter LENNOX and another Lord.

LENNOX My former speeches have but hit your thoughts,
Which can interpret farther. Only I say
Things have been strangely borne. The gracious Duncan
Was pitied of Macbeth. Marry, he was dead.
And the right-valiant Banquo walk'd too late;
Whom, you may say, if't please you, Fleance kill'd,
For Fleance fled. Men must not walk too late.
Who cannot want the thought how monstrous
It was for Malcolm and for Donalbain
To kill their gracious father? Damned fact!
How it did grieve Macbeth! Did he not straight,
In pious rage, the two delinquents tear,
That were the slaves of drink and thralls of sleep?
Was not that nobly done? Ay, and wisely too;
For 'twould have anger'd any heart alive
To hear the men deny't. So that, I say,
He has borne all things well; and I do think
That had he Duncan's sons under his key –
As, an't please heaven, he shall not – they should find
What 'twere to kill a father; so should Fleance.
But peace! For from broad words, and 'cause he fail'd
His presence at the tyrant's feast, I hear,
Macduff lives in disgrace. Sir, can you tell
Where he bestows himself?

LORD The son of Duncan,
From whom this tyrant holds the due of birth,
Lives in the English court, and is receiv'd
Of the most pious Edward with such grace
That the malevolence of fortune nothing
Takes from his high respect; thither Macduff
Is gone to pray the holy King upon his aid
To wake Northumberland and warlike Siward,
That by the help of these – with Him above
To ratify the work – we may again
Give to our tables meat, sleep to our nights,
Free from our feasts and banquets bloody knives,
Do faithful homage and receive free honours –
All which we pine for now. And this report
Hath so exasperate the King that he
Prepares for some attempt of war.

LENNOX Sent he to Macduff?

LORD He did; and with an absolute 'Sir, not I!'
The cloudy messenger turns me his back
And hums, as who should say 'You'll rue the time
That clogs me with this answer'.

LENNOX And that well might
Advise him to a caution t' hold what distance
His wisdom can provide. Some holy angel
Fly to the court of England and unfold
His message ere he come, that a swift blessing
May soon return to this our suffering country
Under a hand accurs'd!

LORD I'll send my prayers with him.
[*Exeunt.*

ACT FOUR

SCENE I. *A dark cave. In the middle, a cauldron boiling.*

Thunder. Enter the three Witches.

1 WITCH Thrice the brinded cat hath mew'd.
2 WITCH Thrice and once the hedge-pig whin'd.
3 WITCH Harpier cries; 'tis time, 'tis time.
1 WITCH Round about the cauldron go;
In the poison'd entrails throw.
Toad that under cold stone
Days and nights has thirty-one
Swelt'red venom sleeping got
Boil thou first i' th' charmed pot.
ALL Double, double toil and trouble;
Fire burn, and cauldron bubble.
2 WITCH Fillet of a fenny snake,
In the cauldron boil and bake;
Eye of newt, and toe of frog,
Wool of bat, and tongue of dog,
Adder's fork, and blind-worm's sting,
Lizard's leg, and howlet's wing –
For a charm of pow'rful trouble,
Like a hell-broth boil and bubble.
ALL Double, double toil and trouble;
Fire burn, and cauldron bubble.
3 WITCH Scale of dragon, tooth of wolf,
Witch's mummy, maw and gulf
Of the ravin'd salt-sea shark,
Root of hemlock digg'd i' th' dark,
Liver of blaspheming Jew,
Gall of goat, and slips of yew
Sliver'd in the moon's eclipse,
Nose of Turk, and Tartar's lips,
Finger of birth-strangled babe
Ditch-deliver'd by a drab –
Make the gruel thick and slab;
Add thereto a tiger's chaudron,
For th' ingredience of our cauldron.
ALL Double, double toil and trouble;
Fire burn, and cauldron bubble.
2 WITCH Cool it with a baboon's blood,
Then the charm is firm and good.

Enter HECATE.

HECATE O, well done! I commend your pains;
And every one shall share i' th' gains.
And now about the cauldron sing,
Like elves and fairies in a ring,
Enchanting all that you put in.

[*Music and a song:* 'Black spirits, etc.' *Exit Hecate.*

2 WITCH By the pricking of my thumbs,
Something wicked this way comes.
Open, locks, whoever knocks.

Enter MACBETH.

MACBETH How now, you secret, black, and midnight hags!
What is't you do?
ALL A deed without a name.
MACBETH I conjure you by that which you profess –
Howe'er you come to know it – answer me.
Though you untie the winds and let them fight
Against the churches; though the yesty waves
Confound and swallow navigation up;
Though bladed corn be lodg'd and trees blown down;
Though castles topple on their warders' heads;
Though palaces and pyramids do slope
Their heads to their foundations; though the treasure
Of nature's germens tumble all together,
Even till destruction sicken – answer me
To what I ask you.
1 WITCH Speak.
2 WITCH Demand.
3 WITCH We'll answer.
1 WITCH Say, if thou'dst rather hear it from our mouths,
Or from our masters?
MACBETH Call 'em; let me see 'em.
1 WITCH Pour in sow's blood that hath eaten
Her nine farrow; grease that's sweaten
From the murderer's gibbet throw
Into the flame.
ALL Come, high or low;
Thyself and office deftly show.

Thunder. First Apparition, an Armed Head.

MACBETH Tell me, thou unknown power –
1 WITCH He knows thy thought.
Hear his speech, but say thou nought.
APPARITION Macbeth! Macbeth! Macbeth!
Beware Macduff;
Beware the Thane of Fife. Dismiss me. Enough.
[*He descends.*
MACBETH Whate'er thou art, for thy good caution, thanks;
Thou hast harp'd my fear aright. But one word more –
1 WITCH He will not be commanded. Here's another,
More potent than the first.

Thunder. Second Apparition, a Bloody Child.

APPARITION Macbeth! Macbeth! Macbeth!
MACBETH Had I three ears, I'd hear thee.
APPARITION Be bloody, bold, and resolute; laugh to scorn
The pow'r of man, for none of woman born
Shall harm Macbeth. [*Descends.*

MACBETH Then live, Macduff; what need I fear of thee?
But yet I'll make assurance double sure
And take a bond of fate. Thou shalt not live;
That I may tell pale-hearted fear it lies,
And sleep in spite of thunder.

Thunder. Third Apparition, a Child Crowned, with a tree in his hand.

What is this
That rises like the issue of a king,
And wears upon his baby brow the round
And top of sovereignty?

ALL Listen, but speak not to't.

APPARITION Be lion-mettled, proud, and take no care
Who chafes, who frets, or where conspirers are;
Macbeth shall never vanquish'd be until
Great Birnam wood to high Dunsinane Hill
Shall come against him. [*Descends.*

MACBETH That will never be.
Who can impress the forest, bid the tree
Unfix his earth-bound root? Sweet bodements, good!
Rebellion's head rise never till the wood
Of Birnam rise, and our high-plac'd Macbeth
Shall live the lease of nature, pay his breath
To time and mortal custom. Yet my heart
Throbs to know one thing; tell me, if your art
Can tell so much – shall Banquo's issue ever
Reign in this kingdom?

ALL Seek to know no more.

MACBETH I will be satisfied. Deny me this,
And an eternal curse fall on you! Let me know.
Why sinks that cauldron, and what noise is this? [*Hautboys.*

1 WITCH Show!

2 WITCH Show!

3 WITCH Show!

ALL Show his eyes, and grieve his heart;
Come like shadows, so depart!

A Show of eight Kings, and BANQUO last; the last king with a glass in his hand.

MACBETH Thou art too like the spirit of Banquo; down!
Thy crown does sear mine eye-balls. And thy hair,
Thou other gold-bound brow, is like the first.
A third is like the former. Filthy hags!
Why do you show me this? A fourth? Start, eyes.
What, will the line stretch out to th' crack of doom?
Another yet? A seventh? I'll see no more.
And yet the eighth appears, who bears a glass
Which shows me many more; and some I see
That twofold balls and treble sceptres carry.
Horrible sight! Now I see 'tis true;
For the blood-bolter'd Banquo smiles upon me,
And points at them for his. [*The show vanishes*]
What! is this so?

1 WITCH Ay, sir, all this is so. But why
Stands Macbeth thus amazedly?
Come, sisters, cheer we up his sprites,
And show the best of our delights;
I'll charm the air to give a sound,
While you perform your antic round;
That this great king may kindly say,
Our duties did his welcome pay.

Music. The Witches dance, and vanish.

MACBETH Where are they? Gone? Let this pernicious hour
Stand aye accursed in the calendar.
Come in, without there.

Enter LENNOX.

LENNOX What's your Grace's will?

MACBETH Saw you the Weird Sisters?

LENNOX No, my lord.

MACBETH Came they not by you?

LENNOX No, indeed, my lord.

MACBETH Infected be the air whereon they ride;
And damn'd all those that trust them! I did hear
The galloping of horse. Who was't came by?

LENNOX 'Tis two or three, my lord, that bring you word
Macduff is fled to England.

MACBETH Fled to England!

LENNOX Ay, my good lord.

MACBETH [*Aside*] Time, thou anticipat'st my dread exploits.
The flighty purpose never is o'ertook
Unless the deed go with it. From this moment
The very firstlings of my heart shall be
The firstlings of my hand. And even now,
To crown my thoughts with acts, be it thought and done:
The castle of Macduff I will surprise,
Seize upon Fife, give to the edge o' th' sword
His wife, his babes, and all unfortunate souls
That trace him in his line. No boasting like a fool:
This deed I'll do before this purpose cool.
But no more sights! – Where are these gentlemen?
Come, bring me where they are. [*Exeunt.*

SCENE II. *Fife. Macduff's castle.*

Enter LADY MACDUFF, her Son, and ROSS.

LADY MACDUFF What had he done to make him fly the land?

ROSS You must have patience, madam.

LADY MACDUFF He had none;
His flight was madness. When our actions do not,
Our fears do make us traitors.
ROSS You know not
Whether it was his wisdom or his fear.
LADY MACDUFF Wisdom! To leave his wife, to leave his babes,
His mansion, and his titles, in a place
From whence himself does fly? He loves us not;
He wants the natural touch; for the poor wren,
The most diminutive of birds, will fight,
Her young ones in her nest, against the owl.
All is the fear, and nothing is the love;
As little is the wisdom, where the flight
So runs against all reason.
ROSS My dearest coz,
I pray you, school yourself. But, for your husband,
He is noble, wise, judicious, and best knows
The fits o' th' season. I dare not speak much further;
But cruel are the times, when we are traitors
And do not know ourselves; when we hold rumour
From what we fear, yet know not what we fear,
But float upon a wild and violent sea
Each way and none. I take my leave of you;
Shall not be long but I'll be here again.
Things at the worst will cease, or else climb upward
To what they were before. – My pretty cousin,
Blessing upon you!
LADY MACDUFF Father'd he is, and yet he's fatherless.
ROSS I am so much a fool, should I stay longer,
It would be my disgrace and your discomfort.
I take my leave at once. [*Exit.*
LADY MACDUFF Sirrah, your father's dead;
And what will you do now? How will you live?
SON As birds do, mother.
LADY MACDUFF What, with worms and flies?
SON With what I get, I mean; and so do they.
LADY MACDUFF Poor bird! thou'dst never fear the net nor lime,
The pitfall nor the gin.
SON Why should I, mother? Poor birds they are not set for.
My father is not dead, for all your saying.
LADY MACDUFF Yes, he is dead. How wilt thou do for a father?
SON Nay, how will you do for a husband?
LADY MACDUFF Why, I can buy me twenty at any market.
SON Then you'll buy 'em to sell again.
LADY MACDUFF Thou speak'st with all thy wit; and yet, i' faith,
With wit enough for thee.
SON Was my father a traitor, mother?
LADY MACDUFF Ay, that he was.
SON What is a traitor?
LADY MACDUFF Why, one that swears and lies.
SON And be all traitors that do so?
LADY MACDUFF Every one that does so is a traitor, and must be hang'd.
SON And must they all be hang'd that swear and lie?
LADY MACDUFF Every one.
SON Who must hang them?
LADY MACDUFF Why, the honest men.
SON Then the liars and swearers are fools; for there are liars and swearers enow to beat the honest men and hang up them.
LADY MACDUFF Now, God help thee, poor monkey! But how wilt thou do for a father?
SON If he were dead, you'd weep for him; if you would not, it were a good sign that I should quickly have a new father.
LADY MACDUFF Poor prattler, how thou talk'st!

Enter a Messenger.

MESSENGER Bless you, fair dame! I am not to you known,
Though in your state of honour I am perfect.
I doubt some danger does approach you nearly.
If you will take a homely man's advice,
Be not found here; hence, with your little ones.
To fright you thus, methinks, I am too savage;
To do worse to you were fell cruelty,
Which is too nigh your person. Heaven preserve you!
I dare abide no longer. [*Exit.*
LADY MACDUFF Whither should I fly?
I have done no harm. But I remember now
I am in this earthly world, where to do harm
Is often laudable, to do good sometime
Accounted dangerous folly. Why then, alas,
Do I put up that womanly defence
To say I have done no harm?

Enter Murderers.

What are these faces?
1 MURDERER Where is your husband?
LADY MACDUFF I hope, in no place so unsanctified
Where such as thou mayst find him.
1 MURDERER He's a traitor.
SON Thou liest, thou shag-ear'd villain.
1 MURDERER What, you egg? [*Stabbing him.*
Young fry of treachery!
SON He has kill'd me, mother.
Run away, I pray you. [*Dies.*
[*Exit Lady Macduff, crying* 'Murder!'

SCENE III. *England. Before King Edward's palace.*

Enter MALCOLM and MACDUFF.

MALCOLM Let us seek out some desolate shade, and there
Weep our sad bosoms empty.
MACDUFF Let us rather
Hold fast the mortal sword, and like good men
Bestride our down-fall'n birthdom. Each new morn
New widows howl, new orphans cry; new sorrows
Strike heaven on the face, that it resounds
As if it felt with Scotland and yell'd out
Like syllable of dolour.
MALCOLM What I believe, I'll wail;
What know, believe; and what I can redress,
As I shall find the time to friend, I will.
What you have spoke, it may be so perchance.
This tyrant, whose sole name blisters our tongues,
Was once thought honest; you have lov'd him well;
He hath not touch'd you yet. I am young; but something
You may deserve of him through me; and wisdom
To offer up a weak, poor, innocent lamb
T' appease an angry god.
MACDUFF I am not treacherous.
MALCOLM But Macbeth is.
A good and virtuous nature may recoil
In an imperial charge. But I shall crave your pardon;
That which you are, my thoughts cannot transpose;
Angels are bright still, though the brightest fell.
Though all things foul would wear the brows of grace,
Yet grace must still look so.
MACDUFF I have lost my hopes.
MALCOLM Perchance even there where I did find my doubts.
Why in that rawness left you wife and child,
Those precious motives, those strong knots of love,
Without leave-taking? I pray you,
Let not my jealousies be your dishonours,
But mine own safeties. You may be rightly just,
Whatever I shall think.
MACDUFF Bleed, bleed, poor country.
Great tyranny, lay thou thy basis sure,
For goodness dare not check thee. Wear thou thy wrongs,
The title is affeer'd. Fare thee well, lord.
I would not be the villain that thou think'st
For the whole space that's in the tyrant's grasp
And the rich East to boot.
MALCOLM Be not offended.
I speak not as in absolute fear of you.
I think our country sinks beneath the yoke;
It weeps, it bleeds; and each new day a gash
Is added to her wounds. I think withal
There would be hands uplifted in my right;
And here, from gracious England, have I offer
Of goodly thousands. But, for all this,
When I shall tread upon the tyrant's head,
Or wear it on my sword, yet my poor country
Shall have more vices than it had before;
More suffer, and more sundry ways than ever,
By him that shall succeed.
MACDUFF What should he be?
MALCOLM It is myself I mean; in whom I know
All the particulars of vice so grafted
That, when they shall be open'd, black Macbeth
Will seem as pure as snow; and the poor state
Esteem him as a lamb, being compar'd
With my confineless harms.
MACDUFF Not in the legions
Of horrid hell can come a devil more damn'd
In evils to top Macbeth.
MALCOLM I grant him bloody,
Luxurious, avaricious, false, deceitful,
Sudden, malicious, smacking of every sin
That has a name; but there's no bottom, none,
In my voluptuousness. Your wives, your daughters,
Your matrons, and your maids, could not fill up
The cistern of my lust; and my desire
All continent impediments would o'erbear
That did oppose my will. Better Macbeth
Than such an one to reign.
MACDUFF Boundless intemperance
In nature is a tyranny; it hath been
Th' untimely emptying of the happy throne
And fall of many kings. But fear not yet
To take upon you what is yours. You may
Convey your pleasures in a spacious plenty,
And yet seem cold, the time you may so hoodwink.
We have willing dames enough; there cannot be
That vulture in you to devour so many
As will to greatness dedicate themselves,
Finding it so inclin'd.
MALCOLM With this there grows
In my most ill-compos'd affection such
A stanchless avarice that, were I King,
I should cut off the nobles for their lands,
Desire his jewels, and this other's house;
And my more-having would be as a sauce

To make me hunger more, that I should forge
Quarrels unjust against the good and loyal,
Destroying them for wealth.
MACDUFF This avarice
Sticks deeper, grows with more pernicious root
Than summer-seeming lust; and it hath been
The sword of our slain kings. Yet do not fear;
Scotland hath foisons to fill up your will
Of your mere own. All these are portable,
With other graces weigh'd.
MALCOLM But I have none. The king-becoming graces,
As justice, verity, temp'rance, stableness,
Bounty, perseverance, mercy, lowliness,
Devotion, patience, courage, fortitude,
I have no relish of them; but abound
In the division of each several crime,
Acting it many ways. Nay, had I pow'r, I should
Pour the sweet milk of concord into hell,
Uproar the universal peace, confound
All unity on earth.
MACDUFF O Scotland, Scotland!
MALCOLM If such a one be fit to govern, speak.
I am as I have spoken.
MACDUFF Fit to govern!
No, not to live! O nation miserable,
With an untitled tyrant bloody-scept'red,
When shalt thou see thy wholesome days again,
Since that the truest issue of thy throne
By his own interdiction stands accurs'd
And does blaspheme his breed? Thy royal father
Was a most sainted king; the queen that bore thee,
Oft'ner upon her knees than on her feet,
Died every day she liv'd. Fare thee well!
These evils thou repeat'st upon thyself
Hath banish'd me from Scotland. O my breast,
Thy hope ends here!
MALCOLM Macduff, this noble passion,
Child of integrity, hath from my soul
Wip'd the black scruples, reconcil'd my thoughts
To thy good truth and honour. Devilish Macbeth
By many of these trains hath sought to win me
Into his power; and modest wisdom plucks me
From over-credulous haste. But God above
Deal between thee and me; for even now
I put myself to thy direction, and
Unspeak mine own detraction, here abjure
The taints and blames I laid upon myself
For strangers to my nature. I am yet
Unknown to woman, never was forsworn,
Scarcely have coveted what was mine own,
At no time broke my faith, would not betray
The devil to his fellow, and delight
No less in truth than life. My first false speaking
Was this upon myself. What I am truly
Is thine and my poor country's to command:
Whither indeed, before thy here-approach,
Old Siward with ten thousand warlike men
Already at a point was setting forth.
Now we'll together; and the chance of goodness
Be like our warranted quarrel! Why are you silent?
MACDUFF Such welcome and unwelcome things at once
'Tis hard to reconcile.

Enter a Doctor.

MALCOLM Well; more anon. Comes the King forth, I pray you?
DOCTOR Ay, sir. There are a crew of wretched souls
That stay his cure. Their malady convinces
The great assay of art; but at his touch,
Such sanctity hath heaven given his hand,
They presently amend.
MALCOLM I thank you, doctor. [*Exit Doctor.*
MACDUFF What's the disease he means?
MALCOLM 'Tis called the evil:
A most miraculous work in this good king;
Which often since my here-remain in England
I have seen him do. How he solicits heaven,
Himself best knows; but strangely-visited people,
All swoln and ulcerous, pitiful to the eye,
The mere despair of surgery, he cures,
Hanging a golden stamp about their necks,
Put on with holy prayers; and 'tis spoken,
To the succeeding royalty he leaves
The healing benediction. With this strange virtue
He hath a heavenly gift of prophecy;
And sundry blessings hang about his throne
That speak him full of grace.

Enter ROSS.

MACDUFF See, who comes here?
MALCOLM My countryman; but yet I know him not.
MACDUFF My ever gentle cousin, welcome hither.
MALCOLM I know him now. Good God betimes remove
The means that makes us strangers!
ROSS Sir, amen.
MACDUFF Stands Scotland where it did?
ROSS Alas, poor country,
Almost afraid to know itself! It cannot
Be call'd our mother, but our grave; where nothing,
But who knows nothing, is once seen to smile;
Where sighs, and groans, and shrieks, that rent the air,

Are made, not mark'd; where violent sorrow seems
A modern ecstasy; the dead man's knell
Is there scarce ask'd for who; and good men's lives
Expire before the flowers in their caps,
Dying or ere they sicken.
MACDUFF O, relation
Too nice, and yet too true!
MALCOLM What's the newest grief?
ROSS That of an hour's age doth hiss the speaker:
Each minute teems a new one.
MACDUFF How does my wife?
ROSS Why, well.
MACDUFF And all my children?
ROSS Well too.
MACDUFF The tyrant has not batter'd at their peace?
ROSS No; they were well at peace when I did leave 'em.
MACDUFF Be not a niggard of your speech. How goes't?
ROSS When I came hither to transport the tidings,
Which I have heavily borne, there ran a rumour
Of many worthy fellows that were out;
Which was to my belief witness'd the rather
For that I saw the tyrant's power afoot.
Now is the time of help; your eye in Scotland
Would create soldiers, make our women fight,
To doff their dire distresses.
MALCOLM Be't their comfort
We are coming thither. Gracious England hath
Lent us good Siward and ten thousand men –
An older and a better soldier none
That Christendom gives out.
ROSS Would I could answer
This comfort with the like! But I have words
That would be howl'd out in the desert air,
Where hearing should not latch them.
MACDUFF What concern they?
The general cause, or is it a fee-grief
Due to some single breast?
ROSS No mind that's honest
But in it shares some woe, though the main part
Pertains to you alone.
MACDUFF If it be mine,
Keep it not from me; quickly let me have it.
ROSS Let not your ears despise my tongue for ever,
Which shall possess them with the heaviest sound
That ever yet they heard.
MACDUFF Humh! I guess at it.
ROSS Your castle is surpris'd; your wife and babes
Savagely slaughter'd. To relate the manner,
Were, on the quarry of these murder'd deer,
To add the death of you.
MALCOLM Merciful heaven!
What, man! Ne'er pull your hat upon your brows;
Give sorrow words. The grief that does not speak
Whispers the o'erfraught heart and bids it break.
MACDUFF My children too?
ROSS Wife, children, servants, all
That could be found.
MACDUFF And I must be from thence!
My wife kill'd too?
ROSS I have said.
MALCOLM Be comforted.
Let's make us med'cines of our great revenge
To cure this deadly grief.
MACDUFF He has no children. All my pretty ones?
Did you say all? O hell-kite! All?
What, all my pretty chickens and their dam
At one fell swoop?
MALCOLM Dispute it like a man.
MACDUFF I shall do so;
But I must also feel it as a man.
I cannot but remember such things were
That were most precious to me. Did heaven look on,
And would not take their part? Sinful Macduff,
They were all struck for thee – nought that I am;
Not for their own demerits, but for mine,
Fell slaughter on their souls. Heaven rest them now!
MALCOLM Be this the whetstone of your sword. Let grief
Convert to anger; blunt not the heart, enrage it.
MACDUFF O, I could play the woman with mine eyes
And braggart with my tongue! But, gentle heavens,
Cut short all intermission; front to front
Bring thou this fiend of Scotland and myself;
Within my sword's length set him; if he scape,
Heaven forgive him too!
MALCOLM This tune goes manly.
Come, go we to the King. Our power is ready;
Our lack is nothing but our leave. Macbeth
Is ripe for shaking, and the pow'rs above
Put on their instruments. Receive what cheer you may;
The night is long that never finds the day.
[*Exeunt.*

ACT FIVE

SCENE I. *Dunsinane. Macbeth's castle.*

Enter a Doctor of Physic and a Waiting-Gentlewoman.

DOCTOR I have two nights watch'd with you, but can perceive no truth in your report. When was it she last walk'd?

GENTLEWOMAN Since his Majesty went into the field, I have seen her rise from her bed, throw her nightgown upon her, unlock her closet, take forth paper, fold it, write upon't, read it, afterwards seal it, and again return to bed; yet all this while in a most fast sleep.

DOCTOR A great perturbation in nature, to receive at once the benefit of sleep and do the effects of watching! In this slumb'ry agitation, besides her walking and other actual performances, what, at any time, have you heard her say?

GENTLEWOMAN That, sir, which I will not report after her.

DOCTOR You may to me; and 'tis most meet you should.

GENTLEWOMAN Neither to you nor any one, having no witness to confirm my speech.

Enter LADY MACBETH, with a taper.

Lo you, here she comes! This is her very guise; and, upon my life, fast asleep. Observe her; stand close.

DOCTOR How came she by that light?

GENTLEWOMAN Why, it stood by her. She has light by her continually; 'tis her command.

DOCTOR You see her eyes are open.

GENTLEWOMAN Ay, but their sense is shut.

DOCTOR What is it she does now? Look how she rubs her hands.

GENTLEWOMAN It is an accustomed action with her, to seem thus washing her hands; I have known her continue in this a quarter of an hour.

LADY MACBETH Yet here's a spot.

DOCTOR Hark, she speaks. I will set down what comes from her, to satisfy my remembrance the more strongly.

LADY MACBETH Out, damned spot! out, I say! One, two; why then 'tis time to do't. Hell is murky. Fie, my lord, fie! a soldier, and afeard? What need we fear who knows it, when none can call our pow'r to account? Yet who would have thought the old man to have had so much blood in him?

DOCTOR Do you mark that?

LADY MACBETH The Thane of Fife had a wife; where is she now? What, will these hands ne'er be clean? No more o' that, my lord, no more o' that; you mar all with this starting.

DOCTOR Go to, go to; you have known what you should not.

GENTLEWOMAN She has spoke what she should not, I am sure of that. Heaven knows what she has known.

LADY MACBETH Here's the smell of the blood still. All the perfumes of Arabia will not sweeten this little hand. Oh, oh, oh!

DOCTOR What a sigh is there! The heart is sorely charg'd.

GENTLEWOMAN I would not have such a heart in my bosom for the dignity of the whole body.

DOCTOR Well, well, well.

GENTLEWOMAN Pray God it be, sir.

DOCTOR This disease is beyond my practice. Yet I have known those which have walk'd in their sleep who have died holily in their beds.

LADY MACBETH Wash your hands, put on your nightgown, look not so pale. I tell you yet again, Banquo's buried; he cannot come out on's grave.

DOCTOR Even so?

LADY MACBETH To bed, to bed; there's knocking at the gate. Come, come, come, come, give me your hand. What's done cannot be undone. To bed, to bed, to bed. [*Exit.*

DOCTOR Will she go now to bed?

GENTLEWOMAN Directly.

DOCTOR Foul whisp'rings are abroad. Unnatural deeds
Do breed unnatural troubles; infected minds
To their deaf pillows will discharge their secrets.
More needs she the divine than the physician.
God, God forgive us all. Look after her;
Remove from her the means of all annoyance,
And still keep eyes upon her. So, good night.
My mind she has mated, and amaz'd my sight.
I think, but dare not speak.

GENTLEWOMAN Good night, good doctor.

[*Exeunt.*

SCENE II. *The country near Dunsinane.*

Drum and colours. Enter MENTEITH, CAITHNESS, ANGUS, LENNOX, and Soldiers.

MENTEITH The English pow'r is near, led on by Malcolm,
His uncle Siward, and the good Macduff.
Revenges burn in them; for their dear causes
Would to the bleeding and the grim alarm
Excite the mortified man.

ANGUS Near Birnam wood
Shall we well meet them; that way are they coming.

CAITHNESS Who knows if Donalbain be with his brother?

LENNOX For certain, sir, he is not; I have a file
Of all the gentry. There is Siward's son,
And many unrough youths that even now
Protest their first of manhood.

MENTEITH What does the tyrant?

CAITHNESS Great Dunsinane he strongly fortifies.
Some say he's mad; others, that lesser hate him,
Do call it valiant fury; but for certain
He cannot buckle his distemper'd cause
Within the belt of rule.

ANGUS Now does he feel
His secret murders sticking on his hands;
Now minutely revolts upbraid his faith-breach;
Those he commands move only in command,
Nothing in love. Now does he feel his title
Hang loose about him, like a giant's robe
Upon a dwarfish thief.

MENTEITH Who then shall blame
His pester'd senses to recoil and start,
When all that is within him does condemn
Itself for being there?

CAITHNESS Well, march we on
To give obedience where 'tis truly ow'd.
Meet we the med'cine of the sickly weal;
And with him pour we in our country's purge
Each drop of us.

LENNOX Or so much as it needs
To dew the sovereign flower and drown the weeds.
Make we our march towards Birnam.

[Exeunt, marching.

SCENE III. *Dunsinane. Macbeth's castle.*

Enter MACBETH, Doctor, and Attendants.

MACBETH Bring me no more reports; let them fly all.
Till Birnam wood remove to Dunsinane
I cannot taint with fear. What's the boy Malcolm?
Was he not born of woman? The spirits that know
All mortal consequences have pronounc'd me thus:
'Fear not, Macbeth; no man that's born of woman
Shall e'er have power upon thee'. Then fly, false thanes,
And mingle with the English epicures.
The mind I sway by and the heart I bear
Shall never sag with doubt nor shake with fear.

Enter Servant.

The devil damn thee black, thou cream-fac'd loon!
Where got'st thou that goose look?

SERVANT There is ten thousand –

MACBETH Geese, villain?

SERVANT Soldiers, sir.

MACBETH Go, prick thy face, and over-red thy fear,
Thou lily-liver'd boy. What soldiers, patch?
Death of thy soul! Those linen cheeks of thine
Are counsellors to fear. What soldiers, whey-face?

SERVANT The English force, so please you.

MACBETH Take thy face hence. *[Exit Servant.*
Seyton! – I am sick at heart,
When I behold – Seyton, I say! – This push
Will cheer me ever, or disseat me now.
I have liv'd long enough. My way of life
Is fall'n into the sear, the yellow leaf;
And that which should accompany old age,
As honour, love, obedience, troops of friends,
I must not look to have; but, in their stead,
Curses not loud but deep, mouth-honour, breath,
Which the poor heart would fain deny, and dare not.
Seyton!

Enter SEYTON.

SEYTON What's your gracious pleasure?

MACBETH What news more?

SEYTON All is confirm'd, my lord, which was reported.

MACBETH I'll fight till from my bones my flesh be hack'd.
Give me my armour.

SEYTON 'Tis not needed yet.

MACBETH I'll put it on.
Send out moe horses, skirr the country round;
Hang those that talk of fear. Give me mine armour.
How does your patient, doctor?

DOCTOR Not so sick, my lord,
As she is troubled with thick-coming fancies
That keep her from her rest.

MACBETH Cure her of that.
Canst thou not minister to a mind diseas'd,
Pluck from the memory a rooted sorrow,
Raze out the written troubles of the brain,
And with some sweet oblivious antidote
Cleanse the stuff'd bosom of that perilous stuff
Which weighs upon the heart?

DOCTOR Therein the patient
Must minister to himself.

MACBETH Throw physic to the dogs – I'll none of it.
Come, put mine armour on; give me my staff.
Seyton, send out. Doctor, the thanes fly from me.

Come, sir, dispatch. If thou couldst, doctor, cast
The water of my land, find her disease,
And purge it to a sound and pristine health,
I would applaud thee to the very echo,
That should applaud again. – Pull't off, I say. –
What rhubarb, senna, or what purgative drug,
Would scour these English hence? Hear'st thou of them?

DOCTOR Ay, my good lord. Your royal preparation
Makes us hear something.

MACBETH Bring it after me.
I will not be afraid of death and bane
Till Birnam Forest come to Dunsinane.

[Exeunt all but the Doctor.

DOCTOR Were I from Dunsinane away and clear,
Profit again should hardly draw me here.

[Exit.

SCENE IV. *Before Birnam Wood.*

Drum and colours. Enter MALCOLM, SIWARD, MACDUFF, Siward's Son, MENTEITH, CAITHNESS, ANGUS, LENNOX, ROSS, and Soldiers, marching.

MALCOLM Cousins, I hope the days are near at hand
That chambers will be safe.

MENTEITH We doubt it nothing.

SIWARD What wood is this before us?

MENTEITH The wood of Birnam.

MALCOLM Let every soldier hew him down a bough
And bear't before him; thereby shall we shadow
The numbers of our host, and make discovery
Err in report of us.

SOLDIERS It shall be done.

SIWARD We learn no other but the confident tyrant
Keeps still in Dunsinane, and will endure
Our setting down before't.

MALCOLM 'Tis his main hope;
For where there is advantage to be given,
Both more and less have given him the revolt;
And none serve with him but constrained things,
Whose hearts are absent too.

MACDUFF Let our just censures
Attend the true event, and put we on
Industrious soldiership.

SIWARD The time approaches
That will with due decision make us know
What we shall say we have, and what we owe.
Thoughts speculative their unsure hopes relate,
But certain issue strokes must arbitrate;
Towards which advance the war.

[Exeunt, marching.

SCENE V. *Dunsinane. Macbeth's castle.*

Enter MACBETH, SEYTON, and Soldiers, with drum and colours.

MACBETH Hang out our banners on the outward walls;
The cry is still 'They come'. Our castle's strength
Will laugh a siege to scorn. Here let them lie
Till famine and the ague eat them up.
Were they not forc'd with those that should be ours,
We might have met them dareful, beard to beard,
And beat them backward home.

[A cry within of women.

What is that noise?

SEYTON It is the cry of women, my good lord.

[Exit.

MACBETH I have almost forgot the taste of fears.
The time has been my senses would have cool'd
To hear a night-shriek, and my fell of hair
Would at a dismal treatise rouse and stir
As life were in't. I have supp'd full with horrors;
Direness, familiar to my slaughterous thoughts,
Cannot once start me.

Re-enter SEYTON.

Wherefore was that cry?

SEYTON The Queen, my lord, is dead.

MACBETH She should have died hereafter;
There would have been a time for such a word.
To-morrow, and to-morrow, and to-morrow,
Creeps in this petty pace from day to day
To the last syllable of recorded time,
And all our yesterdays have lighted fools
The way to dusty death. Out, out, brief candle!
Life's but a walking shadow, a poor player,
That struts and frets his hour upon the stage,
And then is heard no more; it is a tale
Told by an idiot, full of sound and fury,
Signifying nothing.

Enter a Messenger.

Thou com'st to use thy tongue; thy story quickly.

MESSENGER Gracious my lord,
I should report that which I say I saw,
But know not how to do't.

MACBETH Well, say, sir.

MESSENGER As I did stand my watch upon the hill,
I look'd toward Birnam, and anon me-thought
The wood began to move.

MACBETH Liar and slave!

MESSENGER Let me endure your wrath, if't be not so.
Within this three mile may you see it coming;
I say, a moving grove.
MACBETH If thou speak'st false,
Upon the next tree shalt thou hang alive,
Till famine cling thee. If thy speech be sooth,
I care not if thou dost for me as much.
I pull in resolution, and begin
To doubt th' equivocation of the fiend
That lies like truth. 'Fear not, till Birnam wood
Do come to Dunsinane.' And now a wood
Comes toward Dunsinane. Arm, arm, and out.
If this which he avouches does appear,
There is nor flying hence nor tarrying here.
I gin to be aweary of the sun,
And wish th' estate o' th' world were now undone.
Ring the alarum bell. Blow wind, come wrack;
At least we'll die with harness on our back.
[Exeunt.

SCENE VI. *Dunsinane. Before the castle.*

Drum and colours. Enter MALCOLM, SIWARD, MACDUFF, and their Army with boughs.

MALCOLM Now near enough; your leavy screens throw down,
And show like those you are. You, worthy uncle,
Shall with my cousin, your right noble son,
Lead our first battle; worthy Macduff and we
Shall take upon's what else remains to do,
According to our order.
SIWARD Fare you well.
Do we but find the tyrant's power to-night,
Let us be beaten, if we cannot fight.
MACDUFF Make all our trumpets speak; give them all breath,
Those clamorous harbingers of blood and death.
[Exeunt.

SCENE VII. *Another part of the field.*

Enter MACBETH.

MACBETH They have tied me to a stake; I cannot fly,
But bear-like I must fight the course. What's he
That was not born of woman? Such a one
Am I to fear, or none.

Enter young SIWARD.

YOUNG SIWARD What is thy name?
MACBETH Thou'lt be afraid to hear it.
YOUNG SIWARD No; though thou call'st thyself a hotter name
Than any is in hell.
MACBETH My name's Macbeth.
YOUNG SIWARD The devil himself could not pronounce a title
More hateful to mine ear.
MACBETH No, nor more fearful.
YOUNG SIWARD Thou liest, abhorred tyrant; with my sword
I'll prove the lie thou speak'st.
[Fight, and young Siward slain.

MACBETH Thou wast born of woman.
But swords I smile at, weapons laugh to scorn,
Brandish'd by man that's of a woman born.
[Exit.

Alarums. Enter MACDUFF.

MACDUFF That way the noise is. Tyrant, show thy face.
If thou beest slain and with no stroke of mine,
My wife and children's ghosts will haunt me still.
I cannot strike at wretched kerns whose arms
Are hir'd to bear their staves; either thou, Macbeth,
Or else my sword with an unbattered edge
I sheathe again undeeded. There thou shouldst be;
By this great clatter, one of greatest note
Seems bruited. Let me find him, Fortune,
And more I beg not. *[Exit. Alarums.*

Enter MALCOLM and old SIWARD.

SIWARD This way, my lord. The castle's gently rend'red;
The tyrant's people on both sides do fight;
The noble thanes do bravely in the war;
The day almost itself professes yours,
And little is to do.
MALCOLM We have met with foes
That strike beside us.
SIWARD Enter, sir, the castle.
[Exeunt. Alarum.

SCENE VIII. *Another part of the field.*

Enter MACBETH.

MACBETH Why should I play the Roman fool, and die
On mine own sword? Whiles I see lives, the gashes
Do better upon them.

Enter MACDUFF.

MACDUFF Turn, hell-hound, turn.
MACBETH Of all men else I have avoided thee.
But get thee back; my soul is too much charg'd

With blood of thine already.

MACDUFF I have no words –
My voice is in my sword: thou bloodier villain
Than terms can give thee out. [*Fight. Alarum.*

MACBETH Thou losest labour.
As easy mayst thou the intrenchant air
With thy keen sword impress as make me bleed.
Let fall thy blade on vulnerable crests;
I bear a charmed life, which must not yield
To one of woman born.

MACDUFF Despair thy charm;
And let the angel whom thou still hast serv'd
Tell thee Macduff was from his mother's womb
Untimely ripp'd.

MACBETH Accursed be that tongue that tells me so,
For it hath cow'd my better part of man;
And be these juggling fiends no more believ'd
That palter with us in a double sense,
That keep the word of promise to our ear,
And break it to our hope! I'll not fight with thee.

MACDUFF Then yield thee, coward,
And live to be the show and gaze o' th' time.
We'll have thee, as our rarer monsters are,
Painted upon a pole, and underwrit
'Here may you see the tyrant'.

MACBETH I will not yield,
To kiss the ground before young Malcolm's feet
And to be baited with the rabble's curse.
Though Birnam wood be come to Dunsinane,
And thou oppos'd, being of no woman born,
Yet I will try the last. Before my body
I throw my warlike shield. Lay on, Macduff;
And damn'd be him that first cries 'Hold, enough!'
[*Exeunt, fighting. Alarums.*

Retreat and flourish. Enter, with drum and colours, MALCOLM, SIWARD, ROSS, LENNOX, ANGUS, CAITHNESS, MENTEITH, and Soldiers.

MALCOLM I would the friends we miss were safe arriv'd.

SIWARD Some must go off; and yet, by these I see,
So great a day as this is cheaply bought.

MALCOLM Macduff is missing, and your noble son.

ROSS Your son, my lord, has paid a soldier's debt:
He only liv'd but till he was a man;
The which no sooner had his prowess confirm'd
In the unshrinking station where he fought,
But like a man he died.

SIWARD Then he is dead?

ROSS Ay, and brought off the field. Your cause of sorrow
Must not be measur'd by his worth, for then
It hath no end.

SIWARD Had he his hurts before?

ROSS Ay, on the front.

SIWARD Why, then, God's soldier be he!
Had I as many sons as I have hairs,
I would not wish them to a fairer death.
And so his knell is knoll'd.

MALCOLM He's worth more sorrow,
And that I'll spend for him.

SIWARD He's worth no more.
They say he parted well and paid his score;
And so, God be with him! Here comes newer comfort.

Re-enter MACDUFF, with MACBETH'S head.

MACDUFF Hail, King! for so thou art. Behold where stands
Th' usurper's cursed head. The time is free.
I see thee compass'd with thy kingdom's pearl
That speak my salutation in their minds;
Whose voices I desire aloud with mine –
Hail, King of Scotland!

ALL Hail, King of Scotland! [*Flourish.*

MALCOLM We shall not spend a large expense of time
Before we reckon with your several loves,
And make us even with you. My Thanes and kinsmen,
Henceforth be Earls, the first that ever Scotland
In such an honour nam'd. What's more to do,
Which would be planted newly with the time –
As calling home our exil'd friends abroad
That fled the snares of watchful tyranny;
Producing forth the cruel ministers
Of this dead butcher, and his fiend-like queen,
Who, as 'tis thought, by self and violent hands
Took off her life – this, and what needful else
That calls upon us, by the grace of Grace,
We will perform in measure, time, and place.
So thanks to all at once and to each one,
Whom we invite to see us crown'd at Scone.
[*Flourish. Exeunt.*

Hamlet

Introduction by STUART GILLESPIE

Hamlet seems always to have been the most discussed work of literature in the world. The range of possible responses runs from Tolstoy's famously perverse dismissal of the play as unintelligible (Tolstoy, 1937), to the most far-reaching claims for its insight into the Nature of the Cosmos. Understanding of it has been sought from analyses of Hamlet's personality (in our century often in terms of Freudian psychoanalytical theory); of the play's place in a supposed tradition of revenge plays; of Elizabethan pneumatology (the study of ghosts and other spirits); of Shakespeare's biography; and along other routes too numerous even to mention. It has been adapted as play, film, novel, story and cartoon, countless times throughout the world by writers major, minor, and somewhere in between. It has been classed as a tragedy, a 'problem play', a 'revenge play', and seen as entirely *sui generis*. Commentators speak unanimously of its being Shakespeare's most enigmatic work – 'the most problematic play ever written by Shakespeare or any other playwright' (Levin, 1956). Like a black hole, it has tended to assimilate to itself all questions asked of it, so that it seems to anticipate the most bizarre readings and even to sponsor mutally incompatible ones simultaneously. It can be 'insistently incoherent and just as insistently coherent' (Booth, 1969); the audience is drawn into its contradictions, deconstructing and then reconstructing the paradoxes (see Calderwood, 1983). As time has familiarised the play to readers and audiences throughout the world, its performance has become a hallowed ritual – yet this is a work which by Elizabethan standards is remarkable and unconventional, notably in its realism.

In descending to such mundane matters as what happens in the play, readers coming to it for the first time will find themselves pondering many questions. Interpretation of Acts 1–3 involves issues, for example, concerning the nature of the Ghost (is Hamlet's mission divinely or demonically inspired?); the justice of his view of Claudius; whether or not Claudius sees, or understands, the play in Act 3 Scene 2; and whether Hamlet does or does not mistake Polonius for Claudius in Act 3 Scene 4. Readings of later parts turn on, amongst other things, how far Hamlet's madness is considered to be real and how far feigned; whether Fortinbras is seen as an unruly hot-head or a worthy heir to the throne; and whether the Hamlet of Act 5 is the familiar part-failure of the past or the repository of 'a mysterious and beautiful disinterestedness' (Bloom, 1989). All this is to say nothing of the by now ancient question, 'Why does Hamlet delay in killing Claudius?', a question widely posed, frequently but variously answered, and now coming to seem less than useful.

But it would be wrong to lay the stress exclusively on the 'problems', the 'questions', the 'mystery' of *Hamlet*. Though nothing is more certain than that they will continue to engender debate, the play will be read and watched for other reasons. The 'particular excellence' of *Hamlet* was for Johnson its 'variety', its mingling of merriment and solemnity, frivolity and horror (Johnson, 1765). Something of this is echoed in Tillyard's sense that 'simply as a play of things happening, of one event being bred out of another, and of each event being described with appropriate and unwearied brilliance, *Hamlet* is supreme' (Tillyard, 1950). Superlatives seem to come cheap with this play, but *Hamlet*'s readers will undoubtedly continue to find it 'the world's most sheerly entertaining tragedy, the cleverest, perhaps even the funniest' (Everett, 1989); they will also find Shakespeare's power to entertain uniquely combined in it with his power to mean.

Hamlet, Prince of Denmark

DRAMATIS PERSONAE

CLAUDIUS
King of Denmark

HAMLET
son to the former and nephew to the present King

POLONIUS
Lord Chamberlain

HORATIO
friend to Hamlet
LAERTES
son to Polonius

VOLTEMAND, CORNELIUS, ROSENCRANTZ, GUILDENSTERN, OSRIC, *A Gentleman*
courtiers
A Gentleman
A Priest

MARCELLUS, BERNARDO
officers

FRANCISCO
a soldier
REYNALDO
servant to Polonius
Players
Two Clowns grave-diggers
FORTINBRAS
Prince of Norway
A Norwegian Captain
English Ambassadors
GERTRUDE
Queen of Denmark, and mother of Hamlet
OPHELIA
daughter to Polonius
Ghost of Hamlet's Father
Lords, Ladies, Officers, Soldiers, Sailors, Messengers, and Attendants.

THE SCENE: DENMARK.

ACT ONE

SCENE I. *Elsinore. The guard-platform of the Castle.*

FRANCISCO at his post. Enter to him BERNARDO.

BERNARDO Who's there?
FRANCISCO Nay, answer me. Stand and unfold yourself.
BERNARDO Long live the King!
FRANCISCO Bernardo?
BERNARDO He.
FRANCISCO You come most carefully upon your hour.
BERNARDO 'Tis now struck twelve; get thee to bed, Francisco.
FRANCISCO For this relief much thanks. 'Tis bitter cold,
And I am sick at heart.
BERNARDO Have you had quiet guard?
FRANCISCO Not a mouse stirring.
BERNARDO Well, good night.
If you do meet Horatio and Marcellus,
The rivals of my watch, bid them make haste.

Enter HORATIO and MARCELLUS.

FRANCISCO I think I hear them. Stand, ho! Who is there?
HORATIO Friends to this ground.
MARCELLUS And liegemen to the Dane.
FRANCISCO Give you good night.
MARCELLUS O, farewell, honest soldier!
Who hath reliev'd you?
FRANCISCO Bernardo hath my place.
Give you good night. [*Exit.*
MARCELLUS Holla, Bernado!
BERNARDO Say –
What, is Horatio there?
HORATIO A piece of him.
BERNARDO Welcome, Horatio; welcome, good Marcellus.
HORATIO What, has this thing appear'd again to-night?
BERNARDO I have seen nothing.
MARCELLUS Horatio says 'tis but our fantasy,
And will not let belief take hold of him
Touching this dreaded sight, twice seen of us;
Therefore I have entreated him along
With us to watch the minutes of this night,
That, if again this apparition come,
He may approve our eyes and speak to it.
HORATIO Tush, tush, 'twill not appear.
BERNARDO Sit down awhile,
And let us once again assail your ears,
That are so fortified against our story,
What we have two nights seen.
HORATIO Well, sit we down,
And let us hear Bernardo speak of this.
BERNARDO Last night of all,
When yond same star that's westward from the pole
Had made his course t' illume that part of heaven
Where now it burns, Marcellus and myself,

The bell then beating one –
Enter Ghost.
MARCELLUS Peace, break thee off; look where it comes again.
BERNARDO In the same figure, like the King that's dead.
MARCELLUS Thou art a scholar; speak to it, Horatio.
BERNARDO Looks 'a not like the King? Mark it, Horatio.
HORATIO Most like. It harrows me with fear and wonder.
BERNARDO It would be spoke to.
MARCELLUS Question it, Horatio.
HORATIO What art thou that usurp'st this time of night
Together with that fair and warlike form
In which the majesty of buried Denmark
Did sometimes march? By heaven I charge thee, speak!
MARCELLUS It is offended.
BERNARDO See, it stalks away.
HORATIO Stay! speak, speak! I charge thee, speak! [*Exit Ghost.*
MARCELLUS 'Tis gone, and will not answer.
BERNARDO How now, Horatio! You tremble and look pale.
Is not this something more than fantasy?
What think you on't?
HORATIO Before my God, I might not this believe
Without the sensible and true avouch
Of mine own eyes.
MARCELLUS Is it not like the King?
HORATIO As thou art to thyself:
Such was the very armour he had on
When he the ambitious Norway combated;
So frown'd he once when, in an angry parle,
He smote the sledded Polacks on the ice.
'Tis strange.
MARCELLUS Thus twice before, and jump at this dead hour,
With martial stalk hath he gone by our watch.
HORATIO In what particular thought to work I know not;
But, in the gross and scope of mine opinion,
This bodes some strange eruption to our state.
MARCELLUS Good now, sit down, and tell me, he that knows,
Why this same strict and most observant watch
So nightly toils the subject of the land;
And why such daily cast of brazen cannon,
And foreign mart for implements of war;
Why such impress of shipwrights, whose sore task
Does not divide the Sunday from the week;
What might be toward, that this sweaty haste
Doth make the night joint-labourer with the day:
Who is't that can inform me?
HORATIO That can I;
At least, the whisper goes so. Our last king,
Whose image even but now appear'd to us,
Was, as you know, by Fortinbras of Norway,
Thereto prick'd on by a most emulate pride,
Dar'd to the combat; in which our valiant Hamlet –
For so this side of our known world esteem'd him –
Did slay this Fortinbras; who, by a seal'd compact,
Well ratified by law and heraldry,
Did forfeit, with his life, all those his lands
Which he stood seiz'd of, to the conqueror;
Against the which a moiety competent
Was gaged by our king; which had return'd
To the inheritance of Fortinbras,
Had he been vanquisher; as, by the same comart
And carriage of the article design'd,
His fell to Hamlet. Now, sir, young Fortinbras,
Of unimproved mettle hot and full,
Hath in the skirts of Norway, here and there,
Shark'd up a list of lawless resolutes,
For food and diet, to some enterprise
That hath a stomach in't; which is no other,
As it doth well appear unto our state,
But to recover of us, by strong hand
And terms compulsatory, those foresaid lands
So by his father lost; and this, I take it,
Is the main motive of our preparations,
The source of this our watch, and the chief head
Of this post-haste and romage in the land.
BERNARDO I think it be no other but e'en so.
Well may it sort, that this portentous figure
Comes armed through our watch; so like the King
That was and is the question of these wars.
HORATIO A mote it is to trouble the mind's eye.
In the most high and palmy state of Rome,
A little ere the mightiest Julius fell,
The graves stood tenantless, and the sheeted dead
Did squeak and gibber in the Roman streets;
As, stars with trains of fire, and dews of blood,
Disasters in the sun; and the moist star
Upon whose influence Neptune's empire stands
Was sick almost to doomsday with eclipse;
And even the like precurse of fear'd events,
As harbingers preceding still the fates
And prologue to the omen coming on,
Have heaven and earth together demonstrated
Unto our climatures and countrymen.

Re-enter Ghost.

But, soft, behold! Lo, where it comes again!
I'll cross it, though it blast me. Stay, illusion.
[*Ghost spreads its arms.*
If thou hast any sound or use of voice,
Speak to me.
If there be any good thing to be done,
That may to thee do ease and grace to me,
Speak to me.
If thou art privy to thy country's fate,
Which happily foreknowing may avoid,
O, speak!
Or if thou hast uphoarded in thy life
Extorted treasure in the womb of earth,
For which, they say, you spirits oft walk in death,
[*The cock crows.*
Speak of it. Stay, and speak. Stop it, Marcellus.

MARCELLUS Shall I strike at it with my partisan?

HORATIO Do, if it will not stand.

BERNARDO 'Tis here!

HORATIO 'Tis here!

MARCELLUS 'Tis gone! [*Exit Ghost.*
We do it wrong, being so majestical,
To offer it the show of violence;
For it is, as the air, invulnerable,
And our vain blows malicious mockery.

BERNARDO It was about to speak, when the cock crew.

HORATIO And then it started like a guilty thing
Upon a fearful summons. I have heard
The cock, that is the trumpet to the morn,
Doth with his lofty and shrill-sounding throat
Awake the god of day; and at his warning,
Whether in sea or fire, in earth or air,
Th' extravagant and erring spirit hies
To his confine; and of the truth herein
This present object made probation.

MARCELLUS It faded on the crowing of the cock.
Some say that ever 'gainst that season comes
Wherein our Saviour's birth is celebrated,
This bird of dawning singeth all night long;
And then, they say, no spirit dare stir abroad,
The nights are wholesome, then no planets strike,
No fairy takes, nor witch hath power to charm,
So hallowed and so gracious is that time.

HORATIO So have I heard, and do in part believe it.
But look, the morn, in russet mantle clad,
Walks o'er the dew of yon high eastward hill.
Break we our watch up; and, by my advice,
Let us impart what we have seen to-night
Unto young Hamlet; for, upon my life,
This spirit, dumb to us, will speak to him.
Do you consent we shall acquaint him with it,
As needful in our loves, fitting our duty?

MARCELLUS Let's do't, I pray; and I this morning know
Where we shall find him most convenient.
[*Exeunt.*

SCENE II. *Elsinore. The Castle.*

Flourish. Enter CLAUDIUS KING OF DENMARK, GERTRUDE THE QUEEN, and Councillors, including POLONIUS, his son LAERTES, VOLTEMAND, CORNELIUS, and HAMLET.

KING Though yet of Hamlet our dear brother's death
The memory be green; and that it us befitted
To bear our hearts in grief, and our whole kingdom
To be contracted in one brow of woe;
Yet so far hath discretion fought with nature
That we with wisest sorrow think on him,
Together with remembrance of ourselves.
Therefore our sometime sister, now our queen,
Th' imperial jointress to this warlike state,
Have we, as 'twere with a defeated joy,
With an auspicious and a dropping eye,
With mirth in funeral, and with dirge in marriage,
In equal scale weighing delight and dole,
Taken to wife; nor have we herein barr'd
Your better wisdoms, which have freely gone
With this affair along. For all, our thanks.
Now follows that you know: young Fortinbras,
Holding a weak supposal of our worth,
Or thinking by our late dear brother's death
Our state to be disjoint and out of frame,
Co-leagued with this dream of his advantage –
He hath not fail'd to pester us with message
Importing the surrender of those lands
Lost by his father, with all bands of law,
To our most valiant brother. So much for him.
Now for ourself, and for this time of meeting,
Thus much the business is: we have here writ
To Norway, uncle of young Fortinbras –
Who, impotent and bed-rid, scarcely hears
Of this his nephew's purpose – to suppress
His further gait herein, in that the levies,
The lists, and full proportions, are all made
Out of his subject; and we here dispatch
You, good Cornelius, and you, Voltemand,
For bearers of this greeting to old Norway;
Giving to you no further personal power
To business with the King more than the scope
Of these delated articles allow.
Farewell; and let your haste commend your duty.

CORNELIUS, VOLTEMAND In that and all things will we show our duty.
KING We doubt it nothing, heartily farewell.
[*Exeunt Voltemand and Cornelius.*
And now, Laertes, what's the news with you?
You told us of some suit; what is't, Laertes?
You cannot speak of reason to the Dane
And lose your voice. What wouldst thou beg, Laertes,
That shall not be my offer, not thy asking?
The head is not more native to the heart,
The hand more instrumental to the mouth,
Than is the throne of Denmark to thy father.
What wouldst thou have, Laertes?
LAERTES My dread lord,
Your leave and favour to return to France;
From whence though willingly I came to Denmark
To show my duty in your coronation,
Yet now, I must confess, that duty done,
My thoughts and wishes bend again toward France,
And bow them to your gracious leave and pardon.
KING Have you your gracious father's leave? What says Polonius?
POLONIUS 'A hath, my lord, wrung from me my slow leave
By laboursome petition; and at last
Upon his will I seal'd my hard consent.
I do beseech you, give him leave to go.
KING Take thy fair hour, Laertes; time be thine,
And thy best graces spend it at thy will!
But now, my cousin Hamlet, and my son –
HAMLET [*Aside*] A little more than kin, and less than kind.
KING How is it that the clouds still hang on you?
HAMLET Not so, my lord; I am too much in the sun.
QUEEN Good Hamlet, cast thy nighted colour off,
And let thine eye look like a friend on Denmark.
Do not for ever with thy vailed lids
Seek for thy noble father in the dust.
Thou know'st 'tis common – all that lives must die,
Passing through nature to eternity.
HAMLET Ay, madam, it is common.
QUEEN If it be,
Why seems it so particular with thee?
HAMLET Seems, madam! Nay, it is; I know not seems.
'Tis not alone my inky cloak, good mother,
Nor customary suits of solemn black,
Nor windy suspiration of forc'd breath,
No, nor the fruitful river in the eye,
Nor the dejected haviour of the visage,
Together with all forms, moods, shapes of grief,
That can denote me truly. These, indeed, seem;
For they are actions that a man might play;
But I have that within which passes show –
These but the trappings and the suits of woe.
KING 'Tis sweet and commendable in your nature, Hamlet,
To give these mourning duties to your father;
But you must know your father lost a father;
That father lost his; and the survivor bound,
In filial obligation, for some term
To do obsequious sorrow. But to persever
In obstinate condolement is a course
Of impious stubbornness; 'tis unmanly grief;
It shows a will most incorrect to heaven,
A heart unfortified, a mind impatient,
An understanding simple and unschool'd;
For what we know must be, and is as common
As any the most vulgar thing to sense,
Why should we in our peevish opposition
Take it to heart? Fie! 'tis a fault to heaven,
A fault against the dead, a fault to nature,
To reason most absurd; whose common theme
Is death of fathers, and who still hath cried,
From the first corse till he that died to-day,
'This must be so'. We pray you throw to earth
This unprevailing woe, and think of us
As of a father; for let the world take note
You are the most immediate to our throne;
And with no less nobility of love
Than that which dearest father bears his son
Do I impart toward you. For your intent
In going back to school in Wittenberg,
It is most retrograde to our desire;
And we beseech you bend you to remain
Here, in the cheer and comfort of our eye,
Our chiefest courtier, cousin, and our son.
QUEEN Let not thy mother lose her prayers, Hamlet:
I pray thee stay with us; go not to Wittenberg.
HAMLET I shall in all my best obey you, madam.
KING Why, 'tis a loving and a fair reply.
Be as ourself in Denmark. Madam, come;
This gentle and unforc'd accord of Hamlet
Sits smiling to my heart; in grace whereof,
No jocund health that Denmark drinks to-day
But the great cannon to the clouds shall tell,
And the King's rouse the heaven shall bruit again,
Re-speaking earthly thunder. Come away.
[*Flourish. Exeunt all but Hamlet.*
HAMLET O, that this too too solid flesh would melt,
Thaw, and resolve itself into a dew!
Or that the Everlasting had not fix'd
His canon 'gainst self-slaughter! O God! God!

How weary, stale, flat, and unprofitable,
Seem to me all the uses of this world!
Fie on't! Ah, fie! 'tis an unweeded garden,
That grows to seed; things rank and gross in nature
Possess it merely. That it should come to this!
But two months dead! Nay, not so much, not two.
So excellent a king that was to this
Hyperion to a satyr; so loving to my mother,
That he might not beteem the winds of heaven
Visit her face too roughly. Heaven and earth!
Must I remember? Why, she would hang on him
As if increase of appetite had grown
By what it fed on; and yet, within a month –
Let me not think on't. Frailty, thy name is woman! –
A little month, or ere those shoes were old
With which she followed my poor father's body,
Like Niobe, all tears – why she, even she –
O God! a beast that wants discourse of reason
Would have mourn'd longer – married with my uncle,
My father's brother; but no more like my father
Than I to Hercules. Within a month,
Ere yet the salt of most unrighteous tears
Had left the flushing in her galled eyes,
She married. O, most wicked speed, to post
With such dexterity to incestuous sheets!
It is not, nor it cannot come to good.
But break, my heart, for I must hold my tongue.

Enter HORATIO, MARCELLUS, and BERNARDO.

HORATIO Hail to your lordship!
HAMLET I am glad to see you well.
Horatio – or I do forget myself.
HORATIO The same, my lord, and your poor servant ever.
HAMLET Sir, my good friend. I'll change that name with you.
And what make you from Wittenberg, Horatio?
Marcellus?
MARCELLUS My good lord!
HAMLET I am very glad to see you. [*To Bernardo*] Good even, sir. –
But what, in faith, make you from Wittenberg?
HORATIO A truant disposition, good my lord.
HAMLET I would not hear your enemy say so;
Nor shall you do my ear that violence,
To make it truster of your own report
Against yourself. I know you are no truant.
But what is your affair in Elsinore?
We'll teach you to drink deep ere you depart.
HORATIO My lord, I came to see your father's funeral.
HAMLET I prithee do not mock me, fellow student;
I think it was to see my mother's wedding.
HORATIO Indeed, my lord, it followed hard upon.
HAMLET Thrift, thrift, Horatio! The funeral bak'd-meats
Did coldly furnish forth the marriage tables.
Would I had met my dearest foe in heaven
Or ever I had seen that day, Horatio!
My father – methinks I see my father.
HORATIO Where, my lord?
HAMLET In my mind's eye, Horatio.
HORATIO I saw him once; 'a was a goodly king.
HAMLET 'A was a man, take him for all in all,
I shall not look upon his like again.
HORATIO My lord, I think I saw him yester-night.
HAMLET Saw who?
HORATIO My lord, the King your father.
HAMLET The King my father!
HORATIO Season your admiration for a while
With an attent ear, till I may deliver,
Upon the witness of these gentlemen,
This marvel to you.
HAMLET For God's love, let me hear.
HORATIO Two nights together had these gentlemen,
Marcellus and Bernardo, on their watch,
In the dead waste and middle of the night,
Been thus encount'red. A figure like your father,
Armed at point exactly, cap-a-pe,
Appears before them, and with solemn march
Goes slow and stately by them; thrice he walk'd
By their oppress'd and fear-surprised eyes,
Within his truncheon's length; whilst they, distill'd
Almost to jelly with the act of fear,
Stand dumb and speak not to him. This to me
In dreadful secrecy impart they did;
And I with them the third night kept the watch;
Where, as they had delivered, both in time,
Form of the thing, each word made true and good,
The apparition comes. I knew your father;
These hands are not more like.
HAMLET But where was this?
MARCELLUS My lord, upon the platform where we watch.
HAMLET Did you not speak to it?
HORATIO My lord, I did;
But answer made it none; yet once methought
It lifted up it head and did address
Itself to motion, like as it would speak;
But even then the morning cock crew loud,
And at the sound it shrunk in haste away
And vanish'd from our sight.
HAMLET 'Tis very strange.
HORATIO As I do live, my honour'd lord, 'tis true;
And we did think it writ down in our duty
To let you know of it.

HAMLET Indeed, indeed, sirs, but this troubles me.
Hold you the watch to-night?
ALL We do, my lord.
HAMLET Arm'd, say you?
ALL Arm'd, my lord.
HAMLET From top to toe?
ALL My lord, from head to foot.
HAMLET Then saw you not his face?
HORATIO O yes, my lord; he wore his beaver up.
HAMLET What, look'd he frowningly?
HORATIO A countenance more in sorrow than in anger.
HAMLET Pale or red?
HORATIO Nay, very pale.
HAMLET And fix'd his eyes upon you?
HORATIO Most constantly.
HAMLET I would I had been there.
HORATIO It would have much amaz'd you.
HAMLET Very like, very like. Stay'd it long?
HORATIO While one with moderate haste might tell a hundred.
BOTH Longer, longer.
HORATIO Not when I saw't.
HAMLET His beard was grizzl'd – no?
HORATIO It was, as I have seen it in his life,
A sable silver'd.
HAMLET I will watch to-night;
Perchance 'twill walk again.
HORATIO I warr'nt it will.
HAMLET If it assume my noble father's person,
I'll speak to it, though hell itself should gape
And bid me hold my peace. I pray you all,
If you have hitherto conceal'd this sight,
Let it be tenable in your silence still;
And whatsomever else shall hap to-night,
Give it an understanding, but no tongue;
I will requite your loves. So, fare you well –
Upon the platform, 'twixt eleven and twelve,
I'll visit you.
ALL Our duty to your honour.
HAMLET Your loves, as mine to you; farewell.
[Exeunt all but Hamlet.
My father's spirit in arms! All is not well.
I doubt some foul play. Would the night were come!
Till then sit still, my soul. Foul deeds will rise,
Though all the earth o'erwhelm them, to men's eyes. *[Exit.*

SCENE III. *Elsinore. The house of Polonius.*

Enter LAERTES and OPHELIA his sister.

LAERTES My necessaries are embark'd. Farewell.
And, sister, as the winds give benefit
And convoy is assistant, do not sleep,
But let me hear from you.
OPHELIA Do you doubt that?
LAERTES For Hamlet, and the trifling of his favour,
Hold it a fashion and a toy in blood,
A violet in the youth of primy nature,
Forward not permanent, sweet not lasting,
The perfume and suppliance of a minute;
No more.
OPHELIA No more but so?
LAERTES Think it no more;
For nature crescent does not grow alone
In thews and bulk, but as this temple waxes,
The inward service of the mind and soul
Grows wide withal. Perhaps he loves you now,
And now no soil nor cautel doth besmirch
The virtue of his will; but you must fear,
His greatness weigh'd, his will is not his own;
For he himself is subject to his birth:
He may not, as unvalued persons do,
Carve for himself; for on his choice depends
The sanity and health of this whole state;
And therefore must his choice be circumscrib'd
Unto the voice and yielding of that body
Whereof he is the head. Then if he says he loves you,
It fits your wisdom so far to believe it
As he in his particular act and place
May give his saying deed; which is no further
Than the main voice of Denmark goes withal.
Then weigh what loss your honour may sustain,
If with too credent ear you list his songs,
Or lose your heart, or your chaste treasure open
To his unmast'red importunity.
Fear it, Ophelia, fear it, my dear sister;
And keep you in the rear of your affection,
Out of the shot and danger of desire.
The chariest maid is prodigal enough
If she unmask her beauty to the moon.
Virtue itself scapes not calumnious strokes;
The canker galls the infants of the spring
Too oft before their buttons be disclos'd;
And in the morn and liquid dew of youth
Contagious blastments are most imminent.
Be wary, then; best safety lies in fear:
Youth to itself rebels, though none else near.
OPHELIA I shall the effect of this good lesson keep
As watchman to my heart. But, good my brother,
Do not, as some ungracious pastors do,
Show me the steep and thorny way to heaven,
Whiles, like a puff'd and reckless libertine,
Himself the primrose path of dalliance treads
And recks not his own rede.
LAERTES O, fear me not!

Enter POLONIUS.

I stay too long. But here my father comes.
A double blessing is a double grace;
Occasion smiles upon a second leave.

POLONIUS Yet here, Laertes! Aboard, aboard, for shame!
The wind sits in the shoulder of your sail,
And you are stay'd for. There – my blessing with thee!
And these few precepts in thy memory
Look thou character. Give thy thoughts no tongue,
Nor any unproportion'd thought his act.
Be thou familiar, but by no means vulgar.
Those friends thou hast, and their adoption tried,
Grapple them to thy soul with hoops of steel;
But do not dull thy palm with entertainment
Of each new-hatch'd, unfledg'd courage. Beware
Of entrance to a quarrel; but, being in,
Bear't that th' opposed may beware of thee.
Give every man thy ear, but few thy voice;
Take each man's censure, but reserve thy judgment.
Costly thy habit as thy purse can buy,
But not express'd in fancy; rich, not gaudy;
For the apparel oft proclaims the man;
And they in France of the best rank and station
Are of a most select and generous choice in that.
Neither a borrower nor a lender be;
For loan oft loses both itself and friend,
And borrowing dulls the edge of husbandry.
This above all – to thine own self be true,
And it must follow, as the night the day,
Thou canst not then be false to any man.
Farewell; my blessing season this in thee!

LAERTES Most humbly do I take my leave, my lord.

POLONIUS The time invites you; go, your servants tend.

LAERTES Farewell, Ophelia; and remember well
What I have said to you.

OPHELIA 'Tis in my memory lock'd,
And you yourself shall keep the key of it.

LAERTES Farewell. [*Exit.*

POLONIUS What is't, Ophelia, he hath said to you?

OPHELIA So please you, something touching the Lord Hamlet.

POLONIUS Marry, well bethought!
'Tis told me he hath very oft of late
Given private time to you; and you yourself
Have of your audience been most free and bounteous.
If it be so – as so 'tis put on me,
And that in way of caution – I must tell you
You do not understand yourself so clearly
As it behoves my daughter and your honour.
What is between you? Give me up the truth.

OPHELIA He hath, my lord, of late made many tenders
Of his affection to me.

POLONIUS Affection! Pooh! You speak like a green girl,
Unsifted in such perilous circumstance.
Do you believe his tenders, as you call them?

OPHELIA I do not know, my lord, what I should think.

POLONIUS Marry, I will teach you: think yourself a baby
That you have ta'en these tenders for true pay
Which are not sterling. Tender yourself more dearly;
Or – not to crack the wind of the poor phrase,
Running it thus – you'll tender me a fool.

OPHELIA My lord, he hath importun'd me with love
In honourable fashion.

POLONIUS Ay, fashion you may call it; go to, go to.

OPHELIA And hath given countenance to his speech, my lord,
With almost all the holy vows of heaven.

POLONIUS Ay, springes to catch woodcocks! I do know,
When the blood burns, how prodigal the soul
Lends the tongue vows. These blazes, daughter,
Giving more light than heat – extinct in both,
Even in their promise, as it is a-making –
You must not take for fire. From this time
Be something scanter of your maiden presence;
Set your entreatments at a higher rate
Than a command to parle. For Lord Hamlet,
Believe so much in him, that he is young,
And with a larger tether may he walk
Than may be given you. In few, Ophelia,
Do not believe his vows; for they are brokers,
Not of that dye which their investments show,
But mere implorators of unholy suits,
Breathing like sanctified and pious bonds,
The better to beguile. This is for all –
I would not, in plain terms, from this time forth
Have you so slander any moment leisure
As to give words or talk with the Lord Hamlet.
Look to't, I charge you. Come your ways.

OPHELIA I shall obey, my lord. [*Exeunt.*

SCENE IV. *Elsinore. The guard-platform of the Castle.*

Enter HAMLET, HORATIO, and MARCELLUS.

HAMLET The air bites shrewdly; it is very cold.

HORATIO It is a nipping and an eager air.

HAMLET What hour now?
HORATIO I think it lacks of twelve.
MARCELLUS No, it is struck.
HORATIO Indeed? I heard it not. It then draws near the season
Wherein the spirit held his wont to walk.

[A flourish of trumpets, and two pieces go off.

What does this mean, my lord?
HAMLET The King doth wake to-night and takes his rouse,
Keeps wassail, and the swagg'ring up-spring reels,
And, as he drains his draughts of Rhenish down,
The kettle-drum and trumpet thus bray out
The triumph of his pledge.
HORATIO Is it a custom?
HAMLET Ay, marry, is't;
But to my mind, though I am native here
And to the manner born, it is a custom
More honour'd in the breach than the observance.
This heavy-headed revel east and west
Makes us traduc'd and tax'd of other nations;
They clepe us drunkards, and with swinish phrase
Soil our addition; and, indeed, it takes
From our achievements, though perform'd at height,
The pith and marrow of our attribute.
So, oft it chances in particular men
That, for some vicious mole of nature in them,
As in their birth, wherein they are not guilty,
Since nature cannot choose his origin;
By the o'ergrowth of some complexion,
Oft breaking down the pales and forts of reason;
Or by some habit that too much o'er-leavens
The form of plausive manners – that these men,
Carrying, I say, the stamp of one defect,
Being nature's livery or fortune's star,
His virtues else, be they as pure as grace,
As infinite as man may undergo,
Shall in the general censure take corruption
From that particular fault. The dram of eale
Doth all the noble substance of a doubt
To his own scandal.

Enter Ghost.

HORATIO Look, my lord, it comes.
HAMLET Angels and ministers of grace defend us!
Be thou a spirit of health or goblin damn'd,
Bring with thee airs from heaven or blasts from hell,
Be thy intents wicked or charitable,
Thou com'st in such a questionable shape
That I will speak to thee. I'll call thee Hamlet,
King, father, royal Dane. O, answer me!
Let me not burst in ignorance, but tell
Why thy canoniz'd bones, hearsed in death,
Have burst their cerements; why the sepulchre
Wherein we saw thee quietly enurn'd
Hath op'd his ponderous and marble jaws
To cast thee up again. What may this mean
That thou, dead corse, again in complete steel
Revisits thus the glimpses of the moon,
Making night hideous, and we fools of nature
So horridly to shake our disposition
With thoughts beyond the reaches of our souls?
Say, why is this? wherefore? What should we do?

[Ghost beckons Hamlet.

HORATIO It beckons you to go away with it,
As if it some impartment did desire
To you alone.
MARCELLUS Look with what courteous action
It waves you to a more removed ground.
But do not go with it.
HORATIO No, by no means.
HAMLET It will not speak; then I will follow it.
HORATIO Do not, my lord.
HAMLET Why, what should be the fear?
I do not set my life at a pin's fee;
And for my soul, what can it do to that,
Being a thing immortal as itself?
It waves me forth again; I'll follow it.
HORATIO What if it tempt you toward the flood, my lord,
Or to the dreadful summit of the cliff
That beetles o'er his base into the sea,
And there assume some other horrible form,
Which might deprive your sovereignty of reason
And draw you into madness? Think of it:
The very place puts toys of desperation,
Without more motive, into every brain
That looks so many fathoms to the sea
And hears it roar beneath.
HAMLET It waves me still.
Go on; I'll follow thee.
MARCELLUS You shall not go, my lord.
HAMLET Hold off your hands.
HORATIO Be rul'd; you shall not go.
HAMLET My fate cries out,
And makes each petty arture in this body
As hardy as the Nemean lion's nerve.

[Ghost beckons.

Still am I call'd. Unhand me, gentlemen.
By heaven, I'll make a ghost of him that lets me.
I say, away! Go on; I'll follow thee.

[Exeunt Ghost and Hamlet.

HORATIO He waxes desperate with imagination.
MARCELLUS Let's follow; 'tis not fit thus to obey him.

HORATIO Have after. To what issue will this come?
MARCELLUS Something is rotten in the state of Denmark.
HORATIO Heaven will direct it.
MARCELLUS Nay, let's follow him.
[*Exeunt.*

SCENE V. *Elsinore. The battlements of the Castle.*

Enter Ghost and HAMLET.

HAMLET Whither wilt thou lead me? Speak. I'll go no further.
GHOST Mark me.
HAMLET I will.
GHOST My hour is almost come,
When I to sulph'rous and tormenting flames
Must render up myself.
HAMLET Alas, poor ghost!
GHOST Pity me not, but lend thy serious hearing
To what I shall unfold.
HAMLET Speak; I am bound to hear.
GHOST So art thou to revenge, when thou shalt hear.
HAMLET What?
GHOST I am thy father's spirit,
Doom'd for a certain term to walk the night,
And for the day confin'd to fast in fires,
Till the foul crimes done in my days of nature
Are burnt and purg'd away. But that I am forbid
To tell the secrets of my prison-house,
I could a tale unfold whose lightest word
Would harrow up thy soul, freeze thy young blood,
Make thy two eyes, like stars, start from their spheres,
Thy knotted and combined locks to part,
And each particular hair to stand an end,
Like quills upon the fretful porpentine.
But this eternal blazon must not be
To ears of flesh and blood. List, list, O, list!
If thou didst ever thy dear father love –
HAMLET O God!
GHOST Revenge his foul and most unnatural murder.
HAMLET Murder!
GHOST Murder most foul, as in the best it is;
But this most foul, strange, and unnatural.
HAMLET Haste me to know't, that I, with wings as swift
As meditation or the thoughts of love,
May sweep to my revenge.
GHOST I find thee apt;
And duller shouldst thou be than the fat weed
That roots itself in ease on Lethe wharf,
Wouldst thou not stir in this. Now, Hamlet, hear:
'Tis given out that, sleeping in my orchard,
A serpent stung me; so the whole ear of Denmark
Is by a forged process of my death
Rankly abus'd; but know, thou noble youth,
The serpent that did sting thy father's life
Now wears his crown.
HAMLET O my prophetic soul!
My uncle!
GHOST Ay, that incestuous, that adulterate beast,
With witchcraft of his wits, with traitorous gifts –
O wicked wit and gifts that have the power
So to seduce! – won to his shameful lust
The will of my most seeming virtuous queen.
O Hamlet, what a falling off was there,
From me, whose love was of that dignity
That it went hand in hand even with the vow
I made to her in marriage; and to decline
Upon a wretch whose natural gifts were poor
To those of mine!
But virtue, as it never will be moved,
Though lewdness court it in a shape of heaven,
So lust, though to a radiant angel link'd,
Will sate itself in a celestial bed
And prey on garbage.
But soft! methinks I scent the morning air.
Brief let me be. Sleeping within my orchard,
My custom always of the afternoon,
Upon my secure hour thy uncle stole,
With juice of cursed hebona in a vial,
And in the porches of my ears did pour
The leperous distilment; whose effect
Holds such an enmity with blood of man
That swift as quicksilver it courses through
The natural gates and alleys of the body;
And with a sudden vigour it doth posset
And curd, like eager droppings into milk,
The thin and wholesome blood. So did it mine;
And a most instant tetter bark'd about,
Most lazar-like, with vile and loathsome crust,
All my smooth body.
Thus was I, sleeping, by a brother's hand
Of life, of crown, of queen, at once dispatch'd;
Cut off even in the blossoms of my sin,
Unhous'led, disappointed, unanel'd;
No reck'ning made, but sent to my account
With all my imperfections on my head.
O, horrible! O, horrible! most horrible!
If thou hast nature in thee, bear it not;
Let not the royal bed of Denmark be
A couch for luxury and damned incest.
But, howsomever thou pursuest this act,
Taint not thy mind, nor let thy soul contrive
Against thy mother aught; leave her to heaven,

And to those thorns that in her bosom lodge
To prick and sting her. Fare thee well at once.
The glowworm shows the matin to be near,
And gins to pale his uneffectual fire.
Adieu, adieu, adieu! Remember me. [*Exit.*

HAMLET O all you host of heaven! O earth! What else?
And shall I couple hell? O, fie! Hold, hold, my heart;
And you, my sinews, grow not instant old,
But bear me stiffly up. Remember thee!
Ay, thou poor ghost, whiles memory holds a seat
In this distracted globe. Remember thee!
Yea, from the table of my memory
I'll wipe away all trivial fond records,
All saws of books, all forms, all pressures past,
That youth and observation copied there,
And thy commandment all alone shall live
Within the book and volume of my brain,
Unmix'd with baser matter. Yes, by heaven!
O most pernicious woman!
O villain, villain, smiling, damned villain!
My tables – meet it is I set it down
That one may smile, and smile, and be a villain;
At least I am sure it may be so in Denmark.
[*Writing.*
So, uncle, there you are. Now to my word:
It is 'Adieu, adieu! Remember me'.
I have sworn't.

HORATIO [*Within*] My lord, my lord!

Enter HORATIO and MARCELLUS.

MARCELLUS Lord Hamlet!

HORATIO Heavens secure him!

HAMLET So be it!

MARCELLUS Illo, ho, ho, my lord!

HAMLET Hillo, ho, ho, boy! Come, bird, come.

MARCELLUS How is't, my noble lord?

HORATIO What news, my lord?

HAMLET O, wonderful!

HORATIO Good my lord, tell it.

HAMLET No; you will reveal it.

HORATIO Not I, my lord, by heaven!

MARCELLUS Nor I, my lord.

HAMLET How say you, then; would heart of man once think it?
But you'll be secret?

BOTH Ay, by heaven, my lord!

HAMLET There's never a villain dwelling in all Denmark
But he's an arrant knave.

HORATIO There needs no ghost, my lord, come from the grave
To tell us this.

HAMLET Why, right; you are in the right;
And so, without more circumstance at all,
I hold it fit that we shake hands and part;
You, as your business and desire shall point you –
For every man hath business and desire,
Such as it is; and for my own poor part,
Look you, I will go pray.

HORATIO These are but wild and whirling words, my lord.

HAMLET I am sorry they offend you, heartily;
Yes, faith, heartily.

HORATIO There's no offence, my lord.

HAMLET Yes, by Saint Patrick, but there is, Horatio,
And much offence too. Touching this vision here –
It is an honest ghost, that let me tell you.
For your desire to know what is between us,
O'ermaster't as you may. And now, good friends,
As you are friends, scholars, and soldiers,
Give me one poor request.

HORATIO What is't, my lord? We will.

HAMLET Never make known what you have seen to-night.

BOTH My lord, we will not.

HAMLET Nay, but swear't.

HORATIO In faith,
My lord, not I.

MARCELLUS Nor I, my lord, in faith.

HAMLET Upon my sword.

MARCELLUS We have sworn, my lord, already.

HAMLET Indeed, upon my sword, indeed.

GHOST [*Cries under the stage*] Swear.

HAMLET Ha, ha, boy! say'st thou so? Art thou there, truepenny?
Come on. You hear this fellow in the cellarage:
Consent to swear.

HORATIO Propose the oath, my lord.

HAMLET Never to speak of this that you have seen,
Swear by my sword.

GHOST [*Beneath*] Swear.

HAMLET Hic et ubique? Then we'll shift our ground.
Come hither, gentlemen,
And lay your hands again upon my sword.
Swear by my sword
Never to speak of this that you have heard.

GHOST [*Beneath*] Swear, by his sword.

HAMLET Well said, old mole! Canst work i' th' earth so fast?
A worthy pioneer! Once more remove, good friends.

HORATIO O day and night, but this is wondrous strange!

HAMLET And therefore as a stranger give it welcome.

There are more things in heaven and earth, Horatio,
Than are dreamt of in your philosophy.
But come.
Here, as before, never, so help you mercy,
How strange or odd some'er I bear myself –
As I perchance hereafter shall think meet
To put an antic disposition on –
That you, at such times, seeing me, never shall,
With arms encumb'red thus, or this head-shake,
Or by pronouncing of some doubtful phrase,
As 'Well, well, we know' or 'We could, an if we would'
Or 'If we list to speak' or 'There be, an if they might'
Or such ambiguous giving out, to note
That you know aught of me – this do swear,
So grace and mercy at your most need help you.

GHOST [*Beneath*] Swear.

HAMLET Rest, rest, perturbed spirit! So, gentlemen,
With all my love I do commend me to you;
And what so poor a man as Hamlet is
May do t'express his love and friending to you,
God willing, shall not lack. Let us go in together;
And still your fingers on your lips, I pray.
The time is out of joint. O cursed spite,
That ever I was born to set it right!
Nay, come, let's go together. [*Exeunt.*

ACT TWO

SCENE I. *Elsinore. The house of Polonius.*

Enter POLONIUS and REYNALDO.

POLONIUS Give him this money and these notes, Reynaldo.

REYNALDO I will, my lord.

POLONIUS You shall do marvellous wisely, good Reynaldo,
Before you visit him, to make inquire
Of his behaviour.

REYNALDO My lord, I did intend it.

POLONIUS Marry, well said; very well said. Look you, sir,
Enquire me first what Danskers are in Paris;
And how, and who, what means, and where they keep,
What company, at what expense; and finding
By this encompassment and drift of question
That they do know my son, come you more nearer
Than your particular demands will touch it.
Take you, as 'twere, some distant knowledge of him;
As thus: 'I know his father and his friends,
And in part him'. Do you mark this, Reynaldo?

REYNALDO Ay, very well, my lord.

POLONIUS 'And in part him – but' you may say 'not well;
But if't be he I mean, he's very wild;
Addicted so and so'; and there put on him
What forgeries you please; marry, none so rank
As may dishonour him; take heed of that;
But, sir, such wanton, wild, and usual slips
As are companions noted and most known
To youth and liberty.

REYNALDO As gaming, my lord.

POLONIUS Ay, or drinking, fencing, swearing, quarrelling,
Drabbing – you may go so far.

REYNALDO My lord, that would dishonour him.

POLONIUS Faith, no; as you may season it in the charge.
You must not put another scandal on him,
That he is open to incontinency;
That's not my meaning. But breathe his faults so quaintly
That they may seem the taints of liberty;
The flash and outbreak of a fiery mind,
A savageness in unreclaimed blood,
Of general assault.

REYNALDO But, my good lord –

POLONIUS Wherefore should you do this?

REYNALDO Ay, my lord,
I would know that.

POLONIUS Marry, sir, here's my drift,
And I believe it is a fetch of warrant:
You laying these slight sullies on my son,
As 'twere a thing a little soil'd wi' th' working,
Mark you,
Your party in converse, him you would sound,
Having ever seen in the prenominate crimes
The youth you breathe of guilty, be assur'd
He closes with you in this consequence –
'Good sir' or so, or 'friend' or 'gentleman'
According to the phrase or the addition
Of man and country.

REYNALDO Very good, my lord.

POLONIUS And then, sir, does 'a this – 'a does –
What was I about to say? By the mass,
I was about to say something; where did I leave?

REYNALDO At 'closes in the consequence', at

'friend or so' and 'gentleman'.
POLONIUS At 'closes in the consequence' – ay, marry,
He closes thus: 'I know the gentleman;
I saw him yesterday, or t'other day,
Or then, or then; with such, or such; and, as you say,
There was 'a gaming; there o'ertook in's rouse;
There falling out at tennis'; or perchance
'I saw him enter such a house of sale'
Videlicet, a brothel, or so forth. See you now
Your bait of falsehood take this carp of truth;
And thus do we of wisdom and of reach,
With windlasses and with assays of bias,
By indirections find directions out;
So, by my former lecture and advice,
Shall you my son. You have me, have you not?
REYNALDO My lord, I have.
POLONIUS God buy ye; fare ye well.
REYNALDO Good my lord!
POLONIUS Observe his inclination in yourself.
REYNALDO I shall, my lord.
POLONIUS And let him ply his music.
REYNALDO Well, my lord.
POLONIUS Farewell! [*Exit Reynaldo.*

Enter OPHELIA.

How now, Ophelia! What's the matter?
OPHELIA O my lord, my lord, I have been so affrighted!
POLONIUS With what, i' th' name of God?
OPHELIA My lord, as I was sewing in my closet,
Lord Hamlet, with his doublet all unbrac'd,
No hat upon his head, his stockings fouled,
Ungart'red and down-gyved to his ankle;
Pale as his shirt, his knees knocking each other,
And with a look so piteous in purport
As if he had been loosed out of hell
To speak of horrors – he comes before me.
POLONIUS Mad for thy love?
OPHELIA My lord, I do not know,
But truly I do fear it.
POLONIUS What said he?
OPHELIA He took me by the wrist, and held me hard;
Then goes he to the length of all his arm,
And, with his other hand thus o'er his brow,
He falls to such perusal of my face
As 'a would draw it. Long stay'd he so.
At last, a little shaking of mine arm,
And thrice his head thus waving up and down,
He rais'd a sigh so piteous and profound
As it did seem to shatter all his bulk
And end his being. That done, he lets me go,
And, with his head over his shoulder turn'd,
He seem'd to find his way without his eyes;
For out adoors he went without their helps
And to the last bended their light on me.
POLONIUS Come, go with me. I will go seek the King.
This is the very ecstasy of love,
Whose violent property fordoes itself,
And leads the will to desperate undertakings
As oft as any passion under heaven
That does afflict our natures. I am sorry –
What, have you given him any hard words of late?
OPHELIA No, my good lord; but, as you did command,
I did repel his letters, and denied
His access to me.
POLONIUS That hath made him mad.
I am sorry that with better heed and judgment
I had not quoted him. I fear'd he did but trifle,
And meant to wreck thee; but beshrew my jealousy!
By heaven, it is as proper to our age
To cast beyond ourselves in our opinions
As it is common for the younger sort
To lack discretion. Come, go we to the King.
This must be known; which, being kept close, might move
More grief to hide than hate to utter love.
Come. [*Exeunt.*

SCENE II. *Elsinore. The Castle.*

Flourish. Enter KING, QUEEN, ROSENCRANTZ, GUILDENSTERN, and Attendants.

KING Welcome, dear Rosencrantz and Guildenstern!
Moreover that we much did long to see you,
The need we have to use you did provoke
Our hasty sending. Something have you heard
Of Hamlet's transformation; so I call it,
Sith nor th' exterior nor the inward man
Resembles that it was. What it should be,
More than his father's death, that thus hath put him
So much from th' understanding of himself,
I cannot deem of. I entreat you both
That, being of so young days brought up with him,
And sith so neighboured to his youth and haviour,
That you vouchsafe your rest here in our court
Some little time; so by your companies
To draw him on to pleasures, and to gather,
So much as from occasion you may glean,
Whether aught to us unknown afflicts him thus
That, open'd, lies within our remedy.
QUEEN Good gentlemen, he hath much talk'd of you;

And sure I am two men there is not living
To whom he more adheres. If it will please you
To show us so much gentry and good will
As to expend your time with us awhile
For the supply and profit of our hope,
Your visitation shall receive such thanks
As fits a king's remembrance.

ROSENCRANTZ Both your Majesties
Might, by the sovereign power you have of us,
Put your dread pleasures more into command
Than to entreaty.

GUILDENSTERN But we both obey,
And here give up ourselves, in the full bent,
To lay our service freely at your feet,
To be commanded.

KING Thanks, Rosencrantz and gentle Guildenstern.

QUEEN Thanks, Guildenstern and gentle Rosencrantz.
And I beseech you instantly to visit
My too much changed son. Go, some of you,
And bring these gentlemen where Hamlet is.

GUILDENSTERN Heavens make our presence and our practices
Pleasant and helpful to him!

QUEEN Aye amen!

[Exeunt Rosencrantz, Guildenstern, and some Attendants.

Enter POLONIUS.

POLONIUS Th' ambassadors from Norway, my good lord,
Are joyfully return'd.

KING Thou still hast been the father of good news.

POLONIUS Have I, my lord? I assure you, my good liege,
I hold my duty, as I hold my soul,
Both to my God and to my gracious King;
And I do think – or else this brain of mine
Hunts not the trail of policy so sure
As it hath us'd to do – that I have found
The very cause of Hamlet's lunacy.

KING O, speak of that; that do I long to hear.

POLONIUS Give first admittance to th' ambassadors;
My news shall be the fruit to that great feast.

KING Thyself do grace to them, and bring them in. *[Exit Polonius.*
He tells me, my dear Gertrude, he hath found
The head and source of all your son's distemper.

QUEEN I doubt it is no other but the main,
His father's death and our o'erhasty marriage.

KING Well, we shall sift him.

Re-enter POLONIUS, with VOLTEMAND and CORNELIUS.

Welcome, my good friends!
Say, Voltemand, what from our brother Norway?

VOLTEMAND Most fair return of greetings and desires.
Upon our first, he sent out to suppress
His nephew's levies; which to him appear'd
To be a preparation 'gainst the Polack;
But, better look'd into, he truly found
It was against your Highness. Whereat griev'd,
That so his sickness, age, and impotence,
Was falsely borne in hand, sends out arrests
On Fortinbras; which he, in brief, obeys;
Receives rebuke from Norway; and, in fine,
Makes vow before his uncle never more
To give th' assay of arms against your Majesty.
Whereon old Norway, overcome with joy,
Gives him threescore thousand crowns in annual fee,
And his commission to employ those soldiers,
So levied as before, against the Polack;
With an entreaty, herein further shown, *[Gives a paper.*
That it might please you to give quiet pass
Through your dominions for this enterprise,
On such regards of safety and allowance
As therein are set down.

KING It likes us well;
And at our more considered time we'll read,
Answer, and think upon this business.
Meantime we thank you for your well-took labour.
Go to your rest; at night we'll feast together.
Most welcome home!

[Exeunt Ambassadors and Attendants.

POLONIUS This business is well ended.
My liege, and madam, to expostulate
What majesty should be, what duty is,
Why day is day, night is night, and time is time,
Were nothing, but to waste night, day, and time.
Therefore, since brevity is the soul of wit,
And tediousness the limbs and outward flourishes,
I will be brief. Your noble son is mad.
Mad call I it; for, to define true madness,
What is't but to be nothing else but mad?
But let that go.

QUEEN More matter with less art.

POLONIUS Madam, I swear I use no art at all.
That he's mad, 'tis true: 'tis true 'tis pity;
And pity 'tis 'tis true. A foolish figure!
But farewell it, for I will use no art.
Mad let us grant him, then; and now remains

That we find out the cause of this effect;
Or rather say the cause of this defect,
For this effect defective comes by cause.
Thus it remains, and the remainder thus.
Perpend.
I have a daughter – have while she is mine –
Who in her duty and obedience, mark,
Hath given me this. Now gather, and surmise.
[*Reads.*

'To the celestial, and my soul's idol, the most beautified Ophelia.' That's an ill phrase, a vile phrase; 'beautified' is a vile phrase. But you shall hear. Thus: [*Reads*] 'In her excellent white bosom, these, etc.'

QUEEN Came this from Hamlet to her?

POLONIUS Good madam, stay awhile; I will be faithful. [*Reads.*

'Doubt thou the stars are fire;
Doubt that the sun doth move;
Doubt truth to be a liar;
But never doubt I love.

O dear Ophelia, I am ill at these numbers. I have not art to reckon my groans; but that I love thee best, O most best, believe it. Adieu.

Thine evermore, most dear lady, whilst this machine is to him, HAMLET.'

This, in obedience, hath my daughter shown me;
And more above, hath his solicitings,
As they fell out by time, by means, and place,
All given to mine ear.

KING But how hath she
Receiv'd his love?

POLONIUS What do you think of me?

KING As of a man faithful and honourable.

POLONIUS I would fain prove so. But what might you think,
When I had seen this hot love on the wing,
As I perceiv'd it, I must tell you that,
Before my daughter told me – what might you,
Or my dear Majesty your queen here, think,
If I had play'd the desk or table-book;
Or given my heart a winking, mute and dumb;
Or look'd upon this love with idle sight –
What might you think? No, I went round to work,
And my young mistress thus I did bespeak:
'Lord Hamlet is a prince out of thy star;
This must not be'. And then I prescripts gave her,
That she should lock herself from his resort,
Admit no messengers, receive no tokens.
Which done, she took the fruits of my advice;
And he repelled, a short tale to make,
Fell into a sadness, then into a fast,
Thence to a watch, thence into a weakness,
Thence to a lightness, and, by this declension,
Into the madness wherein now he raves
And all we mourn for.

KING Do you think 'tis this?

QUEEN It may be, very like.

POLONIUS Hath there been such a time – I would fain know that –
That I have positively said 'Tis so',
When it prov'd otherwise?

KING Not that I know.

POLONIUS Take this from this, if this be otherwise.
If circumstances lead me, I will find
Where truth is hid, though it were hid indeed
Within the centre.

KING How may we try it further?

POLONIUS You know sometimes he walks four hours together,
Here in the lobby.

QUEEN So he does, indeed.

POLONIUS At such a time I'll loose my daughter to him.
Be you and I behind an arras then;
Mark the encounter: if he love her not,
And be not from his reason fall'n thereon,
Let me be no assistant for a state,
But keep a farm and carters.

KING We will try it.

Enter HAMLET, reading on a book.

QUEEN But look where sadly the poor wretch comes reading.

POLONIUS Away, I do beseech you, both away:
I'll board him presently. O, give me leave.
[*Exeunt King and Queen.*
How does my good Lord Hamlet?

HAMLET Well, God-a-mercy.

POLONIUS Do you know me, my lord?

HAMLET Excellent well; you are a fish-monger.

POLONIUS Not I, my lord.

HAMLET Then I would you were so honest a man.

POLONIUS Honest, my lord!

HAMLET Ay, sir; to be honest, as this world goes, is to be one man pick'd out of ten thousand.

POLONIUS That's very true, my lord.

HAMLET For if the sun breed maggots in a dead dog, being a good kissing carrion – Have you a daughter?

POLONIUS I have, my lord.

HAMLET Let her not walk i' th' sun. Conception is a blessing. But as your daughter may conceive – friend, look to't.

POLONIUS How say you by that? [*Aside*] Still harping on my daughter. Yet he knew me not at first; 'a said I was a fishmonger. 'A is far gone, far gone. And truly in my youth I suff'red much extremity for love. Very near this. I'll speak to him again. – What do you read, my lord?

HAMLET Words, words, words.

POLONIUS What is the matter, my lord?

HAMLET Between who?

POLONIUS I mean, the matter that you read, my lord.

HAMLET Slanders, sir; for the satirical rogue says here that old men have grey beards; that their faces are wrinkled; their eyes purging thick amber and plum-tree gum; and that they have a plentiful lack of wit, together with most weak hams – all which, sir, though I most powerfully and potently believe, yet I hold it not honesty to have it thus set down; for you yourself, sir, shall grow old as I am, if, like a crab, you could go backward.

POLONIUS [*Aside*] Though this be madness, yet there is method in't. – Will you walk out of the air, my lord?

HAMLET Into my grave?

POLONIUS Indeed, that's out of the air. [*Aside*] How pregnant sometimes his replies are! a happiness that often madness hits on, which reason and sanity could not so prosperously be delivered of. I will leave him, and suddenly contrive the means of meeting between him and my daughter. – My lord, I will take my leave of you.

HAMLET You cannot, sir, take from me anything that I will more willingly part withal – except my life, except my life, except my life.

Enter ROSENCRANTZ and GUILDENSTERN.

POLONIUS Fare you well, my lord.

HAMLET These tedious old fools!

POLONIUS You go to seek the Lord Hamlet; there he is.

ROSENCRANTZ [*To Polonius*] God save you, sir!

[*Exit Polonius.*

GUILDENSTERN My honour'd lord!

ROSENCRANTZ My most dear lord!

HAMLET My excellent good friends! How dost thou, Guildenstern? Ah, Rosencrantz! Good lads, how do you both?

ROSENCRANTZ As the indifferent children of the earth.

GUILDENSTERN Happy in that we are not over-happy;
On fortune's cap we are not the very button.

HAMLET Nor the soles of her shoe?

ROSENCRANTZ Neither, my lord.

HAMLET Then you live about her waist, or in the middle of her favours?

GUILDENSTERN Faith, her privates we.

HAMLET In the secret parts of Fortune? O, most true; she is a strumpet. What news?

ROSENCRANTZ None, my lord, but that the world's grown honest.

HAMLET Then is doomsday near. But your news is not true. Let me question more in particular. What have you, my good friends, deserved at the hands of Fortune, that she sends you to prison hither?

GUILDENSTERN Prison, my lord!

HAMLET Denmark's a prison.

ROSENCRANTZ Then is the world one.

HAMLET A goodly one; in which there are many confines, wards, and dungeons, Denmark being one o' th' worst.

ROSENCRANTZ We think not so, my lord.

HAMLET Why, then, 'tis none to you; for there is nothing either good or bad, but thinking makes it so. To me it is a prison.

ROSENCRANTZ Why, then your ambition makes it one; 'tis too narrow for your mind.

HAMLET O God, I could be bounded in a nutshell and count myself a king of infinite space, were it not that I have bad dreams.

GUILDENSTERN Which dreams indeed are ambition; for the very substance of the ambitious is merely the shadow of a dream.

HAMLET A dream itself is but a shadow.

ROSENCRANTZ Truly, and I hold ambition of so airy and light a quality that it is but a shadow's shadow.

HAMLET Then are our beggars bodies, and our monarchs and outstretch'd heroes the beggars' shadows. Shall we to th' court? for, by my fay, I cannot reason.

BOTH We'll wait upon you.

HAMLET No such matter. I will not sort you with the rest of my servants; for, to speak to you like an honest man, I am most dreadfully attended. But, in the beaten way of friendship, what make you at Elsinore?

ROSENCRANTZ To visit you, my lord; no other occasion.

HAMLET Beggar that I am, I am even poor in thanks; but I thank you; and sure, dear friends, my thanks are too dear a half-penny. Were you not sent for? Is it your own inclining? Is it a free visitation? Come, come, deal justly with me. Come, come; nay, speak.

GUILDENSTERN What should we say, my lord?

HAMLET Why any thing. But to th' purpose: you were sent for; and there is a kind of confession in your looks, which your modesties have not craft enough to colour; I know the good King and Queen have sent for you.

ROSENCRANTZ To what end, my lord?

HAMLET That you must teach me. But let me conjure you by the rights of our fellowship, by the consonancy of our youth, by the obligation of our ever-preserved love, and by what more dear a better proposer can charge you withal, be even and direct with me, whether you were sent for or no?

ROSENCRANTZ [*Aside to Guildenstern*] What say you?

HAMLET [*Aside*] Nay, then, I have an eye of you. – If you love me, hold not off.

GUILDENSTERN My lord, we were sent for.

HAMLET I will tell you why; so shall my anticipation prevent your discovery, and your secrecy to the King and Queen moult no feather. I have of late – but wherefore I know not – lost all my mirth, forgone all custom of exercises; and indeed it goes so heavily with my disposition that this goodly frame, the earth, seems to me a sterile promontory; this most excellent canopy the air, look you, this brave o'er-hanging firmament, this majestical roof fretted with golden fire – why, it appeareth no other thing to me than a foul and pestilent congregation of vapours. What a piece of work is a man! How noble in reason! how infinite in faculties! in form and moving, how express and admirable! in action, how like an angel! in apprehension, how like a god! the beauty of the world! the paragon of animals! And yet, to me, what is this quintessence of dust? Man delights not me – no, nor woman neither, though by your smiling you seem to say so.

ROSENCRANTZ My lord, there was no such stuff in my thoughts.

HAMLET Why did ye laugh, then, when I said 'Man delights not me'?

ROSENCRANTZ To think, my lord, if you delight not in man, what lenten entertainment the players shall receive from you. We coted them on the way; and hither are they coming to offer you service.

HAMLET He that plays the king shall be welcome – his Majesty shall have tribute on me; the adventurous knight shall use his foil and target; the lover shall not sigh gratis; the humorous man shall end his part in peace; the clown shall make those laugh whose lungs are tickle a' th' sere; and the lady shall say her mind freely, or the blank verse shall halt for't. What players are they?

ROSENCRANTZ Even those you were wont to take such delight in – the tragedians of the city.

HAMLET How chances it they travel? Their residence, both in reputation and profit, was better both ways.

ROSENCRANTZ I think their inhibition comes by the means of the late innovation.

HAMLET Do they hold the same estimation they did when I was in the city? Are they so followed?

ROSENCRANTZ No, indeed, are they not.

HAMLET How comes it? Do they grow rusty?

ROSENCRANTZ Nay, their endeavour keeps in the wonted pace; but there is, sir, an eyrie of children, little eyases, that cry out on the top of question, and are most tyrannically clapp'd for't. These are now the fashion, and so berattle the common stages – so they call them – that many wearing rapiers are afraid of goose quills and dare scarce come thither.

HAMLET What, are they children? Who maintains 'em? How are they escoted? Will they pursue the quality no longer than they can sing? Will they not say afterwards, if they should grow themselves to common players – as it is most like, if their means are no better – their writers do them wrong to make them exclaim against their own succession?

ROSENCRANTZ Faith, there has been much to-do on both sides; and the nation holds it no sin to tarre them to controversy. There was for a while no money bid for argument, unless the poet and the player went to cuffs in the question.

HAMLET Is't possible?

GUILDENSTERN O, there has been much throwing about of brains.

HAMLET Do the boys carry it away?

ROSENCRANTZ Ay, that they do, my lord – Hercules and his load too.

HAMLET It is not very strange; for my uncle is King of Denmark, and those that would make mows at him while my father lived give twenty, forty, fifty, a hundred ducats apiece for his picture in little. 'Sblood, there is something in this more than natural, if philosophy could find it out. [*A flourish.*

GUILDENSTERN There are the players.

HAMLET Gentlemen, you are welcome to Elsinore. Your hands, come then; th' appurtenance of welcome is fashion and ceremony. Let me comply with you in this garb; lest my extent to the players, which, I tell you, must show fairly outwards, should more appear like entertainment than yours. You are welcome. But my uncle-father and aunt-mother are deceived.

GUILDENSTERN In what, my dear lord?

HAMLET I am but mad north-north-west; when the wind is southerly I know a hawk from a handsaw.

Re-enter POLONIUS.

POLONIUS Well be with you, gentlemen!

HAMLET Hark you, Guildenstern, and you too –

at each ear a hearer: that great baby you see there is not yet out of his swaddling clouts.

ROSENCRANTZ Happily he is the second time come to them; for they say an old man is twice a child.

HAMLET I will prophesy he comes to tell me of the players; mark it. You say right, sir: a Monday morning; 'twas then indeed.

POLONIUS My lord, I have news to tell you.

HAMLET My lord, I have news to tell you. When Roscius was an actor in Rome –

POLONIUS The actors are come hither, my lord.

HAMLET Buzz, buzz!

POLONIUS Upon my honour –

HAMLET Then came each actor on his ass –

POLONIUS The best actors in the world, either for tragedy, comedy, history, pastoral, pastoral-comical, historical-pastoral, tragical-historical, tragical-comical-historical-pastoral, scene individable, or poem unlimited. Seneca cannot be too heavy nor Plautus too light. For the law of writ and the liberty, these are the only men.

HAMLET O Jephthah, judge of Israel, what a treasure hadst thou!

POLONIUS What a treasure had he, my lord?

HAMLET Why –

'One fair daughter, and no more,
The which he loved passing well'.

POLONIUS [*Aside*] Still on my daughter.

HAMLET Am I not i' th' right, old Jephthah?

POLONIUS If you call me Jephthah, my lord, I have a daughter that I love passing well.

HAMLET Nay, that follows not.

POLONIUS What follows then, my lord?

HAMLET Why –

'As by lot, God wot'

and then, you know,

'It came to pass, as most like it was'.

The first row of the pious chanson will show you more; for look where my abridgement comes.

Enter the Players.

You are welcome, masters; welcome, all. – I am glad to see thee well. – Welcome, good friends. – O, my old friend! Why thy face is valanc'd since I saw thee last; com'st thou to beard me in Denmark? – What, my young lady and mistress! By'r lady, your ladyship is nearer to heaven than when I saw you last by the altitude of a chopine. Pray God, your voice, like a piece of uncurrent gold, be not crack'd within the ring. – Masters, you are all welcome. We'll e'en to't like French falconers, fly at anything we see. We'll have a speech straight. Come, give us a taste of your quality; come, a passionate speech.

1 PLAYER What speech, my good lord?

HAMLET I heard thee speak me a speech once, but it was never acted; or, if it was, not above once; for the play, I remember, pleas'd not the million; 'twas caviary to the general. But it was – as I received it, and others whose judgments in such matters cried in the top of mine – an excellent play, well digested in the scenes, set down with as much modesty as cunning. I remember one said there were no sallets in the lines to make the matter savoury, nor no matter in the phrase that might indict the author of affectation; but call'd it an honest method, as wholesome as sweet, and very much more handsome than fine. One speech in it I chiefly lov'd: 'twas Æneas' tale to Dido; and thereabout of it especially where he speaks of Priam's slaughter. If it live in your memory, begin at this line – let me see, let me see:

'The rugged Pyrrhus, like th' Hyrcanian beast,'

'Tis not so; it begins with Pyrrhus.

'The rugged Pyrrhus, he whose sable arms,
Black as his purpose, did the night resemble
When he lay couched in the ominous horse,
Hath now this dread and black complexion smear'd
With heraldry more dismal; head to foot
Now is he total gules, horridly trick'd
With blood of fathers, mothers, daughters, sons,
Bak'd and impasted with the parching streets,
That lend a tyrannous and damned light
To their lord's murder. Roasted in wrath and fire,
And thus o'er-sized with coagulate gore,
With eyes like carbuncles, the hellish Pyrrhus
Old grandsire Priam seeks.'

So proceed you.

POLONIUS For God, my lord, well spoken, with good accent and good discretion.

1 PLAYER 'Anon he finds him
Striking too short at Greeks; his antique sword,
Rebellious to his arm, lies where it falls,
Repugnant to command. Unequal match'd,
Pyrrhus at Priam drives, in rage strikes wide;
But with the whiff and wind of his fell sword
Th' unnerved father falls. Then senseless Ilium,
Seeming to feel this blow, with flaming top
Stoops to his base, and with a hideous crash
Takes prisoner Pyrrhus' ear. For, lo! his sword,
Which was declining on the milky head
Of reverend Priam, seem'd i' th' air to stick.
So, as a painted tyrant, Pyrrhus stood
And, like a neutral to his will and matter,
Did nothing.
But as we often see, against some storm,

A silence in the heavens, the rack stand still,
The bold winds speechless, and the orb below
As hush as death, anon the dreadful thunder
Doth rend the region; so, after Pyrrhus' pause,
A roused vengeance sets him new a-work;
And never did the Cyclops' hammers fall
On Mars's armour, forg'd for proof eterne,
With less remorse than Pyrrhus' bleeding sword
Now falls on Priam.
Out, out, thou strumpet, Fortune! All you gods,
In general synod, take away her power;
Break all the spokes and fellies from her wheel,
And bowl the round nave down the hill of heaven,
As low as to the fiends.'

POLONIUS This is too long.

HAMLET It shall to the barber's, with your beard. Prithee say on. He's for a jig, or a tale of bawdry, or he sleeps. Say on; come to Hecuba.

1 PLAYER 'But who, ah, who had seen the mobled queen –'

HAMLET 'The mobled queen'?

POLONIUS That's good; 'mobled queen' is good.

1 PLAYER 'Run barefoot up and down, threat'ning the flames
With bisson rheum; a clout upon that head
Where late the diadem stood, and for a robe,
About her lank and all o'er-teemed lions,
A blanket, in the alarm of fear caught up –
Who this nad seen, with tongue in venom steep'd,
'Gainst Fortune's state would treason have pronounc'd.
But if the gods themselves did see her then,
When she saw Pyrrhus make malicious sport
In mincing with his sword her husband's limbs,
The instant burst of clamour that she made –
Unless things mortal move them not at all –
Would have made milch the burning eyes of heaven,
And passion in the gods.'

POLONIUS Look whe'er he has not turn'd his colour, and has tears in 's eyes. Prithee no more.

HAMLET 'Tis well; I'll have thee speak out the rest of this soon. – Good my lord, will you see the players well bestowed? Do you hear: let them be well used; for they are the abstract and brief chronicles of the time; after your death you were better have a bad epitaph than their ill report while you live.

POLONIUS My lord, I will use them according to their desert.

HAMLET God's bodykins, man, much better. Use every man after his desert, and who shall scape whipping? Use them after your own honour and dignity: the less they deserve, the more merit is in your bounty. Take them in.

POLONIUS Come, sirs.

HAMLET Follow him, friends. We'll hear a play to-morrow. Dost thou hear me, old friend; can you play 'The Murder of Gonzago'?

1 PLAYER Ay, my lord.

HAMLET We'll ha't to-morrow night. You could, for a need, study a speech of some dozen or sixteen lines which I would set down and insert in't, could you not?

1 PLAYER Ay, my lord.

HAMLET Very well. Follow that lord; and look you mock him not. [*Exeunt Polonius and Players*] My good friends, I'll leave you till night. You are welcome to Elsinore.

ROSENCRANTZ Good my lord!

[*Exeunt Rosencrantz and Guildenstern.*

HAMLET Ay, so God buy to you! Now I am alone.
O, what a rogue and peasant slave am I!
Is it not monstrous that this player here,
But in a fiction, in a dream of passion,
Could force his soul so to his own conceit
That from her working all his visage wann'd;
Tears in his eyes, distraction in's aspect,
A broken voice, and his whole function suiting
With forms to his conceit? And all for nothing!
For Hecuba!
What's Hecuba to him or he to Hecuba,
That he should weep for her? What would he do,
Had he the motive and the cue for passion
That I have? He would drown the stage with tears,
And cleave the general ear with horrid speech;
Make mad the guilty, and appal the free,
Confound the ignorant, and amaze indeed
The very faculties of eyes and ears.
Yet I,
A dull and muddy-mettl'd rascal, peak,
Like John-a-dreams, unpregnant of my cause,
And can say nothing; no, not for a king
Upon whose property and most dear life
A damn'd defeat was made. Am I a coward?
Who calls me villain, breaks my pate across,
Plucks off my beard and blows it in my face,
Tweaks me by the nose, gives me the lie i' th' throat
As deep as to the lungs? Who does me this?
Ha!
'Swounds, I should take it; for it cannot be
But I am pigeon-liver'd and lack gall
To make oppression bitter, or ere this
I should 'a fatted all the region kites
With this slave's offal. Bloody, bawdy villain!
Remorseless, treacherous, lecherous, kindless villain!

O, vengeance!
Why, what an ass am I! This is most brave,
That I, the son of a dear father murder'd,
Prompted to my revenge by heaven and hell,
Must, like a whore, unpack my heart with
words,
And fall a-cursing like a very drab,
A scullion! Fie upon't! foh!
About, my brains. Hum – I have heard
That guilty creatures, sitting at a play,
Have by the very cunning of the scene
Been struck so to the soul that presently
They have proclaim'd their malefactions;
For murder, though it have no tongue, will
speak
With most miraculous organ. I'll have these
players
Play something like the murder of my father
Before mine uncle. I'll observe his looks;
I'll tent him to the quick. If 'a do blench,
I know my course. The spirit that I have seen
May be a devil; and the devil hath power
T' assume a pleasing shape; yea, and perhaps
Out of my weakness and my melancholy,
As he is very potent with such spirits,
Abuses me to damn me. I'll have grounds
More relative than this. The play's the thing
Wherein I'll catch the conscience of the King.
[*Exit*.

ACT THREE

SCENE I. *Elsinore. The Castle.*

Enter KING, QUEEN, POLONIUS, OPHELIA, ROSENCRANTZ, and GUILDENSTERN.

KING And can you by no drift of conference
Get from him why he puts on this confusion,
Grating so harshly all his days of quiet
With turbulent and dangerous lunacy?
ROSENCRANTZ He does confess he feels himself
distracted,
But from what cause 'a will by no means speak.
GUILDENSTERN Nor do we find him forward to
be sounded;
But, with a crafty madness, keeps aloof
When we would bring him on to some
confession
Of his true state.
QUEEN Did he receive you well?
ROSENCRANTZ Most like a gentleman.
GUILDENSTERN But with much forcing of his
disposition.
ROSENCRANTZ Niggard of question; but of our
demands
Most free in his reply.
QUEEN Did you assay him
To any pastime?
ROSENCRANTZ Madam, it so fell out that certain
players
We o'er-raught on the way. Of these we told
him;
And there did seem in him a kind of joy
To hear of it. They are here about the court,
And, as I think, they have already order
This night to play before him.
POLONIUS 'Tis most true;
And he beseech'd me to entreat your Majesties
To hear and see the matter.
KING With all my heart; and it doth much
content me
To hear him so inclin'd.
Good gentlemen, give him a further edge,
And drive his purpose into these delights.
ROSENCRANTZ We shall, my lord.
[*Exeunt Rosencrantz and Guildenstern*.
KING Sweet Gertrude, leave us too;
For we have closely sent for Hamlet hither,
That he, as 'twere by accident, may here
Affront Ophelia.
Her father and myself – lawful espials –
Will so bestow ourselves that, seeing unseen,
We may of their encounter frankly judge,
And gather by him, as he is behav'd,
If't be th' affliction of his love or no
That thus he suffers for.
QUEEN I shall obey you;
And for your part, Ophelia, I do wish
That your good beauties be the happy cause
Of Hamlet's wildness; so shall I hope your
virtues
Will bring him to his wonted way again,
To both your honours.
OPHELIA Madam, I wish it may.
[*Exit Queen*.
POLONIUS Ophelia, walk you here. – Gracious,
so please you,
We will bestow ourselves. – Read on this book;
That show of such an exercise may colour
Your loneliness. – We are oft to blame in this:
'Tis too much prov'd, that with devotion's visage
And pious action we do sugar o'er
The devil himself.
KING [*Aside*] O, 'tis too true!
How smart a lash that speech doth give my
conscience!

The harlot's cheek, beautied with plast'ring art,
Is not more ugly to the thing that helps it
Than is my deed to my most painted word.
O heavy burden!

POLONIUS I hear him coming; let's withdraw, my lord.

[Exeunt King and Polonius.

Enter HAMLET.

HAMLET To be, or not to be – that is the question;
Whether 'tis nobler in the mind to suffer
The slings and arrows of outrageous fortune,
Or to take arms against a sea of troubles,
And by opposing end them? To die, to sleep –
No more; and by a sleep to say we end
The heart-ache and the thousand natural shocks
That flesh is heir to. 'Tis a consummation
Devoutly to be wish'd. To die, to sleep;
To sleep, perchance to dream. Ay, there's the rub;
For in that sleep of death what dreams may come,
When we have shuffled off this mortal coil,
Must give us pause. There's the respect
That makes calamity of so long life;
For who would bear the whips and scorns of time,
Th' oppressor's wrong, the proud man's contumely,
The pangs of despis'd love, the law's delay,
The insolence of office, and the spurns
That patient merit of th' unworthy takes,
When he himself might his quietus make
With a bare bodkin? Who would these fardels bear,
To grunt and sweat under a weary life,
But that the dread of something after death –
The undiscover'd country, from whose bourn
No traveller returns – puzzles the will,
And makes us rather bear those ills we have
Than fly to others that we know not of?
Thus conscience does make cowards of us all;
And thus the native hue of resolution
Is sicklied o'er with the pale cast of thought,
And enterprises of great pitch and moment,
With this regard, their currents turn awry
And lose the name of action. – Soft you now!
The fair Ophelia. – Nymph, in thy orisons
Be all my sins rememb'red.

OPHELIA Good my lord,
How does your honour for this many a day?

HAMLET I humbly thank you; well, well, well.

OPHELIA My lord, I have remembrances of yours
That I have longed long to re-deliver.
I pray you now receive them.

HAMLET No, not I;
I never gave you aught.

OPHELIA My honour'd lord, you know right well you did,
And with them words of so sweet breath compos'd
As made the things more rich; their perfume lost,
Take these again; for to the noble mind
Rich gifts wax poor when givers prove unkind.
There, my lord.

HAMLET Ha, ha! Are you honest?

OPHELIA My lord?

HAMLET Are you fair?

OPHELIA What means your lordship?

HAMLET That if you be honest and fair, your honesty should admit no discourse to your beauty.

OPHELIA Could beauty, my lord, have better commerce than with honesty?

HAMLET Ay, truly; for the power of beauty will sooner transform honesty from what it is to a bawd than the force of honesty can translate beauty into his likeness. This was sometime a paradox, but now the time gives it proof. I did love you once.

OPHELIA Indeed, my lord, you made me believe so.

HAMLET You should not have believ'd me; for virtue cannot so inoculate our old stock but we shall relish of it. I loved you not.

OPHELIA I was the more deceived.

HAMLET Get thee to a nunnery. Why wouldst thou be a breeder of sinners? I am myself indifferent honest, but yet I could accuse me of such things that it were better my mother had not borne me: I am very proud, revengeful, ambitious; with more offences at my beck than I have thoughts to put them in, imagination to give them shape, or time to act them in. What should such fellows as I do crawling between earth and heaven? We are arrant knaves, all; believe none of us. Go thy ways to a nunnery. Where's your father?

OPHELIA At home, my lord.

HAMLET Let the doors be shut upon him, that he may play the fool nowhere but in's own house. Farewell.

OPHELIA O, help him, you sweet heavens!

HAMLET If thou dost marry, I'll give thee this plague for thy dowry: be thou as chaste as ice, as pure as snow, thou shalt not escape calumny. Get thee to a nunnery, go, farewell. Or, if thou wilt needs marry, marry a fool; for wise men know well enough what monsters you make of them. To a nunnery, go; and quickly too. Farewell.

OPHELIA O heavenly powers, restore him!

HAMLET I have heard of your paintings too, well enough; God hath given you one face, and you make yourselves another. You jig and amble, and you lisp, and nickname God's creatures, and make your wantonness your ignorance. Go to, I'll no more on't; it hath made me mad. I say we will have no moe marriage: those that are married already, all but one, shall live; the rest shall keep as they are. To a nunnery, go. [*Exit.*

OPHELIA O, what a noble mind is here o'er-thrown!
The courtier's, soldier's, scholar's, eye, tongue, sword;
Th' expectancy and rose of the fair state,
The glass of fashion and the mould of form,
Th' observ'd of all observers – quite, quite down!
And I, of ladies most deject and wretched,
That suck'd the honey of his music vows,
Now see that noble and most sovereign reason,
Like sweet bells jangled, out of time and harsh;
That unmatch'd form and feature of blown youth
Blasted with ecstasy. O, woe is me
T' have seen what I have seen, see what I see!

Re-enter KING and POLONIUS.

KING Love! His affections do not that way tend;
Nor what he spake, though it lack'd form a little,
Was not like madness. There's something in his soul
O'er which his melancholy sits on brood;
And I do doubt the hatch and the disclose
Will be some danger; which to prevent
I have in quick determination
Thus set it down: he shall with speed to England
For the demand of our neglected tribute.
Haply the seas and countries different,
With variable objects, shall expel
This something-settled matter in his heart
Whereon his brains still beating puts him thus
From fashion of himself. What think you on't?

POLONIUS It shall do well. But yet do I believe
The origin and commencement of his grief
Sprung from neglected love. How now, Ophelia!
You need not tell us what Lord Hamlet said;
We heard it all. My lord, do as you please;
But if you hold it fit, after the play
Let his queen mother all alone entreat him
To show his grief. Let her be round with him;
And I'll be plac'd, so please you, in the ear
Of all their conference. If she find him not,
To England send him; or confine him where
Your wisdom best shall think.

KING It shall be so:
Madness in great ones must not unwatch'd go.
[*Exeunt.*

SCENE II. *Elsinore. The Castle.*

Enter HAMLET and three of the Players.

HAMLET Speak the speech, I pray you, as I pronounc'd it to you, trippingly on the tongue; but if you mouth it, as many of our players do, I had as lief the town-crier spoke my lines. Nor do not saw the air too much with your hand, thus, but use all gently; for in the very torrent, tempest, and, as I may say, whirlwind of your passion, you must acquire and beget a temperance that may give it smoothness. O, it offends me to the soul to hear a robustious periwig-pated fellow tear a passion to tatters, to very rags, to split the ears of the groundlings, who, for the most part, are capable of nothing but inexplicable dumb shows and noise. I would have such a fellow whipp'd for o'erdoing Termagant; it out-herods Herod. Pray you avoid it.

1 PLAYER I warrant your honour.

HAMLET Be not too tame neither, but let your own discretion be your tutor. Suit the action to the word, the word to the action; with this special observance, that you o'er-step not the modesty of nature; for any-thing so o'erdone is from the purpose of playing, whose end, both at the first and now, was and is to hold, as 'twere, the mirror up to nature; to show virtue her own feature, scorn her own image, and the very age and body of the time his form and pressure. Now, this overdone or come tardy off, though it makes the unskilful laugh, cannot but make the judicious grieve; the censure of the which one must, in your allowance, o'erweigh a whole theatre of others. O, there be players that I have seen play – and heard others praise, and that highly – not to speak it profanely, that, neither having th' accent of Christians, nor the gait of Christian, pagan, nor man, have so strutted and bellowed that I have thought some of Nature's journeymen had made men, and not made them well, they imitated humanity so abominably.

1 PLAYER I hope we have reform'd that indifferently with us, sir.

HAMLET O, reform it altogether. And let those that play your clowns speak no more than is set down for them; for there be of them that will themselves laugh, to set on some quantity of barren spectators to laugh too, though in the meantime some necessary question of the play be then to be considered. That's villainous, and shows a most pitiful ambition in the fool that uses it. Go, make you ready. [*Exeunt Players.*

Enter POLONIUS, ROSENCRANTZ, and GUILDENSTERN.

How now, my lord! Will the King hear this piece of work?

POLONIUS And the Queen too, and that presently.

HAMLET Bid the players make haste.

[Exit Polonius.

Will you two help to hasten them?

ROSENCRANTZ Ay, my lord. *[Exeunt they two.*

HAMLET What, ho, Horatio!

Enter HORATIO.

HORATIO Here, sweet lord, at your service.

HAMLET Horatio, thou art e'en as just a man
As e'er my conversation cop'd withal.

HORATIO O my dear lord!

HAMLET Nay, do not think I flatter;
For what advancement may I hope from thee,
That no revenue hast but thy good spirits
To feed and clothe thee? Why should the poor be flatter'd?
No, let the candied tongue lick absurd pomp,
And crook the pregnant hinges of the knee
Where thrift may follow fawning. Dost thou hear?
Since my dear soul was mistress of her choice
And could of men distinguish her election,
Sh'hath seal'd thee for herself; for thou hast been
As one in suff'ring all, that suffers nothing;
A man that Fortune's buffets and rewards
Hast ta'en with equal thanks; and blest are those
Whose blood and judgment are so well comeddled
That they are not a pipe for Fortune's finger
To sound what stop she please. Give me that man
That is not passion's slave, and I will wear him
In my heart's core, ay, in my heart of heart,
As I do thee. Something too much of this.
There is a play to-night before the King;
One scene of it comes near the circumstance
Which I have told thee of my father's death.
I prithee, when thou seest that act afoot,
Even with the very comment of thy soul
Observe my uncle. If his occulted guilt
Do not itself unkennel in one speech,
It is a damned ghost that we have seen,
And my imaginations are as foul
As Vulcan's stithy. Give him heedful note;
For I mine eyes will rivet to his face;
And, after, we will both our judgments join
In censure of his seeming.

HORATIO Well, my lord.
If 'a steal aught the whilst this play is playing,
And scape detecting, I will pay the theft.

Enter trumpets and kettledrums. Danish march. Sound a flourish. Enter KING, QUEEN, POLONIUS, OPHELIA, ROSENCRANTZ, GUILDENSTERN, and other Lords attendant, with the Guard carrying torches.

HAMLET They are coming to the play; I must be idle.
Get you a place.

KING How fares our cousin Hamlet?

HAMLET Excellent, i' faith; of the chameleon's dish. I eat the air, promise-cramm'd; you cannot feed capons so.

KING I have nothing with this answer, Hamlet; these words are not mine.

HAMLET No, nor mine now. *[To Polonius]* My lord, you play'd once i' th' university, you say?

POLONIUS That did I, my lord, and was accounted a good actor.

HAMLET What did you enact?

POLONIUS I did enact Julius Caesar; I was kill'd i' th' Capitol; Brutus kill'd me.

HAMLET It was a brute part of him to kill so capital a calf there. Be the players ready?

ROSENCRANTZ Ay, my lord; they stay upon your patience.

QUEEN Come hither, my dear Hamlet, sit by me.

HAMLET No, good mother; here's metal more attractive.

POLONIUS *[To the King]* O, ho! do you mark that?

HAMLET Lady, shall I lie in your lap?

[Lying down at Ophelia's feet.

OPHELIA No, my lord.

HAMLET I mean, my head upon your lap?

OPHELIA Ay, my lord.

HAMLET Do you think I meant country matters?

OPHELIA I think nothing, my lord.

HAMLET That's a fair thought to lie between maids' legs.

OPHELIA What is, my lord?

HAMLET Nothing.

OPHELIA You are merry, my lord.

HAMLET Who, I?

OPHELIA Ay, my lord.

HAMLET O God, your only jig-maker! What should a man do but be merry? For look you how cheerfully my mother looks, and my father died within's two hours.

OPHELIA Nay, 'tis twice two months, my lord.

HAMLET So long? Nay then, let the devil wear black, for I'll have a suit of sables. O heavens! die two months ago, and not forgotten yet? Then there's hope a great man's memory may outlive his life half a year; but, by'r lady, 'a must build churches, then; or else shall 'a suffer not thinking on, with the hobby-horse, whose epitaph is 'For O, for O, the hobby-horse is forgot!'

The trumpet sounds. Hautboys play. The Dumb Show enters.

Enter a King and a Queen, very lovingly; the Queen embracing him and he her. She kneels, and makes show of protestation unto him. He takes her up, and declines his head upon her neck. He lies him down upon a bank of flowers; she, seeing him asleep, leaves him. Anon comes in a Fellow, takes off his crown, kisses it, pours poison in the sleeper's ears, and leaves him. The Queen returns; finds the King dead, and makes passionate action. The Poisoner, with some two or three Mutes, comes in again, seeming to condole with her. The dead body is carried away. The Poisoner woos the Queen with gifts; she seems harsh awhile, but in the end accepts his love. [*Exeunt.*

OPHELIA What means this, my lord?

HAMLET Marry, this is miching mallecho; it means mischief.

OPHELIA Belike this show imports the argument of the play.

Enter Prologue.

HAMLET We shall know by this fellow: the players cannot keep counsel; they'll tell all.

OPHELIA Will 'a tell us what this show meant?

HAMLET Ay, or any show that you will show him. Be not you asham'd to show, he'll not shame to tell you what it means.

OPHELIA You are naught, you are naught. I'll mark the play.

PROLOGUE *For us, and for our tragedy,*
Here stooping to your clemency,
We beg your hearing patiently. [*Exit.*

HAMLET Is this a prologue, or the posy of a ring?

OPHELIA 'Tis brief, my lord.

HAMLET As woman's love.

Enter the Player King and Queen.

PLAYER KING *Full thirty times hath Phoebus' cart gone round*
Neptune's salt wash and Tellus' orbed ground,
And thirty dozen moons with borrowed sheen
About the world have times twelve thirties been,
Since love our hearts and Hymen did our hands
Unit comutual in most sacred bands.

PLAYER QUEEN *So many journeys may the sun and moon*
Make us again count o'er ere love be done!
But, woe is me, you are so sick of late,
So far from cheer and from your former state,
That I distrust you. Yet, though I distrust,
Discomfort you, my lord, it nothing must;
For women fear too much even as they love,
And women's fear and love hold quantity,
In neither aught, or in extremity.
Now, what my love is, proof hath made you know;
And as my love is siz'd, my fear is so.
Where love is great, the littlest doubts are fear;
Where little fears grow great, great love grows there.

PLAYER KING *Faith, I must leave thee, love, and shortly too:*
My operant powers their functions leave to do;
And thou shalt live in this fair world behind,
Honour'd, belov'd; and haply one as kind
For husband shalt thou –

PLAYER QUEEN *O, confound the rest!*
Such love must needs be treason in my breast.
In second husband let me be accurst!
None wed the second but who kill'd the first.

HAMLET That's wormwood, wormwood.

PLAYER QUEEN *The instances that second marriage move*
Are base respects of thrift, but none of love.
A second time I kill my husband dead,
When second husband kisses me in bed.

PLAYER KING *I do believe you think what now you speak;*
But what we do determine oft we break.
Purpose is but the slave to memory,
Of violent birth, but poor validity;
Which now, the fruit unripe, sticks on the tree;
But fall unshaken when they mellow be.
Most necessary 'tis that we forget
To pay ourselves what to ourselves is debt.
What to ourselves in passion we propose,
The passion ending, doth the purpose lose.
The violence of either grief or joy
Their own enactures with themselves destroy.
Where joy most revels grief doth most lament;
Grief joys, joy grieves, on slender accident.
This world is not for aye; nor 'tis not strange
That even our loves should with our fortunes change;
For 'tis a question left us yet to prove,
Whether love lead fortune or else fortune love.
The great man down, you mark his favourite flies;
The poor advanc'd makes friends of enemies.
And hitherto doth love on fortune tend;
For who not needs shall never lack a friend,
And who in want a hollow friend doth try,
Directly seasons him his enemy.
But, orderly to end where I begun,
Our wills and fates do so contrary run
That our devices still are overthrown;
Our thoughts are ours, their ends none of our own.
So think thou wilt no second husband wed;

But die thy thoughts when thy first lord is dead.

PLAYER QUEEN *Nor earth to me give food, nor heaven light,*
Sport and repose lock from me day and night,
To desperation turn my trust and hope,
An anchor's cheer in prison be my scope,
Each opposite that blanks the face of joy
Meet what I would have well, and it destroy,
Both here and hence pursue me lasting strife,
If, once a widow, ever I be wife!

HAMLET If she should break it now!

PLAYER KING *'Tis deeply sworn. Sweet, leave me here awhile;*
My spirits grow dull, and fain I would beguile
The tedious day with sleep.

[*Sleeps.*

PLAYER QUEEN *Sleep rock thy brain,*
And never come mischance between us twain!

[*Exit.*

HAMLET Madam, how like you this play?

QUEEN The lady doth protest too much, methinks.

HAMLET O, but she'll keep her word.

KING Have you heard the argument? Is there no offence in't?

HAMLET No, no; they do but jest, poison in jest; no offence i' th' world.

KING What do you call the play?

HAMLET 'The Mouse-trap.' Marry, how? Tropically. This play is the image of a murder done in Vienna: Gonzago is the duke's name; his wife, Baptista. You shall see anon. 'Tis a knavish piece of work; but what of that? Your Majesty, and we that have free souls, it touches us not. Let the galled jade wince, our withers are unwrung.

Enter LUCIANUS.

This is one Lucianus, nephew to the King.

OPHELIA You are as good as a chorus, my lord.

HAMLET I could interpret between you and your love, if I could see the puppets dallying.

OPHELIA You are keen, my lord, you are keen.

HAMLET It would cost you a groaning to take off mine edge.

OPHELIA Still better, and worse.

HAMLET So you mis-take your husbands. – Begin, murderer; pox, leave thy damnable faces and begin. Come; the croaking raven doth bellow for revenge.

LUCIANUS *Thoughts black, hands apt, drugs fit, and time agreeing;*
Confederate season, else no creature seeing;
Thou mixture rank, of midnight weeds collected,
With Hecat's ban thrice blasted, thrice infected,
Thy natural magic and dire property
On wholesome life usurps immediately.

[*Pours the poison in his ears.*

HAMLET 'A poisons him i' th' garden for his estate. His name's Gonzago. The story is extant, and written in very choice Italian. You shall see anon how the murderer gets the love of Gonzago's wife.

OPHELIA The King rises.

HAMLET What, frighted with false fire!

QUEEN How fares my lord?

POLONIUS Give o'er the play.

KING Give me some light. Away!

POLONIUS Lights, lights, lights!

[*Exeunt all but Hamlet and Horatio.*

HAMLET Why, let the strucken deer go weep,
The hart ungalled play;
For some must watch, while some must sleep;
Thus runs the world away.
Would not this, sir, and a forest of feathers – if the rest of my fortunes turn Turk with me – with two Provincial roses on my raz'd shoes, get me a fellowship in a cry of players, sir?

HORATIO Half a share.

HAMLET A whole one, I.
For thou dost know, O Damon dear,
This realm dismantled was
Of Jove himself; and now reigns here
A very, very – paiock.

HORATIO You might have rhym'd.

HAMLET O good Horatio, I'll take the ghost's word for a thousand pound. Didst perceive?

HORATIO Very well, my lord.

HAMLET Upon the talk of the poisoning.

HORATIO I did very well note him.

HAMLET Ah, ha! Come, some music. Come, the recorders.
For if the King like not the comedy,
Why, then, belike he likes it not, perdy.
Come, some music.

Re-enter ROSENCRANTZ and GUILDENSTERN.

GUILDENSTERN Good my lord, vouchsafe me a word with you.

HAMLET Sir, a whole history.

GUILDENSTERN The King, sir –

HAMLET Ay, sir, what of him?

GUILDENSTERN Is, in his retirement, marvellous distemp'red.

HAMLET With drink, sir?

GUILDENSTERN No, my lord, rather with choler.

HAMLET Your wisdom should show itself more richer to signify this to his doctor; for for me to put him to his purgation would perhaps plunge him into far more choler.

GUILDENSTERN Good my lord, put your discourse into some frame, and start not so wildly from my affair.

HAMLET I am tame, sir. Pronounce.

GUILDENSTERN The Queen, your mother, in most great affliction of spirit, hath sent me to you.

HAMLET You are welcome.

GUILDENSTERN Nay, good my lord, this courtesy is not of the right breed. If it shall please you to make me a wholesome answer, I will do your mother's commandment; if not, your pardon and my return shall be the end of my business.

HAMLET Sir, I cannot.

ROSENCRANTZ What, my lord?

HAMLET Make you a wholesome answer; my wit's diseas'd. But, sir, such answer as I can make, you shall command; or rather, as you say, my mother. Therefore no more, but to the matter: my mother, you say –

ROSENCRANTZ Then thus she says: your behaviour hath struck her into amazement and admiration.

HAMLET O wonderful son, that can so stonish a mother! But is there no sequel at the heels of this mother's admiration? Impart.

ROSENCRANTZ She desires to speak with you in her closet ere you go to bed.

HAMLET We shall obey, were she ten times our mother. Have you any further trade with us?

ROSENCRANTZ My lord, you once did love me.

HAMLET And do still, by these pickers and stealers.

ROSENCRANTZ Good my lord, what is your cause of distemper? You do surely bar the door upon your own liberty, if you deny your griefs to your friend.

HAMLET Sir, I lack advancement.

ROSENCRANTZ How can that be, when you have the voice of the King himself for your succession in Denmark?

HAMLET Ay, sir, but 'While the grass grows' – the proverb is something musty.

Re-enter the Players, with recorders.

O, the recorders! Let me see one. To withdraw with you – why do you go about to recover the wind of me, as if you would drive me into a toil?

GUILDENSTERN O my lord, if my duty be too bold, my love is too unmannerly.

HAMLET I do not well understand that. Will you play upon this pipe?

GUILDENSTERN My lord, I cannot.

HAMLET I pray you.

GUILDENSTERN Believe me, I cannot.

HAMLET I do beseech you.

GUILDENSTERN I know no touch of it, my lord.

HAMLET It is as easy as lying: govern these ventages with your fingers and thumb, give it breath with your mouth, and it will discourse most eloquent music. Look you, these are the stops.

GUILDENSTERN But these cannot I command to any utterance of harmony; I have not the skill.

HAMLET Why, look you now, how unworthy a thing you make of me! You would play upon me; you would seem to know my stops; you would pluck out the heart of my mystery; you would sound me from my lowest note to the top of my compass; and there is much music, excellent voice, in this little organ, yet cannot you make it speak. 'Sblood, do you think I am easier to be play'd on than a pipe? Call me what instrument you will, though you can fret me, yet you cannot play upon me.

Re-enter POLONIUS.

God bless you, sir!

POLONIUS My lord, the Queen would speak with you, and presently.

HAMLET Do you see yonder cloud that's almost in shape of a camel?

POLONIUS By th' mass, and 'tis like a camel indeed.

HAMLET Methinks it is like a weasel.

POLONIUS It is back'd like a weasel.

HAMLET Or like a whale?

POLONIUS Very like a whale.

HAMLET Then I will come to my mother by and by. [*Aside*] They fool me to the top of my bendt. – I will come by and by.

POLONIUS I will say so. [*Exit Polonius.*

HAMLET 'By and by' is easily said. Leave me, friends. [*Exeunt all but Hamlet.*

'Tis now the very witching time of night,
When churchyards yawn, and hell itself breathes out
Contagion to this world. Now could I drink hot blood,
And do such bitter business as the day
Would quake to look on. Soft! now to my mother.
O heart, lose not thy nature; let not ever
The soul of Nero enter this firm bosom.
Let me be cruel, not unnatural:
I will speak daggers to her, but use none.
My tongue and soul in this be hypocrites –
How in my words somever she be shent,
To give them seals never, my soul, consent!
[*Exit.*

SCENE III. *Elsinore. The Castle.*

Enter KING, ROSENCRANTZ, and GUILDENSTERN.

KING I like him not; nor stands it safe with us.

To let his madness range. Therefore prepare you;
I your commission will forthwith dispatch,
And he to England shall along with you.
The terms of our estate may not endure
Hazard so near's as doth hourly grow
Out of his brows.

GUILDENSTERN We will ourselves provide.
Most holy and religious fear it is
To keep those many many bodies safe
That live and feed upon your Majesty.

ROSENCRANTZ The single and peculiar life is bound
With all the strength and armour of the mind
To keep itself from noyance; but much more
That spirit upon whose weal depends and rests
The lives of many. The cease of majesty
Dies not alone, but like a gulf doth draw
What's near it with it. It is a massy wheel,
Fix'd on the summit of the highest mount,
To whose huge spokes ten thousand lesser things
Are mortis'd and adjoin'd; which when it falls,
Each small annexment, petty consequence,
Attends the boist'rous ruin. Never alone
Did the king sigh, but with a general groan.

KING Arm you, I pray you, to this speedy voyage;
For we will fetters put about this fear,
Which now goes too free-footed.

ROSENCRANTZ We will haste us.

[Exeunt Rosencrantz and Guildenstern.

Enter POLONIUS.

POLONIUS My lord, he's going to his mother's closet.
Behind the arras I'll convey myself
To hear the process. I'll warrant she'll tax him home;
And, as you said, and wisely was it said,
'Tis meet that some more audience than a mother,
Since nature makes them partial, should o'erhear
The speech, of vantage. Fare you well, my liege.
I'll call upon you ere you go to bed,
And tell you what I know.

KING Thanks, dear my lord.

[Exit Polonius.

O, my offence is rank, it smells to heaven;
It hath the primal eldest curse upon't –
A brother's murder! Pray can I not,
Though inclination be as sharp as will.
My stronger guilt defeats my strong intent,
And, like a man to double business bound,
I stand in pause where I shall first begin,
And both neglect. What if this cursed hand
Were thicker than itself with brother's blood,
Is there not rain enough in the sweet heavens
To wash it white as snow? Whereto serves mercy
But to confront the visage of offence?
And what's in prayer but this twofold force,
To be forestalled ere we come to fall,
Or pardon'd being down? Then I'll look up;
My fault is past. But, O, what form of prayer
Can serve my turn? 'Forgive me my foul murder'!
That cannot be; since I am still possess'd
Of those effects for which I did the murder –
My crown, mine own ambition, and my queen.
May one be pardon'd and retain th' offence?
In the corrupted currents of this world
Offence's gilded hand may shove by justice;
And oft 'tis seen the wicked prize itself
Buys out the law. But 'tis not so above:
There is no shuffling; there the action lies
In his true nature; and we ourselves compell'd,
Even to the teeth and forehead of our faults,
To give in evidence. What then? What rests?
Try what repentance can. What can it not?
Yet what can it when one can not repent?
O wretched state! O bosom black as death!
O limed soul, that, struggling to be free,
Art more engag'd! Help, angels. Make assay:
Bow, stubborn knees; and, heart, with strings of steel,
Be soft as sinews of the new-born babe.
All may be well.

[Retires and kneels.

Enter HAMLET.

HAMLET Now might I do it pat, now 'a is a-praying;
And now I'll do't – and so 'a goes to heaven,
And so am I reveng'd. That would be scann'd:
A villain kills my father; and for that,
I, his sole son, do this same villain send
To heaven.
Why, this is hire and salary, not revenge.
'A took my father grossly, full of bread,
With all his crimes broad blown, as flush as May;
And how his audit stands who knows save heaven?
But in our circumstance and course of thought
'Tis heavy with him; and am I then reveng'd
To take him in the purging of his soul,
When he is fit and season'd for his passage?
No.
Up, sword, and know thou a more horrid hent.
When he is drunk asleep, or in his rage;
Or in th' incestuous pleasure of his bed;
At game, a-swearing, or about some act
That has no relish of salvation in't –

Then trip him, that his heels may kick at heaven,
And that his soul may be as damn'd and black
As hell, whereto it goes. My mother stays.
This physic but prolongs thy sickly days.
[Exit.

KING *[Rising]* My words fly up, my thoughts remain below.
Words without thoughts never to heaven go.
[Exit.

SCENE IV. *The Queen's closet.*

Enter QUEEN and POLONIUS.

POLONIUS 'A will come straight. Look you lay home to him;
Tell him his pranks have been too broad to bear with,
And that your Grace hath screen'd and stood between
Much heat and him. I'll silence me even here.
Pray you be round with him.

HAMLET *[Within]* Mother, mother, mother!

QUEEN I'll warrant you. Fear me not.
Withdraw, I hear him coming.
[Polonius goes behind the arras.

Enter HAMLET.

HAMLET Now, mother, what's the matter?

QUEEN Hamlet, thou hast thy father much offended.

HAMLET Mother, you have my father much offended.

QUEEN Come, come, you answer with an idle tongue.

HAMLET Go, go, you question with a wicked tongue.

QUEEN Why, how now, Hamlet!

HAMLET What's the matter now?

QUEEN Have you forgot me?

HAMLET No, by the rood, not so:
You are the Queen, your husband's brother's wife;
And – would it were not so! – you are my mother.

QUEEN Nay then, I'll set those to you that can speak.

HAMLET Come, come, and sit you down; you shall not budge.
You go not till I set you up a glass
Where you may see the inmost part of you.

QUEEN What wilt thou do? Thou wilt not murder me?
Help, help, ho!

POLONIUS *[Behind]* What, ho! help, help, help!

HAMLET *[Draws]* How now! a rat?
Dead, for a ducat, dead! *[Kills Polonius with a pass through the arras.*

POLONIUS *[Behind]* O, I am slain!

QUEEN O me, what hast thou done?

HAMLET Nay, I know not:
Is it the King?

QUEEN O, what a rash and bloody deed is this!

HAMLET A bloody deed! – almost as bad, good mother,
As kill a king and marry with his brother.

QUEEN As kill a king!

HAMLET Ay, lady, it was my word.
[Parting the arras.
Thou wretched, rash, intruding fool, farewell!
I took thee for thy better. Take thy fortune;
Thou find'st to be too busy is some danger.
Leave wringing of your hands. Peace; sit you down,
And let me wring your heart; for so I shall,
If it be made of penetrable stuff;
If damned custom have not braz'd it so
That it be proof and bulwark against sense.

QUEEN What have I done that thou dar'st wag thy tongue
In noise so rude against me?

HAMLET Such an act
That blurs the grace and blush of modesty;
Calls virtue hypocrite; takes off the rose
From the fair forehead of an innocent love,
And sets a blister there; makes marriage-vows
As false as dicers' oaths. O, such a deed
As from the body of contraction plucks
The very soul, and sweet religion makes
A rhapsody of words. Heaven's face does glow
O'er this solidity and compound mass
With heated visage, as against the doom –
Is thought-sick at the act.

QUEEN Ay me, what act,
That roars so loud and thunders in the index?

HAMLET Look here upon this picture and on this,
The counterfeit presentment of two brothers.
See what a grace was seated on this brow;
Hyperion's curls; the front of Jove himself;
An eye like Mars, to threaten and command;
A station like the herald Mercury
New lighted on a heaven-kissing hill –
A combination and a form indeed
Where every god did seem to set his seal,
To give the world assurance of a man.
This was your husband. Look you now what follows:
Here is your husband, like a mildew'd ear
Blasting his wholesome brother. Have you eyes?
Could you on this fair mountain leave to feed,
And batten on this moor? Ha! have you eyes?
You cannot call it love; for at your age

The heyday in the blood is tame, it's humble,
And waits upon the judgment; and what judgment
Would step from this to this? Sense, sure, you have,
Else could you not have motion; but sure that sense
Is apoplex'd; for madness would not err,
Nor sense to ecstasy was ne'er so thrall'd
But it reserv'd some quantity of choice
To serve in such a difference. What devil was't
That thus hath cozen'd you at hoodman-blind?
Eyes without feeling, feeling without sight,
Ears without hands or eyes, smelling sans all,
Or but a sickly part of one true sense
Could not so mope. O shame! where is thy blush?
Rebellious hell,
If thou canst mutine in a matron's bones,
To flaming youth let virtue be as wax
And melt in her own fire; proclaim no shame
When the compulsive ardour gives the charge,
Since frost itself as actively doth burn,
And reason panders will.

QUEEN O Hamlet, speak no more!
Thou turn'st my eyes into my very soul;
And there I see such black and grained spots
As will not leave their tinct.

HAMLET Nay, but to live
In the rank sweat of an enseamed bed,
Stew'd in corruption, honeying and making love
Over the nasty sty!

QUEEN O, speak to me no more!
These words like daggers enter in my ears;
No more, sweet Hamlet.

HAMLET A murderer and a villain!
A slave that is not twentieth part the tithe
Of your precedent lord; a vice of kings;
A cutpurse of the empire and the rule,
That from a shelf the precious diadem stole
And put it in his pocket!

QUEEN No more!

Enter Ghost.

HAMLET A king of shreds and patches –
Save me, and hover o'er me with your wings,
You heavenly guards! What would your gracious figure?

QUEEN Alas, he's mad!

HAMLET Do you not come your tardy son to chide,
That, laps'd in time and passion, lets go by
Th' important acting of your dread command?
O, say!

GHOST Do not forget; this visitation
Is but to whet thy almost blunted purpose.
But look, amazement on thy mother sits.
O, step between her and her fighting soul!
Conceit in weakest bodies strongest works.
Speak to her, Hamlet.

HAMLET How is it with you, lady?

QUEEN Alas, how is't with you,
That you do bend your eye on vacancy,
And with th' incorporal air do hold discourse?
Forth at your eyes your spirits wildly peep;
And, as the sleeping soldiers in th' alarm,
Your bedded hairs like life in excrements
Start up and stand an end. O gentle son,
Upon the heat and flame of thy distemper
Sprinkle cool patience! Whereon do you look?

HAMLET On him, on him! Look you how pale he glares.
His form and cause conjoin'd, preaching to stones,
Would make them capable. – Do not look upon me,
Lest with this piteous action you convert
My stern effects; then what I have to do
Will want true colour – tears perchance for blood.

QUEEN To whom do you speak this?

HAMLET Do you see nothing there?

QUEEN Nothing at all; yet all that is I see.

HAMLET Nor did you nothing hear?

QUEEN No, nothing but ourselves.

HAMLET Why, look you there. Look how it steals away.
My father, in his habit as he liv'd!
Look where he goes even now out at the portal.

[*Exit Ghost.*

QUEEN This is the very coinage of your brain.
This bodiless creation ecstasy
Is very cunning in.

HAMLET Ecstasy!
My pulse as yours doth temperately keep time,
And makes as healthful music. It is not madness
That I have utt'red. Bring me to the test,
And I the matter will re-word which madness
Would gambol from. Mother, for love of grace,
Lay not that flattering unction to your soul,
That not your trespass but my madness speaks:
It will but skin and film the ulcerous place,
Whiles rank corruption, mining all within,
Infects unseen. Confess yourself to heaven;
Repent what's past; avoid what is to come;
And do not spread the compost on the weeds,
To make them ranker. Forgive me this my virtue;
For in the fatness of these pursy times
Virtue itself of vice must pardon beg,
Yea, curb and woo for leave to do him good.

QUEEN O Hamlet, thou hast cleft my heart in twain.

HAMLET O, throw away the worser part of it,
And live the purer with the other half.
Good night – but go not to my uncle's bed;
Assume a virtue, if you have it not.
That monster custom, who all sense doth eat,
Of habits devil, is angel yet in this,
That to the use of actions fair and good
He likewise gives a frock or livery
That aptly is put on. Refrain to-night;
And that shall lend a kind of easiness
To the next abstinence; the next more easy;
For use almost can change the stamp of nature,
And either curb the devil, or throw him out,
With wondrous potency. Once more, good night;
And when you are desirous to be blest,
I'll blessing beg of you. For this same lord
I do repent; but Heaven hath pleas'd it so,
To punish me with this, and this with me,
That I must be their scourge and minister.
I will bestow him, and will answer well
The death I gave him. So, again, good night.
I must be cruel only to be kind;
Thus bad begins and worse remains behind.
One word more, good lady.
QUEEN What shall I do?
HAMLET Not this, by no means, that I bid you do:
Let the bloat King tempt you again to bed;
Pinch wanton on your cheek; call you his mouse;
And let him, for a pair of reechy kisses,
Or paddling in your neck with his damn'd fingers,
Make you to ravel all this matter out,
That I essentially am not in madness,
But mad in craft. 'Twere good you let him know;
For who that's but a queen, fair, sober, wise,
Would from a paddock, from a bat, a gib,
Such dear concernings hide? Who would do so?
No, in despite of sense and secrecy,
Unpeg the basket on the house's top,
Let the birds fly, and, like the famous ape,
To try conclusions, in the basket creep
And break your own neck down.
QUEEN Be thou assur'd, if words be made of breath
And breath of life, I have no life to breathe
What thou hast said to me.
HAMLET I must to England; you know that?
QUEEN Alack,
I had forgot. 'Tis so concluded on.
HAMLET There's letters seal'd; and my two school-fellows,
Whom I will trust as I will adders fang'd –
They bear the mandate; they must sweep my way
And marshal me to knavery. Let it work;
For 'tis the sport to have the engineer
Hoist with his own petar; and't shall go hard
But I will delve one yard below their mines
And blow them at the moon. O, 'tis most sweet
When in one line two crafts directly meet.
This man shall set me packing.
I'll lug the guts into the neighbour room.
Mother, good night. Indeed, this counsellor
Is now most still, most secret, and most grave,
Who was in life a foolish prating knave.
Come, sir, to draw toward an end with you.
Good night, mother.

[*Exeunt severally; Hamlet tugging in Polonius.*

ACT FOUR

SCENE I. *Elsinore. The Castle.*

Enter KING, QUEEN, ROSENCRANTZ, and GUILDENSTERN.

KING There's matter in these sighs, these profound heaves,
You must translate; 'tis fit we understand them.
Where is your son?
QUEEN Bestow this place on us a little while.

[*Exeunt Rosencrantz and Guildenstern.*

Ah, mine own lord, what have I seen to-night!
KING What, Gertrude? How does Hamlet?
QUEEN Mad as the sea and wind, when both contend
Which is the mightier. In his lawless fit,
Behind the arras hearing something stir,
Whips out his rapier, cries 'A rat, a rat!'
And in this brainish apprehension kills
The unseen good old man.
KING O heavy deed!
It had been so with us had we been there.
His liberty is full of threats to all –
To you yourself, to us, to every one.
Alas, how shall this bloody deed be answer'd?
It will be laid to us, whose providence
Should have kept short, restrain'd, and out of haunt,
This mad young man. But so much was our love,
We would not understand what was most fit;
But, like the owner of a foul disease,
To keep it from divulging, let it feed

Even on the pith of life. Where is he gone?
QUEEN To draw apart the body he hath kill'd;
O'er whom his very madness, like some ore
Among a mineral of metals base,
Shows itself pure: 'a weeps for what is done.
KING O Gertrude, come away!
The sun no sooner shall the mountains touch
But we will ship him hence; and this vile deed
We must with all our majesty and skill
Both countenance and excuse. Ho, Guildenstern!

Re-enter ROSENCRANTZ and GUILDENSTERN.

Friends, both go join you with some further aid:
Hamlet in madness hath Polonius slain,
And from his mother's closet hath he dragg'd him;
Go seek him out; speak fair, and bring the body
Into the chapel. I pray you haste in this.
[*Exeunt Rosencrantz and Guildenstern.*

Come, Gertrude, we'll call up our wisest friends
And let them know both what we mean to do
And what's untimely done; so haply slander –
Whose whisper o'er the world's diameter,
As level as the cannon to his blank,
Transports his pois'ned shot – may miss our name,
And hit the woundless air. O, come away!
My soul is full of discord and dismay. [*Exeunt.*

SCENE II. *Elsinore. The Castle.*

Enter HAMLET.

HAMLET Safely stow'd.
GENTLEMEN [*Within*] Hamlet! Lord Hamlet!
HAMLET But soft! What noise? Who calls on Hamlet? O, here they come!

Enter ROSENCRANTZ and GUILDENSTERN.

ROSENCRANTZ What have you done, my lord, with the dead body?
HAMLET Compounded it with dust, whereto 'tis kin.
ROSENCRANTZ Tell us where 'tis, that we may take it thence
And bear it to the chapel.
HAMLET Do not believe it.
ROSENCRANTZ Believe what?
HAMLET That I can keep your counsel, and not mine own. Besides, to be demanded of a sponge – what replication should be made by the son of a king?
ROSENCRANTZ Take you me for a sponge, my lord?
HAMLET Ay, sir; that soaks up the King's countenance, his rewards, his authorities. But such officers do the King best service in the end: he keeps them, like an ape an apple in the corner of his jaw; first mouth'd, to be last swallowed; when he needs what you have glean'd, it is but squeezing you and, sponge, you shall be dry again.
ROSENCRANTZ I understand you not, my lord.
HAMLET I am glad of it; a knavish speech sleeps in a foolish ear.
ROSENCRANTZ My lord, you must tell us where the body is, and go with us to the King.
HAMLET The body is with the King, but the King is not with the body. The King is a thing –
GUILDENSTERN A thing, my lord!
HAMLET Of nothing. Bring me to him.
Hide fox, and all after. [*Exeunt.*

SCENE III. *Elsinore. The Castle.*

Enter KING, attended.

KING I have sent to seek him, and to find the body.
How dangerous is it that this man goes loose!
Yet must not we put the strong law on him:
He's lov'd of the distracted multitude,
Who like not in their judgment but their eyes;
And where 'tis so, th' offender's scourge is weigh'd,
But never the offence. To bear all smooth and even,
This sudden sending him away must seem
Deliberate pause. Diseases desperate grown
By desperate appliance are reliev'd,
Or not at all.

Enter ROSENCRANTZ.

How now! what hath befall'n?
ROSENCRANTZ Where the dead body is bestow'd, my lord,
We cannot get from him.
KING But where is he?
ROSENCRANTZ Without, my lord; guarded, to know your pleasure.
KING Bring him before us.
ROSENCRANTZ Ho, Guildenstern! bring in the lord.

Enter HAMLET and GUILDENSTERN.

KING Now, Hamlet, where's Polonius?
HAMLET At supper.
KING At supper! Where?
HAMLET Not where he eats, but where 'a is eaten; a certain convocation of politic worms are e'en at him. Your worm is your only emperor for diet: we fat all creatures else to fat us, and we fat ourselves for maggots; your fat king and your lean beggar is but variable service – two dishes,

but to one table. That's the end.

KING Alas, alas!

HAMLET A man may fish with the worm that hath eat of a king, and eat of the fish that hath fed of that worm.

KING What dost thou mean by this?

HAMLET Nothing but to show you how a king may go a progress through the guts of a beggar.

KING Where is Polonius?

HAMLET In heaven; send thither to see; if your messenger find him not there, seek him i' th' other place yourself. But if, indeed, you find him not within this month, you shall nose him as you go up the stairs into the lobby.

KING [*To Attendants*] Go seek him there.

HAMLET 'A will stay till you come.

[*Exeunt Attendants.*

KING Hamlet, this deed, for thine especial safety –
Which we do tender, as we dearly grieve
For that which thou hast done – must send thee hence
With fiery quickness. Therefore prepare thyself;
The bark is ready, and the wind at help,
Th' associates tend, and everything is bent
For England.

HAMLET For England!

KING Ay, Hamlet.

HAMLET Good!

KING So is it, if thou knew'st our purposes.

HAMLET I see a cherub that sees them.
But, come; for England! Farewell, dear mother.

KING Thy loving father, Hamlet.

HAMLET My mother: father and mother is man and wife; man and wife is one flesh; and so, my mother. Come, for England. [*Exit.*

KING Follow him at foot; tempt him with speed aboard;
Delay it not; I'll have him hence to-night.
Away! for everything is seal'd and done
That else leans on th' affair. Pray you make haste. [*Exeunt all but the King.*
And, England, if my love thou hold'st at aught –
As my great power thereof may give thee sense,
Since yet thy cicatrice looks raw and red
After the Danish sword, and thy free awe
Pays homage to us – thou mayst not coldly set
Our sovereign process; which imports at full,
By letters congruing to that effect,
The present death of Hamlet. Do it, England:
For like the hectic in my blood he rages,
And thou must cure me. Till I know 'tis done,
Howe'er my haps, my joys were ne'er begun.

[*Exit.*

SCENE IV. *A plain in Denmark.*

Enter FORTINBRAS with his Army over the stage.

FORTINBRAS Go, Captain, from me greet the Danish king.
Tell him that by his licence Fortinbras
Craves the conveyance of a promis'd march
Over his kingdom. You know the rendezvous.
If that his Majesty would aught with us,
We shall express our duty in his eye;
And let him know so.

CAPTAIN I will do't, my lord.

FORTINBRAS Go softly on.

[*Exeunt all but the Captain.*

Enter HAMLET, ROSENCRANTZ, GUILDENSTERN, and Others.

HAMLET Good sir, whose powers are these?

CAPTAIN They are of Norway, sir.

HAMLET How purpos'd, sir, I pray you?

CAPTAIN Against some part of Poland.

HAMLET Who commands them, sir?

CAPTAIN The nephew to old Norway, Fortinbras.

HAMLET Goes it against the main of Poland, sir,
Or for some frontier?

CAPTAIN Truly to speak, and with no addition,
We go to gain a little patch of ground
That hath in it no profit but the name.
To pay five ducats, five, I would not farm it;
Nor will it yield to Norway or the Pole
A ranker rate should it be sold in fee.

HAMLET Why, then the Polack never will defend it.

CAPTAIN Yes, it is already garrison'd.

HAMLET Two thousand souls and twenty thousand ducats
Will not debate the question of this straw.
This is th' imposthume of much wealth and peace,
That inward breaks, and shows no cause without
Why the man dies. I humbly thank you, sir.

CAPTAIN God buy you, sir. [*Exit.*

ROSENCRANTZ Will't please you go, my lord?

HAMLET I'll be with you straight. Go a little before. [*Exeunt all but Hamlet.*

How all occasions do inform against me,
And spur my dull revenge! What is a man,
If his chief good and market of his time
Be but to sleep and feed? A beast, no more!
Sure he that made us with such large discourse,
Looking before and after, gave us not
That capability and godlike reason
To fust in us unus'd. Now, whether it be
Bestial oblivion, or some craven scruple
Of thinking too precisely on th' event –

A thought which, quarter'd, hath but one part wisdom
And ever three parts coward – I do not know
Why yet I live to say 'This thing's to do',
Sith I have cause, and will, and strength, and means,
To do't. Examples gross as earth exhort me:
Witness this army, of such mass and charge,
Led by a delicate and tender prince,
Whose spirit, with divine ambition puff'd,
Makes mouths at the invisible event,
Exposing what is mortal and unsure
To all that fortune, death, and danger, dare,
Even for an egg-shell. Rightly to be great
Is not to stir without great argument,
But greatly to find quarrel in a straw,
When honour's at the stake. How stand I, then,
That have a father kill'd, a mother stain'd,
Excitements of my reason and my blood,
And let all sleep, while to my shame I see
The imminent death of twenty thousand men
That, for a fantasy and trick of fame,
Go to their graves like beds, fight for a plot
Whereon the numbers cannot try the cause,
Which is not tomb enough and continent
To hide the slain? O, from this time forth,
My thoughts be bloody, or be nothing worth!
[*Exit*.

SCENE V. *Elsinore. The Castle.*

Enter QUEEN, HORATIO, and a Gentleman.

QUEEN I will not speak with her.
GENTLEMAN She is importunate, indeed distract.
Her mood will needs be pitied.
QUEEN What would she have?
GENTLEMAN She speaks much of her father; says she hears
There's tricks i' th' world, and hems, and beats her heart;
Spurns enviously at straws; speaks things in doubt,
That carry but half sense. Her speech is nothing,
Yet the unshaped use of it doth move
The hearers to collection; they yawn at it,
And botch the words up fit to their own thoughts;
Which, as her winks and nods and gestures yield them,
Indeed would make one think there might be thought,
Though nothing sure, yet much unhappily.
HORATIO 'Twere good she were spoken with; for she may strew
Dangerous conjectures in ill-breeding minds.
QUEEN Let her come in. [*Exit Gentleman*.
[*Aside*] To my sick soul, as sin's true nature is,
Each toy seems prologue to some great amiss.
So full of artless jealousy is guilt,
It spills itself in fearing to be spilt.

Enter OPHELIA distracted.

OPHELIA Where is the beautous Majesty of Denmark?
QUEEN How now, Ophelia!
OPHELIA [*Sings*] How should I your true love know
From another one?
By his cockle hat and staff,
And his sandal shoon.

QUEEN Alas, sweet lady, what imports this song?
OPHELIA Say you? Nay, pray you mark.
[*Sings*] He is dead and gone, lady,
He is dead and gone;
At his head a grass-green turf,
At his heels a stone.

O, ho!
QUEEN Nay, but, Ophelia –
OPHELIA Pray you mark.
[*Sings*] White his shroud as the mountain snow –

Enter KING.

QUEEN Alas, look here, my lord.
OPHELIA Larded with sweet flowers;
Which bewept to the grave did not go
With true-love showers.
KING How do you, pretty lady?
OPHELIA Well, God dild you! They say the owl was a baker's daughter. Lord, we know what we are, but know not what we may be. God be at your table!
KING Conceit upon her father.
OPHELIA Pray let's have no words of this; but when they ask you what it means, say you this:
[*Sings*] To-morrow is Saint Valentine's day,
All in the morning betime,
And I a maid at your window,
To be your Valentine.

Then up he rose, and donn'd his clothes,
And dupp'd the chamber-door;
Let in the maid, that out a maid
Never departed more.
KING Pretty Ophelia!
OPHELIA Indeed, la, without an oath, I'll make an end on't.
[*Sings*] By Gis and by Saint Charity,
Alack, and fie for shame!
Young men will do't, if they come to't;
By Cock, they are to blame.
Quoth she 'Before you tumbled me,
You promis'd me to wed'.
He answers:

'So would I 'a done, by yonder sun,
An thou hadst not come to my bed'.

KING How long hath she been thus?

OPHELIA I hope all will be well. We must be patient; but I cannot choose but weep to think they would lay him i' th' cold ground. My brother shall know of it; and so I thank you for your good counsel. Come, my coach! Good night, ladies; good night, sweet ladies, good night, good night. [*Exit.*

KING Follow her close; give her good watch, I pray you.

[*Exeunt Horatio and Gentleman.*

O, this is the poison of deep grief; it springs
All from her father's death. And now behold –
O Gertrude, Gertrude!
When sorrows come, they come not single spies,
But in battalions! First, her father slain;
Next, your son gone, and he most violent author
Of his own just remove; the people muddied,
Thick and unwholesome in their thoughts and whispers
For good Polonius' death; and we have done but greenly
In hugger-mugger to inter him; poor Ophelia
Divided from herself and her fair judgment,
Without the which we are pictures, or mere beasts;
Last, and as much containing as all these,
Her brother is in secret come from France;
Feeds on his wonder, keeps himself in clouds,
And wants not buzzers to infect his ear
With pestilent speeches of his father's death;
Wherein necessity, of matter beggar'd,
Will nothing stick our person to arraign
In ear and ear. O my dear Gertrude, this,
Like to a murd'ring piece, in many places
Gives me superfluous death.

[*A noise within.*

QUEEN Alack, what noise is this?

KING Attend!

Enter a Gentleman.

Where are my Switzers? Let them guard the door.
What is the matter?

GENTLEMAN Save yourself, my lord:
The ocean, overpeering of his list,
Eats not the flats with more impitious haste
Than young Laertes, in a riotous head,
O'erbears your officers. The rabble call him lord;
And, as the world were now but to begin,
Antiquity forgot, custom not known,
The ratifiers and props of every word,
They cry 'Choose we; Laertes shall be king'.
Caps, hands, and tongues, applaud it to the clouds,
'Laertes shall be king, Laertes king'.

QUEEN How cheerfully on the false trail they cry!

[*Noise within.*

O, this is counter, you false Danish dogs!

KING The doors are broke.

Enter LAERTES, with Others, in arms.

LAERTES Where is this king? – Sirs, stand you all without.

ALL No, let's come in.

LAERTES I pray you give me leave.

ALL We will, we will. [*Exeunt.*

LAERTES I thank you. Keep the door. – O thou vile king,
Give me my father!

QUEEN Calmly, good Laertes.

LAERTES That drop of blood that's calm proclaims me bastard;
Cries cuckold to my father; brands the harlot
Even here, between the chaste unsmirched brow
Of my true mother.

KING What is the cause, Laertes,
That thy rebellion looks so giant-like?
Let him go, Gertrude; do not fear our person:
There's such divinity doth hedge a king
That treason can but peep to what it would,
Acts little of his will. Tell me, Laertes,
Why thou art thus incens'd. Let him go, Gertrude.
Speak, man.

LAERTES Where is my father?

KING Dead.

QUEEN But not by him.

KING Let him demand his fill.

LAERTES How came he dead? I'll not be juggled with.
To hell, allegiance! Vows, to the blackest devil!
Conscience and grace, to the profoundest pit!
I dare damnation. To this point I stand,
That both the worlds I give to negligence,
Let come what comes; only I'll be reveng'd
Most throughly for my father.

KING Who shall stay you?

LAERTES My will, not all the world's.
And for my means, I'll husband them so well
They shall go far with little.

KING Good Laertes,
If you desire to know the certainty
Of dear father, is't writ in your revenge
That, swoopstake, you will draw both friend and foe,
Winner and loser?

LAERTES None but his enemies.

KING Will you know them, then?

LAERTES To his good friends thus wide I'll ope my arms
And, like the kind life-rend'ring pelican,
Repast them with my blood.

KING Why, now you speak
Like a good child and a true gentleman.
That I am guiltless of your father's death,
And am most sensibly in grief for it,
It shall as level to your judgment 'pear
As day does to your eye.
[*A noise within*: 'Let her come in.'

LAERTES How now! What noise is that?

Re-enter OPHELIA.

O, heat dry up my brains! tears seven times salt
Burn out the sense and virtue of mine eye!
By heaven, thy madness shall be paid with weight
Till our scale turn the beam. O rose of May!
Dear maid, kind sister, sweet Ophelia!
O heavens! is't possible a young maid's wits
Should be as mortal as an old man's life?
Nature is fine in love; and where 'tis fine
It sends some precious instance of itself
After the thing it loves.

OPHELIA [*Sings*] They bore him barefac'd on the bier;
Hey non nonny, nonny, hey nonny;
And in his grave rain'd many a tear –
Fare you well, my dove!

LAERTES Hadst thou thy wits, and didst persuade revenge,
It could not move thus.

OPHELIA You must sing 'A-down, a-down', an you call him a-down-a. O, how the wheel becomes it! It is the false steward, that stole his master's daughter.

LAERTES This nothing's more than matter.

OPHELIA There's rosemary, that's for remembrance; pray you, love, remember. And there is pansies, that's for thoughts.

LAERTES A document in madness – thoughts and remembrance fitted.

OPHELIA There's fennel for you, and columbines. There's rue for you; and here's some for me. We may call it herb of grace a Sundays. O, you must wear your rue with a difference. There's a daisy. I would give you some violets, but they wither'd all when my father died. They say 'a made a good end.

[*Sings*] For bonny sweet Robin is all my joy.

LAERTES Thought and affliction, passion, hell itself,
She turns to favour and to prettiness.

OPHELIA [*Sings*] And will 'a not come again?
And will 'a not come again?
No, no, he is dead,
Go to thy death-bed,
He never will come again.
His beard was as white as snow,
All flaxen was his poll;
He is gone, he is gone,
And we cast away moan:
God-a-mercy on his soul!

And of all Christian souls, I pray God. God buy you. [*Exit.*

LAERTES Do you see this, O God?

KING Laertes, I must commune with your grief,
Or you deny me right. Go but apart,
Make choice of whom your wisest friends you will,
And they shall hear and judge 'twixt you and me.
If by direct or by collateral hand
They find us touch'd, we will our kingdom give,
Our crown, our life, and all that we call ours,
To you in satisfaction; but if not,
Be you content to lend your patience to us,
And we shall jointly labour with your soul
To give it due content.

LAERTES Let this be so.
His means of death, his obscure funeral –
No trophy, sword, nor hatchment, o'er his bones,
No noble rite nor formal ostentation –
Cry to be heard, as 'twere from heaven to earth,
That I must call't in question.

KING So you shall;
And where th' offence is, let the great axe fall.
I pray you go with me. [*Exeunt.*

SCENE VI. *Elsinore. The Castle.*

Enter HORATIO with an Attendant.

HORATIO What are they that would speak with me?

ATTENDANT Sea-faring men, sir; they say they have letters for you.

HORATIO Let them come in. [*Exit Attendant.*

I do not know from what part of the world
I should be greeted, if not from Lord Hamlet.

Enter Sailors.

SAILOR God bless you, sir.

HORATIO Let Him bless thee too.

SAILOR 'A shall, sir, an't please Him. There's a letter for you, sir; it came from th' ambassador that was bound for England – if your name be Horatio, as I am let to know it is.

HORATIO [*Reads*] 'Horatio, when thou shalt have overlook'd this, give these fellows some means

to the King: they have letters for him. Ere we were two days old at sea, a pirate of very warlike appointment gave us chase. Finding ourselves too slow of sail, we put on a compelled valour; and in the grapple I boarded them. On the instant they got clear of our ship; so I alone became their prisoner. They have dealt with me like thieves of mercy; but they knew what they did: I am to do a good turn for them. Let the King have the letters I have sent; and repair thou to me with as much speed as thou wouldest fly death. I have words to speak in thine ear will make thee dumb; yet are they much too light for the bore of the matter. These good fellows will bring thee where I am. Rosencrantz and Guildenstern hold their course for England; of them I have much to tell thee. Farewell.
He that thou knowest thine, HAMLET.'

Come, I will give you way for these your letters,
And do't the speedier that you may direct me
To him from whom you brought them. [*Exeunt.*

SCENE VII. *Elsinore. The Castle.*

Enter KING and LAERTES.

KING Now must your conscience my acquittance seal,
And you must put me in your heart for friend,
Sith you have heard, and with a knowing ear,
That he which hath your noble father slain
Pursu'd my life.

LAERTES It well appears. But tell me
Why you proceeded not against these feats,
So crimeful and so capital in nature,
As by your safety, wisdom, all things else,
You mainly were stirr'd up.

KING O, for two special reasons,
Which may to you, perhaps, seem much unsinew'd,
But yet to me th'are strong. The Queen his mother
Lives almost by his looks; and for myself,
My virtue or my plague, be it either which –
She is so conjunctive to my life and soul
That, as the star moves not but in his sphere,
I could not but by her. The other motive,
Why to a public count I might not go,
Is the great love the general gender bear him;
Who, dipping all his faults in their affection,
Work like the spring that turneth wood to stone,
Convert his gyves to graces; so that my arrows,
Too slightly timber'd for so loud a wind,
Would have reverted to my bow again,
But not where I have aim'd them.

LAERTES And so have I a noble father lost;
A sister driven into desp'rate terms,
Whose worth, if praises may go back again,
Stood challenger on mount of all the age
For her perfections. But my revenge will come.

KING Break not your sleeps for that. You must not think
That we are made of stuff so flat and dull
That we can let our beard be shook with danger,
And think it pastime. You shortly shall hear more.
I lov'd your father, and we love our self;
And that, I hope, will teach you to imagine –

Enter a Messenger with letters.

How now! What news?

MESSENGER Letters, my lord, from Hamlet:
These to your Majesty; this to the Queen.

KING From Hamlet! Who brought them?

MESSENGER Sailors, my lord, they say; I saw them not.
They were given me by Claudio; he receiv'd them
Of him that brought them.

KING Laertes, you shall hear them.
Leave us. [*Exit Messenger.*

[*Reads*] 'High and Mighty. You shall know I am set naked on your kingdom. To-morrow shall I beg leave to see your kingly eyes; when I shall, first asking your pardon thereunto, recount the occasion of my sudden and more strange return.
HAMLET.'

What should this mean? Are all the rest come back?
Or is it some abuse, and no such thing?

LAERTES Know you the hand?

KING 'Tis Hamlet's character. 'Naked'!
And in a postscript here, he says 'alone'.
Can you devise me?

LAERTES I am lost in it, my lord. But let him come;
It warms the very sickness in my heart
That I shall live and tell him to his teeth
'Thus didest thou'.

KING If it be so, Laertes –
As how should it be so, how otherwise? –
Will you be rul'd by me?

LAERTES Ay, my lord;
So you will not o'errule me to a peace.

KING To thine own peace. If he be now return'd,
As checking at his voyage, and that he means
No more to undertake it, I will work him
To an exploit now ripe in my device,
Under the which he shall not choose but fall;
And for his death, no wind of blame shall breathe;
But even his mother shall uncharge the practice
And call it accident.

LAERTES My lord, I will be rul'd
The rather, if you could devise it so
That I might be the organ.
KING It falls right.
You have been talk'd of since your travel much,
And that in Hamlet's hearing, for a quality
Wherein they say you shine. Your sum of parts
Did not together pluck such envy from him
As did that one; and that, in my regard,
Of the unworthiest siege.
LAERTES What part is that, my lord?
KING A very riband in the cap of youth,
Yet needful too; for youth no less becomes
The light and careless livery that it wears
Than settled age his sables and his weeds,
Importing health and graveness. Two months since
Here was a gentleman of Normandy –
I have seen myself, and serv'd against, the French,
And they can well on horseback; but this gallant
Had witchcraft in't; he grew unto his seat,
And to such wondrous doing brought his horse,
As had he been incorps'd and demi-natur'd
With the brave beast. So far he topp'd my thought,
That I, in forgery of shapes and tricks,
Come short of what he did.
LAERTES A Norman was't?
KING A Norman.
LAERTES Upon my life, Lamord.
KING The very same.
LAERTES I know him well. He is the brooch indeed
And gem of all the nation.
KING He made confession of you;
And gave you such a masterly report
For art and exercise in your defence,
And for your rapier most especial,
That he cried out 'twould be a sight indeed
If one could match you. The scrimers of their nation
He swore had neither motion, guard, nor eye,
If you oppos'd them. Sir, this report of his
Did Hamlet so envenom with his envy
That he could nothing do but wish and beg
Your sudden coming o'er, to play with you.
Now, out of this –
LAERTES What out of this, my lord?
KING Laertes, was your father dear to you?
Or are you like the painting of a sorrow,
A face without a heart?
LAERTES Why ask you this?
KING Not that I think you did not love your father;
But that I know love is begun by time,
And that I see, in passages of proof,
Time qualifies the spark and fire of it.
There lives within the very flame of love
A kind of wick or snuff that will abate it;
And nothing is at a like goodness still;
For goodness, growing to a pleurisy,
Dies in his own too much. That we would do,
We should do when we would; for this 'would' changes,
And hath abatements and delays as many
As there are tongues, are hands, are accidents;
And then this 'should' is like a spend-thirft's sigh
That hurts by easing. But to the quick of th' ulcer:
Hamlet comes back; what would you undertake
To show yourself in deed your father's son
More than in words?
LAERTES To cut his throat i' th' church.
KING No place, indeed, should murder sanctuarize;
Revenge should have no bounds. But, good Laertes,
Will you do this? Keep close within your chamber.
Hamlet return'd shall know you are come home.
We'll put on those shall praise your excellence,
And set a double varnish on the fame
The Frenchman gave you; bring you, in fine, together,
And wager on your heads. He, being remiss,
Most generous, and free from all contriving,
Will not peruse the foils; so that with ease
Or with a little shuffling, you may choose
A sword unbated, and, in a pass of practice,
Requite him for your father.
LAERTES I will do't;
And for that purpose I'll anoint my sword.
I bought an unction of a mountebank,
So mortal that but dip a knife in it,
Where it draws blood no cataplasm so rare,
Collected from all simples that have virtue
Under the moon, can save the thing from death
That is but scratch'd withal. I'll touch my point
With this contagion, that, if I gall him slightly,
It may be death.
KING Let's further think of this;
Weigh what convenience both of time and means
May fit us to our shape. If this should fail,
And that our drift look through our bad performance,
'Twere better not assay'd, therefore this project
Should have a back or second, that might hold
If this did blast in proof. Soft! let me see.
We'll make a solemn wager on your cunnings –
I ha't.
When in your motion you are hot and dry –

As make your bouts more violent to that end –
And that he calls for drink, I'll have preferr'd him
A chalice for the nonce; whereon but sipping,
If he by chance escape your venom'd stuck,
Our purpose may hold there. But stay; what noise?

Enter QUEEN.

QUEEN One woe doth tread upon another's heel,
So fast they follow. Your sister's drown'd, Laertes.

LAERTES Drown'd! O, where?

QUEEN There is a willow grows aslant the brook
That shows his hoar leaves in the glassy stream;
Therewith fantastic garlands did she make
Of crowflowers, nettles, daisies, and long purples
That liberal shepherds give a grosser name,
But our cold maids do dead men's fingers call them.
There, on the pendent boughs her coronet weeds
Clamb'ring to hang, an envious sliver broke;
When down her weedy trophies and herself
Fell in the weeping brook. Her clothes spread wide
And, mermaid-like, awhile they bore her up;
Which time she chanted snatches of old lauds,
As one incapable of her own distress,
Or like a creature native and indued
Unto that element; but long it could not be
Till that her garments, heavy with their drink,
Pull'd the poor wretch from her melodious lay
To muddy death.

LAERTES Alas, then she is drown'd!

QUEEN Drown'd, drown'd.

LAERTES Too much of water hast thou, poor Ophelia,
And therefore I forbid my tears; but yet
It is our trick; nature her custom holds,
Let shame say what it will. When these are gone,
The woman will be out. Adieu, my lord.
I have a speech o' fire that fain would blaze
But that this folly douts it. [*Exit.*

KING Let's follow, Gertrude.
How much I had to do to calm his rage!
Now fear I this will give it start again;
Therefore let's follow. [*Exeunt.*

ACT FIVE

SCENE I. *Elsinore. A churchyard.*

Enter two Clowns with spades and picks.

1 CLOWN Is she to be buried in Christian burial when she wilfully seeks her own salvation?

2 CLOWN I tell thee she is; therefore make her grave straight. The crowner hath sat on her, and finds it Christian burial.

1 CLOWN How can that be, unless she drown'd herself in her own defence?

2 CLOWN Why, 'tis found so.

1 CLOWN It must be 'se offendendo'; it cannot be else. For here lies the point: if I drown myself wittingly, it argues an act; and an act hath three branches – it is to act, to do, to perform; argal, she drown'd herself wittingly.

2 CLOWN Nay, but hear you, Goodman Delver.

1 CLOWN Give me leave. Here lies the water; good. Here stands the man; good. If the man go to this water and drown himself, it is, will he, nill he, he goes – mark you that; but if the water come to him and drown him, he drowns not himself. Argal, he that is not guilty of his own death shortens not his own life.

2 CLOWN But is this law?

1 CLOWN Ay, marry, is't; crowner's quest law.

2 CLOWN Will you ha the truth an't? If this had not been a gentlewoman, she should have been buried out a Christian burial.

1 CLOWN Why, there thou say'st; and the more pity that great folk should have count'nance in this world to drown or hang themselves more than their even Christen. Come, my spade. There is no ancient gentlemen but gard'ners, ditchers, and grave-makers; they hold up Adam's profession.

2 CLOWN Was he a gentleman?

1 CLOWN 'A was the first that ever bore arms.

2 CLOWN Why, he had none.

1 CLOWN What, art a heathen? How dost thou understand the Scripture? The Scripture says Adam digg'd. Could he dig without arms? I'll put another question to thee. If thou answerest me not to the purpose, confess thyself –

2 CLOWN Go to.

1 CLOWN What is he that builds stronger than either the mason, the shipwright, or the carpenter?

2 CLOWN The gallows-maker; for that frame outlives a thousand tenants.

1 CLOWN I like thy wit well; in good faith the gallows does well; but how does it well? It does well to those that do ill. Now thou dost ill to say

the gallows is built stronger than the church; argal, the gallows may do well to thee. To't again, come.

2 CLOWN Who builds stronger than a mason, a shipwright, or a carpenter?

1 CLOWN Ay, tell me that, and unyoke.

2 CLOWN Marry, now I can tell.

1 CLOWN To't.

2 CLOWN Mass, I cannot tell.

Enter HAMLET and HORATIO, afar off.

1 CLOWN Cudgel thy brains no more about it, for your dull ass will not mend his pace with beating; and when you are ask'd this question next, say 'a grave-maker': the houses he makes lasts till doomsday. Go, get thee to Yaughan; fetch me a stoup of liquor. [*Exit Second Clown.*

[*Digs and sings*] In youth, when I did love, did love,
Methought it was very sweet,
To contract-o-the time for-a my behove,
O, methought there-a-was nothing-a meet.

HAMLET Has this fellow no feeling of his business, that 'a sings in grave-making?

HORATIO Custom hath made it in him a property of easiness.

HAMLET 'Tis e'en so; the hand of little employment hath the daintier sense.

1 CLOWN [*Sings*] But age, with his stealing steps,
Hath clawed me in his clutch,
And hath shipped me intil the land,
As if I had never been such.

[*Throws up a skull.*

HAMLET That skull had a tongue in it, and could sing once. How the knave jowls it to the ground, as if 'twere Cain's jawbone, that did the first murder! This might be the pate of a politician, which this ass now o'erreaches; one that would circumvent God, might it not?

HORATIO It might, my lord.

HAMLET Or of a courtier; which could say 'Good morrow, sweet lord! How dost thou, sweet lord?' This might be my Lord Such-a-one, that praised my Lord Such-a-one's horse, when 'a meant to beg it – might it not?

HORATIO Ay, my lord.

HAMLET Why, e'en so; and now my Lady Worm's, chapless, and knock'd about the mazard with a sexton's spade. Here's fine revolution, an we had the trick to see't. Did these bones cost no more the breeding but to play at loggats with them? Mine ache to think on't.

1 CLOWN [*Sings*] A pick-axe and a spade, a spade,
For and a shrouding sheet:
O, a pit of clay for to be made
For such a guest is meet.

[*Throws up another skull.*

HAMLET There's another. Why may not that be the skull of a lawyer? Where be his quiddities now, his quillets, his cases, his tenures, and his tricks? Why does he suffer this rude knave now to knock him about the sconce with a dirty shovel, and will not tell him of his action of battery? Hum! This fellow might be in's time a great buyer of land, with his statutes, his recognizances, his fines, his double vouchers, his recoveries. Is this the fine of his fines, and the recovery of his recoveries, to have his fine pate full of fine dirt? Will his vouchers vouch him no more of his purchases, and double ones too, than the length and breadth of a pair of indentures? The very conveyances of his lands will scarcely lie in this box; and must th' inheritor himself have no more, ha?

HORATIO Not a jot more, my lord.

HAMLET Is not parchment made of sheep-skins?

HORATIO Ay, my lord, and of calves' skins too.

HAMLET They are sheep and calves which seek out assurance in that. I will speak to this fellow. Whose grave's this, sirrah?

1 CLOWN Mine, sir.

[*Sings*] O, a pit of clay for to be made
For such a guest is meet.

HAMLET I think it be thine indeed, for thou liest in't.

1 CLOWN You lie out on't, sir, and therefore 'tis not yours. For my part, I do not lie in't, yet it is mine.

HAMLET Thou dost lie in't, to be in't and say it is thine; 'tis for the dead, not for the quick; therefore thou liest.

1 CLOWN 'Tis a quick lie, sir; 'twill away again from me to you.

HAMLET What man dost thou dig it for?

1 CLOWN For no man, sir.

HAMLET What woman, then?

1 CLOWN For none neither.

HAMLET Who is to be buried in't?

1 CLOWN One that was a woman, sir; but, rest her soul, she's dead.

HAMLET How absolute the knave is! We must speak by the card, or equivocation will undo us. By the Lord, Horatio, this three years I have took note of it: the age is grown so picked that the toe of the peasant comes so near the heel of the courtier, he galls his kibe. How long hast thou been a grave-maker?

1 CLOWN Of all the days i' th' year, I came to't

that day that our last King Hamlet overcame Fortinbras.

HAMLET How long is that since?

1 CLOWN Cannot you tell that? Every fool can tell that: it was that very day that young Hamlet was born – he that is mad, and sent into England.

HAMLET Ay, marry, why was he sent into England?

1 CLOWN Why, because 'a was mad: 'a shall recover his wits there; or, if 'a do not, 'tis no great matter there.

HAMLET Why?

1 CLOWN 'Twill not be seen in him there: there the men are as mad as he.

HAMLET How came he mad?

1 CLOWN Very strangely, they say.

HAMLET How strangely?

1 CLOWN Faith, e'en with losing his wits.

HAMLET Upon what ground?

1 CLOWN Why, here in Denmark. I have been sexton here, man and boy, thirty years.

HAMLET How long will a man lie i' th' earth ere he rot?

1 CLOWN Faith, if 'a be not rotten before 'a die – as we have many pocky corses now-a-days that will scarce hold the laying in – 'a will last you some eight year or nine year. A tanner will last you nine year.

HAMLET Why he more than another?

1 CLOWN Why, sir, his hide is so tann'd with his trade that 'a will keep out water a great while; and your water is a sore decayer of your whoreson dead body. Here's a skull now; this skull has lien you i' th' earth three and twenty years.

HAMLET Whose was it?

1 CLOWN A whoreson mad fellow's it was. Whose do you think it was?

HAMLET Nay, I know not.

1 CLOWN A pestilence on him for a mad rogue! 'A poured a flagon of Rhenish on my head once. This same skull, sir, was, sir, Yorick's skull, the King's jester.

HAMLET This?

1 CLOWN E'en that.

HAMLET Let me see. [*Takes the skull*] Alas, poor Yorick! I knew him, Horatio: a fellow of infinite jest, of most excellent fancy; he hath borne me on his back a thousand times. And now how abhorred in my imagination it is! My gorge rises at it. Here hung those lips that I have kiss'd I know not how oft. Where be your gibes now, your gambols, your songs, your flashes of merriment that were wont to set the table on a roar? Not one now to mock your own grinning – quite chap-fall'n? Now get you to my lady's chamber, and tell her, let her paint an inch thick, to this favour she must come; make her laugh at that. Prithee, Horatio, tell me one thing.

HORATIO What's that, my lord?

HAMLET Dost thou think Alexander look'd a this fashion i' th' earth?

HORATIO E'en so.

HAMLET And smelt so? Pah!

[*Throws down the skull.*

HORATIO E'en so, my lord.

HAMLET To what base uses we may return, Horatio! Why may not imagination trace the noble dust of Alexander till 'a find it stopping a bung-hole?

HORATIO 'Twere to consider too curiously to consider so.

HAMLET No, faith, not a jot; but to follow him thither with modesty enough, and likelihood to lead it, as thus: Alexander died, Alexander was buried, Alexander returneth to dust; the dust is earth; of earth we make loam; and why of that loam whereto he was converted might they not stop a beer-barrel?
Imperious Caesar, dead and turn'd to clay,
Might stop a hole to keep the wind away.
O, that that earth which kept the world in awe
Should patch a wall t' expel the winter's flaw!
But soft! but soft! awhile. Here comes the King.

Enter the KING, QUEEN, LAERTES, in funeral procession after the coffin, with Priest and Lords attendant.

The Queen, the courtiers. Who is this they follow?
And with such maimed rites? This doth betoken
The corse they follow did with desperate hand
Fordo it own life. 'Twas of some estate.
Couch we awhile and mark.

[*Retiring with Horatio.*

LAERTES What ceremony else?

HAMLET That is Laertes, a very noble youth. Mark.

LAERTES What ceremony else?

PRIEST Her obsequies have been as far enlarg'd
As we have warrantise. Her death was doubtful;
And, but that great command o'ersways the order,
She should in ground unsanctified have lodg'd
Till the last trumpet; for charitable prayers,
Shards, flints, and pebbles, should be thrown on her;
Yet here she is allow'd her virgin crants,
Her maiden strewments, and the bringing home
Of bell and burial.

LAERTES Must there no more be done?
PRIEST No more be done.
We should profane the service of the dead
To sing sage requiem and such rest to her
As to peace-parted souls.
LAERTES Lay her i' th' earth;
And from her fair and unpolluted flesh
May violets spring! I tell thee, churlish priest,
A minist'ring angel shall my sister be
When thou liest howling.
HAMLET What, the fair Ophelia!
QUEEN Sweets to the sweet; farewell!
[*Scattering flowers.*
I hop'd thou shouldst have been my Hamlet's wife;
I thought thy bride-bed to have deck'd, sweet maid,
And not have strew'd thy grave.
LAERTES O, treble woe
Fall ten times treble on that cursed head
Whose wicked deed thy most ingenious sense
Depriv'd thee of! Hold off the earth awhile,
Till I have caught her once more in mine arms.
[*Leaps into the grave.*
Now pile your dust upon the quick and dead,
Till of this flat a mountain you have made
T' o'er-top old Pelion or the skyish head
Of blue Olympus.
HAMLET [*Advancing*] What is he whose grief
Bears such an emphasis, whose phrase of sorrow
Conjures the wand'ring stars, and makes them stand
Like wonder-wounded hearers? This is I,
Hamlet the Dane. [*Leaps into the grave.*
LAERTES The devil take thy soul!
[*Grappling with him.*
HAMLET Thou pray'st not well.
I prithee take thy fingers from my throat;
For, though I am not splenitive and rash,
Yet have I in me something dangerous,
Which let thy wiseness fear. Hold off thy hand.
KING Pluck them asunder.
QUEEN Hamlet! Hamlet!
ALL Gentlemen!
HORATIO Good my lord, be quiet.

[*The Attendants part them, and they come out of the grave.*

HAMLET Why, I will fight with him upon this theme
Until my eyelids will no longer wag.
QUEEN O my son, what theme?
HAMLET I lov'd Ophelia: forty thousand brothers
Could not, with all their quantity of love,
Make up my sum. What wilt thou do for her?
KING O, he is mad, Laertes.
QUEEN For love of God, forbear him.
HAMLET 'Swounds, show me what th'owt do:
Woo't weep, woo't fight, woo't fast, woo't tear thyself,
Woo't drink up eisel, eat a crocodile?
I'll do't. Dost come here to whine?
To outface me with leaping in her grave?
Be buried quick with her, and so will I;
And, if thou prate of mountains, let them throw
Millions of acres on us, till our ground,
Singeing his pate against the burning zone,
Make Ossa like a wart! Nay, an thou'lt mouth,
I'll rant as well as thou.
QUEEN This is mere madness;
And thus awhile the fit will work on him;
Anon, as patient as the female dove
When that her golden couplets are disclos'd,
His silence will sit drooping.
HAMLET Hear you, sir:
What is the reason that you use me thus?
I lov'd you ever. But it is no matter.
Let Hercules himself do what he may,
The cat will mew, and dog will have his day.
[*Exit.*

KING I pray thee, good Horatio, wait upon him.
[*Exit Horatio.*

[*To Laertes*] Strengthen your patience in our last night's speech;
We'll put the matter to the present push. –
Good Gertrude, set some watch over your son. –
This grave shall have a living monument.
An hour of quiet shortly shall we see;
Till then in patience our proceeding be.
[*Exeunt.*

SCENE II. *Elsinore. The Castle.*

Enter HAMLET and HORATIO.

HAMLET So much for this, sir; now shall you see the other.
You do remember all the circumstance?
HORATIO Remember it, my lord!
HAMLET Sir, in my heart there was a kind of fighting
That would not let me sleep. Methought I lay
Worse than the mutines in the bilboes. Rashly,
And prais'd be rashness for it – let us know,
Our indiscretion sometime serves us well,
When our deep plots do pall; and that should learn us
There's a divinity that shapes our ends,
Rough-hew them how we will.
HORATIO That is most certain.

HAMLET Up from my cabin,
My sea-gown scarf'd about me, in the dark
Grop'd I to find out them; had my desire;
Finger'd their packet, and in fine withdrew
To mine own room again, making so bold,
My fears forgetting manners, to unseal
Their grand commission; where I found, Horatio,
Ah, royal knavery! an exact command,
Larded with many several sorts of reasons,
Importing Denmark's health and England's too,
With, ho! such bugs and goblins in my life –
That, on the supervise, no leisure bated,
No, not to stay the grinding of the axe,
My head should be struck off.

HORATIO Is't possible?

HAMLET Here's the commission; read it at more leisure.
But wilt thou hear now how I did proceed?

HORATIO I beseech you.

HAMLET Being thus benetted round with villainies –
Ere I could make a prologue to my brains,
They had begun the play – I sat me down;
Devis'd a new commission; wrote it fair.
I once did hold it, as our statists do,
A baseness to write fair, and labour'd much
How to forget that learning; but, sir, now
It did me yeoman's service. Wilt thou know
Th' effect of what I wrote?

HORATIO Ay, good my lord.

HAMLET An earnest conjuration from the King,
As England was his faithful tributary,
As love between them like the palm might flourish,
As peace should still her wheaten garland wear
And stand a comma 'tween their amities,
And many such like as-es of great charge,
That, on the view and knowing of these contents,
Without debatement further more or less,
He should those bearers put to sudden death,
Not shriving-time allow'd.

HORATIO How was this seal'd?

HAMLET Why, even in that was heaven ordinant.
I had my father's signet in my purse,
Which was the model of that Danish seal;
Folded the writ up in the form of th' other;
Subscrib'd it, gave't th' impression, plac'd it safely,
The changeling never known. Now, the next day
Was our sea-fight; and what to this was sequent
Thou knowest already.

HORATIO So Guildenstern and Rosencrantz go to't.

HAMLET Why, man, they did make love to this employment;
They are not near my conscience; their defeat
Does by their own insinuation grow:
'Tis dangerous when the baser nature comes
Between the pass and fell incensed points
Of mighty opposites.

HORATIO Why, what a king is this!

HAMLET Does it not, think thee, stand me now upon –
He that hath kill'd my king and whor'd my mother;
Popp'd in between th' election and my hopes;
Thrown out his angle for my proper life,
And with such coz'nage – is't not perfect conscience
To quit him with this arm? And is't not to be damn'd
To let this canker of our nature come
In further evil?

HORATIO It must be shortly known to him from England
What is the issue of the business there.

HAMLET It will be short; the interim is mine,
And a man's life's no more than to say 'one'.
But I am very sorry, good Horatio,
That to Laertes I forgot myself;
For by the image of my cause I see
The portraiture of his. I'll court his favours.
But sure the bravery of his grief did put me
Into a tow'ring passion.

HORATIO Peace; who comes here?

Enter young OSRIC.

OSRIC Your lordship is right welcome back to Denmark.

HAMLET I humbly thank you. sir [*Aside to Horatio*] Dost know this water-fly?

HORATIO [*Aside to Hamlet*] No, my good lord.

HAMLET [*Aside to Horatio*] Thy state is the more gracious; for 'tis a vice to know him. He hath much land, and fertile. Let a beast be lord of beasts, and his crib shall stand at the king's mess. 'Tis a chough; but, as I say, spacious in the possession of dirt.

OSRIC Sweet lord, if your lordship were at leisure, I should impart a thing to you from his Majesty.

HAMLET I will receive it, sir, with all diligence of spirit. Put your bonnet to his right use; 'tis for the head.

OSRIC I thank your lordship; it is very hot.

HAMLET No, believe me, 'tis very cold; the wind is northerly.

OSRIC It is indifferent cold, my lord, indeed.

HAMLET But yet methinks it is very sultry and hot for my complexion.

OSRIC Exceedingly, my lord; it is very sultry, as

'twere – I cannot tell how. But, my lord, his Majesty bade me signify to you that 'a has laid a great wager on your head. Sir, this is the matter –

HAMLET I beseech you, remember.

[Hamlet moves him to put on his hat.

OSRIC Nay, good my lord; for my ease, in good faith. Sir, here is newly come to court Laertes; believe me, an absolute gentleman, full of most excellent differences, of very soft society and great showing. Indeed, to speak feelingly of him, he is the card or calendar of gentry, for you shall find in him the continent of what part a gentleman would see.

HAMLET Sir, his definement suffers no perdition in you; though, I know, to divide him inventorially would dozy th' arithmetic of memory, and yet but yaw neither in respect of his quick sail. But, in the verity of extolment, I take him to be a soul of great article, and his infusion of such dearth and rareness as, to make true diction of him, his semblable is his mirror, and who else would trace him, his umbrage, nothing more.

OSRIC Your lordship speaks most infallibly of him.

HAMLET The concernancy, sir? Why do we wrap the gentleman in our more rawer breath?

OSRIC Sir?

HORATIO [*Aside to Hamlet*] Is't not possible to understand in another tongue? You will to't, sir, really.

HAMLET What imports the nomination of this gentleman?

OSRIC Of Laertes?

HORATIO [*Aside*] His purse is empty already; all's golden words are spent.

HAMLET Of him, sir.

OSRIC I know you are not ignorant –

HAMLET I would you did, sir; yet, in faith, if you did, it would not much approve me. Well, sir.

OSRIC You are not ignorant of what excellence Laertes is –

HAMLET I dare not confess that, lest I should compare with him in excellence; but to know a man well were to know himself.

OSRIC I mean, sir, for his weapon; but in the imputation laid on him by them, in his meed he's unfellowed.

HAMLET What's his weapon?

OSRIC Rapier and dagger.

HAMLET That's two of his weapons – but well.

OSRIC The King, sir, hath wager'd with him six Barbary horses; against the which he has impon'd, as I take it, six French rapiers and poniards, with their assigns, as girdle, hangers, and so – three of the carriages, in faith, are very dear to fancy, very responsive to the hilts, most delicate carriages, and of very liberal conceit.

HAMLET What call you the carriages?

HORATIO [*Aside to Hamlet*] I knew you must be edified by the margent ere you had done.

OSRIC The carriages, sir, are the hangers.

HAMLET The phrase would be more germane to the matter if we could carry a cannon by our sides. I would it might be hangers till then. But on: six Barbary horses against six French swords, their assigns, and three liberal conceited carriages; that's the French bet against the Danish. Why is this all impon'd, as you call it?

OSRIC The King, sir, hath laid, sir, that in a dozen passes between yourself and him he shall not exceed you three hits; he hath laid on twelve for nine, and it would come to immediate trial if your lordship would vouchsafe the answer.

HAMLET How if I answer no?

OSRIC I mean, my lord, the opposition of your person in trial.

HAMLET Sir, I will walk here in the hall. If it please his Majesty, it is the breathing time of day with me; let the foils be brought, the gentleman willing, and the King hold his purpose, I will win for him an I can; if not, I will gain nothing but my shame and the odd hits.

OSRIC Shall I redeliver you e'en so?

HAMLET To this effect, sir, after what flourish your nature will.

OSRIC I commend my duty to your lordship.

HAMLET Yours, yours. [*Exit Osric*] He does well to commend it himself; there are no tongues else for's turn.

HORATIO This lapwing runs away with the shell on his head.

HAMLET 'A did comply, sir, with his dug before 'a suck'd it. Thus has he, and many more of the same bevy, that I know the drossy age dotes on, only got the tune of the time and outward habit of encounter – a kind of yesty collection, which carries them through and through the most fann'd and winnowed opinions; and do but blow them to their trial, the bubbles are out.

Enter a Lord.

LORD My lord, his Majesty commended him to you by young Osric, who brings back to him that you attend him in the hall. He sends to know if your pleasure hold to play with Laertes, or that you will take longer time.

HAMLET I am constant to my purposes; they follow the king's pleasure: if his fitness speaks, mine is ready now – or whensoever, provided I be so able as now.

LORD The King and Queen and all are coming down.

HAMLET In happy time.

LORD The Queen desires you to use some gentle entertainment to Laertes before you fall to play.

HAMLET She well instructs me. *[Exit Lord.*

HORATIO You will lose this wager, my lord.

HAMLET I do not think so; since he went into France I have been in continual practice. I shall win at the odds. But thou wouldst not think how ill all's here about my heart; but it is no matter.

HORATIO Nay, good my lord –

HAMLET It is but foolery; but it is such a kind of gain-giving as would perhaps trouble a woman.

HORATIO If your mind dislike anything, obey it. I will forestall their repair hither, and say you are not fit.

HAMLET Not a whit, we defy augury: there is a special providence in the fall of a sparrow. If it be now, 'tis not to come; if it be not to come, it will be now; if it be not now, yet it will come – the readiness is all. Since no man owes of aught he leaves, what is't to leave betimes? Let be.

A table prepared. Trumpets, Drums, and Officers with cushions, foils and daggers. Enter KING, QUEEN, LAERTES, and all the State.

KING Come, Hamlet, come, and take this hand from me. *[The King puts Laertes's hand into Hamlet's.*

HAMLET Give me your pardon, sir. I have done you wrong;
But pardon 't, as you are a gentleman.
This presence knows,
And you must needs have heard how I am punish'd
With a sore distraction. What I have done
That might your nature, honour, and exception,
Roughly awake, I here proclaim was madness.
Was't Hamlet wrong'd Laertes? Never Hamlet.
If Hamlet from himself be ta'en away,
And when he's not himself does wrong Laertes,
Then Hamlet does it not, Hamlet denies it.
Who does it, then? His madness. If't be so,
Hamlet is of the faction that is wrong'd;
His madness is poor Hamlet's enemy.
Sir, in this audience,
Let my disclaiming from a purpos'd evil
Free me so far in your most generous thoughts
That I have shot my arrow o'er the house
And hurt my brother.

LAERTES I am satisfied in nature,
Whose motive in this case should stir me most
To my revenge; but in my terms of honour
I stand aloof, and will no reconcilement
Till by some elder masters of known honour
I have a voice and precedent of peace
To keep my name ungor'd – but till that time
I do receive your offer'd love like love,
And will not wrong it.

HAMLET I embrace it freely;
And will this brother's wager frankly play.
Give us the foils. Come on.

LAERTES Come, one for me.

HAMLET I'll be your foil, Laertes; in mine ignorance
Your skill shall, like a star i' th' darkest night,
Stick fiery off indeed.

LAERTES You mock me, sir.

HAMLET No, by this hand.

KING Give them the foils, young Osric. Cousin Hamlet,
You know the wager?

HAMLET Very well, my lord;
Your Grace has laid the odds a' th' weaker side.

KING I do not fear it: I have seen you both;
But since he's better'd, we have therefore odds.

LAERTES This is too heavy; let me see another.

HAMLET This likes me well. These foils have all a length? *[They prepare to play.*

OSRIC Ay, my good lord.

KING Set me the stoups of wine upon that table.
If Hamlet give the first or second hit,
Or quit in answer of the third exchange,
Let all the battlements their ordnance fire;
The King shall drink to Hamlet's better breath,
And in the cup an union shall he throw,
Richer than that which four successive kings
In Denmark's crown have worn. Give me the cups;
And let the kettle to the trumpet speak,
The trumpet to the cannoneer without,
The cannons to the heavens, the heaven to earth,
'Now the King drinks to Hamlet'. Come, begin –
And you, the judges, bear a wary eye.

HAMLET Come on, sir.

LAERTES Come, my lord. *[They play.*

HAMLET One.

LAERTES No.

HAMLET Judgment?

OSRIC A hit, a very palpable hit.

LAERTES Well, again.

KING Stay, give me drink. Hamlet, this pearl is thine;
Here's to thy health.
[Drum, trumpets, and shot.
Give him the cup.

HAMLET I'll play this bout first; set it by awhile.
Come. *[They play.*
Another hit; what say you?

LAERTES A touch, a touch, I do confess't.

KING Our son shall win.
QUEEN He's fat, and scant of breath.
Here, Hamlet, take my napkin, rub thy brows.
The Queen carouses to thy fortune, Hamlet.
HAMLET Good madam!
KING Gertrude, do not drink.
QUEEN I will, my lord; I pray you pardon me.
KING [*Aside*] It is the poison'd cup; it is too late.
HAMLET I dare not drink yet, madam; by and by.
QUEEN Come, let me wipe thy face.
LAERTES My lord, I'll hit him now.
KING I do not think't.
LAERTES [*Aside*] And yet it is almost against my conscience.
HAMLET Come, for the third. Laertes, you do but dally;
I pray you pass with your best violence;
I am afeard you make a wanton of me.
LAERTES Say you so? Come on. [*They play.*
OSRIC Nothing, neither way.
LAERTES Have at you now! [*Laertes wounds Hamlet: then, in scuffling, they change rapiers, and Hamlet wounds Laertes.*
KING Part them; they are incens'd.
HAMLET Nay, come again. [*The Queen falls.*
OSRIC Look to the Queen there, ho!
HORATIO They bleed on both sides. How is it, my lord?
OSRIC How is't, Laertes?
LAERTES Why, as a woodcock, to mine own springe, Osric;
I am justly kill'd with mine own treachery.
HAMLET How does the Queen?
KING She swoons to see them bleed.
QUEEN No, no, the drink, the drink! O my dear Hamlet!
The drink, the drink! I am poison'd. [*Dies.*
HAMLET O, villainy! Ho! let the door be lock'd.
Treachery! seek it out. [*Laertes falls.*
LAERTES It is here, Hamlet. Hamlet, thou art slain;
No med'cine in the world can do thee good;
In thee there is not half an hour's life;
The treacherous instrument is in thy hand,
Unbated and envenom'd. The foul practice
Hath turn'd itself on me; lo, here I lie,
Never to rise again. Thy mother's poison'd.
I can no more. The King, the King's to blame.
HAMLET The point envenom'd too!
Then, venom, to thy work. [*Stabs the King.*
ALL Treason! treason!
KING O, yet defend me, friends; I am but hurt.
HAMLET Here, thou incestuous, murd'rous, damned Dane,
Drink off this potion. Is thy union here?
Follow my mother. [*King dies.*
LAERTES He is justly serv'd:
It is a poison temper'd by himself.
Exchange forgiveness with me, noble Hamlet.
Mine and my father's death come not upon thee,
Nor thine on me! [*Dies.*
HAMLET Heaven make thee free of it! I follow thee.
I am dead, Horatio. Wretched queen, adieu!
You that look pale and tremble at this chance,
That are but mutes or audience to this act,
Had I but time, as this fell sergeant Death
Is strict in his arrest, O, I could tell you –
But let it be. Horatio, I am dead:
Thou livest; report me and my cause aright
To the unsatisfied.
HORATIO Never believe it.
I am more an antique Roman than a Dane;
Here's yet some liquor left.
HAMLET As th'art a man,
Give me the cup. Let go. By heaven, I'll ha't.
O God! Horatio, what a wounded name,
Things standing thus unknown, shall live behind me!
If thou didst ever hold me in thy heart,
Absent thee from felicity awhile,
And in this harsh world draw thy breath in pain,
To tell my story.
[*March afar off, and shot within.*
What warlike noise is this?
OSRIC Young Fortinbras, with conquest come from Poland,
To th' ambassadors of England gives
This warlike volley.
HAMLET O, I die, Horatio!
The potent poison quite o'er-crows my spirit.
I cannot live to hear the news from England,
But I do prophesy th' election lights
On Fortinbras; he has my dying voice.
So tell him, with th' occurrents, more and less,
Which have solicited – the rest is silence.
[*Dies.*
HORATIO Now cracks a noble heart. Good night, sweet prince,
And flights of angels sing thee to thy rest!
[*March within.*
Why does the drum come hither?

Enter FORTINBRAS and English Ambassadors, with drum, colours, and Attendants.

FORTINBRAS Where is this sight?
HORATIO What is it you would see?
If aught of woe or wonder, cease your search.
FORTINBRAS This quarry cries on havoc. O proud death,
What feast is toward in thine eternal cell

That thou so many princes at a shot
So bloodily hast struck?
1 AMBASSADOR The sight is dismal;
And our affairs from England come too late:
The ears are senseless that should give us hearing
To tell him his commandment is fulfill'd,
That Rosencrantz and Guildenstern are dead.
Where should we have our thanks?
HORATIO Not from his mouth,
Had it th' ability of life to thank you:
He never gave commandment for their death.
But since, so jump upon this bloody question,
You from the Polack wars, and you from England,
Are here arrived, give order that these bodies
High on a stage be placed to the view;
And let me speak to th' yet unknowing world
How these things came about. So shall you hear
Of carnal, bloody, and unnatural acts;
Of accidental judgments, casual slaughters;
Of deaths put on by cunning and forc'd cause;
And, in this upshot, purposes mistook
Fall'n on th' inventors' heads – all this can I
Truly deliver.
FORTINBRAS Let us haste to hear it,
And call the noblest to the audience.
For me, with sorrow I embrace my fortune;
I have some rights of memory in this kingdom,
Which now to claim my vantage doth invite me.
HORATIO Of that I shall have also cause to speak,
And from his mouth whose voice will draw on more.
But let this same be presently perform'd,
Even while men's minds are wild, lest more mischance
On plots and errors happen.
FORTINBRAS Let four captains
Bear Hamlet like a soldier to the stage;
For he was likely, had he been put on,
To have prov'd most royal; and for his passage
The soldier's music and the rite of war
Speak loudly for him.
Take up the bodies. Such a sight as this
Becomes the field, but here shows much amiss.
Go, bid the soldiers shoot.
[Exeunt marching. A peal of ordnance shot off.

King Lear

Introduction by PHILIP HOBSBAUM

The basic plot of *King Lear* is something like a fairy story. It tells of an old man who casts out his younger daughter and splits his kingdom between the elder two. Summarised in this fashion, the plot can be seen to relate to that of *Cinderella*, a theme that has haunted the human consciousness for hundreds of years.

King Lear, therefore, has its predecessors. There are several versions of the story in medieval chronicles, always involving an old king giving away his domains and then being subject to his unworthy elder daughters. What may have sparked off the intensity of Shakespeare's treatment was the case of an elderly courtier, Sir Bryan Annesley, who was declared insane by an elder daughter, Lady Wildgose, while his youngest daughter petitioned King James VI and I for the restitution of the estate. What seems eerie is that the name of this youngest daughter was Cordell.

The story of King Lear was well known in the sixteenth centry, and Sir Bryan must have named his faithful girl after a legendary creature without realising, of course, that she would grow up to fulfil the legend. The poignancy of the play itself to no small extent depends upon the way it reflects the conflicts that beset us in life. Lear addresses a question to his three daughters in the first scene, 'Which of you shall we say doth love us most?'. Such a question cannot be decently answered. Love cannot be quantified or elicited. That foolish question leads to grave disorder in the realm and to the destruction of Lear and his family. It is mirrored in the sub-plot, where another aged father casts out a virtuous son and is pilloried by one that is unworthy.

Lear descends through inexorable stages. Throughout the drama he is stripped piece by piece of his lands, possessions and followers. By Act 3 he is found raving in a storm, half-naked – 'Off, off, you lendings!' – entering a hovel in company with a feigned madman and a genuine fool. Lear has been reduced to the basic state of 'a poor, bare, forked animal'. This is in order to educate him into a realisation that other people matter as well as himself.

The education of King Lear proves to be an expensive business. The death of Cordelia at the end transpires with the irrationality of a tragic accident. In the chronicles, she survives; in the play, she is eliminated. There can be no greater *coup de théâtre* than that moment when Albany utters the pious hope, 'The gods defend her', just as Lear enters with his youngest daughter dead in his arms.

The death of Cordelia used often to be questioned, particularly in the eighteenth century. One interpretation could be that Lear stands for the obdurate sinner and that Cordelia, as her name would imply, represents the saint or intercessor who has been sent to save him. Those who have mourned the demise of a young colleague may ponder the import of the apparently unnecessary death of Cordelia. Those who have sat by the bedside of an aged relative may gauge the meaning of Lear's own death: 'Vex not his ghost. O let him pass! He hates him/That would upon the rack of this tough world/ Stretch him out longer'.

Lear has been purged by his madness and dies with a kind of hard-won innocence, thinking that he will be at last conjoined with his daughter. Over her prostrate body he seems to receive a revelation to which those others on stage are not parties: 'Look on her. Look, her lips./Look there, look there!'. The key would appear to be the fifteenth verse of the tenth chapter of Luke's Gospel: 'Whoever shall not receive the kingdom of God as a little child, he shall not enter therein'.

King Lear

DRAMATIS PERSONAE

LEAR
King of Britain
KING OF FRANCE
DUKE OF BURGUNDY
DUKE OF CORNWALL
DUKE OF ALBANY
EARL OF KENT
EARL OF GLOUCESTER
EDGAR
son to Gloucester
EDMUND
bastard son to Gloucester
CURAN
a courtier
Old Man, tenant to Gloucester
Doctor
Fool
OSWALD
steward to Goneril
A Captain employed by Edmund
Gentleman attendant on Cordelia
A Herald
Servants to Cornwall
GONERIL, REGAN, CORDELIA
daughters to Lear
Knights attending on Lear, Officers, Messengers, Soldiers, and Attendants.

THE SCENE: BRITAIN.

ACT ONE

SCENE I. *King Lear's palace.*

Enter KENT, GLOUCESTER, and EDMUND.

KENT I thought the King had more affected the Duke of Albany than Cornwall.

GLOUCESTER It did always seem so to us; but now, in the division of the kingdom, it appears not which of the Dukes he values most; for equalities are so weigh'd that curiosity in neither can make choice of either's moiety.

KENT Is not this your son, my lord?

GLOUCESTER His breeding, sir, hath been at my charge. I have so often blush'd to acknowledge him that now I am braz'd to't.

KENT I cannot conceive you.

GLOUCESTER Sir, this young fellow's mother could; whereupon she grew round-womb'd, and had indeed, sir, a son for her cradle ere she had a husband for her bed. Do you smell a fault?

KENT I cannot wish the fault undone, the issue of it being so proper.

GLOUCESTER But I have a son, sir, by order of law, some year elder than this, who yet is no dearer in my account. Though this knave came something saucily to the world before he was sent for, yet was his mother fair; there was good sport at his making, and the whoreson must be acknowledged. – Do you know this noble gentleman, Edmund?

EDMUND No, my lord.

GLOUCESTER My Lord of Kent. Remember him hereafter as my honourable friend.

EDMUND My services to your lordship.

KENT I must love you, and sue to know you better.

EDMUND Sir, I shall study deserving.

GLOUCESTER He hath been out nine years, and away he shall again. [*Sennet*] The King is coming.

Enter One bearing a coronet; then LEAR, then the DUKES OF ALBANY and CORNWALL, next GONERIL, REGAN, CORDELIA, with Followers.

LEAR Attend the Lords of France and Burgundy, Gloucester.

GLOUCESTER I shall, my liege.

[*Exeunt Gloucester and Edmund.*

LEAR Meantime we shall express our darker purpose.
Give me the map there. Know that we have divided
In three our kingdom; and 'tis our fast intent
To shake all cares and business from our age,
Conferring them on younger strengths, while we
Unburden'd crawl toward death. Our son of Cornwall,
And you, our no less loving son of Albany,
We have this hour a constant will to publish
Our daughters' several dowers, that future strife
May be prevented now. The Princes, France and Burgundy,
Great rivals in our youngest daughter's love,
Long in our court have made their amorous sojourn,
And here are to be answer'd. Tell me, my daughters –
Since now we will divest us both of rule,

Interest of territory, cares of state –
Which of you shall we say doth love us most?
That we our largest bounty may extend
Where nature doth with merit challenge.
Goneril,
Our eldest-born, speak first.

GONERIL Sir, I love you more than word can wield the matter;
Dearer than eyesight, space, and liberty;
Beyond what can be valued, rich or rare;
No less than life, with grace, health, beauty, honour;
As much as child e'er lov'd, or father found;
A love that makes breath poor and speech unable:
Beyond all manner of so much I love you.

CORDELIA [*Aside*] What shall Cordelia speak?
Love, and be silent.

LEAR Of all these bounds, even from this line to this,
With shadowy forests and with champains rich'd,
With plenteous rivers and wide-skirted meads,
We make thee lady: to thine and Albany's issues
Be this perpetual. – What says our second daughter,
Our dearest Regan, wife of Cornwall? Speak.

REGAN I am made of that self metal as my sister,
And prize me at her worth. In my true heart
I find she names my very deed of love;
Only she comes too short, that I profess
Myself an enemy to all other joys
Which the most precious square of sense possesses,
And find I am alone felicitate
In your dear Highness' love.

CORDELIA [*Aside*] Then poor Cordelia!
And yet not so; since I am sure my love's
More ponderous than my tongue.

LEAR To thee and thine hereditary ever
Remain this ample third of our fair kingdom;
No less in space, validity, and pleasure,
Than that conferr'd on Goneril. – Now, our joy,
Although our last and least; to whose young love
The vines of France and milk of Burgundy
Strive to be interess'd; what can you say to draw
A third more opulent than your sisters? Speak.

CORDELIA Nothing, my lord.

LEAR Nothing!

CORDELIA Nothing.

LEAR Nothing will come of nothing. Speak again.

CORDELIA Unhappy that I am, I cannot heave
My heart into my mouth. I love your Majesty
According to my bond; no more nor less.

LEAR How, how, Cordelia! Mend your speech a little,
Lest you may mar your fortunes.

CORDELIA Good my lord,
You have begot me, bred me, lov'd me; I
Return those duties back as are right fit,
Obey you, love you, and most honour you.
Why have my sisters husbands, if they say
They love you all? Haply, when I shall wed,
That lord whose hand must take my plight shall carry
Half my love with him, half my care and duty.
Sure I shall never marry like my sisters,
To love my father all.

LEAR But goes thy heart with this?

CORDELIA Ay, my good lord.

LEAR So young and so untender?

CORDELIA So young, my lord, and true.

LEAR Let it be so! Thy truth, then, be thy dower!
For, by the sacred radiance of the sun,
The mysteries of Hecat and the night;
By all the operation of the orbs
From whom we do exist and cease to be;
Here I disclaim all my paternal care,
Propinquity and property of blood,
And as a stranger to my heart and me
Hold thee from this for ever. The barbarous Scythian,
Or he that makes his generation messes
To gorge his appetite, shall to my bosom
Be as well neighbour'd, pitied, and reliev'd,
As thou my sometime daughter.

KENT Good my liege –

LEAR Peace, Kent!
Come not between the dragon and his wrath.
I lov'd her most, and thought to set my rest
On her kind nursery. [*To Cordelia*] Hence, and avoid my sight! –
So be my grave my peace as here I give
Her father's heart from her! Call France – Who stirs?
Call Burgundy. Cornwall and Albany,
With my two daughters' dowers digest this third.
Let pride, which she calls plainness, marry her.
I do invest you jointly with my power,
Pre-eminence, and all the large effects
That troop with what majesty. Ourself, by monthly course,
With reservation of an hundred knights,
By you to be sustain'd, shall our abode
Make with you by due turn. Only we shall retain
The name, and all th' addition to a king:
The sway, revenue, execution of the rest,
Beloved sons, be yours; which to confirm,
This coronet part between you.

KENT Royal Lear,
Whom I have ever honour'd as my king,
Lov'd as my father, as my master follow'd,

As my great patron thought on in my prayers –
LEAR The bow is bent and drawn; make from the shaft.
KENT Let it fall rather, though the fork invade
The region of my heart. Be Kent unmannerly
When Lear is mad. What wouldst thou do, old man?
Think'st thou that duty shall have dread to speak
When power to flattery bows? To plainness honour's bound
When majesty falls to folly. Reserve thy state;
And in thy best consideration check
This hideous rashness. Answer my life my judgment:
Thy youngest daughter does not love thee least;
Nor are those empty-hearted whose low sounds
Reverb no hollowness.
LEAR Kent, on thy life, no more!
KENT My life I never held but as a pawn
To wage against thine enemies; nor fear to lose it,
Thy safety being motive.
LEAR Out of my sight!
KENT See better, Lear; and let me still remain
The true blank of thine eye.
LEAR Now by Apollo –
KENT Now, by Apollo, King,
Thou swear'st thy gods in vain.
LEAR O, vassal! miscreant!
[Laying his hand on his sword.
ALBANY AND CORNWALL Dear sir, forbear.
KENT Do;
Kill thy physician, and the fee bestow
Upon the foul disease. Revoke thy gift,
Or, whilst I can vent clamour from my throat,
I'll tell thee thou dost evil.
LEAR Hear me, recreant;
On thine allegiance, hear me.
That thou hast sought to make us break our vows –
Which we durst never yet – and with strain'd pride
To come betwixt our sentence and our power –
Which nor our nature nor our place can bear;
Our potency made good, take thy reward.
Five days we do allot thee for provision
To shield thee from disasters of the world,
And on the sixth to turn thy hated back
Upon our kingdom; if, on the tenth day following,
Thy banish'd trunk be found in our dominions,
The moment is thy death. Away! by Jupiter,
This shall not be revok'd.
KENT Fare thee well, King. Sith thus thou wilt appear,
Freedom lives hence, and banishment is here.
[To Cordelia] The gods to their dear shelter take thee, maid,
That justly think'st, and hast most rightly said!
[To Regan and Goneril] And your large speeches may your deeds approve,
That good effects may spring from words of love!
Thus Kent, O princes, bids you all adieu;
He'll shape his old course in a country new.
[Exit.

Flourish. Re-enter GLOUCESTER, with FRANCE, BURGUNDY, and Attendants.

GLOUCESTER Here's France and Burgundy, my noble lord.
LEAR My Lord of Burgundy,
We first address toward you, who with this king
Hath rivall'd for our daughter. What in the least
Will you require in present dower with her,
Or cease your quest of love?
BURGUNDY Most royal Majesty,
I crave no more than hath your Highness offer'd,
Nor will you tender less.
LEAR Right noble Burgundy,
When she was dear to us, we did hold her so;
But now her price is fallen. Sir, there she stands:
If aught within that little seeming substance,
Or all of it, with our displeasure piec'd,
And nothing more, may fitly like your Grace,
She's there, and she is yours.
BURGUNDY I know no answer.
LEAR Will you, with those infirmities she owes,
Unfriended, new-adopted to our hate,
Dower'd with our curse, and stranger'd with our oath,
Take her or leave her?
BURGUNDY Pardon me, royal sir;
Election makes not up in such conditions.
LEAR Then leave her, sir; for, by the pow'r that made me,
I tell you all her wealth. *[To France]* For you, great King,
I would not from your love make such a stray
To match you where I hate; therefore beseech you
T'avert your liking a more worthier way,
Than on a wretch whom nature is asham'd
Almost t' acknowledge hers.
FRANCE This is most strange,
That she, whom even but now was your best object,
The argument of your praise, balm of your age,
The best, the dearest, should in this trice of time
Commit a thing so monstrous to dismantle
So many folds of favour. Sure her offence
Must be of such unnatural degree

That monsters it, or your fore-vouch'd affection
Fall into taint – which to believe of her
Must be a faith that reason without miracle
Should never plant in me.

CORDELIA I yet beseech your Majesty –
If for I want that glib and oily art
To speak and purpose not, since what I well intend
I'll do't before I speak – that you make known
It is no vicious blot, murder, or foulness,
No unchaste action or dishonoured step,
That hath depriv'd me of your grace and favour;
But even for want of that for which I am richer –
A still-soliciting eye, and such a tongue
That I am glad I have not, though not to have it
Hath lost me in your liking.

LEAR Better thou
Hadst not been born than not t' have pleas'd me better.

FRANCE Is it but this? A tardiness in nature,
Which often leaves the history unspoke
That it intends to do! My Lord of Burgundy,
What say you to the lady? Love's not love
When it is mingled with regards that stands
Aloof from th' entire point. Will you have her?
She is herself a dowry.

BURGUNDY Royal king,
Give but that portion which yourself propos'd,
And here I take Cordelia by the hand,
Duchess of Burgundy.

LEAR Nothing! I have sworn; I am firm.

BURGUNDY I am sorry, then, you have so lost a father
That you must lose a husband.

CORDELIA Peace be with Burgundy!
Since that respects of fortune are his love
I shall not be his wife.

FRANCE Fairest Cordelia, that art most rich, being poor;
Most choice, forsaken; and most lov'd, despis'd!
Thee and thy virtues here I seize upon,
Be it lawful I take up what's cast away.
Gods, gods! 'tis strange that from their cold'st neglect
My love should kindle to inflam'd respect.
Thy dow'rless daughter, King, thrown to my chance,
Is queen of us, of ours, and our fair France.
Not all the dukes of wat'rish Burgundy
Can buy this unpriz'd precious maid of me.
Bid them farewell, Cordelia, though unkind;
Thou losest here, a better where to find.

LEAR Thou hast her, France; let her be thine; for we
Have no such daughter, nor shall ever see
That face of hers again. [*To Cordelia*] Therefore be gone
Without our grace, our love, our benison.
Come, noble Burgundy.

[*Flourish. Exeunt Lear, Burgundy, Cornwall, Albany, Gloucester, and Attendants.*

FRANCE Bid farewell to your sisters.

CORDELIA The jewels of our father, with wash'd eyes
Cordelia leaves you. I know you what you are;
And, like a sister, am most loath to call
Your faults as they are named. Love well our father.
To your professed bosoms I commit him;
But yet, alas, stood I within his grace,
I would prefer him to a better place.
So, farewell to you both.

REGAN Prescribe not us our duty.

GONERIL Let your study
Be to content your lord, who hath receiv'd you
At fortune's alms. You have obedience scanted,
And well are worth the want that you have wanted.

CORDELIA Time shall unfold what plighted cunning hides,
Who covers faults, at last with shame derides.
Well may you prosper!

FRANCE Come, my fair Cordelia.

[*Exeunt France and Cordelia.*

GONERIL Sister, it is not little I have to say of what most nearly appertains to us both. I think our father will hence to-night.

REGAN That's most certain, and with you; next month with us.

GONERIL You see how full of changes his age is; the observation we have made of it hath not been little. He always lov'd our sister most; and with what poor judgment he hath now cast her off appears too grossly.

REGAN 'Tis the infirmity of his age; yet he hath ever but slenderly known himself.

GONERIL The best and soundest of his time hath been but rash; then must we look from his age to receive not alone the imperfections of long-engraffed condition, but therewithal the unruly waywardness that infirm and choleric years bring with them.

REGAN Such unconstant starts are we like to have from him as this of Kent's banishment.

GONERIL There is further compliment of leave-taking between France and him. Pray you, let us hit together; if our father carry authority with such disposition as he bears, this last surrender of his will but offend us.

REGAN We shall further think of it.

GONERIL We must do something, and i' th' heat.

[*Exeunt.*

SCENE II. *Gloucester's castle.*

Enter EDMUND with a letter.

EDMUND Thou, Nature, art my goddess; to thy law
My services are bound. Wherefore should I
Stand in the plague of custom, and permit
The curiosity of nations to deprive me,
For that I am some twelve or fourteen moonshines
Lag of a brother? Why bastard? Wherefore base?
When my dimensions are as well compact,
My mind as generous, and my shape as true,
As honest madam's issue? Why brand they us
With base? with baseness? bastardy? base, base?
Who, in the lusty stealth of nature, take
More composition and fierce quality
Than doth, within a dull, stale, tired bed,
Go to th' creating a whole tribe of fops
Got 'tween asleep and wake? Well then,
Legitimate Edgar, I must have your land.
Our father's love is to the bastard Edmund
As to th' legitimate. Fine word 'legitimate'!
Well, my legitimate, if this letter speed,
And my invention thrive, Edmund the base
Shall top th' legitimate. I grow; I prosper.
Now, gods, stand up for bastards.

Enter GLOUCESTER.

GLOUCESTER Kent banish'd thus! and France in choler parted!
And the King gone to-night! Prescrib'd his pow'r!
Confin'd to exhibition! All this done
Upon the gad! Edmund, how now! What news?

EDMUND So please your lordship, none.

[Putting up the letter.

GLOUCESTER Why so earnestly seek you to put up that letter?

EDMUND I know no news, my lord.

GLOUCESTER What paper were you reading?

EDMUND Nothing, my lord.

GLOUCESTER No? What needed then that terrible dispatch of it into your pocket? The quality of nothing hath not such need to hide itself. Let's see. Come, if it be nothing, I shall not need spectacles.

EDMUND I beseech you, sir, pardon me. It is a letter from my brother that I have not all o'er-read; and for so much as I have perus'd, I find it not fit for your o'er-looking.

GLOUCESTER Give me the letter, sir.

EDMUND I shall offend either to detain or give it. The contents, as in part I understand them, are to blame.

GLOUCESTER Let's see, let's see.

EDMUND I hope, for my brother's justification, he wrote this but as an essay or taste of my virtue.

GLOUCESTER *[Reads]* 'This policy and reverence of age makes the world bitter to the best of our times; keeps our fortunes from us till our oldness cannot relish them. I begin to find an idle and fond bondage in the oppression of aged tyranny, who sways, not as it hath power, but as it is suffer'd. Come to me, that of this I may speak more. If our father would sleep till I wak'd him, you should enjoy half his revenue for ever, and live the beloved of your brother. EDGAR.' Hum – Conspiracy! 'Sleep till I wak'd him, you should enjoy half his revenue.' My son Edgar! Had he a hand to write this? a heart and a brain to breed it in? When came this to you? Who brought it?

EDMUND It was not brought to me, my lord; there's the cunning of it. I found it thrown in at the casement of my closet.

GLOUCESTER You know the character to be your brother's?

EDMUND If the matter were good, my lord, I durst swear it were his; but in respect of that, I would fain think it were not.

GLOUCESTER It is his.

EDMUND It is his hand, my lord; but I hope his heart is not in the contents.

GLOUCESTER Has he never before sounded you in this business?

EDMUND Never, my lord; but I have heard him oft maintain it to be fit that, sons at perfect age and fathers declin'd, the father should be as ward to the son, and the son manage his revenue.

GLOUCESTER O villain, villain! His very opinion in the letter! Abhorred villain! Unnatural, detested, brutish villain! Worse than brutish! Go, sirrah, seek him; I'll apprehend him. Abominable villain! Where is he?

EDMUND I do not well know, my lord. If it shall please you to suspend your indignation against my brother till you can derive from him better testimony of his intent, you should run a certain course; where, if you violently proceed against him, mistaking his purpose, it would make a great gap in your own honour, and shake in pieces the heart of his obedience. I dare pawn down my life for him that he hath writ this to feel my affection to your honour, and to no other pretence of danger.

GLOUCESTER Think you so?

EDMUND If your honour judge it meet, I will place you where you shall hear us confer of this, and by an auricular assurance have your satisfaction; and that without any further delay than this very evening.

GLOUCESTER He cannot be such a monster.

EDMUND Nor is not, sure.

GLOUCESTER To his father, that so tenderly and entirely loves him. Heaven and earth! Edmund, seek him out; wind me into him, I pray you. Frame the business after your own wisdom. I would unstate myself to be in a due resolution.

EDMUND I will seek him, sir, presently; convey the business as I shall find means, and acquaint you withal.

GLOUCESTER These late eclipses in the sun and moon portend no good to us. Though the wisdom of nature can reason it thus and thus, yet nature finds itself scourg'd by the sequent effects: love cools, friendship falls off, brothers divide; in cities, mutinies; in countries, discord; in palaces, treason; and the bond crack'd 'twixt son and father. This villain of mine comes under the prediction: there's son against father. The King falls from bias of nature: there's father against child. We have seen the best of our time: machinations, hollowness, treachery, and all ruinous disorders, follow us disquietly to our graves. Find out this villain, Edmund; it shall lose thee nothing; do it carefully. And the noble and true-hearted Kent banish'd! His offence, honesty! 'Tis strange. [*Exit.*

EDMUND This is the excellent foppery of the world, that, when we are sick in fortune, often the surfeits of our own behaviour, we make guilty of our disasters the sun, the moon, and stars; as if we were villains on necessity; fools by heavenly compulsion; knaves, thieves, and treachers, by spherical predominance; drunkards, liars, and adulterers, by an enforc'd obedience of planetary influence; and all that we are evil in, by a divine thrusting on – an admirable evasion of whoremaster man, to lay his goatish disposition on the charge of a star! My father compounded with my mother under the Dragon's tail, and my nativity was under Ursa Major, so that it follows I am rough and lecherous. Fut, I should have been that I am, had the maidenliest star in the firmament twinkled on my bastardizing. Edgar!

Enter EDGAR.

Pat! He comes like the catastrophe of the old comedy. My cue is villainous melancholy, with a sigh like Tom o' Bedlam. – O, these eclipses do portend these divisions! fa, sol, la, mi.

EDGAR How now, brother Edmund! What serious contemplation are you in?

EDMUND I am thinking, brother, of a prediction I read this other day what should follow these eclipses.

EDGAR Do you busy yourself with that?

EDMUND I promise you, the effects he writes of succeed unhappily; as of unnaturalness between the child and the parent; death, dearth, dissolutions of ancient amities; divisions in state, menaces and maledictions against king and nobles; needless diffidences, banishment of friends, dissipation of cohorts, nuptial breaches, and I know not what.

EDGAR How long have you been a sectary astronomical?

EDMUND Come, come! When saw you my father last?

EDGAR The night gone by.

EDMUND Spake you with him?

EDGAR Ay, two hours together.

EDMUND Parted you in good terms? Found you no displeasure in him by word nor countenance?

EDGAR None at all.

EDMUND Bethink yourself wherein you may have offended him; and at my entreaty forbear his presence, until some little time hath qualified the heat of his displeasure, which at this instant so rageth in him that with the mischief of your person it would scarcely allay.

EDGAR Some villain hath done me wrong.

EDMUND That's my fear. I pray you have a continent forbearance till the speed of his rage goes slower; and, as I say, retire with me to my lodging, from whence I will fitly bring you to hear my lord speak. Pray ye go; there's my key. If you do stir abroad, go arm'd.

EDGAR Arm'd, brother!

EDMUND Brother, I advise you to the best. I am no honest man if there be any good meaning toward you. I have told you what I have seen and heard – but faintly; nothing like the image and horror of it. Pray you, away.

EDGAR Shall I hear from you anon?

EDMUND I do serve you in this business. [*Exit Edgar.*

A credulous father! and a brother noble,
Whose nature is so far from doing harms
That he suspects none; on whose foolish honesty
My practices ride easy! I see the business.
Let me, if not by birth, have lands by wit:
All with me's meet that I can fashion fit. [*Exit.*

SCENE III. *The Duke of Albany's palace*

Enter GONERIL and OSWALD, her steward.

GONERIL Did my father strike my gentleman for chiding of his fool?

OSWALD Ay, madam.

GONERIL By day and night, he wrongs me; every hour
He flashes into one gross crime or other
That sets us all at odds. I'll not endure it.
His knights grow riotous, and himself upbraids us
On every trifle. When he returns from hunting,
I will not speak with him; say I am sick.
If you come slack of former services,
You shall do well; the fault of it I'll answer.
[Horns within.

OSWALD He's coming, madam; I hear him.

GONERIL Put on what weary negligence you please,
You and your fellows; I'd have it come to question.
If he distaste it, let him to my sister,
Whose mind and mine, I know, in that are one,
Not to be overrul'd. Idle old man,
That still would manage those authorities
That he hath given away! Now, by my life,
Old fools are babes again, and must be us'd
With checks as flatteries, when they are seen abus'd.
Remember what I have said.

OSWALD Well, madam.

GONERIL And let his knights have colder looks among you;
What grows of it, no matter. Advise your fellows so.
I would breed from hence occasions, and I shall,
That I may speak. I'll write straight to my sister
To hold my very course. Prepare for dinner.
[Exeunt.

SCENE IV. *A hall in Albany's palace.*

Enter KENT, disguised.

KENT If but as well I other accents borrow
That can my speech defuse, my good intent
May carry through itself to that full issue
For which I raz'd my likeness. Now, banish'd Kent,
If thou canst serve where thou dost stand condemn'd,
So may it come thy master whom thou lov'st
Shall find thee full of labours.

Horns within. Enter LEAR, Knights, and Attendants.

LEAR Let me not stay a jot for dinner; go get it ready. [*Exit an Attendant*] How now! What art thou?

KENT A man, sir.

LEAR What dost thou profess? What wouldst thou with us?

KENT I do profess to be no less than I seem, to serve him truly that will put me in trust, to love him that is honest, to converse with him that is wise and says little, to fear judgment, to fight when I cannot choose, and to eat no fish.

LEAR What art thou?

KENT A very honest-hearted fellow, and as poor as the King.

LEAR If thou be'st as poor for a subject as he's for a king, thou art poor enough. What wouldst thou?

KENT Service.

LEAR Who wouldst thou serve?

KENT You.

LEAR Dost thou know me, fellow?

KENT No, sir; but you have that in your countenance which I would fain call master.

LEAR What's that?

KENT Authority.

LEAR What services canst thou do?

KENT I can keep honest counsel, ride, run, mar a curious tale in telling it, and deliver a plain message bluntly. That which ordinary men are fit for, I am qualified in; and the best of me is diligence.

LEAR How old art thou?

KENT Not so young, sir, to love a woman for singing, nor so old to dote on her for anything: I have years on my back forty-eight.

LEAR Follow me; thou shalt serve me. If I like thee no worse after dinner, I will not part from thee yet. Dinner, ho, dinner! Where's my knave? my fool? – Go you and call my fool hither. *[Exit an Attendant.*

Enter OSWALD.

You, you, sirrah, where's my daughter?

OSWALD So please you – *[Exit.*

LEAR What says the fellow there? Call the clotpoll back. [*Exit a Knight*] Where's my fool, ho? I think the world's asleep.

Re-enter Knight.

How now! Where's that mongrel?

KNIGHT He says, my lord, your daughter is not well.

LEAR Why came not the slave back to me when I call'd him?

KNIGHT Sir, he answered me in the roundest manner he would not.

LEAR He would not!

KNIGHT My lord, I know not what the matter is; but, to my judgment, your Highness is not entertain'd with that ceremonious affection as you were wont; there's a great abatement of kindness appears as well in the general dependants as in the Duke himself also and your daughter.

LEAR Ha! say'st thou so?

KNIGHT I beseech you pardon me, my lord, if I be mistaken; for my duty cannot be silent when I think your Highness wrong'd.

LEAR Thou but remembr'rest me of mine own conception. I have perceived a most faint neglect of late, which I have rather blamed as mine own jealous curiosity than as a very pretence and purpose of unkindness. I will look further into't. But where's my fool? I have not seen him this two days.

KNIGHT Since my young lady's going into France, sir, the fool hath much pined away.

LEAR No more of that; I have noted it well. Go you and tell my daughter I would speak with her. [*Exit an Attendant*] Go you, call hither my fool. [*Exit another Attendant.*

Re-enter OSWALD.

O, you sir, you! Come you hither, sir.
Who am I, sir?

OSWALD My lady's father.

LEAR 'My lady's father'! my lord's knave! you whoreson dog! you slave! you cur!

OSWALD I am none of these, my lord; I beseech your pardon.

LEAR Do you bandy looks with me, you rascal! [*Striking him.*

OSWALD I'll not be strucken, my lord.

KENT Nor tripp'd neither, you base foot-ball player. [*Tripping up his heels.*

LEAR I thank thee, fellow; thou serv'st me, and I'll love thee.

KENT Come, sir, arise, away! I'll teach you differences. Away, away! If you will measure your lubber's length again, tarry; but away! Go to! Have you wisdom? So. [*Pushes Oswald out.*

LEAR Now, my friendly knave, I thank thee; there's earnest of thy service. [*Giving Kent money.*

Enter FOOL.

FOOL Let me hire him too; here's my coxcomb. [*Offering Kent his cap.*

LEAR How now, my pretty knave! How dost thou?

FOOL Sirrah, you were best take my coxcomb.

KENT Why, fool?

FOOL Why? For taking one's part that's out of favour. Nay, an thou canst not smile as the wind sits, thou'lt catch cold shortly. There, take my coxcomb. Why, this fellow has banish'd two on's daughters, and did the third a blessing against his will; if thou follow him, thou must needs wear my coxcomb. – How now, nuncle! Would I had two coxcombs and two daughters!

LEAR Why, my boy?

FOOL If I gave them all my living, I'd keep my coxcombs myself. There's mine; beg another of thy daughters.

LEAR Take heed, sirrah – the whip.

FOOL Truth's a dog must to kennel; he must be whipp'd out, when Lady the brach may stand by th' fire and stink.

LEAR A pestilent gall to me!

FOOL Sirrah, I'll teach thee a speech.

LEAR Do.

FOOL Mark it, nuncle:
Have more than thou showest,
Speak less than thou knowest,
Lend less than thou owest,
Ride more than thou goest,
Learn more than thou trowest,
Set less than thou throwest;
Leave thy drink and thy whore,
And keep in-a-door,
And thou shalt have more
Than two tens to a score.

KENT This is nothing, fool.

FOOL Then 'tis like the breath of an un-fee'd lawyer – you gave me nothing for't. Can you make no use of nothing, nuncle?

LEAR Why, no, boy; nothing can be made out of nothing.

FOOL [*To Kent*] Prithee tell him, so much the rent of his land comes to; he will not believe a fool.

LEAR A bitter fool!

FOOL Dost thou know the difference, my boy, between a biter bitter fool and a sweet one?

LEAR No, lad; teach me.

FOOL That lord that counsell'd thee
To give away thy land,
Come place him here by me –
Do thou for him stand.
The sweet and bitter fool
Will presently appear;
The one in motley here,
The other found out there.

LEAR Dost thou call me fool, boy?

FOOL All thy other titles thou hast given away; that thou wast born with.

KENT This is not altogether fool, my lord.

FOOL No, faith, lords and great men will not let me; if I had a monopoly out, they would have part on't. And ladies too – they will not let me have all the fool to myself; they'll be snatching. Nuncle, give me an egg, and I'll give thee two crowns.

LEAR What two crowns shall they be?

FOOL Why, after I have cut the egg i' th' middle and eat up the meat, the two crowns of the egg. When thou clovest thy crown i' th' middle, and gav'st away both parts, thou bor'st thine ass on thy back o'er the dirt. Thou hadst little wit in thy bald crown when thou gav'st thy golden one away. If I speak like myself in this, let him be whipp'd that first finds it so.

[*Sings*] Fools had ne'er less grace in a year;
For wise men are grown foppish,
And know not how their wits to wear,
Their manners are so apish.

LEAR When were you wont to be so full of songs, sirrah?

FOOL I have us'd it, nuncle, e'er since thou mad'st thy daughters thy mothers; for when thou gav'st them the rod, and put'st down thine own breeches

[*Sings*] Then they for sudden joy did weep,
And I for sorrow sung,
That such a king should play bo-peep
And go the fools among.

Prithee, nuncle, keep a schoolmaster that can teach thy fool to lie. I would fain learn to lie.

LEAR An you lie, sirrah, we'll have you whipp'd.

FOOL I marvel what kin thou and thy daughters are. They'll have me whipp'd for speaking true: thou'lt have me whipp'd for lying; and sometimes I am whipp'd for holding my peace. I had rather be any kind o' thing than a fool; and yet I would not be thee, nuncle; thou hast pared thy wit o' both sides, and left nothing i' th' middle. Here comes one o' th' parings.

Enter GONERIL.

LEAR How now, daughter! What makes that frontlet on? You are too much of late i' th' frown.

FOOL Thou wast a pretty fellow when thou hadst no need to care for her frowning; now thou art an O without a figure. I am better than thou art now: I am a fool, thou art nothing. [*To Goneril*] Yes, forsooth, I will hold my tongue; so your face bids me, though you say nothing. Mum, mum!

He that keeps nor crust nor crumb,
Weary of all, shall want some.

[*Pointing to Lear*] That's a sheal'd peascod.

GONERIL Not only, sir, this your all-licens'd fool,
But other of your insolent retinue
Do hourly carp and quarrel, breaking forth
In rank and not-to-be-endured riots. Sir,
I had thought, by making this well known unto you,
To have found a safe redress; but now grow fearful,
By what yourself too late have spoke and done,
That you protect this course, and put it on
By your allowance; which if you should, the fault
Would not scape censure, nor the redresses sleep,
Which, in the tender of a wholesome weal,
Might in their working do you that offence
Which else were shame, that then necessity
Will call discreet proceeding.

FOOL For, you know, nuncle,
The hedge-sparrow fed the cuckoo so long
That it had it head bit off by it young.
So, out went the candle, and we were left darkling.

LEAR Are you our daughter?

GONERIL I would you would make use of your good wisdom,
Whereof I know you are fraught, and put away
These dispositions which of late transport you
From what you rightly are.

FOOL May not an ass know when the cart draws the horse? Whoop, Jug! I love thee.

LEAR Does any here know me? This is not Lear.
Does Lear walk thus? speak thus? Where are his eyes?
Either his notion weakens, or his discernings
Are lethargied. – Ha! waking? 'Tis not so. –
Who is it that can tell me who I am?

FOOL Lear's shadow.

LEAR I would learn that; for, by the marks of sovereignty, knowledge, and reason, I should be false persuaded I had daughters.

FOOL Which they will make an obedient father.

LEAR Your name, fair gentlewoman?

GONERIL This admiration, sir, is much o' th' savour
Of other your new pranks. I do beseech you
To understand my purposes aright.
As you are old and reverend, should be wise.
Here do you keep a hundred knights and squires;
Men so disorder'd, so debosh'd and bold,
That this our court, infected with their manners,
Shows like a riotous inn. Epicurism and lust
Makes it more like a tavern or a brothel
Than a grac'd palace. The shame itself doth speak
For instant remedy. Be then desir'd
By her that else will take the thing she begs
A little to disquantity your train;
And the remainders that shall still depend
To be such men as may besort your age,
Which know themselves and you.

LEAR Darkness and devils!
Saddle my horses; call my train together.
Degenerate bastard! I'll not trouble thee;
Yet have I left a daughter.

GONERIL You strike my people; and your disorder'd rabble
Make servants of their betters.

Enter ALBANY.

LEAR Woe that too late repents! – O, sir, are you come?
Is it your will? Speak, sir. – Prepare my horses.
Ingratitude, thou marble-hearted fiend,
More hideous when thou show'st thee in a child
Than the sea-monster!

ALBANY Pray, sir, be patient.

LEAR [*To Goneril*] Detested kite! thou liest:
My train are men of choice and rarest parts,
That all particulars of duty know;
And in the most exact regard support
The worships of their name. – O most small fault,
How ugly didst thou in Cordelia show!
Which, like an engine, wrench'd my frame of nature
From the fix'd place; drew from my heart all love
And added to the gall. O Lear, Lear!
Beat at this gate that let thy folly in [*Striking his head.*
And thy dear judgment out! Go, go, my people. [*Exeunt Kent and Knights.*

ALBANY My lord, I am guiltless, as I am ignorant
Of what hath moved you.

LEAR It may be so, my lord.
Hear, Nature, hear; dear goddess, hear.
Suspend thy purpose, if thou didst intend
To make this creature fruitful.
Into her womb convey sterility;
Dry up in her the organs of increase;
And from her derogate body never spring
A babe to honour her! If she must teem,
Create her child of spleen, that it may live
And be a thwart disnatur'd torment to her.
Let it stamp wrinkles in her brow of youth,
With cadent tears fret channels in her cheeks,
Turn all her mother's pains and benefits
To laughter and contempt, that she may feel
How sharper than a serpent's tooth it is
To have a thankless child. Away, away! [*Exit.*

ALBANY Now, gods that we adore, whereof comes this?

GONERIL Never afflict yourself to know more of it;
But let his disposition have that scope
As dotage gives it.

Re-enter LEAR.

LEAR What, fifty of my followers at a clap!
Within a fortnight!

ALBANY What's the matter, sir?

LEAR I'll tell thee. [*To Goneril*] Life and death! I am asham'd
That thou hast power to shake my manhood thus;
That these hot tears, which break from me perforce,
Should make thee worth them. Blasts and fogs upon thee!
Th' untented woundings of a father's curse
Pierce every sense about thee! – Old fond eyes,
Beweep this cause again, I'll pluck ye out,
And cast you, with the waters that you loose,
To temper clay. Ha! Is't come to this?
Let it be so. I have another daughter,
Who, I am sure, is kind and comfortable.
When she shall hear this of thee, with her nails
She'll flay thy wolfish visage. Thou shalt find
That I'll resume the shape which thou dost think
I have cast off for ever. [*Exit Lear.*

GONERIL Do you mark that?

ALBANY I cannot be so partial, Goneril,
To the great love I bear you –

GONERIL Pray you, content. – What, Oswald, ho!
[*To the Fool*] You, sir, more knave than fool, after your master.

FOOL Nuncle Lear, nuncle Lear, tarry – take the fool with thee.
A fox, when one has caught her,
And such a daughter,
Should sure to the slaughter,
If my cap would buy a halter.
So the fool follows after. [*Exit.*

GONERIL This man hath had good counsel. A hundred knights!
'Tis politic and safe to let him keep
At point a hundred knights – yes, that on every dream,
Each buzz, each fancy, each complaint, dislike,
He may enguard his dotage with their pow'rs,
And hold our lives in mercy. Oswald, I say!

ALBANY Well, you may fear too far.

GONERIL Safer than trust too far.
Let me still take away the harms I fear,
Not fear still to be taken. I know his heart.
What he hath utter'd I have writ my sister.
If she sustain him and his hundred knights,
When I have show'd th' unfitness –

Re-enter OSWALD.

How now, Oswald!
What, have you writ that letter to my sister?

OSWALD Ay, madam.

GONERIL Take you some company, and away to horse;
Inform her full of my particular fear,

And thereto add such reasons of your own
As may compact it more. Get you gone;
And hasten your return. [*Exit Oswald*] No, no, my lord,
This milky gentleness and course of yours,
Though I condemn not, yet, under pardon,
You are much more ataxt for want of wisdom
Than prais'd for harmful mildness.

ALBANY How far your eyes may pierce I cannot tell.
Striving to better, oft we mar what's well.

GONERIL Nay, then –

ALBANY Well, well; th' event. [*Exeunt.*

SCENE V. *Court before the Duke of Albany's palace.*

Enter LEAR, KENT, and FOOL.

LEAR Go you before to Gloucester with these letters. Acquaint my daughter no further with anything you know than comes from her demand out of the letter. If your diligence be not speedy, I shall be there afore you.

KENT I will not sleep, my lord, till I have delivered your letter. [*Exit*

FOOL If a man's brains were in's heels, were't not in danger of kibes?

LEAR Ay, boy.

FOOL Then, I prithee, be merry; thy wit shall not go slipshod.

LEAR Ha, ha, ha!

FOOL Shalt see thy other daughter will use thee kindly; for though she's as like this as a crab's like an apple, yet I can tell what I can tell.

LEAR What canst tell, boy?

FOOL She will taste as like this as a crab does to a crab. Thou canst tell why one's nose stands i' th' middle on's face?

LEAR No.

FOOL Why to keep one's eyes of either side's nose, that what a man cannot smell out, he may spy into.

LEAR I did her wrong.

FOOL Canst tell how an oyster makes his shell?

LEAR No.

FOOL Nor I neither; but I can tell why a snail has a house.

LEAR Why?

FOOL Why, to put's head in; not to give it away to his daughters, and leave his horns without a case.

LEAR I will forget my nature. So kind a father! – Be my horses ready?

FOOL Thy asses are gone about 'em. The reason why the seven stars are no moe than seven is a pretty reason.

LEAR Because they are not eight?

FOOL Yes, indeed. Thou wouldst make a good fool.

LEAR To take't again perforce! Monster ingratitude!

FOOL If thou wert my fool, nuncle, I'd have thee beaten for being old before thy time.

LEAR How's that?

FOOL Thou shouldst not have been old till thou hadst been wise.

LEAR O, let me not be mad, not mad, sweet heaven!
Keep me in temper; I would not be mad!

Enter Gentleman.

How now! are the horses ready?

GENTLEMAN Ready, my lord.

LEAR Come, boy.

FOOL She that's a maid now, and laughs at my departure,
Shall not be a maid long, unless things be cut shorter. [*Exeunt.*

ACT TWO

SCENE I. *A court-yard in the Earl of Gloucester's castle.*

Enter EDMUND and CURAN, meeting.

EDMUND Save thee, Curan.

CURAN And you, sir. I have been with your father, and given him notice that the Duke of Cornwall and Regan his Duchess will be here with him this night.

EDMUND How comes that?

CURAN Nay, I know not. You have heard of the news abroad; I mean the whisper'd one, for they are yet but ear-bussing arguments?

EDMUND Not I. Pray you, what are they?

CURAN Have you heard of no likely wars toward 'twixt the Dukes of Cornwall and Albany?

EDMUND Not a word.

CURAN You may do, then, in time. Fare you well, sir. [*Exit.*

EDMUND The Duke be here to-night? The better! best!
This weaves itself perforce into my business.

My father hath set guard to take my brother;
And I have one thing, of a queasy question,
Which I must act. Briefness and fortune work!
Brother, a word! Descend. Brother, I say!

Enter EDGAR.

My father watches. O sir, fly this place;
Intelligence is given where you are hid;
You have now the good advantage of the night.
Have you not spoken 'gainst the Duke of Cornwall?
He's coming hither, now, i' th' night, i' th' haste,
And Regan with him. Have you nothing said
Upon his party 'gainst the Duke of Albany?
Advise yourself.

EDGAR I am sure on't, not a word.

EDMUND I hear my father coming. Pardon me,
In cunning I must draw my sword upon you.
Draw; seem to defend yourself; now quit you well. –
Yield; come before my father. Light, ho, here! –
Fly, brother. – Torches, torches! – So, farewell.

[*Exit Edgar.*

Some blood drawn on me would beget opinion

[*Wounds his arm.*

Of my more fierce endeavour. I have seen drunkards
Do more than this in sport. – Father, father!
Stop, stop! No help?

Enter GLOUCESTER, and Servants with torches.

GLOUCESTER Now, Edmund, where's the villain?

EDMUND Here stood he in the dark, his sharp sword out,
Mumbling of wicked charms, conjuring the moon
To stand's auspicious mistress.

GLOUCESTER But where is he?

EDMUND Look, sir, I bleed.

GLOUCESTER Where is the villain, Edmund?

EDMUND Fled this way, sir. When by no means he could –

GLOUCESTER Pursue him, ho! Go after. [*Exeunt Servants*] – By no means what?

EDMUND Persuade me to the murder of your lordship;
But that I told him the revenging gods
'Gainst parricides did all their thunders bend;
Spoke with how manifold and strong a bond
The child was bound to th' father. Sir, in fine,
Seeing how loathly opposite I stood
To his unnatural purpose, in fell motion,
With his prepared sword, he charges home
My unprovided body, latch'd mine arm;
But when he saw my best alarum'd spirits,
Bold in the quarrel's right, rous'd to th' encounter,
Or whether gasted by the noise I made,
Full suddenly he fled.

GLOUCESTER Let him fly far.
Not in this land shall he remain uncaught;
And found – dispatch. The noble Duke my master,
My worthy arch and patron, comes to-night;
By his authority I will proclaim it,
That he which finds him shall deserve our thanks,
Bringing the murderous coward to the stake;
He that conceals him, death.

EDMUND When I dissuaded him from his intent,
And found him pight to do it, with curst speech
I threaten'd to discover him; he replied,
'Thou unpossessing bastard! dost thou think,
If I would stand against thee, would the reposure
Of any trust, virtue, or worth, in thee
Make thy words faith'd? No. What I should deny –
As this I would; ay, though thou didst produce
My very character – I'd turn it all
To thy suggestion, plot, and damned practice;
And thou must make a dullard of the world,
If they not thought the profits of my death
Were very pregnant and potential spurs
To make thee seek it'.

GLOUCESTER O strong and fast'ned villain!
Would he deny his letter? – I never got him.

[*Tucket within.*

Hark, the Duke's trumpets! I know not why he comes.
All ports I'll bar; the villain shall not scape;
The Duke must grant me that. Besides, his picture
I will send far and near, that all the kingdom
May have due note of him; and of my land,
Loyal and natural boy, I'll work the means
To make thee capable.

Enter CORNWALL, REGAN, and Attendants.

CORNWALL How now, my noble friend! since I came hither,
Which I can call but now, I have heard strange news.

REGAN If it be true, all vengeance comes too short
Which can pursue th' offender. How dost, my lord?

GLOUCESTER O, madam, my old heart is crack'd, it's crack'd!

REGAN What, did my father's godson seek your life?
He whom my father nam'd? your Edgar?

GLOUCESTER O lady, lady, shame would have it hid!
REGAN Was he not companion with the riotous knights
That tend upon my father?
GLOUCESTER I know not, madam. 'Tis too bad, too bad.
EDMUND Yes, madam, he was of that consort.
REGAN No marvel, then, though he were ill affected.
'Tis they have put him on the old man's death,
To have th' expense and waste of his revenues.
I have this present evening from my sister
Been well inform'd of them; and with such cautions
That, if they come to sojourn at my house,
I'll not be there.
CORNWALL Nor I, assure thee, Regan.
Edmund, I hear that you have shown your father
A child-like office.
EDMUND It was my duty, sir.
GLOUCESTER He did bewray his practice, and receiv'd
This hurt you see, striving to apprehend him.
CORNWALL Is he pursued?
GLOUCESTER Ay, my good lord.
CORNWALL If he be taken, he shall never more
Be fear'd of doing harm. Make your own purpose,
How in my strength you please. For you, Edmund,
Whose virtue and obedience doth this instant
So much commend itself, you shall be ours.
Natures of such deep trust we shall much need;
You we first seize on.
EDMUND I shall serve you, sir,
Truly, however else.
GLOUCESTER For him I thank your Grace.
CORNWALL You know not why we came to visit you –
REGAN Thus out of season, threading dark-ey'd night:
Occasions, noble Gloucester, of some poise,
Wherein we must have use of your advice.
Our father he hath writ, so hath our sister,
Of differences, which I best thought it fit
To answer from our home; the several messengers
From hence attend dispatch. Our good old friend,
Lay comforts to your bosom, and bestow
Your needful counsel to our businesses,
Which craves the instant use.
GLOUCESTER I serve you, madam.
Your Graces are right welcome. [*Exeunt.*

SCENE II. *Before Gloucester's castle.*

Enter KENT and OSWALD severally.

OSWALD Good dawning to thee, friend Art of this house?

KENT Ay.

OSWALD Where may we set our horses?

KENT I' th' mire.

OSWALD Prithee, if thou lov'st me, tell me.

KENT I love thee not.

OSWALD Why then, I care not for thee.

KENT If I had thee in Lipsbury pinfold, I would make thee care for me.

OSWALD Why dost thou use me thus? I know thee not.

KENT Fellow, I know thee.

OSWALD What dost thou know me for?

KENT A knave, a rascal, an eater of broken meats; a base, proud, shallow, beggarly, three-suited, hundred-pound, filthy, worsted-stocking knave; a lily-liver'd, action-taking, whoreson, glass-gazing, superserviceable, finical rogue; one-trunk-inheriting slave; one that wouldst be a bawd in way of good service, and art nothing but the composition of a knave, beggar, coward, pander, and the son and heir of a mongrel bitch; one whom I will beat into clamorous whining, if thou deny'st the least syllable of thy addition.

OSWALD Why, what a monstrous fellow art thou, thus to rail on one that is neither known of thee nor knows thee?

KENT What a brazen-fac'd varlet art thou, to deny thou knowest me! Is it two days since I tripp'd up thy heels and beat thee before the King? Draw, you rogue; for, though it be night, yet the moon shines; I'll make a sop o' th moonshine of you; you whoreson cullionly barber-monger, draw. [*Drawing his sword.*

OSWALD Away! I have nothing to do with thee.

KENT Draw, you rascal. You come with letters against the King, and take Vanity the puppet's part against the royalty of her father. Draw, you rogue, or I'll so carbonado your shanks. Draw, you rascal; come your ways.

OSWALD Help, ho! murder! help.

KENT Strike, you slave; stand, rogue, stand; you neat slave, strike. [*Beating him.*

OSWALD Help, ho! murder! murder!

Enter EDMUND with his rapier drawn, GLOUCESTER, CORNWALL, REGAN, and Servants.

EDMUND How now! What's the matter?
Part!
KENT With you, goodman boy, an you please.
Come, I'll flesh ye; come on, young master.
GLOUCESTER Weapons! arms! What's the matter here?

CORNWALL Keep peace, upon your lives;
He dies that strikes again. What is the matter?

REGAN The messengers from our sister and the King.

CORNWALL What is your difference? Speak.

OSWALD I am scarce in breath, my lord.

KENT No marvel, you have so bestirr'd your valour. You cowardly rascal, nature disclaims in thee: a tailor made thee.

CORNWALL Thou art a strange fellow. A tailor make a man?

KENT Ay, a tailor, sir. A stone-cutter or a painter could not have made him so ill, though they had been but two years o' th' trade.

CORNWALL Speak yet, how grew your quarrel?

OSWALD This ancient ruffian, sir, whose life I have spar'd at suit of his grey beard –

KENT Thou whoreson zed! thou unnecessary letter! My lord, if you will give me leave, I will tread this unbolted villain into mortar, and daub the wall of a jakes with him. – Spare my grey beard, you wagtail?

CORNWALL Peace, sirrah!
You beastly knave, know you no reverence?

KENT Yes, sir; but anger hath a privilege.

CORNWALL Why art thou angry?

KENT That such a slave as this should wear a sword,
Who wears no honesty. Such smiling rogues as these,
Like rats, oft bite the holy cords a-twain
Which are too intrinse t' unloose; smooth every passion
That in the natures of their lords rebel;
Bring oil to fire, snow to their colder moods;
Renege, affirm, and turn their halcyon beaks
With every gale and vary of their masters,
Knowing nought, like dogs, but following.
A plague upon your epileptic visage!
Smile you my speeches, as I were a fool?
Goose, if I had you upon Sarum plain,
I'd drive ye cackling home to Camelot.

CORNWALL What, are thou mad, old fellow?

GLOUCESTER How fell you out? Say that.

KENT No contraries hold more antipathy
Than I and such a knave.

CORNWALL Why dost thou call him knave?
What is his fault?

KENT His countenance likes me not.

CORNWALL No more, perchance, does mine, nor his, nor hers.

KENT Sir, 'tis my occupation to be plain:
I have seen better faces in my time
Than stands on any shoulder that I see
Before me at this instant.

CORNWALL This is some fellow
Who, having been prais'd for bluntness, doth affect
A saucy roughness, and constrains the garb
Quite from his nature. He cannot flatter, he,
An honest mind and plain – he must speak truth.
An they will take it, so; if not, he's plain.
These kind of knaves I know, which in this plainness
Harbour more craft and more corrupter ends
Than twenty silly ducking observants
That stretch their duties nicely.

KENT Sir, in good faith, in sincere verity,
Under th' allowance of your great aspect,
Whose influence, like the wreath of radiant fire
On flickering Phoebus' front –

CORNWALL What mean'st by this?

KENT To go out of my dialect, which you discommend so much. I know, sir, I am no flatterer. He that beguil'd you in a plain accent was a plain knave; which, for my part, I will not be, though I should win your displeasure to entreat me to't.

CORNWALL What was th' offence you gave him?

OSWALD I never gave him any.
It pleas'd the King his master very late
To strike at me, upon his misconstruction;
When he, compact, and flattering his displeasure,
Tripp'd me behind; being down, insulted, rail'd,
And put upon him such a deal of man
That worthied him, got praises of the King
For him attempting who was self-subdu'd;
And in the fleshment of this dread exploit,
Drew on me here again.

KENT None of these rogues and cowards
But Ajax is their fool.

CORNWALL Fetch forth the stocks.
You stubborn ancient knave, you reverend braggart,
We'll teach you.

KENT Sir, I am too old to learn.
Call not your stocks for me; I serve the King,
On whose employment I was sent to you.
You shall do small respect, show too bold malice
Against the grace and person of my master,
Stocking his messenger.

CORNWALL Fetch forth the stocks. As I have life and honour,
There shall he sit till noon.

REGAN Till noon! Till night, my lord; and all night too.

KENT Why, madam, if I were your father's dog,
You should not use me so.

REGAN Sir, being his knave, I will.

CORNWALL This is a fellow of the self-same colour

Our sister speaks of. Come, bring away the
stocks. [*Stocks brought out.*

GLOUCESTER Let me beseech your Grace not to
do so.
His fault is much, and the good King his master
Will check him for't; your purpos'd low
correction
Is such as basest and contemned'st wretches
For pilf'rings and most common trespasses
Are punish'd with. The King must take it ill
That he, so slightly valued in his messenger,
Should have him thus restrained.

CORNWALL I'll answer that.

REGAN My sister may receive it much more
worse
To have her gentleman abus'd, assaulted,
For following her affairs. Put in his legs.
[*Kent is put in the stocks.*
Come, my good lord, away.
[*Exeunt all but Gloucester and Kent.*

GLOUCESTER I am sorry for thee, friend; 'tis the
Duke's pleasure
Whose disposition, all the world well knows,
Will not be rubb'd nor stopp'd. I'll entreat for
thee.

KENT Pray, do not, sir. I have watch'd and
travell'd hard;
Some time I shall sleep out, the rest I'll whistle.
A good man's fortune may grow out at heels.
Give you good morrow!

GLOUCESTER The Duke's to blame in this;
'Twill be ill taken. [*Exit.*

KENT Good King, that must approve the
common saw,
Thou out of heaven's benediction com'st
To the warm sun!
Approach, thou beacon to this under globe,
That by thy comfortable beams I may
Peruse this letter. Nothing almost sees miracles
But misery. I know 'tis from Cordelia,
Who hath most fortunately been inform'd
Of my obscured course. [*Reads*] '– and shall find
time
From this enormous state – seeking to give
Losses their remedies.' All weary and o'er-
watch'd,
Take vantage, heavy eyes, not to behold
This shameful lodging.
Fortune, good night; smile once more; turn thy
wheel. [*He sleeps.*

SCENE III. *The open country.*

Enter EDGAR.

EDGAR I heard myself proclaim'd,
And by the happy hollow of a tree
Escap'd the hunt. No port is free; no place
That guard and most unusual vigilance
Does not attend my taking. Whiles I may scape
I will preserve myself; and am bethought
To take the basest and most poorest shape
That ever penury in contempt of man
Brought near to beast. My face I'll grime with
filth,
Blanket my loins, elf all my hairs in knots,
And with presented nakedness outface
The winds and persecutions of the sky.
The country gives me proof and precedent
Of Bedlam beggars, who, with roaring voices,
Strike in their numb'd and mortified bare arms
Pins, wooden pricks, nails, sprigs of rosemary;
And with this horrible object, from low farms,
Poor pelting villages, sheep-cotes, and mills,
Sometimes with lunatic bans, sometime with
prayers,
Enforce their charity. Poor Turlygod! poor
Tom!
That's something yet. Edgar I nothing am.
[*Exit.*

SCENE IV. *Before Gloucester's castle.*

Enter LEAR Fool, and Gentleman, to KENT in the stocks.

LEAR 'Tis strange that they should so depart from
home,
And not send back my messenger.

GENTLEMAN As I learn'd,
The night before there was no purpose in them
Of this remove.

KENT Hail to thee, noble master!

LEAR Ha!
Mak'st thou this shame thy pastime?

KENT No, my lord.

FOOL Ha, ha! he wears cruel garters.
Horses are tied by the heads, dogs and bears by
th' neck, monkeys by th' loins, and men by th'
legs. When a man's over-lusty at legs, then he
wears wooden netherstocks.

LEAR What's he that hath so much thy place
mistook
To set thee here?

KENT It is both he and she,
Your son and daughter.

LEAR No.

KENT Yes.

LEAR No, I say.

KENT I say, yea.

LEAR No, no; they would not.

KENT Yes, they have.

LEAR By Jupiter, I swear, no.

KENT By Juno, I swear, ay.

LEAR They durst not do't;

They could not, would not do't; 'tis worse than murder
To do upon respect such violent outrage.
Resolve me with all modest haste which way
Thou might'st deserve or they impose this usage,
Coming from us.

KENT My lord, when at their home
I did commend your Highness' letters to them,
Ere I was risen from the place that show'd
My duty kneeling, came there a reeking post,
Stew'd in his haste, half breathless, panting forth
From Goneril his mistress salutations;
Deliver'd letters, spite of intermission,
Which presently they read; on whose contents
They summon'd their meiny, straight took horse,
Commanded me to follow and attend
The leisure of their answer, gave me cold looks;
And meeting here the other messenger,
Whose welcome I perceiv'd had poison'd mine,
Being the very fellow which of late
Display'd so saucily against your Highness,
Having more man than wit about me, drew.
He rais'd the house with loud and coward cries.
Your son and daughter found this trespass worth
The shame which here it suffers.

FOOL Winter's not gone yet, if the wild geese fly that way.

Fathers that wear rags
Do make their children blind;
But fathers that bear bags
Shall see their children kind.
Fortune, that arrant whore,
Ne'er turns the key to th' poor.

But, for all this, thou shalt have as many dolours for thy daughters as thou canst tell in a year.

LEAR O, how this mother swells up toward my heart!
Hysterica passio – down, thou climbing sorrow,
Thy element's below. Where is this daughter?

KENT With the earl, sir, here within.

LEAR Follow me not;
Stay here. [*Exit.*

GENTLEMAN Made you no more offence but what you speak of?

KENT None.
How chance the King comes with so small a number?

FOOL An thou hadst been set i' th' stocks for that question, thou'dst well deserv'd it.

KENT Why, fool?

FOOL We'll set thee to school to an ant, to teach thee there's no labouring i' th' winter. All that follow their noses are led by their eyes but blind men; and there's not a nose among twenty but can smell him that's stinking. Let go thy hold when a great wheel runs down a hill, lest it break thy neck with following; but the great one that goes upward, let him draw thee after. When a wise man gives thee better counsel, give me mine again. I would have none but knaves follow it, since a fool gives it.

That sir which serves and seeks for gain,
And follows but for form,
Will pack when it begins to rain,
And leave thee in the storm.
But I will tarry; the fool will stay
And let the wise man fly.
The knave turns fool that runs away;
The fool no knave, perdy.

KENT Where learn'd you this, fool?

FOOL Not i' th' stocks, fool.

Re-enter LEAR and GLOUCESTER.

LEAR Deny to speak with me! They are sick! They are weary!
They have travell'd all the night! Mere fetches;
The images of revolt and flying off.
Fetch me a better answer.

GLOUCESTER My dear lord,
You know the fiery quality of the Duke;
How unremovable and fix'd he is
In his own course.

LEAR Vengeance! plague! death! confusion!
Fiery? What quality? Why Gloucester, Gloucester,
I'd speak with the Duke of Cornwall and his wife.

GLOUCESTER Well, my good lord, I have inform'd them so.

LEAR Inform'd them! Dost thou understand me, man?

GLOUCESTER Ay, my good lord.

LEAR The King would speak with Cornwall; the dear father
Would with his daughter speak; commands their service.
Are they inform'd of this? My breath and blood!
Fiery? the fiery Duke? Tell the hot Duke that –
No, but not yet. May be he is not well.
Infirmity doth still neglect all office
Whereto our health is bound; we are not ourselves
When nature, being oppress'd, commands the mind
To suffer with the body. I'll forbear;
And am fallen out with my more headier will
To take the indispos'd and sickly fit
For the sound man. Death on my state! Wherefore
Should he sit here? This act persuades me

That this remotion of the Duke and her
Is practice only. Give me my servant forth.
Go tell the Duke and's wife I'd speak with them –
Now, presently. Bid them come forth and hear me,
Or at their chamber door I'll beat the drum
Till it cry sleep to death.

GLOUCESTER I would have all well betwixt you. [*Exit.*

LEAR O me, my heart, my rising heart! But, down.

FOOL Cry to it, nuncle, as the cockney did to the eels when she put 'em i' th' paste alive; she knappp'd 'em o' th' coxcombs with a stick, and cried 'Down, wantons, down'. 'Twas her brother that, in pure kindness to his horse, butter'd his hay.

Enter CORNWELL, REGAN, GLOUCESTER, and Servants.

LEAR Good morrow to you both.

CORNWALL Hail to your Grace!

[*Kent here set at liberty.*

REGAN I am glad to see your Highness.

LEAR Regan, I think you are; I know what reason
I have to think so. If thou shouldst not be glad,
I would divorce me from thy mother's tomb,
Sepulchring an adultress. [*To Kent*] O, are you free?
Some other time for that. – Beloved Regan,
Thy sister's naught. O Regan, she hath tied
Sharp-tooth'd unkindness, like a vulture, here.

[*Points to his heart.*

I can scarce speak to thee; thou'lt not believe
With how deprav'd a quality – O Regan!

REGAN I pray you, sir, take patience. I have hope
You less know how to value her desert
Than she to scant her duty.

LEAR Say, how is that?

REGAN I cannot think my sister in the least
Would fail her obligation. If, sir, perchance
She have restrain'd the riots of your followers,
'Tis on such ground, and to such wholesome end,
As clears her from all blame.

LEAR My curses on her!

REGAN O, sir, you are old;
Nature in you stands on the very verge
Of her confine. You should be rul'd and led
By some discretion that discerns your state
Better than you yourself. Therefore I pray you
That to our sister you do make return;
Say you have wrong'd her, sir.

LEAR Ask her forgiveness?
Do you but mark how this becomes the house:
'Dear daughter, I confess that I am old;

[*Kneeling.*

Age is unnecessary; on my knees I beg
That you'll vouchsafe me raiment, bed, and food'.

REGAN Good sir, no more; these are unsightly tricks.
Return you to my sister.

LEAR [*Rising*] Never, Regan.
She hath abated me of half my train;
Look'd black upon me; struck me with her tongue,
Most serpent-like, upon the very heart.
All the stor'd vengeances of heaven fall
On her ingrateful top! Strike her young bones,
You taking airs, with lameness.

CORNWALL Fie, sir, fie!

LEAR You nimble lightnings, dart your blinding flames
Into her scornful eyes. Infect her beauty,
You fen-suck'd fogs, drawn by the pow'rful sun
To fall and blast her pride.

REGAN O the blest gods!
So will you wish on me when the rash mood is on.

LEAR No, Regan, thou shalt never have my curse:
Thy tender-hefted nature shall not give
Thee o'er to harshness. Her eyes are fierce, but thine
Do comfort and not burn. 'Tis not in thee
To grudge my pleasures, to cut off my train,
To bandy hasty words, to scant my sizes,
And, in conclusion, to oppose the bolt
Against my coming in; thou better know'st
The offices of nature, bond of childhood,
Effects of courtesy, dues of gratitude;
Thy half o' th' kingdom hast thou not forgot,
Wherein I thee endow'd.

REGAN Good sir, to th' purpose.

LEAR Who put my man i' th' stocks?

[*Tucket within.*

CORNWALL What trumpet's that?

REGAN I know't – my sister's. This approves her letter,
That she would soon be here.

Enter OSWALD.

Is your lady come?

LEAR This is a slave whose easy-borrow'd pride
Dwells in the fickle grace of her he follows.
Out, varlet, from my sight!

CORNWALL What means your Grace?

Enter GONERIL.

LEAR Who stock'd my servant? Regan, I have good hope

Thou didst not know on't. – Who comes here? O heavens,
If you do love old men, if your sweet sway
Allow obedience, if you yourselves are old,
Make it your cause; send down, and take my part.
[*To Goneril*] Art not asham'd to look upon this beard? –
O Regan, will you take her by the hand?

GONERIL Why not by th' hand, sir? How have I offended?
All's not offence that indiscretion finds,
And dotage terms so.

LEAR O sides, you are too tough!
Will you yet hold? – How came my man i' th' stocks?

CORNWALL I set him there, sir; but his own disorders
Deserv'd much less advancement.

LEAR You! did you?

REGAN I pray you, father, being weak, seem so.
If, till the expiration of your month,
You will return and sojourn with my sister,
Dismissing half your train, come then to me.
I am now from home, and out of that provision
Which shall be needful for your entertainment.

LEAR Return to her, and fifty men dismiss'd?
No, rather I abjure all roofs, and choose
To wage against the enmity o' th' air,
To be a comrade with the wolf and owl –
Necessity's sharp pinch! Return with her?
Why, the hot-blooded France, that dowerless took
Our youngest born – I could as well be brought
To knee his throne, and, squire-like, pension beg
To keep base life afoot. Return with her?
Persuade me rather to be slave and sumpter
To this detested groom. [*Pointing to Oswald.*

GONERIL At your choice, sir.

LEAR I prithee, daughter, do not make me mad.
I will not trouble thee, my child; farewell.
We'll no more meet, no more see one another.
But yet thou art my flesh, my blood, my daughter;
Or rather a disease that's in my flesh,
Which I must needs call mine; thou art a boil,
A plague-sore, or embossed carbuncle
In my corrupted blood. But I'll not chide thee;
Let shame come when it will, I do not call it;
I do not bid the Thunder-bearer shoot,
Nor tell tales of thee to high-judging Jove.
Mend when thou canst; be better at thy leisure;
I can be patient; I can stay with Regan,
I and my hundred knights.

REGAN Not altogether so.
I look'd not for you yet, nor am provided
For your fit welcome. Give ear, sir, to my sister;
For those that mingle reason with your passion
Must be content to think you old, and so –
But she knows what she does.

LEAR Is this well spoken?

REGAN I dare avouch it, sir. What, fifty followers?
Is it not well? What should you need of more?
Yea, or so many, sith that both charge and danger
Speak 'gainst so great a number? How in one house
Should many people under two commands
Hold amity? 'Tis hard; almost impossible.

GONERIL Why might not you, my lord, receive attendance
From those that she calls servants, or from mine?

REGAN Why not, my lord? If then they chanc'd to slack ye,
We could control them. If you will come to me –
For now I spy a danger – I entreat you
To bring but five and twenty. To no more
Will I give place or notice.

LEAR I gave you all.

REGAN And in good time you gave it.

LEAR Made you my guardians, my depositaries;
But kept a reservation to be followed
With such a number. What, must I come to you
With five and twenty, Regan? Said you so?

REGAN And speak't again, my lord. No more with me.

LEAR Those wicked creatures yet do look well-favour'd
When others are more wicked; not being the worst
Stands in some rank of praise. [*To Goneril*] I'll go with thee.
Thy fifty yet doth double five and twenty,
And thou art twice her love.

GONERIL Hear me, my lord:
What need you five and twenty, ten, or five,
To follow in a house where twice so many
Have a command to tend you?

REGAN What need one?

LEAR O, reason not the need! Our basest beggars
Are in the poorest thing superfluous.
Allow not nature more than nature needs,
Man's life is cheap as beast's. Thou art a lady;
If only to go warm were gorgeous,
Why, nature needs not what thou gorgeous wear'st,
Which scarcely keeps thee warm. But, for true need –
You heavens, give me that patience, patience I need.
You see me here, you gods, a poor old man,

As full of grief as age; wretched in both.
If it be you that stirs these daughters' hearts
Against their father, fool me not so much
To bear it tamely; touch me with noble anger,
And let not women's weapons, water-drops,
Stain my man's cheeks! No, you unnatural hags,
I will have such revenges on you both
That all the world shall – I will do such things –
What they are yet I know not; but they shall be
The terrors of the earth. You think I'll weep.
No, I'll not weep. [*Storm and tempest.*
I have full cause of weeping; but this heart
Shall break into a hundred thousand flaws
Or ere I'll weep. O fool, I shall go mad!
[*Exeunt Lear, Gloucester, Kent, and Fool.*

CORNWALL Let us withdraw; 'twill be a storm.
REGAN This house is little: the old man and's people
Cannot be well bestow'd.
GONERIL 'Tis his own blame; hath put himself from rest,
And must needs taste his folly.
REGAN For his particular, I'll receive him gladly,
But not one follower.
GONERIL So am I purpos'd.
Where is my Lord of Gloucester?
CORNWALL Followed the old man forth.

Re-enter GLOUCESTER.

He is return'd.
GLOUCESTER The King is in high rage.
CORNWALL Whither is he going?
GLOUCESTER He calls to horse; but will I know not whither.
CORNWALL 'Tis best to give him way; he leads himself.
GONERIL My lord, entreat him by no means to stay.
GLOUCESTER Alack, the night comes on, and the high winds
Do sorely ruffle: for many miles about
There's scarce a bush.
REGAN O sir, to wilful men
The injuries that they themselves procure
Must be their schoolmasters. Shut up your doors.
He is attended with a desperate train;
And what they may incense him to, being apt
To have his ear abus'd, wisdom bids fear.
CORNWALL Shut up your doors, my lord; 'tis a wild night.
My Regan counsels well. Come out o' th' storm.
[*Exeunt.*

ACT THREE

SCENE I. *A heath.*

Storm still. Enter KENT and a Gentleman, severally.

KENT Who's there, besides foul weather?
GENTLEMAN One minded like the weather, most unquietly.
KENT I know you. Where's the King?
GENTLEMAN Contending with the fretful elements;
Bids the wind blow the earth into the sea,
Or swell the curled waters 'bove the main,
That things might change or cease; tears his white hair,
Which the impetuous blasts, with eyeless rage,
Catch in their fury, and make nothing of;
Strives in his little world of man to out-scorn
The to-and-fro conflicting wind and rain.
This night, wherein the cub-drawn bear would couch,
The lion and the belly-pinched wolf
Keep their fur dry, unbonneted he runs,
And bids what will take all.
KENT But who is with him?
GENTLEMAN None but the fool; who labours to out-jest
His heart-struck injuries.
KENT Sir, I do know you,
And dare, upon the warrant of my note,
Commend a dear thing to you. There is division,
Although as yet the face of it be cover'd
With mutual cunning, 'twixt Albany and Cornwall;
Who have – as who have not that their great stars
Thron'd and set high? – servants, who seem no less,
Which are to France the spies and speculations
Intelligent of our state. What hath been seen,
Either in snuffs and packings of the Dukes;
Or the hard rein which both of them hath borne
Against the old kind King; or something deeper,
Whereof perchance these are but furnishings –
But true it is from France there comes a power
Into this scatter'd kingdom, who already,
Wise in our negligence, have secret feet
In some of our best ports, and are at point
To show their open banner. Now to you;
If on my credit you dare build so far
To make your speed to Dover, you shall find
Some that will thank you making just report

Of how unnatural and bemadding sorrow
The King hath cause to plain.
I am a gentleman of blood and breeding;
And from some knowledge and assurance offer
This office to you.

GENTLEMAN I will talk further with you.

KENT No, do not.
For confirmation that I am much more
Than my out-wall, open this purse and take
What it contains. If you shall see Cordelia,
As fear not but you shall, show her this ring;
And she will tell you who your fellow is
That yet you do not know. Fie on this storm!
I will go seek the King.

GENTLEMAN Give me your hand. Have you no more to say?

KENT Few words, but, to effect, more than all yet;
That when we have found the King – in which your pain
That way, I'll this – he that first lights on him
Holla the other. [*Exeunt severally.*

SCENE II. *Another part of the heath.*

Storm still. Enter LEAR and Fool.

LEAR Blow, winds, and crack your cheeks; rage, blow.
You cataracts and hurricanoes, spout
Till you have drench'd our steeples, drown'd the cocks.
You sulph'rous and thought-executing fires,
Vaunt-couriers of oak-cleaving thunder-bolts,
Singe my white head. And thou, all-shaking thunder,
Strike flat the thick rotundity o' th' world;
Crack nature's moulds, all germens spill at once,
That makes ingrateful man.

FOOL O nuncle, court holy water in a dry house is better than this rain-water out o' door. Good nuncle, in; ask thy daughters' blessing. Here's a night pities neither wise men nor fools.

LEAR Rumble thy bellyful. Spit, fire; spout, rain.
Nor rain, wind, thunder, fire, are my daughters.
I tax not you, you elements, with unkindness;
I never gave you kingdom, call'd you children;
You owe me no subscription. Then let fall
Your horrible pleasure. Here I stand, your slave,
A poor, infirm, weak and despis'd old man;
But yet I call you servile ministers
That will with two pernicious daughters join
Your high-engender'd battles 'gainst a head
So old and white as this. O, ho! 'tis foul!

FOOL He that has a house to put's head in has a good head-piece.

The cod-piece that will house
Before the head has any,
The head and he shall louse;
So beggars marry many.
The man that makes his toe
What he his heart should make
Shall of a corn cry woe,
And turn his sleep to wake.

For there was never yet fair woman but she made mouths in a glass.

Enter KENT.

LEAR No, I will be the pattern of all patience;
I will say nothing.

KENT Who's there?

FOOL Marry, here's grace and a cod-piece; that's a wise man and a fool.

KENT Alas, sir, are you here? Things that love night
Love not such nights as these; the wrathful skies
Gallow the very wanderers of the dark
And make them keep their caves. Since I was man
Such sheets of fire, such bursts of horrid thunder,
Such groans of roaring wind and rain, I never
Remember to have heard. Man's nature cannot carry
Th' affliction nor the fear.

LEAR Let the great gods,
That keep this dreadful pudder o'er our heads,
Find out their enemies now. Tremble, thou wretch,
That hast within thee undivulged crimes
Unwhipp'd of justice. Hide thee, thou bloody hand;
Thou perjur'd, and thou simular man of virtue
That art incestuous; caitiff, to pieces shake,
That under covert and convenient seeming
Hast practis'd on man's life. Close pent-up guilts,
Rive your concealing continents, and cry
These dreadful summoners grace. I am a man
More sinn'd against than sinning.

KENT Alack, bare-headed!
Gracious my lord, hard by here is a hovel;
Some friendship will it lend you 'gainst the tempest.
Repose you there, while I to this hard house –
More harder than the stones whereof 'tis rais'd;
Which even but now, demanding after you,
Denied me to come in – return, and force
Their scanted courtesy.

LEAR My wits begin to turn.
Come on, my boy. How dost, my boy? Art cold?
I am cold myself. Where is this straw, my fellow?
The art of our necessities is strange
That can make vile things precious. Come, your hovel.

Poor fool and knave, I have one part in my heart
That's sorry yet for thee.

FOOL [*Sings*] He that has and a little tiny wit
With heigh-ho, the wind and the rain –
Must make content with his fortunes fit,
Though the rain it raineth every day.

LEAR True, my good boy. Come, bring us to this
hovel. [*Exeunt Lear and Kent.*

FOOL This is a brave night to cool a courtezan. I'll speak a prophecy ere I go.
When priests are more in word than matter;
When brewers mar their malt with water;
When nobles are their tailors' tutors;
No heretics burn'd, but wenches' suitors;
When every case in law is right;
No squire in debt, nor no poor knight;
When slanders do not live in tongues;
Nor cutpurses come not to throngs;
When usurers tell their gold i' th' field;
And bawds and whores do churches build –
Then shall the realm of Albion
Come to great confusion.
Then comes the time, who lives to see't,
That going shall be us'd with feet.
This prophecy Merlin shall make, for I live before his time. [*Exit.*

SCENE III. *Gloucester's castle.*

Enter GLOUCESTER and EDMUND.

GLOUCESTER Alack, alack, Edmund, I like not this unnatural dealing. When I desired their leave that I might pity him, they took from me the use of mine own house, charg'd me, on pain of perpetual displeasure, neither to speak of him, entreat for him, or any way sustain him.

EDMUND Most savage and unnatural!

GLOUCESTER Go to; say you nothing. There is division between the Dukes; and a worse matter than that. I have received a letter this night – 'tis dangerous to be spoken; I have lock'd the letter in my closet. These injuries the King now bears will be revenged home; there is part of a power already footed. We must incline to the King. I will look him, and privily relieve him. Go you and maintain talk with the Duke, that my charity be not of him perceived; if he ask for me, I am ill, and gone to bed. If I die for it, as no less is threatened me, the King my old master must be relieved. There is strange things toward, Edmund; pray you be careful. [*Exit.*

EDMUND This courtesy forbid thee shall the
Duke
Instantly know, and of that letter too.
This seems a fair deserving, and must draw me
That which my father loses – no less than all.
The younger rises, when the old doth fall. [*Exit.*

SCENE IV. *Before a hovel on the heath.*

Storm still. Enter LEAR, KENT, and Fool.

KENT Here is the place, my lord; good my lord,
enter.
The tyranny of the open night's too rough
For nature to endure.

LEAR Let me alone.

KENT Good my lord, enter here.

LEAR Wilt break my heart?

KENT I had rather break mine own. Good my
lord, enter.

LEAR Thou think'st 'tis much that this
contentious storm
Invades us to the skin; so 'tis to thee,
But where the greater malady is fix'd,
The lesser is scarce felt. Thou'dst shun a bear;
But if thy flight lay toward the roaring sea,
Thou'dst meet the bear i' th' mouth. When the
mind's free
The body's delicate; this tempest in my mind
Doth from my senses take all feeling else,
Save what beats there. Filial ingratitude!
Is it not as this mouth should tear this hand
For lifting food to't? But I will punish home.
No, I will weep no more. In such a night,
To shut me out! Pour on; I will endure.
In such a night as this! O Regan, Goneril!
Your old kind father, whose frank heart gave all!
O, that way madness lies; let me shun that;
No more of that.

KENT Good my lord, enter here.

LEAR Prithee go in thyself; seek thine own ease.
This tempest will not give me leave to ponder
On things would hurt me more. But I'll go in.
[*To the Fool*] In, boy; go first. – You house-less
poverty –
Nay, get thee in. I'll pray, and then I'll sleep.
[*Exit Fool.*

Poor naked wretches, wheresoe'er you are,
That bide the pelting of this pitiless storm,
How shall your houseless heads and unfed
sides,
Your loop'd and window'd raggedness, defend
you
From seasons such as these? O, I have ta'en
Too little care of this! Take physic, pomp;
Expose thyself to feel what wretches feel,
That thou mayst shake the superflux to them,
And show the heavens more just.

EDGAR [*Within*] Fathom and half, fathom and half! Poor Tom!

Enter Fool from the hovel.

FOOL Come not in here, nuncle, here's a spirit.
Help me, help me!

KENT Give me thy hand. Who's there?

FOOL A spirit, a spirit. He says his name's poor Tom.

KENT What art thou that dost grumble there i' th' straw?
Come forth.

Enter EDGAR, disguised as a madman.

EDGAR Away! the foul fiend follows me.
Through the sharp hawthorn blows the cold wind.
Humh! go to thy cold bed and warm thee.

LEAR Didst thou give all to thy daughters? And art thou come to this?

EDGAR Who gives anything to poor Tom? whom the foul fiend hath led through fire and through flame, through ford and whirlpool, o'er bog and quagmire; that hath laid knives under his pillow and halters in his pew, set ratsbane by his porridge; made him proud of heart, to ride on a bay trotting-horse over four-inched bridges, to course his own shadow for a traitor. Bless thy five wits! Tom's a-cold. O, do de, do de, do de. Bless thee from whirlwinds, starblasting, and taking! Do poor Tom some charity, whom the foul fiend vexes. There could I have him now – and there – and there again – and there. [*Storm still.*

LEAR What, has his daughters brought him to this pass?
Could'st thou save nothing? Would'st thou give 'em all?

FOOL Nay, he reserv'd a blanket, else we had been all sham'd.

LEAR Now all the plagues that in the pendulous air
Hang fated o'er men's faults light on thy daughters!

KENT He hath no daughters, sir.

LEAR Death, traitor! Nothing could have subdu'd nature
To such a lowness but his unkind daughters.
Is it the fashion that discarded fathers
Should have thus little mercy on their flesh?
Judicious punishment! 'twas this flesh begot
Those pelican daughters.

EDGAR Pillicock sat on Pillicock-hill. Alow, alow, loo, loo!

FOOL This cold night will turn us all to fools and madmen.

EDGAR Take heed o' th' foul fiend; obey thy parents; keep thy words justly; swear not; commit not with man's sworn spouse; set not thy sweet heart on proud array. Tom's a-cold.

LEAR What hast thou been?

EDGAR A serving-man, proud in heart and mind; that curl'd my hair; wore gloves in my cap; serv'd the lust of my mistress' heart, and did the act of darkness with her; swore as many oaths as I spake words, and broke them in the sweet face of heaven; one that slept in the contriving of lust, and wak'd to do it. Wine lov'd I deeply, dice dearly; and in woman out-paramour'd the Turk. False of heart, light of ear, bloody of hand; hog in sloth, fox in stealth, wolf in greediness, dog in madness, lion in prey. Let not the creaking of shoes nor the rustling of silks betray thy poor heart to woman. Keep thy foot out of brothels, thy hand out of plackets, thy pen from lenders' books, and defy the foul fiend.
Still through the hawthorn blows the cold wind.
Says suum, mun, nonny.
Dolphin my boy, boy, sessa! let him trot by.
[*Storm still.*

LEAR Why, thou wert better in a grave than to answer with thy uncover'd body this extremity of the skies. Is man no more than this? Consider him well. Thou ow'st the worm no silk, the beast no hide, the sheep no wool, the cat no perfume. Ha! here's three on's are sophisticated! Thou art the thing itself: unaccommodated man is no more but such a poor, bare, forked animal as thou art. Off, off, you lendings! Come, unbutton here. [*Tearing off his clothes.*

Enter GLOUCESTER with a torch.

FOOL Prithee, nuncle, be contented; 'tis a naughty night to swim in. Now a little fire in a wild field were like an old lecher's heart – a small spark, all the rest on's body cold. Look, here comes a walking fire.

EDGAR This is the foul fiend Flibbertigibbet; he begins at curfew, and walks till the first cock; he gives the web and the pin, squences the eye, and makes the hare-lip; mildews the white wheat, and hurts the poor creature of earth.
Swithold footed thrice the 'old;
He met the nightmare and her nine-fold;
Bid her alight
And her troth plight,
And aroint thee, witch, aroint thee!

KENT How fares your Grace?

LEAR What's he?

KENT Who's there? What is't you seek?

GLOUCESTER What are you there? Your names?

EDGAR Poor Tom; that eats the swimming frog, the toad, the tadpole, the wall-newt, and the water; that in the fury of his heart, when the

foul fiend rages, eats cow-dung for sallets, swallows the old rat and the ditch-dog, drinks the green mantle of the standing pool; who is whipp'd from tithing to tithing, and stock-punish'd, and imprison'd; who hath had three suits to his back, six shirts to his body –
Horse to ride, and weapon to wear;
But mice and rats, and such small deer,
Have been Tom's food for seven long year.
Beware my follower. Peace, Smulkin; peace, thou fiend!

GLOUCESTER What, hath your Grace no better company?

EDGAR The prince of darkness is a gentleman;
Modo he's call'd, and Mahu.

GLOUCESTER Our flesh and blood, my lord, is grown so vile
That it doth hate what gets it.

EDGAR Poor Tom's a-cold.

GLOUCESTER Go in with me: my duty cannot suffer
T' obey in all your daughters' hard commands.
Though their injunction be to bar my doors,
And let this tyrannous night take hold upon you,
Yet have I ventur'd to come seek you out,
And bring you where both fire and food is ready.

LEAR First let me talk with this philosopher.
What is the cause of thunder?

KENT Good my lord, take this offer; go into th' house.

LEAR I'll talk a word with this same learned Theban.
What is your study?

EDGAR How to prevent the fiend and to kill vermin.

LEAR Let me ask you one word in private.

KENT Importune him once more to go, my lord;
His wits begin t' unsettle. [*Storm still.*

GLOUCESTER Canst thou blame him?
His daughters seek his death. Ah, that good Kent! –
He said it would be thus – poor, banish'd man!
Thou sayest the King grows mad; I'll tell thee, friend,
I am almost mad myself. I had a son,
Now outlaw'd from my blood; he sought my life
But lately, very late. I lov'd him, friend –
No father his son dearer. True to tell thee,
The grief hath craz'd my wits. What a night's this!
I do beseech your Grace –

LEAR O, cry you mercy, sir.
Noble philosopher, your company.

EDGAR Tom's a-cold.

GLOUCESTER In, fellow, there, into th' hovel; keep thee warm.

LEAR Come, let's in all.

KENT This way, my lord.

LEAR With him;
I will keep still with my philosopher.

KENT Good my lord, soothe him; let him take the fellow.

GLOUCESTER Take him you on.

KENT Sirrah, come on; go along with us.

LEAR Come, good Athenian.

GLOUCESTER No words, no words! Hush.

EDGAR Child Rowland to the dark tower came,
His word was still 'Fie, foh, and fum,
I smell the blood of a British man'. [*Exeunt.*

SCENE V. *Gloucester's castle.*

Enter CORNWALL and EDMUND.

CORNWALL I will have my revenge ere I depart his house.

EDMUND How, my lord, I may be censured, that nature thus gives way to loyalty, something fears me to think of.

CORNWALL I now perceive it was not altogether your brother's evil disposition made him seek his death; but a provoking merit, set a-work by a reprovable badness in himself.

EDMUND How malicious is my fortune, that I must repent to be just! This is the letter he spoke of, which approves him an intelligent party to the advantages of France. O heavens! that this treason were not, or not I the detector!

CORNWALL Go with me to the Duchess.

EDGAR If the matter of this paper be certain, you have mighty business in hand.

CORNWALL True or false, it hath made thee Earl of Gloucester. Seek out where thy father is, that he may be ready for our apprehension.

EDMUND [*Aside*] If I find him comforting the King, it will stuff his suspicion more fully. – I will persever in my course of loyalty, though the conflict be sore between that and my blood.

CORNWALL I will lay trust upon thee; and thou shalt find a dearer father in my love. [*Exeunt.*

SCENE VI. *An outhouse of Gloucester's castle.*

Enter KENT and GLOUCESTER.

GLOUCESTER Here is better than the open air; take it thankfully. I will piece out the comfort with what addition I can! I will not be long from you.

KENT All the pow'r of his wits have given way to his impatience. The gods reward your kindness! [*Exit Gloucester.*

Enter LEAR, EDGAR, and Fool.

EDGAR Frateretto calls me, and tells me Nero is an angler in the lake of darkness. Pray, innocent, and beware the foul fiend.

FOOL Prithee, nuncle, tell me whether a madman be a gentleman or a yeoman?

LEAR A king, a king!

FOOL No; he's a yeoman that has a gentleman to his son; for he's a mad yeoman that sees his son a gentleman before him.

LEAR To have a thousand with red burning spits
Come hizzing in upon 'em –

EDGAR The foul fiend bites my back.

FOOL He's mad that trusts in the tameness of a wolf, a horse's health, a boy's love, or a whore's oath.

LEAR It shall be done; I will arraign them straight.
[*To Edgar*] Come, sit thou here, most learned justicer.
[*To the Fool*] Thou, sapient sir, sit here. – Now, you she-foxes!

EDGAR Look where he stands and glares!
Want'st thou eyes at trial, madam?
Come o'er the bourn, Bessy, to me.

FOOL Her boat hath a leak,
And she must not speak,
Why she dares not come over to thee.

EDGAR The foul fiend haunts poor Tom in the voice of a nightingale. Hoppedance cries in Tom's belly for two white herring. Croak not, black angel; I have no food for thee.

KENT How do you, sir? Stand you not so amaz'd.
Will you lie down and rest upon the cushions?

LEAR I'll see their trial first. Bring in their evidence.
[*To Edgar*] Thou robed man of justice, take thy place.
[*To the Fool*] And thou, his yoke-fellow of equity,
Bench by his side. [*To Kent*] You are o' th' commission,
Sit you too.

EDGAR Let us deal justly.
Sleepest or wakest thou, jolly shepherd?
Thy sheep be in the corn;
And for one blast of thy minikin mouth,
Thy sheep shall take no harm.
Pur! the cat is grey.

LEAR Arraign her first; 'tis Goneril. I here take my oath before this honourable assembly she kick'd the poor King her father.

FOOL Come hither, mistress. Is your name Goneril?

LEAR She cannot deny it.

FOOL Cry you mercy, I took you for a joint-stool.

LEAR And here's another, whose warp'd looks proclaim
What store her heart is made on. Stop her there!
Arms, arms, sword, fire! Corruption in the place!
False justicer, why hast thou let her scape?

EDGAR Bless thy five wits!

KENT O pity! Sir, where is the patience now
That you so oft have boasted to retain?

EDGAR [*Aside*] My tears begin to take his part so much
They mar my counterfeiting.

LEAR The little dogs and all,
Tray, Blanch, and Sweetheart, see, they bark at me.

EDGAR Tom will throw his head at them.
Avaunt, you curs!
Be thy mouth or black or white,
Tooth that poisons if it bite;
Mastiff, greyhound, mongrel grim,
Hound or spaniel, brach or lym,
Or bobtail tike or trundle-tail –
Tom will make him weep and wail;
For, with throwing thus my head,
Dogs leapt the hatch, and all are fled.
Do de, de, de. Sessa! Come, march to wakes and fairs and market-towns. Poor Tom, thy horn is dry.

LEAR Then let them anatomize Regan; see what breeds about her heart. Is there any cause in nature that make these hard hearts? [*To Edgar*] You, sir, I entertain for one of my hundred; only I do not like the fashion of your garments. You will say they are Persian, but let them be chang'd.

KENT Now, good my lord, lie here and rest awhile.

LEAR Make no noise, make no noise; draw the curtains. So, so. We'll go to supper i' th' morning.

FOOL And I'll go to bed at noon.

Re-enter GLOUCESTER.

GLOUCESTER Come hither, friend. Where is the King my master?

KENT Here, sir; but trouble him not – his wits are gone.

GLOUCESTER Good friend, I prithee, take him in thy arms;
I have o'erheard a plot of death upon him.
There is a litter ready; lay him in't
And drive toward Dover, friend, where thou shalt meet
Both welcome and protection. Take up thy master;
If thou shouldst dally half an hour, his life,
With thine, and all that offer to defend him,
Stand in assured loss. Take up, take up;

And follow me, that will to some provision
Give thee quick conduct.
KENT Oppressed nature sleeps.
This rest might yet have balm'd thy broken sinews,
Which, if convenience will not allow,
Stand in hard cure. [*To the Fool*] Come, help to bear thy master;
Thou must not stay behind.
GLOUCESTER Come, come, away.
[*Exeunt all but Edgar.*
EDGAR When we our betters see bearing our woes,
We scarcely think our miseries our foes.
Who alone suffers suffers most i' th' mind,
Leaving free things and happy shows behind;
But then the mind much sufferance doth o'erskip
When grief hath mates, and bearing fellowship.
How light and portable my pain seems now,
When that which makes me bend makes the King bow –
He childed as I father'd! Tom, away!
Mark the high noises; and thyself bewray,
When false opinion, whose wrong thoughts defile thee,
In thy just proof repeals and reconciles thee.
What will hap more to-night, safe scape the King!
Lurk, lurk. [*Exit.*

SCENE VII. *Gloucester's castle.*

Enter CORNWALL, REGAN, GONERIL, EDMUND, and Servants.

CORNWALL [*To Goneril*] Post speedily to my lord your husband; show him this letter. The army of France is landed. – Seek out the traitor Gloucester. [*Exeunt some of the Servants.*

REGAN Hang him instantly.
GONERIL Pluck out his eyes.
CORNWALL Leave him to my displeasure.
Edmund, keep you our sister company. The revenges we are bound to take upon your traitorous father are not fit for your beholding. Advise the Duke, where you are going, to a most festinate preparation; we are bound to the like. Our posts shall be swift and intelligent betwixt us. Farewell, dear sister; farewell, my Lord of Gloucester.

Enter OSWALD.

How now! where's the King?
OSWALD My Lord of Gloucester hath convey'd him hence.
Some five or six and thirty of his knights,
Hot questrists after him, met him at gate;
Who, with some other of the lord's dependants,
Are gone with him toward Dover, where they boast
To have well-armed friends.
CORNWALL Get horses for your mistress.
GONERIL Farewell, sweet lord, and sister.
CORNWALL Edmund, farewell. [*Exeunt Goneril, Edmund, and Oswald.*
Go seek the traitor Gloucester,
Pinion him like a thief, bring him before us.
[*Exeunt other Servants.*
Though well we may not pass upon his life
Without the form of justice, yet our power
Shall do a court'sy to our wrath, which men
May blame, but not control.

Enter GLOUCESTER, brought in by two or three.

Who's there? the traitor?
REGAN Ingrateful fox! 'tis he.
CORNWALL Bind fast his corky arms.
GLOUCESTER What means your Graces? Good my friends, consider
You are my guests; do me no foul play, friends.
CORNWALL Bind him, I say. [*Servants bind him.*
REGAN Hard, hard. O filthy traitor!
GLOUCESTER Unmerciful lady as you are, I'm none.
CORNWALL To this chair bind him. Villain, thou shalt find –
[*Regan plucks his beard.*
GLOUCESTER By the kind gods, 'tis most ignobly done
To pluck me by the beard.
REGAN So white, and such a traitor!
GLOUCESTER Naughty lady,
These hairs which thou dost ravish from my chin
Will quicken and accuse thee. I am your host.
With robbers' hands my hospitable favours
You should not ruffle thus. What will you do?
CORNWALL Come, sir, what letters had you late from France?
REGAN Be simple-answer'd, for we know the truth.
CORNWALL And what confederacy have you with the traitors
Late footed in the kingdom?
REGAN To whose hands you have sent the lunatic King:
Speak.
GLOUCESTER I have a letter guessingly set down,
Which came from one that's of a neutral heart,
And not from one oppos'd.
CORNWALL Cunning.
REGAN And false.

CORNWALL Where hast thou sent the King?
GLOUCESTER To Dover.
REGAN Wherefore to Dover? Wast thou not charg'd at peril –
CORNWALL Wherefore to Dover? Let him first answer that.
GLOUCESTER I am tied to the stake, and I must stand the course.
REGAN Wherefore to Dover?
GLOUCESTER Because I would not see thy cruel nails
Pluck out his poor old eyes; nor thy fierce sister
In his anointed flesh rash boarish fangs.
The sea, with such a storm as his bare head
In hell-black night endur'd, would have buoy'd up
And quench'd the stelled fires.
Yet, poor old heart, he holp the heavens to rain.
If wolves had at thy gate howl'd that dern time,
Thou shouldst have said 'Good porter, turn the key'.
All cruels else subscribe, but I shall see
The winged vengeance overtake such children.
CORNWALL See't shalt thou never. Fellows, hold the chair.
Upon these eyes of thine I'll set my foot.
GLOUCESTER He that will think to live till he be old,
Give me some help! – O cruel! O you gods!
REGAN One side will mock another; th' other too.
CORNWALL If you see vengeance –
1 SERVANT Hold your hand, my lord.
I have serv'd you ever since I was a child;
But better service have I never done you,
Than now to bid you hold.
REGAN How now, you dog!
1 SERVANT If you did wear a beard upon your chin
I'd shake it on this quarrel. What do you mean?
CORNWALL My villain! *[They draw and fight.*
1 SERVANT Nay, then come on, and take the chance of anger. *[Cornwall is wounded.*
REGAN Give me thy sword. A peasant stand up thus! *[She takes a sword and stabs him from behind.*
1 SERVANT O, I am slain! My lord, you have one eye left
To see some mischief on him. O! *[Dies.*
CORNWALL Lest it see more, prevent it. Out vile jelly!
Where is thy lustre now?
GLOUCESTER All dark and comfortless! Where's my son Edmund?
Edmund, enkindle all the sparks of nature
To quit this horrid act.
REGAN Out, trecherous villain!
Thou call'st on him that hates thee. It was he
That made the overture of thy treasons to us;
Who is too good to pity thee.
GLOUCESTER O my follies! Then Edgar was abus'd.
Kind gods, forgive me that, and prosper him.
REGAN Go thrust him out at gates and let him smell
His way to Dover. *[Gloucester led out.*
How is't my lord? How look you?
CORNWALL I have receiv'd a hurt. Follow me, lady.
Turn out that eyeless villain; throw this slave
Upon the dunghill. Regan, I bleed apace.
Untimely comes this hurt. Give me your arm.
[Exit Cornwall, led by Regan.
2 SERVANT I'll never care what wickedness I do,
If this man come to good.
3 SERVANT If she live long,
And in the end meet the old course of death,
Women will all turn monsters.
2 SERVANT Let's follow the old Earl and get the Bedlam
To lead him where he would. His roguish madness
Allows itself to anything.
3 SERVANT Go thou. I'll fetch some flax and whites of eggs
To apply to his bleeding face. Now heaven help him! *[Exeunt.*

ACT FOUR

SCENE I. *The Heath.*

Enter EDGAR.

EDGAR Yet better thus and known to be contemn'd,
Than still contemn'd and flatter'd. To be worst,
The lowest and most dejected thing of fortune,
Stands still in esperance, lives not in fear.
The lamentable change is from the best;
The worst returns to laughter. Welcome, then,
Thou unsubstantial air that I embrace!
The wretch that thou hast blown unto the worst
Owes nothing to thy blasts.

Enter GLOUCESTER, led by an Old Man.

But who comes here?
My father, poorly led? World, world, O world!

But that thy strange mutations make us hate thee,
Life would not yield to age.

OLD MAN O my good lord, I have been your tenant, and your father's tenant, these fourscore years.

GLOUCESTER Away, get thee away; good friend, be gone.
Thy comforts can do me no good at all;
Thee they may hurt.

OLD MAN You cannot see your way.

GLOUCESTER I have no way, and therefore want no eyes;
I stumbled when I saw: full oft 'tis seen
Our means secure us, and our mere defects
Prove our commodities. O dear son Edgar,
The food of thy abused father's wrath!
Might I but live to see thee in my touch,
I'd say I had eyes again!

OLD MAN How now! Who's there?

EDGAR [*Aside*] O gods! Who is't can say 'I am at the worst'?
I am worse than e'er I was.

OLD MAN 'Tis poor mad Tom.

EDGAR [*Aside*] And worse I may be yet. The worst is not
So long as we can say 'This is the worst'.

OLD MAN Fellow, where goest?

GLOUCESTER Is it a beggar-man?

OLD MAN Madman and beggar too.

GLOUCESTER He has some reason, else he could not beg.
I' th' last night's storm I such a fellow saw;
Which made me think a man a worm. My son
Came then into my mind; and yet my mind
Was then scarce friends with him. I have heard more since.
As flies to wanton boys are we to th' gods –
They kill us for their sport.

EDGAR [*Aside*] How should this be?
Bad is the trade that must play fool to sorrow,
Ang'ring itself and others. – Bless thee, master!

GLOUCESTER Is that the naked fellow?

OLD MAN Ay, my lord.

GLOUCESTER Then, prithee, get thee away. If for my sake
Thou wilt o'ertake us hence a mile or twain
I' th' way toward Dover, do it for ancient love;
And bring some covering for this naked soul,
Which I'll entreat to lead me.

OLD MAN Alack, sir, he is mad.

GLOUCESTER 'Tis the times' plague when madmen lead the blind.
Do as I bid thee, or rather do thy pleasure;
Above the rest, be gone.

OLD MAN I'll bring him the best 'parel that I have,
Come on't what will. [*Exit.*

GLOUCESTER Sirrah, naked fellow!

EDGAR Poor Tom's a-cold. [*Aside*] I cannot daub it further.

GLOUCESTER Come hither, fellow.

EDGAR [*Aside*] And yet I must. – Bless thy sweet eyes, they bleed.

GLOUCESTER Know'st thou the way to Dover?

EDGAR Both stile and gate, horse-way and footpath. Poor Tom hath been scar'd out of his good wits. Bless thee, good man's son, from the foul fiend! Five fiends have been in poor Tom at once: of lust, as Obidicut; Hobbididence, prince of dumbness; Mahu, of stealing; Modo, of murder; Flibertigibbet, of mopping and mowing, who since possesses chambermaids and waiting-women. So, bless thee, master!

GLOUCESTER Here, take this purse, thou whom the heavens' plagues
Have humbled to all strokes. That I am wretched
Makes thee the happier. Heavens, deal so still!
Let the superfluous and lust-dieted man
That slaves your ordinance, that will not see
Because he does not feel, feel your power quickly;
So distribution should undo excess,
And each man have enough. Dost thou know Dover?

EDGAR Ay, master.

GLOUCESTER There is a cliff whose high and bending head
Looks fearfully in the confined deep:
Bring me but to the very brim of it
And I'll repair the misery thou dost bear
With something rich about me. From that place
I shall no leading need.

EDGAR Give me thy arm;
Poor Tom shall lead thee. [*Exeunt.*

SCENE II. *Before the Duke of Albany's palace.*

Enter GONERIL and EDMUND.

GONERIL Welcome, my lord. I marvel our mild husband
Not met us on the way.

Enter OSWALD.

Now, where's your master?

OSWALD Madam, within, but never man so chang'd.
I told him of the army that was landed;
He smil'd at it. I told him you were coming;
His answer was 'The worse'. Of Gloucester's treachery,
And of the loyal service of his son,
When I inform'd him, then he call'd me sot,

And told me I had turn'd the wrong side out.
What most he should dislike seems pleasant to him;
What like, offensive.

GONERIL [*To Edmund*] Then shall you go no further.
It is the cowish terror of his spirit
That dares not undertake; he'll not feel wrongs
Which tie him to an answer. Our wishes on the way
May prove effects. Back, Edmund, to my brother;
Hasten his musters and conduct his pow'rs.
I must change arms at home, and give the distaff
Into my husband's hands. This trusty servant
Shall pass between us. Ere long you are like to hear,
If you dare venture in your own behalf,
A mistress's command. Wear this; spare speech.
[*Giving a favour.*
Decline your head; this kiss, if it durst speak,
Would stretch thy spirits up into the air.
Conceive, and fare thee well.

EDMUND Yours in the ranks of death.

GONERIL My most dear Gloucester.
[*Exit Edmund.*
O, the difference of man and man!
To thee a woman's services are due.
My fool usurps my body.

OSWALD Madam, here comes my lord.
[*Exit.*

Enter ALBANY.

GONERIL I have been worth the whistle.

ALBANY O Goneril!
You are not worth the dust which the rude wind
Blows in your face. I fear your disposition:
That nature which contemns it origin
Cannot be border'd certain in itself;
She that herself will sliver and disbranch
From her material sap perforce must wither
And come to deadly use.

GONERIL No more; the text is foolish.

ALBANY Wisdom and goodness to the vile seem vile;
Filths savour but themselves. What have you done?
Tigers, not daughters, what have you perform'd?
A father, and a gracious aged man,
Whose reverence even the head-lugg'd bear would lick,
Most barbarous, most degenerate, have you madded.
Could my good brother suffer you to do it?
A man, a Prince, by him so benefited!
If that the heavens do not their visible spirits
Send quickly down to tame these vile offences,
It will come
Humanity must perforce prey on itself,
Like monsters of the deep.

GONERIL Milk-liver'd man!
That bear'st a cheek for blows, a head for wrongs;
Who hast not in thy brows an eye discerning
Thine honour from thy suffering; that not know'st
Fools do those villains pity who are punish'd
Ere they have done their mischief. Where's thy drum?
France spreads his banners in our noiseless land,
With plumed helm thy state begins to threat,
Whil'st thou, a moral fool, sits still, and cries
'Alack, why does he so?'

ALBANY See thyself, devil!
Proper deformity shows not in the fiend
So horrid as in woman.

GONERIL O vain fool!

ALBANY Thou changed and self-cover'd thing, for shame!
Be-monster not thy feature. Were't my fitness
To let these hands obey my blood,
They are apt enough to dislocate and tear
Thy flesh and bones. Howe'er thou art a fiend,
A woman's shape doth shield thee.

GONERIL Marry, your manhood – mew!

Enter a Messenger.

ALBANY What news?

MESSENGER O, my good lord, the Duke of Cornwall's dead,
Slain by his servant, going to put out
The other eye of Gloucester.

ALBANY Gloucester's eyes!

MESSENGER A servant that he bred, thrill'd with remorse,
Oppos'd against the act, bending his sword
To his great master; who, thereat enrag'd,
Flew on him, and amongst them fell'd him dead;
But not without that harmful stroke which since
Hath pluck'd him after.

ALBANY This shows you are above,
You justicers, that these our nether crimes
So speedily can venge! But, O poor Gloucester!
Lost he his other eye?

MESSENGER Both, both, my lord.
This letter, madam, craves a speedy answer;
'Tis from your sister.

GONERIL [*Aside*] One way I like this well;
But being widow, and my Gloucester with her,
May all the building in my fancy pluck

Upon my hateful life. Another way
The news is not so tart. – I'll read, and answer. [*Exit.*

ALBANY Where was his son, when they did take his eyes?
MESSENGER Come with my lady hither.
ALBANY He is not here.
MESSENGER No, my good lord; I met him back again.
ALBANY Knows he the wickedness?
MESSENGER Ay, my good lord; 'twas he inform'd against him
And quit the house on purpose that their punishment
Might have the freer course.
ALBANY Gloucester, I live
To thank thee for the love thou show'dst the King,
And to revenge thine eyes. Come hither, friend:
Tell me what more thou know'st. [*Exeunt.*

SCENE III. *The French camp near Dover.*

Enter KENT and a Gentleman.

KENT Why the King of France is so suddenly gone back know you no reason?

GENTLEMAN Something he left imperfect in the state, which since his coming forth is thought of, which imports to the kingdom so much fear and danger that his personal return was most required and necessary.

KENT Who hath he left behind him general?

GENTLEMAN The Marshal of France, Monsieur La Far.

KENT Did your letters pierce the Queen to any demonstration of grief?

GENTLEMAN Ay, sir; she took them, read them in my presence,
And now and then an ample tear trill'd down
Her delicate cheek. It seem'd she was a queen
Over her passion, who, most rebel-like,
Sought to be king o'er her.
KENT O, then it mov'd her.
GENTLEMAN Not to a rage; patience and sorrow strove
Who should express her goodliest. You have seen
Sunshine and rain at once: her smiles and tears
Were like a better way. Those happy smilets
That play'd on her ripe lip seem'd not to know
What guests were in her eyes, which parted thence
As pearls from diamonds dropp'd. In brief,
Sorrow would be a rarity most beloved
If all could so become it.
KENT Made she no verbal question?
GENTLEMAN Faith, once or twice she heav'd the name of father
Pantingly forth, as if it press'd her heart;
Cried 'Sisters! sisters! Shame of ladies! Sisters!
Kent! father! sisters! What i' th' storm? i' th' night?
Let pity not be believ'd!' There she shook
The holy water from her heavenly eyes,
And clamour moisten'd; then away she started
To deal with grief alone.
KENT It is the stars,
The stars above us, govern our conditions,
Else one self mate and make could not beget
Such different issues. You spoke not with her since?
GENTLEMAN No.
KENT Was this before the King return'd?
GENTLEMAN No, since.
KENT Well, sir, the poor distressed Lear's i' th' town;
Who sometime in his better tune remembers
What we are come about, and by no means
Will yield to see his daughter.
GENTLEMAN Why, good sir?
KENT A sovereign shame so elbows him; his own unkindness,
That stripp'd her from his benediction, turn'd her
To foreign casualties, gave her dear rights
To his dog-hearted daughters – these things sting
His mind so venomously that burning shame
Detains him from Cordelia.
GENTLEMAN Alack, poor gentleman!
KENT Of Albany's and Cornwall's powers you heard not?
GENTLEMAN 'Tis so; they are afoot.
KENT Well, sir, I'll bring you to our master Lear,
And leave you to attend him. Some dear cause
Will in concealment wrap me up awhile;
When I am known aright, you shall not grieve
Lending me this acquaintance. I pray you go
Along with me. [*Exeunt.*

SCENE IV. *The French camp. A tent.*

Enter with drum and colours, CORDELIA, Doctor, and Soldiers.

CORDELIA Alack, 'tis he! Why, he was met even now
As mad as the vex'd sea, singing aloud,
Crown'd with rank fumiter and furrow weeds,
With hardocks, hemlock, nettles, cuckoo-flow'rs,
Darnel, and all the idle weeds that grow
In our sustaining corn. A century send forth;
Search every acre in the high-grown field,
And bring him to our eye. [*Exit an Officer.*

What can man's wisdom,
In the restoring his bereaved sense?
He that helps him, take all my outward worth.

DOCTOR There is means, madam.
Our foster-nurse of nature is repose,
The which he lacks; that to provoke in him
Are many simples operative, whose power
Will close the eye of anguish.

CORDELIA All blest secrets,
All you unpublish'd virtues of the earth,
Spring with my tears; be aidant and remediate,
In the good man's distress. Seek, seek for him;
Lest his ungovern'd rage dissolve the life
That wants the means to lead it.

Enter a Messenger.

MESSENGER News, madam:
The British pow'rs are marching hitherward.

CORDELIA 'Tis known before; our preparation stands
In expectation of them. O dear father!
It is thy business that I go about;
Therefore great France
My mourning and importun'd tears hath pitied.
No blown ambition doth our arms incite,
But love, dear love, and our ag'd father's right.
Soon may I hear and see him! [*Exeunt.*

SCENE V. *Gloucester's castle.*

Enter REGAN and OSWALD.

REGAN But are my brother's pow'rs set forth?

OSWALD Ay madam.

REGAN Himself in person there?

OSWALD Madam, with much ado.
Your sister is the better soldier.

REGAN Lord Edmund spake not with your lord at home?

OSWALD No, madam.

REGAN What might import my sister's letter to him?

OSWALD I know not, lady.

REGAN Faith, he is posted hence on serious matter.
It was great ignorance, Gloucester's eyes being out,
To let him live; where he arrives he moves
All hearts against us. Edmund, I think, is gone
In pity of his misery, to dispatch
His nighted life; moreover, to descry
The strength o' th' enemy.

OSWALD I must needs after him, madam, with my letter.

REGAN Our troops set forth to-morrow: stay with us;
The ways are dangerous.

OSWALD I may not, madam:
My lady charg'd my duty in this business.

REGAN Why should she write to Edmund? Might not you
Transport her purposes by word? Belike
Some things – I know not what. I'll love thee much –
Let me unseal the letter.

OSWALD Madam, I had rather –

REGAN I know your lady does not love her husband;
I am sure of that; and at her late being here
She gave strange oeillades and most speaking looks
To noble Edmund. I know you are of her bosom.

OSWALD I, madam?

REGAN I speak in understanding; y'are, I know't.
Therefore I do advise you take this note.
My lord is dead; Edmund and I have talk'd;
And more convenient is he for my hand
Than for your lady's. You may gather more.
If you do find him, pray you give him this;
And when your mistress hears thus much from you,
I pray desire her call her wisdom to her.
So fare you well.
If you do chance to hear of that blind traitor,
Preferment falls on him that cuts him off.

OSWALD Would I could meet him, madam! I should show
What party I do follow.

REGAN Fare thee well. [*Exeunt.*

SCENE VI. *The country near Dover.*

Enter GLOUCESTER, and EDGAR dressed like a peasant.

GLOUCESTER When shall I come to th' top of that same hill?

EDGAR You do climb up it now; look how we labour.

GLOUCESTER Methinks the ground is even.

EDGAR Horrible steep.
Hark, do you hear the sea?

GLOUCESTER No, truly.

EDGAR Why then, your other senses grow imperfect
By your eyes' anguish.

GLOUCESTER So may it be indeed.
Methinks thy voice is alter'd, and thou speak'st
In better phrase and matter than thou didst.

EDGAR Y'are much deceiv'd: in nothing am I chang'd
But in my garments.

GLOUCESTER Methinks y'are better spoken.

EDGAR Come on, sir; here's the place. Stand still. How fearful

And dizzy 'tis to cast one's eyes so low!
The crows and choughs that wing the mid-way air
Show scarce so gross as beetles. Half-way down
Hangs one that gathers samphire – dreadful trade!
Methinks he seems no bigger than his head.
The fishermen that walk upon the beach
Appear like mice; and yond tall anchoring bark
Diminish'd to her cock; her cock, a buoy
Almost too small for sight. The murmuring surge
That on th' unnumb'red idle pebble chafes
Cannot be heard so high. I'll look no more;
Lest my brain turn, and the deficient sight
Topple down headlong.

GLOUCESTER Set me where you stand.

EDGAR Give me your hand. You are now within a foot
Of th' extreme verge. For all beneath the moon
Would I not leap upright.

GLOUCESTER Let go my hand.
Here, friend, 's another purse; in it a jewel
Well worth a poor man's taking. Fairies and gods
Prosper it with thee! Go thou further off;
Bid me farewell, and let me hear thee going.

EDGAR Now fare ye well, good sir.

GLOUCESTER With all my heart.

EDGAR Why I do trifle thus with his despair
Is done to cure it.

GLOUCESTER [*Kneeling*] O you mighty gods!
This world I do renounce, and in your sights
Shake patiently my great affliction off.
If I could bear it longer, and not fall
To quarrel with your great opposeless wills,
My snuff and loathed part of nature should
Burn itself out. If Edgar live, O, bless him!
[*Rising*] Now, fellow, fare thee well.

EDGAR Gone, sir; farewell,

[*Gloucester casts himself down.*

And yet I know not how conceit may rob
The treasury of life, when life itself
Yields to the theft. Had he been where he thought,
By this had thought been past. – Alive or dead?
Ho, you sir! friend! Hear you, sir! Speak! –
Thus might he pass indeed. Yet he revives –
What are you, sir?

GLOUCESTER Away, and let me die.

EDGAR Hadst thou been aught but gossamer, feathers, air,
So many fathom down precipitating,
Thou'dst shiver'd like an egg; but thou dost breathe,
Hast heavy substance, bleed'st not, speak'st, art sound.
Ten masts at each make not the altitude
Which thou hast perpendicularly fell.
Thy life's a miracle. Speak yet again.

GLOUCESTER But have I fall'n, or no?

EDGAR From the dread summit of this chalky bourn.
Look up a-height; the shrill-gorg'd lark so far
Cannot be seen or heard. Do but look up.

GLOUCESTER Alack, I have no eyes.
Is wretchedness depriv'd that benefit,
To end itself by death? 'Twas yet some comfort,
When misery could beguile the tyrant's rage
And frustrate his proud will.

EDGAR Give me your arm.
Up – so. How is't? Feel you your legs? You stand.

GLOUCESTER Too well, too well.

EDGAR This is above all strangeness.
Upon the crown o' th' cliff what thing was that
Which parted from you?

GLOUCESTER A poor unfortunate beggar.

EDGAR As I stood here below, methought his eyes
Were two full moons; he had a thousand noses,
Horns whelk'd and waved like the enridged sea.
It was some fiend; therefore, thou happy father,
Think that the clearest gods, who make them honours
Of men's impossibilities, have preserved thee.

GLOUCESTER I do remember now. Henceforth I'll bear
Affliction till it do cry out itself
'Enough, enough' and die. That thing you speak of
I took it for a man; often 'twould say,
'The fiend, the fiend'. He led me to that place.

EDGAR Bear free and patient thoughts.

Enter LEAR, fantastically dressed with weeds.

But who comes here?
The safer sense will ne'er accommodate
His master thus.

LEAR No, they cannot touch me for coining; I am the King himself.

EDGAR O thou side-piercing sight!

LEAR Nature's above art in that respect. There's your press-money. That fellow handles his bow like a crow-keeper; draw me a clothier's yard. Look, look, a mouse! Peace, peace; this piece of toasted cheese will do't. There's my gauntlet; I'll prove it on a giant. Bring up the brown bills. O, well flown, bird! i' the clout, i' the clout – hewgh! Give the word.

EDGAR Sweet marjoram.

LEAR Pass.

GLOUCESTER I know that voice.

LEAR Ha! Goneril, with a white beard! They flatter'd me like a dog, and told me I had white hairs in my beard ere the black ones were there. To say 'ay' and 'no' to everything that I said! 'Ay' and 'no' too was no good divinity. When the rain came to wet me once, and the wind to make me chatter; when the thunder would not peace at my bidding; there I found 'em, there I smelt 'em out. Go to, they are not men o' their words. They told me I was everything; 'tis a lie – I am not ague-proof.

GLOUCESTER The trick of that voice I do well remember.
Is't not the King?

LEAR Ay, every inch a king.
When I do stare, see how the subject quakes.
I pardon that man's life. What was thy cause?
Adultery?
Thou shalt not die. Die for adultery? No.
The wren goes to't, and the small gilded fly
Does lecher in my sight.
Let copulation thrive; for Gloucester's bastard son
Was kinder to his father than my daughters
Got 'tween the lawful sheets.
To't, luxury, pell-mell, for I lack soldiers.
Behold yond simp'ring dame
Whose face between her forks presages snow,
That minces virtue and does shake the head
To hear of pleasure's name –
The fitchew nor the soiled horse goes to't
With a more riotous appetite.
Down from the waist they are centaurs,
Though women all above;
But to the girdle do the gods inherit,
Beneath is all the fiends';
There's hell, there's darkness, there is the sulphurous pit –
Burning, scalding, stench, consumption.
Fie, fie, fie! pah, pah! Give me an ounce of civet, good apothecary, to sweeten my imagination.
There's money for thee.

GLOUCESTER O, let me kiss that hand!

LEAR Let me wipe it first; it smells of mortality.

GLOUCESTER O ruin'd piece of nature! This great world
Shall so wear out to nought. Dost thou know me?

LEAR I remember thine eyes well enough. Dost thou squiny at me? No, do thy worst, blind Cupid; I'll not love. Read thou this challenge; mark but the penning of it.

GLOUCESTER Were all thy letters suns, I could not see one.

EDGAR [*Aside*] I would not take this from report. It is,
And my heart breaks at it.

LEAR Read.

GLOUCESTER What, with the case of eyes?

LEAR O, ho, are you there with me? No eyes in your head nor no money in your purse? Your eyes are in a heavy case, your purse in a light; yet you see how this world goes.

GLOUCESTER I see it feelingly.

LEAR What, art mad? A man may see how this world goes with no eyes. Look with thine ears. See how yond justice rails upon yond simple thief. Hark, in thine ear: change places and, handy-dandy, which is the justice, which is the thief? Thou hast seen a farmer's dog bark at a beggar?

GLOUCESTER Ay, sir.

LEAR And the creature run from the cur?
There thou mightst behold the great image of authority: a dog's obey'd in office.
Thou rascal beadle, hold thy bloody hand.
Why dost thou lash that whore? Strip thy own back;
Thou hotly lusts to use her in that kind
For which thou whip'st her. The usurer hangs the cozener.
Through tatter'd clothes small vices do appear;
Robes and furr'd gowns hide all. Plate sin with gold,
And the strong lance of justice hurtless breaks;
Arm it in rags, a pigmy's straw does pierce it.
None does offend, none – I say none; I'll able 'em.
Take that of me, my friend, who have the power
To seal th' accuser's lips. Get thee glass eyes,
And, like a scurvy politician, seem
To see the things thou dost not. Now, now, now, now!
Pull off my boots. Harder, harder – so.

EDGAR O, matter and impertinency mix'd!
Reason in madness!

LEAR If thou wilt weep my fortunes, take my eyes.
I know thee well enough; thy name is Gloucester.
Thou must be patient; we came crying hither.
Thou know'st the first time that we smell the air
We wawl and cry. I will preach to thee. Mark.

GLOUCESTER Alack, alack the day!

LEAR When we are born, we cry that we are come
To this great stage of fools. This a good block!
It were a delicate stratagem to shoe
A troop of horse with felt; I'll put't in proof;
And when I have stol'n upon these son-in-laws,
Then kill, kill, kill, kill, kill, kill!

Enter a Gentleman, with Attendants.

GENTLEMAN O, here he is: lay hand upon him. – Sir,

Your most dear daughter –
LEAR No rescue? What, a prisoner? I am even
The natural fool of fortune. Use me well;
You shall have ransom. Let me have surgeons;
I am cut to th' brains.
GENTLEMAN You shall have any thing.
LEAR No seconds? All myself?
Why, this would make a man a man of salt,
To use his eyes for garden water-pots,
Ay, and laying Autumn's dust.
GENTLEMAN Good sir –
LEAR I will die bravely, like a smug bridegroom.
What!
I will be jovial. Come, come; I am a king,
My masters, know you that.
GENTLEMAN You are a royal one, and we obey
you.
LEAR Then there's life in't. Nay, an you get it, you
shall get it by running. Sa, sa, sa, sa.
[*Exit running; Attendants follow.*
GENTLEMAN A sight most pitiful in the meanest
wretch,
Past speaking of in a king! Thou hast one
daughter
Who redeems nature from the general curse
Which twain have brought her to.
EDGAR Hail, gentle sir.
GENTLEMAN Sir, speed you; what's your will?
EDGAR Do you hear aught, sir, of a battle toward?
GENTLEMAN Most sure and vulgar; every one
hears that
Which can distinguish sound.
EDGAR But, by your favour,
How near's the other army?
GENTLEMAN Near and on speedy foot; the main
descry
Stands on the hourly thought.
EDGAR I thank you, sir; that's all.
GENTLEMAN Though that the Queen on special
cause is here,
Her army is mov'd on.
EDGAR I thank you, sir. [*Exit Gentleman.*
GLOUCESTER You ever-gentle gods, take my
breath from me;
Let not my worser spirit tempt me again
To die before you please.
EDGAR Well pray you, father.
GLOUCESTER Now, good sir, what are you?
EDGAR A most poor man, made tame to fortune's
blows,
Who, by the art of known and feeling sorrows,
Am pregnant to good pity. Give me your hand;
I'll lead you to some biding.
GLOUCESTER Hearty thanks;
The bounty and the benison of heaven
To boot, and boot!

Enter OSWALD.

OSWALD A proclaim'd prize! Most happy!
That eyeless head of thine was first fram'd flesh
To raise my fortunes. Thou old unhappy traitor,
Briefly thyself remember. The sword is out
That must destroy thee.
GLOUCESTER Now let thy friendly hand
Put strength enough to't. [*Edgar interposes.*
OSWALD Wherefore, bold peasant,
Dar'st thou support a publish'd traitor? Hence;
Lest that th' infection of his fortune take
Like hold on thee. Let go his arm.
EDGAR Chill not let go, zir, without vurther
'casion.
OSWALD Let go, slave, or thou diest.
EDGAR Good gentleman, go your gait, and let
poor volk pass. An chud ha' bin zwagger'd out
of my life, 'twould not ha' bin zo long as 'tis by a
vortnight. Nay, come not near th' old man; keep
out, che vor ye, or Ice try whether your costard
or my ballow be the harder. Chill be plain with
you.
OSWALD Out, dunghill!
EDGAR Chill pick your teeth, zir. Come; no
matter vor your foins. [*They fight.*
OSWALD Slave, thou hast slain me. Villain, take
my purse;
If ever thou wilt thrive, bury my body,
And give the letters which thou find'st about me
To Edmund Earl of Gloucester. Seek him out
Upon the English party. O, untimely death!
Death! [*He dies.*
EDGAR I know thee well; a serviceable villain,
As duteous to the vices of thy mistress
As badness would desire.
GLOUCESTER What, is he dead?
EDGAR Sit you down, father; rest you.
Let's see these pockets; the letters that he speaks
of
May be my friends. He's dead; I am only sorry
He had no other death's-man. Let us see.
Leave, gentle wax; and, manners, blame us not:
To know our enemies' minds we'd rip their
hearts;
Their papers is more lawful.
[*Reads*] 'Let our reciprocal vows be rememb'red.
You have many opportunities to cut him off; if
your will want not, time and place will be
fruitfully offer'd. There is nothing done if he
return the conqueror: then am I the prisoner,
and his bed my gaol; from the loathed warmth
whereof deliver me, and supply the place for
your labour.
Your (wife, so I would say) affectionate servant,
GONERIL.'

O indistinguish'd space of woman's will!
A plot upon her virtuous husband's life;
And the exchange my brother! Here, in the sands
Thee I'll rake up, the post unsanctified
Of murderous lechers; and in the mature time
With this ungracious paper strike the sight
Of the death-practis'd duke. For him 'tis well
That of thy death and business I can tell.

GLOUCESTER The King is mad; how stiff is my vile sense,
That I stand up, and have ingenious feeling
Of my huge sorrows! Better I were distract;
So should my thoughts be sever'd from my griefs,
And woes by wrong imaginations lose
The knowledge of themselves. [*Drum afar off.*

EDGAR Give me your hand.
Far off methinks I hear the beaten drum.
Come, father, I'll bestow you with a friend.
[*Exeunt.*

SCENE VII. *A tent in the French camp.*

Music. Enter CORDELIA, KENT, Doctor, and Gentleman.

CORDELIA O thou good Kent, how shall I live and work
To match thy goodness? My life will be too short,
And every measure fail me.

KENT To be acknowledg'd, madam, is o'erpaid.
All my reports go with the modest truth;
Nor more nor clipp'd, but so.

CORDELIA Be better suited.
These weeds are memories of those worser hours;
I prithee put them off.

KENT Pardon, dear madam;
Yet to be known shortens my made intent:
My boon I make it that you know me not
Till time and I think meet.

CORDELIA Then be't so, my good lord. [*To the Doctor*] How does the King?

DOCTOR Madam, sleeps still.

CORDELIA O you kind gods,
Cure this great breach in his abused nature!
Th' untun'd and jarring senses, O, wind up
Of this child-changed father!

DOCTOR So please your Majesty
That we may wake the King; he hath slept long.

CORDELIA Be govern'd by your knowledge, and proceed
I' th' sway of your own will. [*To the Gentleman*] Is he array'd?

GENTLEMAN Ay, madam; in the heaviness of sleep
We put fresh garments on him.

DOCTOR Be by, good madam, when we do awake him;
I doubt not of his temperance.

CORDELIA Very well.

DOCTOR Please you, draw near. Louder the music there!

He draws the curtains and discovers Lear asleep in bed.

CORDELIA O my dear father! Restoration hang
Thy medicine on my lips, and let this kiss
Repair those violent harms that my two sisters
Have in thy reverence made.

KENT Kind and dear princess!

CORDELIA Had you not been their father, these white flakes
Did challenge pity of them. Was this a face
To be oppos'd against the warring winds?
To stand against the deep dread bolted thunder?
In the most terrible and nimble stroke
Of quick cross lightning? to watch – poor perdu! –
With this thin helm? Mine enemy's dog,
Though he had bit me, should have stood that night
Against my fire; and wast thou fain, poor father,
To hovel thee with swine and rogues forlorn,
In short and musty straw? Alack, alack!
'Tis wonder that thy life and wits at once
Had not concluded all. – He wakes; speak to him.

DOCTOR Madam, do you; 'tis fittest.

CORDELIA How does my royal lord? How fares your Majesty?

LEAR You do me wrong to take me out o' th' grave.
Thou art a soul in bliss; but I am bound
Upon a wheel of fire, that mine own tears
Do scald like molten lead.

CORDELIA Sir, do you know me?

LEAR You are a spirit, I know. Where did you die?

CORDELIA Still, still far wide!

DOCTOR He's scarce awake; let him alone awhile.

LEAR Where have I been? Where am I? Fair daylight?
I am mightily abus'd. I should e'en die with pity
To see another thus. I know not what to say.
I will not swear these are my hands. Let's see.
I feel this pin prick. Would I were assur'd
Of my condition!

CORDELIA O, look upon me, sir,
And hold your hands in benediction o'er me.
No, sir, you must not kneel.

LEAR Pray, do not mock me:
I am a very foolish fond old man,

Fourscore and upward, not an hour more nor less;
And, to deal plainly,
I fear I am not in my perfect mind.
Methinks I should know you, and know this man;
Yet I am doubtful; for I am mainly ignorant
What place this is; and all the skill I have
Remembers not these garments; nor I know not
Where I did lodge last night. Do not laugh at me;
For, as I am a man, I think this lady
To be my child Cordelia.

CORDELIA And so I am, I am.

LEAR Be your tears wet? Yes, faith. I pray weep not;
If you have poison for me I will drink it.
I know you do not love me; for your sisters
Have, as I do remember, done me wrong:
You have some cause, they have not.

CORDELIA No cause, no cause.

LEAR Am in France?

KENT In your own kingdom, sir.

LEAR Do not abuse me.

DOCTOR Be comforted, good madam. The great rage,
You see, is kill'd in him; and yet it is danger
To make him even o'er the time he has lost.
Desire him to go in; trouble him no more
Till further settling.

CORDELIA Will't please your Highness walk?

LEAR You must bear with me.
Pray you now, forget and forgive; I am old and foolish. *[Exeunt all but Kent and Gentleman.*

GENTLEMAN Holds it true, sir, that the Duke of Cornwall was so slain?

KENT Most certain, sir.

GENTLEMAN Who is conductor of his people?

KENT As 'tis said, the bastard son of Gloucester.

GENTLEMAN They say Edgar, his banish'd son, is with the Earl of Kent in Germany.

KENT Report is changeable. 'Tis time to look about; the powers of the kingdom approach apace.

GENTLEMAN The arbitrement is like to be bloody. Fare you well, sir. *[Exit.*

KENT My point and period will be throughly wrought,
Or well or ill, as this day's battle's fought. *[Exit.*

ACT FIVE

SCENE I. *The British camp near Dover.*

Enter, with drum and colours, EDMUND, REGAN, Gentlemen, and Soldiers.

EDMUND Know of the Duke if his last purpose hold,
Or whether since he is advis'd by aught
To change the course. He's full of alteration
And self-reproving – bring his constant pleasure. *[Exit an Officer.*

REGAN Our sister's man is certainly miscarried.

EDMUND 'Tis to be doubted, madam.

REGAN Now, sweet lord,
You know the goodness I intend upon you.
Tell me – but truly – but then speak the truth –
Do you not love my sister?

EDMUND In honour'd love.

REGAN But have you never found my brother's way
To the forfended place?

EDMUND That thought abuses you.

REGAN I am doubtful that you have been conjunct
And bosom'd with her, as far as we call hers.

EDMUND No, by mine honour, madam.

REGAN I never shall endure her. Dear my lord,
Be not familiar with her.

EDMUND Fear me not.
She and the Duke her husband!

Enter, with drum and colours, ALBANY, GONERIL, and Soldiers.

GONERIL *[Aside]* I had rather lose the battle than that sister
Should loosen him and me.

ALBANY Our very loving sister, well be-met.
Sir, this I heard: the King is come to his daughter
With others whom the rigour of our state
Forc'd to cry out. Where I could not be honest
I never yet was valiant. For this business,
It touches us as France invades our land,
Not bolds the King, with others whom, I fear,
Most just and heavy causes make oppose.

EDMUND Sir, you speak nobly.

REGAN Why is this reason'd?

GONERIL Combine together 'gainst the enemy;
For these domestic-door particulars
Are not the question here.

ALBANY Let's then determine
With th' ancient of war on our proceeding.

EDMUND I shall attend you presently at your tent.
REGAN Sister, you'll go with us?
GONERIL No.
REGAN 'Tis most convenient; pray you go with us.
GONERIL [*Aside*] O, ho, I know the riddle. – I will go.

As they are going out, enter EDGAR, disguised.

EDGAR If e'er your Grace had speech with man so poor
Hear me one word.
ALBANY I'll overtake you. – Speak.
[*Exeunt all but Albany and Edgar.*

EDGAR Before you fight the battle, ope this letter.
If you have victory, let the trumpet sound
For him that brought it; wretched though I seem
I can produce a champion that will prove
What is avouched there. If you miscarry,
Your business of the world hath so an end,
And machination ceases. Fortune love you!
ALBANY Stay till I have read the letter.
EDGAR I was forbid it.
When time shall serve, let but the herald cry,
And I'll appear again.
ALBANY Why, fare thee well. I will o'erlook thy paper. [*Exit Edgar.*

Re-enter EDMUND.

EDMUND The enemy's in view; draw up your powers.
Here is the guess of their true strength and forces
By diligent discovery; but your haste
Is now urg'd on you.
ALBANY We will greet the time.
[*Exit.*

EDMUND To both these sisters have I sworn my love;
Each jealous of the other, as the stung
Are of the adder. Which of them shall I take?
Both? one? or neither? Neither can be enjoy'd,
If both remain alive: to take the widow,
Exasperates, makes mad her sister Goneril;
And hardly shall I carry out my side,
Her husband being alive. Now then, we'll use
His countenance for the battle; which being done,
Let her who would be rid of him devise
His speedy taking off. As for the mercy
Which he intends to Lear and to Cordelia –
The battle done, and they within our power,
Shall never see his pardon; for my state
Stands on me to defend, not to debate. [*Exit.*

SCENE II. *A field between the two camps.*

Alarum within. Enter, with drum and colours, the Powers of France over the stage, CORDELIA with her Father in her hand, and exeunt.

Enter EDGAR and GLOUCESTER.

EDGAR Here, father, take the shadow of this tree
For your good host; pray that the right may thrive.
If ever I return to you again
I'll bring you comfort.
GLOUCESTER Grace go with you, sir!
[*Exit Edgar.*

Alarum and retreat within. Re-enter EDGAR.

EDGAR Away, old man; give me thy hand; away!
King Lear hath lost, he and his daughter ta'en.
Give me thy hand; come on.
GLOUCESTER No further, sir; a man may rot even here.
EDGAR What, in ill thoughts again? Men must endure
Their going hence, even as their coming hither:
Ripeness is all. Come on.
GLOUCESTER And that's true too.
[*Exeunt.*

SCENE III. *The British camp near Dover.*

Enter, in conquest, with drum and colours, EDMUND; LEAR and CORDELIA prisoners; Soldiers, Captain.

EDMUND Some officers take them away. Good guard,
Until their greater pleasures first be known
That are to censure them.
CORDELIA We are not the first
Who with best meaning have incurr'd the worst.
For thee, oppressed King, am I cast down;
Myself could else out-frown false Fortune's frown.
Shall we not see these daughters and these sisters?
LEAR No, no, no, no! Come, let's away to prison.
We two alone will sing like birds i' th' cage;
When thou dost ask me blessing, I'll kneel down
And ask of thee forgiveness; so we'll live,
And pray, and sing, and tell old tales, and laugh
At gilded butterflies, and hear poor rogues
Talk of court news; and we'll talk with them too –
Who loses and who wins; who's in, who's out –
And take upon's the mystery of things
As if we were God's spies; and we'll wear out
In a wall'd prison packs and sects of great ones
That ebb and flow by th' moon.

EDMUND Take them away.
LEAR Upon such sacrifices, my Cordelia,
The gods themselves throw incense. Have I caught thee?
He that parts us shall bring a brand from heaven
And fire us hence like foxes. Wipe thine eyes;
The good years shall devour them, flesh and fell,
Ere they shall make us weep. We'll see 'em starv'd first.
Come. [*Exeunt Lear and Cordelia, guarded.*
EDMUND Come hither, Captain; hark.
[*Giving a paper*] Take thou this note; go follow them to prison.
One step I have advanc'd thee; if thou dost
As this instructs thee, thou dost make thy way
To noble fortunes. Know thou this, that men
Are as the time is; to be tender-minded
Does not become a sword. Thy great employment
Will not bear question; either say thou'lt do't,
Or thrive by other means.
CAPTAIN I'll do't, my lord.
EDMUND About it; and write happy when th' hast done.
Mark – I say, instantly; and carry it so
As I have set it down.
CAPTAIN I cannot draw a cart nor eat dried oats;
If it be man's work, I'll do't. [*Exit.*

Flourish. Enter ALBANY, GONERIL, REGAN, and Soldiers.

ALBANY Sir, you have show'd to-day your valiant strain,
And fortune led you well. You have the captives
Who were the opposites of this day's strife;
I do require them of you, so to use them
As we shall find their merits and our safety
May equally determine.
EDMUND Sir, I thought it fit
To send the old and miserable king
To some retention and appointed guard;
Whose age has charms in it, whose title more,
To pluck the common bosom on his side,
And turn our impress'd lances in our eyes
Which do command them. With him I sent the Queen,
My reason all the same; and they are ready
To-morrow, or at further space, t' appear
Where you shall hold your session. At this time
We sweat and bleed; the friend hath lost his friend;
And the best quarrels, in the heat, are curs'd
By those that feel their sharpness.
The question of Cordelia and her father
Requires a fitter place.
ALBANY Sir, by your patience,
I hold you but a subject of this war,
Not as a brother.
REGAN That's as we list to grace him.
Methinks our pleasure might have been demanded
Ere you had spoke so far. He led our powers,
Bore the commission of my place and person,
The which immediacy may well stand up
And call itself your brother.
GONERIL Not so hot.
In his own grace he doth exalt himself,
More than in your addition.
REGAN In my rights,
By me invested, he compeers the best.
ALBANY That were the most, if he should husband you.
REGAN Jesters do oft prove prophets.
GONERIL Holla, holla!
That eye that told you so look'd but asquint.
REGAN Lady, I am not well; else I should answer
From a full-flowing stomach. General,
Take thou my soldiers, prisoners, patrimony;
Dispose of them, of me; the walls is thine.
Witness the world that I create thee here
My lord and master.
GONERIL Mean you to enjoy him?
ALBANY The let-alone lies not in your good will.
EDMUND Nor in thine, lord.
ALBANY Half-blooded fellow, yes.
REGAN [*To Edmund*] Let the drum strike, and prove my title thine.
ALBANY Stay yet; hear reason. Edmund, I arrest thee
On capital treason; and, in thy attaint,
[*Pointing to Goneril.*
This gilded serpent. For your claim, fair sister,
I bar it in the interest of my wife;
'Tis she is sub-contracted to this lord,
And I, her husband, contradict your banns.
If you will marry, make your loves to me –
My lady is bespoke.
GONERIL An interlude!
ALBANY Thou art arm'd, Gloster. Let the trumpet sound.
If none appear to prove upon thy person
Thy heinous, manifest, and many treasons,
There is my pledge; [*Throwing down a glove.*
I'll make it on thy heart,
Ere I taste bread, thou art in nothing less
Than I have here proclaim'd thee.
REGAN Sick, O, sick!
GONERIL [*Aside*] If not, I'll ne'er trust medicine.
EDMUND There's my exchange. [*Throwing down a glove*]. What in the world he is
That names me traitor, villain-like he lies.
Call by thy trumpet; he that dares approach,
On him, on you, who not, I will maintain

My truth and honour firmly.
ALBANY A herald, ho!
EDMUND A herald, ho, a herald!
ALBANY Trust to thy single virtue; for thy soldiers,
All levied in my name, have in my name
Took their discharge.
REGAN My sickness grows upon me.
ALBANY She is not well; convey her to my tent.
[Exit Regan, led.

Enter a Herald.

Come hither, herald. Let the trumpet sound,
And read out this.
HERALD *[Reads]* 'If any man of quality or degree within the lists of the army will maintain upon Edmund, supposed Earl of Gloucester, that he is a manifold traitor, let him appear by the third sound of the trumpet. He is bold in his defence.'
Sound, trumpet. *[1 Trumpet.*
HERALD Again! *[2 Trumpet.*
HERALD Again! *[3 Trumpet.*
[Trumpet answers within.

Enter EDGAR, armed, at the third sound, a trumpet before him.

ALBANY Ask him his purposes, why he appears
Upon this call o' th' trumpet.
HERALD What are you?
Your name, your quality, and why you answer
This present summons?
EDGAR Know, my name is lost,
By treason's tooth bare-gnawn and canker-bit;
Yet am I noble as the adversary
I come to cope.
ALBANY Which is that adversary?
EDGAR What's he that speaks for Edmund Earl of Gloucester?
EDMUND Himself. What say'st thou to him?
EDGAR Draw thy sword,
That, if my speech offend a noble heart,
Thy arm may do thee justice; here is mine.
Behold, it is the privilege of mine honours,
My oath, and my profession. I protest –
Maugre thy strength, youth, place, and eminence,
Despite thy victor sword and fire-new fortune,
Thy valour and thy heart – thou art a traitor;
False to thy gods, thy brother, and thy father;
Conspirant 'gainst this high illustrious prince;
And, from th' extremest upward of thy head
To the descent and dust below thy foot,
A most toad-spotted traitor. Say thou 'No',
This sword, this arm, and my best spirits, are bent
To prove upon thy heart, whereto I speak,
Thou liest.
EDMUND In wisdom I should ask thy name;
But, since thy outside looks so fair and warlike,
And that thy tongue some say of breeding breathes,
What safe and nicely I might well delay
By rule of knighthood, I disdain and spurn.
Back do I toss these treasons to thy head;
With the hell-hated lie o'erwhelm thy heart;
Which – for they yet glance by and scarcely bruise –
This sword of mine shall give them instant way
Where they shall rest for ever. Trumpets, speak.
[Alarums. They fight. Edmund falls.
ALBANY Save him, save him!
GONERIL This is practice, Gloucester.
By th' law of war thou wast not bound to answer
An unknown opposite; thou art not vanquish'd,
But cozen'd and beguil'd.
ALBANY Shut your mouth, dame,
Or with this paper shall I stopple it. Hold, sir.
Thou worse than any name, read thine own evil.
No tearing, lady; I perceive you know it.
GONERIL Say, if I do – the laws are mine, not thine.
Who can arraign me for't?
ALBANY Most monstrous! O!
Know'st thou this paper?
GONERIL Ask me not what I know.
[Exit.
ALBANY Go after her. She's desperate; govern her.
[Exit an Officer.
EDMUND What you have charg'd me with, that have I done,
And more, much more; the time will bring it out.
'Tis past, and so am I. But what art thou
That hast this fortune on me? If thou'rt noble,
I do forgive thee.
EDGAR Let's exchange charity.
I am no less in blood than thou art, Edmund;
If more, the more th' hast wrong'd me.
My name is Edgar, and thy father's son.
The gods are just, and of our pleasant vices
Make instruments to plague us:
The dark and vicious place where thee he got
Cost him his eyes.
EDMUND Th' hast spoken right, 'tis true;
The wheel is come full circle; I am here.
ALBANY Methought thy very gait did prophesy
A royal nobleness. I must embrace thee.
Let sorrow split my heart if ever I
Did hate thee or thy father!
EDGAR Worthy prince,
I know't.
ALBANY Where have you hid yourself?

How have you known the miseries of your father?
EDGAR By nursing them, my lord. List a brief tale;
And when 'tis told, O that my heart would burst!
The bloody proclamation to escape
That follow'd me so near – O our lives' sweetness,
That we the pain of death would hourly die
Rather than die at once! – taught me to shift
Into a madman's rags, t' assume a semblance
That very dogs disdain'd; and in this habit
Met I my father with his bleeding rings,
Their precious stones new lost; became his guide,
Led him, begg'd for him, sav'd him from despair;
Never – O fault! – reveal'd myself unto him
Until some half-hour past, when I was arm'd;
Not sure, though hoping, of this good success,
I ask'd his blessing, and from first to last
Told him my pilgrimage. But his flaw'd heart –
Alack, too weak the conflict to support! –
'Twixt two extremes of passion, joy and grief,
Burst smilingly.
EDMUND This speech of your hath mov'd me,
And shall perchance do good; but speak you on;
You look as you had something more to say.
ALBANY If there be more, more woeful, hold it in;
For I am almost ready to dissolve,
Hearing of this.
EDGAR This would have seem'd a period
To such as love not sorrow; but another,
To amplify too much, would make much more,
And top extremity.
Whilst I was big in clamour, came there in a man
Who, having seen me in my worst estate,
Shunn'd my abhorr'd society; but then, finding
Who 'twas that so endur'd, with his strong arms
He fastened on my neck and bellowed out
As he'd burst heaven; threw him on my father;
Told the most piteous tale of Lear and him
That ever ear receiv'd; which in recounting
His grief grew puissant, and the strings of life
Began to crack. Twice then the trumpets sounded
And there I left him tranc'd.
ALBANY But who was this?
EDGAR Kent, sir, the banish'd Kent, who in disguise
Follow'd his enemy king, and did him service
Improper for a slave.

Enter a Gentleman with a bloody knife.

GENTLEMAN Help, help, O, help!
EDGAR What kind of help?
ALBANY Speak, man.
EDGAR What means this bloody knife?
GENTLEMAN 'Tis hot, it smokes;
It came even from the heart of – O, she's dead!
ALBANY Who dead? Speak, man.
GENTLEMAN Your lady, sir, your lady! and her sister
By her is poison'd; she confesses it.
EDMUND I was contracted to them both. All three
Now marry in an instant.
EDGAR Here comes Kent.

Enter KENT.

ALBANY Produce the bodies, be they alive or dead. *[Exit Gentleman.*
This judgment of the heavens, that makes us tremble,
Touches us not with pity. O, is this he?
The time will not allow the compliment
Which very manners urges.
KENT I am come
To bid my king and master aye good night.
Is he not here?
ALBANY Great thing of us forgot!
Speak, Edmund, where's the King? and where's Cordelia? *[The bodies of Goneril and Regan are brought in.*
See'st thou this object, Kent?
KENT Alack, why thus?
EDMUND Yet Edmund was belov'd.
The one the other poison'd for my sake,
And after slew herself.
ALBANY Even so. Cover their faces.
EDMUND I pant for life. Some good I mean to do,
Despite of mine own nature. Quickly send –
Be brief in it – to th' castle; for my writ
Is on the life of Lear and on Cordelia.
Nay, send in time.
ALBANY Run, run, O, run!
EDGAR To who, my lord? Who has the office? Send
Thy token of reprieve.
EDMUND Well thought on. Take my sword;
Give it the Captain.
ALBANY Haste thee, for thy life. *[Exit Edgar.*
EDMUND He hath commission from thy wife and me
To hang Cordelia in the prison, and
To lay the blame upon her own despair,
That she fordid herself.
ALBANY The gods defend her! Bear him hence awhile. *[Edmund is borne off.*

Enter LEAR, with CORDELIA dead in his arms; EDGAR, Captain, and Others following.

LEAR Howl, howl, howl, howl! O, you are men of

stones!
Had I your tongues and eyes, I'd use them so
That heaven's vault should crack. She's gone for ever.
I know when one is dead and when one lives;
She's dead as earth. Lend me a looking-glass;
If that her breath will mist or stain the stone,
Why, then she lives.

KENT Is this the promis'd end?

EDGAR Or image of that horror?

ALBANY Fall and cease!

LEAR This feather stirs; she lives. If it be so,
It is a chance which does redeem all sorrows
That ever I have felt.

KENT O my good master!

[Kneeling.

LEAR Prithee away.

EDGAR 'Tis noble Kent, your friend.

LEAR A plague upon you, murderers, traitors all!
I might have sav'd her; now she's gone for ever.
Cordelia, Cordelia! stay a little. Ha!
What is't thou say'st? Her voice was ever soft,
Gentle, and low – an excellent thing in woman.
I kill'd the slave that was a-hanging thee.

CAPTAIN 'Tis true, my lords, he did.

LEAR Did I not, fellow?
I have seen the day, with my good biting falchion,
I would have made them skip: I am old now,
And these same crosses spoil me. Who are you?
Mine eyes are not o' th' best. I'll tell you straight.

KENT If fortune brag of two she lov'd and hated,
One of them we behold.

LEAR This is a dull sight. Are you not Kent?

KENT The same –
Your servant Kent. Where is your servant Caius?

LEAR He's a good fellow, I can tell you that;
He'll strike, and quickly too. He's dead and rotten.

KENT No, my good lord; I am the very man –

LEAR I'll see that straight.

KENT That from your first of difference and decay
Have follow'd your sad steps.

LEAR You are welcome hither.

KENT Nor no man else! All's cheerless, dark, and deadly.
Your eldest daughters have fordone themselves
And desperately are dead.

LEAR Ay, so I think.

ALBANY He knows not what he says; and vain is it
That we present us to him.

EDGAR Very bootless.

Enter a Messenger.

MESSENGER Edmund is dead, my lord.

ALBANY That's but a trifle here.
You lords and noble friends, know our intent.
What comfort to this great decay may come
Shall be applied. For us, we will resign
During the life of this old Majesty,
To him our absolute power. *[To Edgar and Kent]* You to your rights;
With boot, and such addition as your honours
Have more than merited. All friends shall taste
The wages of their virtue, and all foes
The cup of their deservings. O, see, see!

LEAR And my poor fool is hang'd! No, no, no life?
Why should a dog, a horse, a rat have life,
And thou no breath at all? Thou'lt come no more,
Never, never, never, never, never.
Pray you undo this button. Thank you, sir.
Do you see this? Look on her. Look, her lips.
Look there, look there! *[He dies.*

EDGAR He faints. My lord, my lord!

KENT Break, heart; I prithee break.

EDGAR Look up, my lord.

KENT Vex not his ghost. O, let him pass! He hates him
That would upon the rack of this tough world
Stretch him out longer.

EDGAR He is gone indeed.

KENT The wonder is he hath endur'd so long:
He but usurp'd his life.

ALBANY Bear them from hence. Our present business
Is general woe. *[To Kent and Edgar]* Friends of my soul, you twain
Rule in this realm and the gor'd state sustain.

KENT I have a journey, sir, shortly to go.
My master calls me; I must not say no.

EDGAR The weight of this sad time we must obey;
Speak what we feel, not what we ought to say.
The oldest hath borne most; we that are young
Shall never see so much nor live so long.

[Exeunt with a dead march.

Othello

Introduction by DAVID NEWELL

Othello is a play about a black man in a white man's world. A public servant with a private life, an older man who marries a mere girl, a soldier who exchanges the battlefield for the bedroom: incongruity is pervasive. So too is incomprehension, for if Othello is an unknown quantity because of his mysterious background, Venetian customs are equally outside his experience. Mutual misunderstanding underlies the chaos of this exquisitely painful domestic tragedy.

Our initial perception of Othello is masterminded, as is so much in this drama, by Iago. His opening conversation with Roderigo and his ribald taunting of Brabantio sketch for us a barbaric, incontinent savage, a typical stage negro. But that image is shattered the very first time the audience encounters the Moor. In his calm dignity, courage, and urbane courtesy he seems to step straight off the pages of Castiglione's *Courtier*. Beside him the native Venetians appear trivial, dwarfed by his presence and silenced by his poetry. Othello's life is rooted deep in his language; that is the outward expression of his inner being, a dramatic symbol of the imaginative richness which he represents. Further, he is efficient as a military commander and well respected by the state.

Othello starts the play, then, as an epic warrior hero of classical grandeur, a man of strange experiences, foreign parts, and a distinctive vocal timbre. But the crafty and malicious manipulation of Iago transforms him into the contemptible butt of traditional domestic comedy – the jealous, cuckolded husband. Yet it is not Iago's skill alone which effects this metamorphosis. The entire play seems to undergo a generic shift. It starts at the point where romantic comedy normally ends, with a happy, if unusual, marriage and the marginalising of an irate father. But then a hasty switch of setting to Cyprus, far from replicating the security of a fantasy world like Belmont or the holiday fun of Arden, steers the play into turmoil. Away from Italian civilisation but curiously closer to the forbidding continent of Othello's birth, the lovers are perversely abandoned by Fortune. Events consistently work against them. Cassio is sighted slipping suspiciously away from Othello's house; the handkerchief happens to be dropped and found just when Iago needs tangible proof; Cassio and Bianca converse out of Othello's earshot so that he can misconstrue their meaning. Characters disconcertingly change. Desdemona loses the poise and self-possession which marked her defence before the Venetian Senate, and dwindles into a child-wife, naive, frustratingly inept, and vulnerable.

Most significant of all, Othello himself compromises the heroism of epic warfare with the visual physical frenzy of tawdry comedy: eavesdropping, falling to the ground, beating his wife. Worse, he seems at these moments to be the helpless puppet of Iago. As his actions are cheapened, so too is his speech. Iago was the first to deconstruct Othello's language ('a bombast circumstance/Horribly stuff'd with epithets of war'), and he has not been the last. But then Iago cannot stomach poetry. And what he cannot enjoy he must destroy. But not even Iago can erase the audience's memory, for words once spoken linger, enshrined in a text. At his worst moments we are never allowed to forget what Othello *was*:

> Is this the noble Moor whom our full Senate
> Call all in all sufficient? Is this the nature
> Whom passion could not shake, whose solid virtue
> The shot of accident nor dart of chance
> Could neither graze nor pierce? [4.1.261–5]

Iago's plan to humiliate Othello is ultimately and ironically hijacked by the play itself, which takes on a momentum of its own, bringing Othello through the degradation of comic gull to the new status of tragic hero. The revival of Othello's speech in his last visit to Desdemona's bedchamber, the dawning recognition of his error, and the re-enactment of a past deed of justice in his suicide all combine to make him much more than Iago's dupe. At the very end it is Iago who remains sullenly silent, finally upstaged by Othello, who is allowed the privilege of speaking his own epitaph and passing judgment on his own crime.

The deaths of Brabantio's runaway daughter and the mercenary black soldier create no cosmic ripples. There are no emblematic storms, no upheavals in the body politic. The world outside goes on much as usual. This, far from diminishing, only intensifies the tragedy of two innocents in an unsympathetic, deceiving world. And when misunderstandings are finally over as white girl and black man are reunited in the stage tableau of death, we may find that the only adequate response was uttered long ago:

> O, Iago, the pity of it, Iago! [4.1.191]

Othello, The Moor of Venice

DRAMATIS PERSONAE

DUKE OF VENICE
BRABANTIO
a Senator, father to Desdemona
Other Senators
GRATIANO
brother to Brabantio, two noble Venetians
LODOVICO
kinsman to Brabantio
OTHELLO
the Moor, in the service of Venice
CASSIO
his honourable Lieutenant
IAGO
his Ancient, a villain
RODERIGO
a gull'd Venetian gentleman
MONTANO
Governor of Cyprus, before Othello
Clown servant to Othello
DESDEMONA
daughter to Brabantio, and wife to Othello
EMILIA
wife to Iago
BIANCA
a courtezan, in love with Cassio
Gentlemen of Cyprus, Sailors, Officers, a Messenger, Musicians, a Herald, and Attendants etc.

THE SCENE: VENICE; CYPRUS.

ACT ONE

SCENE I. *Venice. A street.*

Enter RODERIGO and IAGO.

RODERIGO Tush, never tell me; I take it much unkindly
That you, Iago, who has had my purse
As if the strings were thine, shouldst know of this.
IAGO 'Sblood, but you will not hear me.
If ever I did dream of such a matter,
Abhor me.
RODERIGO Thou told'st me thou didst hold him in thy hate.
IAGO Despise me if I do not. Three great ones of the city,
In personal suit to make me his lieutenant,
Off-capp'd to him; and, by the faith of man,
I know my price, I am worth no worse a place.
But he, as loving his own pride and purposes,
Evades them with a bombast circumstance
Horribly stuff'd with epithets of war;
And, in conclusion,
Nonsuits my mediators; 'For, certes,' says he
'I have already chose my officer'.
And what was he?
Forsooth, a great arithmetician,
One Michael Cassio, a Florentine,
A fellow almost damn'd in a fair wife,
That never set a squadron in the field,
Nor the division of a battle knows
More than a spinster; unless the bookish theoric,
Wherein the toged consuls can propose
As masterly as he – mere prattle, without practice,
Is all his soldiership. But he, sir, had the election;
And I, of whom his eyes had seen the proof
At Rhodes, at Cyprus, and on other grounds,
Christian and heathen, must be be-lee'd and calm'd
By debitor and creditor – this counter-caster,
He, in good time, must his lieutenant be,
And I, God bless the mark! his Moorship's ancient.
RODERIGO By heaven, I rather would have been his hangman!
IAGO Why, there's no remedy; 'tis the curse of service:
Preferment goes by letter and affection,
Not by the old gradation, where each second
Stood heir to the first. Now, sir, be judge yourself
Whether I in any just term am affin'd
To love the Moor.
RODERIGO I would not follow him, then.
IAGO O, sir, content you.
I follow him to serve my turn upon him:
We cannot all be masters, nor all masters
Cannot be truly follow'd. You shall mark
Many a duteous and knee-crooking knave
That, doting on his own obsequious bondage,
Wears out his time, much like his master's ass,
For nought but provender; and when he's old, cashier'd.
Whip me such honest knaves. Others there are
Who, trimm'd in forms and visages of duty,

Keep yet their hearts attending on themselves;
And, throwing but shows of service on their lords,
Do well thrive by 'em and, when they have lin'd their coats,
Do themselves homage – these fellows have some soul;
And such a one do I profess myself.
For, sir,
It is as sure as you are Roderigo,
Were I the Moor, I would not be Iago.
In following him I follow but myself –
Heaven is my judge, not I for love and duty,
But seeming so for my peculiar end.
For when my outward action doth demonstrate
The native act and figure of my heart
In compliment extern, 'tis not long after
But I will wear my heart upon my sleeve
For daws to peck at: I am not what I am.

RODERIGO What a full fortune does the thick-lips owe,
If he can carry't thus!

IAGO Call up her father.
Rouse him, make after him, poison his delight,
Proclaim him in the streets; incense her kinsmen,
And, though he in a fertile climate dwell,
Plague him with flies; though that his joy be joy,
Yet throw such changes of vexation on't
As it may lose some colour.

RODERIGO Here is her father's house. I'll call aloud.

IAGO Do, with like timorous accent and dire yell
As when, by night and negligence, the fire
Is spied in populous cities.

RODERIGO What, ho, Brabantio! Signior Brabantio, ho!

IAGO Awake! What, ho, Brabantio! Thieves, thieves, thieves!
Look to your house, your daughter, and your bags.
Thieves! thieves!

BRABANTIO appears above at a window.

BRABANTIO What is the reason of this terrible summons?
What is the matter there?

RODERIGO Signior, is all your family within?

IAGO Are your doors lock'd?

BRABANTIO Why, wherefore ask you this?

IAGO Zounds, sir, you're robb'd; for shame, put on your gown;
Your heart is burst; you have lost half your soul.
Even now, now, very now, an old black ram
Is tupping your white ewe. Arise, arise;
Awake the snorting citizens with the bell,
Or else the devil will make a grandsire of you.
Arise, I say.

BRABANTIO What, have you lost your wits?

RODERIGO Most reverend signior, do you know my voice?

BRABANTIO Not I; what are you?

RODERIGO My name is Roderigo.

BRABANTIO The worser welcome!
I have charg'd thee not to haunt about my doors;
In honest plainness thou hast heard me say
My daughter is not for thee; and now, in madness,
Being full of supper and distempering draughts,
Upon malicious bravery dost thou come
To start my quiet.

RODERIGO Sir, sir, sir –

BRABANTIO But thou must needs be sure
My spirit and my place have in their power
To make this bitter to thee.

RODERIGO Patience, good sir.

BRABANTIO What tell'st thou me of robbing?
This is Venice;
My house is not a grange.

RODERIGO Most grave Brabantio,
In simple and pure soul I come to you.

IAGO Zounds, sir, you are one of those that will not serve God if the devil bid you. Because we come to do you service, and you think we are ruffians, you'll have your daughter cover'd with a Barbary horse; you'll have your nephews neigh to you; you'll have coursers for cousins and gennets for germans.

BRABANTIO What profane wretch art thou?

IAGO I am one, sir, that comes to tell you your daughter and the Moor are now making the beast with two backs.

BRABANTIO Thou art a villain.

IAGO You are – a Senator.

BRABANTIO This thou shalt answer; I know thee, Roderigo.

RODERIGO Sir, I will answer anything. But I beseech you,
If't be your pleasure and most wise consent –
As partly I find it is – that your fair daughter,
At this odd-even and dull watch o' th' night,
Transported with no worse nor better guard
But with a knave of common hire, a gondolier,
To the gross clasps of a lascivious Moor –
If this be known to you, and your allowance,
We then have done you bold and saucy wrongs;
But if you know not this, my manners tell me
We have your wrong rebuke. Do not believe
That, from the sense of all civility,
I thus would play and trifle with your reverence.
Your daughter, if you have not given her leave,
I say again, hath made a gross revolt;
Tying her duty, beauty, wit, and fortunes,

In an extravagant and wheeling stranger
Of here and everywhere. Straight satisfy yourself.
If she be in her chamber or your house,
Let loose on me the justice of the state
For thus deluding you.

BRABANTIO Strike on the tinder, ho! Give me a taper; call up all my people.
This accident is not unlike my dream.
Belief of it oppresses me already.
Light, I say; light!

[Exit from above.

IAGO Farewell; for I must leave you.
It seems not meet nor wholesome to my place
To be producted – as if I stay I shall –
Against the Moor; for I do know the state,
However this may gall him with some check,
Cannot with safety cast him; for he's embark'd
With such loud reason to the Cyprus wars,
Which even now stands in act, that, for their souls,
Another of his fathom they have none
To lead their business; in which regard,
Though I do hate him as I do hell pains,
Yet, for necessity of present life,
I must show out a flag and sign of love,
Which is indeed but sign. That you shall surely find him,
Lead to the Sagittary the raised search;
And there will I be with him. So, farewell.

[Exit.

Enter below, BRABANTIO, in his night gown, and Servants with torches.

BRABANTIO It is too true an evil. Gone she is;
And what's to come of my despised time
Is nought but bitterness. Now, Roderigo,
Where didst thou see her? – O unhappy girl! –
With the Moor, say'st thou? – Who would be a father? –
How didst thou know 'twas she? – O, thou deceivest me
Past thought! – What said she to you? – Get moe tapers;
Raise all my kindred. – Are they married think you?

RODERIGO Truly, I think they are.

BRABANTIO O heaven! How got she out? O treason of the blood!
Fathers, from hence trust not your daughters' minds
By what you see them act. Is there not charms
By which the property of youth and maidhood
May be abus'd? Have you not read, Roderigo,
Of some such thing?

RODERIGO Yes, sir, I have indeed.

BRABANTIO Call up my brother. – O that you had had her! –
Some one way, some another. – Do you know
Where we may apprehend her and the Moor?

RODERIGO I think I can discover him, if you please
To get good guard, and go along with me.

BRABANTIO Pray lead me on. At every house I'll call;
I may command at most. – Get weapons, ho!
And raise some special officers of night. –
On, good Roderigo; I'll deserve your pains.

[Exeunt.

SCENE II. *Venice. Another street.*

Enter OTHELLO, IAGO, and Attendants with torches.

IAGO Though in the trade of war I have slain men,
Yet do I hold it very stuff o' th' conscience
To do no contriv'd murder. I lack iniquity
Sometime to do me service. Nine or ten times
I had thought to have yerk'd him here under the ribs.

OTHELLO 'Tis better as it is.

IAGO Nay, but he prated,
And spoke such scurvy and provoking terms
Against your honour
That, with the little godliness I have,
I did full hard forbear him. But I pray, sir,
Are you fast married? For be assur'd of this,
That the magnifico is much beloved,
And hath in his effect a voice potential
As double as the Duke's. He will divorce you,
Or put upon you what restraint and grievance
That law, with all his might to enforce it on,
Will give him cable.

OTHELLO Let him do his spite.
My services which I have done the signiory
Shall out-tongue his complaints. 'Tis yet to know –
Which, when I know that boasting is an honour,
I shall promulgate – I fetch my life and being
From men of royal siege; and my demerits
May speak unbonneted to as proud a fortune
As this that I have reach'd. For know, Iago,
But that I love the gentle Desdemona,
I would not my unhoused free condition
Put into circumscription and confine
For the seas' worth.

Enter CASSIO and Officers with torches.

But look what lights come yonder.

IAGO Those are the raised father and his friends.
You were best go in.

OTHELLO Not I; I must be found.

My parts, my title, and my perfect soul
Shall manifest me rightly. Is it they?
IAGO By Janus, I think no.
OTHELLO The servants of the Duke and my lieutenant –
The goodness of the night upon you, friends!
What is the news?
CASSIO The Duke does greet you, General;
And he requires your haste-post-haste appearance
Even on the instant.
OTHELLO What is the matter, think you?
CASSIO Something from Cyprus, as I may divine.
It is a business of some heat: the galleys
Have sent a dozen sequent messengers
This very night at one another's heels;
And many of the consuls, rais'd and met,
Are at the Duke's already. You have been hotly call'd for;
When, being not at your lodging to be found,
The Senate hath sent about three several quests
To search you out.
OTHELLO 'Tis well I am found by you.
I will but spend a word here in the house,
And go with you. *[Exit.*
CASSIO Ancient, what makes he here?
IAGO Faith, he to-night hath boarded a land carrack.
If it prove lawful prize, he's made for ever.
CASSIO I do not understand.
IAGO He's married.
CASSIO To who?

Re-enter OTHELLO.

IAGO Marry, to – Come, Captain, will you go?
OTHELLO Have with you.

Enter BRABANTIO, RODERIGO, and Officers with torches and weapons.

CASSIO Here comes another troop to seek for you.
IAGO It is Brabantio. General, be advis'd;
He comes to bad intent.
OTHELLO Holla! stand there.
RODERIGO Signior, it is the Moor.
BRABANTIO Down with him, thief.
[They draw on both sides.
IAGO You, Roderigo; come, sir, I am for you.
OTHELLO Keep up your bright swords, for the dew will rust them.
Good signior, you shall more command with years
Than with your weapons.
BRABANTIO O thou foul thief, where hast thou stow'd my daughter?
Damn'd as thou art, thou hast enchanted her;
For I'll refer me to all things of sense,
If she in chains of magic were not bound,
Whether a maid so tender, fair, and happy,
So opposite to marriage that she shunn'd
The wealthy curled darlings of our nation,
Would ever have, to incur a general mock,
Run from her guardage to the sooty bosom
Of such a thing as thou – to fear, not to delight.
Judge me the world, if 'tis not gross in sense
That thou hast practis'd on her with foul charms,
Abus'd her delicate youth with drugs or minerals
That weakens motion. I'll have't disputed on;
'Tis probable, and palpable to thinking.
I therefore apprehend and do attach thee
For an abuser of the world, a practiser
Of arts inhibited and out of warrant.
Lay hold upon him. If he do resist,
Subdue him at his peril.
OTHELLO Hold your hands,
Both you of my inclining and the rest.
Were it my cue to fight, I should have known it
Without a prompter. Where will you that I go
To answer this your charge?
BRABANTIO To prison; till fit time
Of law and course of direct session
Call thee to answer.
OTHELLO What if I do obey?
How may the Duke be therewith satisfied,
Whose messengers are here about my side,
Upon some present business of the state,
To bring me to him.
OFFICER 'Tis true, most worthy signior;
The Duke's in council, and your noble self,
I am sure, is sent for.
BRABANTIO How! The Duke in council!
In this time of the night! Bring him away.
Mine's not an idle cause. The Duke himself,
Or any of my brothers of the state,
Cannot but feel this wrong as 'twere their own;
For if such actions may have passage free,
Bond-slaves and pagans shall our statesmen be.
[Exeunt.

SCENE III. *Venice. A council-chamber.*

Enter DUKE and Senators, set at a table with lights; and Attendants.

DUKE There is no composition in these news
That gives them credit.
1 SENATOR Indeed, they are disproportion'd;
My letters say a hundred and seven galleys.
DUKE And mine a hundred and forty.
2 SENATOR And mine two hundred.
But though they jump not on a just account –
As in these cases, where the aim reports,
'Tis oft with difference – yet do they all confirm
A Turkish fleet, and bearing up to Cyprus.

DUKE Nay, it is possible enough to judgment.
I do not so secure me in the error
But the main article I do approve
In fearful sense.

SAILOR *[Within]* What, ho! what, ho! what, ho!

Enter Sailor.

OFFICER A messenger from the galleys.

DUKE Now, what's the business?

SAILOR The Turkish preparation makes for Rhodes;
So was I bid report here to the state
By Signior Angelo.

DUKE How say you by this change?

1 SENATOR This cannot be,
By no assay of reason. 'Tis a pageant
To keep us in false gaze. When we consider
The importancy of Cyprus to the Turk,
And let ourselves again but understand
That as it more concerns the Turk than Rhodes,
So may he with more facile question bear it,
For that it stands not in such warlike brace,
But altogether lacks th' abilities
That Rhodes is dress'd in – if we make thought of this,
We must not think the Turk is so unskilful
To leave that latest which concerns him first,
Neglecting an attempt of ease and gain
To wake and wage a danger profitless.

DUKE Nay, in all confidence, he's not for Rhodes.

OFFICER Here is more news.

Enter a Messenger.

MESSENGER The Ottomites, reverend and gracious,
Steering with due course toward the isle of Rhodes,
Have there injointed them with an after fleet.

1 SENATOR Ay, so I thought. How many, as you guess?

MESSENGER Of thirty sail; and now they do restem
Their backward course, bearing with frank appearance
Their purposes toward Cyprus. Signior Montano,
Your trusty and most valiant servitor,
With his free duty recommends you thus,
And prays you to believe him.

DUKE 'Tis certain, then, for Cyprus.
Marcus Lucchese, is not he in town?

1 SENATOR He's now in Florence.

DUKE Write from us: wish him post-post-haste dispatch.

Enter BRABANTIO, OTHELLO, IAGO, RODERIGO, and Officers.

1 SENATOR Here comes Brabantio and the valiant Moor.

DUKE Valiant Othello, we must straight employ you
Against the general enemy Ottoman.
[To Brabantio] I did not see you; welcome, gentle signior;
We lack'd your counsel and your help to-night.

BRABANTIO So did I yours. Good your Grace, pardon me:
Neither my place, nor aught I heard of business,
Hath rais'd me from my bed; nor doth the general care
Take hold on me; for my particular grief
Is of so flood-gate and o'erbearing nature
That it engluts and swallows other sorrows,
And it is still itself.

DUKE Why, what's the matter?

BRABANTIO My daughter! O, my daughter!

ALL Dead?

BRABANTIO Ay, to me.
She is abus'd, stol'n from me, and corrupted,
By spells and medicines bought of mountebanks;
For nature so preposterously to err,
Being not deficient, blind, or lame of sense,
Sans witchcraft could not.

DUKE Whoe'er he be that in this foul proceeding
Hath thus beguil'd your daughter of herself,
And you of her, the bloody book of law
You shall yourself read in the bitter letter
After your own sense; yea, though our proper son
Stood in your action.

BRABANTIO Humbly I thank your Grace.
Here is the man – this Moor whom now, it seems,
Your special mandate for the state affairs
Hath hither brought.

ALL We are very sorry for't.

DUKE *[To Othello]* What, in your own part, can you say to this?

BRABANTIO Nothing, but this is so.

OTHELLO Most potent, grave, and reverend signiors,
My very noble and approv'd good masters:
That I have ta'en away this old man's daughter,
It is most true; true, I have married her –
The very head and front of my offending
Hath this extent, no more. Rude am I in my speech,
And little blest with the soft phrase of peace;
For since these arms of mine had seven years' pith,
Till now some nine moons wasted, they have us'd
Their dearest action in the tented field;
And little of this great world can I speak

More than pertains to feats of broil and battle;
And therefore little shall I grace my cause
In speaking for myself. Yet, by your gracious patience,
I will a round unvarnish'd tale deliver
Of my whole course of love – what drugs, what charms,
What conjuration, and what mighty magic,
For such proceedings am I charg'd withal,
I won his daughter.

BRABANTIO A maiden never bold,
Of spirit so still and quiet that her motion
Blush'd at herself; and she – in spite of nature,
Of years, of country, credit, every thing –
To fall in love with what she fear'd to look on!
It is a judgment maim'd and most imperfect
That will confess perfection so could err
Against all rules of nature, and must be driven
To find out practices of cunning hell,
Why this should be. I therefore vouch again
That with some mixtures powerful o'er the blood,
Or with some dram conjur'd to this effect,
He wrought upon her.

DUKE To vouch this is no proof –
Without more wider and more overt test
Than these thin habits and poor likelihoods
Of modern seeming do prefer against him.

1 SENATOR But, Othello, speak.
Did you by indirect and forced courses
Subdue and poison this young maid's affections?
Or came it by request, and such fair question
As soul to soul affordeth?

OTHELLO I do beseech you,
Send for the lady to the Sagittary,
And let her speak of me before her father.
If you do find me foul in her report,
The trust, the office, I do hold of you
Not only take away, but let your sentence
Even fall upon my life.

DUKE Fetch Desdemona hither.

OTHELLO Ancient, conduct them; you best know the place. [*Exeunt Iago and Attendants.*
And, till she come, as faithful as to heaven
I do confess the vices of my blood,
So justly to your grave ears I'll present
How I did thrive in this fair lady's love,
And she in mine.

DUKE Say it, Othello.

OTHELLO Her father lov'd me, oft invited me;
Still question'd me the story of my life
From year to year – the battles, sieges, fortunes,
That I have pass'd.
I ran it through, even from my boyish days
To th' very moment that he bade me tell it;
Wherein I spake of most disastrous chances,
Of moving accidents by flood and field;
Of hairbreadth scapes i' th' imminent deadly breach;
Of being taken by the insolent foe
And sold to slavery; of my redemption thence,
And portance in my travel's history;
Wherein of antres vast and deserts idle,
Rough quarries, rocks, and hills whose heads touch heaven,
It was my hint to speak – such was the process;
And of the Cannibals that each other eat,
The Anthropophagi, and men whose heads
Do grow beneath their shoulders. This to hear
Would Desdemona seriously incline;
But still the house affairs would draw her thence;
Which ever as she could with haste dispatch,
She'd come again, and with a greedy ear
Devour up my discourse. Which I observing,
Took once a pliant hour, and found good means
To draw from her a prayer of earnest heart
That I would all my pilgrimage dilate,
Whereof by parcels she had something heard,
But not intentively. I did consent,
And often did beguile her of her tears,
When I did speak of some distressful stroke
That my youth suffer'd. My story being done,
She gave me for my pains a world of sighs;
She swore, in faith, 'twas strange, 'twas passing strange;
'Twas pitiful, 'twas wondrous pitiful.
She wish'd she had not heard it; yet she wish'd
That heaven had made her such a man. She thank'd me;
And bade me, if I had a friend that lov'd her,
I should but teach him how to tell my story,
And that would woo her. Upon this hint I spake;
She lov'd me for the dangers I had pass'd;
And I lov'd her that she did pity them.
This only is the witchcraft I have us'd.
Here comes the lady; let her witness it.

Enter DESDEMONA, IAGO, and Attendants.

DUKE I think this tale would win my daughter too.
Good Brabantio,
Take up this mangled matter at the best.
Men do their broken weapons rather use
Than their bare hands.

BRABANTIO I pray you hear her speak.
If she confess that she was half the wooer,
Destruction on my head if my bad blame
Light on the man! Come hither, gentle mistress.
Do you perceive in all this noble company
Where most you owe obedience?

DESDEMONA My noble father,

I do perceive here a divided duty:
To you I am bound for life and education;
My life and education both do learn me
How to respect you; you are the lord of duty –
I am hitherto your daughter; but here's my husband,
And so much duty as my mother show'd
To you, preferring you before her father,
So much I challenge that I may profess
Due to the Moor, my lord.

BRABANTIO God bu'y, I ha done.
Please it your Grace, on to the state affairs –
I had rather to adopt a child than get it.
Come hither, Moor:
I here do give thee that with all my heart
Which, but thou hast already, with all my heart
I would keep from thee. For your sake, jewel,
I am glad at soul I have no other child;
For thy escape would teach me tyranny,
To hang clogs on them. I have done, my lord.

DUKE Let me speak like yourself, and lay a sentence
Which, as a grise or step, may help these lovers
Into your favour.
When remedies are past, the griefs are ended
By seeing the worst, which late on hopes depended.
To mourn a mischief that is past and gone
Is the next way to draw new mischief on.
What cannot be preserv'd when fortune takes,
Patience her injury a mockery makes.
The robb'd that smiles steals something from the thief;
He robs himself that spends a bootless grief.

BRABANTIO So let the Turk of Cyprus us beguile:
We lose it not so long as we can smile.
He bears the sentence well that nothing bears
But the free comfort which from thence he hears;
But he bears both the sentence and the sorrow
That to pay grief must of poor patience borrow.
These sentences, to sugar or to gall,
Being strong on both sides, are equivocal.
But words are words: I never yet did hear
That the bruis'd heart was pierced through the ear.
I humbly beseech you proceed to th' affairs of state.

DUKE The Turk with a most mighty preparation makes for Cyprus. Othello, the fortitude of the place is best known to you; and though we have there a substitute of most allowed sufficiency, yet opinion, a sovereign mistress of effects, throws a more safer voice on you. You must therefore be content to slubber the gloss of your new fortunes with this more stubborn and boisterous expedition.

OTHELLO The tyrant custom, most grave senators,
Hath made the flinty and steel couch of war
My thrice-driven bed of down. I do agnize
A natural and prompt alacrity
I find in hardness; and would undertake
This present wars against the Ottomites.
Most humbly, therefore, bending to your state,
I crave fit disposition for my wife;
Due reference of place and exhibition;
With such accommodation and besort
As levels with her breeding.

DUKE If you please,
Be't at her father's.

BRABANTIO I'll not have it so.

OTHELLO Nor I.

DESDEMONA Nor I. I would not there reside,
To put my father in impatient thoughts
By being in his eye. Most gracious Duke,
To my unfolding lend your prosperous ear,
And let me find a charter in your voice
T' assist my simpleness.

DUKE What would you, Desdemona?

DESDEMONA That I did love the Moor to live with him,
My downright violence and storm of fortunes
May trumpet to the world. My heart's subdu'd
Even to the very quality of my lord:
I saw Othello's visage in his mind;
And to his honours and his valiant parts
Did I my soul and fortunes consecrate.
So that, dear lords, if I be left behind,
A moth of peace, and he go to the war,
The rites for why I love him are bereft me,
And I a heavy interim shall support
By his dear absence. Let me go with him.

OTHELLO Let her have your voice.
Vouch with me, heaven, I therefore beg it not
To please the palate of my appetite;
Nor to comply with heat – the young affects
In me defunct – and proper satisfaction;
But to be free and bounteous to her mind.
And heaven defend your good souls that you think
I will your serious and great business scant
For she is with me. No, when light-wing'd toys
Of feather'd Cupid seel with wanton dullness
My speculative and offic'd instruments,
That my disports corrupt and taint my business,
Let huswives make a skillet of my helm,
And all indign and base adversities
Make head against my estimation!

DUKE Be it as you shall privately determine,
Either for her stay or going. Th' affair cries haste,
And speed must answer it. You must away to-night.

DESDEMONA To-night, my lord!

DUKE This night.

OTHELLO With all my heart.

DUKE At nine i' th' morning here we'll meet again.
Othello, leave some officer behind,
And he shall our commission bring to you;
With such things else of quality and respect
As doth import you.

OTHELLO So please your Grace, my ancient;
A man he is of honesty and trust.
To his conveyance I assign my wife,
With what else needful your good Grace shall think
To be sent after me.

DUKE Let it be so.
Good night to every one. [*To Brabantio*] And, noble signior,
If virtue no delighted beauty lack,
Your son-in-law is far more fair than black.

1 SENATOR Adieu, brave Moor; use Desdemona well.

BRABANTIO Look to her, Moor, if thou hast eyes to see:
She has deceiv'd her father, and may thee.

[*Exeunt Duke, Senators, Officers etc.*

OTHELLO My life upon her faith! – Honest Iago,
My Desdemona must I leave to thee.
I prithee let thy wife attend on her;
And bring them after in the best advantage.
Come, Desdemona, I have but an hour
Of love, of worldly matter and direction,
To spend with thee. We must obey the time.

[*Exeunt Othello and Desdemona.*

RODERIGO Iago!

IAGO What say'st thou, noble heart?

RODERIGO What will I do, thinkest thou?

IAGO Why, go to bed and sleep.

RODERIGO I will incontinently drown myself.

IAGO Well, if thou dost, I shall never love thee after it. Why, thou silly gentleman!

RODERIGO It is silliness to live when to live is torment; and then have we a prescription to die when death is our physician.

IAGO O villainous! I ha look'd upon the world for four times seven years; and since I could distinguish betwixt a benefit and an injury, I never found a man that knew how to love himself. Ere I would say I would drown myself for the love of a guinea-hen, I would change my humanity with a baboon.

RODERIGO What should I do? I confess it is my shame to be so fond, but it is not in my virtue to amend it.

IAGO Virtue? A fig! 'Tis in ourselves that we are thus or thus. Our bodies are our gardens to the which our wills are gardeners; so that if we will plant nettles or sow lettuce, set hyssop and weed up thyme, supply it with one gender of herbs or distract it with many, either to have it sterile with idleness or manur'd with industry – why, the power and corrigible authority of this lies in our wills. If the balance of our lives had not one scale of reason to poise another of sensuality, the blood and baseness of our natures would conduct us to most preposterous conclusions. But we have reason to cool our raging motions, our carnal stings, our unbitted lusts; whereof I take this that you call love to be a sect or scion.

RODERIGO It cannot be.

IAGO It is merely a lust of the blood and a permission of the will. Come, be a man. Drown thyself? Drown cats and blind puppies! I have profess'd me thy friend, and I confess me knit to thy deserving with cables of perdurable toughness. I could never better stead thee than now. Put money in thy purse; follow thou the wars; defeat thy favour with an usurp'd beard. I say, put money in thy purse. It cannot be long that Desdemona should continue her love to the Moor – put money in thy purse – nor he his to her: it was a violent commencement in her, and thou shalt see an answerable sequestration – put but money in thy purse. These Moors are changeable in their wills – fill thy purse with money. The food that to him now is as luscious as locusts shall be to him shortly as acerbe as the coloquintida. She must change for youth; when she is sated with his body, she will find the error of her choice. Therefore put money in thy purse. If thou wilt needs damn thyself, do it a more delicate way than drowning. Make all the money thou canst. If sanctimony and a frail vow betwixt an erring barbarian and a super-subtle Venetian be not too hard for my wits and all the tribe of hell, thou shalt enjoy her; therefore make money. A pox a drowning thyself! 'Tis clean out of the way. Seek thou rather to be hang'd in compassing thy joy than to be drown'd and go without her.

RODERIGO Wilt thou be fast to my hopes, if I depend on the issue?

IAGO Thou art sure of me – go make money. I have told thee often, and I retell thee again and again I hate the Moor. My cause is hearted: thine hath no less reason. Let us be conjunctive in our revenge against him. If thou canst cuckold him, thou dost thyself a pleasure, me a sport. There are many events in the womb of time which will be delivered. Traverse; go; provide thy money. We will have more of this to-morrow. Adieu.

RODERIGO Where shall we meet i' th' morning?
IAGO At my lodging.
RODERIGO I'll be with thee betimes.
IAGO Go to; farewell. Do you hear, Roderigo?
RODERIGO What say you?
IAGO No more of drowning, do you hear?
RODERIGO I am chang'd.
IAGO Go to; farewell. Put money enough in your purse.
RODERIGO I'll sell all my land. [Exit Roderigo.
IAGO Thus do I ever make my fool my purse;
For I mine own gain'd knowledge should profane
If I would time expend with such a snipe
But for my sport and profit. I hate the Moor;
And it is thought abroad that 'twixt my sheets
'Has done my office. I know not if't be true;
Yet I, for mere suspicion in that kind,
Will do as if for surety. He holds me well;
The better shall my purpose work on him.
Cassio's a proper man. Let me see now:
To get his place, and to plume up my will
In double knavery. How, how? Let's see:
After some time to abuse Othello's ear
That he is too familiar with his wife.
He hath a person and a smooth dispose
To be suspected – fram'd to make women false.
The Moor is of a free and open nature
That thinks men honest that but seem to be so;
And will as tenderly be led by th' nose
As asses are.
I ha't – it is engender'd. Hell and night
Must bring this monstrous birth to the world's light. [*Exit.*

ACT TWO

SCENE I. *Cyprus. A sea-port.*

Enter MONTANO, Governor of Cyprus, with two other Gentlemen.

MONTANO What from the cape can you discern at sea?
1 GENTLEMAN Nothing at all; it is a high-wrought flood.
I cannot 'twixt the heaven and the main
Descry a sail.
MONTANO Methinks the wind hath spoke aloud at land;
A fuller blast ne'er shook our battlements.
If it ha ruffian'd so upon the sea,
What ribs of oak, when mountains melt on them,
Can hold the mortise? What shall we hear of this?
2 GENTLEMAN A segregation of the Turkish fleet.
For do but stand upon the banning shore,
The chidden billow seems to pelt the clouds;
The wind-shak'd surge, with high and monstrous mane,
Seems to cast water on the burning Bear,
And quench the guards of th' ever-fired pole.
I never did like molestation view
On the enchafed flood.
MONTANO If that the Turkish fleet
Be not enshelter'd and embay'd, they are drown'd:
It is impossible they bear it out.

Enter a third Gentleman.

3 GENTLEMAN News, lads! Your wars are done.
The desperate tempest hath so bang'd the Turk
That their designment halts. A noble ship of Venice
Hath seen a grievous wreck and sufferance
On most part of their fleet.
MONTANO How! Is this true?
3 GENTLEMAN The ship is here put in,
A Veronesa; Michael Cassio,
Lieutenant to the warlike Moor Othello,
Is come ashore: the Moor himself at sea,
And is in full commission here for Cyprus.
MONTANO I am glad on't; 'tis a worthy governor.
3 GENTLEMAN But this same Cassio, though he speak of comfort
Touching the Turkish loss, yet he looks sadly
And prays the Moor be safe; for they were parted
With foul and violent tempest.
MONTANO Pray heaven he be;
For I have serv'd him, and the man commands
Like a full soldier. Let's to the sea-side, ho!
As well to see the vessel that's come in
As to throw out our eyes for brave Othello,
Even till we make the main and th' aerial blue
An indistinct regard.
3 GENTLEMAN Come, let's do so;
For every minute is expectancy
Of more arrivance.

Enter CASSIO.

CASSIO Thanks you, the valiant of this war-like isle,
That so approve the Moor. O, let the heavens
Give him defence against their elements,
For I have lost him on a dangerous sea!
MONTANO Is he well shipp'd?

CASSIO His bark is stoutly timber'd, and his pilot
Of very expert and approv'd allowance;
Therefore my hopes, not surfeited to death,
Stand in bold cure.
[*Within:* A sail, a sail, a sail!

Enter a Messenger.

CASSIO What noise?
MESSENGER The town is empty; on the brow o' th' sea
Stand ranks of people, and they cry 'A sail!'
CASSIO My hopes do shape him for the Governor. [*A shot.*
2 GENTLEMAN They do discharge the shot of courtesy:
Our friend at least.
CASSIO I pray you, sir, go forth,
And give us truth who 'tis that is arriv'd.
2 GENTLEMAN I shall. [*Exit.*
MONTANO But, good Lieutenant, is your general wiv'd?
CASSIO Most fortunately: he hath achiev'd a maid
That paragons description and wild fame;
One that excels the quirks of blazoning pens,
And in th' essential vesture of creation
Does tire the ingener.

Re-enter second Gentleman.

Now, who has put in?
2 GENTLEMAN 'Tis one Iago, ancient to the General.
CASSIO 'Has had most favourable and happy speed.
Tempests themselves, high seas, and howling winds,
The gutter'd rocks, and congregated sands,
Traitors ensteep'd to enclog the guiltless keel,
As having sense of beauty, do omit
Their mortal natures, letting go safely by
The divine Desdemona.
MONTANO What is she?
CASSIO She that I spake of – our great Captain's Captain,
Left in the conduct of the bold Iago;
Whose footing here anticipates our thoughts
A se'nnight's speed. Great Jove, Othello guard,
And swell his sail with thine own powerful breath,
That he may bless this bay with his tall ship,
Make love's quick pants in Desdemona's arms,
Give renew'd fire to our extincted spirits,
And bring all Cyprus comfort!

Enter DESDEMONA, IAGO, EMILIA, RODERIGO, and Attendants.

O, behold,
The riches of the ship is come ashore!
Ye men of Cyprus, let her have your knees.
Hail to thee, lady! and the grace of heaven,
Before, behind thee, and on every hand,
Enwheel thee round!
DESDEMONA I thank you, valiant Cassio.
What tidings can you tell me of my lord?
CASSIO He is not yet arriv'd; nor know I aught
But that he's well, and will be shortly here.
DESDEMONA O, but I fear! How lost you company?
CASSIO The great contention of the sea and skies
Parted our fellowship.
[*Within:* A sail, a sail!
But hark – 'A sail!' [*A shot.*
2 GENTLEMAN They give their greeting to the citadel:
This likewise is a friend.
CASSIO So speaks this voice.
See for the news. [*Exit Gentleman.*
Good ancient, you are welcome. [*To Emilia*]
Welcome, mistress.
Let it not gall your patience, good Iago,
That I extend my manners; 'tis my breeding
That gives me this bold show of courtesy.
[*Kissing her.*
IAGO Sir, would she give you so much of her lips
As of her tongue she oft bestows on me,
You'd have enough.
DESDEMONA Alas, she has no speech!
IAGO I know too much
I find it aye when I ha list to sleep.
Marry, before your ladyship, I grant,
She puts her tongue a little in her heart
And chides with thinking.
EMILIA You ha little cause to say so.
IAGO Come on, come on; you are pictures out a-doors, bells in your parlours, wildcats in your kitchens, saints in your injuries, devils being offended, players in your huswifery, and huswives in your beds.
DESDEMONA O, fie upon thee, slanderer!
IAGO Nay, it is true, or else I am a Turk:
You rise to play, and go to bed to work.
EMILIA You shall not write my praise.
IAGO No, let me not.
DESDEMONA What wouldst write of me if thou shouldst praise me?
IAGO O gentle lady, do not put me to't;
For I am nothing if not critical.
DESDEMONA Come on, assay. – There's one gone to the harbour?
IAGO Ay, madam.
DESDEMONA I am not merry; but I do beguile
The thing I am by seeming otherwise.
Come, how wouldst thou praise me?

IAGO I am about it; but, indeed, my invention comes from my pate as birdlime does from frieze – it plucks out brains and all. But my Muse labours, and thus she is deliver'd:
If she be fair and wise – fairness and wit,
The one's for use, the other useth it.

DESDEMONA Well prais'd. How if she be black and witty?

IAGO If she be black, and thereto have a wit,
She'll find a white that shall her blackness hit.

DESDEMONA Worse and worse!

EMILIA How if fair and foolish?

IAGO She never yet was foolish that was fair;
For even her folly help'd her to an heir.

DESDEMONA These are old fond paradoxes to make fools laugh i' th' alehouse. What miserable praise hast thou for her that's foul and foolish?

IAGO There's none so foul, and foolish thereunto,
But does foul pranks which fair and wise ones do.

DESDEMONA O heavy ignorance! that praises the worst best. But what praise couldst thou bestow on a deserving woman indeed – one that, in the authority of her merits, did justly put on the vouch of very malice itself?

IAGO She that was ever fair, and never proud;
Had tongue at will, and yet was never loud;
Never lack'd gold, and yet went never gay;
Fled from her wish, and yet said 'Now I may';
She that, being ang'red, her revenge being nigh,
Bade her wrong stay and her displeasure fly;
She that in wisdom never was so frail
To change the cod's head for the salmon's tail;
She that could think, and ne'er disclose her mind;
See suitors following, and not look behind:
She was a wight, if ever such wight were –

DESDEMONA To do what?

IAGO To suckle fools and chronicle small beer.

DESDEMONA O most lame and impotent conclusion! Do not learn of him, Emilia, though he be thy husband. How say you, Cassio? Is he not a most profane and liberal counsellor?

CASSIO He speaks home, madam. You may relish him more in the soldier than in the scholar.

IAGO *[Aside]* He takes her by the palm. Ay, well said, whisper. With as little a web as this will I ensnare as great a fly as Cassio. Ay, smile upon her, do; I will gyve thee in thine own courtship. You say true; 'tis so, indeed. If such tricks as these strip you out of your lieutenantry, it had been better you had not kiss'd your three fingers so oft, which now again you are most apt to play the sir in. Very good; well kissed! and excellent courtesy! 'Tis so, indeed. Yet again your fingers to your lips? Would they were clyster-pipes for your sake!

[Trumpet within.

The Moor! I know his trumpet.

CASSIO 'Tis truly so.

DESDEMONA Let's meet him, and receive him.

CASSIO Lo, where he comes!

Enter OTHELLO and Attendants.

OTHELLO O my fair warrior!

DESDEMONA My dear Othello!

OTHELLO It gives me wonder great as my content
To see you here before me. O my soul's joy!
If after every tempest come such calms,
May the winds blow till they have waken'd death,
And let the labouring bark climb hills of seas
Olympus-high and duck again as low
As hell's from heaven. If it were now to die,
'Twere now to be most happy; for I fear
My soul hath her content so absolute
That not another comfort like to this
Succeeds in unknown fate.

DESDEMONA The heavens forbid
But that our loves and comforts should increase
Even as our days do grow!

OTHELLO Amen to that, sweet powers!
I cannot speak enough of this content;
It stops me here; it is too much of joy.
And this, and this, the greatest discords be

[They kiss.

That e'er our hearts shall make!

IAGO *[Aside]* O, you are well tun'd now!
But I'll set down the pegs that make this music,
As honest as I am.

OTHELLO Come, let us to the castle.
News, friends: our wars are done; the Turks are drown'd.
How do our old acquaintance of the isle?
Honey, you shall be well desir'd in Cyprus;
I have found great love amongst them. O my sweet,
I prattle out of fashion, and I dote
In mine own comforts. I prithee, good Iago,
Go to the bay, and disembark my coffers;
Bring thou the Master to the Citadel;
He is a good one, and his worthiness
Does challenge much respect. Come, Desdemona,
Once more well met at Cyprus.

[Exeunt all but Iago and Roderigo.

IAGO *[To one leaving]* Do thou meet me presently at the harbour. *[To Roderigo]* Come hither. If thou be'st valiant – as they say base men being in love have then a nobility in their natures more than is native to them – list me. The Lieutenant to-night watches on the court of guard. First, I must tell thee this: Desdemona is directly in love with him.

RODERIGO With him! Why, 'tis not possible.

IAGO Lay thy finger thus, and let thy soul be instructed. Mark me with what violence she first lov'd the Moor, but for bragging and telling her fantastical lies. To love him still for prating? – let not thy discreet heart think it. Her eye must be fed; and what delight shall she have to look on the devil? When the blood is made dull with the act of sport, there should be – again to inflame it, and to give satiety a fresh appetite – loveliness in favour, sympathy in years, manners, and beauties – all which the Moor is defective in. Now for want of these requir'd conveniences, her delicate tenderness will find itself abus'd, begin to heave the gorge, disrelish and abhor the Moor; very nature will instruct her in it, and compel her to some second choice. Now, sir, this granted – as it is a most pregnant and unforc'd position – who stands so eminent in the degree of this fortune as Cassio does? A knave very voluble; no further conscionable than in putting on the mere form of civil and humane seeming, for the better compassing of his salt and most hidden loose affection? Why, none; why, none. A slipper and subtle knave; a finder-out of occasion; that has an eye can stamp and counterfeit advantages, though true advantage never present itself; a devilish knave! Besides, the knave is handsome, young, and hath all those requisites in him that folly and green minds look after; a pestilent complete knave, and the woman hath found him already.

RODERIGO I cannot believe that in her; she's full of most blest condition.

IAGO Blest fig's end! The wine she drinks is made of grapes. If she had been blest, she would never have lov'd the Moor. Blest pudding! Didst thou not see her paddle with the palm of his hand? Didst not mark that?

RODERIGO Yes, that I did; but that was but courtesy.

IAGO Lechery, by this hand; an index and obscure prologue to the history of lust and foul thoughts. They met so near with their lips that their breaths embrac'd together. Villainous thoughts, Roderigo! When these mutualities so marshal the way, hard at hand comes the master and main exercise, th' incorporate conclusion. Pish! But, sir, be you rul'd by me; I have brought you from Venice. Watch you to-night; for your command, I'll lay't upon you. Cassio knows you not; I'll not be far from you. Do you find some occasion to anger Cassio, either by speaking too loud, or tainting his discipline, or from what other course you please, which the time shall more favourably minister.

RODERIGO Well.

IAGO Sir, he's rash, and very sudden in choler, and haply with his truncheon may strike at you; provoke him that he may; for even out of that will I cause these of Cyprus to mutiny, whose qualification shall come into no true taste again but by the displanting of Cassio. So shall you have a shorter journey to your desires by the means I shall then have to prefer them; and the impediment most profitably remov'd, without the which there were no expectation of our prosperity.

RODERIGO I will do this, if you can bring it to any opportunity.

IAGO I warrant thee. Meet me by and by at the citadel. I must fetch his necessaries ashore. Farewell.

RODERIGO Adieu. *[Exit.*

IAGO That Cassio loves her, I do well believe it;
That she loves him, 'tis apt and of great credit.
The Moor, howbeit that I endure him not,
Is of a constant, loving, noble nature;
And I dare think he'll prove to Desdemona
A most dear husband. Now I do love her too;
Not out of absolute lust, though per-adventure
I stand accountant for as great a sin,
But partly led to diet my revenge,
For that I do suspect the lustful Moor
Hath leap'd into my seat; the thought whereof
Doth like a poisonous mineral gnaw my inwards;
And nothing can nor shall content my soul
Till I am even'd with him, wife for wife;
Or failing so, yet that I put the Moor
At least into a jealousy so strong
That judgment cannot cure. Which thing to do,
If this poor trash of Venice, whom I trash
For his quick hunting, stand the putting on,
I'll have our Michael Cassio on the hip,
Abuse him to the Moor in the rank garb –
For I fear Cassio with my night-cap too;
Make the Moor thank me, love me, and reward me,
For making him egregiously an ass,
And practising upon his peace and quiet
Even to madness. 'Tis here, but yet confus'd:
Knavery's plain face is never seen till us'd.
[Exit.

SCENE II. *Cyprus. A street.*

Enter Othello's Herald with a proclamation; People following.

HERALD It is Othello's pleasure, our noble and valiant general, that, upon certain tidings now arriv'd, importing the mere perdition of the Turkish fleet, every man put himself into triumph; some to dance, some to make bonfires, each man to what sport and revels his addiction leads him; for, besides these beneficial news, it is the celebration of his nuptial. So much was his pleasure should be proclaimed. All offices are open; and there is full liberty of feasting from this present hour of five till the bell have told eleven. Heaven bless the isle of Cyprus and our noble general Othello! [*Exeunt.*

SCENE III. *Cyprus. The citadel.*

Enter OTHELLO, DESDEMONA, CASSIO, and Attendants.

OTHELLO Good Michael, look you to the guard to-night.
Let's teach ourselves that honourable stop,
Not to outsport discretion.

CASSIO Iago hath direction what to do;
But, notwithstanding, with my personal eye
Will I look to't.

OTHELLO Iago is most honest.
Michael, good night. To-morrow with your earliest
Let me have speech with you. [*To Desdemona*] Come, my dear love,
The purchase made, the fruits are to ensue;
That profit's yet to come twixt me and you. –
Good night. [*Exeunt Othello, Desdemona and Attendants.*

Enter IAGO.

CASSIO Welcome, Iago; we must to the watch.

IAGO Not this hour, Lieutenant; 'tis not yet ten a clock. Our general cast us thus early for the love of his Desdemona; who let us not therefore blame. He hath not yet made wanton the night with her; and she is sport for Jove.

CASSIO She is a most exquisite lady.

IAGO And, I'll warrant her, full of game.

CASSIO Indeed, she is a most fresh and delicate creature.

IAGO What an eye she has! Methinks it sounds a parley to provocation.

CASSIO An inviting eye; and yet methinks right modest.

IAGO And when she speaks, is it not an alarm to love?

CASSIO She is indeed perfection.

IAGO Well, happiness to their sheets! Come, Lieutenant, I have a stoup of wine; and here without are a brace of Cyprus gallants that would fain have a measure to the health of the black Othello.

CASSIO Not to-night, good Iago. I have very poor and unhappy brains for drinking; I could well wish courtesy would invent some other custom of entertainment.

IAGO O, they are our friends – but one cup; I'll drink for you.

CASSIO I have drunk but one cup to-night, and that was craftily qualified too, and behold what innovation it makes here. I am unfortunate in the infirmity, and dare not task my weakness with any more.

IAGO What man! 'Tis a night of revels. The gallants desire it.

CASSIO Where are they?

IAGO Here at the door; I pray you call them in.

CASSIO I'll do't; but it dislikes me. [*Exit.*

IAGO If I can fasten but one cup upon him,
With that which he hath drunk to-night already,
He'll be as full of quarrel and offence
As my young mistress' dog. Now my sick fool Roderigo,
Whom love hath turn'd almost the wrong side outward,
To Desdemona hath to-night carous'd
Potations pottle deep; and he's to watch.
Three else of Cyprus – noble swelling spirits,
That hold their honours in a wary distance,
The very elements of this warlike isle –
Have I to-night fluster'd with flowing cups,
And they watch too. Now, 'mongst this flock of drunkards
Am I to put our Cassio in some action
That may offend the isle – but here they come.

Re-enter CASSIO with MONTANO, and Gentlemen, followed by Servant with wine.

If consequence do but approve my dream,
My boat sails freely, both with wind and stream.

CASSIO Fore God, they have given me a rouse already.

MONTANO Good faith, a little one; not past a pint, as I am a soldier.

IAGO Some wine, ho!
[*Sings*] And let me the canakin clink, clink;
And let me the canakin clink.
A soldier's a man;
O, man's life's but a span;
Why, then, let a soldier drink –
Some wine, boys.

CASSIO Fore God, an excellent song!

IAGO I learn'd it in England, where indeed they are most potent in potting: your Dane, your German, and your swag-bellied Hollander – Drink, ho! – are nothing to your English.

CASSIO Is your Englishman so expert in his drinking?

IAGO Why, he drinks you with facility your Dane dead drunk; he sweats not to overthrow your Almain; he gives your Hollander a vomit ere the

next pottle can be fill'd.
CASSIO To the health of our General!
MONTANO I am for it, Lieutenant; and I'll do you justice.
IAGO O sweet England! [*Sings.*
King Stephen was and a worthy peer,
His breeches cost him but a crown;
He held 'em sixpence all too dear,
With that he call'd the tailor lown.
He was a wight of high renown,
And thou art but of low degree.
'Tis pride that pulls the country down;
Then take thy auld cloak about thee –
Some wine, ho!
CASSIO Fore God, this is a more exquisite song than the other.
IAGO Will you hear't again?
CASSIO No; for I hold him to be unworthy of his place that does those things. Well, God's above all; and there be souls must be saved, and there be souls must not be saved.
IAGO It's true, good Lieutenant.
CASSIO For mine own part – no offence to the General, nor any man of quality – I hope to be saved.
IAGO And so do I too, Lieutenant.
CASSIO Ay, but, by your leave, not before me; the Lieutenant is to be saved before the Ancient. Let's have no more of this; let's to our affairs. God forgive us our sins. Gentlemen, let's look to our business. Do not think, gentlemen, I am drunk. This is my ancient; this is my right hand, and this is my left hand. I am not drunk now; I can stand well enough, and I speak well enough.
ALL Excellent well.
CASSIO Why, very well, then. You must not think, then, that I am drunk. [*Exit.*
MONTANO To the platform, masters; come, let's set the watch.
IAGO You see this fellow that is gone before:
He is a soldier fit to stand by Caesar
And give direction; and do but see his vice;
'Tis to his virtue a just equinox,
The one as long as th' other. 'Tis pity of him.
I fear the trust Othello puts him in,
On some odd time of his infirmity,
Will shake this island.
MONTANO But is he often thus?
IAGO 'Tis evermore the prologue to his sleep:
He'll watch the horologe a double set,
If drink rock not his cradle.
MONTANO It were well
The General were put in mind of it.
Perhaps he sees it not, or his good nature
Prizes the virtue that appears in Cassio,
And looks not on his evils. Is not this true?

Enter RODERIGO.

IAGO [*Aside to him*] How, now, Roderigo!
I pray you, after the Lieutenant; go.
[*Exit Roderigo.*
MONTANO And 'tis great pity that the noble Moor
Should hazard such a place as his own second
With one of an ingraft infirmity:
It were an honest action to say
So to the Moor.
IAGO Not I, for this fair island;
I do love Cassio well; and would do much
To cure him of this evil.
[*Within*: Help, help!
But hark, what noise?

Re-enter CASSIO, driving in RODERIGO.

CASSIO Zounds, you rogue, you rascal!
MONTANO What's the matter, Lieutenant?
CASSIO A knave teach me my duty! But I'll beat the knave into a twiggen bottle.
RODERIGO Beat me!
CASSIO Dost thou prate, rogue? [*Strikes him.*
MONTANO Nay, good Lieutenant; I pray you, sir, hold your hand.
CASSIO Let me go, sir, or I'll knock you o'er the mazard.
MONTANO Come, come, you're drunk.
CASSIO Drunk! [*They fight.*
IAGO [*Aside to Roderigo*] Away, I say!
Go out and cry a mutiny. [*Exit Roderigo.*
Nay, good Lieutenant. God's will, gentlemen!
Help, ho! – Lieutenant – sir – Montano – sir –
Help, masters! Here's a goodly watch indeed!
[*A bell rung.*
Who's that which rings the bell? Diablo, ho!
The town will rise. God's will, Lieutenant, hold.
You'll be asham'd for ever.

Re-enter OTHELLO and Gentlemen, with weapons.

OTHELLO What is the matter here?
MONTANO Zounds, I bleed still; I am hurt to the death – He dies.
OTHELLO Hold, for your lives!
IAGO Hold, ho! Lieutenant – sir – Montano – gentlemen –
Have you forgot all sense of place and duty?
Hold! The General speaks to you; hold, hold, for shame!
OTHELLO Why, how now, ho! From whence ariseth this?
Are we turn'd Turks, and to ourselves do that
Which Heaven hath forbid the Ottomites?
For Christian shame, put by this barbarous brawl.
He that stirs next to carve for his own rage

Holds his soul light: he dies upon his motion.
Silence that dreadful bell; it frights the isle
From her propriety. What's the matter, masters?
Honest Iago, that looks dead with grieving,
Speak. Who began this? On thy love, I charge thee.

IAGO I do not know. Friends all but now, even now,
In quarter, and in terms, like bride and groom
Divesting them for bed; and then, but now,
As if some planet had unwitted men,
Swords out, and tilting one at other's breast
In opposition bloody. I cannot speak
Any beginning to this peevish odds;
And would in action glorious I had lost
These legs that brought me to a part of it!

OTHELLO How comes it, Michael, you are thus forgot?

CASSIO I pray you, pardon me; I cannot speak.

OTHELLO Worthy Montano, you were wont be civil;
The gravity and stillness of your youth
The world hath noted, and your name is great
In mouths of wisest censure – what's the matter
That you unlace your reputation thus,
And spend your rich opinion for the name
Of a night-brawler? Give me answer to't.

MONTANO Worthy Othello, I am hurt to danger;
Your officer Iago can inform you,
While I spare speech, which something now offends me,
Of all that I do know; nor know I aught
By me that's said or done amiss this night,
Unless self-charity be sometimes a vice,
And to defend ourselves it be a sin
When violence assails us.

OTHELLO Now, by heaven,
My blood begins my safer guides to rule;
And passion, having my best judgment collied,
Assays to lead the way. Zounds if I stir
Or do but lift this arm, the best of you
Shall sink in my rebuke. Give me to know
How this foul rout began, who set it on;
And he that is approv'd in this offence,
Though he had twinn'd with me, both at a birth,
Shall lose me. What! in a town of war,
Yet wild, the people's hearts brim full of fear,
To manage private and domestic quarrel,
In night, and on the court and guard of safety!
'Tis monstrous. Iago, who began't?

MONTANO If partially affin'd, or leagu'd in office,
Thou dost deliver more or less than truth,
Thou art no soldier.

IAGO Touch me not so near;
I had rather ha this tongue cut from my mouth
Than it should do offence to Michael Cassio;
Yet, I persuade myself, to speak the truth
Shall nothing wrong him. This it is, General.
Montano and myself being in speech,
There comes a fellow crying out for help,
And Cassio following him with determin'd sword
To execute upon him. Sir, this gentleman
Steps in to Cassio and entreats his pause;
Myself the crying fellow did pursue,
Lest by his clamour, as it so fell out,
The town might fall in fright; he, swift of foot,
Outran my purpose, and I return'd the rather
For that I heard the clink and fall of swords,
And Cassio high in oath; which till to-night
I ne'er might see before. When I came back,
For this was brief, I found them close together
At blow and thrust, even as again they were
When you yourself did part them.
More of this matter can I not report;
But men are men; the best sometimes forget.
Though Cassio did some little wrong to him,
As men in rage strike those that wish them best,
Yet surely Cassio, I believe, receiv'd
From him that fled some strange indignity
Which patience could not pass.

OTHELLO I know, Iago,
Thy honesty and love doth mince this matter,
Making it light to Cassio. Cassio, I love thee;
But never more be officer of mine.

Re-enter DESDEMONA, attended.

Look if my gentle love be not rais'd up.
I'll make thee an example.

DESDEMONA What is the matter, dear?

OTHELLO All's well now, sweeting;
Come away to bed. [*To Montano*] Sir, for your hurts,
Myself will be your surgeon. Lead him off.

[*Montano is led off.*

Iago, look with care about the town,
And silence those whom this vile brawl distracted.
Come, Desdemona; 'tis the soldiers' life
To have their balmy slumbers wak'd with strife.

[*Exeunt all but Iago and Cassio.*

IAGO What, are you hurt, Lieutenant?

CASSIO Ay, past all surgery.

IAGO Marry, God forbid!

CASSIO Reputation, reputation, reputation! O, I have lost my reputation! I have lost the immortal part of myself, and what remains is bestial. My reputation, Iago, my reputation!

IAGO As I am an honest man, I had thought you had receiv'd some bodily wound; there is more sense in that than in reputation. Reputation is an idle and most false imposition; oft got without merit, and lost without deserving. You have lost no reputation at all, unless you repute yourself such a loser. What, man! there are more ways to recover the General again; you are but now cast in his mood, a punishment more in policy than in malice; even so as one would beat his offenceless dog to affright an imperious lion. Sue to him again, and he's yours.

CASSIO I will rather sue to be despis'd than to deceive so good a commander with so slight, so drunken, and so indiscreet an officer. Drunk! And speak parrot! And squabble, swagger, swear! And discourse fustian with one's own shadow! O thou invisible spirit of wine, if thou hast no name to be known by, let us call thee devil!

IAGO What was he that you follow'd with your sword? What had he done to you?

CASSIO I know not.

IAGO Is't possible?

CASSIO I remember a mass of things, but nothing distinctly; a quarrel, but nothing wherefore. O God, that men should put an enemy in their mouths to steal away their brains! That we should with joy, pleasance, revel and applause, transform ourselves into beasts!

IAGO Why, but you are now well enough. How come you thus recovered?

CASSIO It hath pleas'd the devil drunkenness to give place to the devil wrath. One unperfectness shows me another, to make me frankly despise myself.

IAGO Come, you are too severe a moraller. As the time, the place, and the condition of this country stands, I could heartily wish this had not so befall'n; but since it is as it is, mend it for your own good.

CASSIO I will ask him for my place again: he shall tell me I am a drunkard. Had I as many mouths as Hydra, such an answer would stop them all. To be now a sensible man, by and by a fool, and presently a beast! O strange! Every inordinate cup is unblest, and the ingredience is a devil.

IAGO Come, come, good wine is a good familiar creature if it be well us'd; exclaim no more against it. And, good Lieutenant, I think you think I love you.

CASSIO I have well approv'd it, sir. I drunk!

IAGO You or any man living may be drunk at a time, man. I'll tell you what you shall do. Our General's wife is now the General – I may say so in this respect, for that he hath devoted and given up himself to the contemplation, mark, and denotement, of her parts and graces – confess yourself freely to her; importune her help to put you in your place again: she is of so free, so kind, so apt, so blessed a disposition, she holds it a vice in her goodness not to do more than she is requested. This broken joint between you and her husband entreat her to splinter; and, my fortunes against any lay worth naming, this crack of your love shall grow stronger than it was before.

CASSIO You advise me well.

IAGO I protest, in the sincerity of love and honest kindness.

CASSIO I think it freely; and betimes in the morning I will beseech the virtuous Desdemona to undertake for me. I am desperate of my fortunes if they check me here.

IAGO You are in the right. Good night, Lieutenant; I must to the watch.

CASSIO Good night, honest Iago. [*Exit.*

IAGO And what's he, then, that says I play the villain?
When this advice is free I give and honest,
Probal to thinking, and indeed the course
To win the Moor again? For 'tis most easy
The inclining Desdemona to subdue
In any honest suit: she's fram'd as fruitful
As the free elements. And then for her
To win the Moor – were't to renounce his baptism,
All seals and symbols of redeemed sin –
His soul is so enfetter'd to her love
That she may make, unmake, do what she list,
Even as her appetite shall play the god
With his weak function. How am I, then, a villain
To counsel Cassio to this parallel course,
Directly to his good? Divinity of hell!
When devils will their blackest sins put on,
They do suggest at first with heavenly shows,
As I do now; for whiles this honest fool
Plies Desdemona to repair his fortunes,
And she for him pleads strongly to the Moor,
I'll pour this pestilence into his ear –
That she repeals him for her body's lust;
And by how much she strives to do him good
She shall undo her credit with the Moor.
So will I turn her virtue into pitch;
And out of her own goodness make the net
That shall enmesh them all.

Enter RODERIGO.

How now, Roderigo!

RODERIGO I do follow here in the chase, not like a hound that hunts, but one that fills up the cry. My money is almost spent; I have been to-night exceedingly well cudgell'd; and I think the issue will be – I shall have so much experience for my pains as that comes to; and so, with no money at all, and a little more wit, return again to Venice.

IAGO How poor are they that have not patience!

What wound did ever heal but by degrees?
Thou know'st we work by wit, and not by witchcraft;
And wit depends on dilatory time.
Does't not go well? Cassio hath beaten thee,
And thou, by that small hurt, hast cashier'd Cassio.
Though other things grow fair against the sun,
Yet fruits that blossom first will first be ripe.
Content thyself awhile. By th' mass, 'tis morning!
Pleasure and action make the hours seem short.
Retire thee; go where thou art billeted.
Away, I say; thou shalt know more here-after.
Nay, get thee gone. [*Exit Roderigo.*
Two things are to be done:
My wife must move for Cassio to her mistress;
I'll set her on;
Myself awhile to draw the Moor apart
And bring him jump when he may Cassio find
Soliciting his wife. Ay, that's the way;
Dull not device by coldness and delay. [*Exit.*

ACT THREE

SCENE I. *Cyprus. Before the citadel.*

Enter CASSIO, with Musicians.

CASSIO Masters, play here; I will content your pains.
Something that's brief; and bid 'Good morrow, General'. [*Music.*

Enter Clown.

CLOWN Why masters, ha your instruments been in Naples, that they speak i' th' nose thus?

1 MUSICIAN How, sir, how?

CLOWN Are these, I pray, call'd wind instruments?

1 MUSICIAN Ay, marry, are they, sir.

CLOWN O, thereby hangs a tail.

1 MUSICIAN Whereby hangs a tale, sir?

CLOWN Marry, sir, by many a wind instrument that I know. But, masters, here's money for you; and the General so likes your music that he desires you, of all loves, to make no more noise with it.

1 MUSICIAN Well, sir, we will not.

CLOWN If you have any music that may not be heard, to't again; but, as they say, to hear music the General does not greatly care.

1 MUSICIAN We have none such, sir.

CLOWN Then put up your pipes in your bag, for I'll away. Go; vanish into air; away. [*Exeunt Musicians.*

CASSIO Dost thou hear, my honest friend?

CLOWN No, I hear not your honest friend; I hear you.

CASSIO Prithee keep up thy quillets. There's a poor piece of gold for thee. If the gentlewoman that attends the General's wife be stirring, tell her there's one Cassio entreats her a little favour of speech. Wilt thou do this?

CLOWN She is stirring, sir; if she will stir hither, I shall seem to notify unto her.

CASSIO Do, good my friend. [*Exit Clown.*

Enter IAGO.

In happy time, Iago.

IAGO You have not been abed, then?

CASSIO Why, no; the day had broke before we parted.
I have made bold, Iago,
To send in to your wife: my suit to her
Is that she will to virtuous Desdemona
Procure me some access.

IAGO I'll send her to you presently;
And I'll devise a mean to draw the Moor
Out of the way, that your converse and business
May be more free.

CASSIO I humbly thank you for't. [*Exit Iago*] I never knew
A Florentine more kind and honest.

Enter EMILIA.

EMILIA Good morrow, good Lieutenant. I am sorry
For your displeasure; but all will sure be well.
The General and his wife are talking of it;
And she speaks for you stoutly: the Moor replies
That he you hurt is of great fame in Cyprus
And great affinity, and that in wholesome wisdom
He might not but refuse you; but he protests he loves you,
And needs no other suitor but his likings
To take the safest occasion by the front
To bring you in again.

CASSIO Yet, I beseech you,
If you think fit, or that it may be done,
Give me advantage of some brief discourse
With Desdemona alone.

EMILIA Pray you come in.
I will bestow you where you shall have time
To speak your bosom freely.

CASSIO I am much bound to you.
[*Exeunt.*

SCENE II. *Cyprus. The citadel.*

Enter OTHELLO, IAGO, and Gentlemen.

OTHELLO These letters give, Iago, to the pilot;
And by him do my duties to the Senate.
That done, I will be walking on the works;
Repair there to me.

IAGO Well, my good lord, I'll do't.

OTHELLO This fortification, gentlemen – shall we see't?

GENTLEMAN We'll wait upon your lordship.

[*Exeunt.*

SCENE III. *Cyprus. The garden of the citadel.*

Enter DESDEMONA, CASSIO, and EMILIA.

DESDEMONA Be thou assur'd, good Cassio, I will do
All my abilities in thy behalf.

EMILIA Good madam, do. I warrant it grieves my husband
As if the case were his.

DESDEMONA O, that's an honest fellow. Do not doubt, Cassio,
But I will have my lord and you again
As friendly as you were.

CASSIO Bounteous madam,
Whatever shall become of Michael Cassio,
He's never any thing but your true servant.

DESDEMONA I know't – I thank you. You do love my lord;
You have known him long; and be you well assur'd
He shall in strangeness stand no farther off
Than in a politic distance.

CASSIO Ay, but, lady,
That policy may either last so long,
Or feed upon such nice and waterish diet,
Or breed itself so out of circumstances,
That, I being absent, and my place supplied,
My general will forget my love and service.

DESDEMONA Do not doubt that; before Emilia here
I give thee warrant of thy place. Assure thee,
If I do vow a friendship, I'll perform it
To the last article. My lord shall never rest;
I'll watch him tame, and talk him out of patience;
His bed shall seem a school, his board a shrift;
I'll intermingle everything he does
With Cassio's suit. Therefore be merry, Cassio;
For thy solicitor shall rather die
Than give thy cause away.

Enter OTHELLO and IAGO.

EMILIA Madam, here comes my lord.

CASSIO Madam, I'll take my leave.

DESDEMONA Why, stay, and hear me speak.

CASSIO Madam, not now. I am very ill at ease,
Unfit for mine own purposes.

DESDEMONA Well, do your discretion.

[*Exit Cassio.*

IAGO Ha! I like not that.

OTHFLLO What dost thou say?

IAGO Nothing, my lord; or if – I know not what.

OTHELLO Was not that Cassio parted from my wife?

IAGO Cassio, my lord! No, sure, I cannot think it,
That he would sneak away so guilty-like,
Seeing your coming.

OTHELLO I do believe 'twas he.

DESDEMONA How now, my lord!
I have been talking with a suitor here,
A man that languishes in your displeasure.

OTHELLO Who is't you mean?

DESDEMONA Why, your lieutenant, Cassio. Good my lord,
If I have any grace or power to move you,
His present reconciliation take;
For if he be not one that truly loves you,
That errs in ignorance, and not in cunning,
I have no judgment in an honest face.
I prithee call him back.

OTHELLO Went he hence now?

DESDEMONA Yes, faith; so humbled
That he hath left part of his grief with me
To suffer with him. Good love, call him back.

OTHELLO Not now, sweet Desdemona; some other time.

DESDEMONA But shall't be shortly?

OTHELLO The sooner, sweet, for you.

DESDEMONA Shall't be to-night at supper?

OTHELLO No, not to-night.

DESDEMONA To-morrow dinner, then?

OTHELLO I shall not dine at home;
I meet the captains at the citadel.

DESDEMONA Why, then, to-morrow night, or Tuesday morn,
On Tuesday noon or night, on Wednesday morn.
I prithee name the time; but let it not
Exceed three days. I'faith, he's penitent;
And yet his trespass, in our common reason –
Save that, they say, the wars must make example
Out of her best – is not almost a fault
T' incur a private check. When shall he come?
Tell me, Othello – I wonder in my soul
What you would ask me that I should deny,
Or stand so mamm'ring on. What! Michael Cassio,
That came a-wooing with you, and so many a time,

When I have spoke of you dispraisingly,
Hath ta'en your part – to have so much to do
To bring him in! By'r Lady, I could do much –

OTHELLO Prithee, no more; let him come when he will;
I will deny thee nothing.

DESDEMONA Why, this is not a boon;
'Tis as I should entreat you wear your gloves,
Or feed on nourishing dishes, or keep you warm,
Or sue to you to do a peculiar profit
To your own person. Nay, when I have a suit
Wherein I mean to touch your love indeed,
It shall be full of poise and difficult weight,
And fearful to be granted.

OTHELLO I will deny thee nothing.
Whereon I do beseech thee grant me this,
To leave me but a little to myself.

DESDEMONA Shall I deny you? No; farewell, my lord.

OTHELLO Farewell, my Desdemona. I'll come to thee straight.

DESDEMONA Emilia, come. – Be as your fancies teach you;
Whate'er you be, I am obedient.

[*Exeunt Desdemona and Emilia.*

OTHELLO Excellent wretch! Perdition catch my soul
But I do love thee; and when I love thee not
Chaos is come again.

IAGO My noble lord!

OTHELLO What dost thou say, Iago?

IAGO Did Michael Cassio, when you woo'd my lady,
Know of your love?

OTHELLO He did, from first to last. Why dost thou ask?

IAGO But for a satisfaction of my thought –
No further harm.

OTHELLO Why of thy thought, Iago?

IAGO I did not think he had been acquainted with her.

OTHELLO O, yes; and went between us very often.

IAGO Indeed!

OTHELLO Indeed? Ay, indeed. Discern'st thou aught in that?
Is he not honest?

IAGO Honest, my lord?

OTHELLO Honest? Ay, honest.

IAGO My lord, for aught I know.

OTHELLO What dost thou think?

IAGO Think, my lord?

OTHELLO Think, my lord! By heaven, he echoes me,
As if there were some monster in his thought
Too hideous to be shown. Thou dost mean something:
I heard thee say but now thou lik'st not that,
When Cassio left my wife. What didst not like?
And when I told thee he was of my counsel
In my whole course of wooing, thou criedst 'Indeed!'
And didst contract and purse thy brow together,
As if thou then hadst shut up in thy brain
Some horrible conceit. If thou dost love me,
Show me thy thought.

IAGO My lord, you know I love you.

OTHELLO I think thou dost;
And for I know thou art full of love and honesty,
And weigh'st thy words before thou giv'st them breath,
Therefore these stops of thine affright me the more;
For such things in a false disloyal knave
Are tricks of custom; but in a man that's just
They are close delations, working from the heart
That passion cannot rule.

IAGO For Michael Cassio,
I dare presume I think that he is honest.

OTHELLO I think so too.

IAGO Men should be that they seem;
Or those that be not, would they might seem none!

OTHELLO Certain, men should be what they seem.

IAGO Why then, I think Cassio's an honest man.

OTHELLO Nay, yet there's more in this.
I prithee speak to me as to thy thinkings,
As thou dost ruminate; and give thy worst of thoughts
The worst of words.

IAGO Good my lord, pardon me.
Though I am bound to every act of duty,
I am not bound to that all slaves are free to –
Utter my thoughts. Why, say they are vile and false,
As where's that palace whereinto foul things
Sometimes intrude not? Who has that breast so pure
But some uncleanly apprehensions
Keep leets and law-days, and in sessions sit
With meditations lawful?

OTHELLO Thou dost conspire against thy friend, Iago,
If thou but think'st him wrong'd, and mak'st his ear
A stranger to thy thoughts.

IAGO I do beseech you,
Though I perchance am vicious in my guess,
As, I confess, it is my nature's plague
To spy into abuses, and oft my jealousy
Shapes faults that are not – that your wisdom

From one that so imperfectly conjects,
Would take no notice; nor build yourself a trouble.
Out of his scattering and unsure observance.
It were not for your quiet nor your good,
Nor for my manhood, honesty, or wisdom,
To let you know my thoughts.

OTHELLO Zounds! What dost thou mean?

IAGO Good name in man and woman, dear my lord,
Is the immediate jewel of their souls:
Who steals my purse steals trash; 'tis something, nothing;
'Twas mine, 'tis his, and has been slave to thousands;
But he that filches from me my good name
Robs me of that which not enriches him
And makes me poor indeed.

OTHELLO By heaven, I'll know thy thoughts.

IAGO You cannot, if my heart were in your hand;
Nor shall not, whilst 'tis in my custody.

OTHELLO Ha!

IAGO O, beware, my lord, of jealousy;
It is the green-ey'd monster which doth mock
The meat it feeds on. That cuckold lives in bliss
Who, certain of his fate, loves not his wronger;
But, O, what damned minutes tells he o'er
Who dotes, yet doubts, suspects, yet strongly loves!

OTHELLO O misery!

IAGO Poor and content is rich, and rich enough;
But riches fineless is as poor as winter
To him that ever fears he shall be poor.
Good God, the souls of all my tribe defend
From jealousy!

OTHELLO Why, why is this?
Think'st thou I'd make a life of jealousy,
To follow still the changes of the moon
With fresh suspicions? No; to be once in doubt
Is once to be resolv'd. Exchange me for a goat
When I shall turn the business of my soul
To such exsufflicate and blown surmises
Matching thy inference. 'Tis not to make me jealous
To say my wife is fair, feeds well, loves company,
Is free of speech, sings, plays, and dances well;
Where virtue is, these are more virtuous.
Nor from mine own weak merits will I draw
The smallest fear or doubt of her revolt;
For she had eyes, and chose me. No, Iago;
I'll see before I doubt; when I doubt, prove;
And, on the proof, there is no more but this –
Away at once with love or jealousy!

IAGO I am glad of this; for now I shall have reason
To show the love and duty that I bear you
With franker spirit. Therefore, as I am bound,
Receive it from me. I speak not yet of proof.
Look to your wife; observe her well with Cassio;
Wear your eyes thus, not jealous nor secure.
I would not have your free and noble nature
Out of self-bounty be abus'd; look to't.
I know our country disposition well:
In Venice they do let God see the pranks
They dare not show their husbands; their best conscience
Is not to leave't undone, but keep't unknown.

OTHELLO Dost thou say so?

IAGO She did deceive her father, marrying you;
And when she seem'd to shake and fear your looks,
She lov'd them most.

OTHELLO And so she did.

IAGO Why, go to then!
She that, so young, could give out such a seeming,
To seel her father's eyes up close as oak –
He thought 'twas witchcraft. But I am much to blame;
I humbly do beseech you of your pardon
For too much loving you.

OTHELLO I am bound to thee for ever.

IAGO I see this hath a little dash'd your spirits.

OTHELLO Not a jot, not a jot.

IAGO I'faith, I fear it has.
I hope you will consider what is spoke
Comes from my love; but I do see you are mov'd.
I am to pray you not to strain my speech
To grosser issues nor to larger reach
Than to suspicion.

OTHELLO I will not.

IAGO Should you do so, my lord,
My speech should fall into such vile success
Which my thoughts aim'd not. Cassio's my worthy friend –
My lord, I see you are mov'd.

OTHELLO No, not much mov'd.
I do not think but Desdemona's honest.

IAGO Long live she so! and long live you to think so!

OTHELLO And yet, how nature erring from itself –

IAGO Ay, there's the point: as – to be bold with you –
Not to affect many proposed matches
Of her own clime, complexion, and degree,
Whereto we see in all things nature tends –
Foh! one may smell in such a will most rank,
Foul disproportion, thoughts unnatural.
But pardon me – I do not in position
Distinctly speak of her; though I may fear
Her will, recoiling to her better judgment,

May fall to match you with her country forms,
And happily repent.
OTHELLO Farewell, farewell.
If more thou dost perceive, let me know more;
Set on thy wife to observe. Leave me, Iago.
IAGO My lord, I take my leave. [*Going.*
OTHELLO Why did I marry? This honest creature doubtless
Sees and knows more – much more than he unfolds.
IAGO [*Returning*] My lord, I would I might entreat your honour
To scan this thing no further; leave it to time.
Although 'tis fit that Cassio have his place,
For, sure, he fills it up with great ability,
Yet if you please to hold him off awhile,
You shall by that perceive him and his means.
Note if your lady strain his entertainment
With any strong or vehement importunity;
Much will be seen in that. In the mean time
Let me be thought too busy in my fears –
As worthy cause I have to fear I am –
And hold her free, I do beseech your honour.
OTHELLO Fear not my government.
IAGO I once more take my leave. [*Exit.*
OTHELLO This fellow's of exceeding honesty,
And knows all qualities, with a learned spirit,
Of human dealing. If I do prove her haggard,
Though that her jesses were my dear heart-strings,
I'd whistle her off and let her down the wind
To prey at fortune. Haply, for I am black
And have not those soft parts of conversation
That chamberers have, or for I am declin'd
Into the vale of years – yet that's not much –
She's gone; I am abus'd; and my relief
Must be to loathe her. O curse of marriage,
That we can call these delicate creatures ours,
And not their appetites! I had rather be a toad,
And live upon the vapour of a dungeon,
Than keep a corner in the thing I love
For others' uses. Yet 'tis the plague of great ones;
Prerogativ'd are they less than the base;
'Tis destiny unshunnable, like death:
Even then this forked plague is fated to us
When we do quicken. Look where she comes.

Re-enter DESDEMONA and EMILIA.

If she be false, O, then heaven mocks itself!
I'll not believe it.
DESDEMONA How now, my dear Othello?
Your dinner, and the generous islanders
By you invited, do attend your presence.
OTHELLO I am to blame.
DESDEMONA Why do you speak so faintly?
Are you not well?
OTHELLO I have a pain upon my forehead here.
DESDEMONA Faith, that's with watching; 'twill away again.
Let me but bind it hard, within this hour
It will be well.
[*He puts the handkerchief from him, and she drops it.*
OTHELLO Your napkin is too little.
Let it alone. Come, I'll go in with you.
DESDEMONA I am very sorry that you are not well.
[*Exeunt Othello and Desdemona.*
EMILIA I am glad I have found this napkin.
This was her first remembrance from the Moor.
My wayward husband hath a hundred times
Woo'd me to steal it; but she so loves the token –
For he conjur'd her she should ever keep it –
That she reserves it evermore about her
To kiss and talk to. I'll ha the work ta'en out,
And give't Iago. What he'll do with it
Heaven knows, not I;
I nothing but to please his fantasy.

Re-enter IAGO.

IAGO How now! What do you here alone?
EMILIA Do not you chide; I have a thing for you.
IAGO You have a thing for me?
It is a common thing!
EMILIA Ha!
IAGO To have a foolish wife.
EMILIA O, is that all? What will you give me now
For that same handkerchief?
IAGO What handkerchief?
EMILIA What handkerchief!
Why that the Moor first gave to Desdemona;
That which so often you did bid me steal.
IAGO Hast stole it from her?
EMILIA No, faith; she let it drop by negligence,
And to the advantage, I, being here, took't up.
Look, here it is.
IAGO A good wench! Give it me.
EMILIA What will you do with't, that you have been so earnest
To have me filch it?
IAGO Why, what's that to you?
[*Snatching it.*
EMILIA If it be not for some purpose of import,
Give me't again. Poor lady, she'll run mad
When she shall lack it.
IAGO Be not acknown on't; I have use for it.
Go, leave me.
[*Exit Emilia.*
I will in Cassio's lodging lose this napkin,
And let him find it. Trifles light as air
Are to the jealous confirmations strong

As proofs of holy writ; this may do something.
The Moor already changes with my poison.
Dangerous conceits are in their natures poisons
Which at the first are scarce found to distaste
But, with a little act upon the blood,
Burn like the mines of sulphur.

Re-enter OTHELLO.

I did say so.
Look where he comes! Not poppy, nor mandragora,
Nor all the drowsy syrups of the world,
Shall ever medicine thee to that sweet sleep
Which thou owed'st yesterday.

OTHELLO Ha! ha! false to me, to me?

IAGO Why, how now, General? No more of that.

OTHELLO Avaunt! be gone! Thou hast set me on the rack.
I swear 'tis better to be much abus'd
Than but to know 't a little.

IAGO How now, my lord!

OTHELLO What sense had I in her stol'n hours of lust?
I saw 't not, thought it not, it harm'd not me.
I slept the next night well, fed well, was free and merry;
I found not Cassio's kisses on her lips.
He that is robb'd, not wanting what is stol'n,
Let him not know't, and he's not robb'd at all.

IAGO I am sorry to hear this.

OTHELLO I had been happy if the general camp,
Pioneers and all, had tasted her sweet body,
So I had nothing known. O, now for ever
Farewell the tranquil mind! farewell content!
Farewell the plumed troops, and the big wars
That makes ambition virtue! O, farewell!
Farewell the neighing steed and the shrill trump,
The spirit-stirring drum, th' ear-piercing fife,
The royal banner, and all quality,
Pride, pomp, and circumstance, of glorious war!
And O ye mortal engines whose rude throats
Th' immortal Jove's dread clamours counterfeit,
Farewell! Othello's occupation's gone.

IAGO Is't possible, my lord?

OTHELLO Villain, be sure thou prove my love a whore – [*Taking him by the throat.*
Be sure of it; give me the ocular proof;
Or, by the worth of man's eternal soul,
Thou hadst been better have been born a dog
Than answer my wak'd wrath.

IAGO Is't come to this?

OTHELLO Make me to see't; or, at the least, so prove it
That the probation bear no hinge nor loop
To hang a doubt on; or woe upon thy life!

IAGO My noble lord –

OTHELLO If thou dost slander her and torture me,
Never pray more; abandon all remorse;
On horror's head horrors accumulate;
Do deeds to make heaven weep, all earth amaz'd;
For nothing canst thou to damnation add
Greater than that.

IAGO O grace! O heaven forgive me!
Are you a man? Have you a soul or sense? –
God buy you; take mine office. O wretched fool,
That liv'st to make thine honesty a vice!
O monstrous world! Take note, take note, O world,
To be direct and honest is not safe.
I thank you for this profit; and from hence
I'll love no friend, sith love breeds such offence.

OTHELLO Nay, stay. Thou shouldst be honest.

IAGO I should be wise; for honesty's a fool,
And loses that it works for.

OTHELLO By the world,
I think my wife be honest, and think she is not;
I think that thou art just, and think thou art not.
I'll have some proof. Her name, that was as fresh
As Dian's visage, is now begrim'd and black
As mine own face. If there be cords or knives,
Poison, or fire, or suffocating streams,
I'll not endure it. Would I were satisfied!

IAGO I see, sir, you are eaten up with passion;
I do repent me that I put it to you.
You would be satisfied?

OTHELLO Would! Nay, and I will.

IAGO And may; but how – how satisfied, my lord?
Would you, the supervisor, grossly gape on –
Behold her topp'd?

OTHELLO Death and damnation! O!

IAGO It were a tedious difficulty, I think,
To bring them to that prospect. Damn them, then,
If ever mortal eyes do see them bolster
More than their own! What then? How then?
What shall I say? Where's satisfaction?
It is impossible you should see this,
Were they as prime as goats, as hot as monkeys,
As salt as wolves in pride, and fools as gross
As ignorance made drunk. But yet, I say,
If imputation and strong circumstances
Which lead directly to the door of truth
Will give you satisfaction, you might have't.

OTHELLO Give me a living reason she's disloyal.

IAGO I do not like the office;
But, sith I am enter'd in this cause so far,
Prick'd to't by foolish honesty and love,
I will go on. I lay with Cassio lately,
And, being troubled with a raging tooth,

I could not sleep.
There are a kind of men so loose of soul
That in their sleeps will mutter their affairs:
One of this kind is Cassio.
In sleep I heard him say 'Sweet Desdemona,
Let us be wary, let us hide our loves',
And then, sir, would he gripe and wring my hand,
Cry 'O sweet creature!' then kiss me hard,
As if he pluck'd up kisses by the roots,
That grew upon my lips – then laid his leg
Over my thigh – and sigh'd, and kiss'd, and then
Cried 'Cursed fate that gave thee to the Moor!'

OTHELLO O monstrous! monstrous!

IAGO Nay, this was but his dream.

OTHELLO But this denoted a foregone conclusion.

IAGO 'Tis a shrewd doubt, though it be but a dream,
And this may help to thicken other proofs
That do demonstrate thinly.

OTHELLO I'll tear her all to pieces.

IAGO Nay, but be wise; yet we see nothing done;
She may be honest yet. Tell me but this:
Have you not sometimes seen a handkerchief
Spotted with strawberries in your wife's hand?

OTHELLO I gave her such a one; 'twas my first gift.

IAGO I know not that; but such a handkerchief –
I am sure it was your wife's – did I to-day
See Cassio wipe his beard with.

OTHELLO If it be that –

IAGO If it be that, or any that was hers,
It speaks against her with the other proofs.

OTHELLO O that the slave had forty thousand lives!
One is too poor, too weak for my revenge.
Now do I see 'tis true. Look here, Iago –
All my fond love thus do I blow to heaven.
'Tis gone.
Arise, black vengeance, from the hollow hell.
Yield up, O love, thy crown and hearted throne
To tyrannous hate! Swell, bosom, with thy fraught,
For 'tis of aspics' tongues.

IAGO Yet be content.

OTHELLO O, blood, blood, blood!

IAGO Patience, I say; your mind perhaps may change.

OTHELLO Never, Iago. Like to the Pontic sea,
Whose icy current and compulsive course
Ne'er feels retiring ebb, but keeps due on
To the Propontic and the Hellespont;
Even so my bloody thoughts, with violent pace,
Shall ne'er look back, ne'er ebb to humble love,
Till that a capable and wide revenge
Swallow them up. [*He kneels*] Now, by yond marble heaven,
In the due reverence of a sacred vow
I here engage my words.

IAGO [*Kneeling*] Do not rise yet.
Witness, you ever-burning lights above,
You elements that clip us round about,
Witness that here Iago doth give up
The execution of his wit, hands, heart,
To wrong'd Othello's service! Let him command,
And to obey shall be in me remorse,
What bloody business ever. [*They rise.*

OTHELLO I greet thy love,
Not with vain thanks, but with acceptance bounteous,
And will upon the instant put thee to't.
Within these three days let me hear thee say
That Cassio's not alive.

IAGO My friend is dead;
'Tis done at your request. But let her live.

OTHELLO Damn her, lewd minx! O, damn her, damn her!
Come, go with me apart; I will withdraw
To furnish me with some swift means of death
For the fair devil. Now art thou my lieutenant.

IAGO I am your own for ever. [*Exeunt.*

SCENE IV. *Cyprus. Before the citadel.*

Enter DESDEMONA, EMILIA, and Clown.

DESDEMONA Do you know, sirrah, where the Lieutenant Cassio lies?

CLOWN I dare not say he lies anywhere.

DESDEMONA Why, man?

CLOWN He's a soldier; and for one to say a soldier lies, 'tis stabbing.

DESDEMONA Go to. Where lodges he?

CLOWN To tell you where he lodges is to tell you where I lie.

DESDEMONA Can anything be made of this?

CLOWN I know not where he lodges; and for me to devise a lodging, and say he lies here or he lies there, were to lie in mine own throat.

DESDEMONA Can you inquire him out, and be edified by report?

CLOWN I will catechize the world for him; that is, make questions, and by them answer.

DESDEMONA Seek him; bid him come hither: tell him I have mov'd my lord on his behalf, and hope all will be well.

CLOWN To do this is within the compass of man's wit; and therefore I will attempt the doing it. [*Exit.*

DESDEMONA Where should I lose the handkerchief, Emilia?

EMILIA I know not, madam.

DESDEMONA Believe me, I had rather lose my purse
Full of crusadoes; and but my noble Moor
Is true of mind, and made of no such baseness
As jealous creatures are, it were enough
To put him to ill thinking.
EMILIA Is he not jealous?
DESDEMONA Who, he? I think the sun where he was born
Drew all such humours from him.

Enter OTHELLO.

EMILIA Look where he comes.
DESDEMONA I will not leave him now till Cassio
Be call'd to him. How is't with you, my lord?
OTHELLO Well, my good lady. [*Aside*] O, hardness to dissemble! –
How do you, Desdemona?
DESDEMONA Well, my good lord.
OTHELLO Give me your hand. This hand is moist, my lady.
DESDEMONA It yet hath felt no age nor known no sorrow.
OTHELLO This argues fruitfulness and liberal heart:
Hot, hot, and moist. This hand of yours requires
A sequester from liberty, fasting and prayer,
Much castigation, exercise devout;
For here's a young and sweating devil here
That commonly rebels. 'Tis a good hand,
A frank one.
DESDEMONA You may indeed say so;
For 'twas that hand that gave away my heart.
OTHELLO A liberal hand. The hearts of old gave hands;
But our new heraldry is hands, not hearts.
DESDEMONA I cannot speak of this. Come now, your promise.
OTHELLO What promise, chuck?
DESDEMONA I have sent to bid Cassio come speak with you.
OTHELLO I have a salt and sorry rheum offends me;
Lend me thy handkerchief.
DESDEMONA Here, my lord.
OTHELLO That which I gave you.
DESDEMONA I have it not about me.
OTHELLO Not?
DESDEMONA No, faith, my lord.
OTHELLO That's a fault. That handkerchief
Did an Egyptian to my mother give.
She was a charmer, and could almost read
The thoughts of people; she told her, while she kept it,
'Twould make her amiable, and subdue my father
Entirely to her love; but if she lost it,
Or made a gift of it, my father's eye
Should hold her loathely, and his spirits should hunt
After new fancies. She, dying, gave it me,
And bid me, when my fate would have me wive,
To give it her. I did so; and take heed on't;
Make it a darling like your precious eye;
To lose't or give't away were such perdition
As nothing else could match.
DESDEMONA Is't possible?
OTHELLO 'Tis true. There's magic in the web of it.
A sibyl that had numb'red in the world
The sun to course two hundred compasses
In her prophetic fury sew'd the work;
The worms were hallowed that did breed the silk;
And it was dy'd in mummy which the skilful
Conserv'd of maidens' hearts.
DESDEMONA I'faith! Is't true?
OTHELLO Most veritable; therefore look to't well.
DESDEMONA Then would to God that I had never seen't!
OTHELLO Ha! Wherefore?
DESDEMONA Why do you speak so startingly and rash?
OTHELLO Is't lost? Is't gone? Speak. Is 't out o' th' way?
DESDEMONA Heaven bless us!
OTHELLO Say you?
DESDEMONA It is not lost; but what an if it were?
OTHELLO How!
DESDEMONA I say it is not lost.
OTHELLO Fetch't, let me see't.
DESDEMONA Why, so I can, sir, but I will not now.
This is a trick to put me from my suit:
Pray you let Cassio be receiv'd again.
OTHELLO Fetch me the handkerchief: my mind misgives.
DESDEMONA Come, come;
You'll never meet a more sufficient man.
OTHELLO The handkerchief!
DESDEMONA I pray talk me of Cassio.
OTHELLO The handkerchief!
DESDEMONA A man that all his time
Hath founded his good fortunes on your love,
Shar'd dangers with you –
OTHELLO The handkerchief!
DESDEMONA I'faith, you are to blame.
OTHELLO Zounds! [*Exit Othello.*
EMILIA Is not this man jealous?
DESDEMONA I ne'er saw this before.
Sure there's some wonder in this handkerchief;
I am most unhappy in the loss of it.
EMILIA 'Tis not a year or two shows us a man.
They are all but stomachs, and we all but food;
They eat us hungerly, and when they are full,

They belch us.

Enter CASSIO and IAGO.

Look you, Cassio and my husband.

IAGO There is no other way; 'tis she must do 't.
And, lo, the happiness! Go and importune her.

DESDEMONA How now, good Cassio, what's the news with you?

CASSIO Madam, my former suit. I do beseech you
That by your virtuous means I may again
Exist, and be a member of his love
Whom I, with all the office of my heart,
Entirely honour. I would not be delay'd.
If my offence be of such mortal kind
That nor my service past, nor present sorrows,
Nor purpos'd merit in futurity,
Can ransom me into his love again,
But to know so must be my benefit;
So shall I clothe me in a forc'd content,
And shut myself up in some other course,
To fortune's alms.

DESDEMONA Alas, thrice-gentle Cassio!
My advocation is not now in tune;
My lord is not my lord; nor should I know him,
Were he in favour as in humour alter'd.
So help me every spirit sanctified,
As I have spoken for you all my best,
And stood within the blank of his displeasure
For my free speech! You must awhile be patient.
What I can do I will; and more I will
Than for myself I dare; let that suffice you.

IAGO Is my lord angry?

EMILIA He went hence but now,
And certainly in strange unquietness.

IAGO Can he be angry? I have seen the cannon
When it hath blown his ranks into the air,
And, like the devil, from his very arm
Puff'd his own brother – and is he angry?
Something of moment, then. I will go meet him.
There's matter in't indeed, if he be angry.

DESDEMONA I prithee do so. *[Exit Iago.*
Something sure of state
Either from Venice, or some unhatch'd practice
Made demonstrable here in Cyprus to him,
Hath puddled his clear spirit; and in such cases
Men's natures wrangle with inferior things,
Though great ones are their object. 'Tis even so;
For let our finger ache, and it endues
Our other healthful members even to a sense
Of pain. Nay, we must think, men are not gods,
Nor of them look for such observancy
As fits the bridal. Beshrew me much, Emilia,
I was – unhandsome warrior as I am –
Arraigning his unkindness with my soul;
But now I find I had suborn'd the witness,
And he's indicted falsely.

EMILIA Pray heaven it be state matters, as you think,
And no conception nor no jealous toy
Concerning you.

DESDEMONA Alas the day, I never gave him cause!

EMILIA But jealous souls will not be answer'd so;
They are not ever jealous for the cause,
But jealous for they are jealous. 'Tis a monster
Begot upon it self, born on it self.

DESDEMONA Heaven keep that monster from Othello's mind!

EMILIA Lady, amen.

DESDEMONA I will go seek him. Cassio, walk hereabout.
If I do find him fit, I'll move your suit,
And seek to effect it to my uttermost.

CASSIO I humbly thank your ladyship.
[Exeunt Desdemona and Emilia.

Enter BIANCA.

BIANCA Save you, friend Cassio!

CASSIO What make you from home?
How is it with you, my most fair Bianca?
I' faith, sweet love, I was coming to your house.

BIANCA And I was going to your lodging, Cassio.
What, keep a week away? seven days and nights?
Eightscore eight hours? and lovers' absent hours,
More tedious than the dial eight score times?
O weary reckoning!

CASSIO Pardon me, Bianca.
I have this while with leaden thoughts been press'd;
But I shall in a more continuate time
Strike off this score of absence. Sweet Bianca,
[Giving her Desdemona's handkerchief.
Take me this work out.

BIANCA O Cassio, whence came this?
This is some token from a newer friend:
To the felt absence now I feel a cause.
Is't come to this? Well, well.

CASSIO Go to, woman!
Throw your vile guesses in the devil's teeth,
From whence you have them. You are jealous now
That this is from some mistress, some remembrance.
No, by my faith, Bianca.

BIANCA Why, whose is it?

CASSIO I know not neither; I found it in my chamber.
I like the work well; ere it be demanded –

As like enough it will – I would have it copied.
Take it, and do't; and leave me for this time.
BIANCA Leave you! Wherefore?
CASSIO I do attend here on the General;
And think it no addition, nor my wish,
To have him see me woman'd.
BIANCA Why, I pray you?
CASSIO Not that I love you not.
BIANCA But that you do not love me.
I pray you bring me on the way a little;
And say if I shall see you soon at night.
CASSIO 'Tis but a little way that I can bring you,
For I attend here; but I'll see you soon.
BIANCA 'Tis very good; I must be circumstanc'd.
[*Exeunt.*

ACT FOUR

SCENE I. *Cyprus. Before the citadel.*

Enter OTHELLO and IAGO.

IAGO Will you think so?
OTHELLO Think so, Iago?
IAGO What,
To kiss in private?
OTHELLO An unauthoriz'd kiss.
IAGO Or to be naked with her friend abed
An hour or more, not meaning any harm?
OTHELLO Naked abed, Iago, and not mean harm!
It is hypocrisy against the devil.
They that mean virtuously and yet do so,
The devil their virtue tempts, and they tempt heaven.
IAGO So they do nothing, 'tis a venial slip;
But if I give my wife a handkerchief –
OTHELLO What then?
IAGO Why, then 'tis hers, my lord; and, being hers,
She may, I think, bestow't on any man.
OTHELLO She is protectress of her honour too:
May she give that?
IAGO Her honour is an essence that's not seen;
They have it very oft that have it not.
But, for the handkerchief –
OTHELLO By heaven, I would most gladly have forgot it.
Thou said'st – O, it comes o'er my memory
As doth the raven o'er the infected house,
Boding to all – he had my handkerchief.
IAGO Ay, what of that?
OTHELLO That's not so good now.
IAGO What
If I had said I had seen him do you wrong?
Or heard him say – as knaves be such abroad,
Who having, by their own importunate suit,
Or voluntary dotage of some mistress,
Convinced or supplied them, cannot choose
But they must blab –
OTHELLO Hath he said anything?
IAGO He hath, my lord; but be you well assur'd,
No more than he'll unswear.
OTHELLO What hath he said?
IAGO Faith, that he did – I know not what he did.
OTHELLO What? what?
IAGO Lie –
OTHELLO With her?
IAGO With her, on her; what you will.
OTHELLO Lie with her – lie on her? We say lie on her when they belie her. Lie with her. Zounds, that's fulsome. Handkerchief – confessions – handkerchief! To confess, and be hang'd for his labour – first, to be hang'd, and then to confess. I tremble at it. Nature would not invest herself in such shadowing passion without some instruction. It is not words that shakes me thus – pish! – noses, ears, and lips. Is't possible? Confess! Handkerchief! O devil!
[*Falls in a trance.*
IAGO Work on,
My medicine, work. Thus credulous fools are caught;
And many worthy and chaste dames even thus,
All guiltless, meet reproach. What, ho! my lord!
My lord, I say! Othello!

Enter CASSIO.

How now, Cassio!
CASSIO What's the matter?
IAGO My lord is fall'n into an epilepsy.
This is his second fit; he had one yesterday.
CASSIO Rub him about the temples.
IAGO No, forbear.
The lethargy must have his quiet course;
If not, he foams at mouth, and by and by
Breaks out to savage madness. Look, he stirs.
Do you withdraw yourself a little while;
He will recover straight; when he is gone,
I would on great occasion speak with you.
[*Exit Cassio.*
How is it, General? Have you not hurt your head?
OTHELLO Dost thou mock me?
IAGO I mock you? No, by heaven!
Would you would bear your fortune like a man!
OTHELLO A horned man's a monster and a beast.

IAGO There's many a beast then in a populous city,
And many a civil monster.
OTHELLO Did he confess it?
IAGO Good sir, be a man;
Think every bearded fellow that's but yok'd
May draw with you; there's millions now alive
That nightly lie in those unproper beds
Which they dare swear peculiar: your case is better.
O, 'tis the spite of hell, the fiend's arch-mock,
To lip a wanton in a secure couch,
And to suppose her chaste! No, let me know;
And knowing what I am, I know what she shall be.
OTHELLO O, thou art wise; 'tis certain.
IAGO Stand you awhile apart.
Confine yourself but in a patient list.
Whilst you were here o'erwhelmed with your grief –
A passion most unsuiting such a man –
Cassio came hither; I shifted him away,
And laid good 'scuse upon your ecstasy;
Bade him anon return, and here speak with me;
The which he promis'd. Do but encave yourself,
And mark the fleers, the gibes, and notable scorns,
That dwell in every region of his face;
For I will make him tell the tale anew –
Where, how, how oft, how long ago, and when,
He hath, and is again to cope your wife.
I say, but mark his gesture. Marry, patience;
Or I shall say you are all in all in spleen,
And nothing of a man.
OTHELLO Dost thou hear, Iago?
I will be found most cunning in my patience;
But – dost thou hear? – most bloody.
IAGO That's not amiss;
But yet keep time in all. Will you withdraw?
[*Othello withdraws.*
Now will I question Cassio of Bianca,
A huswife that by selling her desires
Buys herself bread and clothes; it is a creature
That dotes on Cassio, as 'tis the strumpet's plague
To beguile many and be beguil'd by one.
He, when he hears of her, cannot restrain
From the excess of laughter.

Re-enter CASSIO.

Here he comes.
As he shall smile Othello shall go mad;
And his unbookish jealousy must construe
Poor Cassio's smiles, gestures, and light behaviours,
Quite in the wrong. How do you now, Lieutenant?
CASSIO The worser that you give me the addition
Whose want even kills me.
IAGO Ply Desdemona well, and you are sure on't.
Now, if this suit lay in Bianca's dower,
How quickly should you speed!
CASSIO Alas, poor caitiff!
OTHELLO Look how he laughs already!
IAGO I never knew a woman love man so.
CASSIO Alas, poor rogue! I think, i' faith, she loves me.
OTHELLO Now he denies it faintly, and laughs it out.
IAGO Do you hear, Cassio?
OTHELLO Now he importunes him
To tell it o'er. Go to; well said, well said.
IAGO She gives it out that you shall marry her.
Do you intend it?
CASSIO Ha, ha, ha!
OTHELLO Do you triumph, Roman? Do you triumph?
CASSIO I marry her! What, a customer! I prithee bear some charity to my wit; do not think it so unwholesome. Ha, ha, ha!
OTHELLO So, so, so, so – they laugh that wins.
IAGO Faith, the cry goes that you marry her.
CASSIO Prithee say true.
IAGO I am a very villain else.
OTHELLO Ha you scor'd me? Well.
CASSIO This is the monkey's own giving out: she is persuaded I will marry her, out of her own love and flattery, not out of my promise.
OTHELLO Iago beckons me; now he begins the story.
CASSIO She was here even now; she haunts me in every place. I was t'other day talking on the sea-bank with certain Venetians, and thither comes the bauble – by this hand, she falls me thus about my neck.
OTHELLO Crying 'O dear Cassio!' as it were: his gesture imports it.
CASSIO So hangs, and lolls, and weeps upon me; so hales, and pulls me. Ha, ha, ha!
OTHELLO Now he tells how she pluck'd him to my chamber. O, I see that nose of yours, but not that dog I shall throw't to.
CASSIO Well, I must leave her company.

Enter BIANCA.

IAGO Before me! Look where she comes.
CASSIO 'Tis such another fitchew! marry, a perfum'd one. What do you mean by this haunting of me?
BIANCA Let the devil and his dam haunt you. What did you mean by that same handkerchief you gave me even now? I was a fine fool to take it. I must take out the whole work – a likely piece of work that you should find it in your

chamber and know not who left it there! This is some minx's token, and I must take out the work? There – give it your hobby-horse. Wheresoever you had it, I'll take out no work on't.

CASSIO How now, my sweet Bianca! how now! how now!

OTHELLO By heaven, that should be my handkerchief!

BIANCA An you'll come to supper to-night, you may; an you will not, come when you are next prepar'd for. *[Exit.*

IAGO After her, after her.

CASSIO Faith, I must; she'll rail i' th' street else.

IAGO Will you sup there?

CASSIO Faith, I intend so.

IAGO Well, I may chance to see you; for I would very fain speak with you.

CASSIO Prithee come; will you?

IAGO Go to; say no more. *[Exit Cassio.*

OTHELLO *[Coming forward]* How shall I murder him, Iago?

IAGO Did you perceive how he laugh'd at his vice?

OTHELLO O Iago!

IAGO And did you see the handkerchief?

OTHELLO Was that mine?

IAGO Yours, by this hand. And to see how he prizes the foolish woman your wife! She gave it him, and he hath giv'n it his whore.

OTHELLO I would have him nine years a-killing. A fine woman! a fair woman! a sweet woman!

IAGO Nay, you must forget that.

OTHELLO Ay, let her rot, and perish, and be damn'd to-night; for she shall not live. No, my heart is turn'd to stone; I strike it, and it hurts my hand. O, the world hath not a sweeter creature; she might lie by an emperor's side and command him tasks.

IAGO Nay, that's not your way.

OTHELLO Hang her! I do but say what she is: so delicate with her needle, an admirable musician – O, she will sing the savageness out of a bear! – of so high and plenteous wit and invention.

IAGO She's the worse for all this.

OTHELLO O, a thousand, a thousand times – and then of so gentle a condition.

IAGO Ay, too gentle.

OTHELLO Nay, that's certain. But yet the pity of it, Iago! O, Iago, the pity of it, Iago!

IAGO If you be so fond over her iniquity, give her patent to offend; for, if it touch not you, it comes near nobody.

OTHELLO I will chop her into messes. Cuckold me!

IAGO O, 'tis foul in her.

OTHELLO With mine officer!

IAGO That's fouler.

OTHELLO Get me some poison, Iago – this night. I'll not expostulate with her, lest her body and beauty unprovide my mind again – this night, Iago.

IAGO Do it not with poison; strangle her in her bed, even the bed she hath contaminated.

OTHELLO Good, good; the justice of it pleases; very good.

IAGO And for Cassio – let me be his undertaker.
You shall hear more by midnight.

OTHELLO Excellent good. *[A trumpet.*
What trumpet is that same?

IAGO I warrant, something from Venice.

Enter LODOVICO, DESDEMONA, and Attendants.

'Tis Lodovico – this comes from the Duke.
See, your wife's with him.

LODOVICO God save thee, worthy General!

OTHELLO With all my heart, sir.

LODOVICO The Duke and Senators of Venice greet you. *[Gives him a packet.*

OTHELLO I kiss the instrument of their pleasures. *[Opens the packet and reads.*

DESDEMONA And what's the news, good cousin Lodovico?

IAGO I am very glad to see you, signior;
Welcome to Cyprus.

LODOVICO I thank you. How does Lieutenant Cassio?

IAGO Lives, sir.

DESDEMONA Cousin, there's fall'n between him and my lord
An unkind breach; but you shall make all well.

OTHELLO Are you sure of that?

DESDEMONA My lord?

OTHELLO *[Reads]* 'This fail you not to do as you will' –

LODOVICO He did not call; he's busy in the paper.
Is there division 'twixt thy lord and Cassio?

DESDEMONA A most unhappy one. I would do much
T' atone them, for the love I bear to Cassio.

OTHELLO Fire and brimstone!

DESDEMONA My lord?

OTHELLO Are you wise?

DESDEMONA What, is he angry?

LODOVICO May be the letter mov'd him;
For, as I think, they do command him home,
Deputing Cassio in his government.

DESDEMONA By my troth, I am glad on't.

OTHELLO Indeed!

DESDEMONA My lord?

OTHELLO I am glad to see you mad.

DESDEMONA Why, sweet Othello?
OTHELLO Devil! *[Striking her.*
DESDEMONA I have not deserv'd this.
LODOVICO My lord, this would not be believ'd in Venice,
Though I should swear I saw't. 'Tis very much.
Make her amends; she weeps.
OTHELLO O devil, devil!
If that the earth could teem with woman's tears,
Each drop she falls would prove a crocodile.
Out of my sight!
DESDEMONA I will not stay to offend you. *[Going.*
LODOVICO Truly, an obedient lady.
I do beseech your lordship, call her back.
OTHELLO Mistress!
DESDEMONA My lord?
OTHELLO What would you with her, sir?
LODOVICO Who, I, my lord?
OTHELLO Ay; you did wish that I would make her turn.
Sir, she can turn, and turn, and yet go on,
And turn again; and she can weep, sir, weep;
And she's obedient, as you say, obedient,
Very obedient. – Proceed you in your tears. –
Concerning this, sir, – O, well-painted passion! –
I am commanded home. – Get you away;
I'll send for you anon. – Sir, I obey the mandate,
And will return to Venice. – Hence, avaunt!
[Exit Desdemona.
Cassio shall have my place. And, sir, to-night,
I do entreat that we may sup together.
You are welcome, sir, to Cyprus. – Goats and monkeys! *[Exit.*
LODOVICO Is this the noble Moor whom our full Senate
Call all in all sufficient? Is this the nature
Whom passion could not shake, whose solid virtue
The shot of accident nor dart of chance
Could neither graze nor pierce?
IAGO He is much chang'd.
LODOVICO Are his wits safe? Is he not light of brain?
IAGO He's that he is. I may not breathe my censure.
What he might be, if what he might he is not,
I would to heaven he were!
LODOVICO What, strike his wife!
IAGO Faith, that was not so well; yet would I knew
That stroke would prove the worst!
LODOVICO Is it his use?
Or did the letters work upon his blood,
And new-create this fault?
IAGO Alas, alas!
It is not honesty in me to speak
What I have seen and known. You shall observe him;
And his own courses will denote him so
That I may save my speech. Do but go after,
And mark how he continues.
LODOVICO I am sorry that I am deceiv'd in him.
[Exeunt.

SCENE II. *Cyprus. The citadel.*

Enter OTHELLO and EMILIA.

OTHELLO You have seen nothing, then?
EMILIA Nor ever heard, nor ever did suspect.
OTHELLO Yes, you have seen Cassio and she together.
EMILIA But then I saw no harm, and then I heard
Each syllable that breath made up between them.
OTHELLO What, did they never whisper?
EMILIA Never, my lord.
OTHELLO Nor send you out o' th' way?
EMILIA Never.
OTHELLO To fetch her fan, her gloves, her mask, nor nothing?
EMILIA Never, my lord.
OTHELLO That's strange.
EMILIA I durst, my lord, to wager she is honest,
Lay down my soul at stake. If you think other,
Remove your thought – it doth abuse your bosom.
If any wretch have put this in your head,
Let heaven requite it with the serpent's curse;
For if she be not honest, chaste, and true,
There's no man happy; the purest of their wives
Is foul as slander.
OTHELLO Bid her come hither. Go.
[Exit Emilia.
She says enough; yet she's a simple bawd
That cannot say as much. This is a subtle whore,
A closet-lock-and-key of villainous secrets;
And yet she'll kneel and pray; I have seen her do't.

Re-enter EMILIA with DESDEMONA.

DESDEMONA My lord, what is your will?
OTHELLO Pray you chuck, come hither.
DESDEMONA What is your pleasure?
OTHELLO Let me see your eyes; look in my face.
DESDEMONA What horrible fancy's this?
OTHELLO *[To Emilia]* Some of your function, mistress:
Leave procreants alone, and shut the door;

Cough, or cry hem, if any body come.
Your mystery, your mystery; nay, dispatch.
[*Exit Emilia.*

DESDEMONA Upon my knees, what doth your speech import?
I understand a fury in your words,
But not the words.

OTHELLO Why, what art thou?

DESDEMONA You wife, my lord; your true and loyal wife.

OTHELLO Come, swear it, damn thyself; lest, being like one of heaven, the devils themselves should fear to seize thee; therefore be double-damn'd – swear thou art honest.

DESDEMONA Heaven doth truly know it.

OTHELLO Heaven truly knows that thou art false as hell.

DESDEMONA To whom, my lord? With whom? How am I false?

OTHELLO Ah, Desdemona! away! away! away!

DESDEMONA Alas the heavy day! Why do you weep?
Am I the motive of these tears, my lord?
If haply you my father do suspect
An instrument of this your calling back,
Lay not your blame on me; If you have lost him,
Why, I have lost him too.

OTHELLO Had it pleas'd heaven
To try me with affliction; had they rain'd
All kind of sores and shames on my bare head,
Steep'd me in poverty to the very lips,
Given to captivity me and my utmost hopes,
I should have found in some place of my soul
A drop of patience; but, alas, to make me
The fixed figure for the time of scorn
To point his slow unmoving finger at! – O, O!
Yet could I bear that too; well, very well;
But there, where I have garner'd up my heart,
Where either I must live or bear no life,
The fountain from the which my current runs,
Or else dries up – to be discarded thence!
Or keep it as a cistern for foul toads
To knot and gender in! Turn thy complexion there,
Patience, thou young and rose-lipp'd cherubin –
Ay, here, look grim as hell.

DESDEMONA I hope my noble lord esteems me honest.

OTHELLO O, ay; as summer flies are in the shambles,
That quicken even with blowing. O thou weed
Who art so lovely fair and smell'st so sweet
That the sense aches at thee!
Would thou had'st never been born!

DESDEMONA Alas, what ignorant sin have I committed?

OTHELLO Was this fair paper, this most goodly book,
Made to write 'whore' upon? What committed!
Committed! O thou public commoner!
I should make very forges of my cheeks
That would to cinders burn up modesty,
Did I but speak thy deeds. What committed!
Heaven stops the nose at it, and the moon winks;
The bawdy wind, that kisses all it meets,
Is hush'd within the hollow mine of earth
And will not hear it. What committed!
Impudent strumpet!

DESDEMONA By heaven, you do me wrong.

OTHELLO Are not you a strumpet?

DESDEMONA No, as I am a Christian.
If to preserve this vessel for my lord
From any other foul unlawful touch
Be not to be a strumpet, I am none.

OTHELLO What, not a whore?

DESDEMONA No, as I shall be sav'd.

OTHELLO Is't possible?

DESDEMONA O, heaven forgive us!

OTHELLO I cry you mercy, then.
I took you for that cunning whore of Venice
That married with Othello. – You, mistress,
That have the office opposite to Saint Peter
And keeps the gate of hell!

Re-enter EMILIA.

You, you, ay you!
We ha done our course; there's money for your pains.
I pray you turn the key, and keep our counsel.
[*Exit.*

EMILIA Alas, what does this gentleman conceive?
How do you, madam? How do you, my good lady?

DESDEMONA Faith, half asleep.

EMILIA Good madam, what's the matter with my lord?

DESDEMONA With who?

EMILIA Why, with my lord, madam.

DESDEMONA Who is thy lord?

EMILIA He that is yours, sweet lady.

DESDEMONA I have none. Do not talk to me, Emilia;
I cannot weep, nor answers have I none
But what should go by water. Prithee, to-night
Lay on my bed my wedding sheets – remember;
And call thy husband hither.

EMILIA Here's a change indeed! [*Exit.*

DESDEMONA 'Tis meet I should be us'd so, very meet.
How have I been behav'd, that he might stick
The small'st opinion on my great'st abuse?

Re-enter EMILIA with IAGO.

IAGO What is your pleasure, madam? How is't with you?
DESDEMONA I cannot tell. Those that do teach young babes
Do it with gentle means and easy tasks.
He might have chid me so; for, in good faith,
I am a child to chiding.
IAGO What is the matter, lady?
EMILIA Alas, Iago, my lord hath so bewhor'd her,
Thrown such despite and heavy terms upon her
That true hearts cannot bear it.
DESDEMONA Am I that name, Iago?
IAGO What name, fair lady?
DESDEMONA Such as she says my lord did say I was.
EMILIA He call'd her whore: A beggar in his drink
Could not have laid such terms upon his callat.
IAGO Why did he so?
DESDEMONA I do not know; I am sure I am none such.
IAGO Do not weep, do not weep. Alas, the day!
EMILIA Hath she forsook so many noble matches,
Her father, and her country, and her friends,
To be call'd whore? Would it not make one weep?
DESDEMONA It is my wretched fortune.
IAGO Beshrew him for't!
How comes this trick upon him?
DESDEMONA Nay, heaven doth know.
EMILIA I will be hang'd if some eternal villain,
Some busy and insinuating rogue,
Some cogging, cozening slave, to get some office,
Have not devis'd this slander; I'll be hang'd else.
IAGO Fie, there is no such man; it is impossible.
DESDEMONA If any such there be, heaven pardon him!
EMILIA A halter pardon him! and hell gnaw his bones!
Why should he call her whore? Who keeps her company?
What place, what time, what form, what likelihood?
The Moor's abus'd by some outrageous knave,
Some base notorious knave, some scurvy fellow.
O heaven, that such companions thou'dst unfold,
And put in every honest hand a whip
To lash the rascals naked through the world
Even from the east to the west!
IAGO Speak within door.
EMILIA O, fie upon them! Some such squire he was
That turn'd your wit the seamy side without
And made you to suspect me with the Moor.
IAGO You are a fool; go to.
DESDEMONA O God! Iago,
What shall I do to win my lord again?
Good friend, go to him; for, by this light of heaven,
I know not how I lost him. Here I kneel.
If e'er my will did trespass 'gainst his love,
Either in discourse of thought or actual deed,
Or that mine eyes, mine ears, or any sense,
Delighted them in any other form,
Or that I do not yet, and ever did,
And ever will – though he do shake me off
To beggarly divorcement – love him dearly,
Comfort forswear me! Unkindness may do much;
And his unkindness may defeat my life,
But never taint my love. I cannot say 'whore';
It does abhor me now I speak the word;
To do the act that might the addition earn,
Not the world's mass of vanity could make me.
IAGO I pray you be content; 'tis but his humour.
The business of the state does him offence,
And he does chide with you.
DESDEMONA If 'twere no other!
IAGO It is but so, I warrant.

[*Trumpets within.*

Hark how these instruments summon you to supper.
The messengers of Venice stay the meat.
Go in, and weep not; all things shall be well.

[*Exeunt Desdemona and Emilia.*

Enter RODERIGO.

How now, Roderigo!

RODERIGO I do not find that thou deal'st justly with me.

IAGO What in the contrary?

RODERIGO Every day thou daff'st me with some device, Iago; and rather, as it seems to me now, keep'st from me all conveniency than suppliest me with the least advantage of hope. I will indeed, no longer endure it; nor am I yet persuaded to put up in peace what already I have foolishly suffer'd.

IAGO Will you hear me, Roderigo?

RODERIGO Faith, I have heard too much; for your words and performances are no kin together.

IAGO You charge me most unjustly.

RODERIGO With nought but truth. I have wasted myself out of my means. The jewels you have had from me to deliver to Desdemona would half have corrupted a votarist. You have told me she hath receiv'd them, and return'd me expectations and comforts of sudden respect and acquaintance; but I find none.

IAGO Well; go to; very well.

RODERIGO Very well! go to! I cannot go to, man, nor 'tis not very well; by this hand, I say 'tis very scurvy, and begin to find myself fopt in it.

IAGO Very well.

RODERIGO I tell you 'tis not very well. I will make myself known to Desdemona. If she will return me my jewels, I will give over my suit and repent my unlawful solicitation; if not, assure yourself I will seek satisfaction of you.

IAGO You have said now.

RODERIGO Ay, and said nothing but what I protest intendment of doing.

IAGO Why, now I see there's mettle in thee; and even from this instant do build on thee a better opinion than ever before. Give me thy hand, Roderigo. Thou hast taken against me a most just exception; but yet, I protest, I have dealt most directly in thy affair.

RODERIGO It hath not appear'd.

IAGO I grant, indeed, it hath not appear'd; and your suspicion is not without wit and judgment. But, Roderigo, if thou hast that in thee indeed, which I have greater reason to believe now than ever – I mean purpose, courage, and valour – this night show it; if thou the next night following enjoy not Desdemona, take me from this world with treachery, and devise engines for my life.

RODERIGO Well, what is it? Is it within reason and compass?

IAGO Sir, there is especial commission come from Venice to depute Cassio in Othello's place.

RODERIGO Is that true? Why, then Othello and Desdemona return again to Venice.

IAGO O, no; he goes into Mauritania, and taketh away with him the fair Desdemona, unless his abode be linger'd here by some accident; wherein none can be so determinate as the removing of Cassio.

RODERIGO How do you mean removing of him?

IAGO Why, by making him uncapable of Othello's place – knocking out his brains.

RODERIGO And that you would have me to do?

IAGO Ay, an if you dare do yourself a profit and right. He sups to-night with a harlotry, and thither will I go to him – he knows not yet of his honourable fortune. If you will watch his going thence, which I will fashion to fall out between twelve and one, you may take him at your pleasure. I will be near to second your attempt, and he shall fall between us. Come, stand not amaz'd at it, but go along with me; I will show you such a necessity in his death that you shall think yourself bound to put it on him. It is now high supper-time, and the night grows to waste. About it.

RODERIGO I will hear further reason for this.

IAGO And you shall be satisfied. [*Exeunt.*

SCENE III. *Cyprus. The citadel.*

Enter OTHELLO, DESDEMONA, LODOVICO, EMILIA, and Attendants.

LODOVICO I do beseech you, sir, trouble yourself no further.

OTHELLO O, pardon me; 'twill do me good to walk.

LODOVICO Madam, good night; I humbly thank your ladyship.

DESDEMONA Your honour is most welcome.

OTHELLO Will you walk, sir? O, Desdemona!

DESDEMONA My lord?

OTHELLO Get you to bed on th' instant; I will be return'd forthwith. Dispatch your attendant there. Look 't be done.

DESDEMONA I will, my lord.

[*Exeunt Othello, Lodovico, and Attendants.*

EMILIA How goes it now? He looks gentler than he did.

DESDEMONA He says he will return incontinent.
He hath commanded me to go to bed,
And bade me to dismiss you.

EMILIA Dismiss me!

DESDEMONA It was his bidding; therefore, good Emilia,
Give me my nightly wearing, and adieu.
We must not now displease him.

EMILIA I would you had never seen him.

DESDEMONA So would not I: my love doth so approve him
That even his stubbornness, his checks, his frowns –
Prithee unpin me – have grace and favour in them.

EMILIA I have laid those sheets you bade me on the bed.

DESDEMONA All's one. Good faith, how foolish are our minds!
If I do die before thee, prithee shroud me
In one of these same sheets.

EMILIA Come, come, you talk.

DESDEMONA My mother had a maid call'd Barbary:
She was in love; and he she lov'd prov'd mad,
And did forsake her. She had a song of 'willow';
An old thing 'twas, but it express'd her fortune,
And she died singing it. That song to-night
Will not go from my mind; I have much to do
But to go hang my head all at one side
And sing it like poor Barbary. Prithee dispatch.

EMILIA Shall I go fetch your night-gown?

DESDEMONA No, unpin me here.
This Lodovico is a proper man.

EMILIA A very handsome man.

DESDEMONA He speaks well.
EMILIA I know a lady in Venice would have walk'd barefoot to Palestine for a touch of his nether lip.
DESDEMONA [*Sings*] The poor soul sat sighing by a sycamore tree,
Sing all a green willow;
Her hand on her bosom, her head on her knee.
Sing willow, willow, willow.
The fresh streams ran by her, and murmur'd her moans;
Sing willow, willow, willow;
Her salt tears fell from her and soft'ned the stones;
Sing willow –
Lay by these –
willow, willow. –
Prithee, hie thee; he'll come anon. –
Sing all a green willow must be my garland.
Let nobody blame him; his scorn I approve –
Nay, that's not next. Hark! who is't that knocks?
EMILIA It is the wind.
DESDEMONA [*Sings*] I call'd my love false love; but what said he then?
Sing willow, willow, willow:
If I court moe women, you'll couch with moe men –
So, get thee gone; good night. Mine eyes do itch;
Doth that bode weeping?
EMILIA 'Tis neither here nor there.
DESDEMONA I have heard it said so. O, these men, these men!
Dost thou in conscience think – tell me, Emilia –
That there be women do abuse their husbands
In such gross kind?
EMILIA There be some such, no question.
DESDEMONA Wouldst thou do such a deed for all the world?
EMILIA Why, would not you?
DESDEMONA No, by this heavenly light!
EMILIA Nor I neither by this heavenly light;
I might do't as well i' th' dark.
DESDEMONA Wouldst thou do such a deed for all the world?
EMILIA The world's a huge thing. It is a great price for a small vice.
DESDEMONA Good troth, I think thou wouldst not.
EMILIA By my troth, I think I should; and undo't when I had done it. Marry, I would not do such a thing for a joint-ring, nor for measures of lawn, nor for gowns, petticoats, nor caps, nor any petty exhibition; but for all the whole world – ud's pity, who would not make her husband a cuckold to make him a monarch? I should venture purgatory for't.
DESDEMONA Beshrew me, if I would do such a wrong for the whole world.
EMILIA Why, the wrong is but a wrong i' th' world; and having the world for your labour, 'tis a wrong in your own world, and you might quickly make it right.
DESDEMONA I do not think there is any such woman.
EMILIA Yes, a dozen; and as many to th' vantage as would store the world they play'd for.
But I do think it is their husbands' faults
If wives do fall. Say that they slack their duties,
And pour our treasures into foreign laps;
Or else break out in peevish jealousies,
Throwing restraint upon us; or say they strike us,
Or scant our former having in despite;
Why, we have galls; and though we have some grace,
Yet have we some revenge. Let husbands know
Their wives have sense like them; they see and smell,
And have their palates both for sweet and sour
As husbands have. What is it that they do
When they change us for others? Is it sport?
I think it is. And doth affection breed it?
I think it doth. Is't frailty that thus errs?
It is so too. And have not we affections,
Desires for sport, and frailty, as men have?
Then let them use us well; else let them know
The ills we do their ills instruct us so.
DESDEMONA Good night, good night. God me such uses send,
Not to pick bad from bad, but by bad mend!
[*Exeunt.*

ACT FIVE

SCENE I. *Cyprus. A street.*

Enter IAGO and RODERIGO.

IAGO Here, stand behind this bulk; straight will he come.
Wear thy good rapier bare, and put it home.
Quick, quick; fear nothing; I'll be at thy elbow.
It makes us or it mars us; think on that,
And fix most firm thy resolution.
RODERIGO Be near at hand; I may miscarry in't.
IAGO Here, at thy hand. Be bold, and take thy stand.
[*Withdraws.*

RODERIGO I have no great devotion to the deed;
And yet he hath given me satisfying reasons –
'Tis but a man gone. Forth, my sword; he dies.

IAGO I have rubb'd this young quat almost to the sense,
And he grows angry. Now, whether he kill Cassio
Or Cassio him, or each do kill the other,
Every way makes my gain. Live Roderigo,
He calls me to a restitution large
Of gold and jewels that I bobb'd from him
As gifts to Desdemona;
It must not be. If Cassio do remain,
He hath a daily beauty in his life
That makes me ugly; and besides, the Moor
May unfold me to him; there stand I in much peril.
No, he must die. Be 't so. I hear him coming.

Enter CASSIO.

RODERIGO I know his gait, 'tis he. Villain, thou diest! [*Thrusts at Cassio.*

CASSIO That thrust had been mine enemy indeed
But that my coat is better than thou know'st.
I will make proof of thine. [*Draws, and wounds Roderigo.*

RODERIGO O, I am slain! [*Iago stabs Cassio from behind in the leg, and exit.*

CASSIO I am maim'd for ever. Help, ho! murder! murder! [*Falls.*

Enter OTHELLO at a distance.

OTHELLO The voice of Cassio. Iago keeps his word.

RODERIGO O, villain that I am!

OTHELLO It is even so.

CASSIO O, help, ho! light! a surgeon!

OTHELLO 'Tis he. O brave Iago, honest and just,
That hast such noble sense of thy friend's wrong!
Thou teachest me – minion, your dear lies dead,
And your unblest fate hies. Strumpet, I come.
Forth of my heart those charms, thine eyes, are blotted;
Thy bed, lust-stain'd, shall with lust's blood be spotted. [*Exit.*

Enter LODOVICO and GRATIANO at a distance.

CASSIO What, ho! No watch? No passage? Murder! murder!

GRATIANO 'Tis some mischance; the voice is very direful.

CASSIO O, help!

LODOVICO Hark!

RODERIGO O wretched villain!

LODOVICO Two or three groan. 'Tis heavy night;
These may be counterfeits; let's think't unsafe
To come in to the cry without more help.

RODERIGO Nobody come? Then shall I bleed to death.

Re-enter IAGO with a light.

LODOVICO Hark!

GRATIANO Here's one comes in his shirt, with light and weapons.

IAGO Who's there? Whose noise is this that cries on murder?

LODOVICO We do not know.

IAGO Did not you hear a cry?

CASSIO Here, here! For heaven's sake, help me!

IAGO What's the matter?

GRATIANO This is Othello's ancient, as I take it.

LODOVICO The same indeed; a very valiant fellow.

IAGO What are you here that cry so grievously?

CASSIO Iago? O, I am spoil'd, undone by villains!
Give me some help.

IAGO O me, Lieutenant! What villains have done this?

CASSIO I think that one of them is hereabout,
And cannot make away.

IAGO O treacherous villains! –
[*To Lodovico and Gratiano*] What are you there? Come in, and give some help.

RODERIGO O, help me there!

CASSIO That's one of them.

IAGO O murd'rous slave! O villian! [*Stabs Roderigo.*

RODERIGO O damn'd Iago! O inhuman dog!

IAGO Kill men i' th' dark! Where be these bloody thieves?
How silent is this town. Ho! murder! murder!
What may you be? Are you of good or evil?

LODOVICO As you shall prove us, praise us.

IAGO Signior Lodovico?

LODOVICO He, sir.

IAGO I cry you mercy. Here's Cassio hurt by villains.

GRATIANO Cassio!

IAGO How is't, brother?

CASSIO My leg is cut in two.

IAGO Marry, heaven forbid!
Light, gentlemen. I'll bind it with my shirt.

Enter BIANCA.

BIANCA What is the matter, ho? Who is't that cried?

IAGO Who is't that cried!

BIANCA O my dear Cassio!
My sweet Cassio! O Cassio, Cassio, Cassio!

IAGO O notable strumpet. Cassio, may you suspect
Who they should be that have thus mangled you?

CASSIO No.
GRATIANO I am sorry to find you thus; I have been to seek you.
IAGO Lend me a garter. So.
O, for a chair, to bear him easily hence!
BIANCA Alas, he faints! O Cassio, Cassio, Cassio!
IAGO Gentlemen all, I do suspect this trash
To be a party in this injury.
Patience awhile, good Cassio. Come, come;
Lend me a light. Know we this face or no?
Alas, my friend and my dear countryman
Roderigo? No – yes, sure; O heaven! Roderigo.
GRATIANO What, of Venice?
IAGO Even he, sir; did you know him?
GRATIANO Know him! Ay.
IAGO Signior Gratiano? I cry your gentle pardon;
These bloody accidents must excuse my manners,
That so neglected you.
GRATIANO I am glad to see you.
IAGO How do you, Cassio? – O, a chair, a chair!
GRATIANO Roderigo!
IAGO He, he, 'tis he. *[A chair brought in.*
O, that's well said; the chair.
Some good man bear him carefully from hence;
I'll fetch the General's surgeon. *[To Bianca]* For you, mistress,
Save you your labour. – He that lies slain here, Cassio,
Was my dear friend. What malice was between you?
CASSIO None in the world; nor do I know the man.
IAGO *[To Bianca]* What, look you pale? – O, bear him out o' th' air.
[Cassio and Roderigo are borne off.
Stay you, good gentlemen. – Look you pale, mistress? –
Do you perceive the gastness of her eye? –
Nay, an you stare, we shall hear more anon. –
Behold her well; I pray you look upon her.
Do you see, gentlemen? Nay, guiltiness will speak
Though tongues were out of use.

Enter EMILIA.

EMILIA 'Las, what's the matter? What's the matter, husband?
IAGO Cassio hath here been set on in the dark
By Roderigo and fellows that are 'scap'd.
He's almost slain, and Roderigo quite dead.
EMILIA Alas, good gentleman! Alas, good Cassio!
IAGO This is the fruits of whoring. Prithee, Emilia,
Go know of Cassio where he supp'd to-night. –
What, do you shake at that?
BIANCA He supp'd at my house; but I therefore shake not.
IAGO O, did he so? I charge you go with me.
EMILIA Fie, fie upon thee, strumpet!
BIANCA I am no strumpet, but of life as honest
As you that thus abuse me.
EMILIA As I! Foh! Fie upon thee!
IAGO Kind gentlemen, let's go see poor Cassio dress'd. –
Come, mistress, you must tell's another tale.
Emilia, run you to the citadel,
And tell my lord and lady what hath happ'd.
Will you go on afore? *[Aside]* This is the night
That either makes me or fordoes me quite.
[Exeunt.

SCENE II. *Cyprus. The citadel.*

DESDEMONA in her bed. Enter OTHELLO with a light.

OTHELLO It is the cause, it is the cause, my soul –
Let me not name it to you, you chaste stars –
It is the cause. Yet I'll not shed her blood,
Nor scar that whiter skin of hers than snow,
And smooth as monumental alabaster.
Yet she must die, else she'll betray more men.
Put out the light, and then put out the light.
If I quench thee, thou flaming minister,
I can again thy former light restore,
Should I repent me; but once put out thy light,
Thou cunning'st pattern of excelling nature,
I know not where is that Promethean heat
That can thy light relume. When I have pluck'd thy rose,
I cannot give it vital growth again;
It needs must wither. I'll smell thee on the tree.
[Kissing her.
O balmy breath, that dost almost persuade
Justice to break her sword! One more, one more.
Be thus when thou art dead, and I will kill thee,
And love thee after. One more, and that's the last:
So sweet was ne'er so fatal. I must weep,
But they are cruel tears. This sorrow's heavenly;
It strikes where it doth love. She wakes.
DESDEMONA Who's there? Othello?
OTHELLO Ay, Desdemona.
DESDEMONA Will you come to bed, my lord?
OTHELLO Have you pray'd to-night, Desdemona?
DESDEMONA Ay, my lord.
OTHELLO If you bethink yourself of any crime
Unreconcil'd as yet to heaven and grace,
Solicit for it straight.
DESDEMONA Alack, my lord,
What may you mean by that?

OTHELLO Well, do it, and be brief; I will walk by.
I would not kill thy unprepared spirit;
No, heaven forfend! – I would not kill thy soul.
DESDEMONA Talk you of killing?
OTHELLO Ay, I do.
DESDEMONA Then heaven
Have mercy on me!
OTHELLO Amen, with all my heart!
DESDEMONA If you say so, I hope you will not kill me.
OTHELLO Humh!
DESDEMONA And yet I fear you; for you're fatal then
When your eyes roll so. Why I should fear I know not,
Since guiltiness I know not; but yet I feel I fear.
OTHELLO Think on thy sins.
DESDEMONA They are loves I bear to you.
OTHELLO Ay, and for that thou diest.
DESDEMONA That death's unnatural that kills for loving.
Alas, why gnaw you so your nether lip?
Some bloody passion shakes your very frame.
These are portents; but yet I hope, I hope,
They do not point on me.
OTHELLO Peace, and be still.
DESDEMONA I will so. What's the matter?
OTHELLO That handkerchief which I so lov'd and gave thee
Thou gav'st to Cassio.
DESDEMONA No, by my life and soul!
Send for the man and ask him.
OTHELLO Sweet soul, take heed,
Take heed of perjury; thou art on thy death-bed.
DESDEMONA Ay, but not yet to die.
OTHELLO Yes, presently.
Therefore confess thee freely of thy sin;
For to deny each article with oath
Cannot remove nor choke the strong conception
That I do groan withal. Thou art to die.
DESDEMONA Then, Lord have mercy on me!
OTHELLO I say, amen.
DESDEMONA And have you mercy too! I never did
Offend you in my life; never lov'd Cassio
But with such general warranty of heaven
As I might love. I never gave him token.
OTHELLO By heaven, I saw my handkerchief in's hand.
O perjur'd woman! thou dost stone my heart,
And mak'st me call what I intend to do
A murder, which I thought a sacrifice.
I saw the handkerchief.
DESDEMONA He found it, then;
I never gave it him. Send for him hither;
Let him confess a truth.
OTHELLO He hath confess'd.
DESDEMONA What, my lord?
OTHELLO That he hath – ud's death! – us'd thee.
DESDEMONA How? unlawfully?
OTHELLO Ay.
DESDEMONA He will not say so.
OTHELLO No, his mouth is stopp'd;
Honest Iago hath ta'en order for't.
DESDEMONA O, my fear interprets! What, is he dead?
OTHELLO Had all his hairs been lives, my great revenge
Had stomach for them all.
DESDEMONA Alas, he is betray'd, and I undone!
OTHELLO Out, strumpet! Weep'st thou for him to my face?
DESDEMONA O, banish me, my lord, but kill me not!
OTHELLO Down, strumpet.
DESDEMONA Kill me to-morrow; let me live to-night.
OTHELLO Nay, an you strive –
DESDEMONA But half an hour!
OTHELLO Being done, there is no pause.
DESDEMONA But while I say one prayer!
OTHELLO It is too late. [*Smothers her.*
DESDEMONA O lord, Lord, Lord!
EMILIA [*Within*] My lord, my lord! what, ho! my lord, my lord!
OTHELLO What voice is this? Not dead? not yet quite dead?
I that am cruel am yet merciful;
I would not have thee linger in thy pain.
So, so.
EMILIA [*Within*] What, ho! my lord, my lord!
OTHELLO Who's there?
EMILIA [*Within*] O, good my lord, I'd speak a word with you!
OTHELLO Yes – 'tis Emilia – by and by. She's dead.
'Tis like she comes to speak of Cassio's death;
The noise was high. Ha! no more moving?
Still as the grave. Shall she come in? Were't good?
I think she stirs again. No. What's the best?
If she come in she'll sure speak to my wife.
My wife! my wife! what wife? I have no wife.
O insupportable! O heavy hour!
Methinks it should be now a huge eclipse
Of sun and moon, and that th' affrighted globe
Did yawn at alteration.
EMILIA [*Within*] I do beseech you that I may speak with you. O good my lord!
OTHELLO I had forgot thee: O, come in, Emilia.

Soft, by and by. Let me the curtains draw.
Where art thou? *[Unlocks the door.*

Enter EMILIA.

What's the matter with thee now?
EMILIA O, my good lord, yonder's foul murders done!
OTHELLO What, now?
EMILIA But now, my lord.
OTHELLO It is the very error of the moon;
She comes more nearer earth than she was wont,
And makes men mad.
EMILIA Cassio, my lord, hath kill'd a young Venetian
Call'd Roderigo.
OTHELLO Roderigo kill'd!
And Cassio kill'd!
EMILIA No, Cassio, is not kill'd.
OTHELLO Not Cassio kill'd! Then murder's out of tune,
And sweet revenge grows harsh.
DESDEMONA O, falsely, falsely murder'd!
EMILIA O Lord, what cry is that?
OTHELLO That! what?
EMILIA Out and alas! that was my lady's voice.
Help! help, ho! help! O lady, speak again!
Sweet Desdemona! O sweet mistress, speak!
DESDEMONA A guiltless death I die.
EMILIA O, who hath done this deed?
DESDEMONA Nobody. I myself. Farewell.
Commend me to my kind lord. O, farewell!
[She dies.
OTHELLO Why, how should she be murd'red?
EMILIA Alas, who knows?
OTHELLO You heard her say herself it was not I.
EMILIA She said so. I must needs report a truth.
OTHELLO She's like a liar gone to burning hell:
'Twas I that kill'd her.
EMILIA O, the more angel she,
And you the blacker devil!
OTHELLO She turn'd to folly, and she was a whore.
EMILIA Thou dost belie her, and thou art a devil.
OTHELLO She was false as water.
EMILIA Thou art rash as fire to say
That she was false. O, she was heavenly true!
OTHELLO Cassio did top her; ask thy husband else.
O, I were damn'd beneath all depth in hell
But that I did proceed upon just grounds
To this extremity. Thy husband knew it all.
EMILIA My husband!
OTHELLO Thy husband.
EMILIA That she was false to wedlock?
OTHELLO Ay, with Cassio. Nay, had she been true,
If heaven would make me such another world
Of one entire and perfect chrysolite,
I'd not have sold her for it.
EMILIA My husband!
OTHELLO Ay, 'twas he that told me on her first.
An honest man he is, and hates the slime
That sticks on filthy deeds.
EMILIA My husband!
OTHELLO What needs this iterance, woman? I say thy husband.
EMILIA O mistress, villainy hath made mocks with love!
My husband say that she was false!
OTHELLO He, woman;
I say thy husband; dost understand the word?
My friend, thy husband – honest, honest Iago.
EMILIA If he say so, may his pernicious soul
Rot half a grain a day! He lies to th' heart.
She was too fond of her most filthy bargain.
OTHELLO Ha!
EMILIA Do thy worst:
This deed of thine is no more worthy heaven
Than thou wast worthy her.
OTHELLO Peace, you were best.
EMILIA Thou hast not half that power to do me harm
As I have to be hurt. O gull! O dolt!
As ignorant as dirt! Thou hast done a deed –
I care not for thy sword; I'll make thee known,
Though I lost twenty lives. Help! help, ho! help!
The Moor hath kill'd my mistress! Murder! murder!

Enter MONTANO, GRATIANO, IAGO, and Others.

MONTANO What is the matter? How now, General!
EMILIA O, are you come, Iago? You have done well,
That men must lay their murders on your neck.
GRATIANO What is the matter?
EMILIA Disprove this villain, if thou be'st a man:
He says thou told'st him that his wife was false.
I know thou didst not; thou'rt not such a villain.
Speak, for my heart is full.
IAGO I told him what I thought, and told no more
Than what he found himself was apt and true.
EMILIA But did you ever tell him she was false?
IAGO I did.
EMILIA You told a lie – an odious, damned lie.
Upon my soul, a lie – a wicked lie.
She false with Cassio! Did you say with Cassio?
IAGO With Cassio, mistress. Go to, charm your tongue.
EMILIA I will not charm my tongue; I am bound to speak:
My mistress here lies murdered in her bed.

ALL O heavens forfend!
EMILIA And your reports have set the murder on.
OTHELLO Nay, stare not, masters: it is true, indeed.
GRATIANO 'Tis a strange truth.
MONTANO O monstrous act!
EMILIA Villainy, villainy, villainy!
I think upon't. I think – I smell't. villainy!
I thought so then. I'll kill myself for grief.
O villainy, villainy!
IAGO What, are you mad? I charge you get you home.
EMILIA Good gentlemen, let me have leave to speak.
'Tis proper I obey him, but not now.
Perchance, Iago, I will ne'er go home.
OTHELLO O! O! O! *[Falls on the bed.*
EMILIA Nay, lay thee down and roar;
For thou hast kill'd the sweetest innocent
That e'er did lift up eye.
OTHELLO *[Rising]* O, she was foul!
I scarce did know you, uncle. There lies your niece,
Whose breath indeed these hands have newly stopp'd.
I know this act shows horrible and grim.
GRATIANO Poor Desdemona! I am glad thy father's dead.
Thy match was mortal to him, and pure grief
Shore his old thread atwain. Did he live now,
This sight would make him do a desperate turn,
Yea, curse his better angel from his side,
And fall to reprobance.
OTHELLO 'Tis pitiful; but yet Iago knows
That she with Cassio hath the act of shame
A thousand times committed; Cassio confess'd it;
And she did gratify his amorous works
With that recognizance and pledge of love
Which I first gave her; I saw it in his hand.
It was a handkerchief, an antique token
My father gave my mother.
EMILIA O God! O heavenly God!
IAGO Zounds, hold your peace.
EMILIA 'Twill out, 'twill out. I, peace!
No, I will speak as liberal as the north.
Let heaven and men and devils, let them all,
All, all, cry shame against me, yet I'll speak.
IAGO Be wise, and get you home.
EMILIA I will not.
[Iago offers to stab his wife.
GRATIANO Fie! Your sword upon a woman?
EMILIA O thou dull Moor! That handkerchief thou speak'st of
I found by fortune, and did give my husband;
For often with a solemn earnestness –
More than indeed belong'd to such a trifle –
He begg'd of me to steal it.
IAGO Villainous whore!
EMILIA She give it Cassio! No, alas, I found it,
And I did give't my husband.
IAGO Filth, thou liest.
EMILIA By heaven, I do not, I do not, gentlemen.
O murderous coxcomb! What should such a fool
Do with so good a wife? *[The Moor runs at Iago; Montano and others disarm the Moor. Iago kills his wife and escapes.*
OTHELLO Are there no stones in heaven but what serves for the thunder? Precious villain!
GRATIANO The woman falls; sure he hath kill'd his wife.
EMILIA Ay, ay. O, lay me by my mistress' side.
GRATIANO He's gone, but his wife's kill'd.
MONTANO 'Tis a notorious villain. Take you this weapon,
Which I have here recover'd from the Moor.
Come, guard the door without; let him not pass,
But kill him rather. I'll after that same villain,
For 'tis a damned slave.

[Exeunt Montano, Gratiano, and others.

OTHELLO I am not valiant neither –
But every puny whipster gets my sword.
But why should honour outlive honesty?
Let it go all.
EMILIA What did thy song bode, lady?
Hark, canst thou hear me? I will play the swan,
And die in music. [*Sings*] Willow, willow, willow. –
Moor, she was chaste; she lov'd thee, cruel Moor;
So come my soul to bliss, as I speak true;
So speaking as I think, alas, I die.

[She dies.

OTHELLO I have another weapon in this chamber;
It was a sword of Spain, the ice-brook's temper.
O, here it is. Uncle, I must come forth.
GRATIANO *[Within]* If thou attempt it, it will cost thee dear;
Thou hast no weapon, and perforce must suffer.
OTHELLO Look in upon me, then, and speak with me,
Or, naked as I am, I will assault thee.

Re-enter GRATIANO.

GRATIANO What is the matter?
OTHELLO Behold, I have a weapon;
A better never did itself sustain
Upon a soldier's thigh. I have seen the day
That with this little arm and this good sword
I have made my way through more impediments

Than twenty times your stop. But, O vain boast!
Who can control his fate? 'Tis not so now.
Be not afraid though you do see me weapon'd;
Here is my journey's end, here is my butt,
And very sea-mark of my utmost sail.
Do you go back dismay'd? 'Tis a lost fear;
Man but a rush against Othello's breast,
And he retires. Where should Othello go?
Now, how dost thou look now? O ill-starr'd wench!
Pale as thy smock! When we shall meet at compt,
This look of thine will hurl my soul from heaven,
And fiends will snatch at it. Cold, cold, my girl!
Even like thy chastity. O cursed, cursed slave!
Whip me, ye devils,
From the possession of this heavenly sight.
Blow me about in winds, roast me in sulphur,
Wash me in steep-down gulfs of liquid fire.
O Desdemona! Dead! Desdemona! Dead!
O! O!

Enter LODOVICO, MONTANO, CASSIO carried in a chair, and Officers, with IAGO prisoner.

LODOVICO Where is this rash and most unfortunate man?
OTHELLO That's he that was Othello – here I am.
LODOVICO Where is that viper? Bring the villain forth.
OTHELLO I look down towards his feet – but that's a fable.
If that thou be'st a devil, I cannot kill thee.
[*Wounds Iago.*
LODOVICO Wrench his sword from him.
IAGO I bleed, sir; but not kill'd.
OTHELLO I am not sorry neither: I'd have thee live;
For, in my sense, 'tis happiness to die.
LODOVICO O thou Othello, that was once so good,
Fall'n in the practice of a damned slave,
What shall be said to thee?
OTHELLO Why, any thing:
An honourable murderer, if you will;
For nought I did in hate, but all in honour.
LODOVICO This wretch hath part confess'd his villainy.
Did you and he consent in Cassio's death?
OTHELLO Ay.
CASSIO Dear General, I never gave you cause.
OTHELLO I do believe it, and I ask your pardon.
Will you, I pray, demand that demi-devil
Why he hath thus ensnar'd my soul and body?
IAGO Demand me nothing. What you know, you know.
From this time forth I never will speak word.
LODOVICO What, not to pray?
GRATIANO Torments will ope your lips.
OTHELLO Well, thou dost best.
LODOVICO Sir, you shall understand what hath befall'n,
Which, as I think, you know not. Here is a letter
Found in the pocket of the slain Roderigo;
And here another: the one of them imports
The death of Cassio to be undertook
By Roderigo.
OTHELLO O villain!
CASSIO Most heathenish and most gross!
LODOVICO Now here's another discontented paper,
Found in his pocket too; and this, it seems,
Roderigo meant t' have sent this damned villain;
But that, belike, Iago in the nick
Came in and satisfied him.
OTHELLO O thou pernicious caitiff!
How came you, Cassio, by that handkerchief
That was my wife's?
CASSIO I found it in my chamber;
And he himself confess'd it even now
That there he dropp'd it for a special purpose
Which wrought to his desire.
OTHELLO O fool! fool! fool!
CASSIO There is besides in Roderigo's letter,
How he upbraids Iago that he made him
Brave me upon the watch; whereon it came
That I was cast; and even but now he spake,
After long seeming dead, Iago hurt him,
Iago set him on.
LODOVICO You must forsake this room and go with us.
Your power and your command is taken off,
And Cassio rules in Cyprus. For this slave,
If there be any cunning cruelty
That can torment him much and hold him long,
It shall be his. You shall close prisoner rest
Till that the nature of your fault be known
To the Venetian state. Come, bring away.
OTHELLO Soft you; a word or two before you go.
I have done the state some service, and they know't –
No more of that. I pray you, in your letters,
When you shall these unlucky deeds relate,
Speak of me as I am; nothing extenuate,
Nor set down aught in malice. Then must you speak
Of one that lov'd not wisely, but too well;
Of one not easily jealous, but, being wrought,
Perplexed in the extreme; of one whose hand,
Like the base Indian, threw a pearl away
Richer than all his tribe; one of whose subdu'd eyes,
Albeit unused to the melting mood,

Drops tears as fast as the Arabian trees
Their med'cinable gum. Set you down this:
And say besides that in Aleppo once,
Where a malignant and a turban'd Turk
Beat a Venetian and traduc'd the state,
I took by th' throat the circumcised dog,
And smote him – thus.

[He stabs himself.

LODOVICO O bloody period!

GRATIANO All that is spoke is marr'd.

OTHELLO I kiss'd thee ere I kill'd thee. No way but this –
Killing my self, to die upon a kiss.

[Falls on the bed and dies.

CASSIO This did I fear, but thought he had no weapon;
For he was great of heart.

LODOVICO *[To Iago]* O Spartan dog,
More fell than anguish, hunger, or the sea!
Look on the tragic loading of this bed.
This is thy work. – The object poisons sight;
Let it be hid. Gratiano, keep the house,
And seize upon the fortunes of the Moor,
For they succeed on you. To you, Lord Governor,
Remains the censure of this hellish villain;
The time, the place, the torture – O, enforce it!
Myself will straight aboard; and to the state
This heavy act with heavy heart relate. *[Exeunt.*

Antony and Cleopatra

Introduction by ROBERT GRANT

Antony and Cleopatra is set at the epicentre of events more momentous even than those described in the second tetralogy (the English history plays from *Richard II* to *Henry V*), written between eight and twelve years previously. Like *Richard II*, the play focuses on a disposition (depicted here in the lovers) to ignore a threatening reality in consequence of a fatal addiction to what, from the point of view of survival, are distractions.

There is also, however, a radical difference. In *Antony and Cleopatra* Shakespeare seems seriously to ask, with the lovers, whether, on the terms dictated by prudence, there really could be anything to live for; that is, whether the supposedly superfluous is not, after all, the *sine qua non* of a meaningful life (a question also raised by King Lear in respect of his hundred knights). The Lancastrian universe may be unattractive (for example, it cannot permanently accommodate free spirits such as Hotspur or Falstaff), but with Richard's defeat nothing very precious has been lost, for Richard had already made nonsense of most of what was worth keeping in the old order (Mowbray's idealism, for example).

What Antony and Cleopatra have stood for, however, *is* precious, and not merely in their own eyes. It is something like W. B. Yeats's aristocratic ideal: life, love, laughter, pleasure, display and military grandeur strenuously and simply pursued for their own sakes, and at their highest pitch of both aesthetic seriousness and glorious inutility. All this is a far cry from Richard's levity, sybaritism, and caprice. But so it is also from Octavius's sober puritanism, self-discipline, conventionality and calculation. There is no room in Octavius's new world order, even in private life, for an Antony or a Cleopatra (he turns down Antony's offer of surrender and retirement).

Octavius stands, at least up to a point, for traditional Rome, whose values he perpetually invokes against Antony's decadence. But it is Rome with the heroism left out. For heroism (which, as Octavius himself concedes, is one of Antony's greatest and most stylish accomplishments) is irrelevant in the coming imperial era of universal peace, justice and prosperity.

With typical Shakespearean ambiguity, however, the play suggests that such 'bourgeois' values and achievements are after all not lightly to be dismissed. If it were not wholly inconceivable, a world permanently under the government of Antony and Cleopatra, like one ruled by Falstaff (with whom the lovers have a certain affinity), would be an intolerable shambles. When the play opens they command enormous power. But both are bohemians and naturally improvident. (Even Antony's wars, like those of Othello or Fortinbras, are undertaken more for glory than for gain.) So neither is greatly concerned to use their power to secure their way of life, which, as already suggested, and equally with Octavius's 'bourgeois' order, is not without its merits. (This is Shakespeare's least puritanical play, and perhaps the furthest in spirit from his Sonnet 129.)

Even while their earthly prospects seem good, the lovers, as in *Tristan und Isolde* and *Wuthering Heights*, seem to live on another plane, notwithstanding that their middle-aged love is anything but Platonic. The play depicts a passion which is fully spiritual yet which never forgets its origins, or its natural and proper realisation, in the body. (It is constantly accompanied by, and likened to, feasting.) It is therefore curious that Antony and Cleopatra, though their love is rooted in the physical, seem almost indifferent to mortality, and thus to prudential considerations. Death, which each embraces with noble resolution, seems in the end no insuperable obstacle to whatever it is they seek, which accordingly, and whatever their detractors say, must be something more than mere animal gratification.

In a sense, *Antony and Cleopatra* is hardly a tragedy at all, since it accords equal weight to the lovers' values and everyday common sense. From the latter point of view, the winner is obviously Octavius; from the former, it is the lovers themselves, since, by dying, they have cheated him of his triumph and achieved their final union in more hospitable surroundings. The play's at times almost unbearable pathos seems to arise from the tension between our imaginative sympathy with the lovers and our simultaneous, contrary conviction that they are quite simply deluded.

Readers have long admired *Antony and Cleopatra* for its profound ethicai insights, its sublime poetry and its brilliantly vivid characterisation, especially of its outrageous, unforgettable heroine. But it has never been a favourite with audiences, and is rarely performed. The locations are too many and too diverse, much of the dialogue is obscure, perfunctory or purely narrative, and there is in any case virtually no plot, the drama consisting mostly in a series of episodes registering the gradual, inexorable closing-in of a hostile reality around a pair of people with more important things to think about, according to their philosophy, than resisting it. It is not surprising, therefore, if the play seems to lack dramatic impetus. Its energy lies elsewhere.

Antony and Cleopatra

DRAMATIS PERSONAE

MARK ANTONY, OCTAVIUS CAESAR, M. AEMILIUS LEPIDUS
Triumvirs
SEXTUS POMPEIUS
DOMITIUS ENOBARBUS, VENTIDIUS, EROS, SCARUS, DERCETAS, DEMETRIUS, PHILO
friends to Antony
MAECENAS, AGRIPPA, DOLABELLA, PROCULEIUS, THYREUS, GALLUS
friends to Caesar
MENAS, MENECRATES, VARRIUS
friends to Pompey
TAURUS
Lieutenant-General to Caesar
CANIDIUS
Lieutenant-General to Antony
SILIUS
an Officer in Ventidius's army
EUPHRONIUS
an ambassador from Antony to Caesar
ALEXAS, MARDIAN, SELEUCUS, DIOMEDES
attendants on Cleopatra
A Soothsayer
A Clown
CLEOPATRA
Queen of Egypt
OCTAVIA
sister to Caesar and wife to Antony
CHARMIAN, IRAS
ladies attending on Cleopatra
Officers, Soldiers, Messengers, and Attendants.

THE SCENE: THE ROMAN EMPIRE.

ACT ONE

SCENE I. *Alexandria. Cleopatra's palace.*

Enter DEMETRIUS and PHILO.

PHILO Nay, but this dotage of our general's
O'erflows the measure. Those his goodly eyes,
That o'er the files and musters of the war
Have glow'd like plated Mars, now bend, now turn,
The office and devotion of their view
Upon a tawny front. His captain's heart,
Which in the scuffles of great fights hath burst
The buckles on his breast, reneges all temper,
And is become the bellows and the fan
To cool a gipsy's lust.

Flourish. Enter ANTONY, CLEOPATRA, her Ladies, the Train, with Eunuchs fanning her.

Look where they come!
Take but good note, and you shall see in him
The triple pillar of the world transform'd
Into a strumpet's fool. Behold and see.

CLEOPATRA If it be love indeed, tell me how much.

ANTONY There's beggary in the love that can be reckon'd.

CLEOPATRA I'll set a bourn how far to be belov'd.

ANTONY Then must thou needs find out new heaven, new earth.

Enter a Messenger.

MESSENGER News, my good lord, from Rome.

ANTONY Grates me the sum.

CLEOPATRA Nay, hear them, Antony.
Fulvia perchance is angry; or who knows
If the scarce-bearded Caesar have not sent
His pow'rful mandate to you: 'Do this or this;
Take in that kingdom and enfranchise that;
Perform't, or else we damn thee'.

ANTONY How, my love?

CLEOPATRA Perchance? Nay, and most like,
You must not stay here longer; your dismission
Is come from Caesar; therefore hear it, Antony.
Where's Fulvia's process? Caesar's I would say? Both?
Call in the messengers. As I am Egypt's queen,
Thou blushest, Antony, and that blood of thine
Is Caesar's homager. Else so thy cheek pays shame
When shrill-tongu'd Fulvia scolds. The messengers!

ANTONY Let Rome in Tiber melt, and the wide arch
Of the rang'd empire fall! Here is my space.
Kingdoms are clay; our dungy earth alike
Feeds beast as man. The nobleness of life
Is to do thus [*embracing*], when such a mutual pair
And such a twain can do't, in which I bind,
On pain of punishment, the world to weet
We stand up peerless.

CLEOPATRA Excellent falsehood!
Why did he marry Fulvia, and not love her?
I'll seem the fool I am not. Antony
Will be himself.

ANTONY But stirr'd by Cleopatra.
Now for the love of Love and her soft hours,
Let's not confound the time with conference harsh;
There's not a minute of our lives should stretch
Without some pleasure now. What sport to-night?

CLEOPATRA Hear the ambassadors.

ANTONY Fie, wrangling queen!
Whom everything becomes – to chide, to laugh,
To weep; whose every passion fully strives
To make itself in thee fair and admir'd.
No messenger but thine, and all alone
To-night we'll wander through the streets and note
The qualities of people. Come, my queen;
Last night you did desire it. Speak not to us.

[Exeunt Antony and Cleopatra, with the Train.

DEMETRIUS Is Caesar with Antonius priz'd so slight?

PHILO Sir, sometimes when he is not Antony,
He comes too short of that great property
Which still should go with Antony.

DEMETRIUS I am full sorry
That he approves the common liar, who
Thus speaks of him at Rome; but I will hope
Of better deeds to-morrow. Rest you happy!

[Exeunt.

SCENE II. *Alexandria. Cleopatra's palace.*

Enter CHARMIAN, IRAS, ALEXAS, and a Soothsayer.

CHARMIAN Lord Alexas, sweet Alexas, most anything Alexas, almost most absolute Alexas, where's the soothsayer that you prais'd so to th' Queen? O that I knew this husband, which you say must charge his horns with garlands!

ALEXAS Soothsayer!

SOOTHSAYER Your will?

CHARMIAN Is this the man? Is't you, sir, that know things?

SOOTHSAYER In nature's infinite book of secrecy
A little I can read.

ALEXAS Show him your hand.

Enter ENOBARBUS.

ENOBARBUS Bring in the banquet quickly; wine enough
Cleopatra's health to drink.

CHARMIAN Good sir, give me good fortune.

SOOTHSAYER I make not, but foresee.

CHARMIAN Pray, then, forsee me one.

SOOTHSAYER You shall be yet far fairer than you are.

CHARMIAN He means in flesh.

IRAS No, you shall paint when you are old.

CHARMIAN Wrinkles forbid!

ALEXAS Vex not his prescience; be attentive.

CHARMIAN Hush!

SOOTHSAYER You shall be more beloving than beloved.

CHARMIAN I had rather heat my liver with drinking.

ALEXAS Nay, hear him.

CHARMIAN Good now, some excellent fortune! Let me be married to three kings in a fore-noon, and widow them all. Let me have a child at fifty, to whom Herod of Jewry may do homage. Find me to marry me with Octavius Caesar, and companion me with my mistress.

SOOTHSAYER You shall outlive the lady whom you serve.

CHARMIAN O, excellent! I love long life better than figs.

SOOTHSAYER You have seen and prov'd a fairer former fortune
Than that which is to approach.

CHARMIAN Then belike my children shall have no names. Prithee, how many boys and wenches must I have?

SOOTHSAYER If every of your wishes had a womb,
And fertile every wish, a million.

CHARMIAN Out, fool! I forgive thee for a witch.

ALEXAS You think none but your sheets are privy to your wishes.

CHARMIAN Nay, come, tell Iras hers.

ALEXAS We'll know all our fortunes.

ENOBARBUS Mine, and most of our fortunes, to-night, shall be – drunk to bed.

IRAS There's a palm presages chastity, if nothing else.

CHARMIAN E'en as the o'erflowing Nilus presageth famine.

IRAS Go, you wild bedfellow, you cannot soothsay.

CHARMIAN Nay, if an oily palm be not a fruitful prognostication, I cannot scratch mine ear. Prithee, tell her but a worky-day fortune.

SOOTHSAYER Your fortunes are alike.

IRAS But how, but how? Give me particulars.

SOOTHSAYER I have said.

IRAS Am I not an inch of fortune better than she?

CHARMIAN Well, if you were but an inch of fortune better than I, where would you choose it?

IRAS Not in my husband's nose.

CHARMIAN Our worser thoughts heavens mend! Alexas – come, his fortune, his fortune! O, let him marry a woman that cannot go, sweet Isis, I beseech thee! And let her die too, and give him a worse! And let worse follow worse, till the worst of all follow him laughing to his grave, fiftyfold a cuckold! Good Isis, hear me this prayer, though thou deny me a matter of more weight; good Isis, I beseech thee!

IRAS Amen. Dear goddess, hear that prayer of the people! For, as it is a heart-breaking to see a handsome man loose-wiv'd, so it is a deadly sorrow to behold a foul knave uncuckolded. Therefore, dear Isis, keep decorum, and fortune him accordingly!

CHARMIAN Amen.

ALEXAS Lo now, if it lay in their hands to make me a cuckold, they would make themselves whores but they'ld do't!

Enter CLEOPATRA.

ENOBARBUS Hush! Here comes Antony.
CHARMIAN Not he; the Queen.
CLEOPATRA Saw you my lord?
ENOBARBUS No, lady.
CLEOPATRA Was he not here?
CHARMIAN No, madam.
CLEOPATRA He was dispos'd to mirth; but on the sudden
A Roman thought hath struck him. Enobarbus!
ENOBARBUS Madam?
CLEOPATRA Seek him, and bring him hither. Where's Alexas?
ALEXAS Here, at your service. My lord approaches.

Enter ANTONY, with a Messenger and Attendants.

CLEOPATRA We will not look upon him. Go with us.
[Exeunt Cleopatra, Enobarbus, and the rest.

MESSENGER Fulvia thy wife first came into the field.
ANTONY Against my brother Lucius?
MESSENGER Ay.
But soon that war had end, and the time's state
Made friends of them, jointing their force 'gainst Caesar,
Whose better issue in the war from Italy
Upon the first encounter drave them.
ANTONY Well, what worst?
MESSENGER The nature of bad news infects the teller.
ANTONY When it concerns the fool or coward. On!
Things that are past are done with me. 'Tis thus:
Who tells me true, though in his tale lie death,
I hear him as he flatter'd.
MESSENGER Labienus –
This is stiff news – hath with his Parthian force
Extended Asia from Euphrates,
His conquering banner shook from Syria
To Lydia and to Ionia,
Whilst –
ANTONY Antony, thou wouldst say.
MESSENGER O, my lord!
ANTONY Speak to me home; mince not the general tongue;
Name Cleopatra as she is call'd in Rome.
Rail thou in Fulvia's phrase, and taunt my faults
With such full licence as both truth and malice
Have power to utter. O, then we bring forth weeds
When our quick minds lie still, and our ills told us
Is as our earing. Fare thee well awhile.
MESSENGER At your noble pleasure. *[Exit.*

ANTONY From Sicyon, ho, the news! Speak there!
1 ATTENDANT The man from Sicyon – is there such an one?
2 ATTENDANT He stays upon your will.
ANTONY Let him appear.
These strong Egyptian fetters I must break,
Or lose myself in dotage.

Enter another Messenger with a letter.

What are you?
2 MESSENGER Fulvia thy wife is dead.
ANTONY Where died she?
2 MESSENGER In Sicyon.
Her length of sickness, with what else more serious
Importeth thee to know, this bears.
[Gives the letter.
ANTONY Forbear me.
[Exit Messenger.
There's a great spirit gone! Thus did I desire it.
What our contempts doth often hurl from us
We wish it ours again; the present pleasure,
By revolution low'ring, does become
The opposite of itself. She's good, being gone;
The hand could pluck her back that shov'd her on.
I must from this enchanting queen break off.
Ten thousand harms, more than the ills I know,
My idleness doth hatch. How now, Enobarbus!

Re-enter ENOBARBUS.

ENOBARBUS What's your pleasure, sir?
ANTONY I must with haste from hence.
ENOBARBUS Why, then we kill all our women. We see how mortal an unkindness is to them; if they suffer our departure, death's the word.
ANTONY I must be gone.
ENOBARBUS Under a compelling occasion, let women die. It were pity to cast them away for nothing, though between them and a great cause they should be esteemed nothing. Cleopatra, catching but the least noise of this,

dies instantly; I have seen her die twenty times upon far poorer moment. I do think there is mettle in death, which commits some loving act upon her, she hath such a celerity in dying.

ANTONY She is cunning past man's thought.

ENOBARBUS Alack, sir, no! Her passions are made of nothing but the finest part of pure love. We cannot call her winds and waters sighs and tears; they are greater storms and tempests then almanacs can report. This cannot be cunning in her; if it be, she makes a show'r of rain as well as Jove.

ANTONY Would I had never seen her!

ENOBARBUS O sir, you had then left unseen a wonderful piece of work, which not to have been blest withal would have discredited your travel.

ANTONY Fulvia is dead.

ENOBARBUS Sir?

ANTONY Fulvia is dead.

ENOBARBUS Fulvia?

ANTONY Dead.

ENOBARBUS Why, sir, give the gods a thankful sacrifice. When it pleaseth their deities to take the wife of a man from him, it shows to man the tailors of the earth; comforting therein that when old robes are worn out there are members to make new. If there were no more women but Fulvia, then had you indeed a cut, and the case to be lamented. This grief is crown'd with consolation: your old smock brings forth a new petticoat; and indeed the tears live in an onion that should water this sorrow.

ANTONY The business she hath broached in the state.
Cannot endure my absence.

ENOBARBUS And the business you have broach'd here cannot be without you; especially that of Cleopatra's, which wholly depends on your abode.

ANTONY No more light answers. Let our officers
Have notice what we purpose. I shall break
The cause of our expedience to the Queen,
And get her leave to part. For not alone
The death of Fulvia, with more urgent touches
Do strongly speak to us; but the letters too
Of many our contriving friends in Rome
Petition us at home. Sextus Pompeius
Hath given the dare to Caesar, and commands
The empire of the sea; our slippery people,
Whose love is never link'd to the deserver
Till his deserts are past, begin to throw
Pompey the Great and all his dignities
Upon his son; who, high in name and power,
Higher than both in blood and life, stands up
For the main soldier; whose quality, going on,
The sides o' th' world may danger. Much is breeding
Which, like the courser's hair, hath yet but life
And not a serpent's poison. Say our pleasure,
To such whose place is under us, requires
Our quick remove from hence.

ENOBARBUS I shall do't. *[Exeunt.*

SCENE III. *Alexandria. Cleopatra's palace.*

Enter CLEOPATRA, CHARMIAN, IRAS, and ALEXAS.

CLEOPATRA Where is he?

CHARMIAN I did not see him since.

CLEOPATRA See where he is, who's with him, what he does.
I did not send you. If you find him sad,
Say I am dancing; if in mirth, report
That I am sudden sick. Quick, and return.
[Exit Alexas.

CHARMIAN Madam, methinks, if you did love him dearly,
You do not hold the method to enforce
The like from him.

CLEOPATRA What should I do I do not?

CHARMIAN In each thing give him way; cross him in nothing.

CLEOPATRA Thou teachest like a fool – the way to lose him.

CHARMIAN Tempt him not so too far; I wish, forbear;
In time we hate that which we often fear.

Enter ANTONY.

But here comes Antony.

CLEOPATRA I am sick and sullen.

ANTONY I am sorry to give breathing to my purpose –

CLEOPATRA Help me away, dear Charmian; I shall fall.
It cannot be thus long; the sides of nature
Will not sustain it.

ANTONY Now, my dearest queen –

CLEOPATRA Pray you, stand farther from me.

ANTONY What's the matter?

CLEOPATRA I know by that same eye there's some good news.
What says the married woman? You may go.
Would she had never given you leave to come!
Let her not say 'tis I that keep you here –
I have no power upon you; hers you are.

ANTONY The gods best know –

CLEOPATRA O, never was there queen
So mightily betray'd! Yet at the first
I saw the treasons planted.

ANTONY Cleopatra –

CLEOPATRA Why should I think you can be mine and true,

Though you in swearing shake the throned gods,
Who have been false to Fulvia? Riotous madness,
To be entangled with those mouth-made vows,
Which break themselves in swearing!

ANTONY Most sweet queen –

CLEOPATRA Nay, pray you seek no colour for your going,
But bid farewell, and go. When you sued staying,
Then was the time for words. No going then!
Eternity was in our lips and eyes,
Bliss in our brows' bent, none our parts so poor
But was a race of heaven. They are so still,
Or thou, the greatest soldier of the world,
Art turn'd the greatest liar.

ANTONY How now, lady!

CLEOPATRA I would I had thy inches. Thou shouldst know
There were a heart in Egypt.

ANTONY Hear me, Queen:
The strong necessity of time commands
Our services awhile; but my full heart
Remains in use with you. Our Italy
Shines o'er with civil swords: Sextus Pompeius
Makes his approaches to the port of Rome;
Equality of two domestic powers
Breed scrupulous faction; the hated, grown to strength,
Are newly grown to love. The condemn'd Pompey,
Rich in his father's honour, creeps apace
Into the hearts of such as have not thrived
Upon the present state, whose numbers threaten;
And quietness, grown sick of rest, would purge
By any desperate change. My more particular,
And that which most with you should safe my going,
Is Fulvia's death.

CLEOPATRA Though age from folly could not give me freedom,
It does from childishness. Can Fulvia die?

ANTONY She's dead, my queen.
Look here, and at thy sovereign leisure read
The garboils she awak'd. At the last, best.
See when and where she died.

CLEOPATRA O most false love!
Where be the sacred vials thou shouldst fill
With sorrowful water? Now I see, I see,
In Fulvia's death how mine receiv'd shall be.

ANTONY Quarrel no more, but be prepar'd to know
The purposes I bear; which are, or cease,
As you shall give th' advice. By the fire
That quickens Nilus' slime, I go from hence
Thy soldier, servant, making peace or war
As thou affects.

CLEOPATRA Cut my lace, Charmian, come!
But let it be; I am quickly ill and well –
So Antony loves.

ANTONY My precious queen, forbear,
And give true evidence to his love, which stands
An honourable trial.

CLEOPATRA So Fulvia told me.
I prithee turn aside and weep for her;
Then bid adieu to me, and say the tears
Belong to Egypt. Good now, play one scene
Of excellent dissembling, and let it look
Like perfect honour.

ANTONY You'll heat my blood; no more.

CLEOPATRA You can do better yet; but this is meetly.

ANTONY Now, by my sword –

CLEOPATRA And target. Still he mends;
But this is not the best. Look, prithee, Charmian,
How this Herculean Roman does become
The carriage of his chafe.

ANTONY I'll leave you, lady.

CLEOPATRA Courteous lord, one word.
Sir, you and I must part – but that's not it.
Sir, you and I have lov'd – but there's not it.
That you know well. Something it is I would –
O my oblivion is a very Antony,
And I am all forgotten!

ANTONY But that your royalty
Holds idleness your subject, I should take you
For idleness itself.

CLEOPATRA 'Tis sweating labour
To bear such idleness so near the heart
As Cleopatra this. But, sir, forgive me;
Since my becomings kill me when they do not
Eye well to you. Your honour calls you hence;
Therefore be deaf to my unpitied folly,
And all the gods go with you! Upon your sword
Sit laurel victory, and smooth success
Be strew'd before your feet!

ANTONY Let us go. Come.
Our separation so abides and flies
That thou, residing here, goes yet with me,
And I, hence fleeting, here remain with thee.
Away! [*Exeunt.*

SCENE IV. *Rome. Caesar's house.*

Enter OCTAVIUS CAESAR, reading a letter; LEPIDUS, and their Train.

CAESAR You may see, Lepidus, and henceforth know,
It is not Caesar's natural vice to hate
Our great competitor. From Alexandria

This is the news: he fishes, drinks, and wastes
The lamps of night in revel; is not more manlike
Than Cleopatra, nor the queen of Ptolemy
More womanly than he; hardly gave audience, or
Vouchsaf'd to think he had partners. You shall find there
A man who is the abstract of all faults
That all men follow.

LEPIDUS I must not think there are
Evils enow to darken all his goodness.
His faults, in him, seem as the spots of heaven,
More fiery by night's blackness; hereditary
Rather than purchas'd; what he cannot change
Than what he chooses.

CAESAR You are too indulgent. Let's grant it is not
Amiss to tumble on the bed of Ptolemy,
To give a kingdom for a mirth, to sit
And keep the turn of tippling with a slave,
To reel the streets at noon, and stand the buffet
With knaves that smell of sweat. Say this becomes him –
As his composure must be rare indeed
Whom these things cannot blemish – yet must Antony
No way excuse his foils when we do bear
So great weight in his lightness. If he fill'd
His vacancy with his voluptuousness,
Full surfeits and the dryness of his bones
Call on him for't! But to confound such time
That drums him from his sport and speaks as loud
As his own state and ours – 'tis to be chid
As we rate boys who, being mature in knowledge,
Pawn their experience to their present pleasure,
And so rebel to judgment.

Enter a Messenger.

LEPIDUS Here's more news.

MESSENGER Thy biddings have been done; and every hour,
Most noble Caesar, shalt thou have report
How 'tis abroad. Pompey is strong at sea,
And it appears he is belov'd of those
That only have fear'd Caesar. To the ports
The discontents repair, and men's reports
Give him much wrong'd.

CAESAR I should have known no less.
It hath been taught us from the primal state
That he which is was wish'd until he were;
And the ebb'd man, ne'er lov'd till ne'er worth love,
Comes dear'd by being lack'd. This common body,
Like to a vagabond flag upon the stream,
Goes to and back, lackeying the varying tide,
To rot itself with motion.

MESSENGER Caesar, I bring thee word
Menecrates and Menas, famous pirates,
Make the sea serve them, which they ear and wound
With keels of every kind. Many hot inroads
They make in Italy; the borders maritime
Lack blood to think on't, and flush youth revolt.
No vessel can peep forth but 'tis as soon
Taken as seen; for Pompey's name strikes more
Than could his war resisted.

CAESAR Antony,
Leave thy lascivious wassails. When thou once
Was beaten from Modena, where thou slew'st
Hirtius and Pansa, consuls, at thy heel
Did famine follow; whom thou fought'st against,
Though daintily brought up, with patience more
Than savages could suffer. Thou didst drink
The stale of horses and the gilded puddle
Which beasts would cough at. Thy palate then did deign
The roughest berry on the rudest hedge;
Yea, like the stag when snow the pasture sheets,
The barks of trees thou brows'd. On the Alps
It is reported thou didst eat strange flesh,
Which some did die to look on. And all this –
It wounds thine honour that I speak it now –
Was borne so like a soldier that thy cheek
So much as lank'd not.

LEPIDUS 'Tis pity of him.

CAESAR Let his shames quickly
Drive him to Rome. 'Tis time we twain
Did show ourselves i' th' field; and to that end
Assemble we immediate council. Pompey
Thrives in our idleness.

LEPIDUS To-morrow, Caesar,
I shall be furnish'd to inform you rightly
Both what by sea and land I can be able
To front this present time.

CAESAR Till which encounter
It is my business too. Farewell.

LEPIDUS Farewell, my lord. What you shall know meantime
Of stirs abroad, I shall beseech you, sir,
To let me be partaker.

CAESAR Doubt not, sir;
I knew it for my bond. [*Exeunt.*

SCENE V. *Alexandria. Cleopatra's palace.*

Enter CLEOPATRA, CHARMIAN, IRAS, and MARDIAN.

CLEOPATRA Charmian!

CHARMIAN Madam?

CLEOPATRA Ha, ha!
Give me to drink mandragora.

CHARMIAN Why, madam?
CLEOPATRA That I might sleep out this great gap of time
My Antony is away.
CHARMIAN You think of him too much.
CLEOPATRA O, 'tis treason!
CHARMIAN Madam, I trust, not so.
CLEOPATRA Thou, eunuch Mardian!
MARDIAN What's your Highness' pleasure?
CLEOPATRA Not now to hear thee sing; I take no pleasure
In aught an eunuch has. 'Tis well for thee
That, being unseminar'd, thy freer thoughts
May not fly forth of Egypt. Hast thou affections?
MARDIAN Yes, gracious madam.
CLEOPATRA Indeed?
MARDIAN Not in deed, madam; for I can do nothing
But what indeed is honest to be done.
Yet have I fierce affections, and think
What Venus did with Mars.
CLEOPATRA O Charmian,
Where think'st thou he is now? Stands he or sits he?
Or does he walk? or is he on his horse?
O happy horse, to bear the weight of Antony!
Do bravely, horse; for wot'st thou whom thou mov'st?
The demi-Atlas of this earth, the arm
And burgonet of men. He's speaking now,
Or murmuring 'Where's my serpent of old Nile?'
For so he calls me. Now I feed myself
With most delicious poison. Think on me,
That am with Phoebus' amorous pinches black,
And wrinkled deep in time? Broad-fronted Caesar,
When thou wast here above the ground, I was
A morsel for a monarch; and great Pompey
Would stand and make his eyes grow in my brow;
There would he anchor his aspect and die
With looking on his life.

Enter ALEXAS.

ALEXAS Sovereign of Egypt, hail!
CLEOPATRA How much unlike art thou Mark Antony!
Yet, coming from him, that great med'cine hath
With his tinct gilded thee.
How goes it with my brave Mark Antony?
ALEXAS Last thing he did, dear Queen,
He kiss'd – the last of many doubled kisses –
This orient pearl. His speech sticks in my heart.
CLEOPATRA Mine ear must pluck it thence.
ALEXAS 'Good friend,' quoth he
'Say the firm Roman to great Egypt sends
This treasure of an oyster; at whose foot,
To mend the petty present, I will piece
Her opulent throne with kingdoms. All the East,
Say thou, shall call her mistress.' So he nodded,
And soberly did mount an arm-gaunt steed,
Who neigh'd so high that what I would have spoke
Was beastly dumb'd by him.
CLEOPATRA What, was he sad or merry.
ALEXAS Like to the time o' th' year between the extremes
Of hot and cold; he was nor sad nor merry?
CLEOPATRA O well-divided disposition! Note him,
Note him, good Charmian; 'tis the man; but note him!
He was not sad, for he would shine on those
That make their looks by his; he was not merry,
Which seem'd to tell them his remembrance lay
In Egypt with his joy; but between both.
O heavenly mingle! Be'st thou sad or merry,
The violence of either thee becomes,
So does it no man else. Met'st thou my posts?
ALEXAS Ay, madam, twenty several messengers.
Why do you send so thick?
CLEOPATRA Who's born that day
When I forget to send to Antony
Shall die a beggar. Ink and paper, Charmian.
Welcome, my good Alexas. Did I, Charmian,
Ever love Caesar so?
CHARMIAN O that brave Caesar!
CLEOPATRA Be chok'd with such another emphasis!
Say 'the brave Antony'.
CHARMIAN The valiant Caesar!
CLEOPATRA By Isis, I will give thee bloody teeth
If thou with Caesar paragon again
My man of men.
CHARMIAN By your most gracious pardon,
I sing but after you.
CLEOPATRA My salad days,
When I was green in judgment, cold in blood,
To say as I said then. But come, away!
Get me ink and paper.
He shall have every day a several greeting,
Or I'll unpeople Egypt. [*Exeunt.*

ACT TWO

SCENE I. *Messina. Pompey's house.*

Enter POMPEY, MENECRATES, and MENAS, in warlike manner.

POMPEY If the great gods be just, they shall assist
The deeds of justest men.
MENECRATES Know, worthy Pompey,
That what they do delay they not deny.
POMPEY Whiles we are suitors to their throne, decays
The thing we sue for.
MENECRATES We, ignorant of ourselves,
Beg often our own harms, which the wise pow'rs
Deny us for our good; so find we profit
By losing of our prayers.
POMPEY I shall do well.
The people love me, and the sea is mine;
My powers are crescent, and my auguring hope
Says it will come to th' full. Mark Antony
In Egypt sits at dinner, and will make
No wars without doors. Caesar gets money where
He loses hearts. Lepidus flatters both,
Of both is flatter'd; but he neither loves,
Nor either cares for him.
MENAS Caesar and Lepidus
Are in the field. A mighty strength they carry.
POMPEY Where have you this? 'Tis false.
MENAS From Silvius, sir.
POMPEY He dreams. I know they are in Rome together,
Looking for Antony. But all the charms of love,
Salt Cleopatra, soften thy wan'd lip!
Let witchcraft join with beauty, lust with both;
Tie up the libertine in a field of feasts,
Keep his brain fuming. Epicurean cooks
Sharpen with cloyless sauce his appetite,
That sleep and feeding may prorogue his honour
Even till a Lethe'd dullness –

Enter VARRIUS.

How now, Varrius!
VARRIUS This is most certain that I shall deliver:
Mark Antony is every hour in Rome
Expected. Since he went from Egypt 'tis
A space for farther travel.
POMPEY I could have given less matter
A better ear. Menas, I did not think
This amorous surfeiter would have donn'd his helm
For such a petty war; his soldiership
Is twice the other twain. But let us rear
The higher our opinion, that our stirring
Can from the lap of Egypt's widow pluck
The ne'er-lust-wearied Antony.
MENAS I cannot hope
Caesar and Antony shall well greet together.
His wife that's dead did trespasses to Caesar;
His brother warr'd upon him; although, I think,
Not mov'd by Antony.
POMPEY I know not, Menas,
How lesser enmities may give way to greater.
Were't not that we stand up against them all,
'Twere pregnant they should square between themselves;
For they have entertained cause enough
To draw their swords. But how the fear of us
May cement their divisions, and bind up
The petty difference we yet not know.
Be't as our gods will have't! It only stands
Our lives upon to use our strongest hands.
Come, Menas. [*Exeunt.*

SCENE II. *Rome. The house of Lepidus.*

Enter ENOBARBUS and LEPIDUS.

LEPIDUS Good Enobarbus, 'tis a worthy deed,
And shall become you well, to entreat your captain
To soft and gentle speech.
ENOBARBUS I shall entreat him
To answer like himself. If Caesar move him,
Let Antony look over Caesar's head
And speak as loud as Mars. By Jupiter,
Were I the wearer of Antonius' beard,
I would not shave't to-day.
LEPIDUS 'Tis not a time
For private stomaching.
ENOBARBUS Every time
Serves for the matter that is then born in't.
LEPIDUS But small to greater matters must give way.
ENOBARBUS Not if the small come first.
LEPIDUS Your speech is passion;
But pray you stir no embers up. Here comes
The noble Antony.

Enter ANTONY and VENTIDIUS.

ENOBARBUS And yonder, Caesar.

Enter CAESAR, MAECENAS, and AGRIPPA.

ANTONY If we compose well here, to Parthia.
Hark, Ventidius.
CAESAR I do not know, Maecenas. Ask Agrippa.
LEPIDUS Noble friends,
That which combin'd us was most great, and let not
A leaner action rend us. What's amiss,
May it be gently heard. When we debate

Our trivial difference loud, we do commit
Murder in healing wounds. Then, noble partners,
The rather for I earnestly beseech,
Touch you the sourest points with sweetest terms,
Nor curstness grow to th' matter.
ANTONY 'Tis spoken well.
Were we before our armies, and to fight,
I should do thus. [*Flourish.*
CAESAR Welcome to Rome.
ANTONY Thank you.
CAESAR Sit.
ANTONY Sit, sir.
CAESAR Nay, then. [*They sit.*
ANTONY I learn you take things ill which are not so,
Or being, concern you not.
CAESAR I must be laugh'd at
If, or for nothing or a little, I
Should say myself offended, and with you
Chiefly i' th' world; more laugh'd at that I should
Once name you derogately when to sound your name
It not concern'd me.
ANTONY My being in Egypt, Caesar,
What was't to you?
CAESAR No more than my residing here at Rome
Might be to you in Egypt. Yet, if you there
Did practise on my state, your being in Egypt
Might be my question.
ANTONY How intend you – practis'd?
CAESAR You may be pleas'd to catch at mine intent
By what did here befall me. Your wife and brother
Made wars upon me, and their contestation
Was theme for you; you were the word of war.
ANTONY You do mistake your business; my brother never
Did urge me in his act. I did inquire it,
And have my learning from some true reports
That drew their swords with you. Did he not rather
Discredit my authority with yours,
And make the wars alike against my stomach,
Having alike your cause? Of this my letters
Before did satisfy you. If you'll patch a quarrel,
As matter whole you have not to make it with,
It must not be with this.
CAESAR You praise yourself
By laying defects of judgement to me; but
You patch'd up your excuses.
ANTONY Not so, not so;
I know you could not lack, I am certain on't,
Very necessity of this thought, that I,
Your partner in the cause 'gainst which he fought,
Could not with graceful eyes attend those wars
Which fronted mine own peace. As for my wife,
I would you had her spirit in such another!
The third o' th' world is yours, which with a snaffle
You may pace easy, but not such a wife.
ENOBARBUS Would we had all such wives, that the men might go to wars with the women!
ANTONY So much uncurbable, her garboils, Caesar,
Made out of her impatience – which not wanted
Shrewdness of policy too – I grieving grant
Did you too much disquiet. For that you must
But say I could not help it.
CAESAR I wrote to you
When rioting in Alexandria; you
Did pocket up my letters, and with taunts
Did gibe my missive out of audience.
ANTONY Sir,
He fell upon me ere admitted. Then
Three kings I had newly feasted, and did want
Of what I was i' th' morning; but next day
I told him of myself, which was as much
As to have ask'd him pardon. Let this fellow
Be nothing of our strife; if we contend,
Out of our question wipe him.
CAESAR You have broken
The article of your oath, which you shall never
Have tongue to charge me with.
LEPIDUS Soft, Caesar!
ANTONY No;
Lepidus, let him speak.
The honour is sacred which he talks on now,
Supposing that I lack'd it. But on, Caesar:
The article of my oath –
CAESAR To lend me arms and aid when I requir'd them,
The which you both denied.
ANTONY Neglected, rather;
And then when poisoned hours had bound me up
From mine own knowledge. As nearly as I may,
I'll play the penitent to you; but mine honesty
Shall not make poor my greatness, nor my power
Work without it. Truth is, that Fulvia,
To have me out of Egypt, made wars here;
For which myself, the ignorant motive, do
So far ask pardon as befits mine honour
To stoop in such a case.
LEPIDUS 'Tis noble spoken.
MAECENAS If it might please you to enforce no further
The griefs between ye – to forget them quite

Were to remember that the present need
Speaks to atone you.

LEPIDUS Worthily spoken, Maecenas.

ENOBARBUS Or, if you borrow one another's love for the instant, you may, when you hear no more words of Pompey, return it again. You shall have time to wrangle in when you have nothing else to do.

ANTONY Thou art a soldier only. Speak no more.

ENOBARBUS That truth should be silent I had almost forgot.

ANTONY You wrong this presence; therefore speak no more.

ENOBARBUS Go to, then – your considerate stone!

CAESAR I do not much dislike the matter, but
The manner of his speech; for't cannot be
We shall remain in friendship, our conditions
So diff'ring in their acts. Yet if I knew
What hoop should hold us stanch, from edge to edge
O' th' world, I would pursue it.

AGRIPPA Give me leave, Caesar.

CAESAR Speak, Agrippa.

AGRIPPA Thou hast a sister by the mother's side,
Admir'd Octavia. Great Mark Antony
Is now a widower.

CAESAR Say not so, Agrippa.
If Cleopatra heard you, your reproof
Were well deserv'd of rashness.

ANTONY I am not married, Caesar. Let me hear
Agrippa further speak.

AGRIPPA To hold you in perpetual amity,
To make you brothers, and to knit your hearts
With an unslipping knot, take Antony
Octavia to his wife; whose beauty claims
No worse a husband than the best of men;
Whose virtue and whose general graces speak
That which none else can utter. By this marriage,
All little jealousies, which now seem great,
And all great fears, which now import their dangers,
Would then be nothing. Truths would be tales,
Where now half tales be truths. Her love to both
Would each to other, and all loves to both,
Draw after her. Pardon what I have spoke;
For 'tis a studied, not a present thought,
By duty ruminated.

ANTONY Will Caesar speak?

CAESAR Not till he hears how Antony is touch'd
With what is spoke already.

ANTONY What power is in Agrippa,
If I would say 'Agrippa, be it so',
To make this good?

CAESAR The power of Caesar, and.
His power unto Octavia.

ANTONY May I never.
To this good purpose, that so fairly shows,
Dream of impediment! Let me have thy hand.
Further this act of grace; and from this hour
The heart of brothers govern in our loves
And sway our great designs!

CAESAR There is my hand.
A sister I bequeath you, whom no brother
Did ever love so dearly. Let her live
To join our kingdoms and our hearts; and never
Fly off our loves again!

LEPIDUS Happily, amen!

ANTONY I did not think to draw my sword 'gainst Pompey;
For he hath laid strange courtesies and great
Of late upon me. I must thank him only,
Lest my remembrance suffer ill report;
At heel of that, defy him.

LEPIDUS Time calls upon's.
Of us must Pompey presently be sought,
Or else he seeks out us.

ANTONY Where lies he?

CAESAR About the Mount Misenum.

ANTONY What is his strength by land?

CAESAR Great and increasing; but by sea
He is an absolute master.

ANTONY So is the fame.
Would we had spoke together! Haste we for it.
Yet, ere we put ourselves in arms, dispatch we
The business we have talk'd of.

CAESAR With most gladness;
And do invite you to my sister's view,
Whither straight I'll lead you.

ANTONY Let us, Lepidus,
Not lack your company.

LEPIDUS Noble Antony,
Not sickness should detain me.

[*Flourish. Exeunt all but Enobarbus, Agrippa, Maecenas.*

MAECENAS Welcome from Egypt, sir.

ENOBARBUS Half the heart of Caesar, worthy Maecenas! My honourable friend, Agrippa!

AGRIPPA Good Enobarbus!

MAECENAS We have cause to be glad that matters are so well digested. You stay'd well by't in Egypt.

ENOBARBUS Ay, sir; we did sleep day out of countenance and made the night light with drinking.

MAECENAS Eight wild boars roasted whole at a breakfast, and but twelve persons there. Is this true?

ENOBARBUS This was but as a fly by an eagle. We had much more monstrous matter of feast, which worthily deserved noting.

MAECENAS She's a most triumphant lady, if report

be square to her.

ENOBARBUS When she first met Mark Antony she purs'd up his heart, upon the river of Cydnus.

AGRIPPA There she appear'd indeed! Or my reporter devis'd well for her.

ENOBARBUS I will tell you.
The barge she sat in, like a burnish'd throne,
Burn'd on the water. The poop was beaten gold;
Purple the sails, and so perfumed that
The winds were love-sick with them; the oars were silver,
Which to the tune of flutes kept stroke, and made
The water which they beat to follow faster,
As amorous of their strokes. For her own person,
It beggar'd all description. She did lie
In her pavilion, cloth-of-gold, of tissue,
O'erpicturing that Venus where we see
The fancy out-work nature. On each side her
Stood pretty dimpled boys, like smiling Cupids,
With divers-colour'd fans, whose wind did seem
To glow the delicate cheeks which they did cool,
And what they undid did.

AGRIPPA O, rare for Antony!

ENOBARBUS Her gentlewomen, like the Nereides,
So many mermaids, tended her i' th' eyes,
And made their bends adornings. At the helm
A seeming mermaid steers. The silken tackle
Swell with the touches of those flower-soft hands
That yarely frame the office. From the barge
A strange invisible perfume hits the sense
Of the adjacent wharfs. The city cast
Her people out upon her; and Antony,
Enthron'd i' th' market-place, did sit alone,
Whistling to th' air; which, but for vacancy,
Had gone to gaze on Cleopatra too,
And made a gap in nature.

AGRIPPA Rare Egyptian!

ENOBARBUS Upon her landing, Antony sent to her,
Invited her to supper. She replied
It should be better he became her guest;
Which she entreated. Our courteous Antony,
Whom ne'er the word of 'No' woman heard speak,
Being barber'd ten times o'er, goes to the feast,
And for his ordinary pays his heart
For what his eyes eat only.

AGRIPPA Royal wench!
She made great Caesar lay his sword to bed.
He ploughed her, and she cropp'd.

ENOBARBUS I saw her once
Hop forty paces through the public street;
And, having lost her breath, she spoke, and panted,
That she did make defect perfection,
And, breathless, pow'r breathe forth.

MAECENAS Now Antony must leave her utterly.

ENOBARBUS Never! He will not.
Age cannot wither her, nor custom stale
Her infinite variety. Other women cloy
The appetites they feed, but she makes hungry
Where most she satisfies; for vilest things
Become themselves in her, that the holy priests
Bless her when she is riggish.

MAECENAS If beauty, wisdom, modesty, can settle
The heart of Antony, Octavia is
A blessed lottery to him.

AGRIPPA Let us go.
Good Enobarbus, make yourself my guest
Whilst you abide here.

ENOBARBUS Humbly, sir, I thank you. [*Exeunt.*

SCENE III. *Rome. Caesar's house.*

Enter ANTONY, CAESAR, OCTAVIA between them.

ANTONY The world and my great office will sometimes
Divide me from your bosom.

OCTAVIA All which time
Before the gods my knee shall bow my prayers
To them for you.

ANTONY Good night, sir. My Octavia,
Read not my blemishes in the world's report.
I have not kept my square; but that to come
Shall all be done by th' rule. Good night, dear lady.

OCTAVIA Good night, sir.

CAESAR Good night.

[*Exeunt Caesar and Octavia.*

Enter Soothsayer.

ANTONY Now, sirrah, you do wish yourself in Egypt?

SOOTHSAYER Would I had never come from thence, nor you thither!

ANTONY If you can – your reason.

SOOTHSAYER I see it in my motion, have it not in my tongue; but yet hie you to Egypt again.

ANTONY Say to me,
Whose fortunes shall rise higher, Caesar's or mine?

SOOTHSAYER Caesar's.
Therefore, O Antony, stay not by his side.
Thy daemon, that thy spirit which keeps thee, is
Noble, courageous, high, unmatchable,
Where Caesar's is not; but near him thy angel
Becomes a fear, as being o'erpow'r'd. Therefore
Make space enough between you.

ANTONY Speak this no more.
SOOTHSAYER To none but thee; no more but when to thee.
If thou dost play with him at any game,
Thou art sure to lose; and of that natural luck
He beats thee 'gainst the odds. Thy lustre thickens
When he shines by. I say again, thy spirit
Is all afraid to govern thee near him;
But, he away, 'tis noble.
ANTONY Get thee gone.
Say to Ventidius I would speak with him.
[Exit Soothsayer.

He shall to Parthia. – Be it art or hap,
He hath spoken true. The very dice obey him;
And in our sports my better cunning faints
Under his chance. If we draw lots, he speeds;
His cocks do win the battle still of mine,
When it is all to nought, and his quails ever
Beat mine, inhoop'd, at odds. I will to Egypt;
And though I make this marriage for my peace,
I' th' East my pleasure lies.

Enter VENTIDIUS.

O, come, Ventidius,
You must to Parthia. Your commission's ready;
Follow me and receive't. *[Exeunt.*

SCENE IV. *Rome. A street.*

Enter LEPIDUS, MAECENAS, and AGRIPPA.

LEPIDUS Trouble yourselves no further. Pray you hasten
Your generals after.
AGRIPPA Sir, Mark Antony
Will e'en but kiss Octavia, and we'll follow.
LEPIDUS Till I shall see in you in your soldier's dress,
Which will become you both, farewell.
MAECENAS We shall,
As I conceive the journey, be at th' Mount
Before you, Lepidus.
LEPIDUS Your way is shorter;
My purposes do draw me much about.
You'll win two days upon me.
BOTH Sir, good success!
LEPIDUS Farewell. *[Exeunt.*

SCENE V. *Alexandria. Cleopatra's palace.*

Enter CLEOPATRA, CHARMIAN, IRAS, and ALEXAS.

CLEOPATRA Give me some music – music, moody food
Of us that trade in love.
ALL The music, ho!

Enter MARDIAN the Eunuch

CLEOPATRA Let it alone! Let's to billiards.
Come, Charmian.
CHARMIAN My arm is sore; best play with Mardian.
CLEOPATRA As well a woman with an eunuch play'd
As with a woman. Come, you'll play with me, sir?
MARDIAN As well as I can, madam.
CLEOPATRA And when good will is show'd, though't come too short,
The actor may plead pardon. I'll none now.
Give me mine angle – we'll to th' river. There,
My music playing far off, I will betray
Tawny-finn'd fishes; my bended hook shall pierce
Their slimy jaws; and as I draw them up
I'll think them every one an Antony,
And say 'Ah ha! Y'are caught'.
CHARMIAN 'Twas merry when
You wager'd on your angling; when your diver
Did hang a salt fish on his hook, which he
With fervency drew up.
CLEOPATRA That time? O times!
I laugh'd him out of patience; and that night
I laugh'd him into patience; and next morn,
Ere the ninth hour, I drunk him to his bed,
Then put my tires and mantles on him, whilst
I wore his sword Philippan.

Enter A Messenger.

O! from Italy?
Ram thou thy fruitful tidings in mine ears,
That long time have been barren.
MESSENGER Madam, madam –
CLEOPATRA Antony's dead! If thou say so, villain,
Thou kill'st thy mistress; but well and free,
If thou so yield him, there is gold, and here
My bluest veins to kiss – a hand that kings
Have lipp'd, and trembled kissing.
MESSENGER First, madam, he is well.
CLEOPATRA Why, there's more gold.
But, sirrah, mark, we use
To say the dead are well. Bring it to that,
The gold I give thee will I melt and pour
Down thy ill-uttering throat.
MESSENGER Good madam, hear me.
CLEOPATRA Well, go to, I will.
But there's no goodness in thy face. If Antony
Be free and healthful – why so tart a favour
To trumpet such good tidings? If not well,
Thou shouldst come like a Fury crown'd with snakes,
Not like a formal man.
MESSENGER Will't please you hear me?
CLEOPATRA I have a mind to strike thee ere thou speak'st.

Yet, if thou say Antony lives, is well,
Or friends with Caesar, or not captive to him,
I'll set thee in a shower of gold, and hail
Rich pearls upon thee.

MESSENGER Madam, he's well.

CLEOPATRA Well said.

MESSENGER And friends with Caesar.

CLEOPATRA Th'art an honest man.

MESSENGER Caesar and he are greater friends than ever.

CLEOPATRA Make thee a fortune from me.

MESSENGER But yet, madam –

CLEOPATRA I do not like 'but yet'. It does allay
The good precedence; fie upon 'but yet'!
'But yet' is as a gaoler to bring forth
Some monstrous malefactor. Prithee, friend,
Pour out the pack of matter to mine ear,
The good and bad together. He's friends with Caesar;
In state of health, thou say'st; and, thou say'st, free.

MESSENGER Free, madam! No; I made no such report.
He's bound unto Octavia.

CLEOPATRA For what good turn?

MESSENGER For the best turn i' th' bed.

CLEOPATRA I am pale, Charmian.

MESSENGER Madam, he's married to Octavia.

CLEOPATRA The most infectious pestilence upon thee! *[Strikes him down.*

MESSENGER Good madam, patience.

CLEOPATRA What say you? Hence, *[Strikes him.*
Horrible villain! or I'll spurn thine eyes
Like balls before me; I'll unhair thy head;
[She hales him up and down.
Thou shalt be whipp'd with wire and stew'd in brine,
Smarting in ling'ring pickle.

MESSENGER Gracious madam,
I that do bring the news made not the match.

CLEOPATRA Say 'tis not so, a province I will give thee,
And make thy fortunes proud. The blow thou hadst
Shall make thy peace for moving me to rage;
And I will boot thee with what gift beside
Thy modesty can beg.

MESSENGER He's married, madam.

CLEOPATRA Rogue, thou hast liv'd too long.
[Draws a knife.

MESSENGER Nay, then I'll run.
What mean you, madam? I have made no fault. *[Exit.*

CHARMIAN Good madam, keep yourself within yourself:
The man is innocent.

CLEOPATRA Some innocents scape not the thunderbolt.
Melt Egypt into Nile! and kindly creatures
Turn all to serpents! Call the slave again.
Though I am mad, I will not bite him. Call!

CHARMIAN He is afear'd to come.

CLEOPATRA I will not hurt him.
These hands do lack nobility, that they strike
A meaner than myself; since I myself
Have given myself the cause.

Enter the Messenger again.

Come hither, sir.
Though it be honest, it is never good
To bring bad news. Give to a gracious message
An host of tongues; but let ill tidings tell
Themselves when they be felt.

MESSENGER I have done my duty.

CLEOPATRA Is he married?
I cannot hate thee worser than I do
If thou again say 'Yes'.

MESSENGER He's married, madam.

CLEOPATRA The gods confound thee! Dost thou hold there still?

MESSENGER Should I lie, madam?

CLEOPATRA O, I would thou didst,
So half my Egypt were submerg'd and made
A cistern for scal'd snakes! Go, get thee hence.
Hadst thou Narcissus in thy face, to me
Thou wouldst appear most ugly. He is married?

MESSENGER I crave your Highness' pardon.

CLEOPATRA He is married?

MESSENGER Take no offence that I would not offend you;
To punish me for what you make me do
Seems much unequal. He's married to Octavia.

CLEOPATRA O, that his fault should make a knave of thee
That art not what th'art sure of! Get thee hence.
The merchandise which thou hast brought from Rome
Are all too dear for me. Lie they upon thy hand,
And be undone by 'em! *[Exit Messenger.*

CHARMIAN Good your Highness, patience.

CLEOPATRA In praising Antony I have disprais'd Caesar.

CHARMIAN Many times, madam.

CLEOPATRA I am paid for't now. Lead me from hence,
I faint. O Iras, Charmian! 'Tis no matter.
Go to the fellow, good Alexas; bid him
Report the feature of Octavia, her years,
Her inclination; let him not leave out
The colour of her hair. Bring me word quickly.
[Exit Alexas.

Let him for ever go – let him not, Charmian –
Though he be painted one way like a Gorgon,
The other way's a Mars. [*To Mardian*] Bid you Alexas
Bring me word how tall she is. – Pity me, Charmian,
But do not speak to me. Lead me to my chamber. [*Exeunt.*

SCENE VI. *Near Misenum.*

Flourish. Enter POMPEY and MENAS at one door, with drum and trumpet; at another, CAESAR, ANTONY, LEPIDUS, ENOBARBUS, MAECENAS, AGRIPPA, with Soldiers marching.

POMPEY Your hostages I have, so have you mine;
And we shall talk before we fight.

CAESAR Most meet
That first we come to words; and therefore have we
Our written purposes before us sent;
Which if thou hast considered, let us know
If 'twill tie up thy discontented sword
And carry back to Sicily much tall youth
That else must perish here.

POMPEY To you all three,
The senators alone of this great world,
Chief factors for the gods: I do not know
Wherefore my father should revengers want,
Having a son and friends, since Julius Caesar,
Who at Philippi the good Brutus ghosted,
There saw you labouring for him. What was't
That mov'd pale Cassius to conspire? and what
Made the all-honour'd honest Roman, Brutus,
With the arm'd rest, courtiers of beauteous freedom,
To drench the Capitol, but that they would
Have one man but a man? And that is it
Hath made me rig my navy, at whose burden
The anger'd ocean foams; with which I meant
To scourge th' ingratitude that despiteful Rome
Cast on my noble father.

CAESAR Take your time.

ANTONY Thou canst not fear us, Pompey, with thy sails;
We'll speak with thee at sea; at land thou know'st
How much we do o'er-count thee.

POMPEY At land, indeed,
Thou dost o'er-count me of my father's house.
But since the cuckoo builds not for himself,
Remain in't as thou mayst.

LEPIDUS Be pleas'd to tell us –
For this is from the present – how you take
The offers we have sent you.

CAESAR There's the point.

ANTONY Which do not be entreated to, but weigh
What it is worth embrac'd.

CAESAR And what may follow,
To try a larger fortune.

POMPEY You have made me offer
Of Sicily, Sardinia; and I must
Rid all the sea of pirates; then to send
Measures of wheat to Rome; this 'greed upon,
To part with unhack'd edges and bear back
Our targes undinted.

ALL That's our offer.

POMPEY Know, then,
I came before you here a man prepar'd
To take this offer; but Mark Antony
Put me to some impatience. Though I lose
The praise of it by telling, you must know,
When Caesar and your brother were at blows,
Your mother came to Sicily and did find
Her welcome friendly.

ANTONY I have heard it, Pompey,
And am well studied for a liberal thanks
Which I do owe you.

POMPEY Let me have your hand.
I did not think, sir, to have met you here.

ANTONY The beds i' th' East are soft; and thanks to you,
That call'd me timelier than my purpose hither;
For I gave gained by't.

CAESAR Since I saw you last
There is a change upon you.

POMPEY Well, I know not
What counts harsh fortune casts upon my face;
But in my bosom shall she never come
To make my heart her vassal.

LEPIDUS Well met here.

POMPEY I hope so, Lepidus. Thus we are agreed.
I crave our composition may be written,
And seal'd between us.

CAESAR That's the next to do.

POMPEY We'll feast each other ere we part, and let's
Draw lots who shall begin.

ANTONY That will I, Pompey.

POMPEY No, Antony, take the lot;
But, first or last, your fine Egyptian cookery
Shall have the fame. I have heard that Julius Caesar
Grew fat with feasting there.

ANTONY You have heard much.

POMPEY I have fair meanings, sir.

ANTONY And fair words to them.

POMPEY Then so much have I heard;
And I have heard Apollodorus carried –

ENOBARBUS No more of that! He did so.

POMPEY What, I pray you?

ENOBARBUS A certain queen to Caesar in a
mattress.
POMPEY I know thee now. How far'st thou,
soldier?
ENOBARBUS Well;
And well am like to do, for I perceive
Four feasts are toward.
POMPEY Let me shake thy hand.
I never hated thee; I have seen thee fight,
When I have envied thy behaviour.
ENOBARBUS Sir,
I never lov'd you much; but I ha' prais'd ye
When you have well deserv'd ten times as much
As I have said you did.
POMPEY Enjoy thy plainness;
It nothing ill becomes thee.
Aboard my galley I invite you all.
Will you lead, lords?
ALL Show's the way sir.
POMPEY Come.
[Exeunt all but Enobarbus and Menas.
MENAS *[Aside]* Thy father, Pompey, would ne'er
have made this treaty. –
You and I have known, sir.
ENOBARBUS At sea, I think.
MENAS We have, sir.
ENOBARBUS You have done well by water.
MENAS And you by land.
ENOBARBUS I will praise any man that will praise me; though it cannot be denied what I have done by land.
MENAS Nor what I have done by water.
ENOBARBUS Yes, something you can deny for your own safety: you have been a great thief by sea.
MENAS And you by land.
ENOBARBUS There I deny my land service. But give me your hand, Menas; if our eyes had authority, here they might take two thieves kissing.
MENAS All men's faces are true, whatsome'er their hands are.
ENOBARBUS But there is never a fair woman has a true face.
MENAS No slander: they steal hearts.
ENOBARBUS We came hither to fight with you.
MENAS For my part, I am sorry it is turn'd to a drinking. Pompey doth this day laugh away his fortune.
ENOBARBUS If he do, sure he cannot weep't back again.
MENAS Y'have said, sir. We look'd not for Mark Antony here. Pray you, is he married to Cleopatra?
ENOBARBUS Caesar's sister is call'd Octavia.
MENAS True, sir; she was the wife of Caius Marcellus.
ENOBARBUS But she is now the wife of Marcus Antonius.
MENAS Pray ye, sir?
ENOBARBUS 'Tis true.
MENAS Then is Caesar and he for ever knit together.
ENOBARBUS If I were bound to divine of this unity, I would not prophesy so.
MENAS I think the policy of that purpose made more in the marriage than the love of the parties.
ENOBARBUS I think so too. But you shall find the band that seems to tie their friendship together will be the very strangler of their amity: Octavia is of a holy, cold, and still conversation.
MENAS Who would not have his wife so?
ENOBARBUS Not he that himself is not so; which is Mark Antony. He will to his Egyptian dish again; then shall the sighs of Octavia blow the fire up in Caesar, and, as I said before, that which is the strength of their amity shall prove the immediate author of their variance. Antony will use his affection where it is; he married but his occasion here.
MENAS And thus it may be. Come, sir, will you aboard? I have a health for you.
ENOBARBUS I shall take it, sir. We have us'd our throats in Egypt.
MENAS Come, let's away. *[Exeunt.*

SCENE VII. *On board Pompey's galley, off Misenum.*

Music plays. Enter two or three Servants with a banquet.

1 SERVANT Here they'll be, man. Some o' their plants are ill-rooted already; the least wind i' th' world will blow them down.
2 SERVANT Lepidus is high-colour'd.
1 SERVANT They have made him drink alms-drink.
2 SERVANT As they pinch one another by the disposition, he cries out 'No more!'; reconciles them to his entreaty and himself to th' drink.
1 SERVANT But it raises the greater war between him and his discretion.
2 SERVANT Why, this it is to have a name in great men's fellowship. I had as lief have a reed that will do me no service as a partizan I could not heave.
1 SERVANT To be call'd into a huge sphere, and not to be seen to move in't, are the holes where eyes should be, which pitifully disaster the cheeks.

A sennet sounded. Enter CAESAR, ANTONY, LEPIDUS, POMPEY, AGRIPPA, MAECENAS, ENOBARBUS, MENAS, with other Captains.

ANTONY [*To Caesar*] Thus do they, sir: they take the flow o' th' Nile
By certain scales i' th' pyramid; they know
By th' height, the lowness, or the mean, if dearth
Or foison follow. The higher Nilus swells
The more it promises; as it ebbs, the seedsman
Upon the slime and ooze scatters his grain,
And shortly comes to harvest.

LEPIDUS Y'have strange serpents there.

ANTONY Ay, Lepidus.

LEPIDUS Your serpent of Egypt is bred now of your mud by the operation of your sun; so is your crocodile.

ANTONY They are so.

POMPEY Sit – and some wine! A health to Lepidus!

LEPIDUS I am not so well as I should be, but I'll ne'er out.

ENOBARBUS Not till you have slept. I fear me you'll be in till then.

LEPIDUS Nay, certainly, I have heard the Ptolemies' pyramises are very goodly things. Without contradiction I have heard that.

MENAS [*Aside to Pompey*] Pompey, a word.

POMPEY [*Aside to Menas*] Say in mine ear; what is't?

MENAS [*Aside to Pompey*] Forsake thy seat, I do beseech thee, Captain,
And hear me speak a word.

POMPEY [*Whispers in's ear*] Forbear me till anon –
This wine for Lepidus!

LEPIDUS What manner o' thing is your crocodile?

ANTONY It is shap'd, sir, like itself, and it is as broad as it hath breadth; it is just so high as it is, and moves with it own organs. It lives by that which nourisheth it, and the elements once out of it, it transmigrates.

LEPIDUS What colour is it of?

ANTONY Of it own colour too.

LEPIDUS 'Tis a strange serpent.

ANTONY 'Tis so. And the tears of it are wet.

CAESAR Will this description satisfy him?

ANTONY With the health that Pompey gives him, else he is a very epicure.

POMPEY [*Aside to Menas*] Go, hang, sir, hang! Tell me of that! Away!
Do as I bid you. – Where's this cup I call'd for?

MENAS [*Aside to Pompey*] If for the sake of merit thou wilt hear me,
Rise from thy stool.

POMPEY [*Aside to Menas*] I think th'art mad.
[*Rises and walks aside*] The matter?

MENAS I have ever held my cap off to thy fortunes.

POMPEY Thou hast serv'd me with much faith.
What's else to say? –
Be jolly, lords.

ANTONY These quicksands, Lepidus,
Keep off them, for you sink.

MENAS Wilt thou be lord of all the world?

POMPEY What say'st thou?

MENAS Wilt thou be lord of the whole world?
That's twice.

POMPEY How should that be?

MENAS But entertain it,
And though thou think me poor, I am the man
Will give thee all the world.

POMPEY Hast thou drunk well?

MENAS No, Pompey, I have kept me from the cup.
Thou art, if thou dar'st be, the earthly Jove;
Whate'er the ocean pales or sky inclips
Is thine, if thou wilt ha't.

POMPEY Show me which way.

MENAS These three world-sharers, these competitors,
Are in thy vessel. Let me cut the cable;
And when we are put off, fall to their throats.
All there is thine.

POMPEY Ah, this thou shouldst have done,
And not have spoke on't. In me 'tis villainy:
In thee't had been good service. Thou must know
'Tis not my profit that does lead mine honour:
Mine honour, it. Repent that e'er thy tongue
Hath so betray'd thine act. Being done unknown,
I should have found it afterwards well done,
But must condemn it now. Desist, and drink.

MENAS [*Aside*] For this,
I'll never follow thy pall'd fortunes more.
Who seeks, and will not take when once 'tis offer'd,
Shall never find it more.

POMPEY This health to Lepidus!

ANTONY Bear him ashore, I'll pledge it for him, Pompey.

ENOBARBUS Here's to thee, Menas!

MENAS Enobarbus, welcome!

POMPEY Fill till the cup be hid.

ENOBARBUS There's a strong fellow, Menas.

[*Pointing to the Servant who carries off Lepidus.*

MENAS Why?

ENOBARBUS 'A bears the third part of the world, man; see'st not?

MENAS The third part, then, is drunk. Would it were all,
That it might go on wheels!

ENOBARBUS Drink thou; increase the reels.
MENAS Come.
POMPEY This is not yet an Alexandrian feast.
ANTONY It ripens towards it. Strike the vessels, ho!
Here's to Caesar!
CAESAR I could well forbear't.
It's monstrous labour when I wash my brain
And it grows fouler.
ANTONY Be a child o' th' time.
CAESAR Possess it, I'll make answer.
But I had rather fast from all four days
Than drink so much in one.
ENOBARBUS *[To Antony]* Ha, my brave emperor!
Shall we dance now the Egyptian Bacchanals
And celebrate our drink?
POMPEY Let's ha't, good soldier.
ANTONY Come, let's all take hands,
Till that the conquering wine hath steep'd our sense
In soft and delicate Lethe.
ENOBARBUS All take hands.
Make battery to our ears with the loud music,
The while I'll place you; then the boy shall sing;
The holding every man shall bear as loud
As his strong sides can volley.
[Music plays. Enobarbus places them hand in hand.

The Song.

Come, thou monarch of the vine,
Plumpy Bacchus with pink eyne!
In thy fats our cares be drown'd,
With thy grapes our hairs be crown'd.
Cup us till the world go round,
Cup us till the world go round!

CAESAR What would you more? Pompey, good night. Good brother,
Let me request you off; our graver business
Frowns at this levity. Gentle lords, let's part;
You see we have burnt our cheeks. Strong Enobarb
Is weaker than the wine, and mine own tongue
Splits what it speaks. The wild disguise hath almost
Antick'd us all. What needs more words? Good night.
Good Antony, your hand.
POMPEY I'll try you on the shore.
ANTONY And shall, sir. Give's your hand.
POMPEY O Antony,
You have my father's house – but what? We are friends.
Come, down into the boat.
ENOBARBUS Take heed you fall not.
[Exeunt all but Enobarbus and Menas.
Menas, I'll not on shore.
MENAS No, to my cabin.
These drums! these trumpets, flutes! what!
Let Neptune hear we bid a loud farewell
To these great fellows. Sound and be hang'd, sound out!
[Sound a flourish, with drums.
ENOBARBUS Hoo! says 'a. There's my cap.
MENAS Hoo! Noble Captain, come. *[Exeunt.*

ACT THREE

SCENE I. *A Plain in Syria.*

Enter VENTIDIUS, as it were in triumph, with SILIUS and other Romans, Officers and Soldiers; the dead body of PACORUS borne before him.

VENTIDIUS Now, darting Parthia, art thou struck, and now
Pleas'd fortune does of Marcus Crassus' death
Make me revenger. Bear the King's son's body
Before our army. Thy Pacorus, Orodes,
Pays this for Marcus Crassus.
SILIUS Noble Ventidius,
Whilst yet with Parthian blood thy sword is warm
The fugitive Parthians follow; spur through Media,
Mesopotamia, and the shelters whither
The routed fly. So thy grand captain, Antony,
Shall set thee on triumphant chariots and
Put garlands on thy head.
VENTIDIUS O Silius, Silius,
I have done enough. A lower place, note well,
May make too great an act; for learn this, Silius:
Better to leave undone than by our deed
Acquire too high a fame when him we serve's away.
Caesar and Antony have ever won
More in their officer, than person. Sossius,
One of my place in Syria, his lieutenant,
For quick accumulation of renown,
Which he achiev'd by th' minute, lost his favour.
Who does i' th' wars more than his captain can
Becomes his captain's captain; and ambition,

The soldier's virtue, rather makes choice of loss
Than gain which darkens him.
I could do more to do Antonius good,
But 'twould offend him; and in his offence
Should my performance perish.

SILIUS Thou hast, Ventidius, that
Without the which a soldier and his sword
Grants scarce distinction. Thou wilt write to
Antony?

VENTIDIUS I'll humbly signify what in his name,
That magical word of war, we have effected;
How, with his banners, and his well-paid ranks,
The ne'er-yet-beaten horse of Parthia
We have jaded out o' th' field.

SILIUS Where is he now?

VENTIDIUS He purposeth to Athens; whither, with what haste
The weight we must convey with's will permit,
We shall appear before him. – On, there; pass
along. [*Exeunt.*

SCENE II. *Rome. Caesar's house.*

Enter AGRIPPA at one door, ENOBARBUS at another.

AGRIPPA What, are the brothers parted?

ENOBARBUS They have dispatch'd with Pompey; he is gone;
The other three are sealing. Octavia weeps
To part from Rome; Caesar is sad; and Lepidus,
Since Pompey's feast, as Menas says, is troubled
With the green sickness.

AGRIPPA 'Tis a noble Lepidus.

ENOBARBUS A very fine one. O, how he loves Caesar!

AGRIPPA Nay, but how dearly he adores Mark Antony!

ENOBARBUS Caesar? Why he's the Jupiter of men.

AGRIPPA What's Antony? The god of Jupiter.

ENOBARBUS Spake you of Caesar? How! the nonpareil!

AGRIPPA O, Antony! O thou Arabian bird!

ENOBARBUS Would you praise Caesar, say 'Caesar' – go no further.

AGRIPPA Indeed, he plied them both with excellent praises.

ENOBARBUS But he loves Caesar best. Yet he loves Antony.
Hoo! hearts, tongues, figures, scribes, bards, poets, cannot
Think, speak, cast, write, sing, number – hoo! –
His love to Antony. But as for Caesar,
Kneel down, kneel down, and wonder.

AGRIPPA Both he loves.

ENOBARBUS They are his shards, and he their beetle. [*Trumpets within*] So –
This is to horse. Adieu, noble Agrippa.

AGRIPPA Good fortune, worthy soldier, and farewell.

Enter CAESAR, ANTONY, LEPIDUS, and OCTAVIA.

ANTONY No further, sir.

CAESAR You take from me a great part of myself;
Use me well in't. Sister, prove such a wife
As my thoughts make thee, and as my farthest band
Shall pass on thy approof. Most noble Antony,
Let not the piece of virtue which is set
Betwixt us as the cement of our love
To keep it builded be the ram to batter
The fortress of it; for better might we
Have lov'd without this mean, if on both parts
This be not cherish'd.

ANTONY Make me not offended
In your distrust.

CAESAR I have said.

ANTONY You shall not find,
Though you be therein curious, the least cause
For what you seem to fear. So the gods keep you,
And make the hearts of Romans serve your ends!
We will here part.

CAESAR Farewell, my dearest sister, fare thee well.
The elements be kind to thee and make
Thy spirits all of comfort! Fare thee well.

OCTAVIA My noble brother!

ANTONY The April's in her eyes. It is love's spring,
And these the showers to bring it on. Be cheerful.

OCTAVIA Sir, look well to my husband's house; and –

CAESAR What, Octavia?

OCTAVIA I'll tell you in your ear.

ANTONY Her tongue will not obey her heart, nor can
Her heart inform her tongue – the swan's down feather,
That stands upon the swell at the full of tide,
And neither way inclines.

ENOBARBUS [*Aside to Agrippa*] Will Caesar weep?

AGRIPPA [*Aside to Enobarbus*] He has a cloud in's face.

ENOBARBUS [*Aside to Agrippa*] He were the worse for that, were he a horse;
So is he, being a man.

AGRIPPA [*Aside to Enobarbus*] Why, Enobarbus,
When Antony found Julius Caesar dead,
He cried almost to roaring; and he wept
When at Philippi he found Brutus slain.

ENOBARBUS [*Aside to Agrippa*] That year, indeed,

he was troubled with a rheum;
What willingly he did confound he wail'd,
Believe't – till I weep too.
CAESAR No, sweet Octavia,
You shall hear from me still; the time shall not
Out-go my thinking on you.
ANTONY Come, sir, come;
I'll wrestle with you in my strength of love.
Look here I have you; thus I let you go,
And give you to the gods.
CAESAR Adieu; be happy!
LEPIDUS Let all the number of the stars give light
To thy fair way!
CAESAR Farewell, farewell! [*Kisses Octavia.*
ANTONY Farewell!
[*Trumpets sound. Exeunt.*

SCENE III. *Alexandria. Cleopatra's palace.*

Enter CLEOPATRA, CHARMIAN, IRAS, and ALEXAS.

CLEOPATRA Where is the fellow?
ALEXAS Half afeard to come.
CLEOPATRA Go to, go to.

Enter the Messenger as before.

Come hither, sir.
ALEXAS Good Majesty,
Herod of Jewry dare not look upon you
But when you are well pleas'd.
CLEOPATRA That Herod's head
I'll have. But how, when Antony is gone,
Through whom I might command it? Come thou near.
MESSENGER Most gracious Majesty!
CLEOPATRA Didst thou behold Octavia?
MESSENGER Ay, dread Queen.
CLEOPATRA Where?
MESSENGER Madam, in Rome
I look'd her in the face, and saw her led
Between her brother and Mark Antony.
CLEOPATRA Is she as tall as me?
MESSENGER She is not, madam.
CLEOPATRA Didst hear her speak? Is she shrill-tongu'd or low?
MESSENGER Madam, I heard her speak: she is low voic'd.
CLEOPATRA That's not so good. He cannot like her long.
CHARMIAN Like her? O Isis! 'tis impossible.
CLEOPATRA I think so, Charmian. Dull of tongue and dwarfish!
What majesty is in her gait? Remember,
If e'er thou look'dst on majesty.
MESSENGER She creeps.
Her motion and her station are as one;
She shows a body rather than a life,
A statue than a breather.
CLEOPATRA Is this certain?
MESSENGER Or I have no observance.
CHARMIAN Three in Egypt
Cannot make better note.
CLEOPATRA He's very knowing;
I do perceive't. There's nothing in her yet.
The fellow has good judgment.
CHARMIAN Excellent.
CLEOPATRA Guess at her years, I prithee.
MESSENGER Madam,
She was a widow.
CLEOPATRA Widow? Charmian, hark!
MESSENGER And I do think she's thirty.
CLEOPATRA Bear'st thou her face in mind? Is't long or round?
MESSENGER Round even to faultiness.
CLEOPATRA For the most part, too, they are foolish that are so.
Her hair, what colour?
MESSENGER Brown, madam; and her forehead
As low as she would wish it.
CLEOPATRA There's gold for thee.
Thou must not take my former sharpness ill.
I will employ thee back again; I find thee
Most fit for business. Go make thee ready;
Our letters are prepar'd.
[*Exit Messenger.*
CHARMIAN A proper man.
CLEOPATRA Indeed, he is so. I repent me much
That so I harried him. Why, methinks, by him,
This creature's no such thing.
CHARMIAN Nothing, madam.
CLEOPATRA The man hath seen some majesty, and should know.
CHARMIAN Hath he seen majesty? Isis else defend,
And serving you so long!
CLEOPATRA I have one thing more to ask him yet, good Charmian.
But 'tis no matter; thou shalt bring him to me
Where I will write. All may be well enough.
CHARMIAN I warrant you, madam. [*Exeunt.*

SCENE IV. *Athens. Antony's house.*

Enter ANTONY and OCTAVIA.

ANTONY Nay, nay, Octavia, not only that –
That were excusable, that and thousands more
Of semblable import – but he hath wag'd
New wars 'gainst Pompey; made his will, and read it
To public ear;
Spoke scantly of me; when perforce he could not
But pay me terms of honour, cold and sickly
He vented them, most narrow measure lent me;

When the best hint was given him, he not took't,
Or did it from his teeth.

OCTAVIA O my good lord,
Believe not all; or if you must believe,
Stomach not all. A more unhappy lady,
If this division chance, ne'er stood between,
Praying for both parts.
The good gods will mock me presently
When I shall pray 'O, bless my lord and husband!'
Undo that prayer by crying out as loud
'O, bless my brother!' Husband win, win brother,
Prays, and destroys the prayer; no mid-way
'Twixt these extremes at all.

ANTONY Gentle Octavia,
Let your best love draw to that point which seeks
Best to preserve it. If I lose mine honour,
I lose myself; better I were not yours
Than yours so branchless. But, as you requested,
Yourself shall go between's. The meantime, lady,
I'll raise the preparation of a war
Shall stain your brother. Make your soonest haste;
So your desires are yours.

OCTAVIA Thanks to my lord.
The Jove of power make me, most weak, most weak,
Your reconciler! Wars 'twixt you twain would be
As if the world should cleave, and that slain men
Should solder up the rift.

ANTONY When it appears to you where this begins,
Turn your displeasure that way, for our faults
Can never be so equal that your love
Can equally move with them. Provide your going;
Choose your own company, and command what cost
Your heart has mind to. [*Exeunt*.

SCENE V. *Athens. Antony's house.*

Enter ENOBARBUS and EROS, meeting.

ENOBARBUS How, now, friend Eros!

EROS There's strange news come, sir.

ENOBARBUS What, man?

EROS Caesar and Lepidus have made wars upon Pompey.

ENOBARBUS This is old. What is the success?

EROS Caesar, having made use of him in the wars 'gainst Pompey, presently denied him rivality, would not let him partake in the glory of the action; and not resting here, accuses him of letters he had formerly wrote to Pompey; upon his own appeal, seizes him. So the poor third is up, till death enlarge his confine.

ENOBARBUS Then, world, thou hast a pair of chaps – no more;
And throw between them all the food thou hast,
They'll grind the one the other. Where's Antony?

EROS He's walking in the garden – thus, and spurns
The rush that lies before him; cries 'Fool Lepidus!'
And threats the throat of that his officer
That murd'red Pompey.

ENOBARBUS Our great navy's rigg'd.

EROS For Italy and Caesar. More, Domitius:
My lord desires you presently; my news
I might have told hereafter.

ENOBARBUS 'Twill be naught;
But let it be. Bring me to Antony.

EROS Come, sir. [*Exeunt*.

SCENE VI. *Rome. Caesar's house.*

Enter CAESAR, AGRIPPA, and MAECENAS.

CAESAR Contemning Rome, he has done all this and more
In Alexandria. Here's the manner of't:
I' th' market-place, on a tribunal silver'd,
Cleopatra and himself in chairs of gold
Were publicly enthron'd; at the feet sat
Caesarion, whom they call my father's son,
And all the unlawful issue that their lust
Since then hath made between them. Unto her
He gave the stablishment of Egypt; made her
Of lower Syria, Cyprus, Lydia,
Absolute queen.

MAECENAS This in the public eye?

CAESAR I' th' common show-place, where they exercise.
His sons he there proclaim'd the kings of kings:
Great Media, Parthia, and Armenia,
He gave to Alexander; to Ptolemy he assign'd
Syria, Cilicia, and Phoenicia. She
In th' habiliments of the goddess Isis
That day appear'd; and oft before gave audience,
As 'tis reported, so.

MAECENAS Let Rome be thus
Inform'd.

AGRIPPA Who, queasy with his insolence
Already, will their good thoughts call from him.

CAESAR The people knows it, and have now receiv'd
His accusations.

AGRIPPA Who does he accuse?

CAESAR Caesar; and that, having in Sicily

Sextus Pompeius spoil'd, we had not rated him
His part o' th' isle. Then does he say he lent me
Some shipping, unrestor'd. Lastly, he frets
That Lepidus of the triumvirate
Should be depos'd; and, being, that we detain
All his revenue.

AGRIPPA Sir, this should be answer'd.

CAESAR 'Tis done already, and the messenger gone.
I have told him Lepidus was grown too cruel,
That he his high authority abus'd,
And did deserve his change. For what I have conquer'd
I grant him part; but then, in his Armenia
And other of his conquer'd kingdoms, I
Demand the like.

MAECENAS He'll never yield to that.

CAESAR Nor must not then be yielded to in this.

Enter OCTAVIA, with her Train.

OCTAVIA Hail, Caesar, and my lord! hail, most dear Caesar!

CAESAR That ever I should call thee castaway!

OCTAVIA You have not call'd me so, nor have you cause.

CAESAR Why have you stol'n upon us thus? You come not
Like Caesar's sister. The wife of Antony
Should have an army for an usher, and
The neighs of horse to tell of her approach
Long ere she did appear. The trees by th' way
Should have borne men, and expectation fainted,
Longing for what it had not. Nay, the dust
Should have ascended to the roof of heaven,
Rais'd by your populous troops. But you are come
A market-maid to Rome, and have prevented
The ostentation of our love, which left unshown
Is often left unlov'd. We should have met you
By sea and land, supplying every stage
With an augmented greeting.

OCTAVIA Good my lord,
To come thus was I not constrain'd, but did it
On my free will. My lord, Mark Antony,
Hearing that you prepar'd for war, acquainted
My grieved ear withal; whereon I begg'd
His pardon for return.

CAESAR Which soon he granted,
Being an obstruct 'tween his lust and him.

OCTAVIA Do not say so, my lord.

CAESAR I have eyes upon him,
And his affairs come to me on the wind.
Where is he now?

OCTAVIA My lord, in Athens.

CAESAR No, my most wronged sister: Cleopatra
Hath nodded him to her. He hath given his empire
Up to a whore, who now are levying
The kings o' th' earth for war. He hath assembled
Bocchus, the king of Libya; Archelaus
Of Cappadocia; Philadelphos, king
Of Paphlagonia; the Thracian King, Adallas;
King Manchus of Arabia; King of Pont;
Herod of Jewry; Mithridates, king
Of Comagene; Polemon and Amyntas,
The kings of Mede and Lycaonia, with a
More larger list of sceptres.

OCTAVIA Ay me most wretched,
That have my heart parted betwixt two friends,
That does afflict each other!

CAESAR Welcome hither.
Your letters did withhold our breaking forth,
Till we perceiv'd both how you were wrong led
And we in negligent danger. Cheer your heart;
Be you not troubled with the time, which drives
O'er your content these strong necessities,
But let determin'd things to destiny
Hold unbewail'd their way. Welcome to Rome;
Nothing more dear to me. You are abus'd
Beyond the mark of thought, and the high gods,
To do you justice, make their ministers
Of us and those that love you. Best of comfort,
And ever welcome to us.

AGRIPPA Welcome, lady.

MAECENAS Welcome, dear madam.
Each heart in Rome does love and pity you;
Only th' adulterous Antony, most large
In his abominations, turns you off,
And gives his potent regiment to a trull
That noises it against us.

OCTAVIA Is it so, sir?

CAESAR Most certain. Sister, welcome. Pray you
Be ever known to patience. My dear'st sister!

[*Exeunt.*

SCENE VII. *Antony's camp near Actium.*

Enter CLEOPATRA and ENOBARBUS.

CLEOPATRA I will be even with thee, doubt it not.

ENOBARBUS But why, why, why?

CLEOPATRA Thou hast forspoke my being in these wars,
And say'st it is not fit.

ENOBARBUS Well, is it, is it?

CLEOPATRA Is't not denounc'd against us? Why should not we
Be there in person?

ENOBARBUS [*Aside*] Well, I could reply:
If we should serve with horse and mares together
The horse were merely lost; the mares would bear

A soldier and his horse.
CLEOPATRA What is't you say?
ENOBARBUS Your presence needs must puzzle Antony;
Take from his heart, take from his brain, from's time,
What should not then be spar'd. He is already
Traduc'd for levity; and 'tis said in Rome
That Photinus an eunuch and your maids
Manage this war.
CLEOPATRA Sink Rome, and their tongues rot
That speak against us! A charge we bear i' th' war,
And, as the president of my kingdom, will
Appear there for a man. Speak not against it;
I will not stay behind.

Enter ANTONY and CANIDIUS.

ENOBARBUS Nay, I have done.
Here comes the Emperor.
ANTONY Is it not strange, Canidius,
That from Tarentum and Brundusium
He could so quickly cut the Ionian sea,
And take it in Toryne? – You have heard on't, sweet?
CLEOPATRA Celerity is never more admir'd
Than by the negligent.
ANTONY A good rebuke,
Which might have well becom'd the best of men
To taunt at slackness. Canidius, we
Will fight with him by sea.
CLEOPATRA By sea! What else?
CANIDIUS Why will my lord do so?
ANTONY For that he dares us to't.
ENOBARBUS So hath my lord dar'd him to single fight.
CANIDIUS Ay, and to wage this battle at Pharsalia,
Where Caesar fought with Pompey. But these offers,
Which serve not for his vantage, he shakes off;
And so should you.
ENOBARBUS Your ships are not well mann'd;
Your mariners are muleteers, reapers, people
Ingross'd by swift impress. In Caesar's fleet
Are those that often have 'gainst Pompey fought;
Their ships are yare; yours heavy. No disgrace
Shall fall you for refusing him at sea,
Being prepar'd for land.
ANTONY By sea, by sea.
ENOBARBUS Most worthy sir, you therein throw away
The absolute soldiership you have by land;
Distract your army, which doth most consist
Of war-mark'd footmen; leave unexecuted
Your own renowned knowledge; quite forgo
The way which promises assurance; and
Give up yourself merely to chance and hazard
From firm security.
ANTONY I'll fight at sea.
CLEOPATRA I have sixty sails, Caesar none better.
ANTONY Our overplus of shipping will we burn,
And, with the rest full-mann'd, from th' head of Actium
Beat th' approaching Caesar. But if we fail,
We then can do't at land.

Enter a Messenger.

Thy business?
MESSENGER The news is true, my lord: he is descried;
Caesar has taken Toryne.
ANTONY Can he be there in person? 'Tis impossible –
Strange that his power should be. Canidius,
Our nineteenth legions thou shalt hold by land,
And our twelve thousand horse. We'll to our ship.
Away, my Thetis!

Enter a Soldier.

How now, worthy soldier?
SOLDIER O noble Emperor, do not fight by sea;
Trust not to rotten planks. Do you misdoubt
This sword and these my wounds? Let th' Egyptians
And the Phoenicians go a-ducking; we
Have us'd to conquer standing on the earth
And fighting foot to foot.
ANTONY Well, well – away.
[*Exeunt Antony, Cleopatra, and Enobarbus.*
SOLDIER By Hercules, I think I am i' th' right.
CANIDIUS Soldier, thou art; but his whole action grows
Not in the power on't. So our leader's led,
And we are women's men.
SOLDIER You keep by land
The legions and the horse whole, do you not?
CANIDIUS Marcus Octavius, Marcus Justeius,
Publicola, and Caelius are for sea;
But we keep whole by land. This speed of Caesar's
Carries beyond belief.
SOLDIER While he was yet in Rome,
His power went out in such distractions as
Beguil'd all spies.
CANIDIUS Who's his lieutenant, hear you?
SOLDIER They say one Taurus.
CANIDIUS Well I know the man.

Enter a Messenger.

MESSENGER The Emperor calls Canidius.
CANIDIUS With news the time's with labour and throes forth
Each minute some. [*Exeunt.*

SCENE VIII. *A plain near Actium.*

Enter CAESAR, with his Army, marching.

CAESAR Taurus!
TAURUS My lord?
CAESAR Strike not by land; keep whole; provoke not battle
Till we have done at sea. Do not exceed
The prescript of this scroll. Our fortune lies
Upon this jump. [*Exeunt.*

SCENE IX. *Another part of the plain.*

Enter ANTONY and ENOBARBUS.

ANTONY Set we our squadrons on yond side o' th' hill,
In eye of Caesar's battle; from which place
We may the number of the ships behold,
And so proceed accordingly. [*Exeunt.*

SCENE X. *Another part of the plain.*

CANIDIUS marcheth with his land Army one way over the stage, and TAURUS, the Lieutenant of Caesar, the other way. After their going in is heard the noise of a sea-fight.

Alarum. Enter ENOBARBUS.

ENOBARBUS Naught, naught, all naught! I can behold no longer.
Th' Antoniad, the Egyptian admiral,
With all their sixty, fly and turn the rudder.
To see't mine eyes are blasted.

Enter SCARUS.

SCARUS Gods and goddesses,
All the whole synod of them!
ENOBARBUS What's thy passion?
SCARUS The greater cantle of the world is lost
With very ignorance; we have kiss'd away
Kingdoms and provinces.
ENOBARBUS How appears the fight?
SCARUS On our side like the token'd pestilence,
Where death is sure. Yon ribaudred nag of Egypt –
Whom leprosy o'ertake! – i' th' midst o' th' fight,
When vantage like a pair of twins appear'd,
Both as the same, or rather ours the elder –
The breeze upon her, like a cow in June –
Hoists sails and flies.
ENOBARBUS That I beheld;
Mine eyes did sicken at the sight and could not
Endure a further view.
SCARUS She once being loof'd,
The noble ruin of her magic, Antony,
Claps on his sea-wing, and, like a doting mallard,
Leaving the fight in height, flies after her.
I never saw an action of such shame;
Experience, manhood, honour, ne'er before
Did violate so itself.
ENOBARBUS Alack, alack!

Enter CANIDIUS.

CANIDIUS Our fortune on the sea is out of breath,
And sinks most lamentably. Had our general
Been what he knew himself, it had gone well.
O, he has given example for our flight
Most grossly by his own!
ENOBARBUS Ay, are you thereabouts?
Why then, good night indeed.
CANIDIUS Toward Peloponnesus are they fled.
SCARUS 'Tis easy to't; and there I will attend
What further comes.
CANIDIUS To Caesar will I render
My legions and my horse; six kings already
Show me the way of yielding.
ENOBARBUS I'll yet follow
The wounded chance of Antony, though my reason
Sits in the wind against me. [*Exeunt.*

SCENE XI. *Alexandria. Cleopatra's palace.*

Enter ANTONY with Attendants.

ANTONY Hark! the land bids me tread no more upon't;
It is asham'd to bear me. Friends, come hither.
I am so lated in the world that I
Have lost my way for ever. I have a ship
Laden with gold; take that; divide it. Fly,
And make your peace with Caesar.
ALL Fly? Not we!
ANTONY I have fled myself, and have instructed cowards
To run and show their shoulders. Friends, be gone;
I have myself resolv'd upon a course
Which has no need of you; be gone.
My treasure's in the harbour, take it. O,
I follow'd that I blush to look upon.
My very hairs do mutiny; for the white
Reprove the brown for rashness, and they them
For fear and doting. Friends, be gone; you shall
Have letters from me to some friends that will
Sweep your way for you. Pray you look not sad,
Nor make replies of loathness; take the hint
Which my despair proclaims. Let that be left
Which leaves itself. To the sea-side straight way.
I will possess you of that ship and treasure.
Leave me, I pray, a little; pray you now;
Nay, do so, for indeed I have lost command;
Therefore I pray you. I'll see you by and by.
[*Sits down.*

Enter CLEOPATRA, led by CHARMIAN and IRAS, EROS following.

EROS Nay, gentle madam, to him! Comfort him.
IRAS Do, most dear Queen.
CHARMIAN Do? Why, what else?
CLEOPATRA Let me sit down. O Juno!
ANTONY No, no, no, no, no.
EROS See you here, sir?
ANTONY O, fie, fie, fie!
CHARMIAN Madam!
IRAS Madam, O good Empress!
EROS Sir, sir!
ANTONY Yes, my lord, yes. He at Philippi kept
His sword e'en like a dancer, while I struck
The lean and wrinkled Cassius; and 'twas I
That the mad Brutus ended; he alone
Dealt on lieutenantry, and no practice had
In the brave squares of war. Yet now – no matter.
CLEOPATRA Ah, stand by!
EROS The Queen, my lord, the Queen!
IRAS Go to him, madam, speak to him.
He is unqualitied with very shame.
CLEOPATRA Well then, sustain me. O!
EROS Most noble sir, arise; the Queen approaches.
Her head's declin'd, and death will seize her but
Your comfort makes the rescue.
ANTONY I have offended reputation –
A most unnoble swerving.
EROS Sir, the Queen.
ANTONY O, whither hast thou led me, Egypt? See
How I convey my shame out of thine eyes
By looking back what I have left behind
'Stroy'd in dishonour.
CLEOPATRA O my lord, my lord,
Forgive my fearful sails! I little thought
You would have followed.
ANTONY Egypt, thou knew'st too well
My heart was to thy rudder tied by th' strings,
And thou shouldst tow me after. O'er my spirit
Thy full supremacy thou knew'st, and that
Thy beck might from the bidding of the gods
Command me.
CLEOPATRA O, my pardon!
ANTONY Now I must
To the young man send humble treaties, dodge
And palter in the shifts of lowness, who
With half the bulk o' th' world play'd as I pleas'd
Making and marring fortunes. You did know
How much you were my conqueror, and that
My sword, made weak by my affection, would
Obey it on all cause.
CLEOPATRA Pardon, pardon!
ANTONY Fall not a tear, I say; one of them rates
All that is won and lost. Give me a kiss;
Even this repays me.
We sent our schoolmaster; is 'a come back?
Love, I am full of lead. Some wine,
Within there, and our viands! Fortune knows
We scorn her most when most she offers blows.
[*Exeunt.*

SCENE XII. *Caesar's camp in Egypt.*

Enter CAESAR, AGRIPPA, DOLABELLA, THYREUS, with Others.

CAESAR Let him appear that's come from Antony.
Know you him?
DOLABELLA Caesar, 'tis his schoolmaster:
An argument that he is pluck'd, when hither
He sends so poor a pinion of his wing,
Which had superfluous kings for messengers
Not many moons gone by.

Enter EUPHRONIUS, Ambassador from Antony.

CAESAR Approach, and speak.
EUPHRONIUS Such as I am, I come from Antony.
I was of late as petty to his ends
As is the morn-dew on the myrtle leaf
To his grand sea.
CAESAR Be't so. Declare thine office.
EUPHRONIUS Lord of his fortunes he salutes thee, and
Requires to live in Egypt; which not granted,
He lessens his requests and to thee sues
To let him breathe between the heavens and earth,
A private man in Athens. This for him.
Next, Cleopatra does confess thy greatness,
Submits her to thy might, and of thee craves
The circle of the Ptolemies for her heirs,
Now hazarded to thy grace.
CAESAR For Antony,
I have no ears to his request. The Queen
Of audience nor desire shall fail, so she
From Egypt drive her all-disgraced friend,
Or take his life there. This if she perform,
She shall not sue unheard. So to them both.
EUPHRONIUS Fortune pursue thee!
CAESAR Bring him through the bands.
[*Exit Euphronius.*
[*To Thyreus*] To try thy eloquence, now 'tis time. Dispatch;
From Antony win Cleopatra. Promise,
And in our name, what she requires; add more,
From thine invention, offers. Women are not
In their best fortunes strong; but want will perjure
The ne'er-touch'd vestal. Try thy cunning, Thyreus;
Make thine own edict for thy pains, which we
Will answer as a law.

THYREUS Caesar, I go.
CAESAR Observe how Antony becomes his flaw,
And what thou think'st his very action speaks
In every power that moves.
THYREUS Caesar, I shall.
[*Exeunt.*

SCENE XIII. *Alexandria. Cleopatra's palace.*

Enter CLEOPATRA, ENOBARBUS, CHARMIAN, and IRAS.

CLEOPATRA What shall we do, Enobarbus?
ENOBARBUS Think, and die.
CLEOPATRA Is Antony or we in fault for this?
ENOBARBUS Antony only, that would make his will
Lord of his reason. What though you fled
From that great face of war, whose several ranges
Frighted each other? Why should he follow?
The itch of his affection should not then
Have nick'd his captainship, at such a point,
When half to half the world oppos'd, he being
The mered question. 'Twas a shame no less
Than was his loss, to course your flying flags
And leave his navy gazing.
CLEOPATRA Prithee, peace.

Enter EUPHRONIUS, the Ambassador; with ANTONY.

ANTONY Is that his answer?
EUPHRONIUS Ay, my lord.
ANTONY The Queen shall then have courtesy, so she
Will yield us up.
EUPHRONIUS He says so.
ANTONY Let her know't.
To the boy Caesar send this grizzled head,
And he will fill thy wishes to the brim
With principalities.
CLEOPATRA That head, my lord?
ANTONY To him again. Tell him he wears the rose
Of youth upon him; from which the world should note
Something particular. His coin, ships, legions,
May be a coward's, whose ministers would prevail
Under the service of a child as soon
As i' th' command of Caesar. I dare him therefore
To lay his gay comparisons apart,
And answer me declin'd, sword against sword,
Ourselves alone. I'll write it. Follow me.
[*Exeunt Antony and Euphronius.*
ENOBARBUS [*Aside*] Yes, like enough high-battled Caesar will
Unstate his happiness, and be stag'd to th' show
Against a sworder! I see men's judgments are
A parcel of their fortunes, and things outward
Do draw the inward quality after them,
To suffer all alike. That he should dream,
Knowing all measures, the full Caesar will
Answer his emptiness! Caesar, thou hast subdu'd
His judgment too.

Enter a Servant.

SERVANT A messenger from Caesar.
CLEOPATRA What, no more ceremony? See, my women!
Against the blown rose may they stop their nose
That kneel'd unto the buds. Admit him, sir.
[*Exit Servant.*
ENOBARBUS [*Aside*] Mine honesty and I begin to square.
The loyalty well held to fools does make
Our faith mere folly. Yet he that can endure
To follow with allegiance a fall'n lord
Does conquer him that did his master conquer,
And earns a place i' th' story.

Enter THYREUS.

CLEOPATRA Caesar's will?
THYREUS Hear it apart.
CLEOPATRA None but friends: say boldly.
THYREUS So, happy, are they friends to Antony.
ENOBARBUS He needs as many, sir, as Caesar has,
Or needs not us. If Caesar please, our master
Will leap to be his friend. For us, you know
Whose he is we are, and that is Caesar's.
THYREUS So.
Thus then, thou most renown'd: Caesar entreats
Not to consider in what case thou stand'st
Further than he is Caesar.
CLEOPATRA Go on. Right royal!
THYREUS He knows that you embrace not Antony
As you did love, but as you fear'd him.
CLEOPATRA O!
THYREUS The scars upon your honour, therefore, he
Does pity, as constrained blemishes,
Not as deserv'd.
CLEOPATRA He is a god, and knows
What is most right. Mine honour was not yielded,
But conquer'd merely.
ENOBARBUS [*Aside*] To be sure of that,
I will ask Antony. Sir, sir, thou art so leaky
That we must leave thee to thy sinking, for
Thy dearest quit thee. [*Exit.*
THYREUS Shall I say to Caesar
What you require of him? For he partly begs

To be desir'd to give. It much would please him
That of his fortunes you should make a staff
To lean upon. But it would warm his spirits
To hear from me you had left Antony,
And put yourself under his shroud,
The universal landlord.

CLEOPATRA What's your name?

THYREUS My name is Thyreus.

CLEOPATRA Most kind messenger,
Say to great Caesar this: in deputation
I kiss his conqu'ring hand. Tell him I am prompt
To lay my crown at's feet, and there to kneel.
Tell him from his all-obeying breath I hear
The doom of Egypt.

THYREUS 'Tis your noblest course.
Wisdom and fortune combating together,
If that the former dare but what it can,
No chance may shake it. Give me grace to lay
My duty on your hand.

CLEOPATRA Your Caesar's father oft,
When he hath mus'd of taking kingdoms in,
Bestow'd his lips on that unworthy place,
As it rain'd kisses.

Re-enter ANTONY and ENOBARBUS.

ANTONY Favours, by Jove that thunders!
What art thou, fellow?

THYREUS One that but performs
The bidding of the fullest man, and worthiest
To have command obey'd.

ENOBARBUS [*Aside*] You will be whipt.

ANTONY Approach there. – Ah, you kite! – Now, gods and devils!
Authority melts from me. Of late, when I cried 'Ho!'
Like boys unto a muss, kings would start forth
And cry 'Your will?' Have you no ears? I am
Antony yet.

Enter Servants.

Take hence this Jack and whip him.

ENOBARBUS 'Tis better playing with a lion's whelp
Than with an old one dying.

ANTONY Moon and stars!
Whip him. Were't twenty of the greatest tributaries
That do acknowledge Caesar, should I find them
So saucy with the hand of she here – what's her name
Since she was Cleopatra? Whip him, fellows,
Till like a boy you see him cringe his face,
And whine aloud for mercy. Take him hence.

THYREUS Mark Antony –

ANTONY Tug him away. Being whipt,
Bring him again: the Jack of Caesar's shall
Bear us an errand to him.

[*Exeunt Servants with Thyreus.*

You were half blasted ere I knew you. Ha!
Have I my pillow left unpress'd in Rome,
Forborne the getting of a lawful race,
And by a gem of women, to be abus'd
By one that looks on feeders?

CLEOPATRA Good my lord –

ANTONY You have been a boggler ever.
But when we in our viciousness grow hard –
O misery on't! – the wise gods seel our eyes,
In our own filth drop our clear judgments, make us
Adore our errors, laugh at's while we strut
To our confusion.

CLEOPATRA O, is't come to this?

ANTONY I found you as a morsel cold upon
Dead Caesar's trencher. Nay, you were a fragment
Of Cneius Pompey's, besides what hotter hours,
Unregist'red in vulgar fame, you have
Luxuriously pick'd out; for I am sure,
Though you can guess what temperance should be,
You know not what it is.

CLEOPATRA Wherefore is this?

ANTONY To let a fellow that will take rewards,
And say 'God quit you!' be familiar with
My playfellow, your hand, this kingly seal
And plighter of high hearts! O that I were
Upon the hill of Basan to outroar
The horned herd! For I have savage cause,
And to proclaim it civilly were like
A halter'd neck which does the hangman thank
For being yare about him.

Re-enter a Servant with THYREUS.

Is he whipt?

SERVANT Soundly, my lord.

ANTONY Cried he? and begg'd 'a pardon?

SERVANT He did ask favour.

ANTONY If that thy father live, let him repent
Thou wast not made his daughter; and be thou sorry
To follow Caesar in his triumph, since
Thou hast been whipt for following him. Henceforth
The white hand of a lady fever thee!
Shake thou to look on't. Get thee back to Caesar;
Tell him thy entertainment; look thou say
He makes me angry with him; for he seems
Proud and disdainful, harping on what I am,
Not what he knew I was. He makes me angry;
And at this time most easy 'tis to do't,
When my good stars, that were my former guides,
Have empty left their orbs and shot their fires
Into th' abysm of hell. If he mislike
My speech and what is done, tell him he has

Hipparchus, my enfranched bondman, whom
He may at pleasure whip or hang or torture,
As he shall like, to quit me. Urge it thou.
Hence with thy stripes, be gone.

[Exit Thyreus.

CLEOPATRA Have you done yet?

ANTONY Alack, our terrene moon
Is now eclips'd, and it portends alone
The fall of Antony.

CLEOPATRA I must stay his time.

ANTONY To flatter Caesar, would you mingle eyes
With one that ties his points?

CLEOPATRA Not know me yet?

ANTONY Cold-hearted toward me?

CLEOPATRA Ah, dear, if I be so,
From my cold heart let heaven engender hail,
And poison it in the source, and the first stone
Drop in my neck; as it determines, so
Dissolve my life! The next Caesarion smite!
Till by degrees the memory of my womb,
Together with my brave Egyptians all,
By the discandying of this pelleted storm,
Lie graveless, till the flies and gnats of Nile
Have buried them for prey.

ANTONY I am satisfied.
Caesar sits down in Alexandria, where
I will oppose his fate. Our force by land
Hath nobly held; our sever'd navy too
Have knit again, and fleet, threat'ning most sea-like.
Where hast thou been, my heart? Dost thou hear, lady?
If from the field I shall return once more
To kiss these lips, I will appear in blood.
I and my sword will earn our chronicle.
There's hope in't yet.

CLEOPATRA That's my brave lord!

ANTONY I will be treble-sinew'd, hearted, breath'd,
And fight maliciously. For when mine hours
Were nice and lucky, men did ransom lives
Of me for jests; but now I'll set my teeth,
And send to darkness all that stop me. Come,
Let's have one other gaudy night. Call to me
All my sad captains; fill our bowls once more;
Let's mock the midnight bell.

CLEOPATRA It is my birthday.
I had thought t'have held it poor; but since my lord
Is Antony again, I will be Cleopatra.

ANTONY We will yet do well.

CLEOPATRA Call all his noble captains to my lord.

ANTONY Do so, we'll speak to them; and to-night I'll force
The wine peep through their scars. Come on, my queen,
There's sap in't yet. The next time I do fight
I'll make death love me; for I will contend
Even with his pestilent scythe.

[Exeunt all but Enobarbus.

ENOBARBUS Now he'll outstare the lightning. To be furious
Is to be frighted out of fear, and in that mood
The dove will peck the estridge; and I see still
A diminution in our captain's brain
Restores his heart. When valour preys on reason,
It eats the sword it fights with. I will seek
Some way to leave him.

[Exit.

ACT FOUR

SCENE I. *Caesar's camp before Alexandria.*

Enter CAESAR, AGRIPPA, and MAECENAS, with his Army; Caesar reading a letter.

CAESAR He calls me boy, and chides as he had power
To beat me out of Egypt. My messenger
He hath whipt with rods; dares me to personal combat,
Caesar to Antony. Let the old ruffian know
I have many other ways to die, meantime
Laugh at his challenge.

MAECENAS Caesar must think,
When one so great begins to rage, he's hunted
Even to falling. Give him no breath, but now
Make boot of his distraction. Never anger
Made good guard for itself.

CAESAR Let our best heads
Know that to-morrow the last of many battles
We mean to fight. Within our files there are
Of those that serv'd Mark Antony but late
Enough to fetch him in. See it done;
And feast the army; we have store to do't,
And they have earn'd the waste. Poor Antony!

[Exeunt.

SCENE II. *Alexandria. Cleopatra's palace.*

Enter ANTONY, CLEOPATRA, ENOBARBUS, CHARMIAN, IRAS, ALEXAS, with Others.

ANTONY He will not fight with me, Domitius.

ENOBARBUS No.

ANTONY Why should he not?

ENOBARBUS He thinks, being twenty times of

better fortune,
He is twenty men to one.

ANTONY To-morrow, soldier,
By sea and land I'll fight. Or I will live,
Or bathe my dying honour in the blood
Shall make it live again. Woo't thou fight well?

ENOBARBUS I'll strike, and cry 'Take all'.

ANTONY Well said; come on.
Call forth my household servants; let's to-night
Be bounteous at our meal.

Enter three or four Servitors.

Give me thy hand,
Thou hast been rightly honest. So hast thou;
Thou, and thou, and thou. You have serv'd me well,
And kings have been your fellows.

CLEOPATRA [*Aside to Enobarbus*] What means this?

ENOBARBUS [*Aside to Cleopatra*] 'Tis one of those odd tricks which sorrow shoots
Out of the mind.

ANTONY And thou art honest too.
I wish I could be made so many men,
And all of you clapp'd up together in
An Antony, that I might do you service
So good as you have done.

SERVANT The gods forbid!

ANTONY Well, my good fellows, wait on me to-night.
Scant not my cups, and make as much of me
As when mine empire was your fellow too,
And suffer'd my command.

CLEOPATRA [*Aside to Enobarbus*] What does he mean?

ENOBARBUS [*Aside to Cleopatra*] To make his followers weep.

ANTONY Tend me to-night;
May be it is the period of your duty.
Haply you shall not see me more; or if,
A mangled shadow. Perchance to-morrow
You'll serve another master. I look on you
As one that takes his leave. Mine honest friends,
I turn you not away; but, like a master
Married to your good service, stay till death.
Tend me to-night two hours, I ask no more,
And the gods yield you for't!

ENOBARBUS What mean you, sir,
To give them this discomfort? Look, they weep;
And I, an ass, am onion-ey'd. For shame!
Transform us not to women.

ANTONY Ho, ho, ho!
Now the witch take me if I meant it thus!
Grace grow where those drops fall! My hearty friends,
You take me in too dolorous a sense;
For I spake to you for your comfort, did desire you
To burn this night with torches. Know, my hearts,
I hope well of to-morrow, and will lead you
Where rather I'll expect victorious life
Than death and honour. Let's to supper, come,
And drown consideration. [*Exeunt.*

SCENE III. *Alexandria. Before Cleopatra's palace.*

Enter a Company of Soldiers.

1 SOLDIER Brother, good night. To-morrow is the day.

2 SOLDIER It will determine one way. Fare you well.
Heard you of nothing strange about the streets?

1 SOLDIER Nothing. What news?

2 SOLDIER Belike 'tis but a rumour. Good night to you.

1 SOLDIER Well, sir, good night.

They meet other Soldiers.

2 SOLDIER Soldiers, have careful watch.

1 SOLDIER And you. Good night, good night.

[*The two companies separate and place themselves in every corner of the stage.*

2 SOLDIER Here we. And if to-morrow
Our navy thrive, I have an absolute hope
Our landmen will stand up.

3 SOLDIER 'Tis a brave army,
And full of purpose.

[*Music of the hautboys is under the stage.*

2 SOLDIER Peace, what noise?

3 SOLDIER List, list!

2 SOLDIER Hark!

3 SOLDIER Music i' th' air.

4 SOLDIER Under the earth.

5 SOLDIER It signs well, does it not?

4 SOLDIER No.

3 SOLDIER Peace, I say!
What should this mean?

2 SOLDIER 'Tis the god Hercules, whom Antony lov'd,
Now leaves him.

3 SOLDIER Walk; let's see if other watchmen
Do hear what we do.

2 SOLDIER How now, masters!

SOLDIERS [*Speaking together*] How now!
How now! Do you hear this?

1 SOLDIER Ay; is't not strange?

3 SOLDIER Do you hear, masters? Do you hear?

1 SOLDIER Follow the noise so far as we have quarter;
Let's see how it will give off.

SOLDIERS Content. 'Tis strange. [*Exeunt.*

SCENE IV. *Alexandria. Cleopatra's palace.*

Enter ANTONY and CLEOPATRA, CHARMIAN, IRAS with Others.

ANTONY Eros! mine armour, Eros!
CLEOPATRA Sleep a little.
ANTONY No, my chuck. Eros! Come, mine armour, Eros!

Enter EROS with armour.

Come, good fellow, put mine iron on.
If fortune be not ours to-day, it is
Because we brave her. Come.
CLEOPATRA Nay, I'll help too.
What's this for?
ANTONY Ah, let be, let be! Thou art
The armourer of my heart. False, false; this, this.
CLEOPATRA Sooth, la, I'll help. Thus it must be.
ANTONY Well, well;
We shall thrive now. Seest thou, my good fellow?
Go put on thy defences.
EROS Briefly, sir.
CLEOPATRA Is not this buckled well?
ANTONY Rarely, rarely!
He that unbuckles this, till we do please
To daff't for our repose, shall hear a storm.
Thou fumblest, Eros, and my queen's a squire
More tight at this than thou. Dispatch. O love,
That thou couldst see my wars to-day, and knew'st
The royal occupation! Thou shouldst see
A workman in't.

Enter an armed Soldier.

Good-morrow to thee. Welcome.
Thou look'st like him that knows a warlike charge.
To business that we love we rise betime,
And go to't with delight.
SOLDIER A thousand, sir,
Early though't be, have on their riveted trim,
And at the port expect you.
[*Shout. Flourish of trumpets within.*

Enter Captains and Soldiers.

CAPTAIN The morn is fair. Good morrow, General.
ALL Good morrow, General.
ANTONY 'Tis well blown, lads.
This morning, like the spirit of a youth
That means to be of note, begins betimes.
So, so. Come, give me that. This way. Well said.
Fare thee well, dame, whate'er becomes of me.
This is a soldier's kiss. Rebukeable,
And worthy shameful check it were, to stand
On more mechanic compliment; I'll leave thee
Now like a man of steel. You that will fight,
Follow me close; I'll bring you to't. Adieu.
[*Exeunt Antony, Eros, Captains and Soldiers.*
CHARMIAN Please you retire to your chamber?
CLEOPATRA Lead me.
He goes forth gallantly. That he and Caesar might
Determine this great war in single fight!
Then, Antony – but now. Well, on. [*Exeunt.*

SCENE V. *Alexandria. Antony's camp.*

Trumpets sound. Enter ANTONY and EROS, a Soldier meeting them.

SOLDIER The gods make this a happy day to Antony!
ANTONY Would thou and those thy scars had once prevail'd
To make me fight at land!
SOLDIER Hadst thou done so
The kings that have revolted, and the soldier
That has this morning left thee, would have still
Followed thy heels.
ANTONY Who's gone this morning?
SOLDIER Who?
One ever near thee. Call for Enobarbus,
He shall not hear thee; or from Caesar's camp
Say 'I am none of thine'.
ANTONY What say'st thou?
SOLDIER Sir,
He is with Caesar.
EROS Sir, his chests and treasure
He has not with him.
ANTONY Is he gone?
SOLDIER Most certain.
ANTONY Go, Eros, send his treasure after; do it;
Detain no jot, I charge thee. Write to him –
I will subscribe – gentle adieus and greetings;
Say that I wish he never find more cause
To change a master. O, my fortunes have
Corrupted honest men! Dispatch. Enobarbus!
[*Exeunt.*

SCENE VI. *Alexandria. Caesar's camp.*

Flourish. Enter AGRIPPA, CAESAR, with DOLABELLA and ENOBARBUS.

CAESAR Go forth, Agrippa, and begin the fight.
Our will is Antony be took alive;
Make it so known.
AGRIPPA Caesar, I shall. [*Exit.*
CAESAR The time of universal peace is near.
Prove this a prosp'rous day, the three-nook'd world
Shall bear the olive freely.

Enter a Messenger.

MESSENGER Antony
Is come into the field.

CAESAR Go charge Agrippa
Plant those that have revolted in the vant,
That Antony may seem to spend his fury
Upon himself. [*Exeunt all but Enobarbus.*

ENOBARBUS Alexas did revolt and went to Jewry on
Affairs of Antony; there did dissuade
Great Herod to incline himself to Caesar
And leave his master Antony. For this pains
Caesar hath hang'd him. Canidius and the rest
That fell away have entertainment, but
No honourable trust. I have done ill,
Of which I do accuse myself so sorely
That I will joy no more.

Enter a Soldier of Caesar's.

SOLDIER Enobarbus, Antony
Hath after thee sent all thy treasure, with
His bounty overplus. The messenger
Came on my guard, and at thy tent is now
Unloading of his mules.

ENOBARBUS I give it you.

SOLDIER Mock not, Enobarbus.
I tell you true. Best you saf'd the bringer
Out of the host. I must attend mine office,
Or would have done't myself. Your emperor
Continues still a Jove. [*Exit.*

ENOBARBUS I am alone the villain of the earth,
And feel I am so most. O Antony,
Thou mine of bounty, how wouldst thou have paid
My better service, when my turpitude
Thou dost so crown with gold! This blows my heart.
If swift thought break it not, a swifter mean
Shall outstrike thought; but thought will do't, I feel.
I fight against thee? No! I will go seek
Some ditch wherein to die; the foul'st best fits
My latter part of life. [*Exit.*

SCENE VII. *Field of battle between the camps.*

Alarum. Drums and trumpets. Enter AGRIPPA and Others.

AGRIPPA Retire. We have engag'd ourselves too far.
Caesar himself has work, and our oppression
Exceeds what we expected. [*Exeunt.*

Alarums. Enter ANTONY, and SCARUS wounded.

SCARUS O my brave Emperor, this is fought indeed!
Had we done so at first, we had droven them home
With clouts about their heads.

ANTONY Thou bleed'st apace.

SCARUS I had a wound here that was like a T,
But now 'tis made an H.

ANTONY They do retire.

SCARUS We'll beat 'em into bench-holes. I have yet
Room for six scotches more.

Enter EROS.

EROS They are beaten, sir, and our advantage serves
For a fair victory.

SCARUS Let us score their backs
And snatch 'em up, as we take hares, behind.
'Tis sport to maul a runner.

ANTONY I will reward thee
Once for thy sprightly comfort, and tenfold
For thy good valour. Come thee on.

SCARUS I'll halt after. [*Exeunt.*

SCENE VIII. *Under the walls of Alexandria.*

Alarum. Enter ANTONY, again in a march; SCARUS with Others.

ANTONY We have beat him to his camp. Run one before
And let the Queen know of our gests.
To-morrow,
Before the sun shall see's, we'll spill the blood
That has to-day escap'd. I thank you all;
For doughty-handed are you, and have fought
Not as you serv'd the cause, but as't had been
Each man's like mine; you have shown all Hectors.
Enter the city, clip your wives, your friends,
Tell them your feats; whilst they with joyful tears
Wash the congealment from your wounds and kiss
The honour'd gashes whole.

Enter CLEOPATRA, attended.

[*To Scarus*] Give me thy hand. –
To this great fairy I'll commend thy acts,
Make her thanks bless thee. O thou day o' th' world,
Chain mine arm'd neck. Leap thou, attire and all,
Through proof of harness to my heart, and there
Ride on the pants triumphing.

CLEOPATRA Lord of lords!
O infinite virtue, com'st thou smiling from
The world's great snare uncaught?

ANTONY Mine nightingale,

We have beat them to their beds. What, girl! though grey
Do something mingle with our younger brown, yet ha' we
A brain that nourishes our nerves, and can
Get goal for goal of youth. Behold this man;
Commend unto his lips thy favouring hand –
Kiss it, my warrior – he hath fought to-day
As if a god in hate of mankind had
Destroyed in such a shape.

CLEOPATRA I'll give thee, friend,
An armour all of gold; it was a king's.

ANTONY He has deserv'd it, were it carbuncled
Like holy Phoebus' car. Give me thy hand.
Through Alexandria make a jolly march;
Bear our hack'd targets like the men that owe them.
Had our great palace the capacity
To camp this host, we all would sup together,
And drink carouses to the next day's fate,
Which promises royal peril. Trumpeters,
With brazen din blast you the city's ear;
Make mingle with our rattling tabourines,
That heaven and earth may strike their sounds together,
Applauding our approach. [*Exeunt*.

SCENE IX. *Caesar's camp.*

Enter a Centurion and his Company; ENOBARBUS follows.

CENTURION If we be not reliev'd within this hour,
We must return to th' court of guard. The night
Is shiny, and they say we shall embattle
By th' second hour i' th' morn.

1 WATCH This last day was
A shrewd one to's.

ENOBARBUS O, bear me witness, night –

2 WATCH What man is this?

1 WATCH Stand close and list him.

ENOBARBUS Be witness to me, O thou blessed moon,
When men revolted shall upon record
Bear hateful memory, poor Enobarbus did
Before thy face repent!

CENTURION Enobarbus?

2 WATCH Peace!
Hark further.

ENOBARBUS O sovereign mistress of true melancholy,
The poisonous damp of night disponge upon me,
That life, a very rebel to my will,
May hang no longer on me. Throw my heart
Against the flint and hardness of my fault,
Which, being dried with grief, will break to powder,
And finish all foul thoughts. O Antony,
Nobler than my revolt is infamous,
Forgive me in thine own particular,
But let the world rank me in register
A master-leaver and a fugitive!
O Antony! O Antony! [*Dies*.

1 WATCH Let's speak to him.

CENTURION Let's hear him, for the things he speaks
May concern Caesar.

2 WATCH Let's do so. But he sleeps.

CENTURION Swoons rather; for so bad a prayer as his
Was never yet for sleep.

1 WATCH Go we to him.

2 WATCH Awake, sir, awake; speak to us.

1 WATCH Hear you, sir?

CENTURION The hand of death hath raught him.
[*Drums afar off*] Hark! the drums
Demurely wake the sleepers. Let us bear him
To th' court of guard; he is of note. Our hour
Is fully out.

2 WATCH Come on, then;
He may recover yet. [*Exeunt with the body*.

SCENE X. *Between the two camps.*

Enter ANTONY and SCARUS, with their Army.

ANTONY Their preparation is to-day by sea;
We please them not by land.

SCARUS For both, my lord.

ANTONY I would they'd fight i' th' fire or i' th' air;
We'd fight there too. But this it is, our foot
Upon the hills adjoining to the city
Shall stay with us – Order for sea is given;
They have put forth the haven –
Where their appointment we may best discover
And look on their endeavour. [*Exeunt*.

SCENE XI. *Between the camps.*

Enter CAESAR and his Army.

CAESAR But being charg'd, we will be still by land,
Which, as I take't, we shall; for his best force
Is forth to man his galleys. To the vales,
And hold our best advantage. [*Exeunt*.

SCENE XII. *A hill near Alexandria.*

Enter ANTONY and SCARUS.

ANTONY Yet they are not join'd. Where yond pine does stand
I shall discover all. I'll bring thee word
Straight how 'tis like to go. [*Exit*.

SCARUS Swallows have built
In Cleopatra's sails their nests. The augurers
Say they know not, they cannot tell; look grimly,
And dare not speak their knowledge. Antony
Is valiant and dejected; and by starts
His fretted fortunes give him hope and fear
Of what he has and has not.

[Alarum afar off, as at a sea-fight.

Re-enter ANTONY.

ANTONY All is lost!
This foul Egyptian hath betrayed me.
My fleet hath yielded to the foe, and yonder
They cast their caps up and carouse together
Like friends long lost. Triple-turn'd whore! 'tis thou
Hast sold me to this novice; and my heart
Makes only wars on thee. Bid them all fly;
For when I am reveng'd upon my charm,
I have done all. Bid them all fly; begone.

[Exit Scarus.

O sun, thy uprise shall I see no more!
Fortune and Antony part here; even here
Do we shake hands. All come to this? The hearts
That spaniel'd me at heels, to whom I gave
Their wishes, do discandy, melt their sweets
On blossoming Caesar; and this pine is bark'd
That overtopp'd them all. Betray'd I am.
O this false soul of Egypt! this grave charm –
Whose eye beck'd forth my wars and call'd them home,
Whose bosom was my crownet, my chief end –
Like a right gipsy hath at fast and loose
Beguil'd me to the very heart of loss.
What, Eros, Eros!

Enter CLEOPATRA.

Ah, thou spell! Avaunt!

CLEOPATRA Why is my lord enrag'd against his love?

ANTONY Vanish, or I shall give thee thy deserving
And blemish Caesar's triumph. Let him take thee
And hoist thee up to the shouting plebeians;
Follow his chariot, like the greatest spot
Of all thy sex; most monster-like, be shown
For poor'st diminutives, for doits, and let
Patient Octavia plough thy visage up
With her prepared nails. *[Exit Cleopatra.*
'Tis well th'art gone,
If it be well to live; but better 'twere
Thou fell'st into my fury, for one death
Might have prevented many. Eros, ho!
The shirt of Nessus is upon me; teach me,
Alcides, thou mine ancestor, thy rage;
Let me lodge Lichas on the horns o' th' moon,
And with those hands that grasp'd the heaviest club
Subdue my worthiest self. The witch shall die.
To the young Roman boy she hath sold me, and I fall
Under this plot. She dies for't. Eros, ho! *[Exit.*

SCENE XIII. *Alexandria. Cleopatra's palace.*

Enter CLEOPATRA, CHARMIAN, IRAS, and MARDIAN.

CLEOPATRA Help me, my women. O, he is more mad
Than Telamon for his shield; the boar of Thessaly
Was never so emboss'd.

CHARMIAN To th' monument!
There lock yourself, and send him word you are dead.
The soul and body rive not more in parting
Than greatness going off.

CLEOPATRA To th' monument!
Mardian, go tell him I have slain myself;
Say that the last I spoke was 'Antony'
And word it, prithee, piteously. Hence, Mardian,
And bring me how he takes my death. To th' monument! *[Exeunt.*

SCENE XIV. *Cleopatra's palace.*

Enter ANTONY and EROS.

ANTONY Eros, thou yet behold'st me?

EROS Ay, noble lord.

ANTONY Sometime we see a cloud that's dragonish;
A vapour sometime like a bear or lion,
A tower'd citadel, a pendent rock,
A forked mountain, or blue promontory
With trees upon't that nod unto the world
And mock our eyes with air. Thou hast seen these signs;
They are black vesper's pageants.

EROS Ay, my lord.

ANTONY That which is now a horse, even with a thought
The rack dislimns, and makes it indistinct,
As water is in water.

EROS It does, my lord.

ANTONY My good knave Eros, now thy captain is
Even such a body. Here I am Antony;
Yet cannot hold this visible shape, my knave.
I made these wars for Egypt; and the Queen –
Whose heart I thought I had, for she had mine,
Which, whilst it was mine, had annex'd unto't

A million moe, now lost – she, Eros, has
Pack'd cards with Caesar, and false-play'd my glory
Unto an enemy's triumph.
Nay, weep not, gentle Eros; there is left us
Ourselves to end ourselves.

Enter MARDIAN.

O, thy vile lady!
She has robb'd me of my sword.

MARDIAN No, Antony;
My mistress lov'd thee, and her fortunes mingled
With thine entirely.

ANTONY Hence, saucy eunuch; peace!
She hath betray'd me, and shall die the death.

MARDIAN Death of one person can be paid but once,
And that she has discharg'd. What thou wouldst do
Is done unto thy hand. The last she spake
Was 'Antony! most noble Antony!'
Then in the midst a tearing groan did break
The name of Antony; it was divided
Between her heart and lips. She rend'red life,
Thy name so buried in her.

ANTONY Dead then?

MARDIAN Dead.

ANTONY Unarm, Eros; the long day's task is done,
And we must sleep. That thou depart'st hence safe
Does pay thy labour richly. Go.

[*Exit Mardian.*

Off, pluck off!
The sevenfold shield of Ajax cannot keep
The battery from my heart. O, cleave, my sides!
Heart, once be stronger than thy continent,
Crack thy frail case. Apace, Eros, apace. –
No more a soldier. Bruised pieces, go;
You have been nobly borne. – From me awhile

[*Exit Eros.*

I will o'ertake thee, Cleopatra, and
Weep for my pardon. So it must be, for now
All length is torture. Since the torch is out,
Lie down, and stray no farther. Now all labour
Mars what it does; yea, very force entangles
Itself with strength. Seal then, and all is done.
Eros ! – I come, my queen. – Eros! – Stay for me;
Where souls do couch on flowers, we'll hand in hand,
And with our sprightly port make the ghosts gaze.
Dido and her AEneas shall want troops,
And all the haunt be ours. – Come, Eros, Eros!

Re-enter EROS.

EROS What would my lord?

ANTONY Since Cleopatra died,
I have liv'd in such dishonour that the gods
Detest my baseness. I, that with my sword
Quarter'd the world, and o'er green Neptune's back
With ships made cities, condemn myself to lack
The courage of a woman; less noble mind
Than she which by her death our Caesar tells
'I am conqueror of myself'. Thou art sworn, Eros,
That, when the exigent should come – which now
Is come indeed – when I should see behind me
Th' inevitable prosecution of
Disgrace and horror, that, on my command,
Thou then wouldst kill me. Do't; the time is come.
Thou strik'st not me; 'tis Caesar thou defeat'st.
Put colour in thy cheek.

EROS The gods withold me!
Shall I do that which all the Parthian darts,
Though enemy, lost aim and could not?

ANTONY Eros,
Wouldst thou be window'd in great Rome and see
Thy master thus with pleach'd arms, bending down
His corrigible neck, his face subdu'd
To penetrative shame, whilst the wheel'd seat
Of fortunate Caesar, drawn before him, branded
His baseness that ensued?

EROS I would not see't.

ANTONY Come, then; for with a wound I must be cur'd.
Draw that thy honest sword, which thou hast worn
Most useful for thy country.

EROS O, sir, pardon me!

ANTONY When I did make thee free, swor'st thou not then
To do this when I bade thee? Do it at once,
Or thy precedent services are all
But accidents unpurpos'd. Draw, and come.

EROS Turn from me then that noble countenance,
Wherein the worship of the whole world lies.

ANTONY Lo thee! [*Turning from him.*

EROS My sword is drawn.

ANTONY Then let it do at once
The thing why thou hast drawn it.

EROS My dear master,
My captain and my emperor, let me say,
Before I strike this bloody stroke, farewell.

ANTONY 'Tis said, man; and farewell.
EROS Farewell, great chief. Shall I strike now?
ANTONY Now, Eros.
EROS Why, there then! Thus do I escape the sorrow
Of Antony's death. [*Kills himself.*
ANTONY Thrice nobler than myself!
Thou teachest me, O valiant Eros, what
I should, and thou couldst not. My queen and Eros
Have, by their brave instruction, got upon me
A nobleness in record. But I will be
A bridegroom in my death, and run into't
As to a lover's bed. Come, then; and, Eros,
Thy master dies thy scholar. To do thus
[*Falling on his sword.*
I learn'd of thee. How? not dead? not dead? –
The guard, ho! O, dispatch me!

Enter DERCETAS and a Guard.

1 GUARD What's the noise?
ANTONY I have done my work ill, friends. O, make an end
Of what I have begun.
2 GUARD The star is fall'n.
1 GUARD And time is at his period.
ALL Alas, and woe!
ANTONY Let him that loves me, strike me dead.
1 GUARD Not I.
2 GUARD Nor I.
3 GUARD Nor any one. [*Exeunt Guard.*
DERCETAS Thy death and fortunes bid thy followers fly.
This sword but shown to Caesar, with this tidings,
Shall enter me with him.

Enter DIOMEDES.

DIOMEDES Where's Antony?
DERCETAS There, Diomed, there.
DIOMEDES Lives he?
Wilt thou not answer, man? [*Exit Dercetas.*
ANTONY Art thou there, Diomed? Draw thy sword and give me
Sufficing strokes for death.
DIOMEDES Most absolute lord,
My mistress Cleopatra sent me to thee.
ANTONY When did she send thee?
DIOMEDES Now, my lord.
ANTONY Where is she?
DIOMEDES Lock'd in her monument. She had a prophesying fear
Of what hath come to pass; for when she saw –
Which never shall be found – you did suspect
She had dispos'd with Caesar, and that your rage
Would not be purg'd, she sent you word she was dead;
But fearing since how it might work, hath sent
Me to proclaim the truth; and I am come,
I dread, too late.
ANTONY Too late, good Diomed. Call my guard, I prithee.
DIOMEDES What, ho! the Emperor's guard! The guard, what ho!
Come, your lord calls!

Enter four or five of the Guard of Antony.

ANTONY Bear me, good friends, where Cleopatra bides;
'Tis the last service that I shall command you.
1 GUARD Woe, woe are we, sir, you may not live to wear
All your true followers out.
ALL Most heavy day!
ANTONY Nay, good my fellows, do not please sharp fate
To grace it with your sorrows. Bid that welcome
Which comes to punish us, and we punish it,
Seeming to bear it lightly. Take me up.
I have led you oft; carry me now, good friends,
And have my thanks for all.
[*Exeunt, bearing Antony.*

SCENE XV. *Alexandria. A monument.*

Enter CLEOPATRA and her Maids aloft, with CHARMIAN and IRAS.

CLEOPATRA O Charmian, I will never go from hence!
CHARMIAN Be comforted, dear madam.
CLEOPATRA No, I will not.
All strange and terrible events are welcome,
But comforts we despise; our size of sorrow,
Proportion'd to our cause, must be as great
As that which makes it.

Enter DIOMEDES, below.

How now! Is he dead?
DIOMEDES His death's upon him, but not dead.
Look out o' th' other side your monument;
His guard have brought him thither.

Enter, below, ANTONY, borne by the Guard.

CLEOPATRA O sun,
Burn the great sphere thou mov'st in! Darkling stand
The varying shore o' th' world. O Antony,
Antony, Antony! Help, Charmian; help, Iras, help;
Help, friends below! Let's draw him hither.
ANTONY Peace!
Not Caesar's valour hath o'erthrown Antony,
But Antony's hath triumph'd on itself.

CLEOPATRA So it should be, that none but Antony
Should conquer Antony; but woe 'tis so!
ANTONY I am dying, Egypt, dying; only
I here importune death awhile, until
Of many thousand kisses the poor last
I lay upon thy lips.
CLEOPATRA I dare not, dear.
Dear my lord, pardon! I dare not,
Lest I be taken. Not th' imperious show
Of the full-fortun'd Caesar ever shall
Be brooch'd with me. If knife, drugs, serpents, have
Edge, sting, or operation, I am safe.
Your wife Octavia, with her modest eyes
And still conclusion, shall acquire no honour
Demuring upon me. But come, come, Antony –
Help me, my women – we must draw thee up;
Assist, good friends.
ANTONY O, quick, or I am gone.
CLEOPATRA Here's sport indeed! How heavy weighs my lord!
Our strength is all gone into heaviness;
That makes the weight. Had I great Juno's power,
The strong-wing'd Mercury should fetch thee up,
And set thee by Jove's side. Yet come a little.
Wishers were ever fools. O come, come, come,

[They heave Antony aloft to Cleopatra.

And welcome, welcome! Die where thou hast liv'd.
Quicken with kissing. Had my lips that power,
Thus would I wear them out.
ALL A heavy sight!
ANTONY I am dying, Egypt, dying.
Give me some wine, and let me speak a little.
CLEOPATRA No, let me speak; and let me rail so high
That the false huswife Fortune break her wheel,
Provok'd by my offence.
ANTONY One word, sweet queen:
Of Caesar seek your honour, with your safety. O!
CLEOPATRA They do not go together.
ANTONY Gentle, hear me:
None about Caesar trust but Proculeius.
CLEOPATRA My resolution and my hands I'll trust;
None about Caesar.
ANTONY The miserable change now at my end
Lament nor sorrow at; but please your thoughts
In feeding them with those my former fortunes
Wherein I liv'd the greatest prince o' th' world,
The noblest; and do now not basely die,
Not cowardly put off my helmet to
My countryman – a Roman by a Roman
Valiantly vanquish'd. Now my spirit is going;
I can no more.
CLEOPATRA Noblest of men, woo't die?
Hast thou no care of me? Shall I abide
In this dull world, which in thy absence is
No better than a sty? O, see my women,

[Antony dies.

The crown o' th' earth doth melt. My lord!
O, wither'd is the garland of the war,
The soldier's pole is fall'n! Young boys and girls
Are level now with men. The odds is gone,
And there is nothing left remarkable
Beneath the visiting moon. *[Swoons.*

CHARMIAN O, quietness, lady!
IRAS She's dead too, our sovereign.
CHARMIAN Lady!
IRAS Madam!
CHARMIAN O madam, madam, madam!
IRAS Royal Egypt, Empress!
CHARMIAN Peace, peace, Iras!
CLEOPATRA No more but e'en a woman, and commanded
By such poor passion as the maid that milks
And does the meanest chares. It were for me
To throw my sceptre at the injurious gods;
To tell them that this world did equal theirs
Till they had stol'n our jewel. All's but nought;
Patience is sottish, and impatience does
Become a dog that's mad. Then is it sin
To rush into the secret house of death
Ere death dare come to us? How do you, women?
What, what! good cheer! Why, how now, Charmian!
My noble girls! Ah, women, women, look,
Our lamp is spent, it's out! Good sirs, take heart.
We'll bury him; and then, what's brave, what's noble,
Let's do it after the high Roman fashion,
And make death proud to take us. Come, away;
This case of that huge spirit now is cold.
Ah, women, women! Come; we have no friend
But resolution and the briefest end.

[Exeunt; those above bearing off Antony's body.

ACT FIVE

SCENE I. *Alexandria. Caesar's camp.*

Enter CAESAR, AGRIPPA, DOLABELLA, MAECENAS, GALLUS, PROCULEIUS, and Others, his Council of War.

CAESAR Go to him, Dolabella, bid him yield;
Being so frustrate, tell him he mocks
The pauses that he makes.

DOLABELLA Caesar, I shall. [*Exit.*

Enter DERCETAS with the sword of Antony.

CAESAR Wherefore is that? And what art thou that dar'st
Appear thus to us?

DERCETAS I am call'd Dercetas;
Mark Antony I serv'd, who best was worthy
Best to be serv'd. Whilst he stood up and spoke,
He was my master, and I wore my life
To spend upon his haters. If thou please
To take me to thee, as I was to him
I'll be to Caesar; if thou pleasest not,
I yield thee up my life.

CAESAR What is't thou say'st?

DERCETAS I say, O Caesar, Antony is dead.

CAESAR The breaking of so great a thing should make
A greater crack. The round world
Should have shook lions into civil streets,
And citizens to their dens. The death of Antony
Is not a single doom: in the name lay
A moiety of the world.

DERCETAS He is dead, Caesar,
Not by a public minister of justice,
Nor by a hired knife; but that self hand
Which writ his honour in the acts it did
Hath, with the courage which the heart did lend it,
Splitted the heart. This is his sword;
I robb'd his wound of it; behold it stain'd
With his most noble blood.

CAESAR Look you sad, friends?
The gods rebuke me, but it is tidings
To wash the eyes of kings.

AGRIPPA And strange it is
That nature must compel us to lament
Our most persisted deeds.

MAECENAS His taints and honours
Wag'd equal with him.

AGRIPPA A rarer spirit never
Did steer humanity. But you gods will give us
Some faults to make us men. Caesar is touch'd.

MAECENAS When such a spacious mirror's set before him,
He needs must see himself.

CAESAR O Antony,
I have follow'd thee to this! But we do lance
Diseases in our bodies. I must perforce
Have shown to thee such a declining day
Or look on thine; we could not stall together
In the whole world. But yet let me lament,
With tears as sovereign as the blood of hearts,
That thou, my brother, my competitor
In top of all design, my mate in empire,
Friend and companion in the front of war,
The arm of mine own body, and the heart
Where mine his thoughts did kindle – that our stars,
Unreconciliable, should divide
Our equalness to this. Hear me, good friends –

Enter an Egyptian.

But I will tell you at some meeter season.
The business of this man looks out of him;
We'll hear him what he says. Whence are you?

EGYPTIAN A poor Egyptian, yet the Queen, my mistress,
Confin'd in all she has, her monument,
Of thy intents desires instruction,
That she preparedly may frame herself
To th' way she's forc'd to.

CAESAR Bid her have good heart.
She soon shall know of us, by some of ours,
How honourable and how kindly we
Determine for her; for Caesar cannot learn
To be ungentle.

EGYPTIAN So the gods preserve thee! [*Exit.*

CAESAR Come hither, Proculeius. Go and say
We purpose her no shame. Give her what comforts
The quality of her passion shall require,
Lest, in her greatness, by some mortal stroke
She do defeat us; for her life in Rome
Would be eternal in our triumph. Go,
And with your speediest bring us what she says,
And how you find of her.

PROCULEIUS Caesar, I shall. [*Exit.*

CAESAR Gallus, go you along. [*Exit Gallus.*
Where's Dolabella,
To second Proculeius?

ALL Dolabella!

CAESAR Let him alone, for I remember now
How he's employ'd; he shall in time be ready.
Go with me to my tent, where you shall see
How hardly I was drawn into this war,
How calm and gentle I proceeded still
In all my writings. Go with me, and see
What I can show in this. [*Exeunt.*

SCENE II. *Alexandria. The monument.*

Enter CLEOPATRA, CHARMIAN, IRAS, and MARDIAN.

CLEOPATRA My desolation does begin to make
A better life. 'Tis paltry to be Caesar:
Not being Fortune, he's but Fortune's knave,
A minister of her will; and it is great
To do that thing that ends all other deeds,
Which shackles accidents and bolts up change,
Which sleeps, and never palates more the dug,
The beggar's nurse and Caesar's.

Enter, to the gates of the monument, PROCULEIUS, GALLUS, and Soldiers.

PROCULEIUS Caesar sends greeting to the Queen of Egypt,
And bids thee study on what fair demands
Thou mean'st to have him grant thee.

CLEOPATRA What's thy name?

PROCULEIUS My name is Proculeius.

CLEOPATRA Antony
Did tell me of you, bade me trust you; but
I do not greatly care to be deceiv'd,
That have no use for trusting. If your master
Would have a queen his beggar, you must tell him
That majesty, to keep decorum, must
No less beg than a kingdom. If he please
To give me conquer'd Egypt for my son,
He gives me so much of mine own as I
Will kneel to him with thanks.

PROCULEIUS Be of good cheer;
Y'are fall'n into a princely hand; fear nothing.
Make your full reference freely to my lord,
Who is so full of grace that it flows over
On all that need. Let me report to him
Your sweet dependency, and you shall find
A conqueror that will pray in aid for kindness
Where he for grace is kneel'd to.

CLEOPATRA Pray you tell him
I am his fortune's vassal and I send him
The greatness he has got. I hourly learn
A doctrine of obedience, and would gladly
Look him i' th' face.

PROCULEIUS This I'll report, dear lady.
Have comfort, for I know your plight is pitied
Of him that caus'd it.

GALLUS You see how easily she may be surpris'd.

[*Here Proculeius and two of the Guard ascend the monument by a ladder placed against a window, and come behind Cleopatra. Some of the Guard unbar and open the gates.*

Guard her till Caesar come. [*Exit.*

IRAS Royal Queen!

CHARMIAN O Cleopatra! thou art taken, Queen!

CLEOPATRA Quick, quick, good hands. [*Drawing a dagger.*

PROCULEIUS Hold, worthy lady, hold, [*Disarms her.*
Do not yourself such wrong, who are in this
Reliev'd, but not betray'd.

CLEOPATRA What, of death too,
That rids our dogs of languish?

PROCULEIUS Cleopatra,
Do not abuse my master's bounty by
Th' undoing of yourself. Let the world see
His nobleness well acted, which your death
Will never let come forth.

CLEOPATRA Where art thou, death?
Come hither, come! Come, come, and take a queen
Worth many babes and beggars!

PROCULEIUS O, temperance, lady!

CLEOPATRA Sir, I will eat no meat; I'll not drink, sir;
If idle talk will once be necessary,
I'll not sleep neither. This mortal house I'll ruin,
Do Caesar what he can. Know, sir, that I
Will not wait pinion'd at your master's court,
Nor once be chastis'd with the sober eye
Of dull Octavia. Shall they hoist me up,
And show me to the shouting varletry
Of censuring Rome? Rather a ditch in Egypt
Be gentle grave unto me! Rather on Nilus' mud
Lay me stark-nak'd, and let the water-flies
Blow me into abhorring! Rather make
My country's high pyramides my gibbet,
And hang me up in chains!

PROCULEIUS You do extend
These thoughts of horror further than you shall
Find cause in Caesar.

Enter DOLABELLA.

DOLABELLA Proculeius,
What thou hast done thy master Caesar knows,
And he hath sent for thee. For the Queen,
I'll take her to my guard.

PROCULEIUS So, Dolabella,
It shall content me best. Be gentle to her.
[*To Cleopatra*] To Caesar I will speak what you shall please,
If you'll employ me to him.

CLEOPATRA Say I would die.

[*Exeunt Proculeius and Soldiers.*

DOLABELLA Most noble Empress, you have heard of me?

CLEOPATRA I cannot tell.

DOLABELLA Assuredly you know me.

CLEOPATRA No matter, sir, what I have heard or known.
You laugh when boys or women tell their dreams;

Is't not your trick?
DOLABELLA I understand not, madam.
CLEOPATRA I dreamt there was an Emperor Antony –
O, such another sleep, that I might see
But such another man!
DOLABELLA If it might please ye –
CLEOPATRA His face was as the heav'ns, and therein stuck
A sun and moon, which kept their course and lighted
The little O, the earth.
DOLABELLA Most sovereign creature –
CLEOPATRA His legs bestrid the ocean; his rear'd arm
Crested the world. His voice was propertied
As all the tuned spheres, and that to friends;
But when he meant to quail and shake the orb,
He was as rattling thunder. For his bounty,
There was no winter in't; an autumn 'twas
That grew the more by reaping. His delights
Were dolphin-like: they show'd his back above
The element they liv'd in. In his livery
Walk'd crowns and crownets; realms and islands were
As plates dropp'd from his pocket.
DOLABELLA Cleopatra –
CLEOPATRA Think you there was or might be such a man
As this I dreamt of?
DOLABELLA Gentle madam, no.
CLEOPATRA You lie, up to the hearing of the gods.
But if there be nor ever were one such,
It's past the size of dreaming. Nature wants stuff
To vie strange forms with fancy; yet t' imagine
An Antony were nature's piece 'gainst fancy,
Condemning shadows quite.
DOLABELLA Hear me, good madam.
Your loss is, as yourself, great; and you bear it
As answering to the weight. Would I might never
O'ertake pursu'd success, but I do feel,
By the rebound of yours, a grief that smites
My very heart at root.
CLEOPATRA I thank you, sir.
Know you what Caesar means to do with me?
DOLABELLA I am loath to tell you what I would you knew.
CLEOPATRA Nay, pray you, sir.
DOLABELLA Though he be honourable –
CLEOPATRA He'll lead me, then, in triumph?
DOLABELLA Madam, he will. I know't. *[Flourish.*
Within. Make way there – Caesar!

Enter CAESAR; GALLUS, PROCULEIUS, MAECENAS, SELEUCUS, and others of his Train.

CAESAR Which is the Queen of Egypt?
DOLABELLA It is the Emperor, madam. *[Cleopatra kneels.*
CAESAR Arise, you shall not kneel.
I pray you, rise; rise, Egypt.
CLEOPATRA Sir, the gods
Will have it thus; my master and my lord
I must obey.
CAESAR Take to you no hard thoughts.
The record of what injuries you did us,
Though written in our flesh, we shall remember
As things but done by chance.
CLEOPATRA Sole sir o' th' world,
I cannot project mine own cause so well
To make it clear, but do confess I have
Been laden with like frailties which before
Have often sham'd our sex.
CAESAR Cleopatra, know
We will extenuate rather than enforce.
If you apply yourself to our intents –
Which towards you are most gentle – you shall find
A benefit in this change; but if you seek
To lay on me a cruelty by taking
Antony's course, you shall bereave yourself
Of my good purposes, and put your children
To that destruction which I'll guard them from,
If thereon you rely. I'll take my leave.
CLEOPATRA And may, through all the world. 'Tis yours, and we,
Your scutcheons and your signs of conquest, shall
Hang in what place you please. Here, my good lord.
CAESAR You shall advise me in all for Cleopatra.
CLEOPATRA This is the brief of money, plate, and jewels,
I am possess'd of. 'Tis exactly valued,
Not petty things admitted. Where's Seleucus?
SELEUCUS Here, madam.
CLEOPATRA This is my treasurer; let him speak, my lord,
Upon his peril, that I have reserv'd
To myself nothing. Speak the truth, Seleucus.
SELEUCUS Madam,
I had rather seal my lips than to my peril
Speak that which is not.
CLEOPATRA What have I kept back?
SELEUCUS Enough to purchase what you have made known.
CAESAR Nay, blush not, Cleopatra; I approve
Your wisdom in the deed.
CLEOPATRA See, Caesar! O, behold,
How pomp is followed! Mine will now be yours;

And, should we shift estates, yours would be mine.
The ingratitude of this Seleucus does
Even make me wild. O slave, of no more trust
Than love that's hir'd! What, goest thou back? Thou shalt
Go back, I warrant thee; but I'll catch thine eyes
Though they had wings. Slave, soulless villain, dog!
O rarely base!

CAESAR Good Queen, let us entreat you.

CLEOPATRA O Caesar, what a wounding shame is this,
That thou vouchsafing here to visit me,
Doing the honour of thy lordliness
To one so meek, that mine own servant should
Parcel the sum of my disgraces by
Addition of his envy! Say, good Caesar,
That I some lady trifles have reserv'd,
Immoment toys, things of such dignity
As we greet modern friends withal; and say
Some nobler token I have kept apart
For Livia and Octavia, to induce
Their mediation – must I be unfolded
With one that I have bred? The gods! It smites me
Beneath the fall I have. [*To Seleucus*] Prithee go hence;
Or I shall show the cinders of my spirits
Through th' ashes of my chance. Wert thou a man,
Thou wouldst have mercy on me.

CAESAR Forbear, Seleucus.

[*Exit Seleucus.*

CLEOPATRA Be it known that we, the greatest, are misthought
For things that others do; and when we fall
We answer others' merits in our name,
Are therefore to be pitied.

CAESAR Cleopatra,
Not what you have reserv'd, nor what acknowledg'd,
Put we i' th' roll of conquest. Still be't yours,
Bestow it at your pleasure; and believe
Caesar's no merchant, to make prize with you
Of things that merchants sold. Therefore be cheer'd;
Make not your thoughts your prisons. No, dear Queen;
For we intend so to dispose you as
Yourself shall give us counsel. Feed and sleep.
Our care and pity is so much upon you
That we remain your friend; and so, adieu.

CLEOPATRA My master and my lord!

CAESAR Not so. Adieu.

[*Flourish. Exeunt Caesar and his Train.*

CLEOPATRA He words me, girls, he words me, that I should not
Be noble to myself. But hark thee, Charmian!

[*Whispers Charmian.*

IRAS Finish, good lady; the bright day is done,
And we are for the dark.

CLEOPATRA Hie thee again.
I have spoke already, and it is provided;
Go put it to the haste.

CHARMIAN Madam, I will.

Re-enter DOLABELLA.

DOLABELLA Where's the Queen?

CHARMIAN Behold, sir. [*Exit.*

CLEOPATRA Dolabella!

DOLABELLA Madam, as thereto sworn by your command,
Which my love makes religion to obey,
I tell you this: Caesar through Syria
Intends his journey, and within three days
You with your children will he send before.
Make your best use of this; I have perform'd
Your pleasure and my promise.

CLEOPATRA Dolabella,
I shall remain your debtor.

DOLABELLA I your servant.
Adieu, good Queen; I must attend on Caesar.

CLEOPATRA Farewell, and thanks.

[*Exit Dolabella.*

Now, Iras, what think'st thou?
Thou an Egyptian puppet shall be shown
In Rome as well as I. Mechanic slaves,
With greasy aprons, rules, and hammers, shall
Uplift us to the view; in their thick breaths,
Rank of gross diet, shall we be enclouded,
And forc'd to drink their vapour.

IRAS The gods forbid!

CLEOPATRA Nay, 'tis most certain, Iras. Saucy lictors
Will catch at us like strumpets, and scald rhymers
Ballad us out o' tune; the quick comedians
Extemporally will stage us, and present
Our Alexandrian revels; Antony
Shall be brought drunken forth, and I shall see
Some squeaking Cleopatra boy my greatness
I' th' posture of a whore.

IRAS O the good gods!

CLEOPATRA Nay, that's certain.

IRAS I'll never see't, for I am sure mine nails
Are stronger than mine eyes.

CLEOPATRA Why, that's the way
To fool their preparation and to conquer
Their most absurd intents.

Enter CHARMIAN.

Now, Charmian!
Show me, my women, like a queen. Go fetch
My best attires. I am again for Cydnus,
To meet Mark Antony. Sirrah, Iras, go.
Now, noble Charmian, we'll dispatch indeed;
And when thou hast done this chare, I'll give thee leave
To play till doomsday. Bring our crown and all.

[*Exit Iras. A noise within.*

Wherefore's this noise?

Enter a Guard.

GUARD Here is a rural fellow
That will not be denied your Highness' presence.
He brings you figs.

CLEOPATRA Let him come in. [*Exit Guard.*
What poor an instrument
May do a noble deed! He brings me liberty.
My resolution's plac'd, and I have nothing
Of woman in me. Now from head to foot
I am marble-constant; now the fleeting moon
No planet is of mine.

Re-enter Guard and Clown, with a basket.

GUARD This is the man.

CLEOPATRA Avoid, and leave him.

[*Exit Guard.*

Hast thou the pretty worm of Nilus there
That kills and pains not?

CLOWN Truly, I have him. But I would not be the party that should desire you to touch him, for his biting is immortal; those that do die of it do seldom or never recover.

CLEOPATRA Remember'st thou any that have died on't?

CLOWN Very many, men and women too. I heard of one of them no longer than yesterday: a very honest woman, but something given to lie, as a woman should not do but in the way of honesty; how she died of the biting of it, what pain she felt – truly she makes a very good report o' th' worm. But he that will believe all that they say shall never be saved by half that they do. But this is most falliable, the worm's an odd worm.

CLEOPATRA Get thee hence; farewell.

CLOWN I wish you all joy of the worm.

[*Sets down the basket.*

CLEOPATRA Farewell.

CLOWN You must think this, look you, that the worm will do his kind.

CLEOPATRA Ay, ay; farewell.

CLOWN Look you, the worm is not to be trusted but in the keeping of wise people; for indeed there is no goodness in the worm.

CLEOPATRA Take thou no care; it shall be heeded.

CLOWN Very good. Give it nothing, I pray you, for it is not worth the feeding.

CLEOPATRA Will it eat me?

CLOWN You must not think I am so simple but I know the devil himself will not eat a woman. I know that a woman is a dish for the gods, if the devil dress her not. But truly, these same whoreson devils do the gods great harm in their women, for in every ten that they make the devils mar five.

CLEOPATRA Well, get thee gone; farewell.

CLOWN Yes, forsooth. I wish you joy o' th' worm.

[*Exit.*

Re-enter IRAS, with a robe, crown, etc.

CLEOPATRA Give me my robe, put on my crown; I have
Immortal longings in me. Now no more
The juice of Egypt's grape shall moist this lip.
Yare, yare, good Iras; quick. Methinks I hear
Antony call. I see him rouse himself
To praise my noble act. I hear him mock
The luck of Caesar, which the gods give men
To excuse their after wrath. Husband, I come.
Now to that name my courage prove my title!
I am fire and air; my other elements
I give to baser life. So, have you done?
Come then, and take the last warmth of my lips.
Farewell, kind Charmian. Iras, long farewell.

[*Kisses them. Iras falls and dies.*

Have I the aspic in my lips? Dost fall?
If thou and nature can so gently part,
The stroke of death is as a lover's pinch,
Which hurts and is desir'd. Dost thou lie still?
If thus thou vanishest, thou tell'st the world
It is not worth leave-taking.

CHARMIAN Dissolve, thick cloud, and rain, that I may say
The gods themselves do weep.

CLEOPATRA This proves me base.
If she first meet the curled Antony,
He'll make demand of her, and spend that kiss
Which is my heaven to have. Come, thou mortal wretch,

[*To an asp, which she applies to her breast.*

With thy sharp teeth this knot intrinsicate
Of life at once untie. Poor venomous fool,
Be angry, and dispatch. O couldst thou speak,
That I might hear thee call great Caesar ass
Unpolicied!

CHARMIAN O Eastern star!

CLEOPATRA Peace, peace!

Dost thou not see my baby at my breast
That sucks the nurse asleep?

CHARMIAN O, break! O, break!

CLEOPATRA As sweet as balm, as soft as air, as gentle –
O Antony! Nay, I will take thee too:

[Applying another asp to her arm.

What should I stay – *[Dies.*

CHARMIAN In this vile world? So, fare thee well.
Now boast thee, death, in thy possession lies
A lass unparallel'd. Downy windows, close;
And golden Phoebus never be beheld
Of eyes again so royal! Your crown's awry;
I'll mend it and then play –

Enter the Guard, rushing in.

1 GUARD Where's the Queen?

CHARMIAN Speak softly, wake her not.

1 GUARD Caesar hath sent –

CHARMIAN Too slow a messenger.

[Applies an asp.

O, come apace, dispatch. I partly feel thee.

1 GUARD Approach, ho! All's not well: Caesar's beguil'd.

2 GUARD There's Dolabella sent from Caesar; call him.

1 GUARD What work is here! Charmian, is this well done?

CHARMIAN It is well done, and fitting for a princess
Descended of so many royal kings.
Ah, soldier! *[Charmian dies.*

Re-enter DOLABELLA.

DOLABELLA How goes it here?

2 GUARD All dead.

DOLABELLA Caesar, thy thoughts
Touch their effects in this. Thyself art coming
To see perform'd the dreaded act which thou
So sought'st to hinder.

Within. A way there, a way for Caesar!

Re-enter CAESAR and all his Train.

DOLABELLA O sir, you are too sure an augurer:
That you did fear is done.

CAESAR Bravest at the last,
She levell'd at our purposes, and being royal,
Took her own way. The manner of their deaths?
I do not see them bleed.

DOLABELLA Who was last with them?

1 GUARD A simple countryman that brought her figs.
This was his basket.

CAESAR Poison'd then.

1 GUARD O Caesar,
This Charmian liv'd but now; she stood and spake.
I found her trimming up the diadem
On her dead mistress. Tremblingly she stood,
And on the sudden dropp'd.

CAESAR O noble weakness!
If they had swallow'd poison 'twould appear
By external swelling; but she looks like sleep,
As she would catch another Antony
In her strong toil of grace.

DOLABELLA Here on her breast
There is a vent of blood, and something blown;
The like is on her arm.

1 GUARD This is an aspic's trail; and these fig-leaves
Have slime upon them, such as th' aspic leaves
Upon the caves of Nile.

CAESAR Most probable
That so she died; for her physician tells me
She hath pursu'd conclusions infinite
Of easy ways to die. Take up her bed,
And bear her women from the monument.
She shall be buried by her Antony;
No grave upon the earth shall clip in it
A pair so famous. High events as these
Strike those that make them; and their story is
No less in pity than his glory which
Brought them to be lamented. Our army shall
In solemn show attend this funeral,
And then to Rome. Come, Dolabella, see
High order in this great solemnity. *[Exeunt.*

Cymbeline

Introduction by DONALD MACKENZIE

Cymbeline is a flamboyant oddity, the Chinese dragon of the Shakespeare canon. It belongs and does not belong with its fellow romances. All of them combine a return to old-fashioned styles and genres and a reaching, through these, to the archaic and the archetypal, with an experimental dramaturgy that recurrently underscores its own artificiality and a verbal art intensely wrought. Rooted in the tragedies, they also tap back, selectively, into Shakespearean comedy, resuming tragic conflict and loss but transcending it in a scene of final restoration first modelled in *The Comedy of Errors* at the opening of Shakespeare's career. *Cymbeline*, however, stands out in the range of earlier Shakespeare it evokes and interlaces. The bedroom scene is sprinkled with recollections of the final scene in *Othello*; but these are elaborated into rococo beauties and touched with echoes of *Macbeth* and, behind it, *Lucrece*. The pastoral scenes can draw equally on *As You Like It* and the anti-pastoral *Lear*. Posthumus' vision [5.4] is framed by gnomic meditations on death that recall *Measure for Measure*. Unlike the other romances *Cymbeline* incorporates historical legend, and the British defiance of Rome returns us (in a compressed, half-incantatory late Shakespearean style) to the patriotism of histories like *Richard II* and *King John*. The play's Italy superimposes a tragicomedy of the contemporary Renaissance on ancient Rome. Imogen is a heroine out of Shakespeare's middle comedies; yet she moves in a play that deploys the romance motifs of the sundered family, chastity threatened by jealousy or brutish violence, averted tragedy and intimations of death and resurrection – but deploys them with an extravagance not found in any of its fellows (consider, e.g., Act 4.2 or compare Posthumus' speech on waking in Act 5.2.123 with Pericles' response to the recovery of Marina).

Some of *Cymbeline*'s oddity might be accounted for by saying that Shakespeare has been content to toss off a sketch of what he had done, or will do, better elsewhere: the Queen is a pantomime Lady Macbeth, Cloten an embryonic Caliban. But over the span of the play the extravagances are too spectacular, the writing too strenuous for that. Its interlacing of earlier Shakespearean styles could be expected to generate discords. But it goes out of its way to heighten the discordant into the bizarre or beyond. In Act 4 Scene2 Imogen (supposed dead) wakes beside the headless body of Cloten whom she takes (in extravagant detail) for his heroic opposite, her husband Posthumus, only because he is wearing the latter's clothes. The episode is preposterous and gruesome; the verse in its twining of the prettified and the intense twirls it up into the wildly grotesque. Yet it can be argued (Taylor, 1983) that the grotesque here brings to a climax and discharges the strained and violent elements in the play's vision which from this point moves increasingly into grace and renewal (one might compare the Dover cliff scene in *King Lear*).

Nonetheless the question persists into the final scene: does the play have any commanding centre or pattern that can bring – even juggle – its discordant multiplicity into coherence? All the romances climax in a reunion that revokes and transfigures past suffering and loss. Shakespeare refashions this scenic form (for the latter concept and its application see Jones, 1971) from *Pericles* through *The Winter's Tale* to *The Tempest*. But in *Cymbeline* he refracts it in a pantomime series of discoveries and reversals and reunions that climax in the astrologer's reading of the tablet left by the ghosts of Posthumus' vision. One can read this scene, and, backwards from it, the play, as Shakespeare's exuberantly taking for a ride the motifs and forms and imaginative preoccupations that command his art in the other romances. Against that, the closing speeches bestow a genuine imaginative weight on the reconciliation of Britain and Rome, as the earlier lines of the reunited Posthumus and Imogen – 'Think that you are upon a rock, and now/Throw me again – Hang there like fruit, my soul,/Till the tree die' – strike home with a brevity intensely potent in this play of shell-whorled verbal elaboration.

Such power (which can be experienced as consummating a good deal that has come earlier) forbids a reading of *Cymbeline* in terms only of self-delighting, self-mocking virtuosity. It enforces the historical motifs that invite interpretation of the play as fashioning a myth of Britain (Wilson Knight, 1947; refined but also muted in Jones, 1961) from which its extravagances finally skate aside. (See, however, the account of 'the play's feeling for compromise' argued by Hill, 1984). In the end *Cymbeline* retains a teasing potency. This may be why it has appealed to poets, specifically, one might venture, to poets engaged by history but drawn, across that engagement, to the pursuit of a haunting and recessive music: Eliot, Geoffrey Hill and, not least, Tennyson who had a copy of *Cymbeline* buried with him.

Cymbeline

DRAMATIS PERSONAE

CYMBELINE
King of Britain
CLOTEN
son to the Queen by a former husband
POSTHUMUS LEONATUS
a gentleman, husband to Imogen
BELARIUS
a banished lord, disguised under the name of MORGAN
GUIDERIUS, ARVIRAGUS
sons to Cymbeline, disguised under the names of POLYDORE and CADWAL, supposed sons to Belarius
PHILARIO
friend to Posthumus
IACHIMO
friend to Philario, Italians
A French Gentleman friend to Philario
CAIUS LUCIUS
General of the Roman Forces
A Roman Captain
Two British Captains
PISANIO
servant to Posthumus
CORNELIUS
a physician
Two Lords of Cymbeline's court
Two Gentlemen of the same
Two Gaolers
QUEEN
wife to Cymbeline
IMOGEN
daughter to Cymbeline by a former queen
HELEN
a lady attending on Imogen
Apparitions
Lords, Ladies, Roman Senators, Tribunes, a Soothsayer, a Dutch Gentleman, a Spanish Gentleman, Musicians, Officers, Captains, Soldiers, Messengers and Attendants.

THE SCENE: BRITAIN; ITALY.

ACT ONE

SCENE I. *Britain. The garden of Cymbeline's palace.*

1 GENTLEMAN You do not meet a man but frowns; our bloods
No more obey the heavens than our courtiers
Still seem as does the King's.
2 GENTLEMAN But what's the matter?
1 GENTLEMAN His daughter, and the heir of's kingdom, whom
He purpos'd to his wife's sole son – a widow
That late he married – hath referr'd herself
Unto a poor but worthy gentleman. She's wedded;
Her husband banish'd; she imprison'd. All
Is outward sorrow, though I think the King
Be touch'd at very heart.
2 GENTLEMAN None but the King?
1 GENTLEMAN He that hath lost her too. So is the Queen,
That most desir'd the match. But not a courtier,
Although they wear their faces to the bent
Of the King's looks, hath a heart that is not
Glad at the thing they scowl at.
2 GENTLEMAN And why so?
1 GENTLEMAN He that hath miss'd the Princess is a thing
Too bad for bad report; and he that hath her –
I mean that married her, alack, good man!
And therefore banish'd – is a creature such
As, to seek through the regions of the earth
For one his like, there would be something failing
In him that should compare. I do not think
So fair an outward and such stuff within
Endows a man but he.
2 GENTLEMAN You speak him far.
1 GENTLEMAN I do extend him, sir, within himself;
Crush him together rather than unfold
His measure duly.
2 GENTLEMAN What's his name and birth?
1 GENTLEMAN I cannot delve him to the root; his father
Was call'd Sicilius, who did join his honour
Against the Romans with Cassibelan,
But had his titles by Tenantius, whom
He serv'd with glory and admir'd success,
So gain'd the sur-addition Leonatus;
And had, besides this gentleman in question,
Two other sons, who, in the wars o' th' time,
Died with their swords in hand; for which their father,
Then old and fond of issue, took such sorrow
That he quit being; and his gentle lady,
Big of this gentleman, our theme, deceas'd
As he was born. The King he takes the babe

To his protection, calls him Posthumus Leonatus,
Breeds him and makes him of his bed-chamber,
Puts to him all the learnings that his time
Could make him the receiver of; which he took,
As we do air, fast as 'twas minist'red,
And in's spring became a harvest, liv'd in court –
Which rare it is to do – most prais'd, most lov'd,
A sample to the youngest; to th' more mature
A glass that feated them; and to the graver
A child that guided dotards. To his mistress,
For whom he now is banish'd – her own price
Proclaims how she esteem'd him and his virtue;
By her election may be truly read
What kind of man he is.

2 GENTLEMAN I honour him
Even out of your report. But pray you tell me,
Is she sole child to th' King?

1 GENTLEMAN His only child.
He had two sons – if this be worth your hearing,
Mark it – the eldest of them at three years old,
I' th' swathing clothes the other, from their nursery
Were stol'n; and to this hour no guess in knowledge
Which way they went.

2 GENTLEMAN How long is this ago?

1 GENTLEMAN Some twenty years.

2 GENTLEMAN That a king's children should be so convey'd,
So slackly guarded, and the search so slow
That could not trace them!

1 GENTLEMAN Howsoe'er 'tis strange,
Or that the negligence may well be laugh'd at,
Yet is it true, sir.

2 GENTLEMAN I do well believe you.

1 GENTLEMAN We must forbear; here comes the gentleman,
The Queen, and Princess. [*Exeunt.*

Enter the QUEEN, POSTHUMUS, and IMOGEN.

QUEEN No, be assur'd you shall not find me, daughter,
After the slander of most stepmothers,
Evil-ey'd unto you. You're my prisoner, but
Your gaoler shall deliver you the keys
That lock up your restraint. For you, Posthumus,
So soon as I can win th' offended King,
I will be known your advocate. Marry, yet
The fire of rage is in him, and 'twere good
You lean'd unto his sentence with what patience
Your wisdom may inform you.

POSTHUMUS Please your Highness,
I will from hence to-day.

QUEEN You know the peril.
I'll fetch a turn about the garden, pitying
The pangs of barr'd affections, though the King
Hath charg'd you should not speak together.
[*Exit.*

IMOGEN O
Dissembling courtesy! How fine this tyrant
Can tickle where she wounds! My dearest husband,
I something fear my father's wrath, but nothing –
Always reserv'd my holy duty – what
His rage can do on me. You must be gone;
And I shall here abide the hourly shot
Of angry eyes, not comforted to live
But that there is this jewel in the world
That I may see again.

POSTHUMUS My queen! my mistress!
O lady, weep no more, lest I give cause
To be suspected of more tenderness
Than doth become a man. I will remain
The loyal'st husband that did e'er plight troth;
My residence in Rome at one Philario's,
Who to my father was a friend, to me
Known but by letter; thither write, my queen,
And with mine eyes I'll drink the words you send,
Though ink be made of gall.

Re-enter QUEEN.

QUEEN Be brief, I pray you.
If the King come, I shall incur I know not
How much of his displeasure. [*Aside*] Yet I'll move him
To walk this way. I never do him wrong
But he does buy my injuries, to be friends;
Pays dear for my offences. [*Exit.*

POSTHUMUS Should we be taking leave
As long a term as yet we have to live,
The loathness to depart would grow. Adieu!

IMOGEN Nay, stay a little.
Were you but riding forth to air yourself,
Such parting were too petty. Look here, love:
This diamond was my mother's; take it, heart;
But keep it till you woo another wife,
When Imogen is dead.

POSTHUMUS How, how? Another?
You gentle gods, give me but this I have,
And cere up my embracements from a next
With bonds of death! Remain, remain thou here
[*Puts on the ring.*
While sense can keep it on. And, sweetest, fairest,
As I my poor self did exchange for you,
To your so infinite loss, so in our trifles
I still win of you. For my sake wear this;
It is a manacle of love; I'll place it
Upon this fairest prisoner. [*Puts a bracelet on her arm.*

IMOGEN O the gods!
When shall we see again?

Enter CYMBELINE and Lords.

POSTHUMUS Alack, the King!

CYMBELINE Thou basest thing, avoid; hence from my sight!
If after this command thou fraught the court
With thy unworthiness, thou diest. Away!
Thou'rt poison to my blood.

POSTHUMUS The gods protect you,
And bless the good remainders of the court!
I am gone. [*Exit.*

IMOGEN There cannot be a pinch in death
More sharp than this is.

CYMBELINE O disloyal thing,
That shouldst repair my youth, thou heap'st
A years' age on me!

IMOGEN I beseech you, sir,
Harm not yourself with your vexation.
I am senseless of your wrath; a touch more rare
Subdues all pangs, all fears.

CYMBELINE Past grace? obedience?

IMOGEN Past hope, and in despair; that way past grace.

CYMBELINE That mightst have had the sole son of my queen!

IMOGEN O blessed that I might not! I chose an eagle,
And did avoid a puttock.

CYMBELINE Thou took'st a beggar, wouldst have made my throne
A seat for baseness.

IMOGEN No; I rather added
A lustre to it.

CYMBELINE O thou vile one!

IMOGEN Sir,
It is your fault that I have lov'd Posthumus.
You bred him as my playfellow, and he is
A man worth any woman; overbuys me
Almost the sum he pays.

CYMBELINE What, art thou mad?

IMOGEN Almost, sir. Heaven restore me! Would I were
A neat-herd's daughter, and my Leonatus
Our neighbour shepherd's son!

Re-enter QUEEN.

CYMBELINE Thou foolish thing!
[*To the Queen*] They were again together. You have done
Not after our command. Away with her,
And pen her up.

QUEEN Beseech your patience. – Peace,
Dear lady daughter, peace! – Sweet sovereign,
Leave us to ourselves, and make yourself some comfort
Out of your best advice.

CYMBELINE Nay, let her languish
A drop of blood a day and, being aged,
Die of this folly. [*Exit, with Lords.*

Enter PISANIO.

QUEEN Fie! you must give way.
Here is your servant. How now, sir! What news?

PISANIO My lord your son drew on my master.

QUEEN Ha!
No harm, I trust, is done?

PISANIO There might have been,
But that my master rather play'd than fought,
And had no help of anger; they were parted
By gentlemen at hand.

QUEEN I am very glad on't.

IMOGEN Your son's my father's friend; he takes his part
To draw upon an exile! O brave sir!
I would they were in Afric both together;
Myself by with a needle, that I might prick
The goer-back. Why came you from your master?

PISANIO On his command. He would not suffer me
To bring him to the haven; left these notes
Of what commands I should be subject to,
When't pleas'd you to employ me.

QUEEN This hath been
Your faithful servant. I dare lay mine honour
He will remain so.

PISANIO I humbly thank your Highness.

QUEEN Pray walk awhile.

IMOGEN About some half-hour hence,
Pray you speak with me. You shall at least
Go see my lord aboard. For this time leave me.
[*Exeunt.*

SCENE II. *Britain. A public place.*

Enter CLOTEN and two Lords.

1 LORD Sir, I would advise you to shift a shirt; the violence of action hath made you reek as a sacrifice. Where air comes out, air comes in; there's none abroad so wholesome as that you vent.

CLOTEN If my shirt were bloody, then to shift it. Have I hurt him?

2 LORD [*Aside*] No, faith; not so much as his patience.

1 LORD Hurt him! His body's a passable carcass if he be not hurt. It is a through-fare for steel if it be not hurt.

2 LORD [*Aside*] His steel was in debt; it went o' th' back side the town.

CLOTEN The villain would not stand me.

2 LORD [*Aside*] No; but he fled forward still, toward your face.

1 LORD Stand you? You have land enough of your own; but he added to your having, gave you some ground.

2 LORD [*Aside*] As many inches as you have oceans. Puppies!

CLOTEN I would they had not come between us.

2 LORD [*Aside*] So would I, till you had measur'd how long a fool you were upon the ground.

CLOTEN And that she should love this fellow, and refuse me!

2 LORD [*Aside*] If it be a sin to make a true election, she is damn'd.

1 LORD Sir, as I told you always, her beauty and her brain go not together; she's a good sign, but I have seen small reflection of her wit.

2 LORD [*Aside*] She shines not upon fools, lest the reflection should hurt her.

CLOTEN Come, I'll to my chamber. Would there had been some hurt done!

2 LORD [*Aside*] I wish not so; unless it had been the fall of an ass, which is no great hurt.

CLOTEN You'll go with us?

1 LORD I'll attend your lordship.

CLOTEN Nay, come, let's go together.

2 LORD Well, my lord. [*Exeunt.*

SCENE III. *Britain, Cymbeline's palace.*

Enter IMOGEN and PISANIO.

IMOGEN I would thou grew'st unto the shores o' th' haven,
And questioned'st every sail; if he should write,
And I not have it, 'twere a paper lost,
As offer'd mercy is. What was the last
That he spake to thee?

PISANIO It was: his queen, his queen!

IMOGEN Then wav'd his handkerchief?

PISANIO And kiss'd it, madam.

IMOGEN Senseless linen, happier therein than I!
And that was all?

PISANIO No, madam; for so long
As he could make me with his eye, or care
Distinguish him from others, he did keep
The deck, with glove, or hat, or handkerchief,
Still waving, as the fits and stirs of's mind
Could best express how slow his soul sail'd on,
How swift his ship.

IMOGEN Thou shouldst have made him
As little as a crow, or less, ere left
To after-eye him.

PISANIO Madam, so I did.

IMOGEN I would have broke mine eye-strings, crack'd them but
To look upon him, till the diminution
Of space had pointed him sharp as my needle;
Nay, followed him till he had melted from
The smallness of a gnat to air, and then
Have turn'd mine eye and wept. But, good Pisanio,
When shall we hear from him?

PISANIO Be assur'd, madam,
With his next vantage.

IMOGEN I did not take my leave of him, but had
Most pretty things to say. Ere I could tell him
How I would think on him at certain hours
Such thoughts and such; or I could make him swear
The shes of Italy should not betray
Mine interest and his honour; or have charg'd him,
At the sixth hour of morn, at noon, at midnight,
T' encounter me with orisons, for then
I am in heaven for him; or ere I could
Give him that parting kiss which I had set
Betwixt two charming words, comes in my father,
And like the tyrannous breathing of the north
Shakes all our buds from growing.

Enter a Lady.

LADY The Queen, madam,
Desires your Highness' company.

IMOGEN Those things I bid you do, get them dispatch'd.
I will attend the Queen.

PISANIO Madam, I shall.
[*Exeunt.*

SCENE IV. *Rome. Philario's house.*

Enter PHILARIO, IACHIMO, a Frenchman, a Dutchman, and a Spaniard.

IACHIMO Believe it, sir, I have seen him in Britain. He was then of a crescent note, expected to prove so worthy as since he hath been allowed the name of. But I could then have look'd on him without the help of admiration, though the catalogue of his endowments had been tabled by his side, and I to persue him by items.

PHILARIO You speak of him when he was less furnish'd than now he is with that which makes him both without and within.

FRENCHMAN I have seen him in France; we had very many there could behold the sun with as firm eyes as he.

IACHIMO This matter of marrying his king's daughter, wherein he must be weighed rather by her value than his own, words him, I doubt not, a great deal from the matter.

FRENCHMAN And then his banishment.

IACHIMO Ay, and the approbation of those that weep this lamentable divorce under her colours are wonderfully to extend him, be it but to

fortify her judgment, which else an easy battery
might lay flat, for taking a beggar, without less
quality. But how comes it he is to sojourn with
22 you? How creeps acquaintance?

PHILARIO His father and I were soldiers together,
to whom I have been often bound for no less
than my life.

Enter POSTHUMUS.

Here comes the Briton. Let him be so
entertained amongst you as suits with
gentlemen of your knowing to a stranger of his
quality. I beseech you all be better known to this
gentleman, whom I commend to you as a noble
friend of mine. How worthy he is I will leave to
appear hereafter, rather than story him
31 in his own hearing.

FRENCHMAN Sir, we have known together in
Orleans.

POSTHUMUS Since when I have been debtor to
you for courtesies, which I will be ever to pay
34 and yet pay still.

FRENCHMAN Sir, you o'errate my poor kindness.
I was glad I did atone my countryman and you;
it had been pity you should have been put
together with so mortal a purpose as then each
bore, upon importance of so slight and trivial a
39 nature.

POSTHUMUS By your pardon, sir, I was then a
young traveller; rather shunn'd to go even with
what I heard than in my every action to be
guided by others' experiences; but upon my
mended judgment – if I offend not to say it is
44 mended – my quarrel was not altogether slight.

FRENCHMAN Faith, yes, to be put to the
arbitrement of swords, and by such two that
would by all likelihood have confounded one
the other or have fall'n both.

IACHIMO Can we, with manners, ask what was
49 the difference?

FRENCHMAN Safely, I think. 'Twas a contention
in public, which may, without contradiction,
suffer the report. It was much like an argument
that fell out last night, where each of us fell in
praise of our country mistresses; this gentleman
at that time vouching – and upon warrant of
bloody affirmation – his to be more fair,
virtuous, wise, chaste, constant, qualified, and
less attemptable, than any the rarest of our
57 ladies in France.

IACHIMO That lady is not now living, or this
gentleman's opinion, by this, worn out.

POSTHUMUS She holds her virtue still, and I my
60 mind.

IACHIMO You must not so far prefer her fore ours
of Italy.

POSTHUMUS Being so far provok'd as I was in
France, I would abate her nothing, though I
profess myself her adorer, not her friend.

IACHIMO As fair and as good – a kind of hand-in-
hand comparison – had been something too fair
and too good for any lady in Britain. If she went
before others I have seen as that diamond of
yours outlustres many I have beheld, I could not
but believe she excelled many; but I have not
seen the most precious diamond that is, nor you
the lady. 72

POSTHUMUS I prais'd her as I rated her. So do I
my stone.

IACHIMO What do you esteem it at?

POSTHUMUS More than the world enjoys. 75

IACHIMO Either your unparagon'd mistress is
dead, or she's outpriz'd by a trifle.

POSTHUMUS You are mistaken: the one may be
sold or given, if there were wealth enough for
the purchase or merit for the gift; the other is
not a thing for sale, and only the gift of the gods. 81

IACHIMO Which the gods have given you?

POSTHUMUS Which by their graces I will keep.

IACHIMO You may wear her in title yours; but
you know strange fowl light upon neighbouring
ponds. Your ring may be stol'n too. So your
brace of unprizable estimations, the one is but
frail and the other casual; a cunning thief, or a
that-way-accomplish'd courtier, would hazard
the winning both of first and last. 89

POSTHUMUS Your Italy contains none so
accomplish'd a courtier to convince the honour
of my mistress, if in the holding or loss of that
you term her frail. I do nothing doubt you have
store of thieves; notwithstanding, I fear not my
ring.

PHILARIO Let us leave here, gentlemen. 95

POSTHUMUS Sir, with all my heart. This worthy
signior, I thank him, makes no stranger of me;
we are familiar at first.

IACHIMO With five times so much conversation I
should get ground of your fair mistress; make
her go back even to the yielding, had I
admittance and opportunity to friend. 102

POSTHUMUS No, no.

IACHIMO I dare thereupon pawn the moiety of
my estate to your ring, which, in my opinion,
o'ervalues it something. But I make my wager
rather against your confidence than her
reputation; and, to bar your offence herein too, I
durst attempt it against any lady in the world.

POSTHUMUS You are a great deal abus'd in too
bold a persuasion, and I doubt not you sustain
what y'are worthy of by your attempt. 111

IACHIMO What's that?

POSTHUMUS A repulse; though your attempt, as
you call it, deserve more – a punishment too.

PHILARIO Gentlemen, enough of this. It came in

too suddenly; let it die as it was born, and I pray you be better acquainted.

IACHIMO Would I had put my estate and my neighbour's on th' approbation of what I have spoke!

POSTHUMUS What lady would you choose to assail?

IACHIMO Yours, whom in constancy you think stands so safe. I will lay you ten thousand ducats to your ring that, commend me to the court where your lady is, with no more advantage than the opportunity of a second conference, and I will bring from thence that honour of hers which you imagine so reserv'd.

POSTHUMUS I will wage against your gold gold to it. My ring I hold dear as my finger; 'tis part of it.

IACHIMO You are a friend, and therein the wiser. If you buy ladies' flesh at a million a dram, you cannot preserve it from tainting. But I see you have some religion in you, that you fear.

POSTHUMUS This is but a custom in your tongue; you bear a graver purpose, I hope.

IACHIMO I am the master of my speeches, and would undergo what's spoken, I swear.

POSTHUMUS Will you? I shall but lend my diamond till your return. Let there be covenants drawn between's. My mistress exceeds in goodness the hugeness of your unworthy thinking. I dare you to this match: here's my ring.

PHILARIO I will have it no lay.

IACHIMO By the gods, it is one. If I bring you no sufficient testimony that I have enjoy'd the dearest bodily part of your mistress, my ten thousand ducats are yours; so is your diamond too. If I come off, and leave her in such honour as you have trust in, she your jewel, this your jewel, and my gold are yours – provided I have your commendation for my more free entertainment.

POSTHUMUS I embrace these conditions; let us have articles betwixt us. Only, thus far you shall answer: if you make your voyage upon her, and give me directly to understand you have prevail'd, I am no further your enemy – she is not worth our debate; if she remain unseduc'd, you not making it appear otherwise, for your ill opinion and th' assault you have made to her chastity you shall answer me with your sword.

IACHIMO Your hand – a covenant! We will have these things set down by lawful counsel, and straight away for Britain, lest the bargain should catch cold and starve. I will fetch my gold and have our two wagers recorded.

POSTHUMUS Agreed. [*Exeunt Posthumus and Iachimo.*

FRENCHMAN Will this hold, think you?

PHILARIO Signior Iachimo will not from it. Pray let us follow 'em. [*Exeunt.*

SCENE V. *Britain. Cymbeline's palace.*

Enter QUEEN, Ladies, and CORNELIUS.

QUEEN Whiles yet the dew's on ground gather those flowers;
Make haste; who has the note of them?
LADY I, madam.
QUEEN Dispatch. [*Exeunt Ladies.*
Now, Master Doctor, have you brought those drugs?
CORNELIUS Pleaseth your Highness, ay. Here they are, madam. [*Presenting a box.*
But I beseech your Grace, without offence –
My conscience bids me ask – wherefore you have
Commanded of me these most poisonous compounds,
Which are the movers of a languishing death,
But, though slow, deadly?
QUEEN I wonder, Doctor,
Thou ask'st me such a question. Have I not been
Thy pupil long? Hast thou not learn'd me how
To make perfumes? distil? preserve? yea, so
That our great king himself doth woo me oft
For my confections? Having thus far proceeded –
Unless thou think'st me devilish – is't not meet
That I did amplify my judgment in
Other conclusions? I will try the forces
Of these thy compounds on such creatures as
We count not worth the hanging – but none human –
To try the vigour of them, and apply
Allayments to their act, and by them gather
Their several virtues and effects.
CORNELIUS Your Highness
Shall from this practice but make hard your heart;
Besides, the seeing these effects will be
Both noisome and infectious.
QUEEN O, content thee.

Enter PISANIO.

[*Aside*] Here comes a flattering rascal; upon him
Will I first work. He's for his master,
And enemy to my son. – How now, Pisanio!
Doctor, your service for this time is ended;
Take your own way.
CORNELIUS [*Aside*] I do suspect you, madam;
But you shall do no harm.
QUEEN [*To Pisanio*] Hark thee, a word.
CORNELIUS [*Aside*] I do not like her. She doth think she has

Strange ling'ring poisons. I do know her spirit,
And will not trust one of her malice with
A drug of such damn'd nature. Those she has
Will stupefy and dull the sense awhile,
Which first perchance she'll prove on cats and dogs,
Then afterward up higher; but there is
No danger in what show of death it makes,
More than the locking up the spirits a time,
To be more fresh, reviving. She is fool'd
With a most false effect; and I the truer
So to be false with her.

QUEEN No further service, Doctor,
Until I send for thee.

CORNELIUS I humbly take my leave. [*Exit*

QUEEN Weeps she still, say'st thou?
Dost thou think in time
She will not quench, and let instructions enter
Where folly now possesses? Do thou work.
When thou shalt bring me word she loves my son,
I'll tell thee on the instant thou art then
As great as is thy master; greater, for
His fortunes all lie speechless, and his name
Is at last gasp. Return he cannot, nor
Continue where he is. To shift his being
Is to exchange one misery with another,
And every day that comes comes to decay
A day's work in him. What shalt thou expect
To be depender on a thing that leans,
Who cannot be new built, nor has no friends
So much as but to prop him?
[*The Queen drops the box. Pisanio takes it up.*
Thou tak'st up
Thou know'st not what; but take it for thy labour.
It is a thing I made, which hath the King
Five times redeem'd from death. I do not know
What is more cordial. Nay, I prithee take it;
It is an earnest of a further good
That I mean to thee. Tell thy mistress how
The case stands with her; do't as from thyself.
Think what a chance thou changest on; but think
Thou hast thy mistress still; to boot, my son,
Who shall take notice of thee. I'll move the King
To any shape of thy preferment, such
As thou'lt desire; and then myself, I chiefly,
That set thee on to this desert, am bound
To load thy merit richly. Call my women.
Think on my words. [*Exit Pisanio.*
A sly and constant knave,
Not to be shak'd; the agent for his master,
And the remembrancer of her to hold
The hand-fast to her lord. I have given him that
Which, if he takes, shall quite unpeople her
Of leigers for her sweet; and which she after,
Except she bend her humour, shall be assur'd
To taste of too.

Re-enter PISANIO and Ladies.

So, so. Well done, well done.
The violets, cowslips, and the primroses,
Bear to my closet. Fare thee well, Pisanio;
Think on my words. [*Exeunt Queen and Ladies.*

PISANIO And shall do.
But when to my good lord I prove untrue
I'll choke myself – there's all I'll do for you.
[*Exit.*

SCENE VI. *Britain. The palace.*

Enter IMOGEN alone.

IMOGEN A father cruel and a step-dame false;
A foolish suitor to a wedded lady
That hath her husband banish'd. O, that husband!
My supreme crown of grief! and those repeated
Vexations of it! Had I been thief-stol'n,
As my two brothers, happy! but most miserable
Is the desire that's glorious. Blessed be those,
How mean soe'er, that have their honest wills,
Which seasons comfort. Who may this be? Fie!

Enter PISANIO and IACHIMO.

PISANIO Madam, a noble gentleman of Rome
Comes from my lord with letters.

IACHIMO Change you, madam?
The worthy Leonatus is in safety,
And greets your Highness dearly. [*Presents a letter.*

IMOGEN Thanks, good sir.
You're kindly welcome.

IACHIMO [*Aside*] All of her that is out of door most rich!
If she be furnish'd with a mind so rare,
She is alone th' Arabian bird, and I
Have lost the wager. Boldness be my friend!
Arm me, audacity, from head to foot!
Or, like the Parthian, I shall flying fight;
Rather, directly fly.

IMOGEN [*Reads*] 'He is one of the noblest note, to whose kindnesses I am most infinitely tied. Reflect upon him accordingly, as you value your trust. LEONATUS.'
So far I read aloud;
But even the very middle of my heart
Is warm'd by th' rest and takes it thankfully.
You are as welcome, worthy sir, as I
Have words to bid you; and shall find it so
In all that I can do.

IACHIMO Thanks, fairest lady.
What, are men mad? Hath nature given them eyes
To see this vaulted arch and the rich crop
Of sea and land, which can distinguish 'twixt
The fiery orbs above and the twinn'd stones
Upon the number'd beach, and can we not
Partition make with spectacles so precious
'Twixt fair and foul?
IMOGEN What makes your admiration?
IACHIMO It cannot be i' th' eye, for apes and monkeys,
'Twixt two such shes, would chatter this way and
Contemn with mows the other; nor i' th' judgment,
For idiots in this case of favour would
Be wisely definite; nor i' th' appetite;
Sluttery, to such neat excellence oppos'd,
Should make desire vomit emptiness,
Not so allur'd to feed.
IMOGEN What is the matter, trow?
IACHIMO The cloyed will –
That satiate yet unsatisfied desire, that tub
Both fill'd and running – ravening first the lamb,
Longs after for the garbage.
IMOGEN What, dear sir,
Thus raps you? Are you well?
IACHIMO Thanks, madam; well. – Beseech you, sir,
Desire my man's abode where I did leave him.
He's strange and peevish.
PISANIO I was going, sir,
To give him welcome. [*Exit*.
IMOGEN Continues well my lord? His health beseech you?
IACHIMO Well, madam.
IMOGEN Is he dispos'd to mirth? I hope he is.
IACHIMO Exceeding pleasant; none a stranger there
So merry and so gamesome. He is call'd
The Britain reveller.
IMOGEN When he was here
He did incline to sadness, and oft-times
Not knowing why.
IACHIMO I never saw him sad.
There is a Frenchman his companion, one
An eminent monsieur that, it seems, much loves
A Gallian girl at home. He furnaces
The thick sighs from him; whiles the jolly Briton –
Your lord, I mean – laughs from's free lungs, cries 'O,
Can my sides hold, to think that man – who knows
By history, report, or his own proof,
What woman is, yea, what she cannot choose
But must be – will's free hours languish for
Assured bondage?'
IMOGEN Will my lord say so?
IACHIMO Ay, madam, with his eyes in flood with laughter.
It is a recreation to be by
And hear him mock the Frenchman. But heavens know
Some men are much to blame.
IMOGEN Not he, I hope.
IACHIMO Not he; but yet heaven's bounty towards him might
Be us'd more thankfully. In himself, 'tis much;
In you, which I account his, beyond all talents.
Whilst I am bound to wonder, I am bound
To pity too.
IMOGEN What do you pity, sir?
IACHIMO Two creatures heartily.
IMOGEN Am I one, sir?
You look on me: what wreck discern you in me
Deserves your pity?
IACHIMO Lamentable! What,
To hide me from the radiant sun and solace
I' th' dungeon by a snuff?
IMOGEN I pray you, sir,
Deliver with more openness your answers
To my demands. Why do you pity me?
IACHIMO That others do,
I was about to say, enjoy your – But
It is an office of the gods to venge it,
Not mine to speak on't.
IMOGEN You do seem to know
Something of me, or what concerns me; pray you –
Since doubting things go ill often hurts more
Than to be sure they do; for certainties
Either are past remedies, or, timely knowing,
The remedy then born – discover to me
What both you spur and stop.
IACHIMO Had I this cheek
To bathe my lips upon; this hand, whose touch,
Whose every touch, would force the feeler's soul
To th' oath of loyalty; this object, which
Takes prisoner the wild motion of mine eye,
Fixing it only here; should I, damn'd then,
Slaver with lips as common as the stairs
That mount the Capitol; join gripes with hands
Made hard with hourly falsehood – falsehood as
With labour; then by-peeping in an eye
Base and illustrious as the smoky light
That's fed with stinking tallow – it were fit
That all the plagues of hell should at one time
Encounter such revolt.
IMOGEN My lord, I fear,
Has forgot Britain.
IACHIMO And himself. Not I

Inclin'd to this intelligence pronounce
The beggary of his change; but 'tis your graces
That from my mutest conscience to my tongue
Charms this report out.

IMOGEN Let me hear no more.

IACHIMO O dearest soul, your cause doth strike my heart
With pity that doth make me sick! A lady
So fair, and fasten'd to an empery,
Would make the great'st king double, to be partner'd
With tomboys hir'd with that self exhibition
Which your own coffers yield! with diseas'd ventures
That play with all infirmities for gold
Which rottenness can lend nature! such boil'd stuff
As well might poison poison! Be reveng'd;
Or she that bore you was no queen, and you
Recoil from your great stock.

IMOGEN Reveng'd?
How should I be reveng'd? If this be true –
As I have such a heart that both mine ears
Must not in haste abuse – if it be true,
How should I be reveng'd?

IACHIMO Should he make me
Live like Diana's priest betwixt cold sheets,
Whiles he is vaulting variable ramps,
In your despite, upon your purse? Revenge it.
I dedicate myself to your sweet pleasure,
More noble than that runagate to your bed,
And will continue fast to your affection,
Still close as sure.

IMOGEN What ho, Pisanio!

IACHIMO Let me my service tender on your lips.

IMOGEN Away! I do condemn mine ears that have
So long attended thee. If thou wert honourable,
Thou wouldst have told this tale for virtue, not
For such an end thou seek'st, as base as strange.
Thou wrong'st a gentleman who is as far
From thy report as thou from honour; and
Solicits here a lady that disdains
Thee and the devil alike. – What ho, Pisanio! –
The King my father shall be made acquainted
Of thy assault. If he shall think it fit
A saucy stranger in his court to mart
As in a Romish stew, and to expound
His beastly mind to us, he hath a court
He little cares for, and a daughter who
He not respects at all. – What ho, Pisanio!

IACHIMO O happy Leonatus! I may say
The credit that thy lady hath of thee
Deserves thy trust, and thy most perfect goodness
Her assur'd credit. Blessed live you long,
A lady to the worthiest sir that ever
Country call'd his! and you his mistress, only
For the most worthiest fit! Give me your pardon.
I have spoke this to know if your affiance
Were deeply rooted, and shall make your lord
That which he is new o'er; and he is one
The truest manner'd, such a holy witch
That he enchants societies into him,
Half all men's hearts are his.

IMOGEN You make amends.

IACHIMO He sits 'mongst men like a descended god:
He hath a kind of honour sets him off
More than a mortal seeming. Be not angry,
Most mighty Princess, that I have adventur'd
To try your taking of a false report, which hath
Honour'd with confirmation your great judgment
In the election of a sir so rare,
Which you know cannot err. The love I bear him
Made me to fan you thus; but the gods made you,
Unlike all others, chaffless. Pray your pardon.

IMOGEN All's well, sir; take my pow'r i' th' court for yours.

IACHIMO My humble thanks. I had almost forgot
T' entreat your Grace but in a small request,
And yet of moment too, for it concerns
Your lord; myself and other noble friends
Are partners in the business.

IMOGEN Pray what is't?

IACHIMO Some dozen Romans of us, and your lord –
The best feather of our wing – have mingled sums
To buy a present for the Emperor;
Which I, the factor for the rest, have done
In France. 'Tis plate of rare device, and jewels
Of rich and exquisite form, their values great;
And I am something curious, being strange,
To have them in safe stowage. May it please you
To take them in protection?

IMOGEN Willingly;
And pawn mine honour for their safety. Since
My lord hath interest in them, I will keep them
In my bedchamber.

IACHIMO They are in a trunk,
Attended by my men. I will make bold
To send them to you only for this night;
I must aboard to-morrow.

IMOGEN O, no, no.

IACHIMO Yes, I beseech; or I shall short my word
By length'ning my return. From Gallia
I cross'd the seas on purpose and on promise
To see your Grace.

IMOGEN I thank you for your pains.

But not away to-morrow!
IACHIMO O, I must, madam.
Therefore I shall beseech you, if you please
To greet your lord with writing, do't to-night.
I have outstood my time, which is material
To th' tender of our present.
IMOGEN I will write.
Send your trunk to me; it shall safe be kept
And truly yielded you. You're very welcome.
[*Exeunt*.

ACT TWO

SCENE I. *Britain. Before Cymbeline's palace.*

Enter CLOTEN and the two Lords.

CLOTEN Was there ever man had such luck! When I kiss'd the jack, upon an up-cast to be hit away! I had a hundred pound on't; and then a whoreson jackanapes must take me up for swearing, as if I borrowed mine oaths of him, and might not spend them at my pleasure.

1 LORD What got he by that? You have broke his pate with your bowl.

2 LORD [*Aside*] If his wit had been like him that broke it, it would have run all out.

CLOTEN When a gentleman is dispos'd to swear, it is not for any standers-by to curtail his oaths. Ha?

2 LORD No, my lord; [*Aside*] nor crop the ears of them.

CLOTEN Whoreson dog! I give him satisfaction? Would he had been one of my rank!

2 LORD [*Aside*] To have smell'd like a fool.

CLOTEN I am not vex'd more at anything in th' earth. A pox on't! I had rather not be so noble as I am; they dare not fight with me, because of the Queen my mother. Every jackslave hath his bellyfull of fighting, and I must go up and down like a cock that nobody can match.

2 LORD [*Aside*] You are cock and capon too; and you crow, cock, with your comb on.

CLOTEN Sayest thou?

2 LORD It is not fit your lordship should undertake every companion that you give offence to.

CLOTEN No, I know that; but it is fit I should commit offence to my inferiors.

2 LORD Ay, it is fit for your lordship only.

CLOTEN Why, so I say.

1 LORD Did you hear of a stranger that's come to court to-night?

CLOTEN A stranger, and I not know on't?

2 LORD [*Aside*] He's a strange fellow himself, and knows it not.

1 LORD There's an Italian come, and, 'tis thought, one of Leonatus' friends.

CLOTEN Leonatus? A banish'd rascal; and he's another, whatsoever he be. Who told you of this stranger?

1 LORD One of your lordship's pages.

CLOTEN Is it fit I went to look upon him? Is there no derogation in't?

2 LORD You cannot derogate, my lord.

CLOTEN Not easily, I think.

2 LORD [*Aside*] You are a fool granted; therefore your issues, being foolish, do not derogate.

CLOTEN Come, I'll go see this Italian. What I have lost to-day at bowls I'll win to-night of him. Come, go.

2 LORD I'll attend your lordship. [*Exeunt Cloten and 1 Lord*.

That such a crafty devil as is his mother
Should yield the world this ass! A woman that
Bears all down with her brain; and this her son
Cannot take two from twenty, for his heart,
And leave eighteen. Alas, poor princess,
Thou divine Imogen, what thou endur'st,
Betwixt a father by thy step-dame govern'd,
A mother hourly coining plots, a wooer
More hateful than the foul expulsion is
Of thy dear husband, than that horrid act
Of the divorce he'd make! The heavens hold firm
The walls of thy dear honour, keep unshak'd
That temple, thy fair mind, that thou mayst stand
T' enjoy thy banish'd lord and this great land!
[*Exit*.

SCENE II. *Britain. Imogen's bedchamber in Cymbeline's palace; a trunk in one corner.*

Enter IMOGEN in her bed, and a Lady attending.

IMOGEN Who's there? My woman? Helen?
LADY Please you, madam.
IMOGEN What hour is it?
LADY Almost midnight, madam.
IMOGEN I have read three hours then. Mine eyes are weak;
Fold down the leaf where I have left. To bed.
Take not away the taper, leave it burning;
And if thou canst awake by four o' th' clock,
I prithee call me. Sleep hath seiz'd me wholly.
[*Exit Lady*.

To your protection I commend me, gods.
From fairies and the tempters of the night
Guard me, beseech ye!
[Sleeps. Iachimo comes from the trunk.

IACHIMO The crickets sing, and man's o'er-labour'd sense
Repairs itself by rest. Our Tarquin thus
Did softly press the rushes ere he waken'd
The chastity he wounded. Cytherea,
How bravely thou becom'st thy bed! fresh lily,
And whiter than the sheets! That I might touch!
But kiss; one kiss! Rubies unparagon'd,
How dearly they do't! 'Tis her breathing that
Perfumes the chamber thus. The flame o' th' taper
Bows toward her and would under-peep her lids
To see th' enclosed lights, now canopied
Under these windows white and azure, lac'd
With blue of heaven's own tinct. But my design
To note the chamber. I will write all down:
Such and such pictures; there the window; such
Th' adornment of her bed; the arras, figures –
Why, such and such; and the contents o' th' story.
Ah, but some natural notes about her body
Above ten thousand meaner movables
Would testify, t' enrich mine inventory.
O sleep, thou ape of death, lie dull upon her!
And be her sense but as a monument,
Thus in a chapel lying! Come off, come off;
[Taking off her bracelet.
As slippery as the Gordian knot was hard!
'Tis mine; and this will witness outwardly,
As strongly as the conscience does within,
To th' madding of her lord. On her left breast
A mole cinque-spotted, like the crimson drops
I' th' bottom of a cowslip. Here's a voucher
Stronger than ever law could make; this secret
Will force him think I have pick'd the lock and ta'en
The treasure of her honour. No more. To what end?
Why should I write this down that's riveted,
Screw'd to my memory? She hath been reading late
The tale of Tereus; here the leaf's turn'd down
Where Philomel gave up. I have enough.
To th' trunk again, and shut the spring of it.
Swift, swift, you dragons of the night, that dawning
May bare the raven's eye! I lodge in fear;
Though this a heavenly angel, hell is here.
[Clock strikes.
One, two, three. Time, time!
[Exit into the trunk.

SCENE III. *Cymbeline's palace. An antechamber adjoining Imogen's apartments.*

Enter CLOTEN and Lords.

1 LORD Your lordship is the most patient man in loss, the most coldest that ever turn'd up ace.

CLOTEN It would make any man cold to lose.

1 LORD But not every man patient after the noble temper of your lordship. You are most hot and furious when you win.

CLOTEN Winning will put any man into courage. If I could get this foolish Imogen, I should have gold enough. It's almost morning, is't not?

1 LORD Day, my lord.

CLOTEN I would this music would come. I am advised to give her music a mornings; they say it will penetrate.

Enter Musicians.

Come on, tune. If you can penetrate her with your fingering, so. We'll try with tongue too. If none will do, let her remain; but I'll never give o'er. First, a very excellent good-conceited thing; after, a wonderful sweet air, with admirable rich words to it – and then let her consider.

Song.

Hark, hark! the lark at heaven's gate sings,
And Phoebus 'gins arise,
His steeds to water at those springs
On chalic'd flow'rs that lies;
And winking Mary-buds begin
To ope their golden eyes.
With everything that pretty bin,
My lady sweet, arise;
Arise, arise!

So, get you gone. If this penetrate, I will consider your music the better; if it do not, it is a vice in her ears which horsehairs and calves' guts, nor the voice of unpaved eunuch to boot, can never amend. *[Exeunt Musicians.*

Enter CYMBELINE and QUEEN.

2 LORD Here comes the King.

CLOTEN I am glad I was up so late, for that's the reason I was up so early. He cannot choose but take this service I have done fatherly. – Good morrow to your Majesty and to my gracious mother.

CYMBELINE Attend you here the door of our stern daughter?
Will she not forth?

CLOTEN I have assail'd her with musics, but she vouchsafes no notice.

CYMBELINE The exile of her minion is too new;
She hath not yet forgot him; some more time

Must wear the print of his remembrance out,
And then she's yours.
QUEEN You are most bound to th' King,
Who lets go by no vantages that may
Prefer you to his daughter. Frame yourself
To orderly solicity, and be friended
With aptness of the season; make denials
Increase your services; so seem as if
You were inspir'd to do those duties which
You tender to her; that you in all obey her,
Save when command to your dismission tends,
And therein you are senseless.
CLOTEN Senseless? Not so.

Enter a Messenger.

MESSENGER So like you, sir, ambassadors from Rome;
The one is Caius Lucius.
CYMBELINE A worthy fellow,
Albeit he comes on angry purpose now;
But that's no fault of his. We must receive him
According to the honour of his sender;
And towards himself, his goodness fore-spent on us,
We must extend our notice. Our dear son,
When you have given good morning to your mistress,
Attend the Queen and us; we shall have need
T' employ you towards this Roman. Come, our queen. [*Exeunt all but Cloten.*
CLOTEN If she be up, I'll speak with her; if not,
Let her lie still and dream. By your leave, ho! [*Knocks.*
I know her women are about her; what
If I do line one of their hands? 'Tis gold
Which buys admittance; oft it doth – yea, and makes
Diana's rangers false themselves, yield up
Their deer to th' stand o' th' stealer; and 'tis gold
Which makes the true man kill'd and saves the thief;
Nay, sometime hangs both thief and true man. What
Can it not do and undo? I will make
One of her women lawyer to me, for
I yet not understand the case myself.
By your leave. [*Knocks.*

Enter a Lady.

LADY Who's there that knocks?
CLOTEN A gentleman.
LADY No more?
CLOTEN Yes, and a gentlewoman's son.
LADY That's more
Than some whose tailors are as dear as yours
Can justly boast of. What's your lordship's pleasure?
CLOTEN Your lady's person; is she ready?
LADY Ay,
To keep her chamber.
CLOTEN There is gold for you; sell me your good report.
LADY How? My good name? or to report of you
What I shall think is good? The Princess!

Enter IMOGEN.

CLOTEN Good morrow, fairest sister. Your sweet hand. [*Exit Lady.*
IMOGEN Good morrow, sir. You lay out too much pains
For purchasing but trouble. The thanks I give
Is telling you that I am poor of thanks,
And scarce can spare them.
CLOTEN Still I swear I love you.
IMOGEN If you but said so, 'twere as deep with me.
If you swear still, your recompense is still
That I regard it not.
CLOTEN This is no answer.
IMOGEN But that you shall not say I yield, being silent,
I would not speak. I pray you spare me. Faith,
I shall unfold equal discourtesy
To your best kindness; one of your great knowing
Should learn, being taught, forbearance.
CLOTEN To leave you in your madness 'twere my sin;
I will not.
IMOGEN Fools are not mad folks.
CLOTEN Do you call me fool?
IMOGEN As I am mad, I do;
If you'll be patient, I'll no more be mad;
That cures us both. I am much sorry, sir,
You put me to forget a lady's manners
By being so verbal; and learn now, for all,
That I, which know my heart, do here pronounce,
By th' very truth of it, I care not for you,
And am so near the lack of charity
To accuse myself I hate you; which I had rather
You felt than make't my boast.
CLOTEN You sin against
Obedience, which you owe your father. For
The contract you pretend with that base wretch,
One bred of alms and foster'd with cold dishes,
With scraps o' th' court – it is no contract, none.
And though it be allowed in meaner parties –
Yet who than he more mean? – to knit their souls –
On whom there is no more dependency
But brats and beggary – in self-figur'd knot,
Yet you are curb'd from that enlargement by
The consequence o' th' crown, and must not foil

The precious note of it with a base slave,
A hilding for a livery, a squire's cloth,
A pantler – not so eminent!
IMOGEN Profane fellow!
Wert thou the son of Jupiter, and no more
But what thou art besides, thou wert too base
To be his groom. Thou wert dignified enough,
Even to the point of envy, if 'twere made
Comparative for your virtues to be styl'd
The under-hangman of his kingdom, and hated
For being preferr'd so well.
CLOTEN The south fog rot him!
IMOGEN He never can meet more mischance than come
To be but nam'd of thee. His mean'st garment
That ever hath but clipp'd his body is dearer
In my respect than all the hairs above thee,
Were they all made such men. How now, Pisanio!

Enter PISANIO.

CLOTEN 'His garments'! Now the devil –
IMOGEN To Dorothy my woman hie thee presently.
CLOTEN 'His garment'!
IMOGEN I am sprited with a fool;
Frighted, and ang'red worse. Go bid my woman
Search for a jewel that too casually
Hath left mine arm. It was thy master's; shrew me,
If I would lose it for a revenue
Of any king's in Europe! I do think
I saw't this morning; confident I am
Last night 'twas on mine arm; I kiss'd it.
I hope it be not gone to tell my lord
That I kiss aught but he.
PISANIO 'Twill not be lost.
IMOGEN I hope so. Go and search. [*Exit Pisanio.*
CLOTEN You have abus'd me.
'His meanest garment'!
IMOGEN Ay, I said so, sir.
If you will make 't an action, call witness to 't.
CLOTEN I will inform your father.
IMOGEN Your mother too.
She's my good lady and will conceive, I hope,
But the worst of me. So I leave you, sir,
To th' worst of discontent. [*Exit.*
CLOTEN I'll be reveng'd.
'His mean'st garment'! Well. [*Exit.*

SCENE IV. *Rome. Philario's house.*

Enter POSTHUMUS and PHILARIO.

POSTHUMUS Fear it not, sir; I would I were so sure
To win the King as I am bold her honour
Will remain hers.
PHILARIO What means do you make to him?
POSTHUMUS Not any; but abide the change of time,
Quake in the present winter's state, and wish
That warmer days would come. In these fear'd hopes
I barely gratify your love; they failing,
I must die much your debtor.
PHILARIO Your very goodness and your company
O'erpays all I can do. By this your king
Hath heard of great Augustus. Caius Lucius
Will do's commission throughly; and I think
He'll grant the tribute, send th' arrearages,
Or look upon our Romans, whose remembrance
Is yet fresh in their grief.
POSTHUMUS I do believe,
Statist though I am none, nor like to be,
That this will prove a war; and you shall hear
The legions now in Gallia sooner landed
In our not-fearing Britain than have tidings
Of any penny tribute paid. Our country-men
Are men more order'd than when Julius Caesar
Smil'd at their lack of skill, but found their courage
Worthy his frowning at. Their discipline,
Now mingled with their courages, will make known
To their approvers they are people such
That mend upon the world.

Enter IACHIMO.

PHILARIO See! Iachimo!
POSTHUMUS The swiftest harts have posted you by land,
And winds of all the corners kiss'd your sails,
To make your vessel nimble.
PHILARIO Welcome, sir.
POSTHUMUS I hope the briefness of your answer made
The speediness of your return.
IACHIMO Your lady
Is one of the fairest that I have look'd upon.
POSTHUMUS And therewithal the best; or let her beauty
Look through a casement to allure false hearts,
And be false with them.
IACHIMO Here are letters for you.
POSTHUMUS Their tenour good, I trust.
IACHIMO 'Tis very like.
PHILARIO Was Caius Lucius in the Britain court
When you were there?
IACHIMO He was expected then,
But not approach'd.
POSTHUMUS All is well yet.
Sparkles this stone as it was wont, or is't not
Too dull for your good wearing?

IACHIMO If I have lost it,
I should have lost the worth of it in gold.
I'll make a journey twice as far t' enjoy
A second night of such sweet shortness which
Was mine in Britain; for the ring is won.
POSTHUMUS The stone's too hard to come by.
IACHIMO Not a whit,
Your lady being so easy.
POSTHUMUS Make not, sir,
Your loss your sport. I hope you know that we
Must not continue friends.
IACHIMO Good sir, we must,
If you keep covenant. Had I not brought
The knowledge of your mistress home, I grant
We were to question farther; but I now
Profess myself the winner of her honour,
Together with your ring; and not the wronger
Of her or you, having proceeded but
By both your wills.
POSTHUMUS If you can make't apparent
That you have tasted her in bed, my hand
And ring is yours. If not, the foul opinion
You had of her pure honour gains or loses
Your sword or mine, or masterless leaves both
To who shall find them.
IACHIMO Sir, my circumstances,
Being so near the truth as I will make them,
Must first induce you to believe – whose strength
I will confirm with oath; which I doubt not
You'll give me leave to spare when you shall find
You need it not.
POSTHUMUS Proceed.
IACHIMO First, her bedchamber,
Where I confess I slept not, but profess
Had that was well worth watching – it was hang'd
With tapestry of silk and silver; the story,
Proud Cleopatra when she met her Roman
And Cydnus swell'd above the banks, or for
The press of boats or pride. A piece of work
So bravely done, so rich, that it did strive
In workmanship and value; which I wonder'd
Could be so rarely and exactly wrought,
Since the true life on't was –
POSTHUMUS This is true;
And this you might have heard of here, by me
Or by some other.
IACHIMO More particulars
Must justify my knowledge.
POSTHUMUS So they must,
Or do your honour injury.
IACHIMO The chimney
Is south the chamber, and the chimney-piece
Chaste Dian bathing. Never saw I figures
So likely to report themselves. The cutter
Was as another nature, dumb; outwent her,
Motion and breath left out.
POSTHUMUS This is a thing
Which you might from relation likewise reap,
Being, as it is, much spoke of.
IACHIMO The roof o' th' chamber
With golden cherubins is fretted; her andirons –
I had forgot them – were two winking Cupids
Of silver, each on one foot standing, nicely
Depending on their brands.
POSTHUMUS This is her honour!
Let it be granted you have seen all this, and praise
Be given to your remembrance; the description
Of what is in her chamber nothing saves
The wager you have laid.
IACHIMO Then, if you can,
[Shows the bracelet.
Be pale. I beg but leave to air this jewel. See!
And now 'tis up again. It must be married
To that your diamond; I'll keep them.
POSTHUMUS Jove!
Once more let me behold it. Is it that
Which I left with her?
IACHIMO Sir – I thank her – that.
She stripp'd it from her arm; I see her yet;
Her pretty action did outsell her gift,
And yet enrich'd it too. She gave it me, and said
She priz'd it once.
POSTHUMUS May be she pluck'd it off
To send it me.
IACHIMO She writes so to you, doth she?
POSTHUMUS O, no, no, no! 'tis true. Here, take this too; *[Gives the ring.*
It is a basilisk unto mine eye,
Kills me to look on't. Let there be no honour
Where there is beauty; truth where semblance; love
Where there's another man. The vows of women
Of no more bondage be to where they are made
Than they are to their virtues, which is nothing.
O, above measure false!
PHILARIO Have patience, sir,
And take your ring again; 'tis not yet won.
It may be probable she lost it, or
Who knows if one her women, being corrupted,
Hath stol'n it from her?
POSTHUMUS Very true;
And so I hope he came by't. Back my ring.
Render to me some corporal sign about her,
More evident than this; for this was stol'n.
IACHIMO By Jupiter, I had it from her arm!
POSTHUMUS Hark you, he swears; by Jupiter he swears.
'Tis true – nay, keep the ring, 'tis true. I am sure
She would not lose it. Her attendants are

All sworn and honourable – they induc'd to steal it!
And by a stranger! No, he hath enjoy'd her.
The cognizance of her incontinency
Is this: she hath bought the name of whore thus dearly.
There, take thy hire; and all the fiends of hell
Divide themselves between you!

PHILARIO Sir, be patient;
This is not strong enough to be believ'd
Of one persuaded well of.

POSTHUMUS Never talk on't;
She hath been colted by him.

IACHIMO If you seek
For further satisfying, under her breast –
Worthy the pressing – lies a mole, right proud
Of that most delicate lodging. By my life,
I kiss'd it; and it gave me present hunger
To feed again, though full. You do remember
This stain upon her?

POSTHUMUS Ay, and it doth confirm
Another stain, as big as hell can hold,
Were there no more but it.

IACHIMO Will you hear more?

POSTHUMUS Spare you arithmetic; never count the turns.
Once, and a million!

IACHIMO I'll be sworn –

POSTHUMUS No swearing.
If you will swear you have not done't, you lie;
And I will kill thee if thou dost deny
Thou'st made me cuckold.

IACHIMO I'll deny nothing.

POSTHUMUS O that I had her here to tear her limb-meal!
I will go there and do't, i' th' court, before
Her father. I'll do something – [*Exit.*

PHILARIO Quite besides
The government of patience! You have won.
Let's follow him and pervert the present wrath
He hath against himself.

IACHIMO With all my heart.
[*Exeunt.*

SCENE V. *Rome. Another room in Philario's house.*

Enter POSTHUMUS.

POSTHUMUS Is there no way for men to be, but women
Must be half-workers? We are all bastards,
And that most venerable man which I
Did call my father was I know not where
When I was stamp'd. Some coiner with his tools
Made me a counterfeit; yet my mother seem'd
The Dian of that time. So doth my wife
The nonpareil of this. O, vengeance, vengeance!
Me of my lawful pleasure she restrain'd,
And pray'd me oft forbearance; did it with
A pudency so rosy, the sweet view on't
Might well have warm'd old Saturn; that I thought her
As chaste as unsunn'd snow. O, all the devils!
This yellow Iachimo in an hour – was't not?
Or less! – at first? Perchance he spoke not, but,
Like a full-acorn'd boar, a German one,
Cried 'O!' and mounted; found no opposition
But what he look'd for should oppose and she
Should from encounter guard. Could I find out
The woman's part in me! For there's no motion
That tends to vice in man but I affirm
It is the woman's part. Be it lying, note it,
The woman's; flattering, hers; deceiving, hers;
Lust and rank thoughts, hers, hers; revenges, hers;
Ambitions, covetings, change of prides, disdain,
Nice longing, slanders, mutability,
All faults that man may name, nay, that hell knows,
Why, hers, in part or all; but rather all;
For even to vice
They are not constant, but are changing still
One vice but of a minute old for one
Not half so old as that. I'll write against them,
Detest them, curse them. Yet 'tis greater skill
In a true hate to pray they have their will:
The very devils cannot plague them better.
[*Exit.*

ACT THREE

SCENE I. *Britain. A hall in Cymbeline's palace.*

Enter in state, CYMBELINE, QUEEN, CLOTEN, and Lords at one door, and at another CAIUS LUCIUS and Attendants.

CYMBELINE Now say, what would Augustus Caesar with us?

LUCIUS When Julius Caesar – whose remembrance yet
Lives in men's eyes, and will to ears and tongues
Be theme and hearing ever – was in this Britain,
And conquer'd it, Cassibelan, thine uncle,
Famous in Caesar's praises no whit less
Than in his feats deserving it, for him
And his succession granted Rome a tribute,

Yearly three thousand pounds, which by thee lately
Is left untender'd.
QUEEN And, to kill the marvel,
Shall be so ever.
CLOTEN There be many Caesars
Ere such another Julius. Britain is
A world by itself, and we will nothing pay
For wearing our own noses.
QUEEN That opportunity,
Which then they had to take from 's, to resume
We have again. Remember, sir, my liege,
The kings your ancestors, together with
The natural bravery of your isle, which stands
As Neptune's park, ribb'd and pal'd in
With rocks unscalable and roaring waters,
With sands that will not bear your enemies' boats
But suck them up to th' top-mast. A kind of conquest
Caesar made here; but made not here his brag
Of 'came, and saw, and overcame'. With shame –
The first that ever touch'd him – he was carried
From off our coast, twice beaten; and his shipping –
Poor ignorant baubles! – on our terrible seas,
Like egg-shells mov'd upon their surges, crack'd
As easily 'gainst our rocks; for joy whereof
The fam'd Cassibelan, who was once at point –
O, giglot fortune! – to master Caesar's sword,
Made Lud's Town with rejoicing fires bright
And Britons strut with courage.

CLOTEN Come, there's no more tribute to be paid. Our kingdom is stronger than it was at that time; and, as I said, there is no moe such Caesars. Other of them may have crook'd noses; but to owe such straight arms, none.

CYMBELINE Son, let your mother end.

CLOTEN We have yet many among us can gripe as hard as Cassibelan. I do not say I am one; but I have a hand. Why tribute? Why should we pay tribute? If Caesar can hide the sun from us with a blanket, or put the moon in his pocket, we will pay him tribute for light; else, sir, no more tribute, pray you now.

CYMBELINE You must know,
Till the injurious Romans did extort
This tribute from us, we were free. Caesar's ambition –
Which swell'd so much that it did almost stretch
The sides o' th' world – against all colour here
Did put the yoke upon's; which to shake off
Becomes a warlike people, whom we reckon
Ourselves to be.
CLOTEN We do.
CYMBELINE Say then to Caesar,
Our ancestor was that Mulmutius which
Ordain'd our laws – whose use the sword of Caesar
Hath too much mangled; whose repair and franchise
Shall, by the power we hold, be our good deed,
Though Rome be therefore angry. Mulmutius made our laws,
Who was the first of Britain which did put
His brows within a golden crown, and call'd
Himself a king.
LUCIUS I am sorry, Cymbeline,
That I am to pronounce Augustus Caesar –
Caesar, that hath more kings his servants than
Thyself domestic officers – thine enemy.
Receive it from me, then: war and confusion
In Caesar's name pronounce I 'gainst thee; look
For fury not to be resisted. Thus defied,
I thank thee for myself.
CYMBELINE Thou art welcome, Caius.
Thy Caesar knighted me; my youth I spent
Much under him; of him I gather'd honour,
Which he to seek of me again, perforce,
Behoves me keep at utterance. I am perfect
That the Pannonians and Dalmatians for
Their liberties are now in arms, a precedent
Which not to read would show the Britons cold;
So Caesar shall not find them.
LUCIUS Let proof speak.

CLOTEN His Majesty bids you welcome. Make pastime with us a day or two, or longer. If you seek us afterwards in other terms, you shall find us in our salt-water girdle. If you beat us out of it, it is yours; if you fall in the adventure, our crows shall fare the better for you; and there's an end.

LUCIUS So, sir.

CYMBELINE I know your master's pleasure, and he mine;
All the remain is, welcome. [*Exeunt.*

SCENE II. *Britain. Another room in Cymbeline's palace.*

Enter PISANIO reading of a letter.

PISANIO How? of adultery? Wherefore write you not
What monsters her accuse? Leonatus!
O master, what a strange infection
Is fall'n into thy ear! What false Italian –
As poisonous-tongu'd as handed – hath prevail'd
On thy too ready hearing? Disloyal? No.
She's punish'd for her truth, and undergoes,
More goddess-like than wife-like, such assaults
As would take in some virtue. O my master!
Thy mind to her is now as low as were
Thy fortunes. How? that I should murder her?

Upon the love, and truth, and vows, which I
Have made to thy command? I, her? Her blood?
If it be so to do good service, never
Let me be counted serviceable. How look I
That I should seem to lack humanity
So much as this fact comes to? [*Reads*] 'Do't.
The letter
That I have sent her, by her own command
Shall give thee opportunity.' O damn'd paper,
Black as the ink that's on thee! Senseless bauble,
Art thou a fedary for this act, and look'st
So virgin-like without? Lo here she comes.

Enter IMOGEN.

I am ignorant in what I am commanded.

IMOGEN How now, Pisanio!

PISANIO Madam, here is a letter from my lord.

IMOGEN Who? thy lord? That is my lord –
Leonatus?
O, learn'd indeed were that astronomer
That knew the stars as I his characters –
He'd lay the future open. You good gods,
Let what is here contain'd relish of love,
Of my lord's health, of his content; yet not
That we two are asunder – let that grieve him!
Some griefs are med'cinable; that is one of them,
For it doth physic love – of his content,
All but in that. Good wax, thy leave. Blest be
You bees that make these locks of counsel!
Lovers
And men in dangerous bonds pray not alike;
Though forfeiters you cast in prison, yet
You clasp young Cupid's tables. Good news,
gods! [*Reads.*

'Justice, and your father's wrath, should he take me in his dominion, could not be so cruel to me as you, O the dearest of creatures, would even renew me with your eyes. Take notice that I am in Cambria, at Milford Haven. What your own love will out of this advise you, follow. So he wishes you all happiness that remains loyal to his vow, and your increasing in love
LEONATUS POSTHUMUS.'

O for a horse with wings! Hear'st thou, Pisanio?
He is at Milford Haven. Read, and tell me
How far 'tis thither. If one of mean affairs
May plod it in a week, why may not I
Glide thither in a day? Then, true Pisanio –
Who long'st like me to see thy lord, who
long'st –
O, let me 'bate! – but not like me, yet long'st,
But in a fainter kind – O, not like me,
For mine's beyond beyond! – say, and speak
thick –
Love's counsellor should fill the bores of
hearing
To th' smothering of the sense – how far it is
To this same blessed Milford. And by th' way
Tell me how Wales was made so happy as
T' inherit such a haven. But first of all,
How we may steal from hence; and for the gap
That we shall make in time from our hence-
going
And our return, to excuse. But first, how get
hence.
Why should excuse be born or ere begot?
We'll talk of that hereafter. Prithee speak,
How many score of miles may we well ride
'Twixt hour and hour?

PISANIO One score 'twixt sun and sun,
Madam, 's enough for you, and too much too.

IMOGEN Why, one that rode to's execution, man,
Could never go so slow. I have heard of riding
wagers
Where horses have been nimbler than the sands
That run i' th' clock's behalf. But this is fool'ry.
Go bid my woman feign a sickness; say
She'll home to her father; and provide me
presently
A riding suit, no costlier than would fit
A franklin's huswife.

PISANIO Madam, you're best consider.

IMOGEN I see before me, man. Nor here, nor
here,
Nor what ensues, but have a fog in them
That I cannot look through. Away, I prithee;
Do as I bid thee. There's no more to say;
Accessible is none but Milford way. [*Exeunt.*

SCENE III. *Wales. A mountainous country with a cave.*

Enter from the cave BELARIUS, GUIDERIUS, and ARVIRAGUS.

BELARIUS A goodly day not to keep house with
such
Whose roof's as low as ours! Stoop, boys; this
gate
Instructs you how t' adore the heavens, and
bows you
To a morning's holy office. The gates of
monarchs
Are arch'd so high that giants may jet through
And keep their impious turbans on without
Good morrow to the sun. Hail, thou fair heaven!
We house i' th' rock, yet use thee not so hardly
As prouder livers do.

GUIDERIUS Hail, heaven!

ARVIRAGUS Hail, heaven!

BELARIUS Now for our mountain sport. Up to
yond hill,
Your legs are young; I'll tread these flats.
Consider,
When you above perceive me like a crow,

That it is place which lessens and sets off;
And you may then revolve what tales I have told you
Of courts, of princes, of the tricks in war.
This service is not service so being done,
But being so allow'd. To apprehend thus
Draws us a profit from all things we see,
And often to our comfort shall we find
The sharded beetle in a safer hold
Than is the full-wing'd eagle. O, this life
Is nobler than attending for a check,
Richer than doing nothing for a bribe,
Prouder than rustling in unpaid-for silk:
Such gain the cap of him that makes him fine,
Yet keeps his book uncross'd. No life to ours!

GUIDERIUS Out of your proof you speak. We, poor unfledg'd,
Have never wing'd from view o' th' nest, nor know not
What air's from home. Haply this life is best,
If quiet life be best; sweeter to you
That have a sharper known; well corresponding
With your stiff age. But unto us it is
A cell of ignorance, travelling abed,
A prison for a debtor that not dares
To stride a limit.

ARVIRAGUS What should we speak of
When we are old as you? When we shall hear
The rain and wind beat dark December, how,
In this our pinching cave, shall we discourse
The freezing hours away? We have seen nothing;
We are beastly: subtle as the fox for prey,
Like warlike as the wolf for what we eat.
Our valour is to chase what flies; our cage
We make a choir, as doth the prison'd bird,
And sing our bondage freely.

BELARIUS How you speak!
Did you but know the city's usuries,
And felt them knowingly – the art o' th' court,
As hard to leave as keep, whose top to climb
Is certain falling, or so slipp'ry that
The fear's as bad as falling; the toil o' th' war,
A pain that only seems to seek out danger
I' th' name of fame and honour, which dies i' th' search,
And hath as oft a sland'rous epitaph
As record of fair act; nay, many times,
Doth ill deserve by doing well; what's worse –
Must curtsy at the censure. O, boys, this story
The world may read in me; my body's mark'd
With Roman swords, and my report was once
First with the best of note. Cymbeline lov'd me;
And when a soldier was the theme, my name
Was not far off. Then was I as a tree
Whose boughs did bend with fruit; but in one night
A storm, or robbery, call it what you will,
Shook down my mellow hangings, nay, my leaves,
And left me bare to weather.

GUIDERIUS Uncertain favour!

BELARIUS My fault being nothing – as I have told you oft –
But that two villains, whose false oaths prevail'd
Before my perfect honour, swore to Cymbeline
I was confederate with the Romans. So
Follow'd my banishment, and this twenty years
This rock and these demesnes have been my world,
Where I have liv'd at honest freedom, paid
More pious debts to heaven than in all
The fore-end of my time. But up to th' mountains!
This is not hunters' language. He that strikes
The venison first shall be the lord o' th' feast;
To him the other two shall minister;
And we will fear no poison, which attends
In place of greater state. I'll meet you in the valleys. [Exeunt Guiderius and Arviragus.
How hard it is to hide the sparks of nature!
These boys know little they are sons to th' King,
Nor Cymbeline dreams that they are alive.
They think they are mine; and though train'd up thus meanly
I' th' cave wherein they bow, their thoughts do hit
The roofs of palaces, and nature prompts them
In simple and low things to prince it much
Beyond the trick of others. This Polydore,
The heir of Cymbeline and Britain, who
The King his father call'd Guiderius – Jove!
When on my three-foot stool I sit and tell
The warlike feats I have done, his spirits fly out
Into my story; say 'Thus mine enemy fell,
And thus I set my foot on's neck'; even then
The princely blood flows in his cheek, he sweats,
Strains his young nerves, and puts himself in posture
That acts my words. The younger brother, Cadwal,
Once Arviragus, in as like a figure
Strikes life into my speech, and shows much more
His own conceiving. Hark, the game is rous'd!
O Cymbeline, heaven and my conscience knows
Thou didst unjustly banish me! Whereon,
At three and two years old, I stole these babes,
Thinking to bar thee of succession as
Thou refts me of my lands. Euriphile,
Thou wast their nurse; they took thee for their mother,
And every day do honour to her grave.

Myself, Belarius, that am Morgan call'd,
They take for natural father. The game is up.
[*Exit*.

SCENE IV. *Wales, near Milford Haven.*

Enter PISANIO and IMOGEN.

IMOGEN Thou told'st me, when we came from horse, the place
Was near at hand. Ne'er long'd my mother so
To see me first as I have now. Pisanio! Man!
Where is Posthumus? What is in thy mind
That makes thee stare thus? Wherefore breaks that sigh
From th' inward of thee? One but painted thus
Would be interpreted a thing perplex'd
Beyond self-explication. Put thyself
Into a haviour of less fear, ere wildness
Vanquish my staider senses. What's the matter?
Why tender'st thou that paper to me with
A look untender? If't be summer news,
Smile to't before; if winterly, thou need'st
But keep that count'nance still. My husband's hand?
That drug-damn'd Italy hath out-craftied him,
And he's at some hard point. Speak, man; thy tongue
May take off some extremity, which to read
Would be even mortal to me.
PISANIO Please you read,
And you shall find me, wretched man, a thing
The most disdain'd of fortune.
IMOGEN [*Reads*] 'Thy mistress, Pisanio, hath play'd the strumpet in my bed, the testimonies whereof lie bleeding in me. I speak not out of weak surmises, but from proof as strong as my grief and as certain as I expect my revenge. That part thou, Pisanio, must act for me, if thy faith be not tainted with the breach of hers. Let thine own hands take away her life; I shall give thee opportunity at Milford Haven; she hath my letter for the purpose; where, if thou fear to strike, and to make me certain it is done, thou art the pander to her dishonour, and equally to me disloyal.'
PISANIO What shall I need to draw my sword? The paper
Hath cut her throat already. No, 'tis slander,
Whose edge is sharper than the sword, whose tongue
Outvenoms all the worms of Nile, whose breath
Rides on the posting winds and doth belie
All corners of the world. Kings, queens, and states,
Maids, matrons, nay, the secrets of the grave,
This viperous slander enters. What cheer, madam?
IMOGEN False to his bed? What is it to be false?
To lie in watch there, and to think on him?
To weep twixt clock and clock? If sleep charge nature,
To break it with a fearful dream of him,
And cry myself awake? That's false to's bed,
Is it?
PISANIO Alas, good lady!
IMOGEN I false! Thy conscience witness! Iachimo,
Thou didst accuse him of incontinency;
Thou then look'dst like a villain; now, methinks,
Thy favour's good enough. Some jay of Italy,
Whose mother was her painting, hath betray'd him.
Poor I am stale, a garment out of fashion,
And for I am richer than to hang by th' walls
I must be ripp'd. To pieces with me! O,
Men's vows are women's traitors! All good seeming,
By thy revolt, O husband, shall be thought
Put on for villainy; not born where't grows,
But worn a bait for ladies.
PISANIO Good madam, hear me.
IMOGEN True honest men being heard, like false Aeneas,
Were, in his time, thought false; and Sinon's weeping
Did scandal many a holy tear, took pity
From most true wretchedness. So thou, Posthumus,
Wilt lay the leaven on all proper men:
Goodly and gallant shall be false and perjur'd
From thy great fail. Come, fellow, be thou honest;
Do thou thy master's bidding; when thou seest him,
A little witness my obedience. Look!
I draw the sword myself; take it, and hit
The innocent mansion of my love, my heart.
Fear not; 'tis empty of all things but grief;
Thy master is not there, who was indeed
The riches of it. Do his bidding; strike.
Thou mayst be valiant in a better cause,
But now thou seem'st a coward.
PISANIO Hence, vile instrument!
Thou shalt not damn my hand.
IMOGEN Why, I must die;
And if I do not by thy hand, thou art
No servant of thy master's. Against self-slaughter
There is a prohibition so divine
That cravens my weak hand. Come, here's my heart –
Something's afore't. Soft, soft! we'll no defence! –

Obedient as the scabbard. What is here?
The scriptures of the loyal Leonatus
All turn'd to heresy? Away, away,
Corrupters of my faith! you shall no more
Be stomachers to my heart. Thus may poor fools
Believe false teachers; though those that are
betray'd
Do feel the treason sharply, yet the traitor
Stands in worse case of woe. And thou,
Posthumus,
That didst set up my disobedience 'gainst the
King
My father, and make me put into contempt the
suits
Of princely fellows, shalt hereafter find
It is no act of common passage but
A strain of rareness; and I grieve myself
To think, when thou shalt be disedg'd by her
That now thou tirest on, how thy memory
Will then be pang'd by me. Prithee dispatch.
The lamb entreats the butcher. Where's thy
knife?
Thou art too slow to do thy master's bidding,
When I desire it too.

PISANIO O gracious lady,
Since I receiv'd command to do this business
I have not slept one wink.

IMOGEN Do't, and to bed then.

PISANIO I'll wake mine eyeballs first.

IMOGEN Wherefore then
Didst undertake it? Why hast thou abus'd
So many miles with a pretence? This place?
Mine action and thine own? our horses' labour?
The time inviting thee? the perturb'd court,
For my being absent? – whereunto I never
Purpose return. Why hast thou gone so far
To be unbent when thou hast ta'en thy stand,
Th' elected deer before thee?

PISANIO But to win time
To lose so bad employment, in the which
I have consider'd of a course. Good lady,
Hear me with patience.

IMOGEN Talk thy tongue weary – speak.
I have heard I am a strumpet, and mine ear,
Therein false struck, can take no greater wound,
Nor tent to bottom that. But speak.

PISANIO Then, madam,
I thought you would not back again.

IMOGEN Most like –
Bringing me here to kill me.

PISANIO Not so, neither;
But if I were as wise as honest, then
My purpose would prove well. It cannot be
But that my master is abus'd. Some villain,
Ay, and singular in his art, hath done you both
This cursed injury.

IMOGEN Some Roman courtezan!

PISANIO No, on my life!
I'll give but notice you are dead, and send him
Some bloody sign of it, for 'tis commanded
I should do so. You shall be miss'd at court,
And that will well confirm it.

IMOGEN Why, good fellow,
What shall I do the while? where bide? how
live?
Or in my life what comfort, when I am
Dead to my husband?

PISANIO If you'll back to th' court –

IMOGEN No court, no father, nor no more ado
With that harsh, noble, simple nothing –
That Cloten, whose love-suit hath been to me
As fearful as a siege.

PISANIO If not at court,
Then not in Britain must you bide.

IMOGEN Where then?
Hath Britain all the sun that shines? Day, night,
Are they not but in Britain? I' th' world's volume
Our Britain seems as of it, but not n't;
In a great pool a swan's nest. Prithee think
There's livers out of Britain.

PISANIO I am most glad
You think of other place. Th' ambassador,
Lucius the Roman, comes to Milford Haven
To-morrow. Now, if you could wear a mind
Dark as your fortune is, and but disguise
That which t' appear itself must not yet be
But by self-danger, you should tread a course
Pretty and full of view; yea, happily, near
The residence of Posthumus; so nigh, at least,
That though his actions were not visible, yet
Report should render him hourly to your ear
As truly as he moves.

IMOGEN O! for such means,
Though peril to my modesty, not death on't,
I would adventure.

PISANIO Well then, here's the point:
You must forget to be a woman; change
Command into obedience; fear and niceness –
The handmaids of all women, or, more truly,
Woman it pretty self – into a waggish courage;
Ready in gibes, quick-answer'd, saucy, and
As quarrelous as the weasel. Nay, you must
Forget that rarest treasure of your cheek,
Exposing it – but, O, the harder heart!
Alack, no remedy! – to the greedy touch
Of common-kissing Titan, and forget
Your laboursome and dainty trims wherein
You made great Juno angry.

IMOGEN Nay, be brief;
I see into thy end, and am almost
A man already.

PISANIO First, make yourself but like one.
Fore-thinking this, I have already fit –
'Tis in my cloak-bag – doublet, hat, hose, all

That answer to them. Would you, in their serving,
And with what imitation you can borrow
From youth of such a season, fore noble Lucius
Present yourself, desire his service, tell him
Wherein you're happy – which will make him know
If that his head have ear in music; doubtless
With joy he will embrace you; for he's honourable,
And, doubling that, most holy. Your means abroad –
You have me, rich; and I will never fail
Beginning nor supplyment.

IMOGEN Thou art all the comfort
The gods will diet me with. Prithee away!
There's more to be consider'd; but we'll even
All that good time will give us. This attempt
I am soldier to, and will abide it with
A prince's courage. Away, I prithee.

PISANIO Well, madam, we must take a short farewell,
Lest, being miss'd, I be suspected of
Your carriage from the court. My noble mistress,
Here is a box; I had it from the Queen.
What's in't is precious. If you are sick at sea
Or stomach-qualm'd at land, a dram of this
Will drive away distemper. To some shade,
And fit you to your manhood. May the gods
Direct you to the best!

IMOGEN Amen. I thank thee.

[*Exeunt severally.*

SCENE V. *Britain. Cymbeline's palace.*

Enter CYMBELINE, QUEEN, CLOTEN, LUCIUS, and Lords.

CYMBELINE Thus far; and so farewell.

LUCIUS Thanks, royal sir.
My emperor hath wrote; I must from hence,
And am right sorry that I must report ye
My master's enemy.

CYMBELINE Our subjects, sir,
Will not endure his yoke; and for ourself
To show less sovereignty than they, must needs
Appear unkinglike.

LUCIUS So, sir. I desire of you
A conduct overland to Milford Haven.
Madam, all joy befall your Grace, and you!

CYMBELINE My lords, you are appointed for that office;
The due of honour in no point omit.
So farewell, noble Lucius.

LUCIUS Your hand, my lord.

CLOTEN Receive it friendly; but from this time forth
I wear it as your enemy.

LUCIUS Sir, the event
Is yet to name the winner. Fare you well.

CYMBELINE Leave not the worthy Lucius, good my lords,
Till he have cross'd the Severn. Happiness!

[*Exeunt Lucius and Lords.*

QUEEN He goes hence frowning; but it honours us
That we have given him cause.

CLOTEN 'Tis all the better;
Your valiant Britons have their wishes in it.

CYMBELINE Lucius hath wrote already to the Emperor
How it goes here. It fits us therefore ripely
Our chariots and our horsemen be in readiness.
The pow'rs that he already hath in Gallia
Will soon be drawn to head, from whence he moves
His war for Britain.

QUEEN 'Tis not sleepy business,
But must be look'd to speedily and strongly.

CYMBELINE Our expectation that it would be thus
Hath made us forward. But, my gentle queen,
Where is our daughter? She hath not appear'd
Before the Roman, nor to us hath tender'd
The duty of the day. She looks us like
A thing more made of malice than of duty;
We have noted it. Call her before us, for
We have been too slight in sufferance.

[*Exit a Messenger.*

QUEEN Royal sir,
Since the exile of Posthumus, most retir'd
Hath her life been; the cure whereof, my lord,
'Tis time must do. Beseech your Majesty,
Forbear sharp speeches to her; she's a lady
So tender of rebukes that words are strokes,
And strokes death to her.

Re-enter Messenger.

CYMBELINE Where is she, sir? How
Can her contempt be answer'd?

MESSENGER Please you, sir,
Her chambers are all lock'd, and there's no answer
That will be given to th' loud noise we make.

QUEEN My lord, when last I went to visit her,
She pray'd me to excuse her keeping close;
Whereto constrain'd by her infirmity
She should that duty leave unpaid to you
Which daily she was bound to proffer. This
She wish'd me to make known; but our great court
Made me to blame in memory.

CYMBELINE Her doors lock'd?

Not seen of late? Grant, heavens, that which I fear
Prove false! [*Exit.*

QUEEN Son, I say, follow the King.

CLOTEN That man of hers, Pisanio, her old servant,
I have not seen these two days.

QUEEN Go, look after.
[*Exit Cloten.*

Pisanio, thou that stand'st so for Posthumus!
He hath a drug of mine. I pray his absence
Proceed by swallowing that; for he believes
It is a thing most precious. But for her,
Where is she gone? Haply despair hath seiz'd her;
Or, wing'd with fervour of her love, she's flown
To her desir'd Posthumus. Gone she is
To death or to dishonour, and my end
Can make good use of either. She being down,
I have the placing of the British crown.

Re-enter CLOTEN.

How now, my son?

CLOTEN 'Tis certain she is fled.
Go in and cheer the King. He rages; none
Dare come about him.

QUEEN All the better. May
This night forestall him of the coming day!
[*Exit.*

CLOTEN I love and hate her; for she's fair and royal,
And that she hath all courtly parts more exquisite
Than lady, ladies, woman. From every one
The best she hath, and she, of all compounded,
Outsells them all. I love her therefore; but
Disdaining me and throwing favours on
The low Posthumus slanders so her judgment
That what's else rare is chok'd; and in that point
I will conclude to hate her, nay, indeed,
To be reveng'd upon her. For when fools
Shall –

Enter PISANIO.

Who is here? What, are you packing, sirrah?
Come hither. Ah, you precious pander! Villain,
Where is thy lady? In a word, or else
Thou art straightway with the fiends.

PISANIO O good my lord!

CLOTEN Where is thy lady? or, by Jupiter –
I will not ask again. Close villain,
I'll have this secret from thy heart, or rip
Thy heart to find it. Is she with Posthumus?
From whose so many weights of baseness cannot
A dram of worth be drawn.

PISANIO Alas, my lord,
How can she be with him? When was she miss'd?
He is in Rome.

CLOTEN Where is she, sir? Come nearer.
No farther halting! Satisfy me home
What is become of her.

PISANIO O my all-worthy lord!

CLOTEN All-worthy villain!
Discover where thy mistress is at once,
At the next word. No more of 'worthy lord'!
Speak, or thy silence on the instant is
Thy condemnation and thy death.

PISANIO Then, sir,
This paper is the history of my knowledge
Touching her flight. [*Presenting a letter.*

CLOTEN Let's see't. I will pursue her
Even to Augustus' throne.

PISANIO [*Aside*] Or this or perish.
She's far enough; and what he learns by this
May prove his travel, not her danger.

CLOTEN Humh!

PISANIO [*Aside*] I'll write to my lord she's dead.
O Imogen,
Safe mayst thou wander, safe return again!

CLOTEN Sirrah, is this letter true?

PISANIO Sir, as I think.

CLOTEN It is Posthumus' hand; I know't. Sirrah, if thou wouldst not be a villain, but do me true service, undergo those employments wherein I should have cause to use thee with a serious industry – that is, what villainy soe'er I bid thee do, to perform it directly and truly – I would think thee an honest man; thou shouldst neither want my means for thy relief nor my voice for thy preferment.

PISANIO Well, my good lord.

CLOTEN Wilt thou serve me? For since patiently and constantly thou hast stuck to the bare fortune of that beggar Posthumus, thou canst not, in the course of gratitude, but be a diligent follower of mine. Wilt thou serve me?

PISANIO Sir, I will.

CLOTEN Give me thy hand; here's my purse. Hast any of thy late master's garments in thy possession?

PISANIO I have, my lord, at my lodging, the same suit he wore when he took leave of my lady and mistress.

CLOTEN The first service thou dost me, fetch that suit hither. Let it be thy first service; go.

PISANIO I shall, my lord. [*Exit.*

CLOTEN Meet thee at Milford Haven! I forgot to ask him one thing; I'll remember't anon. Even there, thou villain Posthumus, will I kill thee. I would these garments were come. She said upon a time – the bitterness of it I now belch from my heart – that she held the very garment of Posthumus in more respect than my noble and natural person, together with the adornment of my qualities. With that suit upon my back will I ravish her; first kill him, and in her eyes. There shall she see my valour, which will then be a torment to her contempt. He on the ground, my speech of insultment ended on his dead body, and when my lust hath dined – which, as I say, to vex her I will execute in the clothes that she so prais'd – to the court I'll knock her back, foot her home again. She hath despis'd me rejoicingly, and I'll be merry in my revenge.

Re-enter PISANIO, with the clothes.

Be those the garments?

PISANIO Ay, my noble lord.

CLOTEN How long is't since she went to Milford Haven?

PISANIO She can scarce be there yet.

CLOTEN Bring this apparel to my chamber; that is the second thing that I have commanded thee. The third is that thou wilt be a voluntary mute to my design. Be but duteous and true, preferment shall tender itself to thee. My revenge is now at Milford; would I had wings to follow it! Come, and be true. [*Exit.*

PISANIO Thou bid'st me to my loss; for true to thee
Were to prove false, which I will never be,
To him that is most true. To Milford go,
And find not her whom thou pursuest. Flow, flow,
You heavenly blessings, on her! This fool's speed
Be cross'd with slowness! Labour be his meed!
[*Exit.*

SCENE VI. *Wales. Before the cave of Belarius.*

Enter IMOGEN alone, in boy's clothes.

IMOGEN I see a man's life is a tedious one.
I have tir'd myself, and for two nights together
Have made the ground my bed. I should be sick
But that my resolution helps me. Milford,
When from the mountain-top Pisanio show'd thee,
Thou wast within a ken. O Jove! I think
Foundations fly the wretched; such, I mean,
Where they should be reliev'd. Two beggars told me
I could not miss my way. Will poor folks lie,
That have afflictions on them, knowing 'tis
A punishment or trial? Yes; no wonder,
When rich ones scarce tell true. To lapse in fulness
Is sorer than to lie for need; and falsehood
Is worse in kings than beggars. My dear lord!
Thou art one o' th' false ones. Now I think on thee
My hunger's gone; but even before, I was
At point to sink for food. But what is this?
Here is a path to't; 'tis some savage hold.
I were best not call; I dare not call. Yet famine,
Ere clean it o'erthrow nature, makes it valiant.
Plenty and peace breeds cowards; hardness ever
Of hardiness is mother. Ho! who's here?
If anything that's civil, speak; if savage,
Take or lend. Ho! No answer? Then I'll enter.
Best draw my sword; and if mine enemy
But fear the sword, like me, he'll scarcely look on't.
Such a foe, good heavens! [*Exit into the cave.*

Enter BELARIUS, GUIDERIUS, and ARVIRAGUS.

BELARIUS You, Polydore, have prov'd best woodman and
Are master of the feast. Cadwal and I
Will play the cook and servant; 'tis our match.
The sweat of industry would dry and die
But for the end it works to. Come, our stomachs
Will make what's homely savoury; weariness
Can snore upon the flint, when resty sloth
Finds the down pillow hard. Now, peace be here,
Poor house, that keep'st thyself!

GUIDERIUS I am throughly weary.

ARVIRAGUS I am weak with toil, yet strong in appetite.

GUIDERIUS There is cold meat i' th' cave; we'll browse on that
Whilst what we have kill'd be cook'd.

BELARIUS [*Looking into the cave*] Stay, come not in.
But that it eats our victuals, I should think
Here were a fairy.

GUIDERIUS What's the matter, sir?

BELARIUS By Jupiter, an angel! or, if not,
An earthly paragon! Behold divineness
No elder than a boy!

Re-enter IMOGEN.

IMOGEN Good masters, harm me not.
Before I enter'd here I call'd, and thought
To have begg'd or bought what I have took. Good troth,
I have stol'n nought; nor would not though I had found
Gold strew'd i' th' floor. Here's money for my meat.
I would have left it on the board, so soon

As I had made my meal, and parted
With pray'rs for the provider.

GUIDERIUS Money, youth?

ARVIRAGUS All gold and silver rather turn to dirt,
As 'tis no better reckon'd but of those
Who worship dirty gods.

IMOGEN I see you're angry.
Know, if you kill me for my fault, I should
Have died had I not made it.

BELARIUS Whither bound?

IMOGEN To Milford Haven.

BELARIUS What's your name?

IMOGEN Fidele, sir. I have a kinsman who
Is bound for Italy; he embark'd at Milford;
To whom being going, almost spent with hunger,
I am fall'n in this offence.

BELARIUS Prithee, fair youth,
Think us no churls, nor measure our good minds
By this rude place we live in. Well encounter'd!
'Tis almost night; you shall have better cheer
Ere you depart, and thanks to stay and eat it.
Boys, bid him welcome.

GUIDERIUS Were you a woman, youth,
I should woo hard but be your groom. In honesty
I bid for you as I'd buy.

ARVIRAGUS I'll make't my comfort
He is a man. I'll love him as my brother;
And such a welcome as I'd give to him
After long absence, such is yours. Most welcome!
Be sprightly, for you fall 'mongst friends.

IMOGEN 'Mongst friends,
If brothers. [*Aside*] Would it had been so that they
Had been my father's sons! Then had my prize
Been less, and so more equal ballasting
To thee, Posthumus.

BELARIUS He wrings at some distress.

GUIDERIUS Would I could free't!

ARVIRAGUS Or I, whate'er it be,
What pain it cost, what danger! Gods!

BELARIUS [*Whispering*] Hark, boys.

IMOGEN [*Aside*] Great men,
That had a court no bigger than this cave,
That did attend themselves, and had the virtue
Which their own conscience seal'd them, laying by
That nothing-gift of differing multitudes,
Could not out-peer these twain. Pardon me, gods!
I'd change my sex to be companion with them,
Since Leonatus' false.

BELARIUS It shall be so.
Boys, we'll go dress our hunt. Fair youth, come in.
Discourse is heavy, fasting; when we have supp'd,
We'll mannerly demand thee of thy story,
So far as thou wilt speak it.

GUIDERIUS Pray draw near.

ARVIRAGUS The night to th' owl and morn to th' lark less welcome.

IMOGEN Thanks, sir.

ARVIRAGUS I pray draw near. [*Exeunt.*

SCENE VII. *Rome. A public place.*

Enter two Roman Senators and Tribunes.

1 SENATOR This is the tenour of the Emperor's writ:
That since the common men are now in action
'Gainst the Pannonians and Dalmatians,
And that the legions now in Gallia are
Full weak to undertake our wars against
The fall'n-off Britons, that we do incite
The gentry to this business. He creates
Lucius proconsul; and to you, the tribunes,
For this immediate levy, he commands
His absolute commission. Long live Caesar!

TRIBUNE Is Lucius general of the forces?

2 SENATOR Ay.

TRIBUNE Remaining now in Gallia?

1 SENATOR With those legions
Which I have spoke of, whereunto your levy
Must be supplyant. The words of your commission
Will tie you to the numbers and the time
Of their dispatch.

TRIBUNE We will discharge our duty. [*Exeunt.*

ACT FOUR

SCENE I. *Wales. Near the cave of Belarius.*

Enter CLOTEN alone.

CLOTEN I am near to th' place where they should meet, if Pisanio have mapp'd it truly. How fit his garments serve me! Why should his mistress, who was made by him that made the tailor, not be fit too? The rather – saving reverence of the word – for 'tis said a woman's fitness comes by fits. Therein I must play the workman. I dare speak it to myself, for it is not vain-glory for a man and his glass to confer in his own chamber – I mean, the lines of my body are as well drawn as his; no less young, more strong, not beneath him in fortunes, beyond him in the advantage of the time, above him in birth, alike conversant in general services, and more remarkable in single oppositions. Yet this imperceiverant thing loves him in my despite. What mortality is! Posthumus, thy head, which now is growing upon thy shoulders, shall within this hour be off; thy mistress enforced; thy garments cut to pieces before her face; and all this done, spurn her home to her father, who may, haply, be a little angry for my so rough usage; but my mother, having power of his testiness, shall turn all into my commendations. My horse is tied up safe. Out, sword, and to a sore purpose! Fortune, put them into my hand. This is the very description of their meeting-place; and the fellow dares not deceive me. [*Exit.*

SCENE II. *Wales. Before the cave of Belarius.*

Enter, from the cave, BELARIUS, GUIDERIUS, ARVIRAGUS, and IMOGEN.

BELARIUS [*To Imogen*] You are not well. Remain here in the cave;
We'll come to you after hunting.
ARVIRAGUS [*To Imogen*] Brother, stay here.
Are we not brothers?
IMOGEN So man and man should be;
But clay and clay differs in dignity,
Whose dust is both alike. I am very sick.
GUIDERIUS Go you to hunting; I'll abide with him.
IMOGEN So sick I am not, yet I am not well;
But not so citizen a wanton as
To seem to die ere sick. So please you, leave me;
Stick to your journal course. The breach of custom
Is breach of all. I am ill, but your being by me
Cannot amend me; society is no comfort
To one not sociable. I am not very sick,
Since I can reason of it. Pray you trust me here.
I'll rob none but myself; and let me die,
Stealing so poorly.
GUIDERIUS I love thee; I have spoke it.
How much the quantity, the weight as much
As I do love my father.
BELARIUS What? how? how?
ARVIRAGUS If it be sin to say so, sir, I yoke me
In my good brother's fault. I know not why
I love this youth, and I have heard you say
Love's reason's without reason. The bier at door,
And a demand who is't shall die, I'd say
'My father, not this youth'.
BELARIUS [*Aside*] O noble strain!
O worthiness of nature! breed of greatness!
Cowards father cowards and base things sire base.
Nature hath meal and bran, contempt and grace.
I'm not their father; yet who this should be
Doth miracle itself, lov'd before me. –
'Tis the ninth hour o' th' morn.
ARVIRAGUS Brother, farewell.
IMOGEN I wish ye sport.
ARVIRAGUS You health. [*To Belarius*] So please you, sir.
IMOGEN [*Aside*] These are kind creatures. Gods, what lies I have heard!
Our courtiers say all's savage but at court.
Experience, O, thou disprov'st report!
Th' imperious seas breed monsters; for the dish,
Poor tributary rivers as sweet fish.
I am sick still; heart-sick. Pisanio,
I'll now taste of thy drug. [*Swallows some.*
GUIDERIUS I could not stir him.
He said he was gentle, but unfortunate;
Dishonestly afflicted, but yet honest.
ARVIRAGUS Thus did he answer me; yet said hereafter
I might know more.
BELARIUS To th' field, to th' field!
We'll leave you for this time. Go in and rest.
ARVIRAGUS We'll not be long away.
BELARIUS Pray be not sick,
For you must be our huswife.
IMOGEN Well, or ill,
I am bound to you.
BELARIUS And shalt be ever.
[*Exit Imogen into the cave.*
This youth, howe'er distress'd, appears he hath had
Good ancestors.
ARVIRAGUS How angel-like he sings!
GUIDERIUS But his neat cookery! He cut our roots in characters,
And sauc'd our broths as Juno had been sick,
And he her dieter.
ARVIRAGUS Nobly he yokes
A smiling with a sigh, as if the sigh
Was that it was for not being such a smile;
The smile mocking the sigh that it would fly
From so divine a temple to commix
With winds that sailors rail at.
GUIDERIUS I do note
That grief and patience, rooted in him both,
Mingle their spurs together.
ARVIRAGUS Grow patience!
And let the stinking elder, grief, untwine
His perishing root with the increasing vine!
BELARIUS It is great morning. Come, away!
Who's there?

Enter CLOTEN.

CLOTEN I cannot find those runagates; that villain
Hath mock'd me. I am faint.
BELARIUS Those runagates?
Means he not us? I partly know him; 'tis
Cloten, the son o' th' Queen. I fear some ambush.
I saw him not these many years, and yet
I know 'tis he. We are held as outlaws. Hence!
GUIDERIUS He is but one; you and my brother search
What companies are near. Pray you away;
Let me alone with him.
[Exeunt Belarius and Arviragus.
CLOTEN Soft! What are you
That fly me thus? Some villain mountaineers?
I have heard of such. What slave art thou?
GUIDERIUS A thing
More slavish did I ne'er than answering
'A slave' without a knock.
CLOTEN Thou art a robber,
A law-breaker, a villain. Yield thee, thief.
GUIDERIUS To who? To thee? What art thou? Have not I
An arm as big as thine, a heart as big?
Thy words, I grant, are bigger, for I wear not
My dagger in my mouth. Say what thou art;
Why I should yield to thee.
CLOTEN Thou villain base,
Know'st me not by my clothes?
GUIDERIUS No, nor thy tailor, rascal,
Who is thy grandfather; he made those clothes,
Which, as it seems, make thee.
CLOTEN Thou precious varlet,
My tailor made them not.
GUIDERIUS Hence, then, and thank
The man that gave them thee. Thou art some fool;
I am loath to beat thee.
CLOTEN Thou injurious thief,
Hear but my name, and tremble.
GUIDERIUS What's thy name?
CLOTEN Cloten, thou villain.
GUIDERIUS Cloten, thou double villain, be thy name,
I cannot tremble at it. Were it toad, or adder, spider,
'Twould move me sooner.
CLOTEN To thy further fear,
Nay, to thy mere confusion, thou shalt know
I am son to th' Queen.
GUIDERIUS I'm sorry for't; not seeming
So worthy as thy birth.
CLOTEN Art not afeard?
GUIDERIUS Those that I reverence, those I fear – the wise:
At fools I laugh, not fear them.
CLOTEN Die the death.
When I have slain thee with my proper hand,
I'll follow those that even now fled hence,
And on the gates of Lud's Town set your heads.
Yield, rustic mountaineer. *[Exeunt, fighting.*

Re-enter BELARIUS and ARVIRAGUS.

BELARIUS No company's abroad.
ARVIRAGUS None in the world; you did mistake him, sure.
BELARIUS I cannot tell; long is it since I saw him,
But time hath nothing blurr'd those lines of favour
Which then he wore; the snatches in his voice,
And burst of speaking, were as his. I am absolute
'Twas very Cloten.
ARVIRAGUS In this place we left them.
I wish my brother make good time with him,
You say he is so fell.
BELARIUS Being scarce made up,
I mean to man, he had not apprehension
Of roaring terrors; for defect of judgment
Is oft the cease of fear.

Re-enter GUIDERIUS with Cloten's head.

But, see, thy brother.
GUIDERIUS This Cloten was a fool, an empty purse;
There was no money in't. Not Hercules
Could have knock'd out his brains, for he had none;
Yet I not doing this, the fool had borne
My head as I do his.
BELARIUS What hast thou done?
GUIDERIUS I am perfect what: cut off one Cloten's head,
Son to the Queen, after his own report;
Who call'd me traitor, mountaineer, and swore
With his own single hand he'd take us in,
Displace our heads where – thank the gods! – they grow,
And set them on Lud's Town.
BELARIUS We are all undone.
GUIDERIUS Why, worthy father, what have we to lose
But that he swore to take, our lives? The law
Protects not us; then why should we be tender
To let an arrogant piece of flesh threat us,
Play judge and executioner all himself,
For we do fear the law? What company
Discover you abroad?
BELARIUS No single soul
Can we set eye on, but in all safe reason

He must have some attendants. Though his
humour
Was nothing but mutation – ay, and that
From one bad thing to worse – not frenzy, not
Absolute madness could so far have rav'd,
To bring him here alone. Although perhaps
It may be heard at court that such as we
Cave here, hunt here, are outlaws, and in time
May make some stronger head – the which he
hearing,
As it is like him, might break out and swear
He'd fetch us in; yet is't not probable
To come alone, either he so undertaking
Or they so suffering. Then on good ground we
fear,
If we do fear this body hath a tail
More perilous than the head.

ARVIRAGUS Let ordinance
Come as the gods foresay it. Howsoe'er,
My brother hath done well.

BELARIUS I had no mind
To hunt this day; the boy Fidele's sickness
Did make my way long forth.

GUIDERIUS With his own sword,
Which he did wave against my throat, I have
ta'en
His head from him. I'll throw't into the creek
Behind our rock, and let it to the sea
And tell the fishes he's the Queen's son, Cloten.
That's all I reck. [*Exit.*

BELARIUS I fear 'twill be reveng'd.
Would, Polydore, thou hadst not done't! though
valour
Becomes thee well enough.

ARVIRAGUS Would I had done't,
So the revenge alone pursu'd me! Polydore,
I love thee brotherly, but envy much
Thou hast robb'd me of this deed. I would
revenges,
That possible strength might meet, would seek
us through,
And put us to our answer.

BELARIUS Well, 'tis done.
We'll hunt no more to-day, nor seek for danger
Where there's no profit. I prithee to our rock.
You and Fidele play the cooks; I'll stay
Till hasty Polydore return, and bring him
To dinner presently.

ARVIRAGUS Poor sick Fidele!
I'll willingly to him; to gain his colour
I'd let a parish of such Clotens' blood,
And praise myself for charity. [*Exit.*

BELARIUS O thou goddess,
Thou divine Nature, thou thyself thou blazon'st
In these two princely boys! They are as gentle
As zephyrs blowing below the violet,
Not wagging his sweet head; and yet as rough,
Their royal blood enchaf'd, as the rud'st wind
That by the top doth take the mountain pine
And make him stoop to th' vale. 'Tis wonder
That an invisible instinct should frame them
To royalty unlearn'd, honour untaught,
Civility not seen from other, valour
That wildly grows in them, but yields a crop
As if it had been sow'd. Yet still it's strange
What Cloten's being here to us portends,
Or what his death will bring us.

Re-enter GUIDERIUS.

GUIDERIUS Where's my brother?
I have sent Cloten's clotpoll down the stream,
In embassy to his mother; his body's hostage
For his return. [*Solemn music.*

BELARIUS My ingenious instrument!
Hark, Polydore, it sounds. But what occasion
Hath Cadwal now to give it motion? Hark!

GUIDERIUS Is he at home?

BELARIUS He went hence even now.

GUIDERIUS What does he mean? Since death of
my dear'st mother
It did not speak before. All solemn things
Should answer solemn accidents. The matter?
Triumphs for nothing and lamenting toys
Is jollity for apes and grief for boys.
Is Cadwal mad?

Re-enter ARVIRAGUS, with IMOGEN as dead, bearing her in his arms.

BELARIUS Look, here he comes,
And brings the dire occasion in his arms
Of what we blame him for!

ARVIRAGUS The bird is dead
That we have made so much on. I had rather
Have skipp'd from sixteen years of age to sixty,
To have turn'd my leaping time into a crutch,
Than have seen this.

GUIDERIUS O sweetest, fairest lily!
My brother wears thee not the one half so well
As when thou grew'st thyself.

BELARIUS O melancholy!
Who ever yet could sound thy bottom? find
The ooze to show what coast thy sluggish crare
Might'st easiliest harbour in? Thou blessed
thing!
Jove knows what man thou mightst have made;
but I,
Thou diedst, a most rare boy, of melancholy.
How found you him?

ARVIRAGUS Stark, as you see;
Thus smiling, as some fly had tickled slumber,
Not as death's dart, being laugh'd at; his right
cheek
Reposing on a cushion.

GUIDERIUS Where?

ARVIRAGUS O' th' floor;
His arms thus leagu'd. I thought he slept, and put
My clouted brogues from off my feet, whose rudeness
Answer'd my steps too loud.
GUIDERIUS Why, he but sleeps.
If he be gone he'll make his grave a bed;
With female fairies will his tomb be haunted,
And worms will not come to thee.
ARVIRAGUS With fairest flowers,
Whilst summer lasts and I live here, Fidele,
I'll sweeten thy sad grave. Thou shalt not lack
The flower that's like thy face, pale primrose; nor
The azur'd hare-bell, like thy veins; no, nor
The leaf of eglantine, whom not to slander,
Out-sweet'ned not thy breath. The ruddock would,
With charitable bill – O bill, sore shaming
Those rich-left heirs that let their fathers lie
Without a monument! – bring thee all this;
Yea, and furr'd moss besides, when flow'rs are none,
To winter-ground thy corse –
GUIDERIUS Prithee have done,
And do not play in wench-like words with that
Which is so serious. Let us bury him,
And not protract with admiration what
Is now due debt. To th' grave.
ARVIRAGUS Say, where shall's lay him?
GUIDERIUS By good Euriphile, our mother.
ARVIRAGUS Be't so;
And let us, Polydore, though now our voices
Have got the mannish crack, sing him to th' ground,
As once to our mother; use like note and words,
Save that Euriphile must be Fidele.
GUIDERIUS Cadwal,
I cannot sing. I'll weep, and word it with thee;
For notes of sorrow out of tune are worse
Than priests and fanes that lie.
ARVIRAGUS We'll speak it, then.
BELARIUS Great griefs, I see, med'cine the less, for Cloten
Is quite forgot. He was a queen's son, boys;
And though he came our enemy, remember
He was paid for that. Though mean and mighty rotting
Together have one dust, yet reverence –
That angel of the world – doth make distinction
Of place 'tween high and low. Our foe was princely;
And though you took his life, as being our foe,
Yet bury him as a prince.
GUIDERIUS Pray you fetch him hither.
Thersites' body is as good as Ajax',
When neither are alive.
ARVIRAGUS If you'll go fetch him,
We'll say our song the whilst. Brother, begin.
[Exit Belarius.
GUIDERIUS Nay, Cadwal, we must lay his head to th' East;
My father hath a reason for't.
ARVIRAGUS 'Tis true.
GUIDERIUS Come on, then, and remove him.
ARVIRAGUS So. Begin.

Song.

GUIDERIUS Fear no more the heat o' th' sun
Nor the furious winter's rages;
Thou thy worldly task hast done,
Home art gone, and ta'en thy wages.
Golden lads and girls all must,
As chimney-sweepers, come to dust.
ARVIRAGUS Fear no more the frown o' th' great;
Thou art past the tyrant's stroke.
Care no more to clothe and eat;
To thee the reed is as the oak.
The sceptre, learning, physic, must
All follow this and come to dust.
GUIDERIUS Fear no more the lightning flash,
ARVIRAGUS Nor th' all-dreaded thunder-stone;
GUIDERIUS Fear not slander, censure rash;
ARVIRAGUS Thou hast finish'd joy and moan.
BOTH All lovers young, all lovers must
Consign to thee and come to dust.
GUIDERIUS No exorciser harm thee!
ARVIRAGUS Nor no witchcraft charm thee!
GUIDERIUS Ghost unlaid forbear thee!
ARVIRAGUS Nothing ill come near thee!
BOTH Quiet consummation have,
And renowned be thy grave!

Re-enter BELARIUS with the body of Cloten.

GUIDERIUS We have done our obsequies. Come, lay him down.
BELARIUS Here's a few flowers; but 'bout midnight, more.
The herbs that have on them cold dew o' th' night
Are strewings fit'st for graves. Upon their faces.
You were as flow'rs, now wither'd. Even so
These herblets shall which we upon you strew.
Come on, away. Apart upon our knees.
The ground that gave them first has them again.
Their pleasures here are past, so is their pain.
[Exeunt all but Imogen.

IMOGEN [*Awaking*] Yes, sir, to Milford Haven. Which is the way?
I thank you. By yond bush? Pray, how far thither?
'Ods pittikins! can it be six mile yet?

I have gone all night. Faith, I'll lie down and
sleep.
But, soft! no bedfellow. O gods and goddesses!
[Seeing the body.
These flow'rs are like the pleasures of the
world;
This bloody man, the care on't. I hope I dream;
For so I thought I was a cave-keeper,
And cook to honest creatures. But 'tis not so;
'Twas but a bolt of nothing, shot at nothing,
Which the brain makes of fumes. Our very
eyes
Are sometimes, like our judgments, blind.
Good faith,
I tremble still with fear; but if there be
Yet left in heaven as small a drop of pity
As a wren's eye, fear'd gods, a part of it!
The dream's here still. Even when I wake it is
Without me, as within me; not imagin'd, felt.
A headless man? The garments of Posthumus?
I know the shape of's leg; this is his hand,
His foot Mercurial, his Martial thigh,
The brawns of Hercules; but his Jovial face –
Murder in heaven! How! 'Tis gone. Pisanio,
All curses madded Hecuba gave the Greeks,
And mine to boot, be darted on thee! Thou,
Conspir'd with that irregulous devil, Cloten,
Hath here cut off my lord. To write and read
Be henceforth treacherous! Damn'd Pisanio
Hath with his forged letters – damn'd Pisanio –
From this most bravest vessel of the world
Struck the main-top. O Posthumus! alas,
Where is thy head? Where's that? Ay me!
where's that?
Pisanio might have kill'd thee at the heart,
And left this head on. How should this be?
Pisanio?
'Tis he and Cloten; malice and lucre in them
Have laid this woe here. O, 'tis pregnant,
pregnant!
The drug he gave me, which he said was
precious
And cordial to me, have I not found it
Murd'rous to th' senses? That confirms it
home.
This is Pisanio's deed, and Cloten. O!
Give colour to my pale cheek with thy blood,
That we the horrider may seem to those
Which chance to find us. O, my lord, my lord!
[Falls fainting on the body.

Enter LUCIUS, Captains, and a Soothsayer.

CAPTAIN To them the legions garrison'd in
Gallia,
After your will, have cross'd the sea, attending
You here at Milford Haven; with your ships,
They are in readiness.

LUCIUS But what from Rome?

CAPTAIN The Senate hath stirr'd up the confiners
And gentlemen of Italy, most willing spirits,
That promise noble service; and they come
Under the conduct of bold Iachimo,
Sienna's brother.

LUCIUS When expect you them?

CAPTAIN With the next benefit o' th' wind.

LUCIUS This forwardness
Makes our hopes fair. Command our present
numbers
Be muster'd; bid the captains look to't. Now, sir,
What have you dream'd of late of this war's
purpose?

SOOTHSAYER Last night the very gods show'd me
a vision –
I fast and pray'd for their intelligence – thus:
I saw Jove's bird, the Roman eagle, wing'd
From the spongy south to this part of the west,
There vanish'd in the sunbeams; which
portends,
Unless my sins abuse my divination,
Success to th' Roman host.

LUCIUS Dream often so,
And never false. Soft, ho! what trunk is here
Without his top? The ruin speaks that sometime
It was a worthy building. How? a page?
Or dead or sleeping on him? But dead, rather;
For nature doth abhor to make his bed
With the defunct, or sleep upon the dead.
Let's see the boy's face.

CAPTAIN He's alive, my lord.

LUCIUS He'll then instruct us of this body. Young
one,
Inform us of thy fortunes; for it seems
They crave to be demanded. Who is this
Thou mak'st thy bloody pillow? Or who was he
That, otherwise than noble nature did,
Hath alter'd that good picture? What's thy
interest
In this sad wreck? How came't? Who is't? What
art thou?

IMOGEN I am nothing; or if not,
Nothing to be were better. This was my master,
A very valiant Briton and a good,
That here by mountaineers lies slain. Alas!
There is no more such masters. I may wander
From east to occident; cry out for service;
Try many, all good; serve truly; never
Find such another master.

LUCIUS 'Lack, good youth!
Thou mov'st no less with thy complaining than
Thy master in bleeding. Say his name, good
friend.

IMOGEN Richard du Champ. *[Aside]* If I do lie,
and do
No harm by it, though the gods hear, I hope

They'll pardon it. – Say you, sir?
LUCIUS Thy name?
IMOGEN Fidele, sir.
LUCIUS Thou dost approve thyself the very same;
Thy name well fits thy faith, thy faith thy name.
Wilt take thy chance with me? I will not say
Thou shalt be so well master'd; but, be sure,
No less belov'd. The Roman Emperor's letters,
Sent by a consul to me, should not sooner
Than thine own worth prefer thee. Go with me.
IMOGEN I'll follow, sir. But first, an't please the gods,
I'll hide my master from the flies, as deep
As these poor pickaxes can dig; and when
With wild wood-leaves and weeds I ha' strew'd his grave,
And on it said a century of prayers,
Such as I can, twice o'er, I'll weep and sigh;
And leaving so his service, follow you,
So please you entertain me.
LUCIUS Ay, good youth;
And rather father thee than master thee.
My friends,
The boy hath taught us manly duties; let us
Find out the prettiest daisied plot we can,
And make him with our pikes and partisans
A grave. Come, arm him. Boy, he is preferr'd
By thee to us; and he shall be interr'd
As soldiers can. Be cheerful; wipe thine eyes.
Some falls are means the happier to arise.
[Exeunt.

SCENE III. *Britain. Cymbeline's palace.*

Enter CYMBELINE, Lords, PISANIO, and Attendants.

CYMBELINE Again! and bring me word how 'tis with her. *[Exit an Attendant.*
A fever with the absence of her son;
A madness, of which her life's in danger. Heavens,
How deeply you at once do touch me! Imogen,
The great part of my comfort, gone; my queen
Upon a desperate bed, and in a time
When fearful wars point at me; her son gone,
So needful for this present. It strikes me past
The hope of comfort. But for thee, fellow,
Who needs must know of her departure and
Dost seem so ignorant, we'll enforce it from thee
By a sharp torture.
PISANIO Sir, my life is yours;
I humbly set it at your will; but for my mistress,
I nothing know where she remains, why gone,
Nor when she purposes return. Beseech your Highness,
Hold me your loyal servant.
LORD Good my liege,
The day that she was missing he was here.
I dare be bound he's true and shall perform
All parts of his subjection loyally. For Cloten,
There wants no diligence in seeking him,
And will no doubt be found.
CYMBELINE The time is troublesome.
[To Pisanio] We'll slip you for a season; but our jealousy
Does yet depend.
LORD So please your Majesty,
The Roman legions, all from Gallia drawn,
Are landed on your coast, with a supply
Of Roman gentlemen by the Senate sent.
CYMBELINE Now for the counsel of my son and queen!
I am amaz'd with matter.
LORD Good my liege,
Your preparation can affront no less
Than what you hear of. Come more, for more you're ready.
The want is but to put those pow'rs in motion
That long to move.
CYMBELINE I thank you. Let's withdraw,
And meet the time as it seeks us. We fear not
What can from Italy annoy us; but
We grieve at chances here. Away!
[Exeunt all but Pisanio.
PISANIO I heard no letter from my master since
I wrote him Imogen was slain. 'Tis strange.
Nor hear I from my mistress, who did promise
To yield me often tidings. Neither know I
What is betid to Cloten, but remain
Perplex'd in all. The heavens still must work.
Wherein I am false I am honest; not true, to be true.
These present wars shall find I love my country,
Even to the note o' th' King, or I'll fall in them.
All other doubts, by time let them be clear'd:
Fortune brings in some boats that are not steer'd. *[Exit.*

SCENE IV. *Wales. Before the cave of Belarius.*

Enter BELARIUS, GUIDERIUS, and ARVIRAGUS.

GUIDERIUS The noise is round about us.
BELARIUS Let us from it.
ARVIRAGUS What pleasure, sir, find we in life, to lock it
From action and adventure?
GUIDERIUS Nay, what hope
Have we in hiding us? This way the Romans
Must or for Britons slay us, or receive us
For barbarous and unnatural revolts
During their use, and slay us after.
BELARIUS Sons,
We'll higher to the mountains; there secure us.
To the King's party there's no going. Newness

Of Cloten's death – we being not known, not
  muster'd
Among the bands – may drive us to a render
Where we have liv'd, and so extort from's that
Which we have done, whose answer would be
  death,
Drawn on with torture.

GUIDERIUS This is, sir, a doubt
In such a time nothing becoming you
Nor satisfying us.

ARVIRAGUS It is not likely
That when they hear the Roman horses neigh,
Behold their quarter'd fires, have both their eyes
And ears so cloy'd importantly as now,
That they will waste their time upon our note,
To know from whence we are.

BELARIUS O, I am known
Of many in the army. Many years,
Though Cloten then but young, you see, not
  wore him
From my remembrance. And, besides, the King
Hath not deserv'd my service nor your loves,
Who find in my exile the want of breeding,
The certainty of this hard life; aye hopeless
To have the courtesy your cradle promis'd,
But to be still hot summer's tanlings and
The shrinking slaves of winter.

GUIDERIUS Than be so,
Better to cease to be. Pray, sir, to th' army.
I and my brother are not known; yourself
So out of thought, and thereto so o'ergrown,
Cannot be question'd.

ARVIRAGUS By this sun that shines,
I'll thither. What thing is't that I never
Did see man die! scarce ever look'd on blood
But that of coward hares, hot goats, and
  venison!
Never bestrid a horse, save one that had
A rider like myself, who ne'er wore rowel
Nor iron on his heel! I am asham'd
To look upon the holy sun, to have
The benefit of his blest beams, remaining
So long a poor unknown.

GUIDERIUS By heavens, I'll go!
If you will bless me, sir, and give me leave,
I'll take the better care; but if you will not,
The hazard therefore due fall on me by
The hands of Romans!

ARVIRAGUS So say I. Amen.

BELARIUS No reason I, since of your lives you set
So slight a valuation, should reserve
My crack'd one to more care. Have with you,
  boys!
If in your country wars you chance to die,
That is my bed too, lads, and there I'll lie.
Lead, lead. [*Aside*] The time seems long; their
  blood thinks scorn
Till it fly out and show them princes born.

[*Exeunt.*

ACT FIVE

SCENE I. *Britain. The Roman camp.*

Enter POSTHUMUS alone, with a bloody handkerchief.

POSTHUMUS Yea, bloody cloth, I'll keep thee; for
  I wish'd
Thou shouldst be colour'd thus. You married
  ones,
If each of you should take this course, how
  many
Must murder wives much better than
  themselves
For wrying but a little! O Pisanio!
Every good servant does not all commands;
No bond but to do just ones. Gods! if you
Should have ta'en vengeance on my faults, I
  never
Had liv'd to put on this; so had you saved
The noble Imogen to repent, and struck
Me, wretch more worth your vengeance. But
  alack,
You snatch some hence for little faults; that's
  love,
To have them fall no more. You some permit
To second ills with ills, each elder worse,
And make them dread it, to the doers' thrift.
But Imogen is your own. Do your best wills,
And make me blest to obey. I am brought hither
Among th' Italian gentry, and to fight
Against my lady's kingdom. 'Tis enough
That, Britain, I have kill'd thy mistress; peace!
I'll give no wound to thee. Therefore, good
  heavens,
Hear patiently my purpose. I'll disrobe me
Of these Italian weeds, and suit myself
As does a Britain peasant. So I'll fight
Against the part I come with; so I'll die
For thee, O Imogen, even for whom my life
Is every breath a death. And thus unknown,
Pitied nor hated, to the face of peril
Myself I'll dedicate. Let me make men know
More valour in me than my habits show.
Gods, put the strength o' th' Leonati in me!

To shame the guise o' th' world, I will begin
The fashion – less without and more within.
[*Exit.*

SCENE II. *Britain. A field of battle between the British and Roman camps.*

Enter LUCIUS, IACHIMO, and the Roman Army at one door, and the Britain Army at another, LEONATUS POSTHUMUS following like a poor soldier. They march over and go out. Alarums. Then enter again, in skirmish, IACHIMO and POSTHUMUS. He vanquisheth and disarmeth Iachimo, and then leaves him.

IACHIMO The heaviness and guilt within my bosom
Takes off my manhood. I have belied a lady,
The Princess of this country, and the air on't
Revengingly enfeebles me; or could this carl,
A very drudge of nature's, have subdu'd me
In my profession? Knighthoods and honours borne
As I wear mine are titles but of scorn.
If that thy gentry, Britain, go before
This lout as he exceeds our lords, the odds
Is that we scarce are men, and you are gods.
[*Exit.*

The battle continues; the Britons fly; CYMBELINE is taken. Then enter to his rescue BELARIUS, GUIDERIUS, and ARVIRAGUS.

BELARIUS Stand, stand! We have th' advantage of the ground;
The lane is guarded; nothing routs us but
The villainy of our fears.
GUIDERIUS AND ARVIRAGUS Stand, stand, and fight!

Re-enter POSTHUMUS, and seconds the Britons; they rescue Cymbeline, and exeunt. Then re-enter LUCIUS and IACHIMO, with IMOGEN.

LUCIUS Away, boy, from the troops, and save thyself;
For friends kill friends, and the disorder's such
As war were hoodwink'd.
IACHIMO 'Tis their fresh supplies.
LUCIUS It is a day turn'd strangely. Or betimes
Let's reinforce or fly. [*Exeunt.*

SCENE III. *Another part of the field.*

Enter POSTHUMUS and a Britain Lord.

LORD Cam'st thou from where they made the stand?
POSTHUMUS I did:
Though you, it seems, come from the fliers.
LORD I did.
POSTHUMUS No blame be to you, sir, for all was lost,
But that the heavens fought. The King himself
Of his wings destitute, the army broken,
And but the backs of Britons seen, all flying,
Through a straight lane – the enemy, full-hearted,
Lolling the tongue with slaught'ring, having work
More plentiful than tools to do't, struck down
Some mortally, some slightly touch'd, some falling
Merely through fear, that the strait path was damm'd
With dead men hurt behind, and cowards living
To die with length'ned shame.
LORD Where was this lane?
POSTHUMUS Close by the battle, ditch'd, and wall'd with turf,
Which gave advantage to an ancient soldier –
An honest one, I warrant, who deserv'd
So long a breeding as his white beard came to,
In doing this for's country. Athwart the lane
He, with two striplings – lads more like to run
The country base than to commit such slaughter;
With faces fit for masks, or rather fairer
Than those for preservation cas'd or shame –
Made good the passage, cried to those that fled
'Our Britain's harts die flying, not our men.
To darkness fleet souls that fly backwards! Stand;
Or we are Romans and will give you that,
Like beasts, which you shun beastly, and may save
But to look back in frown. Stand, stand!' These three,
Three thousand confident, in act as many –
For three performers are the file when all
The rest do nothing – with this word 'Stand, stand!'
Accommodated by the place, more charming
With their own nobleness, which could have turn'd
A distaff to a lance, gilded pale looks,
Part shame, part spirit renew'd; that some turn'd coward
But by example – O, a sin in war
Damn'd in the first beginners! – gan to look
The way that they did and to grin like lions
Upon the pikes o' th' hunters. Then began
A stop i' th' chaser, a retire; anon
A rout, confusion thick. Forthwith they fly,
Chickens, the way which they stoop'd eagles; slaves,
The strides they victors made; and now our cowards,

Like fragments in hard voyages, became
The life o' th' need. Having found the back-door open
Of the unguarded hearts, heavens, how they wound!
Some slain before, some dying, some their friends
O'erborne i' th' former wave. Ten chas'd by one
Are now each one the slaughterman of twenty.
Those that would die or ere resist are grown
The mortal bugs o' th' field.

LORD This was strange chance:
A narrow lane, an old man, and two boys.

POSTHUMUS Nay, do not wonder at it; you are made
Rather to wonder at the things you hear
Than to work any. Will you rhyme upon't,
And vent it for a mock'ry? Here is one:
'Two boys, an old man (twice a boy), a lane,
Preserv'd the Britons, was the Romans' bane'.

LORD Nay, be not angry, sir.

POSTHUMUS 'Lack, to what end?
Who dares not stand his foe I'll be his friend;
For if he'll do as he is made to do,
I know he'll quickly fly my friendship too.
You have put me into rhyme.

LORD Farewell; you're angry. [*Exit.*

POSTHUMUS Still going? This is a lord! O noble misery,
To be i' th' field and ask 'What news?' of me!
To-day how many would have given their honours
To have sav'd their carcasses! took heel to do't,
And yet died too! I, in mine own woe charm'd,
Could not find death where I did hear him groan,
Nor feel him where he struck. Being an ugly monster,
'Tis strange he hides him in fresh cups, soft beds,
Sweet words; or hath moe ministers than we
That draw his knives i' th' war. Well, I will find him;
For being now a favourer to the Briton,
No more a Briton, I have resum'd again
The part I came in. Fight I will no more,
But yield me to the veriest hind that shall
Once touch my shoulder. Great the slaughter is
Here made by th' Roman; great the answer be
Britons must take. For me, my ransom's death;
On either side I come to spend my breath,
Which neither here I'll keep nor bear again,
But end it by some means for Imogen.

Enter two British Captains and Soldiers.

1 CAPTAIN Great Jupiter be prais'd! Lucius is taken.
'Tis thought the old man and his sons were angels.

2 CAPTAIN There was a fourth man, in a silly habit,
That gave th' affront with them.

1 CAPTAIN So 'tis reported;
But none of 'em can be found. Stand! who's there?

POSTHUMUS A Roman,
Who had not now been drooping here if seconds
Had answer'd him.

2 CAPTAIN Lay hands on him; a dog!
A leg of Rome shall not return to tell
What crows have peck'd them here. He brags his service,
As if he were of note. Bring him to th' King.

Enter CYMBELINE, BELARIUS, GUIDERIUS, ARVIRAGUS, PISANIO, and Roman Captives. The Captains present Posthumus to Cymbeline, who delivers him over to a Gaoler. Exeunt omnes.

SCENE IV. *Britain. A prison.*

Enter POSTHUMUS and two Gaolers.

1 GAOLER You shall not now be stol'n, you have locks upon you;
So graze as you find pasture.

2 GAOLER Ay, or a stomach. [*Exeunt Gaolers.*

POSTHUMUS Most welcome, bondage! for thou art a way,
I think, to liberty. Yet am I better
Than one that's sick o' th' gout, since he had rather
Groan so in perpetuity than be cur'd
By th' sure physician death, who is the key
T' unbar these locks. My conscience, thou art fetter'd
More than my shanks and wrists; you good gods, give me
The penitent instrument to pick that bolt,
Then, free for ever! Is't enough I am sorry?
So children temporal fathers do appease;
Gods are more full of mercy. Must I repent,
I cannot do it better than in gyves,
Desir'd more than constrain'd. To satisfy,
If of my freedom 'tis the main part, take
No stricter render of me than my all.
I know you are more clement than vile men,
Who of their broken debtors take a third,
A sixth, a tenth, letting them thrive again
On their abatement; that's not my desire.
For Imogen's dear life take mine; and though
'Tis not so dear, yet 'tis a life; you coin'd it.
'Tween man and man they weigh not every stamp;
Though light, take pieces for the figure's sake;

You rather mine, being yours. And so, great pow'rs,
If you will take this audit, take this life,
And cancel these cold bonds. O Imogen!
I'll speak to thee in silence. [*Sleeps.*

Solemn Music. Enter, as in an apparition, SICILIUS LEONATUS, father to Posthumus, an old man attired like a warrior; leading in his hand an ancient matron, his Wife, and mother to Posthumus, with music before them. Then, after other music, follows the two young LEONATI, brothers to Posthumus, with wounds, as they died in the wars. They circle Posthumus round as he lies sleeping.

SICILIUS LEONATUS No more, thou thunder-master, show
Thy spite on mortal flies.
With Mars fall out, with Juno chide,
That thy adulteries
Rates and revenges.
Hath my poor boy done aught but well,
Whose face I never saw?
I died whilst in the womb he stay'd
Attending nature's law;
Whose father then, as men report
Thou orphans' father art,
Thou shouldst have been, and shielded him
From this earth-vexing smart.

MOTHER Lucina lent not me her aid,
But took me in my throes,
That from me was Posthumus ripp'd,
Came crying 'mongst his foes,
A thing of pity.

SICILIUS LEONATUS Great Nature like his ancestry
Moulded the stuff so fair
That he deserv'd the praise o' th' world
As great Sicilius' heir.

1 BROTHER When once he was mature for man,
In Britain where was he
That could stand up his parallel,
Or fruitful object be
In eye of Imogen, that best
Could deem his dignity?

MOTHER With marriage wherefore was he mock'd,
To be exil'd and thrown
From Leonati seat and cast
From her his dearest one,
Sweet Imogen?

SICILIUS LEONATUS Why did you suffer Iachimo,
Slight thing of Italy,
To taint his nobler heart and brain
With needless jealousy,
And to become the geeck and scorn
O' th' other's villainy?

2 BROTHER For this from stiller seats we came,
Our parents and us twain,
That, striking in our country's cause,
Fell bravely and were slain,
Our fealty and Tenantius' right
With honour to maintain.

1 BROTHER Like hardiment Posthumus hath
To Cymbeline perform'd.
Then, Jupiter, thou king of gods,
Why hast thou thus adjourn'd
The graces for his merits due,
Being all to dolours turn'd?

SICILIUS LEONATUS Thy crystal window ope; look out;
No longer exercise
Upon a valiant race thy harsh
And potent injuries.

MOTHER Since, Jupiter, our son is good,
Take off his miseries.

SICILIUS LEONATUS Peep through thy marble mansion. Help!
Or we poor ghosts will cry
To th' shining synod of the rest
Against thy deity.

BROTHERS Help, Jupiter! or we appeal,
And from thy justice fly.

JUPITER descends in thunder and lightning, sitting upon an eagle. He throws a thunderbolt. The Ghosts fall on their knees.

JUPITER No more, you petty spirits of region low,
Offend our hearing; hush! How dare you ghosts
Accuse the Thunderer whose bolt, you know,
Sky-planted, batters all rebelling coasts?
Poor shadows of Elysium, hence, and rest
Upon your never-withering banks of flow'rs.
Be not with mortal accidents opprest:
No care of yours it is; you know 'tis ours.
Whom best I love I cross; to make my gift,
The more delay'd, delighted. Be content;
Your low-laid son our godhead will uplift;
His comforts thrive, his trials well are spent.
Our Jovial star reign'd at his birth, and in
Our temple was he married. Rise, and fade!
He shall be lord of Lady Imogen,
And happier much by his affliction made.
This tablet lay upon his breast, wherein
Our pleasure his full fortune doth confine;
And so, away; no farther with your din
Express impatience, lest you stir up mine.
Mount, eagle, to my palace crystalline. [*Ascends.*

SICILIUS LEONATUS He came in thunder; his

celestial breath
Was sulphurous to smell; the holy eagle
Stoop'd, as to foot us. His ascension is
More sweet than our blest fields. His royal bird
Prunes the immortal wing, and cloys his beak,
As when his god is pleas'd.

ALL Thanks, Jupiter!

SICILIUS LEONATUS The marble pavement closes, he is enter'd
His radiant roof. Away! and, to be blest,
Let us with care perform his great behest.

[*Ghosts vanish.*

POSTHUMUS [*Waking*] Sleep, thou hast been a grandsire and begot
A father to me; and thou hast created
A mother and two brothers. But, O scorn,
Gone! They went hence so soon as they were born.
And so I am awake. Poor wretches, that depend
On greatness' favour, dream as I have done;
Wake and find nothing. But, alas, I swerve;
Many dream not to find, neither deserve,
And yet are steep'd in favours; so am I,
That have this golden chance, and know not why.
What fairies haunt this ground? A book? O rare one!
Be not, as is our fangled world, a garment
Nobler than that it covers. Let thy effects
So follow to be most unlike our courtiers,
As good as promise.
[*Reads*] 'When as a lion's whelp shall, to himself unknown, without seeking find, and be embrac'd by a piece of tender air; and when from a stately cedar shall be lopp'd branches which, being dead many years, shall after revive, be jointed to the old stock, and freshly grow; then shall Posthumus end his miseries, Britain be fortunate and flourish in peace and plenty.'
'Tis still a dream, or else such stuff as madmen
Tongue, and brain not; either both or nothing,
Or senseless speaking, or a speaking such
As sense cannot untie. Be what it is,
The action of my life is like it, which
I'll keep, if but for sympathy.

Re-enter Gaoler.

GAOLER Come, sir, are you ready for death?

POSTHUMUS Over-roasted rather; ready long ago.

GAOLER Hanging is the word, sir; if you be ready for that, you are well cook'd.

POSTHUMUS So, if I prove a good repast to the spectators, the dish pays the shot.

GAOLER A heavy reckoning for you, sir. But the comfort is, you shall be called to no more payments, fear no more tavern bills, which are often the sadness of parting, as the procuring of mirth. You come in faint for want of meat, depart reeling with too much drink; sorry that you have paid too much, and sorry that you are paid too much; purse and brain both empty; the brain the heavier for being too light, the purse too light, being drawn of heaviness. O, of this contradiction you shall now be quit. O, the charity of a penny cord! It sums up thousands in a trice. You have no true debitor and creditor but it; of what's past, is, and to come, the discharge. Your neck, sir, is pen, book, and counters; so the acquittance follows.

POSTHUMUS I am merrier to die than thou art to live.

GAOLER Indeed, sir, he that sleeps feels not the toothache. But a man that were to sleep your sleep, and a hangman to help him to bed, I think he would change places with his officer; for look you, sir, you know not which way you shall go.

POSTHUMUS Yes indeed do I, fellow.

GAOLER Your death has eyes in's head, then; I have not seen him so pictur'd. You must either be directed by some that take upon them to know, or to take upon yourself that which I am sure you do not know, or jump the after-inquiry on your own peril. And how you shall speed in your journey's end, I think you'll never return to tell one.

POSTHUMUS I tell thee, fellow, there are none want eyes to direct them the way I am going, but such as wink and will not use them.

GAOLER What an infinite mock is this, that a man should have the best use of eyes to see the way of blindness! I am sure hanging's the way of winking.

Enter a Messenger.

MESSENGER Knock off his manacles; bring your prisoner to the King.

POSTHUMUS Thou bring'st good news: I am call'd to be made free.

GAOLER I'll be hang'd, then.

POSTHUMUS Thou shalt be then freer than a gaoler; no bolts for the dead.

[*Exeunt Posthumus and Messenger.*

GAOLER Unless a man would marry a gallows and beget young gibbets, I never saw one so prone. Yet, on my conscience, there are verier knaves desire to live, for all he be a Roman; and there be some of them too that die against their wills; so should I, if I were one. I would we were all of one mind, and one mind good. O, there were desolation of gaolers and gallowses! I speak against my present profit, but my wish hath a preferment in't. [*Exit.*

SCENE V. *Britain. Cymbeline's tent.*

Enter CYMBELINE, BELARIUS, GUIDERIUS, ARVIRAGUS, PISANIO, Lords, Officers, and Attendants.

CYMBELINE Stand by my side, you whom the gods have made
Preservers of my throne. Woe is my heart.
That the poor soldier that so richly fought,
Whose rags sham'd gilded arms, whose naked breast
Stepp'd before targes of proof, cannot be found.
He shall be happy that can find him, if
Our grace can make him so.
BELARIUS I never saw
Such noble fury in so poor a thing;
Such precious deeds in one that promis'd nought
But beggary and poor looks.
CYMBELINE No tidings of him?
PISANIO He hath been search'd among the dead and living,
But no trace of him.
CYMBELINE To my grief, I am
The heir of his reward; [*To Belarius, Guiderius and Arviragus*] which I will add
To you, the liver, heart, and brain, of Britain,
By whom I grant she lives. 'Tis now the time
To ask of whence you are. Report it.
BELARIUS Sir,
In Cambria are we born, and gentlemen;
Further to boast were neither true nor modest,
Unless I add we are honest.
CYMBELINE Bow your knees.
Arise my knights o' th' battle; I create you
Companions to our person, and will fit you
With dignities becoming your estates.

Enter CORNELIUS and Ladies.

There's business in these faces. Why so sadly
Greet you our victory? You look like Romans,
And not o' th' court of Britain.
CORNELIUS Hail, great King!
To sour your happiness I must report
The Queen is dead.
CYMBELINE Who worse than a physician
Would this report become? But I consider
By med'cine life may be prolong'd, yet death
Will seize the doctor too. How ended she?
CORNELIUS With horror, madly dying, like her life;
Which, being cruel to the world, concluded
Most cruel to herself. What she confess'd
I will report, so please you; these her women
Can trip me if I err, who with wet cheeks
Were present when she finish'd.
CYMBELINE Prithee say.
CORNELIUS First, she confess'd she never lov'd you; only
Affected greatness got by you, not you;
Married your royalty, was wife to your place;
Abhorr'd your person.
CYMBELINE She alone knew this;
And but she spoke it dying, I would not
Believe her lips in opening it. Proceed.
CORNELIUS Your daughter, whom she bore in hand to love
With such integrity, she did confess
Was as a scorpion to her sight; whose life,
But that her flight prevented it, she had
Ta'en off by poison.
CYMBELINE O most delicate fiend!
Who is't can read a woman? Is there more?
CORNELIUS More, sir, and worse. She did confess she had
For you a mortal mineral, which, being took,
Should by the minute feed on life, and, ling'ring,
By inches waste you. In which time she purpos'd,
By watching, weeping, tendance, kissing, to
O'ercome you with her show; and in time,
When she had fitted you with her craft, to work
Her son into th' adoption of the crown;
But failing of her end by his strange absence,
Grew shameless-desperate, open'd, in despite
Of heaven and men, her purposes, repented
The evils she hatch'd were not effected; so,
Despairing, died.
CYMBELINE Heard you all this, her women?
LADY We did, so please your Highness.
CYMBELINE Mine eyes
Were not in fault, for she was beautiful;
Mine ears, that heard her flattery; nor my heart,
That thought her like her seeming. It had been vicious
To have mistrusted her; yet, O my daughter!
That it was folly in me thou mayst say,
And prove it in thy feeling. Heaven mend all!

Enter LUCIUS, IACHIMO, the Soothsayer, and other Roman Prisoners, guarded; POSTHUMUS behind, and IMOGENEN.

Thou com'st not, Caius, now for tribute; that
The Britons have raz'd out, though with the loss
Of many a bold one, whose kinsmen have made suit
That their good souls may be appeas'd with slaughter
Of you their captives, which ourself have granted;
So think of your estate.
LUCIUS Consider, sir, the chance of war. The day
Was yours by accident; had it gone with us,

We should not, when the blood was cool, have threaten'd
Our prisoners with the sword. But since the gods
Will have it thus, that nothing but our lives
May be call'd ransom, let it come. Sufficeth
A Roman with a Roman's heart can suffer.
Augustus lives to think on't; and so much
For my peculiar care. This one thing only
I will entreat: my boy, a Briton born,
Let him be ransom'd. Never master had
A page so kind, so duteous, diligent,
So tender over his occasions, true,
So feat, so nurse-like; let his virtue join
With my request, which I'll make bold your Highness
Cannot deny; he hath done no Briton harm
Though he have serv'd a Roman. Save him, sir,
And spare no blood beside.

CYMBELINE I have surely seen him;
His favour is familiar to me. Boy,
Thou hast look'd thyself into my grace,
And art mine own. I know not why, wherefore
To say 'Live, boy'. Ne'er thank thy master. Live;
And ask of Cymbeline what boon thou wilt,
Fitting my bounty and thy state, I'll give it;
Yea, though thou do demand a prisoner,
The noblest ta'en.

IMOGEN I humbly thank your Highness.

LUCIUS I do not bid thee beg my life, good lad,
And yet I know thou wilt.

IMOGEN No, no! Alack,
There's other work in hand. I see a thing
Bitter to me as death; your life, good master,
Must shuffle for itself.

LUCIUS The boy disdains me,
He leaves me, scorns me. Briefly die their joys
That place them on the truth of girls and boys.
Why stands he so perplex'd?

CYMBELINE What wouldst thou, boy?
I love thee more and more; think more and more
What's best to ask. Know'st him thou look'st on? Speak,
Wilt have him live? Is he thy kin? thy friend?

IMOGEN He is a Roman, no more kin to me
Than I to your Highness; who, being born your vassal,
Am something nearer.

CYMBELINE Wherefore ey'st him so?

IMOGEN I'll tell you, sir, in private, if you please
To give me hearing.

CYMBELINE Ay, with all my heart,
And lend my best attention. What's thy name?

IMOGEN Fidele, sir.

CYMBELINE Thou'rt my good youth, my page;
I'll be thy master. Walk with me; speak freely.

[Cymbeline and Imogen converse apart.

BELARIUS Is not this boy reviv'd from death?

ARVIRAGUS One sand another
Not more resembles – that sweet rosy lad
Who died, and was Fidele. What think you?

GUIDERIUS The same dead thing alive.

BELARIUS Peace, peace! see further. He eyes us not; forbear.
Creatures may be alike; were't he, I am sure
He would have spoke to us.

GUIDERIUS But we saw him dead.

BELARIUS Be silent; let's see further.

PISANIO *[Aside]* It is my mistress.
Since she is living, let the time run on
To good or bad.

[Cymbeline and Imogen advance.

CYMBELINE Come, stand thou by our side;
Make thy demand aloud. *[To Iachimo]* Sir, step you forth;
Give answer to this boy, and do it freely,
Or, by our greatness and the grace of it,
Which is our honour, bitter torture shall
Winnow the truth from falsehood. On, speak to him.

IMOGEN My boon is that this gentleman may render
Of whom he had this ring.

POSTHUMUS *[Aside]* What's that to him?

CYMBELINE That diamond upon your finger, say
How came it yours?

IACHIMO Thou'lt torture me to leave unspoken that
Which to be spoke would torture thee.

CYMBELINE How? me?

IACHIMO I am glad to be constrain'd to utter that
Which torments me to conceal. By villainy
I got this ring; 'twas Leonatus' jewel,
Whom thou didst banish; and – which more may grieve thee,
As it doth me – a nobler sir ne'er liv'd
'Twixt sky and ground. Wilt thou hear more, my lord?

CYMBELINE All that belongs to this.

IACHIMO That paragon, thy daughter,
For whom my heart drops blood and my false spirits
Quail to remember – Give me leave, I faint.

CYMBELINE My daughter? What of her? Renew thy strength;
I had rather thou shouldst live while nature will
Than die ere I hear more. Strive, man, and speak.

IACHIMO Upon a time – unhappy was the clock
That struck the hour! – it was in Rome – accurs'd

The mansion where! – 'twas at a feast – O,
would
Our viands had been poison'd, or at least
Those which I heav'd to head! – the good
Posthumus –
What should I say? he was too good to be
Where ill men were, and was the best of all
Amongst the rar'st of good ones – sitting sadly,
Hearing us praise our loves of Italy
For beauty that made barren the swell'd boast
Of him that best could speak; for feature, laming
The shrine of Venus or straight-pight Minerva,
Postures beyond brief nature; for condition,
A shop of all the qualities that man
Loves woman for; besides that hook of wiving,
Fairness which strikes the eye –
CYMBELINE I stand on fire.
Come to the matter.
IACHIMO All too soon I shall,
Unless thou wouldst grieve quickly. This
Posthumus,
Most like a noble lord in love and one
That had a royal lover, took his hint;
And not dispraising whom we prais'd – therein
He was as calm as virtue – he began
His mistress' picture; which by his tongue being
made,
And then a mind put in't, either our brags
Were crack'd of kitchen trulls, or his description
Prov'd us unspeaking sots.
CYMBELINE Nay, nay, to th' purpose.
IACHIMO Your daughter's chastity – there it
begins.
He spake of her as Dian had hot dreams
And she alone were cold; whereat I, wretch,
Made scruple of his praise, and wager'd with
him
Pieces of gold 'gainst this which then he wore
Upon his honour'd finger, to attain
In suit the place of's bed, and win this ring
By hers and mine adultery. He, true knight,
No lesser of her honour confident
Than I did truly find her, stakes this ring;
And would so, had it been a carbuncle
Of Phoebus' wheel; and might so safely, had it
Been all the worth of's car. Away to Britain
Post I in this design. Well may you, sir,
Remember me at court, where I was taught
Of your chaste daughter the wide difference
'Twixt amorous and villainous. Being thus
quench'd
Of hope, not longing, mine Italian brain
Gan in your duller Britain operate
Most vilely; for my vantage, excellent;
And, to be brief, my practice so prevail'd
That I return'd with simular proof enough
To make the noble Leonatus mad,
By wounding his belief in her renown
With tokens thus and thus; averring notes
Of chamber-hanging, pictures, this her
bracelet –
O cunning, how I got it! – nay, some marks
Of secret on her person, that he could not
But think her bond of chastity quite crack'd,
I having ta'en the forfeit. Whereupon –
Methinks I see him now –
POSTHUMUS [*Coming forward*] Ay, so thou dost,
Italian fiend! Ay me, most credulous fool,
Egregious murderer, thief, anything
That's due to all the villains past, in being,
To come! O, give me cord, or knife, or poison,
Some upright justicer! Thou, King, send out
For torturers ingenious. It is I
That all th' abhorred things o' th' earth amend
By being worse than they. I am Posthumus,
That kill'd thy daughter; villain-like, I lie –
That caus'd a lesser villain than myself,
A sacrilegious thief, to do't. The temple
Of virtue was she; yea, and she herself.
Spit, and throw stones, cast mire upon me, set
The dogs o' th' street to bay me. Every villain
Be call'd Posthumus Leonatus, and
Be villainy less than 'twas! O Imogen!
My queen, my life, my wife! O Imogen, Imogen,
Imogen!
IMOGEN Peace, my lord. Hear, hear!
POSTHUMUS Shall's have a play of this? Thou
scornful page,
There lie thy part. [*Strikes her. She falls.*
PISANIO O gentlemen, help!
Mine and your mistress! O, my lord Posthumus!
You ne'er kill'd Imogen till now. Help, help!
Mine honour'd lady!
CYMBELINE Does the world go round?
POSTHUMUS How comes these staggers on me?
PISANIO Wake, my mistress!
CYMBELINE If this be so, the gods do mean to
strike me
To death with mortal joy.
PISANIO How fares my mistress?
IMOGEN O, get thee from my sight;
Thou gav'st me poison. Dangerous fellow,
hence!
Breathe not where princes are.
CYMBELINE The tune of Imogen!
PISANIO Lady,
The gods throw stones of sulphur on me, if
That box I gave you was not thought by me
A precious thing! I had it from the Queen.
CYMBELINE New matter still?
IMOGEN It poison'd me.
CORNELIUS O gods!
I left out one thing which the Queen confess'd,
Which must approve thee honest. 'If Pisanio

Have' said she 'given his mistress that confection
Which I gave him for cordial, she is serv'd
As I would serve a rat.'
CYMBELINE What's this, Cornelius?
CORNELIUS The Queen, sir, very oft importun'd me
To temper poisons for her; still pretending
The satisfaction of her knowledge only
In killing creatures vile, as cats and dogs,
Of no esteem. I, dreading that her purpose
Was of more danger, did compound for her
A certain stuff, which, being ta'en, would cease
The present pow'r of life, but in short time
All offices of nature should again
Do their due functions. Have you ta'en of it?
IMOGEN Most like I did, for I was dead.
BELARIUS My boys,
There was our error.
GUIDERIUS This is sure Fidele.
IMOGEN Why did you throw your wedded lady from you?
Think that you are upon a rock, and now
Throw me again. [*Embracing him.*
POSTHUMUS Hang there like fruit, my soul,
Till the tree die!
CYMBELINE How now, my flesh? my child?
What, mak'st thou me a dullard in this act?
Wilt thou not speak to me?
IMOGEN [*Kneeling*] Your blessing, sir.
BELARIUS [*To Guiderius and Arviragus*]
Though you did love this youth, I blame ye not;
You had a motive for't.
CYMBELINE My tears that fall
Prove holy water on thee! Imogen,
Thy mother's dead.
IMOGEN I am sorry for't, my lord.
CYMBELINE O, she was naught, and long of her it was
That we meet here so strangely; but her son
Is gone, we know not how nor where.
PISANIO My lord,
Now fear is from me, I'll speak troth. Lord Cloten,
Upon my lady's missing, came to me
With his sword drawn, foam'd at the mouth, and swore,
If I discover'd not which way she was gone,
It was my instant death. By accident
I had a feigned letter of my master's
Then in my pocket, which directed him
To seek her on the mountains near to Milford;
Where, in a frenzy, in my master's garments,
Which he enforc'd from me, away he posts
With unchaste purpose, and with oath to violate
My lady's honour. What became of him
I further know not.
GUIDERIUS Let me end the story:
I slew him there.
CYMBELINE Marry, the gods forfend!
I would not thy good deeds should from my lips
Pluck a hard sentence. Prithee, valiant youth,
Deny't again.
GUIDERIUS I have spoke it, and I did it.
CYMBELINE He was a prince.
GUIDERIUS A most incivil one. The wrongs he did me
Were nothing prince-like; for he did provoke me
With language that would make me spurn the sea,
If it could so roar to me. I cut off's head,
And am right glad he is not standing here
To tell this tale of mine.
CYMBELINE I am sorry for thee.
By thine own tongue thou art condemn'd, and must
Endure our law. Thou'rt dead.
IMOGEN That headless man
I thought had been my lord.
CYMBELINE Bind the offender,
And take him from our presence.
BELARIUS Stay, sir King.
This man is better than the man he slew,
As well descended as thyself, and hath
More of thee merited than a band of Clotens
Had ever scar for. [*To the Guard*] Let his arms alone;
They were not born for bondage.
CYMBELINE Why, old soldier,
Wilt thou undo the worth thou art unpaid for
By tasting of our wrath? How of descent
As good as we?
ARVIRAGUS In that he spake too far.
CYMBELINE And thou shalt die for't.
BELARIUS We will die all three;
But I will prove that two on's are as good
As I have given out him. My sons, I must
For mine own part unfold a dangerous speech,
Though haply well for you.
ARVIRAGUS Your danger's ours.
GUIDERIUS And our good his.
BELARIUS Have at it then by leave!
Thou hadst, great King, a subject who
Was call'd Belarius.
CYMBELINE What of him? He is
A banish'd traitor.
BELARIUS He it is that hath
Assum'd this age; indeed a banish'd man;
I know not how a traitor.
CYMBELINE Take him hence,
The whole world shall not save him.
BELARIUS Not too hot.
First pay me for the nursing of thy sons,

And let it be confiscate all, so soon
As I have receiv'd it.

CYMBELINE Nursing of my sons?

BELARIUS I am too blunt and saucy: here's my knee.
Ere I arise I will prefer my sons;
Then spare not the old father. Mighty sir,
These two young gentlemen that call me father,
And think they are my sons, are none of mine;
They are the issue of your loins, my liege,
And blood of your begetting.

CYMBELINE How? my issue?

BELARIUS So sure as you your father's. I, old Morgan,
Am that Belarius whom you sometime banish'd.
Your pleasure was my mere offence, my punishment
Itself, and all my treason; that I suffer'd
Was all the harm I did. These gentle princes –
For such and so they are – these twenty years
Have I train'd up; those arts they have as I
Could put into them. My breeding was, sir, as
Your Highness knows. Their nurse, Euriphile,
Whom for the theft I wedded, stole these children
Upon my banishment; I mov'd her to't,
Having receiv'd the punishment before
For that which I did then. Beaten for loyalty
Excited me to treason. Their dear loss,
The more of you 'twas felt, the more it shap'd
Unto my end of stealing them. But, gracious sir,
Here are your sons again, and I must lose
Two of the sweet'st companions in the world.
The benediction of these covering heavens
Fall on their heads like dew! for they are worthy
To inlay heaven with stars.

CYMBELINE Thou weep'st and speak'st.
The service that you three have done is more
Unlike than this thou tell'st. I lost my children.
If these be they, I know not how to wish
A pair of worthier sons.

BELARIUS Be pleas'd awhile.
This gentleman, whom I call Polydore,
Most worthy, prince, as yours, is true Guiderius;
This gentleman, my Cadwal, Arviragus,
Your younger princely son; he, sir, was lapp'd
In a most curious mantle, wrought by th' hand
Of his queen mother, which for more probation
I can with ease produce.

CYMBELINE Guiderius had
Upon his neck a mole, a sanguine star;
It was a mark of wonder.

BELARIUS This is he,
Who hath upon him still that natural stamp.
It was wise nature's end in the donation,
To be his evidence now.

CYMBELINE O, what am I?
A mother to the birth of three? Ne'er mother
Rejoic'd deliverance more. Blest pray you be,
That, after this strange starting from your orbs,
You may reign in them now! O Imogen,
Thou hast lost by this a kingdom.

IMOGEN No, my lord;
I have got two worlds by't. O my gentle brothers,
Have we thus met? O, never say hereafter
But I am truest speaker! You call'd me brother,
When I was but your sister: I you brothers,
When we were so indeed.

CYMBELINE Did you e'er meet?

ARVIRAGUS Ay, my good lord.

GUIDERIUS And at first meeting lov'd,
Continu'd so until we thought he died.

CORNELIUS By the Queen's dram she swallow'd.

CYMBELINE O rare instinct!
When shall I hear all through? This fierce abridgment
Hath to it circumstantial branches, which
Distinction should be rich in. Where? how liv'd you?
And when came you to serve our Roman captive?
How parted with your brothers? how first met them?
Why fled you from the court? and whither? These,
And your three motives to the battle, with
I know not how much more, should be demanded,
And all the other by-dependances,
From chance to chance; but nor the time nor place
Will serve our long interrogatories. See,
Posthumus anchors upon Imogen;
And she, like harmless lightning, throws her eye
On him, her brothers, me, her master, hitting
Each object with a joy; the counterchange
Is severally in all. Let's quit this ground,
And smoke the temple with our sacrifices.
[*To Belarius*] Thou art my brother; so we'll hold thee ever.

IMOGEN You are my father too, and did relieve me
To see this gracious season.

CYMBELINE All o'erjoy'd
Save these in bonds. Let them be joyful too,
For they shall taste our comfort.

IMOGEN My good master,
I will yet do you service.

LUCIUS Happy be you!

CYMBELINE The forlorn soldier, that so nobly fought,
He would have well becom'd this place and grac'd

The thankings of a king.
POSTHUMUS I am, sir,
The soldier that did company these three
In poor beseeming; 'twas a fitment for
The purpose I then follow'd. That I was he,
Speak, Iachimo. I had you down, and might
Have made you finish.
IACHIMO [*Kneeling*] I am down again;
But now my heavy conscience sinks my knee,
As then your force did. Take that life, beseech you,
Which I so often owe; but your ring first,
And here the bracelet of the truest princess
That ever swore her faith.
POSTHUMUS Kneel not to me.
The pow'r that I have on you is to spare you;
The malice towards you to forgive you. Live,
And deal with others better.
CYMBELINE Nobly doom'd!
We'll learn our freeness of a son-in-law;
Pardon's the word to all.
ARVIRAGUS You holp us, sir,
As you did mean indeed to be our brother;
Joy'd are we that you are.
POSTHUMUS Your servant, Princes. Good my lord of Rome,
Call forth your soothsayer. As I slept, methought
Great Jupiter, upon his eagle back'd,
Appear'd to me, with other spritely shows
Of mine own kindred. When I wak'd, I found
This label on my bosom; whose containing
Is so from sense in hardness that I can
Make no collection of it. Let him show
His skill in the construction.
LUCIUS Philarmonus!
SOOTHSAYER Here, my good lord.
LUCIUS Read, and declare the meaning.
SOOTHSAYER [*Reads*] 'When as a lion's whelp shall, to himself unknown, without seeking find, and be embrac'd by a piece of tender air; and when from a stately cedar shall be lopp'd branches which, being dead many years, shall after revive, be jointed to the old stock, and freshly grow; then shall Posthumus end his miseries, Britain be fortunate and flourish in peace and plenty.'
Thou, Leonatus, art the lion's whelp;
The fit and apt construction of thy name,
Being Leo-natus, doth import so much.
[*To Cymbeline*] The piece of tender air, thy virtuous daughter,
Which we call 'mollis aer', and 'mollis aer'
We term it 'mulier'; which 'mulier' I divine
Is this most constant wife, who even now
Answering the letter of the oracle,
Unknown to you, unsought, were clipp'd about
With this most tender air.
CYMBELINE This hath some seeming.
SOOTHSAYER The lofty cedar, royal Cymbeline,
Personates thee; and thy lopp'd branches point
Thy two sons forth, who, by Belarius stol'n,
For many years thought dead, are now reviv'd,
To the majestic cedar join'd, whose issue
Promises Britain peace and plenty.
CYMBELINE Well,
My peace we will begin. And, Caius Lucius,
Although the victor, we submit to Caesar
And to the Roman empire, promising
To pay our wonted tribute, from the which
We were dissuaded by our wicked queen,
Whom heavens in justice, both on her and hers,
Have laid most heavy hand.
SOOTHSAYER The fingers of the pow'rs above do tune
The harmony of this peace. The vision
Which I made known to Lucius ere the stroke
Of yet this scarce-cold battle, at this instant
Is full accomplish'd; for the Roman eagle,
From south to west on wing soaring aloft,
Lessen'd herself and in the beams o' th' sun
So vanish'd; which foreshow'd our princely eagle,
Th' imperial Caesar, should again unite
His favour with the radiant Cymbeline,
Which shines here in the west.
CYMBELINE Laud we the gods;
And let our crooked smokes climb to their nostrils
From our bless'd altars. Publish we this peace
To all our subjects. Set we forward; let
A Roman and a British ensign wave
Friendly together. So through Lud's Town march;
And in the temple of great Jupiter
Our peace we'll ratify; seal it with feasts.
Set on there! Never was a war did cease,
Ere bloody hands were wash'd, with such a peace. [*Exeunt.*

Pericles, Prince of Tyre

Introduction by ALEC YEARLING

Pericles was popular in its own day, and still tends to be effective in performance – a fact that needs to be borne in mind, since without actors to bring to life its elemental situations of loss, fear, misery and joy, what is liable to strike the reader most forcibly is the ramshackle and arbitrary nature of the whole enterprise. The play may not be wholly Shakespeare's. The text which was printed in various Quartos, and which eventually found its way into the Third Folio, is often chaotically messy, especially in its first two acts: the opening sequences may represent a mangled account of something Shakespeare wrote, or a fractured version of part of someone else's play which Shakespeare completed. Stylistic tests point in the latter direction. Its initial situation is idiotically self-cancelling: suitors may win the hand of King Antiochus's daughter by solving a riddle, the solution to which indicates that the princess is being incestuously enjoyed by her father. Having solved it, and unsurprisingly rejected the daughter, Pericles is on the run from Antiochus's vengeance. The play which ensues is characterised by almost incessant movement as the peripatetic hero gains a family only to lose it in complex circumstances, and to have it restored at the close.

The prince flees and wanders by sea, and the sea predominates as an image of worldly instability, the gulf of loss and separation which may in time give back what it has swallowed. Its poetic and symbolic force overrides any mundane common sense: more than once, the sending of a letter would have prevented years of mistaken heartbreak; but though letters do pass to and fro across this antique Mediterranean world, Pericles and his wife and his daughter have to endure their trials on a more abstracted plane.

Shakespeare shows Providence sundering and healing these people who must endure its trials for no other reason than that life is unstable; unlike Leontes in *The Winter's Tale* and Prospero in *The Tempest*, who respectively err in jealousy and negligence, Pericles is a guiltless sufferer, and his tribulations more closely resemble the hagiography of a saint or martyr than anything springing from the tensions of personality or behaviour. But in a fiction the author necessarily acts as Providence: and here we are faced with a dramatist who in these late plays, the so-called romances, returned repeatedly to an interrelated set of motifs concerning nature, time and endurance, with particular reference to sundered families and the restoration of kinsfolk amidst intimations of rebirth. Perhaps because of its very dramatic looseness, *Pericles* presents these motifs in a notably pure and potent form; and if, as seems likely, the play initiated these 'romances', then one may imagine Shakespeare exploring the possibilities of primal human situations presented with maximum poetic effect. The extended recognition scene of Pericles and his daughter Marina (5.1) is intrinsically moving as the desired climax of an extended action, but also because the playwright takes his time over it, his language essentially plain, but with the psychology of such persons in such a situation so imagined as to move us almost unbearably. The scene recalls other climaxes: the reconciliation of Lear and Cordelia, and the reunion of Viola with her twin in *Twelfth Night*, are both echoed here. Commentators have rightly found the roots of Shakespeare's later work to lie both in his tragedies and comedies, and to find such a blend of joy and pathos here in *Pericles* makes one realise all over again how much may be held in common across the conventional tragic/comic boundary. This play is a 'comedy' only insofar as its resolution is happy – though the presence of Gower as Chorus is a reassuring feature, the storyteller present on stage as controller. Certainly the highly episodic nature of the story, together with its lengthy time-span, allows for unpredictable swings from the casual to the intense, from elevated to earthy. The wooing of Thaisa [2.2] comes garnished with chivalric ceremony, while the Mytilene brothel [4.6] is as coarse-grained in its detail as anything in *Henry IV*'s Eastcheap. That the second of these scenes has worked into it the near-miraculous preservation of the virgin Marina, while the first remains stable in tone and content, is a mark of the play's tonal unpredictability; what finally unites the two is a kind of pious elevation. Chastity, love, proper behaviour, constancy, inner certitude, are what will shine out when the gross and sinful are transcended. A goddess steps into the play to direct Pericles towards his final reward. The crucial fact is that, here, virtue is rewarded, and that is what all centres around. Wish-fulfilment, we may call it; but the play exists to tell us that our salvation may lie in our capacity to harbour such wishes. Gower had intimated as much at the outset: 'The purchase is to make men glorious'.

Pericles, Prince of Tyre

DRAMATIS PERSONAE

GOWER
as Chorus
ANTIOCHUS
King of Antioch
PERICLES
Prince of Tyre
HELICANUS, ESCANES
two lords of Tyre
SIMONIDES
King of Pentapolis
CLEON
Governor of Tharsus
LYSIMACHUS
Governor of Mytilene
CERIMON
a lord of Ephesus
THALIARD
a lord of Antioch
PHILEMON
servant to Cerimon
LEONINE
servant to Dionyza
Marshal
A Pander
BOULT
his servant
The Daughter of Antiochus
DIONYZA
wife to Cleon
THAISA
daughter to Simonides
MARINA
daughter to Pericles and Thaisa
LYCHORIDA
nurse to Marina
A Bawd
DIANA
Lords, Ladies, Knights, Gentlemen, Sailors, Pirates, Fishermen, and Messengers.

THE SCENE: DISPERSEDLY IN VARIOUS COUNTRIES.

ACT ONE

Antioch. Before the palace.

Enter GOWER.

To sing a song that old was sung,
From ashes ancient Gower is come,
Assuming man's infirmities,
To glad your ear and please your eyes.
It hath been sung at festivals,
On ember-eves and holy-ales;
And lords and ladies in their lives
Have read it for restoratives.
The purchase is to make men glorious;
Et bonum quo antiquius, eo melius.
If you, born in those latter times,
When wit's more ripe, accept my rhymes,
And that to hear an old man sing
May to your wishes pleasure bring,
I life would wish, and that I might
Waste it for you, like taper-light.
This Antioch, then, Antiochus the Great
Built up, this city, for his chiefest seat;
The fairest in all Syria –
I tell you what mine authors say.
This king unto him took a fere,
Who died and left a female heir,
So buxom, blithe, and full of face,
As heaven had lent her all his grace;
With whom the father liking took,
And her to incest did provoke.
Bad child! Worse father! To entice his own
To evil should be done by none.
But custom what they did begin
Was with long use account no sin.
The beauty of this sinful dame
Made many princes thither frame
To seek her as a bed-fellow,
In marriage-pleasures play-fellow;
Which to prevent he made a law –
To keep her still, and men in awe –
That whoso ask'd her for his wife,
His riddle told not, lost his life.
So for her many a wight did die,
As yon grim looks do testify.
What now ensues to the judgment of your eye
I give, my cause who best can justify. [*Exit.*

SCENE I. *Antioch. The palace.*

Enter ANTIOCHUS, PRINCE PERICLES, and Followers.

ANTIOCHUS Young Prince of Tyre, you have at large received
The danger of the task you undertake.
PERICLES I have, Antiochus, and, with a soul
Embold'ned with the glory of her praise,

Think death no hazard in this enterprise.
ANTIOCHUS Bring in our daughter, clothed like a bride [*Music.*
For the embracements even of Jove himself;
At whose conception, till Lucina reigned,
Nature this dowry gave to glad her presence:
The senate-house of planets all did sit,
To knit in her their best perfections.

Enter the Daughter of Antiochus.

PERICLES See where she comes, apparell'd like the spring,
Graces her subjects, and her thoughts the king
Of every virtue gives renown to men.
Her face the book of praises, where is read
Nothing but curious pleasures, as from thence
Sorrow were ever raz'd, and testy wrath
Could never be her mild companion.
You gods that made me man, and sway in love,
That have inflam'd desire in my breast
To taste the fruit of yon celestial tree,
Or die in the adventure, be my helps,
As I am son and servant to your will,
To compass such a boundless happiness!
ANTIOCHUS Prince Pericles –
PERICLES That would be son to great Antiochus.
ANTIOCHUS Before thee stands this fair Hesperides,
With golden fruit, but dangerous to be touch'd;
For death-like dragons here affright thee hard.
Her face, like heaven, enticeth thee to view
Her countless glory, which desert must gain;
And which, without desert, because thine eye
Presumes to reach, all the whole heap must die.
Yon sometimes famous princes, like thyself,
Drawn by report, advent'rous by desire,
Tell thee, with speechless tongues and semblance pale,
That, without covering, save yon field of stars,
Here they stand martyrs, slain in Cupid's wars;
And with dead cheeks advise thee to desist
For going on death's net, whom none resist.
PERICLES Antiochus, I thank thee, who hath taught
My frail mortality to know itself,
And by those fearful objects to prepare
This body, like to them, to what I must;
For death remembered should be like a mirror,
Who tells us life's but breath, to trust it error.
I'll make my will then, and, as sick men do,
Who know the world, see heaven, but, feeling woe,
Gripe not at earthly joys as erst they did;
So I bequeath a happy peace to you
And all good men, as every prince should do;
My riches to the earth from whence they came;
[*To the Princess*] But my unspotted fire of love to you.
Thus ready for the way of life or death,
I wait the sharpest blow, Antiochus.
ANTIOCHUS Scorning advice, read the conclusion then:
Which read and not expounded, 'tis decreed,
As these before thee, thou thyself shalt bleed.
DAUGHTER Of all 'say'd yet, mayst thou prove prosperous!
Of all 'say'd yet, I wish thee happiness!
PERICLES Like a bold champion I assume the lists,
Nor ask advice of any other thought
But faithfulness and courage. [*Reads.*

The Riddle.

I am no viper, yet I feed
On mother's flesh which did me breed.
I sought a husband, in which labour
I found that kindness in a father.
He's father, son, and husband mild;
I mother, wife, and yet his child.
How they may be, and yet in two,
As you will live, resolve it you.

[*Aside*] Sharp physic is the last. But, O you powers
That give heaven countless eyes to view men's acts,
Why cloud they not their sights perpetually,
If this be true, which makes me pale to read it?
Fair glass of light, I lov'd you, and could still,
Were not this glorious casket stor'd with ill.
But I must tell you now my thoughts revolt;
For he's no man on whom perfections wait
That, knowing sin within, will touch the gate.
You are a fair viol, and your sense the strings;
Who, finger'd to make man his lawful music,
Would draw heaven down, and all the gods, to hearken;
But, being play'd upon before your time,
Hell only danceth at so harsh a chime.
Good sooth, I care not for you.
ANTIOCHUS Prince Pericles, touch not, upon thy life,
For that's an article within our law
As dangerous as the rest. Your time's expir'd:
Either expound now, or receive your sentence.
PERICLES Great King,
Few love to hear the sins they love to act;
'Twould braid yourself too near for me to tell it.
Who has a book of all that monarchs do,
He's more secure to keep it shut than shown;
For vice repeated is like the wand'ring wind,
Blows dust in others' eyes, to spread itself;
And yet the end of all is bought thus dear,
The breath is gone, and the sore eyes see clear
To stop the air would hurt them. The blind mole casts

Copp'd hills towards heaven, to tell the earth is throng'd
By man's oppression, and the poor worm doth die for't.
Kings are earth's gods; in vice their law's their will;
And if Jove stray, who dares say Jove doth ill?
It is enough you know; and it is fit,
What being more known grows worse, to smother it.
All love the womb that their first being bred;
Then give my tongue like leave to love my head.

ANTIOCHUS [*Aside*] Heaven, that I had thy head!
He has found the meaning.
But I will gloze with him. – Young Prince of Tyre,
Though by the tenour of our strict edict,
Your exposition misinterpreting,
We might proceed to cancel of your days;
Yet hope, succeeding from so fair a tree
As your fair self, doth tune us otherwise.
Forty days longer we do respite you;
If by which time our secret be undone,
This mercy shows we'll joy in such a son;
And until then your entertain shall be
As doth befit our honour and your worth.

[*Exeunt all but Pericles.*

PERICLES How courtesy would seem to cover sin,
When what is done is like an hypocrite,
The which is good in nothing but in sight!
If it be true that I interpret false,
Then were it certain you were not so bad
As with foul incest to abuse your soul;
Where now you're both a father and a son
By your untimely claspings with your child –
Which pleasure fits a husband, not a father –
And she an eater of her mother's flesh
By the defiling of her parent's bed;
And both like serpents are, who, though they feed
On sweetest flowers, yet they poison breed.
Antioch, farewell! for wisdom sees those men
Blush not in actions blacker than the night
Will shun no course to keep them from the light.
One sin I know another doth provoke:
Murder's as near to lust as flame to smoke.
Poison and treason are the hands of sin,
Ay, and the targets to put off the shame.
Then, lest my life be cropp'd to keep you clear,
By flight I'll shun the danger which I fear. [*Exit.*

Re-enter ANTIOCHUS.

ANTIOCHUS He hath found the meaning,
For which we mean to have his head.
He must not live to trumpet forth my infamy,
Nor tell the world Antiochus doth sin
In such a loathed manner;
And therefore instantly this prince must die;
For by his fall my honour must keep high.
Who attends us there?

Enter THALIARD.

THALIARD Doth your Highness call?

ANTIOCHUS Thaliard, you are of our chamber, and our mind partakes
Her private actions to your secrecy;
And for your faithfulness we will advance you.
Thaliard, behold here's poison and here's gold;
We hate the Prince of Tyre, and thou must kill him.
It fits thee not to ask the reason why,
Because we bid it. Say, is it done?

THALIARD My lord,
'Tis done.

ANTIOCHUS Enough.

Enter a Messenger.

Let your breath cool yourself, telling your haste.

MESSENGER My lord, Prince Pericles is fled. [*Exit.*

ANTIOCHUS As thou wilt live, fly after; and like an arrow shot from a well-experienc'd archer hits the mark his eye doth level at, so thou never return unless thou say Prince Pericles is dead.

THALIARD My lord, if I can get him within my pistol's length I'll make him sure enough. So, farewell to your Highness.

ANTIOCHUS Thaliard, adieu! [*Exit Thaliard*] Till Pericles be dead
My heart can lend no succour to my head. [*Exit.*

SCENE II. *Tyre. The palace.*

Enter PERICLES with his Lords.

PERICLES Let none disturb us. [*Exeunt Lords.*
Why should this change of thoughts,
The sad companion, dull-ey'd melancholy,
Be my so us'd a guest as not an hour
In the day's glorious walk, or peaceful night,
The tomb where grief should sleep, can breed me quiet?
Here pleasures court mine eyes, and mine eyes shun them,
And danger, which I fear'd, is at Antioch,
Whose arm seems far too short to hit me here.
Yet neither pleasure's art can joy my spirits,
Nor yet the other's distance comfort me.
Then it is thus: the passions of the mind,
That have their first conception by mis-dread,
Have after-nourishment and life by care;
And what was first but fear what might be done

Grows elder now, and cares it be not done.
And so with me. The great Antiochus –
'Gainst whom I am too little to contend,
Since he's so great can make his will his act –
Will think me speaking, though I swear to silence;
Nor boots it me to say I honour him,
If he suspect I may dishonour him;
And what may make him blush in being known,
He'll stop the course by which it might be known.
With hostile forces he'll o'erspread the land,
And with th' ostent of war will look so huge
Amazement shall drive courage from the state;
Our men be vanquish'd ere they do resist,
And subjects punish'd that ne'er thought offence;
Which care of them, not pity of myself –
Who am no more but as the tops of trees
Which fence the roots they grow by and defend them –
Makes both my body pine and soul to languish,
And punish that before that he would punish.

Enter HELICANUS and all the Lords.

1 LORD Joy and all comfort in your sacred breast!
2 LORD And keep your mind till you return to us,
Peaceful and comfortable!
HELICANUS Peace, peace, and give experience tongue.
They do abuse the king that flatter him,
For flattery is the bellows blows up sin;
The thing the which is flattered but a spark,
To which that blast gives heat and stronger glowing;
Whereas reproof, obedient, and in order,
Fits kings as they are men, for they may err.
When Signior Sooth here does proclaim a peace,
He flatters you, makes war upon your life.
Prince, pardon me, or strike me if you please;
I cannot be much lower than my knees. [*Kneels.*
PERICLES All leave us else; but let your cares o'erlook
What shipping and what lading's in our haven,
And then return to us. [*Exeunt Lords*]
Helicanus, thou
Hast moved us. What seest thou in our looks?
HELICANUS An angry brow, dread lord.
PERICLES If there be such a dart in princes' frowns,
How durst thy tongue move anger to our face?
HELICANUS How dare the plants look up to heaven, from whence
They have their nourishment?
PERICLES Thou know'st I have power
To take thy life from thee.
HELICANUS I have ground the axe myself;
Do but you strike the blow.
PERICLES Rise, prithee, rise.
Sit down. Thou art no flatterer.
I thank thee for't; and heaven forbid
That kings should let their ears hear their faults hid!
Fit counsellor and servant for a prince,
Who by thy wisdom mak'st a prince thy servant,
What wouldst thou have me do?
HELICANUS To bear with patience
Such griefs as you yourself do lay upon yourself.
PERICLES Thou speak'st like a physician, Helicanus,
That ministers a potion unto me
That thou wouldst tremble to receive thyself.
Attend me, then: I went to Antioch,
Where, as thou know'st, against the face of death,
I sought the purchase of a glorious beauty,
From whence an issue I might propagate
Are arms to princes and bring joys to subjects.
Her face was to mine eye beyond all wonder;
The rest – hark in thine ear – as black as incest;
Which by my knowledge found, the sinful father
Seem'd not to strike, but smooth. But thou know'st this,
'Tis time to fear when tyrants seem to kiss.
Which fear so grew in me I hither fled
Under the covering of a careful night,
Who seem'd my good protector; and, being here,
Bethought me what was past, what might succeed.
I knew him tyrannous; and tyrants' fears
Decrease not, but grow faster than the years;
And should he doubt it, as no doubt he doth,
That I should open to the list'ning air
How many worthy princes' bloods were shed
To keep his bed of blackness unlaid ope,
To lop that doubt, he'll fill this land with arms,
And make pretence of wrong that I have done him;
When all, for mine, if I may call offence,
Must feel war's blow, who spares not innocence;
Which love to all, of which thyself art one,
Who now reprov'dst me for't –
HELICANUS Alas, sir!
PERICLES Drew sleep out of mine eyes, blood from my cheeks,
Musings into my mind, with thousand doubts
How I might stop this tempest ere it came;
And, finding little comfort to relieve them,
I thought it princely charity to grieve them.
HELICANUS Well, my lord, since you have given me leave to speak,
Freely will I speak. Antiochus you fear,

And justly too, I think, you fear the tyrant,
Who either by public war or private treason
Will take away your life.
Therefore, my lord, go travel for a while
Till that his rage and anger be forgot,
Or till the Destinies do cut his thread of life.
Your rule direct to any; if to me,
Day serves not light more faithful than I'll be.

PERICLES I do not doubt thy faith;
But should he wrong my liberties in my absence?

HELICANUS We'll mingle our bloods together in the earth,
From whence we had our being and our birth.

PERICLES Tyre, I now look from thee then, and to Tharsus
Intend my travel, where I'll hear from thee;
And by whose letters I'll dispose myself.
The care I had and have of subjects' good
On thee I lay, whose wisdom's strength can bear it.
I'll take thy word for faith, not ask thine oath:
Who shuns not to break one will sure crack both.
But in our orbs we'll live so round and safe
That time of both this truth shall ne'er convince,
Thou show'dst a subject's shine, I a true prince.

[*Exeunt.*

SCENE III. *Tyre. The palace.*

Enter THALIARD.

THALIARD So, this is Tyre, and this the court. Here must I kill King Pericles; and if I do it not, I am sure to be hang'd at home. 'Tis dangerous. Well, I perceive he was a wise fellow and had good discretion that, being bid to ask what he would of the king, desired he might know none of his secrets. Now do I see he had some reason for't; for if a king bid a man be a villain, he's bound by the indenture of his oath to be one. Husht! here comes the lords of Tyre.

Enter HELICANUS, ESCANES, with other Lords.

HELICANUS You shall not need, my fellow peers of Tyre,
Further to question me of your king's departure:
His seal'd commission, left in trust with me,
Does speak sufficiently he's gone to travel.

THALIARD [*Aside*] How! the king gone!

HELICANUS If further yet you will be satisfied
Why, as it were unlicens'd of your loves,
He would depart, I'll give some light unto you.
Being at Antioch –

THALIARD [*Aside*] What from Antioch?

HELICANUS Royal Antiochus, on what cause I know not,
Took some displeasure at him; at least he judg'd so;
And doubting lest that he had err'd or sinn'd,
To show his sorrow, he'd correct himself;
So puts himself unto the shipman's toil,
With whom each minute threatens life or death.

THALIARD [*Aside*] Well, I perceive
I shall not be hang'd now although I would;
But since he's gone, the King's seas must please
He scap'd the land to perish at the seas.
I'll present myself. – Peace to the Lords of Tyre!

HELICANUS Lord Thaliard from Antiochus is welcome.

THALIARD From him I come
With message unto princely Pericles;
But since my landing I have understood
Your lord has betook himself to unknown travels,
Now message must return from whence it came.

HELICANUS We have no reason to desire it,
Commended to our master, not to us;
Yet, ere you shall depart, this we desire –
As friends to Antioch, we may feast in Tyre.

[*Exeunt.*

SCENE IV. *Tharsus. The Governor's house.*

Enter CLEON the Governor of Tharsus, with DIONYZA his wife, and Others.

CLEON My Dionyza, shall we rest us here,
And by relating tales of others' griefs
See if 'twill teach us to forget our own?

DIONYZA That were to blow at fire in hope to quench it;
For who digs hills because they do aspire
Throws down one mountain to cast up a higher.
O my distressed lord, even such our griefs are!
Here they are but felt and seen with mischief's eyes,
But like to groves, being topp'd, they higher rise.

CLEON O Dionyza,
Who wanteth food, and will not say he wants it,
Or can conceal his hunger till he famish?
Our tongues and sorrows to sound deep
Our woes into the air; our eyes to weep?
Till tongues fetch breath that may proclaim them louder;
That, if heaven slumber while their creatures want,
They may awake their helps to comfort them.
I'll then discourse our woes, felt several years,
And, wanting breath to speak, help me with tears.

DIONYZA I'll do my best, sir.

CLEON This Tharsus, o'er which I have the government,
A city on whom plenty held full hand,

For Riches strew'd herself even in her streets;
Whose towers bore heads so high they kiss'd the clouds,
And strangers ne'er beheld but wond'red at;
Whose men and dames so jetted and adorn'd,
Like one another's glass to trim them by;
Their tables were stor'd full, to glad the sight,
And not so much to feed on as delight;
All poverty was scorn'd, and pride so great
The name of help grew odious to repeat.

DIONYZA O, 'tis too true!

CLEON But see what heaven can do! By this our change
These mouths who but of late earth, sea, and air,
Were all too little to content and please,
Although they gave their creatures in abundance,
As houses are defil'd for want of use,
They are now starv'd for want of exercise.
Those palates who, not yet two summers younger,
Must have inventions to delight the taste,
Would now be glad of bread, and beg for it.
Those mothers who to nouzle up their babes
Thought nought too curious are ready now
To eat those little darlings whom they lov'd.
So sharp are hunger's teeth that man and wife
Draw lots who first shall die to lengthen life.
Here stands a lord, and there a lady weeping;
Here many sink, yet those which see them fall
Have scarce strength left to give them burial.
Is not this true?

DIONYZA Our cheeks and hollow eyes do witness it.

CLEON O, let those cities that of Plenty's cup
And her prosperities so largely taste,
With their superfluous riots, hear these tears!
The misery of Tharsus may be theirs.

Enter a Lord.

LORD Where's the Lord Governor?

CLEON Here.
Speak out thy sorrows which thou bring'st in haste,
For comfort is too far for us to expect.

LORD We have descried, upon our neighbouring shore,
A portly sail of ships make hitherward.

CLEON I thought as much.
One sorrow never comes but brings an heir
That may succeed as his inheritor;
And so in ours: some neighbouring nation,
Taking advantage of our misery,
Hath stuff'd the hollow vessels with their power,
To beat us down, the which are down already;
And make a conquest of unhappy me,
Whereas no glory's got to overcome.

LORD That's the least fear; for by the semblance
Of their white flags display'd, they bring us peace,
And come to us as favourers, not as foes.

CLEON Thou speak'st like him's untutor'd to repeat:
Who makes the fairest show means most deceit.
But bring they what they will and what they can,
What need we fear?
Our ground's the lowest, and we are half-way there.
Go tell their general we attend him here,
To know for what he comes, and whence he comes,
And what he craves.

LORD I go, my lord. [*Exit.*

CLEON Welcome is peace, if he on peace consist;
If wars, we are unable to resist.

Enter PERICLES, with Attendants.

PERICLES Lord Governor, for so we hear you are,
Let not our ships and number of our men
Be like a beacon fir'd t' amaze your eyes.
We have heard your miseries as far as Tyre,
And seen the desolation of your streets;
Nor come we to add sorrow to your tears,
But to relieve them of their heavy load;
And these our ships you happily may think
Are like the Troyan horse was stuff'd within
With bloody veins, expecting overthrow,
Are stor'd with corn to make your needy bread,
And give them life whom hunger starv'd half dead.

ALL The gods of Greece protect you!
And we'll pray for you. [*They kneel.*

PERICLES Arise, I pray you, rise.
We do not look for reverence, but for love,
And harbourage for ourself, our ships, and men.

CLEON The which when any shall not gratify,
Or pay you with unthankfulness in thought,
Be it our wives, our children, or ourselves,
The curse of heaven and men succeed their evils!
Till when – the which I hope shall ne'er be seen –
Your Grace is welcome to our town and us.

PERICLES Which welcome we'll accept; feast here awhile,
Until our stars that frown lend us a smile.

[*Exeunt.*

ACT TWO

Enter GOWER.

GOWER Here have you seen a mighty king
His child iwis to incest bring;
A better prince and benign lord,
That will prove awful both in deed and word.
Be quiet then, as men should be,
Till he hath pass'd necessity.
I'll show you those in troubles reign,
Losing a mite, a mountain gain.
The good in conversation,
To whom I give my benison,
Is still at Tharsus, where each man
Thinks all is writ he speken can;
And, to remember what he does,
Build his statue to make him glorious.
But tidings to the contrary
Are brought your eyes. What need speak I?
Dumb show.

Enter, at one door, PERICLES, talking with CLEON; all the Train with them. Enter, at another door, a Gentleman with a letter to Pericles; Pericles shows the letter to Cleon. Pericles gives the Messenger a reward, and knights him. Exit Pericles at one door and Cleon at another.

Good Helicane, that stay'd at home,
Not to eat honey like a drone
From others' labours; for though he strive
To killen bad, keep good alive;
And, to fulfil his prince' desire,
Sends word of all that haps in Tyre:
How Thaliard came full bent with sin
And had intent to murder him;
And that in Tharsus was not best
Longer for him to make his rest.
He, doing so, put forth to seas,
Where when men been, there's seldom ease;
For now the wind begins to blow;
Thunder above and deeps below
Makes such unquiet that the ship
Should house him safe is wreck'd and split;
And he, good prince, having all lost,
By waves from coast to coast is toss'd.
All perishen of man, of pelf,
Ne aught escapen but himself;
Till fortune, tir'd with doing bad,
Threw him ashore, to give him glad.
And here he comes. What shall be next,
Pardon old Gower – this longs the text. [*Exit.*

SCENE I. *Pentapolis. An open place by the seaside.*

Enter PERICLES, wet.

PERICLES Yet cease your ire, you angry stars of heaven!
Wind, rain, and thunder, remember earthly man
Is but a substance that must yield to you;
And I, as fits my nature, do obey you.
Alas, the sea hath cast me on the rocks,
Wash'd me from shore to shore, and left me breath
Nothing to think on but ensuing death.
Let it suffice the greatness of your powers
To have bereft a prince of all his fortunes;
And having thrown him from your wat'ry grave,
Here to have death in peace is all he'll crave.

Enter three Fishermen.

1 FISHERMAN What, ho, Pilch!

2 FISHERMAN Ha, come and bring away the nets.

1 FISHERMAN What, Patchbreech, I say!

3 FISHERMAN What say you, master?

1 FISHERMAN Look how thou stirr'st now. Come away, or I'll fetch thee with a wanion.

3 FISHERMAN Faith, master, I am thinking of the poor men that were cast away before us even now.

1 FISHERMAN Alas, poor souls! It grieved my heart to hear what pitiful cries they made to us to help them, when, well-a-day, we could scarce help ourselves.

3 FISHERMAN Nay, master, said not I as much when I saw the porpas how he bounc'd and tumbled? They say they're half fish, half flesh. A plague on them! They ne'er come but I look to be wash'd. Master, I marvel how the fishes live in the sea.

1 FISHERMAN Why, as men do a-land – the great ones eat up the little ones. I can compare our rich misers to nothing so fitly as to a whale: 'a plays and tumbles, driving the poor fry before him, and at last devours them all at a mouthful. Such whales have I heard on a' th' land, who never leave gaping till they've swallow'd the whole parish, church, steeple, bells, and all.

PERICLES [*Aside*] A pretty moral.

3 FISHERMAN But, master, if I had been the sexton, I would have been that day in the belfry.

2 FISHERMAN Why, man?

3 FISHERMAN Because he should have swallowed me too; and when I had been in his belly I would have kept such a jangling of the bells that he should never have left till he cast bells, steeple, church, and parish up again. But if the good King Simonides were of my mind –

PERICLES [*Aside*] Simonides!

3 FISHERMAN We would purge the land of these drones that rob the bee of her honey.

PERICLES [*Aside*] How from the finny subject of the sea

These fishers tell the infirmities of men,
And from their wat'ry empire recollect
All that may men approve or men detect! –
Peace be at your labour, honest fishermen!

2 FISHERMAN Honest – good fellow! What's that? If it be a day fits you, scratch't out of the calendar, and nobody look after it.

PERICLES May see the sea hath cast upon your coast –

2 FISHERMAN What a drunken knave was the sea to cast thee in our way!

PERICLES A man whom both the waters and the wind
In that vast tennis-court hath made the ball
For them to play upon entreats you pity him;
He asks of you that never us'd to beg.

1 FISHERMAN No, friend, cannot you beg? Here's them in our country of Greece gets more with begging than we can do with working.

2 FISHERMAN Canst thou catch any fishes, then?

PERICLES I never practis'd it.

2 FISHERMAN Nay, then thou wilt starve, sure; for here's nothing to be got now-a-days unless thou canst fish for't.

PERICLES What I have been I have forgot to know;
But what I am want teaches me to think on:
A man throng'd up with cold; my veins are chill,
And have no more of life than may suffice
To give my tongue that heat to ask your help;
Which if you shall refuse, when I am dead,
For that I am a man, pray see me buried.

1 FISHERMAN Die quoth-a? Now gods forbid't! And I have a gown here! Come, put it on; keep thee warm. Now, afore me, a handsome fellow! Come, thou shalt go home, and we'll have flesh for holidays, fish for fasting days, and moreo'er puddings and flapjacks; and thou shalt be welcome.

PERICLES I thank you, sir.

2 FISHERMAN Hark you, my friend; you said you could not beg.

PERICLES I did but crave.

2 FISHERMAN But crave! Then I'll turn craver too, and so I shall scape whipping.

PERICLES Why, are all your beggars whipp'd, then?

2 FISHERMAN O, not all, my friend, not all! For if all your beggars were whipp'd, I would wish no better office than to be beadle. But, master, I'll go draw up the net.

[Exit with Third Fisherman.

PERICLES *[Aside]* How well this honest mirth becomes their labour!

1 FISHERMAN Hark you, sir; do you know where ye are?

PERICLES Not well.

1 FISHERMAN Why, I'll tell you: this is call'd Pentapolis, and our king the good Simonides.

PERICLES The good Simonides, do you call him?

1 FISHERMAN Ay, sir; and he deserves so to be call'd for his peaceable reign and good government.

PERICLES He is a happy king, since he gains from his subjects the name of good by his government. How far is his court distant from this shore?

1 FISHERMAN Marry, sir, half a day's journey; and I'll tell you, he hath a fair daughter, and to-morrow is her birthday, and there are princes and knights come from all parts of the world to joust and tourney for her love.

PERICLES Were my fortunes equal to my desires,
I could wish to make one there.

1 FISHERMAN O sir, things must be as they may; and what a man cannot get he may lawfully deal for – his wife's soul.

Re-enter Second and Third Fishermen, drawing up a net.

2 FISHERMAN Help, master, help! Here's a fish hangs in the net like a poor man's right in the law; 'twill hardly come out. Ha! Bots on't! 'Tis come at last, and 'tis turn'd to a rusty armour.

PERICLES An armour, friends! I pray you let me see it.
Thanks, Fortune, yet, that after all my crosses
Thou givest me somewhat to repair myself;
And though it was mine own, part of my heritage
Which my dead father did bequeath to me,
With this strict charge, even as he left his life:
'Keep it, my Pericles. It hath been a shield
'Twixt me and death;' and pointed to this brace
'For that it sav'd me, keep it. In like necessity –
The which the gods protect thee from! – may't defend thee!'
It kept where I kept, I so dearly lov'd it;
Till the rough seas, that spare not any man,
Took it in rage, though calm'd have given't again –
I thank thee for't. My shipwreck now's no ill,
Since I have here my father's gift in his will.

1 FISHERMAN What mean you, sir?

PERICLES To beg of you, kind friends, this coat of worth,
For it was sometime target to a king;
I know it by this mark. He lov'd me dearly,
And for his sake I wish the having of it;
And that you'd guide me to your sovereign's court,
Where with it I may appear a gentleman;
And if that ever my low fortune's better,

I'll pay your bounties; till then rest your debtor.

1 FISHERMAN Why, wilt thou tourney for the lady?

PERICLES I'll show the virtue I have borne in arms.

1 FISHERMAN Why, do'e take it, and the gods give thee good on't!

2 FISHERMAN Ay, but hark you, my friend; 'twas we that made up this garment through the rough seams of the waters; there are certain condolements, certain vails. I hope, sir, if you thrive, you'll remember from whence you had them.

PERICLES Believe't, I will.
By your furtherance I am cloth'd in steel;
And spite of all the rapture of the sea
This jewel holds his building on my arm.
Unto thy value I will mount myself
Upon a courser whose delightful steps
Shall make the gazer joy to see him tread.
Only, my friend, I yet am unprovided
Of a pair of bases.

2 FISHERMAN We'll sure provide. Thou shalt have my best gown to make thee a pair; and I'll bring thee to the court myself.

PERICLES Then honour be but a goal to my will;
This day I'll rise, or else add ill to ill. [*Exeunt.*

SCENE II. *Pentapolis. A public way or platform leading to the lists. A pavilion by the side of it for the reception of the King, Princess, Lords etc.*

Enter SIMONIDES, THAISA, Lords, and Attendants.

SIMONIDES Are the knights ready to begin the triumph?

1 LORD They are, my liege;
And stay your coming to present themselves.

SIMONIDES Return them we are ready; and our daughter here,
In honour of whose birth these triumphs are,
Sits here like beauty's child, whom nature gat
For men to see, and seeing wonder at.
[*Exit a Lord.*

THAISA It pleaseth you, my royal father, to express
My commendations great, whose merit's less.

SIMONIDES It's fit it should be so; for princes are
A model which heaven makes like to itself:
As jewels lose their glory if neglected,
So princes their renowns if not respected.
'Tis now your honour, daughter, to entertain
The labour of each knight in his device.

THAISA Which, to preserve mine honour, I'll perform.

Enter a Knight; he passes over, and his Squire presents his shield to the Princess.

SIMONIDES Who is the first that doth prefer himself?

THAISA A knight of Sparta, my renowned father;
And the device he bears upon his shield
Is a black Ethiope reaching at the sun;
The word, 'Lux tua vita mihi'.

SIMONIDES He loves you well that holds his life of you.

The Second Knight passes by.

Who is the second that presents himself?

THAISA A prince of Macedon, my royal father;
And the device he bears upon his shield
Is an arm'd knight that's conquer'd by a lady;
The motto thus, in Spanish, 'Piu por dulzura que por fuerza'.

The Third Knight passes by.

SIMONIDES And what's the third?

THAISA The third of Antioch;
And his device a wreath of chivalry;
The word, 'Me pompae provexit apex'.

The Fourth Knight passes by.

SIMONIDES What is the fourth?

THAISA A burning torch that's turned up-side down;
The word, 'Quod me alit, me extinguit'.

SIMONIDES Which shows that beauty hath his power and will,
Which can as well inflame as it can kill.

The Fifth Knight passes by.

THAISA The fifth, an hand environed with clouds,
Holding out gold that's by the touchstone tried;
The motto thus, 'Sic spectanda fides'.

PERICLES as Sixth Knight passes by.

SIMONIDES And what's the sixth and last, the which the knight himself
With such a graceful courtesy deliver'd?

THAISA He seems to be a stranger; but his present is
A withered branch, that's only green at top;
The motto, 'In hac spe vivo'.

SIMONIDES A pretty moral;
From the dejected state wherein he is,
He hopes by you his fortunes yet may flourish.

1 LORD He had need mean better than his outward show
Can any way speak in his just commend;
For by his rusty outside he appears
To have practis'd more the whipstock than the lance.

2 LORD He well may be a stranger, for he comes
To an honour'd triumph strangely furnished.

3 LORD And on set purpose let his armour rust
Until this day, to scour it in the dust.
SIMONIDES Opinion's but a fool, that makes us scan
The outward habit by the inward man.
But stay, the knights are coming. We will withdraw
Into the gallery. [*Exeunt.*

[*Great shouts within, and all cry 'The mean knight!'*

SCENE III. *Pentapolis. A hall of state. A banquet prepared.*

Enter KING SIMONIDES, THAISA, Ladies, Lords, Knights, from tilting, and Attendants.

SIMONIDES Knights!
To say you're welcome were superfluous.
To place upon the volume of your deeds,
As in a title-page, your worth in arms
Were more than you expect, or more than's fit,
Since every worth in show commends itself.
Prepare for mirth, for mirth becomes a feast;
You are princes and my guests.
THAISA But you my knight and guest;
To whom this wreath of victory I give,
And crown you king of this day's happiness.
PERICLES 'Tis more by fortune, lady, than my merit.
SIMONIDES Call it by what you will, the day is yours;
And here I hope is none that envies it.
In framing an artist, art hath thus decreed,
To make some good, but others to exceed;
And you are her labour'd scholar. Come, queen o' th' feast–
For, daughter, so you are – here take your place.
Marshal the rest as they deserve their grace.
KNIGHTS We are honour'd much by good
Simonides.
SIMONIDES Your presence glads our days.
Honour we love;
For who hates honour hates the gods above.
MARSHAL Sir, yonder is your place.
PERICLES Some other is more fit.
1 KNIGHT Contend not, sir; for we are gentlemen
That neither in our hearts nor outward eyes
Envy the great nor shall the low despise.
PERICLES You are right courteous knights.
SIMONIDES Sit, sir, sit.
[*Aside*] By Jove, I wonder, that is king of thoughts,
These cates resist me, he not thought upon.
THAISA [*Aside*] By Juno, that is queen of marriage,
All viands that I eat do seem unsavoury,
Wishing him my meat. – Sure he's a gallant gentleman.
SIMONIDES He's but a country gentleman;
Has done no more than other knights have done;
Has broken a staff or so; so let it pass.
THAISA [*Aside*] To me he seems like diamond to glass.
PERICLES [*Aside*] Yon king's to me like to my father's picture,
Which tells me in that glory once he was;
Had princes sit like stars about his throne,
And he the sun, for them to reverence;
None that beheld him but, like lesser lights,
Did vail their crowns to his supremacy:
Where now his son's like a glowworm in the night,
The which hath fire in darkness, none in light.
Whereby I see that Time's the king of men;
He's both their parent, and he is their grave,
And gives them what he will, not what they crave.
SIMONIDES What, are you merry, knights?
1 KNIGHT Who can be other in this royal presence?
SIMONIDES Here, with a cup that's stor'd unto the brim –
As you do love, fill to your mistress' lips –
We drink this health to you.
KNIGHTS We thank your Grace.
SIMONIDES Yet pause awhile.
Yon knight doth sit too melancholy,
As if the entertainment in our court
Had not a show might countervail his worth.
Note it not you, Thaisa?
THAISA What is't
To me, my father?
SIMONIDES O, attend, my daughter:
Princes, in this, should live like gods above,
Who freely give to every one that comes
To honour them;
And princes not doing so are like to gnats,
Which make a sound, but kill'd are wond'red at.
Therefore to make his entertain more sweet,
Here, say we drink this standing-bowl of wine to him.
THAISA Alas, my father, it befits not me
Unto a stranger knight to be so bold:
He may my proffer take for an offence,
Since men take women's gifts for impudence.
SIMONIDES How!
Do as I bid you, or you'll move me else.
THAISA [*Aside*] Now, by the gods, he could not please me better.
SIMONIDES And furthermore tell him we desire to know of him
Of whence he is, his name and parentage.

THAISA The King my father, sir, has drunk to you.
PERICLES I thank him.
THAISA Wishing it so much blood unto your life.
PERICLES I thank both him and you, and pledge him freely.
THAISA And further he desires to know of you
Of whence you are, your name and parentage.
PERICLES A gentleman of Tyre – my name, Pericles;
My education been in arts and arms;
Who, looking for adventures in the world,
Was by the rough seas reft of ships and men,
And after shipwreck driven upon this shore.
THAISA He thanks your Grace; names himself Pericles,
A gentleman of Tyre,
Who only by misfortune of the seas,
Bereft of ships and men, cast on this shore.
SIMONIDES Now, by the gods, I pity his misfortune,
And will awake him from his melancholy.
Come, gentlemen, we sit too long on trifles
And waste the time which looks for other revels.
Even in your armours, as you are address'd,
Will very well become a soldier's dance.
I will not have excuse, with saying this
Loud music is too harsh for ladies' heads,
Since they love men in arms as well as beds.
[*They dance.*
So, this was well ask'd, 'twas so well perform'd.
Come, sir;
Here is a lady that wants breathing too;
And I have heard you knights of Tyre
Are excellent in making ladies trip;
And that their measures are as excellent.
PERICLES In those that practise them they are, my lord.
SIMONIDES O, that's as much as you would be denied
Of your fair courtesy. [*The Knights and Ladies dance*] Unclasp, unclasp.
Thanks, gentlemen, to all; all have done well,
[*To Pericles*] But you the best. – Pages and lights, to conduct
These knights unto their several lodgings! –
Yours, sir,
We have given order to be next our own.
PERICLES I am at your Grace's pleasure.
SIMONIDES Princes, it is too late to talk of love,
And that's the mark I know you level at.
Therefore each one betake him to his rest;
To-morrow all for speeding do their best.
[*Exeunt.*

SCENE IV. *Tyre. The Governor's house.*

Enter HELICANUS and ESCANES.

HELICANUS No, Escanes; know this of me –
Antiochus from incest liv'd not free;
For which, the most high gods not minding longer
To withhold the vengeance that they had in store,
Due to this heinous capital offence,
Even in the height and pride of all his glory,
When he was seated in a chariot
Of an inestimable value, and his daughter with him,
A fire from heaven came and shrivell'd up
Their bodies, even to loathing; for they so stunk
That all those eyes ador'd them ere their fall
Scorn now their hand should give them burial.
ESCANES 'Twas very strange.
HELICANUS And yet but justice; for though
This king were great, his greatness was no guard
To bar heaven's shaft, but sin had his reward.
ESCANES 'Tis very true.

Enter two or three Lords.

1 LORD See, not a man in private conference
Or council has respect with him but he.
2 LORD It shall no longer grieve without reproof.
3 LORD And curs'd be he that will not second it!
1 LORD Follow me, then. Lord Helicane, a word.
HELICANUS With me? and welcome. Happy day, my lords.
1 LORD Know that our griefs are risen to the top,
And now at length they overflow their banks.
HELICANUS Your griefs! for what? Wrong not your prince you love.
1 LORD Wrong not yourself, then, noble Helicane;
But if the prince do live, let us salute him,
Or know what ground's made happy by his breath.
If in the world he live, we'll seek him out;
If in his grave he rest, we'll find him there;
And be resolv'd he lives to govern us,
Or, dead, give's cause to mourn his funeral,
And leave us to our free election.
2 LORD Whose death's indeed the strongest in our censure;
And knowing this kingdom, if without a head,
Like goodly buildings left without a roof,
Soon fall to ruin, your noble self,
That best know how to rule and how to reign,
We thus submit unto – our sovereign.
ALL Live, noble Helicane!
HELICANUS By honour's cause, forbear your suffrages.
If that you love Prince Pericles, forbear.
Take I your wish, I leap into the seas,

Where's hourly trouble for a minute's ease.
A twelvemonth longer let me entreat you
To forbear the absence of your king;
If in which time expir'd he not return,
I shall with aged patience bear your yoke.
But if I cannot win you to this love,
Go search like nobles, like noble subjects,
And in your search spend your adventurous worth;
Whom if you find, and win unto return,
You shall like diamonds sit about his crown.

1 LORD To wisdom he's a fool that will not yield;
And since Lord Helicane enjoineth us,
We with our travels will endeavour it.

HELICANUS Then you love us, we you, and we'll clasp hands:
When peers thus knit, a kingdom ever stands.

[*Exeunt.*

SCENE V. *Pentapolis. The palace.*

Enter SIMONIDES, reading of a letter, at one door. The Knights meet him.

1 KNIGHT Good morrow to the good Simonides.

SIMONIDES Knights, from my daughter this I let you know,
That for this twelvemonth she'll not undertake
A married life.
Her reason to herself is only known,
Which from her by no means can I get.

2 KNIGHT May we not get access to her, my lord?

SIMONIDES Faith, by no means; she hath so strictly tied her
To her chamber that it is impossible.
One twelve moons more she'll wear Diana's livery.
This by the eye of Cynthia hath she vow'd,
And on her virgin honour will not break it.

3 KNIGHT Loath to bid farewell, we take our leaves. [*Exeunt Knights.*

SIMONIDES So,
They are well despatch'd. Now to my daughter's letter.
She tells me here she'll wed the stranger knight,
Or never more to view nor day nor light.
'Tis well, mistress; your choice agrees with mine;
I like that well. Nay, how absolute she's in't,
Not minding whether I dislike or no!
Well, I do commend her choice;
And will no longer have it be delay'd.
Soft! here he comes: I must dissemble it.

Enter PERICLES.

PERICLES All fortune to the good Simonides!

SIMONIDES To you as much, sir! I am beholding to you
For your sweet music this last night. I do
Protest my ears were never better fed
With such delightful pleasing harmony.

PERICLES It is your Grace's pleasure to commend;
Not my desert.

SIMONIDES Sir, you are music's master.

PERICLES The worst of all her scholars, my good lord.

SIMONIDES Let me ask you one thing:
What do you think of my daughter, sir?

PERICLES A most virtuous princess.

SIMONIDES And she is fair too, is she not?

PERICLES As a fair day in summer – wondrous fair.

SIMONIDES Sir, my daughter thinks very well of you;
Ay, so well that you must be her master,
And she will be your scholar; therefore look to it.

PERICLES I am unworthy for her schoolmaster.

SIMONIDES She thinks not so; peruse this writing else.

PERICLES [*Aside*] What's here?
A letter, that she loves the knight of Tyre.
'Tis the king's subtlety to have my life. –
O, seek not to entrap me, gracious lord,
A stranger and distressed gentleman,
That never aim'd so high to love your daughter,
But bent all offices to honour her!

SIMONIDES Thou hast bewitch'd my daughter, and thou art
A villain.

PERICLES By the gods, I have not.
Never did thought of mine levy offence;
Nor never did my actions yet commence
A deed might gain her love or your displeasure.

SIMONIDES Traitor, thou liest.

PERICLES Traitor!

SIMONIDES Ay, traitor.

PERICLES Even in his throat – unless it be the King –
That calls me traitor I return the lie.

SIMONIDES [*Aside*] Now, by the gods, I do applaud his courage.

PERICLES My actions are as noble as my thoughts,
That never relish'd of a base descent.
I came unto your court for honour's cause,
And not to be a rebel to her state;
And he that otherwise accounts of me,
This sword shall prove he's honour's enemy.

SIMONIDES No?
Here comes my daughter, she can witness it.

Enter THAISA.

PERICLES Then, as you are as virtuous as fair,

Resolve your angry father if my tongue
Did e'er solicit, or my hand subscribe
To any syllable that made love to you.

THAISA Why, sir, say if you had,
Who takes offence at that would make me glad?

SIMONIDES Yea, mistress, are you so peremptory?
[*Aside*] I am glad on't with all my heart. –
I'll tame you; I'll bring you in subjection.
Will you, not having my consent,
Bestow your love and your affections
Upon a stranger? – [*Aside*] who, for aught I know,
May be, nor can I think the contrary,
As great in blood as I myself. –
Therefore, hear you, mistress: either frame
Your will to mine – and you, sir, hear you,
Either be rul'd by me – or I will make you –
Man and wife.
Nay, come, your hands and lips must seal it too;
And being join'd, I'll thus your hopes destroy,
And for further grief – God give you joy!
What, are you both pleas'd?

THAISA Yes, if you love me, sir.

PERICLES Even as my life my blood that fosters it.

SIMONIDES What, are you both agreed?

BOTH Yes, if't please your Majesty.

SIMONIDES It pleaseth me so well that I will see you wed;
And then, with what haste you can, get you to bed. [*Exeunt.*

ACT THREE

Enter GOWER.

GOWER Now sleep yslaked hath the rout;
No din but snores the house about,
Made louder by the o'er-fed breast
Of this most pompous marriage feast.
The cat, with eyne of burning coal,
Now couches fore the mouse's hole;
And crickets sing at the oven's mouth,
Aye the blither for their drouth.
Hymen hath brought the bride to bed,
Where, by the loss of maidenhead,
A babe is moulded. Be attent,
And time that is so briefly spent
With your fine fancies quaintly eche.
What's dumb in show I'll plain with speech.
Dumb Show.

Enter PERICLES and SIMONIDES at one door, with Attendants; a Messenger meets them, kneels, and gives Pericles a letter. Pericles shows it Simonides; the Lords kneel to Pericles. Then enter THAISA, with child, with LYCHORIDA, a nurse. The King shows her the letter; she rejoices. She and Pericles take leave of her father, and depart with Lychorida and their Attendants. Then exeunt Simonides and the rest.

By many a dern and painful perch
Of Pericles the careful search,
By the four opposing coigns
Which the world together joins,
Is made with all due diligence
That horse and sail and high expense
Can stead the quest. At last from Tyre –
Fame answering the most strange inquire –
To the court of King Simonides
Are letters brought, the tenour these:
Antiochus and his daughter dead,
The men of Tyrus on the head
Of Helicanus would set on
The crown of Tyre, but he will none.
The mutiny he there hastes t' oppress;
Says to 'em, if King Pericles
Come not home in twice six moons,
He, obedient to their dooms,
Will take the crown. The sum of this,
Brought hither to Pentapolis,
Y-ravished the regions round,
And every one with claps can sound
'Our heir-apparent is a king!
Who dream'd, who thought of such a thing?'
Brief, he must hence depart to Tyre.
His queen with child makes her desire –
Which who shall cross? – along to go.
Omit we all their dole and woe.
Lychorida, her nurse, she takes,
And so to sea. Their vessel shakes
On Neptune's billow; half the flood
Hath their keel cut: but fortune's mood
Varies again; the grizzled north
Disgorges such a tempest forth
That, as a duck for life that dives,
So up and down the poor ship drives.
The lady shrieks, and, well-a-near,
Does fall in travail with her fear;
And what ensues in this fell storm
Shall for itself itself perform.
I nill relate, action may
Conveniently the rest convey;
Which might not what by me is told.
In your imagination hold
This stage the ship, upon whose deck
The sea-toss'd Pericles appears to speak. [*Exit.*

SCENE I. *Enter PERICLES, a-shipboard.*

PERICLES Thou god of this great vast, rebuke these surges,
Which wash both heaven and hell; and thou that hast
Upon the winds command, bind them in brass,
Having call'd them from the deep! O, still
Thy deaf'ning dreadful thunders; gently quench
Thy nimble sulphurous flashes! – O, how, Lychorida,
How does my queen? – Thou stormest venomously;
Wilt thou spit all thyself? The seaman's whistle
Is as a whisper in the ears of death,
Unheard. – Lychorida! – Lucina, O
Divinest patroness, and midwife gentle
To those that cry by night, convey thy deity
Aboard our dancing boat; make swift the pangs
Of my queen's travails!

Enter LYCHORIDA, with an Infant.

Now, Lychorida!

LYCHORIDA Here is a thing too young for such a place,
Who, if it had conceit, would die, as I
Am like to do. Take in your arms this piece
Of your dead queen.

PERICLES How, how, Lychorida?

LYCHORIDA Patience, good sir; do not assist the storm.
Here's all that is left living of your queen –
A little daughter. For the sake of it,
Be manly, and take comfort.

PERICLES O you gods!
Why do you make us love your goodly gifts,
And snatch them straight away? We here below
Recall not what we give, and therein may
Use honour with you.

LYCHORIDA Patience, good sir, even for this charge.

PERICLES Now, mild may be thy life!
For a more blusterous birth had never babe;
Quiet and gentle thy conditions! for
Thou art the rudeliest welcome to this world
That ever was prince's child. Happy what follows!
Thou hast as chiding a nativity
As fire, air, water, earth, and heaven, can make,
To herald thee from the womb.
Even at the first thy loss is more than can
Thy portage quit with all thou canst find here.
Now the good gods throw their best eyes upon't!

Enter two Sailors.

1 SAILOR What courage, sir? God save you!

PERICLES Courage enough: I do not fear the flaw;
It hath done to me the worst. Yet, for the love
Of this poor infant, this fresh-new seafarer,
I would it would be quiet.

1 SAILOR Slack the bolins there. – Thou wilt not, wilt thou? Blow, and split thyself.

2 SAILOR But sea-room, an the brine and cloudy billow kiss the moon, I care not.

1 SAILOR Sir, your queen must overboard: the sea works high, the wind is loud, and will not lie till the ship be clear'd of the dead.

PERICLES That's your superstition.

1 SAILOR Pardon us, sir; with us at sea it hath been still observed, and we are strong in custom. Therefore briefly yield'er; for she must overboard straight.

PERICLES As you think meet. Most wretched queen!

LYCHORIDA Here she lies, sir.

PERICLES A terrible childbed hast thou had, my dear;
No light, no fire. Th' unfriendly elements
Forgot thee utterly; nor have I time
To give thee hallow'd to thy grave, but straight
Must cast thee, scarcely coffin'd, in the ooze;
Where, for a monument upon thy bones,
And aye-remaining lamps, the belching whale
And humming water must o'erwhelm thy corpse,
Lying with simple shells. O Lychorida,
Bid Nestor bring me spices, ink and paper,
My casket and my jewels; and bid Nicander
Bring me the satin coffer. Lay the babe
Upon the pillow. Hie thee, whiles I say
A priestly farewell to her. Suddenly, woman.
[*Exit Lychorida.*

2 SAILOR Sir, we have a chest beneath the hatches, caulk'd and bitumed ready.

PERICLES I thank thee. Mariner, say what coast is this?

2 SAILOR We are near Tharsus.

PERICLES Thither, gentle mariner,
Alter thy course for Tyre. When canst thou reach it?

2 SAILOR By break of day, if the wind cease.

PERICLES O, make for Tharsus!
There will I visit Cleon, for the babe
Cannot hold out to Tyrus; there I'll leave it
At careful nursing. Go thy ways, good mariner:
I'll bring the body presently. [*Exeunt.*

SCENE II. *Ephesus. Cerimon's house.*

Enter CERIMON, with a Servant, and some Persons who have been shipwrecked.

CERIMON Philemon, ho!

Enter PHILEMON.

PHILEMON Doth my lord call?
CERIMON Get fire and meat for these poor men.
'T'as been a turbulent and stormy night.
SERVANT I have been in many; but such a night as this,
Till now, I ne'er endured.
CERIMON Your master will be dead ere you return;
There's nothing can be minist'red to nature
That can recover him. [*To Philemon*] Give this to the pothecary,
And tell me how it works. [*Exeunt all but Cerimon.*

Enter two Gentlemen.

1 GENTLEMAN Good morrow.
2 GENTLEMAN Good morrow to your lordship.
CERIMON Gentlemen, why do you stir so early?
1 GENTLEMAN Sir,
Our lodgings, standing bleak upon the sea,
Shook as the earth did quake;
The very principals did seem to rend,
And all to topple. Pure surprise and fear
Made me to quit the house.
2 GENTLEMAN That is the cause we trouble you so early;
'Tis not our husbandry.
CERIMON O, you say well.
1 GENTLEMAN But I much marvel that your lordship, having
Rich tire about you, should at these early hours
Shake off the golden slumber of repose.
'Tis most strange
Nature should be so conversant with pain,
Being thereto not compell'd.
CERIMON I hold it ever
Virtue and cunning were endowments greater
Than nobleness and riches: careless heirs
May the two latter darken and expend;
But immortality attends the former,
Making a man a god. 'Tis known I ever
Have studied physic, through which secret art,
By turning o'er authorities, I have,
Together with my practice, made familiar
To me and to my aid the blest infusions
That dwell in vegetives, in metals, stones;
And I can speak of the disturbances
That nature works, and of her cures; which doth give me
A more content in course of true delight
Than to be thirsty after tottering honour,
Or tie my treasure up in silken bags,
To please the fool and death.
2 GENTLEMAN Your honour has through Ephesus pour'd forth
Your charity, and hundreds call themselves
Your creatures, who by you have been restor'd:
And not your knowledge, your personal pain, but even
Your purse, still open, hath built Lord Cerimon
Such strong renown as time shall never raze.

Enter two or three Servants with a chest.

1 SERVANT So, lift there.
CERIMON What's that?
1 SERVANT Sir, even now did the sea toss up upon our shore this chest. 'Tis of some wreck.
CERIMON Set't down, let's look upon't.
2 GENTLEMAN 'Tis like a coffin, sir.
CERIMON Whate'er it be,
'Tis wondrous heavy. Wrench it open straight.
If the sea's stomach be o'ercharg'd with gold,
'Tis a good constraint of fortune it belches upon us.
2 GENTLEMAN 'Tis so, my lord.
CERIMON How close 'tis caulk'd and bitumed!
Did the sea cast it up?
1 SERVANT I never saw so huge a billow, sir, as toss'd it upon shore.
CERIMON Wrench it open. Soft! It smells most sweetly in my sense.
2 GENTLEMAN A delicate odour.
CERIMON As ever hit my nostril. So, up with it.
O you most potent gods! What's here?
A corse!
1 GENTLEMAN Most strange!
CERIMON Shrouded in cloth of state; balm'd and entreasur'd with full bags of spices. A passport too. Apollo, perfect me in the characters! [*Reads from a scroll.*

Here I give to understand –
If e'er this coffin drives a-land –
I, King Pericles, have lost
This queen, worth all our mundane cost.
Who finds her, give her burying;
She was the daughter of a king.
Besides this treasure for a fee,
The gods requite his charity!

If thou livest, Pericles, thou hast a heart
That ever cracks for woe! This chanc'd to-night.
2 GENTLEMAN Most likely, sir.
CERIMON Nay, certainly to-night;
For look how fresh she looks! They were too rough
That threw her in the sea. Make a fire within.
Fetch hither all my boxes in my closet. [*Exit a Servant.*
Death may usurp on nature many hours,

And yet the fire of life kindle again
The o'erpress'd spirits. I heard of an Egyptian
That had nine hours lien dead,
Who was by good appliance recovered.

Re-enter a Servant, with boxes, napkins, and fire.

Well said, well said! The fire and cloths.
The rough and woeful music that we have,
Cause it to sound, beseech you.
The vial once more. How thou stirr'st, thou block!
The music there! I pray you give her air.
Gentlemen,
This queen will live; nature awakes; a warmth
Breathes out of her. She hath not been entranc'd
Above five hours. See how she gins to blow
Into life's flower again!

1 GENTLEMAN The heavens,
Through you, increase our wonder, and set up
Your fame for ever.

CERIMON She is alive. Behold,
Her eyelids, cases to those heavenly jewels
Which Pericles hath lost, begin to part
Their fringes of bright gold; the diamonds
Of a most praised water do appear,
To make the world twice rich. Live, and make
Us weep to hear your fate, fair creature,
Rare as you seem to be. [*She moves.*

THAISA O dear Diana, where am I?
Where's my lord? What world is this?

2 GENTLEMAN Is not this strange?

1 GENTLEMAN Most rare.

CERIMON Hush, my gentle neighbours!
Lend me your hands: to the next chamber bear her;
Get linen. Now this matter must be look'd to,
For her relapse is mortal.
Come, come; and Aesculapius guide us!

[*Exeunt, carrying her away.*

SCENE III. *Tharsus. Cleon's house.*

Enter PERICLES, CLEON, DIONYZA, and LYCHORIDA with MARINA in her arms.

PERICLES Most honour'd Cleon, I must needs be gone;
My twelve months are expir'd, and Tyrus stands
In a litigious peace. You and your lady
Take from my heart all thankfulness! The gods
Make up the rest upon you!

CLEON Your shafts of fortune, though they hurt you mortally,
Yet glance full wand'ringly on us.

DIONYZA O your sweet queen!
That the strict Fates had pleas'd you had brought her hither,
To have bless'd mine eyes with her!

PERICLES We cannot but obey
The powers above us. Could I range and roar
As doth the sea she lies in, yet the end
Must be as 'tis. My gentle babe Marina, whom,
For she was born at sea, I have nam'd so, here
I charge your charity withal, leaving her
The infant of your care; beseeching you
To give her princely training, that she may
Be manner'd as she is born.

CLEON Fear not, my lord, but think
Your grace, that fed my country with your corn,
For which the people's prayers still fall upon you,
Must in your child be thought on. If neglection
Should therein make me vile, the common body,
By you reliev'd, would force me to my duty.
But if to that my nature need a spur,
The gods revenge it upon me and mine
To the end of generation!

PERICLES I believe you;
Your honour and your goodness teach me to't
Without your vows. Till she be married, madam,
By bright Diana, whom we honour all,
Unscissor'd shall this hair of mine remain,
Though I show ill in't. So I take my leave.
Good madam, make me blessed in your care
In bringing up my child.

DIONYZA I have one myself,
Who shall not be more dear to my respect
Than yours, my lord.

PERICLES Madam, my thanks and prayers.

CLEON We'll bring your Grace e'en to the edge o' th' shore,
Then give you up to the mask'd Neptune and
The gentlest winds of heaven.

PERICLES I will embrace
Your offer. Come, dearest madam. O, no tears,
Lychorida, no tears.
Look to your little mistress, on whose grace
You may depend hereafter. Come, my lord.

[*Exeunt.*

SCENE IV. *Ephesus. Cerimon's house.*

Enter CERIMON and THAISA.

CERIMON Madam, this letter, and some certain jewels,
Lay with you in your coffer; which are
At your command. Know you the character?

THAISA It is my lord's.
That I was shipp'd at sea I will remember,
Even on my eaning time; but whether there
Delivered, by the holy gods,
I cannot rightly say. But since King Pericles,

My wedded lord, I ne'er shall see again,
A vestal livery will I take me to,
And never more have joy.

CERIMON Madam, if this you purpose as ye speak,
Diana's temple is not distant far,
Where you may abide till your date expire.
Moreover, if you please, a niece of mine
Shall there attend you.

THAISA My recompense is thanks, that's all;
Yet my good will is great, though the gift small.

[Exeunt.

ACT FOUR

Enter GOWER.

GOWER Imagine Pericles arriv'd at Tyre,
Welcom'd and settled to his own desire.
His woeful queen we leave at Ephesus,
Unto Diana there a votaress.
Now to Marina bend your mind,
Whom our fast-growing scene must find
At Tharsus, and by Cleon train'd
In music, letters; who hath gain'd
Of education all the grace,
Which makes her both the heart and place
Of general wonder. But, alack,
That monster Envy, oft the wrack
Of earned praise, Marina's life
Seeks to take off by treason's knife.
And in this kind hath our Cleon
One daughter, and a wench full grown,
Even ripe for marriage-rite; this maid
Hight Philoten; and it is said
For certain in our story, she
Would ever with Marina be.
Be't when she weav'd the sleided silk
With fingers long, small, white as milk;
Or when she would with sharp needle wound
The cambric, which she made more sound
By hurting it; or when to th' lute
She sung, and made the night-bird mute,
That still records with moan; or when
She would with rich and constant pen
Vail to her mistress Dian; still
This Philoten contends in skill
With absolute Marina. So
The dove of Paphos might with the crow
Vie feathers white. Marina gets
All praises, which are paid as debts,
And not as given. This so darks
In Philoten all graceful marks
That Cleon's wife, with envy rare,
A present murderer does prepare
For good Marina, that her daughter
Might stand peerless by this slaughter.
The sooner her vile thoughts to stead,
Lychorida, our nurse, is dead;
And cursed Dionyza hath
The pregnant instrument of wrath
Prest for this blow. The unborn event
I do commend to your content;
Only I carry winged time
Post on the lame feet of my rhyme;
Which never could I so convey
Unless your thoughts went on my way.
Dionyza does appear,
With Leonine, a murderer. *[Exit.*

SCENE I. *Tharsus. An open place near the seashore.*

Enter DIONYZA and LEONINE.

DIONYZA Thy oath remember; thou hast sworn to do't.
'Tis but a blow, which never shall be known.
Thou canst not do a thing in the world so soon
To yield thee so much profit. Let not conscience,
Which is but cold, inflaming love in thy bosom,
Inflame too nicely; nor let pity, which
Even women have cast off, melt thee, but be
A soldier to thy purpose.

LEONINE I will do't; but yet she is a goodly creature.

DIONYZA The fitter, then, the gods should have her.
Here she comes weeping for her only mistress' death.
Thou art resolv'd?

LEONINE I am resolv'd.

Enter MARINA with a basket of flowers.

MARINA No, I will rob Tellus of her weed,
To strew thy green with flowers. The yellows, blues,
The purple violets, and marigolds,
Shall as a carpet hang upon thy grave
While summer days do last. Ay me! poor maid,
Born in a tempest, when my mother died,
This world to me is like a lasting storm,
Whirring me from my friends.

DIONYZA How now, Marina! Why do you keep alone?
How chance my daughter is not with you? Do not
Consume your blood with sorrowing; you have
A nurse of me. Lord, how your favour's chang'd

With this unprofitable woe! Come,
Give me your flowers. On the sea margent
Walk with Leonine; the air is quick there,
And it pierces and sharpens the stomach. Come,
Leonine, take her by the arm, walk with her.

MARINA No, I pray you;
I'll not bereave you of your servant.

DIONYZA Come, come;
I love the king your father, and yourself,
With more than foreign heart. We every day
Expect him here. When he shall come, and find
Our paragon to all reports thus blasted,
He will repent the breadth of his great voyage;
Blame both my lord and me that we have taken
No care to your best courses. Go, I pray you,
Walk, and be cheerful once again; reserve
That excellent complexion which did steal
The eyes of young and old. Care not for me;
I can go home alone.

MARINA Well, I will go;
But yet I have no desire to it.

DIONYZA Come, come, I know 'tis good for you.
Walk half an hour, Leonine, at the least.
Remember what I have said.

LEONINE I warrant you, madam.

DIONYZA I'll leave you, my sweet lady, for a while.
Pray walk softly; do not heat your blood.
What! I must have care of you.

MARINA My thanks, sweet madam.

[Exit Dionyza.

Is this wind westerly that blows?

LEONINE South-west.

MARINA When I was born the wind was north.

LEONINE Was't so?

MARINA My father, as nurse says, did never fear,
But cried 'Good seamen!' to the sailors, galling
His kingly hands hauling ropes;
And, clasping to the mast, endur'd a sea
That almost burst the deck.

LEONINE When was this?

MARINA When I was born.
Never was waves nor wind more violent;
And from the ladder-tackle washes off
A canvas-climber. 'Ha!' says one 'wolt out?'
And with a dropping industry they skip
From stern to stern; the boatswain whistles, and
The master calls, and trebles their confusion.

LEONINE Come, say your prayers.

MARINA What mean you?

LEONINE If you require a little space for prayer,
I grant it. Pray; but be not tedious, for
The gods are quick of ear, and I am sworn
To do my work with haste.

MARINA Why will you kill me?

LEONINE To satisfy my lady.

MARINA Why would she have me kill'd?
Now, as I can remember, by my troth,
I never did her hurt in all my life.
I never spake bad word, nor did ill turn
To any living creature. Believe me, la,
I never kill'd a mouse, nor hurt a fly;
I trod upon a worm against my will,
But I wept for it. How have I offended,
Wherein my death might yield her any profit,
Or my life imply her any danger?

LEONINE My commission
Is not to reason of the deed, but do't.

MARINA You will not do't for all the world, I hope.
You are well-favour'd, and your looks foreshow
You have a gentle heart. I saw you lately
When you caught hurt in parting two that fought.
Good sooth, it show'd well in you. Do so now:
Your lady seeks my life; come you between,
And save poor me, the weaker.

LEONINE I am sworn,
And will dispatch. *[Seizes her.*

Enter Pirates.

1 PIRATE Hold, villain!

[Leonine runs away.

2 PIRATE A prize! a prize!

3 PIRATE Half part, mates, half part!
Come, let's have her aboard suddenly.

[Exeunt Pirates with Marina.

Re-enter LEONINE.

LEONINE These roguing thieves serve the great pirate Valdes,
And they have seiz'd Marina. Let her go;
There's no hope she will return. I'll swear she's dead
And thrown into the sea. But I'll see further.
Perhaps they will but please themselves upon her,
Not carry her aboard. If she remain,
Whom they have ravish'd must by me be slain.

[Exit.

SCENE II. *Mytilene. A brothel.*

Enter Pander, Bawd, and BOULT.

PANDER Boult!

BOULT Sir?

PANDER Search the market narrowly. Mytilene is full of gallants. We lost too much money this mart by being too wenchless.

BAWD We were never so much out of creatures. We have but poor three, and they can do no more than they can do; and they with continual action are even as good as rotten.

PANDER Therefore let's have fresh ones, whate'er we pay for them. If there be not a conscience to be us'd in every trade, we shall never prosper.

BAWD Thou say'st true; 'tis not our bringing up of poor bastards – as, I think, I have brought up some eleven –

BOULT Ay, to eleven; and brought them down again. But shall I search the market?

BAWD What else, man? The stuff we have, a strong wind will blow it to pieces, they are so pitifully sodden.

PANDER Thou sayest true; they are too unwholesome, o' conscience. The poor Transylvanian is dead that lay with the little baggage.

BOULT Ay, she quickly poop'd him; she made him roast meat for worms. But I'll go search the market. *[Exit.*

PANDER Three or four thousand chequins were as pretty a proportion to live quietly, and so give over.

BAWD Why to give over, I pray you? Is it a shame to get when we are old?

PANDER O, our credit comes not in like the commodity, not the commodity wages not with the danger; therefore, if in our youths we could pick up some pretty estate, 'twere not amiss to keep our door hatch'd. Besides, the sore terms we stand upon with the gods will be strong with us for giving o'er.

BAWD Come, other sorts offend as well as we.

PANDER As well as we! Ay, and better too; we offend worse. Neither is our profession any trade; it's no calling. But here comes Boult.

Re-enter BOULT, with the Pirates and MARINA.

BOULT *[To Marina]* Come your ways. – My masters, you say she's a virgin?

1 PIRATE O, sir, we doubt it not.

BOULT Master, I have gone through for this piece you see. If you like her, so; if not, I have lost my earnest.

BAWD Boult, has she any qualities?

BOULT She has a good face, speaks well, and has excellent good clothes; there's no farther necessity of qualities can make her be refus'd.

BAWD What's her price, Boult?

BOULT I cannot be bated one doit of a thousand pieces.

PANDER Well, follow me, my masters; you shall have your money presently. Wife, take her in; instruct her what she has to do, that she may not be raw in her entertainment.

[Exeunt Pander and Pirates.

BAWD Boult, take you the marks of her – the colour of her hair, complexion, height, her age, with warrant of her virginity; and cry 'He that will give most shall have her first'. Such a maidenhead were no cheap thing, if men were as they have been. Get this done as I command you.

BOULT Performance shall follow. *[Exit.*

MARINA Alack that Leonine was so slack, so slow!
He should have struck, not spoke; or that these pirates,
Not enough barbarous, had not o'erboard thrown me
For to seek my mother!

BAWD Why lament you, pretty one?

MARINA That I am pretty.

BAWD Come, the gods have done their part in you.

MARINA I accuse them not.

BAWD You are light into my hands, where you are like to live.

MARINA The more my fault
To scape his hands where I was like to die.

BAWD Ay, and you shall live in pleasure.

MARINA No.

BAWD Yes, indeed shall you, and taste gentlemen of all fashions. You shall fare well; you shall have the difference of all complexions. What! do you stop your ears?

MARINA Are you a woman?

BAWD What would you have me be, an I be not a woman?

MARINA An honest woman, or not a woman.

BAWD Marry, whip thee, gosling! I think I shall have something to do with you. Come, you're a young foolish sapling, and must be bow'd as I would have you.

MARINA The gods defend me!

BAWD If it please the gods to defend you by men, then men must comfort you, men must feed you, men must stir you up. Boult's return'd.

Re-enter BOULT.

Now, sir, hast thou cried her through the market?

BOULT I have cried her almost to the number of her hairs; I have drawn her picture with my voice.

BAWD And I prithee tell me how dost thou find the inclination of the people, especially of the younger sort?

BOULT Faith, they listened to me as they would have hearkened to their father's testament. There was a Spaniard's mouth so wat'red that he went to bed to her very description.

BAWD We shall have him here to-morrow with his best ruff on.

BOULT To-night, to-night. But, mistress, do you

know the French knight that cowers i' th' hams?

BAWD Who? Monsieur Veroles?

BOULT Ay, he; he offered to cut a caper at the proclamation; but he made a groan at it, and swore he would see her to-morrow.

BAWD Well, well; as for him, he brought his disease hither: here he does but repair it. I know he will come in our shadow to scatter his crowns in the sun.

BOULT Well, if we had of every nation a traveller, we should lodge them with this sign.

BAWD [*To Marina*] Pray you, come hither awhile. You have fortunes coming upon you. Mark me: you must seem to do that fearfully which you commit willingly; to despise profit where you have most gain. To weep that you live as ye do makes pity in your lovers; seldom but that pity begets you a good opinion, and that opinion a mere profit.

MARINA I understand you not.

BOULT O, take her home, mistress, take her home. These blushes of hers must be quench'd with some present practice.

BAWD Thou sayest true, i' faith, so they must; for your bride goes to that with shame which is her way to go with warrant.

BOULT Faith, some do, and some do not. But, mistress, if I have bargain'd for the joint –

BAWD Thou mayst cut a morsel off the spit.

BOULT I may so.

BAWD Who should deny it? Come, young one, I like the manner of your garments well.

BOULT Ay, by my faith, they shall not be chang'd yet.

BAWD Boult, spend thou that in the town; report what a sojourner we have; you'll lose nothing by custom. When nature fram'd this piece she meant thee a good turn; therefore say what a paragon she is, and thou hast the harvest out of thine own report.

BOULT I warrant you, mistress, thunder shall not so awake the beds of eels as my giving out her beauty stir up the lewdly inclined. I'll bring home some to-night.

BAWD Come your ways; follow me.

MARINA If fires be hot, knives sharp, or waters deep,
Untied I still my virgin knot will keep.
Diana aid my purpose!

BAWD What have we to do with Diana?
Pray you will you go with us? [*Exeunt.*

SCENE III. *Tharsus. Cleon's house.*

Enter CLEON and DIONYZA.

DIONYZA Why are you foolish? Can it be undone?

CLEON O Dionyza, such a piece of slaughter
The sun and moon ne'er look'd upon!

DIONYZA I think
You'll turn a child again.

CLEON Were I chief lord of all this spacious world,
I'd give it to undo the deed. O lady,
Much less in blood than virtue, yet a princess
To equal any single crown o' th' earth
I' th' justice of compare! O villain Leonine!
Whom thou hast pois'ned too.
If thou hadst drunk to him, 't had been a kindness
Becoming well thy fact. What canst thou say
When noble Pericles shall demand his child?

DIONYZA That she is dead. Nurses are not the Fates,
To foster it, nor ever to preserve.
She died at night; I'll say so. Who can cross it?
Unless you play the pious innocent,
And for an honest attribute cry out
'She died by foul play'.

CLEON O, go to. Well, well.
Of all the faults beneath the heavens the gods
Do like this worst.

DIONYZA Be one of those that thinks
The petty wrens of Tharsus will fly hence,
And open this to Pericles. I do shame
To think of what a noble strain you are,
And of how coward a spirit.

CLEON To such proceeding
Who ever but his approbation added,
Though not his prime consent, he did not flow
From honourable sources.

DIONYZA Be it so, then.
Yet none does know, but you, how she came dead,
Nor none can know, Leonine being gone.
She did distain my child, and stood between
Her and her fortunes. None would look on her,
But cast their gazes on Marina's face;
Whilst ours was blurted at, and held a mawkin,
Not worth the time of day. It pierc'd me thorough;
And though you call my course unnatural,
You not your child well loving, yet I find
It greets me as an enterprise of kindness
Perform'd to your sole daughter.

CLEON Heavens forgive it!

DIONYZA And as for Pericles,
What should he say? We wept after her hearse,
And yet we mourn; her monument
Is almost finish'd, and her epitaphs
In glittering golden characters express
A general praise to her, and care in us
At whose expense 'tis done.

CLEON Thou art like the harpy,

Which, to betray, dost, with thine angel's face,
Seize with thine eagle's talons.

DIONYZA You are like one that superstitiously
Doth swear to the gods that winter kills the flies;
But yet I know you'll do as I advise. [*Exeunt.*

SCENE IV. *Before Marina's monument at Tharsus.*

Enter GOWER.

GOWER Thus time we waste, and longest leagues make short;
Sail seas in cockles, have an wish but for't;
Making, to take our imagination,
From bourn to bourn, region to region.
By you being pardon'd, we commit no crime
To use one language in each several clime
Where our scenes seem to live. I do beseech you
To learn of me, who stand i' th' gaps to teach you
The stages of our story. Pericles
Is now again thwarting the wayward seas,
Attended on by many a lord and knight,
To see his daughter, all his life's delight.
Old Helicanus goes along. Behind
Is left to govern it, you bear in mind,
Old Escanes, whom Helicanus late
Advanc'd in time to great and high estate.
Well-sailing ships and bounteous winds have brought
This king to Tharsus – think this pilot thought;
So with his steerage shall your thoughts grow on –
To fetch his daughter home, who first is gone.
Like motes and shadows see them move awhile;
Your ears unto your eyes I'll reconcile.

Dumb show.

Enter PERICLES, at one door, with all his Train: CLEON and DIONYZA at the other. Cleon shows Pericles the tomb of Marina, whereat Pericles makes lamentation, puts on sackcloth, and in a mighty passion departs. Then exeunt Cleon and Dionyza.

See how belief may suffer by foul show!
This borrowed passion stands for true old woe;
And Pericles, in sorrow all devour'd,
With sighs shot through and biggest tears o'ershower'd,
Leaves Tharsus, and again embarks. He swears
Never to wash his face nor cut his hairs;
He puts on sackcloth, and to sea. He bears
A tempest which his mortal vessel tears,
And yet he rides it out. Now please you wit
The epitaph is for Marina writ.
By wicked Dionyza. [*Reads the inscription on Marina's monument.*

'The fairest, sweetest, and best lies here,
Who withered in her spring of year.
She was of Tyrus the King's daughter,
On whom foul death hath made this slaughter;
Marina was she call'd; and at her birth,
Thetis, being proud, swallowed some part o' th' earth;
Therefore the earth, fearing to be o'er-flowed,
Hath Thetis' birth-child on the heavens bestowed;
Wherefore she does – and swears she'll never stint –
Make raging battery upon shores of flint.'
No visor does become black villainy
So well as soft and tender flattery.
Let Pericles believe his daughter's dead,
And bear his courses to be ordered
By Lady Fortune; while our scene must play
His daughter's woe and heavy well-a-day
In her unholy service. Patience, then,
And think you now are all in Mytilen. [*Exit.*

SCENE V. *Mytilene. A street before the brothel.*

Enter, from the brothel, two Gentlemen.

1 GENTLEMAN Did you ever hear the like?

2 GENTLEMAN No, nor never shall do in such a place as this, she being once gone.

1 GENTLEMAN But to have divinity preach'd there! Did you ever dream of such a thing?

2 GENTLEMAN No, no. Come, I am for no more bawdy-houses. Shall's go hear the vestals sing?

1 GENTLEMAN I'll do anything now that is virtuous; but I am out of the road of rutting for ever. [*Exeunt.*

SCENE VI. *Mytilene. A room in the brothel.*

Enter Pander, Bawd, and BOULT.

PANDER Well, I had rather than twice the worth of her she had ne'er come here.

BAWD Fie, fie, upon her! She's able to freeze the god Priapus, and undo a whole generation. We must either get her ravished or be rid of her. When she should do for clients her fitment, and do me the kindness of our profession, she has me her quirks, her reasons, her master-reasons, her prayers, her knees; that she would make a puritan of the devil, if he should cheapen a kiss of her.

BOULT Faith, I must ravish her, or she'll disfurnish us of all our cavalleria and make our swearers priests.

PANDER Now the pox upon her green-sickness for me!

BAWD Faith there's no way to be rid on't but by

the way to the pox. Here comes the Lord Lysimachus disguised.

BOULT We should have both lord and lown, if the peevish baggage would but give way to customers.

Enter LYSIMACHUS.

LYSIMACHUS How now! How a dozen of virginities?

BAWD Now, the gods to bless your Honour!

BOULT I am glad to see your Honour in good health.

LYSIMACHUS You may so; 'tis the better for you that your resorters stand upon sound legs. How now! Wholesome iniquity have you, that a man may deal withal and defy the surgeon?

BAWD We have here one, sir, if she would – but there never came her like in Mytilene.

LYSIMACHUS If she'd do the deed of darkness, thou wouldst say.

BAWD Your Honour knows what 'tis to say well enough.

LYSIMACHUS Well, call forth, call forth.

BOULT For flesh and blood, sir, white and red, you shall see a rose; and she were a rose indeed, if she had but –

LYSIMACHUS What, prithee?

BOULT O, sir, I can be modest.

LYSIMACHUS That dignifies the renown of a bawd no less than it gives a good report to a number to be chaste. [*Exit Boult.*

BAWD Here comes that which grows to the stalk – never plucked yet, I can assure you.

Re-enter BOULT with MARINA.

Is she not a fair crature?

LYSIMACHUS Faith, she would serve after a long voyage at sea. Well, there's for you. Leave us.

BAWD I beseech your Honour, give me leave: a word, and I'll have done presently.

LYSIMACHUS I beseech you, do.

BAWD [*Aside to Marina*] First, I would have you note this is an honourable man.

MARINA I desire to find him so, that I may worthily note him.

BAWD Next, he's the governor of this country, and a man whom I am bound to.

MARINA If he govern the country, you are bound to him indeed; but how honourable he is in that I know not.

BAWD Pray you, without any more virginal fencing, will you use him kindly? He will line your apron with gold.

MARINA What he will do graciously I will thankfully receive.

LYSIMACHUS Ha' you done?

BAWD My lord, she's not pac'd yet; you must take some pains to work her to your manage. Come, we will leave his Honour and her together. Go thy ways. [*Exeunt Bawd, Pander, and Boult.*

LYSIMACHUS Now, pretty one, how long have you been at this trade?

MARINA What trade, sir?

LYSIMACHUS Why, I cannot name't but I shall offend.

MARINA I cannot be offended with my trade. Please you to name it.

LYSIMACHUS How long have you been of this profession?

MARINA E'er since I can remember.

LYSIMACHUS Did you go to't so young? Were you a gamester at five or at seven?

MARINA Earlier too, sir, if now I be one.

LYSIMACHUS Why, the house you dwell in proclaims you to be a creature of sale.

MARINA Do you know this house to be a place of such resort, and will come into't? I hear say you're of honourable parts, and are the governor of this place.

LYSIMACHUS Why, hath your principal made known unto you who I am?

MARINA Who is my principal?

LYSIMACHUS Why, your herb-woman; she that sets seeds and roots of shame and iniquity. O, you have heard something of my power, and so stand aloof for more serious wooing. But I protest to thee, pretty one, my authority shall not see thee, or else look friendly upon thee. Come, bring me to some private place. Come, come.

MARINA If you were born to honour, show it now;
If put upon you, make the judgment good
That thought you worthy of it.

LYSIMACHUS How's this? how's this? Some more; be sage.

MARINA For me,
That am a maid, though most ungentle fortune
Have plac'd me in this sty, where, since I came,
Diseases have been sold dearer than physic –
That the gods
Would set me free from this unhallowed place,
Though they did change me to the meanest bird
That flies i' th' purer air!

LYSIMACHUS I did not think
Thou couldst have spoke so well; ne'er dreamt thou couldst.
Had I brought hither a corrupted mind,
Thy speech had altered it. Hold, here's gold for thee:
Persever in that clear way thou goest,
And the gods strengthen thee!

MARINA The good gods preserve you!

LYSIMACHUS For me, be you thoughten

That I came with no ill intent; for to me
The very doors and windows savour vilely.
Fare thee well. Thou art a piece of virtue, and
I doubt not but thy training hath been noble.
Hold, here's more gold for thee.
A curse upon him, die he like a thief,
That robs thee of thy goodness! If thou dost
Hear from me, it shall be for thy good.

Re-enter BOULT.

BOULT I beseech your Honour, one piece for me.

LYSIMACHUS Avaunt, thou damned door keeper!
Your house, but for this virgin that doth prop it,
Would sink and overwhelm you. Away! [*Exit.*

BOULT How's this? We must take another course with you. If your peevish chastity, which is not worth a breakfast in the cheapest country under the cope, shall undo a whole household, let me be gelded like a spaniel. Come your ways.

MARINA Whither would you have me?

BOULT I must have your maidenhead taken off, or the common hangman shall execute it. Come your ways. We'll have no more gentlemen driven away. Come your ways, I say.

Re-enter BAWD.

BAWD How now! What's the matter?

BOULT Worse and worse, mistress; she has here spoken holy words to the Lord Lysimachus.

BAWD O abominable!

BOULT She makes our profession as it were to stink afore the face of the gods.

BAWD Marry, hang her up for ever!

BOULT The nobleman would have dealt with her like a nobleman, and she sent him away as cold as a snowball; saying his prayers too.

BAWD Boult, take her away; use her at thy pleasure. Crack the glass of her virginity, and make the rest malleable.

BOULT An if she were a thornier piece of ground than she is, she shall be ploughed.

MARINA Hark, hark, you gods!

BAWD She conjures. Away with her. Would she had never come within my doors! Marry, hang you! She's born to undo us. Will you not go the way of womenkind? Marry, come up, my dish of chastity with rosemary and bays! [*Exit.*

BOULT Come, mistress; come your ways with me.

MARINA Whither wilt thou have me?

BOULT To take from you the jewel you hold so dear.

MARINA Prithee tell me one thing first.

BOULT Come now, your one thing.

MARINA What canst thou wish thine enemy to be?

BOULT Why, I could wish him to be my master, or, rather, my mistress.

MARINA Neither of these are so bad as thou art,
Since they do better thee in their command.
Thou hold'st a place for which the pained'st fiend
Of hell would not in reputation change;
Thou art the damned doorkeeper to every
Coistrel that comes inquiring for his Tib;
To the choleric fisting of every rogue
Thy ear is liable; thy food is such
As hath been belch'd on by infected lungs.

BOULT What would you have me do? Go to the wars, would you, where a man may serve seven years for the loss of a leg, and have not money enough in the end to buy him a wooden one?

MARINA Do anything but this thou doest. Empty
Old receptacles, or common shores, of filth;
Serve by indenture to the common hangman.
Any of these ways are yet better than this;
For what thou professest, a baboon, could he speak,
Would own a name too dear. That the gods
Would safely deliver me from this place!
Here, here's gold for thee.
If that thy master would gain by me,
Proclaim that I can sing, weave, sew, and dance,
With other virtues which I'll keep from boast;
And I will undertake all these to teach.
I doubt not but this populous city will
Yield many scholars.

BOULT But can you teach all this you speak of?

MARINA Prove that I cannot, take me home again
And prostitute me to the basest groom
That doth frequent your house.

BOULT Well, I will see what I can do for thee. If I can place thee, I will.

MARINA But amongst honest women?

BOULT Faith, my acquaintance lies little amongst them. But since my master and mistress have bought you, there's no going but by their consent. Therefore I will make them acquainted with your purpose, and I doubt not but I shall find them tractable enough. Come, I'll do for thee what I can; come your ways. [*Exeunt.*

ACT FIVE

Enter GOWER.

GOWER Marina thus the brothel scapes and chances
Into an honest house, our story says.
She sings like one immortal, and she dances
As goddess-like to her admired lays;
Deep clerks she dumbs; and with her needle composes
Nature's own shape of bud, bird, branch, or berry,
That even her art sisters the natural roses;
Her inkle, silk, twin with the rubied cherry;
That pupils lacks she none of noble race,
Who pour their bounty on her; and her gain
She gives the cursed bawd. Here we her place;
And to her father turn our thoughts again,
Where we left him on the sea. We there him lost;
Whence, driven before the winds, he is arriv'd
Here where his daughter dwells; and on this coast
Suppose him now at anchor. The city striv'd
God Neptune's annual feast to keep; from whence
Lysimachus our Tyrian ship espies,
His banners sable, trimm'd with rich expense;
And to him in his barge with fervour hies.
In your supposing once more put your sight.
Of heavy Pericles, think this his bark;
Where what is done in action, more, if might,
Shall be discover'd; please you sit and hark.
[*Exit.*

SCENE I. *On board Pericles' ship, off Mytilene. A pavilion on deck with a curtain before it; Pericles within it, reclining on a couch. A barge lying beside the Tyrian vessel.*

Enter two Sailors, one belonging to the Tyrian vessel, the other to the barge; to them HELICANUS.

TYRIAN SAILOR [*To the Sailor of Mytilene*]
Where is Lord Helicanus? He can resolve you.
O, here he is.
Sir, there is a barge put off from Mytilene,
And in it is Lysimachus the Governor,
Who craves to come aboard. What is your will?

HELICANUS That he have his. Call up some gentlemen.

TYRIAN SAILOR Ho, gentlemen! my lord calls.

Enter two or three Gentlemen.

1 GENTLEMAN Doth your lordship call?

HELICANUS Gentlemen, there is some of worth would come aboard;
I pray greet him fairly. [*The Gentlemen and the two Sailors descend, and go on board the barge.*

Enter, from thence, LYSIMACHUS and Lords, with the Gentlemen and the two Sailors.

TYRIAN SAILOR Sir,
This is the man that can, in aught you would,
Resolve you.

LYSIMACHUS Hail, reverend sir! The gods preserve you!

HELICANUS And you, sir, to outlive the age I am,
And die as I would do.

LYSIMACHUS You wish me well.
Being on shore, honouring of Neptune's triumphs,
Seeing this goodly vessel ride before us,
I made to it, to know of whence you are.

HELICANUS First, what is your place?

LYSIMACHUS I am the Governor
Of this place you lie before.

HELICANUS Sir,
Our vessel is of Tyre, in it the King;
A man who for this three months hath not spoken
To any one, nor taken sustenance
But to prorogue his grief.

LYSIMACHUS Upon what ground is his distemperature?

HELICANUS 'Twould be too tedious to repeat;
But the main grief springs from the loss
Of a beloved daughter and a wife.

LYSIMACHUS May we not see him?

HELICANUS You may;
But bootless is your sight – he will not speak
To any.

LYSIMACHUS Yet let me obtain my wish.

HELICANUS Behold him. [*Pericles discovered*]
This was a goodly person
Till the disaster that, one mortal night,
Drove him to this.

LYSIMACHUS Sir King, all hail! The gods preserve you!
Hail, royal sir!

HELICANUS It is in vain; he will not speak to you.

1 LORD Sir, we have a maid in Mytilene, I durst wager,
Would win some words of him.

LYSIMACHUS 'Tis well bethought.
She, questionless, with her sweet harmony
And other chosen attractions, would allure,
And make a batt'ry through his deafen'd parts,
Which now are midway stopp'd.
She is all happy as the fairest of all,
And, with her fellow maids, is now upon
The leafy shelter that abuts against

The island's side. [*He whispers First Lord, who goes off in the barge of Lysimachus.*
HELICANUS Sure, all's effectless; yet nothing we'll omit
That bears recovery's name. But, since your kindness
We have stretch'd thus far, let us beseech you
That for our gold we may provision have,
Wherein we are not destitute for want,
But weary for the staleness.
LYSIMACHUS O sir, a courtesy
Which if we should deny, the most just gods
For every graff would send a caterpillar,
And so inflict our province. Yet once more
Let me entreat to know at large the cause
Of your king's sorrow.
HELICANUS Sit, sir, I will recount it to you.
But, see, I am prevented.

Re-enter, from the barge, First Lord, with MARINA and another Girl.

LYSIMACHUS O, here is
The lady that I sent for. Welcome, fair one!
Is't not a goodly presence?
HELICANUS She's a gallant lady.
LYSIMACHUS She's such a one that, were I well assur'd
Came of gentle kind and noble stock,
I'd wish no better choice, and think me rarely wed.
Fair one, all goodness that consists in bounty
Expect even here, where is a kingly patient.
If that thy prosperous and artificial feat
Can draw him but to answer thee in aught,
Thy sacred physic shall receive such pay
As thy desires can wish.
MARINA Sir, I will use
My utmost skill in his recovery,
Provided
That none but I and my companion maid
Be suffered to come near him.
LYSIMACHUS Come, let us leave her;
And the gods make her prosperous! [*Marina sings.*
LYSIMACHUS Mark'd he your music?
MARINA No, nor look'd on us.
LYSIMACHUS See, she will speak to him.
MARINA Hail sir! my lord, lend ear.
PERICLES Hum, ha!
MARINA I am a maid,
My lord, that ne'er before invited eyes,
But have been gaz'd on like a comet. She speaks,
My lord, that, may be, hath endur'd a grief
Might equal yours, if both were justly weigh'd.
Though wayward fortune did malign my state,
My derivation was from ancestors
Who stood equivalent with mighty kings;
But time hath rooted out my parentage,
And to the world and awkward casualties
Bound me in servitude. [*Aside*] I will desist;
But there is something glows upon my cheek,
And whispers in mine ear 'Go not till he speak'.
PERICLES My fortunes – parentage – good parentage –
To equal mine! – was it not thus? What say you?
MARINA I said, my lord, if you did know my parentage
You would not do me violence.
PERICLES I do think so. Pray you turn your eyes upon me.
You are like something that – What countrywoman?
Here of these shores?
MARINA No, nor of any shores.
Yet I was mortally brought forth, and am
No other than I appear.
PERICLES I am great with woe, and shall deliver weeping.
My dearest wife was like this maid, and such a one
My daughter might have been: my queen's square brows;
Her stature to an inch; as wand-like straight;
As silver voic'd; her eyes as jewel-like,
And cas'd as richly; in pace another Juno;
Who starves the ears she feeds, and makes them hungry
The more she gives them speech. Where do you live?
MARINA Where I am but a stranger. From the deck
You may discern the place.
PERICLES Where were you bred?
And how achiev'd you these endowments, which
You make more rich to owe?
MARINA If I should tell my history, it would seem
Like lies, disdain'd in the reporting.
PERICLES Prithee speak.
Falseness cannot come from thee; for thou lookest
Modest as Justice, and thou seem'st a palace
For the crown'd Truth to dwell in. I will believe thee,
And make my senses credit thy relation
To points that seem impossible; for thou lookest
Like one I lov'd indeed. What were thy friends?
Didst thou not say, when I did push thee back –
Which was when I perceiv'd thee – that thou cam'st?
From good descending?
MARINA So indeed I did.
PERICLES Report thy parentage. I think thou said'st

Thou hadst been toss'd from wrong to injury,
And that thou thought'st thy griefs might equal mine,
If both were opened.

MARINA Some such thing
I said, and said no more but what my thoughts
Did warrant me was likely.

PERICLES Tell thy story;
If thine consider'd prove the thousand part
Of my endurance, thou art a man, and I
Have suffered like a girl. Yet thou dost look
Like Patience gazing on kings' graves, and smiling
Extremity out of act. What were thy friends?
How lost thou them? Thy name, my most kind virgin?
Recount, I do beseech thee. Come, sit by me.

MARINA My name is Marina.

PERICLES O, I am mock'd,
And thou by some incensed god sent hither
To make the world to laugh at me.

MARINA Patience, good sir,
Or here I'll cease.

PERICLES Nay, I'll be patient.
Thou little know'st how thou dost startle me
To call thyself Marina.

MARINA The name
Was given me by one that had some power,
My father, and a king.

PERICLES How! a king's daughter?
And call'd Marina?

MARINA You said you would believe me;
But, not to be a troubler of your peace,
I will end here.

PERICLES But are you flesh and blood?
Have you a working pulse, and are no fairy?
Motion! Well; speak on. Where were you born?
And wherefore call'd Marina?

MARINA Call'd Marina
For I was born at sea.

PERICLES At sea! what mother?

MARINA My mother was the daughter of a king;
Who died the minute I was born,
As my good nurse Lychorida hath oft
Delivered weeping.

PERICLES O, stop there a little!
[*Aside*] This is the rarest dream that e'er dull sleep
Did mock sad fools withal. This cannot be:
My daughter's buried. – Well, where were you bred?
I'll hear you more, to th' bottom of your story,
And never interrupt you.

MARINA You scorn; believe me, 'twere best I did give o'er.

PERICLES I will believe you by the syllable
Of what you shall deliver. Yet give me leave –
How came you in these parts? where were you bred?

MARINA The King my father did in Tharsus leave me;
Till cruel Cleon, with his wicked wife,
Did seek to murder me; and having woo'd
A villain to attempt it, who having drawn to do't,
A crew of pirates came and rescued me;
Brought me to Mytilene. But, good sir,
Whither will you have me? Why do you weep? It may be
You think me an impostor. No, good faith;
I am the daughter to King Pericles,
If good King Pericles be.

PERICLES Ho, Helicanus!

HELICANUS Calls my lord?

PERICLES Thou art a grave and noble counsellor,
Most wise in general. Tell me, if thou canst,
What this maid is, or what is like to be,
That thus hath made me weep?

HELICANUS I know not; but
Here is the regent, sir, of Mytilene
Speaks nobly of her.

LYSIMACHUS She never would tell
Her parentage; being demanded that,
She would sit still and weep.

PERICLES O Helicanus, strike me, honour'd sir;
Give me a gash, put me to present pain,
Lest this great sea of joys rushing upon me
O'erbear the shores of my mortality,
And drown me with their sweetness. O, come hither,
Thou that beget'st him that did thee beget;
Thou that wast born at sea, buried at Tharsus,
And found at sea again! O Helicanus,
Down on thy knees, thank the holy gods as loud
As thunder threatens us. This is Marina.
What was thy mother's name? Tell me but that,
For truth can never be confirm'd enough,
Though doubts did ever sleep.

MARINA First, sir, I pray,
What is your title?

PERICLES I am Pericles of Tyre; but tell me now
My drown'd queen's name, as in the rest you said
Thou hast been godlike perfect,
The heir of kingdoms and another life
To Pericles thy father.

MARINA Is it no more to be your daughter than
To say my mother's name was Thaisa?
Thaisa was my mother, who did end
The minute I began.

PERICLES Now blessing on thee! Rise; thou art my child.
Give me fresh garments. Mine own, Helicanus –

She is not dead at Tharsus, as she should have been
By savage Cleon. She shall tell thee all;
When thou shalt kneel, and justify in knowledge
She is thy very princess. Who is this?

HELICANUS Sir, 'tis the Governor of Mytilene,
Who, hearing of your melancholy state,
Did come to see you.

PERICLES I embrace you.
Give me my robes. I am wild in my beholding.
O heavens bless my girl! But hark, what music?
Tell Helicanus, my Marina, tell him
O'er, point by point, for yet he seems to doubt,
How sure you are my daughter. But, what music?

HELICANUS My lord, I hear none.

PERICLES None?
The music of the spheres! List, my Marina.

LYSIMACHUS It is not good to cross him; give him way.

PERICLES Rarest sounds! Do ye not hear?

LYSIMACHUS My lord, I hear. [*Music.*

PERICLES Most heavenly music!
It nips me unto list'ning, and thick slumber
Hangs upon mine eyes: let me rest. [*Sleeps.*

LYSIMACHUS A pillow for his head.
So, leave him all. Well, my companion-friends,
If this but answer to my just belief,
I'll well remember you. [*Exeunt all but Pericles.*

DIANA appears to Pericles as in a vision.

DIANA My temple stands in Ephesus. Hie thee thither,
And do upon mine altar sacrifice.
There, when my maiden priests are met together,
Before the people all,
Reveal how thou at sea didst lose thy wife.
To mourn thy crosses, with thy daughter's, call,
And give them repetition to the life.
Or perform my bidding or thou liv'st in woe;
Do it, and happy – by my silver bow!
Awake and tell thy dream. [*Disappears.*

PERICLES Celestial Dian, goddess argentine,
I will obey thee. Helicanus!

Re-enter HELICANUS, LYSIMACHUS, MARINA etc.

HELICANUS Sir?

PERICLES My purpose was for Tharsus, there to strike
The inhospitable Cleon; but I am
For other service first: toward Ephesus
Turn our blown sails; eftsoons I'll tell thee why.
[*To Lysimachus*] Shall we refresh us, sir, upon your shore,
And give you gold for such provision
As our intents will need?

LYSIMACHUS Sir,
With all my heart; and when you come ashore
I have another suit.

PERICLES You shall prevail,
Were it to woo my daughter; for it seems
You have been noble towards her.

LYSIMACHUS Sir, lend me your arm.

PERICLES Come, my Marina. [*Exeunt.*

SCENE II. *Ephesus. Before the Temple of Diana.*

Enter GOWER.

GOWER Now our sands are almost run;
More a little, and then dumb.
This, my last boon, give me,
For such kindness must relieve me –
That you aptly will suppose
What pageantry, what feats, what shows,
What minstrelsy, and pretty din,
The regent made in Mytilen
To greet the King. So he thrived,
That he is promis'd to be wived
To fair Marina; but in no wise
Till he had done his sacrifice,
As Dian bade; whereto being bound,
The interim, pray you, all confound.
In feather'd briefness sails are fill'd,
And wishes fall out as they're will'd.
At Ephesus the temple see,
Our king, and all his company.
That he can hither come so soon,
Is by your fancies' thankful doom. [*Exit.*

SCENE III. *Ephesus. The Temple of Diana; THAISA standing near the altar as High Priestess; a number of Virgins on each side; CERIMON and other Inhabitants of Ephesus attending.*

Enter PERICLES, with his Train; LYSIMACHUS, HELICANUS, MARINA, and a Lady.

PERICLES Hail, Dian! to perform thy just command,
I here confess myself the King of Tyre;
Who, frighted from my country, did wed
At Pentapolis the fair Thaisa.
At sea in childbed died she, but brought forth
A maid-child, call'd Marina; who, O goddess,
Wears yet thy silver livery. She at Tharsus
Was nurs'd with Cleon; who at fourteen years
He sought to murder; but her better stars
Brought her to Mytilene; 'gainst whose shore
Riding, her fortunes brought the maid aboard us,
Where, by her own most clear remembrance, she

Made known herself my daughter.
THAISA Voice and favour!
You are, you are – O royal Pericles! [*Swoons.*
PERICLES What means the nun? She dies! Help, gentlemen!
CERIMON Noble sir,
If you have told Diana's altar true,
This is your wife.
PERICLES Reverend appearer, no;
I threw her o'erboard with these very arms.
CERIMON Upon this coast, I warrant you.
PERICLES 'Tis most certain.
CERIMON Look to the lady. O, she's but overjoy'd.
Early in blustering morn this lady was
Thrown upon this shore. I op'd the coffin,
Found there rich jewels; recover'd her, and plac'd her
Here in Diana's temple.
PERICLES May we see them?
CERIMON Great sir, they shall be brought you to my house,
Whither I invite you. Look, Thaisa is
Recovered.
THAISA O, let me look!
If he be none of mine, my sanctity
Will to my sense bend no licentious ear,
But curb it, spite of seeing. O, my lord,
Are you not Pericles? Like him you spake,
Like him you are. Did you not name a tempest,
A birth and death?
PERICLES The voice of dead Thaisa!
THAISA That Thaisa am I, supposed dead
And drown'd.
PERICLES Immortal Dian!
THAISA Now I know you better.
When we with tears parted Pentapolis,
The King my father gave you such a ring.
[*Shows a ring.*
PERICLES This, this! No more, you gods! your present kindness
Makes my past miseries sports. You shall do well
That on the touching of her lips I may
Melt and no more be seen. O, come, be buried
A second time within these arms!
MARINA My heart
Leaps to be gone into my mother's bosom.
[*Kneels to Thaisa.*
PERICLES Look who kneels here! Flesh of thy flesh, Thaisa;
Thy burden at the sea, and call'd Marina,
For she was yielded there.
THAISA Blest and mine own!
HELICANUS Hail, madam, and my queen!
THAISA I know you not.
PERICLES You have heard me say, when I did fly from Tyre,
I left behind an ancient substitute.
Can you remember what I call'd the man?
I have nam'd him oft.
THAISA 'Twas Helicanus then.
PERICLES Still confirmation.
Embrace him, dear Thaisa; this is he.
Now do I long to hear how you were found;
How possibly preserv'd; and who to thank,
Besides the gods, for this great miracle.
THAISA Lord Cerimon, my lord – this man
Through whom the gods have shown their power – that can
From first to last resolve you.
PERICLES Reverend sir,
The gods can have no mortal officer
More like a god than you. Will you deliver
How this dead queen re-lives?
CERIMON I will, my lord.
Beseech you, first, go with me to my house,
Where shall be shown you all was found with her;
How she came plac'd here in the temple;
No needful thing omitted.
PERICLES Pure Dian, bless thee for thy vision! I
Will offer night-oblations to thee. Thaisa,
This Prince, the fair-betrothed of your daughter,
Shall marry her at Pentapolis. And now,
This ornament
Makes me look dismal will I clip to form;
And what this fourteen years no razor touch'd,
To grace thy marriage-day I'll beautify.
THAISA Lord Cerimon hath letters of good credit, sir,
My father's dead.
PERICLES Heavens make a star of him! Yet there, my queen,
We'll celebrate their nuptials, and ourselves
Will in that kingdom spend our following days.
Our son and daughter shall in Tyrus reign.
Lord Cerimon, we do our longing stay
To hear the rest untold. Sir, lead's the way.
[*Exeunt.*

Enter GOWER.

GOWER In Antiochus and his daughter you have heard
Of monstrous lust the due and just reward:
In Pericles, his queen, and daughter, seen,
Although assail'd with fortune fierce and keen,
Virtue preserv'd from fell destruction's blast,
Led on by heaven, and crown'd with joy at last.
In Helicanus may you well descry
A figure of truth, of faith, of loyalty;
In reverend Cerimon there well appears
The worth that learned charity aye wears.

For wicked Cleon and his wife, when fame
Had spread their cursed deed, and honour'd name
Of Pericles, to rage the city turn,
That him and his they in his palace burn;
The gods for murder seemed so content
To punish – although not done, but meant.
So, on your patience evermore attending,
New joy wait on you! Here our play has ending.
[*Exit.*

Shakespeare's Poems

Introduction by Susan Anthony

Apart from *The Phœnix and the Turtle*, a lyric lamenting the death of love's perfection, Shakespeare probably also wrote *A Lover's Complaint*, first published with his *Sonnets*. More widely read are the two major Ovidian narrative poems, *Venus and Adonis* and *The Rape of Lucrece*. Both are moralised sexual tales. Sexual bullying in each confronts passivity, but in one poem the aggressor is female, in the other male. In *Venus and Adonis* Venus is the wooer, 'a bold-faced suitor' frustrated by Adonis' coldness – and ultimately by his death. Lucrece, on the other hand, is so conventionally feminine that she victimises herself after her rape, and feels tragically constrained to repair her husband's honour by suicide.

Venus and Adonis, set in a sunny natural world invaded by death, turns out to be a serio-comic myth about the flawed yet beautiful nature of love. Though moments of lyrical harmony convert their strife to an aesthetically-delightful 'beauteous combat,' the relationship between the goddess and her reluctant 'lovely boy' is frequently bizarre. Adonis, an epicene prig who calls his own self-absorption chastity, lectures the queen of love on her lust. Venus, voluptuous and powerful, at first encounter plucks Adonis from his horse and tucks him beneath her arm.

Painful humour stems from their inverted roles. While Adonis' stallion, mating a wild mare, figures natural passion, his master's obstinate frigidity is disturbing, and makes a fool of Venus, who is helpless to persuade him. The humiliating irony of her position is exploited with tragic absurdity. Pulling Adonis down upon her, she attempts the impossible, a female rape. Such erotic violence is self-defeating. Adonis passively resists arousal. We feel his revulsion as real pain, through images which make our own flesh shrink.

With one of the poem's startling transitions from vulgarity to haunting beauty, Venus loses him forever.

> Look how a bright star shooteth from the sky
> So glides he in the night from Venus' eye [815–6]

Adonis cannot be forced to procreate. Yet the self-willed male who refuses to play his part in natural process destroys himself.

> What is thy body but a swallowing grave? [757]

warns Venus. The Boar, which stands for death, is also part of nature. Hunting him, Adonis pursues his own violent destruction, perceived by Venus, with lyrical perversity, as a kind of rape: the boar

> by a kiss thought to persuade him there,
> And nuzzling in his flank, the loving swine
> Sheathed unaware the tusk in his soft groin [1114–16]

Standing by Adonis' body, Venus identifies her own sensuality with the Boar's:

> Had I been toothed like him, I must confess

With kissing him I should have killed him first. [1117–18]

an image of unrestrained appetite, rather than love. Yet the poem is not a tragedy. Venus laments not so much for Adonis himself as for vanished beauty, and the loss of sexual joy. Finally this strange tale becomes a myth, explaining why human love will always be sorrowful, since Love herself is disappointed. Tragic suffering is displaced. The pain of Adonis' death, and Venus' desire and grief, are delicately transformed, as Adonis' white bloodstained body changes to a chequered flower, which Venus plucks, and sticks within her breast.

The Rape of Lucrece concerns iteself more harshly with erotic violence. In this brutal legend of self-destruction after treacherous rape, there are no half-tones; and though the poem is not without feeling, Lucrece in particular laments and moralises at such weary length that she alienates the reader's sympathy. Yet the poem is a workshop for Shakespearean tragedy. When after her violation Lucrece calls Night to cloud the day,

. . . with rotten damps ravish the morning air,
Let their exhaled unwholesome breaths make sick
The life of purity [778–80]

her diffuse rhetoric palely anticipates the concentrated dramatic symbolism of Shakespeare's mature style. Tarquin, an implacable and yet reluctantly tragic villain, finds that no goodness, neither Lucrece's purity nor his own disabled moral will, can resist the impulsive energy of evil. After her rape, Lucrece too comes to see the universe tragically, as indifferent or ironically hostile.

Though stuffed with these tragic ideas, the poem cannot be read like a play. When in a passage of some tension, Tarquin 'stalks' 'to Lucrece bed,' his progress is charged with figurative significance, in a now-forgotten emblematic style. Forcing symbolic barriers as he goes, the 'locks between her chamber and his will' (both 'chamber' and 'will' are sexual metaphors) he pricks his finger on

Lucretia's glove, wherein her needle sticks. [317]

This accident, which suggests he will be stung by his own violence, ironically leads on to the rape. Lucrece, to whom interest now turns, is presented undramatically as an emblem, 'the picture of pure piety,' in a world of images which reflect her injury and grief. She finds pictured in Hecuba, Troy's mourning queen, a match to heighten her own sorrow. The fall of Troy represents an archetypal tragedy, where lust and treachery cause public ruin: a pattern which is repeated in the history of Lucrece herself.

Lucrece is an example. But when she resolves 'to punish in herself another's fault,' her righteousness, although exemplary, is unsympathetic and unpleasant. Through her rigid virtue a hint of ambivalence enters the poem. Tarquin's tragic evil is now balanced by his victim's obstinate self-destruction. Lucrece's determination 'to clear this spot by death' does not go uncriticised. Her death conceals moral confusion behind an eloquent dramatic pose. Underlying the moral clichés of the poem, which endorse her act, a less simple view is suggested. Pride in her own purity, rather than external and enforced pollution, corrupts Lucrece. Tarquin is not the poem's only tragic sinner.

Venus and Adonis

Vilia miretur vulgus: mihi flavus Apollo
Pocula Castalia plena ministret aqua.

TO THE
RIGHT HONORABLE HENRIE WRIOTHESLEY,
EARLE OF SOUTHAMPTON, AND BARON OF TITCHFIELD.

RIGHT HONOURABLE,

I KNOW not how I shall offend in dedicating my unpolisht lines to your Lordship, nor how the worlde will censure mee for choosing so strong a proppe to support so weake a burthen, onelye if your Honour seeme but pleased, I account my selfe highly praised, and vowe to take advantage of all idle houres, till I have honoured you with some graver labour. But if the first heire of my invention prove deformed, I shall be sorie it had so noble a god-father: and never after eare so barren a land, for feare it yeeld me still so bad a harvest, I leave it to your Honourable survey, and your Honor to your hearts content which I wish may alwaies answere your owne wish, and the worlds hopefull expectation.

Your Honors in all dutie,
WILLIAM SHAKESPEARE

EVEN as the sun with purple-colour'd face
Had ta'en his last leave of the weeping morn,
Rose-cheek'd Adonis hied him to the chase;
Hunting he lov'd, but love he laugh'd to scorn.
Sick-thoughted Venus makes amain unto him,
And like a bold-fac'd suitor gins to woo him.

'Thrice fairer than myself,' thus she began,
'The field's chief flower, sweet above compare,
Stain to all nymphs, more lovely than a man,
More white and red than doves or roses are;
Nature that made thee, with herself at strife,
Saith that the world hath ending with thy life.

'Vouchsafe, thou wonder, to alight thy steed,
And rein his proud head to the saddle-bow;
If thou wilt deign this favour, for thy meed
A thousand honey secrets shalt thou know.
Here come and sit, where never serpent hisses,
And being set, I'll smother thee with kisses;

'And yet not cloy thy lips with loath'd satiety,
But rather famish them amid their plenty,
Making them red and pale with fresh variety –
Ten kisses short as one, one long as twenty.
A summer's day will seem an hour but short,
Being wasted in such time-beguiling sport.'

With this she seizeth on his sweating palm,
The precedent of pith and livelihood,
And, trembling in her passion, calls it balm,
Earth's sovereign salve to do a goddess good.
Being so enrag'd, desire doth lend her force
Courageously to pluck him from his horse.

Over one arm the lusty courser's rein,
Under her other was the tender boy,
Who blush'd and pouted in a dull disdain,
With leaden appetite, unapt to toy;
She red and hot as coals of glowing fire,
He red for shame, but frosty in desire.

The studded bridle on a ragged bough
Nimbly she fastens – O, how quick is love!
The steed is stalled up, and even now
To tie the rider she begins to prove:
Backward she push'd him, as she would be thrust,
And govern'd him in strength, though not in lust.

So soon was she along as he was down,
Each leaning on their elbows and their hips;
Now doth she stroke his cheek, now doth he frown,
And gins to chide, but soon she stops his lips,
And kissing speaks, with lustful language broken:
'If thou wilt chide, thy lips shall never open.'

He burns with bashful shame; she with her tears
Doth quench the maiden burning of his cheeks;
Then with her windy sighs and golden hairs
To fan and blow them dry again she seeks.
He saith she is immodest, blames her miss;
What follows more she murders with a kiss.

Even as an empty eagle, sharp by fast,
Tires with her beak on feathers, flesh, and bone,
Shaking her wings, devouring all in haste,
Till either gorge be stuff'd, or prey be gone;
Even so she kiss'd his brow, his cheek, his chin,
And where she ends she doth anew begin.

Forc'd to content, but never to obey,
Panting he lies and breatheth in her face;
She feedeth on the steam as on a prey,
And calls it heavenly moisture, air of grace,

Wishing her cheeks were gardens full of flowers,
So they were dew'd with such distilling showers.

Look how a bird lies tangled in a net,
So fast'ned in her arms Adonis lies;
Pure shame and aw'd resistance made him fret,
Which bred more beauty in his angry eyes.
Rain added to a river that is rank
Perforce will force it overflow the bank.

Still she entreats, and prettily entreats,
For to a pretty ear she tunes her tale;
Still is he sullen, still he lours and frets,
'Twixt crimson shame and anger ashy-pale;
Being red, she loves him best; and being white,
Her best is better'd with a more delight.

Look how he can, she cannot choose but love;
And by her fair immortal hand she swears
From his soft bosom never to remove
Till he take truce with her contending tears,
Which long have rain'd, making her cheeks all wet;
And one sweet kiss shall pay this countless debt.

Upon this promise did he raise his chin,
Like a dive-dapper peering through a wave,
Who, being look'd on, ducks as quickly in;
So offers he to give what she did crave;
But when her lips were ready for his pay,
He winks, and turns his lips another way.

Never did passenger in summer's heat
More thirst for drink than she for this good turn:
Her help she sees, but help she cannot get;
She bathes in water, yet her fire must burn.
'O, pity,' gan she cry 'flint-hearted boy!
'Tis but a kiss I beg; why art thou coy?

'I have been wooed, as I entreat thee now,
Even by the stern and direful god of war,
Whose sinewy neck in battle ne'er did bow,
Who conquers where he comes in every jar;
Yet hath he been my captive and my slave,
And begg'd for that which thou unask'd shalt have.

'Over my altars hath he hung his lance,
His batt'red shield, his uncontrolled crest,
And for my sake hath learn'd to sport and dance,
To toy, to wanton, dally, smile, and jest,
Scorning his churlish drum and ensign red,
Making my arms his field, his tent my bed.

'Thus he that overrul'd I oversway'd,
Leading him prisoner in a red-rose chain;
Strong-temper'd steel his stronger strength obeyed,
Yet was he servile to my coy disdain.
O, be not proud, nor brag not of thy might,
For mast'ring her that foil'd the god of fight!

'Touch but my lips with those fair lips of thine;
Though mine be not so fair, yet are they red –
The kiss shall be thine own as well as mine.
What seest thou in the ground? Hold up thy head;
Look in mine eyeballs; there thy beauty lies.
Then why not lips on lips, since eyes in eyes?

'Art thou asham'd to kiss? Then wink again,
And I will wink; so shall the day seem night.
Love keeps his revels where there are but twain;
Be bold to play; our sport is not in sight.
These blue-vein'd violets whereon we lean
Never can blab, nor know not what we mean.

'The tender spring upon thy tempting lip
Shows thee unripe; yet mayst thou well be tasted;
Make use of time, let not advantage slip;
Beauty within itself should not be wasted.
Fair flowers that are not gath'red in their prime
Rot and consume themselves in little time.

'Were I hard-favour'd, foul, or wrinkled-old,
Ill-nurtur'd, crooked, churlish, harsh in voice,
O'er-worn, despised, rheumatic, and cold,
Thick-sighted, barren, lean, and lacking juice,
Then mightst thou pause, for then I were not for thee;
But having no defects, why dost abhor me?

'Thou canst not see one wrinkle in my brow;
Mine eyes are grey, and bright, and quick in turning;
My beauty as the spring doth yearly grow,
My flesh is soft and plump, my marrow burning;
My smooth moist hand, were it with thy hand felt,
Would in thy palm dissolve or seem to melt.

'Bid me discourse, I will enchant thine ear,
Or, like a fairy, trip upon the green,
Or, like a nymph, with long dishevelled hair,
Dance on the sands, and yet no footing seen.
Love is a spirit all compact of fire,
Not gross to sink, but light, and will aspire.

'Witness this primrose bank whereon I lie:
These forceless flowers like sturdy trees support me;
Two strengthless doves will draw me through the sky
From morn till night, even where I list to sport me.
Is love so light, sweet boy, and may it be
That thou should think it heavy unto thee?

'Is thine own heart to thine own face affected?
Can thy right hand seize love upon thy left?
Then woo thyself, be of thyself rejected;
Steal thine own freedom, and complain on theft.
Narcissus so himself himself forsook,
And died to kiss his shadow in the brook.

'Torches are made to light, jewels to wear,
Dainties to taste, fresh beauty for the use,

Herbs for their smell, and sappy plants to bear;
Things growing to themselves are growth's abuse.
Seeds spring from seeds, and beauty breedeth beauty;
Thou wast begot – to get it is thy duty.

'Upon the earth's increase why shouldst thou feed,
Unless the earth with thy increase be fed?
By law of nature thou art bound to breed,
That thine may live when thou thyself art dead;
And so in spite of death thou dost survive,
In that thy likeness still is left alive.'

By this the love-sick queen began to sweat,
For where they lay the shadow had forsook them,
And Titan, tired in the mid-day heat,
With burning eye did hotly overlook them;
Wishing Adonis had his team to guide,
So he were like him, and by Venus' side.

And now Adonis, with a lazy sprite,
And with a heavy, dark, disliking eye,
His louring brows o'erwhelming his fair sight,
Like misty vapours when they blot the sky,
Souring his cheeks, cries 'Fie, no more of love!
The sun doth burn my face; I must remove'.

'Ay me,' quoth Venus 'young, and so unkind!
What bare excuses mak'st thou to be gone!
I'll sigh celestial breath, whose gentle wind
Shall cool the heat of this descending sun;
I'll make a shadow for thee of my hairs;
If they burn too, I'll quench them with my tears.

'The sun that shines from heaven shines but warm,
And lo, I lie between that sun and thee;
The heat I have from thence doth little harm;
Thine eye darts forth the fire that burneth me;
And were I not immortal, life were done
Between this heavenly and earthly sun.

'Art thou obdurate, flinty, hard as steel?
Nay, more than flint, for stone at rain relenteth.
Art thou a woman's son, and canst not feel
What 'tis to love? how want of love tormenteth?
O, had thy mother borne so hard a mind,
She had not brought forth thee, but died unkind!

'What am I, that thou shouldst contemn me this?
Or what great danger dwells upon my suit?
What were thy lips the worse for one poor kiss?
Speak, fair; but speak fair words, or else be mute.
Give me one kiss; I'll give it thee again,
And one for int'rest, if thou wilt have twain.

'Fie, lifeless picture, cold and senseless stone,
Well-painted idol, image dull and dead,
Statue contenting but the eye alone,
Thing like a man, but of no woman bred!
Thou art no man, though of a man's complexion,
For men will kiss even by their own direction.'

This said, impatience chokes her pleading tongue,
And swelling passion doth provoke a pause;
Red cheeks and fiery eyes blaze forth her wrong;
Being judge in love, she cannot right her cause;
And now she weeps, and now she fain would speak,
And now her sobs do her intendments break.

Sometime she shakes her head, and then his hand;
Now gazeth she on him, now on the ground;
Sometime her arms infold him like a band;
She would, he will not in her arms be bound;
And when from thence he struggles to be gone,
She locks her lily fingers one in one.

'Fondling,' she saith 'since I have hemm'd thee here
Within the circuit of this ivory pale,
I'll be a park, and thou shalt be my deer;
Feed where thou wilt, on mountain or in dale;
Graze on my lips; and if those hills be dry,
Stray lower, where the pleasant fountains lie.

'Within this limit is relief enough,
Sweet bottom-grass, and high delightful plain,
Round rising hillocks, brakes obscure and rough,
To shelter thee from tempest and from rain;
Then be my deer, since I am such a park;
No dog shall rouse thee, though a thousand bark.'

At this Adonis smiles as in disdain,
That in each cheek appears a pretty dimple.
Love made those hollows, if himself were slain,
He might be buried in a tomb so simple;
Foreknowing well, if there he came to lie,
Why, there Love liv'd and there he could not die.

These lovely caves, these round enchanting pits,
Open'd their mouths to swallow Venus' liking.
Being mad before, how doth she now for wits?
Struck dead at first, what needs a second striking?
Poor queen of love, in thine own law forlorn,
To love a cheek that smiles at thee in scorn!

Now which way shall she turn? What shall she say?
Her words are done, her woes the more increasing;
The time is spent, her object will away,
And from her twining arms doth urge releasing.
'Pity!' she cries 'Some favour, some remorse!'
Away he springs, and hasteth to his horse.

But, lo, from forth a copse that neighbours by,
A breeding jennet, lusty, young, and proud,
Adonis' trampling courser doth espy,
And forth she rushes, snorts, and neighs aloud;
The strong-neck'd steed, being tied unto a tree,
Breaketh his rein, and to her straight goes he.

Imperiously he leaps, he neighs, he bounds,

And now his woven girths he breaks asunder;
The bearing earth with his hard hoof he wounds,
Whose hollow womb resounds like heaven's thunder;
The iron bit he crusheth 'tween his teeth,
Controlling what he was controlled with.

His ears up-prick'd; his braided hanging mane
Upon his compass'd crest now stand on end;
His nostrils drink the air, and forth again,
As from a furnace, vapours doth he send;
His eye, which scornfully glisters like fire,
Shows his hot courage and his high desire.

Sometime he trots, as if he told the steps,
With gentle majesty and modest pride;
Anon he rears upright, curvets, and leaps,
As who should say 'Lo, thus my strength is tried,
And this I do to captivate the eye
Of the fair breeder that is standing by'.

What recketh he his rider's angry stir,
His flattering 'Holla' or his 'Stand, I say'?
What cares he now for curb, or pricking spur?
For rich caparisons, or trappings gay?
He sees his love, and nothing else he sees,
Nor nothing else with his proud sight agrees.

Look when a painter would surpass the life
In limning out a well-proportioned steed,
His art with nature's workmanship at strife,
As if the dead the living should exceed;
So did this horse excel a common one
In shape, in courage, colour, pace, and bone.

Round-hoof'd, short-jointed, fetlocks shag and long,
Broad breast, full eye, small head, and nostril wide,
High crest, short ears, straight legs and passing strong,
Thin mane, thick tail, broad buttock, tender hide;
Look what a horse should have he did not lack,
Save a proud rider on so proud a back.

Sometime he scuds far off, and there he stares;
Anon he starts at stirring of a feather;
To bid the wind a base he now prepares,
And whe'r he run or fly they know not whether;
For through his mane and tail the high wind sings,
Fanning the hairs, who wave like feath'red wings.

He looks upon his love and neighs unto her;
She answers him as if she knew his mind;
Being proud, as females are, to see him woo her,
She puts on outward strangeness, seems unkind,
Spurns at his love, and scorns the heat he feels,
Beating his kind embracements with her heels.

Then, like a melancholy malcontent,
He vails his tail, that, like a falling plume,
Cool shadow to his melting buttock lent
He stamps, and bites the poor flies in his fume.
His love, perceiving how he was enrag'd,
Grew kinder, and his fury was assuag'd.

His testy master goeth about to take him,
When, lo, the unback'd breeder, full of fear,
Jealous of catching, swiftly doth forsake him,
With her the horse, and left Adonis there.
As they were mad, unto the wood they hie them,
Out-stripping crows that strive to overfly them.

All swol'n with chafing, down Adonis sits,
Banning his boist'rous and unruly beast;
And now the happy season once more fits
That love-sick Love by pleading may be blest;
For lovers say the heart hath treble wrong,
When it is barr'd the aidance of the tongue.

An oven that is stopp'd, or river stay'd,
Burneth more hotly, swelleth with more rage;
So of concealed sorrow may be said:
Free vent of words love's fire doth assuage;
But when the heart's attorney once is mute,
The client breaks, as desperate in his suit.

He sees her coming, and begins to glow
Even as a dying coal revives with wind,
And with his bonnet hides his angry brow,
Looks on the dull earth with disturbed mind,
Taking no notice that she is so nigh,
For all askance he holds her in his eye.

O what a sight it was, wistly to view
How she came stealing to the wayward boy!
To note the fighting conflict of her hue!
How white and red each other did destroy!
But now her cheek was pale, and by and by
It flash'd forth fire, as lightning from the sky.

Now was she just before him as he sat,
And like a lowly lover down she kneels;
With one fair hand she heaveth up his hat,
Her other tender hand his fair cheek feels;
His tend'rer cheek receives her soft hand's print
As apt as new-fall'n snow takes any dint.

O, what a war of looks was then between them,
Her eyes, petitioners, to his eyes suing!
His eyes saw her eyes as they had not seen them;
Her eyes wooed still, his eyes disdain'd the wooing;
And all this dumb play had his acts made plain
With tears which chorus-like her eyes did rain.

Full gently now she takes him by the hand,
A lily prison'd in a gaol of snow,
Or ivory in an alabaster band;
So white a friend engirts so white a foe.
This beauteous combat, wilful and unwilling,
Showed like two silver doves that sit a-billing.

Once more the engine of her thoughts began:

'O fairest mover on this mortal round,
Would thou wert as I am, and I a man,
My heart all whole as thine, thy heart my wound!
For one sweet look thy help I would assure thee,
Though nothing but my body's bane would cure thee'.

'Give me my hand' saith he. 'Why dost thou feel it?
'Give me my heart,' saith she 'and thou shalt have it.
O, give it me, lest thy hard heart do steel it,
And being steel'd, soft sighs can never grave it;
Then love's deep groans I never shall regard,
Because Adonis' heart hath made mine hard.'

'For shame,' he cries 'let go, and let me go;
My day's delight is past, my horse is gone,
And 'tis your fault I am bereft him so.
I pray you hence, and leave me here alone;
For all my mind, my thought, my busy care,
Is how to get my palfrey from the mare.'

Thus she replies: 'Thy palfrey, as he should,
Welcomes the warm approach of sweet desire.
Affection is a coal that must be cool'd;
Else, suffer'd, it will set the heart on fire.
The sea hath bounds, but deep desire hath none,
Therefore no marvel though thy horse be gone.

'How like a jade he stood, tied to the tree,
Servilely master'd with a leathern rein!
But when he saw his love, his youth's fair fee,
He held such petty bondage in disdain,
Throwing the base thong from his bending crest,
Enfranchising his mouth, his back, his breast.

'Who sees his true-love in her naked bed,
Teaching the sheets a whiter hue than white,
But, when his glutton eye so full hath fed,
His other agents aim at like delight?
Who is so faint that dares not be so bold
To touch the fire, the weather being cold?

'Let me excuse thy courser, gentle boy;
And learn of him, I heartily beseech thee,
To take advantage on presented joy;
Though I were dumb, yet his proceedings teach thee.
O, learn to love! The lesson is but plain,
And once made perfect never lost again'.

'I know not love,' quoth he 'nor will not know it,
Unless it be a boar, and then I chase it.
'Tis much to borrow, and I will not owe it.
My love to love is love but to disgrace it;
For I have heard it is a life in death,
That laughs, and weeps, and all but with a breath.

'Who wears a garment shapeless and unfinish'd?
Who plucks the bud before one leaf put forth?
If springing things be any jot diminish'd,
They wither in their prime, prove nothing worth.
The colt that's back'd and burden'd being young
Loseth his pride and never waxeth strong.

'You hurt my hand with wringing; let us part,
And leave this idle theme, this bootless chat;
Remove your siege from my unyielding heart;
To love's alarms it will not open the gate.
Dismiss your vows, your feigned tears, your flatt'ry;
For where a heart is hard they make no batt'ry'.

'What! canst thou talk?' quoth she 'Hast thou a tongue?
O, would thou hadst not, or I had no hearing!
Thy mermaid's voice hath done me double wrong;
I had my load before, now press'd with bearing:
Melodious discord, heavenly tune harsh sounding,
Ear's deep-sweet music, and heart's deep-sore wounding.

'Had I no eyes but ears, my ears would love
That inward beauty and invisible;
Or were I deaf, thy outward parts would move
Each part in me that were but sensible.
Though neither eyes nor ears, to hear nor see,
Yet should I be in love by touching thee.

'Say that the sense of feeling were bereft me,
And that I could not see, nor hear, nor touch,
And nothing but the very smell were left me,
Yet would my love to thee be still as much;
For from the stillitory of thy face excelling
Comes breath perfum'd, that breedeth love by smelling.

'But, O, what banquet wert thou to the taste,
Being nurse and feeder of the other four!
Would they not wish the feast might ever last,
And bid Suspicion double-lock the door,
Lest Jealousy, that sour unwelcome guest,
Should by his stealing in disturb the feast?'

Once more the ruby-colour'd portal open'd
Which to his speech did honey passage yield;
Like a red morn, that ever yet betoken'd
Wreck to the seaman, tempest to the field,
Sorrow to shepherds, woe unto the birds,
Gusts and foul flaws to herdmen and to herds.

This ill presage advisedly she marketh.
Even as the wind is hush'd before it raineth,
Or as the wolf doth grin before he barketh,
Or as the berry breaks before it staineth,
Or like the deadly bullet of a gun,
His meaning struck her ere his words begun.

And at his look she flatly falleth down,
For looks kill love, and love by looks reviveth;
A smile recures the wounding of a frown.
But blessed bankrupt that by love so thriveth!
The silly boy, believing she is dead,

Claps her pale cheek till clapping makes it red;
And all-amaz'd brake off his late intent,
For sharply he did think to reprehend her,
Which cunning love did wittily prevent.
Fair fall the wit that can so well defend her!
For on the grass she lies as she were slain,
Till his breath breatheth life in her again.

He wrings her nose, he strikes her on the cheeks,
He bends her fingers, holds her pulses hard,
He chafes her lips, a thousand ways he seeks
To mend the hurt that his unkindness marr'd;
He kisses her; and she, by her good will,
Will never rise, so he will kiss her still.

The night of sorrow now is turn'd to day:
Her two blue windows faintly she up-heaveth,
Like the fair sun when in his fresh array
He cheers the morn and all the earth relieveth;
And as the bright sun glorifies the sky,
So is her face illumin'd with her eye;

Whose beams upon his hairless face are fix'd,
As if from thence they borrowed all their shine.
Were never four such lamps together mix'd,
Had not his clouded with his brows' repine;
But hers, which through the crystal tears gave light,
Shone like the moon in water seen by night.

'O, where am I?' quoth she 'in earth or heaven,
Or in the ocean drench'd, or in the fire?
What hour is this? or morn, or weary even?
Do I delight to die, or life desire?
But now I liv'd, and life was death's annoy;
But now I died, and death was lively joy.

'O, thou didst kill me! Kill me once again.
Thy eyes' shrewd tutor, that hard heart of thine,
Hath taught them scornful tricks, and such disdain
That they have murd'red this poor heart of mine;
And these mine eyes, true leaders to their queen,
But for thy piteous lips no more had seen.

'Long may they kiss each other, for this cure!
O, never let their crimson liveries wear!
And as they last, their verdure still endure,
To drive infection from the dangerous year!
That the star-gazers, having writ on death,
May say the plague is banish'd by thy breath.

'Pure lips, sweet seals in my soft lips imprinted,
What bargains may I make, still to be sealing?
To sell myself I can be well contented,
So thou wilt buy, and pay, and use good dealing;
Which purchase if thou make, for fear of slips
Set thy seal manual on my wax-red lips.

'A thousand kisses buys my heart from me;
And pay them at thy leisure, one by one.
What is ten hundred touches unto thee?
Are they not quickly told, and quickly gone?
Say for non-payment that the debt should double,
Is twenty hundred kisses such a trouble?'

'Fair queen,' quoth he 'if any love you owe me,
Measure my strangeness with my unripe years;
Before I know myself, seek not to know me;
No fisher but the ungrown fry forbears.
The mellow plum doth fall, the green sticks fast,
Or being early pluck'd is sour to taste.

'Look, the world's comforter, with weary gait,
His day's hot task hath ended in the west;
The owl, night's herald, shrieks; 'tis very late;
The sheep are gone to fold, birds to their nest;
And coal-black clouds that shadow heaven's light
Do summon us to part and bid good night.

'Now let me say "good night", and so say you;
If you will say so, you shall have a kiss.'
'Good night' quoth she; and, ere, he says 'adieu',
The honey fee of parting tend'red is:
Her arms do lend his neck a sweet embrace;
Incorporate then they seem; face grows to face.

Till, breathless, he disjoin'd, and backward drew
The heavenly moisture, that sweet coral mouth,
Whose precious taste her thirsty lips well knew,
Whereon they surfeit, yet complain on drouth.
He with her plenty press'd, she faint with dearth.
Their lips together glued, fall to the earth.

Now quick desire hath caught the yielding prey,
And glutton-like she feeds, yet never filleth;
Her lips are conquerors, his lips obey,
Paying what ransom the insulter willeth;
Whose vulture thought doth pitch the price so high
That she will draw his lips' rich treasure dry.

And having felt the sweetness of the spoil,
With blindfold fury she begins to forage;
Her face doth reek and smoke, her blood doth boil,
And careless lust stirs up a desperate courage;
Planting oblivion, beating reason back,
Forgetting shame's pure blush, and honour's wrack.

Hot, faint, and weary, with her hard embracing,
Like a wild bird being tam'd with too much handling,
Or as the fleet-foot roe that's tir'd with chasing,
Or like the froward infant still'd with dandling,
He now obeys and now no more resisteth,
While she takes all she can, not all she listeth.

What wax so frozen but dissolves with temp'ring,
And yields at last to every light impression?
Things out of hope are compass'd oft with vent'ring,

Chiefly in love, whose leave exceeds commission.
Affection faints not like a pale-fac'd coward,
But then wooes best when most his choice is froward.

When he did frown, O, had she then gave over,
Such nectar from his lips she had not suck'd.
Foul words and frowns must not repel a lover;
What though the rose have prickles, yet 'tis pluck'd.
Were beauty under twenty locks kept fast,
Yet love breaks through and picks them all at last.

For pity now she can no more detain him;
The poor fool prays her that he may depart.
She is resolv'd no longer to restrain him;
Bids him farewell, and look well to her heart,
The which, by Cupid's bow she doth protest,
He carries thence incaged in his breast.

'Sweet boy,' she says 'this night I'll waste in sorrow,
For my sick heart commands mine eyes to watch.
Tell me, love's master, shall we meet tomorrow?
Say, shall we? shall we? wilt thou make the match?'
He tells her no; to-morrow he intends
To hunt the boar with certain of his friends.

'The boar!' quoth she, whereat a sudden pale,
Like lawn being spread upon the blushing rose,
Usurps her cheek; she trembles at his tale,
And on his neck her yoking arms she throws;
She sinketh down, still hanging by his neck,
He on her belly falls, she on her back.

Now is she in the very lists of love,
Her champion mounted for the hot encounter.
All is imaginary she doth prove;
He will not manage her, although he mount her.
That worse than Tantalus' is her annoy,
To clip Elysium and to lack her joy.

Even so poor birds, deceiv'd with painted grapes,
Do surfeit by the eye and pine the maw;
Even so she languisheth in her mishaps,
As those poor birds that helpless berries saw.
The warm effects which she in him finds missing
She seeks to kindle with continual kissing.

But all in vain; good queen, it will not be.
She hath assay'd as much as may be prov'd;
Her pleading hath deserv'd a greater fee;
She's Love, she loves, and yet she is not lov'd.
'Fie, fie,' he says 'you crush me; let me go;
You have no reason to withhold me so.'

'Thou hadst been gone,' quoth she 'sweet boy, ere this,
But that thou told'st me thou wouldst hunt the boar.
O, be advis'd! Thou know'st not what it is
With javelin's point a churlish swine to gore,
Whose tushes never sheath'd he whetteth still,
Like to a mortal butcher bent to kill.

'On his bow-back he hath a battle set
Of bristly pikes that ever threat his foes;
His eyes like glow-worms shine when he doth fret;
His snout digs sepulchres where'er he goes;
Being mov'd, he strikes whate'er is in his way,
And whom he strikes his cruel tushes slay.

'His brawny sides, with hairy bristles armed,
Are better proof than thy spear's point can enter;
His short thick neck cannot be easily harmed;
Being ireful, on the lion he will venter.
The thorny brambles and embracing bushes,
As fearful of him, part; through whom he rushes.

'Alas, he nought esteems that face of thine,
To which Love's eyes pays tributary gazes;
Nor thy soft hands, sweet lips, and crystal eyne,
Whose full perfection all the world amazes;
But having thee at vantage – wondrous dread! –
Would root these beauties as he roots the mead.

'O, let him keep his loathsome cabin still!
Beauty hath nought to do with such foul fiends.
Come not within his danger by thy will.
They that thrive well take counsel of their friends.
When thou didst name the boar, not to dissemble,
I fear'd thy fortune, and my joints did tremble.

'Didst thou not mark my face? Was it not white?
Sawest thou not signs of fear lurk in mine eye?
Grew I not faint? And fell I not down-right?
Within my bosom, whereon thou dost lie,
My boding heart pants, beats, and takes no rest,
But, like an earthquake, shakes thee on my breast.

'For where Love reigns, disturbing Jealousy
Doth call himself Affection's sentinel;
Gives false alarms, suggesteth mutiny,
And in a peaceful hour doth cry "Kill, kill!"
Distemp'ring gentle Love in his desire,
As air and water do abate the fire.

'This sour informer, this bate-breeding spy,
This canker that eats up Love's tender spring,
This carry-tale, dissentious Jealousy,
That sometime true news, sometime false doth bring,
Knocks at my heart, and whispers in mine ear,
That if I love thee I thy death should fear;

'And, more than so, presenteth to mine eye
The picture of an angry chafing boar,
Under whose sharp fangs on his back doth lie
An image like thyself, all stain'd with gore;
Whose blood upon the fresh flowers being shed
Doth make them droop with grief and hang the head.

'What should I do, seeing thee so indeed,
That tremble at th' imagination?
The thought of it doth make my faint heart bleed,
And fear doth teach it divination:
I prophesy thy death, my living sorrow,
If thou encounter with the boar tomorrow.

'But if thou needs wilt hunt, be rul'd by me;
Uncouple at the timorous flying hare,
Or at the fox which lives by subtlety,
Or at the roe which no encounter dare.
Pursue these fearful creatures o'er the downs,
And on thy well-breath'd horse keep with thy hounds.

'And when thou hast on foot the purblind hare,
Mark the poor wretch, to overshoot his troubles,
How he outruns the wind, and with what care
He cranks and crosses with a thousand doubles.
The many musits through the which he goes
Are like a labyrinth to amaze his foes.

'Sometime he runs among a flock of sheep,
To make the cunning hounds mistake their smell,
And sometime where earth-delving conies keep,
To stop the loud pursuers in their yell;
And sometime sorteth with a herd of deer.
Danger deviseth shifts; wit waits on fear.

'For there his smell with others being mingled,
The hot scent-snuffing hounds are driven to doubt,
Ceasing their clamorous cry till they have singled
With much ado the cold fault cleanly out.
Then do they spend their mouths; echo replies,
As if another chase were in the skies.

'By this, poor Wat, far off upon a hill,
Stands on his hinder legs with list'ning ear,
To hearken if his foes pursue him still;
Anon their loud alarums he doth hear;
And now his grief may be compared well
To one sore sick that hears the passing-bell.

'Then shalt thou see the dew-bedabbled wretch
Turn and return, indenting with the way;
Each envious briar his weary legs do scratch,
Each shadow makes him stop, each murmur stay;
For misery is trodden on by many,
And being low never reliev'd by any.

'Lie quietly and hear a little more;
Nay, do not struggle, for thou shalt not rise.
To make thee hate the hunting of the boar,
Unlike myself thou hear'st me moralize,
Applying this to that, and so to so;
For love can comment upon every woe.

'Where did I leave?' 'No matter where;' quoth he
'Leave me, and then the story aptly ends.
The night is spent.' 'Why, what of that?' quoth she.
'I am,' quoth he 'expected of my friends;
And now 'tis dark, and going I shall fall.'
'In night,' quoth she 'desire sees best of all.

'But if thou fall, O, then imagine this,
The earth in love with thee thy footing trips,
And all is but to rob thee of a kiss.
Rich preys make true-men thieves; so do thy lips
Make modest Dian cloudy and forlorn,
Lest she should steal a kiss, and die forsworn.

'Now of this dark night I perceive the reason:
Cynthia for shame obscures her silver shine,
Till forging Nature be condemn'd of treason
For stealing moulds from heaven that were divine,
Wherein she fram'd thee in high heaven's despite,
To shame the sun by day and her by night.

'And therefore hath she brib'd the Destinies
To cross the curious workmanship of Nature,
To mingle beauty with infirmities,
And pure perfection with impure defeature,
Making it subject to the tyranny
Of mad mischances and much misery:

'As burning fevers, agues pale and faint,
Life-poisoning pestilence, and frenzies wood,
The marrow-eating sickness whose attaint
Disorder breeds by heating of the blood,
Surfeits, imposthumes, grief, and damn'd despair,
Swear Nature's death for framing thee so fair.

'And not the least of all these maladies
But in one minute's fight brings beauty under.
Both favour, savour, hue, and qualities,
Whereat th' impartial gazer late did wonder,
Are on the sudden wasted, thaw'd, and done,
As mountain snow melts with the midday sun.

'Therefore, despite of fruitless chastity,
Love-lacking vestals, and self-loving nuns,
That on the earth would breed a scarcity
And barren dearth of daughters and of sons,
Be prodigal: the lamp that burns by night
Dries up his oil to lend the world his light.

'What is thy body but a swallowing grave,
Seeming to bury that posterity
Which by the rights of time thou needs must have,
If thou destroy them not in dark obscurity?
If so, the world will hold thee in disdain,
Sith in thy pride so fair a hope is slain.

'So in thyself thyself art made away –
A mischief worse than civil home-bred strife,
Or theirs whose desperate hands themselves do slay,
Or butcher-sire that reaves his son of life.

Foul cank'ring rust the hidden treasure frets,
But gold that's put to use more gold begets.'

'Nay, then,' quoth Adon 'you will fall again
Into your idle over-handled theme;
The kiss I gave you is bestow'd in vain,
And all in vain you strive against the stream;
For, by this black-fac'd night, desire's foul nurse,
Your treatise makes me like you worse and
worse.

'If love have lent you twenty thousand tongues,
And every tongue more moving than your own,
Bewitching like the wanton mermaid's songs,
Yet from mine ear the tempting tune is blown;
For know, my heart stands armed in mine ear,
And will not let a false sound enter there,

'Lest the deceiving harmony should run
Into the quiet closure of my breast;
And then my little heart were quite undone,
In his bedchamber to be barr'd of rest.
No, lady, no; my heart longs not to groan,
But soundly sleeps, while now it sleeps alone.

'What have you urg'd that I cannot reprove?
The path is smooth that leadeth on to danger;
I hate not love, but your device in love,
That lends embracements unto every stranger.
You do it for increase! O strange excuse,
When reason is the bawd to lust's abuse!

'Call it not love, for Love to heaven is fled,
Since sweating lust on earth usurp'd his name;
Under whose simple semblance he hath fed
Upon fresh beauty, blotting it with blame;
Which the hot tyrant stains and soon bereaves,
As caterpillars do the tender leaves.

'Love comforteth like sunshine after rain,
But Lust's effect is tempest after sun;
Love's gentle spring doth always fresh remain:
Lust's winter comes ere summer half be done.
Love surfeits not: Lust like a glutton dies.
Love is all truth: Lust full of forged lies.

'More I could tell, but more I dare not say;
The text is old, the orator too green.
Therefore, in sadness, now I will away;
My face is full of shame, my heart of teen;
Mine ears that to your wanton talk attended
Do burn themselves for having so offended.'

With this he breaketh from the sweet embrace
Of those fair arms which bound him to her breast,
And homeward through the dark laund runs
apace;
Leaves Love upon her back, deeply distress'd.
Look how a bright star shooteth from the sky,
So glides he in the night from Venus' eye;

Which after him she darts, as one on shore
Gazing upon a late-embarked friend,
Till the wild waves will have him seen no more,
Whose ridges with the meeting clouds contend;
So did the merciless and pitchy night
Fold in the object that did feed her sight.

Whereat amaz'd, as one that unaware
Hath dropp'd a precious jewel in the flood,
Or stonish'd as night-wand'rers often are,
Their light blown out in some mistrustful wood;
Even so confounded in the dark she lay,
Having lost the fair discovery of her way.

And now she beats her heart, whereat it groans,
That all the neighbour caves, as seeming troubled,
Make verbal repetition of her moans;
Passion on passion deeply is redoubled:
'Ay me!' she cries, and twenty times, 'Woe, woe!'
And twenty echoes twenty times cry so.

She, marking them, begins a wailing note,
And sings extemporally a woeful ditty –
How love makes young men thrall, and old men
dote;
How love is wise in folly, foolish-witty.
Her heavy anthem still concludes in woe,
And still the choir of echoes answer so.

Her song was tedious, and outwore the night,
For lover's hours are long, though seeming short;
If pleas'd themselves, others, they think, delight
In such-like circumstance, with such-like sport.
Their copious stories, oftentimes begun,
End without audience and are never done.

For who hath she to spend the night withal
But idle sounds resembling parasits,
Like shrill-tongu'd tapsters answering every call,
Soothing the humour of fantastic wits?
She says ''Tis so'; they answer all ''Tis so';
And would say after her, if she said 'No'.

Lo, here the gentle lark, weary of rest,
From his moist cabinet mounts up on high,
And wakes the morning, from whose silver breast
The sun ariseth in his majesty;
Who doth the world so gloriously behold
That cedar-tops and hills seem burnish'd gold.

Venus salutes him with this fair good-morrow:
'O thou clear god, and patron of all light,
From whom each lamp and shining star doth
borrow
The beauteous influence that makes him bright,
There lives a son that suck'd an earthly mother
May lend thee light, as thou dost lend to other'.

This said, she hasteth to a myrtle grove,
Musing the morning is so much o'erworn,
And yet she hears no tidings of her love;
She hearkens for his hounds and for his horn.
Anon she hears them chant it lustily,
And in all haste she coasteth to the cry.

And as she runs, the bushes in the way

Some catch her by the neck, some kiss her face,
Some twine about her thigh to make her stay;
She wildly breaketh from their strict embrace,
Like a milch doe whose swelling dugs do ache
Hasting to feed her fawn hid in some brake.

By this, she hears the hounds are at a bay:
Whereat she starts, like one that spies an adder
Wreath'd up in fatal folds just in his way,
The fear whereof doth make him shake and shudder;
Even so the timorous yelping of the hounds
Appals her senses and her spirit confounds.

For now she knows it is no gentle chase,
But the blunt boar, rough bear, or lion proud,
Because the cry remaineth in one place,
Where fearfully the dogs exclaim aloud.
Finding their enemy to be so curst,
They all strain court'sy who shall cope him first.

This dismal cry rings sadly in her ear,
Through which it enters to surprise her heart,
Who, overcome by doubt and bloodless fear,
With cold-pale weakness numbs each feeling part;
Like soldiers, when their captain once doth yield,
They basely fly and dare not stay the field.

Thus stands she in a trembling ecstasy;
Till, cheering up her senses all dismay'd,
She tells them 'tis a causeless fantasy,
And childish error that they are afraid;
Bids them leave quaking, bids them fear no more –
And with that word she spied the hunted boar,

Whose frothy mouth, bepainted all with red,
Like milk and blood being mingled both together,
A second fear through all her sinews spread,
Which madly hurries her she knows not whither:
This way she runs, and now she will no further,
But back retires to rate the boar for murther.

A thousand spleens bear her a thousand ways;
She treads the path that she untreads again;
Her more than haste is mated with delays,
Like the proceedings of a drunken brain,
Full of respects, yet nought at all respecting,
In hand with all things, nought at all effecting.

Here kennell'd in a brake she finds a hound,
And asks the weary caitiff for his master;
And there another licking of his wound,
'Gainst venom'd sores the only sovereign plaster;
And here she meets another sadly scowling,
To whom she speaks, and he replies with howling.

When he hath ceas'd his ill-resounding noise,
Another flap-mouth'd mourner, black and grim,
Against the welkin volleys out his voice;
Another and another answer him,
Clapping their proud tails to the ground below,
Shaking their scratch'd ears, bleeding as they go.

Look how the world's poor people are amazed
At apparitions, signs, and prodigies,
Whereon with fearful eyes they long have gazed,
Infusing them with dreadful prophecies;
So she at these sad signs draws up her breath,
And, sighing it again, exclaims on Death.

'Hard-favour'd tyrant, ugly, meagre, lean,
Hateful divorce of love,' – thus chides she Death –
'Grim-grinning ghost, earth's worm, what dost thou mean
To stifle beauty, and to steal his breath,
Who when he liv'd, his breath and beauty set
Gloss on the rose, smell to the violet?

'If he be dead – O no, it cannot be,
Seeing his beauty, thou shouldst strike at it,
O yes, it may; thou hast no eyes to see,
But hatefully at random dost thou hit.
Thy mark is feeble age; but thy false dart
Mistakes that aim and cleaves an infant's heart.

'Hadst thou but bid beware, then he had spoke,
And hearing him thy power had lost his power.
The Destinies will curse thee for this stroke:
They bid thee crop a weed; thou pluck'st a flower.
Love's golden arrow at him should have fled,
And not Death's ebon dart, to strike him dead.

'Dost thou drink tears, that thou provok'st such weeping?
What may a heavy groan advantage thee?
Why hast thou cast into eternal sleeping
Those eyes that taught all other eyes to see?
Now Nature cares not for thy mortal vigour,
Since her best work is ruin'd with thy rigour.'

Here overcome, as one full of despair,
She vail'd her eyelids, who, like sluices, stopp'd
The crystal tide that from her two cheeks fair
In the sweet channel of her bosom dropp'd;
But through the floodgates breaks the silver rain,
And with his strong course opens them again.

O, how her eyes and tears did lend and borrow!
Her eye seen in the tears, tears in her eye;
Both crystals, where they view'd each other's sorrow –
Sorrow that friendly sighs sought still to dry;
But like a stormy day, now wind, now rain,
Sighs dry her cheeks, tears make them wet again.

Variable passions throng her constant woe,
As striving who should best become her grief;
All entertain'd, each passion labours so
That every present sorrow seemeth chief,
But none is best. Then join they all together,
Like many clouds consulting for foul weather.

By this, far off she hears some huntsman hollow;

A nurse's song ne'er pleas'd her babe so well.
The dire imagination she did follow
This sound of hope doth labour to expel;
For now reviving joy bids her rejoice,
And flatters her it is Adonis' voice.

Whereat her tears began to turn their tide,
Being prison'd in her eye like pearls in glass;
Yet sometimes falls an orient drop beside,
Which her cheek melts, as scorning it should pass
To wash the foul face of the sluttish ground,
Who is but drunken when she seemeth drown'd.

O hard-believing love, how strange it seems
Not to believe, and yet too credulous!
Thy weal and woe are both of them extremes;
Despair and hope makes thee ridiculous:
The one doth flatter thee in thoughts unlikely,
In likely thoughts the other kills thee quickly.

Now she unweaves the web that she hath wrought:
Adonis lives, and Death is not to blame;
It was not she that call'd him all to nought.
Now she adds honour to his hateful name:
She clepes him king of graves, and grave for kings,
Imperious supreme of all mortal things.

'No, no,' quoth she 'sweet Death, I did but jest;
Yet pardon me I felt a kind of fear
When as I met the boar, that bloody beast
Which knows no pity but is still severe.
Then, gentle shadow – truth I must confess –
I rail'd on thee, fearing my love's decesse.

''Tis not my fault; the boar provok'd my tongue;
Be wreak'd on him, invisible commander;
'Tis he, foul creature, that hath done thee wrong;
I did but act; he's author of thy slander.
Grief hath two tongues, and never woman yet
Could rule them both without ten women's wit.'

Thus, hoping that Adonis is alive,
Her rash suspect she doth extenuate;
And that his beauty may the better thrive,
With Death she humbly doth insinuate;
Tells him of trophies, statues, tombs, and stories,
His victories, his triumphs, and his glories.

'O Jove,' quoth she 'how much a fool was I
To be of such a weak and silly mind
To wail his death who lives, and must not die
Till mutual overthrow of mortal kind!
For he being dead, with him is beauty slain,
And, beauty dead, black chaos comes again.

'Fie, fie, fond love, thou art so full of fear
As one with treasure laden, hemm'd with thieves;
Trifles, unwitnessed with eye or ear,
Thy coward heart with false bethinking grieves.'
Even at this word she hears a merry horn,
Whereat she leaps that was but late forlorn.

As falcons to the lure away she flies;
The grass stoops not, she treads on it so light;
And in her haste unfortunately spies
The foul boar's conquest on her fair delight;
Which seen, her eyes, as murd'red with the view,
Like stars asham'd of day, theselves withdrew;

Or as the snail, whose tender horns being hit,
Shrinks backward in his shelly cave with pain,
And there, all smoth'red up, in shade doth sit,
Long after fearing to creep forth again;
So at his bloody view her eyes are fled
Into the deep-dark cabins of her head;

Where they resign their office and their light
To the disposing of her troubled brain;
Who bids them still consort with ugly night,
And never wound the heart with looks again;
Who, like a king perplexed in his throne,
By their suggestion gives a deadly groan.

Whereat each tributary subject quakes;
As when the wind, imprison'd in the ground,
Struggling for passage, earth's foundation shakes,
Which with cold terror doth men's minds confound.
This mutiny each part doth so surprise
That from their dark beds once more leap her eyes;

And, being open'd, threw unwilling light
Upon the wide wound that the boar had trench'd
In his soft flank; whose wonted lily white
With purple tears that his wound wept was drench'd.
No flow'r was nigh, no grass, herb, leaf, or weed,
But stole his blood and seem'd with him to bleed.

This solemn sympathy poor Venus noteth.
Over one shoulder doth she hang her head;
Dumbly she passions, franticly she doteth;
She thinks he could not die, he is not dead.
Her voice is stopp'd, her joints forget to bow;
Her eyes are mad that they have wept till now.

Upon his hurt she looks so steadfastly
That her sight dazzling makes the wound seem three;
And then she reprehends her mangling eye
That makes more gashes where no breach should be.
His face seems twain, each several limb is doubled;
For oft the eye mistakes, the brain being troubled.

'My tongue cannot express my grief for one,
And yet' quoth she 'behold two Adons dead.
My sighs are blown away, my salt tears gone,
Mine eyes are turn'd to fire, my heart to lead;
Heavy heart's lead melt at mine eyes' red fire!

So shall I die by drops of hot desire.
'Alas, poor world, what treasure hast thou lost!
What face remains alive that's worth the viewing?
Whose tongue is music now? What canst thou boast
Of things long since, or any thing ensuing?
The flowers are sweet, their colours fresh and trim;
But true-sweet beauty liv'd and died with him.

'Bonnet nor veil henceforth no creature wear;
Nor sun nor wind will ever strive to kiss you:
Having no fair to lose, you need not fear;
The sun doth scorn you, and the wind doth hiss you.
But when Adonis liv'd, sun and sharp air
Lurk'd like two thieves to rob him of his fair;

'And therefore would he put his bonnet on,
Under whose brim the gaudy sun would peep;
The wind would blow it off, and, being gone,
Play with his locks. Then would Adonis weep;
And straight, in pity of his tender years,
They both would strive who first should dry his tears.

'To see his face the lion walk'd along
Behind some hedge, because he would not fear him.
To recreate himself when he hath song,
The tiger would be tame and gently hear him.
If he had spoke, the wolf would leave his prey,
And never fright the silly lamb that day.

'When he beheld his shadow in the brook,
The fishes spread on it their golden gills;
When he was by, the birds such pleasure took
That some would sing, some other in their bills
Would bring him mulberries and ripe-red cherries;
He fed them with his sight, they him with berries.

'But this foul, grim, and urchin-snouted boar,
Whose downward eye still looketh for a grave,
Ne'er saw the beauteous livery that he wore:
Witness the entertainment that he gave.
If he did see his face, why then I know
He thought to kiss him, and hath kill'd him so.

''Tis true, 'tis true; thus was Adonis slain:
He ran upon the boar with his sharp spear,
Who did not whet his teeth at him again,
But by a kiss thought to persuade him there;
And nuzzling in his flank, the loving swine
Sheath'd unaware the tusk in his soft groin.

'Had I been tooth'd like him, I must confess,
With kissing him I should have kill'd him first;
But he is dead, and never did he bless
My youth with his; the more am I accurst.'
With this, she falleth in the place she stood,
And stains her face with his congealed blood.

She looks upon his lips, and they are pale;
She takes him by the hand, and that is cold;
She whispers in his ears a heavy tale,
As if they heard the woeful words she told;
She lifts the coffer-lids that close his eyes,
Where, lo, two lamps burnt out in darkness lies;

Two glasses where herself herself beheld
A thousand times, and now no more reflect,
Their virtue lost wherein they late excell'd,
And every beauty robb'd of his effect.
'Wonder of time,' quoth she 'this is my spite,
That, thou being dead, the day should yet be light.

'Since thou art dead, lo, here I prophesy
Sorrow on love hereafter shall attend:
It shall be waited on with jealousy,
Find sweet beginning but unsavoury end,
Ne'er settled equally, but high or low,
That all love's pleasure shall not match his woe.

'It shall be fickle, false, and full of fraud,
Bud and be blasted in a breathing while,
The bottom poison, and the top o'erstraw'd
With sweets that shall the truest sight beguile;
The strongest body shall it make most weak,
Strike the wise dumb, and teach the fool to speak.

'It shall be sparing, and too full of riot,
Teaching decrepit age to tread the measures;
The staring ruffian shall it keep in quiet,
Pluck down the rich, enrich the poor with treasures;
It shall be raging mad, and silly mild,
Make the young old, the old become a child.

'It shall suspect where is no cause of fear;
It shall not fear where it should most mistrust;
It shall be merciful, and too severe,
And most deceiving when it seems most just;
Perverse it shall be where it shows most toward,
Put fear to valour, courage to the coward.

'It shall be cause of war and dire events,
And set dissension 'twixt the son and sire,
Subject and servile to all discontents,
As dry combustious matter is to fire.
Sith in his prime death doth my love destroy,
They that love best their loves shall not enjoy.'

By this, the boy that by her side lay kill'd
Was melted like a vapour from her sight,
And in his blood that on the ground lay spill'd
A purple flow'r sprung up, check'red with white,
Resembling well his pale cheeks, and the blood
Which in round drops upon their whiteness stood.

She bows her head the new-sprung flow'r to smell,

Comparing it to her Adonis' breath;
And says within her bosom it shall dwell,
Since he himself is reft from her by death;
She crops the stalk, and in the breach appears
Green dropping sap, which she compares to tears.

'Poor flow'r,' quoth she 'this was thy father's guise –
Sweet issue of a more sweet-smelling sire –
For every little grief to wet his eyes.
To grow unto himself was his desire,
And so 'tis thine; but know, it is as good
To wither in my breast as in his blood.

'Here was thy father's bed, here in my breast;
Thou art the next of blood, and 'tis thy right.
Lo, in this hollow cradle take thy rest;
My throbbing heart shall rock thee day and night;
There shall not be one minute in an hour
Wherein I will not kiss my sweet love's flow'r.'

Thus weary of the world, away she hies,
And yokes her silver doves; by whose swift aid
Their mistress, mounted, through the empty skies
In her light chariot quickly is convey'd,
Holding their course to Paphos, where their queen
Means to immure herself, and not be seen.

The Rape of Lucrece

TO THE
RIGHT HONOURABLE HENRY WRIOTHESLEY,
EARLE OF SOUTHAMPTON, AND BARON OF TITCHFIELD.

THE love I dedicate to your Lordship is without end: whereof this Pamphlet without beginning is but a superfluous Moity. The warrant I have of your Honourable disposition, not the worth of my untutord Lines makes it assured of acceptance. What I have done is yours, what I have to doe is yours, being part in all I have, devoted yours. Were my worth greater my duety would shew greater, meane time, as it is, it is bound to your Lordship; To whom I wish long life still lengthned with all happinesse.

Your Lordships in all duety.

WILLIAM SHAKESPEARE.

THE ARGUMENT.

LUCIUS TARQUINIUS [for his excessive pride surnamed Superbus), after he had caused his own father-in-law, Servius Tullius, to be cruelly murd'red, and, contrary to the Roman laws and customs, not requiring or staying for the people's suffrages, had possessed himself of the kingdom, went, accompanied with his sons and other noblemen of Rome, to besiege Ardea; during which siege, the principal men of the army meeting one evening at the tent of Sextus Tarquinius, the King's son, in their discourses after supper every one commended the virtues of his own wife; among whom Collatinus extolled the incomparable chastity of his wife Lucretia. In that pleasant humour they all posted to Rome; and intending by their secret and sudden arrival to make trial of that which every one had before avouched, only Collatinus finds his wife [though it were late in the night) spinning amongst her maids; the other ladies were all found dancing and revelling, or in several disports. Whereupon the noblemen yielded Collatinus the victory, and his wife the fame. At that time Sextus Tarquinius, being inflamed with Lucrece' beauty, yet smothering his passions for the present, departed with the rest back to the camp; from whence he shortly after privily withdrew himself, and was [according to his estate) royally entertained and lodged by Lucrece at Collatium. The same night he treacherously stealeth into her chamber, violently ravish'd her, and early in the morning speedeth away. Lucrece, in this lamentable plight, hastily dispatcheth messengers, one to Rome for her father, another to the camp for Collatine. They came, the one accompanied with Junius Brutus, the other with Publius Valerius; and, finding Lucrece attired in mourning habit, demanded the cause of her sorrow. She, first taking an oath of them for her revenge, revealed the actor and whole manner of his dealing, and withal suddenly stabbed herself. Which done, with one consent they all vowed to root out the whole hated family of the Tarquins; and, bearing the dead body to Rome, Brutus acquainted the people with the doer and manner of the vile deed, with a bitter invective against the tyranny of the King; wherewith the people were so moved, that with one consent and a general acclamation the Tarquins were all exiled, and the state government changed from kings to consuls.

FROM the besieged Ardea all in post,
Borne by the trustless wings of false desire,
Lust-breathed Tarquin leaves the Roman host,
And to Collatium bears the lightless fire
Which, in pale embers hid, lurks to aspire
And girdle with embracing flames the waist
Of Collatine's fair love, Lucrece the chaste.

Haply that name of 'chaste' unhap'ly set
This bateless edge on his keen appetite;
When Collatine unwisely did not let
To praise the clear unmatched red and white
Which triumph'd in that sky of his delight,
Where mortal stars, as bright as heaven's beauties,
With pure aspects did him peculiar duties.

For he the night before, in Tarquin's tent,
Unlock'd the treasure of his happy state –
What priceless wealth the heavens had him lent
In the possession of his beauteous mate;
Reck'ning his fortune at such high-proud rate,
That kings might be espoused to more fame,
But king nor peer to such a peerless dame.

O happiness enjoy'd but of a few!
And, if possess'd, as soon decay'd and done
As is the morning's silver-melting dew
Against the golden splendour of the sun!
An expir'd date, cancell'd ere well begun:
Honour and beauty, in the owner's arms,
Are weakly fortress'd from a world of harms.

Beauty itself doth of itself persuade
The eyes of men without an orator;
What needeth then apologies be made
To set forth that which is so singular?
Or why is Collatine the publisher

Of that rich jewel he should keep unknown
From thievish ears, because it is his own?

Perchance his boast of Lucrece' sov'reignty
Suggested this proud issue of a king;
For by our ears our hearts oft tainted be.
Perchance that envy of so rich a thing,
Braving compare, disdainfully did sting
His high-pitch'd thoughts that meaner men should vaunt
That golden hap which their superiors want.

But some untimely thought did instigate
His all-too-timeless speed, if none of those.
His honour, his affairs, his friends, his state,
Neglected all, with swift intent he goes
To quench the coal which in his liver glows.
O rash false heat, wrapp'd in repentant cold,
Thy hasty spring still blasts and ne'er grows old!

When at Collatium this false lord arrived,
Well was he welcom'd by the Roman dame,
Within whose face beauty and virtue strived
Which of them both should underprop her fame:
When virtue bragg'd, beauty would blush for shame;
When beauty boasted blushes, in despite
Virtue would stain that o'er with silver white.

But beauty, in that white intituled,
From Venus' doves doth challenge that fair field;
Then virtue claims from beauty beauty's red,
Which virtue gave the golden age to gild
Their silver cheeks, and call'd it then their shield;
Teaching them thus to use it in the fight,
When shame assail'd, the red should fence the white.

This heraldry in Lucrece' face was seen,
Argued by beauty's red and virtue's white;
Of either's colour was the other queen,
Proving from world's minority their right;
Yet their ambition makes them still to fight,
The sovereignty of either being so great
That oft they interchange each other's seat.

This silent war of lilies and of roses
Which Tarquin view'd in her fair face's field,
In their pure ranks his traitor eye encloses;
Where, lest between them both it should be kill'd,
The coward captive vanquished doth yield
To those two armies that would let him go
Rather than triumph in so false a foe.

Now thinks he that her husband's shallow tongue –
The niggard prodigal that prais'd her so –
In that high task hath done her beauty wrong,
Which far exceeds his barren skill to show;
Therefore that praise which Collatine doth owe
Enchanted Tarquin answers with surmise,
In silent wonder of still-gazing eyes.

This earthly saint, adored by this devil,
Little suspecteth the false worshipper;
For unstain'd thoughts do seldom dream on evil;
Birds never lim'd no secret bushes fear.
So guiltless she securely gives good cheer
And reverend welcome to her princely guest,
Whose inward ill no outward harm express'd;

For that he colour'd with his high estate,
Hiding base sin in pleats of majesty;
That nothing in him seem'd inordinate,
Save sometime too much wonder of his eye,
Which, having all, all could not satisfy;
But, poorly rich, so wanteth in his store
That cloy'd with much he pineth still for more.

But she that never cop'd with stranger eyes
Could pick no meaning from their parling looks,
Nor read the subtle-shining secrecies
Writ in the glassy margents of such books.
She touch'd no unknown baits, nor fear'd no hooks;
Nor could she moralize his wanton sight,
More than his eyes were open'd to the light.

He stories to her ears her husband's fame,
Won in the fields of fruitful Italy;
And decks with praises Collatine's high name,
Made glorious by his manly chivalry,
With bruised arms and wreaths of victory.
Her joy with heav'd-up hand she doth express,
And, wordless, so greets heaven for his success.

Far from the purpose of his coming thither
He makes excuses for his being there.
No cloudy show of stormy blust'ring weather
Doth yet in his fair welkin once appear;
Till sable Night, mother of Dread and Fear,
Upon the world dim darkness doth display,
And in her vaulty prison stows the Day.

For then is Tarquin brought unto his bed,
Intending weariness with heavy sprite;
For, after supper, long he questioned
With modest Lucrece, and wore out the night.
Now leaden slumber with life's strength doth fight;
And every one to rest themselves betake,
Save thieves, and cares, and troubled minds that wake.

As one of which doth Tarquin lie revolving
The sundry dangers of his will's obtaining;
Yet ever to obtain his will resolving,
Though weak-built hopes persuade him to abstaining;
Despair to gain doth traffic oft for gaining;
And when great treasure is the meed proposed,
Though death be adjunct, there's no death supposed.

Those that much covet are with gain so fond

That what they have not, that which they possess
They scatter and unloose it from their bond,
And so, by hoping more, they have but less;
Or, gaining more, the profit of excess
  Is but to surfeit, and such griefs sustain
  That they prove bankrupt in this poor-rich gain.

The aim of all is but to nurse the life
With honour, wealth, and ease in waning age;
And in this aim there is such thwarting strife
That one for all or all for one we gage:
As life for honour in fell battle's rage;
  Honour for wealth; and oft that wealth doth cost
  The death of all, and all together lost.

So that in vent'ring ill we leave to be
The things we are for that which we expect;
And this ambitious foul infirmity,
In having much, torments us with defect
Of that we have; so then we do neglect
  The thing we have and, all for want of wit,
  Make something nothing by augmenting it.

Such hazard now must doting Tarquin make,
Pawning his honour to obtain his lust;
And for himself himself he must forsake –
Then where is truth if there be no self-trust?
When shall he think to find a stranger just,
  When he himself himself confounds, betrays
  To sland'rous tongues and wretched hateful
    days?

Now stole upon the time the dead of night,
When heavy sleep had clos'd up mortal eyes;
No comfortable star did lend his light,
No noise but owls' and wolves' death-boding
  cries;
Now serves the season that they may surprise
  The silly lambs. Pure thoughts are dead and still,
  While lust and murder wake to stain and kill.

And now this lustful lord leap'd from his bed,
Throwing his mantle rudely o'er his arm;
Is madly toss'd between desire and dread;
Th' one sweetly flatters, th' other feareth harm;
But honest Fear, bewitch'd with lust's foul charm,
  Doth too too oft betake him to retire,
  Beaten away by brain-sick rude desire.

His falchion on a flint he softly smiteth,
That from the cold stone sparks of fire do fly,
Whereat a waxen torch forthwith he lighteth,
Which must be lode-star to his lustful eye;
And to the flame thus speaks advisedly:
  'As from this cold flint I enforc'd this fire,
  So Lucrece must I force to my desire'.

Here pale with fear he doth premeditate
The dangers of his loathsome enterprise,
And in his inward mind he doth debate
What following sorrow may on this arise;
Then, looking scornfully, he doth despise
  His naked armour of still-slaughtered lust,
  And justly thus controls his thoughts unjust:

'Fair torch, burn out thy light, and lend it not
To darken her whose light excelleth thine;
And die, unhallowed thoughts, before you blot
With your uncleanness that which is divine;
Offer pure incense to so pure a shrine:
  Let fair humanity abhor the deed
  That spots and stains love's modest snow-white
    weed.

'O shame to knighthood and to shining arms!
O foul dishonour to my household's grave!
O impious act including all foul harms!
A martial man to be soft fancy's slave!
True valour still a true respect should have;
  Then my digression is so vile, so base,
  That it will live engraven in my face.

'Yea, though I die, the scandal will survive
And be an eyesore in my golden coat;
Some loathsome dash the herald will contrive
To cipher me how fondly I did dote;
That my posterity, sham'd with the note,
  Shall curse my bones, and hold it for no sin
  To wish that I their father had not been.

'What win I if I gain the thing I seek?
A dream, a breath, a froth of fleeting joy.
Who buys a minute's mirth to wail a week?
Or sells eternity to get a toy?
For one sweet grape who will the vine destroy?
  Or what fond beggar, but to touch the crown,
  Would with the sceptre straight be strucken
    down?

'If Collatinus dream of my intent,
Will he not wake, and in a desp'rate rage
Post hither, this vile purpose to prevent –
This siege that hath engirt his marriage,
This blur to youth, this sorrow to the sage,
  This dying virtue, this surviving shame,
  Whose crime will bear an ever-during blame?

'O, what excuse can my invention make
When thou shalt charge me with so black a deed?
Will not my tongue be mute, my frail joints
    shake,
Mine eyes forgo their light, my false heart bleed?
The guilt being great, the fear doth still exceed;
  And extreme fear can neither fight nor fly,
  But coward-like with trembling terror die.

'Had Collatinus kill'd my son or sire,
Or lain in ambush to betray my life,
Or were he not my dear friend, this desire
Might have excuse to work upon his wife,
As in revenge or quittal of such strife;
  But as he is my kinsman, my dear friend,
  The shame and fault finds no excuse nor end.

'Shameful it is – ay, if the fact be known;

Hateful it is – there is no hate in loving;
I'll beg her love – but she is not her own –
The worst is but denial and reproving.
My will is strong, past reason's weak removing –
Who fears a sentence or an old man's saw
Shall by a painted cloth be kept in awe.'

Thus, graceless, holds he disputation
'Tween frozen conscience and hot-burning will,
And with good thoughts makes dispensation,
Urging the worser sense for vantage still;
Which in a moment doth confound and kill
All pure effects, and doth so far proceed
That what is vile shows like a virtuous deed.

Quoth he 'She took me kindly by the hand
And gaz'd for tidings in my eager eyes,
Fearing some hard news from the warlike band
Where her beloved Collatinus lies
O how her fear did make her colour rise!
First red as roses that on lawn we lay,
Then white as lawn, the roses took away.

'And how her hand in my hand being lock'd
Forc'd it to tremble with her loyal fear!
Which struck her sad, and then it faster rock'd
Until her husband's welfare she did hear;
Whereat she smiled with so sweet a cheer
That had Narcissus seen her as she stood
Self-love had never drown'd him in the flood.

'Why hunt I then for colour or excuses?
All orators are dumb when beauty pleadeth;
Poor wretches have remorse in poor abuses;
Love thrives not in the heart that shadows dreadeth;
Affection is my captain, and he leadeth;
And when his gaudy banner is display'd,
The coward fights and will not be dismay'd.

'Then, childish fear avaunt! debating die!
Respect and reason wait on wrinkled age!
My heart shall never countermand mine eye;
Sad pause and deep regard beseems the sage;
My part is youth, and beats these from the stage:
Desire my pilot is, beauty my prize;
Then who fears sinking where such treasure lies?'

As corn o'ergrown by weeds, so heedful fear
Is almost chok'd by unresisted lust.
Away he steals with open list'ning ear,
Full of foul hope, and full of fond mistrust;
Both which, as servitors to the unjust,
So cross him with their opposite persuasion
That now he vows a league, and now invasion.

Within his thought her heavenly image sits,
And in the selfsame seat sits Collatine.
That eye which looks on her confounds his wits;
That eye which him beholds, as more divine,
Unto a view so false will not incline;
But with a pure appeal seeks to the heart,
Which once corrupted takes the worser part;

And therein heartens up his servile powers,
Who, flatt'red by their leader's jocund show,
Stuff up his lust, as minutes fill up hours;
And as their captain, so their pride doth grow,
Paying more slavish tribute than they owe.
By reprobate desire thus madly led,
The Roman lord marcheth to Lucrece' bed.

The locks between her chamber and his will,
Each one by him enforc'd, retires his ward;
But, as they open, they all rate his ill,
Which drives the creeping thief to some regard.
The threshold grates the door to have him heard;
Night-wand'ring weasels shriek to see him there;
They fright him, yet he still pursues his fear.

As each unwilling portal yields him way,
Through little vents and crannies of the place
The wind wars with his torch, to make him stay,
And blows the smoke of it into his face,
Extinguishing his conduct in this case;
But his hot heart, which fond desire doth scorch,
Puffs forth another wind that fires the torch;

And, being lighted, by the light he spies,
Lucretia's glove, wherein her needle sticks;
He takes it from the rushes where it lies,
And griping it, the needle his finger pricks,
As who should say 'This glove to wanton tricks.
Is not inur'd. Return again in haste;
Thou seest our mistress' ornaments are chaste'.

But all these poor forbiddings could not stay him;
He in the worst sense consters their denial:
The doors, the wind, the glove that did delay him,
He takes for accidental things of trial;
Or as those bars which stop the hourly dial,
Who with a ling'ring stay his course doth let,
Till every minute pays the hour his debt.

'So, so,' quoth he 'these lets attend the time,
Like little frosts that sometime threat the spring,
To add a more rejoicing to the prime,
And give the sneaped birds more cause to sing.
Pain pays the income of each precious thing:
Huge rocks, high winds, strong pirates, shelves and sands,
The merchant fears, ere rich at home he lands.'

Now is he come unto the chamber door
That shuts him from the heaven of his thought,
Which with a yielding latch, and with no more,
Hath barr'd him from the blessed thing he sought.
So from himself impiety hath wrought
That for his prey to pray he doth begin,
As if the heavens should countenance his sin.

But in the midst of his unfruitful prayer,
Having solicited th' eternal power,
That his foul thoughts might compass his fair fair,

And they would stand auspicious to the hour,
Even there he starts – quoth he 'I must deflow'r.
The powers to whom I pray abhor this fact;
How can they then assist me in the act?

'Then Love and Fortune be my gods, my guide!
My will is back'd with resolution.
Thoughts are but dreams till their effects be tried;
The blackest sin is clear'd with absolution;
Against love's fire fear's frost hath dissolution.
The eye of heaven is out, and misty night
Covers the shame that follows sweet delight.'

This said, his guilty hand pluck'd up the latch,
And with his knee the door he opens wide.
The dove sleeps fast that this night-owl will catch.
Thus treason works ere traitors be espied.
Who sees the lurking serpent steps aside;
But she, sound sleeping, fearing no such thing,
Lies at the mercy of his mortal sting.

Into the chamber wickedly he stalks,
And gazeth on her yet unstained bed.
The curtains being close, about he walks,
Rolling his greedy eyeballs in his head.
By their high treason is his heart misled,
Which gives the watchword to his hand full soon
To draw the cloud that hides the silver moon.

Look as the fair and fiery-pointed sun,
Rushing from forth a cloud, bereaves our sight;
Even so, the curtain drawn, his eyes begun
To wink, being blinded with a greater light;
Whether it is that she reflects so bright
That dazzleth them, or else some shame supposed;
But blind they are, and keep themselves enclosed.

O, had they in that darksome prison died,
Then had they seen the period of their ill!
Then Collatine again by Lucrece' side
In his clear bed might have reposed still;
But they must ope, this blessed league to kill;
And holy-thoughted Lucrece to their sight
Must sell her joy, her life, her world's delight.

Her lily hand her rosy cheek lies under,
Coz'ning the pillow of a lawful kiss;
Who, therefore angry, seems to part in sunder,
Swelling on either side to want his bliss;
Between those hills her head entombed is;
Where, like a virtuous monument, she lies,
To be admir'd of lewd unhallowed eyes.

Without the bed her other fair hand was,
On the green coverlet; whose perfect white
Show'd like an April daisy on the grass,
With pearly sweat, resembling dew of night.
Her eyes, like marigolds, had sheath'd their light,
And canopied in darkness sweetly lay,
Till they might open to adorn the day.

Her hair, like golden threads, play'd with her breath –
O modest wantons! wanton modesty! –
Showing life's triumph in the map of death,
And death's dim look in life's mortality.
Each in her sleep themselves so beautify,
As if between them twain there were no strife.
But that life liv'd in death, and death in life.

Her breasts, like ivory globes circled with blue,
A pair of maiden worlds unconquered,
Save of their lord no bearing yoke they knew,
And him by oath they truly honoured.
These worlds in Tarquin new ambition bred,
Who like a foul usurper went about
From this fair throne to heave the owner out.

What could he see but mightily he noted?
What did he note but strongly he desired?
What he beheld, on that he firmly doted,
And in his will his wilful eye he tired.
With more than admiration he admired
Her azure veins, her alabaster skin,
Her coral lips, her snow-white dimpled chin.

As the grim lion fawneth o'er his prey,
Sharp hunger by the conquest satisfied,
So o'er this sleeping soul doth Tarquin stay,
His rage of lust by gazing qualified;
Slack'd, not suppress'd; for standing by her side,
His eye, which late this mutiny restrains,
Unto a greater uproar tempts his veins;

And they, like straggling slaves for pillage fighting,
Obdurate vassals, fell exploits effecting,
In bloody death and ravishment delighting,
Nor children's tears nor mothers' groans respecting,
Swell in their pride, the onset still expecting.
Anon his beating heart, alarum striking,
Gives the hot charge and bids them do their liking.

His drumming heart cheers up his burning eye,
His eye commends the leading to his hand;
His hand, as proud of such a dignity,
Smoking with pride, march'd on to make his stand
On her bare breast, the heart of all her land;
Whose ranks of blue veins, as his hand did scale,
Left their round turrets destitute and pale.

They, must'ring to the quiet cabinet
Where their dear governess and lady lies,
Do tell her she is dreadfully beset,
And fright her with confusion of their cries:
She, much amaz'd, breaks ope her lock'd-up eyes,
Who, peeping forth this tumult to behold,
Are by his flaming torch dimm'd and controll'd.

Imagine her as one in dead of night
From forth dull sleep by dreadful fancy waking,
That thinks she hath beheld some ghastly sprite
Whose grim aspect sets every joint a-shaking –
What terror 'tis! but she, in worser taking,
From sleep disturbed, heedfully doth view
The sight which makes supposed terror true.

Wrapp'd and confounded in a thousand fears,
Like to a new-kill'd bird she trembling lies;
She dares not look; yet, winking, there appears
Quick-shifting antics, ugly in her eyes.
Such shadows are the weak brain's forgeries,
Who, angry that the eyes fly from their lights,
In darkness daunts them with more dreadful sights.

His hand, that yet remains upon her breast –
Rude ram, to batter such an ivory wall! –
May feel her heart, poor citizen, distress'd.
Wounding itself to death, rise up and fall,
Beating her bulk, that his hand shakes withal.
This moves in him more rage and lesser pity,
To make the breach and enter this sweet city.

First like a trumpet doth his tongue begin
To sound a parley to his heartless foe,
Who o'er the white sheet peers her whiter chin,
The reason of this rash alarm to know,
Which he by dumb demeanour seeks to show;
But she with vehement prayers urgeth still
Under what colour he commits this ill.

Thus he replies: 'The colour in thy face,
That even for anger makes the lily pale
And the red rose blush at her own disgrace,
Shall plead for me and tell my loving tale.
Under that colour am I come to scale
Thy never-conquered fort. The fault is thine,
For those thine eyes betray thee unto mine.

'Thus I forestall thee, if thou mean to chide:
Thy beauty hath ensnar'd thee to this night,
Where thou with patience must my will abide,
My will that marks thee for my earth's delight,
Which I to conquer sought with all my might;
But as reproof and reason beat it dead,
By thy bright beauty was it newly bred.

'I see what crosses my attempt will bring;
I know what thorns the growing rose defends;
I think the honey guarded with a sting:
All this beforehand counsel comprehends.
But Will is deaf and hears no heedful friends;
Only he hath an eye to gaze on beauty,
And dotes on what he looks, 'gainst law or duty.

'I have debated, even in my soul,
What wrong, what shame, what sorrow I shall breed;
But nothing can Affection's course control,
Or stop the headlong fury of his speed.
I know repentant tears ensure the deed,
Reproach, disdain, and deadly enmity;
Yet strive I to embrace mine infamy'.

This said, he shakes aloft his Roman blade,
Which, like a falcon tow'ring in the skies,
Coucheth the fowl below with his wings' shade,
Whose crooked beak threats if he mount he dies.
So under his insulting falchion lies
Harmless Lucretia, marking what he tells
With trembling fear, as fowl hear falcon's bells.

'Lucrece,' quoth he 'this night I must enjoy thee.
If thou deny, then force must work my way,
For in thy bed I purpose to destroy thee;
That done, some worthless slave of thine I'll slay,
To kill thine honour with thy life's decay;
And in thy dead arms do I mean to place him,
Swearing I slew him, seeing thee embrace him.

'So thy surviving husband shall remain
The scornful mark of every open eye;
Thy kinsmen hang their heads at this disdain,
Thy issue blurr'd with nameless bastardy;
And thou, the author of their obloquy,
Shalt have thy trespass cited up in rhymes,
And sung by children in succeeding times.

'But if thou yield, I rest thy secret friend:
The fault unknown is as a thought unacted;
A little harm done to a great good end
For lawful policy remains enacted.
The poisonous simple sometime is compacted
In a pure compound; being so applied,
His venom in effect is purified.

'Then, for thy husband and thy children's sake,
Tender my suit; bequeath not to their lot
The shame that from them no device can take,
The blemish that will never be forgot;
Worse than a slavish wipe or birth-hour's blot;
For marks descried in men's nativity
Are nature's faults, not their own infamy.'

Here with a cockatrice' dead-killing eye
He rouseth up himself, and makes a pause;
While she, the picture of pure piety,
Like a white hind under the grype's sharp claws,
Pleads, in a wilderness where are no laws,
To the rough beast that knows no gentle right,
Nor aught obeys but his foul appetite.

But when a black-fac'd cloud the world doth threat,
In his dim mist th' aspiring mountains hiding,
From earth's dark womb some gentle gust doth get,
Which blows these pitchy vapours from their biding,
Hind'ring their present fall by this dividing;
So his unhallowed haste her words delays,
And moody Pluto winks while Orpheus plays.

Yet, foul night-waking cat, he doth but dally,
While in his holdfast foot the weak mouse panteth;
Her sad behaviour feeds his vulture folly,
A swallowing gulf that even in plenty wanteth;
His ear her prayers admits, but his heart granteth
  No penetrable entrance to her plaining.
  Tears harden lust, though marble wear with raining.

Her pity-pleading eyes are sadly fixed
In the remorseless wrinkles of his face;
Her modest eloquence with sighs is mixed,
Which to her oratory adds more grace.
She puts the period often from his place,
  And midst the sentence so her accent breaks
  That twice she doth begin ere once she speaks.

She conjures him by high almighty Jove,
By knighthood, gentry, and sweet friendship's oath,
By her untimely tears, her husband's love,
By holy human law, and common troth,
By heaven and earth, and all the power of both,
  That to his borrowed bed he make retire,
  And stoop to honour, not to foul desire.

Quoth she 'Reward not hospitality
With such black payment as thou hast pretended;
Mud not the fountain that gave drink to thee;
Mar not the thing that cannot be amended;
End thy ill aim before thy shoot be ended.
  He is no woodman that doth bend his bow
  To strike a poor unseasonable doe.

'My husband is thy friend – for his sake spare me;
Thyself art mighty – for thine own sake leave me;
Myself a weakling – do not then ensnare me;
Thou look'st not like deceit – do not deceive me.
My sighs like whirlwinds labour hence to heave thee.
  If ever man were mov'd with woman's moans,
  Be moved with my tears, my sighs, my groans;

'All which together, like a troubled ocean,
Beat at thy rocky and wrack-threat'ning heart;
To soften it with their continual motion;
For stones dissolv'd to water do convert.
O, if no harder than a stone thou art,
  Melt at my tears, and be compassionate!
  Soft pity enters at an iron gate.

'In Tarquin's likeness I did entertain thee;
Hast thou put on his shape to do him shame?
To all the host of heaven I complain me
Thou wrong'st his honour, wound'st his princely name.
Thou art not what thou seem'st; and if the same,
  Thou seem'st not what thou art, a god, a king;
  For kings like gods should govern everything.

'How will thy shame be seeded in thine age,
When thus thy vices bud before thy spring!
If in thy hope thou dar'st do such outrage,
What dar'st thou not when once thou art a king?
O, be rememb'red, no outrageous thing
  From vassal actors can be wip'd away;
  Then kings' misdeeds cannot be hid in clay.

'This deed will make thee only lov'd for fear,
But happy monarchs still are fear'd for love;
With foul offenders thou perforce must bear,
When they in thee the like offences prove.
If but for fear of this, thy will remove;
  For princes are the glass, the school, the book,
  Where subjects' eyes do learn, do read, do look.

And wilt thou be the school where Lust shall learn?
Must he in thee read lectures of such shame?
Wilt thou be glass wherein it shall discern
Authority for sin, warrant for blame,
To privilege dishonour in thy name?
  Thou back'st reproach against long-living laud,
  And mak'st fair reputation but a bawd.

'Hast thou command? By him that gave it thee,
From a pure heart command thy rebel will;
Draw not thy sword to guard iniquity,
For it was lent thee all that brood to kill.
Thy princely office how canst thou fulfil,
  When, pattern'd by thy fault, foul Sin may say
  He learn'd to sin and thou didst teach the way?

'Think but how vile a spectacle it were
To view thy present trespass in another.
Men's faults do seldom to themselves appear;
Their own transgressions partially they smother:
This guilt would seem death-worthy in thy brother.
  O, how are they wrapp'd in with infamies
  That from their own misdeeds askance their eyes!

'To thee, to thee, my heav'd-up hands appeal,
Not to seducing lust, thy rash relier;
I sue for exil'd majesty's repeal;
Let him return and flatt'ring thoughts retire:
His true respect will prison false desire,
  And wipe the dim mist from thy doting eyne,
  That thou shalt see thy state, and pity mine'.

'Have done;' quoth he 'my uncontrolled tide
Turns not, but swells the higher by this let.
Small lights are soon blown out; huge fires abide,
And with the wind in greater fury fret.
The petty streams that pay a daily debt
  To their salt sovereign, with their fresh falls' haste,
  Add to his flow, but alter not his taste.'

'Thou art' quoth she 'a sea, a sovereign king;
And, lo, there falls into thy boundless flood
Black lust, dishonour, shame, misgoverning,

Who seek to stain the ocean of thy blood.
If all these petty ills shall change thy good,
Thy sea within a puddle's womb is hearsed,
And not the puddle in thy sea dispersed.

'So shall these slaves be king, and thou their slave;
Thou nobly base, they basely dignified;
Thou their fair life, and they thy fouler grave;
Thou loathed in their shame, they in thy pride.
The lesser thing should not the greater hide;
The cedar stoops not to the base shrub's foot,
But low shrubs wither at the cedar's root.

'So let thy thoughts, low vassals to thy state' –
'No more;' quoth he 'by heaven, I will not hear thee!
Yield to my love; if not, enforced hate,
Instead of love's coy touch, shall rudely tear thee;
That done, despitefully I mean to bear thee
Unto the base bed of some rascal groom,
To be thy partner in this shameful doom.'

This said, he sets his foot upon the light,
For light and lust are deadly enemies;
Shame folded up in blind concealing night,
When most unseen, then most doth tyrannize.
The wolf hath seiz'd his prey; the poor lamb cries
Till with her own white fleece her voice controll'd
Entombs her outcry in her lips' sweet fold;

For with the nightly linen that she wears
He pens her piteous clamours in her head,
Cooling his hot face in the chastest tears
That ever modest eyes with sorrow shed.
O, that prone lust should stain so pure a bed!
The spots whereof could weeping purify,
Her tears should drop on them perpetually.

But she hath lost a dearer thing than life,
And he hath won what he would lose again.
This forced league doth force a further strife,
This momentary joy breeds months of pain,
This hot desire converts to cold disdain;
Pure Chastity is rifled of her store,
And Lust, the thief, far poorer than before.

Look as the full-fed hound or gorged hawk,
Unapt for tender smell or speedy flight,
Make slow pursuit, or altogether baulk
The prey wherein by nature they delight;
So surfeit-taking Tarquin fares this night:
His taste delicious, in digestion souring,
Devours his will, that liv'd by foul devouring.

O, deeper sin than bottomless conceit
Can comprehend in still imagination!
Drunken Desire must vomit his receipt,
Ere he can see his own abomination.
While Lust is in his pride, no exclamation
Can curb his heat or rein his rash desire,
Till, like a jade, Self-will himself doth tire.

And then with lank and lean discolour'd cheek,
With heavy eye, knit brow, and strengthless pace,
Feeble Desire, all recreant, poor, and meek,
Like to a bankrupt beggar wails his case.
The flesh being proud, Desire doth fight with Grace,
For there it revels; and when that decays,
The guilty rebel for remission prays.

So fares it with this faultful lord of Rome,
Who this accomplishment so hotly chased;
For now against himself he sounds this doom,
That through the length of times he stands disgraced;
Besides, his soul's fair temple is defaced,
To whose weak ruins muster troops of cares,
To ask the spotted princess how she fares.

She says her subjects with foul insurrection
Have batter'd down her consecrated wall,
And by their mortal fault brought in subjection
Her immortality, and made her thrall
To living death and pain perpetual;
Which in her prescience she controlled still,
But her foresight could not forestall their will.

Ev'n in this thought through the dark night he stealeth,
A captive victor that hath lost in gain;
Bearing away the wound that nothing healeth,
The scar that will despite of cure remain,
Leaving his spoil perplex'd in greater pain.
She bears the load of lust he left behind,
And he the burthen of a guilty mind.

He like a thievish dog creeps sadly thence,
She like a wearied lamb lies panting there;
He scowls and hates himself for his offence,
She, desperate, with her nails her flesh doth tear.
He faintly flies, sweating with guilty fear;
She stays, exclaiming on the direful night;
He runs, and chides his vanish'd loath'd delight.

He thence departs a heavy convertite,
She there remains a hopeless castaway;
He in his speed looks for the morning light;
She prays she never may behold the day.
'For day' quoth she 'night's scapes doth open lay;
And my true eyes have never practis'd how
To cloak offences with a cunning brow.

'They think not but that every eye can see
The same disgrace which they themselves behold;
And therefore would they still in darkness be,
To have their unseen sin remain untold;
For they their guilt with weeping will unfold,
And grave, like water that doth eat in steel,
Upon my cheeks what helpless shame I feel.'

Here she exclaims against repose and rest,
And bids her eyes hereafter still be blind.
She wakes her heart by beating on her breast,

And bids it leap from thence, where it may find
Some purer chest to close so pure a mind.
  Frantic with grief thus breathes she forth her spite
  Against the unseen secrecy of night:

'O comfort-killing Night, image of hell!
Dim register and notary of shame!
Black stage for tragedies and murders fell!
Vast sin-concealing chaos! nurse of blame!
Blind muffled bawd! dark harbour for defame!
  Grim cave of death! whisp'ring conspirator,
  With close-tongu'd treason and the ravisher!

'O hateful, vaporous, and foggy night!
Since thou art guilty of my cureless crime,
Muster thy mists to meet the eastern light,
Make war against proportion'd course of time;
Or if thou wilt permit the sun to climb
  His wonted height, yet ere he go to bed,
  Knit poisonous clouds about his golden head.

'With rotten damps ravish the morning air;
Let their exhal'd unwholesome breaths make sick
The life of purity, the supreme fair,
Ere he arrive his weary noontide prick;
And let thy musty vapours march so thick
  That in their smoky ranks his smoth'red light
  May set at noon and make perpetual night.

'Were Tarquin Night, as he is but Night's child,
The silver-shining queen he would distain;
Her twinkling handmaids too, by him defil'd,
Through Night's black bosom should not peep again;
So should I have co-partners in my pain;
  And fellowship in woe doth woe assuage,
  As palmers' chat makes short their pilgrimage.

'Where now I have no one to blush with me,
To cross their arms and hang their heads with mine,
To mask their brows and hide their infamy;
But I alone alone must sit and pine,
Seasoning the earth with show'rs of silver brine,
  Mingling my talk with tears, my grief with groans,
  Poor wasting monuments of lasting moans.

'O Night, thou furnace of foul reeking smoke,
Let not the jealous Day behold that face
Which underneath thy black all-hiding cloak
Immodestly lies martyr'd with disgrace!
Keep still possession of thy gloomy place,
  That all the faults which in thy reign are made
  May likewise be sepulcher'd in thy shade.

'Make me not object to the tell-tale Day.
The light will show, character'd in my brow,
The story of sweet chastity's decay,
The impious breach of holy wedlock vow;
Yea, the illiterate, that know not how
  To cipher what is writ in learned books,
  Will quote my loathsome trespass in my looks.

'The nurse, to still her child, will tell my story,
And fright her crying babe with Tarquin's name;
The orator, to deck his oratory,
Will couple my reproach to Tarquin's shame;
Feast-finding minstrels, tuning my defame,
  Will tie the hearers to attend each line,
  How Tarquin wronged me, I Collatine.

'Let my good name, that senseless reputation,
For Collatine's dear love be kept unspotted;
If that be made a theme for disputation,
The branches of another root are rotted,
And undeserv'd reproach to him allotted
  That is as clear from this attaint of mine
  As I ere this was pure to Collatine.

'O unseen shame! invisible disgrace!
O unfelt sore! crest-wounding, private scar!
Reproach is stamp'd in Collatinus' face,
And Tarquin's eye may read the mot afar,
How he in peace is wounded, not in war.
  Alas, how many bear such shameful blows,
  Which not themselves but he that gives them knows!

'If, Collatine, thine honour lay in me,
From me by strong assault it is bereft.
My honey lost, and I, a drone-like bee,
Have no perfection of my summer left,
But robb'd and ransack'd by injurious theft.
  In thy weak hive a wand'ring wasp hath crept,
  And suck'd the honey which thy chaste bee kept.

'Yet am I guilty of thy honour's wrack –
Yet for thy honour did I entertain him;
Coming from thee, I could not put him back,
For it had been dishonour to disdain him;
Besides of weariness he did complain him,
  And talk'd of virtue – O unlook'd-for evil,
  When virtue is profan'd in such a devil!

'Why should the worm intrude the maiden bud?
Or hateful cuckoos hatch in sparrows' nests?
Or toads infect fair founts with venom mud?
Or tyrant folly lurk in gentle breasts?
Or kings be breakers of their own behests?
  But no perfection is so absolute
  That some impurity doth not pollute.

'The aged man that coffers up his gold
Is plagu'd with cramps and gouts and painful fits,
And scarce hath eyes his treasure to behold,
But like still-pining Tantalus he sits,
And useless barns the harvest of his wits,
  Having no other pleasure of his gain
  But torment that it cannot cure his pain.

'So then he hath it, when he cannot use it,
And leaves it to be mast'red by his young;
Who in their pride do presently abuse it.

Their father was too weak, and they too strong,
To hold their cursed-blessed fortune long.
The sweets we wish for turn to loathed sours
Even in the moment that we call them ours.

'Unruly blasts wait on the tender spring;
Unwholesome weeds take root with precious flow'rs;
The adder hisses where the sweet birds sing;
What virtue breeds iniquity devours.
We have no good that we can say is ours,
But ill-annexed Opportunity
Or kills his life or else his quality.

'O Opportunity, thy guilt is great!
'Tis thou that execut'st the traitor's treason;
Thou sets the wolf where he the lamb may get;
Whoever plots the sin, thou 'point'st the season;
'Tis thou that spurn'st at right, at law, at reason;
And in thy shady cell, where none may spy him,
Sits Sin, to seize the souls that wander by him.

'Thou makest the vestal violate her oath;
Thou blowest the fire when temperance is thaw'd;
Thou smotherest honesty, thou murth'rest troth;
Thou foul abettor! thou notorious bawd!
Thou plantest scandal and displacest laud.
Thou ravisher, thou traitor, thou false thief,
Thy honey turns to gall, thy joy to grief!

'Thy secret pleasure turns to open shame,
Thy private feasting to a public fast,
Thy smoothing titles to a ragged name,
Thy sug'red tongue to bitter wormwood taste;
Thy violent vanities can never last.
How comes it then, vile Opportunity,
Being so bad, such numbers seek for thee?

'When wilt thou be the humble suppliant's friend,
And bring him where his suit may be obtained?
When wilt thou sort an hour great strifes to end?
Or free that soul which wretchedness hath chained?
Give physic to the sick, ease to the pained?
The poor, lame, blind, halt, creep, cry out for thee;
But they ne'er meet with Opportunity.

'The patient dies while the physician sleeps;
The orphan pines while the oppressor feeds;
Justice is feasting while the widow weeps;
Advice is sporting while infection breeds;
Thou grant'st no time for charitable deeds;
Wrath, envy, treason, rape, and murder's rages,
Thy heinous hours wait on them as their pages.

'When Truth and Virtue have to do with thee,
A thousand crosses keep them from thy aid;
They buy thy help, but Sin ne'er gives a fee;
He gratis comes, and thou art well apaid
As well to hear as grant what he hath said.
My Collatine would else have come to me
When Tarquin did, but he was stay'd by thee.

'Guilty thou art of murder and of theft,
Guilty of perjury and subornation,
Guilty of treason, forgery, and shift,
Guilty of incest, that abomination:
An accessary by thine inclination
To all sins past, and all that are to come,
From the creation to the general doom.

'Mis-shapen Time, copesmate of ugly Night,
Swift subtle post, carrier of grisly care,
Eater of youth, false slave to false delight,
Base watch of woes, sin's packhorse, virtue's snare;
Thou nursest all, and murd'rest all that are.
O hear me then, injurious, shifting Time!
Be guilty of my death, since of my crime.

'Why hath thy servant Opportunity
Betray'd the hours thou gav'st me to repose?
Cancell'd my fortunes and enchained me
To endless date of never-ending woes?
Time's office is to fine the hate of foes,
To eat up errors by opinion bred,
Not spend the dowry of a lawful bed.

'Time's glory is to calm contending kings,
To unmask falsehood, and bring truth to light,
To stamp the seal of time in aged things,
To wake the morn, and sentinel the night,
To wrong the wronger till he render right;
To ruinate proud buildings with thy hours,
And smear with dust their glitt'ring golden tow'rs;

'To fill with worm-holes stately monuments,
To feed oblivion with decay of things,
To blot old books and alter their contents,
To pluck the quills from ancient ravens' wings,
To dry the old oak's sap, and cherish springs;
To spoil antiquities of hammer'd steel,
And turn the giddy round of Fortune's wheel;

'To show the beldam daughters of her daughter,
To make the child a man, the man a child,
To slay the tiger that doth live by slaughter,
To tame the unicorn and lion wild,
To mock the subtle in themselves beguil'd,
To cheer the ploughman with increaseful crops,
And waste huge stones with little waterdrops.

'Why work'st thou mischief in thy pilgrimage,
Unless thou couldst return to make amends?
One poor retiring minute in an age
Would purchase thee a thousand thousand friends,
Lending him wit that to bad debtors lends.
O, this dread night, wouldst thou one hour come back,
I could prevent this storm, and shun thy wrack!

'Thou ceaseless lackey to Eternity,

With some mischance cross Tarquin in his flight;
Devise extremes beyond extremity
To make him curse this cursed crimeful night;
Let ghastly shadows his lewd eyes affright,
And the dire thought of his committed evil
Shape every bush a hideous shapeless devil.

'Disturb his hours of rest with restless trances,
Afflict him in his bed with bedrid groans;
Let there bechance him pitiful mischances
To make him moan, but pity not his moans.
Stone him with hard'ned hearts harder than stones;
And let mild women to him lose their mildness,
Wilder to him than tigers in their wildness.

'Let him have time to tear his curled hair,
Let him have time against himself to rave,
Let him have time of Time's help to despair,
Let him have time to live a loathed slave,
Let him have time a beggar's orts to crave;
And time to see one that by alms doth live
Disdain to him disdained scraps to give.

'Let him have time to see his friends his foes,
And merry fools to mock at him resort;
Let him have time to mark how slow time goes
In time of sorrow, and how swift and short
His time of folly and his time of sport;
And ever let his unrecalling crime
Have time to wail th' abusing of his time.

'O Time, thou tutor both to good and bad,
Teach me to curse him that thou taught'st this ill!
At his own shadow let the thief run mad,
Himself himself seek every hour to kill!
Such wretched hands such wretched blood should spill;
For who so base would such an office have
As sland'rous death's-man to so base a slave?

'The baser is he, coming from a king,
To shame his hope with deeds degenerate.
The mightier man, the mightier is the thing
That makes him honour'd or begets him hate;
For greatest scandal waits on greatest state.
The moon being clouded presently is miss'd,
But little stars may hide them when they list.

'The crow may bathe his coal-black wings in mire
And unperceiv'd fly with the filth away;
But if the like the snow-white swan desire,
The stain upon his silver down will stay.
Poor grooms are sightless night, kings glorious day.
Gnats are unnoted wheresoe'er they fly,
But eagles gaz'd upon with every eye.

'Out, idle words, servants to shallow fools!
Unprofitable sounds, weak arbitrators!
Busy yourselves in skill-contending schools,
Debate where leisure serves with dull debaters;
To trembling clients be you mediators.
For me, I force not argument a straw,
Since that my case is past the help of law.

'In vain I rail at Opportunity,
At Time, at Tarquin, and uncheerful Night;
In vain I cavil with mine infamy,
In vain I spurn at my confirm'd despite:
This helpless smoke of words doth me no right.
The remedy indeed to do me good
Is to let forth my foul defiled blood.

'Poor hand, why quiver'st thou at this decree?
Honour thyself to rid me of this shame;
For if I die my honour lives in thee,
But if I live thou liv'st in my defame.
Since thou couldst not defend thy loyal dame,
And wast afeard to scratch her wicked foe,
Kill both thyself and her for yielding so'.

This said, from her betumbled couch she starteth
To find some desp'rate instrument of death,
But this no slaughterhouse no tool imparteth
To make more vent for passage of her breath.
Which thronging through her lips so vanisheth
As smoke from Ætna, that in air consumes,
Or that which from discharged cannon fumes.

'In vain,' quoth she 'I live, and seek in vain
Some happy mean to end a hapless life.
I fear'd by Tarquin's falchion to be slain,
Yet for the self-same purpose seek a knife;
But when I fear'd I was a loyal wife;
So am I now – O no, that cannot be;
Of that true type hath Tarquin rifled me.

'O, that is gone for which I sought to live,
And therefore now I need not fear to die.
To clear this spot by death, at least I give
A badge of fame to slander's livery;
A dying life to living infamy.
Poor helpless help, the treasure stol'n away,
To burn the guiltless casket where it lay!

'Well, well, dear Collatine, thou shalt not know
The stained taste of violated troth;
I will not wrong thy true affection so
To flatter thee with an infringed oath;
This bastard graff shall never come to growth;
He shall not boast who did thy stock pollute
That thou art doting father of his fruit.

'Nor shall he smile at thee in secret thought,
Nor laugh with his companions at thy state;
But thou shalt know thy interest was not bought
Basely with gold, but stol'n from forth thy gate.
For me, I am the mistress of my fate,
And with my trespass never will dispense,
Till life to death acquit my forc'd offence.

'I will not poison thee with my attaint,
Nor fold my fault in cleanly coin'd excuses;
My sable ground of sin I will not paint

To hide the truth of this false night's abuses.
My tongue shall utter all; mine eyes like sluices,
As from a mountain-spring that feeds a dale,
Shall gush pure streams to purge my impure tale.'

By this, lamenting Philomel had ended
The well-tun'd warble of her nightly sorrow,
And solemn night with slow-sad gait descended
To ugly hell; when lo, the blushing morrow
Lends light to all fair eyes that light will borrow;
But cloudy Lucrece shames herself to see,
And therefore still in night would cloist'red be.

Revealing day through every cranny spies,
And seems to point her out where she sits weeping;
To whom she sobbing speaks: 'O eye of eyes,
Why pry'st thou through my window? Leave thy peeping;
Mock with thy tickling beams eyes that are sleeping;
Brand not my forehead with thy piercing light,
For day hath nought to do what's done by night'.

Thus cavils she with every thing she sees.
True grief is fond and testy as a child,
Who wayward once, his mood with nought agrees.
Old woes, not infant sorrows, bear them mild:
Continuance tames the one; the other wild,
Like an unpractis'd swimmer plunging still
With too much labour drowns for want of skill.

So she, deep drenched in a sea of care,
Holds disputation with each thing she views,
And to herself all sorrow doth compare;
No object but her passion's strength renews,
And as one shifts, another straight ensues.
Sometimes her grief is dumb and hath no words;
Sometime 'tis mad and too much talk affords.

The little birds that tune their morning's joy
Make her moans mad with their sweet melody;
For mirth doth search the bottom of annoy;
Sad souls are slain in merry company;
Grief best is pleas'd with grief's society.
True sorrow then is feelingly suffic'd
When with like semblance it is sympathiz'd.

'Tis double death to drown in ken of shore;
He ten times pines that pines beholding food;
To see the salve doth make the wound ache more;
Great grief grieves most at that would do it good;
Deep woes roll forward like a gentle flood,
Who, being stopp'd, the bounding banks o'erflows;
Grief dallied with nor law nor limit knows.

'You mocking birds,' quoth she 'your tunes entomb
Within your hollow-swelling feathered breasts,
And in my hearing be you mute and dumb.
My restless discord loves no stops nor rests;
A woeful hostess brooks not merry guests.
Relish your nimble notes to pleasing ears;
Distress likes dumps when time is kept with tears.

'Come, Philomel, that sing'st of ravishment,
Make thy sad grove in my dishevell'd hair.
As the dank earth weeps at thy languishment,
So I at each sad strain will strain a tear,
And with deep groans the diapason bear;
For burthen-wise I'll hum on Tarquin still,
While thou on Tereus descants better skill.

'And whiles against a thorn thou bear'st thy part
To keep thy sharp woes waking, wretched I,
To imitate thee well, against my heart
Will fix a sharp knife to affright mine eye;
Who, if it wink, shall thereon fall and die.
These means, as frets upon an instrument,
Shall tune our heartstrings to true languishment.

'And for, poor bird, thou sing'st not in the day,
As shaming any eye should thee behold,
Some dark deep desert, seated from the way,
That knows not parching heat nor freezing cold,
Will we find out; and there we will unfold
To creatures stern sad tunes, to change their kinds.
Since men prove beasts, let beasts bear gentle minds.'

As the poor frighted deer, that stands at gaze,
Wildly determining which way to fly,
Or one encompass'd with a winding maze
That cannot tread the way out readily;
So with herself is she in mutiny,
To live or die which of the twain were better,
When life is sham'd, and death reproach's debtor.

'To kill myself,' quoth she 'alack, what were it,
But with my body my poor soul's pollution?
They that lose half with greater patience bear it
Than they whose whole is swallowed in confusion.
That mother tries a merciless conclusion
Who, having two sweet babes, when death takes one,
Will slay the other and be nurse to none.

'My body or my soul, which was the dearer,
When the one pure, the other made divine?
Whose love of either to myself was nearer,
When both were kept for heaven and Collatine?
Ay me! the bark pill'd from the lofty pine,
His leaves will wither and his sap decay;
So must my soul, her bark being pull'd away.

'Her house is sack'd, her quiet interrupted,
Her mansion batter'd by the enemy;

Her sacred temple spotted, spoil'd corrupted,
Grossly engirt with daring infamy;
Then let it not be call'd impiety
If in this blemish'd fort I make some hole
Through which I may convey this troubled soul.

'Yet die I will not till my Collatine
Have heard the cause of my untimely death;
That he may vow, in that sad hour of mine,
Revenge on him that made me stop my breath.
My stained blood to Tarquin I'll bequeath,
Which by him tainted shall for him be spent,
And as his due writ in my testament.

'My honour I'll bequeath unto the knife
That wounds my body so dishonoured.
'Tis honour to deprive dishonour'd life:
The one will live, the other being dead.
So of shame's ashes shall my fame be bred;
For in my death I murder shameful scorn.
My shame so dead, mine honour is new born.

'Dear lord of that dear jewel I have lost,
What legacy shall I bequeath to thee?
My resolution, love, shall be thy boast,
By whose example thou reveng'd mayst be.
How Tarquin must be us'd, read it in me:
Myself, thy friend, will kill myself, thy foe;
And for my sake serve thou false Tarquin so.

'This brief abridgment of my will I make:
My soul and body to the skies and ground;
My resolutron, husband, do thou take;
Mine honour be the knife's that makes my wound;
My shame be his that did my fame confound;
And all my fame that lives disbursed be
To those that live and think no shame of me.

'Thou, Collatine, shalt oversee this will.
How was I overseen that thou shalt see it!
My blood shall wash the slander of mine ill;
My life's foul deed, my life's fair end shall free it.
Faint not, faint heart, but stoutly say "So be it".
Yield to my hand; my hand shall conquer thee;
Thou dead, both die, and both shall victors be.'

This plot of death when sadly she had laid,
And wip'd the brinish pearl from her bright eyes,
With untun'd tongue she hoarsely calls her maid,
Whose swift obedience to her mistress hies;
For fleet-wing'd duty with thought's feathers flies.
Poor Lucrece' cheeks unto her maid seem so
As winter meads when sun doth melt their snow.

Her mistress she doth give demure good-morrow
With soft-slow tongue, true mark of modesty,
And sorts a sad look to her lady's sorrow,
For why her face wore sorrow's livery;
But durst not ask of her audaciously
Why her two suns were cloud-eclipsed so,
Nor why her fair cheeks over-wash'd with woe.

But as the earth doth weep, the sun being set,
Each flower moist'ned like a melting eye;
Even so the maid with swelling drops gan wet
Her circled eyne, enforc'd by sympathy
Of those fair suns set in her mistress' sky,
Who in a salt-wav'd ocean quench their light,
Which makes the maid weep like the dewy night.

A pretty while these pretty creatures stand,
Like ivory conduits coral cisterns filling:
One justly weeps; the other takes in hand
No cause but company of her drops spilling.
Their gentle sex to weep are often willing;
Grieving themselves to guess at others' smarts,
And then they drown their eyes, or break their hearts.

For men have marble, women waxen minds,
And therefore are they form'd as marble will;
The weak oppress'd, th' impression of strange kinds
Is form'd in them by force, by fraud, or skill.
Then call them not the authors of their ill,
No more than wax shall be accounted evil
Wherein is stamp'd the semblance of a devil.

Their smoothness, like a goodly champaign plain,
Lays open all the little worms that creep;
In men, as in a rough-grown grove, remain
Cave-keeping evils that obscurely sleep.
Through crystal walls each little mote will peep.
Though men can cover crimes with bold stern looks,
Poor women's faces are their own faults' books.

No man inveigh against the withered flow'r,
But chide rough winter that the flow'r hath kill'd.
Not that devour'd, but that which doth devour,
Is worthy blame. O, let it not be hild
Poor women's faults that they are so fulfill'd
With men's abuses! those proud lords to blame
Make weak-made women tenants to their shame.

The precedent whereof in Lucrece view,
Assail'd by night with circumstances strong
Of present death and shame that might ensue
By that her death, to do her husband wrong.
Such danger to resistance did belong
That dying fear through all her body spread;
And who cannot abuse a body dead?

By this, mild patience bid fair Lucrece speak
To the poor counterfeit of her complaining.
'My girl,' quoth she 'on what occasion break
Those tears from thee that down thy cheeks are raining?
If thou dost weep for grief of my sustaining,
Know, gentle wench, it small avails my mood;
If tears could help, mine own would do me good.

'But tell me, girl, when went' – and there she stay'd
Till after a deep groan – 'Tarquin from hence?'
'Madam, ere I was up,' replied the maid
'The more to blame my sluggard negligence.
Yet with the fault I thus far can dispense:
Myself was stirring ere the break of day,
And ere I rose was Tarquin gone away.

'But, lady, if your maid may be so bold,
She would request to know your heaviness.'
'O, peace!' quoth Lucrece 'If it should be told,
The repetition cannot make it less,
For more it is than I can well express;
And that deep torture may be call'd a hell,
When more is felt than one hath power to tell.

'Go get me hither paper, ink, and pen –
Yet save that labour, for I have them here.
What should I say? – One of my husband's men
Bid thou be ready, by and by, to bear
A letter to my lord, my love, my dear.
Bid him with speed prepare to carry it;
The cause craves haste, and it will soon be writ.'

Her maid is gone, and she prepares to write,
First hovering o'er the paper with her quill.
Conceit and grief and eager combat fight;
What wit sets down is blotted straight with will;
This is too curious-good, this blunt and ill:
Much like a press of people at a door,
Throng her inventions, which shall go before.

At last she thus begins: 'Thou worthy lord
Of that unworthy wife that greeteth thee,
Health to thy person! Next vouchsafe t' afford –
If ever, love, thy Lucrece thou wilt see –
Some present speed to come and visit me.
So I commend me from our house in grief;
My woes are tedious, though my words are brief.'

Here folds she up the tenour of her woe,
Her certain sorrow writ uncertainly.
By this short schedule Collatine may know
Her grief, but not her grief's true quality;
She dares not thereof make discovery,
Lest he should hold it her own gross abuse,
Ere she with blood had stain'd her stain'd excuse.

Besides, the life and feeling of her passion
She hoards, to spend when he is by to hear her;
When sighs and groans and tears may grace the fashion
Of her disgrace, the better so to clear her
From that suspicion which the world might bear her.
To shun this blot, she would not blot the letter
With words, till action might become them better.

To see sad sights moves more than hear them told;
For then the eye interprets to the ear
The heavy motion that it doth behold,
When every part a part of woe doth bear.
'Tis but a part of sorrow that we hear:
Deep sounds make lesser noise than shallow fords,
And sorrow ebbs, being blown with wind of words.

Her letter now is seal'd, and on it writ
'At Ardea to my lord with more than haste'.
The post attends, and she delivers it,
Charging the sour-fac'd groom to hie as fast
As lagging fowls before the northern blast.
Speed more than speed but dull and slow she deems:
Extremity still urgeth such extremes.

The homely vallain curtsies to her low;
And blushing on her, with a steadfast eye
Receives the scroll without or yea or no,
And forth with bashful innocence doth hie.
But they whose guilt within their bosoms lie
Imagine every eye beholds their blame;
For Lucrece thought he blush'd to see her shame.

When, silly groom, God wot, it was defect
Of spirit, life, and bold audacity.
Such harmless creatures have a true respect
To talk in deeds, while others saucily
Promise more speed but do it leisurely.
Even so, this pattern of the worn-out age
Pawn'd honest looks, but laid no words to gage.

His kindled duty kindled her mistrust,
That two red fires in both their faces blazed;
She thought he blush'd as knowing Tarquin's lust,
And, blushing with him, wistly on him gazed;
Her earnest eye did make him more amazed;
The more she saw the blood his cheeks replenish,
The more she thought he spied in her some blemish.

But long she thinks till he return again,
And yet the duteous vassal scarce is gone.
The weary time she cannot entertain,
For now 'tis stale to sigh, to weep, and groan;
So woe hath wearied woe, moan tired moan,
That she her plaints a little while doth stay,
Pausing for means to mourn some newer way.

At last she calls to mind where hangs a piece
Of skilful painting, made for Priam's Troy;
Before the which is drawn the power of Greece
For Helen's rape the city to destroy,
Threat'ning cloud-kissing Ilion with annoy;
Which the conceited painter drew so proud,

As heaven, it seem'd, to kiss the turrets bow'd.

A thousand lamentable objects there,
In scorn of nature, art gave lifeless life:
Many a dry drop seem'd a weeping tear
Shed for the slaught'red husband by the wife;
The red blood reek'd to show the painter's strife;
And dying eyes gleam'd forth their ashy lights,
Like dying coals burnt out in tedious nights.

There might you see the labouring pioneer
Begrimed with sweat and smeared all with dust;
And from the towers of Troy there would appear
The very eyes of men through loopholes thrust,
Gazing upon the Greeks with little lust.
Such sweet observance in this work was had
That one might see those far-off eyes look sad.

In great commanders grace and majesty
You might behold, triumphing in their faces;
In youth, quick bearing and dexterity;
And here and there the painter interlaces
Pale cowards marching on with trembling paces,
Which heartless peasants did so well resemble
That one would swear he saw them quake and tremble.

In Ajax and Ulysses, O what art
Of physiognomy might one behold!
The face of either cipher'd either's heart;
Their face their manners most expressly told:
In Ajax' eyes blunt rage and rigour roll'd;
But the mild glance that sly Ulysses lent
Show'd deep regard and smiling government.

There pleading might you see grave Nestor stand,
As 'twere encouraging the Greeks to fight,
Making such sober action with his hand
That it beguil'd attention, charm'd the sight.
In speech, it seem'd, his beard all silver white
Wagg'd up and down, and from his lips did fly
Thin winding breath, which purl'd up to the sky.

About him were a press of gaping faces,
Which seem'd to swallow up his sound advice,
All jointly list'ning, but with several graces,
As if some mermaid did their ears entice;
Some high, some low – the painter was so nice –
The scalps of many, almost hid behind,
To jump up higher seem'd to mock the mind.

Here one man's hand lean'd on another's head,
His nose being shadowed by his neighbour's ear;
Here one being throng'd bears back, all boll'n and red;
Another smother'd seems to pelt and swear;
And in their rage such signs of rage they bear,
As, but for loss of Nestor's golden words,
It seem'd they would debate with angry swords.

For much imaginary work was there;
Conceit deceitful, so compact, so kind,
That for Achilles' image stood his spear,
Grip'd in an an armed hand; himself, behind
Was left unseen, save to the eye of mind:
A hand, a foot, a face a leg, a head,
Stood for the whole to be imagined.

And from the walls of strong-besieged Troy
When their brave hope, bold Hector, march'd to field,
Stood many Troyan mothers, sharing joy
To see their youthful sons bright weapons wield;
And to their hope they such odd action yield
That through their light joy seemed to appear,
Like bright things stain'd, a kind of heavy fear.

And from the strond of Dardan where they fought,
To Simois' reedy banks, the red blood ran,
Whose waves to imitate the battle sought
With swelling ridges; and their ranks began
To break upon the galled shore, and than
Retire again, till meeting greater ranks
They join, and shoot their foam at Simois' banks.

To this well-painted piece is Lucrece come,
To find a face where all distress is stell'd.
Many she sees where cares have carved some,
But none where all distress and dolour dwell'd,
Till she despairing Hecuba beheld,
Staring on Priam's wounds with her old eyes,
Which bleeding under Pyrrhus' proud foot lies.

In her the painter had anatomiz'd
Time's ruin, beauty's wrack, and grim care's reign;
Her cheeks with chaps and wrinkles were disguis'd;
Of what she was no semblance did remain:
Her blue blood chang'd to black in every vein,
Wanting the spring that those shrunk pipes had fed,
Show'd life imprison'd in a body dead.

On this sad shadow Lucrece spends her eyes,
And shapes her sorrow to the beldam's woes,
Who nothing wants to answer her but cries,
And bitter words to ban her cruel foes:
The painter was no god to lend her those;
And therefore Lucrece swears he did her wrong
To give her so much grief and not a tongue.

'Poor instrument, ' quoth she 'without a sound,
I'll tune thy woes with my lamenting tongue,
And drop sweet balm in Priam's painted wound,
And rail on Pyrrhus that hath done him wrong,
And with my tears quench Troy that burns so long;
And with my knife scratch out the angry eyes
Of all the Greeks that are thine enemies.

'Show me the strumpet that began this stir,
That with my nails her beauty I may tear.
Thy heat of lust, fond Paris, did incur
This load of wrath that burning Troy doth bear.

Thy eye kindled the fire that burneth here;
And here in Troy, for trespass of thine eye,
The sire, the son, the dame, and daughter die.

'Why should the private pleasure of some one
Become the public plague of many moe?
Let sin, alone committed, light alone
Upon his head that hath transgressed so;
Let guiltless souls be freed from guilty woe.
For one's offence why should so many fall,
To plague a private sin in general?

'Lo, here weeps Hecuba, here Priam dies,
Here manly Hector faints, here Troilus sounds;
Here friend by friend in bloody channel lies,
And friend to friend gives unadvised wounds,
And one man's lust these many lives confounds.
Had doting Priam check'd his son's desire,
Troy had been bright with fame, and not with fire.'

Here feelingly she weeps Troy's painted woes;
For sorrow, like a heavy-hanging bell,
Once set on ringing, with his own weight goes;
Then little strength rings out the doleful knell;
So Lucrece set a-work sad tales doth tell
To pencill'd pensiveness and colour'd sorrow;
She lends them words, and she their looks doth borrow.

She throws her eyes about the painting round,
And who she finds forlorn she doth lament.
At last she sees a wretched image bound
That piteous looks to Phrygian shepherds lent;
His face, though full of cares, yet show'd content:
Onward to Troy with the blunt swains he goes,
So mild that Patience seem'd to scorn his woes.

In him the painter labour'd with his skill
To hide deceit, and give the harmless show
An humble gait, calm looks, eyes wailing still,
A brow unbent, that seem'd to welcome woe;
Cheeks neither red nor pale, but mingled so
That blushing red no guilty instance gave,
Nor ashy pale the fear that false hearts have;

But, like a constant and confirmed devil,
He entertain'd a show so seeming just,
And therein so ensconc'd his secret evil,
That jealousy itself could not mistrust
False-creeping craft and perjury should thrust
Into so bright a day such black-fac'd storms,
Or blot with hell-born sin such saint-like forms.

The well-skill'd workman this mild image drew
For perjur'd Sinon, whose enchanting story
The credulous old Priam after slew;
Whose words, like wildfire, burnt the shining glory
Of rich-built Ilion, that the skies were sorry,
And little stars shot from their fixed places,
When their glass fell wherein they view'd their faces.

This picture she advisedly perus'd,
And chid the painter for his wondrous skill;
Saying, some shape in Sinon's was abus'd,
So fair a form lodg'd not a mind so ill;
And still on him she gaz'd, and gazing still
Such signs of truth in his plain face she spied
That she concludes the picture was belied.

'It cannot be' quoth she 'that so much guile'
She would have said, 'can lurk in such a look'
But Tarquin's shape came in her mind the while,
And from her tongue 'can lurk' from 'cannot' took;
It cannot be' she in that sense forsook,
And turn'd it thus: 'It cannot be, I find,
But such a face should bear a wicked mind;

'For even as subtle Sinon here is painted,
So sober-sad, so weary, and so mild,
As if with grief or travail he had fainted,
To me came Tarquin armed; so beguil'd
With outward honesty, but yet defil'd
With inward vice. As Priam him did cherish,
So did I Tarquin; so my Troy did perish.

'Look, look, how list'ning Priam wets his eyes,
To see those borrowed tears that Sinon sheds.
Priam, why art thou old, and yet not wise?
For every tear he falls a Troyan bleeds;
His eyes drops fire, no water thence proceeds;
Those round clear pearls of his that move thy pity
Are balls of quenchless fire to burn thy city.

'Such devils steal effects from lightless hell;
For Sinon in his fire doth quake with cold,
And in that cold hot burning fire doth dwell;
These contraries such unity do hold
Only to flatter fools, and make them bold;
So Priam's trust false Sinon's tears doth flatter
That he finds means to burn his Troy with water'.

Here, all enrag'd, such passion her assails
That patience is quite beaten from her breast.
She tears the senseless Sinon with her nails,
Comparing him to that unhappy guest
Whose deed hath made herself herself detest.
At last she smilingly with this gives o'er:
'Fool! fool! ' quoth she 'his wounds will not be sore.'

Thus ebbs and flows the current of her sorrow,
And time doth weary time with her complaining.
She looks for night, and then she longs for morrow,
And both she thinks too long with her remaining.
Short time seems long in sorrow's sharp sustaining;
Though woe be heavy, yet it seldom sleeps;

And they that watch see time how slow it creeps.
Which all this this time hath overslipp'd her thought
That she with painted images hath spent,
Being from the feeling of her own grief brought
By deep surmise of others' detriment,
Losing her woes in shows of discontent.
It easeth some, though none it ever cured,
To think their dolour others have endured.

But now the mindful messenger, come back,
Brings home his lord and other company;
Who finds his Lucrece clad in mouring black,
And round about her tear-distained eye
Blue circles stream'd, like rainbows in the sky.
These water-galls in her dim element
Foretell new storms to those already spent.

Which when her sad-beholding husband saw,
Amazedly in her sad face he stares:
Her eyes, though sod in tears, look'd red and raw,
Her lively colour kill'd with deadly cares.
He hath no power to ask her how she fares;
Both stood like old acquaintance in a trance,
Met far from home, wond'ring each other's chance.

At last he takes her by the bloodless hand,
And thus begins: 'What uncouth ill event
Hath thee befall'n, that thou dost trembling stand?
Sweet love, what spite hath thy fair colour spent?
Why art thou thus attir'd in discontent?
Unmask, dear, dear, this moody heaviness,
And tell thy grief, that we may give redress'.

Three times with sighs she gives her sorrow fire
Ere once she can discharge one word of woe;
At length address'd to answer his desire,
She modestly prepares to let them know
Her honour is ta'en prisoner by the foe;
While Collatine and his consorted lords
With sad attention long to hear her words.

And now this pale swan in her wat'ry nest
Begins the sad dirge of her certain ending.
'Few words' quoth she 'shall fit the trespass best,
Where no excuse can give the fault amending:
In me moe woes than words are now depending;
And my laments would be drawn out too long
To tell them all with one poor tired tongue.

'Then be this all the task it hath to say:
Dear husband, in the interest of thy bed
A stranger came and on that pillow lay
Where thou wast wont to rest thy weary head;
And what wrong else may be imagined
By foul enforcement might be done to me
From that, alas, thy Lucrece is not free.

'For in the dreadful dead of dark midnight,
With shining falchion in my chamber came
A creeping creature with a flaming light,
And softly cried "Awake, thou Roman dame,
And entertain my love; else lasting shame
On thee and thine this night I will inflict,
If thou my love's desire do contradict.

'"For some hard-favour'd groom of thine" quoth he
"Unless thou yoke thy liking to my will,
I'll murder straight, and then I'll slaughter thee,
And swear I found you where you did fulfil
The loathsome act of lust, and so did kill
The lechers in their deed: this act will be
My fame, and thy perpetual infamy".

'With this I did begin to start and cry,
And then against my heart he set his sword,
Swearing, unless I took all patiently,
I should not live to speak another word.
So should my shame still rest upon record,
And never be forgot in mighty Rome
Th' adulterate death of Lucrece and her groom.

'Mine enemy was strong, my poor self weak,
And far the weaker with so strong a fear.
My bloody judge forbade my tongue to speak;
No rightful plea might plead for justice there.
His scarlet lust came evidence to swear
That my poor beauty had purloin'd his eyes,
And when the judge is robb'd, the prisoner dies.

'O, teach me how to make mine own excuse!
Or, at the least, this refuge let me find:
Though my gross blood be stain'd with this abuse,
Immaculate and spotless is my mind;
That was not forc'd; that never was inclin'd
To accessary yieldings, but still pure
Doth in her poison'd closet yet endure.'

Lo, here, the hopeless merchant of this loss,
With head declin'd and voice damm'd up with woe,
With sad-set eyes and wretched arms across,
From lips new-waxen pale begins to blow
The grief away that stops his answer so;
But wretched as he is he strives in vain;
What he breathes out his breath drinks up again.

As though an arch the violent roaring tide
Outruns the eye that doth behold his haste,
Yet in the eddy boundeth in his pride
Back to the strait that forc'd him on so fast,
In rage sent out, recall'd in rage, being past;
Even so his sighs, his sorrows, make a saw,
To push grief on, and back the same grief draw.

Which speechless woe of his poor she attendeth,
And his untimely frenzy thus awaketh:
'Dear lord, thy sorrow to my sorrow lendeth
Another power; no flood by raining slaketh.
My woe too sensible thy passion maketh
More feeling-painful. Let it then suffice

To drown one woe, one pair of weeping eyes.

And for my sake, when I might charm thee so,
For she that was thy Lucrece, now attend me:
Be suddenly revenged on my foe,
Thine, mine, his own; suppose thou dost defend me
From what is past. The help that thou shalt lend me
Comes all too late, yet let the traitor die;
For sparing justice feeds iniquity.

'But ere I name him, you, fair lords,' quoth she,
Speaking to those that came with Collatine,
'Shall plight your honourable faiths to me
With swift pursuit to venge this wrong of mine;
For 'tis a meritorious fair design
To chase injustice with revengeful arms:
Knights, by their oaths, should right poor ladies' harms'.

At this request, with noble disposition
Each present lord began to promise aid,
As bound in knighthood to her imposition,
Longing to hear the hateful foe bewray'd.
But she, that yet her sad task hath not said,
The protestation stops. 'O speak,' quoth she
'How may this forced stain be wip'd from me?

'What is the quality of my offence,
Being constrain'd with dreadful circumstance?
May my pure mind with the foul act dispense,
My low-declined honour to advance?
May any terms acquit me from this chance?
The poisoned fountain clears itself again;
And why not I from this compelled stain?

With this, they all at once began to say
Her body's stain her mind untainted clears;
While with a joyless smile she turns away
The face, that map which deep impression bears
Of hard misfortune, carv'd in it with tears.
'No, no,' quoth she 'no dame hereafter living
By my excuse shall claim excuse's giving.'

Here with a sigh, as if her heart would break,
She throws forth Tarquin's name: 'He, he' she says,
But more than 'he' her poor tongue could not speak;
Till after many accents and delays,
Untimely breathings, sick, and short assays,
She utters this: 'He, he, fair lords, 'tis he,
That guides this hand to give this wound to me.'

Even here she sheathed in her harmless breast
A harmful knife, that thence her soul unsheathed.
That blow did bail it from the deep unrest
Of that polluted prison where it breathed.
Her contrite sighs unto the clouds bequeathed
Her winged sprite, and through her wounds doth fly
Life's lasting date from cancell'd destiny.

Stone-still, astonish'd with this deadly deed,
Stood Collatine and all his lordly crew;
Till Lucrece' father, that beholds her bleed,
Himself on her self-slaught'red body threw,
And from the purple fountain Brutus drew
The murd'rous knife, and, as it left the place,
Her blood, in poor revenge, held it in chase;

And bubbling from her breast, it doth divide
In two slow rivers, that the crimson blood
Circles her body in on every side,
Who like a late-sack'd island vastly stood
Bare and unpeopled in this fearful flood.
Some of her blood still pure and red remain'd,
And some look'd black, and that false Tarquin stain'd.

About the mourning and congealed face
Of that black blood a wat'ry rigol goes,
Which seems to weep upon the tainted place;
And ever since, as pitying Lucrece' woes,
Corrupted blood some watery token shows;
And blood untainted still doth red abide,
Blushing at that which is so putrified.

'Daughter, dear daughter,' old Lucretius cries,
'That life was mine which thou hast here deprived.
If in the child the father's image lies,
Where shall I live now Lucrece is unlived?
Thou wast not to this end from me derived.
If children predecease progenitors,
We are their offspring, and they none of ours.

'Poor broken glass, I often did behold
In thy sweet semblance my old age new born;
But now that fair fresh mirror, dim and old,
Shows me a bare-bon'd death by time outworn;
O, from thy cheeks my image thou hast torn,
And shiver'd all the beauty of my glass
That I no more can see what once I was

'O time, cease thou thy course and last no longer,
If they surcease to be that should survive.
Shall rotten death make conquest of the stronger,
And leave the falt'ring feeble souls alive?
The old bees die, the young possess their hive.
Then live, sweet Lucrece, live again, and see
Thy father die, and not thy father thee.

By this starts Collatine as from a dream,
And bids Lucretius give his sorrow place;
And then in key-cold Lucrece' bleeding stream
He falls, and bathes the pale fear in his face,
And counterfeits to die with her a space;
Till manly shame bids him possess his breath,
And live, to be revenged on her death.

The deep vexation of his inward soul
Hath serv'd a dumb arrest upon his tongue;
Who, mad that sorrow should his use control,

Or keep him from heart-easing words so long,
Begins to talk; but through his lips do throng
Weak words, so thick come, in his poor heart's aid,
That no man could distinguish what he said.

Yet sometime 'Tarquin' was pronounced plain,
But through his teeth, as if the name he tore.
This windy tempest, till it blow up rain,
Held back his sorrow's tide, to make it more;
At last it rains, and busy winds give o'er;
Then son and father weep with equal strife.
Who should weep most for daughter or for wife.

The one doth call her his, the other his,
Yet neither may possess the claim they lay.
The father says 'She's mine'. 'O, mine she is!'
Replies her husband. 'Do not take away
My sorrow's interest; let no mourner say
He weeps for her, for she was only mine,
And only must be wail'd by Collatine.'

'O.' quoth Lucretius 'I did give that life
Which she too early and too late hath spill'd.'
'Woe, woe,' quoth Collatine 'she was my wife,
I owed her, and 'tis mine that she hath kill'd.'
'My daughter!' and 'My wife!' with clamours fill'd
The dispers'd air, who, holding Lucrece' life,
Answer'd their cries, 'My daughter!' and 'My wife!'

Brutus, who pluck'd the knife from Lucrece' side,
Seeing such emulation in their woe,
Began to clothe his wit in state and pride,
Burying in Lucrece' wound his folly's show.
He with the Romans was esteemed so
As silly jeering idiots are with kings,
For sportive words and utt'ring foolish things.

But now he throws that shallow habit by
Wherein deep policy did him disguise,
And arm'd his long-hid wits advisedly
To check the tears in Collatinus' eyes.
'Thou wronged lord of Rome,' quoth he 'arise;
Let my unsounded self, suppos'd a fool,
Now set thy long-experienc'd wit to school.

'Why, Collatine, is woe the cure for woe?
Do wounds help wounds, or grief help grievous deeds?
Is it revenge to give thyself a blow,
For his foul act by whom thy fair wife bleeds?
Such childish humour from weak minds proceeds.
Thy wretched wife mistook the matter so,
To slay herself that should have slain her foe.

'Courageous Roman, do not steep thy heart
In such relenting dew of lamentations,
But kneel with me, and help to bear thy part
To rouse our Roman gods with invocations
That they will suffer these abominations –
Since Rome herself in them doth stand disgraced –
By our strong arms from forth her fair streets chased.

'Now by the Capitol that we adore,
And by this chaste blood so unjustly stained,
By heaven's fair sun that breeds the fat earth's store,
By all our country rights in Rome maintained,
And by chaste Lucrece' soul that late complained
Her wrongs to us, and by this bloody knife,
We will revenge the death of this true wife.'

This said, he struck his hand upon his breast,
And kiss'd the fatal knife to end his vow;
And to his protestation urg'd the rest,
Who, wond'ring at him, did his words allow;
Then jointly to the ground their knees they bow
And that deep vow which Brutus made before
He doth again repeat, and that they swore.

When they had sworn to this advised doom,
They did conclude to bear dead Lucrece thence,
To show her bleeding body thorough Rome,
And so to publish Tarquin's foul offence;
Which being done with speedy diligence,
The Romans plausibly did give consent
To Tarquin's everlasting banishment.

The Sonnets

Introduction by PHILIP HOBSBAUM

The leading figure in Shakespeare's Sonnets is called Will (Sonnet 136). He is, or feels himself to be, stricken in years (Sonnet 73). He is a poet (Sonnet 76). To that extent we can identify this figure, hereinafter called the Speaker, with Shakespeare.

It seems that the Speaker is involved with a fair young man whom he loves but with whom he does not have sexual relations (20), and a dark lady with whom he has sexual relations but whom he does not so much love as lust after (147). One can read the Sonnets as the record of a few turbulent years, most likely the later 1590s, disturbed by two difficult relationships.

The Speaker may have met the Fair Young Man as a result of a commission laid upon him by the Young Man's family. They induce the Speaker to address the Young Man in a series of sonnets (1–17). The purpose is to persuade him to take a wife: 'You had a father: let your son say so' (13).

Those first seventeen sonnets cohere, though the tone becomes appreciably warmer as the sequence progresses. What follows is not a story spelled out but something more akin to a romantic symphony, with themes interrupting and subverting other themes. One idea appearing intermittently in the Sonnets, to some extent contradicting these first seventeen, is this: that the Young Man will be immortalised in the Speaker's verse. Such a certainty will be found in Sonnets 18–19, 55, 59–60, 63, 76–87, 99–102 and 107: 'And thou in this shalt find thy monument,/When tyrants' crests and tombs of brass are spent'. The relationship between the Speaker and the Young Man is celebrated, almost as a kind of wedding: see Sonnets 20–26, 53–54 and 116–126. Sonnet 116, for example, declares with a kind of Old Testament fervour: 'Let me not to the marriage of true minds/Admit impediment'.

But the 'marriage' is not a happy one. The Speaker avers in tones of disillusion that his love is despised: see Sonnets 27–32, 36–39, 56–58, 61–62, 75, 88–91, 97–98, 110–114. Sonnet 27 ends with the nearest poetry can approach to a prolonged groan: 'Lo, thus, by day my limbs, by night my mind,/For thee, and for myself, no quiet find'. The Speaker senses, in his beautiful young friend, the taint of corruption: see Sonnets 33–35, 40–52, 92–96, especially Sonnet 94 – 'Lilies that fester smell far worse than weeds'. Running through the entire cycle is the concept of time as an inexorable destroyer: in Sonnets 64–66, 71–74 and 115 – 'reckoning Time, whose million'd accidents/Creep in 'twixt vows and change decrees of kings'. There is, in spite of this, hope in the Sonnets, but it is frail. The example of the Young Man's beauty is shown as illumining an otherwise desolate world: Sonnets 67–70, 103–106, 108–109 – 'For nothing in this wide universe I call/Save thou, my rose; in it thou art my all'.

The sonnets dealing with the Dark Lady form an uninterrupted sequence, from 127 to 152. There are no words of tenderness here. The Speaker has found himself embroiled with a person who fills him with self-contempt: 'The expense of spirit in a waste of shame/Is lust in action' (129). The anger of the Speaker is made all the more severe by his consciousness that the Dark Lady has forced her seasoned favours upon the Young Man, and so his male lover is also his rival with his female lover. In Sonnet 133 the Speaker demands, 'Is't not enough to torture me alone,/But slave to slavery my sweet'st friend must be?'

So far from reaching a resolution, the cycle ends with two quite irrelevant sonnets, put in as makeweights, it may be, and probably dating from an earlier era. They tell playfully of the love-god, Cupid, and the Speaker's presumed mistress. But this is a mistress of a complexion far other than that of the Dark Lady, and the tone is quite distinct from the tormented utterances of the Sonnets proper.

Sonnets

TO. THE. ONLIE. BEGETTER. OF.
THESE. INSUING. SONNETS.
MR. W. H. ALL. HAPPINESSE.
AND. THAT. ETERNITIE.
PROMISED.
BY.
OUR. EVER-LIVING. POET.
WISHETH.
THE. WELL-WISHING.
ADVENTURER. IN.
SETTING.
FORTH.
T. T.

1

FROM fairest creatures we desire increase,
That thereby beauty's rose might never die,
But as the riper should by time decease,
His tender heir might bear his memory;
But thou, contracted to thine own bright eyes,
Feed'st thy light's flame with self-substantial fuel,
Making a famine where abundance lies,
Thyself thy foe, to thy sweet self too cruel.
Thou that art now the world's fresh ornament
And only herald to the gaudy spring,
Within thine own bud buriest thy content,
And, tender churl, mak'st waste in niggarding.
Pity the world, or else this glutton be,
To eat the world's due, by the grave and thee.

2

When forty winters shall besiege thy brow,
And dig deep trenches in thy beauty's field,
Thy youth's proud livery, so gaz'd on now,
Will be a tatter'd weed of small worth held.
Then being ask'd where all thy beauty lies,
Where all the treasure of thy lusty days,
To say within thine own deep-sunken eyes
Were an all-eating shame and thriftless praise.
How much more praise deserv'd thy beauty's use,
If thou couldst answer 'This fair child of mine
Shall sum my count, and make my old excuse'
Proving his beauty by succession thine!
This were to be new made when thou art old,
And see thy blood warm when thou feel'st it cold.

3

Look in thy glass, and tell the face thou viewest
Now is the time that face should form another;
Whose fresh repair if now thou not renewest,
Thou dost beguile the world, unbless some mother.
For where is she so fair whose unear'd womb
Disdains the tillage of thy husbandry?
Or who is he so fond will be the tomb
Of his self-love, to stop posterity?
Thou art thy mother's glass, and she in thee
Calls back the lovely April of her prime;
So thou through windows of thine age shalt see,
Despite of wrinkles, this thy golden time.
But if thou live rememb'red not to be,
Die single, and thine image dies with thee.

4

Unthrifty loveliness, why dost thou spend
Upon thyself thy beauty's legacy?
Nature's bequest gives nothing, but doth lend,
And, being frank, she lends to those are free.
Then, beauteous niggard, why dost thou abuse
The bounteous largess given thee to give?
Profitless unsurer, why dost thou use
So great a sum of sums, yet canst not live?
For having traffic with thyself alone,
Thou of thyself thy sweet self dost deceive.
Then how when nature calls thee to be gone,
What acceptable audit canst thou leave?
Thy unus'd beauty must be tomb'd with thee,
Which, used, lives th' executor to be.

5

Those hours that with gentle work did frame
The lovely gaze where every eye doth dwell
Will play the tyrants to the very same,
And that unfair which fairly doth excel;
For never-resting time leads summer on
To hideous winter, and confounds him there;
Sap check'd with frost and lusty leaves quite gone,
Beauty o'ersnow'd, and bareness every where.
Then, were not summer's distillation left
A liquid prisoner pent in walls of glass,
Beauty's effect with beauty were bereft,
Nor it, nor no remembrance what it was;
But flowers distill'd, though they with winter meet,
Leese but their show: their substance still lives sweet.

6

Then let not winter's ragged hand deface

In thee thy summer ere thou be distill'd;
Make sweet some vail; treasure thou some place
With beauty's treasure ere it be self-kill'd.
That use is not forbidden usury
Which happies those that pay the willing loan –
That's for thyself to breed an other thee,
Or ten times happier, be it ten for one;
Ten times thyself were happier than thou art,
If ten of thine ten times refigur'd thee.
Then what could Death do if thou shouldst depart,
Leaving thee living in posterity?
Be not self-will'd, for thou art much too fair
To be death's conquest and make worms thine heir.

7

Lo, in the orient when the gracious light
Lifts up his burning head, each under eye
Doth homage to his new-appearing sight,
Serving with looks his sacred majesty;
And having climb'd the steep-up heavenly hill,
Resembling strong youth in his middle age,
Yet mortal looks adore his beauty still,
Attending on his golden pilgrimage;
But when from higmost pitch, with weary car,
Like feeble age he reeleth from the day,
The eyes, 'fore duteous, now converted are
From his low tract and look another way;
So thou, thyself outgoing in thy noon,
Unlook'd on diest, unless thou get a son.

8

Music to hear, why hear'st thou music sadly?
Sweets with sweets war not, joy delights in joy.
Why lov'st thou that which thou receiv'st not gladly,
Or else receiv'st with pleasure thine annoy?
If the true concord of well-tuned sounds,
By unions married, do offend thine ear,
They do but sweetly chide thee, who confounds
In singleness the parts that thou shouldst bear.
Mark how one string, sweet husband to another,
Strikes each in each by mutual ordering;
Resembling sire, and child, and happy mother,
Who, all in one, one pleasing note do sing;
Whose speechless song, being many, seeming one,
Sings this to thee: 'Thou single wilt prove none'.

9

Is it for fear to wet a widow's eye
That thou consum'st thyself in single life?
Ah! if thou issueless shalt hap to die,
The world will wail thee like a makeless wife:
The world will be thy widow, and still weep
That thou no form of thee hast left behind,
When every private widow well may keep,
By children's eyes, her husband's shape in mind.
Look what an unthrift in the world doth spend
Shifts but his place, for still the world enjoys it;
But beauty's waste hath in the world an end,
And kept unus'd, the user so destroys it.
No love toward others in that bosom sits
That on himself such murd'rous shame commits.

10

For shame! deny that thou bear'st love to any,
Who for thy self art so unprovident.
Grant, if thou wilt, thou art belov'd of many,
But that thou none lov'st is most evident;
For thou art so possess'd with murd'rous hate
That 'gainst thyself thou stick'st not to conspire,
Seeking that beauteous roof to ruinate
Which to repair should be thy chief desire.
O, change thy thought, that I may change my mind!
Shall hate be fairer lodg'd than gentle love?
Be, as thy presence is, gracious and kind,
Or to thy self at least kind-hearted prove;
Make thee an other self for love of me,
That beauty still may live in thine or thee.

11

As fast as thou shalt wane, so fast thou grow'st
In one of thine, from that which thou departest;
And that fresh blood which youngly thou bestow'st
Thou mayst call thine when thou from youth convertest.
Herein lives wisdom, beauty, and increase;
Without this folly, age, and cold decay.
If all were minded so, the times should cease,
And threescore year would make the world away.
Let those whom Nature hath not made for store,
Harsh, featureless, and rude, barrenly perish.
Look whom she best endow'd she gave the more;
Which bounteous gift thou shouldst in bounty cherish;
She carv'd thee for her seal, and meant thereby
Thou shouldst print more, not let that copy die.

12

When I do count the clock that tells the time,
And see the brave day sunk in hideous night;
When I behold the violet past prime,
And sable curls all silver'd o'er with white;
When lofty trees I see barren of leaves,
Which erst from heat did canopy the herd,
And summer's green all girded up in sheaves

Borne on the bier with white and bristly beard;
Then of thy beauty do I question make
That thou among the wastes of time must go,
Since sweets and beauties do themselves forsake,
And die as fast as they see others grow;
And nothing 'gainst Time's scythe can make defence
Save breed, to brave him when he takes thee hence.

13

O that you were yourself! But, love, you are
No longer yours than you your self here live.
Against this coming end you should prepare,
And your sweet semblance to some other give,
So should that beauty which you hold in lease
Find no determination; then you were
Your self again, after your self's decease,
When your sweet issue your sweet form should bear.
Who lets so fair a house fall to decay,
Which husbandry in honour might uphold
Against the stormy gusts of winter's day
And barren rage of death's eternal cold?
O, none but unthrifts! Dear my love, you know
You had a father: let your son say so.

14

Not from the stars do I my judgment pluck,
And yet methinks I have astronomy;
But not to tell of good or evil luck,
Of plagues, of dearths, or seasons' quality;
Nor can I fortune to brief minutes tell,
Pointing to each his thunder, rain, and wind,
Or say with princes if it shall go well
By oft predict that I in heaven find;
But from thine eyes my knowledge I derive,
And, constant stars, in them I read such art
As truth and beauty shall together thrive,
If from thy self to store thou wouldst convert.
Or else of thee this I prognosticate:
Thy end is truth's and beauty's doom and date.

15

When I consider every thing that grows
Holds in perfection but a little moment,
That this huge stage presenteth nought but shows
Whereon the stars in secret influence comment:
When I perceive that men as plants increase,
Cheered and check'd even by the self-same sky,
Vaunt in their youthful sap, at height decrease,
And wear their brave state out of memory;
Then the conceit of this inconstant stay
Sets you most rich in youth before my sight,
Where wasteful Time debateth with Decay
To change your day of youth to sullied night;
And all in war with Time for love of you,
As he takes from you, I engraft you new.

16

But wherefore do not you a mightier way
Make war upon this bloody tyrant Time?
And fortify your self in your decay
With means more blessed than my barren rhyme?
Now stand you on the top of happy hours,
And many maiden gardens, yet unset,
With virtuous wish would bear your living flowers,
Much liker than your painted counterfeit;
So should the lines of life that life repair,
Which this, Time's pencil or my pupil pen,
Neither in inward worth, nor outward fair,
Can make you live your self in eyes of men.
To give away your self keeps your self still;
And you must live, drawn by your own sweet skill.

17

Who will believe my verse in time to come,
If it were fill'd with your most high deserts?
Though yet, heaven knows, it is but as a tomb
Which hides your life and shows not half your parts.
If I could write the beauty of your eyes
And in fresh numbers number all your graces,
The age to come would say 'This poet lies;
Such heavenly touches ne'er touch'd earthly faces'.
So should my papers, yellowed with their age,
Be scorn'd, like old men of less truth than tongue;
And your true rights be term'd a poet's rage,
And stretched metre of an antique song.
But were some child of yours alive that time,
You should live twice – in it, and in my rhyme.

18

Shall I compare thee to a summer's day?
Thou art more lovely and more temperate.
Rough winds do shake the darling buds of May,
And summer's lease hath all too short a date:
Sometime too hot the eye of heaven shines,
And often is his gold complexion dimm'd;
And every fair from fair some time declines,
By chance, or nature's changing course, untrimm'd;
But thy eternal summer shall not fade
Nor lose possession of that fair thou ow'st;
Nor shall Death brag thou wand'rest in his shade,
When in eternal lines to time thou grow'st.
So long as men can breathe or eyes can see,
So long lives this, and this gives life to thee.

19

Devouring Time, blunt thou the lion's paws,
And make the earth devour her own sweet brood;
Pluck the keen teeth from the fierce tiger's jaws,
And burn the long-liv'd phoenix in her blood;
Make glad and sorry seasons as thou fleet'st,
And do whate'er thou wilt, swift-footed Time,
To the wide world and all her fading sweets;
But I forbid thee one most heinous crime:
O, carve not with thy hours my love's fair brow,
Nor draw no lines there with thine antique pen;
Him in thy course untainted do allow
For beauty's pattern to succeeding men.
  Yet, do thy worst, old Time. Despite thy wrong,
  My love shall in my verse ever live young.

20

A woman's face, with Nature's own hand painted,
Hast thou, the Master Mistress of my passion;
A woman's gentle heart, but not acquainted
With shifting change, as is false woman's fashion;
An eye more bright than theirs, less false in rolling,
Gilding the object whereupon it gazeth;
A man in hue all hues in his controlling,
Which steals men's eyes and women's souls amazeth.
And for a woman wert thou first created;
Till Nature, as she wrought thee, fell adoting,
And by addition me of thee defeated
By adding one thing to my purpose nothing.
  But since she prick'd thee out for women's pleasure,
  Mine be thy love, and thy love's use their treasure.

21

So is it not with me as with that Muse,
Stirr'd by a painted beauty to his verse;
Who heaven itself for ornament doth use,
And every fair with his fair doth rehearse,
Making a couplement of proud compare
With sun and moon, with earth and sea's rich gems,
With April's first-born flowers, and all things rare
That heaven's air in this huge rondure hems.
O, let me, true in love, but truly write,
And then believe me, my love is as fair
As any mother's child, though not so bright
As those gold candles fix'd in heaven's air.
  Let them say more that like of hearsay well:
  I will not praise that purpose not to sell.

22

My glass shall not persuade me I am old
So long as youth and thou are of one date;
But when in thee time's furrows I behold,
Then look I death my days should expiate.
For all that beauty that doth cover thee
Is but the seemly raiment of my heart,
Which in thy breast doth live, as thine in me;
How can I then be elder than thou art?
O, therefore, love, be of thyself so wary,
As I not for myself but for thee will;
Bearing thy heart, which I will keep so chary
As tender nurse her babe from faring ill.
  Presume not on thy heart when mine is slain;
  Thou gav'st me thine, not to give back again.

23

As an unperfect actor on the stage
Who with his fear is put besides his part,
Or some fierce thing replete with too much rage,
Whose strength's abundance weakens his own heart;
So I, for fear of trust, forget to say
The perfect ceremony of love's rite,
And in mine own love's strength seem to decay,
O'ercharg'd with burthen of mine own love's might.
O, let my looks be then the eloquence
And dumb presagers of my speaking breast;
Who plead for love, and look for recompense,
More than that tongue that more hath more express'd.
  O, learn to read what silent love hath writ!
  To hear with eyes belongs to love's fine wit.

24

Mine eye hath play'd the painter and hath stell'd
Thy beauty's form in table of my heart;
My body is the frame wherein 'tis held,
And perspective it is best painter's art.
For through the painter must you see his skill
To find where your true image pictur'd lies,
Which in my bosom's shop is hanging still,
That hath his windows glazed with thine eyes.
Now see what good turns eyes for eyes have done:
Mine eyes have drawn thy shape, and thine for me
Are windows to my breast, where through the sun
Delights to peep, to gaze therein on thee;
  Yet eyes this cunning want to grace their art:
  They draw but what they see, know not the heart.

25

Let those who are in favour with their stars
Of public honour and proud titles boast,
Whilst I, whom fortune of such triumph bars,
Unlook'd for joy in that I honour most.

Great princes' favourites their fair leaves spread
But as the marigold at the sun's eye;
And in themselves their pride lies buried,
For at a frown they in their glory die.
The painful warrior famoused for fight,
After a thousand victories once foil'd,
Is from the book of honour razed quite,
And all the rest forgot for which he toil'd.
Then happy I, that love and am beloved
Where I may not remove nor be removed.

26

Lord of my love, to whom in vassalage
Thy merit hath my duty strongly knit,
To thee I send this written embassage,
To witness duty, not to show my wit;
Duty so great, which wit so poor as mine
May make seem bare, in wanting words to show it,
But that I hope some good conceit of thine
In thy soul's thought, all naked, will bestow it;
Till whatsoever star that guides my moving
Points on me graciously with fair aspect,
And puts apparel on my tattered loving
To show me worthy of thy sweet respect.
Then may I dare to boast how I do love thee;
Till then not show my head where thou mayst prove me.

27

Weary with toil, I haste me to my bed,
The dear repose for limbs with travel tired;
But then begins a journey in my head
To work my mind when body's work's expired;
For then my thoughts, from far where I abide,
Intend a zealous pilgrimage to thee,
And keep my drooping eyelids open wide,
Looking on darkness which the blind do see;
Save that my soul's imaginary sight
Presents thy shadow to my sightless view,
Which, like a jewel hung in ghastly night,
Makes black night beauteous and her old face new.
Lo, thus, by day my limbs, by night my mind,
For thee, and for myself, no quiet find.

28

How can I then return in happy plight
That am debarr'd the benefit of rest?
When day's oppression is not eas'd by night,
But day by night and night by day oppress'd?
And each, though enemies to either's reign,
Do in consent shake hands to torture me,
The one by toil, the other to complain
How far I toil, still farther off from thee.
I tell the day, to please him, thou art bright
And dost him grace when clouds do blot the heaven;
So flatter I the swart-complexion'd night,
When sparkling stars twire not, thou gild'st the even.
But day doth daily draw my sorrows longer,
And night doth nightly make grief's strength seem stronger.

29

When in disgrace with Fortune and men's eyes,
I all alone beweep my outcast state,
And trouble deaf heaven with my bootless cries,
And look upon myself, and curse my fate,
Wishing me like to one more rich in hope,
Featur'd like him, like him with friends possess'd,
Desiring this man's art, and that man's scope,
With what I most enjoy contented least;
Yet in these thoughts myself almost despising,
Haply I think on thee, and then my state,
Like to the lark at break of day arising
From sullen earth, sings hymns at heaven's gate;
For thy sweet love rememb'red such wealth brings
That then I scorn to change my state with kings.

30

When to the sessions of sweet silent thought
I summon up remembrance of things past,
I sigh the lack of many a thing I sought,
And with old woes new wail my dear time's waste.
Then can I drown an eye, unus'd to flow,
For precious friends hid in death's dateless night,
And weep afresh love's long since cancell'd woe,
And moan th' expense of many a vanish'd sight.
Then can I grieve at grievances foregone,
And heavily from woe to woe tell o'er
The sad account of fore-bemoaned moan,
Which I new pay as if not paid before.
But if the while I think on thee, dear friend,
All losses are restor'd, and sorrows end.

31

Thy bosom is endeared with all hearts
Which I by lacking have supposed dead;
And there reigns love and all love's loving parts,
And all those friends which I thought buried.
How many a holy and obsequious tear
Hath dear religious love stol'n from mine eye,
As interest of the dead, which now appear
But things remov'd that hidden in thee lie!
Thou art the grave where buried love doth live,
Hung with the trophies of my lovers gone,
Who all their parts of me to thee did give;

That due of many now is thine alone.
Their images I lov'd I view in thee,
And thou, all they, hast all the all of me.

32
If thou survive my well-contented day
When that churl Death my bones with dust shall cover,
And shalt by fortune once more re-survey
These poor rude lines of thy deceased lover,
Compare them with the bett'ring of the time,
And though they be outstripp'd by every pen,
Reserve them for my love, not for their rhyme,
Exceeded by the height of happier men.
O, then vouchsafe me but this loving thought:
'Had my friend's Muse grown with this growing age,
A dearer birth than this his love had brought,
To march in ranks of better equipage;
But since he died, and poets better prove,
Theirs for their style I'll read, his for his love'.

33
Full many a glorious morning have I seen
Flatter the mountain-tops with sovereign eye,
Kissing with golden face the meadows green,
Gilding pale streams with heavenly alchemy;
Anon permit the basest clouds to ride
With ugly rack on his celestial face,
And from the forlorn world his visage hide,
Stealing unseen to west with this disgrace.
Even so my sun one early morn did shine
With all triumphant splendour on my brow;
But out, alack! he was but one hour mine,
The region cloud hath mask'd him from me now.
Yet him for this my love no whit disdaineth;
Suns of the world may stain when heaven's sun staineth.

34
Why didst thou promise such a beauteous day,
And make me travel forth without my cloak,
To let base clouds o'ertake me in my way,
Hiding thy brav'ry in their rotten smoke?
'Tis not enough that through the cloud thou break
To dry the rain on my storm-beaten face,
For no man well of such a salve can speak
That heals the wound, and cures not the disgrace.
Nor can thy shame give physic to my grief;
Though thou repent, yet I have still the loss.
Th' offender's sorrow lends but weak relief
To him that bears the strong offence's cross.
Ah! but those tears are pearl which thy love sheds,
And they are rich, and ransom all ill deeds.

35
No more be griev'd at that which thou hast done:
Roses have thorns, and silver fountains mud;
Clouds and eclipses stain both moon and sun,
And loathsome canker lives in sweetest bud.
All men make faults, and even I in this,
Authorizing thy trespass with compare,
Myself corrupting, salving thy amiss,
Excusing thy sins more than thy sins are;
For to thy sensual fault I bring in sense –
Thy adverse party is thy advocate –
And 'gainst myself a lawful plea commence;
Such civil war is in my love and hate
That I an accessary needs must be
To that sweet thief which sourly robs from me.

36
Let me confess that we two must be twain,
Although our undivided loves are one;
So shall those blots that do with me remain,
Without thy help, by me be borne alone.
In our two loves there is but one respect,
Though in our lives a separable spite,
Which though it alter not love's sole effect,
Yet doth it steal sweet hours from love's delight.
I may not evermore acknowledge thee,
Lest my bewailed guilt should do thee shame;
Nor thou with public kindness honour me,
Unless thou take that honour from thy name.
But do not so; I love thee in such sort
As, thou being mine, mine is thy good report.

37
As a decrepit father takes delight
To see his active child do deeds of youth,
So I, made lame by Fortune's dearest spite,
Take all my comfort of thy worth and truth;
For whether beauty, birth, or wealth, or wit,
Or any of these all, or all, or more,
Entitled in thy parts do crowned sit,
I make my love engrafted to this store.
So then I am not lame, poor, nor despis'd,
Whilst that this shadow doth such substance give
That I in thy abundance am suffic'd,
And by a part of all thy glory live.
Look what is best, that best I wish in thee;
This wish I have; then ten times happy me!

38
How can my Muse want subject to invent,
While thou dost breathe that pour'st into my verse
Thine own sweet argument, too excellent

For every vulgar paper to rehearse?
O, give thyself the thanks if aught in me
Worthy perusal stand against thy sight;
For who's so dumb that cannot write to thee,
When thou thy self dost give invention light?
Be thou the tenth Muse, ten times more in worth
Than those old nine which rhymers invocate;
And he that calls on thee, let him bring forth
Eternal numbers to outlive long date.
  If my slight Muse do please these curious days,
  The pain be mine, but thine shall be the praise.

39

O, how thy worth with manners may I sing,
When thou art all the better part of me?
What can mine own praise to mine own self bring?
And what is't but mine own, when I praise thee?
Even for this let us divided live,
And our dear love lose name of single one,
That by this separation I may give
That due to thee which thou deserv'st alone.
O absence, what a torment wouldst thou prove,
Were it not thy sour leisure gave sweet leave
To entertain the time with thoughts of love;
Which time and thoughts so sweetly doth deceive,
  And that thou teachest how to make one twain,
  By praising him here who doth hence remain!

40

Take all my loves, my love, yea, take them all;
What hast thou then more than thou hadst before?
No love, my love, that thou mayst true love call;
All mine was thine before thou hadst this more.
Then if for my love thou my love receivest,
I cannot blame thee, for my love thou usest;
But yet be blam'd, if thou thyself deceivest
By wilful taste of what thyself refusest.
I do forgive thy robb'ry, gentle thief,
Although thou steal thee all my poverty;
And yet love knows it is a greater grief
To bear love's wrong than hate's known injury.
  Lascivious grace, in whom all ill well shows,
  Kill me with spites; yet we must not be foes.

41

Those pretty wrongs that liberty commits
When I am sometime absent from thy heart,
Thy beauty and thy years full well befits,
For still temptation follows where thou art.
Gentle thou art, and therefore to be won,
Beauteous thou art, therefore to be assailed;
And when a woman woos, what woman's son
Will sourly leave her till she have prevailed?
Ay me! but yet thou mightst my seat forbear,
And chide thy beauty and thy straying youth,
Who lead thee in their riot even there
Where thou art forc'd to break a twofold truth:
  Hers, by thy beauty tempting her to thee,
  Thine, by thy beauty being false to me.

42

That thou hast her, it is not all my grief,
And yet it may be said I lov'd her dearly;
That she hath thee is of my wailing chief,
A loss in love that touches me more nearly.
Loving offenders, thus I will excuse ye:
Thou dost love her because thou know'st I love her,
And for my sake even so doth she abuse me.
Suff'ring my friend for my sake to approve her.
If I lose thee, my loss is my love's gain,
And, losing her, my friend hath found that loss;
Both find each other, and I lose both twain,
And both for my sake lay on me this cross.
  But here's the joy: my friend and I are one;
  Sweet flattery! then she loves but me alone.

43

When most I wink, then do mine eyes best see,
For all the day they view things unrespected;
But when I sleep, in dreams they look on thee,
And, darkly bright, are bright in dark directed;
Then thou whose shadow shadows doth make bright,
How would thy shadow's form form happy show
To the clear day with thy much clearer light,
When to unseeing eyes thy shade shines so!
How would, I say, mine eyes be blessed made
By looking on thee in the living day,
When in dead night thy fair imperfect shade
Through heavy sleep on sightless eyes doth stay!
  All days are nights to see till I see thee,
  And nights bright days when dreams do show thee me.

44

If the dull substance of my flesh were thought,
Injurious distance should not stop my way;
For then, despite of space, I would be brought
From limits far remote, where thou dost stay.
No matter then, although my foot did stand
Upon the farthest earth remov'd from thee,
For nimble thought can jump both sea and land
As soon as think the place where he would be.
But ah! thought kills me that I am not thought,
To leap large lengths of miles when thou art gone,
But that, so much of earth and water wrought,

I must attend time's leisure with my moan,
Receiving nought by elements so slow
But heavy tears, badges of either's woe.

45
The other two, slight air and purging fire,
Are both with thee, wherever I abide;
The first my thought, the other my desire,
These present-absent with swift motion slide.
For when these quicker elements are gone
In tender embassy of love to thee,
My life, being made of four, with two alone
Sinks down to death, oppress'd with melancholy;
Until life's composition be recured
By those swift messengers return'd from thee,
Who even but now come back again, assured
Of thy fair health, recounting it to me.
This told, I joy; but then no longer glad,
I send them back again, and straight grow sad.

46
Mine eye and heart are at a mortal war
How to divide the conquest of thy sight;
Mine eye my heart thy picture's sight would bar,
My heart mine eye the freedom of that right.
My heart doth plead that thou in him dost lie,
A closet never pierc'd with crystal eyes;
But the defendant doth that plea deny,
And says in him thy fair appearance lies.
To 'cide this title is impanelled
A quest of thoughts, all tenants to the heart;
And by their verdict is determined
The clear eye's moiety and the dear heart's part –
As thus: mine eye's due is thine outward part,
And my heart's right thine inward love of heart.

47
Betwixt mine eye and heart a league is took,
And each doth good turns now unto the other.
When that mine eye is famish'd for a look,
Or heart in love with sighs himself doth smother;
With my love's picture then my eye doth feast,
And to the painted banquet bids my heart;
Another time mine eye is my heart's guest,
And in his thoughts of love doth share a part;
So, either by thy picture or my love,
Thyself away art present still with me;
For thou not farther than my thoughts canst move,
And I am still with them, and they with thee;
Or if they sleep, thy picture in my sight
Awakes my heart to heart's and eye's delight.

48
How careful was I when I took my way,
Each trifle under truest bars to thrust,
That to my use it might unused stay
From hands of falsehood, in sure wards of trust!
But thou, to whom my jewels trifles are,
Most worthy comfort, now my greatest grief,
Thou, best of dearest, and mine only care,
Art left the prey of every vulgar thief.
Thee have I not lock'd up in any chest,
Save where thou art not, though I feel thou art,
Within the gentle closure of my breast,
From whence at pleasure thou mayst come and part;
And even thence thou wilt be stol'n, I fear,
For truth proves thievish for a prize so dear.

49
Against that time, if ever that time come,
When I shall see thee frown on my defects,
When as thy love hath cast his utmost sum,
Call'd to that audit by advis'd respects;
Against that time when thou shalt strangely pass
And scarcely greet me with that sun, thine eye,
When love, converted from the thing it was,
Shall reasons find of settled gravity –
Against that time do I ensconce me here
Within the knowledge of mine own desert,
And this my hand against myself uprear,
To guard the lawful reasons on thy part:
To leave poor me thou hast the strength of laws,
Since why to love I can allege no cause.

50
How heavy do I journey on the way,
When what I seek – my weary travel's end –
Doth teach that ease and that repose to say
'Thus far the miles are measur'd from thy friend!'
The beast that bears me, tired with my woe,
Plods dully on, to bear that weight in me,
As if by some instinct the wretch did know
His rider lov'd not speed being made from thee.
The bloody spur cannot provoke him on
That sometimes anger thrusts into his hide,
Which heavily he answers with a groan,
More sharp to me than spurring to his side;
For that same groan doth put this in my mind:
My grief lies onward, and my joy behind.

51
Thus can my love excuse the slow offence
Of my dull bearer, when from thee I speed:
From where thou art why should I haste me thence?
Till I return, of posting is no need.
O, what excuse will my poor beast then find,
When swift extremity can seem but slow?

Then should I spur, though mounted on the wind;
In winged speed no motion shall I know.
Then can no horse with my desire keep pace;
Therefore desire, of perfect'st love being made,
Shall weigh no dull flesh in his fiery race;
But love, for love, thus shall excuse my jade:
Since from thee going he went wilful slow,
Towards thee I'll run, and give him leave to go.

52

So am I as the rich whose blessed key
Can bring him to his sweet up-locked treasure,
The which he will not ev'ry hour survey,
For blunting the fine point of seldom pleasure.
Therefore are feasts so solemn and so rare,
Since seldom coming, in the long year set,
Like stones of worth they thinly placed are,
Or captain jewels in the carcanet.
So is the time that keeps you as my chest,
Or as the wardrobe which the robe doth hide,
To make some special instant special blest
By new unfolding his imprison'd pride.
Blessed are you, whose worthiness gives scope,
Being had, to triumph, being lack'd, to hope.

53

What is your substance, whereof are you made,
That millions of strange shadows on you tend?
Since every one hath, every one, one shade,
And you, but one, can every shadow lend.
Describe Adonis, and the counterfeit
Is poorly imitated after you;
On Helen's cheek all art of beauty set,
And you in Grecian tires are painted new.
Speak of the spring and foison of the year:
The one doth shadow of your beauty show,
The other as your bounty doth appear,
And you in every blessed shape we know.
In all external grace you have some part,
But you like none, none you, for constant heart.

54

O, how much more doth beauty beauteous seem
By that sweet ornament which truth doth give!
The rose looks fair, but fairer we it deem
For that sweet odour which doth in it live.
The canker-blooms have full as deep a dye
As the perfumed tincture of the roses,
Hang on such thorns, and play as wantonly
When summer's breath their masked buds discloses;
But for their virtue only is their show,
They lived unwoo'd, and unrespected fade;
Die to themselves. Sweet roses do not so:
Of their sweet deaths are sweetest odours made.
And so of you, beauteous and lovely youth,
When that shall vade, by verse distills your truth.

55

Not marble nor the gilded monuments
Of princes shall outlive this pow'rful rhyme;
But you shall shine more bright in these contents
Than unswept stone, besmear'd with sluttish time.
When wasteful war shall statues overturn,
And broils root out the work of masonry,
Nor Mars his sword nor war's quick fire shall burn
The living record of your memory.
'Gainst death and all-oblivious enmity
Shall you pace forth; your praise shall still find room,
Even in the eyes of all posterity
That wear this world out to the ending doom.
So, till the judgment that yourself arise,
You live in this, and dwell in lovers' eyes.

56

Sweet love, renew thy force; be it not said
Thy edge should blunter be than appetite,
Which but to-day by feeding is allay'd,
To-morrow sharp'ned in his former might.
So, love, be thou; although to-day thou fill
Thy hungry eyes, even till they wink with fulness,
To-morrow see again, and do not kill
The spirit of love with a perpetual dulness.
Let this sad int'rim like the ocean be
Which parts the shore where two contracted new
Come daily to the banks, that, when they see
Return of love, more blest may be the view;
Or call it winter, which, being full of care,
Makes summer's welcome thrice more wish'd, more rare.

57

Being your slave, what should I do but tend
Upon the hours and times of your desire?
I have no precious time at all to spend,
Nor services to do, till you require.
Nor dare I chide the world-without-end hour,
Whilst I, my sovereign, watch the clock for you,
Nor think the bitterness of absence sour,
When you have bid your servant once adieu;
Nor dare I question with my jealous thought
Where you may be, or your affairs suppose,
But, like a sad slave, stay and think of nought
Save where you are how happy you make those.
So true a fool is love that in your will,
Though you do anything, he thinks no ill.

58

That god forbid that made me first your slave
I should in thought control your times of
 pleasure,
Or at your hand th' account of hours to crave,
Being your vassal bound to stay your leisure!
O, let me suffer, being at your beck,
Th' imprison'd absence of your liberty,
And patience, tame to sufferance, bide each check
Without accusing you of injury.
Be where you list; your charter is so strong
That you yourself may privilege your time
To what you will; to you it doth belong
Your self to pardon of self-doing crime.
 I am to wait, though waiting so be hell;
 Not blame your pleasure, be it ill or well.

59

If there be nothing new, but that which is
Hath been before, how are our brains beguil'd,
Which labouring for invention bear amiss
The second burthen of a former child!
O, that record could with a backward look,
Even of five hundred courses of the sun,
Show me your image in some antique book,
Since mind at first in character was done!
That I might see what the old world could say
To this composed wonder of your frame;
Whether we are mended, or whe'er better they,
Or whether revolution be the same.
 O, sure I am, the wits of former days
 To subjects worse have given admiring praise.

60

Like as the waves make towards the pebbled
 shore,
So do our minutes hasten to their end;
Each changing place with that which goes before,
In sequent toil all forwards do contend.
Nativity, once in the main of light,
Crawls to maturity, wherewith being crown'd,
Crooked eclipses 'gainst his glory fight,
And Time that gave doth now his gift confound.
Time doth transfix the flourish set on youth,
And delves the parallels in beauty's brow,
Feeds on the rarities of nature's truth,
And nothing stands but for his scythe to mow.
 And yet to times in hope my verse shall stand,
 Praising thy worth, despite his cruel hand.

61

Is it thy will thy image should keep open
My heavy eyelids to the weary night?
Dost thou desire my slumbers should be broken,
While shadows like to thee do mock my sight?
Is it thy spirit that thou send'st from thee
So far from home into my deeds to pry,
To find out shames and idle hours in me,
The scope and tenour of thy jealousy?
O no! thy love, though much, is not so great:
It is my love that keeps mine eye awake;
Mine own true love that doth my rest defeat
To play the watchman ever for thy sake.
 For thee watch I, whilst thou dost wake
  elsewhere,
 From me far off, with others all too near.

62

Sin of self-love possesseth all mine eye,
And all my soul, and all my every part;
And for this sin there is no remedy,
It is so grounded inward in my heart.
Methinks no face so gracious is as mine,
No shape so true, no truth of such account,
And for myself mine own worth do define
As I all other in all worths surmount.
But when my glass shows me myself indeed,
Beated and chopt with tann'd antiquity,
Mine own self-love quite contrary I read;
Self so self-loving were iniquity.
 'Tis thee, my self, that for myself I praise,
 Painting my age with beauty of thy days.

63

Against my love shall be as I am now,
With Time's injurious hand crush'd and o'erworn;
When hours have drain'd his blood, and fill'd his
 brow
With lines and wrinkles; when his youthful morn
Hath travell'd on to age's steepy night;
And all those beauties whereof now he's king
Are vanishing or vanish'd out of sight,
Stealing away the treasure of his spring –
For such a time do I now fortify
Against confounding age's cruel knife,
That he shall never cut from memory
My sweet love's beauty, though my lover's life.
 His beauty shall in these black lines be seen,
 And they shall live, and he in them still green.

64

When I have seen by Time's fell hand defaced
The rich proud cost of outworn buried age;
When sometime lofty towers I see down-rased,
And brass eternal slave to mortal rage;
When I have seen the hungry ocean gain
Advantage on the kingdom of the shore,
And the firm soil win of the wat'ry main,

Increasing store with loss, and loss with store;
When I have seen such interchange of state,
Or state itself confounded to decay;
Ruin hath taught me thus to ruminate –
That Time will come and take my love away.
This thought is as a death, which cannot choose
But weep to have that which it fears to lose.

65

Since brass, nor stone, nor earth, nor boundless sea,
But sad mortality o'ersways their power,
How with this rage shall beauty hold a plea,
Whose action is no stronger than a flower?
O, how shall summer's honey breath hold out
Against the wrackful siege of batt'ring days,
When rocks impregnable are not so stout,
Nor gates of steel so strong, but Time decays?
O fearful meditation! Where, alack,
Shall Time's best jewel from Time's chest lie hid?
Or what strong hand can hold his swift foot back?
Or who his spoil of beauty can forbid?
O, none, unless this miracle have might,
That in black ink my love may still shine bright.

66

Tir'd with all these, for restful death I cry:
As, to behold desert a beggar born,
And needy nothing trimm'd in jollity,
And purest faith unhappily forsworn,
And gilded honour shamefully misplac'd,
And maiden virtue rudely strumpeted,
And right perfection wrongfully disgrac'd,
And strength by limping sway disabled,
And art made tongue-tied by authority,
And folly, doctor-like, controlling skill,
And simple truth miscall'd simplicity,
And captive good attending captain ill –
Tir'd with all these, from these would I be gone,
Save that, to die, I leave my love alone.

67

Ah! wherefore with infection should he live
And with his presence grace impiety,
That sin by him advantage should achieve,
And lace itself with his society?
Why should false painting imitate his cheek,
And steal dead seeming of his living hue?
Why should poor beauty indirectly seek
Roses of shadow, since his rose is true?
Why should he live now Nature bankrupt is,
Beggar'd of blood to blush through lively veins?
For she hath no exchequer now but his,
And, proud of many, lives upon his gains.
O, him she stores, to show what wealth she had
In days long since, before these last so bad.

68

Thus is his cheek the map of days outworn,
When beauty liv'd and died as flowers do now,
Before these bastard signs of fair were born,
Or durst inhabit on a living brow;
Before the golden tresses of the dead,
The right of sepulchres, were shorn away
To live a second life on second head,
Ere beauty's dead fleece made another gay.
In him those holy antique hours are seen,
Without all ornament, itself and true,
Making no summer of another's green,
Robbing no old to dress his beauty new;
And him as for a map doth Nature store,
To show false Art what beauty was of yore.

69

Those parts of thee that the world's eye doth view
Want nothing that the thought of hearts can mend.
All tongues, the voice of souls, give thee that due,
Utt'ring bare truth, even so as foes commend.
Thine outward thus with outward praise is crown'd;
But those same tongues that give thee so thine own
In other accents do this praise confound
By seeing farther than the eye hath shown.
They look into the beauty of thy mind,
And that, in guess, they measure by thy deeds;
Then, churls, their thoughts, although their eyes were kind,
To thy fair flower add the rank smell of weeds.
But why thy odour matcheth not thy show,
The soil is this – that thou dost common grow.

70

That thou art blam'd shall not be thy defect,
For slander's mark was ever yet the fair;
The ornament of beauty is suspect,
A crow that flies in heaven's sweetest air.
So thou be good, slander doth but approve
Thy worth the greater, being woo'd of time;
For canker vice the sweetest buds doth love,
And thou present'st a pure unstained prime.
Thou hast pass'd by the ambush of young days,
Either not assail'd, or victor being charg'd;
Yet this thy praise cannot be so thy praise
To tie up envy, evermore enlarg'd.
If some suspect of ill mask'd not thy show,
Then thou alone kingdoms of hearts shouldst owe.

71

No longer mourn for me when I am dead

Than you shall hear the surly sullen bell
Give warning to the world that I am fled
From this vile world, with vilest worms to dwell.
Nay, if you read this line, remember not
The hand that writ it; for I love you so,
That I in your sweet thoughts would be forgot,
If thinking on me then should make you woe.
O, if I say, you look upon this verse,
When I perhaps compounded am with clay,
Do not so much as my poor name rehearse,
But let your love even with my life decay;
Lest the wise world should look into your moan,
And mock you with me after I am gone.

72

O, lest the world should task you to recite
What merit liv'd in me, that you should love
After my death, dear love, forget me quite,
For you in me can nothing worthy prove;
Unless you would devise some virtuous lie,
To do more for me than mine own desert,
And hang more praise upon deceased I
Than niggard truth would willingly impart.
O, lest your true love may seem false in this,
That you for love speak well of me untrue,
My name be buried where my body is,
And live no more to shame nor me nor you!
For I am sham'd by that which I bring forth,
And so should you, to love things nothing worth.

73

That time of year thou mayst in me behold
When yellow leaves, or none, or few, do hang
Upon those boughs which shake against the cold,
Bare ruin'd choirs where late the sweet birds sang.
In me thou seest the twilight of such day
As after sunset fadeth in the west,
Which by and by black night doth take away,
Death's second self, that seals up all in rest.
In me thou seest the glowing of such fire
That on the ashes of his youth doth lie,
As the death-bed whereon it must expire,
Consum'd with that which it was nourish'd by.
This thou perceiv'st which makes thy love more strong,
To love that well which thou must leave ere long.

74

But be contented. When that fell arrest
Without all bail shall carry me away,
My life hath in this line some interest,
Which for memorial still with thee shall stay.
When thou reviewest this, thou dost review
The very part was consecrate to thee.
The earth can have but earth, which is his due;
My spirit is thine, the better part of me.
So then thou hast but lost the dregs of life,
The prey of worms, my body being dead;
The coward conquest of a wretch's knife,
Too base of thee to be remembered.
The worth of that is that which it contains,
And that is this, and this with thee remains.

75

So are you to my thoughts as food to life,
Or as sweet-season'd showers are to the ground;
And for the peace of you I hold such strife
As 'twixt a miser and his wealth is found:
Now proud as an enjoyer, and anon
Doubting the filching age will steal his treasure;
Now counting best to be with you alone,
Then better'd that the world may see my pleasure;
Sometime all full with feasting on your sight,
And by and by clean starved for a look;
Possessing or pursuing no delight
Save what is had or must from you be took.
Thus do I pine and surfeit day by day,
Or gluttoning on all, or all away.

76

Why is my verse so barren of new pride?
So far from variation or quick change?
Why, with the time, do I not glance aside
To new-found methods and to compounds strange?
Why write I still all one, ever the same,
And keep invention in a noted weed,
That every word doth almost tell my name,
Showing their birth, and where they did proceed?
O, know, sweet love, I always write of you,
And you and love are still my argument;
So all my best is dressing old words new,
Spending again what is already spent;
For as the sun is daily new and old,
So is my love still telling what is told.

77

Thy glass will show thee how thy beauties wear,
Thy dial how thy precious minutes waste;
The vacant leaves thy mind's imprint will bear,
And of this book this learning mayst thou taste.
The wrinkles which thy glass will truly show
Of mouthed graves will give thee memory;
Thou by thy dial's shady stealth mayst know
Time's thievish progress to eternity.
Look what thy memory cannot contain
Commit to these waste blanks, and thou shalt find.

Those children nurs'd, deliver'd from thy brain,
To take a new acquaintance of thy mind.
These offices, so oft as thou wilt look,
Shall profit thee, and much enrich thy book.

78

So oft have I invok'd thee for my Muse,
And found such fair assistance in my verse,
As every alien pen hath got my use,
And under thee their poesy disperse.
Thine eyes, that taught the dumb on high to sing
And heavy ignorance aloft to fly,
Have added feathers to the learned's wing
And given grace a double majesty.
Yet be most proud of that which I compile,
Whose influence is thine, and born of thee:
In others' works thou dost but mend the style,
And arts with thy sweet graces graced be;
But thou art all my art, and dost advance
As high as learning my rude ignorance.

79

Whilst I alone did call upon thy aid,
My verse alone had all thy gentle grace;
But now my gracious numbers are decay'd,
And my sick Muse doth give another place.
I grant, sweet love, thy lovely argument
Deserves the travail of a worthier pen;
Yet what of thee thy poet doth invent
He robs thee of, and pays it thee again.
He lends thee virtue, and he stole that word
From thy behaviour; beauty doth he give,
And found it in thy cheek; he can afford
No praise to thee but what in thee doth live.
Then thank him not for that which he doth say,
Since what he owes thee thou thyself dost pay.

80

O, how I faint when I of you do write,
Knowing a better spirit doth use your name
And in the praise thereof spends all his might
To make me tongue-tied, speaking of your fame!
But since your worth, wide as the ocean is,
The humble as the proudest sail doth bear,
My saucy bark, inferior far to his,
On your broad main doth wilfully appear.
Your shallowest help will hold me up afloat,
Whilst he upon your soundless deep doth ride;
Or, being wreck'd, I am a worthless boat,
He of tall building and of goodly pride.
Then if he thrive, and I be cast away,
The worst was this: my love was my decay.

81

Or I shall live your epitaph to make,
Or you survive when I in earth am rotten;
From hence your memory death cannot take,
Although in me each part will be forgotten.
Your name from hence immortal life shall have,
Though I, once gone, to all the world must die;
The earth can yield me but a common grave,
When you entombed in men's eyes shall lie.
Your monument shall be my gentle verse,
Which eyes not yet created shall o'er-read;
And tongues to be your being shall rehearse,
When all the breathers of this world are dead.
You still shall live, such virtue hath my pen,
Where breath most breathes, even in the mouths of men.

82

I grant thou wert not married to my Muse,
And therefore mayst without attaint o'er-look
The dedicated words which writers use
Of their fair subject, blessing every book.
Thou art as fair in knowledge as in hue,
Finding thy worth a limit past my praise,
And therefore art enforc'd to seek anew
Some fresher stamp of the time-bettering days.
And do so, love; yet when they have devis'd
What strained touches rhetoric can lend,
Thou truly fair wert truly sympathiz'd
In true plain words by thy true-telling friend;
And their gross painting might be better us'd
Where cheeks need blood; in thee it is abus'd.

83

I never saw that you did painting need,
And therefore to your fair no painting set;
I found, or thought I found, you did exceed
The barren tender of a poet's debt;
And therefore have I slept in your report,
That you your self, being extant, well might show
How far a modern quill doth come too short,
Speaking of worth, what worth in you doth grow.
This silence for my sin you did impute,
Which shall be most my glory, being dumb;
For I impair not beauty, being mute,
When others would give life, and bring a tomb.
There lives more life in one of your fair eyes
Than both your poets can in praise devise.

84

Who is it that says most which can say more
Than this rich praise – that you alone are you?
In whose confine immured is the store
Which should example where your equal grew?
Lean penury within that pen doth dwell
That to his subject lends not some small glory;
But he that writes of you, if he can tell

That you are you, so dignifies his story.
Let him but copy what in you is writ,
Not making worse what nature made so clear,
And such a counterpart shall fame his wit,
Making his style admired every where.
  You to your beauteous blessings add a curse,
  Being fond on praise, which makes your praises worse.

85

My tongue-tied Muse in manners holds her still.
While comments of your praise, richly compil'd,
Reserve their character with golden quill
And precious phrase by all the Muses fil'd.
I think good thoughts, whilst other write good words,
And, like unlettered clerk, still cry 'Amen'
To every hymn that able spirit affords
In polish'd form of well-refined pen.
Hearing you prais'd, I say "Tis so, 'tis true',
And to the most of praise add something more;
But that is in my thought, whose love to you,
Though words come hindmost, holds his rank before.
  Then others for the breath of words respect,
  Me for my dumb thoughts, speaking in effect.

86

Was it the proud full sail of his great verse,
Bound for the prize of all-too-precious you,
That did my ripe thoughts in my brain inhearse,
Making their tomb the womb wherein they grew?
Was it his spirit, by spirits taught to write
Above a mortal pitch, that struck me dead?
No, neither he, nor his compeers by night
Giving him aid, my verse astonished.
He nor that affable familiar ghost
Which nightly gulls him with intelligence,
As victors, of my silence cannot boast:
I was not sick of any fear from thence.
  But when your countenance fill'd up his line,
  Then lack'd I matter; that enfeebled mine.

87

Farewell! thou art too dear for my possessing,
And like enough thou know'st thy estimate.
The charter of thy worth gives thee releasing;
My bonds in thee are all determinate.
For how do I hold thee but by thy granting?
And for that riches where is my deserving?
The cause of this fair gift in me is wanting,
And so my patent back again is swerving.
Thy self thou gav'st, thy own worth then not knowing,
Or me, to whom thou gav'st it, else mistaking;
So thy great gift, upon misprision growing,
Comes home again, on better judgment making.
  Thus have I had thee, as a dream doth flatter:
  In sleep a king, but waking no such matter.

88

When thou shalt be dispos'd to set me light,
And place my merit in the eye of scorn,
Upon thy side against myself I'll fight,
And prove thee virtuous, though thou art forsworn.
With mine own weakness being best acquainted,
Upon thy part I can set down a story
Of faults conceal'd, wherein I am attainted;
That thou, in losing me, shall win much glory.
And I by this will be a gainer too;
For bending all my loving thoughts on thee,
The injuries that to myself I do,
Doing thee vantage, double vantage me.
  Such is my love, to thee I so belong,
  That for thy right myself will bear all wrong.

89

Say that thou didst forsake me for some fault,
And I will comment upon that offence;
Speak of my lameness, and I straight will halt;
Against thy reasons making no defence.
Thou canst not, love, disgrace me half so ill.
To set a form upon desired change,
As I'll myself disgrace, knowing thy will.
I will acquaintance strangle and look strange,
Be absent from thy walks, and in my tongue
Thy sweet beloved name no more shall dwell,
Lest I, too much profane, should do it wrong,
And haply of our old acquaintance tell.
  For thee, against myself I'll vow debate,
  For I must ne'er love him whom thou dost hate.

90

Then hate me when thou wilt; if ever, now;
Now while the world is bent my deeds to cross,
Join with the spite of fortune, make me bow,
And do not drop in for an after-loss.
Ah, do not, when my heart hath scap'd this sorrow,
Come in the rearward of a conquer'd woe;
Give not a windy night a rainy morrow,
To linger out a purpos'd overthrow.
If thou wilt leave me, do not leave me last,
When other petty griefs have done their spite,
But in the onset come; so shall I taste
At first the very worst of fortune's might;
  And other strains of woe, which now seem woe,
  Compar'd with loss of thee will not seem so.

91

Some glory in their birth, some in their skill,

Some in their wealth, some in their body's force;
Some in their garments, though new-fangled ill;
Some in their hawks and hounds, some in their horse;
And every humour hath his adjunct pleasure,
Wherein it finds a joy above the rest;
But these particulars are not my measure:
All these I better in one general best.
Thy love is better than high birth to me,
Richer than wealth, prouder than garments' cost,
Of more delight than hawks and horses be;
And, having thee, of all men's pride I boast –
Wretched in this alone, that thou mayst take
All this away, and me most wretched make.

92

But do thy worst to steal thy self away,
For term of life thou art assured mine;
And life no longer than thy love will stay,
For it depends upon that love of thine.
Then need I not to fear the worst of wrongs,
When in the least of them my life hath end.
I see a better state to me belongs
Than that which on thy humour doth depend.
Thou canst not vex me with inconstant mind,
Since that my life on thy revolt doth lie.
O what a happy title do I find,
Happy to have thy love, happy to die!
But what's so blessed-fair that fears no blot?
Thou mayst be false, and yet I know it not.

93

So shall I live, supposing thou art true,
Like a deceived husband; so love's face
May still seem love to me, though alter'd new –
Thy looks with me, thy heart in other place.
For there can live no hatred in thine eye;
Therefore in that I cannot know thy change.
In many's looks the false heart's history
Is writ in moods and frowns and wrinkles strange;
But heaven in thy creation did decree
That in thy face sweet love should ever dwell;
Whate'er thy thoughts or thy heart's workings be,
Thy looks should nothing thence but sweetness tell.
How like Eve's apple doth thy beauty grow,
If thy sweet virtue answer not thy show!

94

They that have power to hurt and will do none,
That do not do the thing they most do show,
Who, moving others, are themselves as stone,
Unmoved, cold, and to temptation slow –
They rightly do inherit Heaven's graces,
And husband nature's riches from expense;
They are the lords and owners of their faces,
Others but stewards of their excellence.
The summer's flow'r is to the summer sweet
Though to itself it only live and die;
But if that flow'r with base infection meet,
The basest weed outbraves his dignity.
For sweetest things turn sourest by their deeds:
Lilies that fester smell far worse than weeds.

95

How sweet and lovely dost thou make the shame
Which, like a canker in the fragrant rose,
Doth spot the beauty of thy budding name!
O, in what sweets dost thou thy sins enclose!
That tongue that tells the story of thy days,
Making lascivious comments on thy sport,
Cannot dispraise but in a kind of praise:
Naming thy name blesses an ill report.
O, what a mansion have those vices got
Which for their habitation chose out thee,
Where beauty's veil doth cover every blot,
And all things turns to fair that eyes can see!
Take heed, dear heart, of this large privilege;
The hardest knife ill-us'd doth lose his edge.

96

Some say thy fault is youth, some wantonness;
Some say thy grace is youth and gentle sport;
Both grace and faults are lov'd of more and less:
Thou mak'st faults graces that to thee resort.
As on the finger of a throned queen
The basest jewel will be well esteem'd;
So are those errors that in thee are seen
To truths translated and for true things deem'd.
How many lambs might the stern wolf betray,
If like a lamb he could his looks translate!
How many gazers mightst thou lead away,
If thou wouldst use the strength of all thy state!
But do not so; I love thee in such sort,
As, thou being mine, mine is thy good report.

97

How like a winter hath my absence been
From thee, the pleasure of the fleeting year!
What freezings have I felt, what dark days seen!
What old December's bareness everywhere!
And yet this time remov'd was summer's time,
The teeming autumn, big with rich increase,
Bearing the wanton burden of the prime,
Like widowed wombs after their lord's decease;
Yet this abundant issue seem'd to me
But hope of orphans, and unfathered fruit;
For summer and his pleasures wait on thee,
And, thou away, the very birds are mute;
Or, if they sing, 'tis with so dull a cheer
That leaves look pale, dreading the winter's near.

98

From you have I been absent in the spring,
When proud-pied April, dress'd in all his trim,
Hath put a spirit of youth in every thing,
That heavy Saturn laugh'd and leap'd with him.
Yet nor the lays of birds, nor the sweet smell
Of different flowers in odour and in hue,
Could make me any summer's story tell,
Or from their proud lap pluck them where they grew;
Nor did I wonder at the lily's white,
Nor praise the deep vermilion in the rose:
They were but sweet, but figures of delight,
Drawn after you, you pattern of all those.
Yet seem'd it winter still, and, you away,
As with your shadow I with these did play.

99

The forward violet thus did I chide:
Sweet thief, whence didst thou steal thy sweet that smells,
If not from my love's breath? The purple pride
Which on thy soft cheek for complexion dwells
In my love's veins thou hast too grossly dy'd.
The lily I condemned for thy hand,
And buds of marjoram had stol'n thy hair;
The roses fearfully on thorns did stand,
One blushing shame, another white despair;
A third, nor red nor white, had stol'n of both,
And to his robb'ry had annex'd thy breath;
But, for his theft, in pride of all his growth
A vengeful canker eat him up to death.
More flowers I noted, yet I none could see
But sweet or colour it had stol'n from thee.

100

Where art thou, Muse, that thou forget'st so long
To speak of that which gives thee all thy might?
Spend'st thou thy fury on some worthless song,
Dark'ning thy power to lend base subjects light?
Return, forgetful Muse, and straight redeem
In gentle numbers time so idly spent;
Sing to the ear that doth thy lays esteem
And gives thy pen both skill and argument.
Rise, resty Muse, my love's sweet face survey,
If Time have any wrinkle graven there;
If any, be a satire to decay,
And make Time's spoils despised everywhere.
Give my love fame faster than Time wastes life;
So thou prevent'st his scythe and crooked knife.

101

O truant Muse, what shall be thy amends
For thy neglect of truth in beauty dy'd?
Both truth and beauty on my love depends;
So dost thou too, and therein dignified.
Make answer, Muse. Wilt thou not haply say
'Truth needs no colour with his colour fix'd;
Beauty no pencil, beauty's truth to lay;
But best is best, if never intermix'd'?
Because he needs no praise, wilt thou be dumb?
Excuse not silence so; for't lies in thee
To make him much outlive a gilded tomb,
And to be prais'd of ages yet to be.
Then do thy office, Muse. I teach thee how
To make him seem long hence as he shows now.

102

My love is strength'ned, though more weak in seeming;
I love not less, though less the show appear;
That love is merchandiz'd whose rich esteeming
The owner's tongue doth publish every where.
Our love was new, and then but in the spring,
When I was wont to greet it with my lays;
As Philomel in summer's front doth sing,
And stops her pipe in growth of riper days.
Not that the summer is less pleasant now
Than when her mournful hymns did hush the night,
But that wild music burthens every bough,
And sweets grown common lose their dear delight.
Therefore, like her, I sometime hold my tongue,
Because I would not dull you with my song.

103

Alack, what poverty my Muse brings forth,
That, having such a scope to show her pride,
The argument all bare is of more worth
Than when it hath my added praise beside!
O, blame me not, if I no more can write!
Look in your glass, and there appears a face
That over-goes my blunt invention quite,
Dulling my lines, and doing me disgrace.
Were it not sinful then, striving to mend,
To mar the subject that before was well?
For to no other pass my verses tend
Than of your graces and your gifts to tell;
And more, much more, than in my verse can sit
Your own glass shows you, when you look in it.

104

To me, fair friend, you never can be old,
For as you were when first your eye I ey'd,
Such seems your beauty still. Three winters cold
Have from the forests shook three summers' pride,

Three beauteous springs to yellow autumn turn'd
In process of the seasons have I seen,
Three April perfumes in three hot Junes burn'd,
Since first I saw you fresh, which yet are green.
Ah, yet doth beauty, like a dial-hand,
Steal from his figure, and no pace perceiv'd;
So your sweet hue, which methinks still doth stand,
Hath motion, and mine eye may be deceiv'd.
For fear of which, hear this, thou age unbred:
Ere you were born was beauty's summer dead.

105

Let not my love be call'd idolatry,
Nor my beloved as an idol show,
Since all alike my songs and praises be
To one, of one, still such, and ever so.
Kind is my love to-day, to-morrow kind,
Still constant in a wondrous excellence;
Therefore my verse, to constancy confin'd,
One thing expressing, leaves out difference.
'Fair, kind, and true' is all my argument,
'Fair, kind, and true' varying to other words;
And in this change is my invention spent,
Three themes in one, which wondrous scope affords.
Fair, kind, and true, have often liv'd alone,
Which three, till now, never kept seat in one.

106

When in the chronicle of wasted time
I see descriptions of the fairest wights,
And beauty making beautiful old rhyme
In praise of ladies dead and lovely knights,
Then, in the blazon of sweet beauty's best,
Of hand, of foot, of lip, of eye, of brow,
I see their antique pen would have express'd
Even such a beauty as you master now.
So all their praises are but prophecies
Of this our time, all you prefiguring;
And, for they look'd but with divining eyes,
They had not skill enough your worth to sing;
For we, which now behold these present days,
Have eyes to wonder, but lack tongues to praise.

107

Not mine own fears, nor the prophetic soul
Of the wide world dreaming on things to come,
Can yet the lease of my true love control,
Suppos'd as forfeit to a confin'd doom.
The mortal moon hath her eclipse endur'd,
And the sad augurs mock their own presage;
Incertainties now crown themselves assur'd,
And peace proclaims olives of endless age.
Now with the drops of this most balmy time
My love looks fresh, and Death to me subscribes,
Since spite of him I'll live in this poor rhyme,
While he insults o'er dull and speechless tribes.
And thou in this shalt find thy monument,
When tyrants' crests and tombs of brass are spent.

108

What's in the brain that ink may character
Which hath not figur'd to thee my true spirit?
What's new to speak, what new to register,
That may express my love or thy dear merit?
Nothing, sweet boy; but yet, like prayers divine,
I must each day say o'er the very same;
Counting no old thing old, thou mine, I thine,
Even as when first I hallowed thy fair name.
So that eternal love in love's fresh case
Weighs not the dust and injury of age,
Nor gives to necessary wrinkles place,
But makes antiquity for aye his page;
Finding the first conceit of love there bred,
Where time and outward form would show it dead.

109

O, never say that I was false of heart,
Though absence seem'd my flame to qualify!
As easy might I from my self depart
As from my soul, which in thy breast doth lie:
That is my home of love. If I have rang'd,
Like him that travels, I return again,
Just to the time, not with the time exchang'd,
So that my self bring water for my stain.
Never believe, though in my nature reign'd
All frailties that besiege all kinds of blood,
That it could so preposterously be stain'd
To leave for nothing all thy sum of good;
For nothing this wide universe I call
Save thou, my rose; in it thou art my all.

110

Alas, 'tis true I have gone here and there
And made myself a motley to the view,
Gor'd mine own thoughts, sold cheap what is most dear,
Made old offences of affections new.
Most true it is that I have look'd on truth
Askance and strangely; but, by all above,
These blenches gave my heart another youth,
And worse essays prov'd thee my best of love.
Now all is done, have what shall have no end;
Mine appetite I never more will grind
On newer proof, to try an older friend,
A god in love, to whom I am confin'd.
Then give me welcome, next my heaven the best,
Even to thy pure and most most loving breast.

111

O, for my sake do you with Fortune chide,
The guilty goddess of my harmful deeds,
That did not better for my life provide
Than public means which public manners breeds.
Thence comes it that my name receives a brand,
And almost thence my nature is subdu'd
To what it works in, like the dyer's hand.
Pity me then, and wish I were renew'd;
Whilst, like a willing patient, I will drink
Potions of eisel, 'gainst my strong infection;
No bitterness that I will bitter think,
Nor double penance, to correct correction.
Pity me then, dear friend, and I assure ye,
Even that your pity is enough to cure me.

112

Your love and pity doth th' impression fill
Which vulgar scandal stamp'd upon my brow;
For what care I who calls me well or ill,
So you o'ergreen my bad, my good allow?
You are my all the world, and I must strive
To know my shames and praises from your tongue;
None else to me, nor I to none alive,
That my steel'd sense or changes right or wrong.
In so profound abysm I throw all care
Of others' voices that my adder's sense
To critic and to flatterer stopped are.
Mark how with my neglect I do dispense:
You are so strongly in my purpose bred
That all the world besides methinks are dead.

113

Since I left you, mine eye is in my mind;
And that which governs me to go about
Doth part his function, and is partly blind,
Seems seeing, but effectually is out;
For it no form delivers to the heart
Of bird, of flow'r, or shape, which it doth latch;
Of his quick objects hath the mind no part,
Nor his own vision holds what it doth catch;
For if it see the rud'st or gentlest sight,
The most sweet favour or deformed'st creature,
The mountain or the sea, the day or night,
The crow or dove, it shapes them to your feature.
Incapable of more, replete with you,
My most true mind thus mak'th mine eye untrue.

114

Or whether doth my mind, being crown'd with you,
Drink up the monarch's plague, this flattery?
Or whether shall I say mine eye saith true,
And that your love taught it this alchemy
To make of monsters and things indigest
Such cherubins as your sweet self resemble,
Creating every bad a perfect best
As fast as objects to his beams assemble?
O, 'tis the first; 'tis flatt'ry in my seeing,
And my great mind most kingly drinks it up.
Mine eye well knows what with his gust is 'greeing,
And to his palate doth prepare the cup.
If it be poison'd, 'tis the lesser sin
That mine eye loves it, and doth first begin.

115

Those lines that I before have writ do lie;
Even those that said I could not love you dearer;
Yet then my judgment knew no reason why
My most full flame should afterwards burn clearer.
But reckoning Time, whose million'd accidents
Creep in 'twixt vows and change decrees of kings,
Tan sacred beauty, blunt the sharp'st intents,
Divert strong minds to th' course of alt'ring things –
Alas, why, fearing of Time's tyranny,
Might I not then say 'Now I love you best'
When I was certain o'er incertainty,
Crowning the present, doubting of the rest?
Love is a babe; then might I not say so,
To give full growth to that which still doth grow?

116

Let me not to the marriage of true minds
Admit impediments. Love is not love
Which alters when it alteration finds,
Or bends with the remover to remove.
O, no! it is an ever-fixed mark,
That looks on tempests and is never shaken;
It is the star to every wand'ring bark,
Whose worth's unknown, although his height be taken.
Love's not Time's fool, though rosy lips and cheeks
Within his bending sickle's compass come;
Love alters not with his brief hours and weeks,
But bears it out even to the edge of doom.
If this be error, and upon me prov'd,
I never writ, nor no man ever lov'd.

117

Accuse me thus: that I have scanted all
Wherein I should your great deserts repay;

Forgot upon your dearest love to call,
Whereto all bonds do tie me day by day;
That I have frequent been with unknown minds,
And given to time your own dear-purchas'd right;
That I have hoisted sail to all the winds
Which should transport me farthest from your
sight.
Book both my wilfulness and errors down,
And on just proof surmise accumulate;
Bring me within the level of your frown,
But shoot not at me in your wakened hate;
Since my appeal says I did strive to prove
The constancy and virtue of your love.

118

Like as to make our appetites more keen
With eager compounds we our palate urge,
As to prevent our maladies unseen
We sicken to shun sickness when we purge;
Even so, being full of your ne'er-cloying
sweetness,
To bitter sauces did I frame my feeding,
And, sick of welfare, found a kind of meetness
To be diseas'd ere that there was true needing.
Thus policy in love, t' anticipate
The ills that were not, grew to faults assured,
And brought to medicine a healthful state,
Which, rank of goodness, would by ill be cured.
But thence I learn, and find the lesson true,
Drugs poison him that so fell sick of you.

119

What potions have I drunk of Siren tears,
Distill'd from limbecks foul as hell within,
Applying fears to hopes, and hopes to fears,
Still losing when I saw my self to win!
What wretched errors hath my heart committed,
Whilst it hath thought it self so blessed never!
How have mine eyes out of their spheres been
fitted
In the distraction of this madding fever!
O benefit of ill! Now I find true
That better is by evil still made better;
And ruin'd love, when it is built anew,
Grows fairer than at first, more strong, far greater.
So I return rebuk'd to my content,
And gain by ill thrice more than I have spent.

120

That you were once unkind befriends me now,
And for that sorrow which I then did feel
Needs must I under my transgression bow,
Unless my nerves were brass or hammered steel.
For if you were by my unkindness shaken,
As I by yours, y'have pass'd a hell of time;
And I, a tyrant, have no leisure taken
To weigh how once I suffered in your crime.
O that our night of woe might have rememb'red
My deepest sense how hard true sorrow hits,
And soon to you, as you to me, then tend'red
The humble salve which wounded bosoms fits!
But that your trespass now becomes a fee;
Mine ransoms yours, and yours must ransom
me.

121

'Tis better to be vile than vile esteemed,
When not to be receives reproach of being,
And the just pleasure lost, which is so deemed
Not by our feeling, but by others' seeing.
For why should others' false adulterate eyes
Give salutation to my sportive blood?
Or on my frailties why are frailer spies,
Which in their wills count bad what I think good?
No; I am that I am; and they that level
At my abuses reckon up their own.
I may be straight though they themselves be
bevel;
By their rank thoughts my deeds must not be
shown,
Unless this general evil they maintain:
All men are bad, and in their badness reign.

122

Thy gift, thy tables, are within my brain
Full character'd with lasting memory,
Which shall above that idle rank remain
Beyond all date, even to eternity;
Or at the least so long as brain and heart
Have faculty by nature to subsist;
Till each to raz'd oblivion yield his part
Of thee, thy record never can be miss'd.
That poor retention could not so much hold,
Nor need I tallies thy dear love to score;
Therefore to give them from me was I bold,
To trust those tables that receive thee more.
To keep an adjunct to remember thee
Were to import forgetfulness in me.

123

No, Time, thou shalt not boast that I do change.
Thy pyramids built up with newer might
To me are nothing novel, nothing strange;
They are but dressings of a former sight.
Our dates are brief, and therefore we admire
What thou dost foist upon us that is old,
And rather make them born to our desire
Than think that we before have heard them told.
Thy registers and thee I both defy,
Not wond'ring at the present nor the past,

For thy records and what we see doth lie,
Made more or less by thy continual haste.
This I do vow, and this shall ever be:
I will be true, despite thy scythe and thee.

124

If my dear love were but the child of state,
It might for Fortune's bastard be unfather'd,
As subject to Time's love or to Time's hate,
Weeds among weeds, or flowers with flowers gather'd.
No, it was builded far from accident;
It suffers not in smiling pomp, nor falls
Under the blow of thralled discontent,
Whereto th' inviting time our fashion calls.
It fears not Policy, that heretic,
Which works on leases of short-numb'red hours,
But all alone stands hugely politic,
That it nor grows with heat nor drowns with show'rs.
To this I witness call the fools of time,
Which die for goodness, who have liv'd for crime.

125

Were't aught to me I bore the canopy,
With my extern the outward honouring,
Or laid great bases for eternity,
Which proves more short than waste or ruining?
Have I not seen dwellers on form and favour
Lose all, and more, by paying too much rent,
For compound sweet forgoing simple savour –
Pitiful thrivers, in their gazing spent?
No, let me be obsequious in thy heart,
And take thou my oblation, poor but free,
Which is not mix'd with seconds, knows no art
But mutual render, only me for thee.
Hence, thou suborn'd informer! A true soul,
When most impeach'd, stands least in thy control.

126

O thou, my lovely boy, who in thy power
Dost hold Time's fickle glass, his sickle hour;
Who hast by waning grown, and therein show'st
Thy lovers withering as thy sweet self grow'st;
If Nature, sovereign mistress over wrack,
As thou goest onwards, still will pluck thee back,
She keeps thee to this purpose, that her skill
May time disgrace, and wretched minutes kill.
Yet fear her, O thou minion of her pleasure!
She may detain, but not still keep, her treasure;
Her audit, though delay'd, answer'd must be,
And her quietus is to render thee.

127

In the old age black was not counted fair,
Or if it were, it bore not beauty's name;
But now is black beauty's successive heir,
And beauty slander'd with a bastard shame;
For since each hand hath put on nature's power,
Fairing the foul with art's false borrow'd face,
Sweet beauty hath no name, no holy bower,
But is profan'd, if not lives in disgrace.
Therefore my mistress' brows are raven black,
Her eyes so suited, and they mourners seem
At such who, not born fair, no beauty lack,
Sland'ring creation with a false esteem.
Yet so they mourn, becoming of their woe,
That every tongue says beauty should look so.

128

How oft, when thou, my music, music play'st
Upon that blessed wood whose motion sounds
With thy sweet fingers, when thou gently sway'st
The wiry concord that mine ear confounds,
Do I envy those jacks that nimble leap
To kiss the tender inward of thy hand,
Whilst my poor lips, which should that harvest reap,
At the wood's boldness by thee blushing stand!
To be so tickled, they would change their state
And situation with those dancing chips
O'er whom thy fingers walk with gentle gait,
Making dead wood more blest than living lips.
Since saucy jacks so happy are in this,
Give them thy fingers, me thy lips to kiss.

129

Th' expense of spirit in a waste of shame
Is lust in action; and till action, lust
Is perjur'd, murd'rous, bloody, full of blame,
Savage, extreme, rude, cruel, not to trust;
Enjoy'd no sooner but despised straight;
Past reason hunted, and, no sooner had,
Past reason hated, as a swallowed bait,
On purpose laid to make the taker mad –
Mad in pursuit, and in possession so;
Had, having, and in quest to have, extreme;
A bliss in proof, and prov'd, a very woe;
Before, a joy propos'd; behind, a dream.
All this the world well knows; yet none knows well
To shun the heaven that leads men to this hell.

130

My mistress' eyes are nothing like the sun;
Coral is far more red than her lips' red;
If snow be white, why then her breasts are dun;
If hairs be wires, black wires grow on her head.
I have seen roses damask'd, red and white,
But no such roses see I in her cheeks;

And in some perfumes is there more delight
Than in the breath that from my mistress reeks.
I love to hear her speak, yet well I know
That music hath a far more pleasing sound;
I grant I never saw a goddess go –
My mistress when she walks treads on the ground.
And yet, by heaven, I think my love as rare
As any she belied with false compare.

131

Thou art as tyrannous, so as thou art,
As those whose beauties proudly make them cruel;
For well thou know'st to my dear doting heart
Thou art the fairest and most precious jewel.
Yet, in good faith, some say that thee behold
Thy face hath not the power to make love groan.
To say they err I dare not be so bold,
Although I swear it to myself alone.
And, to be sure that is not false I swear,
A thousand groans, but thinking on thy face,
One on another's neck, do witness bear
Thy black is fairest in my judgment's place.
In nothing art thou black save in thy deeds,
And thence this slander, as I think, proceeds.

132

Thine eyes I love, and they, as pitying me,
Knowing thy heart torments me with disdain,
Have put on black, and loving mourners be,
Looking with pretty ruth upon my pain.
And truly not the morning sun of heaven
Better becomes the grey cheeks of the east,
Nor that full star that ushers in the even
Doth half that glory to the sober west,
As those two mourning eyes become thy face.
O, let it then as well beseem thy heart
To mourn for me, since mourning doth thee grace,
And suit thy pity like in every part.
Then will I swear beauty herself is black,
And all they foul that thy complexion lack.

133

Beshrew that heart that makes my heart to groan
For that deep wound it gives my friend and me!
Is't not enough to torture me alone,
But slave to slavery my sweet'st friend must be?
Me from my self thy cruel eye hath taken,
And my next self thou harder hast engrossed;
Of him, my self, and thee, I am forsaken;
A torment thrice three-fold thus to be crossed.
Prison my heart in thy steel bosom's ward,
But then my friend's heart let my poor heart bail;
Whoe'er keeps me, let my heart be his guard;
Thou canst not then use rigour in my gaol.
And yet thou wilt; for I, being pent in thee,
Perforce am thine, and all that is in me.

134

So now I have confess'd that he is thine,
And I myself am mortgag'd to thy will;
My self I'll forfeit, so that other mine
Thou wilt restore to be my comfort still.
But thou wilt not, nor he will not be free,
For thou art covetous, and he is kind;
He learn'd but surety-like to write for me
Under that bond that him as fast doth bind.
The statute of thy beauty thou wilt take,
Thou usurer that put'st forth all to use,
And sue a friend came debtor for my sake;
So him I lose through my unkind abuse.
Him have I lost; thou hast both him and me;
He pays the whole, and yet am I not free.

135

Whoever hath her wish, thou hast thy Will,
And Will to boot, and Will in over-plus;
More than enough am I that vex thee still,
To thy sweet will making addition thus.
Wilt thou, whose will is large and spacious,
Not once vouchsafe to hide my will in thine?
Shall will in others seem right gracious,
And in my will no fair acceptance shine?
The sea, all water, yet receives rain still,
And in abundance addeth to his store;
So thou, being rich in Will, add to thy Will
One will of mine, to make thy large Will more.
Let no unkind, no fair beseechers kill;
Think all but one, and me in that one Will.

136

If thy soul check thee that I come so near,
Swear to thy blind soul that I was thy Will,
And will, thy soul knows, is admitted there;
Thus far for love my love-suit, sweet, fulfil.
Will will fulfil the treasure of thy love,
Ay, fill it full with wills, and my will one.
In things of great receipt with ease we prove
Among a number one is reckon'd none.
Then in the number let me pass untold,
Though in thy store's account I one must be;
For nothing hold me, so it please thee hold
That nothing me, a something sweet to thee;
Make but my name thy love, and love that still,
And then thou lov'st me, for my name is Will.

137

Thou blind fool, Love, what dost thou to mine eyes

That they behold, and see not what they see?
They know what beauty is, see where it lies,
Yet what the best is take the worst to be.
If eyes, corrupt by over-partial looks,
Be anchor'd in the bay where all men ride,
Why of eyes' falsehood hast thou forged hooks,
Whereto the judgment of my heart is tied?
Why should my heart think that a several plot,
Which my heart knows the wide world's common place?
Or mine eyes, seeing this, say this is not,
To put fair truth upon so foul a face?
In things right true my heart and eyes have erred,
And to this false plague are they now transferred.

138

When my love swears that she is made of truth,
I do believe her, though I know she lies,
That she might think me some untutor'd youth,
Unlearned in the world's false subtleties.
Thus vainly thinking that she thinks me young,
Although she knows my days are past the best,
Simply I credit her false-speaking tongue;
On both sides thus is simple truth suppress'd.
But wherefore says she not she is unjust?
And wherefore say not I that I am old?
O, love's best habit is in seeming trust,
And age in love loves not to have years told.
Therefore I lie with her, and she with me,
And in our faults by lies we flattered be.

139

O, call not me to justify the wrong
That thy unkindness lays upon my heart;
Wound me not with thine eye, but with thy tongue;
Use power with power, and slay me not by art.
Tell me thou lov'st elsewhere; but in my sight,
Dear heart, forbear to glance thine eye aside.
What need'st thou wound with cunning, when thy might
Is more than my o'erpress'd defence can bide?
Let me excuse thee: ah! my love well knows
Her pretty looks have been mine enemies;
And therefore from my face she turns my foes,
That they elsewhere might dart their injuries.
Yet do not so; but since I am near slain,
Kill me outright with looks and rid my pain.

140

Be wise as thou art cruel; do not press
My tongue-tied patience with too much disdain;
Lest sorrow lend me words, and words express
The manner of my pity-wanting pain.
If I might teach thee wit, better it were,
Though not to love, yet, love, to tell me so;
As testy sick men, when their deaths be near,
No news but health from their physicians know.
For, if I should despair, I should grow mad,
And in my madness might speak ill of thee.
Now this ill-wresting world is grown so bad
Mad slanderers by mad ears believed be.
That I may not be so, nor thou belied,
Bear thine eyes straight, though thy proud heart go wide.

141

In faith, I do not love thee with mine eyes,
For they in thee a thousand errors note;
But 'tis my heart that loves what they despise,
Who in despite of view is pleas'd to dote.
Nor are mine ears with thy tongue's tune delighted;
Nor tender feeling to base touches prone,
Nor taste nor smell desire to be invited
To any sensual feast with thee alone;
But my five wits nor my five senses can
Dissuade one foolish heart from serving thee,
Who leaves unsway'd the likeness of a man,
Thy proud heart's slave and vassal wretch to be.
Only my plague thus far I count my gain,
That she that makes me sin awards me pain.

142

Love is my sin, and thy dear virtue hate,
Hate of my sin, grounded on sinful loving.
O, but with mine compare thou thine own state,
And thou shalt find it merits not reproving;
Or, if it do, not from those lips of thine,
That have profan'd their scarlet ornaments,
And seal'd false bonds of love as oft as mine;
Robb'd others' beds' revenues of their rents.
Be it lawful I love thee as thou lov'st those
Whom thine eyes woo as mine importune thee.
Root pity in thy heart, that, when it grows,
Thy pity may deserve to pitied be.
If thou dost seek to have what thou dost hide,
By self-example mayst thou be denied!

143

Lo as a careful huswife runs to catch
One of her feathered creatures broke away,
Sets down her babe, and makes all swift dispatch
In pursuit of the thing she would have stay;
Whilst her neglected child holds her in chase,
Cries to catch her whose busy care is bent
To follow that which flies before her face,
Not prizing her poor infant's discontent;

So run'st thou after that which flies from thee,
Whilst I thy babe chase thee afar behind;
But if thou catch thy hope, turn back to me,
And play the mother's part, kiss me, be kind.
So will I pray that thou mayst have thy Will,
If thou turn back and my loud crying still.

144

Two loves I have, of comfort and despair,
Which like two spirits do suggest me still;
The better angel is a man right fair,
The worser spirit a woman colour'd ill.
To win me soon to hell, my female evil
Tempteth my better angel from my side,
And would corrupt my saint to be a devil,
Wooing his purity with her foul pride.
And whether that my angel be turn'd fiend,
Suspect I may, yet not directly tell;
But being both from me, both to each friend,
I guess one angel in another's hell.
Yet this shall I ne'er know, but live in doubt,
Till my bad angel fire my good one out.

145

Those lips that Love's own hand did make
Breath'd forth the sound that said 'I hate'
To me that languish'd for her sake;
But when she saw my woeful state,
Straight in her heart did mercy come,
Chiding that tongue that ever sweet
Was us'd in giving gentle doom;
And taught it thus anew to greet:
'I hate' she alter'd with an end
That follow'd it as gentle day
Doth follow night, who like a fiend
From heaven to hell is flown away:
'I hate' from hate away she threw,
And sav'd my life, saying 'not you'.

146

Poor soul, the centre of my sinful earth,
[My sinful earth] these rebel pow'rs that thee array,
Why dost thou pine within and suffer dearth,
Painting thy outward walls so costly gay?
Why so large cost, having so short a lease,
Dost thou upon thy fading mansion spend?
Shall worms, inheritors of this excess,
Eat up thy charge? Is this thy body's end?
Then, soul, live thou upon thy servant's loss,
And let that pine to aggravate thy store;
Buy terms divine in selling hours of dross;
Within be fed, without be rich no more.
So shalt thou feed on Death, that feeds on men,
And, Death once dead, there's no more dying then.

147

My love is as a fever, longing still
For that which longer nurseth the disease;
Feeding on that which doth preserve the ill,
Th' uncertain sickly appetite to please.
My Reason, the physician to my Love,
Angry that his prescriptions are not kept,
Hath left me, and I desperate now approve
Desire is death, which physic did except.
Past cure I am, now reason is past care,
And frantic mad with evermore unrest;
My thoughts and my discourse as mad men's are,
At random from the truth vainly express'd;
For I have sworn thee fair, and thought thee bright,
Who art as black as hell, as dark as night.

148

O me, what eyes hath Love put in my head,
Which have no correspondence with true sight!
Or, if they have, where is my judgment fled,
That censures falsely what they see aright?
If that be fair whereon my false eyes dote,
What means the world to say it is not so?
If it be not, then love doth well denote
Love's eye is not so true as all men's – no,
How can it? O, how can Love's eye be true,
That is so vex'd with watching and with tears?
No marvel then though I mistake my view:
The sun itself sees not till heaven clears.
O cunning Love! with tears thou keep'st me blind,
Lest eyes well seeing thy foul faults should find.

149

Canst thou, O cruel! say I love thee not,
When I against myself with thee partake?
Do I not think on thee when I forgot
Am of myself, all tyrant, for thy sake?
Who hateth thee that I do call my friend?
On whom frown'st thou that I do fawn upon?
Nay, if thou lour'st on me, do I not spend
Revenge upon myself with present moan?
What merit do I in myself respect
That is so proud thy service to despise,
When all my best doth worship thy defect,
Commanded by the motion of thine eyes?
But, love, hate on, for now I know thy mind:
Those that can see thou lov'st, and I am blind.

150

O, from what pow'r hast thou this pow'rful might
With insufficiency my heart to sway?

To make me give the lie to my true sight,
And swear that brightness doth not grace the day?
Whence hast thou this becoming of things ill,
That in the very refuse of thy deeds
There is such strength and warrantise of skill
That in my mind thy worst all best exceeds?
Who taught thee how to make me love thee more,
The more I hear and see just cause of hate?
O, though I love what others do abhor,
With others thou shouldst not abhor my state;
If thy unworthiness rais'd love in me,
More worthy I to be belov'd of thee.

151

Love is too young to know what conscience is;
Yet who knows not conscience is born of love?
Then, gentle cheater, urge not my amiss,
Lest guilty of my faults thy sweet self prove.
For thou betraying me, I do betray
My nobler part to my gross body's treason;
My soul doth tell my body that he may
Triumph in love; flesh stays no farther reason,
But, rising at thy name, doth point out thee
As his triumphant prize. Proud of this pride,
He is contented thy poor drudge to be,
To stand in thy affairs, fall by thy side.
No want of conscience hold it that I call
Her 'love' for whose dear love I rise and fall.

152

In loving thee thou know'st I am forsworn,
But thou art twice forsworn, to me love swearing;
In act thy bed-vow broke, and new faith torn
In vowing new hate after new love bearing.
But why of two oaths' breach do I accuse thee,
When I break twenty? I am perjur'd most;
For all my vows are oaths but to misuse thee,
And all my honest faith in thee is lost;
For I have sworn deep oaths of thy deep kindness,
Oaths of thy love, thy truth, thy constancy;
And, to enlighten thee, gave eyes to blindness,
Or made them swear against the thing they see;
For I have sworn thee fair – more perjur'd I,
To swear against the truth so foul a lie!

153

Cupid laid by his brand, and fell asleep.
A maid of Dian's this advantage found,
And his love-kindling fire did quickly steep
In a cold valley-fountain of that ground;
Which borrow'd from this holy fire of Love
A dateless lively heat, still to endure,
And grew a seething bath, which yet men prove
Against strange maladies a sovereign cure.
But at my mistress' eye Love's brand new-fired,
The boy for trial needs would touch my breast;
I, sick withal, the help of bath desired,
And thither hied, a sad distemper'd guest,
But found no cure. The bath for my help lies
Where Cupid got new fire – my mistress' eyes.

154

The little love-god, lying once asleep,
Laid by his side his heart-inflaming brand,
Whilst many nymphs that vow'd chaste life to keep
Came tripping by; but in her maiden hand
The fairest votary took up that fire
Which many legions of true hearts had warm'd;
And so the general of hot desire
Was sleeping by a virgin hand disarm'd.
This brand she quenched in a cool well by,
Which from Love's fire took heat perpetual,
Growing a bath and healthful remedy
For men diseas'd; but I, my mistress' thrall,
Came there for cure, and this by that I prove:
Love's fire heats water, water cools not love.

A Lover's Complaint

FROM off a hill whose concave womb reworded
A plaintful story from a sist'ring vale,
My spirits t' attend this double voice accorded,
And down I laid to list the sad-tun'd tale;
Ere long espied a fickle maid full pale,
Tearing of papers, breaking rings a-twain,
Storming her world with sorrow's wind and rain.

Upon her head a platted hive of straw,
Which fortified her visage from the sun,
Whereon the thought might think sometime it saw
The carcase of a beauty spent and done.
Time had not scythed all that youth begun,
Nor youth all quit; but, spite of heaven's fell rage,
Some beauty peep'd through lattice of sear'd age.

Oft did she heave her napkin to her eyne,
Which on it had conceited characters,
Laund'ring the silken figures in the brine
That seasoned woe had pelleted in tears,
And often reading what contents it bears;
As often shrieking undistinguish'd woe,
In clamours of all size, both high and low.

Sometimes her levell'd eyes their carriage ride,
As they did batt'ry to the spheres intend;
Sometime diverted their poor balls are tied
To th' orbed earth; sometimes they do extend
Their view right on; anon their gazes lend
To every place at once, and nowhere fix'd,
The mind and sight distractedly commix'd.

Her hair, nor loose nor tied in formal plat,
Proclaim'd in her a careless hand of pride;
For some, untuck'd, descended her sheav'd hat,
Hanging her pale and pined cheek beside;
Some in her threaden fillet still did bide,
And, true to bondage, would not break from thence,
Though slackly braided in loose negligence.

A thousand favours from a maund she drew
Of amber, crystal, and of beaded jet,
Which one by one she in a river threw,
Upon whose weeping margent she was set;
Like usury, applying wet to wet,
Or monarch's hands that lets not bounty fall
Where want cries some but where excess begs all.

Of folded schedules had she many a one,
Which she perus'd, sigh'd, tore, and gave the flood;
Crack'd many a ring of poised gold and bone,
Bidding them find their sepulchres in mud;
Found yet moe letters sadly penn'd in blood,
With sleided silk feat and affectedly
Enswath'd and seal'd to curious secrecy.

These often bath'd she in her fluxive eyes,
And often kiss'd, and often gan to tear;
Cried 'O false blood, thou register of lies,
What unapproved witness dost thou bear!
Ink would have seem'd more black and damned here!'
This said, in top of rage the lines she rents,
Big discontent so breaking their contents.

A reverend man that graz'd his cattle nigh,
Sometime a blusterer that the ruffle knew
Of court, of city, and had let go by
The swiftest hours observed as they flew,
Towards this afflicted fancy fastly drew;
And, privileg'd by age, desires to know
In brief the grounds and motives of her woe.

So slides he down upon his grained bat,
And comely distant sits he by her side;
When he again desires her, being sat,
Her grievance with his hearing to divide.
If that from him there may be aught applied
Which may her suffering ecstasy assuage,
'Tis promis'd in the charity of age.

'Father,' she says 'though in me you behold
The injury of many a blasting hour,
Let it not tell your judgment I am old;
Not age, but sorrow, over me hath power.
I might as yet have been a spreading flower,
Fresh to myself, if I had self-applied
Love to myself, and to no love beside.

'But woe is me! too early I attended
A youthful suit – it was to gain my grace –
O! one by nature's outwards so commended
That maidens' eyes stuck over all his face.
Love lack'd a dwelling and made him her place;
And when in his fair parts she did abide,
She was new lodg'd and newly deified.

'His browny locks did hang in crooked curls;
And every light occasion of the wind
Upon his lips their silken parcels hurls.
What's sweet to do, to do will aptly find:
Each eye that saw him did enchant the mind;
For on his visage was in little drawn
What largeness thinks in Paradise was sawn.

'Small show of man was yet upon his chin;
His phœnix down began but to appear,
Like unshorn velvet, on that termless skin,

Whose bare out-bragg'd the web it seem'd to
wear;
Yet show'd his visage by that cost more dear;
And nice affections wavering stood in doubt
If best were as it was, or best without.

'His qualities were beauteous as his form,
For maiden-tongu d he was, and thereof free;
Yet, if men mov'd him, was he such a storm
As oft 'twixt May and April is to see,
When winds breathe sweet, unruly though they
be.
His rudeness so with his authoriz'd youth
Did livery falseness in a pride of truth.

'Well could he ride, and often men would say
"That horse his mettle from his rider takes:
Proud of subjection, noble by the sway,
What rounds, what bounds, what course, what
stop he makes!"
And controversy hence a question takes,
Whether the horse by him became his deed,
Or he his manage by th' well-doing steed.

'But quickly on this side the verdict went:
His real habitude gave life and grace
To appertainings and to ornament,
Accomplish'd in himself, not in his case.
All aids, themselves made fairer by their place,
Came for additions; yet their purpos'd trim
Piec'd not his grace, but were all grac'd by him.

'So on the tip of his subduing tongue
All kind of arguments and question deep,
All replication prompt, and reason strong,
For his advantage still did wake and sleep.
To make the weeper laugh, the laugher weep,
He had the dialect and different skill,
Catching all passions in his craft of will;

'That he did in the general bosom reign
Of young, of old, and sexes both enchanted,
To dwell with him in thoughts, or to remain
In personal duty, following where he haunted.
Consents bewitch'd, ere he desire, have granted,
And dialogu'd for him what he would say,
Ask'd their own wills, and made their wills obey.

'Many there were that did his picture get,
To serve their eyes, and in it put their mind;
Like fools that in th' imagination set
The goodly objects which abroad they find
Of lands and mansions, theirs in thought assign'd;
And labouring in moe pleasures to bestow them
Than the true gouty landlord which doth owe
them.

'So many have, that never touch'd his hand,
Sweetly suppos'd them mistress of his heart.
My woeful self, that did in freedom stand,
And was my own fee-simple, not in part,
What with his art in youth, and youth in art,
Threw my affections in his charmed power,
Reserv'd the stalk and gave him all my flower.

'Yet did I not, as some my equals did,
Demand of him, nor being desired yielded;
Finding myself in honour so forbid,
With safest distance I mine honour shielded.
Experience for me many bulwarks builded
Of proofs new-bleeding, which remain'd the foil
Of this false jewel, and his amorous spoil.

'But ah! who ever shunn'd by precedent
The destin'd ill she must herself assay?
Or forc'd examples, 'gainst her own content,
To put the by-past perils in her way?
Counsel may stop awhile what will not stay;
For when we rage, advice is often seen
By blunting us to make our wits more keen.

'Nor gives it satisfaction to our blood
That we must curb it upon others' proof,
To be forbod the sweets that seem so good
For fear of harms that preach in our behoof.
O appetite, from judgment stand aloof!
The one a palate hath that needs will taste,
Though Reason weep, and cry "It is thy last".

'For further I could say "This man's untrue",
And knew the patterns of his foul beguiling;
Heard where his plants in others' orchards grew;
Saw how deceits were gilded in his smiling;
Knew vows were ever brokers to defiling;
Thought characters and words merely but art,
And bastards of his foul adulterate heart.

'And long upon these terms I held my city,
Till thus he gan besiege me: "Gentle maid,
Have of my suffering youth some feeling pity,
And be not of my holy vows afraid.
That's to ye sworn to none was ever said;
For feasts of love I have been call'd unto,
Till now did ne'er invite nor never woo.

'"All my offences that abroad you see
Are errors of the blood, none of the mind;
Love made them not; with acture they may be,
Where neither party is nor true nor kind.
They sought their shame that so their shame did
find;
And so much less of shame in me remains
By how much of me their reproach contains.

'"Among the many that mine eyes have seen,
Not one whose flame my heart so much as
warmed,
Or my affection put to th' smallest teen,
Or any of my leisures ever charmed.
Harm have I done to them, but ne'er was harmed;
Kept hearts in liveries, but mine own was free,
And reign'd commanding in his monarchy.

'"Look here what tributes wounded fancies sent
me,

Of pallid pearls and rubies red as blood;
Figuring that they their passions likewise lent me
Of grief and blushes, aptly understood
In bloodless white and the encrimson'd mood –
Effects of terror and dear modesty,
Encamp'd in hearts, but fighting outwardly.

'"And, lo, behold these talents of their hair,
With twisted metal amorously empleach'd,
I have receiv'd from many a several fair,
Their kind acceptance weepingly beseech'd,
With the annexions of fair gems enrich'd,
And deep-brain'd sonnets that did amplify
Each stone's dear nature, worth, and quality.

'"The diamond – why, 'twas beautiful and hard,
Whereto his invis'd properties did tend;
The deep-green em'rald, in whose fresh regard
Weak sights their sickly radiance do amend;
The heaven-hu'd sapphire and the opal blend
With objects manifold; each several stone,
With wit well blazon'd, smil'd, or made some moan.

'"Lo, all these trophies of affections hot,
Of pensiv'd and subdu'd desires the tender,
Nature hath charg'd me that I hoard them not,
But yield them up where I myself must render –
That is, to you, my origin and ender;
For these, of force, must your oblations be,
Since I their altar, you enpatron me.

'"O, then, advance of yours that phraseless hand
Whose white weighs down the airy scale of praise;
Take all these similes to your own command,
Hallowed with sighs that burning lungs did raise;
What me, your minister, for you obeys,
Works under you; and to your audit comes
Their distract parcels in combined sums.

'"Lo, this device was sent me from a nun,
Or sister sanctified, of holiest note,
Which late her noble suit in court did shun,
Whose rarést havings made the blossoms dote;
For she was sought by spirits of richest coat,
But kept cold distance, and did thence remove
To spend her living in eternal love.

"But, O my sweet, what labour is't to leave
The thing we have not, mast'ring what not strives,
Paling the place which did no form receive,
Playing patient sports in unconstrained gyves!
She that her fame so to herself contrives,
The scars of battle scapeth by the flight,
And makes her absence valiant, not her might.

'"O, pardon me, in that my boast is true!
The accident which brought me to her eye
Upon the moment did her force subdue,
And now she would the caged cloister fly.
Religious love put out religion's eye.
Not to be tempted, would she be immur'd,
And now, to tempt all, liberty procur'd.

'"How mighty then you are, O, hear me tell!
The broken bosoms that to me belong
Have emptied all their fountains in my well,
And mine I pour your ocean all among.
I strong o'er them, and you o'er me being strong,
Must for your victory us all congest,
As compound love to physic your cold breast.

'"My parts had pow'r to charm a sacred nun,
Who, disciplin'd, ay, dieted in grace,
Believ'd her eyes when they t' assail begun,
All vows and consecrations giving place.
O most potential love! vow, bond, nor space,
In thee hath neither sting, knot, nor confine,
For thou art all, and all things else are thine.

'"When thou impressest, what are precepts worth
Of stale example? When thou wilt inflame,
How coldly those impediments stand forth,
Of wealth, of filial fear, law, kindred, fame!
Love's arms are peace, 'gainst rule, 'gainst sense, 'gainst shame,
And sweetens, in the suff'ring pangs it bears,
The aloes of all forces, shocks, and fears.

'"Now all these hearts that do on mine depend,
Feeling it break, with bleeding groans they pine,
And supplicant their sighs to you extend,
To leave the batt'ry that you make 'gainst mine,
Lending soft audience to my sweet design,
And credent soul to that strong-bonded oath,
That shall prefer and undertake my troth".

'This said, his wat'ry eyes he did dismount,
Whose sights till then were levell'd on my face;
Each cheek a river running from a fount
With brinish current downward flow'd apace.
O, how the channel to the stream gave grace!
Who glaz'd with crystal gate the glowing roses
That flame through water which their hue encloses.

'O father, what a hell of witchcraft lies
In the small orb of one particular tear!
But with the inundation of the eyes
What rocky heart to water will not wear?
What breast so cold that is not warmed here?
O cleft effect! cold modesty, hot wrath,
Both fire from hence and chill extincture hath.

'For lo, his passion, but an art of craft,
Even there resolv'd my reason into tears;
There my white stole of chastity I daff'd,
Shook off my sober guards and civil fears;
Appear to him as he to me appears,
All melting; though our drops this diff'rence bore:
His poison'd me, and mine did him restore.

'In him a plenitude of subtle matter,
Applied to cautels, all strange forms receives,
Of burning blushes or of weeping water,

Or swooning paleness; and he takes and leaves,
In either's aptness, as it best deceives,
To blush at speeches rank, to weep at woes,
Or to turn white and swoon at tragic shows;

'That not a heart which in his level came
Could scape the hail of his all-hurting aim,
Showing fair nature is both kind and tame;
And, veil'd in them, did win whom he would maim.
Against the thing he sought he would exclaim;
When he most burn'd in heart-wish'd luxury,
He preach'd pure maid and prais'd cold chastity.

'Thus merely with the garment of a Grace
The naked and concealed fiend he cover'd,
That th' unexperient gave the tempter place,
Which, like a cherubin, above them hover'd.
Who, young and simple, would not be so lover'd?
Ay me! I fell; and yet do question make
What I should do again for such a sake.

'O, that infected moisture of his eye,
O, that false fire which in his cheek so glowed,
O, that forc'd thunder from his heart did fly,
O, that sad breath his spongy lungs bestowed,
O, all that borrowed motion, seeming owed,
Would yet again betray the fore-betray'd,
And new pervert a reconciled maid!'

The Passionate Pilgrim

1

When my love swears that she is made of truth,
I do believe her, though I know she lies,
That she might think me some untutor'd youth,
Unskilful in the world's false forgeries.
Thus vainly thinking that she thinks me young,
Although I know my years be past the best,
I smiling credit her false-speaking tongue,
Outfacing faults in love with love's ill rest.
But wherefore says my love that she is young?
And wherefore say not I that I am old?
O, love's best habit is a soothing tongue,
And age in love loves not to have years told.
  Therefore I'll lie with love, and love with me,
  Since that our faults in love thus smother'd be.

2

Two loves I have, of comfort and despair,
That like two spirits do suggest me still;
My better angel is a man right fair,
My worser spirit a woman colour'd ill.
To win me soon to hell, my female evil
Tempteth my better angel from my side,
And would corrupt my saint to be a devil,
Wooing his purity with her fair pride.
And whether that my angel be turn'd fiend,
Suspect I may, yet not directly tell;
For being both to me, both to each friend,
I guess one angel in another's hell.
  The truth I shall not know, but live in doubt,
  Till my bad angel fire my good one out.

3

Did not the heavenly rhetoric of thine eye,
'Gainst whom the world could not hold argument,
Persuade my heart to this false perjury?
Vows for thee broke deserve not punishment.
A woman I forswore; but I will prove,
Thou being a goddess, I forswore not thee:
My vow was earthly, thou a heavenly love;
Thy grace being gain'd cures all disgrace in me.
My vow was breath, and breath a vapour is;
Then, thou fair sun, that on this earth doth shine,
Exhale this vapour vow; in thee it is:
If broken, then it is no fault of mine.
  If by me broke, what fool is not so wise
  To break an oath, to win a paradise?

4

Sweet Cytherea, sitting by a brook
With young Adonis, lovely, fresh, and green,
Did court the lad with many a lovely look,
Such looks as none could look but beauty's queen.
She told him stories to delight his ear;
She show'd him favours to allure his eye;
To win his heart she touch'd him here and there:
Touches so soft still conquer chastity.
But whether unripe years did want conceit,
Or he refus'd to take her figured proffer,
The tender nibbler would not touch the bait,
But smile and jest at every gentle offer.
  Then fell she on her back, fair queen, and toward:
  He rose and ran away; ah, fool too froward!

5

If love make me forsworn, how shall I swear to love?
O never faith could hold, if not to beauty vowed;
Though to myself forsworn, to thee I'll constant prove;
Those thoughts, to me like oaks, to thee like osiers bowed.
Study his bias leaves and makes his book thine eyes,
Where all those pleasures live that art can comprehend.
If knowledge be the mark, to know thee shall suffice;
Well learned is that tongue that well can thee commend;
All ignorant that soul that sees thee without wonder;
Which is to me some praise, that I thy parts admire.
Thine eye Jove's lightning seems, thy voice his dreadful thunder,
Which, not to anger bent, is music and sweet fire.
  Celestial as thou art, O, do not love that wrong,
  To sing heaven's praise with such an earthly tongue.

6

Scarce had the sun dried up the dewy morn,
And scarce the herd gone to the hedge for shade,
When Cytherea, all in love forlorn,
A longing tarriance for Adonis made
Under an osier growing by a brook,
A brook where Adon us'd to cool his spleen.

Hot was the day; she hotter that did look
For his approach that often there had been.
Anon he comes, and throws his mantle by,
And stood stark naked on the brook's green brim.
The sun look'd on the world with glorious eye,
Yet not so wistly as this queen on him.
He, spying her, bounc'd in whereas he stood;
'O Jove,' quoth she 'why was not I a flood?'

7

Fair is my love, but not so fair as fickle;
Mild as a dove, but neither true nor trusty;
Brighter than glass, and yet, as glass is, brittle;
Softer than wax, and yet, as iron, rusty;
A lily pale, with damask dye to grace her;
None fairer, nor none falser to deface her.

Her lips to mine how often hath she joined,
Between each kiss her oaths of true love swearing!
How many tales to please me hath she coined,
Dreading my love, the loss whereof still fearing!
Yet, in the midst of all her pure protestings,
Her faith, her oaths, her tears, and all, were jestings.

She burn'd with love, as straw with fire flameth;
She burn'd out love, as soon as straw outburneth;
She fram'd the love, and yet she foil'd the framing,
She bade love last, and yet she fell a-turning.
Was this a lover, or a lecher whether?
Bad in the best, though excellent in neither.

8

If music and sweet poetry agree,
As they must needs, the sister and the brother,
Then must the love be great 'twixt thee and me,
Because thou lov'st the one, and I the other.
Dowland to thee is dear, whose heavenly touch
Upon the lute doth ravish human sense;
Spenser to me, whose deep conceit is such
As, passing all conceit, needs no defence.
Thou lov'st to hear the sweet melodious sound
That Phœbus' lute, the queen of music, makes,
And I in deep delight am chiefly drown'd
Whenas himself to singing he betakes.
One god is god of both, as poets feign;
One knight loves both, and both in thee remain.

9

Fair was the morn, when the fair queen of love,
* * * * * * *

Paler for sorrow than her milk-white dove,
For Adon's sake, a youngster proud and wild,
Her stand she takes upon a steep-up hill.
Anon Adonis comes with horn and hounds;
She, silly queen, with more than love's good will,
Forbade the boy he should not pass those grounds.
'Once' quoth she 'did I see a fair sweet youth
Here in these brakes deep-wounded with a boar,
Deep in the thigh, a spectacle of ruth!
See in my thigh,' quoth she 'here was the sore.'
She showed hers; he saw more wounds than one,
And blushing fled, and left her all alone.

10

Sweet rose, fair flower, untimely pluck'd, soon vaded,
Pluck'd in the bud, and vaded in the spring!
Bright orient pearl, alack, too timely shaded!
Fair creature, kill'd too soon by death's sharp sting!
Like a green plum that hangs upon a tree,
And falls, through wind, before the fall should be.
I weep for thee, and yet no cause I have;
For why thou lefts me nothing in thy will.
And yet thou lefts me more than I did crave;
For why I craved nothing of thee still.
O yes, dear friend, I pardon crave of thee!
Thy discontent thou didst bequeath to me.

11

Venus, with Adonis sitting by her,
Under a myrtle shade, began to woo him.
She told the youngling how god Mars did try her,
And as he fell to her, she fell to him.
'Even thus' quoth she 'the warlike god embrac'd me.'
And then she clipp'd Adonis in her arms.
'Even thus' quoth she 'the warlike god unlac'd me'
As if the boy should use like loving charms.
'Even thus' quoth she 'he seized on my lips'
And with her lips on his did act the seizure;
And as she fetched breath, away he skips,
And would not take her meaning nor her pleasure.
Ah! that I had my lady at this bay,
To kiss and clip me till I run away!

12

Crabbed age and youth cannot live together:
Youth is full of pleasance, age is full of care;
Youth like summer morn, age like winter weather;
Youth like summer brave, age like winter bare.
Youth is full of sport, age's breath is short;
Youth is nimble, age is lame;
Youth is hot and bold, age is weak and cold;
Youth is wild, and age is tame.
Age, I do abhor thee; youth, I do adore thee.
O, my love, my love is young!
Age, I do defy thee.

O sweet shepherd, hie thee,
For methinks thou stays too long.

13

Beauty is but a vain and doubtful good,
A shining gloss that vadeth suddenly;
A flower that dies when first it gins to bud;
A brittle glass that's broken presently;
A doubtful good, a gloss, a glass, a flower,
Lost, vaded, broken, dead within an hour.

And as goods lost are seld or never found,
As vaded gloss no rubbing will refresh,
As flowers dead lie withered on the ground,
As broken glass no cement can redress;
So beauty, blemish'd once, for ever lost,
In spite of physic, painting, pain, and cost.

14

Good night, good rest. Ah, neither be my share!
She bade good night that kept my rest away,
And daff'd me to a cabin hang'd with care,
To descant on the doubts of my decay.
'Farewell,' quoth she 'and come again tomorrow.'
Fare well I could not, for I supp'd with sorrow.

Yet at my parting sweetly did she smile,
In scorn or friendship, nill I construe whether:
'T may be she joy'd to jest at my exile;
'T may be again to make me wander thither –
'Wander', a word for shadows like myself
As take the pain but cannot pluck the pelf.

Lord, how mine eyes throw gazes to the east!
My heart doth charge the watch; the morning rise
Doth cite each moving sense from idle rest,
Not daring trust the office of mine eyes.
While Philomela sits and sings, I sit and mark,
And wish her lays were tuned like the lark;

For she doth welcome daylight with her ditty,
And drives away dark dreaming night.
The night so pack'd, I post unto my pretty;
Heart hath his hope, and eyes their wished sight;
Sorrow chang'd to solace, and solace mix'd with sorrow;
For why she sigh'd, and bade me come tomorrow.

Were I with her, the night would post too soon;
But now are minutes added to the hours;
To spite me now, each minute seems a moon;
Yet not for me, shine sun to succour flowers!
Pack night, peep day; good day, of night now borrow;
Short, night, to-night, and length thyself tomorrow.

15

It was a lording's daughter, the fairest one of three,
That liked of her master as well as well might be,
Till looking on an Englishman, the fairest that eye could see,
Her fancy fell a-turning.
Long was the combat doubtful that love with love did fight,
To leave the master loveless, or kill the gallant knight;
To put in practice either, alas, it was a spite
Unto the silly damsel!
But one must be refused; more mickle was the pain
That nothing could be used to turn them both to gain,
For of the two the trusty knight was wounded with disdain.
Alas, she could not help it!
Thus art with arms contending was victor of the day,
Which by a gift of learning did bear the maid away.
Then, lullaby, the learned man hath got the lady gay;
For now my song is ended.

16

On a day, alack the day!
Love, whose month was ever May,
Spied a blossom passing fair,
Playing in the wanton air.
Through the velvet leaves the wind,
All unseen, gan passage find;
That the lover, sick to death,
Wish'd himself the heaven's breath.
'Air,' quoth he 'thy cheeks may blow;
Air, would I might triumph so!
But, alas, my hand hath sworn
Ne'er to pluck thee from thy thorn;
Vow, alack, for youth unmeet,
Youth, so apt to pluck a sweet.
Thou for whom Jove would swear
Juno but an Ethiope were;
And deny himself for Jove,
Turning mortal for thy love.'

17

My flocks feed not,
My ewes breed not,
My rams speed not,
All is amiss;
Love is dying,
Faith's defying,
Heart's denying,
Causer of this.
All my merry jigs are quite forgot,

All my lady's love is lost, God wot.
Where her faith was firmly fix'd in love,
There a nay is plac'd without remove.
One silly cross
Wrought all my loss.
O frowning Fortune, cursed fickle dame!
For now I see
Inconstancy
More in women than in men remain.

In black mourn I,
All fears scorn I,
Love hath forlorn me,
Living in thrall;
Heart is bleeding,
All help needing,
O cruel speeding,
Fraughted with gall!
My shepherd's pipe can sound no deal;
My wether's bell rings doleful knell;
My curtail dog, that wont to have play'd,
Plays not at all, but seems afraid.
With sighs so deep,
Procures to weep,
In howling wise, to see my doleful plight.
How sighs resound
Through heartless ground,
Like a thousand vanquish'd men in bloody fight!

Clear wells spring not,
Sweet birds sing not,
Green plants bring not
Forth their dye.
Herds stand weeping,
Flocks all sleeping,
Nymphs back peeping
Fearfully.
All our pleasure known to us poor swains,
All our merry meetings on the plains,
All our evening sport from us is fled,
All our love is lost, for Love is dead.
Farewell, sweet lass;
Thy like ne'er was
For a sweet content, the cause of all my moan.
Poor Corydon
Must live alone;
Other help for him I see that there is none.

18

When as thine eye hath chose the dame,
And stall'd the deer that thou shouldst strike,
Let reason rule things worthy blame,
As well as fancy, partial wight;
Take counsel of some wiser head,
Neither too young nor yet unwed.

And when thou com'st thy tale to tell,
Smooth not thy tongue with filed talk,
Lest she some subtle practice smell –
A cripple soon can find a halt;
But plainly say thou lov'st her well,
And set her person forth to sell.

And to her will frame all thy ways;
Spare not to spend, and chiefly there
Where thy desert may merit praise
By ringing in thy lady's ear.
The strongest castle, tower, and town,
The golden bullet beats it down.

Serve always with assured trust,
And in thy suit be humble-true;
Unless thy lady prove unjust,
Press never thou to choose a new.
When time shall serve, be thou not slack
To proffer, though she put thee back.

What though her frowning brows be bent,
Her cloudy looks will calm ere night;
And then too late she will repent
That thus dissembled her delight;
And twice desire, ere it be day,
That which with scorn she put away.

What though she strive to try her strength,
And ban and brawl and say thee nay?
Her feeble force will yield at length,
When craft hath taught her thus to say:
'Had women been so strong as men,
In faith, you had not had it then'.

The wiles and guiles that women work,
Dissembled with an outward show,
The tricks and toys that in them lurk,
The cock that treads them shall not know.
Have you not heard it said full oft,
A woman's nay doth stand for nought?

Think women still to strive with men
To sin, and never for to saint;
There is no heaven – be holy then –
When time with age shall them attaint.
Were kisses all the joys in bed,
One woman would another wed.

But soft; enough – too much I fear;
Lest that my mistress hear my song;
She will not stick to round me on th' ear,
To teach my tongue to be so long.
Yet will she blush, here be it said,
To hear her secrets so bewray'd.

19

Live with me, and be my love,
And we will all the pleasures prove
That hills and valleys, dales and fields,
And all the craggy mountains yields.

There will we sit upon the rocks,
And see the shepherds feed their flocks,
By shallow rivers, by whose falls

Melodious birds sing madrigals.

There will I make thee a bed of roses,
With a thousand fragrant posies,
A cap of flowers, and a kirtle
Embroidered all with leaves of myrtle;

A belt of straw and ivy buds,
With coral clasps and amber studs.
And if these pleasures may thee move,
Then live with me and be my love.

LOVE'S ANSWER

If that the world and love were young,
And truth in every shepherd's tongue,
These pretty pleasures might me move,
To live with thee and be thy love.

20

As it fell upon a day,
In the merry month of May,
Sitting in a pleasant shade
Which a grove of myrtles made,
Beasts did leap and birds did sing,
Trees did grow and plants did spring;
Every thing did banish moan,
Save the nightingale alone.
She, poor bird, as all forlorn,
Lean'd her breast up-till a thorn,
And there sung the dolefull'st ditty,
That to hear it was great pity.
'Fie, fie, fie!' now would she cry;
'Teru, Teru!' by and by;
That to hear her so complain
Scarce I could from tears refrain;
For her griefs, so lively shown,
Made me think upon mine own.
Ah, thought I, thou mourn'st in vain;
None takes pity on thy pain:
Senseless trees, they cannot hear thee;
Ruthless bears, they will not cheer thee.
King Pandion, he is dead;
All thy friends are lapp'd in lead:
All thy fellow birds do sing,
Careless of thy sorrowing.
Even so, poor bird, like thee,
None alive will pity me.
Whilst as fickle Fortune smil'd,
Thou and I were both beguil'd.
Every one that flatters thee
Is no friend in misery.
Words are easy, like the wind;
Faithful friends are hard to find.
Every man will be thy friend
Whilst thou hast wherewith to spend;
But if store of crowns be scant,
No man will supply thy want.
If that one be prodigal,
Bountiful they will him call,
And with such-like flattering,
'Pity but he were a king'.
If he be addict to vice,
Quickly him they will entice;
If to women he be bent,
They have at commandement;
But if Fortune once do frown,
Then farewell his great renown.
They that fawn'd on him before
Use his company no more.
He that is thy friend indeed,
He will help thee in thy need;
If thou sorrow, he will weep;
If thou wake, he cannot sleep.
Thus of every grief in heart
He with thee doth bear a part.
These are certain signs to know
Faithful friend from flatt'ring foe.

The Phoenix and Turtle

LET the bird of loudest lay,
On the sole Arabian tree,
Herald sad and trumpet be,
To whose sound chaste wings obey.

But thou shrieking harbinger,
Foul precurrer of the fiend,
Augur of the fever's end,
To this troop come thou not near.

From this session interdict
Every fowl of tyrant wing,
Save the eagle, feath'red king:
Keep the obsequy so strict.

Let the priest in surplice white,
That defunctive music can,
Be the death-divining swan,
Lest the requiem lack his right.

And thou treble-dated crow,
That thy sable gender mak'st
With the breath thou giv'st and tak'st
'Mongst our mourners shalt thou go.

Here the anthem doth commence:
Love and constancy is dead;
Phœnix and the turtle fled
In a mutual flame from hence.

So they lov'd as love in twain
Had the essence but in one;
Two distincts, division none:
Number there in love was slain.

Hearts remote, yet not asunder;
Distance, and no space was seen
'Twixt this turtle and his queen;
But in them it were a wonder.

So between them love did shine
That the turtle saw his right
Flaming in the phœnix' sight:
Either was the other's mine.

Property was thus appalled,
That the self was not the same;
Single nature's double name
Neither two nor one was called.

Reason, in itself confounded,
Saw division grow together,
To themselves yet either neither,
Simple were so well compounded,

That it cried 'How true a twain
Seemeth this concordant one!
Love hath reason, reason none,
If what parts can so remain'.

Whereupon it made this threne
To the phœnix and the dove,
Co-supremes and stars of love,
As chorus to their tragic scene.

THRENOS

Beauty, truth, and rarity,
Grace in all simplicity,
Here enclos'd in cinders lie.

Death is now the phœnix' nest;
And the turtle's loyal breast
To eternity doth rest,

Leaving no posterity –
'Twas not their infirmity,
It was married chastity.

Truth may seem, but cannot be;
Beauty brag, but 'tis not she:
Truth and beauty buried be.

To this urn let those repair
That are either true or fair;
For these dead birds sigh a prayer.

Appendix

THIS transcript, reproduced in type-facsimile, of 147 lines from the manuscript of the play of *Sir Thomas More*, is included by the generous permission of Sir Walter Greg, who made it, and the syndics of the Cambridge University Press. It can be studied with complete advantage only in the context for which Dr. Greg designed it – namely, *Shakespeare's Hand in Sir Thomas More*,* a study from all angles of the authorship of these lines by a group of scholars who proved, beyond reasonable question, that Shakespeare wrote them, and that chance has preserved for us, in addition to the six, possibly seven, genuine signatures, this extensive specimen of the dramatist's handwriting.

*By Alfred W. Pollard, W. W. Greg, E. Maunde Thompson, J. Dover Wilson and R. W. Chambers. Cambridge University Press, 1923.

FOL. 8^{a}

Lincolne — Peace heare me, he that will not ſee [a red] hearing at a harry
grote, butter at a levenpence a pou[nde, meale at]nyne ſhillingę a
Buſhell and Beeff at ſower nob[les a ſtone, lyſ]t to me

~~other~~ Geo bett — yt will Come to that paſſe yf ſtrain[gers be ſu]fferd mark him

Linco — our Countrie is a great eating Country, argo they eate more in
our Countrey then they do in their owne

~~other~~ betts clow — by a half penny loff a day troy waight

Linc — they bring in ſtraing rootes, which is meerly to the vndoing of poor
prentizes, for whatę ~~a watrie~~ a ſorry ꝑſnyp to a good hart

~~oth~~ william — traſh traſh,: they breed ſore eyes and tis enough to infect the
Cytty w^{t} the palſey

Lin — nay yt has infected yt w^{t} the palſey, for theiſe basterdę of dung
as you knowe they growe in Dvng haue infected vs, and yt is our
infeccion will make the Cytty ſhake which ꝑtly Coms through
the eating of ꝑſnyps

~~o~~Clown · betts — rewe and pumpions togeather

Enter ſeriant — what ſay yo^{u} to the mercy of the king do yo^{u} refuſe yt

Lin — yo^{u} woold haue [vs] vppon thipp woold yo^{u} no marry do we not, we
accept of the kingę mercy but wee will ſhowe no mercy vppõ
the ſtraingers

feriaunt — yo^{u} ar the ſimpleſt thingę that eu ſtood in ſuch a queſtion

Lin — how ſay yo^{u} now prenty prentiſſes ſymple downe wth him

3 *Beeff*] the first e has been altered from some other letter. 5 *Linco*] *in* has two minims only but the first is dotted. 8 *of*] the final curl of the *f* has been carried round in such a way as to resemble o. 10 *william*] *m* has two minims only. *traſh,:*] so T, but the lower dot may be accidental: M prints a semi-colon. 12 *dung*] *un* has five minims. 17 The initial letter of the speaker's name, whether it be regarded as minuscule (T) or majuscule (M), is certainly of an Italian type. 18 *haue*] T *have* perhaps by an accidental slip; the word occurs elsewhere eight times always spelt *haue*, Dyce read *haue* here, and the very obscure original seems to me to have *u* rather than *v* 19 *ſhowe*] *w* blotted, possibly altered. 22 The marginal and interlined words were added later. *prenty*] *n* is represented by one minim only, and *y* is doubtful.

Though only a comparison of the transcript with a facsimile of the original will make clear the full implications of this discovery, the reader has here before him a fragment of the master's composition, transcribed with a care that will permit him to understand more adequately than any description the difficulties confronting Heminge and Condell in their editorial labours. The 147 lines occupy both sides of a leaf of paper and one side of a second leaf, and form part of a scene Shakespeare contributed to a piece by some fellow playwrights. The original author or authors had difficulty with the licenser of plays. That official was not troubled by the play's protagonist being More, a martyr to the cause of Catholicism: a Protestant audience under the Protestant Elizabeth had a sufficiently catholic attitude to understand and appreciate his character. But a series of episodes in which he is represented as intervening in person to quell the

all — prentiſles ſymple prentiſles ſymple

Enter the L maier Surrey
Shrewſbury

~~Sher~~ Maior — hold in the kingę name hold

Surrey — frendę maſters Countrymen

mayer — peace how peace J ~~ſh~~ Charg yo^u keep the peace

Shro· — my maſters Countrymen

~~Sher~~ Williamson — The noble Earle of Shrewſbury lettę hear him

Ge bettę — weele heare the Earle of Surrey

Linc — the earle of Shrewſbury

bettę — weele heare both

all — both both both both

Linc — Peace J ſay peace ar yo^u men of Wiſdome ~~ar~~ or what ar yo^u

Surr — ~~But~~ what yo^u will haue them but not men of wiſdome

all — weele not heare my L of Surrey, ~~all~~ no no no no no
Shrewſbury ſhr

moor — whiles they ar ore the banck of their obedyenc
thus will they bere downe all thingę

Line — Shreiff moor ſpeakes ſhall we heare ſhreef moor ſpeake

Doll — Lettę heare him a keepes a plentyfull ſhrevaltry, and a made my

26 *Sher*] this must be a slip for *Shre* 27 The rule has been accidentally omitted after this line. 29 *Shro·*] the last letter certainly seems to be *o* but D always writes *Shrewſbury* elsewhere. 30 C wrote his alternation on the top of D's original. 30, 32 *Shrewſbury*] M, T *Shrowsbury* 38 *all no* … *ſhr*] added later; the deletion is probably by C. *Shrewſbury*] so M: T *Shrowsbury* [the letter is indistinguishable). 40 *thingę*] I am unable to read the end of this word. 42 *ſhrevaltry*,] so M: T *shrevaltry*. but it is clearly a comma I think

'ill May-day' riot of 1517 so disturbed the licenser that after marking several passages for omission he turned back and wrote at the beginning of the manuscript:

'Leave out the insurrection wholly and the cause thereof and begin with Sir Thomas More at the Mayor's sessions with a report afterwards of his good service done being Sheriff of London upon a mutiny against the Lombards. Only by a short report and not otherwise at your own perils. – TYLLNEY'.

The constant danger of attack on the foreign colonies in London from riotous native elements was too present to the licenser's mind to allow him to pass episodes which showed historical precedent for such attempts. At some stage in the struggle to fit the play for official favour the author or authors sought the help of Shakespeare, not as some unknown or prentice playwright, but as one whose

Brother Arther watchin[s] Seriant Safes yeoman letę heare ſhreeve
moore

all — Shreiue moor moor more Shreue moore

moor — [ev]en by the rule yo^{u} haue among yor ſealues — FOL.8b
Comand ſtill audience

all — [S]urrey Sury

all — moor moor

Lincolne bettę — peace peace ſcilens peace

moor — Yo^{u} that haue voyce and Credyt w^{t} the ~~mv~~ nvmber
Comaund them to a ſtilnes

Lincolne — a plaigue on them they will not hold their peace the deule
Cannot rule them

moor — Then what a rough and ryotous charge haue yo^{u}
to Leade thoſe that the deule Cannot rule
good maſters heare me ſpeake

Doll — J byth mas will we moor thart a good howſkeeper and J
thanck thy good worſhip for my Brother Arthur watchins

all — peace peace

moor — look what yo^{u} do offend yo^{u} Cry vppõ
that is the peace; not [on] of yo^{u} heare preſent
had there ſuch fellowes lyvd when yo^{u} wer babes
that coold haue topt the peace, as nowe yo^{u} woold
the peace wherin yo^{u} haue till nowe growne vp
had bin tane from yo^{u}, and the bloody tymes
cold not haue brought yo^{u} to ~~theise~~ the ſtate of men
alas poor thingę what is yt yo^{u} haue gott
although we graunt yo^{u} geat the thing yo^{u} ſeeke

43 *Safes*] *af* seems to me to have disappeared entirely except perhaps for the extreme tail of the *ſ*. *yeoman*] *o* altered, probably by C, from some other small letter. 45 This line with the rule above it was added later. 59 *watchins*] *c* altered, apparently from the beginning of *h*

dexterity and experience would supply the resource required.

Shakespeare's scene opens with the rioters led by Lincoln crying out against the the foreigners. To them enters a Sergeant-at-Arms, followed by the Lord Mayor with the Earls of Surrey and Shrewsbury and Sir Thomas More. The crowd cry down the Mayor and Earls but are willing to give More a hearing. The interpretation of the typographical detail of the transcript will be clear from Dr. Greg's own analysis:

'The author wrote the text, at any rate of the first two pages, continuously, dividing the speeches by rules but without indicating the speakers. He then read it through, inserting the prefixes and at the same time making certain additions to the text, some words at the beginning of l. 22, at the end of l. 38, and the whole of l. 45. . . . The addition of the speakers' names was certainly perfunctory, especially

~~D~~ Bett — marry the removing of the ſtraingers wch cannot chooſe but
much ~~helpe~~ advauntage the poor handycraftes of the Cytty

moor — graunt them remoued and graunt that this yor ~~y~~ noyce
hath Chidd downe all the matie of Jngland
ymagin that yo^{u} ſee the wretched ſtraingers
w^{t}
their babyes at their backę, ~~and~~ their poor lug̃age
plodding tooth portę and coſtę for tranſportacion
and that yo^{u} ſytt as kingę in your deſyres
aucthoryty quyte ſylenct by yor braule
and yo^{u} in ruff of yor ~~yo~~ opynions clothd
what had yo^{u} gott; Jle tell yo^{u}, yo^{u} had taught
how inſolenc and ſtrong hand ſhoold prevayle
how orderd ſhoold be quelld, and by this patterne
not on of yo^{u} ſhoold lyve an aged man
for other ruffians as their fancies wrought
wth ſealf ſame hand ſealf reaſons and ſealf right
woold ſhark on yo^{u} and men lyke ravenous fiſhes
woold feed on on another

Doll — before god thatę as trewe as the goſpell.

Bettę lincoln — nay this a ſound fellowe J tell yo^{u} lets mark him

moor — Let me ſett vp before yor thoughts good freindę
on ſuppoſytion, which if yo^{u} will marke
you ſhall ꝑceaue howe horrible a ſhape
your ynnovation beres, firſt tis a ſinn
which oft thappoſtle did forwarne vs of vrging obedienc to aucthory[ty]
and twere ~~in~~ no error yf J told yo^{u} all yo^{u} wer in armes gainſt g[od]

70 The *D* appears to have been crossed out by both D and C. 71 *handycraftes*] the *e* is represented only by a small blot between *t* and *s* 72 *noyce*] y altered from *w* 73 *matie*] sic, by a slip from *matie* i.e. *maieſtie* [cf. l. 121). 75 *and* was crossed out, and *wt* interlined to replace it, by D. Neither M nor T notices the alteration. 80 *gott;*] so T: M prints a comma, but the original seems to have ·;· 82 *orderd*] so T: M *ordere*: doubtful, but in either case an error for *order* 85 *hand*] there is a very small dot after this word, some stop may possibly be intended. 89 *lincoln*] so M: T *Lincoln* (perhaps a slip). 93 *your*] M, T *yo'* but the reading though indistinct is hardly open to question. 94 *vrging*] so M: T *urging* (an accidental slip).

on the first page, but, apart from the unsatisfactory condition of the deleted passage on the third, I do not find any evidence of haste or carelessness in composition'.

The scene, however, does not stand in its final state exactly as Shakespeare left it. The heavier type indicates additions and alterations by a second hand, that of a playhouse reviser who tried to clarify and pull together certain details of the original. One instance only of his efforts can be commented on here: he has deleted ll. 112–14 and substituted a phrase of his own. Shakespeare's omission of punctuation marks and capital letters, his insertion of the phrase 'in in to your obedience' and the extra-metrical nature of the conclusion of l. 114 puzzled the reviser. He took the phrase 'to kneel to be forgiven' with what goes before instead of with what follows, and in his determination to have it all tidy scored out the

FOL.9^a

all marry god forbid that

moo nay certainly yo^u ar
for to the king god hath his offyc lent
of dread of Juſtyce, power and Comaund
hath bid him rule, and willd yo^u to obay
and to add ampler maṫie to this
he ~~god~~ hath not ~~le~~ only lent the king his figure
&
his throne ~~his~~ ſword, but gyven him his owne name
calls him a god on earth, what do yo^u then
ryſing gainſt him that god himſealf enſtalls
but ryſe gainſt god, what do yo^u to yor ſowles
in doing this o deſperat ~~ar~~ as you are·
waſh your foule mynds w^t teares and thoſe ſame hands
that yo^u lyke rebells lyft againſt the peace
lift vp for peace, and your vnreuerent knees
~~that~~ make them your feet to kneele to be forgyven.
~~is ſafer warrs, then euer yo^u can make~~
~~in in to yor obedienc·~~
~~whoſe discipline is ryot; why euen yor warrs hurly~~
tell me but this
~~cannot pceed but by obediene~~ **what rebell captaine**
n
as mutyes ar incident, by his name
can ſtill the rout who will obay ~~th~~ a traytor
or howe can well that pclamation ſounde
when ther is no adicion but a rebell
to quallyfy a rebell, youle put downe ſtraingers

101 *and*] *n* has three minims. 102 *only*] so M: T *souly* [withdrawn; see above, p. 76, note). 103 *his* [deleted)] so M: T *hys* [withdrawn; see above, p. 76, note). The *&* is really written on the top of *his* not between the lines. 110 *and*] for an attempted alteration see final note. 111 There is a slightly wider space after *feet* and a break may have been intended as in l. 95. *to kneele*] so M: T *fo kneele* [an accidental misprint due to a broken letter). 112–4 With the exception of the single word *warrs* [which he crossed out, adding *hurly* in its place) these lines were left standing by D. All the other deletions are in darker ink, presumably by C, who added the interlined words in the third line. 113 *warrs*] so M: T *warre* altered to *warrs* (see final note). *obedienc·*] T omits the stop, but I do not think that the mark can be accidental. 117 *founde*] *un* has three minims only. 118 *ther*] r altered from *ir*.

troublesome passage and inserted a join of his own contriving.

Had this manuscript gone as it stands to the printer it needs no imagination to picture the difficulties that would have confronted the compositor. It is true that these three pages were composed by Shakespeare in circumstances very different from those in which he wrote his own plays. But the handwriting, with all the difficulties and irregularities recorded in Dr. Greg's notes, would be the same; there would be the same minimum of punctuation and capitalization, and possibly, in places, the same insertions, extra-metrical lines, and loose ends. These by themselves would be sufficient to explain many of the blunders that mar the Good Quartos and that must have stood in the transcripts prepared by scriveners working from Shakespeare's papers. The three pages of Sir Thomas More here transcribed must, when they were new and fresh, have presented an

kill them cutt their throts poſſeſſe their howſes
and leade the matie of lawe in liom
~~alas alas~~
to ſlipp him lyke a hound; ~~fayeng~~ ſay nowe the king
as he is clement,. yf thoffendor moorne
ſhoold ſo much com to ſhort of your great treſpas
    as but to banyſh yo^{u}, whether woold yo^{u} go·
what Country by the nature of yor error
ſhoold gyve you harber go yo^{u} to ffraunc or flanders
to any Jarman pvince, ~~to~~ ſpane or portigall
nay any where ~~why yo^{u}~~ that not adheres to Jngland
why yo^{u} muſt needę be ſtraingers, woold yo^{u} be pleaſd
to find a nation of such barbarous temper
that breaking out in hiddious violence
woold not afoord yo^{u}, an abode on earth
whett their deteſted knyves againſt yor throtes
ſpurne yo^{u} lyke doggę, and lyke as yf that god
owed not nor made not yo^{u}, nor that the elamentę
yor
wer not all appropriat to ~~their~~ Comfortę
but Charterd vnto them, what woold yo^{u} thinck
to be thus vſd, this is the ſtraingers caſe
all and this your momtaniſh inhumanyty

ſayth a ſaies trewe letts ~~vs~~ do as we may be doon by

121 *matie*] contraction mark omitted as in l. 73. 122 *fayeng*] M, T *saying* but there is no doubt of the reading. The substituted words, interlined by D, were deleted by C. 123 *clement*,.] M, T print a comma only, but there seems clearly to be a point after it. 125 The writing avoids a small hole in the paper. 127 *flanders*] the *r* is malformed. 130 *ſtraingers*,] T's comma is better than M's point, but the mark may be accidental. 131 *barbarous*] second *r* altered from *b* [not from *k* as T suggests). 136 *elamentę*] T adds a comma but the mark is in the paper only. 137 *their*] M, T *ther* but there is little doubt of the reading. 140 *all*] belongs properly to the next line where T prints it. *momtaniſh*] T *mountanish* noting '*un* only three minims': the writer's intention is quite obscure. *inhumanyty*] so M: T adds a point but it appears to be no more than a flick of the tail of *y* 141 *vs*] M and T both describe the deletion as being in modern ink, but on re-examination I am unable to distinguish it from that of other deletions and therefore ascribe it to C. The writer probably intended *lett vs* but forgot to cross out the s

appearance that might reasonably be described as scarcely blotted; but careful study can discover beneath the discolourings and blurrings that now overlay them the many pitfalls that would await a printer. We need not therefore be surprised, though we may regret, that even with Shakespeare's papers in their possession Heminge and Condell did not succeed in giving us the perfect text. Only the most unrelaxing vigilance and supervision can arrest the brood of error that haunt the printing-house and the copyist's desk alike. The three pages from Shakespeare's own hand may show the reader some of the loopholes through which those intruders have found their way into Shakespeare's text.

~~all~~ Linco — weele be ruld by yo^{u} maſter moor yf youle ſtand our
freind to pcure our pdon

---

moor — Submyt yo^{u} to theiſe noble gentlemen
entreate their mediation to the kinge
gyve up yor ſealf to forme obay the maieſtrate
and thers no doubt, but mercy may be found yf yo^{u} so seek [yt]

147 *found*] *un* has three minims only. yo^{u}] o^{u} malformed. *yt*] M *it*: T omits. D certainly wrote something after *seek* and the addition seems to me to improve the sense. The visible traces can be read *yt* (hardly *it*), but at the same time they are rather widely separated from the preceding word, and it is possible that they represent an *&* or some other sign indicating that the original text was to resume at this point.

FINAL NOTE ON CERTAIN READINGS IN LL. 103–14.

103 *his* (deleted)] The curious symbol superimposed on this word has certainly not the form of the *&* usual in English hands. It may, however, I think, be a loose attempt at rendering the print form of ampersand, which though rare is not unknown in manuscripts of the period. Since the ink in which the symbol is written is identical with that of the original writing, it seems unlikely that a second hand is involved in the alteration. This also applies to the contraction mark of *matie* in l. 101.

110 *and your*] T notes: 'a word was underlined for insertion between these two words, but it appears to have been wiped out while the ink was still wet. The traces of the letters seem to suggest *bend*.' It appears that *and* was crossed out and the word, whatever it was, interlined to replace it. But the whole alteration, which was probably never completed, has been erased. The traces are very illegible, but to me they suggest the letters *bye* rather than *bend*.

113 *warrs*] T *warre* noting that the writer 'altered *warre* to *warrs* by interlining a long *s*.' I am not myself able to detect any indication of a final *e*, and believe the supposed *ſ* to be the upward curl of the regular English final *s*.

112–4 In these difficult lines, if the original writer intended the interlined words *in in to yor obedienc·* as a substitute for the two half-lines *why euen* ... *by obedienc* (as has been suggested) one would have expected him to delete the latter. But, with the substitution of *hurly* for *warrs* he left the passage as it was, and must, I think, have meant it to stand. I conjecture that a stop was intended after *feet* in l. 111, and that *in in to yor obedienc·* should be inserted between *ryot*; and *why*. The whole passage is clumsy but I no longer think, as I was once inclined to do, that the author was conscious of having left it in confusion.

Glossary

abate to shorten, *Mid. N. Dr.*, 3.ii.432; to except, *L. Lab. Lost*, 5.ii.540; to lessen, *Tam. Shrew*, Ind. 1.135.
abhor to disgust, *Oth.*, 4.ii.163; shudder from, *Mer. Wives Win.*, 3.v.14; to reject, *Hen. 8*, 2.iv.81.
abject *adj.*, despised, *Hen. 8*, 1.i.127; servile, *Mer. Ven.*, 4.i.92; *noun*, contemptible thing, *Jul. Caes.*, 4.i.37.
abode to foretell, *Hen. 8*, 1.i.93.
abortives untimely births, *John*, 3.iv.158.
abram auburn, *Cor.*, 2.iii.18.
abridgement what cuts short or passes the time, *Ham.*, 2.ii.415; *Mid. N. Dr.*, 5.i.39.
abrook to tolerate, *2 Hen. 6*, 2.iv.10.
abruption abrupt breaking off, *Troil. and Cres.*, 3.ii.63.
Absey-book a book to teach the ABC of a subject, *John*, 1.i.196.
absolute perfect, *Hen. 5*, 3.vii.25; positive, *Ham.* 5.i.133; decided, *M. Meas.*, 3.i.5.
aby to pay penalty for, *Mid. N. Dr.*, 3.ii.175.
accite to summon, *Titus*, 1.i.27; to excite, *2 Hen. 4*, 2.ii.56.
accommodate to furnish or equip, *2 Hen. 4*, 3.ii.65.
accomplice comrade (but not in crime), *1 Hen. 6*, 5.ii.9.
accomplish to arm completely, *Hen. 5*, 4. *Prol.* 12; to furnish, *Rich. 2*, 2.i.177.
ache pronounced 'aitch' at *Much Ado*, 3.iv.48, where it is represented by H.
Acheron one of the five rivers of the lower world, but called a lake at *Titus*, 4.iii.44; stands for hell itself at *Mac.*, 3.v.15.
acknown *be not acknown*, admit no knowledge of, *Oth.*, 3.iii.323.
aconitum poison from wolf's-bane, *2 Hen. 4*, 4.iv.48.
action-taking sheltering behind the law, *Lear*, 2.ii.16.
acture action, *Lov. Comp.*, 185.
Adam (i) *the picture of old Adam*, because the officer had a coat of strong leather, and Adam, after the Fall, wore skins, *Com. Err.*, 4.iii.13. (ii) Adam Bell, famous as an archer, *Much Ado*, 1.i.224; *Rom. and Jul.*, 2.i.13.
adamant very hard substance, *1 Hen. 6*, 1.iv.52; lode-stone, *Mid. N. Dr.*, 2.i.195.
addiction natural inclination, *Oth.*, 2.ii.5.
addition description or title acquired by habits or service, *Troil. and Cres.*, 2.iii.241.
address to prepare, *As You Like*, 5.iv.150; to equip, *Troil. and Cres.*, 5.x.14.
admiral flagship, *Ant. and Cleo.*, 3.x.2.
advertisement information, warning, *1 Hen. 4*, 3.ii.172; *All's Well*, 4.iii.197.
advice thought, *Two Gent. Ver.*, 2.iv.203, 204.
aedile Roman official responsible for public order and public works, *Cor.*, 3.i.172.
aery nest and young of eagle, *Rich. 3*, 1.iii.264; applied to the young actors of the boys' companies, *Ham.*, 2.ii.335.
affect aim at, *Cor.*, 3.iii.1; love, *Tw. Night*, 2.v.22.
affection affectation, *L. Lab. Lost*, 5.i.4.
affeer confirm, *Mac.*, 4.iii.34.
affiance trust, *Cym.*, 1.vi.162.
affront to meet, confront, *Ham.*, 3.i.31.
affy to trust, betroth, *Titus*, 4.i.47; *Tam. Shrew*, 4.iv.49.
agate small figure like that cut on stone of seal-ring, *2 Hen. 4*, 1.ii.16.
Agenor King of Tyre and father of Europa, *Tam. Shrew.*, 1.i.163.
aglet-baby small figure on lace-tag, *Tam. Shrew.*, 1.ii.77.
agnize acknowledge, *Oth.*, 1.iii.231.
a-hold directly into the wind, *Tem.*, 1.i.46.
aim conjecture, *Oth.* 1.iii.6; term of encouragement, *John*, 2.i.196.
Ajax Greek hero before Troy with more brawn than brains, *Troil. and Cres.*, 2.i.70; with pun (*see* jakes), *L. Lab. Lost*, 5.ii.572.
alderliefest dearest of all, *2 Hen. 6*, 1.i.28.
Alecto one of the Furies, *2 Hen. 4*, 5.v.37.
a-life dearly, *Win. Tale*, 4.iv.255.
All-hallond eve eve of All Saints' day, *M. Meas.*, 2.i.120.
All-hallowmas 1st Nov., *Mer. Wives Win.*, 1.i.185.
All-hallown summer summer lasting into winter and so vigour of manhood in age, *1 Hen. 4*, 1.ii.153.
all hid hide and seek, *L. Lab. Lost*, 4.iii.74.
allicholy melancholy, *Mer. Wives Win.*, 1.iv.138.
Almain German, *Oth.*, 2.iii.77.
alms drink taken on another's behalf, *Ant. and Cleo.*, 2.vii.5.
ames-ace both aces, lowest throw with two dice, *All's Well*, 2.iii.77.
amort *all amort*, almost dead, *Tam. Shrew*, 4.iii.36.
anchor hermit, *Ham.*, 3.ii.214.
ancient from ensign or standard-bearer, *Oth.*, 1.i.33.
angel gold coin stamped with image of angel, worth about ten shillings, *Mer. Ven.*, 2.vii.55–7.
Anthropophagi cannibals, *Oth.*, 1.iii.144; *Anthropophaginian*, *Mer. Wives Win.*, 4.v.8.
antic odd, unusual, *Ham.*, 1.v.172.
antre cave, *Oth.*, 1.iii.140.
appellant challenger, *Rich. 2*, 1.iii.4.
apple-john a sound but wither'd-looking apple, *1 Hen. 4*, 3.iii.4.
aqua-vitæ whisky, *Mer. Wives Win.*, 2.ii.271.
Aquilon north wind, *Troil. and Cres.*, 4.v.9.
Arabian bird phoenix, *Ant. and Cleo.*, 3.ii.12.
arch patron, *Lear*, 2.i.59.
argal, argo *ergo*, therefore, *Ham.*, 5.i.12.
Ariachne Arachne, changed to a spider for pride in her weaving by Athene, *Troil. and Cres.*, 5.ii.150.
arm-gaunt (doubtful), *Ant. and Cleo.*, 1.v.48.
armipotent strong in arms, *L. Lab. Lost.*, 5.ii.636.
aroint away! *Mac.*, 1.iii.6.
Arthur (i) *Arthur's show*, display of archery by London company called Prince Arthur's Knights, *2 Hen. 4*, 3.ii.272. (ii) *Arthur's bosom*, malapropism for Abraham's bosom, *Hen. 5*, 2.iii.9.

artist learned practitioner, *Troil. and Cres.* 1.iii.24.
assinego ass, *Troil. and Cres.*, 2.i.43.
Astraea goddess of Justice, *Titus*, 4.iii.4.
atone unite, *Cor.*, 4.vi.73.
Atropos one of the Fates, 2 *Hen.* 4, 2.iv.189.
auricular through the ear, *Lear*, 1.ii.88.
bacare go back, *Tam. Shrew.*, 2.i.73.
back-friend the officer who arrests you from behind, *Com. Err.*, 4.ii.37.
backsword-man a single-stick performer, 2 *Hen.* 4, 3.ii.63.
back-trick a movement in some dance, *Tw. Night*, 1.iii.115.
baffle to proclaim one a perjured knight, 1 *Hen.* 4, 1.ii.98; shame, *Tw. Night.*, 2.v.142.
bait to set on dogs to worry an animal, as in a baiting-place, 2 *Hen.* 6, 5.i.150; to catch as with a bait, *Com. Err.*, 2.i.94.
baldrick cross belt from shoulder to carry sword or bugle, *Much Ado*, 1.i.209.
balk to miss an opportunity or prey, *Tw. Night*, 3.ii.23; chop logic, *Tam. Shrew*, 1.i.34.
ballow cudgel, *Lear*, 4.vi.243.
ban prohibit, *Oth.*, 2.i.11; curse, 2 *Hen.* 6, 3.ii.333.
bandy to exchange blows or words or looks (as strokes in a rally at tennis), *Lear*, 1.iv.83.
bank sea-shore, *Troil. and Cres.* 1.iii.328; sand-bank, *Mac.*, 1.vii.6; to take in (as banker at card game), *John*, 5.ii.104.
Barbason a devil, *Mer. Wives Win.*, 2.ii.265.
barbed protected on breast and flanks, of horse, *Rich.* 3, 1.i.10.
barful difficult, *Tw. Night*, 1.iv.40.
barm yeast, *Mid. N. Dr.*, 2.i.38.
barne child, *Much Ado*, 3.iv.42.
barnacle a goose, *Tem.*, 4.1.247.
Bartholomew *-tide*, 24th August, *Hen.* 5, 5.ii.303; *boar-pig*, kind sold at Bartholomew fair, 2 *Hen.* 4. 2.iv.221.
base course, as at game of prisoners' base, *Cym.*, 5.iii.20.
base-court lower court of castle (as *basse-cour* in French), *Rich.* 2, 3.iii.176.
bases cloth extensions to knee, worn by mounted knights, *Per.*, 2.i.159.
Basilisco character in play of 'Soliman and Perseda', *John*, 1.i.244.
basilisk the fabled cockatrice that kills with its look, *Win. Tale*, 1.ii.388; cannon, *Hen.* 5, 5.ii.17.
basimecu corruption of 'baisez ma queue', 2 *Hen.* 6, 4.vii.26.
basta enough! *Tam. Shrew*, 1.i.193.
bastard sweet wine from Spain, 1 *Hen.* 4, 2.iv.25.
bate beat or flutter like a bird's wings, *Rom. and Jul.*, 3.ii.14; to blunt or weaken, *Timon*, 3.iii.26.
bat-fowling catching birds at night by dazzling them with a light, *Tem.*, 2.i.176.
batler wooden instrument for use in washing clothes, *As You Like*, 2.iv.46.
batten eat voraciously, *Ham.*, 3.iv.67.
bavin brushwood, easily kindled, 1 *Hen.* 4, 3.ii.61.
bawbling of little account, *Tw. Night*, 5.i.48.
bawcock stout fellow (French, **beau coq**), *Hen.* 5, 3.ii.24.
bay to pursue with barking, to bring the quarry to a stand, *Mid. N. Dr.*, 4.i.110.
beagle a small type of hound, *Tw. Night*, 2.iii.168.
beam in contrast to the 'mote', as in Matthew's gospel, *L. Lab. Lost*, 4.iii.158.
bear to obtain, *Oth.*, 1.iii.23; to regard with hate, *Jul. Caes.*, 2.i.215.
bear-herd *or* **bear-ward** (berrord), one who keeps a bear for exhibition, *Much Ado*, 2.i.34.
bearing-cloth christening robe, 1 *Hen.* 6, 1.iii.42.
beated (*perhaps*) lined or wrinkled, *Son.*, 62, 10.
beaver face-piece of helmet, *Ham.* 1.ii.229; the helmet as a whole, 1 *Hen.* 4, 4.i.104.
bedlam (i) an asylum, the word being derived from Bethlehem, the name of the London hospital, 2 *Hen.* 6, 5.i.131; (ii) a crazed person, *John* 2.i.183.
beetle (i) a heavy rammer for flattening earth, 2 *Hen.* 4, 1.ii.215. (ii) overhanging, *Rom. and Jul.*, 1.iv.32.
beldam a grandmother, old woman, *Lucrece*, 953.
be-lee'd cut off from the wind and so stationary, *Oth.*, 1.i.30.
bell (book and candle), expression used in excommunication, *John*, 3.iii.12.
bell-wether sheep carrying bell round neck to guide the flock, *As You Like*, 3.ii.71.
be-mete to thrash, *Tam. Shrew*, 4.iii.112.
bench the seat of authority, or those who sit in it, *Cor.*, 3.i.106.
bend glance, *Jul. Caes.*, 1.ii.123.
benevolence a loan exacted by the king on the pretext that the payment is a gesture of good will, *Rich.* 2, 2.i.250.
beray to befoul, *Titus*, 2.iii.222.
bergomask a rustic dance, *Mid. N. Dr.*, 5.i.350.
berrord *see* bear-herd.
beshrew (a good-natured imprecation), plague on or curse whatever follows, *Rom. and Jul.*, 5.ii.26.
beteem to allow, *Ham.*, 1.ii.141.
Bevis of Southampton, whose prodigies were told by the early romancers, *Hen.* 8, 1.i.38.
bezonian a needy rascal, 2 *Hen.* 6, 4.i.134.
bias oblique course, like the curve made by the bowl, *Ham.*, 2.i.65.
bifold twofold, *Troil. and Cres.*, 5.ii.142.
bigamy marriage with a widow as in *Rich.* 3, 3.vii.189.
biggen night-cap, 2 *Hen.* 4, 4.v.27.
bilbo a sword, good swords were made in Bilbao, *Mer. Wives Win.*, 3.v.98.
bilboes irons for mutinous sailors, *Ham.*, 5.ii.6.
bill a weapon like a pole-axe; *bills*, the troops so armed, *Lear*, 4.vi.91.
bird-bolt blunted arrow for shooting birds, *L. Lab. Lost*, 4.iii.20.
bisson blind, blinding, *Ham.*, 2.ii.500.
Black Monday Easter Monday, *Mer. Ven.*, 2.v.24 (from storm of 1360 when English troops outside Paris suffered greatly).
blank (i) white spot in centre of target, aiming point, *Ham.*, 4.i.42; (ii) a document to be filled in as the holder decides, *Rich.* 2, 2.i.250.
blazon (i) coat of arms, *Mer. Wives Win.*, 5.v.62. (ii) from the meaning of describing a coat of arms it comes to mean merely a description or announcement, *Ham.*, 1.v.21.
blear to hoodwink, *Tam. Shrew*, 5.i.104.
blister'd puffed out, *Hen.* 8, 1.iii.31.

block wooden shape on which hats are moulded, *Much Ado*, 1.i.63.
blood-bolter'd the hair matted with blood, *Mac.*, 4.i.123.
blow to puff up, *Tw. Night*, 2.v.40; to burst, *Ant. and Cleo.*, 4.vi.34; to defile with their (flies') eggs, *Ant. and Cleo.*, 5.ii.60.
blue-bottle the beadle, because of his blue coat, 2 *Hen.* 4, 5.iv.20.
blue-caps the Scots with their blue-bonnets, 1 *Hen.* 4, 2.iv.347.
bob a hit or quip, *As You Like*, 2.vii.55.
bob to steal or cheat, *Troil. and Cres.*, 3.i.65.
bodement omen, *Mac.*, 4.i.96.
bodkin dagger, *Ham.*, 3.i.76.
boggler selfishly unstable, *Ant. and Cleo.*, 3.xiii.110.
bollen swollen, *Lucrece*, 1417.
bolt short blunt-headed arrow, *Hen.* 5, 3.vii.119.
bolt to sift, *Win. Tale*, 4.iv.356.
bolter for sifting flour, 1 *Hen.* 4, 3.iii.69.
bombard leather bottle for drink, 1 *Hen.* 4, 2.iv.436.
bombast cotton-wool stuffing, *L. Lab. Lost*, 5.ii.769.
bona-roba showy wanton, 2 *Hen.* 4, 3.ii.22.
bones rural musical instrument, *Mid. N. Dr.*, 4.i.27; bobbins, *Tw. Night*, 2.iv.44.
boot something extra thrown in, *Troil. and Cres.*, 4.v.40; plunder, 2 *Hen.* 6, 4.i.13.
boot-hose a stocking covering the leg like a jack-boot, *Tam. Shrew*, 3.ii.63.
Boreas north wind, *Troil. and Cres.*, 1.iii.38.
bosky with trees and undergrowth, *Tem.*, 4.i.81.
botch (i) *noun*, careless bit in work, *Mac.*, 3.i.133; (ii) *verb*, to patch, *Ham.*, 4.v.10.
bottom (i) valley, *Ven. and Ad.*, 236; (ii) ship, *Mer. Ven.*, 1.i.42; (iii) ball of thread, with *verb* meaning to wind on a core like a ball of thread, *Two Gent. Ver.*, 3.ii.53.
bourn boundary, but brook in *Lear*, 3.vi.25.
bow hand the left hand that holds the bow, *L. Lab. Lost*, 4.i.126.
brace armour for the arms, hence armour as a whole, and state of defence, *Oth.*, 1.iii.24.
brach a kind of hound, *Lear*, 3.vi.68.
bravery show of courage, *Oth.*, 1.i.101; display as of clothes or feelings, *Tam. Shrew*, 4.iii.57.
brawl a dance, *L. Lab. Lost*, 3.i.8.
breese gadfly, *Ant. and Cleo.*, 3.x.14.
Briareus a hundred-handed giant, *Troil. and Cres.*, 1.ii.28.
brib'd stolen, *Mer. Wives Win.*, 5.v.22.
brinded striped, *Mac.*, 4.i.1.
broach to pierce (broach a cask), *Timon*, 2.ii.178; open a discussion, or enter on some business, *Ant. and Cleo.*, 1.ii.165.
brock badger, *Tw. Night*, 2.v.95.
brooch an ornament, so applied to one who is an ornament to his circle, *Ham.*, 4.vii.93.
Brownist an adherent of the Puritan sect which adopted the principles propagated by Robert Browne about 1580, *Tw. Night*, 3.ii.29.
bruit *noun*, report, hearsay, *Troil. and Cres.*, 5.ix.4; *verb*, publish broadcast, *Ham.*, 1.ii.127.
bubukle a portmanteau word from 'bubo', an abscess, and carbuncle, *Hen.* 5, 3.vi.99.
buck the pile of soiled clothes for washing, 2 *Hen.* 6, 4.ii.46; *-ing*, washing, *Mer. Wives Win.*, 3.iii.115; *-basket*, dirty clothes basket, *Mer. Wives Win.*, 3.v.126.
buck a stag, *Troil. and Cres.*, 3.i.110; named by sportsmen according to the year of its age; 1st fawn, 2nd pricket, 3rd sorell, 4th sore, 5th buck of the first head, 6th a buck, *L. Lab. Lost*, 4.ii.54 sqq. plays upon these terms.
Bucklersbury the street where the apothecaries sold herbs, *Mer. Wives Win.*, 3.iii.62.
buckram coarse linen specially treated, 1 *Hen.* 4, 2.iv.186.
buff strong leather from ox-hide, used for jacket of soldiers, bailiffs, *Com. Err.*, 4.ii.36.
bug a thing causing fear, 3 *Hen.* 6, 5.ii.2.
bugle black bead of glass, *As You Like*, 3.v.47.
bulk framework before shop, *Oth.*, 5.i.1.
bully often prefixed to express admiration or affection, *Mid. N. Dr.*, 4.ii.18.
bum-baily bailiff, *Tw. Night*, 3.iv.168.
burden bass accompaniment to tune, *As You Like*, 3.ii.232; refrain, *Tem.*, 1.ii.380.
burgonet light helmet, 2 *Hen.* 6, 5.i.200.
buss *noun* and *verb*, kiss, 2 *Hen.* 4, 2.iv.258.
buzzard a hawk of a type useless for falconry, *Tam. Shrew*, 2.i.206.
cacodemon evil spirit, *Rich.* 3, 1.iii.144.
caddis garter-tape, *Win. Tale*, 4.iv.205.
cade herring-barrel, 2 *Hen.* 6, 4.ii.32.
cadent falling, *Lear*, 1.iv.285.
Cadmus founder and king of Thebes, *Mid. N. Dr.*, 4.i.109.
caduceus Mercury's wand, *Troil. and Cres.*, 2.iii.11.
Cain-coloured reddish, the traditional colour of his hair, *Mer. Wives Win.*, 1.iv.21.
Calipolis wife of Muly Mahamet in Peele's 'Alcazar', 2 *Hen.* 4, 2.iv.169.
caliver musket, 1 *Hen.* 4, 4.ii.19.
call decoy, *John*, 3.iv.174.
callat contemptuous term for a woman, *Win. Tale*, 2.iii.90.
Cambyses vein in the style of the old play 'Cambises, King of Percia', 1 *Hen.* 4, 2.iv.376.
canary (i) sweet wine from the Canaries, *Tw. Night*, 1.iii.79; (ii) Spanish dance, *All's Well*, 2.i.73.
canker ulcer-like evil or sore, 2 *Hen.* 6, 1.ii.18; evil that like caterpillar destroys promise of our nature, *Ham.*, 5.ii.69.
canon church law, then any rule, *e.g.*, grammatical, as in *Cor.*, 3.i.90.
cantle a part cut out, *Ant. and Cleo.*, 3.x.6.
canton song, *Tw. Night*, 1.v.254.
canzonet short song, *L. Lab. Lost*, 4.ii.115.
cap-a-pe from head to foot, *Ham.*, 1.ii.200.
Capitol temple of Jupiter at Rome, *Jul. Caes.*, 1.iii.20.
capocchia simpleton, *Troil. and Cres.*, 4.ii.31.
carack galleon, *Oth.*, 1.ii.50.
carbonado meat prepared for cooking by scoring with knife, *Cor.*, 4.v.187.
carcanet a necklace, *Com. Err.*, 3.i.4.
cardecue 'quart d'ecu', French silver coin, *All's Well*, 4.iii.259.
Carduus Benedictus the blessed thistle, regarded as a kind of cure-all, *Much Ado*, 3.iv.65.
carpet *consideration*, for services not on the field of battle, *Tw. Night*, 3.iv.224.

Cataian a Chinaman, *Tw. Night*, 2.iii.73.
cataplasm poultice, *Ham.*, 4.vii.143.
catch musical composition for several voices, *Tw. Night*, 2.iii.86.
cater-cousins intimates, *Mer. Ven.*, 2.ii.119.
cat-o'-mountain a spotted creature as in Bishop's version of *Jer.*, xiii.23, 'May a man of Inde chaunge his skinne, and the catte of the mountaine her spots', *Tem.*, 4.i.260.
cautel deceit, *Ham.*, 1.iii.15.
cautelous crafty, *Jul. Caes.*, 2.i.129.
caviary salted roe of sturgeon, *Ham.*, 2.ii.430.
cerecloth winding-sheet, *Mer. Ven.*, 2.vii.51.
chace term from tennis, *Hen. 5*, 1.ii.266.
champaign flat country where view is extensive, *Tw. Night*, 2.v.142.
champion to challenge, *Mac.*, 3.i.71.
changeling child left by the fairies for one they have stolen, *Mid. N. Dr.*, 2.i.120 (here, a child adopted by the fairies).
chanson song, *Ham.*, 2.ii.414.
chape the scabbard, or its metal point, *All's Well*, 4.iii.136.
chapless with lower jaw gone, *Ham.*, 5.i.87.
chapman merchant, *L. Lab. Lost*, 2.i.16.
character *noun*, writing; *verb*, to write, *Ham.*, 1.iii.59.
chare chore, *Ant. and Cleo.*, 4.xv.75.
charge-house (doubtful) perhaps a school, *L. Lab. Lost*, 5.i.70.
Chartreux the Charterhouse in London, *Hen. 8*, 1.ii.148.
chaudron entrails, *Mac.*, 4.i.33.
chequin gold coin, *Per.*, 4.ii.25.
cheveril flexible leather, easily manipulated, *Tw. Night*, 3.i.11.
chewet a jackdaw, and so applied to the talkative, *1 Hen. 4*, 5.i.29.
chopine shoe with high sole, *Ham.*, 2.ii.422.
chough crow or jackdaw, *Tem.*, 2.i.257.
chrisom a child still in its christening-robe, *Hen. 5*, 2.iii.11.
chrysolite a precious green stone, *Oth.*, 5.ii.148.
cicatrice a mark of, or like, a scar, *Cor.*, 2.i.140.
cinquepace brisk dance, *Tw. Night*, 1.iii.122.
Cinque-ports five English channel ports, *Hen. 8*, 4.i.49.
Circe the enchantress, a draught from whose cup turned men to swine, *Com. Err.*, 5.i.270.
citizen city-bred, *Cym.*, 4.ii.8.
cittern a guitar-like instrument, often with a curiously carved head, *L. Lab. Lost*, 5.ii.603.
civet perfume, *Lear*, 4.vi.130.
clack-dish beggar's wooden disk with lid for clacking, *M. Meas.*, 3.ii.118.
clearstories upper range of windows in cathedral, *Tw. Night*, 4.ii.37.
clepe to call, *Ham.*, 1.iv.19.
clerk scholar, *Mid. N. Dr.*, 5.i.93.
clew ball of thread, *All's Well*, 1.iii.173.
climatures regions, *Ham.*, 1.i.125.
cling shrivel up, *Mac.*, 5.v.40.
clinquant glittering, *Hen. 8*, 1.i.19.
clip embrace, *John*, 5.ii.34.
clipper one who pares off the edges of coin of the realm, *Hen. 5*, 4.i.225.
clisterpipe syringe, *Oth.*, 2.i.175.
clout mark at archery, *2 Hen. 4*, 3.ii.45.
cobloaf a little loaf with a round head, *Troil. and Cres.*, 2.i.36.
cock perversion of 'God', in oaths, *2 Hen. 4*, v.i.1.
cockatrice *see* basilisk.
cockle the tares that grow with the corn, so of evil disposition, *Cor.*, 3.i.70.
cockle shell scallop shell worn by pilgrims returning from shrine of St. James of Compostella in Spain, *Ham.*, 4.v.25.
cockney useless fellow, *Tw. Night*, 4.i.13.
Cocytus one of the five rivers of the underworld, *Titus*, 2.iii.236.
coffin pie-crust, *Titus*, 5.ii.190.
cog cheat, wheedle, *Timon*, 5.i.93.
cognizance a device worn by a gentleman's retainers, so a token, *1 Hen. 6*, 2.iv.108.
coign projecting corner, *Mac.*, 1.vi.7.
coil troublesome affair, *Ham.*, 3.i.67.
coistrel knave, *Tw. Night*, 1.iii.37.
Colbrand Danish giant, conquered by Sir Guy of Warwick, *Hen. 8*, 5.iv.20.
collection inference, *Ham.*, 4.v.9.
collied overcast and troubled, *Oth.*, 2.iii.198.
Colme-kill Iona (Columba's cell), *Mac.*, 2.iv.33.
coloquintida drug from bitter-apple, *Oth.*, 1.iii.347.
Colossus huge bronze statue of Apollo at harbour of Rhodes, *Jul. Caes.*, 1.ii.136.
colour (often) deceitful appearance, *Two Gent. Ver.* 4.ii.3.
comart bargain, agreement, *Ham.*, 1.i.93.
combination alliance, treaty, *Hen. 8*, 1.i.169.
comedle mingle, *Ham.*, 3.ii.67.
commodity profit, *John*, 2.i.574; merchandise.
competitor partner, *Ant. and Cleo.*, 5.i.42.
complexion appearance as governed by the predominant 'humour', *L. Lab. Lost*, 1.ii.81.
compt reckoning and so Day of Judgment, *Oth.*, 5.ii.276.
con learn, *Jul. Caes.*, 4.iii.97.
conceit thought, *Mer. Ven.*, 1.i.92.
congied taken ceremonious farewell, *All's Well*, 4.iii.83.
conscience knowledge (shading off when of right and wrong into modern meaning), *Ham.*, 3.i.83.
constringe drawn together, *Troil. and Cres.*, 5.ii.171.
contraction pledged faith, *Ham.*, 3.iv.46.
conversion promotion, *John*, 1.i.189.
convince overpower, *Mac.*, 1.vii.64.
cony-catch to cheat, *Mer. Wives Win.*, 1.iii.31.
copatain high-crowned hat, *Tam. Shrew*, 5.i.57.
copp'd pointed, *Per.*, 1.i.101.
copy example to follow, as at head of a copy-book, *All's Well*, 1.ii.46; notion of pattern combined with that of tenure, by copyhold, *Mac.*, 3.ii.38.
coranto a dance, *Hen. 5*, 3.v.33.
Corinth Corinthian, life in Corinth was supposed to be very gay, *1 Hen. 4*, 2.iv.11.
corky pithless, *Lear*, 3.vii.28.
cornet body of mounted troops, *1 Hen. 6*, 4.iii.25.
corollary some extra, *Tem.*, 4.i.57.
corporal a senior rank in Shakespeare's day, *L. Lab. Lost*, 3.i.177.

costard head, from name for large apple, *Rich. 3*, 1.iv.151.
cote pass (from coursing, when one dog outruns the other), *Ham.*, 2.ii.315.
Cotswold, Cotsall this district in Gloucestershire was famous for its coursing contests, *Mer. Wives Win.*, 1.i.80.
counter used with *hunting* when dogs follow the scent in the wrong direction; play on this meaning and counter=debtors' prison in *Com. Err.*, 4.ii.39.
counterfeit portrait, *Mer. Ven.*, 3.ii.115.
counter-gate debtors' prison, *Mer. Wives Win.*, 3.iii.67.
courage disposition, desire, comrade (as Folio reads for 'courage' at *Ham.*, 1.iii.65).
court-hand style of script used in legal documents, *2 Hen.*, 6, 4.ii.89.
cousin, coz a relative of some kind, or courtesy title, *John*, 3.iii.17.
cozen to cheat, *Lucrece*, 387.
cozier cobbler, *Tw. Night*, 2.iii.86.
crack bright lad ('young rascal'), *Cor.*, 1.iii.68.
crank (i) *noun*, twisting passages, *Cor.*, 1.i.135; (ii) *verb*, to twist and turn, *Ven. and Ad.*, 682.
crants a garland, *Ham.*, 5.i.226.
crare small coasting vessel, *Cym.*, 4.ii.206.
cross-row the alphabet, the row in the primer containing it being marked with a cross, *Rich. 3*, 1.i.55.
crow-flower buttercup, or (perhaps) Ragged Robin, *Ham.*, 4.vii.170.
crow-keeper scare-crow, *Lear*, 4.vi.88.
crown-imperial a kind of lily, *Win. Tale*, 4.iv.126.
crusado Portuguese gold coin stamped with a cross, *Oth.*, 3.iv.23.
cry pack of hounds or rascals, *Cor.*, 3.iii.121.
cry aim 'good shot!' *John*, 2.i.196.
cullion low fellow, *Hen. 5*, 3.ii.20.
culverin cannon, long in proportion to its calibre, *1 Hen. 4*, 2.iii.50.
cunning (i) *noun*, knowledge, skill; (ii) *adj.*, learned, clever (not always in bad sense as to-day), *Rom. and Jul.*, 4.ii.2.
Cupid's flower love-in-idleness, the pansy, *Mid. N. Dr.*, 2.i.168 and 4.i.70.
curiosity critical examination, *Lear*, 1.i.6.
curious careful, *All's Well*, 1.ii.20; finely made, *Ven. and Ad.*, 734.
curst sharp in tone or temper, *Tw. Night*, 3.ii.39.
cushes thigh-armour, *1 Hen. 4*, 4.i.105.
custalorum nonsense for 'Custos Rotulorum' Keeper of the Rolls, *Mer. Wives Win.*, 1.i.6.
cut working-horse or gelding, so as term of contempt, and the point of *Tw. Night*, 2.v.81.
cynic blunt fellow like Diogenes, *Jul. Caes.*, 4.iii.131.
cypress garment of crepe, *Tw. Night*, 3.i.118.
daff put off, thrust aside, *1 Hen. 4*, 4.i.96.
Dagonet Arthur's fool, *2 Hen. 4*, 3.ii.272.
Damascus regarded as the place where Cain killed Abel, *1 Hen. 6*, 1.iii.39.
dancing horse a performing horse called Morocco exhibited by its owner Banks about 1590, *L. Lab. Lost*, 1.ii.53.
dancing-rapier for show only, *Titus*, 2.i.39.
Daphne a nymph loved by Apollo and turned to a laurel tree, *Mid. N. Dr.*, 2.i.231.
dare (fowling term) to render the bird immobile by dazzling it by some device, *Hen. 5*, 4.ii.36.
darraign set in order, *3 Hen. 6*, 2.ii.72.
daub keep up the pretence, *Lear*, 4.i.53.
daubery pretence, *Mer. Wives Win.*, 4.ii.155.
day-bed couch, *Tw. Night*, 2.v.45.
dearth value, *Ham.*, 5.ii.117.
death-practis'd marked for death by his enemies, *Lear*, 4.vi.277.
death-token the mark of the plague and so of death, *Troil. and Cres.*, 2.iii.172.
debile feeble, *Cor.*, 1.ix.48.
deboshed debauched, *Lear*, 1.iv.241.
decimation execution of every tenth man, *Timon*, 5.iv.31.
deck pack of cards, *3 Hen. 6*, 5.i.44.
decoct heat up, *Hen. 5*, 3.v.20.
defunctive funereal, *Phoenix*, 13.
degree the principle of order by which persons (or objects) stand in proper relation to one another, *Troil. and Cres.*, 1.iii.109.
delate, dilate express at length, *Ham.*, 1.ii.38.
delation expression of accusation, *Oth.*, 3.iii.127.
demerit (i) merit, *Oth.*, 1.ii.22; (ii) fault, *Mac.*, 4.iii.226.
demi-cannon gun of large calibre, *Tam. Shrew*, 4.iii.88.
denier French copper coin of small value, *Rich. 3*, 1.ii.251.
dependency objects depending, *Cym.*, 2.iii.118.
depose (i) set aside, *Rich. 2*, 3.ii.56; (ii) assert on oath, *M. Meas.*, 5.i.196; (iii) examine on oath, *Rich. 2*, 1.iii.30.
deputation office of deputy, *Troil. and Cres.*, 1.iii.152; *1 Hen. 4*, 4.iii.87.
dern dark, *Lear*, 3.vii.62.
derogate unworthy, to prove unworthy of position or descent, *Lear*, i.iv.280.
descant comment (from the term that refers to the upper and more elaborate part of a musical composition), *Rich. 3*, 3.vii.49.
determinate purposed, conclusive, *Tw. Night*, 2.i.9; *Oth.*, 4.ii.226.
determination decision, *Troil. and Cres.*, 2.ii.170.
determine end, *Cor.*, 3.iii.43.
deuce-ace throw of two and one at dice, *L. Lab. Lost*, 1.ii.46.
dexter right, *Troil. and Cres.*, 4.v.128.
dial watch, *As You Like*, 2.vii.20.
diapason bass part, *Lucrece*, 1132.
difference distinction of rank or descent or character, *All's Well*, 2.iii.119.
diffidence distrust, *1 Hen. 6*, 3.iii.10.
digression transgression, *L. Lab. Lost*, 1.ii.112.
dilate *see* delate.
dilemmas alternatives, *All's Well*, 3.vi.67.
disaster unfavorable aspect, *Ham.*, 1.i.118.
discandy melt, *Ant. and Cleo.*, 4.xii.22.
discernings faculties requisite for judgment, *Lear*, 1.iv.227.
discomfortable discouraging, *Rich. 2*, 3.ii.36.
discontent one not satisfied with his conditions, *Ant. and Cleo.*, 1.iv.39.
discourse power or process of reasoning, *Ham.*, 4.iv.36; *Troil. and Cres.*, 5.ii.140.

discover to reveal what is known to the speaker, *Rom. and Jul.*, 3.i.139; to find out, *Rich. 2*, 2.iii.33.
discovery revelation, *Ham.*, 2.ii.293.
discreet indiscreet, 2 *Hen. 4*, 2.iv.240.
disguise state of drunkenness, *Ant. and Cleo.*, 2.vii.122.
disme tenth man, *Troil. and Cres.*, 2.ii.19.
dismount draw sword from its scabbard, *Tw. Night*, 3.iv.213.
dispark open land to public use, *Rich. 2*, 3.i.23.
dispose *noun*, disposal, *Two Gent. Ver.* 2.vii.86; disposition, *Troil. and Cres.*, 2.iii.159; *verb*, arrange, *John*, 3.iv.11.
disposer one who has the matter in her control, *Troil. and Cres.*, 3.i.81.
disposition arrangement, *Oth.*, 1.iii.236; behaviour, mood, *Ham.*, 1.v.172.
disproperty to take away from their possession, *Cor.*, 2.i.238.
distance dissension, *Mac.*, 3.i.115; space between fencers, *Rom. and Jul.*, 2.iv.21.
distemperature lack of order and so inclemency in weather or illness in man, *Mid. N. Dr.*, 2.i.106; *Per.*, 5.i.27.
distinction judgment, *Troil. and Cres.*, 3.ii.26; the clear and true apprehension of the matter, *Cym.*, 5.v.384.
distinctly in several separate parts, *Tem.*, 1.ii.200.
distinguishment distinction, *Win. Tale*, 2.i.86.
distract *adj.*, divided, and so divided in mind, crazed, *Lov. Comp.*, 231; *Jul. Caes.*, 4.iii.153; *verb*, to divide out, *Oth.*, 1.iii.323.
distrain to take legal possession of goods, etc., to cover debt, to take over, *Rich. 2*, 2.iii.131.
distressful earned by toil and sweat, *Hen. 5*, 4.i.266.
divers diverse, unorthodox in *Hen. 8*, 5.iii.18.
division proper disposition of forces, *Oth.*, 1.i.23; decorative elaboration of a musical theme, 1 *Hen. 4*, 3.i.210.
doctrine precept, principle, learning, *L. Lab. Lost*, 4.iii.346.
document a piece of instruction, *Ham.*, 4.v.175.
doit a Dutch coin of small value, *Cor.*, 4.iv.17.
dollar English name for German thaler, a large silver coin, *Mac.*, 1.ii.64.
dominical letter which was printed in red in the almanacs, so a reference to the lady's hair and complexion, *L. Lab. Lost*, 5.ii.44.
doom judgment, 2 *Hen. 6*, 3.i.281; *day of doom*, *doomsday*, day of one's death, 3 *Hen. 6*, 5.vi.93; *Rom. and Jul.*, 5.iii.233.
double-fatal the yew yielding the wood for bow and poisonous berries, *Rich. 2*, 3.ii.117.
doublet and hose the dress of a man, hence his characteristics, *As You Like*, 3.ii.204; 2 *Hen. 6*, 4.vii.47, implies that plain men have to go simply dressed without a cloak.
dout extinguish, *Hen. 5*, 4.ii.11.
dowlas coarse linen, 1 *Hen. 4*, 3.iii.68.
dowle feather, *Tem.*, 3.iii.65.
doxy beggar's trull, *Win. Tale*, 4.iii.2.
drachma silver coin of antiquity, *Jul. Caes.*, 3.ii.243.
draught cesspool, *Timon*, 5.i.100.
draw dry-foot to track by the scent of the footmarks, *Com. Err.*, 4.ii.39.
drawer tapster, 1 *Hen. 4*, 2.iv.7.
dribbling falling wide of the mark, *M. Meas.*, 1.iii.2.
drift design, intention, *Rom. and Jul.*, 4.i.114; *Troil. and Cres.*, 3.iii.113.
drollery puppet-show, *Tem.*, 3.iii.21.
drumble to move slowly, *Mer. Wives Win.*, 3.iii.130.
ducat gold coin of about ten shillings value, Italian silver coin, *Ham.*, 2.ii.362.
dudgeon kind of wood used in dagger-hilts, so the hilt itself, *Mac.*, 2.i.46.
duello the rules and etiquette of duelling, *L. Lab. Lost*, 1.ii.169.
dump melancholy tune, *Two Gent. Ver.*, 3.ii.85.
dup open, *Ham.*, 4.v.51.
durance lasting nature, *Com. Err.*, 4.iii.24.
eager sharp, cutting, physically or mentally, *Rich. 2*, 1.i.49; acid, *Ham.*, 1.v.69.
eagerly relentlessly, *Hen. 8*, 4.ii.24.
eale (perhaps) for evil at *Ham.*, 1.iv.36.
ean to give birth, *Mer. Ven.*, 1.iii.82.
ear plough, cultivate, *Rich. 2*, 3.ii.212.
earn yearn, *Hen. 5*, 2.iii.3.
earnest token payment as pledge of some service or obligation, *Hen. 5*, 5.i.58.
eche eke out, *Per.*, 3. *Prol.*13.
ecstasy out of one's normal state, madness, stupor, *Tem.* 3.iii.108; *Ham.*, 2.i.102.
effigies image, *As You Like*, 2.vii.193.
eftsoons soon, *Per.*, 5.i.253.
egregious notable, *Cym.*, 5.v.211.
eisel vinegar, *Ham.*, 5.i.270.
eld old age, *M. Meas.*, 3.i.36.
elder-gun child's toy gun, *Hen. 5*, 4.i.196.
elf tangle, *Lear*, 2.iii.10.
elf-locks tangled strands, *Rom. and Jul.*, 1.iv.90.
elm used as a prop for vines, *Com. Err.*, 2.ii.173.
embarquements restraints, *Cor.*, 1.x.22.
embossed (i) swollen, *As You Like*, 2.vii.67; (ii) with mouth covered with foam from exertion, *Tam. Shrew*, Ind.i.15.
empiric, empiricutic unprofessional or quack practitioner and his type of prescription, *All's Well*, 2.i.121; *Cor.*, 2.i.110.
emulous (in both good and bad sense) seeking praise or glory, *Troil. and Cres.*, 2.iii.225.
enew to drive, as the falcon, the prey into the water, *M. Meas.*, 3.i.92.
enfeoff'd became the vassal of, gave himself up to, 1 *Hen. 4*, 3.ii.69.
engine contrivance, weapon of war, *Troil. and Cres.*, 1.iii.208; *Oth.*, 4.ii.216.
engineer, ingener an inventive mind in words or of devices of war, *Oth.*, 2.i.65.
ensconce take shelter, *Mer. Wives Win.*, 3.iii.77.
enseamed greasy, *Ham.*, 3.iv.92.
entertain receive, as a follower, *Lear*, 3.vi.78.
Ephesian companion, *Mer. Wives Win.*, 4.v.16.
epithet, epitheton expression, *Oth.*, 1.i.14.
equinox equal poise, as day and night are equal at the equinox, *Oth.*, 2.iii.116.
ergo therefore, *Com. Err.*, 4.iii.51.
eringo candied sweetmeat, *Mer. Wives Win.*, 5.v.19.
escoted maintained, *Ham.*, 2.ii.342.
esperance hope, *Lear*, 4.i.4; Percy's battle-cry, 1 *Hen. 4*, 5.ii.97.

estridge ostrich, 1 *Hen.* 4, 4.i.98.
even Christian fellow Christian, *Ham.*, 5.i.28.
evitate avoid, *Mer. Wives Win.*, 5.v.215.
exactly completely, *Ham.*, 1.ii.200.
except object, play on legal phrase 'except as before excepted' at *Tw. Night*, 1.iii.6.
exception objection, *Ham.*, 5.ii.223.
excitement encouragement, *Ham.*, 4.iv.58.
excrement what grows from the body as nails or hair, *Ham.*, 3.iv.121.
exempt separated from, free from, *As You Like*, 2.i.15; *Timon*, 4.ii.31.
exhalation meteor, *Jul. Caes.*, 2.1.44.
exhale draw (your sword), *Hen.* 5, 2.i.60.
exhibition a maintenance allowance, *Two Gent. Ver.*, 1.iii.69.
exigent crisis, *Jul. Caes.*, 5.i.19.
exorciser, exorcist one who calls up spirits, *Cym.*, 4.ii.277.
expectancy one in whom hopes are placed, *Ham.*, 3.i.152.
expedience haste, purpose requiring haste, *Ant. and Cleo.*, 1.ii.172.
expiate (literally) ended – the hour of execution has come, *Rich.* 3, 3.iii.23.
expostulate to discuss, *Ham.*, 2.ii.86.
exposture exposure, *Cor.*, 4.i.36.
express (as in 'express likeness') true to divine pattern, *Ham.*, 2.ii.304.
expressure description, *Tw. Night*, 2.iii.147.
exsufficate puffed out, *Oth.*, 3.iii.186.
extemporal extempore, *L. Lab. Lost*, 4.ii.47.
extirp to weed out, *M. Meas.*, 3.ii.95.
extraught descended, 3 *Hen.*, 6, 2.ii.142.
extravagancy, extravagant wandering, *Ham.*, 1.i.154.
eyas young hawk in training, *Ham.*, 2.ii.335; so *eyas-musket* of a boy at *Mer. Wives Win.*, 3.iii.18.
eye-glass lens of eye, *Win. Tale*, 1.ii.268.
face to trim a garment, *Tam. Shrew*, 4.iii.122.
face royal refers to effigy on gold coin called 'a royal', 2 *Hen.* 4, 1.ii.22.
facinerous wicked, *All's Well*, 2.iii.28.
fact what has been done, action, *Mac.*, 3.vi.10; way of acting, *Win. Tale*, 3.ii.83.
faction a party, group, *Jul. Caes.*, 2.i.77.
fadge come off, *Tw. Night*, 2.ii.31.
fading refrain of popular song, *Win. Tale*, 4.iv.193.
fairing present, *L. Lab. Lost*, 5.ii.2.
faitor cheat (but Pistol's meaning, if any, is doubtful), 2 *Hen.* 4, 2.iv.150.
falling sickness epilepsy, *Jul. Caes.*, 1.ii.253.
fame rumour, *Ant. and Cleo.*, 2.ii.167; reputation, *Ant. and Cleo.*, 3.i.15.
fan winnowing-fan, *Troil. and Cres.*, 1.iii.27.
fanatical phantasime individual with crazy but fixed notions, *L. Lab. Lost*, 5.i.16.
fang seize, *Timon*, 4.iii.23.
fantastic merely in the fancy, *Rich.* 2, 1.iii.299; unusual, almost incredible, *Troil. and Cres.*, 5.v.38.
fantastico foolish conceited individual, *Rom. and Jul.*, 2.iv.28.
fantasy mere fancy, *Ham.*, 1.i.54; musings prompted by responsibility or care, *Jul. Caes.*, 2.i.231.
fap drunk, *Mer. Wives Win.*, 1.i.160.
farborough third borough, constable, *L. Lab. Lost*, 1.i.182.
farced stuffed out with the appearance of dignity, *Hen.* 5, 4.i.259.
fardel pack or burden, *Ham.*, 3.i.76.
farrow litter of pigs, *Mac.*, 4.i.65.
farthingale hooped petticoat, *Mer. Wives Win.*, 3.iii.55.
fashions a disease in horses, *Tam. Shrew*, 3.ii.49.
fat hot, 1 *Hen.* 4, 2.iv.1. (*cp. Ham.*, 5.ii.279).
fat vat, *Ant. and Cleo.*, 2.vii.113.
fatigate exhausted, *Cor.*, 2.ii.115.
fault break in the scent in hunting, *Tw. Night*, 2.v.117.
favour mercy, *Ant. and Cleo.*, 3.xiii.133; charm, *Oth.*, 4.iii.20; token of someone's favour, *Rich.* 2, 5.iii.18; features, *Jul. Caes.*, 2.i.76.
feat neat, becoming, *Tem.*, 2.i.264.
featly with neatness and agility, *Tem.*, 1.ii.379.
feature figure (not face), *Much Ado*, 3.i.60.
fedary, federary accomplice, *Win. Tale*, 2.i.90.
fee *sold in fee*, sold with absolute and perpetual possession, *Ham.*, 4.iv.22; *fee-grief*, grief possessed by some individual, *Mac.*, 4.iii.196; *fee-simple*, the most complete and absolute form of tenure or possession, *Rom. and Jul.*, 3.i.31.
feeder servant, *Ant. and Cleo.*, 3.xiii.109.
felicitate happy, *Lear*, 1.i.74.
fere spouse, *Per.*, 1. *Prol.*21.
fern-seed reputed to make the possessor invisible, 1 *Hen.* 4, 2.i.86.
festinate speedy, *Lear*, 3.vii.10.
fetch device, *Ham.*, 2.i.38.
fettle make ready, *Rom. and Jul.*, 3.v.153.
fico, fig, figo contemptuous expression, often accompanied by insulting gesture, 2 *Hen.* 4, 5.iii.117.
fights protective screens used in fighting at sea, *Mer. Wives Win.*, 2.ii.123.
figure appearance, real, imaginary, or assumed, *Much Ado*, 1.i.12; *Mer. Wives Win.*, 4.ii.193; writing, *Timon*, 5.i.152.
file list, *Mac.*, 3.i.94.
fills shafts, *Troil. and Cres.*, 3.ii.44.
film gossamer, *Rom. and Jul.*, 1.iv.63.
fine end, *All's Well*, 4.iv.35; conclusion of legal agreement as in *fine and recovery*, a process to break an entail and convert the tenure to fee-simple, *Mer. Wives Win.*, 4.ii.188.
fineless without end, *Oth.*, 3.iii.177.
fire-drake meteor, and so in slang a red nose, *Hen.* 8, 5.iv.41.
firk beat, *Hen.* 5, 4.iv.28.
fit spasm or attack of some illness, *Ham.*, 4.i.8; trick of grimacing, *Hen.* 8., 1.iii.7; perhaps punning on 'fit' meaning canto or division of a poem, *Troil. and Cres.*, 3.i.54.
fitchew polecat, applied to a courtezan, *Oth.*, 4.i.144.
fives a disease of horses, *Tam. Shrew*, 3.ii.50.
flamen priest in ancient Rome, *Cor.*, 2.i.203.
flap-dragon something served in flaming spirits at Christmas parties, *L. Lab. Lost*, 5.i.38; *verb*, to gulp down, *Win. Tale*, 3.iii.95.
flapjack pancake, *Per.*, 2.i.82.
flaw gust of wind, or passion, *Cor.*, 5.iii.74.
fleckel'd dappled, *Rom. and Jul.*, 2.iii.3.
fleer sneering grimace, *Oth.*, 4.i.82.

flesh (to give a hound the flesh of the victim to rouse its keenness) so to introduce an untried soldier to bloodshed, *Lear*, 2.ii.42; *flesh his sword*, use it in his first fight, 1 *Hen.* 6, 4.vii.36.
fleshment the satisfaction of a first success, *Lear*, 2.ii.118.
flew'd with large chaps, *Mid. N. Dr.*, 4.i.117.
flirt-gill loose woman, *Rom. and Jul.*, 2.iv.149.
flote sea, *Tem.*, 1.ii.234.
flourish embellishment, *L. Lab. Lost*, 2.i.14.
flower-de-luce iris. *Win. Tale*, 4.iv.127; the lily of the French coat of arms, and so applied by Henry to Katherine, *Hen.* 5, 5.ii.208.
flux secretion, *As You Like*, 3.ii.61.
fob set aside by trickery, *Cor.*, 1.i.92.
foil (i) setting of a jewel, so something that shows up the value of an act or accomplishment, *Ham.*, 5.ii.247; (ii) *put to the foil*, deprive of commendation, *Tem.*, 3.i.46.
foin thrust with rapier, *Mer. Wives Win.*, 2.iii.22.
foison harvest, *Tem.*, 4.i.110.
fondly foolishly, 2 *Hen.* 4, 4.ii.119.
foot-cloth saddle-cloth hanging almost to ground, 2 *Hen.* 6, 4.i.54.
foppish foolish, *Lear*, 1.iv.165.
force (*see* 'farce') stuff, *Troil. and Cres.*, 2.iii.217.
forehorse leading horse as in a tandem, *All's Well*, 2.i.30.
forgetive (perhaps from 'forge' *cp. Mer. Wives Win.*, 4.ii.199) shaping, inventive, 2 *Hen.* 4, 4.iii.98.
fosset-seller vendor of taps (faucets) for barrels, *Cor.*, 2.i.65.
fox a sword (some makes were marked with a wolf's head), *Hen.* 5, 4.iv.9.
fracted broken, *Hen.* 5, 2.i.121.
frampold unpleasant, *Mer. Wives Win.*, 2.ii.82.
frank sty, 2 *Hen.* 4, 2.ii.140.
franklin freeholder but not numbered among the county families, *Cym.*, 3.ii.76.
frayed frightened, *Troil. and Cres.*, 3.ii.31.
freshes springs of fresh water, *Tem.*, 3.ii.64.
fret to stop the string (with a pun on the normal meaning of 'fret'), *Ham.*, 3.ii.362.
frets the points marked on the neck of a stringed instrument where the fingers may stop the string, *Lucrece*, 1140.
frieze coarse cloth, *Oth.*, 2.i.126.
frippery old clothes shop, *Tem.*, 4.i.225.
frontier advanced fort, 1 *Hen.* 4 2.iii.49; frontier fortress, *Ham.*, 4.iv.16.
frontlet band on forehead, so frown at *Lear*, 1.iv.187.
frush to batter, *Troil. and Cres.*, 5.vi.29.
fullam kind of loaded dice, *Mer. Wives Win.*, 1.iii.82.
fustian (i) coarse cloth; (ii) ranting, 2 *Hen.* 4, 2.iv.179.
fustilarian (comic formation) 2 *Hen.* 4, 2.i.58.
gaberdine kind of cloak, *Mer. Ven.*, 1.iii.107.
gad sharp metal point, *Titus*, 4.i.104; *upon the gad*, on the spur of the moment, *Lear*, 1.ii.26.
gage pledge, as glove thrown down to pledge the owner to combat, *Rich.* 2, 4.i.25.
gainsay to forbid, to prevent, *Troil. and Cres.*, 4.v.132.
Galen Greek who became physician to the Emperor Marcus Aurelius; his voluminous writings on medical topics were authoritative in Shakespeare's day, *All's Well*, 2.iii.11.
gall bile; as the liver was supposed to provide the capacity for resentment and courage it signifies manly spirit at *Ham.*, 2.ii.572.
Gallian French, *Cym.*, 1.vi.65.
galliard a lively dance usually in triple time, *Tw. Night*, 1.iii.125.
galliass large type of galley, *Tam. Shrew*, 2.i.370.
gallimaufry hotch potch, *Win. Tale*, 4.iv.321.
gallow to terrify, *Lear*, 3.ii.44.
gallowglass heavy-armed footman in army of Irish or from Scottish isles, *Mac.*, 1.ii.13.
gamut musical scale, *Tam. Shrew*, 3.i.65.
garboil disturbance, *Ant. and Cleo.*, 1.iii.61.
gaskins wide breeches, *Tw. Night*, 1.v.23.
gasted frightened, *Lear*, 2.i.55.
gastness signs of fear, *Oth.*, 5.i.106.
gaudy night feast, *Ant. and Cleo.*, 3.xiii.183.
gawds gay trifles, *Mid. N. Dr.*, 1.i.33.
gaze centre of attraction, *Mac.*, 5.viii.24.
geck butt, *Tw. Night*, 5.i.330.
geminy twin pair, *Mer. Wives Win.*, 2.ii.8.
generosity the well born, *Cor.*, 1.i.209.
generous well born, and so acting like a gentleman, *Ham.*, 4.vii.135.
genius the spirit that is assigned to each individual as a guardian, *Mac.*, 3.i.55; so peculiar bent or nature, *Tw. Night*, 3.iv.123.
gennet small horse, *Oth.*, 1.i.114.
gentility gentlemanly conduct, *L. Lab. Lost*, 1.i.127.
gentle of good birth, *Rich.* 3, 1.iii.73.
gentleness courtesy, *Troil. and Cres.*, 4.i.22.
George small figure of St. George slaying the dragon worn as a pendant by Knights of the Garter, *Rich.* 3, 4.iv.366.
german, germane akin, *Oth.*, 1.i.114; *cousin-german*, first cousin, *Troil. and Cres.*, 4.v.121; related to the matter in hand, *Ham.*, 5.ii.155.
germen germ, seed, *Lear*, 3.ii.8.
gest (i) warlike feat, *Ant. and Cleo.*, 4.viii.2; (ii) time limit, *Win. Tale*, 1.ii.41.
ghostly concerned with spiritual welfare, *Rom. and Jul.*, 3.iii.49.
gib male cat, *Ham.*, 3.iv.190.
gig whipping-top, *L. Lab. Lost*, 4.iii.163.
giglet, -ot a wanton, *M. Meas.*, 5.i.345.
gillyvor gillyflower, *Win. Tale*, 4.iv.82.
gimmaled jointed, *Hen.* 5, 4.ii.49.
gimmer links in mechanism of clock, 1 *Hen.* 6, 1.ii.41.
glance satirical comment, *As You Like*, 2.vii.57.
glass hour glass, *Tem.*, 1.ii.240.
glass eyes spectacles, *Lear*, 4.vi.170.
glaze glare, *Jul. Caes.*, 1.iii.21.
gleek to joke, gibe, *Mid. N. Dr.*, 3.i.134.
globe head, *Ham.*, 1.v.97.
gloss explanation, excuse, so fair outward show, *Timon*, 1.ii.16.
gloze to explain, *Hen* 5, 1.ii.40; to comment deceitfully, *Titus*, 4.iv.35.
gobbet portions of flesh, 2 *Hen.* 6, 4.i.85.
God-den, God-i-goden (and similar forms) God give you good even! *Rom. and Jul.*, 1.ii.57 and 3.v.172.
God dild you God yield, or repay, you! *Ham.*, 4.v.40.
good year a common exclamation, without any

particular meaning, *Mer. Wives Win.*, 1.iv.110; used in an imprecation, *Lear*, 5.iii.24.
goose tailor's iron, *Mac.*, 2.iii.15.
gorbellied fat, overfed, 1 *Hen. 4*, 2.ii.85.
Gordian knot an oracle foretold that the man who could unloose this intricate knot, in the acropolis of Gordium, would be ruler of the East; Alexander the Great cut it; so of solving a problem, *Hen. 5*, 1.i.46.
gorget armour for throat, *Troil. and Cres.*, 1.iii.174.
Gorgon a fabulous monster believed able to turn the beholder to stone, *Mac.*, 2.iii.70.
gospell'd like good Christians, *Mac.*, 3.i.87.
goss gorse, *Tem.*, 4.i.180.
gossip one associated with parents at baptism of their child, a godparent, *Hen. 8*, 5.v.12; friend, woman fond of idle talk, *Titus*, 4.ii.151.
gossiping enjoying the 'gossips' feast' at the 'rebirth' of the lost sons, *Com. Err.*, 5.i.418.
gourd loaded dice, *Mer. Wives Win.*, 1.iii.82.
gout drop, *Mac.*, 2.i.46.
government self-control, conduct, *Oth.*, 3.iii.260; accordance with musical requirements, *Mid. N. Dr.*, 5.i.123.
graceful blest with the grace of God, *Win. Tale*, 5.i.171.
graff shoot, scion, *Per.*, 5.i.59.
graft to insert shoots and so to incorporate, *Mac.*, 4.iii.51.
grafter the tree from which the shoot for grafting has been taken, *Hen. 5*, 3.v.9.
grain *in grain*, dyed in a colour that will not wash out, *Tw. Night*, 1.v.222; *against the grain*, contrary to inclination, *Cor.*, 2.iii.230.
gramercy expression of thanks, *Mer. Ven.*, 2.ii.110.
grange a lonely house in the country, *Oth.*, 1.i.107.
grate to fret, annoy, *Ant. and Cleo.*, 1.i.18.
gratulate gratifying, *M. Meas.*, 5.i.527.
greasily indecently, *L. Lab. Lost*, 4.i.130.
great *great morning*, broad day, *Troil. and Cres.*, 4.iii.1; *great belly doublet*, one stuffed with lining; but Falstaff provided the stuffing himself, *Hen. 5*, 4.vii.46.
Greek light fellow or wench, *Tw. Night*, 4.i.17.
Greensleeves a ballad tune not tending to godliness, *Mer. Wives Win.*, 2.i.55.
grievance inconvenience, affliction, *Two Gent. Ver.*, 1.i.17.
grieve regret, *Lear*, 4.iii.53.
gripe vulture, *Lucrece*, 543.
grize step, *Tw. Night*, 3.i.121; *Oth.*, 1.iii.200.
groat fourpenny piece, *Mer. Wives Win.*, 1.i.139.
ground the theme in the bass over which the descant (q.v.) is constructed, so the subject to be elaborated, *Rich. 3*, 3.vii.49.
groundling one who stood in the yard of the theatre, the cheapest part, *Ham.*, 3.ii.10.
guard trimming to a garment, *M. Meas.*, 3.i.98; *guarded*, ornamented, *Hen. 8*, Prol. 16, *velvet-guards*, the women wearing them, 1 *Hen. 4*, 3.i.257.
guardant protector, 1 *Hen. 6*, 4.vii.9.
guidon pennant, *Hen. 5*, 4.ii.60.
guilder Dutch coin, but for money generally, *Com. Err.*, 1.i.8.
guise style, custom, 2 *Hen. 6*, 1.iii.40.
gules heraldic name for 'red', *Ham.*, 2.ii.451.
gurnet fish with large head, 1 *Hen. 4*, 4.ii.12.
gust taste, *Son.*, 114. 11.
gyves fetters, *Ham.*, 4.vii.21.
h *see* ache, *Much Ado*, 3.iv.48.
habiliments costume, *Tam. Shrew*, 4.iii.166.
habit costume, (sometimes combined with idea of corresponding) demeanour, *As You Like*, 3.ii.279.
habited dressed, *Titus*, 2.iii.57.
habitude nature, *Lov. Comp.*, 114.
hack of doubtful meaning, *Mer. Wives Win.*, 2.i.45.
hackney promiscuous wench, *L. Lab. Lost*, 3.i.29.
haggard wild female hawk in training, *Tam. Shrew*, 4.i.177; so as *adj.*, of woman disobedient or unfaithful, *Oth.*, 3.iii.264.
haggled with many wounds, *Hen. 5*, 4.vi.11.
hair *against the hair*, contrary to nature, *Troil. and Cres.*, 1.ii.27; *courser's hair*, supposed to come to life in water, *Ant. and Cleo.*, 1.ii.187.
halberd axe-like weapon with long handle, *Rich. 3*, 1.ii.40.
halcyon (from Halcyone, changed with her husband Ceyx to a type of kingfisher; their breeding season in winter was supposed to be favoured with fine weather) calm, happy, 1 *Hen. 6*, 1.ii.131; a dead kingfisher if hung up was supposed to act as a weather-cock, *Lear*, 2.ii.73.
half-cheek'd applied to inefficient or deficient bit, *Tam. Shrew*, 3.ii.53.
half-faced thin faced (like the profile on the groat, a thin coin), *John*, 1.i.92; half seen, 2 *Hen. 6*, 4.i.98.
half sword most closely engaged, 1 *Hen. 4*, 2.iv.157.
halidom, holidame an oath (on holy relics) reduced by Shakespeare's time to a mere asseveration, *Two Gent. Ver.*, 4.ii.131.
Hallowmas 1st Nov. (All Saints' Day), *Rich. 2*, 5.i.80.
hand fast marriage contract, *Cym.*, 1.v.78.
handsaw (dialect form of 'heronshaw') heron, *Ham.*, 2.ii.375.
hangers straps supporting scabbard, *Ham.*, 5.ii.154.
harbinger forerunner, *Ham.*, 1.i.122.
Harry ten shillings half-sovereign coined in reign of Henry VII, 2 *Hen. 4*, 3.ii.216.
hatchment tablet showing the coat of arms of the deceased, *Ham.*, 4.v.210.
haught haughty, 3 *Hen. 6*, 2.i.169.
haughty ambitious, *Rich. 3*, 4.ii.37.
havoc general slaughter, *Jul. Caes.*, 3.i.274; *Cor.*, 3.i.275; *cries on havoc*, the heap of slain speaks of an indiscriminate slaughter, *Ham.*, 5.ii.356.
hay (i) home thrust in fencing, *Rom. and Jul.*, 2.iv.26; (ii) country dance, *L. Lab. Lost*, 5.i.134.
hazard game with dice, *Hen. 5*, 3.vii.83; risk, *Cor.*, 2.iii.253; term from tennis indicating a scoring stroke, *Hen. 5*, 1.ii.263.
head muster of men, usually soldiers; rioters at *Ham.*, 4.v.98.
headland part of field left, for convenience of working, unploughed till the very end, 2 *Hen. 4*, 5.i.13.
hebona (Folio reads *hebenon*) a poison (perhaps henbane, although there seems some reference to ebony), *Ham.*, 1.v.62.
Hecate divinity of classical antiquity, associated with

ghost world and worshipped in triform shape at cross-roads; *triple Hecate*, as Cynthia in heaven, Diana on earth, and Proserpine in hell, *Mid. N. Dr.*, 5.i.373.
hectic continuous fever, *Ham.*, 4.iii.66.
hedge-pig hedgehog, *Mac.*, 4.i.2.
heft heaving, *Win. Tale*, 2.i.45.
hemp-seed destined for the hangman's hempen rope, 2 *Hen.* 4, 2.i.56.
hent grasp, or possibly occasion (hint), *Ham.*, 3.iii.88.
herbs of grace rue, *Ham.*, 4.v.179.
Hercules and his load, the sign hung outside the Globe Theatre showed Hercules carrying the world on his shoulders, *Ham.*, 2.ii.357.
Herod *see* out-herod.
hest command, *L. Lab. Lost*, 5.ii.65.
hide fox warning in game of hide-and-seek, *Ham.*, 4.ii.29.
high and low dice loaded to throw high or low numbers, *Mer. Wives Win.*, 1.iii.83.
hight named, *L. Lab. Lost*, 1.i.168.
hind female deer, *As You Like*, 3.ii.91.
hint (sometimes spelt 'hent' as at *Oth.*, (Q1) 1.iii.142), occasion, *Tem.*, 1.ii.134.
hipped lame, owing to injury to hip-bone, *Tam. Shrew*, 3.ii.46.
Hiren pun on 'iron' and Hyrin (Irene) a character in a play by Peele, 2 *Hen.* 4, 2.iv.165.
hive straw hat, *Lov. Comp.*, 8.
hoar whitish, *Ham.*, 4.vii.168.
Hobbididence (with Obidicut, Mahu, Modo, Flibberdigibbet), fiends, *Lear*, 4.i.61.
hobby-horse 'the figure of a horse' fastened round the waist of a morris dancer; the antics of this particular character in the dance were offensive to the Puritans, and the part came to be omitted, *Ham.*, 3.ii.130; a loose character, *L. Lab. Lost*, 3.i.27.
holding consistency, *All's Well*, 4.ii.27; chorus of song, *Ant. and Cleo.*, 2.vii.109.
holidame *see* halidom.
holy-ale (a coinage, by analogy with 'church-ale', to rhyme with 'festival'; the text has 'holy dayes'), festivity, *Per.*, 1. *Gower*.6.
holy-rood day 14th Sept., the feast of the Holy Cross, 1 *Hen.* 4, 1.i.52.
holy thistle *see* Carduus Benedictus.
honey stalks clover stalks, *Titus*, 4.iv.91.
honorificabilitudinitatibus stock example of long word, *L. Lab. Lost*, 5.i.37.
hood to blindfold hawk (when unhooded it bates), *Hen.* 5, 3.vii.108.
hoodman blind blind-man's-buff, *Ham.*, 3.iv.77.
horn-book sheet containing alphabet, etc. for children, protected with transparent covering of horn, *L. Lab. Lost*, 5.i.41.
horologe clock, *Oth.*, 2.iii.122.
hose includes various types of breeches and clothing (not stockings) for the lower limbs, 1 *Hen.* 4, 2.iv.208.
howlet owl, *Mac.*, 4.i.17.
hox hamstring, *Win. Tale*, 1.ii.244.
hoy ferry, small vessel, *Com. Err.*, 4.iii.35.
hugger, mugger secretly and without due form, *Ham.*, 4.v.81.
hull to furl sails and drift with the tide, *Tw. Night*, 1.v.191; so of the mind, *Hen.* 8, 2.iv.199.
humorous humid, *Rom. and Jul.*, 2.i.31.
humour corresponding to the four elements (earth, air, fire, water) were the four humours – black bile, blood, bile, phlegm. According as one or other predominated in a man's system so his temperament was choleric or phlegmatic or melancholy, and his complexion in keeping. The term was overworked, and parodied in Nym's use of it, e.g. *Mer. Wives Win.*, 1.i.120.
hunts-up song to rouse hunters, warning of daybreak, *Rom. and Jul.*, 3.v.34.
hurricano waterspout, *Lear*, 3.ii.2.
Hydra many-headed monster, *Oth.*, 2.iii.295.
Hymen whose presence was invoked at Greek marriages, so regarded as god of marriage; the torch was one of his symbols, *Tem.*, 4.i.23.
hyperbole figure of speech characterised by exaggeration, *L. Lab. Lost*, 5.ii.407.
Hyperion god of the sun, *Ham.*, 1.ii.140.
Hyrcania south-east shore of Caspian sea; regarded as wild country and home of savage beasts; *th' Hyrcanian beast*, the tiger, *Ham.*, 2.ii.444. (Virgil mentions tigers of Hyrcania.)
hysterica passio hysteria, *Lear*, 2.iv.56.
Icarus son of Daedalus; father and son imprisoned by Minos of Crete escaped by using artificial wings; Icarus flew too near the sun, the wax of his wings melted and he fell into the Aegean Sea, 3 *Hen.* 6, 5.iv.21.
ice-brook as giving the keenest temper to the sword-blade, *Oth.*, 5.ii.256.
Iceland dog type of pet dog, used in derision at *Hen.* 5, 2.i.40.
idea image, *Rich.* 3, 3.vii.13.
Ides *of March*, 15th March, *Jul. Caes.*, 1.ii.18.
ignominy, ignomy disgrace, *Troil. and Cres.*, 5.x.33.
illness ruthlessness, *Mac.*, 1.v.17.
ill-temper'd the humours being badly mixed, *Jul. Caes.*, 4.iii.114 (*see* humour).
illustrious dim (not lustrous), *Cym.*, 1.vi.108.
imaginary imaginative, *Hen.* 5, *Prol*.18.
imbar to defend, *Hen.* 5, 1.ii.94.
imbrue cover with blood, *Mid. N. Dr.*, 5.i.335.
immanity inhumanity, 1 *Hen.* 6, 5.i.13.
immediately for that particular case, *Mid. N. Dr.*, 1.i.45.
imminence threaten'd evil, *Troil. and Cres.*, 5.x.13.
immoment of no moment, *Ant. and Cleo.*, 5.ii.165.
immures walled confine, *Troil. and Cres.*, Prol., 8.
impale, empale encircle, *Troil. and Cres.*, 5.vii.5.
impasted made into a crust, *Ham.*, 2.ii.453.
impeach charge, ground of question, 3 *Hen.* 6, 1.iv.60.
impeachment interference, *Hen.* 5, 3.vi.137; loss, *Two Gent. Ver.*, 1.iii.15.
impertinency, impertinent what is beside the point, *Lear*, 4.vi.175; *Tem.*, 1.ii.138.
impeticos nonsense formation by fool, *Tw. Night*, 2.iii.25.
impitious relentless and impetuous, *Ham.*, 4.v.97.
implorator one who begs, *Ham.*, 1.iii.129.
impone (Q2 impawn) to stake, *Ham.*, 5.ii.146.
importance importunity, *Tw. Night*, 5.i.350.

important importunate, *Lear*, 4.iv.26.
importune require, *M. Meas.*, 1.i.57.
imposition charge, *M. Meas.*, 1.ii.182.
imposthume septic swelling, so gathering of unhealthy features in body politic, *Ham.*, 4.v.27.
imprese device, family crest, *Rich.* 2, 3.i.25.
impress call up or levy for war, *Mac.*, 4.i.95.
impugn question the process, *Mer. Ven.*, 4.i.174.
imputation prestige, *Troil. and Cres.*, 1.iii.339.
incapable unable to realise, *Ham.*, 4.vii.179; beyond the capacity, *Cor.*, 4.vi.121.
incarnadine dye red, *Mac.*, 2.ii.62.
incarnate in human form, *Hen.* 5, 2.iii.32.
incarnation and similar formations used of the devil are comic versions of 'incarnate', *Mer. Ven.*, 2.ii.23.
inch islet, *Mac.*, 1.ii.63.
income arrival, *Lucrece*, 334.
incomprehensible beyond all bounds, 1 *Hen.* 4, 1.ii.179.
incontinent at once (with pun on normal sense), *As You Like*, 5.ii.36.
incony fine, *L. Lab. Lost*, 3.i.128.
incorporate bound up together, *Cor.*, 1.i.128.
indent to zigzag, *Ven. and Ad.*, 704; (from zigzag tear on matching halves of agreement) make a pact with, 1 *Hen.* 4, 1.iii.87.
index catalogue of contents of work, so indication of what is to follow, *Ham.*, 3.iv.52.
indigested unshaped, 3 *Hen.* 6, 5.vi.51.
indign unworthy, *Oth.*, 1.iii.273.
indirect treacherous, *As You Like*, 1.i.136.
indirection roundabout process, *Ham.*, 2.i.66.
indirectly casually, 1 *Hen.* 4, 1.iii.66.
indistinguish'd boundless, *Lear*, 4.vi.271.
individable *scene individable*, piece in which unity of place is observed, *Ham.*, 2.ii.395.
induction first step, 1 *Hen.* 4, 3.i.2.
industrious skilfully presented, *John*, 2.i.376.
industry skill, 3 *Hen.* 6, 5.iv.11.
infection of a man, unfinished specimen, *Rich.* 3, 1.ii.78.
influence what flows in from the stars and affects character and destiny, *M. Meas.*, 3.i.9.
infer to produce evidence or reason for some conclusion or course, *Rich.* 3, 3.vii.12.
inform to assume material form, *Mac.*, 2.i.48.
informal without reason, *M. Meas.*, 5.i.234.
inginer *see* engineer.
ingenious quick and sensitive, *Ham.*, 5.i.242; cleverly contrived, *Cym.*, 4.ii.187.
ingeniously ingenuously, *Timon*, 2.ii.221.
inhabitable uninhabitable, *Rich.* 2, 1.i.65.
initiate of a beginner, *Mac.*, 3.iv.143.
inkle tape, *Win. Tale*, 4.iv.204; thread, *Per.*, v. *Prol.*8.
inland familiar with good society, *As You Like*, 3.ii.322 (inland, near centres of culture).
insane causing madness, *Mac.*, 1.iii.84.
insinuate to assume a cordial form of address, *Rich.* 2, 4.i.165.
insisture of doubtful meaning. *Troil. and Cres.*, 1.iii.87.
instalment stall, *Mer. Wives Win.*, 5.v.61.
instance reason, *Ham.*, 3.ii.177; example, proof *Ham.*, 4.v.159; 2 *Hen.*, 4, 3.i.103.
instruction significance, *Oth.*, 4.i.41.
intelligent informative, communicative, *Lear*, 3.vii.11.
intentively with full attention to the whole story, *Oth.*, 1.iii.155.
interess'd entitled, *Lear*, 1.i.84.
interest right, title, 1 *Hen.* 4, 3.ii.98.
interlude an early type of dramatic entertainment, so a bit of play-acting, *Lear*, 5.iii.90.
intituled displayed (as in heraldry), *Lucrece*, 57.
intrinse, intrinsicate intricate, *Lear*, 2.ii.70; *Ant. and Cleo.*, 5.ii.302.
investments attire, *Ham.*, 1.iii.128.
iterance repetition, *Oth.*, 5.ii.153.
iwis assuredly, *Rich.* 3, 1.iii.102.
Jack often used to indicate contempt, *Rich.* 3, 1.iii.53; with reference to knave at cards, *Tem.*, 4.i.197; figure on clock, *Rich.* 3, 4.ii.118; associated with 'Jill' as common name and as measure of drink, *Tam. Shrew*, 4.i.43; the keys of the virginal (though the jacks were really only attached to the keys), *Son.*, 128, 5.
Jack-a-lent dummy set up at Lent as a cock-shy. *Mer. Wives Win.*, 5.v.123.
Jack-an-apes a monkey, *Hen.* 5, 5.ii.141; vain fellow, *All's Well*, 3.v.82.
jade poor class of horse, *Tam. Shrew*, 1.ii.245.
jakes privy, *Lear*, 2.ii.61.
jaunce a going backwards and forwards on tiresome journey, *Rom. and Jul.*, 2.v.26.
jay bedizzened wench, *Cym.*, 3.iv.47.
jealous suspicious, *Oth.*, 3.iv.186; on guard against, *Lear*, 5.i.56.
jealous-hood perhaps just jealous woman, *Rom. and Jul.*, 4.iv.13.
jealousy fear, *Tw. Night*, 3.iii.8.
jennet, gennet Spanish horse, *Oth.*, 1.i.114; *Ven. and Ad.*, 260.
jerk sharp stroke of wit or whip, *L. Lab. Lost*, 4.ii.119.
jerkin sleeveless jacket worn over doublet, for hard wear often made of leather, 2 *Hen.* 4, 2.ii.165.
jesses straps on the legs of hawk employed in sport, *Oth.*, 3.iii.265.
jet strut, *Cym.*, 3.iii.5; (jut) intrude upon, *Titus*, 2.i.64.
jig brisk dance, *Much Ado*, 2.i.62; customary after-piece with dancing to a play, *Ham.*, 2.ii.494.
Jill *see* Jack.
Jockey familiar form of Jack or John, *Rich.* 3, 5.iii.304.
joint-ring gimmal-ring, in two or more parts, *Oth*, *4.iii.71*.
joint-stool *(join-, join'd-)* stool carefully carpenter'd, Rom. and Jul, 1.v.5.
jordan chamber-pot, 1 *Hen.* 4, 2.i.18.
journal daily, *Cym.*, 4.ii.10.
Jovial star, Jupiter's planet which conferred on those who were born when it was in the ascendant a jovial nature, *Cym.*, 5.iv.105.
jowl to dash, *Ham.*, 5.i.76.
Judas tradition gave him red hair, *As You Like*, 3.iv.7.
Jug shortened form of Joan, *Lear*, 1.iv.224.
jump *noun*, hazard, *Ant. and Cleo.*, 3.viii.6; *verb*, to risk, *Mac*, 1.*vii.7*; adverb, *precisely*, Ham, 1.i.65.
jutty projection, *Mac*, 1.vi.6; *verb*, overhang, *Hen.* 5, 3.i.13.
juvenal youth, *L. Lab. Lost*, 1.ii.8.
kam contrary, *Cor.*, 3.i.304.
kecksy hemlock-like weed, *Hen.* 5, 5.ii.52.

keech roll of fat; of butcher's wife, 2 *Hen.* 4, 2.i.90; of butcher's son, *Hen.* 8, 1.i.55.
keel cool, keep pot from boiling over, *L. Lab. Lost*, 5.ii.907.
ken range of vision, 2 *Hen.* 4, 4.i.151.
Kendal green coarse cloth made in Westmorland, 1 *Hen.* 4, 2.iv.215.
kennel channel, gutter, 2 *Hen.* 6, 4.i.71.
kern light armed Irish soldier, *Rich.* 2, 2.i.156.
kernel seed, pip, *All's Well*, 2.iii.253.
kersey coarse woollen cloth, *L. Lab. Lost*, 5.ii.413.
kettle kettle-drum, *Ham.*, 5.ii.267.
kibe chilblain on heel, *Ham.*, 5.i.137 (lack of ceremony and respect).
kickshaws fancy trifle of food or deportment, 2 *Hen.* 4, 5.i.27; *Tw. Night*, 1.iii.108.
kicky-wicky wife, *All's Well*, 2.iii.273.
kiln-hole (doubtful), *Mer. Wives Win.*, 4.ii.48.
kindle (term used of the littering of rabbits) born, *As You Like*, 3.ii.317.
kindly according to nature, *Much Ado*, 4.i.73; *adverb*, according to her kind (with ironic suggestion of kindness), *Lear*, 1.v.14.
kirtle skirt, 2 *Hen.* 4, 2.iv.264.
kiss at bowls, balls just touching, *Cym.*, 2.i.2.
kissing-comfit comfit for sweetening breath, *Mer. Wives Win.*, 5.v.19.
kite term expressing abhorrence, *Lear*, 1.iv.262.
knap knock sharply, *Lear*, 2.iv.121.
knot plot in garden, *Rich.* 2, 3.iv.46.
knot-grass a weed thought to check the growth of animals, so derisively at *Mid. N. Dr.*, 3.ii.329.
knotted *curious-knotted*, elaborately laid out, *L. Lab. Lost*, 1.i.236.
label tag to a document to take the seal, *Rom. and Jul.*, 4.i.57.
labras lips (labra), *Mer. Wives Win.* 1.i.147.
lace to trim a garment with, *Much Ado*, 3.iv.18; thread, streak, *Rom. and Jul.*, 3.v.8; *laced mutton*, courtesan, *Two Gent. Ver.*, 1.i.95.
lackey to follow the movements of the tide as a footman to his master, *Ant. and Cleo.*, 1.iv.46.
lade empty by ladling, 3 *Hen.* 6, 3.ii.139.
lady-smock flower, *L. Lab. Lost*, 5.ii.882.
lag suggested for 'legge' in Folio as meaning lowest class of people, *Timon*, 3.vi.80.
lag late, *lag of*, later than, *Lear*, 1.ii.6.
Lammas-tide 1st August, *Rom. and Jul.*, 1.iii.16; *Lammas Eve*, day before Lammas, *Rom. and Jul.*, 1.iii.18.
lampass disease of horses, *Tam. Shrew*, 3.ii.48.
landrakers thieves, 1 *Hen.* 4, 2.i.71.
lank to shrink, *Ant. and Cleo.*, 1.iv.71.
lantern a vaulted chamber in a turret, *Rom. and Jul*, 5.iii.84.
lap to wrap, *Cym.*, 5.v.360; *lapp'd in proof*, clad as in impenetrable armour, *Mac.*, 1.ii.55.
Lapland regarded as the haunt of witches and sorcerers, *Com. Err.*, 4.iii.11.
lapse *lapsed*, arrested, *Tw. Night*, 3.iii.36; *laps'd in time and passion*, having allowed passion to fall off and time to pass idly, *Ham.*, 3.iv.107.
lard to fatten, enrich, *Timon*, 4.iii.12; to cover, *Ham.*, 4.v.36.
latch to catch, *Mac.*, 4.iii.195; to wound, *Lear*, 2.i.52; to touch, *Mid. N. Dr.*, 3.ii.36.
lath *dagger of lath*, of wood, *Tw. Night*, 4.ii.122; so sarcastically of real weapon, *Titus*, 2.i.41.
latten an alloy like brass, *Mer. Wives Win.*, 1.i.146.
lattice *see* red lattice.
laud hymn, *Ham.*, 4.vii.178.
laund clearing in forest, 3 *Hen.* 6, 3.i.2.
lavolt, lavolta lively dance, *Hen.* 5, 3.v.33.
law-day meeting of court *Oth.*, 3.iii.144.
lazar a leper or an afflicted person, *Ham.*, 1.v.72.
leaguer camp, *All's Well*, 3.vi.22.
leaping-house brothel, 1 *Hen.* 4, 1.ii.8.
learn to teach, *Ham.*, 5.ii.9.
leash *leash of drawers*, three tapsters (for hounds were three to a leash), 1 *Hen.* 4, 2.iv.6.
leasing lying, *Tw. Night*, 1.v.91.
leather-coat russet apple, 2 *Hen.* 4, 5.iii.41.
leer complexion, *Titus*, 4.ii.119; glance, *Mer. Wives Win.* 1.iii.42.
lees sediment in wine, *Troil. and Cres.*, 4.i.64.
leet court under jurisdiction of lord of the manor, *Tam. Shrew*, Ind.ii.85.
Legion name taken by unclean spirit in Mark, v.9, 'for we are many'; so host of fiends, *Tw. Night*, 3.iv.80.
legitimation legitimacy, *John*, 1.i.248.
leiger ambassador, representative, *M. Meas.*, 3.i.60; *Cym.*, 1.v.80.
leman sweetheart, *Tw. Night*, 2.iii.24.
lendings *Off, off, you lendings*, clothes, as superfluities not given by nature, but lent by art, *Lear*, 3.iv.107.
Lent forty days fast before Easter, when meat was supposed to be excluded from one's diet, 2 *Hen.* 4, 2.iv.335.
lenten *lenten entertainment*, meagre like the restricted diet of Lent, *Ham.*, 2.ii.314.
l'envoy conclusion of poem, marked off as such by form, *L. Lab. Lost*, 3.i.66.
less (sometimes used in negative or virtual negative expressions where meaning is 'more'), *Win. Tale*, 3.ii.54; *Cym.*, 1.iv.21; *so lesser*, *Troil. and Cres.*, 1.i.28.
let *noun*, impediment, *Hen.* 5, 5.ii.65; *verb*, prevent, *Ham.*, 1.iv.85.
Lethe 'the river of oblivion' in the under-world; *roots itself in ease on Lethe wharf*, as indifferent to the past, *Ham.*, 1.v.33.
letter *affect the letter*, employ alliteration, *L. Lab. Lost*, 4.ii.52.
lettered learned, *L. Lab. Lost*, 5.i.40.
level *noun*, aim (from gunnery), *Hen.* 8, 1.ii.2; *verb*, aim at, *Ant. and Cleo.*, 5.ii.333.
lewd of the baser sort, *Much Ado*, 5.i.316.
lewdster lecherous person, *Mer. Wives Win.* 5.iii.21.
liable subject to, influenced by, *John*, 2.i.490.
libbard leopard, *L. Lab. Lost*, 5.ii.544.
libel lying publication, *Rich.* 3, 1.i.33.
liberal becoming the free man or gentleman, 3 *Hen.* 6, 1.ii.43; *liberal arts*, those suitable for a gentleman, *Tem.*, 1.ii.73; going beyond manners, gross, *Mer. Ven.*, 2.ii.170.
liberty licence, *M. Meas.*, 1.iii.29; *liberties*, individual's rights, *Per.*, 1.ii.112; *the law of writ and the liberty*, classical rule and freedom from these canons of composition, *Ham.*, 2.ii.397.

lief beloved, 2 *Hen. 6*, 3.i.164; *had as lief*, would as willingly, *Ham.*, 3.ii.3.
lifter pun on weight-lifter and thief, *Troil. and Cres.*, 1.ii.112.
lighten enlighten, 2 *Hen. 4*, 2.i.187.
lightning lightening, a rally of the spirit, *Rom. and Jul*, 5.iii.90.
light o'love dance tune, light wench, *Much Ado*, 3.iv.38 and 40.
lily-liver'd cowardly, *Lear*, 2.ii.15 (see liver).
limbeck alembic for distilling, *Mac.*, 1.vii.67.
limber not rigid, *Win. Tale*, 1.ii.47.
Limbo, Limbo patrum the unbaptised and the virtuous pagans were received here after death; slang for prison, *Hen. 8*, 5.iv.61.
lime *limed*, held, as a bird with birdlime, *Ham.*, 3.iii.68; to doctor wine or sack with lime, *Mer. Wives Win.*, 1.iii.14.
line-grove grove of lime-trees, *Tem.*, 5.i.10.
link torch, 1 *Hen. 4*, 3.iii.42; material of, used as blacking, *Tam. Shrew*, 4.i.118.
linsey-woolsey mixture of flax and wool; so unintelligible medley at *All's Well*, 4.i.11.
linstock staff supporting the match with which the gunner touched off the cannon, *Hen. 5*, 3. *Chor.*33.
list strip of cloth, *Tam. Shrew*, 3.ii.64; space enclosed for combat, *Mac.*, 3.i.70.
lither yielding, 1 *Hen. 6*, 4.vii.21.
little *picture in little*, miniature, *Ham.*, 2.ii.362.
livelihood life, animal vigour, *Ven. and Ad.*, 26.
lively like life itself, *Timon*, 5.i.80.
liver regarded as seat of more violent passions: love, courage, anger, *Tw. Night*, 1.i.37; *As You Like*, 3.ii.387; *livers white as milk*, of cowards, *Mer. Ven.*, 3.ii.86.
liver-vein style of a lover, *L. Lab. Lost*, 4.iii.70.
livery *sue my livery*, to take proceedings to regain inheritance, *Rich. 2*, 2.iii.129.
livery to dress as with a livery, *Lov. Comp.*, 105.
lockram coarse kind of linen, *Cor*, 2.i.199.
lode-star guiding-star, *Mid. N. Dr.*, 1.i.183.
lodge *lodg'd*, flatten'd, *Mac.*, 4.i.55.
loggats little logs of wood thrown at mark, *Ham.*, 5.i.90.
London-stone (the central milestone of Roman London from which distances were reckoned), ancient stone in Cannon Street, 2 *Hen. 6*, 4.vi.2.
long purples kind of orchis, *Ham.*, 4.vii.170.
long-staff *sixpenny strikers*, those who would commit robbery with violence for petty sums, 1 *Hen. 4*, 2.i.71.
loof luff, *Ant. and Cleo.*, 3.x.18.
loon, lown useless fellow, *Mac.*, 5.iii.11.
looped full of holes, *Lear*, 3.iv.31.
loose *at his very loose*, at the moment of discharge, *L. Lab. Lost*, 5.ii.730.
lop smaller branches, *Hen. 8*, 1.ii.96.
Lord's sake *for the Lord's sake*, the formula in which those imprisoned for debt begged alms of the passers-by, *M. Meas.*, 4.iii.17.
Love-in-idleness pansy, *Mid. N. Dr.*, 2.i.168.
lozel rascal, *Win. Tale*, 2.iii.108.
lubber lout, *Lear*, 1.iv.89.
luce pike, *Mer. Wives Win.*, 1.i.14.
Lucina goddess presiding over birth, *Per.*, 3.i.10.
lucre gain, 1 *Hen. 6*, 5.iv.141.
Lud's town London (the name of the mythical King Lud is preserved in Ludgate), *Cym*, 3.i.32.
lune mad fit, *Win. Tale*, 2.ii.30.
Lupercal Roman festival on 15th February, connected with fertility rites, *Jul. Caes.*, 3.ii.95.
lurch to deprive, *Cor.*, 2.ii.99.
lure dummy bird to entice hawk to return, *Tam. Shrew*, 4.i.176.
luxurious lascivious, *Mac*, 4.iii.58.
lym bloodhound, *Lear*, 3.vi.68.
Machiavel regarded as the type of ruthless schemer, 3 *Hen. 6*, 3.ii.193.
maculate spotted, impure, *L. Lab. Lost*, 1.ii.88; *maculation*, impurity, *Troil. and Cres.*, 4.iv.63.
madrigal song (though the 'madrigal' was a part-song of a very special type), *Mer. Wives Win.*, 3.i.16.
maggot-pie magpie, *Mac.*, 3.iv.125.
magnanimous great-hearted, *Troil. and Cres*, 2.ii.200.
magnifico Venetian magnate, *Mer. Ven.*, 3.ii.282.
Maid Marian personage in the morris dance, 1 *Hen. 4*, 3.iii.114.
mail *mail'd up*, shrouded in, 2 *Hen. 6*, 2.iv.31.
main the number nominated before casting the dice at the game of hazard, 1 *Hen. 4*, 4.i.47; so *main chance*, 2 *Hen. 4*, 3.i.83.
main-course mainsail, *Tem.*, 1.i.33.
mainly violently, 1 *Hen. 4*, 2.iv.193; strongly, *Ham.*, 4.vii.9.
major *your major*, major premise in syllogism, 1 *Hen. 4*, 2.iv.478.
make *mate and make*, husband and wife, *Lear*, 4.iii.34.
malapert presumptuous, *Rich. 3*, 1.iii.255.
malcontent disgruntled, 3 *Hen. 6*, 4.i.10.
malignant *malignant stars*, exerting evil influence, 1 *Hen. 6*, 4.v.6.
malkin slut, *Cor.*, 2.i.198.
mallard a wild drake, *Ant. and Cleo.*, 3.x.20.
malmsey sweet wine, *Rich. 3*, 1.iv.152.
malt-horse brewer's dray-horse, *Tam. Shrew*, 4.i.113.
malt-worm boozer, 2 *Hen. 4*, 2.iv.322.
mammer stammer, hesitate, *Oth.*, 3.iii.71.
mammet doll, *Rom. and Jul.*, 3.v.185.
mammock pull in pieces, *Cor.*, 1.iii.65.
man (i) to provide a man-servant, 2 *Hen. 4*, 1.ii.15; (ii) to tame a hawk, *Tam. Shrew*, 4.i.177.
manage training or handling of a horse, *Hen. 8*, 5.iii.24; *L. Lab. Lost*, 5.ii.482.
mandragora, mandrake a narcotic, *Oth.*, 3.iii.334; *Ant. and Cleo.*, 1.v.4; the root was thought to resemble the shape of a man and shriek when torn from the earth, *Rom. and Jul.*, 4.iii.47.
manner the stolen article when found on the thief, so caught in the act, 1 *Hen. 4*, 2.iv.306; *L. Lab. Lost*, 1.i.199 (where the company of a woman was the unlawful possession).
mansionry abode, *Mac.*, 1.vi.5.
mantle scum on stagnant water, *Lear*, 3.iv.131.
mappery mere staff-work, *Troil. and Cres.*, 1.iii.205.
marches the English districts adjacent to Scotland and Wales, *Hen. 5*, 1.ii.140.
marchpane a sweetmeat like marzipan, *Rom. and Jul.*, 1.v.7.
margent margin of book, *L. Lab. Lost*, 5.ii.8; commentary or explanation written in margin, *Ham.*, 5.ii.152.

mark a sum of money (not a coin) value 13s. 4d., *Hen. 8*, 5.i.170.
marmoset small monkey, *Tem.*, 2.ii.160.
Martin *Saint Martin's summer*, supposed to run from about 23rd Oct. to 11th Nov., St. Martin's day, *1 Hen. 6*, 1.ii.131.
Martlemas Martinmas, 11th Nov.; animals that could not be fed through the winter were killed at this season, *2 Hen. 4*, 2.ii.98.
martlet house-martin, swallow, *Mac.*, 1.vi.4.
mary-bud marigold bud, *Cym.* 2.iii.23.
mast acorns, food for swine, *Timon*, 4.iii.417.
mastic meaning doubtful, perhaps censorious *Troil. and Cres.*, 1.iii.73.
mate outwit, *2 Hen. 6*, 3.i.265; bewilder, *Mac.*, 5.i.76.
maugre in spite of, *Tw. Night*, 3.i.148.
maund basket, *Lov. Comp.*, 36.
mazard head, *Ham.*, 5.i.87.
meacock feeble, cowardly, *Tam. Shrew*, 2.i.305.
meal stain, *M. Meas.*, 4.ii.79.
mean middle part, tenor or alto, *L. Lab. Lost*, 5.ii.328; singer of such a part, *Win. Tale*, 4.iii.42.
mechanic manual worker, *Cor.*, 5.iii.83.
medicine of chemical preparations other than medicinal, *Oth.*, 1.iii.61; *that great med'cine*, the elixir of life or alchemist's stone that turned all to gold, so figuratively at *Ant. and Cleo.*, 1.v.36; the physician, *Mac.*, 5.ii.27.
meed merit, *3 Hen. 6*, 2.i.36.
meetly not bad, *Ant. and Cleo.*, 1.iii.81.
meiny train, company, *Lear*, 2.iv.34.
melancholy of various kinds, *see As You Like*, 4.i.10.
memorize make memorable, *Mac.*, 1.ii.41.
mercatante merchant, *Tam. Shrew*, 4.ii.63.
Mercury messenger of the gods, so messenger, *Mer. Wives Win.*, 2.ii.72; patron of rogues and cheats, *Win. Tale*, 4.iii.25.
mere complete, absolute, *Mer. Wives Win.*, 4.v.58.
mess four, usual number in sub-divisions of company at banquet, *L. Lab. Lost*, 4.iii.203.
metaphysical supernatural, *Mac.*, 1.v.26.
mete measure, *2 Hen. 4*, 4.iv.77; *mete-yard*, measuring stick, *Tam. Shrew*, 4.iii.149; aim at, *L. Lab. Lost*, 4.i.125.
metheglin spiced drink, *L. Lab. Lost*, 5.ii.233.
mew shut up, *Mid. N. Dr.*, 1.i.71.
micher truant, *1 Hen. 4*, 2.iv.396.
miching mallecho skulking mischief ('mallecho' a Spanish word for 'evil deed'), *Ham.*, 3.ii.132.
might *might not merit*, the intention not the performance, *Mid. N. Dr.*, 5.i.92.
milch used of weeping, *Ham.*, 2.ii.511.
Mile-end Green, where train-bands drilled, *2 Hen. 4*, 3.ii.271.
milk-liver'd cowardly, *Lear*, 4.ii.50.
milliner vendor of gloves, hats, etc., *1 Hen. 4*, 1.iii.36.
mill-sixpence milled coin, not hammered as older pieces, *Mer. Wives Win.*, 1.i.139.
mineral poison, *Oth.*, 2.i.291.
minikin trim and feat, *Lear*, 3.vi.43.
minimus of smallest size, *Mid. N. Dr.*, 3.ii.329.
minute-jacks creatures of the minute, or busy about nothing, *Timon*, 3.vi.97.
minutely every minute, *Mac.*, 5.ii.18.
mirable wonderful, *Troil. and Cres.*, 4.v.142.
Misanthropos the hater of mankind, *Timon*, 4.iii.52.
misgraffed unsuitably mated, *Mid. N. Dr.*, 1.i.137.
misprision (i) undervaluing, scorning, *All's Well*, 2.iii.150; (ii) mistaking, *Mid. N. Dr.*, 3.ii.90.
missive messenger, *Mac.*, 1.v.5.
mistress at game of bowls, the jack, *Troil. and Cres.*, 3.ii.48.
mobled muffled, *Ham.*, 2.ii.496.
model plan, *2 Hen. 4*, 1.iii.42; copy, *Ham.*, 5.ii.50; imperfect manifestation of, *Hen. 5*, 2. *Chor.*16.
modern ordinary, commonplace, *As You Like*, 2.vii.156; *modern grace*, common attractions, *All's Well*, 5.iii.214.
modest reasonable, *Tw. Night*, 1.v.169.
module copy, *All's Well*, 4.iii.94.
moldwarp mole, *1 Hen. 4*, 3.i.149.
mome dolt, *Com. Err.*, 3.i.32.
Monarcho title assumed by mad Italian as emperor of the world, so of those with such notions, *L. Lab. Lost*, 4.i.92.
Monmouth cap commonly worn by soldiers and sailors, *Hen. 5*, 4.vii.97.
monstruosity the great 'snag', *Troil. and Cres.*, 3.ii.78.
montant fencing term for particular thrust, *Mer. Wives Win.*, 2.iii.25.
monumental ring, a momento from the possessor's ancestors, *All's Well*, 4.iii.16.
moonish fickle, *As You Like*, 3.ii.376.
Moor Ditch *melancholy of Moor Ditch*, occasioned by the smell of the ditch, especially when being cleaned out, *1 Hen. 4*, 1.ii.76.
mop grimace, *Tem.*, 4.i.47.
mope wander in body or mind, *Tem.*, 5.i.240; *Ham.*, 3.iv.81.
Morisco a morris-dancer (supposed of Moorish origin), *2 Hen. 6*, 3.i.365.
morris, morris-dance costume dance of fantastic kind; characters included Robin Hood, Maid Marian, *All's Well*, 2.ii.23; *Hen. 5*, 2.iv.25 (*see* hobby horse); *nine men's morris*, a game played on squares cut in the turf, *Mid. N. Dr.*, 2.i.98.
mort the note on the horn that announces the death of the deer, *Win. Tale*, 1.ii.118.
mortise *hold the mortise*, remain with timbers unloosened, *Oth.*, 2.i.9.
mose in the chine, of horses, glanders, *Tam. Shrew*, 3.ii.48.
mot motto, *Lucrece*, 830.
mother hysteria, *Lear*, 2.iv.55.
motion puppet-show, *Win. Tale*, 4.iii.91.
motley fool's particoloured costume, *Lear*, 1.iv.145; one who plays the fool, *Son.*, 110, 2.
mould earth, *Hen. 5*, 3.ii.21.
moulten having moulted, *1 Hen. 4*, 3.i.152.
mountebank to gain by false statements, *Cor.*, 3.ii.132.
mouse to seize in the jaws and rend, *John*, 2.i.354.
mow grimace, *Ham.*, 2.ii.360.
muniments defences, implements, *Cor.*, 1.i.116.
murdering-piece small cannon for grape-shot, *Ham.*, 4.v.92.
mure wall, *2 Hen. 4*, 4.iv.119.
murrain plague, *Troil. and Cres.*, 2.i.19.
muscadel strong sweet wine, *Tam. Shrew*, 3.ii.168.
musit gaps through which hare runs when hunted, *Ven. and Ad.*, 683.

musk secretion from musk-deer, *Mer. Wives Win.* 2.ii.60.
musk-cat musk-deer, *All's Well*, 5.ii.19.
muss a scramble, *Ant. and Cleo.*, 3.xiii.91.
mutine *verb*, to rebel, *Ham.*, 3.iv.83; *noun*, mutineer, *Ham.*, 5.ii.6.
mutiny *verb*, contend, *Ant. and Cleo.*, 3.xi.13; *noun*, dispute, *L. Lab. Lost*, 1.i.167.
mutuality exchange (of intimacy), *Oth.*, 2.i.256.
mynheers (suggested for 'Anheires'), sirs, *Mer. Wives Win.* 2.i.196.
Myrmidon *the great Myrmidon*, Achilles whose followers were the Myrmidons, *Troil. and Cres.*, 1.iii.378.
mystery craft, calling, *M. Meas.*, 4.ii.25; *Timon*, 4.iii.452.
nail measure of length for cloth, one-sixteenth of a yard, *Tam. Shrew*, 4.iii.108.
naked unarmed, *Oth.*, 5.ii.261; *naked bed*, naked, as was the habit, in bed, *Ven. and Ad*, 397.
napless threadbare, *Cor.*, 2.i.224 (the candidates really wore whitened garments to look as fine as possible; North's mistranslation here misled Shakespeare).
nave hub of wheel, *Ham.*, 2.ii.490.
nayward opposite belief, *Win. Tale*, 2.i.64.
nayword byword *Tw. Night*, 2.iii.127, password, *Mer. Wives Win.* 5.ii.5.
Nazarite of Nazareth, *Mer. Ven.*, 1.iii.30 (the term 'Nazarene' was introduced by the Authorized Version of 1611).
neaf fist, 2 *Hen.* 4, 2.iv.176.
Neapolitan bone-ache, venereal disease, *Troil. and Cres.*, 2.iii.17.
near-legged before, fore-legs close, *Tam. Shrew*, 3.ii.52.
neat animal, ox, cow, calf, *Win. Tale*, 1.ii.125; *neat's leather*, shoe leather, *Jul. Caes.*, 1.i.26.
neb mouth, *Win. Tale*, 1.ii.183.
neeze sneeze, *Mid. N. Dr.*, 2.i.56.
nephew a relation – cousin, etc., 1 *Hen.* 6, 2.v.64.
Nereides sea-nymphs, fifty daughters of Nereus, *Ant. and Cleo.*, 2.ii.210.
nether-stocks stockings, 1 *Hen.* 4, 2.iv.111; *wooden nether-stocks*, the stocks, *Lear*, 2.iv.10.
nice coy, shy, mannerly, fastidious, *All's Well*, 5.i.15; *nice wenches*, those affecting shyness, wantons, *L. Lab. Lost*, 3.i.20.
nicely subtly, ingeniously, *Rich.* 2, 2.i.84.
niceness reserve, *Cym.* 3.iv.154.
Nicholas *Saint*, patron saint, of boys and scholars, *Two Gent. Ver.*, 3.i.292; *Saint Nicholas' clerks*, highway robbers, 1 *Hen.* 4, 2.i.60.
nick *out of all nick*, beyond reckoning (nicks used on sticks to keep reckoning), *Two Gent. Ver.*, 4.ii.73; *in the nick*, at the appropriate time (to settle the bill), *Oth.*, 5.ii.320.
nightgown dressing-gown, *Mac.*, 2.ii.70.
nimble-pinion'd swift winged, *Rom. and Jul*, 2.v.7.
noble a gold coin worth 6s. 8d., *Rich.* 2, 1.i.88; the aristocratic party, *Cor*, 3.i.29.
noise often applied to musical sounds, *Ant. and Cleo.*, 4.iii.12; the men who make the noise, the band, 2 *Hen.* 4, 2.iv.11.
nole head, *Mid. N. Dr.*, 3.ii.17.
nonce for this particular purpose or occasion, *Ham.*, 4.vii.160.
non-come Dogberry's term is of doubtful meaning, *Much Ado*, 3.v.57.
nonpareil without an equal, *Tw. Night*, 1.v.238.
nook-shotten all corners and angles, *Hen.* 5, 3.v.14.
nose-herb scented plant, *All's Well*, 4.v.17.
novum a game with dice, in which throws of nine and five were important, *L. Lab. Lost*, 5.ii.540 (the five characters were to enact the Nine Worthies).
nuncio messenger, *Tw. Night*, 1.iv.27.
nut-hook beadle, 2 *Hen.* 4, 5.iv.8.
o *this wooden O*, the theatre (perhaps The Globe), *Hen.* 5, 1. *Chor.*13; *this little O*, the globe itself, the earth, *Ant. and Cleo.*, 5.ii.81; *yon fiery oes and eyes of light*, the stars, *Mid. N. Dr.*, 3.ii.188.
oathable that can be trusted to take an oath, *Timon*, 4.iii.135.
ob abbreviation of 'obolus', a half-penny, 1 *Hen.* 4, 2.iv.521.
objection accusation, 2 *Hen.* 6, 1.iii.153.
obliged *obliged faith*, pledged, *Mer. Ven.*, 2.vi.7.
oblivious causing forgetfulness, *Mac.*, 5.iii.43.
obloquy shame, *All's Well*, 4.ii.44.
obscene abominable, *Rich.* 2, 4.i.131.
obsequious showing proper duty, *M. Meas.*, 2.iv.28; duty or love for the dead, *Ham.*, 1.ii.92.
observance attention required by respect or love, *Troil. and Cres.*, 1.iii.31.
observant one quick to attend to master's wishes, *Lear*, 2.ii.98.
observation of a rite, *Mid. N. Dr.*, 4.i.101; of life itself and compliance with its requirements, *John*, 1.i.208.
observe *Th' observ'd of all observers*, of all courtiers the most reverenced, *Ham.*, 3.i.154.
obstruct obstacle, *Ant. and Cleo.*, 3.vi.61.
obstruction *obstruction in the blood*, hindrance, *Tw. Night*, 3.iv.21; *cold obstruction*, death, where all that makes for life is shut off, *M. Meas.*, 3.i.120.
occasion happenings, 2 *Hen.* 4, 4.i.72; so an opportunity or a reason for something, *he married but his occasion* (took the chance of marriage merely to further his interests), *Ant. and Cleo.*, 2.vi.127; *quarreling with occasion*, deliberately misunderstanding the situation, *Mer. Ven.*, 3.v.48.
occulted hidden, *Ham.*, 3.ii.78.
occupation *voice of occupation*, vote of the manual worker, *Cor*, 4.vi.98.
occupy *as odious as the word 'occupy'*, because it was employed largely in an indecent sense (e.g. *Rom. and Jul.*, 2.iv.96), 2 *Hen.* 4, 2.iv.139.
Od's, Ud's form of 'God' in oaths and exclamations, *As You Like*, 3.v.43; *Oth.*, 5.ii.72.
oeillades inviting glances, *Mer. Wives Win.* 1.iii.57; *Lear*, 4.v.25.
o'erflourish'd decorated outwardly, *Tw. Night*, 3.iv.354.
o'erparted given too difficult a part, *L. Lab. Lost*, 5.ii.578.
o'erpicturing excelling in beauty what the imagination has pictured, *Ant. and Cleo*, 2.ii.204.
o'er-sized besmear'd, *Ham.*, 2.ii.456.
o'er-teemed exhausted with child-bearing, *Ham.*, 2.ii.502.
o'er-wrested seeming, exaggerated acting, *Troil. and Cres.*, 1.iii.157.
off-capp'd stood bare-headed, *Oth.*, 1.i.10.

office function, service, *Rich.* 2, 2.ii.137; the functionary, *Ham.*, 3.i.73.
'old wold, *Lear*, 3.iv.118.
old extreme (in some form), *Tam. Shrew*, 3.ii.31; *Mac.*, 2.iii.2.
oneyer meaning doubtful, 1 *Hen.*, 4, 2.i.74.
operant active, *Ham.*, 3.ii.169.
opposite adversary, *Tw. Night*, 3.iv.255.
opposition *single oppositions*, single combats, *Cym.* 4.i.13.
oppugnancy discord, *Troil. and Cres.*, 1.iii.111.
orb circle, *Mid. N. Dr.*, 2.i.9 (fairy rings); the circle or sphere in which the planets were supposed to move, *Rom. and Jul.*, 2.ii.110.
ordinance what has been ordained in the past or is ordained for the future, *Jul. Caes*, 1.iii.66; *Cym.* 4.ii.146; rank, *Cor*, 3.ii.12.
ordinant provident, *Ham.*, 5.ii.48.
ordinary meal (from name given to meal in a tavern), *Ant. and Cleo*, 2.ii.229.
orgillous proud, *Troil. and Cres.*, Prol. 2.
orifex opening, *Troil. and Cres.*, 5.ii.149.
orison prayer, *Ham.*, 3.i.89.
ort fragment, *Timon*, 4.iii.397.
orthography orthographer, pedantic in his use of words, *Much Ado*, 2.iii.18.
ostent show, appearance, *Mer. Ven.*, 2.ii.181.
ostentation display, *Ham.*, 4.v.211.
othergates in another and very different way, *Tw. Night*, 5.i.186.
ouches ornaments, 2 *Hen.* 4, 2.iv.48.
ought owed, 1 *Hen.* 4, 3.iii.134.
ounce lynx, *Mid. N. Dr.*, 2.ii.30.
ouphe elf, goblin, *Mer. Wives Win.* 5.v.55.
ousel blackbird, *Mid. N. Dr.*, 3.i.114.
out-herod *out-herods Herod*, to rant more outrageously than Herod in the old Mystery plays, *Ham.*, 3.ii.13.
out-peer excel, *Cym.*, 3.vi.86.
out-vie to outbid (as at cards), *Tam. Shrew*, 2.i.377.
overscutch'd huswifes, well-whipped whores, so hardened to the trade, 2 *Hen.* 4, 3.ii.308.
overture disclosure, declaration, *Tw. Night*, 1.v.196.
owe to possess, *Lear*, 1.i.202.
oyes (*Fr.* oyez) the call of the public crier to secure attention, *Mer. Wives Win.* 5.v.39.
pace training (as of horses), discipline, *All's Well*, 4.v.60; *verb*, to train, *Per.*, 4.vi.62.
pack to plot, *Titus*, 4.ii.156; *pack'd*, confederate, *Much Ado*, 5.i.285; *Com. Err.*, 5.i.219; to manipulate the cards dishonestly, to cheat, *Ant. and Cleo.*, 4.xiv.19.
packing plotting, *Tam. Shrew*, 5.i.105.
paddock toad, *Ham.*, 3.iv.190; *paddock calls* the witch's familiar spirit, *Mac.*, 1.i.9.
pageant (the wagon on which a scene in the Miracle plays was staged at the various stations appointed for performance) so of a ship, *Mer. Ven.*, 1.i.11; a show, sometimes with the notion of unreality or deception, *Tem.*, 4.i.155; *Oth.*, 1.iii.18.
pain punishment, *Son.*, 141, 14; toil, *L. Lab. Lost*, 1.i.73.
painful *painful warrior*, enduring toil and danger, *Son.*, 25.9.
painted specious, false, *Ham.*, 3.i.53.
painted cloth canvas hangings painted with figures and moral sentences were a cheap substitute for figures tapestries, 2 *Hen.* 4, 2.i.142; *right painted cloth*, the answer taken from the mottoes, etc. on the hangings, *As You Like*, 3.ii.258; *Lucrece*, 245.
paiock possibly peacock, *Ham.*, 3.ii.278.
palabras *paucas pallabris*, few words, *Tam. Shrew*, Ind.i.5; *Much Ado*, 3.v.16.
pale palisade, so figuratively at *Ham.*, 1.iv.28; *Troil. and Cres.*, 2.iii.243; with idea of winter's whiteness at *Win. Tale*, 4.iii.4; *verb*, to encircle, 3 *Hen.* 6 1.iv.103 (with the crown).
palfrey horse, *Titus*, 5.ii.50.
palisado defence work of stakes, 1 *Hen.* 4, 2.iii.49.
pall (i) fail, *Ham.*, 5.ii.9; *pall'd fortunes*, ruined prospects, *Ant. and Cleo.*, 2.vii.81. (ii) to shroud, *Mac.*, 1.v.48.
pallet bed, 2 *Hen.* 4, 3.i.10.
palliament robe, *Titus*, 1.i.182.
palmy lofty, flourishing, *Ham.*, 1.i.113.
palter deal falsely, *Mac.*, 5.viii.20.
pantaloon originally a stock character in Italian comedy; withered dotard – so figure of old age, *As You Like*, 2.vii.158.
Pantheon temple at Rome (to all the Gods), *Titus*, 1.i.242.
paper to serve with a writ or communication, *Hen.* 8, 1.i.80.
Paracelsus Swiss alchemist of early 16th century; criticised academic medical opinion as represented in Galen; *Both of Galen and Paracelsus*, all schools of medical thought, *All's Well*, 2.iii.11.
paradox contrary to general opinion, *Ham.*, 3.i.114; absurd statement, *Oth.*, 2.i.138.
paragon *paragon'd*, regarded as perfect example of kind, *Hen.* 8, 2.iv.230; *paragons description*, surpasses attempts to describe ideal, *Oth.*, 2.i.62; compare, *Ant. and Cleo.*, 1.v.71.
parcel part, *Oth.*, 1.iii.154; group, *Mer. Ven.*, 1.ii.97; *verb*, (perhaps) add to, *Ant. and Cleo.*, 5.ii.62; *parcell'd*, particular, *Rich.* 3, 2.ii.81.
pard panther or leopard, *Tem.*, 4.i.260.
Paris balls tennis balls, *Hen.* 5, 2.iv.131.
Paris garden a bear-garden (for in this liberty on the Bankside was situated the ring for bear baiting), *Hen.* 8, 5.iv.2.
parish-top kept to provide recreation in cold weather, *Tw. Night*, 1.iii.38.
paritor summoner to the Bishop's court (the pranks inspired by Cupid giving him most work), *L. Lab. Lost*, 3.i.176.
parle conversation (with pun on 'parle'= truce for discussion of terms), *Ham.*, 1.iii.123; *angry parle*, perhaps just a sharp encounter, *Ham.*, 1.i.62.
parlous perilous, *As You Like*, 3.ii.40; shrewd, *Rich.* 3, 2.iv.35.
parmaceti spermaceti, 1 *Hen.* 4, 1.iii.58.
partial *a partial slander*, the accusation of partiality, *Rich.* 2, 1.iii.241.
partialize affect with partiality, *Rich.* 2, 1.i.120.
partially affin'd, bound by desire to favour a colleague, *Oth.*, 2.iii.210.
parti-coated motley, the garb of the fool, *L. Lab. Lost*, 5.ii.754.
partisan a blade mounted on a long pole, common weapon for guards, *Ham.*, 1.i.140.

Partlet *Dame Partlet*, traditional name for the hen, *Win. Tale*, 2.iii.75.

party-verdict individual's contribution to common decision, *Rich. 2*, 1.iii.234.

pash (i) *noun*, head, *Win. Tale*, 1.ii.128; (ii) *verb*, strike, *Troil. and Cres.*, 2.iii.198.

passado a lunge in rapier fighting, *Rom. and Jul.*, 3.i.82.

passant (of heraldic figures), walking, *Mer. Wives Win.*, 1.i.17.

passion Christ's sufferings (in oaths, etc.), *Mer. Wives Win.*, 3.i.57; physical or mental pain, 1 *Hen. 4*, 3.i.35; love, *Titus*, 2.i.36; a passionate speech, *Mid N. Dr.*, 5.i.307; *Ham.*, 3.ii.9; *verb*, feel sorrow, *Tem.*, 5.i.24.

passy measures pavin (from Italian passamezzo pavana), a variety of pavan, which was slow and stately, *Tw. Night*, 5.i.192.

patch fool, *Mid. N. Dr.*, 3.ii.9.

patchery roguery, *Troil. and Cres.*, 2.iii.67.

patent *virgin patent*, privilege of liberty as maid, *Mid. N. Dr.*, 1.i.80.

patine circular metal plate (patine, plate used in the Eucharist), *Mer. Ven.*, 5.i.59.

patronage maintain, 1 *Hen. 6*, 3.i.48.

Paul's *known as well as Paul's*, as familiar as the old St. Paul's cathedral which was the 'Bond Street of London' till the days of the Commonwealth, the haunt of idlers and centre of commerce, 1 *Hen. 4*, 2.iv.508.

paunch pierce his belly, *Tem.*, 3.ii.86.

pavin *see* passy.

pax representation of the Crucifixion, or reliquary, kissed by the celebrant and people at mass, *Hen. 5*, 3.vi.39.

peach to give away one's confederates, 1 *Hen. 4*, 2.ii.43; proclaim, *M. Meas.*, 4.iii.10.

peak to droop in spirit or strength, *Ham.*, 2.ii.561; *Mac.*, 1.iii.23.

pearl cataract (with play on usual sense), *Two Gent. Ver.*, 5.ii.12.

peck you o'er the pales, pitch you over the railings, *Hen. 8*, 5.iv.87.

peculiar belonging to particular individual, personal, *M. Meas.*, 1.ii.86; *Troil. and Cres.*, 2.iii.161.

pedant schoolmaster *Tw. Night*, 3.ii.70; *pedascule* pedant, *Tam. Shrew*, 3.i.48.

peel'd tonsured, 1 *Hen. 6*, 1.iii.30.

peise *peised well*, well balanced, *John*, 2.i.575; *peize the time*, make it heavy and slow, *Mer. Ven.*, 3.ii.22.

pelican (the pelican was supposed to feed her young with her blood), *Ham*, 4.v.143.

Pelion the giants placed mount Ossa on mount Pelion in their attempt to scale the heavens, *Ham.*, 5.i.247.

pelting *pelting wars*, poor fighting, *Troil. and Cres.*, 4.v.267; paltry, *Lear*, 2.iii.18.

pendulous suspended overhead, *Lear*, 3.iv.66.

pensioners royal body-guard, formed by Henry VIII, *Mer. Wives Win.*, 2.ii.70.

Pepin father of Charlemagne, and so someone who lived long ago, *L. Lab. Lost*, 4.i.113.

perdu a soldier on a post or task of special danger, so as good as lost, *Lear*, 4.vii.35.

perdurably *fin'd*, eternally punished, *M. Meas.*, 3.i.116.

perdy (French, *par dieu*), *Tw. Night*, 4.ii.73; *Ham.*, 3.ii.288.

peregrinate with the affectations of one who has seen the world, *L. Lab. Lost*, 5.i.12.

peremptory determined, *Cor*, 3.i.286.

perfect certain, *Cym.*, 3.i.71; *perfect soul*, sound conscience, *Oth.*, 1.ii.31; *verb*, to instruct, *M. Meas.*, 4.iii.138.

perfection performance, *Troil. and Cres.*, 3.ii.83.

perfumer one who kept the rooms fresh with perfume, *Much Ado*, 1.iii.50.

periapt a charm carried on the person, 1 *Hen. 6*, 5.iii.2.

perjure *noun*, a perjurer, *L. Lab. Lost*, 4.iii.43; *perjur'd note*, the paper pinned to the perjurer setting out his guilt, *L. Lab. Lost*, 4.iii.121.

peroration studied harangue, 2 *Hen. 6*, 1.i.100.

perpend ponder, *As You Like*, 3.ii.60.

Persian rich and ornate, *Lear*, 3.vi.79 (Edgar being in rags).

perspective a picture that appeared coherent and intelligible only from one particular point of view, *Rich. 2*, 2.ii.18; illusion, *Tw. Night*, v.i.209.

pertaunt-like 'pertaunt' was perhaps a winning declaration at the card game of Post and Pair – perhaps a hand of four Queens (*see* Dr. Percy Simpson's letter, *T.L.S.*, 24 Feb. 45), *L. Lab. Lost*, 5.ii.67.

petar a bomb or charge for blowing in gates, *Ham.*, 3.iv.207.

pew *pew-fellow*, associate, *Rich. 3*, 4.iv.58.

phantasime a fantastic fellow, *L. Lab. Lost*, 4.i.92.

phantasma nightmare, *Jul. Caes.*, 2.i.65.

pheeze castigate, *Tam. Shrew*, Ind.i.1; *Pheazar*, comic formation, *Mer. Wives Win.*, 1.iii.9.

Philip name for sparrow, *John*, 1.i.231.

Philip and Jacob 1st May, feast of Philip and James, *M. Meas.*, 3.ii.189.

Philip, Saint *Saint Philip's daughters*, the daughters of Philip the Evangelist (Acts xxi, 8–9) had the gift of prophecy, 1 *Hen. 6*, 1.ii.143.

Philippan *sword Philippan*, the sword he used in the victory at Philippi, *Ant. and Cleo.*, 2.v.23.

Philomel-a the nightingale; according to the legend, Pandion, king of Attica, had two daughters, Philomel and Procne; Procne was married to Tereus who ravished Philomel and cut out her tongue to conceal his sin; she was changed to a nightingale, *Titus*, 4.i.48.

philosopher *philosopher's two stones*, even better than the philosopher's stone that was supposed to turn base metals to gold, 2 *Hen. 4*, 3.ii.320.

Phoebe, Phoebus the moon-goddess, the sun-god, *Mid. N. Dr.*, 1.i.209 and 1.ii.29 (Phibbus).

phoenix a unique wonder, *Hen. 8*, 5.v.40.

phraseless beyond description, *Lor. Comp.*, 225.

physical good for the health, *Jul. Caes.*, 2.i.261.

pia mater brain, *Tw. Night*, 1.v.108.

pick pitch, *Cor.*, 1.i.198.

picked finical, *L. Lab. Lost*, 5.i.11.

pickers and stealers hands ('to keep my hand from picking and stealing' *Catechism*), *Ham.*, 3.ii.327.

pick-thank toady, 1 *Hen. 4*, 3.ii.25.

Pickt-hatch a quarter of ill-repute in London, *Mer. Wives Win.*, 2.ii.16.

pigeon-liver'd spiritless, tame, *Ham.*, 2.ii.572.

pight pitched, *Troil. and Cres*, 5.x.24; fixed, *Lear*, 2.i.65.
pike spike on buckler, *Much Ado*, 5.ii.19.
pilcher (i) pilchard, *Tw. Night*, 3.i.32; (ii) scabbard, *Rom. and Jul.*, 3.i.78.
pill plunder, *Timon*, 4.i.12.
pin peg in the centre of target, *L. Lab. Lost*, 4.i.129; *pin and web*, cataract, blindness, *Win. Tale*, 1.ii.291; *pin buttock*, narrow buttock, *All's Well*, 2.ii.17.
pinfold pound for stray animals, *Lear*, 2.ii.8.
pink'd *pink'd porringer* a cap, *Hen. 8*, 5.iv.45.
pioned *pioned and twilled brims*, meaning doubtful, *Tem.*, 4.i.64.
pip *a pip out*, thirty-two when thirty-one (at card game) is needed *Tam. Shrew*, 1.ii.32.
pipe-wine wine from cask, *Mer. Wives Win.*, 3.ii.77.
pismire ant, 1 *Hen. 4*, 1.iii.240.
pitch height, *Ham.*, 3.i.86.
place *pride of place*, the height from which hawk strikes, *Mac.*, 2.iv.12.
placket slit in petticoat to allow it to slip on, so woman *Troil. and Cres.*, 2.iii.19.
plain-song *the very plain-song of it*, the simple truth, *Hen. 5*, 3.ii.5.
planched of boards, *M. Meas.*, 4.i.28.
plantage vegetation (supposed to be affected by phases of moon), *Troil. and Cres.*, 3.ii.173.
plantain plant with broad flat leaves, thought good for wounds, *L. Lab. Lost*, 3.i.68.
plantation settlement, *Tem.*, 2.i.137.
plash pool, *Tam. Shrew*, 1.i.23.
plate silver coin, *Ant. and Cleo.*, 5.ii.92.
plate to cover with armour, *Lear*, 4.vi.165; *plated Mars*, armed for battle, *Ant. and Cleo.*, 1.i.4.
plausive pleasing, acceptable, *Ham.*, 1.iv.30; plausible, cunning, *All's Well*, 4.i.25.
pleached *thick-pleached alley*, the boughs closely intertwined, *Much Ado*, 1.ii.8; *pleach'd arms*, folded arms, *Ant. and Cleo.*, 4.xiv.73.
please-man toady, *L. Lab. Lost*, 5.ii.463.
pleurisy a plethora or excess, *Ham.*, 4.vii.117.
plighted wrapped as in pleats, folded, *Lear*, 1.i.280.
plume plumage, *Tem.*, 3.iii.65; *plume up*, dress up, express, *Oth.*, 1.iii.387. *plume-pluck'd*, dispossessed, *Rich. 2*, 4.i.108.
point *point of war*, trumpet-call, 2 *Hen. 4*, 4.i.52; lace for keeping hose attached to doublet, 1 *Hen. 4*, 2.iv.207 (pun on 'point'=sword-point); *armed at point exactly*, completely, *Ham.*, 1.ii.200; (in falconry) the height to which the hawk climbs before striking, 2 *Hen. 6*, 2.i.5; *point-devise*, in all particulars, precisely, *Tw. Night*, 2.v.145.
poise weight, *Lear*, 2.i.120; momentum, *Troil. and Cres.*, 1.iii.207; *verb*, to weight, estimate, *Troil. and Cres.*, 1.iii.339.
poke pocket, *As You Like*, 2.vii.20.
poking-sticks for ruffs *Win. Tale*, 4.iv.223.
Polacks Poles, *Ham.*, 1.i.63.
pole pole-star, *Oth.*, 2.i.15.
pole-clipt vineyard, the poles perhaps for the vines to climb on, *Tem.*, 4.i.68.
politic *politic authors*, writers on state affairs, *Tw. Night*, 2.v.143.
politician a political intriguer, *Lear*, 4.vi.171; *Ham.*, 5.i.78.
pomander scent-ball, *Win. Tale*, 4.iv.590.
pomewater kind of apple, *L. Lab. Lost*, 4.ii.4.
Pomgarnet pomegranate, rooms in inns often having names, 1 *Hen. 4*, 2.iv.36.
Pontic sea Black Sea, *Oth.*, 3.iii.457.
Poor-John salted fish, *Tem.*, 2.ii.26.
pop'rin pear kind of pear (from Poperinghe near Ypres), *Rom. and Jul.*, 2.i.38.
popularity contact with the common people, 1 *Hen. 4*, 3.ii.69.
porpentine porcupine, *Ham.*, 1.v.20.
porridge pottage or soup, 1 *Hen. 6*, 1.ii.9.
port (i) gate, *Troil. and Cres.*, 4.iv.110; (ii) bearing, *Hen. 5*, 1. *Chor*.6; rank, wealth, *Mer. Ven.*, 3.ii.283.
portage (i) venture (what the sailor traded on his own), *Per.*, 3.i.35; (ii) port-holes, *Hen. 5*, 3.i.10.
portance bearing, conduct, *Oth*, 1.iii.139.
posied *see* posy, *Lov. Comp.*, 45.
position argument, assertion, *Troil. and Cres.*, 3.iii.112; *in position*, in the statement, *Oth.*, 3.iii.238.
possession possessed as by an evil spirit, *Com. Err.*, 5.i.44.
posset *noun*, 'night-cap' of hot milk and spiced liquor, *Mac.*, 2.ii.6; *verb*, curdle, *Ham.*, 1.v.68.
post *sheriff's post*, sheriff's notice-board, *Tw. Night*, 1.v.140; door-post of tavern, *Com. Err.*, 1.ii.64.
postern side-door, *Win. Tale*, 1.ii.438.
post-haste speeding-up, *Ham.*, 1.i.107; *haste-post-haste*, immediate, *Oth.*, 1.ii.37.
posy inscription inside a ring (e.g. *Mer. Ven.*, 5.i.150), *Ham.*, 3.ii.147.
potch stab, *Cor.*, 1.x.15.
potential powerful, *Oth.*, 1.ii.13.
potents potentates, *John*, 2.i.358.
pother commotion, *Cor.*, 2.i.208.
potting drinking, *Oth.*, 2.iii.72.
pottle two-quart measure so tankard, *Oth.*, 2.iii.78.
pouncet-box perforated scent-box, 1 *Hen. 4*, 1.iii.38.
powder salt, 1 *Hen. 4*, 5.iv.112; *powdering-tub*, brine-tub (used of treatment for venereal disease), *Hen. 5*, 2.i.73.
practic practical, *Hen. 5*, 1.i.51.
practice intrigue, treachery, *Tw. Night*, 5.i.339; *Lear*, 1.ii.173.
practisant performer of a stratagem, 1 *Hen. 6*, 3.ii.20.
practise use some device, *Lear*, 3.ii.57; plot, *John*, 4.i.20.
praemunire *compass of a praemunire*, open to a charge of maintaining papal authority in England, *Hen. 8*, 3.ii.340.
prætor Roman magistrate, chiefly concerned with law, *Jul. Caes.*, 2.iv.34.
preambulate to go before *L. Lab. Lost*, 5.i.68.
precedence what is said before, *Ant. and Cleo.*, 2.v.51.
precedent original, *Rich. 3*, 3.vi.7; token, *Ven. and Ad.*, 26; *adj*, earlier, *Ham.*, 3.iv.98.
preceptial *preceptial medicine*, suitable precepts or advice on conduct, *Much Ado*, 5.i.24.
precipitate fall headlong, *Lear*, 4.vi.50.
precipitation extent of the fall, *Cor.*, 3.ii.4.
precise scrupulous, puritanical, *M. Meas.*, 1.iii.50 (also at 3.i.95 and 98, where the Folio reads 'prenzie').
precisian puritan-like adviser, *Mer. Wives Win.*, 2.i.5.
pre-contract engagement of marriage, *M. Meas.*, 4.i.70.

precurrer forerunner, *Phoenix*, 6.
precurse foreshadowing, *Ham.*, 1.i.121.
predominance *spherical predominance*, compulsion of planetary influence, *Lear*, 1.ii.118.
predominant in the ascendant or influential position, *All's Well* 1.i.185.
pregnancy ingenuity, wit, 2 *Hen. 4*, 1.ii.160.
pregnant (i) clear, *Oth.*, 2.i.232; weighty, significant, *Ham.*, 2.ii.207; apt to respond or act, *Ham.*, 3.ii.59.
prejudicate pass judgment on a matter before it is formally raised, *All's Well*, 1.ii.8.
premeditation *cold premeditation*, discouraging consideration for any future scheme, 3 *Hen. 6*, 3.ii.133.
premised sent before their time, 2 *Hen. 6*, 5.ii.41.
prenominate name beforehand, *Troil. and Cres.*, 4.v.250; *prenominate crimes*, already mentioned, *Ham.*, 2.i.43.
pre-ordinance decree already made, *Jul. Caes.*, 3.i.38.
preparations accomplishments, *Mer. Wives Win.*, 2.ii.206.
prerogative precedence, *Tam. Shrew*, 3.i.6; *All's Well*, 2.iv.39.
presage prophecy, signs of future happenings, presentiment, *Son.*, 107, 6; *Rich. 2*, 2.ii.142.
prescript *prescript praise*, praise as required by the subject of it, *Hen. 5*, 3.vii.45.
prescription title founded on usage or antiquity, 3 *Hen. 6*, 3.iii.94.
present immediate, *Ham.*, 4.iii.65; *present money*, ready money, *Mer. Ven.*, 3.ii.275.
presentation show, disguise, *As You Like*, 5.iv.101.
presentment dedication of book to patron, *Timon*, 1.i.29.
press authority to impress soldiers, 1 *Hen. 4*, 4.ii.12.
press *pressing to death*, refers to the pressing to death, with weights, of accused who would not plead, *M. Meas.*, 5.i.520.
pressure impression, *Ham.*, 3.ii.24.
Prester John a fabled and mysterious king of the East or Ethiopia, *Much Ado*, 2.i.238.
presuppos'd *forms presuppos'd*, dressed as the false letter suggested, *Tw. Night*, 5.i.337.
pretence purpose, *Cor.*, 1.ii.20; *pretence of danger*, malicious intention, *Lear*, 1.ii.84.
prevent anticipate, *Ham.*, 2.ii.293.
prevention interference, anticipatory counteraction, *Jul. Caes.*, 3.i.19.
prick *noun*, mark on dial of clock, against hour, 3 *Hen. 6*, 1.iv.34; to mark centre of target, *L. Lab. Lost*, 4.i.125; *verb*, mark off on a list, *Jul. Caes.*, 4.i.1.
pricket *see* buck.
prick-song song set out in notation, *Rom. and Jul.*, 2.iv.21.
prig thief, *Win. Tale*, 4.iii.96.
primero card-game, *Hen. 8*, 5.i.7.
primogenity legal right of elder, *Troil. and Cres.*, 1.iii.106.
principality Principalities, Archangels and Angels formed the third order of Heavenly beings, *Two Gent. Ver.*, 2.iv.148.
princox forward fellow, *Rom. and Jul.*, 1.v.84.
Priscian Roman grammarian, *a little scratch'd*, his rules violated somewhat, *L. Lab. Lost*, 5.i.25.
pristine former, ancient, *Hen. 5*, 3.ii.77.
privilege justification, explanation, *Mid. N. Dr.*, 2.i.220.
prize contest, *play'd your prize*, played your game, *Titus*, 1.i.339.
prizer (i) prize-fighter, *As You Like*, 2.iii.8; (ii) valuer, *Troil. and Cres.*, 2.ii.56.
probation examination, *Tw. Night*, 2.v.119; proof, *Ham.*, 1.i.156.
proceeder *quick proceeders*, with play on idea of proceeding to a university degree in Arts, *Tam. Shrew*, 4.ii.11.
process account, *Ham.*, 1.v.37; mandate, *Ham.*, 4.iii.63; by legal process, *Cor.*, 3.i.314.
proditor traitor, 1 *Hen. 6*, 1.iii.31.
proface may it do you good! (formula before a meal), 2 *Hen. 4*, 5.iii.28.
progeny race, *Cor.*, 1.viii.12; descent, 1 *Hen. 6*, 3.iii.61.
prognostication according to the almanac's forecast, *Win. Tale*, 4.iv.778; *fruitful prognostication*, sign of future fertility, *Ant. and Cleo.*, 1.ii.49.
prolixious time-wasting, *M. Meas.*, 2.iv.162.
Promethean heat, life-giving fire, such as Prometheus took from Heaven, *Oth.*, 5.ii.12.
promulgate announce, *Oth.*, 1.ii.21.
proof of armour, fitness to be put to the proof, impenetrability, *Rich. 2*, 1.iii.73.
propend incline, *Troil. and Cres.*, 2.ii.190.
propension inclination, *Troil. and Cres.*, 2.ii.133.
proper-false good-looking but deceitful at heart, *Tw. Night*, 2.ii.27.
property a mere tool, *Jul. Caes*, 4.i.40; *property of blood*, kinship, *Lear*, 1.i.113; *verb*, to treat as some inanimate object, *Tw. Night*, 4.ii.88.
Propontic Sea of Marmora, *Oth.*, 3.iii.460.
propose purpose, *Much Ado*, 3.i.12.
propugnation protection, *Troil. and Cres.*, 2.ii.136.
prorogue postpone, *Rom. and Jul.*, 2.ii.78.
Proteus sea-god who assumed various forms, 3 *Hen. 6*, 3.ii.192.
proud-pied with many fine colours, *Son.*, 98, 2.
provincial of a particular province, *M. Meas.*, 5.i.314.
Provincial roses rosettes covering the laces (Provencal roses), *Ham.*, 3.ii.270.
prune preen, *Cym.*, 5.iv.118.
psaltery stringed instrument, *Cor.*, 5.iv.48.
pudder commotion, *Lear*, 3.ii.50.
pugging thieving (doubtful), *Win. Tale*, 4.iii.7.
puissance power, army, *John*, 3.i.339.
puke-stocking cloth stocking, 1 *Hen. 4*, 2.iv.67.
punk harlot, *Mer. Wives Win.*, 2.ii.122.
punto thrust in fencing, *Mer. Wives Win.*, 2.iii.24; *punto reverso*, backhanded thrust, *Rom. and Jul.*, 2.iv.26.
purchas'd acquired as opposed to possession by descent, e.g. *hereditary rather than purchas'd*, *Ant. and Cleo.*, 1.iv.14.
purgation clearance of guilt, *Win. Tale*, 3.ii.7.
purl flow, *Lucrece*, 1407.
purlieu land bordering forest, *As You Like*, 4.iii.75.
purple-in-grain *see* grain.
pursuivant messenger, *Rich. 3*, 3.iv.90.
purveyor officer who went ahead to see to lodging, etc., *Mac.*, 1.vi.22.
push attack, 1 *Hen. 4*, 3.ii.66.

push-pin children's game, *L. Lab. Lost*, 4.iii.165.
putter-out of five for one, the voyager who put down a sum with a dealer on condition that he obtained on return five times the original, but forfeited the lot if he failed to return or keep the date fixed, *Tem.*, 3.iii.48.
puttock bird of prey, kite, *Cym.*, 1.i.140.
puzzel a drab, 1 *Hen.* 6, 1.iv.107.
quail a loose woman, *Troil. and Cres.*, 5.i.50.
quaint clever, 2 *Hen.* 6, 3.ii.274; charming, delicate, *Mid. N. Dr.*, 2.ii.7; *quaint mazes*, intricate paths, *Mid. N. Dr.*, 2.i.99.
quaintly artfully, *Ham.*, 2.i.31; *Mer. Ven.*, 2.iv.6.
qualification condition, *Oth.*, 2.i.269.
qualified possessed, endowed, *Win. Tale*, 2.i.113; competent, *Lear*, 1.iv.34.
qualify to moderate, *Lear*, 1.ii.153; dilute, *Oth.*, 2.iii.36; diminish, *Ham.*, 4.vii.113.
quality natural parts, *Troil. and Cres.*, 4.iv.75; social position, *Lear*, 5.iii.120; acquired skill, profession (especially of actor), *Ham.*, 2.ii.426.
quarrel cause for strife, *Ham.*, 4.iv.55.
quarry heap of dead (from term used of deer killed in sport), *Ham.*, 5.ii.356.
quarter area of camp or town assigned to a body of troops, 1 *Hen.* 6, 2.i.63 and 68; *keep good quarter*, watchful guard, *John*, 5.v.20; *have quarter*, have entrusted for protection, *Ant. and Cleo.*, 4.iii.24; on amicable terms, *Oth.*, 2.iii.172; *quarter'd fires*, camp fires, *Cym.*, 4.iv.18; dead, *Cor.*, 1.i.197.
quat pimple, so contemptuously of a person, *Oth.*, 5.i.11.
quean female, scold, 2 *Hen.* 4, 2.i.45.
queasy *of a queasy question*, difficult nature, *Lear*, 2.i.17; upset, disgusted, *Ant. and Cleo.*, 3.vi.20.
quell slaughter, *Mac.*, 1.vii.72.
quest *crowner's quest law*, law as laid down at the coroner's inquest, *Ham.*, 5.i.22; party to make inquiry, *Oth.*, 1.ii.46.
questant seeker for fame, *All's Well*, 2.i.16.
questrists searchers, *Lear*, 3.vii.16.
quick living, *Ham.*, 5.i.122; pregnant, *L. Lab. Lost*, 5.ii.665; sensitive part, *Ham.*, 2.ii.593; sharp, *Per.*, 4.i.28.
quicken are born, *Oth.*, 3.iii.281; come to life again, *Ant. and Cleo.*, 4.xv.39.
quiddities fine-spun arguments, *Ham.*, 5.i.96.
quietus term signifying the discharge of a debt, *Son.*, 126, 12; release from the bondage of life, *Ham.*, 3.i.75.
quillet legal quibble, *Ham.*, 5.i.97.
quintain an object for tilting at, *As You Like*, 1.ii.230.
quintessence the fifth essence, underlying the four elements (earth, air, fire, water), and forming the stars; so the most subtle extract or manifestation, *Ham.*, 2.ii.307.
quip retort, sharp remark, *As You Like*, 5.iv.71.
quirk clever stroke, *Oth.*, 2.i.63; shock, *All's Well*, 3.ii.47; turn of mind, *Tw. Night*, 3.iv.233.
quit *adj., quit with, of*, even with, *Cor.*, 4.v.83.
quit *verb*, release, *Tw. Night*, 5.i.308; release from, *Hen.* 8, 5.i.70; to remit, *Mer. Ven.*, 4.i.376; to requite, *Ham.*, 5.ii.68.
quittance like for like, 2 *Hen.* 4, 1.i.108; recompense, *Hen.* 5, 2.ii.34.
quiver agile, 2 *Hen.* 4, 3.ii.273.
quoif close-fitting cap, *Win. Tale*, 4.iv.221.
quoit cast, 2 *Hen.* 4, 2.iv.182.
quondam former, *Troil. and Cres.*, 4.v.179.
quoniam since, because, *L. Lab. Lost*, 5.ii.585.
quote indicate (as a reference in a book), *L. Lab. Lost*, 2.i.245; mark out, *John*, 4.ii.222; observe, *Ham.*, 2.i.112; regard, *L. Lab. Lost*, 5.ii.774.
quotidian *quotidian of love*, a fever that recurs daily, *As You Like*, 3.ii.339; *quotidian tertian*, Mistress Quickly's terminology (a tertian fever recurred every second day), *Hen.* 5, 2.i.116.
R *the dog's name*, or letter, because 'arre' is like a dog's snarl, *Rom. and Jul.*, 2.iv.203.
rabato kind of stiff collar, *Much Ado*, 3.iv.6.
rabbit-sucker baby rabbit, 1 *Hen.* 4, 2.iv.422.
race course, *John*, 3.iii.39.
race herd, *Mer. Ven.*, 5.i.72; strain, e.g. *sensual race*, lust, *M. Meas.*, 2.iv.160; *race of heaven*, of heavenly descent, *Ant. and Cleo.*, 1.iii.37.
race, raze *race of ginger*, root of ginger, *Win. Tale*, 4.iii.45.
rack clouds drifting with the wind, *Ham.*, 2.ii.478; *leave not a rack behind*, no trace, even as unsubstantial as a cloud, *Tem.*, 4.i.156.; *verb*, stretch, *Mer. Ven.*, 1.i.181; distort, misrepresent, *M. Meas.*, 4.i.63.
rackers distorters, *L. Lab. Lost*, 5.i.17.
rage madness, *Lear*, 4.vii.78; martial ardour, *John*, 2.i.265; *a poet's rage*, poet's enthusiasm, *Son.*, 17.11; *verb*, act madly, *Ant. and Cleo.*, 4.i.7.
raging-wood raging mad, 1 *Hen.* 6, 4.vii.35.
raisins o'th'sun sun-dried grapes, *Win. Tale*, 4.iii.46.
ramp harlot, *Cym.*, 1.vi.133.
rampallian of a woman, scoundrel, 2 *Hen.* 4, 2.i.57.
ramping on hind legs in fighting attitude, 1 *Hen.* 4, 3.i.153.
rampir'd fortified, *Timon*, 5.iv.47.
rangers *Diana's rangers*, her virgin nymphs, *Cym.*, 2.iii.69.
rank perhaps for 'rack' = easy pace, *As You Like*, 3.ii.88.
rank *adj., rank Achilles*, overgrown in pride, *Troil. and Cres.*, 1.iii.318; *rank corruption*, uncheck'd, *Ham.*, 3.iv.148; *ranker rate*, greater price, *Ham*, *4.iv.22*; adv., completely, *Troil. and Cres.*, 1.iii.196.
rankle inflict a wound that festers, *Rich.* 2, 1.iii.302.
ransack'd *queen*, carried off, *Troil. and Cres.*, 2.ii.150.
rap *thus raps you*, moves you to this strange fit, *Cym.*, 1.vi.50.
rapture forcible seizure, *Per.*, 2.i.153; fit, *Cor.*, 2.i.197.
rascal a lean and worthless deer, so term of contempt, *Cor.*, 1.i.157.
rash sudden in operation, 2 *Hen.* 4, 4.iv.48; hasty, demanding haste, *Troil. and Cres.*, 4.ii.60; *verb*, stick, *Lear*, 3.vii.57.
rate price, *Ham.*, 4.iv.22; estimation, *Tem.*, 2.i.103; way of living, *Mer. Ven.*, 1.i.127.
rather *the rather*, the sooner, *All's Well*, 3.v.39; *ratherest*, most of all, *L. Lab. Lost*, 4.ii.16.
ratify *only numbers ratified*, correct in form only, *L. Lab. Lost*, 4.ii.116.
Ratolorum corruption of Custos Rotulorum (Keeper of the Rolls), *Mer. Wives Win.*, 1.i.7.
ravel *ravell'd sleave*, tangled skein (*see* sleid), *Mac.*,

2.ii.37; *Two Gent. Ver.*, 3.ii.52.
ravin *adj*, ravenous, *All's Well*, 3.ii.116; *verb*, devour, *M. Meas.*, 1.ii.123; *ravin'd shark*, devouring, *Mac.*, 4.i.24.
ravish to infect, *Lucrece*, 778; tear out, *Lear*, 3.vii.37; *ravish'd queen*, carried off by force or guile, *Troil. and Cres.*, Prol. 8; *ravishing strides*, steps of the ravisher, *Mac.*, 2.i.55.
rawness unprotected condition, *Mac.*, 4.iii.26.
ray'd bemired, *Tam. Shrew*, 4.i.3.
raze obliterate, *Mac.*, 5.iii.42; pluck off, *Rich.* 3, 3.iv.84; lay flat, *M. Meas.*, 2.ii.171.
raz'd *raz'd shoes*, uppers cut pattern-wise, *Ham.*, 3.ii.271.
razure obliteration, *M. Meas.*, 5.i.13.
reach attainment, *Ham.*, 2.i.64.
reach *verb*, *raught* (participle), taken hold of, *Ant. and Cleo.*, 4.ix.29; attain to in duration or numbers, *L. Lab. Lost*, 4.ii.38.
read give learned instruction, 1 *Hen.* 4, 3.i.46.
re-answer give compensation, *Hen.* 5, 3.vi.124.
reason *noun*, observation, *L. Lab. Lost*, 5.i.2; justice, *Titus*, 1.i.279; *verb*, discuss, *Lear*, 2.iv.263.
reave reft (participle), taken away, *Ven. and Adon.*, 1174.
rebate blunt, *M. Meas.*, 1.iv.60.
rebeck fiddle with three strings, used as name of musician, *Rom. and Jul.*, 4.v.130.
recheat call on horn for hounds, so of cuckold's horns, *Much Ado*, 1.i.208.
reck *recks not his own rede*, heeds not his own advice, *Ham*, 1.iii.51.
reckless regardless of duty, 3 *Hen.* 6, 5.vi.7.
reclaim subdue, 1 *Hen.* 6, 3.iv.5.
recognizance a legal bond, defining a debt, *Ham.*, 5.i.101; token, *Oth.*, 5.ii.217.
recoil to degenerate, *Cym.*, 1.vi.127; to go back in thought, *Win. Tale*, 1.ii.154.
recollect *recollected terms*, studied diction, *Tw. Night*, 2.iv.5.
recommend deliver, *Tw. Night*, 5.i.85; inform, *Oth.*, 1.iii.41.
record sing, *Two Gent. Ver.*, 5.iv.6; *recorded*, witness'd for, *Timon*, 4.ii.4.
recorder kind of flageolet, *Ham.*, 3.ii.286.
recourse flow, *Troil. and Cres.*, 5.iii.55; admittance, *Rich.* 3, 3.v.109.
recoverable able to be repeated, *Timon*, 3.iv.13.
recovery *see* fine.
recreation taking food, *L. Lab. Lost*, 4.ii.156.
rector ruler, *All's Well*, 4.iii.56; *rectorship*, rule, *Cor.*, 2.iii.202.
rede counsel, *Ham*, 1.iii.51.
red lattice window of alehouse, 2 *Hen.* 4, 2.ii.76; *red-lattice phrases*, language of alehouse, *Mer. Wives Win.*, 2.ii.23.
reduce bring again, *Rich.* 3, 5.v.36.
reechy smoky unclean, *Cor.*, 2.i.199.
reed voice piping voice, *Mer. Ven.*, 3.iv.67.
re-edify rebuild, *Titus*, 1.i.351.
refel refute, *M. Meas.*, 5.i.94.
refuge hide away, *Rich.* 2, 5.v.26.
regard object to the eye, *Oth.*, 2.i.40; observance of duty, *Lear*, 1.iv.265; estimation, *Troil. and Cres.*, 3.iii.128.
regiment government, *Ant. and Cleo.*, 3.vi.95.
region the heavens, *Ham.*, 2.ii.481; *region kites*, of the air, *Ham.*, 2.ii.574.
reguerdon *noun*, reward, 1 *Hen.* 6, 3.i.170; *verb*, to reward, 1 *Hen.* 6, 3.iv.23.
reins loins, *Mer. Wives Win.*, 3.v.20.
rejoindure union, *Troil. and Cres.*, 4.iv.35.
rejourn adjourn, *Cor.*, 2.i.65.
relation application, *Mer. Ven.*, 4.i.243; *understood relations*, combinations rightly interpreted, *Mac.*, 3.iv.124.
religious conscientious, *Tw. Night*, 3.iv.373.
relinquish *relinquish'd of the artists*, given up by doctors, *All's Well*, 2.iii.10.
relish *noun*, *grafted to your relish*, changed to your quality, *Cor.*, 2.i.180; characteristic mark or flavour, *Ham.*, 3.iii.92; sing, *Two Gent. Ver.*, 2.i.18.
relume rekindle, *Oth.*, 5.ii.13.
remainder *cut the entail from all remainders*, (legal terms) give away also anything that may remain after he has parted with his (inheritance) salvation, *All's Well*, 4.iii.261; *remainder viands*, food left over, *Troil. and Cres.*, 2.ii.70; *remainder biscuit*, *As You Like*, 2.vii.39.
remediate remedial, *Lear*, 4.iv.17.
remission *apt remission*, ready pardon, *M. Meas.*, 5.i.496.
remonstrance *rash remonstrance*, sudden demonstration, *M. Meas.*, 5.i.390.
remorse pity, *Lear*, 4.ii.73; *remorseful*, compassionate, *Two Gent. Ver.*, 4.iii.13; *remorseless*, without pity, *Ham.*, 2.ii.576.
remotion flight, holding aloof, *Timon*, 4.iii.339; *Lear*, 2.iv.112.
render *noun*, settlement of a debt or obligation, *Cym.*, 5.iv.17; confession, admission, *Timon*, 5.i.147; *verb*, give an account of, characterize, *As You Like*, 4.iii.121; *Cym.*, 2.iv.119.
rendez-vous meeting place, *Ham.*, 4.iv.4.
renege deny, *Lear*, 2.ii.73; resigns, *Ant. and Cleo.*, 1.i.8.
renew repeat, *Hen.* 5, 1.ii.116.
repair *noun*, resort, *Ham.*, 5.ii.210; *verb*, return, *Mid. N. Dr.*, 4.i.64.
repasture food, *L. Lab. Lost*, 4.i.86.
repetition reference to the past, *All's Well*, 5.iii.22.
repining reluctant to praise, *Troil. and Cres.*, 1.iii.243.
replenished full, complete, *Win. Tale*, 2.i.79.
replication reply, *Ham.*, 4.ii.13; echo, reverberation, *Jul. Caes.*, 1.i.47.
reposure placing, *Lear*, 2.i.68.
reprisal prize, 1 *Hen.* 4, 4.i.118.
reprobance damnation, *Oth.*, 5.ii.212.
reprove disprove, 2 *Hen.* 6, 3.i.40.
repugn resist, 1 *Hen.* 6, 4.i.94.
repugnancy resistance, *Timon*, 3.v.45.
repure purify again, *Troil. and Cres.*, 3.ii.21.
repute value, 2 *Hen.*. 6, 3.i.48.
require to request, *Cor.*, 2.iii.1.
requiring request, *M. Meas.*, 3.i.235.
requit repaid, *Tem.*, 3.iii.71.
rere-mice bats, *Mid. N. Dr.*, 2.ii.4.
resemblance probability, *M. Meas.*, 4.ii.178.
resist repel, *Per.*, 2.iii.29.
resolution certainty, *Lear*, 1.ii.96.
resolve dissolve, *Timon*, 4.iii.437; free from doubt,

answer a question, *Jul. Caes.*, 3.i.132; *resolv'd correction*, purposed chastisement, 2 *Hen.* 4, 4.i.213.
respect *noun, without respect*, apart from its context, *Mer. Ven.*, 5.i.99; rank, estimation, *Jul. Caes.*, 1.ii.59; *base respects of thrift*, considerations of profit, *Ham.*, 3.ii.178; deliberation, *Troil. and Cres.*, 2.ii.49; *upon respect*, deliberately, *Lear*, 2.iv.23; *verb*, consider, *Mid. N. Dr.*, 1.i.160; *respecting*, remembering, in comparison with, *Win. Tale*, 5.i.35.
respective *respective lenity*, deliberate forbearance, *Rom. and Jul.*, 3.i.120; courteous, *John*, 1.i.188; to be admired, *Two Gent. Ver.*, 4.iv.191.
respectively very warmly, *Timon*, 3.i.8.
respite delay, 1 *Hen.* 6, 4.i.170; *determin'd respite*, appointed end of the time (in which my crimes went unpunished), *Rich.* 3, 5.i.19.
rest term from card game of primero signifying the stake on which the game turned, the loss of which ended the game – so hazard everything, make an end of matter, *Rom. and Jul.*, 5.iii.110.
resting immovable, *Jul. Caes.*, 3.i.61.
resty sluggish, *Troil. and Cres.*, 1.iii.263; *Son*, 100, 9.
retreat withdrawal from pursuit, 2 *Hen.* 4, 4.iii.71.
retrograde with apparent backward motion in the heavens, *All's Well*, 1.i.186; contrary, *Ham.*, 1.ii.114.
return *noun*, reply, *Hen.* 5, 2.iv.127; *verb*, to send back someone, *Timon*, 3.vi.37; to be handed over, *Ham.*, 1.i.91.
reverb reverberate, *Lear*, 1.i.153.
reverberate hills, re-echoing, *Tw. Night*, 1.v.256.
reverse back-handed thrust in fencing, *Mer. Wives Win.*, 2.iii.24.
reversion *in reversion*, in the future, *Troil. and Cres.*, 3.ii.89.
review see again, *Win. Tale*, 4.iv.656.
revolution change, as made by time or the turning of Fortune's wheel, *Ham.*, 5.i.88.
revolve turn over in mind, *Tw. Night*, 2.v.128.
rhapsody meaningless verbiage, *Ham.*, 3.iv.48.
Rhenish Rhine wine, *Ham.*, 1.iv.10.
rheum a flow of tears, saliva, etc., *bisson rheum*, blinding tears, *Ham.*, 2.ii.500; *Mer. Ven.*, 1.iii.112; a disease characterized by such an excessive flow, *Ant. and Cleo.*, 3.ii.57; *rheumatic diseases*, diseases brought on by an excessive flow, *Mid. N. Dr.*, 2.i.105; *rheumy*, causing the morbid condition, *Jul. Caes.*, 2.i.266.
ribaudred *ribaudred nag of Egypt*, Egyptian harlot, *Ant. and Cleo.*, 3.x.10.
riggish wantonly inclined, *Ant. and Cleo.*, 2.ii.244.
right *adv*, exactly, to the life, *Troil. and Cres.*, 1.iii.170.
right-hand *right-hand file*, patricians, *Cor.*, 2.i.21.
rigol circle, *golden rigol*, crown, 2 *Hen.* 4, 4.v.36.
rim lining of belly, *Hen.* 5, 4.iv.14.
ring *crack'd within the ring*, coin rendered uncurrent by a crack extending inside the ring round the sovereign's effigy, *Ham.*, 2.ii.423.
ring-carrier a go-between, *All's Well*, 3.v.89.
ripe *sinking-ripe*, ready to sink, *Com. Err.*, 1.i.78; ready prepared, *Mid. N. Dr.*, 5.i.42.
rivage shore, *Hen.* 5, 3. *Chor.*14.
rival partner, *Ham.*, 1.i.13; *rivality*, partnership, *Ant. and Cleo.*, 3.v.8.
rivelled wrinkled, *Troil. and Cres.*, 5.i.21.
rivo a toper's exclamation, 1 *Hen.* 4, 2.iv.107.
road roadstead, *Mer. Ven.*, 1.i.19.
robustious violent (in action or declamation), *Ham.*, 3.ii.9.
rogue vagrant, *Lear*, 4.vii.39; *roguing*, wandering, *Per.*, 4.i.98.
roisting rousing, *Troil. and Cres.*, 2.ii.208.
romage turmoil, *Ham.*, 1.i.107.
Roman *Roman hand*, the style of handwriting called Roman or Italian that replaced the English hand, *Tw. Night*, 3.iv.28.
rondure sphere, *Son.*, 21, 8.
ronyon scabby creature, *Mac.*, 1.iii.6.
rook squat, 3 *Hen.* 6, 5.vi.47.
ropery knavery, *Rom. and Jul.*, 2.iv.142; *rope-tricks* (may be connected with 'ropery'), *Tam. Shrew*, 1.ii.109.
roted learnt by rote, *Cor.*, 3.ii.55.
rother ox, *Timon*, 4.iii.12.
round *adj.*, *roundest manner*, plainest, *Lear*, 1.iv.53.
round to whisper, *John*, 2.i.566.
roundel a dance in a circle, *Mid. N. Dr.*, 2.ii.1.
roundly unceremoniously, *Rich.* 2, 2.i.122.
roundure circuit, *John*, 2.i.259.
rouse a bumper, *Oth.*, 2.iii.60; carouse, *Ham.*, 2.i.58.
royal gold coin, value 10 shillings, 1 *Hen.* 4, 1.ii.136; (punning on royal = 10 shillings, noble = 6s. 8d., difference = 40 pence = ten groats), *Rich.* 2, 5.v.67.
roynish scurvy, *As You Like*, 2.ii.8.
rub *noun*, impediment (from game of bowls), *Cor.*, 3.i.60; *verb*, *rubb'd*, diverted from his course, *Lear*, 2.ii.149.
rubious ruby-coloured, *Tw. Night*, 1.iv.31.
ruddock robin, *Cym.*, 4.ii.225.
rudesby rude fellow, *Tam. Shrew*, 3.ii.10.
rue pity, *Titus*, 1.i.105.
ruffle *noun*, ostentation, *Lov. Comp.*, 58; bluster, swagger, *Titus*, 1.i.313.
rug-headed shaggy-hair'd, *Rich.* 2, 2.i.156.
rump-fed fat-rumped, well-fed (but other suggestions put forward), *Mac.*, 1.iii.6.
runagate deserter, fugitive, *Rom. and Jul.*, 3.v.89.
runaways (not satisfactorily explained), *Rom. and Jul.*, 3.ii.6 (cp. *vagabonds, rascals, and runaways*, *Rich* 3, 5.iii.316).
russet homespun cloth, so plain, genuine, *L. Lab. Lost*, 5.ii.413; *russet-pated*, grey-headed, *Mid. N. Dr.*, 3.ii.21.
ruth pity, *ruthful*, pitiable, *Troil. and Cres.*, 5.iii.48.
Saba Queen of Sheba; 'Saba' is the spelling used in the Bishops' Bible, *Hen.* 8, 5.v.23.
sable black, *Ham.*, 2.ii.446.
sables garment trimmed with a brown fur, for ceremonial or leisure, *Ham.*, 3.ii.125; 4.vii.80.
sack a white wine of Sherry class from Spain or Canaries, 1 *Hen.* 4, 1.ii.7.
sackbut musical instrument of brass group, like trombone, *Cor.*, 5.iv.48.
Sackerson a performing bear at Paris garden, *Mer. Wives Win.*, 1.i.269.
sacring bell during Mass, the bell rung at elevation of Host; or bell calling to morning prayer, *Hen.* 8, 3.ii.295.
sad serious, grave; *speak sad brow and true maid*, in all truth and sincerity, *As You Like*, 3.ii.200; *Jul. Caes.*, 1.ii.217; *sad-ey'd*, of serious countenance, *Hen.* 5, 1.ii.202; *sadness*, gravity, 3 *Hen.* 6, 3.ii.77.

safe sane, sound, *Oth.*, 4.i.266.
saffron crocus-yellow (alluding to yellow starch'd ruffs, etc.), *All's Well*, 4.v.2.
Sagittary (i) the Centaur whom medieval romancers represent as fighting as an archer for the Trojans, *Troil. and Cres.*, 5.v.14; (ii) An inn with the sign of Sagittarius (but there are other explanations), *Oth.*, 1.i.159.
sail ships, *armado of convicted sail*, defeated fleet, *John*, 3.iv.2.
sain *tofore been sain*, said before, *L. Lab. Lost*, 3.i.77.
salad days youth, *Ant. and Cleo*, 1.v.73.
salamander fabled to live in fire, so of toper's red face, 1 *Hen.* 4, 3.iii.46.
sale-work ordinary ready-made quality, *As You Like*, 3.v.43.
Salique *Salique law*, law limiting succession to heirs male, *Hen.* 5, 1.ii.54.
sallet (i) salad, 2 *Hen.* 6, 4.x.8; *sallets*, spicy or bawdy lines, *Ham.*, 2.ii.435; (ii) light helmet, 2 *Hen.* 6, 4.x.10.
salt *man of salt*, tearful, *Lear*, 4.vi.196; biting, *Troil. and Cres.*, 1.iii.371; wanton, *Ant. and Cleo.*, 2.i.21.
Saltiers perhaps for 'Satyrs', *Win. Tale*, 4.iv.320.
salute excite, please, *Hen.* 8, 2.iii.103.
sanctimonious sacred, *Tem.*, 4.i.16.
sanctuarize shelter, *Ham.*, 4.vii.127.
sandblind almost blind, *Mer. Ven.*, 2.ii.31.
sanded sand coloured, *Mid. N. Dr.*, 4.i.117.
sandy *sandy hour*, hour marked by the falling sand in hour-glass, 1 *Hen.* 6, 4.ii.36.
sanguine *sanguine coward*, full-blooded coward, 1 *Hen.* 4, 2.iv.235; pink (and white) cheek'd, *Titus*, 4.ii.97.
sans without, *As You Like*, 2.vii.166.
sarcenet *adj.*, made of flimsy silk (Saracenic), *Troil. and Cres.*, 5.i.29; flimsy, 1 *Hen.* 4, 3.i.252
Sarum *Sarum plain*, Salisbury plain, *Lear*, 2.ii.78.
Saturn planet under which saturnine characters were born, revengeful, *Much Ado*, 1.iii.10; *Titus*, 2.iii.31.
Savoy palace in Strand, 2 *Hen.* 6, 4.vii.1.
say (i) serge, 2 *Hen.* 6, 4.vii.23; (ii) accent, quality, *Lear*, 5.iii.144.
'Sblood by God's blood, *Ham.*, 2.ii.362.
scaffoldage the boards of the stage, *Troil. and Cres.*, 1.iii.156.
scald scurvy, *Ant. and Cleo.*, 5.ii.214.
scale *scaled sculls*, scattered shoals, *Troil. and Cres.*, 5.v.22.
scamble scramble, *John*, 4.iii.146.
scamels (various suggestions, e.g. seamells, seamews), *Tem.*, 2.ii.162.
scantling sample, *Troil. and Cres.*, 1.iii.341.
scantly depreciatingly, *Ant. and Cleo.*, 3.iv.6.
scarre (meaning doubtful), *All's Well*, 4.ii.38.
scathe *noun*, injury, *John*, 2.i.75; *verb*, to injure, *Rom. and Jul.*, 1.v.82.
scatter *scatter'd kingdom*, disunited realm, *Lear*, 3.i.31.
scene *scene individable*, the locality of events unchanged, unity of place, *Ham.*, 2.ii.395.
schedule document, *Jul. Caes.*, 3.i.3.
school university, *Ham.*, 1.ii.113; the learned faculties, *All's Well*, 1.iii.231.
science knowledge, *All's Well*, 5.iii.103.
scion cutting for grafting, *Win. Tale*, 4.iv.93; bud, *Oth.*, 1.iii.331.
sconce fort, *Hen.* 5, 3.vi.71; protection, *Com. Err.*, 2.ii.34; head, *Ham.*, 5.i.99.
scorch cut, *Com. Err.*, 5.i.183.
score *the score and the tally*, reckonings kept by notching a stick, 2 *Hen.* 6, 4.vii.32; *on the score*, in debt, *Tam. Shrew*, Ind.ii.21.
scot *scot and lot*, in full, 1 *Hen.* 4, 5.iv.114.
scotch *noun*, gash, wound, *Ant. and Cleo.*, 4.vii.10; *verb*, to cut, wound, *Cor.*, 4.v.186; *Mac.*, 3.ii.13 (where Folio reads scorch'd – *see* scorch).
scrimer fencer, *Ham.*, 4.vii.100.
scrip document, *Mid. N. Dr.*, 1.ii.3.
scrip *scrip and scrippage*, shepherd's pouch (the second element being a nonce formation), *As You Like*, 3.ii.152.
scriptures writings, letter (with reference to holy writ), *Cym.*, 3.iv.79.
scrowl indicate roughly (as a scrawl may), *Titus*, 2.iv.5.
scroyle rascal, *John*, 2.i.373.
scrubbed undersized, *Mer. Ven.*, 5.i.162.
scrupulous *scrupulous faction*, hesitating allegiance, *Ant. and Cleo.*, 1.iii.48.
sculls shoals, *Troil. and Cres.*, 5.v.22.
scullion kitchen drudge, *Ham.*, 2.ii.583.
scut tail of a deer, *Mer. Wives Win.*, 5.v.17.
'Sdeath by God's death, *Cor.*, 1.i.215.
sea-coal pit coal (not charcoal), so called being brought to London by sea from Newcastle, 2 *Hen.* 4, 2.i.85.
seal *seal'd quarts*, measures officially stamped as correct, *Tam. Shrew*, Ind.ii.86.
seam fat, *Troil. and Cres.*, 2.iii.180.
sea-maid mermaid, *Mid. N. Dr.*, 2.i.154.
sea-monster that to which Hesione daughter of Laomedon King of Troy was exposed and from which she was delivered by Hercules, not for love but for a gift of horses, *Mer. Ven.*, 3.ii.57.
seamy *seamy side*, worst side, *Oth.*, 4.ii.147.
sear, sere sere or withered state, *Mac.*, 5.iii.23; *sear'd*, withered, *Lov. Comp.*, 14.
searcher officer that reported on the cause of death and kept watch for cases of plague, *Rom. and Jul.*, 5.ii.8.
searching *searching terms*, invective, 2 *Hen.* 6, 3.ii.311; *searching wine*, intoxicating, 2 *Hen.* 4, 2.iv.27.
second supporter, *Lear*, 4.vi.195.
sect (i) a cutting, *Oth.*, 1.iii.331; (ii) a division, party, *Lear*, 5.iii.18; womankind, 2 *Hen.* 4, 2.iv.37.
sectary *sectary astronomical*, an astrologer, *Lear*, 1.ii.143.
secure *adj.*, free from all suspicion or care, *secure hour*, fearing no danger, *Ham.*, 1.v.61; *Oth.*, 3.iii.202; *verb*, to make careless, *Lear*, 4.i.21; *secure thy heart*, free it from anxiety, *Timon*, 2.ii.177.
security *security is mortal's chiefest enemy*, lack of vigilance, *Mac.*, 3.v.32.
See *the See*, Rome, *M. Meas.*, 3.ii.206.
seeded come to a head, active, *Troil. and Cres.*, 1.iii.316.
seedness sowing, *M. Meas.*, 1.iv.42.
seel to close the eyes of a captured falcon by a thread through its eyelids, so to blind, *Oth.*, 3.iii.214; *Mac.*, 3.ii.46.
seeming appearance, outward show true or false, *Win. Tale*, 4.iv.75; *Much Ado*, 4.i.55.
seld *seld-shown flamens*, priests who seldom appear in public, *Cor.*, 2.i.203.

semblable *adj.*, similar, 2 *Hen.* 4, 5.i.62; *noun, his semblable*, his like, *Timon*, 4.iii.22.
sennet (in stage directions) trumpet notes to mark entrance or exit of a procession, *Mac.*, 3.i.10 (S.D.).
se'nnight week (from ancient custom of beginning day at sunset), *Oth.*, 2.i.77.
senseless *senseless things*, objects without feeling, *Jul. Caes.*, 1.i.36; *senseless conjuration*, addressed to the inanimate earth, *Rich.* 2, 3.ii.23.
sensible *the sensible avouch*, the evidence of one of the senses, *Ham.*, 1.i.57; capable of physical or spiritual feeling, *Mid. N. Dr.*, 5.i.180; *Mer. Ven.*, 2.viii.48; capable of being felt, *Mac.*, 2.i.36.
sensibly *sensibly in grief*, affected by grief, *Ham.*, 4.v.147; *sensibly outdares*, in spite of being subject to pain, wounds, etc., *Cor.*, 1.iv.54.
sentence moral saying, maxim, *Mer. Ven.*, 1.ii.9.
sententious full of wise saws, *As You Like*, 5.iv.60.
septentrion the north, 3 *Hen.* 6, 1.iv.136.
sequent following, *Oth.*, 1.ii.41; consequent, *Lear*, 1.ii.102.
sequester *noun*, separation, *Oth.*, 3.iv.37; *verb, sequest'red*, separated, *As You Like*, 2.i.33.
sequestration separation, *Oth.*, 1.iii.343 (perhaps sequel).
sere *tickle o'th' sere*, easily set off (like a gun with a low trigger pressure, the sere being part of the trigger mechanism), *Ham.*, 2.ii.322.
sergeant bailiff, *Ham.*, 5.ii.328.
serpigo skin disease, *Troil. and Cres.*, 2.iii.70.
servant avowed lover, *Two Gent. Ver.*, 2.i.97.
set stake, *Who sets me else?* Who puts down a stake (challenge) against me, *Rich.* 2, 4.i.57; (as in music), *Two Gent. Ver.*, 1.ii.81.
setter spy for thieves, 1 *Hen.* 4, 2.ii.49.
several *adj., a several plot*, a private enclosure, *Son.*, 137.9; as opposed to common land, *L. Lab. Lost*, 2.i.222; *noun, severals*, particulars, *Hen.* 5, 1.i.86.
sewer butler, servant responsible for service at table, *Mac.*, 1.vii.1 (S.D.).
'Sfoot by God's foot, *Troil. and Cres.*, 2.iii.5.
shag hairy, *shag-hair'd kern*, 2 *Hen.* 6, 3.i.367.
shale shell, *Hen.* 5, 4.ii.18.
shamefac'd modest, backward, *Rich.* 3, 1.iv.137.
shard (i) broken bit of pottery, *Ham.*, 5.i.225; (ii) wing-case or wing of beetle, *Ant. and Cleo.*, 3.ii.20; *shard-borne*, *Mac.*, 3.ii.42; *sharded*, *Cym.*, 3.iii.20.
shark *shark up*, gather as chance offers, *Ham.*, 1.i.98.
sheal'd shell'd, *Lear*, 1.iv.198.
shearman cloth-cutter, 2 *Hen.* 6, 4.ii.128.
sheav'd *sheav'd hat*, straw hat, *Lov. Comp.*, 31.
sheep-biter term of abuse, *Tw. Night*, 2.v.5.
sheer pure, *Rich.* 2, 5.iii.61; *for sheer ale*, for ale alone, *Tam. Shrew*, Ind.ii.22.
shent blamed, *Ham.*, 3.ii.388.
sherris sack, from Xeres in Spain, 2 *Hen.* 4, 4.iii.101.
shift trick, *John*, 4.iii.7.
ship-tire elaborate head-dress, *Mer. Wives Win.*, 3.iii.48.
shive slice, *Titus*, 2.i.87.
shoal shallow, *Mac.*, 1.vii.6 (Folio reads 'school'); *Hen.* 8, 3.ii.436.
shoon shoes, 2 *Hen.* 6, 4.ii.180.
shot reckoning, *Cym.*, 5.iv.155; *shot-free*, without paying, 1 *Hen.* 4, 5.iii.30.
shotten *shotten herring*, herring that has shed its roe and is of little value, 1 *Hen.* 4, 2.iv.122.
shough shaggy dog, *Mac.*, 3.i.93.
shoulder-shotten damaged in the shoulder, *Tam. Shrew*, 3.ii.52.
shove-groat *shove-groat shilling* (same as an *Edward shovel-board*, *Mer. Wives Win.*, 1.i.139), smooth shilling for game of shove-halfpenny, 2 *Hen.* 4, 2.iv.182.
shrewd shrewish, *Mid. N. Dr.*, 3.ii.323; malicious, *All's Well*, 3.v.65; evil, *Ant. and Cleo.*, 4.ix.5.
shrieve sheriff, *All's Well*, 4.iii.174.
shrift confession and absolution, *Rom. and Jul.*, 2.iii.56.
shrill-gorged shrill-throated, *Lear*, 4.vi.58.
shrine image, *Rom. and Jul.*, 1.v.92.
shroud shelter, *Ant. and Cleo.*, 3.xiii.71.
shrouds ropes supporting mast, *John*, 5.vii.53.
shrow shrew, *L. Lab. Lost*, 5.ii.46.
sicle shekel, *M. Meas.*, 2.ii.149.
siege seat, *M. Meas.*, 4.ii.94; *men of royal siege*, royal ancestors, *Oth.*, 1.ii.22.
silly helpless, *Two Gent. Ver.*, 4.i.72.
simple medicinal herbs were called simples because they were ingredients in medieval compounds, *Lear*, 4.iv.14; *Ham.*, 4.vii.144.
simplicity folly, *Son.*, 66, 11.
simular *simular man of virtue*, hypocrite, *Lear*, 3.ii.54; specious, *Cym.*, 5.v.200.
singule to single out, *L. Lab. Lost*, 5.i.68.
sinister left, *Troil. and Cres.*, 4.v.128; discourteous, *Tw. Night*, 1.v.165.
sir-reverence corruption of 'save your reverence', *Rom. and Jul.*, 1.iv.42; *Com. Err.*, 3.ii.90.
sister *Sisters Three*, the three Fates, *Mid. N. Dr.*, 5.i.327.
size *sizes*, allowances, *Lear*, 2.iv.174; share, *Ant. and Cleo.*, 4.xv.4.
skains-mates unexplained term of reproach, *Rom. and Jul.*, 2.iv.150.
skillet kitchen pot, *Oth.*, 1.iii.272.
skipper giddy youth, *Tam. Shrew*, 2.i.331.
skirr scour, *Mac.*, 5.iii.35.
slab sticky, *Mac.*, 4.i.32.
sleave skein of silk, *Mac.*, 2.ii.37.
sledded *sledded Polacks*, Poles on sledges, *Ham.*, 1.i.63.
sleeve-hand wristband, *Win. Tale*, 4.iv.207.
sleid *sleid silk*, untwisted silk, *Troil. and Cres.*, 5.i.29.
'Slid By God's eyelid (*cp. Troil. and Cres.*, 1.ii.203); *Tw. Night*, 3.iv.374.
'Slight By God's light, *Tw. Night*, 2.v.30.
slip counterfeit coin, *Rom. and Jul.*, 2.iv.48 (with similar pun at *Troil. and Cres.*, 2.iii.24).
slipper slippery, *Oth.*, 2.i.238.
slipshod in slippers, *Lear*, 1.v.11.
sliver *noun*, small branch, *Ham.*, 4.vii.174; *verb*, tear away, *Lear*, 4.ii.34.
slops wide breeches, 2 *Hen.* 4, 1.ii.28.
slubber to scamp, *Mer. Ven.*, 2.viii.39.
smatch taste, *Jul. Caes.*, 5.v.46.
smock woman's undergarment, so a woman, *a shirt and a smock*, a man and woman, *Rom. and Jul.*, 2.iv.99.
smoke drive from hiding with smoke, so show up faults, *All's Well*, 3.vi.93.

smooth flatter, *Rich. 3*, 1.iii.48.
smug spick and span, *Lear*, 4.vi.200.
sneap snub, *2 Hen. 4*, 2.i.118.
sneck-up expression of contempt, *Tw. Night*, 2.iii.90.
snipt-taffeta *snipt-taffeta fellow*, over-dressed creature, *All's Well*, 4.v.2.
snuff huff, *Lear*, 3.i.26; *to take in snuff*, to resent, *1 Hen. 4*, 1.iii.41.
sob a rest during which a horse recovers its wind, so punningly at *Com. Err.*, 4.iii.22.
soiled *soiled horse*, over-fed, *Lear*, 4.vi.122.
sole unique, *John*, 4.iii.52.
solemnity festivity, *Rom. and Jul.*, 1.v.61.
solidare coin, *Timon*, 3.i.43.
sonties saints, *Mer. Ven.*, 2.ii.39.
sooth truth, *Mac.*, 1.ii.36; flattery, *Rich. 2*, 3.iii.136.
sop cake or wafer in wine, *Tam. Shrew*, 3.ii.172.
sophister one who makes wrong appear right, *2 Hen. 6*, 5.i.191.
sophisticated disguised (by clothes), *Lear*, 3.iv.105.
Sophy Shah of Persia, *Tw. Night*, 2.v.161.
sore *see* buck.
sorel *see* buck.
sort *noun* (i) lot, *Troil. and Cres.*, 1.iii.376; (ii) rank, *M. Meas.*, 4.iv.15; collection, *Mid. N. Dr.*, 3.ii.13; *many in sort*, many together, *Mid. N. Dr.*, 3.ii.21; *verb*, ordain, *Rich. 3*, 2.iii.36; choose, *Two Gent. Ver.*, 3.ii.92; put among, *Ham.*, 2.ii.266; suit, *Ham.*, 1.i.109.
sortance agreement, *2 Hen. 4*, 4.i.11.
souse swoop down on, *John*, 5.ii.150.
sous'd *sous'd gurnet*, fish treated in brine, *1 Hen. 4*, 4.ii.12.
South Sea a *South Sea of Discovery*, a lengthy voyage in the unknown Pacific, *As You Like*, 3.ii.183.
sowl pull, *Cor.*, 4.v.200.
Sowter cobbler as name of hound, *Tw. Night*, 2.v.113.
span-counter game in which a coin is thrown to hit or lie beside another, *2 Hen. 6*, 4.ii.152.
spavins joint-disease of horse, *Tam. Shrew*, 3.ii.50.
spectacles the eyes, *2 Hen. 6*, 3.ii.112.
speculation vision, *Mac.*, 3.iv.95.
speculative with power of seeing, *Oth.*, 1.iii.270.
sperr *sperr up*, shut up, *Troil. and Cres.*, Prol. 19.
sphere *the tuned spheres*, the Sun, Moon and Planets were considered to be carried round the earth by transparent concentric spheres, whose motions produced a harmonious sound, *Ant. and Cleo.*, 5.ii.84.
spherical *spherical predominance*, influence of planets, *Lear*, 1.ii.118.
spill kill, *Lear*, 3.ii.8.
spital hospital, *Hen. 5*, 5.i.75.
spleen regarded as seat of anger, pugnacity, violent laughter, *M. Meas.*, 2.ii.122.
splinter join (as with splints), *Oth.*, 2.iii.313.
spongy soaked in drink, *Mac.*, 1.vii.71.
spot pattern, *Oth.*, 3.iii.439.
sprag quick, *Mer. Wives Win.*, 4.i.75.
springe snare, *Ham.*, 1.iii.115.
springhalt leg-disease in horse, *Hen. 8*, 1.iii.13.
square to measure, *Troil. and Cres.*, 5.ii.130; to quarrel, *Mid. N. Dr.*, 2.i.30.
squarer quarreller, *Much Ado*, 1.i.66.
squash unripe peascod, *Mid. N. Dr.*, 3.i.172.
squene squint, *Lear*, 3.iv.115.
squier carpenter's rule, *L. Lab. Lost*, 5.ii.474.
squiny squint, *Lear*, 4.vi.137.
staff *staves*, lance shafts, *Rich. 3*, 5.iii.65.
staggers disease in animals accompanied by giddiness, *Tam. Shrew*, 3.ii.51.
stale (i) bait, *Tem.*, 4.i.187; dupe, *Titus*, 1.i.304; (ii) urine, *Ant. and Cleo.*, 1.iv.62.
stamp coin, medal, *Mac.*, 4.iii.153.
stanchless insatiable, *Mac.*, 4.iii.78.
standing-bed bed on legs, *Mer. Wives Win.*, 4.v.6.
staniel poor type of hawk, *Tw. Night*, 2.v.105.
staple wool before spinning into yarn, *L. Lab. Lost*, 5.i.15.
starting-hole refuge, *Hen. 4*, 2.iv.255.
state *cons state*, get up matters of state, *Tw. Night*, 2.iii.139; chair of authority or dignity, *Tw. Night*, 2.v.42.
statist statesman, *Ham.*, 5.ii.33.
statute-cap to help the wool trade Parliament made the wearing of woollen caps compulsory on Sundays, *L. Lab. Lost*, 5.ii.281.
stickler-like as an umpire, *Troil. and Cres.*, 5.viii.18.
stigmatic marked out as wicked by some deformity, *2 Hen. 6*, 5.i.215.
still *adverb*, always, *still-vex'd Bermoothes*, always storm bound, *Tem.*, 1.ii.229.
stillitory a still, *Ven. and Adon.*, 443.
stint to cause to cease, *Troil. and Cres.*, 4.v.93; to cease, *Rom. and Jul.*, 1.iii.49.
stithy smithy, *Ham.*, 3.ii.82.
stoccado thrust, *Mer. Wives Win.*, 2.i.201; *alla stoccata*, at the thrust, *Rom. and Jul.*, 3.i.72.
stock *see* stoccado.
stock-fish dried cod, softened before cooking with beating, *Tem.*, 3.ii.67.
stole garment, *Lov. Comp.*, 297.
stomach *noun*, inclination, *As You Like*, 3.ii.20; courage, ambition, *Ham.*, 1.i.100.
stone-bow cross-bow for discharging stones, *Tw. Night*, 2.v.43.
stoop to descend upon prey, *Hen. 5*, 4.i.107.
store increase, *Son.*, 11.9.
stoup flagon, *Ham.*, 5.i.60.
stover fodder, *Tem.*, 4.i.63.
straight-pight erect, *Cym.*, 5.v.164.
strangeness aloofness, *Troil. and Cres.*, 2.iii.122.
strappado a punishment in which the victim is hoisted by a rope, let fall, and then brought up with a jerk, to dislocate his joints, *1 Hen. 4*, 2.iv.230.
strike shed evil influence, *Ham.*, 1.i.162; *strike the vessels*, tap the casks, *Ant. and Cleo.*, 2.vii.95.
strossers *strait strossers*, narrow trousers, *Hen. 5*, 3.vii.53.
stuck *see* stoccado, *Tw. Night*, 3.iv.263.
Stygian of Styx, river of hell, *Troil. and Cres.*, 3.ii.9.
style title, *1 Hen. 6*, 4.vii.72.
subscribe sign to, sign away, *Lear*, 1.ii.24; assess, characterize, *Rich. 2*, 1.iv.50; *Much Ado*, 5.ii.51; admit, *M. Meas.*, 2.iv.89; *all cruels else subscribe*, write off all other cruelties, *Lear*, 3.vii.64.
subscription obedience, *Lear*, 3.ii.18.
succeed follow as a natural or legal consequence, *Lear*, 1.ii.137; *bloody succeeding*, inevitable duel, *All's Well*, 2.iii.189.

success *in whose success*, as their issue, *Win. Tale*, 1.ii.394; *success of mischief*, disastrous consequences, 2 *Hen.* 4, 4.ii.47.
succession those coming after in like condition, *All's Well*, 3.v.21; after condition, inheritance, *Ham.*, 2.ii.347.
sufferance forbearance, *Hen.* 5, 3.vi.121.
suggest persuade, instruct, *Son.*, 144, 2; *Cor.*, 2.i.235; seduce, *Oth.*, 2.iii.341.
suggestion incitement, *Lear*, 2.i.73.
summoner officer who cited persons before ecclestiastical courts, *Lear*, 3.ii.59.
sumpter pack-horse, so drudge, *Lear*, 2.iv.215.
suppose *counterfeit supposes*, deceptive substitutions, *Tam. Shrew*, 5.i.104.
surcease *noun*, cessation, *Mac.*, 1.vii.4.
sur-rein'd overridden, *Hen.* 5, 3.v.19.
suspiration breathing, *Ham.*, 1.ii.79.
sutler camp follower, *Hen.* 5, 2.i.108.
swabber sailor who cleans up, *Tw. Night*, 1.v.191.
swaddling *swaddling clouts*, wrappings for new-born infants, *Ham.*, 2.ii.379.
swarth swath, *Tw. Night*, 2.iii.139.
swarth *adj.*, dark, *Titus*, 2.iii.72.
swath, swathing *see* swaddling, *Timon*, 4.iii.251.
sway'd *sway'd in the back* (of horse), weak-backed, *Tam. Shrew*, 3.ii.52.
sweeting apple, *Rom. and Jul.*, 2.iv.77.
swinge *noun*, blow, *Troil. and Cres.*, 1.iii.207; *verb*, thrash, 2 *Hen.* 4, 5.iv.20.
swinge-bucklers bold sparks, 2 *Hen.* 4, 3.ii.20.
Swithold Saint Vitalis, invoked as protection against nightmare, *Lear*, 3.iv.118.
swoopstake to take all, *Ham.*, 4.v.139.
sword-and-buckler arms of lower ranks, so, as epithet, common, 1 *Hen.* 4, 1.iii.230.
'Swounds by God's wounds, *Ham.*, 2.ii.571.
sympathise share nature, *Hen.* 5, 3.vii.143; *symphathized error*, error shared in, *Com. Err.*, 5.i.396.
table (-s) *noun*, wood or canvas for painting on, *John*, 2.i.503; note-book (so, *table-book*), *Ham.*, 1.v.107; palm of hand, *Mer. Ven.*, 2.ii.145; backgammon, *L. Lab. Lost*, 5.ii.326; *verb*, listed, *Cym.*, 1.iv.5.
tabor drum, *Tw. Night*, 3.i.9.
tabourine soldier's side-drum, *Troil. and Cres.*, 4.v.275.
taffeta *changeable taffeta*, shot silk, *Tw. Night*, 2.iv.73.
tag rabble, *Cor.*, 3.i.248.
taint *noun*, disgrace, *Troil. and Cres.*, 1.iii.374; *tainture*, evil state, 2 *Hen.* 6, 2.i.183; *verb*, discredit, *Oth.*, 2.i.262; to be affected, *Mac.*, 5.iii.3.
take bewitch, *Ham.*, 1.i.163; *take out*, copy, *Oth.*, 3.iii.300.
tall of a fine specimen of manhood or shipping, *Ant. and Cleo.*, 2.vi.7; *Mer. Ven.*, 3.i.5.
tame *tamed piece*, broached cask of wine, *Troil. and Cres.*, 4.i.64.
tarre to incite (as a dog), *Ham.*, 2.ii.349.
Tartar Tartarus, hell, *Tw. Night*, 2.v.184.
task to contract, *Cor.*, 1.iii.36; challenge, 1 *Hen.* 4, 5.ii.51.
tassel-gentle tercel male hawk, *Rom. and Jul.*, 2.ii.159.
tawdry-lace necklace (originally from Saint Audrey's fair), *Win. Tale*, 4.iv.244.
tax *noun*, censure, *All's Well*, 2.i.169; *verb*, to censure, *Ham.*, 1.iv.18.
taxation censure, *As You Like*, 1.ii.76; demand, *Tw. Night*, 1.v.197.
teen grief, *Tem.*, 1.ii.64.
tender (i) regard, *Lear*, 1.iv.209; (ii) offer, *Ham.*, 1.iii.99.
tent *noun*, roll of linen for cleaning out a wound, *Troil. and Cres.*, 2.ii.16; *verb*, to probe, *Ham.*, 2.ii.593.
tercel male goshawk, *Troil. and Cres.*, 3.ii.51.
Termagant a ranting part in the Mystery cycles, thought to be a Mohammedan deity, *Ham.*, 3.ii.13.
termination word, *Much Ado*, 2.i.221.
termless beyond words, *Lov. Comp.*, 94.
tertian occurring every other day, *Hen.* 5, 2.i.116.
tester sixpence, *Mer. Wives Win.*, 1.iii.84.
testril *see* tester.
tetchy peevish, *Troil. and Cres.*, 1.i.95.
tetter *noun*, scurf, *Ham.*, 1.v.71; *verb*, affice as with the tetter, *Cor.*, 3.i.79.
thane Scots title (the thanes become earls in last scene), *Mac.*, 5.viii.62.
Thessaly *the boar of Thessaly*, the Calydonian boar that ravaged Thessaly, slain by Meleager, *Ant. and Cleo.*, 4.xiii.2.
Thetis mother of Achilles, *Troil. and Cres.*, 1.iii.212.
thick *thick-ey'd*, dim unheeding eyes, 1 *Hen.* 4, 2.iii.43; *thick-pleached*, with dense intertwining branches, *Much Ado*, 1.ii.8.
thin-belly *thin-belly doublet*, unlined over belly, *L. Lab. Lost*, 3.i.17.
third thread, *Tem.*, 4.i.3.
thirdborough constable, *Tam. Shrew*, Ind.i.9.
Thracian *Thracian singer*, Orpheus, *Mid. N. Dr.*, 5.i.49.
thrasonical boastful (from Thraso, bragging soldier in *Eunuchus* of Terence), *As You Like*, 5.ii.29.
three-man song-men singers of three-part catches, *Win. Tale*, 4.iii.40.
three-pile rich velvet, *Win. Tale*, 4.iii.14; *three-pil'd hyperboles*, extravagant exaggerations, *L. Lab. Lost*, 5.ii.407.
threne dirge (threnos), *Phoenix*, 49.
thrice-crowned *see* Hecate.
thrift profit, *Ham.*, 3.ii.60.
throe pain, *Tem.*, 2.i.222.
thrum *thread and thrum*, good and bad, *Mid. N. Dr.*, 5.i.278; *thrumm'd hat*, witch-cap of weaver's ends, *Mer. Wives Win.*, 4.ii.66.
thwart perverse, *Lear*, 1.iv.283; *adv.*, against intention, *Troil. and Cres.*, 1.iii.15.
tickle so delicately adjusted as to be unsafe, 2 *Hen.* 6, 1.i.211.
tight (i) (of ship) sound, *Tem.*, 5.i.224; (ii) swift, *Ant. and Cleo.*, 4.iv.15.
tinct colour, *Ham.*, 3.iv.91; the golden colour given by the alchemists' grand elixir to base metal, *Ant. and Cleo.*, 1.v.36; the elixir itself, *All's Well*, 5.iii.102.
tinctures *tinctures, stains*, on handkerchiefs which would be dipped in the blood and kept as relics, *Jul. Caes.*, 2.ii.89.
tire head-dress, *Mer. Wives Win.*, 3.iii.49 (so *tire-valiant* indicates a particular style).
tire *tire on*, to devour (as a bird of prey), 3 *Hen.* 6, 1.i.269; *Cym.*, 3.iv.93.
tiring-house dressing-room, *Mid. N. Dr.*, 3.i.4.
tisick cough, *Troil. and Cres.*, 5.iii.101.
tissue fabric woven of gold thread and silk, *Ant. and*

Cleo., 2.ii.203.
tithe tenth, *Troil. and Cres.*, 2.ii.19.
tithing locality (originally containing some ten families, or tenth of a hundred), *Lear*, 3.iv.132.
toast toast in wine, *Mer. Wives Win.*, 3.v.3.
toaze, touze draw, *Win. Tale*, 4.iv.724.
tod *noun*, 28 lbs. of wool; *verb*, to make up a tod, *Win. Tale*, 4.iii.31.
toil net, trap, *Ham.*, 3.ii.338.
token *Lord's tokens*, marks of plague and so of death, of infection of love, *L. Lab. Lost*, 5.ii.423.
toll pay the seller's due on a sale at market, *All's Well*, 5.iii.146.
tomboys harlots, *Cym.*, 1.vi.121.
tongs *the tongs and the bones*, a percussion instrument like the triangle, and clappers, *Mid. N. Dr.*, 4.i.27.
top-gallant mast above top-mast, so the very height, *Rom. and Jul.*, 2.iv.184.
tortive twisted, *Troil. and Cres.*, 1.iii.9.
touch *noun*, inward sense or feeling, *Cym.*, 1.i.135; *one touch of nature*, a common characteristic, *Troil. and Cres.*, 3.iii.175; touchstone, *Timon*, 4.iii.387; *of noble touch*, of proved nobility, *Cor.*, 4.i.49; *verb*, to test, *Timon*, 3.iii.6; to infect, *John*, 5.vii.2.
touze to tear, *M. Meas.*, 5.i.309.
train *noun*, bait to trap, *Mac.*, 4.iii.118; *verb*, entice, *Com. Err.*, 3.ii.45.
trammel up catch as in a net, so dispose of, *Mac.*, 1.vii.3.
translate transform, *Mid. N. Dr.*, 3.i.108.
trash to curb a hound's impetuosity by adding weight to the collar, so *Oth.*, 2.i.297.
traverse soldier's drill order, *Oth.*, 1.iii.367; *adv.*, *quite traverse*, missing aim with the lance at tilting and breaking it crosswise on the opponent, so *As You Like*, 3.iv.38.
tray-trip game with dice in which three (trey) was the important throw, *Tw. Night*, 2.v.170.
treatise recital, *Mac.*, 5.v.12.
treble-dated with thrice man's span of life, *Phoenix*, 17.
trey throw of three with dice, *L. Lab. Lost*, 5.ii.232.
tribunal dais, *Ant. and Cleo.*, 3.vi.3.
tribune officer elected by commons in Rome, *Cor.*, 1.i.213.
trick *noun*, fashion, *M. Meas.*, 5.i.503; characteristic, *Lear*, 4.vi.106; gift, *Ham.*, 5.i.88; *verb*, cover (with reference to heralds' designs and their hatchings to indicate colours), *Ham.*, 2.ii.451.
tricking furnishings, *Mer. Wives Win.*, 4.iv.78.
Trigon the twelve signs of the Zodiac were grouped in threes (trigons) to correspond to the elements of earth, air, water, fire. 2 *Hen. 4*, 2.iv.255.
triple the third, or one of three, *Ant. and Cleo.*, 1.i.12.
triumph occasion of public rejoicing or recreation 3 *Hen. 6*, 5.vii.43; trump-card, *Ant. and Cleo.*, 4.xiv.20.
trophy token, *Lov. Comp.*, 218; memorial, *Ham.*, 4.v.210.
tropically metaphorically, *Ham.*, 3.ii.232.
truckle-bed low bed that could be pushed under standing-bed, *Mer. Wives Win.*, 4.v.6.
truepenny trusty fellow, *Ham.*, 1.v.150.
trundle-tail long-tail'd dog, *Lear*, 3.vi.69.
trunk sleeve wide sleeve, *Tam. Shrew*, 4.iii.138.
try *bring her to try*, into the wind, *Tem.*, 1.i.33.
tucket signal on trumpet, *Hen. 5*, 4.ii.35.
tuition protection, *Much Ado*, 1.i.244.
Tully *Tully's Orator*, Cicero's *De Oratore*, *Titus*, 4.i.14.
tun-dish funnel, *M. Meas.*, 3.ii.161.
twiggen wicker covering, *Oth.*, 2.iii.140.
twire twinkle, *Son.*, 28.12.
umber earthy brown colour, *As You Like*, 1.iii.108; *umber'd*, showing dark in the fire-light, *Hen. 5*, 4. *Chor.*9.
umbrage shadow, *Ham.*, 5.ii.119.
unable weak, inadequate, *Lear*, 1.i.59.
unaccommodated unprovided with what civilization gives, *Lear*, 3.iv.106.
unadvis'd unconsidered, *Rom. and Jul.*, 2.ii.118.
unanel'd without receiving extreme unction, *Ham.*, 1.v.77.
unattainted impartial, *Rom. and Jul.*, 1.ii.85.
unavoided not to be escaped, *Rich. 3*, 4.iv.217.
unbarb'd unprotected, bare, *Cor.*, 3.ii.99.
unbated unblunted, so of rapier without button on point, *Ham.*, 4.vii.138.
unbolt explain, *Timon*, 1.i.54; *unbolted*, unsifted, so crude, *Lear*, 2.ii.61.
unbonneted without removing the bonnet (*cp. Cor.*, 2.ii.25, where 'bonneted' means with cap in hand), *Oth.*, 1.ii.23.
unbookish *unbookish jealousy*, uninstructed in ways of society, *Oth.*, 4.i.101.
unbraided fresh and new, *Win. Tale*, 4.iv.201.
uncase undress, *Tam. Shrew*, 1.i.202.
unclew undo, *Timon*, 1.i.171.
uncoined *uncoined constancy*, pure metal needing no formal stamp to give it worth, *Hen. 5*, 5.ii.153.
unconfirmed uninstructed, *Much Ado*, 3.iii.107.
uncouth unfamiliar and fearsome, *Titus*, 2.iii.211.
unction ointment, *Ham.*, 3.iv.145.
underborne lined, *Much Ado*, 3.iv.20.
undercrest support worthily, *Cor.*, 1.ix.72.
under-skinker tapster, 1 *Hen. 4*, 2.iv.22.
undertaker venturer, *Tw. Night*, 3.iv.302.
undoubted fearless, 3 *Hen. 6*, 5.vii.6.
unexpressive beyond all praise, *As You Like*, 3.ii.10.
unhair'd too young for a beard, *John*, 5.ii.133.
unhoused without domestic responsibility, *Oth.*, 1.ii.26.
unhous'led not have taken the sacrament, *Ham.*, 1.v.77.
unimproved waiting to be given shape or purpose, *Ham.*, 1.i.96.
union pearl, *Ham.*, 5.ii.264.
unkennel disclose itself, *Ham.*, 3.ii.79.
unkind unnatural, *Lear*, 3.iv.70; *Timon*, 2.ii.217.
unlimited *poem unlimited*, drama not observing unities of time and place, *Ham.*, 2.ii.395.
unmann'd (of a hawk), still untrained by man, *Rom. and Jul.*, 3.ii.14.
unmoving as if unmoving, *Oth.*, 4.ii.56.
unpaved castrated, *Cym.*, 2.iii.31.
unpink'd still lacking their pierced pattern, *Tam. Shrew*, 4.i.117.
unpregnant barren of purpose, *Ham.*, 2.ii.562.
unprizable beyond price, in value or worthlessness, *Cym.*, 1.iv.86; *Tw. Night*, 5.i.49.
unproper not reserved for one man, *Oth.*, 4.i.68.

unrespective thoughtless, *Rich.* 3, 4.ii.29; *unrespective sieve*, for what we no longer heed, *Troil. and Cres.*, 2.ii.71.
unseminar'd castrated, *Ant. and Cleo.*, 1.v.11.
untented incurable, too deep for the tent to clean and cure, *Lear*, 1.iv.300.
unvalued priceless, *Rich.* 3, 1.iv.27; of no worth or rank, *Ham.*, 1.iii.19.
unyok'd *unyok'd humour*, unrestrained mood, 1 *Hen.* 4, 1.ii.189.
upcast throw at bowls, *Cym.*, 2.i.2.
upshoot winning shot, *L. Lab. Lost*, 4.i.129.
up-spring *up-spring reels*, a style of dance, *Ham.*, 1.iv.9.
urchin hedgehog, *Titus*, 2.iii.101; hobgoblin *Mer. Wives Win.*, 4.iv.48.
urinal doctor's glass for testing urine, *Two Gent. Ver.* 2.i.35.
usance interest, *Mer. Ven.*, 1.iii.40.
use custom, *Ham.*, 1.ii.134; *in use*, in trust, *Mer. Ven.*, 4.i.378; interest, *Son.*, 6.5.
usuring profiteering, *Timon*, 3.v.110.
usurp'd *usurp'd beard*, new-acquired beard, like a soldier's, *Oth.*, 1.iii.339.
utis week beginning with a feast-day, so frolic, 2 *Hen.* 4, 2.iv.19.
utter sell, *Rom. and Jul.*, 5.i.67.
utterance *to th' utterance (à outrance)*, in a fight to the death, *Mac.*, 3.i.71.
vade fade, *Son.*, 54, 14.
vail *noun*, sinking, *Troil. and Cres.*, 5.viii.7; *verb*, lower, *M. Meas.*, 5.i.20; lower in token of submission, *Cor.*, 3.i.98.
vails dues, *Per.*, 2.i.148.
valanc'd fringed (with a beard), *Ham.*, 2.ii.418.
validity worth, *All's Well*, 5.iii.190; strength, *Ham.*, 3.ii.184.
value *valued file*, the list giving the gift valued in each item, *Mac.*, 3.i.94.
Vanity *Vanity the puppet*, Lady Vanity was a character in Morality plays, *Lear*, 2.ii.33.
vantbrace armour for forearm, *Troil. and Cres.*, 1.iii.297.
varlet squire, *Troil. and Cres.*, 1.i.1; but often used abusively; *varletry*, mob, *Ant. and Cleo.*, 5.ii.56.
vastidity measureless space, *M. Meas.*, 3.i.70.
vaunt first part, *Troil. and Cres.*, Prol.27.
vaunt-couriers forerunners, *Lear*, 3.ii.5.
vaward advance-guard, *Hen.* 5, 4.iii.130.
velure velvet, *Tam. Shrew*, 3.ii.57.
velvet-guards *see* guard.
vent (i) *vent of hearing*, ear, 2 *Hen.* 4, Ind. 2; (ii) *full of vent*, hot on the scent, *Cor.*, 4.v.223.
ventage stops of wind-instrument, *Ham.*, 3.ii.348.
ventricle one of the three divisions into which the brain was held to be divided, *L. Lab. Lost*, 4.ii.66.
venue, veney thrust, *L. Lab. Lost*, 5.i.52; hit at fencing, *Mer. Wives Win.*, 1.i.259.
verbatim orally, 1 *Hen.* 6, 3.i.13.
verge circle, limit, 2 *Hen.* 6, 1.iv.22.
Veronesa a ship charter'd from Verona, *Oth.*, 2.i.26.
via *interjection*, go on, 3 *Hen.* 6, 2.i.182.
vice The Vice was a character in the Morality plays, presented often as a buffoon, so *Ham.*, 3.iv.98.
vie to call against or stake at cards, so to compete with, *Ant. and Cleo.*, 5.ii.98.
vigil eve of a feast-day, *Hen.* 5, 4.iii.45.
Villiago villain, slave, 2 *Hen.* 6, 4.viii.45.
viol-de-gamboys *viol da gamba*, being held between the knees like the cello, *Tw. Night*, 1.iii.24.
virginalling fingering, as if playing on the virginals, *Win. Tale*, 1.ii.125.
virtue valour, *Lear*, 5.iii.104; the most excellent characteristic, *Timon*, 3.v.8.
virtuous potent, *Mid. N. Dr.*, 3.ii.367.
visit *strangely-visited*, terribly afflicted, *Mac.*, 4.iii.150; punish, *John*, 2.i.179.
visitation (in two senses), affliction (of love) and visit, *Tem.*, 3.i.32.
visitor like clergyman coming to console the afflicted, *Tem.*, 2.i.11.
visor, vizard mask, *Rom. and Jul.*, 1.iv.30.
voiding-lobby waiting-room, 2 *Hen.* 6, 4.i.61.
vouch testimony, *Oth.*, 2.i.146.
waft carry by sea, *John*, 2.i.73; beckon, *Mer. Ven.*, 5.i.11; move, *Win. Tale*, 1.ii.372.
waftage transport (by ferry), *Troil. and Cres.*, 3.ii.10.
wafture motion, *Jul. Caes.*, 2.i.246.
wag to go about, *Titus*, 5.ii.87.
wage *wag'd equal*, met on equal terms (like equal stakes), *Ant. and Cleo.*, 5.i.31.
waist of ship, mid part, *Tem.*, 1.ii.197.
wake *noun*, celebration on some holy day, beginning the evening before, *Lear*, 3.vi.73; *verb*, hold night revel, *Ham.*, 1.iv.8.
wall-ey'd discolouration of eye, giving it threatening look, *John*, 4.iii.49.
wan go pale, *Ham.*, 2.ii.547; *Ant. and Cleo.*, 2.i.21 (may mean: lost its youthful colour).
wappen'd worn out, *Timon*, 4.iii.38.
ward cell, *Ham.*, 2.ii.245; defence, *Mer. Wives Win.*, 2.ii.222.
warden pear, *Win. Tale*, 4.iii.44.
warder baton of rank, *Rich.* 2, 1.iii.118.
Ware *bed of Ware*, bed from Ware in Hertfordshire, famous for its size (now in the Victoria and Albert museum), *Tw. Night*, 3.ii.44.
warp distort, *All's Well*, 5.iii.49; change, *As You Like*, 2.vii.187; *warp'd*, distorted, *Lear*, 3.vi.52.
warrantise authority, *Ham.*, 5.i.221.
warranty permission, *Oth.*, 5.ii.63.
warren game preserve, *Much Ado*, 2.i.191.
warrener game-keeper, *Mer. Wives Win.*, 1.iv.25.
wassail (originally the salutation on drinking) carousing, *Ham.*, 1.iv.9.
waste *waste blanks*, unused pages, *Son.*, 77, 10.
waste *noun*, what is damaged (as in legal sense of damage to an estate by owner), *Rich.* 2, 2.i.103; desolation, *Ham.*, 1.ii.198; *verb*, *wasted time*, past time, *Son.*, 106, 1.
Wat hare, *Ven. and Adon.*, 697.
watch *a watch*, insomnia, *Ham.*, 2.ii.147; timepiece, *L. Lab. Lost*, 3.i.182; *verb*, to tame hawk by denying it sleep, *Tam. Shrew*, 4.i.179.
water brilliance of diamond, *Timon*, 1.i.20.
water-gall secondary bow, *Lucrece*, 1588.
watering drinking, 1 *Hen.*, 4, 2.iv.15.
water-rug hairy water-dog, *Mac.*, 3.i.93.
water-work water-colours, 2 *Hen.* 4, 2.i.141.

weal state, *Mac.*, 3.iv.76.
wealsmen statesman, *Cor.*, 2.i.50.
weather *keep the weather of*, control (as holding windward position at sea), *Troil. and Cres.*, 5.iii.26.
weather-fend shelter, *Tem.*, 5.i.10.
weed garment, *Mid. N. Dr.*, 2.i.256.
weet to know, *Ant. and Cleo.*, 1.i.39.
weird *Weird Sisters*, the Fates, *Mac.*, 1.iii.32.
welkin sky, *Tem.*, 1.ii.4.
westward-ho cry of boatmen going up Thames, *Tw. Night*, 3.i.131.
wezand windpipe, *Tem.*, 3.ii.87.
wharf river-bank, *Ham.*, 1.v.33.
Wheeson Whitsun, 2 *Hen.* 4, 2.i.85.
whelk pimple, *Hen.* 5, 3.vi.99.
whelk'd in spirals, *Lear*, 4.vi.71.
whey-face pale, *Mac.*, 5.iii.17.
whiffler official who goes ahead of procession to clear the way, *Hen.* 5, 5. *Chor.*12.
whinid'st very mouldy, *Troil. and Cres.*, 2.i.14.
whipping-cheer served with the lash, 2 *Hen.* 4, 5.iv.5.
whipster insignificant enough to be whipt, *Oth.*, 5.ii.247.
whirligig like Fortune's wheel, *Tw. Night*, 5.i.362.
whist hushed, *Tem.*, 1.ii.378.
white *noun*, play on white on target and name of Bianca, *Tam. Shrew*, 5.ii.186; *adj.*, fresh (not cured), *Lear*, 3.vi.31.
white-lim'd white-washed, *Titus*, 4.ii.98.
whiting-time bleaching-time, *Mer. Wives Win.*, 3.iii.115.
whitster bleacher, *Mer. Wives Win.*, 3.iii.12.
whittle small knife, *Timon*, 5.i.178.
whoreson bastard, *Lear*, 1.i.22.
wild weald, 1 *Hen.* 4, 2.i.54.
wild-goose chase form of cross-country horse-racing, *Rom. and Jul.*, 2.iv.69.
wild mare see-saw, 2 *Hen.* 4, 2.iv.237.
wilful-blame deliberately culpable, 1 *Hen.* 4, 3.i.177.
wimpled hooded, blind, *L. Lab. Lost*, 3.i.169.
Winchester *goose* (the liberty of the Bankside, under the jurisdiction of the Bishop of Winchester, sheltered many brothels; so the disease and its victims were named after him), *Troil. and Cres.*, 5.x.53.
Wincot Wilmecot (home of Shakespeare's mother), *Tam. Shrew*, Ind.ii.20.
wind *have the wind of*, have controlling position, *Titus*, 4.ii.133; *windy side of*, safe side of, *Tw. Night*, 3.iv.156.
windgalls disease of horse's fetlock, *Tam. Shrew*, 3.ii.49.
windlass means of winding, *Ham.*, 2.i.65.
wind'ring (perhaps wandering or winding), *Tem.*, 4.i.128.
winking blind spell, *Ham.*, 2.ii.136.
winnowed select, *Ham.*, 5.ii.187.
winter-ground cover as against winter's frost, *Cym.*, 4.ii.230.
wise woman witch, *Tw. Night*, 3.iv.97.
wittol complacent cuckold, *Mer. Wives Win.*, 2.ii.267.
wood mad, frantic, *Mid. N. Dr.*, 2.i.192.
woodcock a fool (like the stupid bird), *Ham.*, 1.iii.115.
woodman hunter, *Cym.*, 3.vi.28; so, of women, *M. Meas.*, 4.iii.158.
woollen *lie in the woollen*, in blankets and no sheets, or in the grave (the shroud being by law of wool), *Much Ado*, 2.i.26.
woolward with woollen inner garment, *L. Lab. Lost*, 5.ii.698.
working causing a working of the feelings, *Hen.* 8, Prol. 3.
world *go to the world*, marry, *Much Ado*, 2.i.287; *woman of the world*, married woman, *As You Like*, 5.iii.4.
worm small snake, *Ant. and Cleo.*, 5.ii.242.
wort (i) vegetable, *Mer. Wives Win.*, 1.i.110; (ii) unfermented beer, *L. Lab. Lost*, 5.ii.233.
worthy deserved, of praise or blame, *All's Well*, 4.iii.5.
wrangler opponent, *Hen.* 5, 1.ii.264.
wrest *noun*, key for tightening harp-strings, *Troil. and Cres.*, 3.iii.23; *verb*, draw out, *Titus*, 3.ii.44; misconstrue, *Much Ado*, 3.iv.30.
writ document, *Ham.*, 5.ii.51.
writhled wrinkled, 1 *Hen.* 6, 2.iii.23.
wroth misfortune, *Mer. Ven.*, 2.ix.78.
wry leaving path of virtue, *Cym.*, 5.i.5.
wry-neck'd fife, played with the head turned away, *Mer. Ven.*, 2.v.29.
yare quick and efficient, *Ant. and Cleo.*, 3.vii.38 (of ships); *M. Meas.*, 4.ii.53; *yarely*, *Ant. and Cleo.*, 2.ii.215.
yaw (of ship) to steer unsteadily, *Ham.*, 5.ii.114.
yawn gape in surmise, *Ham.*, 4.v.9.
yclad clad, 2 *Hen.* 6, 1.i.33.
ycleped called, *L. Lab. Lost*, 1.i.231.
Yead, Yedward Edward, *Mer. Wives Win.*, 1.i.140; 1 *Hen.* 4, 1.ii.129.
yearn grieve, *Hen.* 5, 4.iii.26.
yellowness jealousy, *Mer. Wives Win.*, 1.iii.97.
yellows jaundice (of horses), *Tam. Shrew*, 3.ii.50.
yeoman *yeoman's service*, invaluable service (from the reputation the yeoman class had won in war), *Ham.*, 5.ii.36.
yerk stab, *Oth.*, 1.ii.5.
yest, yeast, froth, *Win. Tale*, 3.iii.91; *yesty*, frothy, showy, *Ham.*, 5.ii.186.
yoke *noun*, pair, *Mer. Wives Win.*, 2.i.156; *verb*, pair, *yok'd*, married, *Oth.*, 4.i.66.
younker younger son, novice, *Mer. Ven.*, 2.vi.14.
yravish ravish, *Per.*, 3. *Gower*.35.
yslaked silenced, *Per.*, 3. *Gower*.1.
zany a fool's 'stooge', *Tw. Night*, 1.v.84.
zenith the culmination of his life, *Tem.*, 1.ii.181.
zodiac year (in which sun completes its course through the Zodiac), *M. Meas.*, 1.ii.161.
Zounds by God's wounds, *Oth.*, 1.i.87.

Shakespearian websites

The internet has a vast amount of information on the life and work of Shakespeare for those who enjoy and are studying Shakespeare. Finding reliable and free data should not be difficult, although a few points need to be borne in mind. Make sure to look at the 'Last updated' section of the main website page before using any data. Try clicking on the links to make sure that they have been maintained properly and do not result in error messages. Ideally information should be obtained from websites run by universities, research institutes, and other reputable organizations. Websites maintained by individuals may not be up to date and comprehensive. It is also possible that the prejudices of those maintaining the websites will be reflected in the content and list of links. The first selection of sites below act as gateways to a wide variety of sites about Shakespeare and provide a good starting point. The last section contains a small selection of some of the more unusual sites.

Introductory sites

http://shakespeare.palomar.edu
Mr William Shakespeare and the Internet: a gateway site that provides valuable introductory material and links to many Shakespeare sites. It includes a selection of oddities along with many invaluable academic sites.

http://ise.uvic.ca/index.html
Internet Shakespeare Editions: a site from the University of Victoria in Canada, for the student, scholar, actor, and general reader. It contains annotated texts of Shakespeare's plays, multimedia explorations of the context of Shakespeare's life and works, records of his plays in performance, and links to many sites, from critical academic papers to parodies of Shakespeare.

www.folger.edu
The Folger Shakespeare Library, located on Capitol Hill in Washington, DC, is a world-class research centre on Shakespeare. It is home to the world's largest and finest collection of Shakespeare materials. Its website has lots of material on Shakespeare's life and works, including a digitised version of the First Folio.

www.touchstone.bham.ac.uk
The British Library's research tool for Shakespeare: information on productions, resources, meetings, groups, and questions.

http://search.eb.com/shakespeare/esa/660007.html
Encyclopaedia Britannica site on Shakespeare.

www.talkingto.co.uk/ttws
A site called Talking to William Shakespeare, maintained by *The Times Educational Supplement*. It provides answers to hundreds of Shakespeare questions.

http://pages.unibas.ch/shine
Shakespeare in Europe: criticism, research material, sources and links, maintained by the English Department, University of Basel.

http://www.shakespeare.com/
This site contains thousands of pages of content on Shakespeare's life and work.

www.about-shakespeare.com
General facts about Shakespeare and links.

http://shakespeare.about.com
A site covering many aspects of Shakespeare and his writing , plus some fun, such as most frequently asked Shakespeare questions.

Shakespeare's life and times

http://shakespeare.palomar.edu/timeline/summarychart.htm
A timeline for Shakespeare's life and contemporary events.

www.likesnail.org.uk/welcome-es.htm
Educating Shakespeare: school life in Shakespeare's day.

http://shakespeare.about.com/library/weekly/aa101000a.htm
Shakespeare's will.

www.william-shakespeare.info/william-shakespeare-children-and-grandchildren.htm
The story of Shakespeare's descendants.

www.william-shakespeare.info/william-shakespeare-pictures.htm
Survey of the portraits of Shakespeare.

Shakespeare and Stratford-upon-Avon

www.stratford-upon-avon.co.uk/kes
A brief history of the town in Shakespeare's day with illustrations.

www.stratford.co.uk/shakespeare.asp
Town history and buildings important in Shakespeare's life.

www.shakespeare.org.uk
Shakespeare Birthplace Trust., with information on the life of Shakespeare and on the buildings in Stratford-upon-Avon that are connected with Shakespeare, including his birthplace.

www.stratford-upon-avon.org/bard.html
History of Holy Trinity Church, where Shakespeare was baptised and buried.

The Globe Theatre

www.shakespeares-globe.org
General site for the rebuilt Globe Theatre.

www.allshakespeare.com/globe/
Introduction to and history of the Globe Theatre.

www.bardweb.net/globe.html
Investigation of the history of the Globe with links.

http://virtual.clemson.edu/caah/Shakespr/VRGLOBE/tourst.htm
A virtual tour of the Globe.

www.greatbuildings.com/buildings/Globe_Theater.html
Pictures and links.

http://absoluteshakespeare.com/trivia/globe/globe.htm
How the original Globe was financed and built.

http://shakespeare.palomar.edu/theatre.htm
Elizabethan theatre and many links.

Theatre companies

www.rsc.org.uk/
The Royal Shakespeare Company.

http://btsc.homestead.com
The British Touring Shakespeare Company.

www.shakespearedc.org
Shakespeare Theatre Company, Washington, DC.

www.reducedshakespeare.com
The Reduced Shakespeare Company: a three-man comedy troupe taking plays by Shakespeare and others and reducing them to short, sharp comedies.

Shakespeare organizations

www.arts.unsw.edu.au/conferences/anzsa/index.html
The Australian and New Zealand Shakespeare Association

http://britishshakespeare.ws
British Shakespeare Association.

www.shakespeare.org.uk/main/7/78
International Shakespeare Association

www.ShakespeareAssociation.org/
Shakespeare Association of America

www.shakespeare.org.uk
The Shakespeare Birthplace Trust, Stratford-upon-Avon.

www.shakespeare.bham.ac.uk
The Shakespeare Institute: a centre for postgraduate study of Shakespeare and his contemporaries.

www.shakespearesociety.org
Society based in New York: a non-academic, membership organization formed to increase the enjoyment, understanding, and appreciation of Shakespeare.

www.shakespearemag.com
An online magazine for Shakespeare teachers and enthusiasts.

The language of Shakespeare

www.bardweb.net/words.html
A look at Shakespeare's language, with links.

http://quarles.unbc.ca/shakescan
Concordance-like tool for searching Shakespeare's works for particular words.

www.rhymezone.com/shakespeare
Site that allows you to search for words and phrases in Shakespeare's works.

www.online-literature.com/shakespeare
Another site that allows you to search for words and phrases.

http://absoluteshakespeare.com/trivia/quotes/quotes.htm
List of famous quotes from the plays.

www.allshakespeare.com/quotes/
Searchable database of quotes.

http://www.shakespeare-online.com/faq/misquotesfaq.html
A selection of quotes which we mistakenly think are by Shakespeare.

The authorship debate

http://shakespeareauthorship.com/
The Shakespeare Authorship page, dedicated to the proposition that Shakespeare wrote Shakespeare.

http://www.shakespeare-oxford.com/
A site that advocates the Earl of Oxford as the author.

http://www.princeton.edu/~rbivens/shakespeare/
The Shakespeare Question, a site that looks at who really wrote the works of Shakespeare.

www.bbc.co.uk/history/programmes/shakespeare/index.shtml
Site linked to the BBC series *In Search of Shakespeare.*

www.pbs.org/wgbh/pages/frontline/shakespeare/index.html
The Shakespeare Mystery: information on and responses to this PBS programme.

The plays

www.bl.uk/treasures/shakespeare/homepage.html
Digitised online versions of Shakespeare's plays at British Library.

http://the-tech.mit.edu/Shakespeare
Full versions of the plays online at the Massachusetts Institute of Technology

http://etext.virginia.edu/shakespeare/works
Full versions of the plays online at the University of Virginia

www.folger.edu/template.cfm?cid=930
Information on the First Folio from the Folger Library, including a digital version of the complete First Folio.

Studying the plays

www.bardweb.net/plays.html
Introduction to the plays and links to useful sites.

http://aboutshakepeare.com
Site containing the plays, summaries, and study guides for school students.

www.cummingsstudyguides.net/
Shake Sphere: a study guide to Shakespeare, primarily for schools, with links to many other sites.

www.shakespeare-online.com/
Analysis of all the plays given on this site.

www.william-shakespeare.info/
Text and analysis of all plays given on this site.

www.sparknotes.com/shakespeare/
Study notes on all plays given on this site.

www.online-literature.com/shakespeare/
Text and analysis of all the plays given on this site.

The sonnets

www.shakespeare-sonnets.com/
Texts of sonnets, with descriptive commentary and sonnets by contemporaries.

www.shakespeare-online.com/sonnets/
Texts of sonnets with analysis and modern English versions.

www.allshakespeare.com/sonnets/
Background, analysis and critical assessment.

http://town.hall.org/Archives/radio/IMS/HarperAudio/020994_harp_ITH.html
John Gielgud reads the sonnets.

Other poetry

http://shakespeare.about.com/od/shakespearespoems/
Complete texts of Shakespeare's other major poetic works.

www.william-shakespeare.info/william-shakespeare-poems.htm
Texts and analysis of longer poems.

http://darkwing.uoregon.edu/~rbear/ren.htm
Full text versions of the poems and other Shakespearian works.

Shakespeare on film

http://absoluteshakespeare.com/trivia/films/films.htm
List of major film productions of Shakespeare plays.

www.pbs.org/shakespeare/educators/film/indepth.html
A historical survey of Shakespeare in the cinema.

http://bardcentral.com
Listing of Shakespeare plays available on film

A selection of surprising sites

Herbs and plants
www.chennaionline.com/columns/variety/05botanic.asp

Insults
www.insults.net/html/shakespeare/
www.pangloss.com/seidel/Shaker/

Music
www.onlineshakespeare.com/music.htm

Quizzes and trivia
www.shax.net/
www.barcelonareview.com/mis/shquiz.htm
http://shakespeare.about.com/library/weekly/aa073101a.htm

Shakespeare and food
www.soupsong.com/ibard.html

Shakespeare parodies
www.shakespeare-parodies.com/